Praise for *Cuba or The Pursuit of Freedom*

"Scholarly in concept yet easy to read." —*New York Times Book Review*

"Both an incisive analysis and a moving evocation of a diverse and tragic history. If possible, Hugh Thomas has excelled his brilliant book on the Spanish Civil War." —**Arthur Schlesinger, Jr.**

"Those who are unfamiliar with Cuban history will be amazed at its richness, color, and drama—qualities which Thomas, a master stylist, knows how to use. . . . [This book's] literary qualities, its solid scholarship, its urbane judgments make it worthy of a place in any library. Highly recommended." —*Library Journal*

"A remarkable book . . . balanced and insightful. For the decade from 1952 to 1962 it might be considered definitive. . . . This study goes far toward clarifying the colors in the confused kaleidoscope that is contemporary Cuba." —*American Historical Review*

"[Thomas] shares a loving interest in the Cuban people; he writes sensitively about their sufferings and aspirations." —*Dissent*

"An impressive work, thoroughly researched, immense in its canvas, brilliant in its superabundance of detail. . . . Thomas seems to have missed nothing of relevance in Cuba's multidimensional political, social, and economic history. . . . An engrossing and very nearly definitive work." —*Publishers Weekly*

"The great value of *Cuba* is that it puts an appalling story together in one place for the first time." —*Time*

"A monumental history of the Caribbean's largest and most prosperous island. . . . Thomas presents a balanced account of revolutionary Cuba, showing both its administrative injustices and its social achievements. . . . An extremely useful and wide-ranging account of the Cuban drama." —*Times Literary Supplement*

"Fascinating and scholarly. . . . The epic proportions of this work are fully justified, and in the reflective passages the author's great strengths as an interpret~~ historian emerge.~~" —*Contemporary Review*

D1343245

Cuba

or
The Pursuit of Freedom

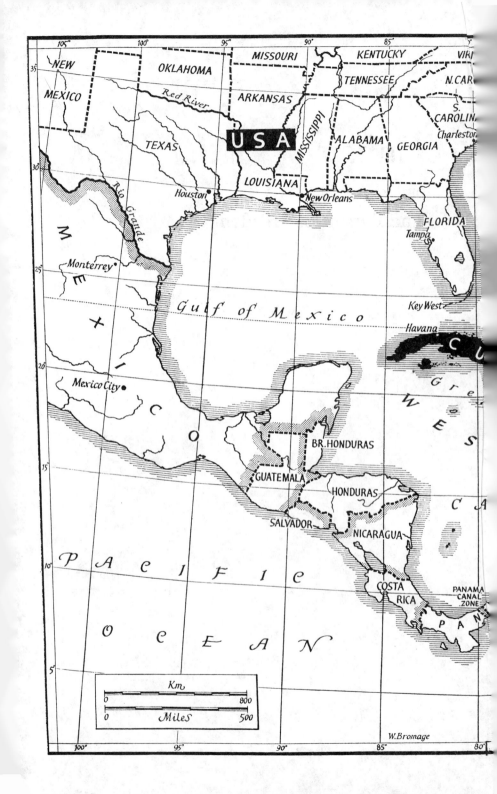

Cuba

or
The Pursuit of Freedom

HUGH THOMAS

UPDATED EDITION

DA CAPO PRESS • NEW YORK

Y00522O8

Library of Congress Cataloging-in-Publication Data
Thomas, Hugh, 1931–
    Cuba, or, The pursuit of freedom / Hugh Thomas.–Updated ed.
    p.   cm.
    Includes bibliographical references and index.
    ISBN 0-306-80827-7 (alk. paper)
    1. Cuba–History–1959– . 2. Cuba–History. I. Title.
F1788.T47   1998
972.91–dc21   97-52949
                                                                    CIP

First Da Capo Press edition 1998

This Da Capo Press paperback edition of *Cuba* is an unabridged
republication of the edition first published in New York in 1971,
here updated with a new afterword. It is reprinted by arrangement
with the author.

Published by Da Capo Press, Inc.
A Subsidiary of Plenum Publishing Corporation
233 Spring Street, New York, N.Y. 10013

Manufactured in the United States of America

DEDICATION

'Yet, Freedom! yet, thy banner, torn, but flying,
Streams like the thunder-storm *against* the wind.'

Byron, *Childe Harold*

CONTENTS

Preface   page xxi
Acknowledgements   xxiv
Abbreviations   xxv
PROLOGUE *With Albemarle to Havana, 1762*
   I   The English Expedition   1
  II   The Spanish Colony   12
 III   Sugar and Society   27
 IV   The Victors and the Creoles   42

BOOK I *The Great Leap Forward, 1763–1825*
   V   Enter North America   61
  VI   The Challenge of Haiti   72
 VII   Rebellion in South America   85
VIII   The Ever-faithful Isle   93

BOOK II *The Golden Age, 1825–68*
  IX   The World of Sugar   109
   X   Coffee   128
  XI   The Planters   136
 XII   The Slave Merchants   156
XIII   The Slaves   168
XIV   The Decline of Slavery   184

BOOK III *The Political Struggle, 1823–98*
  XV   Captains-General in Search of Wealth   193
 XVI   The Politics of Abolitionism   200
XVII   Manifest Destiny   207

vii

XVIII	Annexationism	218
XIX	Reformism	233
XX	The War of 1868: I	245
XXI	The War of 1868: II	254
XXII	The Spanish Counter-Revolution	264
XXIII	The Sugar Crisis of the 1880s	271
XXIV	The End of Slavery	281
XXV	José Martí	293
XXVI	The New America	310
XXVII	The War of 1895	316
XXVIII	General Weyler	328
XXIX	Cuba and U.S. Public Opinion	339
XXX	The *Maine*	356
XXXI	McKinley and the War	367
XXXII	The Spanish-American War	381
XXXIII	San Juan Hill and Santiago	390
XXXIV	End of Empire	402

BOOK IV *From Occupation to Occupation, 1899–1909*

XXXV	Cuba Prostrate	417
XXXVI	The Proconsuls, I: General Brooke	436
XXXVII	The Proconsuls, II: General Wood	444
XXXVIII	The U.S. Stake in Cuba, 1899–1902	463
XXXIX	Don Tomás	471
XL	The Second Intervention: Magoon	481

BOOK V *The Young Republic, 1909–32*

XLI	Cuba in 1909	497
XLII	Gómez and the Good Life	504
XLIII	The Negro Protest	514
XLIV	Menocal	525
XLV	Sugar, 1906–20	536
XLVI	The Dance of the Millions	544
XLVII	The Sugar Troubles of the 1920s	557

XLVIII   Zayas   564

XLIX   Machado: I   569

L   Machado: II   586

BOOK VI *The Revolution of 1933*

LI   Sumner Welles   605

LII   The Fall of Machado   615

LIII   The Middle-Class Government   626

LIV   The Sergeants' Revolution   634

LV   Grau's Girondin Revolution   650

LVI   The Battle of the Hotel Nacional   658

LVII   The November Revolt   666

LVIII   The Counter-Revolution   678

BOOK VII *The Age of Democracy, 1934–52*

LIX   Batista and the Puppet Presidents   691

LX   Batista and the Communists   706

LXI   The Constitution of 1940   716

LXII   Batista: the Democratic President   724

LXIII   Grau   737

LXIV   Prío 'el Presidente de la Cordialidad'   759

LXV   The Fall of Prío   775

BOOK VIII *The Struggle, 1952–9*

LXVI   Batista: II   789

LXVII   Fidel Castro: Childhood and Youth   803

LXVIII   Moncada: the Idea   824

LXIX   Moncada: the Fight   835

LXX   Indian Summer   845

LXXI   The Civic Dialogue   863

LXXII   Castro in Mexico   876

LXXIII   The *Granma* and the Sierra Maestra   894

LXXIV   Herbert Matthews goes to the Sierra   909

LXXV   The Attack on the Palace   925

LXXVI   War in the Sierra (March–May 1957)   934
LXXVII   The U.S. enters the Controversy   942
LXXVIII   Miami and Santiago   950
LXXIX   The Naval Mutiny at Cienfuegos   961
LXXX   The Arms Embargo   974
LXXXI   The Strike of 9 April   988
LXXXII   Batista's 'Big Push' of May 1958   996
LXXXIII   The Collapse   1005
LXXXIV   How Batista Fell   1020

BOOK IX *Victory:* L'Illusion Lyrique, 1959

LXXXV   Springs of Victory   1037
LXXXVI   Castro and the Americas in 1959   1048
LXXXVII   *L'Illusion Lyrique*   1065
LXXXVIII   First Shadows   1078

BOOK X *Old Cuba at Sunset*

LXXXIX   The Island   1093
XC   The Class Structure of Cuba   1108
XCI   Black Cuba   1117
XCII   The Church   1127
XCIII   Education   1131
XCIV   Sugar   1138
XCV   Tobacco and other Industries   1158
XCVI   The Economy: Labour   1173
XCVII   The Economy: the Central Neurosis   1180

BOOK XI *The Clash, 1959–62*

XCVIII   Castro in America   1193
XCIX   Agrarian Reform: Politics and Crisis   1215
C   The Eclipse of the Liberals   1234
CI   A Sword is Drawn   1255
CII   The End of Capitalist Cuba   1272
CIII   The U.S. Prepares for Battle   1300

CIV   Cuba Socialista: I   1312
CV   Cuba Socialista: II   1339
CVI   Battle of Cochinos Bay   1355
CVII Between the Crises   1372
CVIII The Missile Crisis: I   1385
CIX   The Missile Crisis: II   1395
CX   The Missile Crisis: III   1406

EPILOGUE

CXI   The Utopians   1423
CXII The 'Ten Million Ton Harvest' and its
          Implications   1436
CXIII The New Men   1445
CXIV The Guardians   1453
CXV   New Friends and Old   1474
CXVI The Pursuit of Freedom   1483

AFTERWORD   1495

APPENDICES

    I   The Cuban Oligarchy   1510
   II   Cuban Governors and Presidents   1522
  III   Who were the Cuban Indians?   1525
   IV   Kennion's Slave Concession   1544
    V   Estimated Cuban Slave Imports   1546
   VI   Outfit of a Slave Ship, 1825   1548
  VII   Slave Ships from Havana, 1825   1549
 VIII   Affidavit of Lieutenant Nott   1551
   IX   Chinese Imports to Cuba, 1847–73   1555
    X   The Last Slave Journey across the Atlantic, 1865   1557
   XI   The Attack on Moncada and Bayamo   1560
  XII   The State of Agriculture in 1959   1562
 XIII   Cuban and World Sugar Production, 1770–1970   1574
  XIV   World Raw Sugar Prices, 1900–1962   1579

Glossary   1583
Bibliographical Note   1587
General Bibliography   1593
Index   1615

PLATES

---

1 View of Havana, 1762   facing page 34
2 The British land in Cuba, 1762   35
3 The British Commanders, 1762:   66
   a Lord Albemarle
   b Admiral Sir George Pocock
   c Admiral Keppel
   d General William Keppel

4 a Francisco Arango, c. 1800   67
   b The market-place at Havana
5 Four Spanish Captains-General: 226
   a General Tacón
   b General O'Donnell
   c General Martínez Campos
   d General Weyler

6 The Tinguaro sugar mill, c. 1860   227

7 Four U.S. Presidents who tried to buy Cuba: 258
   a James K. Polk, 1845–1849
   b James Buchanan, 1857–1861
   c Ulysses S. Grant, 1869–1877
   d William McKinley, 1897–1901

xiii

8 Four Cuban liberators: 259
   a Carlos Manuel de Céspedes
   b Antonio Maceo
   c Calixto García
   d Máximo Gómez

9 José Martí: 386
   a In New York
   b In Kingston, Jamaica
10 Theodore Roosevelt: 387
   a The Colonel
   b With the Roughriders
11 a Santiago Bay from the Morro Castle   418
   b The U.S. battleship *Maine* enters Havana Bay, 1898
12 a The U.S. flag is raised over Santiago de Cuba, 1898   419
   b General Miles
   c General Brooke

13 Two U.S. Proconsuls: 482
   a General Wood
   b General Crowder

14 Four Cuban Presidents: 483
   a Estrada Palma, 1902–1906
   b José Miguel Gómez, 1909–1913
   c Mario García Menocal, 1913–1921
   d Alfredo Zayas, 1921–1925

15 a General Machado, President of Cuba 1925–1933   514
   b The Machados and the Calvin Coolidges, 1928
16 Sergeant Batista greets Dr Grau San Martín, 1933   515
17 a The Hotel Nacional   642
   b Colonel Batista, Dr Grau San Martín, Colonel Blas
      Hernández

18 Five U.S. Ambassadors: 643
   a Sumner Welles, 1933
   b Jefferson Caffery, 1933–1936
   c Arthur Gardner, 1953–1957
   d Earl Smith, 1957–1959
   e Philip Bonsal, 1959–1961

19 1952:   674
   a Batista comes in
   b Prío goes out

20 a Batista as President   675
   b Rolando Masferrer
   c Eddy Chibás

21 The Moncada attack: 930
   a Fidel Castro and other prisoners
   b The barracks after the attack

22 a The Sierra Maestra   931
   b The Rebels in their stronghold

23 Rebel Commanders: 962
   a Raúl Castro and 'Che' Guevara
   b Guevara later, as a Minister
   c Camilo Cienfuegos

24 The Honeymoon period, abroad and at home: 963
   a Castro and Nixon, Washington, April 1959
   b The first cabinet after the fall of Batista

25 Peasants come to Havana   1186

26 Interrogation of the prisoners after the Bay of Pigs   1187

27 U.2. photograph of missile base at San Cristóbal   1218

xvi · PLATES

28 The withdrawal of the missiles: 1219
   a The Soviet vessel *Fizik Kurchatov* at sea
   b The U.S. navy radar ship *Vesole* alongside the
      Soviet vessel *Volgoles*

29 Castro in the Plaza de la Revolución, 1964   1442

30 a Castro cuts cane, 1965   1443
   b Castro explains a new dam

31 Revolutionary Diplomacy: 1474
   a Castro in Russia, 1964
   b Castro with Le Thanh Nghi, 1967

32 View of Havana, 1962   1475

Acknowledgements for the Plates

Acknowledgements and thanks for permission to reproduce the photographs are due to the British Museum for plates 1 and 6; the Mansell Collection for plate 2; Goodwood House for plate 3a; the National Portrait Gallery for plate 3b; the National Maritime Museum for plate 3c; Lord Albemarle for plate 3d; Ampliaciones y Reproducciones MAS for plates 4a, 5a, 8b, 8d, 14c, 15a, 15b, 18c, 23c and 24b; Studio M Photography for plate 4b; the Radio Times Hulton Picture Library for plates 5b, 5c, 5d, 7c, 11b, 12b, 14d and 18a; The Polk Home for plate 7a; the New York Historical Review for plates 7b and 7d; Fine Art Engravings Ltd for plates 8a, 12c and 14a; Sr Guillermo Cabrera Infante for plates 9b and 22a; the Library of Congress for plate 10a; the Bettmann Archive Inc. for plates 10b and 12a; Acme Photography Inc. for plates 16 and 17b; United Press International Inc. for plates 18b, 18d, 18e, 20a, 22b and 28b; Associated Press Ltd for plates 19a, 20b and 23a; Pix Photography for plates 21a, 21b and 26; Camera Press Ltd for plates 23b and 30b; the Keystone Press Agency for plates 24a, 27, 30a and 31b; United Press International Ltd for plates 28a, 31a and 32; and Photo Pic (France) for plate 29.

MAPS

Endpaper – Cuba in relation to North and South America
    and the West Indies

1	Cuba	Page xxvi–vii
2	The English Capture of Havana, 1762	8–9
3	The Caribbean in 1796	14–15
4	Major Sugar Mills, *c.* 1860	138–9
5	The Atlantic Slave Trade, *c.* 1850	157
6	The War of 1868–1878	246
7	The War of 1895–1898	318
8	The Santiago Campaign, 1898	392
9	The Naval Battle of Santiago, 1898	394–5
10	Sugar Mills in the Banagüises Area, *c.* 1860	426–7
11	The Castro Country	806
12	Havana in the 1950s	865
13	The Sierra Maestra, 1956–1959	905
14	Sugar in 1959	1140–41
15	World Sugar, 1959	1156
16	Caribbean Populations, 1959	1194
17	The Bay of Pigs, 1961	1362
18	The Missile Crisis, 1962	1405

All the maps, including the endpaper, were drawn by William
Bromage

Cuba

or
The Pursuit of Freedom

PREFACE

I began to write this book on an evening in Havana in July 1961. I stood in the Plaza de la Revolución listening to a speech by Fidel Castro. The immense crowd were treating the occasion as a picnic, despite the sombre tones of the impassioned orator. Small boys sold drinks and hats from stalls and brilliantly dressed girls shook with pleasure as the 'maximum leader of the revolution' lashed himself into a fury against the government of President Kennedy. At about a quarter past eight in the evening, when the sun was beginning to die behind the statue to the Cuban liberator, José Martí, Castro's voice began to give out and it was clear that, though he had not finished his speech (it had by then lasted only four hours), he needed a rest. Doubtless by prearrangement with cheerleaders, the orator allowed one of his remarks to be drowned by shouts and the singing first of the Cuban national anthem, then of the International.

In the section of the crowd where I stood, a group of Cubans, some white, some mulatto, some Negro, a few women, began to sing and dance the International to a cha-cha-cha rhythm, the song itself being sung by a huge Negress in the centre, the choruses by a laughing circle round her. The words came over with bizarre syncopation, '*arriba hijos, de la tierra . . .*'. As André Breton years before said to the Cuban painter, Wilfredo Lam, '*Ce pays est vraiment trop surréaliste pour y habiter*'.

The consequence was that I, who had gone to Cuba that summer with the intention of writing a short book about the current scene, embarked on a longer project, in order to explore the springs of this curious event at which I had participated. In the course of the work, I extended the starting point further and further backwards; originally I had thought that the book should begin with Batista's *coup d'état* in 1952. But this seemed to miss too much and so I looked backwards further to that morning in January 1899 when the last Spanish Captain-General of Cuba sadly handed over power to an Anglo-Saxon, North American General. But that also omitted the absorbing question of slavery and how that decisively affected the character of Cuba, not to speak of the golden age of Cuban sugar in the nineteenth century; and so, after wondering whether there could be such a thing at all as a starting point to the book I had in mind (other than Columbus's journey to Cuba in 1492), I finally selected 1762, the year of the first Anglo-Saxon capture of Havana – a year of great importance in the history of Cuba and of the Spanish Empire, though just how important is controversial. Afterwards, it seemed to me in Cuba that this decision was wise since so much that seems obscure in the present Cuban scene becomes more comprehensible if set against the experiences of the previous four or five generations.

The outcome is a long book. Half of it, plainly, is history; but, in the second half, I enter upon contemporary politics, and by the time the Revolution of 1959 is reached I am in a no-man's-land between history, politics, sociology and journalism. This raises special questions: some will say that it is premature to write this part of the story, at least as 'history', since the necessary historical perspective does not exist. Of course it is harder to write of the recent past with an historian's eye than of a more distant time. But all happenings, from the moment they cease to be future possibilities, are historical events. Often, indeed, they are allowed to suffer from neglect for some decades before being subjected to historical attention. An event is often a wound which, temporarily bound up by the journalist as if he were a field doctor, is then allowed to wait, even to fester, till it is treated by the surgeon at the hospital, the 'professor of history'. As a result, a paradox arises: journalists and newspaper proprietors concern themselves with the immediate present and the future; historians prefer the safe frontiers of remoteness, where nearly all the facts seem at hand – or are irretrievably lost – and when those who played a part in the events described are dead and unable to answer. The recent past is thus often less studied than almost any other age.

This does not in general derive from any timidity on the part of historians. Much material, possibly crucial material, is indeed often not available. Would it not be better to wait, for that reason, it might be said, to write about the Revolution in Cuba till, say, the despatches of North American ambassadors in Havana are duly printed, along with Washington's replies and instructions; till all the Eisenhower, Dulles and Kennedy papers can be examined at ease in the cool libraries of still non-existent research foundations; and till the private papers of Fidel Castro and of the Cuban Communist Party, of the Soviet government, the files of several leading American companies, not to speak of the Central Intelligence Agency, may all be studied comparatively and without strong political bias, in the calm of some international Castro institute?

Yet, what is available is already considerable. The richness of newspaper material is great, and there is much material in articles, books, periodicals and pamphlets about the events in Cuba during and immediately before the Revolution. Some private papers have been available to me. There are also the memories of many of the leading actors in the events, and few of these are reluctant to talk of what they have seen or done. Many of the actors in the drama have unburdened themselves, to a lesser or a greater extent, particularly Fidel Castro, whose speeches have dealt not only with future plans but also, and often at length, with almost every aspect of his life and career – not dispassionately, but with much detail. A careful analysis of all published evidence, checked against the memory of a number of individuals and treated patiently, can now be made which, if still incomplete and tentative, must nevertheless be a contribution to knowledge.

The chief gaps, indeed, do not lie in lack of access to United States diplomatic papers, for the account of a revolution is not an essay in bureaucratic history. The gaps are on the Cuban and the Soviet side, and there is a strong possibility that these papers may never be available. It seems doubtful whether even the Cuban government archives document completely the change of life between the old and the new Cuba. Thus an historian in fifty years might be in the same position as a contemporary one, with the disadvantage that he will be less able to make up for documentary deficiencies by personal exploration. I hope, in short, that the last section of the book describing President Kennedy's unsuccessful expedition to Cuba in 1961 (if that is a fair way of describing it) is as respectable as that of Lord Albemarle's triumphant one two hundred years before. It is, of course, an illusion to suppose that history gives an answer to everything.

During the course of writing, the missile crisis of 1962 intervened; and this momentous event marks the terminal point of the main part of the book – appropriately so, since, if events even between 1959 and 1962 are difficult to disentangle, after 1962 it is difficult to be certain of anything. The hold of the present regime on the country seemed by then firm. The Revolution might not be complete but the revolutionaries were in power. 1962 also marks a date when Cuba's relations with the rest of the Americas, including the Caribbean, were quite cut; so that if Cuba had been a kingdom in an old-fashioned pantomime, the appealing programme note, *'During this act, the curtain will fall in order to indicate the passage of two hundred years,'* would be appropriate: for the old, closed empire of Spain has been substituted the new economic bloc directed by Russia; and statistics of Cuba since 1962 are almost as questionable as were those in the age of smuggling before 1762.

ACKNOWLEDGEMENTS

This book owes a great deal to many Cubans and others who in some cases have become friends. In the latter part of the book many of these have given actual historical evidence. Some of these informants remain anonymous for the purposes of their own safety or comfort, even though the anonymous reference, 'private information', may be irritating to the reader. However, I should like to thank them all for their assistance though probably few of them will entirely approve what I have written. When in Cuba, I should add, I have had the assistance of the press department of the Foreign Ministry and I am grateful to them.

I must also thank Mr Theodore Draper for most generously making available to me his own collection of Cuban newspapers, interviews and manuscript sources, in particular the unpublished memorials and papers of Dr Justo Carrillo, Sr Mario Llerena, Sr Raúl Chibas and Sr Luis Simón. This material, now deposited in the Hoover Library of War, Revolution and Peace, at Stanford, was originally intended for a book on the coming of the Cuban Revolution which was never written. Mr Cass Canfield, jr, of Harper & Row is in many ways the godfather of the book and I thank him for his valuable advice over several years.

Mr Theodore Draper, Mr Robin Blackburn, Dr Eric Jones, Dr E. A. Smith, Dr Alastair Hennessy, Mr Stephen Clissold, Dr Felipe Pazos, Dr Javier Pazos, Sr Guillermo Cabrera Infante, Sr Luis Anguilar Leon, Professor Arthur Schlesinger Jr and Lord Gladwyn all read part of the book in proof or MSS and made many valuable suggestions; I am very grateful to them. I am particularly grateful to Sr Cabrera Infante who is such a mine of information on so many aspects of Cuban history. Finally, I thank Mrs Hugh Pennant Williams, Mrs Janet Cory and Miss Griselda Grimond who typed the book at different stages and did much other work.

Hugh Thomas
London, April 1970

ABBREVIATIONS

The following abbreviations are used:

Foreign Relations : Foreign Relations of the U.S. (State Department Papers published annually)
HAHR : Hispanic American Historical Review
HAR : Hispanic American Report
PP : Parliamentary Papers (Commercial and consular reports)
PRO : Public Record Office, London
WB : World Bank (i.e. International Bank for Reconstruction and Development) Report on Cuba, 1952

The first reference to a work gives author, full title, and place and date of publication. Full references can be discovered thereafter by consulting the Bibliography (page 1579)

(Note on currencies)

In the earlier part of this book, where dollar, peso and sterling conversions are very unlike contemporary ones, the sterling and/or dollar equivalents are usually given to assist the reader. After about 1880 these conversions are not made, and the conventional equivalents should be reckoned.

HAVANA

Sabana Archip

Varadero
Cárdenas
La Isabel

Matanzas

San Cristóbal
Artemisa
Güines
Colón
Sagua
la Gr

D E L R I O

Surgidero
debatabano

Jagüey
Grande

San Juan
Martínez
Pinar del
Río

Santa Clara
Plac

La
Coloma

Cienfuegos

Nueva-
Gerona

Bay of
Cochinos

Sierra de
Escambray

Island
of
Pines

Trinidad

C A R I B B E A

CUBA

Principal roads
Railways

Miles
0   50   100

0   50   100
Kilometres

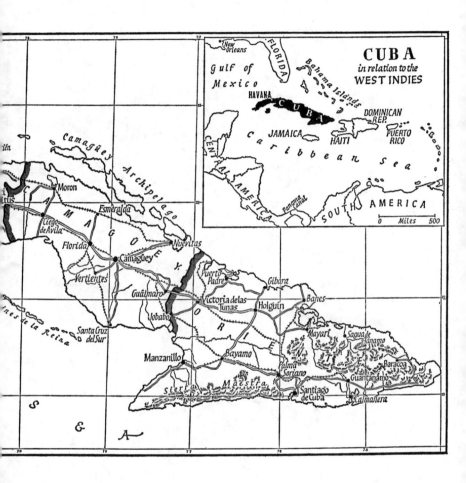

CUBA
in relation to the
WEST INDIES

New Orleans

Gulf of Mexico

FLORIDA

Bahama Islands

HAVANA

CUBA

DOMINICAN REP.

JAMAICA

HAITI

PUERTO RICO

CENTRAL AMERICA

Caribbean Sea

Panama Canal

SOUTH AMERICA

0   Miles   500

Camagüey   Archipelago

Moron

Esmeralda

Ciego de Avila

Florida

Nuevitas

Camaguey

Vertientes

Guáimaro

Jobabo

Puerto Padre

Gibara

Victoria de las Tunas

Holguin

Banes

Santa Cruz del Sur

Manzanillo

Bayamo

Mayari

Sagua de Tanamo

Palma Soriano

Baracoa

Guantánamo

Sierra Maestra

Santiago de Cuba

Caimanera

nes de la Reina

S   E   A

With Albemarle to Havana 1762

'The multitude of palm trees of various forms, the highest
and most beautiful I have ever met with, and an infinity
of other great and green trees; the birds in rich plumage
and the verdure of the fields; render this country, most
serene princes, of such marvellous beauty that it surpasses
all others in charms and graces as the day doth the night
in lustre. I have been so overwhelmed at the sight of so
much beauty that I have not known how to relate it.'

COLUMBUS
TO KING FERDINAND AND QUEEN ISABELLA, 1492

CHAPTER I

The English Expedition

'I own I am shock'd at the purchase of slaves,
And fear those who buy them and sell them are knaves;
What I hear of their hardships, their tortures and groans,
Is almost enough to draw pity from stones.
I pity them greatly but I must be mum,
For how could we do without sugar and rum?'
Pity for Poor Africans, WILLIAM COWPER (1788)

On 5 March 1762 an English expedition secretly left Portsmouth to capture Havana, capital of the Spanish colony of Cuba. It was the last campaign of a great war. England had won Canada and India from France. France, to stave off catastrophe, had badgered Spain to help her. England had declared war on Spain on 4 January.

Havana had been for two centuries the place of rendezvous for the Spanish treasure fleets from South and Central America. It was the military port of the New World; it was considered impregnable. It lay in a place of commanding importance in the Caribbean; and it had not been taken since being sacked by French pirates in the sixteenth century, though the English had mounted an unsuccessful attack twenty-one years before. With a population of thirty or forty thousand, larger than either Boston or New York, Havana was the third largest city of the New World, ranking after Lima and Mexico.[1] Its capture would strike a powerful blow at French morale and destroy Spanish imperial communication. It would interrupt the flow of bullion to Spain and France. Admiral Rodney had recently won several French islands in the Caribbean; his West Indian fleet was poised to capture Martinique.[2] Perhaps here then was a chance for the Caribbean islands to be united under a single, and English, flag.

Glory thus lay ahead of the English commanders, but also profit. Profit was a matter of concern to the English commander-in-chief on land, Lord Albemarle,[3] as it was to his younger brothers, Commodore

[1] The population of Spanish and Portuguese America was probably fifteen million in the 1760s, that of North America a mere one and a half to two million. That of Europe was perhaps a hundred and fifty million.

[2] George Brydges Rodney (1719–92), naval hero and prize-hunter, later Lord Rodney.

[3] George, third earl of Albemarle (1724–72), previously M.P. for Chichester, a borough controlled by his cousin the duke of Richmond.

Keppel and Major-General Keppel, who, by the happy fortune of eighteenth-century politics, were respectively second-in-command of the naval forces and one of the two divisional commanders on land.[4] Their father, an extravagant courtier, 'the spendthrift earl', had died after running through £90,000, leaving his sons only 'a house in the Hague let at £200 a year'.[5] But Albemarle was political secretary and 'chief favourite'[6] of the duke of Cumberland, King George's uncle, whose A.D.C. he had been at Fontenoy and Culloden;[7] he had a reputation, at least with General Wolfe, the recently dead hero of Quebec, of being 'one of those showy men who are seen in palaces . . . [who] never desires to see his regiment'.[8] His portraits by Reynolds, a family friend and protégé, show him to be plump, fair and unimaginative. But he was also brave and self-confident and Cumberland, thanks to the young King George III's respect for his uncle as a military authority (combined with dislike of him as a person and as a political influence), had been permitted to choose the officers for the expedition to Havana.[9] Albemarle was Cumberland's first choice, though he had never before held a field command. No doubt Cumberland thought him to be a good officer but his military qualities were, like Cumberland's own, conventional and European in outlook, and not easily adaptable to the amphibious and sub-tropical enterprise now embarked upon.

The spoils of a captured city were at that time paid to the captors in accordance with rank: the commander-in-chief might get a third of the profits, the rest being divided up. So the younger Keppels, as well as their brother, might expect rewards. The Commodore had, when fifteen years of age, sailed round the world with the legendary Anson. Helped on by Anson, but anyway resolute and decisive, he had commanded the English Mediterranean squadron when under thirty. In 1758, with an expedition which gave a foretaste of that against Havana, he had captured the French slave-trading station of Goree, off Senegal.[10] He

---

[4] Augustus, later Admiral Viscount Keppel (1725–86), and William Keppel (1727–82).
[5] *The House of Commons, 1754–90 (History of Parliament)*, ed. Sir Lewis Namier and John Brooke, 3 vols (1964), III, 11; G.E.C., *Complete Peerage*, Albemarle. The first Albemarle's fortune had included a legacy of 200,000 guilders from William III. The second Albemarle had been Cumberland's successor as commander-in-chief in Scotland after Culloden and twice ambassador in Paris.
[6] Horace Walpole, qu. Namier, *loc. cit.*
[7] William Augustus, duke of Cumberland (1721–65), the 'Butcher' of Culloden and after, abandoned military career, 1757.
[8] Robert Wright, *Life of Major-General James Wolfe* (1864), ch. ix.
[9] See G. T. Keppel, *Memoirs of the Marquess of Rockingham and his Contemporaries*, 2 vols (1852), by a nineteenth-century Lord Albemarle, I, 87.
[10] The prize money at Goree and Fort Louis totalled £20,000 but of course this had had to be divided up among the expedition (Elizabeth Donnan, *Documents illustrative of the slave trade to America*, 4 vols (Carnegie Institution, 1930), II, 513). Commodore Keppel had been an M.P. since 1755, at first for his brother's old seat at Chichester, then for Windsor, in Cumberland's interest.

deserved his post as second-in-command of the fleet, though Rodney, already in the West Indies, had strictly a better claim.[11] The third brother, Major-General William Keppel, though he had had a less dramatic life than his brothers, was also penniless.

Sir George Pocock, the commanding admiral of the expedition to Havana, was in less desperate financial straits than the Keppels.[12] Now fifty-six, he had seen forty-four years of hard fighting in the West and East Indies. He had just returned from India, and gained his command in the Havana expedition on his merits as did the second-in-command of the army, another veteran of Fontenoy, General George Eliott.[13]

Also attached to the expedition were a painter, Dominic Serres, who knew Havana and who was now commissioned to record in oil the victories which it was hoped would follow,[14] and John Kennion, a thirty-six-year-old Unitarian merchant of Liverpool and Jamaica, who as 'commissary' had secured the valuable contract of victualling, arming and clothing the expedition.[15] Such contracts were then the best way in England to make a great fortune as well as a great family, while Liverpool (partly through smuggling to Cuba and the Spanish empire in the preceding decades, partly through lower costs and closer access to the growing industrial centres of Lancashire and the Midlands) had already overtaken Bristol as the main English Atlantic and African port. Kennion then had a part share in about ten slave ships.[16] He played a minor part in Liverpool public life, having been trustee of the workhouse in 1750. Most of the big slave merchants of Liverpool, the premier slaving port of Europe, were men of greater consequence than

[11] Sir Julian Corbett, *England in the Seven Years War*, 2 vols (1907), II, 249. Keppel had been a member of the tribunal which tried poor Admiral Byng in 1757 and afterwards sought to secure him a pardon. A patron and friend of Sir Joshua Reynolds, Keppel took Reynolds on his ship when he was commander in the Mediterranean. The Keppel brothers were great-grandchildren of Charles II through their mother; their grandfather on the other side, the first earl of Albemarle, a Dutchman, had been a special friend of William III; and these facts, together with General Lord Albemarle's close attachment to the duke of Cumberland, gave the expedition to Havana a semi-royal flavour.

[12] Sir George Pocock (1706–92), M.P. for Plymouth, an Admiralty borough.

[13] George Eliott (1717–90), later defender of Gibraltar and made Lord Heathfield. An intelligent officer who had been educated at Leyden and La Fère.

[14] Dominic Serres (1722–93), born at Auch, Gascony. He had been captain of a French merchant ship in Havana and began his career as a maritime painter after his capture.

[15] John Kennion (1726–85), Jamaican landowner and afterwards Collector of Customs at Liverpool.

[16] The Liverpool register of shipping gives ten ships part-owned by Kennion and registered between 1748 and 1758. These vessels varied between 20 and 120 tons in weight. Three were French prizes from either the War of Austrian Succession or the Seven Years War. Even the smallest of these ships, the *Mercury* of 20 tons, carried a hundred slaves, according to Gomer Williams (*History of the Liverpool Privateers*, London 1897, 676). Kennion owned one of these ships as partner of the famous Samuel Touchet, who was himself separately represented in 1762 in Havana and for whom see below, p. 49 fn. 31. See also Holt and Gregson MSS., 335.

he, dominating the corporation as mayors and bailiffs, even as M.P.s.[17] Kennion, a Unitarian, was outside the inner group of mainly Anglican Liverpool merchants, and unconnected with them either by blood or apparently close financial association. He invested his profits from slave voyages neither in grand houses near Liverpool, nor canals or other industrial activity, as did many of his confrères;[18] he bought plantations in Jamaica, the main English sugar colony,[19] then at the peak of prosperity, the main-spring of English imperial wealth, sugar being then by far the largest English import.[20] In 1760 he had become a member of the Jamaica Council.[21]

The British government which dispatched the expedition to Havana was pacific. The great William Pitt, architect of earlier victories in the war, had resigned the previous autumn, since he had wished to strike at Spain there and then. The cabinet thereafter had been headed by the sixty-nine-year-old duke of Newcastle, master of political corruption, and the earl of Bute, the king's intimate friend; the former at least was inclined to peace at almost any price; Newcastle thought the expedition to Havana 'most *expensive*, hazardous, uncertain . . . when both men and ships are wanted elsewhere, a wild goose chase (as I now understand) afterwards, after Mexico, St Augustin [Florida] and God knows what'.[22]

These apprehensions were real, since Albemarle's instructions left

[17] At least sixty out of eighty-one mayors of Liverpool between 1726 and 1807 engaged in the slave trade as owners of slaveships. The rest almost certainly participated in its consequences in one way or another, supplying cord, wine, linen, wood, etc. The mayor in 1762–3 was William Gregson, later renowned as the notorious owner of the *Zong*.

[18] For instance, John Ashton, member of the Company of Merchants trading to Africa in 1752, had been in 1755 the financial backer of the first canal in England – the Sankey Brook Canal, from the Mersey to St Helens (see James Touzeau, *The Rise and Progress of Liverpool, 1551–1835*, 2 vols (1910), II, 498). Almost all the country houses just outside Liverpool (such as Everton House, Santo Domingo House, Walton Hall, etc.) were owned by merchants who had made money in the slave boom of the mid-eighteenth century.

[19] In 1765 his 'kinsman', Edward Kennion, a minor water-colourist who accompanied him, aged eighteen, on the Havana expedition, was looking after John Kennion's estates at Hallhead in St Thomas in Jamaica but these may have been bought after the Havana expedition. Nevertheless, in Albemarle's accounts Kennion is referred to as 'John Kennion of the Island of Jamaica' (*Documentos Inéditos sobre la toma de la Habana por los Ingleses en 1762* (1963), 53). It is typical of the attitude of nineteenth-century intellectuals towards trade, that the water-colourist appears in the *Dictionary of National Biography*, while the millionaire merchant does not.

[20] In 1755, the last year of peace, English sugar imports amounted to £M1.6 while its nearest rivals, tobacco and tea, reached only £460,000 and £400,000 respectively (*Abstract of British Historical Statistics*, ed. B. R. Mitchell and Phyllis Deane (1962), 286–8). British West Indian imports totalled £M1.9, compared with £M1.2 from Asia (including India), and a mere £986,000 from North America. R. B. Sheridan, 'The Wealth of Jamaica in the 18th Century: a rejoinder,' *Economic History Review*, 2nd series, XVIII (1965), 292–311, argues that the West Indies now provided at least 8% to 10% of British wealth – an argument he sustains in controversy with R. P. Thomas 'The sugar colonies of the old empire: Profit or loss for Great Britain' (*ibid.*, XXI (1968), 30.) Bristol merchants seem to have more often bought West Indian plantations than Liverpool ones, which were *nouveaux riches* in comparison.

[21] *Journal of the Commissioners for Trade and Plantations 1759–63*, 181.

[22] Newcastle to Lord Hardwicke, 12 February 1762, qu. Namier, *England*, 311.

him at liberty, after taking Havana, to go to Vera Cruz or any other part of the Spanish colonies and 'reduce all, or any, of the Said Places, to Our Obedience'.[23] Pitt perhaps wanted to take Panamá as well as Havana.[24] The decision for war, and to send the expedition at all, had been forced through by the military and naval commanders, men still in touch with Pitt, such as the great if aged admiral, Lord Anson, against the inclinations of the politicians who even doubted if they could thereby gain worthwhile bargaining counters at the peace conference, which they greatly hoped would not be long delayed: 'I never saw this nation so near its ruin as at present ... Peace, my dear Lord, is the only remedy ... victories hurt us, as they make the peace more difficult'. In this doubting mood did the English Prime Minister, the duke of Newcastle, dispatch this expedition.[25]

Five warships left Portsmouth with thirty transport ships (carrying 4,000 troops), nineteen supply ships, and eight bearing cannon. Many of the troops were veterans, at their head Guy Carleton, quartermaster to Wolfe at Quebec.[26] Off the Barbados, the commanders heard the news of Rodney's capture of Martinique.[27] But Rodney, against explicit instructions from the Admiralty, immediately dispersed his fleet, some ships sailing under Commodore James Douglas to comfort Jamaica (whose planters thought themselves about to be attacked by the French), some sailing south to seek more prizes.[28] Maybe Rodney so behaved from pique at not having gained the command given to Commodore Keppel, an attitude no doubt increased when Pocock took from him his flagship, the *Marlborough*. At Barbados meantime the fleet picked up 11,000 gallons of rum, 100 hogshead of claret and 900 casks of wine with some beef, and sailed on[29] – a gallon of rum per soldier, 500 gallons of wine per officer. Off Hispaniola, Albemarle and Pocock were joined by a contingent from Jamaica, including 700 Negroes, under Commodore Douglas with nine of Rodney's ships of the line, including

---

[23] Secret Instructions for ... Ld Albemarle, 15 Day of February 1762 (CO 117/1, f. 29).

[24] Richard Pares, *War and Trade in the West Indies*, new edn. (1963), 582.

[25] Qu. Namier, *England*, 293, 307.

[26] Guy Carleton (1724–1808), later general, governor of Quebec and first Lord Dorchester.

[27] The route had been carefully worked out before the expedition left London (see instructions to Pocock, 18 February 1762, ADM 2/1332, 25–33). The plan for the attack on Havana was that of Anson, based on ideas of Sir Charles Knowles (d. 1777) who had led the unsuccessful expedition of 1741 and who later, when governor of Jamaica, had been round Havana's defences (Corbett, II, 246).

[28] See ADM 1/237 and 1/307, May 1762. James Douglas (1703–87) was, like Keppel, Pocock and Rodney, an M.P.; like Keppel, he had sat in judgment on Byng. Later admiral and baronet. (Orders to Rodney, *ibid.* 2/1332, 17.)

[29] And paid Mr Gedney Clarke the sum of £7,819 7s 0d for it. Rum was 3d a gallon. (*Cf. Documentos Inéditos*, 41.) Clarke had wide interests, being regarded as the father of British planting, of sugar cane in the colony of Demerara (Guiana). See Noël Deerr, *The History of Sugar*, 2 vols (1949, 1950), 209–10. See also Richard Pares, 'A London West India Merchant House', *Essays presented to Sir Lewis Namier*, 80 (1956).

the *Dragon* under Captain Augustus Hervey, an old companion of Keppel's in the English Channel and Belle Isle in 1758 and 1760.[30] These reinforcements included a number of slaves to work for the army.[31]

The main danger to the Havana expedition now was a French fleet under Admiral Blénac[32] (almost the last French squadron then at sea anywhere) which had sailed from France to try to prevent the capture of Martinique: the French, unlike the English, did not keep a fleet permanently in the West Indies. But Blénac had many sick. He was angry that the Spaniards showed no sign of helping him and so he did not move from Cap François, the capital city of the rich French colony of Saint Domingue. He had been ordered to cooperate with the Spaniards and try to conquer Jamaica. This might have been possible (Jamaica being poorly defended) had he acted firmly, before the English fleet from home joined with that already in the West Indies. He failed to do this.[33] The English fleet sailed between him and Cuba, and then along the north coast of Cuba westward to Havana.

This route – which was not the usual southerly one, with a rendezvous at Port Royal, Jamaica, but a difficult east–west journey through the Bahama Sound – had the advantage of surprise.

On 6 June Albemarle began to land troops at the mouth of the river Cojímar, fifteen miles east of Havana, being covered at sea by his brother the commodore. Pocock carried on with the main fleet towards the harbour of Havana, and effected a simple decoy west of the city to divert attention from Albemarle's activities. This scheme worked well. A Spanish force under Colonel Caro set off in pursuit of Pocock, while Albemarle's army landed without opposition.

The captain-general of Cuba, Juan de Prado,[34] held a hasty war council in Havana on the night of 6 June. He had heard of the proximity of the English expedition for the first time only a day or two before, from a Spanish frigate which escaped into the little port of Matanzas. Even then Prado had not taken the rumour seriously; no one thought that a major English fleet could go through the Bahama Sound. Present at the war council were the retiring viceroy of Peru, the Conde de Superunda, and the retiring governor of Cartagena (Colombia), Diego de Tabares, who both chanced to be in Havana on their way to Spain. Their presence was expressive of the immense slowness of imperial com-

---

[30] Augustus Hervey (1724–79), later third earl of Bristol, son of Lord Hervey of Ickworth, the gossip; husband of the notorious Elizabeth Chudleigh. Like other commanders on this expedition, Hervey was an M.P., for the family seat of Bury St Edmunds. 'Active and brave but reckless and over confident', was a contemporary verdict.

[31] *Journal of the Commissioners for Trade and Plantations 1759–63*, 299.

[32] Admiral Jean Sophie Courbon, Comte de Blénac (1710–66).

[33] Pares, *War and Trade in the West Indies*, 592.

[34] Juan de Prado y Malleza Portocarrero (1716–c. 1770). He had been captain-general since 1760.

munication in Spanish America: Tabares had left Cartagena in August 1761; Superunda had been ordered home as early as June 1760 and had received the order in April 1761. Both had been waiting in Havana for months for an escort to take them home to Spain. The admiral in command at Havana, the Marqués del Real Transporte,[35] and the captains of the twenty ships in the harbour, of which only twelve were 'of the line', were also present at this council.

The council decided to block the entrance of Havana harbour with two large ships, and to use the sailors and the guns on them and on other vessels to reinforce the land defences. The Spanish fleet would thus not sally out and engage the English, who were accordingly left to choose their own time for their attack, and to let reinforcements arrive. Although timid, this plan was in keeping with orders received by Real Transporte in November.[36] The Spanish decision was influenced by the presence in the harbour of a hundred merchant vessels, a rich haul to lose in any war.[37]

The Spanish command placed their hopes, then, on defence, to be conducted by 3,000 regular soldiers (the garrison had been reduced by yellow fever the previous year), 9,000 sailors (of whom only a few would stay on the boats) and perhaps 15,000 militia; but, when it came to the test, the militia did not number more than 3,000, and only 2,000 muskets were available,[38] though there were a number of machetes and pikes. Many militiamen were Negro or mulatto, and Captain-General Prado also armed many slaves and promised them their freedom if they fought.[39] (The promise was kept.) The Spaniards decided to defend with cannon the long ridge, known as La Cabaña, which commanded Havana, falling back on El Morro, a castle on the seaward end built in the 1590s as a defence against Sir Francis Drake.

Albemarle proceeded slowly from Cojímar, his delay being due to outbreaks of malaria and dysentery. Though General Eliott captured Guanabacoa, a village some miles beyond the eastward head of Havana Bay, Albemarle was expecting a siege, not a *coup de main*, and prepared battery engines. Only on 1 July, nearly a month after landing, was an attack made in earnest and perhaps only then because Albemarle feared the loss of all his men from disease if he did not act soon. English

[35] Gutierre de Hevia y Bustamente (1720–72); he was also Vizconde Buen Viaje. He had been given these silly titles for escorting Charles III from Naples to Spain two years earlier.
[36] Cesáreo Fernández Duro, *Armada española desde la unión de los reinos de Castilla y de León*, 9 vols (1895–1903), VII, 43. Later orders to Havana had been intercepted by Rodney and indeed Havana only heard of the declaration of war by the chance of getting a copy of the *Gaceta de Madrid* containing the news.
[37] Admiral Pocock's report, ADM 1/237, 19 August 1762.
[38] See the discussion of these figures in Jacobo de la Pezuela, *Sitio y Rendición de la Habana en 1762* (1859), 24; and Corbett, 269, fn.
[39] José Antonio Saco, *Historia de la esclavitud de la raza africana en el nuevo mundo* (1879), I, 317.

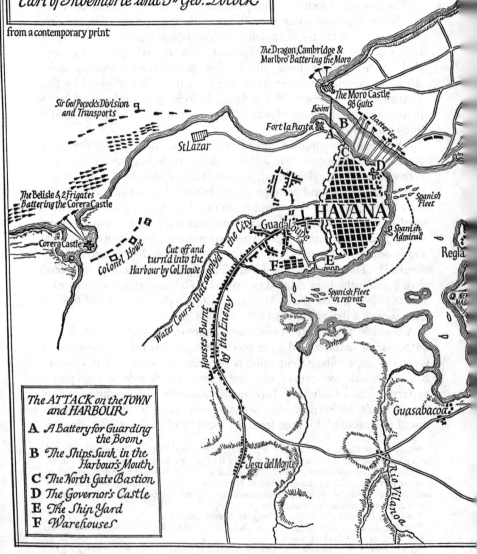

THE CAPTURE OF HAVANA, 13ᵗʰ August, 1762

by the BRITISH FORCES
under the Command of the
Earl of Albemarle and Sʳ Geo: Pocock

from a contemporary print

The Dragon, Cambridge & Marlbro' Battering the Moro

The Moro Castle 98 Guns

Sir Geo Pocock's Division and Transports

Boom

Fort la Punta

Batteries

St Lazar

The Belisle & 2 Frigates Battering the Corera Castle

Corera Castle

Colonel Howe

Cut off and turn'd into the Harbour by Col. Howe

Water Course that supply'd the City

Guadaloupe

HAVANA

Spanish Fleet

Spanish Admirall

Regla

Houses Burnt by the Enemy

Spanish Fleet in retreat

Guasabacoa

Jesu del Monte

Rio Vilaroa

The ATTACK on the TOWN and HARBOUR

A A Battery for Guarding the Boom
B The Ships Sunk in the Harbour's Mouth
C The North Gate Bastion
D The Governor's Castle
E The Ship Yard
F Warehouses

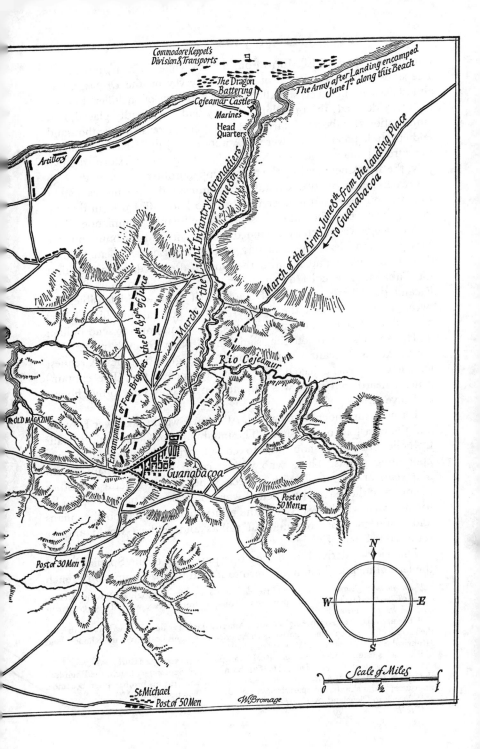

Commodore Keppel's
Division & Transports

The Army after Landing encamped
June 7th along this Beach

The Dragon
Battering

Cojeamar Castle

Marines

Head
Quarters

Artillery

March of the Army June 8th from the landing Place
to Guanabacoa

June 8th

March of the Light Infantry & Grenadiers

Rio Cojeamur

OLD MAGAZINE

Encampment of Four Brigades. the 6th & 9th of June

Guanabacoa

Post of
50 Men

Post of 30 Men

N

W   E

S

Post of
50 Men

St Michael
Post of 50 Men

W. Bromage

Scale of Miles

0   ½   1

warships bombarded El Morro from the sea while the army advanced. The ships drew a good deal of the fire. Hervey on the *Dragon*, while almost destroyed, suavely signalled that he had been 'often duller', but still the army delayed; the breaching battery had been badly placed, and ammunition was short. Malaria and dysentery increased. Five thousand soldiers and 3,000 sailors were sick about 25 July.[40] Reinforcements came from Jamaica and from New York.[41] El Morro was stormed on 30 July, the attack being led by the third Keppel brother, William, through a breach made by two carefully laid mines: the Spaniards fought gallantly but were outnumbered. They too had suffered from disease. Perhaps 200 were killed in the assault.[42] The Spanish commander, Luis de Velasco,[43] was mortally wounded with his second-in-command, the Marqués González. The next day or two the English spent lobbing shells into Havana and counting their losses, afterwards moving against La Cabaña. The chief of engineers, a French technician, Baltasar Ricaud de Tirgale, reported Havana itself as now indefensible. Between 1 and 7 August the Spanish captain-general and his advisers decided on surrender and made hasty but vain attempts to send bullion in Havana elsewhere on the island or to other Spanish possessions. On 11 August Havana was surrounded by English batteries. A request for surrender was rejected. The batteries opened fire. The captain-general heard that there was ammunition for only four to five hours; and gave in.[44]

Terms of surrender were agreed. Albemarle would take over Havana and the west part of the island. The inhabitants of Cuba could remain Catholic but the bishop had to consult with the governor before appointing priests. Those who wished could return to Spain within four years or become English subjects. The captain-general and other members of the Havana council of war would be sent back to Spain by frigate. Men who had served in the militia would be reckoned civilians and could therefore remain, but sailors and soldiers would also be returned to Spain.[45]

This victory derived from the ill-preparedness of the Spaniards and the lack of men and ammunition. Prado had had with him two French

---

[40] *An Authentic Journal of the Siege of the Havana*, by an officer (1762). As Raymond Carr, *Spain 1808–1939* (1966), 384, fn., points out, casualties from disease were always greater in colonial wars than from battle.

[41] The arrival of troops from English North America has led zealous U.S. writers to attribute the success of the expedition to 'native-born Americans' (*cf.* publications of the Rhode Island Historical Society, new series, V, 1, April 1898).

[42] Pocock's estimate was 1,000, but Real Transporte reported 132 (Duro, 65).

[43] Luis Vicente de Velasco Isla (1711–62), born at Noja, Santander; fought the English in the war of 1739–48. After his death he became a Spanish hero; his brother Iñigo became a marquess; and a ship of the Spanish navy has always since been called Velasco.

[44] Pocock to Cleveland, ADM 1/237.

[45] *Ibid.*

engineers and careful directions for the defence of Havana. But nothing had been done. Spain had been preparing for war for years but had wasted them. On return to Spain, Prado and his colleagues of the war council were brought before a tribunal as scapegoats; Prado was condemned to death for negligence but this sentence was commuted to ten years of exile, loss of employment and all rights. He died in disgrace.[46]

[46] His trial is summarized in Duro, 75 ff.

CHAPTER II

The Spanish Colony

Since he arrived in the hot season and since he, like most of his men, was sick, Albemarle did not leave any such lyrical expressions of pleasure as Columbus had when he first saw the island. Cuba had not, however, changed much in two and a half centuries: the Spanish empire as a whole had indeed 'developed with a truly majestic slowness'. Perhaps a quarter of the population of Cuba in 1762 lived in the city of Havana.[1] For a hundred and fifty years, the four to five thousand sailors of the Spanish grand fleet had waited at Havana for about six weeks a year, in order to meet the treasure ships bearing half the world's precious metals, coming from Vera Cruz or Portobello, and to escort them back through the Bahama Channel to Seville or Cádiz.[2] Havana was also a shipyard, building small ships as auxiliaries to the Cádiz fleet, and a purveyor of food – salt beef, green vegetables and fruit for the homeward journey.[3] These commercial activities had given Havana its special character. When this grand fleet arrived, uncontrolled gambling had been allowed, brothels sprang up, the rate of crime rose. The city (which had a permanent garrison of Spanish soldiers) seemed truly the 'boulevard of the New World', as the Abbé Raynal[4] had put it; 'one of the gayest and most picturesque [ports] on the shore of equinoctial America', as Baron Humboldt would later do so, filled with riff-raff, deserters, escaped slaves, gamblers, escaping crooks, sailors looking for ships, prostitutes for sailors, and 'friars without fixed destination'. The regular sailing of the fleet had admittedly ceased fifty years before and attempts to revive the old timetables had failed. But Havana was still a military port and had already that unique, easy-going, brilliant but semi-criminal, maritime and cosmopolitan character that has marked it ever since. The *habaneros* seemed to a North American, Major

[1] The census of 1774 gave Havana province a population of 75,618 out of 172,620. The white population of Havana was 43,392, the slave, 21,291. Havana and suburbs were 50,000 in 1792.

[2] The average stay was forty-four days, the longest 198. (Figures for 1561–1650 in H. and P. Chaunu, *Séville et l'Atlantique (1504–1650)* (1956), VI, 280.) Cádiz had been the official port of the Spanish Indies since 1680, when it was recognized that Seville was drying up.

[3] C. H. Haring, *Trade and navigation between Spain and the Indies in the time of the Hapsburgs*, (1918), 268; Heinrich Friedländer, *Historia económica de Cuba* (1944), 22.

[4] Guillaume Raynal (1713–96), author of *L'histoire philosophique et politique des établissements et du commerce des Européens dans les deux Indes* (Amsterdam, 1776); philosopher and liberal.

Gosham, who came in with Albemarle, to be 'as bad a Mongrel Crew perhaps as any on earth'.[5] They had, however, the grace of diversity: unlike the British islands of the West Indies, there was a large free mulatto or Negro community in Cuba – in Havana reaching 10,000, a third of the mulatto or Negro population of the city. Such things must have seemed specially odd to Major Gosham, since in some colonies in English North America there was severe legislation against 'miscegenation' and there were few free Negroes.

Havana was walled, and built like most Spanish-American cities round a central Plaza de Armas. There was as yet no cathedral, though plans for one existed; when in Havana, the bishop (whose seat was in Santiago) preached in a parish church of mixed date, partly sixteenth-century. But there were several imposing religious buildings, built with stone brought from Mexico, most already battered by storms and hurricanes so that they appeared very ancient, the wood dampened, the copper turned green, and which were filled with wounded after the fall of Havana: Santo Domingo, the Dominican monastery (described in a list of ecclesiastical houses in the city prepared for the English as 'rich'), which had been founded in the late sixteenth century; the similarly 'rich' nunnery of Santa Catalina, whither rich girls could flee the world, built in the late seventeenth century; a tall-towered 'poor' Franciscan convent which, begun in the sixteenth century, was only finished in the 1730s and was damaged in the siege (this had been the burial place of rich Havana families for several generations; Albemarle used it later as a barracks). There was a second, 'very, very rich' Franciscan monastery, and a 'very poor' Belemite one with a school (later taken over by the Jesuits),[6] and another older, 'rich' convent, dedicated to Santa Clara, in whose cemetery most of the dead were buried after the fall of Havana in 1762. Havana had a university, founded in 1728 by the Dominicans, which, like all eighteenth-century universities, was far from enlightened; the professor of mathematics taught 'astronomy and its consequences for Our Lord and King'; his Chair was often vacant. Mulattoes and Negroes, slave and free, were, like Jews and Moors, excluded, though some free mulattoes avoided this regulation.[7] There was also a Jesuit college, of San Ambrosio and San Ignacio, attached to the Jesuit monastery, and founded on the wreck of various older schools, victims of quarrels between the Jesuits and the other orders. The most beautiful church in Havana was that of

[5] That is, *mestizos* (mixture of whites and Indians); *mulattos* (or *pardos*) (whites and blacks); *zambos* (blacks and Indians); and many varieties of the white-black mixture, quadroons and octaroons. (*Cinco diarios del sitio de la Habana* (1963), 198.)

[6] Afterwards the famous Jesuit school of Belén.

[7] Several eighteenth-century instances have been dug out of the Archivo de Indias by Herbert S. Klein, *Slavery in the Americas* (1967), 207–8.

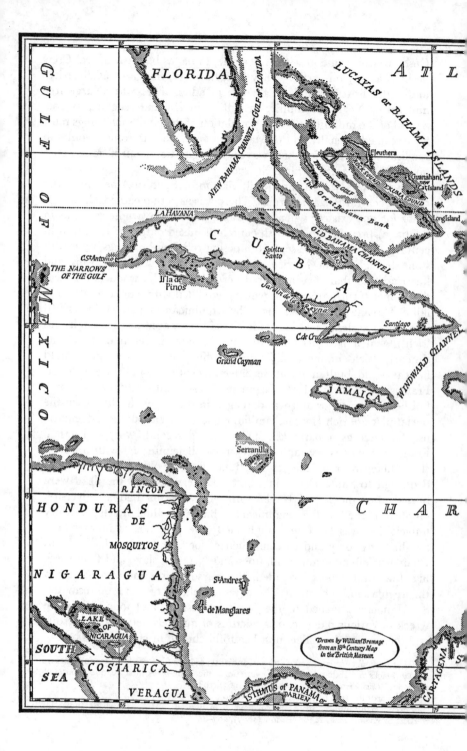

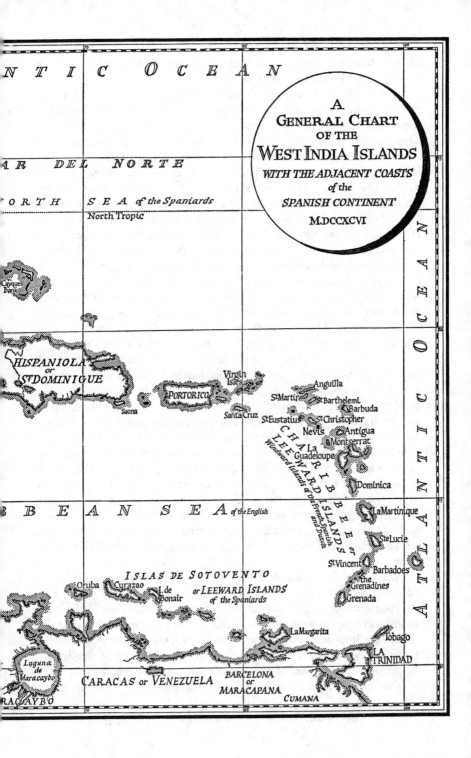

NTIC OCEAN

A GENERAL CHART OF THE WEST INDIA ISLANDS WITH THE ADJACENT COASTS of the SPANISH CONTINENT M.DCCXCVI

AR DEL NORTE

ORTH SEA of the Spaniards

North Tropic

Cayque Bank

HISPANIOLA or St DOMINIGUE

Saona

PORTORICO

Virgin Isles

Santa Cruz

Anguilla

St Martin St Barthelemi Barbuda

St Eustatius St Christopher

Nevis Antigua Montserrat

La Guadeloupe

CHARIBBEE LEEWARD ISLANDS Windward Islands of the French, Spanish and Dutch

Dominica

BBEAN SEA of the English

La Martinique

Ste Lucie

St Vincent Barbadoes the Grenadines

ISLAS DE SOTOVENTO or LEEWARD ISLANDS of the Spaniards

Oruba Curazao I. de Bonair

Grenada

La Margarita

Tobago

LA TRINIDAD

Laguna de Maracaybo

RACAYBO

CARACAS or VENEZUELA BARCELONA or MARACAPANA

CUMANA

ATLANTIC OCEAN

the hospital of San Francisco de Perla, which had a fine dome like that of the church of La Misericordia in Mexico.

A Belgian had set up a printing press in Havana in 1723, and one or two other presses existed. There were as yet no newspapers but a few poems and pamphlets occasionally appeared, and some of the quite large number of Spanish periodicals were sometimes distributed.

Outside Havana, several churches were of interest; thus the architect Hernández, of the parish church at Guanabacoa, the village captured by General Eliott, had begun to span naves by transverse arches covered with panelling. Cuban churches also often had unusual pyramidical stone spires, with arched dormer windows projecting from the bays, as in the famous church of La Merced in Puerto Príncipe.[8] Cuba had, however, far fewer buildings of quality than, for instance, Mexico or Peru, with their innumerable baroque churches and pre-Columbian monuments. Apart from churches, the interesting buildings of the island were indeed mainly forts, the characteristic Caribbean architecture, dominating the cities, which were thus products of European military engineering: El Morro, the sixteenth-century place of battle in 1762 and badly battered in the siege; San Diego, in ruins along the Havana river; La Fuerza, in Havana itself, begun in 1538, the 'oldest inhabited building in the New World', the residence of the Spanish governor and from whose eyelet windows, in the sixteenth century, the wife of Hernando de Soto watched for three years while waiting vainly for her husband to return from his discovery of the Mississippi; and La Punta, opposite El Morro on the other side of the harbour, beyond the city walls, built in the 1630s. The most opulent edifice in Cuba was however the cathedral at Santiago, seat of the bishopric of the island, built in the sixteenth century; there was also a cathedral at Puerto Príncipe, the work being still under way though begun in 1616. The most important shrine, that of Our Lady of Charity at El Cobre, the copper mine near Santiago, was simple, being stone with a cedar-wood roof, a single nave and blue and white tiles on the floor.

Such were the monuments of the island now penetrated by the English: a few towers rising above walled cities, most of whose back streets, unpaved, unlit and uncleaned, might seem familiar in the 1960s to anyone who walks about the slums of South American capitals. But there were important differences; thus the cities were planned. The cities of British North America rose to serve the countryside; in the Spanish empire the population of the countryside grew to answer the needs of the cities.[9] The cities of Spanish America (unlike those of the

[8] Now known as Camagüey.
[9] Bernard Moses, *Spanish Dependencies in South America*, 2 vols (1914), II, 370.

Anglo-Saxon north) were built according to specific architectural rules,[10] the church here, the plaza there: for safety, few buildings straggled outside the city walls. The whitewashed houses with red-tiled roofs were more reminiscent of Andalusia than of North America. There were in Havana perhaps fifty grandees' houses resembling those of Seville, with large courtyards, carved *mudéjar* ceilings and heavy doors, the oldest owned by the Sotolongos and the Recios who had founded Havana in the sixteenth century; within, a count and his family, his slaves, his bastards and cousins of various shades (each, in contrast to British North America, with precise names for their precise shades), would live most of the year – though their income derived, as in Spain, from the largely unknown and despised countryside. The strait-laced North American Major Gosham in 1762 found these people 'indolently fond of rich and gaudy furniture and apparel'.[11] The houses of Havana had on the other hand seemed to Sir Charles Knowles in 1756 to 'stand thick and well built'.[12] The most ambitious of these houses were the fine mid-eighteenth-century palaces in what is now the Cathedral Square, such as the great house of José Pedroso, today known as the Palacio de Lombillo.[13] There was much dirt in the muddy streets and disease, especially yellow fever, in the houses. Baron Humboldt in 1800 found that 'the multitude of *caleches* or *volantes* [the large-wheeled carriage characteristic of Cuba], of carts loaded with casks of sugar and porters elbowing passengers, rendered walking most disagreeable. The smell of *tasajo* [jerked beef] often poisons the houses and the winding streets'.[14] At night, wild dogs and runaway slaves would try to enter the city to search through garbage for food; few people after dark would go into the streets unarmed, or without a lantern and escort.

Beyond the walls of Havana and the few other such smaller cities lay a largely virgin countryside. Over half the island (an eighth smaller

[10] 'In inland towns the main plaza should be in the centre of the town and of an oblong shape, its length being equal to at least 1½ times its width, as this proportion is best for festivals in which horses are used and any other celebrations ... the plaza is to be planned with reference to the possible growth of the town. It shall not be smaller than 200 ft wide and 300 ft long or bigger than 800 ft long and 300 ft wide. A well-proportioned, medium-size plaza is 600 ft long by 400 ft wide. The four principal streets are to leave the plaza from the middle of each of its sides and two streets are to meet at each of its corners. The four corners of the plaza are to face the four points of the compass, so that the streets leaving the plaza will not be exposed to the four principal winds. The plaza and the four main streets leading off it are to have arcades for convenience of trade', etc. (Ordinance of Philip II, 3 July 1573, *Contribuciones a la Historia Municipal de América*, 18, qu. *Documents of West Indian History*, vol. 1, 1492–1655, ed. Eric Williams (1963), 192.)

[11] Gosham, *Diary*, in *Cinco Diarios*, 198.

[12] *Documentos Inéditos*, 187.

[13] Because it later passed to the Lombillo family. José Pedroso, brother of the merchant and *regidor perpetuo*, Mateo Pedroso, became attorney-general (*sindico procurador*) in 1763.

[14] Alexander von Humboldt and Bonpland, *Personal narrative of travels to the equinoctial regions of The New Continent, 1799–1804*, trans. T. Ross, 3 vols (1852–3), 157. Humboldt (1769–1859) was in Cuba between 1800 and 1801.

than England in extent, though longer and narrower) was forest, with many fine trees – cedar, mahogany, other cabinet woods and some pines, though much cedar and mahogany had been either used for ships or exported to Spain, particularly in the 1580s, to provide furniture and panelling for the Escorial or doors for San Francisco el Grande in Madrid, and not replaced. There were many wild fruit trees – mangoes and oranges (both originally imported from Europe or Africa), lemons, pineapples, bananas, along with wild indigo and cotton – and everywhere, over forests and plantations, marvellous royal palms sixty to eighty feet high, a tree very useful as well as beautiful since the heart at the centre of the palm makes a good salad, and since the seeds can be used for feeding pigs or as a substitute for coffee. The trunks form natural thin boards for use in houses, and the branches can be used for roofs and the fibre in them for string.

There were a few ranges of mountains in Cuba such as the 150-mile-long Sierra Maestra, near Santiago in the east; the Sierra de Escambray, in the south near Trinidad; and the Sierra de Organos in the west; these were forested. The highest mountain, Pico Turquino in the Sierra Maestra, rose a mere 6,000 feet. The soft, though rich, vegetation was reflected by the fauna: there were no snakes or large wild animals and few big reptiles, apart from occasional crocodiles in the marshes along the south coast. There were, however, deer, parrots, green pigeon, cuckoos, owls, wild duck, humming birds and vultures, hawks and buzzards. The worst natural enemies were the small sand fly (*jején*), the mosquito, the biggest local ant (*bibijagua*) and the scorpion.

Rainfall was constant and there were few droughts. East Cuba was often ravaged by hurricanes, but the rain did not often wash soil away completely as occurred in similar latitudes in Africa. The Cuban climate was equable, save for the summer, the time when Albemarle arrived, when it became humid and stormy. For the rest of the year the sky was blue and the heat rarely troublesome. It was not usually as hot as Seville can be in the summer. Although Spaniards were less interested in natural beauties than the English, even their stony imaginations were excited by Havana sunsets, dropping over the ocean skyline like a vast red sail. (The ocean itself is often obscured from the main island, for Cuba is an archipelago more than a single island, with a long indented coast with a thousand offshore coral islands and keys.)

There were no good roads in Cuba. Communication was mostly by sea, though a postal service went once a month from Havana to Santiago. This journey took the postman fourteen days, changing horses. (The first general post office had been inaugurated only seven years before, in 1755, by the *correo mayor*, postmaster-general, José Cipriano de La Luz, in a suite of rooms in his own house.) The countryside had few inhabitants. Probably less than a tenth of the total population remained there all the time. Even the overall density of population was only about three to the square mile – smaller than any country in the world in 1960 save for Australia. Those who did live in the country were escaped slaves, primitive Indians, tobacco farmers with their servants and families; the slaves who worked on the few sugar plantations, their overseers and, occasionally, their owners; and a number of cattle ranchers where these were not rich enough either to go over to sugar production or to build houses in Havana.

Of these, the last had been politically and socially the most important for generations. Lacking good maps, regular landholding habits and articulate knowledge of the country, the Spanish Crown had devised in the sixteenth century a simple method of giving the land in the Caribbean to their followers. Grants (*mercedes*) were made in the form of circles:[15] a proprietor was allotted land to a certain radius from a given point. The proprietor received the usufruct of the land on condition that he provided the nearby town or settlement with the beef it needed and maintained an inn in the centre of the circle. These circles of land were therefore less grants of property than plans for food. But they did not suffice. Other enticements to settlers were prepared: lands, tax rebates, animals, farm buildings, and prizes for the first Spaniard who grew a new crop in the island. Few Spaniards came, for there was also a shortage of labour in Spain; the indentured labourer of the English colonies had no Spanish equivalent. Then disputes began as to where one grant-in-circle ended, where another started. Many grants were vague in territorial definition. Some had ambiguous radii, such as the distance that a cow bell or a cock crow could be heard. Titular owners without land squabbled with cultivators without title. Attempts to rationalize the matter – such as by squaring the circle, with sixty-four sides – succeeded only in giving money to clerks. Divisions of lands in circles, small or large (*corrales* or *hatos*), continued to be granted,

---

[15] Roughly, of three types: the *hato*, for cattle, of two leagues' radius; *corrales*, for pigs, of one league radius; and *estancias*, for minor activities which might be established within the other larger areas. All were known as *haciendas* or farms. Land was originally granted in terms of what was usually needed for a specific amount of produce or cattle-grazing; for example, 'pasture-land for 10 breeding pigs, 20 cows, 5 mares, 100 sheep and 20 goats'. These livestock, together with land 'adequate to grow 100 *fanegas* (hundredweight) of wheat and barley and 10 of maize, 2 *huebra* (the approximate amount of land which 2 yoke of oxen could cover in a single day = 1 *huebra*) for market gardening and 8 for trees', were regarded as adequate to support a '*peón*' – literally, an ex-infantry man or common soldier, hence any common man who wanted to set up on his own account (*cf.* 'pawn'). This land was known as *peonía*. A gentleman (*caballero*) would get a *caballería* of land, five times larger than a *peonía*. But this system of distribution of land never got under way. The Spanish colonisers were interested in cattle, not agriculture. The *peonía* and *caballería* disappeared, though the word *caballería* survives as the most frequently used Cuban measure of land, equivalent to 33⅓ acres, rather smaller than the sixteenth-century *caballería* (and also different from the *caballería* elsewhere in Spanish America).

despite this, until the eighteenth century. A map of Cuba which marks the *mercedes* shows some circles overlapping, some tangential to each other, some inside each other. Many ranches were never surveyed.

These circular grants made a lasting impression on Cuban geography. Any detailed map even of twentieth-century Cuba shows how farms, roads, city boundaries, have been determined by these circles. Towns still appear at the centre of circles; paths or cart tracks resemble ring roads. Further, the grants were made to all descendants of a particular person, as holdings in common: therefore all the heirs, generation after generation, assumed the use of the land, sometimes all trying to live in the central house, more often establishing houses at different points, though all sharing in the profits of the whole estate.

The segments of land which were not granted between circles re-mained technically with the Crown, a so-called *realengo*; and until the late 1720s, the city councils (*cabildos*) could dispose of this land to a likely applicant on the payment of an appropriate tax. Then the confusion became so great that the Council of the Indies took over the task. Finally, eight years before the fall of Havana to Albemarle, the captain-general took over the impossible responsibility (acting on behalf of the court of Audiencia in Santo Domingo). Meantime, many squatters settled in the *realengos* without money or will to secure a formal grant, gaining from their farms a bare living without any incentive to improve them.[16] Thirty years later, the king of Spain's chief administrative officer in Cuba, the *intendente*,[17] was asked by Madrid whether it would not be wise to have the island surveyed and to delineate clearly what land belonged to the king and what to this or that Cuban landholder. The *intendente* replied that the idea was 'useless, prejudicial and terrible'; there were of course many boundary disputes, but most of them were dormant; a great survey would lead to trouble and bloodshed; the expense and the confusion would be enormous; it would take three months to survey a single *hato*.

These *haciendas* [he added] have no visible demarcations or boundaries other than some prominent trees and on one side or the other the sea, a river or a brook or some other natural mark. In the centre there is a house of wood, mud or straw which is called the seat of the ranch and usually the hand of man is seen in nothing else.

---

[16] All these grants were made without prejudice to woods, meadows, allotments, etc., around established villages or towns, which were in various ways farmed in common. See D. C. Corbitt, 'Mercedes and realengos', *Hispanic American Historical Review*, XIX (1939), 262–85; and Franscisco Pérez de la Riva, *Origen y Régimen de la Propiedad Territorial en Cuba* (1946). There are traces of circular grants in the Dominican Republic and, slightly, in Mexico (*cf.* François Chevalier, *La Formation des grands domaines au Méxique* (1952), 112).

[17] See below, p. 65.

Everything is forest, save some meadows or natural clearings called savannah ... upon these savannahs the animals graze, and also on the fruit which falls from the trees, the leaves and on other grasses and bushes. They often mix with animals from neighbouring *haciendas* to graze and drink but afterwards return to their haunts; and all of this shows that on the point of demarcation of boundaries the ranchers observe no exactitude because of the low value of the *haciendas* and the expense of fencing or surveying makes a quarter of a league of no great importance.[18]

The native Indians, never numerous, who had lived in Cuba before the arrival of Columbus (and from whom Europe gained the benefits of both tobacco and syphilis[19]) had by this time dwindled into a few thousand isolated peasants, some living nomadically in caves in West Cuba beside the escaped slaves, some gathered in townships in the east.[20] However few there originally were – perhaps 60,000, perhaps even fewer – they had been diminished by overwork looking for the elusive gold which the early Spaniards believed must be present; by European diseases (particularly the plagues of 1517 and 1528); and by famine caused by the collapse of their old institutions and customs. It was much the same elsewhere in Spanish America: a total population of about forty million probably vanished to a tenth of that within fifty years of the conquest. Many, however, were undoubtedly absorbed in Cuba as elsewhere into Spanish families and, because of the whiteness of their skin, were regarded as Spanish (or creoles), though sometimes their small hands or feet, their slight beard or their oblique eyes betrayed their real origin.[21] The Cuban census-makers of the 1770s treated Indians as 'white', and indeed they never figured as a separate minority in any later reckoning of the population. But certain places such as Guanabacoa, where the Indians near Havana had been congregated in the 1540s, and Jiguaní, a largely Indian township founded in the 1740s in Oriente, were without doubt Indian in formation.[22]

The Indians left other marks on the island: their *bohío*, the small hut

[18] Qu. Corbitt, 'Mercedes and realengos', *op. cit.*, 274.

[19] The Cuban origin of syphilis appears to be finally confirmed by the analysis in S. E. Morison, *Admiral of the Ocean Sea*, 2 vols (1942), II, 201–3, 212–13.

[20] See Appendix III for a study of the Cuban Indians.

[21] This side of the origins of the Cuban people appears to have been ignored by most Cuban historians though it is clearly reflected by archaeological inquiries. See M. R. L. Harrington, *Indians in Cuba*, and Felipe Pichardo Moya, *Los Indiós de Cuba en sus tiempos históricos* (Academía de la Historia de Cuba, Havana, 1945). For the Mexican experience, see C. E. Marshall, 'Birth of the Mestizo in New Spain', *Hispanic American Historical Review*, vol. 19 (1934), 161–84.

[22] See Hortensia Pichardo, *Los orígenes de Jiguaní*, *Boletín del Instituto de Historia y del Archivo Nacional*, Jan–June 1964.

made of palm leaves and wood, remained the distinctive Cuban peasant house. They contributed words, too, such as *batey*, for the group of buildings round a sugar mill; *huracán*, for the whirlwind which often destroyed Cuban harvests; *hamaca*, the hammock, the most practical bed in the tropics; *canoa*, the most practical boat; and *guajiro*, the small subsistence farmer, such as most of them were, growing yucca, maize, avocado and sweet potato, all indigenous Cuban vegetables. They also contributed place names, including that of 'Cuba' itself and 'Havana' (the same word as 'Savannah', signifying a treeless plain[23]); and the art of cultivating tobacco (*tabaco* too was an Indian word).

Columbus was presented with tobacco leaves on his first stop at an inhabited island across the Atlantic, in the Bahamas; but the first Europeans to smoke tobacco (or see it being smoked) were an Andalusian, Rodrigo de Jerez, and a Jew from Murcia, Columbus's interpreter, Luis Torres, on a mission inland in Cuba on behalf of the admiral.[24] The Spaniards in the New World were, however, like most empire builders, bad at learning from the people whom they conquered, and they wished to cultivate vines, wheat and olives, none of which prospered in the Caribbean. But the art of cultivation of tobacco, the drying and the fermentation, was gradually acquired by Spaniards along with the afterwards famous method of rolling the leaves, while tobacco during the sixteenth century established itself in Europe. In Cuba, many allegedly 'white' Spanish tobacco growers (*vegueros*, so named since they were the only regular cultivators of the *vega*, or plain[25]) were probably half Indian, or wholly so; and others from the sixteenth century were Canary Islanders.

The Spaniards cultivated tobacco in accessible places, such as along the banks of the river Almendares, near Havana, or of the river Arimao, near Trinidad. Cuban tobacco, however, had been much sold (sometimes as snuff) to the Dutch, French or English pirates and smugglers who flocked round the coast till the end of the seventeenth century. Snuff 'mills' were numerous in Havana, while the south-east of Cuba, particularly the towns of Bayamo and Manzanillo, became, despite

[23] The city of Havana is formally the city of San Cristóbal de la Habana, San Cristobal of the Plain, and is still referred to always in Spanish as 'La Habana'. The 'b' in Habana came in in the mid-eighteenth century, the word being always previously spelt with a 'v', like most spanish 'b's till then.

[24] *Diary of Columbus*. Rodrigo came from Ayamonte (Huelva); Torres knew Latin and Hebrew. Jews were in the van of many Spanish adventures. They found Indians smoking tobacco near what is now Holguín. The Indian mode of smoking was by inhalation through the nostrils by means of a hollow forked cane, the forked ends being inserted in the nostrils, the other end being placed on the burning tobacco leaves.

[25] An early usage for a tobacco plantation was *tabacal*. *Vega* is found in use for the first time in 1654 (Rivero Muñiz, 30).

severe penalties, a great contraband market where European smugglers exchanged woods, dyes, salt-meats and slaves.[26] Officials in Havana were also implicated; a governor of Cuba was sacked in the seventeenth century for admitting Dutch and other traders into port. But Seville was still the largest consumer of Cuban tobacco, and in Seville was founded the royal tobacco factory (tobacco began to be grown in Spain and it appears that the word 'cigarro' was first used by the inhabitants of Toledo for the plant which they grew in their gardens, where there were so many *cigarras* (cicadas)).

Spain, in decline at home, finding that a sparse population was a serious risk in defending the island against foreigners, tried to encourage more colonists from Spain by giving them tobacco farms either free or at a peppercorn rent. This was unsuccessful. There were also difficulties deriving from the circular system of landholding. *Vegueros* wanted river valleys, not arbitrary tracts between vaguely known circles. Some proprietors allowed them on to their land, but they could not prevent tobacco from being trampled down by cattle which ranged wild. There were endless quarrels between tobacco men and cattle farmers, small men and big. In the absence of law, force won. The Havana oligarchy and council (*cabildo*) were dominated by cattle ranchers. Tobacco farmers sought the help of pirates, ultimately of the Crown.

The representatives of the Crown, the captain-general and his staff, tried to guarantee the estates of the tobacco farmers, but, once implicated in this quarrel, could not withdraw. Tobacco was now much the most profitable Cuban crop. *Vegueros* were forbidden to sell their product (snuff included) to anyone save the government, who set up a monopoly company (the *estanco*, literally, a place where privileged goods are sold) to handle the crop and to manufacture cigars in a royal factory. Many *vegueros*, supported by some churchmen and aldermen, resented this. There were protests, finally rebellions, particularly in 1717 and 1723, when three hundred armed men burned the farms of those who collaborated with the government and marched on Havana. This assertion of private enterprise was ultimately crushed and the ringleaders hanged. The *estanco* however did not alter much. In theory all Cuban tobacco was supposed to go to Cádiz; in practice, much of it (perhaps most of it) went to smugglers. According to statistics, Cuban

[26] Pezuela, *Historia de la Isla de Cuba*, I, 343. A smuggler captain would approach the port and send a note to the governor saying he needed to repair – accompanying the note with a gift. The ship would enter, and the cargo be placed in a stone house with the door locked; but a back door would remain unsealed and the goods would be taken out, and tobacco, or coin or gold, hides or cocoa, substituted. Or the cargo would be shipped into small boats and the inhabitants would come out at night to take the cargo off, after a cannon had announced the arrival. (C. H. Haring, *The Buccaneers in the West Indies in the 17th century* (1910), 26 ff.)

tobacco production did not increase during the eighteenth century;[27] in reality it doubtless doubled. Many mills were founded for the manufacture of snuff, some of them by cattle ranchers, one even by the two agents of the English South Sea Company who had the monopoly between 1713 and 1739 of importing slaves.[28] At the same time many *vegueros* of the Havana neighbourhood left the district for the interior or the extremities of the island, in particular going to the hitherto inaccessible far west where they began to cultivate the tobacco of the special quality, aroma and taste associated with the Vuelta Abajo. The extensive settlement along the banks of the river Cuyaguateje, whence derives the tobacco for all quality Havana cigars, begins indeed in this period. But there were also settlements in the east, around Bayamo, Holguín and Yara, and for a time the tobacco of the latter enjoyed a special fame in north Europe. Güines near Havana was the main producer of tobacco for the snuff factories, which by 1760 numbered forty.

There was some other small husbandry in Cuba; the Indians had shown the way to the cultivation of *boniato* (sweet potato), yam, maize, yucca, pumpkin, several sorts of beans and various medicinal plants, as well as tobacco. Necessarily, they passed on less to Spain in Cuba than they did on the mainland where substantial Indian majorities survived. The Incas and their vassals, for instance, had developed an irrigation system, fertilizers from bird droppings, and methods of storing surplus grain. The Cubans scarcely learned these techniques before the 1960s.

The ranches of central Cuba produced leather and beef; most of it was sold to the treasure fleets or exported to Spain: the demand for leather was great, while dried or jerked beef was the staple diet on all old sea voyages.[29] Official figures probably reflect the reality; hides were Cuba's main export till the eighteenth-century tobacco boom. The breeding of cattle was in fact an appropriate pursuit for a Spanish gentleman, since it then demanded little save good horsemanship, sporadic bursts of work and the pursuit of escaped animals.

[27] See Ramiro Guerra, J. M. Pérez Cabrera, J. J. Remos and E. S. Santovenia, *Historia de la Nación Cubana*, 10 vols (1952) (hereafter, Guerra and Santovenia), II, 140–2, 170–2. Rivero Muñiz, 58–126, gives the best detailed study.
[28] This was the mill *El Inglés* of Nicolson and Tassel near Havana (Rivero Muñiz, 137). For the South Sea Company, see below, p. 31
[29] The word 'jerked' is the only English one of Inca origin: it derives from the Quechua, *ccharqui*, flesh dried in the sun. Caracas and Buenos Aires were the main sources of this in the Spanish empire though Cuba was an exporter too at this time.

The Tobacco Process in Cuba

(This description is intended to be a general one, not confined to any special date)

The tobacco plant has many very small seeds. One ounce of seed can in theory produce 300,000 plants. It is an indigenous Cuban plant: or, at least, existed in Cuba before Columbus.

Each seed, being delicate, benefits from individual care. Indeed only in this way can the best grade cigar tobacco be produced. Flavour also depends, like that of wine, on climate and soil. It is no good trying to produce 'Havana' cigars in Virginia. Virginia, due to less good soil and a different climate, has always concentrated on quantity and large plantations. Cuban tobacco growers have been gardeners more than farmers.

Tobacco is planted in furrows on flat ground, to avoid anything being washed away by rain. The furrows are covered with cloth to prevent excessive light and heat. After five to eight days, the seed germinates. The cloth is taken off by stages, the planter taking great care to get rid of voracious insects: in the nineteenth century planters might often pass nights cleaning the buds as they opened. In the twentieth century the *veguero* applies wheat mixed with arsenic to kill insects. The worst enemy of the tobacco plant is, however, a large ant, the *bibijagua*.

After thirty-five days the plant is six inches high. It is then transplanted to a new bed, usually in the last half of October in Cuba. (New insecticides are now applied.) Then comes the unbuttoning (*desbotonado*): the bud is taken out to avoid flowering, to discourage growth and the loss of aromatic substances. Thirty days after this, with the plant now six to nine feet high, the oblong, spear-shaped dark green leaves are cut and are left to dry in a hut, sometimes in sun, always fermenting, sometimes a selection of leaves being already made (leaves at the top of the plant, *desecho*, being of the best quality). Bunches of leaves are tied together in a bundle (*gavilla*) and left to ferment again, before being placed in a succession of boxes, one stage being to allow the leaves to dry in bark of royal palms.

This description leaves out several minor stages. Each stage has a separate name and so have the different leaves from top to bottom of the plant (*desecho*, *desechito*, *libra*, *injuriado*,the last being nearest the root). October to January has been for a long time the most active season.

The bundles go off tied together in bales (*tercios*) to Havana or another town. They can then be made into cigars – a number of dried tobacco leaves rolled up in another leaf (*capa*); or into *andullo*, a plug of tobacco for eating or chewing; or *picadura*, fine, cut tobacco to be smoked in a pipe or a twist of paper; or a *cigarrillo*, the cigarette of cut tobacco wrapped in paper. All these types were available in the late eighteenth century. There was also powdered tobacco (snuff, or *rapé*). Due to mixing of different sorts of leaf, there were infinite varieties, at that time chosen and selected by the planters. Already there was one 'particularly thick and of superior quality . . . made for Priests'.

As yet there were no private tobacco factories apart from mills to make snuff. Officially all leaf had for generations to be sent to Seville. In practice, cigars were rolled by workers in their homes, either as a task supplementary to their normal lives or as their only job. (Women probably already wrapped cigarettes, a less demanding task than cigars.) There was further selection of leaves within classes, and finally the rolling of cigars. Bundles of finished cigars and cigarettes were then delivered to merchants. In 1761 the Crown established a new monopoly factory in Havana. This too failed in its purpose: cottage industry survived.

CHAPTER III

Sugar and Society

Cuba, unlike the mainland of South America, had never been held by Spain for the value of its exports. It had now no gold and had never had much. It was a service colony, kept up, like Aden in the nineteenth-century British empire, for the fleets carrying home the main imperial products. Even the mainland was still expected to produce precious metals rather than crops: Spaniards 'wanted gold, not to till the earth like a peasant', Cortés remarked in 1504.[1] Cuba, unlike the other Caribbean islands, as yet produced little cotton or coffee; nor had she yet been persuaded into the manufacture on a large scale of that originally South-Pacific product for which she was to be specially renowned and in respect of which the Caribbean was already pre-eminent, cane sugar.[2] The English found about six thousand boxes of sugar in the harbour of Havana – the year's export[3] or about 500 tons – a hundredth of the then production of Jamaica. But the grounds for expansion were already there (as there were in the equally neglected Spanish colonies of Puerto Rico and Santo Domingo); the Spanish market at home was growing, due to increased prosperity and increased population, while Spanish sugar production, once of importance under the Moors, was actually in decline in the eighteenth century, with fewer than ten sugar mills and not much more than 1,000 acres of cane.[4] Cuban production was also much greater than the formal export figures suggest.[5] The cane area amounted to 10,000 acres, which, if nothing compared to Jamaica, was clearly a beginning.[6] What was perhaps needed was some sudden shock, 'ideas from abroad', and, even more important than psychological encouragement, more labour.

There were in fact already over a hundred sugar plantations in

[1] W. H. Prescott, *History of the Conquest of Mexico* (Everyman edn), 149.

[2] That sugar cane derives from the South Pacific is evident from the arguments and evidence in Deerr, 13 ff.

[3] 5,841 boxes, each containing 16 *arrobas* (*Documentos Inéditos*, 17, fn. 23). An *arroba* was about 25 lb, so that each box contained about 400 lb of sugar.

[4] Some cane fields were planted with cotton or mulberries in Spain, see Deerr, 81. There were only four mills in the Canaries in 1752.

[5] On the basis of a newly discovered list of mills between 1759 and 1762 (*Arch. Nac. Misc. de Libros*, 2646), Moreno Fraginals, *El Ingenio*, 3, estimates Cuban sugar production at almost half a million *arrobas* (5,500 tons) in the 1750s. *Cf.* Arango's 200 tons (*Obras*, II, 18).

[6] Manuel Moreno Fraginals, *El Ingenio*, Tomo I, 1760–1860 (1964), 10.

Cuba.[7] These plantations had changed little since the sixteenth century. Most were near Havana, some near other cities, and most had mills moved by six often lethargic oxen or sometimes horses, egged on by small black boys, rather than the doubly more powerful and more expensive water-driven mills which were bringing wealth to the English islands of the Caribbean and the French (above all Saint Domingue). There were some Cuban watermills but Cuba had few powerful rivers. Production of sugar had indeed scarcely increased since the end of the sixteenth century.[8]

The machinery in all these mills was of course wooden: usually three vertical rollers turning to crush, under a cover like that of a merry-go-round, long stalks of cane carried by Negro slaves. The liquid thereby produced, *guarapo*, a greyish olive-green juice, was boiled at the *casa de calderas* (boiling house) in a series of five open copper kettles (the 'train') of decreasing size, each tended by separate slaves, while it thickened through evaporation into syrup.[9] Lye, an alkalized water obtained from vegetable ashes, was also put into the juice at this point. Each kettle had its own separate wood fire. The syrup in its turn was poured into hogsheads, clay moulds or barrels, and left there in the refining house (*casa de purga*) for some weeks to harden, the coarsest syrup, the molasses, dropping by weight through a hole in the bottom of the mould into a bowl beneath, afterwards in the distillery to be made into rum. The finished sugar came in the form of loaves, the best quality being from the top of the hogshead, the worst from the lowest.[10] The process was not hygienic. The mills made an extraordinarily vivid impression on those who saw them: the *casa de purga* seemed a veritable palace of Pluto, enveloped in sulphurous smoke, far indeed from the terrestrial paradise which America represented in so much European

[7] Compare this with the 599 plantations at the French colony at Saint Domingue in 1754 and 648 in Jamaica in 1768. The *cabildo* (municipality) of Havana spoke of 'over 100', Colección del Bicentenario de 1762, *La Dominación Inglesa en la Habana, Libro de Cabildos, 1762–63* (1962), 75–6. Moreno Fraginals speaks of 89, 93, 98, in 1759, 1761, in the Havana jurisdiction, on the basis of new material (*op. cit.*, 15).

[8] Columbus (whose first mother-in-law owned a sugar estate in Madeira) took cane to the Caribbean on his second voyage. After a few mills were founded in Cuba in the 1520s, there had been a spurt of mill-building at the end of the sixteenth century under the impetus of the slave imports of a Portuguese, Gómez Reynal, the monopolist of the period. Some early sugar barons were Portuguese, as were also some sugar technicians (*maestros de azúcar*), *cf.* Ramiro Guerra, *Manual de Historia de Cuba*, 2nd edn (1964), 97. Sugar production attained 312 tons in the early seventeenth century, from the 37 mills then founded in East Cuba. See Deerr, I, 128.

[9] Some older mills of Brazil or the other Antilles had as many as seven kettles in the 1760s. Five was the usual number in the eighteenth century, deriving from the '*équipage du Père Labat*', each with distinctive names, these being the *grand, propre, flambeau, sirope* and *batterie* in French colonies; there appear to have been no distinctive names in Spanish or English colonies, except for the last and smallest – the '*batterie*' being the 'strike-pan' in Jamaica, the *tacho* in Cuba.

[10] See below, p. 40.

literature: Negroes, naked to the waist, their bodies lit by the fire of the ovens; the splash of boiling liquid; cries of the slaves who fed the kettles and the orders of the overseer (*E-cha can-de-la* or *Puer-ta*); the lugubrious songs of the slaves, inside and outside; a cutlass ever ready to cut off the hands of slaves if caught in the rollers; and the simultaneous crunch of cane.[11]

These mills (known generally as *trapiches*, from the Italian or Sicilian *trapetto*, the roller mill devised in the fifteenth century in Sicily) had a life of about forty years at most. The land would by then have deteriorated, since it received no fertilizer. It had probably anyway only been roughly cleared and never ploughed and, not surprisingly, two or three sowings of canes (each lasting about fifteen to twenty years) were the most that it could stand. All the nearby available wood too would by then have been cut for fuel. The cost in labour of carrying both cut cane and firewood from farther afield would have been too much. So the planter would either close down completely or move on to other land. The price of virgin land after all was low – $500 (£120) per *caballería* (under £4 per acre) at the end of the eighteenth century,[12] and only a short time before, it could have been had, free for the asking, by anyone able to develop it.[13]

Sugar mills were as a rule set amidst a group of buildings (the *batey*), consisting of the *casa de vivienda*, the house of the owner (or his administrator), some small houses for the salaried workers, a kitchen, and a nursery and a hospital for the slaves; there would also be a carpenter's shop, a blacksmith's forge, a cooper's shed, stables, perhaps a distillery to make *aguardiente* (a cane brandy, much liked by the slaves) and lodgings for the slaves, usually at this time a group of little primitive houses. Sugar plantations were customarily divided into two sections: the cane area (*cañaveral*), and the *potrero*, the larger reserve area kept for vegetables and pasturage for oxen. The mills worked only during the four- to five-month harvest (February to June) but for the rest of the year there was much other work – weeding, the building of paths, clearing jungle and planting new cane. Harvest was the hardest but also the gayest time, since the slaves had more *aguardiente* than usual, cane to suck and more *fiestas*. As important agriculturally was the time of planting or re-planting (in the rainy season of July to October) for, though cane roots could be left in the ground after being cut, the new shoots (ratoons) which they yielded produced each year less and less

[11] e.g. Mrs W. M. L. Jay, *My Winter in Cuba* (1871), 219–20.

[12] F. H. A. von Humboldt, *The Island of Cuba* (English edn, 1856), 261. *Cf.* p. 63 for further discussion of land prices.

[13] The royal decrees of 1729 and 1739 forbade further distribution of *realengos*, i.e. undistributed territory regarded as royal. But some continued by the local *cabildos* acting on their own.

sugar; though in Cuba they continued to do well even after the tenth year. But perhaps a tenth of the cane fields was replanted annually, after 'holing': slaves dug a hole four feet square and about nine inches deep (into which manure as well as cane cuttings might be put). No ploughs were used anywhere in the Caribbean at this time, and indeed with small variations (except in Cuba, cane rarely lasted longer than seven years) this manner of organizing sugar production was common to the entire archipelago.

Such plantations were usually maintained to produce sugar only. There was no thought of diversification. Rarely even was food grown to feed the slaves. Sometimes they were fed simply by killing cattle. Clothes, food and medicine had usually to be bought and so the beginning of the sugar industry was accompanied by the further expansion of the merchant classes of the colony concerned. Though Cuba had yet to reach this stage of mono-culture and indeed Cuban sugar plantations produced vegetables for Havana, this process was already beginning there also, in imitation of Jamaica or the other colonies; and in Havana, because of the fleets and their needs, the resident merchant class had always been disproportionately large. Some merchants were mere pedlars, others great men with palatial residences in the city, such as, in the 1760s, Mateo Pedroso, a permanent member of the *cabildo* (town council) and the most prominent merchant of the city.[14]

At least a third and probably half the cost of founding a sugar plantation must then have derived from the cost of slaves. In Cuba, as in the other West Indian islands, slaves were the most valuable part of a planter's investment, more so than either the land or the machinery and buildings. To found a plantation it was thus necessary first to have access to a slave market and second to find money both to buy them and the other necessary capital investments, as well as to maintain slaves and keep the plantation running for perhaps one season when there were no profits. The growth of the industry thus depended upon supply of slaves.[15] Of course, there were other necessities: fertile land close to a port whence to embark the sugar; woods with trees of good quality for buildings as well as to provide fuel; cattle to feed the slaves and to work the machinery; and nearness to a centre of manufacture such as the shipyard and arsenal at Havana, whose workshops could be turned over to the manufacture of wooden sugar machinery or copper saucepans. All these were fully available in the neighbourhood of Havana partly

[14] Mateo Pedroso y Florencia (1719–1800). His father had been municipal treasurer, and he was himself a fourth-generation *criollo*, his ancestor, Pablo Pedroso, having come to Havana as a lay official of the Inquisition at the end of the sixteenth century. He was brother to José Pedroso, owner of the Lombillo palace previously mentioned.

[15] As Moreno Fraginals, 5, says explicitly 'The number of slaves decided the volume of the production'.

because of demand from the already thriving sugar industry in the rest of the West Indies.[16] Still, labour – that is, slave labour – was the crux.

The Spaniards had hitherto kept, partly through self-interest, partly through lack of capital to do otherwise, the old papal regulation whereby the West African coast was regarded as a Portuguese zone of influence. Even by the mid-eighteenth century they had no trading establishments on the African coast, though most other European nations had, and though Spanish writers were urging that Spain should too.[17] No Spanish ship had indeed been to Africa to buy or to kidnap slaves. The Spanish colonies had had, therefore, always to rely on foreign slaves – now above all on the English who, dominating the carrier trade of the world, also dominated the slave trade. The South Sea Company of London had had an exclusive licence (*asiento*) to sell slaves to Cuba and to the Spanish empire from 1713 to 1739, though afterwards a monopoly of providing slaves for Cuba was allocated to a Spanish national company which itself bought from the South Sea Company or other English merchants in Jamaica. Neither system was satisfactory. Cuban planters could not get as many slaves as they wanted. Neither the South Sea Company nor the Havana Monopoly Company did well: the latter sold about 5,000 slaves (mostly bought in Jamaica) in Cuba between 1740 and 1760 at $144 (£33) each.[18] Smuggling may have accounted for another 5,000 in the same period, but the Cuban planters remained dissatisfied. They needed not only slaves for new plantations but a regular supply thereafter; for Caribbean planters of all nationalities in the eighteenth century bought an overwhelming majority of male slaves first because, they believed, female slaves could not work so well on the sugar plantations, and second, because they thought the import of a regular replacement – say 10 per cent – was less costly than rearing slave children. Pregnant slaves, after all, were useless for heavy work though they consumed food.[19] There were therefore probably only a third as many female slaves as male in Cuba.

Even supposing slaves were available, how could they be paid for? How could the machinery and land be paid for? Capital was rare. So far as land was concerned, those who founded new sugar plantations in Cuba between 1750 and 1770 were usually creole families who already held land and who, beginning to realize that sugar would make them better off than cattle did, turned over their estates to cane. A few, like the Englishmen Nicolson and Tassel, who had represented the South

---

[16] *Ibid.*, 4. One of the reasons for the decline of the Havana shipyard (after 1763) was the dedication of its workers to tasks connected with sugar.

[17] e.g. Miguel Antonio Gándara in 1762 in a memorandum circulated in MSS., qu. Richard Herr, *The Eighteenth-Century Revolution in Spain* (1958), 48.

[18] Saco, *Historia de la esclavitud de la raza africana en el nuevo mondo y en especial en los países américo-hispanos*, vol. I (1879), 312. This price was not high, prices in 1755-7 varied between £33 and £50 each (see Donnan, II, 510, 511).

[19] The Jesuits and Bethlemite monks were an exception to this practice (Humboldt, 241).

Sea Company, built sugar mills and snuff factories on the same estate. These creole families included most of the older established families of Cuba to whose ancestors original grants of land had been made in the sixteenth and seventeenth centuries: those of Pedroso or Calvo de la Puerta, Cárdenas or Recio, Betancourt, Chacón, Sotolongo or Peñalver, and others more recently established such as the Herreras or O'Farrills (descendants of the South Sea Company's Havana factor in 1718)[20] and the Núñez del Castillo, whose head, the Marqués de San Felipe, was the highest-ranking creole Spanish nobleman. Some of these were families who had previously grown tobacco and ceased to do so with the coming of the state monopoly factory. Those who turned over cattle estates, or a section of them, to sugar were also technically in breach of the law which had obliged them and their ancestors to raise cattle for beef to serve the nearby township.[21] This conversion of the landowners between 1750 and 1770 to sugar production reflected the similar conversion of English landowners to scientific farming a generation earlier, though in the case of Cuba there was always an industrial side to the development of sugar cane. This first Cuban industrial revolution was essentially aristocratic, carried out, too, by families who stayed on the island; for these aristocrats were not absentee landlords in the same way as were the English landlords in Jamaica who were off to Dorset or Wiltshire as soon as they could. Cuban entrepreneurs or their families on the other hand often spent most of the year in Havana where they would have palaces or houses.[22]

Buildings were not really a separate item of expenditure for sugar entrepreneurs at this time, since they were built by slaves and chiefly from locally obtained wood. But slaves, machinery, sugar equipment such as cauldrons; food, clothing, wages for the few salaried workers who attended even a modest plantation; all these things demanded money. If the plantation owner was an ex-cattle farmer, perhaps he could gradually kill off cattle to feed the new slaves in the first years, but not for long.

Most frequently, these things were not immediately paid for. Though there were no banks in Cuba till the nineteenth century, it was possible to obtain goods, or slaves, on credit. Out of the five thousand[23] slaves

[20] However, he had become a Spanish citizen in 1722 and was not mentioned in the list of South Sea Company's agents in that year (Donnan, II, 295, fn). He married a young Cuban widow, a daughter of the oligarchy, Teresa Arriola de Ambulodi. This was no doubt the secret of his success.

[21] Another reason, incidentally, to distrust official statistics.

[22] The largest mill in the 1761 harvest was owned by Pedro Beltrán de Santa Cruz, and produced 165 tons of sugar (16, 612 *arrobas*). There were eight other mills in that year which produced over 100 tons, these being owned in order of production, by Gonzalo de Herrera (Marqués de Villalta), Ignacio Peñalver, the Marqués de San Felipe, Francisco Oseguera, Ignacio de Cárdenas, Juan O'Farrill, José Ambrosio Zayas, and María Teresa Chacón. (The list in Moreno Fraginals, 15, is misleading.)

[23] Actually 4,986 (Saco, *Historia de la esclavitud*, I, 312).

introduced by the Havana Monopoly Company between 1740 and 1760, 80 per cent, or 4,000, were bought on credit (or by barter for tobacco). Planters usually borrowed money from some merchant. In both instances the planter mortgaged fractions of his future sugar crop to the merchant, usually for large interest rates. Sometimes as much as half the crop was paid to the merchant, simply as interest: the question of repayment of the principal was deferred indefinitely. Such high interest rates seem more comprehensible if it is realized that sugar mills could not, by an old law of Charles V, be attached for debt. This protective device in fact had a counter-productive effect: by raising interest rates, it forced mill owners more and more towards what Humboldt would describe as a state of 'absolute dependence' on the merchants.[24] But once again in the 1760s this development was a matter for the future.

The merchants of Cuba were general traders, dealing in everything from slaves to hats, wheat and wine. Such explicitly *slave* traders as did exist were agents of foreign merchants, who acted on behalf of a slave merchant or shipowner of Kingston, Jamaica, Liverpool or Cádiz; though any trade with England, the main slave seller, was technically illegal before Albemarle's victory and the only legal slave-selling agency was the State Monopoly Company, with headquarters in Cádiz.[25] Others traded illegally off the coast, particularly the south coast, so close to Jamaica, the main slave mart of the Caribbean. The leading merchant of Havana, Mateo Pedroso (in fact of aristocratic origin), like the Beckfords in Jamaica, not only lent money to his planter cousins and friends but from early on also bought lands himself which were valued at his death at $M2.[26] His own capital derived either from the money made by his ancestors who came to Cuba as lay officials for the Inquisition or by his father who was for many years municipal treasurer; his movement into business from bureaucracy was a sign of the times. In these ways were laid the foundations of many merchant fortunes, such as those of the Poeys (by origin French merchants) or the Iznagas of Trinidad. Merchants tempted sugar planters by loans of capital and promises of labour in order precisely to stimulate the slave trade at the same time.

Yet, despite smuggling, in the years before the English invasion they could not always supply slave labour when it was demanded. Indeed, Cuba remained a colony with fewer slaves per European than anywhere else in the Caribbean except Puerto Rico (which the Spaniards used as a convict colony). Less than half the population of Cuba were slaves in

[24] Humboldt, *Travels*, 280–1.

[25] Other monopoly companies (which broke Cádiz's monopoly of trade to the Indies) were the Real Compañía Guipuzcoana of San Sebastián for trade with Venezuela (founded 1728) and the Catalan Company for trade with Puerto Rico, Santo Domingo, Honduras and La Margarita.

[26] Humboldt, *Travels*, 312.

1762, whereas in such economically successful islands as Jamaica, Saint Domingue, Barbados and Antigua, the white population constituted small armed garrisons surrounded by hordes of slaves, these islands consisting less of coherent societies than centres for a number of autonomous, powerful sugar enterprises.[27] The consequence was that Cuba, though doubtless 'backward', was more homogeneous than elsewhere in the Caribbean : slaves were on balance treated better, though because of economic underdevelopment rather than of true magnanimity. For treatment of slaves in the Americas depended on the work upon which they were engaged and the type of property on which they worked; a slave on a sugar plantation in Jamaica lived worse than one on a tobacco plantation in Virginia; a house slave in Charleston or Havana perhaps better than either. There was one other difference : slavery had died in England; but neither slavery itself nor specifically Negro slavery had ceased in Spain and in the Mediterranean countries.[28] Consequently, the Spaniards had in the sixteenth century a detailed code for the treatment of slaves derived from the famous Castillian collection of laws, the *Siete Partidas* of Alfonso the Wise; and these laws were naturally introduced into the New World. The English had no such code upon which to base themselves and indeed England herself continued to ignore the question, leaving it to the separate colonial assemblies to make the appropriate legislation : thus Virginia recognized slavery in 1661, made it an hereditary state in 1662, established in 1667 that baptism did not alter slave conditions, and so on. These laws were formulated with the immediate interest of North American planters as the decid-

[27] Rough estimates for the British West Indies in the mid-eighteenth century were:

Jamaica (1762):	15,000 white	146,805 Negro slaves
Antigua (1756):	3,412	31,428
Montserrat (1756):	1,430	8,833
Nevis (1756):	1,058	8,380
St Kitts (1756):	2,713	21,891
Virgin Is (1756):	1,263	6,121
Barbados (1757):	16,772	63,645

For the French:

St Domingue (1754):	14,253	172,188
Guadeloupe (1754):	10,538	45,653
Martinique (1751):	12,068	65,905
Grenada (1753):	1,262	11,991
St Vincent (1763):	695	3,430

(See Deerr, 278–80; Sir Alan Burns, *History of the British West Indies* (1954), 196–9.) In North America at this time, due to different use of land, the whites were, as in Cuba, in a majority. Even in Virginia the Negro population (140,570) was out-distanced by the white (199,156). Only South Carolina, of the thirteen colonies, had a Negro majority (*Historical Statistics of the U.S.* (1961), 756.) The North American estimate for 1760 is: Negro 325,806; white 1,267,820.

[28] But see D. Brion Davis, *The Problem of Slavery in Western Culture* (1966), 40–2 for a synoptic view of the matter; and Anthony Luttrell, 'Slavery and Slaving in the Portuguese Atlantic', a paper read to the Edinburgh seminar on the slave trade (1965).

1   View of Havana, 1762

2   The British land in Cuba, 1762

ing factor; slaves could not therefore marry; they had no legal right to possessions; they could not sue; they could not buy their freedom; they had in short no legal being and were chattels. Slaves in Cuba, as in all Spanish colonies, had the benefit of hispanic, and hence Roman law (with, of course, its modifications and subsequent changes); the Church knew them; they could have and exchange property; they could marry; they were legal personalities, even if their rights were often only theoretically guaranteed by law. Time, custom, humanity and interest might mitigate Anglo-Saxon severity, and the practice of law under Spain often deny utterly the formal theory of codes. But law did have a number of precise consequences which coloured Spanish slave life.

Another contrast between Spanish and North American practice is that though, perhaps, so far as brutality of treatment is concerned it is difficult to make much distinction between them, the North American church and white master class, by denying to the slave real rights as Christians, were often found proclaiming that Negroes were accursed of God, being descended either from Cain or from the serpent who tempted Eve – and who was supposed to be the Negro incarnate. Of this odd theological attitude there is no trace in Spanish slave society.[29]

Cuban slaves could also buy their own freedom or that of their children or parents. This was by means of the *coartación*, obligation, the legal right possessed by slaves to pay a sum of money to their master, so guaranteeing first that they could not be sold save at a fixed price (usually the average price for slaves in the market), second that the slave could buy his freedom after he had paid, by instalments, the difference between his original down payment and the agreed fixed price. These rights naturally necessitated another, namely the right of slaves to possess or to accumulate capital and property by, for instance, the cultivation of vegetables on the side, or extra work in the cities, or even by theft. Slaves could also be freed by the benevolence of a master or protector or other friend: these acts of emancipation occurred usually but not exclusively in the cities. Masters would often free their illegitimate children. There were various limitations in practice upon these rights: *bozales*, or slaves direct from Africa, could not purchase freedom or enrol themselves as *coartados* until seven years after they had arrived in Cuba. Many slaves were incapable of counting or were so feckless or

[29] See Harry McNeill, 'No "Curse" on the Negro', *Negro World Digest* (1940), I, 40–2, qu. Herbert Aptheker, *American Slave Revolts* (1944) 53. The question of whether Negroes were better treated in North America by Anglo-Saxons or in South America by Latins is debated by Frank Tannenbaum, *Slave and Citizen, The Negro in the Americas* (1947), and by Klein (both pro-Latins), against D. Brion Davis in *Slavery in Western Culture* (basically pro-Anglo-Saxon), far the most sophisticated treatment of an interesting topic. None I think pays adequate attention to the sheer economic and organizational factors which made any sugar plantation something like a concentration camp, though Stanley Elkins, in his admirable work *Slavery* (1953), makes the analogy, falsely surely, about the whole slave process.

so disturbed by the psychological consequences of capture, sale and passage as to be unable to begin to think of accumulating capital. Some masters showed ill faith. In the cities the *síndico*, the member of the city council supposed to deal with these matters, might be generally accessible to an intelligent slave but in the country it was harder for slaves to reach the *capitán de partido*, the official responsible there. Slaves could not pass on their property to their children, only to their masters who usually but not invariably would themselves give it to the children. As soon as the first instalment was paid by the *coartado* to the master, however, a slave could leave home and work on his own in conditions almost the same as those of a free Negro.

This right of *coartación* – of accepting, that is, the virtual freedom of the slave after receiving a fraction of his value – was a Hispano-American institution, and not a Spanish or Mediterranean one. It had no equivalent in North America where indeed planters often did not even recognize their own illegitimate children, much less emancipate them.[30] *Coartación* seems to have originated in Cuba in the 1520s and to have spread from there with some variations to other Spanish colonies. Other rights possessed by slaves in Cuba as in other Spanish colonies included that of changing their master for a new one if such could be found, while the children of slaves by free women (and men) became automatically free.[31]

The consequence was a substantial number of free Negroes and mulattoes in Cuba: possibly 20,000 in comparison with a slave population of 32,000. This again was a complete contrast with the British and French West Indian islands where the free black population was insignificant. In Cuba these were chiefly concentrated in the cities; there were only very few black smallholders, though at least one sugar mill had been owned by a mulatto in 1760. In the cities these free men worked in the shipyards in various capacities, rolled tobacco, were shoemakers, carpenters, tailors and indeed had already begun to establish themselves in the trades in which they were to be dominant in the twentieth century. Some mulattoes also had Indian blood so that, by the terminology then in use, they were technically *zambos*.

City slaves, especially domestic slaves, lived a different life from those of the plantation. They may have numbered only a quarter of the slaves of the island, but they lived alongside free mulattoes or Negroes, and often enjoyed the affection of their masters and mistresses, and returned it, serving often as friend or accomplice of the children of the household.

[30] Some instances exist of North American slaves buying their freedom but not as of right. The question is discussed in Elkins, *Slavery*, 59, fn. 64.

[31] The legal position of slaves in Cuba, with texts of laws from the *Siete Partidas* onwards, can be seen in Fernando Ortiz, *Hampa Afrocubana: Los Negros Esclavos* (1916), ch. xix, and appendices. See also below, ch. xiii.

Few of the punishments meted out by the overseer in the country were given to the city slaves. One can glimpse something of the life of these from the advertisements, thus (one deriving from the nineteenth century) : 'For sale: a magnificent Negress of 24 years, of fine and handsome presence, excellent laundress and cook, can iron well, above average seamstress, born *en la casa*, accustomed to good relations with her masters, particularly with children, always has been in the towns on the island, has no vices, blemishes nor illnesses, very strong and healthy.'[32] Town slaves could enjoy many urban entertainments, drinking in the *bodegas* with friends or *carabelas* (Negroes who arrived in Cuba in the same slave-ship),[33] or dancing in clubs for people of the same African origin. Negresses might settle down with a white man, such as a soldier or shopkeeper. A town slave could benefit much more than one from the country from the possibility available to him of being hired out by his master to a third person; and conditions of work under the third person would approximate more to normal labour. Town slaves could more easily gather capital, either by loan from free Negroes or perhaps by thefts: and, in this way, work on their own in conditions close to liberty. On the other hand, the slaves themselves often considered it indecorous to hire themselves or be hired, since it suggested that their masters were of poor social position.[34]

Despite these evident advantages, there were of course slave protests: and these took the form of, first, suicide; second, escape; and third, open rebellion. Suicide was appealing since Negroes often believed that they would thereby return to Africa; and this could be done by hanging themselves, or by eating earth, or by poison – making use of either the *curamagüey* or the *guao*, a tree whose flowers had a fatal scent. Slaves were also known to asphyxiate themselves with their own tongues.[35] Suicides by drowning were frequent on the journey from Africa. Slaves also escaped fairly often, living as *cimarrones* (that is, escaped slaves) in the forests, eating herbs or killing animals, often making for stockaded settlements (*palenques*) known to Negroes which had permanent existence in the hills of the far west, east and south of the island.[36]

[32] 'Se vende una magnífica negra de 24 años de edad, de hermosa y bonita presencia, excelente lavandera, planchadora y cocinera, más que regular costurera, nacida en la casa, *acostumbrada a buenas maneras con sus amos*, y particularmente con los niños, siempre ha estado en las poblaciones de la isla; no tiene vicios, tacha, ni enfermedades, muy robusta y sana. Calle de Manrique, num 17, impondrán', *El Siglo* (Habana, 1865).

[33] *Malungo* was the equivalent word in Brazil. There appears to have been no such word in North America. '*Carabela*' is a corruption of 'caravel'.

[34] See Ortiz, 313; Cirilo Villaverde, *Cecilia Valdés* (1941), 516.

[35] Cirilo Villaverde, *op. cit.*, p. 132, has a nineteenth-century instance. This appears to have been done by throwing the tongue backwards into the throat.

[36] For a general consideration, see R. Bastide, *Les Amériques Noires*, 51–75 (1967); for a careful consideration in Cuba, see José L. Franco, *Cuatro siglos de Lucha por la Libertad: Los Palenques* (Revista de la Biblioteca Nacional José Martí, Año 58, No. 1).

Professional searchers for slaves (*rancheadores*) existed in most townships, supported by bloodhounds well known for their efficiency throughout the Caribbean (the earl of Balcarres, governor of Jamaica, for instance, sent for a shipload of Cuban mastiffs during a major slave revolt in the 1790s). The *rancheadores* were paid not only for bringing slaves back but also for dead slaves, since neighbourhoods wanted a settlement of bandit slaves nearby even less than they wanted their property destroyed. The *rancheadores* themselves inevitably were often feared for their arbitrary behaviour in certain places. The right of disposing ultimately of captured slaves was hereditary in Havana province – that is, the west of the island captured by Albemarle – in the family of the condes de Casa Barreto.

Finally, there were outright insurrections. These had begun almost as soon as slaves were taken to Cuba and in the sixteenth century slaves and Indians had joined forces against the first generation of *conquistadores*. There had also been occasional mutinies on slave-ships coming from Africa. In 1538 the slaves had joined forces with the French and sacked Havana. But by the eighteenth century such occurrences were rare. When the English Admiral Hosier had threatened Havana in the early years of the century, the slaves of the district had admittedly believed, with varying degrees of enthusiasm or anxiety, that the hour of liberation was near and had made an abortive attempt to rise; the slaves of the copper mines of Santiago had risen in 1731; a slave had been in 1736 condemned to death (but pardoned after the intercession, it was said, of Our Lady of Rosario) for burning cane fields belonging to Juan de la Barrera. Nevertheless, the fear of insurrection was not a continuous one, and no special precautions were taken against it even in sugar plantations. Later on, such slave revolts as there were would often be directed by free Negroes.

This apparently tolerant society, in comparison with the English colonies, does not alter the fact that Cuban planters hoped to build on their island the rich tyrannies which they could increasingly admire elsewhere; absence of opportunity, not innate Spanish good will towards humanity, had hitherto delayed a sugar-rush.

Lack of adequate labour was critical, but there were other sides to the question; among them the still stifling Spanish commercial restrictions which formally limited Spanish colonial trade not only to Spain but to a limited Spanish market; where Cuba was concerned, to Cádiz. At the same time, Spanish demand for sugar was still low, with consumption of coffee or tea – the main concomitants of a substantial sugar import – much lower than in northern Europe. This too was changing. Population in the eighteenth century in Spain as elsewhere in Europe was at last increasing, as was industrial activity, at least in the years immediately before the war.[37] The sugar enterprises in the French and English colonies had demanded a whole series of home industries, from the manufacture of copper cauldrons to hats and clothes for slaves, ladles and machetes, not to speak of chains for recalcitrant slaves. Previously, Spain would have been unable to provide such services, nor was her political and commercial French ally able to produce these things in sufficient quantity to satisfy her own colonial demand. By 1760 this situation was changing fast in Spain. At the same time too, the illegal markets of English North America and even of Spanish South America were growing. In many ways the time was ripe for a radical shock such as the English occupation of Havana.

The Church's attitude to slavery in Cuba was not progressive. Most priests would still have given willingly and with sincerity the reply given to King Louis XIII of France by the Dominicans, that slavery was the best way of ensuring that Africans could be shown the way to the true God. But the priests of Cuba carried this interpretation little further than baptism and the giving to the slave of a Christian first name. (The Protestants of the English and Dutch colonies, believing that baptism was equivalent to freedom and knowing from experience that God could be subversive if used intelligently, usually did not even go as far as that.)[38]

One exception to Catholic neglect was important: Juan Matienzo, in a famous textbook of Peruvian administration, had in 1570 warned Spaniards never 'to try and change the customs abruptly' of the Indians of Peru, since 'one must first accommodate oneself to the customs of those one wishes to govern'.[39] From the sixteenth century onwards, priests had in this spirit encouraged Negroes, slaves and freed men, to seek some blend between Catholic and African religious practices, so that Christian saints could, in processions and ritual, receive the enthusiastic adoration which Africans in their native land lavished on their own gods. Perhaps the idolatrous nature of much of Catholic practice, the beards on the figures of the painted Christs, the baroque and golden saints, the dragons and the marvellous animals, the incense and the gloom, was more sympathetic to Africans, themselves dominated by mysterious signs and omens, than was the clean, sparer Christianity of the Anglo-Saxon north. These matters are difficult to resolve: the slave-ships carried not only men but gods and beliefs. Some Africans, even some slaves, may have been genuinely Christians: but most of those who seemed to be or said they were continued to worship African deities. In the eighteenth century, African *cofradías* (religious brotherhoods)

[37] Jaime Vicens Vives, *Manual de Historia Económica de España* (1959), 506.
[38] Klein, 117.
[39] Qu. Haring, 110.

were vigorously encouraged by the bishop, Mgr Morell de Santa Cruz (as a result partly of his experience in 1730 of coping with a slave rebellion in El Cobre). The *Día de los Reyes* (Epiphany) was a time of unbridled license at which Africans of different tribes would select chiefs, dress them up lavishly and celebrate the arrival of the 'kings' with bands, drinking, dancing and drums; an English traveller in 1820 drily commented, 'The only *civilized* part of the entertainment is – *drinking rum*'.[40] In this way were Negroes drawn into Spanish fiestas and fiestas partly Africanized.[41]

The monasteries survived, as rich as or richer than any *latifundista*: eight Franciscan, four Dominican, two Jesuit – twenty in all. Inside were about 150 monks only, mostly of upper class *criollo* background, all needing to pay at least $300 (£70) a year to enter, and, technically, all save Jesuits having to prove purity of blood: no Jewish or African blood up to the fourth generation. The Jesuits were exempt from this rule but even they were nearly all Spaniards.[42] All these monastic houses had enriched themselves extensively over many generations, owning sugar mills, cattle farms, slaves and large tracts of uncultivated land. (Enemies would calculate that the Dominicans, in about 1830, owned $M25 (£M6), and the Franciscans and Jesuits $M20 (£M4½), all in the prosperous west of Cuba.)[43] The secular clergy on the other hand were poor and no one took much notice of them.

Cuba had some things in common with the rest of the West Indies. Despite the introduction from the early sixteenth century of European or Asiatic crops, such as sugar and European animals, the island was not self-supporting. The colonists could not, at least did not, change their eating habits. They did not like fish. Wine, rice, bread (made from wheat, not yucca as the Indians were used to) and other food, drink, clothes and weapons, all instruments from knives to wheels, paper and church ornaments, all had to be brought in from outside, as were slaves. The other West Indian islands were sugar factories, Cuba a roadhouse, but each depended on the outside world for its livelihood.

The Sugar Process

In the late summer, slaves with sharp sticks make six-inch to twelve-inch holes, two and a half feet wide, about four feet apart. (About a hundred holes a day was considered the right number: a hard, but by no means over-whelmingly hard day.) Other slaves follow, with short cuttings of cane (the cane top and one or two joints), which they plant in the holes, two cuttings

---

[40] Robert Francis Jameson, *Letters from the Havana during the year 1820* . . . (1820), 22.

[41] See below, ch. xi, xiii and xliii, for more extensive consideration.

[42] General Miguel Tacón, *Correspondencia Reservada, 1834–6*, ed. J. Pérez de la Riva (1963) 46.

[43] *Ibid.*, 48.

in each hole horizontally, and make firm by stamping round. Cane sprouts within two weeks from the eyes of the sections, more earth is put on, and in eighteen months the cane has grown to about eight feet, ready for cutting. In Cuba, the original plants lasted five to twenty-five years, though elsewhere less long. Some cane fields produced crops of a sort in Cuba after sixty years. (Second-year growth is known as ratooning.)

The soil becomes exhausted long before that without fertilizer. If the soil is new and rich, fifteen good harvests are possible.

Cane grows with little attention. In harvest, after Christmas, the waving cane stalks are cut to the ground by machete, stripped of leaves and cut into pieces about three feet long.

Once the cane is cut, it should be ground within two days to avoid fermentation. In the eighteenth century, the mill therefore had to be close to the cane field and, in practice, cane was grown by the man who owned the mill (in the late nineteenth century private railways would make it possible for cane to be taken many miles in the two days. This would lead to both an increase in the size of mills and to a division of responsibilities between cane grower and miller.)

Cane is hauled to the mill by the best means available – oxcarts in the eighteenth century, by railways in the nineteenth and twentieth. (Even in the twentieth century, oxcarts would be used to take the cane to the railway station or on short journeys to the mill.) Other carts would collect the cane leaves for fodder.

Because of the need for speed, the workmen who do the cutting cannot be the same as those who grind the cane and boil the juice. Thus while one group of workers cut a cane field, another is busy converting the produce of another field into a sack of sugar. Cheap labour was necessary. So was access to water and to forests, for the large fires. There had to be large well-built sheds for sugar-making and for storing it, as well as a great number of wagons for hauling cane to the mill and to fetch wood, along with an uninterrupted supply of food for the workers.

There were in the eighteenth century four qualities of sugar in Cuba, according to the degree of purity attained by refining; in every sugar loaf the upper part yielded the white sugar (*blanco*); the middle part, the yellow sugar (*quebrado*); and the brownest, lowest part, the *cucurucho* (sometimes *cogucho, culo* or *puntas*). There were also coarse and quite unrefined sugars, *mascabado* and *raspadura*, the sugar of the poor (figures for this category did not usually occur in the statistics). The sugar *maestros* tried to make every loaf of sugar for export yield $\frac{5}{9}$ of white, $\frac{3}{9}$ of *quebrado* and $\frac{1}{9}$ of *cucurucho*. Sometimes the white and yellow sugar would be sold together, when it would be known as *surtido*. The division into different types was done by eye and much therefore depended on the individual *maestro de azúcar*.

CHAPTER IV

The Victors and the Creoles

The news of the fall of Havana to Lord Albemarle reached London on 27 September, just seven weeks after the event: then a fast time for a west-east Atlantic crossing. The news intoxicated the capital. The French diplomat, the Duc de Nivernais (present in London to discuss peace terms), chanced to be at dinner with the earl of Bute and other ministers and passed '*une heure bien cruelle*' to see the toasting and celebration after the news was brought, during the middle of the meal, by the heroic Captain Lord Hervey in person.[1] Nivernais 'was reduced to the awkward necessity of picking his Teeth'.[2] The duke of Cumberland told old Lady Albemarle, the victorious Keppels' mother: 'If it was not ... the drawing room, I would kiss you.'[3] People in London wrote letters congratulating each other, in a mood of high complacency: 'Our fears for the Havannah are now over by the surrender of that place with eleven men of war ... three more sunk and one million and a half sterling in money.' Thus the old duke of Newcastle (who had recently resigned) wrote to his old ally, ex-Lord Chancellor Hardwicke, thus forgetting his hostility to expeditions and even victories.[4]

> The great news of our success at the Havannah upon which I most heartily congratulate you ... the Nation in general will expect something very advantageous in the future treaty with Spain in exchange for such a conquest; and it is well if the old cry of '*Take and Hold*' is not revived ...

Thus Hardwicke's son to a friend.[5] In Philadelphia Benjamin Franklin

---

[1] Nivernais to Choiseul, 29 September 1762, qu. *Documentos Inéditos*, 231. Nivernais (1716–98) was in London to discuss peace terms. As 'Citizen Mancini', this nobleman remained in Paris during the revolution.

[2] Lord Bath to Mrs Elizabeth Montagu, qu. Reginald Blunt, *Mrs Montagu ... her letters and friendships from 1762 to 1800* (1923), I, 35.

[3] Horace Walpole to Sir H. Mann, 28 October 1762 (Horace Walpole, *Letters to Horace Mann*, ed. W. S. Lewis, VI, 94).

[4] Newcastle to Hardwicke in Albemarle, *Memoirs of Rockingham*, I, 122. His accounting was, however, wrong, though both Horace Walpole (*Letters to Horace Mann*, ed. Lewis, VI, 83) and Vickers to Newcastle (Add. MSS, 32. 942. f. 412) make the same mistake. See below, p. 56.

[5] Lord Royston to Dr Birch (Albemarle, *op. cit.*), 123–4.

wrote to George Whitefield to congratulate *him*, saying the conquest would 'doubtless contribute a due share of weight in procuring us reasonable Terms of Peace if John Bull does not get drunk with victory, double his Fists and bid all the world kiss his Arse'.[6]

It was left, however, to the duke of Cumberland to express himself most fulsomely in his letter to Albemarle:

> You have made me the happiest man existing ... you have done your king and country the most material service that any military man has ever done since we were a nation ... all this I knew was in you but now the world sees it ... Militarily speaking, I took your siege to have been the most difficult that has been since the invention of artillery. 68 days in that climate is alone prodigious ... we make you as rich as Croesus, I hope ... health and owned merit are sufficient ingredients for the happiness, so much the better if you add wealth to it.[7]

As it turned out, the prize money found in Havana in the coffers of public bodies[8] amounted to \$1,882,116 (about £440,000). Ships, brass cannon, sugar, tobacco and other goods raised the total to about £750,000. Of this Admiral Pocock and Albemarle got £122,697 10s 6d each, the other two Keppel brothers £25,000 each; naval captains got £1,600, the rest being divided according to rank: ordinary soldiers and sailors received £4 1s 8d and £3 14s 9¾d respectively.[9] Thus the fortunes of the Keppel family were repaired.

Albemarle proclaimed himself captain-general and governor. Cuba had before been a sub-satrapy of the viceroyalty of New Spain (Mexico): the link with Mexico was of course now broken and the main upholders of Spanish imperial government, the *peninsulares*, such as the governor, Prado, the treasurer, the accountant and others charged with supervising customs and taxes vanished in disgrace; the creoles – those, that is, who, though of Spanish origin, were colonists born and bred in Cuba – remained, many of them delighted. Their harmonious collaboration with the English is suggestive of the bad relations between them and the *peninsulares* (though there had always been inter-marriage between the two groups, sometimes creoles had been *tesorero* or *contador*, and every year some *peninsular* – particular *oidores*, or judges – would think it more profitable to remain in the Americas with their children). Sebastián de Peñalver, a fifty-four-year-old *regidor* (alderman) and an ex-mayor, a third generation creole, took over as lieutenant-governor, acting as

---

[6] *Documentos Inéditos*, 234.
[7] Cumberland to Albemarle (Albemarle, *op. cit.*), 125–7.
[8] i.e. the State Slave Monopoly Company, the municipal treasury, etc.
[9] Corbett, 283; CO 117.

Albemarle's deputy in all civil matters.[10] After some weeks he was replaced by the grandest of *habaneros*, the municipal *alférez* (herald), Gonzalo Recio de Oquendo, a man of great wealth, interested above all in keeping it (though nearly seventy years old and childless), with a small amount of Indian blood.[11] Both of these acted in Albemarle's name in presiding over the town council, the *cabildo*.[12]

The two *alcaldes* (magistrates) of Havana, Pedro José Calvo de la Puerta and Pedro Beltrán de Santa Cruz,[13] continued in their posts, holding *audiencias* (courts) every afternoon at a given time, as did the six *regidores* (aldermen) and the other members of the *cabildo* who had specific jobs. Now, as indeed ever since 1574, the *cabildo* met (unarmed) weekly in Havana, on Fridays, at eight in the morning. These meetings were supposed to last an hour 'even if there is nothing to do' (the governor or one of the *alcaldes* with three of the *regidores* constituted a quorum). A scrupulous regard for precedent had for generations animated (if that is not too extravagant a word) these discussions. Theoretically, if there were a clash between governor and council, the vote of a two-thirds majority would prevail. Under Albemarle, as under Captain-General Prado, the governor's will usually carried the day. But under Spain the governor always had had to take his oath of office before the *cabildo*. Some governors had been hurriedly removed or died, and so in the ensuing interregnum the *cabildo* wielded full power. Absentees from the *cabildo* were fined unless they were ill. The *cabildo* of 1762 were mostly elderly men, much of whose lives had been spent disputing over what should happen to the sale of tobacco and over the Havana Monopoly Company. Most were closely related: thus the two *alcaldes ordinarios*, Calvo de la Puerta and Beltrán de Santa Cruz, were both cousins and brothers-in-law; the brother of Calvo was the *alguacil mayor*, or chief constable; Sebastián Peñalver, Albemarle's chief collaborator, had also married a sister of the Calvos de la Puerta; Peñalver's son Gabriel was already a *regidor*, and his daughter Josefa had married Jacinto Tomás Barreto, another member of the *cabildo*, as hereditary *alcalde mayor de la Hermandad*, or justice of the rural district around Havana, one of whose daughters by a previous marriage had recently married the richest merchant of Havana, Mateo Pedroso,

[10] Sebastián Peñalver y Angulo (1708–72); his grandfather had been governor of Jamaica when captured by the English and then left for Cuba; his great-grandfather came from Valdeolivas in Cuenca province, Spain.

[11] Gonzalo Recio de Oquendo (1701–73); a seventh generation Cuban, he handed over to Peñalver again on 1 January 1763. In the 1580s one of the founders of Havana, Antón Recio, married Cucanda, daughter of the Indian Cacique of Guanabacoa (see García Carraffa, *Enciclopedia Heráldica, y Genealógica Hispano-Americana*, vol. 77, 116–17).

[12] *Cabildo* meant any council, e.g. a cathedral chapter, and the word was also used by Negroes to describe their clubs.

[13] Elected on 1 January 1761 for their two years as *alcaldes ordinarios* or magistrates of first instance. The *alcalde* was something less than a mayor, more than a justice.

himself a *regidor perpetuo* (and incidentally a first cousin of Barreto); while Pedroso's first wife had been a sister of Cristóbal Zayas Bazán, the *síndico* or receiver of fines.[14]

These town councils for a short time, long ago, had been chosen by election by property-owners but for generations money had been decisive. As early as the late sixteenth century, the Crown sold office (for life) by public auction; the job-holders and life aldermen, the rulers of cities, had thus become, with their families, self-perpetuating oligarchies, distributing land, fixing prices, directing justice, given a free hand by the Crown, with jobs passing down from father to son as often as not. Sebastián Peñalver, Albemarle's chief friend in Havana, for instance, had been a *regidor* for twenty years, as had the merchant Pedroso and the Calvo de la Puerta brothers. Half the members of the *cabildo* were owners of sugar mills. Similar councils, similarly elected, existed all over Spanish America, varying only in the numbers of *regidores* (sometimes as few as four, sometimes twelve, depending on the size of the city).

To cut links in 1762 with the viceroy in Mexico and the king in Spain meant of course a sharp change in the fabric of the Spanish empire. Government in this empire was primarily judicial. The supreme institution was the *audiencia,* a high court first used to enforce law in territories reconquered from the Moors, and now in the Americas the court of appeal from the *alcalde ordinario.* Three or four superior judges (*oidores*), almost always born in Spain, usually professional lawyers, were allocated to each of fourteen *audiencias* in Spanish America. The viceroy in Mexico and Peru or the captain-general in Cuba or Santo Domingo presided. Appeals might be made from one *audiencia* to a higher one, but the faraway king was the only authority above the *audiencia* of New Spain. The *audiencia* was also consultative and even administrative: it advised the viceroy on general matters and, when a viceroy died, it assumed his powers. Cuba was only a captaincy-general, nominally subordinate to the viceroy of New Spain in Mexico City, its *audiencia* established anyway in Santo Domingo, the old first colony of

[14] The *cabildo* consisted in 1762 of: *alcaldes ordinarios* – Pedro Beltrán de Santa Cruz and Miguel Calvo de la Puerta; *alférez mayor* (herald or municipal standard bearer and chairman in the absences of the *alcaldes*) – Gonzalo Recio de Oquendo; *alguacil* (chief constable) – Pedro José Calvo de la Puerta; *alcalde mayor de la Santa Hermandad* (justice of the rural areas around Havana and head of the constabulary to keep order in it) – Jacinto Tomás Barreto; *correo mayor* (postmaster) – José Cipriano de la Luz; *síndico* (receiver of fines) – Cristóbal Zayas Bazán; *fiel ejecutor* (inspector of weights and measures and in charge of food prices and food supplies) – Luis José de Aguiar; *síndico procurador* (attorney-general) – Felipe José de Zequeira; *regidores* (aldermen) – José Martín Félix de Arrate, Sebastián Peñalver, Gabriel Peñalver, Miguel Sotolongo and Laureano Chacón; *regidores perpetuos* – Pedro Beltrán de Santa Cruz and Mateo Pedroso; *Depositor-General* (Public Trustee) – Félix José de Acosta; *escribano* (secretary) – Antonio Ignacio de Ayala. The proceedings of the council were published as *La Dominación Inglesa, op. cit.*

Spain in the New World but now poor and miserable. So the relation to both political and legal authority anyway had been remote. In practice, the Cuban captain-general conducted himself independently: Prado had received his instructions to fortify Havana direct from Madrid, and even strong viceroys had their margin of activity limited by the vast number of regulations on every subject under the sun issued by the Council of the Indies at Seville.

The main mark of the Spanish empire until now had been formally its centralization. In contrast with Anglo-Saxon America, the Crown had been the decisive factor in colonization, government and town planning. For the first hundred years of the empire, laws and decrees arrived from Spain by every ship, deriving from the Board of Trade at Seville, or the supreme Council of the Indies. By 1635 over 400,000 decrees (*cédulas*) had been issued – 2,500 a year since Columbus sailed. They were later reduced to a code of 6,400 decrees (*recopilación*). The colonies were theoretically regarded as equivalent to provinces of Spain; in practice, they were treated more arbitrarily than Spanish provinces, though the arbitrary laws could rarely be fulfilled. No part of the Spanish empire had anything like the *fueros* of the Basques; but the delays in dealing with business were great. Thus when Lorenzo Montalvo, *comisario* of the navy in 1762, had bought an estate in 1746, it was only in 1752 that the Council of the Indies decided that the procedure which he had followed was wrong (in fact, since he had wisely already paid taxes he was allowed to keep the land). Captains-general in Cuba were of course nominated by the king, to whom they reported. Beneath them (and also appointed in Madrid) were numerous minor officials: such as the governor in Santiago at the far east of Cuba, still holding out for Spain in 1762 against the English after the fall of Havana, or the *alcaldes* who presided over the local town councils in smaller towns such as Matanzas or Sancti Spiritus. Apart from the top officials, no one was paid enough. All were corrupt.

Thus already in the history of South America and Cuba certain familiar characteristics were apparent: centralization; reliance on a remote sovereign authority; corruption; and confusion between, or blur between, the executive and the judicial authority.

The creoles, who always resented control from Madrid and could never do anything about it, were, as Major Gosham put it, a 'mongrel crew'. The first big estate in Cuba after the conquest had been established by a ruined bastard of the family of the dukes of Feria, Vasco Porcayo de Figueroa, one of the villains of the 'black legend' of the assassination of Indians, who seemed certainly to combine the barbarity of the Middle Ages with the refinement of the Renaissance; his daughter married an Indian chief, and thereby inherited vast estates in the region of Camagüey. Some creoles, such as the Herreras and Núñez de Castillo,[15] were already ennobled by the eighteenth century and were large landowners in Cuba, though their lands were close to Havana, where they had their town houses. Those who, less fruitfully, had estates in East Cuba had town houses in Santiago or Puerto Príncipe and rarely if ever went to Havana. Some creoles were merchants made good, some peasants; some were the heirs of that first generation of adventurers who descended on the Caribbean in the sixteenth century with nothing to lose and now, two hundred years later, seemed pillars of the small Havana society; the ancestors of some had as soldiers of Charles V forced Indians to sieve rivers for gold, while others were descended from seamen who had, as distant agents of a crumbling empire, hung on in Havana rather than return to the Spain of Charles II. They had come in the early days mostly from Andalusia, and latterly more often from the northern coast of Spain.[16] Some were descendants of Jews who had chosen to leave Spain, like the brothers of St Teresa, on the expectation that the laws regarding purity of blood would be less likely to be applied in the Indies – though other laws, even less applied, banned the emigration of Jews to the New World completely. The much inter-married creole *haute bourgeoisie* now rarely left Cuba: Calvos de la Puerta and Peñalvers, Beltráns de la Cruz and Recios de Oquendo, Pedrosos and Herreras, they already ran the economy of Cuba and were preparing to enrich themselves from its development on a substantial scale.

In 1762 only a few *peninsulares* such as the *comisario* of the navy, Lorenzo Montalvo, who had come to Cuba from Castille in 1734, collaborated with the English and remained in their posts; and even Montalvo had already laid plans to settle down in Cuba, having bought a huge estate of three *hatos* and five *potreros* (on which, however, he would establish sugar mills) at Macuriges, thirty miles from Matanzas.[17] Merchants such as Pedroso or Pedro de Estrada (who had been imprisoned during the siege of Havana for trying to help the English) immediately saw their chance. Only the remarkable bishop of Havana, Morell de Santa Cruz, aged seventy-two, intransigent but enlightened, born, as it happened, in Santo Domingo (but holding a post usually filled by *peninsulares*),[18] offered defiance; and, after disputes with Albemarle as to which church could be used for Anglican services and

---

[15] Captain Juan Núñez de Castillo owed his title to his activity in support of the Crown's policies against the tobacco farmers in 1710–20. See Rivero Muñiz, 88.

[16] See V. Aubrey Neasham, 'Spain's Emigrants to the New World', *Hispanic American Historical Review*, xix (1939), 147–60. Spanish emigration to the Americas may not have been much more than 1,000–1,500 a year in the sixteenth century (*ibid.*, 179).

[17] Corbitt, 'Mercedes and Realengos', 270. He paid $33,071, plus $1,500 and $239 for various taxes. This land had previously been a *merced*, not a *realengo*.

[18] It might be that *criollos* might serve on these posts but almost always away from their home province.

another over the appointment of priests, he was dispatched to Florida.[19] Their relations were bad from the beginning, due to Albemarle's extra demands for tribute from the church: 'the least you can give is $10,000,' said Albemarle, 'as a donation to the conquering general'; whether for his personal use or for his country was uncertain.[20] Some anti-English inhabitants of Havana went to the interior and, led by Martín Esteban de Aróstegui, the governor of Puerto Príncipe, and Luis de Aguiar, the *fiel ejecutor,* or director of supply in the *cabildo* of Havana, plotted unsuccessfully the recapture of the city.[21] Nevertheless, with only five thousand troops (after Pocock, the navy and the North American troops had left), the English could hardly have maintained themselves without creole acceptance, explicitly and actively articulated by the *cabildo*. Social contact with the English began when Albemarle gave a series of balls. There was speculation as to whether Havana might not be turned into another Jamaica or Gibraltar: and the *alférez* or standard bearer, Recio de Oquendo, apparently thought so.[22]

Outside Havana the situation was less promising. In Santiago the governor of the province, Lorenzo de Madariaga, maintained the Spanish flag, assuming the functions of captain-general. Albemarle announced on 1 September that England would not attack the eastern part of the island, nor indeed any other part of the Spanish empire. Apart from the ports of Matanzas and Mariel, the English kept to the area near Havana, though being ready to 'bring to reason' the inhabitants of Trinidad or Sancti Spiritus (formally within the Havana jurisdiction) if they should interrupt the supply of beef for Havana.[23]

The harbour of Havana was cleared by 21 August. But the main problem was disease. 'Havana is taken,' remarked Dr Johnson, 'but it is a conquest too dear, for Bathurst is dead in it': dead, needless to say, of fever.[24] Up till 8 October, Albemarle lost 560 killed in action and 4,708 from sickness – or well over one third of the total force; Pocock lost 186 killed and 1,300 seamen and marines dead from sickness.[25]

[19] Pedro Agustín Morell de Santa Cruz (1644–1768). Born Santiago de los Caballeros. Ordained Havana 1718. Bishop of León de Nicaragua 1745–53 and of Cuba 1753–68.

[20] Mgr Morell de Santa Cruz had vigorously encouraged the merger of African with Catholic practices which is such a remarkable characteristic of Negro life in Cuba. See above, 39, and Klein, 101. Other difficulties derived from Albemarle's insistence on an English church. See A. Bachiller y Morales, *Cuba: monografía histórica que comprende desde la pérdida de la Habana hasta la restauración española* (1883), 114. The bishop came back in April 1763.

[21] See Guerra and Santovenia, II, 46. Not to be confused with his brother, the Martín de Aróstegui who had been president of the Havana Company in the 1750s. Luis José de Aguiar (1710–66) was the only member of the *cabildo* to oppose the English regime outright.

[22] García Carraffa, vol. 77, 120.

[23] Havana jurisdiction extended '60 leagues east of the city' – i.e. just about to Sancti Spiritus. (See note of Prado defining the limits, 14 August 1762, CO 117/1, f. 102.)

[24] Richard Bathurst, army physician and essayist, Johnson's 'beloved friend', whose father brought back Johnson's Negro servant, Francis Barber, from Jamaica.

[25] CO 117. This did not include slaves who died.

'It is not to be described all we have gone through,' Albemarle wrote to Newcastle.[26]

Despite the bad conditions in Havana, the British capture of the city was the signal, as it had been in the case of the capture of Guadeloupe and Martinique, for an immediate descent on the island by English merchants. From North America came food, horses, and grain merchants and, direct from England, linen, cloth and wool sellers, and dealers in sugar equipment. Goods long coveted by frustrated Cubans flooded in. First in order of importance among the English traders was the commissary John Kennion, to whom Albemarle gave the exclusive right to import two thousand slaves a year, of whom 1,500 were to be males and 500 females. The price would be determined by the market. Albemarle asked a duty to be paid by the importer of $40 (£9) per adult slave and $20 (£4 10s) per child slave, along with other duties on other merchandise.[27] He had later to admit that these duties were illegally imposed and had to return what he had received to the merchants. 'Send someone here that understands trade and will not cheat the King,' Albemarle pettishly wrote back to England. (A Mr William Michie became Collector of Customs in December.[28]) But of course Spanish taxes ceased to be paid. Those extraordinarily wearisome dues, *almojarifazgos* (payable on goods coming in from Spain), *avería* (payable to the navy), *alcabalas* (payable on exports to Spain) and *donativos* (extra levies), paid by the Indies to finance the impoverished government of Madrid, vanished.[29]

Though Kennion was the largest single importer of slaves, he did not maintain his monopoly. 'The acquisition of Havana will give great spirits to the planters in Georgia and this province [South Carolina] to purchase Negroes,' wrote the South Carolina slave dealer, Henry Laurens, to his agent in Liverpool.[30] All the large English or West Indian merchants turned their ships towards Havana on hearing of its surrender.[31] But when they reached Havana, they discovered Kennion's

[26] *Loc. cit.*, letter received 29 September. He meant illness not military action. He himself was sick for the rest of his life (Corbett, II, 292).

[27] Albemarle's formal concession to Kennion is in the Liverpool Papers in the British Museum (Add. MSS., 38201, f. 299), dated 23 October 1762. See also CO 117/248 and *Nuevos Papeles sobre la toma de la Habana por los Ingleses en 1762* (1951), 131. The concession is printed as Appendix IV.

[28] BM, Add. MSS., 38, 201, f. 301.

[29] *Ibid.*, 32, 942, item 388; Albemarle to Newcastle.

[30] Donnan, IV, 380. Laurens later became a politician; president of the Continental Congress; U.S. minister to Holland; he signed the preliminaries of peace with England in 1781.

[31] The merchants who with Kennion led the trade with Havana in 1762-3 were the ubiquitous Samuel Touchet, cotton spinner and shipowner, government adviser and slave merchant; Robert Grant; Alexander Grant (presumably the Sir Alexander Grant who, an M.P. in 1761, had spent years in Jamaica where he made his fortune); Charles Ogilvie; Maltby and Dyer; James Christie; Alexander Anderson and Davidson; William Wright & Co.; John Gregg; a representative of Hutchinson & Co.; Richard Atkinson; and William

monopoly and therefore they had to sell their cargo at a low price on a black market; thereafter they avoided Havana in general.[32] Even so, very many slaves were now sold. Some were sold from among those brought in to service the English army; Albemarle himself had paid $60,000 for about 1,200 slaves while *en route* to Havana and these became available for Cuban buyers during his sojourn in Havana.[33] The precise number of slaves is impossible to calculate but it may well have approached 4,000 during the eleven months from August 1762 to July 1763.[34]

This importation did not bring such profit to the English slave merchants as similar expeditions had done in the past or as they had done in the French islands,[35] even to John Kennion. The Spanish empire's wealth had for generations been over-estimated by foreigners, particularly the English. The old *asiento* to supply the Spanish market with slaves had been foolishly reckoned a kind of 'commercial eldorado',[36] certain to enrich all who held it. One attraction of the market had been that Spaniards paid in gold. But in 1762–3, there was little spare cash in Cuba. Prices of slaves sagged: the old State Monopoly Company had sold slaves at over $200 (£46);[37] the price obtained by the English merchants was $90 (£21) as compared with the £25 to £35 a head elsewhere in the islands at this time.[38]

With slave prices at £12 a head on the Nigerian and Angola coasts

[32] See the case of the *Africa*: 'The Apellant [Jasper Hall of Jamaica] received Advice from his Agent at the Havannah to whose care he had in the previous October sent a cargo of two hundred slaves for Sale that it would not be prudent or advisable for him to send this cargo thither on Account of the Governor of Havannah's Grant to a person resident there of an Exclusive Right of importing and vending slaves whereby this Correspondent had been . . . laid under the necessity of selling the whole cargo . . . at an under price . . . so the Apellant . . . sent the *Africa* . . . to Hispaniola' (qu. Donnan, II, 535).

[33] *Documentos Inéditos*, 204; see also *Papeles sobre la toma de la Habana por los Ingleses en 1762* (1948), 103.

[34] Kennion, officially, had sold 1,700 slaves by April 1763, not 10,700 as the U.S. historian H. S. Aimes said in his *History of Slavery in Cuba, 1511–1868* (1907), 33, countless other historians following him. (Aimes also got the citation of the document wrong: it should have been Est. 84, caja 7, leg. 23', not 'leg. 13', and anyway has been renumbered Santo Domingo 2210, letter of the fiscal, Francisco López Gamarra to Julián de Arriaga, Madrid, dated 27 April, 1763.) On the other hand it would be false to suppose that the 1,700 *'cabezas de negros bozales'* here mentioned were all that the English sold, or even all that Kennion sold. No exact figure is likely to be found, though I should be surprised if it was under 4,000.

[35] In Guadeloupe 12,347 slaves from 41 ships were sold for £334,605 11s 2d (John Entick, *The General History of the Late War*, 5 vols (1763), V, 433–4), i.e., £22 10s a head.

[36] As Professors P. M. Parry and J. H. Sherlock, *A Short History of the West Indies*, 2nd edn (1963), put it.

[37] 1754 prices had been $210 to $225 for a *muleque* (six to fourteen years), $250 to $270 for a *mulecón* (fourteen to eighteen years), and $280 to $300 for a *pieza de Indias* (eighteen to thirty-five years). Archivo de Indias, qu. Aimes, 267.

[38] Albemarle was in fact paying up to £50 per Negro earlier in the year (*cf. Documentos Inéditos*, 43).

Bond (CO 117/1, 295). It appears that Kennion and Touchet alone came from Lancashire, the rest from London, Glasgow, Kingston, Jamaica, or North America.

and nearly £17 for the more sought-after Gold Coast Negroes,[39] after paying crews and maintenance bills, Kennion could therefore have made only a small profit; though, since Albemarle had paid him £98,000 during recent weeks for supplies, there is no reason to think that he was out of pocket on the whole enterprise.[40] In a memorandum to the secretary of state, Lord Egremont, meantime, in November 1762, 145 of the principal slave merchants of Liverpool begged the British government to keep at least Guadeloupe at the forthcoming Peace, because of their great profits from selling slaves there and from the stimulus this trade had been to English manufacturers; the slaves themselves as usual had been exchanged in Africa for manufactured goods, not cash.[41] These merchants admittedly did not mention Havana. But in the eleven months of English occupation of that city, apparently over 700 merchant ships entered the port which previously never in one year had been entered by more than fifteen, apart from treasure fleets under royal control.[42] Of these ships, probably twenty, or one in forty, would have been slaveships.[43] Almost a quarter of the total were probably English North-American vessels.[44] A great many also were ships bringing supplies, while others took off wounded and other soldiers.

[39] As qu., Donnan, II, 516, fn., from a contemporary pamphlet. *Cf.* prices in *Report to the Privy Council, 1788,* Pt V; £17 was high, the average being £12 to £14. Most slaves were bought in Africa, few were kidnapped ('*panyared*').

[40] See accounts in *Documentos Inéditos.*

[41] This memorandum, published in *London Magazine,* November 1762, is reprinted in Donnan, 514–15. It was not, however, presented since it was apparently finished too late to influence events.

[42] Figures in Guerra and Santovenia, etc., II, 51.

[43] i.e., assuming a load of 250 slaves per ship. The exports to Cuba this year are reflected in British Board of Trade figures. Their reliability is not absolute but the trend is obvious:

| | Imports | | Exports | |
| | | (in £1,000) | | |
	Total S. America and foreign W. Indies	Havana	Total S. America and foreign W. Indies	Havana
Last year of peace (1755)	0	0	0	0
1757	1	0	0	0
1759 (i.e. Guadeloupe)	93	0	61	0
1760	424	0	120	0
1761	491	0	140	0
1762	827	0	460	117
1763	1,036	249	32	6

(*Abstract of English Historical Statistics,* 310; Havana figures: Sir Charles Whitworth, *State of Trade of Great Britain in its imports and exports...from the year 1762.* 2 Pts (1726), Pt II, 89.) These figures do not take account of the curious circumstances of the triangular trade to the West Indies via Africa. But the British exports to Africa in 1763 went up by 70%, from £273,000 to £464,000 – *cf.* £174,000 in 1755, the last year of peace – a sure index of increased slave purchases.

[44] Thirty ships from New York sailed in 1763 alone and 150 may have sailed from Boston, Philadelphia and Charleston. *New York Gazette,* 3 January 1763 (NN. 201763), qu. Harry Bernstein, *Origins of Inter-American Interest, 1700–1812* (1945), 22: the other ports are guesses. Few of the slaveships would have been North American based.

There were probably no more than 32,000 slaves in Cuba previously.[45] During the whole period since the Spanish arrival in Cuba perhaps only 60,000 slaves had been imported.[46] Thus the slaves brought in this year by the English possibly numbered an eighth of the total previously on the island. Without much doubt the slaves mostly came from the Nigerian ports, in the Bight of Benin, probably most of the slaves being Ibos, but Yorubas forming a substantial minority. The slave coast (Dahomey and Lagos) and the Gold Coast closely followed the Bight of Benin in satisfying the labour demands of Cuba.

This import of cheap labour helped Cuba further on her remarkable and sustained, if politically melancholy, sugar career so that, within thirty years, she, like South Carolina and the other imperial islands in the Caribbean, but unlike any Spanish possession on the mainland or the rest of North America, would have a black or mulatto majority in the population. No doubt the Spanish planters in Cuba would have tried to embark on large-scale purchases of slaves anyway; but they had not been able to do so before and in the late 1750s an application by José Pico Villanueva to import a thousand slaves a year had been rejected on the specific ground that it would be dangerous to have so many potentially rebellious slaves on the island.[47]

This import of slaves, combined with the long-term commercial arrangements then established (including debts), was the distinguishing characteristic of Albemarle's expedition to Havana.[48] It is doubtless true that had it not been for the existence of conditions favourable to the absorption of an increased labour force – eager landowners, woods, cattle and land itself – the sugar industry would not have developed even so; and that therefore the English occupation may be said to have

[45] 32,000 is the figure accepted by Donnan (II, xlviii) and given for 1763 by Humboldt, (*Travels* (Bohn edn, 1853), III, 243), though it is unclear how he reached this figure. Much higher estimates have been given, but the census of 1774 gives a total of 44,000. Slave importation between 1763 and 1774 could hardly have been more than 1,500 a year; at the same time we hear of a great plague in 1770 which allegedly killed 17,000 slaves – doubtless an exaggeration. More important, there is also a letter from Governor Cagigal in 1753 in which he said that since eight to ten out of 80 slaves died every year, Cuba needed 600–800 slaves. These would give figures of about 32,000. Imports between 1756 and 1761 were notoriously unsatisfactory, due to the war.

[46] A calculation of 1811, by the Real Consulado, says 60,000 between 1521 and 1762 inclusive (Ramón de la Sagra, *Historia económico–política y estadística de la isla de Cuba*, 10).

[47] The English incidentally took 10,000 slaves to Guadeloupe in each of the four years that they occupied that island. On the other hand all pre-1760 estimates for Cuban slaves are open to doubt: thus the English South Sea factor in Kingston claimed in 1748 to have sold 3,700 slaves to Havana in eighteen months (*H.A.H.R.*, xviii, 117).

[48] The importance of this aspect of the matter was recognized by Francisco Pérez de la Riva alone of Cuban historians (*Origen y Régimen de la Propiedad Territorial en Cuba* (1946), 73–4, 123–4). See also Moreno Fraginals, 5.

accelerated an inevitable historical process.[49] But the acceleration was so important as to be itself almost a revolution.

The English occupants also imported so many goods that they could not be disposed of by Havana shopkeepers for years, many being distributed slowly throughout the Spanish empire.[50] Many of these goods must have been sugar equipment such as machetes, cauldrons and ladles cheaper than those manufactured in Havana itself, as well as the hats, stockings, cottons and linens mentioned as being the largest single group. The importing merchants found it hard to get paid, and thus began a long period of indebtedness of Havana shopkeepers and landowners towards them or towards their factors or agents in Jamaica.

There were some other changes: in November Albemarle explained that the custom of making large cash presents to the governor of the island in return for a favourable conclusion of lawsuits would now end; he would rule impartially, favouring neither rich nor poor, superior nor inferior.[51] The English also seem to have introduced freemasonry into Cuba. But the arrogant invaders were unpopular with a lower class which, if scarcely patriotic, did not welcome change. Only the *haute bourgeoisie* can really have hoped the English would stay.

Peace between Britain, France and Spain was now imminent. Preliminaries of peace were signed in early November 1762, the treaty itself in February. Commodore Keppel had earlier left to command the Jamaica squadron and in January 1763 Albemarle himself, with the colonial troops, left Havana. The youngest Keppel on the expedition, the general, William, took over as military governor. On 1 January 1763, as on every alternate New Year's day, two new mayors (*alcaldes ordinarios*) were elected – Laureano Chacón and José Cipriano de la Luz, as usual, all the aldermen in the *cabildo* voted for the same men (as in other offices), the discussion having been settled beforehand.[52] The old Spanish system continued. Negotiations in Paris made England's gains in the war seem like temporary advantages gained at chess. What would be the position of Havana, as well as of Guadeloupe and Martinique, the other sugar colonies of the Caribbean? The English attitude was determined partly by the mood of the new prime minister,

[49] As argued by Moreno Fraginals, 4. Similar consequences followed in Guadeloupe where 18,721 slaves had been imported during the occupation. It rapidly overtook Martinique.

[50] This was realized at the time by the Fiscal who so wrote to his government in April 1763 (Santo Domingo, 2210, A de I). The quantity was so great as to disrupt trade between Cuba and Jamaica for years afterwards (see Allan Cristelow, 'Contraband Trade between Jamaica and the Spanish Main' *H.A.H.R.* xxii, p. 309; and Richard Pares's contribution to *Essays presented to Sir Lewis Namier*, where the difficulties of getting paid are described).

[51] Actas del Cabildo de la Habana, No. 4, 1762, qu. *La Dominación Inglesa*, 48.

[52] Actually on this occasion there was a second vote since at first the Marqués de Villalta was elected instead of de la Luz; he was not acceptable, being too closely related to Chacón, his brother-in-law. Chacón, whose family had been in Cuba since the early seventeenth century, had been identified with Luis José de Aguiar in protest against the English.

Lord Bute, no friend of 'Take and Hold', and partly by the attitude of Jamaica and her friends in London. There seems never to have been any serious disposition on Britain's part to keep Havana; the main controversy was between the French sugar islands and Canada; and even that had really been resolved before Albemarle's expedition had set out.[53]

Jamaica, the queen of sugar at that time, lay a bare eighty miles to the south of Cuba. But while economic prosperity lay ahead for Cuba, in Jamaica the greatest age of expansion was already past. Many Jamaican sugar plantations were mature. Their soil had often been used up. Manure was expensive and required more slaves than was economical for it to be used effectively. Planters might abandon old mills and move to new ones in virgin land; that also involved expenditure of capital and higher costs; and there was now little virgin land still in Jamaica, since much of the island, being mountainous, was unsuitable for the cultivation of cane. Available land was therefore expensive. Ahead of Jamaica, indeed, there seemed to lie the fate of Barbados and Antigua, which had both had their day as golden sugar colonies; both had fallen behind, also because of lack of land. Already the cost of English West Indian sugar was higher than that of French sugar from Martinique, Guadeloupe or Saint Domingue. Buyers of sugar in English North America already illegally bought French sugar if they could. English consumers (particularly industrial consumers) at home were also complaining at the laws which forbade them to buy anything but English.

The economic success of the French islands was due to Martinique and Guadeloupe being bigger than Barbados and Antigua, while Saint Domingue was bigger than Jamaica. The virgin lands on which cane grew almost without attention seemed endless. The French colonies were also enabled by law to refine sugar on the spot; whilst English law, supported by refiners at London and Bristol, forbade refineries (like other industries) in the colonies. So, stimulated by the illegal North American markets, the French had been already poised, before the war, to overtake the English in production.

The prospect of an English acquisition of Cuba as a result of Lord Albemarle's expedition thus could not be welcome in Jamaica. True, Commodore Keppel's capture of Goree in West Africa had disrupted the French slave trade, seriously damaging the work on sugar plantations in the French West Indies.[54] The French West Indian economy was

[53] The cabinet decision to prefer to keep Canada and Cape Breton was taken on 24 June 1761, but the question was nevertheless open all through 1762, and revived when peace negotiations began. See Namier, *England*, 279–80.

[54] Samuel Touchet, the great cotton merchant, patron of Paul's spinning machine, M.P., one of the merchants trading to Havana, and aggressive entrepreneur, tried to get the

so closely linked with Africa for labour that even a year's interruption in the slave supply caused havoc.[55] (Planters often spoke of a *penurie effrayante* of slaves, as twentieth-century farmers speak of terrible weather.) But when Guadeloupe and Martinique fell to the English, their planters had been allowed to continue to grow sugar on terms which the English planters of neighbouring islands considered all too favourable. They retained French law. Their slaves were guaranteed to them. Their sugar was even allowed free into English markets.[56] English and North American merchants poured in food, timber and slaves, as they later did into Havana.[57] Some French planters were enabled to escape their debts and run up new ones with English merchants. In the English home market, flooded with French sugar, sugar prices indeed dropped (from a range of between thirty and fifty shillings a hundredweight to below thirty to forty).[58]

Where Cuba was concerned, it was not indeed what she was but what she might become if developed that disturbed the planters of Jamaica. Their friends were strong in parliament: indeed, since many of them were absentees, they were strong in parliament themselves. There were at Westminster at least twenty 'West Indian' members and about fifty general merchants (of whom ten had connections with the West Indies).[59] Apprehensive of the consequences for their wealth if England became responsible for further islands in the Caribbean, their influence was critical, even though William Pitt argued forcefully against the surrender of these prizes. There were in the winter of 1762–3, apparently, only two men prominent in, or knowledgeable of, the British North American colonies to counterbalance those 'pampered creoles', as the North Americans called the West Indian lobby.[60] The English were, therefore, ready to surrender Havana, provided Spain were to give way on other matters, such as the rights of the baymen of Honduras and of English merchants in Cuba afterwards. Yet it is hard

[55] Gaston Martin, *Histoire de l'Esclavage dans les colonies françaises* (1948).
[56] See M. Satineau, *Histoire de la Guadeloupe sous l'ancien régime, 1635–1789* (1928).
[57] 40,000 slaves were imported by the English to Guadeloupe between 1759 and 1763.
[58] See the tables in Deerr, *History of Sugar*.
[59] Namier, *England*, 234ff., corrected older impressions that there were fifty or sixty 'West Indians' in the House of Commons in 1761. Some of the merchants might, however, have supported 'Take and Hold' since they often had interests in the North American colonies as well as the West Indies.
[60] *Ibid.*, 229–30; of these one was only returned in December 1762. There were no Americans at all. William Beckford had 22,022 acres, his two brothers 8,000 and 9,000 acres respectively (*ibid.*, 237). He did however vote with Pitt in the minority against surrendering the sugar islands (the vote being 319 to 65).

monopoly of trade to and from Goree, but it was decided that this would have been an infringement of the licence granted to the Company of Merchants trading to Africa. See discussion of his tempestuous career in A. P. Wadsworth and J. de L. Mann, *The Cotton Trade and Industrial Lancashire, 1600–1780* (1931) and in Namier, *History of Parliament*.

to reach a firm conclusion about the interests of the West Indian merchants in this matter. The merchants trading to Havana, headed by John Kennion and Alexander Grant, had also Jamaican interests in the form of plantations; Kennion also traded with North America, as did Sir Ellis Cunliffe, the M.P. for Liverpool, whose slave-selling interests were, however, centred in Jamaica. Whatever the motives, which must have been mixed, of these men, those who were planters in Jamaica and not traders, and particularly those who in England lived off Jamaican income, were opponents of 'Take and Hold'.

King Charles III of Spain was at first inclined to a heroic posture and to fight on, rather than give way on anything. But the French persuaded their ally that unless he made peace now he might lose Mexico or other parts of South America. The French ministers were anxious to re-establish themselves in Martinique and in Guadeloupe and in the all-important slave labour supplies of Goree in West Africa.[61] Even the Foreign Minister, the Duc de Choiseul, had a family link with the slave trade and hence with West Indian prosperity.[62] Peace was signed in February: the English would leave Havana by July. The Spanish Crown would resume control, after western Cuba had received the profound shock of attachment to the British empire and to British commerce.

As for the conquerors, Albemarle remained the political agent of the duke of Cumberland, transferred his allegiance afterwards to Lord Rockingham, never again saw military action, remained ill for the rest of his life, and died in 1772 aged forty-eight, having only in 1770 married a girl from Chichester (his old constituency), leaving an only son and heir.[63] With his prize money, meantime, he had bought the estate of Quidenham in Norfolk from John Bristowe, the chairman of the South Sea Company, the leading British trader to Portugal and to South America. Bristowe had made a fortune out of supplying and provisioning Minorca and Gibraltar in the War of Austrian Succession but lost much of it in the Lisbon earthquake in 1755. He valued Quidenham at £36,000 in August 1761 but Albemarle paid £63,000. Norfolk land values had risen enormously in the thirty years 1730–60, so Bristowe may have undervalued and Albemarle even so may have made a

[61] Though they surrendered trading rights in Senegal.

[62] Choiseul's two cousins had married into the rich slave-trading family of Walsh, whose most prominent representative was Antoine Walsh, the biggest slave merchant of Nantes, and who, after founding the Compagnie des Indes, provided the ship which carried Bonnie Prince Charlie to Scotland. He died, ennobled, in Saint Domingue in 1762. (All Frenchmen who built sugar mills received a title.)

[63] While all the three Keppels who had been in the expedition to Havana were for years happy bachelors living with mistresses and illegitimate children, the fourth brother Frederic, the bishop, was married to a wife (Laura Walpole) whom the others cordially disliked for her pomposity. When it became clear that, unless another brother married, the bishop (and Laura) would inherit the title and property, the brothers drew lots as to who should marry to thwart their sister-in-law. The earl won and duly carried out his part of the bargain.

bargain. The whole exchange was typical of the eighteenth-century inter-relation between commerce and war: the old manager of the company which in the past had sent slaves to Cuba sold his estate to the prize winner of Havana, much of whose prize money itself came from the Spanish State Slave Company's coffers. The estate itself was ripe for development along the lines of scientific farming.[64]

Commodore Keppel became commander-in-chief of the fleet in the American war and was court-martialled for his mishandling of operations against Brest in 1779. Found innocent, he became a viscount but died shortly afterwards in 1786 aged sixty-one. The youngest brother, General William Keppel, became an M.P., commander-in-chief in Ireland and governor of Jersey, also never married and also died quite young, like his brother happy in the affections of a convenient mistress. Sir George Pocock retired from the navy in 1766 but, although much older, outlived all the Keppels, dying at the age of eighty-six in 1792. John Kennion kept his sugar estates in Jamaica but, becoming an absentee, like many English proprietors there, had turned by 1774, like other successful slave merchants of Liverpool, insurance broker,[65] and afterwards Collector of Customs; he died at the age of fifty-nine in 1785,[66] and, as befitted a successful West Indian merchant, left an endowment of apprenticeships for children in Rochdale, valued in 1826 as £6,365 worth of consols.[67]

The fortunes made by these men foreshadowed others which would be made directly or indirectly out of Cuba by Anglo-Saxons, chiefly from North America, some from England. One elegiac memorial to the expedition is a painting by a Norfolk painter named Gilpin. Albemarle is depicted out shooting on his new estate of Quidenham, whose church tower is seen through a break in the trees. There are dogs and the beaters are in olive-green livery. Albemarle himself is depicted teaching his illegitimate son George Keppel (a future admiral) how to shoot. The scene must have occurred between 1764 and 1770. It was not the last tranquil scene in an Anglo-Saxon country financed by bloodshed in Cuba or the Caribbean.

[64] See Namier and Brooke, *History of Parliament*, II, 119; and GEC Complete Peerage, Albemarle. Quidenham is now a nunnery.

[65] He was established at 1 Peter Street, College Lane (*Gore's Liverpool Directory*, 1774). In 1781 he was on the committee for the Chamber of Commerce (*ibid.*, 1781, 112) and in that year he had a counting house. Kennion's Jamaican plantation was at Hallhead, St Thomas in the East (see his will, probate 12 December 1785). Eight ships were registered in his name in Liverpool between 1772 and 1785 and of these he was mostly sole owner. All were over 100 tons in weight.

[66] He died 20 June 1785 and his wife Alice died in 1813 aged eighty-three. Both were buried in the Unitarian Ancient Chapel of Toxteth, where Kennion's uncle had long been minister.

[67] *Victoria County History of Lancashire*, Vol. V (1911), 201.

BOOK I

The Great Leap Forward
1763 - 1825

'The Island of Cuba alone might be worth a kingdom
to Spain.'

ABBÉ RAYNAL

CHAPTER V

Enter North America

The English left and the *cabildo*, its reputation scarcely enhanced, received the new Spanish governor with as much show of enthusiasm as it had received Lord Albemarle a year before. But though most of these *criollos* made their peace with Spain, Sebastián Peñalver and Gonzalo Recio de Oquendo were both sent back to Spain and there tried and imprisoned. Peñalver died in disgrace in Ceuta, but Gonzalo Recio was pardoned after some years and indeed received when over seventy the title of Marqués de la Real Proclamación. Their families and connections flourished in liberated Cuba: of the other members of the council in 1762, four were surprisingly ennobled for their 'valiant service against the English'.[1] The collaborators reaped honours of realism – or should one say of wealth? – for these men were very exactly sugar barons. All remained in Cuba, providing the island with an aristocracy, however *nouveau*, that the English islands always lacked.

Sugar production now moved forward at an extraordinary pace. In the seven years before 1760, official exports had averaged about 300 tons a year, with production at the most reaching 5,000 tons;[2] between 1764 and 1769 exports were officially over 2,000 tons a year, seven times what they had been in the 1750s. In the 1770s, an average export of over 10,000 tons a year meant that Cuba was exporting officially five times what it had done in the 1760s and over thirty times what it had exported officially in the 1750s. Thereafter, Cuban sugar production rose further, unsteadily (wars and blockades caused irregularities in the world demand for sugar and the world slave market), till in the late 1820s Cuba had become the richest colony and the largest sugar producer in the world.[3]

These great steps forward should be attributed partly, of course, to a

[1] Felipe José de Zequeira became Conde de Lagunillas; Gabriel Peñalver, Sebastián's rich son, became Marqués de Casa Peñalver; Jacinto Barreto became Conde de Casa Barreto; Pedro Calvo de la Puerta became Conde de Buena Vista; while the son of Pedro Beltrán de Santa Cruz became Conde de Jaruco.

[2] Exports *officially* were 2,200 tons in the seven years 1754–60. See above, p. 30. As there suggested, old figures deriving from Arango have consistently underestimated Cuban sugar production before 1762, neglecting both home consumption and illegal exports. Moreno Fraginals calculates (p. 3) total production to have been *c.* 5,500 tons before then.

[3] In 1829, Cuban production reached 73,000 tons of sugar, while Jamaica's was 69,000; by 1836, Cuban production had attained 160,000 tons (compared with Jamaica's maximum of 1805 of 99,000 tons), while Jamaica's had fallen to 53,000 (*cf.* Deerr, I, 199 and 131).

change from illegal to legal trade (made possible by legalization of other markets than simply Cádiz) but also to the English Negroes, to the continuance of the slave traffic thereafter, to the further spread of English ideas of development (and English sugar equipment), the increase in the Spanish home market (coupled with, for ten years, relatively stable prices[4]), the greatly increased demand and accessibility of the North American market, and the virtual collapse of Havana ship-building activities: cordwainers, carpenters, coopers, beef-salters began to service a sugar industry financed by merchants similarly changing their main direction of interest. Of these elements, the increase in the North-American market offered far more commercial opportunities than Spain, where prices dropped markedly in the late 1760s.[5] Augustin Cochin once wrote: '*L'histoire d'un morceau de sucre est toute une leçon d'économie politique, de politique et aussi de morale.*'[6] The history of how Cuba became the world's largest producer of such sugar-lumps is also a history of the world.

To begin with, there was a fourfold increase in the amount of cane land: 10,000 acres were planted with cane in 1762; by 1792 the total was over 160,000;[7] and whereas in the 1750s and 1760s plantations numbered little more than a hundred, as early as 1774 there were nearly 500.[8] There was, however, no technical break-through, and the new mills were scarcely more productive than the old: their average production was still between forty and fifty tons each per year.[9]

There had therefore been little change in the character of sugar mills since the sixteenth century, when there had already been mills capable of producing sugar at the rate of one ton a year per slave – a rate scarcely exceeded till the nineteenth century. Such improvements as did occur were primarily due to the use of new land (where cane always grew best, and where firewood was easier to come by). But in the late eighteenth century bigger mills were being built: whereas some old mills employed only half a dozen slaves, some new ones would soon employ well over a hundred, and the average about 1790 would be eighty. An average sugar plantation in 1762 was about 320 acres (four *caballería*),

[4] Except for 1766, see table in Earl J. Hamilton, *War and Prices in Spain 1651–1800* (1947), 155. The mid-1760s were years of bad harvests.

[5] Prices of loaf sugar stood at 140 *maravedís* per lb in 1764 in New Castille and were under 100 *maravedís* till 1776; white sugar prices increased slightly in the 1760s and fell in the 1770s (*ibid.*, 254–5).

[6] Augustin Cochin (1823–72), French abolitionist, politician and philanthropist.

[7] Moreno Fraginals, 10.

[8] The census of 1774 gave 478 mills. The *Cuadro Estadístico* of 1827, 428; and 453 mills for 1775. The *Guía de Forasteros* of 1781 speaks of 480 mills in 1780 (qu. Roland T. Ely, *Cuando Reinaba su Majestad el Azúcar*, 107, fn. 220). Moreno Fraginals, 15, has 106 for Havana jurisdiction in 1764, 227 in 1792.

[9] Average capacity of sugar mills: 1761 – 40 tons; 1792 – 55 tons; 1804 – 130 tons; 1827 – 170 tons (adapted from Moreno Fraginals, 83).

in the 1790s nearly 700 (over twenty *caballería*). The price of land leapt up: in Havana province prices rose from thirteen shillings to £13 an acre ($100 (£23) to $2,000 (nearly £500) a *caballería*) in fifteen years.[10] Whereas in the past some sugar mills had been almost self-sufficient – growing some maize and vegetables, burning their own woods, killing their own cattle – the new ones were often dependent on provisions from outside. Less and less care was paid to the Church's explicit regulation (which alone justified slavery, in its eyes) that Negroes should be instructed in Christianity on the plantations. The last occasion when a mulatto, much less a Negro, owned a sugar mill was in 1760.[11] Slaves often lost the little plots (*conucos*) on which they could grow their own cassava bread or keep chickens.[12] Increases in the numbers of slaves necessitated both hospitals and more guards and finally barracks, instead of huts. These changes did not, however, prevent sugar mills being, as usual, named after saints. But whereas old sugar mills had lived up to this nomenclature at least to the extent of having chapels, many newer ones did not. It would seem likely that though there was some increase in the number of owners of sugar properties, in general there was a rise also in the number of planters who possessed two or three or more mills: the Conde de Casa Montalvo, for instance, on his huge estate at Macuriges had nine mills in 1792 whereas his father had only two in 1762. Meantime, many small old mills employing, say, five slaves dropped out and did not seek to make sugar for export, but made *raspadura*, or rough sugar, for consumption by slaves.

So far as slaves were concerned, some factors other than commercial played a part. The Spaniards were determined in 1763 that Havana should not fall again. New fortifications were begun under the first new Spanish captain-general, the Conde de Ricla,[13] and with him the Irish soldier Marshal Alejandro O'Reilly, an expert in fortifications.[14] Another castle was built up the river from El Morro – La Cabaña (or San Carlos de la Cabaña), of gloomy fame later, and another on the Atarés hill at the head of the harbour. These public works also meant heavy imports of slaves and also misappropriation of funds for sugar purposes.[15] These slaves (bought, like most Cuban slaves till the 1790s, from Jamaica) were afterwards free for sale in the market. The fortifications created work for many *habaneros*, and this in itself led to

[10] *Ibid.*, 14.
[11] *Nuestra Señora de la Candelaria*, owned by Rosendo de Neyra.
[12] These often became unproductive.
[13] Ambrosio de Funes y Villalpando, Conde de Ricla (1720–80), son of Conde de Atarés; governor 1763–6.
[14] Alejandro O'Reilly (1725–94), born in Dublin; joined the Spanish army aged ten; later Conde de O'Reilly.
[15] The money to buy the slaves was lent to the Crown by two Cuban creoles, Gonzalo Herrera, Marqués de Villalta, and Domingo Veitía (Guerra and Santovenia, II, 55).

further sums for investment in plantations. At the same time, the now two-hundred-year-old convoy system for the treasure fleet was dropped formally, the Spanish government seeking a more flexible defence, with new attention to Puerto Rico: the old role of Havana vanished, a new one grew. The old dockyard in Havana became more and more used for the manufacture of sugar-mill machinery.

The English occupation also temporarily left behind fourteen merchants in Havana – John Kennion the richest of them; he told the Colonial Office that his goods were of equal value to that of all other British merchants together.[16] Some were men who had realized the possibilities of trade with Cuba in sugar, tobacco and, in particular, snuff. All these merchants were supposed to withdraw from Havana within eight months after the peace treaty, together with all their goods. But their prolonged stay had a decided effect upon the Cuban merchant, with whom they left behind credits as well as theories.

Soon after the peace, the French (following the Dutch example at St Eustatius and Curaçao) opened free ports in their newly regained colonies of Martinique and Guadeloupe: their aim was to get food, cattle, timber and sugar machinery illegally from English North America and more slaves, in English boats as well as French, from Africa. Môle San Nicholas in Saint Domingue and Sainte Lucia became free ports in 1767. Partly as a result the French West Indies shot ahead of the British colonies in sugar production, exporting 77,000 tons (nearly half semi-refined) compared with the British 72,000.[17] With heavy imports of slaves, Saint Domingue became queen of sugar, as Barbados and Jamaica had been before. Prices meantime remained relatively stable. North Americans annually bought more and more French sugar, getting cash, not sugar, for what they sold in the English islands, which gave less and less yield except in Jamaica. The new English islands (gained by the Peace) in the Windwards, on the other hand, avoided sugar, so far as they could, but Barbados and the Leewards remained sugar-bound, as did Jamaica. English free ports established in 1766 (four in Jamaica, two in Dominica) stimulated the slave trade to Saint Domingue and to Cuba, but restrictions (intended to prohibit re-export to English North America) prevented other business.

In 1765, the right of Spaniards to trade in the Caribbean was extended to seven Spanish ports apart from Cádiz.[18] A regular monthly mail packet service was introduced between Corunna and Havana. These steps towards general freedom of trade were interpreted, even by officials, as legalizing general commercial activity within the Caribbean.

16 CO 117/1, 295–7.
17 Parry and Sherlock, 129, figures for 1767.
18 Barcelona, Málaga, Alicante, Cartagena, Corunna, Gijón and Santander.

Illegal trading in slaves with Jamaica thrived in south and east Cuba. The authorities in Havana did not exert themselves to stop it: Louisiana, huge but depopulated, which fell to Spain at the Peace of Paris (and was incorporated with Cuba administratively as a new captaincy-general),[19] was a good channel for smuggling between the British and Spanish colonial empires. (Spain did little more with it: Admiral Rodney, always concerned with economic interpretation, commented that Spain had added another desert to her empire.)[20] Some Spaniards left Florida for Cuba rather than live under the English, and were settled at Ceiba Mocha, Matanzas.[21]

In Havana, the new governor, the Conde de Ricla, imposed new taxes to take advantage of the much improved economic position: and in the nine years 1766–74 these annually brought to Spain over three times what they had from 1759 to 1760.[22] There were administrative changes: in Cuba, as in the rest of the empire, the Crown would be served by an intendant (*intendente*), or general financial commissioner, also in charge of the interminable land question, and taking over responsibility for many of the old activities of the *cabildo*, whose members were increasingly preoccupied with the pursuit of private affluence: this idea was taken from France, though put into effect by the Spaniards before the French.

In 1774 the first rough Cuban census was held – itself an indication of the growing wealth of the colony, since it was needed for the purpose of taxation.[23] Though inaccurate, no doubt (the total population was probably at least a tenth larger than this figure), this roll-call gave the first even remotely serious estimate of the population of Cuba. The total reached 170,000 of whom nearly 100,000 or about 60 per cent were white, the rest being black or mulatto. Of the Negroes or mulattoes, two-thirds were slaves, of whom only a third were women. Of the free Negro

[19] The French gave it to their Spanish ally after conceding the territory east of the Mississippi to England – a concession which troubled the Spaniards for geographic reasons, though in the event these arrangements made things difficult for the English.

[20] On the other hand, in the 1790s it was a Spaniard who with French help founded the Louisiana sugar industry. See Deerr, 248. Louisiana remained Spanish till 1803 when it became French before being sold by Napoleon to the U.S.

[21] D. C. Corbitt, 'Immigration in Cuba' *HAHR*, xxii, 280. A hundred families were given farms of one *caballería* each and loans to buy a slave each and implements.

[22] $532,512 (£125,000) in place of $63,605 (£15,000) p.a. (De la Sagra, 278.)

[23] For a discussion of the authenticity of the 1774 census, see *Census of 1899*, 703–4. The ensuing figures derive from the summary in Sagra, *Historia*, 3. A similar census was also held in 1775, to check that of 1774: the results were (1774 figures in brackets):

	Men		Women		Total	
Whites	54,555		40,864	(40,864)	95,419	(96,440)
Free people of colour	10,021		9,006		19,027	
Free Negroes	5,959		5,629	} 14,698	11,588	} 30,000
Negro and mulatto slaves	28,774	(29,366)	15,562	(15,562)	44,336	(44,928)
	99,309		71,061		170,370	(171,368)

or mulatto, about 2,000 were in the army.[24] Compared with the rest of the Caribbean, Cuba was still untypical; the British colonies had a white population of about 60,000 all told.[25] Elsewhere the free Negroes were almost negligible.

Cuba in 1774 was thus (compared with her neighbours) still a country with a well-balanced population. She was economically on the move, with this increased prosperity relatively well balanced socially also, since the growth of sugar production was the result of an increase in the number of sugar plantations, rather than in the size and power of individual ones. But this advance was already neurotically driven, since probably a majority of the new plantations had been at least partly founded on loans from merchants such as Mateo Pedroso at huge interest rates. There was too a dominant source of anxiety in the reliance on a constant supply of slave labour not only to expand but merely to maintain the existing labour force. But for the majority of planters there could be no going back: interest had to be paid, eventually (perhaps at a time of high sugar prices) the principal had to be returned. Big debts could only be coped with by still further expansion.[26] In 1773, the British West Indian merchants secured, against much opposition, an act enabling Spaniards and other foreigners to make loans in the English islands. Cuba was thus becoming dependent on the world market, not only in respect of sugar prices but also in respect of both capital and labour.

This indebtedness of the founders of Cuban sugar production was nothing unusual in the West Indies. A visitor to Jamaica in the good days in the 1750s had noted that the planters, 'though rich and in easy circumstances, are seldom out of debt, for the charges attending a sugar settlement are very considerable and their natural propensity to increase their possessions constantly engage them in new disbursements'.[27]

A new problem loomed: a fundamental cause of the revolt of the British North American colonies in the 1770s was their desire to trade with Cuba and the French West Indies. For two generations Massachusetts had made the best 'Antilles rum'. Expansion of this manufacture could now only come from the French or Spanish colonies, not from Jamaica with its tired soil. 'I know not why we should blush to confess

[24] See figures in Klein, 218, from *Archivo de Indias*. Some officers were also mulatto or Negro (Klein, 223).

[25] In the Long Papers (Add. MSS., 12438, f. 22, qu. Namier, *England*, 236) a computation for whites in 1773 gave a total of 58,000 of whom 20,000 were in the Barbados and 16,000 in Jamaica.

[26] The historian of the British West Indies, Bryan Edwards (*History, Civil and Commercial of the British Colonies in the West Indies*, 3rd edn, 3 vols (1801), II, 290), wrote, about 1790: 'The business of sugar planting is a sort of adventure in which the man that engages, must engage deeply. There is no medium [path], and very seldom the possibility of retreat . . . it requires a capital of no less than £30,000 to embark.'

[27] Patrick Browne, *Civil and Natural History of Jamaica* (1756), qu. Parry and Sherlock, 145.

a   *b*

British Commanders in the Havana Expedition, 1762
3*a* Lord Albemarle (from a painting by Romney)
  b Admiral Sir George Pocock (from a painting by Hudson)
  c Admiral Keppel (Reynolds)
  d General William Keppel (Reynolds)

c   *d*

4a Francisco Arango, the econom

4b The market-place at Havana in the late eighteenth century

that molasses was an essential ingredient in American independence,'
said John Adams later. Typical of the commercial interests behind the
American revolution was Robert Morris, the warden of the port of
Philadelphia and the revolution's financier: himself a Liverpool-born
man, Morris's father had gone to Philadelphia in the 1730s and in his
first business, Willing and Morris, was both arms dealer and slave
trader,[28] being prominent among those who in 1761 protested against a
new tax on slaves.[29] Morris, in the years leading up to the war, was a
leader in the illegal trade to Cuba and later his agent in Havana,
Robert Smith, was named by the U.S. Congress as their commercial
representative – the first in a long line of controversial North American
envoys to Cuba.[30]

The English West Indian colonies did not join those in North America,
for they still needed British imperial defence against Spain and France
(though, otherwise with many of the same grievances, perhaps they
might have done so). Bermuda, however, sent representatives to the first
U.S. Congress. In this major world conflict the winds of war afterwards
swept across the Caribbean, as across North America; supplies failed,
food prices rose, slaves died, Rodney won more prizes. Spain issued
paper money for the first time, to finance the war. Merchants of Nantes
and Liverpool turned themselves into privateers and fought to capture
merchant vessels, not to carry slaves. Deprived of access to Jamaican
slave markets, the Cubans were permitted to buy slaves from the French
colonies, paying in either money or sugar. Neutral nations (Dutch and
Danes) were allowed to bring in slaves as well. One more fortress was
built in Havana, the Príncipe, on a hill to the south of the city. War
gave some benefits to the Caribbean: to meet the risk of famine from
blockade the ackee tree was brought to Jamaica in 1778, the mango
in 1782: two afterwards decisive developments in the diet of West
Indians, slaves and free.

Peace returned in 1783, the English got back the islands which they
had lost to the revivified French and Spanish navies, but not their sugar

[28] Donnan, III, 455.
[29] *Ibid.*, IV, 37. Morris's family money was originally made on the Maryland shores of the
Chesapeake, first as agent to the Liverpool slave merchant Foster Cunliffe, then trading in
tobacco, and afterwards in company with Anthony Bacon, Manx merchant and slave dealer,
victualler of the British army in countless fights, M.P., who eventually turned his fortune to
iron works in South Wales, and from those works to supplying indeed Britain with cannon
in this very American war (he obtained the contract) wherein his old partner was the financier
of his enemies. See Lawrence C. Wroth, 'A Maryland Merchant and his friends in 1750',
Maryland Historical Magazine, September 1911. He was factor to Foster Cunliffe & Co.
1740–50 in Maryland, apparently dealing mostly in tobacco. For Bacon, see Namier, *Harvard
Journal of Economic and Business History*, II, No. 1, November 1929. His brother was a Maryland
clergyman, author of *Laws of Maryland*. Bacon was the founder of the iron trade in South
Wales, with his great estate at Cyfarthfa, Merthyr Tydfil.
[30] Basil Rauch, *American Interest in Cuba, 1848–1855* (1948), 12. He was later expelled.

pre-eminence: Saint Domingue now exported nearly as much sugar in the 1780s as all the English West Indies. English duties increased greatly at home.[31] The English had also grudgingly to allow the merchants of free North America to continue to trade in the West Indies, since the colonies needed the food. Even before 1776, a third of the ships leaving New York or Boston went to English or foreign West Indian islands. Such vessels did not have to be so large as those engaged in the triangular trade of manufactured goods, slaves and sugar.[32] During the war, this trade greatly increased. Most of the increase of sugar produced by Cuba between 1779 and 1785 went not to Spain but to the U.S.

During the American revolutionary war, Spanish and Cuban merchants at last contemplated embarking on the slave trade: two trading stations off the West African coast were bought in 1778 (from Portugal), the islands of Fernando Po and Annobon, and a company was formed.[33] Some North American merchants began to establish themselves in Cuba – providing food, money and slaves as well. A *reglamento* of 1778 allowed Spanish ports to trade with all the Americas save Mexico and Venezuela, where Cádiz and San Sebastián maintained rickety monopolies. But the expansion of the Cuban sugar industry did not continue so fast as in the preceding decade. The number of plantations remained much the same. Prices of imports consistently rose. The problem for the planters continued to be one of labour: they could in fact only expand to the full if the Spanish government permitted a free trade in slaves. In 1780, the Cuban planters presented a memorial to King Charles III, complaining at the high price of slaves and begging that Havana and Santiago might be opened to foreign traders permanently.[34] The next year, the Crown circulated a long memorandum admitting that slaves were needed in great abundance, and suggesting a regular Spanish traffic.[35] But a monopoly contract and a ban on further imports were confirmed till the end of the 1780s; the Marqués de Casa Enrile was succeeded as slave monopolist in Cuba by a Liverpool firm, Baker and Dawson, who sold at least 5,768 slaves between 1786 and 1789 at £35 ($155) and later £42 ($175–$185).[36] About a third of

[31] See L. J. Ragatz, *The Fall of the Planter Class in the British Caribbean, 1763–1833* (1928), 380.

[32] See *Historical Statistics*, 758; Ely, 57.

[33] Even so the first Spanish slaveship did not sail till 1792. The Slave Trading Company formed by the Marqués de Cárdenas de Montehermoso, the Condes de Lagunillas, Vallellano and Gibacoa and an agent of the Belén and San Francisco monasteries, never got under way.

[34] Qu. Saco, *Papeles sobre Cuba*, 3 vols (1962), I, 406.

[35] BM, MS. Eg.520, ff. 215–28, qu. Aimes, 40.

[36] See *Report of the Privy Council on the African Trade 1788*, Pt VI; Humboldt, 142–3; and Aimes, 36–7. Prices given by Madden, *The Island of Cuba* (1849) 28, $175 being for '*piezas* and *mulecones*', $185 for 'the public'. (A *mulecón* was a male slave of between fourteen and eighteen years old.) Miguel de Uriarte a large shipbuilder of Cadiz sold 4,957 slave at the same time as Baker and Dawson. Peter Baker was then probably the biggest shipbuilder in Liverpool. He built four ships for the navy between 1778 and 1781. He went into slaving at least as

these slaves were women and none was older than thirty (or under four feet six inches high); most of them were purchased at Bonny, and Baker and Dawson brought back from this contract £100,000 to £120,000 a year.[37] Altogether 60,000 to 70,000 slaves were probably sold in Cuba, legally or illegally, between 1763 and 1789, though many of these were resold elsewhere in Spanish America.[38] Another Liverpool firm, Tarleton & Co., had a similar contract to supply other Spanish colonies,[39] and it is probable that some Bristol firms also engaged (illicitly) in the Spanish trade.[40]

These figures, as the Cuban planters realized, were nothing compared with the huge waves of Africans brought every year to Saint Domingue – 30,839 in 1787, 29,506 in 1788.[41] In Cuba in 1787, due to deaths, there appear to have been still only 50,000 slaves,[42] compared with over 450,000 in the English islands.[43] In 1788 Baker and Dawson made a bid to renew their Cuban contract to bring in 3,000 slaves a year at £48 ($200) each. But the Spanish government now surrendered to the planters' pressure and, for a trial period of two years to begin with, allowed the free entry to Havana and Santiago de Cuba of as many slaves as were demanded, from whatever source. As under Baker and Dawson, a third of each shipload were to be women and, if not being used for sugar or agriculture, a selective employment tax of 9s 4d ($2) per slave had to be paid.[44] In the next year and a half 4,000 slaves were imported under this law, over half, as it happened, by Baker and Dawson through their agent, Philip Allwood (known also for his introduction to Cuba of the mango).[45] The critical argument against a new monopoly contract with the Liverpool traders was, first of all,

[37] Dawson's evidence to the Privy Council in 1788.

[38] Moreno Fraginals calculates 2,000 a year, pointing out that official figures suggesting half this number were probably false.

[39] Donnan, II, 577.

[40] Ibid., 582, fn.

[41] Bryan Edwards, III, 13, 143.

[42] Report of the Privy Council, loc. cit.

[43] 461,684 valued at £40 each (Bermuda £45), ibid., Pt IV.

[44] Ibid., Pt VI.

[45] Allwood first became concerned in Cuba during the American revolutionary war when as a Kingston merchant he was prevailed upon by Francisco Miranda the liberator (then in Jamaica on a dubious mission) to lend money to Spanish prisoners. He went to Cuba to reclaim these debts in 1783. See 'Note on Miranda's Guilt', Salvador de Madariaga, Fall of the Spanish Empire (1947), 412–16.

early as 1773 when his then partner Barton built the Princess Royal (376 tons). His only daughter Margaret married Captain James Dawson, who commanded his father-in-law's ships; he had captured the richest prize ever won by a Liverpool privateer, a French ship with £135,000 worth of diamonds on board. Baker and Dawson bought a big estate, Mossley Hill, outside Liverpool and built the famous 'Carnatic Hall' (after the name of the French prize), Baker being mayor of Liverpool when he died aged sixty-four in 1796. Just before, he had sent a petition to the House of Commons opposing limitation of the slave trade, representing that he had over £500,000 invested in eighteen slaveships 'for the service of Spain' (see A. Mackenzie Grieve, The last years of the English Slave Trade, Liverpool 1750–1807 (1941), 269).

jealousy on the part of Cádiz merchants[46] and second, that while England did not allow import of foreign sugar, the government in Madrid did not permit export of tobacco except to Spain; so that the only commodities which legally could be exchanged for slaves were hides, which the English did not much want, or cotton, of which Cuban production was slender. In fact, therefore, the inference was that Baker and Dawson wanted cash, which was in short supply, or cotton – which would thereby have all gone to England, not to Spanish mills.[47] It is apparent, from Dawson's evidence to the Privy Council in 1788, that he had wished to establish a branch of his firm in Cádiz; had he been so allowed, he expected to dominate the trade there within ten years.[48] It should also be appreciated that between 1786 and 1788 there was for the first time in the late eighteenth century the only major drop in international sugar prices. This harmed many small producers, played into the hands more than ever of merchants, and helped to persuade the major producers that the only secure course was to create large mills able to weather through sheer wealth any future storm.

When these trial two years of unlimited slave import ended, the concession was re-allowed for six years till 1798.[49] Other goods were also brought to Havana in the slaveships, and slave traders were able to take away from Cuba in their empty bottoms as much rum and some other commodities as they wanted, without payment of tax. As well as enabling any foreign slaver to set up shop in Havana (the most prominent of these was William Woodville of London),[50] these regulations helped to make of Cuba the best international slave market at the turn of the century, profits per slave shipped being £62 compared to £58 or £56 being sometimes achieved elsewhere.[51] A 'New Commercial Company' was founded consisting of twelve leading merchants and planters, with the right to buy slaves from traders and re-sell them to the planters.[52] A Spanish slave-ship, the Cometa, belonging to a Spanish

[46] Dawson's evidence to the Privy Council.

[47] Other goods exported from Cuba in 1788 were tobacco, oil de camme, cane brandy (aguardiente), cacao, coffee, tortoiseshell, copper, dried fruit, log wood and other timber, nuts, pepper and sarsaparilla. From the analysis of the quantities of these which arrived in Barcelona (Pierre Vilar, La Catalogne dans l'Espagne moderne, III, 504–5), it is clear that none of them could compare with sugar or hides (500 tons valued at 1.6 M pesos and at 1 M pesos respectively). Cuba exported a substantial quantity of wax to Mexico, used in the churches there: the bees did well round sugar factories.

[48] Report to the Privy Council, Pt VI.

[49] Aimes, 50. The proportion of women was now left to the buyer and the selective employment tax withdrawn. On one mill, Arango's Ninfa, the cutting of cane was done entirely by women.

[50] Member of the English Company of Merchants trading to Africa at the end of the English slave trade, in 1807 (Donnan, II, 656).

[51] See Gomer Williams.

[52] Papel periódico de la Habana No. 27, qu. Friedländer, 98; Trelles, Biblioteca Histórica Cubana, II, 3 vols. (1922–6), 378, qu. Ely.

merchant, was in 1792 sent to the coast of Africa, its insurance placed in Liverpool.[53] English merchants such as Baker and Dawson, Woodville, Philip Allwood and later Thomas Leyland, continued to trade, but now U.S. traders were also moving into the market, carrying rum to Africa, exchanging it there for slaves and exchanging the slaves in Havana for molasses, to make more rum. The most prominent of these newcomers were the de Wolfs, Jewish merchants of Bristol, Rhode Island, of whom James de Wolf, a slave captain in the 1790s, had become himself owner of ten slaveships by 1800 and who later, out of his profits, built one of the earliest cotton mills in the U.S. (Later still, after thirty years in the Rhode Island legislature, he entered the U.S. Senate.)[54] It is harder to say whence the slaves themselves came; we hear of slave vessels from Goree, Mozambique, Guinea, Congo, in fact everywhere that slaves were then sent from. Many still came on from the West Indies, some from North America.

Meantime, to show that Cuba now had as much claim to piety as anywhere else in the Americas, the cathedral in Havana was finally completed under the supervision of the vicar-general of the diocese, Luis Peñalver (a nephew of Albemarle's lieutenant-governor), the façade being the work of a popular architect from Cádiz, Pedro Medina;[55] and Havana itself received a bishopric, while Santiago de Cuba boasted henceforth an archbishop.

[53] Donnan, II, 624 and xlvi; Ortiz, *Negros Esclavos*, 86. Note that Moreno Fraginals, 8, falsely says that the first Spanish slaveship to arrive in Havana was that which Luis Beltrán Gonet brought in 1798.

[54] See discussion of the De Wolfs in Donnan, III, 380, 340.

[55] Luis Peñalver (1749–1810), then vicar-general of Havana, later bishop of New Orleans and archbishop of Guatemala, was one of the few *criollos* to find episcopal preferment. Havana only became the seat of the bishopric in 1788, until then having been under the bishop of Santiago. Cuba and Louisiana, with Florida, were under the archbishop of Santo Domingo till 1804 when Santiago became an archbishopric.

CHAPTER VI

The Challenge of Haiti

The leader of the expansionist movement in Cuba was a young creole planter with unusual understanding of economics, Francisco de Arango.[1] He and his friends were frankly anxious to create a rich sugar colony, a new Saint Domingue, in Cuba, and they succeeded in persuading the captain-general, Luis de las Casas,[2] to back this adventure to the hilt. The wealth deriving from the fast developing sugar industry gave birth to a certain intellectual activity in Havana which, if it scarcely deserves to be known as 'the great enlightenment',[3] undoubtedly led to a hard-headed appraisal of Cuba's economic possibilities. Influenced by the arguments in Madrid of Jovellanos and Campomanes, Arango was busy in the late 1780s making a careful study of why the French and English colonies could produce more sugar, and at less cost. He and the Conde de Casa Montalvo (son of the *Comisario* of the navy at the time of the English capture of Havana) visited England in 1788 to see how the English ran their slave trade; they and three merchants from Cádiz went to Liverpool and asked many pertinent questions:

> How many hands each vessel carried out; lists of the cargoes necessary to purchase slaves on different parts of the coast of Africa; which goods might be procured in Spain, which goods must be purchased in England and which were East India goods; whether the Slave Trade had been profitable to the Town of Liverpool at large [and] whether the English manufacturers had been gainers by supplying the Merchants with goods . . .[4]

Las Casas and Arango were afterwards associated with the foundation

---

[1] Francisco de Arango y Parreño (1765–1839). His great-grandfather had come to Cuba in the seventeenth century from Navarre. He was not by birth a member of the inner *criollo* oligarchy, but he and his near relations soon became so by marriage. He presented in Madrid the memorial to the government asking for a free trade in slaves and the rejection of Baker and Dawson's tender. See W. W. Pierson, 'Francisco Arango', *H.A.H.R.*, xvi, 451, and A L. Valverde in *Revista Bimestre*, XXVIII (No. 2), 238.

[2] Luis de las Casas y Aragorri (1745–1807), born Sopuerta, Vizcaya; a protégé of Aranda, he had accompanied his brother, the Spanish ambassador, to Moscow, and had fought in various wars, before going to Havana; he was brother-in-law to O'Reilly, the fortifier of Havana, whom he had accompanied in battle.

[3] The phrase is that of the North American writer, Philip Foner.

[4] *Report to the Privy Council 1788*, Pt VI; also printed in Donnan, II, 575–6. A long article in the *Papel Periódico de la Habana*, 26 December 1799, was devoted to the English slave trade. It is quoted almost in full in Ortiz, *Negros Esclavos*, 154 ff.

in 1792 of the part club, part college, part board of inquiry, known as La Sociedad Económica de Amigos del País – modelled on similar organizations in other parts of the Spanish empire[5] – the agricultural board known as the Junta de Fomento (Development Board), the commercial tribunal and centre of information, the Real Consulado, and Cuba's first newspaper, *Papel Periódico*, a weekly founded in 1791 which became a daily in 1793. Of these institutions, the Real Consulado was a modernized version of a medieval Catalan institution and the Sociedad Económica was the favourite hispanicization of the French encyclopedists which the Spanish government hoped would satisfy all 'liberal' demands in their colonies. The Junta de Fomento was Arango's own idea, a 'Ministry of Industries' in embryo, but headed not by Spanish merchants but by Cuban entrepreneurs. These institutions expressed a body of opinion specifically Cuban rather than Spanish; even Captain-General de las Casas, though a Spaniard by birth, settled down after his term of office on a sugar plantation and died there. There was movement of ideas in all directions – thus the *intendente* of Havana in the 1790s, José Pablo Valiente, was later associated with the Economical Society in Seville, after he had enriched himself in Cuba.[6]

The respectable faces of all these founders of the Cuban liberal economy – Arango, de las Casas, Montalvo, José Ricardo O'Farrill, Nicolás Calvo, Luis Peñalver (the first director of the Economical Society) – stare out from nineteenth-century portraits, portentous, solemn, almost noble. They not only made but wrote history, and few future historians of Cuba have escaped their influence. It was they who first made it possible for the Cuban administration to finance itself: previously, Cuban governments had subsisted on *situados* (grants) from the vice-royalty of Mexico. The Economical Society opened its library to the public and so created the first public library in the island; they also created a girls' school and other benefits.[7] Las Casas built schools, roads and bridges, an aqueduct, hospitals and asylums. Yet he and his generation were concerned primarily with the pursuit of wealth, regardless of social consequences, neglectful of other advice (by, for example, the economist Arrate) that slavery was wasteful and expensive, and careless of the unreliable basis of slavery itself. Further, the old small, semi-patriarchal, often self-sufficient sugar plantation of thirty

---

[5] The first society was the Basque (founded in 1765 by sixteen Basque noblemen influenced by French ideas); the first abroad, that at Manila, the first in Spanish America that at Mompox in 1783; a society had been formed in Santiago de Cuba in 1787 but it was not active and published little. The Basque Society had specially interested itself in iron (see R. J. Shafer, *Economic Societies in the Spanish World (1763–1821)* (1958), 35). According to Shafer, there were eleven members of the Basque Society resident in Havana in 1775 (*ibid.*, 45).

[6] José Pablo Valiente y Bravo (1740–1818), previously *oidor* in Mexico.

[7] The library had 1,500 volumes in 1794 (Shafer, 305).

slaves and less was finally killed by them: henceforth Cuba produced not for English smugglers nor poor Spain but specifically for the world market, absolutely relying, therefore, on the world slave labour market. They enriched but, after a few generations, ruined the whole aristocracy of Cuba, and laid the foundation for what Cuba later became – a sugar prison rather than a sugar palace. Henceforth too, slaves, brutalized by routine and force, lost most of such dignity as they previously possessed. Sugar mills increasingly had lay names, masters began to refuse to send slaves on Sundays to mass, and sought first permission to build chapels at their mills in order to avoid interference of the parish, and finally to cease any pretence at religious instruction for slaves. The Church lost other battles: dried meat (*tasajo*) could be eaten on Fridays by slaves except in Lent, slaves could be buried in unconsecrated burial grounds, the priest turned a blind eye to work on Sundays and allowed masters to get away with 'one Sunday every ten days'. The new slave code of 1789, the Spanish *Code Noir*, high-minded though it was in intention, was largely a dead-letter: instruction in the Catholic religion and attendance of priests on feast days; the proportion of men to women and hours and years of work; the punishment and the health provisions – all these were ignored.[8] It is true that the law in theory was more enlightened than any other slave code; but it is also true that few laws have ever been so openly and completely ignored.[9] It was not even promulgated in Cuba, for the slave owners appealed to the government that to do so would be to encourage dangerous attitudes among the slaves. Meantime, what the Church lost on the one hand it gained on the other; for monasteries and churches found themselves profiting from the sugar boom: the Havana monastery of Santa Clara owned twenty mills at the end of the century; Saint Ignatius himself was a part owner of the mill *San Juan Nepomuceno* in 1772; and the seminary of Havana also had two mills of its own.[10]

Arango and his generation were liberals *par excellence*, concerned with the relation between freedom and riches, pursued with all the energy and also the naïvety with which a new discovery is often pursued, oblivious of any discrepancy between free trade and forced labour. They achieved a semi-industrial revolution without encouragement from and indeed in many ways despite what was happening in Spain itself – a great contrast from the British or French sugar islands which, of course, depended on home backing and initiative. Las Casas, on arrival, was suborned by the gift, from the oligarchy of Havana, of a rich sugar mill in the old tobacco zone of Güines, *Amistad*, one of the

[8] For a discussion, see Ortiz, *Negros Esclavos*, 255 ff.
[9] The comment of Klein, 78, on this subject is perhaps over-optimistic.
[10] Moreno Fraginals, 54.

few mills not to be called after a saint.[11] These men were the incarnation of the dictum of the Spanish minister, Floridablanca, in his judgement that 'greed and interest are the main incentive for all human toil and they should only be checked in public matters when they are prejudicial to other persons or to the State'.[12] No doubt they should be judged 'according to the standards of their time'; but this hardly justifies much applause for their policies. Growing to maturity in the age of Wilberforce and Clarkson, they plunged into a whole series of schemes which vastly extended the commitment of their society to slaves. If 'new ideas' about cane cultivation and milling reached Cuba, it is hard to believe that similar concepts of philanthropy could not also have been introduced. Arango and Montalvo, after all, visited England where abolitionism was already the cry of a large and vociferous pressure group.[13] They knew what they were doing; they surrendered to the pulsing drive for wealth which they identified with progress; they did exactly what English pioneers had done in Jamaica two or three generations before.

Of course there were side benefits: thus the men of the Economic Society were aware that education was economically advantageous and in consequence a primary education reform plan, after inquiry into the real state of things, was introduced to the Society in 1794. Two free schools were founded, for white children only however, and these limited to two hundred each. These institutions were added to the thirty-nine previously existing Havana schools – mostly 'primitive little tutorial groups directed by mulatto women',[14] often scarcely literate themselves – in which about 1,700 children were then enrolled (of these, 600 were boys at the *convento* of Belén). This marked the beginning of the free education system in Cuba.

In 1791 the history of the Caribbean was further decisively altered by the first fully successful slave revolution in European colonies (or, indeed in history), in Saint Domingue. This really derived from the French planters' attempt to wring from the National Assembly in Paris an interpretation of 'liberty, equality and fraternity', which would have enabled them to act authoritatively against slaves and free Negroes.[15]

[11] See discussion in *ibid.*, 12–13. Since he could not legally run it as captain-general, this mill was held for him by Joaquín de Ayesterán; he later developed a second mill near by, *Alejandría*, held for him by his nephew, Alejandro O'Reilly.

[12] In a report on sheep-raising in Estremadura, qu. Herr, 50.

[13] These two pioneers visited England the same year that the House of Commons set up a Select Committee on the slave trade.

[14] Shafer, 308.

[15] There were half a million slaves in Saint Domingue, 31,000 white men and women, and 24,000 freed slaves. F. H. A. von Humboldt, *Essai politique sur le royaume de la Nouvelle Espagne* 2 vols (1811), II, 98, says he thought the French in the West Indies treated their slaves worst of all: after them, in ascending order, the English and Spaniards of the West Indies, and after them the slave owners of the U.S. South. Best treated of all, in his view, were the few slaves in

The protest came in August with the revolt of slaves, under voodoo inspiration, the destruction of 180 sugar and 900 coffee plantations, the death of 2,000 whites and 10,000 Negroes – as many planters, even, as victims who fell under the guillotine in Paris.[16] The Jacobins sent from France an army whose leader, Sonthonax, proclaimed emancipation. The surviving whites fled, many to Cuba, some to Jamaica, some to Puerto Rico. The planter president of the island assembly secretly offered the colony to England, and Pitt, though less mesmerized than most statesmen of the age by West Indian wealth, accepted the idea, a decision warily backed by the planters of all the West Indies, aghast at the prospects for themselves of a successful slave revolt : the threat seemed international – several of the Haitian slave leaders had come from Jamaica or the Windward Islands.[17] An English army occupied Port au Prince. Six years of war followed – the slaves being led by Toussaint, a brilliant general of whom it might have been said (as was later said of Abd-el-Krim) that he 'first taught men of colour that imperialism was not invincible'.[18] Wordsworth's sonnet to him made the point at the time :

> Thou hast left behind
> Powers that will work for thee; air, earth and skies;
> There's not a breathing of the common wind
> That will forget thee: thou hast great allies;
> Thy friends are exultations, agonies,
> And love, and man's unconquerable mind.

Sir John Fortescue, the historian of the British army, wrote that the secret of England's impotence 'may be said to lie in the two fatal words, Saint Domingue'.[19] The English certainly failed and the sugar bowl of Saint Domingue was destroyed in the process and by the radical agrarian reform which followed.

The revolution in Haiti (an old Arawak Indian word for 'mountainous' which Toussaint's successor, Dessalines, gave to Saint Domingue) continued. Napoleon failed to reduce the slaves, though he kidnapped Toussaint. The independent Republic divided the big estates. Sugar exports of Haiti sank from 70,000 tons in 1791 to 25,000 in 1802 and

[16] Bryan Edwards's estimates. He was at Cap Français at the time.

[17] Chatham Papers, G.D. 8/349, W. Indian islands, papers relating to Jamaica and Santo Domingo. The president was De Cadusey. See Eric Williams's *Capitalism and Slavery* (1949), 147 and 247.

[18] *African Revolution*, May 1963, in memory of Abd-el-Krim.

[19] *History of the British Army*, IV, Pt I, 565.

Mexico. But he did not go to Brazil. As has been previously suggested, this matter really depends on what was grown by what planter: sugar plantations were necessarily worse than cotton or tobacco. But it would seem that a slave on a French sugar plantation during the overwhelmingly rich period 1760–90 was treated worse than one on a Jamaican plantation at the same time.

only 2,020 lbs in 1825.[20] The standard of living of the country remains in 1970 below what it was two hundred years before.[21]

The consequences for Cuba of this great event were many: first, the French sugar trade was ruined, so destroying Cuba's biggest rival in the sugar world of that day. Second, Napoleon, after his failure to recapture the colony, gave the first and decisive impetus to the manufacture of sugar from beet in Europe,[22] so firing the first shot in the great 'war of the two sugars'.[23] Third, the collapse of French West Indian sugar did not avert the decline of English: between 1799 and 1807, sixty-five plantations in Jamaica were abandoned, thirty-two sold for debts, and in 1807 suits were pending against 115 others.[24] Fourth, the price of sugar doubled in the European market between 1788 and 1795[25] – so that, though Cuban production remained much as before, the planters could make a much bigger profit, giving them a first taste of that volatility of the market which characterized the rest of their history. (This event incidentally spelled the final ruin of tobacco in the old Güines area, tobacco plantations being actually burned.)[26] Finally, many exiles fled from Saint Domingue to Cuba, particularly to the neighbourhood of Santiago, but also to other places in the island.[27] These exiles brought with them not only the *passepied* and the *contredanse*, the powdered wig and Parisian dress (and the French habit of turning their feet outward to show off their slippers), but also terrible stories of rape, murder, looting and destruction which were enough to keep Cuban planters from giving an inch to their slaves for nearly a hundred years.

This was not, after all, the first slave revolt even if it was the only successful one: in 1657 the Negroes of St Vincent had allied with the Caribs; in the 1720s Negroes in Carolina had aided Lower Creek Indians; in 1733 the slaves on the Danish island of St John had killed all the planters except a few who escaped to St Thomas. There had been several earlier rebellions in Saint Domingue and, in Jamaica, escaped slaves had established themselves so effectively in the mountains that a

[20] Figures in Parry and Sherlock, 170.

[21] Sugar production was reckoned as producing less than 70,000 tons in the late 1960s.

[22] Napoleon's decree of 11 March 1811, drawing attention to the cost of importing sugar and indigo, drew up plans for planting 80,000 acres of beetroot.

[23] The phrase is Eric Williams's. For sugar beet, its challenge and characteristics, see p. 125.

[24] Ragatz, 308.

[25] Deerr, II, 530–1. Amsterdam prices were 25s maximum in 1788, 35s–49s in 1795, and up to 93s in 1797; London prices were 34s–46s in 1788, 42s–75s in 1795. New Castille prices for white sugar rose from 2,691 *maravedis* per 25lb box in 1788 to 6,392 in 1799 (Hamilton, *War and Prices in Spain*, 255).

[26] Thus José de Coca burned eleven tobacco fields and built on their site a large sugar mill, *Nuestra Señora de las Mercedes* (Moreno Fraginals, 12).

[27] Massé, *L'isle de Cuba et la Havane* (1825), 248–50. Miss Irene Wright spoke of 27,000 of them (*Cuba* (1910), 361).

regular war was needed to restrict (not to crush) them in both the 1730s and 1795. (The descendants of the rebellious slaves in these struggles retained afterwards the character of a secret society.) In 1760 in Jamaica, the Coromantee slaves prepared what later occurred in Saint Domingue – 'a total massacre of whites and . . . a Negro colony'. There had been many minor outbursts in Cuba. The long saga of slave revolts in Brazil was already legendary. Indeed, the slave revolution in Saint Domingue was in many respects the culmination of a chain of slave revolts, mostly in the West Indies, some in North America.[28] The savagery and the completeness of the revolution in Saint Domingue was, however, a revelation, though it would not have occurred in a colony less filled with feverish hatreds, itself deriving from the recent import of a huge mass of new slaves and the arrival of new and anxious money-grubbing proprietors.[29]

The French immigrants to Cuba also brought, with their own recollections of prosperity (and sometimes a few slaves who in their turn brought the elements of voodoo to East Cuba), schemes for coffee and sugar development in Cuba such as overshot water mills with horizontal rollers. Some brought capital. French sugar technicians were soon to be found in all the bigger Cuban sugar mills and indeed the biggest mills of all were built by them. They brought, too, ideas of how sugar might be refined in Cuba itself.[30] The French engineer Esteban Lafaye came from Haiti to tempt the oligarchy with a scheme for grinding sugar without using either oxen or water – a pendular machine which, however, failed. Soon after the Haitian revolution, duties on the import of machinery for sugar (and coffee)[31] were nevertheless abandoned. North American foundries began to sell iron machinery to replace the old wooden material. There was also introduced the so-called 'Jamaican train' which, despite its name, followed the technique of Saint Domingue; by this, the long train of copper cauldrons could be heated over a single fire at the same time and at the same temperature. This was economical in wood (essential in less forested islands than Cuba) and could be run entirely on the cane waste (*bagasse*) left over from milling.[32] It saved labour too, even though it

[28] The legend of the rarity of slave revolts in North America propagated by, e.g., Ulrich Phillips (*American Negro Slavery* (1918), 341–2), is exposed by Herbert Aptheker (*American Negro Slave Revolts*, 13), who found records of *c.* 250 revolts and conspiracies in North American slave history.

[29] For a vivid description of French immigrants in Santiago, see Alejo Carpentier's novel, *El Reino de este Mundo* (*The Kingdom of this World* (1967), Pt II, ch. V).

[30] Many of these exiles remained, though some were expelled when Spain and France were at war in 1808–14. Technicians like Lafaye, Bardière and Lage crop up as owners of sugar mills by 1820. A French influence in the Santiago dialect can still be detected.

[31] See ch. VIII.

[32] Moreno Fraginals, 75, calculates that at the end of the eighteenth century in Cuba 500 cabs (16,500 acres) of wood a year were used for fuel.

was a little slower than its predecessor. The pioneer here was again the Conde of Casa Montalvo, now owner of 180,000 acres and nine sugar mills, who had accompanied Arango to Europe.[33]

There were further innovations. The first steam-powered mill, bought by Arango in London in 1794 from the Reinold firm, was used experimentally in 1797 at the Seybabo plantation by Montalvo's son-in-law, the Conde de Jaruco,[34] grandson of one of the *regidores* during the English occupation, and an intimate of Godoy's.[35] This was one of the earliest steam engines exported, though an attempt to use steam power in the sugar industry had been made by John Stewart in Jamaica in 1768,[36] and by a French planter in Saint Domingue. Unfortunately Jaruco's experiment was not fully successful since, though the steam worked perfectly the mill itself was ill-fitted to the experiment. Further, such engines could not be bought in large numbers for another twenty-five years, for only England made them and the French revolutionary wars were to prevent further shipments to Cuba. But though this development was delayed, water mills were at last successfully constructed in the Güines district, along the river Mayabeque; the new overshot water wheel worked where old wheels had failed; the lead here being taken by Nicolás Calvo[37] who built a model mill (with a French architect), *La Holanda*. In 1794 the so-called *volvedora* (turner) was introduced; this much improved the conditions of labour: previously, slaves had laboriously introduced each cane separately twice through the rollers by hand. Now the second action at least could be done by machine, saving many hands of slaves. In some places, mules successfully replaced oxen as the motor power in milling. In 1798 bigger cauldrons (*clarificadoras*) were introduced in place of the 'train', so simplifying the evaporation process. Lime began to be used at this stage also.[38]

[33] J. de la Pezuela, *Diccionario geográfico, estadístico, histórico de la isla de Cuba*, 4 vols (1859), I, 57; Moreno Fraginals, 16, 31. A variety of this had been used in the 1780s, but with the destruction of forest in the Havana–Güines area it became much more used.

[34] Joaquín Santa Cruz de Cárdenas, second Conde de San Juan de Jaruco y Santa Cruz de Mopox (1769–1807). Jaruco had travelled all over Europe. Restless and intelligent, his other projects included ideas for a port at Mariel, a Havana–Batabanó canal, cartography of *realengos*, etc. He was sub-inspector of the royal troops in Cuba. Like Las Casas, he died poor, leaving a daughter, María de la Mercedes, who married the French General Merlin and wrote a famous travelogue of the Caribbean.

[35] Deerr, II, 552; Humboldt, *Travels*, 266. See also Deerr and Alex. Brooks, 'The Early Use of Steam Power in the Cane Sugar Industry', *Publications of the Newcomen Society*, XXI (1943), 15–16; and comment in Ely, 510; and Moreno Fraginals, 23, 30. Humboldt visited the count's estate in 1800.

[36] See Deerr, 549.

[37] Nicolás Calvo de la Puerta y O'Farrill (d. 1802), similarly son of one of the *regidores* of 1762, doctor of Theology at the University of Havana, a brilliant chemist and all-round scholar. He was a brother-in-law of the Conde de Casa Montalvo, since they both married sisters of José Ricardo O'Farrill.

[38] That is, in place of lye. This was a standardized product rather than one made locally from a variety of substances, as Moreno Fraginals (32–3) points out.

Arango, who was responsible for this innovation, began also to argue for the more economical use of land; other West Indian planters believed already that with scientific agriculture, and some rotation of crops, sugar plantations could last for ever, instead of a mere forty years. In 1798 either Nicolás Calvo or Arango brought to Cuba (through the persuasion of Philip Allwood, Baker and Dawson's astute agent in Havana) from the Danish island of Santa Cruz a new cane variety, Bourbon or Otaheite, a fresher green cane which proved very successful, in Cuba as elsewhere, by furnishing on the same amount of soil both a quarter more juice and a stem more woody and thicker, and therefore of more use as firewood.[39]

By a mixture of patronage and bullying the sugar-obsessed aristocrats of creole society had now completely pushed out the tobacco farmers in the province of Havana. Roads began to be built, to cut the huge cost of transporting sugar to Havana or other ports simply by oxen. Arango proposed to build canals. Allwood, pioneer of the mango and Otaheite, also helped introduce mills with horizontal rather than vertical rollers. Finally, as the commercial concomitant of this increased expansion, U.S. merchants were permitted to sell food and clothing in Cuba for slaves. Foundries sold iron gudgeons and cogs for machinery. The eccentric Timothy Dexter[40] sold 42,000 warming-pans as frying-pans in Cuba – perhaps for use in sugar mills; and Humboldt speaks of 'light and elegant' houses ordered from the U.S., 'like pieces of furniture' in the already large suburbs outside the walls of Havana.[41]

The response by Arango and the creole 'liberals' to the collapse in Haiti was less, at first, one of fear lest Cuba might follow the same road, than a sense of opportunity that the Cubans now almost had the world sugar market in their hands. Certainly prosperity followed from the sensational rise in sugar prices in the 1790s. Great trees were indiscriminately felled. Jerked beef was now imported, not exported. To serve the sugar industry, capital from all over the Caribbean poured into Havana. Between 1792 and 1806, 179 new mills were founded in the jurisdiction of Havana: and, while an average mill in 1792 produced about fifty-five tons a year, in 1804 it had gone up to over 130. By 1800 sugar fields extended beyond the immediate neighbourhood of Havana

[39] First used in the 1780s, it passed into general use after 1797. It had been brought from the South Seas by the French to the Antilles, and now replaced the old *criollo* (or *puri*) cane which had been the standard variety in both the New World and the Old, apparently leaving India in the early middle ages. Since Bougainville took the cane first to Bourbon (Réunion), this cane is also known as Bourbon. See Deerr, 19; and D. C. Corbitt, *Revista Bimestre Cubana*, XLVII, No. 3 (May–June 1941); Ely, *Cuando reinaba*, 94; and Moreno Fraginals, 20, 26. Ragatz (*Fall of the Planter Class*, 90) falsely attributes to this cane the decline of the British West Indies. If he had looked from Jamaica to Cuba he would have seen the folly of this argument.

[40] Timothy Dexter (1747–1806) of Newburyport.

[41] Humboldt, *Travels*, 159.

well into what is now the province of Matanzas. Other mills sprang up around the old smugglers' port of Trinidad, so close to Jamaica. Down the island, in the Puerto Príncipe region, there subsisted only fifty-five mills, slightly less than had been working thirty years before. But this area had lived on smuggling, now no longer necessary.[42] Oriente remained backward: a few mills around Bayamo, Holguín and Santiago, with perhaps fifty slaves each and producing 250 hogsheads of rough sugar, produced in all under 6,000 tons.

Some planters of the west in these years even felt able to settle a part of their accumulated debts. Underlying this confidence was a realization that the whites in Cuba still were far more numerous than they had ever been in Saint Domingue, even though the census of 1792 gave evidence for the first time of an overall black or mulatto majority.[43] Arango and his friends thought that they could import slaves in unlimited numbers because they believed that the government would always have troops (and dogs) to crush any serious revolt, as they indeed did crush the Negro conspiracy of 1795, led by a would-be Cuban Toussaint, Nicolás Morales.[44]

Morales, a freed Negro (like most leaders of Cuban slave revolts he was the son of a slave), set up a network of conspirators to demand equality between black and white, the abolition of taxes and the distribution of plantations to the slaves: that is, a radical agrarian revolution. The creoles relied on the government. But the government stood to gain anyway. Controlling the army, Spanish colonial ministers, captains-general and *intendentes* knew that the fear of a slave revolution would hold the 'liberals' to Spain.

At home, Spain embarked on a policy of giving 'every encouragement . . . to the manufacturing in old Spain of all goods proper for the African Trade' and an ex-Jesuit, Raimundo Hormaza, remained in Liverpool as a permanent Spanish representative.[45] He also wrote pamphlets attacking abolitionism under the more acceptable name of 'Rev. Raymond Harris'; his *Scriptural Researches into the Licitness of the Slave Trade* was highly regarded by Liverpool slave traders.

[42] Moreno Fraginals, 69. These produced altogether about 430 tons a year.

[43] 138,742 black or mulatto to 133,559 white. It is just possible that the inaccuracy, if real, in this respect derived from a desire on the part of the government to give the impression that the blacks were in the majority when they were not. The consequent sense of fear would add authority to governmental actions.

[44] There was also a serious slave revolt in Jamaica this year which the governor, Lord Balcarres, supposed to have been inspired by Haiti (Orlando Patterson, *The Sociology of Slavery*, 279). Cuban *bloodhounds* were imported, despite the Franco-Spanish alliance against England. Ortiz (406, fn.) quotes a long account of the English Colonel Quarrel's visit to Cuba, his reception by de las Casas and the ball given by the Marquesa de San Felipe at Bejucal to bid goodbye to the Cuban dogs and their attendants, some of the best *slave-catchers* in the island.

[45] Donnan, II, 577.

Arango's policy, of course, depended on the merchants of Havana.[46] For the basic structure of the sugar industry remained the same: to start a new plantation, to pay for new equipment, to pay for new slaves or to replace old ones who had died or become incapable, the only recourse was to borrow money or to get goods on credit. The average number of slaves per mill was now about eighty, though already huge mills such as *La Ninfa*, founded jointly by Arango and the *intendente* Valiente (doubtless with money belonging to the Crown, and with French technical assistance), employed 350 slaves.[47] If this had been the position in the 1760s, it was even more so in the 1790s. As ever, sugar mills remained unattachable for debt. Interest rates remained huge. It was now that the great Humboldt, travelling in Cuba, observed that the Cuban planters were in 'absolute dependence' on the merchants.[48] Merchants as everywhere at the time, in England and in North America, often ran in effect a private bank, keeping large stores of cash in their cellars. Without advances on earnings from their crop, planters often could not dress or feed their slaves or buy a 'Jamaican train', much less buy slaves to begin with. Many Cuban planters now were resigned never to be able to free themselves of debts since, however great their production, they could never hope to pay off more than the accumulated interest, at 18 or 20 per cent. Merchants such as Allwood (ultimately expelled for reasons of jealousy on the part of his Cuban rivals), Pedro Juan de Erice (who made loans of over £500,000 ($M2) in three years), Bonifacio González Larriñaga (with loans of over £250,000 ($M1)), Juan de Santa María or Bernabé Martínez de Pinillos, continued to advance money, year after year, waiting for a time of high prices when they could collect at least the interest on their debt. They forced planters to use their boxes and hogsheads in which to carry sugar to Havana, and even planters who established a relative degree of independence had to pay a commission to these merchants to ship their goods.

One casualty of these developments was the Church's old rights to *Diezmos* (tithes), a tenth of all profits: these had been generally paid till about 1750 but by 1790 only thirty out of 193 mills in the bishopric

[46] It is hard to believe they did not realize this since Arango and Nicolás Calvo accompanied Humboldt on his visit round Cuba and Humboldt's views were clear on the subject (see above).

[47] The five biggest mills in the 1804 harvest were: *San José de los Dolores* (belonging to the Marqués de Arcos), producing 430 tons a year; *San Miguel* (belonging to Bonifacio Duarte), 400 tons; *Ninfa*, 380 tons; *San Cristóbal de Baracoa* (belonging to the Reverend Fathers of Belén), 350 tons; and *La Asunción* (belonging to José Ignacio Echegoyen), producing 350 tons. The Marqués de Arcos (otherwise Ignacio Peñalver) had also owned the third biggest mill in 1761. All these mills had over 300 slaves (Moreno Fraginals, 19). In 1761 no mill had produced more than 165 tons in a year.

[48] Humboldt, *Travels*, 280–1. As previously described, Friedrich, Baron von Humboldt travelled in South America throughout 1799–1804. His *Travels* though on occasion inaccurate in detail, are a monument of meticulous observation.

of Havana were still paying. By the end of the century indeed the planters were refusing to open their books to the Church. The bishop protested but eventually gave in. Feudalism had been worsted by capitalism, though the blow was softened by the fact that the Church itself retained many mills; for instance, the monastery of Santa Clara alone owned twenty while the Reverend Fathers of Belén owned the third most productive mill in the harvest of 1804.[49]

Most merchants were at least partially slave traders. Cubans or Spaniards were now setting out for Africa; even Arango sent an expedition. After 1807, when the British abolished the slave trade, Cubans learned the trade with English crews to begin with, and by 1810 there were about thirty successful expeditions a year.[50]

Cost of sugar estates, c. 1800 Hüne's estimate *				
	Total cost of plantation	Number of slaves	Overheads	Slave renewal	Interest on capital
1780	£35,000	220	£1,200	£600 (12 @ £50 a head)	£2,600 (8% interest)

* *Vollständige historisch-philosophische Darstellung aller veränderungen des Negersclavenhandels*, 2 vols (1820), qu. Deerr, I, 129.

This was beginning to bring really large quantities of spare cash.[51] The effect of the freeing of the slave trade in 1790 was indeed to make Havana merchants themselves very rich, in contrast to the days before when the Cuban slave trade gave wealth particularly to others, notably the English. An Italian traveller of the 1840s noted that all the great fortunes of Havana had been made from trading human flesh.[52] Successful merchants themselves often bought plantations, establishing a junior member of the family or some other colleague as administrator on the land. In this way, some of the largest (and later model) plantations were founded. Thus, among the grand slavers of the late eighteenth century was the half-French firm of Poey and Hernández: a generation later, the Poeys were to be found showing admiring foreign visitors round their model mill, *Las Cañas*.[53] The Iznagas of Trinidad accumulated a huge fortune from slaving which they afterwards invested in nine famous sugar mills. By now too, symptomatically, the family of O'Farrill (grandchildren of the agent of the South Sea Company in

[49] Moreno Fraginals, 54. For the Church and the growth of the sugar industry see also Moreno Fraginals' article in the *Revista de la Biblioteca Nacional January-December, 1963.*
[50] *Ibid.,* 143.
[51] See, for instance, Ortiz's account of a journey in 1807.
[52] Carlo Barinetti, *A Voyage to Mexico and Havana*, 135, qu. Ely, *Cuando reinaba*, 1841, 101.
[53] Ely, *Cuanda reinaba*, 64, 797.

Havana after the treaty of Utrecht) was well on the way to being regarded as 'among the six best families in Cuba' and indeed their daughters married into all the grand Cuban families; the Conde de Casa Montalvo, innovator of the Jamaican train, married one O'Farrill; Nicolás Calvo, another innovator, had both an O'Farrill mother and wife; the Conde de Jaruco y Mopox married Casa Montalvo's daughter, an O'Farrill grand-daughter; Juan O'Farrill would receive the first licence for a steamboat service (in 1819), while General Gonzalo O'Farrill, his brother, became Spanish Minister of War during the Bonaparte usurpation in 1810. By the mid-nineteenth century the O'Farrills would be found with six big mills altogether worth £400,000 ($1,730,000), owning 1,458 slaves and 620 pairs of oxen, with an annual profit (after deduction of expenses) of £65,000 ($277,491).[54] The exact relationship between the accumulation of the original capital necessary to launch the Cuban sugar industry and the slave trade is impossible to define in terms of the last peso; but the slave trade, now as at the beginning in the 1760s, often provided not only the labour for the advancement of this industry but the capital as well; and the merchant, slaver or not, who also had a plantation was in a sense the only free planter.[55]

[54] *Ibid.*, quoting Moses Taylor Papers, 452.

[55] This situation was reflected in all slave-marketing countries. The links between slave dealing and manufacturers (the Hardman brothers of Liverpool and Rochdale, Bacon of Senegal and South Wales, Touchett of Liverpool and Manchester, Ashton of the Sankey Brook Canal, the Montaudoins of Nantes, James de Wolf of Rhode Island) and bankers or insurers (Leyland, Kennion, Gregson, Heywood, all of Liverpool, not to mention the Sun and Royal Exchange insurance companies) were close enough to make it a temptation to suppose that the slave trade was a strong stimulus to manufacture to whomever it brought profits. Liverpool slave merchants, when the question of abolition came up for the first time, themselves insisted that the slave trade stimulated manufacture in Manchester, while the abolitionists depreciated that matter, to prevent it being thought that abolition would indeed ruin industry. There is more therefore, to Eric Williams's argument about the slave-trading basis of industrialism than allowed for by e.g. M. W. Flinn, *Origins of the Industrial Revolution* (1966), 45–6.

CHAPTER VII

Rebellion in South America

During the Napoleonic Wars, Cuba had her first taste of those extreme fluctuations in sugar prices which have bedevilled her economy ever since. After the high prices of the 1790s and during the Peace of Amiens, sugar dropped to under thirty shillings a hundredweight, but rose when war began again. In 1807 prices fell once more, due partly to the British conquest yet again of Martinique and Guadeloupe, but they rose again the next year, stimulated by both American and British political behaviour and eventually by the Anglo-American war. In 1814 the raw sugar price reached nearly £5 a hundredweight.[1]

In the face of this unstable, even if, for Cuba, intermittently rewarding international situation, the Spanish government followed an erratic and politically disastrous course. Spain gained nothing from her brief alliance with England (1793–5), and less from her enmity with her (1799–1801). The planters of Cuba in 1796 met lower prices for sugar with complaints of ruin, and secured lower taxes. Arango, who had often attacked monopoly where Spanish merchants were concerned, became, with the Conde de Jaruco, monopolist for the import of wheat, in a scandal which implicated the Spanish ambassador to the U.S. (Carlos Martínez de Irujo) and the U.S. Consul in Cádiz (José Martínez Iznardi).[2] In 1799, the government reimposed the old prohibitions against foreign trade. Neither the captain-general of Cuba[3] nor Pablo José Valiente, the *intendente*, obeyed these bans, suggesting the first whisper of an independent policy on Cuba's part in the slow road to nationalism. The U.S.'s share meantime of the Cuban harvest increased ten times: 16 tons in 1790, nearly 160 in 1795.[4]

With rising prosperity, more schools were founded; in 1801 there were seventeen in Havana, with 2,000 pupils, though, commented a North American later with some accuracy, most 'were not under the Government and were taught by ignorant coloured women who had

---

[1] Deerr, II, 531.

[2] This wheat scandal and its implications throughout Cuban–Spanish society is skilfully disentangled by Moreno Fraginals, 36–7.

[3] De Las Casas had given way to Juan Bassecourt in 1796.

[4] American State Papers: *Commerce and Napoleon*, class IV, vol. 1 (1832), 367; qu. Ely, *Cuando reinaba*, 61.

neither method nor order.'[5] A course of anatomy was begun at the university and at the seminary of San Carlos logic began to be taught. In 1811 Fr Félix Varela took the revolutionary step of dropping the use of Latin for his lectures in philosophy. More and more great houses were built in Havana.

The coming of peace in 1801 enabled the Spanish government to re-enact the prohibition on trade with the U.S. – the U.S. Consul Blakely (the first permanent U.S. diplomat in Cuba) being imprisoned.[6] But at the same time peace brought new prosperity – a record figure of nearly 14,000 slaves being introduced in the year of the Peace of Amiens.[7] Havana merchants such as Joaquín de Urria & Co. were making a great deal of money, as well as their Liverpool suppliers, such as Thomas Leyland & Co.,[8] and also North Americans.[9] In 1804 the Council of the Indies in Seville, though specifically alluding to the fate of Haiti, gave permission for twelve years of free trade to Spaniards and to foreigners to introduce slaves direct from Africa – bozals who, it was thought, were more likely to attach themselves to the religion of Cuba than slaves brought in from English or English-speaking America. Planters who had tried to bring in only male slaves were instructed to import women to encourage families and also to enable slaves generally to benefit from the presence of Negresses in illness and other matters.[10]

War returned. The battle of Trafalgar in 1805 shattered the Spanish navy and made communication between Spain and her American empire almost impossible. (Nelson's last fight was thus in some respects the first battle in the war of Latin American independence since, during the following years of neglect, the mainland colonies of Latin America at last began to assume a separate identity.) Under the stress of war the

[5] *Census of Cuba*, 1899, 568.

[6] H. Portell Vilá, *Historia de Cuba en sus relaciones con los Estados Unidos y España*, 4 vols (1938), 133.

[7] Aimes's figure was 13,832. The figures available for English trade to Africa naturally shot up in 1804.

[8] Leyland had a copybook career of the successful slave merchant. In about 1752 he was in business in the Irish trade with Gerald Dillon. In 1776 he won £20,000 ($85,000) in a lottery and went into ship-owning, buying $\frac{2}{16}$ of a privateer, the *Enterprise*, belonging to Francis Ingram. In 1780 he entered the slave trade and soon bought a stately home, Walton Park, outside Liverpool. He was mayor of Liverpool in 1798. In 1802 he entered banking, though keeping his slaveships – the *Enterprise* reached Havana with 412 Negroes for Pérez de Urría in 1803 – and though one of his partners was the abolitionist, Roscoe. In 1807 he founded an independent bank. Mayor again in 1814 and 1820, he stood unsuccessfully for parliament against Canning and died in 1827 leaving £600,000 ($M2.6). His bank held part of the corporation account of Liverpool, and in the late nineteenth century merged with the Bank of North and South Wales. See John Hughes, *Liverpool Banks and Bankers*.

[9] The figures for North American slavers entering Havana are not yet obtainable, but in Montevideo twenty out of thirty U.S. ships were slavers in 1806 (*cf.* A. P. Whitaker, *The U.S. and the Independence of Latin America, 1800–1830*, 2nd edn (1964), 16).

[10] *Recueil de diverses pièces*, 133. This cedula was not published for fear that the slaves might understand it and so cause trouble.

Spanish imperial system really broke down. North Americans who broke into ports technically out of bounds were treated leniently. Cuba now relied on U.S. boats for food supplies. In 1806, in fact, all Cuban trade was carried on by non-Spanish vessels.[11]

The abolition of the slave trade in England in 1807 caused a marked drop in the availability of slaves; between 1790 and 1807 most slaves had been brought to Cuba in English vessels.[12] Further, in 1807, President Jefferson, angry at the losses of U.S. shipping in the war, took reprisals, with an Embargo Act, attempting to suppress all commercial interchange between the belligerents. U.S.-Cuban trade dropped by half and prices of imported goods tripled in Havana. Two-thirds of the sugar harvest of 1808 went unsold, and fifty good sugar mills were reported ruined.[13] Pöey and Hernández, slave merchants, said that many slaves were unsold too.[14] The aged Gabriel, Marqués de Casa Peñalver, one of the pioneers of the 1760s and 1770s, complained that he had lost sixty slaves in the last two years and had not replaced them because his estates did not pay.[15] Of course, receipts at the Customs House dropped too, from £420,000 ($2,400,932) in 1802 to £280,000 ($1,178,974) in 1808.[16] The Embargo Act was abandoned in 1809 but further growth in the sugar industry, despite the high prices obtainable, was delayed, since the British-American war of 1812–14, though raising prices, broke U.S. commerce. The consequences of Jefferson's policies were thus to let England even farther into South America. The English (due to their alliance with Bourbon Spain against Napoleon) were also able to use Cuban ports in their attacks on North America: a fact which strategic-minded North Americans never forgot.

Such was the commercial background to four epoch-making political events: first, in 1808 the Spanish Crown collapsed before Napoleon, who placed his brother, Joseph, on the Spanish throne. The English went to Spain to fight with the populace against the French along with the liberal wing of the upper class (supported by several members of the Cuban oligarchy such as the Marqués de Casa Calvo and General

[11] Sagra, *Historia*, 142. In the first four months of 1805, Consul Hill announced that 175 U.S. ships had left Havana harbour and only 25 Spanish, with three Danish ones (American State Papers, *Commission of Navigation*, I, 696, qu. Ely, *Cuando reinaba*, 64). In 1806, North American sales to Cuba reached £2,500 ($11,000). In 1800 the U.S.A. took in return 13,000 tons of refined sugar and 9,500 tons of crude; in 1806, she took 15,000 tons of refined and 18,000 of crude sugar. The U.S. also imported hides for the shoe industry of Pennsylvania (*ibid.*, 470–2, 705–6, qu. Ely, 64; figures adjusted). Before 1790, of course, the U.S. took much more sugar from Haiti than from Cuba.

[12] Between 1795 and 1804, England carried a total of nearly 400,000 slaves to the Americas, over 300,000 in Liverpool ships (Gomer Williams, 632).

[13] American State Papers, *Commerce and Navigation*, I, 815, 851–57, qu. Ely, 65.

[14] *Recueil de diverses pièces*, 133, et seq. papers, qu. Aimes, 61.

[15] Aimes, 61. This was the same Gabriel de Peñalver who already as a young man in 1762 had been a *regidor*.

[16] Humboldt, *Travels* (Spanish edn.), 253.

Gonzalo O'Farrill, who became Joseph Bonaparte's war minister).[17] Until 1814 war ravaged Spain, leaving Cuba under an independent-minded captain-general, Someruelos,[18] virtually free to act as he wished.

Also in 1808, President Jefferson for the first time played on what was to be a recurrent theme in American history: the willingness of the U.S. to purchase Cuba, just as they had taken over Louisiana (by buying it in 1803 from Napoleon, who had received it from Spain in 1800). The president sent General James Wilkinson (who had appropriately taken physical possession of Louisiana for the U.S.) to Captain-General Someruelos, to explain that the U.S. would very much prefer Cuba and Mexico to remain under Spain rather than pass under British or French control but if Spain could not maintain herself there, the U.S. would be ready to buy the island.[19] The mission failed to make headway but Jefferson, despite North American ignorance of and distrust for Catholic Cuba, continued to hanker after the idea of close association with the island; did not all men of the New World partake of the same natural goodness? he wrote to James Madison in 1809, adding that he thought Napoleon (supposedly in control of Spain and her empire) might agree to give Cuba to the U.S. in return for the U.S. permitting France a free hand elsewhere in Spanish America.[20] In 1810 the *cabildo* at Havana began secret negotiations with William Shaler, the American Consul in the city:[21] in the cause of preserving slavery (beginning to be threatened by the abolitionism preached at the Cortes of Cádiz), they said they would be ready to organize the annexation of Cuba to the U.S. But they wanted first a U.S. guarantee against intervention by Britain. This was not forthcoming.[22] The planters were led by José de Arango y Núñez de Castillo, first cousin of Arango the economist, and himself reckoned to be the 'father of statistics' in Cuba and treasurer of Havana 1799–1800. He had been involved in the political tumult of Madrid in 1807–8, condemned to death in Seville and later escaped.

The third epoch-making event was the formation, in 1809, of the first movement for outright independence in Cuba – led by Román de la Luz, a mason. The planter classes and the leaders of Cuban intellectual society, such as it was, refused to back the project and the plot was

[17] Gonzalo O'Farrill y Herrera (1754–1831) took part in siege of Gibraltar, 1782. Active in Napoleonic Wars, Minister of War, 1807. Afterwards exile in Paris, where he died.

[18] Salvador de Muro, Marqués de Someruelos (1754–1813), captain-general 1799–1812.

[19] See Isaac Cox, 'The Pan-American Policy of Jefferson and Wilkinson', *Mississippi Valley Historical Review*, I, 212–39; Whitaker, 42–3. General James Wilkinson (1757–1825) had an adventurous career, first with Benedict Arnold, then in the Conway scandal in 1777, then apparently a Spanish agent in 1784, and a witness against Aaron Burr. Died in Mexico.

[20] *The Writings of Thomas Jefferson*, ed. P. L. Ford, 10 vols (1893-9), IX, 252.

[21] William Shaler (1773–1833), ex-South Sea captain and trader; U.S. Consul in Havana 1810 and 1830–3.

[22] Consular Dispatches Havana, II, U.S. National Archives, 24 October 1810; Portell Vilá, I, 167.

discovered and broken. Among the cattlemen of Puerto Príncipe, down the island, similar thoughts directed at the idea of a specifically Cuban nationality had already been expressed.[23] But these views did not commend themselves to the cosmopolitan sugar barons of Havana and Matanzas who, if and when they looked away from Spain, looked northwards to the U.S.

The fourth great event was the beginning of the continental Spanish-American war of independence with the declaration of the provincial junta of Caracas on 9 April 1810, the deposition of the viceroys of Buenos Aires and New Granada in May and July, and the popular rising in Mexico the same year. The Cuban upper class might, almost certainly would, have sided with the rest of Spanish America (the *cabildo* of Havana playing the same decisive part as that of Caracas or Lima) had it not been for anxiety about their slaves, and the spectre of Haiti.[24] The slaves represented wealth. The value of the 88,000 slaves in 1792 in Cuba – based on what it would have cost to replace them – was about £M4 ($M17·6); the value of the 147,000 slaves in 1817 would be about £M11 ($M54·5).[25] The thought of the disappearance of these great assets was not agreeable.

Where the slaves were concerned the population was changing fundamentally: male slaves in 1792 numbered 50,000, but in 1817, 125,000; at the same time the female slave population dropped from just under 40,000 in 1792 to an intolerable minority in 1817 of less than 25,000.[26] Such an imbalance must have at the very least caused an acute sexual strain and made it less easy to care for sick slaves. It also increased crime. Therefore, the planters' anxiety rose the richer they got.

The last years of the old, united Spanish empire thus brought to Cuba not only relative wealth (in comparison both with the other islands and her own past) but also the expectation of still greater wealth to come.[27] Hence the reluctance of the planters and the merchants of Havana to back any revolutionary independence movement such as that which triumphed on the mainland, and the reason why the same

[23] See *Informe* Directed to the *Real Consulado* by Ignacio Zarragoitia, 5 March 1805, qu. Moreno Fraginals, 69.

[24] (Just as the planters of the English West Indies would have liked to have sided with the North American revolutionists of the 1770s.) The Cuban creoles had been even further disillusioned by the general collapse to the east of Haiti: the oldest Spanish colony, Santo Domingo, after two hundred years of inactivity, was rudely disturbed by marauding mobs from Haiti in 1801 and in succeeding years by further plunder till the temporary reinstatement of first French, then Spanish rule in 1805–8. Afterwards, Santo Domingo attempted independence, returned to Spain (1814), once again proclaimed independence in 1821 but was absorbed by Haiti from 1822–44.

[25] Calculated from Aimes's estimate of the cost of bozals in 1792 at 200 pesos and 300–450 pesos (average 375 pesos) in 1818 (Aimes, 267–8).

[26] These censuses are given in Sagra, *Historia*, 4–5.

[27] The sudden rise of coffee in Cuba during the time of the wars is discussed in ch. X.

class toyed as early as 1810 with the idea of unification with the U.S. Rising wealth rather than mere strategic importance also explains why the second and fourth presidents of the U.S. played with the scheme of absorbing Cuba. It is true that Spanish America in general since 1760 had, like Cuba, experienced similar changes in the direction of a new prosperity; the *intendentes* in Peru and in Mexico had cleaned and lit streets; Las Casas in Cuba had his equivalent or superior in Revilla- gigedo in Mexico; but this prosperity of the mainland had not been based upon potentially insurrectionary slave labour.

In May 1810 the Cuban *junta superior*, set up in 1808 to manage the island while sovereign power was almost in abeyance in Spain, did receive an invitation from Caracas to take part in the great revolt but, after some discussion and some popular enthusiasm for acceptance, the invitation was finally rejected. The sheer physical difficulties of joining the independence movement played a part. Cuba was an island, easily cut off by a Spanish fleet (had there been one). The Crown could act more harshly and effectively in Cuba since the territory was smaller and, then as now, it was harder for political opponents to escape across a frontier. On the other hand, royalist refugees from the mainland began to arrive in Cuba – 20,000 between 1810 and 1826 – helping to swell pro-Spanish sentiments. Some later came too from Florida, sold to the U.S. in 1819, and some from Louisiana.[28] There was also an institutional hindrance to revolution: while by 1810 on the mainland many of the lower clergy were creoles who often, like the Mexican Fr Miguel Hidalgo, gave the incentive to the revolutionaries, in Cuba they were mainly *peninsulares* and pro-Spanish.

Another reminder was given of the risks of independence by a Negro wood-carver from Havana, José Antonio Aponte, who, somewhat in- fluenced by the memory of Moses and his mission 'to lead his people out of bondage', like de la Luz and Nicolás Morales, prepared an elaborate conspiracy, with tentacles all over the island, to burn both the cane and coffee fields (so making an end of the wealth necessary to buy slaves). Worst of all, he made contact with the dreaded Haitians. Meetings were held, as they had been in Haiti before the Revolution, in Aponte's house which was also the seat of the African deity, Changó, and political happening were plotted under the guise of religious festi- vals (Aponte was a *santero*, or priest, in this rite). Though he was be- trayed and hanged, Aponte's conspiracy appears to have been on a national scale. There was a minor rising, some *mayorales* and land- owners being killed, while there were riots in several mills and cities.[29]

---

[28] Just as the more conservative settlers in Kenya moved in the 1960s after independence to Rhodesia, so helping to delay the revolution in that outpost of the British empire.
[29] See José L. Franco, *La Conspiración de Aponte* (1963). Whites also were involved.

This caused a chill down the spine for the creoles. It drove those Cuban deputies who were returned to the Spanish Constitutional Cortes between 1811 and 1813 to argue consistently and successfully for a postponement even of any discussion of the abolition of slavery. In March 1811 one Spanish deputy, Alcocer, however, did propose a ban on the slave trade, which would leave existing slaves with their masters and render children free at birth; slaves thereafter would be treated like domestic servants and paid wages to be fixed by judges. This plan was supported by another deputy, the 'divine' Argüelles (future tutor to Queen Isabella II), with his eye on 'liberal' Spain's English ally. The Cortes then heard an appeal by Arango from the town of Havana on the importance of the slave trade for its commerce: not one estate on the island had enough Negroes; very few had enough females; it was not the fault of the present generation of planters that there were slaves in Cuba, but now, like it or not, the island depended on slaves; and it was not right to condemn existing slaves to celibacy. More slaves were accordingly needed, not fewer. Las Casas (the bishop) was blamed for starting the slave trade. Cuba was beginning to awake from 'three centuries of exhaustion and neglect'; it was unjust to prevent this.[30] The Cortes therefore dismissed the matter: Cuba would remain Spanish, and slavery would survive. Arango's economic revolution therefore survived too.

THE CENSUS OF 1791 AND 1792

Despite the remarks in the American Census of 1899 (p. 704), it is clear that two separate counts were taken in 1791 and 1792 in Cuba (the same occurred in 1774 and 1775). De La Sagra says clearly that he saw them both and, though admitting that it has errors, says he preferred that of 1792. Both counts were made for the purposes of coordinating taxation. The figures were 255,860 and 272,301 for 1791 and 1792, a difference of 17,481 in the two years. One must assume, therefore, that it was the second one which was seen by Humboldt, who stated the total as 272,141, but suggested that it erred by 25% and that it should be 362,700. Humboldt, however, was not faultless. (For instance, his estimate of the average investment needed to set up a sugar plantation seems to have gone seriously wrong in estimating the cost of slaves per head as £20 ($90). This was the figure in 1762–3 under the English, but otherwise would have been more likely in the seventeenth than in the eighteenth century.) The acceptance by near contemporary authorities such as De La Sagra (who wrote after Humboldt) of the figures 255,860 and 272,301 respectively for 1791 and 1792 suggests that here too the baron may have gone wrong.

[30] A translation can be found in Aimes, 65–71.

De La Sagra's figures make clear that Pezuela (in his note made in 1866) on the county 792 has simply either himself made errors of transcription or has relied on false figures:

	La Sagra	Pezuela
Total Population	272,301	272,300
Whites	133,559	153,559
males	72,299	82,299(!)
females	61,260	72,209
Mulatto or Negro	138,742	116,741
free	54,142	54,151
slave	84,590	64,590(!)

CHAPTER VIII

The Ever-faithful Isle

A new challenge came to Cuba from the proposed international abolition of the slave trade itself. The abolitionist movement in England derived from economic opposition to the West Indian monopoly, from a powerful humanitarian movement, and from a pronounced shift in general attitudes to sin, human nature and progress.[1] It gathered momentum from the decline in British West Indian prosperity and the shift in Liverpool commerce towards cotton and away from slaves. (Since palm oil was the chief, if inadequate, substitute for slaves as a West African export, it might be said that the slave trade could not have been abolished by England before the English became interested in washing, for palm oil is the chief constituent of soap.) Denmark was the first European country to abolish the slave trade. In 1808 this trade was formally abolished by both England and the U.S. Sweden and Holland followed, then France at the Congress of Vienna. But some North Americans, some Englishmen, many Frenchmen and many Portuguese and Spaniards continued to trade, though the English were faced with increasing penalties such as, after 1811, transportation, and were faced, too, by the British navy, brought in to enforce these acts of abolition: for clearly any abolition, to be effective would have both to be international and be policed. But the sheer respectability of those who controlled the trade in England was another factor: Liverpool slave merchants were too grand to break the law; and they had also other interests, not only in palm oil import but in banking and insurance. Some English traders changed their nationalities and names: Captain Philip Drake of Bristol turned up as Don Felipe Drax of Brazil.[2] On the other hand, the African economy was so geared to slaving that the trade could not be abolished overnight. In 1816 in Spain the right to free trade, approved in 1804, expired and the Council of the Indies recommended abolition. But this recommendation was made with one eye on England, and with a powerful dissenting report, signed by Arango and others. The arguments varied a little from those of 1811 – if the trade were abolished the same amount of work would have to be done by fewer

---

[1] D. Brion Davis (*Slavery in Western Culture*, 363) develops this aspect of the matter.
[2] G. F. Dow, *Slave Ships and Slaving*, Vol. 11, 209. This volume includes a long extract from Drake's own 'memoirs'.

slaves; the value of slaves would go up and so it would be harder for them to buy freedom. The dissentient members also said menacingly that abolition might be resisted by force and lead to the loss of the island. In theory, they admitted, the slave trade might have eventually to be banned, but even England had delayed twenty years after the idea was first suggested.[3]

In 1817 the Spanish government, however, was finally persuaded by the English, commercially and politically dominant in the peninsula after 1815, formally to abolish the slave trade as from 1820. The Spaniards would be paid £400,000 ($M1·7) to compensate those who might lose by abolition. The Portuguese agreed to do the same, though restricting their obligation to the territory and seas north of the Equator;[4] they would receive £300,000 ($M1.3), together with a £600,000 ($M2.6) loan.[5] The right of the British navy to stop slaveships was accepted but not that to search vessels merely suspected of trading slaves. Courts were set up, in Sierra Leone (the uneasily established English freed slave colony), and afterwards at Havana, Loanda, Río de Janeiro and Surinam, to judge seized vessels and cargoes. If a vessel were condemned, the slaves were taken to the court and would be maintained free by the government for a year. Afterwards, they were to be left to their own resources, unless they volunteered to work in Cuba or the British West Indies as apprentices (*emancipados*). Alongside abolition, came a new decree to promote emigrant labour ('Catholic labour') from Spain.

Three years' grace was thus given to the Cuban slave merchants and planters who made as much use as possible of their last legal opportunity. This was a period of much economic activity in Havana led by another astute *intendente*, Alejandro Ramírez, under whose influence the Economic Society was kept busy with innumerable projects – encouraging small farming and diversification, studying Adam Smith, abolishing the tobacco monopoly (in 1817) and growing trees.[6] The critical decisions at this time were those between 1814 and 1816 which formally permitted the cutting of trees and which allowed holders of *mercedes* to devote their land to any purpose which they liked – absolving them of any formal requirement (in many cases long since ignored) to supply beef to any city. Formal ownership was also given to any landholder who could prove his family to have been in possession for ninety years and to have

---

[3] See *British and Foreign State Papers*, IV, 543–9.

[4] They had agreed to abolish the slave trade north of the Equator in 1810, but this ban came into full existence in 1820.

[5] *British and Foreign State Papers*, IV, 33 ff.

[6] See Shafer, 323, for summary of the *Memorias* of the Economic Society in these years. Alejandro Ramírez (1777–1821) was previously in Guatemala and Puerto Rico. Intendente in Havana 1816–1821. Founder of the Botanical Gardens in Havana.

been cultivating it for forty years. Finally, in 1819 those who held communal holdings were enabled to divide them up or to found sugar mills on their own. All further circular grants were forbidden. Owners of *mercedes* who had been holding *realengos* for over forty years could sue for ownership of them.[7]

These liberating decrees for better or worse gave to many Cubans much unexpected wealth with corresponding benefit to the state in the form of increased revenue. It may be that as many as 10,000 Cubans converted themselves in this way into full-scale landowners, whereas in the past they had technically merely enjoyed a usufruct.[8] On the other hand, disputes over land continued for many years to come.

Against this background, the supply of slaves had picked up in the first years after the Peace of 1815; over 9,000 were said to have arrived in 1815 and over 17,000 in 1816 – the latter a record, above the previous peak level of the year of the Peace of Amiens.[9] In 1817 slave imports reached 25,000; in 1818, nearly 20,000; 15,000 in 1819 and 17,000 in 1820 itself.[10] Thus the five years 1816–20 saw the import of at least 100,000 slaves – more, probably, than were imported in the whole period before 1790.[11] Prices also greatly increased: the 1815–20 price being between £70 ($300) and £115 ($500) for a *bozal* (slave brought direct from Africa). The slaves imported between 1816 and 1820 therefore must have cost about £M12 ($M50) in all – approximately the value of the entire slave population some years before. Other figures suggest that total slave imports between 1803 and 1816 inclusive totalled $M20.[12] But it seems clear that, though prices of slaves rose in Cuba after abolition, their cost to the slave merchants in Africa fell considerably.[13] This was because of the serious economic crisis which faced Africa after English abolition. English exports to Africa fell by a third.[14] Many Africans were ruined.[15] Substitute exports such as palm oil or

---

[7] Corbitt, 'Mercedes and Realengos', *H.A.H.R.* xix, 278.

[8] Pezuela, *Historia,* IV, 62–3; Guerra, 241.

[9] Even this high figure was considerably less than the average import into Saint Domingue in the years before the revolution – which had approached 40,000. Philip Drake says he and his uncle, of Villeño & Co., established at 'New Tyre' on the River Basso, sent 43,000 slaves to Cuba and Brazil in 1816 (*op cit.*, 221). All slave import figures are suspect.

[10] Aimes, 269.

[11] The total number of slaves imported between 1512 and 1798 was supposed (by Aimes (*loc. cit.*)) to be about 90,000. Aimes's figures for the period before 1760 seem likely to be modest; thus he gave a total of 60,000 for all imports of slaves before 1760 – though about 1711 Matthew Prior, English plenipotentiary in France, estimated an import to Havana of about 1,000 a year, apart from smuggled slaves (see Donnan, II, 142).

[12] Sagra, *Historia,* 136, gives value of imports from Africa for these years.

[13] Who the slave merchants were is discussed further below, Chapter xii.

[14] See *Abstract of English Historical Statistics,* 311; levels of exports to Africa reached in 1806 (admittedly a very high year) were not repeated till 1835, without even taking into account variation in value and money.

[15] See W. E. F. Ward, *A History of Ghana,* rev. 2nd edn (1958).

cocoa could not for many years take the slave's place. For several years during the war the slave trade almost faded away, with the English blockading the seas. Consequently slave prices in Africa were very low between 1810 and 1820; and it seems that these low prices continued for most of the next half-century, providing without any doubt whatever the main single reason for the continuance of the slave trade.

The population of Africa also seems to have begun to rise slowly at the beginning of the nineteenth century, for the first time – in the same way as the population of Europe in the early eighteenth century had done – so further depressing slave prices. Costs in Africa were reckoned as under £4 ($16) a head, and prices in Havana no less than £84 ($360) in 1835.[16] The only hurdle was the voyage – which, if successful, could mean profits in that year of £20,000 or $100,000 per journey. By this time there were in Havana twenty-two rich slave merchants, many of them in origin from Cádiz, who were taking the place completely of the old foreign merchants; alongside them were also many merchants from the South of the U.S. who had transferred to Havana.[17]

Before the law forbidding the trade was finally enacted in 1820, a revolution in Spain temporarily transformed the situation. In the most radical *pronunciamiento* of the century, liberal officers headed by Captain Riesgo from the Corunna garrison marched on Madrid. A constitution was then imposed on King Ferdinand. This also applied to Cuba; 'the ever faithful isle' was henceforth to be regarded as a regular province of Spain. Monasteries were (temporarily) abolished, the chapel of one of the Augustinians became a school, political prisoners were freed, and newspapers were quickly founded and filled with radical articles and editorials. Exiles returned from the U.S. and the mainland empire, while secret reform societies, especially masons, proliferated. The political atmosphere of Havana was electric. The cork drawn, it was amazing to see how many radicals there seemed to be among the lower ranks of the Cuban oligarchy and the poorer white population of Havana. Deputies went to the Cortes in Madrid and, although a majority argued for a delay in the application of the ban on the slave trade, one of them, Fr Félix Varela[18] proposed firmly not only immediate application but the abolition of all slavery in Cuba, with compensation. Despite the anger of his Cuban colleagues, the liberal Cortes asked him to prepare a project to carry this out. Meantime, the growth of white immigration into Cuba flagged.

[16] Drake, qu. Dow, 247.
[17] Moreno Fraginals, 143.
[18] Félix Varela y Morales (1788–1853); first professor of philosophy in Havana, 1811. See José Ignacio Rodríguez, *Vida del Presbítero Don Félix Varela* (1944), 113–22.

Such schemes were not acceptable to the planters in Cuba. The five years since the end of the Napoleonic wars had seen a new leap forward in sugar and also coffee production. U.S.–Cuban trade had resumed fast after 1815, due partly to the commercial rivalries of Britain and the U.S. Freedom of commerce had been finally permitted (having been really tolerated since 1800) in the Spanish empire in 1818 – though not commerce without tariffs (a duty was imposed on non-Spanish articles not arriving in Spanish ships). This enabled legal access for Cuban merchants on a permanent basis to the expanding North American market. The sugar plantations now numbered 800, and most new ones had installed Jamaican trains with imported machinery. In the years between 1815 and 1820 sugar production per mill seems to have been about fifty tons – an advance of 50 per cent on levels obtained at the start of the era of Arango in 1790. In 1818 four planters installed steam engines at their mills equivalent to the energy of perhaps twenty oxen: it is instructive that of these technical adventurers only one (Nicolás Peñalver) was a member of the old oligarchy which had carried out the sugar revolutions of the 1760s and 1790s. The others were immigrants, and it would be they who in the future would play a major part in similar advances.[19] Of these men, Diago had previously been the first and only Cuban who attempted to grind sugar by wind-mill, a method much in use in wind-swept Barbados. Within a few years most new plantations would establish steam mills as a matter of course.

These engines, though labour-saving in many ways, had to be stoked; bagasse left over from cane harvesting and wood from near-by forests came to be inadequate. Thus coal even had to be imported, especially in wet years.[20] Cuba was entering the industrial revolution with a vengeance, though older, poorer, smaller mills, such as persisted in Oriente, continued to use cattle. The most significant development after 1815, however, was that of the port of Matanzas in the beautiful bay of that name at the mouth of the rivers San Juan and Yumurí. Its wealth derived, to begin with, from the settlement there of various 'European capitalists' who, we are told, could not go back to Spain after its invasion by the French.[21] They converted the previously small town (founded in 1693 by about thirty Canary Island families) into the second port of Cuba: its population would double from 20,000 in 1817 to 45,000

[19] These were Joaquín Pérez de Urría, originally a slave merchant from Cádiz; Pedro Diago, an immigrant from the Basque provinces; Juan Madrazo; and Nicolás Peñalver. These mills, it seems, came from Fawcett Preston of England, despite the suggestion of Rauch (*American Interest in Cuba 1848–55*, 20) to the contrary (see Moreno Fraginals, 108; Deerr, 553; and Ely, 512, fn. 11). Most of the early steam mills came from Fawcett Preston & Co. Diago is wrongly credited with having been the first to undertake this invention.

[20] A gas mill was installed later to avoid this.

[21] The remark is Sagra's (*Historia*, 183).

in 1827.[22] In 1816 Matanzas exported 20,000 boxes of sugar; in 1827 nearly 100,000. In 1816, 400 tons of coffee left Matanzas; in 1827, 5,000 tons.[23]

But it was not only 'foreigners' from Spain who then crowded into Cuba; from 1815 an increasing tide of North American merchants reached Havana, Trinidad, Matanzas and Santiago. From Louisiana came a number of Frenchmen, as well as Spaniards. It is to Louisianan Frenchmen that the foundation was due, in what had previously been a *realengo*, of the port of Cienfuegos in the bay of Jagua, in South Cuba, in 1817–19: their leaders were Louis de Clouet, the first mayor of the city, and Andrés Dorticós, a merchant whose daughter Teresa married the multi-millionaire planter and merchant in slaves, Tomás Terry, originally from Venezuela.[24] U.S. citizens were specially favoured since they were free of many taxes and restrictions affecting the Spaniards. Nor was it only merchants who came to Cuba in the second decade of the nineteenth century. The *Memorias* of the Economic Society of Havana indicate for instance that in the twelve months 1 December 1818 to 30 November 1819, 1,332 immigrants came to Cuba, of whom 416 were Spaniards, 389 Frenchmen, 65 Englishmen, 126 Anglo-Americans, along with a few Portuguese, Germans, Irish, Italians, Serbs and others; of these, 722, we are told, were 'farmers', 266 carpenters, 79 masons, 30 bakers and 25 coopers.[25]

It was this expanding, acquisitive, wealthy and remarkably cosmopolitan society, with slaves the most valuable item of everyone's equipment, and refugees or emigrants flocking from all over the Spanish and French empires in America, which had to bear the formal ban on the slave trade in 1820. The planters responded in two ways; first, they tried to ensure that captains-general and other officials from Madrid would ignore the ban. It became an accepted matter that the captains-general should personally receive a bribe from the illegal import of slaves. Other officials were also appropriately rewarded. Such bribes naturally raised the price of slaves, a cost borne by planters rather than traders. Numbers temporarily dropped, only about 6,000 allegedly arriving in 1821, 2,500 in 1822, but the demand for replacement was partly kept

[22] *Ibid.*, 6, 7.
[23] *Ibid.*, 184. A box of sugar normally carried between 16 and 22 *arrobas*, or 400 lb. to 450 lb.
[24] Ely, *Cuando reinaba*, 388–9; Edwin F. Atkins, *Sixty Years in Cuba* (1926), 57; Corbitt, 'Immigration in Cuba', *HAHR*, xxii, 290; 'Mercedes and Realengos' *ibid.*, 939, 290. Osvaldo Dorticós, president of Cuba from 1959, was of this family. In these days the Spanish government gave a *caballería* of land to any white man of sixteen or over, his passage to Cuba and enough to live on until the first crop was in. Other settlements founded at this time included Santo Domingo (Santa Clara), Mariel, Guantánamo and Nuevitas.
[25] See D. C. Corbitt, 'Immigration in Cuba', *HAHR*, xxii, 280–308; see also discussion in Shafer, 283.

up with.[26] The Spanish government was too weak and too far away to insist on execution of the ban in 1820, and in this they had the encouragement of knowing that, despite the French formal ban of 1818, slave-ships sailed regularly from Nantes, Bordeaux and Le Havre to such an extent that the British abruptly told the French government in 1824 that their flag covered 'the villains of all nations'.[27] (The English had by now almost wholly given up the trade, though a few Englishmen were active under false colours.)

The government in Spain had indeed too much on hand in these years, with the formalization of Latin American independence; Peru was declared independent in July 1821; in September a declaration was issued setting up the United Provinces of Central America; in May 1822, Mexico became independent; while, in the same month, the U.S. recognized these declarations. In these circumstances, the Madrid government, however 'liberal', was absolutely unwilling to antagonize the planters of the 'ever-faithful isle'. Public feeling in Spain and Portugal, as in Cuba and Brazil, was that the English interest in abolition was hypocritical; that, having carried an immense number of slaves, they had turned against the trade so as to prevent the competition of Cuban and Brazilian sugar; that they had done so due to economic pressures of East Indian interests at a time when the English West Indies were in decline; that, by not discriminating against slave-grown cotton from the U.S. South, they showed insincerity; and that, by maintaining slavery in their own islands while abolishing the trade, they were simply forcing up the price of slaves without abolishing slavery:[28] English goods were anyway used by slavers in buying slaves in Africa, as English manufacturers knew. English capital was invested in slave-owning concerns (the gold mines of Brazil, the copper mines near Santiago de Cuba, and several plantations in Cuba).

The planters of Cuba were of course in the hands of the government in that they still relied on the captain-general to retain an army adequate to maintain the subjection of their slave labour force; but they had still another card to play. Not, to be sure, independence: that would be too dangerous, it would risk war, and hence revolution such as had ruined Haiti. But could they not follow Florida into the U.S.?

This did not mean precisely that the planters now wished to join the U.S. They preferred the *status quo*. But to preserve slavery (the essence

---

[26] Aimes, *loc. cit.* (Pezuela, II, 285–7, says that 600,000 slaves arrived between 1821 and 1823; a wild overestimate (a misprint for 6,000?) though it is probable that Aimes's figures are too low.)

[27] W. L. Mathieson, *Great Britain and the Slave Trade, 1839–1865, etc.* (1929), 10.

[28] These were very roughly the arguments used by Eric Williams in *Capitalism and Slavery* in 1949.

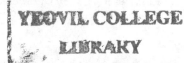

of the *status quo*), they would have liked more to join the Union than to become independent; and in 1820, as in 1808, they would have wished to join the Union if Madrid had insisted that they honour their agreement with the English to ban the slave trade.

These matters were delicately explored again when Bernabé Sánchez, a native of Camagüey, representing several planters, arrived in Washington in September 1822 to offer annexation *as a state*.[29] The U.S. cabinet assembled, undecided. John Quincy Adams, secretary of state, wrote in his diary:

> The question was discussed what was to be done. Mr Calhoun[30] has a most ardent desire that the island should become a part of the United States and says that Mr Jefferson[31] has the same. There are two dangers to be averted ... one that the island should fall into the hands of Gt Britain; the other that it should be revolutionized by the Negroes. Calhoun says Mr Jefferson told him two years ago that we ought, at the first possible opportunity, to take Cuba, though at the cost of a war with England; but as we are now not prepared for this, and as our great object must be to gain time, he thought we should answer this overture [from the planters] by dissuading them from their present purpose and urging them to adhere at present to their connection with Spain.[32]

The U.S. cabinet's reply to the Cuban planters was then a rejection but also an inquiry as to the real state of opinion in Havana. Bernabé Sánchez turned out an unreliable source, being condemned by a correspondent of Joel Poinsett as 'a silly fellow, without education, without judgement and unauthorized'.[33] But it is obvious that some people at least in the North American government believed ultimately that Cuba should join the Union. This was put at its most succinct by Adams in a famous letter to the U.S. minister in Spain, Hugh Nelson:[34]

> Cuba ... has become an object of transcendent importance to the commercial and political interests of our Union. Its commanding position ... its safe and capacious harbour of the Havana ... the nature of its productions and of its wants ... give it an importance in the sum of our national interests with which that of no other foreign

[29] Portell Vilá, I, 210, 215–16, 223; J. Fred Rippy, *British Investments in Latin America, 1822–1949* (1959), 80–82; see also J. L. Franco, *La Batalla por el dominio del Caribe y el Golfo de México*, 3 vols (1964–68), 302, n. 534.

[30] U.S. Secretary of War.

[31] Then still alive.

[32] *Memoirs of J. Q. Adams*, ed C. F. Adams (1874), VI, 70–4; see also 112–13; J. R. Poinsett to Monroe, 7 May 1823; and José del Castillo to Poinsett, 16 April 1823, in National Archives.

[33] Poinsett to Monroe, 7 May 1823. See also Castillo's letters to Poinsett which the latter sent to Monroe.

[34] Hugh Nelson (1768–1836), Congressman for Virginia, 1811–23.

territory can be compared and little inferior to that which binds the different members of this Union together ... It is scarcely possible to resist the conviction that the annexation of Cuba to our federal Republic will be indispensable to the continuance and integrity of the Union itself ... There are laws of political as well as of physical gravitation; and if an apple severed by the tempest from its native tree cannot choose but fall to the ground, Cuba, forcibly disjoined from its own unnatural connection with Spain, and incapable of self support, can gravitate only towards the North American Union which by the same law of nature cannot cast her off from its bosom.[35]

This letter meant that, unless the English struck, the U.S. would play a waiting game, expecting eventually to acquire the island without effort; this policy formed the basis of U.S. policy for half a century since, despite a plan for the seizure of Cuba presented to Canning by Colonel de Lacy Evans in April 1823, England never did strike.[36]

Back in Cuba, with constitutional freedom still miraculously and uniquely surviving, a new and formidable movement for actual independence had by this time grown up. It was led by José Francisco Lemus, a republican who, though a *habanero*, had risen to a colonelcy in the Colombian Army of Independence backed by other Colombian reformers. He had also a lieutenant from Haiti. His movement, the Soles y Rayos de Bolívar, was carefully organized chiefly by masons throughout Cuba on a cell basis, appealing primarily to students and to the poorer white Cubans, urging them to unite with the Negroes, slave and free. In early 1823 a mission of this group left for Colombia to discuss a Cuban revolution with Bolívar, who, however, said the time was not ripe. Posters, nevertheless, were designed with the proclamation: *Independencia o muerte* – independence or death.

Spaniards [Lemus appealed], we do not wish to part from growing friendship, nor to break the sweet ties of language, blood and religion. But we will never return to dependence on you ... Sons of Cubanacán [the Indian name for Cuba], let us make known to the entire world our undertakings to get rid of ridiculous ranks and hierarchies that foster ignorance and stultify the virtuous character of free men. We do not acknowledge any distinction other than that owed to true merit. Let us treat the unfortunate slaves generously, alleviating

[35] *Writings of J. Q. Adams*, ed. W. Chauncey Ford (1913), VII, 369–421. There is also a letter from Monroe to ex-President Jefferson: 'I have always concurred ... that too much importance could not be attached to that Island ... we ought, if possible, to incorporate it' (*Writings of James Monroe*, ed. S. M. Hamilton, 7 vols (1898–1903), VI, 312); see also Jefferson to Monroe, 24 October 1823: 'I have ever looked on Cuba as the most interesting addition which would ever be made to our system' (*Writings of Jefferson*, ed. Ford, X, 278).

[36] *Some Official Correspondence of George Canning*, ed. Edward J. Stapleton, 2 vols (1887) I, 116–18.

their frightful lot until the representatives of our country propose the means of happy redemption, without prejudice against individual interests. They are children of our own God ... Ministers of the Altar! Do not forget that the law of the good Jesus is purely Republican.[37]

While the grandest Cuban planters were thus toying with annexation to the U.S., the leaders of the lower middle class, such as it was, were attempting radical, even multi-racial policies, to gather the support of the slave masses.

The conspiracy of Lemus was given extra point by the collapse of constitutional government in Spain in April 1823. King Ferdinand successfully outwitted his Liberal advisers and overthrew them by a blatant appeal to his cousin the king of France and his conservative foreign minister, Chateaubriand. The Liberal government was unable to organize any resistance and the king of France's outrageously-nick-named '100,000 sons of St Louis' marched to impose an authoritarian regime in place of the Constitution of 1820. Executions and exiles followed. An autocratic captain-general, Dionisio Vives,[38] was sent to Havana where the constitutional liberty of the last three years was quickly abrogated. Monasteries, for instance, got back their properties; and Vives began a systematic programme to crush Cuban liberalism.

Lemus then decided a date for a rising of his conspiracy, but Vives was able to trap him first, as a result of an intensive programme of bribery and treachery. On 1 August 1823 Lemus was captured with most of his lieutenants, and was imprisoned.[39] Others escaped abroad. Several slaves rose without leadership, but were quickly shot. Cuban liberals, such as the abolitionist priest, Fr Félix Varela, and the poet José María de Heredia,[40] fled abroad. The captain-general was in May 1825 given '*facultades omnímodas*' – an authority to do much as he liked; residents of Cuba lost the protection of what law there was. In April 1826 a decree forbade the import of books which opposed 'the Catholic religion, monarchy, or which in any other way advocated the rebellion of Vassals or nations'. A few more conspiracies spluttered on in 1826 and 1827. They were smashed, their leaders hanged. Forty thousand Spanish troops thronged Cuba and the country swarmed with government spies

[37] See Rodrigo Garriga, *Historia Documentada de la Conspiración de los Soles y Rayos de Bolívar* (1927).

[38] General Francisco Dionisio Vives (1735-1840). Fought under O'Farrill in Tuscany, 1866; captain-general of Cuba, 1822-32.

[39] He was confined in Seville, escaped, went to Mexico where he became a general, and died in 1832.

[40] José María Heredia y Campuzano (1803-39) romantic poet known for his *Himno del desterrado* and the famous Ode to Niagara, arguably the most famous poem by a Cuban. Not to be confused with José María de Heredia (1842-1905) who, although Cuban-born, is known as a master of the French sonnet.

and informers. The laws preventing Cuban-born persons from serving in the army or the civil service were rigidly maintained. Cuba was an armed camp. Martial law lasted in effect fifty years.

The situation was accepted internationally. In the summer of 1823 the British foreign minister, Canning, had proposed to the U.S. minister in London, Richard Rush, a joint U.S.-British policy for Latin America. Canning wanted a declaration that any recovery of the Spanish-American colonies by Spain was hopeless, that at the same time neither the U.S. nor Britain coveted them for themselves, and that neither wanted ('would not view with indifference') the transfer of any of them to any other power.[41] To secure this he was willing to bury the hatchet with the U.S. over a variety of issues. One might well find in Canning's speech in his Liverpool constituency (suitably) on 25 August the origins of the famous 'special relationship': the U.S. and Britain were united by 'a common language, a common spirit of commercial enterprise and a common regard to well regulated liberty'.[42] This policy was approved in another form by Monroe in his message to Congress on 2 December 1823, adding that, while the United Kingdom had agreed not to interfere in the ex-Spanish colonial world, the U.S. undertook to take no action in the old world. This message (which later of course became known as the Monroe doctrine) made no mention of Cuba and the Spanish presence was thus tacitly accepted there.[43]

One chance remained for a Cuban independence movement: the new Spanish-American countries might intervene. On 7 December 1824 Bolívar convoked a congress at Panama to take place in 1826 to form a federation of Spanish-speaking republics. On 9 December he decisively defeated the last Spanish army of South America at Ayacucho, forcing a surprisingly indifferent Spain to face the reality of the extinction of the mainland empire. Ten days later he wrote to General Santander (vice-president of Colombia) from Lima:

> The Government should let Spain know that if in a specific space of time Colombia is not recognized and peace made, our troops will go immediately to Havana and Puerto Rico. It is more important to have peace than to liberate these islands; an independent Cuba would take us a great deal of work . . . but if the Spaniards are obstinate we shall move.[44]

At the same time, the new president of Mexico permitted the formation

[41] Dexter Perkins, *The Monroe Doctrine, 1867–1907* (1937), 200–2.

[42] Temperley, 112. Considering the close relationship between Liverpool and the U.S. east coast ports, this was no more than the truth.

[43] For various accounts, see Whitaker, 429–563.

[44] Simón Bolívar, *Cartas del Libertador, corregidas conforme a los originales (1799–1830)*, 10 vols (1929) vol. xxx.

of a 'Junta for the Liberation of Cuba' to be formed of Cubans in Mexico.

But these projects did not mature. Nothing had happened by April 1825 when the new U.S. secretary of state, Henry Clay, with all the moral authority that the U.S. government then had among the southern American liberators, announced: 'This country prefers that Cuba and Puerto Rico should remain dependent on Spain. This government desires no political change in that condition.'[45] Clay told Mexico and Colombia that the U.S. could not tolerate any change in the status of the Spanish West Indies. He told the U.S. representative in Madrid, Nelson that, only by making peace on the Spanish-American continent, could Spain hope to retain Cuba and Puerto Rico. He also appealed to the other European countries to try to bring pressure on Spain to make this peace. In London, Canning was also known not to favour a Mexican-Colombian expedition against Cuba. In December of the same year Clay asked both Mexico and Colombia to suspend their projected expeditions against Cuba and Puerto Rico.

The reason why the U.S. government followed this policy is clear. Clay not only desired to keep clear the possibility of Cuba's eventual entry into the Union; he was also afraid, as were the Cuban planters, lest a revolution against Spain would be followed by 'the tragic scenes which were formerly exhibited in a neighbouring island' – i.e. Haiti.

> Would not the freed slaves of Cuba be tempted by the very fact of that independence to employ all the means which vicinity, similarity of origin and sympathy could supply, to foment and stimulate insurrection, in order to join ultimate strength to their cause [to stir up insurrection, that is, among the slaves in the southern states of the U.S.]. The U.S. have too much at stake in the fortunes of Cuba to allow them to see . . . a war of invasion.[46]

The seventy years of international change in the Caribbean from 1760 to 1830 thus ended with an event which was to cast its shadow across the relations of Cuba with the United States for the rest of their history: the action by Clay and the earlier policy as declared by Monroe were naturally construed by Cuban historians as acts preventing the independence of Cuba at the same time as that of the rest of Spanish America. The arguments for this point of view are indeed strong: General Páez, named as commander of the proposed Mexican-Colombian expedition by Bolívar, stated firmly in his memoirs that the U.S. 'blocked the independence of Cuba'. But it is at least possible that

[45] Henry Clay (1777-1852), previously senator; Secretary of State, 1825-9, under John Quincy Adams.
[46] Clay's instructions to the U.S. representatives at the Panama Congress.

the expedition would not have got under way anyway; Clay's behaviour was in truth probably seized on as an excuse for inaction by Bolívar and new southern American governments scarcely anxious for further hard fighting. Would a South American revolutionary movement which was really dynamic have been held up by this U.S. attitude? The U.S. was not strong militarily in 1825 and Clay's attitude was not generally supported, as suggested by a speech by Representative John Holmes of Maine:

> My life, you could not maintain such a way; public opinion would not sustain you. A war out of the limits of the United States, a foreign war, to reduce men to servitude? Not an arm and scarcely a voice north of the Potomac would be raised in your behalf. An administration which should attempt it would seal its own destruction.

He was right: if Bolívar had called the U.S. bluff it is hard to think that Clay's policy would have been upheld. In fact, Bolívar did not want to go on fighting and had no desire to free Cuba, as is suggested in letter after letter of his.[47]

It is also possible that even if the expedition had got under way it might have been defeated by General Vives in Havana. All the obvious independence leaders in Cuba were either dead, in prison or in exile: most important, the master class of Cuba, the counts, the marquises and the natives of Cádiz, the planters and the merchants, were, if often divided, at least behind Vives in their hostility to independence, for fear of its consequences for slave-holding. Annexation to the U.S. was for them the only alternative to Spanish rule.

Vives, it should be noted, had gone out of his way to make easy the flow of (illegal) slave labour: at least 50,000 slaves were known to have been imported between 1823 and 1831 – or an average of 6,250 a year, about as high as any year during the Napoleonic period except 1802. The continued flow kept merchants as well as slave owners loyal to Spain: an abandonment of the slave labour force would have threatened the collection of loans; and such an abandonment would certainly have followed a revolutionary war.

At all events, the crisis of 1825–6 passed. Spain made peace with her ex-colonies, who jettisoned expansionist leaders. The possibility of aid for Cuba from the rest of Latin America, always remote, disappeared. The Latin-American countries looked inward for the rest of the nineteenth century. Cuba remained a political anomaly, increasingly rich but practically under martial law.

[47] e.g. 'I would rather go to Mexico than to Havana . . .' 'I believe our league can maintain itself perfectly well without embracing the extremes of the South . . . and without creating another Republic of Haiti [in Cuba] . . . do not attempt to liberate Havana . . . should it prove necessary we shall yet go there but I prefer peace . . .' (extracts from letters, 1824).

BOOK II

The Golden Age
1825 - 68

"The irresistible voice of Nature claims that the island of Cuba ought to be happy."

FÉLIX VARELA

Spanish dollar (also Mexican and South American dollar) sterling ($£$ 1,500 = $7,200) usually $1 = 4$s$ 2d

$\frac{1}{8}$ dollar = *real de plata* (8 *reales* to $1, piece of 8)

Onza de oro (Spanish doubloon) = $£$3 10s 0d = 17 hard dollars ($\frac{1}{2}$, $\frac{1}{4}$, $\frac{1}{8}$, $\frac{1}{16}$ doubloon in circulation) known as *media onza, doblón, escudo;* i.e. *doblón* would normally mean $4.25, rather than doubloon. Doubloon always known as *onza.*

Also

peso	=	$1·00
Medio peso	=	50¢
Peseta fuerte	=	25¢
Peseta sencilla	=	20¢
Real fuerte	=	12$\frac{1}{2}$¢
real sencillo	=	10¢
medio fuerte	=	6$\frac{1}{4}$¢
medio sencillo	=	5¢

Arroba = 25$\frac{7}{16}$ lbs English and approximately $\frac{1}{90}$ ton

Box of sugar	= 16 to 22 *arrobas*
Estuche of sugar	= 10 to 15 ,,
Cajita (little box)	= 5 to 6 ,,

Bocoy (hogshead) (barrel for sugar *mascabado* = 40–60 *arrobas*)

CHAPTER IX

The World of Sugar

The wealth of Cuba between 1825 and the end of the nineteenth century grew to first class levels. The prolonged absolute powers of the captains-general also grew to a real dictatorship, different in kind from the incompetent autocracies of the eighteenth and previous centuries. Cuban wealth contrived to grow, and the Cuban dictatorship to flourish, alongside relative stagnation in Spain, the mother country. Slavery and the slave trade, even though the latter was illegal, were the institutions which held these things together.

The wealth of Cuba depended partially on coffee (between the 1820s and 1840s), mostly on sugar. Sugar continued to depend until the late 1860s on slave labour. Slaves could be obtained illegally, for neither the British navy nor the anyway reluctant Spanish authorities could control the coast. One British Consul in Havana, David Turnbull, suggested that in 1837–40 each slave cost the importer a doubloon ($17 or £3 10s 10d) of which a quarter went to the captain-general, a quarter to the coastguard, a quarter to the harbour master, and a quarter to the local customs officer.[1] Thus sugar planters and government were driven by self-interest to give each other continuous support. In consequence, between 1823 and 1865 perhaps 400,000 slaves were imported.[2] Planters depended on the non-fulfilment of the anti-slave trade laws by the government; and the government came to rely on protection money as much as on the taxes they could get out of the rising sugar industry. The slave traders continued to be closely linked with the planters and the most successful merchants continued to invest their money in plantations.

Law and government continued in Cuba to be coterminous, both without much moral sanction, either for *criollos* or for slaves. The municipality and the *cabildo*, the jurisdiction and the *audiencia*, continued with only a few changes from the eighteenth century. Havana remained a great city, with a population of over 100,000 in 1827.[3] New towns

---

[1] David Turnbull, *Travels in the West* (1840), 156. This corrects the impression left, for example, by Ely, *Cuando reinaba*, (585), that the captain-general would take the whole doubloon. Madden, 32, alleged that Captain-General Tacón got 28,000 doubloons (£100,000 or $500,000) from the trade, see below, 156.

[2] See below, p. 194 for discussion.

[3] 112,000, according to the Census of 1827: within the walls 39,980, suburbs bringing it up to 94,023. Whites 46,621, free Negroes 15,347, free mulattoes 8,215, Negro slaves 22,830, mulatto slaves 1,010.

were founded: the Isle of Pines, with a population of under a hundred in 1800, a garrison for the first time in 1826, got a 'capital' the next year: this was Nueva Gerona (since Captain-General Vives gained his 'laurels' at the famous siege of Gerona); two large buildings of clay and palm leaves were christened Vatican and Quirinal.[4] The Spaniards were still building to stay.

The state also continued to provide the forces of order to restrain any slaves or free Negro revolt as well, of course, as any external threat. As in the British and French islands, planters could not serve except under special circumstances (as in 1762) even as militiamen, for that would mean abandoning their estates to the slaves. The captain-general, as commander-in-chief of the army in the island, supported by his brigadier and his *mariscales de campo* (as the sub-inspectors of artillery and engineers were called) therefore held the island in his hands. For most of the nineteenth century the Spanish garrison consisted of 25,000 to 30,000 men, and from the 1840s there was also the civil guard, the half-military police corps founded to crush banditry in Spain and in Cuba used to unearth conspiracies and rebellion. From time to time the captain-general's dictatorship was such that private citizens were supposed to give notice to the *celador,* a local alderman, not only of the arrival of guests but of any intended party or gathering. Licences were needed for opening shops, or holding a theatrical performance and theoretically even to build a house. It should be appreciated, of course, that the army played a no less pre-eminent role in Spain itself in the nineteenth century, as the institution of national arbitration.

Commercially, the state, despite bureaucracy and corruption, did its best nevertheless, to free business to pursue wealth without encumbrances or ideological preconceptions. The dissolution of monastic lands in 1840 also increased the patronage, and hence the stature, of the captain-general; even charitable educational establishments founded for religious ends became his responsibility. The institutions founded by Captain-General Las Casas were maintained throughout the nineteenth century as educative centres of information: thus the Junta de Fomento stimulated the first railways and sent an agent to China to look for labour to replace slaves; the library of the Economical Society continued as the chief centre of information.

There were considerable returns. In 1759–60 taxes collected in Cuba had amounted to about £37,500 ($160,000);[5] by 1777 £250,000 (1,000,000 pesos); by 1825, Cuba (taxing perhaps 400,000 people) actually made money for the king: £M2 ($M8) taxes were collected

---

[4] *Cf.* Irene Wright, *Cuba,* 306.

[5] Sagra, *Historia,* who has $163,605 (£37,000). All the figures in this paragraph came from him or (after 1831) Pezuela, IV.

annually. In the 1860s over £M5 ($M20) was taken. A far cry from the days before 1800 when Cuba had been unable to finance even herself regularly, having to use '*situados*' from the viceroyalty of Mexico.

Had the captains-general fulfilled their obligations and undertaken to abolish the slave trade, they would have either lost the whole colony (to the U.S. doubtless) or certainly a large percentage of its revenues. Further, the whole administrative structure was dependent on fraud: smuggling (not merely of slaves) by even the most respectable import houses was general. Spanish officials, from the highest to the lowest, encouraged and shared in the illegal profiteering; salaries were as ever small, appointments often short and it was expected in Madrid that such impecunious imperial officials would live off their corrupt practices.

The gap between the prosperous oligarchic capitalists of Cuba and their compatriots at home in Spain was large and grew bigger during the century. Both sides suspected each other. Spain provided officials, clergy, judiciary, army officers and much of the rank and file of the army also. The *criollos* were still usually unable to enter these professions except the last. They still therefore confined their interests to plantations and cattle farming, commerce and the law. There were some break-throughs; for instance, the intelligent *intendente* Claudio Martínez Pinillos (Conde de Villanueva) in the 1830s and 1840s, was Cuban, the son of a rich merchant.[6] But in general, antagonism mounted, while captains-general and others returned to Spain to use the fortunes they had made to finance political careers and other undertakings in Catalonia or the Basque provinces.

For a long time unification with the U.S. seemed the rational alternative to remaining Spanish. To join the Union (till 1861) would guarantee the continuance of slavery. It would restrain the English from forcing the Madrid government to abolish the slave trade but, important also, would not enforce the freedom of slaves who had entered the island since 1820. Refined sugar would be able to be sold to the U.S. market without crossing a tariff wall while North American wheat could feed the slaves in Cuba without meeting Spanish taxes *en route*; the wheat interests of Castile would no longer be preferred nor would the merchants of Santander be able to sell their corn at high prices. Such was the political pattern and conflict at the heart of Cuba during what was, by world standards, her golden age as a provider of sugar.

In the late 1820s sugar was produced on about 1,000 plantations,[7]

---

[6] Claudio Martínez Pinillos (1782–1853).

[7] I have adopted the figure of 1,000 in the 1827 census, *Cuadro Estadístico de 1827*, 28, qu. Turnbull, 126, even though the usually reliable Sagra, *Historia*, 110, gave a lower estimate – 510. This chapter of De La Sagra, though in many respects useful (see below) contains some definite errors, for example, he overestimated the average price of land at $1,500 to $1,800 (£350 to £420) per cab, as he later admitted. See Pezuela, *Diccionario*, I, 60.

still concentrated in the western central part of the island. The most usual type of mill was still mostly operated by oxen, sometimes horse or water, and its machinery made of wood. But there were already perhaps fifty steam-driven mills, with some iron attachments. The plantations were still limited in size, since cane had as always to be got to the mill within at least two days of being cut. Even in steam-driven mills, oxen played a great part: they drew carts carrying cane from the fields, they carried the raw sugar to the port, their hide was sold as a by-product and their flesh eaten by slaves. Large herds of cattle – 120 pairs if the mill was steam or water-driven, many more if oxen were the only source of power – demanded large pastures (Guinea grass had been profitably introduced at the end of the eighteenth century). The average size of a plantation was therefore now about 160 acres of cane, with perhaps 750 acres more in wood or pasture – the wood being used gradually for firewood and the ground so cleared used for cane. An average planta-tion in 1830 might produce seventy-two tons of sugar a year,[8] and employ about seventy slaves – each ton of sugar could still thus be regarded as needing one slave. Below these 1,000 plantations, and not figuring in the statistics, were perhaps another 750 to 1,000 much smaller mills (*trapiches*). A small *trapiche* might have about ten slaves and be founded on only one *caballería* (33 acres) of land. This would still produce only the inferior sugar known as *mascabado* (dark and rough sugar) or *raspadura* (pan sugar) or cane brandy, which was sold cheaply to the poor and would not be exported.

About 1830 some 500,000 acres were in sugar plantations, of which 125,000 were sown with cane, the rest being forest or reserve. This compared with a total cultivated area of over a million acres, with 300,000 in pasture, and with a total uncultivated land area still of about fifteen million acres of forest and mountain.

INVENTORY OF INGENIO SARATOGA, OWNED BY THOMAS DUGGAN (1846)

		$
LAND	1850 acres @ $1,000 per cab (33 acres), of which 933 in cane, 267 in pasture, 67 in ground provisions, 100 in fallow, 433 in woods	55,000
CROPS	667 acres of good cane @ $1,200 per acre, 267 acres in poor condition @ $500 per acre, 25,000 plantation trees @ 12½¢ each, orchard trees @ $100	31,225

[8] Sagra erroneously speaks of his 510 mills producing on an average 155 tons. See Moreno Fraginals's table, op. cit., 93.

ANIMALS	Oxen 12½ pairs @ $59.50 each, mules 30 @ $34 each, cows 25 @ $25 each, calves 24 @ $5 each, sheep 267 @ $1	9,929
NEGROES	Drivers 4 @ $600, engineers 1 @ $650, first class prime Negroes 11 @ $550, first class able Negroes 112 @ $150 to $400, boys 16 @ $50 to $100	70,000
NEGRO WOMEN	Prime wenches 6 @ $400, wenches 80 @ $250 to $350, girls 38 @ $50 to $200	32,380
BUILDINGS	1 Engine House, boiling house, two steam engines and mills, and four Jamaica trains	38,000
	2 Two purging houses with room for claying, 11,144 sugar pots with tramway and hoisting plant	25,000
	3 Drying and packing house, *bagasse* logie, brick kilns, lime kiln and tramway about factory	10,000
	4 Dwelling houses, Negro quarters, hospital, stables, wash houses, clock tower, small buildings	16,025
	5 Reservoirs, wells and pumping house	10,045
	6 Boundary wall and fencing	6,133
	7 Embankments and bridges	2,000
	8 Fire engines	1,000
	9 34 ox carts	1,581
	10 Sundries	640
	Total	$308,958
ANNUAL EXPENSES	Cattle, horses and mules	2,300
	Food and clothing for Negroes	6,174
	Salaries for white employees	7,340
	Containers, transport and replenishment of Negroes	21,337
	Total	$37,151
RECEIPTS	226 tons white sugar (*blanco*)	18,326
	266 tons brown sugar (*quebrado*)	16,996
	267 tons low grade sugar (*cucurucho*)	14,174
	800 hogsheads molasses	2,000
	4,000 containers, cost paid by merchants	13,000
	Total	$64,495
PROFIT (less interest)		$27,344

(*Select committee on Sugar and Coffee Planting* (1848), 4th report, 86, qu. Deerr, II, 339.)

Talk of 'the average plantation' is somewhat confusing since the sugar plantation system consisted by now of a patchwork of different sized plantations at several different stages of development – both in respect of technology and labour: old mills with vertical rollers moved by oxen survived alongside new mills equipped with high pressure steam; while salaried labourers from the Canaries, freed Negroes and, later, slaves hired from other plantations, jostled with the plantation slaves, presenting a pattern of employment as diverse as the colour of those employed, or indeed as the different types of sugar produced. But, whatever the size of the estate, the sugar plantations almost always had as the centre the *casa de vivienda*, the stone country house of the owner or the *administrador*, with tiled floor (unless marble), huge windows without glass, usually one storey high, built round a patio sometimes laid out with jasmine or heliotrope, usually full of Negro children and horses. Other buildings would include normally a chapel, houses for the white labourers and technicians,[9] the hospital, the slaves' quarters, the nursery, and the establishments of the cooper, the carpenter and the blacksmith. Included in the estate there would be the *potrero*, a word now generally used for the area in which cattle would be kept either for hauling cane or other work or for beef. The dimensions of estates were often rather inadequately drawn but the most usual differentiation was a hedge of rough pine with deep green exterior leaves and intense vermilion interior ones, or of the spiky *maguey* [agave].

There had always been a number of usually white salaried workers on the sugar plantations: first, the *mayoral* or overseer, whose task was to discipline the slaves; he carried at all times a whip and a sword. In the eighteenth century this post sometimes went to a mulatto or even a Negro, but in the nineteenth it always went to a white man, most often a Canary Islander. No one had a good word for any *mayoral*. In 1830 he seems to have got about $500 to $700 a year; in 1863 under the same circumstances his pay appears to have reached $1,000.[10] Small planters would of course run their own estates but the bigger plantations always had a *mayoral*. He was assisted on larger plantations still by a 'contra mayoral'. He was customarily authoritarian: in the 1870s the *mayoral* on the *Soledad* mill was an ex-slave trader, on a small scale presumably; when the mill was taken over by the American E. Atkins, he urged the new owner to fit out an expedition for Africa rather than instal new machinery.[11] Many were men of great brutality,[12] and often were somewhat pompously dressed, for instance in a blue striped linen suit, straw hat and silk scarf.

[9] See below, 115.

[10] Sagra, *Historia*, 109.

[11] Atkins, 92. Edwin Atkins (1850–1926), President, Bay State Sugar Refinery, 1875–88. Chairman, American Sugar Refining Co. lived in Boston.

[12] Ortiz, *Negros Esclavos*, 222. He prints a revealing instruction by a *mayoral* of 1791 to his heirs.

The other jobs on the plantation were all paid less,[13] except for those who looked after the steam engine, and for the sugar master (*maestro de azúcar*), the expert technician who attended to the details of the manufacture, both as regards the heat and the mixture of the syrup. In 1830 this industrial chemist was found with the same salary as the *mayoral* ($700). In 1860 he was getting $750 for the six months of harvest. These were often, on the most successful estates, under the direction of North American, German or English technicians whose salary seems to have been as much as $1,200 to $1,500 for the six months of harvest, sometimes as high as $2,500. Doctors made occasional visits, though on large estates they were permanently, perhaps attending several plantations in the neighbourhood. The hospital would be run by a steward and the nursery by slave women too old to work.[14]

In the eighteenth century big planters, to increase production, had merely added two or three new sugar mills to their original one: a solution which doubled or trebled the slaves needed, their food, the oxen and the general overhead expenses. The old mills with 150 slaves produced, say, 150 tons of sugar; if there were two mills on an estate, production would merely rise to 350 tons, if three, to 500. But now the sugar plantation underwent a full technological revolution in at least its industrial or manufacturing stage.

It has been seen how in the 1790s the Jamaican train cut down the work and the slaves needed for the evaporation phase of manufacture; and how steam came in as a force to drive mills in substantial numbers after 1818. The first industrial development in the mill itself meantime had been the iron drums and gudgeons to protect the old wooden rollers, which seem to have been introduced in the 1790s; then came iron rollers instead of wooden rollers, horizontal or vertical, as the case might be; afterwards, iron horizontal rollers, one above and two beneath, in a pyramidical shape (the opening between the upper and first lower one being larger than that between the upper and second lower one) which could cope better with irregularly sized cane. They were also safer: thus a 'dumb turner' or *volvedora* could be introduced into these machines to save the slaves from guiding the stalk to the roller.[15] These machines, manufactured in England or the U.S., came in during the 1820s, particularly from the English firm of Fawcett Preston & Co. and later Merrick & Sons of Philadelphia, but at all events from non-

[13] See analysis, p. 281.

[14] See below, for slaves and their life. The cost of these salaried workers is best estimated against the total product. To produce 1,000 boxes of sugar, wages of $1,900 were paid in 1830 (De La Sagra's estimate), or about 12% of the total annual costs of the farm ($13,600). To produce 6,000 boxes in 1863, on what Pezuela called an economical hacienda, costs were generally lower thanks to mechanization, but wages cost $7,500, or 20% of the annual costs ($36,500).

[15] Introduced by Bell of Barbados in 1805.

Spanish sources. Substantially the mill had then reached the form existing in the twentieth century. But of course these changes did not reach all or even most sugar estates and, throughout the nineteenth century, there would remain wooden or vertical sugar mills, left behind from an earlier stage of development, like stone axes in the age of bronze.[16]

Even these 'new' mills were not new in the sense of demanding new technological understanding or new organization of labour. They were merely more efficient versions of the old mills and they needed fewer slaves. They were, however, all imported machines, whereas old small wooden *trapiches* would have been constructed in Cuba. It is instructive that, though many Cuban entrepreneurs imported technologically advanced sugar equipment at an early date, none of the major advances was achieved in Cuba: whereas such advances did occur in Martinique and Guadeloupe, though they were smaller centres of production.[17]

Some of these rollers had been driven by steam since 1818, but most of them by oxen. At this stage, it scarcely mattered which was used: it was the quality of the rollers in the mill which counted:[18] in the 1830s it was even still argued that the oxen-driven mill was better suited to Cuba. But steam engines did save oxen, and therefore slaves (who would otherwise be looking after those animals).

Meantime, a new vacuum boiler, the first application of steam to evaporate liquid, had been patented by Edward Howard in England.[19] This 'vacuum pan' (patented in 1812), an airtight copper vessel, began to be used in Cuba in the early 1830s.[20] It could be heated by the same fire that drove the steam engine for the mill, and thus the first two stages of sugar manufacture (grinding and evaporating) were almost merged, greatly cutting labour. The number of slaves necessary for stoking dropped considerably. The concentration of the ovens meant that *bagasse* (the cane waste after the juice has been taken out) began to be used as the only fuel, saving wood and in yet another way the cost of labour;[21] huge droves of oxen had previously been required to drag firewood to the mill.

---

[16] See Deerr, 536–7. Later changes were concerned mainly in the reduction of the form of headstock to a sound engineering model.

[17] e.g. the three roller mill was reduced to its present shape by a Martinique engineer, Théophile Rousselot, in 1871.

[18] See the illuminating paragraphs on this theme by Moreno Fraginals, 107–8.

[19] Edward Howard (1774–1816) became interested in sugar through marriage to a daughter of a refiner, William Maycock. He was brother of the twelfth duke of Norfolk but as Nöel Deerr points out he does not get a mention in *DNB*, 'unlike 54 other far less creative scions of the house of Howard'.

[20] J. G. Cantero, *Los Ingenios* (1857), and Deerr following him, place the use of these to 1835. To use the pan, a quantity of liquid sugar was admitted and the air pump set to work to exhaust all the air from the pan so that the contents could boil at a low temperature.

[21] J. García de Arboleya, *Manual de la Isla de Cuba* (1859), 136.

At the end of the 1830s yet another decisive development became available. On the designs and ideas of the Louisianan mulatto Norbert Rillieux,[22] the engineer Charles Derosne[23] brought out a quite new vacuum boiler, essentially a refinement of Howard's, but incorporating the grinding and evaporating not merely in the same oven but the same steam engine. Derosne was really marketing a 'sugar machine' co-ordinating all aspects of the manufacturing process.[24] A similar and cheaper machine was marketed by Rillieux in New Orleans (and also by Pontifex and Wood of England) at much the same time. Derosne, how-ever, first caught the Cuban market – due to the translation of Derosne's manual by the then outstanding sugar chemist of Havana, José Luis Casaseca, a protégé of old Arango.[25] Derosne in 1841 personally installed the first Cuban model on the plantation *La Mella*, in Matanzas, owned by Wenceslao Villa-urrutia, another of those first generation Spanish immigrants who did so much for Cuban development in the nineteenth century.[26] This machine was an immediate success. In the harvest of 1843, Villa-urrutia produced a far higher yield of sugar in a shorter time than ever before. More significant still, Derosne himself pointed out that his machine required only one white and salaried attendant – the sugar master.[27] There was yet another new saving of slaves: the Derosne machine produced four and a half tons per slave, while older types of mill only made two tons.[28] Further, the Derosne mills could produce a new and iridescent white sugar ('*blanco del tren Derosne*' became mentioned on the advertisements) which was much sought after. In effect the manufacturing side of the sugar industry was already al-most out of slave hands; enough slaves were still responsible for harvest-ing and tending cattle, with a myriad other odd jobs, before and after the actual manufacture of sugar.

At the same time the Derosne machines gave a fillip to native refining of sugar, since they made that more economical. The enterprising Diago brothers even began to find it profitable to refine other planters' raw sugar. This was an important step towards the totally capitalized sugar

[22] Norbert Rillieux (1806–94), son of a quadroon, eventually went to Paris in 1861 because of colour prejudice in Louisiana. Rillieux said that he told Derosne of his ideas.

[23] Charles Derosne (1780–1846), born Paris; partner of Cail from 1824.

[24] See Deerr, 562; including the insertion into the syrup of animal charcoal to complete the decolourization process.

[25] José Luis Casaseca, born Madrid, studied in Paris, reached Cuba 1825.

[26] Wenceslao Villa-urrutia y Puente (1816–62), born in Spain at Alcalá de Henares; arrived in Cuba with *intendente* Ramírez, his brother-in-law, in 1816; secretary of the Real Junta de Fomento 1836; married a Montalvo, and therefore became a nephew by marriage of the pioneer of the Jamaican train; established the Derosne machine by means of a loan of $9,000 from the Junta de Fomento. The complicated investigations into this process are explained by Moreno Fraginals, 117–18, with his customary skill.

[27] C. M. Derosne, *De la elaboración del azúcar en las colonias* (Spanish trans. José Luis Casaseca), 24.

[28] García de Arboleya, 138.

mill of the late nineteenth and twentieth century. Ayesterán, the Diagos' nephew, was in fact the pioneer of the next step forward. Less than ten years after Derosne's revolution another new device enabled the sugar planter to convert the juice immediately it left the rollers into a clear, loose, dry and fine sugar, in place of the old sugar loaf which had retained a quantity of liquid. This was the 'centrifugal' machine – an iron cylinder, with a metal drum within, which, when connected with a steam engine, could turn at two thousand revolutions a minute. The centrifugal machine was of German origin, patented by Penzoldt of Silesia in 1837 in connection with drying textiles but developed by Derosne, and introduced to Cuba by Ayesterán in 1850 on the mill *Amistad* (on extended credit from Drake & Co. 'We have had to write hundreds of letters to make Ayesterán sign cheques,' one of the banker Drake's partners, José María Morales, wrote in 1853).[29] Fewer still of the Cuban planters were able to buy these centrifugal machines than had managed the Derosne or Rillieux machinery. Many smaller mills faced ruin or resigned themselves to make only *mascabado* but those who could find or borrow the capital were sure of immense rewards. This development was only the most recent in a long line of saccharial inventions causing a series of revolutions in chemical engineering, which thus owed much to the sugar industry.

These technical developments are evident in such statistics as are available in respect of costs. In 1830, when the vacuum boiler was coming in, sugar buildings were reckoned as being worth $22·9 million, in 1859 $30 million; machinery was reckoned at $6·8 million in 1830. $15 million in 1859.[30] But despite the doubling of its value in these thirty years, machinery represented a slightly smaller percentage of total investments in sugar plantations in 1859 than it had done in 1830, 8·3% in place of 8·75%. The reason was the extraordinary increase of the nominal value of slaves.

By 1860 55 mills out of 1,365 in the island were equipped with modern machinery, that is, Derosne- or Rillieux-type sugar machines; they produced nearly 90,000 tons out of almost 450,000,[31] or 4% of the mills produced 20% of the sugar. Of these, as can be expected, most were concentrated in the Matanzas-Cárdenas-Colón triangle.[32] Well over

[29] To his New York partner, Coit (Coit papers, qu. Ely, *Cuando reinaba*, 557.) Morales was founder of two famous Havana insurance companies: *El Iris*, which lasted into the twentieth century; and *La Protectora*, founded in 1856 to assure the lives of slaves.

[30] Sagra *Historia*, and García de Arboleya, 140; estimates combined and compared.

[31] Rebello figures (C. Rebello, *Estadísticos relativos a la producción azucarera de la Isla de Cuba* (1860)), calculated by the author.

[32] Six were in the Cabañas-San Diego de Núñez area to the west of Havana; four were in the Rancho Veloz area on the north coast; one, *Santa Susana*, was in Cienfuegos and one, Cantero's *Guinia de Soto*, was near Trinidad. Four only were in the Havana-Güines area, the main sugar district of the late eighteenth century. Two were in the far east. The remaining thirty-three were in what is now the province of Matanzas.

half the mills (949) by this time were driven by some sort of steam; 409 by oxen, only seven by water. Sugar plantations were now far the most important sector of the economy. Indeed the figure of 1,365 mills in 1860 did not include 750 or so, still surviving, of the old small ten-slave *trapiches* which produced *mascabado* for the poor.[33]

Little attention was paid to the cane fields themselves since it was still possible to extend them merely by burning 500 to 650 acres of virgin forest and applying 200 slaves and 100 pairs of oxen.[34] No rotation of crops and no manure were the rules.[35] Guano from Peru, or elsewhere, though now available, was both expensive and not popular. Virgin land continued to be regarded as the only real place for new cane. In consequence, the price of land (though varying in proportion to distance from the coast) does not seem to have greatly increased in the middle of the century.[36] The consequence in turn was that by now sugar was no longer concentrated around Havana: new ports such as Matanzas, Cárdenas and Cienfuegos served as the lodge-gates to rich new hinterlands of immense wealth, as new planters – immigrants or Havana merchants anxious to invest in land – moved steadily eastwards, cutting forests as they went. The destruction of the great mahogany and cedar trees of Cuba begun by the navy and the builders of the Escorial, was thus continued in the cause of sugar, to some extent as a result losing the famous fertility of the soil.

By 1827 Matanzas exported a quarter of the sugar in Cuba. In the Cienfuegos and Trinidad region in the south, heir of generations of contraband with Jamaica across the sea, there were some of the largest mills in the 1820s, many built on the profits of the slave trade – such as the Iznagas' *Manacas* and *Guinia de Soto* and José Borrel's *Guáimaro,* which in 1827 produced the largest harvest of any sugar mill in the world: nearly 1,000 tons.[37] Both the Matanzas and the Trinidad regions were easy of access for landing new slaves from Africa.

[33] *Cf.* Pezuela who gave 2,050 sugar mills copying official figures for the year, while Rebello gave 1,305. *Cf.* the illuminating comment by Moreno Fraginals, 82.

[34] Ramón de la Sagra, *Cuba en 1860* (1863), 141.

[35] *Cf.* E. D. Genovese, *Political Economy of Slavery* (1966), for comparable conditions in the U.S.

[36] Turnbull, 261. Representative estimates are:

    c. 1800: $500 a cab (£3 10*s* an acre) (Humboldt)
    c. 1827 $1,000 a cab (£7 an acre) (De la Sagra, as revised 1860)
    c. 1838 $500 a cab (£3 10*s* an acre) (Turnbull)
    c. 1846 $1,000 a cab (£7 an acre) (McCulloch, *Commercial Dictionary*)
    c. 1859 $1,500 a cab (£10 10*s* an acre) (García de la Arboleya)
    c. 1863 $1,000(!) a cab (£7 an acre) (Pezuela)

On the other hand estimates for 'good' (i.e. cleared) land reached $3,000 a cab. The clearing of virgin land including tree-cutting was reckoned in 1830 as costing generally $300 to $400 (£70 to £95) per *caballería*, or, taking one man three months, the price to cover food (De la Sagra, 84). Turnbull, 262, had $300 (£70), without cost of tools.

[37] Moreno Fraginals, 65.

INVESTMENT IN SUGAR MILLS ABOUT 1830

	Average-to-large mill producing about 180 tons of sugar		All Cuba	
Land @ $1,000* per cab	1,000 acres	$30,000	520,000 acres	$15,300,000
Value of cane	As sown over 6 cabs	$12,000	As sown over 200,000 acres (3,600 cabs)	$6,068,877
Buildings		$45,000		$22,950,000
Machines		$13,500		$6,885,000
Slaves @ $350*	90 slaves	$31,000	70,000 slaves	$24,500,000
Oxen @ $117 a pair*	50 pairs	$5,850	25,500 oxen (pair)	$3,033,500
Horses and mules @ $55 each	4 horses	$220	2,040 horses and mules	$112,000
Vegetables, bananas, etc., for use on plantation	12,000 cooking banana plants	$2,510		$1,275,000
		$140,080†		$80,124,377

* These figures, though deriving from Sagra, *Historia* 108–10, have been standardized. The price of land has been reckoned not at $1,800 but at $1,000 per cab. Slaves are reckoned @ $350 each (in place of $300 and $400), oxen @ $117 (in place of $100 and $135 the pair), horses and mules @ $55 each in place of $50 and $60. Otherwise the figures are Sagra's.

† Sagra worked out $170,000 (£40,000) for the reasons given in fn. *.

The average production of sugar per acre between 1820 and 1830 seems to have been about half a ton, then worth about £17.[38] Compared with this an acre of land on a coffee plantation would only have produced £4 or less than one quarter. The figures suggest that in 1830 a total of about £20 million ($80 million) had now been invested in sugar plantations in Cuba, much the same, that year, in coffee plantations, together making up about a quarter of the total invested in agriculture.

'Whirr, whirr! All by wheels! – whizz, whizz! All by steam!' Kinglake made his Turkish Pasha exclaim in 1844 in *Eothen*. By then, Derosne had sold eight of his machines in Cuba – out of a total of twenty-six.[39] They cost $60,000 (£14,000) each. Only a minority naturally could hope to buy them, an important factor in Cuban social history in ensuing years: this machine would lead in the end to the disappearance of the old sort of sugar mill.

By the mid-century there was thus a most complicated disorganization of sugar production in Cuba: some small *trapiches*, with about ten

[38] 1,500 *arrobas* (13.3 tons) per *caballería*, then worth about $2,500.
[39] The others went to Java (7); Mauritius (4); Guadeloupe (5); Surinam (1); Mexico (1) (Ely, *Cuando reinaba*, 535).

slaves; some bigger mills, with animal power; and mills at various stages of mechanization – all producing different sorts of sugar and using in fact by now five different types of sugar cane.[40]

Another change which was transforming Cuba was the world railway revolution. In the past, mills on rivers had an overwhelming advantage since boxes of sugar could be much more easily shipped along them and down the coast to Havana or Matanzas. Otherwise, the boxes were carried by oxen in carts on long journeys, often prolonged by bad weather. A journey of sixty miles might take three weeks.[41] Planters reckoned that the cost of transport might equal almost a quarter of the sale of their product in Havana.[42]

The consequence of these high costs was to bring steam transport early to Cuba – long before it came to Spain. The first steamboat appeared about the same time as the steam-powered mill – a concession being granted to Juan O'Farrill in 1819. As early as 1823 three steamboats plied regularly between Havana, Matanzas, Cárdenas, S. Juan de los Remedios and Bahía Honda;[43] later, another ran between Santiago and Batabanó, while in the 1830s another line was founded between Havana and New Orleans; though this was of no help for sugar distribution, it was for slave-marketing: steamers often met the African slavers and took the slaves into harbour.[44]

It was the railway, however, which brought major changes. In the early 1830s a plan and a company for a Havana railway took shape, under the inspiration of the *intendente*, Martínez de Pinillos. A loan of $M2 (£450,450 negotiated at 75%, i.e. totalling £337,337 10*s*) was raised from Alexander Robertson & Co. of London (to be paid for by a special import/export tax);[45] and a thousand Irishmen, with a number of Canary Islanders, some Spanish convicts, some *emancipados* and slaves, all directed by an American engineer, Alfred Kruger, began to build

[40] These were

(*i*) *Caña criolla;* the old sixteenth-century cane, six to seven feet high, cut in Cuba every year; ideal for old wooden *trapiches*; its *bagasse* poor as firewood. Continued to be used in old mills.

(*ii*) *Caña de Otahití* (Bourbon). (a) White. This is usually what is meant by Otaheite in Cuba in the nineteenth century; grew to 12 feet; strong and tough *bagasse* useful for firewood; used in iron mills. (b) Yellow. Began to be used in mid-nineteenth century.

(*iii*) *Caña cristalina* or Batavian cane, introduced about 1820–30; much easier to grow in overworked land; otherwise inferior to Otaheite, but by late nineteenth century, indeed till about 1920, the chief variety grown.

(*iv*) *Caña de Cinta* (or *caña listada* or *caña de Batavia*), introduced between 1795 and 1810; reddish, 9 feet; used instead of Otaheite in overworked land.

(*v*) *Caña Morada* (also confusingly known as *Caña de Batavia*), introduced 1820.

[41] Ely, *Cuando reinaba*, 621.

[42] Sagra, *Historia*, II, 244, qu. Ely, *Cuando reinaba*, 621, fn.

[43] García de Arboleya, 215.

[44] Turnbull, 186–7.

[45] Attempts to raise a Paris and a Madrid loan had failed.

the first railway in Latin America, indeed in the Spanish-speaking world or West Indies. Sixteen miles of line, at a cost of $28,000 (£6,500) per mile, were completed by 1837.[46] The technological advance of the Cubans was thus great, since Brunel had not then completed the Great Western as far as Taplow. The costs in labour were not reckoned; the Irishmen at least suffered greatly and were left to beggary.[47] The line extended forty-five miles from Havana to Güines by 1838, touching Bejucal and San Felipe. In 1942 a line to Júcaro began to be built. By 1860 there were nearly 400 miles of railway in Cuba, owned by fifteen companies, of which the Havana Railway Company was the biggest. Most of the rolling stock and the lines came originally from England, but this equipment was treated so carelessly that English machinery got a bad name and afterwards U.S. stock was relied on – this possibly being due to sabotage by Kruger's subordinates interested in providing U.S. capital with another good outlet.[48]

Control of the railways rested from the beginning with the big planters and their agents. Thus in 1842 the Havana Railway Company was bought by a company backed by the Alfonsos, an old Matanzas family (proprietors of the *Santa Isabel* mill, near Sagua la Grande), the Drakes (proprietors of the *Saratoga* and *Júcaro* mills but also creditors-in-chief of many of the leading planters) and the Aldamas (proprietors of the *Armonía, Concepción* and *Unión* mills).[49] The first president was the proprietor of the *Santa Isabel* mill, Gonzalo Alfonso, and a vice-president was his brother, José Luis Alfonso. Another vice-president was Juan Poey,[51] and the secretary Felipe Poey,[51] joint owners of the *Las Cañas* mill and sons of a famous slave merchant. The treasurer was Juan Espiño, agent and administrator of the Drakes' estates. The extension of this line to Güines favoured another prominent planter and shareholder, Joaquín de Ayesterán, whose plantation, *Amistad* (first financed by Governor de Las Casas), was close to that city, and the Drakes' cousins, the old family of Núñez del Castillo, with their estates at Bejucal, also on the line.

The second railway in Cuba, the Júcaro line, was similarly built by and for the convenience of sugar interests. The line began near the three Diago brothers' estates (*Santa Elena, Tinguaro*[52] and *Ponina*), passed the *Alava* mill and near *Flor de Cuba*, and ended at Júcaro where, again, the

[46] Ely, *Cuando reinaba*, 629; see D. C. Corbitt, 'El primer ferrocarril construido en Cuba', *Revista Cubana*, xii, April–June 1938, 179–95.

[47] Turnbull, 191.

[48] *Ibid.*, 193. Ely, *Cuando reinaba*, 645–6, adds that drivers also came from the U.S.

[49] José Luis Alfonso was part-owner of the *Armonía* mill with Miguel Aldama.

[50] Juan Pöey (d. 1876), a tireless experimenter.

[51] Felipe Poey y Aloy (1799–1885); brilliant entomologist; brought up in Pau, studied in France and Spain; joined constitutional movement (1822–3); went to Havana 1824.

[52] Called after Tinguaro, the last Guanche leader to hold out in the Canary Islands in the 1490s against the Spaniards.

Drakes had an interest: in this case, their *Vega Mar* plantation. Though the Diagos gave titular chieftainship of the line to noblemen such as the Conde de Peñalver[53] (president), and the Marqués de la Real Proclamación (a director), they provided the main directors, and their nephew, Ayesterán, was secretary.[54] One can contrast these developments, controlled by Cubans and undertaken by them, with comparable Spanish development: there, most of the capital in the railway development (which did not occur till the 1850s) was French and the network was in effect run from Paris.[55]

The immediate effect of the railways was to cut the cost of transporting sugar enormously. In 1830 the average cost of carrying a three- to four-hundredweight box of sugar from Güines to Havana, by mule or oxen, was estimated at $12·50. By train this dropped to $1.25 and would drop in 1863 to $1 only.[56] No one lost money: thus the mule-king of Cienfuegos, Tomás Terry, was a leading railway backer. On the other hand, cane continued to be drawn to the mill from the field itself largely by oxen; yet even here there was experiment: thirty-six camels were imported by Patricio de la Guardia for the *San Ignacio* mill in the vale of Yumurí, Matanzas.[57]

Another consequence of railways was the establishment of a huge warehouse, at the railway head, for keeping sugar in the port of Havana – the *Almacén de Regla* – by an Andalusian, Eduardo Fesser, who married into a family of immigrants a generation before: the Diagos of Cárdenas.[58]

By 1860 the money invested in sugar plantations reached about $M185 (£M42), by then many times more than in coffee ($M40·55 (£10,600,000)) or tobacco ($M17·3 (£M4)).[60] The number of mills altogether had only increased during the past forty years from about 1,000 to 1,400; but output per mill had increased phenomenally: from 72 tons a mill in 1827–30, the average nearly doubled (120 tons) by 1841 and more than doubled again by 1860 (316 tons).

This was chiefly due to mechanization. The Cuban sugar industry had in this middle stage of development a history which would have

[53] Nicolás Peñalver y Cárdenas, first Conde de Peñalver, 1835; son of the only aristocrat among the first steam-engine users.

[54] *Guía de forasteros* (1846), 327–8. Other friends and neighbours, also planters, who received directorships were Ezra Dodd (North American proprietor of a near-by mill) and Tomas de Juara y Soler (proprietor of *La Conchita de Banagüises*). See Ely, *Cuando reinaba*, 639–40.

[55] Cf. Carr, *Spain*, 265–7.

[56] J. R. L. McCulloch, *A Dictionary Practical Theoretical and Historical of Commerce and Commercial Navigation* (1840); and Pezuela, II, 252; Turnbull, 194.

[57] Moreno Fraginals, 98, 186.

[58] See Cantero, *Los Ingenios*, and S. Hazard, *Cuba with Pen and Pencil* (1871), 267–8, for description and pictures.

[59] García de Arboleya, 140. This is no doubt a very rough estimate since his figure for land owned by sugar plantations is 30% out (see below).

delighted Marx, though the decisive changes in the means of production themselves derived from critical scientific inventions (and those outside the society concerned). The difference in average production between the most up-to-date mills and the old ones was phenomenal; an oxen-powered mill thus produced 130 tons a year in 1860, a fully mechanized one almost 1,000 tons. Such inventions became necessary in Cuba since the price of slave labour was mounting and by the 1860s was becoming prohibitive for small planters.[60] The centre of activity lay now in the Matanzas-Cárdenàs-Colón triangle: 400 mills lay in those three 'jurisdictions',[61] alone producing over half the sugar in Cuba.

A prosperous plantation about 1860 would consist of first and fore-most the building of the mill itself, usually a large roof only, supported by pillars but open on all sides, the floor paved with brick, usually well kept 'in the most scrupulously clean order', Samuel Hazard, a keen observer, said 'equal to a man-of-war'.[62] Next in importance would be the *Casa de Purga*, usually of two storeys, of which the upper would consist simply of a kind of pavement of apertures through which the sugar was placed in funnels (*hormas*) to drain. In big mills there would be some 20,000 apertures. Beneath the *hormas* on the ground floor of the building, there would be the hogsheads (*bocoyes*) for coarse sugar.

Sugar was still far from being an absolute: different types of mill still produced different sugars, ranging from the *blancos del Tren Derosne,* superlative white sugar, through a variety of *blancos* (white) and brown sugars (*quebrados*) and dark, coarse cone-shaped *cucuruchos* to rough *mascabados corrientes* made in old-fashioned small *trapiches* (an inter-national convention, the Dutch treaty of 1850, tried to standardize export sugars, and Cuba adhered, though without much success). Sugar was still marketed in large boxes (made of imported wood from the U.S.) with capacity of between sixteen and twenty-two *arrobas* or 400lbs and 650lbs.[63] *Mascabado*, with its great quantity of rough *mieles en suspensión* (molasses), was still marketed in barrels – normally the *hogshead* with capacity of 1,000 lbs to 1,500 lbs. Many mills also had established distilleries in which to manufacture rum, competing with North-American rum makers.

Cuba remained a protected island in the mid-nineteenth century. Duty on Spanish flour was $2.90 a barrel, on U.S., $9.20; French wines, English hardware, German linens, received a duty of 34%, while similar Spanish products paid only 7%. Foreign vessels were

---

[60] This was, it would seem, 'a period when the scale of productive economic activity reaches a critical level and produces changes which lead to a massive and progressive structural, transformation' in society, as W. W. Rostow put it (*The Process of Economic Growth* (1953), 40).

[61] i.e. in 1859–60.

[62] Samuel Hazard, 178.

[63] Also *cajitas* of 5 to 6 *arrobas* and *estuches* of 10 to 15 *arrobas*.

charged $1.45 per ton, Spanish 60 cents.[64] Still Cuba bought many articles of primary necessity from abroad – clothing as well as much food, except for a little beef and some roots and vegetables. Foreign merchants also realized that, despite protection, the quantity of soft goods (flour, rice, lard, salt fish, salt beef, cheese, wine) sold in Cuba per head of the population greatly exceeded that of any other country in the Caribbean. Already each Cuban probably consumed $80 (£18) a year per head, of foreign produce – an amazing figure for the nineteenth century.

To earn this of course there was the ever expanding sugar trade with coffee, tobacco, some honey, wax, a little indigo; but sugar above all by 1840. The pattern was set.

A new international challenge to Cuba's own best product was, however, already appearing: beet. As long ago as 1747 a German chemist, Marggraaf, had told the Royal Academy of Sciences and Literature in Berlin that there were some sweet beetroots, long grown in Silesia, though deriving from Sicily, out of which sugar crystals could be prised.[65] His pupil, another German, Achard,[66] began to experiment in the late eighteenth century, also in Berlin, and produced the first sugar loaf from beet in 1799. Napoleon, finding the route to the French West Indies barred by the British blockade, decided to stimulate continental sugar beet production; by 1836 a third of the sugar refined in France came from beet.[67] Of course, sugar can be obtained from palms, fruits, maize and maple, not to speak of honey, but nothing was so productive as beet. The beet method of sugar-making seemed, furthermore, to remove sugar in Europe from the consequences of war;[68] it also involved no plantation or slave problem since beet was from the start grown by peasants alongside other crops. Finally, it began to be protected. On the other hand, beet sugar was expensive. Beet had to be planted annually, cane every seven years or more. The process of washing to separate the beet sugar from the waste was costly and complicated. Still, by 1857, out of 200,000 tons of sugar consumed in France, 132,000 tons (66 per cent) came from beet. Cane sugar provided 86% of world sugar production in 1850, but had dropped to 64% by 1870.[69]

In the early years after 1815, demand for sugar (above all in the U.S. and Europe) was expanding fast enough, apparently, to banish all fear

[64] Turnbull, 139.
[65] Andraeas Sigismund Marggraaf (1709–82), son of the Königlichen Hofapotheker Christian Marggraaf.
[66] Franz Carl Achard (1753–1821), a Prussian of Huguenot origin.
[67] H. C. P. Geerligs, *Cane sugar and its manufacture* (1909), 13–17; Deerr, 474ff.
[68] But see below, p. 537, for the effect on French beet of the First World War.
[69] Deerr, 490–1; Geerligs, 21.

of competition for the Cubans. But the situation changed. There was increased consumption in the mid-century, though only because of lower prices. Thus in England and the U.S. (by far the two largest consumers) consumption doubled–from 17 lbs per head to 34 lbs in England and from 13½ lbs to 34 lbs in the U.S. between 1841 and 1854. But prices were dropping all through the 1840s: in 1860 indeed sugar fetched barely half the prices of 1840. Consumption was still rising faster than prices were dropping but not much more.[70]

The anxiety beginning to be felt in the 1850s by the Cubans was, admittedly, nothing to that felt by the sugar planters in other West Indian islands. The long decline in the British West Indian trade, hastened by the abolition of slavery, had been completed by the British Sugar Act, 1846, which fully opened the British market to Cuban

WORLD SUGAR PRODUCTION IN THE MID-NINETEENTH CENTURY

	1849		1856	
CANE	Products in tons	% of world production	Products in tons	% of world production
Cuba	220,000	21	359,397	25
British West Indies	142,000	14	147,911	10
Brazil	121,509	12	105,603	7
U.S. (Louisiana)	99,180	10	132,468	9
Java	90,200	9	68,240	4
British East Indies	73,600	7	58,383	4
French West Indies	56,300	5	110,000	7
Mauritius	44,900	4	115,000	8
Puerto Rico	43,600	4	53,377	5
Philippines	20,400	2	48,422	3
Dutch West Indies	13,000	1	18,291	1
Danish West Indies	7,900	1	11,204	1
	932,789		1,228,296	
BEET				
France	38,000	4	95,100	7
German states	33,000	3	80,753	6
Russia	13,000	1	21,207	1
Austria	6,500	1	19,102	1
Belgium	5,000	1	9,180	1
	95,500		225,342	
	1,028,259		1,453,638	

[70] See the tables in Deerr, II, 531. According to Julio Brusone, *Trimestre Económico* II (1944–5), 62, average world sugar consumption was 9.9 lbs in 1854 – less than one third of U.K. consumption. Compare this with average *per capita* consumption in 1958; less than 32 lbs, or still under one third of U.K. consumption. See p. 1138 below.

sugar. The British West Indies produced 142,000 tons of sugar in 1849 and 148,000 tons in 1856, declining from 14% of world sugar to 10% while Cuba's increase in the same years took her from a contribution of 21% to 25%,[71] even though the British West Indies remained the second largest exporter of sugar in the world.

Another anxiety for the Cuban sugar producers came from the sustained rise of Louisiana, whose production leapt up to over a third of Cuban output by 1859.[72] But the possibility of cold and frost always meant that Louisiana was a little more hazardous than Cuba and in fact several Cuban merchants, such as the Drakes, established New Orleans branches themselves as re-insurance.[73] Also, when the biggest Louisianan harvest of 250,000 long tons was achieved in 1861 (Cuban production being in that year almost double, at 449,000 tons), the American civil war prevented its marketing and afterwards the whole sugar export of the state was ruined, so much so that it did not recover till the Cubans' own civil war at the end of the century.

[71] Table in Ely, *Cuanda reinaba*, 427, from Erenchun, 831.
[72] Bouchneau, *Statement of the Sugar and Rice Crops Made in Louisiana 1874-5*, V, qu. Ely, *Cuando reinaba*, 431, fn. 52.
[73] Ely, 434, fn. 42.

CHAPTER X

Coffee

The whole of Cuba in the mid-nineteenth century did not go over to sugar production. About 1860 there were 6,000 cattle farms (*potreros*) and 34,000 other smaller farms, supporting some 300,000 people of whom a tenth were slaves. Of these, perhaps 1,100 were cattle farms 'of the first class' and 6,200 'inferior' breeding farms.[1] Most travellers, however, found the beef in Cuba very poor, and indeed there was no scientific attempt at improving herds at all. In many senses cattle was merely a subsidiary activity to sugar: the beef being eaten by the slaves, the animals themselves being useful on the plantation, and their bones being required for 'bone black' used to whiten the sugar. Some experiments were tried, in bringing in Hereford or Durham cattle, along with Guinea and Para grass, but on the whole this was very much an inferior activity to sugar making.

The second quarter of the nineteenth century, however, saw in Cuba not only the lavish development of sugar, but also both the climax and decline of the coffee crop; thus in 1829 slightly more capital was invested in coffee than in sugar, though the return was never anything like as high.

Coffee, apparently native to Abyssinia, spread in a north-westerly direction, reaching England about 1615, through Constantinople, Venice and the Danube cities.[2] The coffee plant (*coffea arabica*), small, slight and evergreen, flourishing in a damp temperature fairly consistent between 75° and 80° – most appropriately therefore in regions which are tropical, rainy and between 2,000 and 3,000 feet high – was apparently introduced into the West Indies by the French (into Martinique) in 1727 and by the English into Jamaica the following year. Demand for coffee grew in Europe very quickly in the eighteenth century and a large coffee industry grew up in the English and French colonies, particularly in Saint Domingue, alongside sugar. A variety of coffee known as 'Hope of Asabiaca' was apparently brought to Cuba in 1748 by a Havana municipal official named José Gelabert.[3]

[1] Figures in García de Arboleya. Cuban farm names are confusing. See glossary at end of the volume.

[2] This was *coffea arabica*. Other indigenous plants are *coffea robusta*, from the Congo, and *coffea liberica* from West Africa.

[3] Gelabert was municipal accountant. See Francisco Pérez de la Riva, *El Café* (1944), 7, the best study of Cuban coffee. Other varieties were grown too, later on.

Coffee was not, however, extensively developed in Cuba for a generation after this, the coffee plant in the late eighteenth century being chiefly grown around the *casas de vivienda* of sugar mills by planters who liked the beauty of the tree and flowers – and not for commercial purposes. But a few cafés were founded in Havana, the first by a native of Navarre, Juan Bautista Tabernas.[4]

The Haitian revolution threw forth a flood of exiles, among them many experienced French coffee growers. Many of these families established themselves first in central and afterwards in east Cuba. In 1792 a royal decree exempted coffee from the taxes *alcabala* and *diezmo*, first for ten years, then indefinitely, so greatly stimulating production: the Patriotic Society gave full support to coffee production, as to sugar. Where as exports were under 80 tons in 1790–2, they rose to over 550 tons by 1804. From then they doubled every three or four years, reaching 10,000 tons in 1815. Coffee prices rose too, like sugar prices, in the Napoleonic wars, doubling between 1792 and 1796.[5]

With the coming of peace, Cuban coffee exports had a lower average, of about 8,000 tons; but in 1823 exports reached 12,000 tons, and in 1827 rose to over 20,000 tons. From then till 1844 exports were never less than 12,000 tons;[6] the coffee habit seized Cuba for good while cafés in Havana, such as the Café de Copas in Oficios Street, the Café de los Franceses and the Café La Dominica became famous as centres of liberalism.

Cafetales (coffee farms) in Cuba in the high period of expansion numbered about 2,000.[7] The land in Cuba which was sown with coffee then just exceeded that in cane – 192,000 acres in *cafetales,* 180,000 acres in sugar cane.[8] Machinery and other equipment on *cafetales* was valued at roughly 70% of that on sugar estates ($M20 to $M29·8).

The most favoured areas for growing coffee in the early nineteenth century were in the Pinar del Río area in the west, near Santiago in the Sierra Maestra and in Guantánamo, and also in the districts of Alquízar (thirty miles south-west of Havana) and of San Marcos, between Colón

<hr>

[4] Tacón, *Correspondencia,* ed. Pérez de la Riva, 178.
[5] Parry, and Sherlock 172.
[6] Pezuela, *Diccionario,* qu. *Estudio Sobre Cuba* (1963), 155:

    1825–30 : 2,055,000 *arrobas*
    1831–5 : 2,260,000 „
    1836–40 : 2,397,000 „
    1841–5 : 1,800,000 „
    1846–50 : 1,288,000 „
    1851–4 : 1,047,000 „

[7] 2,067 in 1827, to be precise. Turnbull, 126, qu. *Census.*
[8] Though the land belonging to coffee farms (300,000 acres) was less than that in sugar plantations (510,000 acres), Sagra, 122. In 1958 only 150,000 acres were dedicated to coffee (A. Núñez Jiménez, *Geografía de Cuba,* 2nd edn, 3rd imp. (1961) 229) and in 1936–7 the same, according to the World Bank (824–5).

and Sagua la Grande. The size of such estates varied from 100 to 1,000 acres and most *cafetales* grew a little rice, plantains, potatoes, chocolate and so on. Like the sugar mill, the *cafetal* had its *batey* or group of buildings which included a *casa de vivienda* (dwelling house), *tendal* (stone house) and *secadero* or stone terrace for drying coffee. There were usually also a small white or, at any rate, free, staff, though the *mayoral* seems less invariably to have been a white man than on a sugar plantation. He was sometimes 'the most intelligent Negro on the place'.[9]

Cafetales were less rivals of sugar plantations than extra or parallel activities for the great planters whose land was sown with sugar or coffee, as the local conditions varied: thus slaves in *cafetales* numbered officially about the same as on sugar plantations – 50,000 – probably a few less. The average *cafetal* probably had about fifty to sixty slaves. The capital invested in coffee in 1829 was slightly over $M85 compared with $M84 invested in sugar; but the total value of the coffee produced was only half that of the sugar crop – $M4·3 (£M1) compared with just over $M8 (£1,875,000);[10] that is, in rough terms, coffee gave a return on capital of about 5%, while sugar gave a return of nearly 10%.

These facts were soon realized. Within a few years the coffee industry was in rapid decline and primarily for this reason, though there were others.[11] By 1846 the numbers of *cafetales* had dropped to 1,670. In 1859 another estimate placed total investment in coffee at about half that in 1829, or $M40.[12]

A typical *cafetal* would resemble the one in Havana province described by the assiduous Turnbull, the Ubajay plantation, owned by Antonio García, with 110 slaves and 200,000 coffee trees producing 60 tons a year. His slaves had two meals a day, one of which consisted of about a pound of jerked beef, and plantains, and the other, a pound of yucca or yams.[13] Coffee farms would often be in themselves places of great beauty, sometimes with a splendid ironwork entrance and a long avenue of royal palms. The *cafetal* could be begun less ambitiously than a sugar plantation; perhaps the first year the proprietor would begin with ten slaves – purchased for, say, £500, who would clear two cabs (64 acres). The second year the slaves would be doubled; the third year a Gallego carpenter and a Canary Island mason might be hired, along with a *mayoral* and more slaves. (It is only at the end of the third year

[9] Hazard, 481.

[10] All these figures are in Sagra, *Historia*, 121–7. By 1837, 22,300 tons of coffee produced at a dollar an *arroba* (just over 2d a lb) or $2,133,567 (£M5) (Turnbull, 45), whereas just over nine million *arrobas* (100,000 tons) of sugar made just under $M8 (over £1,700,000).

[11] See below, 131. That the relative advantages of investment in sugar and coffee indicated that sugar did twice as well became clear with the publication of Ramón de la Sagra's *Historia* in 1831.

[12] García de Arboleya, 142.

[13] Turnbull, 296; i.e. perhaps slightly above that on a sugar plantation.

that coffee begins to bear anything and only at the end of the fourth that it can be harvested.) By the fifth year there would be perhaps 40,000 four-year-old coffee trees, 60,000 three-year-old and 10,000 of two years or less: this forest would produce 400 quintals and be worth $2,400 (£560). By the seventh year the estate would be in full bearing, with seventy slaves, costing $200 in clothing, $150 in medical attendance and $10 in medicines a year; the *mayoral* would get $500, and other miscellaneous costs ($115) would raise annual expenses to $1,800 (£420). The original coffee plants might then last twenty-five years in all, though good crops would only be produced every other year after the tenth.

The success of the Cuban coffee farms scarcely lasted more than the one generation of Haitian immigrants. This was partly (as suggested above) because of the evidently greater profits obtained from sugar. From the 1840s onwards more and more coffee farms were being bought up for cane. The higher costs of coffee farming naturally seemed not to be worth the smaller profit. *Cafetales* were also unable to pay the cost of slaves, even though their price remained constant between the mid-1820s and mid-1840s. In 1845 *bozales* were still quoted at 300 to 350 pesos (£70 to £82). Secondly, in 1834 the U.S. imposed a high tariff on coffee imports and tonnage duties on all Spanish ships entering U.S. waters: this was a reaction to the new Spanish tariff on U.S. goods – a move intended, like most Spanish fiscal activities, to raise cash.[14] Thirdly, there was a series of terrible hurricanes, particularly in 1844 and 1846, worse than had occurred at any time since the rise of coffee. These wreaked havoc on the crops of 1845 and 1847, especially in west Cuba and, after 1844, exports of coffee never again topped 12,000 tons.[15]

A fourth factor was international competition. After 1840 Brazil began to expand production enormously.[16]

The most important of all these challenges, however, was that afforded in Cuba itself by sugar. Many *cafetales* had been owned by people who also owned sugar estates: such people realized very clearly the relative advantages. Some such were U.S. citizens – for instance Gardiner Greene and Samuel Shaw Howland owned the sugar plantation of *El*

[14] Pezuela, *Diccionario*;.

[15] See Tacón, *Correspondencia*, ed. Pérez de la Riva 70–1.

[16] In 1855 de la Sagra (*Cuba en 1860*, 146) calculated world production (in million lbs) as:

Brazil	320	Sumatra	10
Java	110	Costa Rica	5
Haiti	35	Moka	5
Ceylon	35	British West Indies	5
Guiana	30	Dutch and French West Indies	3
Cuba and Puerto Rico	25	Philippines	2
		Total *c.*	585

The main consumers were the U.S.: 200 Mlbs; France and Italy, 110 Mlbs; Germany 100 Mlbs; England with 33 Mlbs was behind both Benelux (80 Mlbs) and Austria (65 Mlbs).

Dorado near Sagua la Grande, and the *cafetales Ontario* and *Mount Vernon* near Matanzas. Others were Cuban aristocrats. Joaquín Gómez, the big slave dealer, was a coffee planter, as was the banker Manuel Calvo. A member of the Herrera family possessed the biggest coffee estate (*La Gratitud*, in the district of El Cuzco), just as another member of the family possessed the largest sugar mill (*Sansom y Unión*).

By 1860 coffee production had dropped to 8,000 tons, or a fall of almost half in the figures for fifteen years before. But this fall in production was limited entirely to the western part of Cuba: east Cuba actually produced more in 1862 than in 1846; while the drop in the western department was of the order of 300%. In western Cuba the sugar planters were in fact still extending their hold. It is a commentary on the lack of morale, at least, among the *cafetales* of west Cuba, that in 1862 the numbers employed remained actually higher than in east Cuba (the white population of the *cafetales* being three times higher), though production was so much less.[17]

The coffee farms did not cease production though their numbers and stake in the economy decreased enormously. In 1860 there were about 1,000 estates,[18] but in 1877 only 192. In 1899 there would be 425 *caballería* (over 14,000 acres) given over to coffee, or less than a tenth of the land used for the same purpose in 1827.[19]

The tragedy for Cuba in the decline of coffee is that this product could have been developed much more easily by white farmers or small black freeholders than sugar could. As it was, coffee was produced by some without the intention or the means of selling it. Others took the newly-gathered fruit to the nearest *cafetal* where, for the newly-dried fruit with the musk still on it, they would get half the current price of coffee.[20]

The swift rise and decline of the coffee industry created in east Cuba a discontented class of rural gentry, closer to local conditions than the sugar planters and therefore more potentially dangerous to the social order. Such men believed that they had been ruined by sugar. It is scarcely surprising that several of them should adopt from the mid-1860s a revolutionary attitude which not only would express itself against the Spanish military government but also against an economy dominated by sugar. They would therefore be able to envisage, from the

[17] *Ibid.*, qu., 157. The figures were:

Population	West Cuba	East Cuba
White	4,194	1,488
Free Black	469	1,348
Freed	55	17
Slave	12,141	13,801
Total	16,859	16,654

[18] F. Pérez de la Riva, *El Café*, 78. Of these 437 were in the region of Santiago.
[19] *Census of Cuba 1899.*
[20] Turnbull, 314-16.

depths of their own economic ruin, the abolition not only of the slave trade but also of slavery itself.

These events are also important since they gave rise to yet another half truth about U.S. influence over Cuban development. Thus it is the clear implication in much Cuban historical interpretation that the U.S. tariff of 1835 'ruined' Cuban coffee; whereas this Act – itself a *quid pro quo* for Spanish behaviour[21] – was only one of several causes and not the most prominent; as can be seen from the fact that Cuban coffee production did not decline but merely failed to expand after 1834; the catastrophic drop only came in the mid-1840s after the combined effects of hurricanes and of much sugar investment.

The French influence in the island, mainly deriving from the coffee boom sponsored by immigrants from Saint Domingue, also died, except in the east: but there the dialect retained French words, in Santiago there was a famous French club and considerable French or Franco-Cuban influence among, for instance, the hoteliers and launderers. French coffee growers in the mountains of Guantánamo survived, Rousseaus and Carpentiers continuing till the end of the century at least to entertain travellers in a 'French style', their black servants or slaves still greeting visitors as '*maître*', and the mountains around Guantánamo now known as Yateras being referred to for many years as the coffee mountains. In this region the traveller Hazard was given to understand that the transporting of coffee to market was generally carried on by Indians who owned trains of mules for this purpose: if so, coffee in Cuba can be seen to be more than even a multi-racial project.

Tobacco increased in production and return throughout the early nineteenth century. In 1817 the old royal monopoly was abolished, and in 1821 the royal tobacco factory which had been established in 1765 disappeared to become the Military Hospital. There was now free trade in tobacco and freedom for all to manufacture cigars and cigarettes. But this made rather less difference than would have been the case thirty years before. The society of Cuba was now completely organized around sugar or coffee. Tobacco growers started far behind the sugar men. Many of them carried out their work with only their families to help. In 1827 their slaves were valued at not much more than $M2 (£500,000), while the land, at $700 per cab (nearly £5 or $21 an acre), was reckoned as well under that sum.[22] There were then apparently about 3,500 tobacco farms (*vegas*).

---

[21] In 1834 the Spanish government in Madrid, alarmed by the big decline of import of Spanish flour, placed a tax of $6 a barrel on foreign flour, $2 only on Spanish; the U.S. government insisted that all Spanish vessels should pay on entering U.S. harbours a tonnage duty equal to what their cargoes would have paid had they been exported from Cuba or Puerto Rico in U.S. ships.

[22] *Cuadro Estadístico de 1846*, 42.

Twenty years later, however, with coffee in decline, this number had gone up to 9,000 and by 1860 there were 11,500 *vegas* – of which most were still in east Cuba. The total product was then apparently worth about $M18 to $M20. Although the number of slaves had increased, at 18,000 these remained below the total for free Negro tobacco labour (30,000) and the two were well below the 75,000 whites understood to work on tobacco estates, often on fairly menial jobs.[23] So tobacco was mostly still cultivated by free labour. The size of such estates was usually small; scarcely more than a *caballería* – 33 acres – being the average, and of that perhaps as much as a half was customarily devoted to growing *plantains* or other minor vegetables. Such an estate might produce about 9,000 lbs of tobacco.

The quantity of tobacco smoked in Cuba amazed all visitors; even elderly women smoked, sometimes between courses at meals; even lunatics in the Mazorra asylum chain-smoked cigars. All visitors had thrust upon them two or three cigars. Cubans seem to have devised in the 1850s the first cigarette holder: an elaborate form of tongs (*tenacina*) made of silver or gold – one end with little claws to grasp the cigarette, the other with a small ring to put over the finger.[24] About three times as much tobacco was exported in the 1850s as in the 1830s. Most went to Europe: the high comfortable tide of English Victorian cigar consumption doubled the incomes of small tobacco men of the Vuelta Abajo and also of the 'Yara' region in the east, Cuban tobacco being by now the acknowledged master of the tobacco world and a Havana cigar being the supreme pleasure after dinner in a self-confident London or New York.

Many private factories were springing up. Some of the manufacturers were, like most businessmen in Havana, and nearly all of the enlightened sugar planters, recent Spanish immigrants. From this time indeed many of the best-known Cuban tobacco manufacturers, from Larrañaga to Uppman and Ramón Allones, were Spaniards of nineteenth-century immigration. In 1860 there were about 130 cigar factories and twenty cigarette factories in Havana,[25] of which the biggest was the Susini family's cigarette factory known as *La Honradez*, partly mechanized (in its printing department), and a major employer of Chinese labourers, many of whom lived in the factory's dormitories.[26] This firm also produced cigars and snuff.[27]

There were then in Havana more cigar workers than there were a hundred years later, and from the start these were more expert and

[23] Qu. *Estudio*, 147; Hazard, 330.
[24] Hazard, 154–5.
[25] Ortiz, *Cuban Counterpoint*, 84; Hazard, 216.
[26] For Chinese labour, see below, p. 186.
[27] Hazard, 145ff., describes a visit.

better organized than any other group: at that time, all were men. In 1857 the American President Buchanan's government announced that they would raise the tariff. In the year before this came into force 360 million cigars were exported – an all-time record, comparing very grandly with the puny thirty to forty million normal in the 1950s. Afterwards, a panic ensued. Many cigar factories went bankrupt. Many workers became unemployed. Some fled to the U.S. – the first group of Cuban cigar workers had set up at Key West (working at Tampa with imported Cuban tobacco leaves) as long ago as the early 1830s.[28]

There were, of course, some other activities in Cuba apart from sugar, tobacco, coffee and cattle, or their interchange: thus the old copper mines of El Cobre, now mostly owned by the English firm of Consolidated Copper, and also run by Englishmen, still produced fifty tons a day, mostly shipped to Europe to be smelted.[29] Conditions were gloomy, since the workers had to go up and down shafts of 1,000 feet by ladder; the temperature in the lowest shaft often attained 140°. Workers (and visitors) were indeed expected to bath when they reached the top. Such mining interests were, however, very small and made no contribution to the wealth of the great Cuban planter class during the nineteenth century.

[28] Ortiz, *Cuban Counterpoint*, 79.
[29] Hazard, 447, describes a visit.

CHAPTER XI

The Planters

The victorious sugar planters continued for many years to depend on merchants, for their capital as for labour, since, though the population of Havana reached 150,000 by about 1840 and though 1,000 to 2,000 ships now entered the harbour of Havana each year, there were still no banks for credit: the Royal Bank of Ferdinand VII, founded in 1827, with a capital of $M1 provided by the Spanish government, was restricted to exchange and paying letters of credit and forbidden to indulge in any loans over $10,000 or in speculation.[1] Nor were there any commercial banks in Spain. The merchants thus remained the effective bankers till after the middle of the century, though the two insurance companies of Havana did some private banking. As in the past, merchants continued to supply planters with money, although often even interest had not been paid, till a year of high prices gave them a chance of recovering the consolidated interest.[2]

Several of the largest planters were in fact merchants, and most even of those who were simply great landowners had a commercial origin. This was partly because the actual running of some estates passed (despite the laws against attachment) into the hands of the creditors; and, as had been seen earlier, traders in slaves were merely the richest of merchants. Often their owners, to cut costs, would themselves fit out slaving expeditions and at their own expense, at every stage of the slave process, ship the labour to the plantations direct from Africa. A notorious example was Julián de Zulueta,[3] founder in 1845 of the huge *Alava* mill with 600 slaves and a production of nearly 100,000 tons of

---

[1] Set up by *intendente* Martínez Pinillos, the counts of Santovenia and Reunión, and Joaquín Gómez, were the first directors, with the Spanish colonial minister as president. Gómez a, slave merchant of Gaditano origin, owned the *Perla* and *San Ignacio* mills in Pinar del Río; Santovenia the *Seibabo* mill in Bejucal, the *Montserrate* mill near Colome and *Santa Rita* near Guanabacoa; and the Conde de la Reunión owned the *Dos Hermanos* mill in Guanajay.

[2] Drake & Co. had to badger Joaquín de Ayesterán for what was due to them as a result of his purchase of a centrifugal machine; his uncle Fernando Diago had by 1853 a debt of $M2 owing to Drake & Co. also – paying $100,000 a year interest; the O'Farrill family owed $860,000 to the Drakes about the same time (Ely, *Cuando reinaba*, 339–40, 411, fn.).

[3] Julián de Zulueta (1814–78), native of Anucita (Álava), Spain; arrived in Cuba penniless in 1832, but was left a fortune by his uncle; accumulated a vast capital; stood by Spain in the first Cuban war of independence and became Marqués de Alava; married a Cuban. He owned two other mills in the Macagua region, the *Habana* and *Vizcaya* mills, each with advanced Derosne machines.

sugar about 1860,[4] making a profit per year of almost £50,000 ($200,000).[5] Zulueta had connections in London, where his cousin Pedro de Zulueta (son of the president of the Cortes and representative for Cádiz) was a merchant and shipper of goods for Africa, often going to Pedro Blanco's well-known slave factories on the river Gallinas. Julián de Zulueta also bought ships through Pedro's firm. He was in fact one of the last operators of the triangular trade, for by now most of the slave trade went direct Havana-Africa-Havana or Brazil-Africa-Brazil.[6] There were others no less prominent, such as José Luis Baró, proprietor of the *Luisa* and four other plantations, who employed large steamers to carry slaves to Cuba,[7] and Antonio Parejo, who came to Cuba from Cádiz about 1840 with 'a very immense capital', apparently the property of the queen mother of Spain, María Cristina, for whom Parejo acted as Cuban agent and for whom he founded the huge *Santa Susana* mill.[8] Other planters who made their original capital from selling slaves after the formal ban on the trade were Pedro Forcade of Forcade and Font, slavers of Cádiz, Joaquín Gómez, Antonio Pastor, the Iznagas of Trinidad, originally Basques, and the Borells, of the same town.[9]

Alongside the planters who bought or sold slaves direct were those whose fortunes were founded in one side or another of the slave trade. The most outrageous of these (if his own account is true) was Philip Drake or Felipe Drax, originally of Stockford, Lancashire, who bought a sugar plantation for $20,000 (£4,700) near Matanzas about 1820; he had made his money as a factor in his uncle's firm, of Villeño & Co. (an assumed name) at New Tyre on the river Basso in the Sierra Leone area.[10] The most successful of this group, however, was Tomás Terry, of Venezuelan origin, who made his first and critical $10,000 in a Gogolesque manner, by buying sick slaves and reselling them at a great profit after helping them back to health.[11] His favourite mill, *Caracas* (which was the first in Cuba to introduce electricity), cost him $23,000 (£5,000). Banker, importer, slave merchant and sugar grower, he

[4] E. Duvergier de Hauranne, *Huit mois en Amérique*, 2 vols (1866), 633–7; Gallega, 95–7; Rebello, 17.

[5] Pezuela, I, 59.

[6] See 'Trial of Pedro de Zulueta [on a charge of slave trading] at the Old Bailey' (1843), published by the British & Foreign Anti-Slaving Society. Zulueta was closely involved with Blanco and Cavallo, and Pedro Martínez & Co., both of Havana. Zulueta was found innocent.

[7] Aimes, 207.

[8] It is significant that as regent in 1840, the year that Parejo seems to have reached Cuba, María Cristina left Spanish politics for good, thereafter devoting herself to making a private fortune in conjunction with her ex-sergeant morganatic husband, Muñoz.

[9] W. H. Reed, *Reminiscences of Alisha Atkins* (1890), 67–9, qu. Ely, 767, gives details of Borell. The slave trade to Cuba in the nineteenth century is considered in greater detail in ch. XII.

[10] See Dow, 233.

[11] Atkins, 57–8.

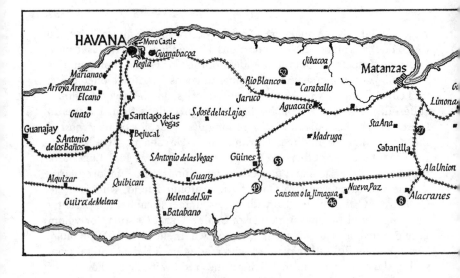

MAP KEY [Numbers refer to place on map]

This map shows the whereabouts of leading Cuban Sugar mills possessing Derosne (D) or Rillieux (R) centrifugal machines in 1860. They are listed in order of performance in the harvest of 1860.

	Mill		Owner	Production	
				Boxes	*Hogsheads*
1	San Martín (Guamutas)	D	La Gran Azucarera (i.e. Queen Mother of Spain)	13,837	1,644
2	Flor de Cuba (Macagua)	D	Arrieta heirs	11,300	1,360
3	Alava (Macagua)*	D	Julián de Zulueta	10,450	1,200
4	Alcancia (Cimarrones)	D	Conde de s. Fernando (Juan Peñalver)	7,850	
5	Sta. Teresa (Macagua)	R	Conde de Fernandina (Jº Mª Herrera)	7,840	
6	Andrea (Macuriges)	R	Noriega, Olmo & Co.	7,390	
7	Luisa (Cimarrones)	D	José Baró	7,278	
8	Las Cañas (Alacranes)	R	Juan Poey	7,182	659
9	Sta. Rita (Jiquimas)*	D	José Baró	6,972	981
10	Asunción (Cabañas)	R	Lorenzo Pedro heirs	6,700	
11	Sta. Elena (Jiquimas)	R	La Perseverencia (i.e. Diago Brothers)	6,550	705
12	Casualidad (Guamutas)	R	Marqués Duquesne	6,424	
13	Porvenir (Palmillas)	D	Pedro Forcade	6,242	408
14	Ponina (Macagua)	R	La Perseverencia (i.e. Diago Brothers)	5,951	566
15	Sta Isabel (Guamutas)	D	Greg. Menéndez	5,944	
16	Concepción (Macagua)	D	Marquesa de Urria	5,888	
17	Atrevido Nuevo (Macuriges)		José G. Chavez	5,841	200
18	Bramales (Cabañas)	D	Luis Amyot	5,721	615
19	Urumea (Macagua)		Stgo. Zuaznavar	5,578	383
20	Manuelita (Jiquimas)	D	Antonio Ma. Ventosinos	5,500	
21	Habana (Macagua)	D	Julián de Zulueta	5,487	532
22	Unión (Jiquimas)	D	Lamberto Fernández	5,162	363
23	Sta. Lutgarda (Ceja de Pablo)*	D	José Eusebio Alfonso	5,068	
24	Sta. Clara (Rancho Veloz)	D	José Mazorra	5,006	303
25	Julia (Sabanilla)	R	Julia Alfonso de Moliner	4,969	808
26	Aurora (Guamutas)	R	Nicolás Valdivieso	4,825	
27	Antonio (Guamacaro)	D	Heirs of Julián Alfonso	4,872	391
28	Vizcaya (Macagua)	D	Julián de Zulueta	4,780	490
29	Sta. Tomás or Descanso (Macuriges)	D	Joaquín Pedroso	4,417	416
30	Tinguaro (Jiquimas)*	R	La Perseverencia (i.e. Diago Brothers)	4,208	419
31	La Panchita (Rancho Veloz)	D	Pedro Gutiérrez	4,200	
32	San Silvestre (Sta. Ana)	D	José Eusebio Alfonso	4,069	
33	Sta. Gertrudes (Guamutas)	D	José Manuel Espelius	4,039	204
34	Arcos Yris (Alacranes)	R	Compañía Teritorial Cubana	4,064	795
35	Guinia de Töto (Río de Ay)		Justo Germán Cantero	4,011	300
36	Santiago (Macagua)	D	Marquesa de Urria & Sister	3,782	
37	Dos Hermanos (Cabañas)	R	Conde de la Reunión	3,714	

* Still in being 1959.

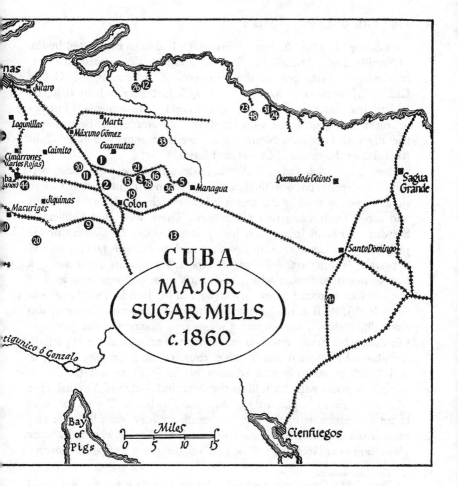

	Mill		Owner	Production	
				Boxes	Hogsheads
38	Chucha (Jiquimas)	R	Juan Bautista Lanz	3,544	
39	Manuelita (Cabañas)	R	Juan Aguirre	3,512	
40	Dos Hermanos (Macuriges)	D	Joaquín Pedroso	3,296	302
41	Sta. Susana (S. Isabel de las Lajas)	D	La Gran Azucarera (i.e. Queen Mother of Spain)	3,258	
42	Petrona (Guamacaro)	D	Petrona Milian	3,012	
43	Jesús Nazareno (S. Diego de Núñez)	R	Miguel Hano y Vega	2,822	
44	Sta. Victoria (Jiquimas)		Simon P. de Terán	2,713	195
45	San Agustín (Cabañas)	R	Antonio Ecay	2,508	
46	Armonía (Nueva Paz)	R	Widow Schull	2,497	
47	S. Joaquín (or Azopardo) (Macuriges)	R	Compañía Territorial Cubana	2,451	1,315
48	Sta. Rosa (Ceja de Pablo)	R	Heirs of James Lawton	2,398	
49	Providencia (Güines)*	D	Fco. de Arango	2,225	
50	S. Joaquín (Macuriges)	R	Joaquín Pedroso	2,168	1,098
51	Descanso (Guamacaro)	D	Pedro de la Rudée	1,950	136
52	Dolores (Río Blanco del Sur)	D	Luisa Calvo	1,784	
53	Amistad (Güines)*	D	Ayesterán heirs		1,246
54	Río Grande (Santiago de Cuba)		Ursula Repilado		1,218
55	Cercado (Maraguan, Puerto Principe)		Tomás Betancourt		443

263,249

* Still in being 1959.

consolidated in 1869 the large debts which had been contracted by the O'Farrills, and of which the firm of Drake & Co. wished to divest themselves.[12] Terry became the great boss of Cienfuegos, the 'Cuban Croesus', leaving over \$25M (nearly £6M) at his death in 1886, by which time much of his money was in foreign investments,[13] but enjoying a very good name with his slaves and employees: he was very friendly with Congolese Negroes and gave them money to found clubs (*cabildos*) in the towns of Cruces and Lajas.[14]

Ever since 1818 (when indiscriminate commerce was finally permitted with other nations) foreigners had been buying interests in Cuban sugar as well as establishing themselves as merchants. Many Americans and some Englishmen had plantations. There was 'Don Guillermo' Stewart of Philadelphia, who had a large estate, *La Carolina* in the jurisdiction of Cienfuegos, of two thousand acres, with 500 slaves and a private landing stage for sugar export;[15] Augustus Hemenway, a ship-owner from Boston with Chilean interests, but also proprietor of the eighteen-hundred acre mill *San Jorge* in the jurisdiction of Sagua la Grande;[16] J. W. Baker, who later hispanicized his name to Bécquer, also from Philadelphia, who owned a prosperous plantation, *San José* near Cienfuegos, of twelve hundred acres with 700 all male slaves;[17] perhaps the absence of women was the chief cause of the large slave revolt, in which Baker narrowly escaped with his life.[18] There was the North American Jenks with his mill in the beautiful valley of Yumurí near Matanzas. From England there were the Fowlers of Cienfuegos, who came as merchants in the late eighteenth century but who were also proprietors of a mill (*La Narcisa*);[19] and J. G. Taylor who had a poor plantation near Holguín,[20] till he gave up, disgusted by Spanish govern-

---

[12] Ely, *Cuando reinaba*, 412–13.

[13] Not bad for a Cuban, when it is recalled that putatively the richest man in the world at the time, William Backhouse Astor, left only \$M50. Ely, 406, gives this instructive picture of Terry's total wealth at different years:

	Total capital \$	Foreign investments \$	Debts in his favour \$	Invested in sugar mills \$	Miscellaneous \$
1851	724,180	20,888	256,204	193,098	187,810
1860	3,090,593	79,621	701,333	1,303,114	382,346
1870	7,891,784	2,467,843	2,034,752	1,344,701	1,118,344
1880	13,763,594	9,383,373	2,139,083	1,482,906	364,926

[14] Esteban Montejo, *The Autobiography of a Runaway Slave* (1968), 144, who added, 'I wish all the slave-owners had been like him and his sons'.

[15] Hazard, 402, describes a visit; Rebello, 15.

[16] Rebello, 53. Augustus Hemenway (1805–76); see Frederic Eustis, *Augustus Hemenway* [Sagua la Grande], *1805–1876* (Salem, Mass., 1955), 81, 102 fn. Hemenway bought the *San Jorge* estate for 'over \$50,000', (£12,000).

[17] Turnbull, 146; Rebello, 13.

[18] Madden, 171. He later gave himself an 'English' title, 'Sir William Bécquer'.

[19] See Ely, *Cuando reinaba*, 83; Atkins, 58–9.

[20] J. G. Taylor, *The U.S. and Cuba* (1851).

mental interference, and went to grow tea in Ceylon. Another early U.S. merchant was Frederick Freeman who established himself in Trinidad about 1835.[21] Among others were the Phinneys of Bristol (Rhode Island), who developed interests in several sugar plantations (*La Palma, Roble, La Sonora*) near Cárdenas;[22] James Burnham of Matanzas, Thomas Brooks of Santiago, Francis Adams of Matanzas, and the Drakes of Havana, whose English founder James (Santiago) Drake had come to Cuba in the 1790s.[23] The rise of this family was indeed swift; James Drake married a Núñez del Castillo, cousin of the Marqués de San Felipe, then Cuba's only 'Grandee of Spain'; their son, Carlos, became a count, married a De La Cerda, a cousin of the Empress Eugénie; and their son Emilio, totally hispanicized, became a marquess in the 1890s. The Drakes, though retaining their counting house in Havana, ran several plantations, and later bought estates in Spain.

There was an English sugar refinery near Matanzas run by George and Burnell.[24] There were a gathering of English merchants in Santiago, headed by Richard Bell and the Consul and the copper mine manager, Hardy. J. G. Taylor of Holguín found a group of English merchants all drunk one breakfast time at the only good hotel in the city, Madame Sauce's.[25] (Many hotels throughout Cuba were run by Frenchmen or North Americans by the 1860s, such as Colonel Lay's establishment in Havana, Mrs Woodbury's in Cárdenas or Mme Lescailles's in Santiago.)

Some planters came from other less prosperous parts of Spanish America as Tomás Terry had done. Prominent among these was Justo Germán Cantero, a penniless doctor from Santo Domingo, who gained his plantations of Buena Vista and Guinia de Soto by poisoning the rich old ex-slaver Pedro Iznaga of Trinidad and marrying his widow (who also opportunely disappeared).[26] Cantero became a model planter, buying all the latest machinery, and produced a beautifully illustrated work on Cuban sugar mills, *Los Ingenios*.

Very many nineteenth-century planters in Cuba came from Spain, such as Villaurrutia, the Diagos, Baró, the Aldamas (who had arrived in 1808) and Julián Zulueta, but in general they were, as in these instances, primarily merchants to begin with. In the 1860s the leading merchants of Cienfuegos were all Spaniards, headed by the De La

[21] Uncle by marriage of Elisha Atkins, later founder of one of the biggest Cuban-American fortunes.
[22] Ely, *Cuando reinaba*, 187, fn.
[23] He was from Devon and his family claimed descent from the Drakes of Ashe House, baronets.
[24] Turnbull, 219.
[25] J. G. Taylor, *op cit.*, 160.
[26] Reed, 67–9.

Torriente brothers from Santander.[27] The Spanish arrivals were mostly Catalans or Basques, who, as reported by Rev. Abbot, 'arrive in poverty, begin with a shop six or eight feet square, live on a biscuit and rise by patience, industry and economy to wealth and, unlike the Yankees, never fail.'[28] Almost all shops were owned by Catalans and of one Negro in Santiago who had a shop it was said that he was a 'black Catalan'.[29] These of course should be distinguished from the large number of families of 'loyal Spaniards' who had emigrated from the rest of South America – defeated officers and disgruntled officials – who received special favours despite their contemptuous name of '*ayacuchos*', often living on the lottery or prostitution.

Cuban sugar planters still customarily lived on the island, though, as they got richer, not usually on their plantations.[30] Esteban Montejo, a slave whose 'autobiography' was published in the 1960s, recalls a planter riding past in his carriage 'with his wife and smart friends through the canefields waving a handkerchief but that was as near as he ever got to us'.[31] Most planters had town houses in Havana or perhaps Santiago or Matanzas. By the 1860s some great proprietors were however beginning to be found in Paris or New York. Other planters with houses and families in Havana might spend a few weeks, especially during harvest, on their estates. Those who did not do so would appoint administrators (sometimes younger members of the family) and leave the running even of the harvest to them.

The wealth obtained through the immense development of sugar reached lavish proportions; and the opulence created a magnificent if somewhat demoralized society. Money seems often to have been treated as a kind of miracle or incitement to spending and dissipation. Many planters bought titles. It was possible to become a marquess by paying $45,000 (£10,000), a count for $25,000 to $30,000 (£6,000 to £7,000).[32] In this way Nicolás Martínez de Campos became Conde de Santovenia in 1824; José Ramón de Alfonso became in 1834 Marqués de Montelo; Carlos Pedroso became in 1832 Conde de Casa Pedroso; the *regidor decano* of Santiago de Cuba, Bartolomé Portuondo, a great slave dealer and scandalous judge of the Mixed Court set up in fact to ban slave trafficking, became Marqués de las Delicias in 1832;[33] the *parvenu* Drakes became counts (of Vega Mar) in the 1840s. The Montalvos picked up two titles (Condes de Macuriges and Casa Montalvo),

[27] Atkins, 12.
[28] Qu. *ibid.*, 65.
[29] Cristóbal C. M. F. Fernández, *El confesor de Isabel II y sus actividades en Madrid* (1964), 187.
[30] Turnbull, 47–8.
[31] Montejo, 19.
[32] See discussion in Ely, *Cuando reinaba*, 719, fn. 1.
[33] See J. G. Taylor's scornful remarks about him in *The U.S. and Cuba*, 283.

the Peñalvers four (Marqués de Arcos and de Casa Peñalver, Conde de San Fernando and Peñalver), the Calvos two (Marqués de Buena Vista and Casa Calvo), the Herreras four (Marqués de Almendares and Villalta, Conde de Jibacoa and Fernandina). In the 1840s in Cuba there were thirty-four marquesses and thirty-two counts; three of these were now grandees of Spain – the Marqués de San Felipe; the Count of Villanueva (the *intendente*, Martínez de Pinillos), his title dating from 1845; and the Conde of Fernandina, dating from 1819 (Gonzalo José de Herrera).[34] Titles were not quite honorific. They gave some social stature. They gave freedom from arrest for debt and some other crimes, though not treason. Even minor titles such as Gentleman of the Bed-chamber of the Queen (of whom there were many, including the sinister Cantero and the Philadelphia business man Baker-Bécquer) enabled the holder to transfer litigation pending against him to Spain, there to be subject to delays even more useful and inexplicable than in Havana.

Havana, throughout the nineteenth century was, very much a Spanish city. The old walls were only removed in 1863. The many coloured red-roofed houses were almost all slightly different, though built on the same general plan, painted green or blue, built round a court-yard, the enormous windows without glass but with iron bars, single-storeyed, with huge doorways and heavy doors studded with knobs and decorations 'all bearing the appearance of having been built for defence against outside attack'.[35] The courtyard took the place of the gardens beloved by Anglo-Saxons but these often had, as in Spain, fountains, oranges, pomegranates or mignonette trees. The dining room, however well furnished, was usually so placed immediately behind the front door that everything passing from street to courtyard, including horses, had to go through it. In the houses there was much white marble, some of it from Genoa, more from the Isle of Pines, but a billiard room was more frequent than a library. In the salon, there were the inevitable rocking chairs, a long mirror or two in richer houses, a portrait of an ancestor perhaps and sometimes, in the houses of a Montalvo or a Pedroso, a chandelier; no carpets, though sometimes a rug; and often a *candela*, a silver or plated dish filled with wood ashes, in which a live coal burned, to light cigars.

North Americans found Havana 'apparently feudal'[36] or 'reminding me of Eastern bazaars'.[37] Pavements were narrow, 'seldom used', though cleaned nightly by chain-gangs of Chinamen and Negroes. The streets of Old Havana had by now most of the names which they

[34] *Guía de los Forasteros* (1864), 77–9. See J. de Atienza, *Nobiliario Español*, 2nd edn (1954); and García de Arboleya, 279–80.
[35] Hazard, 142.
[36] Atkins, 2.
[37] Hazard, 163.

afterwards retained: Muralla, where the walls used to run; Obispo, after the bishop (Morell de Santa Cruz) who used to walk there; Amargura, bitterness, as part of the Via Crucis used in religious procession; Inquisidor, from the stay there of an inquisitor; Damas, because of its pretty girls on the balconies; Refugio, where in the 1830s Governor Ricafort took refuge and other comfort in the house of a beautiful mulatto widow; Empedrado, because it was the first paved street; O'Reilly, after the Irish marshal; Obrapia, because in the seventeenth century Martín Calvo de la Puerta had obliged it to endow five orphans a year.[38] The streets as in Spain had their watchmen (*serenos*) after the 1830s. The size of these streets was a persistent argument for the first thirty years of the century: sugar barons wanted to take their ox carts of sugar through narrow streets to the dock, when only mules were allowed. Anthony Trollope, visiting Cuba in the 1840s, commented that the streets were 'narrow, dirty and foul'.[39] There were however a series of squares and parks – from the Plaza de Armas, still the main square, to Colón Park, on the grounds of the Conde de Villanueva's old country house; Campo Marte, previously used as a drill ground; Captain-General Tacón's big square, the Parque Central; the Botanical Gardens; and the Quinta de los Molinos, the country house of the captain-general on the edge of the city. All were dominated by magnificent palms. The Paseo, built by Captain-General Tacón, became the pride of the city and on Sunday afternoons was crowded by *volantes*. The city increased by the 1860s to contain 140,000 people, occupying some two square miles, stretching to what is now the Calzada de Galiano, compared with 30,000 to 50,000 occupying about threequarters of a square mile in 1760. Several *haciendas* near the city, such as those of the Conde de Pozos Dulces, Juan Espino or Domingo Trigo, in what is now called the Vedado district, were by the 1860s beginning to be laid out as residential districts and, for the first time, in the blocks of a hundred yards square which have since become typical of the district. In the neighbourhood of what had once been the village of Cerro, there were now many beautiful *quintas* or country residences, some with famous mango avenues (such as the Conde de Peñalver's) or great cactuses.

Even in a period of normal peace, Spanish soldiers in seersucker uniforms and straw hats with red cockades were seen all the time in Havana. The city seemed indeed to simmer permanently with violence and colour, every scene contriving to emphasize contrasts between luxury and violence. Aristocrats sought to excel each other in glorious

---

[38] See E. Roig de Leuchsenring, *La Habana, Apantes Históricos*, 2 vols (1964), II, 31, for a full interpretation of Havana street names.

[39] A. Trollope, *West Indies and The Spanish Main* (1862), 147.

équipage for their carriages, and the jewellery and silver shops were increasingly famous in North America. There were a very large number of tailors, milliners, hatters, artificial-flower makers, furnishing shops, with Frenchmen well established among shoemakers and perfumers. Havana was also known for its fans and the beauty of certain types of lawn cloth and organdies. *Criollo* or Spanish women were, however, rarely seen on the street and when aristocrats went shopping the shop assistants would customarily bring their goods to the carriages in the road. There were of course no fixed prices, and arguments were usual.

Much meat was available in Havana, but covered with dirt, sold by half-naked Negroes, their skin glistening with sweat. There was much poultry also, sold alive. Jerked beef and fish were sold in huge quantities, these with plantain being the chief food of the poor. There were few vegetables, but much fruit such as pineapples, oranges and bananas. Sugar cane itself was sucked with zest and *guarapo*, cane juice, drunk in the harvest. Beggars and prostitutes abounded as never elsewhere in the West Indies. Both smoked incessantly, however, like the rest of the population.[40] The best café for a long time was the Dominica, where both men and women drank their *refrescos*, such as orangeade or *panales* (white of eggs and sugar) or *limonada*, sometimes with rum. The Dominica was a large marble-floored room with a fountain in the middle, but the most celebrated for 'ices and sherbets' was El Louvre. (Ice had been introduced to Havana in 1806 though it was rare in the country.) *The Times* correspondent Gallenga thought that he had never seen even in Paris 'so many or proportionately such sumptuous and constantly crowded cafés'. Immense quantities of cheap Spanish wine (*vino Catalán*) were drunk, and there was also already almost as much beer. Coffee, on the other hand, was for any *criollo* the first drink of the morning and the last at night, as well as little cups (*jícaras*) of chocolate (no Cuban had breakfast). There were four markets, including Captain-General Tacón's big fish market, selling perhaps a hundred species.

By the 1860s there were many hotels. The Santa Isabel, in what had been the palace of the Condes de Santovenia, had been fitted up as a hotel by Colonel Lay of New Orleans. Another North American, Mrs Almy, ran the *Hotel de Europa* ('for those who like a quiet listless life'), but a Cuban later took it over. Some large boarding houses were kept by American ladies. The Inglaterra, in Tacón's Paseo, was a grander affair, as was the Telegráfico. Anthony Trollope, however, found it unusual to have a bedroom (to himself) in any hotel.[41] There were several good restaurants, such as the Tuileries, the Noble Havana, the

[40] See Hazard 215.
[41] Trollope, 146.

Crystal Palace and the Restaurant Français. Several of the hotels had baths and, scattered through Havana, there were also public baths at thirty cents a time, some, such as El Louvre, rather grand. These establishments were chiefly frequented by men: it was assumed in Havana that women rarely went out and rarely washed, instead rubbing their faces with cane brandy. Some upper class women in fact avoided washing except in *la temporada*, the season for medicinal waters. No one ever swam in the sea for fear of sharks, though there were one or two large swimming baths of sea water near the ocean, hollowed out of rocks at great cost which, during the *temporada*, were even patronized by upper-class women.[42] But dirt and disease were still rampant, yellow fever being still put down to the former but little being done about it.

Tidy-minded North American visitors as ever found it curious that the grand houses of the old nobility should be jumbled up with markets and shops; thus the Santovenia Palace, both when the old count still lived there and when it had become an hotel, had shops on the ground floor. The New York artist Samuel Hazard kept looking for a 'west end', the quarter of the 'best society', but discovered that 'people of the best class live here, there, everywhere ... some in warehouses, some over warehouses'.[43] To such visitors Havana seemed intolerably noisy, incessant church bells mingling with new street cars, ferry boat and mail boat booms, clatter of horses and *volantes*,[44] Negroes selling milk from tin cans, crying '*Leche, leche!*' or oranges ('*Naranjas! naranjas!*') lottery ticket sellers ('*Lotería, lotería*'), Chinamen selling crockery, innumerable guitars and trumpets of soldiers at drill. The markets were always full of mounted country people. Meantime, next to *mudéjar* palaces of the sixteenth and seventeenth centuries, and baroque adaptations of the eighteenth, there now arose classical palaces inspired by the French Revolution, of which Miguel Aldama's new palace remains the best example.

Many planters behaved with amazing absence of foresight. A Spanish clerk once pointed out to the North American merchant Atkins a plumed Cuban grandee passing in a *volante* and asked, 'Why don't you ride like that instead of walking and carrying your bag?' 'I could,' replied Atkins, 'if he would pay what he owes me.'[45] Justo Cantero,

[42] Hazard, 29–54.
[43] *Ibid.*, 66.
[44] A *volante* was a carriage with wheels so wide apart that it was almost impossible to over-turn even on Cuba's very bumpy roads. The wheels themselves were 6 to 7 feet in diameter. The body lay low between the shafts, so that the heads of travellers were always below the top of the wheels. The *volante*, drawn by a single horse in towns, would have two outriders in addition and on these the *calesero* would sit. Later, the top of this vehicle could be moved up or down, being then referred to as a *quitrín*, the most usual word for a Cuban carriage in the 1860s.
[45] Atkins, 66.

when he had got hold of part of the Iznaga fortune, probably by poison, built a house in Trinidad with a Roman marble bath and two cherub heads which spouted gin (for men) and eau de cologne (for women). Cantero also had a *quinta* overlooking Trinidad, 'rivalling in beauty' that of the captain-general. The Cantero regime went out with a bang in one last great extravagant banquet: afterwards, ruin and bailiffs.[46]

Much money was spent on lavish entertainment. Dancing was a passion for all and, as well as the famous slow *danza criolla* or *habanera*, there was the *contradanza* (an import from Saint Domingue).[47] The Pedrosos and Montalvos and so on, even took up fashionable dances of North America such as the Lancers (*Lanza*), converted by the Cubans into what one North American thought 'one of the most indecent spectacles I have ever seen'.[48]

On sugar and coffee plantations, owners and overseers frequently attended the much more exciting *bailes de tambor* (drum dances) held by the Negro *cabildos* on Sundays or fiestas. In the country the most customary dance was the *zapateo*, danced to the harp or guitar, but sung by all present too. There were innumerable balls in Havana, often costume or masked, and some town balls for all classes (a *máscara*), as well as many theatrical performances, with some European *artistes* brought over, at the large Tacón theatre. To these occasions the *haut-monde* of Havana would drive in *volantes*, conducted by a Negro footman (*calesero*), dressed in high boots and heavy silver spurs, perched on a silver-mounted saddle on the shaft horse. The theatres were elaborate costume occasions, attended by soldiers in full dress, the civil guard and Negro pages. Havana men-about-town wore white suits and panama hats, their wives mantillas, and before them on a little seat there would doubtless be their daughter, an overdressed little Lolita or Rosita.[49] (The seat itself came to be known as la *Niña Bonita*.) There were also great funerals – that of Antonio Parejo, the queen mother's agent, cost $10,000. The females of the upper class, very attractive as many travellers noted, had very little to do, especially if they lived on the plantations, but they seem to have read but rarely, and occupied their time managing their powdered eggshell cosmetic (*cascarilla*) and their fans – unless they had been educated abroad. In Cuba education was certainly not a way of filling in the time. In 1833 there were less than 10,000 children even registered in schools on the island, out of 200,000 under fifteen years old.[50] On the other hand, in most towns of

---

[46] For Cantero, see Atkins, 68; Hazard, 419.

[47] *Contradanza* or *contredanse*, originally however derived from the English 'country dance'.

[48] Hazard, 197.

[49] By the late 1860s *volantes* were giving way to victorias used as taxis, often run by Frenchmen.

[50] *Census of 1899*, 570.

any importance there was an association of young men, known as *El Liceo*, organized for general artistic and literary purposes and for recreation.

Great sums were also spent on houses, fountains, renaissance ceilings, marble staircases and baths. Miguel Aldama had a water closet in his palace long before such things existed anywhere save in England.[51] Bécquer (Baker) proposed to lay a mosaic of doubloons in the floor of the dining room; the authorities suggested that it would be improper to walk on the Spanish coat of arms, and so, with a rare excess of loyal extravagance, he suggested that the coins might go on their edges.[52] Planters were immensely hospitable alike to friends and passing strangers, who were infrequent enough to contribute to the information and the amusement of the family, always handing them, to Anthony Trollope in Cienfuegos, to Ampère, to other travellers, as Cubans do still, innumerable cigars.[53] After 1835 or so, this hospitality became more circumspect; planters were afraid lest an unannounced stranger might be a snooper for the British Consul or the Permanent Court of Arbitration at Havana to discover who had new slaves and who had not.

As the accounts of Tomás Terry suggest, much money was invested abroad. The permanent fear of a slave revolution for instance caused the Drakes to invest heavily in the U.S. and Europe. One son of Tomás Terry bought the Château of Chenonceaux on the Loire, another a $150,000 house on Fifth Avenue. Once planters had made money and placed their fortune, as they supposed, beyond the possibility of ruin (for their own generation anyway), they travelled, went to the waters at Madruga or San Diego or to the Isle of Pines or Saratoga Springs, employed North American or European governesses, from whom their children learnt French (governesses might be paid $25 a month and all found). Some went to great lengths to avoid miscegenation: 'The parents want to avoid contacts between the children and persons of colour', wrote one businessman to New York in 1849, explaining why one of his friends needed a North American nanny.[54] But on the other hand no one seemed to mind about inbreeding; so first cousins married first cousins again and again, Pedrosos y Pedroso marrying Pedrosos y Pedroso, and unbelievably often uncles marrying nieces, on occasion uncles marrying nieces who were also, on the other side, first cousins.

Wealth did not bring intelligence. In Cienfuegos in the 1870s there was a rich ex-cooper, Manuel Blanco, who spent nothing and whose

---

[51] Letter to Domingo del Monte, qu. Moreno Fraginals, 56. Miguel de Aldama, 1821-88, oligarch and patriot.
[52] Atkins, 124.
[53] Trollope, *West Indies*, 133.
[54] J. M. Morales to Colt, 7 October 1849, qu. Ely, *Cuando reinaba*, 681.

balance kept accumulating in the house of Atkins & Co. in Cienfuegos. He never made a will, preferring to think of his relatives fighting over his money after he had died. His last instruction to his sister Cándida was never to put her name to any document: an unnecessary charge since she could not write. The balance continued to accrue and the firm of Atkins could never persuade the Blanco heirs to invest anything or spend it.

This Cuban aristocracy lacked public spirit. No sacrifice was too much for families or friends: '*La vie de famille, à la Havane*', wrote la Comtesse Merlin, '*renouvelle les charmes de l'age d'or*';[55] any service was too great for the community. A particular symptom of this was the state of the roads. As Trollope found out in 1859, the conveyance from Cienfuegos to Havana, the main ports of the colony, went only once a week.[56] Paths between even very rich plantations were often non-existent and dangerous. In the 1820s and early 1830s (before the arrival of the disciplinarian Captain-General Tacón) Cuba presented a lurid picture of persistent robbery and highway assassination. No doubt this attitude was partly though not wholly explained by the continued government ban on *criollo* political activity.

Litigation really took the place of public service. This was endless, chiefly because of the immense confusion in which almost all land titles rested after the gradual collapse of the old circular grants and their polygonal successors. The law was neither cheap nor honest, verdicts being bought and sold 'with as much scandalous publicity as the bozal slaves are bought and sold in the barracoons'.[57] Judges were paid little and even that small amount had often to be sent to Madrid to the politician who had helped the judge to get his job. In the 1830s the pay of judges depended on the length of their sittings: a *Juez Letrado* got $10 a day or part of a day in which his services were required,[58] and lawyers were paid according to the number of pages of their briefs (two *reales* per folio). Witnesses too were paid by the hour. Other court officials were also paid, though not much. Corruption was the only way for these people to survive. In smaller towns, judges (*alcaldes mayores*) would often be little more than clerks, with hardly any knowledge of the law. In Cienfuegos, the merchants once subscribed to pay a judge's salary so that he could live. When two such merchants were in conflict the judge had a difficult decision. It was common to seek the opinion of a judge to know first, before beginning suit, what his decision would be.[59]

[55] Comtesse Merlin, *La Havane*, 3 vols (1844), I, 310. She returned to Cuba from France in 1840 after many years.
[56] Trollope, 5.
[57] Madden, 124.
[58] Turnbull, 94.
[59] Atkins, 69.

Legal proceedings were also usually conducted in writing and could always be enormously long drawn out, so again favouring the rich. In no other country, an English planter noted, is 'the pure vexation' of the law more manifest.[60]

The lottery (established 1812) also used up a good deal of money in Havana – a million dollars a year, thought Richard Madden[61]; a universal indulgence, thought Samuel Hazard – as did bullfights, goosefights (in the country) and cockfights, in theory a royal monopoly.[62] English breeds were considered the best for cocks, and the export of birds from England must have been substantial (particularly after this sport was made illegal in England in 1849). 'Now I know you, and can trust you,' said a Cuban to the English planter J. G. Taylor in the 1840s, 'if you bring me a bird from Liverpool, I will give you $200.'[63] Bullfights were confined to the Plaza de Toros in Havana, and the matadors were usually Spanish: but there was also a bullfight season in Santiago at Easter. Though sporadically illegal, in private houses gambling was persistent. Slaves, estates, pictures, were all staked on cockfights as on Monte, Faro, Piquet, Burro or sometimes Até.[64] Monte was a game which passed from popularity among the Havana aristocracy to the slaves.[65]

Apart from affording the excuse and justification for fiestas and carnivals (at which the Santiago Virgin or the Black Virgin of Regla, or some other local saint would be carried by slaves around the town), the Church played little part. The island might have some eighty parish churches. But the lay nature of fiestas surpassed Spain: thus the custom of forming altars in the houses in the first week of May (*altares de Cruz*) was an excuse only for drinking and eating in many places.[66] In 1859 Trollope thought 'Roman Catholic worship at a lower ebb in Cuba than almost anywhere else.'[67] His view was shared by Archbishop Claret a few years before. No priest would dare to admonish his flock for buying slaves on Sunday; none would confront the captain-general with the Spanish law of 1820 abolishing the slave trade. Village priests were as ignorant and as poor as they were in Spain. One priest, *en route* for a Sunday cock fight, told Richard Madden: 'The system is so bad that the

[60] J. G. Taylor, *op. cit.*, 257.
[61] Richard Robert Madden (1798–1886), surgeon and writer; superintendent of *emancipados* in Havana, 1836–40. Colonial Secretary of Western Australia, 1847–50. Secretary of Loan Fund Board, Dublin, 1850–80. Author of *The United Irishmen*, and many other works.
[62] The treasury issued about 500,000 lottery tickets a year; there were twenty drawings a year, the tickets varying from $100,000 to $10,000, each being divided up. (Details in Hazard, 171–2.)
[63] J. G. Taylor, 310. Hazard, 190–290, has a description.
[64] Rules in J. G. Taylor, 314–15.
[65] Montejo, 108.
[66] Hazard, 539–40.
[67] Trollope, 123.

very ministers at the altar must sell the holy things for money.'[68] It has been shown how tithes were abolished. The nineteenth century saw such an alignment of religion with slavery that slaves were announced in church as to be sold 'on the following Sunday, during the celebration of Mass, before the church doors'.[69] Priests were unable to instruct in anything slaves who worked up to twenty hours during the harvest. Nor were there adequate numbers of priests. Madden heard of only two estates in all Cuba where Negroes were able to go to mass on Sundays and on feast days and only on one plantation (*Santa Ana de Aguiar*, belonging to José de Luz, at Bejucal) did there seem to be regularly a chaplain.[70] Slaves could marry; that was a notable contrast with North America; but sacraments did not otherwise play a big part in the life of most slaves.[71] One archbishop, Antonio María Claret, alone stands out as an enlightened pastor and missionary.[72] His attempts at improvement in the manners of Cubans led to his attempted assassination and return to Spain. In Cuba too there were fewer missionaries than there had been in the British West Indies. Some North American Baptists did reach Cuba in the mid-nineteenth century but their work had little effect. The Virgin of El Cobre remained the most prominent and beloved sanctuary. The monasteries and convents disappeared after the liberal legislation of the 1830s but their land as in Spain was sold to new men and only about 1,000 monks and nuns were dispossessed, mostly returning to Spain.

Chaplains were rather rare visitors to plantations, even though the Code of 1789 and that of 1842 technically still provided that slaves should be instructed in Christianity. The slave Montejo recalls visiting priests as very delicate individuals who never under any circumstances entered the slave barracoons.[73] (The priest at *Santa Ana* said incidentally that he had never once seen a freed Negro in church all his life, save at his baptism.)[74]

These inadequacies were also seen in the newer towns; churches had not kept pace with the buildings; thus in Manzanillo or Cienfuegos, Sagua or Villaclara, there was still only one church with three priests, though populations were now 12,000 to 15,000.[75] On some mills, 'Sundays' appear simply to have been days of rest, sometimes every week, sometimes every ten or fourteen days, according to the whim or

[68] Madden, 110.
[69] *Ibid.*, 112.
[70] *Ibid.*, 164.
[71] For an opposing view, see Klein, 86–105.
[72] See Cristóbal Fernández, *San Antonio María Claret*. Saint Antonio Claret y Clara, 1807–70, confessor to Isabella II, was canonized 1950.
[73] Montejo, 360.
[74] Turnbull, 285.
[75] A. C. N. Gallenga, *The Pearl of the Antilles* (1873), 155.

calculation of the owner or administrator. On the other hand there was still much instinctual religion. Hazard saw the population kneeling in the streets of Santiago in prayer during an earthquake, and the fiestas were of course popular occasions.[76] On one Easter Thursday the Conde de Casa Bayona humiliated himself, washed the feet of twelve slaves, and personally served them at his table: unfortunately this did not prevent the excited slaves from rebelling nor the *rancheadores* from afterwards pursuing and killing them.[77]

By 1860 mechanization, imagination, luck and money had established a number of distinct groups among the planters: first, the old oligarchic families of Cuba whose ancestors had acquired estates in the eighteenth century or before and different members of whom owned many mills and vast acres. These were concentrated mostly in the region of Havana and to a lesser extent in Matanzas. Of them, the Cárdenas family owned twenty-one mills and 30,000 acres in sugar farms alone, not to speak of three marquesates, though they were by no means technologically advanced: a visit by Turnbull and Madden in 1838 to an estate belonging to Joaquín de Cárdenas was one of their most gloomy experiences, being the 'most imperfect' mill mechanically they had seen, and there having been no slave births there in the previous year – a sure sign of bad conditions.[78] Indeed, though these families had been innovators in the eighteenth century, by the nineteenth they were already as a general rule old-fashioned. Of the other families, the Alfonsos owned seventeen mills and 21,000 acres, and the Herreras thirteen mills and 24,000 acres, including the vast plantation proudly named *Sansom y Unión*, at Nueva Paz; the Betancourts of Puerto Príncipe had nine old poor mills – seven oxen-driven – but with 20,000 acres;[79] the O'Farrills ran these close, with eleven mills and 19,000 acres; the Pedrosos had ten mills and 16,500 acres; while the Iznagas, the Arangos and the Calvos de la Puerta each had about 12,500 acres, with ten, seven and eight mills respectively; with slightly smaller estates there were the Peñalvers, the O'Reillys and the Montalvos. All of these, save those of the Betancourts, lay in the west.[80] Though so many estates were concentrated in families, the mills were themselves controlled by single men, of whom the greatest pluralists were José Eusebio Alfonso; the Marqués de Campo Florido (a Cárdenas); Pedro Iznaga; and the Marqués de Almendares (a Herrera).

Some of these families dated their inheritances from original grants from the Crown, though perhaps not until the mid-eighteenth century.

[76] Hazard, 439–40.
[77] Moreno Fraginals, 49.
[78] Madden, 166.
[79] José Betancourt had a mill in the west, *Merced*, at Lagunillas, Matanzas.
[80] The Arangos had two small mills in the east.

All were still closely connected by marriage, so that indeed, like the Habsburgs and Bourbons, it is hard to consider this sugar oligarchy[81] separate families. Of these, the Alfonsos, long established in Matanzas, did not prosper until the irresistable tide of sugar riches reached that region in the 1830s. Many aristocratic estates were already in decay by 1840; thus Madden and Turnbull were told that the Conde de O'Reilly (grandson of the marshal) had 102 slaves, of whom only thirty-five were fit for work, the soil being worn out too. Did the count sell Negroes? No, the Conde was in debt; he did not sell any hands off, but he bought no new ones.[82] At least one of the Montalvo estates, *La Holanda*, was in a similar bad state by the 1840s. One branch of the Calvos, on the other hand, were thriving international capitalists. By 1850 they owned a weekly steamship from Batabanó to the Isle of Pines; and by the 1870s Manuel Calvo was a financier of revolution in Spain itself. The O'Farrills, though in debt, were public benefactors, one member having given to the watering place of Madruga all its public buildings.

The second class of big planters in 1860 were the recent self-made immigrants, men without *hidalguía*: the Aldama brothers; Tomás Terry; José Baró; Julián Zulueta; the Diagos; Wenceslao Villa-urrutia; the de la Torrientes; Justo Germán Cantero; the Apezteguías at *Constancia;* and Alvaro Reynoso, the writer. It is appropriate to refer to them as a separate class from the Pedrosos, Montalvos and their cousins since, until the end of the century, there are almost no instances of these newcomers marrying into older and nobler families.[83] These families might in fact own several mills and several thousand acres – thus Zulueta had three mills, all close together and 10,000 acres, and the Aldamas had five mills (two shared). But they were not pluralists on the indiscriminate or wasteful scale of the Cárdenases. The Diagos, with their nephew Joaquín de Ayesterán, had four mills, all large, modern and important.

The most productive mill of all, however, was the Spanish queen mother's *San Martín*, with 1,000 acres, employing 800 slaves and alone producing 2,670 tons a year; and her company also owned the mill with the most land, *Santa Susana* in the south, with 6,000 acres. Very slightly larger though less productive than *San Martín* was the Herreras' *Sansom y Unión* – also over 6,000 acres.[84] In comparison the biggest Jamaican plantation in the golden days of that island, belonging to Philip

[81] *Sacroacia*, as they are called by Moreno Fraginals. See genealogy in Appendix I of this work.
[82] Madden, 167.
[83] This seems to be so after an analysis of the genealogies in García Carraffa's monumental work.
[84] See Cantero for a study of the biggest sugar mills of the mid-century, and J. Pérez de la Riva, '*Riesgo y ventura de San Martín*', Revista de la Biblioteca Nacional, June 1967.

Pittucks, had been a mere 2,900 acres large, had employed 280 slaves and produced only 184 tons of sugar a year.

The immigrants' mills were in general the sites of technological innovation. It was on their mills that were first seen Derosne's and Rillieux's great machines. Miguel Aldama at *Concepción* made use of a U.S. steam plough, though this was not a profitable venture. Socially, people like Zulueta and Aldama were on the other hand already jumping into the ranks of the oligarchy; already Miguel Aldama had refused a marquesate (offered to keep him from plotting) though Zulueta later received one. Within a generation, none would distinguish between a Zulueta and an O'Farrill, just as, a hundred years before, the O'Farrills and Arangos came to be accepted by the Montalvos and Calvos. Some vague stigma seems to have attached socially to men who had made fortunes through the slave trade; thus when Joaquín Gómez was blinded by a deranged doctor who threw vitriol in his face when leaving church, it was said that it was an act of God.[85] But all still bought slaves if they could: people were easily able to make moral distinctions between men who lived off selling slaves and those who bought them to live.

In the 1850s mills were beginning to be owned by companies rather than individuals. The queen mother here led the way since after the death of her agent in Cuba, Antonio Parejo, her interests were grouped together as *La Gran Azucarera* with a number of other prominent shareholders from Spain such as Atilano Colomé and the Conde Ibáñez.[86] Scarcely less important was La Compañía Territorial Cubana owned by the firm of Noriega Olmo & Co. of Havana and Barcelona. Analysis of the ownership of the most technologically advanced mills shows that only two of the ten most productive belonged to members of the old oligarchy, and perhaps only fifteen out of the first fifty-five belonged to that class. Peninsulares, of the first or second generations (Zulueta, Diago, Arrieta, Baró, Poey, Forcade) dominate the list, along with the queen mother María Cristina through *La Gran Azucarera*. Men whose fortunes derived in the recent past from slave trading are also well up in the list; if *La Gran Azucarera* is counted within that category, as it should be, five out of the first ten most productive sugar mills can be described as being built on slave fortunes.[87]

In the 1850s the planters were freed from their last inconvenient legal encumbrance. For years the sixteenth century provision that sugar mills could not be attached for debt had actually been an inconvenience

[85] Tacón *Correspondencia*, ed. Pérez de la Riva. See Philalethes, *Letters from Havana*, for another version of this.

[86] See Juan Pérez de la Riva, *'Riesgo y ventura de San Martín'* in Revista de la Biblioteca Nacional, June 1967.

[87] This excludes Lorenzo Pedro, the origins of whose fortune is as yet unknown to me. A list of those mills with Derosne or Rillieux machines in 1860 can be seen in the key to the map on p. 138.

to planters since it sent up the rate of interest for loans. Hence in 1852 all new mills became subject to the ordinary law, a revision which made loans easier to come by. After 1865 even old mills were able to be attached. This also had the consequence of stimulating a sensation of economy among the planters, who before had been notable for their great dissipation. The immense wealth of many Cubans on the other hand was beginning to have consequences for Spain itself. Rich men from Cuba – or, at least, men who had made money out of Cuba – more and more influenced the economic and even the political development of Spain. Thus Juan Güell y Ferrer invested his Cuban fortune in Catalan cotton manufacture and became the first Catalan industrialist to take a title; Pablo de Espalza, first president of the Banco de Bilbao (founded in 1857 with a capital of eight million pesetas) had made his fortune in Cuba as adviser of the friend of the royal family, Antonio López, Marqués de Comillas, himself a self-made Spanish millionaire from the carrying trade to Cuba; Manuel Calvo of the famous Calvos de la Puerta helped finance the election of King Amadeo in 1870; the greatest fortune in Spain in the early nineteenth century was that of Xifré who made his money originally in the Cuban trade; while captain-general after captain-general would return to the poor peninsula with his pockets well enough lined from bribes to embark on well-financed political careers.

CHAPTER XII

The Slave Merchants

'Ebony', or 'sacks of coal', or simply 'bales' (*bultos*), as slaves were now described by those who sold them, partly in jest, partly in order to defeat the moralistic English, were still wholly bought directly by planters from merchants (*negreros*), who specialized in the trade. Sometimes, as in Liverpool or Nantes in the past, the slave voyage from Havana would be a joint stock enterprise, with numerous shareholders, some shares worth as little as $100.[1] On the African side of the Atlantic, most of the dealings were through factors residing permanently there and professionally occupied with the problems of dealing with African kings. Journeys were now usually direct trips to and from Africa, though sometimes North America came into the route. Often the ships were built in North America and often the insurance for the voyage was raised in New York. Occasionally ships were fitted out at, and returned to, Cádiz. Most merchants of Havana had Spanish connections: indeed, the biggest of them had almost always in the nineteenth century started life in Spain, being usually regarded and regarding themselves as members of the Spanish section of the Havana community: *negrero* was even a slang word for a peninsular Spaniard in the 1870s.[2]

About twenty important Havana merchants had now almost completely displaced foreigners in the traffic in slaves. The biggest slave merchant in the 1830s was probably Joaquín Gómez, a native of Cádiz, co-founder of the first bank in Havana, an anti-clerical and freemason whose masonic name was 'Aristides the Just' and who 'arrived at Havana – about the age of thirteen or fourteen years old, almost naked'; he was the first importer of horizontal sugar mills with iron rollers from Fawcett and Preston of England in 1830 and bought several productive *cafetales* and sugar mills himself.[3] After him came Manuel Cardozo, a Portuguese, and Francisco Marty y Torrens and Manuel Pastor, both Spaniards of great riches, the former a retired bandit, both later associated with Antonio Parejo and the Spanish queen mother in slave traffic in the 1840s and 1850s on the very largest scale, in fast steamers (Pastor later became a count, his heirs became bankers in Madrid and

[1] In 1821, *P.P.* (1822), *Accounts and Papers*, XXII, 540–1.
[2] See Gallenga, 87.
[3] Moreno Fraginals, 107; see also Philalethes, *Letters from the Havana*, 62.

another generation established a munificent foundation from the remaining millions). There were also Pedro Forcade, of French origin and his partner Antonio Font, both of whom soon appear, like nearly all their predecessors, in lists of sugar planters (Forcade founded *Porvenir*, near Colón, Font *Caridad*, near Cienfuegos). Forcade apparently had both English capital and some English partners.[4] Darthez and Brothers

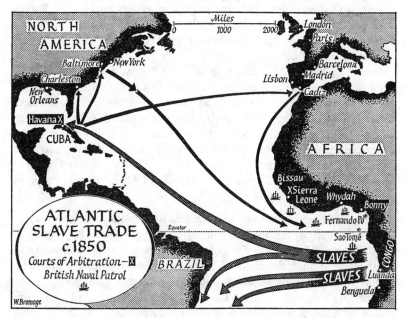

of London had a Havana representative, with exclusive concern with slaving. Cunha Reis, slavers of New York, had a Havana man. Pedro Martínez of Cádiz was also represented in Havana, sometimes by himself. Another firm established on both sides of the Atlantic was Pedro Blanco and Carballo, of whom Blanco, a native of Málaga, at first a captain of slave ships, lived near the Gallinas lagoon with a large harem and many luxuries,[5] and later retired in 1839 to Barcelona with over $M4, where he became a major figure on the Stock Exchange.[6] Others active were Julián Zulueta, also with a London connection in the person of his cousin Pedro, though by 1840 this skilful Basque entrepreneur had become a planter and local grandee; and José Baró, a man

[4] Turnbull, 312.

[5] Theodore Canot, *Revelations of a Slave Trader or Twenty Years Adventures of Captain Canot* (1954), 115; *cf. Parliamentary Papers*, XXIX, 349, where he is captain of the *Barbarita*, and *ibid.*, 358, where he stayed at Gallinas; *ibid.* (1828), XXVI, *Correspondence with British Commissionaries*, 128, shows him as captain of the *Hermosa Dolorita*.

[6] He figures in Texidó's novel in the style of Eugene Süe, *Barcelona y sus misterios* and in Lino Nová's Calvo's fictionalised biography, *Pedro Blanco, el negrero* (Buenos Aires, 1941)

of much the same origin and position as Zulueta who in addition to his mills and his slave ships controlled the supply, manufacture and repair of moulds for use in sugar manufacture.[7] Ships could still be built in Liverpool for Havana merchant houses. Portuguese traders were still very large importers of slaves into Brazil, and also often sold to Havana: in 1837 the English Consul, David Turnbull, calculated that out of seventy-one slave ships operating on Cuban coasts, forty were Portuguese, nineteen Spanish, eleven U.S. and one Swedish;[8] in 1820–1, eighteen had been Spanish, five French, two Portuguese and one U.S. – if flags were to be believed.[9]

However, exact nationalities should not be considered too closely. Because of the international interference by the English, ships sailed under several flags. We hear, for instance, that the ship *Fanny* cleared out of Santiago de Cuba in 1827 under Dutch colours; on her arrival at Calabar she raised a French flag; she sailed back to the Americas with 238 slaves under that flag but she would have hoisted a new Dutch flag had the pursuing English frigate turned out to be French.[10] One instruction from Blanco and Carballo of Cádiz to their captain sailing for Africa ran thus:

> From the moment that you sail and lose sight of the Morro, you must use no other papers but Portuguese, unless you should be obliged to put into any of the ports of the island [of Cuba], in which case you will make use of Spanish papers. Your route to the coast of Africa must be that which you think the safest; you will touch in going at the Gallinas; there you will see Don Pablo Alvarez; you will hear from him if he will give you the cargo for the merchandise which you will carry, which cargo must be from 200 [slaves] upwards; and the said Pablo ought also to provide provisions for them ... Should you at last not be able to arrange the business you will set sail without losing a moment and continue your voyage towards the south, where you will settle the matter according to circumstances, taking care to visit the points of Loanda, Ambriz and all other trading places throughout the Congo.[11]

This instruction also makes clear that now as ever the slaves brought over in the mid-nineteenth century derived from all parts of Africa, and that rather more may have come from the Congo than is sometimes imagined. Few of the Cuban slaves came from the old Gold Coast, the preferred slaving ground of the previous century; the river Bonny was

[7] Moreno Fraginals, 123.
[8] Turnbull, 456.
[9] *P.P.* (1822), XXII, 540–1.
[10] *Ibid.* (1827), 225.
[11] Turnbull, 425–6.

the slave centre in the 1820s, Gallinas or Dahomey in the 1830s. The Guinea centre had shifted north towards the Río Pongo, the Gallinas lagoon and the river Sulima – all in the Senegal-Gambia region.[12] A list of merchandise in the slave ship *L'Oiseau*, a French vessel leaving Guadeloupe for Africa in 1825, shows 220 muskets as the largest single item out of a total of $8,600 worth of goods.[13]

The most important slave dealers on the other side of the Atlantic in Africa (some also dealt in 'legitimate trade' such as palm oil) were Antoine Léger, a French-born nationalized Portuguese, active in the Cape Verde Islands in the 1820s,[14] 'Dos Amigos' of Lagos, Caefano Nozzolino at the Cape Verde Islands, Pablo Frexas at Brass on the Niger Delta,[15] Louis Seminaire at Gallinas, Pedro Blanco when he was at Gallinas, but above all the scarcely credible figure of the Portuguese mulatto, Francisco Félix Da Souza, active from the 1820s to the late 1840s.[16] Da Souza, after starting life apparently in Cuba,[17] was for a time commander of the Portuguese fort at Whydah. After working for some time as a slaver on his own account, he gained a monopoly of slave exports from Ghezo, king of Dahomey, the monster of West Africa whose income from his export tax on slaves amounted in 1849 alone to £300,000 ($1,300,000). His slaves were guarded by a powerful force of Amazons, wearing war caps made in Manchester. With Da Souza's financial help, Ghezo built up a military suzerainty over the old Slave Coast between 1818 and 1858.[18] Da Souza's funeral rites at Whydah in 1849 lasted six months, during which time King Ghezo in honour of his old friend enthusiastically had a boy and a girl beheaded and three men burned alive. (But Da Souza died much in debt.) The forty Portuguese ships for instance which arrived in Havana in 1837 no doubt carried Da Souza's slaves – probably in all over 12,000 slaves that year.[19] Most of Da Souza's exports, of course, went to Brazil. Scarcely less important in the slave trade to Brazil was Diego Martínez of Lagos, originally a protégé of Da Souza's who flourished in the late 1840s and in reality succeeded Da Souza, despite the survival of the latter's sons in the coast till 1858–60.[20] Both these men lived in a style of unbridled luxury, their hospitality to all save the English being legendary along the coast.

---

[12] Dow, *Slaves, Ships and Slaving*, 15. See also the maps and diagrams derived from Koelle's enquiry into the tribal origins of Sierra Leone Africans in *Journal of African History*, V (1964), No. 2, 185–208.

[13] *P.P.* (1826), 225. See Appendix, VI, for full list.

[14] *Papers on the Slave Trade* (1826), XXIX, 309.

[15] K. Onwuka Dike, *Trade and Politics in the Niger Delta, 1830–1885* (1956), 52.

[16] *Cf. Accounts and Papers* (1826–7), XXVI, 147.

[17] Dow, 252.

[18] See Newbury, *The Western Slave Coast and its Rulers*, 37.

[19] Turnbull, 154, i.e. at 300 slaves per ship (Consul Tolmé's reckoning).

[20] See David Moses, 'Diego Martínez in the Bight of Benin', *Journal of African History*, VI (1965), 79–90.

The European or mulatto factors on the coast of Africa were, of course, only the last stations in an immense organization. Europeans had never been permitted by African rulers to go far beyond the coast and, since they were interested in commerce (even if commerce in men), not conquest, this had suited them. Perhaps many slave traders of Liverpool or Cádiz genuinely knew nothing of the complicated arrangements of which they were the final, but by no means the only benefactors: thus in the region of the Niger delta a large trading organization was run by a branch of the Ibos, the Aros, whose influence was based on the Aro Chukwu Oracle, everywhere respected and feared in East Nigeria. The Aros exploited these feelings in order to dominate the economic life of the region and they became the sole middlemen of the hinterland trade, by establishing colonies along the trade routes. Other tribes came to believe that this monopoly was divinely appointed and in addition accepted Aro judicial and political arrangements. The consequence was that the Aros sold most of the slaves at Bonny, which in the 1820s was the most prominent slave port of West Africa; and that the slaves were captured by means of oracular devices. For instance, the oracle levied fines of slaves on certain communities and groups; these groups believed that the oracle would eat them; whereas in fact the Aros sold them to Da Souza or Diego Martínez and other factors on the coast.[21] It might also be added that, bloody though the journey in the Middle Passage certainly was, it was shorter as a rule and perhaps often less intolerable than the journeys from the interior of Africa to the coast, often on foot, often by river, and organized by Africans.[22] Another prominent slave trading race were the tiny tribe of Efiks of old Calabar, who also enslaved those of their own people who were guilty of adultery or theft and whose descendants in Cuba founded the most persistent of the Cuban sacred cults, the Abakuá.[23]

Many professional slave merchants in the nineteenth century were semi-gangsters like Mungo John (alias John Ormond), the half-caste ex-Liverpool slave-trader of the Río Pongo,[24] Pedro Blanco himself, or Theodore Canot, a half-Italian, half-French sailor who described how his first view of the slave ships in Havana harbour dazzled him: 'These dashing slavers, with their arrowy hulls and raking masts, got complete possession of my fancy'.[25] Some captains combined slaving with piracy.

[21] Dike, *Trade and Politics in the Niger Delta*, 156.

[22] See Summary in Elkins, *Slavery*, 99.

[23] See below, 521. For the Efiks, see C. Daryll Forde, ed., *Efik Traders of Old Calabar* (1956), in which is included Antera Duke's diary for 1785-8, one of the most extraordinary documents preserved from pre-colonial Africa.

[24] Father and son, John Ormond dominated the Río Pongo for two generations; see C. Fyfe, *A History of Sierra Leone* (1962), 66, 185.

[25] Canot, *Captain Canot*, 50.

Baltimore or New York-made clippers were usually too fast to be easily caught by the British naval vessels, heavily loaded as they were with food and armaments.[26] With these new clippers it was possible to cross the Atlantic several times a year. Joseph Gurney, visiting Cuba in 1841, was told that nine tenths of the vessels employed in the Cuban slave trade were built in North America.[27] The trade increasingly relied indeed on U.S. shipbuilders and U.S. capital, and there was no prosecution at any time under the U.S.'s own anti-slave trade laws. It was this continuing U.S. trade that really prevented English action from being effective, though U.S. ships sailed under several flags, constantly changing to suit circumstances (even some French men fitting out ships in Baltimore).[28] The Brazilian slave merchants, though condemned by the English Consul as 'twenty to thirty men, principally adventurers of foreign extraction of the basest class – the worst pariahs of the human race' – were far the largest capitalists in the country. Much the same comment could have been made in respect of Havana except that the North American connection was stronger.

Few instances are recorded of English ships engaging in the trade in the mid-century though in 1826 the master of an English palm oil ship the *Matta* was nevertheless found guilty of selling four female Negroes to a Spanish captain in the old Calabar river.[29] Occasionally, someone under English protection might also do some selling.[30] English half-castes such as the Ormonds, Fabers and Skeltons, were active, however, on the West African coast as was Mrs Lightburn, half-African, half-North American.[31] Because of the number of U.S. ships anyway in Brazilian waters, sometimes with 'double papers, double captains and a double flag', the Royal Navy had a far more delicate task in stopping them.[32] Slaves were even taken on board Spanish mail vessels, according to one English commander.[33] But most English officers assumed that about half the slave trade to Cuba was, during the 1850s at least, in U.S. hands, an adjunct of the still grandiose slave trade to Texas and the U.S. south (perhaps 300,000 slaves were brought into the U.S. south between 1808 and 1860).[34] A number of them came from Cuba, even though the

[26] C. Lloyd, *The Navy and the Slave Trade* (1949), 34. These were usually 300 tons, averaging 100 feet long, with a crew of 40.

[27] J. J. Gurney, *A Winter in the West Indies* (1840), 213. J. J. Gurney (1788–1847) was a philanthropist and the brother of Elizabeth Fry.

[28] *Cf.* the case of the *Guadeloupe* (*P.P.* (1826), XXI, 551).

[29] *Ibid.*, *Accounts and Papers* (1828), XXVI, 91.

[30] Fyfe, *Sierra Leone*, 225.

[31] *Ibid.*, 100.

[32] Turnbull, 459. The navy's role is considered in Chapter XVI.

[33] *P.P.* (1852–3), XXXIX, 8.

[34] W. E. B. du Bois, *The Suppression of the African Slave Trade to the United States of America, 1638–1870*, vol. 1 (1896), 178; Soulsby 169. For figures, see *ibid.*, 110–12; also *cf.* Mathieson, 138.

figure may not have been as high as the 15,000 a year estimated by the Dutch Consul-General in Havana, Mr Lobé.[35]

Despite the continuance of the slave trade in Cuba, the situation was nevertheless slowly changing; thus by 1840 it was already impossible to insure slave ships in Havana since the two main insurance companies (*Compañía de Seguros Marítimos* and *Especulación*), which had begun business almost exclusively with slavers, found that the risks were too great, despite premiums varying from 25% to 40%. But U.S. insurance continued on these ships, at only $2\frac{1}{2}$% (it was no doubt mainly for that reason that the Havana firms went out of business), and Brazilian ships at a higher rate, though less than Cuban.[36]

There were of course still insurrections on slave ships, as in the eighteenth century and before. The best known was that of the slave cargo belonging to two planters of Puerto Príncipe, José Ruiz and Pedro Mantes, which was being carried along the Cuban coast on the Havana vessel *Amistad* in very bad weather. The Spanish mulatto cook told the slaves (pointing to some barrels of beef and then to an empty barrel) that on arrival at Puerto Príncipe they would be chopped up and made into salt meat. One master spirit among the slaves (all bozals from different tribes near Sierra Leone) named Cingues, therefore, led a revolt, broke the slaves' irons and, after throwing captain and crew overboard, directed Ruiz and Mantes (who had once himself been a sea captain) to sail to Africa, always towards the rising sun. But Ruiz and Mantes secured that they sailed out of course at night so that, after two months, with water and food short, they landed in the U.S. near New York. There the Negroes were accused of piracy and murder, while the Spaniards demanded the return of their property. The question was complicated by the fact that there were three little girls and one small boy (*mulecón*) among the slaves, against whom a plaint of piracy could not legally be preferred. Eventually the slaves were acquitted and thirty-five (out of an original fifty-three, the rest having died) sent to Sierra Leone by friends of the anti-slavery cause.[37]

Such accounts of the slave ships as exist suggest that profits remained high and that still, if one ship out of three or four came home, the owners would be in pocket. Thus the *Firme*, captured at Havana with 484 slaves in 1829, had been financed as follows:[38]

[35] Turnbull, 149.

[36] *Ibid.*, 463. Private underwriters still guaranteed Havana slavers at between 33% and 36% (Madden, 33). As the ships were often U.S. owned and U.S. built it is natural that they should have been underwritten there.

[37] Madden, 228–41; see also Fyfe, *Sierra Leone*, 222–3. Richard Robert Madden (1798–1886), magistrate appointed to supervise abolition of slavery in Jamaica 1833–41; superintendent of Liberated Africans and judge arbitrator in Mixed Court, Havana, 1836–40; afterwards Colonial Secretary of Western Australia.

[38] *Parl. Report* (1829), Class A, 115.

EXPENSES	COSTS	SLAVES	TOTAL
Outward cargo for slave purchase ($\frac{1}{2}$ in coin, $\frac{1}{2}$ in spirits, gunpowder, calicoes, handkerchiefs)	$28,000	484 slaves sold at Havana @ $300[39] a head	$145,200
16 able seamen at $40 a month			
20 ordinary seamen at $35 a month			
Vessel 10 months absent, and wages if capture had been avoided would have been	$13,400		
Wear and tear of voyage	$10,600		
Deduct expenses	$52,000		$52,000
		Net profit on voyage	$93,200

There is no evidence to suggest that mortality *en passage* had lessened in the nineteenth century. Seventy-two slaves out of 258 died on the *Segunda María* (1825); 73 on the *Orestes* out of 285 (1826); 47 out of 300 on the *Campeador* (1826); 271 out of 562 on the *Midas* (1829); 680 out of 983 on the *Fama de Cádiz* (1829); 126 out of 348 on the *Cristina* (1829); 39 out of 144 on the *Santiago* (1830); 216 out of 422 on the *Umbelina* (1831).[40] All these were on boats captured by the English and afterwards condemned. There were now no clear regulations for carrying slaves, as there had been in England during the legal period. The vessels were built, in Baltimore or elsewhere, to be as fast as possible and were driven, especially when chased, with the hatches closed down. If anything went wrong and the crew had to abandon ship, they would do so without providing for the slaves, and in most nineteenth-century memoirs of this business there is some such remark as 'I shall never forget the dreadful shriek of the panic-stricken blacks' in respect of some atrocious behaviour or other.[41] No doubt the sick as well as the dead were thrown overboard.[42] There are several instances of slaveships sinking,[43] while the macabre voyage of the *Rodeur* is perhaps symbolic of the whole trade in the nineteenth century. This was a French ship which sailed from the river Bonny to Guadeloupe in 1819: the captain, 'very good tempered, he drinks a lot of brandy', told a young planter's son his views on slave treatment: 'Flog them as well as feed them . . . of course not maim them . . . for then they would not work; but if you do not

---

[39] Lieut. Jackson 'just returned from the coast' told *The Times* (29 January 1849) that slaves cost a doubloon (£3 8s) only in Africa. Sir Thomas Buxton spoke of slaves costing £4 ($17) in 1838 (*The African Slave Trade* (1839), 57, fn.)

[40] Madden, qu. 48–9.

[41] Dow, 215, qu. Drake's memoir.

[42] M. M. Ballou, *Due South; or, Cuba past and present* (1885), 297.

[43] See list in Ortiz, *Negros Esclavos*, 151.

make them feel to the marrow, you might as well throw them into the sea.' The Negroes' howls at nights kept the boy awake. 'One day, one of the blacks whom they were forcing into the hold suddenly knocked down a sailor and attempted to leap overboard. He was caught, however, by the leg by another of the crew and the sailor, rising up in a passion, hamstrung him with a cutlass. The captain, seeing this, knocked the butcher flat upon the deck with a handspike. "I will teach you to keep your temper," he said with an oath, "he was the best slave of the lot!" I ran to the main chains and looked over; for they had dropped the black into the sea when they saw that he was useless. He continued to swim even after he had sunk under water, for I saw the red track extending shorewards, but by and by it stopped, widened, faded and I saw it no more.'

Later, there was a successful attempt by some Negroes to throw themselves overboard and, 'from the waves came what seemed ... a song of triumph' in which they were joined by their comrades on the deck. The captain then made an example of six slaves, shooting three and hanging three. After that, the Negroes were kept in the hold. Ophthalmia broke out and spread. Soon 'all the slaves and some of the crew are blind. The captain, the surgeon and the mate are blind. There is hardly enough men left out of our twenty-two, to work the ship'. Then a few days later, the boy noted 'All the crew are now blind but one man. The rest work under his orders like unconscious machines; the captain standing by with a thick rope ... yet had hopes of recovering his sight ... A guard was continually placed with drawn swords at the storeroom to prevent the men getting at the spirit casks ...'

Though it is hard to believe, the *Rodeur* was later nearly run down by another ship, the *San León* from Cádiz, bound for Havana, whose crew turned out to be entirely infected by ophthalmia. At this discovery, the crew of the *Rodeur* broke into macabre laughter, and the two ships drifted apart. Eventually some of the crew recovered. The captain lost an eye, but the other recovered. After being reminded that the cargo was fully insured, the captain threw the thirty-nine wholly blind slaves overboard and put in successfully to Guadeloupe.[44] Upon curious similar voyages was the Cuban economy for the first two-thirds of the nineteenth century essentially based; and it would seem that, with the activities of abolitionists, conditions got worse rather than better.

In the first period of illegal trade (1820–35), before the Royal Navy were entitled to check on the 'equipment' of the slave vessel, slavers bound to Cuba would usually land slaves somewhere on 'the back of the island'. The ship would then travel round empty to Havana and announce her arrival to the merchants by raising a red flag. The British

[44] Diary of the *Rodeur*, qu. Dow, xxvii–xxxv.

commissioner or Consul would then report the ship's arrival to the captain-general, who would gravely cause her to be inspected and then announce with satisfaction and injured innocence that there was no proof that the ship had been engaged in slaving. The merchants would meantime dispose of their slaves through factors. In 1836 the red flag was banned, but regulations were relaxed so much that slavers sometimes sailed straight into Havana itself after dark.[45]

The size of the financial interest involved in slaves suggests why the efforts of the English were defeated by the organization of planters, hand-in-glove with traders and officials. The Cuban coast line was long, the possibilities of fraud limitless. Illegal and legal slave trading (that is, internal traffic within the western hemisphere) were difficult to disentangle. But an immense catalogue of facts was collected by British consuls and commissionaries proving illegal trading. It was want of will on the Spaniards' part, not want of adequate information, that prevented them from effectively extinguishing the trade. The traders were helped by officials and even by U.S. Consul Trist – himself a failed planter – who in the 1830s enabled U.S. shipping papers to be quite easily available.[46]

Cotton was booming in the U.S. south, the conditions which had prevailed in 1808 and enabled Jefferson to agree to the abolition of the trade no longer prevailed and a U.S. official who connived at the slave trade had nothing to fear.[47] The Cuban slave trade was very busy in these years, Governor Maclean of Cape Coast estimating that three out of five slaves leaving the Gulf of Benin were bound for Cuba about 1834–5.[48]

The British Consul, Turnbull, who made courageous efforts to bring an end to the slave trade by public exposure, wrote in respect of 1838–9:

> As if to throw ridicule on the grave denials of all knowledge of the slave trade which are forced from successive captains-general by the unwearied denunciations of the British authorities, two extensive depots for the reception and sale of newly imported Africans have lately been erected at the further end of the Paseo, just under the windows of his Excellency's residence, the one capable of containing 1,000 and the other 1,500, slaves; and I may add, that these were

---

[45] *Cf.* accounts in *P.P.* (1826), XXX, 37. An interesting account of the landing of a slave ship is given by Ballou (*Due South*, 285ff.): how 'with a look of treacherous tranquillity the dark, low hull of a brigantine' would suddenly appear ... 'the rakish craft was of Baltimore build, and about 200 tons and narrowly escaped a French cruiser. The slaves were apparently Ashantis, the cargo reaching 350 of whom between 30 and 40 had died'.

[46] See below, 199.

[47] See report of British Consul at Cape Verde Island, 31 December 1838 (Class B, 1839, F.S., 110, qu. Buxton, 40).

[48] Buxton, 47.

constantly full during the greater part of the time that I remained in Havana. As the barracoon or depot serves the purpose of a market place as well as a prison these two have, doubtless for the sake of readier access and to save the expense of advertising in the journals, been placed at the point of greatest attraction, where the Paseo ends, where the grounds of the Captain-General begin, and where the new railroad passes into the interior, from the carriages of which the passengers are horrified at the unearthly shouts of the thoughtless inmates.[49]

These barracoons, kept by a certain Riera, were often thought to be the real showpieces of Havana, and were shown with pride to foreign visitors. They had taken the place of older barracoons which, lining what is now the Prado, had originally been built as barracks for the Spanish navy in 1781.[50]

The actual illegality of the trade in the nineteenth century caused it to assume some of the outward (as well as, in English eyes, the formal) characteristics of piracy. Thus one slave captain might be robbed of his slaves by another and recoup himself by pillaging a third.[51] Armed vessels might leave Havana and simply attack Portuguese slavers or even ordinary traders or, in one instance in 1825, a British brigantine escorting two prizes. A whole fleet of fast pirates was established at Galveston, Texas, in the 1820s.[52]

It is hard to imagine the manner in which, whatever the intolerable practices which occurred in Africa itself, the labour force of Cuba was dragged out of the dark continent into America, half tortured and in the general belief that numbers only mattered, there to be branded with iron.[53] The instances recorded, mostly deriving, of course, from accounts of English captures, leave no doubt at all that the Spanish slave trade in the nineteenth century, under whatever flag, was handled with at least as great brutality as at any previous time. The decisive factors in enabling it to survive in the nineteenth century were however African conditions themselves. The economy of that continent had been organized for so long for the slave trade that it was everywhere the staple item of trade; yet the English, for a hundred years the biggest shippers, had now changed their policy, and turned policeman. Slaves could therefore be bought for very little in an Africa whose economy was half shattered by English abolition – half the price payable in the 1780s; but they could be sold, due to the insatiable demands of Cuban

---

[49] Turnbull, 60.
[50] Ortiz, *Negros Esclavos*, 166.
[51] See Gurney, *A Winter in the West Indies* (1840).
[52] Mathieson, 25–6.
[53] See Ortiz, *Negros Esclavos*, 164–5, for a description.

and Brazilian planters, at a price several times that which obtained in the eighteenth century. The collapse in Africa and the conversion of what had hitherto been from the European point of view a respectable trade to semi-gangsterism was the most remarkable consequence of abolition.[54] But the worm was turning; and even Francisco Arango, who had done so much to initiate the trade in the 1790s, died as an old man in 1840 – with the title of Marqués de la Gratitud – writing a tract against the trade and encouraging his countrymen to procreate mulattoes in order to 'whiten' (*blanquear*) the island.

[54] See for instance Ward, *A History of Ghana*, 160. 'A heavy blow was struck at the economic system of the country. In 1807 the British Government abolished the slave trade . . . There existed a vast organisation of wholesale dealers, brokers, depots for the collection of slaves. The slave trade . . . was a trade in which the small man could share. The purchasing power of the people depended on it. Petty chiefs could sell into slavery people who lost their cases in their courts and could not pay . . . not only European, but African fortunes were founded on the slave trade'.

CHAPTER XIII

The Slaves

During the first half of the nineteenth century Cuba had always a black or mulatto majority. But this majority was never greater than a 60 % to 40 % balance – this being achieved about 1840; by the 1850s the Negro majority was slender and by 1859 the whites were officially at least in the lead. Such official statistics no doubt underestimate the real numbers of slaves but at least give a rough guide.[1]

These same figures suggest that in 1840 there were 280,000 male slaves, compared to 150,000 female, in 1855 220,000 males and 150,000 female; the difference between the sexes therefore fell from a little over 125,000 to 70,000.[2]

About a third of the slaves in Cuba worked on sugar plantations – 100,000 out of 300,000 being a likely figure for 1830, 150,000 out of 400,000 being likely for 1860.[3] In 1827, another third of the slaves may have been employed on prosperous coffee estates but by 1860 this proportion had dropped to about 3 %. Nevertheless, even then it would seem that well over three-quarters of the total slave population worked in the country in this or in some other employment; and such figures as are available show, as one would expect, very heavy slave concentrations in the Matanzas-Cárdenas-Colón triangle and in the Guanajay-San Diego area.[4]

The sugar industry naturally absorbed the activities of very many

[1] See figures in Ortiz, *Negros Esclavos*, 21.

[2] 281,250 to 155,245 in 1841, to be precise; 218,722 to 151,831 in 1855. Mulatto slaves ranked with Negroes. In 1841, 54,515 (20%) of the males and 44,483 (29%) of the females were under fifteen. 6,954 (2½%) of the male slaves and 2,434 (1½%) of the female slaves were over sixty. Thus 219,781 (78%) of the male slaves and 108,328 of the females (70%) were between sixteen and sixty or the most valuable class of slave. 28,808 slaves were said to have been married, or 9% of the total slaves over sixteen (337,495). These figures may have been exaggerated, or may have related only to those slaves married to non-slaves. Of course there were many other unions between men and women not ranked as marriages. There were 7,644 slaves officially ranked as widowed (as summarized in *Census of 1899*). The advantage of marriage by the Church, was that though expensive, legally wed wives and children were rarely separated from the husband – formally being forbidden to be.

[3] For 1827, Sagra has 70,000 out of 286,942 but this was based on official figures, universally regarded as an underestimate, in order to avoid the English Consul's earnest complaints. Similar errors have been taken into account to correct García de Arboleya's figure of 370,553 (120,000 in sugar) for 1859–61. See Table, p. 169 for García de Arboleya's figures, 90,000 were supposed to be in their prime and 30,000 either very young or very old, and valued, as previously indicated, at less than half the others.

[4] One series of figures for 1855 give 311,245 slaves in the country, 65,539 in the towns. (Erenchun, *Anales de la Isla de Cuba*, qu. Ortiz, *Negros Esclavos*, 306.)

OFFICIAL OR CONVENTIONAL FIGURES FOR SLAVES IN CUBA

	Male slaves	Female slaves	Male superiority of number over women
1774	28,771	15,562	13,209
1792	47,424	37,166	10,258
1817	124,324	74,821	49,503
1827	183,290	103,652	79,638
1841	281,250	155,245	126,005
1861	218,722	151,831	66,891

	Slaves in Cuba	In sugar plantations	Total population	Slaves as % of total population
1774	44,333		171,620	20
1792	84,590		272,301	25
1817	199,145		553,033	44
1827	286,942	70,000	704,487	42
1841	436,495		1,007,624	43·5
1861	370,553	120,000 (1859)	1,396,530	26·5

The British Consul Tolmé estimated the total slave population in 1838 as 360,000, and free Negro or mulatto people as 110,000, with a white population of 400,000, totalling 870,000 – a likely estimate (Turnbull, 151). The slave population of Jamaica was nearly 350,000 at its height, in 1817 and 1820.

* Sources: for 1774–1827, Sagra *Historia*; for 1841–61, Census of 1899; for 1859, García de la Arboleya, 140.

others besides those working on plantations. The rest remained in the cities or on coffee, tobacco or cattle estates, and those in the city often came by enough money to purchase freedom or the opportunity to escape in some other way. Indeed Negroes, slave or free, were in the eighteenth century already well established in a number of trades in Havana, Santiago, Guantánamo and other cities (laundering, carpentering, cigar-making, building and tailoring) where they would always remain prominent or perhaps dominant, even in the twentieth century.[5]

A substantial proportion of this large slave labour force was illegally obtained. The number of slaves introduced into Cuba in the forty-five years after 1820 may have exceeded 500,000:[6] the last slave reported

[5] Klein, 162–3, rightly emphasizes this.

[6] Aimes's estimate, however, was 200,000: the British Foreign Office and the navy together estimated that 360,000 slaves were imported into Spanish colonies between 1835 and 1864, mostly to Cuba (see tabulation in Lloyd, 275–6), which in view of the care with which such estimates were made and in default of better evidence than Aimes presents, I am inclined to accept; anyway, Aimes's figures are not always reliable, see above, 50 fn 34. The British commissioners estimated that 130,797 slaves were brought in between 1817 and 1827 (Turnbull, 150) and 122,500 between 1827 and 1837.

brought from Africa was in 1865–70.[7] The average price could never have been less than $450 and latterly reached $1,000;[8] a total illegal investment over half a century of $M100 (£M23) was thus likely. Rather more than half these new slaves were taken by the sugar plantations: towards the end of the era of slave import indeed, only sugar planters (and latterly only big sugar planters) could afford the high prices – $700 to $750 for a *bozal* in 1856, even higher ($1,250 to $1,500) in 1864. But there remained many slaves at work in minor manufacturing, such as shoes or tobacco, in Havana, and others working in small tobacco farms or on the large cattle estates; precisely how many or what percentage of the total it is hard to say.[9] Many of these worked on matters connected with ship building and sugar traffic.

Slavery in Cuba was also complicated by the fact that, because of the need for replacement of 8% to 10% each year, the end of the slave trade meant the end of slavery. Cuban experience was in this respect different from that in North America, where in 1808 (when the U.S. formally abolished the slave trade) there were already half a million quite well acclimatized slaves, some of them Americans of the second or third generation. There were, in addition to new illegal sales, also slave breeding farms in Virginia, described by their proprietors as 'another Africa' in the 1850s.[10] In Cuba there were perhaps 200,000 slaves when Spain formally banned the trade;[11] and of these the vast majority had entered Cuba in the preceding thirty years: perhaps as many as 75% were in fact African-born.[12] On top of these something between 200,000 and 300,000 were introduced, mostly from Africa, in the next generation or so. Few therefore were acclimatized and breeding was not easy. Children born to slaves were often neglected abominably, left without hygiene or even much maternal attention after the third day of birth, and infant mortality reached extraordinary numbers.[13] If they survived this experience slave children began to work at five or six years.

Few Cuban planters had foresight enough even for a breeding farm such as existed in Virginia – perhaps because the chief suppliers of capital were slave traders or had trade with them. Nevertheless, Tomás Terry of Cienfuegos and José Suárez Argudín at Bacuranao did experi-

[7] But see below, 235, for further discussion of this point.
[8] Analysis of Aimes's estimates; £100 or £230.
[9] See Klein, who bravely relies on the figures provided by García de la Arboleya, 186. But see Moreno Fraginals' comments.
[10] Broadus and Louis P. Mitchell, *American Economic History Review* (1947), 494–6. Captain Drake gives an account of a visit to a Virginia breeding farm: 'on a farm, near Alexandria, I counted 30 about to become mothers and the huts swarmed with pickaninnies of different shades' (qu. Dow, 240).
[11] Census of 1817 had 199,145.
[12] Aimes has 185,000.
[13] *Cf.* Moreno Fraginals, 157.

ment in this manner (the former being recognized as enlightened as well as rich), as did Esteban Santa Cruz de Oviedo at Trinidad.[14]

Work on a nineteenth-century sugar plantation was also such that only men could really carry it out – unlike that on a cotton plantation. Female labour had always fetched a lower price in Cuba than in the U.S. and mothers were sometimes sold away from their infants: thus Turnbull saw an advertisement for *'una nodriza de dos meses de parida, con su cría o sin ella'*.[15] Always, more males had been brought from Africa than females. The regulations of 1790, it will be recalled, had specifically provided for more men than women but these had soon been dropped. There was some homosexuality. It is also likely that the hard work in the sugar mills prevented breeding even where there was anything approaching a balance of numbers.[16]

Cuban slaves (unlike their fellows in the north) could still legally purchase their freedom by the old system of *coartación*.[17] Mothers could thus purchase the freedom of their unborn children for $25 (£6) and any babies between birth and baptism could be freed for $50 (£12). In the nineteenth century there were, however, comparatively few *coartados*. Slaves in their prime were generally valued at $500 (£120) in the 1830s or 1840s, a large sum for a slave to gather. Then, so many children died on sugar plantations – perhaps as many as 200 per 1,000 – that the mother's right to purchase a child's freedom often seemed scarcely worthwhile. Some slaves did gather money by doing extra work out of harvest, or by selling stolen goods to Catalan merchants, and so obtained at least the first down payment for freedom, but these resourceful slaves were naturally exceptional.[18] The right of *coartación* was also only now regularly observed in the towns and was usually ignored by *mayorales* on plantations: another reason for the popularity of slave assignments in towns. Here however Cuba still scored (because of pre-nineteenth century behaviour in this respect) in comparison with, say, the U.S.: in Virginia, in 1860–1 the Negro or mulatto freemen constituted only 11 % of the total population of African origin; in Cuba they constituted now 35 %, or over 200,000 covering between 14 % and 16 % of the total population.[19] Negroes in Cuba still could also become free men because their masters might free them believing it to be

---

[14] Cantero on the Ingenio *Trinidad* in his book.

[15] A nursing mother two months from the child's birth, with or without child.

[16] J. G. F. Wurdermann, *Notes on Cuba* (1844), 153.

[17] See above, 36.

[18] Aimes, 'Coartación', *Yale Review*, XVII (February 1909), argues that in the 1850s, 6.2% of the slave population embarked on this process each year or about 2,000 a year. Klein accepts this but I suspect that both underestimate the size of the slave population. To say as Aimes does that 'in character Spanish slave legislation was a continuation of that of the Divine Emperors' (*op. cit.*, 421) is grossly overdoing it.

[19] Klein, 312.

virtuous to do so in a way that North Americans appear not to have done; this, like *coartación*, was less frequent in the nineteenth century than in the eighteenth, as can be seen from the fact that, whereas in 1774 free men constituted 40 % of the black or mulatto population, between 1820 and 1840 the percentage fell to a mere 25 % with indeed an absolute fall in the number of free Negroes or mulattoes apparently being registered. *Coartación* was still however sufficiently frequent for it to be an occasional alternative to buying a slave or an *emancipado*: a *coartado* might be bought for, say $350 (£80), instead of a slave for $700 (£160) and therefore to hard pressed employers, always at their witts end for cash, an acceptable if in the long term uneconomic bargain.

| | Free People of Colour | | | |
| | Free Negroes | | Free mulattoes | |
	Male	Female	Male	Female
1774	5,951	5,689	10,210	9,006
1792	9,366	10,900	15,845	18,041
1817	28,373	26,003	30,512	29,170
1827	23,904	25,176	28,158	29,456

| | Total free Negro or mulatto | | Grand Total | Total population | Approx. total free Negro or mulatto as % of total population |
	Male	Female			
1774	16,161	14,695	30,856	171,620	17
1792	25,211	28,941	54,152	272,301	16
1817	58,885	55,173	114,058	553,033	21
1827	52,062	54,632	106,694	704,487	14·3
1841	75,703	77,135	152,838	1,007,624	15
1861	109,027	118,816	227,843	1,396,530	16

Once free there naturally remained other obstructions to equality but since the end of the eighteenth century it had been possible to dispense even of these by payment. Here the nineteenth century was an improvement on the previous one. Intelligent mulattoes could buy their way into the bureaucracy, the university, or even the professions, perhaps being allowed to regard themselves as white. Some priests undoubtedly had some black blood, while the nineteenth century saw the beginning of a whole school of Negro or mulatto poets and writers among whom Plácido (Gabriel de la Concepción Valdés) was pre-eminent.[20] On the other hand the percentage of freed Negroes in the army diminished in the nineteenth century because of the increased fears of Negro risings.

[20] Gabriel de la Concepción Valdés (1809–44), son of a mulatto barber and a Spanish girl from Burgos. Poet of Matanzas, executed in the Escalera conspiracy.

Any new slave could theoretically also become free if he was able to denounce to the international permanent tribunal at Havana the slave ship which had brought him. But this was difficult since the newly imported slaves (who usually knew no Spanish)[21] were kept in a state of virtual imprisonment from the moment they arrived in Havana. Local courts were naturally composed of slave owners, and could be easily bribed if that were necessary. Even so, the fear that ultimately Britain or a reforming government in Madrid might force Cuba to fulfil the treaty obligations and free all slaves imported since 1820 kept the planters in acute anxiety, almost as strong as their anxiety that the slaves would themselves stage a successful rebellion à la Haiti.

The extent to which white masters took Negro mistresses is not easy to disentangle: but all the evidence of rumour and hearsay suggest that it occurred on a lavish scale in both plantations and cities. The census figures for mulattoes (who must have mostly descended from one

	MULATTOES						
	Free (male)	*Free (female)*	*Slave (male)*	*Slave (female)*	*Total* *Male*	*Female*	*TOTAL*
1774	10,210	9,006	3,518	2,206	13,728	11,212	*24,940*
1792	15,845	18,041	5,769	10,900	25,614	24,941	*50,555*
1817	30,512	29,170	17,803	14,499	48,315	43,669	*91,984*
1827	28,158	29,456	....		not reckoned separately		
1841	43,396	44,396	5,868	5,106	49,264	49,502	*98,766*

irregular union or other – few between free Negroes and poor whites) suggest that: the two generations 1774–1841 showed a consistent increase over the first fifty years, almost doubling twice in just over forty years.[22] Consul Turnbull (like Major Gosham two generations before) describes a big house in Havana as being likely to be lived in by a very large number of mulattoes, in colour variations from near-white to near-ebony.[23] The substantial number of free mulattoes compared with the very low figures of mulatto slaves – nearly 6,000 in 1774, nearly 11,000 in 1841 – suggests that the majority of masters did indeed free their slaves if they were their own children. But always a number of mulattoes were the consequence of brief promiscuous relations between passing Spanish sailors or soldiers and Havana girls, between small shopkeepers from the Canaries and laundresses or fruit-sellers.

Cuba, as indeed so often in her history, was isolated from the rest of Spanish America in all these matters; the newly independent states of

[21] Though Madden (*op. cit.*, 240) testified in the *Amistad* case that slaves very quickly learnt Spanish and dropped their own language.

[22] 'White woman for marriage, mulatto woman for love, black woman for work' was a Brazilian saying.

[23] Turnbull, 53.

South America proclaimed abolition in the 1820s, since they had a plentiful supply of labour.

Slaves were the biggest single investment on all Cuban sugar plantations.[24] One can assume that in most cases they constituted about 30 % to 33 % of the cost. In 1829 slaves appear to have been just over 25 % of the total investment on plantations – $M24 out of $M80.[25] A *bozal* slave direct from Africa then cost $300 to $320 or $68 or so more than local slaves.[26] In 1846 the total value of slaves on 'a first-class mill' was over $100,000 or about a third of the total investment of $310,000 – these prices then varying between a maximum of $650 (£150) and $50 (£12) (for children).[27]

Mechanization caused the total numbers of slaves per plantation to be much smaller but their continued rise in cost increased the proportion of their value compared to other items. Even in 1859, when almost three-quarters of the plantations of Cuba had steam engines and fifty had Derosne or other vacuum boilers, the total estimate for buildings and machinery only amounted to about $M45, with slaves amounting to $M76·5;[28] on a comparatively large and modern plantation (three times the average size) in 1863, the value of the slaves was equal to that of the machinery and buildings combined ($105,000 (£24,500) each).[29] If a Derosne 'sugar machine' cost $60,000 (£14,000), the same sum could buy about 100 slaves. In 1859, the total slave population of sugar estates was estimated as being worth $76,500,000 (£17,900,000) or not far off 40 % of the total investment in sugar mills of $M185 (£M43).[30]

Slaves on sugar plantations worked unbelievably hard during the six months' harvest, perhaps sleeping only four hours a day. This method of using labour derived from the illusion, first, that kettles and sugar pans ought never to be allowed to cool from beginning to end of the harvest and, second, that 'four hours' sleep is sufficient for a slave'. There is too much evidence to suppose that these figures are exaggerated. At *La Lima*

[24] On a new mill in 1800 a modest estimate made them worth $27,000 (300 slaves @ $90 each, though never after 1763 were full grown slaves so cheap) or a quarter of the total cost of the farm ($94,000), slightly more than either the land (50 cabs @ $500 each, or $25,000), and the animals ($26,000) (Humboldt's estimate).

[25] Sagra's estimate, revised to take into account the probable cost of land and slaves ($1,000 (£230) per cab; $350 each slave (£82), instead of $1,500 (£350) and $300 (£70)).

[26] Turnbull, 65 ($70 to $75 or £16).

[27] McCulloch.

[28] García de Arboleya, 140.

[29] Pezuela, *loc. cit.*

[30] García de Arboleya, 140 (in 1859), speaks of 90,000 slaves @ $750 (£175) and 30,000 young or very old slaves @ $300 (£70). The figure was apparently much the same in 1863 when on a largish estate producing 1,158 tons a year, with a total investment of about $350,000 (£82,000), 150 slaves were valued @ $700 (£162) each, or $105,000 (£24,500). Two insurance companies (Morales's *La Protectora* and Miguel Embil's *La Providencia*) insured the lives of a certain number of slaves for $M14 (Ortiz, *Negros Esclavos*, 302).

mill six hours' sleep was allowed, but described as a most philanthropic system.[31] 'Out of crop time' slaves usually assembled at 3 a.m., sometimes at 2 a.m. with an Ave Maria. They would then be employed cleaning the workhouse or courtyards for an hour and a half. Then, with the ringing of another bell, they would go to the fields to work till noon, when they would have an hour for dinner (jerked beef and plantains, six to eight ounces of the first, three of the latter). From one to eight o'clock they worked again in the fields, finishing by cutting and carrying grass for cattle. They would go to their barracoons or huts at about 8.30 p.m. But on 'bad estates' these hours would be exceeded, even out of harvest.

Harvest lasted five or six out of twelve months. The slaves would be divided into gangs and put to work twenty-five at a time. Those who began at 8 p.m. continued till 12 p.m. at the mill. They then slept till 4 a.m. when they would be sent to the field where they would cut cane all day till 8 p.m. when perhaps they might go to the mill tavern and drink cane brandy. A tenth of the slaves would probably be at work in the boiling house, and their rota there would vary.[32] One visitor describes how he heard the 'cane-crushing machine grinding and groaning till two or three o'clock after midnight.'[33] (The autobiography of the slave Montejo suggests that hours of work by slaves were probably better in the 1860s than they had been in the 1840s.)[34] An American observer who probably favoured slavery estimated that 10% of slaves died during the harvest before the appearance of the steam mills.[35] Similar hours were clearly worked on French or on Jamaican plantations in the eighteenth century. On the other hand, it is evident that some slaves during the harvest could idle away some of the time; and the digging of one hundred small holes was a full day's work during the planting season, which does not indicate overwhelming labour.

As well as deaths from sheer overwork, there were many accidents: sometimes in the middle of manufacture there would come a terrible cry, the oxen would halt and a mangled African (who had perhaps fallen asleep) would be drawn out of the machinery or out of a stream of boiling sugar. Epidemics were often very serious – in particular yellow fever (*vómito negro*) and occasionally cholera. There were also severe punishments: the stocks were constantly used (Madden and Turnbull

[31] Landa, *El administrador de ingenio*, ch. 8, qu. Moreno Fraginals, 167.
[32] All this from Madden, 174–6.
[33] Gallenga, 127.
[34] Montejo, 24.
[35] Wurdermann, 153. Turnbull's estimate was 10% a year in 1839–40 based on discussion with *mayorales* (*op. cit.*, 150). For Jamaica, see Orlando Patterson, *Sociology and Slavery* (1965), 66–9.

met two Negroes and a mulatto boy who had spent the nights in the stocks for two months at the Montalvo estate, *La Holanda*, near Güines). Slaves were sometimes killed by their masters for quite trivial offences: Juan Sarriá, for instance, founder of the *Soledad* mill (Cienfuegos) killed a slave waitress simply because he was impatient to be served.[36] Philip Drake (not of the merchant family) says his wife beat a slave to death about 1820.[37] One North American woman long resident in Havana had a girl slave murdered out of jealousy by being chained to a wall.[38] A well-known Havana lawyer named Machado had a slave flogged to death for suspected theft.[39] Such people would with the help of bribes escape scot-free in Cuba though this was not invariably the case in English colonies where there are two instances of planters who killed slaves being executed.[40] But in general to kill a Negro did not seem a crime, even if he were free: a Spanish civil guard might hang a number of Negroes himself if he suspected them of stealing.[41] A *mayoral* might flog a slave to death and, thanks to the general refusal to bring any white man into trouble because of a dead Negro, escape all blame. The normal punishment for slaves was of course some variety or other of flogging.[42] In Havana there was a special building just outside the old gates of the city to which town slaves might be sent to be whipped – sometimes they seem to have been in fact sent regularly, month by month, to keep them subservient.[43] There can too be no doubt that slaves on efficient modern plantations with steam-driven mills were treated more inhumanely than those on the old oxen-driven mills: they were confined to menial and manual labour; and they were regarded and treated as economic rather than human units; hence the greater number of slave revolts on large and rich mills.

The slaves, in these circumstances, would attempt to revenge themselves on their masters, by various charms in which it would seem they believed completely.[44] Slaves on plantations were also supposed to be allowed a leave of absence of four days once in twelve months if they wished to seek a new master. Since owners did not like discontented slaves, this rule was quite often fulfilled. But if the request under the letter of the law was made to a *mayoral*, the slave would be more

[36] Atkins, 91.
[37] Dow, 234.
[38] Madden, 152–3. Orlando Patterson (*Sociology and Slavery*, 58) says 'white women in the slave colonies tended to be more sadistic than their male counterparts'.
[39] Madden, 147.
[40] In 1776 and 1811 in Tobago and Tortola, see Deerr, 351.
[41] *Ibid.*, 92.
[42] Ortiz, *Negros Esclavos*, 247, makes his usual exhaustive classification.
[43] Turnbull, 278–9; Madden, 149–50. This was at *La Holanda*, Güines.
[44] Montejo, 26, describes a sacred pot into which earth was put and while it was inside it was supposed to keep a master ill. For an argument that Cuban punishments were less severe than elsewhere in the Antilles, see Ortiz, *Negros Esclavos*, 262ff.

likely to be flogged. Most slaves in fact would not set out on this project till they had by hook or by crook found a new master.[45]

In different sugar mills different recollections of African religion would survive, sometimes Yoruba, sometimes Congolese, depending on which was the dominant influence at the time; so that a survey of mills would have presented a baffling anthropological confusion, ceremonials, dances, games all blending with snatches of Catholicism under whose auspices all was supposed to take place: thus the slave Montejo gives a picture of the *mayombé* cult at the *Flor de Sagua* plantation (in the 1860s and 1870s) in which white overseers joined.[46] Such fiestas, for such they became, customarily occurred on Sundays and indeed in and out of harvest, Sunday was a day of drinking, love, drumming and dancing, dressing up and washing. African magic also survived in different forms, the overseers treating *mayombero* African medicine men with great care and consideration and permitting them access to sacred thickets or trees around the plantations.[47] In the course of all these changes the slaves naturally created, alongside their memories of Africa, a folklore of the plantation, with new songs and dances which were specifically Negro Cuban (or Negro American) manifestations and in no way African any more.

The main pleasure was of course dancing, and here the variety was enormous; there were the loud drum dances which were sometimes used to pass revolutionary messages to slaves in next-door plantations and were accordingly sometimes banned; the *tumba*, an eastern Cuban parody of the minuet from Saint Domingue of which the novelist Bacardí gives a good picture in his novel *Via Crucis*:

> 'Master the tumba is going to begin',
> '*Bueno*, let it begin; let's go there'.

The coffee threshing room had been converted into a dance hall. The cutting tables had been dismantled, already placed against the walls, and against them were placed benches full of girls. On a species of dais, 'the king and queen', elected by the slaves; a little further down the master of ceremonies; next to them men and women fitted out with various hierarchical titles and in the rest of the room, fairly large in size, were spread out almost the entire personnel [of the *cafetal*] ...

---

[45] *Ibid.*, 218. See Madden, 122–3. However, Ortiz, *Negros Esclavos*, 177, publishes an advertisement in *El Siglo (Havana)* of 1865 describing a slave to be sold at his own request.

[46] *Mayombé* (Bantu in origin) eventually became generally subordinate to Yamamba. Its principal deities were (and are) Sarabanda (identified with St Peter), the Mother of Waters (Our Lady of Charity), Kisimba (the same as St Francis). See Lachatañeré, *Rasgos bantú en la Santería, Les Amériques Noires*, 181–3, qu. Bastide, 118. This religion consisted of a pact (or a dialogue) with the dead and since bodies lay in cemeteries and in trees, *mayomberos* divided their time between cemeteries and woods.

[47] Montejo, 141.

On one side the musicians with their *drums* and *chachás*;[48] on the other,
the Negresses with their pairs of *maracas*[49], beating with them the time
of the music and the songs. Some palm leaves, a Spanish flag and a
French one, both discoloured and various little lanterns of yellow wax,
were the decorations . . . 'the king and queen' occupied leather chairs,
the master of ceremonies a similar one but smaller . . .

The cymbals played by the hard hands of toil at last grow silent and
the echo of the drums, falling back into the room, madden some
specially fanatical dancers. The *chachá* . . . shook frantically in the
hands of the accompanists. And the slow and monotonous song of the
Negresses filled the musicians and dancers with intoxication.

Then the *babul*[50] began with its exquisite cadence and the most
lively of the young Negresses inaugurated the dance . . . her companion was a Negro of a certain age, but the best dancer of the *hacienda*.

After a long description of the dance, Bacardí records that the song
sung 'with incomparable brio' was in a mixture of French and Spanish:

> *Blanca yo qui sot en Frans; oh jele!*
> *Yo pran madan yo serví sorelle*
> *Pu yo caresé negués.*[51]

It was in dancing that the two cultures of Cuba in the nineteenth century contrasted most exactly: in the palaces the Spaniards danced the
quadrille or the lancers, outside the Congolese danced their early
rumbas.

Slaves had as ever to be fed, clothed, kept medically fit, housed and
of course supervised. A certain number still had to be bought each year –
6% according to most estimates. Maintenance charges are hard to disentangle, for most accountings place the maintenance of slaves and
animals under the same heading. But it appears that in 1863 renewal
charges were \$5,000 on a plantation producing 4,000 boxes of sugar and
feeding and clothing for 150 slaves, together with medical attention,
seems to have been \$6,000 or \$40 a year per slave.[52] In 1838 at the well-
run plantation of *Santa Ana*, belonging to José de la Luz, slaves had
three meals a day, with four ounces of either salted cod or jerked beef.[53]
In 1846 the slaves on a 'first class farm' got 140 lbs of meat (at 6¢ ($3\frac{1}{2}d$) a
pound) each during the year (six to eight ounces a day) – a rate of con-

[48] *Chachá* was a type of cymbal, African in origin.
[49] A pair of rattles with pebbles and a shot inside.
[50] *Babul* was an African dance of Oriente province.
[51] Emilio Bacardí Moreau, *Via Crucis* (c. 1860)
> White am I who leave France, oh cry it loud!
> I take my wife to serve as a pillow,
> Then I caress my Negresses.
[52] Pezuela, *loc. cit.*
[53] Turnbull, 283.

sumption which compares with that of England of the 1950s.[54] 325 lbs of maize were used on the plantation each day at 12¢ (6½d) a pound, but it is obscure how much the slaves had and how much the animals.

It seems possible that slaves in Cuba ate a little better than their cousins in Virginia. The meat was sometimes fresh, particularly in the Trinidad or Sancti Spiritus area, more usually jerked beef from Buenos Aires or Tampico, particularly in Matanzas. In addition, there would be likely to be plantains, yam, sweet potato, and half a pound of rice and twelve ounces of maize – out of which the slave would make two or three meals a day.[55] All these matters varied according to time and place, even in the island.

Very hard work itself however necessitated adequate food and medical care. A sick slave was worthless. There was no point in starving a valuable possession. So there was of course the doctor, often a Spaniard, the hospital and its steward and apothecary. There was also the nursery, in which slave children would be kept, usually under the eye of elderly slave women too old to work; mothers would come back two or three times a day to suckle their children.

In most big sugar mills the slaves were now housed in barracks (*barracones*) rather than in the little huts which had been customary in the eighteenth century. The purpose was of course security: males and females were kept apart in small cells with earth floors. *Barracones* were always of one floor only and usually built round a courtyard with a well in the centre. The *contramayoral*, the overseer's assistant, would normally sleep in one room near the locked main gate.[56] There did remain in the nineteenth century some huts (*bohíos*), and there were still sugar plantations which enabled slaves to have their own small plots (*conucos*) on which to grow their own vegetables and keep a pig.[57]

Slaves were also naturally given clothing (*esquifación*): usually, two changes of underwear a year (*lienzo de cañamazo*), sometimes a jacket of baize (*bayetón*), a night cap for the winter, one handkerchief and a blanket for their bed, a hat, one shirt and pair of trousers.[58] Of course these things varied from plantation to plantation and from time to time. The slave code provided that this minimum should be fulfilled but it was sometimes not. Few slaves had shoes.

A *cafetal* often seems to have been a more homogeneous community than a sugar mill – a happier one it is possible to say. The slaves worked far less hard due to the much less demanding daily and harvest arrangements. The novelist Cirilo Villaverde acutely compared the difference

[54] See below, Epilogue, for meat consumption in Cuba in 1970.
[55] Saco, *Apuntes autográficos inéditos*.
[56] See plan of barracoon in Ortiz, *Negros Esclavos*, 213.
[57] See Montejo, 26; Ortiz, *Negros Esclavos*, 226.
[58] Ortiz, *Negros Esclavos*, 217–18.

in the cemeteries on coffee farms with those on sugar mills: the sugar mill cemetery was a deserted spot abandoned in the centre of pasture land, where slaves were buried in common graves without names; but graves on *cafetals* were in a prized and central place in the farm. Slaves had names on their graves, and owners were often buried there too, being attached to their farms – either by poverty or affection, especially if they were of the first generation of immigrants from Haiti. Some coffee farmers during the 1830s were rich enough to live in Havana, but many lived in nearby villages or towns. Smaller immigrants often lacked the resources to buy a vault in the local church; also *cafetals* were in more mountainous areas than sugar plantations and it was therefore harder and more expensive to carry bodies into the towns.[59] (Coffee farmers would also often plant vegetables and fruit for their own use or, in the nineteenth century, for their slaves.) For slaves, the turning-over of coffee and its submission to machinery when sufficiently dry was easier work than the labour of ladling and feeding fires in the sugar mill. On *cafetals* slaves worked for only fifteen hours or so in harvest in place of nineteen or even twenty on sugar estates. They had, therefore, a longer life as well as better cemeteries, the annual loss being only $3\frac{3}{4}\%$ compared with almost 10% in sugar plantations.

In the nineteenth century as in the eighteenth, slaves of the city enjoyed a life which, by comparison with those of the country, was eminently desirable. The African clubs and bars had increased in numbers, *coartación* and emancipation was, in the cities, much more frequent and possible, the presence of an increasing free black or mulatto population was both comforting and helpful and there were many more activities possible than in the plantation – from theft to dancing: in the 1820s a secret society of Havana city slaves, the *negros curros*, exercised a semi-mastery over certain streets in the oldest quarter.[60] The clubs acted as the centres for preservation of African religion and twice a year, at Epiphany and during the carnival, slaves would sally out into the streets to enact masques which were a replica of what occurred in Africa; save that the government forbade the establishment of Catholic saints in the clubs and the carrying round of dead bodies which some tribes desired.[61] There were also instances of loyalty by town slaves to their masters and their families: there was a famous instance of a slave chef employed by the daughter of the Marqués de Casa Calvo refusing to cook at a banquet organized by Captain-General Tacón who had exiled the marqués: he even refused a bribe

[59] Cirilo Villaverde. There is also a moving description of a sugar mill cemetery by Anselmo Suárez, qu. Ortiz, *Negros Esclavos*, 302.
[60] Fernando Ortiz completed a major study of this phenomenon before he died but it has not yet been published.
[61] Ortiz, *Los Cabildos Afrocubanos* (1921).

and offer of his own freedom, with the comment, 'Tell the Governor that I prefer slavery and poverty with my masters to riches and liberty without them'.[62]

There is no reason to doubt that old and sick slaves were often, even usually, cared for: they were treated paternally like tired horses, with occasional affection. The labour force of England at the same time was undeniably treated often worse or no better than slaves on a sugar plantation – a fact which slave merchants frequently pointed out at the time as a justification for slavery.[63] Negro slaves in Cuba probably lived better than, say, the nominally free Indian peasants in Mexico who in the 1750s had 'offered their labour at a price less than the cost of maintenance of slaves'.[64] Gallenga, a *Times* correspondent (of Italian nationality) who visited Cuba in 1872, thought that 'There can be no doubt whatever that the condition of the Cuban slave is in every material respect better than that of the free cultivator on the plains of Lombardy'.[65] It also seems evident that, in Cuba (as in Jamaica), slaves seemed least unhappy during the harvest-time, despite the extra work: this being due not only to the excitement and the tension of keeping the rollers going but because there were ample opportunities of drinking cane brandy (*aguardiente*) and eating cane and the anticipation of the fiesta at the end of the harvest. None of such comments takes into account the moral degradation, for master as well as slave, of the absence of liberty.

Nevertheless, disagreeable though the life of slaves might be, it is melancholy to realize that that of slaves freed as a result of British or international intervention seems to have been worse. The case of the *emancipados* is one of the larger scandals of the nineteenth century. If the slaves were freed at Havana, they were at first handed over to the Spanish authorities who, through the merciless brokerage of Francisco Marty y Torrens, slave merchant and intimate of Captain-General Tacón, hired them out for seven years to the highest bidder. The employer who hired them thus had no interest in keeping them alive after seven years, and no obligation to support them if sick or disabled. Some *emancipados* were placed also with hospitals, the botanical garden, or the municipal authorities, some with private persons (such as widows of officers who could not afford to buy slaves) as servants.[66] Further, any who survived this seven-year period might be re-hired without asking their consent. Their pay was not always given. The *emancipados* had even less status than a slave and no backing from custom or Spanish law. Slaves despised *emancipados*. At first *emancipados* were supposed not to be

[62] Comtesse Merlin, *La Havane*, II, 169. The daughter was Luisa Marquesa de Arcos.
[63] Moreno Fraginals, 142.
[64] *Cf.* José Martín Félix de Arrate, *Llave del nuevo mundo*, qu. *ibid.*, 142.
[65] Gallenga, 80.
[66] *Cf.* Aimes, 224–7, where a defence of the system occurs.

sent out of Havana, being used as lamplighters or scavengers, but under the captaincy-general of Tacón in the late 1830s, the temptation to profit became too much, the *emancipados* became too many, and the authorities in practice sold them to employers in the hinterland for work on plantations – at a price reckoned as three to six *onzas de oro* (£10 10*s* to £20) for women, six to ten *onzas de oro* (£20 to £27) for men. The English Superintendent of Freed Slaves (for some years in Havana the enlightened Richard Madden) did his best to alleviate the situation but his position was hopeless.[67] He himself said that the *emancipados* were sold virtually into slavery for ever. At the end of seven years it was almost always found that the *emancipados* appeared on the books of the estate as dead.[68]

Madden's aim was to try to recover these *emancipados* and, after a while, the captain-general began handing them over to him at between twelve and twenty a month; they were then dispatched to the British West Indies where they apparently made 'very undesirable immigrants'.[69] The British arranged later that liberated slaves should be assigned to the government whose ship had captured the slaver and placed an old warship, the *Romney*, in Havana harbour to deal with this. But after about 1838 these became much less numerous, since the Portuguese flag began to be used for slaving itself; later, the Spanish authorities began themselves to 'emancipate' slaves, turning them into contract labourers with no status who could be and usually were treated abominably. The *emancipados* in Brazil, by now the only other large slave society south of the Río Grande, had similar experiences, save that the nominal period of apprenticeship was fourteen rather than seven years.

It is thus fanciful to suppose (as many have argued and as de Tocqueville even assured the French parliament in 1839) that the Spaniards treated their slaves specially mildly. Laws might be mild deriving from Castillian, and ultimately Roman codes, but particularly after 1800 they were rarely enforced, only serving to deceive casual visitors or even permanent residents of Havana who could not or did not disembarrass themselves of the merchant-slaver influence, that 'deadening influence of slavery which steals so imperceptibly over the feelings of strangers in the West Indies', and led people to justify cruelty. The great age of Cuban sugar – when the island produced for the world market – was a hundred years later than elsewhere, and that meant that comparisons made with the eighteenth century inevitably reflected well on the Spaniards (and badly on the English or French). On the other hand, the

[67] See Turnbull, 161–2. Madden had previously been a magistrate in Jamaica.
[68] Madden, 39.
[69] See Mrs Henry Cust, *Wanderers: episodes from the Travels of Lady Emmeline Stuart Victoria Wortley and her daughter 1849–55* (1928), 114.

cruelty and tedium of unremitting toil was probably mitigated by a more violently exciting cultural life than in Jamaica. Slaves could no doubt expect better treatment from resident owners (more common in Cuba than in Jamaica) than from agents. Household and stable slaves evolved affections and loyalties. As in some other West Indian islands, house slaves and slaves of the city considered sugar mills to be places of punishment.[70] (Beckford, however, noted that in Jamaica slaves tended to regard 'domestic service as more honourable and the field as more independent' and that most slaves preferred therefore the stability of a plantation to the capriciousness of being a house slave).[71]

It is also difficult to avoid the conclusion that the lives of most slaves in Cuba in the nineteenth century, particularly those working on the large modern sugar estates, had declined and was getting worse; that international humanitarianism was one reason why this had occurred, at any event so far as the *emancipados* were concerned; and that this treatment in Cuba reflected that in the U.S. also, where a reaction had set in, in contrast with the more enlightened if patriarchal attitudes of the late eighteenth century.

The tribal origins of the Cuban Negroes are not very easy to resolve and since for so many years the planters depended upon non-Spanish shippers, it would seem that the Cuban Negro population derived from the whole range of African slave ports from Senegal in the north to the Congo and Angola in the south. The Dutch and Portuguese shippers of the seventeenth century had concentrated on the Gold Coast and Angola; the British in the eighteenth century concentrated on the Slave Coast (Dahomey and Lagos), with their wares usually shipped from Jamaica; the Spaniards and Portuguese of the early nineteenth century concentrated to begin with in the Cameroons but afterwards returned to the Niger Delta, the Slave Coast and Angola. They also went to East Africa. Most Cuban Negroes descend from the nineteenth-century imports of slaves and since a wide variety of slaves were shipped even then it would be rash to say that a larger proportion were Yoruba or Ashanti, Carabalí or Popo; but it seems likely that the Congolese and the Yoruba cultural influences were in the long run the strongest.[72]

[70] Turnbull, 53.

[71] See Patterson, 58.

[72] Contrary views are expressed by Wurdemann, 153; and more recently Klein, 152–5. Cuban names for different African tribes are often technically inaccurate. Thus the Cubans called the natives of Calabar 'Carabalí' a corruption of the English 'calabary' and most of these were probably Ibos. The word 'Lucumí' describes Yorubas. The Moslem Haussas appear in Cuba as 'Appapas'. These were old names. See Ortiz, *Negros Esclavos*, 25ff. In 1833 out of a list of 2,583 Negroes dead in Havana from cholera, 536 were Carabalí (Ibo), 457 Congolese, 285 Ganga, 258 Lucumí (Yoruba), 213 Mandinga, 128 Mina, 49 Arará, 20 Macua and 637 of indeterminate origin. (Saco, *Papeles sobre Cuba*, II, 343.)

CHAPTER XIV

The Decline of Slavery

By the late 1850s and early 1860s, at long last, some planters, though of course still prisoners of their prejudices, were hoping on economic grounds that contract labour might eventually replace slavery. A prize essay by Pedro José Morillas in the 1830s had suggested that white labour was as capable of hard work as black. The Alfonsos and Aldamas had even tried unsuccessfully to found a mill with only white labour. Some smaller planters were now shutting their mills and hiring their slaves out to bigger plantations at $30 or $40 a month. The Cuban planters, however, did not quickly learn from the experience of British West Indian planters: that slave labour was in fact more expensive than contract and, despite the many favourable conditions in Cuba for a successful slave society, was fundamentally irrational when allied to comparatively sophisticated capitalism. Cubans identified British West Indian decline with British West Indian emancipation, and feared (as Jamaican and British Guianian planters feared) that in Cuba there was so much land that they would have no labour at all unless they controlled it by force.[1]

The British West Indies had also undergone disaster after disaster in the 1840s and 1850s, partly from natural reasons, partly because of social dislocation.[2] (After emancipation in Jamaica there had been a swift exodus from sugar plantations to the unoccupied hill country). Slavery certainly delayed labour-saving agriculture. Slaves thus looked after animals badly; the pressure of the slave system often prevented fertilization and any variation of crops was unthinkable.[3] Since the slaves were on the plantation always, harvest and non-harvest, they might as

---

[1] In Antigua and small islands the British planters were able to pay a wage less than the cost of slave maintenance – there was no more land for any new farmer. In Jamaica, Trinidad and British Guiana a tax was laid on all crop land so that Negroes would be compelled to work as wage-paid workers; another device was to charge a high rent on the ex-slaves' huts on the plantations. Money from English abolitionist societies helped to set up independent communities in Jamaica (see Mathieson, *British Slave Emancipation*, 61).

[2] A number of English West Indian planters withdrew their capital and migrated to India (see Deerr, 56).

[3] See E. Genovese, *The Political Economy of Slavery*, 26ff., for discussion of these matters in the U.S. South, though it is of course clear that the planters of that region retained slavery as a definition of their way of life even when it was uneconomic. For an opposing view there is the famous article of A. Conrad and J. Meyer, *Journal of Political Economy* (1958) vol. 66, No. 2, 95–130.

well be employed: why import a plough for replanting when a slave was there to dig? One sees here the beginning of a marked difference between a sophisticated treatment of the manufacturing side of the industry and a continued unsophisticated and primitive treatment of the harvesting and agricultural side, so pronounced later that slaves who worked in the mills would despise and boycott those who worked in the fields, even refusing to shake their hornier hands.

Another economic activity of slaves – to dig up new land – declined as the price of land at last began to rise, and it became more sensible to fertilize old land than buy new. In 1862 an astute planter, Alvaro Reynoso, published what has been in fact Cuba's chief contribution to research on sugar: a book recommending a method of intensive treatment of land;[4] by 1863 Domingo Aldama (brother of Miguel Aldama) was proving such methods successful at his plantation, *Concepción* at Sabanilla (Matanzas).[5] This book afterwards had a great influence on Java where deep trenching cultivation continues to be referred to as the Reynoso system.

There were several alternative new sources of labour: vagrants, of whom there were always an immense number in Cuba, could be despatched to sugar plantations; Gallegos or Andalusians, direct from Spain, lured by interested Catalans to Cuba by inviting laws (intended to balance the white and Negro population) and attracted by the prospect of high wages in this now richest of Spanish provinces – the Spanish population had increased to about 16 million in 1860 from 10 million in 1800.[6] Canary Islanders came like indentured labourers to the British colonies of the past, contracted to work for a specific period but afterwards free, even if this only meant in practice that they could aspire to become *mayoral* (overseer) on estates where they had once been labourer. The 1861 census listed 41,661 free white labourers working alongside slaves during the harvest. However, this immigration undertaken as a commercial venture by, for instance, the firm of González y Torstall of Barcelona, was not enough to fill the gaps caused by the high price of slaves.[7] Nor were the other encouragements, including prizes, offered to white labourers. For, of course, as always, no Castillian peasant, however poor, wished to work in a sugar plantation. Miguel Aldama thus made an abortive effort to found a sugar mill with Basques from Vizcaya.

One group who could only occasionally be drawn on for contract

---

[4] Alvaro Reynoso (1829–78), educated in Paris, held chair of chemistry, Madrid, and owned the *San Francisco de Asís* mill at Rancho Veloz, Sagua la Grande; retired to Cuba 1858 and after exile 1875–78 became commissioner for agriculture.

[5] Alvaro Reynoso, *Ensayo sobre el cultivo de la caña de azúcar*, 5th edn. (Havana, 1954), 598.

[6] Carr, 197.

[7] *Cf.* Moreno Fraginals, 147–9.

labour were free Negroes or mulattoes. Although there seem to have been 200,000 of them in 1861, they generally would do anything, even nothing, rather than work on sugar plantations: far better sit and starve in Havana than work in any capacity on a sugar estate (partly because relations between plantation slaves and house slaves were bad). Many in fact neither sat nor starved: freed Negroes or mulattoes were now even further entrenched in what became distinctive Cuban Negro crafts, constituting already in 1861 a majority of Havana builders, carpenters, tailors, chauffeurs of *volantes* and cooks, seamstresses and laundresses.[8] There were also many involved in minor crafts such as shoe-making and, after the panic deriving from the *Escalera* and other slave revolts had died down, some were again found in militia regiments.

The result of the slave shortage was that other foreign labour was sought. Irishmen had worked on the railways, but they were fairly expensive labour. The planters turned first to the South American continent and an experiment was made by Tacon's old friend 'Pancho' Marty with Indian labourers from Yucatan. A number were imported, treated physically as slaves or, in many cases, since they were not an article of value for their masters to sell, doubtless worse. These poor Indians, like their ancient Arawak relations, were either too weak or able to give the impression of so being and they mostly went back.[9] Zorrilla, the poet and author of *Don Juan Tenorio*, unsuccessfully sought to engage in this commerce.

Then a more sustained attempt was made on that new source of labour already begun in China after the country had been fully prised open to European influence by the English in 1840. (Chinese labour first reached the West Indies in 1806 when 182 coolies and one woman were taken to Trinidad.) After enquiries by the Junta de Fomento in 1844, 206 Chinese were brought from Amoy to Cuba in 1847 by Zulueta & Co. of London on the Spanish boat *Oquendo*, followed by 365 Chinese on an English vessel, the *Duke of Argyll*. Among those who first used this new source of labour were the captain-general, the Diago brothers, the Conde de Peñalver, Julián de Zulueta and Martín Pedroso.[10] During the next twenty years over 140,000 labourers were brought in from China, perhaps more – though the serious trading only began in 1853. They came as immigrants, usually on an eight-year contract, and therefore they were not to be regarded as slaves barred under the treaty of 1817. But the difference was really one in name only. The Chinese were per-

[8] Pezuela, *Diccionario*, III, 350–72, qu. Klein, 203.

[9] See Juan Pérez de la Riva, *Documentos para la historia de las gentes sin historia* and the same author's 'Demografía de los Culíes Chinos en Cuba', *Revista de la Biblioteca Nacional*, Año 57, No. 4; and Juan Jiménez Pastrana, *Los Chinos en las Luchas por la liberación Cubana, 1847–1930* (1963).

[10] Jiménez Pastrana, 26.

suaded, press-ganged, or told that they would be sent to *Tay Lloy Sun* (the Great Spain), or deluded by the merchants' Chinese agents by promises of a good life, shown Mexican coins and sweets in a tea house, taken in the ports of southern China proper or in Macao and carried in bad conditions (sometimes via Manila) across the Pacific. They were unshipped at Panama, sent across the isthmus by rail and reshipped to Cuba. This voyage was handled by merchants who hardly differed from slavers, and indeed they were often, as in the case of Zulueta & Co., the same men. These sold contracts to prospective employers at $150 to $250 (£35 to £58) (which included their fare to Cuba)[11] and, as the house of Fernández Shimper & Co. blandly added, '$100 (£23) for each ill or blind Chinaman'. Of 132,435 brought between 1853 and 1872, some 13,973 (13%) probably died, either *en route* or shortly after their arrival – if anything slightly higher than slave mortality.[12] The leading merchants in this traffic were, in addition to Zulueta of London, Matias Menchaca Torre of Manila; Tait & Co., English merchants of Amoy; and Syme Muir of Canton; Manuel Pereda (whose partners included the ubiquitous and powerful Juan Espino, the Drakes' plantation manager and treasurer of the Havana railway); together with some representatives of the Pedroso family.[13] The Drakes themselves were also involved.[14]

Arrived in Havana the Chinese were distributed to the plantations where they received 20 to 30¢ (1s to 1s 6d) a day, 1½ lbs of potatoes or other food, 1½ lbs of salt meat a day, and two cotton suits a year.[15] They also had a blanket and medical attendance. This was for a working day, and in fact hours of work probably meant the Chinese got about $4 (18s) a month to begin with. However, as in the case of the Yucatan Indian, they seem to have been treated as badly as, and probably worse than the slaves, since they had no economic value after eight years.[16] 'No Cuban going to the barracoon to contract for the services of a Chinese coolie ever talks about "hiring"; he bluntly says he is *buying* a Chinese', reported the correspondent of *The Times* in 1872.[17] The consequence was remarkably similar to what occurred with Negroes: there were escapes, revolts, suicides, assassinations, acts of arson – and a Spanish '*reglamento*' prescribing duties and punishments. The Spaniards accused the

[11] Morales's letter to H. Coit, qu. Ely, *Cuando reinaba*, 609.
[12] Census of 1899, 71.
[13] Ely, *Cuando reinaba*, 611, 616.
[14] Jiménez Pastrana, 40, cites fuller list. No effort seems to have been made to bring Indians (from India) to Cuba, as Mauritius and Guianian sugar planters (headed by Sir John Gladstone) were embarking upon.
[15] Census of 1899, 69.
[16] See report of Commissioner Ch'an, Macpherson & Ruber, qu. H. B. Morse, *International Relations of the Chinese Empire*, 3 vols (1910–18), II, 179.
[17] Gallenga, 88.

Chinese as they had once the Arawak Indians; they were thieves, rebels, suicides and homosexuals – the last scarcely fair, even if true, since the traders in Chinamen introduced almost no women. The slaves did not get on well with the Chinese ('those pederasts had no ear for drums', the slave Montejo commented, 'and they stayed in their little corners'),[18] while a Spanish *reglamento* forbade – ineffectively – intermarriage between 'Asiatics and people of colour'.[19] After their eight years, if they survived, most Chinese went back to China, though after 1870 they were allowed to stay in Cuba.[20] Again, as with the Negroes, those who killed themselves believed that they would be carried back after death to their homes across the sea, and there appear to have been many of these: 173 suicides in 1862 out of a total of 346 in Cuba – exactly half.[21] As in the case of Africans, many wild rumours circulated in China – that Europeans ate them, boiled them down for soap, or killed them in order to extract a special ointment or substance from their bodies. Nevertheless, in Cuba these Chinese played an essential role; they were allotted tasks of a limited technological importance, on the assumption that, as salaried workers, they were capable of an intelligence which it would be both unprofitable and dangerous to foster among slaves. The census of 1861 lists 34,834 'Asiatics' of whom only 57 were women, the rest men; the 1877 census speaks of 40,261, of whom 66 were women. After that date the Chinese trade was officially ended by treaty between Spain and China after much discussion as to its immorality.[22] Long before then, Chinese were already established in a number of Cuban professions apart from sugar estates: fruit-sellers in the streets or restaurateurs – the first Chinese restaurant being established as early as 1858. A society to protect Chinese interests had been founded in 1867 and indeed, by 1870, there were already three separate such societies.

About 1860 in Cuba the numbers of black or mulatto had fallen in proportion to white, so that, for the first time for sixty years, there were more 'white' persons in Cuba than black and mulatto put together. This was partly due to natural increase (particularly strong among whites), partly to increased Spanish immigration, partly to higher slave prices, and a consequent diminution of the slave trade. The Chinese and Mexican contract labourers from Yucatan were clearly pointing the way to a change of labour conditions and some slave owners were already renting their slaves as day-labourers in the harvests. Nevertheless, the years 1859–61 saw a great increase in slave importation (chiefly

[18] Montejo, 29.

[19] Jiménez Pastrana, 69.

[20] Census of 1899, 71. The number who went back was however only between 10% and 20%.

[21] Saco, qu. Ortiz, *Negros Esclavos*, 392.

[22] Census of 1899, 71.

from the 500 miles between the Equator and Ambriz) partly due to the absence in the Far East of the regular British anti-slaving garrison,[23] but afterwards slaves were few and far between, since Cuban traders were cut off from their North American bases and could only operate in a hole-and-corner fashion – partly from European ports (a new fast ship got away even from Liverpool and another from Hartlepool) perhaps under French colours. In Marseilles some 'splendid vessels' were fitted out and also some from Fécamp and from the old centre at Cádiz.[24] Now only the richest planters could afford to buy slaves, but at the same time it was only they who could afford the heavy machinery to take the place of slaves. Smaller plantations required more slaves if they were to survive.

Thus although the American civil war made the preservation of slavery through annexation to the U.S. anyway impossible, the mechanization of sugar production was making slavery less necessary. The centrifugal machine (admittedly only for those who could afford it) enabled sugar to be refined much more cheaply; it therefore began to be competitive even in the U.S. Meanwhile the civil war ruined the Louisiana sugar plantations; only 175 out of 1,200 in 1861 were still in existence in 1864.[25]

[23] Mathieson, 166, estimates the number of slaves imported as, in 1859, 30,000; 18,000 in 1860; and 24,000 in 1861 (*ibid.*, 174).
[24] *Ibid.*, 179.
[25] Walter Prichard, 'Effects of the Civil War on the Louisiana Sugar Industry', *Journal of Southern History*, V (August 1939), 316–20.

BOOK III

The Political Struggle 1823-98

'Honour is more important than success'

GENERAL MARTÍNEZ CAMPOS, INTERVIEW WITH *New York World*, 26 OCTOBER, 1895.

CHAPTER XV

Captains-General in Search of Wealth

The first two captains-general of Cuba after the general disintegration of the rest of the Spanish empire in the 1820s, Vives and Ricafort,[1] were, though ruthless to liberals, otherwise amiable and lazy, disinclined to make difficulties with the increasingly rich sugar and coffee oligarchy. Their letters to the English Commissioners and Consuls, disclaiming knowledge of the slave trade, are masterpieces of dissembling. Stiff in manners, dissolute in habits, these captains-general from poor Spanish provinces laid enough personally aside to keep them thereafter very well in their retirement: *'Si vives como Vives, vivirás'* ('if you live as Vives does, you will live well)', people in Havana were accustomed to say. Vives, an ex-Spanish minister in Washington, was the more astute, Ricafort the more agreeable; Ricafort enriched his relations, Vives helped his friends.[2] In their day Cuba overtook Jamaica as the greatest producer of sugar in the world and moved into that position of saccharine pre-eminence which she has known for most of the time since. The yellow stone house of the captain-general, at once the town house and the office of the Crown's representative, was the centre of favour, interest and fashion. Under them, Cubans became rich not only in terms of their own past experience and in that of Spanish incomes, but according to the best international criteria. Slaves flooded in all along the coast, regardless of the British navy. In the cities, whole classes seemed able to live for the lottery or for gambling games, men for prostitutes, women for dancing, all for cigars. In the countryside escaped slaves or free mulattoes often roamed as bandits, while other gangs stole slaves from one plantation and sold them to another, and while murder and robbery on the rotten muddy track which passed as the highway were persistent and only checked by semi-independent bands led by commissioned officers out for their own loot. There was also violence in Havana, where the English traveller Patterson reported in 1820, 'assassinations have been frightfully frequent . . . on 18th of June [last] no less than seven people, "whites", were assassinated in the streets'.[3]

---

[1] Mariano Ricafort Palacín y Abarca (1776–1846), born Huesca; fought in Peninsular War and in the South American wars of independence; governor-general of the Philippines, 1825–30.

[2] See, e.g., Philalethes, *Yankee Travels through the Island of Cuba* (1856), 95.

[3] R. Patterson, *Letters from the Havana*, 64.

The island was more and more the trading partner of the U.S. American ships numbered 783 out of the 964 that entered the port of Havana in 1826.[4] The Spanish government was in no way disturbed by this development; bankrupt herself, unable to raise loans, she saw in it a means of raising revenue. Thus in 1832 Spain placed discriminatory tariffs on imports. The United States in reply raised the tonnage duties on Spanish ships coming from Cuba or Puerto Rico. In 1834 Spain in return raised still further the duty on U.S. flour brought to Cuba in U.S. vessels and in their turn the United States responded (not at all understanding Spanish motives) by raising tonnage duties and levying a special duty on Cuban coffee (though not on sugar). This opened a time of political crisis between Spain and the United States, during which, in 1834, Captain-General Ricafort was succeeded by one of the most remarkable proconsuls whom Spain had sent to a dominion overseas. This was Tacón,[5] a sixty-year-old widower and despot of great persistence, a passionate Spanish patriot, spectacled, the survivor of a hundred fights in Colombia and Peru on behalf of the Crown against independent South America and veteran in particular of an extraordinary ride across the Andes from Colombia to Lima. In Spain he passed for a liberal but in Cuba he was far from one. He hated the *criollo* oligarchy (who seemed all too like the *criollos* who had rebelled elsewhere in the empire), surrounded himself with a group of Spanish merchants, mostly *negreros* and, though accepting without cavil the usual captain-general's cut from the slave trade ($100,000 a year, reputedly), embarked on a policy of administrative reform designed to establish order in the countryside and law in the city. His instructions from Madrid were not unnaturally more severe than those of his predecessors, since the Restoration settlement in Spain itself was breaking down with the death of King Ferdinand, and the Carlists were preparing to rise in civil war against the infant Queen Isabella and her mother, the Regent María Cristina.

In his first months, the captain-general successfully avoided a major struggle with the Cuban oligarchy, being busy with the establishment of a nocturnal police force, with plans for street-cleaning and general sanitation, with sewers and firemen, with the macadamizing of roads, the numbering of houses in the streets, and the destruction of a number of murderous gangs previously active in Havana itself, particularly in the neighbourhood of the docks. Weapons were forbidden in Havana,

---

[4] It is perhaps worth pointing out that the Cuban proportion of U.S. dealings with Latin America actually dropped during the first quarter of the century: from 545 out of 802 ships in 1806 and 1808–9, to 638 in 1826–31 out of 1,758 (Harry Bernstein, *Origins of Interamerican Interest*, 91).

[5] Miguel Tacón y Rosique (1775–1855). See *Correspondencia Reservada, 1834–6*, ed. Juan Pérez de la Riva (1963).

except for soldiers, and new military courts were established which were both more efficient and less corrupt than the old *audiencia*. A large sanitary fish market was built by Manuel Pastor, a *negrero* who was, in addition, Tacón's most intimate financial adviser, and Tacón himself set about the construction, just outside Havana, of a huge new prison, the largest in Latin America (240 feet by 300 feet), enabling such improvements as the separation of black and white prisoners and the removal of those who had until then languished, as in so many Spanish-American capitals, in the dungeons under his own palace. On the terraced roof of this prison, Tacón and his Spanish *negrero* friends, such as Manuel Pastor, the banker Joaquín Gómez, the Marqués de las Delicias (José Antonio Portuondo, the senior alderman in Santiago) and Francisco Marty, would meet daily to smoke cigars, drink champagne and discuss politics and plans.

These developments did not much worry the Cuban oligarchy, though the spectre of action of any sort on the part of a captain-general was mildly disturbing. More irritating, however, was Tacón's scheme for driving a fine new avenue, the Paseo, through the middle of Havana, which, though not actually destroying any of the Montalvos' or Calvos' palaces, did make it difficult for them to get to their front doors from somewhat narrow pavements. Nevertheless, these families were placated by Tacón's next and highly publicized act: the expulsion of the writer José Antonio Saco[6] for spreading abolitionist doctrines such as were now prevailing in the British West Indies.

Saco was at this time the editor of a recently founded magazine, the *Revista Bimestre Cubana*, one of a number which had sprung up in the lax days at the end of Vives's captaincy-general. Eight newspapers now flourished in Cuba, four daily (*Diario de la Marina* and *Noticioso y Lucero* of Havana, *Aurora* of Matanzas and *Redactor de Cuba* at Santiago).[7] Saco, a brilliant journalist, was the favourite writer of all the younger Cubans who were in any way disgruntled with the existing order. In a famous article in the *Revista* on Brazil, he had argued that the slave trade was a serious threat to the future of Cuba, on the old ground that so large an influx of Africans would be certain to lead to revolution. This was of course neither a humanitarian point of view nor a new one; indeed, the novelty lies more in the fact that Saco himself opposed the slave trade more because he distrusted the whole black race of than through any sense of humanity.[8]

[6] José Antonio Saco (1797–1879) from a family of small means in Bayamo. A bigamist. Maintained for forty years in exile in Paris by rich friends in Cuba. Never associated explicitly with separatist plots but always persecuted.

[7] The other newspapers were occasional, at Villa Clara, Trinidad, Sancti Spiritus, and Puerto Príncipe.

[8] This argument is convincingly developed at length by Moreno Fraginals.

This was, however, an ill-chosen moment to show any criticism of the slave trade for whatever motive: in 1833 the perfidious English had at long last actually embarked on the risky business of freeing their own slaves completely,[9] and the contamination which Cuban slaveholders feared might drift over from Jamaica as a result seemed very threatening. Saco had also for the first time in a Spanish colony produced arguments which calculated that free labour was really cheaper than slave labour.[10] He himself argued that the government of Spain was actually interested in promoting the slave trade to Cuba since, the larger the black population, the more Cuba would have to rely on the Spanish army: and though Spain itself was incapable of any such long-term planning, some Spanish merchants of Cádiz or Havana, who were occupied with the slave trade, may perhaps have thought so.

Tacón was persuaded to send Saco to exile by the omnicompetent Martínez de Pinillos, now Conde de Villanueva,[11] who had been *intendente* for ten years, spokesman of the oligarchy, a *peninsular* who was beloved by the *criollos*, a man who, thanks to the sugar boom, had become a financier of international importance, since he controlled the dispatch of $4M (nearly £1M) a year sent to Spain in taxes: indeed, many Cubans believed that Spanish ministers owed their salary entirely to him. Certainly, the Cuban revenue was almost the one sure guarantee for potential creditors, such as the Rothschilds or other London bankers, that the government of Spain could offer. Villanueva and the old families of Havana wanted Saco out of Cuba, and Tacón, still in the honeymoon of his relationship with Cuban society, agreed, though, showing a delicacy rarely shared by future Cuban tyrants, he allowed him to leave in his own time. For the rest of his life Saco, maintained in Spain or in Paris by money sent from the more enlightened of the planters he had left behind in Cuba (the Aldamas, the Alfonsos of Matanzas and the Del Montes), remained a centre of criticism, speculation and controversy directed against the Spanish authorities in Cuba

---

[9] 660,000 slave holders of the British West Indies were paid £20M ($85M) compensation.

[10] Thus:

Maintenance, clothing, medicine for 100 slaves for 1 year		$4,562	(£1,000)
Interest on capital borrowed to buy 100 slaves		$4,000	(£950)
Loss by deaths and old age		$4,000	(£950)
Charges arising from child rearing, runaways, baptisms, etc.		$800	(£190)
		$13,362	(£3,100)
Compare: 50 men at $12 (£2 16s) per month for 12 months	..	$7,200	(£1,700)
50 women at $10 (£2 7s) per month for 12 months	..	$6,000	(£1,400)
		$13,200	(£3,100)

[11] Claudio Martínez Pinillos, Conde de Villanueva (1782-1853). Fought in Spain against Napoleon, including Bailén; deputy for Havana, 1813; treasurer of Havana, 1814; *intendente*, 1825.

and against the slave trade, on the grounds of its wastefulness and economic shortcomings, rather than its immorality.

Over the affair of Saco the two most powerful men in Cuba, Tacón and Villanueva, had worked in relative harmony. But they soon quarrelled. Villanueva was an ardent advocate for (and shareholder in) railways. Tacón, outraged that the invention should come to Cuba before the motherland of Spain, but also, contradictorily, contemptuous of this 'Anglo-Saxon ironmongery', delayed for months before agreeing to the siting of the Havana railway station. Two or three other bones of contention cropped up. Villanueva, from long friendship with the religious order, did his best to delay the Liberal government's order to dismantle the monasteries, delaying in fact till the monks themselves had sold off large sections of their great estates. Another somewhat curious quarrel followed Tacón's accusation that the municipality (with Villanueva's connivance) was allowing the denizens of his new prison to starve. A further problem arose from Tacón's limited welcome to a number of real liberals, such as the poet Heredia.

All these disputes led to the growth of utter distrust between the captain-general on the one hand and the *intendente* and the oligarchy on the other. The great families of Havana boycotted the palace and were then outraged when Tacón filled the building with 'plebeians'. Tacón responded by a series of questionable ripostes, such as the expulsion of the dashing young Marqués de Casa Calvo for holding a gaming house in his palace in Havana: a rigid interpretation of the law which infuriated a capital so long used to licence that it knew no other liberty.

At the height of these quarrels came two major constitutional problems. In 1836 elections were ordered in Madrid. Tacón paid no attention, basing his action on the curious law of 1825 which enabled any captain-general to set aside instructions from Madrid if it seemed in the best interests of Cuba. The municipal council of Havana (to whom the election of deputies was formally entrusted) was therefore forbidden to arrange the election. But in east Cuba, the commanding general, General Manuel Lorenzo, a friend of Mendizábal, the outstanding liberal politician in Madrid, and a veteran of the peninsular war, openly proclaimed the Constitution of 1812, and called for elections.

Santiago was then underdeveloped in comparison with Havana, being the centre of a semi-pastoral community with no modern sugar mills. It nevertheless responded to the call, partly influenced by a long-term dislike of rule from Havana and from jealousy of the new rich planters of the west. 'Liberalism' lasted three months in east Cuba. But the threat of a military intervention by Tacón, the fear of a blockade at sea and the gradual decline of Lorenzo's support in the countryside and in the other barracks of the region, finally forced a surrender. Captain Jones of the British naval frigate *Vestal* played with the British consul in Santiago a somewhat curious intermediary role on Tacón's behalf, and eventually the constitutional leaders were carried off in the *Vestal* and allowed to go back to Europe. Commander Dallas of the U.S. navy lent his friendly support to the authoritarian captain-general. The liberals of Madrid, crushed by their own troubles, unable politically to give any encouragement to any form of Cuban self-determination (which they anyway disliked), refused to seat the three deputies from Cuba who claimed to represent the east of the island. The Cortes, liberals and conservatives alike, believed as a body that any representation of Cuba was bound to be 'a step towards' independence and that 'all steps towards independence were but a step away from the extermination and ruin of capital and people . . . The island of Cuba, if it does not remain Spanish, is bound to become Negro, inevitably Negro.'[12] As a result a special law was rushed through the Cortes confirming that henceforth the Constitution would not apply to Cuba and that the island would be governed by 'special laws'.

These events should have seemed a triumph for Tacón, but the Conde de Villanueva, to dull his success, saw to it that all sorts of accusations were raised about graft in the dispatch of the armed force to the east of Cuba, and accused the captain-general of using the crisis to further his own smuggling interests. A new crisis undid all the good that Tacón's handling of the affair of Santiago had done him. He received a somewhat mysterious message that an 'English agent' was on his way to Cuba to attempt to persuade him and the island to remain neutral in the Carlist wars. On receipt of this news, the Spanish government therefore instructed Tacón immediately to arrest and expel the archbishop of Santiago, a known supporter of the Carlist cause.[13] Tacón did this with as much tact as possible, Captain Jones and the *Vestal* once more proving invaluable at one stage of the drama, but unfortunately the government in Madrid went through a series of crises of its own, and the order against the archbishop was countermanded. Tacón was disowned by his government and so subject to the bitter criticism of Villanueva and the oligarchy for what they represented as an unnecessary insult to a prince of the Church.

The accusations sent to Madrid from various opponents of Tacón were now so numerous as to place his appointment in jeopardy. Groups of exiles in Cádiz and elsewhere published brochure upon brochure

[12] Vicente Sancho, *Diario de las Sesiones*, III, 1836-7, qu. Tacón, *Correspondencia*, ed. Pérez de la Riva, 69.

[13] Cirilo de Alameda y Breay, archbishop since 1832, an intimate of Ferdinand VII, returned to Spain later to become archbishop of Toledo and cardinal primate of Spain, dying aged ninety-one in 1872.

attacking him as a 'sanguinary tyrant' and plotting his downfall as best they might; although the various alleged attempts at his assassination in 1837 were apparently all unreal, being concocted by his own police to discredit his enemies. Tacón was violently criticized when an English Methodist, George Davidson, was expelled from the island after merely being suspected of proselytizing for abolition; Tacón was also criticized for his tolerance, even encouragement, of African cultural activities. Dances, religious music, even drums were permitted and from 1836 onwards the most complicated Afro-Cuban ritual, Abakuá (whose adherents are known as ñáñigos) has had a continuous history, with mulatto and some white members.[14]

In the end Tacón who, like Holstein in Germany, often gave his resignation to his monarch but never dreamt that one day it might be accepted, found that his offer had been taken seriously. This was due to a persistent series of intrigues in Madrid, including the bribing of deputies, by Saco's friends the Aldamas and Alfonsos and by the *intendente*, Villanueva. Tacón returned to Spain Vizconde de Bayamo and Marqués de la Unión de Cuba, more loaded with honours than any of his predecessors, and with a huge fortune gathered from his slave merchant friends such as Pastor and Gómez. He left behind streets, theatres, markets called after him and a curiously ambivalent historical reputation. He passed the last years of his life in a palace in Majorca, built with the profits that he had made out of his proconsulship.

One bizarre sequence of events during his captaincy-general remains to be recounted. In 1833 Nicolas Trist, private secretary to President Andrew Jackson, had been appointed consul in Havana. He respected and liked Tacón and collaborated closely with him in the illegal slaving, making the U.S. flag available to slavers who would otherwise have met difficulties with the British. The U.S. Secretary of State, Forsyth,[15] eventually heard so many accusations against Trist that he dispatched Alexander Everett,[16] then editor of the *North American Review*, to investigate: he reported that Trist had provided papers to sixty-one out of the seventy-one slavers known to have put into Cuban ports in 1838. Accused, Trist replied by proposing to his chief a plan for the U.S. purchase of Cuba.[17] Trist was then relieved, though later he was promoted to advantageous posts in U.S. diplomacy, the idea of purchase being not forgotten.

---

[14] See below, p. 521.

[15] John Forsyth (1780–1841), senator and Secretary of State.

[16] Alexander Everett (1790–1847), writer and diplomat.

[17] Forsyth to Trist, 19 March 1839, Dept of State Special Missions, I. See discussion in Warren S. Howard, *American Slavers and the Federal Law, 1837–1862* (1963), 33ff.

CHAPTER XVI

The Politics of Abolitionism

It had become swiftly clear after 1820, the much trumpeted year of Spain's abolition of the slave trade, that in fact it was continuing at least as strongly as ever, and indeed had even increased. Year after year British Consuls reported slavers leaving Havana; for instance, 63 in 1828, 45 in 1829 and 80 in 1835. The Spanish laws on the subject were found by the British Consul never to have been promulgated in Cuba. In 1825 the consul wrote to Canning that 2,642 slaves had been landed at Cabañas within two months, and that 'the success of the illicit slave traders has completely relieved them from all apprehension ... transactions of this nature are now public and notorious, no mystery being found necessary'.[1] Ten years later the Consul – a careful and hard-working symbol of international justice in Havana, as in Brazil, throughout most of the nineteenth century – wrote that the total import that year of slaves must have been about 24,000, representing $2.7M (£630,000).[2]

The British formally complained again and again:

> Vessel after vessel clears out from Cuba regularly for the coast of Africa: and ... returns laden with slaves, lands them at the back of the island and puts into the Havannah, declaring herself to have returned in ballast. The representations of His Majesty's Commissary Judge at the Havannah are of no effect ... he is referred from one authority to another.

Thus Frederick Lamb at Madrid in 1825;[3] there were other complaints, to the French government, to the captain-general at Havana and to the Spanish foreign ministry, to no avail.

Some international events helped to make the ban slightly less of a dead letter: in 1831, the French government, now a constitutional monarchy, instituted harsher measures against slaving – acutely realizing that their new sugar-beet industry required some measure of help against the sugar men of Martinique and Guadeloupe.[4] But there was little more to help the English. The navy had too few ships and these

[1] H. T. Kilbee to Canning, 25 February 1825 (Parliamentary papers 1825, 341).

[2] *Ibid*, 1835, 413.

[3] *Slave Population*, 1826, XXIX, 415.

[4] The beet problem is discussed on p. 125. There had been substantial French slave-trading in the 1820s.

were except for captured slavers, often, too slow. African kings refused to give up the trade except with great reluctance and for large bribes. Bounties (rewards to officers per head of slave rescued) were cut when abolitionist zeal in England flagged. The rights of the naval patrol were at least until 1835 completely inadequate: in that year the Spaniards agreed to the so-called 'Equipment Treaty', by which slaveships could be captured and condemned by one of the courts (Havana or Sierra Leone) if articles obviously needed for slaving were found on board, not simply slaves.[5] But Spain's only concern in accepting this treaty was the hope of her government for a loan from England to raise a new army to fight the Carlists and, when the government realized that English investors were now more interested in foreign railways (including Cuban ones) than in Spanish loans, there was little incentive for them to implement that treaty fully.[6] Afterwards, Spanish vessels changed to U.S. or Portuguese flags, while the U.S. never agreed to give England the right of search (or 'visit') in the years before the American Civil War.[7] The British government was often ambiguous in giving instructions, and there were disputes between the Foreign Office and the navy. Still the navy stuck to their task, treaties were slowly concluded with African kings and Britain caused enough difficulties at least to alter slave prices in Havana. (In Brazil the navy could not act at all before 1842, since the treaties with Portugal only covered activities north of the Equator.) In so far as Cuba was concerned, they could not cover the 1,500–2,000 ships now leaving Havana each year, nor the rest of the coast, and so concentrated on the African rather than the American end of the trade.

The condition of slaves who had been freed *(emancipados)* as a result of the Havana Mixed Commission's findings, usually after the intervention of a British naval ship, continued as, has been suggested, in some ways worse than that of a slave.[8] So, except for the slaves, this Equipment Treaty was not as the *Edinburgh Review* enthusiastically put it, 'a fatal blow' – partly because of the planters' feverish desire to replenish their stock of slaves after the cholera epidemic of 1833–4. In 1840 the famous traveller and abolitionist David Turnbull arrived as British Consul in Havana, appointed by Palmerston, the Foreign Secretary. He had worked for the English Anti-Slavery Society and had published a travelogue about Cuba which was violently critical of the

[5] Equipment was 'hatches with open gratings; divisions or bulkheads in the hold; spare planks for making a second or slave deck; shackles, bolts, handcuffs; more water, water casks, mess tubs, and mats than required for the crew; an unusually large boiler or more than one boiler; and an extraordinary quantity of rice'.

[6] *Cf.* Carr, 171.

[7] A small U.S. squadron was supposed to assist the British navy but it did little. See Howard, *American Slavers and the Federal Law*, 41ff., for a U.S. interpretation.

[8] See above, p. 181.

Spanish government.[9] The Spanish government protested against this appointment but did not expel him and, with their eyes on the City of London and their own debts, gave him an *exequatur*. The bizarre experiment of an abolitionist appointment in the chief slave colony of the world was begun. It was as if Father Huddleston were nominated to the consulate at Johannesburg in the 1960s.

Turnbull's arrival astounded Cuba. The *Junta de Fomento* protested, once again raising the cry of Haiti. It was a bad moment in Havana, since Captain Denman had recently destroyed the big slave barracoons on the river Gallinas, for a long time the centre of operations of Pedro Blanco: Turnbull, no doubt exaggeratedly, reported that Havana merchants besieged him, begging him to put them into an honest line of business.[10] The Spanish members of the Mixed Commission on the implementation of the ban on the slave trade were Juan Montalvo (arbitrator), and the Conde de Fernandina (commissary judge), both big plantation owners naturally, the first a son of the pioneer of the 1790s, the Conde de Casa Montalvo, the second, one of the huge Herrera clan, while the British commissary judge was Kennedy, ex-member of parliament for Tiverton who gave up his seat for the Foreign Secretary and took up this £1,600 a year appointment (together with a rent-free house).[11] The arbitrator for Britain was a Scot, Dalrymple. Turnbull proposed a census of slaves to decide which had come since 1820; those who had done so should be freed. The Spaniards refused, saying that the treaties were being fulfilled and that the recent increases of slaves derived from breeding – obviously a lie. The *Junta de Fomento* meanwhile again warned the government that 'from the moment that "Turnbull's system" was established, production [of sugar] would stop . . . leaving the territory to the disaster of general misery and the commotions of Negro against white'. At this moment came the surprising fall of Tacón.

A new captain-general, Valdés,[12] arrived with instructions to try to avoid a slave rebellion by means of encouraging white immigration; owing his appointment apparently to the friendship of his sister (the

---

[9] *Travels in the West, op. cit.*, published 1840.

[10] *P.P.*, 1850, IX, 651 (Turnbull before the House of Lords, 7 May 1850).

[11] This court gradually fell out of use as the navy concentrated more and more on the coast of Africa. Since the judges rarely agreed, it became anyway increasingly necessary to have recourse to the arbitrators; which of the two, British or Spanish, was decided by dice (Turnbull, 41).

[12] Geronimo Valdés y Sierra (1784–1855). In between, there had been Captain-General Espeleta, mild, gentle and weak and in the hands of Villanueva. Of him it was said, contrasting him with Tacón –

> El General Tacón
> Vale un Doblón
> El General Espeleta
> No vale una peseta.

Marquesa de Santa Cruz) with María Cristina, the Queen Regent, Valdés nevertheless recognized Turnbull and announced briefly that the treaties would be implemented. The British position was at this moment rubbed home by a particularly exciting chase (and capture) by H.M.S. *Fantôme* of one of Da Souza's cargoes from Whydah in the fast brig *Josephine*[13] and by several new destructions of slave barracoons belonging to Spaniards (on the river Shebar by Captain Hill, on the river Pongo by Captain Nurse, and on the Kabenda and Ambriz factories by Captain Matson).

Valdés's declaration stimulated a good deal of discontent among the slaves in the summer and autumn of 1841 partly inspired no doubt by revolts in the British West Indies, particularly Jamaica, in the early 1830s, just before abolition. There had also been a recent major slave revolt in Texas. In Cuba, some slaves building a palace for Miguel Aldama in Havana rebelled and fought a pitched battle with Spanish troops. Turnbull was blamed. Valdés received another order from Madrid (that is, from the Progressive government of General Espartero), telling him to go ahead with the emancipation of all slaves brought in since 1820; under the influence of the *intendente* Villanueva and his own instincts and interests, he made every excuse to avoid publishing this order. Palmerston backed Turnbull and dispatched warships to stand off Havana, though their commander, Vice-Admiral Hyde Parker, procrastinated when he got there. This was the closest yet that Cuba had got to abolition and indeed the closest that Britain got to war with Spain after 1815. Lord Aberdeen then succeeded Palmerston in London, and he withdrew Admiral Parker, agreeing not to press for a census of slaves for the moment and telling Turnbull also to stop pressing for it.[14] The reason was the acutely bad relationship between Britain and the U.S. at that period, chiefly over the British desire to search ships at sea for slave 'equipment' – U.S. ships as well as Spanish. Palmerston had left the subject near to war by his adjuration to the U.S. that they would soon 'look to things, not words'.[15] This was a year when nearly every slaver carried U.S. colours even when they were not U.S. ships.[16]

Turnbull, scarcely an orthodox civil servant, now began to overplay his hand. He apparently started to organize a revolt against Spain and the slave holders to abolish slavery.[17] He was finally arrested at Cárdenas

[13] Lloyd, *The Navy and the Slave Trade*, 91.
[14] See Mario Hernández y Sánchez Barba, 'David Turnbull y el problema de la esclavitud en Cuba', *Anuario de Estudios Americanos*, XIV (1937), 288–9.
[15] As quoted, H. G. Soulsby, *The Right of Search and the Slave Trade in Anglo-American Relations, 1814–1862* (1933), 60.
[16] *P.P.*, 1842, XI, 137, 182.
[17] U.S. Consul Calhoun to Daniel Webster, 4 and 6 November 1842, qu. Rauch, 40.

and expelled from Cuba, while Vice-Consul Francis Cocking and a freed Negro named José Miguel Mitchell later travelled farther inland and looked for support. But Mitchell was shortly arrested. Meantime a certain agreement was reached between the U.S. and Britain, but not on the right of search: the Ashburton Treaty of 1842 obliged the U.S. to maintain at least eighty guns on the African coast, though not to collaborate with Britain. The slave trade was in no way injured, and Aberdeen, capitulating to criticisms by free trade members of parliament such as Cobden, declared a ban on further destruction of slave factories on the African coast. By the end of 1842 the ruined factories on the river Gallinas had consequently been rebuilt, and Burón, the owner of those destroyed, was suing Captain Denman for £180,000 for loss of slaves and other property. A succession of U.S. consuls and other agents assured the Cubans that the U.S. would protect the *status quo* in Havana against the English.

These incidents were followed in Cuba by the provision of a new slave code, aimed primarily at preventing revolts. It was really a reissue of the flouted laws of 1789, rendered more strict and more systematic. Slaves could not visit plantations other than their own without permission. Slaves informing on a conspiracy were given freedom and $500.[18] Later the same year, a new captain-general, O'Donnell,[19] with an iron but greedy hand, more resolute than Valdés, more conventional than Tacón, arrived to satisfy the planters by stationing troops everywhere on the island (though 1842 was a bad year for the slave trade: perhaps only three slavers left Havana).[20] O'Donnell summed up the situation quickly: Cuba, he said, could be very easily governed with a fiddle and a fighting cock *(un violín y un gallo)*.

Early in 1843 there were new slave revolts – to begin with at the Alcancia plantation (Cárdenas) owned by Joaquín Peñalver.[21] The whole mill was wrecked except the *'casa de purga'*. The slaves moved on to the near-by *Luisa* and the *Trinidad* plantations, owned by José Baró (the slave trader), to the *'Moscú'* coffee plantation and the horse-breeding ranch at Ranchuelo. The slaves on the Cárdenas railway also rebelled, but they failed to unite with those on the plantations. A great many slaves were killed, whilst others fled into the interior[22] and were pursued as usual by bloodhounds, carefully trained for the business of tracking escaped slaves.[23]

[18] See Ortiz, *Negros Esclavos*, 370.

[19] Leopoldo O'Donnell, duke of Tetuan (1808-67) had helped overthrow Espartero the previous year.

[20] Lloyd, *The Navy and the Slave Trade*, 90.

[21] Joaquín Peñalver y O'Farrill, son of the second Marqués de Casa Peñalver; distinguished by inbreeding to such an extent that his wife, María Michela, was his sister's daughter by his uncle.

[22] Morales to Coit, 1 April 1843, qu. Ely, *Cuando reinaba*, 497.

[23] See Ballou, *Due South*, 270.

Later that year another slave revolt broke out in the *Triunvirato* mill (owned by the comparatively enlightened Alfonsos), not far from the previous year's outbursts at Santa Ana, Matanzas; 400 slaves mastered the mill, burned the cane, and marched on the neighbours, wrecking five mills before being cornered by a peasant militia. These events were however only the preliminaries to what for long has been celebrated as the most famous of all Negro and slave conspiracies, apparently betrayed to O'Donnell by a female slave.[24]

In early 1844, about 4,000 people (in Matanzas) were suddenly arrested, including over 2,000 free Negroes, over 1,000 slaves and at least seventy whites.[25] Negroes believed to be guilty of plotting were tied to ladders and whipped to confess – the name *La Escalera* thus becoming notorious, though this had been for a long time the name for a recognized type of punishment. Seventy-eight were shot, and perhaps 100 more whipped to death.[26] The period of acute repression continued for half a year. Among those shot was the mulatto poet 'Placido',[27] the musician Román and others of the more brilliant and attractive free Negroes. José de la Luz y Caballero, Professor of Philosophy at the College of San Francisco, was among those accused though he was acquitted.[28] The Negro or mulatto regiments in the militia were abolished and dispersed. Turnbull, then in Jamaica, was accused of abetting the conspiracy. It seems that in fact there was an elaborate conspiracy in Matanzas, organized through the *cabildos* and drum dances of the sugar estates, the 'king' and 'queen' of the weekly dance being the agents of conspiracy. One slave testified that poison was contemplated as a weapon, 'more effective than war'. On the other hand, it seems evident that the authorities used the occasion to disembarrass themselves of all trouble-makers, real and potential.[29] The consequence was that the small mulatto or Negro *bourgeoisie* of Matanzas was destroyed and even those who were not shot but merely imprisoned for a time were unwilling or unable to take any further part in conspiracy: thus

[24] A mulatto sergeant had warned O'Donnell the year before of a plot. A description of a slave revolt on the estate of Rafael Montalvo is given by Comtesse Merlin, *La Havane*, II, 157. The interesting part of this tale is that both Montalvo and his nearest neighbour, the Marqués de Cárdenas, were living on their estates.

[25] Aimes, 146; Vidal Morales y Morales, *Iniciadores y Primeros Mártires de la Revolución Cubana*, 3 vols (1931), 147; Guerra and Santovenia, IV, 71.

[26] Vidal Morales, I, 335.

[27] The *nom de plume* of Gabriel de la Concepción Valdés (1809–44), illegitimate child of a mulatto barber of Havana and a Spanish dancer from Burgos. Worked as a printer's apprentice, won Havana poetry prize, 1834. Practised as a romantic poet in Havana and Matanzas in late 1830s and till 1844.

[28] José de la Luz y Caballero (1800–62). Afterwards founder and president of the College San Salvador. One of the great intellectual influences in Cuba, a liberal of courage, learning and resilience.

[29] See Ortiz, *Negros Esclavos*, 434; José Ignacio Rodríguez, *Vida de Don José de la Luz y Caballero*, 143.

the poet Manzano even abandoned poetry after being in prison and ended his life as an obscure cook. Captain-General O'Donnell, meantime, was investing some of his profits from bribes in a great mill with North American machinery on the Isle of Pines to procure gold from some interesting but deceptive quartz.[30]

This policy, carried out with a severity which Tacón never approached, had the effect of preventing further revolts for some time. Most planters enthusiastically backed the policy and those who did not, such as Domingo del Monte, were sent into exile. Even stricter regulations for slaves followed. All African religious ceremonies, such as those sponsored by Tacón, were banned. Plantations became even more prison-like. The series of incidents, however, gave a violent shock to the planters. It actually made them for the first time almost inclined to listen to arguments designed to end the slave trade, since that seemed (as men such as the still-exiled Saco put it once more, in his *La Supresión del Tráfico*, published in Paris in 1845) the only way to keep Cuba from a racial revolution. The numbers of slaves imported in the years immediately after *La Escalera* seem to have dropped considerably;[31] but, of course, prices and profits (on slave trading) rose to such an extent that in this curious tropical world of suspected conspiracies it almost seemed that the whole crisis had been devised by men like Zulueta or Pastor to inflate the value of the slaves they could offer in the market. Freed slaves (*emancipados*) were resold, Captain-General O'Donnell making a good profit (according to the British Commissioners)[32] but the English, still affected by Lord Aberdeen's timidity, would only exert diplomatic pressure. A commission in Havana was set up to report on the application of a new Spanish law banning the slave trade – a commission ironically composed of Joaquin Gomez, the Marques de Estevez, the Conde de Fernandina, Brigadier-General Juan O'Farrill and Jose de Arango – all of course slave owners and Gomez a retired slave-dealer. O'Donnell thought that a ban on slave traffic would not only ruin the Cuban economy but cause the creoles to seek to escape from Spanish rule, on the grounds that, outnumbering Negroes, they would have no need of the Spanish army.[33] But anyway no slaves were to be touched in plantations. The personnel of the commission made nonsense of the law. The Spanish government toyed with slave breeding on the Birginian model, while some planters once again began to look northwards as a means of preserving their hold upon the island whose wealth had now gone up by at least a half since the idea of joining the U.S. was mooted.

[30] *Cf.* Wright, *Cuba*, 288.

[31] Aimes, 170.

[32] See Palmerston's letter to Bulmer, 3 August 1846 (Madrid).

[33] O'Donnell to the Spanish Secretary of State, July 1846, quoted in A. F. Corwin, *Spain and the Abolition of Slavery in Cuba* (1968), 86.

CHAPTER XVII

Manifest Destiny

Not long after the slave revolts near Matanzas, the U.S. Secretary of State, Daniel Webster, received an alarming communication from one of the Cuban planters exiled after *La Escalera*, Domingo del Monte, a literary member of a rich though *nouveau* Cuban family and secretary of the Cárdenas to Soledad de Bemba railway.[1] Del Monte said that the English, wearying of unavailing efforts to secure the abolition of the slave trade, intended 'to seize Cuba, free the Negroes and establish a black military Republic under British protection'.[2]

The report (unfortunately for the black majority in Cuba) was baseless, but its views showed the extent to which even enlightened Cuban planters, terrified of abolitionism, were prepared now to drag the United States into the struggle for their own preservation. The U.S. administration on the other hand also feared that the English were about to enforce abolition even in Texas.[3] Washington Irving, the U.S. minister in Madrid, was instructed to find out all English moves in respect of Cuba.[4]

The centre of what became known as Cuban '*anexionismo*' was the Club de la Habana; among its leaders was Carlos Núñez del Castillo, Director of the Savings Bank of Havana, son of the Núñez del Castillo who had laboured for the same end in 1822. His cousins the Drakes were also concerned in the cause. There was also Domingo del Monte's brother-in-law, Miguel Aldama, Saco's chief financial helper, now owner of five fine mills[5] and one of the original backers of the Havana railway. On one of his plantations one of the worst slave

---

[1] Domingo del Monte y Aponte (1804–53). Owner of the *Ceres* sugar plantation, 900 acres at Cimarrones (Cárdenas). He had been an intimate friend of the poet Heredia and had himself written poetry. Famous for his *tertulias* to which young Cuban writers would come. Married Rosa Aldama, sister of Miguel. Known for his correspondence. The del Montes came originally from Alava, like so many Cuban families, and thereafter passed to Santo Domingo. Domingo's father, Leonardo del Monte y Medrano (d. 1820), a Spanish colonial official, had been *Oidor* of Havana, 1810–20. Delmonte, with Francisco Pobeda, is regarded as the first *Cuban* poet in the sense of looking to the island for a unique experience rather than to Europe or elsewhere in the Americas.

[2] Webster to Robert B. Campbell, U.S. Consul in Havana. House Executive Documents, 32: 1 doc. 121, 38–40.

[3] See A. A. Ettinger, *The Mission to Spain of Pierre Soulé, 1853–1855* (1932), 21–2.

[4] State Dept. Instructions, 9 January 1844.

[5] *Concepción, Santa Rosa, Santo Domingo, San José* (Sabanilla, Matanzas) *Armonía* (Alacranes, Güines).

revolts had occurred. Through sheer wealth, apparently, he became effectively the leader of the group.[6] Another member was Cristóbal Madán, a powerful and articulate merchant and planter of Matanzas (owner of the *Rosa* sugar mill, Cimarrones), a Cuban who made himself an American citizen, simply, apparently, in order to escape the number of Spanish taxes otherwise payable.[7] He was a vigorous critic of allowing 'idle' free Negroes to sit about doing nothing in Havana instead of dragging them into the fields as workmen and, like the others, an early backer of the railway, though his pet idea of a line from Matanzas to Coliseo (with Joaquín de Arrieta of the *Flor de Cuba* mill farther east of Coliseo) had not yet materialized.[8] Another member of the club was John S. Thrasher, as American journalist with a Cuban mother, living in Havana, editor of *El Faro Industrial,* known for his annotated edition of Humboldt's study on Cuba (which, however, carefully omitted the sections which criticized slavery).[9] There were also José María Sánchez y Iznaga and his cousin José Aniceto Iznaga, members of the large clan of Iznagas of Trinidad, and the enlightened planter Francisco de Frías, Count of Pozos Dulces,[10] specially hypno- tized by the experience of Texas which, after seceding from Mexico in 1835 and existing for a short while independently, joined the U.S. in 1845. Others included Gaspar Betancourt Cisneros,[11] of a prominent Camagüey landed family. These were only the articulate members of a wide section of *criollo* opinion, though, apart from José Luis Alfonso and Carlos Nuñez de Castillo, few of the older Cuban families such as the Montalvos or the O'Farrills played a part. The Drake family, however, played an essential role as a means of communication with New York and of distributing literature.

The purpose of these men was to preserve slavery and so safeguard the chase for wealth in the future. They were leaders in the develop- ment both of Cuban railways and of trade with the U.S. The abolition of English tariffs in 1846–8 was opening the English market, then the biggest in the world, to foreign grown sugar. The end of the British

[6] He was the son of Domingo Aldama, an originally poor Basque who had founded the *Santa Rosa* mill in 1818.
[7] See Madan, *Llamamiento de la isla de Cuba a la nación españda, etc.* (1855?), 13–17. He was the 'mentor' of the U.S. Consul in Havana, W. H. Robertson (Portell Vilá, II, 78).
[8] See Ely, *Cuando reinabe,* 634.
[9] For Thrasher, see Portell Vilá, II, 129.
[10] Francisco de Frías y Jacob, second Conde de Pozos Dulces (1809–77). Educated in Baltimore. Succeeded his father in the family estates, 1829. Travelled in Europe, 1832–3, studied science in Paris, 1842–6.
[11] Gaspar Betancourt Cisneros (1803–66). The Betancourts were an immense clan originally settled in the Canary Islands, conquered in 1404 by the French adventurer Jean de Bethen- court, from Normandy. Gaspar's family was well-known in Puerto Príncipe (Camagüey), for several generations. He had been educated in the U.S., and returned to write a brilliant series of descriptive articles in the *Gaceta de Puerto Príncipe* under the pseudonym *El Lugareño.*

West Indian monopoly had come. The slave trade to Cuba was thereby given an immense shot in the arm at a time when it had otherwise been in decline (possibly no slave cargo was landed in 1845 and only two in 1846).[12] Gaspar Betancourt Cisneros expressed the Cuban planters' doctrine in its purest form: 'The English Cabinet asked several years ago that liberty be given to all slaves introduced into Cuba since 1820; and since it is very much to be feared she will renew her request and that Spain will now consent to it, the annexationist revolution is essential for saving us.'[13] Some, educated in the U.S., also wished explicitly to share in the vast adventure of North American capitalist enterprise; some merely wished to preserve and extend existing commercial relations, since now the U.S. had long been Cuba's largest trading partner, much more than Spain. Much of the machinery used on the sugar mills, the railway lines, the engines, some of the technicians, and the loans attached to capital in sugar plantations were now often North American. In 1844 the streets of Havana had gas lighting provided by a New Orleans company.

The 'annexationists' were at this time undoubtedly the most enterprising and the most realistic of the Cuban planters. Intelligent Cubans had been sending their sons to U.S. schools or universities for a generation, and Cuban and U.S. freemasons were formally connected. In the 1840s the annexationists had essentially simple motives; comparatively young men, having sided with the cause of wealth, they were determined to make the cause work more effectively. Had they wished to join the U.S. for the sake of the inspiring idea that that country represented in the 1840s to say, the Germans or the Irish, rather than because they wished to preserve their wealth, they might perhaps have triumphed; and, if Cuba had joined the Union in 1845–50, she would have later been ranked with the slave states and the Confederacy. This might itself have had considerable and distressing consequences in the Civil War.

Not all Cubans, of course, backed these schemes and not even most articulate ones. Saco, in Paris, believed that 'a war for annexation would be ... a certain way of losing our slaves', as the Spaniards would probably free the Negroes if the planters rebelled.[14] On these grounds Saco, who never agreed with anyone, had a vigorous controversy with the annexationists for some years.

The annexationist movement however would not have gathered much momentum had it not struck a vigorous response in the U.S. The U.S. Secretary of State, J. C. Calhoun, was an inveterate champion of slavery. At a public dinner in 1845 the Vice-President, George Dallas,

[12] *P.P.*, XV, 437, and *ibid.*, 1847–8, XVIII, 65.
[13] In a letter, quoted by Saco, *Contra La Anexión*, (1835), I 184.
[14] Letter, 10 March 1848, qu. Vidal Morales, II, 94–101.

publicly toasted 'the annexation of Cuba'.[15] 1846–8 saw the U.S. war with Mexico. The treaty of Guadelupe Hidalgo brought California and New Mexico to the U.S. – a total of 918,000 square miles – an area whose potential wealth to the victor was symbolized within a few months of the treaty's signature by the great gold rush to California of 1849.[16] In the south of the United States, newspaper opinion, at least, was heady with grasping and guileful expansionism. Texas's attachment to the Union in 1845 had already meant one increase in the number of slave states. This seemed to suggest final victory for the new world opened up by the wealth brought by sugar from Louisiana.[17] Havana and New Orleans merchants were closely connected; the Drakes had a branch there. The American South was not in the 1840s an old world, jealously preserving traditional customs; but a new, restless one, economically awakening, imbued with the frontier rather than a settled spirit, less anxious to preserve old ways than to gain a new victory, more a military dictatorship of white men over black than a liberal democracy. Even slavery was less a time-honoured institution based on generations of mutual cohabitation between black and white, than a system of forced labour completely renewed due to the recent development of cotton on a large scale.

Later, in the 1850s, some Americans of the South would hanker after an immense Caribbean military empire, based on slavery, rich from its sugar and cotton. A dreamy racism indeed caught hold of some Southern intellectuals. These were mostly young men, ambitious romantics with a streak of violence which was specially marked where the idea of the annexation of Cuba was concerned: 'This full-blooded Anglo-American race is destined to sweep over the world with the might of a tornado. The Hispano-Morescan (*sic*) race will quail.' (Thus the *New Orleans Creole Courier*, 27 January 1855.) The *New Orleans Delta* went further: the Cuban language would disappear.

> For the bastard Latin of their nation cannot stand for any time against the conquering power of the robust and hardy English . . . Their political sentimentalism and anarchical tendencies follow rapidly after the language and by degrees the absorption of the people becomes complete – all due to the inevitable dominance of the American mind over an inferior race.[18]

In 1845 John L. O'Sullivan, sometime 'Barnburner' and 'Free soiler',

[15] J. M. Callahan, *Cuba and International Relations* (1899), 195.
[16] The U.S. Commissioner in Mexico was none other than the wily Nicolas Trist, who left his Havana consul-generalship after being implicated in the slaving scandals. California is of course naturally as much a part of Mexico as of the U.S.
[17] See above, p. 127.
[18] *New Orleans Delta*, 3 January 1853, Quoted Foner.

editor of the *Democratic Review*, coined the phrase 'manifest destiny' to describe the expectation that the U.S., thanks to the superior qualities of the Anglo-Saxons as such (including presumably the Irish) and to their democratic institutions, would inevitably absorb their neighbours.

O'Sullivan was brother-in-law to the Cuban planter Cristóbal Madán who had set up as the leader of the annexationist lobby in New York early in the same year.[19] Indeed Madán, inferior Hispano-Morescan though he was, himself may have been the inspiration of this all-American phrase.[20]

In early 1847 O'Sullivan went to Havana with the editor of the *New York Sun*, Moses Yale Beach.[21] They met Madán's friends of the Habana Club, in Miguel Aldama's new palace (now finished, despite the slave revolts). When they returned, they launched a campaign for the U.S. to buy Cuba, just as Consul Trist had suggested and as the U.S. had bought Louisiana and Florida in 1804 and 1819, and were to buy Alaska in 1867.[22] On 6 July 1847, O'Sullivan wrote to the Secretary of State, James Buchanan, telling him that many rich Cubans wanted to join the Union rather than be independent and that they were ready to contribute largely towards purchase by the USA.[23] O'Sullivan had been a distributor of patronage for President Polk and knew Washington well[24] but he was nevertheless inclined to romanticism, being 'full of grand and world-embracing schemes which seemed to him, and which he made appear to others, vastly practicable and alluring but which invariably miscarried'.[25] Two weeks later Beach in the *New York Sun* came out with a demand: 'Cuba by geographical position necessity and right . . . must be ours . . . give us Cuba and our possessions are complete': Cuba was 'the garden of the world, the key to the Gulf'.[26]

During the rest of 1847 Buchanan and President Polk were occupied

[19]. J. L. O'Sullivan (1813–95), born in Gibraltar.

[20] But see J. W. Pratt, 'Origin of Manifest Destiny', *American Historical Review*, XXXII (July 1927), in which it is argued that O'Sullivan coined it in the *Morning News*, July 1845.

[21] Moses Yale Beach (1800–68). A man of parts. Invented a machine powered by gunpowder explosion, 1819. Invented rag cutting machine. Entered newspapers from owning a paper mill. Special emissary of President to Mexico 1846. First U.S. publisher to use syndicated articles or a foreign edition. In the Mexican war organized a news service for his paper 78 hours faster than the mails. (*Cf.* Frank M. O'Brien, *The Story of 'The Sun' New York 1833–1928* (1928), 139ff.)

[22] Senator David Yulee of Florida (born David Levy, in the British West Indies) had made a similar but less publicized proposal in 1845. See Rauch, 45.

[23] James Buchanan (1791–1868), afterwards President. Pennsylvania lawyer. Senator, 1837–46: 'There is nothing in his conduct which indicates political wisdom' was the verdict on his presidency by Carl Russell Fish.

[24] Rauch, 49.

[25] Julian Hawthorne, *Nathaniel Hawthorne and His Wife* (Cambridge, 1844), I, 160. O'Sullivan was a great friend of Hawthorne's.

[26] *New York Sun*, 23 July 1847, quoted in Rauch, 59.

with winding up the Mexican war. Beach's plan was greeted with ridicule, at first, though less so after the English Conservative leader, Lord George Bentinck, Disraeli's artificial hero, had told the House of Commons that Britain ought to seize Cuba to pay Spain's debts to her.[27] In 1848, a contrived tide of enthusiasm began to sweep the U.S. for the annexation of Cuba. A semi-monthly, *La Verdad*, edited by Gaspar Betancourt Cisneros along with Moses Beach's daughter, Cora Montgomery, devoted itself exclusively to annexation. (The Drake brothers ensured distribution in Havana.) It was an election year and Senator Lewis Cass already had his eye on the democratic candidacy (which he obtained), when in May he proposed the purchase of Cuba.[28] Senator Jefferson Davis, a hero of the Mexican war (where he had been wounded as brigadier under his ex-father-in-law, Zachary Taylor) also urged the capture of Cuba, though with Yucatán too, while Senator Westcott of Florida justified the idea of annexation by announcing that Britain 'sought to emancipate the slaves in Cuba and to strike at the southern portion of this confederacy through its domestic institutions . . . Are [the U.S.] prepared to see the slaves in Cuba emancipated by the efforts of Great Britain? My state will not assent to such a state of things.'[29]

Meantime the Cuban annexationists also issued a proclamation:

> Cuba, united to this strong and respected nation [U.S.], whose southern interests would be identified with hers, would be assured serenity and future prosperity; her riches would increase, *her farms and slaves would double their value*[30] and her whole territory treble its value. Liberty would be given to private enterprise and the system of hateful and harmful restrictions which paralysed commerce would be destroyed.

On 10 May Senator Stephen Douglas, whose political career had been founded on the idea of expansion, saw President Polk with John O'Sullivan to urge the purchase of Cuba; Polk, a secretive man – he was known as 'the mole' – said nothing, though he explicitly thought the plan good.[31] On 18 May the U.S. Consul in Havana, General Robert Campbell, wrote to Secretary of State Buchanan that a 'certain Spanish general' would shortly stage a revolt; if it were successful, immediate application would be made to the U.S. for annexation.[32] This Spanish general was Narciso López who had distinguished

[27] Hansard, 3rd Series, XCIII, 1286–1303.
[28] Lewis Cass (1782–1866). Lawyer, previously Secretary for War under Andrew Jackson.
[29] *Congressional Globe* (30:1), Appendix, 608.
[30] Author's italics.
[31] *The Diary of James K. Polk, 1845–1849*, ed. M. M. Quaife, 4 vols (1910), III, 446.
[32] Robert Blair Campbell (1809–62), consul and congressman.

himself fighting against Bolívar and the Carlists and, going to Cuba with Captain-General Valdés, had been President of the Military Commission, being known for the severity of his sentences against free Negroes. Narciso López, though Venezuelan born, and now in his 'fifties, was related to at least two powerful planter families – the Iznagas (his uncle was José María Sánchez Iznaga), and his brother-in-law was the progressive planter, Pozos Dulces.[33]

On 30 May Polk proposed the purchase of Cuba to his cabinet; the Secretary of the Treasury, Robert Walker (leader of Polk's cabinet), and the Secretary of the Navy, John Y. Mason, both from the South, agreed. The Attorney-General, Cave Johnson from Tennessee, opposed the idea and the Secretary of State, Buchanan, always cautious, gave general but rather vague approval.[34] As a result, Buchanan instructed the U.S. minister in Madrid, Romulus M. Sanders, to open negotiations with the Spanish government: the President was willing to pay \$100M (£23½M).[35] Simultaneously, General Narciso López was apparently betrayed by Buchanan, who allowed the Spanish authorities to discover too what was planned;[36] anyway López fled and escaped, and his aides were captured and tried, though no one was shot – an unusual consequence in Cuban revolutions, and one which may have been itself caused by the U.S. connivance in its discovery. Among others who escaped was the Costumbrista novelist, Cirilo Villaverde, whose *Cecilia Valdés* had been published ten years before and who was in fact condemned to the *garrote vil*.[37]

But President Polk's plan to buy Cuba directly failed. Romulus Sanders received his instructions to buy the island in June 1848 and, shortly afterwards, Polk's vice-president, Dallas, received a visit from an agent of María Cristina, the queen mother of Spain, in the person of a Philadelphia lawyer though a Spaniard, who said that the queen would herself make the sale.[38] In Madrid Sanders went about his delicate business with the maximum procrastination, indiscretion and incompetence. The Spanish government fell. The *New York Herald* published a letter from a correspondent in Madrid revealing that these negotiations were going on. Uproar followed in Madrid as soon as this

[33] See R. G. Caldwell, *The López Expeditions to Cuba, 1848–51* (1915). Narciso López, 1798–1851, born in Venezuela. Governor of Valencia, 1839, General, 1840; Married a Cuban.

[34] *Polk Diary*, III, 469. *Cf.* William E. Dodd, *Robert James Walker, Imperialist* (Chicago, 1913).

[35] *Polk Diary*, III, 468–93; Buchanan to Sanders, 17 June 1848, House Doc., 121, 42–9.

[36] *Polk Diary*, III, 478–88. The U.S. minister in Madrid told the Spanish government and Buchanan told Calderón de la Barca (*cf.* Rauch, 77).

[37] Villaverde (1802–94) was the most famous of the Costumbrista novelists and *Cecilia Valdés* is probably the most famous Cuban novel; it describes the love of the young son of a *negrero*, Leonardo Gamboa, for a young mulata, Cecilia Valdés, who turns out to be his bastard sister. The canvas is large. The influence of Scott and Manzoni is evident, the latter through the inspiration of the Tuscan Consul in Havana, Pablo Veglia.

[38] *Polk Diary*, IV, 4–5.

was known. The new Spanish Foreign Minister, Pedro Pidal, told Romulus Sanders that 'sooner than see the island transferred to *any power* [*sic*] they would prefer to see it sunk in the Ocean'.[39]

No doubt the price offered was indeed derisory; already taxes alone brought Spain $10M (£2,350,000) a year. This was a serious blow for President Polk and the Democrats; two weeks later their candidate, Senator Cass, was defeated in the presidential election, and General Zachary Taylor, the successful commander in the Mexican war, became president in March 1849.

Narciso López, the discomfited rebel of June 1848, was nevertheless still at large and so of course were his powerful backers. By July 1849 he had fitted out an expedition of liberation from Round Island, New Orleans. Several U.S. veterans of the Mexican war agreed to serve. Others were attracted by an offer of $1,000 (£235) and 160 acres in Cuba if they were successful. López offered the command to Jefferson Davis who recommended Colonel Robert E. Lee. Lee refused and López decided to take command himself.[40] But the U.S. government ultimately decided to step in to break up the expedition as 'grossly' violating neutrality laws.[41] President Taylor, though a Mississippi slave owner, was not keen on Polk's idea; if Cuba were going to join the U.S., the government should surely buy it honestly rather than let it free itself in a war which might destroy its slaves.[42]

Federico Roncali, Conde de Alcoy, one of the more intelligent Spanish captains-general of Cuba, had meantime arrived in Havana – in succession to O'Donnell; he wrote to his masters on 29 September, in complete seriousness, that, after all, 'emancipation [of slaves] might be the only means of preventing the island's take-over by the annexationists ... this terrible weapon could ... prevent the loss of the island.'[43] Roncali was certainly regarded in Havana as attempting to end the slave trade and in 1848 he even dared to interfere with a supply of slaves being sent to the millionaire Zulueta, ineffectually since Zulueta and the slaves were allowed to go to New York.[44] On the other hand too, Roncali found it difficult to act because of the heightened activities of the Spanish queen mother's slave agent Parejo.[45] (France released

[39] For these negotiations, see Rauch, 81-97.
[40] Caldwell, *The López Expeditions to Cuba*, 49.
[41] *Cf.* Rauch, 101-20.
[42] Some controversy attaches to this action; Portell Vilá and Narciso López's admirers say that President Taylor acted as he did because he feared López was at heart for Cuban independence not annexation. But P. Foner (*A History of Cuba and its Relations with The U.S.*, II 1962, 46) appears to be correct when he says that Taylor was involved in the conference of 1850 and did not want to antagonize the North when he was trying to save the Union.
[43] *Boletín del Archivo Nacional*, XVL (Madrid) No. 4, 281.
[44] Report of H.M. Commissary Judge, 1 January 1849, qu. Madden, 193-4.
[45] See Mathieson, 142-3, for comment.

the slaves in her West Indian colonies in 1848, thus increasing the Cuban slaveholders' sense of isolation and the drive to get as many slaves in before such a disaster befell them too.)

But for the next few years English efforts to end the slave trade flagged a good deal. Some free traders, and even some philanthropists, still opposed coercion or the use of force, such as the destruction of barracoons. The Royal Navy was divided over the tactics, 'close blockade', or 'distant cruising'. There was also doubt over the desirability of steam vessels. Palmerston and Russell had lost prestige since, though advocates of abolition and the continuance of the squadron off West Africa, they had also defended free trade and hence the entry of foreign, that is Cuban and Brazilian, slave sugar (as well of course as southern cotton). The cost of the West African squadron was attacked, in men and revenue. Others, such as Wilberforce's successor Buxton, were preoccupied by alternative trades for Africa. There was hostility to any idea that the British might become permanently responsible for the territory around the African slave ports. Meantime, there was also a temporary absence of anxiety in the sugar planters' efforts to continue the trade in Cuba since about 30,000 slaves who had been working on coffee plantations became available in 1848.[46] In the early 1850s some of the fast clippers which had been used in North America for trade with Cuba were turned over to slaving; thus the *Sunny South*, sold at Havana for $18,000 (£4,400), became the *Emanuel* and was caught with 800 slaves on board.[47] Palmerston now pointed out to Spain that the best way to ensure control of Cuba was to institute reform so that the island would lose its attraction to the U.S. South.[48]

The discomfiture of López's second attempt led to the break-up of the annexationist group. The 'responsible' and richer planters such as Madán and Betancourt Cisneros concluded that the *status quo* could be preserved indefinitely since, though the Spanish government had refused to declare the slave trade to be piracy, as the British demanded, the rise of free trade suggested the British were not going to act either. López, on the other hand, was heading in a more and more violent direction, linking himself with more extreme Southern politicians, especially with the truculent and violent Governor Quitman of Mississippi.[49]

Quitman had been military governor of Mexico City after its surrender in 1847 and wanted the U.S. to absorb Mexico as well as Cuba.[50] In mid 1850, one of his close friends (later his biographer) was to express succinctly what he felt:

[46] Madden, 194.
[47] Dow, 276.
[48] See Ettinger, 43.
[49] John Anthony Quitman (1798–1858), mason and lawyer.
[50] John F. H. Claiborne, *Life and Correspondence of John A. Quitman* (1860).

Our people want Cuba free not only because they detest the Despotism of its government but for reasons of political necessity. If the Cubans wish to become free and to be admitted to share our civil rights, very well. *If not they must go away from Cuba*, which must be ours, whether its present inhabitants desire it or not.[51]

López proposed that Quitman should lead the next expedition against the Spaniards in Cuba. Quitman decided he could serve the cause better by remaining governor in Mississippi. But he allowed López to gather a new expedition, backed by leading Mississippi and Louisiana slave owners (such as Laurence Sigur, editor of the *New Orleans Delta*). New Orleans had long loved romantic and piratical causes. Bank's Arcade in Magazine Street had been the established centre for wild expeditions since Davy Crockett organized his raids into Texas in the 1830s. The port authorities were easily suborned. Freemasonry provided a strong link between López, Quitman and other Cubans and Louisianans.[52] In April 1850 López issued a new proclamation, ending with the ringing words: 'The star of Cuba ... will emerge beautiful and shining on being admitted with glory into the splendid North American constellation where [*sic*] destiny leads it.'

A month later the 600-strong expedition landed near Cárdenas and captured the Spanish garrison and the governor. But the Cubans took to the hills, not rallying to what seemed to them an American expedition. López then decided to re-embark and he returned to Key West, pursued by Spanish ships. Back in Key West and greeted curiously as a hero, he and his backers were accused of a breach of the American neutrality laws.[53]

Nothing daunted, however, López sailed again in August with a fourth expedition of about 400 men, including many Hungarian exiles as well as Cuban; López was clearly influenced by the romantic appeal of Kossuth, who had received an official welcome in New Orleans in 1850.[54] This time this romancer and dreamer at last came up against political reality. Two internal Cuban risings planned for the same time were crushed and its leaders captured and executed – the chief, Joaquín de Agüero (a freemason) being betrayed by his wife's confessor.[55] The flags of independence – a single star like that of Texas on the background of a Masonic triangle – were unwisely laid on altars

[51] 14 June 1850, Claiborne Papers, University of North Carolina, qu. Rauch, 158.
[52] *Cf.* James B. Scott, *Outline of the Rise and Progress of Freemasonry in Louisiana* (1925), 61–5.
[53] *Cf.* Rauch, 128–50.
[54] Ettinger, 314.
[55] Joaquín de Agüero (1816–52) came of an old Camagüey family, many of whom became associated with this revolution and most of whom were poets. The first Agüero in Cuba was Fernando, established in 1620, coming from Burgos.

ready to be blessed. López meantime landed at Bahía Honda, with Colonel Crittenden, a veteran of the Mexican war, like most others involved in these ideas, and nephew of the U.S. Attorney-General, as his second-in-command.

Almost immediately, the two commanders were separated. Crittenden lost most of his men, returned to the sea, and embarked in small boats. They were captured and quickly shot in the Plaza Major in Havana. López was taken shortly afterwards with 160 men. After trial for treason, he was publicly garrotted and all his followers, except four, were sent to work in the quicksilver mines of Spain, being ultimately pardoned.[56] There were prolonged riots in New Orleans at this news. The Spanish consulate was wrecked. But the U.S. government was not prepared to do anything to protest against the persecution of an expedition of which it disapproved. The planters of Cuba and their friends seem not to have been displeased either. One merchant, José M. Morales, a partner in the house of Drake, wrote to his North American correspondent: 'Our Government was perfectly justified in not giving quarter to the filibusters . . . though modern times demand conciliatory measures.'[57] Merchants were as anxious as the U.S. government to avoid the liberation of Cuba by war, which would risk the slave properties; they too wanted liberation by cash.

The career of Narciso López added another element to the confused history of U.S.–Cuban relations; for some Cubans, such as the eminent and influential Professor Portell Vilá, he was a hero and a martyr for Cuban liberty; but in truth he was an agent of annexation, and to the South. More curious still, the Cuban flag from the day of independence in 1902 to the present day is one designed by Lopez: a single white star on a red background, the whole against blue stripes – a visual suggestion of Cuba's aspiration to join the Union.

[56] Vidal Morales, II, 128ff.; Ettinger, 46; Portell Vilá, I, 457–61.
[57] Morales to Coit, qu. Ely, *Cuando reinaba*, 658–9.

CHAPTER XVIII

Annexationism

The death of López, however, was not at all the end of *anexionismo*. Cuba could still satisfy the land-hunger of the planters of the U.S. south and so guarantee perhaps the preservation of southern slavery. Jean Jacques Ampère, travelling in the 1840s, was told that Cuba had been detached from the U.S. by the Gulf Stream and that Cuba had to be annexed to provide a sanatorium for U.S. consumptives.[1] New Orleans continued to be a centre of agitation to absorb Cuba, powerfully backed by economic interest. Newspapers such as *De Bow's Review* and the *New Orleans Courier* continued their propaganda, calling for most unusual action in most bizarre causes:

> We have a destiny to perform, a manifest destiny over all Mexico, over South America, over the West Indies and Canada. The Sandwich islands are as necessary to our Eastern, as the isles of the gulf to our western, command. The gates of the Chinese Empire must be thrown down. . . . The people stand ready to hail tomorrow . . . a collision with the mightiest empire upon earth . . . [and] a successor to Washington [shall] ascend the chair of universal empire.[2]

The *Richmond Enquirer* in 1854 imagined that a political union could be forged between the U.S. South and Brazil.[3]

The fact indeed that the most prominent Southern ideologues in the U.S. coveted territory to preserve their civilization is the best proof that the desire to expand was at the heart of the crisis which led to the American Civil War.[4]

In September 1851 a new Cuban conspiracy against Spain took form led by Francisco de Frías. Frías, whose father had bought himself the title of Count of Pozos Dulces (Sweet Wells), was Narciso López's brother-in-law. Quitman was head of the 'supreme council' of this conspiracy in New Orleans. They gathered 'chapters' in many North American states till a branch of the conspiracy was unearthed in Cuba in mid-1852. Eduardo Facciolo, one of the leaders (an editor of *La Voz*

---

[1] *Promenade en Amérique, Etats-Unis, Cuba, Mexique*, 2 vols (1855), II, 223-4.
[2] *De Bow's Review*, August 1850, qu. Rauch, 187.
[3] Qu. Genovese, 249.
[4] See Genovese, 254ff. for a refutation of the argument that the Southern slave-owners were 'just' capitalists who happened to have money in slaves.

del Pueblo Cubano, the first revolutionary paper of Cuba), was garrotted and Pozos Dulces imprisoned.[5] A little later, the extent of backing of annexationism in North America and of Pozos Dulces's organization, 'the Order of the Lone Star', was revealed, after the Spaniards gave out that they would refuse permission to berth to the North American mail steamer, the *Crescent City*, because the purser William Smith was a conspirator. Another riot followed in New Orleans, egged on by the owner of the steamer, George Law, president of the U.S. Mail Steamship Company (which, since 1847, had a contract to carry mail twice a month from Panama to New York via Havana and New Orleans). Law was the outstanding shipping magnate interested in annexation, leader of the 'steamboat crowd' – 'Live Oak George' – a powerful man in the politics of New York.[6] Crowds in New Orleans called for war; Law himself perhaps hoped that war between the U.S. and Spain would swiftly follow and the subsequent peace would give him a chance to extend passenger traffic to the island.[7] The Spaniards delicately avoided grounds for war by finally allowing the ship and the purser to enter Havana but it was nevertheless in a decidedly bellicose atmosphere that Franklin Pierce and the Democrats fought and won the presidential elections of November 1852. Stephen Douglas, a candidate for the Democratic nomination, backed by Law and Young America, offered the single platform of Cuba. Meanwhile slave trading to Cuba had received a fresh fillip by the establishment of the new 'Portuguese Company' in New York, backed by well-known Eurafrican and Portuguese financiers[8].

The somewhat second-rate administration of Franklin Pierce returned immediately, so far as Cuba was concerned, to the purchase policy of James Polk. The U.S. Secretary at War – influential over the President – was now ex-senator Jefferson Davis, an annexationist. Pierce appointed as Minister to Spain Senator Pierre Soulé, a flamboyant and eloquent New Orleans lawyer of French birth[9] who had in the previous congress been already an advocate of secession by the southern states. In January 1853, before his appointment, he had assured the Senate that, to guarantee slavery in the USA, Cuba should be acquired, if possible by negotiation, if not by conquest.[10]

[5] Vidal Morales, II, 359–89.

[6] George Law (1806–81). President of Dry Dock Bank, afterwards of 8th and 9th Avenue Railway, New York City.

[7] This is Rauch's interpretation (Rauch, 232).

[8] See Howard, *American Slavers and the Federal Law*, 50ff.

[9] Pierre Soulé (1801–70). A young lawyer in Paris, and a friend of Dumas, he had been arrested for political activities in 1825 and went to the U.S. where he practised law at New Orleans. In the U.S. Senate in 1847, he led the 'right' wing of Southern democracy. See the sketch of his career in Ettinger, 100–13, 'of swarthy complexion, black flashing eyes, and Frenchified dress and speech'.

[10] Ettinger, 99–100. In the same speech he warmly praised López and the filibusters.

A radical in Paris, Soulé had become an imperialist in New Orleans. Cured completely of his 'dreams of liberty' by a short stay in Haiti, then slumbering nervelessly under the corrupt tyranny of President Boyer, Soulé had already had an extraordinary career; his appointment to Madrid was almost as provocative a step as it had been to appoint Turnbull to Havana; his chief, the new Secretary of State, the New York politician William Marcy, was also known to back annexation. Horace Greeley's *New York Tribune* had no doubt that 'if every other expedient fails to acquire Cuba, our new minister will not hesitate to do his best to get up a war between us and Spain'.[11] Still, beneath Soulé's tactless and flamboyant manner, it is clear that he maintained an at least theoretical devotion to Republican sentiments, and a hostility towards monarchical systems, though these views stopped short of disapproving slavery.[12]

Soulé left for Madrid in the middle of the year, however, without any purchase instructions.[13] A little later, in New York on 18 August, Governor Quitman of Mississippi accepted an invitation from the most powerful organization of Cuban exiles, the Junta Cubana, to lead a new expedition to Cuba: he would get $M1 (£230,000) if successful. A large demonstration cheered him, some carrying banners bidding the Spaniards:

> O pray ye doomed tyrants
> Your fate's not afar
> A dreaded Order now watches you –
> It is the Lone Star!

The plan now was for Cuba, like Texas, to proclaim itself first independent, and later apply to join the U.S. Slavery would of course be preserved: Quitman's agreement made specific mention of the need to preserve the 'domestic institutions of the country' – slavery being, of course, the main one.

Ironically, the Spanish government, under the temporarily robust control of Narváez, at the same moment appointed its first captain-general who was both humane and strong: the Marqués de la Pezuela, an anti-slaver and personally incorruptible, in fact regarded in Spain

---

[11] 8 April 1853, quoted Ettinger, 159.

[12] Other friends of expansion or members of Young America such as Daniel Sickles, George Sanders and John O'Sullivan also got diplomatic jobs under Pierce (minister in London, consul in London, and minister in Lisbon). All were both friends of European revolutionaries and of the secession of the U.S. South: a revealing conjunction which reached its apogee at George Sanders' famous dinner in London where Mazzini, Kossuth, Ledru-Rollin, Garibaldi, Orsini, Ruge and Herzen drank healths with Buchanan and Sanders to 'a future alliance of America with a federation of the free peoples of Europe'.

[13] Ettinger 171–2.

as ultra-conservative and very much a political general.[14] He arrived in December 1853 and immediately inspired a series of articles in the *Diario de la Marina* which discussed slavery and called for the implementation of the treaties banning the slave trade. They also praised the archbishop, Monsignor Claret, known for his opposition to the trade. On 23 December a decree was issued which proclaimed that all *emancipados* should be freed; that slave importers would henceforth be fined and banished; that intermarriage between black and white would be encouraged; and that governors and lieutenant-governors who did not inform on slavers would be dismissed.

Cuba reeled under the impact of this decree. The grander planters became once again drawn towards the machinations of the annexationists, and General Quitman in New Orleans prepared a great invasion for February 1854. Cuban exiles in the U.S., still not knowing quite what they wanted, persuaded him to delay till March at least, so that the bulk of the sugar harvest might be securely in.[15] Meantime, in Madrid, the third centre of decision in the affairs of Cuba, a curious drama was being played out.

The U.S. minister Soulé, after visiting both Kossuth and Mazzini in London, and his old friend Alexandre Dumas in Paris, had reached Madrid with the background information that 'in one way or another' the Pierce government expected Cuba to 'release itself or be released'.[16] The Spanish government had unwisely agreed to receive Soulé. His first weeks in Madrid were occupied in showing off his new ambassadorial uniform, designed to copy the clothes of Benjamin Franklin at the court of Louis XVI, and in private scandals, culminating in a duel between his son and the duke of Alba and then another between himself and the French Ambassador.[17] Soulé then tried to persuade the queen mother María Cristina that her extensive Cuban interests, such as her four mills in *La Gran Azucarera*, organized by the slave trader, Antonio Parejo, would be best served by a sale of the island to the U.S.[18] The queen mother liked Soulé, or at least for a time regarded his presence as a balance to the extensive influence of the French court, greatly increased after Napoleon III's marriage to a sister-in-law of the duke of Alba. She seems to have now approved the scheme to sell

---

[14] Juan Manuel de la Pezuela y Ceballos Escalera, Marqués de la Pezuela (1810–75). Son of the last Viceroy of Peru, poet and soldier, and cousin of the economist Jacobo de la Pezuela.

[15] See Rauch, 264ff.

[16] Marcy to Soulé, Washington, 23 July 1853, qu. Rauch, 263.

[17] Ettinger, 229–31. See also *The Attaché in Madrid* (1856), a picture of Madrid society by the English wife of the Spanish foreign minister; Frédéric Gaillardet, *L'Aristocratie en Amérique* (1883); and Maunsell B. Field, *Memories of Many Men and Some Women* (1874).

[18] See above. With 8,700 acres in these four plantations, she was now probably the biggest single sugar planter of the island.

Cuba.[19] In March 1854, while Quitman was still busy organizing in Louisiana, Soulé offered Spain, without instructions from Washington, a loan of $M 400, whose guarantee would be Cuba. He knew that Spain's debts, mainly to British citizens, reached that figure and that she found it hard even to pay the interest. Though the Spanish regime and ministry, torn by scandals and permanent crises, was weak, its Foreign Minister refused.

A month later a new incident gave the Pierce administration an opportunity for tougher tactics. The U.S. steamship *Black Warrior*, which regularly plied between New York and Mobile, docked at Havana for passengers and mail. The law demanded a manifest of the cargo, but since this usually was a formality it was often forgotten. In the case of the *Black Warrior*, no mention had been made of the cargo of cotton and the ship was arrested by a pedantic harbourmaster. A violent correspondence ensued between Soulé and the Spanish government, and it seemed that Pierce, egged on by Jefferson Davis and Caleb Cushing, was tempted by the idea of war.[20] But he was restrained by a hostile congress.

Captain-General Pezuela was meantime doggedly maintaining his drive against the slave trade. The governors of Trinidad and Sancti Spiritus had been dismissed for failing to report slave importations and in March a decree opened up sugar plantations to investigation. Enthusiasm for U.S. action mounted. Quitman was only persuaded to delay his invasion for a few more weeks by the prestigious General Sam Houston, ex-president of the republic of Texas. But there was no slackening in the opinion of the South as to the desirability of acquiring Cuba: even the *New York Herald* said firmly on 13 March, 'Now is the time to get Cuba', and on 17 March 1854, a famous editorial appeared in the *Richmond Enquirer* (Virginia) entitled 'Cuba and Slavery':

> It is because we regard the acquisition of Cuba as essential to the stability of the system of slavery and to the just ascendancy of the South that we consent to forego our habitual repugnance to political change . . . if we would restore to the South its proper position in the Confederacy and the means of protecting its constitutional rights, we must reinforce the power of slavery as an element of political control. And this can only be done by the annexation of Cuba. In no other direction is there a chance for the aggrandisement of slavery.

Pierce reacted strongly to the *Black Warrior* affair; in a message to the House of Representatives on 15 March, he said darkly: 'I shall not hesitate . . . to insure the observance of our just rights to obtain redress

[19] Ettinger, 245-6.
[20] For this incident, see H. L. James, *H.A.H.R.*, 280-98; Ettinger, 254ff; Rauch, 279ff.

for injuries received and to vindicate the honor of our fiat',[21] just as if he were Soulé challenging the French ambassador to another duel. The Pierce administration believed they had popular backing in the South adequate to send a new and precise instruction to Soulé in Madrid – instructions which Soulé himself had subtly asked for. On 3 April, Secretary of State Marcy told Soulé to offer \$M130 (£M31) for Cuba (i.e. \$M30 (£M7) more than offered by Buchanan) and also empowered him to 'detach that island' in any other way if purchase failed.[22] Soulé was also told to press for \$300,000 (£70,000) indemnity on the *Black Warrior* – a demand which was held off by the Spanish Foreign Minister Calderón de la Barca with the excuse that he had no news from Cuba.[23] An agent of Marcy's, Charles W. Davis, had also arrived in Cuba to discover the significance of Pezuela's policies: was it true, as some slave owners wildly alleged, that the Spanish government was determined to send large quantities of Negroes to the island, free them after a short period of enforced labour and so ultimately 'Africanize' the island, creating a free apprentice African republic to be guaranteed by Britain?[24] On 3 May in Havana Pezuela issued a new decree by which an annual registration of slaves would have to be made every August, after the sugar harvest. Any slave whose master could not show a registered title for him would be free. This would involve the emancipation of all slaves brought in since 1820.[25]

This measure caused near panic among the Cuban planters. A number of them in April had called on U.S. Consul William Robertson to urge the dispatch of the U.S. army to Havana. On 22 May 1854, three weeks after Pezuela's decree, Marcy's private agent Davis dispatched a report which echoed the most sensational of the slave-owners' charges: 'Africanization' was a real danger, since it was the only positive policy of the Spaniards; emancipation would undoubtedly lead to black revolution and the creation of a new Haiti. The English were primarily to blame for their malign influence over successive Spanish governments.[26] 'Africanization' became a major propaganda weapon among the Cuban annexationists established in New York: 'Better Cuba were obliterated than "Jamaicanized" by negrophilism';[27]

[21] J. D. Richardson, *A Compilation of The Messages and Papers of The Presidents 1789–1897* (1896), V, 234–5.
[22] *The American Secretaries of State and their Diplomacy*, ed. Samuel F. Bemis, 10 vols, V, 193 (essay by H. B. Learned on Marcy). U. S. State Dept, Instructions, Spain, XV, Marcy-Soulé, No. 13. William Marcy (1786–1857) is perhaps best known for his invention of the phrase 'spoils system' in 1832.
[23] Ettinger, 265.
[24] Ettinger, 248, 256.
[25] *Cf.* Rauch, 285.
[26] Davis to March, 22 May 1854, *Consular Despatches*, Havana, XXIX, qu. Ettinger, 275.
[27] *De Bow's Review*, XVII (1854), 222.

and O'Sullivan's *Democratic Review* trumpeted, 'This continent is for white people, and not only the continent but the islands adjacent, and the Negro must be kept in slavery . . .'[28]

The administration's reaction was not, however, to give full freedom to Governor Quitman and the Cuban junta, but to press Soulé on with negotiations in Madrid. The Finance Minister of Spain was influenced by Pierce's message in March to back the plan of a sale. At the end of May, President Pierce explicitly declared private expeditions against foreign countries to be illegal. The following day, however, he committed one of the major blunders of U.S. history by signing the Kansas-Nebraska Act; it was left to these two states themselves to decide whether they should be slave or free; the effect was to make their future a matter for controversy and immediately to divert public opinion from foreign to domestic matters.

Negotiations continued in Madrid, but were hopelessly confused in midsummer by the collapse of the government and the outbreak of near civil war there.

On 28 June 1854 General O'Donnell, the most rapacious of recent captains-general in Cuba, rose against the government at the head of a regiment and several squadrons of cavalry. But Madrid did not join him. A popular revolution gathered momentum. Two Liberal ministries collapsed. For the first time in Spanish history the populace gained control of the capital: the Queen Mother's palace was pillaged, while she and the young Queen had to barricade themselves in the Royal Palace. A revolutionary junta was formed in Madrid and in other towns. Soulé, who had friends among the revolutionaries, was suspected of paying crowds to demonstrate, 'distributing cigars and . . . cakes of chocolate'.[29] In early August, with Spain still in confusion, the Assistant Secretary of State, Dudley Mann, wrote to Marcy that the purchase of Cuba was 'as good as accomplished'. But at the end of August the leaders of the Spanish revolution delivered power over to the 'democratic' General Espartero, who was reluctantly accepted by the Queen; he rapidly restored order, although the Liberal clubs and journals, so long banned, returned. Soulé was everywhere thought to be implicated in an abortive uprising in August: indeed, Orense, a leading Republican conspirator, had hidden in his house.[30] As a result, Marcy instructed Soulé to confer with the U.S. ministers in London and Paris to consult on a new Cuban policy to fit the changed circumstances.[31] The procrastinatory Quitman and his supporters, now supposed to be

[28] *Democratic Review*, XXXI, November–December 1852, 440.
[29] *Charivari of Paris*, qu. *New York Times*, 13 August 1854. See V. G. Kiernan, *The Spanish Revolution of 1854* (1966); and Carr, 246–7.
[30] Ettinger, 306.
[31] Rauch, 292.

50,000 strong, were meantime bound over for $3,000 (£700) not to break the Neutrality Act.

The three diplomats met at Ostend in October. The minister in London, James Buchanan, had, as President Polk's Secretary of State, been the main agent in Polk's $M100 offer for Cuba. As eager and ambitious as Soulé, but more respectable and conservative, he vigorously agreed that the policy of the U.S. towards Cuba should consist of purchase, accompanied by threats:[32] $M120 ($M10 less than Soulé had already proposed) should be offered. If Spain were to refuse this price ('far beyond its [Cuba's] present value'), the U.S. would, by every law human and divine, 'be justified in wresting it from her', Spanish actions would endanger 'our internal peace and the possession of our beloved Union'.[33] A preamble stated Cuba to be as important to the U.S. 'as any of its present members', and that:

> We should be unworthy of our gallant forefathers and commit base treason against our posterity if Cuba were to be 'Africanized' and become another Santo Domingo [Haiti], with all its attendant horrors to the white race, and suffer the flames to extend to our neighbouring shores, seriously to endanger or actually destroy the fabric of our Union:[34]

This belligerence was no greater than anything which Quitman or the Mississippi and Louisiana press had been saying for months. But it was surprising to see it on the lips of U.S. diplomats and, thanks to Buchanan (an aspirant to the Democratic nomination for presidency in 1856), the public soon knew of it through a leak to the *New York Herald*. The general reaction, however, was critical. U.S. diplomacy was scornfully characterized as 'a very singular profession which combines with the utmost publicity the habitual pursuit of dishonourable objects by clandestine means'. In the congressional elections of November 1854 Pierce and the Democrats lost control of Congress and the Administration dared not back the 'Ostend Manifesto' even if it had wanted to.[35] On 13 November the Secretary of State, Marcy, repudiating his own instructions of six months before,[36] wrote to Soulé that if Spain refused to sell, negotiations were to be discontinued; but the U.S. would not seize the island even if she did refuse.[37] Spain did refuse and Soulé, astounded, disappointed and impatient, resigned as

[32] Ettinger (365) thinks Soulé wrote the policy and beguiled Buchanan into accepting it.
[33] *The Works of James Buchanan*, ed. J. B. Moore, 12 vols (1908–11), IX, 260–6.
[34] See discussion in Ettinger, 361ff.
[35] Ettinger, 379.
[36] But see H. B. Learned in Bemis, *American Secretaries of State*, V, 194, where it is argued that Marcy nodded when giving his earlier instructions to the Ostend conspirators.
[37] *Loc. cit.* But see the discussion in Rauch, 295, fn. 1, where contradictory interpretations (e.g. H. B. Learned, *William Learned Marcy, Secretary of State* (1928), 209) are discussed.

minister, refusing to stay in what he called 'languid impotence'.[38] But by this time the urgency for a 'solution' to the Cuban problem seemed to have passed.

On her own initiative the new Spanish government (radical at home, cautious abroad) had already dismissed the enlightened Captain-General Pezuela, replacing him with General Gutiérrez de la Concha: within weeks Pezuela's persecution of the slave trade would be quietly dropped. This indeed was the main reason for the comparative withdrawal by the U.S. government over the Ostend Manifesto. It was no longer urgent. 'Africanization' had been staved off. The Spanish government paid $53,000 (£12,400), to compensate for the *Black Warrior*.[39] On 26 August 1855, General Dodge,[40] Soulé's successor as minister in Madrid told the Spanish Foreign Minister that his government wished to impress how important it was that there should be no return to Pezuela's policies, instigated by the 'abolitionists of Great Britain and elsewhere . . . seeking . . . to interfere with and undermine or abolish slavery in the southern states'. The Spanish Foreign Minister, General Zabala, a heavy-handed autocrat, who apparently got his job because he was an aristocrat,[41] gravely replied that Spain regarded slavery as 'an indispensable element for the prosperous development of the resources of Cuba'. Soulé resumed his law practice and took no further active part in public life.[42] With the achievement of a temporary *modus vivendi*, between the U.S. and Spain, the stage seemed set for the culmination of Governor Quitman's imperial if dilatory career.

Fifty thousand volunteers and one million dollars had now been gathered. Senator Alexander Stephens, future vice-president of the Confederacy in the Civil War, urged Quitman to act 'while England and France have their hands full in the East' (the Crimea). But the prolonged delays had soured relations between Quitman and the Cuban junta, especially a powerful group led by Domingo Goicuría of Goicuría & Co. of Havana, also with a branch in New Orleans;[43] and José Elías Hernández.[44] They broke with Quitman and dispatched their own expedition to Cuba. This was quickly cut up by the Spaniards. General Gutiérrez de la Concha also broke up a freedom conspiracy led in

[38] State Dept, *P.P.*, vol. 39, No. 42, qu. Ettinger, 382. Maunsell Field, 80–4, gives an entertaining picture of Soulé at this time.

[39] Ettinger, 290.

[40] Augustus Dodge (1812–83), senator, Ia, 1848–55; author of *The Mediator's Kingdom not of This World*.

[41] Kiernan, 151.

[42] In the Civil War he was arrested, taken prisoner to New York, broke his parole, became an honorary brigadier and died mad in 1870 in New Orleans.

[43] Domingo Goicuría (1804–70), tireless opponent of Spain, and agitator for white colonization. He made money later from the Civil War, running supplies from Matamoros, Mexico, to Brownsville, Texas. See Ely, *Cuando reinaba*, 604. For his frightful end, see below, p. 257.

[44] José Elías Hernández, Doctor of Law, old friend of the poet Heredia.

a

b

Four nineteenth-century Spanish Captains-General :
    5*a* General Tacón
     b General O'Donnell
     c General Martínez Campos
     d General Weyler

c

d

6 Tinguaro Sugar mill, c. 1860. The picture shows the layout of the mill buildings in a typical large mill in central Cuba

Havana by a Spaniard, Ramón Pintó, a businessman, with a career behind him fit to please Stendhal,[45] and another by Francisco Estrampes: both were executed and their followers imprisoned. At the end of February 1855 Quitman went to Washington, where he met Pierce, Marcy and the Spanish minister, Calderón de la Barca. They finally dissuaded him from going ahead. Quitman, it turned out, was a firebrand from whom it was easy to draw the fire, an impresario of vain illusions. The Junta Cubana, infuriated, began to think not surprisingly that they were merely being used as pawns in U.S. politics. Quitman resigned from his post as general in command on 30 April 1855. The junta tried without success to get back the million dollars entrusted to him; while he, however, disbanded his followers and became, no doubt by arrangement, a representative in Congress for the Democrats.[46]

The Cuban annexationists were nevertheless not yet ruined, even though the new captain-general in Cuba was making it clear that he was going to present difficulties for neither slaves nor slave traders. The decree making compulsory the investigation of slaves in the plantations themselves was abrogated. There began a shift by the men of the junta towards the idea of independence, and in June 1855 Goicuría issued a manifesto announcing that since the U.S. had failed them, the Cubans had no alternative to independence even if emancipation was thereby made inevitable. Shortly afterwards Goicuría joined forces with the Southern American adventurer, William Walker.[47] Walker was fitting out an expedition to invade Nicaragua. Goicuría offered Walker money in return for a pledge to invade Cuba as soon as his conquest of Nicaragua should be consolidated. 'Commodore' Cornelius Vanderbilt also helped to finance Walker.[48]

Early in 1856 Goicuría's adventurers set off, 250 strong, Goicuría himself a brigadier-general. The capital of Nicaragua, Granada, fell easily, a Nicaraguan puppet was named head of state and Walker became effective ruler. In May President Pierce boasted of the new

[45] Ramón Pintó y López (1802–55), a Catalan, began life as a jeronomite monk but, being dragged into the political struggles of Madrid in 1820–3, fled to Cuba as a tutor to the sons of Baron de Kessel, a sugar planter in Pinar del Río. Pardoned in 1833, he became a businessman, later Director of the Liceo of Havana. Became intimate friend of Governor de la Concha, who nevertheless eventually had him shot. His daughter, América, married into the oligarchy, in the person of Laureano Chacón. See his last letter to Wenceslao Villaurrutia in Vidal Morales, III, 29ff.

[46] Cf. Rauch, 299.

[47] William Walker (1824–62), lawyer at New Orleans; editor of New Orleans Daily Crescent, 1848; in Gold Rush California, 1850; led armed expedition to Mexico, 1853; proclaimed Lower California a republic and himself president, 1853; forced out by Mexican army. See W. O. Scroggs, 'William Walker's Designs on Cuba', Mississippi Valley Historical Review, I, 198ff.

[48] His Accessory Transit Company had a monopoly of the steamship navigation in Nicaraguan waters.

government as being helped to power by U.S. citizens and officially recognized it – to the anger of other Latin American states whose most articulate spokesman, Martínez Irisarri, took the opportunity to point out that the famous Monroe doctrine was proving to be merely a means to establish puppet governments.[49]

This state, run by a Cuban merchant and a North American mercenary did not last long. Goicuría, appointed minister to London, quarrelled with Walker once the latter made clear that his next plan was to conquer the whole of central America, and thereafter the Caribbean. In September 1856, Walker restored slavery in Nicaragua and opened the slave trade to Africa again. Within a few months Costa Rica had declared war on Nicaragua, feeling its independence threatened, and not much longer after that, in March 1857, the U.S. fleet intervened. Walker surrendered, but he returned nevertheless to New Orleans a hero.

James Buchanan, now president (he owed his elevation partly to his co-authorship of that manly stand, the Ostend Manifesto), had meanwhile added fuel to the national desire for expansion. He said in his inauguration speech that if he could 'settle' slavery and then add Cuba to the Union he would be 'willing to give up the ghost and let the vice-president succeed'. In December 1857 he began the third attempt by a U.S. president to buy Cuba. Christopher Falcon, a Philadelphia banker and one of the financial advisers of Queen María Cristina, proposed that he should make use of his connections with European bankers who held Spanish bonds – Rothschilds, Barings of London and Leon Loth of Paris. (Spain was in debt $M400 [£M93], half of it to Britain.) With money from the sale of Cuba Spain would be able to pay her accumulated interest and a part even of the principal. Falcon was authorized to go ahead on these lines and later reported that the European bankers would be delighted to help; but a number of Spanish politicians would have to be bought too. He proposed a new minister should be sent to Madrid with a large secret service fund for the purposes of bribery. Buchanan agreed and it was at first proposed that an annexationist banker, August Belmont, until recently ambassador in the Netherlands, should be appointed.[50] But the Senate refused to approve the appointment. William Preston, ex-congressman for Kentucky, was finally chosen.[51]

[49] In 1858 the presidents of Costa Rica and Nicaragua were to place themselves under the protection of the U.K., France and Sardinia, for fear of U.S. annexation.

[50] Belmont, banker of German origin, nephew by marriage of Senator Slidell of Louisiana, had helped finance Pierce's electoral campaign and had been making private proposals for Cuban purchase for some years. See Rauch, 227, and Irving Katz, *August Belmont, A Political Biography* (1968).

[51] William Preston (1816–87), at Louisville Bar; Lieut.-Col. in Mexican War; U.S. House of Representatives, 1852–5.

The money for Cuba was not found, despite continued popular backing in the South. Albert Gallatin Brown announced in 1858, 'I want Cuba, I want Tamaulipas, Potosí and one or two Mexican states, and I want them all for the same reason – for the planting or spreading of slavery'.[52] But only in his 1858 message to Congress did Buchanan ask for an appropriation on the ground that 'the success of the negotiations might depend on an advance payment to the Spanish Government immediately after the Treaty was signed'. A month later, in January 1859, Senator Slidell, the political chieftain of Louisiana, put before the Foreign Relations Committee of the Senate a formal bill asking for $M30 (£M7) for Buchanan, accompanied by this jargon:

> The ultimate acquisition of Cuba may be considered a . . . purpose [of all parties] . . . and in regard to which the popular voice has been expressed with a unanimity unsurpassed on any question of national policy that has heretofore engaged the public mind. The purchase and annexation of Louisiana led as a necessary corollary to that of Florida and both point with unerring certainty to the acquisition of Cuba.

He added by way of explanation:

> The white creole is as free from all taint of African blood as the descendant of the Goth . . . Hundreds of their youths are acquiring our language and fitting themselves to play a distinguished part in their own legislative halls or in the Council of the Nation.[53]

The Republican party, however, was not going to accept this proposal. Though possessing only a third of seats in the Senate they were nevertheless able to block the Democrats successfully. Even so, Preston was sent to Madrid with full powers and he reported back that he was sure that the purchase of Cuba could be arranged by means of bribes of $M30 (£M7). But nothing further transpired and in December 1859 Buchanan was still pursuing what was now a $M30 bill in the midst of his other searing problems.

In Madrid meanwhile the ex-captain-general in Cuba, O'Donnell, sent one of the most intelligent of his colleagues, General Serrano, to Cuba. Serrano, an ex-lover of Queen Isabella and himself half-Cuban, embarked on a series of discussions with the planters, including the reformers and annexationists, in the house of Miguel Aldama.[54] Serrano sought to help the planters over the slave trade by encouraging

[52] Speech at Hazlehurst, Mississippi, qu. Genovese, 258.
[53] Sen. Rep., 361, 35th Cong., 2nd session, qu. Jenks, 316.
[54] General Francisco Serrano (1810–85).

the import of Chinese, at the same time as suggesting measures to end the trade; not perhaps with the vigour of Pezuela but, at least, with his own brand of diplomacy.

Cuba in 1859 was in fact back to high slave imports, probably at least 40,000 a year,[55] and about 85 slavers were fitted out in New York alone for Cuba in 1859–60.[56] Though these were among the last slave ships fitted out in the U.S., there is no suggestion that the slaves were treated any better than in the sixteenth century. The description of a journey on a slaveship in 1860 made by Edward Manning reads as appallingly as any in the 1560s, showing if anything a greater indifference to lives and sensitivities.[57]

The U.S. slid into civil war at a time when the South still hoped that the acquisition of Cuba would enable them to perpetuate slavery inside or outside the Union. Senator Slidell acknowledged defeat over the $M30 bill in May 1860 but promised to reintroduce it. In July Jefferson Davis, already leader of the South and already hinting that the South would secede if a Republican president were elected in November, told the Democratic Convention that after secession Cuba would certainly be acquired. The South would no more haggle with Spain, they would simply conquer Cuba. In November Abraham Lincoln was elected President; he had announced before that the U.S. could not think of acquiring Cuba so long as slavery lasted there. The annexationists were thereby defeated, though President Buchanan, in his last message to Congress, repeated his recommendation that Cuba should be acquired.[58] When Senator Slidell reintroduced the $M30 bill in January 1861, after South Carolina had already seceded from the Union, there was a great protest, the northern senators saying that they could not think of buying with millions of dollars a country which would doubtless afterwards assert its right of secession.[59] An unsuccessful compromise by the ex-Attorney-General Crittenden proposed permission of slavery in all land south of the latitude 36° 30′, so enabling the South to expand into Cuba, Mexico and South America. Lincoln would not accept it. Later, Lincoln's Secretary of State, William Seward, suggested that the U.S. might take Cuba as a sop to keep the South in the Union. Again Lincoln refused. The dream of annexation was finally dropped, when in March 1861 Jefferson Davis and A. H. Stephens, ardent annexationists both of them, became president and vice-president

[55] Lloyd, *The Navy and the Slave Trade*, 116.

[56] *Ibid.*, 171; see Howard, *American Slavers and the Federal Law*, 54, for identity of these New York slavers.

[57] See Dow, 294ff. There are two long descriptions of slave voyages to South Cuba in this book. The Spanish captain only revealed himself as such to the crew and what the journey was for on the African coast.

[58] J. D. Richardson, *Messages and Papers*, V, 642.

[59] Howard C. Perkins, *Northern Editorials on Secession*, 2 vols (1942), I, 390, qu. Foner, 121.

respectively of the Confederate states. In order to win friends in Europe and diplomatic recognition, the Confederacy disclaimed all plans of annexing Cuba. The slave trade to the Southern states died. In 1862 Lincoln's government with some reluctance finally conceded the right of search to the British,[60] while for the first time a U.S. slave captain was hanged for piracy;[61] simultaneously Lincoln set out, successfully, to crush the New York slave traffic. In May 1862 the British commodore reported that though the barracoons on the Congo were crammed with slaves, there were no vessels to take them off.[62]

One question remains to be answered: why did the English fail so patently to enforce their demands earlier? Why did successive administrations, including even that of Palmerston, allow the Spaniards to escape without paying the cost of their illegality? It was not that the British governments did not know of the extent of evasion. The explanation is that, due to the ambiguous position of the U.S., the English government never felt able to make a final *démarche* over Cuba which might lead to war with Spain. Far better to attempt slowly to seal off the sources of supply in Africa by blockade, bribery, the establishment of alternative and more lasting if less immediately profitable commerce, and hence of territorial occupation. To 'stop the bung-holes through which the Dahomey slave trade issues', as Palmerston put it, meant, it became increasingly evident, British occupation of Lagos.[63] No wonder the remains of the old West Indian interest complained that the English were hypocritical. Not only did they after 1848 merrily eat slave-grown sugar, but they failed to enforce the abolition even of the trade which had been legally banned by most countries in 1820. Over Brazil the British were much tougher than over Cuba and these actions gave added weight to the not inconsiderable group of Brazilian abolitionists and to those Brazilians anxious to restrict the number of Negroes in the country: the spectre once more of Haiti. The trade in fact ended there by 1851-2.[64]

[60] Cruisers of both nations were entitled to visit and search suspected slave ships anywhere south of Latitude 32°N – though still not within 200 miles of the U.S. and within 30 leagues of the Cuban coast. Mixed Commissions were set up at New York, the Cape of Good Hope and Sierra Leone. In November 1862 the British Consul at New York reported that there had been no slave expedition from that port for many months. (See Lloyd, *The Navy and the Slave Trade*, 59, for discussion, and Howard, *American Slavers and the Federal Law*, 60–1, for the U.S. point of view.)

[61] Captain Nathaniel Gordon, in February 1862 (see Howard, *op cit.*, 201). He was carrying 890 slaves on the *Erie*, bound for Havana. There had been about 80 prosecutions under the slave trade acts (see list in *ibid.*, 224).

[62] Mathieson, 177. But 88 ships were still understood to be involved in the trade.

[63] Letter to Russell, 13 August 1862 (P.R.O., Russell Papers), qu. Lloyd, 158.

[64] See Laurence F. Hill, 'Abolition of the African slave trade to Brazil', *H.A.H.R.*, XI (May 1931); and Percy A. Masten, 'Slavery and Abolition in Brazil', *ibid.*, XIII (May 1933). Consul-General Turnbull (*op. cit.*, ix) makes a general accusation against British shipping as providing the means for slave dealing (e.g. Pedro de Zulueta's supply of goods for exchange in

The failure of the South to implicate Cuba in any North American political grouping seems, a century later, to have been a mere inevitable acceptance of geographical and social or economic differences: in fact there are no such inevitabilities, certainly not in the Caribbean. The U.S. absorbed Texas, California and New Mexico, with populations totalling over 350,000 in the 1850s or equivalent to about a quarter of the population of Cuba. In the ten years between 1850 and 1860 the U.S. absorbed well over two million immigrants of diverse nationalities. It would have been as natural for a state to grow around the shores of the northern Caribbean as for one to develop in the land-locked north. Who knows whether it would not in the long run have been better for all concerned if William Walker had achieved his ends and established a military empire based on black slavery, extending throughout the Caribbean? Such an empire would in the long run have fallen and led to the creation of a homogeneous black republic of sufficient size to be viable.

Cuba is closer to the U.S. than Corsica is to France. The Caribbean seaboard, like the Mediterranean, has common economic problems and common traditions: a fact which those who come from the region continue to appreciate in defiance of remote bureaucracies in distant capitals.

Africa), but the pressure of that lobby can hardly have been critical. Another Englishman in Cuba, J. G. Taylor (*op. cit.*, 215), suggests the governments were afraid of higher sugar prices. Such an economist's interpretation was unlikely for governments headed by Palmerston or Aberdeen but of course these governments were all subject to the pressure of free traders such as Bright and Cobden who regarded Brazil and Cuba, Spain and Portugal, as good customers and trading partners.

CHAPTER XIX

Reformism

After the collapse of the idea of annexation, most prominent creole planters prepared to contemplate indefinite Spanish rule, while seeking those constitutional reforms which would give them political control of Cuba, as well as the economic control which they possessed.

Their first step was the foundation of a Havana Reform Club (*Círculo Reformista*). The leaders of this were, first, ex-annexationists – Miguel Aldama,[1] José Antonio Echevarría[2] and Pozos Dulces.[3] Others were José Morales Lemus,[4] José Ricardo O'Farrill,[5] Antonio Fernández Bramosio[6] and José Manuel Mestre.[7] Except for Miguel Aldama none of these men had taken a leading part in the annexationist movement though they may perhaps have favoured it. Some (such as Fernández Bramosio) were active in municipal administration in Havana. These men were all rich, although it is relevant that none of them, even Aldama, was so up-to-date as to have a Derosne or a Rillieux machine on their plantations. Their policy was a return to the reformism of the 1820s. They wanted a cut in the powers of the captain-general and the extension to Cuba of such political rights as there in Spain. Taxation, in short, would be accompanied by representation. But these powerful slaveholders also became committed to some solution of the evident political problem of slavery. They were convinced that the slave trade would ultimately cease and that Cuba would have to face the possibility that, deprived of regular replenishment in the number of slaves, slavery itself would be abandoned. They reached this conclusion without romanticism or humanitarianism. They

---

[1] See above, 207.

[2] José Antonio Echevarría (1815–85). Born in Venezuela, went as a boy to Cuba. A poet (author of a lyric commentary on the birth of Isabella II) and *littérateur*.

[3] See above, 208.

[4] José Morales Lemus (1810–71), lawyer. Born Nuevitas, or perhaps on the boat which brought his parents from the Canary Isles. Self-made, practised law, freed his own slaves. Involved in the Pintó conspiracy, and afterwards in exile.

[5] His family needs no introduction. He was a very large mill owner particularly in the Güines area. See Appendix I.

[6] Antonio Fernández Bramosio (d. 1878), a Havana lawyer, novelist, merchant and *regidor* of Havana municipality.

[7] José Manuel Mestre (1832–?), Havana-born Professor of Logic (1856–66); lawyer too, becoming famous as the defender of the attempted assassin of Mgr Claret (1856); *Alcalde Mayor* of Havana, 1858; *Regidor* of Havana, emigrated afterwards.

looked forward to a settlement which would not injure slave-holders, and being themselves rich men, they contemplated that this, as in the British and French colonies, would be achieved by compensation. In these plans they were assisted by the new captain-general Domingo Dulce who though an old friend and follower of O'Donnell, showed himself ready to act even against Julián de Zulueta, expelled a number of slave merchants in 1863, and imprisoned some local governors, including the political governor of Havana province.[8] Some of these reformers looked forward to a quite new development in sugar manufacture: that not all those who grew cane need grind it. The development of railways meant that cane could be taken a longer distance before being ground. Why therefore should not a manufacturer act as a common factory to which many growers who could not afford to finance a mill could bring their cane? Would not this sort of opportunity help to develop white immigration also, since it provided a chance for Castillian peasants to establish themselves as small holders? Finally, would this not enable the mill owners, increasingly alarmed by the competition of beet and therefore by the low prices of the early 1860s, to cut the costs of harvesting – the most expensive side of sugar manufacturing and the one which had had no mechanization – by handing over responsibility to the peasants? The early 1860s saw at the same time the formation in Madrid of something of a Cuban lobby, composed of wheat, textile and shipping interests. Many of these men had been concerned with Cuba all their lives and were now anxious to keep the island Spanish not only by political pressure but by white immigration.

A curious incident occurred in 1863. A cargo of 1,105 slaves was landed at a beach near Matanzas from the steamer *Cicerón*, owned partially (as part of a fleet of four) by Zulueta, José Baró, José Carreras of Havana and José Rousel of Cárdenas. The slaves were intercepted and captured by the lieutenant-governor of Colón, Colonel Argüelles, who received $15,000 as prize money. He himself sold 141 of the slaves he had captured at between $700 and $750 (£160–£175) – and then went to New York to try to buy the newspaper *La Crónica*. The Spanish authorities found out Argüelles's treachery, had him extradited and later condemned to the galleys.[9] The size of this boatload, the great sums invested, show that only very rich men indeed could embark upon the trade; for even men such as the O'Farrills, the Conde de Pozos Dulces, the Marqueses de la Real Proclamación and Duquesne, the Condes de O'Reilly and la Reunión, all came out against a traffic in which they, not now in the first rank of sugar growers, could no longer

[8] Mathieson, 178.
[9] *P.P.*, 1865, LVI, 59.

participate.[10] Their animosity towards successful neighbours and rivals such as Zulueta or Baró must have been great.

The Reformers maintained relations with both Captains-General Serrano and Domingo Dulce, even though under the martial laws existing since 1825 no political parties were legally permitted. They ran a paper, *El Siglo*, edited by Pozos Dulces, which throughout the early 1860s carried on a vigorous debate on constitutional issues with the conservatives of the so-called *Partido Incondicional Español*, the name of which roughly expressed their dreams at least of integration with Spain and who expressed themselves in the *Diario de la Marina*. But these men were all aristocratic reformers. Lincoln's proclamation of the emancipation of slaves on 1 January 1863 left them uneasy since it was clear he had caused great enthusiasm among Cuban Negroes. Lincoln's death also brought immense and spontaneous grief to the Negroes of Cuba and once again the slave-owners were disturbed.

The Reformers were not all for abolition. In early 1865 (when the slave trade had died down despite some activity based on Cádiz in 1864) a meeting was held of Reformers at the house of José Ricardo O'Farrill. The editor of *La Prensa*, Francisco Montaos,[11] proposed the gradual emancipation of slaves with graduated compensation. But the Reformers opposed this scheme. O'Farrill – at that time owing $600,000 (£140,000) to J. M. Morales & Co.[12] and facing considerable difficulties with Chinese labour on his mill *Esperanza*[13] – urged Captain-General Dulce to have nothing to do with the Montaos proposal on the grounds that it would totally antagonize the *Partido Incondicional Español*. A petition was afterwards sent to General Serrano in Spain, congratulating him on a recent speech in the Cortes which had been progressive in respect of Cuba and urging three demands: (1) a reform of the tariff to stimulate commerce with the U.S.; (2) Cuban representation in the Cortes; and (3) abolition of the slave trade.

In fact, 1865 did see the last definitely authenticated recorded slave voyage to Cuba carried out for the benefit of 'Pancho' Marty;[14] it

---

[10] Sedana, *Cuba*, 274ff., qu. Aimes, 209.

[11] Born in the Philippines, cavalry colonel and publisher. Later director of the *Diario de la Marina* and later still returned to the Canaries to practise agriculture.

[12] A debt he successfully transferred in 1869 to Tomás Terry (Ely, *Cuando reinaba*, 412).

[13] *Ibid.*, 614.

[14] See Appendix X. This was the clear impression of the British Consuls, and September 18 appears to have been the last occasion when a slaver definitely arrived. On the other hand, rumours of landings continued till as late as 1872. See *P.P.*, 1872, LIV, 763, where Acting Consul-General Crawford says, 'since ... 1870 ... there has not been any well authenticated case of Negro slaves having been introduced ... from Africa though as usual rumours of such importations have not been wanting; in fact five cargoes are reported to have been successfully run'. Gallenga in 1872 thought that 'slaves ... to some extent, still continue to be imported into Cuba'. See also *Accounts and Papers*, 1870, LVI, 850; 1873, LXI, 651, for evidence of some imports in June 1869 and June 1872. There is also discussion in Corwin, 183.

was also the last authenticated journey of any slaveship to the New World; thereafter the price of slaves, already very high at $750 (£175), rose to prohibitive levels of over $1,000 (£230). In 1872 Gallenga, *The Times* correspondent, found slaves being sold at £400 ($1,700) a head.[15] Small planters were unable to keep up with this, and the years 1865–8 saw them meeting great economic difficulties, while the big ones, headed by the reformers, increasingly prospered, as sugar production leapt to over 500,000 tons between 1862 and 1864 and an average of over 600,000 between 1865 and 1867. As usual in political or economic crises, it was the small men, not the big, who suffered.

But all was certainly far from quiet on the plantations of the big men also: in 1865–6 there came the first instance of an actual strike by slaves: on Miguel Aldama's plantation, *Unión*, and more appropriately on Zulueta's *Alava* plantation the slaves struck, 'demanding payment for their work', and calmly saying that since they had arrived in Cuba after 1820, they must be legally free. The strikers showed no violence but refused for a time to work as slaves. Troops had to be sent to force them to work. The *New York Times* commented: 'If the mania of not wishing to work without money is extended to other farms, the proprietors will find it hard to accustom themselves to such a revolutionary state of affairs.'[16]

The drive towards organization of labour came in the section of Cuban society which was most socially advanced:[17] the tobacco factories. The crisis of the late 1850s led to an attempt by many workers to found some sort of mutual aid societies.[18] Workers were now actually suffering a decline in their standard of living and their general status after the 1840s. The pioneer of union organization was Adolfo Ramos, who, in 1857, got permission to found a 'Mutual Aid Society of Honest Workers and Day Labourers' in the parish of Our Lady of El Pilar, Havana. Pointedly, the society admitted only 'all-white people of good education'. The aim was simply to help those who were sick out of the contributions of the able-bodied, but it was a semi-religious organization, under the aegis of a patron saint, and confined to the parish. Later, a group of Negro workers gained permission to form a 'Mutual Aid Society in the Havana parish of S. Nicolás de Bari'. Here the pioneer was Antonio Mora, a free Negro. Neither of these projects was specifically concerned with tobacco workers, though in both they predominated. Within a few years, during the relatively mild cap-

[15] Gallenga, 78.

[16] *New York Times*, 3 April 1866, qu. Ely, 495.

[17] As usual: the first instance of organization in England was that of the well-off wool combers of Yorkshire.

[18] See above, p. 186.

taincies-general of Serrano and Domingo Dulce, the Mutual Aid societies proliferated, all confined to parishes.

The next step was the foundation of a newspaper, *La Aurora*, 'a weekly newspaper dedicated to artisans'. Its founder was Saturnino Martínez, who came from Asturias to work from an early age in Jaime Partagás's cigar factory, Havana. Asturias had a strong tradition of emigration at an early age both to Madrid and abroad.[19] Self-educated, himself a poet – like most Cuban revolutionaries – he interested the more radical members of *La Sociedad Económica* in whose library he for a time worked. The first number of *La Aurora* appeared on 22 October 1865, being sold chiefly to tobacco workers. It gave some attention to literature (in which Martínez was more interested than in politics) but concentrated on general studies of working class conditions. There were articles by various Cuban writers of the time but also translations of foreign writers. *La Aurora* campaigned for Mutual Aid societies on the model of those founded in the late 1850s.

La Aurora also argued from its inception for a remarkable experiment in self-improvement which had apparently begun in the prison of the Arsenal of Havana, where prison cigar-makers had organized readings during their work.[20] The practice began on a permanent basis at the Viñas cigar factory at Bejucal in 1864, the first reader being named as Antonio Leal.[21] It was a custom, no doubt, adapted from the refectories of convents or prison dining rooms. Certainly, it caught on. It was in the same town, Bejucal, that a reader first mounted on to a platform for his reading, in the factory of Facundo Acosta.[22] The workers agreed to contribute to the wages of the reader.

In January 1866, partly as a result of the campaigns of *La Aurora*, partly because of the interest in the whole idea by Nicolás de Azcárate, the enlightened headmaster of the Liceo at Guanabacoa, an experimental reading occurred for the first time in Havana at the tobacco factory *El Fígaro*, on the same basis as at Bejucal: the owners agreed. On 7 January 1866 *La Aurora* announced with justifiable pride:

> Reading . . . has been started for the first time among us . . . This constitutes a giant step in the march of progress and the general advance of the artisans because in this way . . . they will gradually get to know books, so that ultimately they will become their best friends.[23]

[19] Carr, 11.
[20] Fernando Ortiz, *Cuban Counterpoint. Tobacco and Sugar*, trans. Harriet de Onís (1947), 89.
[21] Fr Manuel Deulofeu, as qu. *ibid.*, 89.
[22] *Ibid.*, 90.
[23] *La Aurora*, 7 January 1866, qu. Foner.

The *Partagás* factory followed, on 3 February 1866, and Saturnino Martínez, still a worker there, made a speech:

> If we had a Cobden or a Bright who had made us familiar with the great questions with which we are dealing, perhaps we would have succeeded in getting rid of the iron cloak which oppresses us (i.e. ignorance) . . . But thanks to the great step we have taken we shall not stay long in darkness.

Other factories followed the example of *El Figaro* and *Partagás*.

But the seeds of confusion were already sown, since the books which were read in those first months of active education in the tobacco factories were not quite innocent. *La Aurora* carried weekly reports of the books being read – *Political Economy* by Núñez y Estrada; the six-volume *History of Spain* of Galeano; the *Key of the World* by Fernández y González; and the reformers' newspaper *El Siglo*.[24]

The first crisis for the readings did not, however, come before the reformers gained a notable victory. In November 1865, the Spanish government agreed that a Cuban commission should be elected to go to Spain to discuss the constitutional development of the island. This proposal was due to the presence of the intelligent and still youthful Antonio Cánovas del Castillo as Minister of the Colonies under ex-Captain-General O'Donnell as premier.[25]

Moderation no doubt seemed necessary even to O'Donnell, who was dour and narrow, in consequence of the recent disastrous events in Santo Domingo (the eastern half of the island had petitioned to return to Spain in 1861 but, infuriated to find the Spanish authorities had learnt nothing, broke away again in 1865). Cánovas acted in the knowledge that after the Civil War the administration of the U.S. was now at one with the United Kingdom on slavery. In March 1866 elections in Cuba were at last held, with a high property qualification. Leading Reformers were elected – José Morales Lemus, José Antonio Echevarría, Pozos Dulces – and with them the now aged Saco, the Reformer of the 1830s, still in exile in Paris. Tomás Terry, now probably the richest of all the planters in Cuba (being worth about $7M (or over £M1½)), was returned for Cienfuegos; the enlightened Director of the Liceo at Guanabacoa, Azcárate, went to Madrid on behalf of the electors of Güines as did the multi-plantation owner José Luis Alfonso (recently made Marqués de Montelo) for Matanzas.[26] A similar reforming majority was gained in Puerto Rico. (It was precisely at this time

[24] Ortiz, 90.

[25] Antonio Cánovas del Castillo (1828–97), historian, afterwards architect of the Restoration settlement.

[26] List as in Antonio Pirala, *Anales de la Guerra de Cuba*, 3 vols (1896), I, 206, fn. 1. Terry was at this time heavily investing in non-Cuban securities; see Ely, 407.

that slave strikes were breaking out on Aldama's plantation, giving him added cause for attempting a solution of the labour question.)

Before they left, crisis had come to the tobacco factories. The manager of the Caruncho factory refused to allow readings. *La Aurora* denounced the ban. *El Siglo* supported *La Aurora* and was in turn denounced in *Diario de la Marina*. On 14 May 1866 the authorities banned readings on the ground that 'meetings of the artisans were converted into political clubs'; books were being read which 'contain sophisms or maxims prejudicial to the weak intelligence of persons who do not possess the critical faculties and the learning necessary to judge with accuracy.'[27] But some readings continued and indeed there is evidence that the movement actually spread during 1866 among tobacco pickers as well as in factories. *La Aurora* meanwhile continued, though censored. Saturnino Martínez directed a strike in the cigar factory of Cabañas y Carvajal, and narrowly escaped deportation.

In the summer of 1866 the reformers were given their opportunity to negotiate with the government. But on 9 July, even before they reached Madrid, the Cortes passed a law which finally aimed to end the slave trade in all seriousness. Heavy fines and imprisonment would be the punishment for those who broke the law. Death was promised to those who resisted arrest or who caused death or injury to slaves. Immediately after, however, O'Donnell's government was dismissed, the queen's confidence being shattered by a revolt of sergeants in the San Gil barracks in Madrid. Narváez, the 'strong general', was the only alternative: the Cortes was suspended for six months, Cánovas del Castillo fled Madrid. There were many detentions, even Serrano (who with O'Donnell had crushed the sergeants) being exiled to the Canaries. Liberal professors were expelled from their Chairs. This was a bad moment for the arrival in Madrid of Cuban and Puerto Rican Liberals. But Narváez allowed them to meet the Colonies Minister, Alejandro de Castro. At their third meeting the Puerto Rican representatives proposed abolition of slavery.[28]

The proposal horrified the Cubans. Echevarría ironically congratulated Puerto Rico on their good fortune in being able to contemplate such a measure. Other criticism was expressed by all the Cuban representatives – even by Luis María Pastor and Domingo Sterling, who were essentially abolitionists. They did not defend slavery as such but demanded that first the *criollos* should gain political power; afterwards they would consider the question of slavery with, of course, compensation. Eventually they drew up a scheme for gradual emancipation over seven years with compensation at an average of $450 per slave: José

[27] Foner, 145.
[28] Much the best description of the work of the Commission is in Corwin, 189ff.

Antonio Saco refused to back this as being too radical ('Remember Haiti,' he repeated) but the other Cubans signed. By this time a Spanish abolitionist movement headed by the Havana-born Rafael María Labra with much support from Puerto Ricans and Spanish anti-clerical Liberals had at last come into being.[29]

The commission adjourned in April 1867, having apparently accomplished an immense amount of work. Every demand of the representatives had been discussed. There had also been extensive discussion of the problem of Chinese labour.[30] The Cubans were led to believe that action would follow. It did not. Narváez had never intended the commission to be more than a talking shop. By this time a new and vigorous reactionary captain-general, Lersundi, had established himself in Cuba.[31] The Colonial Minister, Alejandro de Castro, resigned in anger. Nobody, however, was able to discuss Cuba or Puerto Rico with Narváez. The Reform Movement of moderate men and rich planters cracked. They no longer had any solution to offer.

Back in Cuba it appeared, ironically, that one at least of the proposals of the Reformers was going to be fulfilled. On 12 February 1867 Captain-General Lersundi imposed a new tax of 6% on income, giving himself the alternative of a 12% tax 'if necessary'. This appeared to be a final insult, since the Reformers had proposed this instead of, and not as well as, the old customs and other taxes.

Millionaires such as José Morales Lemus or Miguel Aldama could of course survive well enough even the short-sightedness of General Narváez. The steady march to greater and greater wealth of Tomás Terry, for instance, was unchecked during the autumn and winter of 1867-8; he was at that time buying North American bonds, paying in gold and getting nearly 25% discount.[32] Sugar production in the harvest of 1867 was just under 600,000; in the harvest which ended in June 1868 it was just under 750,000, a great record marking double what it had been even in the years 1850-4. Between September 1866 and April 1868 over 17,000 Chinese had been imported to Havana, bringing the grand total of Chinese imported to Cuba to almost 100,000.[33]

Of the alternatives to a temporary acceptance of the situation, annexation to the U.S. seemed now out of the question, though General

[29] See *ibid.*, 154ff. Rafael María Labra (1841–1918). Already deputy for Puerto Rico and Asturias; afterwards autonomist and independent Republican. A very productive writer.
[30] See Jiménez Pastrana, 52–64.
[31] General Francisco Lersundi, ex-Carlist and Minister of War, who had suppressed a revolt in Spain in 1848 with skill.
[32] Tomás Terry, *Diario*, qu. Ely, *Cuando reinaba*, 407, fn. 331.
[33] Actual figures, 17,721 and 96,581, respectively, *Accounts and Papers*, 1868–9, LVI, 789. By December 1868 the figure reached 101,597, though perhaps 30,000 had died. The ships bringing them were of all nations.

Sherman, no less, paid a friendly visit to Miguel Aldama's estates in the winter of 1866, and though Morales Lemus was to toy once again with the idea for some months in 1868. There remained only the possibility of armed revolt. But a rebellion could not hope to triumph fast. Cuba might be devastated, and the Reformers, who were all rich men, had much to lose. Even more important, a civil war against the Spaniards would risk slavery. If the planters attempted to retain their slaves, Spain could beat them as Lincoln did the South in the U.S., by 'the terrible weapon' of emancipation. The only way to stage a successful rebellion against Spain would be to gain Negro support by freeing the slaves. But the main argument, from the Reformers' point of view, in a rebellion at all was to preserve slavery or at least to delay its abolition till it was no longer economically necessary. Hence the Reformers had, after they returned from Spain, no policy.

But others had a policy. These were the smaller planters of the east. Long neglected, parochial and impoverished, they were ready for rebellion. The wealth brought in by the great sugar crops of the 1860s had passed them by, since they had money for neither machinery nor slaves. The Betancourt family, for instance, in 1860 had had nine mills in Oriente and Camagüey; of these six were still oxen-powered.[34] They were too far from Havana – there was no good road, no railways reached the east as yet – to be able to command huge loans from big merchants. In 1860 the 284 sugar mills of Oriente (an area which then comprised the present provinces of Oriente and Camagüey or half the island) produced only 9% of the total production of sugar: nearly two-thirds[35] of the mills there were old fashioned and oxen-driven compared with a fifth in the western department.[36] Out of 942 steam-powered mills, 118 only were in the east. The average yield of sugar per *caballería* in the west was eighteen tons, five in the east; the average yield per mill in the east was 164 tons, 438 in the west. Even the production of ox-powered mills was three times higher per mill in the west. In 1860 only three mills in all the eastern province had Derosne-type vacuum boilers: in the west there were fifty-two.

Some of the planters of the east had already anticipated the emancipation of slaves by letting them out for wages during the harvest. Some planters were coffee farmers, grandsons of French immigrants from Haiti, who had seen their farms decline into providing a third-rate crop, or had gone over unsuccessfully to small-scale sugar production.[37] Others were cattle farmers in the same position. Some of them, not

[34] Statistics from Rebello.
[35] 57·75% to be precise.
[36] 21·44%.
[37] About 40 to 50 sugar owners in 1860 in Oriente had names which seem to be obviously of French origin. See Rebello.

at first all by any means, were prepared to take the great leap into the unknown of emancipation. Or was it unknown? Was it not an even chance that Negroes under contract labour for six months of harvest would actually cost less than slaves? Probably the smaller sugar planters who backed the idea of rebellion did so, however, more because their fortunes were in decline than because they saw rebellion as a means of increasing their wealth; doubtless they were dimly aware of impending great changes in the sugar industry, they knew that the bigger plantations of the west were more profitable because they could afford more equipment and machinery as well as slaves at $1,000 (£235). Thus, aware of an impending economic revolution, they launched a political rebellion.

1867–8 was a year of revolutionary formation. The centres, as in rebellious Spain, were the masonic lodges, well established in the eastern province, especially in Bayamo. An exile society in New York, the Republican Society of Cuba and Puerto Rico, backed by North American abolitionists, secured circulation of their paper, *The Voice of America*, which demanded liberty of white and black.[38] The newly formed *Junta Revolucionaria* of Bayamo (organized by the masonic lodge) sent an emissary, Pedro Figueredo, to negotiate with the Reformers. Bayamo, an Indian *cacicazgo* occupied in 1512 by Pánfilo de Narváez, appeared a conventional Spanish provincial town, with 10,000 people, a town hall, church, prison, barracks, and Philharmonic society surrounding the large Plaza Isabella II. The big families of the region – Tamayos, Aguileras, Céspedes, Figueredos and Palmas – nevertheless often sent their children to Europe or the U.S.; they returned to the *patria chica* disturbed by colonial conventions and methods of government. The revolutionary movement of Bayamo had a somewhat literary as well as an aristocratic air. Its leaders thought in poems. The priest, Fr Diego Batista, was a sympathizer and allowed a revolutionary march composed by Pedro Figueredo to be played in the church. The *Junta Revolucionaria* of Bayamo was composed of one rich landowner, Francisco Vicente Aguilera; a lawyer, Francisco Maceo; and Pedro Figueredo. In that municipality in 1860 there had been twenty-three sugar mills, but the only steam-driven one, that owned by the Figueredo family, was the biggest in size and output. All the rest were oxen-driven.[39]

Morales Lemus from Havana at first promised support, and money, on behalf of the reformers; later they withdrew, apparently persuaded that General Grant in the U.S. would come to their aid. Rebuffed, the rebels turned for help to a number of exiles from the Dominican Repub-

[38] There were now seven shipping lines running between Havana and New York.
[39] See Rebello, 89.

lic, who had fought the Spaniards. Similar activities were at this time continuing in Puerto Rico.

A meeting of the new rebels of Oriente occurred on a farm named *San Miguel de Rompe* in Las Tuñas (Oriente). Presiding was Carlos Manuel de Céspedes, aged just under fifty, who had spent most of his youth taking part in revolutionary activity in Spain; he was, however, a native of Bayamo and his family owned a small sugar plantation, *La Demajagua*, near Yara. Since returning to Cuba in the 1850s Céspedes had been a fairly consistent critic of Spanish policy.[40] In 1851 he had been detained for reciting an improvised poem demanding freedom, at a banquet where the military governor of the town was present. He was a mason.[41] His family had been in the district ever since 1517 when the Spanish government granted a large estate, covering much of the Sierra Maestra, to Javier de Céspedes.

Céspedes made a very successful speech at the meeting of San Miguel, ending with the fine phrase: 'Gentlemen . . . the power of Spain is decrepit and worm eaten. If it still appears strong and great, it is because for over three centuries we have regarded it from our knees. Let us rise!'[42] This speech, with stirring echoes from French revolutionary connections, was adequate to give Céspedes the leadership for the time being of the rebellious movement. But no decision whatever was reached on slavery. There were even still some annexationists at this meeting.

Nothing might have happened immediately had it not been for the outbreak of a new revolution in Spain which finally disposed of Queen Isabella II. The revolt began on 18 September. On 3 October General Serrano forced his way into Madrid. The Queen left Spain. On 8 October Serrano formed a government, with General Prim as Minister of War, intending to carry on the 'revolutionary work' (*obra revolucionaria*) already, as he believed, so admired by Europe.[43] Then came news of a revolution in Puerto Rico, on 23 September. Still the men of Oriente hesitated. The final event was the symbolic act of Luis Figueredo in hanging a Spanish tax-collector on his plantation *El Mijial*: a gratuitous act of violence which forced the *Junta Revolucionaria* into the condition of outlaws.

More meetings were held by the Cuban conspirators and areas of

[40] *Demajagua* had a Jamaican train and was steam-powered. In 1860 it consisted of 100 acres sown and 433 acres not, and produced 212 hogsheads (Rebello, 100). Céspedes (1819–74), brought up in the country, travelled and married his cousin.

[41] M. Fernández Almagro, *Historia Política de la España moderna y contemporánea*, 2 vols (1946, 1959), I, 82. See Portell Vilá, *Céspedes, el Padre de la Patria Cubana* (1931) and the admirable edition of his letters to his wife published in Havana in 1964.

[42] Pirala, I, 249.

[43] Fernández Almagro, I, 12. Juan Prim, 1814–70, son of a lawyer from Reus. Hero of Carlist wars. Captain-General of Puerto Rico. Deputy and commander in African war.

command were allocated. No decision was reached on slavery. The rebellion was planned to begin at Christmas, or perhaps before. But then came a move which even those reluctant rebels could hardly evade. The wife of one of the conspirators, Trinidad Ramírez, told of the plots to her confessor, and the news reached the authorities. Immediately Captain-General Lersundi sent word to arrest the leading plotters.

In the confusion of Spain and the remains of the Spanish empire, both among rebels and supporters of the new government in Madrid, the captains-general in Havana and Puerto Rico, Lersundi and Pavía, were alone sure of what they wanted: to keep the two islands Spanish. Lersundi, appealed to by both Queen Isabella and Don Carlos, the Carlist claimant, maintained iron control. *La Aurora*, forced to become little more than a literary weekly earlier in the year, was totally banned. Lersundi's attempted arrest of the plotters in the east forced them either to rise or fly. They rose.

CHAPTER XX

The War of 1868: I

The planters of the east rose against Spain in early October 1868. Céspedes was named as commander in the Bayamo area. On 10 October at his plantation, *La Demajagua*, he freed his thirty slaves, and enrolled them in his small army, now totalling 147 men. At the same time he issued a proclamation which, after explaining that an appeal to argument had failed, announced: 'We only want to be free and equal, as the Creator intended all mankind to be . . . we believe that all men were created equal.' But having apparently grasped the nettle of slavery he retreated: 'We desire the gradual, indemnified emancipation of slaves.'[1] This *'grito de Yara'*, despite its ambiguity on the central issue, had the immediate effect of rallying men to him in large numbers. In early October Céspedes had been merely a farmer who had decided to take on the government, accompanied by his friends. By the end of the month he had 12,000 men and had captured Bayamo and Holguín, his follower Pedro Figueredo proclaiming a martial song which afterwards became the Cuban national anthem:

Al combate corred bayameses
Que la patria os contempla orgullosa
No temáis una muerte gloriosa
Que morir por la patria es vivir.

To the battle, Bayameses!
Let the fatherland proudly observe you!
Do not fear a glorious death,
To die for the fatherland is to live!

With enthusiasm and machetes, this amateur army swept their way through Oriente, their ignorance of war corrected by a group of veterans of the war against Spain in Santo Domingo. In November, while Lersundi was still preparing a force in Havana to relieve his commanders, the cattle farmer Ignacio Agramonte raised the standard of revolt in the region of Puerto Príncipe, assisted by a Cuban veteran of the U.S.–Mexican war, General Manuel de Quesada.

[1] Text in Vidal Morales, III, 501ff.

This rising was led by the white population of Oriente, mostly countrymen. To them a great many of the free mulatto population of east Cuba quickly rallied, 'men of colour' whose formal civil liberty had given them no means of abandoning their insecurity and poverty. Later, some slaves followed, but in the earlier stages they were always few.[2] In many respects this war was a conflict between *criollos* and *penin-*

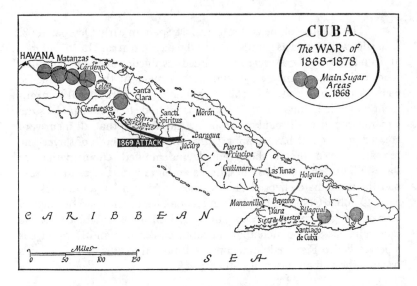

sulares, a conflict always endemic in Cuba and exacerbated by the fortunes made by the latter in the last half century. Though the rebels were in fact ultimately backed by some outstanding rich men of the west, the Spanish resistance was always supported at local level by Spanish merchants and their families.

Céspedes's caution on the subject of slavery had positive results. On 24 October 1868, the leading businessmen of west Cuba, including such men as Julián de Zulueta, Miguel Angel de Herrera, Miguel Aldama, José Morales Lemus and José Manuel Mestre – some forty in all – called on Captain-General Lersundi. The latter denounced the Oriente rebels in bitter terms. Mestre urged Lersundi to permit the Cubans publicly to discuss the various problems facing them in the island and in Spain, but he was refused. Thereafter, the meeting broke up angrily, and later Mestre, Morales Lemus, Miguel Aldama, with several other Reformers, crossed the Rubicon and publicly backed the rebellion; they went to New York and began collecting money and support. Perhaps if Céspedes had denounced slavery from the beginning they

[2] See R. Guerra y Sánchez, *Guerra de los Diez Años, 1868-1878*, 2nd edn (1900), 30-2.

would not have done so. (Aldama was most bizarrely offered the governorship of Cuba by the Carlist Pretender, an honour he refused.) Others at the meeting on 24 October, such as, not surprisingly, Zulueta and Miguel Angel Herrera, stood by Lersundi, and the new government in Madrid, not knowing what to do in the state of confusion at home, allowed Lersundi to remain.[3]

Céspedes was encouraged by the rallying of the Reformers to the cause and as a result his proclamation of Bayamo on 27 December on the question of slavery still burked the issue (though the aldermen of Bayamo had proclaimed abolition). Abolition would be contingent on the final success of the rebellion. In the meantime the rebels' Republic would recognize slavery. Escaped slaves would not even be accepted in the army of rebellion without the agreement of their owners, unless they were the property of those hostile to the rebellion or, if they were the property of rebel planters, had permission to do so.[4]

The end of 1868 found Céspedes and the Oriente rebels having constituted themselves as a formal if unorthodox Republic and nominated a rebel parliament. They controlled a handful of towns and farms. A similar though smaller group under Agramonte was established in Puerto Príncipe. Of its followers, a small minority consisted of freed slaves; a larger minority was white; and the majority was free Negroes. Agramonte, in the cattle districts of Puerto Príncipe, had some horses; Céspedes had very few. In New York powerful friends were beginning to assemble but their very existence hampered Céspedes and the rebels in Cuba from taking the decisive step of freeing the slaves.

Captain-General Lersundi on the other hand had only about 7,000 troops in the island and therefore could launch no serious attack.[5] No one had thought that military action would be needed in Oriente; most available troops were in the prosperous and potentially incendiary slave plantation areas around Cárdenas and Colón where, rebellion or confusion in Spain notwithstanding, a new sugar harvest was about to begin; in 1869 a total production of 726,000 tons would be ground, only a little less than in the record year of 1868.

In Spain, meantime, the successive governments of Generals Serrano and Prim, in search of a monarch, bitterly criticized by Republicans and Federalists to the left of them and by the Carlists to the right, with mounting disorder in the countryside, were not at all anxious for a violent crisis in Cuba. Though potentially sympathetic to constitutional change in Cuba, they were anxious to maintain the *status quo* there

[3] Pirala, I, 298.
[4] See text in Vidal Morales, III, 198ff.; and *Accounts and Papers*, 1870, LXI, 681. The British Consul Crawford denounced this statement as 'a miserable farce'.
[5] Fernández Almagro, I, 86.

at least until they had effectively established themselves and a constitutional monarchy in Madrid. But this golden moment seemed to arrive only slowly. Even so, Serrano took the important step late in December of sending his friend and fellow-abolitionist, Domingo Dulce, back to Havana as captain-general in place of Lersundi.[6]

Dulce arrived on 4 January 1869, with a programme of moderate reform: freedom of the press, freedom of assembly and representation for Cuba in the Cortes. He proclaimed an amnesty for all rebels who would surrender in forty days and sent peace commissioners to talk with Céspedes. With the end of censorship, a flood of newspapers and periodicals rushed into print. Dulce, however, had acted without realizing the intensity of pro-Spanish feeling among prosperous *habaneros* of Spanish origin. These groups, headed now by Julián de Zulueta, wished to have no truck whatsoever with the rebels, specially not with Céspedes who, ambiguous though he might be over slavery, had freed his own slaves, and therefore seemed a most dangerous firebrand. These *peninsulares* were elated by the news in late January that Generals Valmaseda and Weyler had succeeded in coming face to face with a main body of 4,000 rebels, led by Donato Mármol, not far from Bayamo. It had been the first proper battle of the war and the rebels had lost perhaps 2,000 men, fleeing in confusion, allowing the Spanish to re-enter Bayamo. The victory added power to the arguments of those who believed that the war could be won by military force. The idea of negotiations was finally even rejected by the rebels when one of the Puerto Príncipe leaders, Augusto Arango, was assassinated despite a safe conduct, by apparently civilian peninsular volunteers.[7]

These volunteers became rapidly almost as serious a problem for Captain-General Dulce as the rebels. In Havana, militia cadres had been formed by Captain-General de la Concha, fifteen years before, to resist Narciso López, as they had been in 1762 to fight Albemarle and the English. They were now reorganized. Mostly middle- or upper-class *peninsulares*, they were able by sheer force of numbers to cow Dulce into acceptance of their views. They sacked Miguel Aldama's palace. They shot up a theatre where rebel songs were being sung. They attempted to block the gates of Havana to prevent people leaving the city to join Céspedes. Their journal, *La Voz de Cuba*, accused Dulce of working for the rebels. Within a month of arrival the captain-general had capitulated to the *habaneros*. Political guarantees were suspended. Anyone suspected of being favourable to the rebels was interrogated and

[6] *Ibid.*, 86-7. Dulce had been captain-general in the 1860s and had married a Cuban, the Condesa de Santovenia. The rebellion in Puerto Rico had already been crushed by General Pavía.

[7] Pirala, I, 402-4.

imprisoned. The press was censored. The volunteers had a free rein.[8] The noise of their trumpets at drill in the morning added to the cacophony of sounds already dominating the capital. Enmities between Spanish *peninsulares* and Cuban creoles reached heights rarely achieved in the rest of Spanish America, almost obliterating colour prejudice.

The volunteers were a foretaste of those twentieth century lower middle-class mobs of young men who often protest violently against the end of empire. Shouting *Viva España!* in the Villanueva Theatre, foreshadowing the *pieds noirs* of Algeria, they bridge the gap between Carlism and Fascism. They were clearly in some instances *agents provocateurs*: was there really fire from Aldama's house before it was sacked? Were some not anxious to provoke tumult in Havana so as to give the impression that Spain could only govern Cuba in a state of siege?

The strength of the volunteers amounted on 1 January 1869 to over 20,000 infantry and 13,500 cavalry.[9] Their leaders were usually prominent merchants, the commanders in Cienfuegos, for instance, being the Spanish merchant brothers, Ramón and Esteban de la Torriente.[10] Zulueta played the principal role in financing the volunteers in Havana. In Cienfuegos at least the volunteers held bizarre ceremonies, their womenfolk lying on the floor of the church while drums, bells and bugles sounded imposing and quasi-religious calls to action.[11]

The acceptance of the volunteers by a Spanish government still headed by 'liberals', and by Captain-General Dulce, would have seemed impossible a year before. But, so far as Empire was concerned, by early 1869 there seemed scarcely any difference between Serrano or Prim and their predecessors. The Cortes were preoccupied with prolonged debates on the constitution. In the countryside of Spain the civil guard continued to shoot peasants while trying to escape. The link between the Spanish federalists and trade unions with anarchism began effectively in December 1868, when Bakunin's emissary Fanelli arrived in Madrid to found the first nucleus of the Spanish section of the International Association of Workers. The war in Cuba seemed far away, though in the long run Fanelli's ideas would influence Cuba almost as much as Spain.

The volunteers were forcing Spain's hand in Havana towards intransigence; on the rebel side, the abolitionists were attempting less successfully to force Céspedes towards radicalism. The abolitionists often hailed from Camagüey, mainly cattle country and therefore with few slaves to lose. At the end of February 1869 a revolutionary

[8] *Ibid*, I, 498–9.
[9] *Ibid.*, I, 385.
[10] Atkins, 28.
[11] *Ibid.*, 29.

assembly of rebel leaders from Camagüey criticized Céspedes' policy towards slavery and themselves abolished slavery in the area which they commanded. Slave owners were eventually to be indemnified. All slaves so liberated would be welcome in the revolutionary army. This act forced Céspedes to some form of *riposte*. A constitutional convention was convened at Guámairo in April 1869. A democratic constitution was accepted by delegates from the different areas of Cuba then fighting. There was to be a House of Representatives, Céspedes to be president and Manuel de Quesada commander-in-chief. Article 24 of the proposed constitution announced: 'All the inhabitants of the Republic are absolutely free.' But a later meeting of the rebel House of Representatives provided that slavery would be followed by a *Reglamento de Libertos* (Rule of the Freed). The ex-slave (*liberto*) would work for his previous master and the master would be obliged not only to pay him, but also to feed and clothe him. This compromise was evidently intended to satisfy the planters of the west. But by in effect turning slaves into *emancipados*, the rebellion still could not catch the support of slaves or free Negroes there. Some rebel commanders, particularly the mulatto captain, Antonio Maceo, made a special point of freeing slaves whenever possible by raiding plantations, but this was not a regular practice, nor was there yet any fighting in areas of large plantations.

The convention of Guámairo in April 1869 was not only conservative in its social policy. It declared formally in favour of annexation to the U.S. (Alaska had been bought in 1869 by the U.S.) A month before, General Grant's cabinet had decided not to receive Morales as the rebel representative; Secretary of State Hamilton Fish 'informally' told Morales that he wanted to keep faith with Spain.[12] On April 6 1869 Fish recommended to the U.S. cabinet that its best policy would be to allow the 'madness and fatuity of the Spanish dominion in Cuba' to continue until a time when all nations 'would be glad that we should impose and regulate the control of the island.'[13]

Fish thus seems to have been as interested as most of his predecessors in eventually obtaining Cuba and, like them, he would have preferred to buy rather than liberate it. Also like them he was in no hurry: the cabinet had been told that the U.S. received over $M30 worth of import duties from Cuba: 'an important item in the present condition of the Treasury'.[14] Cuba could obviously not enter the Union with slaves, and the representatives of the Cuban rebels in New York were only reluctant abolitionists. In Cuba itself the issue of slavery had simply

[12] Hamilton Fish (1808–93) senator, 1851–3; Secretary of State, 1869–77, throughout Grant's administration.
[13] J. A. Nevins, *Hamilton Fish* (1937), 191.
[14] *Ibid.*, 125.

not been worked out by the rebels in the field. Procrastination seemed the only possible tactic, and Cuban historians who have reproached the Grant administration for machiavellian diplomacy have overlooked this central and embarrassing issue. In Grant's cabinet, the President himself was willing to assist the Cubans but was easily deflected; Secretary of War Rawlins, Grant's old chief of staff in the Civil War, vigorously backed the rebels but his motives were mixed in that he had received $28,000 in Cuban bonds from the New York junta.[15] The Attorney-General Creswell was also moderately pro-Cuban.[16] The rest were unconcerned.

The issue was not simply one of annexation or acquiescence, aid or aloofness, but also of whether the U.S. should recognize a state of war in Cuba and so accord to the rebels the full rights of a belligerent. President Juárez in Mexico and some other Latin American republics had indeed recognized a state of belligerency. President Grant, Rawlins and Creswell were willing to do so too, but Fish and the rest of the cabinet were not, on grounds which implied that the issue in Cuba had to be settled by force of arms. (It would also embarrass the U.S. in their relation to Britain over the Alabama claims.) Fish had other ideas. His plan was to buy the independence of Cuba by means of a cash payment to Spain, to be made by U.S. bankers as a loan to the Cubans; the price would be $M100, as before the Civil War. Other conditions were the abolition of slavery and an armistice during the negotiations.

After prolonged discussion, the New York junta of Cubans, headed by Morales and Miguel Aldama, agreed to support this plan. From Madrid Paul Forbes, representative of several European bankers who held Spanish bonds, reported that General Prim was ready to re-negotiate[17] and in midsummer 1869 another envoy, General Daniel Sickles, set off for Madrid.

Sickles was even more bizarre a man than Pierre Soulé to find as U.S. minister to Spain.[18] Once a member of Young America, he had been secretary of the legation in London under Buchanan and had backed the Ostend Manifesto; he was hence familiar with the role of Cuba in U.S. politics in the past. From 1857–61 he had been a Democratic representative in Congress, and had been involved in a larceny scandal; in 1859 he murdered his wife's lover and was acquitted after a sensational trial in which he pleaded temporary insanity. In 1861 he appeared as brigadier-general of volunteers, but surprisingly on the Northern side; he fought through the war and lost a leg at Gettysburg.

[15] John Aaron Rawlins (1831–69), at the Illinois Bar before the Civil War; A.D.C. to Grant, later chief of staff of army. For Rawlins's Cuban holdings, see *ibid.*, 184.
[16] John Creswell (1828–91), earlier senator, later a noted Postmaster-General.
[17] Nevins, *Hamilton Fish*, 191.
[18] Daniel Sickles (1825–1914).

He was known as having been one of the harshest governors in the South during Reconstruction. In 1869, retired from the army, he set off as minister to Madrid to buy Cuba from Spain. While negotiations were beginning, the administration did their best to prevent filibustering or arms expeditions leaving Florida or New York and indeed did intercept a large expedition containing the 'First New York Cavalry Cuban Liberators' with two batteries of 12-pounder guns and a vast quantity of other arms.

Before Sickles reached Madrid, there had been a hardening in Spain's Cuban policy. After February, Captain-General Domingo Dulce had been in most respects a prisoner of the volunteers, but his aims were still moderate and he much desired to wage the war in a humane fashion, keeping open the *possibility* of negotiations. This approach had been actually disobeyed by his subordinate military commanders, in particular by the order of General Valmaseda on 4 April that in the eastern province all males over fifteen found away from home without cause would be shot. All women and children not living in their houses were to be concentrated in fortified towns. All houses were either to carry a white flag or be burned down (unless occupied by Spanish troops). In late May a group of militant volunteers broke into the captain-general's residence and insisted on Dulce's resignation. He decided to agree. Lacking all authority, he left Havana on 5 June.[19]

A new captain-general, General Caballero de Rodas, was soon named, but there was a gap of several weeks before he arrived and in the interim the volunteers established themselves as the effective authority in Havana, finding a headquarters in the Casino Español, which had branches in the larger cities. Led now by the two most powerful sugar planters, Manuel Calvo and Julián de Zulueta, the volunteers could dictate policy. The new captain-general was a right-wing but popular and subversive critic of Prim's policy at home who thereafter took his place beside the volunteers: he had crushed rebellion in southern Spain by disobeying the government whenever it suited him on the principle of 'if we don't devour them, they will devour us'.[20] In Spain itself a group of Barcelona businessmen meantime set up a 'permanent commission for the Defence of Spanish Interests in Cuba',[21] that is, their partners and in some cases their relations.

Paul Forbes and Daniel Sickles arrived in Madrid, the latter on 21 July, unfortunately a week after the Cortes had closed for the summer. Prim had been prime minister now since mid-June (Serrano had become regent). His chief preoccupation was to find a king for Spain. But he

[19] Pirala, I, 552.
[20] Carr, 315.
[21] J. Carrera Pujal, *Historia política y económica de Cataluña*, 4 vols (1946, 7), V, 347–71.

was nevertheless prepared to negotiate over Cuba with the U.S. He first proposed an amnesty; the rebels would give up their arms, and Cuban deputies would be elected to the Cortes in Madrid. The Cortes would supervise a plebiscite in Cuba; if a majority desired independence, they could have it, though the new Cuba would in return give Spain a cash sum – perhaps $M125 – to be guaranteed by the U.S.[22] Prim assured Sickles that the Spaniards wanted nothing better than to leave Cuba, provided they could do this in an honourable way.[23]

The offer at least had the effect of delaying U.S. recognition of rebel belligerence. In August, Grant (under General Rawlins's influence) had actually signed a proclamation accepting belligerence but Fish had delayed issuing it.[24] At the end of that month, Rawlins denounced Fish for opportunism in a full cabinet meeting, but Fish again dissuaded Grant from acting, though he did send an offer to Spain to mediate which he made clear would have to be taken up by 1 October at latest.[25] On 6 September, however, Cuba's chief friend in the cabinet, Rawlins, died of consumption, though only thirty-eight years old, still holding his Cuban bonds and from his death-bed still vigorously urging his only ally Creswell 'to stand by the Cubans. Cuba must be free. Her tyrannical enemy must be crushed. Cuba must not only be free but all her sister islands'.[26]

What did this hectic death-rattle signify? The U.S. annexation of the whole Caribbean? For Grant was preoccupied with an idea for the annexation of Santo Domingo into the Union: General Babcock had indeed signed a treaty on 4 September which provided for the absorption of that Republic, and which caused a prolonged Caribbean crisis in its own right. Meantime the Sickles-Fish scheme for Cuba received a death-blow when the new Spanish Colonial Minister, Manuel Becerra, leaked news of the negotiations to the press. In Prim's cabinet, both he and Manuel Silvela were vigorous opponents of Prim, being explicitly 'partisans of blood and war'.[27] Among Spaniards, only the federalist Pi y Margall openly backed Prim. The Madrid papers made clear their opposition to his ideas, and the New York junta also publicly denounced Prim's *riposte*. Prim's Unionist opponents denounced him for betraying Spanish interests to the U.S.[28] Even the Republicans accused him of secrecy.

[22] Nevins, *Hamilton Fish*, 240. The sum was not mentioned but it would be clearly in the radius of this, as was made clear from other communications.
[23] E. S. Santovenia y Echaide, *Prim, el Caudillo Estadista* (1933), 219–47. See Fernández Almagro, 90.
[24] Hamilton Fish, *Diary*, 10 July 1870, in Nevins, *Hamilton Fish*.
[25] Nevins, *Hamilton Fish*, 243–5.
[26] *Ibid.*, 247. The centenary of his birth in 1931 was enthusiastically celebrated in Cuba.
[27] Fernández Almagro, 91.
[28] See C. A. M. Hennessy, *The Federal Republic in Spain* (1962), 127.

CHAPTER XXI

The War of 1868: II

The field of battle in Cuba remained unchanged throughout the first year of war. The rebels, now between 10,000 and 20,000 strong, remained confined to the east, with various small enclaves of fighting in Puerto Príncipe, but failed altogether to raise the prosperous west, where the sugar harvest of 1869 was brought home most successfully.[1] The rebels sought to avoid contact with the Spanish army and, living off the land in remote regions, carried on sabotage more than war, trying to confine the Spanish army to the cities by cutting roads and railway lines. Sugar plantations in the east were more and more converted into fortified encampments in which, of course, the owner's word was law. Still only about one-quarter of rebel troops had rifles, the rest machetes, or perhaps daggers made out of indigo wood and dipped in poison, if they were Congolese.[2] A few Chinese had also incorporated themselves in the 'Army of Liberation', and indeed constituted whole companies under several leaders.[3] The Spaniards numbered about 40,000 trained soldiers by late 1869. They were supplemented by volunteers in the cities and paid *guerrilleros* in the country, many of whom were ex-rebels who had deserted or been captured.[4]

To a great extent the war consisted of a formalization of the violent banditry that had gone on through much of the early nineteenth century; escaped slaves now proclaimed themselves rebels and in place of *rancheadores* sent by the Conde de Casa Barreto, the Spanish army and its allies (themselves half bandits) pursued them half-heartedly while regaling themselves with rum at the Spanish government's cost. Desertions were frequent in both directions. In many ways it was less a war than a breakdown of order. A more typical rebel leader than gentlemen such as Céspedes or Agramonte was the gigantic ex-slave 'Guillermón', described by the Irish journalist, O'Kelly, with his harem in the Sierra Maestra. On the other hand, the social conditions in Cuba remained the same: O'Kelly described how in war as in peace:

[1] It totalled 726,000 tons.
[2] Montejo, 168.
[3] Jiménez Pastrana, 71–5.
[4] See the description in J. J. O'Kelly, *The Mambi-Land, or, Adventures of a Herald Correspondent in Cuba* (1874), 118–20.

Dancing appears to be the one absorbing passion of the Cuban soul. Suffering, fatigues, dangers are all forgotten . . . wherever the encampment is established for even a few days this passion must be satisfied. The families scattered about in the wood seem to know by instinct when a long halt is . . . made and crowd in . . . the Commander . . . immediately organizes the dance.[5]

The rebel bands were divided into small mobile units in some cases hardly bigger than gangs, among whom immunity to disease, and knowledge of vegetation and of local social and geographical circumstances, counted most: 'Every tree and flower and grass had a use or virtue with which they seemed acquainted', reported O'Kelly. In these circumstances, the older rebel leaders, intellectuals, *littérateurs* and poets of Havana, lost prestige, while new and younger men gained, particularly the dashing mulatto Captain Antonio Maceo, who set up a kind of command post in an old shelter (*palenque*) built by escaped slaves (*cimarrones*) where the wives of his followers established primitive hospitals, workshops and centres of supply.[6] The outstanding leader of the rebels, however, was the Dominican Máximo Gómez, an ex-commander in the Spanish army, sprung from the savagery of politics in the Santo Domingo of the 1860s; his evident mastery of guerrilla war and his 'character of iron' never, however, quite succeeded in giving him the confidence of the majority of the Cubans.[7] From the start he and Maceo were closely associated, not simply in their tactical understanding but in their political belief that the rebellion could only be successful by carrying fire and sword indiscriminately into the west of the island. They were a brilliant combination: the character of the one was all craft, persistence, calculation and capacity for endurance; and that of the other was all dash, audacity, willingness to take all risks, and pleasure in danger. They, with José Martí, would become in the 1890s the outstanding men of the Cuban independence movement.

The guerrilla policy gained in favour during 1869 so that by October Céspedes, still nominally chief of the rebels, decreed the attempted destruction of the sugar plantations: 'Better . . . that Cuba should be free even if we have to burn every vestige of civilization'. This lurch into revolutionary absolutism began immediately to be carried out by

[5] *Ibid.*, 222–3. For conditions of living of the leaders and much other interesting information, see also the letters from Céspedes to his wife and his diary.

[6] Antonio Maceo (1848–96), born in Santiago. Had been a groom. Later known as 'The Titan of Bronze', and one of the great heroes of Cuban nationalism.

[7] Máximo Gómez (1836–1905), born in Bani, Santo Domingo, child of a prosperous family, and had a good education. Fought the Haitians and lost all his property in the Civil War of 1866 in Santo Domingo. Became a farmer near Bayamo and enlisted with Céspedes as sergeant. Another hero of Cuban nationalism.

Federico Cavada, the rebel commander in the mountains of Escambray around Cienfuegos. (These mountains, far to the west of most of
the rebels' activities, afforded the one good area for guerrilla activity
near the most prosperous region of Cuba.) He set to work on the destruction of some of the famous mills, and in November Céspedes agreed for
the first time that slaves should be encouraged to rise. A letter from the
Cienfuegos merchant, Ramón de la Torriente, the Spanish volunteer
leader, described how 'burned cane gives good sugar only during eight
or ten days – afterwards it becomes dry and produces [only bad
molasses]'. De la Torriente continued, 'Lately we are receiving plenty
of troops from home; all of us expect for an early end of the robbers
who are all badly tiring us further than men's patience can endure.'[8]

Soon a powerful drive by the Spaniards dislodged Cavada and his
followers from Cienfuegos. The inhabitants of Santiago and Manzanillo, Bayamo and Puerto Príncipe, were held in near-concentration
camps. There were innumerable instances of Spanish brutality, and
arrests were frequent up and down the island. A schoolboy, José
Martí, got six months' forced labour merely for writing a letter which
accused a fellow student of treachery for walking in a Spanish parade.
The war settled into a chronic state of violence, seeming to justify
arbitrary rule by the Spaniards. The volunteers in different towns of
central Cuba shot all the rebels whom they caught with arms in their
hands, but also shot innocent fugitives. In the east of the island arrests
and even executions on suspicion were frequent.[9] Similar events
occurred on the other side. Both sides acquired such skill in the use of
the machete as to rival that of 'professional executioners'. Women
occasionally acted as spies, sometimes changing sides if their husbands
were murdered.[10] The rebels remained in loose control of large areas in
the east but shortage of arms and new indecision over whether or not
to ruin the western plantations prevented any new movement west and
therefore any further success. As it was, sugar production in 1870 was
well up to that of 1869 and even in 1871, when production dropped to
547,000 tons, a hurricane, not the action of the revolutionary army,
was the main cause of failure. The price of slaves, meantime, reported
the British Consul, 'kept up wonderfully' – £500 to £650.[11]

How could this intolerable stalemate in the war be broken? The
rebels' first plan – preferred by the leaders to any advance by Gómez
and Maceo to burn up the prosperity of the west – was to secure
recognition as belligerents from the U.S. The rich junta in New York
did its utmost but without success. Men such as Senator Sherman and

[8] Atkins, 23.
[9] See, for example, O'Kelly, 81.
[10] *Cf.* Gallenga, 170.
[11] *Accounts and Papers,* LXI, 687.

Representative Bailey helped them in Congress. Horace Greeley (Karl Marx's editor) proclaimed, 'Something must be done for Cuba',[12] placing the issue so far as possible on the plane of freedom versus slavery. Much publicity was given to the undoubted brutalities practised by the Spaniards. Petitions were presented and bribes distributed. But the administration continued to oppose any kind of intervention. Hamilton Fish desired still to limit and if possible to end the war, if necessary by spending money. Filibustering expeditions continued to be intercepted. A presidential message to Congress on 14 June 1870 opposed recognition of belligerents on the grounds that U.S. holders of Cuban bonds were behind the agitation to help the rebels. Each side, Grant pointed out, was committing atrocities. Recognition would also injure commerce. The Opposition press decided that Grant was 'sold to Spain',[13] but the exile junta in New York continued merely to argue. Rich men, they themselves would doubtless profit from the independence of Cuba even if it meant the abolition of slavery. They could afford to buy machines. But their lesser followers, including some who were in the lead in the rebellion itself, could not be so optimistic; the Spanish captain-general had too many successes; thus in late April, Caballero de Rodas had captured the rich rebel merchant, Domingo Goicuría, leader of the filibustering expeditions of the 1850s; he was garrotted in public on 6 May.

Prim had not lost hope of 'solving' the Cuban problem. In May his new Minister of the Colonies, Moret, wrote to Captain-General Caballero de Rodas: 'France and Britain will not help us while we are slave-holders, and this one word [slavery] gives North America the right to hold a suspended threat above our heads'.[14] On 28 May Moret introduced a new law abolishing slavery under certain conditions.[15] This document was criticized by even so convinced a conservative as Hamilton Fish as 'a project for relieving the slave-owners from the necessity of supporting the infants and aged slaves who can only be a burden and of prolonging the institution as to the able bodied'.[16] In fact, this was not quite true. All children of slave mothers would be henceforth free. All baby slaves born in the last eighteen months would be bought by the state for $125. Both these categories would remain to be fed, brought up, and trained to a craft, and kept, up to the age of eighteen, by their old masters in a state of patronage (*patronato*). Slaves over sixty would be freed, as would be all slaves who had served under

[12] *New York Tribune*, 23 February 1870.
[13] Nevins, *Hamilton Fish*, 361.
[14] Qu. Foner, II, 220. Segismundo Moret (1838–1913), Gaditano lawyer and economist; an anglophil and indeed half English.
[15] Quoted in full, Pirala, I, 830; see also Ortiz, *Negros Esclavos*.
[16] Nevins, *Hamilton Fish*, 345.

the Spanish flag or had in any other way helped the army in the war: the first group would be freed without compensation, the latter would be compensated for by the state. If such slaves' masters had served the rebellion – an improbable eventuality – there would be no compensation. Slaves freed under the second heading would be under state protection and the state would have to look after them until they were able to do so themselves: 'Those who prefer to go back to Africa will be taken there', Article 13 stated firmly. Over-age slaves would stay in their old masters' houses, and would remain in a state of patronage. The old master would have to feed, dress and look after them, if they could not do so themselves. But if such slaves once left they could not go back. The compensation required by this law would be paid by means of a tax on able-bodied slaves still working and the government undertook (Article 21) to present to the Cortes a law with compensation and emancipation for all those who remained in slavery after the fulfilment of the act; until then, whipping was to be forbidden, as was the sale of slaves away from their wives, or of those less than fourteen years old away from their mothers.

Tentative though this law was, it was a real beginning of the end of slavery; even if no other law had followed, it would have meant ultimate abolition. Moret's law was, further, only intended as a first step, but it was all that the Spanish government could at that moment politically afford. Compensation for all slaves at market price would cost too much, whilst freedom without compensation was obviously unacceptable in terms of contemporary Cuban society. The Spaniards were anxious to bring about abolition with minimum disturbance.

At all events the measure evidently served one essential purpose. Though incomplete, it promised at least as much as did the rebels, for all their fine words. Gómez and Maceo might desire to free slaves when they came to them but they had not been given their heads.

Moret's slavery law was followed by a renewed attempt by Prim to negotiate a Cuban peace. First, he secured the Cortes' approval to his nominee for a king in Spain – Amadeo, duke of Aosta, brother of the king of Italy. The Cortes' agreement was helped through the financial activity among the representatives of Manuel Calvo, the Cuban merchant and financier, then representative in Madrid of the intransigent *peninsulares* of Havana. Then in November (before Amadeo had landed in Italy) Prim sent the Cuban educationalist Nicolás Azcárate to try to start peace negotiations with the New York junta – Azcárate was an old friend of Moret.[17] Another of Prim's agents was Miguel Jorro, a Spaniard living in Cuba, who was instructed to propose an independent

[17] Pirala, II, 81.

Four U.S. Presidents who tried to buy Cuba:
7a James K. Polk, 1845–1849
 b James Buchanan, 1857–1861
 c Ulysses S. Grant, 1869–1877
 d William McKinley, 1897–1901

Four Cuban liberators:
8*a* Carlos Manuel de Céspedes
 b Antonio Maceo
 c Calixto García
 d Máximo Gómez

Cuba to the Cubans at a cost of $M200 guaranteed by the U.S.[18] 'If the situation in Cuba is prolonged,' Prim wrote on 28 October, 'the result would be fatal for the great Spanish interests there.' A representative of the junta, the lyric poet, Juan Clemente Zenea, set off for Cuba.[19] The purpose of this new negotiation was not independence but autonomy – the establishment in Cuba of 'a constitution similar to that of Canada'.[20] But though Aldama, Morales and others in New York accepted this plan at least as a basis for negotiations, the rebels in Cuba did not. They were too close to violence for any solution other than victory, and the atrocities of Spanish soldiers as well as their own retaliation had made negotiation almost impossible.[21] Then Prim himself was murdered in Madrid, on 27 December.[22] His go-between in Cuba, Zenea, was captured and later shot – his safe conduct, issued by the Spanish legation in Washington, being dishonoured in the field. The succeeding Spanish governments maintained themselves with great difficulty, King Amadeo being hardly accepted anywhere and with rising disorders. The Carlist rebellion isolated the north and parts of the Levante, and Republican Federalism was already taking hold of the south and east.

The rule of King Amadeo in Madrid left the captains-general of Havana with *de facto* autonomy: the brutal Caballero de Rodas gave way to the even tougher General Valmaseda in December 1870, and he, in mid-1872, when he reached the date by which he had sworn to finish the war, to General Francisco de Ceballos. Valmaseda's deputy, General Crespo, was responsible for the most outrageous single injustice of the war in shooting eight students accused, wrongly in at least one instance, of desecrating the tomb in the cemetery of Gonzalo Castañón, the founder of *La Voz de Cuba*, the Volunteer paper. One English merchant selling clothes in Havana, however, thought this 'a capital job', establishing order through terror.[23]

The generals in the field faced the guerrilla war in the east in the only way possible – defence of cities by martial law and the sealing off of the area of fighting by an immense fortified ditch (*trocha*) running the width of the island at its narrowest point – a mere thirty miles – so cutting off Oriente from the centre and the prosperous west. The

[18] Fernández Almagro, 92; Nevins, *Hamilton Fish*, 617.

[19] Juan Clemente Zenea (1832–71). Associated with Facciolo in *Voz del Pueblo*. His most famous poem was '*Fidelia*'.

[20] Fernández Almagro, 91.

[21] *Ibid.*, 95.

[22] Presumably by the federalist, José Paúl y Angulo. See Hennessy, 141, fn; Fernández Almagro, 75–7; and R. Olivar Bertrand, *El Caballero Prim*, 2 vols (1952), II, 317. There is also the theory that Prim was killed by the agency of Cuban slave-owners, fearing for their future under his reforms. For a discussion, see Santovenia, *Prim*, 277–82.

[23] Gallenga, 75.

rebels themselves remained incapable of initiative, throughout 1871. Puerto Príncipe was now maintained only by Ignacio Agramonte and a few other guerrilla fighters. Las Villas was abandoned. Máximo Gómez continued to urge on Céspedes the need for a big invasion of the west, so causing chaos, but again his plan was rejected – as was a similar scheme put forward by General Federico Cavada. These ideas were based on the campaign of the Union army in the American Civil War after emancipation. Gómez withdrew in dudgeon to an area near Guantánamo. The policy of the rebels surprisingly was now less forthcoming on slavery even than that of the Spanish government. In 1872, when a modified version of Gómez's plan did gain a measure of acceptance, Gómez himself was removed from command in Oriente province for refusing to guard the persons of the revolutionary government. There were several military successes thereafter in Oriente, but discontent within the rebel camp was now general. An immense number of brave leaders of the rebels had been shot. Violence and atrocity were the work of both sides, prisoners being executed without mercy. About 1,500–2,000 rebels fled from Cuba to Jamaica,[24] and the total number dropped to between 10,000 and 12,000 at most.[25]

For all these failures Céspedes was made the scapegoat; though he had angered his conservative backers by his inclination to risk abolition, his opportunism had unfortunately lost the support of the radicals. Surrounded by rivals, nearly blind, ill-dressed and ill-fed, attempting to sustain a ghostly government through arrogance and pride alone, he nevertheless often seemed dictatorial. In late October 1873 he appealed for even greater powers.[26] On 27 October a rump meeting of the revolutionary House of Representatives assembled, accompanied by most of the military leaders, at Bijagual. Céspedes was removed from office *in absentia*, and was later killed by the Spaniards in an ambush at San Lorenzo (Oriente) in March 1874.

The new President, Salvador Cisneros Betancourt, was a cattle farmer from Camagüey. His 'government' was composed exclusively of planters. From them Gómez received less shrift than ever. It seemed that the revolution, strong as it was in Oriente, had simply lost momentum, waiting vainly for the U.S. to give it an *imprimatur*. The Spaniards, firmly maintained in the West, also lacked vigorous direction at a time when the peninsula was once more itself divided by civil war after Don Carlos had raised the Carlist flag of insurrection on 14 April 1872.[27]

U.S. support never came. Fish remained Secretary of State through-

[24] *Ibid.*, 147.
[25] So Céspedes told O'Kelly in 1873 (O'Kelly, 249).
[26] Pirala, II, 611.
[27] Fernández Almagro, 127, 134–5.

out Grant's administration (1869–77). His principal concern in respect of Cuba was to do nothing to make difficulties for the Liberals in Spain nor (in 1873) for the Republic which ensued after Amadeo had abdicated in February 1873 – an event greeted in Havana with 'the utmost tranquillity and apathy'.[28] (The U.S. was by far the first power to recognize the Spanish Republic, though conservative opposition to the abolition of slavery in Cuba had been a main reason for the fall of Amadeo.) Fish also successfully steered public opinion and the president away from their intermittent enthusiasm for recognizing belligerence.[29]

The new Republican government in Madrid in 1873 could not maintain peninsular cohesion. The Republic no doubt would have attempted to negotiate on Cuba on the basis of Prim's initiative but they were preoccupied with the continuing Carlist war in the north and the rural violence in the south. In the army, there were signs of disaffection: General Moriones refused to hand over command to his successor, General Pavía; soldiers sent the reply 'Let them dance' to orders by their officers in certain garrisons. The capture of the state by the Madrid militia was narrowly avoided. Cantonal insurrections ensued in Andalucía and the Levante; cities asserted their independence. The president, Castelar, noted:

> There were days in that summer [1873] when we believed our Spain was completely dissolved ... It was not a question of substituting an existing Ministry nor of forming a government in an agreed form. It was a question of dividing the fatherland into a thousand portions, similar to what occurred at the collapse of the Caliphate of Córdoba. .... Some said that they were going to resuscitate the ancient crown of Aragón ... others an independent Galicia under British protection. Jaén prepared a war against Granada. Rivalries ill covered over by national unity during long centuries were renewed ... Universal war [seemed to beckon] ... insignificant towns, hardly marked in the map, summoned constituent assemblies. These risings were ironically against the most federally inclined of all governments.[30]

In these circumstances the Republic had no time to cope with Cuba, apart from replacing Captain-General Ceballos – who had followed the example of Valmaseda in closely identifying himself with the *status quo*, by his pronouncement against anything which could endanger the integrity of the territory. His successor was General Pieltaín,[31] who like all his predecessors began with a carefully planned and much publicized campaign, which led in this instance on 11 May 1873 to the death of

[28] Gallenga, 72.
[29] See Nevins, *Hamilton Fish*, 615–37.
[30] Castelar, 'La España Moderna', *Crítica internacional* (June, 1893), 192–3.
[31] General Cándido Pieltaín (1822–1888). Fought Carlists in Catalonia, friend of Prim.

the soul of rebellion in Puerto Príncipe, Ignacio Agramonte. But there came nothing further: Pieltaín soon asked for his release and was followed by General Jovellar, previously Minister of War (a post in which he was followed by ex-Captain-General Ceballos).[32] These captains-general made no progress against the rebels, but they did not lose ground in the west and, most important, sugar production was maintained: 1873 incredibly saw a record harvest – 775,000 tons.

Martial law was no doubt very disagreeable and there were sporadic outbursts of brutality, but in this fourth year of war Cuba was richer than ever. The Carnival in Havana in 1873, for instance, was celebrated with as much energy as usual: the Montalvos, Alfonsos and other grand families turning out as ever with a long line of coaches-and-six, bewigged coachmen, belaced footmen, postillions and outriders.[33] Slavery, these people believed, was 'as safe under Castelar as it ever was'. 'There is not a man likely to come into power in Madrid,' Zulueta happily remarked to The Times correspondent sent from London to report the war, 'but has his price'.[34] Zulueta with his four great mills employing 500 men each was now at the height of his reputation and power, and Gallenga commented that the captain-general would 'as little venture upon any measure without consulting him as the Priori . . . of Florence would have dreamt of issuing a decree without the sanction of the elder Cosimo de Medici'. The Casino Español was the real centre of authority in the island.

This serenity was not seriously interrupted even by the incident of the Virginius in October 1873 when a rebel supply ship of that name, owned by the New York junta but sailing under the U.S. flag, was captured by the Spaniards off Oriente. All fifty-three persons on board, including its North American captain, several U.S. and British citizens, together with a brother of Céspedes and one prominent rebel general (Bernabé Varona), were shot; many more might also have been had not the British frigate Niobe under Captain Lambton Lorraine appeared from Jamaica and threatened to bombard Santiago.[35] But Fish, Sickles, and the skilful Spanish ambassador in Washington, Polo de Bernabé,[36] succeeded in preventing either war, the recognition of belligerent rights or any change in the status quo. Much to the fury of volunteers and Spaniards in Cuba, the government of Spain made apology, handed

[32] General Joaquín Jovellar (1819–92), served in Cuba under O'Donnell 1842–49, and in Morocco. Under-Secretary of War, 1864. Director-General of Military Administration, 1869. Afterwards Senator.

[33] Gallenga, 71.

[34] Ibid., 73. Gallenga speaks of 'The prince of slave owners' but it is clear that it is of Zulueta that he is speaking.

[35] Sir Lambton Lorraine (1838–1917), baronet and admiral, long remembered with affection in Santiago.

[36] Polo de Bernabé, Admiral José (1821–95), Minister in Washington, 1872–4.

over the *Virginius*, paid $80,000 as indemnity and agreed to punish the responsible officer, General Burriel.[37]

On 3 January 1874, General Pavía, captain-general of Madrid, the successful repressor of Puerto Rico, staged a famous *golpe* against the Republic in Madrid, surrounding the Cortes and capturing the deputies. Thereafter, the government of Spain was republican only in name: and this 'Republic of Dukes' gave way, after a year of reconsolidation of state power in the peninsula, to the restored monarchy under the young Alfonso XII at the end of December 1874. It was thus not perhaps surprising to find old Concha, in Havana in the 1850s and ex-Queen Isabella's last prime minister, returning to Cuba as captain-general from 1874.

[37] See Nevins, *Hamilton Fish*, 667–94. Burriel was never punished, however.

CHAPTER XXII

The Spanish Counter-Revolution

The rebels after five years of ambiguity had still not grasped the nettle of revolutionary realism. In February 1874 Gómez, with Maceo as his second-in-command, had it is true been at last permitted to 'invade' the west; they won two almost pitched battles but had to retire due to casualties and lack of ammunition. When Gómez desired to set out once more in midsummer, his old enemies had gathered their old arguments together again and, even more, the rebel chiefs in the province of Las Villas had started a campaign of defamation against Maceo, evidence of a new fear that the victory of this brilliant and courageous mulatto might after all lead to a 'black republic'. Maceo was forced out of his second position in Gómez's army and a less prominent Negro, Cecilio González, took his place. Even so, the revolutionary government, still influenced by exiles such as José Morales Lemus, combined to withhold approval from any new plan of invasion. It was not till January 1875 that Gómez succeeded in crossing the *trocha*, leaving behind much of the countryside of Oriente and Camagüey in rebel hands, though not the cities.

The revolutionary impact of this move was immediate. Gómez burned eighty-three plantations in the Sancti Spiritus area in six weeks, including Julián de Zulueta's new mill *Zaza*.[1] Their slaves were freed. Alarm spread through the sugar plantations of the centre of the island and to Havana. But, once again, political confusion made further advance impossible. In April a new general assembly of rebels under conservative influence detached a large number of men from Gómez's army. The consequences of Gómez's offensive were thus far less marked than expected. The great sugar triangle Matanzas-Cárdenas-Colón was unharmed and the sugar harvest remained well over 700,000 tons. There was a renewed 'Cuban crisis' in the U.S. in 1875 but once again Fish, this time skilfully backed by Caleb Cushing, his minister in Madrid, held off demands for the recognition of belligerence.[2]

The rebel commanders were beginning to admit the possibility of defeat. In early 1876 a new whispering campaign was launched by the conservatives to ruin the prestige of Maceo, and later in the year

[1] Fernández Almagro, I, 322.
[2] Nevins, *Hamilton Fish*, 873ff.

General Carlos Roloff (of Polish origin) told Máximo Gómez that the officers in Las Villas would not accept their commander since he was a Dominican. 'I did not answer a word,' Máximo Gómez recorded later, 'and immediately turned over to him the command of the force with which I expected to fight the last battle against the Spanish Army.'[3] Maceo had recently reacted to his persecution by the conservatives in the following terms (writing to the new president of the rebel Republic, Estrada Palma):

> I have known for some time Mr President that . . . a small circle exists which has indicated that it did not wish to serve under my orders because I belong to the coloured race . . . I have learned that they are now releasing me and show favouritism to the coloured over the white officers in my command. . . . And since I do belong to the coloured race, without considering myself worth more or less than other men, I cannot and must not consent to the continued growth of this ugly rumour. Since I form a not unappreciable part of this democratic republic, which has for its basis the fundamental principles of liberty, equality and fraternity, I must protest energetically with all my strength that neither now nor at any time am I to be regarded as an advocate of a Negro Republic or anything of that sort. . . . Those who are to mould the future nation must declare themselves now. The men who act in the manner I have described can never form a part of the sort of country for which we are fighting. They are as much the enemies of the revolution as those who are fighting openly and directly against us . . . if politics are to have the upper hand, I must ask for my passport to some civilized land . . .[4]

But Maceo remained unsatisfied; and it became evident on every side that the rich exiles of New York were ceasing their active financial support of the rebellion. Other Negroes began to waver too from their backing of the rebels; thus, after the death of the Negro leader, Donato Mármol, one of his followers, Policarpo Rustán, a *mestizo* from Oriente, turned his arms against the Cubans and proclaimed his support (with a few dozen followers) of the mulatto Doroteo, a slave from Cienfuegos whom he proclaimed emperor of Cuba.

In the winter of 1876, with the Spanish monarchy now firmly re-established, and with the tenacious General Jovellar as captain-general in Havana for the third time, General Arsenio Martínez Campos, who had been the first officer two years before to declare for the King, who had served as chief of staff to General Valmaseda in his first period

---

[3] Roloff was a Polish Jew by birth who became a U.S. citizen and who had first gone to Cuba as a clerk in the house of Bishop & Co. at Cabarién.

[4] *Documentos, Manuscritos del Interior* (Habana, 1885), I, 44, qu. Foner, II, 260,

in Havana, and who had been the commander of the Alphonsist forces in Catalonia against the Carlists, arrived in Cuba with 25,000 men as reinforcement.[5] He had worked well with Jovellar before. His mission was a subtle one, of pursuing a vigorous offensive but at the same time (now that Spain was master of her own house at home) attempting to negotiate. The plan was soon successful since the astute Spanish Prime Minister Cánovas had given him plenty of room to negotiate. Martínez Campos had a total of 70,000 men which he distributed between the eight main Spanish commands. Morale among the rebels was anyway low after eight years of conflict. Some officers deserted. Others left the rebels when Martínez Campos proclaimed an amnesty for all except the leaders who surrendered before the end of the war. The Spanish offensive caused many losses and drove back the rebels behind the line of the *trocha*. Martínez Campos offered land on the old royal lands (*realengos*) to all 'ex-soldiers, volunteers . . . needy residents who had remained faithful', and revolutionaries who deserted.[6] In September Maceo was nearly captured, while in October the new rebel President, Estrada Palma, was indeed captured. The President of the so-called rebel legislative chamber, Eduardo Machado, was killed. Gómez's leading antagonist in the councils of the rebels, Vicente García, took over from Estrada, and in mid-December he let it be known that he was willing to discuss terms.[7] On 9 February Martínez Campos proposed a 'general pardon', the political equality of Cuba with Puerto Rico, the liberation of those slaves and Chinese who had fought with the rebels, and the freedom for all leaders who agreed to leave Cuba. Ultimately, the phrase 'forgetting the past' was substituted for the amnesty.[8] On 11 February an armistice was finally signed at Zanjón, embodying these terms. Some further clauses were added: no action would be taken against anyone for any political offence since 1868, nor against Spanish army deserters, and anyone who wanted to leave Cuba would be allowed to do so.

In February 1878, a few rebels headed by Maceo announced that they could not accept the terms of Zanjón, since they did not provide for the abolition of slavery nor for Cuban independence. Maceo wrote to Martínez Campos and asked to see him. Martínez Campos agreed: 'This Negro is the key to a real peace,' he reflected.[9] On 16 March Maceo went to Baraguá near Santiago for the curious conference – other Cuban leaders all distrusting the scheme. Maceo was nevertheless backed by about 1,500 men from Oriente, to whom he explained his

---

[5] Arsenio Martínez Campos (1831–1900). In the Moroccan war 1864. In Cuba 1869–72.
[6] See Corbitt, *H.A.H.R.* (1939), 280.
[7] Fernández Almagro, 329.
[8] *Ibid.*, 332.
[9] J. M. Figueredo, *La Revolución de Yara* (*c.* 1880), 200.

hostility to the pact of Zanjón and his long-standing dislike of the rich planters among the rebels.

The interview between Maceo, the mulatto 'titan of bronze', and Martínez Campos, kingmaker and arch negotiator, was dramatic. Martínez Campos began the discussion by urging that there had been enough war, and that it was time for Cuba to unite with Spain in a march towards progress and civilization. His aide, General Polavieja, then read out the Zanjón treaty. Maceo said that without the abolition of slavery it was impossible to take the pact seriously, and Dr Félix Figueredo, Maceo's political mentor, said that the rebels wanted independence. Martínez Campos said he would not have come to the meeting if he had thought that Maceo and his friends would only settle for independence. As for slavery, he personally was in favour of abolition but, since it was a controversial issue, it would have to be discussed by the Cortes. The Cuban general said again that independence and peace were inseparable. Martínez Campos then said, 'Hostilities will be renewed?' Maceo agreed. 'How much time do you need?' asked Martínez Campos with courtesy. Maceo replied that war could be renewed immediately. But an eight-day truce was agreed.

This 'Protest of Baraguá' excited general enthusiasm and made Maceo a hero throughout America. But it was hard for Maceo to carry his undertaking into action. The reorganization of the rebel army (with, surprisingly, General Vicente García, Gómez's old enemy, as commander-in-chief and General Jesús ('Tito') Galván as president) was not complete before Martínez Campos renewed the offensive. At first he and General Polavieja, beneath him, had told his men merely to meet Cuban firing passively and with shouts of compromise (*Viva Cuba! Viva la Paz!* Don't shoot, we are brothers!). But this did not last. A vigorous campaign followed and by May capitulation was inevitable. Maceo had refused to accept a bribe to surrender. Now he was allowed by Martínez Campos quietly to leave Santiago in a Spanish cruiser while the 'government' which he left behind accepted the armistice of Zanjón.

The war over, Jovellar gave way to Martínez Campos as captain-general. In July Cánovas dismantled the old dictatorial governmental machinery of Cuba and allowed the island to elect forty deputies to the Cortes and the island (previously divided into two) was divided into six provinces for that purpose.[10] Municipal elections were also introduced for local councils (though mayors were appointed by civil governors). But the Negro and poorer Cubans had no vote since the property qualification was high – taxpayers paying $25 a year. The followers of

[10] For the politics of the 1880s and 1890, see Francis Lambert's Oxford thesis, 'The Cuban Question in Spanish Restoration Politics' (1969).

Martínez Campos among the Spaniards – a small group of conciliators – formed a party which later became the Liberal or Autonomist party, designed to realize Martínez Campos's programme. Its chiefs were Vicente de Galarza, later Conde de Galarza; José Bruzón, Raimundo Cabrera, Demetrio Pérez de la Riva, Carlos Zaldo and Emilio Terry; on its left wing there were a number of masons.[11] Their programme was to extend civil rights to provide equal possibilities for Spaniards and Cubans to hold office; and permanent guarantees for freedom of speech, assembly and press. The slaves would be freed; when that would occur was left vague, though no more slaves would be allowed in. Commercial preference would be given to Cuba by Spain but tariffs would not exclude the U.S. Most of these Liberals were Cubans who had taken little or no part in the war or some who had backed Zanjón. In essence they were reformists who had been brushed aside by the war's extremism and who, with the peace, saw an opportunity for new leadership. They were in general middle class people who wanted the same rights in Cuba – no more – as Spaniards already had. In class origins they were petty *bourgeois*, some of them being *peninsulares*, and some were very keen on white immigration to Cuba.

In August the formation of the Liberal party was followed by that of a 'Spanish party', officially called the Constitutional Union party, whose design was to guarantee that Cuba would be 'always part of Spain'. They feared that autonomy would lead to separatism, and they desired a customs union between Cuba and Spain as well as a commercial treaty with the U.S. The rest of their programme even accepted Moret's slavery law and some limited civil rights. Here were found many ex-'volunteers', young *peninsulares* who had recently reached Cuba, together with planters such as the Marqués de Apezteguía and the philanthropic first leader of the party, the Conde de Casa Moré, the most prominent sugar proprietor and benefactor of Sagua la Grande.[12] Both these parties entered the Spanish Cortes in 1879.

The only other political group in Cuba was a small separatist one headed by the educationalist and mediator of 1871, Nicolás Azcárate, and the editor of *La Libertad*, Adolfo Márquez Sterling, with some other Havana intellectuals; among these was the young writer, José Martí, who returned in September from exile in Mexico and Guatemala.

The only group which had no part in this new political alignment were the amnestied ex-heroes of the 'Ten Years' War'. From late 1878 there was the general suspicion that the Spanish government was not

---

[11] Fernández Almagro, I, 340; R. Cabrera y Bosch, *Cuba y sus Jueces* (1887), 135. Galarza went on to become president of the Constitutional Union party but was forced out by the Right Wing.

[12] José Eugenio Moré (1810–90), Conde de Casa Moré, philanthropist and millionaire, born in Colombia, emigrated to Cuba in poverty as a child.

going to honour its promises in the Zanjón agreement. The leaders had no desire to accept permanent exile in Jamaica or the U.S. Martínez Campos, who alone had the political skill to win the peace as well as the war, returned to Madrid to become prime minister, being succeeded by General Ramón Blanco, a successful commander against the Carlists in the Basque provinces and Navarre, but of no great political understanding.

Elaborate plans were therefore made for a new rising for the summer of 1879. Its leader, General Calixto García in New York, had escaped from a Spanish prison. General Máximo Gómez believed the time not ripe for a new rising. In this scheme, once again Maceo was the victim of conspiracy among those who distrusted his skin: he was promised command of the army in Oriente but did not get it. But the series of conspiracies in Puerto Príncipe and Oriente were betrayed to the Spanish police and the rebels had as so often before 1868 to take action before they had co-ordinated their plans. Many escaped slaves flooded to the old commanders. For some weeks East Cuba seemed much as it had been two or three years before – in full war. But the Spaniards under Blanco as captain-general and Polavieja, in command in Oriente, acted with speed and decision. The rebels were isolated, suddenly appearing without the old leaders to be no more than bandits, and many were captured. Maceo's arrival was delayed until it was too late. General Calixto García was captured in August, only a few weeks after he had landed. He and the other leaders were despatched by warship back to prison in Spain. The *Guerra Chiquita* petered out.

The cost of this conflict along with the ten years' war was reckoned at $M300. This sum was added to the Cuban debt. Total Spanish deaths were reckoned at 208,000, Cuban deaths at less than one quarter of that number – 50,000. The war was rhetorically characterized by José Martí, the young revolutionary of Azcárate's group, who had been in exile or prison for most of it, as 'that wonderful and sudden emergence of a people apparently servile only a short time before, who made heroic feats a daily occurrence, hunger a banquet, the extraordinary a commonplace'.[13] More accurately, however, it can be seen as a middle-class and liberal venture which failed because the leaders were never willing to risk the extension of the war to the west and so risk freeing the slaves and destroying the country's prosperity. The internal dissensions between the rebels revolved round the question of slavery. The preoccupation of the rebel commanders throughout was the need to avoid angering the rich planters of the west, for it was the exiles from this class in New York who men such as Céspedes and Estrada Palma hoped would give money for the cause. In these circumstances it was easy for the Spaniards and the planters of the west to maintain

[13] J. Martí, *Obras Completas* (1931, etc.), 675–6.

their economic strength. The only possible change in the course of the war could have been avoided by external action but the Grant administration was not prepared to risk its excellent relations with its protégés, the Spanish constitutional monarchists, nor with the Republicans; while in Madrid until 1874 the government was too weak to hold its own even in the peninsula, much less in Cuba, and none dared risk a progressive colonial policy – few even wanted such a thing – for fear of antagonizing public opinion to frenzy. The government never had enough money to think seriously of abolition with compensation; abolition without compensation was politically inconceivable.

The war added an extra chapter to the Cubans' compendium of historic charges against the U.S. If Fish had granted belligerent rights; if Fish had allowed filibustering expeditions free rein; if Fish had brought pressure on the Spaniards; even, if Fish had allowed Céspedes to adhere to the U.S. But here the central ambiguity of the rebels' position on slavery played into the Spaniards' hands: the U.S. after their own civil war could not back a rebellion which still was less than frank on slavery.

Whatever economic motives may have underlain the actions of the participants, however, political attitudes were nevertheless engendered: the liberation of slaves, however incomplete; the sacrifice on the part of men such as Aldama and Morales of most of their wealth (Aldama was ruined by the war, having been one of the richest planters: he died in poverty in a friend's house in Havana in 1888); the inclusion of several sections of society in the ranks of the rebel army – rich and poor, black and white, Chinese and mulatto, peasants and workers – created in Cuba a strong nationalistic spirit which has never since quite died though it has often burned under curious auspices.

CHAPTER XXIII

The Sugar Crisis of the 1880s

The last three years of the Ten Years' War, unlike the first seven, had at last made a mark on sugar production; many mills had been ruined in the region of Cienfuegos, and in Oriente: production fell and, though the crop of 1879 was high,[1] the early 1880s saw a drop back to the averages reached in the 1860s, of a little over 500,000 tons per year.[2] There was a rise in the late 1880s, but even so the average in the six years 1885–90[3] lay below that in the last years of the 1860s or even the war years.[4] In the 1890s, there was a new leap forward, so that the average between 1891 and 1895 exceeded 900,000 tons a year, with bumper crops in 1894–5, when for the first time production of Cuban sugar attained a million tons.

Behind these bland figures lies a revolution in labour, in technique, and in the social and political circumstances of production.

At the end of the Ten Years' War, the financial condition of most planters remained what it had been throughout the century, even in the best days: hopelessly indebted to merchants, with interest rates running as high as 18%, or even 30%.[5] Many mills in the Cienfuegos area changed hands between 1870 and 1883 because of debts,[6] which were partly due to ruin in the war, particularly during Gómez's expedition. But everywhere planters who had been paying exorbitant interest but living well found that further credit was unobtainable. This was not only because of the war: the end of the slave trade meant the gradual disappearance of those powerful merchants who had always had a double interest in making loans to sugar planters; and now sugar mills could be attached for debt.

By the 1880s, further, even the largest plantations had mortgaged

[1] 670,000 in 1860; 20,757 cabs were in cane, and another 38,689 were in sugar plantations (Rebelló); in 1877, 17,701 cabs were in cane while the remainder of the land in cane farms dropped to 25,804 cabs (*Revista de Agricultura*, 31 March 1877, 75).

[2] 504,000 tons in 1860–4, 527,400 tons per year in 1880–4.

[3] 647,000 tons.

[4] The average 1865–75 was 676,000 tons.

[5] Report by Consul Vickers (Matanzas), 3 July 1888 (*Consular Reports*, 1884, No. 43, 481, qu. *Estudio*).

[6] Report by Consul William P. Prince of Cienfuegos, 10 August 1883 (*ibid.*, 485, qu. *Estudio*, 198). He says 'nearly all'. Some Cuban planters went to the Dominican Republic where they assisted the regeneration of sugar in that country. These were Carlos Loynaz, Joaquín Delgado and Enrique Lamar (Deerr, 123).

themselves to the hilt, for original capital, for supplies or for cooperage; and in 1880 a new mortgage law enabled creditors to seize land as well (as was previously possible) produce.[7]

But this was a time when a sugar mill, to keep going at all, had to expand. During the Cuban civil war, beet had crept up on cane to gain what seemed a winning advantage: in 1840 less than a fifth of the world's sugar came from beet; in 1884 just over half.[8] Beet was protected in Europe by bounties, so that in effect between 1850 and 1900 over sixty million tons of sugar were put on the market at less than the cost of production.[9] During the Ten Years' War, Germany had become the world's largest sugar producer. Worse still, U.S. cane sugar was recovering from the North American Civil War, so that from 1875 the Department of Agriculture in Washington began not only to experiment with beet but also, about the same time, to try out in Louisiana a new sorghum cane. President Rutherford Hayes prophesied that by 1884 the U.S. would no longer need sugar from abroad.[10] This hope was not fulfilled, but since Europe's sugar needs were being increasingly satisfied at home, Cuba depended on the U.S. market. In the 1880s even Spain developed a beet sugar industry. Two beet factories were established at Granada and Córdoba in 1882; ten years later the industry was further extended, at Zaragoza and Aranjuez. In 1883 this industry produced 35,000 tons, in 1895 over 400,000.[11]

The result was that from early 1884 sugar prices dropped sharply, permanently and alarmingly so for Cuba and they had already been slackening for decades. Prices had fallen during the 1850s, and certainly did not rise during the 1860s. Still, in 1870–2 the average price of sugar in London was about twenty-four shillings a hundredweight. In 1883 the average price stood at nineteen shillings. By 1884, it had fallen by a third, to thirteen shillings and threepence, and except for a brief rise at the end of the decade stayed at that level for several years. Indeed, prices never returned to the figures of pre-1884 except during the exceptional years of the First World War and immediately afterwards. But any price less than three cents per pound was found to bring really unacceptable losses to small or inefficient mills, and prices such as 2·50 cents per pound, which were now encountered for the first time, were bound to bring losses to a far greater number of mills – perhaps a majority – and suddenly.

[7] Cf. Atkins, 52, 69, for some consequences.
[8] 14% and 53%, to be precise.
[9] Deerr, 504.
[10] H. Jenks, Our Cuban Colony (1928), 28.
[11] 409,000 tons (M. Tuñón de Lara, La España del siglo XIX, 1808–1914 (1961), 218). After 1898 Spain, behind a high tariff, would produce more beet sugar than her home market could absorb though its high price made it impossible to export (see Carr, 402).

This was far the most harsh trial experienced by Cuba in her economic history since the eighteenth century, and indeed it quite overshadowed in importance the end of slavery. Alongside sugar, there was in Cuba only tobacco, coffee being now hardly existent. No planter had developed secondary crops to fall back on; if they had, where could they be sold? Also, what other crop could stand transport along Cuban roads? Certainly not citrus fruit. Some sugar plantations went over to cattle. Further, the old economic anomalies, typical of slave societies, remained (despite the erosion of the slave system): even the rural population did not grow minor crops for subsistence. Nor did villages and towns. The tradition of Cuba, like the rest of the West Indies, was still to buy food in bulk from the north or from Europe, to feed the slaves who drove the plantations which made the money to buy, *inter alia*, the food. This was slavery's most lasting contribution to Cuban society.

But now a sugar mill, to keep going at all, had absolutely to cut costs and to mechanize. It was also a difficult time to obtain capital, yet technological innovations were becoming the indispensable conditions of survival.

One innovation was more significant than all others, a factor independent of both beet sugar development and slavery, which enabled at least some mills to save themselves from the wreck. This affected railways, and derived from a decisive change in the technology of steel. In 1850 steel had been almost a precious metal. But in 1856 Sir Henry Bessemer[12] opened up the prospect of cheap mass production with his new process. England was in the lead but the U.S. soon leapt ahead after 1870: from just under 20,000 tons in 1867 they produced well over 500,000 in 1877, and over a million by 1880. At the same time, therefore, the price of steel rails dropped from $166 per hundred pounds (in 1867) to $46 (in 1877) and, after a brief rise, to $30 or below in the 1880s.[13] So railways in the 1880s could be built for a fifth of what they had cost ten years earlier. In Cuba this had three critical consequences: first, cane could now be carried to be milled much further on economically worthwhile private railways; hence, plantations could be bigger. Second, the finished sugar could be carried by railway to the sea by private rail to private wharves. Planters were thus able to escape the tentacles of Havana. Port merchants in the past had taken their cut even from those rich planters who owed them nothing. Third, it was of course U.S. steel rails which were exported to Cuba, not Basque or Spanish: a further step in the North Americanization of the 'ever-faithful isle'.

[12] Sir Henry Bessemer (1813–98), a prolific inventor, himself concerned with sugar.
[13] See *Historical Statistics of the U.S.*, 123, 416–17.

The private railway boom began in the 1880s and lasted all the first half of the 1890s. By 1895 there were 350 miles of private railways, compared with 150 miles semi-private and only 800 miles of public railway.[14]

Two classes of the Cuban *bourgeoisie* lost money: the small planters who could not afford these railways; and the smaller merchants.[15]

All these developments spelled the end of the old sugar oligarchy, and the entrance into the Cuban economic field of a new factor: the U.S. The precise effects of all these demands were shown by the misfortunes of the Sarriá family who in the past had had five good mills in the Cienfuegos area, as well as, in 1884, an outstanding debt of $750,000 to Torriente Brothers of Cienfuegos, who for a long time had been shippers and merchants. All went well until the death of Juan Sarriá, the founder of this empire. Then the eldest son, Domingo, left his half-brother to run his estates and went to live in Spain. Disillusioned, he later sent his own son to take over in Cuba; but Domingo Sarriá II, used to Spain and to luxury, lived in Cienfuegos in such magnificence – his horses were shod with silver – that he was taken for a member of the royal family. These extravagant sugar kings were ill-fitted to face the crisis of 1883. In 1884 Atkins & Co. (acting as the Torrientes' receiver) closed the mortgage on the plantations and became sole proprietors of the *Soledad* plantation.[16] Atkins & Co. improved and developed it to one of the largest sugar plantations in the world by 1893: 12,000 acres, twenty-three miles of private railway, 5,000 acres of cane, and 1,200 men employed in harvest time. This plantation represented the largest U.S. investment in Cuban sugar.

A branch of the De la Torriente family – Sarriá's old mercantile contacts – meanwhile ruined themselves at the nearby *Carlota* plantation. In 1879 they owed $600,000, much of it spent on grottoes, fountains and marble baths.[17] This mill also passed to Atkins by default. The *Soledad* plantation was further developed by the inclusion in its boundaries of the *Caledonia* mill and plantation, taken over from the

[14] Brooke Report, 285, 320.

[15] In addition to railways, centrifugal machines costing $30,000 for a 'triple effect' were now essential for an up-to-date mill. In the 1870s, two Scots, Duncan Stewart and Macdonald, devised a new hydraulic pressure system giving the rollers automatic elasticity, so demanding new application of steam. Chemical engineering altered the process once more; by the late 1880s sugar refineries began to popularize granulated sugar in standard packages. Other new technological changes included Watson's modern 'dumb turner' of 1871, experiments with six or five rollers instead of three, heavily indented rollers, special 'crushers' to treat the cane before introduction to the rollers, and the use of green bagasse as fuel.

[16] 1884 was the most disastrous year, since mass beet production then really hit sugar prices; if the price of sugar halved, it meant that the actual cost of interest, reckoned in terms of the year's harvest, doubled; i.e. the Sarriás's loan meant an interest of, say, 20% of the 1883 harvest but 40% of that of 1884.

[17] Atkins, 38.

heirs of Diego Julián Sánchez;[18] Atkins then bought the *Limones* and the *Brazo* mills from other heirs of Diego Julián Sánchez, leasing the *Limones* mill to the second of them. Thus the large estates of the Sánchez family were absorbed as well as those of the Sarriás. Atkins finally broke into the declining fortune of the Iznagas, buying a half interest in *Vega Vieja* from Carlos Iznaga, and leasing the other half from his sister, Dina Barrieta, and also bought the *Santa Teresa* estate from Juan Pérez Galdós, brother of the novelist,[19] turning both this and the nearby *Veguitas* estate into a cattle ranch.

This story illustrates one decisive change in Cuban society in the 1880s. Since there were no more fortunes to be made from slave trading, there was no more idle capital: capital had to come from elsewhere. Despite the great superiority of Britain and France in most foreign investments at that time, even in South America, the proximity of the U.S. and her dominant part in Cuban trade made her far the most likely source.[20]

Atkins's *Soledad* in 1893 was a powerful new society within a society. Such concentrations of capital, technological and social organization, the product of union between several old large plantations, became known as a *central*, a centre of grinding linked with other plantations by rail and perhaps with the sea. Most of the cane used came from tenants of *Soledad*.[21]

The essential mark of this system of economic organization was, however, less its size, its origin, its high capital cost or its technological efficiency than the fact that, for the first time since sugar had been grown in the Antilles, sugar grinding was no longer carried out by the person who grew it.

From the 1840s, the stimulus of white immigration had been a major aim of the Havana worthies who made up the *Junta de Fomento*. Prizes were offered to planters who established white families on their estates. In 1857, the Conde de Pozos Dulces had written firmly that the separation of cane cultivation from sugar manufacture was the best means of solving the terrible question of slavery; white immigrants should be encouraged to plant cane and sell it to large sugar factories; and after the failure of the attempt to bring in Mexicans and Chinese to replace slaves, and the appreciation by the planters that mechanization of the

[18] Partly belonging for a time to another receiving merchant, Manuel Blanco.

[19] Atkins, 111.

[20] Others who played the same role as Atkins were the U.S. bankers Eaton Stafford & Co and the Danish Guillermo Schmidt; the Germans, Fritze & Co., and their successors, Meyer Thode, who gained hold of much of the old Iznaga empire by the marriage of Meyer with Belencita Iznaga. Schmidt had also married the heiress of a comparable family, the Malibráns, previously owners of the *Canamabo* plantation. These firms later combined with Atkins and H. O. Havemeyer, the biggest U.S. sugar refiner, to found the Trinidad Sugar Co.

[21] Atkins, 209.

harvesting side of cane cultivation was unlikely at least in the near future, that is what happened. There always had been, in fact since the first big sugar boom of the 1790s, a small number of peasants who had grown some sugar cane and sold it to be ground.[22]

There were three aspects of this development. First, proprietors, both of old, small, ox-driven mills, incapable of raising the money to modernize them, and of modern mills which would have been reckoned advanced in the 1860s, decided to abandon grinding and to sell their cane to the nearest undertaking sufficiently big to be able to take more cane than their owners grew themselves. Then, some landowners, including cattle farmers, who owned land near a mill which needed more cane, simply began to grow it; and third, the mill, which became known as the *central*, itself let out some of its lands to *colonos*.

The war of 1868-78 favoured this development of the *colonato*, as it was called, partly because of the physical damage caused to some central and eastern plantations. Some royal lands (*realengos*) were distributed to volunteers or pardoned revolutionaries under Martínez Campos's law, so swelling the ranks of smallholders. Planters whose mills were actually destroyed might give up the attempt to rebuild their machinery and concentrate exclusively on growing cane. The war also made slaves difficult to come by. Planters whose slaves had fought in the rebel army lost their source of labour entirely. *Colonos* from now on got a specific percentage (*arrobaje*) of sugar per hundred arrobas of cane delivered – usually four or five arrobas (about 100-125 lbs). By 1887 a third to two-fifths of Cuban sugar was grown by the *colono* system, and the percentage was every year increasing.

Colonos as a rule lacked capital, like the mill-owners they – in some cases – had been. But they too had expenses, especially in respect of personnel: even small *colonias* had to provide food and lodging for labourers. So the *central* would often advance money to the *colonos*. They were therefore generally indebted. This system of payment, the so-called 'truck system', has usually been regarded as inequitable wherever it has occurred – for instance in the London lace industry; and indeed it has been illegal in England since 1701. On the other hand, in Cuba it did stimulate white immigration from Spain and it did allow a much smoother transition from both slavery and the old sugar system than would otherwise have been possible. In 1886 the Spanish government announced its willingness to pay the passage to Cuba of all workers who went there for a year and the consequence was a flood of immigrants far greater than any previously known.[23]

[22] Moreno Fraginals, 34.

[23] Official statistics say that 224,000 arrived in Cuba from Spain between 1882 and 1894 (excluding 1888), of whom only 142,000 ever returned (D. C. Corbitt, 'Immigration in Cuba' *H.A.H.R.*, xxi, 304).

The size of the *colonia* varied. There were a few very big *colonia* by the end of the 1890s having 3,000 or more acres, producing 40,000 or 50,000 tons of sugar. The slave Montejo speaks of the 'typical' *colono* as having ten or fifteen *besanas* (furrows).[24] Smaller owners, however, spoke of the system as 'plunging into deep misery those who were before . . . wealthy landowners'. It is true that families such as the Pedrosos, Diagos or Arrietas, old oligarchs or nineteenth-century *peninsulares* alike, were reduced in circumstances. But most *colonos* were new men, immigrants from Spain or from other small farms: after all, the actual number of sugar plantations had never exceeded 1,500. In 1894 there were still reckoned to be over 1,000 mills, but many were already ruined, so 500 would be a more accurate estimate. The number of *colonos* on the other hand probably exceeded 15,000 by 1895.[25]

In general only the owners of large *colonia* could really be satisfied. The manager of one reported: 'I have never known a single instance where a small *colonia* prospered or was able to extricate itself from debt'; for a large farm could buy wholesale, while a small one had to buy retail at 15% or 30% more. A large farm also employed scarcely more salaried employees than a small one.[26]

These developments occurred in nearly all sugar-cane-growing countries, including other areas of Spanish America such as Argentina and Peru. Indeed it seems to have been in Martinique that a *central* system was first used.[27] But in Brazil the *centrales*, organized, inspired and partly financed by the government in several instances, co-existed alongside still surviving small *engenhos*; the same occurred in India which still indeed has many bullock mills alongside modern factories. Similarly, Barbados remained a colony of self-contained properties of individual proprietors. In Peru the distance from the U.S. was no doubt one reason for the maintenance of the old oligarchy in its old place.

The straightened circumstances of the 1880s did not seem to have any consequence on the private life of those planters who did keep above water: reports are still common of planters keeping 'open house . . . often entertained as many as twenty', of balls with Chinese lanterns, of visits to operas, and of sailing parties: '*Elles pratiquent l'hospitalité avec une largesse magnifique.*'[28] But perhaps there were fewer instances of

[24] Montejo, 108.
[25] Deerr's figure (I, 130), which I accept. See, however, W. J. Clark, *Commercial Cuba*, 212, who speaks of 1,100. There had been 1,190 in 1879, *Anuario Estadístico* (1914), 96.
[26] Census of 1899, 532.
[27] Deerr, 235.
[28] H. Piron, *L'Ile de Cuba* (1876), 30. Consuelo Iznaga had enough money to go to England, dazzle London society of the 1880s, and marry the eighth duke of Manchester:

> 'And next with all her wealth of hair unroll'd
> Was Lady Mandeville, bright-eyed and witty;
> And Miss Iznaga, whose dark cheek recalled
> Lord Byron's Spanish ditty.'

fantastic luxury. That exquisite carriage, the *volante*, was rare in Trinidad in 1892, rare in Havana by 1884. Indeed Trinidad itself had been in decay since the economic crisis of the late 1850s.

Some really large mills survived to become *centrales*. This was true of Zulueta's *Alava*, two of the Diago and Ayesterán mills (*Amistad* and *Tinguaro*), *Constancia*, and Tomás Terry's *Caracas*. The Montalvos maintained themselves in their Cienfuegos estates, founding indeed a new mill (*Andreita* at Cruces), and taking over two new ones in addition to their old holding at *Concepción*.[29] But the Arrietas's old pride, *Flor de Cuba*, went down, with many others, though the moment of final defeat was put off. The *Gran Azucarera*, Queen María Cristina's old company, also lost its mills.

Indeed the more the matter is examined the more it seems that this revolution of the 1880s, as it is often regarded, was the most important social change that the island of Cuba has experienced; for it was then that Cuba lost her old upper-class based on land, so that, alone of the South American states, she would later embark on independence with her social revolution already accomplished. Certainly the changes that Cuba underwent have yet to occur in most of her neighbours, except Mexico, Bolivia and Argentina. In Peru, for instance, the equivalent of the Montalvo–O'Farrill–Pedroso connection continues to control vast estates and economic power. In Cuba these related families admittedly continued to play a part in history; thus a Montalvo became a minister in the 1930s and a Pedroso was a bank president in the 1950s. But they owed these positions to their membership of the *bourgeoisie* rather than to landed aristocracy.

The disappearance of this aristocracy was not an unmixed blessing. Foolish, indulgent, over-generous and extravagant though these old families often were, they set an unmistakable national social tone, *criollo* or Cuban, rather than North American. They may have treated their slaves indifferently or badly, but they did create a society with its own often brilliant characteristics. Many of them were public benefactors: Miguel del Monte left money to give a free European education to five pupils in agricultural science; the O'Farrills munificently endowed Managua; the Conde de Casa Moré gave $200,000 for a school of agriculture; the Terrys and Abreus built theatres; the list is endless. When they had been depressed to the status of an urban *bourgeoisie*, or of a small farmer, or had gone away for ever, back to a Spain that neither they nor their fathers had thought of before as home, they left the island of Cuba open to penetration by North Americans, culturally and economically as well as in the long run politically.

In the 1880s Spanish wealth increased in the peninsula on its own

[29] Atkins, 47; and Rebello, for old holdings.

account. The Bessemer steel process and phylloxera in France made an unprecedented demand for both iron ore and wine from Spain. Railway building developed fast. After 1882 the home market (as well as the Cuban) grew immensely, causing a 'euphoria of cotton' in Catalonia,[30] deriving partly from the management of those fortunes made originally out of Cuba. In Cuba, however, for the first time the rate of economic growth was falling behind that of the home country.

Slavery in Cuba meantime came to an end, with a whimper not a bang, and certainly without the celebrations which occurred when the institution was abolished in Brazil in 1890. The social implications of this momentous step indeed seemed in Cuba disappointingly slight. In November 1879 General Martínez Campos, now prime minister in Madrid, formally abolished slavery in Cuba as from 1888, completing the promise contained in the Moret Law. There would be no compensation as there had been in the British and French colonies, instead, an eight-year *patronato* or time of apprenticeship for all liberated slaves. (Puerto Rican slaveholders had been compensated in 1873, but there had been only 31,000 slaves.) The Cuban *patronato* was bitterly criticized, particularly the provision that Negroes were able to buy their liberty out of the *patronato* for $30–$50 a year. But many masters, believing that paying for free labour was cheaper than maintaining Negroes in the *patronato*, freed their slaves before the proper day. In 1880, there were apparently about 200,000 slaves in Cuba, with 3,500 *coartados* and 270,000 free black or mulatto;[31] in September 1886 there were only about 26,000 slaves held on the *patronato* and in that year, by general agreement, the *patronato* was abolished two years early. Four years later the slaves were also freed in Brazil, and the African Negro at long last had achieved everywhere in the Americas what liberals at least have termed liberty. Ex-slaves now usually added to the Christian names which they had been given at baptism the surname of their old master: thus a new generation of Pedrosos, Peñalvers, O'Reillys and O'Farrills made its appearance.

As had been found elsewhere in the Caribbean by other colonists, employment of contract labour was indeed a saving over employment of slaves. 'Slave labour is more costly than any other, all things considered', one planter of the region of Cienfuegos remarked to an American traveller in 1884.[32] The consequence was bizarre; in the 1880s slaves became quite cheap to buy – averaging a mere $50 or $60 at the time of final emancipation. In many places life seemed, to begin with, to go on much as before, the slaves staying in their barracoons,

[30] J. Vicens Vives, *Els Catalans en el siglo XIX* (1961), 60–1, qu. Carr, 391.

[31] Salví, *Anunciador General de la Habana*, qu. Aimes, 'Coartación', *Yale Review*, XVII (1909). Actual figures: 196,359, 3,526 and 269,547.

[32] Ballou, *Due South*, 61.

but with no locks on the doors and able to leave if they wished – though many with no initiative and fearful of freedom, did not.[33] On a typical large *colonia* in 1895, 150 permanent workers and 200 others were employed from 1 December to 1 June (during the harvest, that is). Of the latter, 10% were Spaniards or Canary Islanders; 10% Negresses or boys; 20% white Cubans; and 60% Negroes or mulattoes. This *colonia* thus exactly resembled in the organization of its labour a large plantation in the days of slavery. The permanent workers got different wages, varying from $85 a month for the *mayoral*, to $15 a month for an assistant groom. An average wage for the permanent worker was $288 a year. In addition, the maintenance of workers was paid at $12 a month. So the total cost in wages at this farm reached $4,320, and in maintenance, $3,600; about $7,920, that is, in all.

The harvest workers got an average of $20 a month (or $120 for the six months of work), together with maintenance of $7.50 a month. Three hundred harvest workers thus received annually $4,000 in wages and $1,500 in maintenance – $5,500 in all. The total costs of this 'free labour' *colonia* therefore reached $13,420.

The maintenance of a slave labour force approximately similar would, in 1865, have been $9,000; allowing for the fall in the value of the peso between 1865 and 1895, for the cost of the initial purchase of slaves and for the annual replacement of slaves (usually calculated at 6%), the cost of labour in 1895 could have amounted to about $8,400 (reckoning slaves as costing $700 a head). This sum at least was pure gain to the planter or *colono*. It is hard to believe that his saving from employing cheap contract labour rather than expensive slaves could have been less than 50%.[34]

Thus the standard of living of those who were slaves in the 1870s actually fell, in Cuba as elsewhere in the Caribbean, after the coming of freedom. Freedom gave no greater stability to Negro families,[35] even if there were clearly other improvements.

[33] See Montejo, 66.

[34] The figures in these paragraphs derive from Mr P. M. Beal's statements in the Guamairo Colonia, near Soledad, in the Census of 1899, and from Pezuela's figures for an average plantation in 1863. The old question of the low productivity of Southern slave labour is explored fruitfully by Genovese, 46–7.

[35] It is alas quite impossible to accept Elkins's view (*Slavery*, 79) that in all Latin countries there was a transition from slavery that was 'smooth, organic and continuing'.

CHAPTER XXIV

The End of Slavery

Thus slavery and the slave trade from Africa to the Americas came to an end and it is perhaps desirable, after all that has been said, to make some final judgment upon the matter. First, though all sorts of contrasting judgments may be made about the diverse behaviour of different European colonizers, and though some might argue that it would be preferable, say, to be a slave on a Cuban plantation in the eighteenth century than on a Jamaican one at the same time, or to be a house slave in Virginia than a mining slave in Brazil (all of which, for reasons previously suggested, is no doubt true), the judgment of Baron Humboldt is surely the most appropriate, namely, 'what a melancholy spectacle is that of Christian and civilized nations discussing which of them has caused the fewest Africans to perish during the interval of three centuries by reducing them to slavery'. Humboldt added, 'The slave who has a hut and a family is less miserable than he who is purchased as if he formed part of a flock.'[1] This qualification is an absolute one and cuts across any differentiation of place or type of labour or nationality of master. Otherwise, the different points cancel each other out: the English feared Negroes but often treated them correctly, the Portuguese felt no repulsion but worked them to death; the Spaniards had no abolition movement but encouraged and developed the marriage of African and Catholic religions, while the English refused to recognize even their own bastards; it was much easier to become free if one were a Spanish slave; but it seems fair to point out despite the Anglo-Saxon carriage of so many slaves themselves, particularly in the eighteenth century, that, had it not been for Anglo-Saxon abolitionism, slavery might well have lasted several generations more in the Spanish and Portuguese colonies, despite the increasingly strong economic arguments against it.[2]

The chief iniquity of slavery was that it handed over to the master complete power over the slave's sexual and family life, including the possibility of such a thing: man and woman might very well be

---

[1] Humboldt, *Travels*, III, 244. In his discussion of the matter (*Slavery in Western Culture*, 227ff) Brion Davis presents arguments that 'lead us to suspect that Negro bondage was a single phenomenon, or *Gestalt*, whose variations were less significant than underlying patterns'.

[2] Travellers to Cuba in the 1870s were still reporting frightful tales of ill treatment of slaves by masters or mistresses, e.g. Piron, *L'Ile de Cuba*, 184.

separated for ever, sold in different places and by different masters, separated even from their children. The plantation or the *cafetal* was in fact a private feud where, despite the formal law, the master (or his representative, the *administrador* or the *mayoral*) could be as brutal or on occasion as humane as he liked. In these circumstances the formal possibility of buying freedom, getting a new master and accumulating a small capital was delusory. In the cities and on tobacco plantations life was, of course, very much better.

The essence of slavery, however, was the plantation both in Cuba and elsewhere; for this was work which would have been refused by the poorest free men; given the great availability of land, there was never any possibility of holding men in the conditions of a large sugar plantation except by force. Even so, slaves from time to time escaped.

Slavery is as old as society itself; but it seems offensive, however evil conditions undoubtedly were in Africa, that western Europe, having in the late middle ages retreated from that form of labour, should sink back into tolerance of and then reliance upon it during the four centuries following the Renaissance.

Perhaps fifteen million people were carried across the Atlantic from the early sixteenth to the late nineteenth centuries.[3] The vast majority

[3] See figures in R. R. Kuczynski, *Population Movements* (1936), 26; Deerr, II, 284, has 12·4 million, together with 10% mortality on the voyage and perhaps another five million dead *en route* in Africa; see also Hugh Thomas, 'The Dark Millions', *Observer*, 17 October 1965, in which the fifteen million figure is accepted and broken down nationally as follows:

Probable shipments		Average per year (slaves)	Average voyages per year (average 300 boatload)
Sixteenth century	900,000	9,000	30
Seventeenth century	2,750,000	27,500	92
Eighteenth century	7,000,000	70,000	233
Nineteenth century	4,000,000	60,000	200
TOTAL about	15,000,000	40,000	138

Probable shippers	Number of slaves	Estimated number of voyages
British (including U.S. to 1783)	4,500,000	15,000
Portuguese	4,500,000	15,000
Dutch	1,800,000	6,000
French	2,000,000	6,667
Spanish	1,000,000	3,333
Danish	100,000	333
U.S. after 1783	1,000,000	3,333
German and others	100,000	333
	15,000,000	50,000

Of these tables, that entitled 'Probable shipments' derives from Kuczynski while the rest are my own computations. Brion Davis, *Slavery in Western Culture*, 9, accepts fifteen million as a conservative estimate. Tannenbaum, *Slave and Citizen*, 29-33, explores figures without reaching any decision. Pope-Hennessy, *Sins of the Fathers* (1967), 2, accepts fifteen million. The *Catholic Encyclopaedia* has twelve million. Dike, *Trade and Politics in the Niger Delta*, 3, thinks five to six million is 'nearer the mark'.

of these were sold by Africans rather than *panyared* (the English seven-teenth-century term for kidnapping), and probably a majority of them were already slaves in Africa beforehand. There is no doubt, of course, that the Atlantic slave trade stimulated internal African slave traffic, just as, by introducing gunpowder, guns, gin and Indian cottons, it transformed Africa and deprived it of other, more creative, commerce with Europe. On the other hand, it is not inconceivable that, as bland historians have suggested, given economic and social conditions in Africa, many Africans, offered a possibility of being fed and housed in return for labour, might have actually chosen to go to America, even under eighteenth-century conditions of voyage which were, of course, bad for all. The food available to nineteenth-century sugar workers in Cuba was superior to that available to nineteenth-century workers in industrial conditions in England.[4] Africans might also have generally preferred to have been slaves to Europeans than to Arabs and that perhaps might have been their fate otherwise. The problem of Ibo over-population has not been solved since the end of the trade. These facts in no way excuse the behaviour of Europeans, though it was more difficult than might be supposed to withdraw from the trade once it had begun and had been in existence for several generations; no doubt the same sort of judgment will eventually be made about the conditions in South Africa and the continued investment in it by humane men and women in England. In 1511 King Ferdinand the Catholic wrote to an official in Santo Domingo: 'I do not understand how so many Negroes have died; take much care of them'. Later kings in Europe were less considerate. Most Europeans who thought about the matter in any reflective spirit believed that they were saving Africans in large numbers for contact at least with Christianity and anyway from a fate worse than death.

Whatever moral, social or economic judgments are made, the Americas now had, by the 1880s, a substantial Negro or mulatto population: probably, however, because of the great superiority in numbers of men over women carried from Africa, only about fifteen million in all,[5] and these mostly concentrated around the Caribbean, or the Atlantic seaboard of Brazil. Many of these Africans and their descendants were survivors of the economic circumstances that had created them: their future in the British Caribbean had no economic meaning; they had served their purpose at one stage of development and, almost always with no sense of either paternity or property

---

[4] E.g., 'The victims of the rapine were quite possibly better off on the American plantations than the captives who remained in the African jungle', Ulrich Phillips, *American Negro Slavery*, 45.

[5] Kuczynski, *Population Movements* 7, speaks of 'nearly ten million' in 1835, and 'between thirty-six and forty-two million' in 1935.

(often with long-standing habits of thievery and violence), were now superfluous. Had they not been available in their millions in the first place, no doubt the goods which they produced would either not have been grown at all (such as tobacco or cotton in the U.S. south) or (like sugar and Caribbean cotton) would have been provided by India. Indeed, it is the loss to Asia of the investment and employment which went into the Americas that must be the most lasting effect of the slave trade: on the one hand an empty continent to which labour had to be brought to develop imported crops; on the other hand, a continent already over full and under-employed. Of Africa it should suffice to say that the export of slaves became slowly almost a monocrop during the seven centuries of Arab and European slave traffic; that kingdoms and societies were organized around this monocrop; and that when it ceased these systems collapsed: the collapse of the trade brought in the imperial flags in the 1880s.

Overall nineteenth-century standards of living are impossible to establish in Cuba. Death rate figures are nevertheless indicative, and for Havana there is a rough guide based on returns in the registry.[6] This suggests little improvement during the century, though suicide figures for Negroes fell swiftly in the last years of slavery.[7] The volatility of the figures was, of course, due to the epidemics: yellow fever, cholera and smallpox. Except in the war years, the death rate was probably higher in Havana than outside the city.[8] No single country anywhere in the world which recorded statistics in the 1960s produced any figures which resembled these.[9]

[6] *Death rate in Havana:*

	(per 1,000)	
1801–10:	37.96	
1811–20:	46.70	(yellow fever epidemic 1816–20)
1821–30:	36.17	
1831–40:	32.34	(cholera epidemic 1833, 1834, 1835, 1836)
1841–50:	23.27	(yellow fever epidemic 1844)
1851–60:	26.17	(Asiatic cholera epidemic 1850–4)
1861–70:	42.04	(Asiatic cholera epidemic 1867–8; yellow fever epidemic 1861)
1871–80:	44.97	(yellow fever epidemic 1873–7; smallpox epidemic 1871, 1872, 1874, 1875, 1878–81)
1881–90:	34.18	(smallpox epidemic 1887–8)
1891–1900:	43.81	(rose to 89.19 per 1,000 in 1898; yellow fever epidemic 1895–8; smallpox epidemic 1891 and 1894–8)
1901–10:	20.56 ⎱ (for comparison)	
1911–20:	19.85 ⎰	

(*Source:* Census of 1919, 252).

[7] In the twentieth century the Havana figures were always 50%–75% higher than the country.

[8] See figures in Ortiz, *Negros Esclavos*, 396.

[9] Not once was a figure of over twenty deaths per 1,000 recorded (*UN Statistical Yearbook 1961*, 46–7). The average annual death rate in England and Wales in the second part of the nineteenth century was about twenty, or half the Cuban rate, the highest figures being 24.7 per 1,000 in 1847. Of course, such figures only give an adequate gauge of the trend of mortality if the age structure of the population did not change: of this there is no clear evidence.

Other figures in Cuba, however tentatively they are approached, suggest the same stagnation or even decline. Thus the number of cattle in the country seems to have increased from about one million in 1827 to just over two million in 1894. But the population rose over four times in this period. The availability of fresh milk and fresh meat therefore decreased fairly substantially. In absolute terms, there were well over 50% more pigs in 1827 than in 1894: in 1827 there were about three pigs per head of population, in 1894 there were nearly three people per pig.

These gloomy truths were confirmed by the evidence of visitors. Clean-living North Americans described the island in the 1880s as 'thoroughly demoralized',[10] venal in everything, running with beggars, often Chinese, often blind. Such travellers complained much of the time they were there: at the dirt and misery they met everywhere; at the meat – game, usually, due to the continued decline of cattle; at the 'inveterate gaming propensities of the people'. The press is full of accounts of murders, as much in the 1880s as before.

The same judgments appear dimly out of other statistics. In 1827 we find thirty hospitals in Cuba; even in 1919 there were only twenty-one. In 1827 there were 504 physicians and in 1860 230 doctors or oculists in Havana alone;[11] however elementary their training, this meant that there was one per 600 of the population; in 1907 there would be one doctor per 1,700. Cuba was, in fact, better off from the point of view of accessibility of doctors in the early nineteenth century than at any other period afterwards. In 1827 there were 222 primary schools, still mostly 'primitive little tutorial groups taught by mulatto women'[12] except for the *convento* at Belén and seven free schools for white children founded by the Economical Society. There were also six schools for black or mulatto boys and eight for black or mulatto girls. No slaves went to school. About a tenth of the *free* children of school age probably went to school (6,000 white boys, 450 black or mulatto; 2,500 white girls, 180 black or mulatto). Of this number over half had their own education paid for by parents, whilst a small number were paid for by sympathizers such as the Economical Society and others by taxation. Only in the 1880s was this pattern radically altered, when an educational reform (of 1880) decreed the co-ordination of Cuban with Spanish educational practice: a twelve-member Board of Education was set up, along with other boards in each of the now six provinces, and yet further local or municipal boards, consisting of three fathers of families, the priest, mayor and an alderman. The priest went to the schools

[10] Ballou, *Due South*, 57.
[11] *Directorio de la Habana* (1860), 129.
[12] Shafer, 308.

once a week to give religious instruction. Teachers were henceforth paid by the municipalities. Every town or village with 500 people was supposed to have two public schools, one for boys, one for girls. An institute of secondary education would be set up in the capital of each Cuban province, with a grant from the central government; religious colleges might be substituted for the public ones if none such were forthcoming.

There were as a result about 500 public schools in the island, together with nearly 200 private; between then and 1895 the number of public schools nearly doubled and private schools went up three times in number.[13] In 1895, 36,000 children were being taught by 1,000 teachers in the public schools, while 25,000 were going to private schools. Maybe this was only about one-fifth to one-sixth of those of school age. Still, the advance was undeniable, even if the provisions of the law presented compulsory school for all between nine and thirteen. Nor, despite the segregation in the early nineteenth century even between free Negro or mulatto and white, was there now any division between the races.[14] Education was not, however, good. All teachers could nominate substitutes, who would be paid, whatever their qualities, by the regular incumbent: and some schools were without their regular teacher for years.

Before these problems, social and hygienic, the Roman Catholic Church was not active. Bells might ring incessantly in Havana 'with their superfluous summons to matins which no one attended'; Sunday services might be little carnivals; but religion played scarcely more than a ceremonial part. In Holy Week the cathedral would be full, the procession to the cathedral square watched by thousands. But this barely went even skin deep. In general the Church was poor and of very low quality. The English historian, Froude, who visited Cuba in 1887, was told that in Havana 'there was no preaching, famous or otherwise'; he found the Jesuit church in Havana attended only by women.[15]

[13] Schools 1880–1895

	Public		Private	
	1883	1895	1883	1895
Havana	173	219	101	329
Matanzas	95	143	22	117
Pinar del Río	82	159	18	33
Santa Clara	103	221	18	100
Puerto Príncipe	24	37	4	41
Santiago	58	125	21	120
	535	904	184	740

In 1895 there were also 2,265 pupils at seventy colleges, 671 students and 58 professors at the university and 1,186 children at the secondary education institutes (Census of 1899, 581, 584).

[14] 'The pupils, *without respect to race, blacks and whites mixed* [author's italics], sat on benches with no backs for five or six hours consecutively', Census of 1899, 581.

[15] J. A. Froude, *The English in the West Indies* (1888), 304. The remark about matins is his too (310). He also noticed that in the Havana cemetery there were no inscriptions.

Many priests led undisguised domestic lives with mistresses, visiting cock fights, bullfights[16] and gambling. They had little integrity. Only the Jesuits seemed even interested in social welfare, and only they ran a good secondary school.

Havana remained, however, the gayest city of the Caribbean as it was indeed ten times the largest. The most fashionable square was now the Plaza de Isabel II in front of the Teatro Tacón. Here music played almost continuously; here, despite the fall of sugar prices, there remained chess players, domino players, drinkers, men in evening dress with *demi-mondaines*, buying ices, cake and champagne. The terraced cafés were famous and indeed many new ones opened in the 1880s and here always were beggars loitering in the shadows, the lame and the blind, Chinese and Negro, particularly hanging round men whom they knew to have been successful in the lottery. In 1885 there were 200 registered brothels in Havana, mostly filled with Canary Islanders and black girls.[17] Cuban women always seemed immodest to North Americans (as indeed to Spaniards) since the climate made cloaks or shawls unnecessary. The popular place for a drive was still the Paseo de Tacón whose hibiscus and carolina bushes had now grown up well. During the carnival season in Havana in March there were very successful masked balls at the Teatro Tacón lasting all night. Popular North American singers such as Jenny Lind or Adelaide Phillips often visited Havana. Matanzas, too, had numerous cafés, though Santiago had none and no other town was well-furnished with them.

The appearance of prosperity thus remained. But there had disappeared in Cuba any clear idea of what the future held for the country. Old Cuba, based on slavery and aristocracy, had vanished. Reprehensible though that society was in many respects, it was at least, like the old South in the U.S., a self-sufficient community with recognizable rules and expectations; the post-1880 society in Cuba did not have a clear picture of the future. The only Cubans who did have such a picture were the exiles from the Ten Years' War in the U.S.; and it was indeed they who in the end were to impose their picture on the island. Yet when it came to the point it was much more confused and muddy than it seemed in the rhetorical speeches of the would-be liberators. The explanation lay with geography.

Throughout the nineteenth century Cuba exported much more to the U.S. than to Spain.[18] Indeed as early as 1841–5 even England had topped Spain as a customer for Cuba. After 1878 Cuba became even more closely linked with the U.S. Spain sought to direct Cuban demand

---

[16] Bullfights were held in Havana on Sundays in winter.
[17] Cabrera, *Cuba y sus Jueces*, 141.
[18] See above, 126.

towards herself by dropping any duties on trade between Cuba and
Spain, but the pattern of U.S. commercial friendship was already too
strong. Travellers from North America began often to visit Cuba in the
winter, expressing anxious surprise to find the streets of Santiago as
sleepy as Córdoba, the inhabitants beginning the day with 'a very
liberal dram' of gin, indeed 'tippling at every convenient opportunity',
and resolving to do something about it.[19] They were shocked to find that
black children under eight years old went about naked and that in the
country this scandalous custom even extended to some white children.
They were appalled by the fact that 'a brief period of the day only [in
Havana] is given to business, the rest of the day and night to melting
lassitude, smoking and luxurious ease. Evidence of satiety, languor and
dullness, the weakened capacity for enjoyment' were, they thought,
sadly conspicuous. They were still disturbed to discover Cubans, even
women, smoking all day, even at meals, even at funerals; slaves and
masters, mulatto and mulata; and to find that children of twelve years
old went to balls, decked out just as their elders were and 'knowing the
delicate relations of the sexes as well as they would ever know them.
What else could be expected in an atmosphere so wretchedly immoral?'[20] Despite this high-mindedness, there was a great deal of
smuggling from the U.S. By 1894 indeed official Cuban exports
accounted for three-quarters of all South and Central American exports
to the U.S.,[21] and Cuban imports from the U.S. were more than half all
Latin American imports from the U.S.[22] Cuban exports to Spain were
ten times smaller than her exports to the U.S.[23]

Cuban-American trade was given even further impetus by the wide-
reaching tariff reforms in the U.S. carried out under the lead of William
McKinley in October 1890.[24] U.S. tariffs were in general reduced and
abandoned entirely on such goods as raw sugar and molasses (and also
tea). This move was probably at least partly due to Atkins, proprietor
of *central Soledad*, who had suggested it to Secretary of State Blaine
some years before,[25] and here is to be seen the beginning of private
commercial influence on U.S. foreign policy so far as Cuba is concerned.
But an amendment by Senator Nelson Aldrich imposed complementary tariffs on goods which came from countries which did not grant
reciprocal advantages to the U.S. This amendment forced Spain to

[19] Ballou, *Due South*, 38.
[20] cf. in Brazil where the concern of ten-year-olds was to 'syphilize themselves as soon as
possible' (Freyne, *The Masters and Slaves*, New York 1946, 404).
[21] $53,801 out of $97,758 in 1890; $75,678 out of $109,916 in 1894.
[22] $20,125 out of $37,443.
[23] 1894 figures were $7,265 to Spain, $75,678 to the U.S.
[24] McKinley (1843-1901), later president, was then Chairman of Ways and Means in the
House of Representatives.
[25] Atkins, 81, 108.

some reaction and in June 1891 Blaine's successor as Secretary of State, John Foster, and the Spanish premier, Cánovas, signed an agreement by which the McKinley tariff would indeed become applicable to Cuba while Spain dropped, in respect of Cuba and Puerto Rico, her traditional protectionism. This treaty remained in force from September 1891 to August 1894. Cuban imports from the U.S. doubled,[26] while of course exports also increased.[27]

The McKinley tariff meant that Cuba now provided the U.S. with 10% of her total imports, being exceeded only by England and Germany. The tariff was doubtless the main factor in enabling Cuban sugar production to top a million tons in 1894. It certainly took the Cuban sugar industry out of the doldrums. In 1894 the U.S. took 87% of Cuba's total exports,[28] and provided her with 38% of her imports;[29] the Spanish figures were respectively a mere 6% and 35%. The only loser was the Spanish government who lost its substantial income from duties on U.S. imports.

The tariff also cheapened the price of wheat and provided an extra argument in Cuba against any attempt at diversification. But it also cheapened the price of U.S. machinery and weakened the stranglehold over Cuban food supplies of the rapacious wheat merchants of Castille. The consequences must therefore have been balanced, despite, once again, much play on the iniquities of this policy later by Cuban nationalist historians. Tobacco was not included on the free list for the U.S., though already half of the Cuban tobacco trade was with the U.S.

American influence grew not only where commerce was concerned. Many more engineers and merchants came in from the U.S. with the new machinery of the *centrales*. In 1885 two hundred 'Bostonians' were found on Cuban sugar estates.[30] The later giant company which became known as Bethlehem Steel had already staked claims in Oriente. But even more important, while the U.S. became far the most important customer for Cuban sugar, the Cuban sugar producers were increasingly at the mercy of the U.S. manufacturers to whom they sold their raw sugar – particularly, the consortium of eight major sugar refiners combined in 1888 by Henry Osborne Havemeyer into the American Sugar Refining Company (the so-called Sugar Trust).[31] They agreed to reduce production until prices improved and closed

---

[26] From $12,224 in 1891 to $24,157 in 1893.

[27] $61,714 in 1891 to $78,766 in 1893.

[28] $98,000 out of $116,000.

[29] $38,508 out of $96,793.

[30] Jenks, *Our Cuban Colony*, 123.

[31] Henry Osborne Havemeyer (1847–1907). He also had huge coffee interests, being president of the American Coffee Co. He belonged to a famous family of sugar kings of German origin, who began operations in New York in 1805. The other major companies were Mathiesen & Weichers and the Brooklyn Sugar Refining Company.

down ten out of twenty plants. This group soon captured between 70%
and 90% of the refined sugar eaten in the U.S.[32] This trust was fought
by the remaining refineries, and finally the Supreme Court denounced
the organization as a monopoly. But after reorganization Atkins & Co.
of Boston joined in and in 1892 Havemeyer and Atkins went together
into Cuba to found the Trinidad Sugar Company on the old estates of
the Iznaga family.[33] Other North Americans bought *El Triunfo* – 1,553
acres – in 1892. The minority refineries led by Claus Sprechels (of the
California beet sugar industry) combined to fight and the U.S. Mapos
Company bought a 2,800 acre estate near Sancti Spiritus, producing
6,000 tons. In 1893 the powerful New York Cubans, the Rionda family,
organized the *Tuinicú* Cane Sugar Company,[34] and the *Hormiguero* mill
(previously owned by the old Boston family of Ponvert),[35] was also
bought by a new U.S. company. A West Indian trader, Hugh Kelly,
with Franklin Famel, an iron man, founded the *central Santa Teresa*
near Güines. Kelly was also Atkins's New York agent; another example
of a merchant becoming a landowner. The richest catch by the U.S. at
this time was, however, the *central Constancia* which had previously
belonged to Julio, Marqués de Apezteguía, leader of the Cuban
Constitutional Union party in the Cortes,[36] and which was then the
biggest sugar plantation in the world (producing 135,000 sacks of sugar
a year).[37] This was bought by Perkins and Welsh. Such developments
were paralleled elsewhere at this time in the sugar world; for instance in
the British West Indies, the refiners Tate and Lyle appear as producers
of sugar cane in Jamaica.

All in all, U.S. investment in Cuba amounted to about $M30 in
1895.[38] These included the Havana waterworks, built in 1893, and the
Havana lighting system, belonging to the Spanish-American Light and
Power Company.

The McKinley tariff was dropped in 1894. The succeeding Wilson
tariff imposed a duty of 40% on all sugar entering the U.S., raw and

[32] Jenks, *Our Cuban Colony*, 28-9; Deerr, 462-4.
[33] One daughter of Pedro Iznaga married, first Queen Isabella's favourite, General
Riquelme, and later Sebastian Montalvo, a connection of the Cienfuegos Montalvos. Sebastian Montalvo ran the plantation for a time, became indebted to Atkins and later handed
over control to Atkins on a long lease (Atkins, 131-2).
[34] Jenks, *Our Cuban Colony*, 35.
[35] See Ely, *Cuando reinaba*, 461, fn. 105.
[36] Apezteguía's father, Martín Felipe de Apezteguía, came from Aranaz (Navarre) and
married a rich Cuban widow, Josefa Mariana Tarafa, in Trinidad in 1835. Julio and his
step-brother, Eduardo del Camino, operating their mother's sugar estates, transformed
Constancia into the 'biggest sugar plantation in the world'. Julio was a deputy representing
Santa Clara between 1879 and 1890. He was a vigorous opponent of liberalism and abolition,
and like the Drakes and others was really more Spanish than Cuban by 1894. *Constancia* was
the only plantation which milled cane in 1896, thanks to Spanish soldiers guarding it.
[37] Ortiz, *Cuban Counterpoint*, 50.
[38] Atkins's estimate in letter to Secretary of State Olney in 1897 (Atkins, 208-9).

refined, together with an extra 8% on refined. Cuban sugar was therefore seriously affected, though that of Hawaii (then about to join the Union)[39] was not. Exports to Spain itself increased in 1895. But the U.S. remained the only possible large customer.

So far as tobacco was concerned, there had been substantial damage in the course of the Ten Years' War. Many of the *vegas* in Oriente such as Mayarí and Cauto had been almost destroyed. Many tobacco workers fled to Florida: in 1868 there had been 3,000 in Key West, in 1870, 18,000. Many contributed monthly to the revolutionary cause in the war and remained afterwards in Florida – a permanent Cuban colony straddling the narrow sea. In 1881 in consequence there were 2,000 fewer tobacco farms in Cuba than in 1862;[40] though now the pre-eminence of Pinar del Río was firmly established. In Havana one interesting change had occurred: a woman went to work in a tobacco factory for the first time in 1873, at *La Africana* cigarette factory.[41] She was the first of many, giving rise to the happy myth that Havana cigars were rolled on the thighs of Cuban girls. By now the Cuban cigar industry had been favoured with much jargon and different words for different techniques: most of its traditions dated from the 1820s at earliest, after the end of the Estanco, but anyone would have supposed that the cigar manufacturers as well as their habits derived from an ancient medieval guild.

Meantime, a new movement was gathering momentum in the Cuban working class: this was anarcho-syndicalism, already strong in Spain since the 1870s and now, with new Spanish immigrants and a big influx of literature, threatening to destroy utterly the worthy, non-political trade unionism of Saturnino Martínez. The outstanding anarchist convert was Enrique Roig, a sugar technician, who as propagandist and spokesman from the early 1880s carried on a vigorous campaign, backed by young workers, against Martínez's old-fashioned 'Reformism'. In 1885 the anarchists founded the *Círculo de Trabajadores*, the first important workers' club in Havana, and two years later a newspaper, *El Productor*, appeared, while the first national Labour Congress was also held. This adopted a specifically anarchist programme[42] and inaugurated a bitter struggle between Saturnino Martínez and Roig for control of the Cuban working class organizations. Unions split, one faction often acting as strike breakers against the other. Roig died in 1889 but in 1892 the conflict was decided in favour of the anarchists at another congress which resolved formally that 'the

[39] See below, 312.
[40] 9,715 (*Estudio*, 148), of which 6,746 in Pinar del Río.
[41] Ortiz, *op. cit.* 84. Women in the Casa de Beneficiencia in 1810–20 had produced cigars however before this.
[42] Despite later suggestions by Cuban Communists to reckon Roig as a forerunner of theirs.

working class will not emancipate itself until it embraces the ideas of revolutionary socialism'. But this victory, though decisive, brought the Spanish authorities down on the heads of the anarchist leaders and many of them were imprisoned or deported to Spain and their headquarters closed down. Martínez abandoned the Labour movement altogether and became secretary to the Chamber of Commerce. Thus the increasing prosperity of the mid-1890s found the Cuban working class virtually inactive.

CHAPTER XXV

José Martí

'There was a time,' said a Cuban planter in 1884 to a North American traveller, 'when [the] threat [of a war of races] had great force . . . but that time is past. The slaves are . . . amalgamating with the rest of the populace.'[1] This was a hasty judgment: a general impression of the transition to freedom suggests that slaves were coping, with almost as much difficulty as elsewhere, with the psychological and social problems of emancipation. One slave secret society, the Ñáñigos, or Abakuá, founded by the Efiks, seems to have degenerated for a time into banditry in the 1880s.[2] Nothing illustrates the problem more vividly than the controversy in the 1880s between two mulattoes, Juan Gualberto Gómez and Bernabeu, in the columns of the newspaper *La Unión*, as to whether mulattoes should ostracize Negroes as well as whites.[3]

On the other hand, thanks to the campaign led by Gómez, many important steps towards racial integration were taken: thus discrimination in theatres was disallowed as from 1889, nobody could be excluded from public service for racial reasons after 1887, state schools accepted black or mulatto children on the same basis as white as from 1893, cafés and bars could not exclude blacks or mulattoes after 1889. In some cases these laws, like most Spanish laws, were not fully carried out, yet in general they were. Gómez, the son of a slave on a Santa Ana sugar mill, now entered Arango's famous Economical Society. On the other hand, '*la gente de color*' still used separate swimming pools on the sea coast.

By the 1890s even the richest Cuban planters had no need to rely on the army of Spain to protect them from their slaves. They also had nothing to gain from Cuban independence. The merchants, both Spanish and foreign, probably echoed Ramón de la Torriente's frank remark in a letter in 1878: 'The majority of us are conservative and desire no reforms at all.'[4] Such men considered the timid governments of the Spanish republic of the 1870s to have been explicitly 'Communist'.[5]

---

[1] Ballou, *Due South*, 134.
[2] See below, 521.
[3] See L. Horrego Estuch, *Martín Morúa Delgado: vida y mensaje* (1954), 17. Juan Gualberto Gómez (1854–1930), born Havana, and away from Cuba during ten years' war.
[4] Atkins, 35.
[5] *Ibid.*, 36.

The *colonos*, both new men and ex-planters, were generally politically inactive, since their status was new and ambiguous. The Autonomist or ex-Liberal party remained the critical movement of the day; could it succeed? In demanding 'the liberty of Cuba legally within Spanish nationality' these Autonomists already seemed to many out of date, cut off between the revolutionaries in exile and the pro-Spanish die-hards. Most Autonomist politicians were isolated from the main stream of Spanish politics and some could not afford to pass much time in Madrid. They only at best had seven deputies out of 450 in the Cortes while the conservative Constitutional Union party, backed by Spanish merchants and with close links with Catalan shipping and industry and controlling the electoral machinery of Cuba, controlled also the formal election of members of the legislature from Cuba and therefore the real political life of the country. For in April 1881, seven months after the last rebel in the *Guerra Chiquita* had given himself up, the Spanish Constitution of 1876 was formally promulgated in Cuba. But the captain-general still had the right to ban public meetings. Elections were often as corrupt in Havana as they were in Spain. The possibility of real criticism of the government was even less in Cuba than in Spain. Critics could be exiled. Further the predominance of *peninsulares* among the voters, especially in Havana and the bigger towns often made corrupt voting procedure unnecessary; for a majority for the Spanish party was often the natural one. By 1884 still nothing had radically altered, so that in March of that year, when sugar prices were falling and there was widespread discontent, the exiled heroes of the previous war began to recover their nerve. Many returned under an amnesty of 1885. No doubt, had there been real constitutional development in Cuba these men might have come to terms with Spain. As it was they were for a time divided and quarrelsome. A rich backer in New York, for instance, Félix Govín, promised $200,000 to Máximo Gómez and Antonio Maceo for a new revolution and at the last went back on the promise. There were many such incidents. Máximo Gómez in New York quarrelled with the brilliant thirty-year-old pamphleteer and agitator, José Martí, who, having left Havana and Azcárate's group, was swiftly establishing himself as the leader of Cuban exiles in the U.S., the spokesman for a new and radical revolutionary movement. 'One does not found a nation, General,' wrote Martí, 'with commands as issued in an army camp . . . Are you trying to suffocate thought even before you have got yourself to the front of a grateful and enthusiastic populace?'[6]

---

[6] Martí, *Obras Completas*, vol. XXI. For the political discussions of the exiles in the 1880s, see the life of the mulatto Martín Morúa Delgado by Leopoldo Horrego Estuch, 35–92.

José [Martí (1853–95) was the most brilliant of Cubans.[7] The number of photographs and busts of him which adorn Cuban houses, squares, and public buildings for many years rivalled by far those of anyone else. The absence of constraint with which he was customarily referred to by Cubans should not blind others to his virtues.

It is none the less appropriate that, despite Martí's sacramental role in Cuban history, both Martí's parents should have been Spaniards: his father was a sergeant in the artillery from Valencia, his mother a Canary Islander from Tenerife; indeed part of Martí's childhood was passed in Spain. His father ultimately became a 'minor city official', and then a policeman in Havana, and, besides José, had six daughters.

Martí's mind was formed less by his home, which offered little of either intelligence or interest, than by his school where he came under the influence of Rafael María Mendive, a romantic poet, cosmopolitan and backer of Cuban independence, as well as a schoolmaster, who offered to support Martí through high school when his father was reluctant.[8] Martí was at school at the start of the Cuban war of 1868 and, like many schoolchildren of that time, passionately supported the cause of independence. In January 1869, aged sixteen, Martí founded his first newspaper, *Patria Libre*, to which he contributed romantic writings on behalf of the rebels. Disaster followed: Mendive was accused of being present at an anti-Spanish rally and exiled to Spain; Martí was arrested for having written a letter which accused an old friend of being a backer of Spain. On this trivial charge, he was sentenced to six years in prison and dispatched to the stone quarry of St Lázaro in Havana. Thence, through the influence of his father, he was transferred to the Isle of Pines and finally in 1871 sent to Spain where he was left at liberty, aged eighteen, to do what he liked provided that he did not return to Cuba.

This merely placed the young Cuban in the heady atmosphere of revolutionary Madrid. He went to the university, studying law, like most revolutionaries, and moved to the University of Saragossa where he gained a degree in 1874. All the time he wrote articles, poems and, as was characteristic of nineteenth-century romantics, plays on the theme of national independence. In early 1875 he went, via Paris, to Mexico where his parents were then living and where he remained

---

[7] There are several lives of Martí, particularly those by Jorge Mañach, *Martí Apostle of Freedom*, trans. Coley Taylor, (1950); and Félix Lizaso, *Martí, místico del deber* (1952). All are romanticized. His works have been published complete in two separate sets. For a useful bibliography see Richard Butler Gray, *José Martí, Cuban Patriot* (1962), 285ff., which is also an interesting general introduction to the cult of Martí. Manuel Pedro González's *José Martí, Epic Chronicler of the U.S. in the Eighties* (1953), is well done. See also impressions in Horatio Rubens, *Liberty, The Story of Cuba* (1932), 23ff.

[8] Rafael María Mendive (1821–86), translated 'Irish Melodies' of Thomas Moore, Byron, Longfellow, etc.; wrote poems, plays; founder of *Revista de la Habana*.

several years, his great literary fluency establishing him as a coming young man, with articles for the *Revista Universal*, a translation of Hugo's *Mes Fils*, and a play of his own – *Amor con amor se paga*, a derivative play in Hugo's style. This energetic and restless young Cuban with slanted intelligent eyes, who always wore a small black bow tie and a black suit, became a familiar figure in Mexican literary circles.

By 1877 Martí had been an exile for eight years, much of which time had been spent in agitation for a free Cuba, but he had lost touch with Cuba itself. He returned to Havana under a false name for a month, hated it and quickly moved on to Guatemala, where he settled for a time as a teacher of languages and philosophy, and where he fell in love with a daughter of an ex-president but whom un-romantically he abjured in favour of a more suitable girl, Carmen Zayas Bazán, daughter of a rich Cuban sugar family, whom he married in Mexico.[9] This linked Martí by marriage at least with the Cuban oligarchy now about to disappear. At last in 1878 Martí, now twenty-five, returned to Cuba under a general amnesty and worked as a clerk in the law firm which had been founded by the educationalist Nicolás Azcárate, now an Autonomist. However, once again Martí did not take much to Havana. He found what seemed the excessively conservative and hispanic atmosphere of Havana as intolerable as its political repression: 'If Cuba were not so unfortunate, I would love Mexico more than Cuba,' he rhetorically and typically wrote to a friend in 1879.[10]

Martí therefore once again entered conspiracy, hoping to convert Cuba into a new free American state; most of 1879 he passed making contacts with young people and specifically quarrelling with Autonomists, tempting fate by outspoken and romantic statements in favour of independence. The consequence, as might have been expected, was renewed deportation, once again to Spain. He left his wife behind.

Martí did not remain long in Spain. Passing once again through Paris he made his way back to the New World, and arrived at New York, from then on busying himself with the activities of exiles, and undertaking a vast quantity of journalism, much of it for Charles Dana's *Sun*. He became co-ordinator and president of the Cuban revolutionary committee of New York and spent the next ten years based there, undertaking many journeys both inside the U.S. and in south and central America, living for some months in Venezuela in 1881. He quarrelled finally with his wife, who preferred Cuba, and took up with other Cuban women such as Carmen Miyares with whom he lived in a boarding house in New York. He contributed to many South American

---

[9] See David Vela, *Martí en Guatemala* (1954). The girl, María García Granados, is the girl in Martí's poem *La Niña de Guatemala*.
[10] Martí, *Obras Completas*, LXVIII, 79, qu. Gray, *Martí*, 11.

newspapers, many of his articles describing the grandeur and miseries of life in the U.S., with whom his relations were already ambiguous: he was impressed by the haste and bustle, the work, the enterprise, the individualism, in comparison with lazy Spanish cities where nothing was ever completed and where the dead hand of catholicism stifled opportunity; but he mistrusted the materialism, and found no North American woman whom he could seduce.

His writing at this time was becoming less romantic and more critical. Articles appeared on a vast quantity of subjects, and that which introduced Walt Whitman to Spanish and South American readers (in 1887) was deservedly famous. Such activities made him so well-known in South America that Uruguay named him their Vice-Consul in New York in 1884 – a nominal job which gave him a regular salary. A novel, *Amistad funesta*, written in seven days, did very badly. It was clearly autobiographical:

> He travelled because he was full of eagles which gnawed at his body and wanted wide spaces. He travelled because he was married to a woman whom he thought he had loved and whom he found then like an insensible asp, in which the harmonies of his soul found no echo.[11]

He wrote as a journalist for a decade, covering every great event, electoral, cultural, economic; South American readers learnt for the first time through him the reality of North American life – and not only of Whitman but also of Emerson, Longfellow and Wendell Phillips. Martí despised the cult of wealth in the U.S.; he distrusted the alliances between politicians and bankers, as exemplified above all by James G. Blaine; he found the presidential elections nauseating; he thought that the educational system stifled the individual; but always he regarded the U.S. as an astonishing experiment and adventure in democracy. Martí appears to have been a freemason[12] and an agnostic though his attitude to religion was one of unconcern, not of hatred.

From early on he was very successful and popular with the Cuban tobacco workers in Key West, Florida, whom he visited to get contributions, but their contributions were small, and well into 1886 Martí and Máximo Gómez were squabbling over money. The abolition of slavery in October 1886 was a serious blow to the revolutionary cause. But even so the Autonomists in Cuba were unable to make headway. Partly they were distrusted by everyone in Madrid because they seemed to be Republican as well as Autonomist; they had no friends in the established

[11] As qu. Gray, *Martí*, 18.
[12] *Cf.* discussion in *ibid.* 119–21.

Spanish scene except among the few followers of the discredited Pi y Margall. The conservatives thought that independence would inevitably follow autonomy and, being businessmen and merchants themselves, they thought that there would then be no chance of maintaining any customs union with Spain.

The decisive achievement of Martí, however, not only lay in cultivating distrust of the Autonomists, but in creating hostility to annexationism, based on years of having lived in the U.S. Before him, there had been many Cuban revolutionaries who overtly or implicitly longed to join the world's most powerful and indeed most progressive nation. Many Cubans might not have admitted this to themselves but until Martí this was clearly their real passion. For good or evil, Martí's stay in New York led to a fundamental change.

With their enemies at loggerheads, successive Spanish ministries tried to reach some degree of compromise over Cuba. These attempts failed because the Spaniards could not attain the flexibility which made the Canadian experiment successful within the British empire. This in its turn derived from the absence of a firmly established political order in Spain itself. The restored monarchy did not command the same unshakeable respect that Victoria's throne did in England and the Crown could not by itself serve as a force of unity. Further, the Crown was represented from 1874 to 1885 by a young king without an heir, and from 1885 onwards by yet another Queen Regent and, first, an unborn child, then an infant (Alfonso XIII). In 1886 an unsuccessful military coup by Brigadier Villacampa had ended with the cry of *Viva la República*. Nor was the Cortes a realistic organ of government since it was clear, even at the time, that the elections which were celebrated so regularly were comedies managed by the Ministry of the Interior, even if they were serious comedies deliberately planned to provide the framework of a future system: as if a sporting contest could gradually ripen into a legislative process. Outside the electoral game, the rise of anarchism and socialism on the one hand and Catalan and Basque separatism on the other suggested many further possibilities for disintegration; thus in 1888 Sabino de Arana published his Basque grammar, in the same year as the socialist trade union, the *Unión General de Trabajadores* (UGT), was first established. Separatism in Cuba was unlikely to get any hearing from governments reluctant even to consider the question of autonomy in Barcelona or Bilbao. There was also a fundamental economic anomaly: Spanish merchants in both Spain and Cuba hoped that the latter could become a full member of the Spanish economy; but Cubans required to trade with the U.S., and Cuba was drawing closer to the U.S. throughout the fifteen years 1880–95. Catalonia, on the other hand, knew that 60% of her external commerce was with

Cuba,[13] and a British Consul in Corunna thought that the export trade of his region 'would certainly be almost entirely extinguished by the loss of Cuba'.[14]

Most of the Spanish proconsuls, not unworthy successors of the great administrators of the sixteenth century, fully appreciated the position of the Cubans. General Salamanca attempted to bring in reforms but died mysteriously before he had been in office a year;[15] General Polavieja, at the very moment of crushing the *Guerra Chiquita* in Oriente, had written to General Blanco:

> Martínez Campos has been able to subjugate this people, to give a truce to inflamed passions, has assuaged old hatreds, but he has not been able to go against the nature of an entire people. Having conquered them, we should . . . instead of wishing to prevent for all time and at all costs the independence of Cuba, which would be a vain project, prepare for it, staying in the island only as long as we reasonably can and establish ways whereby we are not expelled violently with prejudice to our interests and the decay of our honour . . .[16]

Polavieja himself, captain-general from 1890-2, resigned on account of the corruption in Cuba which he was powerless to control.[17]

This Cuban faith in the future was accompanied, also, by the actually increasing corruption in the Spanish administration on the island, so that the desire for purification accompanied the drive for political change. Corruption as usual was accompanied by virtual bankruptcy: all income derived only from the customs but duties constantly varied.

Despite continued wealth, a certain seediness had come over Havana by the 1890s: carriages seemed worn out, streets ill-repaired and badly lit and cleaned. It was true that the sugar industry was being modernized by U.S. capital but the profits were not coming, as they had in the 1840s or 1850s, to help beautify Havana. The sheer inconvenience of being run by a far-away government in Madrid struck home more and more in these years too: 'there is not a wheel in our administrative machinery which runs smoothly'.[18] Spaniards were favoured by

[13] Carr, 397; equal to that of France and Britain.
[14] *P.P.* (1897), 539, qu. Carr, 398, fn.
[15] See Tesifonte Gallego, *La Insurrección Cubana* (1897), 85-125. It was rumoured that Salamanca was poisoned. General Salamanca (1831-91), active in second Carlist war, deputy, passed the nights painting and engraving, made the longest speeches in the Cortes.
[16] García de Polavieja, *Relación documentada de mi política en Cuba* (1898), 32-40. General Camilo García de Polavieja (1838-1914), aide to Martínez Campos in the civil wars of the 1870s. Crushed Cuban rebels in Las Villas, 1876.
[17] *Ibid.*
[18] Cabrera, *Cuba y sus Jueces*, 179. However Cabrera was violently prejudiced.

captains-general at all levels of the administration. In Havana in 1891 twenty-seven *regidores* out of twenty-eight were Spaniards; Cubans scarcely figured at all in the Constitutional Union party; 75% of mayors up and down Cuba were Spaniards.[19] If anything, indeed, relations between *peninsulares* and *criollos* were getting worse, not better. Meantime, the Autonomists became finally disillusioned when the Liberal government in Madrid tried to rearrange the voting system to favour the Conservatives; they even withdrew from the Cortes of Madrid though the proposal was in fact dropped in the Senate. In fact the Autonomists had run out of ideas and their backing in Cuba was really dwindling. All the advances of the last fifteen years, such as they were, were the achievements of the Constitutional Union party rather than of them.[20]

Such circumstances gave new heart to the exiled separatist or independence movement. In January 1890 José Martí founded in New York a new and unconventional movement, *La Liga de Instrucción*, to act as a kind of training school for revolutionaries. There would be lectures for Cuban exiles, chiefly Negro workers, in New York. Martí himself talked to thousands, explaining his reasons for rejecting any solution for Cuba save that of outright independence. The next struggle, he said, would be not of the planters but of the people; his backer in this was nevertheless a rich exile, Rafael Serra. Meanwhile Maceo, the 'Titan of bronze', was most surprisingly permitted to go to Cuba with a safe conduct, nominally to inspect property, in fact to make contact with potential revolutionaries. Creoles (as well as Negroes) visited him in his hotel at Havana. At a banquet in his honour at Santiago a young Cuban, José Hernández, proclaimed fervently that he hoped that Cuba would soon be annexed to the U.S. Maceo replied: 'Young man, I believe that in such circumstances I would be on the side of the Spaniards.' Maceo made various plans for a new rising perhaps even for that year but these leaked to the Spaniards and Maceo, with several of his followers (such as Flor Crombet), was hastily deported. But there was from then on much discussion of a new rebellion, partly stimulated by literature (such as Fermín Valdés Domínguez's book about the execution of the students in 1871), partly by the mere fact that, after fifteen years, people were beginning to forget anew how unpleasant war could be.

Martí's fame in the U.S. and South America grew and he became more economically independent when he added the consulship of Argentina and of Paraguay to his bow, while he was also representative of Uruguay to the first Inter-American money conference, on bi-

---

[19] *Ibid.*, 192–4.

[20] E.g. the introduction of the Spanish Constitution to the Antilles, the law of 1882 (*Cabotaje*) abolishing duties between Cuba and Spain, the electoral laws of 1890 and 1885, and the tariff reform of 1892.

metallism, to meet in Washington in 1891. This conference concerned the policy of the U.S. to support equal and worldwide circulation of both gold and silver. The U.S. produced silver and so would have profited. Martí took a vigorous part in opposing this, 'thwarted the design of the Department of State', and in so doing entered the public eye in the U.S. more than he had ever done. The report which he prepared on behalf of the Latin American delegations included some afterwards famous sentences:

> It is not the province of the American continent to disturb the world with new factors of rivalry and discord, nor to re-establish, with new methods and names, the imperial system through which republics come to corruption and death . . .[21] [and] The hands of every nation must remain free for the untrammelled development of the country in accordance with its distinctive nature and with its individual elements.[22]

In 1891 Martí extended his programme of revolutionary instruction to the tobacco workers in Tampa. He reorganized his followers as the Cuban Revolutionary party in January 1892 and persuaded many Cuban workers in the U.S., including those in Florida, to contribute one-tenth of their earnings. Martí became respected as an orator as much as a writer. In early 1892 he founded a newspaper, *Patria*, in New York, edited by a Puerto Rican Negro, Sotero Figueredo. In April the different Cuban-exile political clubs of the U.S. adopted a revolutionary programme embodied in a document devised in March ('the Bases'). This foreshadowed 'a brief and generous war' of 'republican spirit and method', to achieve a state capable of ensuring the permanent prosperity of Cubans and fulfilling in the 'historical life of the Continent the difficult charges laid on [Cuba] . . . by her geographical position'. This state would free the island from dependence on the outside world, and substitute for the economic confusion of the present a public financial administration which would 'immediately open up the country to the diverse potentialities of its inhabitants.'

These 'Bases' of Martí's party were adopted in the same month as the Bases of Manresa, adopted by the Catalan nationalists. To some extent they were in the same tradition. On the other hand, Martí's document already showed that concern with complete freedom, the desire to escape from both Spain and the U.S., which has preoccupied Cubans

---

[21] *Minutes of the International American Monetary Commission*, 3 April 1891, 44, qu. Manuel Pedro González, *José Martí*.

[22] The first meeting of North and South American governments on a formal basis had occurred in 1889 at a conference called by Blaine intended to promote a customs union and some sort of arbitration system. This failed but it did lead to the formation of an International Bureau of American Republics, afterwards the Pan-American Union, afterwards the Organization of American States.

ever since. Martí also had (which neither Catalonia nor, twenty-five years before, Céspedes had) the support of the fledgeling socialist groups among the tobacco workers of Tampa. The most prominent of these, Carlos Baliño and Diego Vicente Tejera, were associated with Martí, and Baliño signed the 'Bases'.

Baliño was one of the most remarkable of Cuban revolutionaries.[23] In the 1890s he was already over forty. His father had vanished after being deported for political activities against the Spaniards under Domingo Dulce. Baliño was a tobacco worker in Florida and represented the *escogedores* (selectors of tobacco leaf) in the revolutionary movement. He also worked as director of *La Tribuna del Pueblo* of Tampa and by the time that he signed Martí's document it would be appropriate to regard him as an anarchist, a follower of Fanelli more than Marx. Thus in the only speech of his which seems to have survived from this period, that of October 1892, there are quotations almost exclusively from anarchists such as Pedro Estévez in Spain or Fanelli in Italy, and Bakunin in Russia, reserving a kind word for Byron but not for Marx. He was the inspiration of many small clubs in Florida dedicated to this ideal, particularly the Enrique Roig Club which included all the socialist or anarchist supporters of Martí.[24] All these clubs gave money – theoretically 10% of their wages – to the independence movement.

In August 1892 Martí was authorized by his colleagues to go to the old veteran of the 1870s, Máximo Gómez, then in Santo Domingo, and to offer him the post of military commander. Martí had purposely delayed an approach to any military commander until he had firmly established the party. Gómez wisely laid aside his past difficulties with Martí who, he admitted, came 'in the name of Cuba', and accepted the invitation.[25] Martí also went to Maceo, then in Costa Rica, where he had established himself as a banana grower, and who appeared at the beginning reluctant to countenance further warfare. Eventually he agreed to do so.[26] Meantime Cuba itself was already disturbed by much sporadic banditry, some of it of a vague politically radical nature, particularly by Manuel García in the centre of the island[27] who claimed to despoil the rich for the benefit of the poor. He and other bandits asserted that they were in favour of Cuban independence and were revolutionaries but even the poor and the Negroes knew of the falsity of

[23] Carlos Baliño (1848-1926). See *Documentos de Carlos Baliño* (1964); Blas Roca, *El Recuerdo de Carlos Baliño, Hoy*, 13 February 1945.
[24] *Documentos de Carlos Baliño*, 12.
[25] Gómez, *Diario de Campaña* (1940), 273.
[26] Carlos Jinesta, *José Martí en Costa Rica* (1933), 19-20.
[27] See Atkins, 141-2, where there is a description of a demand for protection money to be paid at *central Soledad*; Montejo gives the slaves' attitude (p. 114) and says that the hearsay was that García gave money to Máximo Gómez. However Montejo disliked Gómez.

this claim.[28] García offered money to Martí for the cause of independence but Martí refused it with the rhetorical reply, 'The tree must grow clean from the root.'[29]

A final effort was being made in Madrid to secure the peaceful evolution of Cuba within Spanish rule. Manuel Becerra, a progressive Minister for Overseas Territories, introduced one proposal to extend the franchise in Cuba and Puerto Rico in 1888. But this had lapsed after the revelation of a scandal about a scheme for a Cuban central railway. Further reforms were introduced by Romero Robledo. On 9 December 1892 the Liberal, Sagasta, became prime minister again and appointed the brilliant Antonio Maura as successor to Becerra. Maura, of Majorcan Jewish origin, though a firm Catholic and inflexible, embarked on a programme of constitutional change chiefly because he saw the impossibility of governing Cuba at all unless the Autonomists ceased to boycott the Cortes.[30] In January 1893 he wrote to the Cuban leaders of the conservative Constitutional Union, such as Apezteguía, Ramón Herrera, the Conde de Galarza and others, urging them to accept the Autonomists as legitimate opponents within the electoral fabric. The reformist plans of Maura were assisted by a disorganized anti-Spanish rising of the brothers Sartorius, Manuel and Ricardo, at Holguín. After this failure, contributions to the revolutionary cause in New York dropped and the world financial panic of May 1893 set Martí back further. Sugar prices fell and caused distress in Cuba: tobacco factories closed in Florida and workers were unable to continue with their contributions to Martí's party.

In June meantime Maura replanned the civil administration of Cuba and Puerto Rico. Military and foreign affairs, justice, public order and finance would remain the responsibility of Madrid; public works, communications, education, health, questions of production would be undertaken by an autonomous island government to be elected by an assembly of Cubans.[31] These reforms were denounced as 'traps for the gullible' by Martí in *Patria*, and by Martí's chief political follower in Cuba itself – the spokesman of the black or mulatto minority, the mulatto ex-autonomist Juan Gualberto Gómez – in a famous article *Por Qué Somos Separatistas?* (Why are we Separatists?) in the *Revista Cubana*.[32] They were also criticized, less openly, by the conservative constitutional

---

[28] Montejo, 118.

[29] *'El árbol debe venir sano desde la raíz.'*

[30] See Lambert, and Carr, 381. Antonio Maura (1853–1925), Conservative statesman outstanding in Spain in the first quarter of the twentieth century.

[31] Fernández Almagro, II, 193–4.

[32] The nature of the debate on the racial question in Cuba can be seen from Juan Gualberto Gómez's remark that the reason why an independent Cuba would not turn into a Haiti was that the Haitian Negroes came from bellicose tribes of Africa while the Cuban came from the peaceful Gulf of Guinea! (L. Horrego Estuch, *Juan Gualberto Gómez* (1954), 99.)

Union as too extreme. The only party which showed any support for Maura were the Liberal-Autonomists, though there was little enthusiasm in Cuba itself. Also Maura's arrogant presentation of the reforms to the Cortes was calculated to anger rather than please. But a section of the Conservatives, led by Maura's friend, Ramón Herrera, were induced to break away from their negative colleagues and establish a little group of 'Reformistas' to back reform. For some months there was a chance that Maura's scheme might work; even Máximo Gómez was later to admit that if these reforms had come earlier, there might have been no new rebellion.[33] But, as in the case of most moderate reforms put forward by imperial governments, there was little support for Maura even among his own administration.

1893 was a year of difficulty for the Spanish politicians. In the middle of the summer there were a series of riots in San Sebastián in favour of Basque autonomy, and those who opposed Maura argued that his proposed autonomy in Cuba could lead to the disintegration of Spain. In September came an Arab attack on the Spanish Moroccan outpost of Melilla and the consequent beginning of a new war there: Martínez Campos, kingmaker and pacifier of the Cubans, went to Melilla to command a new Spanish expeditionary army. Some weeks before, an attempt had been made on his life by a young anarchist, Paulino Pallás: in November another young anarchist, Santiago Salvador, attempted to take revenge on the society which had condemned his friend Pallás (to death), and threw a bomb, in the Teatro del Liceo in Barcelona, during the second act of Rossini's *William Tell*: thirty people were killed, eighty wounded.[34] All the threats of ruin, internal and external, which then seemed to threaten Spain, thus glowed violently in the course of a few months, and these events could only have a conservatizing influence on Prime Minister Sagasta. In March 1894, Sagasta abandoned Maura's reform project and Maura himself resigned.[35] A new, less extreme, plan was embarked on however by Maura's successor, Abárzuza, a man more capable temperamentally of securing support by a saner and less unyielding presentation.

While the government in Madrid was still pursuing its goal of a settlement, their antagonists were once more prospering. In the autumn of 1893 the tobacco factories of Florida, which had closed during the financial panic of May, reopened. The Cuban employers, taking advantage of the depression, attempted to cut wages. The workers struck. The employers then agreed with the Spanish authorities in Havana to bring labour from Cuba into Florida. The workers appealed

[33] See Luis Estévez Romero, *Desde el Zanjón hasta Baire*, 143; and Guerra and Santovenia (1899), VI, 96.
[34] Fernández Almagro, 209.
[35] *Ibid.*, II, 199.

to Martí as leader of the Cuban revolutionary movement. Martí and a young New York lawyer, Horatio Rubens, succeeded in proving that the import of labour was against the U.S. Contract Labour Act of 1885. The strikers thus won a complete victory.[36] After this success, more Cuban revolutionary clubs proliferated while socialist and anarchist clubs continued active and, in conjunction with them, among the tobacco workers of Florida: thus one club named after the great Spanish anarchist Fermín Salvoechea was founded, with Carlos Baliño its president.[37]

With these successes to his credit, Martí originally desired to name February 1894 as the date for the next and, as he hoped, final rising in Cuba against Spain. But those planters (particularly in Puerto Príncipe) who were on the side of rebellion were anxious to finish the harvest, and once again economic or commercial motives delayed a Cuban rebellion. Puerto Príncipe was an essential province, and Martí and Máximo Gómez (in New York from April 1894) therefore waited, but this postponement confirmed both in their belief that they could not once again wait for the rich. On 30 September 1894, Gómez wrote to Maceo, then in Costa Rica recovering from a wound, allegedly inflicted by Spanish would-be assassins, but otherwise in the same superb physical state as in the 1870s, 'After November 15 we must be prepared to move immediately.'

During late 1894 Martí, impoverished, often ill, probably suffering from tuberculosis, 'laboured as one inspired . . . The organization of the conspiracy in Cuba was crystallizing . . . Cigar workers responded nobly . . . At the end of October Martí let it be known he would have $5,000 more.'[38] Working with the recollection of innumerable past mistakes, from Narciso López onwards, it was agreed that no rising would begin until at least four provinces (out of the six) were reliably reported ready for revolution and one province as well as Oriente was ready for the reception of rebel officers. Three expeditions were meantime gathered together in the Florida port of Fernandina, near Jacksonville. But thanks to the carelessness or treachery of their field commander, Colonel López Queralta, the U.S. authorities caught the whole group on 14 January 1895. This was a bad blow. In fact it also served as a stimulus. Before, no one had thought that Martí could assemble such a large force and in secret. Those who had believed Martí to be a poet and a dreamer were more impressed by 'the imaginative promise of his plan than by its temporary frustration'.[39]

Two weeks later, on 29 January, Martí, with a representative from

[36] Rubens, *Liberty*, 15–16.
[37] *Documentos de Carlos Baliño*, 13.
[38] Rubens, *Liberty*, 72–3.
[39] *Ibid.*, 74.

the Cuban interior (Mayía Rodríguez), signed an order for the beginning of the new rebellion for 24 February. A message was dispatched
immediately to the exiles' agent in Havana, Juan Gualberto Gómez,
and on 31 January Martí left New York to join Máximo Gómez in
Santo Domingo. On 24 March at the small Dominican port of Montecristi, on the north of Hispaniola near the Haitian border, Martí and
Gómez issued a manifesto. This promised a 'civilized war' in which
private rural property would be respected and non-combatant Spaniards
would not be attacked. Negroes would be welcome to take part and
those who spoke of the Negro race as a threat to free Cuba were dismissed as wanting to maintain Spanish rule indefinitely. At the end,
Cuba would be a republic 'different from the feudal and theoretical
ones of Hispano-America'; for Cuba was 'different from the peoples
previously liberated'. This was due to the 'civic responsibility of its
warriors; the culture and magnanimity of its artisans; the appropriate
and most up-to-date use of a vast number of skills and riches; the
strange moderation of the peasant, seasoned by both exile and war'.
There would be a new economic system, which would give work for all,
and therefore a free nation, well situated between the industrial and
the agriculturally productive parts of the world, which would stand in
place of a humiliated country whose prosperity could be obtained only
with the connivance of tyranny and of hungry exploiters.[40] The document
ended with the words *La Victoria o el Sepulcro* (Victory or the Tomb),
harking back appropriately to Garibaldi's cry of *Roma o Mòrte*.[41]

This ebullient nationalism was the work primarily of Martí himself.
Of the other leaders, Bartolomé Masó and José Miró Argenter were
born in Catalonia. Máximo Gómez was, of course, Dominican. Carlos
Roloff, another veteran of the 1870s, was of Polish origin. Others –
Sanguily, the Marqués de Santa Lucía (Cisneros Betancourt), Calixto
García, survivors of the Ten Years' War – were Cuban creoles. Antonio
and José Maceo, and Juan Gualberto Gómez, were mulattoes. Flor
Crombet and 'Périco' Pérez were Negroes (Crombet descended from
Haitian Negroes). All, including those of recent arrival in Cuba, were
evidently convinced of the unique possibilities of achieving a 'new
country' in Cuba and all were critical of the existing economic structure
as well as the Spanish political system. Some leading members of the
old plantation class were with them, particularly those ruined in the
1880s, or their sons, such as Cosme de la Torriente, a connection of
Atkins's old partners. Indeed the fundamental differences between the
rebellion which began in 1895 and that of 1868 was that the old master

---

[40] This was actually issued on 25 March.
[41] Castro's *Patria o Muerte* is a composite of two old slogans: *Indepencia o muerte* and *Patria y Libertad*.

class, which had for so long dominated the Cuban economy, was now broken and that already some of the largest plantations were in the hands of planters from the north. It is ironical that Abárzuza, the Minister of Colonies in Madrid (and the only Cuban to hold that post), presented his version of Cuban reform on 15 February while the civil war was beginning: a reform which would certainly have satisfied many of the Separatist rebels.[41A]

Some new economic problems too disturbed Cuba on this new eve of conflict. Sugar production had been inflated by the false dawn of McKinley's tariff and depressed by that of Wilson. Cuban sugar, over-extended in 1891–4, felt a cold wind in the winter of 1894–5 when world prices dropped even further to a level of ten shillings a hundredweight in the London exchange. 1893 had seen a crash on the New York Stock Exchange, a serious blow to capitalist confidence which led to a general shrinking in New World trade – largely affecting Cuba. At the same time, tobacco merchants had not been favoured by the tariff changes of the 1890s, though they desired to be. The cost of the Ten Years' War had also been saddled on the Cubans: a large debt which demanded an annual interest payment of $M10·5. Between 1893 and 1898, this amounted to nearly half the total revenue of the country (from the Havana lottery and duties, this averaged $M25).[42] Another $M12 was spent on the Spanish army. Only $M2·5 was left for all public works including education.[43]

Like most Cuban rebellions, the War of Independence began at half-cock. The rebel commanders in the western region, 'Generals' Julio and Manuel Sanguily, Pedro Betancourt, with Juan Gualberto Gómez, were arrested in Havana by the Spanish authorities. There were, however, various risings in the east of the island which gained immediate local mastery. A delphic exchange occurred between Máximo Gómez who wrote 'Gunfire can already be smelt in Cuba, the blood of our comrades is already being shed', and Maceo who replied: 'Once in Cuba we can depend on the machete to open the breach.'[44] The Autonomists made an offer of mediation and were brushed aside.

The Spanish captain-general, Calleja, evidently believed, to begin with, that his 16,000 troops were adequate to reduce the new rising. Even so, an expeditionary force of 9,000 was immediately sent out from Spain, constitutional guarantees were suspended, and the press in

[41A] Buenaventura de Abárzuza (1841–1910), son of a Cádiz shipowner, returned from Havana when young. Diplomat and Deputy.

[42] Census of 1899, 38. 1860 revenue was $M29·6, 1880 $M40, 1882 $M35·86.

[43] The price of land was also higher in 1895 than at any previous time of the century. The cost of leasing a *caballería* ready for cutting was calculated at $1,400 to $1,600, or nearly four times the estimated cost in 1830. It certainly was no longer more worth while buying new land than treating old (Beal Report, Census of 1899, 532).

[44] Archivo Nacional, qu. Foner, II, 350.

Havana censored. *La Epoca* of Madrid commented: 'The press has disguised, in general, the bad effect produced by the aspect of the troops who today set off for Cuba. The trouble is that these grey uniforms, these discoloured barrack-room caps, the lack of flags and armaments, robbed the soldiers of any martial brilliance . . . they appeared simply to be uniformed masses.'[45] A few days later another Madrid paper, *El Resumen*, published an article suggesting that the lack of volunteers for places as subalterns should be settled by a lottery. A group of young officers demanded an explanation from the director, Angel de Luque. He refused. The officers broke up the editorial offices and later the printing works. Next day *El Globo* gave a version of these events which the officers considered unjust and they broke up *El Globo* offices too. Demands began to be made that all offences against the Spanish army, including libel, should be heard by military courts.[46]

A few days later the affair was raised in the Cortes, and the old trouble-shooter, Martínez Campos, became captain-general of Madrid; even so the general mood of discontent was such that the prime minister, Sagasta, felt incapable of meeting the crisis. Though he had gone back on Maura's reforms he was unwilling to fight a war again in Cuba as he had had to do for a time twenty years before. At the end of the month he gave way to Cánovas, who re-introduced a Conservative administration.[47]

Cánovas prepared to meet the crisis of 1895 with confidence. He had been re-invigorated by his new marriage to a young wife (who however cut him off from his old intellectual friends); and the nation had recently cheered Martínez Campos to a military victory in Morocco. Cánovas nevertheless was at the mercy of conflicting pressures, particularly that of 'the Joe Chamberlain of Spain',[48] his own one-time chief organizer, Romero Robledo,[49] now an enemy, supported by the imperialists; one historian explains Cánovas's policy as comprehensible solely 'as steering between the varying pressure groups in Madrid in order to retain the leadership of his party',[50] and indeed his difficulties in Cuba always took second place to those within Spain.[51]

Constant efforts by politicians during the last fifteen years to achieve Cuban reform within the Spanish system had now failed. Constitutional Unionists were brushed aside. Abárzuza's reforms were suspended. On

[45] *La Epoca*, 9 March 1895, qu. Fernández Almagro, II, 232–3.
[46] See *Diario Universal de Madrid*, 30 December 1904, article by Angel de Luque, qu. Fernández Almagro, II, 224–5. The incident is known to connoisseurs of intervention by Spanish officers in civil life as the '*tenientada*' or the lieutenants' (*tenientes*) riots.
[47] Fernández Almagro, II, 236.
[48] Carr's phrase, 382.
[49] Francisco Romero Robledo (1838–1906). Married to a daughter of Julián de Zulueta.
[50] Carr, 382.
[51] With the Silbetistas and the Pedalistas as well as the Romeristas.

28 March Cánovas predictably nominated Martínez Campos, the grand defender of the Spanish imperium in its last days, to succeed Calleja as captain-general, and arranged for the dispatch of 7,000 men, armed with Remingtons rather than Mausers.[52] The general of victory (perhaps appointed by Cánovas to get him out of Spain) left Cádiz on 4 April. By that date, Maceo, Flor Crombet and Maceo's brother José had set out from Costa Rica and, on 1 April, Martí, with Máximo Gómez and four companions, had left Santo Domingo: two groups of brave and intelligent men crossing the seas, one side in small boats, one in a great convoy, to engage in war in Cuba, a trysting place named for them by several generations of short-sighted planters and politicians.

[52] Fernández Almagro, 239.

CHAPTER XXVI

The New America

José Martí had acted fast, for more than one reason. In May he was to write:

> It is my duty ... to prevent, through the independence of Cuba, the U.S.A. from spreading over the West Indies and falling with added weight upon other lands of Our America. All I have done up to now and shall do hereafter is to that end ... I know the Monster, because I have lived in its lair – and my weapon is only the slingshot of David.[1]

The U.S., the nation where he had been living for fourteen years, was indeed in a new mood, akin to that Southern expansionism which had dogged U.S. foreign policy before the Civil War, but now more powerful and, though often as strident or more so, more widely backed.[2] The massacre of Wounded Knee in 1890 marked a watershed in U.S. history. The frontier no longer existed. Henceforth it seemed that there was no more land available for conquest in the far west. Already by the 1870s more people were working in the city than in farms.[3] In 1890 Captain Mahan published his famous book describing sea power as the key to greatness in nations, and the U.S. built its first battleship. The year before, a meeting with the German navy at Samoa had suggested that these 'vast castles of steel' were indeed necessary, even for so eminently peaceable a country as the U.S.; but, was the U.S. peaceful after all? A new generation of North Americans was now reaching maturity who had known the Civil War only from the sidelines. Such young men (and jingoism was far more popular among young than old) began to feel that they too had to prove themselves as courageous as the

---

[1] Letter to his old friend, Manuel Mercado, Martí, *Obras Completas*, I, 271–3. This was Martí's last letter and was not finished.

[2] For analysis of the roots of U.S. expansionism and of U.S. imperial motives, see a number of recent works such as W. Mayne Morgan, *William McKinley and his America*; Ernest May, *Imperial Democracy*; Walter Lafeber, *The New Empire* (1963); and J. A. S. Grenville and G. B. Young, *Politics, Strategy and American Diplomacy* (1967). The essay by Richard Hofstadfer *The Paranoid Style in American Politics* (reprint, 1967) is also illuminating.

[3] In 1870, just under seven million worked in farms but just over six million already were employed in industry or services; in 1880, the figures were 8·5M to 8·8M, in 1890 9·9M to 13·4M (*Historical Statistics*, 72).

fathers from whose lips they had heard incessantly of Appomattox and Gettysburg. The young Theodore Roosevelt, the New York police chief, was representative of many.[4] Other Americans, such as John Fiske, John Burgess and Josiah Strong, gave some degree of intellectual backing for the idea of expansion. Roosevelt (a pupil of Burgess) in later life said that no one had appealed to him so much as 'Uncle Bullock', who had been an officer in the confederate navy.

> What is the occasion for all this militant insanity we do not know [declared the *Journal of Commerce* in late 1895]. Some of it is probably due to the fact that a generation has elapsed since we have had a war and its unspeakable horrors are largely forgotten. Undoubtedly, the reconstruction of the navy has done much; naval officers are impatient to use their new fighting machines.[5]

The word 'manifest destiny' was on every lip, though stretched to mean a great deal more than it had signified in the 1840s and 1850s; in 1884 one American traveller used it to mean the emancipation of slaves even in Brazil.[6]

This mood was more than simply the reflection of young men feeling their oats. All through the years that Martí was living in New York the immigrant ships were arriving in hundreds; half a million immigrants a year came into the U.S. between 1880 and 1893 (when the world panic caused numbers to drop). In 1882, 250,000 immigrants came from Germany alone. The U.S. had of course long ago overtaken England in population,[7] and with almost seventy million people in 1890 was already larger than any single European country. The tensions within this society were considerable. In 1892 the U.S. overtook England in the annual production of steel and thereafter bid fair to be already, before the beginning of the twentieth century, the most powerful industrial country in the world. Production and sea power together spelled commerce and, in the curious words of Senator Beveridge[8] in 1898, it was realized that American factories

---

[4] Theodore Roosevelt (1858–1919), member of New York Legislature, 1882–4; U.S. Civil Service Commissioner, 1889–95; president New York Police Board, 1895–7; Assistant Secretary of the Navy, 1897–8; governor of New York State, 1899–1900; vice-president, 1900–1; president, 1901–9.

[5] As qu. W. Millis, *The Martial Spirit* (1931), 35.

[6] Ballou, *Due South*, 62. Albert Weinberg has pointed out that whereas in the 1840s or 1850s the phrase meant that North American expansion could not be resisted when North Americans desired it, in the 1890s it suggested that even North Americans would not be able to resist it.

[7] This occurred between 1840 and 1850 when the populations of the two were each about twenty million.

[8] Albert Jeremiah Beveridge (1862–1927), senator from Indiana, 1889–1911.

are making more than the American people can use ... Fate has written our policy ... the trade of the world must and can be ours. And we shall get it, as our Mother England has told us how. ... We will cover the ocean with our merchant marine. We will build a navy to the measure of our greatness. Great colonies, governing themselves, flying our flag, and trading with us, will grow about our ports of trade. Our institutions will follow ... And American law, American order, American civilization and the American flag will plant themselves on shores hitherto bloody and benighted by those agents of God henceforth made beautiful and bright.[9]

Dreams of hegemony indeed swept the United States of America. In 1892 Theodore Roosevelt earned the nickname 'The Chilean Volunteer' from his wife and their close friend, Spring Rice, the English minister,[10] when he had rigorously approved the rather extravagant U.S. demands that an indemnity be paid by Chile for injustices to U.S. sailors in Valparaiso. Then there was the controversy as to whether the U.S. should annex Hawaii. In January 1893 while a U.S. cruiser lay in the harbour, a 'committee of safety' backed by the U.S. minister John Stevens, took over power from Queen Liliuokalani and installed a U.S. citizen, Sanford Dole, as head of government.[11] A detachment of marines landed to preserve lives and property. Roosevelt was among many who demanded immediate annexation, adding an insistence on an oceanic canal at Nicaragua. Roosevelt significantly also began an intellectual friendship with Kipling from 1895 and considered him 'a genius'.[12] An increasingly powerful pressure group grew up, with Roosevelt among the leaders, who were generally expansionist. They considered that the U.S. should abandon its inward-looking 'materialism' and exert the power that it actually possessed.[13]

Was this expansionism an excuse, explicit or implicit, for a failure to assure the unity of the races in the U.S. itself? Imperialism helped to heal surviving sores between old Confederates and Union men. Jingoism diverted men away from reflection on the slump of the mid-1890s. But it seems also to have diverted North Americans away from any

[9] C. G. Bowers, *Beveridge and the Progressive Era* (1932), 69.

[10] *Letters and Friendship of Sir Cecil Spring Rice*, ed. Gwynn S. P. Stephen, I, 326.

[11] Sanford Dole (1844–1926), of missionary parents in Hawaii.

[12] As qu. Howard K. Beale, *T. Roosevelt and the Rise of America to World Power* (1956), 21. His original dislike of Kipling derived obviously from Kipling's contemptuous attitude to America.

[13] This group included Senator Lodge; various professional diplomats such as William Rockhill; Senators Fry and Chandler (Harrison's Secretary of the Navy and founder of the U.S. Navy in 1890); Secretary of the Navy Benjamin Tracy; Chief of Naval Intelligence Charles Davis; Admiral Mahan himself; and, to some extent, John Hay and Henry and Brooks Adams.

serious attempt at integration of the Negro race in the U.S. at a time when it was perhaps possible. Of course not all North Americans were jingoes and at their head was the President Grover Cleveland, a man of caution. But in an adventurous time he was increasingly isolated.[13A]

This euphoric if somewhat rootless expansionism had an effect also on Cuba. The unsettled condition of the island partly invited such sentiments, although even the serene state of Mexico, calm under the dictatorship of Porfirio Díaz, received attention from the expansionists. But chiefly it was Cuban wealth which seemed delectable. An American financier wrote in early 1895: 'It makes the water come to my mouth when I think of the state of Cuba as one in our family.'[14] In 1887 Senator John Sherman represented, after a visit to Cuba, that 'the inhabitants to a man' were in favour of annexation.[15] Other optimistic statements followed, suggesting with as much confidence as in the 1850s that ultimately Cuba would join the Union – one in the authoritative voice of General Thomas Jordan, a Civil War veteran but also for a time chief of staff to Céspedes in the Cuban Ten Years' War. He called for the incorporation of Cuba into the U.S. to strengthen the U.S. defence system.[16]

This America had a new collective voice in the 'new journalism'. For in the U.S. press a new race had begun for big circulations. The great contest was between Hearst's *Journal* and Dana's *World* with the *Sun*, edited by Martí's friend Dana, struggling behind. The battleground for the critical years 1895–8 would be Cuba, as it was Martí's and Martínez Campos's. Hearst, in the *Journal*, stated his ideology clearly in an article on 25 September 1898:

> Under republican government, newspapers form and express public opinion. They suggest and control legislation. They declare wars. They punish criminals, especially the powerful. They reward with approving publicity the good deeds of citizens everywhere. The newspapers control the nation . . .[17]

The new journalism supported the Cuban rebels from the start; only the *Evening Post*, sanely edited by E. R. Godkin, and the *New York Herald*, run by Whitelaw Reid from Paris, were in any way circumspect.

[13A] Grover Cleveland (1837–1908). President of the U.S. 1885–9 and 1893–7. Son of a New Jersey parson.

[14] In a symposium in the *American Magazine of Civics*, VII, 561–86.

[15] C. E. Chapman, *A History of the Cuban Republic* (1927), 72. John Sherman (1823–1900), U.S. senator, 1861–77; Secretary of Treasury, 1877–81; U.S. senator, 1881–97; Secretary of State, 1897–8.

[16] *Forum Magazine*, qu. Foner, II, 345.

[17] *New York Journal*, 25 September 1898, qu. W. A. Swanberg, *Citizen Hearst* (1962), 168.

Dana's *Sun* announced on 28 February: 'Why should the Spanish monarchy any longer exercise despotic authority over the people of this radiant island? . . . we wish success to every struggle for emancipation.'[18] Shortly, a familiar but, in March 1895, a somewhat old-fashioned note, was struck by Henry Cabot Lodge, an intimate friend of Theodore Roosevelt: 'From the Río Grande to the Arctic Ocean there should be but one flag . . . when the Nicaragua Canal is built, the island of Cuba, still sparsely settled and of almost unbounded fertility, will become a necessity',[19] and when on 8 March a Spanish gunboat fired on the U.S. merchant ship *Alliance* there were familiar expostulations: 'Our flag fired on! . . . Wilful insult . . . it makes my blood boil.'[20] The *Post* retorted soberly on 15 March: 'Nothing is more shocking . . . than the preparation of the public mind for hostilities by persons who do not propose to fight themselves but do expect to make money out of the spectacle of other men's deaths and destruction.'[21] But even the comparatively quiet *Tribune* reasoned on 27 March: 'If Cuba desires to be annexed to the U.S. . . . and if the people of the island are found knocking at the door for admission to the Union, it will not be easy to keep them out.'[22]

Speculation will continue as to why precisely these jingoistic ideas caught on so successfully then and there. Did the press create, or respond to, a mood? Doubtless the whole trend of North American politics in the early 1890s was towards a situation where such a yellow press could exert an influence out of all proportion to what could have occurred ten years before.

These newspapers had helping them, in their task of building circulation by means of sensation, the services of the information bureau of the Cuban junta in New York. At the head of this impoverished body was Tomás Estrada Palma who had been briefly 'President' of the Cuban rebels in the previous war, and who had spent the interval running a private Quaker school for Cuban boys in Central Valley, Upper State New York. Estrada Palma and his assistants (at the Raleigh Hotel in Washington or in 120 Front Street, New York) busily fed Pulitzer of the *World*, Hearst and others with invigorating, heroic and sometimes truthful tales of victory and atrocity. A Cuban league of pro-Cuban U.S. citizens organized clubs throughout the U.S. Estrada Palma and

[18] *Sun*, 28 February 1895, qu. Wisan, 42. For newspaper opinion in 1895-8, see also Marcus M. Wilkerson, *Public Opinion and the Spanish–American War* (1932).

[19] *Forum*, March 1895, qu. Millis, *The Martial Spirit*, 27. Henry Cabot Lodge (1850–1924), lecturer in American history, Harvard, 1876–9; U.S. senator, 1893–1924; author; led fight against the treaty of Versailles, 1919.

[20] J. E. Wisan, *The Cuban Crisis as reflected in the New York Press (1895–1898)* (reprint, 1965), 70-2.

[21] *New York Post*, 15 March 1895, qu. *ibid.*, 73.

[22] *Ibid.*, 44-5.

his two main deputies, Benjamín Guerra and Gonzalo de Quesada, were in fact themselves naturalized U.S. citizens along with many of their supporters (who were occupied with sending arms to as well as organizing news from Cuba). Cuban-American relations as ever stood in the shadow of ambiguity.[23]

[23] The activities of the Junta are investigated by George W. Auxier, *H.A.H.R.*, XIX (1939), 286–305. The legal adviser of the Cuban junta was Horatio Rubens, Martí's friend. The activities of the Cubans in the direction of the unions in the U.S. is well emphasized by May, *Imperial Democracy*, 70.

CHAPTER XXVII

The War of 1895

The main protagonists in the renewed Cuban war – Martí and Máximo Gómez, the brothers Maceo, Martínez Campos – reached the island in early April, but in differing circumstances. The Maceo brothers landed at Playa de Derata. They were pursued, and divided. Antonio Maceo lived for some days on sour wild oranges, and it was only after thirteen days that they were reunited with some of their few followers. Flor Crombet was killed. Martí landed at Playitas, on the far south-east of Cuba, in great difficulty, and wrote of the occasion in his diary:

> They lower the boat. Raining hard as we push off. Set course wrong. Conflicting opinions in the boat. Another downpour. Rudder lost. We get on course. I take forward oar. Salas rows steadily. 'Paquita' Bornero and the General help in the stern. We strap on our revolvers. Steer towards clearing. Moon comes up red . . . we land on a rocky beach . . .[1]

Martínez Campos on the other hand arrived with great style on 15 April at Havana, commander-in-chief and captain-general as he had been nearly twenty years previously: bands, salutes, and cheering Spaniards greeted him along open avenues. The great proconsul had returned to the last frontier of the Spanish empire.

At the beginning of May, Martí, Máximo Gómez and Maceo succeeded in meeting at the *central La Mejorana*. They discussed the critical question of civilian or military control. Maceo wanted a military junta to control everything till victory. Martí disagreed. There was no agreement. Martí, disheartened, gave an interview to the *New York Herald* and went off with Gómez to meet the Cuban-Catalan, Bartolomé Masó. On 19 May a Spanish colonel, Ximénez de Sandoval, surprised Gómez, and in a skirmish at Dos Ríos ten miles east of Bayamo, Martí, conspicuous on a white horse, was killed. The rebels thus lost their most prominent civilian leader and far their best pamphleteer and organizer. Had he lived he would doubtless have been the first

---

[1] Martí, Journal, *Obras Completas*, vol. XXI, 17.

president of an independent Cuba, and it is impossible to believe that Cuban history would have been the same thereafter. But his death gave the Cubans a martyr. He left a large body of writings, chiefly articles, to which future generations would refer as others would to Marx or the Bible. Sentences have been extracted from the immense bulk of his work to prove almost any point of view.[2]

He was a perplexing and often contradictory figure: did he really believe that, as he said in his most famous poem, *The White Rose*, one should turn the other cheek to the cruel? 'That grief is life; . . . that man needs to suffer' . . . that death is the 'sublime bosom where all the sublime kingdoms are wrought' . . . It is improbable. His religious views were ambiguous: 'Religion is the form of natural belief in God.' It is clear that for years he was preoccupied by death, second only to Cuba:

> 'I am good and, like a good being,
> I shall die with my face to the Sun',

the last line of which was fitted out forty years later by Dionisio Ridruejo and others to be the opening line (*Cara al sol*) of the 'hymn' of the Spanish Falange.

Martí undoubtedly went further than most of his contemporaries to affirm the equality of races and it is here and in his hostility to any relation with the U.S. that his originality lies. His precise views of the future of Cuba were always romantic, never clear. Cuba was to be free of the U.S. as well as of Spain, there would be education on a large scale, and Cuba would establish herself pre-eminent for numerous virtues alongside the other South American republics. There was no thought of Socialism, and Martí seems to have believed that the cultivation of land was the only really honest activity, while the planting of trees would entitle men to extra benefits. He had thus strong though ill-organized social principles, and from his writings seems a contemporary of Rousseau rather than of Marx; and although he sided with the anarchists hanged after the Haymarket riots in Chicago of 1886, he did not side with anarchism.

His extraordinary appeal among Cubans is explained by his great energy, his organizing ability, his sensuous proclamation of Cuban identity apart from that of the U.S. and by the belief that, despite his pure European origin and his long residence in North America, he was a true 'son of the tropics', the most Cuban of Cubans. Yet he spoke always as a Spanish American, not as a parochial Cuban. He was an ardent and generous soul, though full of contradictions and unclear in his political aims.

Martí's successor as provisional president of the rebel republic was

[2] See Gray, *Martí*, 35–82.

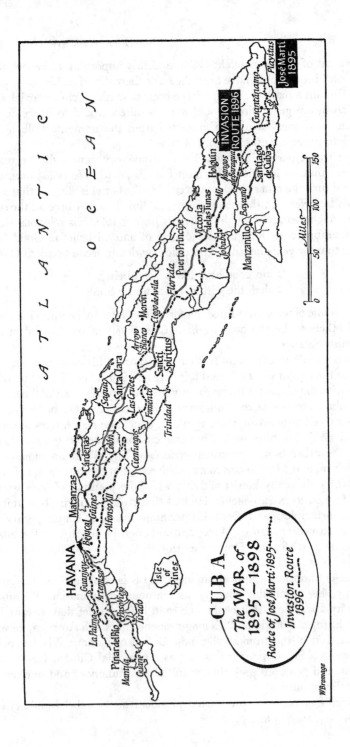

ATLANTIC OCEAN

José Martí
1895

Playitas

Guantánamo

INVASION
ROUTE 1896

Santiago
de Cuba

Baraguá
Mangos
Mir
Holguín

Bayamó

Manzanillo

Victoria
de las Tunas

Jobabo

Puerto Príncipe

Florida

Ciego de Ávila

Morón

Arroyo
Blanco

Sancti
Spíritus

Fomento

Trinidad

Las Cruces

Santa Clara

Cienfuegos

Saguá

Colón

Cárdenas

Alfonso XII

Güines

Bejucal

Matanzas

HAVANA

Guayjay

Artemisa

La Palma

Pinar del Río

Sábalo

Tirado

Isle
of
Pines

Mantua

Guane

CUBA
The WAR of
1895 – 1898

Route of José Martí 1895 ....

Invasion Route
1896 _ _ _ _

W. Bromage

Miles
0   50   100   150

Salvador Betancourt Cisneros, Marqués de Santa Lucía, a figure-head merely. Power, such as it was, rested on a tacit understanding between the generals – Máximo Gómez, Maceo and, later, Calixto García – and some civilians, led by Bartolomé Masó, who was elected president of the rebel 'House of Representatives'. The generals were really in control. Their task was never easy. Though they were not faced with the rankling criticism from slave-owners which marked the war of 1868–78, the Spanish forces from the start presented a more formidable military problem. In June 1895 there seem to have been for instance some 6,000 to 8,000 revolutionaries, but 52,000 Spaniards, along with nineteen warships, of which six were over 1,000 tons.[3] However, this difference in numbers was illusory. The Spaniards seemed almost from the beginning to be fighting a revolution, not a war. In the east of Cuba all classes openly or secretly backed the rebellion – even sometimes members of the Civil Guard.[4] The different units of the rebel army (sometimes with several hundred mounted men operating independently) held out without much difficulty in high lands, with their headquarters at remote farms and villages, occasionally sallying down to threaten roads between towns such as Bayamo or Santiago; recruiting or being joined by many of the 'revolutionary' bandits who had terrorized central Cuba in the years before the war. (The most famous bandit, Manuel García, was killed on the first day of the war after robbing a ship as his first act of commitment to the rebel cause.) Outright criminals like Aranda, afterwards president of the War Veterans' Council, fought in order to escape justice – he had murdered his wife. Esteban Montejo recalled that 'stealing animals was what I did most of during the war'.[5] Combatants often noted going for thirty hours without eating.[6] The Spanish army, without heavy reinforcements, kept to the roads and towns for fear of damage to these, while the countryside quickly lapsed into a state of anarchy.

In September the political organization of the rebel cause was formalized, with a cabinet (consejo de Gobierno), the Marqués de Santa Lucía (Salvador Betancourt Cisneros) being President (Prime Minister), Bartolomé Masó, Vice-Premier, and the Polish veteran of the 1870s, Carlos Roloff, Secretary for War along with other 'ministers'. Máximo Gómez was General-in-Chief, Maceo second-in-command and in command in the province of Oriente. Estrada Palma remained agent in New York. This 'government' met rarely and, when it did, in rough circumstances, in safe farmhouses. But they took themselves seriously.

[3] G. Maura Gamazo, Historia Crítica del Reinado de Don Alfonso XIII, 2 vols (1919, 1925), 235.
[4] E.g. the case of the Spaniard Grande, commander of the rebels in Cienfuegos, who had been a corporal in the Civil Guard before (Atkins, 173).
[5] Montejo, 193.
[6] Horacio Ferrer, Con el rifle al hombro (1950), 23.

They occupied their first meeting by the re-enactment of all laws promulgated during the Ten Years' War, such as the establishment of tribunals, a civil registry, civil marriage and so on. There was also a recruitment law and one which obliged Cubans in the U.S. to contribute to the cause. The firm stand of the Church beside the Spanish authority left the rebellion no alternative save to fight it. It was implicit that any government which would be established after victory would be democratic, but there was no other commitment. Máximo Gómez busied himself with shooting various famous bandit leaders such as Tuerto Matos and Roberto Bermúdez, but his authority was not absolute.

Despite the remoteness and ineffectiveness of the rebellion, it was clear from the beginning that most Cubans placed great hopes in it. Martínez Campos wrote in June 1895 to Cánovas:

> The few Spaniards in the island alone proclaim themselves as such ... the rest ... hate Spain; the masses, as a result of the activity of the press and the clubs ... and the abandonment of the island since Polavieja [i.e. in the early 1890s] have taken to resignation and license out of ... fear ... even the timid will soon follow the orders of the insurrectionary chiefs. Passing by bohíos in the country there are no men to be seen, and women, on being asked after their husbands and sons, reply with terrible frankness: 'in the mountains, with So and So'.

In these circumstances, Martínez Campos added, the only effective policy was one of complete ruthlessness. But he went on:

> I cannot, as a representative of a civilized country, be the first to give an example of ... intransigence. I must hope that they begin it. We could reconcentrate the families of the countryside in the towns [as had occurred in the 1870s in the east], but much force would be needed to compel them, since already there are very few in the interior who want to be [Spanish] volunteers ... the misery and hunger would be terrible: I would then have to give rations, which reached 40,000 a day in the last war. It would isolate the country from the towns but it would not prevent espionage, which would be done by women and children. Perhaps we will come to this, but only in a last resort and I think I lack the qualities to carry through such a policy. Among our present generals only Weyler has the necessary capacity for such a policy, since only he combines the necessary intelligence, courage and knowledge of war.

> Reflect my dear friend and if after discussion you approve the policy I have described, do not delay in recalling me. We are gambling with the destiny of Spain; but I retain certain beliefs and

they are superior to everything; they forbid me to carry out summary executions and similar acts. The insurrection today is more serious and more powerful than early in 1876. The leaders know more and their manner of waging war is different from what it was then ...

Finally, General Martínez Campos concluded:

Even if we win in the field and suppress the rebels, since the country wishes to have neither an amnesty for our enemies nor an extermination of them, my loyal and sincere opinion is that, with reforms or without reforms, before twelve years we shall have another war.[7]

This wise general, rare among European colonial commanders in his sensitivity, intelligence and understanding, remained as captain-general for some months more. His short-term aim was to prevent Máximo Gómez's prime purpose, to extend the war into the west. Gómez however had already left Oriente, and Maceo was busy training men in the hills, though the men of Oriente showed some reluctance to march out of their own province: even Maceo's brother José demurred at the idea.[8] In July Martínez Campos was in Oriente, and nearly cut off Maceo between Bayamo and Manzanillo: but he failed and a full Spanish general, Santocildes, was killed in the attempt. He himself narrowly escaped capture at Peralejo.[9] Spanish casualties mounted in the hot summer, perhaps a fifth of the new men dispatched to Spain being ill in August, chiefly from yellow fever.[10] Gómez meantime was riding round Puerto Príncipe, busily burning and destroying canefields in what was, of course, the least productive of sugar provinces. Further up the island there was as yet no great alarm. In June Edwin Atkins wrote from his great *Soledad* estate, near Cienfuegos, 'Everything is going well on our estates.'[11]

In mid-October Gómez took the critical decision to extend the war there and then to the west, that is after six months only of conflict, in contrast to the seven years' procrastination during the previous war. Even now there was some complaint, since the civilian Vice-President Masó supported the idea of guerrilla war alone. Gómez and Maceo, nevertheless, with 500 infantry and over 1,000 cavalrymen, broke out of the old line of *trochas* from Júcaro to Morón, outmanoeuvring the Spaniards by sheer speed, working in many, often ill-coordinated, bands, concentrating on the destruction of property, usually ordering the

[7] *Apuntes del ex-Ministro de Estado, Duque de Tetuán, para la defensa de la política internacional y gestión diplomática del gobierno liberal-conservador desde el 28 de marzo de 1895 al 29 septiembre de 1897*, II, 114–16, qu. Fernández Almagro, II, 246–7.
[8] Rubens, *Liberty*, 110–13.
[9] Fernández Almagro, II, 246.
[10] *Ibid.*, 149.
[11] Atkins, 161.

inhabitants out of their houses before they were burned and their possessions looted. The rebels rode onwards to a good tune, the *Himno Invasor*, composed by Loynaz del Castillo, the banners of liberty flying, living off the land, creating an inextinguishable legend.

At the end of November the Cuban provisional government followed the generals into Las Villas while, by Christmas, columns led by Gómez and Maceo were at Coliseo, not far short of Matanzas.[12] The really rich plantation area, the old fiefs of Zulueta and Baró, Antonio Parejo and Pedroso, were starting to suffer. Several rich little towns such as Cidra, which had grown up in the 1850s and 1860s in Matanzas, were wrecked. This was the moment of truth for which the rebels of the 1870s had longed in vain. There was little major fighting, since the Cubans carefully avoided anything approaching a pitched battle. Even so, however, Havana seemed threatened and it appeared certain that the sugar harvest of 1896 would be ruined. Many labourers, ex-slaves and whites, were now taking to the hills and, only very unofficially part of the rebellion, were living by pillage, as there was still much cattle.[13] The island seemed indeed in a ferment, small parties gathering everywhere, Spanish and insurgent, hurrying off in all directions, taking their machetes with them.

Edwin Atkins, from the start favouring autonomy, tried, like many planters, to steer a middle course:

> Orders sent to Soledad are to show respect for civil and military orders of the Spanish authorities and to render every assistance for transportation of troops, to deny all demands for money from insurgents and report same by cable but at the same time not to offer any resistance to [the] latter if they appear.[14]

When General Roloff tried to forbid the grinding of cane and demanded contributions to the rebel cause, from U.S. holdings as from Cuban, much cane was burnt, a loss at the *Soledad* plantation of between seven and eight million *arrobas* of cane, burned, Atkins thought, by a few Negroes only with a high wind to help them.[15] The old Terry estates also suffered greatly, despite the fact that Francesca Terry, one of the Terry heiresses, had married the Cienfuegos rebel leader Cabrera.[16] Atkins's local representative, Williams, wrote home on 24 November:

> It is apparent that the scheme of holding to the middle course is no longer tenable. For the protection of your large interests and our own

[12] Fernández Almagro, II, 258.
[13] Atkins, 162.
[14] *Ibid.*, 164-5.
[15] *Ibid.*, 174-7.
[16] *Ibid.*, 274.

lives it now becomes necessary that we join with that side which stands for law and order.[17]

Such indeed were the views of most planters.

In December a representative of Atkins (Walter Beal) went to New York to complain to Estrada Palma of the burning of property. Estrada answered that the property of U.S. citizens would be respected only after the formal recognition of the rebels as belligerents by the U.S.[18] The burning therefore continued: 'It has been a perfect roaring hell of fires all the way to the hills of Trinidad and the sea,' wrote Captain Beal to Atkins on 27 December, 'and we could see nothing but smoke and smouldering ruins, groups of poor people on foot . . . homes burned and clothing stolen.' Plantations established militia forces, of themselves and a number of others, making deals with the local Spanish forces. Even so, the gloom was everywhere considerable; the agent at *central Soledad* wrote on the last day of 1895: 'It would certainly seem as though the end cannot be far off.'[19]

The character of the rebels now became clearer. Some estimates gave 80 % as the proportion of Negroes.[20] Afterwards they themselves claimed to constitute 85 % of those present in rebel ranks. A number of rebels at least seem to have fought in and pillaged the areas where they had previously worked: *central Soledad*, for instance, was in constant fear of a Negro named Claudio Sarriá, born on the estate (taking the old Cuban planter's name) and also of a certain Torres, who 'used to work in the machinery department'. The rebel commander in the area of the Parque Alto plantation had similarly once been a slave in its owner's family.[21] This was therefore a revolutionary war, not simply one of independence.

A distinction should be drawn between the local rebels or bandits and the main forces under Gómez and Maceo. Captain Beal said of 150 cavalry and infantry under Quintín Banderas:

I cannot speak in too high terms of their exceptional behaviour and good discipline. They were here under trying circumstances, hungry, barefooted and half naked, yet not one of them appropriated the smallest thing to himself without permission – and not one of them entered a building. They are begging their officers to lead them to the attack of some town so that they may clothe themselves.[22]

[17] *Ibid.*, 179.
[18] *Ibid.*, 180.
[19] *Ibid.*, 188.
[20] *Ibid.*, 178.
[21] *Ibid.*, 186.
[22] Qu. Atkins, 196.

On the other hand Captain Beal suffered from the attentions of a local guerrilla leader known as El Mejicano: on 21 January 1896 he arrived about midday in the Guabairo *batey.*

Fighting crazy drunk, [he] ordered for oxen to be killed and breakfast made for all the force. He was so drunk that he had forgotten that they had already breakfasted. He informed me that he had information that I had offered $10,000 for his head and that he had come . . . on purpose to take my life . . . Once he handed out his machete and handed it to one of his men as if he were afraid to trust himself with it. However being there two hours drinking *aguardiente,* at short intervals, he got so completely drunk that he forgot what he came for, asked me for three centimos and left . . .

Afterwards the whole San Francisco plantation was completely burned, for El Mejicano ordered his men to draw their machetes and 'burn right and left'.[23]

CUBAN REBEL NUMBERS, DECEMBER 1895

Máximo Gómez (Matanzas)	5,000	Vidal (Sagua)	600
Antonio Maceo (Matanzas)	4,000	Cebreco (Santiago de Cuba)	500
José Maceo (Santiago de Cuba)	3,000	Zayas (Havana)	500
Lacret (Santa Clara)	2,500	Rafael Socorro (Cienfuegos)	200
Núñez (Havana)	1,600	Ruen (Guantánamo)	200
Roloff (Santa Clara)	1,500	Miró (Santiago de Cuba)	400
Rabí (Santiago de Cuba)	1,000	Ignacio Súarez (Sagua)	200
Cortina (Santa Clara)	1,000	Juan Bravo (Trinidad)	200
Quintín Banderas (Sancti Spiritus)	1,000	Pajarito (Remedios)	200
Bermúdez (Havana)	500	Muñoz (Cienfuegos)	50
Pancho Pérez (Santa Clara)	800	Clotilde García (Cárdenas)	600
Perico Díaz (Santa Clara)	500	Luis Chapotín (Cárdenas)	400
Basilio Guerra (Las Villas)	800	Perico Cárdenas (Cárdenas)	500
Lino Pérez (Trinidad)	700	Robau (Cárdenas)	500
Castillo (Sagua)	500	R. Carrillo (Matanzas)	400

TOTAL: 29,850

(Estimate by Havana correspondent of *Le Temps,* qu. A. S. Rowan and M. M. Ramsey, *The Island of Cuba* (1898), 166-7. A similar distribution published in the U.S. Congressional Record, 23 March 1896 (p. 3424) gave a total of 42,800. But the maximum number of fighting men probably never exceeded 25,000.)

Maceo's column deserves special notice. They were mostly Negroes, armed with machetes and a few rifles, cut short to make them more effective. They were not regularly provisioned but, accustomed to living in the woods, lived off the country. Expert horsemen, they were mounted on horses captured on the line of march. Other forces, however,

[23] *Ibid.,* 156-7. Possibly not céntimos, which were worth nothing, but gold *centenes,* worth $5.

especially those established in provinces such as Cienfuegos on a permanent basis, were organized on an elaborate system of hilltop sentinels,
with vegetables planted, regular cockfights and dances, and families
established. Down the hill and in the towns the Spanish army tried
ineffectively to maintain normal life. Recruits from Catalonia or
Castile behaved foolishly and irregularly. Officers despaired. Local
businesses closed. Bankruptcies increased.

Meantime, Christmas of 1895 saw the U.S. also in a strangely agitated
state. A minor quarrel with Britain over the Venezuela–British Guiana
boundary threatened to be explosive. War was not quite excluded; the
thought was agreeable in some quarters. Theodore Roosevelt, for
instance, had written to his friend, Lodge:

> Let the fight come if it must. I don't care whether our sea-coast cities
> are bombarded or not; we would take Canada ... Personally I
> rather hope the fight will come soon. The clamour of the peace
> faction has convinced me that this country needs a war.[24]

In the *New York Evening Sun* of 23 December, Roosevelt embroidered the
theme:

> American cities may possibly be bombarded but no ransom will be
> paid for them. It is infinitely better to see the cities laid level than to
> see a dollar paid to any foe to buy their safety.[25] [Later he wrote
> privately:] It is very difficult for me not to wish a war with Spain, for
> such a war would result at once in getting a proper Navy.[26]

Such sentiments were not confined to the New York police chief.
President Cleveland, in his congressional message, had appeared
similarly bellicose: 'It will in my opinion be the duty of the U.S. to
resist by every means in its power . . . the appropriation by Great
Britain of any lands . . . which belong . . . to Venezuela.'[27] However,
Roosevelt seemed not to care whether the purgative war was against
Britain or Spain or perhaps both at once; while Cleveland at least felt it
necessary to add:

> Whatever may be the traditional sympathy of our countrymen as
> individuals with a people who seem to be struggling for larger
> autonomy and greater freedom ... yet the plain duty of this govern-
> ment is to observe in good faith the recognized obligations of inter-
> national relationships.[28]

[24] Roosevelt and Lodge, *Correspondence*, I, 204.
[25] Qu. H. F. Pringle, *Theodore Roosevelt* (1932).
[26] Theodore Roosevelt to A. T. Cowles, 9 March 1896 (Cowles MSS, qu. Beal, *op. cit.* 37).
[27] Congressional Message. This message was in fact really a climb-down and was thus
interpreted by most diplomats.
[28] *Loc. cit.*

The violence of the American scene had now been immensely heightened by Hearst's *New York Journal*.[29] Accounts had begun to appear in the New York and particularly the Mid West press purporting to describe Spanish cruelty; the *Journal* led the way. All in fact were less founded on reality than on the enterprising falsifications emanating from Estrada Palma and the Cuban junta. Nevertheless they were adequate to create a general demand for 'action' in Congress as well as outside. These demands were also stimulated by the Spaniards themselves, whose press related constant news of victory – no less false than the news of atrocity. U.S. journalists found it hard to penetrate to the actual scenes of fighting and, sitting in Havana, relayed all sorts of reports from bars. The confusion between truth and reality was never greater as new and ill-managed mass communications began to play over a war whose intensity of civilian involvement reflected the twentieth rather than the nineteenth century. But deception was everywhere. Thus the young Winston Churchill, a volunteer who saw service this winter with the Spanish army in Las Villas (and indeed was there first under fire), was impressed by Spanish propaganda and wrote on return: 'The Cuban rebels give themselves the name of heroes and only are boastful and braggarts. If the Revolution triumphs, Cuba will be a black Republic';[30] and: 'They neither fight bravely nor do they use their weapons effectively . . . Their army, consisting to a large extent of coloured men, is an undisciplined rabble.'[31] It is clear however that Churchill had second thoughts about Cuba. He wrote to his mother a year later:

> I reproach myself somewhat for having written a little uncandidly and for having perhaps done injustice to the insurgents. I rather tried to make out, and in some measure succeeded in making out, a case for Spain. It was politic and did not expose me to the charge of being ungrateful to my hosts but I am not quite clear whether it was right.[32]

General Martínez Campos had now to resolve his difficult choice: to answer a mobile war with the toughest measures, a war of terror with terror, or to resign. He chose the latter course on 16 January 1896. By this time Maceo had by-passed Havana and almost attained the westernmost tip of the island; Gómez was in the neighbourhood of Havana. 'If I have failed,' Martínez Campos telegraphed to Cánovas on 20 January, 'the unique responsibility is mine. The government has in no way restricted my action, neither political nor military. I have not happened

[29] Hearst bought it in October 1895.
[30] *Saturday Review*, 15 February 1896; see also *Bohemia*, 27 September 1952.
[31] *Ibid.*, 6 March 1896.
[32] Randolph Churchill, *Winston S. Churchill*, vol. I, *Youth, 1874–1900* (1966), 279.

to have used the means and the full powers which have been conceded to me.'

Who would succeed Martínez Campos? The only way to win the war was evidently to adopt the tactic suggested by him; and the 'only man' for this was the then captain-general of Barcelona, Valeriano Weyler, Marqués de Tenerife. Cánovas was a pragmatist. When he appointed Martínez Campos he no doubt hoped that a conciliation of the type reached at Zanjón might be possible.[33] Since Martínez Campos had been unable even to broach this, the only alternative was to appoint a general able to achieve victory – though Cánovas, from his knowledge of the past history of Spain's decline, must have realized in his heart that there was a strong chance at least that Martínez Campos had been right in his letter of the previous year and that even a short-term victory would be followed by another war years later. His actions were of course influenced by their possible effect on the U.S. and the chance of their intervention, and on internal Spanish politics. He, like President Cleveland, had his nationalistic opposition to cope with – expressed at its most strident by the Carlist 'theoretician' Vázquez de Mella: 'This Spain most glorious and all-powerful in better days cannot leave a red blot in the middle of the ocean.'[34] There remained a chance too that if all available Spanish troops were sent off to Cuba there would be a *pronunciamiento* in Spain – perhaps a republican one – and the elaborate constitutional monarchical structure in Spain which Cánovas had been trying all his life to build would collapse. A military collapse in Cuba could also bring military action, perhaps from the Carlists or the critics on the orthodox Right who were far more powerful politically than the very few Left Republicans or federalists (such as Pi y Margall) who believed Cuba should be free. That subject was indeed hardly mentioned, even by socialists or anarchists: for most Spaniards, Cuba was a province of Spain and could never be anything else.[35] This proprietary attitude was reflected in the quiet 1896 general elections, when the socialists received only 600 votes, and Pi only 700. No doubt the figures were false but they reflected a reality.

[33] Fernández Almagro, II, 367–8.
[34] *Ibid.*, 375.
[35] See *ibid.*, 267–8.

CHAPTER XXVIII

General Weyler

General Weyler went to Cuba. Severe, single-minded and ruthless, he was intelligent and serious, responding not only to his orders but to the type of warfare which had already been imposed on him by his opponents. He had been Spanish military attaché in Washington during the American Civil War, and much admired Sherman. He was puritanical in private habits, being fully able to satisfy his hunger in the field with a lump of bread, a tin of sardines and a pitcher of wine. He habitually slept on the mattress of a private soldier. He never smoked nor took hard liquor. He was dry and uncommunicative, authoritarian but anticlerical. He dressed very carelessly and in later life his clothes were filthy from spilling food down the front. He had German blood, and was tenacious. Ruthless to men he loved horses and in Madrid kept a horses' home to save them from the knacker.[1] He had a great influence over the Spanish army, especially among young ambitious officers including, some years ahead, the puritanical Franco. His sound health and constitution enabled him to carry on tropical warfare as if he had been born in a swamp.[2] He had fought in the first Cuban war and also against the Carlists.

Weyler's first dispatch clearly reflected the severity of the situation:

When I took command Maceo was still in Pinar del Río being on that day at Sabana del Mar and on the 11th in the Laborí sugar mill near Artemisa. Máximo Gómez was moving towards Guayabal [20 miles west of Havana] from the Jamaica mill. He encamped near the Portugalete mill, well known as the property of Don Manuel Calvo [the financier who had been representative in Madrid of the 'volunteers' in the previous war] and for being very close to the capital ... [where] terror reigned, my predecessor having taken dispositions against an enemy attack ... teams of 'volunteers' and firemen were in the post office and the main public buildings, and every night these admirable corps guarded the external section of the city, to avoid attack ... food from the countryside could only enter

---

[1] Sir J. R. Shane Leslie, *Long Shadows* (1966), 155. General Valeriano Weyler (1838–1930), see his life by his grandson, *En los Archivos de mi abuelo*, Madrid 1946.
[2] Luis de Armiñán Pérez, *Weyler, el Gran Capitán* (1946), 74–5 and 94–6.

after paying the rebels the duty which they demanded ... The day after my arrival they prevented milk coming in. I should add that in the capital itself there were conspiracies, that munitions of various types went in and out, and that ... all respect for authority had vanished. There was public muttering everywhere against Spain, everywhere criticism and complaint ... [Our] various columns, formed of isolated contingents from different corps and commanded by officers unknown to them, had no spirit and they were only fed irregularly. There was such anarchy that the officers, passing by one military post, would leave behind some men and pick up new ones. The troops had to cover an immense number of farms and villages ... so that when one contingent was attacked by the enemy, it lacked any positive reinforcement and so was constrained to watch the canefields burning in front of them. Finally, the ease with which guerrillas and volunteer forces could be formed [on the Spanish side], granting ranks as Captain or Major to any who ask, produced ... a great lack of unity in the command, many of them shortly afterwards giving up and passing over to the enemy with arms and ammunition ... And as in the headquarters there was inadequate intelligence about all this, it will be realized that the work awaiting me was hard and laborious.[3]

Weyler set out first of all to try to isolate Maceo in Pinar del Río by fortifying a new north–south line. He then proposed to divide the island into further sections by other north–south lines, also re-equipping the Júcaro-Morón *trocha* of the last war. He cut the cavalry to give it greater mobility, substituting the regulation sabre for the machete, which even some Spanish squadrons still used. The battalions were reorganized to form columns self-sufficient for each area. The army posts in the country-side were reduced to the smallest number, the defence of small towns being confined to groups of volunteers. Cuban counter-guerrillas were recruited to fight and scavenge in the countryside, these being often much more feared than the Spaniards by the rebels. But Weyler's most controversial step (as seen from Martínez Campos's letter of the previous August, almost inevitable) was the order concentrating the whole population of towns or villages in 'military areas', in specific and well-defended outposts, to be served by special zones of cultivation. Since the greater part of Cuba in early 1896 was 'a military area', the whole island would become little more than an immense concentration camp.[4] These plans were accompanied by decrees defining treason as punishable by death; ordering the registration of the population of all the eastern

[3] Armiñán Pérez, I, 129–31.
[4] Fernández Almagro, II, 282.

provinces; and giving military commanders extraordinary judicial powers to try and punish, including execute, any who contravened these decrees. This policy (begun in a small way by the rebels) has since been found to be the only effective one against guerrilla war, as the British were soon to find in South Africa and Castro in the war of Escambray in 1960–1.[5]

This policy, steadily and vigorously pursued throughout 1896, implied the destruction of the agricultural wealth of the country; and indeed the damage caused in the course of 1896 was estimated at $M40, the total loss being evidently much more, since sugar mills and tobacco factories were at a standstill. The total production of sugar in 1896 fell to 225,000 tons – only the great *Constancia* mill (the old property of the conservative leader, the Marqués de Apezteguía, and now leased by the U.S. Constancia Co.) having an uninterrupted harvest among the larger mills: and this thanks to being guarded by Spanish soldiers,[6] a service for which Apezteguía was responsible. On many plantations an acute problem was presented: to start grinding and thus risk an attack and complete destruction; or to do nothing, and let the *colonos* who had sugar cane to be ground sue them. Atkins, for instance, at *Soledad* decided to attempt to grind and on 27 February sent down as usual the 'sugar men', the *maestros de azúcar*. A day or two later, the biggest sugar *colono*, Captain Beal, received a note from the local rebel Captain Rego saying that the rebels had valued his *batey* at $10,000, and that he was required to pay 2%. When he refused, a messenger arrived to say that the rebels had had orders to burn the dwelling house. Even so, grinding began, carefully guarded by an armed force under the command of the ex-timekeeper: most of the men were 'old hands . . . who have an interest in the place'. But it was very difficult to get new workers since they feared death at rebel hands if caught. 'All possible expenses . . . were cut . . . no attention was paid to decrees from either side and we worked steadily on, determined to yield only to direct printed orders of the government or to force.'[7] So at *Soledad* not only was some cane ground but the fields got ready for the 1897 crop. Meantime general conditions were very bad; even the birth rate in the city of Havana was dropping;[8] people had the impression that the countryside, unique source of national wealth, was waging war on the cities.

Weyler's initial scheme to isolate Maceo was defeated, since Maceo, in a bold drive eastwards, returned to the neighbourhood of Havana, reaching the Havana-Batabanó railway line. General Linares set out

[5] Lee Lockwood, *Castro's Cuba: Cuba's Fidel* (1967), 268. Weyler himself pointed out the South African parallel (*Mi mando en Cuba*, 6 vols (1910), I, 11).

[6] Ely, *Cuando reinaba*, 691.

[7] Atkins, 240.

[8] Census of 1899, 716.

from Havana to attempt to prevent Maceo from joining up with Gómez, who was now at Quivicán. Linares engaged Maceo on 19 February and the latter withdrew, leaving fifty dead out of his 300 men but, even so, the two columns of Cuban rebels succeeded in meeting in Matanzas, encamping at San Pablo. Much skirmishing followed. Maceo eventually returned to Havana province while Gómez went back into Las Villas, pursued but elusive. Weyler doggedly dedicated his main effort to Maceo, giving each of his columns the task of operating in a rough square of 200 kilometres. As a result Maceo, then with 6,000 men heading westwards, brushed during March three times against columns headed by different Spanish officers, but continued to burn canefields, *bateys* and mills on plantations which did not pay the contribution which he demanded, releasing the oxen, sacking the shops and cutting down with machetes those who continued to cut cane or who worked railway lines. Telegraph wires were cut, bridges destroyed, trains blown up from a distance. This spring campaign of Maceo's in 1897 was one of the most effective guerrilla strikes. The Spanish Command regarded even Gómez as more humane than Maceo, whom they feared as a Negro as well as a commander. They saw in him the spirit of elemental Negro energy, the wave of a terrible future. But the arrival of Weyler nevertheless transformed the morale of the *habaneros* as well as of the Spanish community in general.

Weyler's arrival also transformed the junta in New York, who both attempted to send more and more equipment and arms to Cuba and redoubled their efforts to place stories of atrocities, which Hearst's *Journal* and Pulitzer's *World* (Charles Dana's *Sun* was no longer in the race) so coveted. Occupied primarily with the battle of circulation, Hearst and Pulitzer failed to see, and did not care, that they were being used as catspaws. On 23 February 1896 the *Journal* told its readers that Weyler was a 'fiendish despot . . . a brute, the devastator of *haciendas* . . . pitiless, cold, an exterminator of men . . . there is nothing to prevent his carnal, animal brain from running riot with itself in inventing tortures and infamies of bloody debauchery.'[9] This description was, of course, incorrect. It was a successful story to run, however, since it helped to create an atmosphere whereby it was hoped the U.S. government and judiciary would overlook the organization in New York set up that same month to dispatch material to Cuba. To a great extent this campaign was successful. From this time any rebel leader from Cuba who left the island on a diplomatic or commercial errand would return at the head of new expeditions, with rifles, dynamite, machetes and ammunition.

There were other motives in the junta's propaganda against Weyler:

[9] As qu. Wisan, 204.

to raise money (and sums far greater than had been raised in the 1870s were now available) and to secure recognition of belligerent rights for the rebels, the same issue, that is, that had occupied Hamilton Fish throughout the Ten Years' War. At the end of February the persistent 'sympathy meetings', 'Cuban-American fairs' in Madison Square Gardens, New York and elsewhere, advertisements organized by the junta's representatives as well as the general sympathies increasing in Congress, resulted in a resolution by the Senate recommending the recognition of belligerency. But President Cleveland opposed this. He had often refused to follow the Senate, even though several speakers, such as the aged Senator John Sherman, spoke with an almost obsessive violence against Spain.

The only consequence was in fact that the Secretary of State, Olney, dispatched a note to Madrid on 4 April 1896 offering his 'good offices': 'The existing situation [in Cuba] is of the greatest importance for the people of the U.S. [since] the U.S. is concerned in all struggles for freedom . . .'; if the struggle were prolonged the U.S. would be inevitably drawn in; therefore, the U.S. would try to agree with Spain an immediate pacification of the island, on the basis of the recognition of Spain's sovereign rights and the concession to Cuba of all reasonable local rights.[10] Olney, an old friend of the Atkins family, was throughout this time in touch with Edwin Atkins who, from New York and Boston, used his considerable influence as the most prominent U.S. planter in Cuba in favour of autonomy and against belligerent rights.[11] Atkins argued that the grant of belligerent rights by the U.S. would ruin U.S. interests in Cuba, since they could not thereafter be legally defended by Spanish troops. Atkins in person was a very active lobbyist. Olney himself, however, needed little encouragement and bluntly told the junta to their faces that he considered their policy of burning estates to be arson. Atkins was offered a bribe of $100,000 by the junta to cease his activities, and he was also promised that his property would be left alone. But he refused to accept the bribe.[12]

The policy of Olney and Atkins pre-supposed a Canadian solution for Cuba, but such a scheme was still unacceptable both to Spain and to the Cubans. Because of the long war in the 1870s and of the involvement in 1895-6 of the whole island in the struggle, Cuban nationalism was now aflame and could scarcely be satisfied with anything less than

[10] Spanish Diplomatic Correspondence and Documents, 1896-1900 (Washington, D.C., 1905). Grenville and Young (*Politics, Strategy and American Diplomacy*, 190) point out this document repudiated the historic mission of the U.S. of placing herself on the side of the colonial people of the hemisphere and argued strictly from the point of view of U.S. interests.

[11] Atkins, 157. Richard Olney (1835-1917), attorney-general 1893-5. A lawyer from Massachusetts.

[12] *Ibid.*, 214.

independence. At the same time, Cánovas still had no intention of negotiating with the Cubans until peace had been established. He intended to negotiate from strength. Obstinate by nature, he felt able to take this policy since the resolution of the U.S. and the anti-Spanish philippics in the New York *Journal* and the *World* had led even the Spanish Left, even Spanish republicans, to protest against the 'most frivolous proposition' that any foreign power could argue over 'indisputable Spanish sovereign rights'. Again, as in the past, only the aged federalist, Pi y Margall, stood out. The bellicose American press, indeed, had the effect of inflating the bellicosity of the Spanish: the Liberal *Heraldo de Madrid* thus had a headline on 19 March proclaiming the need for 'Guns, not reforms' and saying 'we are ready for anything, including a conflict with the U.S.'[13]

So Cánovas rejected Olney's note,[14] raising, as he did so, the old hare that 'given the combination of races, the withdrawal of Spain from Cuba would deprive the island of the only unifying bond, giving rise to an inevitable war between men of different colour, contrary to the spirit of Christian civilization'.[15] Cánovas was convinced that Weyler would in fact win the war and he believed that to surrender to pressure by the U.S. would not only bring down his government but wreck his Constitution. He believed that once victory was attained, he could give administrative reforms to Cuba.

The early months of 1896 suggested that this policy might just work. Cleveland reconfirmed his neutral position, promising to prosecute any U.S. citizen who assisted 'any' rebels. Of the governments of Latin America, only President Eloy Alfaro of Ecuador gave any backing to the rebellion.[16] Porfirio Díaz in Mexico had his foreign minister tell Gonzalo de Quesada that he believed a Spanish victory to be inevitable.[17] An appeal by a young Cuban man of letters, Enrique Varona, probably the outstanding Cuban polemicist now that Martí was dead, to the 'peoples of Latin America' was fruitless.[18] Slumbering under the rule of bloody dictators, themselves sustained by barefoot armies, most of South America responded to the war of Cuban independence as if Bolívar had been a legendary eponymous hero and San Martín an obscure martyr in a forgotten century.

The war in Cuba continued with singular ferocity. On 15 April, Máximo Gómez dispatched from his headquarters a circular announcing, in respect of the sugar harvest: 'The proprietors of mills who go on

[13] Fernández Almagro, II, 293.
[14] On 22 May.
[15] Cánovas's reply in Fernández Almagro, II, 810–15.
[16] *Ibid.*, 297.
[17] *Loc. cit.*
[18] *Contra España* (New York, 1895, also English, French and Italian versions).

milling . . . will be immediately hung. Identification only is necessary.'[19] Maceo still evaded a pitched battle, though at times hard pressed. He was eventually forced to a big skirmish at Cacarajícara where he lost about 200 out of 1,500 men (30 April 1896), and another at Las Lajas in mid-May, where he lost 39 dead. Weyler had now constructed a small defence system across the island from Mariel south to Las Mangas, and Máximo Gómez was prevented for the moment from thinking of rejoining him after a setback at Ciego Montero on 12 May in Las Villas. All summer, Maceo's marches and counter-marches continued, superior manoeuvrability being always the reason for the successes which he achieved, bad weather, disease and inflexibility being the chief reasons for Weyler's failure to press home his growing advantage (at least as far as the west was concerned).

Weyler also had difficulties inside Havana, where he found, according to his own account:

> Many germs of separatism, conspiring to aid the rebels by all means, the tobacco factories being the official centres, since there readers read separatist books and articles, together with news, false or exaggerated, of the war and the revolution, thus fomenting among the workers hatred for Spain . . . On Saturdays, after getting their weekly wage, a collection for the rebels is made. All this, given . . . the destruction of the . . . tobacco plantations principally in Pinar del Río, can only result in a fall in work in the factories, leaving unemployed thousands of workers which, with the propaganda which has already occurred, naturally goes to enlarge the ranks of the insurrection . . .[20]

Weyler proceeded to ban the export of tobacco in leaf from Pinar del Río, so as to make more available for Havana and to try to ruin the cigar workers in Florida who were irretrievably pro-rebel. This was followed in June 1896 by a similar ban on banana exports through the closing of the small Northern Oriente ports of Samá and Banes (surrounded and burned by the rebels). In August coffee and sugar exports were also forbidden except with prior authorization.

Thus Cuba in mid-1896 presented a desolate picture. Many sugar estates were idle. Most of the male population had joined either the rebels or the Spanish guerrilla forces, as an alternative to starvation.[21] As yet no general order for reconcentration had been given, but most of the population was already confined. Captain Beal, the *colono* of Cienfuegos, wrote to Atkins on 11 July:

[19] Fernández Almagro, II, 307.
[20] Weyler, *Mi mando en Cuba*, I, 341.
[21] Atkins, 199.

No sanitary measures have been adopted. Smallpox extends to all parts of the city [Cienfuegos] where there are tenements. The rags used for the sick are thrown into the streets, where they are carried up and down by the wind and curs ... Smallpox and pernicious fevers are very fatal, particularly to children. I am informed that a large trench has been dug in the cemetery, where the dead are thrown in during the night and covered with quick lime. Both of our contractors succumbed to the smallpox. The death rate from this disease is now on the wane, [but] I suppose from lack of victims. Yellow fever is very epidemic and of an alarming type and many of the troops are dying.[22]

Despite Weyler, in the areas of central Cuba to which he had not attended, the officers of the Spanish army still scandalously sought at every point to make money. Some Spanish commanders withdrew their troops from guarding plantations unless they were well paid by the owner: in this way a certain General Pin made a good deal out of Atkins & Co.[23] A judge in Manzanillo made a large sum by arresting various citizens, letting them out after they had paid a fine, and reimprisoning them. Later there were rumours of the same procedure in Cienfuegos when 169 people were arrested on suspicion, including the administrators of both of Emilio Terry's sugar estates.[24]

Weyler's duel with Maceo continued into the autumn, though fighting was delayed by the heavy rains of midsummer. Maceo remained in Pinar del Río, unable to break out to the east through the line which began at Mariel. Weyler on 21 October brought in the first of his famous concentration orders – though the vigilant New York press were slow to grasp the significance of the instruction:[25] the entire population of Pinar del Río who lived outside the fortifications of towns would have to move into those towns in a space of eight days. Anyone found outside a fortified town would thereafter be considered a rebel and treated as such. All unauthorized food distribution from place to place would be forbidden. Cattle were to be taken by their owners to the nearest town.[26] Two weeks later Weyler himself set off for Mariel in search of Maceo.

As in the 1850s, Cuba was meantime a leading issue in the hectic U.S. elections in 1896 when, as a consequence of the depression of the 1890s, a radical section of the Democratic party had captured the nomination. The war had by November in fact come to seem almost as critical for the honour of the U.S. as for that of Spain. After Olney's abortive attempt

[22] *Ibid.*, 242–3.
[23] *Ibid.*, 244.
[24] *Ibid.*, 246. This matter was never quite cleared up.
[25] Wisan, 205–6. It took the *World* nearly a month (until 16 November) to take it in.
[26] Fernández Almagro, II, 306–7.

to negotiate on the matter, reports of atrocities and bloodshed continued increasingly in the press, although in a confused fashion, so that it seemed almost that it was Weyler who was burning canefields, not Maceo. The *World* correspondent in Havana, Creelman,[27] wrote on 17 May: 'Blood on the roadsides, blood in the fields, blood on the doorsteps, blood, blood, blood. The old, the young, the weak, the crippled, all are butchered without mercy.'[28] The capture by the Spaniards of a U.S. vessel loaded with arms for the rebels, and the subsequent condemnation to death of two U.S. citizens, caused such a storm of protest that Weyler had eventually to agree to a delay.[29] A campaign against the president for 'doing nothing about Cuba' preoccupied several papers. If President Cleveland, carolled the *Mail & Express*, is giving secret comfort to Spain in her barbarous treatment of our courageous, liberty-loving Cuban neighbours, he is betraying this country.[30] The Republican candidate in the 1896 elections, McKinley, was contrasted with Cleveland: 'That McKinley's heart beats warmly for the Cuban cause is as certain as that he is loyal and true to his native land . . .'[31] But it was not only honour that was at stake. Sugar had been the one major import which McKinley's Act of 1892 had rendered duty free. The Democrats in 1894 had reinstated some duties, including one on sugar, and McKinley desired to remove them in the interest of consumers; but this could not be done while the Cuban war was under way, since the absence of Cuban production would evidently let beet sugar from Germany or central Europe into the U.S. and so wreck the politically important beet farmers of the middle and far west. The barons of the sugar trust, Atkins and Havemeyer, were also of course interested in the restoration of peace, as were those senators and congressmen who were close to them.[32] These men were not specially interested in intervention by the U.S., but they did want peace, even if it could only be secured by intervention.[33] Meantime, as early as June 1896 the office of naval intelligence had drawn up possible war plans for use against Spain.[34]

Weyler was now well established as the villain – 'the Butcher'. On

[27] James Creelman (1854–1915), Canadian by birth.

[28] Qu. Wisan, 203.

[29] *Ibid.*, 149–50. This was 29 April.

[30] *Mail & Express*, 9 May 1896, qu. *ibid.*, 137.

[31] *Mail & Express*, 15 June 1896, qu. *ibid.*, 171. William McKinley (1843–1901). A lawyer from Ohio. Methodist and champion of protection. President, 1897–1901.

[32] See May, 115–16; Senators Aldrich, Achison and Quay were all supposed to receive cash from the sugar trust. See Nathaniel Stephenson, *Nelson W. Aldrich* (1930), 111–20.

[33] See Pratt, *Expansionists of 1898*, 248, for discussion and note of a memorial presented by George Mosler, August Belmont, Lawrence Turnure, etc., to this end in May 1897.

[34] See Grenville and Young, *Politics, Strategy and American Diplomacy*, 272–6. The author was Lieut. W. W. Kimball. The assumption was to 'liberate Cuba', but action against the far east Spanish possessions as against Spain was also contemplated.

7 May Hearst's *Journal* had noted with self-satisfaction Máximo Gómez's order to destroy towns and villages ('leave nothing un-destroyed');[35] the same paper on 11 May announced that Weyler would resign unless he was 'allowed to quench his thirst with American gore' (this was *à propos* of the captured U.S. boat).[36] On 10 July the *New York Tribune* noted a speech in the Cortes by the Carlist, Mella, in which he had urged preparation for the inevitable conflict with the U.S., in which 'Spain would prove her virility and her greatness'.[37]

What exactly the New York press wanted in Cuba was not, however, quite certain. The *Journal* had hectically promised: 'we are ready, for the country's sake, to accede to any treaty in which independence is granted, even paying Spain an indemnity, but we shall not hear any other proposals based on home rule or reforms'.[38] The *Sun* said: 'Spain must abandon Cuba if either is to be saved. If she does not act, a power greater than Spain should give notice that the war must come to an end.'[39] For a while it was believed that action, nameless, undefined but decisive – and who could doubt that this would mean Cuba's direct involvement with the U.S.? – would be taken once McKinley had won the election and taken office.

McKinley did win against the whirlwind figure of William Jennings Bryan, in November, and the *Journal* on 6 November urged that: 'No surer road is open for popularity for the new President than the abandon-ment of the cold-blooded indifference to Cuba to which Cleveland has committed our government.'[40] And popularity was what McKinley, God-intoxicated, with his sick and possessive wife, especially craved.[41]

In mid-November 1896 there was indeed a real war scare, after a new congressional demand for the recognition of belligerency. Several papers drew back: 'This country has done nothing to provoke a war.'[42] The *Commercial Advertiser* declared: 'Some of the newspapers that flourish by dragging the sewers for filth and crime have undertaken to perpetuate a quarrel with Spain.'[43] The *Sun* and the *Journal* soon returned to the attack, however, and, vigorously blaming Cleveland for going far 'in making statute law subservient to Spain's interests', declared that 'Spain's lone ally is in the White House'.[44]

[35] Wisan, 199.
[36] *Ibid.*, 153.
[37] *Op. cit.*, 166.
[38] 20 April 1896, qu. Wisan, 177.
[39] *Sun*, 5 May 1896, qu. *ibid.*, 162.
[40] *Ibid.*, 172.
[41] *Cf.* Margaret Leech, *In the Days of McKinley* (1959), H. Wayne Morgan's attempt, in *William McKinley and his America*, to reassess this president is valiant but unsuccessful. See also Grenville and Young, *op. cit.*, 239ff.; and Walter Lafeber, *The New Empire*, 327ff.
[42] 13 November, qu. Wisan, 167.
[43] Qu. *ibid.*, 168.
[44] *Sun*, 15 November 1896 and *Journal*, 17 November 1896, qu. *ibid.*, 139.

At the end of the month Senator Lodge wrote to the bellicose Theodore Roosevelt, after lunching with McKinley;[45]

He naturally does not want to be obliged to go to war as soon as he comes in, for ... his great ambition is to restore business and bring back good times and he dislikes the idea of such an interruption. He would like the crisis to come this winter and be settled one way or the other before he takes up the reins:[46]

that is, get into war there and then, before inauguration in March. What sort of conflict would it be? The *World* had foreshadowed it:

Any armed conflict would be short, sharp and decisive, and it would lead the U.S. to assume a protectorate over Cuba ... that would ensure the freedom of that unhappy island. And that is a consummation most devoutly to be wished by every true American.[47]

Meantime Olney was employing the last months of his administration trying secretly to persuade the Cuban rebels to accept the wisdom of an autonomous solution.[48]

[45] Who would be inaugurated only in March 1897.
[46] Roosevelt and Lodge, *Correspondence.*
[47] Qu. Wisan, 169.
[48] This mission was carried out by the planter Oscar Stillman (see Grenville and Young, 197). It was not successful.

CHAPTER XXIX

Cuba and U.S. Public Opinion

The Spanish tactics were beginning to pay off. In the east a number of leaders were killed – including Maceo's brother José. Though Máximo Gómez and Calixto García exercised local mastery in the centre and east respectively, they were unable to mount offensive action. Weyler, moving back and forth from Havana, diligently pursued his plans to force Maceo to capitulate or attempt to cross the Mariel lines. Eventually Maceo and a small group did get across the line but, shortly after, a Spanish column under Major Cirugeda surprised them, and Maceo fell from his horse, mortally wounded, being killed by another shot. His aide, 'Pancho' Gomez, son of Máximo, also died in the ensuing skirmish, just possibly by his own hand.

This was the biggest victory obtained by the Spaniards since the death of Martí. The end of 1896 saw indeed the gradual pacification of the three western provinces of Pinar del Río, Havana and Matanzas. In the east, depression among the rebels was widespread, and the dry and uncommunicative personality of Máximo Gómez caused incessant difficulties with the civilian leaders and with the more open-minded and humane commander, Calixto García, in Oriente. Several rebel leaders deserted to the Spaniards, particularly some of the ex-bandits.[1] In New York, Estrada Palma resigned from the leadership of the New York junta. It appeared to Weyler, and to Cánovas in Madrid, that the surrender of the Cubans was merely a matter of time.[2]

The death of Maceo led to the most lavish misrepresentation till that date of the news from Cuba in the New York press. It was said that he had been murdered by trickery or that he had been invited to a parley and then killed.[3] Congress was highly animated and a new resolution demanding belligerent rights was introduced.[4] Cleveland, still with a few months of his presidency to run, as ever sought to hold back the flood of belligerence; though even he felt bound to admit in his message to Congress on the day Maceo died:

---

[1] Montejo, 199, describes how one leader, Cayito Alvarez, was killed by his own men for so deserting.

[2] Fernández Almagro, II, 312–16.

[3] Wisan, 192–3.

[4] The Cameron Resolution.

When the inability of Spain to deal successfully with the insurrection has become manifest ... our obligation to the sovereignty of Spain will be superseded by higher obligations which we can hardly hesitate to recognise and discharge. [He did however add:] If Spain should offer to Cuba genuine autonomy – a measure of home rule which, while preserving the sovereignty of Spain, would satisfy all rational requirements of her Spanish subjects – there should be no just reason why the pacification of the island might not be effected.[5]

This was not very satisfactory to those anxious for 'action'. Senator Cameron rushed through a resolution to recognize the 'Cuban Republic' and this passed, under the influence of the garbled version prevalent about Maceo's death; but Olney pointed out that recognition depended on the president.[6] Hearst was still very dissatisfied. Earlier, he had sent two hot-blooded and able men, Frederic Remington, his ace cartoonist,[7] and Richard Harding Davis, the best known freelance journalist of the day[8] (each paid $3,000 a month), to Havana.[9] Hearst hoped that their presence would make up for some of the prestige gained by the *World* whose correspondent, Sylvester Scovel,[10] to Pulitzer's great satisfaction had been gaoled by the Spaniards for constantly repeating such stories as 'the Spanish soldiers habitually cut off the ears of the Cuban dead and retain them as trophies'.[11] But there were inexplicable delays in getting passes to 'the front' and Davis and Remington spent all their time drinking in the Hotel Inglaterra – a familiar predicament for journalists in Havana.[12] From February 1897 Weyler had prohibited reporters from accompanying troops.[13] In a famous exchange, Remington telegraphed to Hearst: 'Everything is quiet ... There will be no war. I wish to return.' Hearst answered: 'Please remain. You furnish the pictures and I'll furnish the war.'[14] Remington did furnish a picture. In February 1897 the *Journal* featured a five-column headline, *Does Our Flag Protect Women?* Underneath was a story of how three Cuban girls had been stripped by Spanish policemen in search of secret documents on the U.S. ship *Olivette*. Beneath, Remington had drawn a demure and naked girl surrounded by policemen.[15]

[5] Message to Congress, December 1896.
[6] Atkins, 245.
[7] Frederic Remington (1861–1909), clerk, cowboy, stockman, before turning cartoonist and artist.
[8] Richard Harding Davis (1864–1916). Afterwards in South Africa and in France.
[9] Swanberg, 104.
[10] Sylvester Scovel (1869–1905), time-keeper in blast surface, 1888–95; sent to Cuba, 1895.
[11] *New York World*, 29 May 1896.
[12] Swanberg, 107–8.
[13] Wisan, 194.
[14] J. Creelman, *On the Great Highway* (1901), 177–8.
[15] *Journal*, 12 February 1897.

This picture caused a major sensation. The Republicans were pleased to find another opportunity of attacking Cleveland; resolutions were presented in both houses. But when the girls arrived in New York, they denied to the *World* that they had been searched by men. Davis sent a muddled apology from Havana. The storm died out when Hearst took up another Cuban cause – the death of a Cuban dentist accused of train robbery, who had become a U.S. citizen, and who either died or was beaten to death in a Havana gaol. Old Senator Sherman, still bellicose in his old age, and already appointed Secretary of State in McKinley's cabinet, was quoted (though he later denied it) by a Hearst Washington correspondent as saying: 'If the facts are true . . . and American citizens are being murdered in Cuba in cold blood, the only way to put an end to the atrocities is to declare war on Spain.'[16] The *Journal* editorial on that day proudly said: 'War is a dreadful thing but there are things more dreadful even than war and one of them is dishonour.'[17] Hearst had already given a jewelled sword to another journalist-adventurer, Ralph Paine,[18] to be handed to Máximo Gómez if he were able to get through to him. Several yachts in Hearst's pay also hung about the coast of Florida waiting for a gap in the U.S. coastguard sloops which might let them through, with cargoes of medicine, reporters and ammunition.

It was not only Hearst who now trumpeted war but also Pulitzer, moving restlessly from one to another of his mansions in the country or in France, or in his yacht *Liberty*. He later freely admitted that he backed war because of its possible effects on his paper's circulation.[19] In 1897 Pulitzer's papers had a circulation of over 800,000 a day, and Hearst's 700,000. The *Sun*, also pro-war in theory at least, had merely 80,000.[20] Anti-war papers (*Herald, Tribune, Post* and *Times*) had a total circulation of 225,000.[21] Further, in early March 1897, after McKinley's inauguration, the Cuban junta had friends in Washington as well as in the New York press. True, the new Secretary of State, Sherman, was as usual in such instances more cautious in office than he had been in opposition. Nevertheless he appears to have thought war with Spain inevitable though, as one author put it, in Sherman it 'was not possible to discern the outlines of a policy'.[22] Real power in the State Department lay more with the first and second Assistant Secretaries, Day[23] and Adee.[24] The

[16] *Ibid.*, 22 February.
[17] *Loc. cit.*
[18] Ralph Paine (1871–1925).
[19] W. G. Bleyer, *Main Currents in the History of American Journalism* (1927), 342.
[20] Swanberg, 116.
[21] Wisan, 231.
[22] Leech, *In the Days of McKinley*, 151.
[23] William Rufus Day (1849–1923), lawyer and judge.
[24] Alvey Adee (1842–1924), ex-secretary of legation in Madrid.

other members of the cabinet were scarcely men of vigour: typical of them all was the old-fashioned Naval Secretary Long, dreaming of his farm at Buckfield, Maine.[25] President McKinley himself seemed less of a friend of the Cubans in March than he had in December: he did not mention Cuba in his inaugural speech, besides rather disappointingly saying 'the U.S. will never undertake a war without exhausting all ways of avoiding it'. Before inauguration he had remarked to outgoing President Cleveland: 'If I can only go out of office ... with the know-ledge that I have done what lay in my power to arrest this terrible calamity [i.e. war] ... I shall be the happiest man in the world.'[26]

But if the president and the elderly cabinet members were distinctly calmer (or more vacillating) than might have been anticipated, younger members of the administration were not, in particular the new Assistant Secretary of the Navy, old Long's aide, Theodore Roosevelt: 'Roosevelt came down here [i.e. to Washington] looking for war,' reported the Pennsylvania congressman Thomas Butler years later;[27] 'he did not care whom he fought so long as there was a scrap.' Why? In an address to the Naval War College on 2 June, Roosevelt explained:

> A wealthy nation is an easy prey for any people which still retains the most valuable of all qualities, the soldierly virtues ... Peace is a goddess only when she comes with sword girt on thigh ... No triumph of peace is quite so great as the supreme triumphs of war ... the diplo-mat is the servant, not the master of the soldier.[28] [Later in the year he explained in private in greater detail:] I would regard the war with Spain from two viewpoints: first the advisability, on the ground of humanity and self interest, of interfering on behalf of the Cubans and taking one more step toward the complete freedom of America from European domination; *second, the benefit done to our people by giving them something to think of which isn't material gain and especially the benefit done our military forces by trying both the army and the navy in actual practice.*[29]

McKinley had not wanted to appoint Roosevelt: 'He is too pugnacious ... I want peace,' he said. But Senator Lodge, Maria Stoner and Judge William Taft all urged Roosevelt's nomination and McKinley, ready to please these powerful lobbyists, eventually agreed.[30]

Roosevelt by now desired a stronger and more competent navy for

[25] John Davis Long (1838–1915), lawyer; ex-governor of Massachusetts.
[26] J. F. Rhodes, *The McKinley and Roosevelt Administrations, 1897–1909* (1932), 41.
[27] In a letter to H. F. Pringle, Roosevelt's biographer; Pringle, 71.
[28] *The Works of Theodore Roosevelt*, ed. H. Hagedorn, 20 vols (1926), XIV, 182–99; Roosevelt won the Nobel Peace Prize in 1906.
[29] In a letter to Commander Kimball (the author of the 1896 war plans of naval intelli-gence), qu. Pringle, 175–6.
[30] Beale, 55. A more sophisticated version appears in May, 121–2.

several reasons. He had always made a hobby of naval matters. He co-operated with Captain Mahan ('To no one else except Lodge do I talk like this,' he said).[31] He wanted a Central American isthmus canal and to promote independent-minded admirals such as Dewey, who he believed should lead the Far East Squadron. He was disturbed by German and other countries' behaviour in the Caribbean;[32] and he also wanted action himself and gave their head to the ambitious and far-sighted group of naval officers working under him.[33]

The McKinley administration was also served by another firebrand in a then critical position: General Fitzhugh Lee, Consul-General in Havana and nephew of Robert E. Lee, who had commanded a division of Confederate cavalry in the civil war, later being governor of Virginia.[34] Like Hearst's men, Davis and Remington, and other journalists, Lee lived at the Hotel Inglaterra in Havana. Like them, he sympathized with the rebels without venturing much out of Havana. His fat figure decked out in a white suit and panama hat, from the moment he arrived at Havana in April 1896 he worked for intervention by the U.S. in the war,[35] 'rolling intervention like a sweet morsel under his tongue', as Cleveland put it; he even suggested that Cleveland should foment a war over Cuba as a means of diverting the public imagination from unreal ills.[36] McKinley kept him on, though he also sent a private emissary, William J. Calhoun, on a secret mission to report conditions in Cuba.[37]

What, meantime, of the war situation? Weyler was now facing the problem of the sugar harvest of 1897. His plan was to ban grinding and to restrict the payment of funds to the rebels, except with official permission. Atkins elicited from him personally an agreement not to take action against him if he did grind.[38] In fact Weyler told Pin, his general at Cienfuegos, not to ban grinding, but to impede it by driving off cattle and cutting supplies. Atkins began to grind on a limited scale, hampered in this way. He wrote to the Spanish minister in Washington, De Lôme: 'As very many planters are absolutely without resources

[31] *Ibid.*, 56.
[32] Justifiably in the Luders case of 1897; Luders, son of a German and a Haitian, was imprisoned and fined for attacking a policeman in Haiti. Though he was released and allowed to leave, the German navy arrived at Port au Prince and threatened to shell the town unless a $30,000 indemnity was paid on the nail; the Haitians paid up (D. Munro, *Intervention and Dollar Diplomacy*, 14). Debt collection by force was a major international scandal.
[33] See J. A. Grenville, 'American Naval Preparations for War', *American Studies*, vol. 2, 1, 39.
[34] Fitzhugh Lee (1834–1905), governor of Virginia, 1886–90; he had three horses shot under him and was severely wounded at Winchester, Virginia.
[35] Atkins, 249.
[36] Lee to Cleveland, qu. May, *Imperial Democracy*, 89.
[37] H. Wayne Morgan, *William McKinley and his America*, 339. Calhoun (1848–1916) had previously been at the Illinois Bar and now began a diplomatic life.
[38] Atkins, 251.

either to make new plantings or to care for the few fields that are still left, they will have no crop another year and I can see little chance of their grinding again. The estates must pass into fresh hands with fresh capital.'[39] He was right.

After Maceo's death Weyler had first sought to establish the complete pacification of the west before turning to deal with Máximo Gómez. An instruction by him of 19 December 1896 gives a good impression of his tactics:

> I observe that the columns operating in Havana and Matanzas provinces, instead of camping in places or mountains frequented by the enemy, go nightly to the towns or mills in their zone to sleep. This has grave consequences for the operations, since it makes it easier for the enemy to know the route which the columns will take the next day, and also their number and morale. At the same time, the soldiers are more tired: ... for these reasons, please arrange that all columns of both provinces, when setting out for operations, take with them three days' worth of rations and four of biscuits; with these, and with the cattle that abound in these provinces, it is easy to sustain the forces for six days in operations, camping on the mountains and at crossroads being able from the encampments to send picked troops swiftly for reconnaissance for four kilometres around, while the encampment is being prepared. In this way the enemy will be kept in a constant state of uneasiness ... My aim is that during my stay in Pinar del Río there should not remain a place or a mountain which will not have been crossed by the responsible column, while all really suspicious places will have been camped in.[40]

Máximo Gómez had received the news of Maceo's death, and that of his son, when in Oriente. For a long time he assumed that Hearst had been right and that both had been murdered. His reserve and his ferocious desire to beat the Spaniards both received added strength; and his immediate reaction was to cross the Morón-Júcaro *trocha* back towards the west, aiming to return the war to the central provinces of Matanzas and Havana, which hitherto had suffered rather less than the extremities of the island. Gómez believed single-mindedly that the destruction of commerce could not fail to bring eventual defeat for the Spaniards. His aim in fact was to win without combat.

In early 1897 a Spanish Republican journalist, Luis Morote of *El Liberal* of Havana, succeeded in forcing his way into the presence of Gómez, who at first submitted him to court-martial and then sent him away with a letter, read after he was *en route* for Havana:

[39] Letter, qu. *ibid.*, 256.
[40] Fernández Almagro, II, 318.

Señor ... After your departure from my presence, I owe you an explanation, even though you write for a paper which condemns and wishes to bathe our most just aspiration in blood. I cannot be bloody; my temperament and education oppose this; yet I confess to you sincerely that in the circumstances [of his arrest] I feel there ought to have been no court-martial but ... that you ought to have been summarily executed as an act of true justice and national decorum ... I feel this because I have a natural need to shed Spanish blood to cure me of the grief caused by the events in Punta Brava [where his son was killed] ... The *machetazo* which killed Francisco Gómez will not be forgotten ... So go back to Spain. And tell your queen and the wife of the assassin [Colonel] Cirugeda that ... America is used to grief and sadness at Spain's hands, having had it since the days of Columbus, Ovando and Bobadilla ... And when you receive your fee for having visited me, please do not forget that we shall continue fighting for liberty and that justice from on high will eventually finish this cruel and bloody war which is carried on by Spain to its dishonour and ruin.[41]

Gómez was now seventy-three. Few commanders have ever been successful at his age. Yet he still showed himself a master of protecting his supplies, caring for his wounded, burying his dead. Weyler too was old and gave an example to the young officers under his command in resilience; Gómez was older still yet taught tenacity no less strongly. At the end of January 1897 he was encamped at Remedios with 3,000 men, awaiting another force of equal number being sent by Calixto García.[42] On 3 February he wrote to José de Jesús Monteagudo: 'The hour has come to fight with absolute tenacity. Don't waste men ... or horses and make use of the night. In these circumstances twenty men can easily conquer 1,000.'[43] But the arrival of Weyler with heavy reinforcements prevented any new invasion of the west. On 26 February 1897, Weyler could telegraph the Ministry of War saying that Pinar del Río, Havana and Matanzas were completely pacified; that the recent defeats of Máximo Gómez could have left him with only about fifty horses; that he expected that by the middle of March Las Villas, including Sancti Spiritus and Remedios, would also be pacified; and that in all provinces save Oriente, grinding could begin.[44] But this estimate was shown to be over-optimistic: a new rebellion gathered momentum in the province of Havana and sporadic fighting once more occurred everywhere in Matanzas and Las Villas. Even so, Gómez, Calixto

[41] Qu. Luis Morote, *Sagasta, Melilla, Cuba* (1908), 291–375.
[42] Fernández Almagro, 300.
[43] B. Souza, *Máximo Gómez, el Generalísimo* (1936), 185.
[44] Fernández Almagro, II, 325.

García and Quintín Banderas (in command in Matanzas) were cut off from each other, and the equipment of the *trocha* of Júcaro was so strong as to prevent movement very effectively.

By mid-1897 this line consisted of a complete chain of forts and battlements with local headquarters throughout its length. At Ciego de Avila in the centre there were six mobile pieces of mountain artillery ready to be taken where any breach of the *trocha* might be made. The country beyond the *trocha* was covered with wire and undergrowth for six kilometres to make surprise impossible. This prevented Calixto García from sending Gómez the aid he expected. The depression in the Cuban camp was such that on 28 April, Calixto García wrote complainingly to Gómez:

When can I try a new advance and what will the result be? Our remaining forces, already reduced by long and continuous marches as much as by battles, are fading away now ... it is essential to give them some rest, the shortest possible no doubt: and what I call rest, improperly ... is to let the men go back to their own homes, so that they at least may get clothes and so on ... I don't believe that even Maceo, who once took two or three thousand men west from Oriente, could today raise as many as five hundred ... In Maceo's invasion the troops went enthusiastically, in search of the unknown, experiencing that spirit of adventure which marks to a great extent the beginning of every revolution, believing they would find extraordinary rewards, attracted in the most part by the appeal of unusual noise and movement and galloping; it owed much to the imagination and to a certain, shall we say, *tropical* curiosity. Today, this region does not have the enthusiasm for invasion that it had then. It has lost the enchantment of the unknown, the adventurous spirit ... hundreds and hundreds of stragglers and others now repent of their past commitment; the rewards, after all, have not yet arrived ... and I know very many officers and leaders who, after very tough campaigns and truly uncountable sufferings, have returned to Oriente with the same rank with which they set out, disillusioned ... All this ... makes a return to the past impossible ... the natural desire to stay at home ... in the area where you have been brought up, and born and bred, and to have a family, all deriving from the parochialism and the love of home so highly developed in Cuba ... all this, and other reasons which I omit in order not to appear prolix, make it impossible, in my judgment, to take people from Oriente again to the West ... It was an effort in which Maceo after all failed and in which I would fail and in which I believe even you, with all your popularity, would fail ... I believe in short that you should disband the Army

of invasion . . . I desire as much as anyone that the day will come
when our army, duly disciplined and organised, is equipped so as to
move everywhere on the orders of its chief but . . . this is unhappily
far from reality and this cannot be changed in a day.[45]

There were already many divergencies in the rebel camp. Both
Gómez and García were naturally irritable old men – the latter had
now a bodyguard muttering *Ave Marías* behind his head whenever he
seemed likely to lose his temper.[46] García was indeed accused of having
promoted the deposition of Céspedes in 1874. The civilian president,
Cisneros Betancourt, was at loggerheads with Máximo Gómez. Máximo
Gómez indeed contemplated a kind of *golpe* to establish himself as
military dictator, and he seems not to have done so because of inadequate
forces rather than because of loyalty to the revolutionary government.
On 26 May Weyler could report to Madrid that even in Las Villas,
where Gómez still glowered in the far north-east corner, the trains were
now reaching the end of their lines. It seemed now that Weyler would
be able to finish off the war.

But he could not be left to himself. He was now the object of vociferous
attack by most liberal newspapers in Madrid such as *El Imparcial* and
Heraldo de Madrid. Secondly, a new colonial war had opened for Spain
in the Philippines, Spain's only other large colony: the expense and
strain of two such running conflicts was immense. The Philippine
captains-general – Blanco, Polavieja, Primo de Rivera[47] – needed men
and supplies as much as Weyler. Their troops were worn down by
yellow fever just as those in Cuba were. They too were trapped into a
permanent expense of effort and money against an elusive enemy able
to rely on the nearly unanimous support of the local population.

At the same time, it was realized in Madrid that even though Weyler
might succeed in Cuba, the real question concerned more and more
Washington. The only hope for Spanish public opinion therefore was
that the war should end quickly. Weyler's methods seemed too slow.
The government was confused since health in the army left so much to
be desired, although elaborate diagrams were prepared which proved
that the incidence of death from yellow fever was lower than in the last
year of the last war, 1876–7.[48] The military administration in Cuba
was accused of many enormities, most of them justified. Costs seemed
enormous, and the only satisfaction was that derived by the Marqués de
Comillas's *Compañía Transatlántica*, which dealt with shipping to Cuba.
But there was still hardly any criticism from the Left. Only Pi y Margall

[45] Weyler, *Mi mando en Cuba*, IV, 289–92.
[46] Leech, 123.
[47] Uncle of the future dictator.
[48] See the diagram at the back of Weyler, *Memoirs*, III.

mentioned independence and even he suggested that any new republic should take on the Cuban debt – including the costs of war.[49] Both Carlists and Republicans believed that the prolongation of the war would mean the collapse of the constitutional monarchy.[50] In early 1897 the returning captain-general of the Philippines, Polavieja, was greeted as a possible dictator to succeed Cánovas and pushed as such by the Catholic Right headed by the archbishop of Valladolid. The Catalan separatist movement also regarded the possible grant of autonomy in Cuba as immensely encouraging to themselves.

Cánovas had been waiting, in fact, for a favourable opportunity to introduce constitutional reforms for Cuba and in February 1897 these were announced: fairly strong powers to local governments and mayors; a numerical superiority (21 to 14) of elected over nominated members of a legislature; two years' residence only would constitute eligibility to vote; there would be a measure of fiscal independence; local administrators would be mostly locally born, though not the captain-general. Cuba would continue to be represented in the Cortes. These reforms were perhaps primarily introduced to indicate to the McKinley administration that something was being done, and they certainly went further than the reforms of Abárzuza. President McKinley and his Secretary of State Sherman nevertheless admitted that the reforms were 'as much as could be asked for and more than could be expected'.[51] As for the press, the *World*, *Journal* and the *Sun* predictably denounced the reforms as bogus, but the *Herald*, *Evening Post* and *New York Times* were generally favourable.[52] No doubt the administration's views were at least partly dictated by the visits paid by the ever diligent Edwin Atkins to the 'President and some of his cabinet, who seemed much interested in learning about the actual condition of affairs on the island'.[53] This response encouraged both Cánovas and Weyler to suppose that the U.S. might even be prepared to restrict the activities of the junta in New York from, for instance, sending supplies and new men to Cuba. A Senate debate urging the release of U.S. citizens in Spanish hands revealed that many were in fact really Cuban, and for several months to McKinley's relief this discredited the cause of Cuba, even in the columns of the *Journal* and the *World*.

By early summer Weyler's optimism about ending the war quickly was considerable. The only outstanding rebel leader left in west Cuba,

[49] Interview reported in *La Patrie* (Paris), 23 January 1897, qu. Fernández Almagro, II, 389.
[50] Fernández Almagro, II, 397.
[51] Dupuy de Lôme to Duque de Tetuán, *Documentos presentados a las Cortes en La Legislatura de 1898 por el Ministro de Estado*, 14, 21, qu. *ibid.*, 391. In Spain the proposed reforms were supported by men as varied as Maura and Labra.
[52] 5 February 1897, qu. Wisan.
[53] Atkins, 263.

Quintin Banderas, was surrounded. Maximo Gomez in Santa Clara had a very limited following and beyond that only Oriente (outside the towns) remained to be subdued, although, of course, that province is always the most difficult to conquer. Spanish optimism had been generally raised by the virtual extinction of the Philippine rebellion. The cost of the war in men and in cash, however, weighed on all minds: 200,000 men had been sent to Cuba, a larger army than had ever crossed the Atlantic and huge bond issues had been sold. The danger of U.S. intervention was known. The consequence was that the war in mid 1897 undoubtedly still posed a menace to the Restoration political system.

On 17 June Estrada Palma from New York, still President of the Cuban Junta in New York, wrote to General Calixto García:

I understand . . . your difficult situation. The truth is that the forces of Oriente and Camagüey are the only ones which have been fully mobilised – in this war as in the last. General Roloff you remember had the idea of crossing from Las Villas to Camagüey to arm himself and arrange from there a convoy of munitions. Unarmed men cannot of course now cross the *trocha* . . . otherwise that would have been the rational way to increase the Las Villas forces. . . . I am now making a special appeal to emigrants for funds. I have little confidence in the result because in truth those who have any patriotic ardour left have small and diminishing financial resources and the rich, with few exceptions, are deaf to the voice of duty. Many of them, no doubt. would see Cuba submitted anew to Spain with pleasure . . . In the provinces of Las Villas, Matanzas and Havana the proprietors of sugar mills who have been able to grind cane have done so without contributing a peso to the Treasury of the Republic. In Camagüey one single *ingenio*, mostly owned by Americans, has paid regularly a monthly contribution in accord with the agreement made by the owners last September . . . At the end of August, I made an agreement with another New York house and I got over 30,000 pesos promised. If the harvest is carried out, we must at all costs ensure the destruction of some great *ingenio* in Cienfuegos, such as that of the American Atkins who has been so hostile to our cause . . . or that of Apezteguía . . . I have a list of the *ingenios* who are grinding cane and I am sending them a letter demanding contributions.[54]

A week later, the Secretary of State, Sherman, was found sending a note to Spain protesting against Weyler's methods. The Duque de Tetuán, Cánovas's Foreign Minister (nephew of the ex-captain-general

[54] Letter in Fernández Almagro, II, 831–4.

O'Donnell), replied that the protest must surely have been inspired by incorrect information in Washington. Admitting that the war was hard, he pointed out that the American Civil War had also been hard; he referred to the invasion of Generals Hunter and Sheridan down the Shenandoah, to the activities of General Sherman in Georgia and to other dark memories in U.S. history. He even quoted from Sherman's memoirs to justify Weyler; and he referred to the fact that Máximo Gómez had first ordered the firing of canefields, and had been the first therefore to declare total war.[55]

Four days after the date this despatch was signed, Cánovas, the architect of the constitutional restoration, was murdered by an Italian anarchist, Miguel Angiolillo, in an hotel at Santa Agueda in northern Spain. The assassin later told Cánovas's widow that he had acted to avenge the death of the anarchist prisoners in Montjuich.[56] Angiolillo, a railwayman, was a dedicated regicide and apparently left Italy with the firm intention of putting an end, by a single blow, to at least one evil regime. But it seems that the Cuban rebels were also involved in this murder: for in Paris, Angiolillo had met several times Dr Ramón Emeterio Betances, the Cuban agent. Betances, a doctor born in Puerto Rico, was, according to one colleague, a man very much of the generation of 1848, a romantic exile with heavy beard, flowing hair and sonorous conversation. He gave Angiolillo 500 francs to go to Spain, and explained too that it would not profit his cause to kill the king or the queen mother of Spain, since the death of a woman and a child would cause horror; further, the monarch and his mother had now no real influence on the government of Spain. 'The name of Cánovas then came up spontaneously in the course of the conversation', and Angiolillo, his fare paid by the Cuban representative, then travelled from Paris to Spain and made Cánovas his first victim.[57]

Betances undeniably served his cause well, though he was at pains later to point out that he was not wholly responsible. Still, had it not been for him, the assassin would not have reached Spain and would not have killed Cánovas. Cánovas was the ablest statesman in Spain and Cuba's most redoubtable enemy, as much even as Weyler, for Weyler needed Cánovas to sustain him.

A cabinet crisis in Spain naturally followed. After a series of short-lived attempts at Conservative government, the queen mother sent

[55] Qu. *ibid.*, 835–41.

[56] *Ibid.*, 624–8, 'Cánovas, su vida y política'. On 30 April 1897, the Spanish cabinet had approved the execution of five anarchists, the perpetual imprisonment of thirteen, ten years for seven, as a result of the recent anarchist crimes in the Calle de Cambios Nuevos, Barcelona.

[57] Orestes Ferrara, *Mis Relaciones con Máximo Gómez* (1942), 49–52. Estrada Palma told the *World*: 'While I have no sympathy with the assassin, I cannot help but feel that the act was one of retribution. He [Cánovas] was the cause of the cruelties of the Spanish troops in Cuba. I cannot help but feel I am benefited by it.' (*World*, 9 August 1897.)

finally for the old Liberal leader, Sagasta, the only real alternative even though he had recently become convinced of the desirability of autonomy for Cuba. The astute Moret, author of the slavery law of 1870, became Minister of the Colonies, a clear sign of a changed policy since he had always been a friend of the Autonomists and in July had stated in a speech at Saragossa that Cuba ought to get the same dominion status as Canada.[58]

When Cánovas died, Weyler was at Aguacate, preparing for an autumn campaign against Oriente. He made no change in his dispositions, though he must have felt that recall was near. Sagasta disliked Weyler and his policy. Calixto García meantime initiated an attack in Puerto Príncipe with 5,000 men, with five cannon commanded by a young colleague, General Mario Menocal, capturing the centrally placed town of Victoria de la Tunas (so named by the Spaniards after their victory there in the previous war).[59] But he was still far from Máximo Gómez in Remedios. And in September a new revolutionary government had to be elected, for it was two years since the start of the war. There was a nearly complete change in personnel: Masó, old rival of Maceo, became President; Professor Domingo Méndez Capote became the Vice-President; the Secretaries of War, External Affairs, Interior and Finance were respectively José Alemán, Andrés Moreno de la Torre, Manuel Silva and Ernesto Font. All these men were ciphers. They played no part in the conflict, and merely hoped for a victory which seemed increasingly remote unless the U.S. acted.

But the only possibility for action in mid-1897 seemed (at least before Canovas's murder) to be a revival of the old idea of purchase: a syndicate of U.S. bankers headed by Samuel Janney and Colonel John McCook, a prominent Republican and friend of McKinley,[60] agreed in August 1897 with the Cuban junta to make arrangements to pay off the Cuban debt to Spain by a fifty-year lien on Cuban customs. But negotiations in this delicate matter were not formal till the end of the year.[61]

A new exploit of the *Journal* had taken precedence over the conflict, in the eyes of North Americans at least. In August a Cuban girl, Evangelina Cisneros, daughter of a rebel imprisoned since June 1895, had first secured her father's removal from Ceuta (Morocco) to the Isle of Pines and then attempted to effect his escape by kidnapping the commander of the island, Colonel Berris. Evangelina was then caught herself and

[58] Fernández Almagro, II, 423–4.
[59] See description of this battle in Ferrer, *Con el rifle al hombro*, 78–91.
[60] John James McCook (1845–1911), youngest of the Ohio 'fighting McCooks' in the Civil War; lawyer.
[61] See Portell Vilá, *Historia* III, 348–61; Santovenia, *Actas de las Asambleas de Representantes y del Consejó de Gobierno, etc.* (Havana, 1932), III, 68–70.

sent for trial. The *Journal* took up her case with gusto: 'This tenderly nurtured girl was imprisoned at eighteen among the most depraved Negresses of Havana. Now she is about to be sent in mockery to spend years in a servitude that will kill her in a year ...'[62] Hearst instructed his drunken but loyal toady Sam Chamberlain, to 'get up a petition to the Queen Regent of Spain ... Enlist the women of America ... Wake up our correspondents all over the country.'[63] All two hundred Hearst correspondents in the U.S. called on prominent local women to get their support. This was forthcoming, from women as various as the mother of President McKinley, the widow of President Grant, Mrs Mark Hanna, Frances Hodgson Burnett and Julia Ward Howe;[64] the last named sent a petition to Pope Leo XIII.

Evangelina Cisneros however was still only awaiting trial. Nor, as even Fitzhugh Lee admitted, was she badly treated. The small circulation papers of the U.S. pointed out that 'nine-tenths of the statements about Miss Cisneros ... seem to have been sheer falsehood'.[65] But Hearst decided to rescue her. He sent another reporter, Karl Decker, to do so, by bribing the prison guards at Las Recojidas prison. Decker pulled this off, smuggling her, dressed as a sailor, to an American steamer and landing her successfully in New York to face an open-air reception on Madison Square. Hearst's euphoria was predictable: 'An American Newspaper Accomplishes at a Single Stroke what the best efforts of diplomacy failed utterly to bring about in many months.'[66] It was a brilliant move in the *Journal*'s war against the *World*. An editor remarked later that Hearst took

> the whole affair with the utmost seriousness ... if ever for a moment he doubted that he was battering a powerful state to save the life and liberty of a sorely persecuted girl martyr, he gave no sign of it. It was the one dominating, all compelling issue ... and he brooked no indifference on the part of his employees ...[67]

While the *Journal* with energy and vulgarity was inflating its circulation at Weyler's expense ('BAFFLED WEYLER RAGES AT THE JOURNAL')[68] General Weyler finally resigned on the ground that he knew of the predisposition of Moret and Sagasta in favour of Autonomy. The resignation was accepted by Sagasta and Moret in the face of impas-

[62] *Journal*, 18 August 1899.

[63] Creelman, 180. Sam Chamberlain (1851-1916), afterwards supervising editor of all Hearst's papers.

[64] Julia Ward Howe, author of the Battle Hymn of the Republic; the most famous North American woman of her time.

[65] *Commercial Advertiser*, 9 September 1897.

[66] *Journal*, 10 October.

[67] W. J. Abbott, *Watching the World Go By*, 216.

[68] *Journal*, 12 October 1897.

sioned pleas from merchants and business men of Havana for Weyler to stay. Sagasta wanted a captain-general who would lead the way to autonomy and, more important still, who would avoid antagonizing the U.S. quite to the point of intervention. Weyler's reputation in the U.S. was so terrible as by itself to make war with them more likely. His successor was General Ramón Blanco, indecisive and an appeaser, who had been in command in the Philippines before the last insurrection. Weyler returned to Spain to be widely cheered, but he conducted himself quietly and with dignity, avoided antagonizing anyone and made no attempt to capitalize on his great reputation. Attempts by the Carlists to secure his backing failed even after he had agreed to meet Don Carlos on an English yacht.[69]

Blanco announced in his first address to the Cubans that his government had completely changed its policy and that he had come to give them self-government – to sweep away all who had taken up arms against the country but to embrace anew all who lived 'within the law'.[70] His instructions were to drop all new attempts at offensives and to maintain the lines as they then were. On 6 November Moret in Madrid announced a full amnesty for all political prisoners in both Cuba and Puerto Rico: Máximo Gómez replied with a command which promised a court-martial to any Cuban officer who availed himself of it.

The mood in Spain in the winter of 1897–8 was one of growing realism. It began to be appreciated that self-government would in the end be granted: it was a question of what sort. The losses of Spanish men were recognized. In November it was announced that 200,000 officers and men had left for Cuba since the beginning of the rebellion, all singing 'the March of Cádiz', setting off with mixed enthusiasm and fear. Of these, only 53,000 were still in the front line in Cuba: over 26,000 were sick; over 35,000 were doing other duties. Where were the rest? – asked *El Imparcial* of Havana at the end of November:[71] the only positive answer seemed to be: dead, from disease, and not from action.

It is impossible to know what would have been the consequence of this new mood in Spain, had it not been for changes in the U.S. But in its first nine months of office McKinley's administration, though less active than it had promised to be before capturing power, had not been idle. The new envoy to Spain, General Stewart L. Woodford, arrived in San Sebastián on 13 September 1897, and presented to the government a long Note stating in firm terms that unless by 31 October peaceful measures were taken to end the conflict in Cuba, the U.S. herself would

---

[69] F. M. Melgar, *Veinte Años con Don Carlos* (1940), 216–17. Weyler refused to meet Don Carlos if anyone else was present but the latter's wife, María Berta de Rohán, a French woman of interfering habits, refused to let her husband out of her sight.

[70] Fernández Almagro, II, 431.

[71] 30 November 1897, qu. *ibid.*, 434.

have to take steps to see that that occurred.[72] On 23 October the new Spanish Foreign Minister, Pío Gullón, answered by promising that the new ministry had indeed embarked on a change of 'immense scope'. There would be 'real self-government', whereby the Cubans would be both the 'regulators' of their own life and also partake of the 'integral nationality' of Spain. In the meantime, military operations would be kept as humane as possible. The situation was anyway very different from what it had been when 'the hosts of Maceo and Máximo Gómez' were overrunning the provinces of Havana and Pinar del Río. Gullón also asked for a 'clarification' of the U.S. Note's mention of its duty to make the strongest effort towards peace. U.S. recognition of belligerency of the Cubans for instance would be so unjust, so unjustifiable, so contrary to the correct procedure that it was dismissed as 'utterly improbable'. Meantime, the Spaniard went on, Cuba's economic recovery had begun.[73]

On 22 November Moret told the Cortes of the projected reformed Constitution, which would apply to all colonies. It went further than the programme of the old Autonomist party. There would be equal rights between Spaniards and Cubans: both could vote. There would be universal suffrage and a local parliament divided into two chambers, the first freely elected, for five years, the second partly nominated by the captain-general. The Cubans and the Puerto Ricans (who had as yet experienced no rebellion since 1869) would have local governmental powers, including even the right to draw up their own budget, but the captain-general would be responsible for internal order and for foreign affairs.[74]

This new scheme was an attempt therefore to embrace Cuba in a modified version of the Spanish Constitution of 1876. Whether this could work in 1897–8 depended simply on whether it would be accepted by Gómez and the rebels. For the rebellion, though weakened and incapable of military victory, was still strong enough to prevent a peaceful settlement and to ensure a continuation of the vile conditions of the concentration; their spirit of resistance was maintained, partly by the U.S. press. Though the *Herald* was favourable to the proposals for autonomy,[75] the *Journal* said the Cubans would be fools to trust the Spaniards, and the *Mail-Express* spoke of Liberty still in chains.[76]

---

[72] *Foreign Relations of the U.S. transmitted to Congress*, 5 December 1898, 567–8. Stewart Lyndon Woodford (1835–1913), lawyer and soldier; McKinley's private agent; made much, in conversations with the Spanish government and with his fellow ambassadors, of the fact that Cuba was the source of yellow fever in the Southern U.S. (*ibid.*, 573).

[73] *Ibid.*, 582–9.

[74] Text of these plans signed by the queen regent on 25 November can be most easily found in *ibid.*, 617–44.

[75] 27 November 1897.

[76] Wisan, 351.

McKinley, on the other hand, in his annual address on 6 December though he spent some time deploring Weyler's brutality, urged that the Sagasta administration be given a

> reasonable chance to realise her expectations ... The near future will demonstrate whether the indispensable condition of a righteous peace just alike to Cubans and to Spaniards ... is likely to be obtained. If not, the exigency of further and other action by the U.S. will remain to be taken. When that time comes [McKinley continued ponderously if delphically] that action will be determined in the line of indisputable right and duty ... *If it shall hereafter appear to be a duty*[77] imposed on us by our obligations to ourselves, to civilisation, and to humanity, to intervene with force, it shall be without fault on our part and only because the necessity for such action will be so clear as to command the support and approval of the civilised world.[78]

Most Americans and most American papers were satisfied with these responsible words, although as usual the *Sun*, the *World* and the *Journal* gave some criticism. The Assistant Secretary of the Navy, Theodore Roosevelt, however, had already dispatched Commodore Dewey to the Asiatic Squadron with orders to attack Manila if war came.[79] In Cuba itself, Moret's plans were gravely hampered by the fact that opinion was nicely divided between loyalists and separatists with very little real support being available for Autonomy.

[77] Author's italics.
[78] Messages of the Presidents. This had also been the spirit of Sherman's dispatch of 20 November to Woodford in Madrid (*Foreign Relations* (1898), 603–11).
[79] See the Sicard war plan, Appendix III to J. A. Grenville, 'American Naval Preparations or War with Spain 1896–1898', *American Studies*, vol. 2, 1, 33–47.

CHAPTER XXX

The Maine

In early December 1897 General Fitzhugh Lee, U.S. Consul at Havana, sent back a message about rumours of 'an extensive and dangerous' anti-American conspiracy in Havana and urged that a strong naval force be concentrated off the Florida Keys 'ready to move here at short notice'.[1] He had previously made such a suggestion and had been repelled.[2] The battleship *Maine*, which had been launched in 1890 and embodied the very idea of the new navy, was therefore ordered to Key West, ready to go to Havana when Fitzhugh Lee gave the word, to protect U.S. lives and property if it should be necessary. (Lee was told to communicate every day with the *Maine*; if a day passed without a message, the *Maine* would sail.)

Lee had thus laid the fuse which would ultimately realize Theodore Roosevelt's dream of strife. But for a little time more there was no bellicosity. The rumour of which Lee talked was not substantiated, nor substantiable. President McKinley made an appeal for contributions of food, money and clothing to be sent to Cuba for the sufferers in the war. Godkin in the *Evening Post* once again denounced the jingoes: 'What of those single-minded, single-gaitered patriots who announced their willingness to wade knee-deep in blood for the salvation of their brothers of the machete?'[3] Hearst meantime had been temporarily diverted to organize a celebration to mark the formal merger of Brooklyn with New York City, while the junta in New York was still privately negotiating with the banker Janney for the purchase of Cuban independence.

In Havana the first home rule government was duly constituted, under the aegis of Spain, its leaders being a coalition of the old Autonomist party and the Reformists. The prime minister, José María Gálvez, had been an Autonomist leader from the beginning in the 1870s. Other ministers were Antonio Govín (Interior and Justice), a lawyer, previously of the radical wing of the Autonomist party and an exile in New York during Weyler's command; Dr Francisco Zayas, a physician (Education); the Marqués de Montoro (Treasury); Dr Eduardo Dolz

---

[1] C. D. Sigsbee, *The 'Maine' : an account of her destruction in Havana Harbor, etc.* (1899) 23.
[2] May, 91.
[3] *Evening Post*, 4 January 1898.

(Communications and Transport), a leading *Reformista*; and Laureano Rodríguez, a prominent merchant, Secretary for Agriculture, also a *Reformista*. Edwin Atkins, arriving in Havana in mid-January, wrote that after talking with Montoro and another autonomist, Fernández de Castro, 'all autonomists feel hopeful over the situation but the public generally does not feel so, because the insurgents hold out. I found no opposition to autonomy anywhere, but a general sentiment now pervades the whole community for annexation . . . All the better class Cubans fear independence.'[4]

This autonomist government was of course not backed by the conservatives of the Constitutional Union, to whom the word autonomy was as bad as independence. They remained inexorably assimilationist, knowing that they had many friends in Madrid, from the Carlists to the industrialists of Barcelona. In fact, many newspapers in Spain, even the Liberal *Heraldo*, opposed autonomy. *El Nacional* complained that the government was ensuring 'for the Antilles, all the benefits. For Spain, all the inconveniences'.[5] In Havana, the Constitutional Union organized a large demonstration against the new administration, and this went to the editorial offices of the conservative *Diario de la Marina*, crying 'Long Live the Volunteers!' and 'Down with Autonomy!'[6] The condition of Cuba this winter indeed gave no reason for optimism of any kind; deaths in the concentration camps from starvation were daily occurrences. In Matanzas several thousand women raided the market in October, pandemonium lasting an hour or more. Coffins ran out in interior towns.[7] In Havana homeless vagrants from the country spent the day begging, and slept in doorways at night. The authorities made space for some of these in the old city walls and distributed some rough *rancho* soup to them – beans, pork, potatoes, lentils and so on.[8] Out of the 50,000 to 60,000 people then in Matanzas 14,000 were 'absolutely without food and clothing, and 11,000 without homes or shelter'.[9]

The riots in Havana against autonomy were renewed on 12 January with remarkable and indeed, irreversible consequences. A new pro-Spanish but anti-military paper, *El Reconcentrado*, published a short paragraph headed 'Flight of the scoundrels', which ran: 'In the steamer *Monserrat* there left for the mother country Captain Sánchez, executor of those terrible orders of Senor Maruri, whom we all remember.'[10] This captain had been a close collaborator of Weyler and the

[4] Atkins, 266.
[5] Qu. Fernández Almagro, II, 443.
[6] *Ibid.*, 443–4.
[7] *Foreign Relations* 1898 (report of U.S. Consul Brice, *El Correo de Matanzas*, 30 September 1898).
[8] Report of Vice-Consul-General Joseph Springer, 20 October 1897, *ibid.*, 598–9.
[9] Report of commanding officer of *USS Montgomery*, 6 February 1898, *ibid.*, 669.
[10] Qu. Fernández Almagro, II, 454.

article of course implied criticism of the army. A group of officers, remembering no doubt the *tenientada* of nearly three years before in Madrid, went to beat up the offices of *El Reconcentrado*. They caused little damage, but there were further angry crowds in the streets, and gatherings of people who wanted to protest against the army, some Spaniards, some Cubans.[11] General Fitzhugh Lee was purposefully about in the crowd, looking at this man or that with Anglo-Saxon impatience, and it is evident that, either wilfully or innocently, he overestimated the crisis. He telegraphed: 'Mobs, led by Spanish officers, attacked today the offices of the four newspapers here advocating autonomy.'[12] Later he telegraphed 'much excitement, which may develop into serious disturbances' which no doubt could have been construed as threatening U.S. interests.[13] At the same time, he also sent the word to Captain Sigsbee, commander of the *Maine*, to prepare for the voyage to Havana to protect U.S. interests.[14]

The next day the *Journal*, under the headline 'NEXT DOOR TO WAR WITH SPAIN', ran a story of U.S. citizens taking refuge with the consul.[15] This was not true. The *World* announced 'THE RIOTS IN HAVANA MEAN REVOLUTION'. The *Sun* reported the continuation of the riots for the next four days. All this was quite untrue.[16] On 14 January even Fitzhugh Lee reported all quiet, and repeated this in succeeding days. Even so, the administration in Washington thought that U.S. lives and property must be in danger: should not the *Maine* go to Havana? On 24 January, Judge Day of the State Department asked the Spanish minister if the administration could send the *Maine* to Havana, 'purely as a mark of friendship', and to 'please Spanish opinion, disturbed by speeches in the Spanish legislature'.[17] The Spanish government eventually agreed and the Secretary of the Navy, Long, and Day both went to McKinley. McKinley believed that the most serious threat of war derived from the possible injury to U.S. citizens in Havana. So to fulfil this aim, he dispatched the *Maine* on its way.[18] Spain got permission, also, for the cruiser *Vizcaya* to go to New York, on a friendly visit.

Fitzhugh Lee was alarmed, or at least said he was, and urged delay.

---

[11] See also Atkins.

[12] *Foreign Relations*, 671.

[13] *Loc. cit.*

[14] See C. D. Sigsbee, *Personal Narrative of the Battleship Maine*, 11. Charles Dwight Sigsbee (1845-1923); at Mobile Bay, 1864; later admiral; author of *Deep Sea Sounding and Dredging* (1880).

[15] *Journal*, 13 January 1898.

[16] Wisan, 324-5. For Wayne Morgan (*ibid.*, 352) to argue that these riots could shake McKinley's 'faith in Spanish ability to reform Cuba' is utterly misleading.

[17] Telegram from Ministerio del Ultramar to Secretary General, Habana, 25 January 1898, '*desagraviar opinión española por discursos Cámaras españolas*'; cf. *Foreign Relations*, 1025.

[18] D. Long, *The New American Navy*, 2 vols (1909), I, 134-7; Chadwick, *Diplomacy*, 533-5; *Foreign Relations*, 1026-8.

Looking into the abyss which by exaggeration, self-importance and intolerance he himself had opened up, did this old warrior have second thoughts? But the *Maine* was at sea.

The *Maine* was well received in Havana and its captain went to the bullfight with the Spanish commander. By this time the autonomist government in Havana had settled in well and had issued a first appeal, sober and balanced, to the best-intentioned citizens. The Cuban shadow government in the hills meantime formally approved a contract with the banker Janney of New York by which this financier and his friends undertook less to buy Cuba from Spain than to bribe Washington opinion to get the administration to cajole the Spaniards out of Cuba.[19] President McKinley and the Spanish minister to Washington, Dupuy de Lôme,[20] meanwhile, exchanged friendly words at a diplomatic dinner on 26 January.[21] On 17 January the Spanish queen mother had, in a secret interview with the U.S. minister, requested McKinley to denounce the rebels publicly and break up the Junta, in return for the dismissal of Weyler and the establishment of autonomy which she said had been concessions to the U.S.[22] The Junta in New York, on the other hand, was still busy: on 1 February 1898 Estrada Palma wrote to a companion:

> The notes which have been weekly reaching the hands of the President ... will contribute sharply to making up his mind. All of them have set out to demonstrate that, while the Cuban people do not now desire annexation to the U.S. or even need it, *they are desirous that the American government in some manner manage to provide a guarantee for the internal peace of our country,* so that the Republic of Cuba will inspire sufficient confidence among foreign capitalists.[23]

This was a point of view firmly expressed in a letter by a committee of New York businessmen on 9 February.[24]

It was, however, another letter which finally brought on the crisis. Early in December Dupuy de Lôme had written to the brilliant editor of the Madrid *El Heraldo*, Canalejas, who was then in New York, attempting to negotiate unofficially on Spain's behalf with the Junta.[25] He had not answered Dupuy's letter before he left for Havana. In Havana he rashly engaged a temporary secretary, Gustavo Escoto, who

[19] See David Healy, *The U.S. in Cuba 1898–1902* (1963), 15.
[20] Enrique Dupuy de Lôme (1851–1904).
[21] *Spanish Correspondence* (1898), para. 54.
[22] Woodford to McKinley, qu. May, 162–3.
[23] Manuel Sanguily, in a review of '*La Enmienda Platt*' in *Cuba Contemporánea*, XXX, 123. This was perhaps the genesis of the Platt Amendment.
[24] 70 New York, 40 Philadelphia, 64 Mobile firms signed (J. W. Pratt, *Expansionists of 1898* (1936), 250).
[25] Canalejas, later prime minister, murdered by an anarchist in 1912.

was in sympathy with the rebels. Escoto came across the minister's letter in a file, read it and passed it to his friends of the junta.[26] Estrada Palma immediately took the letter to the *Journal* and thereafter to all the newspapers of New York, though the *Journal* alone was given the right to publish a facsimile.[27] At the same time, the junta's lawyer, Horatio Rubens, took a copy of the letter to Judge Day at the State Department in Washington, telling him it would appear in print the next day. Day went to confront Dupuy de Lôme, who admitted it was his, and resigned before even the U.S. could ask for his recall.[28]

The letter ran:[29]

My dear friend,

You haven't got to make excuses for not having written. I should have written myself but did not, due to pressure of work. We are quits. Here, the situation is unchanged. All depends on what happens, politically and militarily in Cuba ... The prologue to all this, this second stage. of the war, will come to an end when the colonial [Autonomist] cabinet is named and we rid ourselves, in the eyes of the Americans, of responsibility for what is happening and what must befall the Cubans, who believe themselves so immaculate. Up till now, we cannot see clearly; I consider it a waste of time to despatch emissaries to the rebel camp on a false basis ...

The message [of President McKinley to Congress] *has disabused the rebels who hoped for something more and has also paralysed Congress: but I consider it bad. In addition to the natural and inevitable coarseness with which the message repeats everything said about Weyler by the Press and by Spanish public opinion, it shows once more McKinley for what he is, weak and popularity-seeking* [débil y populachero[30]] *and in addition a hack politician* [politicastro[31]] *who wants to keep all his options open and stand well with the jingoes of his party. But in practice, if things turn out ill and contrary to our interests, it will be our fault. I am in complete agreement with you: with no military success, nothing will happen here and, without a political as well as military success, there is always a danger of driving a section of public opinion, now not in favour of the government, towards the rebels.*

I don't believe that enough is made of the role of England. Almost all the journalistic rabble [*canalla periodística*] who infest this hotel are English and, in addition to the *Journal* correspondents, there are those from the most serious London newspapers. So far as I can see,

---

[26] Rubens, *Liberty*, 298.
[27] Abbott, 217–18, qu. Swanberg, 135.
[28] Rubens, *Liberty*, *loc. cit.*
[29] Author's translation from the text in Fernández Almagro, II, 458–9.
[30] The New York *Journal* translated this as 'weak and catering to the rabble'.
[31] Translated by the New York *Journal* as a 'low politician'.

the unique desire of England is that the Americans should amuse themselves with us and leave them in peace and, if there is a war, so much the better. That would remove what threatens them . . .

It would be very important (even if only for this reason) to concern ourselves with commercial relations and to send here a man of importance to make propaganda among senators and others who oppose the [Cuban] junta and to go on gathering the support of exiles. At present there is only Amblard, who I think gets too mixed up in minor politics. We must do something very big or we are lost.

Adela sends you her greetings and all we desire is that next year [i.e. 1898] may be the harbinger of peace and that it gives that New Year present to poor Spain.

Always your friend . . .
Enrique Dupuy de Lôme.

The main passage[32] in this letter caused a scandal when it was splattered all over the front page by the *Journal* on 11 February under the headline 'THE WORST INSULT TO THE UNITED STATES IN ITS HISTORY'. Along with insulting cartoons, the *Journal* appealed: 'Now let us have action immediate and decisive . . . the Flag of *Cuba Libre* ought to float over Morro Castle within a week.'[33] But the storm settled somewhat when Dupuy de Lôme left Washington; and Godkin's *Evening Post* spoke of an 'experienced diplomat who had maintained himself in a position of extreme difficulty with great resource and skill . . . brought low by a petty thief'. It scarcely seems appropriate indeed that a diplomat should be asked to leave Washington for calling McKinley a hack when members of his administration were calling him far worse.

Perhaps war could still now have been avoided. Perhaps the war-dreams of Roosevelt and Hearst, differently inspired but with the same goal, could have been thwarted. Perhaps Gálvez's autonomous government could still have proved itself. But four days later, the atmosphere changed radically for the worse when at 9.40 p.m. on the evening of 15 February 1898 the U.S. battleship *Maine*, still in Havana harbour on her mission of security, was blown up. There was a sudden explosion, the whole of the fore part of the ship was wrecked; the stern began to sink; two officers and 258 men out of the ship's company of 355 were killed. Captain Sigsbee was saved. Many others were injured.

How did it happen? The Assistant Secretary of the U.S. navy, Roosevelt, seems to have had no doubts: 'The *Maine* was sunk by an act of dirty treachery,' he wrote privately the next day.[34] The *Journal*, of

[32] Italicized.
[33] *Journal*, 11 February 1898.
[34] Theodore Roosevelt to Dibdee, 16 February 1898.

course, agreed; the explosion of the *Maine* gave Hearst an opportunity to stretch his warlike imagination beyond all previous limits: on 17 February the *Journal* carried a headline: 'THE WARSHIP MAINE WAS SPLIT IN TWO BY AN ENEMY'S SECRET INFERNAL MACHINE'. Beneath was a drawing of the ship anchored over mines and a diagram, showing wires leading to the Cabaña.[35] But Sigsbee, in his first telegram from Havana, after explaining the help which the Spanish authorities gave in searching for survivors, adjured his superiors: 'Public opinion should be suspended until further report.'

There were in fact to be two enquiries; one by a U.S. court, the other by Spain. The U.S. government refused to collaborate with the Spanish commission. The U.S. report was straightforward:

> In the opinion of the Court, the *Maine* was destroyed by the explosion of a submarine mine which caused the partial explosion of two or more of the forward magazines. The court has been unable to obtain evidence fixing the responsibility for the destruction of the *Maine* upon any person or persons.[36]

This enquiry had made an examination of affairs on board from survivors and a somewhat amateurish examination of the wreckage carried out by inadequate divers. Fitzhugh Lee placed the responsibility on some 'unknown conspirators', who might have planted a mine at a point where the hull of the *Maine* would hit it, as she swung at her buoy; the explosion, he believed, had set off the powder magazine; McKinley, Long and Judge Day accepted this explanation as 'probable',[37] and Sigsbee in the end concluded that the cause of the explosion came from under the bottom of the ship.[38] A seaman from the Ward Line ship *Saratoga* which was in port at the time gave the New York *World* a block of cement allegedly from the bottom of the *Maine* purporting to prove an upward and external explosion.[39]

The Spanish court of enquiry was hampered by the need for diplomatic correctness in the examination of a U.S. vessel. It concluded that the explosion had an internal origin[40] – a view shared by the French engineer, Admiral Dupont.[41]

In 1911 the *Maine* was raised and a new (U.S.) court of enquiry examined the vessel. This reached the conclusion that 'a charge of a low form of explosive exterior to the ship' had been detonated, though

---

[35] *Journal*, 17 February 1898.
[36] Report of Enquiry on the *Maine*, qu. Sigsbee, 212.
[37] *Foreign Relations*, 686, 692; J. D. Long, *America of Yesterday*, ed. L. S. Mayo (1923), 171-2.
[38] Sigsbee, 58.
[39] D. C. Seitz, *Joseph Pulitzer: his life and letters* (1926), 239.
[40] Telegram of Gullón to Washington, qu. Fernández Almagro, 467, fn. 8. The report of the Spanish commission is printed as Appendix F (p. 231) to Sigsbee, the *Maine*.
[41] *Le Gaulois* (Paris), qu. Fernández Almagro, II, 470.

apparently not at the same point as the court of enquiry had thought in 1898.[42] After that, the *Maine* was ceremoniously sunk at sea. The Spanish court of enquiry thus left responsibility with the U.S.; and the U.S. left it open that Spanish negligence, if not worse, was responsible.

The official enquiries were therefore not conclusive. The Spanish government, of course, desired to improve relations with the U.S. and could have had in truth nothing to do with it. The first reaction of the Spanish authority was to explain it as 'indisputably accidental'.[43] Possibly some of the younger Spaniards, whom General Fitzhugh Lee had thought were threatening U.S. lives in Havana, could have contemplated such a crime, driven to fury as many were by the *Journal* and the *World*. Many officers of the Spanish army evidently hated the U.S.: General Pin, commander of the Cienfuegos region in 1896, had told Atkins how easy it would be to capture Boston, New York and Washington and how he hoped the opportunity would offer itself to him.[44] But there is no evidence of any sort implicating them and in default of it, 'the Spaniards' would seem to be exonerated from guilt.

One alternative possibility is that some U.S. citizen, anxious for war, or some friend of the Cuban revolutionaries, was responsible. A finger was once pointed at Hearst[45] but his conduct on the night of the explosion seems to suggest the contrary.[46] Nor was Hearst actually a murderer, despite other faults. Still, he gained; the *Journal*'s circulation for the first time rose to over one million on 17 February.[47] No doubt, however, had Hearst been responsible the story would somehow have come out later. But it is possible that if indeed a single person exploded the *Maine* he may have expected the destruction of the ship but not of lives.

If there is any serious possibility of individual responsibility, it is most likely to lie with the Cuban revolutionaries. Their position had not improved during the last two months and they were now fully prepared to accept U.S. help, even if there was a chance that annexation might follow. The most vigorous opponents of annexation among them had been Martí and Maceo, but they were dead. The Cubans were capable of such action, as anyone might be after three years of pitiless war (as the murder of Cánovas suggests). The establishment of the autonomist government in Havana was a serious political threat, for there was a chance that it might succeed. Even so,

[42] Enquiry of 1911.
[43] Telegram, 15 February, Ministerio de Ultramar, 60, in the library of the Ministerio del Ejército, Madrid.
[44] Atkins, 213.
[45] Ferdinand Lundberg, *Imperial Hearst* (New York, 1936), 81.
[46] E. D. Coblentz, ed., *William Randolph Hearst* (1952), 59.
[47] Wisan, 395.

N*

there is no evidence to link the Cubans with the blowing up of the *Maine*.

One story suggests that she was blown up by a mine planted by a U.S. millionaire and eccentric, William Astor Chanler,[48] after discussion with Máximo Gómez. Six weeks before on 23 December 1897, Theodore Roosevelt had written to Chanler ('as strong in [his] views of foreign policy as Cabot and [Roosevelt]'[49]) 'I do not believe that Cuba can be pacified by autonomy and I earnestly hope that events will so shape themselves that we must interfere some time in the not distant future.'[50] Chanler and his brother Lewis were already engaged in gun-running to Cuba.[51]

The most likely explanation however is that the *Maine* blew up due to the carriage within it of quantities of the new gunpowder needed for heavier guns and which often caused explosions in its first years. Later events suggest that the U.S. armed forces were so badly organized that bad packing was possible. As the Spanish minister of Overseas Territories telegraphed, the officers of the *Maine* as well as the U.S. government had 'a great interest in hiding the truth'.[52]

At all events, no evidence was forthcoming to discredit any single party at the time. Nevertheless the weeks following the explosion of the *Maine* were marked by hysteria in the U.S., inflamed by the yellow press and by younger members of the government and public opinion; and, in the end, the McKinley administration surrendered to the prevailing mood. At the same time the Cuban illusion has remained that the U.S. 'blew up the ship themselves and then accused Spain', as 'a pretext for intervention'.[53]

On 16 February President McKinley was appalled, and by no means prepared to commit himself immediately to war: 'The President has no more backbone than a chocolate éclair,' exploded Roosevelt.[54] On 17 February excitement was such that the Associated Press News Agency had to despatch the denial: 'The Cruiser *New York* has not been

[48] William Astor Chanler (1867–1934), explorer, romantic and in 1897 member of Congress for New York State; a great-nephew of Julia Ward Howe.
[49] *The Letters of Theodore Roosevelt*, ed. E. E. Morison, 8 vols (1951–4), I, 744.
[50] *Ibid.*, 747.
[51] This story owes its genesis to William C. Bullitt, U.S. ambassador in Paris, who was told it by Chanler in Paris many years later. But Chanler was clearly a romancer and it is possible that the tale may have become confused with an incident in which a third Chanler brother, Winthrop, some time a colonel in the Mexican army, was blown up off Havana when he took over the gun-running business after the two elder brothers had joined Roosevelt's rough riders. Winthrop Chanler escaped the Spaniards and joined Gómez (*cf. ibid.*, 352).
[52] Telegram, 26 February 1898, Ministerio de Ultramar to Gobernador de Cuba, in library of Ministerio del Ejército, Madrid.
[53] The remarks occurred in Miguel Barnet's introduction to Esteban Montejo, *Autobiography of a Runaway Slave*, 11; Montejo, 217, said the same: 'Any fool here knew that the Americans blew up the *Maine* themselves so as to get into the war.'
[54] Letter to Dibdee, *loc. cit.*

ordered to Havana. Consul General Lee has not been assassinated. There is no conference of the cabinet. Congress is not in session . . .'[55] Hearst did not mind; he sent two yachts to Havana carrying all his star correspondents, including the d'Artagnan of 1897, Karl Decker, and Frederic Remington. On the 18th, the *World* described mass meetings in Buffalo, urging McKinley to declare war,[56] and the same day the *Journal* said: 'The whole country thrills with war fever.'[57] This was, however, not quite true since clergy and businessmen throughout the U.S. were now appealing for peace.[58] It would be quite false to assume that economic interests wanted war: indeed, as Atkins's activities show, this was the last thing most U.S. men with Cuban interests desired. There were, of course, exceptions but in general the interventionists were polemicists, romantics and enthusiasts, not calculating machines.[59]

On 25 February the sleepy naval secretary, Long, overworked, nervous and ill took a day off: he returned to find that Roosevelt, his deputy, had

> come very near causing more of an explosion than happened to the *Maine* . . . the very devil seemed to possess him . . . he immediately began to launch peremptory orders, distributing ships, ordering ammunition, which there was no means to move, to places where there is no means to store it;[60]

in particular, Roosevelt cabled to Commodore Dewey in Hong Kong that, in the event of war, his duty was 'to see that the Spanish [naval] squadron does not leave the Asiatic coast', and then to carry out the previously agreed offensive operations in the Philippines.[61] Long seems to have assumed that Roosevelt was acting impulsively; in fact he was carrying out long-prearranged plans even if made less by him than by his department but never hidden from him.[62] Meanwhile the inimitable *Journal* happily denounced

> eminently respectable porcine citizens who, for dollars in the money-grubbing sty, support 'conservative' newspapers and consider the starvation of . . . inoffensive men, women and children and the murder of 250 American sailors . . . of less importance than the fall of two points in the price of stock.[63]

[55] Qu. Millis, 108.
[56] Wisan, 403.
[57] *Ibid.*, 399.
[58] See, e.g., May, 140–1.
[59] See Pratt, 252.
[60] Long, *America of Yesterday*, 169.
[61] G. Dewey, *Autobiography of George Dewey* (1913), 179. *Cf.* Roosevelt, *Letters*, 784, and comment there by Professor Morison. (Senator Lodge had called in at the Navy Department during the afternoon.)
[62] See the article re-assessing Roosevelt's 'plot', J. Grenville, *American Studies*, 2, 1, 33–47.
[63] *Journal*, 24 February. Roosevelt was also preoccupied at this time by the extent to which 'Big Business' opposed war.

Such propaganda began to have a great effect. Theatre audiences wept on hearing the 'Star Spangled Banner'. Secretary Long rashly said that Spanish official reponsibility for the *Maine* explosion could be discounted, and was placed on the *Journal*'s list of those who had sold out to pacific Wall Street.[64] Hearst arranged to send a group of jingoistic senators and representatives to Havana with their wives, to make a survey on conditions in Cuba as 'journal commissioners', with, as Godkin in the *Post* pointed out, 'free wine, rum and cigars';[65] while the Methodist Bishop McCabe told an excited congregation: 'There are many things worse than war. It may be that the U.S. is to become the Knight Errant of the world. War with Spain may put her in a position to demand civil and religious liberty for the oppressed of every nation.'[66]

[64] *Ibid.*, 8 March 1898, qu. Swanberg.
[65] *Evening Post*, 17 March 1898.
[66] Qu. May, 141.

CHAPTER XXXI

McKinley and the War

President McKinley made one last attempt to settle the Cuban question without war. After a good deal of financial negotiation with old friends such as Myron Herick (who had saved him from bankruptcy in 1893) the president sent a private message to the queen regent in Madrid (quite independently of the banker Janney's dealings with the junta), saying that the U.S. would pay $M300 for Cuba. Six million dollars would be available to the Spanish mediators personally: 'very American that,' commented the Marqués de Lema. The idea was already much canvassed in Madrid. María Cristina, after some days of agonizing doubt, told her prime minister and also the heads of other Spanish political parties (including the Republican Rafael María de Labra) that she would give office to any party prepared to accept McKinley's peace proposals. But none of them agreed to take responsibility, though those consulted included Republicans such as Salmerón, though none opposed the idea outright and though María Cristina herself had certainly now accustomed herself to the idea of Cuban independence. She had also established a friendship with Ambassador Woodford. Still the Spanish reply in the end was negative to this fourth main offer to buy Cuba from Spain, either for incorporation into the Union or for independence.[1] The Spanish Government was still transfixed by fear of a *golpe* from the Right perhaps carried out by Weyler, perhaps by Polavieja.

The news of this offer was not made public in the U.S.: one can imagine the treatment that it would have received from the *Journal*.[2] Woodford had cabled on 26 February, after a discussion the day before with Gullón and Moret:

I think that I have now secured the practical adjustment of every important matter which has been entrusted to me ... Autonomy cannot go backward. It must go forward and its results must be

---

[1] The first three being Polk's, Buchanan's and Grant's. See May, 150 and 167, for a discussion of this; Marqués de Lema, *Mis Recuerdos, 1880–1901* (1930), 239–40, gives the Spanish side.

[2] See Gabriel Maura Gamazo, *Historia crítica del reinado de Don Alfonso XIII*, 359–60; Romanones, *Doña María Cristina*, 144; H. E. Flack, *Spanish-American Diplomatic Relations Preceding the War of 1898* (1882), 86–90.

worked out in Cuba ... They [Sagasta administration] cannot go further without being overthrown by their own people in Spain ... They [certainly] prefer the chance of war, with the certain loss of Cuba, to the overthrow of the dynasty.[3]

(Martínez Campos had earlier said that the only way Spain could get out of the Cuban war with honour was for it to be expanded to cover the U.S.)

The U.S. was theoretically, like Spain, still waiting for the result of the naval enquiry. President McKinley might still have withstood the tides of war fever rising round him. He told Senator Fairbanks:

I don't propose to be swept off my feet by the catastrophe. My duty is plain. We must learn the truth and endeavour, if possible, to fix the responsibility ... The Administration will go on preparing for war but still hoping to avert it.[4]

But on 6 March McKinley, apparently without anything new having occurred to cause him to be more decided, sent for the chairman of the House Appropriations Committee and said: 'Cameron, I must have money to get ready for war. I am doing everything possible to prevent war, but it must come and we are not prepared ... it may be more than a war with Spain. How can I get this money?' McKinley could not appeal openly for money to Congress, since he was still negotiating with Spain. So Cameron, on his own, introduced a bill asking $M50 for national defence and the money was granted on 9 March by 311 to nil in the House of Representatives and in the Senate by 76 to nil, after scenes of 'more unanimity, more harmony and more real enthusiasm' than Cameron had 'ever known or was ever to know again'.[5] Thereafter, North American papers were full of news of war preparations (as well as further denunciations of 'hesitations, delay, deficiency and idle talk'[6]), though none of the money was spent on mobilizing the U.S. army which, presumably, would be sent to Cuba if war did come: the whole went to Atlantic sea defences.[7] A Chippewa chief proposed to enlist 500 braves.[8] 'Whatever the report of the Naval Court of Inquiry,' the *Journal* stated, 'our moral right ... [and] political duty [will be] to say to Spain that the day of her rule in the Western Hemisphere is over.'[9] 'Everything is ready,' the *World* said (it was now merely an echo of its

[3] *Foreign Relations*, 665.
[4] Olcott, *Talks with Fairbanks*, II, 12–13, qu. Leech, 168.
[5] Qu. Millis, 115–16.
[6] Wisan, 404. This was the Reverend Thomas Dixon in the *World*.
[7] *Loc. cit.*
[8] *Journal*, 11 March.
[9] 13 March 1898, see Wisan, 401.

rival), 'the Army, the Navy, the Treasury . . . the Naval Court of Enquiry . . . the people.'[10] The *Journal*'s tame senators had now returned with full reports of the ruined state of Cuba: the wife of Senator Thurston had unfortunately died *en route*, in Matanzas, and Hearst blamed this on the frightful poverty which she had seen.[11] The *Evening Post* pointed out:[12] 'No one – absolutely no one – supposes a yellow journal cares five cents about the Cubans, the *Maine* victims or anything else . . .'. But it was still clear that war was close, the nation being utterly trapped by its sources of information, though at this distance of time it becomes difficult to see what the war was really about.

Into the highly charged atmosphere the Senate Foreign Relations Committee injected, on 16 March, the scarcely urgent or relevant question of Hawaii, recommending annexation. Senator Proctor of Vermont, on 17 March, who had been on Hearst's senatorial expedition to Cuba, gave a powerful and distressing description of what he had seen. Autonomy was a failure and 'the fear that a free Cuba would be revolutionary' was 'not so well-founded'.[13] His speech was a strong argument for war and made a great impression: the Spanish government could not keep order in Cuba and, even if they had not blown up the *Maine* themselves, plainly they could not prevent chaos in their principal harbour, whatever the cause. The U.S. therefore had a definite right to demand action, and if not, to impose it.

In Madrid the situation was seen differently by everyone, including the U.S. minister who had been approached by many, private and official, to seek to avoid war. On 17 March, the day of Proctor's speech, he saw the Spanish Colonial Minister, Moret. Moret told him: 'A single word from McKinley would assure the success of the [autonomist] regime' (Moret cleverly made himself out as leader of a peace faction to the cabinet opposed to the Foreign Minister Pío Gullón). Woodford said that he did not think that autonomy could bring peace to Cuba under the flag of Spain: 'There is but one power and one flag that can secure peace: that is the U.S. and that flag is our flag.' Moret 'paled and said, "Who knows then what will happen?"' Woodford said the U.S. could only negotiate on the basis of a payment to Spain. The sale should be effected secretly and any disagreement would be submitted to the arbitration of the queen of England.[14] In a later interview, the Foreign Minister Gullón repeated however that the queen regent would leave her throne before selling any part of Spain.

[10] *World*, 16 March 1898.
[11] Swanberg, 140.
[12] 12 March.
[13] Wisan, 418. Redfield Proctor (1831–1908), fought in Civil War; lawyer, businessman; Governor of Vermont, 1878–80; Secretary of War, 1889–91; Senator, 1891–1908.
[14] *Foreign Relations*, 689–90.

Woodford argued hard and earnestly:

Our responsibility and duty are precisely what would be the duty of the Minister himself in case there was a penthouse next door to his own residence . . . I next told him that we raise in the U.S. about one-tenth of the sugar we consume . . . that we must purchase from abroad the nine-tenths; that, before the present [Cuban] civil war, we drew much of our supply from Cuba and so sold to Cuba . . . flour, meat, and manufactures; that all this commerce is practically destroyed. I then called his attention to the large amounts of American capital invested in Cuba, partly in actual ownership of Cuban property, partly as loans to Cuban corporations and residents and pointed out how valueless are such holdings and securities while this civil war continues. I emphasised the tremendous pecuniary loss which the people of the U.S. suffer.[15]

On 23 March Woodford made a curious new approach: by then the report on the *Maine* was in the hands of the President. Woodford was not authorized to describe it in detail. But he was to say that, unless within a very few days a satisfactory agreement was reached, the President could only submit the question of U.S.-Spanish relations to Congress, including also that of the *Maine*.[16]

This meant that it was now up to Spain to make the next gesture, and Spain said that the Cuban Autonomists would of course also have to be consulted. On 29 March Woodford came back with another major proposal from McKinley, for an armistice till 1 October. During the interval, peace would be negotiated between Spain and the rebels, with McKinley using his good offices; the *reconcentrados* would be sent to their homes and the U.S. promised to help them.[17] On 31 March the Spaniards replied that they would certainly submit the *Maine* question to arbitration; but the *reconcentrados* had already been allowed to return to west Cuba, and the government had placed three million pesetas at the disposal of the governor for their relief. The Cuban legislature was, as it happened, to meet on 4 May. It would prepare a peace treaty and the Spanish government would be ready for an armistice if the rebels arranged it through Captain-General Blanco.[18]

The Spanish government was playing a bad hand carefully and cleverly, conscious of the real danger of war and of the likely inequality of such a conflict. But Spanish public opinion, as expressed in the press, seemed not to realize how long the odds were against Spain; national

---

[15] *Ibid.*, 698-700.
[16] Fernández Almagro, II, 466; *Foreign Relations*, 718-19.
[17] *Foreign Relations*, 720. The origins of this three-point offer are discussed by May, 152-3; see also Grenville and Young, 257.
[18] Fernández Almagro, II, 472.

pride seemed inflated rather than depressed by the diplomatic isolation of the country. But Spain had some friends: for instance, on 25 March the papal Secretary of State, Cardinal Rampolla, told the Spanish ambassador to the Holy See, Merry del Val, that he at least recognized the calm and the moderation of the Spanish government. He suggested that France, 'animated by great sentiments of friendship towards Spain', might help.

But the grave ways of European diplomacy had little place in the new America of Hearst and Roosevelt. On 20 March the *Journal* announced that when war came it would raise a regiment of giants – composed of the world heavyweight champion, Bob Fitzsimmons, ex-champions Sullivan and Corbett, the champion hammer-thrower Jim Mitchell, and Red Water, the Indian football player. 'Think of a regiment composed of magnificent men of this ilk. They would overawe any Spanish regiment by their mere appearance.'[19] Senator Thurston put his view bluntly on 25 March when he said:

War with Spain would increase the business and earnings of every American railroad, it would increase the output of every American factory, it would stimulate every branch of industry and domestic commerce, it would greatly increase the demand for American labour and in the end every certificate that represented a share in any American business enterprise would be worth more money than it is today.[20]

It is hard indeed to find a parallel outside Germany for such simple belief in the advantages of conflict.

On 28 March the report of the naval court of enquiry was delivered to Congress. The finding that the *Maine* had been destroyed from without was generally taken as a conviction of the Spaniards. Yet the *Journal* seemed dissatisfied: truth was being 'suppressed' by peacemongers.[21] McKinley told Congress with his customary vagueness that he expected Spain to do what honour and justice required.[22] On 29 March Roosevelt wrote:

Personally I cannot understand how the bulk of our people can tolerate the hideous infamy that has attended the last two years of Spanish rule in Cuba and still more how they can tolerate the treacherous destruction of the *Maine*. I feel so deeply that it is with very great difficulty I can control myself;[23]

[19] *Journal*, 20 March, qu. Wisan, 404.
[20] Congressional record, 3165. Congressman Peters of Kansas said that war would put the divine right of kings against the divine right of man: such a war would be a blessing to the world (*ibid.*, 3263). There is no evidence that any of this was true, as most U.S. businessmen knew.
[21] *Journal*, 2 April.
[22] Leech, 177.
[23] Roosevelt, *Letters*, 803.

and on 31 March even William Jennings Bryan, still the nominal leader of the Democratic party, who had never backed expansionism, spoke: 'The time for intervention has arrived ... Humanity demands that we shall act.'[24]

This last comment, in fact, suggests a possible further motive in President McKinley's mind – a motive explained perfectly by the Chicago *Times-Tribune*:

> Let President McKinley hesitate to rise to the just expectations of the American people, and who can doubt that the war for Cuban liberty will be the crown of thorns [that] the free silver Democrats and Populists will adopt ... this fall ... that by that sign, held aloft and proclaimed by such magnetic orators as William Jennings Bryan, they will sweep the country like a cyclone?[25]

Thus political calculation may have played a part in the judgment of the president.

On 3 April the Roman Catholic archbishop of New York went to see the president on the pope's behalf. McKinley told him that he personally was still for peace but that Congress would vote for war.[26] In Madrid the Foreign Minister of Spain, Gullón, was still hoping that the pope would propose mediation. The Spanish government looked on this idea as a way out, though they asked that surrender be made easier for them by the withdrawal of the U.S. fleet mobilized at Key West. Woodford cabled:

> [Gullón] asks your immediate answer as to withdrawal of warships at once after proclamation of armistice. I still believe that immediate armistice will secure permanent and honourable peace to Cuba ... if conditions in Washington still enable you to give me the necessary time. I am sure that before next October I will get peace in Cuba with justice.[27]

The State Department telegraphed back:

> The disposition of our fleet must be left to us. An armistice, to be effective, must be immediately proffered and accepted by insurgents. Would the peace you are so confident of securing mean the independence of Cuba? The President cannot hold his message [to Congress] longer than Tuesday [i.e. the 6th].[28]

On 6 April McKinley had planned to ask Congress for authority to use military and naval forces 'as might be necessary to secure peace and

[24] As qu. Jenks, 55.
[25] As qu. Millis, 124.
[26] Fernández Almagro, II, 470.
[27] *Foreign Relations*, 731-2.
[28] *Ibid.*, 733.

a stable government in Cuba'. Another appeal for understanding of the Spanish position by Woodford was not heeded.[29] At the last minute, however, the president received an appeal from General Fitzhugh Lee asking for the message to be delayed to permit U.S. citizens to leave Havana, and so it was: McKinley delayed. In the circumstances Congress was put off, though with great difficulty. McKinley became once more suspect on Capitol Hill: for the legislature was now for war, Republicans as well as Democrats. An ex-governor of New York, Morton, asked 'Czar' Reed, Speaker of the House, to try to dissuade his colleagues: 'He might as well ask me to stand out in the middle of a Kansas waste and control a cyclone.'[30] Even so, he did not try. Edwin Atkins, back from Cuba, spent hours lobbying president, cabinet, senators and representatives, in favour of peace. Atkins met Reed who was introduced as one who had 'the right views' on Cuba, Reed said: 'What is the *use* of being right when everyone else is wrong?'[31] On 6 April McKinley saw the ambassadors from Europe; the British Ambassador, Sir Julian Pauncefote, presented a note saying Europe hoped 'for humanity's sake you will not go to war'. McKinley replied: 'We hope if we do you will understand it is for humanity's sake.'[32]

On 9 April the European powers made a more important *démarche* in Madrid, asking that the Spanish government accept the U.S. mediation offer 'in the name of the Vatican' and the same day the Spanish cabinet (agreeing that it would be acceptable and honourable to accept from Europe what could not be accepted from the U.S.) accepted the U.S. demands almost in full: Spain would agree to an immediate, unconditional armistice; Captain-General Blanco indeed had already decreed an end of hostilities; the reconcentration orders had been withdrawn; the question of the *Maine* would be submitted to arbitration; the U.S. government would be asked to advise upon the nature and length of the proposed armistice; and the future of Cuba would lie with the Autonomist government. Only the last qualification could possibly disturb the U.S. Woodford accordingly telegraphed: 'I hope that nothing will now be done to humiliate Spain, as I am satisfied that the present government is going, and is loyally ready to go, as fast and as far as it can. With your power of action sufficiently free, you will win the fight on your own lines.'[33] Woodford was perhaps now believing what he wanted to believe.[34]

[29] *Ibid.*, 735.
[30] *New York Times*, 4 April 1898.
[31] Atkins, 280.
[32] *Foreign Relations*, 741; May, *Imperial Democracy*, 181, describes this rather extravagantly as Europe's 'one united response to the emergence of America as a great power'.
[33] *Foreign Relations*, 746–7.
[34] Grenville and Young, 259.

These telegrams were discussed by the U.S. cabinet on Easter Sunday, 10 April. Spain had yielded on all points save that of the U.S. president's desire to determine the future sovereignty of Cuba. That of course was the rub. The cabinet decided that McKinley's message would still be sent to Congress the next day. The news of Spain's concessions would be mentioned at the end of the speech, though the early section of it (already written) would assume that she had not done so. The cabinet apparently 'met twice on Easter Sunday', but its deliberations were fruitless.[35] The decision to accept the demands of mob orators and to go to war had already really been made ten days before.[36] The Naval Secretary, Long, on whose old shoulders would fall the task of accoutrement of the U.S. fleet, wrote a few days later privately to the editor of the *Boston Journal* and put the position plainly:

> Do you realise the President has succeeded in gaining from Spain a concession upon every ground which he has asked: that Spain has yielded everything up to the present time except the last item of independence for Cuba; that she has released every American prisoner; recalled Weyler; recalled De Lôme; changed her reconcentration order; agreed to furnish food; and ordered an armistice ... I honestly believe that if the country and Congress had been content to leave the matter in his [McKinley's] hands, independence would have come without a drop of bloodshed as naturally as an apple falls from a tree.[37]

Other forces for peace in the administration, such as Secretary Gage and Judge Day however had given up,[38] being browbeaten by senators who insisted that the 'war-declaring power' was lodged in the Senate anyway, and by Hearst's continued chauvinism: on 9 April a series of interviews were published with mothers of men killed on the *Maine*: 'How would President McKinley have felt, I wonder, if *he* had a son murdered on the *Maine* ... I ask that mine and other mothers' sons be avenged ... I ask it for justice' sake [*sic*] and the honour of the flag.'[39] The Secretary of War Alger, lazy but spiteful, meantime had only 'his war days and his anti-war days'.[40]

The lack of a strong opposition was also critical: ex-President Cleve-

[35] Leech, 186. See also Ernest May, 157. Hofstadter, 158, wisely says that at this point McKinley 'passed up his chance for one final statesmanlike act'.

[36] Secretary of State Sherman was now in the last stages of senility: shortly he would be replaced, after 'a lapse of memory in a conversation with the Austrian Minister of so serious a nature that the President had to put in [Judge] Day without an instant's delay'.

[37] Long, *America of Yesterday*, 179–82.

[38] See Theodore Roosevelt's letter to Root, 15 April.

[39] *Journal*, 9 April 1898.

[40] McKinley papers, qu. Leech, 201. Russell Alger 1836–1907. Lumberman and lawyer from Ohio, major general in civil war, governor of Michigan 1885, Senator 1902–1907.

land, opposed to war, did not speak out, but wrote privately to his old Secretary of State Olney:

> I cannot avoid a feeling of shame and humiliation ... McKinley is not a victim of ignorance but of amiable weakness, not unmixed with political ambition. He ... was abundantly warned against [Fitzhugh] Lee ... Roosevelt too will have his share of strut and sensation ... My only relief consists in the reflection that ... the war will be short and that the result may not be much worse than a depreciation of our national standing abroad and at home, demoralisation of our people's character, much demagogy and humbug, great additions to our public burdens and the exposure of scandalous operations.[41]

The final collapse into war, however, was still some days ahead. On 11 April, Easter Monday, McKinley's message was finally sent to Congress. It demanded authorization for the president

> To take measures to secure a full and final termination of hostilities between the government of Spain and the people of Cuba ... to secure in the island a stable government ... and to use the military and naval forces of the U.S. as may be necessary.

The justification was described as the losses of the war, the cruelty of Spanish policy and the damage to U.S. property (the loss of the *Maine* was attributed to the prevailing disorder). McKinley described his diplomatic efforts to secure settlement down to 31 March (when the message had been drafted), but, as expected by his cabinet colleagues, only after his peroration ('The issue is now with the Congress. It is a solemn responsibility. I have exhausted every effort to relieve the intolerable condition ... at our doors ... I await your action') did he say:

> Yesterday and since the preparation of the foregoing ... official information was received by me that the latest decree of the Queen Regent of Spain directs General Blanco, in order to prepare and facilitate peace, to proclaim a suspension of hostilities the duration and details of which have not yet been communicated to me ... This fact ... will, I am sure, have your just and careful attention.[42]

It did not do so.

The week after the president's message, Senator Foraker said that he wanted 'immediate recognition' of Masó's rebel Cuban government. His amendment embodying this was adopted in the Senate by 67 votes to 21 on 17 April, but later dropped after careful manipulation by

[41] Qu. Millis, 161.
[42] Message of President McKinley, as qu. *Foreign Relations*, 751–68.

McKinley's friends in the House. This concession was accepted by Foraker in return for McKinley's acceptance of a more strongly worded general resolution tantamount to a declaration of war, which demanded Spain's immediate relinquishment of authority in Cuba. Another amendment was then slipped in by Senator Teller on the urgent suggestion of the Cuban junta's lawyer, Horatio Rubens, the old lawyer friend of José Martí. Teller (previously an advocate of annexation) 'wanted to do something for Cuba'.[43] Rubens said: 'Let there be a declaration of the purpose of the U.S. to make Cuba an independent nation . . . Cuba will be absorbed as a colony against her will if we are not careful. I tell you, Senator, they intend to steal the island of Cuba. The way to stop a theft is to cry "stop thief"'.'[44] So an amendment was introduced by which the U.S. government would disclaim any 'disposition or interest to exercise sovereignty, jurisdiction or control over the said island except for the pacification thereof and assert its determination, when that is accomplished, to leave the government and the control of the island to its people.' Apparently the banker Janney distributed a good deal of money – perhaps $M2 – to senators in order to allow this critical amendment through without discussion, on behalf of the Cuban junta[45] in New York. Horatio Rubens could count himself as one of the real fathers of Cuban independence. So perhaps could the sugar beet industry in the U.S., though there is no direct evidence to suggest their involvement.[46]

In these circumstances, on 19 April the resolutions were passed, by majorities of 310 to 6 in the House, by 42 to 35 in the Senate. The Senate had actually wished to recognize the Cuban rebel government but the House refused this. The votes were greeted with great enthusiasm, and the Capitol rang with men singing. 'The Battle Hymn of the Republic' was sung by General Henderson, representative of Iowa, and 'Dixie' by ex-Confederates. An improvisation, 'Hang General Weyler on a sour apple tree', also rang out vigorously, regardless of the fact that Weyler had been home in Madrid looking after his horses for months. On 20 April McKinley signed the resolution and also an ultimatum to Spain, instructing General Woodford to demand that 'the Government of Spain at once relinquish its authority and government in the island of Cuba'. But this ultimatum was not delivered, since Sagasta had

[43] Henry Moore Teller (1830–1914), senator for Colorado, 1876–82, 1887–1909; Secretary of the Interior to Arthur, 1883–6.

[44] Rubens, *Liberty*, 341–2; see also L. B. Richardson, *William E. Chandler, Republican* (1940), 580–2, and N. W. Stephenson, *Nelson W. Aldrich*, 156ff.

[45] The Cuban junta paid $M2 to Janney. The matter later came up and was publicly denied. But the evidence presented by Healy, *The U.S. in Cuba*, 26–7, on the basis of unpublished material in the National Archives (U.S. Minister Squiers to Secretary of State Hay, 9 September 1904), seems incontrovertible.

[46] See G. W. Auxier, 'Propaganda Activities of the Cuban Junta', *H.A.H.R.*, vol. 19, 304.

decided to interpret the congressional resolution itself as a declaration of war. Woodford was told that the time for diplomatic activity was past. The Spanish minister in Washington also asked for his passports. Then, on 21 April, McKinley ordered Captain Sampson's fleet at Key West to blockade Havana. Sampson, who had presided at the *Maine* enquiry, became an admiral. Congress declared war on 25 April, though stating, so confusing future lawyers, that there had been a 'state of war' since the blockade had begun.

The autonomist government of Cuba had on 7 April meantime sent a message to McKinley:

> Even though there are some Cubans now in arms, there are an immense number who accept autonomy and are disposed to work with zeal, under this form of government, to re-establish peace and prosperity ... The Cuban people are an American people and have as a result a perfect right to govern themselves, according to their desires and aspirations; it would not be in any way right that a foreign power should impose on them a political regime which they consider contrary to their happiness and conscience ... The Government of Cuba very much hope that the President of the U.S. will contribute by the use of his power to re-establish peace in Cuba under the sovereignty of the mother country ... The autonomist government of Cuba ... protests energetically against the falsities of a part of the section of the American press which is published with the evil purpose of encouraging passions, making it appear that in Cuba injustice and brute force alone reign and that autonomy has failed – and this even before the colonial parliament has been constituted, and when it has not yet been shown whether the new regime will produce the expected results. As the immortal Washington put it: honesty is the best policy.[47]

This message appears not to have been answered.

The queen mother of Spain and the three most responsible ministers in Madrid – Sagasta, Moret and Gullón – had sought in the first part of April to find a diplomatic solution to the crisis. But there was mounting popular outcry against the U.S. Crowds filled the streets, carrying banners and flags. The march of Cádiz was incessantly played. Don Carlos, from his pretender's safe retreat, demanded war at all costs.[48] But though Sagasta understood war to be unavoidable, his main preoccupation, like Cánovas's, was to avoid the collapse of the dynasty and of the system. A long war would bring revolution at home. A dishonourable peace would do the same. The only possibility therefore was a swift

---

[47] Fernández Almagro, II, 479.
[48] F. G. Bruguera, *Histoire contemporaine d'Espagne* (1953), 320.

defeat, in which the army and the navy might seem to come out with honour.

Before all hope of avoiding conflict however had been abandoned, the Spaniards played their last card: a sad if dignified attempt to save themselves. On 11 April Captain-General Blanco announced an armistice in Cuba, 'because of the repeated desires of Pope Leo XIII and earnestly recommended by the ambassadors of six great European powers'. But it was in vain. On 19 April Calixto García, still the rebel commander in the east, sent a circular to the commanders of the three rebel armies that they should under no circumstances accept the truce:

> As it is necessary for both parties to accept the agreement for it to be put into effect, and since up till now our government [i.e. the rebel provisional government] has communicated nothing to us on this subject, you should go on shooting up pueblos as before and attacking any column which comes out, with greater ardour than ever, causing as much damage as possible. Any individual who leaves our camp with the aim of conferring with the enemy on any basis except the absolute independence of Cuba will be judged with all the rigour of the law.[49]

But the captain-general returned to the matter with an astounding proposal.

On 22 April Blanco – whether with or without Spanish official backing is obscure – on the brink of disaster and after the U.S. fleet had already appeared on the horizon outside Havana, wrote to Máximo Gómez to propose that a 'supreme moment' had arrived, in which Cuban-Spanish differences should be forgotten. An alliance between Cubans and Spaniards should be achieved in Santa Clara. 'The Cubans will receive arms from the Spanish army and, with the cry "Hurrah for Spain, Hurrah for Cuba" we will repel the [North American] invader, and keep free from a foreign yoke the descendants of a single race.'

Máximo Gómez, however, was not prepared to discuss the idea in any way, though the tone of his letter suggested he appreciated the point made:

> You represent an old and discredited monarchy and we fight for the same principles as Bolívar and Washington. You say we belong to the same race and invite me to fight against a foreign invader. I only know one race, humanity, and for me there exist only good nations and bad ones. Spain has done badly here and the U.S. are carrying out for Cuba a duty of humanity and civilisation ... Up till now I have only had motives of admiration for the United States. I have written to President McKinley and General Miles thanking them for the

[49] Fernández Almagro, II, 478, fn. 11.

American intervention . . . I do not see the danger of our extermination by the U.S. to which you refer . . . If that should come to pass, history will judge. For the present I have only to repeat to you that it is too late for understandings between your army and mine.[50]

With this letter Máximo Gómez sealed the fate of Spain in the New World, and also that of Cuba. It was the decisive act of welcome to the U.S. which dictated Cuban history for the next sixty years.

The leaders of the Cuban rebellion were indeed quite uninformed about U.S. moves: they learned of them from newspapers and private letters. But after some reflection, and recognition of political realities, Bartolomé Masó proclaimed a *de facto* alliance of Cubans and Americans: 'The most glorious revolution begun by José Martí on February 24 1895 is about to triumph, thanks to the magnanimous assistance of the U.S.A.; our arms which were never conquered by the Spaniards in three years of war, will soon have gained their victory.'[51] Martí and Maceo would doubtless have rejected the idea of the U.S. as an ally against Spain; but they were dead. The torch had passed to those who were oblivious of these delicate matters.

The motives of the U.S. in embarking on this war appear somewhat trivial and selfish: trivial, since it is improbable that Hearst, Roosevelt and the other men of war would have been so bellicose had their enemy been a stronger power than was Spain; selfish, since real concern in the U.S. for the Cubans was not much marked before the explosion of the *Maine* killed some Americans. Yet 'outraged humanity' did play a part and indeed the interest of the war is that it enabled North Americans to articulate their new imperialism by presenting it, not entirely hypocritically, as a humanitarian crusade.[52] The surrender first of the legislature to the mood created by Hearst and then of the administration to the legislature was however pitiful. There were men who thought differently from Hearst, including indeed McKinley, most of the cabinet and most of the older generation, who actually knew what war was like from personal experience. These surrendered. The existence of the yellow press as of the navy rendered the Cuban crisis of the 1890s quite different from that of the 1870s, when for instance the incident of the *Virginius* offered almost as good an excuse for war as the *Maine* later did. This war may not have been wholly caused by the press; but it was more a newspaper war than an economic conflict.[53] The Secretary of War, Alger, himself said of McKinley: 'He has many lovable qualities, but he lacks backbone and nothing can make up for the lack of

[50] Rubens, *Liberty*, 347.
[51] As qu. Guerra and Santovenia, VI, 423–4.
[52] Hofstadter, *Paranoid Style*, 161.
[53] *Ibid.*, 151, fn. 2. The first Cuban war had seen a good deal of 'yellow' journalism.

backbone.'[54] In the circumstances the Spanish government deserve some sympathy, even admiration, for their dignified handling of the crisis. The Spanish government had done all in its power to avoid war; but it preferred war to a *coup d'état* from the Right, which would have been a likely consequence of any further concession.

Viewed from a distance, Spain had of course a heavy responsibility. Yet the margins within which Spain could move were narrow. With continued threats from Left and Right, no Spanish government was strong enough to contemplate a progressive settlement for Cuba, when the most powerful Cubans themselves after all were anxious to maintain the *status quo*. Still, Spain should have been warned by the Ten Years' War, and the dispatches of her generals, that the forces making for independence were resolute and single-minded. The lesson of Canada, which the Spaniards belatedly remembered, had been clear since 1868: colonies which had attained a certain degree of economic development could move towards home rule without catastrophe, indeed had to do so, if they were to remain friends with the home country. The black population of Cuba certainly presented a difficulty for the *criollos*, but the danger of independence now was less that it might bring a 'black republic' than that, a foretaste of Rhodesia, the Negroes might be denied all civil rights. This possibility seems never to have been taken into any account by the Spanish government. It is possible that autonomy, even the limited scheme proposed by Maura in 1892–3, might have been ultimately successful. In the long term autonomy would perhaps have been the solution to guarantee a permanent political and economic structure in Cuba better designed than independence to secure a consistently rising standard of living, accompanied by cultural and social homogeneity.

[54] Leech, 367. Grenville and Young, 263–6, make a spirited defence of McKinley and say 'Evidence suggests that McKinley's policy was steadily moving to the point where he would have presented an ultimatum to Spain quite independently of the *Maine* disaster'.

CHAPTER XXXII

The Spanish-American War

The war between Spain and the U.S. in 1898 foreshadowed the clash between the U.S. and the U.S.S.R. in 1962: Cuba was the cause of fighting, but in the moment of crisis the island was half forgotten. The Cubans themselves stood apart, almost neglected. In 1898 neither of the somewhat shadowy governments then constituted for the island, neither the autonomist government of José María Gálvez nor the rebel 'provisional government' of Bartolomé Masó – had a role.

Passive also were the Cubans in New York, the famous junta led by Estrada Palma, Quesada and Benjamín Guerra. By this time the last-named, however, had sold $122,400 worth of Cuban bonds at prices ranging from 25% to par. In April 1898 they stood at 40%. Another $M3 of Cuban independence bonds had been deposited with the old firm of August Belmont & Co.[1] All could only watch passively while the two war machines of Spain and the U.S., both rusty, were wheeled into clumsy action.

There was some similarity between the Spanish and the U.S. attitudes to the conflict. While Spain did not doubt they would be defeated, the U.S. had no doubt of victory. Neither country wanted a long war. Both wanted honour more than substantial gains.

In Madrid reaction to war had a certain elegiac grace: Sagasta eloquently told the Cortes how peace had been sought. The queen regent and the boy king, Alfonso, appeared on distant balconies; there were street demonstrations. Those who opposed war were silenced by the impossibility of avoiding it. The socialists were unable to claim that this conflict had been sought by a *bourgeois* government. The conservative opposition rallied to the Liberal government. In Havana, Captain-General Blanco proclaimed a call to arms:

Without reason or pretext, and after the U.S. had received proofs of friendship from us, they declared war precisely when we had started to re-establish peace, and when commerce and industry were reviving ... Perhaps, however, these American Carthaginians will now meet their Rome in this Spanish territory, which was

[1] The head of the firm, August Belmont II (1853–1924), was the son of the emissary of President Pierce with Spain over Cuba.

discovered, peopled and civilized by Spain and will always be Spanish.[2]

Popular reaction, though patriotic in Havana, had in Spain a bitter flavour. One song ran:

> *'Colores de sangre y oro*
> *Tiene la hispana bandera;*
> *No hay oro para comprarla*
> *Ni sangre para venderla.'*[3]

And Pierre Loti, in Madrid at the time, heard a singer in a café:

> *'Tienen muchos barcos*
> *Nosotros, razón*
> *Ellos armamentos,*
> *Nosotros, honor.'*[4]

The Spanish army in Cuba at this time numbered 80,000. Its strength could be supplemented by the fleet, but the very existence of the fleet was deplored by the Minister of War, General Correa, for what he feared most of all was the effect on morale of an American flag on a captured Spanish vessel: 'If only we had had none, we could say to the U.S., from Cuba as from the peninsula: "Here we are! Come when you want to!"'[5] As it was, the government ordered Admiral Cervera to take the two cruisers *María Teresa* and *Cristóbal Colón* from Cádiz to the Cape Verde Islands, where he was joined by a flotilla of three torpedo boats, three destroyers and two other cruisers, the *Almirante Oquendo* and the *Vizcaya*.[6] Admiral Cervera was instructed to take this fleet to Puerto Rico (still with no rebellion) and thence to Cuba, there to accept or to avoid battle with the U.S. as he should judge right.

Given these orders, Cervera assembled the chiefs of his squadron on 20 April, on board his flagship the *Colón*. These officers were gloomy. They knew that 'the naval forces of the U.S. are so immensely superior to ours in the number and class of boats … and in preparations made … that they could easily attack us in the Antilles, the Peninsula or its islands [Canaries] as well as in the Philippines'. These commanders were

---

[2] Fernández Almagro, II, 500.

[3] *Ibid.*, 593.   'Blood red and gold
Flies the Spanish pennon;
But there's no gold to pay for it
Nor blood to sell for it.'

[4] *Loc. cit.*   'They have many ships,
We, the Right;
They have armaments;
And we, honour.'

[5] According to *El Imparcial*, this robust language, 'manly and dignified, produced everywhere a very good impression … we have always felt and talked like that. That is how our country is'.

[6] Admiral Pascual Cervera (1839–1909). Ex-Minister of Marine. Born Jérez de la Frontera.

intelligent and politically knowledgeable men. Two had been Liberal deputies. It seemed obvious to them that they should stay in the Canaries, in order if need be to defend Spain but also ready to go to the Antilles if and when it became evident that the U.S. fleet would remain in those waters. Cervera appealed to the Spanish Admiralty. But after several hours' discussion in Madrid the admirals dispatched Cervera's squadron to the Antilles, despite appeals by dissentients to the queen regent and to the new Conservative opposition leader, Silvela,[7] and even threats to disobey orders by the political officers. Cervera set out on the morning of 29 April, sending back home as he did so a famous telegram: 'With a calm conscience I set off for the sacrifice, without having the reasons of the Admiralty explained to me and knowing that my own recommendations have been discounted.'[8] Fernando Villaamil wrote to Sagasta: 'You should know . . . that while as seamen we are ready to die with honour in the fulfilment of our duty . . . the sacrifice of these naval forces will be as certain as it will be pointless and useless.'[9] The U.S. press watched the ships sail off, as they excitedly predicted, for the east coast of the U.S. itself, where the owners of empty summer hotels appealed to the administration for naval protection.[10]

The U.S. preparations for war in 1898 will always seem a subject for high comedy. The cabinet, a group of dignified but elderly men, were caught up in the turmoil of a patriotic war in the industrial age. They were overwhelmed by the problems of organization, and often yielded to personal arguments. The Secretary of War, Alger, complained:

> The life of the Secretary of War was not a happy one in those days of active military operations . . . It seemed as if there was hardly a family in the U.S. that did not have a friend or a relative in the service and . . . for one reason or another some member from each of these found it necessary to write to, or personally visit, the War Office. Members of Congress, departmental and state officials, cannot as a rule be denied audience. The office of the Secretary was daily visited by not less than one hundred persons whose business or position entitled them to a personal hearing. So urgent was the pressure that almost the entire day was given to them. It therefore became necessary to devote the greater part of the night and Sundays to the consideration of department work.[11]

[7] Francisco Silvela (1845–1905), historian and for a time disciple of Cánovas.
[8] Fernández Almagro, II, 490. See also Víctor Concás, *The Squadron of Admiral Cervera* (1900) where the telegrams between the Admiral and Madrid are reproduced; F. Camba Andrell, *Fernando Villaamil* (1954), 177–81.
[9] Qu. Millis, 170; Camba, 136. In fact Villaamil was killed.
[10] Swanberg, 150.
[11] R. A. Alger, *The Spanish-American War* (1901), 29.

Long, the Secretary of the Navy, also made a memorable comment: 'It is interesting to note how every section of the country, although all are patriotic, has an eye to the main chance.'[12]

The commander-in-chief of the U.S. army in 1898 was the ambitious and vain General Nelson A. Miles – a 'brave peacock' as Roosevelt put it – married to a niece of Secretary of State Sherman, and much embroiled in politics.[13] The regular army then numbered 28,000 men. Despite the 'useful battle experience of the Indian wars' of the 1880s, most of the U.S. generals were living strictly on their Civil War pasts. The National Guard numbered perhaps 100,000. But these knew nothing of war, were badly equipped, and were legally under the orders of state governors. On 23 April, when President McKinley called up the National Guard, it was made immediately obvious that even if states sent their quotas they would refuse to be commanded by 'West Point martinets'. In these circumstances the question arose: should not any offensive be delayed till December? General Miles pointed out that it was 'extremely hazardous . . . and injudicious to put an Army on [Cuba] at this time of the year as it would undoubtedly be decimated by . . . deadly disease'. Congress, however, authorized the recruitment in the south-west and in the Rockies of three new cavalry regiments. Alger offered Theodore Roosevelt a command of one, as he had earlier promised; Roosevelt refused on grounds of inexperience. Even so, a few days later he is found telegraphing to Brooks Brothers for a 'blue cravenette regular Lieutenant-Colonel's uniform without yellow on the collar and with leggings',[14] and he accepted the deputy commandership of one regiment. Fitzhugh Lee had to find accommodation somewhere since he had naturally given up being consul in Havana. He rejoined the colours as a major-general, along with another ex-Confederate general, Representative Joe Wheeler of Alabama. The reception of these two ex-Southern cavalry commanders into the Union army was greeted as proving finally that the old great quarrel of America was over, even if a new one had begun.

On 26 April McKinley gave orders to Brigadier-General Rufus Shafter, the fattest man in the army, to take a reconnaissance force of 4,000 to Cuba the following month. Miles succeeded in raising the figure to 10,000. The war had become a great popular issue. Buoyed by an extraordinary tide of enthusiasm, millionaires offered great sums to help the war preparations. Hearst offered first a regiment of cavalry (to be financed by himself) – the offer was rejected – and then proposed

[12] Long, *America of Yesterday*, 376.
[13] General Nelson Miles (1839–1925); he had made a great name when he commanded troops against Sitting Bull, Crazy Horse, Geronimo and Natchez; major-general at twenty-six; author of *Personal Recollections* or *From New England to the Golden Gate*.
[14] Pringle, 183.

to the navy a steam yacht on which he himself would serve.[15] William Astor Chanler, whether or no he was the creative spirit behind the *Maine* crime, offered a regiment too, and his cousin John Jacob Astor[16] a battery of artillery. War correspondents described every move of the preparations with an exultation which served as a substitute for security. The *World* was selling 1,300,000 a day by late April and the *Journal* – 'HOW DO YOU LIKE THE JOURNAL'S WAR?' it asked unashamedly on 9 and 10 May – sold a million.

The war began with Commodore Dewey.[17] He had sailed on 27 April to Manila, in accordance with orders issued long ago in February by the Navy Department. He carried with him two rebel Filipinos so as to make clear that the U.S. was going to free the Philippines as well as Cuba. This course of action was reluctantly accepted by the Philippine patriots, led by the indomitable General Aguinaldo, whose conversations with U.S. Consul Pratt in Singapore had been anything but reassuring on the question of what the U.S. might do with the islands after victory. On 1 May, anyway, Dewey destroyed the small Spanish fleet in Manila Bay, without a single casualty to man or ship, and so immediately became, thanks to the yellow press, a national hero, renowned for his serenity ('You may fire when ready, Gridley') and his stern blue eyes. After this great victory, the east coast of the U.S. ceased immediately its anxiety about Admiral Cervera's 'swift and powerful cruisers . . . flashing across the Atlantic to lay American ports in ruin'.[18] On 4 May, McKinley sent an army of occupation of 5,000 under General Merritt to establish land control of the Philippines.[19] This force would administer the territory but the Philippines would not, it was plainly stated, join the Union. Still, the Filipino patriots were not happy, and rightly so.

A decision now came about Cuba too. At a war conference on 8 May, McKinley agreed that 70,000 troops should be prepared in Florida to land at Mariel in north Cuba and then 'on to Havana'.

The disaster of Manila caused an immense heave of despair in Madrid; as usual in Spanish political crises, crowds assembled in the Puerta del Sol, and demonstrated before the houses of Sagasta, Moret and General Weyler. There were riots elsewhere in Spain. The government feared revolution but neither the Republican leader, Salmerón, nor the aged federalist, Pi, were ready for action. Don Carlos in Paris

---

[15] Swanberg, 146–7.

[16] J. J. Astor (1864–1912), capitalist and inventor of the steamship chair held in place by suction.

[17] Admiral George Dewey (1837–1917), fought in the battle of New Orleans and Port Hudson (1862).

[18] The phrase is Miss Leech's (p. 203).

[19] The number was later increased to 20,000, chiefly western volunteers.

thought that he had only to wait for military disaster to be able to take over the throne, and so remained silent, though his rhetorical spokesman, Vázquez de Mella, in a scandalous speech in the Cortes, quoted from Ecclesiastes to prove how unhappy are countries when in crises they are ruled by a woman and a child.[20]

Meantime, a modest step had already been taken by the U.S. to establish relations with the Cuban rebels. Lieutenant Andrew Rowan (who had previously written a short topographical study of the island) put ashore secretly near the Turquino peak to confer with General Calixto García.[21] García felt, or at least appeared, 'embarrassed' since he thought that Gómez or the Masó government should have been consulted first. It would seem, however, that although Máximo Gómez's prestige had diminished and the putative government was merely a shadow, the U.S. sought out García because of his area of command, not to bring about disruption among the rebel cause.[22] But he nevertheless sent back General Enrique Collazo and Colonel Charles Hernández to the U.S.; and some days later Hernández returned to Cuba with a message from Miles asking García to maintain 5,000 Cubans in the Santiago area.[23] The *New York Tribune* noted on 23 May that

> For nearly two years [there have been] positive assertions . . . that the Cubans with merely the moral encouragement of the U.S. think a recognition of belligerency could quickly encompass their own independence . . . it is now definitely known that little or no assistance from the 'vaunted armies of liberation' need be expected.

On 13 May Admiral Cervera's naval squadron appeared off Martinique and the fears of an attack on the U.S. east coast finally evaporated. On 19 May this squadron reached Santiago Bay without being seen by the U.S.

On 19 May Admiral Sampson received a secret report that Cervera was in Santiago. He ordered Commodore Schley to establish a blockade. Schley and Sampson were contrasting and competitive men; Schley was an extrovert, a 'hearty old sea dog',[24] but foppish and vain, well known in Washington and a public hero since his modest action off Chile defending U.S. seamen in 1892. Sampson was retiring, intellectual, impassive, with no friends in Congress. But his orders were unfortunately

[20] *Diario de Sesiones*, qu. Fernández Almagro.
[21] *Cf.* Rowan, *The Island of Cuba 1898: How I Carried the Message to García.* Rowan (1857–1943) retired early from the army in 1909.
[22] Portell Vilá, *Historia*, III, 465, takes a different view.
[23] Rubens, *Liberty*, 349. See also Ulises Cruz Bastillo, *El Mensaje a García* (1943); and Guerra and Santovenia, etc., VI, 423–4.
[24] Leech, 197.

José Martí:
9*a* In New York
   b In Kingston, Jamaica

Theodore Roosevelt:
10a The Colonel
  b With the Roughriders

vague: 'Spanish squadron probably at Santiago . . . If you are satisfied they are not at Cienfuegos, proceed with all dispatch . . . continuing to Santiago . . . and, if the enemy is there, blockade him in front.'

On 26 May Commodore Schley did 'cautiously' reach Santiago. He did not realize that Cervera was already there. Three 'fast scouts' had gone ahead and had found nothing. Schley was worried about his coal supply. He headed back to Key West. Washington cabled: 'All the department's information indicates Spanish division is still at Santiago de Cuba.' Schley cabled: 'Cannot remain off Santiago . . . on account of coal . . . Much to be regretted, cannot obey orders of the Department. Have striven earnestly.' Long in Washington thought this 'incomprehensible . . . fleet flinching . . . the darkest day of the war', and cabled: 'You must not leave the vicinity of Santiago de Cuba unless it is unsafe.' In fact by then Schley had managed to fuel and was heading back; on 29 May at dawn he looked into Santiago and to his surprise saw Cervera's flagship unconcealed in the harbour. The Spanish fleet lay in the bay because of its need for fuel, though the vacillating Minister of Marine in Madrid had now ordered it to return to the peninsula.

At this the U.S. finally decided not only to attempt to blockade the Spanish fleet where it was but also to land the main bulk of the army now ready at Santiago. General Miles left Washington for Tampa to supervise the embarkation.[25] But not Miles but General Shafter, older still at sixty-three, slow-moving and unimaginative as well as immensely fat, would be the field commander. At least he had the realism not to have political ambitions.[26] On 3 June Colonels Roosevelt and Wood, President McKinley's physician and in command of a volunteer regiment, arrived at Tampa with their regiment the Rough-Riders: 'The railway system was in the wildest confusion; it took us twelve hours to get into camp with our baggage.'[27] The same day Admiral Sampson dispatched Lieutenant Hobson to sink the blockship *Merrimac* across the narrowest part of the way out of the harbour in Santiago to prevent Cervera escaping. Nothing happened till the afternoon when Cervera's chief of staff came out of the harbour with a white flag to tell Sampson that Hobson's boat had capsized and that he was a prisoner. The Spanish commander warmly praised Hobson's bravery and Sampson was enthusiastic in his thanks to Cervera. Hobson, though he had utterly failed, became a hero to the press.

[25] Accompanied by, as the press noted with glee, Mrs Miles, Miss Miles and Sherman Miles, from the 6th Street Station.

[26] General William Rufus Shafter (1835–1906), Colonel in the Civil War. Previously a Michigan schoolmaster.

[27] Leonard Wood (1860–1927) was among the many who made their careers in the forthcoming war. He had helped in the 1880s to destroy the Apache Indians in a campaign of great toughness. He played a great part later in Cuban history.

On 8 June the U.S. army began to set off from Tampa. No one was ready. Tampa was a bad embarkation port. Confusion (no water supply, no pilots) delayed departure till 14 June. Roosevelt as usual was the most vivid witness:

> After an hour's industrious and rapid search through this antheap of humanity, Wood and I, who had been separated, found Colonel Humphrey at nearly the same time and were allotted a transport – the *Yucatan*. She was out in midstream, so Wood seized a stray launch and boarded her.

Roosevelt dropped a hasty line to Lodge describing the 'frightful mismanagement'[28] and then they were off – the 5th Army Corps under General Shafter, composed of eighty-five officers, 16,000 men and ninety journalists on thirty-two coastal ships. Wood wrote presciently to his wife:

> Hard it is to realise that this is the commencement of a new policy and that this is the first great expedition our country has ever sent oversea and marks the commencement of a new era in our relations with the world. For all the world the ocean reminds one of dear old Vineyard sound . . .[29]

At this time Senator Lodge was writing to Roosevelt:

> Porto Rico [*sic*] is not forgotten and we mean to have it. Unless I am utterly and profoundly mistaken, the Administration is now fully committed to *the large policy* that we both desire. We have had some dark days since you left and my very humdrum and unexciting part in the struggle has been one of constant work and anxiety.[30]

The armada appeared off Santiago on 20 June. That day Admiral Sampson and General Shafter landed to visit General Calixto García. Shafter announced he was going to the village of Daiquirí, about sixteen miles east of Santiago – Sampson was amazed and angry that he was not going to land nearer the bay – where he might have assisted the army. Shafter even refused to send troops to destroy the coastal batteries training on the bay, though he needed the navy to help him disembark. The landing followed – Shafter brushing with R. H. Davis who protested that, as a 'descriptive writer', he was exempt from the order preventing the other reporters from landing till later.[31] On 22 June 6,000 men set foot on Cuban soil, with great difficulty. The Spaniard,

[28] *Letters*, vol. II, 830,

[29] H. Hagedorn, *Leonard Wood*, 2 vols (1931), I, 160.

[30] This was in reply to Roosevelt's 'Give my best love to Nannie and do not make peace until we get Porto Rico while Cuba is independent and the Philippines at any rate taken from the Spaniards'.

[31] Stewart Holbrook, *Lost Men of American History* (1947), 288-9.

had several hundred men near by but failed, either by design or inertia, to make any attempt at preventing them. It was as if Sagasta's decision to lose the war in the shortest time had become known to every soldier. In Santiago, General Arsenio Linares had about 8,000 men and twenty bronze cannon[32] and, of course, Admiral Cervera's fleet; but Cervera and Captain-General Blanco in Havana were on almost as bad terms as were Shafter and Sampson.

[32] Fernández Almagro, 529.

CHAPTER XXXIII

San Juan Hill and Santiago

General Shafter's plan was to get to Santiago as soon as possible. He was deeply worried lest his men would succumb to disease as indeed he himself already had, suffering 'from gout and some malaria. It was a dash or nothing'.[1] At 9.20 p.m. anyway on the day of arrival General Lawton,[2] in command of the first infantry division, drove forward to the little town of Siboney and the small Spanish garrison withdrew. In the early hours of the next day 23 June, Lawton was surprised to be visited by ex-Confederate General Wheeler,[3] in command of the cavalry, Theodore Roosevelt, Colonel Wood, R. H. Davis and, behind them, the Rough-Riders: 'In their anxiety to be well forward they had reached Siboney by a forced march', Roosevelt explained. Even more surprising, General Wheeler thereafter actually overtook Lawton. A vigorous clash between a Union and a Confederate officer then occurred.

On 24 June Wheeler came upon earthworks breast-high about half a mile short of the village of Siboney. Secretary of State Fish's grandson, Hamilton Fish, was shot dead, the first U.S. casualty of the war. Spanish defensive firing brought the cavalry to a halt.

> What to do then [Roosevelt later wrote] I had not an idea . . . There was nothing but jungle . . . I was afraid I might get out of touch with everybody and not be going in the right direction . . . I was wearing my sword which in thick jungle now and then got between my legs.[4]

Later Roosevelt charged a small farmstead (known in U.S. military histories as Las Guasimas) and caught up with the main advance. By then General Wheeler however had been compelled, to his irritation, to send back for General Lawton's help. Wheeler then sent off an infantry regiment into Siboney. The Spaniards withdrew. 'We've got the damn Yankees on the run,' shouted Wheeler. Roosevelt wrote the next day:

> Yesterday we struck the Spaniards and had a brisk fight for two and a half hours . . . we lost a dozen men killed or mortally wounded

[1] Shafter's words reported in R. H. Titherington, *A History of the Spanish American War* (1900), 233.
[2] General Lawton (d. 1899), fought for the Union, 1863–6; died of drink in the Philippines.
[3] Joseph Wheeler (1836–1906); sixteen horses were shot under him in the Civil War.
[4] *Autobiography* (1913), 258.

[actually 16] and sixty severely or slightly wounded [actually 52] ...
the fire was heavy at one or two points where the men around me
went down like ninepins ... The Spaniards shot well but they did
not stand when we rushed. It was a good fight.[5]

From 25 to 29 June Shafter sought to consolidate his landing, secure
his rear and supplies, and prevent his over-eager commanders from
re-engaging. Generals Lawton and Wheeler quarrelled again over who
was to be in the advance. Shafter finally went down with fever and
directed the rest of the campaign with a high temperature from a camp
bed. On 30 June he ordered an attempt on the Spanish position at El
Caney in front of Santiago the next day. Roosevelt reported his men
'greatly overjoyed'.[6]

A U.S. message also requested General Calixto García to advance
with 4,000 men to protect El Caney and San Juan.[7] García's relations
with Shafter were bad but in these weeks it is clear that García felt such
contempt for the Cuban provisional government that he thought the
main aim of the Cuban rebels should be to prove their worth alongside
their new allies.[8] García was visited on 28 June by William Randolph
Hearst himself. García presented to Hearst a tattered battle flag, in
commemoration of the *Journal*'s services to liberty: 'Its colours are
faded but it is the best thing the Cuban Republic can offer its best
friend.'[9] García assured Hearst that the *Journal* had been the 'most
potent influence' in bringing the U.S. to the help of Cuba.[10] Under what
curious colours did liberty then ride!

Hearst had been active. When a rumour came that another Spanish
squadron was about to leave Cádiz for the Philippines, he had telegraphed
his favourite reporter, James Creelman, then in London: 'Make preparations so that in case the Spanish fleet actually starts for Manila we
can buy some big English steamer ... take her to ... the Suez Canal ...
sink her and obstruct the passage.'[11] Later, thwarted of a commission in
the navy, Hearst sailed for the U.S. landing stage in Cuba on the yacht
Sylvia; he interviewed Sampson personally ('a tea-going admiral – a

[5] *Letters*, 844–5.
[6] Roosevelt had now been appointed full colonel in command of the Rough-Riders since
Wood had been promoted, due to General Young's illness (Pringle, 194). His impatience
during the last few days had grown, especially against General Shafter, whose gout had
prevented him from wearing boots for a week. Roosevelt himself was very active, working
'like a cider press ... let him be a politician if he likes,' noted Stephen Crane, 'he was a
gentleman down here'. (Thomas Beer, *Stephen Crane* (1924), 197.)
[7] Roig, 89.
[8] García's letter to Estrada Palma, 27 June 1898, *Boletín del Archivo Nacional* (Havana, 1936),
110–12.
[9] *Evening Journal*, 29 June 1898, qu. Swanberg, 153.
[10] W. R. Hearst, letter to his mother, qu. *ibid.*, 154–5.
[11] Creelman, *On the Great Highway*, 190.

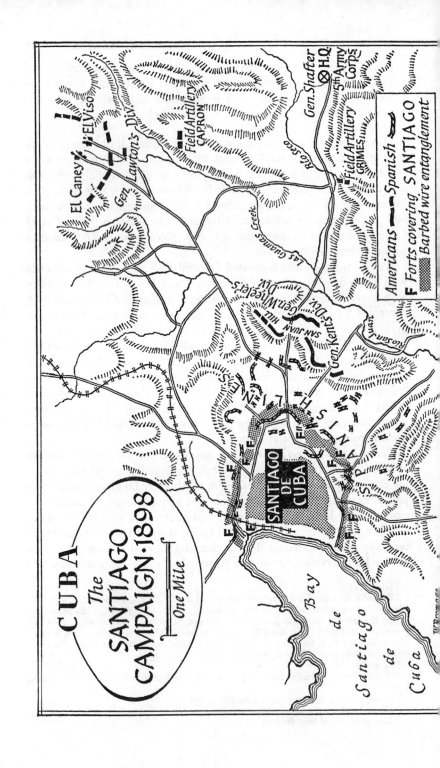

CUBA

The SANTIAGO CAMPAIGN · 1898

One Mile

El Caney
El Viso
Field Artillery CAPRON
Gen. Lawton's Div.
Gen. Shafter ⊗ H.Q.
5th Army Corps
Rio Seco
Field Artillery GRIMES
Las Guamas Creek
Gen. Wheeler's Div.
SAN JUAN HILL
Gen. Kent's Div.
San Juan River
SPANISH LINES
SANTIAGO DE CUBA
Bay de Santiago de Cuba

Americans ⌇ Spanish
F Forts covering SANTIAGO
▨ Barbed wire entanglement

W. Browne

rear-admiral, always in the rear'[12]) and made ready a printing press to print the *Journal-Examiner* for U.S. troops in Cuba. Hearst made himself war-correspondent-in-chief. In addition, he supplied the army surgeons with the ice which they had forgotten.[13] He had watched the first action, at Las Guasimas, from a near-by hill, being rebuked for 'drawing the fire' from the enemy.[14]

On 1 July the only major land battle of the Spanish-American war occurred, in face of the Spanish position on San Juan heights. It was a confused affair. Lawton's division set out for El Caney. Generals Kent and Wheeler were ordered to attack the hill known as San Juan.[15] Lawton faced only a company of Spaniards, 600 men with two cannons; Kent and Wheeler faced 250.[16] But this inequality of numbers did not make for a short battle. At 7 a.m. on the San Juan front, a U.S. battery opened fire on the Spanish position. Two hours later Kent's infantry was ordered to advance. About 3,000 men moved forward along a narrow track, scarcely broad enough in some places to permit the passage of a column of fours. The cavalry, including the Rough-Riders, now headed by General Sumner (Wheeler being ill), came up. Kent and Sumner carried out a reconnaissance. The advance continued, the fire becoming heavier.[17]

The fighting was concluded by a battery of Gatling guns on the Spanish position in the south. This kept the Spaniards' heads down, while first the infantry and then two regular cavalry regiments (one Negro) charged; Roosevelt with the Rough-Riders followed. The Spaniards withdrew to their next line of defence. The U.S. had thus captured at some cost the city's outer defences. The U.S. dead were 223, and wounded 1,243, with 79 missing; Spanish were 102 dead and 552 wounded. The U.S. thus lost a total of 1,591, or 10% of the total effective U.S. force.[18] For Roosevelt personally, an architect of the war, and the man perhaps best remembered in connection with it, the charge on 1 July was the final triumph of will over frail physique, as of the energy

---

[12] Swanberg, 151.

[13] George Clarke Musgrave, *Under Three Flags in Cuba* (1899), 327.

[14] J. C. Hemment, *Cannon and Camera* (1898), 148. Hemment was Hearst's cameraman.

[15] General Kent was the first infantry commander.

[16] Fernández Almagro, II, 531.

[17] The Spaniards were guided to their target by the U.S. raising an observation balloon.

[18] Fernández Almagro, 533. In retrospect this charge was a great moment: in Roosevelt's mind, it assumed immense importance: 'I waved my hat and we went up the hill with a rush' (*Autobiography*, 242); 'I rose over those regular officers like a balloon' (to Hagedorn, 13 August 1918); 'Did I tell you that I killed a Spaniard with my own hand?' (Roosevelt to Lodge, *Correspondence*, I, 325–8). A friend, R. H. M. Ferguson, wrote to Mrs Roosevelt: 'No hunting trip so far has ever equalled it in Theodore's eyes . . . when I caught him up the day of the charge . . . [he] was revelling in victory and gore. He had just doubled up a Spanish officer like a "jack-rabbit" as he retired from a block house and he encouraged us to look at those "damned Spanish dead"' (Pringle, 195). Roosevelt had six pairs of spectacles ready for the action.

of a young nation against a decadent old one. However, it would be more appropriate to recall the whole day as an occasion when 700 Spaniards held up 6,000 North Americans and inflicted very heavy damages upon them.

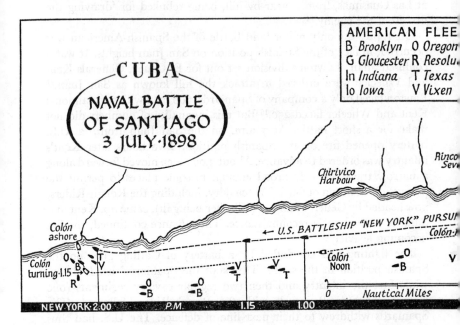

It would seem appropriate also to recall that another of the main architects of the war was in action too. Creelman, Hearst's ace reporter, hot-foot from London, also charged and was wounded:

> Someone knelt down in the grass beside me and put his hand on my fevered head. Opening my eyes I saw Mr Hearst . . . a straw hat with a bright ribbon on his head, a revolver at his belt, and a pencil and notebook in his hand . . . Slowly he took down my story of the fight. Again and again the ting of Mauser bullets interrupted. 'I'm sorry you're hurt, but,' his face was radiant, 'wasn't it a splendid fight? We must beat every paper in the world.'[19]

Even so, the historical recollection of victory differed in most minds from what really occurred after the battle. As usual in battles in Cuba, malaria and dysentery were gaining ground. General Shafter believed he had sustained a defeat, and lying on his bed contemplating retreat he could not visit the front. His divisional commanders, Wheeler and Young, were too ill to do anything. Theodore Roosevelt wrote to

[19] J. Creelman, 210-12.

Senator Lodge: 'Tell the President for heaven's sake to send us every regiment and above all every battery possible. We have won so far at a heavy cost ... We are within measurable distance of a terrible military disaster.'[20]

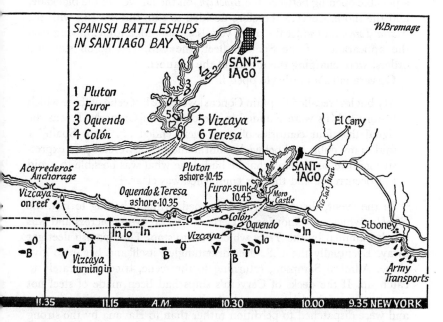

Had the Spaniards counter-attacked, they must have obtained a substantial victory. But they were in poor morale. There was no food in Santiago save rice. Captain-General Blanco too had ordered Admiral Cervera to leave port, and the admiral was complaining that the 'blockading fleet is four times superior to ours; our destruction is absolutely certain if we leave port'. Cervera appealed to the queen regent who, however, only implored for divine mercy. Blanco's insistence derived from his conviction that Spain might recover from the loss of a city but not from that of the fleet. On 3 July, then, the Spanish battle fleet steamed out of harbour determined to break the U.S. naval blockade, which consisted of a half-circle of powerful vessels ending appropriately on the east shoreward side with the *Gloucester* (in peace time, J. P. Morgan's yacht the *Corsair*).

One new element of comedy was forthcoming. The day that Cervera left port Admiral Sampson had already left for Siboney to confer with General Shafter. Hence neither he nor his flagship was present at this crucial engagement between the Anglo-Saxon and the Latin races: his rival, the discredited Commodore Schley, was in command.

The Spanish fleet left Santiago with Admiral Cervera and his flagship, the *María Teresa*, at its head. His aide, Captain Concás, had seen a possible opening between the *Brooklyn*, on the far west of the blockade, and the shore. Cervera therefore decided to ram the *Brooklyn* with the *María Teresa* and so let the other vessels escape. Meantime, having seen the appearance of the Spanish fleet, the U.S. vessels, on standing orders, were charging the mouth of the channel.

Cervera gave an order to open fire.

> My bugles [recalled Captain Concás] were the last echo of those which history tells us were sounded in the capture of Granada. It was the signal that four centuries of glory were ended ... 'Poor Spain,' I said to my noble and beloved admiral and he answered by an expressive gesture, as if to say that he had done what was possible to avoid this occurrence and that his conscience was clear.[21]

In the event, the *María Teresa* escaped, without having to ram the *Brooklyn* which, not knowing of Cervera's tactic, swung across and was nearly rammed by the *Texas* which had to stop. The Spanish fleet got away. Eventually the U.S. fleet disentangled itself and began to give chase. Admiral Sampson, returning to the scene, tried desperately to catch up. If the decks of Cervera's ships had been made of steel not wood, they might have escaped. As it was, they were easily set afire and were dispatched to perdition rather than to Havana by the strong following wind. The *María Teresa* ran aground in flames six miles west of the exit to the channel, Cervera himself swimming ashore. There he set up a temporary hospital till his surrender later to the U.S. naval command. The *Oquendo* followed, and then the *Vizcaya*. The commander of the first killed himself after directing the evacuation of his crew. *Colón* alone escaped altogether, but she ran out of coal and ran to shore after a short battle. The victory was as complete as Dewey's in Manila; but whose was it? Schley sent to Sampson the tactless signal: 'Have gained a great victory. Details will be communicated.' Sampson, appalled at the victory which had occurred in his absence, cabled Washington and did not speak of Schley: 'The fleet under my command offers the nation as a 4th of July present the whole of Cervera's fleet.' The total dead were: 350 Spaniards out of 2,225, and 1,670 prisoners; and only 1 dead, 2 wounded, in the U.S. fleet.[22] The Spanish officers mostly behaved with their usual gallantry: Lieutenant Fajardo lost an arm

---

[21] Víctor Concás, *The Squadron of Admiral Cervera*.
[22] See Cervera's dispatch of 9 July, qu. Fernández Almagro, II, 859–65; in addition, works cited, *ibid.*, 540, fn. 22.

but exclaimed amid horrible sufferings: 'There is still another to serve the country.' 'Do you believe, father, I have done my duty?' Midshipman Saralegui asked the naval chaplain, after his legs were cut off. Hearst toured the battleground in a yacht the next day, captured some Spanish sailors who, he noticed with interest, 'seemed to dread the Cubans far more than the Americans'.[23]

There had been meantime new developments on land. Shafter, appalled by the lack of morale and his weak position, had begun the day with a telegram to Washington suggesting a withdrawal of five miles. But his adjutant McClernand said, 'General, let us make a demand on them to surrender.'[24]

> Shafter was still ill and lying on his cot. He looked at me for perhaps a full minute and I thought he was going to offer a rebuke ... but finally he said, 'We'll do it.' I went ... and wrote the demand at 8.30 a.m. addressed to the commanding general of the Spanish forces ... He was told that unless he surrendered we would shell the city.

There was no immediate response, but at 6.30 General Toral said the city would not give in.[25] But in fact the fighting was not begun again. Four foreign consuls in Santiago came out with Shafter's messenger and begged for respite: about 20,000 persons wished to leave the city; they suggested non-combatants should be allowed to go to the village of Caney, and there be supplied with food. A truce was therefore agreed till 5 July.

On 4 July Shafter was still undecided what to do. Though he believed he could reduce the city, he knew that casualties would be heavy and that he could not even look after those of his men who were already sick. Sanitation in the U.S. camp was non-existent. Refugees mingled with soldiers in incessant rain. General Shafter cabled to Admiral Sampson: 'Now if you will force your way into that harbour, the town will surrender without any further sacrifice of life.' Sampson, frozen in hatred of Schley, again refused and Shafter telegraphed to Secretary of War Alger. Alger went to the president, with the naval expert Mahan present, and also Secretary of the Navy, Long.

> I remember a pretty scrimmage [wrote Long] between [Alger] and Captain Mahan ... the Secretary of War was complaining because we did not take the risk of blowing up our ships by going over the mines at Santiago ... Mahan at last sailed into him, telling him

[23] *Journal*, 6 July 1898, qu. Swanberg, 158.
[24] Edward John McClernand (1848–1926), hero of the Indian wars.
[25] Juan José Toral (1832–1904), a conventional Spanish officer.

he didn't know anything about the use or purpose of the Navy, which rather amused the President, who always liked a little badinage.[26]

McKinley ordered Shafter and Sampson to confer. Toral, appalled at the loss of the fleet, had spent the night of 4 July trying to sink the last cruiser in Santiago, the *Reina Mercedes*, in the channel. He was successful, though, thanks to U.S. crossfire from the *Texas* and *Indiana*, it went down in the wrong spot.

The role of the Cuban rebels and in particular of Calixto García in these events was obscure. In the battle of San Juan hill Cuban forces had had only 10 casualties. On 2 July at dawn they dislodged the Spaniards from Chabitas and Boniato, eventually covering the road from Holguín. Entrusted with 40 Spanish prisoners by the Americans at Caney, they cut off their heads – an atrocity defended by Hearst as the natural result of Spanish oppression, partly perhaps because the officer in charge, Colonel Honoré Laine, was a part-time Hearst correspondent: 'One seldom finds a man of more generous and gracious impulses than this same Laine. His hour has come and he is lost in almost savage enjoyment of it.'[27]

The sight however of the Cuban rebels under Calixto García appears to have disillusioned the U.S. forces. The U.S. army was mostly white, the Cuban almost entirely Negro. The U.S., even before their recent victory, felt more drawn to the chivalrous enemy than to their Cuban allies. The U.S. regular troops suffered from a shortage of supplies (especially tobacco) and it angered them to see the Cubans eating U.S. army stores and smoking tobacco. Already Spanish prisoners had struck up intense friendships with their captors. García was treated with contempt by Shafter who even suggested that, instead of battle, the guerrillas should work as labourers.[28]

In the evening of 3 July, Colonel Escario's Spanish relief column from Manzanillo reached Santiago along the Cobre road, without being prevented by Calixto García. He was evidently reluctant to lift a finger to help – an error of judgement which finally diverted the U.S. army from sympathy with the Cubans. But Escario's arrival made the Spanish position worse rather than better, for he brought neither munitions nor food.[29] This reinforcement therefore added to Toral's supply difficulties. In the meantime Shafter was establishing himself effectively around the city. On 8 July Shafter was visited by Captain Chadwick, on behalf of Sampson (nominally ill), and another surrender demand was decided

[26] Long, *America of Yesterday*, 326.
[27] *New York Journal*, 6 July 1898, qu. Swanberg, 156.
[28] Leech, 273.
[29] Fernández Almagro, II, 536.

upon. Unless terms were agreed by the next day, the navy would open fire. This gave no time for communication with Madrid. On 8 July Toral offered to surrender the city and the eastern part of the province, on condition that he should be allowed to withdraw with full equipment to Holguín. Shafter telegraphed Washington to secure agreement to this but Alger refused and the truce accordingly ended on 10 July. That day and the next there was artillery fire, destroying some houses in the now almost deserted city of Santiago and disabling most of Toral's artillery. On 11 July Shafter suggested, on Washington's proposal, that Toral's army would be returned to Spain at U.S. expense if they surrendered unconditionally.

On 12 July the commander-in-chief General Miles arrived in Siboney from Florida with reinforcements. He found the U.S. troops in an even worse position than he had supposed. Three cases of yellow fever had been established; malaria, dysentery and typhoid dominated the rainy forest; journalists were turning their mood from triumph to revelation of the misery on the U.S. lines. Miles took vigorous action in burning the village of Siboney to the ground, destroying the infected huts which passed for houses. Miles, Shafter and Toral met and on 14 July Toral told Shafter that Captain-General Blanco had referred the subject of surrender to Madrid. Meanwhile discussions could continue. Blanco himself argued for resistance à l'outrance: 'The Army in general desires to continue the war . . . it would be tragic to give up now without fighting a territory which it has kept through so many years at the cost of so much blood . . .' But General Correa, Minister of War, telegraphed back on 12 July:

> I am surprised that the honour of your indomitable Army being already saved – as it indubitably is to the admiration of the whole world . . . you should persist in urging the forces in the province of Santiago to continue a war in which they cannot, certainly, gain more laurels . . . *neither can I explain to myself your tenacity in maintaining our position in so ungrateful a territory, a territory which repels us and makes itself hateful to us through its desire to separate from the mother country.*

Blanco replied that the army in Cuba wished to continue the war but that it would 'of course' never present obstacles to the full execution of the government's order.[30] But even so there was considerable fear in Washington that the Spaniards might merely be playing for time.

They were not. On 12 July Captain-General Blanco suggested that Toral should break through the U.S. lines by attacking in conjunction with the troops at Holguín. General Linares ('confined to my bed by great weakness and much pain') replied:

[30] *Ibid.*, 544.

Enemy's position very close to precinct of city, favoured by nature of ground; ours spread out over fourteen kilometres. Large number sick, not sent to hospital because necessary to retain them in trenches. Horses and mules without food or shelter. Rain has been flowing into the trenches incessantly for twenty hours . . . [Therefore] impossible to open passage, because one third of our men would be unable to go out . . . Santiago de Cuba is not Gerona, a walled city, on the soil of the mother country, to be defended inch by inch by her own sons . . .[31] Here there is solitude, the complete exodus of the population, insular as well as peninsular . . . only the clergy remain and they intend to leave tomorrow . . . The defenders . . . have been fighting for three years against the climate, other privations and fatigue.

On 14 July Miles and Shafter saw Toral again, telling him that the only condition of surrender could be the safe return of his troops to Spain. Generals Wheeler and Lawton, General Escario and Colonel Fontán, and the British Vice-Consul Mason were then appointed commissioners to draw up terms. There was no Cuban rebel representative. Negotiations continued but were delayed by Toral's requirement to communicate with Madrid. It was believed in the U.S. camp that an attack on Santiago would ultimately be necessary, and everything was prepared. But on 17 July the final terms of surrender were agreed. Toral handed over Santiago and its province to 'the authority of the U.S.' (Blanco later assured his government in Madrid that the surrender had been carried out without 'the intervention of my authority'.[32]) Shafter and Toral rode into Santiago and at noon the U.S. flag rose over the governor's palace. As ever in this conflict the press intervened: Sylvester Scovel of the *World* tried to be photographed with the flag rising behind him. He was arrested in time but spoiled the day for Shafter. Posters were distributed quickly throughout the city: '*Remember the Maine. Buy the Journal*' – the Cuban edition, that is. General Calixto García, though orally invited to attend by Shafter, refused on the grounds that the Spanish municipal officials had not been removed. His men were not asked, in fact, on the grounds that 'the entering of Cuban troops into the city would not be tolerated for the obvious fear of reprisals'.[33] General Shafter had some outstanding quarrels with Admiral Sampson but the conquest of Santiago and Oriente was now

[31] As occurred in the case of Gerona in both 1708 and 1809.

[32] Fernández Almagro, II 544.

[33] Rubens, *Liberty*, 378, puts the last point; for the first, see Shafter, *Century* magazine; Shafter-Alger, 29 July 1898, *Corres. Rel.*, I, 185; ref. Leech, 638. A note in the Communist newspaper *Hoy* after Castro's revolution says that the 'troops of the U.S. who had intervened to frustrate the true independence of Cuba kept the Cuban military leaders to whom the Spaniards owed their defeat out of the negotiations' (*cf. Hoy*, 17 July 1965). The inaccuracy of this statement can be seen.

complete.[34] 'I feel that I now leave the children a memory that will partly offset the fact that I do not leave them much money,' wrote Roosevelt.[35] General Miles, angered by the ambiguity of his relationship with Shafter, left for Puerto Rico with a small force of volunteers, with Sampson's help and quite contrary to the expressed wishes of Alger and McKinley. Once more, field officers were exceeding their instructions.

[34] The U.S. took 30,000 prisoners, with arms – 100 cannon, 6,800 charges, 15lbs of gunpowder, 25,114 rifles, 1½ million cartridges and 19 machine-guns.
[35] *Letters*, II, 854.

CHAPTER XXXIV

End of Empire

The war between the U.S. and Spain now came to an end. General Miles, with less than 3,000 men, himself landed in Puerto Rico and began to advance towards the centre of the island with the verve of one who had to gain a great success to justify his criticism of others. There was no resistance. General Miles told Puertorriqueños to their surprise: 'The just effect of this occupation will be the immediate release from your former political relations and, it is hoped, a cheerful acceptance of the government of the U.S.' No one knew till that moment that the U.S. had any designs on Puerto Rico. In the Philippines the second U.S. army, of 35,000 men, also arrived; the patriot leader, General Aguinaldo, had proclaimed himself president of a Philippine republic but the U.S. General Anderson told him to 'inform your people that we are here for their good and that they must supply us with labour and material at current market prices'. On 26 July Admiral Dewey wrote home that the land army's 'most difficult problem will be how to deal with insurgents under Aguinaldo who had now become aggressive and even threatening towards our Army'.[1]

McKinley suggested to his cabinet a trip down the Potomac to discuss the peace proposals. What status should be given to Cuba? What should the U.S. do with the Philippines? And Puerto Rico? On 30 July terms were decided; the U.S. would offer guidance in establishing an independent Cuban government. Spain would drop all claims on Cuba. Puerto Rico, together with other Spanish small islands in the West Indies, together with the largest island in the Ladrones (the later famous Guam),[2] would be ceded to the U.S. as indemnification as a result of war. The U.S. would keep Manila till the future status of the Philippines was decided.[3]

These were high-handed demands. The imperial mood in the U.S. was irresistible. On 7 July, almost unnoticed, all opposition to the annexation of Hawaii had collapsed and the cruiser *Philadelphia* had gone off to take formal possession of the island. ('We need Hawaii just

[1] Millis, 334–5.

[2] Also known as the Marianas; fifteen islands in the Pacific discovered by Magellan. Spain sold the other islands to Germany in 1899, and these were later put under a Japanese mandate.

[3] See Eugenio Montero Ríos, *El Tratado de París* (1904), 34.

as much and a good deal more than we did California,' muttered McKinley to his secretary, 'it is manifest destiny.'[4])

Cuba was confused. General Lawton was appointed governor of the province of Oriente and on 20 July Colonel (now acting General) Wood became governor of the city of Santiago. But Calixto García insisted that 'by the nature of the intervention [the administration] should be turned over to the Cubans'. Shafter told García that the Cubans might direct the Civil administration and named General Demetrio Castillo as mayor. However this arrangement did not last more than a few days since though Castillo impressed the U.S. officers as an excellent man, at his back there seemed 'to be only a hungry, vengeful horde'.[5] McKinley then agreed that Spanish officials should where possible remain: Leonardo Ros, mayor of Santiago in the past, resumed his old position, to the fury of the Cubans. It was a terrible insult. García took his troops up to the hills in dudgeon. The augury was disagreeable.

Wood, as effective ruler of Santiago, found himself with 'the very air ... laden with death'.[6] The death rate from dysentery or yellow fever was 200 a day. Corpses had been lying unburied for days. The charnel houses were full. Cremation was essential to kill germs, but one day in late July the rain quenched the smoke of all fires. Wood summoned the merchants of the city and lectured them: 'We have come to Cuba at your call to relieve your distress. You are repaying our efforts by trying to make money out of us.'[7] Wood himself shortly succumbed to yellow fever, but he maintained morale and work. His biographer says that 'he received no help from the people of Santiago, Cubans or Spaniards ... the Spanish officials, the priests, the friars, were callous; the old archbishop was concerned only about the $18,000 in salary which the Spanish government had hitherto paid him ...' Wood himself wrote: 'The people are entirely brutalized and not a Cuban, with one or two exceptions, has come forward to do anything for his people ... The conditions here are something frightful and the civil hospital crowded. Small children may be seen any day striving to waken their mother already dead or dying.'[8] The only possible Cuban administration could have been provided by the Cuban rebel army and they, disillusioned and disgruntled, were permitted no role.

What also was going to happen to the Cuban rebel provisional government? In late July a Nebraska lawyer, Charles Magoon, went to

---

[4] Cortelyou MSS, as qu. Leech, 213. Thomas Bailey (*Am. Hist. Rev.*, xxxvl, 560) thought that had it not been for the war Hawaii would never have been annexed.

[5] Hagedorn, *Wood*, I, 199.

[6] *Ibid.*, 185.

[7] *Ibid.*, 189.

[8] *Ibid.*, 196–8.

inform the junta in New York of the ceasefire, on behalf of the McKinley administration, but Estrada Palma insisted that the notification be made to the provisional government.[9] Nevertheless, this clarified nothing. Calixto García marched his threadbare army to Holguín and Gibara to secure the surrender of the Spanish forces there. Then he handed over to the shadow government.[10]

A similar situation persisted in the Philippines, where the other group of patriots helped by the U.S. were also feeling cheated. General Aguinaldo had won several victories but had surrendered Manila to the U.S. generals. He wrote to the U.S. Consul Williams that the Filipinos would not believe in the benefits to be obtained by joining the U.S.:

> You say all this and more will result from annexing ourselves to your people and I believe the same myself, since you are my friend and the friend of the Filipinos ... But will ... my people believe it? I have full confidence in the generosity and philanthropy which shine in letters of gold in the history of the privileged U.S. people and for that reason ... I pray you earnestly ... to recognise the revolutionary government of the Filipinos.[11]

Yet even so, ominously, three more U.S. armies shortly landed, under Generals Anderson, Greene and MacArthur.

This anxiety on the part of the peoples allegedly freed by the U.S. made the thoughts of the U.S. governing class seem curiously ill-informed. Ambassador John Hay (in London) wrote a famous letter to Theodore Roosevelt:

> It has been a splendid little war; begun with the highest motives, carried on with magnificent intelligence and spirit, favoured by that fortune which loves the brave. It is now to be concluded, I hope, with that firm good nature which is after all the distinguishing trait of our American character.[12]

Hay shortly became Secretary of State.[13]

As with the English in 1762, and indeed as with most armies in the Caribbean 'splendid' though the war may have been, the victory was less so for the U.S. forces (like those of Albemarle) which were now losing more casualties from malaria than they had done in battle. The 24th Infantry, supposedly immune by reason of their black skin, were immediately sent to Cuba to help the medical staff: all went down.

[9] Rubens, 382-3.
[10] *Ibid.*, 380. For Charles Magoon (1861-1920), see below Chapter XL.
[11] Qu. Millis.
[12] Hay to Roosevelt.
[13] In August, succeeding Judge Day.

General Shafter cabled on 2 August: 'I advise that the troops be moved as rapidly as possible while the sickness is of a mild type.' But what could be done with the Spanish prisoners? Washington suggested that the army move up to the hills – a long march impossible for fever-ravaged men. The consequence was near panic in the U.S. command. Shafter called a staff meeting at the palace in Santiago at which all the commanders and the medical officers insisted that the army be moved. Wood drafted a protest in the form of a letter to Shafter signed by all commanders[14] demanding recall. Shafter sent the letter to Washington to substantiate his recommendations, and either Roosevelt or Wood gave the letter to the correspondent of Associated Press.[15] This 'Round Robin' was couched in rather sensational terms: Roosevelt's cavalry brigade was described as 'dying like rotten sheep';

The Army should be at once taken out of . . . Cuba and sent to some port on the north coast of the U.S. . . . the Army is disabled by malarial fever to the extent that its efficiency is destroyed and that it is in a condition to be practically entirely destroyed by an epidemic of yellow fever which is sure to come in the near future.[16]

The document (which appeared in the U.S. press on 4 August) was quite truthful: double the number of men had died since the fighting had ended than had died in action.[17] McKinley and Alger were indignant; for it left the suggestion that, while still negotiating with Spain, the U.S. might not be able to hold the territory they had won. Even so, transport of troops back to the U.S. began on 7 August, though the camps in the U.S. were not ready to receive them. Millionaires once more stepped in, this time with cooks.

So the coming of peace occurred against a background of protest, counter-protest, enquiries, press arguments[18] and recrimination. The

[14] Except Lawton who criticized the 'mandatory language'.
[15] This was never substantiated.
[16] Roosevelt, *Letters*, 864–5.
[17] The *Report of the Adjutant-General 1898–99* (facing p. 10) gives this breakdown of losses for March 1898–June 1899:

	Officers			Men		
	Killed in action	Died of wounds	Died of disease	Killed in action	Died of wounds	Died of disease
Regular army	24	7	51	270	114	1,524
Volunteers	17	3	114	188	78	3,820
	38*	10	165	458	192	5,344

* 3 officers of regular army also held commissions in volunteer regiments and are deducted from the total.

[18] 'Many of the Nebraska volunteers,' said William Jennings Bryan (who had insisted on becoming a colonel of the National Guard enrolled as the 3rd Nebraska regiment), 'feel they have a right to be mustered out, on the ground that the issues of the war have changed. They volunteered to break the yoke of Spain in Cuba and for nothing else. They did not volunteer to attempt the subjugation of other peoples . . .'; qu. Leech, 338, from McKinley papers.

U.S. press, losing interest in the war, was beginning to lose money, finding that the scandals of the army sold newspapers less than pre-. paration for conflict. The cost of maintaining the fleet of tugs and of sending incessant cables had wiped out much of the *World*'s profits. Pulitzer had been jaded with the war since he had been exposed by Hearst for stealing his news,[19] and demanded the return of the troops.[20]

On 11 August the Spanish cabinet accepted the U.S. peace terms, but pointed out that 'the ground on which the U.S. believe themselves entitled to ... Manila cannot be that of conquest' since it had not yet been occupied: Dewey's fleet was merely anchored outside and General Aguinaldo had declared the Philippines independent. The Spaniards apparently hoped even then to preserve the Philippines as Spanish by surrendering Cuba. Of Spanish generals and politicians consulted by Sagasta, only one, Romero Robledo, thought that war should be continued, though General Azcárraga thought it tragic that all the Spanish troops in central and west Cuba should not be tested against the U.S. Weyler also appears not to have accepted the idea of peace.[21] On 15 August Manila surrendered to the U.S. and the campaign in Puerto Rico also ended. U.S. and Spanish commissions met in Paris on 1 October: before they set out the U.S. commissioners were addressed by McKinley:

The march of events rules and over-rules human action ... we cannot be unmindful that without any desire or design on our part the war has brought us new duties and responsibilities which we must meet and discharge as becomes a great nation, on whose growth and career, from the beginning, the Ruler of Nations had plainly written a high command and pledge of civilisation. Incidental to our tenure in the Philippines is the commercial opportunity to which American statesmanship cannot be indifferent.[22]

Few voices rose to challenge this view.

[19] The *Journal*, 8 June, published a story of the death of 'an Austrian Colonel, Reflipe W. Thenuz', from wounds, and the *World* also reported this on 9 June. On 10 June the *Journal* revealed that the name was an invention, being an anagram of 'we pilfer the news'. This excellent joke was rubbed in for a month, with cartoons of Colonel Thenuz 'especially taken for the *World*' and speaking of 'a monument to Colonel Thenuz's memory' (Swanberg, 148-9).
[20] Pulitzer's boldest bid for attention – the hiring of Stephen Crane as a correspondent – went wrong, for Crane's longest dispatch spoke of the shortcomings under fire of the 71st New York regiment. This was seized on by Hearst as slandering the honour of New York. When Pulitzer attempted to make amends by starting a fund for a war memorial to the dead of the 71st, Hearst poured scorn on this change of front and Roosevelt, back from Cuba in early August, announced that no dead Rough-Rider could possibly lie in the same grave as one of the 71st. See D. C. Seitz, *Joseph Pulitzer*, 241.
[21] Fernández Almagro II, 567-8.
[22] Qu. Millis, 374.

Spain undertook to evacuate Cuba by 1 January. The Spaniards tried to get the U.S. to assume responsibility for the Cuban debt, that is, about $M400 spent in Cuba by the Spanish government. After much debate, and anguish on the part of Spain, the question was left for future settlement: the U.S. refused responsibility. Then, after weeks of indecision and praying, McKinley yielded to popular demand and accepted the expansionists' desire to absorb the Philippines: the only alternative to U.S. rule seemed to be General Aguinaldo and in Washington it was supposed that Aguinaldo could not hold the archipelago together, thereby rendering conquest by new European powers (Germany for instance) likely. McKinley ... 'walked the floor of the White House night after night until after midnight', and

> I am not ashamed to tell you gentlemen [he told the General Missionary Committee of the Methodist Episcopal Church], that I went down on my knees and prayed Almighty God for ... guidance ... And one night late it came ... there was nothing left for us to do but to take them all, and to educate the Filipinos and uplift them ... And then I went to bed ... and the next morning I sent for the chief engineer of the War Department (our mapmaker) and I told him to put the Philippines on the map of the U.S.[23]

Ecclesiastical and missionary support for the annexationism was now strong.[24]

The Spanish government was equally self-satisfied: 'Moved by lofty reasons of patriotism and humanity' they would 'not assume the responsibility of again bringing upon Spain all the horrors of war. In order to avoid them it resigns itself to the painful strait of submitting to the law of the victor, however harsh it may be ...'. Spain would be paid $M20 by the U.S. for the cession of the Philippines. The peace treaty was signed on 10 December and, after what Lodge termed the 'closest, hardest fight', ratified by Congress – a few hours after actual fighting had broken out between the rebel Filipinos under Aguinaldo and the Americans. This did not, however, later prevent McKinley appearing in a big hall in Boston on the anniversary of the *Maine* explosion in early 1899, under portraits of himself, Lincoln and Washington, all three being described as 'liberators'. Senator Hoare, the leader of the anti-expansionists, was dispatched to London as ambassador to succeed John Hay.

[23] Leech, 345. This was in the course of the 1898 congressional elections. Earlier he had remarked, 'I must learn a great deal of geography in this war' (qu. Wayne Morgan, 387).

[24] See Pratt, *Expansionists*, 315ff. Much the most interesting account of the pressures behind the move to take the Philippines is in Grenville and Young.

In Spain these events called forth a whole series of self-questioning reflections and doubts, beginning with a famous article by the Conservative leader, Silvela, entitled *Sin Pulso*[25] in August in *El Tiempo*:

> Peace is being made, reason counsels it, men of right minds do not even discuss it. But it signifies our surrender, the final expulsion of our flag from lands which we discovered and conquered; everyone can see that a little more application on the part of our leaders, a little more foresight by our governments, would have sufficed to wrest some moment of glory for us, a date or a victory to arrest such universal decay, and to enable us to close our eyes and those of our children with confidence in our race. But all await and all fear some trembling of the national conscience; it is only averted by a general cloud of melancholy silence, which like a grey background in a portrait, does not alter our life, our customs, our habits, nor the act of surrender with which, without knowing why or wherefore, the government is concerned. Some say that materialism has overtaken us; some, that egotism has killed us; that ideas of duty, glory, national honour have passed ... we must stop lying to ourselves and face facts ... reconstituting all the organisms of our national life, on the basis, modest but firm, that our means provide.

This appeal inaugurated the national soul-searching of Spain in 1898-1900, which to some extent has never ceased and which was partly echoed by the similar post-imperial soul-searching in Britain during the 1960s. The generals returned, to meet, like Toral at Vigo, various popular manifestations of hostility or, like Cervera at Madrid, respectful silence. There were rumours of *pronunciamientos*: would General Polavieja, the hero of a 'forward' policy in the Philippines, rise with Republican support? Would Weyler join Don Carlos? Did Polavieja have Catalan backing? But evidently the sense of loss among the crowds shouting '*muera*' outside the house of an unpopular general or reeling back from the Plaza de Toros (the news of Manila Bay began to circulate round the crowd at a *corrida* in Madrid) was greater than this mere political anxiety. The mood in Madrid was more profound than had occurred after Bolívar's victory at Ayacucho. There was a sensation of stupor, of pointlessness, of nothing to fall back upon; to think of all the armies dying, the ships sunk, the gold wasted – and what was left, besides a few broken politicians, some calling themselves Liberals, some Conservatives? And how could republicanism or Carlism be a satisfactory solution? Hence the swift rise of Catalan and Basque nationalism, of socialism through the U.G.T. and anarcho-syndicalism through the C.N.T. The failure of the State appeared patent. It was appropriate

[25] 'No pulse', qu. as Appendix 32 to Fernández Almagro, II.

that Sabino de Arana should achieve a municipal councillorship for the Basque National party in 1898.

Across the Atlantic, the Cubans accepted the *diktat* presented to them, not joyfully but reluctantly, trusting in the Teller amendment.[26] Had they been in a fit condition to fight the U.S. they might have continued to do so, as Aguinaldo was preparing to do in the Philippines. But Máximo Gómez and García had fought much longer and harder than Aguinaldo. Many of their outstanding lieutenants were dead. They were themselves now old men. They lacked the critical support of U.S. newspapers. U.S. news dispatches indeed depicted them and the other rebels as greedy adventurers or ruthless killers of chivalrous Spaniards.[27]

The period between the signature of the protocol of peace on 12 August and the establishment of U.S. control in Cuba in January was one of disorder in all Cuba except in the east:

> There was little semblance of . . . government and no security . . . the Spanish guerillas have been disbanded; some have been paid partially, and others not at all. They have taken to marauding and in small bands take from the poor whatever they have; they slaughter all the cattle they find quite close up to the town and send this meat to market . . .[28]

In west Cuba, 'the most unclean and repugnant animals were devoured with delight and . . . hunted with frenzied zeal. Roots, branches and herbs . . . also.'[29] Havana depended on the U.S. exclusively for food.[30]

The Spaniards 'to a man', reported Atkins's Cienfuegos manager, now wanted only annexation and 'unless this is obtained or the island is to remain under control of the U.S., they will give up their business and return to Spain'. One Cuban rebel officer also said:

> 'God grant the [North] Americans will soon take possession of the government and let us go home and do something different . . .' That was the general desire of their people here.[31] The insurgents in camps near here are being fed by Cienfuegos people but how long this constitution can continue is a question . . . there is extreme suffering among the insurgents coming in from the hills . . . the [Spanish] troops are still concentrated on and near this city, anxious to return to Spain. I hear the guerillas have not been paid for six

[26] See above, 376.
[27] See New York *Evening Post*, 19 and 21 July 1898; New York *Tribune*, 7 and 20 July.
[28] Cabada (agent) to Atkins, Atkins, 286.
[29] R. Martínez Ortíz, *Cuba: los primeros años de independencia*, 2 vols (2nd edn, 1921), I, 15.
[30] *Ibid.*
[31] Atkins, 290.

months. Will our governments have to assist them as well as the insurgents? . . .[32]

In general the relations between Americans and Spaniards in Cuba were excellent, while those between Cubans and Americans were almost invariably bad. General Young was found speaking of Calixto García's army as 'a lot of degenerates, absolutely devoid of honour or gratitude. They are no more capable of self government than the savages.'[33] Montejo thought the 'Americans didn't like the Negroes much. They used to shout "nigger nigger" and burst out laughing.'[34] Spanish officers in contrast were greeted as chivalrous brothers in arms: Admiral Cervera received a great welcome in New Hampshire when he visited Spanish prisoners there.

The Spaniards drew out of the towns of Oriente with bitterness and sometimes with spite – filling water cisterns with manure and killing cattle, almost invariably leaving behind disease. In September General Leonard Wood took over as governor of all Oriente.[35] Again the Cubans were not consulted. Wood wrote to his wife that Santiago 'is at least clean and we are down, so to speak, to *modern* dirt . . . of a less offensive character than that of 1520'.[36] The water system was restored, garbage collected, but misery remained in outer districts. However, according to Wood, 'agitators' were already saying that if only Cubans had been in control there would be adequate food. Wood found himself restraining two Cubans from beginning a Radical newspaper. Accusations of corruption accompanied denunciations of agitation: 'You would be amazed at the frankness of some of the people who want to buy favors or influence,' Wood wrote to his wife. 'They are so absolutely corrupt.'[37] Wood set to work cutting municipal salaries right and left, especially the archbishop's down to one-third of what it had been; and an Irish Major McCleary from Texas, who spoke Spanish, became mayor.

These measures scarcely helped relations with the Cubans. As early as mid-September there were strong rumours of an anti-U.S. *pronunciamiento*. On 22 September Calixto García was at last allowed to enter Santiago as a U.S. guest: there were great celebrations by the Cubans who had to be prevented by force from breaking up the *Casino Español*.[38] At the beginning of October, Wood was asked by García to provide

> Work and rations for his men. I told him they could have neither while they remained under arms. He threatened war and I told him

[32] *Ibid.*, 289.
[33] *loc. cit.*
[34] Montejo, 216. Direct reportage in Montejo may not be accurate.
[35] Lawton went to the Philippines.
[36] Hagedorn, I, 202.
[37] *Ibid.*, 207.
[38] *Ibid.*, 205.

the sooner he began the better because, as we had taken a mean job on our hands, that might be the best way out of it.

After this, the Cubans gave up their arms slowly: some became brigands. Colonel Francisco Valiente cleverly suggested to Wood that he should try to organize these into a form of rural guard: he did so, quite successfully. Wood as a result 'agreed to avoid U.S. soldiers having to fight Cubans';[39] and in November Wood appointed the 'ablest' citizen of Santiago, Emilio Bacardí, a rum merchant, as the fourth mayor of the city since July.[40]

On 27 November Wood wrote personally to his ex-patient, President McKinley:

> The plan of administration has been one of personal supervision to the greatest extent possible. I inspect, advise, and counsel with hundreds of people daily . . . getting them to disband, getting them to work, and impressing upon them the necessity of recognising the absolute authority of the civil law.[41]

He worked indefatigably – bringing back the public records of the city from the refuse dump, appointing judges, attorneys, a court, issuing a bill of rights: 'ever since I have been in Santiago I have prescribed liberal doses of the U.S. Constitution and the treatment has been remarkably efficacious'.[42] He appointed a committee of fifty Cubans to select honest and efficient public servants. This 'stirred Cubans' to 'self sacrifice'. He imposed a tax on all trade licences – that is, all gainful occupations – raising the city of Santiago's income from $200,000 to $240,000. He embarked on building limestone highways along old Cuban trails, and a new wall along the waterfront; he extended the government wharf in the port, dredging where the sewers flowed out; he renovated the gaol, the slaughter houses, the markets and the military hospital; he built an ice plant, a new orphanage, and a grammar school for girls. He banned bullfighting and public gambling, secured that all livestock owners should register their animals, prosecuted bakers and merchants for falsifying weights and scales, inspected steamers going north with sick soldiers, prepared a code of Spanish and Cuban laws, engaged engineers to plan a new water system and eventually abolished free rations except for the totally destitute.[43] It was as if an immense machine was at work: the competent and dedicated North American in Latin surroundings.

[39] *Ibid.*, 214.
[40] *Ibid.*, 217.
[41] *Ibid.*, 216
[42] *Ibid.*, 21£
[43] *Ibid.*, ££¢

Wood's effect was less marked outside Santiago but still vigorous. He found one small town in north Oriente which had three mayors, and about fifteen officials each; each proposed to spend $10,000 a year on salaries out of an annual income of $4,000. Wood said: 'You are not very patriotic.' The mayors said they had each served in the revolution. Wood said: 'Is there a man in this town . . . patriotic enough to serve as mayor without a salary?' A man who had not fought in the revolution was found and Wood made him mayor.[44]

Meantime the Cuban provisional government dissolved itself but Gómez continued as commander-in-chief of the army, while the army assembly – which had passed during both the Ten Years' War and the recent war as a legislature – appointed a special committee to look after Cuban interests during the U.S. control. A committee also went to New York to raise funds to pay the rebel army so that it could indeed be formally disbanded – this being headed by García. García was well treated. He met Shafter and McKinley at the White House and at the Gridiron Club dinner, then suddenly died in Washington on 11 December. Cuban independence seemed a forgotten matter of the past, while the island waited for the Spanish authorities to withdraw completely and for a North American military governor to arrive in Havana itself. The employees of the National Archives had ample time to sell off large quantities of official documents to the paper factory at Puentes Grandes.[45] 'Self-government,' the liberator Shafter remarked in mid-December, 'why, these people are no more fit for self-government than gun-powder is for hell.'[46]

So ended Cuba's long experience of Spanish rule, along with the Spanish colonial empire. Corrupt, inefficient and short-sighted the Spanish captains-general and ministers of overseas territories had been for many generations, but much of the vilification latterly heaped upon them by both Cubans and North Americans was not deserved; for, despite every frustration, by the 1890s they had created (or at least not prevented the creation of) a society of a distinctive, recognizable Spanish type in Cuba, one which was reasonably balanced between Negro and white and where the relations between the races were, if elusive, evidently less tense than in the Anglo-Saxon societies of America. Despite wars, persistent conspiracies and continual economic crises, prosperity and production had grown steadily. The emancipation of slaves had finally been achieved, with relative serenity. In addition by the 1890s there did exist a political life within the island underpinning strong political parties, with clear rights and possibilities, even with

[44] *Ibid.*, 214.
[45] Serie Archivos, No. 1, *Guía del Archivo Nacional*.
[46] New York *Tribune*, 19 December, 1898.

friends as well as representation in Madrid. Constitutional evolution between 1878 and 1895 was quite fast by most colonial standards. Indeed, Spain's general achievements in Cuba compare most favourably with those of Britain in Jamaica and the other islands of the West Indies at the same time, as was pointed out by the English historian Froude after his Cuban visit in 1887:

> Be the faults of their administration as heavy as they are alleged to be, the Spaniards have done more to Europeanise their islands than we have done with ours . . . Cuba is a second home to the Spaniards, a permanent addition to their soil. We are as birds of passage, temporary residents for transient purposes with no home in our islands at all.[47]

The vast number of poets left behind by the independence movement, rhetorical and repetitious though they were, some martyrs, some opportunists, left behind a real national tradition, even if it was a little operatic, an affair of gestures and cloaks.

The trouble however was that there was no real long-term solution to the problem of Cuba within the Spanish empire. Cuba was already as closely connected with the U.S. economy as with the Spanish. The U.S. was Cuba's greatest customer. It was thus appropriate as well as symptomatic that despite the understandable protestations of Cuban historians to the contrary, it was either intervention or the fear of it which actually decided the issue in the second war of independence. Had it not been for the U.S. Weyler would not have been recalled; had it not been for the intervention by the U.S., the Autonomist government would have established itself while Ramón Blanco would ultimately have achieved a new Zanjón or even a more conclusive peace. Whether in the long run an autonomous government would have been very different from what actually transpired cannot be known. The slender following for such a party in peacetime conditions was evident. But even had such an autonomist government been established it would have continued to depend on the U.S. Such a government would no doubt have welcomed U.S. investment, would have looked for U.S. help in reconstructing the country and would have sold its sugar to the U.S. The Cuban oligarchy of the early nineteenth century had been severely bruised by the sugar crisis of the 1880s and their destruction as a master class would have been completed by the civil war of 1895–8, however it ended. Still, such an autonomous Cuban state would nevertheless have been Spanish in authorship, and it might have preserved the island and people from the disconcerting and ambiguous experiences of U.S. intervention and military rule afterwards.

[47] Froude, *The English in the West Indies*, 332.

COST TO SPAIN OF THE CUBAN WAR, 1895–8

From 4 May 1895 to 30 June 1898: 1,554,447,449.64 pesetas

180,431 soldiers
6,222 *oficiales*
6,015 *jefes* } sent on expeditions
20 generals
12,000 already there

over 200,000

	Killed in battle with the enemy	Died of wounds	Died of yellow fever	Died of other diseases
Casualties	1 general			
	81 *oficiales*	463	313	127
	704 soldiers	8,164	13,000	40,000

BOOK IV

From Occupation to Occupation
1899–1909

'The work called for and accomplished was the building
up of a Republic, by Anglo-Saxons, in a Latin country . . .
a Republic modelled closely upon the lines of our Great
Republic . . . in one of the most unhealthy countries.'

CIVIL REPORT OF GENERAL LEONARD WOOD FOR 1902, PT I, 217

CHAPTER XXXV

Cuba Prostrate

The outstanding U.S. hero of the Spanish-American war, Theodore Roosevelt, was elected governor of New York State in November 1898.[1] The Cuban war made Roosevelt's political career, and through him it helped therefore to create the modern U.S. presidency. It launched the U.S. on a policy of increasing commitment in world affairs. It helped to create a united U.S.: in the autumn of 1898 President McKinley was cheered in the south, to the sound of 'Dixie', with General Joe Wheeler, the old Confederate, at his side as well as Shafter, the Yankee. But it was much more doubtful whether the Cuban war had made Cuba, even though it had given the island a heroic revolutionary saga to tell, re-tell, even re-enact, in the years to come, a recollection of combat against great odds and a literary, romantic tradition imposed on many garibaldiesque events of the nineteenth century.

The very mood of self-analysis and rediscovery which marked Spain in 1898–9 (and which affected much of Spanish America) threw a question-mark over the U.S. achievement. Thus in a famous article, 'The Triumph of Caliban', the golden poet of Nicaragua, Rubén Darío,[2] wrote, 'no no, I cannot, I don't want to be part of these buffaloes with silver teeth'. He recalled Martí, and speculated 'what that Cuban would say today in seeing that under the cover of aid to the grief-stricken pearl of the Antilles, the "monster" gobbles it up, oyster and all . . .'[3] ('Monster' was Martí's word for the U.S.) This point of view was repeated by José Enrique Rodó in his book, *Ariel*, published in 1900. The Cuban war was already altering the view of the South Americans towards the North. In the nineteenth century there had been almost universal admiration for the U.S.; in the twentieth there would be apprehension, even fear, and hence stirrings of Latin unity against Anglo-Saxon hegemony. Martí was the catalyst of this mood: the Spanish Cuban who had lived in Mexico and the

---

[1] By 17,000 votes – a narrow majority in a year when his party's majority generally was cut.

[2] Rubén Darío, the first Spanish–American writer since Garcilaso El Inca to have an effect on Spain itself.

[3] Published in *El Tiempo* (Buenos Aires) and reprinted 20 August 1898 in *La Época* (Madrid).

U.S. almost all his adult life had believed that 'our fatherland ... begins at the Río Grande and ends in the muddy woodlands of Patagonia'.[4]

This was a hispanic view. Grandson of Valencianos, graduate of Madrid, eloquent writer of Castillian prose, Martí did not look towards those other islands of the sugar sea whose economies and social circumstances seemed so similar to Cuba. He looked south and west.

The North Americans looked south, though askance, since there was a strong sense of superiority in the way that they treated the Cubans during their occupation of the island between 1898 and 1902, explicit both in what they wrote and also in what they did not mention. Roosevelt, for instance, believed in the Anglo-Saxons' duty to help backward races, whose incapacity to govern themselves effectively he despised.[5] He had spoken vigorously of the Spanish ill-treatment of the Cubans; indeed he had helped to take the U.S. to war over this question. In January 1897 he wrote to his sister, 'I am a quietly rampant *Cuba Libre* man';[6] but, a U.S. patriot above all, he never showed much interest in the Cubans themselves. The name of Martí, for instance, was never mentioned in anything he wrote. When as president in 1904 he secured, by political sleight of hand, the Panama Canal, he justified his neglect of the Colombians (who owned the territory) by saying that the Colombians were an inferior people.[7] It was not that he despised individual members of any race, and he would never have stooped to persecute them; but he regarded it as his duty to help the backward even if they resented it. This meant not only a toleration of the idea of war, but, particularly before he was actually involved in one, a pleasure in it. Logic did not always enter into Roosevelt's thought, 'I don't want to see our flag hauled down where it has been hauled up,' he wrote about Hawaii, 'it was a curse against ... white civilisation not to annex it in 1893'.[8] Hot-blooded but unsure of themselves, both Lodge and Roosevelt excused themselves for their imperialism with the thought that Britain, in fact already satiated, was interested in extending her possessions in South America.

The mild yet undeniable racism of Anglo-Saxon Americans was evident not only in speeches of politicians; it entered bureaucratic analyses. Thus the hard working American census-takers who worked

---

[4] *Obras* (Trópico, 1941 edn), XXXIII, 55.

[5] See Beal, 27-9.

[6] Cowles MSS, qu. *ibid.*, 59.

[7] See below, p. 468; Beal, 33, 'to talk of Colombia as a responsible power to be dealt with as we would deal with Holland or Belgium or Switzerland or Denmark is a mere absurdity'.

[8] *Op. cit.*, 47.

1a Santiago Bay from
the Morro Castle
b The U.S. battleship
Maine enters
Havana Bay, 1898

12a The U.S. flag is raised over Santiago de Cuba, 1898

12b General Miles, Commander-in-chief of the U.S. forces, 1898

12c General Brooke, military governor of Cuba, 1899

effectively in Cuba in 1899 argued that the decline of the black race in Cuba in proportion to the total population was 'doubtless but another illustration of the inability of an inferior race to hold its own in competition with a superior one, a truth which is being illustrated on a much larger scale in the U.S.'[9] This decline derived in Cuba in fact from the end of the slave trade. Juan Gualberto Gómez, the leading Negro spokesman after 1898, feared the U.S. and the possibility of annexation less for itself than for its racism.[10] Even so humane a North American observer of Cuba as Irene Wright thought that the 'decadence and depravity in Cuba are due, largely, to the too free commingling of black blood with white'.[11]

Some North Americans, however, were conscious of the ambiguity of their position. In April, Senator Spooner of Wisconsin noted: 'I dread war and looking beyond tomorrow, I dread what is to follow . . . I fear Cuba, having been rescued from Spain, may more than once demand rescue from the Cubans.'[12] Others doubted the whole imperialistic policy of expansion which men like Roosevelt, Hearst and Lodge were successfully foisting on the nation.

In Cuba the situation was rendered specially ambiguous by the links connecting so many Cubans with the U.S. Not only had many lived there for long periods, but many had actually become U.S. citizens, partly perhaps to benefit from various tax advantages available to North Americans in Spanish Cuba; nevertheless, their commitment had been definite. The first U.S. minister after Cuban independence, Squiers, wrote, no doubt exaggeratedly, that Juan Gualberto Gómez was the only editor of an anti-American Cuban paper who had never held U.S. citizenship.[13]

Were U.S. motives 'naval' (concerned, that is, with power politics) or did they have a rationale of their own? In 1897, Captain Mahan had suggested that a U.S. naval base in Cuba would be desirable.[14] Roosevelt answered on 10 April 1899: 'If we are to hold our own in the struggle for naval and commercial supremacy, we must build up our power without our own borders. We must build the Isthmian Canal and . . . grasp the points of vantage which will enable us to have our say in deciding the destiny of the ocean.'[15] Did this merely signify that, since the activities of great powers nowadays extended across oceans, the U.S. had to have a world policy? Did the U.S. realize that because of

[9] Census of 1899, 97.
[10] C. A. Gauld, *The Last Titan: Percival Farquhar, American Entrepreneur in Latin America* (1964), 35.
[11] Wright, *Cuba*, 95.
[12] Spooner MSS, qu. Beal, 17.
[13] Squiers dispatch No. 64 to Hay, 11–7–1902, qu. Gauld, *The Last Titan*, 45.
[14] A. F. Mahan, *The Interest of America in Sea Power, Present and Future* (1897), 313.
[15] *Public Papers of T. Roosevelt, Governor*, p. 298.

British economic weakness[16] they would be unable to depend upon British strategic superiority for ever? These problems were never satisfactorily resolved. Perhaps the simplest explanation gets nearest the truth: 'The American people of that day, or at least many of their more influential spokesmen, simply liked the smell of empire and felt an urge to range themselves among the colonial powers . . . to feel the thrill of foreign adventure and authority.'[17]

The general truth of another remark of George Kennan's is also obvious: that the Spanish-American war, the occasion of which was Martí's rebellion against Spain, 'represented a turning-point . . . in the whole concept of the American political system'.[18] The U.S. acquired not only the Philippines but also Guam, Puerto Rico and Hawaii – the first territorial extensions of U.S. sovereignty outside the North American continent: further, these territorial acquisitions were merely the outward expression of a new attitude by administrations in the U.S., leading directly if slowly to a firm commitment to international action, responsible or irresponsible, in the second half of the twentieth century. This imperialism followed directly, just as the expansion of Spain into the New World followed directly, from the final conquest of the home country: the tears of Bobadilla in 1492 heralded Columbus's expedition from Palos just as the massacre of Wounded Knee in 1890 heralded the expansion of North America.

The U.S. took over Cuba 'temporarily' in January 1899. General Brooke, one of the three most senior officers of the U.S. army before the war, arrived as military governor, formally receiving the keys of Havana from the last Spanish captain-general, Jiménez Castellanos.[19] On that day the Spanish American empire ended, only one cry apparently being heard of '*Viva España*' in the streets of Havana. General Brooke had, however, no specific instructions from McKinley. The administration and the president were vague as to what they wanted of Cuba. Spanish laws were to remain in force unless countermanded or revised. In practice, U.S. officers, with largely Negro or mulatto troops (because of the climate[20]), merely took over from their Spanish predecessors.

U.S. relations with the Cubans continued to be bad. The greater part of the rebel army had remained in existence, carrying out police

[16] 'Eccentricity' is Brooks Adams's phrase in *America's Economic Supremacy*, that work of perceptiveness published in 1900.

[17] George Kennan, *American Diplomacy, 1900–1950* (1951), 22.

[18] *Ibid.*, 19.

[19] General John Rutter Brooke (1838–1926), brigadier-general of Volunteers in the Civil War.

[20] The surgeon-general of the U.S. army specifically recommended 'coloured' troops, after a visit to Jamaica to see what the British did there.

duty: only those few who had properties or jobs disbanded. (There were originally 48,000 men to be disbanded.) The Cuban army's request to take part in the farewell to the Spaniards was rejected; in Havana, as in Santiago, the U.S. announced that 'the danger to life and property was too great';[21] celebrations ('when the excitement had cooled off and the passions of the people would be under control') only occurred on Máximo Gómez's entry into Havana on 24 February 1899. Gómez was met by the U.S. General Ludlow[22] at the city limits and later occupied the Spanish captain-general's old summer residence at Quinta de los Molinos. Meantime, the original declaration made by Brooke studiously avoided any indication of what would happen to Cuba eventually: the object of his rule would be 'to give protection . . . security . . . restore confidence' and so on. When in February a state funeral had to be held for General Calixto García, it was at first arranged that the Assembly of the Cuban army – the remains, that is, of the old rebel legislature – should march behind the U.S. military authorities; but when Brooke's carriage appeared, it was seen that he was followed by his staff and a military escort. Therefore the Cuban officers, led by General Freyre de Andrade, refused to take part.

Brooke's appointments had a familiar ring. Colonel Chaffee, who had commanded a brigade at Santiago, was his chief-of-staff while General James Wilson, who had commanded in Puerto Rico, became military governor of Santa Clara and Matanzas;[23] Leonard Wood remained in Santiago, taking in Puerto Príncipe too; General Ludlow was military governor of the city of Havana; and ex-Consul-General General Fitzhugh Lee took over as military governor of Havana (province) with Pinar del Río. Lee's was not the only specifically political appointment. A hatchetman of the Republican party, and a close friend of the party boss Mark Hanna, Estes Rathbone, became controller of posts and telegraphs.

The civil government was left in structure much as the Spaniards had left it under the Autonomists, though the departments of state were reduced to four. These were headed by Cubans: the secretary of the Interior (*Gobernación*) was Domingo Méndez Capote, who had been vice-president in the last rebel provisional government.[24] The secretary of finance was Pablo Desvernine, a lawyer who had been (and apparently remained) Havana representative of the New York firm of Condert;[25] the secretary of justice and education was José Antonio González

[21] Brooke Report, 7. Nine Cuban generals, however, attended as guests.
[22] General William Ludlow (1843–1901), chief engineer in Atlanta campaign and under Sherman. Commander in Santiago campaign.
[23] In the Civil War he had captured Jefferson Davis.
[24] Domingo Méndez Capote (1863–1933), lawyer, general, afterwards vice-president.
[25] Gauld, *The Last Titan*, 22 fn. 17

Lanuza;[26] and the secretary of agriculture, industry, commerce and public works, Adolfo Sáenz Yáñez, who was somewhat unpopular due to his devotion to the defunct regime. The customs on the other hand were placed under the military control of Major Tasker Bliss.[27] At local level, the U.S. military authorities accepted the *status quo*, not anywhere attempting much change in the old order of things in Cuban society. Thus Saturnino Sánchez Iznaga was appointed mayor of Trinidad and Armando Sánchez Agramonte mayor of Puerto Príncipe – both representatives of well-known families in those cities. Lope Recio, a member of one of the oldest Cuban families, became civil governor of Puerto Príncipe. A Betancourt became civil governor of Matanzas. Rewards were also found for many of those who made their name in the war. The civil governor of Santa Clara was thus General José Miguel Gómez, with Orestes Ferrara, a young Italian ex-anarchist from Naples as his secretary; the civil governor of Havana province was Maceo's old second-in-command and successor in the western command, General Juan Rius Rivera; Ricardo Céspedes (son of the leader in the first civil war) was mayor of Manzanillo; Cosme de la Torriente, related to Atkins's old partners in Cienfuegos, and auditor-general at Máximo Gómez's headquarters, became a judge in Santa Clara province; General Freyre de Andrade, a backer of Máximo Gómez in his anxieties in 1897, became a judge in Havana. These rewards all went without much question. It was nevertheless surprising to find the ex-*World* journalist, Sylvester Scovel, established as a contracting engineer in Havana.[28]

Brooke's military government was benevolent, without being assertive. When he arrived, 'a state of desolation, starvation, and anarchy prevailed almost everywhere'.[29] On the other hand, the ex-slave Montejo in a vivid passage described how 'Havana was in those days of victory like a fair-ground . . . old and young danced till they dropped. The clubs of the ñáñigos were all lit up . . . People kept on inventing new rumbas . . . I must have had more than fifty Negresses in one week.'[30] Anyway, between 1 January and the end of August 1899 six and a half million complete rations were distributed.[31] Real destitution, then reported Colonel Chaffee,

in such form as to require the issue of food supplies is fast disappearing

---

[26] José Antonio González Lanuza (1865–1917), exile under Spain, lawyer, afterwards Deputy.

[27] Tasker Bliss (1853–1930), later general and chief of staff of the U.S. army in the First World War, military member of the U.S. delegation to the Paris peace conference.

[28] Atkins, 312.

[29] Brooke Report, 9.

[30] Montejo, 212.

[31] Brooke Report, 129.

... such as remains outside of Havana is confined almost entirely to the aid of institutions for the care of the sick, poor and old persons, and orphans. The number of the latter is large and the expense, either to the state or municipal governments, for support of orphans is ... a charge that must continue for at least ten years.

To Major Dudley, the judge advocate, fell the task of reorganizing Cuban law. He reported that the laws themselves in most instances gave proper remedies for 'injustices', but that the procedure in the courts and the administration of the laws were intolerable. The courts were found to be corrupt 'largely due to the methods pursued in criminal cases'.[32] Cordell Hull, a young Tennessee lawyer who had raised a regiment of volunteers and was temporarily posted to Santa Clara, described such corruption as being actually justified on the grounds of the need to hire more help to get through the documentation.[33]

As a result, existing Spanish taxes were retained, or were revised: jurisdiction of several local courts was altered. A stream of decrees, more or less arbitrary, was issued, affecting property, rents, past taxes and past crimes, procedure in courts, appeals, import of meat and insurance. Thus the decrepit O'Reilly family lost their monopoly of slaughtering cattle in Havana. A supreme court was established, composed of a president and six associate justices (paid $6,000 and $5,500). Beneath him there were to be six *audiencias* or courts based on the six old provinces, Havana to be in two parts, civil and criminal, the rest to combine these functions.

The North Americans patiently went about their business of discovering the Cubans, and duly reported what they found. The Cubans in 1899 numbered a million and a half.[34] Probably in 1895 they had reached 1,800,000. The losses of the war, either in action or more likely in consequence of the concentration policy (including a decrease of births and an increase of deaths) were therefore 300,000,[35] or well over a tenth of the population. This was a severe loss; few nations had lost so high a proportion of population in a war before that date.[36] That Cuba as a nation was born in such violence gave it a special character thereafter. Another consequence was the immense number of children who failed to survive their earliest years, due to war and its effects. Thus no other country for which figures are available had in 1899 so

---

[32] *Ibid.*, 163.
[33] *The Memoirs of Cordell Hull*, 2 vols (1948), 36.
[34] Exactly 1,572,797.
[35] Census of 1899, 72.
[36] It compares to Russia's losses in the Second World War, Serbia's in the First World War, and probably double the proportion in the Spanish or the American Civil Wars.

small a proportion of children under five.[37] In every census afterwards too the absence of men and women born in 1895-8 made its grim mark. By the Revolution of 1959, for instance, there was a notable lack of men and women in their early sixties.[38]

POPULATION OF CUBA BY PROVINCES

	1861	1887	1899
Havana	393,789	451,928	424,811
Matanzas	234,524	259,578	202,462
Pinar del Río	146,685	225,891	173,082
Puerto Príncipe	85,702	67,789	88,237
Santa Clara	272,310	354,122	356,537
Santiago	264,520	272,379	327,716
	1,397,530	1,631,687	1,572,845

In general, such increases of population as there were came in cities which had been fortified during the war.[39] This war, like most, increased the size and hence the power of cities. Havana itself almost reached 250,000, a city now occupying six square miles or nearly seven times the area it had occupied in 1762.[40]

The ruin caused by the war was everywhere visible. Thus the number of schools open in 1898 was almost half that open in 1895;[41] before the war there were 90,000 farms and plantations in Cuba; in 1899 only 60,000;[42] 900,000 acres were cultivated in 1899, compared with well over 1,300,000 in 1895.[43] Havana and Matanzas were the worst hit, each cultivating less than one half what they did before. Only the province of Pinar del Río cultivated more in 1899 than 1895, though many towns of Pinar del Río had been reduced to ashes by Maceo.

[37] In 1899 there were 130,878 children aged 0 to 4 in Cuba, and 226,109 aged 5 to 9.

[38] Notable, since these are men just retired from their main life's work but still active, often politically very active. In 1899 incidentally the U.S. census-makers noted a small ratio of adults 20 to 35 years old in Camagüey and Oriente – an echo no doubt of a lower birth rate in the war of 1868-78. But in the second war of independence the losses in the east were smaller than in the west; the children of school age in 1907 in Camagüey and Oriente averaged 29·25% of the population, whereas the overall average was 26·4%. (Census of 1907, 270.)

[39] [In addition to Havana] Pinar del Río (up 8,846 to 38,343); Viñales (up 6,150 to 17,700); Puerto Príncipe (up 12,182 to 53,140) and Nuevitas (up 3,737 to 10,355); Cienfuegos (up 18,164 to 39,128); Manzanillo and Santiago were also certainly up, but how much is hard to see.

[40] E. Roig de Leuchsenring, La Habana, Apuntes Históricos, 3 vols (2nd edn, 1964), II, 14.

[41] 541 in place of 904 public primary schools. See Census of 1899, 584, 585.

[42] 90,960 and 60,711, to be precise.

[43] Census of 1899, 543 and 553. The 1895 figure is approximate, since no statistics for Puerto Príncipe were available for 1895. Also, these figures only consider farms which were still in existence in 1899; so the 1895 estimate is undoubtedly low.

Even more than in the past, tenure was uncertain or unknown: many tracts of land were held by squatters without title; many people did not know how large their farms were; when asked, they gave measurements in many different units – varas and cordels, hectares and kilometres, often without knowing what they meant.[44]

Everywhere, more farms were rented than were owned, in most cases far more. This was because of the terrible tangles in which the old laws had left land-holding. For years, titles and surveys had been in such a state that legal transfers could not be made. Outright sale was almost impossible. In the cattle area of Camagüey, two-fifths of the great pasture lands there were owned by their farmers, about a third rented – the rest being difficult to establish.[45] White owners outnumbered black and mulatto everywhere, usually many times, except in Santiago, where there were three white owners to two black or mulatto.[46]

As might be expected, many owners had very small farms and a few great landowners had huge tracts. This tendency had been greatly increased in the last quarter of a century, during the sugar revolutions of the 1880s and 1890s. Thus in 1899 two-thirds[47] of the farms were under about eight acres, and over 80%[48] under sixteen acres. At the other end of the scale, 2% of the farms were over a hundred acres, but they consisted of over 40% of the land.[49]

Nearly half the cultivated area[50] was now given over to sugar cane. The next most important crop was sweet potato,[51] and after that came tobacco.[52] Lesser crops were bananas and Indian corn. Coffee accounted in 1899 for less than 2% of the cultivated area.

In 1899, there were only a few more than 200 sugar mills in any state worth reviving, compared with 1,100 in 1894.[53] Matanzas, the old sugar centre, had by now collapsed in the most spectacular way: there

[44] In 1899 just under one third of Cuba was in farms, but only a tenth of that was culti-vated – 3% of the total area. In 1895 at least 5% had been cultivated. Camagüey, the great cattle area, had the largest area in farms but the smallest area cultivated, and its 2,582 farms were the largest – 850 acres, on the average, six times the average size in the country. Santiago had the smallest farms; the average was only 80 acres, with a very small area cultivated per farm – 10 acres. Matanzas, still the great sugar area, had the highest average area cultivated per farm – 40 acres – and the highest number of hands per farm, 35: Santiago had only 13 (Census of 1899, 543–4).

[45] Census of 1899, 551.

[46] See p. 429 for further discussion of race and agriculture. If occupancy alone is reckoned, white occupants comprised nearly 90% in Havana and Matanzas whereas in Santiago the proportions were 53·3% to 40·8%.

[47] 63·5%.

[48] 82·7%. And this 82·7% of the farms only controlled some 28% of the cultivated area.

[49] 41·9%.

[50] 47%.

[51] About 414·262 acres.

[52] 11% of the cultivated area.

[53] 207, to be precise. But see above, p. 277, for 1890–5 estimates.

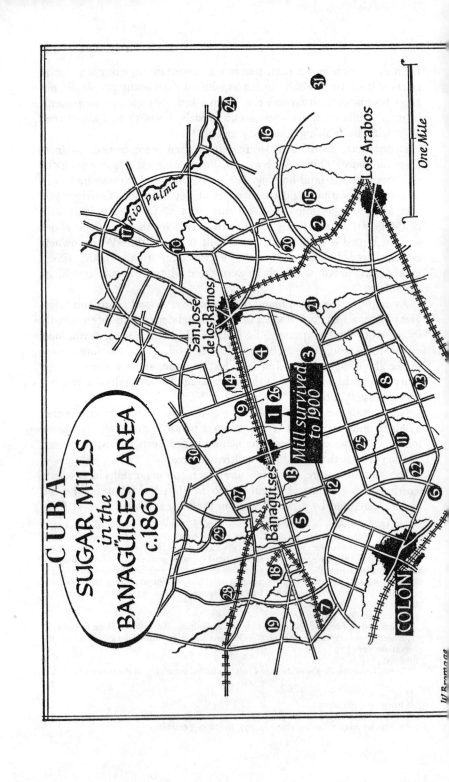

CUBA

SUGAR MILLS
in the
BANAGÜISES AREA
c.1860

Mill survived to 1900

One Mile

Río Palma

San José de los Ramos

Banagüises

Los Arabos

COLON

W.R.

KEY to the preceding map. Numbers indicate mills which existed in 1860. Only Alava (Number 1) lasted into the 20th century. Note that this map gives a good impression of the surviving influence on the geography of Cuba of the old circular *mercedes* (see pp. 19–20). The circles here, of course, indicate roads, most of which are still in use.

1 *Alava* Julián Zulueta
2 *Caridad* Bacallado
3 *Carmelo* Carmen Zequeira
4 *Concepción* Marquesa de Urria & Conde de la Reunión
5 *Conchita* Tomás de Juara
6 *Desengaño* Rafael de Quesalta
7 *Flor de Cuba* Arrieta Brothers
8 *Gran Antilla* Marqués de Almendares
9 *Habana* Julián Zulueta
10 *Hatuey* Vicente de la Guardia
11 *Montserrate* Conde de Santovenia
12 *Panchita* Francisco Gispert
13 *Ponina* Francisco Diago
14 *Progreso* family of Marqués de los Arcos
15 *Recompensa* Fidel Zuaznavar
16 *Reserva* Antonio Benítez

17 *S. Felipe* Josefa A. de Delgado
18 *S. Isidro* Mariana Hernández
19 *Sta. María de Neda* Francisco Gómez de Criado
20 *Santa Teresa* Conde de Fernandina
21 *Santiago* Marquesa de Urria
22 *Santo Domingo* Domingo García Capote
23 *Serafina* Marqués de Almendares
24 *Sociedad* Camilo Feijoo de Sotomayor
25 *Urumea* Santiago Zuaznavar
26 *Vizcaya* Julián Zulueta
27 *La Marquesita*
28 *San Martín* La Gran Azucarera
29 *Nueva Echevarría* La Gran Azucarera
30 *El Líbano* Francisca Herrera de Morales
31 *Zorrilla*

were now only 62 mills in place of 434; but even in Santa Clara there were only 73 in place of 332.

Not even all these mills would take part in post-war harvests: in 1901 only 168 mills ground. The social consequences can be seen most easily from the map (on pages 426 to 427), showing a part of Matanzas which in 1877 had had thirty mills. In this area of approximately 300 square miles there was in the twentieth century only one *central*: *Alava*. Distinguished names in the history of sugar and society, such as Pedroso, Diago, Arrieta, Cárdenas, can be seen to have sunk to the rank of *colonos* serving *Alava*, now a North American-owned mill.

In Oriente, plantations belonging to *reconcentrados* had in many cases been burned by Cubans; those belonging to Cubans had by now been burned by Spaniards. The jungle had crept up.

Around these mills there were now established, either on their own or on rented land, a great army of 15,000 small sugar cane estates.[54] Of these, a third[55] were owner-managed, the remainder[56] being under various forms of rent. The average owner-run sugar estate was about fifty acres, while the average rented estate was sixteen.[57]

There were in 1899 six estates over 3,240 acres in size (all owner-managed), fifteen between that and 1,620 acres (all but two owner-managed); but most (13,517) were under thirty acres. Most of these planters (*colonos*) now lived on their estates. A few on the other hand kept their families in Havana, where they went for the dead season, their arrival at the family house being treated as if it were the return of the lord from the wars.

The war had of course told specially hard on livestock. There were under a sixth of the horses in 1899 that there were before the war, and only an eighth of the cattle.[58]

[54] 15,521.

[55] 5,061, covering 230,000 acres.

[56] Covering 165,000 acres.

[57] There were 520 black or mulatto owners, all but 37 of whom had estates smaller than 323 cordels (32 acres); one estate alone belonging to a black person lay between the 324 and 800 acre mark. (Census of 1899, 560.) The 520 black owners controlled only 3,680 acres and 2,645 black renters covered 1,500 acres. (Census of 1899, 558, 560.)

[58] *Total Livestock*

	1894		1899	
	584,725	Horses	88,001
	value: $20,466,377	Mules	18,474
		Asses	1,842
	570,194	Pigs	358,868
	value: $5,700,000		
		Goats	18,564
	78,494	Sheep	9,982
	value: $393,000		
		Chickens	1,517,892
	2,485,766	Cattle	376,650
	value: $74,572,980		

Source: Census of 1899, 512, 540.

In 1899 just under 300,000 persons in Cuba were occupied in one way or another with agriculture.[59] Of these, a third were Negro or mulatto.[60] There were 60,000 farms, so the average farm employed five men. But the big farms still employed armies of men.[61]

The black or mulatto minority apparently constituted 32 % of the population; the Chinese, 1 %. In every province Cuban-born whites constituted a majority, except in Havana where, due to the large element of Spaniards who stayed on in Havana and who kept Spanish nationality, they were not quite one half. Cuban-born whites were most numerous in the still chiefly cattle-breeding province of Camagüey.[62] The black or mulatto percentage ranged from 20% in Camagüey to 45% in Santiago, being also large in Matanzas (40%) and Santa Clara (30%); the proportion in the city of Havana was 27%.

The black or mulatto half-million was very slightly less in proportion than it had been in 1887, and some 20,000 fewer in number.[63] The black percentage had never been smaller since censuses began to be taken in Cuba in the 1770s. Of those with some African blood, over half (327,000) had been born since the abolition of slavery in 1880; perhaps only 70,000 were ex-slaves, the rest of the over-twenty-year-olds having always been free. Just under 13,000[64] had actually been born in Africa, being therefore ex-*bozales*, first generation slaves,[65] and now old.[66] No trace was seen of the old emphasis on males in the slave trade; there were indeed more female Negroes than males.[67]

Most Negroes lived in Havana province and most mulattoes in

[59] Census of 1899, 403, says 299,197 were concerned with agriculture, mining and fishing; but the latter groups comprised only 854 and 2,262 respectively.

[60] Census of 1899, 405, describes total in the big class as 100,967. It is necessary therefore to subtract 314 fishermen and 122 miners, i.e. 436.

[61] Figures for the provinces are more revealing:

	Total Agriculturalists	Total farms	Men per farm
Pinar del Río	48,450	10,408	5
Havana	31,422	6,159	8
Matanzas	50,588	4,083	13
Santa Clara	81,231	16,129	5
Puerto Príncipe	16,911	2,382	8
Santiago	67,509	21,550	3

[62] 75·2 %.

[63] 505,443 instead of 528,798. The total whites had been 67·6% in 1887 and were 67·9 in 1899, but were only 1,067,354 instead of 1,102,889 (Census of 1899, 96–8).

[64] Estimate from Census of 1899, 206.

[65] *Ibid.*, 98, 99.

[66] Of the 12,898 Negroes in 1899 born in Africa, 1,784 lived in Havana, 4,390 in Matanzas, 1,302 in Pinar del Río, 674 in Puerto Príncipe, 4,159 in Santa Clara, and 589 in Santiago (Tables, Census of 1899, 221–3). In the cities, 144 were found in Cienfuegos, 836 in Havana, 244 in Matanzas, 189 in Puerto Príncipe, 70 in Santiago (*ibid.*, 223–5); in all these, except Puerto Príncipe, there were more females than males, reflecting their use as domestics. Of this number, 7,288 males (out of 7,613) and 1,592 females (out of 5,284) were in employment in 1899 (*ibid.* 220, 472–4).

[67] Table, Census of 1899, 206 (268,308 to 252,092).

Oriente.[68] The majority of black or mulatto thus lived in Oriente, with Santa Clara and Havana close behind, followed by Matanzas. Most Chinese were in Santa Clara. Only twenty-one districts had a black or mulatto majority in 1899: nine were in Matanzas,[69] three in Pinar del Río,[70] and nine in Oriente.[71] These certainly were among the most primitive places in Cuba in 1899; in the whole district of Alto Songo, for instance, with a total population of nearly 13,000, only eleven out of 3,600 children under ten were going to school.

There were more black or mulatto people over sixty than whites but in all other age groups there were more whites.[72] In 1899 the number of farms owned by black or mulatto people were 5% of the total[73] and they rented $18\frac{1}{2}$%[74] – a total of just under a quarter.[75] These farms were generally small and poor, covering in all only 11% of the cultivated land.[76] No Negro or mulatto owned a farm larger than 100 acres or rented one larger than 165 acres.[77] Most of the very small farms – those under eight acres – were owned or rented by them.[78] Of the farms owned by Negro or mulatto families, nearly all (96·4%) were less than twenty-five acres, and even more in respect of those rented (97·2%). But the concentration of large properties in few hands made this almost true of the whites too (85·5% of white owners had land under twenty-five acres, 90·1 of white renters).[79]

Nine-tenths of the sugar cane was produced by white farmers; tobacco production was similarly white-controlled.[80] Indeed, the only

[68] Census of 1899, 195.

	Negroes	Mixed	Rough Total	Chinese
Havana	54,849	53,479	107,000	3,886
(City of Havana)	(28,750)	(36,004)	(64,000)	(2,794)
Matanzas	47,793	32,528	79,000	4,199
Pinar del Río	28,811	18,025	46,000	575
Puerto Príncipe	6,975	10,400	16,000	462
Santa Clara	48,524	58,050	106,000	5,194
Santiago	47,786	98,323	145,000	496
	234,738	270,805	c. 500,000	14,812

[69] Carlos Rojas, Guamacaro, Jovellanos, Macuriges, Martí, Máximo Gómez, Palmillas, Perico, S. José de los Ramos.

[70] Cabañas, Bahía Honda, S. Diego de Núñez.

[71] These were Alto Songo, Baracoa, Caney, Cobre – with the highest black population percentage, 76·7%, of Cuba – Cristo, Guantánamo, Palma Soriano, Santiago – including the city – and San Luis.

[72] Table, Census of 1899, 206.

[73] 3,092.

[74] 11,247.

[75] 14,339 out of 69,711.

[76] See tables and figures, Census of 1899, 544.

[77] Census of 1899, 546, 555.

[78] 75·6% of the owners under $\frac{3}{4}$ cab were black or mulatto, 77% of the renters.

[79] Census of 1899, 546.

[80] Census of 1899, 548.

crops where black or mulatto people were substantial producers were coffee (43% of the total), cocoa (58%), coconuts (30%), and yams (30%).[81] Black or mulatto people had very little hold in the cattle area of Camagüey, owning or renting less than 30,000 acres between them, or 5% of the total.[82] Thus it was true in Cuba as elsewhere in the West Indies that 'racial distinction ... was only the superficial visible symbol of a distinction which in reality was based on the ownership of properties'.[83]

It was evident that many (white) Cubans wished to increase the proportion of whites to Negroes. Thus the following note appeared in the *Cuban Financier and Havana Advertiser* of 4 August 1900: 'Recently at the demand of the press of Santiago, [Major] Tasker H. Bliss asked officials there to stop the importation by local planters and mining companies of contract labour from Haiti, Jamaica and Turks Island, whence had come over a thousand Negroes since January 1900.'[84] During the railway building of 1900–1[85] the 'Santiago authorities' (i.e. Cuban) protested against a plan to import 4,000 Jamaicans.[86] Frank Steinhart, General Brook's A.D.C., later consul-general and later still a boss of the Havana Electric Co., was thought to favour 'white immigration only', from Northern Spain.[87]

Black or mulatto farmers controlled only a small percentage of the livestock then existing in Cuban farms,[88] so that in nearly every instance the Negro percentage of farm possession was greater than its percentage of animals.

[81] *Loc. cit.*
[82] *Ibid.*, 551.
[83] Eric Williams, 'Race Relations in Caribbean Society', in *Caribbean Studies*, 54.
[84] Quoted Gauld, *The Last Titan*, 44.
[85] See below, p. 465.
[86] Gauld, *The Last Titan*, 44.
[87] *Ibid.*, 46.
[88]

	Total	Black or mulatto possession
Horses	58,064	6,777
Mules	8,569	776
Asses	1,249	112
Pigs	290,973	36,022
Goats	11,565	1,207
Sheep	7,231	653
Fowl	1,145,474	59,166
Oxen	136,268	6,929
Steers	7,652	285
Bulls	8,744	323
Heifers	9,282	342
Young bulls	21,339	657
Cows	56,796	1,912
Yearling calves	11,542	355
Other animals	892	86

Source: Census of 1899, 562.

In respect of professions generally, Negroes or mulattoes were well established among bakers, barbers, carpenters, launderers, builders, shoemakers, seamstresses, and domestic servants.[89]

Illiteracy in Cuba embraced about three-fifths of the population.[90] Of the literate, only 1% had any higher education. Havana had the largest and Pinar del Río the lowest percentage of literates, reflecting the extent to which the provinces had an urban population. Two-thirds of the population of Havana city could read. Just over half of white males over ten could read, compared with 28% of black or mulatto males over ten. Among the white population, literacy was slightly greater among men than women but among the Negroes the opposite was the case (26% of black or mulatto males could read, 30% of females). The largest literate group in 1899 were, as might be expected, those aged between twenty and twenty-four, the class whose school years were between the wars, 1878 and 1895.[91]

The overall rate of school attendance was naturally low in 1899, something under 90,000[92] out of the 550,000 children aged between five and seventeen.[93] The figures were naturally higher in cities than in the country, the proportion in the large cities being almost three times that of the rest of the island: outside the five cities with over 25,000 population, the proportion was about 11% of the school age

[89] The professions where black or mulatto men are listed as outnumbering or roughly equalling white in Cuba in 1899 and 1907 were bakers (2,097 to 2,105 native white, though this does not take into account 1,231 foreign white); in 1907 the split was much the same; barbers (1,459 to 1,420, with 470 foreign white); carpenters (6,326 to 5,120, 2,758 foreign white); charcoal burners (668 to 450, with 490 foreign white); confectioners (48, 30, 38); coopers (521 to 351 and 77); firemen and engine men (233 to 64 and 202); gardeners and florists (106 to 35 and 169); ostlers (123 to 91 and 183); hucksters (787 to 455 and 400); labourers (144,208 male with 7,394 female to 192,737 male and 1,346 female and 43,572 male with 120 female); launderers (17,555 Negresses were occupied here, and 415 Negroes, out of a total of 22,218); dressmakers (251, compared with 107 female white and 61 foreign whites); builders (4,486 to 1,173 and 898); musicians (260, compared with 180 and 190); seamstresses (5,286 to 2,833 and 210); servants (as we have seen: 11,289 and 17,390 male and female coloured to 3,171 and 4,267 native white male and female; 4,197 and 1,150 foreign); shoemakers (3,441 compared with 1,823 and 1,046); woodcutters (100 out of 191); apprentices (1,164 out of 2,543).

The Negroes were ill-established in several key areas: 3,453 merchants out of a total of 47,265; government officials, 17 out of 473; 10 physicians out of 1,223; 29 dentists out of 354; 794 policemen out of 4,824; 73 printers out of 1,481; 314 out of 2,262 fishermen; 488 sailors and boatmen out of 4,820; 11 saloon keepers out of 73; 1,950 out of 3,481 factory workers; 102 (71 female) out of 1,708 teachers; 4 veterinary surgeons out of 63; 27 watchmakers out of 255; 8 architects and draftsmen out of 162; 20 out of 241 artists; 815 out of 2,328 blacksmiths; 17 journalists out of 245; 52 clerks and copyists out of 2,248. In 1899 there were one Negro stenographer (male), one telephone and telegraph employee, 3 lawyers (out of 1,406).

[90] This includes as literate the small (2·1%) percentage of those able to read but not write (Census of 1899, 148).

[91] Census of 1899, 152–4.

[92] Actually 87,935.

[93] 552,928; i.e. 15·7% went to school.

population. School attendance of whites was a little higher than black, though not much so.[94]

Havana, with a population of about 240,000, was still one of the great cities of America. The once forbidden (*vedado*) area of woodland to the west had already before the war become a handsome suburb and afterwards developed greatly with most rich families moving out there. The North American colony began to live there in 1899. Villages such as Jesús del Monte and Cerro had become suburbs too, as Edgware or Lambeth had done in London. The 'old city' of narrow streets was now only a small part of the new big capital. Its streets were cobbled, and the pavements were still only curbs to keep carriage wheels from scraping houses. On the skyline, a new National Bank building – a five-storey block – would soon compete with the old tower of San Francisco. Houses were still built of brick or stone but now were almost always plastered and painted – white, lavender, pink or green. Many old palaces had become business houses. Much remained for a long time of the *reconcentrados* – tenements and desperate dwellings all along the old walls of the city. The old university reopened after the war, and kept for a few years the adjective 'royal'; since the Dominicans had not thought of banning women, one-seventh of its members in 1899 were girls – mostly in the teachers' faculty, though some in medicine and later, law.

Havana had done better in the war than most places in Cuba. Many small towns had been sacked and were uninhabitable. Others could only be rebuilt in new places. Essential links had been destroyed. Society could not recover quickly and in some ways never did. Resorts like San Diego de los Baños and Viñales could be rebuilt. But other, less attractive towns were rebuilt, if at all, hastily, shoddily and without plan: on the North American habit of confused spread, not the Spanish one of controlled order.

Five-sixths of the houses in Havana now got water from Albear's famous municipal aqueduct. Everywhere else the proportion from aqueducts was less than a seventh. Water carriers abounded in most cities, Havana included, since only half the houses were actually connected to the main water supply. Wells were everywhere suspect, and owners of underground cisterns made a handsome profit from selling water. In the larger cities, seven out of eight of the houses had some kind of municipal garbage collection. Half the Cubans had no lavatory arrangements of any formal kind. All but 3 % of the houses in Havana had some kind of lavatory. The *escusado Inglés*, the English W.C., was, however, still unusual in Havana and unknown elsewhere.[95]

[94] Census of 1899, 152.
[95] Census of 1899.

Cuba in 1899–1900 was an island heavily in debt. This is most vividly seen in respect of property: approximate figures given to the U.S. military authorities suggest that the amount of cash advanced on mortgages in Havana was rather more than the total value of properties in the cities ($M89 guaranteed by $M85). The total urban indebtedness was about two-thirds of the total declared value of property and, where owned property was declared, it reached over half.[96] Of course, the real value of property was greater than was declared but so doubtless was the real extent of the indebtedness.[97]

Tobacco in 1898

In 1899, three-quarters of the tobacco in Cuba was grown on land rented by the growers (74·0%); the rest was produced by the owners. Both groups were mostly white, though less universally so than the sugar producers. Nine per cent of the tobacco was produced by black or mulatto people, nearly all renters. The tobacco territory comprised 9% of the cultivated land.[98]

Pinar del Río was established by 1899 as the great tobacco area of Cuba as of the world, producing 72·2% of the total in Cuba. 42·4% of the cultivated area of Pinar del Río was given over to tobacco and the best tobacco was of course still grown in Vuelta Abajo, the marvellously favoured territory on the banks of the Cuyaguateje. Vain attempts had been made to transplant the tobacco plants of the region elsewhere. Endless discussions were held over mechanization, irrigation, professionalism. Cuban planters resisted steel ploughs on the ground that they 'extracted the virtue from the soil'.[99]

In 1899 there were about 80,000 persons employed in the agricultural side of the tobacco industry on some 16,000 vegas. The crop in 1899–1900 was 460,000 bales (of 51 lbs each), or well below the crop of 1894–5 when it reached 560,000 bales or 62 million lbs of leaf, valued at $M22. Of this, in 1895, 220,000 bales (40%) were valued at $M10. In the years before the war some 20 million lbs of tobacco leaf were exported to the U.S., valued at approximately $M10. This was maintained in 1895 and 1896 (Pinar del Río was the last region to be hit by war) but it dropped in the next years and did not pick up in 1899 and 1900. Still, tobacco suffered less from the war than sugar, and since the harvest only required four or five months it rapidly recovered.

Till 1895 the first selection and weeding out of the leaves was made by the planter. After the war, this was done in towns nearest the tobacco field. This

[96] See property mortgage figures in Census of 1899, 41.

[97]
Rural Real Estate Value	Amount of indebtedness	Quit Rents
$184,724,836	$106,897,249	$25,679,452
Urban Real Estate		
$138,917,059·70	$100,729,943·5	$14,608,850

[98] Census of 1899, 548.

[99] They were right to criticize steel ploughs, for the wrong reasons: the steel sometimes cut too deep.

was a promising development. It brought life to several previously dull rural centres.

	Crop (bales)	Exports to U.S. million lbs	value
1892–3		21·69	$M8·9
1893–4		14·58	$M5·8
1894–5	560,000	20	$M7·3
1895–6		26·7	$M10·6
1896–7	375,000	4·4	$M2·3
1897–8	88,000	4·7	$M4·3
1898–9	220,000	8·1	$M6·9
1899–1900	460,000	11·8	$M9·7

Quoted from Census of Cuba 1899, 535.

CHAPTER XXXVI

The Proconsuls I: General Brooke

Between 1 January 1899 and May 1902, Cuba was run by a U.S. military government. To begin with, it was unclear what the future status of the island would be. A Cuban Commission in Washington in late 1898 said that, on the question of payment of the Cuban army,[1] 'it was absolutely impossible ... to obtain any explanations, only vague manifestations'.[2] McKinley, in his message to Congress in December 1898, said military government would continue in Cuba 'until there is complete tranquillity in the island and a stable government inaugurated'. Some of the North American officers who constituted the military government supposed, and hoped, that the 'pearl of the Antilles' would soon be annexed to the U.S., maybe as a state, maybe as a dependency. In the light of this expectation, and of their own prejudices, these officers sought with dedication and without sparing themselves, to recast Cuban society, such as it was, in the mould of North America; all the corruption, the incompetence and makeshift devices lying between law and custom were to be swept immediately away; and from this well-meant effort much ill was later to flow.[3]

The great material help afforded by the U.S. in the first weeks cannot of course be gainsaid. Further, Brooke also had to report that 'many requests have been made by the planters and farmers to be assisted in the way of supplying capital, farming implements and money ... the conclusion [was] reached that aid could not be given in that direction'.[4] General Brooke added:

> The limit has been reached in other means of assistance, to the verge of encouraging or inducing pauperism, and to destroy the self-respect of the people by this system of paternalism is thought to be a most dangerous implanting of a spirit alien to a free people. ... There is enough capital lying idle in Cuba today to supply all that is needed were the capitalists assured as to the future.

[1] See below, p. 438.
[2] *Actas de las Asambleas de Representantes y del Consejo de Gobierno durante la Guerrade Independencia*, 3 vols (1930), V, 157.
[3] Healy points out that London newspapers such as the *Daily Telegraph* remarked the similarity between U.S. language in respect of Cuba and British in respect of Egypt.
[4] Brooke Report, 13.

General Brooke, an old soldier of much experience, was in fact less aggressively proconsular in his nature than some of his subordinates.

His attitude to law was revealing. Instead of a complete revision of the existing code, the U.S. military authorities modified each existing law as the need arose. A great difficulty was met, however, in finding what law did exist since the royal decrees were not collected: a complete file of the *Official Gazette* was not available to Brooke and his advisers. Brooke also met immediately the problem of judges, who had been for generations used to accepting illegal fees not only to find in favour of such and such a client but merely to bring an action to court at all. 'This opportunity for corruption will disappear,' Brooke reported confidently, after a regular system of salaries had been set up.[5]

All the way through Brooke's report to the War Office runs an echo of 1865: to him, Havana resembled Richmond, Virginia, after the civil war;[6] Cuba was a land to be reclaimed from sin.

Brooke's reign in Havana began, however, with a serious insult to the Cubans. The rebels had planned a great celebration in honour of the final withdrawal of the Spaniards. This was banned because of fear of riots: there had been a little bloodshed in December. A few rebel leaders were present at the transfer of power, but not Máximo Gómez and not the army as such. This arrogant attitude naturally caused dismay among Cuban patriot leaders but, debilitated by war and unused to politics, they did not know how to act for the best and for a time kept their complaints to murmurings *sotto voce*. There were submerged stirrings. Máximo Gómez travelled to Cienfuegos surrounded by a Negro escort; at the speeches made at a celebratory breakfast 'nothing was said about the Americans, only that the Cubans could have conquered Spain without assistance from us'.[7] There was some mingling with U.S. troops though the rebels appeared in poor military fettle. In Havana there were some street fights, U.S. troops being attacked and being exasperated 'waiting for a chance to sail into the Cubans'.[8] The ex-slave Montejo recalls a similar incident in Cienfuegos in which he took part.[9]

The U.S. took over the old Spanish administration root and branch. The old municipalities and mayors, the six provincial governments and governors, and the Secretary of the Interior were in form all precisely as before, as were the other hierarchies of Law and Education. The difference was the imposition on top of this system of a military government, with subdivisions corresponding to the civil governments, and

[5] *Ibid.*, 11.
[6] E.g., *ibid.*, 14.
[7] Atkins, 300.
[8] *Ibid.*, 303.
[9] This was an attack on U.S. soldiers who were trying to seduce Creole girls, led by the ex-slave Claudio Sarriá.

incorporating 24,000 U.S. servicemen at the beginning of 1899.[10] The civil administration was staffed by Cubans, except in one or two important instances, and in many cases at low levels the old officials merely stayed at their old posts.

There was never a real chance that the Cuban armed forces would behave like the ungrateful Filipinos and fight, since it was known that eventually the North Americans planned to leave. But they would not disband until they were paid. It was hoped that a loan on the security of the future Cuban customs might be raised to cover this. The U.S. however offered a mere $M3 out of the surplus which Congress had granted for war and suggested a division of it among those Cubans who turned in their arms. Máximo Gómez, to whom money meant nothing, but who did not wish to saddle Cuba with vast obligations, eventually agreed; his followers were furious. The Assembly of the Cuban army, led by Manuel Sanguily, Freyre de Andrade and Martí's old friend Juan Gualberto Gómez, therefore met to depose Gómez from his supreme command. Gómez was unpopular already because of his evident lack of vengefulness and his speech at Quinta de los Molinos at which he had said that in Cuba there were neither victors nor vanquished.[11] Gonzalo de Quesada was also deprived of his post as Cuban representative in Washington.

Negotiations continued, U.S. senators were lobbied, other loans canvassed[12] and ultimately the soldiers were paid $75 each if they could prove they had been fighting before the end of hostilities with Spain – a modest requirement, it might have been thought, though one which excluded a number of expectant soldiers. After dispute, the figure of 33,390 such soldiers was eventually agreed.[13] The Cuban Assembly abandoned its struggle for better terms and indeed abandoned the position entirely, dissolving itself. Payment of the Cuban army began at the end of May.

The arrival of the U.S. in Cuba might have been expected to herald the arrival of U.S. business. So the most controversial measure of the first months of occupation was Senator Foraker's amendment (to the Army Bill), by which no commercial concession was granted by the military government in Cuba: this passed the U.S. Senate by 47 to 11 in March 1899. Foraker believed that if it were possible for business to receive contracts or concessions, the U.S. would never get out of Cuba.

[10] This number was raised to 45,000 in March and fell to 11,000 later in the year.
[11] *Cf.* Montejo, 827; Martínez Ortiz, 56–7. Colonel Orestes Ferrara told the author (letter, 28 April 1964) that Máximo Gómez ordered him to keep his brigade in being after the peace, in case it should be necessary to fight the U.S.
[12] *Cf. Actas de las Asambleas representantes*, V, 102; there is a good discussion of the dealings between the Cuban army and the financier, C. M Cohen.
[13] R. P. Porter, *Industrial Cuba* (1899), 204–10.

This move prevented the prospect of great wealth arising in Cuba, and also the possibility of much U.S. capital investment during their political control of the island.[14]

The severance of the Catholic Church from the new state was accomplished easily. Cemeteries maintained by public funds were handed to the municipalities. All divorce questions were henceforth to be settled by civil courts[15] and all marriages had to be civil even if ecclesiastical as well.[16] Religious processions were banned, including funerals, although this regulation was not fully kept and funerals themselves continued on a grand scale, as in the past no women attending.

Brooke's moderate attempt to coordinate U.S. and Cuban customs, while disturbing Cubans, also upset his most powerful subordinate, the herculean General Wood, for the continuation of Spanish law meant an abandonment of some of the things he had already done in Santiago. Brooke also decreed quickly that Santiago post revenues should be sent to Havana, so cutting off Wood's supply of ready cash. Wood, unforgivably from the point of view of military etiquette, cabled to Secretary Alger who supported him, despite Brooke's protests.[17] But it was impossible for Wood to resist Brooke's control over all appointments or his insistence that plans for local taxation should be placed in abeyance until a national plan was agreed. Brooke naturally regarded Wood with distaste and the latter wrote to Theodore Roosevelt in February: 'I am kept extremely busy doing all I can to preserve order and harmony in this part of the island. The new order of things is not conducive to such conditions here.'[18] That Brooke's suspicion about Wood was not misplaced is proved by a remark made later by President Wilson when rejecting the pressure in 1917 to give Wood the supreme American command in Europe in place of Pershing: 'I have had a great deal of experience with General Wood. He is a man of unusual ability but apparently absolutely unable to submit his judgement to those who are superior in command.'[19] But in 1898 Wood had friends. Roosevelt, now governor of New York State, wrote to him on 1 March: 'Lodge and I went to see the President and told him that we thought you ought to be in command of the whole island.'[20] Nothing happened immediately to secure this, but Roosevelt wrote quite often to Wood: 'I send you

[14] J. B. Foraker, *Notes of a Busy Life*, 2 vols (1916), II, 42, 46–9. Fitzhugh Lee commented to Foraker (in November) that 'outside capital must be employed for Cuba's development'·
[15] Order of 12 May 1899, Brooke Report, 41.
[16] *Ibid.*, 42.
[17] Hagedorn, I, 226. It is clear from Wood's papers that he had a paid agent lobbying for him in the U.S. in late 1898 (see Healy, 89–90).
[18] Hagedorn, 236.
[19] Rubens, *Liberty*, 415: Letter 5 June 1918 to the editor of the Springfield (Mass) *Republican*.
[20] Roosevelt, *Letters*, II, 955.

herewith a copy of Bonsal's book which contains a really outrageous account of the Guasimas fight.'[21] In June, Wood went to America and rejected an offer of the presidency of the Washington Railway and Electric Company at $25,000 a year (he was then getting $5,500 as a major-general of volunteers). McKinley gave him assurances about his career in the army and even promised him the command of the island after Brooke, 'though the crisis over Alger had to be settled first'.[22] Wood returned to Santiago, where another yellow fever epidemic had broken out.

Wood's overall views at this stage were roughly typical of U.S. officers in Cuba:

> [He] believed that after a brief period of independence, which would satisfy the sentiment for theoretical liberty, the Cubans would voluntarily ask to be admitted to the Union ... annexation by acclamation had been his dream from the beginning. Behind the ardour, the endeavour, had been the aspiration to make the American rule so kindly, so just, and so productive of ... well-being that the Cubans would not consent to let the Americans go ...

His grievance against Brooke was that the 'well-intentioned stupid man had by his surrender to the Cuban politicians made the fulfilment of his dream next to impossible'.[23] That Wood had these views in mid-1899 is clear from a letter which Roosevelt wrote to Lodge on 21 July:

> Wood believes that we should not promise or give the Cubans independence: that we should govern them justly and equitably, giving them all possible opportunity for civil and military advancement and that in two or three years they will insist upon being part of us. [General] Wilson [governor of Matanzas and Santa Clara] believes [however] that we should now leave the island, establishing a Republican form of government and keeping a coaling station, etc., together with tariff arrangements which would include them with us as against outsiders and he thinks that in a very few years they would drop into our hands of their own accord.[24]

Whether Wilson's views really deserve to be described as 'utterly different' from Wood's – Roosevelt thought so – is doubtful. It is certainly clear that Wilson too was full of letters and memoranda on the subject of Cuba's future – in which he showed himself rather more con-

---

[21] *Ibid.*, 957. This was Stephen Bonsal's *The Fight for Santiago*. Bonsal (1865–1951) was an east coast journalist; his son was U.S. ambassador to Havana, 1959–61.
[22] Hagedorn, 241.
[23] This is Wood's biographer speaking, *ibid.*, I, 371.
[24] Roosevelt, *Letters*, II, 1,038.

cerned with independence than Roosevelt credited him.[25] The ambitious Wilson, like Wood a man with many connections in Washington, himself coveted Brooke's job as governor.[26] But it was Wood who had the more powerful friends; no one wrote to any other officer as Roosevelt did on 10 July to Wood, 'I had a very enjoyable night at the White House last Saturday ... but I could not get [McKinley] to take my view. He believes things in Cuba are satisfactory!'[27] To this Wood replied: 'The so-called cabinet at Havana is establishing in all their old details the old Spanish laws and customs. Nothing more idiotic can be imagined than the attempt to establish a liberal government under Spanish laws.'[28] Roosevelt in consequence told Secretary of State Hay:

> In Cuba we may lay up for ourselves infinite trouble if we do not handle the people with a proper mixture of firmness, courtesy and patience ... I most earnestly urge the wisdom of the President putting Major-General Leonard Wood in immediate command of all Cuba with a complete liberty to do what he deems is wisest ... I question if any nation in the world has now or has had within recent time anyone so nearly approaching the ideal of a military administrator of the kind now required in Cuba. Perhaps one or two ... Englishmen who have appeared in India ... but only one or two.[29]

Henry Adams, wryly sitting in Washington, noted that 'a dozen Major-Generals are all pulling different ways in Cuba, Brooke and Ludlow and Lee, Jim Wilson, Wood and I don't know how many more are pulling different ways on totally different lines'.[30] Indeed, all these officers had different ideas for Cuba's future and did not shrink from proselytizing in Washington by means of an endless stream of letters.

But the next move was Brooke's: a critical telegram from him arrived in Wood's office saying his accounts were wrong. Wood requested a Court of Enquiry and only General Chaffee succeeded in smoothing matters over.[31] Wood wrote to his wife on 3 August: 'I have had a good deal of trouble with Brooke, who has toiled in every way to hamper,

[25] E.g. his report of 20 June published in Hagedorn, I, 421.

[26] See Healy, 92–3, for a study of this officer, and also Roosevelt's letter of 5 August 1899 (ibid., 103) in which he says, 'I have on different occasions applied on your behalf for the Administration to give you the Secretaryship of War, the governor-generalship of the Philippines ... of Cuba ... in Puerto Rico. But my dear General you know that when official recommendations are not taken ... it is not possible to make the same suggestions over again.'

[27] Roosevelt, Letters, II, 1,032.

[28] Hagedorn, I, 250–1.

[29] Roosevelt, Letters, II, 1,025. Lord Cromer later told St Loe Strachey (editor of the Spectator) that Wood would be the best man to succeed him in Egypt (Hagedorn, I, 375).

[30] Ford, Letters of Henry Adams, II, 218.

[31] Hagedorn, I, 249.

hinder and discredit my work here ...'[32] On the 18th he wrote to
Roosevelt:

> Clean government, quick decisive action and absolute control in the
> hands of trustworthy men, establishment of needed legal and educa-
> tional reform and I do not believe you could shake Cuba loose if you
> wanted to. But dilly-dallying and talking politics will play the devil
> with people of this temperament. Every café loafer and political
> demagogue floats on top ... The condition of this island is dis-
> heartening ... no single reform has been instituted which amounts to
> anything ... educational matters are where they were last year. The
> criminal courts are swarming with untried cases; ordinary criminals
> have to wait from three to seven months for trial ... Every large
> municipality in this province has tendered directly or indirectly its
> resignation, as they were bankrupt owing to the re-establishment of
> this idiotic system of taxation. [And ...] generations of misrule and
> duplicity have produced a type of man whose loyalty is always at the
> command of the man on top whoever or whatever he may be. These
> men, who a few months ago were fighting the Spaniards, are now
> intriguing vigorously against each other. Many of the best men here
> are men whom I myself appointed and they will be good, energetic
> and faithful just so long as they know that I have the power to
> suspend them.[33]

There had been trouble of one sort or another therefore throughout
the year, beginning with strikes for more money by the dockers of
Cárdenas, Regla and Havana in January and leading to the reformation
of a new Labour organization, founded as the Liga General de Trabajadores de Cuba, once again as in the 1890s under anarchist leadership.[34]
In August there were more strikes of builders and tobacco workers,
almost reaching the dimensions of a general strike in September and
some demands were met.[35] In October 1899 a newspaper, the *Cubano
Libre* in Santiago, urged a revolutionary though nationalist insurrection
in the hills. Wood was attacked as the embodiment of a perfidious U.S.
Violence was narrowly avoided. On 20 November Fitzhugh Lee
entered the controversy in a letter to Senator Foraker; he pointed out
that the 'Spaniards ... own most of the property and are doing most of
the commercial business and must therefore remain in Cuba so long as
Cuba has a [capable] government ... They are annexationists but of

[32] *Loc. cit.*
[33] *Ibid.*, 282.
[34] The first president was 'an active anarchist', Enrique Messonier (Serviat, *40 aniversario
de la fundación del Partido Comunista*, 18).
[35] There was thereafter much internal dissension as to why all the demands had not been
gained, the jettisoning of Messonier and the temporary breakdown of the Liga.

course keep quite quiet.' Lee urged that no U.S. soldier should be withdrawn 'till after the experiment of free government has been tried and
failed';[36] on 21 November Foraker replied that in his opinion the sooner
the U.S. handed over the better, and urged that the Cubans had been
'splendid'. Surprisingly Lee came back with 'You and I are not far
apart ... Let the U.S. government carry out its pledge to give the
people of Cuba a government of their own. If the experiment fails, the
U.S. ... must guide the Cuban ship of state.'[37] But Wood meantime
was writing to McKinley himself: 'I am giving the Cubans every
chance,' he wrote, 'to show what is in them, in order that they may
either demonstrate their fitness or their unfitness for government.'[38]
McKinley seemed to respond: at least in his personal address to Congress of 5 December he said: 'The new Cuba yet to arise from the ashes
of the past must needs be bound to us by ties of singular intimacy.'[39]
Rumours that the U.S. was about to hand over Cuba from its temporary
military government to a permanent civil one had caused terrible alarm
in Cuba and helped to discredit Brooke. On 13 December the intrigues
of Roosevelt, Lodge and Wood himself were at last successful: Wood
was appointed to succeed Brooke, and the well-meaning General
Brooke lumbered off to retirement.

> I want you to go down there [said McKinley to Wood] to get the
> people ready for a Republican form of government. I leave the
> details of procedure to you. Give them a good school system, try to
> straighten out their courts, put them on their feet as best you can.
> We want to do all we can for them and to get out of the island as soon
> as we safely can.[40]

This new attitude on McKinley's part was partly due to his realization
that in fact he had a new real war on his hands in the Philippines; there
was even a desperate note in the instructions to the Philippine Commission itself: 'Bear in mind that the government ... is ... designed not
for our satisfaction ... but for the happiness, peace and prosperity of the
people ... and the measures adopted should be made to conform to
their customs, their habits and even their prejudices ...'[41] With such
anxious steps did the U.S. embark upon her imperial mission.

[36] Foraker, II, 49.
[37] *Ibid.*, 56.
[38] Hagedorn, I, 257. Letter of 27 November 1899.
[39] Qu. Jenks, 72.
[40] Wood in speech at Williamsburg, Mass, 25 June 1902, qu. Hagedorn, I, 261.
[41] I, 261.

CHAPTER XXXVII

The Proconsuls II: General Wood

'The native hogs have such filthy food that fresh pork is to be absolutely prohibited.'

SURGEON-GENERAL'S REPORT, 1899, 482.

Wood took over Cuba on 20 December 1899. He kept Brooke's military staff, but appointed a new cabinet of Cubans with a slightly different administrative form.[1] Within a few weeks, he took a trip down the island:

> Generally speaking [he wrote to Elihu Root, Alger's successor as Secretary for War], everything is all right.[2] Everywhere one sees small patches of land under cultivation and all the sugar mills which are grinding are going to turn a comparatively large increase over last year's crop . . . practically no hunger . . . no beggars . . . There is of course an opposition element, led by *La Discusión* and small papers of the same political stripe but their importance is very small and their capacity for doing harm is not great . . . eight out of ten people are . . . friends of good government and of what we are doing . . . There is not a sensible man who thinks we can leave for a long time, not measured by months but by years, several . . . at least. I have consulted all classes, the Spaniards and the conservative element: property holders as well as foreigners. They trust absolutely in the good faith of the American government not to leave here until an absolutely stable government is established.

Wood still 'inclined to the opinion that the Cubans themselves would ask to be annexed'.[3] Presumably this was one reason why, in June, he

[1] These were: José Ramón Villalón (Public Works), a rebel general; Diego Tamayo (Interior); Enrique José Varona (1849–1933) (Finance), Cuba's leading intellectual, an economist and pamphleteer of a high quality; Luis Estévez Romero (Justice), during 1899 an associate judge of the Supreme Court; Juan Rius Rivera (Agriculture), Maceo's successor in command of the rebels based on the west of Cuba; and Juan Bautista Barreiro (Education). The previous cabinet had, to Wood's relief, resigned; he thought them 'little rascals'.

[2] Root (1845–1937), future Secretary of State and senator, had been a lawyer of the Ryan Whitney syndicate's American Indies Co. who had been beaten by Farquhar in the struggle for the Havana Electric Railway contract and later played a role in the Van Horne Railway (see below).

[3] Hagedorn, I, 277–8.

reorganized the schools 'adapting them as far as practicable to the public school system of the U.S.'[4]

But already he had talked with Cuban generals about the suffrage for the forthcoming local elections. An attempt in effect to bribe Máximo Gómez into friendship by means of a sinecure failed; and Bartolomé Masó, the old president of the rebel government, General Miró and others (all suspected that Wood favoured annexation) criticized Wood vigorously, demanding universal suffrage where Wood had argued for limited property suffrage. Wood said that people who could not meet his demands were 'a social element unworthy to be counted upon for collective purposes'.[5] In April 1900, Wood promulgated the election law in the form in which he had proposed.[6] General Rius Rivera demanded immediate independence. Wood refused to countenance the idea, and Rius Rivera resigned from the government. A meeting of 'notables' was called to discuss the election law and agreed with the generals. Wood nevertheless did not give way. On 12 April Wood wrote to McKinley:

The great mass of public opinion is perfectly inert; especially ... among the professional classes. The passive inactivity of 150 years has settled over them and it is hard to get them out of old ruts and old grooves ... For three months I have had commissions at work, on law, taxation, electoral law, etc., and after all this time, the only result is the adoption of practically the original plans submitted by the Americans on the commissions as working models ... The people here, Mr President, know that they are not ready for self-government and those who are honest make no attempt to disguise the fact. *We are going ahead as fast as we can but we are dealing with a race that has been steadily going downhill for a hundred years* and into which we have got to infuse new life, new principles, and new methods ...[7]

Within a fortnight of this self-confident and contemptuous letter, an incident occurred which caused the Cubans to wonder whether the Anglo-Saxon race were not themselves in decline. Estes Rathbone, Mark Hanna's appointee in charge of the Cuban post office, was found to be drawing a salary equivalent to 10% of the total income of his department. He refused to have an inquiry.[8] On 5 May, Wood also had to tell Root that Charles Neely, head of the finance department of the Post Office, was

[4] Census of 1899, 585.
[5] Hagedorn, I, 267.
[6] The publication of the great Cuban Census of 1899 in April, showing that two-thirds of adult Cubans were illiterate, helped Wood's point of view.
[7] Hagedorn, I, 285 (author's italics).
[8] *Ibid.*, 294.

a defaulter to the extent of probably $100,000 ... we can find no records at all for the finance department of the post office for the past year[9] ... whether there is criminal responsibility on [Rathbone's] part or not I should hesitate to say; but there is every indication of either the grossest ignorance or total neglect of proper supervision ...[10]

Root cabled back, 'I want you to scrape to the bone, no matter whose nerves are hurt.'[11] And eventually Neely was caught in Rochester, U.S., and Rathbone, too, both being sent to prison for embezzlement.

These events disillusioned Wood. In June there came another crisis. General Brooke in 1899 had taken over 541 primary schools from the Spaniards.[12] There were also 400 private schools including some good ones, most of them ecclesiastically directed. Brooke tried to carry on from Spanish customs but Wood began to reorganize the education system.[13] The new public school law was written by Lieutenant Hanna of Wood's staff, based on the law of Ohio.[14] New school equipment was bought in the U.S. Textbooks were translated direct from English, with no attempt to make them comprehensible in Cuban terms.[15] Cuban teachers were given instruction in U.S. teaching methods, some of them being sent to the U.S. A superintendent of schools and a board of education would arrange syllabuses, grades and textbooks. The Boards of Education would be locally elected, at the same time as the municipal elections. Schools would normally divide the sexes, but not necessarily in remote districts. Substitute teachers, the curse of Spanish Cuba, were abolished. All children between six and fourteen were to go to school for at least twenty weeks a year. No children under fourteen were to be employed.[16]

To carry out his own instructions Wood had of course to found an immense number of schools. By June there were 3,000 public schools, 3,500 teachers, and 130,000 pupils under instruction. Wood's agent was an educational eccentric of great brilliance, Alexis Frye. No doubt he was obsessed with numbers, as Wood found out after three months;

[9] Loc. cit.
[10] Ibid., I, 294-5.
[11] Ibid., 295.
[12] There had been 904 in 1895.
[13] Census of 1899, 585. In 1899 out of a total of 2,708 teachers in all Cuba 1,206 were male, 1,502 female: 102 were coloured; 144 of the men and 643 of the women (a majority) had no higher education (302 of the men and 115 of the women had been born in Spain). Nearly half were in Havana province, 824 being in the city of Havana, or about one quarter of the whole.
[14] D. A. Lockmiller, Magoon in Cuba, 1906-1909 (1938), 134.
[15] Annual Reports of the Secretary of War, 1899-1903, 111: Civil Report of Gen. Leonard Wood for 1900, I part 1, 97-112.
[16] See decree in census of 1899, 585-615.

nevertheless, abandoned buildings, ex-barracks, warehouses, and old houses became schools. Then Wood and Frye quarrelled – Wood accusing Frye of spreading the 'most intense radicalism as to the future relations between Cuba and the U.S.'[17] Even so, in two years, 140,000 pupils were going regularly to public schools. The University of Havana had been reinaugurated. Private schools had been inspired by the state inspection system. But afterwards there was no consolidation, and no improvement: in December 1906 a new North American proconsul found fewer children at school than in 1899.[18] Frye admittedly had been arguing that Wood was a tyrant, in company with 1,500 Cuban schoolteachers who went to Boston on a conference. This threatened a breakdown till Wood astutely sent to Wilson Gill, an educational enthusiast after Frye's heart, a plan to organize Cuban schools as miniature cities.[19] But Wood's sense of mission seemed dimmed, and he wrote to Root: 'If there is going to be a war in China I want to go. I do not want to be left here to fossilize.'[20] This disillusionment, however, led to the beginning of realism in his attitude to the Cubans. He began seriously to envisage independence, and even began to show cordiality towards his old antagonist General Wilson, who, he even suggested, should replace him in his post. 'I think on the 1st July it will be a good idea to ... authorise the floating of the Cuban flag from all municipal and civil buildings.'[21] It was not the first time that countries so far apart and so different in size as Cuba and China had found their fates implicated.[22] But it is ironical that Cuban independence should depend upon a North American's concern to command there.[23]

On 16 June municipal elections were held – the first free elections in Cuba, with three parties contesting. First, there were the Republicans, based on Santa Clara, who said that they wanted immediate independence, but also giving emphasis to a degree of devolution into provinces. Their leader was General José Miguel Gómez, civil governor of Santa Clara, naturally (like all the leaders), a veteran of the war. Second, there were the Nationalists of Havana, favouring the idea of central government, allegedly too the party of Máximo Gómez; they too favoured immediate independence. Finally there was the Unión Democrática, a conservative grouping, to whom some ex-Autonomists rallied: their standpoint was one of some hostility to immediate

[17] Wood-Root in Root papers; 8 January 1901, qu. Healy, 181.
[18] 122,214, Lockmiller, 134.
[19] Hagedorn, I, 303–4.
[20] *Ibid.*, 302. Roosevelt wrote to Root urging that Wood should go to China if he wanted to, on 20 July (Roosevelt, *Letters*, II, 1,357). This was the Boxer rebellion.
[21] Hagedorn, I, 299.
[22] See above, p. 186.
[23] Actually the command went to General Chaffee, Brooke's old chief of staff, and General Wilson became No. 2.

independence, and indeed some expectation that annexation would come.[24]

The result was an expected one: Nationalists won in Havana, Republicans in Santa Clara and Matanzas. Elsewhere, regional candidates won. Root wrote:

> It was a great thing to secure the peaceful adoption of the basis of suffrage upon which we had agreed and to carry the Cubans through their first election so quietly and satisfactorily ... when the history of the new Cuba comes to be written, the establishment of popular self-government based on a limited suffrage, *excluding so great a proportion of the elements which have brought ruin to Haiti and Santo Domingo will be regarded as ... of the first importance.*[25]

Wood, encouraged, moved on to organize a national electoral system.

> I am going to work on a constitution [he told Root] ... similar to our own and embody in the organic act certain definite relations and agreements between the U.S. and Cuba ...[26] My idea is to call [a] constitutional convention right away ... Have a Constitution adopted and simultaneously with the adoption of the constitution get a treaty ... signed ... which will definitely bind [our] ... two countries and definitely state their relations. ... we can if deemed advisable [hold on to] ... the collectorship of customs and the military commander representing the U.S. holding if necessary the veto power ...[27]

On 25 July Wood called for the election of delegates to frame a constitution, 'and as a part thereof to provide for and agree with the government of the U.S. ... the relations to exist between that government and the government of Cuba'.

The qualification caused a sensation. It seemed to the Cubans merely to form the basis for annexation. Nine Cuban political groups sent a message to Wood pointing out that relations between Cuba and the U.S. were not constitutional questions. But Wood's hand had meantime been strengthened by the departure of General Fitzhugh Lee, following that of Generals Wilson and Ludlow, so that the whole island was now run by him with no eminent feuding officers beneath him – very satisfactory from his point of view, despite his arguments for decentralization

---

[24] Chapman, 131. (General Máximo Gómez (1836–1905), General José Miguel Gómez (1858–1921) and Juan Gualberto Gómez (1854–1933), mulatto, politician and journalist, are of course all separate people.)

[25] Hagedorn, I, 299. Author's italics. These elements were, of course, the Negroes and mulattoes. If these were excluded from Haiti, who would be left?

[26] *Loc. cit.*

[27] *Ibid.*, 302.

in the days of Brooke.[28] On 15 September, nevertheless, the delegates to the constitutional convention were elected. Many were regarded as vaguely radical. On 5 November they met: there was an initial clash over the question of invoking the word God in the preamble. General Sanguily and Salvador Cisneros desired the word to be left out, Pedro Llorente wanted it in. There was a dispute over the qualifications which presidents of Cuba were supposed to have, owing to the claims of Máximo Gómez, a Dominican. Eventually it was decided that any native-born citizen as well as any naturalized citizen who had served ten years in the Cuban wars would be eligible. There was to be universal manhood suffrage – including Negroes and illiterates. The establishment of a state church was firmly abolished – and in this respect the Cubans went even further than the U.S., making civil marriage essential, not merely possible: but the main question was the qualification affecting the future relations of Cuba and the U.S., and that of the possible maintenance by the U.S. of a naval station in the island.[29] This matter preoccupied the convention from December 1900 to May 1901.

The crux was one of those fundamental procedural points which, as so often in politics of the twentieth century, become matters of substance. This was whether the relationship with the U.S. should be inscribed in the Constitution or not. The ideas of Elihu Root were put in a letter to Wood dated 9 January 1901:

> If we . . . simply turn the government over to the Cuban administration, retire from the island, and then turn round to make a treaty with the new Government, just as we would with Venezuela, Brazil, etc. . . . no foreign government would recognise any longer a right on our part to interfere in any quarrel which she might have with Cuba, unless that interference were based upon an assertion of the Monroe doctrine. But the Monroe doctrine is not a part of international law and has never been recognised by European nations. [Nor, he might have added, did the Monroe doctrine apply to Cuba, since it was concerned with the *status quo* of 1823.] How soon someone of these nations may feel inclined to test the willingness of the U.S. to make war in support of her assertion of that doctrine no one can tell. It would be quite unfortunate for Cuba if it should be tested there.[30]

[28] Wood's biographer noted with satisfaction, 'He was convinced that, at the moment, a dictatorship was necessary in Cuba. Circumstances indeed were pressing him more and more toward autocracy' (*ibid.*, I, 274); Portell Vilá, *Historia*, IV, 82, notes the comment, with equal satisfaction.
[29] The idea of buying 'land for a naval station at Guantánamo' had been mooted by Admiral Bradford in June 1898. *Cf.* Root papers, qu. Healy, 143.
[30] Hagedorn, I, 341.

Root was in fact suspicious of Germany, and thought that the U.S. had an obligation to Spain to secure protection for Spanish interests, being apparently less worried about U.S. interests.[31]

It seems important [he continued], that the Convention shall be required either to take the initiative in stating what they want the relations to be or to definitely refuse it. It might be wise ... in talking with members of the Convention ... to disabuse their minds of the idea that they are certain to be protected by the U.S., no matter what they do or refuse to do. If Cuba declines to accord to this government the authority and facilities for her protection, she will have to look out for herself in case of possible war with any other nation.[32]

Two days later, Root suggested to Secretary of State Hay:

Could you turn over in your mind ... the *advisability of incorporating into the fundamental law of Cuba a provision to the following effect*: (1) that ... the U.S. reserves and retains the right of intervention for the preservation of Cuban independence and the maintenance of a stable government ... (2) that no government organised under the Constitution should be deemed to have authority to enter into any treaty or engagement with any foreign power which may tend to impair or interfere with the independence of Cuba ... (3) that to facilitate the U.S. in the performance of such duties as may devolve upon her under the foregoing ... and for her own defence, the U.S. navy may acquire and hold the title to land and maintain naval stations at certain specified ports ...[33]

Root was explicitly interested in whether British behaviour in Egypt could yield any fruitful example for Cuban–U.S. relations.

For Root's ideas there was much support in the U.S. Even Godkin's Liberal *Evening Post* announced: 'In spite of all the talk [of] *Cuba Libre* ... few Cubans have at all expected to see a day of unabridged Cuban sovereignty and it is also very doubtful if more than a small minority really desire that day.'[34] As for Cuba, on 8 February Wood was writing to Root:

It is my opinion that at the next municipal elections we shall get hold of a better class of people. If we do not, we must choose between establishing a central American republic or retaining some sort of control for the time necessary to establish a stable government. The

[31] P. C. Jessup, *Elihu Root*, 2 vols (1938), I, 313–15.
[32] Hagedorn, I, 341.
[33] *Ibid.*, I, 422.
[34] *Op. cit.*, 345.

time has been very short to convert a people into a Republic who have always existed as a military colony, 60% of whom are illiterate and many sons and daughters of Africans ... To go further without giving them time to organise and get rid of the adventurers who are now on top simply means to ruin the whole proposition of any Cuban government either for them or under the protection of our own country, unless we again assume entire control ... Gómez said that to get out now will cause fighting and bloodshed here inside of sixty days. This would come not from any desire for fighting but simply because the present leaders suspect each other and each one would make a grab for the first place. All Cubans want independence as a matter of sentiment but all the thoughtful ones are very much in doubt as to the success of an independent government ...[35]

But the next day Root, in a letter which deserves to be fully quoted sent to Wood the considered view of McKinley's administration on what policy should be adopted towards Cuba:[36]

No one familiar with the traditional and established policy of this country in respect to Cuba can find cause for doubt as to our remaining duty ... the U.S. would not in any circumstances permit any foreign power other than Spain to acquire possession of the island of Cuba ... the U.S. has therefore not merely a moral obligation arising from her destruction of Spanish authority in Cuba and the obligations of the Treaty of Paris for the establishment of a stable and adequate government ... but it has a substantial interest in the maintenance of such a government ... [Therefore] the people of Cuba should desire to have incorporated in her fundamental law provisions ... as follows:

(1) no government ... shall ... have any authority to enter into any treaty or engagement with any foreign power which may tend to impair or interfere with the independence of Cuba or to confer upon such foreign power any special right or privilege without the consent of the U.S.;

(2) no government ... shall ... assume or contract any public debt in excess of the capacity of the ordinary revenues of the island after defraying the current expenses of government to pay the interest;

(3) that upon transfer of the control of Cuba to the government established under the new Constitution, Cuba consents that the U.S. reserve and retain the right of intervention for the preservation of Cuban independence and the maintenance of stable

[35] Hagedorn, I, 348.
[36] There had been discussion with the senate leader and the president.

government, adequately protecting life, property and individual
liberty and discharging the obligations with respect to Cuba
imposed by the Treaty of Paris on the United States;

(4) that all the acts of the military government and all rights acquired thereunder shall be valid;

(5) that to facilitate the U.S. in her performance of such duties as
may devolve under the foregoing provisions and for her own
defence the U.S. may acquire and hold the title to land for naval
stations and maintain the same at certain specific points.[37]

Root added, graciously: 'It is not in our purpose at this time to discuss
the cost of our intervention and occupation or advancement of money
for disarmament or our assumption under the Treaty of Paris of the
claims of our citizens against Spain for losses which they had incurred
in Cuba.'[38]

This letter reached Havana on 18 February 1901. Wood wrote the
next day:

In my opinion the demands are liberal, equitable and just and should
be insisted on throughout. It is very probable that we shall have to
exercise directly the intervention provided for ... and it is certain
that we should, were it not known in Cuba that in case of lack of
stability and failure to observe the provisions ... [of] the Treaty ...
the U.S. would promptly intervene.[39]

Wood took these terms to be discussed by the appropriate committee of the Cuban Constitutional Convention – the conference, somewhat bizarrely, was summoned for the edge of the Zapata swamp at
Batabanó, while waiting to shoot crocodile. At first, the sporting
Cubans seemed to Wood to make 'no serious objection ... excepting the
reference to naval stations ... some apparent objection to the third
article'. But when Wood returned to Havana there was great confusion. The committee announced that they had been insulted by
Wood's manner as much as by the substance of what he said. Juan
Gualberto Gómez and *Patria* demanded Wood's recall.[40] But the proconsul was unmoved. He was merely busy adding a provision on the
question of sanitation to be added to the law on U.S.–Cuban relations:
if the Cubans did not keep Havana clean that too would justify intervention.[41] He added a private comment: 'Among the elements now
dominating in the politics of the island there is little or no gratitude for
what has been done by the U.S. Among the bulk of the people there is a

[37] Hagedorn, I, 349.
[38] As qu., Jenks, 66.
[39] Qu., Chapman, 139–40.
[40] Hagedorn, I, 352.
[41] *Ibid.*, 353.

feeling of appreciation and gratitude.' At the same time in Washington Senator Orville Platt of the Foreign Relations Committee went ahead with the formulation of a bill embodying both Root's proposals and Wood's latest suggestion; it was introduced as an amendment to the Army Appropriations Bill.

On 25 February this so-called Platt amendment went to the Senate. It was not greeted with unanimous approval. Senator Morgan said, 'This is . . . a legislative ultimatum to Cuba.' Senator Foraker wisely and accurately predicted,

> If we adopt this amendment . . . [it] would seem to invite intervention. Suppose they have an election. One party or the other will be defeated. The party that is out is apt to complain and with this kind of provision . . . it would be thought that by making objections, by making trouble and creating difficulties they would make a condition that would lead to an intervention by the U.S. to put the successful party out. It seems that instead of having a restraining influence it would have an exciting influence and that the very result the committee evidently sought to accomplish would be defeated and the opposite would be the result.[42]

But Senator Teller, without whom perhaps the U.S. would have been in the same state of war as they were with the Philippines, thought the amendment 'not so drastic or so severe as I had supposed'. Senator Tillman thought Cuba 'a ward in chancery of the U.S.' The anti-imperialists in general thought the amendment a compromise.[43] On 27 February the Senate passed the amendment after two hours' debate, and on 1 March the House of Representatives did so too.

But Havana was seething. A torchlight procession gave a formal protest to Wood, who however wrote: 'The political element are a mean, ungrateful lot and they appreciate only one thing . . . the strong hand of authority, and if necessary we must show it.'[44] Máximo Gómez, much jaded, agreed:

> We must not think of getting out under any circumstances at present. He [Gómez] knows the people and knows that things will go to pieces if we move just now. He says that he does not want to be president [himself] but that he wants Estrada Palma to be . . . This government he says could not be established within a year or two years. Gómez leaves for the U.S. within a few days to see Palma. They will meet in Washington.[45]

[42] Congressional Record, XXXIV, 3038, 3340.
[43] Cf. Healy, 168–9.
[44] Hagedorn, I, 358–9.
[45] Ibid., 360.

But even though Gómez might differ from them, the Cuban Convention was determined to oppose the amendment: they firmly announced that

> Some of these stipulations are not acceptable, exactly because they impair the independence and sovereignty of Cuba. Our duty consists in making Cuba independent of every other nation, the great and noble American nation included, and if we bind ourselves to ask the governments of the U.S. for their consent to our international dealings, if we admit that they shall receive and retain the right to intervene in our country to maintain or precipitate conditions and fulfil duties pertaining solely to Cuban governments and ... if we grant them the right to acquire and preserve titles to lands for naval stations and maintain these in determined places along our coast, it is clear that we would seem independent of the rest of the world although we were not in reality, but never would be in reference to the U.S.[46]

The Cubans proposed an alternative, whereby no Cuban governments would enter into a treaty limiting the independence of Cuba or in any way alienating Cuban soil; Cuba would not permit its soil to be used as a basis for war operations against the U.S. or any other foreign nation; the goverment of Cuba would accept in full the Treaty of Paris; Cuba would recognize the legal validity of the acts of the U.S. military government; and the U.S. and Cuba would regulate their commercial relations on the basis of reciprocity.[47] This was put to Wood by Méndez Capote but Wood, in passing it on to Washington, warned that it was doomed to failure.[48] A Cuban delegation ultimately set out for Washington to discuss the Platt amendment; but they were presented with a *fait accompli*: McKinley had signed the bill (of which it was an amendment) into law. On 26 March Juan Gualberto Gómez again denounced the amendment in the Convention:

> To reserve to the U.S. the faculty of deciding for themselves when independence is menaced and when therefore they ought to intervene to preserve it is equivalent to delivering up the key of our house so that they can enter it at all hours when the desire takes them, day or night ...[49]

A cartoon, on Good Friday (12 April), in the Cuban paper *La Discusión* showed Cuba crucified between two thieves, Wood and McKinley: Senator Platt stood by nearby with a spear. Wood arrested

[46] House Document No. 1, I, 362. H. C. Hill, *Roosevelt and the Caribbean* (1927), 74.
[47] *Loc. cit.*, 364.
[48] Hagedorn, I, 358.
[49] Senado, *Memoria*, 1902-1904.

the editor, but, thinking better of it, released him the next day. Yet press attacks continued, and Root, therefore, was hoping for a good deal when he wrote to Wood:

> I hope you have been able to disabuse the minds of members of the convention of the idea that the intervention described in the Platt amendment is synonymous with intermeddling or interference with the affairs of a Cuban government. It of course means only the formal actions of the government of the U.S.A. based upon just grounds of actual failure or imminent danger and is in fact but a declaration of acknowledgement of the right to do what the U.S.A. did in April 1898 as the result of the failure of Spain to govern Cuba. It gives to the U.S. no right which she does not already possess and which she would not exercise but it gives her, for the benefit of Cuba, a standing as between herself and foreign nations in the exercise of that right which may be of immense value in enabling the U.S. to protect the independence of Cuba.[50]

In late April a delegation of five members of the Convention went to Washington and were given a great deal of hospitality and flattery by the administration. Root made the Platt amendment sound much like the Monroe doctrine.[51] It was a classic example of diplomacy by entertainment. On their return to Cuba the delegation appeared won over. Diego Tamayo and Méndez Capote told Wood that they 'realised they had made a mistake in rushing through proposals of their own and that the majority in their committee were now looking for a way of accepting the Amendment with dignity'. The Convention in fact was soon ready to accept the amendment, adding an interpretation to the third and seventh clauses. Wood agreed.

Wood wrote similarly, wishfully as ever, but nevertheless explaining some of the reasons for the Convention's change of front:

> There is a very strong annexationist sentiment growing up everywhere and, unless the Convention accepts the Platt amendment very quickly, sufficient influence will be brought to bear . . . through commercial interests and great agricultural concerns to defeat it. They want the American military government to stay.[52]

Finally, on 28 May, the Convention was brought to accept the Platt amendment, by one vote,[53] with however a vast interpretative qualification – said to be a quotation from Root's remarks in Washington to the delegation of Cubans, though Root had said his remarks were not

[50] This was on 29 March (Hagedorn, I, 362).
[51] Senado, *Memoria*, 469 ff.
[52] Hagedorn, I, 364.
[53] 15 to 14 votes.

for publication.[54] But Washington was not prepared to accept any qualification. Wood told Root:

> We have done all that we can ... Any further discussion or any more communications, explanations or attempts to assist the Convention out of its difficulties will in my opinion be a mistake. The time has come to state clearly the position of the government and to state it as an ultimatum of which there will be no further reconsideration or discussion.[55]

Wood then showed the Convention a section from a recent letter in which Root said that McKinley would not change or modify the amendment as passed by Congress nor withdraw the army from Cuba till the amendment was accepted. Therefore the Platt amendment was resubmitted to the Convention; it passed by sixteen to eleven, with four absent. It was to be added as an appendage to the Constitution, together with a permanent treaty securing it.[56]

This done, Wood had also to secure the carrying into effect of a constitution and, hardly less important than the Platt amendment, the essential *quid pro quo* of a treaty enabling Cuban sugar to enter the U.S. at an advantage over beet. There were, however, interruptions. Wood was himself ill with typhoid in July and went north to recuperate. When in Washington in August, he found Mark Hanna at work doing his best to get his friend Rathbone out of the Cuban postal scandal. McKinley was believed to be weakening under pressure from the man who after all had made him president. Wood bluntly told McKinley:

> We have gone into Cuba to give these people an example of good government. These thefts in the Post Office are so far the only blot on our record. Our honour as a nation demands that we bring the thieves to trial ... I think you ought to see that leaders of the Republican party – even Senators and people close to you – are interfering with my efforts in this direction. If it is embarrassing to you to have me persist in this matter, I will resign ...

McKinley replied, 'Wood, I want you to uphold the honour of our country, whoever you may hit, even though it may destroy one of the pillars of the Republican temple.'[57] In October, the postal case came up. $100,000 and $200,000 were involved. The defence contended that

[54] Hagedorn, I, 364.

[55] *Ibid.*, 368.

[56] The Cuban account in Martínez Ortiz (I, 300 ff) is the clearest. Those voted for included José Miguel Gómez, General Monteagudo, the mulatto Morúa Delgado, Pedro González Llorente, Gonzalo de Quesada, Diego Tamayo, Manuel Sanguily, Emilio Núñez and Méndez Capote: those against, José Alemán, Salvador Cisneros Betancourt, Juan Gualberto Gómez, Rafael Manduley, Alfredo Zayas and J. Fernández de Castro.

[57] Hagedorn, I, 369.

Wood had used his power to determine the course of the trial. Rathbone and his associate Neely were in the end found guilty of conspiracy to defraud, and were given ten years imprisonment, with heavy fines. A third person involved, Reeves, on turning state's evidence, was pardoned.[58]

By now however McKinley himself had dropped out of history. On 7 September 1901 a Polish anarchist, Leon Czolgosz, possessed of much the same notions as Angiolillo only four years before in the murder of McKinley's old antagonist Cánovas, shot the president at the Temple of Music in the Pan-American Exposition at Buffalo. On 14 September McKinley died of his wound. The vice-president, Theodore Roosevelt, became president. Wood went to McKinley's funeral. Riding in Rock Creek park, the ex-colonel and the lieutenant-colonel of volunteers, now governor-general of Cuba and president of the U.S., respectively, asked themselves: 'how did we ever do it?'

Wood now returned to Havana to embark upon the difficult task of assisting the revival of the sugar industry.

In 1899 each pound of sugar cost roughly 1 to $1\frac{1}{4}$ cents to make. The world price of sugar per pound was about $2\frac{1}{4}$ cents. The manufacturer had therefore only a little over 1 cent per pound to cover expenses, including freight, and many mills were operating at a loss. Atkins reported explicitly[59] that the situation was 'not such as to invite any large investment of new capital in sugar manufacturing'. He added: 'The future values of sugar in Cuba are dependent not upon the cost of production in that island but rather upon the cost in Germany and to the extent to which free sugars are to be admitted into the U.S. from the Sandwich islands, Porto Rico and the Philippines.'[60]

The U.S. tax structure, however, had recently been revised by the Dingley Act.[61] This put German and European sugar (which had subsidies from their home country) on the same level[62] as Cuban and other cane sugar, though the cost of production in Cuba was lower than beet sugar. So Cuba seemed likely to be able to recapture her pre-1895 position in the sugar world, provided that the U.S. did not give any special advantage to sugar from any other country.[63] But revision did not come in 1899–1900, though Puerto Rico, previously in the same plight as Cuba and with a likely sugar future, was allowed into the U.S. system immediately without difficulty.[64]

[58] *Ibid.*, 378.

[59] In a note for the Census authorities, qu. Atkins, 526.

[60] These had of course been assimilated into the U.S. after the Treaty of Paris.

[61] Of 1897.

[62] A tariff of 1.685 cents per pound.

[63] Census of 1899, 527.

[64] In 1893 there had been 341 sugar mills in Puerto Rico, but they produced barely a tenth of Cuban production and hardly any of it was centrifugal.

Total Cuban production therefore reached about 335,000 tons in 1899 and 285,000 in 1900 – a sad drop to $3\frac{1}{2}$% of world sugar as compared with about 13% in 1894. The main reason for the continued decline, as put clearly by Perfecto Lacoste, the Cuban Secretary of Agriculture and Industry, was that *'the Cuban planters have to depend on their own resources for the development of their plantations, without the necessary implements or the help* of agricultural banks or similar establishments of credit . . .'[65] General Brooke similarly noted that the reason the sugar industry was slow to revive was lack of capital. 'The quick return from tobacco and food crops will, it is believed, deter many from entering upon cane growing.'[66] But the American Census makers of 1899 realized that the existing sugar crop was only grown on a small percentage of the land on which sugar could be grown, and that therefore Cuba could 'easily become the greatest sugar producing country of the world' – an odd remark since of course except since 1880 Cuba had been so during most of the nineteenth century.[67]

There was another point. The Cuban war had given general encouragement both to European beet growers and to beet farmers of the U.S. Thirty-five new U.S. beet factories were built between 1896 and 1902. $M21 had been invested.[68] Cuba had thus a new rival, not on, but beyond the doorstep of her main customer, and a rival who would seek to influence the tariff itself, and oppose any concession over 'reciprocity'. Oxnard, the president of the U.S. Beet Sugar Company, indeed spent 'long days on Capitol Hill' in the winter of 1901–2 arguing against any relaxation of the tariff.[69]

He was, however, up against General Wood. On 28 October Wood was writing to President Roosevelt to complain that 'the U.S.A. had not taken any action . . . to stimulate the two great industries whose increase will speedily put Cuba on her feet. . . .'[70] In the next few months Wood then set in train his most controversial measure: the devotion of $15,000 of Cuban state funds to publicize Cuba's economic needs in the U.S. – that is, to lower tariffs on sugar and tobacco. Root had after all

[65] Census of 1899, 533.
[66] Brooke Report, 12.
[67] Census of 1899, 533.
[68] 1900 Census of U.S., qu. Jenks, 128.
[69] Hagedorn, I, 383. The U.S. beet sugar industry had begun in earnest in 1897 when the Department of Agriculture began to import European beet seeds and send them free to farmers. Henry Thomas Oxnard (1860–1922), Benjamin Oxnard (1855–1929), and Robert Oxnard (1853–1930), brothers coming from Louisiana, established a strong hold over the U.S. sugar world; Henry was vice-president of the American Beet Sugar Co., director of Central Sugar Corporation and the Savannah Sugar Refining Corporation. Benjamin had been refining sugar in Brooklyn till 1889. Afterwards he was president of the Savannah Corporation, and Adeline Sugar Corporation, New Orleans. Robert worked at first with Zaldo Brothers in Havana and became president of the American Sugar Refining Co., of the American Beet Sugar Co., and vice-president of Savannah.
[70] *Ibid.*, I, 382.

written to him as early as January: 'we cannot justify the demand that
Cuba shall treat us as a kind of foster-mother ... to whom she is to give
special privileges in the way of naval stations and rights of suspension
and intervention, while we are prepared to treat her commercially at
arm's length'.[71] Republicans, however, saw in the sugar issue a means of
holding down Roosevelt, at a time when Roosevelt himself realized
that there were many people 'who feared for the office [of President]
in the hand of this navy man'.[72] Roosevelt's message to Congress in
December might argue for tariff reduction, but there was nothing to
make this as attractive politically to his followers. Ex-President Cleveland backed Roosevelt, but despite this the Senate delayed, was
deluged with pro-beet propaganda, and eventually rejected the
proposal.[73]

Controversy over the sugar tariff continued throughout 1902. Wood
wrote to Root on 30 March: 'The situation here cannot continue much
longer. Enormous amounts of sugar are being held and the delay in
granting reciprocity is causing loss of confidence.'[74] On 9 April Roosevelt said in Charleston, South Carolina:

> Cuba is so near us that we can never be indifferent to misgovernment
> and disaster within its limits ... Cuba's position makes it necessary
> that her political relations with us should differ from her political
> relations with other powers. This fact has been formulated by us and
> accepted by the Cubans ... in return ... we must give to Cuba a
> different, that is, a better position economically in her relations with
> us than we give to other powers.[75]

Against this unpromising background, Wood issued an order for
Cuban elections on 31 December 1901, to settle the future presidency.
Máximo Gómez refused to run for President, formally at least with the
explanation, 'men of war for war, and those of peace for peace', and
threw his support to Estrada Palma, the old chief of the Cuban Junta
in New York, who had held the shadowy role of president of the provisional rebel government as long ago as 1876. He was also supported
by most of the leaders of Cuban opinion, such as José Miguel Gómez,
Alfredo Zayas, Domingo Méndez Capote, Emilio Núñez, Manuel
Sanguily, Ricardo Dolz, Martín Morúa Delgado, and Gonzalo de
Quesada; but Bartolomé Masó, the most recent ex-president of the

[71] *Ibid.*, I, 343.
[72] Thomas Beer, *Hanna* (1929), 236.
[73] *Cf.* Ray Stannard Baker, 'How the Beet Sugar Industry is growing', *Review of Reviews*,
XXII (March, 1901).
[74] Hagedorn, I, 384.
[75] *Addresses and Presidential Messages of Theodore Roosevelt, 1902–1904*, intro. H. C. Lodge
(1904), 7 ff.

shadow government in the hills, between Martí's death and 1898, stood firmly as an anti-Platt Amendment candidate. He made a series of violent speeches, full of promises to Spaniards, autonomists and Negroes. But the election campaign did not get under way. After a number of tactical errors, Masó objected that the Central Board of Scrutiny did not have any representative of his upon it and he withdrew from the election. Somewhat unfortunately, therefore, for the future of Cuban democratic institutions, Estrada Palma (who was still in the U.S.) was elected first Cuban president without opposition.

In March, Root, Wood and Estrada Palma met in Washington to discuss the transfer of power; the plan was that U.S. troops would be withdrawn save for a small number to man the coastal defences till Cuba developed an artillery of her own. On 5 May 1902 Wood convened the new Cuban congress to pass their own credentials; and on 20 May with enthusiasm, the Cuban flag was hoisted. Wood handed over power to Estrada, and, without drama or romanticism, withdrew.

Wood did not think that this U.S. withdrawal would be permanent. Up to the last, he had seized on small indications of opinion to construe them as signs of 'an extremely strong sentiment for annexation'.[76] Powerful senators such as Senator E. Payne, chairman of the Ways and Means Committee, still comforted themselves with the thought that 'the time will come when Cuba will be annexed to the U.S.A.'[77] Even Estrada Palma seems himself eventually to have expected 'annexation through acclamation'.[78] No doubt his Protestantism, his years spent with a Quaker family while teaching in New York State, all helped to prompt this conclusion. That Wood for much of his period of rule in Cuba expected and planned for eventual annexation is suggested by his education policy – having Lieutenant Hanna to write the schools law on the model of Ohio for ease of translation – as by his unfulfilled policy towards law.

One major achievement of the U.S. military government remains: the conquest of yellow fever. This disease had been a chronic affliction of the Spanish empire, its first incidence apparently being in Yucatan in 1648; it was regarded as the hopeless scourge of the Caribbean.[79] It was universally believed that it had been caused by filth, and under Wood, the epidemics in Santiago had been crushed. In 1900 Havana was effectively cleaned up, but immediately a new epidemic broke out.

[76] e.g., letter to Root, 16 October 1901.

[77] Congressional Record, XXXV, 3,850, 3,854, 3,856. Qu. Jenks, 71.

[78] See Camacho, *Retrato de Estrada Palma* (1938), 176–7.

[79] It appears to have begun in Africa and to have been taken to America with the slave trade. Its symptoms are: onset of severe headache, pains in back and neck, a rise in temperature, vomiting of blood which turns black (and hence for a long time known as 'black vomit'), increase of pulse, jaundice, death in the sixth or seventh day after delirium and coma.

Wood, a doctor by training, realized that this proved that the usual supposition for the origins of yellow fever was wrong. In fact, Carlos Finlay, a Cuban of Scottish origin, had earlier, eccentrically, said that the fever was transmitted by the stegomyia mosquito.[80] A commission under Dr Walter Reed was appointed by Wood to investigate. Two American doctors, Dr Jesse Lazear and Dr James Carroll, volunteered as guinea-pigs; both caught the disease; Carroll recovered, Lazear died. It transpired in the end that one major means of transmitting the disease was through the female stegomyia, who had to have bitten an infected person during the first three days of an attack. Dr William Crawford Gorgas, an old friend of Wood's, came out to Havana to embark on the systematic destruction of the mosquitos.[81] As a result, yellow fever, which had previously struck Havana every year since 1761,[82] fell from 1,400 cases in 1900 to 37 in 1901 and none in 1902.[83] It struck no more.

On other matters decisions were left in the air: in 1899 the U.S. Judge Advocate in Cuba (Major Edgar Dudley) had speculated on how difficult it was being shown to be to combine the Spanish law and the U.S., deriving from Roman law on the one hand and English common law on the other.[84] But, apart from an abortive attempt to introduce the jury system and a more successful one to introduce habeas corpus, the U.S. left the Cubans carrying on with Spanish customs in 1902.

The electoral system

The electorate of 1900 was based on male literacy. Of the total number of males of voting age (418,000), or 26% of the population, of these 200,631 or a little less than half were able to read, of whom just under 70% were white and just over 30% coloured. Of the Negroes of voting age (127,298), 96,463 could not vote since they could not read (i.e. 75% of the male Negroes of voting age). The total Negroes who could vote in 1899–1900 amounted to only about 31,000. The exclusion of women from the roll affected the Negroes more than it did the whites, since by 1899 there were more female Negroes and mulattoes than men, whereas there were more white males than females. Only 35,000 out of 145,000 black or mulatto women over twenty could read – approximately the same percentage as men. White women over twenty who could read amounted to 118,805, out of a total of 371,896.[85]

[80] Carlos Finlay (1833–1915) had never really been given the credit in North America for what was, all things considered, a major contribution in this field.

[81] William Crawford Gorgas (1854–1920), surgeon-general of the U.S. army in the First World War; also worked on tropical diseases in Panama.

[82] Surgeon-General's Report, 1899, Report of the War Dept, Vol. I, Pt II, 491.

[83] It was however not till 1928 that it was eventually found that the yellow fever virus could be carried by other agents than the mosquito. See article of Dr R. M. Taylor (of International Health Division of the Rockefeller Foundation) in *Encyclopedia Americana*.

[84] Report of the War Dept for 1899, Vol. II, 143.

[85] Worked out from figures in Census of 1900, 195, 361–2.

Wood and Church lands

During the Liberal government of Mendizábal in Spain (coinciding with Tacón's rule at Havana) the government had confiscated all Church lands, all the property, that is, which was not specifically used for masses or for housing priests.[86] By a compromise between Church and State in 1861 (ten years after a similar compromise reached in Spain), all property which the government had sold was to be excluded from consideration; all land the government 'did not need' was handed back to the Church; the rest was leased by the state – and rent between then and 1899 had totalled $M21. Most of this land was urban property in Havana and Santiago, on which had been built the Havana customs house, the Academy of Studies, the Havana high school and other important institutions. This Havana property was valued at $M1½. Wood agreed that the government would in Havana then go on paying 5% of this a year, though the total rentals would be deducted from the total price if the future government decided to pay. In Oriente the government paid 3% a year on property valued a $535,000. The question as to whether or not the state should settle the controversy by buying the property was left undecided.[87] Many believed that these payments were unnecessary, arguing that Church property belonged to the state. This problem was handed down for the future to resolve.

[86] Pezuela, estimated that in the mid-seventeenth century the Church had a capital of $M4, or one third of the public wealth of Cuba.

[87] See Hagedorn, I, 316–18.

CHAPTER XXXVIII

The U.S. Stake in Cuba, 1899–1902

One of the hardest features of my work [Wood wrote] was to prevent the looting of Cuba by men who were presumed respectable. Men came down there apparently with the best recommendations and wanted me to further the most infamous of schemes. They expected to profit by sharp business practices at the expense of the people of the island and were naturally embittered in their failure . . . and came home with all sorts of tales of highhandedness.

A typical case was that of Michael Dady of Brooklyn, who had had a contract in 1895 to pave Havana's streets; by Spanish law, his estimate gave him the right to *tanteo*, that is, the right to take the contract on the terms of the next bidder or to oblige him to pay a percentage of the difference. General Ludlow, governor of Havana, became embroiled against Dady and set about banning newspapers which defended him, and had to be sent on leave.[1]

Wood made an enquiry, so offending not only Dady but his friends the Brooklyn Republicans. Wood eventually paid Dady $250,000 to settle his claims.[2]

Wood had, however, always opposed the Foraker amendment which prevented the grant of contracts to U.S. citizens by the military government. Indeed, he had written to Foraker urging the withdrawal of the resolution, but in fact this was not done: this regulation was only applied for the first time in early 1900 and by that time there were many financial adventurers on the scene. First in order of audacity was the thirty-four-year-old Quaker financier, Perceval Farquhar, who had arrived in Havana in the summer of 1898 determined to electrify Havana's horse-driven tramways. There had then been 250 buses in bad condition, covering twenty-seven miles, three horses per bus, owned under a concession of 1859 by the *Ferrocarril Urbano y Omnibus de la Habana*.[3] A Cuban-Spanish financier, Tiburicio Castañeda, and

---

[1] 'Do give the General some good advice,' Wood wrote to Root, 'and keep him in the States for a couple of weeks until things cool off.' In fact, Ludlow went off to become president of the War College Board and never returned to Havana, which was administratively incorporated in the province.

[2] Hagedorn, I, 332, 281–2.

[3] Porter, *Industrial Cuba*, 139–53.

Farquhar first clashed over the electrification project, then divided it between them, defeating various other syndicates also anxious for the concession. Castañeda and Farquhar browbeat the shareholders of the old company to vote them into control. A Quaker, Farquhar would not bribe; but he did not mind bullying, by hiring a strong-voiced man to shout down disaffected stockholders. At this point rivals, led by another North American, Robert A. C. Smith, the manager of the Havana Gas Company, kidnapped Castañeda. Farquhar persuaded the Spanish captain-general still in control to free him. Smith's lawyers in New York, the Conderts, led by their Havana representative, Pablo Desver-nine, attempted to break Farquhar, till eventually after a year of litigation Wood had to force a compromise.⁴ (Desvernine later himself became Wood's First Secretary of the Treasury.) Farquhar went ahead, the value of the Urbano concession rose from $M1 to $M3, and the electrification was carried out by the engineers Pearson and Billings. But rivalry between Farquhar and Smith continued over subsidiary projects during the rest of Wood's government.

Farquhar afterwards had moved on to bigger game. The obvious and dramatic possibility for Cuba in 1898 was a railway line from Havana to Oriente and Santiago. Spanish coastal shipping interests had always prevented Spain going ahead with such a project, which might have made a considerable difference to the war of 1895–8. Such a railway evidently would open up vast new territories for sugar produc-tion and for creating wealth. First Farquhar, with a Wall Street associate, Samuel Thomas, and the rich Zaldo brothers of Havana, formed a syndicate to buy the small Matanzas–Sabanilla railway.⁵ Henry O. Havemeyer of the 'Sugar Trust' shared in this until he, with all the others save Thomas, dropped out when all share prices were upset by the Boer War. Thomas then introduced Farquhar to Sir William Van Horne, founder of the Canadian-Pacific Railway, who became interested in January 1900.⁶ Abandoning a plan to build a railway in British Guiana, Van Horne embarked on the Cuban project with enthusiasm. U.S. concessions were, of course, forbidden under the Foraker amendment. But what was there to prevent the purchase of land and the construction of a railway on it without a concession? In April 1900 the Cuba Company was formed, with Van Horne as president and Farquhar as his aide. Recalling his difficulty over the

⁴ See Gauld, *The Last Titan*, 11–16. An agent of Desvernine's, José A. Marx, attempted to 'line up property owners along the tram lines to sue for damages', and tried to bribe the A.P. correspondent, C. M. Dobson, with $500 to spread his stories (U.S., M.G. Records, 1517–25. See Gauld, 22, fn. 17).

⁵ Guillermo de Zaldo had had his Pinar del Río sugar plantation destroyed in the war.

⁶ Sir William van Horne (1843–1915), born Illinois, started life as telegraph operator on the Illinois Central Railroad; went to Canada 1881, afterwards knighted by the English.

multitude of shareholders in the Canadian-Pacific, Van Horne issued only 160 $50,000 shares.[7]

At this time, Oriente had only a hundred miles of railroad, mostly private company railroads.[8] The new line was begun in Oriente and also in Santa Clara. A branch led up to Antilla, headquarters of the newly developing United Fruit Co., who bought 90,000 acres in 1900. Farquhar went down the country buying land, asking from landowners three times what he needed because of overlapping land titles and inaccurate maps. The Cubans Teodoro de Zaldo and Manuel Manduley[9] (the latter an ex-captain in the liberation army) travelled by buggy and horseback to reassure landowners that this was not the first step to annexation. Some land was even secured by gift, as that of a Catalan merchant, Balbín, at Ciego de Avila. Wood assisted by granting, despite the Foraker amendment, revocable permits to cross rivers and roads. The Cuban Central Railroad attempted to halt the development as contrary to law, arguing that they anyway had the concession. Wood replied that 'no central railroad as such was being built', only a private one on private land with no concession. Van Horne and Farquhar also secured petitions for the continuance of the railroad from many farms by the simple device of sporadically laying off labour. They bought two sugar mills in Oriente and the small private Guantánamo-San Luis railway; they founded lumber mills; they drafted a Cuban Railway Law; and they persuaded Wood to let them import Canary Island workers and *gallegos*, since the North American labourers, of the American Bridge Company, drank too much rum and delayed labour. Farquhar also persuaded Juan Gualberto Gómez not to attack the Railway Law which he had intended to do, since he thought the railroad would give the U.S. excessive economic power;[10] perhaps he was also afraid that if there should ever be a Negro revolt in the east, such a railway would enable it to be easily crushed.

Early in 1902 new capital was needed. Thomas Ryan, Widener and

[7] Early shareholders included: Samuel Thomas of Wall Street, ex-president of several U.S. railroads; Thomas Ryan of the Morton Trust Co., with Levi Morton (see below); William and Henry Whitney; Widener and Elkins – all members of the American Indies Co., whom Farquhar had beaten in 1898–9 over the Havana electric (in addition to Smith); Farquhar's father; Jacob Schiff and Lanman Bull of Wall Street; the rail and coal king, E. J. Berwind; August Belmont, the Cuban rebel banker during the war of 1895–8; E. H. Harriman of Canadian Pacific (father of Averell Harriman); the gas tycoon, Anthony Brady (see below); the Union Pacific builder, Grenville Dodge; Henry M. Flagler; and J. J. Hill, Van Horne's old enemy in Canada.

[8] The Jaragua Iron Co. of Philadelphia had 28 km. of narrow-gauge lines; its subsidiary, the Cuban Steel Ore Co., had 8 km. at Guamá; the Spanish American Iron Co. at Daiquirí had 6 km. Also several cane plantations had a few narrow-gauge lines.

[9] Manuel Manduley (1866–1947), born in Holguín, adviser to Wood, prepared a penal code for the U.S. military government; he was also a constituent assemblyman.

[10] See Gauld, *The Last Titan*, 45, and references: Ben B. Shaw, 'Building a Railway: Unusual Circumstances', *Railway Age*, 31 October 1925.

Elkins sold their shares – as part of the original arrangement by Van Horne which provided that shareholders when asked had either to put up 40% more or sell. The buyer was Robert Fleming of London. Thereafter everything went very fast. With grading complete, construction began, and 1 December was announced as inauguration day. Fleming meantime succeeded in enlarging his share, so that ultimately he gained control – obliging Van Horne in the end to appoint as a director, a young protégé of his, George Whigham.[11]

This railroad cost $M10½ to equip. Travelling time from Havana to Santiago was thereby cut from a sea voyage of ten days to twenty-four hours.[12]

In 1902, when Wood withdrew, U.S. capital in Cuba totalled $M100, of which $M45 was in tobacco, $M25 in sugar. Farquhar by then had moved on, thanks to a chance meeting with Minor Keith of United Fruit, to begin work on the Guatemala Railway, and thence to titanic struggles throughout Latin America.

U.S. business reached specially far into Cuban tobacco. Before 1899 there had been one English-owned cigar factory group, Henry Clay and Block; there were some German factories; otherwise all were Spanish or Cuban. In 1899 the Havana Commercial Company promoted by H. B. Hollins of New York and a Cuban American, Rafael Govín, bought twelve cigar factories and a cigarette factory in Havana. They also bought tobacco plantations, keeping the share croppers and helping them with advances of $M1·3 by December 1900. Next, the American Tobacco Co.[13] combined twenty U.S. owned Cuban tobacco factories as the American Cigar Company. In early 1902 they forced British tobacco interests to accept an alliance with them, and afterwards, in May 1902, swallowed the Havana Commercial Co., which had already gobbled up Henry Clay and Block. This meant that 90% of the export trade in Havana cigars passed into North American control, along with half the entire manufacture of Cuban cigars and cigarettes.[14]

North Americans also interested themselves in Cuba's mineral resources. Wood commissioned a report from three prominent U.S. geologists on the geological resources of Cuba. Afterwards, Wood granted 218 mining concessions, mostly to U.S. companies, who were exempted from the annual property tax.[15]

[11] Whigham succeeded Van Horne as president from 1915–19. Then Herbert C. Lakin of Wall Street succeeded from 1919–30, after the provision by which the British had to sell their stocks abroad during the First World War.

[12] For all the above, see Gauld, *The Last Titan*, 26–37; Wright, *Cuba*, 354.

[13] Controlled by James B. Duke, Thomas F. Ryan, P. A. B. Widener, Anthony N. Brady, and Grant Schley. Ryan, Widener and Brady were all stockholders in the railway.

[14] Jenks, 155–6.

[15] These concessions were made much of by Núñez Jiménez in his 'revolutionary' *Geografía de Cuba*, 212.

In 1899 two sugar mills had been founded,[16] and 1901 had seen the foundation on the north coast of Oriente of two huge mills, *Boston*, by the United Fruit Company, and *Chaparra*, by a new company formed under the aegis of the first Republican U.S. congressman for Texas, Representative R. B. Hawley – the Cuban American Company.

The United Fruit Company incorporated in 1899 had already begun its long history of adventurous commerce and controversial land-holding.[17] It was already far the biggest U.S. enterprise in Central America. Minor Keith, its piratical chairman, carried off a superlative triumph in buying, for a mere $400,000, 200,000 acres on Nipe Bay through a syndicate.[18] No doubt he would have been more reluctant had he not known, through Perceval Farquhar, that a railway would shortly be driven into the heart of this virgin territory. Indeed, Keith had shares in Farquhar and Van Horne's Cuba Company, though he was also president of the rival Cuban Central Railway Company, and therefore crossed swords as to who would build the railway. The United Fruit Company, whose concern in Cuba was formed out of the com-bination of several interests, among them the Dumois brothers' citrus and banana plantations founded in 1889, began by continuing the banana business, but, finding it less profitable than they had supposed, began work in 1901 on their first great sugar mill in Cuba, the *central Boston*, on the edge of the bay of Banes.[19] So a new satrapy was added to the far-reaching United Company served by the 'white fleet', and by a growing though dormant body of North American stockholders. Its assets rose from $M17 in 1900 to $M82 in 1913.[20] In Cuba as elsewhere it operated in regions where there were few inhabitants and, in addition to providing foreign capital, often brought into Cuba foreign labour, in the form of British West Indians, just as the old slave plantations had done.[21]

R. B. Hawley's investment had a different inspiration. Its promoter was himself a Cuban, Mario García Menocal,[22] a young officer in the

[16] *Washington* and *Francisco*.

[17] See Stacy May and Galo Plaza, *The United Fruit Company in Latin America* (1958); Biography of Minor Keith in German by Hermann Bitter. C. D. Kepner and J. H. Soothill, *The Banana Empire* (1914). F. U. Adams, *The Conquest of the Tropics* (1935).

[18] Beals, 405; Jenks, 130; Minor Keith (1848–1929) was nephew and protégé of Henry Meiggs, the Chilean and Peruvian railway builder; he married the daughter of the president of Costa Rica; built Costa Rican railroad, 1871–82; organized Tropical Trading Transport Co. for banana interests, Costa Rica; 1899 united with Boston Fruit to form United Fruit Co. 1908; built Guatemala railway; 1912–28 president of International Railways of Guate-mala; left $3,336,507.

[19] Wright, *Cuba*, 464. The birth of the Boston mill almost coincided exactly in place and time with that of Fulgencio Batista, in the village of Veguitas, Banes.

[20] Adams, *Conquest of the Tropics*, 332.

[21] Munro, *Dollar Diplomacy*, 19.

[22] General Mario García Menocal y Deop (1866–1941), always known as Menocal and hereafter so described; born at Jagüey Grande; spent childhood in U.S. and Mexico, during ten years' war. Afterwards president of Cuba.

war of independence. Earlier an engineer at Cornell and with experience in Nicaragua, he joined the *mambises* as a private, and ended the war as a general, having fought a good deal, mostly under Calixto García. He had supervised the trench construction at the siege of Cascorro; and there was later a famous picture of him leading the capture of a block-house at Vitoria de las Tunas, bought later by a grateful nation for an absurd sum. For a time in 1898–9 Menocal was chief of police in Havana and inspector of public works, but he quickly realized where power would lie in the new Cuba. He resigned to help found, with Hawley, the Cuban American Company, with its main mill, *Chaparra*, near a village of that name on the north coast of Cuba, fifty miles or so west of the United Fruit Company's plantations. Even larger than the United Fruit Company's establishment, *Chaparra*, under Menocal's management, became the largest sugar estate in the world.

Thus U.S. capital showed its confidence in Cuban sugar as an exciting commercial venture, even before any reciprocatory treaty had been signed and even despite the very low figures attained by sugar production at the end of the South African war – Wood in fact left Cuba with sugar piling up unbought in the warehouses.[23] Atkins, as usual, was working away in Washington to counter the influence of Oxnard and the beet lobby[24] while the new president, Roosevelt, was a strong partisan of assuming an obligation to the Cubans. On 2 December 1902, in his annual message to Congress, he would demand a treaty:

> Not only because it is enormously in our interest to control the Cuban market and by every means to foster our supremacy in the tropical lands and waters south of us, but also because we . . . should make all our sister nations of the American continent feel that . . . we desire to show ourselves disinterestedly and effectively their friend.[25]

Roosevelt admittedly was then about to embark on the final stage of his Panamanian adventure and no doubt wished this Cuban problem out of the way first.[26] At all events, thanks partly no doubt to General

---

[23] The lowest figure was 1·56 cents per pound; average for the year, 1·84.

[24] Atkins, 308.

[25] Roosevelt, *Addresses and Presidential Messages*.

[26] In late 1902 Hay and Roosevelt hatched a plan by which Colombia would be paid $M10 in gold and $250,000 a year for a licence to build the canal and to construct a canal zone three miles each side of it. The Colombian *chargé d'affaires* in Washington accepted this in January 1903, but his parliament, engaged in much internal dispute, refused it. 'Those contemptible little creatures in Bogota,' Roosevelt exploded to Secretary of State Hay, 'ought to understand how much they are jeopardising . . . their own future.' On 14 October 1902 Dr Manuel Amador, physician to the U.S. Panamá Railroad and Steamship Company, visited the French adventurer and inspiration of the canal project, Bunau-Varilla, at the Waldorf Hotel in New York. The latter promised $100,000 for the preliminary expenses of a revolution to be staged on 3 November (election day in the U.S.), whose aim was to break

Wood's expense of Cuban government funds to publicize the cause,[27] a reciprocity treaty was finally signed on 11 December; on 19 March 1903, the Senate ratified it and the treaty, not without further hostility, became law in December 1903 – hardly noticed in the U.S. thanks to the triumph of Roosevelt's Panamá policy. This treaty gave Cuba a 20% tariff preference over other countries, in the U.S.; in return, Cuba gave U.S. shippers a reduction varying between 25% and 40% of normal.

This was a signal for big further investment. The investment was almost all in sugar; but whatever remote hope there might have been that the old sugar economy might be replaced by a more balanced system was lost.[28] Root and Roosevelt were giving Cuban mills a chance to expand production till they supplied all the sugar the U.S. needed. Both politicians, however, believed they were helping Cuba, not ruining it, and most Cubans agreed, at the time. U.S. sugar consumption was meantime leaping ahead: the average North American ate 63 lbs of sugar in 1899, 75 lbs in 1904, and, just before the First World War, 81 lbs a year.[29] During 1903 two new U.S. companies were founded, one in Oriente, the other in Camagüey. In 1904, with sugar prices picking up to an average of 2·6 cents a pound,[30] and production topping a million tons for the first time since 1895, the United Fruit Company began work on the *central Preston*, their second big mill on their

[27] See above, p. 458.
[28] Portell Vilá, IV, 317, 379–80. But was such hope genuine?
[29] *Historical Statistics*, 187.
[30] All sugar prices raw unless stated.

Panamá away from Colombia. He was given a draft of Panamá's new constitution, a code with which to contact the U.S. fleet, a proclamation of independence, and a message appealing to Bunau-Varilla to become the first minister to the U.S.: Bunau Varilla wrote: 'I am going tomorrow to join my family ... [where] I shall find ... agile and discreet fingers that will make a new flag.' Next day Mme Bunau-Varilla stitched the flag of Panamanian Liberation. In Panamá, the Colombian general was given $50,000, officers $30,000 or $10,000, soldiers, $50 a head. The Panamanian governor agreed to a friendly arrest, and Colonel Shaler of the Panamá Railroad prepared to block the railway lines. All turned out as planned. On 4 November Dr Amador proclaimed the independence of Panamá: 'The world is astounded at our heroism. Yesterday we were but the slaves of Colombia. Today we are free ... free sons of Panamá I salute you, long live the Republic ... Long live President Roosevelt.' There was some popular support for this in the region; Panamá had had an autonomous government in the past and was a remote province. The security of the old 'transit route' had always been regarded as an international concern accepted by Colombia who had in the past asked the U.S. to send troops. On 17 November Panamá and the U.S. signed a treaty enabling the canal to be built. $M40 was distributed to stockholders of the new Panamá Canal Co. by J. P. Morgan & Co.; who they were remains a secret. The 'jack-rabbits', the 'foolish and homicidal corruptionists', as Roosevelt described the Colombians, were paid $M25 compensation in 1921. Panamá, who gave up a zone ten miles wide to the U.S., were paid $M10 and $250,000 a year thereafter. (See Pringle, *Roosevelt*, 320 ff; *New York Times*, 24 March 1911; P. Bunau-Varilla, *The Great Adventure of Panamá* (1920), 328; D. C. Miner, *The Fight for the Panamá Route* (1940).) A judicious account giving the U.S. position in its best light appears in Munro, *Dollar Diplomacy*, 57.

stretch of new land in north Oriente, and their banana groves were forever covered with cane. They now had 25,000 acres of cane, had bought 1,500 acres of cane from *colonos*, and gave over 15,000 acres to 4,400 head of cattle; they had over 100 miles of private railway, 17 locomotives, 640 cane wagons, and employed 5,000 during harvest.[31] Though two other mills were founded that year, one Spanish, this investment was the emblem of the time, the symbol of a North American penetration of the last Spanish dominion in the New World.

U.S. political concern for the future good government of Cuba was sincere and well meant. General Wood's anxiety about the character of the Cuban politicians who had survived the war of independence was well based: many were rogues. Many North American businessmen were at least half interested in the development of the prize which was now at their mercy, as well as in their profits. But the mixture of political control, as expressed by the Platt Amendment, and economic penetration was certain to rouse animosity among those Cubans who had hoped and planned for a more heroic independence. The Platt Amendment, though well intentioned, was an unhappy compromise, patronising and counter-productive, as indeed one U.S. senator had predicted. With the benefit of hindsight, it is possible to say that it would have been far better for the U.S. to have taken over full responsibility for Cuba for a time as she did in respect of Puerto Rico and the Philippines and afterwards move either to full independence or perhaps annexation; as it was, the relationship achieved between the U.S. and Cuba resembled that between England and Egypt or other Arab countries, the U.S. preening herself on her help to Cuba to achieve independence from Spain as the English did in respect of their help to the Arabs against the Turks, that help being itself an unacceptable memory piled on top of an intolerable present.

[31] Wright, *Cuba*, 470.

CHAPTER XXXIX

Don Tomás

Political independence in Cuba began quite promisingly due to the evident disinterestedness of the president of Cuba, the Quaker ex-schoolmaster of Happy Valley, Tomás Estrada Palma. Liberation also coincided with a period of increasing prosperity, natural enough, considering the rapid investment from abroad and the general recovery after the war. Spanish immigration began on a lavish scale, a bizarre consequence of the severance of Cuba's last formal ties with the homeland. Domestic animals were imported to make up for losses. New houses went up in the Vedado. Land prices went up seven times between 1902 and 1905. Between 1902 and 1905 Estrada Palma built 328 kilometres of roads, compared with 98 kilometres under Brooke and Wood. 'Don Tomás could govern Cuba with coffee cups', it was pointed out.

The Cuban Congress, however, embarked upon democracy with a scandal fit to discredit it. Having first passed a bill giving lavish salaries to public office holders, another was introduced to give extra payments to the army of liberation: one dollar was promised to privates for each day of service, and lavish sums to officers. This opened the way to a sensational speculation on the part of a number of politicians, who let it be understood that the delays in settling this question would be endless, and persuaded half the soldiers with claims to sell these at half their proper price. Afterwards, when the bill had been in the event quickly passed, the new politicians (headed by Colonel Miguel Tarafa) drew in the profit without shame. There were other scandals. Imaginary names were given; people made up campaigns in which they said they had served. Among those who went to prison as a result was Alfredo Zayas, the rebels' chief representative at Havana during part of the war.

Then there were serious unresolved discrepancies in Cuban law. Wood had left the very status of the judiciary in doubt, since by the old Spanish law judges and magistrates were appointed by, and therefore subordinate to, the governor-general. The Constitution of 1902 provided in theory for separation of powers, but Estrada's Congress met so infrequently and unsatisfactorily that the laws enabling the implementation of the Constitution were not carried out. The executive was thus able to browbeat the judiciary between 1902 and 1906 much as

they had done in colonial days. Similarly, the Constitution of 1902 gave
provinces and municipalities considerable powers of self-government in
the U.S. spirit; the previous municipal law, however, had been based
on the much criticized Spanish law of 1877. Wood had supposed the
Cuban Congress would pass the necessary enabling laws to be carried
out, but it did not, and the 1877 law remained in practice. When later
Estrada's ministers removed certain municipal officials of whom they
personally disapproved, they could claim they were acting legally, even
if unconstitutionally.

In addition the U.S., through its representatives in Cuba, had scarcely
set a good example. General Wood unthinkingly and autocratically had
presented 'heavy doses of the U.S. constitution', and had persuaded
himself and others that the medicine worked, without realizing that
institutional development must come from within and not from without;
nor was there, in the early days, much evidence that U.S. citizens
respected the democratic procedure, about which they talked so
grandly, when it came to the point; thus even the upright Atkins
recalled that in 1900 he was sent for by Wood, who

> asked me to use my influence in support of a very respectable man
> whom he wished to elect as mayor of Cienfuegos. I sent for one of the
> *alcaldes de barrio* and told him my wishes. He told me to have no
> anxiety: it was a simple matter; they would take possession of the
> ballot boxes and destroy the ballots of the opposition candidates. I
> told him it was a magnificent idea and worthy of Tammany Hall.[1]

While democracy had such friends there was hardly need of enemies.

The course of electoral history was therefore scarcely surprising. The
first elections in free Cuba for a national Congress came in February
1904. Two parties had quickly taken shape from the ruins of the Cuban
past, gaseous clouds hardening into mineral but brittle substances; they
were entitled 'Republicans', who were, roughly speaking, Conservatives and included several prominent autonomists of the past, and
'Nationals' or 'National Liberals', who were more of a popular party
and whose interests were in the direction of substantial local autonomy;
both really gangs of friends and pursuers of spoils rather than advocates
of principle, ex-generals turned *políticos* who were exhausted by war and
determined to share in the plenty of peace. From the beginning, the
Cuban parliamentary parties seized on the worst aspects of the Spanish
and American systems. The first election of the Republic in February
1904 was 'a farce represented with less shame than in the times of the
colony'. Both sides sought to win by means of *el copo*, that is, a fraud to
prevent the minority from any representation. Thus in Pinar del Río

[1] Atkins, 322.

two electoral boards flourished separately. Even Martí's chosen heir, the Negro polemicist, Juan Gualberto Gómez, got more votes than were cast. There was a good deal of sporadic violence. Though the Republicans seemed to have gained the day, their opponents did not concede. When Congress opened in April, the Liberals did not attend, so preventing the legislature from meeting, since two-thirds of the members had to be present for a quorum. A temporary solution was achieved when, in order to pass the all-important bill giving more pay for the veterans, the old members of the previous House were brought in, together with those new members who were veterans: but the credentials of these latter had never been approved. In September, the Republican leader Ricardo Dolz (an ex-autonomist), eventually engineered a compromise. But by then Dolz's party itself was beginning to melt away.

By now the dominant question in Cuban politics were the next presidential elections, of 1905; the popular Liberal leader, ex-civil governor of Santa Clara, General José Miguel Gómez was the obvious candidate. The argument ranged over a question of equality of representation for each province. Gómez's opponents, including some of the Liberals and the Republicans who jointly reformed themselves as the Moderate party, found that the only strong candidate for the presidency whom they could find was the sitting president, Estrada Palma, who despite age and manifest incapacity to lead was at least well known and was believed to be honest.[2] He was willing to stand again since he was understandably afraid that Gómez and his corrupt vice-presidential running mate, Alfredo Zayas, would spend the surplus which he, Estrada Palma, had managed to amass in the Treasury.[3] In March, General Freyre de Andrade, Secretary of the Interior, a leading Moderate, and far the strongest character among the president's ministers, began a systematic programme of dismissals of government employees, even schoolmasters, who were not Moderates; and by September it became clear that Freyre de Andrade was ready to use the force of police and rural guards (there being as yet no army) to ensure victory for Estrada Palma.[4] On 22 September, the day before the date of preliminary elections, an unexplained murder occurred in Santa Clara. A meeting of Liberals was being held in the Hotel Suiza. The chief of police went to the hotel, allegedly acting on a report that arms had been found there. A brawl followed in which both the police chief and a much loved Liberal leader in Santa Clara, Enrique Villuendas, were killed. The next day the Liberals, echoing Bartolomé Masó in

[2] General Máximo Gómez died in 1905.

[3] Alfredo Zayas (1861–1934), lawyer, autonomist under Spain, joined Martí 1895; subsequently Justice under Wood; president of Cuba 1921–5.

[4] Fernando Freyre de Andrade (1863–1929), lawyer, general in legal corps of the rebel army, afterwards magistrate; mayor of Havana, 1912–16.

1901, declared they would call off their candidates altogether and abstain, since it had become clear that they would be beaten by force. The Moderates went ahead, and steadily built up an electoral registry of 432,000, of whom 150,000 were invented. Estrada Palma was thus re-elected president without opposition on 1 December 1905.

Did no issue other than self-interest divide these parties? On the Platt Amendment, the Moderates advocated eventual, the Liberals immediate, abrogation. But José Miguel Gómez explained ambiguously in New York on 5 October:

> The U.S. has a direct responsibility concerning what is going on in Cuba ... Estrada Palma continues at the head of the government only by telling the people that in case of disorder or revolution the U.S. will immediately send troops to chastise the 'insurrectionists' ... The U.S. is under the duty of putting an end to this situation which if it continues any longer will oblige us to go to the government of Theodore Roosevelt with a petition for it to do so. If the U.S. would intervene and insist that the presidential elections should be held honestly, it would prove that 80% of the Cuban people were Liberal.[5]

However, what was it to be Liberal? Little more than to support José Miguel and through him at least to support a kind of popular, almost populist, *caudillismo* based on his warm, generous, extrovert, *simpático* character. José Miguel was for a time the centre of attraction for all those who thought that independence had let them down – articulating the 'growing feeling among Negroes against white Cubans who they say have robbed them of the spoils of war'.[6] The Republicans opposed this in the name of the creole *haute bourgeoisie*. Neither party was dedicated to the democratic experiment, none feeling that the U.S.-style Constitution meant much.[7] The U.S. Legation appeared completely in the dark, or at least pretended to be so: the minister, Morgan, went off to Europe for a long holiday in the early summer. However, it was rumoured – though never confirmed – that his predecessor Squiers had given money to the Liberals.[8]

By April 1906, Liberal veterans, like General Pino Guerra, were darkly talking that they 'must seek justice somewhere else', that is

---

[5] *Diario de la Marina*, 4 October 1905.

[6] Atkins's comment in February 1900 (Atkins, 313).

[7] *Cf.* Enrique Barbarosa, *El proceso de la República, etc.* (1911), 65, who argues that only the conquest of the Treasury was at stake.

[8] See Roosevelt, *Letters*, V, 426. Roosevelt later complained of Morgan to Root. 'Apparently Mr Morgan did not leave Cuba until the latter part of July. At that time ... most observers of intelligence saw that grave trouble was impending ... yet he gave no syllabub of warning ... and ... went not to the U.S. but to Europe.' But Morgan stayed as minister in Cuba till 1910, thereafter going to Uruguay and Paraguay (*ibid.*, V, 440–1). Squiers had been in the army where his career had been notable for several refusals to obey orders.

outside Congress.[9] They knew that if they were to act at all they would have to do so swiftly if they were going to avoid U.S. intervention. They prepared carefully all the summer and, on 16 August, 'Pino' Guerra raised the standard of revolt. Eduardo Guzmán and Orestes Ferrara headed columns in Santa Clara, while Colonel Asbert and General Loynaz del Castillo did so in the province of Havana. The rebels seemed everywhere likely to win with a total force of perhaps 24,000 opposed to no army, only about 600 artillerymen, and 3,000 dispersed rural guards. Both Juan Gualberto and José Miguel Gómez together with generals Monteaguado and Castillo Duany however were arrested, and their presence in government hands as hostages might have tipped the balance if real war had come.

The Liberal rebels of 1905 raised the flag of insurrection on a broad front, in the hallowed tradition of Cuban history of the past forty years – actually a Cuban flag draped in black; most of the rebels had taken an active part in the second war of independence, some in the first. Their predecessors had acted similarly in Spain throughout the nineteenth century until the Restoration of 1875 and the Liberal rising was a *pronunciamiento* on a Spanish, not a Latin-American, model. There were several fights along the railway lines, rightly considered the key to victory.

At this point, the rich General Mario Menocal arrived in Havana from his great sugar *central Chaparra* on behalf of a number of other ex-leaders of the war of independence. He saw President Estrada and begged him to achieve a compromise based on honest elections. But Estrada dithered. On 8 September he told Menocal that he could not talk with the rebels till they had laid down their arms. Civil war was joined, though the rebels for a few days merely busied themselves capturing horses and issuing proclamations. There was much sporadic fighting. The U.S. *chargé d'affaires*, James Sleeper, a young man acting in the stead of Minister Morgan on holiday, telegraphed Washington the agreeable news: 'Revolution spreading. Everything quiet.' On the other hand, the American colony in Havana, particularly the press, longed for intervention, even annexation; 'it was our policy to whoop the row along until American intervention occurred', recalled a journalist in the Havana *Telégrafo*.[10]

A few hours later, a sterner telegram was sent to Washington. This was from Consul-General Steinhart.[11] It ran:

[9] Guerra was thought to be after money, *cf*. Wright, *Cuba*, 178.

[10] *Ibid.*, 175. *La Lucha*, the Spanish paper, did the same.

[11] Frank Steinhart (1864–1938), a remarkable man, born in Munich, educated there, and read law; went to U.S. and enlisted as a private, became sergeant-clerk; chief clerk to General Brooke in Puerto Rico, later chief clerk under him and Wood in Cuba; U.S. consul-general 1903–7; afterwards entered business and became president of Havana Electric Railways.

[Cuban] Secretary of State ... has requested me in the name of President Palma [*sic*] to ask President Roosevelt to send immediately two vessels: one to Havana, the other to Cienfuegos. Government forces are unable to ... protect property ... Congress will ask for our further intervention.[12]

This request was 'emphatically' not welcome to President Roosevelt,[13] who at that moment was anxiously trying to persuade South and Central America in general that, Panamá notwithstanding, the U.S. had no imperialistic intentions. He was also concerned to keep other powers, such as Germany, out of the Caribbean. At that very moment his Secretary of State, Elihu Root, was in Buenos Aires making that point with his customary lucid if legalistic responsibility, and wondering if his constitution could stand 'the sweet champagne of our sister Republics'.[14] Roosevelt had no desire to spread U.S. direct rule southwards, and in his inaugural address of December 1904 he had glowingly described how 'if every country washed by the Caribbean ... would show the progress in stable and just civilisation which with the aid of the Platt Amendment Cuba has shown ... all questions of interference by this nation would be at an end.'[15] Nevertheless in his famous 'Corollary' to the Monroe doctrine Roosevelt had acknowledged that the U.S. would always intervene in South America in instances of 'brutal wrongdoing or an impotence which results in a general loosening of the ties of civilised society'.[16] He believed that unless the U.S. took a line, Britain or Germany probably would.[17]

On 10 September 1906 Roosevelt asked Root's deputy, Bacon, to telegraph Consul-General Steinhart: 'Perhaps you do not yourself appreciate the reluctance with which this country would intervene.'[18] Confirming this in a letter on 11 September, the president thought 'actual immediate intervention' to be out of the question. But on 12 September Estrada pathetically begged Roosevelt to send 2,000–3,000 men 'with the greatest secrecy and rapidity',[19] telling Steinhart that he could not any more prevent the rebels from 'entering cities and burning property'. The same day, Estrada persuaded Sleeper to ask on his own the nearest U.S. destroyer, the *Denver*, to land at Havana and put ashore 125 men, which was done. A few hours later Sleeper received a

[12] Taft-Bacon Report, 444–51.
[13] See letter to Sir G. Trevelyan, Roosevelt, *Letters*, V, 401.
[14] *Ibid.*, V, 396.
[15] T. Roosevelt, *State Papers as Governor and President*, 257.
[16] Letter read 20 May 1904 at dinner in New York to celebrate the first anniversary of Cuban independence, qu. Munro, 77.
[17] See his message of 3 December (Annual Message to Congress).
[18] *Taft-Bacon Report*, 445.
[19] *Ibid.*, 207.

telegram telling him not to do anything in the way of intervention, and Sleeper had to rouse his 125 marines and send them back again, gaining the description from Roosevelt of a 'wretched and worthless creature'.[20] In fact in Havana all was quiet.[21] Estrada, however, had obviously now decided on the course to be followed: he told the rump of the Cuban Congress on 14 September that the revolution threw 'doubt on the seriousness of our institutions', raising mistrust in 'our capacity for self-government'. The same day Roosevelt, evidently with immense reluctance, wrote to Gonzalo de Quesada, still the Cuban representative in Washington, and said that he would 'aid the Cubans in reaching a peaceful solution' by sending Taft the Secretary for War and Bacon the Under-Secretary of State to Havana: 'our intervention in Cuban affairs will only come if Cuba herself shows that she has fallen into the revolutionary habit, that she lacks the self-restraint necessary to ensure peaceful self-government and that her contending factions have plunged the country into anarchy.'[22]

By 19 September Taft and Bacon were in Havana, and immediately they saw Estrada. He seemed unctuous and pathetic. He described his efforts to teach his people 'the knowledge of self-government which by twenty years of residence in the U.S.A. he had gained from association with the American people, of his successful handling of the finances . . . of the encouragement he had given to the investment of foreign capital and of the consequent prosperity'.[23] The next day, the two American politicians were in touch with the Liberal 'revolutionaries', through their ex-vice-presidential candidate, the slippery Zayas. Zayas agreed that the rebels would lay down arms if all 1905 officials resigned, except for the president and vice-president, and if other laws relating to judiciary, municipal government and elections were re-examined. Estrada, however, refused to treat with Zayas till the Liberals had laid down their arms, but Zayas in his turn refused. On 20 September Taft wrote two letters; first to Roosevelt: 'the best solution [is] to permit Palma to resign and select an impartial Cuban for temporary chief executive'; and second to his wife: 'the great trouble is that unless we can secure peace some $M200 of American property will go up in smoke'.[24] By 21 September Taft was reporting that 'we would be fighting the whole Cuban people in effect by . . . [trying] to maintain this

[20] Roosevelt, *Letters*, V, 402.

[21] Wright, *Cuba*, 180.

[22] Roosevelt, *Letters*, V, 411–13. The letter was also published immediately. William Howard Taft (1857–1930) succeeded Roosevelt as president in 1909. Robert Bacon (1860–1919), member of J. P. Morgan's Bank, 1894–1903, Assistant Secretary of State, 1905–9), ambassador to France, 1909–12.

[23] Taft-Bacon correspondence.

[24] H. F. Pringle, *Life and Times of William Howard Taft*, 2 vols (1939), II, 41, and I, 305.

government',[25] but on 22 September, 'nobody in the Liberals is fit to be President'.[26] To his wife he described Estrada as 'a good deal of an old ass . . . obstinate . . . and difficult . . . and doesn't take in the situation at all'.[27] On 24 September Estrada refused to take part in any conference based on any previous proposals of Taft's – 'in their characteristic Spanish way,' Taft commented contemptuously, 'Palma and the moderates now take away their dolls and not play [*sic*].'[28] But in another letter to his president he wrote of the Liberals:

> The even remote possibility suggested in your telegram of last night that . . . the present insurrectionary force [may] be treated as a government *de facto* makes me shiver . . . It is not a government . . . only an undisciplined horde of men under partisan leaders. The movement is large and formidable and commands the sympathy of a majority of the people of Cuba but they are the poorer classes and uneducated.[29]

That day in fact Zayas had already really accepted intervention on behalf of the Liberals. On 27 September Taft told his wife that Roosevelt was 'supporting me well, though some of his telegrams have been a little extreme' (i.e. on the side of avoiding intervention),[30] and Roosevelt was busy explaining away the need for intervention to Senator Foraker:

> Palma sent us a series of appeals asking for immediate armed intervention, saying that if it was delayed, his government would fall and chaos would ensue . . . The Palma government has . . . been evidently bent on forcing us to an armed intervention in their support . . . when Taft got the insurgents to a very good compromise . . . Palma bluntly repudiated the agreement.[31]

On 25 September meantime Roosevelt had sent a message to Estrada through Taft:

> I most earnestly ask that you sacrifice your own feeling on the altar of your country's good and yield to Mr Taft's request by continuing in the Presidency a sufficient length of time to in his judgement inaugurate the new temporary government . . . I adjure you for your own fair fame not to so conduct yourself that the responsibility if such there be for the death of the Republic can be put at your door. I pray that you will act so that it shall appear that you at least have

[25] Taft-Bacon correspondence, 470.
[26] Pringle, *Taft*, I, 309.
[27] *Ibid.*, 308.
[28] *Ibid.*, 309.
[29] Taft-Bacon correspondence, 475–7.
[30] Pringle, *Taft*, I, 310.
[31] *Foraker*, II, 57–9. The telegram is also in Roosevelt, *Letters*, 429 ff.

sacrificed yourself for your country and that when you leave office you leave your country still free.[32]

On 28 September, however, Estrada went to the Congress and resigned, together with his vice-president, Méndez Capote. All the Moderates then left the Congress, and Cuba was left with no government. Estrada Palma had given up without a fight.

Intervention was then inevitable, though Roosevelt was still cabling Taft, 'I earnestly hope you can persuade the two parties themselves to agree'.[33] Nevertheless on 29 September 2,000 U.S. marines landed, and were sent by Taft to a camp just outside Havana – Columbia. Taft issued a proclamation:

> The failure of Congress to act on the irrevocable resignation of the President of the Republic . . . leaves this country without a government at a time when great disorder prevails and requires that pursuant to a request of President Palma, the necessary steps be taken in the name and by the authority of the President of the U.S. to restore order . . . The Provisional Government hereby established . . . will be maintained only long enough to order . . . and to hold elections . . . Insofar as this is consistent with the nature of a provisional government established under the authority of the U.S., this will be a Cuban government, conforming as far as may be to the constitution of Cuba. The Cuban flag will be hoisted . . . the country will continue to administer justice.[34]

On 30 September Enrique José Varona, a survivor from Wood's cabinet and the outstanding Cuban man of letters, wrote (approvingly) in *Le Figaro* that the U.S. had acted to avoid civil war and the destruction of foreign capital and property. Once violence had begun, most businessmen wanted swift intervention and some might have contemplated British or German alternatives if the U.S. had not acted. Estrada himself later put his position clearly: the Liberals were perfectly happy to disband now that Estrada and the Moderates were gone – providing, as it later turned out, they were allowed to keep their horses:

> When I saw the insurrection take serious proportions, my soul was overcome with profound disenchantment, contemplating the patient and glorious work of four years overthrown . . . The conscience of a superior duty, one of those duties which cause the heart to bleed and give rise to unpopularity and hate, imposed on me as the only

[32] Roosevelt, *Letters*, V, 422.
[33] *Ibid.*, V, 434.
[34] Taft-Bacon, 486.

measure of salvation, the necessity of acquainting the Washington government with the true situation ... and *with the lack of means of my government to give protection to property and to say that I considered* that an occasion had risen for the U.S. to make use of the right granted them by the Platt amendment. I did so, consulting few people since it was not a time to expose myself to contradiction, not in order to seek partners in this responsibility but to assume the responsibility entirely ..., [after all] a political dependence which assures us the fecund bonus of liberty is a hundred times preferable for our beloved Cuba to a sovereign and independent Republic discredited and made miserable by the baneful action of ... civil wars.[35]

On 2 October Estrada left Havana for Matanzas by train and so also left Cuban history. He left a reputation for financial integrity never repeated thereafter by any Cuban administration before the Revolution of 1959. But he did not show that he believed in the future of Cuba as a separate state. Nor did he show his dislike of the methods of the Moderates, such as General Freyre de Andrade, nominally acting in his cause.

But the main reason for the successful rebellion of the Liberals in 1905 was the absence of a standing army.

[35] Report of the Provisional Administration, 13 October 1906 to 1 December 1907, 13 ff.

CHAPTER XL

The Second Intervention: Magoon

President Roosevelt in October 1906 picked up the reins of rule in Cuba where he had left them in 1902. By 1906 he had enjoyed six years of a brilliantly creative presidency. His internal and external policies were intimately related. He rebuked, verbally but effectively, 'our men of vast wealth [who] do not fully realise that great responsibility must always go hand in hand with great privilege'.[1] In the same way he believed that great countries, wherever they were, had great responsibilities. Constantly brooding over the decline of empires and the purpose of political ambition, Roosevelt's conception of the U.S. was not its expansion through the capture or purchase of greater territory but the responsible articulation of its own already existing strength. His energy touched every aspect of the nation's life. He was however uninterested in the annexation of Cuba; Roosevelt remarked, 'not a European nation would have given up Cuba as we gave it up';[2] his view was widely shared: Senator Lodge wrote on 16 September:

> Disgust with the Cubans is very general. Nobody wants to annex them but the general feeling is that they ought to be taken by the scruff of the neck and shaken until they behave themselves ... I should think that this ... would make the anti-imperialists think that some peoples were less capable of self-government than others.[3]

In his annual message of December 1906 Roosevelt explained the U.S. wanted nothing of Cuba except that the island should 'prosper morally and materially'.[4]

Roosevelt's policy towards the new situation in Cuba was put by him in his usual forceful way in a telegram to Taft on 26 September:

> It is undoubtedly a very evil thing that the revolutionists should be encouraged and by the dreadful example afforded the island of success in remedying wrongs by violence and treason to the government. If the Palma government had shown any real capacity for

[1] Letter to King Edward VII, Roosevelt, *Letters*, VI, 941.
[2] *Ibid.*, V, 775 (August 1907).
[3] *Selections from the Correspondence of Theodore Roosevelt and Henry Cabot Lodge, 1884–1918*, ed. H. C. Lodge (1925), 233.
[4] Roosevelt, *Autobiography* (1913), 390.

self-defence and ability to sustain itself and a sincere purpose to remedy the wrongs of which your telegrams show them to have been guilty, I should have been inclined to stand by them no matter to what extent, including armed intervention. But as things already are we do not have the chance of following any such course ... [since] they absolutely decline either to endeavour to remedy the wrongs they have done or to so much as lift a hand in their own defence ... we must simply put ourselves ... in Palma's place, land a sufficient force to restore order and notify the insurgents that we will carry thru[5] the program in which you and they are agreed ... I do not have much hope that with the example before them of such success in an insurrection the people who grow discontented with the new government will refrain from insurrection and disturbance some time in the future but there is a slight chance and in my opinion we should give them this chance. Then if the new government sooner or later falls to pieces under the stress of another insurrection, not only will our duty be clearer but we will have removed all chance of any honest people thinking we have failed to do our best to establish peace and order in the island without depriving it of its independence.[6]

Opinion in the U.S. was mostly with Roosevelt, though the ineffable Senator Beveridge thought that the U.S. 'should at once take the island'.[7] William Jennings Bryan thought that they should declare that they would never use force and Foraker continued to argue that everything should be left to Congress. Roosevelt admitted, 'our permanent policy toward the island must depend absolutely upon the action of Congress. No matter what construction is given the Platt amendment, Congress has nothing to do but to refuse appropriations to put it into effect ...'[8] In the interim, in early October, Roosevelt and Taft acted; officers who had before served in Cuba were sent back. Though Roosevelt had been urged to send back Wood, he chose instead a civilian judge, Charles Magoon: for this time it was a civilian not a military rule, and the Cuban flag, the single white star, flew throughout the new occupations and not the stars and stripes. Five to six thousand troops remained in Cuba, but they never appeared in Havana in uniform. There was no serious suggestion at any time that politically there should be any form of integration with the U.S.

Charles Magoon has reaped a vast number of lurid accusations at the hands of Cuban writers: 'gross in character, rude of manner, of a

[5] This was part of Roosevelt's spelling reform campaign.
[6] Roosevelt, *Letters*, 425–6.
[7] *Ibid.*, 428.
[8] *Loc. cit.*

Two U.S. Proconsuls:
13*a* General Wood (military governor of Cuba 1900–1902)
  b General Crowder (Special representative and ambassador 1921–1927)

a

b

Four Cuban Presidents:
14a Estrada Palma, 1902–1906
 b José Miguel Gómez, 1909–1913
 c Mario García Menocal, 1913–1921
 d Alfredo Zayas, 1921–1925

c

d

profound ambition, greedy for despoilment. He falls like a buzzard on the treasury of Cuba and devours it . . . a Jew who fondles gold like a sweetheart'.[9] 'Morally a man of wax . . . pliant and amiable . . . tall and fat.'[10] Magoon 'began to write the annals of the dilapidations of the Cuban treasury'.[11] The distinguished Cuban scholar Trelles wrote: 'The American governor . . . profoundly corrupted the Cuban nation and on account of his venality was looked upon with contempt by the honourable element of the great American confederation where he died a short time ago completely obscured.'[12] More soberly, Ramiro Guerra, in his *Historia elemental de Cuba*, described Magoon as 'very wasteful':

He not only spent the whole public income each year but also spent $M12 which he found in the Treasury that had been saved by Don Tomás. Mr Magoon was very prodigal with pardons and although he attended to the development of public works these were often not completed in due form. The administration of Mr Magoon left a bad memory and a bad example in the country.[13]

Martínez Ortiz, the orthodox Cuban historian of this time, wrote:[14]

The government opened its hands and let loose the purse strings without any regard. It had no idea other than pleasing the committee on jobs . . . Magoon did not know how to say 'no', he always said 'amen' and in this way the money so carefully saved by Don Tomás Estrada Palma gradually disappeared. The governor defended himself from his critics saying he was doing nothing but granting the requests of the great Cuban politicians. His kindness in granting *botellas* – i.e. sinecures – became a public scandal . . . the administration in general returned to the corrupt practices of colonial times.

In the same vein, Mr Herbert Matthews, godfather of the Revolution of 1959, spoke of 'a shameful administration'.[15] What is the truth?

Magoon was a dull man from Minnesota, aged forty-five in 1906 and apparently worth about $100,000, chiefly in property. He had accumulated this fortune by his own efforts, in land speculation and law practice. He had come into government business through an interest in military affairs, becoming a mayor and judge-advocate of the Nebraska National Guard. In 1899 he joined the War department and worked there on legal questions deriving from the acquisition of Spanish

[9] M. Lozana Casado, *La Personalidad del General José Miguel Gómez* (1913), 17.
[10] Barbarosa, 88–9.
[11] E. Varona, *De la Colonia a la República* (1919).
[12] Trelles, 9.
[13] Qu., Martínez Ortiz, 243–4.
[14] *Ibid.*, 487–8.
[15] Matthews, 242.

property. He had visited Estrada Palma on McKinley's behalf in 1898.[16] From 1905 to 1906 he was governor of the Panama Canal Zone. He never married.

Magoon was not, in fact, corrupt. None of his Cuban accusers can point to a single instance of graft.[17] His most criticized step was to adopt the view that the ex-revolutionary Liberals had a right to posts in government. But he did not wish to sack all the existing civil servants who, though mostly Moderates, represented the idea of continuity with the Estrada regime. Accordingly he set up a committee of the prominent Liberals to recommend names whenever a vacancy occurred.[18] Thus, all vacancies were filled by Liberals; and after a time the widening differences between Alfredo Zayas and José Miguel Gómez (held by some of his followers to have been captured somewhat too quickly in the Revolution) led to an immense series of intrigues between Miguelistas and Zayistas.[19] No doubt Magoon should have planted in Cuba the idea of a permanent civil service, faithful to all governments. But once the principle of political spoils is admitted, Magoon had a good case, since the Liberals stood for an unrepresented popular force although their capacity for government was far from clear. So far as his own administration was concerned, Magoon kept the old chiefs of the departments as he found them and gave them U.S. aides – all U.S. officers of whom two out of seven had served in Cuba under Wood. So far as the future was concerned, Magoon did attempt in 1908 to establish a permanent civil service, though he could not create any tradition of behaviour for it. A civil service law was established, prescribing rules for examinations, giving, it is true, security of tenure to those with jobs already, and preference to veterans.[20] This law was promulgated on 11 January 1909. Here was an attempt to establish in Cuba at least the outlines of responsible bureaucracy. If it did not work perfectly thereafter, the mistake was mostly that of the Cubans, who continued to treat the civil service as an opportunity for political pickings. Probably also it was a political error to permit the Spaniards still in the Cuban administration, carrying on from colonial days, to remain: it led to a long wrangle over the political pasts of civil servants which further weakened their loyalty. But this was an error, not a crime. It is incorrect to speak of Magoon as approaching the 'problem of administering Cuba

[16] See above, p. 404.

[17] For evidence of his character, see his aide General Ryan's letter to Lockmiller (*op. cit.*, 216–17); and others, such as Judge Otto Schoenrich, the Cuban Manuel Lando, and General Pershing.

[18] The committee was Faustino Guerra, Eduardo Guzmán, Ernesto Asbert, Alfredo Zayas, José Miguel Gómez and Juan Gualberto Gómez, Tomás Rico, Demetrio Castillo, Gen. Monteagudo and Gen. García Vélez. (Magoon Report, I, 16–17.)

[19] See Lockmiller, 79–80.

[20] *Ibid.*, 166–7.

as a problem of patronage'.[21] The arguments of Cuban historians, later copied by guilt-ridden North Americans, that Magoon taught the Cubans corruption are among the most hilarious examples ever of self-deception.[22]

Roosevelt understood Magoon most satisfactorily when he described him as getting on 'beautifully with the Cuban; he has done his work well but he is not a man of masterful type ... and he shrinks from following any course to which he thinks any considerable number of Cubans would object, whether rightly or wrongly'.[23] Magoon was also reproached for granting an excessive number of pardons. After a general amnesty to all who took part in the August Revolution, Magoon certainly behaved often as if he were the final court of appeal, mitigating the severity of Spanish law and the corruptibility of the judiciary. There is no proof, though, that he sold pardons. Maybe, as in other things, he was over-magnanimous.[24]

Two other accusations remain. The first was that in the course of 1908, after the date when the U.S. would again leave Cuba had been settled, Magoon issued a number of contracts for work which would be carried out after he had left. These were mainly to U.S. firms. Afterwards, the State Department exerted itself to ensure that these contracts were honoured. To cover these Magoon issued authority for a forty-year $4\frac{1}{2}\%$ bond issue of $M16·5; the loan was assured by Speyer and Co., whose representatives in Cuba were none other than Frank Steinhart, until recently U.S. Consul-General in Havana, and Henry W. Taft, brother of the then president-elect.[25]

The second accusation is that among these contracts was one for the extension of the Havana Electric Railway – a franchise extended on 30 July 1908 also to Frank Steinhart.

Steinhart, now forty-five, had come a long way from the poor Munich suburb where he was born. In 1906 he had become interested in the possibilities opening up for Havana Electric. At that time a group of Montreal financiers was in control, with shares held widely in Cuba and Spain. Its plant however was deteriorating and complaints were being brought to the U.S. Consulate. Steinhart took the complaints to Montreal and the president of the company told him he would only be entitled to complain if he had enough stock to qualify as a director. Steinhart took up the challenge and made a heavy investment, becoming the largest stockholder. At this the directors told him that the company

[21] Jenks, 96–7.

[22] Yet they persist. Thus Roig Leuchsenring in his history of Havana: 'The unscrupulous individual who governed or better misgoverned Cuba ... only merits the contempt of Cubans' (*La Habana*, II, 279); in the history of the Cuban Communist party, Magoon appears (1968) as '*el corrompido reaccionario*' (p. 25).

[23] Roosevelt, *Letters*, VI, 1,037.

[24] For a discussion, see Lockmiller, 95–6.

[25] *Ibid.*, 159. Taft had been elected as Roosevelt's successor in November 1908.

owed them $750,000 and was in effect bankrupt. They told him that if he turned them out, they would demand payment. They would be willing to stay and market the bonds (which guaranteed their credits) only if they were able to stay where they were for another year. But Steinhart was not ready to take such blackmail. He borrowed $M1 from, of all people, Archbishop Farley of New York, resigned the consulate-general and went into business with Havana Electric. His first step was to secure the promise of favourable treatment from Magoon for the extension of the railway.[26]

Steinhart's relations with Magoon were close. He played an important advisory role on the Committee of Liberals to advise who should get what appointments. General Crowder (who worked closely with both) later said Steinhart 'actually controlled Magoon and was the invisible government'.[27] This meant that public opinion was bound to watch any financial arrangement between them very closely. Certainly Magoon's actual conduct was above suspicion – but it did not appear to be so and, as a result, Magoon deserves condemnation. He and the U.S. administration should have known that there was a serious danger that future Cuban governments would relapse into old Spanish ways, and that this was something particularly to guard against, by an example of impeccable conduct. It was known too in Havana that Steinhart was no friend of the idea of scuttle; at the end of the first intervention in 1902, he had written: 'it was like bringing a shipwrecked crew within sight of sandy Hook and then telling them to swim . . .'[28] The combination of Steinhart's reputation and his economic power – he became vice-president of the new luxury hotel Sevilla Biltmore, as well as a big investor in other concerns – created a bad impression.

Magoon's civil service sprang from the work of a commission set up within a few weeks of his arrival in Cuba, aiming to revise the whole field of Cuban law. The commission set out to work over the most serious lacuna of the Wood era – law reform. In 1906 the law of Cuba consisted of an immense rabbit warren of Spanish statutes and customs, modified by various royal decrees in the nineteenth century, by various acts of the first U.S. occupation and some of Estrada's. The Constitution of 1902 contradicted the law in some respects. The confusion was particularly intense in municipal government, since Spanish law had given Havana control of all aspects of government whereas the Constitution gave considerable powers to municipalities. But in 1906 these

[26] See *ibid.*; Jenks.

[27] NA 837 51/632, qu. Smith, 25. Enoch Crowder (1859–1932), in Judge-Advocate's department, commander of troop in Sitting Bull and Geronimo campaigns; served in the Philippines, 1898–1901; Secretary of Justice under Magoon, 1906–8, Provost-Marshal of the U.S., 1917–19, ambassador to Cuba, 1923–7; never married.

[28] Jenks, 263.

lacked resources for tax-gathering. Magoon entrusted Colonel Enoch
Crowder to carry out the necessary reform, starting with electoral law
and working through all aspects of social behaviour.

Most of the work was done in sub-committees: Colonel Crowder
wrote the first draft of the electoral law; Francisco Carrera Justiz, a
Cuban lawyer, prepared that of the provincial and municipal laws;[29]
another American military lawyer, Blanton Winship,[30] prepared the
civil service law; and Judge Otto Schoenrich wrote the law on the
judiciary. These high-minded men proceeded in a straightforward and
sensible way. After the laws had been discussed in committees, they
were published and allowed to stand or be revised in accord with the
criticisms received. A proposed telephone law was dropped, and the
electoral law revised.[31] The four sub-committees were led by North
Americans, but Cubans had a majority on each. However, 'some of the
Cuban members often missed meetings . . . especially toward the latter
part of the . . . work when political aspirations took much time'.[32] It
was no doubt disadvantageous that the Cubans concerned should have
been politically ambitious – such as Rafael Montoro (once a leading
Autonomist), on the electoral law committee; Alfredo Zayas with
Carrera Justiz on the municipal and provincial law; García Kohly, a
Conservative, on the civil service committee; and Juan Gualberto
Gómez with Manuel Colorado, editor of *La Discusión*, on the judicial
committee.

The judiciary had careful though unfortunately not final treatment.
Crowder and Schoenrich worked through the inconsistencies, slipping
in here and there a pinch of U.S. practice and phrasing: the Supreme
Court was to be appointed by the president with 'advice and consent'
of the Senate; other judges would be appointed by the president, from
names submitted by the Supreme Court. Judges could not be removed
except by impeachment. Judicial districts were re-defined, as were the
fields of jurisdiction of the Supreme Court, of the provincial *audiencias*,
of the municipal courts, judges had to be Cuban, over twenty-three,
sane and solvent; they were appointed after an examination, as a
career.

The electoral law was the most ambitious of Magoon's and Crowder's
plans – justifiably, since it had been the failure of the electoral system
that brought the U.S. again to Cuba in the first place. It was to be a
'perfect electoral instrument or at least proof against frauds and electoral

---

[29] Francisco Carrera Justiz (b. 1857), lawyer, author of a hundred books, diplomat.

[30] Blanton Winship (1869–1947), captain in the Philippines; Assistant Secretary of State
to Magoon, 1906–9; in France, 1917–23; Judge-Advocate of the U.S. army in Germany;
military aide to Coolidge, 1927–8; governor of Puerto Rico, 1934.

[31] Magoon Report, II, 19–20.

[32] Judge Schoenrich to Lockmiller, Lockmiller, 149, fn.

abuses', and aimed to equip Cuba with 'governmental machinery that would not go wrong'.[33] Crowder, it is disconcerting to discover, drew his inspiration from the Australian system; permanent electoral boards in each municipality would control elections. A central board would sit in Havana. Every board would have two members representing the two main political parties. The others would be delegates from universities, high schools or the judiciary. The board's role would be to keep a registered list of those entitled to vote as found by the census – the task carried out in England by local government officers, and one not done at all in the U.S. In this way all male Cubans over twenty-one, except criminals and members of the (as yet unachieved) armed forces would be registered. Nominations were to be made either by official party conventions or, as in England, by a fixed number of registered voters in the provinces. The numbers required for independent nominations varied according to populations of provinces – 800 in Havana, 200 in Camagüey. Literacy was made a condition of public office, presidential candidates had to be over forty, and to be Cuban by birth or naturalization; if the latter they had to have served at least ten years in Cuban wars. Senators had to be thirty-five and be Cuban-born, whilst Representatives had to be twenty-five years old and Cuban born or naturalized, in which case they had to have lived eight years in Cuba.[34]

Crowder and his advisers also made a 'thorough study of proportional representation as it existed in Belgium and Switzerland'. Voters chose several candidates, numbering them in order of preference. The total of all valid votes cast would be divided by the number of places to be filled so giving that desperate formula, the 'quotient'. This decided the number of votes needed for election. Candidates with votes equal to or above the quotient were declared elected. As for the procedure within Congress, the old disastrous quorum law was rescinded.

This plan was promulgated on 1 April 1908. Tried out in provincial and municipal elections in August 1908, it was modified, and reissued the following month.

The U.S. was now anxious once again to leave. Indeed, Magoon's first words in Cuba were: 'As soon as it shall prove to be consistent with the attainment of these ends, I shall seek to bring about the restoration of the ordinary agencies and methods of government under the other and general provisions of the Cuban constitution.'[35] At first Magoon seems to have believed that these elections could be held on New Year's day, 1907. But this date was advanced, after Magoon had consulted

[33] Jenks, 100.
[34] Lockmiller, 150.
[35] *Ibid.*, 72.

with Taft, in order to 'secure calm during the sugar harvest'.[36] Further delay was caused by divisions and unreadiness among the Liberals. By mid-1907, the Liberals' extraordinary confusion was causing a definite revival of their opponents: a new Conservative party was formed, which insisted it had no relations with the old Moderates. The leader was that energetic captain of industry, Menocal, and the ex-Autonomist of the 1890s, Rafael Montoro. In May there were municipal elections. But not till January 1908 did Roosevelt clearly decide that the intervention should end in February 1909 – just before, in fact, the end of his own term of office;[37] the decision was reached just when a new wave of *anexionismo* was detectable. An English resident in Cuba wrote that 'Spaniards clearly seem to favour annexation'; he discussed the possibility of Cubans getting dual U.S. and Spanish citizenship.[38] But there was no real chance of this. Roosevelt told Root, 'we ought to communicate to them in great seriousness and in a manner that will impress them our earnest desire that the new government will be perpetual', though he added that he hoped to guarantee independence 'by leaving certain assistants in the island' to ensure 'that the finances be kept straight' and 'that order be maintained' (that is, by a military adviser). 'Our sole and genuine purpose is to help them to manage their affairs so that there won't be the slightest need of further interference on our part.'[39]

In August 1908 there were local elections; 270,000 votes (60%) were cast. The two Liberal groups, Miguelistas and Zayistas, ran separately, and though they respectively gained 35 and 18 mayoralties compared to 28 for the Conservatives, the Conservatives won three out of the six provincial governorships. The Liberals, realizing that they had lost votes because of their split, and accepting the moral for almost the only occasion in Cuban history, therefore went united into the national elections with José Miguel Gómez for president and Zayas for vice-president, as had occurred in 1905. These elections were held on 14 November. Crowder worked indefatigably behind the scenes, distributing 8,000 voting books and 1,650 ballot boxes to the municipalities. The campaign was reckoned fair. Gómez and Zayas won by a little over 200,000 votes to 130,000 for Menocal and Montoro. Just over 70% of the votes was cast.[40] Magoon, therefore, was able to hand over to a man who, despite his faults, was far the most popular candidate

[36] Chapman, 213.
[37] 'If it can be turned over earlier I shall be glad; but under no circumstances and for no reason will the date be later than 1 Feb 1909' (Roosevelt, *Letters*, VI, 967). Till the days of F. D. Roosevelt, inauguration was of course in March.
[38] *Lippincott's*, May–June 1908, qu. Chapman, 264.
[39] Roosevelt, *Letters*, VI, 1,138. In fact U.S. troops drew out entirely in April 1909.
[40] Total electorate was 466,745 out of a total population of 2,048,980. (Magoon Report, II, 73.)

for president and who almost certainly had been the real victim in 1905.[41]

Magoon further laid the foundations for a Cuban army. Rural guards were first increased to 5,200 and General Pino Guerra, the successful Liberal leader in 1906, given command. The small artillery force inherited from Estrada was slightly increased. Three officer schools were established, under U.S. officers, to serve the rural guards. It was clearly understood that one of the next independent Cuban government's acts would be to increase the army to 5,000 men, and a law of Magoon's was passed in April 1908 making this clear.[42] Pino Guerra was made commander of the whole army in April 1908, General Monteagudo taking over the rural guards.

All these were serious contributions to Cuban development, although they can be criticized as incomplete and inadequate. The army was a necessity, pinpointed as such by the statistic that, though in August 1906 there appear to have been 25,000 members of the revolutionary forces, only 3,152 handed in arms, to be dropped ceremoniously at the Morro Castle for the sharks to eat (Magoon himself ruled with 5,000 U.S. soldiers at hand throughout his stay under the command of General Bell[43]). The judicial law can be criticized as concentrating on rendering the judges independent of the executive, and ignoring other almost equally pressing demands, such as procedure, treatment of witnesses, civil appeals, and so forth. But Crowder and Magoon, like Wood before them, believed that the Cubans might be able to do these things themselves. The electoral law, it was true, was painfully complicated and theoretical. Few people ever understood this system either at the time or later. The 'quotient' made Cuba's search for political leadership resemble a dull arithmetic lesson. The shortcomings of the civil service derived from excessive generosity. It is possible to accuse this U.S. intervention of vanity in supposing that the customs of North America were universally applicable, and in thinking, like Locke in Carolina, that an ideal electoral system is devisable; but it is not

[41] For discussion about the form of Cuban government after the Americans left, see Roosevelt, *Letters*, VI, 994.

[42] Lockmiller, 117; see also R. Adam y Silva, *La Gran mentira, 4 de Septiembre de 1933* (1947), 10–15. The total police and army in 1907 reached 8,238 of whom most (5,204) were bachelors; 2,486 were married and 425 lived with wives-by-consent. 543 were posted in Camagüey, 3,109 in Havana (2,245 in Havana city), 855 in Matanzas, 1,451 in Oriente, 630 in Pinar del Río, 1,650 in Santa Clara. 1,101 were born in Spain (6 in the U.S., 3 in China). Half the Spanish-born policemen (513) were in Havana City. 7,901 knew how to read, only 337 – at least officially – did not. Most policemen were between twenty and thirty-five, though 30 were younger, 1,045 between thirty-five and forty-four, 489 between forty-five and sixty-four, and 43 over sixty-five. 1,718 were black or mulatto, 1,135 foreign white, the rest (5,385) were white natives. (Census of 1907, 551–76.)

[43] Afterwards under General Thomas Barry. They were stationed at 27 points, and never marched into Havana. They were mostly occupied with revising the map of Cuba, while the Medical Corps did much work.

possible on this score to suppose them corrupt or dishonest. After all, there were Cubans on all the law commissions, and they had a chance to alter or form the laws. It was not Magoon's fault that they did not go to committee meetings.

Two extra-constitutional forms of protest occurred in Magoon's time: first, political violence, on a very small scale. One or two sporadic outbursts occurred in 1906–7: people 'took to the hills', attempted to 'raise towns' and conspired openly in the name of Cuban nationalism. But nothing came of such events. A bandit, 'General' Masó Parra, who had played a minor if ambiguous role in the war of independence, tried vainly to stage a 'great revolution' in 1907, in the interests of whom it is unclear although he was evidently intending to arrange a St Bartholomew's Eve for the entire U.S. population resident in Cuba.[44]

There were also several important labour strikes in the same year as Masó's attempt; in particular, in the famous *Huelga de la Moneda*, the cigar workers made a demand for a 10% increase in wages, which they desired to be paid in U.S. money. (Since 1899 both U.S. and Cuban money had been current in Cuba but 25 Cuban pesos were worth $26½ in U.S. money.) The tobacco trade was in fact in the doldrums. In 1905 independent tobacco firms had tried to throw out the giant American Cigar Company. The Cigar Company was hampered by a major strike, well organized and financed, lasting 145 days. The company was ultimately successful, but many workers moved to Tampa.[45] Prices of cigars rose after the 1907 strike, and Cuban exports of cigars slumped, both to the U.S. and to England, which was still the biggest importer (though in 1910 she would take only sixty million, instead of nearly a hundred million in 1902).[46]

Other strikes followed with similar demands. Stevedores, bus drivers, box makers, plumbers, broom makers and carpenters urgently insisted on being paid in dollars, not pesos. The organization of these men was primitive in the extreme: indeed, except for the cigar workers all forms of union organization appear to have been *ad hoc*, and to have been confined to Havana. The political consciousness of the 1880s and 1890s had evaporated and in most respects labour was less well organized than it had been twenty years earlier. Magoon's dislike of doing anything which displeased the Cubans here showed itself to good effect. He declined to intervene, telling the cigar makers:

> The strikers decline to work unless they are paid the prices fixed by them for their labour. This is a right which every free man possesses.

[44] Lockmiller, 144. He had fought for the Cubans, joined the Spaniards, and remained in Spain till 1907.
[45] Jenks, 159–60.
[46] Estimates, 500.

R*

They offer no obstacles to the manufacturers' employment of others and they have not resorted to violence or other unlawful means of coercing the manufacturers ... Their refusal to work may be ill-advised ... but so long as they conduct themselves in an orderly manner as peaceable law-abiding citizens I cannot interfere officially, for the occasion for the exercise of official powers is not presented.[47]

In the end, the cigar makers gave in: 30,000 workers held a fiesta on 21 July 1907 celebrating Magoon's stand,[48] but railway and other strikes followed.

Magoon's educational policy was less sensational than Wood's, but in some ways more effective. An inventory of schools was made. Children between six and fourteen were arrested if found in the street in school hours. Factories or shops which employed children would be charged. The policy worked. In November 1908 there were nearly 200,000 pupils in the state system, and nearly 15,000 in private schools. Even so, teachers were scarce; many had joined the 1906 Revolution, and the question of their reinstatement raised political difficulties. School boards had become centres of politics. There were complaints of *botellas*: a certain Gustavo Escoto was discharged from the Ministry of Education for having his mother-in-law on the payroll. Magoon did little to stop these complaints. Perhaps he was incapable of doing so.[49]

Magoon's general administrative conduct was neither inspired nor specially creative in spirit, but it was never outrageous. It lacked the autocracy of Wood's rule; even so Magoon never became popular. His generosity of conduct smacked a little of laxity. His agreement that the rebels of 1905 should retain their horses unless their old owners could prove ownership suggested that the U.S. approved horse-stealing – an impression not quite removed by a U.S. commission's payment of over $400,000 to 5,500 claimants demanding restitution for damage caused in the Revolution, of which one-third went to foreigners.[50] Some corruption persisted in the civil service, as is seen from the sacking of Miguel de la Trope, who embezzled almost $200,000 of public money.[51] Magoon's financial measures were criticized as 'spending all Don Tomás saved'; but to those who realize the unsophisticated character of a balanced budget, there is everything to praise in Magoon's use of revenue. The Church property in Havana and in Oriente which was outstanding after the first intervention was bought by the state. Magoon's road-building was as great a contribution to the Cuban economy

[47] Magoon Report, I, 66.
[48] Lockmiller, 91.
[49] *Cf. ibid.*; Magoon Report 135–6.
[50] Lockmiller, 83.
[51] *Havana Post*, 20 October 1908; Magoon Report, II.

as his law-giving had been to society, as well as being less ambiguous: over $M11 were spent on roads, creating almost as many miles in two years as had previously been built in two centuries.[52] Unfortunately, the grand design of building a central highway from Santiago to the far west of Pinar del Río was shelved; Magoon concentrated on Pinar del Río, because of the tobacco crop, and perhaps because of the ease with which Pino Guerra had gathered his troops there in 1906. Magoon cut the expenditure of the Department of Posts and Telegraphs, as well as that of the presidential palace. But he mishandled a number of matters, such as the contorted affair of the Cienfuegos water project.[53] His contract with McGivney-Rokeby in the U.S. for the paving and sewering of Havana was so fulfilled as to give the U.S. a bad name.

Magoon was, finally, unfortunate in that his period of power in Havana coincided with a depression culminating in the New York stock panic of late 1907. There was also a short tobacco crop in 1906 and cyclones ruined the fruit trees the following year. Bad weather caused a drop in the sugar crop in 1908 – the total falling away from 1·4 million to 960,000 tons. Consequently he was always associated afterwards with a time of ill-luck, although these conditions were not in his gift.

[52] See Jenks, 99; 256 km. of road had been built under Spain; Brooke and Wood built 98 km.; Estrada Palma built 382; and Magoon 608 km. together with 120 new bridges. These were good strong roads, reducing costs of sugar transport from 90 cents to 50 cents a bag, with Public Works blockhouses every 8 km. and with trees planted to give shade. The Pinar del Río-Viñales road reduced passenger transport from $15.00 to $1.50. See Lockmiller, 163. There were then 10,113 km. of road in Jamaica, one-fifth of the size (*ibid.*, 242).

[53] In 1905 the city of Cienfuegos voted to raise a loan of $M3 at 5% to establish a new sewer and water system. The city made a contract with Hugh Reilly, a North American, before the August revolution, and he began work in November 1906. Later the Liberals captured the Cienfuegos council and suspended the loan. Reilly appealed to Magoon, but Magoon backed the council. Crowder recommended new tenders. Taft and Roosevelt overrode their Cuban representatives and Reilly got the job, even though it was clear the decision was very unpopular in Cienfuegos itself (see Lockmiller, 121).

BOOK V

The Young Republic
1909–32

Para Vigo me voy!
Mi negra, dime adiós!

Words of a Cuban rumba c.1930

CHAPTER XLI

Cuba in 1909

The Cuba which Magoon handed over to José Miguel Gómez was by no means the ruined country which limped out of the war of independence with U.S. help. All provinces had increased their population, the smallest rise being registered in the economically declining Matanzas, the biggest in Oriente, opened up by the railway. Economic recovery from the war and improved medicine and health were partly responsible, but immigration from Spain was almost as important: between 1902 and 1910 almost 200,000 Spaniards, mostly Gallegos or Asturians, emigrated to Cuba,[1] attracted by opportunities of high wages. Spanish emigration in these years was ironically higher than at any time when she herself owned the colonies. (Indeed total Spanish emigration to Cuba between 1511 and 1899 was probably below the number attained between 1900 and 1925.) Havana's population meantime exceeded 300,000, compared with about 240,000 in 1899 – an increase slightly smaller than the national average, due to the number of *reconcentrados* included in 1899. But new buildings and roads had almost doubled its geographical size. The pretty farms and town houses just outside the city walls, such as the *Quintas* of Arango or Villanueva in the Cerro district, had become absorbed by the city.

The suburb Vedado was now the centre of social life, the favoured place for leaders of the rebel army to invest their money, though even the new houses there did not have panes in their windows. Old Havana was mainly the centre of business. Coachmen had been joined by taxis and a few cars were on the streets, most of which were now paved, not cobbled. There were also motor buses, known as *guaguas*, a Havana word of English origin, some of which went into the country round Havana, taking tourists – 'Florida ducks' – to beaches or hotels.[2] Havana was still a Spanish city but one on the brink of change superficially into a North American. Gas lights continued alongside policemen in capes; there were *serenos* as in Madrid but commissionaires, as in New York; a profusion of fruit, fish, cafés, toll of church bells for compline,

[1] Census of 1919, 173, 176.
[2] *Guagua* seems to derive from the English 'wagon' on account of the first omnibuses in Havana about 1900 being horse wagons. It afterwards became assimilated to an Indian word, *guagua*, a parasite on the tobacco leaf (wagon = *guagón* = *guagua*). There are other uses of this word in other parts of South America: e.g. in Peru a *guagua* is a baby.

bugles for Reveille at La Cabaña, but also a few phonographs and hooters, alongside mango-sellers, orange-sellers and pedlars. Havana still had an afternoon siesta, though less than under Spain. U.S. influence had had a benevolent effect on the status of women, but Cuban women still married to escape from home; courting lasted a long time, as in Spain; many wives had hours of boredom, with literally nothing to do and forbidden to go out by their husbands. Women used cosmetics lavishly, far more so than in North America, and now went out walking, at least to the smart shops of Obispo Street. Bargaining there was frequent. There were many dressmakers, though many Cubans had sewing-machines manufactured in the U.S. In some respects, such as fashion, Cuba still looked to Europe more than to the U.S., but many people sent their children to be educated in the U.S., and often stayed there themselves.

There were about five theatres in Havana, where every winter outstanding international actors or singers would appear. Bernhardt, Réjane, Patti and Tetrazzini all came to Havana. Plays, however, were in general bad, and the theatres too hot. In the Havana carnival, public masked balls continued to be held at the Hotel Nacional, though they were considered low by good Havana society: they were places where silver-buckled *jeunesse dorée* could pick up attractive black laundresses. Dancing was as popular as in the nineteenth century, sometimes in private houses, sometimes in clubs such as the Centro Asturiano or the Casino Español. At carnival, children went to *bailes infantiles*, though the carnivals were less glittering than in the past. There were innumerable prostitutes. Most intelligent visitors shared the view of Miss Irene Wright: 'Havana is rotten and rotting.'[3] Few houses in Cuba had hot water yet, for Havana got nearly all its water by aqueduct, some by pipe, some by street sellers. There was no effective sewerage. Most houses, even of the rich, were bare and comfortless, though many were brightly painted. The splendid old colonial palaces were now mostly deserted; and in their place came new fashions: under the occupation there had been much silly imitation of North American practices, leading to light, wood, hot houses without an internal courtyard, most unsuitable for hurricanes; then there had been under Estrada and even under Magoon a 'Catalan phase', inspired by Spanish immigrants themselves influenced by the contemporary flourishing of *art nouveau*, Gaudí and many fantasies beloved by the Barcelona *bourgeoisie*. Contorted pillars and excessive decoration had its day in Havana as elsewhere, particularly, as can be observed, in the Vedado. Within, decorations were few, flowers were far more frequent than pictures, books were rare, floors were tiled but turned to marble if

[3] Wright, *Cuba*, 97.

the family grew richer. The salon was a dark stuffy room kept for grand occasions which occurred too rarely for the room to seem lived in.

The country towns resembled Havana in decoration; those who lived in the country still usually lived in *bohíos*, perhaps of two to three rooms, unless they were administrators or grandees, when a ranch house would be created, maybe with a mosquito net round the outside. Food was still Spanish rather than North American: soup twice a day, always four courses, and almost always, as the second course, fried eggs with rice. Breakfast was almost non-existent, as in Europe. Bread came in long flutes; a frequent joke was that it was bought by the yard.

The land question was still in confusion. Little work had been done in respect of surveys and titles. For that reason alone more land was rented than owned: to sell outright remained almost an impossibility. Due to the opening up of the East, probably more people worked on the land in 1909 than in 1899. Maybe there were a few more farms too, though probably still fewer than before 1895. Probably the number of squatters had increased; later, the owner might set a rent, which might or might not be paid. If he could not pay, the squatter moved on. Hence rural housing remained bad; why improve, if you might have to leave at a moment's notice? Further, was there not a chance that soldiers might return, or rebels or patriots, and destroy whatever existed?

> Only those travellers who see Cuba – who ride over mile after mile of her rich, undeveloped territory; who see her common people (living wretchedly from hand to mouth, ambitionless, because they have inherited a realisation of the uselessness of striving) can comprehend what detriment the present situation with regard to land, lack of surveys, uncleared titles, community holdings and improperly adjusted taxation is to the island.[4]

Neither Magoon nor Wood had done anything to change the situation, even from the legal point of view.

Cuba in 1910 was to an almost unsurpassed extent owned by foreigners, including those with Spanish passports. Even without them North Americans had great holdings. The Spaniards remained the dominant mercantile influence, both in the cities and in the country. Nearly a quarter of the population had been born in Spain, though not all of these now had Spanish nationality. Out of 50,000 big or small merchants, almost half were Spaniards;[5] out of 32,000 describing themselves as salesmen, over 20,000 were Spaniards;[6] Spaniards owned a

[4] Wright, *Cuba*, 197.
[5] 23,973 to 50,856.
[6] 32,324 to 20,787.

quarter of the sugar mills[7] and had considerable investments in tobacco. The groceries found at crossroads in the country usually belonged to Spaniards. As in the past, this sort of grocer was a banker and money-lender, at a usurious rate; and often they monopolized local trade, taking crops from their debtors. In Spain, Spaniards were thought lazy; in Cuba, they were regarded as hard-working and efficient business men. Many expected to go home when they had made money. Many had apprentices living with them, sent from Spain by their parents to learn business.

The chief paper for Spaniards was the *Diario de la Marina*, run by Nicolás Rivero, a paternalistic and patriarchal Castillian whose vast family considered themselves Cuban, and whose policy was to support as a matter of course every government, Spanish, Autonomist, North American, interventionist, Don Tomás and Don José Miguel. Another paper, *La Lucha*, was run by an inveterate pro-Spaniard, San Miguel, who, when asked on Independence day 1902 why he stayed, pointed to the procession passing in front and said, 'I stay to be present at the funeral – of this'.[8]

There were only 6,700 North American residents, but many birds of passage, and *la présence américaine*, after two long periods of occupation, was strong. The American minister was the most powerful foreigner: indeed to say that he was the most powerful man in Cuba after the president was in a way an understatement, for he not only repre-sented a country which regarded itself as the special protector of Cuba under the Platt Amendment, as well as one whose citizens were each year owning more of Cuba; he also represented Cuba's largest customer, the U.S. sugar eater. Many enlightened North Americans (living in Cuba, like Miss Wright) still believed that the only answer for Cuba in the end was to join the U.S., though perhaps not as a state.

In Havana North Americans, where they could, lived upstairs, because they thought ground floors damp. Some lived in lodging houses. Their greater social freedom had some slight effects on *habaneros*; some North American typists lived alone in rooms, insisting on using latchkeys and receiving visitors at all hours, to the surprise of the 'cultivated Spanish family' who had let a 'pleasant front room facing the Ocean'. The North Americans of the 'Vedado set' with the English and the Canadians behaved in the same way as empire builders any-where: they played bridge, and looked forward to going north for their holidays. The American Club was their social centre, though the ocean terrace of the Hotel Miramar (at the foot of the Prado) ran it close. For

[7] See p. 425.
[8] Wright, *Cuba*, 142–6.

Cuba was in many respects now a North American dependency. Miss Irene Wright wrote:

> This republic is not a creature of Cubans – it was neither fashioned by them nor by them influenced – but on the contrary it is of all-American manufacture. Americans built it. Americans set it up again when it fell flat. American influence is all that sustains it to this moment. If they discover anything to criticise in it, or its failure, let Americans remember in so criticising that they are dealing with the work of their own hands.[9]

Doubtless most taxes in this period were paid by foreigners rather than Cubans. Doubtless too this had a certain effect on the attitude, explicit or implicit, of successive governments to revenue. It was not as if taxes were high enough to pay for adequate municipal or national government. Eighty-five per cent of the administration's income came from duties on imports; in 1909 the total income from customs reached just under $M25, or $12.10 per head of the population. Few countries had such a high rate. Of course, the goods in question were almost always the manufactured goods of the U.S. It was not that Cuba had industries to protect. Nor were these luxuries. They were clothes (or cloth) and food. Hence the cost of living was very high.

The sugar harvest, always the main event in each year, was now, with the reduced number of mills, something like a race: one day in November, one manager would give the signal. There would be headlines in the papers. Those who sold the machinery to the mill in question would go to see it work. Other mills joined in. Bets were placed, on which mills would grind most, on whether one mill would beat its record. The mills, and the workers, worked day and night; trains arriving at dusk would bring enough cane to keep the mill going all night. A broken roller spelt idleness, the loss of a fortune, telegrams to Europe or the U.S. The pace of, and the stage reached by, each mill was anxiously observed by brokers in London and New York. The increased size of mills and the swifter communications made the matter seem more urgent. Managers now had several thousand men under their command – armies not by any means battered down, but sometimes as enthusiastic to surpass a rival mill as the bettors. In 1909, with 170 mills grinding, 34% of the sugar came from U.S.-owned mills, 35% from Spanish or other European, 31% from Cuban: some of the Spanish group among the Europeans were really Cuban, but then some Cuban mills had U.S.-guaranteed mortgages.

Two sources of Cuban hostility to North America dated from the earliest days of the Republic. In November 1902, in the first year of

[9] *Ibid.*, 152–3.

independence, the U.S. had suggested that the bases on Cuban territory to which she was 'entitled', to fulfil the 'guarantee of independence' which she had assumed under the Platt Amendment, should be the bays of Guantánamo, Cienfuegos, Bahía Honda and Nipe. Estrada Palma ensured that this demand was cut to Guantánamo and Bahía Honda, and that the bays should be rented, not ceded. Eventually, Bahía Honda was cut out in 1912, the size of the Guantánamo lease being increased. However, the rent paid for this forty-five square mile site was only $2,000 a year and the lease stipulated no terminal date. This Gibraltar in the east end of the island, covering the exit to the sea of one of the old and surviving centres of sugar, was a permanent, irritating reminder of the U.S.'s superior position.

The other irritant was even more delicate: it affected the status of the Isle of Pines. Should this be regarded as a part of Cuba, or, like other small Caribbean islands – such as Vieques, or Puerto Rico – as legitimate conquests from Spain by the U.S.? These developments were an interesting case history of mismanagement. Since the Isle of Pines had been reckoned part of Cuba under Spain, it was so after 1902. In 1903 the U.S. signed a treaty with Cuba confirming this arrangement. But it was not ratified in the time prescribed. Another treaty in 1904 left the ratification date unnamed and the Senate did nothing. Already U.S. property developers, led by S. H. Pearcy of Nashville, had been selling Spanish property to North Americans. Hotels and parks were planned. Journalists as prominent as R. H. Davis and Nicholas Biddle argued in November 1905 that the Isle of Pines should belong to the U.S., and the first U.S. Minister to Havana, Squiers, left Havana in a hurry after an indiscretion to the same effect. No doubt such rumours assisted Pearcy in his sales of land. The only bank in Nueva Gerona was North American. In 1907 the U.S. Supreme Court pronounced that the Isle of Pines was *de facto* Cuban territory, but it was not till 1925 that finally the 1904 treaty was ratified by the Senate. This also gave rise to intense irritation.[10] (By 1919 nearly a quarter of the population were in fact U.S. citizens.[11])

In all save name the Isle of Pines had become a North American community. The North Americans were even annoyed that government education in English was discontinued. They had built new towns – McKinley being under construction in 1909. Most North Americans were new frontiersmen, 'by no means afraid of work . . . sons and daughters help . . .' They already had, however, the Embroidery Club, the Hibiscus Club and the Pioneer Club, in Santa Fé or Nueva Gerona, to fall back on, when their citrus fruit wearied them. As in the rest of

[10] See Jenks, 148–9; Chapman, 157–9.
[11] Census of 1919.

Cuba, fresh foodstuffs were rare: the farmers sold to the North and received back tinned food, if not the jerked beef of the past. Even tinned tomatoes were eaten. The North Americans had surrendered to the Caribbean economic rhythm.[12] Meantime, the old Cuban oligarchy had vanished: the Duartes and Acostas who had divided up the island had vanished, along with a 1,600 acre sugar estate which had flourished before the war. Henceforth the Isle of Pines remained outside the great sugar adventures of the main island.

Many North Americans had now also bought land in Cuba itself: often not from Cubans but from U.S. land companies who bought large tracts at cheap prices, and who earned their profit by arranging for the extraordinarily complicated and tedious matter of title and survey. Some North Americans bought without seeing their future property from a picture in a brochure. Such ventures usually made the adventurers rich. Sometimes they sank into the landscape, unable to cope, and either went home or were reduced to the status of poor whites. Such ventures were usually citrus fruit farms. Some buyers were Swedish- or German-born North Americans, of whom the first went out of their way to break the rhythm of monoculture, and kept a cow and chickens as well as fruit farms.

Cuba in 1909, with two million inhabitants, was the most populous of the small states around the Caribbean: Guatemala was about the same, but all others, including Venezuela, were smaller. Of her reasonably near neighbours only Colombia, with about five million, exceeded her. All the English and other colonial islands were tiny. The big Cuban population rise since 1900 had principally been because of the disappearance of yellow fever and generally improved health conditions since the end of Spanish rule.

[12] Wright, *Cuba*, 330–3. Tinned vegetables, tinned fruit, condensed milk, figure high on the list of imports.

CHAPTER XLII

Gómez and the Good Life

José Miguel Gómez had at long last achieved his ambition. He was the most sympathetic of all the presidents of Cuba. Large, easy-going, tolerant, loving the good life, he was to the Cubans the archetype of their own ideal personalities, the fulfilment of their expansive cigar-smoke daydreams. He ended his presidency a millionaire after having entered it quite poor, but in a time of prosperity, rising production and high sugar prices (the average per pound reached 3 cents in 1911 for the first time since 1893, while the total value of the crop for the first time exceeded $M100 in the years of his presidency), these things were tolerated. Known as the Shark (*Tiburón*), of him the phrase was coined *Tiburón se baña pero salpica* (the Shark goes swimming but he makes a nice splash: that is, he knew how to be a friend to friends, a Cuban virtue). Almost alone of Cuban politicians of the Republic, Gómez had a strong personal base, in Santa Clara; here he resembled Latin American politicians more than his Cuban colleagues, most of whom, even those born in the provinces, made their names and fortunes in the great wen of Havana. When he saw Magoon off to the U.S. on the new battleship *Maine*, he announced, 'Once again we are completely free.' His friends knew that the freedom concerned was license.

Theodore Roosevelt, speculating on the likely course of events, argued that the 'inertia and governmental incapacity of the new Cuban Congress, if it is like the preceding Cuban Congresses, may very possibly prevent their re-enacting the [Crowder and Magoon] laws even if they really wished to do so'.[1] The president's prognostication was sound so far as Cuban practice was concerned: a long list might be drawn up of government contracts where government officials, president or cabinet ministers, congressmen or local officials, made money. These were all humdrum contracts; yet vast sums began soon illegally to be made from the purchase of ships for the navy, for dredging Havana harbour, for making a new railway along the line of Weyler's *trocha* from Júcaro to Morón, from the monopolization of collectorships and from other operations of the newly restored national lottery. Pardons, sewerage, telephone concessions, bridge building, barracks, all yielded lavish

[1] Roosevelt, *Letters*, 1136.

profits to those who surrounded the president: the building of a presidential palace was particularly lucrative and so, no doubt, was the building of two new ministries of the Interior and Justice, in the style of the Italian renaissance.[2] The word summing up the Gómez years was *chivo*, a goat; but since it is slang for 'crumbs', its colloquial usage is graft. The word went from lip to lip evoking hilarity as often as condemnation, for graft of course, like goat, can be smelled far off. Congress, since its members profited from these transactions, complained least. Many Cubans regarded *chivo* as a way of making an extra slice out of the U.S., and of course little of the money of the poorer Cubans was involved since income tax was so low and most taxes were indirect. Of the leading men in the first days of the Republic, only Enrique Varona was in a strong enough position to denounce what was happening; few listened to him. He had also become identified with the Conservative ultra-Spanish cause.

The origins of these corrupt habits are easily comprehended. Under Spain, officials had been paid little. The task of merely keeping jobs often involved such men in lavish social activity, and those who sought promotion were obliged to give really splendid entertainments, which could only be afforded by corrupt practices. The king had also been looked on as the source of patronage, and some of this attitude rubbed off on civil servants, however humble. Thus corruption in the Spanish empire was in origin a means whereby men of commerce were made to pay an extra tax to supplement officials' salaries; since the social exigencies of the situation obliged as a rule the recipient of bribes to spend, the money he gained was at least ploughed back into the economy.[3]

Of course industrialization and independence changed matters, but not the motives of the parties concerned. Politicians and civil servants in the new Cuba were ill-paid in comparison with those men of business reaping rich profits from the new prosperity, and so the old temptation survived in new clothes. Under José Miguel Gómez there began an advanced system of political corruption whereby all newspapers were recipients of government subsidies and so could never be regarded as arguing their own point of view. A decade later *La Lucha* specifically announced that they were not going to defend the project of President Zayas to buy the Santa Clara convent[4] 'simply because we have not been given money to defend it. Everyone knows . . . that when lances are broken in favour of this or that transaction it is because money has been given or else that the newspaper or newspapermen have not been

[2] See discussion in Chapman, 290.
[3] For a discussion of the sixteenth and seventeenth centuries, see J. H. Elliott, *Imperial Spain, 1469–1716* (1963), 171–2.
[4] See below, p. 555.

considered in the division'.[5] Within a few years, it was also estimated that the Customs lost between 15% and 25% of its revenues through corruption.[6]

The first of the three main scandals of Gómez's time related to that unfortunate loan which Charles Magoon had raised with Speyer and Co., the German bankers (whom President Taft's brother and Frank Steinhart represented in Havana). The purpose of this loan had been to continue the financing of the sewerage of Havana and Cienfuegos, the paving of Havana, and the building of an aqueduct in Cienfuegos. These capacious works had already swallowed an immense quantity of the Cuban revenues.[7] In June 1912 Gómez announced that another $M13 was needed to finish the work: uproar and protests followed.

The second great scandal concerned the Arsenal Lands – thirty evidently rich acres near Havana harbour. On 19 April 1909, two and a half months after Magoon's departure, Gómez announced that, in order to beautify the city, the English-owned United Railway had agreed to move its main station from Villanueva; the government would build a beautiful new block of public buildings there for Congress, for the president, for departments of government, costing $M6½; the railways would build five new docks and an incinerator for refuse at $M1½. There was an immediate wave of public enthusiasm until it became apparent that the whole scheme was fraudulent. Thus the Arsenal Lands turned out to be far larger than Gómez had said; and therefore worth far more. The project went ahead, but no buildings were finished and the only positive result, and that of dubious advantage, was that the railway station was moved away from the centre of the town.

Whatever Gómez and his ministers made out of these projects it was nothing to what they made out of the third scandalous project – the Ports Company. This derived from the evident need of the Cuban ports to be dredged. A number of Liberals, friends of the president, such as Carlos Miguel de Céspedes and Orestes Ferrara, president of the House of Representatives, formed a company whose aim was to take over the business of clearance. Gómez willingly agreed that the company should be formed and given a contract, but he stipulated that the work must be done. He proposed that the company should employ a crony of his, Colonel Tillinghurst Hommedien Huston, president of the Huston Contracting Company (and a future part-owner of the New York Yankee baseball club). Huston and another friend, Norman Davis, president of the Trust Company of Cuba, previously a partner of 'Tilly'

[5] *Lucha*, 18 May 1923, qu. Chapman, 519.
[6] Chapman, 430.
[7] There had also been a long and costly strike against low pay and bad conditions in 1911 led by anarchists such as Saavedra among the workers and with the support of the recently formed Partido Socialista de Cuba.

Huston and still a stockholder in his business, then organized the Ports Company.[8] Carlos Miguel de Céspedes became manager, Huston president. The Ports Company, formally approved in Congress in February 1911, was given a contract to dredge Havana and several other harbours, the work to be done within six years. In return, it would receive 75 cents a ton on all goods brought into Cuba for thirty years. The company was authorized to raise $M10 in stock and $M10 in bonds. In March 1911 the company began work and became a public concern: many foreigners, particularly English and Spanish shareholders, invested. Carlos Miguel de Céspedes and other Liberal politicians then sold out, taking their profits with them. A few months later an ominous and partially true rumour spread that the U.S. administration did not approve of the concession on the grounds that it clashed with the Platt Amendment.[9] The company therefore agreed to reduce its costs and began to negotiate with the U.S. government as to what it should compensate the shareholders 'if the Ports Company did not go ahead'. Shares fell alarmingly and English stockholders complained to their brokers. But the work continued, and so did the payments by importers to the company.

The final act to the drama occurred after Gómez had left the presidency. His successor annulled the Ports Company as illegal; orders were given that there should be no more payment to it. The government took over the works. Accusations were made in every direction. It turned out that Huston had received 900 shares 'for services'; that the company had been paid $M3, not $850,000 as they had announced, in the twenty-seven-month period of their operation; and that the company had spent $M9 on unspecified advances, so that there remained a deficit of $M6. The newspapers, paid lavishly by President Menocal, described the scandal in full detail. The Department of Public Works took over; work stopped. Shareholders complained to the U.S. government who eventually, in 1916–17, persuaded Menocal to pay compensation: payment was ultimately made in April 1918: $M7 in 5% bonds was paid out in return for the same number of bonds of the Ports Company.[10]

It was scarcely surprising that the reign of *Tiburón* should also be marked by a revival of violence, which had in the past never been far from the surface. Although trivial, these occurrences were just a little

---

[8] Norman H. Davis (1878–1944), began business career in Cuba, 1902; organized Trust Co. of Cuba, 1905, later adviser to U.S. Secretary of Treasury; Assistant Secretary of Treasury, 1919–20; diplomat under Roosevelt.

[9] The U.S. government contained members who believed that a new intervention was inevitable and that it was therefore in the U.S. interest that the government of Cuba should not be saddled with improvident contracts. See Munro, *Dollar Diplomacy*, 470–4.

[10] Discussed in Jenks, 123–5; Chapman, 332–9.

more serious than had occurred in Magoon's time and suggested a pattern of decay. In March 1909, there was the affair of Captain Manuel Lavastida, previously of the Rural Guard, arrested for 'plotting' and then shot 'while trying to escape'. This relapse towards Spanish colonial behaviour caused a scandal. The captain of the Rural Guard responsible, Captain Cortés, was arrested with his companions, and condemned to death. The *audiencia* of Santa Clara, however, set him free. President Gómez was furious and removed the judges – the law of the irremovability of judges only came into effect in July 1909. Already bricks were dropping away from Crowder and Magoon's patched-up fabric of Republican constitutionality: the judges were legally sacked but their dismissal was not in the spirit of the law. Their own action was mistaken; the 'mistakes' of the police were sinister.

Another step in the swift decline came in January 1910. Orestes Ferrara introduced, on behalf of Gómez, a law 'of National Defence' which aimed to muzzle the press. All newspapers protested, except Gómez's own friends on *El Triunfo*. The law was eventually withdrawn, but a week or so later the editors of two papers, *El Gordo* and *La Prensa*, were imprisoned on account of articles which appeared in their papers, and other editors were fined. One editor was accused but was not tried since he was a congressman.

This led to further trouble. General Vicente Miret denounced the government as tyrannical and in July 1912 took to the hills. He was captured at El Caney, but thereafter the atmosphere was full of rumours. Was he in league with the Conservatives, or the Veteran Association? In September a trunk was found mysteriously full of arms. The next month, General Pino Guerra, the chief of the army, was mysteriously shot in the leg leaving the presidential palace where he had been playing billiards. Gómez himself was believed to have been involved. Pino Guerra resigned and was succeeded by General Monteagudo. The next year another general, Guillermo Acevedo, attempted a revolution in Havana province, and old General Emilio Núñez, hero of the Little War of 1879, led the veterans to a demonstration of protest. On 5 September the veterans launched a full-scale attack on the Spanish sympathizers and Spaniards who had remained in the civil service since before 1895 – though only about forty civil servants of that time had actually been born in Spain.[11] General uproar continued most of the autumn on this score – so much so that on 17 January 1911 President Taft's Secretary of State, Philander Knox, sent a note to Gómez that the situation in Cuba was causing 'grave concern'.[12] This was evidently

[11] Census of 1907 says 42.

[12] Philander Knox (1853–1921), Secretary of State, 1909–13; lawyer; attorney-general under Roosevelt and McKinley; senator before and after. The U.S. attitude is discussed in Munro, 474–7.

a threat of intervention, and probably it had much to do with the compromise shortly reached, in March 1912. The veterans agreed to abandon their campaign against Spanish office holders and to behave in future as a benevolent association; Gómez for his part sacked two cabinet members and a number of civil servants, suspending the civil service law.

No one was satisfied by this. Nor were tempers assuaged by a visit paid to Havana by Knox himself in April. At a banquet in his honour he lectured: 'In Cuba, as in all republics, all classes should be alert in their consciousness of their civil duties, and should not remit the destinies of their country to the hands of a few who with nothing to lose and everything to gain make a business of the politics of their country'.[13] In fact his audience were by that time concentrating on the revival of an old hatred: the Gómez–Zayas hostility. Alfredo Zayas, the vice-president, desired the Liberal nomination for president, but Gómez himself had not decided if he would stand again. At the end of May, General Machado, one of Gómez's oldest followers, resigned from the Cabinet by writing an ornate letter arguing that Gómez's hatred of Zayas was causing Cuba to head once again for intervention.[14] In May, Zayas was definitely nominated by the Liberals as their candidate. Gómez's friends were appalled; some of them, such as the powerful General Asbert, governor of Havana province, began to shift their allegiance towards Menocal and the Conservatives: better an open enemy than an ally you hate.

This shift certainly lost Zayas the election. Both General Monteagudo, in command of Oriente, and General Asbert in Havana made certain, with Gómez's connivance, that those important provinces rallied to Menocal, by the simple expedients of fraud already only too well-known under Estrada Palma. Elsewhere it appears that the election was relatively free from corruption.

Philander Knox and the Taft administration meantime had devised what they called 'the preventive policy'. Taft himself defined this, in March 1913, as 'doing all within [our] power to induce Cuba to avoid every reason that would make intervention possible at any time'.[15] U.S. property in Cuba was assuming formidable proportions, so that an umbrella of governmental protection was sought for by many U.S. men of business. Four events in 1912 showed 'the preventive policy' in action.

First, there was the bizarre affair of the forest privileges of the Zapata swamp. Gómez allocated the right to cut the timber in this desolate area to a company of his friends, on the condition that they cleared it

---

[13] *Cuba Review*, April 1912, qu. Jenks, 325.
[14] Gerardo Machado, afterwards Cuban president. See below, p. 569, for life story.
[15] Qu. Jenks, 325.

within eight years. Beaupré, the U.S. minister, always quick to panic, became disturbed simply on grounds of waste, and Knox telegraphed to him:

> You will address a note to the government of Cuba saying that to the department . . . the Zapata swamp concession seems to be so clearly ill-advised . . . so reckless a waste of revenue and natural resources that the government is impelled to express to the government of Cuba its emphatic disapproval . . . and its firm conviction that a measure so inimical to the interests of the Cuban people will not be suffered by the government of Cuba.[16]

Gómez, occupied that summer with the Negro revolt,[17] could only back down. He annulled the concession. Some curious facts later seeped out: and Hugh Gibson, the U.S. *chargé d'affaires*, reported that there was in fact very little timber on the Zapata swamp.[18]

Second, there was the odd business of the Nuevitas–Caibarién railway. One day in March 1912 an anxious telegram arrived from Washington at the U.S. Legation in Havana:

> Information received by department foreshadows an attempt to renew a project of British capitalists to rush through the Cuban Congress a concession for a railroad from Nuevitas to Caibarién [a long stretch along the north coast of Cuba in the centre of the island]. You will earnestly urge upon the President the desirability of postponing final action on this bill sufficiently to allow the fullest investigation . . . emphasising the burden it would impose on the Cuban Treasury in favor of capital . . . neither American nor Cuban . . .[19]

A later telegram confirmed the act of interference, if not of intervention: the U.S. 'cannot give its approval to the railroad project in its present form'.[20] So much for private enterprise. The prospect of English capital expansion in Cuba was almost as intolerable to the State Department as was revolution. The incident indicates a certain element of truth in the analysis of one Marxist historian who anticipated open war between the U.S. and Britain as a result of rival economic interests in Latin America.

The third item was the question of a new loan. Gómez began to talk of the need for such a thing in mid-1912. The U.S. minister Beaupré telegraphed Washington:

---

[16] Foreign Relations, 1912, 309–10. Arthur Matthias Beaupré (1853–1919), barrister, consul in Guatemala, then Colombia; minister to Cuba, 1911–13.
[17] See below, p. 523.
[18] See Munro, 480–2.
[19] Foreign Relations, 1912, 381.
[20] *Ibid.*, 384.

The floating of a new loan would offer us an extremely good opportunity to be of real assistance to the Cuban people by putting our own conditions upon the granting of the loan in order to make sure of its honest application. It would seem that this might be readily made to entail some more or less active fiscal control which would protect the Cuban treasury against the wholesale looting to which it has hitherto been subjected.[21]

Here then was yet another idea, though scarcely a new one: interference in the name of honesty.

Finally in December 1912 came the Guantánamo treaty, the consequences of which were that the U.S. surrendered all interest in the useless Bahía Honda base while Cuba handed over that outside Guantánamo indefinitely, at the absurd rent of $2,000 a year.

Such were the diplomatic consequences of President William Howard Taft, whose diplomacy towards Cuba was a touchstone of his general relations with foreign countries. The 'preventive policy' was the backcloth to a great further increase of U.S. investment in Cuba. Taft was himself not afraid of the description 'dollar diplomacy': better dollars than bullets, and no doubt he saw the increase of commerce as an improvement of the chances of peace. But there is no doubt that both he and Philander Knox interpreted 'the national interest almost exclusively in the terms of the interests of the business community'.[22]

To Gómez finally was due the reinstatement of two of the most typical social activities of old Cuba: cock-fighting and the lottery. In the old days, the cock fight had been at the heart of country life. Wood had abolished it, along with bull fights. In 1908 there had been demonstrations in favour of its re-establishment. Gómez's Liberals had used a cock on a plough as a party symbol. It had been interpreted as a promise to 'bring back the cock'. It was indeed almost his first governmental act to revive this.

José Miguel's second legacy was the restoration of the national lottery, banned since 1898. In 1904, during one of the Congress's rare meetings, the mulatto Senator Morúa Delgado had rushed through a lottery re-establishment act. A surprise vote got it through, but Estrada vetoed it, pointing out that Morúa Delgado had in 1891 referred to the lottery as 'social gangrene' and adding: 'If the lottery should now become established as a speculation of the State, we might be able to say that an insurmountable wall has been raised to separate the nation

[21] Foreign Relations, 395.
[22] See Foster Rhea Dulles, *America's Rise to World Power, 1898–1954*, 81; Pringle, *Taft*, II, 737; etc. Dana Munro's comments (*Dollar Diplomacy*) are illuminating.

of which we dreamed in the revolutionary epoch from that which really exists.'[23]

In 1909 Morúa Delgado was president of the Senate, a post with different social obligations, and José Miguel was not Estrada. On 17 February 1909 the historian Martínez Ortiz introduced a bill to restore the lottery, with the proviso that the proceeds would go to bridges, building and roads. His belief was that the restoration of the lottery was inevitable and that his bill would at least render it benevolent. Senator Gonzalo Pérez proclaimed that the bill 'gave hope of wealth to the poor man, sustaining him, animating him'. Others argued that the gambling instinct was so set among Cubans that the people would use foreign lotteries if that at Havana were not restored.

The system now inaugurated dominated Cuban life for many people for the next fifty years. It provided for four draws each month, every Saturday afternoon, an extra Christmas draw, 30,000 tickets costing between $20 and $50, usually bought in fractions. Collectors were appointed to help boost the sale of tickets. Fifteen whole tickets would be allotted to them, and they would get 3% of the face value of a ticket. People could regularly subscribe to a single number. The draws were made by a child from one of the Havana orphanages. The child would draw first a ball from a globe carrying all the numbers in the lottery, and second, from another globe, a ball bearing the details of the prize. In that way draws would carry on until all the prizes were drawn.

The details of the lottery were framed and reframed with the solicitude that in other countries is devoted to the details of pensions. The lottery was provided with a director-general and an assistant director-general, neither of whom could be removed except by an elaborate process. These posts were among the most sought after in Cuba. There would be one collector per 3,000 inhabitants, these being appointed by the Treasury. Soon there appeared dealers (*acaparadores*), often Spaniards,[24] who would buy tickets in advance from the collectors and sell them to the general public at a higher price. In good times (the *bonanza*) the price of the whole ticket might fetch three, four or even five times the proper price. Though initially the collectorships were intended for the widows and families of the war of independence, they became sinecures zealously sought by politicians. Though there were about 2,000 nominal collectors, about 800 to 900 of these were latterly often taken up by the director-general of the lottery, for whom the profits of cheating were always too much to be resisted, and who by 1920 might expect an income of over $M2½ a year. About 500 collectorships meantime were distributed among congressmen. The average number of

[23] Chapman, 169.
[24] Gonzalo de Quesada y Miranda, *En Cuba libre* (1925), 29-30.

collectorships held by a senator in the 1920s was perhaps eight. In 1927 there were apparently only two senators who had no collectorships.[25] The rest of these desirable posts were divided among other political hangers-on.

Within a few years of Gómez's law, the lottery was known to be the most efficient method of illegal enrichment, and above all for buying the silence or the support of the legislature or press. Under Gómez's successor, Menocal, the *colecturía* indeed became so normal a route to easy wealth that 'people in the best society claimed their cut (*basurita*) as if it were the most normal thing in the world'. As for the lottery proper, people would often weekly 'devote a specified percentage of their earnings to lottery tickets'. It was useless to argue, a North American sociologist pointed out in the 1940s, that 'the same amount placed in a savings account would in time provide a competence in old age ... the remote chance of winning as much as $100,000 with an investment of 20 cents has too strong a pull ... the Lottery,' added that serious and sanguine American, 'is the most potent enemy of progress designed to promote thrift among the population. It encourages a sort of chance-boom psychosis ... where everyone lives in a bubble which for most investors bursts every Saturday.'[26] 'It takes the rent money,' wrote Miss Wright, 'the money due to the groceryman and the money needed to buy the family clothing.'[27]

The restoration of the lottery was the most dazzling achievement of President José Miguel Gómez. Two congas commemorate him:

Ya ha llegado Tiburón	Tiburón has come back
De viajar por tierra extraña	From his grand tour
Y le ha dicho a Menocal	He has told Menocal:[28]
Para que hagas un caudal	'To make your fortune
Tienes que chivar con saña.	You must take graft really seriously.'

and

La otra Tarde en el Senado	The other evening in the Senate
Puede oir esta canción	I could hear this song:
'No se apuren, caballeros,	'Don't worry, gentlemen,
que si hoy no hay chilindrón	If there's no *fricassée* today
Comeremos chivo fresco	We'll have fresh crumbs
cuanda suba Tiburón'.	When Tiburón comes up for air.'

[25] Chapman, 328.
[26] L. Nelson, *Rural Cuba* (1950), 218. He is writing of the forties but the habits became ingrained in the earlier days.
[27] Wright, *Cuba*, 198.
[28] i.e. his successor.

CHAPTER XLIII

The Negro Protest

In 1907 there had been founded in Cuba a threateningly named Independent Party of Colour. Its leader was Evaristo Estenoz, a Liberal leader of the 1906 Revolution, a Negro of intelligence and imagination but also an opportunist. His plan was to articulate the grievances felt throughout the first ten years after the end of the war of independence: that the Negroes of Cuba 'had been robbed . . . of all the fruits of victory,'[1] when they had in fact provided, as they claimed, 85% of the rank and file in the war.[2] Certainly, there had been much fighting in Oriente province, and in other rural areas which had a strong Negro population. Certainly too the Negro population had dropped from about half the population to a third between 1887 and 1899.

During the election campaign of 1908 Gómez and the Liberals had been generous in their promises to satisfy these grievances. 1909 saw no fulfilment. Agitation grew. In April 1910, Estenoz and his aide Ivonet were arrested, charged with disturbing the peace, but released. In May a law was introduced banning political parties formed on any colour basis. But Estenoz and Ivonet continued to plot, though they often went to see Gómez also. Nevertheless, the Negroes felt there was little to hope from Gómez. Like Maceo, their hero, or Martí, from whom they drew intellectual inspiration, or like the famous slave rebels of the past, they therefore planned a revolution.

In fact this question was more complicated than it appeared. Racial feeling was not strong in Cuba. The best families had mulatto cousins: the better the family, the more probable this was. The flood of new immigrants from Spain was more likely to be intolerant than families who had been in Cuba for generations. The black or mulatto minority was less in proportion to what it had been in 1899 – just under 30% instead of 32%, due to Spanish immigration and to the high average age of Negroes in 1899;[3] but the total number had increased by 100,000 to a little over 600,000.[4]

[1] Atkins, 312; see also Montejo, 216 ff.

[2] The claim was repeated in Chapman, 310, and Wright, *Cuba*, 144.

[3] i.e. in the Census of 1907. By 1907 the age structure was clearly seen in that 65% of those over eighty were black or mulatto, 47·2% of those over seventy-five and 52·6% of those over fifty. Thereafter, far more were white. (Negroes also tend to exaggerate their age.) (Census, 226.) In 1907 only 7,867 Negroes were said to have been born in Africa (*ibid.*, 340); of these the majority (3,965) were classified as being farmers (*agricultores*); the only other significant groups were gardeners (352) and servants (118).

[4] 608,967 to be precise (Census of 1907).

General Machado, President of Cuba,
1925–1933
The Machados and the Calvin Coolidges
at the Pan-American Conference, 1928
left to right, Señora de Machado,
Coolidge, Mrs Coolidge, Machado

16 Sergeant Batista greets Dr Grau San Martín, September 1933

In the professions, Negroes still played a very small part, much fewer than their percentage of the population: in the whole country there were only four lawyers, nine doctors, forty dentists, fifteen architects, fourteen engineers, and only 430 teachers. This represented little improvement upon their fate in 1899;[5] indeed, there were nominally fewer black or mulatto doctors in 1907 than eight years before. In every profession of standing there were more Spaniards even than Negroes. On the other hand, thanks to the existence for many years of so many freed Negroes, Negroes were already predominant in a few crafts – coopers, laundresses, dressmakers, builders, shoemakers, woodcutters, tailors, musicians and domestic servants, and they were also entrenched in other jobs – such as bakers, barbers and carpenters. Negro or mulatto tobacco workers comprised between a third and half of the total. Blacks as well as whites had found jobs in towns in the interior. In Cuba there was, as perhaps elsewhere, an internal caste division between the descendants of recently freed slaves and those of long free Negroes. But there is no reason to doubt that (as in 1899) the farms and plots owned or rented by the black population were smaller and less productive than those of the whites.[6] Some of the Negroes who had gone into towns became policemen; already 1,700 of the police (out of 6,400) were black – and the proportion was increasing.[7] Three relatively large towns (i.e. those over 8,000 strong) had a Negro or mulatto majority (Santiago de Cuba, Jovellanos, Guantánamo),[8] as had nine municipal districts, all in Oriente except Jovellanos (Matanzas).[9] Oriente was still the poorest area of Cuba, though Van Horne's railway had brought in new jobs and capital.

The Cuban black population, therefore, had genuine grounds for grievance. The ex-slave, Esteban Montejo, had joined the war to be free of bondage as well as of Spaniards. Yet the gains registered in the 1880s and 1890s remained: segregation did not exist in schools, theatres and bars practised no colour bar, and so on. The chief explanation of Negro difficulties derived not from any government action or any omission but from the difficulties met by all Negroes in dealing with freedom after generations of slavery. Partly, no doubt, the continued presence of the Spaniards, together with the increased immigration

[5] Three lawyers, ten doctors.
[6] There was no agricultural census in 1907, nor indeed until 1946. But in 1907 we find 105,915 black and mulatto males and 2,143 females classified as *agricultores*; most of these were in Oriente (33,410), and after that Santa Clara (25,768) and Matanzas (19,496). It would seem likely that the same share of the nation's wealth went to those people in 1910 as in 1899, though it is possible that they fell behind.
[7] Census of 1907.
[8] 56·7%, 58% and 60·6%, respectively.
[9] These were: Alto Songo, Baracoa, Caney, Cobre, Guantánamo, Palma Soriano, Santiago, San Luis, Jovellanos (Census of 1900, 306).

from Spain, was to blame. The governments of Estrada Palma and Gómez admittedly sought always to mitigate racialism. Such prejudice as there was derived from an unthinking inheritance from old days of anxiety about a slave revolt, and partly too from a desire to imitate the U.S. and so prove U.S. investments safe.

On the other hand, despite Maceo and various Negro leaders since, Negro and white did not much mix. In the 1940s the 'visiting pattern' seemed to a sociologist to be entirely uniracial while only mulattoes were able to go between: and though he was a North American drawing his morals from the west and centre, not the east, of the island, it is clear that though marriages between white men and Negresses were frequent, those between black men and white women were rare. (This is, however, normal in most multiracial societies.) Cock-fighting was the only social occasion which was always mixed[10] – if one excludes the African religious cults.[11] Otherwise, a colour bar of a kind did erect itself, self-arranged, instinctive, often barely perceptible. The blacks lived in a world apart: they felt different from others and they were forced – or preferred – to keep to themselves. North American influence somewhat exacerbated this. There were some clubs where the blacks could not go and private schools where it would be unthinkable they should go. There were also illegal but effective restrictions against entry into some new restaurants and hotels. Negro politicians did not make much of these matters. Morúa Delgado (a would-be 'Zola of the black people'), president of the Cuban Senate in 1909 and later Secretary of Agriculture (who in the 1880s and 1890s had explored all the matters raised by a mixed society in his newspapers) would say that he expected political but not social equality; he had himself however been offended by Estrada Palma's refusal to ask his wife to official banquets.[12]

Many echoes of slavery survived. Slavery had broken up the usual ties of affection in families for so long that instability, irresponsibility, delinquency and reluctance to accept property or *bourgeois* values was traditional. Indeed, for many ex-slaves (like Esteban Montejo, who gave a version of his autobiography in the 1960s) hostility to property seems to have extended to a virtual incapacity to accept any form of family ties or settled way of life; he never knew whether he had children or not. If this was an extreme example, the absent father was a common phenomenon, as was a marked lack of responsibility on the part of fathers towards children (much contrasting with the patriarchal attitude of Spanish fathers to their families); hence what Fernando Ortiz described as that special 'delinquency' of Havana, corrupting and

---

[10] Nelson, 170; Ortiz, *Negros Esclavos*.
[11] See below, p. 519.
[12] *Cf.* Wright, *Cuba*, 95; see Horrego Estuch's life, *Martín Morúa Delgado*.

pervasive, deriving from the part played by the mother (and the ambivalent role often of her brothers). Many more black people lived together in 'consensual marriages' than white; indeed the figures suggest much greater casualness in personal relations of all sorts than among whites. Roger Bastide later argued that 'the black family ignored romantic love', or rather, looked on romantic love as only a kind of folk-lore, borrowed from the whites. Black families were on average smaller than white,[13] but the illegitimacy rate was double that of whites.[14] In 1907 55 % of blacks or mulattoes were illiterate, compared with 26 % of whites, though the percentage would improve by 1919 (to 47%). Just under 8,000 of the Negro population in 1907 meantime had been born in Africa, elderly ex-*bozales* who might still recall at least a real if shadowy and mysterious homeland, and could transmit memories of it.[15]

Public celebration of all religious ceremonies and festivals both Afri-can and Catholic, had been banned by the U.S. military government. But this ban could be evaded by Negroes with the argument, sometimes sincere, that their fiestas were under Catholic auspices. Those could be more easily overlooked. St Barbara, St Joseph, Our Lady of Mercy, were brought in now even more than in the nineteenth century, to act as supervisors of the festivities of Changó, the god of war, Yoruba god of lightning and storms, or Obatalá, an Africanized Our Lady of Mercy (popularly, La Mercé or Merced). Recent immigrants from Galicia might suddenly look out from their stuffy salons into the hot street to observe processions celebrating a, to them, unknown festival to an equally unknown god, including doubtless sacrifices of white cocks to Christian saints.[16] A North American traveller, such as Irene Wright was de-lighted to be taken to a Yoruba *cabildo* licensed by the municipality, under the name of St Joseph, to observe what appears to be the initiation of a female *dévouée*:

We were accompanied by a member, a mulatto, the leader of an orchestra well known in Havana. Before we reached the house, we heard the nervous beat of the drum which takes the place of the tom-tom, forbidden by law, and the accompanying rattle of gourds shaken up and down inside a beaded net. Three young Negroes standing on a bench manipulated the gourds; another seated below them pounded the drum . . . The music was unquestionably African. In the open space on the stone floor, before the players, members of the organisation danced, not together, but singly, jerking and gesticulating in a circle

[13] 4·2 to 4·8, Census of 1907, 586.
[14] Based on 1919 census; since 1907 the figures are not accurate.
[15] Evidence of their experiences was given by Ortiz, *Negros Esclavos*, 163, who examined an old Congo slave brought presumably in the 1860s.
[16] Bastide, 163, has a key to the transculturation of saints.

round and round. They sang in an African dialect. We were told that one song, movements to which simulated snatching from above, was a prayer to Saint Barbara for blessings. In an adjoining room, we were shown altars. One was to our Lady of Mercy, one to Saint Joseph, and one to Saint Barbara at the base of whose shrine was an iron image of a black jockey ... These altars were decorated with cheap hangings and tawdry trinkets ... In another room, in which also was a bed, elaborately trimmed with yellow satin and ribbon, was an altar to the Virgin of Cobre.[17] There were dishes of food before it, in the process of being blessed ... and there was a covered soup tureen which, we were given to understand, held a holy secret. We returned to the dancing in time to see one apt performer throw a fit [that is, she was being subjected to a series of rites which made the profanity leave her]. 'The saint' had entered into her. Immediately, another woman unbound her hair and removed her shoes. They hustled her into the other room and she returned clad in a garment which seemed to imitate the robes and altar images of the Virgin and Saints ... She wore gold and brass bracelets which jingled as she danced ... She proceeded to salute all present by throwing her arms about the shoulders of men and women alike, one after another, kissing them on the cheek, if they were women, and rubbing each of her shoulders to each of theirs in turn, if they were men. As she went she collected pennies and dimes ... Sometimes in this condition, those who 'had' the 'saint' prophesied and prescribed remedies for the sick.[18]

This particular ceremony was probably Yoruba. One can imagine the surprised and shocked faces of observers from New England at these 'nefarious mysteries and trickeries of witchcraft', but they were of course simply survivals or distortions (themselves changing in the new circumstances of formal emancipation) of African religion, such as existed in the rest of black America to a lesser or greater extent. Doubtless these cults survived more in Cuba (as in Brazil) because slavery had lasted until recently there (it was still only twenty years dead in Brazil, twenty-five in Cuba); because therefore some surviving Africans had lived through the whole process of capture, enslavement, emancipation, war (in the case of Cuba) and disillusion; because these were the territories which had absorbed most slaves from Africa in the nineteenth century; and, as suggested earlier, because it was possible in those countries (thanks partly to the good offices of Mgr Morell de Santa Cruz) more easily to combine the celebration of diverse African gods with that of Roman Catholic saints. The *cabildos* devoted to separate

[17] Yellow was the colour of Our Lady of Cobre, white for Our Lady of Mercies, purple and green for St Joseph, red for the favourite, St Barbara.
[18] Wright, *Cuba*, 149. A scene similar in details was witnessed by the author in 1969.

religions survived, despite a ban on their emergence into the streets at Epiphany or Carnival.[19] But Cuba was in some ways closer to Africa even than Brazil. It is the only place in America where African proverbs survive in common parlance.[20] Many African words are used in Cuba more usually than their hispanic equivalent: thus *jimagua* of African origin, a twin, is more frequent than the Castillian *gemelo*. Catholics had usually baptized slaves, and had for several generations made little fuss if, for instance, the Yoruba Changó became Santa Barbara. Thus the uneasy blend of Spanish or *criollo* and North American in Cuba was imposed on an even uneasier one between African and Hispanic.[21]

By 1910 it was becoming clear how much of Africa remained in Cuba.[22] One can also contrast this with the U.S. where the Negroes, mostly Fanti or Ashanti in origin (so far as Virginia was concerned) or Dahomean and sometimes Angolan (Bantu) in Louisiana or Mississippi, had lost, or been forced to lose, much more of their native African culture. A number of Cuban place names (such as Songo, Cambute, Zaza, even the heroic Yara) were of African origin.[23] In Cuba, attendance at and participation in African ceremonies was not confined to pure Negroes. Mulattoes, even sometimes whites, took part; Mohammedan Negroes, or Cuban Africans who were descended from Mohammedans, must have felt as excluded from these occasions as most Castillians. (Since Mohammedan Negroes appear to have reached the New World later than the rest, there was undoubtedly a substantial Cuban Negro population of this origin, who appear to have lost all contact with Islam before emancipation.)

The Yoruba was the dominant influence in Cuba, though the partially subordinate (Bantu) Mayombé influence lasted too, and there was also the *Zarabanda*, a mixture between Yoruba and Congo religion – Zarabanda being himself the Congo equivalent of Changó, the Yoruba god of war. Another Congolese mixture with Yoruba was the acceptance by the former of the latter's vegetable deity Osain, at least in the search for medicinal plants.[24]

[19] In protestant North America and the British West Indies no comparable religious experiences survived apart from Protestant revivalism, with some similar characteristics, enough to confuse the anthropologists, inadequate to illuminate them. See discussion by George E. Simpson and Peter B. Hammond in *Caribbean Studies*, 49. Bastide (168 ff) also discusses it.

[20] Bastide, 183.

[21] As in Trinidad and in some parts of Brazil, Yoruba traditions apparently dominated Afro-Cuban behaviour even if the Yoruba were not numerically dominant among Cuban slave imports. The provenance of the first, not the most, Negroes, is perhaps the most important factor. See Bastide, 18.

[22] But *cf.* M. G. Smith, 'The African Heritage in the Caribbean' where it is pointed out that there are numerous tribes of West Africa where 'spirit possession is not to be found' (*Caribbean Studies*, 36). The word Afro-, as a prefix (Afro-American, Afro-Cuban), seems to have been coined about 1910 by Fernando Ortiz.

[23] Ortiz, *Negros Esclavos*, 51.

[24] Lydia Cabrera, *El Monte* (1954).

Yoruba religion in America seems to have remained closer than any of its rivals to its African ancestors. This is equally true of its Cuban, Brazilian or Trinidadian manifestations – for what is known in Cuba as *Santería*, in Brazil as *candomblés pagos*, *Changó* or *Batuque*, or as *Changó* in Trinidad is much the same. There were some differences between the *Santería* (literally, cult of gods, or *orishas*) in the Americas and in Africa: thus, in the former, slavery destroyed the element of lineage and the recounting of ancestors; and while in Africa the Yorubas as a tribe had been close to a nation, almost a state, with a religious element binding together many villages and cities, in Cuba the priests of the *santería* could only operate in small units on single plantations or in certain quarters of specific towns. In Cuba this apparently led to many more people being possessed of divine souls during the celebration.[25] Otherwise the list of *orishas* celebrated was much as in Nigeria,[26] while the Cuban Yorubas seem to have retained more gods than the Brazilians whose mythology in general was less diverse or rich. In all places the activities were much the same: the gods were mimed in dancing, their life stories persistently re-enacted, with drums perhaps playing an even greater part in Cuba than in Brazil (all with their own names, magic properties and, sometimes, secrets). The initiation of women took several months – since the initiate was supposed to learn African dancing and language, to go through several tests, to be bathed in blood, to appear in a trance (*éré*) before the society, and so on.

Christ appeared under the Yorubas as Obatalá, given the task of finishing the creation; his colour, significantly one supposes, was white; he was married to Odudúa, dark goddess of the underworld, and was a critic of alcohol; Odudúa was also identified with Our Lady and the Holy Ghost at times and she received white chickens monthly; Ogún, a drunkard, was identified with St John the Baptist, and was the patron of blacksmiths, soldiers and huntsmen; Yemayá, her favourite colours blue and white, was Our Lady of Regla who lived in the sea and behaved as the goddess of sailors and fresh water; while Oshún, known for love affairs and beauty, with yellow her colour, was the very important *Virgen de la Caridad del Cobre*, or Caridá, also familiarly known as Cachita, – the patron saint of Cuba.

Orishas were not expected to know everything but they could pick up new knowledge and new beliefs. Every participant in the cults had his patrons, carefully selected, or decided on because various families regarded a particular Orisha as an ancestor. The ritual varied. Sometimes it appeared as almost completely Catholic, with Hail Marys, Our

[25] Bastide, 124.
[26] Bastide, 125, has a list, with slight differences.

Father, candles and incense. Sometimes an especially hysterical occasion developed, various worshippers becoming possessed, putting on the clothes of Orishas, and being recognized as such by the spectators.

The French who had come to Cuba from Saint Domingue in the late eighteenth century brought with them certain slaves who were practitioners of voodoo; so that this religion had a specific Cuban variety already in the nineteenth century.[27] There was also to be found in post-slave Cuba a form of spiritualism known as the *cordoneros de Orilé* (the Orilé ropemakers), of whose practice less is known.[28] Fernando Ortiz has described the importance in Cuba too of Negro literary tournaments, entertainments rather than religious admittedly, long collective literary improvisations on specific themes, directed perhaps against some institution or person who had committed an offence against the Negro way of life. From these entertainments developed some of the specifically entertaining, that is non-religious dances, such as the rumba, for which Cuba is famous, but the most distinct and original cult or reminiscence of Africa in Cuba was that of the Ñáñigo (or Abakuá), which unlike the *Santería* is not found anywhere but in Cuba. Abakuá is the name of the society, Ñáñigo is the popular name of its adepts.

Fernando Ortiz, the most persistent and distinguished Cuban anthropologist, once remarked that in a lifetime of study he failed to discover the precise meaning of this society. But its broad outlines are clear: Abakuá was a secret society of the Efors and Efiks, small but independent people settled along the estuary of the Cross River on the Niger Delta, who presumed themselves a specially chosen race in Africa. Their role in slave-trading and commerce had been pre-eminent.[29] They enacted as a part of their religious rite a long saga whose most interesting aspect was that it enabled souls to rest permanently in limbo rather than pursue for ever the path of reincarnation. The cult was carried to Cuba by the Efiks, where it became a secret society, whose adepts became known in the nineteenth century as Ñáñigos.[30]

[27] See H. Perou, *L'Ile de Cuba* (1889).

[28] Fernando Ortiz, *La Africanía de la Música Folklórica de Cuba*, 450–6; Bastide, 173–4.

[29] See above, p. 160.

[30] The legend at the basis of Abakuá was that a woman of the Efors, Sikán, went to look for water in a river at the foot of a palm tree. She felt something move and murmur in her water bucket – the mysterious voice Ekué. Her father, King Mikuire, ordered her to keep this secret and made Ekué carry out his designs. However, since all women were considered gossips, Sikán was sent away into the forest. Ekué (presumed a fish) eventually died but its spirit was preserved and kept in an Ekón drum. Seven priests (children of Ekué) were chosen to guard this spirit: they condemned Sikán to death on suspicion of treachery, her blood and bones being used to ward off enemies. But her spirit also survived and became the mother who collected souls of the dead, and preserved them from persistent reincarnation.

The rival tribe of Efiks meantime became jealous of the Ekué and by means of magic induced by plants, a group of them obtained the mysterious Ekué, whom they also shut up in a drum. They introduced into the cult the figure of Morúa Yuansá, apparently the same as Sikán in her first appearance; 'she sought souls' and brought people together, for mar-

In Cuba the Ñáñigos held their meetings in a temple (*fambá*), and enacted the story of the discovery of the voice Ekué. The different participants in the ceremony took the parts of the different protagonists in the tale (Ekueñon, the slave; Ekorié, the master of the sect; Morúa Yuansá, the priest; Nasakó, *el brujo* (witchdoctor); Aberisún the executioner, and so on). Initiates were known as Okobio. The Ñáñigos had lavishly adorned flags and other permanent objects of veneration. Once a Ñáñigo, always a Ñáñigo. The Ñáñigos (unlike the practitioners of Santería) refused to allow women or homosexuals to take part, or even to touch the drums or other instruments. One other unusual character-istic was the existence alongside it of a white secret society which, initiated by a Frenchman perhaps from Saint Domingue, exactly copied its rites without being in any way affiliated.[31]

It is unfortunately obscure whether this cult in all its details (reminis-cent, as Roger Bastide pointed out, of the Eleusinian mysteries) was transported from Africa; in outline it was clearly African, but there remains a doubt whether this serene element of resting, away from the struggles of reincarnation, did not derive from Christian embroidery in Cuba itself. At all events it was flourishing, particularly at Regla near Havana, in 1900, as it had been on several plantations in the past.

During the late nineteenth century, when slavery was ending, the Ñáñigos seem to have gone through a semi-criminal phase since new members were also obliged to go out and kill the first passer-by they met after initiation. Different lodges of the society fought each other and made forays on the cartloads of meat coming to the Havana slaughterhouse. But this phase appears to have passed by 1900.

Another characteristic of Negro attitudes was frequent attention to more than one religion: Catholic on Sunday, Pentecostal in the week, Afro-Cuban on specific days. Catholicism was of course socially domi-nant but frequently remote, and in the country often non-existent.

Against this extremely complicated and often ambiguous religious, social and moral scene (in which one could say that 'the man without an adjective', as Juan Gualberto Gómez put it, was nearer achievement than in most other countries), the truth of the political events leading to the black revolution of 1912 is hard to disentangle. Accusations were rife at the time that President Gómez encouraged the revolutionaries, in order later to gain a spurious credit for putting down the revolution.

[31] See Lydia Cabrera, *La Sociedad secreta Abakuá narrada por viejos adeptos* (1958); Fernando Ortiz, *Los Bailes y el teatro de los negros en el folklore de Cuba* (1951), and a summary in Bastide, 120-2. Some members of *Santería* cults are also members of Abakuá, particularly drummers.

riage. The enactment of this rite consisted first of the initiation of a new candidate by killing him in theory (he being represented by a goat). The blood is offered to Ekué and then to the others. There are other celebrations, dances, the charade of the stealing of the goat meat and the pursuit of the thief, and the ventilation of a cock to represent purification (perhaps it should be added that there are several other versions of this legend).

At all events, on 20 May 1912 a Negro rising began, with demonstrations and strikes throughout the island, just when the harvest (larger than ever before) was coming to an end. The movement was crushed immediately everywhere except in Oriente, especially in the Guantánamo region. The alarm was nevertheless immense, Havana being overwhelmed by panic. Everyone had feared a 'Negro uprising' for years. The atmosphere resembled the 'Great Fear' in the French Revolution. Gómez ordered his aides to form volunteer forces, for which the government would supply arms and ammunition.[32] The U.S. Secretary of State, Philander Knox, was worried, too, and told the U.S. minister in Havana:

> The *Nebraska* should arrive at Havana tomorrow and a large naval force will be assembled at a convenient point, probably Key West. A gunboat will be ordered to Nipe ... You will inform the Cuban government that in the event of its inability or failure to protect the lives or property of American citizens in Cuba, the government of the U.S. will land forces ...[33]

On 31 May a body of U.S. marines did land at Daiquirí in Oriente, the beach where the U.S. landed in Cuba fourteen years before, aiming, they said, 'to protect sugar estates', though this was not the great sugar area. Gómez 'gave his consent' to the landing a few minutes before it occurred: in fact, it does not seem that his permission was asked.[34] But against whom were these forces arrayed? On 2 June a Negro leader, Isidro Santos Carrera, sacked *La Maya* sugar mill. General Monteagudo suspended constitutional guarantees throughout Oriente. On 15 June General Menocal, from the grandeur of his great *Chaparra* sugar mill, sent a message to Gómez, offering to supply 1,000 cavalrymen. But by then Monteagudo's rural guard and soldiers had defeated 4,000 Negroes under Estenoz in a pitched battle and was then embarking on the pursuit of small bands of guerrillas. Monteagudo spent the next month doing his best to extirpate the revolution, and claimed he killed 3,000. The movement fell away, almost as mysteriously as it had begun. Estenoz, the central organizer, was dead.

The U.S. government's policy in this 'revolution' received the name of 'preventive' from its initiator, Philander Knox; that is, the U.S. would act, if necessary intervene, before real intervention was necessary.

The consequences were of importance for the Cuban Negroes and their relations with the rest of the population. No Negro politician before 1959 played on the theme of Negro ill-treatment. Indeed, almost all

[32] Sanjenis, *Tiburón*, 150.
[33] Foreign Relations, 1912, 248.
[34] See Chapman, 312.

Negro or coloured politicians, such as they were, concentrated on close alignment with the existing political structure. There were in fact no outstanding Negro politicians after Juan Gualberto Gómez, and he, already old, suspect and suspecting, did little more in Cuban public life.[35] José Miguel Gómez gave Negroes government posts, consciously, but they did not often run for elective office. No Negro ever stood for the presidency. Negroes as a whole were driven in on themselves more and more and excluded from the general political and cultural development of the country the further they got away from the revolutionary wars, the age of Maceo. Apart from the shining exception of the historian and anthropologist Fernando Ortiz, and some disciples (mostly of the Cuban *haute bourgeoisie*), little attempt was made to absorb Cuban Negro life with that of the rest of the island. In the heady era of sugar expansion which followed, few cared about Afro-Cuban culture, though soon the 'whitest' themselves danced to Afro-Cuban rhythms. This did not mean that Afro-Cuban cults disappeared; they flourished, Negroes finding in them the means of security and social mobility. These religions were the expression of a private world whose persistence helps to explain the curiously opaque nature of Cuban society in the rest of the century. The arrival of many Haitians between 1913 and 1925 increased also the voodoo element in Afro-Cuban religions (voodoo is a powerful magic, of which even the Ñáñigos were a little apprehensive).

Since 1898 there had been a general ban on black immigration to Cuba; but in late 1912, after the Negro revolt, the United Fruit Company asked if they could bring in 1,400 Haitians to work on their plantations in Oriente. Gómez agreed. In succeeding years, a torrent of black labourers came, Haitians and Jamaicans. All were supposed to come for the harvest and return, but they did not always do so. Many went into the cities. Wages were far higher than in Haiti and in the English West Indies, left behind on the edge of another empire. Within the next ten years, over 150,000 Negroes were brought in, but while the black or mulatto population of Cuba increased, the new arrivals diminished rather than increased Negro political solidarity.

[35] The exceptions were the Communists of the post-1933 generation. See below. But even they did not argue that Negroes were worse treated than the rest of the Cuban poor.

CHAPTER XLIV

Menocal

Appropriately, the president of Cuba during the years of the swiftest advance in the sugar industry, the twentieth century, was General Mario García Menocal.[1] In 1913 Menocal was forty-six. He had managed the huge *Chaparra* mill and plantation with verve, the sugar produced being in 1910 almost 70,000 tons. This was as much as was produced in all Cuba in the 1830s, and was possible because of the new elaborate and expensive machinery introduced, which could masticate cane very quickly. (The yield incidentally from the cane was not very impressive in the *Chaparra* mill, being always among the least economical in Cuba.[2])

Before he gained power, Menocal was respected as an able man, but distrusted for being excessively identified with the U.S. As president he became known as a man more utterly committed to bribery and corruption than even Gómez. He was understood to have possessed $M1 in 1913 when he became president; when he left in 1921 he had perhaps $M40.[3] Menocal was reserved, unlike Gómez, who talked all the time. He was an autocrat without the charm of Gómez; he was corrupt without Gómez's love of life; his desire for wealth was cold and calculating, whereas Gómez's was expansive and generous; and as a result no doubt his wealth was greater in the end, since he worked very hard, both at administration and on his sugar mill.

Menocal began his rule with a promising display of honesty, repudiating Gómez's contracts, such as the Ports Company and another interesting idea which gave rich jobs to 'provincial sanitary inspectors': 'in the majority of cases in the works undertaken by the previous administration a larger amount has been invested in general expenses and personnel than on the works themselves', the new government sententiously pointed out. In 1915 came a number of positive measures: compulsory workers' insurance; an effective monetary system placing the dollar and peso on a par; and provision for state mediation in labour disputes. Although Menocal, following Gómez, permitted the United Fruit Company in 1913 to introduce its labour force of Haitians, he also encouraged white immigration.

[1] Always referred to as Menocal. See above, p. 468, for early career.
[2] See *Anuario Estadístico 1914*, 103.
[3] Chapman's sober estimate, 395.

There were, however, bad signs early on. The new president raised the salary and expenses (covering the 'secret service') of the Ministry of the Interior to $75,000. He followed Gómez's U.S. loan of $M1½ with a request for another of the same sum and then yet another for $M15 – $M10 for the same old work of Gómez's, $M5 for repayment of old debts. The Liberals successfully prevented a vote, but Menocal, by judicious bribes, eventually received authority for $M10. J. P. Morgan lent the sum at 5%, to mature in 1949. The president knew that a foreign loan was the swiftest means to a private fortune. On 4 December 1915 he also exempted the lottery from national accounting, having earlier promised to abolish it: office taught him the truth in that department also. The world war meantime was causing a general rise in sugar profits: in 1914 the harvest brought in $M163; in 1915, $M202; in 1916, $M308 – almost three times more than the prices under Gómez. With the collapse of the European beet production, Cuba was once again the greatest sugar producer in the world, as she had been between 1830 and 1880. War brought back plenty.[4]

In this heady atmosphere an undercurrent of violence remained. The Liberals were much divided. A majority still backed Zayas, but there were sizable minorities behind José Miguel, General Asbert, General Pino Guerra and a small Unionist group headed by General Machado and Colonel Mendieta. Asbert's popularity however waned a little after a desperate brawl in 1913 when he shot dead the Chief of Havana police, General Armando Riva, in broad daylight for trying to close certain gambling dens which he protected: Asbert was suspended for two years but was amnestied and got back to politics by 1917 though he never again could aspire to be José Miguel's nominee for his successor. In November 1913 there was an obscure mulatto rising in Santa Clara: but Zayas and the leading Liberals were kept happy by being enabled to keep their *botellas*; Zayas himself was living well on a salary of $6,000 a year for writing a history of Cuba, together with expenses and the right to go wherever he wished to collect material. This had been Gómez's farewell *douceur*.[5]

In January 1916 Menocal and his friends began work on a campaign for his re-election. Emilio Núñez, old rebel since the 1880s, was for a time Menocal's strongest rival on the Right, although eventually he was persuaded to stand as vice-president. In return he elicited from Menocal a meaningless promise as it transpired, for support in 1921. A number of civil servants were given *ex-officio* seats at the Convention. Even so, votes 'had to be lost', before Menocal won by 92–71.[6] Meantime Zayas was

---

[4] The question of sugar development, 1905–20, is separately considered in the next chapter.
[5] See L. Primelles, *Crónica Cubana*, 2 vols (1955, 7), II, 7.
[6] See Chapman, 348–9.

nominated once more for the Liberals: it was his fifth campaign either as president or vice-president. The so-called Unionist wing of the Liberals – Machado and Mendieta – now rallied to him. Gómez remained outside. The Congress voted a law providing that presidents standing for re-election should stand down during the campaign; Menocal vetoed it. As a result Gómez then joined forces with Zayas, enabling him to receive Zayas's support for certain of his friends looking for congressional posts.

The elections did not come till November but the summer of 1916 was passed in an atmosphere of tumult. Prosperity did not pacify political emotion; it stimulated it. Threats abounded. 'Either Zayas or Revolution', carolled the Liberals. Did Gómez really shoot up the Conservative headquarters in Santa Clara? In August there was shooting almost daily at election meetings. On 17 September Asbert's candidate for the mayoralty of Güines shot his opponent dead. The same month there was a pitched battle at Camajuaní in which twenty-eight men were killed. Fifty people were probably killed before the elections, mostly Conservatives.

The warring groups of Liberals also continued to fight among themselves, and although Asbert came round to Zayas, another group, the Hernández Liberals, went over to the Conservatives. Menocal secured that 'military supervisors' appointed by the government would be able to rig the election in many places. Election day itself, 1 November 1916, was like a huge rodeo with live rounds in all the guns: three Conservative presidents of electoral boards were shot. To the amazement of the Liberals, 800,000 votes were cast, whereas there were less than 500,000 eligible. The elections had in fact been relatively honest, but fraud came when, in the afternoon of 2 November, the earliest results indicated an electoral defeat. Menocal, his wife and daughters were appalled at the prospect of leaving the presidency. A wholesale effort at fraud was set on foot, involving the 'losing' of masses of votes and the invention of innumerable new voting papers. The results were not finally declared until December when Menocal was announced as having won. The Central Electoral Board immediately issued a disclaimer.

This defeat placed the Liberals in a difficult position. They were willing to resist Menocal's fraud by force but they knew that the U.S. minister Gonzales (a North Carolinian of Cuban origin) believed 'any electoral improprieties should be corrected by legal methods'.[7] The general attitude in Washington had always been that Menocal was upright and that Gómez and the Liberals were corrupt. Had not

[7] William Gonzales (1866–1937), served in Cuba in 1898–99; journalist, editor-in-chief of the *State*, Columbia, South Carolina; appointed minister to Cuba by Wilson, 1913.

Menocal been educated in the U.S.? Had he not been manager of the great U.S.-owned *Chaparra* mill? The State Department could not face the fact that where corruption was concerned there was nothing to choose between Menocal and Gómez, Conservative or Liberal. Further, in threatening 'the peace', the Liberals were behaving most inconveniently, at a moment when the United States were moving towards the unknown abyss of a war in Europe.

To the Liberals, the U.S. seemed purblind. This was the second occasion in the fifteen years since General Wood left that the Liberals appeared to have been defrauded of an electoral victory through the action of a Conservative government backed by the U.S. The resulting anxieties were compounded when they saw Menocal and his friends evidently gathering great wealth: the value of the sugar crop would rise even higher in 1917. Even the Supreme Court recommended an appeal that the elections had been falsified. But in January rumours spread that, in the supplementary elections in Santa Clara and Oriente proposed by the Central Electoral Board for mid February, the Conservatives were distributing arms and money.

So a new Liberal revolution was prepared. Lists were made of Liberal supporters in the army. Plans were made to burn cane fields. At the right moment, the conspirators supposed, the plantation owners would demand U.S. intervention, and the recently elected President Wilson would surely decide on enquiry that the Liberals had been cheated of victory.[8] José Miguel Gómez got ready to march on Havana from Santa Clara. Zayas, Asbert, Machado, Ferrara, were all agreed on the desirability of insurrection. Old General Pino Guerra and Costa, the mayor of rapidly growing Marianao, were also in favour, and in arms. On 4 February Orestes Ferrara and Raimundo Cabrera left for the U.S. so as to be ready to exert the right pressure in Washington when the time came. José Miguel left Havana in his yacht *Julito*: on 10 February he landed at Juan Hernández Bay near Tunas de Zaza, on the south coast of Cuba, close to the *Natividad* and *Amazonas* sugar mills. Immediately he raised the standard of revolt. Zayas did the same in Santa Clara, with Machado, Mendieta and other Liberal leaders at his side.[9] Two army commanders, Colonels Quiñones and Rigoberto Fernández, also declared against Menocal, in Camagüey and in Santiago. The same day, Ferrara and Raimundo Cabrera sent a letter to President Wilson asking for intervention to avoid further illegality in the supplementary elections (planned for 14 February in Santa Clara, for 20 February in Oriente); two days later

[8] B. Merino and F. Ibarzabal, *La revolución de febrero; datos para la historia*, 2nd edn (1918), 86.

[9] Cabrera, *Mis Malos Tiempos*, 190–3.

they dispatched a telegram to Menocal from Washington demanding his resignation.

Would the U.S. act? On 12 February, Colonel Fernández in Santiago succeeded in persuading a local U.S. naval commander to do so by preventing the Menocalista fleet from arriving. Wilson and his Secretary of State, Lansing, disavowed this action however.[10] While they were hesitating, Menocal was making his position strong in Havana. He issued a call for volunteers, on the slogan of avoiding intervention, and ordered the blowing-up of the rail bridge at Jatibonico, which divided Camagüey from Santa Clara and which therefore would place a serious barrier in Gómez's scheme to advance on Havana with a united revolutionary force.

On 14 February the U.S. government announced grandly, but ambiguously, that the U.S. only 'gave confidence and support' to constitutional governments and so would oppose governments which came to power unconstitutionally. This was the day that the supplementary elections were to be held in Santa Clara: in the circumstances, the Liberals did not vote, and whether many Conservatives actually went to the polls or not, they certainly received an immense paper majority. Five days of uneasy calm passed, while Gómez wondered whether to advance westwards without his full strength. On 19 February another U.S. Note openly condemned the Liberal revolution, stressed its support for Menocal and stated that it would hold the leaders of the revolt responsible for any damage to property.[11] The U.S. government also sold Menocal 10,000 rifles and 2 million cartridges.[12] In the last week of February it became clear that the U.S. action, or rather inaction, had saved the day for Menocal. On 26 February government troops under Colonel Eduardo Pujol captured Camagüey from the Liberal leader Gustavo Caballero. Various skirmishes followed, by which Menocal eventually crushed the rebellion. On 5 March Menocal solemnly asked Congress for a suspension of constitutional guarantees – having previously bullied or bribed the few Liberal deputies in Havana not to attend: the most intractable individual, Alberto Barreras, governor-elect of Havana, was imprisoned for several days.[13] On 7 March, José Miguel Gómez was captured by Colonel Collazo at Cascaje and sent to gaol at El Príncipe in Havana. But all was not yet lost. On 8 March the temporary Liberal governor of Oriente, García Muñoz, asked Commodore Belknep to land 500 men from U.S. ships off Santiago, as he could not protect the city. And that night

[10] Robert Lansing (1864–1928), Secretary of State, 1915–20; son-in-law of John Foster, Harrison's Secretary of State and uncle of John Foster Dulles and Allen Dulles.

[11] See Cabrera, 154–5; Merino and Ibarzabal, 108–9.

[12] Munro, 492.

[13] Cabrera, 200–5.

500 marines did land, though most either quickly withdrew or went to occupy several other points – Guantánamo, El Cobre and even later on Manzanillo and Nuevitas. The Liberals were not the gainers from this intervention: the U.S. marines simply made it possible for Colonel Miguel Varona to enter Santiago on behalf of the Menocalistas.

U.S. action in 1917 was entirely determined by questions of general diplomacy. For on 6 April she would declare war on Germany. It seemed to the busy president and secretary of State that the Cuban Liberals were acting in the interests only of the Germans. In 1917 rumours of German spies were everywhere. It was also a principal interest of the U.S. that if she were to go to war, Cuba would have to do so too: not, admittedly, that President Wilson contemplated the dispatch of such gallant officers as General Pino Guerra, General Monteagudo or General José Miguel Gómez to the western front. But if the U.S. were at war and Cuba remained neutral, the economic consequences for the U.S. would be serious or, even, intolerable; for, under the terms of international law, Cuba would be obliged to treat Germany and the U.S. as equals. But in 1916 and even more in 1917 Cuba was the main sugar purveyor of the allies. The armies in France marched on stomachs filled from Havana. Hence a Cuban declaration of war was essential. Which president would best toe the line, Menocal or Gómez? From all the North Americans knew of Menocal's solid and impressive work at the *Chaparra*, there was no doubt in their mind that he, rather than the mercurial José Miguel, was their man. With great satisfaction, therefore, they welcomed Menocal's message of 7 April to the Cuban Congress: 'Cuba cannot remain neutral in this supreme conflict for . . . this would be contrary to the essence of the pacts and obligations . . . which bind us to the U.S.'[14]

This commitment enabled the U.S. to look with equanimity on a series of threatening events which suggested that the confusion in Cuba was not going to be easily overcome. On 9 April, the long-postponed elections in Oriente were held and, though Menocal already held an immense if bogus majority everywhere else, he and his minions went again through the dreary farce of faking even that poll so that, as in Santa Clara, more voted than were registered. Ten days later, the Liberal chief in Camagüey, Gustavo Caballero, a senator-elect, was captured by Colonel Pujol: he was sent, wounded, to Havana by train under armed escort. On arrival he was dead. It is almost certain that he had been murdered in the carriage. Thus ended the Revolution

[14] *Boletín Oficial del Secretario de Estado 1917*, 217, qu. Jenks, 194. Among the U.S. advisers responsible for these matters was Secretary of State Lansing's nephew, John Foster Dulles, a young special counsellor for Latin American Division.

known as 'La Chambelona' from the Liberal conga sung during the campaign.[15]

The Liberal revolution had now been destroyed. On 8 May Menocal and Emilio Núñez were formally proclaimed as the new president and vice-president. Immediately after his inauguration on 20 May, Menocal made it plain he was going to keep the extraordinary powers granted to him after the revolution of February: the World War seemed adequate justification. At the same time, Menocal also requested the U.S. to retain troops in Cuba, not only in Oriente but in Camagüey too. So 1,600 marines were established in the former province, 1,000 in the latter. They remained till 1923. Menocal reigned for another four years also, more or less as a dictator, governing largely by decree, drawing huge private profits for himself and his family, while Cuba itself embarked on a drive for unprecedented wealth – 1917 was the year when the great new sugar plantations of Oriente began to bear fruit for the first time, already overtaking Matanzas as the second most productive province after Las Villas. On the other hand, from May 1917 till 1925 at least, remarked one historian,[16] 'it is hard to find anything good to say about anybody or anything in the conduct of the Cuban state'.

The war gave the Menocal regime a curious constitutional and social character. Immediately after the declaration, in April 1917, Cuban exports were placed under a licensing system similar to that prevailing in the U.S. There was even a press censorship and a postal and telegraph censorship, organized by a series of U.S. officers. Other U.S. legislation was copied – such as the Alien Property Act and the Espionage Act. Soon the U.S. Food Administration and War Trade Board, set up by the Lever Act of August 1916, was extended to cover Cuba: the Cuban government was therefore asked to impose a maximum price for sugar, at 4·6 cents per lb. Meantime Herbert Hoover, controller of the Food Board,[17] arranged with his English colleague first that Britain would get Canada to back out of the Cuban sugar market; second, that

---

[15] The song ran:

Ae, ae, ae!	Ae, ae, ae!
Ae La Chambelona!	Ae the lollipop!
Ae, ae, ae!	Ae, ae, ae!
Ae la chambelona!	Ae the lollipop!
El Rey de España mandó un mensaje,	The king of Spain sent a message
El Rey de España mandó un mensaje:	The king of Spain sent a message:
Diciéndole a Menocal	Telling Menocal
Devuélveme mi caballo	Give me back my horse
Que no lo sabes montar.	Which you don't know how to ride.
A pie, A pie, A pie . . .	On foot, on foot, on foot . . .

[16] Chapman.

[17] Herbert Hoover (1874–1964), mining engineer, 1895–1913; U.S. food administrator, 1917–19; chairman, European Relief Council; president of the U.S., 1929–33.

Britain and the U.S. would place their sugar orders with a committee of the Food Board in New York; and third, that that committee would set a price for raw sugar purchases and divide up the Cuban crop among participating nations.[18]

It was of course difficult to get the Cuban producers to agree on a price. 4·6 cents seemed too low, since, though higher than any pre-war average, the 1917 price had reached 5·2 cents, and that of 1916 4·8; also all prices were rising during the war, so that the real value of the price offered could not have been much more than 3·8 cents by the standards of 1914.[19] Meantime, with the question still undecided, President Menocal set what seemed a good example by beginning grinding in his own mill, *Palma*, on the unprecedentedly early date of 16 November – aiming, of course, to put his crop on the market before the price was agreed.[20] On 24 November Hoover angrily asked the State Department to help 'force the Cubans into line',[21] but a month later the Cubans were still complaining – having shifted their attack to criticism of the proposed membership of the committee of five: they argued that it was overheavy with refining interests, being headed by Earl Babst, president of the American Sugar Refining Company.[22] Finally, economic blackmail was used: the U.S. made clear that unless the Cubans accepted a figure of 4·6 cents they would cut off supplies of wheat and coal.[23] Already there was a shortage of flour in Havana. Licences for shipment were specifically delayed. Frankly held up to ransom, the Cubans agreed to sign; those acting in their name were Manuel Rionda, of Cuba Cane, and R. B. Hawley of Cuban-American.[24] This arrogant behaviour was perhaps an inappropriate background to the formulation by Woodrow Wilson of his fourteen points to Congress on 8 January 1918.

The sugar harvest of 1918 was entirely bought by the allies, through a Sugar Equalization Board set up in New York, and in the event they paid 5·5 cents per lb.

Sugar apart, Cuba's part in the First World War was limited. The president's wife did Red Cross work. There were contributions to U.S. 'liberty loans'. A hundred doctors and nurses went to France. There were meatless days. Some talk came of sending troops to France – but only the anthropologist, Fernando Ortiz, was really in favour.

[18] See Foreign Relations, 1917, I, 65.
[19] See Foreign Relations, 1918, I, 347.
[20] Jenks, 199.
[21] Foreign Relations, 1918, 349.
[22] Earl Babst (1870-1967), lawyer and also sometime editor of the *Michigan Farmer*. The other refiners were William A. Jamison and George N. Rolph. (Foreign Relations, 1917, 350-3.)
[23] Foreign Relations, 353-4.
[24] Jenks, 199. See *El Mundo*, 14 January 1918.

The U.S. troops who remained in Cuba after the revolution of 1917 pretended to train Cubans for war. A revealing dispatch of Minister Gonzales to Lansing, 14 July 1917, describes how in order to salve Cuban feelings a plan had been devised whereby Menocal would offer 'training camps' in 'the mild winter climate' 'so useful for battle training for France'. This would 'impress' eastern Cuba with the fact of the presence of U.S. troops.[25] An even more frank statement appears in a letter from Hubert Lakin of the Cuba company: the U.S. intervention was necessary to 'aid in the protection of sugar properties and mining properties and in restoring complete order in Oriente province'.[26] A U.S. officer even took charge of a factory making uniforms for Cuban soldiers.[27]

The U.S. economic blackmail of Cuba in Menocal's day was not confined to sugar. Two questions were outstanding in 1917: the old Ports Company had not yet been compensated for, and the Cuba Railroad had filed a demand for damages of $M25 suffered in the course of the revolution to 1917. Not long after his second inauguration in May 1917, Menocal appealed for a U.S. loan, of $M15. On 13 August 1917, Lansing wrote to the Secretary of the Treasury, McAdoo, explaining that 'Cuba's application for a $M15 loan offers a good opportunity to press[28] Cuba for a favourable settlement of the claims of the Ports Company and the Cuba Railroad ... the loan should not be made till these questions are settled.'[29] On 29 August Lansing's nephew, Foster Dulles, from the Latin American division, reported that Cuba was willing to lend money to the company but that the government did not admit their indebtedness.[30] In fact, Cuba Railroad eventually got only $M3, the Ports Company shareholders were paid, and Menocal got his loan.[31]

After the defeat of the Liberal revolution, Menocal 'unapproachable, dignified, lavish', entered into his own as president and crook, with 'several tricks that even Gómez had not thought of'. There was enormous activity in the department of Public Works, where plans and estimates were made for innumerable imaginary roads and mythical bridges over non-existent rivers. Congressmen were corrupted wholesale by the apportionment of lottery collectorships. Government revenue of course was leaping with sugar prosperity. Fortunes were made everywhere. Several ministers and public officials began businesses of their

[25] NA 837.00/1407, qu. Robert F. Smith, *The U.S. and Cuba, 1917–1960* (1960), 18.
[26] Lakin to Charles Hughes, 29 August 1921, NA 837.00/2155, qu. Smith, 18–19.
[27] *Evening News of Havana*, 25 May 1917, qu. Jenks, 195.
[28] Lansing wrote 'pressure'.
[29] Foreign Relations, 1918, 298.
[30] *Ibid.*, 301, 331.
[31] See Jenks, 125; Smith, 20.

own without abandoning their official positions. Fascinated by the steady rise in incomes, the country became gradually money-mad. In May 1918 Menocal bought General Asbert's palace in Havana province for the State for $M3·75: $100,000 was spent on linen alone for this. $60,000 out of State funds were spent on a heroic picture of Menocal himself winning the battle of Victoria de las Tunas – the scene of Menocal's triumph in 1897.[32] In 1919, after the World War was over, fresh areas for enrichment were opened up by a tourist law enabling bets on *jai-alai*, gambling and horse-racing. There was a vast property boom. Every sugar planter felt that he could afford a house in Vedado or in Marianao, where new developments were being corruptly planned by Liberal businessmen. A vast complex of new U.S. shops and firms was set up, owned by North Americans, managed by Cubans.

The great plunge for wealth continued despite public denunciation. One of the Liberal leaders, Colonel Mendieta, wrote several famous articles in 1919 describing Menocal as having converted 'Cuba into . . . a theatre of caprices, dilapidation, insanity. His work of destruction is almost impossible to repair. He has virtually enthroned the greed for money.'[33] Menocal seemed only able to reply that deposits in banks and saving institutions had increased one thousand per cent since he came to office, while land values had advanced 500%.[34] Yet the Liberals hardly seemed able to offer a real alternative. In September 1917 José Miguel Gómez was allowed to leave prison for his hacienda and in March 1918 an amnesty (perhaps on U.S. insistence) freed all those imprisoned after the 1917 revolt.[35] Nevertheless by early 1919 Alfredo Zayas was once again preparing to break with Gómez; raising political opportunism to a fine art by the middle of the year, he and his friends founded the Popular party – a party ready to jump either way, and in fact ready to come over to Menocal himself, providing Menocal backed Zayas for the elusive presidency. Menocal also skilfully bought off Gervasio Sierra, the leader of the Anarchist trade unionists, who had caused a good deal of trouble in the docks throughout the war, though this did not entirely quieten the Labour movement.

As Menocal's second term reached half-way, the future course of politics became an obsessive question. To avoid further accusations of fraud, he willingly accepted the proposal that General Crowder, the

[32] Told to Chapman by reliable witness, *op. cit.*, 394.

[33] Qu. *ibid.*, 389, 396. Colonel Carlos Mendieta Montefur (1873–1960), colonel in war of independence; House of Representatives, 1901–23; vice-presidential candidate, 1916; 'white hope' of the Republic off and on until president, 1934–6.

[34] *Ibid.*, 397.

[35] It was believed that Wilson insisted 'there was to be no blood' to Pablo Desvernine, Menocal's Foreign Minister.

old legislator of Magoon's time, should return to Cuba to advise on the electoral organization. Crowder, now nationally famous as the father of the U.S. draft, came in March 1919, working on the census and the electoral role all that summer. But by this time the pursuit of wealth at last reached its term and *hubris* overtook the gamblers who were most implicated.

CHAPTER XLV

Sugar, 1906–20

The economic crisis of 1919 which smashed the Menocalian prosperity with greater swiftness than the South Sea Bubble, owed its origin to the curious developments in the sugar industry both before and after the First World War. Apart from the Atlantic Sugar Company of the Gulf (*Cía Azucarera Atlántica del Golfo*) which had moved in during Magoon's time (founding a huge mill, the *Stewart*, not far from Ciego de Avila, in Camagüey, and *Jagüeyal*, nearby), there was no further heavy investment till 1911 when the Cuban American Company, founded just after Wood's departure, established the even larger *central Delicias*, along the north coast of Oriente, next door to *Chaparra*. The same year, the U.S.-owned Cuban Company founded *Jobabo*, also in Oriente. In 1913, along with one smaller Cuban *central* (the only one founded with Cuban money in these years) two new big U.S. mills were set up, one new one by the Atlantic Gulf Company – together with a new Canadian mill. By 1913 U.S. investment in Cuba, mostly in sugar, was reckoned as being worth $M200 or 18% of all U.S. investments in the twenty-two countries of Latin America.[1] The pattern of these investments were of course entirely decided by the health or ill will of the New York Stock Exchange, which had bad times during 1908 and 1909.

Sugar production in Cuba meantime rose steadily, in 1913 exceeding two million tons for the first time. Cuba was then producing 12 % of the total world supply which, if hardly yet equalling the golden days of the 1850s when she produced a quarter of world sugar, was a great advance on 1896–1910. Germany still exceeded Cuba as a producer though not as an exporter. By 1912 the reciprocity treaty with the U.S. had worked: Cuban sugar had driven out all European, West Indian or other unfavoured sugar from the U.S. market; and while previously all Cuban exports had gone to the U.S., she was now seeking other markets such as Britain. There were technological changes too; thus multiple rollers were introduced from the U.S. in 1914, being first used at *Amistad*, which also introduced the first electrically driven mills; once again as in the nineteenth century, however, Cuba was the beneficiary, and not the initiator, of these changes.[2]

---

[1] Winkler, *Investment of U.S. Capital in Latin America*, 275.
[2] Deerr, 546.

It had also by then become clear that the reciprocity treaty had other and odder consequences. The closer Cuba got to satisfying the entire sugar demand of the U.S., the more it had to accept what were in effect world prices, since the world price with the Cuban duty added became the usual New York price. So Cuba, with a preferred market, did not really get a preferred price after all.[3]

This fact was not really appreciated before the First World War, though had it not been for the war there would within a few years have been a Cuban economic crisis, deriving from over-production of sugar. The war delayed the crisis and made it ultimately more desperate. The immediate consequence was that until July 1914 the price of sugar stood at 1·93 cents a pound. In August, it had nearly doubled to 3·66 cents. The main reason was that in 1913 Britain had taken two-thirds of her total sugar from either Germany or Austria-Hungary. In the first year of war Cuba sold 2·6 million tons of raw sugar at an average of 3.31 cents, much of it to the new English Royal Commission set up to buy, sell and regulate sugar distribution – a state trading project which lasted throughout the war.[4] In 1915 meantime it had become clear that the war was destroying or dislocating the European beet fields. The western front lay across the French beet area,[5] and German and Austrian farmers were in the armies. The Allies therefore became increasingly dependent on Cuban sugar while the central powers starved. England took 450,000 tons of sugar from Cuba in 1914–15 and 550,000, 780,000 and 883,000 tons in the succeeding years.[6] The message was plain for North American, Cuban and even Spanish capital. Who did not know that in east Cuba vast forests, cheaply bought, lay on top of rich land, potentially immensely productive?

The last great expansion of Caribbean sugar into virgin land was now undertaken, as a direct consequence of the European war. In 1914, three *centrales* had been founded – two Spanish, one Canadian.[7] In 1915 twelve mills were founded – eight U.S., one Cuban, two Spanish, one Canadian – five in Camagüey, three in Oriente, one in Santa Clara, two even in Pinar del Río. One Cuban mill was *Palma*, in Oriente, the work of President Menocal himself.[8]

These U.S. foundations were large investments. The Punta Alegre Company, founded by old Edwin Atkins's son Robert, with old Atkins (now president also of the American Sugar Refining Company) himself

---

[3] Lockmiller, 21; Philip G. Wright, *The Cuban situation and our treaty relations* (1931), 21.

[4] A. J. P. Taylor, *English History 1914–1945* (1965), 5.

[5] Of 206 factories producing beet in France in 1913–14 only 5% were working in 1918–19 producing 100,000 tons instead of 800,000 (*Estudio*, 445, fn. 1).

[6] Geerligs, 10.

[7] *Borjita* (Canadian), *La Vega* and *Ulacio* (Spanish).

[8] The other enterprise was the creating of a Cuban Food Company headed by the engineer Eduardo Chibás, Luis Fernández Marcané and José Hill.

its president, had three of these mills. But there was a further development. In 1915 the Cuban Cane Sugar Corporation was founded in New York by two men, one born Spanish, one Cuban, both in fact cosmopolitan bankers, Manuel Rionda and Miguel Arango. Rionda was then managing partner in New York of Czarnikow Ltd of London, the largest dealer in European beet and other sugars. His family had reconstructed the *central Tuinicú* in the 1890s, and he himself had already had one success in interesting New York bankers in sugar investment in Cuba: in 1912 he had persuaded a New York bank to found a 70,000 acre estate and mill at Manatí.[9] Cuba Cane formed a syndicate in New York to invest $M50 in Cuban sugar mills and sell securities to that amount in New York.[10] The conclusion reached in Cuba when this news reached there was that the *centrales* must in general be undervalued. In January 1916 Cuba Cane's representatives appeared in Havana to buy mills. They bought straight off fourteen mills at prices ranging from 60% to 100% over their cost before 1914. Among their purchases were the *centrales Conchita* and *Asunción*, gained for $M6 from the director of the National Bank, a Spanish adventurer named 'Poté' Rodríguez. Others in 1916 were *Mercedes, San Ignacio, Agramonte, Jaguayal, Lugareño*. 'Poté' himself had only the year before bought *Conchita* and *Asunción* from Juan Pedro Baró for $M3½.[11] In general the mill management was not changed, and the old owners in some cases continued to run the mills with a salary.[12] Cuba Cane's interest was not the establishment of new mills but the capture and take-over of old ones.

Cuba Cane was the biggest sugar enterprise in the world by 1918. Its directors had prominent positions in New York business,[13] but management remained with Czarnikow and Rionda. Other U.S. firms also bought *centrales*, rather than build them,[14] Milton Hershey[15] bought *San Juan Bautista* (Canasí) in 1916; so did some Cubans, such as the Liberal politician, Machado, who bought *Carmita* (Vueltas), near Santa Clara.[16]

Meantime, all went well for production. In 1916, with 189 mills grinding, three million tons was reached, sold at 4·37 cents per pound.

[9] He also had connections with McCahan Sugar Refining Co. of Philadelphia.
[10] J. W. Seligman's were the main bankers.
[11] Baró, a grandson of the *negrero* of the 1860s, lived then in Paris and came from there grandiosely to sign the contract of sale and returned (Primelles, I, 64).
[12] *Ibid.*, I, 183. See Jenks, 179–80.
[13] For instance, E. W. Stetson, of tobacco and Coca-Cola; Irenée Dupont (of Dupont de Nemours); Matthew Chauncey Brush (of the Boston elevated railroad).
[14] e.g., *Jesús María* was bought from Segundo Botet for $850,000 by a U.S. company in 1915. In the same year Enrique Andino sold *Rendención* (Camagüey) to Rafael Fernández. In 1917 José María Espinoza sold the *central Fé* for $M3 to a U.S. company.
[15] Milton Hershey (1857–1945), began chocolate manufacture, 1893; gave $M60 in 1918 to Hershey Industrial School for orphan boys.
[16] Primelles, I.

The new *centrales* were built at great speed. The forests of eastern Cuba were engulfed. 'I remember in Oriente,' noted Teresa Casuso, daughter of a disgruntled Oriente tobacco farmer:

> ... the great impenetrable forests that were set aflame, whole jungles that were fired and razed to the ground to make way for the sugar cane. My parents were in despair for that most beautiful and fragrant tropical wood – cedar and mahogany and mastic, and magnificent pomegranate – blazing in sacrifice to the frenzy to cover the countryside with sugar cane. In the nights the sight of that flaming horizon affected me with a strange, fearful anxiety and the aroma of burning wood floating down from so far away was like the incense one smells inside churches. But the house we lived in was made entirely of cedar and was like a great perfumed chest.[17]

Cane was sometimes grown around the tree trunks, without any ploughing.[18] *El Mundo* remarked, 'If things go on at this rate we'll be sowing cane in the patios of our houses.'[19]

The war brought prosperity, but also state intervention. This was true of all industries in England, but also of Cuban sugar. Once the U.S. (and Cuba following her) was in the war, an international committee was set up with two English and two U.S. members to supervise the sugar supply to the Allies. By early 1918, this committee fixed the price of raw sugar at 4·6 cents per pound, and undertook to buy the whole of Cuban production at that price. Whether this was fair or not is beside the point: but had there been no fixed price, the price would have risen, perhaps to double that figure. The agreed fixed price was high in relation to the pre-1914 average, but prices, especially of imports, were also high, and the handling of the crop caused difficulties with the settlement of what was due to *colonos*.[20]

In the increase since 1907 Oriente had seen the biggest surge forward.[21] The largest mill by far, *Delicias* (Puerto Padre), was grinding 100,000 tons in 1919 from well over a million tons of cane. After that came *Chaparra, Manatí, Boston, Santa Lucía, Jobabo,* and *Preston.* Of these, *Delicias, Manatí* and *Jobabo* had not been in existence in 1907. Altogether twenty-one new mills were constructed in the period 1907–19.

[17] Teresa Casuso, *Cuba and Castro*, trans. E. Grossberg (1961), 92.
[18] Jenks's comment.
[19] 30 April 1916, qu. Primelles, I, 182.
[20] In the 1919 harvest, 2,203,630 acres were planted with cane. 36,800,629 tons of cane were milled, and from this 4,104,205 tons of sugar only, or 27·4%, were milled in Cuban-owned mills; 51·4% came from U.S. mills, 13·9% from Spanish, and 2% from British. Production of molasses and rum was also high. The total value reached $536,851,717. 3,944,860 tons of raw sugar were exported, including 9,593 of refined.
[21] See tabulation of Oriente mills, Census of 1919, 959.

A major problem now was labour. Some effort was made to supplement labour demands in Cuba by increased settlement of farmers from Spain. This was only a partial success since, though Spaniards continued to flock to Cuba, they generally did not desire to be farmers but to earn immediate high wages in cities; they did not often get further than Havana. The sugar managers of Oriente had to turn to the rest of the West Indies. Already in 1912 the United Fruit Company had been allowed to import 1,400 Haitians. During the war Haiti and Jamaica provided thousands of Negroes, and the old source, China, was also tapped. 27,000 Haitians came in between 1914 and 1918, and nearly 23,000 Jamaicans.[22] In 1919 alone, almost 24,000 Jamaicans arrived, along with 10,000 Haitians.[23] In the same period, also, nearly 30,000 Spaniards came each year, though this was no change – if anything a little less than during the previous ten years.

There is a sense therefore in which this great leap forward in Cuban sugar – made possible in the first instance because of the melancholy follies of Europe – was carried on not only by foreign mills, capital and management, but also by foreign labour. Even those capitalists who were Cuban in origin, such as Rionda, became increasingly North American in outlook and sensitivity. Cuba was thus a spectator in the transformation of her own destiny. The great forests of Oriente did not burn for her own carnival.

Colonos became almost as rich as mill-owners. Receiving eight pounds of cane for every hundred pounds which they delivered,[24] more arrived than ever before. Many successfully cleared their debts to the mills – though as often running into even greater obligations through receiving advances to plant a larger crop next year. Some *colonos* even bought mills themselves.[25] Others invested their profits in handsome mansions in Havana, dispatching their large families to Rome, Paris and London, and themselves purchasing lavish cars. They and their families returned to attempt to recreate in the Vedado the architecture of the Italian Renaissance, laced by the style of Louis XVI, or even Florentine Gothic; towers, miradors, minarets, replaced flat roofs – the Villa Medici everywhere, bankers of the new world pursuing the idiosyncrasies of their predecessors. The Vedado became a very metropolis of marble palaces, while a sumptuous new suburb, Miramar, with houses with large gardens, sprang up across the Almendares river, facing the ocean, being financed by Ramón Mendoza and José ('Poté') López. Further still, even grander houses were built round the Country Club, now accessible because of the arrival of the motor car, itself available

[22] Both years inclusive Census of 1919, 173, 176.
[23] *Loc. cit.*
[24] This odd rent system is explained on p. 276, above.
[25] So Jenks says, p. 222.

to richer bankers. Consumption of cigars rose to 118 a year per man, woman and child. In early 1919 U.S. tourists returned. At the same time a continuing influx of Spaniards came to Cuba escaping from their own invertebrate social structure, bringing besides their skills various convictions about the power of organized labour.[26]

The great boom intensified an already existing trend: companies involved in one stage of sugar production sought to gain control of the remaining stages. Great combinations of distributors tried to guarantee their own supplies. Czarnikow-Rionda in 1920 gained control of W. J. McCahan of Philadelphia; Atkins captured the Philadelphia Sugar Refinery. Industrial consumers of sugar already in the market also tried to control it; the Coca-Cola Company made plans to buy raw sugar direct from Cuba; the Charles Hires Company, manufacturers of the famous root beer, bought the old *central Dos Rosas* of Cardenas; Hershey's, the chocolate kings, bought not only a sugar mill, but the Havana-Matanzas electric railway which carried its high salaried executives there.[27] Some fifty mills changed hands altogether, at the height of the boom.

It is a little difficult to know exactly how many mills at this time were Cuban, how many U.S., since nominal ownership meant little; many mills had partially Cuban, partially U.S. capital: many of the so-called Cubans were often more North American than Cuban, and sometimes *vice versa*. The National City Bank estimated that in 1919 between 40% and 50% of the mills were North American; *The Times* of Cuba thought that the figure was nearer 35% (71 out of a total of 209), but that they produced over 50% of the sugar. There was equal confusion among Spanish and Cuban ownership since, while most North American mills were owned by large joint stock companies with shares diversely owned, most Spanish ones were still owned by single families in the nineteenth-century style. The same was true of French mills, and some Cuban ones. Many of the Spanish owners had in fact lived in Cuba for many years, even a generation or two, and were possibly more Cuban than Spanish; more Cuban perhaps, in some sense, than some, particularly some New York, Cubans. A 'Spaniard' such as Manuel Rionda broke all generalizations. Over all, at least half the Cuban sugar production in 1919-20 was probably controlled by North Americans and the actual ownership was spread among a large number of stockholders. In 1919 the North American company Cuban Cane, itself owned mills which produced 16·7% of the sugar made in Cuba.[28]

In the short run, of course, these important foreign investments had

[26] See below, p. 575.
[27] Chapman, 14; South, 30.
[28] See discussion in *Estudio*, 448.

revolutionary consequences, on society and the standard of living. Most of the big *centrales* were established in areas previously deserted or which had had a small population, and so they fomented new towns out of what were previously hamlets, creating work and to some extent centres of culture and education. The new *centrales* probably made possible a higher standard of living than in other industries. These investments by U.S. companies and citizens seemed also to be reinforcing Cuba's position *vis-à-vis* her major market, the U.S., although this connection was noticeably unimportant when it came to the point of negotiations for favourable duties.

But the longer Cuba remained the major world sugar producer, the more she was to be ultimately at the mercy of the winds of world demand. The U.S. profit-seekers did not create the problem; they confirmed it. Furthermore, though they created much work for Cubans, the big *centrales* of East Cuba came in this golden period to rely very much on the cheap labour from Haiti or Jamaica. These immigrant masses created their own problems.

1918 and 1919 saw enthusiasm still at its height. In 1919 'Poté' declared that his mill, *España*, would soon produce a million sacks.[29] President Menocal bought all the outstanding shares in the *central Palma*. *Central Pilar* was sold for $900,000 by Fermín Goicoechea to Pedro Laborde.[30] Although the First World War was now over, the European sugar beet fields were still at a low ebb. In 1919-20 they produced barely $2\frac{1}{2}$ million tons in place of 8 million in 1913-14. Of the sugar beet producers of the old world, Russia was still dislocated, Austria-Hungary disastrously split up, with few of the successor states having access to the sea, while Germany remained short of labour and capital. World demand for sugar was evidently high. Believing that here was one of their chances of making a really giant profit, the Cuban sugar producers, U.S. and Cuban, Spanish and Canadian, began to demand an end to the control of prices. Other wartime practices were abandoned: why not sugar control? The Sugar Equalization Board was undecided. The decision was sent up to President Wilson in July 1919, but the president had many preoccupations and a decision was slow to come. In August, therefore, an association of sugar growers was formed to campaign for the end of price control.

The pressure of this powerful lobby eventually told. The Sugar Equalization Board informed U.S. refiners that they were free to buy raw sugar in 1920 at whatever price they could. Attorney General Palmer on 8 November announced in Louisiana (still struggling to recapture her pre-1861 eminence) that sugar could be sold at 7

[29] Primelles, I, 471.
[30] *Ibid.*, 473-4.

cents. In 1919 indeed the average price of sugar was 6·65 cents per pound.

1920 was the grand climacteric in the history of Cuban sugar, and a landmark in the history of capitalism. The sugar harvest began at the usual date, but by 18 February the world price of sugar had already risen to $9\frac{1}{8}$ cents. This was well above any previous price ever obtained. Previously in Cuba it had been assumed that $5\frac{1}{2}$ cents was enough to 'stimulate the island to extreme prosperity'. At this point a mania set in. The rest of 1920 was passed, day by day, in a dream-like atmosphere more reminiscent of a film comedy than real life. Up, up, up, went the prices. On 2 March, sugar sold at 10 cents; on 18 March, at 11 cents; on 27 March, at 12 cents; on 8 April at $15\frac{1}{2}$ cents, and on 15 April, at 18 cents.

The 'dance of the millions' continued. On 12 May sugar stood at 19 cents. On 14 May it rose to $20\frac{1}{2}$ cents, on 17 May to $21\frac{1}{2}$ cents, on 18 May to 22 cents, and on 19 May 1920 to $22\frac{1}{2}$ cents.

CHAPTER XLVI

The Dance of the Millions

In fact there was plenty of sugar in the world in 1920. Europe was recovering. Prices in Cuba soon dropped. By the end of June sugar sold at a mere $17\frac{1}{4}$ cents, by the end of July at $15\frac{1}{4}$ cents, and by late August at 11 cents. In September it had dropped to 8 cents. By late November, sugar sold at only $4\frac{3}{4}$ cents and by Christmas the price stood at $3\frac{3}{4}$ cents. The sugar surplus in Cuba had been calculated in June as 460,000 tons, worth $M230; in September 335,000 tons were left, worth only $M75.[1]

Of course many people had made money: the average selling price during the year was 11·35 cents, nearly double any previous or future year's price. The 1920 harvest had been $3\frac{3}{4}$ million tons, higher than any other except 1919. The total value of the harvest, therefore, was about $M1,000. Even the closing price of $3\frac{3}{4}$ cents a pound was higher than any price reached between 1885 and 1915. 180,000 tons of sugar had been sold to the U.S. at as high as 19·38 cents.[2] But this extreme volatility of price, as usual, brought ruin in its trail, though primarily to owners of mills, not to *colonos*. Further, the great price rise had occurred during the harvest; the *colonos* were paid every five years. So the mid-1920 settlement gave them very considerable income. The workers did quite well also and were not much immediately affected by the crash.

The first sign of disaster for the mill owners came in July when the euphoria was only just below its peak. Firms which had ordered goods two months before when prices were at their height refused to accept them. The congestion at Havana docks was such that a U.S. commission had to be sent to enquire into its causes. In August Cuban sugar producers sought unsuccessfully to hold back their sugar and restrain the fall of prices. By September the banks were facing a crisis, due to over-commitment when prices were high. They delayed, however, any mutual action between them until it was late, in the interests of ruining their rivals. On 6 October the Banco Mercantil Americano gave borrowers a few hours only to clear off their debts. The same day there was a run on the Banco Español: big depositors withdrew their accounts. On 8 October there came a run on the Banco Internacional: it closed on 9 October, and on that day bankers, at last acting together,

---

[1] J. W. Connor, *Bankers' Magazine*, October 1920, qu. *Estudio*, 460.
[2] *Anuario Azucarero de Cuba* (1959), 93.

asked President Menocal to declare a general moratorium. This was done on 10 October, to last till 1 December, and extended thereafter to 1 February.

The question now was: could the banks be saved? In 1920 the dominant bank in Cuba was the Banco Nacional. This was not merely an institution to guarantee the currency; it had 130 branches throughout Cuba.[3] At the end of June 1920 its deposits were reckoned at \$M194.[4] It had been founded by U.S. capital after the Spanish-American war, being, in its first incarnation, the North American Trust Company.[5] In 1901 it had been reorganized as the Banco Nacional. Shares were issued, fairly widely, some bought in Cuba, some in the U.S. – some by J. P. Morgan. The president was at first E. Granghan, son-in-law of old Jarvis. The vice-president was an amiable English West Indian banker, W. Merchant, a self-made man and ex-railway telegrapher who from 1905 had been responsible for making loans on sugar collateral.[6] The bank was established in a fine sober building built by the Cuban architect Toraya, one of the few semi-classical buildings of Havana's Catalan period. After 1911, the situation of this respectable institution radically changed: the Gallego, José López Rodríguez (Poté), secured from it – through Merchant's connivance – a large overdraft which sometimes reached \$M5.[7] With this, he proceeded to buy the bank itself, starting off with the Morgan shares, and moving on to a majority holding of the other shares. Poté was a pioneer among developers of the Miramar suburb. In 1913 Poté's friend, Merchant, succeeded as head of the bank, despite marital unorthodoxies which caused him to be regarded askance by the American colony. The economic historian, Jenks, describes Merchant:

> He was a big, broad-shouldered, deep-chested man, warm and hearty, with a fluent command of Spanish. He was *simpático*. His avowed policy of friendliness to the sugar planters made him a figure of national importance. His reception at provincial towns rivalled that of President Menocal ... Merchant's arm round his shoulder satisfied many a struggling branch manager better than a rise in salary.

Merchant trained young Cubans in banking methods, and under his Caribbean temperament the bank began to lose its North American

[3] Census of 1919, 221–2.
[4] *Loc. cit.*
[5] Its inspirers had been Samuel Jarvis (1853–1913) and R. R. Conklin (1858–1938), previously in the Missouri valley. Conklin was also president of the Júcaro and Morón railway and of the Havana Telephone Co. as well as being vice-president of the Central Cuba Sugar Co.
[6] This was the year of the Ports scandal (Cabrera, *El Libro de Cuba*, 1925).
[7] Jenks, 210.

character, though two U.S. directors remained on the board – Andrew Preston of United Fruit and L. E. Bronson of Purdy and Henderson.[8] Poté, meantime, as controlling shareholder, was able to increase his overdraft by geometric progression: it rose to $M25, unsecured. This gave him enough cash to buy several mills, and to plunge into much other speculation.

There were other banks in Cuba in 1920, though none so important. Some dated from the colonial epoch, such as the Banco Español, with fifty-five branches and deposits of $M112. Some merchants of the old style hung over from the pre-banking era such as the Zaldos, the German cigar makers the Upmanns, or the Gelats. The Zaldo interest became merged in the Banco de la Habana, of which Carlos Zaldo became president: Upmanns' joined Speyer's of New York, London and Frankfurt. Several foreign banks got their foot in the door during Wood's day: the Royal Bank of Canada, emerging with Chicago capital from the parochiality of Merchant's Bank of Nova Scotia, absorbed the old Spanish Banco de Comercio in Havana and set up forty-six branches in Cuba as in the rest of the Caribbean. In 1905 the Trust Company of Cuba was set up, and after 1912 (when Poté bought J. P. Morgan out of the National Bank), it became Morgan's leading representative. The National City Bank expanded during 1914–18, having earlier controlled Zaldo's Banco de la Habana. Later still the Banco Internacional de Cuba was organized by a group of Cuban bank clerks, developing 104 branches and deposits of $M30 in a very short time.[9]

All these banks, Cuban and U.S., had encouraged Cuban planters and farmers to borrow indiscriminately for five years before 1920. Bank managers had appeared during the golden days of wartime expansion of wealth as salesmen – and competitive salesmen too.[10] In late 1920 there were understood to be $M80 loans outstanding made on the price of sugar at 15 cents to 20 cents per pound.[11]

From 1915 a new Cuban monetary system based on the peso was introduced, identical with the dollar, but still both Cuban and U.S. money was current,[12] and workers still far preferred the latter.

The first move to save the banks of Cuba was a proposal by a group of New York banks to make a $M100 loan to the Cuban government. But President Menocal announced that Cuba had no intention of saving the banks from the consequences of their own folly: the president was in fact at that time passing through anxieties involved in the election

[8] Andrew Preston (1846–1924) was president of the United Fruit Company from its foundation.
[9] Ibid.
[10] Jenks, 213.
[11] Ibid., 214.
[12] Census of 1919, 220–1.

of his own candidate, his ex-rival, Alfredo Zayas, as the next president, and was in no mood to help Poté or Merchant.[13] But after the election the Cubans did approach J. P. Morgan for a loan. Morgan agreed to lend \$M50 with the qualification that a committee of New York bankers should manage it. The State department in its turn proposed that financial reform should accompany the negotiations for the loan and suggested a former Assistant Secretary of the Treasury, Albert Rathbone, as 'financial adviser' to the Cuban government.[14] Rathbone's appointment was indeed suddenly announced on 30 November. The Cuban Secretary of the Treasury, Cancio, complained angrily that he had not been consulted, and very properly resigned.[15]

Rathbone set a bad example. He arrived in early December, sat down at Cancio's desk, stayed two weeks, gave orders, wrote a memorandum recommending that a foreign loan should be sought specifically to save the Havana banks and left for New York, whence he sent the Cuban government a bill for his services for \$50,000. He was paid \$15,000.[16]

Meantime the elections of 1 November had resulted in the victory of Menocal's candidate, Zayas, over ex-president José Miguel Gómez, '*Tiburón*', but there was no reason to believe that they were fairly conducted. The government had said that in 112 municipalities there were 73 'military advisers' – that is, thugs instructed to follow the regime's line. Many older officers refused to act in this way, but lesser officers and sergeants were easily come by. In many places, the start of the poll was delayed or the poll was closed early. There were instances, clearly documented, of sergeants burning the votes when a Liberal victory was indicated. In Santa Clara, fourteen people were killed. In several places the electoral fraud was, as in 1916, such that the total votes cast were greater than the total on the register. In some places where it was known that Gómez had had enrolment of 80 votes over Zayas, the booth never opened.[17] In the end, Zayas was declared the winner but again, as in 1905, under fair conditions Gómez would probably have won.[18]

Gómez, of course, like all other Cuban politicians, was acutely concerned in the sugar crisis. In the course of 1920, sugar refining had been revived, and he and Orestes Ferrara had inspired a grand new

[13] See below, p. 549.

[14] NA 837.51/362; *ibid.*, 367, qu. Smith, 86, 209.

[15] *La Prensa*, 30 November 1920. Leopoldo Cancio (1851–1927), Autonomist in 1878, deputy in Cortes 1879, Secretary of Treasury under Wood, Professor of Economics.

[16] *Gaceta Oficial*, 31 January 1921, qu. Jenks, 334, 233.

[17] See Chapman, 403–6, who adds that 335 criminals, including 44 murderers, had been amnested in the six months before the poll – for use as gunmen.

[18] Zayas scorned the support in this campaign of a miniscule Partido Socialista Radical, founded in 1920, whose leaders Arévalo and Fabregat had afterwards offered themselves to Gómez.

refinery. Gómez's running mate, the vice-presidential candidate, was Miguel Arango, vice-president of Cuba Cane, and therefore intricately involved in the whole Czarnikow-Rionda interests. Neither of them was disposed to accept this election fraud without protest. The Liberal party launched a whole series of demands for an enquiry. On 7 November they even suggested a U.S. provisional intervention to supervise new elections.

This situation began to force the hand of the administration in Washington. The U.S. minister, Boaz Long, had reported Menocal's views in October that intervention would bring wholesale attacks on U.S. property.[19] On 19 September Long had, however, requested that the marines still stationed in Camagüey should be increased to 500 men, explaining that the request derived from the need to protect U.S. sugar interests in the east: 'He assured Washington that partisans of both sides in Cuba had announced that if disturbances or revolution were to come, U.S. interests would be the first to be destroyed.'[20] But earlier still, Boaz Long's second-in-command, Francis White, had specifically told Menocal's government that the U.S. regarded it as a duty to 'observe the manner in which the precepts of the electoral law are complied with . . . it is bound by treaty to maintain government in Cuba which is adequate for the protection of lives and property'.[21]

The U.S. position hardened while the electoral protests showed no signs of dying down and while no one showed any signs of being able to solve the bank crisis. On 4 January 1921 Norman Davis, still Wilson's under-secretary in the Treasury, but still with financial interests in Cuba, acutely affected by the course of policy which he was recommending, sharply told Boaz Long to 'take immediate and forceful steps' to end Cuban press attacks on the National City Bank and the Royal Bank of Canada – the two major foreign banks then still financially reputable.[22] But by then Lansing had already decided to send back Crowder to Cuba, without apparently any consultation: this was, as Crowder's biographer notes, an 'intervention in fact if not in name'.[23] Crowder arrived in Havana on the battleship *Minnesota* on 6 January 1921.

Crowder at this time was being spoken of as a possible Secretary of War for the new president, the unsatisfactory Warren G. Harding. He was also contemplating retirement. He had recently opposed his old commander General Wood's nomination for the U.S. presidency on the ground that Wood was ignorant of constitutional government; he was a

[19] Foreign Relations, 1920, II, 24.
[20] Ibid., 22–3.
[21] Qu. Jenks, 235–6.
[22] Foreign Relations 1921, I, 773.
[23] Lockmiller, 229.

storm centre, if 'a great sanitary engineer'.[24] But in Havana Crowder hardly conducted himself like a parliamentarian. He kept his head-quarters on the *Minnesota*, issuing recommendations to Menocal which were 'in effect orders'.[25] There should be a further extension of the moratorium on debts, with a provision for gradual payments over six months: 15 May would be the closing day for paying merchants, 15 June for banks. Elections in a fifth of the electoral districts would be annulled, and new elections would be held there in March: unless this question was settled, 'intervention' would be 'difficult, if not impossible, to avoid'.[26] R. B. Hawley and Manuel Rionda, the bosses of Cuban American and Cuba Cane respectively, came down from New York to try to revivify the sugar market.[27] On 26 February Menocal, Zayas and Gómez, the three most powerful individuals in Cuban politics, were prevailed on to meet with Crowder. Menocal agreed not to have military advisers in March's little election.[28] A new board took over from Merchant at the Banco Nacional, headed by the honourable figure of Porfirio Franca, previously manager of the National City Bank; and on 1 March 1921 a new future Proconsul delivered himself in the State Department, Washington, of his memorandum, the first of many, on Cuban affairs: young Sumner Welles drew up a list of the six most desirable characteristics for a Cuban president to have, to be intimated to Zayas or Gómez, whoever should win in March. The first and sixth were: 'His thorough acquaintance with the desires of this [the U.S.] government . . . [and] his amenability to suggestion of advice which might be made to him by the American legation.'[29]

Was all going well? It was not. On 9 March firing broke out again between Liberals and Conservatives, and the Liberals accordingly refused to go to the polls on 15 March. Zayas therefore won, but Gómez and the Liberals were not totally estranged. Crowder had not solved the constitutional question, nor the financial one. A new bank board did not create new money. On 28 March, Poté Rodríguez was either murdered or killed himself: he was found hanging from the balcony of his flat. On 9 April the Banco Nacional closed its doors, admitting liabilities of $M67·66, with a mere $M1½ cash in hand. The leading sugar speculator, José Lezama, declared himself bankrupt – being in deficit of $M24. A warrant was issued for his arrest for forgery,

---

[24] Crowder to Governor Frank Lowden (Wood's leading opponent at the first ballot of the Chicago convention, 1920) qu. Lockmiller, 226.

[25] Lockmiller's phrase, 231.

[26] Foreign Relations, 1921, I, 674.

[27] Jenks, 242.

[28] Chapman, 408.

[29] NA 837·00 (2216), qu. Smith 87. Sumner Welles (1892–1962), Secretary of Embassy, Tokyo, 1915–17, Buenos Aires, 1917–19, afterwards Under Secretary of State, plays a great part in this history. See Book VI.

but he, with ex-president Merchant of the Banco Nacional, and José Mariman, fled abroad. Banks collapsed all over Cuba, eighteen of them by the end of June, with a total indebtedness of $M130. The only credit-worthy institutions were foreign – the National City Bank and the Royal Bank of Canada, specially protected, as Boaz Long had demanded in January, by an instruction from Menocal on 13 April to the Cuban press not to 'annoy the banks'.[30] These two banks met their obligations and lived on, greatly profiting as a result. Crowder, with no permanent status, was master of political power in Havana.

This did not mean, however, that the U.S. had now decided on a co-ordinated and enlightened policy for Cuba. On the contrary, they chose in April 1921 to impose a new emergency tariff, affecting Cuban sugar, of just over one cent per pound. This did not cover the U.S. island dependencies of the Philippines, Hawaii and Puerto Rico, and there, after 1921, production was stimulated to Cuba's disadvantage.

Crowder had come, of course, for military reasons. But his old friend and collaborator under Magoon, Frank Steinhart, still general manager of Havana Electric, still 'no friend of scuttle', wrote on 28 April to the new Secretary of State, Charles Hughes, that it was absolutely necessary for Crowder to stay, 'for the financial betterment and stabilisation of commercial conditions in Cuba'.[31] President-elect Zayas took the situation admittedly in his stride, nervous, no doubt, about the con-tinuance of political trouble from the Liberals: his secretary was mur-dered in May. He wrote to *Heraldo de Cuba* saying he would be happy to 'use' Crowder, just as Menocal had.[32] Crowder replied that in addition to everything else all the scandals associated with public works would have to be cleared up before Cuba got a loan.[33] Once inaugurated, Zayas gave Congress a message inspired by Crowder: a cut in the budget, a new electoral code, presidents to be elected for one term only, a central highway to be built, secretaries of government departments liable to be summoned to appear before Congress as occurred in the U.S.[34] Very soon, therefore, in June, there were new discussions between J. P. Morgan and the State Department on the subject of a loan – even though Zayas spoiled the good impression by curious behaviour over his own expenses: when Zayas came to power he found unpaid hundreds of bills for food and drink consumed by Menocal at the palace. One bill was for $800 for a month's supply of eggs. There was another for $20,000 for 'pheasants and roses'. To settle these, Zayas demanded an increase of $180,000 or over 50%, for his

[30] Foreign Relations, 1921, I, 793.
[31] NA 837.00 (2102), qu. Smith, 87.
[32] *Heraldo de Cuba*, 13 May 1921, qu. Chapman, 423.
[33] *Ibid.*, 425.
[34] *Ibid.*, 453.

executive expenses per year. When Congress demurred, Zayas hinted that he would sack all the palace servants and close the palace. Eventually Zayas merely ordered the Treasury to pay him what he wanted, and it did. José Miguel Gómez, who had gone to Washington to complain to President Harding, died in New York on 13 June, removing Zayas's most serious political opponent. On 3 July Crowder suggested to Washington that a loan should be made, though with conditions that the U.S. should be able to inspect the annual budget and that any additional credits be cleared with the U.S. too.[35]

The subject was discussed between Sumner Welles, Norman Davis and J. P. Morgan's representatives on 28 July.[36] But nothing had been decided before an ugly little incident occurred on the Cuba Railroad. In July Secretary of State Hughes had ordered the navy to keep the marines at Camagüey because of Crowder's reports of labour agitation on the railway,[37] and in August two men who had been sacked for striking, physically attacked the (American) assistant general manager. The marines stepped in and forced their way into the house of the assailants.[38] The president of the Cuba Company wrote to Secretary of State Hughes that the marines 'have been of very material assistance to us at various times and their presence there has saved us from much more trouble ... That section of Cuba,' he added expansively, 'is a hotbed of Bolshevism. The Bolshevists are inclined to destroy property. The presence of the marines has prevented them.'[39] No one suggested removing the marines. Zayas had not declared his hand on that score. Anxious above all to secure a loan, in the interests of an appearance of sound finance, he decreed the annulment of several of Menocal's contracts and allowed the U.S. military attaché, Lyman, to investigate the legality of others. He discovered, needless to say, a far greater commitment than had been authorized.[40]

It remained to reach some sort of agreement on the sugar question. The 1921 sugar crop was disposed of for a total of $M273, or a smaller sum than any year since 1915, even though the quantity was greater than any year except 1919. In the course of the year the National City Bank had taken over direction of nearly sixty sugar mills, due to bankruptcy of the old owners.[41] The bank crash, interestingly enough, had not dissuaded further investment in Cuba: in 1921 six new mills, including the huge *Vertientes*, ground cane for the first time. Senator

[35] Foreign Relations, 1921, 362.
[36] *Ibid.*, I, 711.
[37] NA 837.00/2140, qu. Smith, 165.
[38] NA 837.00/2155, qu. Smith, 106.
[39] NA 837.00/2155, qu. Smith, 105. The question whether 'Bolshevists' was an accurate description is explored on p. 575.
[40] Chapman, 420.
[41] Jenks, 285.

Smoot on the other hand was urging Crowder to ensure the limitation of the Cuban crop to 2½ million tons. Meantime U.S. sugar users and sugar makers continued to oppose the tariff of the previous April, forming a powerful committee to co-ordinate action.[42] Early in 1922 hearings began in the Senate: the Cuban cause – that of the reduction of the tariff – ironically, was put by old Edwin Atkins, with Edwin Shattuck, lawyer for the American producers of Cuban sugar. Horatio Rubens, Martí's lawyer, the author of the Teller amendment and now president of Consolidated Railways of Cuba, president and chairman of the board of the Cuban Railroad, director of the Cuba Company, and chairman of the board of Cuba Railways Company and having received from Habaneros the title of 'adopted son of Havana', represented the American committee just described. Their arguments were twofold. First, the tariff would provoke political disturbances and so risk not merely sugar but all North American property in Cuba; second, U.S. exports would be severely affected by the inevitable Cuban counter moves against the tariff. The matter hung fire, but meantime several large U.S.-owned sugar producers in Cuba (United Fruit, Cuban-American, American Sugar Refining, and B. H. Howell) formed themselves into an 'Export Sugar Company' in December 1921, which would buy 500,000 tons of unsold Cuban sugar, refine it and ship it to Europe. The refineries would get a toll of 90 cents per 100 pounds of sugar. Horace Havemeyer, son of Henry Osborne Havemeyer, himself controlling 73% of the U.S. beet sugar production, as well as extensive Cuban holdings, began negotiations with the beet sugar industry, but Senator Smoot then re-entered the controversy and said he would back a 1·4 cent tariff if Cuba cut her production to 2½ million tons. The Export Sugar Company refused and the tariff (Fordney-McCumber tariff of September 1922) was therefore fixed at 1·765 cents. The Export Sugar Company then put the Cuban surplus on to the market in New York, the price of sugar dropped (the average price in 1922 was 2·80 cents, the lowest since before the war), and Smoot went off with the curious belief that Cuba had concocted a Wall Street plot to ruin the beet men.[43]

By now the sugar crop of 1921 was clearly approaching four million tons, a little more than 1920 had produced. Nothing had been done about a loan, or about the banks. Worse, in April, by a curious ineptitude in timing, the U.S. general tariff had been raised from 1·0048 cents to 1·60 cents – so virtually rendering irrelevant a minor improvement in prices of sugar. Of course, the U.S. sugar lobby (headed by Atkins and the Warner Sugar Refinery) had opposed this, Atkins telling the

[42] Represented were: Westinghouse Electric (of which Atkins was president); the Belmont-White Coal Mining Company; the American Trading Co; Coca-Cola; American Iron and Foundry Company; and Baldwin Locomotive.
[43] Smith, 48.

House of Representatives that the Cuban revolution of 1895 had been caused by a rise in the sugar tariff. But this was to no avail. A Cuban sugar delegation went off to Washington in midsummer to try to secure more favourable treatment. It discovered that the men concerned on Capitol Hill were all acutely conscious, at the very least, of the importance of U.S. beet interests: both Senator Smoot, chairman of the Senate Finance Committee, and Representative Joseph Fordney, chairman of the Home Ways and Means Committee, came from the beet areas of Utah and Michigan. The Secretary of Commerce, Hoover, airily suggested to the Cubans that they should reach some agreement with the beet men, who were then proposing that Cuba should limit her production to 2½ million tons the next year, and Fordney was actually demanding a tariff of 2·50 cents.

By September 1921 Cuba had large stocks of unsold sugar lying in her warehouses. Nearly all mill owners, even those whose fathers had successfully weathered the alarms of war in the nineteenth century, could not now continue. The National City Bank and the Chase National Bank received the titles of many mills in return for settlement of debts. Workers who had come to Havana in the good times streamed back to Spain. Schoolteachers, postmasters, all civil servants, remained without pay for weeks, as government reserves, always dependent on taxes on sugar sales, rapidly dropped.[44] Crowder meanwhile watched impassively from the battleship *Minnesota* in Havana harbour.[45]

Only now, when the heart of Cuba had fallen out, was the U.S. Government prepared to act. On 24 September Secretary of State Hughes told Crowder that the bankers were ready for a short-term loan of $M5 'if it were the first step in constructive (financial) reform'.[46] Under-Secretary Norman Davis and the most humane and intelligent of the men at J. P. Morgan's, Dwight Morrow, went to Havana. Zayas promised to cut the budget. Morgan's agreed to lend $M5, as the first part of a much bigger loan of $M50.[47] Though Hughes said he was satisfied with Zayas's promises, Crowder was not.[48] The loan was delayed. Hoover urged its immediate acceptance,[49] and the matter was resolved in January. The same month, despite renewed protests by

[44] Jenks, 250–2.
[45] Lockmiller is curiously silent on this section of Crowder's life.
[46] Foreign Relations 1921, I, 733.
[47] See NA 837.51/624, and Smith, 210, fn 37; Foreign Relations 1921, I, 759.
[48] Foreign Relations 1921, I, 757, 656.
[49] Maybe he had seen a memorandum by the U.S. Commercial Attaché in Havana, Chester Lloyd Jones (10 November): 'Capital investment should be encouraged when it will, through the business connections established, help to increase the market for American goods in Cuba. Capital investment should be encouraged in Cuba to a greater extent than in any other foreign countries; because of the political arrangements existing between the two republics and through the proximity of the island to the U.S. it is easier to guarantee the rights of the investors than is the case in other countries.' (MS. qu. Smith, 82.)

the fearful but impetuous railway king, Herbert Lakin, the marines were finally withdrawn from Camagüey.[50]

Crowder was still in Cuba. In the course of the first half of 1922 he sent Zayas a whole series of memoranda making recommendations for reform in nearly every aspect of Cuban life: electoral reform, grafts, auditing, the lottery, commercial and financial reform. The first of these memoranda, based on much careful research by officials of the Embassy, was dispatched on 24 February 1922, the fifteenth and last on 15 August.[51] Crowder had wished the memoranda on budget reform to be accompanied by the threat of intervention. But Secretary of State Hughes demurred.[52] Sporadic negotiations meantime continued between the Cuban government and the U.S. banks on plans to re-establish a Cuban national reserve bank, but they broke down early in 1922 on a straightforward issue of nationalism. The Cubans desired to appoint a majority of the directors, while the U.S. wanted a final sanction to remain with the Federal Reserve Banks of the U.S. Winds of nationalism blew harder each month: in April a magazine published a cartoon echoing a famous insult of the time of Wood: a Cuban martyr was depicted hanging between two thieves, the bank speculators Merchant and Marimán while Menocal and Crowder, as centurions, stood by.[53]

Zayas's response to Crowder was astute. Many of Crowder's plans had been foreshadowed in Zayas's inaugural speech, which had been partly written by Crowder. But there was no great desire on anyone's part to enact any proposal which emanated from the haughty Proconsul, even if his power was such that Zayas himself, interested above all in the accumulation of personal riches, had no desire to offend him. Zayas's replies were therefore conciliatory and seemingly anxious to negotiate, while egging the press on to fume on the subject of 'U.S. imperialism'. On 16 July *Política Cómica* had a cartoon depicting Zayas signing a paper with Crowder holding his hand. 'Which name shall I sign, Crowder's or mine?' Zayas's treatment of Memorandum 10 (on the lottery) was typical: Crowder had not demanded the abolition of the lottery, only its 'purification'. Zayas therefore sent Crowder a copy of a decree mitigating some of the lottery's shortcomings but not abolishing the advantageous sinecure of *colecturía*. Crowder complained in his Memorandum 11, and sent a revised decree; but Zayas published his version of the decree just before he received Crowder's reply. Zayas's son, Alfredo Zayas jr, was therefore suffered to remain with his responsibilities as assistant director of the lottery.[54]

---

[50] NA 837.51/1027, qu. Smith, 106.
[51] Copies are in the Crowder Papers. See summary in Lockmiller, 233-41.
[52] Foreign Relations 1922, I, 1023.
[53] *La Política Cómica*, 16 April 1922.
[54] See Lockmiller, 237.

Memorandum 13, 'Conditions precedent to approval of a loan', reached Zayas on 21 July. Zayas, or someone close to him, allowed its contents to leak to the press. It was published in Orestes Ferrara's paper *Heraldo de Cuba* on 5 August, and summarized in other papers. A wave of anti-Americanism spread through Cuba.

Crowder doggedly went on. He seemed to have gained the upper hand for good when he insisted that Zayas should sack those of his ministers who had been associated with corruption. Zayas agreed and a so-called 'Honest Cabinet' came in. Its members included Aristides Agramonte, Manuel Despaigne, and Ricardo Lancís Castillo, all honest men, all approved or even suggested by Crowder. They went to work 'with a will':[55] the budget was cut by 50%; unnecessary government employees were rendered redundant; many public works contracts were cut – though a scandalous paving contract in Cienfuegos went to a company in which Zayas's son was a leading stockholder, and another for dredging Havana harbour went to a bad U.S. company whose chief claim was that it had been a client of Zayas's law firm. The president of the Senate also received a paving contract in Camagüey. Nevertheless the cabinet gave general confidence to Crowder. The bankers of New York still hesitated over the loan. Dwight Morrow told Secretary of State Hughes that Morgan's would like Crowder to remain in Cuba for at least another two years, preferably with his status regularized as ambassador.[56] This was done. The loan was then agreed. $M50 was lent for thirty years at 5½% interest; $M7 was lent to pay Cuban war debts, and $M6 for public works debts. The rest would go to a floating debt. What folly on the part of Morgan's and Crowder to suppose that the money would be spent by Zayas in a fair and honest way! Crowder meantime assumed the post of ambassador, being specially allowed by President Harding to retire from the army, and he thenceforth received diplomatic status and a salary of $17,500.[57]

Immediately the loan was final, Zayas embarked on an unrestrained crusade of personal enrichment. First, in March, he bought for $M2½ on the State's behalf the ruined convent of Santa Clara on a most valuable site in Havana, the profits of that advantageous exchange going to a close supporter of the administration. Zayas himself probably made a million dollars from the deal.[58] In April he devised a cabinet crisis, and sacked all the Honest Cabinet; its disappearance naturally aroused Crowder's anger, but he found to his surprise that from the post of ambassador he could do nothing. Zayas protested that he could not,

[55] *Ibid.*, 240. Manuel Despaigne had a high reputation for probity. Lancís was director of *El Mundo*. Agramonte was a distinguished physician.
[56] Hughes MSS, qu. Smith, 93.
[57] Lockmiller, 242.
[58] Chapman, 458.

from the point of view of national dignity, keep indefinitely the ministers whom Crowder had imposed on him. This attitude carried the day. Fortunately for Zayas, sugar prices were reviving. The 1922 harvest reached four million tons – though the low prices had kept its value to \$M240. In 1923 (partly due to the crisis in the Rhineland) the average price was up to 5 cents a pound, as high as any year in living memory save the freakish 1920, and higher than any year in the future till 1956. There were fewer mills grinding in 1923 than in any year since 1916 (182), but this fact seemed simply to be identified with higher production per mill. Zayas was riding high. Fourteen members of his family obtained advantageous or strategic positions. Not only the rest of the loan but in addition the annual revenue of \$M81 was used up before further employees could be paid, and bogus bridges were once again provided for in lavish maintenance grants, as in Menocal's day.

CHAPTER XLVII

The Sugar Troubles of the 1920s

For the remainder of the 1920s, sugar history is an unedifying tale of decline and squabble for cash. Cuban interests clashed with those of the beet men of the U.S. middle West, but with over 60% of the industry in U.S. hands and the U.S. taking 95% of the crop, Cuba was primarily represented by U.S. businessmen and particularly by U.S. bankers, from their new buildings in classical style in old Havana in the so-called 'Distrito Bancario'. Cuban sugar, the island's staple, became the shuttlecock of U.S. internal political and economic policy. It was surprising in the circumstances that these businessmen did not do better.

Maybe in fact they had drawn ultimately depressing conclusions for themselves from an incident at the beginning of the 1920s, when the whole Cuban sugar world was shaken by the effect of a decision by General Sugar (the National City Bank's group) and American Sugar to abandon the public railroad and go over to a private system. This was a serious matter for the Cuban Northern Railroad, run then by Colonel Joseph Tarafa, who had earlier made his fortune by bribes to the rebel army in 1902. He immediately introduced a bill in the Senate to provide for the closing of private railways and ports. In seeking support for this bill, the resolute colonel spent $500,000 in bribes among the congressmen. Eventually it was introduced without notice in the early hours of the morning of 10 August 1923. U.S. opinion, with belief in the virtues of the unbridled free market at its height, felt outraged. The U.S. sugar companies went to the State Department, being represented by Elihu Root. Ultimately a concession was made; private ports and railways which existed before 1923 would survive. But no new one would be built. The public railways would therefore get the benefit of any further development of the sugar industry. Later Tarafa successfully merged his Cuba Northern Railroad with the Cuba Railway, which also owned the Camagüey and Nuevitas lines; the merger, Consolidated Railways, later absorbed 86% of the other outstanding railway in East Cuba – the Guantánamo and Western Railroad Company. After Tarafa, power in this new unit rested with U.S. directors such as the ubiquitous 'friend of Havana' (Horatio Rubens)[1] and

[1] Its president after 1933.

W. H. Woodin,[2] who in 1933 became F. D. Roosevelt's Secretary of the Treasury. But despite this law, the vast majority of the high Cuban railway kilometrage remained private sugar railways.[3] By 1950, for instance, out of 11,000 miles of railway, 7,000 were sugar rails, though they were partially open to public use.[4]

In 1924, the sugar harvest again topped four million tons, with an average price of 3·82 cents.[5] The sugar companies raked in $M352, less than 1923 with a slightly smaller crop, but still high. But the U.S. tariff was clearly damaging Cuba in the U.S. A National Defence Committee was therefore formed to fight it, with Horatio Rubens taking the lead. The situation became more urgent still in 1925 when a record-breaking five million tons (21 % of total world sugar) were achieved, but even this record was a smaller percentage of the total world production, now leaping ahead, than the harvest of 1920 (22·4 %). In this happy Locarno period, sugar prices dropped to below 3 cents a pound (for the first time since 1914). The actual return was $M260. Sugar manufacturers, *colonos* and mill owners, American and Cuban, Spanish and Canadian, began to wonder whether the game was worth the candle. U.S. sugar consumption, though still going up as the population grew, was no longer rising per head of population: by the early 1920s the average U.S. citizen, eating about a hundred pounds a year (compared to eighty pounds just before the war), had reached his fill. For the next forty years his intake would if anything mildly drop as dentists and nutrition experts devised new dogmas on diet. This too marked the end of an epoch.[6]

In 1926, both harvest and takings dropped slightly. With sugar at 2·22 cents the 4·9 million ton crop made less than any year of the last ten. 1926 saw the foundation of the *central Santa María* near Santa Cruz del Sur in Camagüey: it was the last mill to be founded in Cuba. Thereafter there would only be closures. In May 1926 the slow process of state intervention in the sugar industry began, leading ultimately to the control of output and in the distant future to nationalization. Was Senator Smoot perhaps not right and the reduction of output the only way to increase profits? The Verdeja Act (so-called after the minister responsible) was thus introduced to the Cuban Congress, calling, in the interests of a good price, for a 10 % cut of production in 1926, and for the limitation of the 1927 crop to 4½ million tons. It was suggested that grinding should start in all mills on 1 January, so as to

[2] President of Consolidated Railways till 1933.
[3] In 1950 there were 3·4 km. of rail per 1,000 people in Cuba; the U.S. kilometrage per 1,000 was 2·4 (W.B., 241).
[4] W.B., 241.
[5] For all below, see Smith, 42–71; W.B., 812 ff; Jenks, 275–8.
[6] *Cf. Historical Statistics*, 187.

prevent any single mill getting ahead of the others and having sugar in hand to sell at an early date. Each mill would receive a production quota, taking into account past production and the number of *colonos* responsible to it. The president would decide which mill got what quota, though this of course imposed irresistible temptations on all Cuban politicians.

The next year, however, after the end of the harvest, and when prices had only risen to 2·64 cents, this first attempt at control was lifted and a free market restored; the announcement of the quotas for mills had been delayed till the beginning of the harvest, and only the harvest of 1927 was affected by the restrictions. But a pattern had been set which would affect the future.

In the autumn of 1927 Colonel Tarafa, the powerful victor of the railroad merger three years before, introduced, with Cuban government backing, a new suggestion providing that the crop limitation by the president should be renewed for six years.[7] The five advisers (the Sugar Defence Commission, headed by Tarafa himself) would advise the president on what to do. The Cuban sugar crop would be divided into three before harvesting began: three million tons or so would be set aside for the U.S., and 150,000 for Cuban home consumption. The rest would be sold in the world market by a national 'Cuban Sugar Export Company' which would have a number of shares, to be distributed among the sugar mills of Cuba in proportion to the harvest of 1927. Nor were the *colonos* left out of the labyrinth: they could jointly subscribe up to 10% of the shares allocated to each mill. The government lent founding capital of $250,000. Tarafa was also president of this unit. Total production for 1927–8 would be limited to four million tons. In November Tarafa set off for Paris and Berlin to try to secure that European beet producers would not expand either; he secured, during rather bad conditions for European agriculture, what he thought were agreements with Germany, Poland and Czechoslovakia,[8] but neither Cuba nor any of these countries, when it came to the point, was prepared to keep to the agreements. Internationalism burns low among men of agriculture. The Cuban government thereby 'freed' the 1928 harvest, but it turned out to be not much over four million tons.

In 1928, Orestes Ferrara, José Miguel's old friend, now, in a new incarnation, ambassador in Washington, warned rather desperately at the National Trade Convention that, unless the U.S. changed its sugar policy, Cuba would 'try and industrialise'. Vain threat, vain hope, though the Cubans did bring in a protective tariff to stimulate diversification in Cuba. By then, U.S. beet men were agitating for an increase in

[7] The Tarafa Law, 4 October 1927; also known as Sugar Defence Act.
[8] Jenks, 276–7.

the sugar tariff, perhaps to 3 cents. The average sugar price in 1928 was a miserable 2·18 cents. At this price, even U.S. beet men were unable to make a profit. Producing only 18% of the U.S. sugar consumption, they could not keep their eyes from Cuba, which still supplied 49%. The U.S.'s island dependencies (the Philippines, Hawaii, Puerto Rico), stimulated by the tariff, were also making a substantial contribution – 32% – and from now on entered the field as a recognizable force.

From 1928 to 1930 there was a struggle in Washington between no less than five lobbies: the first two were the beet men of the middle West and the cane interests of the U.S. islands, acting together to try to reduce the Cuban slice of the U.S. market. The third lobby was the American Chamber of Commerce in Cuba (that is, non-sugar U.S. interests in Cuba, such as the railway bosses, with H. C. Lakin, of the Cuba Railway, at their head), together with the U.S. Sugar Association, composed of all the main U.S. sugar companies of Cuba – Hershey, W. J. McCahan (that is, Rionda and Czarnikow), Punta Alegre, Tuinicú, and others. This group of course took, and led, the Cuban side. But the fourth and fifth lobbies were also pro-Cuban: namely, those interested in a low price of sugar in the U.S. (the American Bottlers of Carbonated Beverages, Hershey in its mainland role as chocolate men and H. H. Pike, the sugar brokers) and those interested in higher duties on refined, rather than raw, sugar (the east coast sugar refineries). This alliance of the three last lobbies came into being in late 1928, when a record crop in Cuba seemed in prospect: Lakin raised a fighting fund of $95,000 and retained the lawyer Edwin Shattuck – a fortunate choice since he was the 'closest legal friend' to President-elect Hoover. A tortuous intrigue followed. Shattuck played with all kinds of proposals – such as a limitation on the free import of Philippine sugar; of the acceptance of a 3 cent tariff, with however 2½ million tons of Cuban sugar allowed in at 1·5 cents; while Hoover and the beet senator, Smoot, desired the tariff to fluctuate with the sugar price. The Cuban lobby began to accept the principle of restriction, but the presence of an ex-governor-general of the Philippines, Henry Stimson, as Secretary of State, made difficulties in the way of his acceptance of this scheme for that island dependency. Lakin meantime had a very useful informant in the House, Cordell Hull of Tennessee, who leaked to him all discussions in the Committee of Ways and Means.

Despite this impressive array of influence, the House committee eventually presented a bill, whose purpose was to increase the tariff to 2·4 cents. Hull, the lonely leader of the opposition to the bill, described the plan as an 'economic outrage'. Congresswoman Ruth Pratt ('ambitious to be one of the outstanding women of America') was prevailed on to 'rally the women of America to defend their sugar bowls'. She accord-

ingly delivered an impassioned attack on the beet-sugar producers –
Lakin and Shattuck being partly responsible for the text of the gallant
speech. But this eloquence did not prevent the 2·4 cent duty becoming
law. Other last-minute efforts were made: the Cuban lobbyists paid for
a holiday in Havana for an editor of the new magazine *Time*, but he
wrote a disappointing article, while his wife stayed on living well in
Havana at Lakin's cost. Shortly, too, the alliance of Cuban interests
broke up, since the bottlers, previously content to leave negotiations
with Lakin and Shattuck, discovered that the latter were trying to
increase the price of sugar as well as to cut the tariff. This quarrel was
inauspicious for the opening of discussions in the Senate on 13 June.
The egregious Smoot produced an elaborate scheme for a sliding scale
duty of 1 cent to 3 cents, to go up as the price went down and *vice versa*.
H. H. Pike, jr, the sugar broker, with an engaging touch of fantasy,
described this as 'a dangerous step towards Communism'. In mid-
August 1929 the Republicans in the Senate did persuade Smoot to
drop the scheme, and a tactical compromise of 2·2 cents was reached.
Lakin, however, renewed his attack and, working with the Democrats
and rebel Republicans, was ultimately able, after four years of incessant
labour, to get a tariff passed at 2 cents – this becoming known as the
Hawley-Smoot tariff of August 1929.[9]

It satisfied nobody. The price of sugar was dropping badly in these
years – to 1·72 cents in all 1929 – while Cuban production kept gamely
up, topping five million tons, if not quite breaking the 1925 record. An
attempt was made to market the large unsold portion of the 1929 crop
by bulk-selling. But the agency so formed (the Vendendor Único,
under Rionda's inspiration and headed by Tarafa) turned out a fiasco
since it could give no advance to sugar mill owners; that was the only
advantage they would have gained from the necessary co-operation.
The agency was dissolved and the *central* owners returned to private
selling. In 1930 Cuban sugar leaders (North Americans, of course, since
at this point U.S. firms produced well over two-thirds of Cuban sugar)
tried once more to work out a sugar policy. Led by the banks, they met
in August in New York under the direction of the chairman of the
Matanzas Sugar Company, Thomas Chadbourne, who was believed
to have invested over $M2 in Cuban sugar in the crisis of 1920–1.[10] At
this conference, Dr Viriato Gutiérrez, for the Cuban government, proposed that in 1931 Cuba would limit her exports to the U.S. to M2·8
tons, with a proportionate increase thereafter if consumption rose; but
this proposal was conditional on similar restrictions being accepted by the
'islands' and by the beet men in the U.S. These were not forthcoming.

[9] See Hull, *Memoirs*, 132–3.
[10] Beals, 88.

The 'Cuban' interests then launched an alternative plan, for a general international conference on sugar stabilization. First, a Sugar Stabilization Act was passed in November 1930, enabling a hastily formed New Sugar Export Corporation to buy 1½ million tons of sugar at $4 a bag – all left over from the 1929 crop. Export quotas were introduced, including one for the U.S. Four U.S. mill owners, four Cuban, were nominated with a representative of the *colonos* to serve on this exporters' junta. Chadbourne[11] went to Europe in November 1930. He secured undertakings (signed in Brussels in May 1931) by Germany, Czechoslovakia, Poland, Belgium, Hungary, Java (Dutch, of course) as well as Cuba that they would restrict exports for five years. Alas, this merely offered disastrous opportunities for the U.S. and the 'islands' to increase production: the Cuban share of the U.S. market therefore dropped from 49·4% in 1930 to 25·3% in 1933, while the domestic share rose from 31·8% to 47·9%. The islands replaced Cuba as the main sugar suppliers of the U.S. Nor did the Brussels agreement succeed in raising sugar prices which, in the hurrying clouds of the international economic depression, dropped further and further: the average price in 1930 had been 1·23 cents and in 1931 was to be barely a cent a pound. These were prices lower than had been recorded at any previous period. World consumption of sugar per head began to drop, as it continued to do through the next ten years.[12] The golden years were over. Surplus sugar in warehouses from Havana to Batavia remained. Similarly, the Chadbourne agreement was between producers, not governments, and therefore was not binding. In 1932, in an effort at least to get over this weakness, the governments of Cuba and the Netherlands (Java) both ordered a reduction of production by some 60%, the Cubans acting under the umbrella afforded by the Verdeja Act. But this did nothing for prices: in 1932, the average world price was 0·71 of a cent, and the greatly reduced Cuban harvest, of 2·6 million tons, produced a total income of a mere $M41·8 – the lowest recorded, even reckoning money values constant, since 1901, and, in real terms of what it would buy, much lower than that. The last time that Cuba had produced about that quantity of sugar, in 1915, the value of the harvest had been four and a half times more. In 1929–30, the countries represented at the Chadbourne Conference had produced almost half the world sugar: in 1932–3 they would produce less than a quarter[13] – though there were some other factors involved, such as protectionism in India and Japan. So much for the 'laws of international supply and demand'. Cuba too (like Java) was able to produce sugar at a lower cost than anywhere else. But now it was

[11] With Viriato Gutiérrez, José Gómez Mena, José María López Ochoa, and William Douglas (*Estudio*, 622).

[12] A. Vitón and F. Pignalosa, *Trends and Forces of World Sugar Consumption* (1961), 7.

[13] See B. C. Swerling, *International Control of Sugar, 1918–41* (1949), 46.

clear that the price basis, even in a capitalist world, could not be the deciding factor in what share Cuba had of the market.[14] Meantime, in 1930 only 157 mills were at work in place of 163 in 1929; in 1931 only 140 mills ground; and in 1932, only 133. The government attempted to keep the smaller mills going by giving them preferences, at least ensuring their production. The unemployed in the sugar industry grew to great regiments; most of those even who had work in 1932 had a total of a bare eighty days.

Here then was a revolutionary economic situation: mills closing, work and capital unobtainable, the international market at its lowest point, everywhere decay and misery.

The world's restrictions forced a restrictive policy upon Cuba though her society had been built upon the dream of maximum production. But the law of capital, as Pierre Mantoux reminds us, is the law of profit 'which urges it ceaselessly to produce, in order ceaselessly to grow'.[15] If only restriction could guarantee profit, was not something very wrong? The sugar production of Cuba between 1850 and 1925 mounted by an average of 8% a year, even though the country had suffered two serious civil wars, one of them ruinous. This advance could be maintained if the world's buying power increased; and it did not. Hence the origin of a whole series of fantasies which Fidel Castro, Cuba's first international political figure, would eventually satisfy.

[14] See World Bank, *Report on Cuba* (1951).
[15] *The Industrial Revolution in the 18th Century*, 26. Mantoux goes on: 'Left entirely to itself, production would rush on to excess, until it became ruinous over-production . . . the instinctive tendency of capitalism ends in self destruction.'

CHAPTER XLVIII

Zayas

The events of the 1920s in the political life of Cuba followed a turbulent course largely unrelated to what was happening to the country's main crop. This turbulence began in the university when, at the end of 1922, the students in Havana demonstrated in violence against the incompetence and corruption of many of their professors, many of whom were simply sinecure holders. University reform became the burning question.

This university revolt owed much to the revolution of March 1918 of students in Argentina. A new romantic, messianic generation of students stalked Latin America,[1] interested in reform of society as much as of the university, but seeing in an attack on the university a means of criticizing society. José Arce, the first reformist rector of the University of Buenos Aires, had visited Cuba in 1922. At the inaugural session of the Sixth Latin American Medical Federation he had, with his eloquent references to the danger of imperialism and his air of being quite different to other more conventional rectors, won much sympathy. The rector of Havana University, Carlos de la Torre, an eminent malacologist, was won over to the cause of reform, together with his few progressive colleagues.[2] It was scandals in the university maintained by the state that caused the movement for university reform; but university reformers soon came to denounce the state. Thus the university was a good example of corruption, with many 'professors' being paid without teaching, being merely political henchmen or relations of the president. There was a big demonstration against the usual inaugural address by the Minister of Education, while a minor dispute in the Faculty of Medicine led to the formation of the first organized Students' Federation (FEU),[3] whose first manifesto of 10 January 1923 made seven demands, which, though concerned with purely university matters, in such a centralized state nevertheless represented a challenge to the government. On 12 January, a meeting of the students was held along with the progressive professors – headed by the aged friend of Martí,

---

[1] *Cf.* Germán Arciniegas, *El Estudiante de la Mesa redonda* (1933), 230.

[2] Carlos de la Torre (1858–1930), succeeded Felipe Poey in the chair of Zoology, 1885; lost his chair, 1896, but restored to it, 1898.

[3] President, Felio Marinello; vice-presidents: José A. Estévez, Ramón Calvo, Bernabé G. Madrigal and Camilo Hidalgo; secretary, Julio Antonio Mella; treasurer, Félix Guardiola.

ex-Secretary of Education under Wood, Enrique José Varona. Demands were repeated for the withdrawal of corrupt teachers. The secretary of the Students' Federation, Mella, went rather far for the rector: 'I have seen with pleasure the file of students – their discipline, their order and their composure have moved me, for which I congratulate both students and professors, for this discipline is what makes people great and nations strong.' But the tone of speeches of even the professors was full of bellicosity. Their enemies threatened to close the university. A huge Cuban flag was then extended over the steps up to the university from the street, and a tribunal to purge the university was formed. President Zayas, always able to see how the wind blew, received a delegation of students. On 30 January Fernando Ortiz, representative and professor of anthropology, presented to the legislature a draft law conceding autonomy to the university. The Rector resigned, and his interim successor, Dr José Antolín del Cueto, tried to close the university.[4] A tumultuous assembly of students followed. This agreed to suspend classes for three days and to renew them under the authority of the federation. The acting rector and university council resolved to ask the government to close the federation, which promptly, in a heady moment, named the secretary of the FEU, Mella, as rector. Finally, after interminable negotiations, the government intervened and gave in; at the end of 1923 over a hundred corrupt 'professors' left the university. Thereafter the rector of the university would be elected every two years by the faculty, the students and the ex-students – all of whom would have an equal vote.

The students had always been a potentially explosive force: in 1910 an observant American had written that nobody should ever antagonize the students of the University of Havana, since once aroused no other body could make its opinions felt so much.[5] But in late 1923 the students entered the political stage with a vengeance. They were not to leave it for any length of time till 1960.

Julio Antonio Mella was thus the first student leader who became at the same time a national figure.[6] He had been throughout the guiding spirit of the Cuban university reform movement. His mother was Irish, his father Dominican in origin. He was of the middle class and went to a Catholic private school whence he was expelled after many disputes with the teachers. A teacher at a state secondary school imparted to him some of the political and social ideas of the Mexican revolution.

[4] José Antolín del Cueto (1854–1929), autonomist deputy in the 1880s, president of the Chamber in the Autonomist Constitution of 1898; president of the Supreme Court under Menocal.

[5] Wright, *Cuba*, 35–7.

[6] Julio Antonio Mella (1905–29), outstanding student leader and an heroic memory on the Left in Cuba till this day.

Entering the university in September 1921, he soon acquired a mesmeric influence over his generation: 'young, beautiful and insolent, like a Homeric hero', one contemporary recalled.[7] He had a strong and deep voice, capable of projection from within his chest. When he began to speak under the great laurel bush in the university courtyard, lecture halls would empty, leaving the professors talking to empty chairs. He was a militant atheist, and a dogmatist; he once berated a fellow student for advocating the abolition of the Platt Amendment simply on the grounds that he came from a Catholic school and therefore could not know anything.[8] The physical strength which he had developed in rowing he afterwards used to break the line of police demonstrating in front of the presidential palace.[9] He later organized an ambitious Revolutionary Students' Congress at Havana which led to the foundation (along the lines of others inspired in Peru by José Carlos Mariátegui) of an adult education institute to which he gave the resounding name of Universidad Popular José Martí, of which he was secretary-general, while a young poet, Tallet, was president. The name was significant: Mella admired Martí and said a little sententiously of him much the same as Lenin had recently remarked of Sun Yat Sen: 'Though representative of a bourgeois democracy [he is] still capable of doing much because he had not fitted into its historic mission.'[10] For by this time Mella, who had earlier on been influenced by the Peruvian Social Democratic movement, APRA, was moving towards the far left, and thereafter every night, at various places in the city of Havana and nearby, Mella or Tallet, or some other intellectual, would give lessons in Marxism before interested audiences of workers. None of these men were as yet Communist, but soon they would begin to abandon purely literary pretensions for 'revolutionary' ones.

1923, reasonably prosperous though it was, saw the beginning of a serious movement of protest against the corrupt and seemingly incapable political system. The corrupt sale of the Santa Clara convent was bitterly denounced by the students in a famous 'protest of the 13', headed by a brilliant young poet, Ruben Martínez Villena.[11] Their mood, like that of Cuban radicals of the nineteenth century, was literary but also unmistakably millenarian: thus Martínez Villena:

[7] Pablo de la Torriente Brau, *Ahora* (1934), reprinted in *Revolución*, 15 January 1962.

[8] Evidence of Herminio Portell Vilá.

[9] Article by Portell Vilá, 'Cuban Students and Machado's Bloody Tyranny' (Washington, D.C., Cuban Information Service, 1932, mimeographed, p. 2). See also *Julio A. Mella, Documentos para su vida* (1964).

[10] Quoted from *La Lucha Revolucionaria contra el Imperialismo*.

[11] The '*Protesta de los Trece*' was signed by José Manuel Acosta, José Antonio Fernández de Castro, José Ramón Martínez Pedrosa, Luis Gómez Wangüemert, Alberto Lamar Schweyer, Primitivo Cordero Leyva, Félix Lizaso, Francisco Ichaso, Jorge Mañach, Juan Marinello, Calixto Masó, José Z. Tallet, Guillermo Martínez Márquez and Andres Núñez Olano.

Nuestra Cuba bien sabes cuan propicia a la caza
De naciones y cómo soporta la amenaza
Permanente del Norte que su ambición incuba
La Florida es un índice que señala hacia Cuba.[12]

Martínez Villena became the centre of other movements of protest too, of which the first was the so-called Grupo Minorista, also young men who founded a Liga Anticlerical whose aim was to fight Catholic influence.[13] In April 1923 adult protest groups began to be organized. The Cuban Committee of National and Civil Renovation launched a brilliant manifesto denouncing corruption in government, which it described in bravura terms as 'inefficient from lack of culture, rotten in character, ready to compromise with every sort of delinquency . . . an unbridled pilferer from the public treasury . . .'[14] The author was Fernando Ortiz, the anthropologist for whom Martínez Villena worked as secretary. On 14 April another famous pamphlet denouncing the decay of Cuban society was published by the historian Carlos Manuel Trelles.[15]

Finally, on 12 August 1923, the Veterans' and Patriots' Association was launched against the evils of corrupt government. Yet one more of the politically maleficent generals of the revolutionary army of 1898, Carlos García Vélez (son of the great Calixto García), though scarcely a new political figure, strode on to the political stage, burning with righteous patriotism, at the Maxim Theatre, Havana, and in a violent speech gave the old warning: the Republic was in danger. The movement he founded, with himself, of course, as president, had the admirable ex-Secretary of the Treasury of the Honest Cabinet, Manuel Despaigne, as its treasurer and Oscar Soto as its secretary. The ubiquitous Ruben Martínez Villena ran the propaganda – the 'Saint Just of the movement', a friend later and, typically romantically, recalled: typically, for all these Cubans saw themselves in heroic eighteenth-century roles.

Other tumultuous meetings were held at the end of August, and in October: by then, other distinguished Cubans such as Manuel Sanguily, Colonel Mendieta, Maza y Arbola, Hernández Cartaya and Enrique

[12]   Our Cuba, how well you know when the hunting
        Of nations is in season and how
        The menace of the North is prepared
        Florida is a finger which points to Cuba.

[13] Others involved were Juan Marinello, Emilio Roig, José A. Fernández de Castro, Alejo Carpentier, Luis Gómez Wangüemert, Andres Núñez Olano, Maria Villar Buceta and Mariblanca Sabas Aloma. See Roa, *Retorno a la Alborada*, 115.

[14] Ortiz, *La Decadencia Cubana*.

[15] Carlos Manuel Trelles (1866–1941), famous bibliophile, member of Revolutionary Committee of Matanzas.

Varona rallied to the cause. Long lists of accusations were prepared against President Zayas. Revolution seemed just round the corner again, so much so that General Gerardo Machado (a contender for the presidency in 1924) telephoned Frank Steinhart to request (on his own behalf) that the U.S. should take preventive action against the Veterans.[16] The winter fizzled on, with rising discontent everywhere, particularly at the university: Mella held a national students' congress in October at which heroic and far-reaching goals were announced: the FEU would regard as their first task the organization of a Latin American students' league, whose first aim would be to realize Bolívar's dream: the Latin Republic of America.[17] But the Veterans were not quite decided on an explosion, even though Martínez Villena was gathering the dynamite. An impatient section of Veterans under Colonel Laredo Brú rose in Las Villas and marched on Santa Clara.[18] His force was dispersed without difficulty. Recriminations followed. Martínez Villena was put in prison for gun-running. García Vélez disowned these actions and, despite brilliant appeals to patriotism, the Movement fell away. President Zayas meantime drove on furiously towards greater accumulation of wealth, corrupting the legislature as Menocal had done before him so that in June the House of Representatives met in secret in order the more easily to dispose of twenty-nine bills spending public funds in ways benefiting themselves. The only setback Zayas experienced was his rejection by the Conservative party as their candidate in the following election. They chose Menocal once again. Zayas began to move back towards the Liberals, in particular towards the rising figure of General Machado.[19]

[16] NA 837.00/2419, qu. Smith, 216.

[17] Serviat, *40 Aniversario de la fundación del Partido Comunista* (1965), 85.

[18] Federico Laredo Brú (1875–1950), colonel in the war, president of the *Audiencia* of Santa Clara, secretary of the Interior under Gómez.

[19] Gerardo Machado (1871–1939), a by-word of iniquity but probably the ablest president Cuba has had.

CHAPTER XLIX

Machado: I

Gerardo Machado, like his friend and previous patron, José Miguel Gómez, came from the province of Las Villas. His origins were rough and crooked. He began life in a butcher's shop in Camajuaní, and always thereafter bore the macabre marks of that trade: his left hand had only three fingers.[1] Before the war of independence he and his father were cattle robbers, and one of the first events during his mayoralty of Santa Clara after 1899 was the mysterious burning of the *audiencia* which contained records of his criminal activities.[2] He had spent most of the war of independence in Santa Clara, except for a time when he was employed in Sagua for the purchase of arms. Later he supervised all disbursements of the army in Santa Clara, from which activity it may be surmised that he did not neglect opportunities for private enrichment.[3] Machado's career in Liberal politics took him into Gómez's cabinet, from which he resigned in spectacular style in 1911, and caused some to forget his somewhat brutal repression of the anarchist strike of the sewage workers a few months before.[4] Back with José Miguel in the revolution of 1917, he broke with him finally in 1921; but after his death, Machado made an attempt to pose as Gómez's spiritual successor; he was delighted to find himself sketched in the pages of *La Política Cómica* wearing Gómez's old sombrero. But their relations had never been the same after 1917, since Gómez believed Machado had let him down at the critical moment.

Machado had also a continuously expanding business life. In the first years of the century he managed a small electric light company in Santa Clara; later he ran a sugar mill, as Menocal had done. Later still, he joined Cuban Electric – the Havana subsidiary of the great Electric Bond and Share Company – and became its vice-president. From 1921 this company began to buy up Cuban electric supply businesses on a lavish scale, so that by 1924 they controlled nearly the whole of these utilities in Havana. It seems probable that, as Machado's enemies alleged, the president of the Electric Bond and

[1] See the photograph on p. 31 of *Bohemia*, 1 October 1933.
[2] Beals, *The Crime of Cuba*, 241–2. As mayor he also helped Van Horne get the central railway through (see Martínez Ortiz, I, 331).
[3] Rubens, *Liberty*, 116.
[4] See above, p. 509.

Share Company, Catlin, gave Machado half a million dollars for his electoral expenses.[5]

In 1924 Machado appeared to those who knew him to be an amiable rogue, a good business man, somewhat given over to the fleshpots, pleased to own (through his barber) the Moulin Rouge theatre where pornographic shows were shown, and enjoying the illusion that he was a great dancer: 'Machado imagines that it is enough to be a thief to equal Machiavelli'.[6] There seemed every chance that Machado in the presidency would steal the government funds; that he would enrich his friends and relations as Zayas, Menocal and Gómez had done; but nothing more sinister was expected.

This is to anticipate: for in mid-1924 it seemed to the majority of literate, professional, decent Cuban opinion that the best Liberal candidate for the presidency was Colonel Carlos Mendieta, the current idol of the masses, the hero of the *guajiro*, apparently honest, dedicated, energetic, a man capable of cleaning up the country at last. As director of the *Heraldo de Cuba* in the time of Menocal, his brave articles entitled '*Abajo la Dictadura!*' had seemed a blast of hope. Earlier, during the revolution of 1917, he had continued to fight even after José Miguel Gómez had been captured, so that he appeared to incarnate persistence as well as courage. Indeed, he believed himself to be the only possible candidate for the Liberals; Machado had been his own lieutenant and besides was a man of little reputation and did not seem in any way honest. But while Mendieta rested, during the summer of 1924, on his reputation, taking his nomination for granted, Machado was busy seeking support, greatly helped by his electoral manager, Vázquez Bello: '*Chico*, come and see me!' he would say to everyone up and down Havana, taking them warmly by the arm, and holding out infinite possibilities for the future should he become president. This simple policy worked wonders.[7]

In July the convention of the Liberal party was held with old General Pino Guerra in the chair. Orestes Ferrara, the friend and manager of Mendieta, found that Machado had a good deal more support than he had expected, for not only the chairman but his brilliant brother, the historian Ramiro Guerra, had changed sides. There were several squabbles over voting and, while the disputes dragged on and on, the expansive character of Machado seemed to glow brighter and brighter. One delegate leant over the chair in which Gonzalo de Quesada, disgruntled and alarmed, was sitting, and pointing to Machado remarked: 'If *he* becomes President, the palace gates will always be open.' Rumours

[5] See Beals, 101.
[6] Quesada, 44.
[7] Gonzalo de Quesada, 20–1.

abounded. Agreement was difficult. Finally the leader of the Matanzas delegation, the mayor, Carlos de la Rosa, was prevailed upon to change his allegiance in return for the vice-presidency, and Machado became the candidate.[8] Within weeks President Zayas had turned over his support to Machado also, and it hardly mattered that Juan Gualberto Gómez, the ancient liberal spokesman of the Negroes, turned in disgust back to Menocal: the outgoing president's blessing was hard to beat, since it included the support of rural guards and sergeants' rifles at the polls. Of course, Machado had a price to pay, if he won: Zayas's popular party would have to have three ministerial posts, half the senatorial seats of the four eastern provinces and many minor jobs. But this was not too much. Machado hired a 'victory train' and began to travel about Cuba promising Roads, Water and Schools.

Menocal set off looking for votes too. But his trip down the island was anything but a triumph. His train itself was shot up near Esmeralda and eventually derailed at Florida. Undaunted, Menocal continued by road. At Camagüey, the governor, Zayas Bazán, and the mayor, Domingo de Parra, announced they would turn that capital into a Cuban Verdun: 'They will not pass'. Camagüey Liberals hung the walls of their houses with skulls and crossbones, and with slogans recalling Menocal's brutal treatment of the 1917 revolution and the death of the Liberal, Gustavo Caballero. Menocal, however, arrived and made a tour of the city. Then came shots. Alberto Agüero, the deputy police chief, was killed. Gravely wounded was Pepe Magriñat, a Menocalista *político*. Menocal complained to Colonel Quero, the police commander, that he was not keeping order, and then enthusiastic Menocalistas imprisoned Quero in the military headquarters. Rumours spread that Menocal was about to '*dar un golpe*'. But he was not; he left for Oriente, and appeared on a huge white horse; his supporters popularized the cry: *a caballo*. The Liberals retorted *a pie?*, recalling the *conga liberal* of 1916–17, with the slogan 'Honour, Peace, and Work'. The actual elections were held in surprising calm, and probably fewer votes than usual were bought.[9] Machado gained votes everywhere except in the historically Conservative Pinar del Río. It was clear to the crowds in the Havana streets (even on the night of 1 November) that he had won. Menocal and his vice-president, Méndez Capote, denounced the election as illegal, but after a conference with the now powerless General Crowder, conceded defeat.[10]

Machado thus became president-elect and prepared to take office in May 1925. In the meantime his predecessor used his last months of

[8] *Ibid.*, 22–5.
[9] Such is the judgement of Chapman (p. 490), an observer, and of Gonzalo de Quesada.
[10] Chapman, 490–1.

office to good advantage: when a $M2·7 contract for dredging Cárdenas Bay had been passed by the Senate in secret session, Zayas insolently said he had 300,000 good reasons for signing it. Another scandal affected a motor drive along the Malecón, or Vedado seafront, in Havana. In November Zayas decreed the expense of $36,000 to build a statue of himself in front of the presidential palace: the legend would read, 'Restorer of the Liberties of the country'. One writer commented: 'The monument ought to be made not of marble, but of slime . . . in that way his memory will be perpetuated, not in the imperishable bronze as befits his frauds, but in the . . . mud that is so congenial to him.'[11]

Everyone now waited for Machado. He travelled to the U.S. speaking unctuously of President Coolidge as 'this great man who knows how to love liberty and practises the civil virtues'. He assured the Arbitration Society of America that after four years of his government the capacity of Cubans to govern themselves would be assured.[12] At a banquet offered by the president of the National City Bank (Charles E. Mitchell), he said: 'I wish to say that in my administration there will be absolute guarantees for all businesses . . . there are sufficient forces to repress all disorder.' To businessmen he said firmly: 'There will be no more strikes.' But to workers, he said: 'The right to strike is defensible when the worker finds his daily wage is inadequate to live on.'[13] At a banquet offered in Havana by the army officers he dressed as a brigadier, accompanied by his chief associate among the officers, General Herrera; since it was known that the officers had previously supported Menocal Machado promised never to think of the past: 'I only know the future'.[14]

In this way, Machado charmed everyone. The defeated Conservatives might accuse him of already showing dictatorial signs,[15] but his other old enemies, from Mendieta's wing of the Liberal party, began to praise him. The impression spread that Machado was, after all, 'the man the young Republic had been waiting for'.

Machado's programme, announced after his inauguration, pleased most people: no presidential re-election; end of the Platt Amendment; a new commercial treaty with the U.S.; the suppression of the Lottery; judicial reforms; educational reform; and the establishment of autonomy for the university. Orestes Ferrara, Mendieta's old lieutenant, praised Machado as a statesman and spoke of him as 'almost Apollo-like', spruce, tall, vigorous, of penetrating glance, 'still gay and decisive as when, though barely twenty-five years old, he had worn the braid of a

[11] Qu. Chapman, 502. The statue was put up in May 1925.
[12] Quesada, 84–6.
[13] Ibid., 63.
[14] Ibid., 54.
[15] See the files of La Discusión and La Tarde of this time.

general'.[16] Some even complained of an excessive Puritanism in Machado's programme.[17] Others saw a connection with Fascism and Mussolini in Machado's declared aim to 'discipline these Cubans', these 'Italians of America';[18] and this too was not unappealing.

To implement his programme, Machado made up his cabinet of a contrasting group of men: the secretary to the presidency, and ultimately the most powerful man in the administration, was Viriato Gutiérrez, son-in-law and eventually heir of Laureano Falla Gutiérrez, the biggest Spanish sugar mill owner in Cuba. He represented Machado's best link with the important Spanish colony and also with the sugar dealers. Viriato Gutiérrez also acted as a kind of breakwater for the tide of place-seekers who day and night soon swept into the palace, and thereby contributed a useful new verb to Cuban Spanish: *viriatear* – to hold back ardent sycophants.

Nominated Minister of Education, to convert Cuba into 'the Athens of America', was Guillermo Fernández Mascaró. Public works were handed over to Carlos Miguel de Céspedes,[19] brother-in-arms of Machado in *La Chambelona*, a lawyer who had become famous in the great struggle over the Ports Company. Later, he had formed a company with José María Cortina to build Marianao into an unrivalled pleasure centre. When minister, he worked feverishly at his luxurious villa in Miramar, near the mouth of the Almendares, surrounded by engineers and contractors, devising in public Aladdinesque plans for the beautification of cities and the conquest of nature, being consequently nicknamed by the press (which he paid) 'El Julio Verne Cubano' or 'El Dinámico'.[20]

The Minister of the Interior, and the man whose declared aim was to stamp out evil living, was Rogerio Zayas Bazán, an odd choice – even though he had so greatly helped Machado against Menocal when governor of Camagüey – since, a scion of the old aristocracy, he prided himself on being an invincible domino and poker player. Nevertheless, he began vigorously enough, despite the contrasting goals of Céspedes. Numerous *jai-alai* halls were closed, as were hundreds of bars and gambling joints. He even devised a special police force to persuade prostitutes to return to the honest life. He attacked the bogus dancing schools, created a film censorship board, drove out palmists and fortune tellers, and imposed fines on the eternal street vendors and stallholders at the corner of San Rafael and Galiano streets. Inevitably, a North American 'expert' was needed; he arrived in the shape of August Voll-

[16] *Revue de l'Amérique Latine* (1925).
[17] Quesada, 60.
[18] Aldo Baroni, *Cuba, país de poca memoria* (1944), 26.
[19] No relation of Carlos Manuel.
[20] Quesada, 52.

mer from Berkeley, California, who came to advise on methods of detection. Zayas Bazán also built a model prison on the Isle of Pines.

The Secretary of Justice, Jesús María Barraqué, was the first of Machado's men to meet trouble. A short, grey-whiskered man dispensing justice on the ground floor of the palace, he was considered 'the most Cuban' of the ministers – a description which Cuban newspapers usually used approvingly in respect of someone with each administration. He began his tenure of office by saying that he would end the scandals of bribed amnesties, and that he would always abandon the sweet pleasure of pardon for the bitterness of refusing one; and within a few months, the *vil garrote*, the distasteful Spanish death penalty machine, was brought out and dusted.

The reality behind Machado's golden promises swiftly became clear. Corruption persisted from the start and in a worsening economic situation labour troubles multiplied: 1925 was a great year for sugar production – over five million tons being produced – but prices had fallen severely. In August, after Machado had been in power for three months only, came two significant though quite separate events: on 15 August the foundation of the Cuban Communist party in Havana,[21] and on 20 August the murder of Armando André, a distinguished Conservative newspaper proprietor and veteran of the war of independence, famous for the bomb which he had thrown at General Weyler in Havana in 1897 and for his work under Menocal in the First World War as president of the Commission of Subsistences. André was shot while turning the key of his front door. The evidence suggested that the police had been responsible, and that they were acting on Machado's orders to destroy a man who had hinted in a newspaper article that Machado's daughter was a lesbian. But perhaps even more disconcerting than this state crime was the calm and the cold indifference with which it was treated almost as a matter of course. Ex-President Menocal did not care to interrupt his improving relations with Machado. Conservative deputies only felt it necessary to pass a colourless resolution of regret. Already Machado, through the promise of jobs and hints of possible graft, was half-way to buying the allegiance of the legislature. Ex-President Zayas meantime watched (from his splendid country house, La Villa María in the *nouveau riche* suburb of El Wajay) with cynicism and pleasure, the further disintegration of the Cuban Republic.

The chief labour movement in Cuba was still, as it had been since 1880, led by the anarcho-syndicalists. It was closely connected with the Spanish movement of the same romantic persuasion, they read Spanish papers, and exchanged Spanish proposals and Spanish ideas. There had

[21] See below, p. 576.

been much sporadic strike activity, particularly under Menocal, and now the maritime, the railway, the restaurant and the tobacco manufacturing workers were controlled by anarchists. But only in 1925 did the Cuban anarchists found a general labour federation on the model of the CNT,[22] the Spanish general union (as they had often tried before). This Cuban version was called the Confederación Nacional Obrera Cubana (CNOC). The first secretary-general was a typographer, Alfredo López, a member of a profession often in the van of syndical organization in Spanish countries. There were various socialist or Communist groups as well as anarchists involved in this federation, and in August 1925 a number of them formed the Communist party of Cuba.[23]

This institution, which later had moments of power, derived from the combination of several small Communist groups in Cuba, themselves the outcrop of small socialist groups roughly affiliated with the Partido Obrero Socialista, founded in 1905 by an old friend of Martí's, the ex-anarchist, Carlos Baliño. All the running, such as there was, in Cuban labour organization had been made between then and 1925 by the anarchists, and what socialists there were were isolated and few. A new Partido Socialista Radical had in fact been founded in 1920[24] but this was from the beginning collaborationist: having been declined an alliance by Gómez, they had supported Zayas and now, still very small, had an understanding with Machado. But some socialist groups had become carried away with enthusiasm for the Russian revolution in 1918 and 1919, as occurred in Spain and in Europe generally, and between then and 1923 a quantity of revolutionary literature in Spanish was brought to Cuba by Communist sympathizers among seamen.[25] A number of prominent anarchists, men who had taken part in many strikes and labour fights over the last fifteen years, also came to be attracted by the idea of a disciplined state party which would operate unlike the anarchist movement, with real support, as they supposed it would be, from Russia. Also, the anarchist movement had been so severely damaged as a result of the struggles in the time of Menocal – either by *colaboracionismo* by the leaders, by deportation of others to Spain, or by police repression – that many anarchists were indeed anxious for a tighter and more efficient organization: even Alfredo López appears to have been undergoing a definite intellectual development in 1920–3 away from the old idea of craft unions (*gremios*),

[22] Confederación Nacional del Trabajo, founded 1910. There had been in Cuba earlier attempts to found a general union under anarchist auspices, in 1891 and 1899.

[23] F. Grobart, *XV Años de Lucha* (1940), 13; *Fundamentos*, September–October 1946, 103, and November 1949, 920; *Voprosi istorii*, No. 9 of 1949, 91 inaccurately gives July 1925.

[24] By Juan Arévalo, Luis Fabregat and Luis Domenech.

[25] Justo González in *Hoy*, 20 August 1963.

towards that of *sindicatos*, or unions based on a specific factory or industry regardless of craft.

Despite this evolution among the anarchists, the initiative to form a Communist party in Cuba, to be affiliated to the new Russian Third (Communist) International, or 'Comintern', came from the socialists. The president of the Agrupación Socialista of Havana, Carlos Baliño, now over seventy, was aware of the different currents of opinion among his members and began a series of debates. In these the same occurred as in Spain and other countries: most of the socialists took the path towards what the Communists later scornfully called 'politics', or *colaboracionismo*. Only four men followed Baliño to found an Agrupación Comunista, which was formally constituted in March 1923. The four were the national secretary-general of house painters, José Peña Vilaboa, then working as a decorator in the presidential palace and previously nominated as secretary-general of the abortive Havana Workers' Federation in 1920; José Miguel Pérez, a Canary Isle school-teacher; Alejandro Barreiro, an ex-anarchist, tobacco worker and a veteran of the Havana strikes in 1911; and a marble-cutter, José Vilasuso.[26]

In the next two years several other Agrupaciónes Comunistas were founded: in San Antonio de los Baños and Guanabacoa in Havana province, and in Manzanillo and Media Luna in Oriente. There was also a Communist group established among the recent Jewish immigrants of Havana, mostly Poles.[27] In 1924 Julio Antonio Mella, the brilliant and dominant student leader, joined the Havana Communists, along with a number of his fellow student friends.[28] Mella with his oratory, physical strength and charm, soon triumphed over the initial hostility of the working-class membership to the idea of an intellectual leader.[29] Mella's earliest exploit with the party is enshrined in legend: the Agrupación Comunista in Havana instructed him to greet the first Soviet Russian vessel to come to Cuba, but the Havana port authorities refused to let it dock and forced it to go to Cárdenas. Mella quickly went there and, escaping the police guard and finding a convenient launch, spent 'four hours under the Red Flag', as he later told an admiring audience in the cigar-workers' headquarters.[30]

In early August 1925 representatives of the Communists attended the

[26] Serviat, *40 Aniversario*, 92. See also interview with José Rego, a survivor of these days, in *Revolución*, 16 August 1963.

[27] Serviat, *40 Aniversario*, 94.

[28] These included Alfonso Bernal del Riesgo, Francisco Pérez Escudero, and Gerardo Manuel Hernández.

[29] Justo González (in *Hoy*, 20 August 1963) says that he at first felt animosity towards the idea of Mella but that he was soon 'dazzled' (*desumbrado*) by Mella's eloquence.

[30] He did not swim out, as legend has it, but went in a launch. See his article, reprinted in *Granma*, 10 January, 1970.

founding Congress in Camagüey of CNOC, still under strong anarchist influence; and later the same month the six then existing Agrupaciónes Comunistas formed themselves into a single Communist party at a series of meetings held in Havana. (There could then have been hardly a hundred members, since the Havana Agrupación numbered only 27.[31]) Present on this occasion was a representative of the Communist party of Mexico, Enrique Flores Magón, and this representative of the strongest Communist party of the Caribbean area played an important part in persuading the separate Cuban groups to unite. Thirteen others were present at this sacramental meeting: Mella, Baliño and Alejandro Barreiro, on behalf of the Havana Communists; two Polish Jews, members of the *sección Hebrea* of the Havana Communist Agrupación – Yotshka Grinberg and Yunger Semjovich (later known as Fabio Grobart); Félix Gurbich, representing the Jewish Communist youth; three Communists from Guanabacoa and San Antonio de los Baños:[32] and three officers of the Havana Communist group, present *ex officio*.[33] Representatives from Oriente could not come for financial reasons, and a certain Waserman acted as interpreter for the Jewish delegates, who could, bizarrely, speak Yiddish and no Spanish.[34]

Flores Magón explained to the ignorant delegates such matters as what a 'cell' was and how to organize *'núcleos'* inside unions, clubs, sporting groups and so on; 'of the internal democracy of the party, when it may be possible'; and so on. The party formally accepted the leadership of the Comintern in Moscow, rejected the idea of taking part in elections, discussed agricultural workers' conditions, founded a youth movement and a weekly journal, and elected a central committee and officers. José Miguel Pérez, the first secretary-general, did not last as such more than a fortnight, since on 31 August he was arrested and thereafter transported home to Spain, whence he never returned (he died ten years afterwards in the Spanish Civil War, falling a prisoner to the Nationalists, who had him shot)[35]; so that effectively the first secretary-general was the house-painter, José Peña Vilaboa.[36]

This first Communist Congress decided to concentrate its efforts on railwaymen and dockworkers, and to publish a paper, *Justicia*, to replace

[31] Serviat, *40 Aniversario*, 94.

[32] Venancio Rodríguez, a tobacco worker from Guanabacoa; Miguel Valdés, a cigar worker; and Emilio Rodríguez from San Antonio.

[33] Francisco Pérez Escudero; José Miguel Pérez and José Rego, secretary-general, vice-secretary-general and financial secretary, respectively.

[34] Others present who were not delegates were José Peña Vilaboa, Alfonso Bernal del Riesgo; Rafael Sáinz; and a certain Ruiz.

[35] He was then secretary-general of the Communist party of Santa Cruz de las Palmas. A prisoner on 18 August 1936, he was shot in early September. His wife, daughter and grandchildren survive in Cuba (1968).

[36] The first central committee was composed of Mella, Peña Vilaboa, Barreiro, Valdés, Baliño, Venancio Rodríguez, Rafael Sáinz and Yotshka (Serviat, *40 Aniversario*, 117).

a sheet already distributed by the Havana Communists, *La Lucha de Clases*. From the beginning Semjovich was the main link between the party and the Comintern in Moscow, the Latin secretary-generalship of which rested in the hands, under Zinoviev, of the capable Swiss, Jules Humbert-Droz.[37] Semjovich himself, before 1925 a member of the Jewish sub-department of the Havana Communist group (*sección Hebrea*), probably only came to Cuba a short time before this congress, at which he does not seem to have spoken. Perhaps this somewhat uncertain national identity was one reason why the Cuban Communist party was not admitted even to provisional membership of the Comintern until 1927 and not to full membership until 1928.[38]

The CNOC meantime remained very small: in the late 1920s it comprised thirty-five unions, of all trades. The Havana branch had 8,000 members in thirty unions.[39] CNOC was affiliated to the Profintern, the 'Red Union' organization in Moscow, but this did not mean that its organization was specifically Moscow-directed.

Other Communist activity was through the Anti-Imperialist League (a world-wide Comintern front activity) and the distribution of the small *El Comunista*, which sold about 1,000 to 1,500 copies. The head of the Comintern trade union bureaucracy in Moscow, Alexander Lozovsky, admitted that so far as Latin America was concerned:

> Only in 1927 or 1928 did we begin to see in the majority of countries an ideological crisis among the anarchists, which brought a certain number of anarchist or anarcho-syndicalist comrades to understand that the revolution cannot be made by proclamations, that strikes cannot be made every twenty-four hours and that, to combat the *bourgeoisie*, it was not sufficient to have a weekly paper and a few hundred members, but it was necessary to have a sufficiently strong organisation eventually to combat and finally to overthrow the capitalist state.[40]

The anarchist experience in Cuba was similar to the general pattern of Latin American labour movements in the early twentieth century; everywhere the Russian revolution caused, as in Spain, intense interest: the Brazilian anarchist paper *A Plebe* published a passionate pro-Russian appeal by Gorki in February 1919,[41] and several anarchists in Brazil founded the Brazilian Communist party in 1921.[42] The Bolivian

[37] The Comintern itself had only been organized according to national groups since early 1925 – Humbert-Droz being from the first the Latin secretary (Humbert-Droz to the author, 9 July 1965).

[38] *Imprecorr*, 21 November 1928, and 23 November 1928 (pp. 1545 and 1575).

[39] See Beals, 248.

[40] Lozovsky, *El Movimiento sindical Latino Americano – sus virtudes y sus defectos* (1928), qu. R. J. Alexander, *Communism in Latin America* (1957), p. 47.

[41] See Alexander, 93.

[42] *Ibid.*, 94.

so-called Communist party was anarchist in outlook throughout most of the 1920s, and in Paraguay the anarchists completely controlled such organized labour as did exist. The Mexican Communists, though deriving from socialist origins, had anarchist leanings, though from about 1922 they were dominated by the famous social realist painters, Diego de Rivera, Siqueiros and Orozco.

Some Communist parties had admittedly been founded with pre-ponderant socialist origins – such as the Uruguayan (in 1921), the Argentinian (in 1918), and the Chilean (in 1921). The Peruvian Communist party broke out of a section of Victor Haya de la Torre's APRA, with new intellectual backers (especially José Carlos Mariátegui) in 1928. The Communists of Ecuador grew up round the paper *La Antorcha* in 1924, behind Ricardo Paredes, a doctor. In Colombia, the party sprang up around a Russian immigrant, Silvestre Savisky, in 1924, though it was only affiliated to the Comintern in 1927. In Venezuela there was no real Communist party till 1931, but some students of the generation of 1928, such as Romulo Betancourt, were party members and a Venezuelan, Ricardo Martínez, was the Latin American representative on the Profintern from 1928. The Haitian Communist party on the other hand did not appear till 1930, when it was founded by intellectuals with no working-class base. In Costa Rica, where Romulo Betancourt helped to found the party with Manuel Mora, the basis was also intellectual, but socialist. In Panama labour dominated. The Dominican Republic had no Communist party in the 1920s at all.[43] Nor really did Nicaragua, but some Puerto Rican comrades were active in the early 1930s. Finally, the Guatemalan party had a primarily working-class origin, mostly socialist, as did those of El Salvador and Honduras.

Relations between these parties and Moscow were never close. The direction of Latin American Communist politics, like that of Spain, remained under the control of the two Swiss, Alfred Stirner and Jules Humbert-Droz. Local area chiefs stayed for a time in Mexico, headed by Borodin and Vittorio Vidali. The Tass News Agency, though under a near-anarchist, Arnold Roller, was a useful source of information. International Red Aid was another unifying institution. From 1922 Communist leaders streamed off annually to Moscow, the first visitor being Recabarren from Chile.

During the autumn of 1925 there was a wave of strikes in Cuba, the most important being that of the textile workers (Sindicato de la Industria Fábrica) against the Asociación Patronal de Cuba: it was

---

[43] It was eventually founded by exiles from the Spanish Civil War. About that time, in the years immediately before the Second World War, there began, unconnected with all this, various minor Communist movements in the colonial Antilles.

broken by bullets – the railway workers' leader Enrique Varona fell in Morón, and Santiago Esteban Brooks was shot in Puerto Tarafa. Bloody noises continued in obscure fields. Mella, returning to the university (where the government was trying to arrange for safe men to be in control both of the professorships and of the Students' Federation), made a fine speech denouncing the president. He left little doubt that these shootings were not just sporadic firing by the police – which would have been bad enough – but that in the case at least of Varona they were clear attempts to destroy the most outstanding labour leaders. Mella was arrested; he went on an eighteen-day hunger strike, and was eventually released only on the protest of his comrade Martínez Villena and others. They saw Machado himself, in the course of which interview the general said, 'You are right – I don't know what anarchism is, what socialism is, what communism is. For me they are all the same. All bad patriots.' Martínez Villena called Machado, to his face, an ass with claws.[44] At this stage Machado shrank from shooting members of the middle class whilst in prison; but throughout the autumn, labour agitators were rounded up. Spanish anarchists were deported immediately – several hundred indeed were expelled in a single month. 'The Red Flag cannot fly in Cuba,' noted a writer in the *Cuba Review*.[45]

In December 1925 Machado, with promises still on his lips of creating an Antillean Switzerland, was far ahead in the development of a new Italy instead. Impressed by the example of Mussolini, he secured that the Congress should pass a resolution providing that existing political parties should not be reorganized, or new ones created. Party control was carefully arranged to be in the hands of congressional members, and all nonconformist deputies were systematically ejected from party leadership. Machado in practice took over all party names, headquarters and machinery. The Conservative party found itself absolutely proscribed in practice and then even in name. Obscure shooting continued in the provinces. The anarchist organization in the island was mercilessly persecuted and, if ultimately it vanished effectively as any kind of rival to Communism in the struggle for the control of the working classes, this was Machado's achievement.

Thus the anarchist secretary-general of CNOC, Alfredo López, was thrown to the sharks by the police in 1926; and he was succeeded by his deputy, a young Communist called César Vilar, a railwayman and an ex-anarchist from Manzanillo. This initiated a long struggle for the Communists against the anarchists for the control of CNOC. The anarchists were now led by a Spaniard named Antonio Gaona.[46]

[44] Roa, *Retorno a la Alborada*, 118.
[45] *Cuba Review*, October 1925.
[46] Mujal memorandum, 4.

Communist groups were organized among railway workers, weavers and tobacco workers, to some extent among sugar workers and other farm workers by means of regional peasants' leagues. An unsuccessful effort was made to penetrate the army. With César Vilar as secretary-general of CNOC after the end of 1926, the Communists had apparently the way to control open for them. But Vilar did not entirely break with his old ex-anarchist friends. The day of reckoning was delayed.[47]

Machado seemed borne onwards irresistibly by successive waves of violence, as if the comparatively calm years between the end of the war of independence and the present had been an untypical and meaningless interlude. Though General Crowder lingered on, a ghost in his battleship, the Crowder election law was set aside.

How was all this possible? Only by colossal corruption. Senators found it impossible not to accept the distribution of lottery collectorships with the right to sell 30 % or 50 % above the marked price. The president and his friends absorbed a graft equivalent to a fifth of the national product, or $M10 a year. Most politicians, like most Cubans, had over-extended themselves in the boom years; prices were now falling, and so those who could grasped at corruption in order to help themselves, even if they had previously not stooped so low. Thugs invaded the Bar Association to terrify lesser members of the profession into acquiescence in these intolerable conditions.[48]

Like his mentor in Rome, with the sugar restrictions named in the Verdeja Act, Machado sought to promote prosperity by a vast programme of public works. This was to have been backed by a financial plan in July 1925, prescribing extra taxes; but, needless to say, a new loan was needed. The Chase National Bank had talks in March 1926 to discuss a loan for road building. In September of that year, Carlos Miguel de Céspedes launched the public works programme in, appropriately, the restored convent of Santa Clara; the main plan was the creation of a first-class road all the way through the island, linking the capitals of all the provinces. Fourteen tenders were soon made for this in itself admirable project, of which eight were native. The leading bidders were the National City Bank and Ulen and Company. However, due to the 'persuasion' of Machado's son-in-law, José Enrique Obregón (manager of the Cuban branch of Chase National Bank) and of H. C. Catlin, Machado's old boss in Havana Electric, the contract finally went to the little-known Warren Bros, who handed over construction rights in the *central* provinces of Matanzas and Santa Clara to a Cuban company in which Machado himself had a strong interest.

[47] Mujal memorandum, 10.
[48] *Ibid.*, 244–5.

At the same time Warren Bros arranged a $M10 loan from the Chase National Bank.[49]

Despite this Machado still managed to preserve his reputation for honesty among the *bourgeoisie* and with the U.S. The nation seemed elated by the building programme. Machado carefully cultivated his public reputation, being often seen walking in the street, giving $100 to a beggar or waving to a pretty girl. The Public Works department made a road to his country estate, but he paid the $734 bill. He gave a piano to a rural school, founded a women's tennis club, sent a poor girl to Europe to be taught music, and everyone said, 'The General paid out of his own pocket'. Machado assured the city of Santiago that he would pay himself if they did not have enough to settle the bill for an aqueduct. The idea was propagated that Machado was working himself to death, sacrificing his health to the country. Almost weekly he swore he would never stand for re-election: 'My ambition is not to be re-elected but to be applauded and praised by all my countrymen the day I cease to hold this post ... [then] however I shall not return to my own house to rest ... [but] will go back to my own people to serve as the mayor of Santa Clara, my native city.'[50]

Let us observe Machado one night in the summer of 1926 at a great party in a famous night club – his face resplendent with smiles, a full moon beaming at a crowded table, his soft, maimed white hand drooped round 'one of the most beautiful girls of the Antilles'. A journalist summoned to the table asked him how he always maintained such an impeccably starched white shirt front even in the steamy heat. He releases the banal secret explanation as if it were a diamond-sharp epigram: he had always a valet somewhere near with a clean shirt; and he changed often. An Italian editor approaches him, champagne glass in hand: 'General, this wonderful fiesta reminds me of the great "Ball of the Century", given by General Díaz to the foreign missions in September 1910' (just before the final collapse of the Díaz regime in Mexico). Machado takes him aside: 'You can be certain that my future will be quite different from what happened to Don Porfirio'.[51]

In truth, Machado by this time based his power on the army, which he had successfully suborned by a skilful mixture of threats and bribery. All 'difficult' officers had been got rid of, or given unimportant posts; the rest received lavish rewards – a minimum of 38 cents a day, plus food, even for other ranks. Military supervisors were installed in schools. Machado began to use the army in effect as an extra civil service, officers becoming overseers in all government departments, national and

[49] Quesada, 79.
[50] *Ibid.*, 81.
[51] Baroni, 26.

local, in a kind of parody of the Russian commissar system. Even the meat and milk monopolies were run by the army. Military 'mayors', even, later became the rule. Graft surrounded the army; one firm secured the right in 1926 to provision the army, and so remained till 1933, heaven knows what sum passing to Machado in return, heaven knows how many horses receiving full rations. A military tailor ensured that uniforms should cost more than civilian clothes – thus a dozen *pañuelos* at El Encanto's cost $2.80, but $8.01 in San Ambrosio. An airman's jacket cost $13.00 in civilian stores, $25.00 in a military one.[52] If a company was 150 men strong, the commander received pay for that amount, even though the actual personnel almost certainly fell short.[53]

The structure of the Cuban army in the late 1920s lent itself particularly to such graft. The army was still only twenty years old. The relation between officers and non-commissioned officers seemed especially close by Latin American standards; being based on the U.S. system, sergeants were enabled to move easily into the officer ranks. Contrary to what was later argued during the famous sergeants' revolt in 1933, a majority of officers under Machado were enlisted men: 417 out of 757 or 56% in 1933.[54] Some of the inefficiencies of the first years of the Cuban army were abolished, but the result had been favouritism. By 1932–3, the last year of Machado's rule, the army budget was $M10, or nearly a quarter of the total national income.[55]

There were admittedly some officers whom Machado was unable to suborn, chiefly the 150 or so younger men, career officers, trained in U.S. military schools; when he found these men intractable, he went over their heads by appealing to the interests of sergeants, thus severely weakening their discipline with interesting results in the future. The Army numbered 12,000 in all.

In February 1927, the contract for the Central Highway was signed with theatrical ceremony. Work on the road began in March. The minister responsible, the indefatigable Carlos Miguel de Céspedes, dug the early turves dressed as a *guajiro*, in an ancient Texan hat. There was much discussion about the possibility of making tourism the second industry of Cuba: a French architect, Forestier, flew over Havana and announced that the streets were too narrow. Céspedes embarked on the solution of this 'colonial defect', destroying shops, uprooting pretty squares, pushing back doors, conducting himself as the Haussmann of Cuba. Daily he became himself more publicity-conscious: in diver's clothes, he inspected the dredging of the bay; he mounted the works of the new Capitol; and he personally closed the United Railways when

[52] See Adam y Silva, 59–60.
[53] See Arthur, *A Sergeant called Batista*, 57
[54] Adam y Silva, 27.
[55] Ruby Phillips, 37.

they refused to build a viaduct in accordance with the law.[56] The new Capitolio was opened. There was a big new private building boom: the Condesa de Buena Vista had a palace built for her in 5th Avenue Miramar by Leonardo Morales in a 'neo-baroque' style; the telephone company built a *campanile* in old Havana; and Florentine villas once more sprang up in new suburbs. The Minister of Public Works himself had a Swiss chalet built in *El Country Club*, and another palace on the Almendares River.

The reality behind this euphoria was not much questioned yet by the U.S. Two prominent North American writers on the history of Cuba at that time had few doubts on Machado's score: Professor Charles Chapman wrote in 1926: 'It may confidently be asserted that Cuba already has the elements within her own body politic that could make Government attain to the level of decency that most other factors in Cuban life have already reached';[57] and Professor Leland Jenks wrote, 'Cuban leadership as exemplied in Ferrara, Tarafa, Carlos Miguel de Céspedes and Cortina, is today a far different thing from the dull though honest incompetence of Estrada Palma ... There are few American cities that could not profit from a study of the police and sanitary arrangements of Havana.'[58] General Crowder, who remained as ambassador till the summer of 1927, wrote to the U.S. Secretary of State, Kellogg, in February of that year that 'most Cubans favoured a second term for Machado' and said that the State Department should give the president an 'informal' assurance that they were not opposed to re-election since, after all, Machado continually and indeed accurately was saying that he favoured the 'closest possible co-operation' with the U.S.[59]

But a month later Crowder was reporting that Machado's behaviour 'cannot be interpreted otherwise than as savouring of dictatorship' and that he feared that 'the reaction upon the popular mind will ... lend itself ... to upsetting the stability of the island.'[60] One State Department memorandum, by the then chief of the Latin American affairs division (Stokeley Morgan), said that the U.S. would 'seriously object' if Machado went ahead with any constitutional revision.[61]

A different report from these was provided by an intrepid reporter from Washington, Chester Wright, editor of *International Labour News*, the organ of the AFL, who returned in early 1927 from Cuba to tell his readers that Machado had by then killed no fewer than 147 persons.

[56] Quesada, 82.
[57] Chapman, vii.
[58] Jenks, 304–6. Though Jenks did admit that freedom of speech only existed 'when it supports Machado'.
[59] Crowder-Kellogg, NA 837.00/2627, qu. Smith, 116.
[60] Crowder, NA 837.00/2646, qu. Wood, *The Making of the Good Neighbour policy*, 51.
[61] 11 April 1927, NA 837.011/128, qu. Wood, 51.

The allegation created much publicity and the New York port workers made a feeble but unfulfilled effort to boycott Cuban sugar coming in to the harbour. William Green of the AFL publicly denounced the murders of labour leaders in Cuba and complained of 'a condition of virtual terrorism'.[62]

These denunciations and rumours had no effect on Machado's schemes to preserve his power. As was now long expected, in April 1927 the corrupted Congress, despite the denials, called for a constitutional change: the presidential term would be extended from four to six years; Machado's term would be extended two years without a new election; senators and representatives would serve the same.

[62] In February. See Buell, *Cuba and the Platt Amendment*, 42–3.

CHAPTER L

Machado: II

The date was now approaching for the Sixth Pan American Conference, to be held in Havana. In the heady atmosphere of the late 1920s (still hardly marred, so far as Cuba was concerned, except by a few students and persecuted labour leaders) it seemed natural that Machado should go to Washington to invite President Calvin Coolidge to come to Havana in person to inaugurate the conference. Many thought that Machado would make use of this opportunity to ask for an end to the Platt Amendment. This did not occur, though few visits by Latin American presidents to the U.S. have gone off with quite such panache: luncheons were given by the Chase National Bank, by Electric Bond and Share, by J. P. Morgan, by the New York Chamber of Commerce, by Sosthenes Behn, by the National City Bank, and by the mayor of New York, Jimmy Walker. William H. Woodin, president of the American Car and Foundry Company (among other concerns), announced with the fervour of one who had extensive investments in Cuba himself that it was a fine thing to have a businessman as president of Cuba;[1] President Coolidge spoke warmly of the moral responsibility which the U.S. felt towards governments 'this side of the Panama Canal';[2] and Thomas Lamont of Morgan's said that he hoped the Cubans would find a way of keeping Machado in power indefinitely.[3] On Machado's return to Cuba, the State Department told J. P. Morgan that it had 'no objection' to a further $M9 loan to Cuba, even though the future would have been allowable under the terms of the Platt Amendment.[4] This decision meant a change in the government's Cuban policy from the definite if guarded criticism of the era of Crowder; and Coolidge privately told Machado that his plans to revise the constitution were for Cuba to decide and that they certainly did not clash with the Platt Amendment.[5] Just as interventionism in the 1890s could be argued as being in the cause of freedom, so too could this withdrawal. If the Cubans wanted to make difficulties for themselves was it not fairer to let them?

[1] *New York Times*, 28 April 1927, 22.
[2] Jenks, 315.
[3] *New York Times*, 29 April 1927.
[4] Qu. Smith, 125.
[5] Foreign Relations, 1927, II, 527.

On 5 October 1927, Harold Williamson, U.S. *chargé d'affaires* in Havana (Crowder had at last left), reported that there was now little doubt that the amendments revising the Cuban constitution would be adopted: 'If [Machado] continues to govern as heretofore he will have an ample and unfettered opportunity to accomplish for Cuba what only an intelligent executive in a position of semi-dictatorial authority can in the present state of politics in this island';[6] Cuban-U.S. relations continued on this plane: Coolidge did go to Havana for the Pan-American Conference and announced: Cuba's people are 'independent, free, prosperous, peaceful, and enjoying the advantages of self-government . . . They have reached a position of stability of their government in the genuine expression of their public opinion at the ballot box.'[7]

But no sooner had Coolidge and his entourage gone home than the real political struggle in Cuba took a repellent and outrageous turn: four students – Claudio Brouzón, Noske Yalob, Puerto Reyes and Manuel Cotoño – accused of being Communists, were dropped out of the Morro castle, tied to weights, to be eaten by sharks.[8]

From then on the struggle between Machado and his enemies was violent. These enemies were thereafter middle class, professional men, together with (in many instances) their sons, students anyway, combined with labour leaders through the agency of the Communist party. The bloodshed fed on the persistent instability of the period since 1902 and on the recollection of the habits of violence during the rebellion against Spain. Indeed, it was all too easy for both government and opposition to slip into the role of Spaniards and Nationalists – with the U.S. playing a similar if more ambiguous role than in the 1890s, its home territory acting as a base for rebels, its citizens in Cuba being a support of the Cuban government, both helping to provide specific financial assistance and giving general political backing.

In April 1928 Machado finally threw down the gauntlet before the opposition by assembling first a packed constitutional convention which, presided over by his friend Sánchez Bustamente, first abolished the vice-presidency and secondly gave Machado his new six-year period of power to run, without re-election, from the day his first administration was supposed to end, 20 May 1929, until 30 May 1935.[9] This unexpected illegal extension of powers in effect forced many people not automatically opposed to Machado into active opposition. Machado also conferred on himself the title of 'Illustrious and Exemplary Citizen'. The same month saw the murder of a rebellious pilot, Néstor Ponce de

[6] NA 711.37/109, qu. Smith, 117.
[7] Qu. Beals, 270.
[8] See *El País*, 5 March 1928, and 15 March 1928; *Diario de la Marina*, 10 March 1928; Beals, 270; González Pereda, 17.
[9] See Beals, 255.

Léon, and another student, Pérez Terradas. At the end of May an attempt at an uprising by certain officers failed; the ringleader, Iturralde, escaped, but Colonel Blas Masó was shot dead. Two more police murders followed in the summer: that of Esteban Delgado in July and the deputy Bartolomé Sagaró in August. In June Machado nevertheless secured a new $M60 loan from the Chase Bank,[10] while in the autumn of that year he both defended the Platt Amendment and secured his own re-election.

Early in 1929 came the sinister murder of Julio Antonio Mella, who had gone into exile in 1927. After a visit to the 'Anti-Imperialist' conference in Brussels and afterwards to Moscow,[11] Mella had established himself in Mexico where he founded periodicals (*Cuba Libre*) and an exile association – as well as working for the revolutionary Escuela Emiliano Zapata and for International Red Help. For a time Mella was apparently a member of the Mexican Communist party and helped to organize the Mexican branch of the Liga Antimperialista. On the night of 10 January 1929 he was shot down while walking arm-in-arm with his beautiful *compañera*, Tina Modotti, an Italian Communist and photographer. Despite difficulties between Mella and the Communists before his death,[12] all the evidence suggests that this crime was committed by a Cuban hatchetman of Machado's, Magriñat, who, after pro-Menocalista incidents in the 1924 election, had joined the new president and who appears to have gone to Mexico City, together with Antonio Sanabria, specifically in order to kill Mella on Machado's orders. José Agustín López Valinas, a Mexican gunman without political affiliation, was later charged with the actual murder. Mella was taken back to the apartment of the painter Diego de Rivera, where he died.[13]

Back in Cuba, the Communists had been led in turn by Mella's comrade, the ever active poet Ruben Martínez Villena who, in his

[10] Of this, $M20 of deferred payment work certificates were converted into certificates with 5½% interest, sold on the New York stock market (see Smith, 125).
[11] E. Ravines, *La Gran Estafa*, 138, says he nearly remained in Moscow, and was prevented from doing so by the arguments of Codovilla, the Argentinian leader. The leaders of the Communists of South America were in Moscow to celebrate the tenth anniversary of the Russian Revolution (see Alexander, 35).
[12] As explained by his daughter Natasha Mella, *Avance* (Miami), 24 March 1961.
[13] See Beals, 267, who was present at Mella's deathbed, with Tina Modotti, Rivera and Francis Toor, editor of *Mexican Folkways*. Mella appears to have been expelled from the (Mexican) Communist party in late 1928 as a Trotskyist but re-admitted two weeks before his death. See the New York Trotskyist paper, the *Militant*, 15 January 1931. López Valinas was denounced to the police by his wife. During his trial Rafael Iturriaga, previously a member of Machado's cabinet, accused Machado of sending gunmen to Mexico to kill Mella. For the evidence against Magriñat, see the *New York Times*, 15 May 1932, giving testimony of Aurelio Alvarez de la Vega, Angel Utol, José Magriñat, José Agustín López Valinas, Antonio Sanabria, etc. Other discussion is in Beals, 267-9; Alberto Baeza Flores, *Las Cadenas vienen de lejos* (1960), 81-3; Ravines, 58; Alexander, 271; and S. C. Blasier, *The Cuban and Chilean Communist Parties, etc.*, (1956), 133.

footsteps, had joined the party after the closing of Universidad Popular two years before. His movement towards Communism had been slow and methodical. Though he gave up his poetry ('I will never write poetry as I have done up to now ... I no longer feel my personal tragedy. I am now of them and of my party') he was a good leader – an attractive and eloquent front for the more serious conspirators behind him.[14] Afterwards in 1928 there came another young intellectual, Leonardo Fernández Sánchez, and then for two years a cigar worker Joaquín Valdés.[15] Canary Islanders and Spaniards persisted among the leaders; thus the future Spanish Communist general, Enrique Lister, who came to work in Cuba in 1927 learned about socialism and the Soviet Union from an *isleño* on the *capitolio* building site.[16]

The first occasion on which the government of the U.S. seemed interested in any protest against the iniquities of Machado's rule came in April 1929, when the Under-Secretary of State, J. Reuben Clark, suggested that the department should take steps to correct conditions in Cuba; failure to do so, he said, would constitute support for Machado.[17] In July, Francis White, Assistant Secretary of State, was told pointedly by W. W. Lancaster of the National City Bank that Machado was becoming both dictatorial and corrupt and that the U.S. ambassador, Judah, was 'a stuffed shirt' since he did not exercise adequate influence over Machado.[18] A resolution alleging that Machado was corrupt was indeed put to the Senate Foreign Relations Committee in September, suggesting that the U.S. should intervene and 'clean up Cuba'.[19] The committee appointed a sub-committee to investigate. Immediately, distinguished U.S. businessmen began to lobby on behalf of Machado.[20] Colonel John Carroll of the Cuban (Railway) Company told Senator Moses that his company wanted to keep Machado.[21] Warren Bros, already at work building the Central Highway, also protested. The American Chamber of Commerce complained to the Cuban Chamber of Commerce. Secretary of State Stimson spoke quite favourably of

[14] See Raúl Roa, *el Pupila Insomne* (*c.* 1960), 51–2.

[15] Martínez Villena had apparently succeeded Peña Vilata in mid-1926.

[16] Enrique Lister, *Nuestra Guerra* (1966), 21; Lister went back to Spain after only six months. Lister's father had been eight times to Cuba to work and return to Galicia.

[17] NA 837.00/2749, qu. Smith, 218. Machado was clearly benefiting from the wave of non-interventionism in the U.S. deriving from the anxieties over Nicaragua.

[18] NA 837.00/2755, cited, *loc. cit.*

[19] See *New York Times*, 20 September 1929.

[20] See letters to Stimson from R. A. Anderson (American Club of Havana), 23 September 1929, NA 837.00/2760; Gustavo Lobo (Cuban Chamber of Commerce in the U.S.), 24 September 1929, NA 837.00/2762, etc. See other references in Smith, 217–18; Senate Lobby Investigation, Pt 2, 1,220–1.

[21] Carroll had been legal adviser to the Cuban embassy in Washington and now looked after the affairs of six railways, the UFCO and Royal Dutch Shell. He had been the leading spirit behind Machado's invitation to the U.S. in 1924.

Machado in his testimony to the Senate, saying that few Americans [sic] had been ill-treated in Cuba. This Senate resolution therefore never got any further, and the Senate even approved, after some initial delay, the appointment of a rich businessman, Henry Guggenheim, as the new U.S. ambassador to Havana.[22]

By the time of Guggenheim's arrival the minor anxiety about a possible change of policy in the U.S. had died down, and Machado was evidently attempting to set out once again to try to please, chiefly since he was again running short of money. The $M60 Chase credit of 1928 had nearly gone, and the Central Highway was not complete. Before Guggenheim reached Havana, Machado had already approached the U.S. administration for another loan, and the U.S. *chargé d'affaires*, Charles B. Curtis, had recommended to Washington that they could not refuse loans to Cuba, since otherwise the economic distress already evident from laying off labour would increase and provoke revolution. (The price of sugar in 1929 fell to below 2 cents.) Cuba certainly needed reforms, he added, but these would be difficult to force on Machado. The substance of this advice was that the U.S. should in fact try to tide Cuba over the depression.[23]

In February therefore, the Chase Bank negotiated a loan of another $M20 (by then they had $M80 indebtedness from Cuba, but 1930 was a hard year). The opposition parties were daily gathering adherents, though in the face of Machado's Olympian insolence they made little progress: the president still adopted a policy of arbitrary assassination, killing in August the editor of *La Voz del Pueblo*, Abelardo Pacheco, who some months earlier had requested intervention under the Platt Amendment in order to preserve life and property, he himself believing that he was threatened at this time.[24] The orthodox opposition, now headed by Colonel Mendieta and Menocal, found themselves faced with a dilemma: they had either to negotiate with Machado or they had to place all hopes on the U.S., who might possibly get them out of their difficulties, but by so doing would deal a serious blow to their pride.[25] The revolutionary opposition, on the other hand, was, first, divided and, second, poor. Strike funds were almost non-existent, though CNOC, led by the Communists, did stage a successful one-day strike against the regime on 20 March 1930. In the latter part of that year, Colonel Mendieta sought to collect the nucleus of a new united anti-Machado movement by a series of speeches, after first approaching

---

[22] Harry F. Guggenheim (b. 1890) had spent a long time in business in Mexico and Chile; chairman of the Solomon Guggenheim Foundation.

[23] NA 837.51/1360, qu. Smith, 126.

[24] See 837.00/2825, qu. Bryce Wood, *The Making of the Good Neighbour Policy* (1961), 377.

[25] See Lamar Schweyer, *Como Cayó el Presidente Machado*, 12; *cf.* the position of the exiles of the 'sixties against Castro.

Guggenheim to suggest U.S. intervention to restore constitutional government.[26] In September 1930, however, at the end of a big rally at Artemisa, on the road to Pinar del Río from Havana, a corporal stepped forward to arrest Mendieta. In the ensuing meleé, Lieutenant Silva of that section of the army which supported Machado to the hilt was killed. A *pronunciamiento* against the dictator was seriously prepared by several officers headed by Colonel Collazo, with some civilian backers, such as Justo Luis del Pozo, but it became known and the backers had to hasten into exile.[27] On 28 January the Havana Yacht Club was closed. All newspapers were suppressed for a month.

Far the most vociferous and dangerous opponents of Machado remained the students, led often by men who were themselves no longer at the university, or by professors. Hitherto, some had disappeared mysteriously, apparently murdered. On 30 September 1930 the president of the Law school, a much more prominent student, Rafael Trejo, from a small *bourgeois* family, was killed by the police during a large demonstration honouring the work of Enrique José Varona. Trejo was not a man of the left; but he became a leftist martyr.[28] Shortly after, a large meeting of students, attended by one professor – the young historian, Herminio Portell Vilá – called for Machado's resignation.[29] The university was immediately closed and fifty-two members of the staff sacked, 300 teachers met in the Engineering School to affirm their solidarity with the students. They were all gaoled and, though most were later allowed out, the closing of the university meant that they had no work and no pay.[30] On 2 October 1930 the U.S. Secretary of State, Henry Stimson, permitted himself to admit that the situation in Cuba was serious, but that the U.S. were 'following Root's interpretation of the Platt Amendment' and therefore would not intervene.[31] The next month, however, his ambassador, Henry Guggenheim, reported that the Opposition – the supporters, that is, of Colonel Mendieta and ex-President Menocal – had privately asked him for 'preventive intervention'.[32]

The closing of the university did not mean the dispersal of the students. On the contrary, with no need to attend classes, they were developing into articulate political parties, as separate from Colonel Mendieta and the other older groups as from the dictatorship. Three student parties prevailed: the Directorio Estudiantil of 1927, composed of the student

[26] NA 837.00/2808, qu. Wood, 377.
[27] Edelmira González, *La Revolución en Cuba* (1934), 22–4.
[28] *Cf.* Roa, *Retorno a la Alborada*, 21, qu. from article written in prison.
[29] See Portell Vilá's article in *Bohemia*, 23 March 1953.
[30] See Beals, 284.
[31] Smith, 127.
[32] Foreign Relations, 1930, II, 673.

leaders of three years before, nearly all expelled in 1927;[33] the similar student leaders of 1930;[34] and the Ala Izquierda Estudiantil,[35] a more leftist group, some of whom later joined the Communist party. Members of Ala Izquierda Estudiantil certainly wrote in Marxist terms: 'the history, already extensive and rich, of peoples submitted to imperialist oppression, has in Cuba one of its bloodiest and most shameful chapters' – thus Raúl Roa (who thirty years on became Foreign Minister in Communist Cuba).[36] Concerned to secure 'absolute economic and political liberation from the foreign yoke and the native tyranny',[37] they were less students than full-time revolutionaries, organized and disciplined political parties, controlled by the leaders, with secrecy attaching to membership.[38] Between October and December the students mounted an elaborate series of demonstrations, minor bomb attacks, protests in theatres and cinemas. These students regarded themselves as the real heirs of Martí and Máximo Gómez, revolting against the actual survivors of the war of independence who, the students believed, had as políticos exploited the national revolutionary tradition for their own ends.

In February 1931 yet another emissary from the U.S., James Bruce of the Chase National Bank, told Machado that the state of the U.S. stock market made any new bond issue impossible, but nevertheless promised $M20 in ninety days. He told Machado that he should try to cut the budget and restore political calm even if that could 'only be done by making a compromise with his political enemies';[39] so far as Machado's 'personal expenses' were concerned, Bruce reported that there was no prospect of repayment of a personal loan of $130,000 or of any other loans to Machado's construction company. As for the

[33] Gabriel Barceló, Manuel Cotoño (who had already been murdered), Aureliano Sánchez Arango, Manuel Guillot, Porfirio Pendás, Luis Avisso, Reinaldo Jordán, Rogelio Portuondo, Eduardo Chibás, Leopoldo Figueroa, Ramón Hermida, Edgardo Buttari, Inocente Alvarez, Rodolfo Enríquez, Antonio Guiteras and Antonio Viejo.

[34] Fernando López Fernández, Roberto Lago Pereda, Rafael Escalona Almeida, Juan Antonio Rubio Padilla, Ruben León García, José Lleiva Gordil, Carlos Guerrero Costales, José Sergio Velázquez, Raúl Ruiz Hernández, Justo Carrillo Hernández, Augustín V. Miranda, Manuel Varona, Sarah del Llano, Virginia Pego, José Morell Romero, Alberto Espinosa Bravo, Francisco Suárez Lopeteguí, Carlos Prío Socorrás, Antonio Viejo, Rafael Sardiñas, Carlos Fuertes, Ramiro Valdés Daussa, Ramón Miyar and Felipe Pazos.

[35] This was: Juan Luis Rodríguez, Eugenio Silva, Manuel Marsal, Justino Lizcano, Rafael García Barcena, Carlos Fuertes (of the 1930 group), Juan Mendoza, José María Sanblette, Ignacio González de Mendoza, Manuel de Jesús Lefrán, José Antonio Guerra (son of Machado's minister, the historian Ramiro Guerra), Porfirio Pendás (of the 1927 group) and Raúl Roa.

[36] Roa, *Retorno a la Alborada*, 15.

[37] *Ibid.*, 21.

[38] Recruitment was personal: thus apparently Sánchez Arango recruited Juan Ramón Breá; Breá recruited Carlos Prío; Prío recruited Rafael Trejo; Trejo, Augustín Valdés Miranda; Valdés Miranda, Justo Carrillo; and so on.

[39] James Bruce to Jos. Rosenberg, qu. Smith, 128.

president's son-in-law José Obregón, the Chase Bank thought it would be best to retain him even though he was 'perfectly useless' from 'any business standpoint', since Machado would have to provide for him if he were dropped.[40] But, as the year wore on, even though the Central Highway was completed, the Chase Bank began to consider the country to be near bankruptcy.

But political bankruptcy was, if anything, nearer. In August the old opposition, consisting of orthodox professional politicians, some Conservatives, some non-party men, headed by ex-President Menocal but backed by Colonel Mendieta, staged a full-scale attempt to overthrow General Machado. Forty volunteers landed at Gibara in north Oriente with a large quantity of arms and ammunition. Among the volunteers were Sergio Carbó, the newspaper proprietor, Aurelio Hevia (ex-colonel in the war of 1895-8), his son Carlos, an engineer, Gustavo Aldereguía, Natalia Collazo, Eduardo Machado, one of the Agramontes, Lucilo de la Peña, and Julio Gaunard. The leader was Emilio Laurent, a decent and determined man but naïve. On arrival, there was a brief scuffle with the rural guards guarding the pier, and one guard was killed. The expeditionaries captured the police station, telephone exchange and town hall of Gibara and then proceeded to distribute arms to the citizens (*'repartir armas al heroico pueblo gibareño'*). Laurent telephoned the colonel at Holguín, the big city in the centre of Oriente, and called on him to surrender. The colonel agreed but in fact telephoned to warn Havana. Machado then sent an *élite* repressive force to Gibara by rail and blockaded the harbour with the cruiser *Patria*. Laurent set off for Holguín by train, his men crowding the wagons and travelling on top of the train, only to meet with, and be totally defeated by, the army in a big palm grove some miles away. Though Laurent and some other leaders escaped, many of their followers were caught, tortured and shot, and many innocent people in Gibara itself were also killed afterwards. The town was heavily bombed by the air force, so that Gibara became the first place in the Americas to suffer from this new form of warfare. Elsewhere in Cuba, the two leaders, Menocal and Mendieta, were arrested without a shot being fired.

The failure caused general disillusion with the men of 1895 and with all the old leaders surviving from the war of independence; after this date, it was impossible for well-intentioned members of the Cuban liberal professions to believe in anything, much less any survivor from the war of independence. There was trust only in what one observer of this time refers to as the inevitable fatalism caused by the Platt Amendment of 'placing the solution of Cuban problems in the hands of

[40] Smith, 229.

foreigners'.[41] Students, however, still spoke of 'a revolt of the masses against Yankee imperialism and its hangman Machado; Comrade Mauser has the floor!'[42] Many of those who took part, such as Gustavo Aldereguía, moved afterwards steadily leftwards.[43]

The immediate consequence of the political bankruptcy was the foundation in the last part of 1931 of a new middle-class opposition force, grouped as a secret society, the so-called ABC. The founders of this movement, young lawyers such as Joaquín Martínez Sáenz or Carlos Saladrigas, had only one real aim: to destroy Machado, on middle-class terms. To do this they were perfectly prepared for U.S. intervention and, indeed, they expected it. No one really knew what else the ABC stood for, if anything. Its organization was copied from Italian and Russian secret societies of an older epoch. Its members were mostly young men of the professional middle class, some of whom worked in government departments during the day. A programme was drawn up by the brilliant writer Jorge Mañach, a graduate of Harvard and Paris, 'not quite clear perhaps but full of beautiful promises'.[44] There was in this programme a slight hint of radicalism and it speci-fically spoke of youth as playing an important part, since the generation of 1895 was inclined to exclude from the old political parties all who were not its contemporaries, or at least its contemporaries' sons.[45] In general, the supporters of ABC were serious idealists, interested in the regeneration of Cuban life. Though they collaborated in a New York junta of exiles co-ordinating opposition to Machado, in Cuba itself their relations were restricted to the students. Their seventeen original points proposed elimination of *latifundias*, restriction on the acquisition of land by U.S. companies, producers' co-operatives, nationalization of the public services, preference for Cubans in business appointments, and new men, new ideas, political liberty, social justice, and recovery of the land.[46]

ABC's methods, however, were revolutionary and more important than its manifestos. Organized in cells, its members were linked with

---

[41] See A. Lamar Schweyer, *Cómo cayó el presidente Machado; una página oscura de la diplomacia norteamericana* (1938), 51–2.

[42] *Línea*, 10 July 1931, article by R. Roa, qu. *Retorno a la Alborada*, 15.

[43] In prison with members of the Ala Izquierda Estudiantil, such as Roa (Roa, 39), Aldereguía later became a distinguished doctor, a Communist, and served Communist Cuba as ambassador to Yugoslavia. As often, the prisons were libraries, almost universities of revolution. Roa recorded in the Presidio Modelo: '6 a.m. The Karl Marx academy begins its daily task. The moral strength and desire for knowledge of these comrades is admirable. Gab-riel reads and explains . . . the obscure points of *Das Kapital* . . . At night the materialist Academy functions at 7 p.m.'

[44] See Lamar Schweyer, 27.

[45] See González Peraza, 218.

[46] *Ibid.*, 115–50 gives the full text. A slander probably put out by the Communists was that ABC stood for Asociación Blanca de Cuba. This did it much harm.

each other only by middle men whose real names they did not know. Their aim was less to overthrow the government by force – a hard task since Machado was still supported at least nominally by one of the most powerful armies in Latin America – than by the deliberate creation of terror to cause a breakdown in governmental activities, so, they assumed, making action of some sort by Washington inevitable.[47]

In this aim they were successful. Even before they were properly organized, Ambassador Guggenheim had admitted that Machado would 'eventually have to go'.[48] This attitude became a conviction during early 1932, when the ABC's tactics became clear. On 25 January 1932 Guggenheim urged Secretary of State Stimson publicly to announce that Machado was not supported by the U.S. Guggenheim suggested it might be possible to shock Machado into a desire for compromise.[49] ABC's first serious move meantime was the mining of a house in Flores Street, where an anonymous telephone call warned the notorious police chief, Captain Miguel Calvo Herrera, of an arms dump. Calvo Herrera and a small force went there. One of his lieutenants and a private were blown up when they tried to telephone. 'The success of this venture delighted its directors but they were disappointed to know that Calvo had escaped. The women especially were disappointed and all news-paper offices were besieged with telephone calls making new threats against him.'[50]

Thereafter violence began in earnest, the ABC and students returning *coup* for *coup* the brutalities of police and army. Bombs were laid nightly. Real experts in explosives such as López Rubio advised enthusiastic amateurs such as the Valdés Daussa brothers, Félix Alpízar, Gonzalo Gutiérrez, Ruben de León, Carlos Prío, Manuel Fuertes, and others. The police arrested the Valdés brothers and Alpízar, but the judge released them due to absence of proof. Thereupon the police, who had followed orders to behave legally for some months, started to kill again. In response, Captain Calvo was finally caught by ABC and killed, while Carlos García Sierra, a Machadista político, was blown up in his study. The ABC's bomb explosive expert, López Rubio, was killed in return. On 20 May 1932, the student Ignacio Mendoza and his friends blew up Lieutenant Díaz, Chief of Police at Artemisa, with a parcel bomb, and several other police chiefs were also killed. Mendoza planned too an enormous bomb plot against Machado's life in a house in 5th Avenue, Miramar. But a participant warned Machado, who in turn rather unexpectedly merely gaoled Mendoza and his

[47] See also U. Vega Cobiellas, *Los doctores Ramón Grau San Martín y Carlos Saladrigas Zayas* (1944), 10 ff.
[48] Smith, 130.
[49] Foreign Relations, 1932, V, 533.
[50] Lamar Schweyer, 31.

colleagues: 'that night the servants of the Mendoza family had to take from the refrigerator the bottles of champagne which were being got ready to celebrate the death of the dictator'.[51]

By now a situation of semi-civil war obtained. The law, always limping in Cuba, hardly existed: when the chief justice of the Supreme Court, Juan Gutiérrez, resigned at the end of March 1932 he was merely admitting reality.

If the upper middle class, faced with the failure of Mendieta, Menocal and the old parties, turned to the ABC, others in the lower middle class had turned to the Communist party. Thus in early 1930, even before the *bagarre* at Gibara, Eusebio Mujal, a young Catalan baker's son from Guantánamo, joined the party – because, he later recalled, 'my formation and character derived from people of the organising type, disciplined and studious people'.[52] According to one Cuban Communist, the party could reckon on several hundred members in 1929 – almost as many as in Spain itself.[53] The Communists were, on the other hand, still preoccupied with the anarchists as much as with Machado; the anarchists seemed inactive talkers, rather than men of action (unlike their comrades in Spain); and in 1930–1 the Communists successfully broke the anarchist control of CNOC, winning union after union in succession and finally crowning their success at a conference of five days in a farm near Morón attended by 400 delegates, by foul means rather than by fair.[54] Party policy was to destroy all members of CNOC who were not Communists, even by betraying them to Machado's police. Several Spanish anarchist leaders were murdered, by Machado, it is charitable to suppose, and most of the others went back to Spain, particularly after the coming of the Republic there in April 1931.

This period of extreme Communist sectarianism so far as other parties were concerned coincided with the secretary-generalship of a lawyer, Jorge Antonio Vivó,[55] and with the replacement of the Swiss Humbert-Droz by the Italian Togliatti, at the head of the Latin secretariat of the Comintern in Moscow – including all Spanish American countries.[56]

---

[51] *Ibid.*, 32–3.

[52] In memorandum to the author. Mujal was born in Santiago de Cuba in 1915, but both his parents were Catalan.

[53] Juárez at the conference of Latin-American Communist parties at Montevideo in mid-1929 (evidence of Humbert-Droz who was present under the name of Luis).

[54] Mujal describes the Communist technique as being to face the conference with roughly equal anarchist and Communist delegates, but with also a large number of neutral delegates who had pledged themselves secretly to the Communist party.

[55] Mujal, 2.

[56] Humbert-Droz to the author, July 1965. In 1929, the 'Latin Secretariat' had been divided into two – Latin America on the one hand, European countries (France, Italy, Spain) on the other. The Latin American secretariat was headed at the start by the Bulgar Stepanov (also known as Lebedev, Vanion, and Minieff, his real name) whose job was partly to keep a watch on his chief Humbert-Droz who was already distrusted.

The poet Martínez Villena had left Havana after the strike of March 1930, condemned to death *in absentia*, and went, ill, to a sanatorium in the Caucasus, 'his memory floating over us like a flag', noted one of his friends in prison, Raúl Roa.[57] Vivó's aides included several men who later proved faithful advocates of the Communist cause in Cuba, such as Aníbal Escalante, then known as 'Cid', and his brother César – from a middle-class family.[58] César Escalante said years afterwards that he became a Communist after being in prison in the Príncipe (for having taken part in several of the revolutionary actions of students after Trejo's murder) where he met 'fishermen ... [and] sugar workers' and then began to realize 'that the struggle was not against Machado only but that [it was also] ... against imperialism'. He thereupon entered the Young Communist League. Other young men joining the party at this time were a shoemaker from Manzanillo, Francisco Calderío, later better known as Blas Roca, and an ex-anarchist, Joaquín Ordoqui.[59]

The still very small Cuban Communist party did not maintain itself without further divisions. One of its earliest Negro members, Sandalio Junco, was expelled in 1932 for 'mistakenly maintaining that a revolution in the U.S.A. was an essential prerequisite for a revolution in Cuba';[60] and the number of arrests was such that the greatest difficulty was experienced in finding men able to serve as secretary-general. In those years, the Jewish group of Communists in Havana, headed by Semjovich, did most of the work for the party, contributing most money and being better at avoiding the police.[61] But Semjovich was himself arrested and imprisoned in 1930.[62]

This was the political background to the poor, sad harvest of 1932: the total was the lowest since 1915, with an annual sugar price of less than a cent. In June 1932 a small group of New York bankers did extend to Cuba a small new credit which enabled Machado to meet at least the interest repayments on his old debts, and in December another plan was prepared to help him pay the next instalment of that month: another $M4.[63] But by then the violence in the cities was hard to ignore. The president of the Senate, Machado's close friend, Clemente Vázquez

[57] Roa, *Retorno a la Alborada*, 45. He left on 1 April 1930, taking with him his wife Asela Jiménez and holding a meeting of denunciation in New York on the way.

[58] '*Una familia acomodada*' as César put it in 1964 at the famous Marquitos trial in March 1964.

[59] See Mujal memorandum. Ordoqui joined in 1927. Calderío was imprisoned also in 1930. He changed his name later legally to Blas Roca (Blas the Rock).

[60] Blasier, 23. Mujal says that the expulsion was due to the fact that Junco, then in Moscow, denounced Stalin to his face as 'betrayer of the world working-class movement'; Junco was then abandoned without papers or money in Hamburg, but not killed, as Stalin did not then wish to embroil himself in racial questions. But he was later killed by the Communists in Cuba.

[61] Private information coming from a member of the Cuban Communist party at that time who wishes to remain anonymous.

[62] Jiménez Pastrana, 197.

[63] See Smith, 131.

Bello, had been shot leaving the Yacht Club, still in yachting clothes as the outraged government newspapers recounted. The ABC's aim had in fact been to kill someone so important that the government would attend the funeral, and Havana Cemetery had already been filled with high explosives. But Vázquez Bello was buried in the family vault in Santa Clara and it was left to a gardener to discover the explosives. Meantime, the day after the Vázquez Bello murder, three eminent members of the Conservative opposition, the Freyre de Andrade brothers,[64] and Miguel Angel Aguiar, a deputy, were in reprisal shot by the police, apparently on the orders of the Secretary of the Interior, Octavio Zubizarreta.

By October 1932 murders were happening almost daily. Policemen were everywhere shot down. Machado's chief hatchetman in Oriente, Arsenio Ortiz, only avoided death by being warned by a certain Manuel Cepero; Ortiz killed his potential assailant, Argelio Puig Jordán, and some nights later Manuel Cepero was found with his throat cut, his tongue and ears cut off, adorned with a message: 'The punishment of ABC on those who see and talk too much'.[65] The situation in the countryside was now intolerable. The prospect of another harvest in the same conditions as that of 1932 was discomforting. In December 1932, CNOC organized a conference of sugar workers, and delegations arrived from thirty-two sugar mills. A strike was prepared. In early 1933 it began: 20,000 sugar workers walked out, leaving only 125 mills even partially active.[66]

But a great event had now occurred, affecting Cuba as much as North America: Franklin Roosevelt had been elected U.S. president. Cuban exiles in New York or Washington were looking forward to his inauguration in March 1933, without hiding their enthusiasm. Many articles about Machado's Cuba were appearing in the North American press. In December 1932 Roosevelt's close foreign policy advisers, members of his famous Brains Trust, Adolf A. Berle, Junior and Charles Taussig, went to Cuba to 'study the situation'. Taussig knew something of Cuba, since he was president of the American Molasses Company, and Berle was its legal adviser. (A third member of the Brains Trust was vice-president of American Molasses – Rexford Tugwell.[67]) A number of other leading Democrats were known to have been interested in Cuba, though the extent to which Roosevelt's first cabinet had at one time been implicated in Cuba could not have been foreseen.[68]

---

[64] Brothers of Estrada's minister.

[65] This was January 1933. See Foreign Relations for 1933, 270; and Lamar Schweyer, 39

[66] It goes without saying that similar conditions existed everywhere in the sugar world – for instance in Java only 97 out of 176 mills were active in 1933 (Geerlig, 91).

[67] See Chas. W. Taussig, Some Notes on Sugar and Molasses (1910), 23.

[68] See below, p. 686.

As a result, in this 'tepid winter' of 1932–3, few in Cuba troubled really to deny the extent to which intervention was longed for. Only Machado, on the one hand, and the students on the other, the former through the *Heraldo de Cuba*, the latter through their secretly distributed organ *Alma Mater*, took a consistent line opposing intervention. Bombs continued to explode, and there were more murders. Machado and Guggenheim, described mockingly in view of their supposed close friendship as Machaheim and Guggenado, appeared already to have been forced to retire from the control of events. The future seemed to be with Roosevelt.

During the first thirty years or so of independence from Spain, Cuba, led by ex-soldiers of the war of 1895–8[69] had failed to create a credible political system. Partly the fault lay in old Spanish habits of corruption and desire for personal gain. But blame lay also with the U.S. who with a dominant economic position did not see the evils of an ambiguous political one. Thus several times U.S. action or threat of action prevented the seizure or the legitimate capture of power by the Liberal party which, for all its evident faults, under José Miguel Gómez was a genuine popular movement; finally, when the Liberals gained power in 1925, José Miguel was dead and his successor Gerardo Machado was unable to resist the blandishments of autocracy and, ultimately, tyranny. This tyranny was underwritten by the U.S. in the 1920s in the interests of a quiet life and business confidence, but the attraction of U.S. power was too great for Cubans, so that by 1933 it was Washington rather than Havana which, again as in the 1890s, held the key to Cuba.

The direct relation between political and economic events is always obscure: often the ultimate link is evident, often such and such a political happening, when examined, is traceable in the long run to certain economic anxieties, to a rise or fall in production, share values, employment, or the price of land; but the train of causation usually resembles a mountain whose peak and foothills are evident but whose middle slopes are hidden by fog.

In Cuba there was a great rise in sugar production after the war of 1895–8, more particularly after the end of U.S. occupation in 1902. The merits of victory or defeat as an impetus to economic health is impossible to resolve without reference to the history of the society concerned,[70] and the Cubans in this instance had neither lost nor really won the war.

U.S. investment was to a certain extent an intensification of the

[69] Only Zayas of Cuban presidents, 1902 to 1933, had not been a general and he had been a civilian agent in the first insurrection in Havana.

[70] e.g. victory by Germany in 1870 and the U.S. in 1945 was the prelude to a great economic advance, though British victory in 1945 was hardly so, nor was French in 1918.

habits of the nineteenth century, heightened by the swifter communications now possible, and by the natural expansion into a territory close to the U.S. – a territory bound, as it would seem, by what were now long ties of common commerce. Unlike the situation of the other Caribbean islands, there was no apparent limit to the expansion of sugar cane in Cuba. Nor was it only sugar that could expand: railways, oil, electricity, telephones, banks – all could receive in Cuba the injection of dollar investment, which, unlike medical injections, seemed therapeutic at the time and only hurt later on.

Land could also be bought in Cuba by North Americans, whether or not it was later used for sugar. In November 1905, for instance, 13,000 Americans had bought land in Cuba worth $M50, perhaps half the province of Camagüey, perhaps a tenth of all the land in Cuba.[71] In 1913 U.S. investments in Cuba would total about $M220 – 18% of all her investments in Latin America.[72] By 1923 this investment had risen by the foundation or capture of so many great mills to over a quarter of U.S. investments in the republics to the south of her;[73] and at this time the U.S. invested more in South America than anywhere else in the world. Throughout these years U.S. capital was 'usually welcome, anxiously sought'.[74] Already before the First World War, new standards of living were being created in much of Cuba, new thirsts which could be slaked only with U.S. goods: already even U.S. companies were finding it economic to pay U.S. managers $500 a month in Cuba rather than Cubans $250. But the war encouraged headlong expansion, bringing astonishing heights of growth for which the country was not ready, intensifying reliance on expensive techniques and heavy overheads, causing the critical decisions affecting Cuban society as a whole to be transferred to Wall Street – even when occasionally a 'Latin' such as Manuel Rionda was in the thick of things.

Foreign investment, particularly by the U.S., has been seriously attacked in the era since 1945. Thus it takes an effort of imagination to picture how during the U.S. occupation there were patriotic Cubans who anxiously criticized the Foraker Law which restricted U.S. investments in that period. Cuba in general clearly benefited from Farquhar's reorganization of the lighting system in Havana, from Sir William Van Horne's railway, from Morgan's original investment in the Banco Nacional – even if aspects of these investments were open to criticism. But the construction of the great sugar mills of the east seems more open to question. It is not an invariable rule that the major industrial

[71] *Cuba Review*, November 1905, qu. Jenks, 144.
[72] Winkler, *U.S. Investments in Latin America*, 275.
[73] Chapman, 610.
[74] As Leland Jenks put it in 1927, summarizing the developments of 1902–27, in a famous passage to which I shall refer again.

undertakings of a country should be, if not in public hands, at the very least in the hands of natives of the country? Is this not even more necessary when there is, as in Cuba, to all intents and purposes only one industry in the country? Of course, mismanagement or delay in development may be inevitable, but are not these things preferable to foreign efficiency? The reason is, of course, not that there is any virtue in economic nationalism but that foreign interests are likely to have foreign priorities. Thus Cuba's involvement in the First World War was unnecessary, and even if no Cuban blood was actually wasted in Flanders the development of Cuban society during and immediately after the war had as a direct consequence a drunken folly that left the history of the other 'victors' far behind.

The capture by North Americans of vast tracts of Cuban territory, as well as of such important industrial concerns, had two effects, both of which were felt politically. First, the old Cuban masters of society were overwhelmed, tempted by the great profits available to them if they sold their mills. Thus old creole society, already deeply injured by the wars of independence, disappeared, and those members of the old master class who survived did so increasingly by assuming North American habits. The surrender of the sugar mill *Asunción* to a U.S. company by Baró who came specially from Paris to sign the documents (and returned there) in 1915 was a symbolic event. Of course, the old society of the Barós and Pedrosos had itself been restless, incoherent, unstable: but Spanish colonial Cuba had traditions and customs nevertheless, even if these were sometimes ruinous and self-defeating. Of course, many, perhaps most, famous or infamous Cuban families of the nineteenth century had given up long before the First World War. The richer Terrys were well settled in Chenonceaux. But the American invasion enhanced this. Many captains of Cuban industry were henceforth non-Cuban. Cuban delegations would be led to international conferences in the 1920s by North Americans. Thus old Cuba lurched further away, to be replaced at the level of command by international free enterprise.

The second development was the increasing identification of the nation of Cuba, such as it was, with the people, the workers, the millworkers, the Negroes, *los humildes*. Foreigners might control the means of production but Cubans on the whole worked for it (on the whole, since even this was far from being entirely true due to the import of other West Indian labour). The continuing commercial role of Spaniards – persons who retained Spanish nationality at independence – was a further de-nationalizing factor. Among intellectuals and writers, such as they were, already by 1920 there was a tendency to identify the 'real' Cuba with the Negroes, the slaves who had made the sugar industry, especially after the dawning realization of the contribution made to Cuban rhythm, dancing, folklore, generally by Negroes – a realization which began seriously to gather weight from about 1906 under the inspiration of Fernando Ortiz.[75] The sense of outrage, the sense that the high if amorphous ideals of Martí had been forgotten, grew greatly in intellectual circles from the end of the First World War, though during the prosperity of this time they were confined to a small group. This sense of outrage became partly concerned to create in Cuba a genuinely Latin American state, not an Anglo Saxon one.

Power confers responsibility, whether desired or not. Overwhelming economic strength in a country gives its holder political power. It is difficult to see that the U.S. was aware of its responsibility in Cuba in the early twentieth century, of its duty, that is, to Cuba – to Cuba as a political organism with a future and a past as well as a present, to Cuba as something more than an economic colony. As earlier suggested it might have been in the long run more beneficial to the lives of both communities, Cuban and U.S., if in 1902, say, or in 1905 the U.S. had directly taken over the government of Cuba. She was reluctant to do this because, of course, of the Teller amendment binding her not to, and of the fear of the charge of empire-building which would have been laid against her by Europeans vis-à-vis whom she desired to feel virtuous. But it is hard to believe that the consequences would not have been better than the untidy compromise eventually found.

The threat of, or fear of, or desire for, a U.S. intervention was the dominating theme of Cuban politics for thirty years after 1902. Few Cubans seriously wished for political absorption by the U.S., but they were anxious to use the U.S.'s apparently legal power (under the Platt Amendment) to intervene as a means of ruining their political opponents.

[75]His first volume of *Hampa Afro-Cubana, Los Negros Brujos,* appeared in 1906.

BOOK VI

The Revolution of 1933

'Like bone to the human body, and the axle to a wheel, and the song to a bird, and air to the wing, thus is liberty the essence of life. Whatever is done without it, is imperfect.'

JOSÉ MARTÍ

CHAPTER LI

Sumner Welles

The revolution of 1959 followed in the wake of that of 1933 as the Second World War followed the First, or the revolution in Russia in 1917 followed that in 1905. The middle class of Cuba received a warning, to which they paid little attention. Afterwards, it was much less easy to expect their radical sons to place faith in liberal solutions.

In early March 1933, Cuba was waiting. *Denuncia*, the secretly distributed organ of the middle-class ABC, was full of threats. *Alma Mater*, the students' equally secret news-sheet, attacked Ambassador Guggenheim. The sugar harvest was hardly under way, with only 125 mills working, but it was not clear how far this was due to the efficiency of the strike and how far to a reluctance of owners to finance work while the price of sugar stayed low. The British minister, Sir John Broderick, began his report for the year early in 1933 with the comment that in the economic as in the political sphere 'the situation grew steadily worse'.[1] He believed that the U.S. would not even try to 'ease' Machado out of the government until their bankers had been repaid. Machado telegraphed to Roosevelt on inauguration day: 'At this hour, difficult everywhere, good wishes for your complete success go to you from this Republic which owes its birth not only to the sacrifice of its sons but to the noble and decisive help of the U.S.'[2]

But a bizarre change was coming over Cuban politics: the passionate interventionism of the ABC and of the orthodox opposition was leading Machado to take up a nationalistic position, to drive him into a position with some points of contact with that of the extreme left. The Communists, for instance, had no sooner launched the great sugar strike than they began to appreciate more clearly that the consequence of the war *à l'outrance* against Machado would be intervention, even occupation; and so gradually within a few weeks a pact was concluded by a visit to Machado by César Vilar, secretary-general of CNOC, together with another comrade, Vicente Alvarez, a Communist cigar worker from Havana.[3]

This agreement was naturally, in the circumstances, denounced by

[1] FO 371/165.77.
[2] Roosevelt papers, Hyde Park, OF 159.
[3] Mujal memorandum, 4.

the democratic left, but for the Cuban Communists it did have a certain mad logic: they later recalled, 'The central committee considered that the armed struggle against Machado will lead to impending intervention. Therefore from early April onwards CNOC called for an end to the great strike, though candidly it was unsuccessful in this.'[4] At the same time, the machinery of Communist propaganda swivelled round to be ready to denounce ABC as 'fascist', while at the same time 'responsible' foreign opinion, such as the British Embassy, regarded ABC as extremely dangerous and irresponsible.

One interesting sign of the extremely volatile state of Cuban political strength was the incessant rumour that the black or mulatto people of Cuba were 'behind Machado'. The Opposition were held to think, 'if you have food to spare, give it to a dog but not to a Negro'.[5] Certainly, many of Machado's police were mulattoes and he, like other political leaders in Cuba, had always been careful to give approval and money to the African cults.

There was meanwhile much speculation in Washington as to who would be the new American ambassador in Havana. General McCoy? Mr White, Under-Secretary of State? A letter reached Roosevelt from a certain Mr Caldwell Pérez, an 'old Yank', as he called himself, living in Cuba for twenty-five years: 'Cuba is dying with hunger ... I beg you Mr President to do something for her. Pay attention to the voice of common sense ...' He urged Roosevelt to send 'some friend' to Cuba for a week to work out something with honest Cubans and 'money will cease to flow out ... and there will be peace and the American government, recognizing the new government, will save Cuba's soul, and, like in fairy tales, everything will be all right'.[6]

Within a few days Roosevelt, after having to pledge in his famous inaugural speech that his own country would 'endure', applied for diplomatic acceptance for his old friend, Sumner Welles, not as ambassador but as 'special envoy'. But Machado's Foreign Minister, Ferrara, made clear that this could not be agreed and Welles came as an ordinary ambassador.[7] The curiosity as to what Welles would actually do in Havana was not satisfied; and on 3 April the Cuban government instituted a mortgage moratorium suspending all interest and mortgage payments, railways and sugar companies alike.

Sumner Welles, who now became for some months the arbiter of Cuba's destinies, was experienced in diplomacy, rich, able, proud and ambitious. He was tall in build and immaculately dressed, and had been a friend of Roosevelt since they had been at school at Groton. He had

[4] *Imprecorr*, qu. Baeza Flores, 87.
[5] Lamar Schweyer, 57.
[6] FDR Papers, F.159.
[7] Evidence of Orestes Ferrara in letter to the author, 1964.

made his name as the author of *Naboth's Vineyard*, a careful history of the Dominican Republic. More a Proconsul than an ambassador, a politician than a civil servant, it was evident from the start that Welles's personality would make on Havana a strong impression for good or evil. While Havana waited for his arrival, new bloodshed swept across the island. Machado had organized under a friend, Leopoldo Fernández Ros, ex-journalist and old Liberal, ex-editor of a sensationalist evening paper, *El Imparcial*, a gang of private killers known as *La Porra* (the Big Stick), hence *porristas*, to fight both the ABC and the students. On 6 April a lieutenant of police was shot and wounded by unidentified people in a car. The same day Carlos María Fuertes, of the Students' Directorate of 1929, was arrested and later shot, because of his participation in the murder of Vázquez Bello. On 14 April, Good Friday, there were many bomb explosions in different parts of the city. Two well-known students, also members of the Directorio, the Valdés Daussá brothers, José Antonio and Solano, were shot by the police in broad daylight, in sight of the *New York Times* correspondent, Phillips, whose wife, Ruby Hart Phillips, reported in her diary:[8]

> The sunshine makes the streets and buildings seem much more white than they are. We saw a youth come running. He was alone in the street, his shadow the only other moving thing. He was weaving wildly from side to side, as if he did not know where he was going. Then I saw him halt, raise his arms and wave them. In the still, hot afternoon, his voice was perfectly audible as he cried: '*No tire más, no tire más*' (Don't shoot any more). Several men posted on the cliff nearest our house raised their rifles. The first fusillade struck him in the back ... the second smashed through his head and shoulders. He fell in front of the huge statue [of] ... José Miguel Gómez ... the mulattoes who had shot the boy leisurely strolled down the cliff with trailing rifles. They paused and looked at the dying boy without the slightest emotion.

This crime was fully reported in the *New York Times* and as a result Phillips and his wife were themselves menaced by *porristas*.

On 1 May 1933 the new U.S. Secretary of State, Cordell Hull (a captain in Cuba in 1898 and the useful friend of Lakin in the House of Representatives), issued a long instruction to Welles.[9] This described

[8] See R. H. Phillips, *Cuba, Island of Paradox* (1959), 7; Foreign Relations, II (1933), 275–7.

[9] Perhaps written in fact by Welles himself, though Hull does not say so. Welles and Hull were never on very good terms: 'I found myself in agreement with my other associates more often than with Welles on important questions,' Hull said in his memoirs (*op. cit.*, I, 213). Welles believed that he should and soon would take the place of Hull. Hull was a sound administrator but an uninspired Secretary of State, whom Roosevelt kept in this post for political reasons for over ten years.

in detail Machado's breach of the Cuban Constitution, repeated and confirmed the Platt Amendment, told Welles to say that the incessant murders in Cuba had outraged the public opinion of the U.S., that President Roosevelt's new government required the end of such atrocities, that the U.S. was ready to mediate ('the nature of such mediation and the form in which it may be exercised must necessarily be left to your discretion'), and that the U.S. desired to alleviate the 'distressing economic situation' in Cuba. 'You will recall,' Cordell Hull nevertheless added, 'that relations between the U.S. and Cuba are those of sovereign independent powers'.[10]

Welles did not pay much heed to that last sentence. He arrived on 8 May, awaited on the quay by a vast multitude which thereafter followed him everywhere. The Cuban newspapers described his every movement, details of his clothes, the cost and diet of his dog. On 13 May Welles gave Machado an amiable private letter from Roosevelt in which, along with various good wishes, he assured Machado that what he said to Welles could be considered as said 'to him'. Machado was 'deeply appreciative'. He told Welles that the opposition had no constructive programme or any plan other than his own overthrow. Machado said that he desired to re-establish the Constitution, and to lift the censorship, and that he had already freed many political prisoners. He would personally welcome any mediation by the U.S. There followed some discussion of a future economic agreement between the two countries. Welles, after this first interview, came away thinking that now 'is not the time for change. President Machado is able to preserve order, because of the unquestioned loyalty and discipline of the Cuban army'. He was 'hopeful of concessions by Machado', and reported that a reciprocal trade agreement would 'not only revivify Cuba but will give us practical control of a market [that] we have been steadily losing for the past ten years not only for our own manufacturing products but for our own agricultural exports . . .'[11] Welles was able to act more or less freely during these weeks since his superior, Hull, was all the summer at the London economic conference (as was the Cuban Foreign Minister, Orestes Ferrara), while Roosevelt was absorbed in domestic matters.

But Welles could not settle down quietly to commercial diplomacy. On 15 May came the news of a minor revolution in Santa Clara. Rebels gathered in the hills, swooped on a village guard post, killed soldiers and returned to the hills with their arms and supplies.[12] On 19 May Mr F. Adair Munroe, president of the Cuban (Railway) Co., and Mr

[10] Foreign Relations (1933), II, 279–86. This was in reality an extreme form of Philander Knox's preventive policy, that is action to the extent necessary to avoid intervention.
[11] See ibid., 287–8. He was alluding to Japanese competition.
[12] Phillips, 14.

Schneider, manager of the *Jatibonico* mill, called on Welles: to complain that three guards in their service had been shot by Major Arsenio Ortiz on suspicion of being opposition men. Welles immediately raised the question with Ferrara, who promised a full investigation; and on 25 May Machado glibly assured Welles that Ortiz would be punished.

By then, however, Welles had already opened negotiations with the opposition. He first approached the opposition newspaper editors; then he saw Cosme de la Torriente, a sixty-year-old Cuban of the generation of the war of independence but of impeccable reputation, ex-Secretary of State and ambassador to the U.S. under Zayas and to the League of Nations under Menocal.[13] The press began to speculate again: 'Welles sees Dr Zayas'; 'Welles two hours with Torriente'. Welles laid special emphasis on the fact that the embassy of the U.S. was open to all, and from late May visitors from all sides (except the students, the government, the Communists and the Menocalistas who were in Miami) began to come regularly. De la Torriente remained the main contact, though he was himself opposed to intervention. On 27 May Machado for his part put out an interview with the editor of the *Diario de la Marina*: 'I wish my opponents would be willing, like good Cubans, to discuss, without prejudice, the problems at issue ... If they convince me I am wrong they would save themselves from the hardships of exile, and they would save the country from the furious effects of prolonged agitation.'[14]

On 28 May Welles saw both Ferrara and De la Torriente: the latter told him that he had had assurance from the ABC and another middle-class secret society, the Organización Celular Radical Revolucionaria (OCRR), that they would accept him as a negotiator. Meantime, as an earnest of government goodwill, Major Arsenio Ortiz was once more brought back from Oriente to answer charges of murdering innocent men; once again he escaped justice – this time for good: the government allowed him to leave for Germany on a feeble excuse and he never returned to Cuba, passing the remainder of his days as a successful hotel proprietor in the Dominican Republic under the benevolent guardianship of General Leonidas Trujillo.[15]

On 2 June Welles and Machado had a second interview; Welles said that the only hope for Cuba was a new electoral code based on the recommendations of a constitutional expert, such as he, Welles, could obtain. This would involve complete liberty for the reorganization of

[13] Cosme de la Torriente (1872-1957) was also the mediator in the 1950s between Batista and the opposition.
[14] Qu. Foreign Relations (1933), II, 296–7.
[15] He died in 1949.

electoral parties, together with various other reforms such as limitation of terms of presidents to five years. Machado agreed with everything, and said that he would be willing to resign from the presidency 'after the election of a Vice President'. 'I did not,' Welles told Hull, 'indicate ... when I thought such retirement on his part ... desirable.'[16]

In about a week, an invitation to Professor McBain[17] of Columbia University was formally sent, asking him to come to Cuba. Machado, on the other hand, had recreated a potentially provocative situation by publicly stating that he would not leave the presidency till 1938, saying that the opposition was negligible and that the majority of Cubans supported him. Welles complained to Machado, saying that this interview 'caused ... the greatest personal effort' to restrain the opposition leaders. Welles saw Machado again on 5 June: he told him that the students, the professors and the ABC all now supported the mediation of the U.S., and suggested that he, Welles, should announce that a political solution could be reached through swift revision of the existing constitution, that 'in his opinion the suppression of the Vice-Presidency ... had been a fundamental error and that the Vice-Presidency should be restored not only for the constitutional term commencing in 1935 but through ... the remainder of the existing Presidential term', and thirdly that the vice-president should be 'a citizen of outstanding reputation'. Again Machado agreed.

Welles was now confident of the support of all the *bourgeois* opposition group, Mendieta, Méndez Peñate and Miguel Mariano Gómez of the New York junta included. Of this group, only Menocal in Miami remained recalcitrant. De la Torriente was, however, undoubtedly the central person in Welles's calculations, as one who had not taken part in recent politics. On 7 June Machado gave the assurances that Welles had demanded, and on 10 June De la Torriente published a statement which argued for negotiations between all parties and implicitly backed Welles as a mediator. On 16 June the ABC leaders gave Welles a memorandum 'accepting my friendly mediation ... on the understanding that [it] ... had no aspect of intervention but was to be interpreted as the friendly effort of the representative of a friendly government'. The ABC also promised not to agitate any more, unless the negotiations were unduly prolonged. On 15 June Menocal also accepted Welles's mediation; the OCRR, the high school teachers' organization, and the university professors also agreed, and on 21 June Roosevelt gave a statement welcoming the general agreement.[18] Machado, too, welcomed

---

[16] Foreign Relations (1933), II, 299–310.

[17] Howard Lee McBain (1880–1936), for a long time a teacher of political and constitutional history.

[18] Actually Roosevelt said that he had 'been so darn busy with other things that I have not read a single dispatch from Welles' (Press Conference, 9 June, No. 28, FDR papers).

Welles, in guarded terms, in an editorial in Ferrara's *Heraldo de Cuba* on 22 June.[19]

Active mediation therefore began in July, at a series of meetings between government, opposition and Welles: Machado was represented by Averhoff, the Secretary of the Treasury, Dr Ruiz Meza (an ex-Secretary of Justice) and the chief of staff, General Herrera; of the opposition there came De la Torriente (of Unión Nacionalista); Martínez Sáenz, the lawyer, who led ABC; and Wilfredo Albanés, of the Conservative opposition; Dr Rafael Santos Jiménez, an old admirer of José Miguel, represented the Liberal opposition; Dr Dorta Duque came for the university, Luis Baralt and Dr Aragón for the teachers, Dr Nicasio Silverio for OCRR, and María Corominas and Hortensia Lamarr for the women's organizations. These people repaired to the U.S. Embassy in the morning of 1 July. But the preparations were not complete, and the first meeting was postponed till 3 July.[20] On that day, in intense heat, big crowds lined the road to the U.S. Embassy. The opposition began with a series of good conduct demands from the government. But these negotiations were not accepted by the Radical wing of the ABC or by the students; the latter had begun clearly to abandon hope for negotiation, though they did say that they would not raise obstacles. But bombs began to be thrown again – one in the American Club on 11 July.[21] Welles pooh-poohed this student opposition and also the renewed hostility to intervention voiced by Menocal.[22] But then mediation came almost to a halt thanks to the refusal of the government to release a political prisoner, Dr Castellano of ABC, and ABC's consequent reluctance to attend.

On 11 July Machado released Castellano, and afterwards there was discussion of a revised Constitution. The opposition, however, was slow in making up its mind. On 14 July Welles saw the editors of the leading newspapers (*La Voz, El Mundo, Diario de la Marina*), and asked explicitly for their support: they agreed not to publish comment or information which 'would excite public sentiment and provoke public disorder'; attacks on Machado would be dropped; rumours would not be spread. In return Machado was persuaded by Welles to drop the censorship commission.[23]

On 17 July Welles personally summed up to Roosevelt:

[19] Machado said, 'the Ambassador does not prejudice our sovereignty'.
[20] See Lamar Schweyer, 91.
[21] *Ibid.*, 100. Welles reported, probably accurately, that this bomb was placed by monarchists, headed by engineer Nogueira, 320.
[22] Foreign Relations (1933), II, 318.
[23] Lamar Schweyer, 106; Foreign Relations (1933), II, 322–3. Among the editors Welles saw frequently was the young editor of the *Havana Post*, Mr William Wieland, a man whose fate was inextricably involved in future events in Cuba (U.S. Senate, *Communist Threat to the U.S.A. through the Caribbean* (1959–62), 619).

Machado and the three organised political parties of the Republic have formally accepted my tender of good offices and every important faction in the opposition has taken the same action with the exception of the small and constantly diminishing group which surrounds General Menocal. I am unable to attach very much importance to the student groups. While they have not expressed their approval of what we are trying to do, they at least have declared that they will suspend all terroristic activities.

Welles speculated on the likely course of action over constitutional change, asked for permission to urge that the next election should take place in 1936, and made one or two suggestions for a new commercial treaty to be concluded after the constitutional crisis was over.[24] But when it came to the essential question of the restoration of ordinary civil guarantees, Machado stalled, saying that this could not be done unless the opposition gave a promise not to disturb public order. Welles telegraphed Machado to insist, but Machado refused to accept such orders: and when Welles demanded an interview, Machado announced that he was ill.[25] An amnesty bill affecting both sides – Machado's men and the opposition (however much the opposition disliked the idea of abandoning vengeance) – was the only way whereby Machado could be prevailed on to give way on constitutional guarantees. This was quietly put to and passed by the opposition. In the morning of 26 July Machado promulgated the amnesty law; he also saw Welles, who urged that Mendieta, Méndez Peñate and Miguel Mariano Gómez should be allowed to return to Cuba, but Machado told Welles he could have no personal dealings with Gómez whom he understood to be planning the murder of himself and his family.[26]

At this point Machado began to find his position well-nigh intolerable. Senator Wilfredo Fernández asked Machado's press officers whether Ambassador Welles's behaviour ought not to be taken up by the U.S. Congress. Machado's press officer, Lamar Schweyer, went accordingly to the president's palace, where he found 'the halls of the palace facing the private offices of General Machado ... congested. Awaiting their turn to see Machado could be found the political negotiators of the intervention, some cabinet ministers, police chiefs, newspaper men and intimate friends of Machado ... all faces reflected an expression ... of anguish ...'. Lamar Schweyer sent in his request, and in reply he was told Machado would speak in congress that afternoon. There was general astonishment. At 3 p.m. Machado arrived and

[24] Foreign Relations (1933), II, 323–5.

[25] Lamar Schweyer, 114–15. No notice of these incidents occurs in the Foreign Relations publications.

[26] Foreign Relations (1933), II, 329.

thanked the Senate for its swift approval of the amnesty law. Then he said:

> I wish also to speak of the work of mediation of Mr Welles. The object of this mediation was the re-establishment of peace and it is for that reason that I accepted it. The mediation of Mr Welles in no way diminishes our freedom, because his cooperation is of his own free will and he does not obey instructions from the government of the U.S.A. If it were otherwise I would have ceased to be President before accepting it.

Later Machado went to the House of Representatives, where he said:

> You may have the assurance that the mediation does not mean any act which diminishes the sovereignty of this chamber, because if that were attempted, the Executive would not permit it, since we are free men of an independent nation. The mediation does not represent any foreign government ... it is the work of a friend of the Cubans.[27]

These statements were warmly welcomed by huge numbers of people, and, outside, the president stood for twenty minutes 'facing the multitude'.[28] Welles was irritated, of course, and urged the State Department to say somewhere that 'while of course my tender of good offices has been spontaneously welcomed ... it could not have been made other than with full authorisation of my government'.[29] However, negotiations went on with the main political groups: discussion began on constitutional reform; on 28 July the telegraph operators showed that they knew where power lay by going to Welles to demand their back pay,[30] and shortly Welles found it necessary to set up a committee of complaints, run by two ABC representatives Guillermo Belt and Orosman Viadenibule, to deal with all accusations and demands, whether they had to do with mediation or not;[31] Welles even had to see the relations of a man murdered in a *crime passionel* on 31 July.

On 29 July the ABC chiefs Saladrigas and Martínez Sáenz stated publicly that given the delays, the new threatening labour situation, and the pressure of events, 'Machado would not last for two weeks more'.[32] Certainly on 30 July, the strike seemed very grave. Had the U.S. ambassador and the ABC together reached the rough conclusion that in fact Machado would have to be got out and that the way to do this was through the manipulation of the strike? The ABC was Welles's

[27] Qu. Lamar Schweyer, 124.
[28] *Ibid.*, 125.
[29] Foreign Relations (1933), II, 330. Welles also sent Machado a note to this effect.
[30] Lamar Schweyer, 127.
[31] *Ibid.*, 108.
[32] *Ibid.*, 131.

niña bonita, as José Manuel Valdés Rodríguez put it. It seems at least possible that this change on Welles's side was due to some hints thrown out to his military attaché, Colonel Gimperly, by a young Cuban officer, Captain Andrés Angulo, that the younger officers were by now in favour of Machado's overthrow.[33]

Relations between Machado and Welles continued to deteriorate. In Washington, the diplomat Jefferson Caffery (who had already been named Welles's successor and was now acting as assistant Under-Secretary till he should return), was called on by the Cuban ambassador, Oscar Cintas, who complained that Welles was refusing to negotiate a new economic treaty until after political discussions were settled, thereby using the economic distress in Cuba to bring pressure on Machado to carry out Welles's wishes. Cintas said in these circumstances either Machado would be shot or the marines would have to land. Caffery denied this without convincing Cintas.[34] Meantime Welles was again with Machado, who regretted his speech of 27 July, saying 'almost invariably when he spoke in public he made statements which he did not intend'. Welles accepted this resignedly, but then complained that there were strong rumours that members of the government opposed to mediation, such as the Minister of the Interior, Zubizarreta, were using 'the secret police to stir up . . . popular demonstrations and are trying to obtain a general strike . . . which would presumably result in such disorder that the government would once more be obliged to declare a state of martial law'.[35] Uncertainty reigned.

[33] See a discussion in Adam y Silva, 40.

[34] Foreign Relations (1933), II, 331–2. This interview was probably on 2 August. Cintas had been a young man of good looks and poor family who after an English education entered business, married a daughter of Colonel Tarafa, became a protégé of W. H. Woodin, who made him vice-president of the American Car and Foundry Co., before he became ambassador.

[35] *Ibid.,* 333.

CHAPTER LII

The Fall of Machado

In early August 1933 Cuba presented a desolate and disconcerting picture; there were serious strikes in all service sections of Havana, with the railway workers out for the first time. Newspapers were also shutting down. The bars and cafés were closed for the first time in history. Food was scarce. Most shops were shut, and there were few people on the streets. Everyone was asking 'when the American marines' would land.[1] In Havana there were no milk or ice deliveries. The situation in other cities was much the same. In Cienfuegos, 'shortly after noon, mobs commenced to parade in the streets armed with large sticks and wherever they found a wastepaper receptacle they attacked it . . . until it was destroyed'. Plate glass and windows were also broken.[2] In particular, Spanish shops were attacked. No one quite knew how the strikers were organized, and Gonzalo de Quesada, then working with ABC, spoke of it to the *New York Times* as spontaneous. The ABC denied they had anything to do with it. The Communist party on the other hand certainly backed the strike, and Martínez Villena, far the most intelligent of the Communist leaders at this time (though seriously ill with tuberculosis), had in May returned secretly from Russia.[3] They were protesting against Welles's mediation and urging 'the revolutionary seizure of land belonging to the large landowners and imperialists'. Soldiers were urged to 'fraternize with your class brothers and poor peasants and refuse to persecute and attack them'. There were numerous armed but sporadic insurrections of workers, echoes of the slave revolts of the 1840s, and there were also demands for an eight-hour day, an end to the Platt Amendment, and 'the formation of a Red Army'.[4] These exhortations to assist the collapse of the regime encouraged Machado, since he could justifiably claim that martial law was necessary. But it would be a mistake to think (as Welles did) that these strikes were part of a great prearranged plan. On the contrary, by 4 August, printers approached Welles demanding Machado's collapse as a price for return to work: they feared, and Welles does not seem to have discouraged them in that fear, that intervention would be inevitable if

[1] Phillips, *Island of Paradox*, 27–9.
[2] FO 371/16573, f. 260, telegram 4 August from British vice-consul Cienfuegos.
[3] Lamar Schweyer, 136.
[4] From a Central Committee manifesto in *Imprecorr*, No. 39 (1933), 848–9, 887.

Machado were to remain: one printer said that they had only really included the demand for Machado's overthrow for fear of the 'Thompsons of the ABC'.[5]

In these circumstances, Welles lunched with Machado[6] who was 'in a highly nervous and excitable condition', though in conversation courteous. He said that the mediation had much weakened government authority; he personally was ready now for any fair solution provided he was not 'thrown into the street'. Welles, behaving more as if he were the leader of the opposition than an ambassador, agreed that the opposition should be prevented for a time from publishing in the newspapers complaints against the government. Meantime, the 'Mixed Commission' of Constitution-reformers remained in almost continual session,[7] while the strikes in Havana settled into a general strike. Mrs Phillips, the wife of the *New York Times* correspondent, noted in her diary:

> A marvellous thing, a whole nation folds its arms and quits work. I don't know exactly what they can accomplish ... They intend either to starve themselves to death or force the U.S.A. to take pity on them and intervene ... There is no leadership ... it is entirely spontaneous – a nation without a leader, acting in perfect accord, waiters, cooks, bellboys, room service and other employees of all hotels walked out this morning ... Welles has now bluntly ordered Machado to resign.[8]

That was almost true. Welles spent much of the night of 5 August and all the morning of 6 August in 'continuous interviews' with the opposition bosses. By now he was firmly committed to getting rid of Machado without actual intervention. Machado, on the other hand, could see that the fear of intervention was one strong card in his favour. For the next week, therefore, the two men fought, as in a wrestling match, each realizing that their careers and in Machado's case his life were so far committed that neither could give way. Neither knew whether time was in his favour but each suspected that it might be in the other's. On the afternoon of 6 August, Welles saw Machado again and gave him a five-point plan as the 'only possible solution to prevent a state of utter chaos in the Republic': (1) The appointment of an impartial Secretary of State (this was a quite new proposal: the actual Secretary of State, Ferrara, was in London still at the World Economic Conference); (2) Request by the president for 'leave of absence' and his permission to the Secretary of State to reorganize the cabinet; (3) and, (4) Immediate passage by Congress of the Mixed Commission's pro-

[5] Lamar Schweyer, 141.
[6] Still 4 August.
[7] Foreign Relations (1933), II, 334–5.
[8] Phillips, 30–1.

posed reforms, by which representatives would shorten their terms, so that half the House of Representatives and the Senate would be renewed in the national elections of 1934 and the rest would cut their terms by the same percentage; and (5), Revival of the vice-presidency, whose first incumbent would shortly become president.

Machado agreed to create a vice-presidency, but opposed the first provision, which he curiously said would bring anarchy. He also said that Congress desired to suspend constitutional guarantees; Welles said that he had 'no objection thereto provided that the guarantees were suspended for a limited and fixed period'.[9]

Shortly after Welles's interview, the ABC broadcast the false news of Machado's resignation; their announcer said, 'It is necessary for the multitude to go out into the streets so that Machado may see his unpopularity.' At this, the silence and emptiness which had lasted for several days was broken, huge crowds gathered, and a great demonstration moved towards the Capitol, with songs and slogans. (Machado himself was in the country.) This faced the chief of police, Ainciart, with the serious problem of whether to allow the demonstrators into the palace or to fire on them. First, however, he sent out 'experts to go out and dissolve the groups'.[10] Police then fired in the air. There was a general panic. The crowd began to run, and a policeman was killed by a shot from the Gallegand Club. This brought reprisals. Within the next few hours eighteen people were killed, a hundred wounded. Machado returned from the country, to speak on the radio of the police headquarters; he repeated his general position as one of accepting mediation but added that, if the U.S. were to disembark a single soldier, Cuba would resist in arms.[11]

After this, Machado refused to see Welles, feigning illness, until 8 August when he saw him at 9.30 a.m., on a morning already terribly hot; Welles came in walking rigidly in black clothes, not inclining his head for anyone, keeping his arms close to his body. Servants carrying huge glasses of iced water stood to attention by the wall; on either side walked General Herrera and the president's ADC, the latter without gloves; a grave breach of etiquette, noted one observer. Welles had now Roosevelt's specific backing for his five-point plan, which he presented in writing; he carried this 'ultimatum' through the crowds of senators and *políticos* gathered along the corridors, so that all could see it. Machado, however, told Welles he could not accept the solution, and that he would prefer armed intervention to any such proposal. 'It was evident,' Welles reported, 'that he was in a state of

[9] Foreign Relations (1933), II, 337.
[10] Lamar Schweyer, 149.
[11] *Ibid.*, 149–54. Welles has 17 killed and over 100 wounded

mental disturbance bordering on hysteria.' After a while, Machado said he had counter-proposals which he would soon communicate and Welles left unsatisfied. He noted that Machado had not seemed upset about those killed the previous day: 'As a matter of fact,' he assured Welles airily, 'more than half of those killed were not even Cubans, they were foreigners.'[12] Yet, Welles added, he had once seen Machado with tears running down his cheeks on finding a dead dove, killed by flying against its cage. In the afternoon, Machado telephoned Washington and told his ambassador that 'there had been a meeting of workers at the palace and that the strike had been called off; all the workers, he said, had agreed to go back to work and complete tranquillity existed throughout Cuba'. He also told Cintas that Welles had 'presented this morning in writing a communication which in fact meant the overthrow of the government'; Machado had said that he could not and would not be 'pushed out by the U.S.'. Cintas added (when reporting this conversation to Under-Secretary Phillips) that 'though he knew Mr Welles had this in mind for a long time, this was the first proposal he had made of it directly to the President'.[13]

But what was this 'meeting of workers'? It was in fact a meeting with leaders of the CNOC: César Vilar, the secretary-general, and Vicente Álvarez, one of the Communist cigar workers of Havana, had come to Machado and had undertaken to call off the strike in return for a promise to recognize the CNOC. Machado perhaps did not appreciate that the strike extended far beyond what could be controlled by that organization.[14] The Communists had in fact decided that the danger of U.S. intervention was such that any recourse, even a temporary alliance with Machado, was licit in order to try to avoid it.

In the latter part of the day opposition to Welles's ultimatum mounted; Machado also told Congress that Welles's behaviour was not supported by Roosevelt. Welles telegraphed to his president begging him to tell Ambassador Cintas that he was firmly behind him.[15] Conservative *políticos* meantime allowed it to be known that they refused to consider the shortening of Machado's term by one minute. Old Liberal leaders, old friends of José Miguel, declared themselves opposed to the 'courteous indication of the Mediator'. Representative García Ramos put down a resolution deploring Welles's behaviour and asking for help from other American states. On the other hand, Colonel Gimperling, the U.S. attaché, bluntly told 'various army officers' that intervention would come unless Machado resigned.[16] Welles by this

---

[12] Sumner Welles, *The Time for Decision* (1944), 196.
[13] Foreign Relations (1933), II, 339–40.
[14] See Mujal memorandum, 2.
[15] Foreign Relations (1933), II, 339–40.
[16] Lamar Schweyer, 157–9.

time had concluded that 'forceful and positive action by the government of the U.S. was necessary in order that our prestige both here and
in the rest of the continent, may not be seriously prejudiced'. He had
come to the view that:

> If President Machado remains in power, he can only continue
> through the . . . most brutal methods . . . If the present condition is
> permitted to continue . . . I am positive that a state of complete
> anarchy will result, which might force the Government of the U.S.,
> against its will, to intervene. [He added:] I should like further to
> emphasize . . . that . . . the permanent treaty [i.e. of 1902] imposes
> upon us responsibilities as regards the Cuban people. I do not see
> how the government of the U.S. can, in view of its treaty obligations,
> continue its formal support of a Cuban government, which has con-
> sistently deprived the Cuban people of their constitutional rights,
> which has been guilty of atrocities which have shocked the entire
> continent and which refused to consider the acceptance of a fair
> *and Cuban*[17] solution of this disastrous situation . . . I believe that
> should President Machado positively refuse to agree to the solution
> . . . the government of the U.S. should . . . withdraw recognition. I
> do not believe that [this] . . . would force us to intervene; I think that
> if the President himself was advised that we would withdraw recog-
> nition . . . he would be obliged to accept [the] . . . proposed solution
> by most of the members of his Cabinet, by the Army and by the great
> majority of Congress . . . If, however, he persists . . . I do not believe
> that his government [would] be able to maintain itself for more than
> an extremely brief period . . . [after which] I have every reason [from
> the ABC] to believe that the situation would continue sufficiently
> within control to make it unnecessary for the U.S. government to
> undertake even a brief armed intervention.[18]

On the next day, 9 August, however, Machado seems to have decided
to resign. Despite his agreement with the Communists, the strikes were
going on. Yet he had not decided to leave at short notice. In the course
of the morning, Orestes Ferrara at last arrived back from Europe. He
went first to the palace and then to Welles. He began the conversation
with the comment that in his opinion there was more disorder in New
York than in Havana; he then asked Welles whether he had sent his
'ultimatum' as the mediator under the Platt Amendment or under
international law. 'Have I sent you an ultimatum?' Welles asked disin-
genuously. Ferrara then said that as mediator Welles surely could not
offer solutions, he could only harmonize the work of the two parties.

[17] Author's italics.
[18] Foreign Relations (1933), II, 340–3.

They made an appointment for the next day.[19] Meantime the Spanish ambassador complained to Welles; three Spaniards had been killed by the police, sixty had been arrested in Havana for refusing to open their shops.[20] Property was being damaged in the interior.

Roosevelt now stepped into the crisis; he saw Ambassador Cintas in the afternoon. He said that Machado could go down in Cuban history as a great patriot if he would only accept Welles's plan; Welles was acting with full presidential approval; he personally had 'no desire to intervene but that it was our duty to do what we could so that there should be no starvation and chaos among the Cuban people'. Cintas said that Machado could not let himself be forced out of the presidency. Roosevelt suggested the economic not the political crisis should be used to save Machado's face; if Machado were to leave in order to save the Cubans from starvation, he would be performing an act of nobility; a shipload of supplies might then be sent to Havana for the benefit of the Cubans.[21] Cordell Hull of course sent Welles an account of this conversation, adding that he and Roosevelt thought that Welles should not press Machado too much, because of a possible counter-proposal. But Welles was then busy dealing with the rumours of threatened assassinations of himself – in particular by ex-chief of police, Ainciart, whom Machado had just removed on Welles's proposal.[22] Even more vigorous opposition to Welles was being organized in the House of Representatives at Havana, where a motion was tabled:

> That the activities of H.E. the Ambassador of the U.S. . . . . interfering in the interior problems of the government, have caused a deep perturbation of public order and the threat embodied in his insinuations of possible intervention in our country are a violation upon our rights as a free and independent people and an aggression upon the sovereignty of small nationalities.[23]

On the morning of 10 August, this nationalistic mood was successfully maintained. Machado, with Ferrara's help, forced through the executive committee of the Liberal party a resolution regretting the Welles mediation. The Conservatives and Popular parties, however, refused to back this: and Senator Alberto Barreras, Liberal president of the Senate, and the governor of Oriente, José Barceló, president of the Liberal party, both privately told Welles that they backed his solution.

---

[19] Account of conversation in Lamar Schweyer, 176.

[20] There is no truth in the suggestion that the British minister also complained. See British correspondence, FO 371/16573.

[21] Ibid., 347–8. Lamar Schweyer says that Roosevelt offered Machado a military aeroplane on which to leave. There seems no evidence of this offer in the U.S. archives.

[22] Ibid., 346.

[23] Loc. cit.

Welles showed Ferrara the report on Roosevelt's talk with Cintas, but refused him permission to keep a copy; on the other hand the opposition received a copy, and loose sheets giving the text of the telegram began to circulate in Havana.[24] It turned out that Ferrara's proposals to Welles were: an indefinite extension of time before reaching a decision; and U.S. acquiescence in the suppression of the general strike by any means possible. Ferrara added that Roosevelt's offer of food was a futile gesture and suggested instead a generous loan. If this were done, Ferrara would advise Machado to resign some time later after the effects of the U.S. action permitted him, Machado, to regain his lost popularity. Welles refused, saying he had decided that 'normal conditions' could not exist so long as Machado continued and that 'as soon as there existed in Cuba a constitutional government which merited the confidence of all of the Cuban people, the Government of the U.S. would be disposed to consider favourably any reasonable requests for economic assistance'. Ferrara then said he wanted to 'think things over', and would return next day when he had seen Machado again.[25] Welles meantime apparently talked a good deal of intervention, even to foreign diplomats; López Ferrer, the Spanish ambassador, told Ferrara that Welles had spoken in this vein to him.[26] In Washington, Ambassador Cintas told Cordell Hull that he thought Welles should be recalled to Washington for consultations, so perhaps making concessions by Machado easier; but Roosevelt rejected this.[27] He did, however, cause Hull to send a telegram telling Welles to 'bear in mind' rumours that the U.S. was trying to 'coerce, not persuade' in Havana.

Now more was afoot in Havana than Welles had as yet reported. Late on the night of 10 August he spoke a long time with General Herrera, to whom he sketched the idea that Machado should request leave of absence until a vice-president was inaugurated; then would come the immediate resignation of all the members of the cabinet except General Herrera himself, who should act as head of government until the inauguration of a vice-president. Herrera accepted this scheme with alacrity, and Welles decided to propose it to Ferrara the next afternoon. (This seemed to promise that Herrera would become acting head of government till February.) This new scheme of Welles's would save Machado's face since he would be handing over to one of his own cabinet ministers (Welles's other considered proposal for acting president, Céspedes, ambassador in Mexico, grandson of the liberator of 1898, being a man without much strength). Machado's life would be guaranteed and so would those of the other Liberal politicians; the plan would

[24] Lamar Schweyer, 180-2.
[25] Foreign Relations (1933), II, 351-2.
[26] Lamar Schweyer, 183.
[27] Foreign Relations (1933), II, 352-3.

also guarantee public order since the army was known to respect Herrera. 'The powerful leaders of the opposition,' Welles said, 'have unanimously decided to accept this proposal since, in their belief, it is the only method of obtaining Machado's resignation and of avoiding American intervention, which in their opinion Machado is at present determined to force.'[28]

In the morning of 11 August, Welles apparently had a preliminary meeting with Colonel Sanguily ('Sanguilito', to distinguish him from his father, the hero of 1868 and 1895); at this meeting in the house of Antonio González de Mendoza, one of the most important lawyers in Havana, the eventual *pronunciamiento* against Machado, such as it was, was planned. Sanguily said that the army had been offended by Machado, since it had not been a party to the mediation.[29] Rumour spread of an officers' revolt. Troops were observed moving about. The palace guard was tripled. Machine guns were mounted on the top of the buildings and in Zayas Park. Cavalry and infantry were drawn up ready for action at Campo Colombia.

In the afternoon of 11 August, however, Ferrara told Welles that Machado would accept the ambassador's latest scheme and ask leave of absence from Congress not later than Wednesday of the next week; he would also request the resignation of the cabinet except Herrera, and would effectively resign when the latter was inaugurated as vice-president. But Machado also had another idea, which he was still canvassing, demanding a new version of the Platt Amendment, the indefinite prolongation of the existing administration, and a request for economic aid. Once this had been rejected, Ferrara assured Welles, Machado would go ahead with the request for leave of absence. Ferrara also wanted guarantees of public order given by the ABC. Welles's latest brainwave was meantime exciting much adverse comment among the opposition. Ferrara and Ramiro Guerra, Machado's secretary, then began to draw up a document to be signed by the president, in which the key phrase was: 'If the U.S.A. desires the good of Cuba, they should make my departure concur with a series of indispensable provisions', such as the 'approval of a reciprocity treaty, a fifty per cent reduction of North American duties on Cuban products', and a revision of the Platt Amendment.[30] Machado was determined thus to go down fighting. While this document was being drawn up, however, there were clear signs that unless Machado went soon, he would certainly go down altogether.

---

[28] *Ibid.*, 355–6.
[29] Adam y Silva, 48. See also Arthur Krock, *New York Times*, 17 August, in which he says that Welles 'was able to report before Machado himself knew it that the Army was about to desert the Cuban President'; and the *New York Times*, 13 August.
[30] Document in Lamar Schweyer, 190.

The army had of course been Machado's main support. Many officers had been accused by the opposition of breaking the law to serve the president. With Machado's resignation they would be defenceless: this predisposed many officers to make every effort, even at this late hour, to change sides. About 1 p.m. on 11 August, Colonel Erasmo Delgado went to the Máximo Gómez Barracks, where the artillery regiment keeping guard over public palaces was lodged. He openly urged these troops to rebellion, and this movement soon spread. Several higher army commanders were imprisoned. Machado even left the palace for Campo Colombia for fear of finding himself made prisoner. There Colonel Castillo guaranteed the president support, and so did other barracks in and around Havana (Cabañas, Atarés, San Ambrosio). At this point General Herrera, still provisional president-elect under Welles's plan, hearing of the rebels, went alone to the Máximo Gómez Barracks, where Delgado told him that he and his friends were rising in order to stave off intervention. All seemed to support the idea of Herrera taking over provisionally. Herrera returned to Machado and Machado returned to the palace.

That night, 11–12 August, was utterly silent. The streets were deserted. Herrera seemed to be in control. Machado was preparing to leave,[31] having been told at some point, bluntly, that the higher officers were unanimous in demanding that he should leave during the course of the next day.[32]

But Welles was now having second thoughts about Herrera. His original choice had been the colourless diplomat Céspedes (who had nothing to contribute save his name) and it was to Céspedes that he was now beginning to return. At twelve midnight, Welles met with the three leaders of the dissident group of officers – Colonels Delgado, Sanguily and Horacio Ferrer. Welles led them to understand that intervention would follow Herrera's acceptance of the presidency. Lieutenant Zayas Bazán of the Aviation Corps, and his brother, a civilian in the radio business, set up an improvised radio which demanded that Machado should be forced to hand over to 'an impartial civilian'. Herrera and Machado were amazed: the former telephoned Welles, who said he knew nothing of this idea. But at 1 a.m. the two met, with De la Torriente, at Herrera's house. Welles assured Herrera that it was not he but the army who impeded the keeping of the earlier bargain. Herrera telephoned Orestes Ferrara, who demanded that the pact should be kept, saying that the army would accept whoever Welles wanted. Welles therefore once again agreed to accept Herrera, and at 4 a.m. Sanguily and Delgado assured Welles that they would

[31] *Ibid.*, 200.
[32] Foreign Relations (1933), II, 357.

accept any Cuban, provided Machado would go; it was on this understanding that all the parties went to bed.[33]

Two hours later, at six o'clock in the morning of 12 August, the
Aviation Corps' radio and ABC Radical once more came on the air.
They proclaimed that Machado had already resigned in favour of
Herrera. But at 7 a.m., Welles was told that Sanguily and the officers
had changed their minds again, and that they could not accept Herrera,
since they feared that most of the opposition thought him too closely
involved with Machado.[34] The public received the news of Machado's
resignation calmly: they were used to rumours without foundation.
Early in the morning, however, it became clear that this time the
rumour was firmly based. Welles appeared shortly on the balcony of
the U.S. Embassy accompanied by Sanguily, Tina Forcade, Hortensia
Lamarr and Raúl de Cárdenas. Cheering began. The flag of the ABC
was brought on to the balcony by Martínez Sáenz, Saladrigas, Guillermo Belt and Erasmo Delgado. At the same time, the corridors in the
palace which for so long had been full of ardent visitors were deserted:

> In the great central courtyard the soldiers could be heard hitting the
> ground with the butts of their rifles in order to render the last salute
> ... through the wide windows ... could be seen to one side at a
> distance of less than three blocks, the conquerors [the ABC, that is]
> still fearful of leaving the protection of the American flag. And on all
> sides large numbers of people were crying out in enthusiasm and
> shouting against Machado ...

At 9.30 Machado calmly descended in the lift. Ferrara, Ramiro Guerra,
Lamar Schweyer, all three distinguished historians, stood on the
balcony to watch the president leave. In the street the multitude broke
into two to allow Machado's cars to pass in dead silence. The cars
vanished, always opening waves of deep silence. The police abandoned
their guard, fearful of the ABC. Guerra meantime drew up a decree
whereby Machado accepted the resignation of all ministers except
Herrera, and Ferrara drew up a statement by which Machado asked
leave of absence from Congress. The crowd gathered outside ever more
closely. Lamar Schweyer telephoned Welles saying that their lives were
in danger. Welles said he could do nothing. Ferrara took the telephone
and said: 'You, Ambassador, are the only one who can today prevent a
spectacle such as has never occurred even in our history. Otherwise a
great many people will die. See what a state the public are in.' 'Oh
doctor,' Welles said, 'these are just manifestations of joy.' Ferrara hung
up violently after Welles told him to take these documents of abdication

---

[33] *Ibid.*, 359.
[34] *Ibid.*, 205.

to Herrera's house. But he agreed to do so nevertheless and, with Ramiro Guerra and Lamar Schweyer, bravely sallied out by car; like Machado, they created silence as they drove along. Behind them, the multitude turned away from the palace, placing the notice 'To Let' on the great front door. The three old supporters of Machado soon began to pass cars flying the green flag of the ABC: 'Seeing these men, enraged, sweating, hoarse from shouting, eyes bulging from their sockets, thirsty for vengeance, and waving their green flag like Mahomet's, we knew we were lost.' A bloodbath was inevitable.

At Herrera's house several officers and congressmen were waiting. Herrera could no longer control himself. Welles arrived and urged Herrera to resign by first appointing Céspedes Secretary of State and then giving up in his favour. Sanguily and Erasmo Delgado, Céspedes and Torriente also appeared and backed this course. Herrera carried out his charade, though he was not legally president since Congress had not yet granted Machado his solicited leave of absence. Undismayed, Welles saluted Céspedes as president. Sanguily and Delgado looked smug at having 'saved their country from intervention'. An announcement was then made to the public summarizing the events.

This was the signal for violence. The masses broke into the empty presidential palace and sacked the lower two floors. Books, pianos, typewriters, vases, furniture, all were thrown out of windows or otherwise destroyed. ABC's green flag was seen everywhere in the city. The first victim was the chief of the Porra, Colonel José Antonio Jiménez, upon whom the crowd closed in at the corner of Virtudes and the Prado: he was lynched. Students set off to kill policemen everywhere, and the lives and the houses of all the politicians of the Machado era, the remains of the Conservative as well as of the Liberal party, became immediately in danger. A quivering group of three congressmen went to accept Machado's request for a leave of absence, meeting by candlelight for fear of attracting attention.[35] Ferrara, Averhoff, and most of the leaders, however, escaped by air, though General Herrera found himself hiding for several days in the Hotel Nacional. Finally, in the night of 12–13 August Machado himself flew to Nassau, carrying five revolvers, seven bags of gold and five friends in pyjamas; he arrived at dawn, and later in the day his family was escorted from Havana by ship.[36]

[35] Phillips, 38–9.
[36] i.e. his wife Elvira, and his three sons-in-law and their families – Obregón, Baldomero Grau and Rafael Jorge Sánchez.

CHAPTER LIII

The Middle-Class Government

During the early twentieth century the U.S. intervened in the affairs of many countries, not only of Cuba. U.S. armed forces entered the territories of foreign states twenty times between 1898 and 1920[1] mostly as a result of 'disturbed conditions' or threats of 'utter chaos' which usually involved the U.S. Legation, 'the American colony', and U.S. business interests. Since 1920 such occasions had been less frequent, partly as a result of President Wilson's championship of democratic principles, partly as a result of political opposition to the support of business interests by marines.[2] But there had been no specific change of policy. Marines landed in Honduras in 1924; they ruled Nicaragua from 1912 to 1925, the Dominican Republic from 1916 till 1930 and Haiti from 1915 till 1934 – their original intervention there being partly at least inspired by fear of German or even French occupation.[3]

The Nicaraguan experience of 1926–7 was a turning-point; few interventions were so opportunistic as this one carried out by Secretary of State Kellogg, the planner of perpetual peace, to prevent the Liberal president from winning the election.[4]

This experience exerted a profound influence on Stimson and on the State Department as a whole. It had been found that mere electoral supervision was not enough, and that intervention involved the U.S. in a whole range of complicated activities – above all, from the long-term point of view, in fighting the revolutionary patriot, or bandit, self-proclaimed saviour of Nicaragua, and a man of popular appeal, 'General' Sandino.[5]

---

[1] See Captain H. A. Ellsworth, *180 Landings of the U.S. Marines, 1800–1934*, 2 vols (1934). There was also the pursuit of Pancho Villa into Mexico in 1916.

[2] Bryce Wood argues thus (*op. cit.*, 4–5).

[3] See H. Herring, *A History of Latin America*, 2nd edn (1961), 430.

[4] 'It would have been a serious blow to the prestige of the U.S. in the Caribbean area and in the world as a whole if its presidential choice for Nicaragua had been overthrown by Mexico's candidate,' says Professor Bryce Wood, baldly (*op. cit.*, 17). In both the Dominican Republic and Nicaragua the U.S. was thus ultimately responsible for establishing dictators. Both were murdered, Somoza in 1956, Trujillo in 1961.

[5] See Wood, 26 ff. Over 100 marines were killed in Nicaragua. Sandino was described by the U.S. diplomats as 'an erratic Nicaraguan about 30 years of age with wild Communist ideas acquired largely in Mexico'. He was killed in 1934.

Franklin Roosevelt had many advantages over his predecessor where consideration of Latin America was concerned. He knew Central and South America well, had visited Cuba and Panamá as Assistant Secretary of the Navy, and was well acquainted with Haiti and the Dominican Republic. He also read Spanish. Likewise he was more interested in the problems of South America than any other President before or since, save perhaps his cousin Theodore, and Kennedy.

During the nineteenth century the U.S. had successfully defended the principles of the Monroe doctrine, occasionally elaborating it (as when President Grant said that his government regarded it as a principle that 'hereafter no territory on this continent shall be regarded as subject to a European power'.)[6] This policy had always been adopted in the name of liberty; and until the 1890s, until indeed the Spanish-American war and the age of Martí, this interpretation had been widely approved by the South American republics. The North American stand against French intervention in Mexico, for instance, and the Spanish return to the Dominican Republic was generally approved. Blaine's customs and monetary proposals had marked the beginning of a new attitude, however, and throughout the first quarter of the twentieth century doubts about U.S. altruism had grown, during the era of commercial expansion and occasional political intervention.

In the course of 1933 in Cuba, a new type of intervention occurred: the U.S. ambassador secured the withdrawal of one relatively unpopular government and placed power in the hands of a neutral successor who enjoyed no general backing. The consequence was a new revolution and the accession temporarily to power of a radical government which despite the anarchic conditions seemed to promise well. The reluctance of the U.S. administration to recognize this government caused its downfall – an act which cast long shadows over events in the 1950s a generation later.

In Cuba in mid-1933 it seemed at first sight as if Sumner Welles had gained a great victory. 'Warm congratulations' came from Roosevelt and Cordell Hull. Welles seemed happy, Céspedes was busy forming his government. 'The situation in all of the larger cities including Havana [is] very well under control,' Welles telegraphed on 13 August; but the next day he spoke more circumspectly: 'Better control,' ₁he reported, though 'looting and burning of houses was extensive.' Even so the 'situation now however is well in hand throughout the city'.[7] Though admitting that 'in Marianao, a suburb, several casualties occurred', he never gave the State Department a true picture of Havana on 12 and

---

[6] Qu. Foster Rhea Dulles, *Prelude to World Power* (1965), 36.
[7] Foreign Relations (1933), II, 361–3.

13 August. At least a thousand were killed and three hundred houses were sacked. The British minister gave a far more truthful picture to his government:

> The scenes of vengeance which were enacted ... will remain for ever a painful recollection for those who beheld them ... The bodies of the most famous *porristas* were even dragged in triumph through the streets.[8]
>
> Shortly after dinner [he reported] I saw the street outside H.M. Legation fill with frenzied people who, at that moment were directing their imprecations against the police on guard ... and threatening to lynch them but they were passing on to the beautiful house of my neighbour, a prominent senator. ... The sackage ... was a revolting sight for while Negroes fought for gramophones and nursemaids for shawls, well-dressed families drove up in Packards and Cadillacs, seized Louis XV cabinets and gilded chairs.[9]

No one did anything to contain what was in effect an avalanche. Céspedes, impeccably dressed in white, kept on being photographed embracing Welles and receiving the good wishes of the U.S. military attaché, Colonel Gimperling. But beyond the radius embraced by the camera, 'civilisation was stripped away at one stroke'. 'Relations of boys who had been tortured and killed started on vengeance hunts ... they knew the men they were seeking [because] the *porristas* had never kept it a secret when they killed. ... The masses, as well as the ABC, demanded blood.'[10] The ABC had in fact a list of active *porristas* and all connected with them, and after Machado fell there occurred a man-hunt. One *porrista*, Leblanc, was murdered in front of the Hotel Pasaje. Machado's Chief of Police Ainciart was traced and killed on 19 August. The offices of Ferrara's *Heraldo de Cuba* were looted and smashed, as were the houses of Ferrara himself, Secretary Averhoff, General Molinet, Zubizarreta, Viriato Gutiérrez, Ramiro Guerra and Carlos Miguel de Céspedes. Daily for a week at least, at dawn, drums would be heard summoning people to witness a sacking or an execution; a few shots from a Springfield rifle with its unmistakable whistle, and, then, silence. The least cry of accusation (*porrista!*) could release terrible violence.[11] At the same time there began, not for the first time in Havana and certainly not for the last, the 'amusing and embarrassing period in which the Americans here turn about face ... the managers of the American companies [who] usually gathered at the American Club [and who had] refused to believe ... that Machado committed murders,

[8] Dispatch of Grant Watson, 21 August 1933.
[9] *Ibid.*
[10] Phillips, 45.
[11] Phillips, 52.

[thinking that it was] ... all a newspaper invention'.[12] These changes were made easier by the arrival in port of U.S. ships *Taylor* and *Claxton*: Welles assured Commander Howard that there was 'no reason now to contemplate ... landing even one man'; though he added in his report to Hull: 'I feel very confident that the visit of these ships was essential for its moral effect alone.'[13]

The new provisional president, Céspedes, formed his cabinet on 14 August: he included three ABC leaders (Joaquín Martínez Sáenz, Carlos Saladrigas and Guillermo Belt); Laredo Bru (the hero of the Unión Nacionalista of 1923); the rich engineer Eduardo Chibás; Rafael Santos Jiménez (an old follower and biographer of José Miguel Gómez); Nicasio Silverio (of the OCRR); Raúl Cárdenas (a Menocalista, a deputy first in 1911); Dr Presno (of the University of Havana);[14] and the old aide and friend of Crowder and Wood, Demetrio Castillo Pokorny, without a party. Two further members of the old Liberal party (Estanislao Cortina and Miguel Angel Cisneros), who had managed to save something from the wreck of their party by Machado, became respectively mayor of Havana and chairman of the municipal council.[15] Welles commented: 'There is not a man ... who is not of high personal integrity.'[16] Did his double negative, one wonders, hide the fact that even the Proconsul judged something lacking. These new ministers from the president downwards were very North American in outlook; Céspedes himself had been born and educated in the U.S.; Chibás had been ADC to General Ludlow in the U.S. army in Cuba in 1898; Castillo Pokorny was almost more North American than Cuban. The ABC men were most of them devoted admirers of North America.

Welles seems to have had no doubt about the importance of OCRR and ABC and of keeping them within the system. He appears, however, to have completely ignored not only the Communists and the CNOC but also the students, the ABC Radical and the small group, Ley y Justicia,[17] headed by the survivor of the Valdés Daussá brothers who, if relatively few in number, were aggressive, uncontrolled and very active. He took comfort from the fact that 'a good many omnibuses and taxis are circulating ... many of the stores have re-opened ... streetcars will be in operation by noon today ... railroads will be operating by nightfall'.

[12] *Ibid.*, 46.
[13] Foreign Relations (1933), II, 363.
[14] José Antonio Presno (1876–1950), professor of the Medical School, surgeon.
[15] Castillo became Minister of Agriculture on 30 August in place of Santos Jiménez who had become mayor of Havana. Castillo's place as war minister was taken by the ex-Surgeon-General, Horacio Ferrer.
[16] Foreign Relations (1933), II, 363–4.
[17] Properly, Agrupación Revolucionaria pro Ley y Justicia.

Nevertheless his Olympian enthusiasm soon waned: Demetrio Castillo, who had taken over the War Department, came to his house on 15 August at 8 a.m. and said the situation

> was most disquieting ... public opinion was rolling up [*sic*] increasingly against the continuation in office of any national, provincial or municipal executive or legislative authorities who held office under the old regime ... this feeling was shared by the majority of the younger officers ... resignations of certain provincial governors have been forced ... or they have been violently removed ... if the government insisted upon replacing the former officials ... by force, the Army in many districts would refuse to carry out orders ... agitation was spreading against the Government for having permitted the departure ... of so many officials of the old regime who were connected in the public mind with the atrocities performed by the Machado administration.

The Proconsul drew a deep breath and went there and then to see Céspedes, urging 'immediate energetic action', consisting, he suggested, of declarations that all guilty of crimes would be tried while there was a 'truce with regard to the removal ... of unpopular officials'. Céspedes agreed and issued the announcement; meantime, Castillo 'urged me to leave the *Taylor* in the harbour ... and has also requested me ... that ... reinforcements should be at hand both at Key West and at Guantánamo.'[18]

Another North American comment seems appropriate.

> The Cuban people [recorded Ruby Hart Phillips at this time] are like children who have suddenly entered fairy land. They have a new government making new promises, and now, to hear the Cuban tell it, all they have to do is to sit back and wait for the miraculous recovery of business and watch the dollars roll in ... They confidently expect a loan of fifteen million dollars although the island cannot pay what it [already] owes. Foreign obligations total ... $M160. [She added] Cubans are getting drunk day after day – something never seen before on this island ... terrorists spend their days and nights ... drinking.[19]

Welles soon apparently reached much the same judgement: almost every Cuban expected 'the government to perform miracles without a moment's delay'.[20] But even Céspedes, dry civil servant that he was,

[18] Foreign Relations (1933), II, 363–6. The *Taylor* and the *Claxton*, both destroyers, had arrived in Havana on 14 August.
[19] Phillips, 52.
[20] Telegram on 20 August, NA 837.00/3685, qu. Wood, 70.

pointed out that poverty existed throughout the country to such an extent that no government could really stand.[21]

As early as 17 August, there were rumours of further plots by the students and Communists against Céspedes and the army.[22] NCOs in the army were for the first time mentioned in these rumours, although no one paid any attention to them. On 18 August, a sergeant stenographer, Fulgencio Batista, made a somewhat menacing speech at the funeral of one of the soldiers killed by Machado, demanding better conditions for the enlisted men.[23] On 20 August, Menocal, still an opponent of Céspedes, returned to Cuba without ceremony – a threatening sign in no way counterbalanced by the return on 22 August of two other exiles, Colonels Carlos Mendieta and Méndez Peñate.[24] On 24 August Céspedes took a firm step towards the restoration of normality by formally re-establishing the constitution of 1902 and dissolving Machado's old Congress: new elections would be held in February. Both students, however, and Menocal were asking for a 'firmly *revolutionary* government',[25] using the adjective which had already passed into Cuban speech as signifying patriotism. The students also desired a new constitution 'totally unconnected with the past'.[26]

By that day Welles seems inexplicably to have abandoned hope that Céspedes and the ABC could govern constitutionally: Menocal, he said, was attempting to suborn the army; Sanguily, the 'only officer of quality', was ill:

> Students and radicals of every shade are breaking into houses, promoting lynchings, forcing resignations from ex-senators . . . congressmen . . . other public officials . . . and only this morning forced the resignation of the [new] Sub-Secretary of Communications. The labour situation is of course disquieting . . . conditions on the sugar plantations are very grave and it was only through acceptance of all the demands presented by the strikers that collected on the *Punta Alegre* sugar estate . . . that destruction of the property and possible loss of life of the American manager and his family was averted.[27]

Similar reports came from all over the island: the British vice-consul in Cienfuegos reported that 'a large number of strikers are visiting the sugar mills with demands for higher wages etc. . . . The men go in large numbers armed with heavy sticks and some have guns; up to 1000

[21] *Loc. cit.*
[22] This is again Ruby Hart Phillips's belief. Her husband told Welles of a possible plot against the government.
[23] Adam y Silva, 321.
[24] Foreign Relations (1933), II, 369.
[25] *Ibid.*, 369–70. See also despatch of Grant Watson, 29 August.
[26] Conte Agüero, *Eduardo Chibás, el adalid de Cuba* (1955), 182.
[27] Foreign Relations (1933), II, 371–3.

strong'. In Cienfuegos itself a baker's strike was also maintained by the use of sticks against black-legs.[28] More and more mills passed into the hands of workers, often outsiders, sometimes tenants, but rarely actually employees of the mill. On Céspedes's urgent invitation, a three-man mission from Washington composed of Adolf A. Berle, Jr,[29] John Laylin[30] and James H. Edwards, came down to Havana to see what they could do to help Cuban finances. They gave a workmanlike preliminary report;[31] but nothing had been done before a ferocious hurricane dislocated communications throughout the island for three days – Havana had a wind of 98 m.p.h., while the little town of Isabella had one of 145 m.p.h., and hardly a house was left standing.[32]

Welles himself was in despair. His moment of triumph was turning sour; he had already telegraphed home asking to be replaced by 1 September.[33] But Roosevelt insisted that he should stay on till 15 September. He agreed, unfortunately for him. His close personal relationship with all members of the Céspedes government meant that he was being 'daily requested for decisions on all matters'. The ABC to his sorrow seemed to have no more positive policy than to persecute old *porristas* or other supporters of the *Machadato*. On 29 August, thirty 'of the most prominent American businessmen in Cuba' came to see him, certain of them 'firmly of the opinion that communist agitators "in the pay of Russia" are seizing this opportunity through the formation of unions and the promotion of syndicalism to [instal] ... a communist regime.' Welles, not entirely correctly, assured them that Communism 'did not yet have any support among the laboring class'. A 'small number of foreign agitators are availing themselves of this opportunity to stir up strikes and labor unrest ... [but] I cannot see any indications of the "red menace" '.[34]

At this point in fact the Cuban Communist party was not in a strong position strategically, owing to their last-minute change of policy towards a pact with Machado.[35] Ruben Martínez Villena had been forced to admit his mistake in order to stay in the party and had given way to the unknown shoemaker from Manzanillo, Francisco Calderío, who under the name of Blas Roca took over the secretaryship-general (Manzanillo was now one of the biggest centres of the party). This

[28] Dispatch of 4 September 1933, G. W. Bradley, Cienfuegos.
[29] Adolf Augustus Berle (born 1895), lawyer; diplomat at Paris Peace Treaty; afterwards Assistant Secretary of State, under Roosevelt and Kennedy, ambassador, author, etc.
[30] John Gallup Laylin (born 1902), lawyer, legal adviser to Dwight Morrow in Mexico and afterwards to many governments.
[31] See Foreign Relations (1933), II, 583–5.
[32] Nelson, 56.
[33] See Foreign Relations (1933), II, 367–8.
[34] *Ibid.* (1933), II, 370.
[35] See Mujas MSS.

change was presided over by a Comintern representative of Polish-Jewish origin who went under the name of 'Juan'.[36] The Communists had not, needless to say, wasted any opportunities to settle old scores; Julio Antonio Mella's presumed assassin, the *político*, Magriñat, was among the many murdered in these weeks.

[36] Evidence of anonymous member of Cuban Communist party. This was not, apparently, Fabio Grobart (Semjovich).

CHAPTER LIV

The Sergeants' Revolution

To the general surprise, the outcry against Céspedes's middle of the road and middle-class government was led not by students nor by other disaffected opponents of General Machado but by a group which had been his closest supporters, the non-commissioned officers of the army. The 'sergeants' conspiracy' of September 1933 was, to begin with, led by Sergeant Pablo Rodríguez, president of the Enlisted Men's Club. He was an *oficinista* – a man who wanted to be an officer, but had failed his examinations – who had been working recently at a company headquarters. Second in importance in the plot was Sergeant José Pedraza, an enlisted man from Santa Clara, the most strictly military of the group. Though he had served in Santa Clara throughout the time that the butcher Arsenio Ortiz commanded there, he seems not to have served under Ortiz directly. Manuel López Migoya, another sergeant from Pinar del Río was the most discreet of the group; and finally, in the inner circle, there was Fulgencio Batista, the sergeant stenographer from Oriente who had made the menacing speech at Alpízar's funeral on 18 August, who at first acted as the secretary of the group. They were joined by three ordinary soldiers – Mario Alfonso Hernández, Ramón Cruz Vidal and Juan Estévez; and a corporal, Angel Echevarría. These men became known as the first Junta de Defensa, or the Unión Militar Revolucionaria, or the Junta de los Ocho.[1]

This group had come together in order primarily to avoid any purge of enlisted men on the ground of having backed Machado, and to try to raise these sergeants without examinations to officer rank. Apparently the movement did not exist before Machado fell.[2] Plotting began after rumours that, in the extremely tight financial circumstances, the salaries of enlisted men were about to be cut. Batista tried to see Martínez Sáenz, the ABC Minister of Finance, and failed. The plotters also

[1] Adam y Silva, 101. Several of these men played a major part in the future governments of Batista: thus Pedraza became chief of staff of the army under Batista in 1940, was sacked by him after an attempted *coup* in 1941 and was brought back in 1958 to command in Santa Clara in an attempt to withstand Guevara; Cruz Vidal became chief of the SIM (special police) in the 1950s and commanded against Castro in the Sierra Maestra; López Migoya was chief of staff, 1941–5, in succession to Pedraza.

[2] Evidence of Rodríguez and Echevarría to Adam y Silva.

approached a Radical newspaper-owner, Sergio Carbó, owner and director of *La Semana*, with the idea that he might speak of their grievances in his paper. Finally, the group of students and recent ex-students of the Ley y Justicia movement, headed by Ramiro Valdés Daussá, were also in touch with the sergeants after the end of August. But as for most of the student groups, Batista told Welles later that 'the students did not even know of the movement until 24 hours before it took place ... they and the radical professors were not called in until the sergeants felt [that] they dared not carry out their protest mutiny [*sic*] without civilian support.'[3] The left-wing students of Ala Izquierda Estudiantil held aloof.

The plot might not have come to anything had it not been for the foolishness of a corporal, Capote, who rashly approached a popular captain, Torres Menier, to join the enlisted men's plans. Captain Torres Menier went down to the Enlisted Men's Club to investigate the complaints. He was met by Sergeant Stenographer Batista. Captain Torres Menier denied that soldiers' wages were going to be cut. Batista on behalf of the men demanded better conditions. Torres Menier withdrew and returned with other officers who, seeing how the temper of the gathering was shaping, offered to mediate. Batista refused these offers and appointed, on his own initiative, other NCOs to take command of each company, instructing them thereafter not to take the orders of their own officers. Torres Menier and his colleagues pleaded moderation. Batista, however, without violence and without hostility, handed over the command of Campamen to Columbia to Sergeant Jos Pedraza. He himself went to the barracks of the first infantry battalion at Maestranza, where several sergeants refused to join the revolution. Batista told his friend there, Corporal Oscar Diaz, to assemble the whole battalion and to harangue them, and later he did so himself, in the old cinema of Campamento Columbia. He spoke of the disorders of the past which the officers had done nothing to counteract. He berated the U.S. government. He told the men that their officers were under surveillance, not arrest. Finally, he issued a manifesto to the general public. By this moment Batista had really taken command of the revolt, leaving all his colleagues behind in audacity, rhetoric and resolution.[4] In fact it seems that the soldiers themselves supported the rebel cause chiefly because they had expectations of better boots.

Fulgencio Batista thus made his bow in Cuban politics, which he was to dominate for much of the next twenty-five years. He was the son of Belisario Batista, a sugar worker of north-east Cuba, apparently being born at Veguitas near Antilla, the sugar port which served the United

---

[3] Foreign Relations (1933), II, 488.
[4] See Edmund A. Chester, *A Sergeant named Batista* (1954), 67–8.

Fruit Company.[5] Batista's birth had been during the year that the *Boston* mill had been built by the United Fruit Company, so that it is reasonable to suppose that his father had gone there to seek work. Both Batista's parents appear to have been mulatto and one or other of them may have had some Indian blood. Belisario Batista was supposed to have fought in the war of 1895–8 under José Maceo.[6] The young Fulgencio had had a childhood both varied and disorganized. He went to a public school at Banes and afterwards to a Quaker school at night: in the day he was already cutting cane. He left home at the age of fourteen when his mother, Carmela, died, and worked on a sugar plantation at Holguín. Then he became water-boy at a plantation in San Germán and afterwards the timekeeper of a workgang. Thereafter, he went back to Banes and once more worked as a cane cutter. After that, he lingered around the railway station at Dumois for some time doing odd jobs, and then went to the sugar port of Antilla. There a contingent of the army was posted, because of a threatened strike, real or suspected. Batista then began to work for the army, washing bridles and again doing odd jobs. He was known there as the '*mulato lindo*'.[7] He went on to Alto Cedro, working again as a cane cutter, and then returned to Holguín, where he became first a tailor's, and then a carpenter's, apprentice, and after that a hand boy at a barber's. He also for a time found work as a brakeman on the Consolidated Railways. This shiftlessness and feckless career was unusual only in that most Cubans did not have such good fortune at finding new work as soon as they had lost their old employment. No doubt Batista's good looks and charm helped him.

In April 1921, aged twenty, Fulgencio Batista, with this wide experience of life behind him, joined the Cuban army as a private. In the army he learned shorthand and studied law and typing. So equipped, he left the army for a few months in 1923 and worked as a teacher in stenography, but soon afterwards re-enlisted, joining the Guardia Rural, near Zayas's *finca*. Later he transferred to the regular army, becoming a corporal and secretary to Colonel Federico Rasco. In 1926 he married a girl from El Wajay, Elisa Godínez, who lived near Zayas's *finca*.

In the last year of the *Machadato*, Batista became sergeant stenographer of the 7th District (La Cabaña) and as such worked for councils of war. From this position, he began to see that the regime was collapsing, and he appears to have joined the ABC, 7th Branch, led by a certain Manuel Martí. But he was not at all active in the ABC and such prominence as

[5] There were later rumours that Batista had not been born in Cuba at all but in Central America. No evidence for this was ever forthcoming.

[6] Batista said so, see Chester, 94.

[7] The pretty mulatto.

he gained before 4 September derived from his connection with the defence lawyers in the incident at Artemisa of early May 1933.[8]

His activities at the time of the fall of Machado are obscure. But on 18 August 1933 he is found making his fluent and successful funeral oration commemorating three NCOs killed under Machado. At this he hinted that NCOs would ultimately lead a national revolutionary democracy. He was already known among officers for his unusual quickness and wide interests.

In fact he was more than these things. With his Indian blood, he was almost red in complexion, with great personal charm. He impressed the *New York Times* correspondent as having a mind 'which moves like lightning. He smiles readily and often, gives his complete attention to the person addressing him ... he seemed plausible in the superlative degree ...'[9] With his charm, in fact, he was able to give the impression to anyone whom he saw that he regarded him as the most important person in the world; in this he resembled great seducers rather than most politicians. His varied experience, his knowledge of all parts of Cuba and all sections of society, would make him when he gained revolutionary power a most formidable opponent – particularly since it was clear that he was no mere bureaucratic officer but a self-made man of the people, who hoped to be worshipped by them.

After Batista had won over Campamento Columbia with such astonishing ease, Pablo Rodríguez resigned his nominal leadership of the revolt. Some officers at Campamento Columbia were imprisoned. Some left quietly. Others were detained in the barracks. Batista named himself chief of staff. The new chief of police of Havana, Major Botifoll, was arrested, being replaced by Captain Emilio Laurent, an ex-soldier who had been the leader of the Gibara expedition of 1931 against Machado.

But Campamento Columbia was one thing, control of Havana another. After the meeting with Torres Menier many sergeants thought that they were lost. They therefore approached Colonel Blas Hernández, an eccentric and independent officer who had for some time been holding out as a bandit in Havana province, who offered them 150 to 200 men. Meantime, Radio Havana broadcast the news that there had been an unsuccessful *golpe*. The officers appear to have refused to believe in the possibility of a successful strike against them, and the older officers even restrained younger ones from organizing resistance.[10]

The students were prepared to collaborate with Batista, as were the ABC Radical and those university professors who had not been given

[8] See the description in Edmund Chester, 27–8.
[9] Phillips, 157–8.
[10] Foreign Relations (1933), II, 379.

any part in Céspedes's government. The cabinet showed itself nerveless. Céspedes himself was away in Oriente, observing the hurricane. In Havana the cabinet broke up, 'fearing an attack'. Ferrer, the Secretary of War, telephoned Sumner Welles saying that in his judgement 'there was no hope of solution'. After 10 p.m. the embattled warriors of the Directorio Estudiantil began to arrive at Columbia, as well as Santiago Alvarez and Ramiro Valdés Daussá of Ley y Justicia; there came also students such as Justo Carrillo, Rafael García Barcena, Juan Antonio Rubio Padilla, and a well-known Radical lawyer, José María Irisarri. The latter, a partner in the law firm of Menocal's son-in-law, wrote: 'I passed to the office of Sergeant Batista ... I did not know him and I was presented by Pepín Leyva ... he did not seem a leader, rather the secretary of a revolutionary committee. But he appeared listo.'[11]

Among the civilians only Sergio Carbó knew Batista, and it was apparently Carbó who persuaded him to drop both his demand for a Radical revolution immediately, and his idea of eventually collaborating with officers, as desired probably by the majority of all ranks of the army.[12] It was also Carbó who prepared the 'Proclamation of the Revolutionaries': the reorganization of the economic and political system of Cuba, through a constituent assembly; the immediate punishment of 'the guilty during the previous regime'; the acceptance of all past national debts; and 'to take all steps not herein described leading to the creation of a new Cuba, built on the solid foundations of justice and in accordance with the most modern conception of democracy'. This document was signed by nineteen men: Carbó, Batista, Professor Grau San Martín, Dean of the Medical Faculty in the university, and fifteen other students or professors.[13] It was Carbó who in La Semana, Danton-like, called for 'All power to the Revolution' – though, as left-wing students noted, workers and peasants were far from the theatre of action.[14]

Quite quickly a five-man group was formed prepared to take over the government: Professor Grau San Martín, a fashionable doctor and exile under the last half of the Machado regime; an honest banker, Porfirio Franca, who having been manager of the National City Bank

[11] i.e. shrewd. See Bohemia, 30 September 1934: 'Como nació y como fué asesinada la Comisión Ejecutiva'.
[12] Adam y Silva, 178.
[13] These included: Carlos Prío (student leader of 1930), José Morell y Romero, Justo Carrillo, Guillermo Barrientos, Juan A. Rubio Padilla, Laudelino H. González, José María Irisarri Oscar de la Torre, Carlos Hevia (ex-sugar colono leader and participant in the Gibara expedition of 1931); Emilio Laurent (the new police chief), Roberto Lago, Ramiro Valdés Daussá, Gustavo Cuervo Rubio (gynaecologist and professor at the University of Havana) and Guillermo Portela (El Mundo, 5 September 1933).
[14] Roa, Retorno a la Alborada, 62.

branch in Havana afterwards took over as director of the National Bank in 1920 when 'Poté' and Merchant were disgraced; the journalist, Carbó; the lawyer Irisarri and a professor of criminal law, Guillermo Portela. All these began to talk as if portfolios of government would soon be theirs. Students settled down in the ministries. Batista refused the Ministry of War, but remained in command of the army. Eduardo Chibás, the young leader of Directorio Estudiantil of 1927 and a son of one of the ministers in the Céspedes government, prepared to take over the much needed task of government press relations. In consequence of this, Carbó told Phillips of the *New York Times*: 'At day-break on September 5 1933, the Republic came of age and, with cries of joy, escaped from the American embassy.'[15] Some members of Ala Izquierda Estudiantil (Gustavo Aldereguía, Raúl Roa, Aureliano Sánchez Arango and José Tallet), present at the nomination of the Pentarquía, as it became known, reflected, though they disliked people such as Franca and Carbó, that for the first time Cuba had 'an authentically revolutionary government backed and nourished by the great popular masses without the previous authorization of Washington and its agent in Cuba'.[16] This was a brief moment of national euphoria, and one which was never forgotten.

At the American Embassy, meantime, Sumner Welles, for obvious reasons, was extremely gloomy and anxious. The Proconsul's first reaction to the events at Columbia had been to report that 'by morning in all likelihood there will be a complete collapse of government throughout the island . . . I recommend the immediate necessity of sending at least two warships to Havana and one to Santiago de Cuba at the earliest moment'.[17] Welles also panicked by describing the first revolutionary proclamation as signed by 'the most extreme radicals of the student organization and three university professors whose theories are frankly communistic'.[18] That red peril whose evils the Proconsul had discounted a few days before was soon to dominate his imagination. At eight in the morning of 5 September Welles talked with Secretary of State Cordell Hull on the telephone and said: 'Disorders [were] more or less prevalent wherever his limited advices came from, all over the island' due to activities by 'radical citizens'; but that information, however, was itself more or less sporadic on account of the destruction of communications by storm. 'It was [furthermore] very important that a battle cruiser be sent to Havana at once . . . the small destroyers we were sending would be of some help in the meantime, but not of sufficient use.'

[15] Phillips, 66.
[16] Roa, *Retorno a la Alborada*, 62.
[17] Foreign Relations (1933), II, 379.
[18] *Ibid.*, 381–3.

Hull asked if these ships should not 'stand outside the Havana harbour, lest irresponsible individuals might fire on such vessels if close in the harbour'. Welles thought they 'should go in'.[19] In a few hours' time, however, Batista himself, accompanied by a sergeant, paid his first call on Welles; neither seemed to Welles to have 'any clear conception of what the movement of the soldiers and the NCOs is responsible to'. They wanted to know what the U.S. attitude was to the revolutionary government. Welles said he had 'no comment though he [said] that he would be glad to see them at any time'.[20] He had already proposed that all U.S. citizens should concentrate at the Hotel Nacional, a rather panicky plan which led to the arrival of a hundred and fifty North American families in various stages of distress.

A little later, Céspedes's Secretary of War, Ferrer, saw Welles and told him that the old cabinet was going to tell Céspedes to 'make no effort to maintain himself . . . since all the armed forces of the Republic are in mutiny and he can count on only moral support'; and indeed at 1 p.m. Céspedes handed over to the five-member committee, who formally took possession of the palace and thenceforward regarded themselves, and were regarded as, the government. One of Céspedes's secretaries said to Grau San Martín: 'Don't you think we could agree?' Grau replied: 'Agree? What for? You have still not understood that it is not a question of sharing the jobs between you, the old politicians, and us, the revolutionaries. You must understand that we are making a Revolution.' The secretary asked timidly: 'You believe that the people will understand?' Grau replied: 'I am sure that they will understand. The Cuban people are tired of being exploited, they are tired of hearing the lies of politicians, the Cuban people are in misery and wish to rise and be free';[21] and afterwards the Directorio Estudiantil issued a statement, signed by the student leaders of the faculties of medicine, law, letters and science:

The Directorio . . . is against the whole unhappy business of mediation and the inanimate government named by the U.S. Ambassador . . . With this chaotic state in the country, without principle of authority and with many Machado-stained men still in the armed forces, the Directorio decided to launch its revolutionary action, with the relatively untarnished section of the armed forces [i.e. the Other Ranks] who, with great patriotic organisation and responsibility, acted energetically but without needing to fire a single gun, cleansing

[19] *Ibid.*, 381.
[20] *Ibid.*, 383.
[21] Eddy Chibás's article in *Prensa Libre*, 24 May 1944, qu. Adam y Silva, 188. See also *El Mundo*, 6 September 1933. It is appropriate to doubt whether Dr Grau spoke so clearly.

in this way the glorious uniform of the Army, which was on the edge of dishonour, because of the collaboration of its leaders with the *Machadato*.

People of Cuba! Here is your immense, your patriotic Cuban task, to be carried out without the suspicion of intervention, disguised or open. You have at last entered the list of free peoples and you will be respected by all. Help then the Revolution, your own Revolution, and co-operate in the maintenance of order. Long live Cuba free and sovereign.[22]

A similar statement was issued by the university faculties, which 'unanimously' agreed that 'the present provisional revolutionary government represents the ideals of the Cuban people and, in virtue of this, offers to the same their most decided support'.[23] The fact was that now the university was the only surviving institution in the country, apart from the army, and it hastened to fill the vacuum left by the dissolution of the old legislature as if it were itself a constitutional convention.

Welles meantime was seeing his old friends – such as Colonel Mendieta, Méndez Peñate, ex-President Menocal, Miguel Mariano Gómez (mayor of Havana), Martínez Sáenz and Saladrigas of the ABC. All agreed that 'the only possibility of avoiding American intervention was ... the installation of a government composed of the chiefs of all of the political groups'. Everyone thought that Colonel Mendieta should head this government and that the ranks would support the officers if the NCOs could be got out of the way. '*It was the unanimous opinion likewise that the only way in which a government of the character proposed could be maintained in power until a new Army could be organised ... was for the maintenance of order in Havana and Santiago de Cuba, and perhaps one or two other points in the island, by the American marines.*' All believed that the present revolutionary group could not remain in control for more than a few days and would then in turn be forced to give way to an entirely

---

[22] This was signed by the following: *Faculty of Law*: Carlos Prío Socarrás, Manuel Varona Loreda, Augusto Valdés Miranda, Justo Carrillo, Raúl Ruiz Hernández, José Morell Romero, Sara de Llano y Clavijo, Felipe Martínez Araujo and Felipe de Pazos y Roque; *Faculty of Medicine*: José Leiva y Cordillo, Rafael Escalona y Almeida, Juan Rubio Padilla, Roberto Lago, Carlos Guerrero Cortel, Fernando López del Castillo, Clara Luz Durán y Guerrero, Luis Barreras y López del Castillo, Guillermo Barrientes y Schweyer, Juan Febles Secretal, Laudelino H. González, Fernando González Pérez, Raúl Oms y Narbona and Antonio Medina; *Faculty of Letters and Sciences*: Ramón Miyar, Ramiro Valdés Daussá, José A. Viejo Delgado, Inés Segura Bustamente, Silvia Martell y Bracho, Agustín Guitart and Benigno Recarey y Corono; *Delegates of the Directorio of 1927*: Eduardo Chibás and Reinaldo Jordán.

[23] Signing this were: Francisco Carrera, Reinaldo Marqués, Carlos Coro, Ramiro Capablanca, José Guerra, Miguel Fernández de Castro, S. Massip, Nicolás Puente Duany, Carlos Finlay, Aurelio Fernández Conchoso, María Tapia Ruano, María Ampudia, José Pereda Carreras, Emilio Romero and Elpidio Stincer.

Communist organization.[24] Even so, Martinez Sáenz and Saladrigas restrained their ABC followers from marching on Campamento Columbia. About 1,500 had assembled, fully armed, at their headquarters in the early afternoon with this in mind.[25]

Thus the middle-class politicians were once again using the appeal for intervention as a final sanction. They probably knew quite well that their rivals in the government were not themselves 'Communists', though their fear of the real if still small Communist party and the CNOC may have been almost as strong as they intimated. José Mariano Gómez therefore shortly afterwards visited Dr Grau San Martín and Porfirio Franca of the Pentarquía, but these two rejected the idea of a 'government of concentration'. Later Grau visited Welles. The Proconsul found Grau 'utterly impractical . . . [He] appears to be obsessed with the idea that the soldiers are so devoted to the ideal of the "revolution", as he terms the military rising, that they will take it upon themselves without any orders to maintain order and to guarantee life and property.'

At 5.30 Welles once more spoke to Hull on the telephone. The following conversation ensued:

HULL: How are things coming along by this time?

WELLES: I think that the situation is gradually getting worse. I have had a conference with the political leaders of the Republic and they are of the opinion that it would be wise to land a certain number of troops from the American ship. It would be my idea that what we would do in that case would be to have a certain number come to the Embassy as a guard and a . . . certain number to the National Hotel . . . The difficulty is that we have only fifty men on the *McFarland*, which is now in port, to be brought ashore. That number is not sufficient to make it wise to bring them ashore. Is the *Richmond* arriving tomorrow?

HULL: I do not think it can get there before tomorrow morning. That is, the *Richmond* from the Canal Zone. There is no other battleship on the way just yet. We can take this matter up and have a conference about it. How could we define our policy?

WELLES: Our policy would simply be on the ground of protection of the American Embassy and the protection of American nationals.

HULL: Have you any other suggestions?

WELLES: The political leaders say that a government will be restored with the support of all the army officers but this can only

[24] *Foreign Relations* (1933), II, 388.
[25] *Ibid.*, 392.

17a The Hotel Nacional
 b Colonel Batista, Dr
   Grau San Martín,
   and Colonel Blas
   Hernández

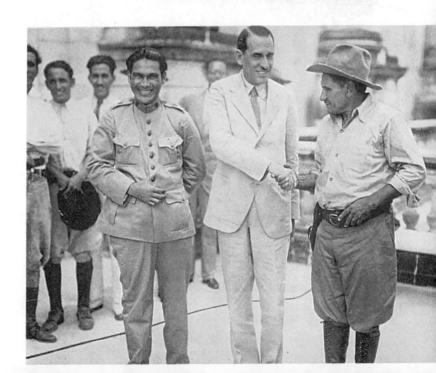

Five U.S. Ambassadors:
18a Sumner Welles, 1933
 b Jefferson Caffery, 1933–1936
 c Arthur Gardner, 1953–1957
 d Earl Smith, 1957–1959
 e Philip Bonsal, 1959–1961

be accomplished with the aid of an American guard and the present small number of men offshore is insufficient.

[At this point Hull was replaced on the line by his subordinate, Caffery.]

WELLES: I think it is absolutely indispensable that men be brought from the ship to the Embassy and to the hotel. A crowd is gathering in front of the Embassy now and there is no protection whatever except a few policemen we have in the Embassy building. I am not at all certain what will happen before long as we do not have any men here.

CAFFERY: You have no guard there?

WELLES: No guard anywhere. There is absolutely no semblance of order of any kind ... I could not hear whether the Secretary said the *Richmond* was arriving tomorrow.

CAFFERY: No, the *Richmond* is not due to arrive till Thursday. I think in the early afternoon.

WELLES: What time does the *Bainbridge* get here? Tomorrow in the early afternoon?

CAFFERY: Not early – I think late afternoon. Now the *Mississippi* is on the way. She is 32,000 tons [a very large battleship].

WELLES: The situation is increasingly serious here. What time will the *Mississippi* get here?

CAFFERY: She cannot make it in under three days. She is at Hampton Roads.

WELLES: I have just had another meeting with the political leaders and they seem to be all of the opinion that the only possible way is for a temporary landing of possibly a thousand men, until a new government can be restored with the co-operation of all of them – with all of the officers who are loyal to the constitutional government and who have not gone over to the other side.

[Interruption.]

CAFFERY: It is better to cable the whole thing. We miss words.

WELLES: All right ... I think we will have some men come from the *McFarland* to the Embassy ... There is absolutely no evidence of any intention to maintain order. The soldiers are going anywhere that they want and pay no attention whatever to anyone's objections.

CAFFERY: ... The Secretary who is here now asks if you know whether [Grau and Franca] ... have any intention of trying to see you again.

WELLES: I am unable to hear what you say ...

'Alas, alas, Mr Welles's position is decidedly unenviable,' an English official minuted in the Foreign Office, not without satisfaction.[26] After this, Cordell Hull consulted with President Roosevelt and it was decided that, contrary to Welles's request, no marines would go ashore unless Welles and his staff were in physical danger. Then, and in succeeding days, Mexico, through the U.S. ambassador there, the brilliant Josephus Daniels, and the Mexican *chargé d'affaires* in Washington, Padilla Nervo, exercised a beneficently moderating influence – pointing out that whatever Welles might think the supposed 'Communist influence' in the Pentarquía and among the students was exaggerated.[27] But at the same time U.S. naval vessels did begin to surround Cuba so that within a week all big harbours had at least one destroyer from the U.S.

Later that night, Welles had two more meetings with his old political friends. He told them that no marines would land for the time being. The ABC and the other backers of Céspedes's government told Grau and Franca that they would support them to 'maintain order'. Grau said that officers of the rank of major and below would soon be reinstated. But General Sanguily at this point went to stay at the Hotel Nacional, not apparently because Welles was there, but because he was ill, and already that night a number of other officers followed him.[28]

This curious movement of officers from their barracks to the hotel continued till 7 September. There were constant discussions, but the officers had not thought to stay there for more than a day, from the point of view of expense alone. Some of them went there without knowing that Welles was living there also. But some did know and some no doubt thought to use him as a shield.[29] The Hotel Nacional, a large modern building on the sea in the style of Spanish plateresque, thus became the rendezvous of counter-revolution.[30]

Welles, by 6 September, was a little less desperate: he had had 'four hours of sleep ... and ... [felt] somewhat better', he assured Hull by telephone in the morning. He was still discussing the possibility of U.S. military intervention but thought that 'if we go in ... we will never be able to come out'.[31] Naturally, the U.S. Chamber of Commerce and others were urging intervention. In East Cuba, there came an urgent demand from Bethlehem Steel to ask for 'protection' for their mines:

[26] Minute of 'G.M.', 23 September 1933 on Grant Watson dispatch (FO 371/16574, f. 31).

[27] See Foreign Relations (1933), II, 380; see also memoirs of Josephus Daniels, *Shirt-Sleeve Diplomat* (1947).

[28] See *Carteles*, 18 February 1934.

[29] See article by Captain Aniceto Sosa Cabrera, *ibid*. Welles himself denied that any direct contact was made.

[30] Built in 1930, by a U.S. company.

[31] See Foreign Relations (1933), II, 389. The Latin American representatives in Washington seemed to accept intervention and the Guatemalan minister actually thought it 'essential'. The Mexican government however voiced strong protests through the U.S. ambassador there, Josephus Daniels (see *ibid.*, 394) and their *chargé d'affaires* in Washington, Padilla Nervo.

again this had to be rejected.[32] But a U.S. destroyer continued in Havana bay, and the papers were full of the fact that three other U.S. warships were on their way.

Late on 6 September Horacio Ferrer, ex-Secretary of War under Céspedes, once more called to see Welles. He gave an optimistic account of the possibilities of rallying the old regime. The sergeants in the Cabaña had made a written statement pledging themselves to Céspedes. Céspedes planned to go with eighty loyal officers on Sunday to that impregnable fortress, where there was 'food and water and sufficient ammunition for them to hold out for . . . at least two months'. Ferrer 'had already been in touch with the officers of the military forces of Matanzas and Pinar del Río . . . and . . . as soon as the proclamation from Cabaña has been issued the loyal troops and officers throughout the country would make a simultaneous proclamation . . . the present regime would be overthrown'. Welles told Ferrer he 'deeply appreciated his advising me of his intentions; that of course it was impossible for me to participate even tacitly . . . and that I could make no commitment to him at this time with regard to the landing of American troops'. But in fact Welles clearly recommended to Washington that if these events did come to pass then the U.S. should do what they could to help it, *including backing by force*:

> It is obvious [he told Hull on 7 September] that with a great portion of the Army in mutiny it could not maintain itself in power in any satisfactory manner unless the U.S. government were willing . . . to lend its assistance in the maintenance of public order . . . Such policy on our part would presumably entail the landing of a considerable force at Havana and lesser forces in certain of the more important ports of the Republic.[33]

This was in effect the second suggestion in 1933 that the U.S. should intervene.

Cordell Hull once more consulted Roosevelt and 'strongly expressed to him' his opinion that 'we could not and should not think of intervening in Cuba even to a limited extent'. It seemed to Hull that 'Welles was over-influenced by local conditions in Cuba and misjudged the disastrous reaction that would follow throughout Latin America'.[34] Roosevelt agreed with Hull, as usual, and fortunately so on this occasion. Once again, Welles's plan was rejected. The cock would crow a third time, however.

Early on 7 September nothing was clear in Cuba: several privates,

---

[32] NA 837.000/3891, qu. Smith, 151.
[33] Foreign Relations (1933), II, 396–7.
[34] Hull, *Memoirs*, 315.

of the same views as the men of *La Cabaña*, and led by sergeant of engineers Matías Hendel, called on Céspedes, offering him the presidency, in the name of Batista, on the condition that Batista could remain head of the army until the purge of officers was complete, and that the new Secretary of War would be named by the Junta Militar. Céspedes said that the officers would first have to have their jobs returned to them; then he himself would carry out the purge. This showed no basis for agreement.[35] Shortly afterwards, Batista gave the order for the encirclement of the Hotel Nacional, where the officers were still gathered. Saladrigas and Domingo Ramos of the ABC chanced to be at the bar of the hotel at the time, and Ramos was held as a hostage.

At the same time, at the meeting of the Pentarquía in the National Palace, Sergio Carbó proposed the immediate reorganization of the army. He successfully brought together Batista and Colonel Hector de Quesada and Colonel Perdomo. Carbó proposed that the command of the army should be reorganized under a committee of five at the top, to be composed of Batista, two officers, and two 'sergeants of the Revolution', selected by the other three members. Foolishly, as it turned out, the officers rejected this, counterproposing the reinstatement of all officers except those actually charged with crimes under Machado and simply 'an annuity to all enlisted men'.[36] The next stage was perhaps foreseeable: Batista raised himself to the rank of colonel 'for merits of war and exceptional services to the country'. The other leading sergeants were made captains.[37] The new regime then attempted to arrest Martínez Sáenz, Saladrigas and other previous backers of Céspedes, such as Mendieta and Torriente. All these, however, were in secure hiding. Even so, throughout 7 September, Welles continued to believe, on inaccurate information, that Batista and the army would come round to Céspedes as president. Certainly, all political groups other than the students and the professors urged the Pentarquía to resign in favour of Céspedes, but a meeting at the National Palace, lasting from 10 p.m. to 4 a.m., failed to decide this, and Menocal and Mendieta left in disgust. Welles remained in some anxiety: 'Another group who are in close touch with the communist leaders in Havana

[35] Adam y Silva, 184.
[36] See Edmund Chester, 72.
[37] These were (and most of them would crop up in the history of the next twenty-five years of Cuba): Pablo Rodríguez, Evelio Alvarez Mieres, Manuel López Migoya, José Pedraza, Ernesto Pérez Chavez, Herberto Marchena Montero, Francisco Tarrau, Manuel Miranda Herrera and Manuel Castillo García. The following became first lieutenants: Sergeant Pedro Santán, Corporal Angel Echevarría, Sergeant Gonzalo García Pedroso, Sergeant Octavio Soca Llanez, Soldado Mario Alfonso Hernández and Sergeant Arturo Díaz Calderón. Second lieutenants: Corporal Oscar T. Díaz Martínez, Ignacio Galíndez and José Rodríguez Corzo. Captain of Marine: Overseer Angel Aurelio González y Fernández (see Adam y Silva, 493).

may resort to desperate measures if they become sufficiently drunk.'[38] He was still receiving constant requests for protection from U.S. property holders: the United Fruit Company, for instance, argued that this could be easily done, since its property was on the coast and therefore within reach of the navy's comforting arm.[39]

The Pentarquía and the students spent 8 September 1933 in prolonged discussion, beginning with the bombshell that the most respectable of their members, Porfirio Franca, had resigned in protest against the nomination of Batista as chief of staff. Two other members of the Pentarquía, Guillermo Portela and José Irisarri, were also scarcely enthusiastic. Both argued in prolonged speeches that the delays and the uncertainty over the future of the army were bound to provoke U.S. intervention. Irisarri suggested handing over power to a committee of notables comprising, say, ex-President Menocal, Colonel Mendieta and Miguel Mariano Gómez. Grau, the students, and Carbó vigorously opposed this scheme.[40] Irisarri then spoke again, in tones of such immense pessimism as to bring a chill for the first time to the hearts of the student directorate: was it possible, as they sat there in the summer night in the president's palace, with U.S. destroyers ringing the island, that the country would really disintegrate?[41] The U.S. Secretary of the Navy meantime arrived in Havana on the *Indianapolis* but did not land. Outside in the streets, there were Colonel Batista's soldiers, at Columbia there was Colonel Batista himself, his motives obscure, but obviously not the man to shrink from a *golpe de estado* if it were necessary. Irisarri then turned to Grau and argued that if he were not perturbed then he should take over the provisional presidency. But Carbó announced that he had nominated Batista to prevent the total dissolution of the country, in a situation where the U.S. fleet was in the bay and where no one else would take on the job. Grau explained that the revolution – whatever was meant by that enigmatic word – was being carried out in order to destroy traditional politics. He said that his duty as a professor was to guide and support his students and that he could not abandon them at this time. A vote was later taken giving the Pentarquía power to elect a president.[42]

An increasingly bizarre situation was now developing at the Hotel Nacional. 250 officers were gathered there. A little before midnight on 8 September, a commission of sergeants arrived at the hotel with orders to search it for arms. The officers moved to the upper floor, ready to

[38] Foreign Relations (1933), II, 404–5.
[39] NA 837.00/3793, qu. Smith, 151.
[40] See article by Chibás in *Prensa Libre*, 24 May 1944; see also Conte Agüero, *Eduardo Chibás*, 188 f.
[41] Recollection of Felipe Pazos.
[42] Chibás's resolution, *Prensa Libre*, 24 May 1944.

defend themselves, accompanied by several civilians and U.S. citizens. Welles, naturally, was brought in. He told Sergeant Díaz that if his men tried to enter the hotel they would certainly be shot at and 'the lives of the North American residents in the hotel would be unquestionably endangered'. Within a few minutes a telephone call came from the palace that all troops would be withdrawn: so they were, but a similar scene occurred again at four in the morning.

These swift changes meant only one thing: Batista and the Pentarquía were no longer acting together. Welles, reporting 'cumulative evidence from every province that complete anarchy exists in Cuba', therefore made yet another appeal for U.S. intervention, his third since 4 September, though he now merely asked for a number of marines 'affording police service'.[43] Roosevelt immediately telephoned Havana. As a result of their unrecorded conversation, Welles changed his view to accepting 'watchful expectancy'. Roosevelt doubtless spoke sharply to change Welles's views so radically.[44] Thereafter, indeed, Welles dropped appeals for intervention unless essential to save U.S. lives, telling this to the press and to U.S. sugar farm managers.[45] The U.S., nevertheless, did shortly have about thirty warships surrounding the island, mostly small vessels and moving out of actual sight of Cuba. Their purpose seems to have been to make the Cubans think that they might intervene if disorder became too great; and it would seem that in a number of instances the presence of a warship in a particular port did have an effect; thus, a U.S. destroyer sent to the port of Manatí appeared to prevent the capture of the U.S. owned mill *Manatí* by armed strikers.[46]

That the Pentarquía and Batista were no longer on good terms became even more clear in the morning of 9 September, when a number of sergeants called on Céspedes to say simply that Batista would back Céspedes for president if the latter were to confirm him as chief of staff. Céspedes refused to bind himself but the approach was significant.[47] Batista appears to have done nothing throughout that day. In the evening, at another mammoth meeting, the possibility of a *rapprochement* was closed to him: the Pentarquía, such as it was, met on the third floor of the National Palace, the students met on the second. The meeting of the latter was presided over by the youthful Ramón Miyar, who announced, without any evidence, that a plot by Portela and Irisarri

[43] Foreign Relations (1933), II, 405–7.
[44] See the allusion to the conversation in *ibid.*, 417–18, and comments by Bryce Wood, 75.
[45] See NA, qu. Bryce Wood, 76. There were perhaps 5,500 U.S. citizens in Cuba at this time, no more.
[46] See dispatch of Grant Watson, 19 September.
[47] Foreign Relations (1933), II, 414.

had been discovered 'to hand over power to the *políticos*'. Another speaker said: 'They are trying to return the command to the officers, to arrest Batista and the other sergeants and, after a summary council of war, shoot them at dawn.' Carlos Prío, a prominent student, said: 'I propose we rescind the vote of confidence which we gave the Pentarquía and ourselves name the President.' Miyar put this idea to the meeting and it was agreed. Various nominations were then made: Ruben de León proposed Professor José Antonio Presno, Felipe Pazos Professor Cuervo Rubio, another university teacher who had backed the students. Chibás proposed Grau, who was duly elected. Prío, Rubio Padilla, and Ruben de León were selected to go up to tell the Pentarquía what had happened. On entry they found these men still arguing. Portela angrily told the three students: 'We, members of the Executive Commission of the Government, have a transcendent mission, a historic mission, and a very serious mission: to elect the President. I ask the *señores estudiantes* to withdraw.' At this, Prío said: 'In the name of the Directorio Universitario, we have come to tell you, Dr Portela, that this transcendent, this historic mission, has been withdrawn from you. The Directorio has withdrawn its vote of confidence in the Pentarquía and has elected Dr Grau President.'[48] Amid tumult, with other students crowding in, Grau duly became president by acclamation.[49]

[48] Chibás, *Prensa Libre*, 24 May 1944.

[49] It is not without interest that Welles in his memoirs, *The Time for Decision*, 196, otherwise usually accurate, speaks of the five days between the sergeants' revolt and Grau's take-over of power as 'some disorderly and sterile *weeks*' (author's italics).

CHAPTER LV

Grau's Girondin Revolution

Dr Grau became president of Cuba at 2.30 a.m. on 10 September 1933. He was unknown to more than a small circle. He seemed to be a new man, respectable and scholarly, with some knowledge of the world derived from an extensive medical practice in Havana. He looked nervous and emotional, but at that time that was attributed to his excessive honesty and dedication to the cause of authentic revolution. Effeminate in looks yet lecherous, seemingly earnest but a brilliant and malicious wit, Grau San Martín appeared indecisive and weak though was actually ruthless, cunning and brave. He was then aged forty-six.

Dr Grau immediately nominated four men to his cabinet: Eduardo Chibás (the son) as Secretary of Public Works; Carlos Finlay, a teacher in the university's medical faculty, son of the yellow fever pioneer, Secretary of Sanitation; José Barquín, Secretary of the Treasury; and Antonio Guiteras, Secretary of the Interior.

The last named was the most outstanding of the youthful Cuban leaders, a gifted member of the gifted university generation of 1927. Unlike many of his comrades, he had never been a Communist nor even a member of the *comunizante* Ala Izquierda Estudiantil. He was a socialist and had been partly brought up in the U.S., the son of a teacher of French and, like Julio Antonio Mella, of an English mother (his full name was Antonio Guiteras Holmes). Guiteras had been a student in chemistry before launching into full-time politics. Now twenty-seven, known as the man with only one suit (*hombre de un solo traje*), he was regarded as incorruptible; strong, but Liberal; a patriot evidently and with already much support from the masses. The government, therefore, in fact became fundamentally the Grau-Guiteras coalition.

Grau took over power formally in mid-morning on 10 September, but he refused to swear an oath of office before the Supreme Tribunal of the Republic who had awkwardly assembled in their black clothes: he would not accept the Constitution of 1902 with the Platt Amendment written into it; instead, he took a public oath in spectacular style on the balcony of the palace, swearing before the multitude of people congregated below. Dr Grau enjoyed this, his first appearance as a demagogue. Phillips of the *New York Times* wrote that he had 'never seen such a mad mob, especially the women'. After this, Grau, his ministers, and the students of the Directorio, occupied the offices of the government: Carlos Manuel de Céspedes went into asylum in the embassy of Brazil; the press was censored as severely as in Machado's day, and the leaders sought to prevent Associated Press reports of bad conditions in Cuba. Both the U.S. and the other American governments were denounced for refraining from immediate recognition.[1]

The enemies of the new government began to show their hand. Horacio Ferrer went once more to Welles, and this time he asked explicitly for U.S. intervention against Batista and the army. The Proconsul this time replied: 'I would not even receive such a petition; and it was absurd to imagine that the government of the U.S. would undertake [such action] ... at the request of two hundred deposed army officers.' This did not prevent the Directorio Estudiantil from cabling Latin-American universities that the U.S. ambassador was inciting the officers in the Hotel Nacional to 'disturb public order ... to find a pretext for landing marines'.[2] At the same time, the Communists, expressing themselves at a meeting of the Liga Anti-Imperialista in Central Park, staged their first demonstration since the overthrow of Céspedes: they denounced everything – Yankee imperialism, Welles, the new government, the ABC, all.[3] At Campamento Columbia the sergeants, including several Spanish in origin, continued to make passionate speeches about Cuba's historic role and their unique mission.[4] The ABC meantime prepared a long denunciation of the new order, and published it on the morning of 11 September. Mendieta and OCRR, the Unión Nacionalista and Menocal, took the same view. But control remained with the army. Though Welles reported almost hourly that discipline was collapsing,[5] it became clear that Batista was daily strengthening his hold.

Grau was meantime completing his cabinet. Young Chibás decided after all not to take part as had the banker Barquín. In the end the portfolio of the Treasury was filled by Colonel Manuel Despaigne, who had occupied that post in Zayas's short-lived 'Honest Cabinet'. Gustavo Moreno, a representative of the small Unión Revolucionaria, which had taken part in the meditation, became Secretary of Communications. In addition to Grau himself and Finlay, two other university professors

[1] Adam y Silva, 278; Phillips, 70.
[2] Foreign Relations (1933), II, 418–19.
[3] Phillips, 70.
[4] Adam y Silva, 278.
[5] Here is a selection of his comments: 10 September (2 p.m.): 'Even the appearance of discipline among the troops of Havana has vanished.' 11 September (12 noon): 'The discipline of the Army is daily slipping and rivalry and dissension between the various sergeants is on the increase.' 11 September (6 p.m.): 'Discipline in the Army is vanishing rapidly.' 12 September (1 p.m.): 'Discipline within the ranks of the troops is degenerating.'

joined the government – Ramiro Capablanca of the law faculty (Secretary of the Cabinet) and Manuel Costales Latatú, a stomach surgeon (Secretary of Education). The Secretary of Justice, Joaquín del Río Balmaseda, a judge in Santiago, had valiantly tried to maintain standards in the age of Comandante Ortiz. The Minister of the Army, an important appointment, was Colonel Julio Aguado, a regular officer who had conspired against Machado in 1931. Before that, however, he had been in command in La Cabaña, so it was believed that his hands were not quite free from blood. The Secretary for Foreign Affairs, Manuel Márquez Sterling, had been minister in Washington and belonged to a family well known in politics and journalism.[6] The Directorio Estudiantil meanwhile remained in existence as a kind of legislature, and Grau owed his position to their continued support. Outside Havana, the writ of the new government seemed, however, not to run far: most sugar mills for instance recorded stories of visits by armed strikers demanding more money and better conditions and even in Havana the English ambassador's cook took to bed on threat of being beaten up.[7]

The curious situation in the Hotel Nacional seemed to have hardened to the extent that Welles and the Americans who were still there decided to move out, because of the departure of the servants and the cutting off of electricity and water by orders of the sergeants surrounding the hotel. The manager of the hotel (a U.S. citizen) said that his life was being threatened, and the property inside too, unless he cut off the hotel from external assistance.[8] But the officers were able to store enough water in tanks to keep themselves going and, during 13 September, they also received arms, reinforcements of men from the interior and supplies of food. Batista's invitations to the officers to withdraw to their homes were rejected. Similarly, the ABC moved into a posture of outright antagonism to Batista and Grau by allowing Dr Martínez Sáenz to become the virtual dictator of the party, and by entering close relations with ex-President Menocal.[9] At the same time, nothing seemed in any way fixed at the National Palace. Mrs Phillips called there on the afternoon of 14 September:

Amid the screams ... of urchins who demand [one] to *cuida la máquina* [take care of the machine] ... knowing I can't possibly get near the elevator, I take to the stairs and on the second floor find myself ... in another crowd. Finally I arrive at the Cabinet room

[6] Manuel Márquez Sterling (1872–1934), founder of *Heraldo de Cuba*, minister in Mexico, 1911.

[7] Grant Watson dispatch, 26 September.

[8] Foreign Relations (1933), II, 428.

[9] *Ibid.*, 935–6.

where President Grau receives everyone. It is a long narrow table. The President sits at the head of the table surrounded by the Directorio ... A couple of hours later, I had progressed several places towards the head of the table where Grau is now totally obscured from my view by excited, youthful nation-savers. Eventually, I get within striking distance and, finding that a woman's voice will make itself distinct ... I ask a question. The President replies, looking right at me but not in answer to ... [my] question ... No one around the President pays the slightest attention to him.[10]

Conversations were in fact going on between the Directorio and the old politicians.[11] These seem to have been made more urgent by a revolt in Pinar del Río led by a dismissed officer, Captain Arán, who had taken over the garrison at Consolación del Sur. Two hundred troops set out to counter this. Eventually, after his troops deserted, Arán surrendered. But disorders now seemed to be spreading with a hurricane of force through the Republic: there were other rumours of revolt in Havana, strikers were beginning to break into shops, sugar mills were still in a state of revolutionary effervescence, urged on by the CNOC. Some sugar mills were taken over by workers: for instance, at the Cuban-owned *central Mabay*, near Bayamo, founded in 1918, a Soviet was set up and lasted several weeks.[12] On 14 September Roosevelt's special representative A. A. Berle had a long conversation with several members of the Directorio and on 15 September Welles himself met the whole Directorio at the house of Eduardo Chibás, Sr, the rich engineer who had been in Céspedes's cabinet, father of the student leader. Berle and Welles denied the allegations of U.S. interference since 5 September, and appealed for reason and compromise: 'The interview was extremely cordial,' said Welles, adding dryly, 'and most of the lady members were not unreasonable.'[13] But nothing followed from this. The situation at the Hotel Nacional was all the time hardening. The ex-Secretary for War, Horacio Ferrer, had now explicitly joined the officers, General Sanguily was in overall command (except for the small number of naval officers who had elected their own commander), and it was evident that the Hotel Nacional had become, half by accident, a counter-revolutionary redoubt. The manager had begun to accept his alarming guests: two officers were established in each room. Some rich officers established a fund for food. But families were prevented from entering. On 15 September, Grau and the old political leaders met in the

10 Phillips, 73.
11 Foreign Relations (1933), II, 438.
12 See Roa, 63.
13 Foreign Relations (1933), II, 438-9. Chibás's account of this interview is in Conte Agüero, *Eduardo Chibás*, 192.

evening and continued to talk till three o'clock the next morning.
Mendieta and the ABC now seemed to be united; but Menocal, Miguel
Mariano Gómez and the OCRR acted independently. Mendieta tried
to persuade Grau to resign his presidency in favour of a 'government of
national concentration'. It seemed just possible that a new administration of that character might be set up, since several members of the
Directorio Estudiantil had begun to suspect the intentions of Batista:
others had been impressed by Adolf Berle's gloomy report to them that
the Treasury would be empty within a few weeks and that stores of food
in Havana and elsewhere would barely last ten days. Grau and Welles
finally met secretly on the morning of 17 September. Welles began with
a statement that:

> The attitude now assumed by financial, commercial and agricultural
> elements in refusing to pay taxes, in closing down or in cancelling
> orders wherever possible . . . must certainly convince [Grau] . . . that
> the Government was not supported by exceedingly important ele-
> ments . . . in my opinion lack of confidence was not directed . . .
> against him personally . . . but in the basic fact that his government
> had been installed as the result of a mutiny in the Army . . . and . . .
> that it was responsible solely to . . . the [students] . . . I knew and I
> had no doubt that he knew that disorders were increasing every
> moment . . . I was by no means certain that the lives and properties
> of American citizens at the present time were safe . . . except in those
> ports where American warships were stationed.

Grau admitted all this frankly but argued with Welles regarding his
popular support. He thought that everyone would support the government if the U.S. would only accord recognition. Welles said that U.S.
recognition could not be employed as a means of obtaining popular
support. His conversations, he said, with the political groups opposed to
Grau convinced him that they agreed with the main features of the
programme which Grau had announced as the ideal of his government,
but that they felt him to be subservient to the students. What possible
objection could the students or he himself have to a government of concentration? Grau said that in truth he believed such a solution to be
necessary – that is, the opposite of what he had previously promised
repeatedly to the political leaders. Grau, like the students, was beginning
to be apprehensive of the power wielded by the sergeants. As early as
16 September he had reached the conclusion that Batista wanted to be
president, though from what he had seen of Batista he thought that he
'would try and gain popular support' from the working classes and
would not attempt a *coup d'état*. Grau had thus changed his view of a
few days before that the soldiers who had joined in the mutiny were so

pure in mind and so devoted to the ideals of the students that they could have no ulterior ambitions.[14]

The Calvary of Cuban political disintegration continued. No doubt the persistent U.S. withholding of recognition from the government of Grau prevented not only the stabilization of the regime but the achievement of a Cuban government of any kind. Welles was indeed probably correct in saying that at that stage anyway of Cuban history 'no government here can survive for a protracted period without recognition by the U.S.'[15] On 17 September, Grau told the *políticos* that he *would* resign, if the army and students would let him (it was on that day significantly that a special cloakroom for revolvers was made at the palace).[16] That night, the Unión Nacionalista, ABC, OCRR and Menocalistas, with Miguel Mariano Gómez, at last united in a common front. They appeared to have decided by now that the U.S. government was not going to help them out of their difficulties and that the responsibility for action lay entirely with them. They issued, therefore, what was in a sense an ultimatum to Grau, demanding a 'non-partisan government', nominated by themselves, together with the Directorio and the professors. Three old members of the Pentarquía (Irisarri, Franca and Portela) sought to persuade Grau to accept this compromise. Grau seemed for a time ready to give in and indeed told the students so; but one of the latter, Rafael Escalona y Almeida, who was standing behind Grau, forced him back into his chair by physical force and told him brusquely that he had to remain president so long as the Directorio wanted him to, whether he liked it or not. Antonio Varona, another student leader, was so angry at Grau's statement that he broke several pieces of furniture. During the next few days, negotiations continued therefore between the Directorio and the *políticos*. Meantime, the Directorio halted press attacks on Welles and the U.S. Outside Havana, Colonel Blas Hernández, a veteran of 1895, a famous rural gangster and a guerrilla fighter against Machado, turned his gangs of bandits into an army of 500 men in Santa Clara: in Oriente, near Antilla, Major Balán rose with 800 men, marching along the north coast of the country to take Gibara and then turning inland to take Holguín.[17] Grau in Havana, however, attempted desperately to please everyone – anti-imperialist with the students, *bourgeois* with Welles and the business men, man of all the people with crowds.

Batista, on the other hand, continued to say nothing, still consolidating his position in Havana, and sending small detachments to try to contain the rebels in the country. In a conversation with Welles on 21

[14] Foreign Relations (1933), II, 493–5.
[15] *Ibid.*, 417.
[16] Phillips, 76.
[17] Foreign Relations (1933), II, 448–50.

September, Batista seemed in favour of compromise with the old regime and the ABC, and told the ambassador he would try to influence the students to accept one. But the students insisted on Grau's retention as president. This, though accepted by Colonel Mendieta and some others, was not agreed by all. On the afternoon of 22 September, the students veered away again from compromise. Throughout these days, confused reports came of risings and hurried marches in the interior by Blas Hernández and others. There were strikes at most sugar mills, though, of course, there was not much work at this time of the year anyway. Rumours spread, as often in these confused conditions, of Negro riots, and wild tales were told of notices at sugar mills calling on workers to: 'Pick your own white woman.' On 25 September the *políticos* broke off all negotiations, though naming the lawyer Antonio de González Mendoza and Dr Granados of the Rotary Club as their representatives if anyone wanted to negotiate again. Meantime, Dr Cuervo Rubio, previously identified with the students, and indeed Felipe Pazos's candidate for the presidency on 9 September, launched a bitter attack against the government on the radio on 25 September.[18]

The following day, a large crowd organized by the Communists assembled in Havana to welcome back from Mexico the ashes of Julio Antonio Mella; on 29 September, however, there were riots and running street fights when the remains were carried to final interment at Fraternity Park. The government had prohibited any burial except in the cemetery and also the display of red flags. But the demonstration took place, shots were fired at the soldiers and fighting became general. Mella's friend, Martínez Villena, the sick Communist leader, addressed a fighting throng.[19] The ashes were lost in the fighting, the monument destroyed, the red flags captured, six people killed and twenty-seven wounded. Soldiers then broke up the headquarters of the Liga Anti-imperialista,[20] but numerous 'revolutionary organizations', armed with guns which they had bought from the army, had a wild day of uncontrolled firing.

By the end of September there thus appeared an armed political stalemate. Despite dire prophecies, Havana still ate. The students and the cabinet still hung on to power. In the country, however, nearly forty sugar mills were in the hands of the workers. Various foreign diplomats were busy offering to negotiate. The U.S. administration was still refraining from public comment, though Welles naturally remained a centre of intrigue. Blas Hernández's revolt had died down, apparently because the colonel's one-time political boss, Mendieta, asked him to

[18] Adam y Silva, 301.
[19] It was his last speech; in January 1934 he died in a tuberculosis sanatorium.
[20] Phillips, 80–2; Roa, 66; Grant Watson's dispatch of 4 October.

surrender: in the East isolated fighting and rioting continued. In all cities cases of armed robbery and other acts of violence had much increased. In several sugar mills managers had been held prisoner by groups of armed workers till their demands for higher wages had been agreed. At *Agramonte*, a Polish worker dismissed in 1923 gave the manager twenty-four hours to leave and had become in effect the local dictator. The English minister reported:

> Student delegations and rural guards move from point to point, strikes are settled and fresh strikes break out elsewhere. All the provinces are equally affected though there seems to be more unrest in Oriente province than elsewhere ... Usually the soldiers are mere onlookers and remain passive in the midst of a mob ... The Banks at present are refusing to grant credits to the mills which, without such credit, will not be able to grind the cane and if present conditions continue for another month or so the mills will be unable to grind.[21]

At this point came the long-delayed explosion between the old officers and Batista's men.

[21] Dispatch of Grant Watson, 9 October 1933.

CHAPTER LVI

The Battle of the Hotel Nacional

There were now about 300 officers in the Hotel Nacional,[1] together with one cavalryman named Rojas, who had joined the officers in late September, and several sailors.[2] The hotel was the obvious centre of hostility to the regime, of whose provisional status it was a reminder, a menace too to the new ranks assumed by the ex-sergeants. On 1 October Batista summoned a council of war to decide whether or not an attack on the hotel should be made. Carbó and Guiteras of the civilian government leaders, but surprisingly enough not Grau, were present, along with Batista, Pablo Rodríguez (the first leader on 4 September), and Captains Raimundo Ferrer and Manuel Benítez, two of the small number of officers who had taken Batista's side a month previously. These last were the most vigorous for an attack; Batista seemed indecisive; Pablo Rodríguez was opposed.[3] It is unclear what the civilians desired.

Grau and the Directorio Estudiantil were not specifically consulted by Batista on this occasion. The students' criticism of the NCOs was indeed already reciprocated in army circles. Even Carbó, describing military views to Welles on 1 October, spoke of a 'healthy reaction among the soldiers against . . . those members of the Student Council whom they consider identified with the Communist organization'. Carbó himself still seemed to retain a hold over Batista, and indeed was himself toying with the idea of a replacement of Grau by some new national movement in which the ABC, the less radical section of the Directorio, the progressive section of OCRR, and some others would be merged, to be backed by Batista's new army: he told Welles, 'the Army leaders were no longer willing to stand the attempt on the part of the students to dominate . . . the soldiers were already disarming students as well as other civilians and intended to disband the small semi-armed militia of about 2,000 students.'

This conversation, held in the afternoon of 1 October, was doubtless

---

[1] Out of a total of about 1,000 officers in all services. Of these, less than 30 supported Batista.

[2] Adam y Silva, 301.

[3] *Ibid.*, 318.

intended by Carbó to soothe Welles's reactions to an attack on the palace the next day.[4]

At dawn on 2 October an armoured car drove to the gate of the Hotel Nacional in 23rd Street. The officers gave an order to the driver to halt; he replied by firing.[5] This was the signal for firing on the hotel from all sides. About 6 a.m. light artillery opened up. The officers continued to shoot with rifles. Since many were excellent shots, they cleared the surroundings of the hotel by 8 a.m., at least fifteen soldiers were killed and a much greater number seriously wounded. During the course of firing one U.S. citizen, Robert Lotspicht,[6] was killed; he had been watching the fight from his apartment in the López Serrano block of flats. At 8 a.m. Welles received a message from Grau telling him that the soldiers intended to bring heavy artillery into play and asking if there were any Americans left there. When Welles told him no, the heavy bombardment began, and the cruiser *Cuba* began to shell the hotel, inaccurately, from the sea.[7] General Sanguily got a message to Welles saying that the officers were determined to resist and to reinstall the legitimate government of Carlos Manuel de Céspedes. By noon only one officer had been killed – Veterinary Lieutenant Abelardo Fernández.[8]

In the middle of the morning the Red Cross successfully established an armistice, whereby a number of wounded officers and officers' wives were escorted from the hotel; some civilians in the neighbourhood also moved to safety. Batista now offered terms to the officers: they could leave the hotel unarmed, by fives, and their lives and persons would be guaranteed. There followed a poll among the officers as to whether this proposal should be accepted, but the poll took a long time, since the hotel lifts no longer worked. The armistice was due to expire at 3.30: at 3 p.m., however, Captain Cossío Betancourt was treacherously shot, and the firing began again.[9] This time the artillery was much better directed, casualties were extensive and at 4.45 the officers, despite their fine talk of the middle of the day, decided to give in. A critical fact was the failure of the ABC organization to make any common cause with the officers: the English minister reported that 'the members stood ready to take action [but] no orders were

[4] I have found no proof of the alleged meeting on 1 October between Welles and Batista at the Restaurant Kohly, at which Batista allegedly asked 'if he could attack the hotel' and Welles said, 'Do as you wish.' This is alleged in *ibid.*, 320.

[5] There is as usual some doubt as to who opened fire on whom; but since Batista had decided to launch an attack this question is irrelevant.

[6] Manager of the Swift and Co. plant. He was the only U.S. citizen killed during the Grau regime.

[7] The Cuban navy consisted then of 13 ships, 11 gunboats, one training ship and one so-called cruiser 1,500 tons. All were in bad condition save the gunboat and the cruiser.

[8] See Adam y Silva, 312; Foreign Relations (1933), II, 463.

[9] It is doubtful who began again. Batista said it was the officers (Edmund Chester, 113).

given'.[10] Also many officers had no doubt supposed that by now the U.S. would have intervened.

The soldiers lined up the officers as they came out, in twos. A large crowd gathered, and several people egged it on to kill the officers. The soldiers opened fire over the crowd and later a number of shots were also fired on the surrendered officers, particularly on those who left the hotel last, who happened to be medical officers. Eleven were killed, including three doctors, and twenty-two wounded.[11] Those who fired on the officers seem to have been members of the organizations known as Pro Ley y Justicia or the ABC Radical. The other officers were dispatched to La Cabaña. There was much shooting in Havana for the rest of the day, while the soldiers were busy looting the cellars of the Hotel Nacional. The total number of soldiers killed was four times the number of officers – eighty dead and 200 wounded.[12] The hotel (which had been insured by two English companies) suffered between £25,000 and £35,000 damages.[13]

A certain section of the students and soldiers wanted to execute the officers. Francisco Gramero proposed that they should be dropped in the ocean to the sharks, but when Batista went to see Welles on 4 October he gave his word that the officers would not be molested, and that he would delay the court martial until passions cooled: they would, however, be transferred to the Isle of Pines. In practice the prisoners were treated with minimum courtesy. Carlos Prío, the student leader, and Manuel Benítez, the renegade officer, visited the Cabaña on 3 October; Prío at least was impressed by the irony of the situation, for he himself had been in that gaol two years previously, and had even shared a cell with one of those captains now there again – Adam y Silva. As before, a cage hung from the ceiling in which to keep the incorrigible prisoners. Prío assured the officers that their lives would be preserved.[14] Meanwhile, a delegation of officers' wives called on Welles and asked him to intervene, as did the French minister: Welles said that the decision was Roosevelt's alone.[15]

---

[10] Grant Watson's dispatch of 4 October. One English official, R. R. Craigie, questioned, 'I should like to know how Mr Welles and Mr Hull defend their policy – first intervening when they ought to have stood clear then holding aloof when their former meddling made them morally responsible for the mess?'

[11] Those killed were: Lieut.-Col. (Medical) Miguel A. Céspedes, Major Alfredo Buffil, Captain (Medical) Miguel Dobal, Lieut. of Infantry Juan S. Rojo Grau, Lieut. of Infantry Rafael Sebasco, Lieut. of Artillery Cándido Gómez Viera, Sub-Lieut. of Navy Jacinto Folch, 2nd Lieut. of Artillery Manuel Girón Guerra, 2nd Lieut. of Infantry Enrique Campo Abadía, Captain (Medical) Armando de la Torre and Captain of Infantry Evelio Piña (Adam y Silva, 312).

[12] Foreign Relations, 467–8.

[13] Grant Watson, telegram 98, 4 October.

[14] Adam y Silva, 317.

[15] Grant Watson's dispatch, 4 October.

Batista's interview with Welles on 4 October 1933, when the fighting was over, was of decisive importance, since the new commander-in-chief was told by the Proconsul that he was 'the only individual in Cuba . . . who represented authority'. Welles said, presumably on good information, that, save for Menocal, all the *políticos* now accepted him as chief of staff and that Batista's refusal to hand over the printing presses to the students had endeared him to the old press interests and, through them, to the commercial and financial forces in Cuba as well. Batista himself seemed quite disillusioned with the students and entirely willing, even anxious, to work with the ABC, and other *políticos*.[16] Welles reported to Washington that the defeat of the officers, so far from being a confirmation in power of the government, marked only a rise in Batista's prestige and not in Grau's: Welles still bitterly opposed the idea of recognition, with which his enemy and rival Hull seemed to be toying.[17]

It is significant that the English minister, a sound observer, had said on 4 October that Batista had already 'become the real Dictator of Cuba'.[18]

On 6 October meantime, a meeting of the Student Directorate decided that they would have to try to rid themselves of Batista, because of his popularity and his ambition, of which the students were both jealous and fearful. Batista for his part sent the students a message that they should withdraw from the government and allow a 'cabinet of concentration' to be formed. (Carbó was behind Batista in this.) Further meetings followed between Batista and Welles: the former promised many things, particularly to arrest the 'communist agitators' on the U.S.-owned sugar plantations, and to send the Directorio back to the University. These things made a deep impression on Welles. Dr Carlos Finlay then came back from Washington, where he had seen the Under-Secretary of State, Jefferson Caffery, who, he claimed, had told him that the inclusion in Grau's government of three members of the opposition would lead to U.S. recognition. (Caffery later denied that he said this.) The Directorio busily circulated a rumour, however, that a change of government would be followed by an immediate landing of U.S. troops. Grau, believing himself at the last ditch, announced that he was making an important cabinet change, in order to replace Guiteras and Colonel Aguado, who had resigned. Batista rejected this. By 14 October no real progress had been made; the U.S. Consul in Santiago was no doubt right when he wrote unhappily that in his bailiwick there was 'universal dissatisfaction and expectancy

[16] Foreign Relations (1933), II, 472–3.
[17] *Ibid.*, 471.
[18] Grant Watson dispatch, 4 October 1933.

and no harmony of opinion'.[19] Welles meantime maintained his government's refusal to recognize Grau as best he could, being slightly discouraged (as were the Spanish colony and the Spanish minister) by the decision of the new Spanish government to recognize Grau.[20] Rumours persisted too of Welles's responsibility for everything from petrol shortages to revolution in Pinar del Río. He was accused of being bribed by the National City Bank and by the American Sugar Refining Company, of having instigated the gathering of officers in the Hotel Nacional and, especially by the wives, of letting down the officers.[21]

During the six weeks since 5 September each government department had been run by a purging committee which had not only expelled the Machadistas but also members of ABC and in reality anyone not a student.[22] This meant that civil servants who had been in their apparently safe jobs for decades were replaced by very young men whose chief contribution was enthusiasm. In the interior of the country, taxpayers were in consequence refusing taxes and, though hundreds of decrees had been published, most of them had been ignored. Only the Treasury, under the reasonably honest and firm hand of Captain Despaigne, maintained a certain style and isolation, rejecting on occasion at least the demands of young revolutionaries seeking new jobs. An air of insecurity persisted everywhere: there were arbitrary arrests, unexplained house-searchings, seizures of properties, occasional assassinations. Grau and the students drove about in armoured cars, surrounded by machine guns. The 'revolutionary organizations' and their splinter groups maintained their arms and their pretensions, determined to fight their way if need be to power and jobs.

On 16 October Welles explicitly advised Hull to refuse recognition 'until a provisional government is constituted offering guarantees acceptable both to the political and non-political forces of the Republic': whatever this Delphic phrase meant, the U.S. government's acceptance of this recommendation was a major reason for the continuance of the very unstable conditions which Welles deplored. Welles and the U.S. were therefore positively engaged in the search for a new government.[23]

The crisis between Batista and Grau took a surprisingly long time to mature. There were all sorts of minor disputes, chiefly over appointments: Batista, for instance, had appointed a Captain Franco to head the police in Havana; the students desired to replace him by a twenty-seven-year-old member of Ley y Justicia, Mario Labourdette. Welles

[19] Foreign Relations (1933), II, 481.
[20] A new government headed by the Radical Lerroux had been formed in early October 1933 with three Catholic deputies joining the cabinet.
[21] Foreign Relations (1933), II, 486–7; cf. Grant Watson's dispatches.
[22] Cf. Phillips, 99.
[23] See Foreign Relations (1933), II, 488–90.

clearly feared Labourdette as a kind of gangster but the students had their way. The Directorio tried to take a firm line against Batista, demanding that Grau should choose whether he would leave the government or cease subservience to his chief of staff. ABC Radical at this moment chose to announce the cessation of its backing of the government and its re-adherence to the ABC proper (except for a splinter group led by Oscar de la Torre). ABC Radical took with it, and handed over to its central headquarters, a large quantity of arms given to it by Batista immediately after the events of 4 September. ABC itself sought to renew its attraction by ordering its members to leap on to the stages of the theatres of Havana, surrounded by bodyguards, proclaiming their programme, often to tremendous applause. Fear of physical reprisals, however, led some leaders, headed by Martínez Sáenz, to flee to Miami, although common fear of Batista led the Directorio on the other hand to approach ABC to ask for their backing for a change of government. But the ABC steadily refused anything to do with the Directorio. There matters rested for several more days, still unresolved, incoherent and tense.

The situation altered for the worse during the night of 25–6 October, when a large time-bomb exploded in the front of Colonel Mendieta's house as he was returning at 2 a.m. after a conversation with Batista. A return to chaos and violence seemed possible. Batista's position now suddenly seemed to weaken, because of hostility within the barracks: his old comrade Pablo Rodríguez, in charge of Campamento Columbia, was scheming to make Colonel Perdomo (commander at Columbia under Céspedes) chief of staff. Many soldiers and others were being arrested daily for conspiracy – perhaps 200 others were in prison. In these deteriorating circumstances, Mendieta, ABC and Batista began to negotiate the idea of a provisional government to be headed by the first, but then Mendieta had cold feet about accepting Batista as chief of staff, observing that he would in fact turn out merely as Batista's prisoner. Welles began to think again about Grau's compromise plan which would keep Grau as president, though with a new cabinet except for Despaigne. Batista still backed the reluctant Mendieta. On 30 October the Student Assembly met, in continuous disorder. Chibás announced that the Directorio had asked Grau 'to change the identity of the Government' before 4 November. Then he and about a hundred others, including all the leaders, left the hall, leaving the rest debating whether or not they should continue to support the Directorio. They appeared not to have reached a decision.[24] But meantime the new police commanders and some ex-army officers were imploring Mendieta to take over, by whatever means, with or without

[24] Foreign Relations (1933), II, 505.

a military *coup*, and at the same time to establish a certain degree of press censorship.[25] Every newspaper nevertheless urged Mendieta, the only surviving symbol of decency and strength, to take the presidency. On 2 November bombs exploded all over Havana, killing one policeman, and destroying the offices of Carbó's *La Semana*.

On the following day in the afternoon Grau received the written resignation of all his ministers and himself prepared to resign. The Directorio also undertook to withdraw. Then *País Libre*, an evening paper, announced, with the help of a bogus telegram, that U.S. intervention was at long last coming. A mutiny broke out in the navy barracks and there was violent agitation at Campamento Columbia. Welles quickly denied the allegation of *País Libre* and Batista read the denial over the loudspeaker at Campamento Columbia, but much damage had been done. At a long meeting that night in a crowded room at Carbó's house between the student leaders, Grau and Batista, Grau withdrew any thought of resignation on, surprisingly, the urgent demands of the ex-pentarchs Irisarri and Portela. Several speeches followed, notably by Carbó and the student Lucilo de la Peña, who said 'the people are not in contact with the revolution'. Grau described the political aims of himself and his movement and their achievements, and accused Batista of secret understandings with the U.S., with Welles, and of selling the national heritage. He said that he would have liked to dismiss him, Batista then made an attempt at reparation, with an apology and an effort at self-abasement. He begged forgiveness.[26] Grau upbraided Batista for seeking to overthrow him; he could not continue, he said, in these conditions. A clash was in fact averted. Grau, Batista and the students each separately hung on, and Grau finally admitted Batista to have been 'the soul of the revolution', and confirmed him as chief of staff.[27]

This unexpected *rapprochement* brought the resignation of the powerful Guiteras from the Ministry of the Interior: the failure of the government, he said, was that it had not turned sharply enough to the left. He announced his intention of working for a government of 'soldiers, sailors, small shopkeepers and workers'. He held out the idea of a genuine social democratic political force; Welles, with little understanding of the extraordinary rivalries which divided the world's working-class forces, henceforth referred to him specifically as 'Communist',[28] but Guiteras nevertheless withdrew his resignation.

[25] See *ibid.*, 503–6.

[26] '*Pide perdón*' (Justo Carrillo, Papers, Memoirs, etc., MSS).

[27] For different accounts of these events see Edmund Chester, 126; Adam y Silva, 361; and Foreign Relations (1933), II, 511–12. I have benefited from a memorandum by Justo Carrillo.

[28] Foreign Relations (1933), II, 512.

The same day, 4 November, the students at the University of Havana held a referendum among themselves on the activities of their leaders, the Directorio, and finally voted against them. The Directorio dissolved itself. Some members announced that they would remain in the palace 'as individuals', to advise Grau. The opposition to the Directorio from the students also derived from the growing strength of Guiteras. This was also backed by a number of letters from imprisoned officers confessing that their actions had been inspired by Welles or, more truthfully, by hopes that they had falsely laid in Welles. At that moment, the Proconsul himself, infuriated by these accusations, was being visited by two men whom he described in a dispatch as 'the two foremost leaders of the groups in Oriente province'[29] which had been organized against the Machado government.

> They stated that they were supported by all of the soldiers in the province [except for] 250 men recently sent to Santiago from Havana; that the old officers were ready to take charge of the troops . . . and that approximately 11,000 men were under orders . . . whether the government in Havana was overturned or not, the revolution in Oriente would break out; that the situation there was absolutely intolerable and that it had only been with the utmost difficulty that the movement had been so far controlled . . . I did my utmost to persuade them to hold back.

> Welles told them that in Cuba's present condition civil war would have 'almost fatal effects and in any event make infinitely more difficult the process of economic rehabilitation . . . They assured me that they would make one last effort . . . for a pacific settlement. . . .'

But it was in fact too late.

[29] It is not clear who these were; but it seems almost certain that they were Mendieta's men.

CHAPTER LVII

The November Revolt

The attempted revolution of 8–9 November 1933 resembled that of 4 September in that it was entirely unexpected by the Proconsul of the U.S., Sumner Welles. It was organized not by ABC or Mendieta or Guiteras – though any of these might as well have acted at this point – but by a group of enlisted men in Campamento Columbia and the Aviation Corps. From these small beginnings, the revolt had extraordinary consequences. The central figures were Lieutenant of Aviation José Barrientos and the new Lieutenant Faustino Collazo, ex-sergeant of aviation before 5 September. These individuals appear to have been acting with patriotic as well as ambitious designs: they thought that the 'present state of affairs could not go on since it did not offer a possibility of taking the Republic along the path of legality and order'.[1] The fact also that Batista, through superior cunning, had elevated himself to a position of general command, led to expectations by the soldiers that their new 'officers' too would one day capture power, and so advance themselves. *Cuadrillas* of plotters gathered round prominent new officers such as Emiliano Pérez Leiva, Homoboro Rodríguez, Alejo Sánchez, or Armengol Rodríguez in Battalion No. 3, and in Battalion No. 1 around Corporal Julio Rodríguez and machine-gunner Angel Pons. Some established contact with Colonel Miguel Guerra, an older regular officer (not implicated in recent politics) lately named to be in command at Campamento Columbia. Several plotters were arrested on charges of conspiracy during October. This did not dissuade aviation officers from planning to capture Campamento Columbia from the air. Many regular officers of the past who had not been in the Hotel Nacional joined the plot, including a captain who told his followers, encouragingly, that he personally would prefer to be a sergeant in the old army than a captain under Batista.

A number of these conspirators had been members of ABC, and hence the ABC leader, Dr Saladrigas, came to hear of it. Saladrigas seems to have believed that he could use the conspiracy to capture control of ABC from his colleague Dr Martínez Sáenz, national head of the movement, then in Miami. But civilians were not kept abreast of the plot and, though some of ABC's branches were implicated, its national leadership was not.

[1] Article by ex-sergeant of Aviation Corps, *Bohemia*, 4 March 1934.

The plan for a *pronunciamiento* was laid for 8 November, when it was thought that Batista would be in Matanzas. The conspirators were, however, betrayed, by a young mulatto corporal, whose task was to burn down the old wooden barracks. After the final meeting between Colonel Miguel Guerra, Captain Isidro Cordobés, and Ricardo Cobián, of ABC, the corporal slunk away to Major Ignacio Galíndez, who immediately went to Batista. Batista swiftly returned to Havana and decreed the detention of all old officers. The plotters heard of Fajardo's treachery and tried to postpone or cancel their plans. But their collaborators had gone too far, the airport had already been taken over, and Lieutenant Miguel Hernández, a newly commissioned officer, had been arrested. The insurrectionary lieutenants Barrientos and Agüero reached the airport to find five aircraft ready: three Corsairs, with ten 25-pounder bombs, and two small fighters, with two 20-pounders. The moon was full. Barrientos set off for Columbia and bombed it. He was attacked by anti-aircraft guns but the confusion and panic which he caused were enormous. It was indeed Havana's first limited taste of war in the air. Batista went down to the cellars in a highly anxious state, even promising, according to one account, that he would hand back power to the old officers.[2] Agüero, who followed Barrientos, unaccountably dropped no bombs, landed in the sea and was later picked up. A third aviator, Montall, arrived over Columbia in a fighter, but he too could not bring himself to drop any bombs: he flew off to land at Batabanó, and eventually escaped abroad.[3]

About two thousand members of ABC had meantime gathered at the Miramar Yacht Club, where they were armed and harangued by Saladrigas, before advancing to the airport, where they placed themselves under the command of the rebellious officers, with Captain José Herrera y Roig at their head. Their aim was to advance on Columbia once its morale had been crushed by bombing. Alas, they were unable to do this, or even to leave the airport, since, while they continued to deliberate, a large force of Batista's army had surrounded the airport itself. There was a good deal of intermittent firing between dawn and 9 a.m., but about the latter hour Herrera surrendered, some 20 men being killed and 400 being made prisoner. The other members of ABC made good their escape.

In the rest of Havana there was lack of cohesion among the conspirators, though many buildings were occupied, including the headquarters of the police, and some other police stations. The head of the national police, Gonzalo García Pedroso, was among those arrested. The most important victory achieved by the rebels was in the San

[2] So Adam y Silva was told by an officer present there.
[3] Adam y Silva, 337–40.

Ambrosio and Dragonès barracks, where a motley gathering assembled, commanded by Lieutenant José Ovares, an old officer who had left the Hotel Nacional during the middle of the siege, on Sanguily's instructions. Backing him were ex-Colonel Collazo, Dr Rafael Iturralde, Secretary for War in Machado's first cabinet, and Colonel Blas Hernández, the famous Mendietista guerrilla. By 10 a.m. the revolt had been joined by many of those who, survivors of this regime or that, had nothing to gain from parley with either Grau or Batista.[4]

The failure of the revolt at the airport, however, caused a sickening shudder of fear to run through the rebels, and in mid-morning Major Leonard, in command at the Ambrosio barracks, decided that he would not be able to hold that position. He accordingly proposed a withdrawal to the Atarés Castle, just beyond Havana inland on a small hill dominating the harbour. Blas Hernández and Otero opposed this, fearful of another Hotel Nacional: Leonard showed them a telegram purporting to come from Colonel Amiel in Las Villas who urged a concentration in Atarés, where he promised to come also. Hence the disastrous evacuation of the barracks in Havana and the establishment at Atarés.

Atarés was guarded by squadron No. 5 of the Guardia Rural, an excellent unit manned by selected enlisted men, often used in the past for a presidential escort. This force had completely rallied to the rebellion. One thousand men were now established there.[5]

By 9 November the remainder of the rebels had moved to Atarés. But Batista also began to move. He concentrated all the artillery in Havana before the fortress and began to shell it. The vessels *Patria* and *Cuba* were also brought up. The rebels inside the fort had some long-distance guns and silenced the *Patria*, hitting too the U.S. ferry boat *Morro Castle*, of the Ward Line. For six hours, guns roared. During this time, however, the inside of the Atarés fortress was gradually destroyed. The cook was killed; his body fell into the large pot of rice and black beans which he had been stirring; he was lifted out and the food continued to cook. At two o'clock Major Leonard killed himself. Captain of Artillery Felipe Domínguez tried to rally the morale of those remaining, but despite his efforts and those of Colonel Blas Hernández, a white flag was raised.[6] Batista's soldiers advanced. This time there was no peaceful surrender as after the Hotel Nacional. The conquerors indeed took no notice of the white flag for some time. One fifteen-year-old boy, son of the ABC newspaperman, Pizzi de Porra, shot himself.[7] The gates were opened, prisoners came out with their hands raised and

---

[4] *Ibid.*, 337–44; Foreign Relations (1933), II, 517
[5] Adam y Silva, 345. Another account has 600. There were two anti-aircraft guns, twenty to twenty-five machine-guns, and 15,000 rounds of ammunition.
[6] Edmund Chester in his hagiography of Batista incorrectly says that Atarés was stormed.
[7] Phillips, 111. She was watching.

were mown down by machine-guns. Nearly all the prisoners were killed in a cowardly fashion, mostly against a wall. Old Colonel Blas Hernández was shot by the new Captain Mario Alfonso Hernández, Hernández slaying Hernández – the killer himself soon to die also in civil conflict.

One rebel lieutenant gave the *New York Times* correspondent an account of what occurred:

> After the surrender we were marched outside the fort and were standing under guard near the gate. Colonel Blas Hernández was standing beside me. A captain [Mario Alfonso Hernández] walked up and asked 'Is Blas Hernández here?' The old Colonel replied, 'I am Blas Hernández.' Without a word the Captain pulled out his revolver and shot the colonel. We were so horror-struck that none of us moved, not even the soldier guarding us. The Captain demanded: 'Is Lieutenant A—— here?' That was my name. Although I had never seen the Captain before and knew of no grudge he could have against me, I said, 'I think I saw the Lieutenant go with the first group of prisoners . . .'[8]

That night in Havana the hospitals and first-aid stations were overflowing. People sought their relations everywhere. Rifle fire continued most of the night. Snipers on roofs shot civilians. The students turned on the lights of the Capitol to celebrate 'their' victory. Though firing continued the next day all over Cuba, this fourth revolution within four months was clearly over. At least two hundred had been killed.[9] Court martials followed, but for the time being there were few executions, the exceptions being Private Homobono Rodríguez and Sergeant Basilio González. The Secretary for Justice, Joaquín del Río Balmaseda, resigned. All ABC leaders went into hiding or exile.

With his most recent compromise solution now in ruins, Sumner Welles was most restive. His own position was increasingly uncomfortable; the Minister of Agriculture, Hevia, had visited Washington to say that Grau desired to name Welles *persona non grata*; the British now believed that they ought to recognize the government, but it was confidence in Batista not Grau that characterized their attitude.[10] On 20 November, with the situation still unsettled, Welles visited Roosevelt, in Warm Springs, Georgia, to answer among other things a charge made directly to Roosevelt by Grau that Welles 'had repeatedly disclosed his partiality'.

Welles and Roosevelt issued a long statement from Warm Springs on

[8] *Ibid.*, 112–13.
[9] 500 according to Edmund Chester, 130–9. But the British Legation had 200: 32 government troops, 6 rebel civilians, 30 rebel soldiers, 60 unclassified and 17 civilians.
[10] Grant Watson dispatch, 15 November.

23 November, repeating the tenor of Welles's statement over the past few weeks that the U.S. could only re-negotiate their old political and economic treaties with a provisional government in which the Cuban people really showed confidence. Welles, it was explicitly agreed, would shortly return to Washington and be replaced in Havana by Jefferson Caffery. The State Department at the same time let it be clearly known that they hoped that other Latin American countries would still not recognize the Grau regime.[11] This statement clearly showed that Roosevelt was not intending to support Grau: it was indeed an 'invitation' to the Cuban opposition to continue their remorseless hostility to him.[12] Roosevelt, however, declared to the press: 'We are not taking sides . . . we haven't yet got a provisional government that clearly has the support of the majority of the Cuban people. What can we do? We can't do anything. The matter rests.'[13] This confession of impotence was of course Welles's view; and the view gained of Dr Grau's character by Welles and by Roosevelt was closer to the truth than that propagated by Grau's perfervid supporters.

Welles returned to Cuba for the last weeks of his stay there. During this time, there was increasing recognition that, as the magazine *Bohemia* put it, 'One voice strikes a different note from all others . . with the metallic accent of rifles and machine-gun: that of Fulgencio Batista.'[14] Many agreed with the U.S. Consul General Dumont, who believed Batista to be 'the only one in the government with any brains'.[15] There was still sporadic violence: Pro Ley y Justicia and a newly formed political semi-gangster group, composed of students, the so-called Ejercito del Caribe, kidnapped and killed five former army officers, including Colonel Herrera, in transit from Havana to Santa Clara for trial, for their alleged part in the murder of the Alvarez brothers in July 1932. The government proceeded with a much-discussed and highly nationalistic decree by which employers would have to hire 50% of Cuban-born labour. Many Spaniards, Jamaicans, Haitians, not to speak of North Americans, Englishmen and Germans, had thereby to be dropped. Another decree ordered the Cía Cubana de Electricidad (much compromised through its and its parent company's[16] relationship with Machado) to cut its prices by 45%.

Welles persisted in early December with renewed discussions for a stronger government, helped by no consistent line on anyone's part.

[11] Foreign Relations (1933), II, 526–9. There is no record of Welles's and FDR's talk at Warm Springs.

[12] See Bryce Wood, 95.

[13] Press Conference, 24 November 1933; F. D. Roosevelt, *Public Papers and Addresses*, comp. S. Rosenman, 13 vols (1938).

[14] Qu. from 26 November issue.

[15] Phillips, 124.

[16] Electric Bond and Share.

Ex-President Menocal, for instance, issued a statement from Miami which denounced any solution approving of either Grau's government or the army as then constituted under Batista. Some in the opposition thought that Grau's aim was to hang on by hook or by crook until he had bought enough arms from Europe. Others thought that Batista would take over completely were it not for his fear of a revolution, headed by Antonio Guiteras: Guiteras, who had returned to the Ministry of the Interior, was plotting with some sections of the army. Colonel Mendieta and José Mariano Gómez, who had returned as mayor of Havana, hung about in the wings, each posing as a saviour. Hull meanwhile warded off attempts by the Cuban delegation at the Montevideo conference to denounce the U.S. for not recognizing Grau.[17]

Welles had yet another secret midnight talk with Grau on 6 December. Grau spoke bitterly of the 'international conspiracy' which had prevented recognition of his government – an accusation partly true in that though Grant Watson, the British minister, along with other Europeans, had recommended recognition, his government had decided it better to risk offending Latin America than the U.S.[18] On 7 December, Cosme de la Torriente, representing the 'best elements in Cuban public life', a man certainly unbesmirched by collaboration with either Machado, Céspedes or Grau, saw Welles, Grau again being present. Grau said that he was willing to resign after the convocation of a constitutional convention. De la Torriente argued that the existing government, because of the extra-constitutional role of the army and because of the continuing disturbances, could not convoke such a convention. The press, however, was still strongly in favour of Colonel Mendieta's assumption of power, a compromise supported apparently by both Batista and De la Torriente. Grau at first listened to this and Welles could speak for at least one day of meeting an 'entirely conciliatory spirit'. Alas, the next day, 12 December, this telegram left Havana:

Personal for the Acting Secretary. In view of the unexpected and complete collapse of negotiations this afternoon, shall leave Havana by aeroplane Wednesday, arriving Washington Friday morning.[19]

[17] Foreign Relations (1933), II, 531–3; Phillips, 125–6. Cuba was there represented by Grau's Labour secretary, Dr Angel Alberto Giraudy; the historian, Dr Portell Vilá, and Dr Alfredo Nogueira, with the student leaders Carlos Prío and Rubio Padilla.

[18] See ibid., 529, and Grant Watson's dispatch making this recommendation on 30 November.

[19] Foreign Relations (1933), II, 539. In the British Foreign Office the Permanent Under-Secretary wrote, 'This looks like a most futile and undignified proceeding. Is this all the U.S. can do?' But his subordinate, R. R. Craigie, replied. 'I agree, but we have got rid of Mr Sumner Welles. That is the important thing.' (Minutes on Grant Watson telegram No. 143, of 14 December.)

Grau had in fact been told by Carbó and by Guiteras that they could not support a national government under Mendieta; they threatened immediate revolt.[20] Second, Batista seems to have decided again to veer round to Grau for the time being.[21] In these confused, bitterly disheartening and undecided circumstances Welles at last and for good left Havana, taking up the post of Assistant Secretary of State at the State Department and remaining therefore in general control of Cuban policy.

Before his successor, Jefferson Caffery, arrived,[22] on 8 December, Batista and the student chief, Rubén de León, jointly assured his (and Welles's) deputy, Matthews,[23] that the Grau government was now stable, that schools and university would be working properly from January onwards and that no 'communism' was to be found among the government supporters.[24] Indeed, the Communist party was in reality strongly opposed to Grau. Batista urged that recognition by the U.S. would soon secure the diminution of the opposition, but his game was still obscure.

Welles's motives in his persistent hostility to Grau are, however, not obscure. He was clearly less concerned about U.S. property or his physical security than to back his friends, and he seems to have genuinely confused their interests with 'the will of the people'. He was a man who always suspected popular emotion and demonstrations of crowds. He was right to distrust the personality of Grau, yet, though progressive and well intentioned, he distrusted the social revolution which Grau was nominally attempting to enact. He thought Grau's pursuit of pure freedom hypothetical; when Grau said to him that 'Cuba could get along without the recognition of foreign powers and even without foreign commercial interchanges', he might very well be expressing an age-old Cuban desire, but Welles thought him absurd.[25] Welles's actions and the action of the U.S. government to which he was responsible clearly constituted a real if disguised intervention: he explained in retrospect that he could not recommend recognition of any regime which 'was not approved by the great majority',[26] yet Welles did not love that majority overmuch, being happier with an *élite*.

By this time there were other political anxieties: another sugar

[20] Foreign Relations (1933), II, 540.

[21] Phillips, 128.

[22] Foreign Relations, 541. Caffery (born 1886) had been in the Department of State since 1913 and had served in Paris, Madrid, Bogotá, etc To Cuba he came as special representative of Roosevelt, to avoid being ambassador to a country which the U.S. had not recognized.

[23] H. Freeman Matthews (born 1899), in U.S. diplomatic service since 1924; served later in Vichy France, London, on Eisenhower's staff, Yalta, and the Netherlands.

[24] Foreign Relations (1933), II, 541–3.

[25] Grant Watson dispatch of December 18.

[26] Welles, *Time for Decision*, 198.

harvest was about to begin. Should this be unrestricted? Could the harvest be carried out in existing political conditions? Would the banks give credit to mills which had overthrown the managers? On 21 December the government took over the stagnant mills of the Cuban American Co., the giants *Chaparra* and *Delicias*, which might not otherwise have ground cane in 1934. A purge of the army continued.[27] There were constant riots against the 'fifty per cent' law: the CNOC rioted on 17 December, in protest against Spanish shops which were closed, *El País* newspaper offices being burned in the mêlée, and several people killed. On 19 December, Spanish commercial employees rioted in the same cause.[28] Many Spanish employees were threatened with unemployment and repatriation. A U.S. journalist, George Miller, of the *Detroit News*, sent Roosevelt a passionate description of Cuba – the cities swarming with hungry, idle men, thoughtful citizens praying for U.S. intervention.[29] On the same day, the government declared that it would not refund any part of Machado's $M60 loan, on the grounds that it was illegally contracted. But Grau nevertheless showed himself Machado's pupil in, at least, his sugar policy. Machado had attempted to keep all the sugar mills going by paternalism. Grau divided sugar mills into two categories: those whose quota had in 1933 been less than 60,000 sacks, and those who had more. The first were now authorized to have a free harvest up to that number. Otherwise Machado's quotas were kept.[30]

The New Year came in with amnesties for prisoners involved in the Atarés revolution of November, with the Uruguayan minister at work as he had been before, between the Cuban parties, on conciliation. It was time. High School children in Havana were holding a series of anti-Grau meetings. Anyone over thirteen had a revolver. Schoolteachers were on strike from 8 January. One group of children blew up the doorway of the Spanish Asturiano Club. Violence between Negroes and whites broke out in Trinidad. On 14 January the government took over the Compañía Cubana de Electricidad. But now Batista was ready once again (with the 'cleansing of the army' the chief event of the previous two weeks and with Batista in an even stronger position) to negotiate an agreement with Mendieta. This time, at last, with the sugar harvest in the balance, Grau was unable to maintain himself. Batista had no doubt decided from Caffery's aloof and calm manner that the Roosevelt administration would never recognize Grau: on 10 January, he had seen Caffery, who merely said: 'I will lay down no specific terms: the matter of your government is a Cuban matter and it is for you to

[27] 7 colonels, 16 lieutenant-colonels, 41 majors, 124 captains, 160 lieutenants, 67 second lieutenants and 99 ensigns all lost their ranks on 15 December (Adam y Silva, 499–505).
[28] Phillips, 131.
[29] F. D. Roosevelt, *Papers*, 179.
[30] *Estudio*, 641.

decide.'[31] On 13 January, the Secretary of State, Manuel Márquez Sterling, returned from Washington and convinced Grau that he could not secure recognition from the U.S.[32]

Caffery's attitude appears also to have been more that of an observer than Welles's had been. Maybe the absence in Washington of that opinionated and ever-active Proconsul afforded a little will-power to the Cuban politicians. Batista and Colonel Mendieta also appear to have been persuaded of the desirability of firm action by the menacing and verbally revolutionary conclusions of the fourth congress of CNOC in the first week of 1934, at which 10,000 delegates were assembled. But Caffery clearly agreed with Welles as to the 'inefficiency, ineptitude and unpopularity with all the better classes in the country of the *de facto* government. *It is supported only by the Army and ignorant masses who have been misled by Utopian promises.*'[33] On 13 January Grau and Batista had their last interview as colleagues on Enrique Pedro's *hacienda* outside Havana. Mendieta also was present. Batista bluntly told Grau that he knew the U.S. would recognize a government headed by Colonel Mendieta: he therefore asked Grau to resign.[34] Grau replied that, though he would not stand in the way of any patriotic solution, he could only resign to those nineteen students and pentarchs which had elected him in September.[35]

The following day there was a large meeting of the most prominent persons, politicians and students who had come into places of importance since September. Most of the government's old backers were present.[36] The student leader, Rubén de León, now shuttled into a prominent place by the pressure of student politics, arrived late, bent on making a denunciation of Batista. Batista came up to him smiling, saying, '*Caramba*, you don't want to greet me?' 'No,' replied Rubén de León with spirit, 'since you have conspired against those who gave you responsibility, you have betrayed the revolution, betrayed your friends,

[31] Foreign Relations, V, 97.

[32] Grant Watson dispatch, 14 January 1934.

[33] Foreign Relations, V, 95. He later pointed out that the 'ignorant masses reach . . . a very high number', NA 837.00/3931, qu. Wood, 85.

[34] Adam y Silva, 376; Phillips, 142. See also *Ahora*, 22 January 1934, for the Secretary of Justice Luis Almagro's account. Grau later said that Caffery had requested to see him but that he had refused, unless Caffery wished to talk of international affairs. (see *El País/Información*, Havana, 8 November 1934). Caffery said nothing to Washington of this.

[35] Edmund Chester, 155-6.

[36] These were, apparently: Fernández Velasco, Secretary of Labour; José Antonio González Rubiera, Secretary of Education; Reinaldo Jordán, Sub-Secretary of Education (of the Directorio of 1927); Luis Almagro, Secretary of Justice; Carrera Justiz, Secretary of the Presidency (he would become Batista's Minister of Communications in 1952); Pablo Beola, Secretary of Public Works; Carbó, Lucilo de la Peña, Alejandro Vergara, Major Pablo Rodríguez; Colonel López Migoya; Juan Govea, President of *ABC Radical*; Mario Labourdette, Chief of Police; Dr Trejo, the new mayor of Havana; Rubén de León, Eddy Chibás, Lincoln Rodón and Segundo Curti, of the Directorio Estudiantil of 1927 and 1930.

1952:
Batista comes in
Prío goes out (Señora
de Prío in foreground)

20a Batista as President, 1956

20b Rolando Masferrer,
after Cayo Confites, 1947

20c Eddy Chibás

shown cowardice before your duties, and panic in the face of the possible landing of the Yankee marines.'[37] Batista nevertheless took the chair, sitting between Dr Fernández Velasco, Secretary of Labour, and Carbó, and began to speak at about 1.30 a.m. He gave a short account of recent events and talked no longer against the old *políticos* and reactionaries but in the solemn measured tones of a father and saviour of the nation; he said that he was forgiving all and understanding all. Rubén de León again denounced Batista, accusing him of betraying the Revolution, of being ungrateful, ambitious, and a president-maker. He challenged Batista to drop his mask and reveal himself as he was – a would-be dictator.[38] The meeting not surprisingly broke off without reaching any decision, at 5 a.m.

On 15 January, it seemed that some kind of compromise would have to be reached: the students were not going to accept Mendieta; nor was Batista any more going to accept Grau. Guiteras threatened that he and organized labour would under no circumstances accept a solution which was not accepted by the committee. The police seemed to be likely to follow Guiteras. The compromise candidate was the honest engineer, Carlos Hevia, revolutionary of Gibara in 1931, Secretary of Agriculture in Grau's cabinet, son of Aurelio Hevia, a well-known officer of the revolutionary war and afterwards a Conservative politician. Batista then suddenly called a few members of the committee[39] to Campamento Columbia. Rubén de León, not knowing how Batista's mind was changing, launched into another rhetorical attack, this time on Colonel Mendieta as a tarnished representative of the old politique. This gave Batista a chance to announce his conversion to Hevia, and the Junta immediately named Hevia president.[40] A group of students rushed to Mendieta. The colonel said that if the country needed it, he would in fact back Hevía. But the rest of the committee (waking about noon) refused to accept the scheme, since it seemed Batista had devised it as a temporary expedient. Guiteras contemplated backing Hevia, provided Hevia replaced Batista as Chief of Staff by Pablo Rodríguez, the old sergeants' leader whom Batista had sidestepped. Grau appeared at the National Palace in the afternoon, exhausted: Rubén de León proposed that the students refused to accept his resignation. But the Secretary of Justice, Almagro, wrote out the abdication in a document which de León ripped across, shouting, 'Grau is not quitting.'[41] Everyone got up, shouting and waving their hands. Almagro said, 'Well, what about Batista? Batista will not accept

[37] This is Rubén de León's account. *Bohemia*, 18 March 1934.
[38] *Carteles*, 11 March 1934.
[39] Hevia himself, de la Peña, Carbó, Ferrer, Mariné, and Rubén de León.
[40] See *Bohemia*, 18 March 1934, article by Rubén de León.
[41] Phillips, 145.

Grau.' Rubén de León called Almagro a traitor, and they came to blows. A growing number of persons gathered around Grau shouting '*Que no se vaya! Abajo los políticos! Mueran los traidores!*' They all went into the adjoining office, leaving the UP correspondent to steal the key of the president's desk ('I hadn't collected a single souvenir in the whole revolution,' he excused himself).[42] Eventually, at 5 p.m. Grau resigned in favour of Hevia and, at long last, after four months of anxiety, dispute and controversy, went home to his own house in Vedado.[43]

On 16 January, at noon, Carlos Hevia took the oath as president before Chief Justice Edelman, his father-in-law. His first move was to confirm several of Grau's ministers in office.[44] He immediately began negotiations with Mendieta's group for their possible membership of the cabinet. Casanova, president of the Association of Cuban Landowners, assured Caffery that he and his friends would accept Hevia. Guiteras, contrariwise, now observed that the game was up, so far as Hevia was concerned, and seems to have decided to stake all on a popular challenge to Batista. He promptly prepared to arrange a general strike directed against the participation of Batista in the government. By 17 January Guiteras's strike, of public utilities, was firmly under way. This strike had counterproductive results, however. At 2 p.m. on 17 January Batista told Caffery simply that 'in view of the very precarious strike situation (seriously endangering enormous American properties) provoked by Guiteras and also in view of Hevia's inability to secure the full support of Mendieta's group, he has decided to declare Mendieta President'.[45] This was easily accomplished. Hevia began drafting his resignation in the evening. It proved impossible to call the Revolutionary committee, since most of them did not wish to have a new meeting at Campamento Columbia and the rest did not want in any way to play Batista's game. A group headed by de la Torriente and Méndez Peñate tried at the last minute to inveigle the Secretary of State, Márquez Sterling, into accepting the presidency. But now at last there was no holding Mendieta, with Batista behind him. Mendieta's house, according to Mrs Phillips, quickly began to resemble a camp before the battle, full of job-hunters flattering the man they knew would now be bound to be able, if he so wished, to help them.[46]

Hevia left the palace early on the morning of 18 January. Colonel Mendieta took over at noon, amid scenes of amazing jubilation which astonished and greatly surprised Guiteras and the radicals. The crowds thronged the streets round the National Palace. A salute was fired.

[42] *Ibid.*, 146.
[43] Foreign Relations (1934), II, 101; Phillips, 146.
[44] Adam y Silva, 384.
[45] Foreign Relations (1934), II, 104.
[46] *Ibid.*, 148. See also *Bohemia*, 28 January 1934.

Whistles blew. Those with revolvers – they were many – let them off into the air in enthusiasm. The bars were full. 'The fatigue of the long struggle against Machado and the vertiginous tumult of the hundred or so days of Grau's regime' converted the people into an ally of Batista; they believed that peace would at last come.[47] Surely the golden age would now return. Dr Cosme de la Torriente agreed to become Secretary of the Presidency. The upright Colonel Méndez Peñate became Minister of Justice. Guiteras left secretly for Oriente, intending to stir up trouble, while the strike collapsed slowly in Havana. In the country, the CNOC decided to continue to strike and many mills and other sectors of work remained idle. But even so, on 23 January the U.S. government recognized Colonel Mendieta's regime, and in consequence the banks agreed to finance the harvesting of the 1934 sugar crop,[48] while Dr Grau left for a holiday in Mexico.

A crowd of his adherents gathered at the wharf [wrote Grant Watson] and as the vessel steamed down the harbour they ran along the quayside. They belonged to the poorer classes and were very enthusiastic. They regarded the impractical consumptive doctor as their champion. He had been in office for only 4½ months and yet he made reforms some of which will last. Students of Cuban history will remember his term because a great change came over Cuba. The rule of the sugar magnates was shaken at any rate for the present – perhaps for ever.[49]

[47] Carrillo MSS.
[48] See Foreign Relations (1933), II, 104–7; Phillips, 150–3.
[49] Dispatch, 29 January 1934.

CHAPTER LVIII

The Counter-Revolution

Unfortunately for Cuba, Colonel Mendieta, the new president, was not José Martí, just as Dr Grau, General Machado and General José Miguel Gómez had in their time turned out not to be 'the Apostle' or even his heir, spiritual or material. In 1934 Mendieta was just sixty years old. He had been a member of the Cuban House of Representatives throughout the first twenty years of the Republic from 1901 till 1923; he had been vice-presidential candidate in 1916 with Zayas, and in those days he had been associated with Machado on the so-called Unionist wing of the Liberals. His attacks against Menocal's autocratic behaviour had made him famous and he had been in prison under Machado. He was in the public mind the outstanding, the best, the most honest of the old *políticos*, but he was certainly one of them, in his light grey suit and light green tie, with his courtesy and air of distinction. In character, he vacillated. His administrative skill turned out to be limited to a facility for organizing compromises among the party leaders. To begin with, this enabled him to build a comparatively strong cabinet, composed mostly of men who had been associated with him in the interminable discussions with Welles and Caffery. These included his own party friends, De la Torriente and Méndez Peñate; Rafael Santos Jiménez of *Acción Republicana*; Conservatives such as Carlos Manuel de la Cruz (a well-known politician of the early 1920s, who as a barrister had defended many of Machado's opponents in the courts); Dr Cuervo Rubio, the gynaecologist who had been associated with the September revolution in the beginning; a member of ABC Radical (José Becquer) and of the well-named 'Conservative Revolutionary Party' (Colonel Rafael Peña); and, from the ABC itself, Dr Martínez Sáenz came from Miami to take over as Secretary of Finance, a post he had filled under Carlos Manuel de Céspedes. Miguel Mariano Gómez returned as mayor of Havana.

But it shortly became clear that the real centre of power in Cuba from 15 January 1934 at least was Batista. If decisions had to be made, he made them. If there was a strike, Batista decided how it should be settled, or crushed. Batista's personality firstly explains this, for it was a mixture of strength and superficiality, of desire to please and willingness to repress, of love of acclaim and contempt for individual protest. The only effective parties of the past, the Liberals and Conservatives, creations of Gómez and Menocal during the first two decades of the Republic, had been smashed by the autocracy of Machado during the third decade, when the Liberals had gradually been bribed or bullied into executants or collaborators of tyranny. The two parties had always lacked effective national organization. Now Menocal was a conspirator in Miami, rich, but whose wealth was without roots in Cuba; Gómez was dead; Machado was in exile. Gómez's friends, such as Orestes Ferrara, had either been with Machado and were therefore discredited, or were hopelessly divided. The groups who surrounded Mendieta or Miguel Mariano Gómez (Gómez's son) were comrades in arms not political forces, and who knew whether their hands might not be stretched out as Machado's, Zayas's or Gómez's had been, when it came to the point, towards the Lottery or the Treasury itself in search of jobs and riches? The only effective political unit in Cuba was now the army, which, young though it might be and however bereft of tradition, had a national organization and had its armed representatives at least in all the cities. It also had a revolutionary ideology, for Batista's army was, of course, founded on the victory of September; it was an army which still believed or was told that it was carrying on a revolution. If Grau's friends thought that Batista and the army were betraying the revolution, the army believed that Grau had betrayed it first.

There was, too, a sense in which Batista and the army were right about themselves. Not only were they at that time the only effective political institution, but they were genuinely revolutionary and even egalitarian. They had broken the old officer corps in the successive blows of 4 September, at the Hotel Nacional and at Atarés. Nearly all Batista's officers were working-class in origin, as was Batista himself. Negroes and mulattoes were freely admitted as officers. Batista was not proposing the repeal of all Grau's decrees. His declared intention, on the contrary, was to go further still, to break the Platt Amendment for good and to negotiate an equitable sugar arrangement with the U.S. Treading gently, at this stage of his life he was anxious for a revolution, but one run by himself. For the time being Colonel Mendieta was a necessary front. But Batista was less concerned with the appearance than the reality of power and of decision-making, while Mendieta and the old-style *políticos* desired the contrary.

It would be foolish to belittle Batista's achievement. In a few weeks he had overthrown an officer class, as well as the government which backed it and which was itself the creation of the U.S. administration; he had nevertheless been able to charm the U.S. ambassador, a man of astuteness and intelligence. No similarly successful NCOs' revolt can be found anywhere else though it may be added that 'in these armies of nations where there is no chance of war the sergeants are the only people to have any real functions'.[1]

By January 1935 Batista was acknowledged, *faute de mieux* but nevertheless securely, as the only source of authority in the whole country, a man who ruled certainly through the army but who was not really a military man at all: rather was he a civilian in uniform who owed his rise to political finesse.

Yet though much was due to Batista's native intelligence and vigour, he merely represented a strong force, perhaps the only strong force, in a society whose old bonds had largely disintegrated. The Cuban army had been founded in 1909, at the end of Magoon's administration, with the candid realization that, thanks to the heritage of Cuban wars and rebellions in the time of the Spanish dominion, political parties would come to blows with each other if there were no public force in addition to the police.[2] But the army was nevertheless founded in the shadow of the war of independence; the political leaders – Menocal, Gómez, Mendieta, Asbert, Machado and even Orestes Ferrara – had all been generals or other officers in the war of 1895–8. How could the new officers who came out of the military academies of the years after 1911 compete with such legendary men? Their position was weak from the start.

Thus the army, brought into being for political reasons, was always political. Gómez, the president at the time of the army's inception, gave the high commands exclusively to his friends; Pino Guerra and Monteagudo were in name professional officers but they were also politicians just as Gómez and Menocal were in name politicians if also generals. Menocal tried to do the same, though, since Gómez's officers had not actually committed treason, they could not be disposed of at once or completely. But afterwards officers were mostly Menocalistas, Miguelistas, or Zayistas, labels which they upheld as passionately as most political persons did. The officer corps could not speak with a single voice, but had loyalties less to its own chiefs than to outside political bosses who were, after all, mostly generals or military commanders with experience of combat in the most glorious of all wars, the struggle for national liberation.

The army in 1933 was not only political but had been tarnished by long association with Machado. Under Machado, some officers remained Menocalistas; some of those had gone away, others had remained to conspire, more or less ineffectively. Others still, ex-Liberals or Miguelistas, made one sort of protest or another. But the majority

[1] Letter to the author from Orestes Ferrara, 26 July 1964.
[2] See above, p. 490.

remained, either through loyalty to the state, inertia or opportunism. Machado had favoured his army with lavish pay, good conditions and privileged treatment of several kinds. Inevitably, therefore, the officers as such were implicated in Machado's repression: not simply the known killers such as Captain Arsenio Ortiz but others who followed outrageous orders, or heard of them and did nothing. It was true, of course, that the officer corps finally changed its front and helped to expel Machado, but only at the very end. This change did something to restore the officers' prestige and self-respect but it did not do so completely and there were still many men guilty of murder in the army in September 1933. Machado's dictatorship had been to a great extent a military dictatorship: the military 'superiors' in the schools, in the city council halls and in the government departments, were the means of Machado's control of the state. Even the milk and meat deliveries had been controlled by the army. By 1932 martial law was more or less normal, under military 'mayors' such as Colonel Federico Rasco, a Liberal officer who had once been dismissed by Menocal for refusing to fake elections on Menocal's behalf. So the revolution of 1933, if it was to be a real protest against the past, had to be a protest against the old army too.

By September 1933, the Cuban regular army was only one more group among many accustomed to bear arms. The various revolutionary parties, ABC, ABC Radical and OCRR, Pro Ley y Justicia, La Legión del Caribe, the Directorio Estudiantil of 1927 and of 1929, the political bandits associated with Colonel Blas Hernández, the Communists too, had all fought against Machado, after their fashion, often bravely. They too had their martyrs and their epics. They considered themselves no less worthy of public acclaim than the men of an earlier generation who had fought against Spain. Significantly, perhaps the first man to be murdered by Machado, the journalist Armando André, had tried to place a bomb under Weyler in 1896, and was regarded as a hero for so doing. Of course some members of the army were associated with ABC and some had taken part in the OCRR. But in September 1933 the old regular army, founded in 1909, could be seen as only one among several competing armed forces – a situation symbolic of a national tradition which supposed that in fact soldiering and fighting was something done by everybody: 'With a rifle and a machete everything is resolved.' Thus in Cuba there survived on the one hand a distrust of soldiering and on the other a respect for weapons.

A military caste can only be created when the officers come from one class. This was not so in Cuba. First, a number of officers at the beginning had come from the old rural guard, and were really a kind

682 · THE REVOLUTION OF 1933

of peasant policemen. Second, a large number of officers had been promoted from the ranks, as a result of examinations by tribunals.[3] There was therefore in the Cuban Officer Corps before 1933 none of the camaraderie based on total social acceptance which characterizes so many similar forces.

The weakness of the corps of regular officers led to the strength of the NCOs and even of enlisted men. Most came from the same class in the admittedly limited sense that they were men who had no stake in, and certainly no capital in Cuba. They were men who knew that many of their superiors, like them, had come up from nothing. Everything was open to them. They had carried out the orders of Machado and Ortiz but not being officers they had not had to take responsibility for them; the *porristas*, after all, had done more killing than the army.

There had been an occasion in 1930 when the sergeants, Pablo Rodríguez included, had specifically rallied to Machado, but this was more easily overlooked than such action by the officers. Further, there was something to be said for the sincerity of the sergeants. Some of them were honest when they talked about the Revolution. Some thought that their mission was to cleanse Cuba. For a while at least, Batista himself seemed to be among these.

As with the army, so with the old parties. The sergeants and the students broke the Céspedes government with such ease because the parties behind Céspedes, like the officers, were without substance. Thus the old Liberal party, José Miguel Gómez's creation, a group for a while with great populist appeal, a movement which had embodied hopes of all classes in the community, had crashed with the conversion of Machado, its last leader, to tyranny and self-indulgence. Colonel Mendieta's Unión Nacional had roots within the Liberal party but, due partly to the colourless characteristics of its chief, it never gathered much more following: it never seemed more than an agglomeration of interests, some doubtless decent, in pursuit of jobs in the old style rather than ideals. It would survive only a short time, after the assumption of the presidency by the colonel: to describe it as Welles did, as the most important political force in Cuba, was utterly misleading.

To a lesser extent, the other political groups of the pre-Machado era also collapsed, partly because they had failed to restrain Machado and because even many Conservatives had handsomely profited by his regime. All members of the 1925 and 1927 legislatures had received Machado's money, sliced off the lottery, or the Chase Bank loan, or the National Highways Bill or some other national enterprise financed by custom duties on U.S. goods.

[3] See above, p. 583.

At a deeper level, too, it was clear that whatever following these parties, including the Liberal, might have among the *guajiros*, none had any support among the Negro masses. The Negro issue, real or false, was ignored. The colour bar was hardly a reality in Machado's Cuba; the army and the police were full of Negroes; but in a sense the Negro community was ignored, held apart and holding itself apart, and really supporting Machado more than the 'better classes' surrounding Mendieta. Machado had given support to the African fiestas and cults. Here too the revolutionary parties themselves were lacking. The ABC, the ABC Radical, the OCRR, the Directorio Estudiantil, had an almost entirely professional middle-class and mostly white membership. The Communist party, though much more multi-racial, was too small, its bluff having been called when Machado placed his faith in them to end the strike of August. They also were somewhat compromised by their past relationship with Machado and were undergoing now their own major crisis. The Church had many of the weaknesses of political parties. It suffered still from having made no contribution at all to Cuba's struggle against Spain not to speak of having played no part in the fight against Machado. Throughout most of the early history of the Republic, the men of the Church had remained Spanish in nationality. In Menocal's day about two-thirds of the churchmen in Cuba were non-Cuban, mostly Spanish, and few black or mulatto.[4]

Among the upper classes, among the Spaniards and among the still fairly rich children of the old sugar kings, the Church retained a social importance. Well-off people living in Vedado or Miramar had church weddings. But among farmers religion by now meant little: they rarely had contact with a church in a town and even town churches failed to adapt themselves from Spanish conditions.[5] There were never any churches at modern sugar mills and the church played no part in the gathering of the great harvests of Cuba. Some of the priests sent to Cuba were ecclesiastical exiles, sent there from Spain because of various 'offences'.[6] The quality of the priesthood was low; pastoral visits of priests in remote areas were rare, perhaps once a year to some places for baptisms, at $3 a head. Perhaps during the carnival of the patron saint at some nearby village the farmers might have their children

---

[4] According to the Census of 1919, churchmen numbered 880, of whom 667 were men, 213 women. 482 men and 160 women were foreign white; 147 men and 52 women white Cubans; 38 men and one woman black or mulatto. Nearly half lived in Havana. Of the men, two-thirds (426) were born in Spain, only 156 in Cuba. 17 were born in the U.S., 38 elsewhere; 28 of the women were born in Spain, 43 in Cuba, 1 in the U.S., 78 elsewhere (Census of 1919, 662, 677, 695–6, 731–3).

[5] Few Spanish farmers live in the country, and the Church, as indeed Spanish life in general, is centred on the towns.

[6] Nelson, 174.

baptized, and though the ceremony might be done *en masse*, the $3 would still be charged.[7] This would do nothing to endear the priest to the 'parishioner'.[8] The bishops had little effect on social welfare in the island, nor did most priests, with a few exceptions.

Not surprisingly, therefore, during the first thirty years of Cuban independence, there was little increase in the number of legal marriages in the island, although even secular weddings had been legalized in 1901. The North American sociologist, Nelson, even wrote that 'usually those who get married do so through the intervention of some politician whose candidates take advantage of the event as an act of propaganda'.[9]

But while neither Church nor army was able to give strength to the political Liberals of Céspedes's government, and the political parties were really mere shadowy groups of friends without organization, the commercial and economically powerful groups in Cuba were also peculiarly unable to shore up the political system – for one main reason: they were chiefly foreigners. It was not simply that so much of the sugar industry was, after the débâcle of 1921, almost entirely in U.S. hands and that even other Cubans involved were completely orientated towards New York, but that the merchant class was still dominated by Spaniards, even if less so than in the first decade of the Republic.[10] In 1931, no fewer than 21·5 % of the whole population were foreigners, compared with 18·5 % in 1919 and 13 % in 1907.[11] Of course, Spaniards were in many ways only nominally alien, but they were people nevertheless with often a real foreign allegiance or at least with a far from positive Cuban one. Many of the foreigners were West Indians and Haitian labourers, who also had loyalties elsewhere. None of this 21·5 % really cared what happened in the Cuban body politic. In many professions there was a constant rise in the Spanish-born participation throughout the first years of the century, and though Cuban nationalism in the twentieth century was generally directed against the U.S., it nevertheless gathered much of its real momentum at lower levels from hostility to the sur-

[7] *Loc. cit.*, and 218. Chapman in his history of Cuba, published in 1927, hardly mentions the Church in 655 pages, besides idly mentioning that it seemed 'to have lost its grip' (*op. cit.*, 604).

[8] This instance described by Nelson of a period some years later, in the area south-east of Cienfuegos (op. cit., 268–9).

[9] *Ibid.*, 269.

[10] 1931 figures for breakdown not available. 1919 figures are a total of 67,483 merchants, of whom 32,726 were foreign and 27,501 Cuban white, the rest (7,256) being Cuban Negro – i.e. an actual Cuban majority though only just in terms of man for man. This was not at all reflected in wealth (Census of 1919, 662).

[11] In 1907, 268,352; in 1919, 535,950; in 1931, 850,413 were foreigners, of whom in 1919 and 1931, 404,674 and 625,449 were Spanish citizens. Of these 'foreigners', however, by no means all had been born outside Cuba. The population born in Spain in 1931 was 257,596. Thus nearly two-thirds of the Spaniards were merely children of Spaniards who had chosen to keep their nationality. (See Censuses of 1907, 1919, 1931.)

viving Spanish influence in the Republic. This hostility also gathered further from the skill with which the various Spanish clubs in Cuba managed to secure extra funds for Spanish indigent and unemployed during the depression and there were various quarrels arising from difficulties over the repatriation of poor Spaniards. The consequence was that in 1933 there were specific anti-Spanish riots and the destruction of Spanish property.[12]

Had there been institutions to contain it or even to express it, had there not been desperate poverty, of course, nationalism would have been weaker. As it was, it was the dominant political philosophy of the students in the revolution, and because they articulated it in its purest form and because of their unrivalled place in the struggle against Machado, their position had been strong in September. No election had occurred to test Grau's position, nor were there any other means to test opinion. It can never really be known how strongly Grau was supported. Welles's and Caffery's views were based on what they described as 'the best people', though Caffery at least specifically accepted that the 'ignorant masses' were behind Grau *en masse*.[13] Welles on the other hand thought that 'an overwhelming majority were for Mendieta' while Grau never had 'the great majority'.[14]

The students of 1933 were older than would normally be understood by that word, since they were those who went to the university in the late 1920s. Since then no one had gone to the university. Most were, however, men in their twenties: Eduardo Chibás junior, for instance, was still only twenty-six in 1933. Although students, such as those associated with the Ala Izquierda Estudiantil, for instance, were willing to compromise with the Communists, this was not their general position. Even the Ala Izquierda had adopted some of Mella's arguments but not his final intellectual conclusion. The students were anti-American primarily because Machado had been so closely connected with the U.S. and had been elected in the first place with U.S. money: 'It is for no one a secret that the murderous and rapacious oligarchy which captured power on 20 May 1925 with the direct support of Wall Street is near its tragic final leap,' remarked the student Raúl Roa in *Línea*, the organ of Ala Izquierda Estudiantil, on 10 July 1931;[15] the revelations of the Senate enquiry into the Chase National Bank as to the extent of their bribery of the press and their help to Machado's son-in-law added fuel to this fire; partly then students interpreted the collapse of the Cuban economy as the consequence of U.S. lack of vision and understanding;

---

[12] See reprint of report of British Vice-Consul, Cienfuegos, 5 August 1933, for description of attack on Spanish shops there.

[13] See Wood, 85.

[14] See Welles, *Time for Decision*, 199, 198.

[15] Roa, *Retorno a la Alborada*, 15.

partly they saw the whole instability of sugar prices as making Cuba the victim of an international financial system of which the U.S. was the upholder; partly they inherited a multitude of ideas from Martí, from Bartolomé Masó or Juan Gualberto Gómez directed against 'the Monster', the Platt Amendment, and U.S. 'dollar diplomacy' in Cuba and elsewhere in the Caribbean and Latin America. They believed that in their revolution they would fulfil Martí's dreams, though their knowledge of economic history since Martí's death made them more radical, more socialist, at least in theory, than Martí had been.

Martí's unachieved revolution, so far as 1933 was concerned, spelled regeneration: regeneration in face of the failure of the old liberalism, in Cuba as in Europe, and in Spain. It was of course also interpreted as a demand for regeneration after Machado, and in face of the political world of the history of the Republic to date, but it was also the idea of regeneration against Spain which the war of 1895–8 and its aftermath had not fulfilled.

The students played on many themes both political and economic. Politically, there were many instances when the broad lines of U.S. policy towards Cuba had been directed mainly in the interests of U.S. property holders there; the U.S. marines had been in Camagüey from 1917 to 1922 in order to preserve Herbert Lakin's railway line. It was known too that U.S. policy towards Cuba was often formed, partially or entirely, by persons who at least had once had a financial interest in Cuba. Norman Davis, general manager of the Trust Company of Cuba, acutely involved in the scandal of the Ports Company, was still close to the nerve-centres of Democratic 'power' in 1933,[16] had been Under-Secretary and financial adviser to the Treasury under Wilson and was probably instrumental in the traumatic despatch of General Crowder to Havana in January 1921. The career of Frank Steinhart set a bad example: Magoon had given him a contract to develop Havana Electric after he had been the very powerful Consul-General; Gómez's 1909 loan had been contracted with Steinhart's firm Speyer and Co: it had been scarcely reassuring to know that President Taft's brother was Steinhart's partner; and Steinhart had desired intervention during the Negro revolt of 1912. Later, the Secretary of State, Cordell Hull, had been lobbyist for Lakin and his friends during 1929–30. Several members even of Roosevelt's government had been involved in Cuban finances: Woodin, the First Secretary of the Treasury, had been indeed director of Consolidated Railways and of the Cuba Co., and president of the American Car and Foundry Co.; Charles Taussig, president of the great sugar-refiners, the American Molasses Co., was a 'marginal'

[16] He would later be U.S. representative at the 1937 Sugar Conference.

member of the Brains Trust,[17] and Rexford Tugwell, vice-president of American Molasses, became Under-Secretary of Agriculture and one of the great names of the New Deal; even Adolf Berle was a legal adviser of American Molasses.[18]

The attitude towards the U.S. in Cuba during the first thirty years of the Republic had never really been other than ambiguous and nervous, while hostility to Machado was not confined to the Left. Hardly indeed had Magoon's battleship left Havana Bay than Senator Emilio Arteaga introduced a bill limiting the purchase of property by foreigners; but it was rejected as seeming likely to cause a flight of capital.[19] In 1915 there had been general clamour over the consequences of mass sale of Cuban mills and lands to Americans, and considerable speculation over the patriotism of so doing. In November 1915 the formation of the giant combine Cuba Cane had been arrested by a resolution in the Cuban Senate, backed by several orthodox politicians such as Wilfredo Fernández and Carlos Mendieta. But even then there was doubt about resisting the trend: an impeccable and honest nationalist of the old school, such as Varona, was arguing that Cuba needed all the capital she could get in order to develop.[20] In the Chamber, anti-Americanism had then been attacked by Ferrara and Betancourt Manduley. These problems had been intensified during the twenties, especially after the 'dance of the millions', when Cuban property passed on an even greater scale to U.S. banks. There were many instances of tactless, overbearing and arrogant behaviour by U.S. officials, not only private business men: and others asked why Crowder kept his headquarters on the battleship *Minnesota* in 1921, and why Coolidge's administration did not at least answer the Cuban requests for a revision of the sugar tariff in 1926–8.

One party or other had often played on the threat of provoking U.S intervention as a major factor in the development of events. Estrada Palma had begun the rot by begging for intervention in 1905.[21] In August 1920 the Liberals, faced with the likelihood of electoral fraud by President Menocal, had hinted that they would not take part in the elections, thereby clearly threatening to provoke either revolution or intervention.[22] In October 1923 General Machado, later president, had telephoned Frank Steinhart to request that the U.S. take preventive

[17] A. Schlesinger, *The Age of Roosevelt*, vol. I, *The Crisis of the Old Order 1919–1933* (1957), 427.

[18] The chairman of the Democratic Convention of 1932, Senator Thomas Walsh, married a Cuban, Mina Pérez Chaumont, a rich society patroness, in February 1933; though appointed to Roosevelt's cabinet, he died in March.

[19] Chapman, 621.

[20] Primelles, 183.

[21] See above, p. 476.

[22] Chapman, 402; Primelles, II, 177.

action against the insubordinate and semi-rebellious Veterans' Association.[23] During 1933 the threat of U.S. intervention was the central point of anxiety among all Cuban political parties; indeed between 1927 and 1933, the non-revolutionary parties were constantly appealing for intervention, so that Secretary of State Stimson was actually embarrassed, for his experience in Nicaragua had disillusioned him as to the possible achievements of U.S. intervention.[24] Stimson indeed, by his reluctance to act, had more or less foreshadowed the abrogation of the Platt Amendment; he had seen in July 1932 that intervention under the agreement would probably 'break down all feeling of responsibility on the part of the people of Cuba to mend their own affairs, and to conduct a responsible government'.[25] Paradoxically, therefore, the U.S.'s reluctance to use the Platt Amendment had helped to keep Machado in power.

Welles's refusal to recognize Grau laid the foundations for radical anti-Americanism in the future, as was in fact admitted by the then State Department representative at the Latin American desk, Laurence Duggan, in his book published ten years later: 'Batista . . . saw it was hopeless for Cuba, whose life depended on a restored sugar market with the U.S., to risk our disapproval.'[26]

At the same time, the economic hardship of the majority of Cubans was always a dominant factor in the minds of Grau and his collaborators. Statistics, accounts of travellers and photographs testify to the desperate conditions in 1933. The general standard of living fell by about a fifth from what the Cubans were used to in 1925; the countryside was impoverished and a perpetual prey to the chronic banditry that had characterized it off and on since the days of slavery; the sugar mills were silent, plantations idle. United Railways in the autumn had noted a fall in receipts since 1929 to less than 30% of their receipts of that year, their employees were down by 60%, their passengers down about 70%.[27]

The events of 1933 finally created a revolutionary generation which, despite some real achievements, regarded itself as thwarted, and its appetite whetted for both power and social change, carried on its desires and its methods, particularly the use of weapons, into the succeeding years; for the revolutionary organizations which helped to overthrow Machado never properly disbanded or laid down their arms.

[23] NA 837.00/2419, qu. Smith, 216.

[24] See Wood, 54 ff.

[25] NA 837.00/3454, qu. Wood, 56.

[26] L. Duggan, *The Americans: The Search for Hemisphere Security* (1945), 62. Laurence Duggan (1905–48), a gifted and progressive public servant, committed suicide to avoid investigation by HUAC in 1948.

[27] Report of L. Simpson to British Minister, 20 October 1933. Total receipts in 1929 were (to October) $18,785,000; in 1933 $4,997,000.

BOOK VII

The Age of Democracy
1934 - 52

'Strangers praised the town's colour and gaiety after
spending three days visiting its dance halls, saloons,
taverns and gambling dens, where innumerable
orchestras incited sailors to spend their money . . .
But those who had to put up with the place all the
year round knew about the mud and the dust, and
how the saltpetre turned the door-knockers green, ate
away the ironwork, made silver sweat, brought mildew
out on old engravings . . .'

ALEJO CARPENTIER,
Explosion in a Cathedral

CHAPTER LIX

Batista and the Puppet Presidents

When, in January 1934, Colonel Batista took over government through Colonel Mendieta, he found a nation either resigned to or expectant of radical reform; he had himself the support of several middle-class parties such as ABC; he had too in his favour a desire from almost all sections of opinion for an end to disorder and instability, at almost any price; and he expected a benevolent attitude from the U.S., whose Secretary of State, Cordell Hull, was soon speaking (no doubt on Sumner Welles's suggestion) of the 'almost universal support' by the people of Cuba for Mendieta. The *Wyoming*, however, remained in Havana, keeping its marines ready to land. At the same time the Roosevelt administration made an offer of food, clothing and medicine;[1] and in February hearings began in the U.S. House Committee on Agriculture about the Jones-Cooligan Act for a possible establishment of a 'closed sugar area' to supply the U.S. with whatever it needed, but thereby offering Cuba a 'new deal' in sugar also. In March, Batista was received on board the *Wyoming* as if he were head of state. On 9 March the U.S. created a new Export-Import bank to lend money to Cuba.[2] Recognition therefore completed its work.

But in fact the events of 1927 to 1933, and particularly the experiences of 1933, had created tensions and forces which could not be easily satisfied. Revolutionary demands existed on all sides; all parties declared themselves to be revolutionary, and protests continued. In February 30,000 tobacco workers struck. Various strikes continued in the sugar mills, and even doctors and nurses struck against Spanish private medical schemes, with extraordinary scenes at hospitals: patients were turned away, while doctors were seen stamping up and down the Prado singing the *International*. No death certificates were given and coffins piled up. One doctor was shot and buried in a red flag. Bombs exploded throughout the island, mostly organized by Guiteras's organization. On 7 March, President Mendieta was persuaded to suspend constitutional guarantees, so placing the army formally as well as effectively

---

[1] F. D. Roosevelt, *Papers*.

[2] With a capital of $M2·75 of which $250,000 was common stock held by the U.S. Secretaries of State and of Commerce. See Martínez Sáenz's letter of 9 March to Welles (Roosevelt, *Papers*), in which he explained that, as secretary of the Cuban Treasury, he desired to increase the money in circulation to pay arrears of salary to public employees; to found a government agency to buy land to be distributed; and to found an agricultural financing bank.

in control of Cuba. Then he decreed the dissolution of all unions which refused to accept the regulations governing strikes. A dock strike was broken up. That the army was in control was evident to all: many despaired who had actually put their faith in Mendieta. No move was made to introduce parliaments or elections or establish constitutional behaviour. On 4 April, the Secretary of Justice, the persistent opponent of Machado, Colonel Méndez Peñate, killed himself. He was for a time succeeded by the ABC second-in-command, Saladrigas: but the ABC now refused to back the government, and Saladrigas resigned both from the government and the ABC itself. On 1 May, there was some shooting and a few deaths, while on 3 May demonstrations protesting against what occurred on 1 May were also shot up.[3] The disillusion was considerable among all liberals, while approval in the U.S. was confirmed. Corruption had also returned: Batista, for instance, sent for Rafael Montalvo, who had had the commission to supply Machado's army with uniforms, and told him that all uniforms henceforth would have to cost 15 cents a piece more, for Batista's own benefit.[4]

The Communist party meantime held their second main congress from 20 April to 22 April. It was still an illegal party, but the occurrence of the congress was well-known. Sixty-seven were present, of whom fourteen were Negroes.[5] The meeting was addressed by Bob Minor of the U.S. Communist party, and from this time relations between U.S. and Cuban Communists were close – more so than Cuban Communist relations were with brother parties of South America. The slogan of the Congress was: 'Workers' control, confiscation and distribution of the land of the Yankee and native landlords'. They urged self-determination for Negroes in Oriente province. During the spring of 1934, however, after the death of Martínez Villena, a visit by Comintern representatives brought a formal purge of the entire party which embraced nearly all the intellectual middle-class Communists associated with Martínez Villena – always excepting Grobart. The secretary-general remained Blas Roca.[6]

In May in the U.S. the Jones-Cooligan Act became law, and so determined sugar policy in Cuba for the next twenty-five years: the U.S. Secretary for Agriculture would forecast each year the quantity of sugar needed by the U.S.; each sugar-producing area, foreign and domestic, would then receive a quota, consisting of a specific percentage of this quantity. The quota would be fixed according to marketing in the course of 1931–3: this favoured the U.S. beet sugar growers more

---

[3] See Roa, 74.

[4] Private information.

[5] *Imprecorr*, 14 June 1934. There were 13 sugar workers, 9 tobacco workers, 6 transport workers.

[6] The purge is described, rather mysteriously, in Suárez, 3 fn.

than Roosevelt had intended, since those years had been even less satisfactory for foreign than for domestic U.S. producers.[7] Though later attacked for restricting the production of Cuban sugar, the law, inspired by Welles among others, was undoubtedly an attempt by the U.S. to help the Cubans, but alas like all such efforts ultimately turned very sour. The short-term effects were, however, to raise the then ominously low price of sugar. But Cuba lost the opportunity to compete with the U.S. home industry on a purely economic basis, since Cuban sales were now limited, and by the fiat of a North American politician himself not always uninfluenced by U.S. commercial interests. The consequences were to cause new debate and controversy, and in the 1960s pre-revolutionary Cuba would denounce this Act as leading to 'economic servitude'.

The good intentions of the U.S. government in 1934 were also spoiled by a rather over-nice attention to detail. U.S. commercial policy was then generally actuated by anxiety arising from Japanese competition; Cuba indeed had, under the U.S.'s nose, already become a battlefield between these powers. In early 1934 several Japanese firms were in Havana offering a variety of goods which competed with U.S. exports, often offering prices much below those current in the U.S. Some U.S. firms had had to purchase Japanese raw materials in order to compete. Thus, the new U.S. textile mill founded by Dayton Hedges of New York had placed large orders for Japanese yarn in order to cut the price of its finished products. The U.S. government, therefore, 'acting simply as the agent of its commercial representatives', asked Cuba to make an increase of 100% in the general duty on cotton yarn, but with a 50% preference for the U.S. No increase was demanded for cotton textiles, since the only possible tariff would have provided 'so much additional protection as to encourage the establishment of new mills in Cuba'.[8] Similarly, the only worth-while rayon tariff would have encouraged a native Cuban rayon textile industry, and would be 'as detrimental to American trade as is the Japanese competition'.[9] Japan could, however, be excluded from the rayon yarn market in Cuba by a similar provision to that covering cotton yarn. In both these instances, Japanese prices were respectively 20% and 50% below the U.S. prices.[10]

[7] The Act also restricted the import of Cuban refined sugar to 22% of the total Cuban allocation.

[8] Foreign Relations, 1934, V, 130.

[9] Ibid.

[10] Loc. cit. These conditions also affected other goods; thus in 1930 the U.S. had provided Cuba with 56% of its electric light bulbs, and Japan 4%; but in 1933 Japanese participation had reached 60·7% and U.S. fallen to 17%. The Japanese were able to sell at $2.72 per 100 bulbs, the U.S. had to sell at $12.87. Other areas of anxiety included copper wire (95% sold by the U.S. in 1929, only 39% in 1932), cellophane, and iron and steel, where Belgium as well as Japan were strong competitors. Indeed, in 1933, the U.S. share had dropped to 10% of the iron and steel imports, and Belgian prices were again far lower than U.S. prices.

These kitchen sink statistics show how General Electric and Westinghouse had a strong need to be on intimate terms with the U.S. commercial attaché. Sale of electric light bulbs was the main skirmishing ground with Japan, since other electric equipment seemed to depend on what happened there. The U.S. commercial representatives argued very strongly that the new commercial treaty with Cuba should not 'make the same mistakes' as the old, and permit foreign competition.

These proposals were, however, severely criticized by Welles, who pointed out that all governments, including Roosevelt's, had undertaken, at the Montevideo and London conferences, to increase the volume of international trade. The State Department would therefore have to refuse the higher rates suggested. A critical concession was the reduction in the duty on sugar to nine-tenths of a cent per pound, with a preference of 20% – a virtual abolition, that is, of the old Hawley-Smoot Act. Another concession was made in respect of tobacco, applying a quota of 18% of the total quantity of tobacco used in the U.S. in the manufacture of cigars. But the U.S. kept stringent demands on industrial and agricultural goods. There was also much haggling over cigarettes, avocados, pig products and petrol.[11]

The agreement was finally signed on 24 August 1934.[12] In return for the sugar arrangements, Cuba made six main concessions to the U.S.: import duties on a large variety of U.S. goods were cut; Cuba agreed not to increase her existing duties on a number of other products; Cuban internal taxes on U.S. goods would be cut or reduced; there would be no other restrictions; no qualitative restriction would be placed on any article receiving benefit of tariff reduction. This was in fact the first of Hull's series of bilateral treaties to enlarge U.S. trade. Sumner Welles, Hull recalled, made an earnest plea to 'be allowed the privilege of signing it with me, although this was not customary. He had taken a considerable part in the negotiations, hence I agreed.'[13]

This treaty was in some respects beneficial in that it did secure a stable market for Cuban sugar and tobacco; but it also bound Cuba even more closely to the U.S., and to the use of U.S. goods, instead of encouraging home manufacture. Although it enabled Cuba to rise to supplying over 30% of U.S. sugar in 1937, there was now no possibility ever of returning to the good days before the Hawley-Smoot legislation of the 1920s, when Philippine and Hawaiian sugar could hope for no *entrée* and when Cuba supplied half the U.S. market.

At the same time, a complementary treaty finally abrogating the hated Platt Amendment was signed on 29 May. The 1903 treaty was

[11] For the negotiations see Foreign Relations (1934), V, 140–68.
[12] Text in *ibid.*, 169 ff.
[13] Hull, *Memoirs*, I, 527.

abolished, except for the Guantánamo provisions which remained.[14] The future relations of Cuba and the U.S. would formally at least be those 'normal' between 'independent though friendly states'. But the word *plattista* continued to be an adjective of denunciation in the vocabulary of the Cuban Left. Some questions remained to antagonize Cuban-U.S. relations: were the big loans of Machado from the Chase Bank legal or illegal? What lay behind an attempted assassination of Jefferson Caffery on 27 May? With a sugar harvest in 1934 of M2·26 tons selling at $M73 – only slightly above the dismal years of 1932–3 – could the economy really be regarded as on the mend, whatever reservations one might have about the government? During the summer the fever of political activity did not much drop, there was further violence and shooting of students on 7 August, and Cuba approached the first anniversary of the sergeants' revolt, on 4 September, too undecided and too unsettled to take in the full implications of the fact that that day would be henceforth called the 'Day of the Constitutional Soldier'. The old student Left, outraged by the backing given to the regime by old allies, such as Jorge Mañach and Martínez Sáenz, declared that they were facing 'a dictatorship more irresponsible than that of Gerardo Machado',[15] and the young poet Pablo de la Torriente Brau declared that 3 May, the date of the death of a young student named Rubiera, should be, 'the 30th of September [the date when the student Trejo died in 1930] of a new stage in the student struggle against imperialism and tyranny'.[16]

Born in violence, ex-sergeant Batista's control of Cuba could, in fact, only use violence to consolidate itself. All the summer of 1934 there were sporadic risings and shootings, fights and rumours. None of the political action groups accepted Batista's army as representing the authority of the state: Ejercito del Caribe, OCRR, ABC Radical, Pro Ley y Justicia, and, above all, Antonio Guiteras's Joven Cuba, each consisting of violent groups of more or less educated men used to struggle, both fighting Machado and later settling scores against the *porristas* and the army. Joven Cuba and most of the others had genuine grievances against the new regime; Joven Cuba in fact was still trying to offer a fundamentally social democrat if nevertheless verbally revolutionary alternative to Batista, to the Communists, and even to Grau, though Grau's followers and Guiteras saw eye to eye throughout most of 1934. With Grau himself in Mexico, indeed, many of the old student leaders were collaborating with Guiteras, though some of them disliked the gun-happy side of some of those who surrounded him. There were

---

[14] Foreign Relations (1934), V, 183–4. Welles commented in 1948 that this treaty was concluded almost without negotiation (see *Time for Decision*, note, 185.)

[15] Roa, *Retorno a la Alborada*, 76.

[16] Qu. *ibid.*, 77.

frequent gun-fights, clashes with police, and occasional political murders. The old students were now divided between the democratic Left headed by Chibás, and the Communists, of the Ala Izquierda Estudiantil, and much eloquent oratory and many exhausting arguments were spent in sterile fights between the two. In the background of this complicated and often bloody picture, there also remained in opposition ex-President Menocal, still prudently in Miami and still rich, ambitious and active. Beyond, on the Left, there was the Communist party, still in control, through its secretary-general, César Vilar of the unrecognized labour federation CNOC, which was itself still very small. Treading his way through these violent opponents was by no means easy for Batista, but gradually, as the summer continued, he began to gather the general backing of many of those 'better classes' in whom Sumner Welles and after him Jefferson Caffery placed faith. This change of heart was partly because of Batista's own qualities, but also because he had become a man whom the U.S. ambassador would accept.

There was elsewhere, in the autumn, a mood of despair.

Was it this that the Cuban people aspired to [*Bohemia* asked on 14 October, with its customary panache] when breast to breast, as the Spartans joined their shields, they fought to overthrow the corruptions and diseases of the old regime? Was it for this that the revolutionary nuclei paid with blood and heroism for the fall of the old intolerable system? Was it for this that we lit the torch of popular anger, offering a new Cuba as a tribute?

The only answer received to such questions was a suspension by Mendieta of *habeas corpus*. In January 1935 constitutional guarantees were again suspended for three months – penalties of death and life imprisonment being imposed for such acts as cane burning – and the editor of *Bohemia* was himself detained, with other journalists.

Occupied in the re-coordination, even the preservation, of the North American Union, Roosevelt's administration meanwhile had little time for Cuba. Provided that the confusion did not become unconfined, provided that there was no intolerable threat to U.S. property and lives, what could be done by a power which had explicitly and recently renounced intervention? There is no evidence that, except for discussion of the sugar quota, Cuba ever figured again in the agenda of the U.S. cabinet under Roosevelt.[17]

If Washington's attitude was remarkably static, the attitude of the

---

[17] See H. L. Ickes, II, *The Secret Diary of Harold L. Ickes* (1955), I, 128. Cuba never afterwards reappears in the memoirs of Sumner Welles and only in passing in those of Cordell Hull.

international Communist movement was changing. In late 1935, Blas Roca, the new secretary-general of the Cuban party, attended a meeting in Moscow of all the Latin American Communist parties under the chairmanship of the Comintern chiefs, Manuilsky, Dimitrov, and Togliatti, the 'Latin secretary'. Present also were Luis Carlos Prestes and Da Silva from Brazil; Rodolfo Ghioldi and Victorio Codovilla, from Argentine; Eudocio Ravines, from Peru; and Guralsky, a Jewish Lett who had directed the South American bureau of the Comintern from 1930–4. In practice, the conference decided to seek to order its members to follow a Popular Front line – though there were differences. Thus, in Peru, the Communist party would try and succeed with an experimental Popular Front (under Ravines), while in Brazil Prestes would back the idea of an uprising. Another meeting also occurred in Moscow with Earl Browder, secretary-general of the U.S. Communist party. The Latin American parties proposed that Browder should become the general adviser of these groups, and Browder accepted, becoming in consequence the virtual chief of all the parties in the Latin American west coast and Caribbean – or at least the channel of communications from Moscow.[18] Among the parties of the Caribbean, the Cuban party had already established a perilous eminence: at this time there were no Communist organizations in the Dominican Republic, nor in the still colonial West Indian islands. In Haiti, the Communist party had been organized illegally in 1930 but its two earliest leaders, the poet Jacques Roumains and Max Hudicourt, were in exile in Mexico and the U.S. In Puerto Rico, a small Communist organization was founded in September 1934, the leader being a worker in the U.S., Alberto Sánchez, secretary-general of the large Taxidrivers' Union.[19]

The change to the Popular Front policy of seeking allies from among the other parties, including middle-class parties, came too late to prevent a final philippic against Guiteras and Grau from the young Communist, Joaquín Ordoqui, in December 1934:

> The Party ... has exposed the policy of Grau San Martín and Guiteras as a policy of 'Retreat', that is, of support for the policy of the ruling classes. Guiteras calls upon the masses to trust that he, with his 'revolution' will solve the situation. As the Communist party of Cuba has correctly stated, what Guiteras with his Left demagogy is preparing is a *coup d'état* in which a faction of Cuban elements of the army that are antagonistic to Batista will take part.[20]

[18] See Alexander, 38. Earl Browder testified to this (evidence of Theodore Draper).
[19] Alexander, 304–5.
[20] *The Communist*, December 1934.

But, within two months, the fourth plenum of the Central Committee of the party had opportunistically swung the Cuban Communists away from this intransigence: the Communist attitude towards Guiteras and Grau changed in both language and action. They now began to conceive of a different interpretation of their rivals' qualities.

Colonel Mendieta, provisional president, spoke from time to time of approaching elections and of an impending constituent assembly. Such plans were constantly discussed, and, as usual, had there been a greater general agreement among the opposition, no doubt he would have had to act faster; but the antagonism between the parties gave the impression that the divisions were unconquerable. Yet there were advances. A university reform was finally put into effect following the recommendations of a mixed commission of students and professors. After weeks of riots, bloodshed, strikes, and rumours that the state was about to take over the university, Mendieta formally handed over the title deeds of the university autonomy to the student leaders. This meant that thereafter the university, though paid for by the state, was within its precincts free from the writ of the ministries of the Interior and Education. It seemed a great victory, as indeed it was: but once outside the flights of steps leading to the university, students could still be hunted, and they still were. The freedom within the university, combined with the often frivolous violence and authoritarian cynicism outside, contributed to a new tension in Havana: this was a town-and-gown squabble with revolvers, since in 1934 the university was the only place where political meetings could be freely held, and it soon became a place where arms could best be stored also.

In 1934 a minimum wage law was also introduced, paying a minimum of 80 cents a day in the country, $1 a day in cities or sugar mills. Admittedly, enforcement took a long time, and indeed was never complete. Another law of January 1934 provided that no employee should be dismissed without cause; again, this was not enforced immediately and the level of labour was so low that in practice it was not effective.

The change in the Communist line was much too late for full cooperation between Batista's opponents in the famous strike movement of March 1935. Beginning with a series of bombs exploding during the carnival of February 1935, this economic and political protest against the delay in establishing a constitution absorbed many trades and communities throughout Cuba in the first week of March. The strike organization was now mostly in the hands neither of the Anarchists nor of the Communists, but of a new generation of students at the re-opened university. Government employees, railway workers, public service workers were all implicated, and for several days Cuba was at a standstill as complete as that in August 1933. The ABC, the Communist party and Grau's supporters collaborated, though they were not agreed on any common programme.

It was supposed in Cuba that the U.S. ambassador, Jefferson Caffery, played a decisive role during these weeks; in one account it was even suggested that Batista had decided to flee but that Caffery prevented him, encouraging him to use his army to crush the rebels.[21] But in fact he played a moderating role, urging on Batista the importance of holding a constituent assembly providing Mendieta would resign.[22] As often before, the fear of 'chaos' was a leading factor in the U.S. appreciation of the situation – a situation which would certainly severely threaten U.S. property, whatever else happened. In Oriente many sugar mills had lost control of their plantations; thus the United Fruit Company found their mills occupied by a group of men never employed by them. In the end, the Army did indeed end the strike. There was a great deal of shooting. Batista's old ally, José Eleuterio Pedraza, ex-sergeant and colonel, became military governor of Havana, and there was some police irresponsibility; the numbers shot by the police and army could not have been less than a hundred though the *Preston* and *Boston* mills were recovered without bloodshed. As usual, innocent men such as Armando Feito, a student, were killed.[23] Eddy Chibás and others were arrested. Immediately afterwards, all trade unions which had taken part in the strike were declared illegal and their funds confiscated. All constitutional laws were again suspended. The university was occupied by soldiers. On 10 March Mendieta declared Cuba in a 'state of siege'. On 11 March the Sub-Secretary of the Interior under Guiteras, Enrique Fernández, was murdered by the police 'trying to resist arrest'. Batista was in complete command, and his authoritarian brutality was now backed by those 'better classes' who previous to January 1934 had despised him: indeed, as early as June 1934, some such had suggested to Caffery that the only way for Cuba was for Batista to become unashamedly military dictator.[24]

The failure of the strike brought recriminations. The parties of Grau and Guiteras claimed that CNOC and the Communists had taken action too late. Blas Roca claimed that on the contrary the Communists had done their best to secure an alliance with Grau but that the latter's intransigence had prevented it.[25] Internal disputes among the opposition evidently hindered any unity: it could hardly have helped that the secretary-general of Guiteras's Joven Cuba was at this moment

[21] See the version in Casuso, 75.
[22] NA 837.00/6123 and 6124, qu. Wood, 108.
[23] Casuso, 76.
[24] NA 837.00/5196, qu. Wood, 108.
[25] See article in *Imprecorr*, No. 62 (1935), 1,540.

an ex-Communist from Guantánamo, Eusebio Mujal.[26] Meantime, among the democratic middle-class and radical circles there was increased despair. Many now went abroad to exile. Guiteras, still on the run, was shortly afterwards hunted down. Surrounded in an old fort while waiting for a ship to carry them to Mexico, Guiteras and a small group of comrades held off several hundred soldiers in a long battle before he was eventually killed, together with a Venezuelan exile, General Carlos Aponte. Though Guiteras was dead his organization lived on: and Joven Cuba killed nearly everyone who had anything to do with this murder within the next few years, the police violence seeming to make licit even to the professional middle class the political terrorism practised by the revolutionaries.

In 1935, the sugar harvest, though still only $2\frac{1}{2}$ million tons (and therefore 50% below the 1929 figures), was nevertheless well sold.[27] The economy, therefore, began to pick up, though only 133 mills were grinding. There came comforting mutters from the American Chamber of Commerce: 'Importers of American goods report considerable increase in sales throughout the island.'[28] This modest improvement meant that what impetus there might be for social advances had almost vanished; the crisis was over; and the only critical measure in mid-1935 which, despite Batista's heroic speeches, could be really regarded as carrying on 'the Revolution', was the enfranchisement of women on 12 June. Batista's speech of 6 September 1935 was, however, typical:

> The triumphant movement of the other ranks and soldiers of the army and navy has consolidated itself thanks to the conduct of the citizens . . . the representative of the United States of North America [*sic*] has accepted the facts – we can affirm that there is no danger of intervention. . . . Neither exists there a communist danger, which has always been a fantasy with which public opinion has been stifled for years. The country demands a change of front. The Revolution was not made to force one dictator to disappear, but finally to abolish the colonial system which thirty-one years after 20 May 1902 continued to suffocate the country. Now only has the Republic been born, founded on immovable bases, its form dictated by the free will of the country. It will not be a fascist republic, nor socialist, nor communist, but it will have the orientation which the will of the people desire to give it.[29]

With this sort of rhetoric and a slowly improving economy, it was

---

[26] Mujal took no part in the strike, being shot in the back just before in Guantánamo, by the army, after he had killed a soldier. (Mujal, *Memorandum*, 6.)
[27] 2·33 cents per pound.
[28] Phillips, 169.
[29] Qu. Adam y Silva, 489–90.

easy to imagine how Batista became increasingly popular among the masses.

By now conditions seemed 'normal' enough for elections to be held. But only the old parties, and not Grau, nor Joven Cuba, nor even ABC, took any part: Menocal appeared as the leader of the 'Democrats'; against him stood José Miguel's son, Miguel Mariano Gómez, behind whom a number of smaller middle-class parties also sheltered. But they could not agree, and the disputes were such that Mendieta decided to postpone the elections. He was inspired to do this by Batista, who was anxious lest Menocal in fact should get elected, for he assumed – rightly no doubt – that he would not be able to run Menocal as he could Mendieta.

Mendieta's postponement was a confession of failure on his part: he also coupled it with an invitation to Dr Harold Willis Dodds, president of Princeton,[30] to act as constitutional adviser to the government – a curious act on the part of a free nation. Secondly, Mendieta himself also resigned after failing to get the parties to agree on 10 January 1936 as an election date: 'Some political parties are now alleging my occupancy of the office of Chief Executive is their reason for not participating in elections, claiming a non-existent partiality on my part. . . .' Mendieta had shown himself in two years of compromises an honest man among thieves, who could not, however, bring himself to believe that the thieves were less honest than he.

Mendieta's sudden resignation gave the provisional presidency to the Secretary of State, José Antonio Barnet. He was able to confirm that the elections would be held on 10 January. There was some further muffled disputation. Professor Willis Dodds was accused of entangling himself in politics. The U.S. Foreign Policy Association (of New York) said that unless Batista's rule was replaced, 'the U.S. has employed its influence to overthrow one dictatorship – that of Machado – only to have it succeeded by another'.

In the event, the elections were held, and Cuban women voted for the first time. Miguel Mariano Gómez beat Menocal and was elected president, with Colonel Federico Laredo Bru vice-president. Thus José Miguel's son had returned to the post which his father had so enjoyed, accompanied by yet another ex-colonel of the wars of independence. The latter had been in all the legislatures of the Republic, as had Mendieta; he had been in the 1920s the white hope of the Veterans' Association,[31] and once too was in Céspedes' middle-class cabinet. But until inauguration in May, Barnet remained provisional president. Congressional elections gave a majority to men who had backed the

---

[30] Harold Willis Dodds (born 1889). Also professor of politics and an economist, who had advised Nicaraguan elections.

[31] See above, p. 567.

Mendieta-Batista regime. It was evident from the start, therefore, that Gómez would not necessarily have a working majority.

It was hard for a casual traveller to Cuba in 1936 or 1937 to see that the social structure of Cuba had changed much since the late 1920s. Yet organized labour was far more powerful. The 50% law, the minimum wage law and the law relating to dismissals had struck a severe psychological blow on labour's behalf. It was not that labour leaders felt more hostile to employers but that employers for the first time had been forced to give in, at least in theory. Educational improvements were being not only demanded but seriously considered.

This last matter caused a new explosion in Cuba's frail institutional organization during 1936. Barnet, while still in office, approved a decree which enabled Batista as chief of staff to name members of the army to serve as teachers in new rural schools. To many this seemed a further, perhaps irreversible, drive of the army into control of Cuban politics. It was of course desirable to have new schools, and there was no reason why in an emergency such schools should not be looked after by soldiers, but it was a move which in so far as it had any lineage threatened the re-establishment of Machado's military supervisors in civil life. No doubt Batista's motives were mixed, half concerned to carry education into remote areas, half concerned to expand both his own power and the army's, but this move was accompanied by other developments designed to help the army, such as new barracks for the enlisted men at Columbia and new recreation clubs; Batista had built himself a splendid house at Campamento Columbia; there were new military hospitals, military orphanages, and much propaganda was distributed praising not only the military view of life but also the army as such, and indeed a military dictatorship.

These rural schools customarily consisted of one room only where the same teacher taught all forms. Batista wanted to organize these on the basis of military zones. The schools themselves would be run by NCOs. Thus in the sergeants' regime the teachers too would be sergeants, paid by the army, answerable to the army, and only remotely connected with the Ministry of Education and the civil power. Perhaps the idea behind this expansion of schools echoed, as much did in Cuba in the 1930s, the Mexican rural schools started in 1923 under José Vasconcelos.[32] Whatever their purpose and origin, the military character of the schools immediately offended the in-coming President, Miguel Mariano Gómez, and disturbed much of the country during the second half of 1936.

---

[32] In Mexico over 6,000 schools were built by the villages themselves, without cost, by men on holiday, according to the ideas of a 'missionary' turned architect. *Anexos* (in the shape of shower baths, sports fields, kitchen, etc.) were sometimes added.

There continued some sporadic violence: Joven Cuba remained in being. In April a leading follower of Grau, Octavio Seigle, was murdered; in September, the offices of *El Pais*, a right-wing newspaper, were blown up by a lorry loaded with dynamite, four people being killed, twenty-seven wounded, and several nearby buildings wrecked:[33] it seemed that the explosion was due to some members of Grau's party who had been angered by *El Pais*'s advocacy of the Nationalist cause in the Spanish Civil War which had broken out in July. A number of young Cubans, meanwhile, mostly combatant communists such as Pablo de la Torriente Brau, Rolando Masferrer and Joaquin Ordoqui, went to Spain to fight on the Republican side; the mulatto Communist poet, Nicolas Guillen, accompanied them.[34]

Miguel Mariano Gómez had meanwhile shown that he had some at least of the qualities of his father. He was, however, more honest, though he had had less time to become popular. He lacked too that extra portion of energy which, despite his weaknesses, had made his father one of the most appealing of Cubans. Miguel Mariano was nevertheless determined to overcome the threat so evidently presented to the idea of civil life by Batista and the army; indeed, in his inaugural address he remarked: 'Force alone is precarious if it is not animated and authorized by reason and justice, without which firm and permanent peace cannot exist.' But his cabinet contained at least one good friend of Batista: the old general, Rafael Montalvo, who had first been in the cabinet of Cuba under Estrada Palma, previously a veteran of 1895, latterly a possible presidential candidate against Menocal and once himself a candidate to be the 'strong man that Cuba needed'. A man of the 'best class', as Caffery would have put it, he was in fact completely behind Batista: an oligarch and descendant of the great nineteenth-century sugar kings, his friendship with Batista finally symbolized the acceptance by that class of Batista.[35] Interested in securing the maximum civilian support, Batista proclaimed in September an amnesty on all political exiles and prisoners; everyone could return except actual officials of Machado. The revolutionary groups were not satisfied, however, that they would be free from reprisals. None gave in its arms.

At the end of June 1936[36] President Gómez attempted to show Cuba that he desired to detach himself from Batista, by dismissing 3,000

[33] See Phillips, 176.

[34] Ruby Hart Phillips, 176, says nearly 100 Cubans fought in Spain. Another Cuban was Rodolfo de Armas (killed at Jarama; see Edwin Rolfe *The Lincoln Battalion* (1939), 42). The Cubans in general were regarded as North Americans and served with them, and as a link in interpreting for them with Spaniards.

[35] *Cf.* in the Dominican Republic the friendship between the Cabrals and other good families with the other mountebank of the Caribbean, Trujillo.

[36] In this month Batista formally married Elisa Godónez, by whom he had had a son in November 1933 (*cf.* his will revealed by *Revolución*, 24 January 1959, 15).

government employees, mostly military reservists. Batista reacted strongly by sending word to his commanders that the dismissed men should be given 'every attention'.[37] The clash came, however, as everyone thought it would, over the rural schools. In mid-December the Senate, packed with many of Batista's friends, approved a new tax on sugar of one cent a bag, so providing $M1·5, out of which another 2,300 military rural schools could be paid for. Gómez opposed the bill on the simple ground that the military should not interfere with education. The secretary to the presidency, Domingo Macías, announced that President Gómez thought that Cuban education was turning Fascist. Batista's friends worked hard to get the bill passed. The sugar *colonos* backed it. There were animated meetings up and down the country and the bill was finally passed by 106 to 43 in the Lower House. Gómez vetoed it. Immediately the House of Representatives passed a petition accusing him of partiality, and there were proposals for an impeachment. Gómez sent his ambassador in Washington to see President Roosevelt and gave him a 'purely informative' memorandum, describing what he thought to be a threat to 'democratic and constitutional government'.[38] Gómez's Secretary of the Treasury also appealed to Ambassador Caffery who, however, merely replied that Washington 'could not intervene'.[39] Roosevelt later confirmed this but did say that Gómez seemed to him to be acting in much the same way as he himself, and other presidents, often did, without giving ground for a charge of 'infringement of legislative prerogatives'. Caffery replied that the Cuban opposition to Gómez had given little attention to such representation from him.

An impeachment trial duly followed, on 22–4 December. In a sensational hearing, Gómez was voted out by 22 to 12 in the Senate (the army using what even Caffery called 'intimidation'). Gómez vainly protested that his impeachment marked a victory for military forces 'determined' to control the country. His supporters put about rumours that the U.S. would exert economic pressure on Cuba in retaliation for the impeachment. But the U.S. had no such intentions. Roosevelt and Hull were clearly disappointed,[40] but, immersed in so many other matters, would do nothing. The *New York Times* correspondent, Phillips, remarked that 'the military clique is convinced that the U.S. government dare not intervene in any manner in Cuban affairs for fear of endangering the good neighbour policy'.[41]

[37] Phillips, 175.
[38] 837.00/7770 B, qu. Wood, 114.
[39] *Loc. cit.*
[40] Memorandum by Duggan, 9 September 1938. See NA 837.00/8383–1/2, qu. Wood, 116.
[41] *New York Times*, 27 December 1936.

Two days later, Laredo Bru, the vice-president, was installed as president. He was pleased to surrender his soul completely to Batista. His cabinet was composed only of Batista's friends, of whom only the treacherous Secretary of State, General Montalvo, the old survivor of the oligarchy and of pre-Machado politics, had been in Miguel Mariano's government. Dr Juan J. Remos, director of the Civil-Military Institute, newly founded by Batista, became Minister of Education. A major in the reserve, Dr Zenón Zamora, became Secretary of Health. A close friend of Batista, Amadeo López Castro, became Secretary of Agriculture. President Laredo Bru was the happiest of figureheads, 'tall, austere, with a dry sense of humour'.[42] He was a new Chilperic of the Caribbean, before Batista's Carolingian hammer.

[42]Phillips, 182.

CHAPTER LX

Batista and the Communists

Batista made no secret that he was in control. He, not Laredo Bru, announced the programme of the 'new' government:

> Two things are imperative, the calling of a constituent assembly and the approval of the educational law . . . with the administration and Congress identified with these two promising proposals and with the armed forces complying with and enforcing the laws, the people of Cuba are to be congratulated.[1]

Throughout the following months, life was calm in Cuba; only Miguel Mariano Gómez and Menocal of the old Cuban parties remained outside the embrace of the new military system. In April the Communist party attempted to rally all anti-Batista forces into a Popular Front alliance, charging Batista with imitating Hitler and Mussolini.[2] But this was scarcely possible. Grau, the Communists' natural ally, was still abroad in exile and only now reorganizing his scattered and warring followers into a new force, the Partido Revolucionario Cubano Auténtico, known as the Auténticos, claiming in this way to be the real representatives of Martí. He still had not incorporated many of the more militant would-be revolutionaries, surviving members of political action groups such as Joven Cuba, though they were in a tactical alliance with him. Grau recognized, however, the disadvantage of being a reforming party with Communist allies, and the only group which did join forces with him was that of democratic left ex-students, the Izquierda Revolucionaria, led by Eduardo Chibás.

After this attempt, the Communist party made the first of a number of gestures towards the government; the consequence was the permission granted in the middle of 1937 to organize what was essentially a front party, the Partido Unión Revolucionaria (PUR). In this party the leadership was in the hands of Juan Marinello, a poet and writer of Julio Antonio Mella's generation at the university, the son of a rich family with sugar connections;[3] Salvador García Agüero, a leading

---

[1] Qu. Phillips, 183.

[2] See P. Pavio, 'The Military dictatorship in Cuba', *Communist*, April 1937.

[3] Juan Marinello (born 1898), at University of Madrid, 1921; professor of literature at Escuela Normal, Havana; co-editor of *Revista de Avance*, 1927–39; in exile, 1930–3; author of poems and essays.

Negro teacher and writer; Augusto Rodríguez Miranda, a leading mason;[4] and Antonio Macías, a leading intellectual in Matanzas. To this party also adhered the small socialist group headed by Juan Arévalo, now secretary-general of the Maritime Union, the Labour leader who ten years before had organized for Machado a kind of bogus union system. The PUR was always a front for the Communists, who never denied that they controlled it. All the leaders were, if not members of the Cuban Communist party, so close to it as to make no difference. At a different level the Communist-controlled Ala Izquierda Estudiantil dominated life at the university.

Batista was in these months moving leftwards in a manner which in the 1960s would have suggested an element of Nasserism in his programme: the socially conscious military ruler. On 25 July 1937 he announced a three-year plan, so extensive in ambition as to be nicknamed 'the 300-year plan'. The sugar and tobacco industries would be brought under closer state direction; workers would receive insurance, paid holidays and other advantages. Plans were confidently announced for forest conservation, for a new currency, for water supply, for distribution of state lands, reorganization of agriculture, mining and oil, a great new health plan, a merchant marine, even a new tax system. In keeping with the new nationalism, there would be a registration tax on all foreigners of from $1.40 to $5.

As for sugar, in May a conference of twenty-three major sugar countries assembled in London. More comprehensive than the ill-fated Chadbourne meeting of 1930, this conference once again tried to secure the 'orderly liquidation of sugar surpluses'. The major exporters accepted a quota for their world market exports – Cuba 940,000 tons a year (over and above her exports to the U.S., which were not considered, any more than were the European imperial sugar systems). An International Sugar Council was set up to administer the agreement but, in the event, war (or the fear of it) dictated what was exported and what was not. Meantime the U.S. pushed through a new sugar law. By this, 56% of the U.S. sugar market would be reserved to the 'domestic producers' (Hawaii, Puerto Rico, the home beet men and so on); the rest would be divided between Cuba and the Philippines, in the proportion of 64% and 36% each. But this left Cuba with only an assured 29% of the total U.S. market – more than the islands certainly or than U.S. cane, or the beet men, but even further behind her old position: her export to the U.S. of two million tons in 1937 was just under half her total in 1929.

So far as production was concerned Batista followed his predecessors since 1930 in attempting above all to help the smaller mills keep

[4] R. J. Alexander speaks of him as 'head of the Grand Lodge of Cuban Masonry'.

going, whatever their economic conditions, and in some cases at the cost of the larger ones. Such a policy had a political as well as a social purpose. The mill was the centre of a community; to let it vanish would have revolutionary consequences.[5] But at the same time he introduced in September 1937 a new Sugar Co-ordination Law, the effects of which were important and widespread.

This law, chiefly the work of the Secretary for Agriculture, López Castro, was intended to allay the anxieties of the *colonos* and the mill workers in recollection of the depression which was indeed still partly persisting. The law organized the Cuban sugar industry to such an extent that henceforth it would be misleading to regard it as a normal part of the system of private enterprise. Much of the law went to guarantee the rights of the small *colono* – that is, any farmer who normally produced less than 30,000 *arrobas* (330 tons) of sugar. It was now assured that, whoever the mill might wish to lay off, it would not be the small *colono*. The small *colono* could also vary his production below the 30,000 *arroba* level. In return, his obligation was to grow minor crops on at least a section of land.[6] The law simplified the rather complicated methods by which sugar mills settled their accounts with *colonos*,[7] and guaranteed against the possible loss of an estate due to the depression. It provided that, so long as a *colono* kept his land cultivated with cane and delivered the right quantity to the appropriate *central*, he should never have to give it up: this meant that, if he were a lessee, his lease was underwritten by the state. The million and a half or so acres rented by *colonos* from the sugar mills were thus guaranteed to the lessees in perpetuity.[8]

By this time, the U.S. owned sixty-nine mills, producing about 56% of the total of Cuban sugar. Spaniards still owned thirty-six mills, accounting for another 17% of the total. Canadians owned eleven mills, English four, French and Dutch both two, together producing another 7% of the total. The approximately fifty Cuban-owned mills, therefore, still produced under a fifth of the total production of Cuba.[9]

Other benevolent laws were passed. Just before Christmas an amnesty permitted the return to Cuba of all exiles, even members of the Machado regime, even Machado himself – though the old tyrant was by this time actually dying in the U.S. But others of his government, such as Orestes Ferrara, did return. The government recognized the debts

[5] *Cf.* Guerra, *Ramiro Azúcar y Población en las Antillas*, 1940 edn, Appendix 5.
[6] On at least 25 cordels.
[7] See p. 276.
[8] i.e. 50,000 *caballeria*. *Cf.* discussion of this law in *Estudio*, 642–58.
[9] *Anuario Azucarero*, 1937, 38. Half the sixty-nine U.S. mills belonged to companies who owned more than one mill: three large companies, Compañía Azucarera Atlántico de Golfo, Cuban American Sugar and General Sugar Estates, had nine, six and eight *centrales*, producing 1,650,299, 1,134,513, and 1,139,162 bags of sugar in 1937.

contracted by Machado, making an $M85 issue to repay the bond-holders. Batista continued with a number of popular statutes – founding a National Transport Commission, and a law for the distribution of state lands and *realengos*, promising at long last an end to interminable disputes over land titles. This law echoed that of Mexico in that to receive land people had to apply for it. No one was supposed to receive more than one *caballería* of arable land above that on which the farmhouse and other buildings were to be built. Recipients had to live on their land for six years, cultivate them with the intention of thereby keeping their families, plant fruit orchards and keep to the rules laid down by the Department of Agriculture. Such farms could not be sold and could change hands only by inheritance. In April 1938, an old *realengo* near Mariel in Pinar del Río was indeed handed out in the first *reparto de tierras*. During the rest of 1938 and 1939 other *realengos* were divided and it certainly seemed that in a modest way an agrarian reform had been begun, in a style reminiscent of that happening under Cárdenas in Mexico.[10]

In April 1938 meantime Batista used the occasion of a demonstration before the presidential palace, in favour of mortgage credits, to make his most vigorous appeal yet to mass support, speaking in almost sacramental terms of '*los humildes*' (the humble), and adding, however: 'What a beautiful thing is peace and quiet obtained through the means of labour! . . . What an inspiration!'[11] Later that month he had to announce the delay of his three-year plan until after a constituent assembly had been attained.[12]

Despite much lip service to progress, attended by some real achievements, Batista had nevertheless by mid-1938 alienated most of the respectable representatives of Cuban public life and all the old middle-class and professional groups; but he had popular support, he was admired and even, in a way, loved by the masses; the middle-class parties knew it and were paralysed by their own weakness from doing anything about it. Only Dr Grau San Martín remained a threat through the memory of his government in the past, a hint of future disturbance, since the failure of that government could be attributed to the U.S.

The long delayed elections for the House of Representatives on 5 March 1938 showed Batista that Grau represented the only real centre of opposition to him. Menocal and Miguel Mariano Gómez he could discount. Immediately after these elections, however, Batista announced that he had 'unearthed a revolutionary plot'. He described a motley

[10] Corbitt, 'Mercedes and Realengos', HAHR, vol. 19 (1939), 283–4.
[11] F. D. Roosevelt, *Papers*, Hyde Park.
[12] See Phillips, 186–7.

collection of ex-ABC leaders, professional men and old *políticos*, such as Dr Guillermo Belt, Dr Alfredo Reguero and Cosme de la Torriente as being in some way involved. The truth was that these men certainly met to discuss common political action in the semi-authoritarian circumstances then persisting. Batista as certainly used the knowledge of these meetings for his own ends, and, in an unsubtle attempt to stimulate national support, accused the U.S. Embassy of being involved. The new ambassador, Caffery's successor, J. Butler Wright,[13] denied the charge with vehemence, but Batista's utterance carried weight in Cuba.[14]

In this mood and with this background, seeking to woo organized labour, playing on the expectations of the masses, Batista now began to turn, as Machado had before him when *in extremis*, towards the Communists. Already he had allowed Marinello's PUR a legal existence. From May 1938 he permitted the publication of the Communist paper *Hoy*, which thereafter appeared daily under the editorship of Aníbal Escalante, an able if overbearing organizer. In July, the Communists began to respond; they dropped their own approaches to Grau, who with Chibás and others remained firmly opposed to any idea of a Communist party alliance. He pointed out that the Communists could join the Auténticos if they felt so enthusiastic about his programme.[15] At the Xth Plenum of the party in July, the Communists resolved that they should 'adopt a more positive attitude towards Colonel Batista, compelling him as a result to take up even more positively democratic attitudes'. Batista began then to be described in party publications as being no longer 'the focal point of reaction, but the focal point of democracy'.[16] Blas Roca later put it blandly: 'When Batista found the path to democracy, the Party helped him.'[17] Though Batista had enriched himself, like almost all the new officialdom, very rapidly, Blas Roca went on, so that he could already consider himself as belonging to the 'haves', nevertheless, for certain reactionary groups of the *bourgeoisie*, '"the sergeant" is still the man who cannot be trusted . . . on the other hand, his links with the revolutionary movement are still very close, he is still surrounded by ex-sergeants, corporals and soldiers who have heard his vows of fidelity to the interests of Cuba.' Blas Roca accompanied these remarks with demands for a

[13] Joshua Butler Wright (1877–1939), banker, joined diplomatic service 1909, wide general experience.

[14] Caffery had been sent off on a highly successful career in the U.S. foreign service, being ambassador in Brazil, in France after the liberation, and afterwards in Egypt where he became a friend of both Neguib and finally Nasser before retiring in 1955. He seems to have had a definite feeling for radical officers (see H. Finer, *Dulles over Suez* (1964), 23).

[15] See Blasier, Ph.D. thesis, 36.

[16] *New York Daily Worker*, 1 October 1939.

[17] Arthur Pincus, *Nation*, 17 December 1938, qu. Alexander, 278.

new constitution, another for an effective alliance with the 'democratic forces', and another still for a United Party of the Revolution.[18]

Admittedly, Blas Roca, as secretary-general of the Communist party, had been supporting formally constitutional demands for some time: as long ago as May 1936 he had declared: 'Today it is necessary to name the centre of our work the struggle for the sovereign constitution.'[19] Roca, a curious combination of *apparatchik* and Cuban *político*, was proving a good choice for secretary-general of the party, whose disparate elements he held together for many years by serving as a middle man rather than by acting as a strong man. He had an amiable, even jovial personality, so that few disliked him for any but political reasons and many people did not take him seriously enough as a political thinker to dislike him even for that.

A week after the Communist Xth Plenum, Blas Roca and his comrade, Joaquín Ordoqui went to confer with Batista at Campamento Columbia. At this curious meeting, an echo of that between Machado and César Vilar five years before, the Communists agreed to support Batista's plans for a new constitutional assembly, and even to back Batista's friends in it; in return, Batista would legalize the Communist party and give to it the right to reorganize the union movement under its control.[20] The two Communists also undertook to try to form a united revolutionary party which would include Grau's followers; but Grau once again rejected this idea. Soon afterwards, Batista was found telling reporters that in his view, 'the Communist party, according to its constitution, is a democratic party which pursues its ends within the framework of a capitalist regime and has renounced violence as a political means; consequently, it is entitled to the same status as that of any other party.'[21] The party was in fact then inscribed, on 13 September 1938, on the electoral rolls of Havana province. Batista also removed the restrictions on union organization. The Comintern's journal *World News and Views* happily commented: 'Batista . . . no longer represents the centre of reaction', and added 'the people who are working for the overthrow of Batista are no longer acting in the interests of the Cuban people'.[22]

This was, then, a close attachment between Batista and the Communists, not a mere flirtation. Ironically the attachment was even more closely cemented by a visit paid by Batista to the U.S. in the autumn of 1938. (Blas Roca had preceded him to the U.S., publicly praising Roosevelt's Good Neighbour policy and admitting to the *New*

---

[18] Speech later published as: 'For a Constitution which would assure Democracy, the Popular Improvement and the Defence of the Economy'.

[19] Blas Roca, 'El Pueblo y la nueva constitución', *Bandera Roja*, No. 7, p. 4.

[20] See Alexander, 378, based on Fausto Waterman interview.

[21] *Ibid.*, 278–9.

[22] *World News and Views*, No. 60 (1938), 1,370.

York Times that he was in the U.S. in order to ensure 'continued financial aid' from the U.S. Communists.)[23] Invited by the U.S. chief of staff, General Malin Craig,[24] Batista was met at Washington by his old friend Sumner Welles, and talked with both Roosevelt and Hull.[25] Nothing of moment was discussed, though Batista 'heard something about the commercial policy of the U.S. and some guarded suggestions concerning Washington's hopes for the progressive development of democratic institutions in Cuba'.[26] Roosevelt said he was afraid that Cuba might become a victim of 'totalitarian influences'. Batista replied that on the contrary the island would certainly cling to democratic principles. There was also an oral agreement that the U.S. and Cuba would embark on a new round of tariff negotiations, to lower the duties on both countries' exports.[27] Batista visited West Point, watched the Armistice Day celebrations at Arlington and saw snow for the first time. He returned to Havana with his prestige high. An immense crowd greeted him, led by the puppet president Laredo Bru. A public holiday was proclaimed. Banners and flags flew. The Communist party naturally demonstrated in Batista's honour, and Blas Roca once more proclaimed, 'Batista has begun to cease to be the centre of reaction.'[28] While Batista was in the U.S. the first great public rally of the Communist party, after its legalization, had been held in the Polar Stadium, and while Batista and Roosevelt were in discussion in Washington Cuban crowds were addressed in Havana not only by Blas Roca and Joaquín Ordoqui (the two Communist leaders most associated with the new policy), but also by James W. Ford of the U.S. Communist party.

The new attachment flowered further in the spring of 1939. From 10–15 January the 3rd National Congress of the Communist party was held openly, at Santa Clara. 347 delegates were present,[29] claiming that the party now numbered 23,300. If true, the party already represented the largest paid-up political force in Cuba. Marinello's Partido Unión Revolucionaria virtually disappeared, merging with the Communist party in name as it always had been in private and planning to run in common at the forthcoming general election for the constituent assembly.[30] Blas Roca described the programme of the party in its new guise:

[23] *New York Times*, 21 October 1939.
[24] General Malin Craig (1875–1945). He had been in the Santiago campaign in 1898 and was chief of staff of the 1st Corps in France, 1918.
[25] No mention of this visit in Hull's memoirs. See Chester, 174.
[26] The phrase is Bryce Wood's, *Making of the Good Neighbour Policy*, 117.
[27] *New York Times*, 26 November 1938, 30 November 1938, qu. from Batista's speech of the 25th.
[28] *Por una constitución que sigue la democracia*, 16.
[29] 25 peasants, 259 workers.
[30] *World News and Views*, 18 February 1939.

We fight for the unity of the people of Cuba, for the unity of the revolutionaries and for a great united national front, to realise immediately an urgent practical programme; to achieve a free and sovereign Constituent Assembly; to establish democracy, with equal rights for Negroes and women: to aid the unemployed; to protect the peasant against evictions; to enact the social laws; to increase education; to save thousands of Cuban debtors by a mortgage revaluation law; to defend the national economy, and the country from Nazi-Fascist invasion; help for Spain and China; and collaboration with the democracies.

Then, a little over a week later, the old CNOC disappeared, like the PUR, and a new Labour confederation, directed by the Communists, was established. This was the Confederación de Trabajadores de Cuba (CTC), with a Negro tobacco workers' leader, Lázaro Peña, as its first secretary-general. This organization, with Batista's encouragement, became immediately the favourite son of the Ministry of Labour. The CTC became in effect the state trade union. From the beginning, the new leaders, instead of bargaining with employers, went direct to the ministry; and summing up all these developments, Colonel Batista also had his word of praise: 'The Communist party, as in Mexico, the USA and in France, is recognised, and communism, as a legal instead of a disturbing force, has become the promoter of democratic formulae.'[31]

In February 1939 Batista went to visit President Cárdenas in Mexico – another gesture popular with the masses though not with industry and commerce, since Cárdenas was believed to be a real revolutionary and a passionate enemy of capital.[32] Though President Laredo Bru again declared the day of Batista's return a holiday, the streets were emptier; only Labour greeted him and so it was to Labour that he spoke from the balcony of the palace: 'Capital should not fear the spoliation of property but, if it does not wish to respect the desires and rights of the people, the resulting confusion will work against its own aspirations.'[33]

These developments did not occur without a continuing assertion of executive power, both legal and illegal. Thus in the autumn of 1938 Laredo Bru signed a decree which made possible the suspension of any newspaper. In May 1939 Felipe Rivero, editor of a weekly magazine *Jorobemos* which had criticized the government, was forced to drink a large bottle of castor oil by four unidentified thugs, undoubtedly in

[31] Fulgencio Batista, *Estoy con el pueblo* (1939), 36.
[32] General Lázaro Cárdenas, president of Mexico, 1934–40.
[33] Phillips, 188–9.

the government's pay. An undercurrent of violence stayed: the political gangster organizations remained, though some members of Joven Cuba and other para-political forces were in exile and others moved during 1938 into Grau's Auténtico party, among them the ex-Communist leader from Guantánamo, Eusebio Mujal.[34]

Batista and his ex-NCOs and the Communists were of course partly tarnished by collaboration with Machado, and like Machado himself, were firmly opposed by the Liberal middle classes, by 'all that was best in public life'. 'I accuse Blas Roca of being a traitor,' thundered the eloquent and mercurial Eddy Chibás, Grau's most brilliant follower, in an article in *Bohemia* on 14 May 1939, inviting a libel suit, which failed. But the hostility of the Auténticos did not seem to shake the new alliance. 'We want a Cuba free from the economic imperialism of Wall Street and the political imperialism of Rome, Berlin and Moscow', Chibás had continued.[35] But the pursuit of pure freedom was as ever impossible from the state of opposition in which Chibás then found himself.

These developments were not occurring *in vacuo*. Plans for the new CTC had indeed been laid at the Latin American Labour Congress in Mexico in September 1938. Here had been present not only Communists such as Lázaro Peña, but other Labour leaders who were moving towards the Auténticos, such as Sandalio Junco and Mujal, (both ex-Communists). All the Latin American Labour confederations which then existed were represented there, so becoming founder members of the Confederación de Trabajadores de América Latina (CTAL). This meeting had been concerned partly to restore the prestige of Cárdenas's government, but nevertheless, it did mark a peak in the cooperation between Labour unions. The Peruvians were represented by Apristas as well as Communists, for instance, and most countries dispatched varied delegations, though no anarchists or Catholics seem to have been present.[36] Communist strength was considerable but not dominant, though the president, Lombardo Toledano,[37] gradually moved during the following months to a generally Communist position, even denouncing Trotsky's presence in Mexico.

Meantime the relationship which Batista and the Communists were working out in Cuba had echoes throughout the continent. In Peru, for instance, the dictator Prado also gave the Communists a strong voice in the Labour movements; in Chile, President Aguirre Cerda had even invited the Communists to join his government: they had

[34] Mujal memorandum.
[35] Conte Agüero, *Eduardo Chibás*, 255.
[36] See Alexander, 55.
[37] Lombardo Toledano, the dominant Labour influence in Mexico in the mid-twentieth century.

refused, preferring certain subordinate positions in the administration, although Pedro Pacheco, famous as the mutineer of the Chilean fleet, took the sensitive place of mayor of Santiago de Chile; while in Mexico, Lombardo Toledano's leadership of the Labour force pushed Cárdenas into relations with the Communist party. Thus the events in Havana were not isolated but part of a continent-wide swing.[38]

[38] For the 1938 discussions between the Cuban government and the U.S. over the Public Works debts (to Warren and Co. and to Pindy and Henderson), see Foreign Relations (1938), V, 475–90.

CHAPTER LXI

The Constitution of 1940

With a firm ally in the Communists and in organized labour Batista's political position was strong in the first months of 1939. His only anxiety was economic. There was some difficulty in disposing of the sugar crop. The value of Cuban exports in fact fell between 1937 and 1939 from $M187 to $M147. Excessive peso issues caused some capital flight. The national income in these years declined about 20%, and food prices fell 6%. 1939 found Cuban economic activity at a low level, prices declining, gold and dollar holdings of the Treasury reaching only $M7·5.[1] Nor had the negotiations with the U.S. over the debts contracted by Machado yet been resolved. In February, U.S. Ambassador Wright had explained to the secretary of the Cuban Treasury, Jorge García Montes, on the basis of a conversation with Warren Pierson, the president of the Export–Import Bank,[2] that unless or until Machado's public works debt was fully paid no further credits could be extended to Cuba.

> [García Montes], a very cautious man, said that the financial situation of Cuba was growing worse; I replied that I was unfortunately aware of it. He said that the opposition . . . contended that the Government should not incur further obligations. . . . I replied I had been informed of his unfortunate situation. . . . He said that the remainder of the $M85 issue was not sufficient to meet these obligations, a supplemental issue was necessary; I replied that I was of course fully aware of this fact. . . .[3]

Discussion of how this debt might be repaid took up most of 1939, together with outstanding claims from Purdy and Co. and Warren Bros. On 20 July the State Department issued a virtual ultimatum to Cuba: negotiations on a supplemental trade agreement would be indefinitely delayed until Cuba had settled these old bills, and also until they had dealt with the credit moratorium and the revaluation bill.[4] On 7 August the Cuban ambassador in Washington, Martínez

---

[1] World Bank, 530–1.

[2] Warren Pierson (b. 1896) afterwards a director, among many other things, of the Vertientes-Camagüey Sugar Company.

[3] Foreign Relations (1939), V, 522–4.

[4] This required exporters in Cuba to exchange a certain percentage of dollars earned for pesos at par (*ibid.*, 1939, V, 531–2).

Fraga,[5] said that the Cuban government would certainly assume the public works obligations, but asked for $M20 if they did so. Welles, still the responsible under-secretary in Washington, refused to have anything to do with such a deal.[6]

On 29 August, after much press speculation about a new U.S. loan, the Cuban Secretary of State, Miguel Angel Campa,[7] told Ambassador Wright that he would 'have to have something to show to the Cuban people' in return for the passage of the *obligaciones*.

> He then handed me the . . . draft of a proposed statement to the press. . . . After reading it, hurriedly, I informed him that there was no possibility that my government would acquiesce in the statement therein concerning any agreement to contribute towards the [sugar] stabilisation fund . . . with regard to the allusion to the $M50 credit I said that I thought the time had come for me to inquire where and at what time that figure had arisen: the Secretary made the astounding reply that he really did not know. . . I said – as emphatically as I could – that there was no ground whatsoever for any such figure, or for that matter any specified figures: that we had ignored its continual appearance in the press in Cuba because it hardly seemed worthwhile . . . but . . . I could state categorically that there was no ground for the mention of such a sum.[8]

After this, the U.S. government announced that on 1 September negotiations on the supplementary trade agreement would be dropped. Campa requested delay and Sumner Welles agreed to delay a decision till 11 September, on the grounds that a European war would give Cuba a higher and practically limitless demand for sugar. But by 11 September nothing had been done and on that day Roosevelt announced unilaterally that as a result of the war all sugar quotas would be suspended: and this would mean an immediate increase in the Cuban sugar quota price sold in the U.S. of 1·5 cents a pound.[9]

Conflict in fact made the U.S. more conciliatory. The State Department realized that in this, as in all wars, Cuba might be able to find quite new commercial partners for sugar – perhaps even Germany.[10] In December a supplementary trade agreement was signed.[11] This was an interim measure designed to restore the tariff to 0·9 of a cent. It

[5] Pedro Martínez Fraga (born 1889), lawyer, representative in Machado's legislature 1931; diplomat since 1934; ambassador to U.S., 1937–44.
[6] Foreign Relations (1939), V, 540–1.
[7] Miguel Angel Campa (born 1882), regular diplomat till 1934; represented Cuba at Paris peace conference.
[8] Foreign Relations (1939), V, 546–8.
[9] *Ibid.*, 567–8.
[10] See Smith, 174.
[11] On the 18th.

was too late to assist the 1940 harvest, and even the 1941 harvest would be unsatisfactory due to other reasons, but afterwards the recovery was complete.

In November 1939, meanwhile, the long apprehension as to whether elections were or were not going to be held was at last laid; for on 15 November elections were held for a Constituent Assembly, with the understanding that elections for the office of president would follow in February. In the intervening period the constituent assembly would frame a new Constitution, and President Laredo Bru and the existing administration would remain in power. Batista held these elections on the assumption that his 'mass support', through the CTC, would enable him to win. He was making the same mistake as Machado, who believed the Communists when they promised to call off the strike in August 1933. When it came to the polls, apparently fairly conducted, Dr Grau San Martín and his allies (Auténticos, the ABC, Menocal's Demócrata Republicano and Acción Republicana), 'economically in rags, morally in gala dress', emerged as the victors, winning 41 seats out of 76; Batista and the Communists gained only 35 seats. Blas Roca was reduced to saying that Grau's victory was itself evidence of Batista's devotion to democracy.[12] There was, however, no slackening of Communist backing for Batista: 'We must work openly for support of Batista's policies,' the Comintern announced;[13] and in January a congress of the Communist party announced it still had 'a general attitude of support towards Batista while criticising him for his failure to fight for his own project'.

Batista had greeted his defeat with equanimity, and attributed it to his own failure to identify himself completely with the government. On 6 December he publicly announced he would stand as a candidate for the presidency in the general elections of 1940 and there and then resigned from command as chief of staff. Most of his staff also retired, after six good years as officers, and thereafter formed his election campaign staff.

Batista's platform was much the same as his three-year plan in 1937: a promise to reorganize the tax structure; the stabilization of the peso; and a new pledge for new circumstances – neutrality in the World War. He seemed to think it possible to delay the meeting of the Constituent Assembly,[14] but this played into the opposition's hands, enabling it to justify delays in the presidential election. On 11 January, the Senate

[12] Blas Roca *Por la consolidación de la República Democrática y Los Avances Obtenidos* (1939), 113. There had been 916 candidates for the 73 places. See *Diario de la Marina* 21 November 1939. In fact the difference between the two groups was more than the number of seats indicated, since Grau and his allies got 225,223 votes and Batista 97,944.

[13] *World News and Views*, No. 18 (1939), 368.

[14] See Foreign Relations (1940), V, 173–8.

passed a bill of postponement until the end of February, while Laredo
Bru was clearly planning a delay till the middle of the year, ensuring
that the Constituent Assembly would not do anything to exclude
Batista as a presidential candidate.

The U.S. attitude to developments in Cuba had by now, January
1940, become once more the real issue in Cuban internal politics. On
11 January ex-President Menocal accused Martínez Fraga of 'withholding from the Government the circumstances that the Government
of the U.S. would not recognise the results of an election in which the
opposition did not participate'. 'General Menocal's impression of our
attitude,' said Willard Beaulac, the U.S. *chargé d'affaires* in Havana,[15]
'is partly responsible for the failure of the government and opposition to
reach an agreement on the several matters in dispute.'

Cordell Hull seems to have taken the hint and pointed out to the
Cuban ambassador that:

> This Government would under no conditions give any indication of
> whether it would or would not recognise a future Government of
> Cuba. I stressed the fact that our relations with Cuba today were
> exactly the same as . . . with any other American Republic and that
> the time had passed since . . . any special relationship existed.[16]

On 9 February, with the position clear at least to the government,
the Constituent Assembly held its first meeting. A boy scout from Regla
inaugurated the session, presenting a Cuban flag. There were speeches
evoking Martí and the other founders of the nation: the country of
Martí could not remain a country of fratricide; the task of the constituent Assembly was the preparation of a new constitution, to revise
that of 1902, and to incorporate in it the benevolent laws and the
distinct improvements in social conditions achieved since the revolution
of 1933. This new Constitution was one of the most serious political
achievements of the Cubans, and it was certainly achieved as a result
of an unusual degree of co-operation between the different politicians.
It looked back, that is, to the Spanish Constitution of 1931 and the
Weimar Constitution of 1920. On the other hand the text also provided
explicitly for suspension of all political rights for forty-five days whenever 'security' required it. A fixed arrangement for elections was not
laid down. Political rights, according to the Constitution, involved
freedom to vote in 'elections and referendums' and freedom of association, but political movements based on sex, class or race were not to be
allowed. The Constitution provided for the use of a referendum. It

---

[15] Ambassador Butler Wright had died in Havana in December 1939. Willard Beaulac
(born 1899) later became U.S. ambassador to Cuba, 1951–3.

[16] Foreign Relations (1946), V, 740.

envisaged the state as playing a positive role in economic and social development. It was very much a post-New Deal document; the 'subsoil belongs to the state' (Article 88); the state should prevent unemployment (Article 60); Article 90 provided that a property maximum should be laid down for 'each person . . . [and] for each type of exploitation'. The planting and grinding of cane would be regulated or restricted (Article 275). Expropriation would be justified (Article 24). The Constitution spoke also of compulsory social insurance, accident compensation, pensions, a minimum wage, an eight-hour day, a forty-four hour week and paid holidays lasting a month.

The shortcomings of this Constitution were of course considerable, as the fates of the Weimar and Spanish models might have suggested. It is not, as English people often suppose, that there is anything specially doomed about the idea of a written Constitution as such, for countries which do not have strong political traditions and entrenched customs require guides to action and to collaboration, and many written Constitutions have worked well. But to implicate controversial legislative ideas in the text of a Constitution means that opposition to that measure may lead to discussion, criticism or even denunciation of the Constitution itself. Legitimate political controversy, being forced to play over constitutional reform, can therefore lead directly to a general argument about the very bases of the regime.

Similarly, the high-sounding principles embodied in this constitutional arrangement meant potential disillusionment: some articles of the Constitution of 1940 laid down as a general principle (to be implemented by subsequent legislation) that all children were entitled to eight years of primary education. Unless these principles were fulfilled, there would be a danger that the omission to enact the article would bring the Constitution itself into disrepute.[17] In addition there were a number of pernickety, though sometimes well-meant clauses. Of these, the most curious was the provision that teachers should receive a salary never less than a millionth part of the national budget.

Despite these shortcomings, the Constitution of 1940 marked a real attempt at social democracy.[18] It was, however, rarely read after it was written.

The Communist attitude was favourable. Blas Roca summarized the situation in a speech to his comrades:[19]

At last today we have a constitution, today the great assembly

---

[17] *Business Week*, 12 October 1940, commented, 'Sudden and drastic enforcement of the new regulations is not anticipated. Cuba is too closely tied to the U.S., both economically and politically' (qu. W. A. Williams, *The U.S., Cuba and Castro* (1962), 67).

[18] See *The Constitutions of the Americas*, ed. R. H. Fitzgibbon (1948), for text.

[19] Actually the plenary of the National Executive Committee of the Unión Revolucionaria.

[*Magna Asamblea*] has finished its labours: to achieve this, we had to defeat the capitulationist tendencies of Vivó and Martín Castellanos[20] as well as '*putchismo, insurrecionalismo* and infantile extremism'.

The Constitution, he said, in words which echoed Roosevelt, 'closed the revolutionary cycle which began in 1933', establishing a regime with institutions and legal validity, 'confirming the most important conquests of the revolutionary period' and guaranteeing the new regime from intervention. In general, the 1940 Constitution seemed to the Communists 'progressive and in some respects really advanced'. For instance, it made clear that segregation was illegal. In other respects, it was no advance on 'democratic *bourgeois* constitutions'. Nevertheless, '*Viva* the 1940 Constitution! *Viva* the glorious URC! *Viva* President Batista! *Viva* Mayor Marinello!'[21] Blas Roca also made a fervent appeal that the flag of the sergeants' revolt of 4 September 1933 should be allowed to be raised alongside the Cuban flag on barracks, an appeal which was as fervently opposed by Chibás.[22]

But it was still premature to hail Batista as president. Elections were in June. The Communists proved his strongest supporters, though they clearly disliked their leader's newest alliance with ex-President Menocal, not least because Batista had naturally to make some sort of arrangement with the hero of Victoria de las Tunas: Menocal's party in fact supplied Batista's running-mate, and Batista allocated to the Menocalistas six senatorial seats from his list.

When it came to the day of reckoning, there were 25,000 candidates for 2,343 offices. A large body of police, though fewer than a tenth of the number of candidates, were on duty. The elections seemed 'impartial and fair'[23] though Batista had been able to mount what seemed then an amazingly elaborate campaign, making use of films, radio soundtracks, campaign songs, and telephone calls. Batista himself toured the island in a special train, the 'train of victory'. On 9 March, the new U.S. Ambassador Messersmith telegraphed Hull:

I have the honour to report that ex-President Menocal endeavoured yesterday through an intermediary in whom I have complete confidence to ascertain from me whether the government of the U.S. would like him to join forces with Colonel Batista or with Dr Grau. General Menocal also expressed to the same intermediary his belief that Colonel Batista would resign his candidacy if he received an

---

[20] Vivó had been Blas Roca's predecessor as secretary-general of the party. Martín Castellanos was a Communist Negro doctor who had supported Blas Roca in 1933, but was later pushed aside.

[21] Blas Roca, *El Pueblo y la Nueva Constitución.*

[22] Conte Agüero, 278.

[23] Phillips, 198–9.

indication that this would be pleasing to the government of the U.S.[24]

Other political leaders also approached the ambassador to try to see what wishes the U.S. had. Messersmith succeeded in avoiding entanglement by declining discussion till after he had presented his letters. In fact Menocal decided to back Batista; this really left Grau in a small minority even in the Constituent Assembly.

Grau campaigned more modestly than Batista, backed by Chibás, Prío and other old supporters of 1933; though his private fortune was certainly considerable he lacked the vast number of opportunistic and rich bankers assembled by Batista, who played skilfully on their (actually baseless) fear that Grau would bring social revolution. Even so, Grau eventually won over two-fifths of the total votes, nearly half a million in all; Batista and his allies got just under three-fifths, the Communists 73,000, of which half were from Havana.[25] Batista therefore was fairly elected president of Cuba, the first man to be so for at least sixteen years, and in reality almost the first reasonably honest election since that of 1912.[26]

Meantime, both Cuba and the U.S. lived in the darkening world atmosphere caused by the Second World War in Europe. The Cubans dangled their strategic position before the U.S. (as well as their old sugar role in the First World War) to get further delay still in payment of the vexed question of the Machado debts. Batista announced: 'The U.S. can count on us as a factor in their plans for the defence of the Caribbean.'[27] On 24 May Nazi and also Communist propaganda were banned; and on 29 May Welles cabled Messersmith that two U.S. officers would arrive in Havana on 7 June with 'special passports' for secret military and naval talks with the U.S. and other Latin American governments, about the sort of co-operation which the American republics could have in the event of any aggression against Latin America. Then came the central point:

What we particularly need so far as Cuba is concerned is: (1) the construction of adequate airfields (which we would be prepared to

[24] Foreign Relations, V, 742.

[25] *Diario de la Marina*, 23 July 1940, 2.

[26] Till 1940 women did not have the vote. From 1901 till then, theoretically, every male over twenty-one who was not foreign, absent, or a member of the Rural Guard, had the right to vote. The electoral system established by the Constitution of 1940 (and reproduced in Batista's system in 1952) provided that all Cubans over twenty, men and women, had the vote, except for men in the services, the mad, and the criminal: the voters' lists would be prepared, as in the U.S., by registration of electors, but once on the list there was no need to register again. To avoid fraud, the Constitution of 1940 provided for electoral cards with photographs and fingerprints. See description in Census of 1953, xlvi. In 1953 the Census made out that there were 2,787,534 electors.

[27] Qu. Phillips, 197.

finance, although they would of course be entirely under the sovereignty of the Cuban government); (2) the use of Cuban ports in time of need, and (3) adequate protection and vigilance by Cuba of her own coastal waters and of other activities within the Republic.

These military talks took place successfully on 10 June, Batista and Pedraza meeting Colonels P. A. del Valle and Archibald Randolph of the U.S. Legation: they reached 'complete agreement', opening 'the way to staff conferences'. But the question of the debts still hung on. On 30 July Cordell Hull, in Cuba for the Havana conference on the consequences of the Second World War for the western hemisphere,[28] spoke to Laredo Bru 'of the importance of orderly and stable governments in this hemisphere and of the governments maintaining their obligations. Bru [*sic*] took the point.'[29] Some discussion followed between the Cubans and Messersmith, but the former were once again dilatory. On military matters they were much more forthcoming, and the U.S. military authorities received from Batista an agreement 'in writing that our government shall have full use of Cuban territory not only in the defence of the U.S. and Cuba but of the other American Republics.'[30] As a result, even before the debts were settled, Laurence Duggan could tell the Cuban *chargé d'affaires* in Washington on 3 September, 'we were giving the most careful consideration to his request for credit':[31] in fact, by then the Cubans knew that they would receive further loans (Messersmith had approved), so that the Casanova bill for paying these interminable debts was finally passed.[32] Laredo Bru signed the bill on 16 September, while on 14 September Welles had asked the Secretary of Treasury Morgenthau:

> Now that the public works debt is out of the way, could the Treasury not undertake a broad study of the Cuban monetary, banking and fiscal situations in relation to the whole Cuban economic structure?[33]

Of course, why not? On 4 October a Cuban delegation of financial experts arrived in Washington to discuss agriculture and the monetary system,[34] and on 10 October Fulgencio Batista took over as legally elected president of Cuba. The age of *présidents fainéants* was over; Batista was in control.

[28] The U.S. delegation included Berle, Duggan and Harry Dexter White. It was Hull's first visit to Cuba, 'since I went there as a mustached infantry captain in 1898' (Hull, *Memoirs*, 822).
[29] *Ibid.*
[30] Foreign Relations (1940), V, 99–100.
[31] *Ibid.*, 776.
[32] *Ibid.*, 767.
[33] *Ibid.*, 776.
[34] They were Amadeo López Castro, Eduardo Montalbán (who would be Secretary of the Treasury in a few days when Batista took office), Oscar García Montes, and Major Antonio Bolet of the Army Engineering Corps.

CHAPTER LXII

Batista: the Democratic President

The day that Batista took office a casual traveller in Havana would have thought the Saviour had indeed come. The bands, the artillery salutes, the crowds in the streets, the president on the balcony – the atmosphere was one of carnival and optimism. There were soothing words:

'the close relationship between international security and the normal economic development of our democratic peoples demands that Americanism cease to be a concept of protocol and become an understanding of economic, social and political need'.[1]

Batista began his presidency in the happy position of being supported by representatives of all classes, capitalists and Communists. Though he did not at first give posts to the latter in the cabinet, they maintained their general backing, while continuing to oppose the 'imperialistic war'. Batista's cabinet was headed as premier by Carlos Saladrigas, the old ABC chief, now an independent man. The Secretary of State was Cortina.[2] There were other figures increasingly familiar as Batista supporters, such as the sugar expert, Amadeo López Castro (Minister of the Presidency), Andrés Morales del Castillo and Oscar García Montes. Some younger members were ex-collaborators at least of Machado.[3]

The cabinet was composed of docile men. Less so were the new president's old comrades-in-arms, the ex-sergeants of 1934, now at the head of the armed forces, who believed that they had a right to all the profits of the administration.[4] These, jealous of the new 'civilian' president (who now confined himself to civil matters) objected in particular to Batista's delivering of the departments dealing with posts, fishing, lighthouses, port police, and so on, from military to civil control. On 31 January 1941 Batista summarily dismissed the police chief, Bernardo García, for 'negligence in seeking out the guilty in a number

---

[1] Qu. Phillips, 206.

[2] José Manuel Cortina (b. 1880), lawyer, Havana municipal councillor, author, orator, secretary to the presidency under Zayas.

[3] e.g. Juan M. Alfonso y Peña, representative, 1925–31, consultant to the municipality, 1936–40, Under-Secretary of Justice, 1941–3.

[4] See Barrera Pérez, *Bohemia Libre*, 19 July 1961.

of recent crimes'. Batista complained that García was always unavailable when he wanted him, either in Miami or at Varadero Beach. The appointment of Colonel Manuel Benítez as García's successor provoked the open enmity of the chief of staff, Colonel Pedraza, and of Angel Anselmo González, the naval chief of staff, a naval overseer before being promoted captain on 8 September 1933. Benítez heard of this opposition to his appointment and offered to resign. Pedraza meantime drove immediately to Campamento Columbia, where he persuaded some of his officer friends to draw up a formal document of complaint of Batista's recent measures of demilitarization. Batista was confronted by a group of these officers. He tore up the document in their presence and they went away even more discontented. At the same time a scandal broke over a merchant ship, which was supposed to bring in petrol to Havana: the master claimed that he had to jettison his cargo due to bad conditions; it seemed certain that it had been smuggled in as contraband. Batista's immediate reaction was to dismiss the already semi-insurrectionary Gonzalez.

These measures forced into the open a dispute between Batista and his old followers. Pedraza drove to the National Palace, accompanied by thirty cars filled with bodyguards and officers with machine-guns. The old cycle of violence and irresponsibility seemed about to begin anew. Pedraza met Batista face to face and demanded control of the armed forces, navy and army. Batista temporized. He asked for twenty-four hours' reflection. Pedraza agreed, foolishly for him, and went away. Immediately, Batista began to barricade himself in around the palace. Sandbags and machine-guns reasserted themselves. However, the police seemed committed against Batista, backing Bernardo García, under whom they had enjoyed the fruits of good living. At this point Batista saved himself by a decisive act of self-assertion. Wearing an open shirt and leather jacket (*el yaque*, which he used afterwards as a symbol of his autocracy) he drove to Campamento Columbia accompanied by Manuel Benítez and Colonel Ignacio Galíndez, another close comrade in 1933. There he summoned a large parade of the soldiers and told them that because of disaffection among the officers he himself would once more be taking over Columbia. It became immediately clear that the soldiers would not resist him. The colonel in command of San Ambrosio barracks, López Migoya, arrested Pedraza, and afterwards Bernardo García and González were also captured. All three were placed on an aeroplane bound for Miami. Men who had stood with Batista moved into their places: López Migoya became chief of the army, and Ignacio Galíndez took over at Columbia; Jesús Gómez Calvo, an ex-corporal of 1933, took over the navy; Manuel Benítez was confirmed in command of the police. Batista spoke on the wireless to the nation, telling them that Pedraza and his friends had wanted to make him into a puppet president, but assuring them that legality had been preserved.

The incident indicated not only Batista's intelligence and resolution but also the almost frivolous fragility of the system over which he presided: the sergeants, having captured power, were falling out, disputing over the essential commands in the country as if they were prostitutes available in the Sergeants' Mess.

Despite this thin constitutional surface, Batista was able to profit from the world war so as to enjoy a close relationship with the U.S. On 3 December 1940 a close programme of economic co-operation had been mooted: budgetary problems, mineral legislation, credit for more public works in Havana, such as the waterworks.[5] On 24 December came a proposal for an advance credit for agricultural development.[6] The U.S. first offered to fix their quota at $2\frac{1}{2}$ million tons of sugar in 1941 and to make available credit of $M10 for agricultural projects and $M20 for public works projects. In fact the fall of France had removed from the market one of Cuba's most valued customers. Only England remained, apart from the U.S. Lack of ocean transport increased difficulties of sales, though England could get her sugar more easily from Cuba than from Australia or Java. In March the Export-Import Bank lent Cuba $M11, to be spent on ensuring an increased sugar crop, and this was balanced by a sugar law which gave the control of the crop a permanent form.[7] A little later, a Cuban request for loans co-ordinating the requests of the last few months was sent over by Hull to his colleague at the Department of Commerce.[8] Batista's last serious intervention in the economy meanwhile was his decree of 18 January fixing sugar workers' wages for 1941 at the same level as for 1940: sugar prices had dropped and employers desired to reduce wages. Batista's action may indeed have avoided a strike.

Cuba was then the sixth most important exporter to the U.S. There were no restrictions in U.S.–Cuban trade and Cuba was the best field for U.S. investments in Latin America, with a total of $M733. The Cuban government had recently been helpful to the U.S. especially in respect of 'hemisphere defence', and had shown some intention of reorganizing its administrative machinery. The U.S. Department of State therefore believed that the time had come for a 'broad programme of economic co-operation', and proposed that the Export-Import Bank should immediately give credit to Cuba of $M30, of which

[5] See Foreign Relations (1940), V, 785-8.
[6] Ibid., 788-91.
[7] World Bank, 804.
[8] Jesse H. Jones (1874-1956), banker and minister, Secretary of Commerce, 1940-5.

$M15 would be for agricultural development and diversification.[9] In reply Batista was soon telling the U.S. ambassador that Cuba was ready 'to enter into a far-reaching military alliance with [the U.S.] for an indefinite period'. The Cuban people would wholeheartedly be behind such an alliance 'and would welcome it'.[10] This was true, judging from the vigorous response of Cuban public opinion to Roosevelt's famous 'last call' to the Americas on 27 May for a joint defence of democracy – a broadcast heard everywhere in the streets of the cities.[11] By June, after Germany had attacked Russia, there was even stronger feeling for the U.S. alliance; thereafter the Communist party of Cuba, as of other South American countries, seemed the bravest of the brave so far as denunciation of Germany was concerned. The Chilean Communist, Escobar, set the tune: 'We are in the middle of a just war which the workers and the people of the entire world should support and sustain with all their strength.'[12] Roosevelt began to be described as one of the greatest statesmen, and another Chilean Communist, Contreras Labarca, attacked the 'reactionary forces' for 'discrediting the good neighbour policy of President Roosevelt by an anti-imperialist campaign'.[13]

But Welles threw cold water on the idea of any formal alliance between the U.S. and South America: 'I am of the opinion . . . that an alliance of this nature would not materially assist in advancing the defence arrangements of this hemisphere.'[14] Even so, the sunny atmosphere between Cuba and the U.S. continued: Messersmith talked with the Mayor of Havana, Raúl Menocal,[15] about the Havana waterworks;[16] meetings occurred between Pierson of the Export-Import Bank and Saladrigas, and with other cabinet ministers.[17] Batista also saw Messersmith often. On 13 June he told him he was:

. . . greatly impressed by the necessities of more active co-operation between Cuba and the U.S. in . . . defence [matters]. . . . He saw the war coming closer and closer and it seemed almost inevitable that the U.S. would take an active part in it.

Batista wanted airfields more than public works.[18] Messersmith backed

[9] Foreign Relations (1941), V, 153–6.
[10] In mid-May 1941, ibid., 97–101.
[11] Phillips, 209.
[12] Escobar, Unidad Nacional contra el Fascismo, etc., 3.
[13] Contreras Labarca, Unión Nacional y el partido único, 43.
[14] Foreign Relations (1941), V, 102–3.
[15] Raúl (García) Menocal (born 1910), son of the president, owner of Santa Marta sugar mill, mayor of Havana, 1942–6.
[16] Foreign Relations (1941), V, 172–6.
[17] Ibid., 172–83.
[18] Ibid., 104–7.

the idea, and in early July there were discussions with Philip Bonsal,[19] in the Under-Secretary's office about the possible extension of the base at Guantánamo Bay. Bonsal found García Montes, the Cuban Secretary of Finance, in Washington wanting a $M25 credit immediately. A National Development Corporation to dispose of it was set up but there was delay in final settlement.

This, and inaction over the $M25 public works loan, upset the honeymoon between Batista and the U.S. Batista and his cabinet reported themselves 'profoundly disturbed by the allocations for Cuba, since the amounts were only a fraction of the requests submitted'.[20] A note of complaint followed. The U.S. office of price administration had fixed a price ceiling on sugar as they had done during the First World War. The sugar industry had denounced the ceiling as unfair. Food too began to increase in price. Of course, as during the First World War, the cigar world suffered from the closure of the European market: cigar factories closed, though exports of leaf tobacco to the U.S. increased. Cuban domestic cigar consumption remained the same, but that of cigarettes, both Cuban and U.S., went up.

All the errors of 1915-17 began now to be repeated. Batista established a decree providing a profit of 10% for wholesalers and 20% for retailers. A commission was set up to control all products subject to any U.S. 'priorities'. In early October 1941 Harry Dexter White and a mission of the U.S. Treasury arrived in Havana on a Cuban invitation to talk about a scheme for a central bank. The U.S. next offered to buy the entire 1942 sugar crop (less 200,000 tons for Cuba itself), in order to get the Cubans out of their anxieties, at a price of 2·9 cents per pound, a price higher than any since 1927.[21] Russia by this time also required Cuban sugar, since the Ukrainian beet fields had fallen to Germany: 70,000 tons a month were sent via the Allies.[22] On 27 October, arms valued at $M7·2, or nearly twice the original commitment, were finally made available to Cuba under the lend-lease agreement.[23]

Batista was thus enjoying good fortune. On 10 October, the first anniversary of his assumption of the presidency, the Communist party president, Juan Marinello, said handsomely that Batista would be the 'first president of Cuba' able to say on leaving office that 'his electoral promises had not been inflated boasts but were drawn from the impulse

[19] Philip Bonsal, son of Stephen Bonsal, acting as chief of the Latin American division of the State Department in the absence of Laurence Duggan. Born 1903, himself an old Havana hand, having been both in the Cuban Telephone Company in the 1920s and in the embassy as vice-consul and Third Secretary, 1938-9; ambassador to Cuba, 1959.

[20] Foreign Relations (1941), V, 118 (9 August 1941).

[21] A trickle of 65,000 tons was allowed for the world market, and molasses requirements for Cuban distilleries (ibid., 1941, 242-3).

[22] Estudio, 934; see also Timoshenko and Swerling.

[23] Foreign Relations (1941), V, 122-5.

of popular service';[24] the Communists had thus rallied gamely to the concept of national unity.[25]

The sugar industry was even now not quite so pleased as the Communists were. The Cane Planters' Association said that, due to past restrictions, they could produce only 3·4 million tons in 1942. The industry desired more money than the ceiling price suggested by the U.S.; they thought that they could get a larger profit from selling what they had on the world market. The question was poised delicately when the Japanese solved the problem by attacking Pearl Harbor. Cortina, the Cuban Secretary of State, immediately asked Ambassador Messersmith to call, saying that Cuba considered . . .

> The dastardly and unprovoked attack made by the Japanese . . . as an attack against Cuba and as against every one of the American states. The Cuban government considered the unprovoked attack on us by Japan as calling for an immediate declaration of war on the part of Cuba against Japan.

The next day, 9 December, the Cuban Congress declared war against Japan, and on 11 December Cuba declared war also against Germany and Italy. This was highly gratifying to the U.S. and it enabled Batista to confiscate German, Italian and Japanese balances; it gave him cause to ask for and be quickly granted emergency powers – an internment camp was established at the Hacienda Torrens, twenty-five miles from Havana, where 1,370 Italians and 3,000 Germans were held for the duration of the war.[26]

This posture led to the swift conclusion of a second trade agreement between the U.S. and Cuba,[27] and to Cuban agreement to a host of military facilities,[28] including the stationing of detachments from the aviation corps in Cuban airfields; the extension of overflights in Cuba; the use of landing fields and repair shops; permission for 'armed and uniformed' U.S. personnel to go where they wanted and to photograph Cuban territory.[29] Finally, on 28 January, the Cuban–U.S. sugar deal was signed, Batista authorizing the sale of the whole harvest at 2·65 cents a pound. The crop was in February fixed at 3·6 million tons and later raised to 3·95 million. England for her part bought the entire 1942 sugar harvests of Haiti and the Dominican Republic.[30] In Cuba the sale

[24] *Cuba en su puesto*, 7.
[25] See also Report to the Executive Committee of the URC, in Blas Roca, *Por la defensa nacional y el progreso de Cuba* (1941).
[26] Phillips, 212.
[27] Negotiations described in Foreign Relations (1941), V, 196–227.
[28] *Ibid.*, 114–15.
[29] *Ibid.*, 253–4.
[30] *Cf.* Sir Eric Roll, *The Combined Food Board: A study in wartime international planning* (1956), 38–40.

was not popular: Dr Viriato Gutiérrez denounced it as imposing an excessive sacrifice for Cuba. Batista had previously imposed a large number of higher taxes to 'help him with the war', such as income and luxury taxes, a 20% surcharge on all existing taxes, taxes on foreigners' registration and so on, most of which brought protests, though not from the Communists. The entry of both Russia and the U.S. into the war in alliance brought a curious sense of both relief and unreality to the Cuban Communists.

On 6 April 1942, the Cuban ambassador in Washington, Concheso, with López Castro and García Montes, called on Sumner Welles. The Cubans desired to conclude the $M25 loan negotiations on the ground that Batista wished to start work on the projects concerned – the repair and widening of the central highway, the construction of small distributory roads, new water systems in Santiago and Guantán-amo, along with two hospitals each in these towns: Batista 'felt he had a moral obligation to leave behind these hospitals in Cuba'. Welles said that he wanted to do his best but war priorities had to be kept. Concheso asked 'if . . . Cuba would have some preferential position in connection with the requirements of the other American Republics'. Welles said that they would not.[31] But in fact the $M25 loan was very soon agreed and signed. There remained some disputes – such as that between Mayor Raúl Menocal and the president of the Export-Import Bank over the Havana water supply – but there was no further delay.

This was a satisfactory omen for the arrival in Cuba of the next in that long line of envoys extraordinary, or Proconsuls, Spruille Braden.[32] Braden was an intelligent man, with considerable Latin American experience. Educated for a business career, he had begun life as a mining engineer, advising on the electrification of the Chilean railways before plunging into New York in the 1920s. Retaining a strong interest in South America (he married a Chilean), after an evident business success, at the age of forty he began representing the U.S. at various congresses, being chairman of the U.S. delegation at the Chaco conference. Afterwards, from 1939 to 1942, he was ambassador to Colombia.[33] Braden was a distinctly Radical diplomat, with strong views on social reform. He was regarded by many Cubans as the best ambassador that the U.S. ever sent to Havana. Most of his activity, however, was necessarily military: his first instructions from Hull told him that the War Department wanted 'to establish with the least delay possible a heavy bombardment and operational training unit' under

[31] Foreign Relations, 291-3.
[32] Spruille Braden (born 1894).
[33] With him came a new and intelligent staff, among it, Gustavo Durán, an exile from Spain where, in the civil war, he had distinguished himself as a divisional commander on the Republican side.

U.S. officers, to train U.S. and British RAF personnel.[34] This was quickly agreed, and San Antonio and San Julián in Pinar del Río became centres for allied training. Braden received instructions in July to ask permission to buy land at San Julián to construct at least one 7,000-foot runway, and to station 500 men there, with the U.S. having operational and administrative control. The Cubans agreed, their willingness to co-operate being encouraged by their loss at sea, through German submarine action, of two freighters in August 1942. There were several other torpedoings around Cuba, and for a week or so an ineffective blackout was imposed.[35]

By late 1942 there were nine military arrangements between the U.S. and Cuba using Cuban territory; in addition to the San Antonio and San Julián air bases, there was a base for seaplanes and a communication project at La Fé (Pinar del Río), naval patrol stations, extended landing stations and emergency airfields.[36] A leading German spy in the Caribbean, August Luning, the 'canary man' (because he used canaries to disguise his transmitter), was executed in Havana – the only spy executed in Latin America in the Second World War.[37] Cuban diplomatic relations with the U.S.S.R. were also opened, as befitted two separate states of the great alliance. The following year Stalin received Secretary of State Concheso in Moscow, and the Soviet ambassador in Washington, Litvinov, came to Havana to open a Soviet Embassy for the first time. An emergency military service law prepared for the reconstruction of the Cuban war machine on a war footing. A submarine sold to Cuba by the U.S. sank a German submarine. Cuba even began to organize a FBI, under U.S. training. German submarine activity in the Caribbean continued spasmodically, several sugar tankers being sunk. Several hundred Cubans volunteered to fight for the U.S., though only a few exceptional cases were enlisted.

Some clouds, however, remained. The first related to the recommendation by Harry Dexter White that a central bank of issue should be created in Cuba. Braden was critical. He told the premier, Saladrigas, that 'honest and competent management' was a *sine qua non* for the successful operation of the proposed central bank: 'The only assurance he could give me was that Dr Oscar García Montes . . . and Sr Eduardo Durutti would be top executives of the new institution for at least five years.' He commented: 'As the department is aware, honest and competent administrators in government-controlled organisations have been and are a rarity in Cuba . . . the volume and potency of corruption' was

[34] Foreign Relations (1941), V, 265–6.
[35] The Cubans also made requests for further lend-lease allocation. See Duggan's memorandum, 9 July 1942, Foreign Relations, 276–7. This was rejected.
[36] *Ibid.*, 287–9.
[37] Phillips, 217. Luning was detected through Anglo-American counter espionage.

such that he could not think it was the time to create a new institution.[38] The U.S. financial experts reacted sharply: Luthringer, of the Financial Division in the State Department, wrote:

> Fears of the possible incapacity of the Cuban government in these matters would not in my opinion justify an attempt on the part of the Department to prevent Cuba joining the vast majority of her sister Republics which have an independent currency and a central bank. . . . The establishment of its own monetary system is as much a prerogative of Cuban sovereignty as the establishment of its own army, police forces and courts.[39]

Welles backed this, but Braden kept on:

> The technical mission did not study the political aspects of this matter and therefore did not go into the repercussions which the widespread corruption in Cuba might have on the proposed banking and monetary reforms. These *unique conditions of corruption* must inevitably have an important bearing on the success or failure of the pending legislation.

In the end, Braden triumphed; the creation of the National Bank was again postponed.

The other cloud related to sugar. The 1942 harvest reached nearly four million tons,[40] bringing in $M256, or nearly double that brought by the 1941 crop. An ebullient mood was present everywhere in Cuba Braden was found on 2 September 1942 telling Washington that . . .

> The past few days have witnessed the inauguration of a local campaign for the apparent purpose of establishing a conviction in the mind of the Cuban people that Cuba has a vested right to a 1943 sugar crop of approximately the same size as the 1942 *zafra* . . . with the implication that the U.S. government has some moral obligation to make such a crop possible in order to maintain the Cuban economy.

Dr Zaydín (the new premier) told the Lions' Club:

> It is said . . . the harvest will be reduced and in the name of the government I declare that this cannot and will not be. A reduction of the sugar crop will bring about a civil war. With the misery existing in the fields, with the national economy battered, workers and the entire people would establish a protest based on reason.[41]

[38] Braden, 30 July 1942.
[39] Foreign Relations (1942), V, 301–6.
[40] 3,975,000 tons.
[41] Foreign Relations (1942), V, 330–1.

On 25 September, however, Braden handed over a memorandum saying that Cuba should produce in 1943 a maximum of 2·6 million tons, of which two million would be taken by the U.S. The U.S. government appreciated the 'problems which may arise from the reduction'[42] but this had to be Cuba's contribution to the Allied cause. The Cubans were highly pessimistic. On 15 October a hot-tempered note reached the U.S. Embassy; this was later withdrawn and 'more moderate negotiations followed'. On 5 December the U.S. proposed that they would pay 2·65 cents per pound for 2½ million tons in 1943.[43] In the end the harvest was as a compromise limited to 2·8 million tons, and the average price was agreed at 2·99 cents, about the same as the 1942 price. The total, after Cuban home needs had been satisfied, was sold to the U.S. Commodity Credit Corporation.

Since August 1942 Batista's loyal allies, the Communists, had been proposing their entry into the government; they had also in the course of the previous two years consolidated their pre-eminent position in the unions. In February 1942, therefore, Juan Marinello, the dilettante Communist leader, finally entered the cabinet as minister without portfolio. The CTC was given official status in April. Afterwards, another, younger Communist, the thirty-one year old Carlos Rafael Rodríguez, joined the cabinet – 'a most interesting experience,' he later recalled, with some understatement; of *bourgeois* origin also, he had entered the Communist movement after being a leader of the Directorio Estudiantil in Cienfuegos, where he had been a compromise candidate for mayor in September 1933. Later resigning because of the corruption of a number of students, he then went to Havana and worked there with the strike committee of May 1935. From then till 1939 he had remained most of the time at the university.[44] The most sophisticated Communist of his generation, his entry into the government marked the high tide of Communist collaboration with Batista's regime. In early 1944 the Communists changed the formal name of their party from Unión Revolucionaria Comunista to Partido Socialista Popular (PSP). 'The immediate historical task of our party,' explained Marinello at this time,[45] 'is not the establishment of Communism but the struggle for complete liberation which ought to culminate in the . . . establishment of socialism.' Their slogan would now be 'Economic Progress, Social Security, Victory and "a People's Peace"'. 'Our change of name . . . is a far-reaching change, not a matter of labels. The cell would be replaced by the socialist committee.' An attempt would

[42] *Ibid.*, 332–3.
[43] Short tons.
[44] Carlos Rafael Rodríguez (born 1913), writer and economist. This paragraph is based on a conversation the author had with Carlos Rafael Rodríguez, June 1966.
[45] In a pamphlet, *El PSP* (1944).

be made to make all who enrolled as party supporters into members. A goal of 400,000 members was set as a long-term aim. The Communists meantime were not pressing for radical changes in Cuban society. Their programme in 1943-4 was mild, calling merely for racial equality, and rights for women, but not even for land reform, nor for nationalization on a large scale.

Indeed at this period the Cuban Communists were closer than almost any other world Communist party to the repudiation of Marx's or Lenin's theories of imperialism and of class struggle. They showed great enthusiasm for co-operation with the U.N. and the U.S. Blas Roca wrote:

> We must of course increase our efforts to inform our people of the possibilities of a profitable collaboration with England and the U.S. on a joint plan, for resolving harmoniously our most acute and urgent economic problems. . . .[46] Teheran [i.e. where the Big Three met] offered a lasting peace for many generations.[47]

In another pamphlet of 1944 Blas Roca said: 'The imperialist era has ended, as Sumner Welles has pointed out.'[48] The Communist party was looking forward to 'the possibility of a long period of a flourishing economy . . . of substantive social reforms in benefit of the masses'[49] and hoped that the U.S. would find means of containing any renewed depression.[50] Blas Roca abandoned his statements of the past on nationalization of foreign investments, indicating that the nationalization of public services would be adequate. Lázaro Peña, as secretary-general of the CTC, spoke of the profound change recently in the attitude of the Cuban upper classes and offered 'severe and patriotic collaboration to the other classes'. Carlos Rafael Rodríguez believed that the entry of the Communists into the government had some effect on stopping corruption and self-enrichment.[51]

For the Cubans the war was thus a time of compromise between nearly every interest. While the Communists were in the government, 4 July was publicly celebrated with great zeal. 80,000 Cubans paraded in the streets, and Batista, his breast clinking with North American medals, visited the *Maine* memorial. Havana newspapers published celebration issues and the Havana Rotary Club sent ten tons of sweets to the American soldiers at Guantánamo. In this politically sugary atmosphere there were of course some shortages, some economic dis-

---

[46] See Roca, *Estados Unidos, Teheran*, 30.
[47] *Los Socialistas y la Realidad Cubana*, 87.
[48] *Los Fundamentos del Socialismo*, 11.
[49] *Fundamentos*, February 1944, 89.
[50] *Los Socialistas y la Realidad Cubana*, 88.
[51] Evidence of Carlos Rafael Rodríguez.

tortions: no petrol for private cars and bad posts. The unemployment in the tobacco industry was not made up for by the heavy shipments to the U.S. of leaf tobacco. Fruit and vegetable growers could not export more than two-thirds of their usual produce to the U.S. due to lack of shipping. Supplies of machinery dropped. Spare parts ran out and were impossible to replace. Prices rose almost 100 % between 1940 and 1945. Lack of iron and steel threatened to paralyse the building industry, suggesting unemployment. Tourists were rare and several famous bars closed. There were continuous beef shortages and a flourishing black market.

The continuation of the war, fortunately for Cuba, caused greater shortages of sugar than had been anticipated. The U.S. government therefore permitted Batista to fix the 1944 sugar crop at 4·25 million tons, the biggest figure since 1930. In the event the harvest reached a little under five million tons,[52] fetching $M330, the highest price gained since 1924, and on the level with the big prices reached in the First World War. Sugar workers' wages were increased by 10 % in 1944 too, so that some claim could be made that the profits were distributed. Admittedly, German submarine activity forced the enshipment of most sugar from Havana under convoy, so that dock workers were idle in other parts of Cuba, though railways were active. In these years, especially 1944, the increased activity in the now fifty-year-old[53] Bethlehem steel-manganese mines brought a further wind of prosperity to blow through Oriente: in 1944, over 400,000 tons of raw manganese were exported, bringing in $M11.

The nation calmly and optimistically approached the elections of 1944. Batista, anxious now to appear the good democrat, stood down in favour of his friend Dr Saladrigas, the prime minister and ex-ABC leader. No doubt, had Saladrigas won, as everyone in the government assumed he would, Batista would have continued to play an important part behind the scenes, almost as important a part perhaps as he had done between 1934 and 1940 or as General Trujillo played behind the different presidents whom he nominated in the Dominican Republic. But Batista miscalculated. He did not use the armed forces to secure a corrupt election; and, despite vigorous Communist support for Saladrigas and Batista's own remarkable prestige with all the publicity the regime could organize, Grau and the Auténticos were able to mount a formidable campaign, 'promising everyone a pot of gold and an easy chair', touring the country indefatigably, speaking on every subject under the sun. It mattered little that his opponents christened Grau 'the divine gibberer'. The country suddenly became obsessed with the election.

[52] 4,996,841.
[53] Founded 1888.

Cars swept along the prados and across the plazas of Cuba with flags
and slogans flying. Grau's promises became more and more elaborate.
The workers would have a fair deal. Corruption would end. Cuba
would be for the Cubans. The Auténticos would make Cuba economically independent. Grau won. The old university leader himself, now
almost sixty, persuaded that he could be the saviour of the nation,
and his party of now ageing students, professors, lawyers or university
lecturers, captured real power at last.

A new stipulation in the Constitution of 1940 had, however, made
vote-splitting possible and Grau did not receive a majority in Congress
or in the municipal or provincial governments. Thus, though personally
popular, he had from the beginning no solid basis for his administration
and no solid anti-Batistiano majority.

Batista's national regime left behind a state where, it seemed, in
the shadow of the New Deal, the most overt and outrageous side of
U.S. involvement in Cuba had been removed and where the state had
made an apparently decisive step towards a form at least of socialism.
There were few countries in the Americas where the trade unions were
so well established and exercised such a powerful role. Of course, some
of Batista's acts had been reprehensible, such as killing Guiteras, forcing
castor oil down the throats of opponents and using the army to crush the
general strike of 1935, but those had been early days and Guiteras in retrospect seemed almost as much a gangster as a socialist. Batista had not
destroyed gangsterism or corruption of government officials, and he
certainly left office himself a rich man – perhaps amassing as much as
$M20 since 1933.[54] It was widely assumed, for instance, that out of
$M20 spent on new government buildings, $M12 was spent on graft.
Much of Batista's wealth was in urban property.[55] Further, the experience of the war had made it clear that, whether the Platt Amendment was still in force or not, the U.S. government remained the
effective master of the Cuban economy. Batista's departure was much
regretted by the Communists. For them he had been the father of the
Cuban Popular Front, 'the people's idol, the great man of our national
politics', and even Blas Roca hinted that, when he went, he might
not be gone for ever, and described him as 'this magnificent reserve of
Cuban democracy'.[56]

[54] This was the estimate of his cabinet colleague Carlos Rafael Rodríguez to the author,
June 1966.
[55] Chibás gave a list of Batista's property in Havana in 1949, see Conte Agüero, *Eduardo
Chibás*, 609.
[56] Blas Roca, Carlos Rafael Rodríguez, *En Defensa del Pueblo* (1945), 41–3.

CHAPTER LXIII

Grau

Ramón Grau San Martín was inaugurated on 10 October 1944, amid three days of celebrations. A chorus of a thousand male voices sang the hymn of the Auténticos. Church bells rang. Bars and hotels were crowded. Huge pictures of the new saviour looked down upon seething masses. Boats and launches blew whistles. Idle to say it all seemed familiar! Idle to say that Grau seemed to parody even himself when he announced: 'It is not I who have taken office today, but the people.'[1] The effect of this was scarcely spoiled by the immediate outbreak of one of the worst hurricanes that Cuba had known.

Grau's cabinet brought back into the public eye many of those associated with the revolutionary aspirations of 1933–5, and for a time the Conservative classes, the U.S. property owners and the merchants experienced some uncertainty for the future. They need not have worried. The Authentic Revolutionary movement was neither authentic nor revolutionary. It was a democratic party but most of the leaders were anxious to enjoy the fruits of power more than to press through such reforms as were needed by Cuban society. They already possessed beautiful houses in Marianao or Miramar, which they aspired to render more exotic and amusing. Their programme turned out to be words.

Dr Ramon Grau San Martín was now almost sixty years old. He embodied in 1944 the hopes of hundreds of thousands of Cubans who wanted a secure future for themselves and their children, a serious and socially conscious government free from corruption, and one which was essentially, in some clear if undefined or 'Martían' way, Cuban. He betrayed these hopes utterly. The trust which the people of Cuba had in him was wasted in a revel of corrupt government which rivalled the era of Zayas and exceeded that of Batista. Already a rich man due to an extensive private practice and the fortune which he inherited from his father (a tobacco salesman from the Vuelta Abajo), Grau turned his presidency into an orgy of theft, ill-disguised by emotional nationalistic speeches. He did more than any other single man to kill the hope of democratic practice in Cuba.

[1] Phillips, 224.

It was his good luck to rule in Cuba during a new golden era of sugar expansion. By the winter of 1944–5 much of Europe and North Africa had been liberated, and the Allied governments were wondering how these devastated areas might be fed. The U.S. Commodity Credit Corporation once more bought the whole 1945 harvest, as it had done during the rest of the war, but at 3·10 cents a pound – an increase due to the rise in prices in the U.S.[2] Both the 1946 and 1947 harvests were sold in the same way. In the last of these years, a new U.S. sugar law produced a new quota to Cuba – a minimum of 28·6% of the total consumption of the U.S., which could be increased if the other countries involved in the arrangements did not fulfil their quotas. All these events gave rising prosperity to Cuba. Production in the rest of the world remained at very low levels, so that the era of Grau became once more the time of *vacas gordas*.

Corruption, of course, is a complicated matter and is hardly explained by merely saying that the rulers could not restrain themselves from putting their hands in the till. What was the exact style of the corruption, who did precisely what? No less important, how did they get away with it, why did no vigilant member of the opposition, newspaper or legislator, make an effective protest? There is also the question, how did the corruption effect the life of the state in the long term?

In general, these frauds had their origin in Spanish practice whereby civil servants and judges were paid so little, or had themselves paid so much for their jobs that corruption was the only effective method of recompense. There was also the lottery which, under Spain, had given many opportunities for enrichment. That had been further used under the Republic, by means of the collectorship system which, farmed out among senators and newspapermen, explains much of the second question under discussion: critics were in fact silenced by being allocated lottery collectorships. Others were threatened by physical reprisals, by the dismissal of their friends, or by visits of unmistakable menace by police officers or hired gunmen. There were few public men who did not themselves look forward to their period in power as a time when they too would be able to make their thousands of pesos through some agreement to provide food for the army, through control of customs houses or even through the establishment of a series of imaginary jobs in, for instance, the Bureau of Communications.

How governments carried out corruption varied. There were the bogus jobs in government departments. Pardons could be bought.

---

[2] Sugar being the first product to be controlled in the U.S., its variation of price (32%) between 1939 and 1944 was less than most products: e.g. fats (45%), cheese (91%), eggs (160%), wheat (144%).

Buildings could be rented to the government (particularly as schools). Old government stores could be sold. Contracts for public works (as well as concessions for development) were given to favoured builders or engineers without tenders being made. The money passed directly to the politician responsible. (This practice is no doubt the commonest form of graft in Latin-American as in European and North American politics.) There were, finally, actual thefts or misappropriations of public funds. This last technique of enrichment at the public cost is rarer than the others, though Grau was to refine its use. Grau himself would publicly try to stand aside from corruption: 'You can't do any dirty business with me,' he would say, 'but how about a word with Paulina?' Paulina, his mistress and sister-in-law, would then enter into contact with this or that enterprising business man.[3]

Not all criticism was silenced, and indeed by 1947 those members of Grau's own party who found what was happening intolerable were thinking of breaking away into a separate entity, under the leadership of Senator Eduardo Chibás, who had followed Grau for many years, and who was himself free at least from the most obvious temptation of corruption by the possession of considerable wealth, inherited from his engineer father, one of Céspedes's ministers in 1933.

There were other more profound causes for corruption. By the last years of the Second World War Cuba had depended for one hundred years almost exclusively on sugar for its wealth. Tied to the vagaries of the world market, and to the hopes and fears engendered by world war and economic crisis, even with matters only remotely connected with sugar dependent to an astonishing extent upon sugar, the whole economy swayed to the rhythm of the sugar industry. The impression was widespread that no individual effort could be as profitable or as damaging as the rise or the fall of a percentage of a cent in the world price of sugar.[4] The Cuban economy in fact, resembled a lottery; indeed it was hardly surprising that the entire population was geared to the lottery itself, poor families waiting pathetically each week as the results came out, in the hope that at last their number would spring up first and provide a new world for them – rather in the same mood with which they also optimistically waited for a new leader, for Grau or for Mendieta, for Machado or for Batista, in the expectation that a

---

[3] Comment of Julio Lobo. Paulina Alsina de Grau was secretary to the Presidency, 1944–8. She had been married to Grau's brother Francisco, a journalist who shot himself in the fencing room of the Centro de Dependientes, perhaps through jealousy of his brother's affair with his wife. Paulina, who was greedy, exerted a great influence over Grau, and was partly responsible for the change that occurred in Grau from the revolutionary leader of 1933 to the corrupt politician of 1944.

[4] As the famous World Bank report pointed out.

lucky number would come up to incarnate, like a panacea, the spirit of José Martí.

There need be, of course, no particular link between a nation addicted to gambling and one whose government is given to corruption, but the anxiety inculcated by the unreliability of the sugar economy communicated itself to the political master class. No one felt secure. Some believed that Cuban sugar wealth was already in permanent decline, and that it was essential to take advantage of the opportunities for enrichment, never to recur, provided by the Second World War and its immediate aftermath. During the Second World War, world sugar production had fallen by 20 %; the pre-war average of 24·6 million tons was not repeated till 1947–8. Even then *per capita* consumption throughout the world was lower than it had been in 1937–9 or 1928–30. Immense opportunities therefore opened before Cuba. No unshaven warriors had spoiled her *centrales*. Who could forget the riches made under Menocal? Onwards, onwards, once more to wealth! And who could really count himself well off in Cuba unless he had a reasonable investment in property in Florida?

Further, by 1944–5 corruption had gone so far at so many levels in Cuba that the complete change of personnel provided by revolution seemed essential to secure any real change. An astute international observer in 1950 noted: 'Many . . . inspectors who . . . visit factories expect to be paid for not making bad reports. The factories pay them, moreover, and so they do not even make the inspections. The Government in Havana [therefore] finds it unnecessary in many cases to pay the inspectors more than token salaries.'[5] It was not just the president and a few ministers who helped themselves to cash which was not theirs – that was a comparatively minor problem – but everyone, in any official position: mayors, sub-mayors, governors and lieutenant-governors of provinces, treasurers, accountants of small towns such as Batabanó,[6] school inspectors and school teachers. There was no social stigma to graft. It resembled the non-payment of taxes in Italy. Of course, it extended to law as well as to government. The American historian Chapman, for instance, had been told in the 1920s:

> Graft is . . . constantly thrust at you. I don't like it but I have paid it and taken my profit rather than suffer the annoyance that would surely follow if I refused. On one occasion . . . an underling of the judge came to see me and said he could get a decision for me if I could give him $50. Otherwise it looked as if I would lose. I told him I would make him a present of $50 if I won. And I won . . . If you

[5] World Bank, 190.
[6] See instance described in *El Mundo* 10, January 1946.

decline to enter a graft deal with them, they do not attribute it to honesty. They think you are afraid you may get caught and are at great pains to explain how safe it is.[7]

Corruption coincided with violence. The various political action groups, who owed their origin to the struggle against Machado and the revolution of 1933–4 had mostly lost any real ideological content that they might have had, though they kept their formal protestations. When Grau took office, there were at least ten political semi-gangster groups in Cuba, most of them being the product of splits in the old left-wing organizations. The chief of them was Acción Revolucionaria Guiteras(ARG), known under Antonio Guiteras as Joven Cuba, now led by two contrasting men. The first was Dr Eufemio Fernández Ortega, a soft-spoken lawyer who had fought in Spain and was loved by all, an occasional contributor to the periodical *Bohemia* (run by his friend Quevedo); the second was a bizarre thug named Jesús González Cartas, *El Extraño* (the odd man out), a man skilled in violence, incapable of oratory, though as leader of a nominally social democratic sect he was responsible for the latter as often as the former. This group had about 800 members in 1944. They had trade union links through the busmen's leader, Marco Antonio Hirigoyen. One leader, Fabio Ruiz, had been made chief of police in Havana by Grau in return for support in the elections.

Second in importance, numbering perhaps 300, was the Movimiento Socialista Revolucionario (MSR) founded quite recently by Rolando Masferrer, a prodigy of a sort who had fought as a schoolboy against Machado, joined Guiteras in 1933–4, and fought in Spain during 1937–8 where he became a Communist and remained so until 1944 when, still only thirty, he set out to establish an anti-Communist action group. Masferrer was wounded in the battle of the Ebro and ever afterwards was known as *El Cojo*, the cripple. He was used by the Communists as the leader of their militant action group in the 1940s, graduated well at university, fancied himself as a man of letters and broke with the party over the question of the planned agreement with Grau San Martín. His colleagues were, in the early days, Carlos Montenegro and Roberto Pérez Santisteban. Montenegro, a novelist and short story writer, had, like Masferrer, once been a Communist and, also like Masferrer, been expelled from the party, along with his wife, the poetess Emma Pérez. Pérez Santisteban had been a Trotskyist, and was the most serious and intelligent of the group; his reputation encouraged many younger Radicals to become associated with the MSR for a time, among them Rolando Meruelos, Boris Goldenberg, an ex-Communist from Germany

[7] Chapman, 542.

and France of Russian Jewish origin, and two student leaders, Faure Chaumón and Manolo Castro. The latter was a brilliant, handsome, attractive gunman whose career, like Masferrer's, characterizes his generation of Cubans. A student who fought Machado (belonging to an organization named the Legión Revolucionaria) under Grau's regime in 1933, he became a police lieutenant. Afterwards, he returned to the School of Engineering in the university and acted as second in command to Ramiro Valdés Daussá when he was head of the university police. Finally (in 1945) he was named by Grau president of the Students Union. All Cuban presidents knew that the students carried political weight and they tried to have a man of their own political views at their head, if only to discourage political demonstrations against the government. Afterwards, in 1947, Grau named Castro State Director of Sports (despite his evident implication in a number of crimes, such as the murder in the Bar Criollo of the young student Hugo Dupotey). But, though a member of the government and now over thirty, he remained registered in the University School of Engineering, where he taught in the design department. He still regarded himself as a member of the Legión Revolucionaria but collaborated with Masferrer.[8]

A critical member of the MSR was Mario Salabarría, a friend of Grau, who appointed him chief of secret police (Buró de Investigaciones) as a counter to Fabio Ruiz of the ARG. For a time, partly through semi-Nazi style meetings in which the red letters MSR blazed at large audiences as if they were an open fire, partly through the magazine *Tiempo en Cuba*, Masferrer's group clearly showed a genuine if highly theatrical social purpose. But after a while, as so often in Cuban politics, murder and thuggery caught hold of the movement. This was in no way prevented and was even exacerbated by the fact that this group, like the Acción Revolucionaria Guiteras, was personally implicated with the authorities.

A third revolutionary action group, the Unión Insurrecional Revolucionaria (UIR), also had friends at court. The leader of this gang was Emilio Tró, the bitter enemy of both Salabarría and Fabio Ruiz, who became under Grau the chief of police in Marianao, by now a huge city. Like ARG and MSR, the UIR had its ultimate origins in Guiteras's Joven Cuba, and its leaders seem at one time to have been Communists, though by 1946 they were far from being so. They had the habit of leaving the note 'Justice is slow but sure' beside the bodies of

[8] From an obituary 24 February 1948, *El Mundo*. For what seems to be a description, see Ernest Hemingway, 'The Shot', in *By Line*, 422-3. 'This friend, who had been shot dead had been a beautiful backfield man on the local university team. He was a fine quarterback and he could play half back. He was director of sports of the Republic when he died. No one was ever punished.'

their victims. The UIR appears after 1946 to have been the closest action group to Grau himself, sometimes acting as his bodyguard, but all these groups, with 0·45 pistols the symbol of their 'arguments', had in fact helped Grau in his election campaign, many of their members having some connection with the Auténticos, and after he had taken office all of them moved in, as it were, on the government.

All these groups also had links with the university. University politics indeed became itself so gangster-ridden that it was an open question whether gangsterism was more a problem of rival university politicians than rival police forces. The presidency of the FEU (students union) had been settled more than once at the point of a revolver. Indeed, since the university was beyond the bounds of police intervention, and since it was full of tough young men anxious to get hold of their first machine-guns, the university was an ideal place for the operation of the 'action groups', who could also make money by monopolizing the sale of textbooks, by selling examination papers and marks and raiding the office of the bursar. The education minister under Grau, Alemán, recognized this and seems to have made payments to the action group in the university for his own purposes. Meetings and even lectures were sometimes interrupted by shots. Several people (such as Ramiro Valdés Daussá, the chief of the university police till 1940) had been murdered for vaguely political reasons in the past few years, giving rise to a series of interlocking vendettas.[9]

The centre of this picture and, despite the extremely elusive nature of his politics, the commanding figure, was Dr Grau San Martín himself, surrounded in the National Palace, just as President Zayas had been, by his innumerable relations and friends. For Grau, tall and severe in looks and always talking, was still influenced by his sister-in-law, Paulina Alsina de Grau, 'the first lady of the Republic'. He was always able to attribute blame for inaction to the fact that he did not have a majority in the Congress.[10] Other friends and ministers, such as

[9] *Cf.* articles by Raúl Roa, *Retorno a la Alborada*, 208. In the late 1930s the Ala Izquierda Estudiantil, led by the Communists (Carlos Rafael Rodríguez and Ladislao González Carvajal) had controlled the university: they had then been beaten out by a group of 'politicians' including El Bonche Universitario, a political group led by an *auténtico*, Luis Orlando Rodríguez, which started out as anti-Batista or anti-dictatorship but gradually became corrupted and ended in near-gangsterism. The Bonche (literally 'bunch') rode high until 1944 when, with Batista's abandonment of power, it suffered a decline. The fight against the Bonche was led by Manolo Castro. Luis Orlando Rodríguez, who will crop up again in this account, had started life in the struggle against Machado, had been wounded in an attempt on the life of Major Arsenio Ortiz and afterwards joined the *Pro Ley y Justicia* organization. From 1944 to 1945 he was Grau's Director of Sports, preceding Manolo Castro, his rival.

[10] His first cabinet found posts for many of his old friends of 1933. Prime Minister was Félix Lancís Sánchez, son of Ricardo Lancís who had been in Crowder's Honest Cabinet of 1922–3; Foreign Minister, Cuervo Rubio, co-professor with him in 1933, gynaecologist turned *político*; Minister of Labour, Carlos Azcárate Rosell; Minister of Finance,

Antonio (Tony) Varona, Carlos Prío Socarrás, Porfirio Pendás – all members of the Auténtico party – attempted various arrangements with the ABC and other groups. They were not successful, though Grau himself, just before he was inaugurated, did reach a compromise with the ever-malleable Communists. Afterwards, the Communists announced that they would not be an 'obstacle' to Grau – thereby suggesting the voting collaboration of their three members in the legislature.[11] Grau in return recognized the CTC and undertook to continue assisting it with money. The Auténticos in the CTC would collaborate with the Communist leadership, and Grau promised to complete the great 'workers' palace' projected by Batista.[12] The CTC lumbered on with the Negro Lázaro Peña still at its head, but with tension beneath the surface, its rivalries being pointed with the violence and corrupt practices which stained the roots of all Cuban politics. There was indeed much shooting in the unions in 1944 and 1945, with the Auténticos employing gunmen attached to the revolutionary organizations.

The Communists were going through a curious stage, thanks primarily to the inevitable unpredictability of Stalin's policy as the Second World War moved towards its end. Thus on 12 January 1945 Blas Roca was found 'fully approving' the anticipation by Earl Browder, still secretary-general of the U.S. Communist party, of an era of sunny co-operation between the U.S. and U.S.S.R.[13] In March President Grau seemed to seal the new sympathies between Auténticos and Communists, at the top at least, by presenting the CTC with $750,000 to convert the Havana Jai-alai headquarters into the 'workers' palace'.[14] But the next month came the famous attack on Earl Browder by the French Communist, Jacques Duclos, in *Cahiers du Comunisme*, criticizing him for his 'notorious revisionism' and his acceptance of the Teheran conference – a mere 'diplomatic document', he said scornfully. Duclos also attacked the Latin

[11] *Los Socialistas y La Realidad Cubana*, 24.
[12] *Fundamentos*, March 1945, 181–2.
[13] See *Political Affairs*, March 1945, qu. Browder, 95.
[14] Phillips, 229.

Manuel Fernández Supervielle, an honest man who had been dean of the Havana Bar Association and president of the Inter-American Bar Association; Minister of Health, José Antonio Presno who had been rector of the university in the time of his first government; Minister of Justice, Carlos Eduardo de la Cruz; Minister of Public Works, Gustavo Moreno Lastres, also Secretary of Public Works in Grau's 1933 cabinet, and Auténtico vice-presidential candidate in 1940; Minister of Defence, Salvador Ménendez Villoch, an ex-marine officer retired by Machado; Minister of Agriculture, Germán Alvarez Fuentes; Minister of Communications, engineer Sergio Clark Díaz; Minister to the Presidency, young Dr Julián Solorzano; Minister of the Interior, Segundo Curti, an old collaborator of Grau's in 1933; Minister of Commerce, Alberto Inocente Alvarez, a co-founder of the Directorio in 1927; Minister of Education, Luis Pérez Espinós, superintendent-general of schools, 1933-4, later with Guiteras in Joven Cuba, having been before a member of ABC, a young but volatile man who had passed his childhood selling newspapers.

American Communist parties for following Browder's line, mentioning the Cuban and Colombian parties by name.[15] Blas Roca and the Cuban leaders rallied to Duclos' side and quickly denounced Teheran and Yalta. Alas, they acted too fast: within a month Blas Roca had to eat humble pie again, apologizing at the National Executive Committee of the party in June[16] for his previous criticism of the Teheran and Yalta conferences; contrary to what they had previously said, these agreements were after all the basis of hope. 'It is possible to hope for peace. Dimitrov in May 1938 criticized those who argued that peace was impossible; Dimitrov was right. As for Roosevelt, recently dead, there is no doubt he was a democratic and progressive force (great applause).'[17] The July issue of *Fundamentos*, the party's theoretical journal, however, switched the line yet once more: Duclos had underestimated the significance of Teheran and only provided ammunition for the enemies of Communism. But 'we must revise all our views of recent times'. Blas Roca had previously made an exaggerated estimate of 'the possible results of the [Yalta and Teheran] agreements ... in the field of world economics'. Socialism and capitalism could not after all live together; Britain and the U.S. 'would not carry out their Teheran and Yalta agreements'.[18]

For this essentially doctrinal reason the Communist party remained passive during the first year of Grau's presidency. By late 1945 the cold war had already extended to the Caribbean as *Fundamentos* began to differentiate the Rooseveltian foreign policy of international collaboration for peace from the imperialistic tendencies under Harry S. Truman seeking an 'American century'.[19] On 28 October 1945, *Hoy* noted that the end of the war and the elimination of the common danger cleared the way for increasing imperialist influences on American policy in general.[20] But at this time Grau's attitude to the U.S. and international affairs in general had been left vague, even though until August 1945 Cuba remained formally a state at war.

Grau began his administration with a careful reorganization of the higher commands in the army. Most of Batista's friends, such as the commanders of the Campamento Columbia (Ignacio Galíndez) and of La Cabaña (Tabernilla Dolz), the chief of police, and the chief of the army staff (Lopez Migoya), were replaced, under a scheme worked out by Grau's sub-secretary of defence Luis Collado, and a Grauista officer, Major Pérez Dámera, who was soon promoted to the rank of general and chief of staff. However, this did not halt the grumbling among officers;

[15] *Cahiers du Comunisme*, April 1945.
[16] It was still known as the PSP (Partido Socialista Popular).
[17] Blas Roca, *Por la defensa del pueblo*.
[18] *Fundamentos*, July 1945. See also *ibid.*, August 1945.
[19] *Fundamentos*, September–October 1945.
[20] Qu. Blaiser, 192.

indeed it increased it, since Pérez Dámera was much despised (he was a fat young officer of good looks and conventional Latin American military attitudes) and in February, predictably, a plot to kill Grau was discovered. A number of old Batista supporters including Colonel Pedraza, the protagonist in the affair of 1940, were arrested and spent time in prison, though the evidence of attempted assassination seemed slender, as did the sentences for such a serious accusation. No doubt they were innocent, but in April the chief of the secret police, Enrique Enríquez Ravena, was murdered, apparently on the ground that Acción Revolucionaria Guiteras blamed him for failing to release one of its number, imprisoned under Batista, who later, seemingly genuinely, was shot while trying to escape.[21]

By 1945 Cuba was once more, as in 1919-20, being swept by a warm wave of prosperity attributable to the end of a world war. Even the cathedral was carefully and expensively restored. The national income was already approaching double what it had been in 1939. Real incomes seem to have increased 40% between 1939 and 1947. The steadily rising sugar exports, combined with the import scarcities caused by the war, brought a big balance of payments surplus, averaging $M120 annually between 1943 and 1947.[22] At the same time, money of foreign origin increased fifteen-fold between 1939 and 1947, constituting over 80% of the total money supply in 1947 against 40% in 1939. Most of this, of course, was dollars. Government revenues were also rising steadily from taxation. Food prices had risen substantially to well over double their 1939 level, but this inflation was less than it would have been had it not been for the wartime import shortages and for the Cuban habit of keeping savings in idle balances; money supply in fact rose by 500% while the cost of living rose 145%. Between 1939 and 1947 the dollar gold and silver holdings of the Cuban treasury rose from $M25 to $M402; Cuban banks' holdings abroad rose to $M200 (from $M6) and private dollar holdings mounted probably to a little more (from $M14).[23]

Grau's government recklessly dissipated these advantages, however, although it always remained in credit. Much revenue went on unfinished construction projects. Much also took the form of transferred payments to political protégés. Despite its immense revenue the government nevertheless shortly embarked on the most daring and contemptible of its frauds – the theft of the reserve of non-governmental pension and social security funds lodged with the Treasury. This scandal was not immediately appreciated. The facts were, however, that on 30 June

[21] According to Chibás, the murderers were three members of the ARG, González Cartas, Antonio de Cárdenas ('Cuchiféo') and Luis Salazar ('Guichi').

[22] World Bank, 531-2.

[23] Ibid., 534.

1945 these sums amounted to $M8. Between then and 30 June 1950, another $M42 was deposited in the Cuban treasury, making $M50. Most of this, perhaps $M46·5, derived from the Sugar Workers' Union. But after a report on 30 June 1950, it transpired that the available resources of the Treasury amounted to $M40, against which there was already an outstanding short-term debt of $M134. The World Bank put it politely: 'It is evident that the Cuban government levied a forced loan on non-governmental pension funds lodged with them, without formal acknowledgment of the debt, and without paying interest.'[24]

Grau's political conduct must be judged against these acts of spoliage. In November 1945 he intervened in a major wage dispute, and actually seized the Havana Electric Railway Company, making use of wartime powers assumed by Batista which had never been rescinded, so as to enforce high increases which the company said they could not afford.[25] In December a beginning was made of the Auténticos' plan for pensions for all professions, beginning with a scheme for dentists.

In December 1945 that increasingly *bourgeois* and formalistic group, the Cuban Communist party, joined the government coalition, lending Grau support in the Chamber on all normal occasions, and, though no Communist actually joined the cabinet (as under Batista), the poet Marinello became vice-president of the Senate. In that body, since the Auténticos and Republicans had only twenty-four seats and the opposition twenty-seven, three Communist senators (Marinello himself, César Vilar and García Agüero) held the balance of power.[26] As part of this arrangement the Communists backed the Auténtico candidate for the presidency of the Senate. These cynical understandings caused bitterness: the outgoing president of the Senate, Eduardo Suárez Rivas, recalled how at the 4 July celebrations in 1944, just after the elections:

> The Cuban people had paraded along the Martí Paseo in honour of the people of America. Forming part of the file, the P.S.P.[27] came angrily marching past, with their fists clenched, shouting, 'Unity, unity, unity!' Someone said to Grau, 'President, see how angry they are!' And Grau said, with that special psychological air of his, 'Don't worry, my friend, tomorrow they will open their fists.'[28]

[24] *Ibid.*, 486–7.
[25] Phillips, 238.
[26] There were nine Communists in the House of Representatives.
[27] i.e. Communists.
[28] E. Suárez Rivas, *Un Pueblo Crucificado* (1964), 18. In Chile too there remained strong Popular Front representation, Contreras being appointed to the Chilean cabinet. Contreras was actually under fire at this moment in the Communist movement for, though he attended the San Francisco conference on the U.N. as member of the Chilean delegation, he was thought not to have supported the U.S.S.R. enough – e.g. by opposing Argentinian membership.

This prophecy was now fulfilled.

Suárez Rivas also complained that those who had criticized a recent rice barter with Ecuador and a candle-grease agreement with Argentina had suffered reprisals. 'Many people who had voted for the motion expressing lack of confidence in that Minister [Inocente Alvarez] have been answered with the dismissal of their friends in the Foreign Office or in other government departments.'[29]

1946 was the first full post-war year for the sugar industry, and there was naturally speculation about the attitude of the U.S., who of course would remain the dominating customer in the sugar market. Prices were generally high: producers could expect to get 6 cents per pound from England or Mexico, for instance. In the event, a two-year agreement was reached with the U.S. whereby the latter would purchase the whole harvest for two years at 3·675 cents, that is, the same as during the war, with a slightly higher price in the third and fourth quarters of the year in proportion to any rise in the price of goods imported by Cuba from the U.S. The U.S. also agreed to buy at least 115 million gallons of blackstrap molasses in 1946 and 165 million in 1947, with 40 million gallons of alcohol over the two years – a transaction, that is, involving $M1,000.[30] A little later Earl Wilson, director of sugar in the Commodity Credit Corporation of the U.S., made clear that the old 1937 quotas would not be reimposed[31] and the Senate in Cuba recommended the revision of the 1934 Reciprocity Treaty.[32]

The alliance between Auténticos and Communists lasted the winter of 1945-6 and past the XIth National Congress of the CTC in February, despite a protest from the Education Association of Cuba denouncing Communist control of teachers' associations. But early in 1946 a group of CTC Auténticos, including Eusebio Mujal, Juan Arévalo (the Maritime Union leader with a highly chequered past), and Francisco Aguirre (leader of the Waiters' and Restaurant Workers' Union) met in Miami; there or soon afterwards they took a decision to work consistently towards the exclusion of the Communists in the union – whether or no they were 'suborned by American spies', as was later argued by Blas Roca.[33] Even so, the political leaders of both parties remained in alliance throughout the year, the Communists still backing Grau in the congressional elections in the summer. As a result, Grau won for the first time a majority of seats in Congress, as did his candidate for the

[29] *Ibid.*
[30] See *El Mundo*, 1 January 1946. Phillips, 236, comments.
[31] *El Mundo*, 6 January 1946. Earl Wilson (born 1891) had been in the sugar business since 1920, and had been vice-president of the National Sugar Refining Co. Later as president of the Californian and Hawaiian Sugar Corporation (1946-51), he played an important part in directing U.S. sugar supply away from Cuba.
[32] *El Mundo*, 11 January 1946.
[33] *Fundamentos*, May 1947, 41 ff. Anything is possible.

supremely important mayoralty of Havana – Manuel Fernández Supervielle, previously Secretary of Finance.

In most respects 1946, the midway year of Grau's term, signified the moment of truth for many ordinary backers of the Auténticos – not the party chiefs but the rank and file of unidentified followers, who, hopeful till now, were increasingly disillusioned. One sign was that a substantial black market had survived the war, and whenever the government fixed the price for an article, that article would disappear from the shops to be found on the black market only at a high price.

There was also much criticism of a decree that a substantial portion of cargo arriving in Cuba should be unloaded on the dock before going on to the sea train, which ran up to the wharfs; this created unnecessary jobs by 'featherbedding' the maritime workers, causing delays; the government seemed to have surrendered completely to the maritime workers. The management of the sea train answered that the new system could not work, and accordingly the government first suspended the regulations for six months and then provided for a subsidy to be paid to the port workers.[34] The port of Havana, however, was a perpetual problem for all governments.

The 1946 sugar crop of just under four million tons was back at pre-depression figures. The continuing world shortages gave a sale exceeding \$M400 and it was only in the autumn that the economic policy of the government – a failure to stop the black market, breakdown of the public works schemes, beef shortages (due to reluctance of cattlemen to sell at the low government prices) – caused a major crisis. In October six of the 'Big Nine' revolutionary organizations, including Acción Revolucionaria Guiteras, withheld backing for Grau, yet, with its new legislative majority, the government was able to maintain itself without difficulty. But meantime the Auténtico movement was beginning to split up, thanks to the rhetorical and incendiary behaviour of Eduardo Chibás.

Chibás, now forty, was the son of a rich, public-spirited religious and well-connected family originally from Guantánamo. His grandmother was an Agramonte.[35] His father, Eduardo Chibás, Sr, had prospered having been part owner of the *Central Oriente*, director of tramways and electricity in Santiago and proprietor of a *cafetal* at Yateras. Educated at the Colegio de Dolores in Santiago and at Belén, the two most famous schools of Cuba, he had travelled to Europe and to the U.S. and from his youth had enjoyed all the advantages of privilege, such as membership of the Havana Yacht Club; nevertheless from the age of

[34] World Bank, 393.
[35] Thus Chibás's great-uncle Eduardo had been Secretary of Foreign Relations to Céspedes in the first war of independence, and Chibás learned of the heroic deeds of the Agramontes then ('*Todos los Agramontes murieron en la guerra*') from his grandmother.

twenty he had been associated with radical politics and counted himself a revolutionary, being in his twentieth year a leading member (treasurer) of the Directorio Estudiantil opposed to Machado. As with most of his generation the experience of fighting as a revolutionary conspirator, almost full time between 1927 and 1933, was unforgettable; Chibás himself was in exile some of this time, in prison from January 1931 (an opponent however of the terrorism of the ABC[36]), and in prison again with his father and brother; he had been a prominent student leader and frequent orator during the extraordinary debates which had led to the formation of the government of Dr Grau San Martín, whom indeed he had nominated for the presidency. In the numerous public speeches which he made during Grau's first government he had persistently explained that the fight against Machado had not been simply a revolt but 'a revolution which seeks a change in the economic structure of the regime . . . to destroy the great foreign monopolies, to eliminate their indigenous servitors, and to reunite with the people the properties robbed from them by political hacks'.[37] His oratory was always demagogic, inspiring emotions and creating desires which he could not fully satisfy. After the end of the exhausting and distressing Grau administration Chibás took the lead of the democratic wing of the ex-students of the struggle against Machado, and from the start was a prominent opponent of the Communists – whose Cuban leadership however he contrasted with that offered by Lenin and the Bolsheviks, and whom he seemed in some speeches at least theoretically to defend.[38] His language was always laced with Marxism even if he was not at all a determinist. As leader of the democratic Left he took a major part in the strike of February and March 1935, and was accordingly arrested and imprisoned for six months. On coming out in September 1935 he and his friends (who had set themselves up in yet another secret political organization called Izquierda Revolucionaria) made a tactical pact with the remains of Guiteras's Joven Cuba and with Grau's Auténticos, though he condemned the political gangsterism of the first. He always spoke, in print or in speeches, of 'the Cuban revolution', as if it was a continuing process; expelled from Izquierda Revolucionaria for advocating unification with Grau, he became known in the late 1930s and 1940s as an uncontrollable firebrand, fighting several duels, a slight embarrassment as well as of great assistance to Dr Grau San Martín, whose main disciple he became in the elections of 1939 and 1940, as well as in 1944.

[36] See conversation in Conte Agüero, *Eduardo Chibás*, 156-7.
[37] Qu. *ibid.*, 193.
[38] See speech commemorating Gabriel Barceló, a Communist friend who was expelled from the party before his death in January 1934 (*ibid.*, 211-12); '*lidercillos tropicales*' were his words for the Communists in Ala Izquierda Estudiantil.

Chibás did not enter Grau's administration but he remained for two years its most eloquent advocate. However, he always had around him a group of friends of his own, such as Luis Orlando Rodríguez, the youth leader, his secretaries, Consuelo Murillo or Conchita Fernández, Luis Conte Agüero, a journalist, or Manuel Bisbé, a scholarly politician of his own party,[39] a *camarilla* devoted and admiring, ready to act as Chibás's seconds in a duel, or to shield him from enemies. From 1945 meantime Chibás was building up a strong national following by his broadcast addresses, being one of the first politicians in the world to make use of this instrument. On this, he courageously attacked corruption and *gangsterismo*, not fearing to make personal accusations of murder where he knew the names of those guilty. On the other hand, it was becoming evident that despite his great gifts, his strong mesmeric wireless personality, the streak of irrationality in him was growing stronger with age: he would often fast, he would invite women to lunch with him and appear at five o'clock, he would remain in the bath under water for long periods, his telephoning of friends was frenetic, his speeches had more and more the hysteria of madness as much as of genius. He became engaged in persistent personal scandals and crises: the president of the Senate charged him with setting the multitude against the legislature; he personally attacked Blas Roca with his fists and there were often violent incidents at his meetings; yet all the time he spoke of the need for continuing the 'Cuban revolution', for public beaches for the people and ending corruption in government. His national name and his own evident freedom from corruption, made him an obvious possible successor to Grau as president in 1948, but he was opposed by the regular Auténtico politicians, and slowly but surely this led to a split in the Auténtico movement: the regular Auténticos feared and distrusted Chibás as a megalomaniac, while Chibás's own friends saw in him a new saviour of the nation. The drive to form a separate party became stronger when, despite promises to the contrary, Grau seemed to be trying to have himself re-elected: until this time Chibás had often attacked Grau's ministers but not Grau himself. In January 1947 Chibás wrote to Grau that if the latter disavowed his corrupt ministers such as César Casas, Minister of Commerce, and Inocente Alvarez, Secretary of State, he would continue to support him but otherwise he could not do so and, after further open polemic, Chibás challenged Alvarez to a duel (his sixth), but Alvarez called off the challenge at the last minute. All the spring of 1947, Chibás and his followers debated the desirability of breaking with the government – the Auténticos of Oriente province, the youth movement and the women's section of the Auténticos being the keenest for a breach, the

[39] Others included Orlando Castro, Leonardo Fernández Sánchez and Arturo Gil.

issue turning from re-electionism to the black market and general corruption.

Chibás could not be regarded as speaking with any personal axe to grind. Nor did his money, deriving from his engineer father, have any dishonest genealogy, and this gave him a firm moral position from which to launch his famous slogan *vergüenza contra dinero* 'Honour against Money'. However, he was also ugly, being very short-sighted and with a squint, so that it was never possible to know in which direction he was looking. These physical characteristics seem to have led him to suppose people were laughing at him – which indeed they often did. It was also difficult to avoid feeling that he was in some way in love with himself. He was undoubtedly a showman of neurotic persistence. He was perhaps influenced by Perón, though his political philosophy concentrated upon the single idea of uprooting corruption. Otherwise, he voiced strong, vague but familiar nationalistic desires, demanding a Cuba 'free from the economic imperialism of Wall Street and from the political imperialism of Rome, Berlin or Moscow'. He had now had a long time in politics. 'One of the first into Columbia in September 4 1933', Chibás had always firmly opposed the Communists. But it is possible that if Grau had made him his heir to the Auténtico leadership in place of Prío he would have behaved differently. Certainly he spoke enough on Grau's behalf in the early 1940s to earn the nickname 'Grau's Goebbels' and he did much to sustain the national desire for revolution, the cult of which still dominated the youth of the country. On the other hand he was at heart a constitutionalist.

Although the Communists also attacked the black market, they had still been able as late as November 1946 to praise Grau's government as 'oriented in a democratic progressive way for the people's benefit'.[40] But during the spring of 1947 the cold war was casting shadows over Cuban politics and therefore over the Communist–Auténtico alliance. The Auténticos had successfully established themselves as the dominant force among the sugar workers, with Emilio Surí Castillo at their head, and among the port workers, led by Gilberto Goliat. Several prominent Communist union leaders, such as León Rentería and Vicente Rubiera, joined the Auténticos. A critical point in this rivalry came when, at a national sugar workers' conference, an Auténtico trade unionist, Félix Palau, was shot.[41] In March the Communists presented a list of demands to Grau who, according to them, agreed to check inflation and corruption but refused to break diplomatic relations with Spain.[42] In April Blas Roca was still saying the party

[40] *Fundamentos*, December 1946.
[41] Mujal memorandum, 9.
[42] *Fundamentos*, March 1947, 217 ff.

should support Grau, despite the 'strain',[43] but by this time Grau had stated his policy definitively, calling the Auténticos to oppose the election of Lázaro Peña as secretary-general of the CTC at its impending fifth Congress.[44]

The Congress was therefore delayed. Just before it started, leaders of both factions became involved in gunfights. The Auténtico leaders seem to have called in a number of gunmen from the UIR and MSR. One more Auténtico leader was killed while leaving the Credentials Committee the night before the beginning of the Congress. Carlos Prío, then the most favoured of Grau's ministers, who on 30 April had taken over as Minister of Labour, indefinitely postponed the Congress, proposing instead a Credentials Committee which would be composed of an equal number of representatives from the Auténticos, Communists and the government. The Communists charged the government with trying to break the Cuban labour movement. The Auténticos were in fact still negotiating to secure the election as Peña's successor of Angel Cofiño, a socialist and therefore nominally independent, though an ex-Communist who had stood unsuccessfully as a Communist candidate for the Chamber in the early 1940s and therefore specially unacceptable to the Communist party.

Prío's manœuvres were very successful. First he suggested that the Credentials Committee should decide a time for the CTC meeting. The Auténticos agreed, though not the Communists, who went ahead and held what turned out to be a rump general meeting of the union, only a few Auténticos attending. Peña was elected secretary-general, and there was in fact a strong Communist majority on the new Executive Committee.[45] Mujal and the Auténticos held their meeting in mid-summer and duly elected Cofiño as secretary-general, with no Communists on any committee. Thus Cuba now had two general Labour unions, with most of the important Labour federations undecided as to which finally to join.

Grau's government waited uneasily for the outcome, its prestige low, Chibás having embarked on a violent campaign against the corruption of Prío's brother, Francisco, now a senator, but a man with an ambiguous record in his career in the municipal government under Machado. On 4 May the new mayor of Havana, Fernández Supervielle, ex-president of the Inter-American Bar Association, killed himself due to

[43] *Ibid.*, April 1947.

[44] Mujal memorandum, 9. Those who believe that this policy must have been decided with the connivance of the U.S. government receive some backing from the recollection that it was of course in March 1947 that President Truman called for U.S. military aid to Greece and Turkey. Cuban events also, as so often at this time, were reflected in Chile, where in mid-April the Liberals forced the Communists out of President González's cabinet – despite the fact that González probably owed his presidency to Communist backing.

[45] Alexander, 287.

the 'insurmountable difficulties' which he had encountered in his task of administering the capital – above all in providing an ample water supply: at every turn he had been blocked by graft. The atmosphere of tension was considerable, due to the increased opposition to the government of its old friends, the revolutionary-gangster groups. Thus 8 May, the day of Guiteras's death in 1935, was celebrated in 1947 with extraordinary panache by the Acción Revolucionaria Guiteras (ARG); not only the leader, González Cartas (*El Extraño*), spoke but also Marco Antonio Hirigoyen, the flamboyant leader of the bus drivers' union;[46] also present were Alfonso Bernal del Riesgo, professor of psychology at Havana University, a founder member, as it happened, of the Cuban Communist party, and Colonel Fabio Ruiz, the police chief, who appeared on the platform in full uniform. Present too, as invited guests, were members of the MSR, among them Masferrer, Goldenberg, and Pérez Santisteban. The MSR, especially its police friend Salabarría, were contemplating some *coup* or capture of power, although they were also evidently concerned to partake of the profits to be got from a recent rice scandal.[47]

A week later on 15 May, by long prearranged agreement, Chibás and his friends took the critical step of forming publicly his breakaway party – the Cuban People's Party[48] or Ortodoxos – implying they were repositories of the real revolutionary tradition in place of the Auténticos.

The next stage in the fight against the Communists came at the height of summer. The government had on 17 July sent troops to the Havana docks when the Communist stevedores struck. On 29 July Prío (after being wounded twice in a duel two weeks before with Chibás) took over the CTC headquarters by force from Lázaro Peña and handed the building over, palace as it was, to the Auténtico unionists. With this high-handed act, the government gained control of the union organization of Cuba.

This certainly strengthened the government. It was in search of further popularity still that the new education minister, José Manuel Alemán, an intimate friend of Grau's, sponsored a filibustering expedition against the dictatorship of Trujillo in the Dominican Republic. Many Dominican exiles had been living in Cuba, among them Juan Bosch, the writer who would eventually lead the Partido Revolucionario

[46] An ex-Communist having joined the party youth when a child.

[47] Evidence of Goldenberg.

[48] Partido del Pueblo Cubano (PPC). Chibás was backed from the beginning by other members of the anti-Machado generation, such as Emilio Ochoa, Manuel Bisbé, Luis Orlando Rodríguez, Rafael García Bárcena, Roberto Agramonte, Herminio Portell Vilá, Jorge Mañach and Luis Conte Agüero – the first secretary to the party – with many of the old Auténtico youth and most of its Oriente chapter. See Conte Agüero, *Eduardo Chibás*, 508, for list of founders.

Dominicano to its short-lived and bitter victory in 1962; Bosch indeed had worked with Prío. Havana was the biggest centre of Dominican exiles.[49] There was general sympathy between the Auténticos and the Dominican exiles, and the former, with their friendship with the gangster revolutionaries, were able to interest the latter in a scheme to land about 1,200 armed young men on the coast of Trujillo's republic as an advance guard of a liberating army. The leading spirits of this expedition were, on the Dominican side, Juan Bosch and Juan Rodríguez,[50] and among Cubans Manolo Castro and Rolando Masferrer of MSR and Eufemio Fernández of the ARG as well as one man attached to UIR.[51] The arms were obtained from Argentina and concealed in school buildings which were then closed for the holidays, and the men gathered at the *finca* San Ramón, in Oriente province, and afterwards moved to Cayo Confites, a wild island off the coast of Camagüey. (They had been transferred there by order of the Cuban chief of staff, Pérez Dámera, who had desired not to have so many Cubans together, armed on the mainland.)

This expedition was still gathered at Cayo Confites waiting to depart when one of the most famous gangster battles occurred. The leader of the MSR, Mario Salabarría, chief of the secret police, went to Orfila, a neighbourhood of Marianao, to attempt to force the resignation of Emilio Tró, the police chief of that suburban city and acknowledged chief of MSR's rival, UIR, who had sometime before been responsible for the death of Captain Avila, a noted gang leader. Tró refused to resign and there followed a regular battle in which ultimately Tró and four others, including a woman, were killed. This pointless bloodshed caused a scandal even in the blasé Cuban society, hardly reassured by the thirty-year gaol sentence imposed on Salabarría, or by the realization that one of the most important gangster leaders was now removed from the scene.

The 'events at Orfila' gave General Pérez Dámera the excuse to insist to Grau that the expedition of Cayo Confites be disbanded, as a danger to the state. In addition Trujillo had heard of the expedition and complained to President Truman through the Organization of American States: and Truman had ordered his chief of staff, General Eisenhower, to summon General Pérez Dámera and demand the cessation of the expedition. Juan Rodríguez was summoned to Havana but in his absence the rest of the expedition set off under the command of Juan Bosch. However, contrary to the latter's orders, the ships sailed westward towards Havana – suggesting indeed to the Dominicans that the

---

[49] See Galíndez, *La Era de Trujillo*, 440.
[50] These two composed the Junta Militar. Other members of the Dominican Junta were Leovigildo Cuello, Angel Morales and Juan Isidro Jiménez-Guillón.
[51] This was Fidel Castro. See below, p. 812.

expedition was primarily concerned with Cuban politics – where it was intercepted by a frigate off Cayo Winche, itself off Caibarien. The expedition was then transported back eastwards to Antilla, in the Bay of Nipe, and disbanded, some escaping, others being transported to Havana.[52]

Prío took the opportunity of the general disarray to declare that thereafter the only CTC which he as Minister of Labour recognized was the Auténtico one. In the autumn most of the larger unions came over to the anti-Communist side, Surí Castillo bringing over the sugar workers, though leaving an intransigent minority behind under Jesús Menéndez. The Maritime Federation and even the tobacco workers' federation, of which Lázaro Peña had been the leader, also came over to the Auténticos. This meant that the Communists moved finally into opposition, though as late as October 1947 the political leadership at least was prepared to grant that Grau had 'not surrendered completely to imperialism and reaction' and that they would support Grau's 'progressive measures'.[53] But by November matters had gone further and the Communists claimed they were being 'cruelly persecuted', just at the moment when it was necessary for them to register for the 1948 elections;[54] in the circumstances they pronounced themselves satisfied with the slender increase in their registration of from 152,000 to 158,000 – though they were at this stage well behind all the other parties, including even Chibás's new Ortodoxos.[55]

Grau had now to look for new allies both immediately and for the general elections of 1948, in which as yet it was not known who would be the Auténtico candidate: he was clearly aiming at re-election in the beginning, and, to secure this, formed a brief alliance with his colleague Alemán and his nephew Grau Alsiña. This grouping failed when it became evident that even the Auténticos were disillusioned with Grau, and Grau began to prepare his eminently successful Minister of Labour, Prío, the most successful of the generation of students of 1933, as dauphin.

The Communists were in the same position. On 2 March 1948 they wrote to the president of the Senate, Miguel Suárez Fernández, one of Chibás's friends, offering to withdraw Marinello and Lázaro Peña, their

[52] From a memorandum by Juan Bosch. See also articles in *El Tiempo* (New York), 24 and 28 August 1966, by Colonel Esteban Ventura and Rolando Masferrer. The future of the participants in this expedition constitutes alone a history of Cuba: some, like Rolando Masferrer, backed Batista's second dictatorship; some, headed by Fidel Castro, directed the revolution of 1959 (apart from Castro, admittedly, the revolutionaries were all relatively unimportant); some were killed in a famous assassination attempt on Batista in 1957; and some were shot by Castro as counter-revolutionaries in the 1960s.

[53] *Fundamentos*, October 1947.

[54] *Ibid.*, November 1947.

[55] See Blasier, 127.

presidential and vice-presidential candidates, in favour of the Ortodoxos, if the Ortodoxos would 'carry out a third front programme', declaring that their support of the Ortodoxos would not be contingent on government or senatorial jobs. Suárez Fernández politely refused after consultation with Chibás, so disappointing the Communists.[56] (According to one source, Suárez himself had tried to use the action group UIR to intimidate delegates to the 1947 Auténtico convention and secure the nomination for himself.[57]) A month later, in early May, the Minister of Communications took over the Communist radio station 1010 (Mil Diez) by force, on the bogus grounds that it had deviated from its wavelength.[58] In early June the party tried to make an arrangement with the democratic and liberal parties, on the basis that all should 'labour for the unity of all the civil and electoral forces opposed to the government'.[59] But again they failed. The Communists went into the 1948 presidential election isolated for the first time in ten years.

This electoral campaign, the eighth since 1902, and, as it has turned out, the last that Cuba has yet experienced, was fought with great energy and some violence between Prío for the Auténticos, Eduardo Chibás and Ricardo Núñez Portuondo, representative of the old Liberal, Democratic and Republican parties, and representative also of Batista's interests. Batista himself had been urged by several friends to stand – ultimately indeed he entered his name for a senatorship for Las Villas. The campaign was marked by much gangsterism, Prío being accompanied as bodyguard by one of the leaders of Acción Revolucionaria Guiteras, Dr Eufemio Fernández, who was later given Salabarría's old job of chief of the secret police. It was obvious that Chibás's Ortodoxos would trail some way behind and that Marinello, the Communist candidate, would be last: in the event Prío won, on a minority vote however: he gained 900,000 votes, Núñez Portuondo 600,000, Chibás 325,000 and Marinello 142,000. The Communists lost their three seats in the Senate, retaining nine deputies. Their presidential poll nevertheless was 20% more than it had been in 1944. Batista was elected a senator and so returned from Florida, where he had been living since 1944.

Grau's rule, therefore, drew to an end after four years of deception and disappointment. Trampling on the expectations of the many people who placed faith in his promises, he did a great disservice to the cause of democratic reform, not only in Cuba but in the whole western hemisphere. His period of power is appropriately commemorated by the

[56] *Fundamentos*, January–March 1948, 104–6.
[57] Fernando Freyre evidence.
[58] *Gaceta Oficial*, 6 May 1948.
[59] *Hoy*, 20 June 1948.

career of his old friend José Manuel Alemán, in 1944 a minor official at the Ministry of Education, who arrived in Miami in 1948 after two years as minister with $M20 in notes in his suitcase,[60] not to speak of thousands of *caballerías* of land, sugar mills, air companies and a chain of houses left behind.

[60] Evidence of Arthur Gardner, later ambassador to Cuba, to whom fell the task of deciding what should be done: he was then working as a dollar-a-year man in the Treasury.

CHAPTER LXIV

Prío, 'el Presidente de la Cordialidad'

Carlos Prío had been Grau's colleague and backer in the government of 1933. He had also, as a graduate student in his late twenties, been a leader of the student 'generation of 1930' in the struggle against Machado. He was attractive, still young at forty-five, handsome, *simpático*, very well-meaning.[1] But many years had passed since those heroic days when he stood at the deathbed of Rafael Trejo, victim of Machado's police. Already he was known to be extraordinarily attracted by the idea of money. This he would be likely to admit: at the time of Prío's election, Felipe Pazos, a contemporary in the university, the outstanding Cuban economist of his generation, then working in the fledgling International Monetary Fund, went to see him for a long discussion about the economy.[2] Pazos did not raise the question of corruption, since he knew Prío's weaknesses. But at the end, with one of those charming smiles that the Cubans later learned to distrust, Prío told Pazos, 'Believe me, I am going to create the most honest government that it is possible for a *criollo* to do.'[3]

Prío had, it is true, a certain toughness in his character, as suggested by his skilful manipulation of the Communists from their position of power in the union. He was a genuine Democrat who did his best for social democratic movements in countries nearby, giving asylum to their exiles. Throughout the time he was in power he supported, morally and with money, an action group, La Legión del Caribe, a skeleton army of armed democrats who, it was hoped, would provide the *élite* firepower needed to topple tyrants: it is clear that they were in a position to help Figueres in Costa Rica and to threaten Trujillo in the Dominican Republic. Prío, in short, loved liberty, though it was unfortunately difficult for him to distinguish between liberty and licence. His tastes were if anything more luxurious than Grau's; Grau accumulated money without apparent pleasure, perhaps chiefly to satisfy or to entertain his female relations: a Puritan air of hypocrisy dominated his relentless pursuit of other people's money. Prío, on the contrary, enjoyed whatever

---

[1] Carlos Prío Socarrás (b. 1903), born Bahía Honda, Pinar del Río; member of Constitutent Assembly, 1939, Senator, 1940–8; Prime Minister, 1945; Minister of Labour, 1947–8.

[2] Felipe Pazos, president, Cuban National Bank, 1950–2, and 1959; in exile, 1930–3, 1952–9, and since 1960.

[3] Evidence of Felipe Pazos.

he laid his hands on. His supreme delight was his farm La Chata, outside Havana, where throughout his reign favoured guests would drink *daiquirís* by the side of the great swimming-pool into which an artificial waterfall fell from a tall hill nearby. The farm had a barber's shop of its own, where Prío and his friends could lie in adjacent chairs and discuss politics, or, better, appointments, barely disturbed by the discreet interruptions of razor, manicurist or masseuse.[4] It was difficult to dislike Prío, and difficult to take him quite seriously. In 1956 he wrote to an old friend, Teresa Casuso, then emerging as a playwright in Mexico, and explained, 'I envy you, because my lifelong dream was to be an actor and if my dull wits had not brought me to the presidency, that is what I would have been.'[5] Further, he entered on his period of power 'saturated with *compromisos*' to action groups to whom he always thereafter had to pay subventions.[6] His 'law against *gangsterismo*' merely sent to prison a few innocent men while Prío entered into excellent relations with their leaders.

Grau and Prío had one thing in common, relations – though whereas Grau had cousins and in-laws, Prío had brothers. 'Paco' (Francisco) Prío and Antonio Prío were both interested in the good life as well, though Antonio's passion was to become mayor of Havana and Paco's was less politically orientated: he was primarily concerned to amass a fortune out of the import of a large variety of drugs – a task lightened by the presence as chief of police of the ARG chieftain, Eufemio Fernández, his brother Carlos's old friend.

Thus merrily Prío entered his heritage on 10 October 1948, careful, like his predecessor, to ensure that the student leaders all got good jobs to keep them at least happy.

All this is not to deny that Prío had some idea of putting into effect the good intentions which he had paraded before the Cuban people and electorate. He appointed Aureliano Sánchez Arango as Minister of Education, an honest and intelligent man who announced himself determined to clean up the scandal left behind by Alemán. Prío pressed forward the long discussed idea of a Central Bank, announcing this within two months of taking office and securing its establishment in early 1950: his student contemporary, Felipe Pazos, returned from the IMF to take over as its first director. Then too there was a new Land Law, thereby further putting into effect the 1940 constitution; owners of over fifty acres of good land which were not being cultivated were obliged to let it to farmers or companies or collective groups. The sugar boom continued: 1948 had seen the end of the wartime controls. Even so,

---

[4] See pictures and description of La Chata in *Bohemia*, 6 April 1953.
[5] Casuso, 90.
[6] See the article by Fidel Castro, *Alerta*, 4 March 1952.

the U.S. Commodity Credit Corporation continued to make purchases: chiefly for the areas occupied by U.S. troops in Europe and Asia. Towards the end of the year sugar prices dropped towards 4 cents a pound but prosperity continued all through 1949. Only in 1950 did doubts about the future begin to be raised. The critical political event, however, was that Prío broke with ex-President Grau, attempting to force him to face the consequences of his four years' thieving.

This odd struggle began on 15 January 1949 when Grau demanded, with an air of moral superiority, that Prío should 'clear up the responsibilities' of a $M84 government deficit. Within a month, however, Grau himself was forced to appear before the courts, accused by the government of having misappropriated $M174. Grau naturally denied these charges. Chibás and the Ortodoxos at this entered the lists by accusing Prío's government of being also involved and by alleging that the national lottery was still a scandal. Next month, Chibás accused the Supreme Court of accepting $300,000 in bribes from the Cuban Electric Company in return for reaching decisions favourable to them. Chibás was immediately cited for contempt. At the same time one of his associates, Pelayo Cuervo, was fined $150 for accusing Grau of having stolen $M175. The fat now was in the fire, with the Ortodoxos mounting a major attack on the somewhat diseased institutions of the regime itself as well as on the administrations of Grau and Prío.

Despite the 'law against *gangsterismo*', there had been no pause in the political gang-warfare. Masferrer, now a senator for the Auténticos, rode round Cuba in his Cadillac like a pirate king, surrounded by bodyguards. Deaths were increasingly frequent, in the union movement and among the students, though Prío's Minister of Education, Sánchez Arango, had stopped the subsidies paid by his predecessor to the gangster representatives in the university. 1948 had seen the murder among others by the UIR of first, Manolo Castro, Grau's Secretary of State for sports and MSR's blue-eyed boy, one of those implicated being Gustavo Ortiz Faes, a student aged twenty, an adopted son of Grau;[7] second, two prominent Communists, Jesús Menéndez, the Negro sugar workers' leader, by an army captain, Casillas, near a sugar plantation; and Aracelio Iglesias Díaz, the secretary of the Communist Maritime Workers' Union, by an old rival for that appointment – perhaps as a result of a private feud. In early 1949, the vice-president of the student union, Justo Fuentes, a member of the UIR, was murdered by the gang led by *el Colorado*, Orlando León Lemus, in revenge for the

---

[7] See below, p. 813. The career of this individual illuminates the history of the Caribbean. Pardoned through the influence of his adopted father, he was head of the political police (G2) in Matanzas under Fidel Castro and then became bodyguard to President Betancourt of Venezuela. (See *El Tiempo* (Caracas), 12 December 1963.)

762 · THE AGE OF DEMOCRACY 1934-52

death of Manolo Castro. His body lay in state in the Aula Magna as Manolo Castro's had done a year before.[8] The School of Agronomy in the university was revealed as a veritable arsenal. The university seemed in total decomposition.

The murder of Fuentes aroused a great deal of anger in Cuba, more particularly since the presumed murderer was observed to be in hiding in the house of Prío's brother, Senator 'Paco' Prío; the students themselves, politically active and politically organized as ever, voted to suspend attendance until the murderers were arrested. They even visited Prío, who promised action, and said that he would secure that those allegedly already in the U.S. were extradited. One rich landowner suggested a practical solution to the problem of gangsterism by offering to transport all the political gangsters to his plantation and then to supply them with ammunition so that all could shoot out their quarrels till only one survived.

In May Prío met with some members of the cabinet (the prime minister Varona, the Interior minister Ruben de León, and the Minister of Communications Carlos Maristany) and discussed the question. They proposed to found a special police force to fight gangsterism. This idea was vigorously attacked on grounds of civil liberties, as a return to the hated SIM of the past. The plan hung fire for a while. The political tension was kept up by the imprisonment for contempt of Eddy Chibás. (Chibás was saved by Gustavo Ortiz Faes from assassination in gaol by a group of *pistoleros* then also incarcerated.) Chibás was shortly afterwards freed by presidential pardon. Once out of gaol Chibás charged Senator José María Casanova, a leading sugar magnate, with conspiring his downfall and fought his eighth duel at the *finca* Plasencia, arguing in the Senate for the revision of the clause in the Constitution which disallowed any man with a prison record from running for president.

Prío attempted to divert attention from this public confusion by announcing, in the style of most Cuban presidents, a public works programme. A new aqueduct in Havana (such as poor Fernández Supervielle had promised) and a dredge of the harbour would be among the projects. Private capital seemed ready to lend the necessary cash. In September Oscar Gans, the Cuban ambassador in the U.S., announced that Cuba would within a week begin negotiating for a $M200 loan for public works. But this was not everywhere accepted. Chibás had already made invidious comparisons with Machado. Batista, back in Cuba as a senator, living in his farm the Kuquine, denounced the loan: he

<hr/>

[8] Roa, *Retorno a la Alborada*, 223. The actual assassins appear to have been Policarpo Soler, afterwards killed in St Domingo, and Evaristo Venero, of the university police, later killed by Castro in the Sierra Maestra, as a spy.

pointed out how many projects of Grau's were unfinished due to lack of funds. Was it not bad to incur a huge new U.S. debt? Batista, on the look-out for popularity, had backed the recent anti-U.S. Peace Congress in Mexico.

Chibás remained on the warpath. In an open letter to Prío, at the end of July, he asked:

> Tell me, Carlos Prío, how you can buy so many farms and build in them so many and various things while at the same time you say that there is no money and no material to build roads or carry out state public works, that there is nothing with which to pay the veterans of the War of Independence nor for the costs of schools . . . tell me why you suddenly put at liberty the famous international drug trafficker whom you arrested in the Hotel Nacional with a cargo of drugs for the head of the secret police?[9]

Nor was Prío free from the threat of actual military upheaval. In mid-August, he received news of contentiousness among the officers and, taking advantage of the absence of General Pérez Dámera, the chief of staff, at his *hacienda*, on 24 August the president and an escort arrived at military headquarters at dead of night and announced the succession of General Ruperto Cabrera, the adjutant-general, to Pérez Dámera's job. A number of intelligent and able young officers, such as Major Ramón Barquín, Lieutenants Orihuela and Borbonnet, and Captain Monteagudo Fleites, had in fact contemplated a *golpe de estado* against Prío and Pérez Dámera, but they desired to use Cabrera as their leader, and he had explained their antagonism to Pérez Dámera to the president. These officers, instead of being punished, were promoted.[10] For some weeks afterwards, Prío was seen to be acting quite firmly. He issued a decree declaring duels to be a crime. After the murder of yet another student Gustavo Adolfo Mejía, president of the Social Science faculty,[11] eleven students accused of gangsterism were sent to prison while a number of under-age gunmen were dispatched to reformatories. As for the gangs themselves, Prío arranged a so-called 'Pact of *grupos*' by which each action group undertook to cease activities in return for government posts and subsidies. Prío was believed to have distributed in consequence over 2,000 separate posts: the group of Guillermo Comellas received 60 posts; the Tribunal Ejecutor Revolucionario, 120; UIR, 120; ARG, 200; the MSR splinter group led by *'el Colorado'*, 400; Masferrer's MSR itself, 500; and the group led by

[9] Qu. Ernesto de la Fé, *Bohemia*, 12 October 1952.
[10] See F. Batista y Zaldívar, *Cuba Betrayed* (1962), 233–4; Phillips, 252; Barrera Pérez, *Bohemia Libre*, 19 July 1961.
[11] This did not pass without protest in the university. The Dean of the Faculty of Social Sciences, Raúl Roa, resigned in despair.

Policarpo Soler received 600 posts – all these being sinecures in the ministries of Health, Labour, the Interior, and Public Works.[12]

After continued attacks throughout the winter, Prío slightly reformed his cabinet, keeping Varona as premier.[13] The House of Representatives passed Prío's scheme for a public works loan; Batista, the Communists and Chibás, in an unlikely alliance, staged a demonstration of protest. Prío's chief preoccupation now was the fate of his brother Antonio in the elections for the mayoralty of Havana in June, for his enemies, who now included Grau as well as Batista, were backing Nicolás Castellanos, a man without much promise of integrity. Prío sought to do what he could to suck some prestige for himself out of the meeting in May 1950 of the Inter-American Conference for Democracy and Freedom at Havana and out of the formal opening of the National Bank in April. There was also an unprecedented amount of bribery, kidnapping and other violence, but this could not prevent Castellanos from winning the election on 1 June: he gained 52 % of the votes against Antonio Prío's 37 % while Manuel Bisbé, the Ortodoxo candidate, got 11 %. The rest of the voting, however, gave the Auténticos a solid majority in the House of Representatives, with over one hundred mayoralties out of 126. Castellanos' victory could be considered by most standards as a freak due to the alliance, not repeated elsewhere in the country, between Batista, Grau and, at the last minute, the Communists.[14]

Prío's somewhat desperate attempt to place all blame for the country's ills on Grau and bring him to book was making little progress. Grau demanded a complete investigation to clear his name, and he promised to stay in Cuba to see that justice was done. But this hardly seemed so honest an undertaking when on 4 July the court in which his case was being heard was broken into by six masked men who, holding the court officers at gun point, stole thirty-five files of documents relating to the proceedings. No one was ever arrested for this and the files were never seen again. This naturally delayed the trial. It also delayed the general process of clearing Cuba from robbery and deception – in so far, that is, as the government wished to do such a thing. Even the Supreme Court's order at the end of July to Panchín Batista, the ex-president's brother, now governor of Havana province, to submit to investigation in respect of an alleged misappropriation of between $M50 and $M150

[12] See speech by Fidel Castro before Tribunal de Cuentas, March 1952, *Alerta*, 4 March 1952.

[13] New members of the cabinet were the ex-ambassador in Washington, Oscar Gans (who had been in Batista's cabinet in 1940), Evelio Rodríguez, Sergio Clark and José Morell Romero. Dihigo stayed as Foreign Minister. Gans was proving one of the Cuban politicians with most staying power since he had also served Machado and been in exile after 1933.

[14] See Phillips, 253; Batista, *Cuba Betrayed*, 226.

fell rather flat. The presumption was that Grau had prevented his trial by force: if that could happen without difficulty, and almost without protest, had public morality any chance whatever? The final insult to public morality seemed given by the gift, in the will of Grau's thieving education minister Alemán, of $M5 for the foundation of an infant hospital.[15]

Had Cuba been a normal country, the persistent ill-management of the state, so widely known, would have had serious economic consequences. It would have led in 1950 or 1951 to extraordinary revolutionary demands from those who naturally suffered most – the poor. But these governments of Grau and Prío continued against a background of rising prosperity. The price of sugar remained over 5 cents a pound and in 1950, when recovery of the sugar areas (such as the Philippines) devastated in the war seemed likely to depress prices, the Korean war broke out, once again causing a sharp rise. The U.S. continued to make purchases to assist European recovery. Hence Cuba was always able to exceed her minimum export quota to the U.S.

There were as always at such times in Cuba ostentatious signs of this new wealth. New cars filled the streets of Havana. Wages went up in proportion to the increase of sugar prices in early 1951, to 4·96 cents a pound. Korea indeed brought happiness to almost all the political parties and sugar men of Cuba. The Communists' violent attacks on the U.S. appeared to redound against them: members were thought to be leaving. Prío was delighted to take advantage of this situation: *Hoy* and *América Deportiva* (a sporting weekly edited by Joaquín Ordoqui) were suddenly suspended on 24 August 1950. The Communist daily radio broadcast over the station 1010 was banned and so was the Chinese Communist publication *Kwong Was*. One minister, the opportunistic mulatto journalist Ramón Vasconcelos, resigned from the cabinet in protest against an invasion of human rights. Police, however, went on to search local Communist headquarters. Tony Varona, the prime minister, accused the Communists of being 'the centre of Russian espionage in the U.S.A.', but in support of the charge could only display a number of envelopes bearing the letterhead 'Prensa Continental'. Rumours were rife that U.S. troops were searching Oriente for hidden radio transmitters, and the U.S. also provided that thereafter all Cubans had to have visas to enter the U.S.: an attempt to restrict the illegal entry of Cuban and other Communists who had previously found the Havana–Miami route an easy way of penetration. The Communist party remained a legal entity, but in November over 150 members were arrested, after a meeting with various Mexican Communists to discuss the Sheffield Peace Conference – including Lázaro

[15] Roa, *Retorno a la Alborada*, I, 229.

Peña, still shadow leader of the shadow Labour Federation, and Juan Marinello, still president of the party.

Prío was not without labour troubles, though his friends controlled the unions. In September 1950, the dock dispute entered a newly tense phase when the new Maritime Federation proved as awkward as the old over the question of the sea train.[16] Next month, there was an ineffective but menacing general strike by the CTC against the formation of an employers' union, the Confederación Patronal. The Havana Aliados Omnibus Company announced that it would strike if management were to abolish the seven-hour pay for six-hour work formula. Prío ended a strike in 1951 by railworkers and dockworkers by simply increasing their pay and adding the necessary balance from state funds. Political violence continued: in September, the Under-Secretary of the Treasury and secretary to the president of the Senate, Julio Paniagua, was shot dead by gunmen – and it seemed likely that this incident was involved with the quarrel between Paniagua and one of his superiors at the Treasury. The Senate president, Suárez Fernández, resigned in anger, but again nothing was done to detect the assassins. In early 1951 a bomb was found in the house of one of Chibás's closest followers, Roberto Agramonte. Chibás denounced the MSR and Masferrer on the radio, and Masferrer demanded that he should have equal right of reply. On 18 February Chibás attempted to prevent Masferrer reaching the radio station, and afterwards Masferrer challenged Chibás to settle their differences in a duel. For once, Chibás refused. At the same time ARG, MSR, UIR and other groups made almost daily attacks on Communist party offices up and down the country. A feeling of political hopelessness spread through Cuba, in no way assuaged by the continuing prosperity and by such technological turning-points – of special importance in Cuba, as it turned out – as the first television broadcast on 24 October 1950, inaugurated by Prío; with money around, a rush began to buy television sets, dealers buying large stocks on account, and restaurants, bars and shops beginning to install sets.[17]

It was still however the age of radio, and in 1950 to 1951, wireless was still giving a platform to Chibás, one of its most successful and practised orators.[18]

Every week on Sunday night, Chibás spoke. Crowds flocked to cafés or hotels to hear him. He spoke with extraordinary passion and energy, denouncing the unbridled corruption of the regime and the

[16] See World Bank, 393.

[17] By February 1951 when Prío opened the CMQ television station there were already 14,000 television sets in Cuba.

[18] There were in 1949, 575,000 radio sets in Cuba, already nearly one per family (*UN Statistical Yearbook* (1963), 684).

gangsterismo associated with it. During the early months of 1951 he appeared as a real demagogue, half preacher, half scourge, one of the most effective destructive orators in Latin American history; by his accusations, week after week, he effectively completed the discrediting of all surviving political institutions in Cuba, describing this, the last democratic government in Cuba, as 'a scandalous bacchanalia of crimes, robberies and mismanagement'. The symbol of his party was a broom. By 1950 *el Adalid*, the chief, was the most powerful voice of opposition in the land. It was impossible not to listen to him. The vagueness of his ultimate programme, his omission to mention any precise policies of economic or social control (save criticism of certain foreign companies such as the Cuban Electricity Company) meant that many people of differing long-term views could assemble behind him. Thus there were many on the right of the Ortodoxos, who, ex-Auténtico politicians like Ochoa who could not stomach Prío, thought that all that was needed in Cuba was to remove dishonesty from public life; while there were others on the left (such as Dr Eduardo Corona, Marta Frayde and Vicentina Atuña) who, distrusting a *laissez-faire* solution, were more serious social reformers looking forward to a vigorous reorganization of the whole of Cuban society; some were even prepared for collaboration to this effect with the Communist party – though Chibás was an inveterate anti-Communist – but since both Grau and Batista had also had their time of collaboration this seemed rather different than it might seem in other countries. Chibás's attacks on the government were balanced by a movement in the university, led by supporters of his with the Catholic students (Agrupación Católica Universitaria), the 'Pro-Dignidad Estudiantil' movement.[19] Chibás had a programme for agrarian reform, like most other Latin politicians: this, as usual was 'land for those who work it' and the distribution of '*latifundios*' to landless peasants.

All through early 1951, Chibás's attacks on the government and on Cuban political institutions rolled on, against the unedifying and unconvincing spectacle of the administration trying to bring ex-President Grau to book despite the disappearance of the essential evidence, and despite a certain *rapprochement* between Prío and Grau against the threat of the elections of 1952, which seemed to afford Chibás a strong chance of victory.

In mid-December 1950, Prío had captured Gregorio Simonovich, the king of the Caribbean drug smugglers, and in January the Minister

---

[19] Pro-Dignidad Estudiantil and the 'established' forces in the university clashed so violently on the critical election day, 10 December 1949, that the university was closed for a month and the authorities declared that there would be no FEU (students' union) in 1950. This ruined Ovares and the established group and they were succeeded in 1951 by a cleaner set. During these struggles, the Communists in the university backed Ovares against the dangerous alliance of Ortodoxos and Catholics.

of the Interior, Lomberto Díaz, opened an anti-vice drive in Havana. No one took such moves seriously. There was a resurgence of police violence and after one exchange a young Ortodoxo, Otero Ben, died. Batista meantime announced that he would himself stand for the presidency in 1952, and soon began to allege that people round Prío – particularly the police chief, Dr Eufemio Fernández – were planning a *coup d'état*. In February 1951, Batista embarked on an attempt at the unification of the older opposition parties, entering into a tactical alliance with the new mayor of Havana, Nicolás Castellanos. A month later Grau was finally indicted with ten of his ex-ministers (two existing congressmen among them) for the theft of $M40 – a smaller sum, it is true, than he had been accused of the previous year. The widow of the Secretary of Education, Alemán, was also charged.

This case for a time dominated political speculation. Grau's lawyers alleged that the judge, Federico Justiniani, was incompetent on the ground that the alleged crimes occurred during Grau's presidency: Grau thought that he ought to be tried by the Supreme Court. The judge was eventually changed, but his successor was intimidated and forced to withdraw. *His* successor, Judge Riera Medina, immediately issued a writ of attachment for Grau's $M2 house in 5th Avenue. But as all expected this was contested. The trial was constantly delayed on trivial charges. In the summer Grau challenged one of his principal Ortodoxo accusers, Pelayo Cuervo, to a duel which was disallowed on the chivalric ground that duels were improper when criminal charges were pending. On 17 June a bomb exploded in the home of Dr A. Vignier, one of the several ex-judges in the Grau case: was it possible that the ex-president was prepared to kill as well as to steal?

All this time Prío continued afloat despite the need to reshuffle his government,[20] due to the resignation of his finance minister, Bosch, as a result of the Paniagua murder. Prío's efforts seemed to be merely attempts to survive rather than to create anything lasting. What else could be the meaning of his request to Congress to send 1,000 men to Korea? Some measures, however, had practical benefit – the establishment, for instance, of a new Agricultural and Development Bank under the presidency of another economist of the 1933 student generation, Justo Carrillo. During most of 1951 there were some signs of industrial and economic revival: some commercial banks bought new sites and opened new branches. The appointment to the cabinet of Luis Casero, Mayor of Santiago, shipbuilder, and believed to be incorruptible, was of some strength to the administration.[21] Even so, Chibás went thunder-

---

[20] Now with seven non-Auténticos to twelve Auténticos.

[21] Luis Casero (b. 1902), administrator and vice-president, *La Marítima* S.A.; mayor of Santiago, 1945-51.

ing on, insults on the air flying as frequently as fists and guns in the streets, and by the middle of the year sugar prices were slackening due to hopes of peace in Korea.

In June 1951 people were beginning to think once more of elections, and above all of who should succeed Prío as the Auténtico presidential candidate. Masferrer, influential through the MSR, proposed Ruben de León, Prío's Defence Minister and one of the two or three leading members of the 1933 students' directorate. In an interesting exchange, Goldenberg, no longer a member of MSR (he had broken over the issue of violence), protested, as the two drove in a huge Cadillac along the Malecón, guarded by machine gunners: 'But he's a gangster,' said Goldenberg. 'Yes, *chico*,' replied Masferrer, 'but we're all gangsters. What do you expect? This isn't Europe. Only Chibás is not a gangster and he's mad. Anyway before he does anything, I'll deal with him.'[22]

In the latter part of June, Aureliano Sánchez Arango, the Minister of Education, launched a strong counter-attack on Chibás on behalf of the government, accusing him *inter alia* of speculating in coffee, and describing him as a leader of defamation, a would-be dictator, apostle of untruth. Chibás in reply accused the minister of stealing public money to develop timber in the Central American Republic of Guatemala. He had not previously attacked this minister on his programmes, though he always disliked him, perhaps being jealous of his success and poise.[23] The vituperation between the two one time colleagues of the famous students' directorate of 1927, lasted for weeks, being carried on in the press, on the air, in public speeches and in interviews and correspondence. Sánchez Arango made an immense parade of evidence to prove his innocence of all charges, and challenged Chibás to a four-day wireless debate. Chibás in reply said that he would bring the evidence for what he had charged to the Ministry of Education on 21 July. He did so but was refused entry to the ministry, and thereupon pledged that:

> Next Sunday at half past nine at night before the television cameras and the microphones, I shall be ready to open my portmanteau and show the nation the proofs of the embezzlement in respect of the school textbooks, furniture and meals, the Guatemala district and other things even worse to prove that this government of Carlos Prío is the most corrupt in the history of the Republic.[24]

But when it came to the point most of the 'evidence' incriminated not Sánchez Arango but an associate.

It became clear that Chibás had committed an error. On 5 August

[22] Goldenberg evidence.
[23] Aureliano Sánchez Arango had been on the Left as a student but had moved to the Right in the late 1930s, receiving a post under President Laredo Bru.
[24] Conte Agüero, 772.

he went to the CMQ radio station highly distraught, in an atmosphere of tension. The nation was waiting for a spectacular reply. Chibás on this occasion spoke only a few moments, said that Galileo had been right to point out that the earth went round the sun even though he lacked the evidence to prove it, warned against Batista and the 'castor oil colonels' and ended: 'Comrades of Ortodoxia, forward! For economic liberty, political liberty and social justice! Sweep away the thieves in the government! People of Cuba, arise and walk! People of Cuba, keep awake. This is my last knock at your door [*aldabonazo*]!' With this he went off the air and immediately shot himself in the stomach with a 0·38 pistol.

Chibás had apparently desired the sound of the shot to ring over the radio, a kind of last desperate appeal for sanity; and he apparently had wished merely to wound himself.[25] If so, he was doubly thwarted; for the shot went off after he was no longer on the air; and, though he lingered for ten days, the wound was fatal. He died on 15 August 1951, in the arms of the Church as of a crowd of despairing admirers.

This sensational event naturally caused much scandal. It seemed to complete Chibás's work of bringing discredit on all established institutions. It even deprived Sánchez Arango of the moral victory over Chibás which he deserved. Chibás, given the honours of a colonel killed in the line of duty, at a tumultuous funeral, accomplished in his own death the destruction of Cuban political life – even ruining his own party, for they never recovered from his death, finding a worthy successor impossible to decide on.

The political disintegration after the death of Chibás was everywhere notable. Prío himself on 20 September desperately accused capital of creating economic uncertainty and labour of striking and threatening to influence the government. The Communists, he said, were responsible. He himself would eradicate insults to Cuban institutions. The next day Mujal and other Labour leaders called on Prío to protest against the implication that there were any more Communists in the CTC. Two days later, masked gunmen broke up the printing plant of the Communists' paper *Hoy*: Escalante, the editor, succeeded in getting out a one-page denunciation of Prío. The Communists then launched a similar accusation against the CTC, suing them for $80,000 damages. A week or so later Escalante was himself shot up by machine guns, nineteen

[25] This is the view of Portell Vilá who was close to him at this time. Portell Vilá discussed with him one week before he died the idea that he might kill himself. Portell Vilá tried to dissuade him, but afterwards they left the house and saw a group of workers at the roadside who seemed to laugh at him. 'You see,' said Chibás, 'they are laughing.' (Testimony of Portell Vilá.) Chibás may have got the idea of this spectacular act from a wireless satire of some years before in which a mock Chibás did indeed kill himself on the air (see Conte Agüero, 439).

bullets being fired at him. Miraculously he escaped and levied a specific charge that his would-be assassin had been a prominent leader of the Chemical Workers' Union. Nothing was proved, and nothing done. On 3 October 1951 a newspaper strike halted the innumerable government attacks on the press. But no one felt safe; the arrest of Policarpo Soler, the most scandalous, outrageous and bloody of the Auténtico gangsters, was swiftly followed by his escape and his own subsequent announcement on a secret radio that he would campaign as senator in 1952. The government seemed impotent but ubiquitous: for example, the $M10 Orange Crush Company dissolved itself because of alleged government partiality to labour; in November the Cuban National Association of Industrialists pronounced Cuba to be stagnant because capital, foreign and Cuban, was given no government encouragement. Corruption continued: persons close to president Prío were believed to have retained a large quantity of notes, perhaps $M3 worth, which were supposed to have been handed back to the treasury by the banks.

Malaise, too, affected the sugar industry: the U.S. Congress introduced amendments to its quota law; Cuba still only had 29% of the U.S. market, but extras were easily picked up from other countries. An attempt was next made on the life of the Cuban chief of staff, General Ruperto Cabrera, and also on Masferrer, the latter by the Guiteras organization. This did not restrain Prío from going ahead – in, as it seemed, the most acute stage of the cold war – with a scheme to bring Cuba into close alliance with the U.S. In February 1952 a visit was paid to Cuba by a delegation of the Inter-American Board for Defence of the Western Hemisphere, led by a young and ambitious general, Gustavo Rojas Pinilla, a Colombian, who said gratifyingly that he believed Cuba to be ready 'to carry out whatever duties it might be entrusted with for the defence of the Western Hemisphere . . . the Cuban people are definitely behind the government in the fight against Communism'.[26] There were talks under way between the U.S. ambassador, Willard Beaulac, and Sánchez Arango who had succeeded as Foreign Minister; and in the early days of March 1952 a U.S.–Cuban military agreement was signed. By its first article Cuba undertook to make use of all assistance received . . . for the purpose of defence plans worked out between the two governments. A U.S. military mission prepared to embark for Cuba[27] and in January a U.S. congressional mission visited the island to investigate the possibility of producing new strategic raw materials: of course they should already have known that Cuba's nickel and iron ore could be fruitfully developed. The sugar malaise

---

[26] *HAR*, March 1952.
[27] Text in *Communist Threat to the U.S. through the Caribbean*, 586.

was overcome by a sale of one and a half million tons over three years to England, and arrangements were made for sales to West Germany – although England still had sugar rationing and although the German beet fields were picking up, under the stimulus of the Marshall Plan.

By now, the political parties were embarking on the long period of alliance-making and intriguing which preceded any Cuban election. The Ortodoxos were in some uncertainty for months after Chibás's death; only in December did Dr Roberto Agramonte, Chibás's cousin, of the University of Havana, finally appear as his successor. Agramonte was a pleasing, honourable man of no great ability; his main published work on sociology was a very vague document. Aged forty-four, he was the son of a colonel in the war of independence,[28] a scion of the Agramontes of Camagüey, and, like Chibás, had been expelled from the University of Havana in 1927 by Machado. Under Grau he had been ambassador to Mexico. He commanded the support, though scarcely the enthusiasm, of most middle-class Liberal Cubans. There was little feeling that he could win the election, as Chibás might have done, nor that he would make a strong president if he did. While his leadership was becoming accepted one prominent intellectual supporter, Jorge Mañach, once a member of ABC, left the movement on the simple ground that it was becoming faction-ridden. Agramonte was Chibás's heir but even his most vigorous speeches sounded mere shadows of the master.

The Auténtico candidate for the presidential election was Carlos Hevia, who had already been president of Cuba, if only for seventy-two hours, between Grau San Martín and Colonel Mendieta in 1934. Hevia was now forty-eight, an engineer, and, though closely connected with the Bacardí Rum Company, believed to be honest. This indeed was his main quality, though he had also several years of competent administration to his credit, as director of Supplies and Prices during the war and in Prío's cabinet as Secretary of State, Minister of Agriculture, and president of the Development Commission[29] under Prío. But he owed his nomination to his reputation for honesty; the Auténticos badly needed a respectable candidate in 1952.

The Communists reacted violently against Hevia's candidacy, particularly since he had been specially critical of the USSR in his first statement of views:

The programme of the Auténtico convention [the Communists said] rejects the Nationalist and progressive Auténtico programme of 1934 . . . it betrays anti-imperialism, it betrays Cuba . . . the candidacy

[28] Colonel Frank Agramonte, ADC to Flor Crombet.
[29] He now resigned these appointments to fight the campaign.

of Hevia is not only the candidacy imposed by the Presidential Palace, it is a symbol of the surrender to imperialism, since Hevia is the nominee of Annapolis and the Bacardí Rum Company, which has long since ceased to be Cuban, being more American than Cuban.[30]

The Communists themselves announced that they would not run a candidate, urging a united front of all opposition parties. But this did not mature, since the Ortodoxos and Batista refused to collaborate, either with the Communists or with each other. The Communists ultimately urged their followers to support the Ortodoxos, since the death of Chibás had removed the strongest anti-Communist in that movement;[31] towards the end of 1951 there was some interchange of ideas between the left of the Ortodoxos and the Communist party in the face of the declining character of political life in Cuba.

The third candidate in 1952 was Batista. He had announced his candidature in response to what he claimed to be appeals from all sections of the community. He was at first well fancied but in December 1951 his associate, Castellanos, the mayor of Havana, and his followers,[32] were successfully suborned by Prío on the condition, it seemed, that his followers would get seven senatorships as well as the provincial governorship of Havana. Batista then made various proposals to the Communists for an alliance, but Blas Roca refused on the ground that in a third world war the Communists would back the U.S.S.R. while Batista had announced specifically that in those circumstances he would back the U.S. Prío meantime visited Grau, who afterwards announced his backing for Hevia. Agramonte denounced this pact as showing that Hevia was 'in open complicity with the squanderers of our national Treasury'.[33] The Ortodoxos announced that on Inauguration Day Prío would go to La Cabaña to answer for his vandalism;[34] Batista launched into a personal attack on Agramonte, alleging that he had sheltered 'gunmen' of UIR and MSR in the Cuban Embassy in Mexico and so had had to resign. Batista also accused Prío and his brothers of stealing $M47 in notes which were announced as having been withdrawn and burnt.[35]

By February 1952 Cuba was already suffused with election fever. The election itself was in May. Several minor candidates for the presidency withdrew, trying instead to get themselves nominated for Congress. The Ortodoxos were confident that they would win the

[30] Blas Roca, *Fundamentos*, February 1952, qu. Alexander, 289.
[31] VIIth National Congress of the PSP, speech by Blas Roca, p. 7. See also *HAR*, March 1952, which contradicts Alexander's account (*Communism in Latin America*, 290).
[32] The so-called National party.
[33] *HAR*, February 1952.
[34] Batista, *Cuba Betrayed*, 235.
[35] *Ibid.*, 226.

national elections, but this was not altogether clear. There was a new outburst of violence. UIR gunmen shot and killed Alejo Cossío del Pino, ex-minister and representative, owner of Radio Havana, apparently because of his alleged part in the death of Emilio Tró in 1947. A policeman of the Machado regime, Segundo Prendes Fernández, was also shot in a final act of revenge nearly twenty years after his crimes. Some arrests were made of those who had attempted the assassination of Pérez Dámera.

An effort was made by the Auténticos to indicate that matters were going well. The cabinet announced that 1952 production of sugar would be about 5·9 million tons. There were rumours that the Philippines would not be able to fulfil their quota in the U.S. sugar market. With a big harvest coming, it seemed possible that in a mood of general prosperity Cuba might after all vote to return the Auténticos, despite the violence and the rapacity with which they were associated.

Whether Cuba would have so acted, we shall never know. No doubt the number of political affiliations registered in October 1951 is one indication, for this gave the Auténticos a long lead over any other group.[36] But it is hard to know whether this could have been transferred into political reality at the polls.

[36] Thus (*HAR*, November 1951):

Auténticos	621,000
Partido Ortodoxo	94,000
Nacional Cubano	189,000
Acción Unitaria (Batistianos)	204,000
Republicans	40,000
Liberals	185,000
Democrats	195,000
Communists	53,000

CHAPTER LXV

The Fall of Prío

Prío's cabinet, as it faced the last six months of office in early 1952, was still chiefly composed of survivors of the student generation of 1930 and of the 'struggle against Machado' – men such as Rubén de León, José Antonio Rubio Padilla and Aureliano Sánchez Arango.[1] Oscar Gans, the premier, had twenty years before led the ABC Radical. To a great extent these men had now failed in their life's work. The Auténtico party, despite much attraction, was discredited throughout the country, especially among intellectuals, but also among the *haute bourgeoisie* and the survivors of the old Conservative society. The reason was the gangsterism and corruption which pervaded legislature and executive. Many even on the right were hoping for some Radical solution, and some of these appear to have hoped that the Ortodoxos would win the elections. Others doubted whether that party had sufficient force to carry through even their limited programme of purges. But those devoted, intelligent and energetic Ortodoxos, men of real sincerity and patriotism, looked to the Ortodoxo victory with vast enthusiasm, as the longed-for time of liberation, the long-anticipated creative moment, hour of hope, when at long last dedicated, intelligent, generous and honest men would propel the ship of state into progressive channels. There seemed, after all, reason for optimism: the National Bank and the Agricultural Bank, both achieved under Prío, had been competently

[1] Full list:

Prime Minister:	Oscar Gans
Foreign Minister:	Aureliano Sánchez Arango
Education:	Félix Lancís
Interior:	Edgardo Buttari
Treasury:	José Alvarez Díaz (resigned January 1952)
Defence:	Rubén de Léon
Communications:	Sergio Mejías
Agriculture:	Eduardo Suárez Rivas
Commerce:	Ramón Zaydín
Health:	José Andreu
Public Works:	Luis Casero
Ministers without Portfolio:	Carlos Hevia (resigned November 1951)
	Mariblanca Sabés
	Angel Ferro
	José Antonio Rubio Padilla
	Orlando Puente
	José Manuel Casado

administered by Ortodoxos of integrity. The Ortodoxo movement had at its back many able managers and administrators and some capable politicians who had played a part in government. Maybe it would indeed have won the elections of 1952; but these hopes were frustrated.

According to Batista, three visits were made to him in March 1952 by different people who alleged that Prío was not going to accept the defeat of his party in the elections, indeed that on the contrary he was going to stage a *coup d'état*, and establish himself unconstitutionally as dictator. But Prío, despite his condonation of gangsterism and graft, retained certain democratic predilections which make it unlikely that he seriously wished to interfere with the constitution and postpone the election. It is possible that he may have talked about such a project, and that his idle or impatient remarks may have been eagerly reported by men anxious to provide Batista with some pretext for action of his own. But there is slight evidence to convict Prío: the first of the three visits allegedly made to Batista was in February 1952 by an unnamed officer who said that Prío had a plan for a *coup* to prevent the election. Of this conversation Batista only was the witness.[2] The second visit was by Dr Juan José Remos, a professor and author who had been Minister of Education during Batista's first period, in 1936 and 1940, and also Foreign Minister in 1937.[3] Remos alleged that Prío was seriously contemplating a *pronunciamiento*. Batista therefore sent a message via Remos seeking to dissuade him. Of this, Batista and Remos are the only witnesses; Prío denied any such behaviour and denied receiving any visit from Remos. There is no evidence which helps the decision whether in this matter Prío, or Remos and Batista, were witnesses of truth.

The alleged third[4] visit poses more problems still. Dr Anselmo Alliegro, Batista's prime minister and finance minister in the 1940s, who was standing in 1952 as a senator, said that on 2 March 1952 he went to a cattle fair at Rancho Boyeros, near the airport at Havana; he was thinking of buying a brown Swiss cow for his farm at Baracoa, on the extreme east of the island. He was making his way round the stands when he met Prío, dressed in a sports shirt, grey trousers, no tie, dark jacket and Texan hat. The following conversation reportedly ensued:

A: How are you [*usted*], Mr President?
Prío: Don't be so fastidious, *chico*. I always *tutoyer* you.

[2] Batista, *Cuba Betrayed*, 235–6.
[3] Juan José Remos y Rubio (born 1896). His works included a history of the fall of the Bastille written when he was fifteen, and a life of Donizetti.
[4] It occurred after 2 March 1952, and must have been the last of the three, though Batista in *Cuba Betrayed* puts it earlier.

A: Well, thank you.

Prío: Come and sit down with me.

A: With great pleasure but only a few minutes, because I wish to look around – there is a bull which interests me.

Prío [after some talk]: For many months I have asked you to lunch or suggested we dine, but you have always made me some excuse. Aren't you brave enough to accept my invitation?

A: No, no, but . . .

After this, a chestnut mare was brought forward in which Prío in his turn was interested and Prío was photographed, smiling, next to it. Prío then said that he had to go home; he insisted that Alliegro came too; they went to his *hacienda*, La Chata, sat in one of the summer houses, and a servant brought highballs.

At this point Prío talked of the Ortodoxos who, he said, were placing no limits on their hatreds and resentments. They would not stop even at civil war. They calumniated, intrigued, and did not respect the family.

> I have thought about the problem [said Prío, according to Alliegro] and *I have decided that unless Hevia's electoral position is not improved by April 15 I swear to you that I shall take all the decisions* which may be necessary . . . so that they will not be permitted in any way to reach power. I am at a crossroads [*encrucijada*], and I don't think that I can let these people take power. I won't commit the folly [*bobería*] of Batista of giving up without knowing what will happen afterwards . . . I would like things to be resolved constitutionally but with these people I don't see any possible understanding. They are irresponsible. They are blinded by hatred. If I have to finish by giving the ——,[5] I have the support of the Army.

At this Alliegro began to speak of Batista. Prío replied: 'But you can't deny that I have been a generous friend of Batista. Precisely one of the reasons for my quarrel with Grau was the guarantee which I gave him to allow him to return.'

Afterwards the two went to see a champion dairy cow and Prío said that 'in order to keep this government coalition going, we must have bigger udders than this cow'.[6]

Prío denied that this conversation ever took place, and said that it was an invention of Alliegro. But though it is hard to believe that it was a total invention, it may have been intended more as a warning to Batista – for Prío must have suspected that Alliegro would report the conversation – that the government was strong and that he, Prío, was

[5] Omitted presumably because obscene.
[6] Article by Alliegro, *Bohemia*, 14 September 1952.

aware of the challenge of the Ortodoxos. If so, it had a counterproductive sequel.

The beginning of March 1952 saw more politicking. On 5 March an attempt was made on the life of Pelayo Cuervo, a prominent Ortodoxo; the same day, Ramón Hermida, one of the ex-ABC politicians who now favoured Batista, told Batista that the Auténticos would offer him $M8 to $M10 if he would only withdraw and back Hevia; Hermida had replied with dignity to the Auténticos that Batista preferred physical death to moral death. Batista congratulated Hermida, telling him that he had done all he could with the government. On 6 March Batista was at a congo fiesta at Guanabacoa. By then a conspiracy had clearly been formed to take over the power of the state in Batista's name.

The conspirators in 1952 against the Prío government and the prospect of the elections were all army officers; some of them had profited in the past under Batista and stood to lose if Batista did not return. The conspiracy was directly attributable to the political complexion of the Cuban army: thus Prío had appointed Ruperto Cabrera chief of staff in place of Pérez Dámera, whom Grau in turn had appointed in place of Batista's intimate, López Migoya; the latter therefore belonged essentially to a different caste within the officer hierarchy. In 1952 there was a strong possibility that the Batistiano officers of the past would, after a third victory either by the Auténticos or by the Ortodoxos, be permanently excluded from participation in the spoils of office. No doubt they felt it riling that General Cabrera or Admiral Pedro Pascual Borges, chief of the navy, should be in a position to enrich themselves indefinitely whilst they seemed indefinitely excluded. Here again corruption played a part. But on the other hand there is no doubt that some among the plotters thought that they had a duty to save Cuba from a government of thievery; they had to 'restore order', against politicians in whom there was every justification for having no confidence; and, Batista added in his memoir of the time, they had to prevent Prío from setting up 'a savage dictatorship'. The conspirators were mostly captains or lieutenants: maybe they were impatient too for promotion, as well as for riches.[7] There is evidence for thinking that Batista was pushed into rebellion by men younger than himself.[8] They had earlier canvassed Colonel Ramón Barquín whom some among them believed to be the

---

[7] See *Bohemia*, 30 March 1952, for a discussion of the meeting on 8 March, at which plans were made to take over the telephone company, the police, army and navy headquarters.

[8] In an article, *Bohemia*, 30 October 1952, the United Press correspondent, Francis McCarthy, described how as long as eight months before 10 March 1952 Batista was visited by several young officers who suggested he headed a *coup*. Batista refused, being still then democratically concerned.

'ideal' candidate for chairman of a military junta but they doubted whether he would be able to 'control' public reaction so well as Batista.[9] Batista meantime was doing less well in the electoral battle than he had hoped, and the suggestion at a meeting in early February by young officers of a *pronunciamiento* apparently presented him with a difficult decision.[10] This was the first time he had considered over-throwing 'the constitution [of 1940] which he had given to the people'. He told the officers that he personally was not interested in becoming president in such circumstances, but that someone such as Carlos Saladrigas should be brought in. Batista thought over the matter. Two more groups of conspirators arrived, not knowing of the first group. Their plan was a *golpe* to destroy corruption in the government. Batista decided finally to go ahead, bringing together the groups who had called on him, and hopefully embarked on a plan by which bloodshed would be avoided, gambling on Prío's vacillation and known weakness.

The conspiracy became more and more widespread, the commander-in-chief, General Cabrera being asked to join, and though he refused he did nothing against it; one colonel, Lázaro Landeira, apparently gave some information to Prío, who was informed by Cabrera that all was well. Batista had the highest opinion of his own capacities 'to save Cuba'. He was far the best known Cuban internationally. His conduct of affairs during the war had made him many friends in the U.S. He realized that the circumstances of the cold war gave him new opportunities for ingratiation with the U.S. The widespread dislike of the Auténticos combined with the uncertainty, beyond a certain point, of just what the Ortodoxos would actually do, conspired to provide him with a great temptation as well as a great opportunity. To this temptation he surrendered. He was not the initiator of the conspiracy, but he was the man who made it different from the other splintering plots which stained the record of the Cuban army during the regimes of Prío and Grau. Afterwards, like some sorry or reformed crooks, he attempted to do what he could to make up for the crime: but he was never able to expiate it, since he hung on to the position which he usurped by every means, fair and foul alike, and increasingly foul.[11]

Sometime in early March (perhaps after Alliegro's visit), Batista convoked a new meeting in the house of ex-Captain Fernández Miranda,

[9] Colonel Barrera Pérez, *Bohemia Libre*, 28 July 1961.
[10] F. McCarthy, *Bohemia*, 30 October 1952.
[11] Barrera Pérez, *op. cit.* The officers present at this meeting in the house of ex-captain Fernández Miranda were in addition to Batista, Lieut. Barrera Pérez, later a field commander against Castro in the Sierra Maestra, Dr Nicolás (Colao) Hernández, ex-General Tabernilla Dolz, comrade-in-arms of Batista's since 1933, ex-Captain Rodríguez Calderón, Captains Robaina, Jorge García Tunón and Juan Rojas González, Lieutenants Artemio Pérez Díaz, Ignacio Leonard Castell and Armando Echemendía Leyva, and retired Lieutenant Francisco Tabernilla.

at which not only the conspiratorial serving officers were present but a number of those now ex-officers purged by Grau on the grounds of being Batista's men: these included Captain Cruz Vidal and Díaz Tamayo, along with some admirers of Batista still serving, such as Lieutenant Salas Cañizares and Captain Dámaso Sogo – all of whom later played a prominent role in the second *Batistato*. On this occasion Batista explained that Prío was contemplating a *golpe de estado* in order to prevent the Ortodoxos taking power. Whatever Batista himself believed, some of the officers clearly believed him. On 8 March final plans were laid, dispositions being made for the new commands in the police and the army.[12]

On 9 March Batista went to an outdoor election meeting at Matanzas. There was no untoward sign of illegal activity. That night, however, three large Buicks assembled at Batista's villa, the Kuquine, outside Havana, and left about midnight for separate destinations, four officers in the first car, four retired officers in the second, and Batista and two officers still on active service in the third. Prío was at La Chata. Antonio Prío, the president's brother, was dancing at the Sans Souci night club. Segundo Curti and Orlando Puente were dining at Río Mar with other cabinet ministers. One of Batista's big cars, with Lieutenant Negrete on board, circled round the presidential palace to ensure that there was nothing untoward to guard against. The three Buicks of rebellion met and left for Campamento Columbia. They arrived at the gate of the headquarters and were allowed in by the officer on duty, Captain Dámaso Sogo, who was party to the plot. The officers in the first car got out and covered the entry of the other two. Batista went to the headquarters of Regiment No. 6, where the guard immediately handed over to him. Officers whom he trusted went to assume command of the four battalions of infantry. The troops were mobilized, the houses of their recent commanders – within the camp – being surrounded. At 3 a.m. almost all was done. A handful of young officers arrested the principal generals of Cuba – Ruperto Cabrera, the chief of staff, Quirino Uría, inspector-general of the army, Rogelio Soca Llanes, adjutant-general, and some others. They made no resistance. When Cabrera's wife encouraged him to fight he replied, '*Chica*, when things have reached this pass, all is lost.' General Tabernilla took command in La Cabaña; Lieutenant Rodríguez Calderón took over command of the navy. He and the other officers named to the key commands were immediately promoted. Police Lieutenant Salas took over the telephone exchange, and became himself the new head of the police.

At a quarter to three in the morning of 10 March, Cabrera's wife telephoned her daughter to say that Cabrera had been arrested, and the daughter's *novio* telephoned the presidential palace; someone there

[12] Barrera Pérez, *op. cit.*

spoke to two ministers, Diego Vicente Tejera and Sergio Mejías, who immediately telephoned Prío. Prío drove quickly from La Chata to the presidential palace, where the cabinet assembled. The president's publicity adviser, René Fiallo, urged Prío to take command of the regiment of Matanzas. But as yet Prío's information was imprecise. He did not know that Batista's men had taken over the telephone head-quarters and therefore could listen in to the almost hysterical exchanges between Prío and his friends. He knew, for instance, that at the moment anyway the generals in charge of Las Villas and Matanzas were loyal to the government, and had telephoned to this effect. At six in the morning Prío issued a manifesto: 'I have heard that the Chief of Staff of the army has been arrested by officers under General Batista. The leading commands of the Army in the provinces have reaffirmed their loyalty to the legally constituted regime . . . I trust in the morality and valour of Cubans to oppose this attempt of a single ambitious man.'[13] Soon after this, Lieutenant Negrete arrived at the palace, with a small group of soldiers, saying he had come to reinforce the president. Prío realized that they were sent by Batista and had the soldiers disarmed. Negrete tried to demand the surrender of the guard, and an aide of Prío shot him dead: first blood, therefore, to Prío.[14]

Batista's next move was to dispatch tanks to the palace, to have them half surround it and then to withdraw them. What next? Would the palace be assaulted? There were more hysterical conversations inside. Prío contemplated surrender. Then there arrived a delegation of students headed by Álvaro Barba, president of the students' union. Barba said:

> Mr President, you know that on many occasions we have censured you publicly when we have thought that your conduct deserved it but on this occasion the FEU comes to offer you its support in defence of the Constitution. We have come to say that the University, faithful to its revolutionary and civilian traditions, must confirm by action its backing of democratic rights.

Prío appeared sincerely moved, but his answer was vague: 'I believe the people will back me at this historic moment . . . Yes we shall resist this *golpe*. But everything depends on the attitude of the workers – the people – the students. But I thank you for this gesture.'

One student, José Hidalgo, asked abruptly: '*Presidente*, are you going to fight against this barrack rebellion?'

Prío answered, 'Yes, *claro*, I am going to fight.'

Hidalgo asked, 'But have you any idea how to do so?'

[13] *Bohemia*, 16 March 1952.
[14] Francis McCarthy, *ibid.*, 30 March 1952.

Prío said, 'We are studying the situation, how to go about things in the best way, I will fight in the best place, not the palace because it is very vulnerable to attack.'

Barba asked, 'But what exactly are you going to do?'

Prío said, 'I am going to one of the loyal garrisons and there I will start the fight. I think there is no other way out.'

An officer entered at this point: '*Presidente, presidente,* a soldier of Colonel Calleja says that tanks are moving from Campamento Columbia towards the palace. What are we going to do?'

There was silence. At last Agustín Valero of the FEU said, 'We came here to discuss how to organise resistance to this *golpe.* In the university there are no arms. You must distribute arms to the students to defend the legally constituted power. We merely wish to fight.'

Prío said: '*Está bien,* Dieguito [that is, Diego Tejera, Minister of Education], see that a cargo of arms is sent to the University – whatever they have need of. Gentlemen, the meeting is over. We must act fast.'

The students left for the university in great enthusiasm, to await the arrival of arms. In a few minutes, however, without having done anything, Prío left the palace in a Buick sedan.[15]

He drove towards Matanzas with 'Tony' Varona, his prime minister. *En route* out of Havana they were stopped and asked who they were by a guard of corporals. The driver said that he was taking an old man to the doctor. They drove on. But by the time they got to Matanzas, the Plácido regiment had gone over to Batista, Colonel Martín Elena, loyal to Prío, being arrested.[16] The multicolour Septiembrista banner flew over the barracks. Prío and Varona drove towards Camagüey, but on the way they heard that Bilbatúa, an old crony of Batista's, had taken over the barracks. 'Millo' Ochoa, the rich leader of one of the factions of the Ortodoxos, offered to fly Prío to Santiago. But he had already decided to return to Havana. The Buick sedan turned round and the president and the prime minister, quivering with fear, drove to the Mexican Embassy, where he already found, not wholly to his surprise, a curious group of frightened men: the Foreign Minister, Aureliano Sánchez Arango, who had fired a shot at a policeman and escaped to this sanctuary; Segundo Curti (Minister of the Interior, nominally head of the police); Rafael Trejo; and Ricardo Artigas, chief of the national lottery. Artigas was at once the most agitated and then the most resigned of the asylees. 'Are you sure that nothing will happen here?' he said tremblingly to the ambassador of Mexico, 'Batista is capable of any barbarity.' 'Rest tranquil,' replied the ambassador, 'the Mexican flag flies here, nothing can happen.' 'Good,'

[15] *Ibid.,* 16 March 1952.
[16] Later chief of staff to the anti-Castro Frente in 1961.

Artigas breathed, 'once in Mexico, I shall fly to Miami. There I have all my interests. I knew that this would happen and I told that gentleman [Prío] but he would do nothing; I, on the other hand, I have saved my money and I shall establish residence in the U.S.A.' There is no reason to believe that the funds of Major Artigas were small.[17]

Thus died the administration of Carlos Prío. But was all lost, even though the government had fled its posts? The few possible centres of resistance waited for Prío and waited in vain. All was quiet. The CTC called a general strike. Banks, offices, government departments, did not open, soldiers standing outside doors to prevent office workers from arriving. Batista's ends were indeed served by this action of the CTC more than hindered. Newspapers were not distributed. The 'workers' palace', the Communist headquarters, the Ortodoxo and Auténtico headquarters in all cities were all guarded and men were turned politely but firmly away. Only the university remained as a possible centre of opposition. No arms arrived, despite the president's promise. The dean of the medical faculty, Dr Angel Vieta,[18] said that there would be no classes till the return of constitutional integrity. Various politicians and Labour leaders inclined to resist went to the university during the course of the day – including Masferrer, Pablo Balbuena, and Marcos Hirigoyen of the CTC. The last, with Calixto Sánchez and Pascasio Linares, assured Mujal, the secretary-general of the CTC and until now the Auténticos' most vigorous defender, that the buses and the airlines would be kept from service by a continuation of the general strike. But later Hirigoyen and Linares were arrested. Mujal, after the surrender of the cabinet, chose to regard the *golpe* as a merely political event which he as a union leader could ignore,[19] and he was shortly in touch with Portocarrero, Batista's nominee as Minister of Labour. At 1 p.m. on 10 March, Radio Havana announced the new government, with various well-worn old friends of Batista in key positions – Miguel Angel Campa, for instance, was back as Foreign Minister, Ramón Hermida came in as Minister of the Interior, Miguel Angel de Céspedes as Minister of Justice.[20] The political origin of these

---

[17] Years later, on behalf of democratic Cubans, Artigas went to the State Department to urge the U.S. to intervene to overthrow Castro.

[18] Dr Angel Vieta (born 1891), dentist and bacteriologist, Dean, 1934 and 1940–52.

[19] According to Mujal, the CTC had in some places requested arms from the military commanders but had been refused.

[20] Full list: Miguel Angel Campa, Foreign Secretary; Miguel Angel de Céspedes, Minister of Justice; Ramón Hermida, Minister of the Interior; José A. Mendigutia, Minister of Public Works; Alfredo Jacomino, Minister of Agriculture; López Blanco, Minister of Finance; Andrés Rivero Agüero, Minister of Education; Oscar de la Torre, Minister of Commerce; Pablo Carrera Justiz, Minister of Communications; Andrés Domingo Morales del Castillo, Minister of the Presidency; Nicolás Pérez Hernández, Minister of Defence; Ernesto de la Fe, Minister of Information; Enrique Saladrigas, Minister of Health; and Jesús Portocarrero, Minister of Labour.

men were various: some were straightforward bureaucrats who, like Campa, had served Batista before; Dr Nicolás Hernández at the Defence Ministry had throughout been involved in the successful conspiracy; Hermida and Saladrigas were ex-members of the now defunct ABC (as was Martínez Sáenz, who became president of the National Bank). Oscar de la Torre, the new Minister of Commerce, had been the leader of ABC Radical who in the 1930s had refused, on radical grounds, to rejoin his old comrades; Hermida had been a member of the famous Directorio Estudiantil of 1927 and had once even solicited entry into the Ortodoxo party.

At 3 p.m. Batista's emissaries promised Mujal that all the labour laws of the past ten years would be respected, and the other leading Labour leaders seem to have wished to agree to accept Batista's promises. Mujal telephoned Prío at the Mexican Embassy to see whether he had really abandoned the struggle. It was clear he had. At 4 p.m. a manifesto to the people was issued by Batista:

> The military junta have acted to avoid the regime of blood and corruption which has destroyed institutions, created disorder and mockery in the State, aggravated by the sinister plans of the Government which intended to continue further beyond its constitutional terms, for which President Prío had placed himself in agreement with various military leaders, preparing a military *golpe* before the elections.

Batista promised that elections with full guarantees would follow, suspending constitutional guarantees for forty-five days. Most of the leading army and navy officers of the Prío era were dismissed from their commands, some going into business, others into journalism or retirement. Their posts were taken over by Batista's friends. But this did not happen with all: thus the able Colonel Barquín and his group of officers, nicknamed the *puros*, who had nearly staged a *golpe* against Prío a year before, were confirmed in their posts and did not resign. The government ordered all government employees and mayors and municipal employees to remain at their posts, although Castellanos was immediately dismissed from the mayoralty of Havana to be succeeded by Justo Luis Pozo and although Pazos, Carrillo and Irisarri, all progressive men, resigned from the presidencies of the National Bank, the Agricultural Development Bank and the Tobacco Stabilization Board. Batista's brother 'Panchín' became governor of Havana province again. Congressional rights were suspended, though members would receive salaries till further notice. Some days later a number of legislators made their way to the Capitol in defiance. Two gunshots were fired, and they scurried home, for good. Legislative power henceforth lay with the government. There was also a temporary prohibition of the right to strike.[21] The *coup d'état* of 10 March was complete. Oriente collapsed within hours. On 11 March Batista and Mujal met at dawn and Mujal undertook to remain the boss of the CTC; at 2 p.m. the nine-man executive committee of the CTC accepted this. The general strike was called off.

These events, however apocalyptic in their ultimate consequences, were greeted with remarkable tranquility. The passivity of those against whom the *coup* had been directed drew the contempt of public opinion. One group who were specially disillusioned were the young officers who had actually initiated the conspiracy; they felt 'defrauded' when they heard the names of the new government, and General García Tuñón led a protest to Batista. The Ortodoxos, of course, condemned the *coup*, but their reaction, inevitably in view of Prío's nervelessness, was delayed. The Communists proclaimed that the new regime was in no way different from the old, thereby implying at least that it was no worse.[22] (Eight years later, it is true, they gave a rather more heroic account of their behaviour on 10 March.)[23] Only the students remained in a posture of real hostility. A firm statement appeared on 14 March, signed by all the student leaders.[24] As to mass opinion, Liberals underestimated the degree of acceptance and even approval with which many members of the working class approached the '*golpe libertador*' or, as it was also known, due to the current popularity of a song of that name, the '*golpe de la sunsundamba*'. Batista had always been popular outside educated circles in the past and something remained of that popularity; and then, who cared about the fall of Prío outside the constitutional middle class? Chibás had done his work of destruction too well: no one believed in Prío's system. Most indeed settled to accept Batista with relief.

Prío himself left by air for Mexico on 13 March under safe conduct, with Sánchez Arango and Curti. A reporter caught him on arrival at the Hotel Continental Reforma: 'Did you suspect a *golpe*?'

'No – that is, yes, I had some suspicions. Some days before it, I asked the high command of the army to see me, and I said I had had confidential information something was up.'

[21] *Bohemia*, 16 March 1952.

[22] *Ibid.*

[23] The Communists, Blas Roca would tell the 8th Congress of the party, were 'the first of all the organised parties . . . to denounce the *golpe* of March 10 . . . In the provinces of Oriente, Camagüey and Las Villas our organisations brought out the masses into the streets on March 10 and mobilised actively to resist until the local military commander had surrendered . . .' However, these masses were few in reality.

[24] These were: Alvaro Barba, Quinto Peláez, Julio Castañeda, Orestes Robledo, Agustín Valero, Sigismundo Parés, Andrés Rodríguez Fraga, Antonio Cisneros, Antonio Torres Villa, Eduardo Santés, Edelberto Ciré, Ismael Hernández, Vilma Garrido, José Hidalgo Peraza, Aurora Cueva, Juan Mena Ortiz, Pedro García Mellado, Ramiro Baeza, Eduardo Hart, Armando Prieto, Mario Chaple and José Antonio Echevarría (*Bohemia*, 23 March 1952).

786 · THE AGE OF DEMOCRACY 1934–52

'And they replied?'

'They said they would investigate. Some days later they returned to say that I could sleep peacefully.'

'Are you going to form a government in exile?'

'No, it is pointless.'

'What about your personal fortune? Is it here or abroad?'

'I don't have a single *centavo* in foreign banks. All my money is in Cuba. Invested.'

'Now you are in the same boat as the Ortodoxos and Communists. Will you join up with them?'

'I am ready to join anyone except the Communists.'

'It has been said you were in cahoots with Batista?'

'It is a bloody lie.'

However, it would be misleading to give the Prío administration an epitaph in such manly language. In its issue following the *golpe*, *Bohemia* published a quotation from the Mexican educationalist Vasconcelos which almost in the style of Junius, aptly summed up Prío's constitution:

> He fell like a rotten fruit, almost by his own weight, victim of his own intrigues, of his uneven ambitions and of his contempt for public opinion . . . like other climbers, he recognised public office only as a ladder for rapid enrichment and he recognised his closest collaborators only as helpers to make a fortune. Talkative in the moment of action, tortuous in his private relations, superficial in his affections, he was as inept for crime as he was condescending towards criminals.[25]

Thus constitutional rule died in Cuba.

[25] *Bohemia*, 16 March 1952.

BOOK VIII

The Struggle
1952 - 9

'*Los Camiros de mi Cuba, Nunca van a dande deben.*'

SONG OF CARLOS PUEBLA, *c* 1955

(The roads of my Cuba never lead where they should)

CHAPTER LXVI

Batista: II

In the spring of 1952 the Cuban political system, such as it was, had already been tortured to death. The accumulated follies of fifty years were bearing their rotten fruit. The overthrow of Prío passed easily, the scarcely melancholy cry of '*Prío sale!*' (Prío quits!) echoing throughout the cigar-smoking and rum-drenched streets of old Havana. The prostitutes of Virtue Street knew that the substitution of Batista for Prío in the National Palace would make little difference to them. But Batista's easy triumph spelled tragedy to those who hoped, through the constitutional process enshrined in 1940 and through the Ortodoxo party, to create by the next elections a new Cuba, a decent and happy country. For all interested in political decency Batista's *golpe* in 1952 was intolerable, an event comparable in the life of an individual to a nervous breakdown after years of chronic illness. Thus to men of the generation of the directors of the Agricultural and National Banks, Carrillo and Pazos, this event represented, at the least, a new monstrous interruption in their careers, already gravely injured by the interruptions of the 1930s, of the *Machadato* and afterwards under Batista in his first incarnation. To such people, often temperamentally sensitive, it seemed the final insult that *Time* magazine, the dream machine of the north, should in April for the first time feature Cuba on its cover with a specially effulgent representation of the head of Batista, the Cuban flag behind him spread like a halo, accompanied by the bright comment, 'Cuba's Batista: he got past Democracy's sentries'.[1]

The stamp of acceptance had indeed by this time been given to Batista. On 12 March Elliott Roosevelt, son of Franklin, visited Batista on behalf of a television company.[2] On 23 March the Ortodoxo politicians made a vain appeal to the OAS and to the UN for help.[3] But on 27 March Willard Beaulac, the U.S. ambassador in Havana, visited the new Foreign Minister, Campa, to give U.S. recognition. A less official, but no less welcome and significant move, was a visit by officials of the United States Steel Co. to Ernesto de la Fe, Minister of Information, to say that U.S. capital 'responded favourably' to U.S.

---

[1] *Time*, 9 April 1952.
[2] *Bohemia*, 13 March 1952.
[3] The Ortodoxo politician, Buenaventura Dellundé, went to the U.S. on behalf of their cause to see John Dreir, U.S. ambassador to the OAS.

recognition of Batista; U.S. capital, they assured the minister, could supply Cuba with whatever was needed. On the other hand, the *chargé d'affaires* at the embassy on 10 March itself later assured Carlos Hevía the Auténtico candidate for the presidency that if Prío had held out in any part of the island, the U.S. would not have recognized Batista.[4]

But what was this new government, how was it sustained? The government itself was made up of loyal Batista men or opportunists. On the other hand there is some evidence to suggest that Batista did his best to get Carlos Saladrigas or Emeterio Santovenia or Jorge García Montes to take over the presidency: the last named refused by saying, 'Batista has caught a lion by the tail, let's see how it will escape.'[5] Batista declared that he was loyal to the 1940 Constitution, but that he had nevertheless suspended constitutional guarantees, as well as the right to strike. In April however he proclaimed a new constitutional code of 275 articles, *estatutos de gobierno*, claiming that the 'democratic and progressive essence' of the 1940 Constitution was preserved in the new law. But rights of speech, of assembly and of press could be automatically suspended at any time for forty-five-day periods. New elections would be held, but not before November 1953, eighteen months ahead. Until then, all parties would be suspended, and it was suspected that they would only be reorganized on Batista's terms. The old Congress also was suspended, though congressmen were to draw their salaries for another six months. For the time being the premiership and vice-premiership would be abolished. Batista would govern as president. There would also be an eighty-member *consultative council* to take the place of the legislature, since Batista knew that the old assembly would not support him. Batista's old friend, Carlos Saladrigas, the ex-ABC ex-premier of 1940–4 and his unsuccessful presidential candidate in 1944, would become president, and Oscar García Montes, another old crony, vice-president. This group of legislators would hold at least fifteen sessions a month and be paid $30 per session they attended, though not more than $600 in all.

Batista was full of promises: he would honour international agreements: guarantee all lives and property; fulfil public works contracts (the new president of the development commission, the sugar administrator Amadeo López Castro, said that all projects already begun would be finished in six months). The economy would be strengthened through foreign investments. Cuba would send men to Korea 'if needed', and build 12,000 houses. 'The people and I are the dictators,' Batista explained.

[4] HAR, December 1952. López Fresquet, 31. Ambassador Beaulac told the author that he had been apprised of the imminence of a *coup* by the U.S. businessman, Hodges.

[5] José Suárez Núñez, *El Gran Culpable* (1963), 9.

The conventional *bourgeoisie* rallied quite quickly round the new regime. Batista's past democratic record did not make it far-fetched to suppose that ultimately some constitutional restoration would be achieved. The ex-mayor of Havana, Castellanos, offered to collaborate. The Veterans' Association (a shadow of its once powerful political force), the Bankers' Association, and the Asociación de Colonos y Hacendados (*colonos* and sugar planters) offered co-operation. The CTC gave practical co-operation. A circular from the National Federation of Sugar Workers asked members to 'maintain cordial relations' with the new government.[6] Many isolated Labour leaders – such as Pascasio Linares, Jesús Artigas, Calixto Sánchez (textile, medicine and airway workers' leaders, respectively) – denounced the regime; they were in the minority. Within a few weeks even some parties which had backed Prío or contributed to his cabinets, such as the Democrats and Radicals, were scurrying round to Batista. Marta Fernández de Batista began to make gifts to charity in the style of Evita Perón, stretching out the hand of a First Lady in the hope of soothing disturbed political sensibilities.

But it immediately became clear even to old admirers of Batista that in the years of exile the ex-sergeant had changed. He was far lazier than he had been in the 1940s. He spent an inordinate amount of time in peripheral matters such as the punctuation of a letter, the correct tying of a tie, and changing his clothes. He was fascinated by the private life of his opponents or even of ordinary people in Cuban society and spent hours listening to their tapped telephone conversations: in particular the correspondence of Aureliano Sánchez Arango obsessed him. He ate sumptuously. He spent hours playing canasta with his military friends and hours watching horror films.[7] He seemed more snobbish than he had been before, cultivating the friendship of the heirs of the old Cuban oligarchy and inviting them to splendid banquets even if he knew from their tapped telephones or their intercepted letters that they opposed him. It was popularly suggested that 'Batista worked sixteen hours a day'. This was quite false.

Some new arrangement of public force was judged necessary and the pay of the army was increased. There were a large number of shifts in the disposition of both police and military commands: in April the new police chief, Brigadier Rafael Salas Cañizares (who had taken over the radio station on 10 March), announced openings for 2,000 more men in the police: all police would get new weapons, new cars, new motor cycles. The rank and file of both army and police accepted the new regime with satisfaction even if they had been mostly recruited under Grau and Prío.[8]

But one beneficial consequence of the *Batistato* was the virtual demise of private political gangsterism. Policarpo Soler was allowed to leave Cuba for more promising shores – Spain and later the Dominican Republic. Rolando Masferrer, the MSR chief, now a senator, was willing to throw in his hand with Batista, and became a pillar of the regime though he retained a considerable private army in Santiago. The truth was that the abolition of political life partly meant the abolition of the violence and the opportunities for corruption which went with it, while the old members of UIR, MSR and ARG took up positions as defenders or opponents of Batista. In a way Batista's *golpe* formalized gangsterism: the machine gun in the big car became the symbol not only of settling scores but of an approaching change of government.

The opposition to Batista was slow to gather shape but it never really died. For the next six and a half years, though Batista was always apparently confident in the Capitol, there was never an occasion when it could be said, 'Cuba is at peace'.

The Auténticos were divided, their followers almost equally furious with Prío as with Mujal. Mujal replied to an attack by Varona with the evasion that the Auténticos had failed to represent the interests of the workers. The Ortodoxos meantime refused to accept their dissolution: Carlos Márquez Sterling, on their behalf, denounced the idea of taking part in elections in 1953.[9] They tried, unsuccessfully, to expel the mayor of Camagüey for swearing allegiance to the new government. On 6 April the Ortodoxo presidential candidate, Agramonte, and several others (Márquez Sterling, Manuel Bisbé, and Luis Orlando Rodríguez), were taken with Pardo Llada before Colonel Cruz Vidal, the new chief of the SIM (the special political police).[10] Cruz Vidal threatened them, accusing them of plotting with the students, but let them go. By this cat-and-mouse procedure, the police and the administration kept the Ortodoxos on the hop. A lack of robustness as well as opportunity on the part of Agramonte and the leaders restrained them from action. Nor were the Communists an effective centre of opposition. Rebuffed by all other parties in the election campaign before the *golpe*, the leaders of course denounced Batista but were slow to do anything more: Marinello, who was still the party's

---

[8] To Batista's surprise, according to Suárez Núñez, 19.

[9] Carlos Márquez Sterling (born 1899), son of Manuel Márquez Sterling (see above, p. 674); lawyer, diplomat, representative, 1936–48.

[10] Cruz Vidal, a special follower of Batista, had become sergeant, lieutenant and captain in swift succession between September and December 1933; he was retired from the army in 1944, and now at the age of forty-six had been recalled to the colours to head this investigation squadron.

formal president, merely assured a visiting U.S. historian that the party would probably not resume its old alliance with Batista, though they did have some friendships which he believed might be useful to him.[11] For a few weeks, Batista and the Communists held back in their attitudes to each other: several Communists remained in the Ministry of Labour and in other posts in the administration, whilst others were newly appointed. Cuban-Russian diplomatic relations admittedly were interrupted, after a Russian diplomatic courier's bags were inspected in Havana: the Cubans refused to apologize and Russia broke off relations. But the Communists remained free and well-considered. Some went abroad, most remained. Communist magazines and newspapers still circulated. The historian, Portell Vilá, now an Ortodoxo, even complained that while Communist newspapers such as *Hoy* could easily be bought, he, Portell Vilá, could not be heard on the radio.[12] This ambivalent situation persisted, though in May the police raided Communist headquarters in Havana and forty-three branch offices to prevent any demonstration on Guiteras's anniversary – a curious move since no such demonstration would have been then likely by the party, whose leaders hated Guiteras dead as they had hated him alive.

As usual the Church in Cuba was as ambiguous as the Communists: Cardinal Arteaga congratulated Batista, and other bishops backed him. Two or three opposed and a Franciscan priest, Fr Bastarrica, publicly denounced the *golpe*, as did several prominent Catholic lay leaders, such as Andrés Valdespino, president of Juventud Católica, and Angel del Cerro. In June a Catholic Action meeting at Guanajay was broken up by the police. It became clear that while some members of the hierarchy and the regular clergy would tolerate the new order only too easily, most Catholic laymen and priests would not. Communists and Catholics separately showed themselves ambiguous.[13]

The students provided Batista's main source of worry. Anxious for their own future, many had been thwarted by the *golpe* of the fine future which must have awaited them in Auténtico or Ortodoxo governments. They felt strongly on the issues involved, and demanded the dismissals of professors who had accepted jobs with Batista – such as Carrera Justiz, the new Minister of Communications, and Saladrigas, the president of the new legislature. Batista let it be known that he would give $M10 to build a new 'Ciudad Universitaria' with boarding houses for the students; they replied heroically, '*La Universidad ni se vende ni se*

---

[11] Alexander, 293.

[12] *Bohemia*, 7 April 1952.

[13] So much for the often quoted remarks of Dr Magiot in Graham Greene's *The Comedians* (1966): 'Catholics and Communists have committed great crimes but at least they have not stood aside ... and been indifferent' (p. 312).

rende.' On 2 April the police found out that the student leaders were planning a massive demonstration for the following Sunday, at which a copy of the 1940 Constitution would be symbolically buried. Four of them were arrested and taken personally before Batista.

Batista said ingratiatingly, if royally, 'We have an enormous desire to talk with you.'

Alvaro Barba replied, 'Fine, but first we want to know why we have been detained.'

Batista denied that they had been detained. He said that he wished that he could describe the chaos which had existed before 10 March. Prío had been planning a *coup.* Another student, Robledo, spoke of the military *golpe.* Batista interrupted to explain that he had not carried out a *golpe* but a revolutionary movement, to avoid a civil war.

Baeza: 'Yes, a *madrugonazo!'*

Batista: 'No, no, not a *madrugonazo,*[14] but a *madrugón.'*

The student Baeza answered that it might have been a fresh spring morning for Batista but it had not been so for him. Batista said that he needed the co-operation of all Cubans to reorganize the institutional life of the nation, and that the students could not bury the Constitution, because it had not died.

'Precisely,' returned Barba, 'it has been murdered.'

Batista appealed to the need to maintain public order.

Robledo asked, 'But General, are you going to ban all opposition?'

'Opposition is a necessity,' replied Batista, charmingly, 'a constructive opposition is more beneficial to the government than a good minister. This is why I admire you so much . . . if I were a student, I would be in the FEU doing what you do . . . I am not against this demonstration for itself [i.e. the burying of the Constitution] but against the professional agitators who will make capital out of the occasion . . .'

But the students said that they would have to persist in their plan: 'General, we must continue this till the end.'

'Then Colonel Salas [the police chief] will have to act,' said Batista, who thereupon let them free.[15]

The students had every intention of carrying out their plans. On 4 April at three o'clock in the afternoon the chief of the university police, always a key figure, telephoned the FEU leaders and said that two armoured lorries were on their way. Alvaro Barba said, 'Comrades, we must advance the hour of the burial to avoid being shut up in here.' So immediately, instead of waiting for 4 p.m., two hundred

[14] There have been so many early morning *golpes* in Latin American history that the Spanish word for a very early rising or an early bird, *madrugón* has received the suffix *-azo,* from *cuartelazo* (a military *coup d'état*), to indicate a rising at dawn against the government.

[15] *Bohemia,* 6 April 1952.

students stood by while their leaders solemnly interred the 1940 Constitution before the bust of Martí at the corner of 25th and Hospital streets. This act of opposition was thus brought to a triumphant conclusion.

The next month, on 20 May, the students staged a massive demonstration to commemorate the fiftieth anniversary of Cuban independence. The meeting was held on the stone staircase, the famous *escalinata*, on the way up to the university: Barba and Mañach, the writer, defended the Constitution in impassioned speeches. 'Cuba can live without meat, water, even dancing,' proclaimed Mañach, 'but not without liberty.' There were cries of 'Chibás, Chibás, Chibás', and demands that the U.S. should boycott the regime.[16] The students, secure in the sanctuary of their autonomous university, were thus able to maintain a front of hostility. In June they proposed that the solution to the political problem in Cuba should be the resignation of Batista, followed by a provisional presidency, to be appointed, as Grau had been in 1933, by the FEU till elections were held. Students called on the public (usually through loudspeakers) to reject Batista's Constitution and swear support of the 1940 Constitution.

With the legislature dormant, there remained only one institution which reflected representative opinion – the municipalities or the mayoralties. Here all stood or fell by what happened in Havana. The Havana municipal council included several prominent citizens some of whom, like the historian Portell Vilá, had tried unsuccessfully to build up Cuban politics from that level. On the municipal council there was also César Escalante, a Communist of long standing and of *bourgeois* origins, brother of the editor of *Hoy*, Aníbal Escalante. Here if anywhere a stand might perhaps still be made. All the elected councillors refused to swear the Batista statutes. But a few weeks later César Escalante was arrested with Nila Ortega, leading a demonstration outside the city hall. Portell Vilá was stopped by Lieutenant Chorro, armed with a machine gun. He was never able to return.[17] Thereafter opponents of Batista did not go to Havana or any other city hall.

By midsummer Batista had thus survived the storms which had followed his insolent capture of power in March. In June he tried to define to the country more precisely why he at least thought he should remain in the President's Palace: he made three speeches, explaining that his 'liberation movement' had made an end of a disastrous regime of disorder, anarchy, concupiscence, vice, venality and ineptitude; and that he, Batista, needed time to study the 'tremendous problems' facing Cuba. Violence, he explained, derived from the opposition; he

[16] *Ibid.*, 22 May 1953.
[17] Evidence of Herminio Portell Vilá.

personally had ended gangsterism as well as suppressing smuggling
and bribery, and allowing the reorganization of government departments. He promised agrarian reform, public beaches, public works,
cheap housing, honest government and educational reforms (a 'school
wardrobe' for school children). Constantly, he blamed Prío for all
shortcomings. On 4 July Batista told the *Havana Post* that his revolution
was intended to 'eliminate the cancer which was consuming the vital
organs of the nation' – that is, the conspirators and gangsters of the past.
As an earnest of its high intentions, the government had decided to
revive the Grau case once again; and both Grau and his Minister of
Agriculture, Germán Álvarez Fuentes, were brought up on a new charge
and forced to deposit $40,000 to enjoy provisional liberty.[18] Other
'cancers', however, still flourished. *Botellas* (sinecures) increased. In
the countryside landowners connected with the regime or the army
were able to do much as they liked, living outside the law: thus in
Oriente some landowners were able to take over the property of
peasants by sheer force of arms: in the *hacienda* Arroyo del Medio,
in Mayarí Arriba, seven families were evicted, their houses wrecked, and
700 *caballerías* taken over in mid-1953 by a certain Baldomero Casas
and his nephew Álvaro;[19] while from the very beginning every public
work contract, of which there were many, brought its 30 per cent commission to various secretaries and assistants of the President and thence
to Batista's bank account.[20] On 14 June the students took advantage
of another famous anniversary, Maceo's birthday, to march up the
Prado in Havana making protest, in elaborate mourning for the recently
dead horse 'Caporal' which had belonged to Eddy Chibás. That night
a U.S. Embassy official did a disproportionate amount of harm to
Cuban–U.S. relations by drunkenly driving his car into the police
across red lights, and, when finally captured, by announcing, 'I am a
North American citizen and no authority of a country of Indians can
detain me.'[21]

The Auténticos began a lengthy attempt to lure the Ortodoxos
into collaboration, proposing a 'civic front' of resistance to Batista.
The Ortodoxos were, however, themselves divided in this matter –
Mañach and Márquez Sterling leading those in favour of an alliance.
But, alas, while the Auténticos, in their humiliation, were surprisingly
united, the Ortodoxos were proudly split. The heritage of Chibás had
many heads. What did Agramonte stand for, what did Márquez Sterling, and what about 'Millo' Ochoa?

Another movement altogether was being formed by Dr Rafael

[18] HAR, July 1952.
[19] *Revolución*, 27 January 1959, 5.
[20] Suárez Núñez, 21.
[21] *Bohemia*, 29 June 1952.

García Barcena, one of the most attractive and intelligent of the generation of 1933, who as professor of the Escuela Superior de Guerra (a post given to him by Grau) had already tried to form a conspiracy of officers against Prío, and who now prepared a gathering of liberal officers against Batista. García Barcena, noted for his anti-Communism and his nationalism, had some almost Fascist characteristics – particularly a reliance on demagogy and eloquence and a personal clique of devoted friends (without ideology but with loyalty to him), desiring power though lacking administrative experience. His movement, the Movimiento Nacional Revolucionaria (MNR), gathered momentum among students and younger professional people in Havana for a time. It seemed to satisfy their demands for 'action', rather than discussions of ideology. The only other movement was led by Prío's Minister of Education, Sánchez Arango, whose organization, the triple A (a codeword, nicknamed Amigos de Aureliano Arango), represented the most respectable of those who were actually trying to do something more than talk.

García Barcena's was an interesting movement. Mario Llerena, one of its central committee members, who had at first been impressed by García Barcena himself because of his 'charming personality', and 'sympathised right away with his idea of organising armed action against the Batista government', later 'came to realise that the MNR was not entirely democratic':

> Two of the members of the central committee betrayed a definite fascist mentality. Another . . . was, as it turned out later, a Marxist. García Barcena himself, while looking and sounding like a true freedom-loving man, was somewhat lax and sceptical in regard to democratic procedure. Whether he felt the same way about the democratic philosophy itself I never knew. His immediate political objective seemed to amount to something like a moral, constructive dictatorship.[22]

The MNR was indeed one of the many tributary movements of what ultimately became Castroism, or, as it was later re-christened, Cuban Communism, both so far as its ideology and its intellectual approach is concerned and in respect of its actual membership.

There were meantime constant arrests: Jorge Agostini, for a time chief of Prío's secret service, was accused of arms smuggling; Hevia, the Auténtico presidential candidate in March, was for a time imprisoned on a trumped-up charge of gangsterism. The secretary-general of the Transport Workers, Marco Antonio Hirigoyen, was arrested for the murder in a gang battle in 1947 of Manuel Montero Castillo, a tramway

[22] Mario Llerena, Memoir (unpublished MSS), p. 3.

worker; his lawyers, Arnaldo Escalona (a Communist)[23] and Jesús Rolando Valera, were detained too.

Batista and those around him were thus shown to be nervous, insecure and suspicious, even by their own definition, of many whom they should have sought to placate. The top ranks of the military were from the start disgruntled: the chief of staff, Tabernilla Dolz, was at odds with the Minister of Defence, Nicolás Hernández ('Colacho'); the chief of police, Salas Cañizares, took orders not from the Ministry of the Interior nor the head of the army, but only from Batista. Soon the army was dominated by a net of intrigue and distrust, exacerbated by Tabernilla's recall of all officers dismissed by Grau in 1944-5, who were given their back pay over seven or eight years as well. Tabernilla was concerned to establish a network of officers loyal to him – an activity which made enemies not only of the professional group of officers, the *puros*, who had joined since 1945 but of those – the *tanquistas* – who had begun the conspiracy against Prío and who now were increasingly disillusioned, having hoped for a tougher, stricter and more puritanical regime. The only real protests were made by the articulate but relatively small professional middle class. As for the masses, unawakened, their imaginations concentrated on the lottery and on the harvest, and their long unsatisfied thirst for a miraculous cure of their ills seemed briefly assuaged by the extraordinary success of a self-styled faith healer, a singer named Clavelito, who would appear either in life or on the wireless armed with a glass of water and bring almost immediate healing to all disease. The programme was so successful that Unión Radio, which refused to ban Clavelito's programme, was eventually suspended.

The largest sugar harvest in Cuban history had meantime been reaped. Its size was due to excessive sowing in the first days of the Korean War as well as to the coincidence of specially good weather. Restriction of the harvest was politically unpopular; hence Prío had shrunk from it. Nor did Batista's government face the problem: by March, indeed, it would have been difficult to restrict the harvest fairly. There was a feeling that the larger the surplus, the larger the quota would be at the next world conference (planned for 1953). Yet as production went up, prices, partly for that reason, partly due to the decline of world tension after Korea, went down. The government decided finally to keep back 1·7 million tons as a reserve to be sold over the next five years and to restrict the next year's harvest. This plan was vigorously attacked by, among others, Lobo, the biggest Cuban mill owner.

The summer was full of plots and rumours as this great harvest came

[23] His wife was director of the Escuela Normal in Havana. Longstanding party members, the Escalonas were examples of the best sort of progressive and humane Cubans.

in. The chief of police accused nearly every politician of some sort of plot during August: a meeting in Santiago commemorating the anniversary of the death of Chibás was broken up by the arrest of Roberto Agramonte, with Raúl Chibás, Eddy's brother, Luis Conte Agüero and Luis Orlando Rodríguez, all Ortodoxo writers and leaders. Ochoa too was once again arrested on a charge of using television to incite the public to revolt. Tried and found guilty, he refused to pay a fine and so remained in prison. On 17 August a new and sinister event occurred, intolerably reminiscent of the era of Machado: a leading opposition half-Chinese journalist, Mario Kuchilán, who worked on the paper *La Calle*, was called out of his house in Havana at about nine o'clock in the evening, pushed into an Oldsmobile, driven into the Country Club district and beaten, the blows being punctuated with demands for news of the whereabouts of Aureliano Sánchez Arango. Kuchilán escaped alive and got home. The Journalists' Association demanded a seventy-two hour strike of newspapers. The Information Minister, Ernesto de la Fe, blandly said that the Legión Caribe, Prío's famous democratic international squadron, must be responsible. Batista himself spoke of this 'indescribable brutality', and let it be understood that he personally thought the attack had been framed by his enemies to discredit the regime. He said he would fight *gangsterismo* everywhere, 'even in the circle of my friends'. Some attempt was made to carry this into effect: police who beat two photographers for trying to photograph others while being beaten up were suspended. There was also an amnesty cutting sentences for minor offences by a third; but this was, of course, an attempt to please, not to make political concessions.

In October the new Batista constitutional code was published: anyone wishing to organize a party had to gather 5,000 signatures and, after January 1953 parties could act normally, preparing for the elections in November 1953. There would be nine senators for each province, six for the party or *bloc* which gained a majority of votes there, and three for the minority or runner-up. Parties which had been dissolved in March could reorganize themselves providing they could boast 6% of the electorate. The president would be elected by direct vote, and would take office in May 1954. There would be one member of the House of Representatives for each 45,000 inhabitants, each to serve four years. Half would be renewed every two years. Political meetings could be held, provided that those who requested them 'observed the law'. They also had to 'recognise and respect' the existing government and to refrain from inflammatory statements.[24]

All parties of the opposition found this too insulting to take much

[24] HAR, November 1952.

notice of: besides, they had other plans. $240,000 to buy arms for action against Batista were stolen from the friends of Prío in a hotel at Fort Worth, Florida: about half of this sum was later found in a thermos flask in Texas. Another incident occurred in New York State, where police discovered $10,000 worth of arms for Cuba. The Auténticos' hand, mildly fortified by the adherence of an old enemy leader from the Liberals, Eduardo Suárez Rivas, and by some co-operation between Varona and Grau, was once more stretched out to the Ortodoxos. It remained unclasped. Among the Ortodoxos, Agramonte and Ochoa were still at loggerheads, and on 7 October, Agramonte challenged Ochoa to a duel over this very question of alliance with the Auténticos. After elaborate preparations, made in the full glare of public knowledge, the duel was called off. Ochoa resigned his position in the movement and then withdrew his resignation.

There was of course widespread disillusion with this prevaricating and ineffective Ortodoxo leadership; some members of the Young Ortodoxos joined the Communist Youth (Juventud Socialista).[25] Still the press (to which, of course, many political leaders contributed as individuals) remained the most important institution of critical comment and opposition. On 14 October 1952 most of the leading newspapers demanded immediate elections and announced that Cuba was in economic and political peril; and it was in *Bohemia* that Agramonte on 10 November dispatched an open letter to Batista:

> If our country which was born with the most generous democratic ideals, in a heroic fight against abuse and despotism, has to return to the dark and sombre days of the *Machadato*, the fault will be yours, General Batista . . . I accuse you, Fulgencio Batista, of being the great obstacle for the happiness of the poor crushed Cuban people.[26]

And it was in *Bohemia* also that Dr Pelayo Cuervo revealed curious details of the new regime; how interesting, he pointed out, that Francisco Blanco, manager of Batista's own sugar *central, Washington*, had paid $M24 to Dr Jorge Barroso, the Sugar Board chief, and how almost every morning Blanco went to visit Amadeo López Castro, the government's representative at the committee on sugar sales. Was it as a result of this that the Vendedor Único, the single Cuban selling agency, dominated by Blanco, had been set up?

Nothing happened to Pelayo Cuervo for the moment. But Batista made an effort to tighten censorship. Grau meantime continued to keep the Auténticos in the same fissiparous condition as the Ortodoxos

[25] Raúl Castro, *Fundamentos*, June–July 1961, 8–9.
[26] *Bohemia*, 16 November 1952.

by claiming to be their new leader through getting 12,300 signatures in his support.

The first martyr in the struggle against the new dictatorship came on 15 January 1953, when a student named Batista (Rubén Batista) was shot when taking part in a banned student procession in memory of Mella; he later died. 'The blood of good men does not flow in vain,' announced with bravura the student leader Barba at the funeral. Another demonstration shared in by all classes occurred at the centenary of the death of Martí on 28 January. On 10 March there were riots inspired by the students in protest against the first anniversary of the *golpe*. As expected, Batista made a speech, only promising, however, maintenance of high police and army salaries. He accused Prío and his brother of stealing $M20 from the Treasury: they replied from Mexico that it had been lent to them. Batista also announced that Prío could return when he wished. Prío said that he would not dream of doing so until Batista had left.

In April 1953 more serious events occurred. On Easter Sunday Professor García Barcena's MNR finally took action and a large group of students and lecturers, armed with knives and guns, marched on Campamento Columbia with a plan to try to persuade the military there to rise against Batista.[27] The government was appraised of the plot and was ready. All were arrested, as were García Barcena and José Pardo Llada, who had been on the movement's fringes. A week later the police dispersed two hundred students who had gathered to place a wreath on the tomb of Rubén Batista. There was also a demonstration at the Medical School, where two students were shot and ten others beaten by the police. On 14 April the university was summarily closed by its council (dominated by Batista men), but even so the police had to arrest another 175 students, including thirty-two girls, at the Faculty of Arts on 23 April. On 27 April García Barcena and sixty-nine others were tried, García Barcena having been tortured so vilely that his spirit and any political career that he might have had were finished; even so he was sentenced to two years' imprisonment and twelve others were given provisional terms of one year. His movement col- lapsed.[28] Resignations followed from the medical faculty. When the university was reopened, the students went on strike. In May Pelayo Cuervo made another violent attack on Batista in *Bohemia*, saying that the only way to oust him was through force of arms. He also accused

[27] The Central Committee of the MNR had been divided between 'electoralists' and 'insurrectionists'; the latter won.

[28] And his followers, young men such as Armando Hart, Faustino Pérez, Manuel Fer- nández, Frank País, Mario Llerena – all future followers of Castro to one point or another – had to seek another star. García Barcena obtained liberty on the undertaking that he would do no more against the regime – which undertaking he fulfilled.

officers in the new army of the old crime of swindling the lottery. He was arrested and charged with inciting a revolt.

The atmosphere was thus everywhere warming up. No doubt this was responsible for at least a degree of agreement being reached at last by the Ortodoxos and Auténticos on some sort of common action. Prío and Ochoa signed an agreement at Montreal by which they undertook to aim to restore the 1940 Constitution. They called for a new provisional government, as well as a committee to coordinate action. But this was all that occurred, either in Montreal or in subsequent meetings at the Hotel Plaza in New York and the Ritz Carlton, and not all the leading Ortodoxos signed: Cuervo after all was in prison, Agramonte was being accused of *colaboracionismo* – i.e. considering taking part in the 1954 elections, while Prío was criticized from the left of the Ortodoxos as interested only in restoration, not renewal (*restauracionismo*).[29] Despite this, the situation, violent and unpromising though it might remain, was better in July 1953 from the point of view of the opposition than it had been for some time. Meanwhile, a new grouping, *Acción Libertadora*, was formed in May under the leadership of the ex-head of the agricultural development bank, Carrillo, with the backing of some students such as Barba and Baeza, some trade unionists such as Calixto Sánchez, and some professional men.

[29] The Montreal document was signed by Prío, Ochoa, Varona, Parda Llada, Alonso Pujol, Isidoro Figuera, Hevia, José Manuel Gutiérrez and Eduardo Suárez Rivas.

CHAPTER LXVII

Fidel Castro: Childhood and Youth

In the early summer of 1953 the historian of Cuban–U.S. relations, Portell Vilá, was sitting in a bar in Havana when a young ex-pupil of his at the university passing by told him that he was planning an attack on the Moncada barracks at Santiago de Cuba, a gloomy pile named after a Negro commander in the war of 1895. Portell Vilá tried to dissuade the conspirator but he was adamant, explaining how he had the arms, the volunteers, and the enthusiasm, and how the attack would be a great moral blow against the regime.[1]

The ex-pupil was Fidel Castro Ruz, then just under twenty-seven years old,[2] and at that time a member of the left wing of the Ortodoxos, known for his energy and gift of language. His character since that time has become widely known, but while few have been so vilified few have also been so praised. It is desirable therefore to gain some impression of his earlier life and experiences.

Castro's father, Angel Castro, like the father of so many Cubans, had come from Galicia in north-west Spain, with the Spanish army at the time of the Spanish-American war. He was a strong man, in physique and in character, willing to do anything, suited to do well out of the general social collapse that attended the end of Spanish rule and the coming of the Americans and the independent Republic. He worked on the United Fruit Company railway in 1904, and otherwise as a day labourer near Antilla,[3] but despite this (or perhaps because of it) he always had a violent hispanic antipathy towards the North Americans, who, he thought, rightly, had cheated the Spaniards out of victory over the Cuban rebels: an odd origin, but no doubt genuine, for his son's similarly hispanic dislike of the Monster of the North.[4] By one means or

---

[1] Portell Vilá, evidence to the author. There are already several lives of Fidel Castro. The most favourable is that by Herbert Matthews, *Castro, a Political Biography* (London, 1969), and the most hostile are the works of his old friend, Luis Conte Agüero, *Los Dos Rostros de Fidel Castro* (Mexico, 1960), and a new edition, *Fidel Castro, Psiquiatría y Política* (Mexico, 1968). Castro's autobiograpy, long expected, has yet to appear.

[2] Castro was born on 13 August 1926, despite rumours that he was actually born a year later.

[3] According to a vice-president of the United Fruit Company to the author, Angel Castro had been a checker of sugar and had been charged with systematic theft, though the charge was dropped.

[4] A rather wild but suggestive biographical article by Julio del Mar in *El Diario de Nueva York*, 20 July 1962, hints that Castro's family were *integristas*, i.e. Right-wing Carlists, in politics: The village from which they came was Lanteira (Lugo).

another Angel Castro accumulated money enough to buy land, and later succeeded in expanding it, by what means is somewhat speculatory. He appears to have been able to profit by the revolution of 1917 through looking after United Fruit Company property and increasing his own estate at the cost of the company. He worked, perhaps not always honestly, but anyway no less so than, say, H. E. Catlin, or Perceval Farquhar. He hacked his farm out of forest, perhaps sometimes on moonless nights, perhaps by stealing title deeds. His son admitted that Angel Castro paid 'no taxes on his land or income'.[5] His farm, a mixed farm but one which grew cane, lay at a village named Birán near Mayarí, twenty miles inland, in a countryside which till the twentieth century had remained unsubdued, virgin soil; the region had, however, been opened up by the Antilla railway and by the foundation in 1901 and 1904 of the United Fruit Company's great sugar mills, *Boston* and *Preston*. Mayarí, the municipality, increased in population ten times between 1899 and 1953; the village and surroundings of Birán, a United Fruit Company town in every respect, increased no less than sixteen times in the same period, from 529 to 8,305.[6]

The land lying round the Bay of Nipe is among the most beautiful in Cuba. The town of Mayari, inland from the centre of the bay, is old; that of Antilla, on the west, is twentieth-century, being founded as the northern end of the Cuban railway system. The river Mayarí meanders into the bay, its banks being one of the oldest tobacco regions of Cuba, though latterly neglected. However, in the twentieth century there was some diversification of agriculture in the neighbourhood: some cattle, even some corn. Once there had been two small sugar mills in the valley. In the twentieth century the whole area was dominated by four great U.S. companies – not just the United Fruit, but also the Dumois–Nipe Company,[7] the Spanish–American Iron Company and the Cuba Railroad Company.[8] Beyond was forest, except where men such as Angel Castro had carved a *colonia*.

Few places in Cuba were quite so dominated by the North American presence. The United Fruit Company's employees had a polo club, swimming pools, shops for U.S. goods. Even the post office and rural guard headquarters were on company land. The company had its own force of twenty field soldiers, licensed to bear arms. At both *Boston* and *Preston* there were schools and hospitals, and every possible amenity. From Antilla to New York the Munson line maintained a fortnightly service. Only a few miles along the coast were the Nicaro nickel deposits, developed in the Second World War – probably the most

[5] Lee Lockwood, *Castro's Cuba, Cuba's Fidel*, 25.
[6] See Census of 1899, 189, and census of 1953, 193.
[7] Bananas, grapefruit, oranges, sugar cane.
[8] The Nipe Bay Co. in which the *Preston* was vested, was owned by the UFCO.

valuable industrial plant in Cuba, with an estimated capital of $M85. It was owned by the U.S. government itself and was not now working. At Felton, the Spanish–American Iron Company also presided for years over deposits which, at the time, it was uneconomic to mine.[9] Work had gone on at Felton from 1908 till 1917, and then closed.[10]

In 1953 the municipality of Mayarí had a working population of 24,000, of which 15,000 were engaged in agriculture, 3,000 in manufacture, and nearly 2,000 in shopkeeping or some kind of trading.[11] There were about twice as many white as black or mulatto (54,000 to 27,000).[12] Under 250 (1 % of the adult population) had attended a university course. 30,000 out of a total population of nearly 70,000 over six years old had not even made the first grade in education. It was therefore a poor area; Castro himself said that most of his companions at the village school went barefoot.[13] Very few of Mayarí's 15,000 houses had lavatories, baths or showers.[14] Fourteen per cent of the people were said to be unemployed or 'looking for a job'.[15]

Angel Castro's *hacienda*, Manacas, grew to about 10,000 acres and dominated the surrounding area.[16] According to his daughter Juana, it employed 500 men.[17] Though the farm produced mixed crops its main activity was growing sugar cane to be sold to the *Central Miranda* ten miles to the south. In the 1950s its quota was about 18,000 tons of cane a year.

Angel Castro made two marriages. By the first, a school teacher – most school teachers in Cuba were women – there were a son and a daughter (Pedro Emilio and Lidia; the former became an Auténtico politician, the latter married an army officer). Afterwards, the great sugar boom during the First World War brought many living in Pinar del Río or Matanzas eastwards in search of work, amid the crashing trees of East Cuba and the foundation of new sugar principalities. Among them was Lina Ruz González, a girl from Pinar del Río who worked for a time as a cook in Angel's house and later (while the first

[9] The Spanish–American Iron Co. was a subsidiary of Bethlehem Steel.

[10] *Cf.* description in Wright, 494–501; World Bank, 211, 996–7; Jenks, 292.

[11] Census of 1953, 193.

[12] More Negroes were 'urban' than 'rural'.

[13] Letter, qu. Robert Merle, *Moncada, premier combat de Fidel Castro* (1965), 342.

[14] Census of 1953, 248. B. Goldenberg, *The Cuban Revolution and Latin America* (1965), 148 says Castro's house did not have a bathroom or an indoor lavatory.

[15] Census of 1953, 160. In 1899 the population of the municipality of Mayarí reached 8,504; in Birán, the second *barrio* in the district, where Angel Castro eventually placed his farm, 529 (Census of 1899, 189). In 1907 Mayarí reached 17,628 and Birán 2,280; Mayarí reached 45,126 in 1931, Birán 3,787. By 1943 Mayarí had a population of 61,172 and Birán 4,505 (Census of 1943, summary, i.e. Birán doubled in size between 1943 and 1953).

[16] Lee Lockwood (*Castro's Cuba, Cuba's Fidel*, 25), has a story of Fidel and Raúl Castro disputing, in May 1965, how many *caballería* of land their father owned. The above is a rough calculation.

[17] *Life*, 28 August 1964.

wife still lived) gave Angel Castro five more children: Ramón, Fidel, Juana, Emma and Raúl. It does not seem, however, that Angel Castro ever settled down with one woman.

The early lives of men who become famous are often shrouded in

myth; that of Castro is more obscure than usual due to the break that he made afterwards with his upbringing and with his parents' world. In some ways, of course, his parents did not have a world: they were both *nouveau*, both in different ways ambitious and greedy, both restless and insecure, he an immigrant from Spain and a self-made rich man, she an internal immigrant from the country of tobacco, both now living in the profitable but savage sugar territory of Oriente, where the few villages were formless shanty gatherings without traditions or churches, where bandits of various types persisted into the 1950s and where the dominant institution was the United Fruit Company's mills with their private railways, their wharves and their seemingly insatiable demands on the soil.

It is easy to picture the exciting childhood led by the Castro family – fishing, hunting, shooting, surrounded by dogs. The atmosphere in the household was evidently savage: Angel, reticent, violent, hard-working, and rich, resembling *le père* Grandet, though more generous with money, or the father of Cirilo Villaverde, the novelist, who is described as having 'neither time nor inclination to talk with his sons':[18] no emphasis on comfort: poverty and squalor nearby, unredeemed by even the minor advantages that long traditions may bring. Castro's mother liked money and possessions; thus in 1957, after her husband was dead, she visited Mexico when her son was fighting a guerrilla war in the hills of Cuba. She complained to a group of Castro's supporters that her cane fields had been burned, and she had spent $26,000 having them weeded. She asked for it to be arranged that her crop should be left alone, though she did not help her cause when she explained that Batista's soldiery dropped in to see her for coffee.[19]

However it was accumulated, Angel Castro's fortune enabled him to circumvent the depression. In the early 1930s he began to consider the question of the education of his second family,[20] who previously had only been to the hardly existent local school. He called on the college of La Salle in Santiago de Cuba, directed by the Marianist brothers, where many upper-class boys of Oriente went: the registrar insisted on baptism and confirmation, and also on his religious marriage to his new wife, since the first wife had now died. This was arranged by the bishop of Camagüey, Enrique Pérez Serantes, from Galicia like Angel Castro, and an old friend.[21] Ramón, Fidel and later Raúl then went to the Colegio La Salle, later to the Colegio Dolores, Santiago, and after to Belén, the famous Jesuit school in Havana – an educational path which had been followed twenty years before by Eddy Chibás. It is perhaps possible to trace in Castro's father's hostility to legal forms in both property and personal relations his son's lack of interest in constitutionalism, bureaucracy and formality of any kind.

The Jesuit education made a strong impression on Castro. He became known there as a debater and athlete, and as the owner of an excellent memory. He gained a prize in 1943–4 as Cuba's best all-round school athlete. Here again myth takes over: 'He had many heroes during his boyhood and youth . . . Lenin, Hitler, José Antonio Primo de Rivera . . . Mussolini . . . Perón . . . He knew the speeches of José Antonio by memory . . . He knew *Mein Kampf* and also Lenin's *What is to be Done?*'[22] Thus one recollection; and it is clear from the internal evidence of Castro's speeches that José Antonio was an inspiration to

[18] In *Nota Biográfica* to the 1941 edition of Cecilia Valdés.
[19] Casuso, 131.
[20] i.e. by Lina Ruz de Castro.
[21] This derives from a reliable source, an attorney who watched the Castro estates grow.
[22] José Antonio Rasco to Daniel James, *Cuba: the First Satellite in the Americas* (New York, 1961), 34. Also told to me by Portell Vilá.

him. 'The first time I heard of him was when he wrote to President Roosevelt asking for $20 and congratulating him on his victory in 1940. The State Department's answer was posted up on the door, giving thanks and regrets that no money could be sent.'[23] One school contemporary commented: 'The Jesuits were training him to be the white hope of the right.' School stories are not easy to disentangle. One priest, Fr Jean Marie Ramousse, who claimed to have taught him at La Salle, said that though Castro worked quite hard in the classes, outside he was 'insupportable', being always surrounded by a gang of followers and eventually he was removed to the Jesuits who, the Marianists supposed, could do better with him.[24] Evidently, though, he was not an insistent rebel, accepting much of his conventional education with a good grace. His brother Raúl is perhaps a reliable witness here: 'He succeeded in everything. In sport, in study. And every day he fought. He had a very explosive nature. He defied the most powerful and the strongest and when he was beaten he began again the next day. He never gave up.'[25] At least it is evident that Castro seemed then strong, ambitious, well read; a host of historical allusions crop up all the time in his later revolutionary speeches. It also seems that so far as the family was concerned Castro was rebellious: in 1940, aged thirteen, he tried to organize a strike of sugar workers against his father; when he was eighteen there were many quarrels, Castro calling his father to his face 'one of those who abuse the powers they wrench from the people with deceitful promises'.[26] Even so, he continued to expect and to receive financial support from his father.[27] He was following partly, perhaps, his elder brother, Pedro Emilio, who had broken with the father in 1940 and denounced him over the radio in Santiago as a thief, and partly perhaps a Spaniard named Salazar, a teacher, hired as a tutor by Mayarí families and a survivor of the Spanish Civil War. Pedro Emilio was by the 1950s a minor Auténtico politician in Oriente.[28]

Castro's early impressions and ambitions were mostly therefore formed by conditions in Oriente province, the most savage part of Cuba, where gun-law often reigned; the area where the U.S. influence was strongest and most brutally exercised; where the doctors, teachers, dentists and indeed all social professions were least

[23] Told me by a school friend of Castro's at Colegio Dolores, Santiago.
[24] Fr Ramousse, *Bohemia Libre*, 3 September 1961.
[25] To Robert Merle (Merle, *op. cit.*, 90).
[26] But Juana Castro (*Life*, 28 August 1964) says that Castro never showed interest in the *guajiros* on their father's farm; he is alleged even to have criticized his father for over-generosity to these peasants. This is not very reliable evidence.
[27] See comment by the Wohlstetters, *Controlling the risks in Cuba* (Adelphi Papers (Institute for Strategic Studies) April 1965), 7. See also the somewhat unreliable article by Emma and Lidia Castro, as told to Michael Erice, '*Vida de Fidel Castro*', *El Diario de Nueva York*, 22 April–1 May 1957.
[28] *Cartas del Presidio*, 32.

numerous in proportion to the population. Castro could have known little of Matanzas or Pinar del Río (save through his mother), the old sugar and tobacco areas. Nor could the memory of slavery have been a dominant one among those who were living around him. Many Spanish rather than explicitly Cuban traditions came to him either through his father, or perhaps through the Spaniard Salazar, or the Jesuits: thus he is found saying, as he watched the elections of 1954 from prison: 'what good luck to watch the bulls from the good seats':[29] Cuba of course had no bullfights after 1898.

At the same time his curious family background was certainly unrestful and insecure: the Balzac-like father, like so many characters out of those Latin-American novels which Anglo-Saxons and Europeans find difficult to read; the wildness of the family plantation; the link which the family had perforce with the *Central Miranda*, the medium-size U.S.-owned mill to which the Castros sent their sugar; the fact indeed that this mill had been founded in the great boom of 1917, and was an efficient mill, with its high yield[30] and increasing production from an increasing number of *colonia* – in 1958 there would be 374 *colonia*, in 1937, 73;[31] the fact that Castro's father had not only fought for the Spaniards (against Martí, Maceo, Gómez) but had worked for the United Fruit Co.; the intellectual agility prized by the Jesuit schools; and the disputes within the Castro family; all these influences blended to create the mercurial but forceful character which Fidel Castro now proceeded to display.[32]

Castro went to the University of Havana in October 1945, in a car given to him by his father.[33] He appeared from the beginning possessed with desire to triumph at all costs and always over the most heavily weighted odds. Within a week of the beginning of the term at the university Professor Portell Vilá, the same who saw him in July 1953, was greeted by a porter who said: 'Don't you know there are no students, everyone has gone to watch the fight – the President of the FEU [Student Federation] has been challenged by a freshman, Fidel Castro.'[34] The pattern became settled: Castro drove a bicycle hard into a brick wall to prove to onlookers he had the willpower to do something they would never do.

Castro chose to study law without much more appreciation of what

[29] *Loc. cit.*
[30] In 1937 its yield was 14·54%, higher than anywhere else in Oriente.
[31] *Anuario Azucarero*, 1937, 1959.
[32] An ex-police officer of President Prío, Salvador Díaz Versón, claims that Castro was recruited as a Soviet agent in 1943 by the Russian diplomat Bashirov. See his article in *El Mundo* (Miami), 9 December 1961. No one who has known Castro at any time could believe this.
[33] Juana Castro, *Life*, 28 August 1964.
[34] Evidence of Professor Portell Vilá.

810 · THE STRUGGLE 1952-9

it would lead to than many English students who choose that faculty.[35] In 1961 he said, 'I ask myself why I studied law. I don't know. I attribute it partly to those who said "He talks a lot, he ought to be a lawyer". Because I had the habit of debating and discussing, I was persuaded I was qualified to be a lawyer.'[36] But he was a student who 'never went to lectures, never opened a book except just before examinations';[37] 'how often have I not regretted that I was not made to study something else.'[38]

From the beginning at the university, in fact, Castro spent his time in political activity. For his first two years he was elected 'class delegate' in the Law School – partly at least as a result of his athletic prowess at school. Among his friends were Alfredo Guevara and Leonel Soto, already members of the Communist youth, the first being then president of the Social Sciences Faculty Students and secretary of the FEU in 1948, the latter president of the School of Philosophy and Letters. Castro entered politics at the university as he had been athletically active at school, because it was 'the favourite hobby or obsession. It was the anteroom to power . . . There was nothing odd or unusual about this. The political atmosphere in the University was so charged and pervasive that many were caught up in it.'[39] Thus from 1946 onwards Castro belonged to the millenarian minority of the population of Cuba, phrasing heroic slogans, recalling past heroes, an active political minority: it is as a representative of the law faculty in September 1946, supporting Chibás and in January 1947, criticizing Grau's 're-electionism', that Castro first appears as a politician.[40] In this speech, Castro is found talking of the '*pléiade*' of students who faced the dictatorship (of Machado).[41] From the second term of his university career, Castro had also, like most of his fellow student leaders, a connection with at least two of the revolutionary organizations which dominated university politics and threatened national affairs.

His university career was, therefore, already extraordinary, and it became more so. Castro himself later spoke of the time in fairly candid terms:

The political atmosphere in the University of Havana had been contaminated by the national disorder. My impetuosity, my desire

[35] Theodore Draper is scornful of Castro's decision to read law. 'He chose a field of study in which the standards were notoriously low, the pressure to study minimal and his future profession already over-crowded.' (*Castroism: theory and practice* (1965), 114.)
[36] *Revolución*, 10 April 1961.
[37] *Ibid.*, 7 March 1964.
[38] *Ibid.*, 14 March 1964.
[39] Comments of Fructuoso Pérez.
[40] Conte Agüero, 457.
[41] *El Mundo*, 17 January 1947, and 17 July 1947.

to excel fed and inspired the character of my struggle. My straightforward character made me enter rapidly into conflict with the *milieu*, the venal authorities, the corruption and the gang-ridden system which dominated the university atmosphere. The pressure groups of corrupt politicians made the gangs threaten me and led to a prohibition on my entering the University. This was a great moment of decision. The conflict struck my personality like a cyclone. Alone, on the beach, facing the sea, I examined the situation. Personal danger, physical risk made my return to the University an act of unheard-of temerity. But not to return would be to give in to threats, to give in before bullies, to abandon my own ideals and aspirations. I decided to go back and I went back . . . *with arms in my hand* . . .[42] Naturally I did not find myself fully prepared to understand exactly the roots of the profound crisis which disfigured the country. This resulted in my resistance being centred on the idea of personal valour.[43]

Reading between the lines, it is clear that Castro must have indeed been threatened, that perhaps to begin with against his will he joined in the extraordinary gang warfare in which against his better judgement he excelled. It should be remembered too that the 'action groups', though they had degenerated into *gangsterismo*, were not even in 1948 wholly bereft of idealism and political romanticism.

The two groups with whom Castro was in any way implicated were, first, Rolando Masferrer's MSR, and the UIR, led, until his murder, by Emilio Tró, the police boss of Marianao. The revolutionary violence which characterized the students who had overthrown Machado never lost its fundamentally romantic appeal. The future leader of the Cuban socialist revolution was blooded in politics during the machine-gun and big car era in the time of Grau and, whatever part he personally played it is evident that he learned much about the nature of Cuban political institutions, their feebleness, their susceptibility to violence and their corruption.[44] On the other hand, though Castro used all the action groups, he failed to be elected either president of the Law Students or president of the FEU.

Elections in student politics at Havana were often settled by fists, guns and kidnappings. Some shootings were attributed to Castro. Thus in December 1946 Leonel Gómez, president of the Student Federation at the (first) Havana High School, and a member of the UIR, was wounded in Rionda Street. This attack had apparently been

[42] Author's italics.
[43] Remarks to Gloria Gaitán de Valencia, *América Libre* (Bogotá), 22–8 May 1961.
[44] This is well put by Suárez, *Cuba: Castroism and Communism* (MIT Press, 1967), 18.

engineered by Manolo Castro, the president of the Students' Union, since Gómez had bragged that he was going to enter the university and take over power there. At this time Fidel Castro was anxious to gain the confidence of Manolo Castro in order to help him in his own university ambitions, and (according to another student who was wounded)[45] Fidel Castro and some others were apparently responsible for the shooting.

When still a friend of Manolo Castro, Fidel Castro also took part in the abortive invasion of the Dominican Republic organized by the MSR and other 'action groups' in the summer of 1947.[46] Castro was placed in command of a group of Dominican exiles;[47] but since he was the only member of the UIR on this expedition he was in a delicate position. When the expedition was called off the participants were mostly arrested. Castro was among those who escaped; he swam, carrying an Argentinian sub-machine gun and a pistol, across the Bay of Nipe, known to be infested with sharks, but arrived safely at his father's farm.[48]

By this time, however, it had become clear that Manolo Castro was not going to help Fidel Castro much in his quest for university political leadership, and so he joined his enemies, the UIR, the action group led by Emilio Tró until his death in open battle in Marianao at the hands of Manolo Castro's friends, the Salabarrías. At the same time, through a friendship with Enrique Ovares, Manolo Castro's successor as president of the students' union, Fidel Castro succeeded in being nominated as president of one of the university specialist committees on legal affairs.

In the autumn of the same year, with a group of students (financed by Chibás), Castro went on a wild expedition to Manzanillo to bring back to the students of Havana, as a symbol of a new revolt, the bell which Céspedes had rung as a tocsin in 1868 – which the owners, the surviving veterans of 1898 in the town, had refused to present to the city of Havana.[49] On 12 February 1948 he was involved in a famous clash with the police outside the university in protest again at the invasion of university autonomy.[50] Ten days later, on 22 February 1948, Manolo Castro, State Secretary of Sports, president of the FEU some time before, 'handsome as a picture postcard but a paranoiac', the virtual tyrant of the university, a close friend of the Education Minister Alemán and other Auténtico leaders, was lured out of a cinema (of which he was part-owner) and shot down. Fidel Castro was accused of

[45] Fernando Freyre.
[46] See above, p. 755.
[47] Rolando Masferrer, in a letter to Theodore Draper.
[48] The shark swim is confirmed by Juan Bosch, the Dominican commander who attempted to dissuade him (memorandum of Juan Bosch).
[49] Evidence of Max Lesnick.
[50] Hoy, 13 February 1948.

being implicated in this assassination. He was arrested at the airport, appeared before a judge and had his passport removed.[51] It seems probable that Castro did not participate in the attempt itself nor did he fire a shot in the next street to distract attention, as alleged, but that he was present at the meeting of the UIR which agreed to undertake the attempt.[52] The evidence, however, is inconclusive. The UIR was a group given to black humour – the killers each received engaging nicknames such as Billykin, Bright Eyes, Patachula – and the idea of one Castro killing another would have appealed to the then leader, Justo Fuentes, a Negro gangster and part-time student. It is not a matter on which Fidel Castro has bothered to dwell much in his speeches. (Manolo Castro was, of course, avenged in 1949 by the assassination of Justo Fuentes.[53])

This was certainly the most sensational act of the political gang warfare to date. (Fidel Castro as a suspect told the judge in March that he believed that some of Manolo Castro's friends were out to kill him.) It would not be out of character if Fidel Castro had been involved, and in equity it is not inappropriate to add that in some ways Manolo Castro deserved his fate. Castro gave later an analysis of this stage in his career:

> Without experience but full of youthful rebelliousness, [he had fought] against the imperium of Mario Salabarría . . . This evil which culminated in *autenticismo* had its origins in the resentment and hatred which Batista sowed during [his first] eleven years of abuses and injustices. Those who saw their comrades assassinated wished to avenge them, and a regime which was incapable of imposing justice, permitted vengeance. The blame lies not with those young men who, distracted by their natural anxieties and by the legend of a heroic epoch, desired to make a revolution which had not been achieved, at a moment when it could not be done. *Many of those who, victims of illusion, died as gangsters, would today be heroes.*[54]

On another occasion he remarked, 'When the worst is enthroned, a pistol at his belt, it is necessary to carry pistols oneself in order to fight for the best.'[55]

[51] *Noticias de Hoy*, 21 March 1948 (the Communist paper). Ma nolo Castro's friend, Carlo Puchol Samper, was also killed, and others.

[52] Evidence of Enrique Barroso. Osvaldo Soto (then president of the Law School students) says that Castro invited him and another student (Benito Besada) to a café that night and left a few minutes after arriving (Soto memorandum).

[53] Manuel Corrales, who is believed to have accompanied Manolo Castro from the cinema into the street on this occasion, was appointed by Castro in 1959 to the Cuban delegation to UNESCO. Those who appeared before a court accused of the crime were Fidel Castro, Justo Fuentes, Pedro Mirassón, Armando Galí Menéndez and Gustavo Ortiz Faes.

[54] *Bohemia*, 25 December 1955 (author's italics).

[55] '*Cuando lo peor está entronizado con la pistola al cinto, para luchar por lo mejor hay que portar la pistola también.*' (Remark to Carrillo, September 1955, Carrillo MSS, *Información Histórica*, 8.)

Whatever Castro's part in the death of Manolo Castro, a month later he was implicated in a still more sensational event – the famous 'Bogotazo', as it is now known. Here again rumour and fear have fed fantastically on tragedy: here those who find comfort in seeing themselves threatened by a single, centrally directed minority conspiracy allow Fidel Castro to appear on the scene for the first time, outrageously garbed, the assassin of the Americas, professional subverter of private enterprise.

In April 1948 a Pan-American Conference had been arranged to be held in Bogotá, the capital of Colombia, to reform the old Pan-American Union of American states into a more closely knit organization, the Organization of American States (OAS). General Marshall would arrive representing the U.S. and all other American states would be represented by Foreign Ministers.

A protest to coincide with this assembly was planned by Cuban and Argentinian students, with a sprinkling of others from other parts of Latin America. The fares of many students, including those of the student delegation from Cuba, were paid by Perón, the Argentinian dictator, anxious to make trouble for the U.S. in Latin America.[56] Perón also desired an attack on British imperialism to try to force Britain to return the Falkland Islands to him. Among those asked from Cuba were the president and the secretary of the FEU, Enrique Ovarcs and Alfredo Guevara (the Communist leader in the University of Havana), along with Castro, representing the law faculty of the University of Havana, and Rafael del Pino, a Cuban-American who registered every year as a student but did not attempt much to study, also like Castro a member of UIR. Their meeting at Bogotá was to prepare for a full meeting inaugurating a new inter-American student organization to be held in the autumn, in which Castro had always been interested.[57] Both Communists and Peronists throughout South America collaborated in these student plans.

Castro and del Pino arrived in Bogotá on 29 March 1948, armed with various documents including a letter of introduction from Rómulo Betancourt, the Venezuelan Social Democrat president whom they had visited en route.[58] During the next week they had discussions with other student leaders in Bogotá; on 3 April the Pan-American meeting

[56] Evidence of Max Lesnick, president of Ortodoxo Youth, in letter dated 20 August 1963 to Draper. The Peronist representative in the University of Havana was Santiago Tourino and, according to Carlos Reyes Posada (*El Espectador*, Bogotá, 10 December 1961), the chairman of the Argentinian Senate Foreign Relations Committee, Diego Molinari, visited Havana in February 1948 to arrange the Cuban delegation's expenses.

[57] 'When we were still on good terms with him during his second year . . . we asked him why he wanted to be President of the Law School . . . he would always say that time was running out, that his true ambition was not merely to be president of the FEU but to organize a Federation of Latin American students which would be a tremendous political instrument in South America.' (Memorandum of Fernando Freyre.)

[58] *La República* (Bogotá, 21 January 1959), in *Communist Threat to the Caribbean*, 277.

began and the two groups – the established world of statesmen and diplomats and the new world of placeless and ambitious students – swung towards each other, and clashed for the first time, though gently, as if irregulated pendulums. At a public ceremony in the Teatro Colono attended by the most prominent members of Colombian society and the government, leaflets were dropped in thousands from the balconies, attacking U.S. colonialism. Many of these leaflets were printed in Havana and some were dropped by Castro and del Pino. Interrogated, these two students were ordered to report to the police two days later: when they did not do so, their hotel rooms were searched and more so-called Communist leaflets were found. On 6 April both were taken to the police headquarters and ordered to cease '*actos hostiles*'.

On 9 April the worlds of statesmen and students clashed again, much more severely. At about 1.20 p.m. the much-loved Colombian Liberal demagogue Jorge Eliécer Gaitán, the Chibás of Colombia it might be argued, was murdered, in the course of a demonstration, by a lunatic, Juan Roa Sierra.[59] Gaitán had been the great hope for Colombian social reform. His speeches had roused the masses of Colombia and, if he were not precisely a democrat in the European tradition ('there are roads more advisable than those of the ballot boxes' was one of his more famous remarks), he had a generous heart.[60] His death cast Bogotá into a spasm of fury and fear: Roa Sierra was lynched. Processions were formed, rioting began and, by the evening, Bogotá was out of control. Shops were looted, and burned, police stations blown up, and there was much sporadic firing and fighting. Police gave arms to rioters anxious to overthrow the government. The Communists tried to seize advantage of the confusion, but failed. For several days the violence continued, an earthquake uncontrolled and undirected, resembling the tragic week of Barcelona of 1909, though estimates of the numbers killed in Bogotá reached 3,000, far higher than had occurred in Spain. Afterwards, as usual in such circumstances, scapegoats were sought. General Marshall and the majority of the statesmen attending the Pan-American Conference blamed the Communists. The U.S. ambassador to the U.N., Pawley, a veteran anti-Communist who was in Bogotá,[61] later recalled: 'We had information that there was a Cuban there, a very young man who appeared to us not to be the real threat.' Later, he said that he heard a voice on the radio just after Gaitán's

---

[59] That Roa Sierra was the sole assassin is accepted in the report by the Scotland Yard chief, Sir Norman Smith, who says that Roa's motives derived from Gaitán's reiterated refusal to receive him.

[60] See *La Nueva Prensa* (Bogotá), 6–9 April 1963, for Gaitán's programme.

[61] William D. Pawley (born 1896), founder of Cubana Airlines, businessman, ambassador to Peru and Brazil; in 1949 he took over the Havana Trolley Co., and in 1950–1 founded Havana's Autobuses Modernos.

murder: 'This is Fidel Castro from Cuba. This is a Communist revolution. The President has been killed, all the military establishments in Colombia are now in our hands, the Navy has capitulated to us and this Revolution has been a success.'[62] This report must surely have owed much to imagination. But the Colombian chief of police, Alberto Niño, also later claimed that Castro and del Pino were Communist agents sent in to organize the riots and others have claimed that Castro killed thirty-two people in these days.[63] A guest at the Hotel Claridge heard Castro and del Pino boasting about their success: Castro is even believed to have shown Colombian detectives a pass book which identified himself as 'Grade I agent of the Third Front of the U.S.S.R. in South America'.[64] Another, perhaps more reliable report described how the two Cubans arrived at their hotel on 9 April 'bringing a large quantity of arms and staying there for many hours, talking on the phone, in English, with various people.'[65] It is true that Castro did get involved in the riots, but obscure how much fighting he did; it is evidently incorrect to suppose that Castro was the agent of the riots, and it is not a subject upon which he, usually garrulous, has enlightened the world. Castro had a *rendezvous* with Gaitán about the hour of his death but he apparently wished to ask advice about booking a theatre for a meeting.[66] On 13 April Castro and Rafael del Pino were taken to the Cuban Embassy by an Argentinian secretary of embassy, and the ambassador, Dr Guillermo Belt, an old ABC leader, gave them sanctuary and enabled them to return to Havana in a cargo plane.[67]

These events of course made an impression on Castro: the crowds, the violence, the destruction, the oratory of Gaitán and his magnetic personality – Castro met him before 9 April – all played their part.[68] He commented later that the Colombian masses failed to gain power 'because they were betrayed by false leaders'.[69] Doubtless he felt as Napoleon did when observing the Swiss guards fighting to the last man

[62] *Communist Threat*, 724–5.
[63] *Antecedentes y secretos del 9 de Abril.*
[64] *Ibid*, 278.
[65] Report by Sir Norman Smith of Scotland Yard, as reported in *El Tiempo* (Bogotá), 12 April 1961.
[66] Comment of Gloria Gaitán de Valencia in *América Libre*, 22 May 1961.
[67] The author has encountered no evidence that, as argued by his enemies, Castro's life was spared on the intervention of the Russian ambassador. There were other scapegoats. Thus: 'Romulo Betancourt headed a plot against the Nation on April 9 . . . it was prepared in the city of Havana.' See *El Siglo* (Bogotá, 2 July 1948), qu. *Communist Threat*, 278. A Colombian detective claimed to have seen Castro with Roa Sierra on the morning of the 9th (*La República*, Bogotá, 10 April 1961). See also Francisco Sandiño Silva, *La Penetración Soviética en América y el 9 de Abril* (Colección Nuevos Tiempos, Bogotá, 1949).
[68] '*Tuve oportunidad de oír a Gaitán. Su voz, su personalidad impresionante, y el movimiento popular vigoroso que acaudillaba, lucía como la salvación de ese gran pueblo colombiano. Por eso lo asesinaron . . .*' (interview with Gaitán's daughter, *América Libre*, 22 May 1961).
[69] *Ibid.*

at the Tuileries: that these 'masses' could win when they were well led.

On return from Bogotá, Castro for a time turned to a conventional life. He married, when just twenty-two, Mirta, sister of Rafael Díaz Balart, a friend in the law faculty at the university, also of the UIR, of the same age as himself. The Díaz Balart family disapproved of the engagement, but the marriage occurred on 10 October 1948, the day of the inauguration of Prío as president. For the rest of that year and till 1952 Castro was a member of Chibás's Ortodoxo party, which he had formally joined in 1947. Indeed, he had been to its foundation meeting in Havana in May 1947. He followed Chibás with immense enthusiasm, regarding him as the man of the future, and seems to have dropped what little feeling for Marxism he may have had: maybe the absence in Moscow of his university Communist friends, Soto and Alfredo Guevara, helped. He also dropped out of the action group UIR, after another fracas in the university resulting in an armed attack on a member of the university police, Sergeant Fernández Cabral[70] and a final fling at his old enemy Masferrer in 1949 in which one man was killed.[71] Justo Fuentes, the UIR leader, meantime was killed when leaving the radio station COCO on which he and Fidel Castro had a daily programme: Fidel Castro did not reach the station that day and so escaped. At the same time, in the first two years of marriage, he worked, and graduated as a doctor of law in 1950.

There was one other interesting incident. Batista returned to Cuba after the election of 1948, and one of his friends, Leopoldo Pío Elizalde, hearing of Castro as an exceptionally promising and wild student, thought that he might draw him into Batista's new Partido de Acción Unitaria. According to Pío Elizalde, Castro said that he personally had no animosity against Batista, that his father knew him and owed him gratitude, but that for 'generational reasons' he could not link himself politically to the ex-president. If Batista had come back with insurrectionary (*golpista*) intentions, he could count on him. Pío Elizalde then primly told Castro that Batista expected to get back to power by vote (*con las urnas*).[72]

This curious tale is so fully in character that it is difficult not to accept it: Castro has so evidently believed in insurrection rather than election campaigns. Pío Elizalde told Batista, and some months later

---

[70] See *Hoy*, 8 July 1948, and *El Mundo*, 7 July 1948. Fernández Cabral was one of Salabarría's men and was shot by the UIR including José de Jesús Ginjaume who claimed to have been in the house of the Minister of Education at the time.

[71] Castro was accused, along with surviving members of the Acción Revolucionaria Guiteras and UIR, such as 'Billiken' (Guillermo García Riestra), Rafael del Pino (his collaborator at Bogotá), José de Jesús Ginjaume, etc.

[72] '*Si Batista ha regresado de Daytona con una intención golpista, que cuente conmigo*', L. Pío Elizalde, *La Tragedia de Cuba* (1959), 225–6.

Castro's brother-in-law, Rafael Díaz Balart, who had joined Batista from the UIR, persuaded Castro to visit Batista in his estate, *Kuquine*. The two then talked in the library on 'literary and historical themes without the host giving [Castro] a chance to begin a political discussion'.[73]

On this period of his life Castro later remarked, perhaps forgetting, certainly rationalizing:

> At the time I passed the baccalaureat I was a political illiterate. My first contacts at the university with middle class economics showed me some of its contradictions and I got to know some revolutionary ideas . . . Afterwards, naturally, [there was] University politics. We [that is, himself or perhaps himself and his intimates] began at that time to have our first contacts with the communist manifesto, with the works of Marx, Engels, Lenin. This was a very clearly defined stage of development. Of course, many of the things which we did at the university were not devised by us, certainly not. When we left the University, I myself particularly, we were already greatly influenced [by Marxism]; I am not going to say I was already a Marxist–Leninist; possibly I had two million petty *bourgeois* prejudices . . . At best I can say that if I had not had all those prejudices I would not have been in a condition to make a contribution to the Revolution in the way I have now been able to . . .[74]

A little later, in an interview with an American journalist, Castro said that his 'first questionings of an economic and social kind arose when I was a student . . . [The] problems posed by overproduction and the struggle between the workers and the machines . . . aroused my attention extraordinarily.'[75] Castro explained that he had read as far as page 370 in *Das Kapital* at this period[76] and had 'studied' the Communist manifesto and some of the works of Marx, Engels and Lenin:[77] but page 370 is not so very far in most editions of *Das Kapital* and it is perhaps unexpected to hear that 'the Marxist point of view . . . captivated me and awakened my curiosity'.[78]

All this surely was to say at some length that at the university Castro was influenced in a modest and superficial way by Marxism and nationalism. By the former he perhaps meant no more than that he

[73] *Loc. cit*; Batista gave himself a guarded account of the meeting saying he had avoided talking of political matters because he knew of Castro's '*antecedentes gangsteriles*' (*Respuesta*, 325). To Suárez Núñez (*El Gran Culpable*, 12), Batista said, 'I had to tell Díaz Balart not to bring Fidel Castro to my house because he was a *pistolero*'.

[74] Castro speech, 2 December 1961 (*Obra Revolucionaria*, 1961, No. 46, p. 38).

[75] Lockwood, 138. (This was in 1965.)

[76] *Obra Revolucionaria*, 1961, No. 46, p. 35.

[77] *Loc. cit.*

[78] Lockwood, 139.

heard for the first time the theory that society is divided into antagonistic classes. Yet if he only got to page 370 in *Das Kapital*, he seems to
have reached further in Thiers's and Jaurés's histories of the French
Revolution and also Macchiavelli and Malaparte's *Technique of the
Coup d'Etat*. Later on, he was anxious to give the impression that he had
been a good revolutionary for as long as possible. It would be appropriate to point out that several of Castro's contemporaries at the university
regarded him as 'a power-hungry person, completely unprincipled,
who would throw in his lot with any group he felt could help his political
career',[79] and not long before the famous confessional speech of December 1961, quoted above, Castro explained that 'the knowledge gained
from a revolutionary work, from . . . Marx or . . . Lenin cannot be the
same when we read it without having any experience of government . . .
we once read them [i.e. Marx and Lenin] for general interest, for curiosity. . . .'[80] Yet one further comment might be suggested: the culmination of his university experiences and those of his childhood appear for
whatever reason – a desire to carry on a student tradition of tyrannicide,
revolution and insurrection, an identification conscious or unconscious
with the seething crowds in Bogotá, a challenge to his father or a pursuit
of intellectual systemization – to have led him to what he would later
refer to as the 'vocation of revolution'. 'What made us revolutionaries?'
he demanded rhetorically in 1961, and answered, first, the vocation
of 'being a revolutionary':[81] and perhaps revolution for revolution's
sake, not any particular revolution.

Afterwards anyway his life seems to have been ever preoccupied
with politics. He hardly became at all involved in the career of the law.
Though he worked in a law firm named Azpiazu, Castro and Resende,
his clients were mostly few and poor. One case only caught public
attention: at a student meeting called to protest against an increase in
bus fares a police lieutenant, Salas Cañizares (afterwards chief of
Batista's police) hit a young worker, who later died of his wounds.
Castro volunteered to act as prosecutor. Meantime, it seems that
money was short: he recalled later that milk was often short for his
son, that the electricity company cut off his light, that he could not
find an apartment and that he was always in debt, when not to the
grocer, to the butcher.[82] He was anxious to stand for Congress, but
his old history teacher, Portell Vilá, refused to champion him, on
the grounds that he associated with the left wing of the Ortodoxos.[83]

[79] From a memorandum by Fernando Freyre, a fellow law student.
[80] Speech at 1st National Congress of Responsables del Trabajo de Orientación Revolucionaria, *Revolución*, 11 November 1961, 8.
[81] *Obra Revolucionaria*, 2 December 1961.
[82] *Ibid.*
[83] Evidence of Dr Portell Vilá, repeated by him in *Avance* (Miami), 5 January 1962.

An active member of the Ortodoxo party, he carried out in 1950 a famous raid on Prío's villa, where he took compromising photographs afterwards published in the newspaper *Alerta*.[84] In the 1952 election campaign, Castro, having specifically denounced his old friends in the political gangster groups in *Alerta*,[85] spoke on behalf of the senatorial aspirations of Chibás's old friend Leonardo Fernández Sánchez and was himself later nominated, under the sponsorship of the mulatto editor of *Alerta*, Vasconcelos, as Ortodoxo candidate for the House of Representatives for one of the Havana municipalities. He later explained, not entirely convincingly, that, though he had been thinking of using parliament . . .

> as a point of departure from which I might establish a revolutionary platform . . . I didn't believe that my programme could be realized in a legal, parliamentary way . . . already I believed then that I had to do it in a revolutionary way . . . once in parliament I would break party discipline and present a programme embracing practically all the measures that later on were contained in our Moncada programme and which [after the Revolution were] . . . turned into laws.[86]

He added also (but this was in 1965) that to gain power he would need the support of a section of the army.

Castro's writings at this time often appeared in *Alerta*, whose editor, Vasconcelos, can, despite his own ambiguous past,[87] be considered one of his mentors. In June 1951 we hear of an attack by him on *latifundistas* and a demand for 'justice for the workers and Cuban peasantry';[88] in November 1950 came a demand for the independence of Puerto Rico and a statement that 'the students of Cuba are united against the tyrants . . . of America'.[89] A week before Batista's *golpe*, Castro accused Prío of distributing $18,000 a month to action groups – to one of which at least he had himself once belonged but which he now castigated: 'The mystique and past struggles gave [these groups] access to the organs of propaganda . . . young men attracted by a false concept of heroism and of the revolution . . . The regime degenerated and all those organisations sooner or later lost . . . their ideological concept . . . But the apparatus of terror and death cannot be sustained without vast financial means.' Castro's speech before the Tribunal de

[84] *Mártires del Moncada*, 90.
[85] 28 January 1952.
[86] Lockwood, 140.
[87] An opponent of Machado, he was later persuaded to join Machado as a diplomat and acted as a spy for the government on Cuban exiles in Europe (see Conte Agüero, *Eduardo Chibás*, 343–4). He had also had a similar career with respect to Batista.
[88] *Alerta*, 6 June 1951.
[89] *Ibid.*, 4 March 1952.

Cuentas, making detailed accusations against President Prío for financing the *grupos de acción*, reads well, a long and sustained philippic by an apparently highly articulate patriot.[90] On the other hand, it would seem that he really attacked the groups led by El Colorado and Masferrer, not UIR.

It was in this mood that the *golpe* of the *sunsundamba* of 10 March found him. On that day, he was at the university and helped to distribute arms to the students and others with them.[91] Several days later, he distributed a manifesto entitled *Zarpazo*,[92] which, while challenging Batista in vigorous terms, is significant as Castro's first independent political statement:[93] it ended with a call to struggle: '*La hora es de lucha*; to live in chains is to live in shame!' It called on Cubans to restore the constitution of 1940.[94] His own response to this injunction was first to write a personal letter warning Batista of the dire consequences of his action, second to file a suit with the court of Constitutional Guarantees demanding Batista's punishment for crimes against the Constitution. No one listened, though these acts gave publicity to Castro's somewhat new-found devotion to the old constitution.

Castro was now a politician without a platform as well as a lawyer without clients,[95] although his brother-in-law, Díaz Balart, who had become a supporter of Batista, tried unsuccessfully to persuade him to back the *cuartelazo*.[96] He was nearing thirty, his father was still vaguely supporting him, his marriage was not very successful (though he had had a son, Fidelito, in September 1949). Something had to be done if the chance of a political career was not to slip through his fingers. He had a reputation already as a man who loved risks: one who wished to assert his quality and his individuality in a world where other politicians seemed powerless. He had already, as he had always had since the university, a group round him who regarded him as a leader, who either discounted or even admired his exhibitionist side; a Negro admirer once described how Castro ate enormously, and thought, 'This *blanco* eats like a *negro*.'[97] He always had fine thoughts (in his mind): 'Those who march towards death with the smile of supreme happiness on

---

[90] *Ibid.*

[91] C. Franqui, *Le Livre des Douze* (1965); also article by José Rebellón, *Revolución*, 24 July 1962.

[92] The word means the blow of a wild cat's paw.

[93] See Castro's speech in Venezuela in 1959; in 1960 he referred to it as his '*primer manifiesto*' (*La Calle*, 30 March 1960).

[94] Full text republished in Castro's speech at Matos trial (*Revolución*, 20 December 1959).

[95] In 1943 there were 6,000 lawyers in Cuba, plus 625 judges and 1,300 involved in some side of legal work – i.e. a total of about 8,000 persons living off the law, or one per 900 of the population.

[96] Evidence of Raúl Martínez Arará. Díaz Balart had been for a time secretary of the Juventud Ortodoxo of Banes, but had moved over to Batista about a year before the *golpe de estado*.

[97] Merle, 143.

their lips embraced by the call of duty.'[98] '[Men] not born to resign themselves to the hypocritical and miserable life of these times', a sentence which recalls some of the better passages in the works of José Antonio Primo de Rivera. His reading and his language were full of 'the manly thoughts which agitate unquiet souls'.[99] At the rally on 28 January 1953 to commemorate the centenary of Martí's birth, Castro had led, he said, 'an erect group of ex-students and others in military style parade'[100] – again, an expression which perhaps owed something to José Antonio.[101]

Fidel Castro in 1953 was a restless and energetic nationalist with a sound education behind him. Although it doubtless misses the point to charge so ardent a patriot with insincerity, he was able to deceive, though often, like Lloyd George, the first person he deceived was himself.[102] He found it impossible to fit in with García Barcena, Sánchez Arango and Carrillo, the only politically promising groups of the years 1952–3. He revelled in action and in crowds and sometimes seemed to regard politics, even violence, as hunting carried on by other means. He had as strong a sense of humour as of history but he lacked magnanimity, and while he might enjoy laughing at others, he rarely did so at himself. He had evident gaps in his imagination; for instance, he had never had anything yet to say on the problem of the Negro in Cuba, and he had only a sporadic economic understanding. His closest followers, however, already regarded him as a potential saviour of the nation. His chance might come in certain extreme circumstances which in their turn could only be achieved by the maintenance in power of Batista, the increase in support of Batista by the business community and, despite this, the collapse of Batista at Castro's own hands. Western countries, recalling the experience of Lenin, have come to expect from revolutionary leaders a consistency and a ruthless integrity which they would not demand from more conventional leaders; Castro, with his many changes of mind and of front, may have been a man almost incapable of consistency, therefore difficult for conventional Liberals or Conservatives to understand. Obviously, power meant much to him: before 1952 Alfredo Guevara had done his best to convert Castro to Communism. Castro allegedly replied gaily, 'I'd be a Communist if I were Stalin'.[103]

[98] *Cartas del Presidio*, 18.

[99] *Ibid.*, 19.

[100] Raúl Castro, *Fundamentos*, June–July 1961, 10–11.

[101] For what it is worth, Pardo Llada later said that he found Primo de Rivera's complete works in Castro's camp in the Sierra Maestra (*Bohemia Libre*, December 1961).

[102] There were other aspects of Castro's character which recall Lloyd George: *c.f.* F. E. Smith's remark, 'The man who enters into real and fierce controversy with Mr Lloyd George must think clearly, think deeply and think ahead. Otherwise he will think too late.'

[103] *Sería comunista si yo fuera Stalin*. (Private Information.)

At the beginning of this second *Batistato*, Castro's idea probably was, as he said himself:

> Not to organise a movement but to try to unite all the different forces against Batista. I intended to participate in that struggle simply as one more soldier. I began to organise the first action cells, hoping to work alongside those leaders of the [Ortodoxo] party who might be ready to fulfil the elemental duty of fighting against Batista . . . But when none of these leaders showed that they had the ability, the resolution, the seriousness of purpose or the means to overthrow Batista it was then that I finally worked out a strategy on my own.[104]

[104] Lockwood, 141.

CHAPTER LXVIII

Moncada: the Idea

By the middle of 1953 Castro was the centre of a group of young men, and a few women, whose aim was to carry on the struggle against Batista with greater energy than the conventional politicians. Those who had any formal political loyalty were, like Castro himself, members of the Ortodoxo Youth Movement, though these were in a minority. By accident of acquaintance, the Pinar del Río section of the Juventud Ortodoxia was, however, captured by Castro, and its leader, José Suárez, brought in to Castro's group a number of friends who lived near him in Artemisa. Hence Artemisa, a town founded by Arango in 1803 on the main highway to the west, became by chance a stronghold of followers of Castro. The meetings of these men at Artemisa took place in the masonic lodge because one of the Members (the printer Ponce) was a Mason: the others were not.[1]

Those who followed Castro in 1953 were almost entirely men of the lower middle class or working class.[2] Few were students, and only a small minority had been to the university.[3] Out of 150 or so who took part in the attacks on the barracks, most were factory workers, agricultural workers and shop assistants. Four only seem to have been directly involved in the sugar industry, and there was one schoolboy. The others worked in a wide diversity of professions: there was one watchmaker, a teacher, a taxi-driver, a doctor, a dentist, a bookshop assistant, a chimney sweep, three carpenters, a butcher, an oyster seller and a male nurse.[4] Only one or two appear to have been unemployed. Nearly sixty came from Havana and twenty-four from

[1] Franqui, 16. There were some others who had been active in the Masonic movement.
[2] To Lockwood, Castro said that 90% of his followers were 'workers and farmers' (p. 146). He seems to have been right.
[3] Herbert L. Matthews (*The Cuban Story* (1961), 144) thus errs in speaking of Castro's followers as then 'nearly all university students'. At Moncada the explicitly 'university group', four students of Havana led by the wooden-legged 'Patachula', son of a rich advocate of Havana, and an ex-member like Castro of the UIR, withdrew at the last minute. Castro himself, his brother Raúl, Dr Muñoz, Jesús Montané (in 1953 an accountant at General Motors in Havana) and Miret were apparently the only members who had completed a higher education. Raúl de Aguiar, Hector de Armas and Lester Rodríguez could still be regarded as students. Abelardo Crespo was a part-time student. Gustavo Arcos, often listed as a student, was in fact a shop assistant in the Calle Muralla, having come to Havana to study but having failed.
[4] See Appendix XI for detailed analysis.

Artemisa or Guanajay. Few came from the province of Oriente. Of the *habaneros*, however, about twenty-five had been born elsewhere in the island and like so many citizens of the capital had migrated there since. Of those whose ages are known, eleven were under twenty, fifty-two between twenty and thirty, seventeen in their thirties, five over forty. A large number had been active in one branch or other of the Ortodoxo Youth. Judging from photographs, it would seem that a maximum of twenty-five might have had some Negro or Indian blood, mostly Negro, but this may be to over-estimate the right number. A few – perhaps twenty – were married. So far as can be seen none of these men had been associated with Castro in his gangster days in the university and none except Castro had been a member of UIR or MSR except for the so called 'Patachula'.

These men were in fact mostly camp-followers of industrial civilization and some had direct experience of U.S. firms – Santamaría had worked at the *Central Constancia* owned by the U.S. Cuban–American Co., Montané worked as an accountant in General Motors, and 'Nico' López in the Nela milk factory. They came together under Castro partly fortuitously (he was friend of a friend) or because he evidently had gifts at least for gang leadership. Some of the Artemisa group had been part of García Barcena's movement for a few months.[5] Ernesto Tizol had tried unsuccessfully to lead his own group before.[6] Montané and Santamaría had run a clandestine political news letter, *Son Los Mismos*, before Castro had joined them and founded *El Acusador*. Tasende had been somewhat involved with Castro since the days of Cayo Confites,[7] while two of Castro's followers, the Gómez brothers, had been cooks at the Jesuit school of Belén and had followed him, in all the vicissitudes of his career, ever since:[8] these two had been political 'militants' since the struggle against Machado, when they had been in the ABC. Castro's movement in 1953, then, was the merger of several small groups, each following a minor leader who in turn accepted Castro as the over-all chief. They had little ideology save hostility to Batista, though in most of the leaders the notion of revolution, patriotic and social, burned fiercely, if vaguely. Several of the older of these men had made the far from untypical intellectual journey from support of the Auténticos to the Ortodoxos and then, with disillusionment, to Castro.

One group almost unrepresented among Castro's followers was the Juventud Socialista, the Communist Youth movement. On the contrary, while some members of the Ortodoxo Youth were joining Castro,

[5] See statements made by Angel Eros in the magazine *Cuba*, March 1965, 3.
[6] Tizol to Merle, Merle, 87.
[7] *Mártires del Moncada* (1965) p. 90.
[8] *Ibid.*, 222. The Colegio Belén is now (1967) called after these revolutionary cooks and is known as Gómez Brothers Technical Institute.

others, as an alternative, were moving towards the Communists.[9] Castro's younger brother Raúl was among these, though he only left the university in 1953 and had little political experience with the Ortodoxos behind him. He visited the World Youth Congress at Vienna in February 1953. Afterwards he went to Bucharest and Prague as well as Paris. Travelling home with a Russian and two young Guatemalan Communists, he solicited entry to the Communist Youth on his return to Havana in June 1953 (after a few days in gaol for having Communist literature on him).[10] But Raúl Castro was not a supporter of his brother's movement till July 1953. When he joined in, he did so on brotherly rather than ideological grounds, as he was not a leader, and he did not tell the Communist party what he was doing.[11] Fernando Chenard, the photographer, had also once been a member of Juventud Socialista, but he was now thirty-four and an Ortodoxo.[12] One man, José Luis López, who followed Castro in 1953, had voted Communist in the past and accordingly had had difficulties with his employers.[13] The only member of the Cuban Communist party was Luciano González Camejo, a forty-year-old sugar mechanic from Bayamo.[14] Some of the other Fidelistas of 1953 may have had philo-Communist outlooks in the sense that they were vaguely familiar with Communist textbooks; among these were the Santamaría brother and sister, 'Nico' López and Ramiro Valdés, but none of these had formal relations with the party.[15]

These men had as yet no name (though for a time they were referred to as the Youth of the Centenary – that is, of José Martí's birth), calling themselves simply the Movement.[16] Castro provided them with arms, bought by well-wishers (the Ortodoxo leaders refused to help). Castro apparently only received $140 instead of the $3,000 from his father he had demanded.[17] Cuba was never short of guns, particularly the university, and many of the hangers-on of one or another of the old

[9] See article by Raúl Castro, *Fundamentos*, June–July 1961.

[10] Merle, 121. Fidel Castro confirmed this to Lee Lockwood in 1965: 'Raúl completely on his own . . . had joined the Communist Youth' (Lockwood, 144). Raúl Castro himself attributed his early radicalism to the fact that when he got home from his vacations, he saw that of 'thousands of peasants, the only ones who could study were those of my family' (*Obra Revolucionaria*, 1960, No. 2, p. 3).

[11] Lockwood and Merle, *loc. cit.* Raúl Castro had had a childhood which contrasted with that of Fidel Castro: his break with religion at the Colegio Dolores, for instance, seems to have been more anguished than his brother's. He was less successful, being less strong and prominent physically; he took up a totally hostile attitude to Belén and left when quite young to work in the estate office at Birán, afterwards joining the law faculty at the University of Havana.

[12] Merle, 154.

[13] Merle, *op. cit.*

[14] *Mártires del Moncada*, 164.

[15] Martínez Arará's evidence.

[16] Raúl Castro, *Fundamentos*, June–July 1961, 11.

[17] Martínez Arará's evidence: he and Castro visited Castro's father at this time.

gangster groups had all sorts of weapons for sale. By late 1952 there were a number of young women also attached to the Castro group.[18]

Castro was nominally still an Ortodoxo, but he did not consult with the Ortodoxo leadership in deciding what to do. He had already expressed his personal dissatisfaction, indeed, with the Ortodoxos, in his mimeographed sheet, *El Acusador*:

> Whoever thinks that up to now everything has been done well, that we have nothing with which to reproach ourselves, such a man is one very tender to his conscience. These sterile fights which followed the death of Chibás, these colossal commotions for reasons scarcely ideological, but of a purely egoistical and personal nature, even now resound like bitter hammer blows in our conscience. This most funereal proceeding of going to the public tribunal to elucidate Byzantine[19] quarrels was a grave symptom of indiscipline and irresponsibility. Unexpectedly, there came the *golpe* of 10 March. One might have hoped that such a grave happening would eradicate from the party the petty rancours and the sterile private empire-building . . . [but] the stupid quarrels returned. The madness of the idiots did not give heed that the doorway of the Press was too narrow to enable a full attack on the regime but on the other hand it was all too broad for an attack on the Ortodoxos themselves . . . nevertheless the immense mass of the Ortodoxo party is ready, more so than ever, demanding sacrifice . . .
>
> Those who have a traditional concept of politics feel themselves pessimists in the present situation. But those who in contrast have faith in the masses, those who believe in the indestructible force of great ideas, will not be affected by the vacillation and gloom of the leaders. For this vacuum will soon be filled by tougher men from the ranks. The moment is revolutionary, not political. Politics means the consecration of the opportunism of those who have means . . . Revolution opens the way to true merit – to those who have valour and sincere ideals, to those who carry their breast uncovered, and who take up the battle standard in their hands. To a revolutionary party there must correspond a young and revolutionary leadership, of popular origin, which will save Cuba.[20]

Stirring words such as these had of course often appeared on the

---

[18] Before 26 July 1953 there would appear to have been six – Haydée Santamaría, Melba Hernández, Elda Pérez, Natividad ('Naty') Revuelta, Elisa Dubois, and an 'old Spanish revolutionary', Josefa. Natividad Revuelta, of good family, was married to a prosperous doctor and worked for a U.S. oil company.

[19] A favourite adjective with Castro (as with other Cuban political orators): for instance, he repudiated the Sino-Soviet breach as such in 1965.

[20] Qu., Raúl Castro, *Fundamentos*, June 1961, 8–9.

lips of Cuban politicians: a speech by Grau or Laredo Bru, Gómez or even Machado or the young Batista would hardly have been complete without them. The political thought was scarcely detailed, and the sentiments would have been little different if they had been expressed by Eddy Chibás.

There was, however, a difference. The project which Castro had in mind was a desperate one, an attack on two barracks in Oriente, at Santiago and at Bayamo. The purpose of this was primarily to capture an arsenal, to arm his movement for future exploits. If he won, he hoped to arm many volunteers from the ranks of anti-Batistianos in Santiago. Santiago was after all far from Havana: the barracks had normally a thousand men who might just be overwhelmed by a hundred if taken by surprise.[21]

There was also another purpose: the attack might lead to a spectacular and heroic success which could spark off a popular rising everywhere in Oriente – 'to light the flame of a general rising in the country: to be the initiators'.[22] This attempt had a certain affinity, conscious or unconscious, with the old anarchist idea of propaganda of the deed, a single act which would lead, if not to the millennium, at least to revolution. Castro was not an anarchist by traditional standards but his methods had affinities with anarchism, as was his expectation that the country would fall into the hands of revolution by a single act. Also, unconsciously Castro's movement took for its colours the black and red of the anarchist flag.

Oriente, of course, was the old traditional centre of Cuban revolution, in 1868 and 1895. Castro wished naturally to gain prestige for himself as a major revolutionary leader by a sensational gesture. The allegation that he met with the Communist party in order to plan an attempt on Batista's life seems to be certainly false.[23] Castro was probably further from the Communists than he had been at any time since arriving at the university: and afterwards the Communist party dismissed the attack on the Moncada barracks as futile.[24] It is true that Castro now lived in a circle which regarded it as ignorant not to read Lenin; Abel Santamaría, one of his followers with whom he really discussed matters, was 'an impassioned reader of Lenin and Soviet revolutionaries', according to his sister, and at the Moncada carried a

[21] This is the case put forward by Merle, 102–3.
[22] Martínez Arará's comment.
[23] The full range of fancy is shown in Nathaniel Weyl, *Red Star over Cuba* (1960), 122, allegedly basing himself on reports of Batista's new anti-Communist investigation and police force, Buró de Represión Actividades Comunistas (BRAC). But BRAC was not founded till 1954.
[24] See below, p. 842. Juan Almeida later said, however, of this stage of Castro's life that he always carried a book by Lenin about with him: 'a blue book with a portrait of Lenin on the front' (Franqui, 15).

book of Lenin's with him;[25] but this is indeed far from saying that they were Communists, for Santamaría was also, like Castro, 'a fanatic of Martí'.

The theoretical ideas of Castro and his friends in 1953 can be gauged most exactly from the proclamation to be read after the capture of the radio station:

> The Revolution declares its firm intention to establish Cuba on a plan of welfare and economic prosperity that ensures the survival of its rich subsoil, its geographical position, diversified agriculture and industrialisation . . . The Revolution declares its respect for the workers . . . and . . . the establishment of total and definitive social justice, based on economic and industrial progress under a well-organised and timed national plan . . . The Revolution . . . recognises and bases itself on the ideals of Martí . . . and it adopts as its own the revolutionary programme of Joven Cuba, the ABC Radical and the PPC [Ortodoxos] . . . The Revolution declares its absolute and reverent respect for the Constitution which was given to the people in 1940 . . . In the name of the martyrs, in the name of the sacred rights of the fatherland . . .[26]

Castro also had ready to play a recording of Chibás's last speech.[27]

Was this the real programme of Castro's movement on 26 July 1953? If so, what are we to make of his self-questioning in December 1961: 'Did I believe in [Marxism] on the 26th of July [1953]? I believed on the 26th of July. Did I understand it as I understand it today after ten years of struggle? No, I did not understand it as I understand it today . . . There is a great difference. Did I have prejudices? Yes, I had prejudices; yes I had them on the 26th of July.'[28] The truth though is that Castro was in no way a Marxist in 1953, even if he had some superficial knowledge of those matters. He did, perhaps, have slightly more radical views than he gave out, yet if the previously described programme was actually to be implemented, the changes in Cuba's condition would be radical: 'The ideals of Martí'? 'Joven Cuba' – Guiteras's old programme? In fact, any of these, if precisely defined, might result in perhaps not a Communist revolution, but one certainly more 'revolutionary' than that in Mexico under Cárdenas. It may very well be that, as Martínez Arará recalled, there was 'never any type of ideological discussion', but this comment need only apply to Martínez Arará.

---

[25] *Ibid.*, 69; *Obra Revolucionaria* (1961), No. 46, 35.
[26] As qu., Du Bois, 34; complete text in *Bohemia*, 15 February 1959. Conte Agüero (*Los dos rostros de Fidel Castro* (1960) says that it was written by Raúl Gómez García.
[27] So Castro himself said, *History will absolve me* (1961).
[28] *Obra Revolucionaria, loc. cit.*

Castro explained[29] later that he had in fact five revolutionary laws which would have been immediately proclaimed had he conquered the barracks:

First, a restoration of the 1940 Constitution, and, until elections, the Revolutionary Movement – that is, he and his friends, presumably – would have itself assumed all legislative, executive and judicial powers, except the power to modify the Constitution. There was, of course, a contradiction here since the Constitution of 1940 naturally divided these powers. This law would have meant too that Castro would have immediately either seized power from his nominal Ortodoxo leaders or that they would have been impressed into the revolutionary movement. (This was roughly what occurred when finally Batista withdrew in 1959.)

Second, all property 'not mortgageable and not transferable' would be handed over to planters, sub-planters, squatters or others who had less than 150 acres. The State would pay the old owners on the basis of rent which they would have received over ten years. This would, of course, have been a genuine if somewhat conventional land reform. In 1946 there had been 140,000 farms of this size in Cuba out of a total of 160,000, or about 80 % of the farms.[30]

Third, workers and employers would have been able to share a third of the profits of all sugar mills and other 'large' non-agricultural concerns. Such a profit-sharing scheme fitted in more with Chibás's ideas than with any other intellectual ancestor.

Fourth, sugar *colonos* would receive henceforth a minimum quota of about 450 tons of cane a year and the *colonos* would have a right to 55 % of the total production. This was a sugar reform law of a modest kind in the tradition of Batista's laws of the late 1930s. There were about 50,000 *colonos* in 1950.[31]

Fifth, all land illegally obtained and all other property or cash obtained by fraud would be confiscated.

Castro added that these laws would be followed by further laws for agrarian and educational reform, by the nationalization of the utilities and the telephones, and even by a refund of some of what had been paid to these U.S. owned companies in the past. There would also be a housing reform. The agrarian reform would reflect the Constitution of 1940 in that a maximum area of land would be indicated for each agricultural project. Measures would be adopted to make land 'tend to revert to the Cubans', though this was a general tendency anyway

[29] In the pamphlet based on his speech in his own defence at his trial in September. I have assumed that the main parts in the pamphlet were included in the speech; but that the general language and argument of the pamphlet should be considered later.
[30] See Agricultural Census of 1946. No later figures available.
[31] World Bank, 798.

since 1934. Small farmers working on rented land would receive that land as owners. Castro spoke of these as numbering 100,000, showing that he included all squatters, share-croppers and sub-renters. Swamp would be filled in, there would be reafforestation and the establishment of centres of research. Agricultural cooperatives would be encouraged, to help the use of costly equipment, cold storage and scientific farming generally. These cooperatives were intended to help individual land-owners; they did not foreshadow any nationalization of land.

The educational reform he envisaged seems to have meant an increase of pay to teachers. Rural teachers would have free travel and every five years all teachers would have a sabbatical six months, to keep up to date in their subjects at home or abroad. An 'integral reform' of education was intended, but nothing more specific than this was mentioned.

The housing reform would involve a cut in rent of 50 %. Tax exemptions on owner-occupied houses; triple taxes on rented homes; slum clearance and redevelopment with 'multiple dwelling buildings' – all aimed to create and to encourage the ownership of one's own house or flat.

These different projects would be financed by the end of corruption and the end of the purchase of expensive armaments. There was also a plan to 'mobilize all inactive capital', estimated at $M500, for the industrialization of the country. Details of this topic, and of the manner of nationalization of the utilities and telephone company were not provided. There was no mention of compensation, except to those whose lands were being given to small farmers.

This programme could not in itself be described as supporting any single political philosophy, though it was evidently close to the ideas of Chibás. It concentrated on the aspects of Cuban society which Castro himself knew – farming and education, housing and social conditions. The plans must have been Castro's own, and it seems likely that he did not consult anyone. None of the distinguished economists such as Cuervo or Pazos who were connected with the Ortodoxo movement was consulted. The idea of the division of land, the *repartimiento* beloved of the Spanish anarchists of the 1920s, would of course have led to the increase of the number of plots beyond an economically desirable point. Small estates, even of 150 acres, are not easier to run than large, particularly if they produce sugar. Indeed, what seems surprising is the modesty of Castro's approach towards the sugar problem. Workers' shares in profits; encouragement of Cuban ownership (already increasing); guaranteed 55% *colono* participation in cane production (already normal); movement towards a *colonia* between 150 acres and (say) 1,000 acres – all this was scarcely radical, and by itself would not have fulfilled the demand that Cuba should become internationally independent. There was no mention of nationalization of the sugar industry – a measure which might certainly have been justified by its curious structure and the extent to which the nation depended on it. The English Labour party, for instance, would have placed that demand high on a list of prescriptions. Any social democratic economist, on the other hand, would have been doubtful about the proposed 50% cut in rents, the tax exemptions on owner-occupier houses and the increased taxes on rented houses: these measures would all be ones which would antagonize the *bourgeoisie*, without in themselves leading to a larger number of houses available.

Later on, Castro implied that these proposals of 1953 contained less radical views that he had actually had at that time. In 1961 he said in a famous speech:[32]

> People have asked me if my thinking at the time of Moncada was what it is today. I have replied 'I thought very much then as I think today' . . . Whoever reads what we said on that occasion will see very many fundamental things of the Revolution . . . That is a document further written with care. It was written with a care adequate to express a series of fundamental points, avoiding at the same time making commitments which would limit the field of action within the Revolution . . . That is, one had to try and make the movement the most broad-based as possible. If we had not written this document with care, if it had been a more radical programme (even though it is certain that many people were a trifle sceptical of programmes and did not pay them much attention) the revolutionary movement of struggle against Batista could not afterwards have acquired the breadth that it afterwards did and which made victory possible. Anyone reading the manifesto, the speech of that occasion, will understand our fundamental ideas. There are certain things, like various pledges which we made on that occasion, such as the increase to the *colonos* (at least 55% of the quota) . . . and which, afterwards, in certain conferences of *colonos*, were pointed out to me: they said *Bueno*, and aren't you going to mention the increase. I told them: Yes, but in that period we could not think of what we can talk of today and we have converted these *colonos* into proprietors of lands and that is much more than to have conceded them an increase in the proportion of sugar in the quota. Some pledges of that time were made simply with the concern of not harming the breadth of the revolutionary movement.[33]

On the other hand, some devoted supporters of Castro at that time and

[32] 2 December 1962.
[33] *Obra Revolucionaria*, 1961, No. 46, 34–5.

since believe that 'the Revolution . . . is always the same as that which we directed at Moncada'.[34]

In addition to this reform programme, Castro and his comrades were suffused by an heroic picture of their own actions in the tradition of the Cuban revolution against Spain: Castro made much of the cry of Yara and Baire, of Martí and Maceo; Castro might know something of Marx, might regard those who did not know Lenin as ignoramuses, but he evidently knew Martí much better. Like others before him, he saw himself indeed as Martí, the young man who forced the different groups opposed to Spain into a single movement, the man of heroic phrases as well as deeds, speaker and soldier, enemy of tyrants *par excellence*, incorruptible renewer. Castro embarked on the Moncada attack without indeed a very carefully worked-out ideology, only a desire to overthrow the 'tyrant' Batista and also move on to destroy the whole rotten society, the institutionalized, 'normal' violence of old Cuba of which Batista was a symptom not a cause. The 'Hymn of Liberty',[35] composed a few days before the attack on the Moncada barracks, with its emphasis on liberty, not bread or gold, made the point despite its English seaside rhythm.[36]

THE HYMN OF THE 26 JULY

Marchando vamos hacia un ideal	Marching towards an ideal
Sabiendo que vamos a triunfar	Knowing very well we are going to win;
Además de paz y prosperidad	More than peace and prosperity
Lucharemos todos por la libertad.	We will all fight for liberty.
Adelante Cubanos!	Onwards Cubans!
Que Cuba premiara nuestro heroismo	Let Cuba give you a prize for heroism.
Pues somos soldados	For we are soldiers
Que vamos a la patria a liberar	Going to free the country
Limpiando con fuego	Cleansing with fire
Que arrase con esa plaga infernal	Which will destroy this infernal plague
De gobernantes indeseables	Of bad governments
Y de Tiranos insaciables	And insatiable tyrants
Que a Cuba han sumido en el mal.	Who have plunged Cuba into evil.

[34] Haydée Santamaría, in Franqui, 54.

[35] Afterwards, 'Hymn of 26 July'.

[36] Composed by the mulatto singer Agustín Díaz Cartaya, who took part in the Bayamo attack (*Revolución*, 26 July 1963). The similarity with 'We do like to be beside the seaside' is marked.

La sangre que en Cuba se derramó	The blood which flowed in Cuba
Nosotros no debemos olvidar	We must never forget
Por eso unidos debemos estar	For that reason we must stay united
Recordando a aquellos	In remembrance of those
Que muertos están.	Who died.
El pueblo de Cuba	The Cuban people
Sumido en su dolor se siente herido	Drowned in grief feels itself wounded
Y se ha decidido	And has decided
A hallar sin tregua una solución	To pursue without respite a solution
Que sirva de ejemplo	Which will serve as an example
A esos que no tienen compasión	To those who don't have pity
Y arriesguemos decididos	And we risk, resolved
Por esta causa dar la vida:	For this cause to give our life:
Que viva la Revolución!	'Long live the Revolution!'

CHAPTER LXIX

Moncada: the Fight

Castro's plan, worked out in the offices of Abel Santamaría at Sosa brothers, in Havana,[1] was to attack two military barracks in Oriente, the Moncada barracks at Santiago and the Bayamo barracks. The main force of his supporters, 134 men, would attack at Santiago: 28 would fall on Bayamo.[2] The men would force entrance by surprise, capture the barracks and distribute arms to other volunteers who, it was supposed, would then crowd to their support. The attack would occur at dawn. The date, 26 July, was suitable because it coincided with the carnival at Santiago. Many soldiers, including the officers, would be going to the public dances of the carnival on the night of 25 July, and might be expected to be unready for fighting at 5.30 a.m. on 26 July. Castro had secured the use of a farm near Siboney as a base and several rooms had been rented in Santiago itself.

The attack was, of course, an act of war. Castro was outnumbered by about ten to one (the barracks held about 1,000 soldiers) but he banked on surprise, confusion and superior morale among his men. (Castro had apparently visited his brother-in-law, Rafael Díaz Balart, the sub-secretary for the Interior, a week before, to make sure that the police suspected nothing of his plans.)[3] Castro's armaments were limited to three U.S. army rifles, six old Winchester rifles, one old machine gun and a large number of game rifles. 'I awaited my rifle as if it had been a Messiah,' Almeida said ten years later, 'when I saw it was a 0·22, I froze.'[4] There were also some revolvers and a certain quantity of ammunition. Some small arms had been bought from soldiers, and so had about one hundred military uniforms; others had been made.[5] Castro himself spoke of the expedition as costing less than $20,000,[6] which appears to have been the sum collected by his followers beforehand,[7]

---

[1] In Consulado, No. 9.

[2] Castro speaks of 27 at Bayamo. (*History will absolve me*, 25.) Martínez Arará, the commander at Bayamo, has 28.

[3] Martínez Arará's evidence (Raúl Martínez Arará was present at Castro's talk with Díaz Balart and Orlando Pietra on 19 or 20 July).

[4] Franqui, 18.

[5] Merle, 111–13, has interesting details.

[6] *History will absolve me*, 44.

[7] Merle, 102. Martínez Arará said that some $3,000 of the money was obtained by Santamaría by means of a fraudulent signature on a cheque drawn on his firm, Sosa Bros. But this cheque seems to have been cashed nevertheless after the revolution.

of which the arms cost $5,000, the rifles costing $80 each.[8]

Nine volunteers fell out through fear, at the last minute; these included some of the few students in the expedition. Others of the group were vaguely religious and visited the Virgin del Cobre on the eve of the fight, though fortuitously. Most had driven down from Havana in cars, while some had come by train or *guagua*. Only six knew precisely what was afoot before the hour of combat,[9] and few knew each other.[10] One man at least (Almeida) thought they were going to the carnival at Santiago, as a prize for successes at earlier weapon training.[11] Others appear to have been only told that they were going to embark on some more intense shooting practice.[12] The farm at Siboney was attended by two women, Melba Hernández and Haydée Santamaría, the *fiancées* of two of the combatants, Jesús Montané and Boris Santa Colona. In his harangue of encouragement before they set out, Castro seems to have dwelt particularly on the 'historic' importance of their exploit more than the social and political.[13] Several of the participants clearly envisaged that they would be killed,[14] and one participant, Dr Muñoz, is understood to have told Castro that it was a crime to deceive so many men into so perilous an enterprise.[15]

Night of Carnival turned to revolutionary dawn: at 5.30 a.m. twenty-six cars bearing a hundred and eleven men (all dressed as sergeants) and two women drove into Santiago from Siboney. Castro was in the second car. The next car contained Raúl Castro, who, with ten men,[16] was supposed to take over the Palace of Justice overlooking the barracks; from the roof he would be in an excellent position to give covering fire to his brother in the central courtyard of the barracks. Another three cars contained Abel Santamaría, Castro's second-in-command, the two women and Dr Muñoz, twenty-two men in all.[17] They would take the civil hospital nearby and be available to treat the wounded. One car had a puncture and was left behind. According to Castro himself, 'Due to a most unfortunate error, half our forces – and the better armed half at that – went astray at the entrance to the city

---

[8] Marta Rojas, *Verde Olivo*, 29 July 1962.

[9] Merle, 143, says these were Castro, Santamaría, Alcalde, Tizol, Tasende and Guitart. Martínez Arará claims, no doubt rightly, he also knew everything.

[10] Thus the printer José Ponce remarked, 'There were so many unknown faces. No one really knew each other.' Franqui, 13.

[11] *Ibid.*, 17.

[12] Martínez Arará's evidence.

[13] Almeida in Franqui, 18.

[14] *Cf. ibid.* 54–5.

[15] Martínez Arará's evidence. Another account makes Gustavo Arcos, a young shop assistant, say the same thing.

[16] Castro, *History will absolve me*, 23.

[17] *Ibid.*, 23–5, speaks of 'Santamaría and 21 men'. Merle speaks of 20 men at the hospital and six at the law courts (p. 167).

and were not on hand to help us at the decisive moment.'[18] But the group of university students who had withdrawn at the last minute had been ordered by Castro to follow the motorcade; they moved up into the middle in a Chrysler and it was they who diverted several cars from the route to Moncada.[19]

The first car halted at the gate of the barracks. Six men[20] got out and their leader, Guitart, called on the sentry to 'make way for the general'. The three sentries, deceived by the sergeants' uniforms, which they 'did not recognize but which they momentarily assumed were those of a military band', presented arms, and these weapons, Springfield rifles, were seized from them. The rebels then burst into the barracks upstairs, pushing the sentries before them. Outside, Castro in the second car had been held up by two unexpected encounters: two soldiers with machine guns and an armed sergeant. Castro ran his car against the machine gunners and the sergeant fled. But he could clearly give the alarm. Following previous orders, once Castro's car stopped, the men in the following cars all leapt out and attacked the buildings to their left. Castro tried unsuccessfully to regroup his men. Inside the barracks, the men of the first car, having bewildered a dormitory of undressed soldiers, found themselves cut off, and, having shot down a number of sergeants, as well as the officer of the day, Lieutenant Morales, withdrew. The alarm being given, a general fusillade followed from the first floors into the street. The attackers protected themselves behind parked cars. What precisely occurred in any such event is bound to be a matter of controversy afterwards: another account has it that Castro drove his car on to the pavement, hitting the kerb violently, and so attracting the attention of the guard who thereupon shot at and wounded Gustavo Arcos.

The other two sections of the attack in Santiago had been successful; Raúl Castro captured the almost unguarded Palace of Justice, and Abel Santamaría the Civil Hospital, with no losses to themselves or to the army. But this meant little while the advantage of surprise at Moncada had been lost and when the attack had turned into an uneven battle between one hundred men armed with sporting guns and one thousand well-armed soldiers, rallied by Major Morales, a brother of the dead officer of the day. Castro quickly gave the order to retire, and he and his men did so, leaving behind some wounded and some others to be captured. As usual in such circumstances there were later allegations that the leaders fled first. Raúl Castro and the victors of the Palace of Justice also withdrew, but those in the Civil Hospital did not know

[18] *History will absolve me*, 23.
[19] Merle, 254.
[20] José Suárez, Ramiro Valdés, José Luis Tasende, Rigoberto Corcho, Carmelo Noa and Renato Guitart.

of the order to retreat and afterwards hid, disguised as patients, in the hospital itself. At this stage it seems that Castro had lost only two men killed[21] and one mortally wounded;[22] the army had lost three officers and sixteen men killed.[23] Both sides had a substantial number of wounded. The battle had lasted about one hour.

At Bayamo also the attack failed, horses apparently giving the alarm. The leader, Raúl Martínez Arará, delayed in giving the order for withdrawal, but the battle nonetheless lasted only fifteen minutes.[24] It was an even more complete fiasco than Moncada. It is clear that there had been some political dispute and argument among the Bayamo fighters, several disapproving of Fidel Castro as leader.[25] Six were killed.

The aftermath of the attacks on the barracks had crucial consequences for the history of Cuba. Some, such as Martínez Arará of the Bayamo attack, escaped to foreign embassies. Perhaps eighty of the original 160 rebels were captured either on 26 July or in the following days; most of these who were captured the first day or two were murdered. Those who, like Castro himself, managed to hold out a few days in the forests, escaped this death. But altogether sixty-eight prisoners appear to have been killed, including even three young men (the 'Almendares' group of Víctor Escalona) who had withdrawn from the attack at the last minute. Most of these prisoners were beaten with rifle butts before being shot and some were tortured in other ways. Some died during the course of brutal treatment. Three prisoners at Bayamo were dragged along for miles behind a jeep. The two women, Haydée Santamaría and Melba Hernández, were not themselves tortured; but Abel Santamaría, the brother of the former and *novio* of the latter, was apparently tortured to death in their hearing, as was Boris Santa Coloma, Haydée Santamaría's *novio*. Thirty-two prisoners survived to be brought to trial while forty-eight escaped altogether, returning to Havana by bus or escaping to friends' houses.[26]

This brutality was initially a spontaneous reaction of frightened and angry soldiery, backed by their NCOs. The accusations later made by Batistiano officers of brutality on the part of the rebels (such as knifing patients in the military hospital) appear false.[27] The com-

---

[21] Gildo Fleitas and Guillermo Granados.

[22] Rigoberto Corcho.

[23] *Avance*, 27 July, speaks of 16 soldiers dead. The most immediate press reports seem in the circumstances the most likely.

[24] See Merle, 213–15.

[25] Evidence of Martínez Arará, who adds, '*casi todos los compañeros de mi grupo sentían cierta repugnancia por Fidel Castro*'. This may have been an afterthought.

[26] An incomplete list of killed first appeared in *Revolución*, 15 January 1959, 14. In 1967 Castro argued (at the first conference of the Latin American Solidarity Organisation) that the attack was a mistake and that he should have embarked on guerrilla warfare at the start.

[27] The commander of the military hospital said at the trial of some of the rebels that no one was killed there except one patient who rashly put his head out of the window.

manders of the Moncada barracks (Colonel del Río Chaviano and Captain Pérez Chaumont), also frightened and also angry, with the scent of rum and cigars from the carnival still in their nostrils and no doubt heavy hangovers, arriving on the scene of battle after the last shot had been fired, not only made no attempt to restrain the brutalities but encouraged them and afterwards helped cover them up.[28] The military intelligence (SIM) at Moncada, under Captain Lavastida, also took a prominent part in the repression. A few doctors and officers (such as Captain Tamayo, Major Morales and Lieutenant Sarriá) tried to save several lives and did so. But this was hard since in so doing they themselves risked ill treatment.

Finally, this brutality was underwritten by the government itself though the governor of Oriente, Pérez Almaguer, later said that Batista did not know what was being done in his name.[29] On 26 July the cabinet hastily approved a decree suspending Article 26 of the Prison Statute making the prison officers responsible for the lives of their prisoners. Batista himself and the officer corps were evidently as frightened and as angry as the soldiery and their officers. If rebels could make an onslaught on the second biggest barracks in Cuba, who was safe? The government panicked, the army throughout the island was placed on the alert, and hundreds of people were detained. Since some *Fidelistas* were known to be wounded, anyone with a wound, even from a road accident, was in danger of interrogation and ill treatment. A Santiago citizen whose arm was in plaster was for that reason taken to Moncada and badly beaten.[30] This ruthless and reckless behaviour caused public opinion to forget entirely the doubtful morality of the original attack.

The Moncada attack occurred at a bad moment in the life of Batista's administration since the intrigues and struggles in the armed forces had been almost uncontrolled: Tabernilla as chief of staff was more and more unpopular but more and more ambitious, now seeking to arrange the ruin of three ministers – Nicolás Hernández, Ramón Hermida and Pablo Carrera Justiz, who had been architects on the civilian side of the 10 March plot. He had already successfully disposed of the able General García Tuñón, who had been Hernández's own candidate for the chief army command, to be military attaché in Chile; another disappointed *Batistiano*, Colonel Lambea, had pulled a pistol on Tabernilla in his office and been disposed of to a similar job in Costa Rica; an unconditional friend, Ugalde Carrillo, had been given the important post of command of the SIM, and two of Tabernilla's sons, 'Wince' and

---

[28] The governor of Oriente province, Waldo Pérez Almaguer, who tried unsuccessfully to stop the bloodshed and who visited the barracks early in the morning of 26 July, confirms the personal responsibility of Del Río Chaviano (*La Calle*, 3 June 1956).

[29] *Ibid.*, 3 June 1955.

[30] Merle, 249.

'Silito', had been promoted beyond all possible deserts; while other representatives of the Tabernilla faction had been given command of the rural guard up and down the island. These appointments had naturally antagonized the rest of the civil and military administration, particularly the officers who had manned the 10 March plot and who had been excluded from the benefits in a signal manner: they had after all many of them quite serious if autocratic desires for the regeneration of the country, and were affronted by the use to which Tabernilla's men put their power, in particular by the network of protection rackets and gambling dens which they had organized throughout the country. One minister, Ernesto de la Fe, had had an open scene with Batista on this matter, pointing out to the president that the military commands in all the six provinces were held by intimate friends of Tabernilla[31] and saying that the government could only hold its backing in public opinion by getting rid of these men as of the chief of police, Salas Cañizares, and the head of the SIM, Ugalde Carrillo.[32]

Batista had then agreed at least to make an inquiry into these charges and appointed Colonel Fermín Cowley to investigate. Cowley had confirmed them while Colonel Barrera, a member of the 10 March group, had told Batista of a particularly scandalous instance of the misuse of power, whereby Ugalde Carrillo was using his influence in the rural guards to force a lorry company to sell out to a friend of his for an absurdly low sum; the rural guards were forcing the lorries to stop, subjecting them to all sorts of delays and thereby causing the company to lose the confidence of their customers. Batista had just agreed that as a result of all these charges, there should be a general reorganization of the military commands when the Moncada crisis began.[33]

The attack was something bigger than even the gangster attack on the police headquarters of Marianao in 1948; any army would have reacted fairly strongly. But the savagery of the repression exceeded normal expectations. The consequences were critical. The facts of torture and murder became quickly known, both through gossip and afterwards, despite censorship, through the press: *Bohemia* published on 2 August a large number of photographs of bodies, many dressed up in clean clothes after being killed, to give an impression that they had been killed in fighting.[34] Before then a meeting had occurred between several Santiago notables – the bishop (Angel Castro's old friend, Pérez Serantes), the rector of the university, a judge, a large department store owner, Enrique

---

[31] Colonels José Fernández Rey, Dámaso Sogo (Soguito), Pilar García, Aquilino Guerra, and Alberto del Río Chaviano, in the provinces running west to east.

[32] Barrera Pérez, *Bohemia Libre*, August 1961. Barrera was present at the interview.

[33] *Loc. cit.*

[34] These photographs were taken by one of a group of journalists to whom Colonel del Río Chaviano spoke on the day of the attack on the Moncada barracks.

Canto – with Batista's principal secretary, Morales del Castillo.[35] The notables demanded an end to the massacre of prisoners, and Batista shortly gave the proper order. Pérez Serantes gave a press conference announcing the agreement, but in setting out himself (with Judge Subirats and Enrique Canto) for La Gran Piedra, a mountain where Castro was thought (rightly) to be hiding, he showed his lack of faith in the regime's word: his intention was personally to find those who surrendered and hand them over to the army. The bishop drove, and then walked, several hours over the mountainside, calling through a megaphone that he guaranteed the lives of those who surrendered. Though unsuccessful immediately, his gesture led to the surrender of several rebels; shortly after, Castro was himself captured by the humane army lieutenant, Sarriá, with two followers, while sleeping.[36]

Officials of Batista's regime had thus swung backwards to the era of Machado and of Spain, equalling or even exceeding in their behaviour the worst excesses of those dark days. Partly, no doubt, they saw in Castro and his friends the outriders of a movement which threatened them personally: they had a real interest in serving the regime and, being poor and ill-educated, they reacted in the most brutal way possible. It is also clear that they would not have so acted had it not been for their presumption that their superior officers would not cause them to bear responsibility for their actions: the Cuban army, first, partook of the easy-going character of Cubans in general, so that indiscipline was normal: many officers acted in all matters as if they owned private fiefs. The officers also served a regime from which they hoped much. The condition of the law and its relation to the administration was such that there was only a remote chance that they would be faced with charges as a result. Indeed, some were promoted.[37] Recalling atrocious precedents, insecure, hating a revolt which seemed led by middle-class people more than they would have hated a working-class explosion, they did not scruple to react in a way which seriously affected Cuba for years to come.

The commander in Santiago was Alberto del Río Chaviano, then thirty-eight, commander of the Maceo Regiment No 1, who had entered the army at eighteen in November 1933, presumably attracted by the prospects apparently opening up after the sergeants' revolt of September. In 1938 he entered the cadet school; while there, he had led the cadets loyal to Batista in opposition and protest to the attempted Pedraza golpe in 1941. He remained in the army during the Auténtico governments, and indeed had on that account been briefly detained on

[35] Usually in Cuba a member of the cabinet.
[36] See Fidel Castro's account, *La Calle*, 30 May 1955.
[37] *Bohemia*, 2 August 1953.

10 March 1952. But, due to his friendship with General Tabernilla, his brother-in-law, he was soon released, promoted and sent back to an active command in Santiago. The SIM commander, Captain Lavastida, had been only a sergeant at Camagüey before 1952[38] and owed his promotion to his knowledge of the drug traffic. Captain Pérez Chaumont, under thirty, known as '*Ojos Bellos*', who shot many prisoners on the outskirts of El Caney, had already in the last few years made enough out of protection rackets to buy a $100,000 house in Miramar, near Santiago.

A number of leading Communists were also arrested at this time. These included Lázaro Peña, Blas Roca, Carlos Rafael Rodríguez and others who chanced to be in Santiago at the time in order to celebrate Blas Roca's birthday. This always sounded suspicious, and their presence has been naturally used further to implicate Castro with long-standing Communist associations: Blas Roca, after all, lived in Havana and his home town was Manzanillo. But their presence was fortuitous. They 'knew nothing of the Moncada plan'[39] and actually most of the party leaders left the town on 25 July. Afterwards they repudiated the attack on the Moncada:

> We repudiate [they said] the Putschist methods, peculiar to *bourgeois* factions, of the action in Santiago de Cuba and Bayamo, an adventurist attempt to capture the two military headquarters. The heroism displayed by the participants in this action is false and sterile, as it is guided by mistaken *bourgeois* conceptions. But even more we repudiate the repression directed by the government with the revolt as a pretext . . . The entire country knows who organised, inspired and directed the action against the barracks and that the communists had nothing to do with it. The line of the Communist party and of the masses had been to combat the Batista tyranny seriously and to unmask the *putschistas* and adventurers as being against the interests of the people. The Communist party poses the necessity of creating a united front of the masses against the government, for a democratic way out of the Cuban situation, restoration of the constitution of 1940, civil liberties, general elections, and the establishment of a National Democratic Front government, with a programme of national independence, peace, democracy, and agrarian reform.[40]

[38] Merle, 256.

[39] Carlos Rafael Rodríguez to the author, June 1966.

[40] *Daily Worker* (New York), 5 and 10 August. The statement could not be published in Havana. It is interesting to compare this attitude with that of the established Communist parties towards the guerrilla struggles in the 1950s: thus the Communist leader in Ceylon Sanmugathasan said that Guevara in Bolivia failed because his method was 'the romantic and petty bourgeois ideology which places its main reliance on a band of swashbuckling "Three Musketeers" type of bravados who one expected to perform miraculous feats against terrific odds'. (*Ceylon Daily News*, 5 November 1967.)

Moncada had found Batista at Varadero beach. He gave no sign of concern but showed himself a great deal to the crowd, appearing on television, giving prizes at a regatta, claiming later he knew himself to be a target for an assassin. On 2 August he arrived in Santiago to commiserate with the soldiers. Constitutional guarantees were suspended. On the 6th a more vigorous public order law was decreed, aimed specially at the press. As a result the press all but dried up. Batista also rearranged his cabinet to give an impression at least of vitality: and to the newly created Transport Ministry went Castro's father-in-law.[41] But there were no changes in the army command. Batista went back on his plan to weaken the empire of Tabernilla, thinking it best in these abnormal circumstances to keep such commanders as there were where they were.[42] Nor were there any changes in the police command who despite their obsession with the telephone calls of the opposition, had failed to predict this event.

In October Castro and his comrades were tried. An attempt was made either to poison Castro or to prevent him from appearing by alleging that he was sick. In the event he appeared, on 21 September and 16 October (on the first occasion as a witness), and made a brilliant speech in his own defence.[43] He was sentenced to fifteen years' imprisonment, Raúl Castro to thirteen years, others to lesser terms. The case against the Communists was dismissed.[44]

The consequences on public opinion of Moncada and its aftermath were considerable. Had it not been for the repression, the Moncada attack would doubtless have been dismissed as one more wild and semi-gangster incident in the life of Fidel Castro. The repression and the trial made Castro appear henceforth something of a hero. Professional, catholic, liberal or middle class opinion was outraged. A Santiago judge on 27 July telephoned Andrés Domingo, Batista's presidential secretary, and asked 'Are you trying to revive the epoch of Machado

[41] The new ministers were: Rafael Díaz Balart (Transport); Gustavo Gutiérrez (Finance); José E. Olivella (Health); Rafael Guas Inclán (Communications); Santiago Rey (without Portfolio); Radio Cremata Valdés (Secretary of the Consultative Council); César Camacho Govani (Chairman of Social Security); Marino López Blanco (in charge of United Railways). Arsenio González remained at the Ministry of Labour – a lawyer who had been the Communists' adviser in their struggles against Prío; he was said to be a Communist himself, by, for example, R. J. Alexander.

[42] Barrera Pérez, *Bohemia Libre*, August 1961.

[43] Roughly, one may assume, similar to the text of the pamphlet, *History will absolve me*. But see below, p. 848.

[44] See description, *Bohemia*, 22 May 1955. The judges were A. Nieto Piñeiro Osorio, Juan Francisco Mejías Valdivieso and Ricardo Díaz Oliveira. Present also were three journalists and fifty soldiers. Others imprisoned at the time of Moncada were also put at liberty, these were Dr 'Millo' Ochoa, Dr O. Alvarado and R. Arango Alsina, of the Ortodoxos; Ordoqui and Lázaro Peña, Communists; and Auténticos – Aracelio Azcuy, Roberto García Ibáñez, Sergio Mejías, José Manuel Gutiérrez, Arturo Hernández Tellaheche and Luis Casero (*ibid.*, October 1953).

with all these assassinations?'[45] Professional people in Santiago, people who had either seen or had met someone who had seen something of what happened, turned almost without exception away from Batista. The part played by the bishop, Pérez Serantes, was also important, both for the Church and for the upper class Catholics: if Castro's life could be saved by the bishop, then his cause seemed almost respectable. For Castro himself, the attack had overwhelming consequences: exposure to the imminent threat of death, the death of so many of his associates, led by him into an action of his planning, both isolated him from other young Ortodoxo leaders and heightened his own sense of mission. Afterwards, it seemed symbolic that the first peasant he should meet in the Sierra Maestra should have been an old woman who apparently recalled helping the *mambises* of the war of independence. At the end of his period of hiding he was toying with the idea of moving up into the Sierra Maestra on the other side of Santiago. The future seemed to have no alternative except further action, 'the continuance of the struggle'. On the other hand, the morale of Batista's army sank lower, not only because of the widespread hostility to the treatment by Río Chaviano of the prisoners but because of his happy acceptance of the role of hero and victor in this contest: so much so that he began to persecute the real victor, Major Morales, and sent him under guard to Havana as an enemy of the people.[46]

[45] Baudilio Castellanos to Merle (Merle, 282).
[46] Barrera Pérez, *Bohemia Libre*, 6 August 1961. For Pérez Serantes's account, see Herbert Matthews, *Castro*, 61.

CHAPTER LXX

Indian Summer

In October 1953, ten days after the trial of the survivors of Moncada, Batista announced that there would be general elections a year later, on 1 November 1954. All parties would have till February 1954 to register. Censorship was soon lifted and on 28 October the ninety-day decree suspending civil rights came to an end. Batista coyly refused to say whether he would be a presidential candidate: 'The grapes are still green,' he told audiences, usually whipped up by Díaz Balart, Castro's brother-in-law, and still youth leader of Batista's movement. Other crowds cheered Señora de Batista, shouting on her public appearances as if she were indeed Evita Perón: '*Martha del pobre, Martha del Pueblo*'.[1] Martha Batista went to Washington, where she was received by Mrs Eisenhower and Secretary Hobby of the Department of Health, Education and Welfare. With Prío forced to register as an agent of a foreign political party, the star of Batista seemed to be rising. Indeed, the regime seemed outwardly solid and self-confident, lapped in the arms of U.S. acceptance, its enemies in gaol or in exile. The new ambassador, Arthur Gardner, was a vigorous and unashamed friend of both the regime and of Batista. Gardner, an appointee of the new President Eisenhower (who had been inaugurated six months before Moncada, in January 1953), had been Assistant Secretary of the Treasury under President Truman, 1947–8: as such, it had fallen to him to receive the news of the arrival at Miami of Grau's Minister of Education, Alemán, with $M20 of Cuban government funds[2] in his suitcase. Perhaps this experience caused him to look on the Auténticos and politicians of the old order with special suspicion, and to regard Batista as the saviour which Cuba needed. Amiable and agreeable, he gave Batista much self-confidence, though the *New York Times* correspondent, Mrs Phillips, noted that his fulsome admiration for the general sometimes caused its object some embarrassment.[3]

[1] She was Batista's second wife, having married him in November 1945; he divorced his first wife, Elisa Godínez, in October 1945. By her he had had three children – Mirta Caridad, Fulgencio and Elisa Aleida. By Martha, he had Jorge (born 1942), Roberto (born 1947), Carlos Manuel (born 1950), Fulgencio José (born 1953). He also recognized in his will an illegitimate daughter Fermina Lázara, born 1935 (*cf.* will published in *Revolución*, 24 January 1959). He was evidently a generous father and treated all his children, of both marriages, with equal generosity.

[2] Evidence of Ambassador Gardner.

[3] R. H. Phillips, *Island of Paradox*.

A big sugar conference had meanwhile been successfully held in London, binding its seventy-eight national participants for five years to keep to certain quantities in the world market. Cuba received $2\frac{1}{4}$ million tons or slightly under half the whole free market (40 %) over and above her sales to the U.S. However some exporting countries (India, Indonesia, Peru) did not sign the convention. Nor were the importing countries constrained to restrict their imports in the same way as the exporters had to restrict theirs. Yet the Cuban share was, of course infinitely superior to that handed out in 1937 (940,000 tons), and the 1954 harvest was fixed firmly at $4\frac{3}{4}$ million tons; most people believed that, despite the long-term uncertainty – could the standard of living be maintained unless sugar production went up steadily? – the government had done well.

Gardner's arrival in Havana coincided with a firmer hand towards the Communists than Batista had hitherto ventured towards his old friends. On 10 November the Communist party was outlawed. Its appendages, such as the newspapers *Hoy* and *Ultima Hora*, the Federation of Democratic Women, and the youth movement Juventud Socialista, were banned. The weekly magazine *Carta Semanal* and the theoretical monthly *Fundamentos* continued to be produced, however, and were sold, the former at least quite easily, though under the counter. Batista and his ministers, in fact, maintained a deliberately agreeable and relaxed attitude to the Communists, at least towards those with whom they had once had dealings: Ramón Vasconcelos, for instance, the journalist and afterwards Minister of Communications, concerned himself with the interests of Negro Communist leaders. There was not much persecution of any of them except that they were occasionally detained and questioned on their arrival from Mexico, Prague or elsewhere. Fabio Grobart, for so long *éminence grise* of the Communist party, left Cuba in this period, profiting thereby since he was able to refresh his views in the relatively new atmosphere in Moscow which opened up after Stalin's death.[4] The Cuban Communists in general were in semi-retirement during most of these years, recovering their health and energies, and so preparing themselves effectively for the future. Blas Roca, the old secretary-general, was ill and day-to-day control rested in the hands of a five-man junta composed of Carlos Rafael Rodríguez, Aníbal Escalante, Lázaro Peña, Manuel Luzardo and Severo Aguirre.[5]

---

[4] Luis Serrano Romayo told Alexander that Grobart had already left in the time of Prío (Alexander, 293).

[5] Evidence in Marquitos trial, 1964. Some isolated Communist party members, however, were later persecuted by the police: thus a young Negro athlete Chicqui Hernández was murdered later in the 9th police station, and José María Pérez, the Communist transport workers' leader, disappeared without a trace. Some students or ex-students such as Valdés Vivo and Leonel Soto were brutally tortured.

Their policy eddied between different aims. Some Communists expected that Batista would over-reach himself and so create an acute crisis from which they would profit. Some seem to have expected that, with Stalin dead, a Soviet–U.S. *rapprochement* was possible, in turn making possible a renewed deal between themselves and Batista, perhaps leading to their capture of power through Batista rather than against him. The inaction necessitated by this policy was as early as 1953–4 resented by younger members of the party, members of Juventud Socialista, and particularly by its members who had been contemporaries of Fidel Castro or his brother Raúl – himself, after all, a member, if then an errant one, of Juventud Socialista – at the university.

Fidel Castro, on the other hand, now in prison in the Isle of Pines, was still closely linked to the Ortodoxos – perhaps closer to them than he had been at Moncada. On 12 December 1953, in a letter to an old friend, the journalist Luis Conte Agüero, the secretary-general of Ortodoxo youth in the beginning, he wrote:

> If our revolutionary effort had triumphed, our plan was to put power in the hands of the most fervent Ortodoxos. Our triumph would have meant the immediate rise to power of Ortodoxia, first provisionally, afterwards via general elections . . . so inevitable was this that despite our failure, our sacrifice has strengthened the cause of the ideals of Chibás . . . speak to Agramonte, show him this letter, express to him our most loyal sentiments towards the most pure ideals of Chibás.[6]

Castro was bitter about the role of the Communists:

> We would never have had . . . inappropriate and sterile theories about a *putsch* or a revolution, at the very moment when it was right to denounce monstrous crimes . . . do you think, Luis, that we would have called a *putsch* your effort to raise the Maceo Regiment on the morning of March 10?[7]

Immediately after this letter, a pamphlet on its general lines was prepared by Luis Conte Agüero, Melba Hernández (freed after the Moncada trial) and other supporters of Castro in Havana, with Castro's aid from prison. They followed the outlines of Castro's speech in self defence in Santiago, and it was in that form that the pamphlet was eventually published. Nevertheless, the feel, the mood, even on occasion the language and allusions echo more the letter of 12 December 1953.

[6] L. Conte Agüero, *Cartas del Presidio* (1959), 20–1. 'Our' meant 'my'. Castro early adopted this royal first person plural which he would use afterwards in speeches though in his speech at the trial he spoke of 'History' absolving 'me' not 'us', a *personalismo* which was at the time resented by his friends.
[7] Conte Agüero, *Cartas del Presidio*, 22.

The pamphlet was clearly based on the letter. An edition prepared in 1964 argued that it was a 'reconstruction' of the speech made 'little by little' without apparently the shorthand notes of what was said being available.[8]

Whether written at this time or not, this famous pamphlet began as a speech in self-defence: 'Never has a lawyer had to practise his profession under more difficult conditions . . . As attorney for the defence I have been denied even a look at the indictment . . . As the accused, I have been for the past seventy-six days shut away in solitary confinement.'[9] The speech was carefully formal, appealing to precedent, looking back at the past as if there had indeed been a time in Cuba when law and liberty had marched together. Thus we hear of a right 'sanctified by long tradition in Cuba', namely that of an accused's right to plead in his own defence, and:

> Once upon a time there was a Republic. It had its constitution, its laws, its civil rights, a president, a Congress and law courts. Everyone could assemble, associate, speak and write with complete freedom. The people were not satisfied with the government officials at that time but . . . had power to elect new officials and only a few days remained before they were going to do so . . . There existed a public opinion both respected and heeded: all problems of common interest were freely discussed . . . the whole nation throbbed with enthusiasm . . . they felt confident that no one would dare commit the crime of violating their democratic institutions. They desired a change for the better . . . and they saw all this at hand.[10]

This indeed was an extravagant over-romanticism of the age of Prío, to highlight the monstrosity of Batista's regime, with which Chibás for one would not have agreed.

Castro attempted too to depict Batista not only as a tyrant but as the

[8] See appendix to 1964 edition (Havana, *Ediciones Política*) of speech, and article by Francisco de Armas in *Hoy*, 21 July 1963, 2–3. The information derived from Melba Hernández. But shorthand notes taken by the *Bohemia* reporter Marta Rojas must have been available (*cf.* Merle, 333, and Draper's comments, *Castroism*, 5). The pamphlet was first circulated in June 1954, when it said that 'A group of Cuban intellectuals . . . have decided to publish the complete text of Dr Fidel Castro's defence plea'. But see also the version given by Castro to Robert Taber in a foreword to the New York edition in the spring of 1957: Castro spoke of 'a "little book" that he had written several years before . . . He showed obvious pleasure and no little pride in describing the ingenuity with which while in solitary confinement and under close guard . . . he had set down his thoughts invisibly in lime juice between the lines of ordinary letters'. 'You would be surprised how much trouble it was. I could write for only twenty minutes or so each evening at sunset when the sun slanted across the paper . . . to make the letters visible.' (p. 7). This last account perhaps owes something to romantic imagination.

[9] Dr Paglieri of Santiago was not allowed to visit Castro in gaol except once with a SIM sergeant present.

[10] *Ibid.*, 16.

worst dictator in all Cuba's history, or indeed in Latin American history.

> *Monstrum horrendum* . . . a man named Batista . . .[11] The man who encouraged the atrocious acts in Santiago . . . has not even human entrails . . .[12] has furthermore, never been sincere, loyal, honest or chivalrous for a single minute of his public life . . .[13] Only one man in all these centuries has stained with blood two separate periods of our historic existence and has dug his claws into the flesh of two generations of Cubans . . .[14] That grip, those claws, were familiar: those jaws, those death-dealing scythes, those boots . . .[15]

Castro did not omit, either, to revive memory of the murders of officers after the surrender of the Hotel Nacional in 1933 and of Blas Hernández and others, after the surrender of Fort Atarés the same year.[16] Batista, he said, was not content with 'the treachery of December 1933, the crimes of March 1935 and the $M40 fortune that crowned his first regime'.[17]

Revolutionary appeals were almost non-existent:

> The *people* means the vast unredeemed masses, to whom all make promises and whom all deceive; we mean the people who yearn for a better, more dignified and more just nation; who are moved by ancestral aspirations of justice, for they have suffered injustice and mockery, generation after generation; who long for great and wise changes in all aspects of their life . . .[18]

The speech spoke of '700,000 Cubans without work'[19] – a rough approximation of numbers of unemployed during the dead season; of 500,000 farm labourers inhabiting miserable shacks;[20] of 400,000 industrial labourers and stevedores whose pension funds had been stolen and whose life was otherwise intolerable – again, perhaps an overstatement; there were 275,000[21] supposed to be involved in manufactures (not including sugar). Builders (50,000)[22] and transport workers (75,000)[23] might bring the total up to 400,000. Not all these

[11] *Ibid.*, 18.
[12] *Ibid.*, 49.
[13] *Loc. cit.*
[14] *Loc. cit.*
[15] *Ibid.*, 62.
[16] *Ibid.*, 48.
[17] *Ibid.*, 49.
[18] *Ibid.*, 33–4.
[19] *Ibid.*, 34.
[20] Possibly an exaggeration, since the 1953 census makers thought there were only 118,000 houses in really bad condition (Census, p. 212). The number of agricultural labourers in 1953 totalled 510,016.
[21] Exact number 272,569.
[22] 51,263.
[23] 76,378.

people's lives were intolerable and not all of their pension funds had been stolen. Castro also spoke of 100,000 small farmers working land which was not their own, 200,000 peasant families without an acre of land, much good but uncultivated land, 30,000 underpaid teachers, 20,000 small debt-ridden businessmen, 10,000 young professionals – all fairly accurate approximations. He contended that 85 % of small farmers paid rent and lived under the threat of being dispossessed, that over half the best cultivated land belonged to foreigners, while in Oriente the United Fruit Company's lands and the West India Sugar Corporation joined the north with the south coast.[24]

Castro pointed out what he judged the anomaly of exporting sugar in order to import sweets, hides to import shoes, iron to import ploughs. He urged the planned manufacture of steel, paper and chemicals, and the improvement of cattle food and grain products, to compete with Europe in cheese, condensed milk, wine and oil, and with the U.S. in tinned goods. Tourism should bring 'an enormous revenue'. But, said Castro, 'the capitalists insist that the workers remain under a Claudian yoke; the state folds its arms and industrialization can wait for the Greek Calends.'[25] This was Castro's only reference to 'capitalism' or indeed his only use of the jargon of Marxism or the class war.

Castro also launched a general attack on inadequate schooling, health, child welfare, and rural unemployment, while complaining that the rich could buy as much justice as they wanted, 'like Balzac's *taillefer*'. Cuba, he said, could easily feed a population three times as great – 'markets should be overflowing with produce ... all hands should be full, all hands should be working'. What seemed to him intolerable was that '30 % of our farm people cannot write their names and that 99 % of them know nothing of Cuba's history' – a somewhat curious bracketing.

Initially there was a series of legal arguments based on Cuban law, and upon historical arguments about the morality of the overthrow of tyrants: the authority of Montesquieu, John of Salisbury, St Thomas, Luther, Melanchthon, Calvin, Milton, Locke, Rousseau and Tom Paine were invoked for rebellion; the American, English and French revolutions were mentioned, as well as the Cuban leaders of 1868–98 (Agramonte, Céspedes, Maceo, Gómez and Martí). Always there was a hint of the role played by fighting: Maceo was quoted as saying liberty is 'not begged for but won with the blow of a machete'.[26]

Finally came the rhetorical conclusion:

[24] The West India Sugar Corporation, which had just over one million shares in 1957, had $M35 worth of land in the Dominican Republic also, according to a Dow Jones estimate in 1957 (*Havana Post*, 1 May 1957).
[25] *Op. cit.*, 38.
[26] 77.

I know that imprisonment will be as hard for me as it has ever been for anyone – filled with cowardly threats and wicked torture. But I do not fear prison, just as I do not fear the fury of the miserable tyrant who snuffed life out of seventy brothers of mine. Sentence me, I don't mind. History will absolve me.

Thus in the winter of 1953–4 Castro and his friends out of prison were at work on an eloquent denunciation of the regime, supported by a multiplicity of historical and social arguments, which was not only an attack on the Batista government but more profoundly was an attempt to plant a land-mine beneath the entire structure of Cuban society as it was then organized. The statistics were loosely gathered but roughly accurate and the drive of the pamphlet's social demands chiefly reflected Castro's own knowledge of the countryside of Oriente. There was as ever lacking any mention of racial intolerance; indeed, it would have been possible to have read *History will absolve me* without knowing there were Negroes at all in Cuba. But Castro knew that Batista was quite popular among Negroes and mulattoes. He gave consistent support to various Afro-Cuban cults. Several of his own black or mulatto followers had been taunted by their black soldier captors at the time of Moncada for following a white leader against Batista, the friend of the Negroes. Some soldiers had shown genuine surprise that there were any 'black revolutionaries'. A Negro brick-layer, Armando Mestre, maltreated by the police at Moncada, was told 'You a revolutionary, you? You don't know that Negroes can't be revolutionaries? Negroes are either thieves or partisans of Batista, not revolutionaries.'[27] When Lieutenant Sarriá and his men came upon the sleeping Castro and his two followers, their shout was, 'They are white!', '*Son Blancos*,' as if proof that they were revolutionaries, not *guajiros* or workers.[28]

Three further points might be made about this famous statement: first, there was no major attack on the U.S. – indeed, Castro spoke less violently of the 'colossus of the north' than most Cuban nationalist politicians of the previous fifty years; second, unlike the rhetorical statements of his fellows in Cuban politics, the speech included a considerable panoply of statistical material; and third, much of this statistical material seems from internal evidence to have come from a famous popularizing work, *Los Fundamentos del Socialismo*, by the secretary general of the Cuban Communist party, Blas Roca.[29]

With every month after Moncada, and despite Castro's literary activities, Batista improved his position. The man in the street told

[27] Almeida to Francqui, 18.
[28] See Merle, 268.
[29] I am indebted for this last point to Mr Robin Blackburn.

himself that political gangsterism and graft had been reduced. Labour relations seemed good and the foreign exchange situation excellent. An occasional ugly incident could be ignored if it remained unexplained – such as the mysterious murder of Mario Fortuny, a journalist who had worked with Sánchez Arango in the Ministry of Education. There were anyway fewer political murders than in the days of the Auténticos. In December the regime received a fillip from the arrest of ex-President Prío in Florida, on charges of violating the U.S. Neutrality Law of 1939. Released on a $50,000 charge, he was arraigned on 14 December with various followers, finger-printed and sent for trial. Such events might cause merriment to Batista. They exacerbated U.S. relations with the opposition. Jorge Mañach sent an open letter to Eisenhower accusing him of intervening in Cuban affairs.

But in the army the animosities and intrigues continued. General del Río Chaviano, it will be remembered, had sent Major Morales, the real victor of Moncada, back to Havana under lock and key, as a conspirator: but Morales had successfully got a letter to Batista explaining the truth of the matter, adding that del Río Chaviano was running a big gambling and protection racket in Santiago, that there were almost daily drunken orgies in the barracks, and that he had made vast profits from smuggling; he added too that if on investigation these things were not found to be true, he personally would shoot himself in Batista's presence. Batista did make an investigation. Morales was freed and became head of the Cuban military archives but nothing was done to del Río Chaviano; the scandals associated with Tabernilla and the officers so well placed and so near to him continued.

The reason for this was that Tabernilla's eldest son, the young Lieutenant 'Silito', had successfully manœuvred his way from being simply a military aide of the president to being his chief secretary, securing the dispatch of Dr Raúl Acosta Rubio who had held this post for years, including during the time when Batista was in exile, to the appointment of Cuban minister to Honduras. This had led to various changes and promotions in the military commands, designed to establish further Tabernilla in a powerful position.

In January 1954 an embarrassing event occurred: Grau San Martín announced his candidacy in the Batista presidential elections for November. He was naturally criticized, even by his relations, for deigning to collaborate with the new constitutional laws – a criticism in no way removed by Batista's 'pledge' that the old constitution would be restored piecemeal after the elections, beginning with the articles that dealt with local government.[30] The articles on the Congress

[30] Several supporters of Grau left him, among them Primitivo Rodríguez, Hugo Alvarez, Edgardo Buttari and Antonio Fernández Macho.

would apply after January 1955, when that body would meet again. The whole constitution would function after the new president had taken office on 20 February 1955.

The Communists were not among those groups who trifled to register for the elections. They urged their followers to back Dr Grau San Martín and later explained:

> We said to the masses: since we have to vote, let us vote against Batista's tyrannical and anti-popular government. We explained publicly that Grau could not supply any solution; that we were not calling for a vote for him but for a vote against Batista, though the only way possible to vote against Batista . . . was to mark a cross against Batista's name. The slogan of the negative vote [Blas Roca self-importantly added] had profound repercussions amongst the masses. Under that slogan . . . the masses of all tendencies and parties of the opposition united . . . the meetings that Grau called in the election campaign became against those who called them, militant mass demonstrations against the tyranny.[31]

The nation was thus faced by the bizarre alliance of the Communists and Auténticos, with Ortodoxos holding aloof. Whether as a result or not, only 210,000 registered for Grau: and only 20,000 for the single splinter group of the Ortodoxos who were interested in participating. Nearly 1·7 million allegedly registered for the pro-Batista parties,[32] but the chances of this being in any way a truthful reflection of Batista's following are remote; the total electorate in mid-1954 did not attain 2,800,000.

Raúl Chibás, Eddy's brother, finally took over the leadership of the Ortodoxos in February, as a compromise leader. Another letter from Castro in prison, this time to Melba Hernández, should be judged against this background.

> One should not abandon propaganda for one moment because it is the soul of all struggles [he wrote in February], ours must have its own style and adjust to circumstances. We must continue ceaselessly denouncing the assassinations. Mirta [his wife] will speak to you of a document of decisive importance for its ideological content and for its tremendous accusations [i.e. the 'speech', *History will absolve me*] . . . whatever happens a demonstration on the university *escalinata* is

[31] Blas Roca at the 8th Congress of the PSP in 1960, 35–6.
[32] Batista's PAP: 945,555
    Liberals: 279,542
    Democrats: 250,190
    Radicals: 211,058.

essential . . . Gustavo Arcos[33] must speak with the FEU leaders about it.

Secondly, we must co-ordinate the work between our people here and abroad. Prepare to this end . . . a voyage to Mexico to meet there with Raúl Martínez [the Bayamo leader] and Lester Rodríguez.[34] We must arrange with great care whatever proposition may be made for co-ordination with other groups, lest they simply make use of our name, as Pardo Llada[35] has been doing . . . It is preferable to go alone . . . you keep the flag flying until the *muchachos* now in prison come out . . . To know how to wait, said Martí, is the great secret of success.

Thirdly, show much guile [*mano izquierda*] and smiles to everybody. Follow the same course which we followed in the trial: defend our points of view without wounding others. We will have time later on to trample underfoot all the cockroaches . . . Accept all sorts of help, but, remember, trust in no one. Mirta has instructions to help you with all her soul.[36]

A little later, on 15 April 1954, he wrote:

With what joy would I bring revolution to this country from top to bottom . . . I would be disposed to draw on me the hate and ill will of one or two thousand people, among them some relations, half my friends, two-thirds of my colleagues, and four-fifths of my old comrades at university . . . Have you noticed the number of invisible links which a man who is anxious to live in accord with his ideas must break? What makes me suffer most, is to think that if all the generous men there are on earth were to respond to our appeal, all the charlatans, parasites, mediocrities, and egoists of every kidney would vanish at once.[37]

Castro was thus able to communicate easily with his co-conspirators. Letters flowed regularly. He was able also to read extensively in prison: books flowed in all the time. He read *Les Misérables*, and, though contrasting the novel unfavourably with *Le 18 Brumaire de Louis Bonaparte*, admitted that 'the phrases of Hugo . . . remind me of our own speeches, full of poetic faith in liberty, and holy indignation against outrages . . .'[38]

Back in Havana meantime Sánchez Arango, the most active of Prío's old lieutenants, and believed to be in exile, was discovered in the

[33] One of the Moncadaistas then free. Afterwards Cuban ambassador to Belgium, and apparently in confinement since 1966.
[34] Another Moncadaista from Santiago, also escaped without arrest.
[35] The Ortodoxo radio writer.
[36] Conte Agüero, *Cartas del Presidio*, 37–8.
[37] Qu. Merle, 347–8.
[38] Qu. *ibid*. (date, 1 March 1954).

Country Club district of Havana. Pursued by police, he took refuge in the Uruguayan Embassy, with various followers, mostly ex-officials of the Ministry of Education such as Carlos Enrique Alfonso Varela or Guillermo Barrientos and Prío's ex-Communications Minister, Sergio Mejías. He was later allowed to go abroad. A list of Aureliano's followers fell into the hands of the police: the simply named Asociación de Amigos de Aureliano (AAA) seemed larger than had been anticipated and a curious panic overcame the police for some months. Still, Batista continued to treat his opponents warily: thus in May an amnesty was offered to all exiles except to those who had taken part in the attack on the Moncada, but at the same time, due to 'hemispheric anxiety', Batista declared a new anti-Communist decree by which Communist activity in any form was declared a sufficient cause for dismissal from, for instance, the Civil Service, the universities, and the Labour unions. But this seemed a mere token act of solidarity with the U.S. at the moment when the latter was about to commit itself to the overthrow of the Guatemalan government of Colonel Arbenz.[39] About this time too there came the more serious foundation of a special committee of the Ministry of War to 'fight' the Communists, the Buró de Represión a las Actividades Comunistas (BRAC). This owed much to U.S. representations: the U.S. ambassador, Arthur Gardner, regarded himself as 'the father of the BRAC';[40] Batista had promised Foster Dulles that he 'would organize an effective agency to cope with Communist activities in Cuba'; and Allen Dulles, the new director of the Central Intelligence Agency, had a long conversation with Batista about this time, being 'not unfavourably impressed': the U.S., according to Allen Dulles, helped Batista's intelligence organization, though quite soon it declined in quality,[41] and for the next two years 'most of the money' meant for the BRAC 'never reached the proper destination'.[42]

In June 1954 Castro's *History will absolve me* finally appeared as a pamphlet and circulated clandestinely. In two more letters written in that month, from his sunless cell, to Conte Agüero, Castro further explained how he read all day; how his only companions were the bodies of fellow prisoners who had mysteriously died and were hanging on the other side of his cell: but even these, he added with a somewhat self-defeating excess of drama, he could not see because of a wall separating him from them; the theme of the seventy prisoners killed in Moncada recurred; he recalled again 'the beloved and unforgettable shape of the masses of our party, always vibrant and enthusiastic . . . the soul incarnate of the great leader' (Chibás); while praising some

---

[39] This was done by clandestine support to Guatemalan exiles.
[40] In a conversation with the author, 1962.
[41] These words were also in a conversation with the author in 1962.
[42] Lyman B. Kirkpatrick, *The Real CIA* (1968), 157.

Ortodoxo leaders, he denounced others who were prostituting Ortodoxia, 'landowners, millionaires and exploiters of the peasants' – what
were they doing inside a party whose first duty was social justice? With
increasing bitterness he referred to the Auténticos' disputes with
Batista as a battle between the robbers of yesterday against the robber
of today. There was more than ever about the importance of 'principles'.
'All will save themselves if they save their principles: from the deepest
dregs of corruption will come more purified and clean the ideal re-
deemer; sacrifice is now our only duty.' During some months he was
treated very harshly in gaol but this ceased after the representations of
the richest of his fellow prisoners, Enrique Sánchez del Monte, who
threatened to cut off his monthly bribe to the governor if they did not
cease.[43]

Castro now became far more famous than he had been when free.
In the elections of 1954 he was already an unseen candidate, the spirit
of liberty incarcerated and of Martí reincarnated. Among those who
sang, revived and warmed the flame of hope was Carlos Puebla, a
mulatto, who nightly, with elegiac grace, aroused memories and
expectations in *La Bodeguita del Medio*, a Bohemian restaurant off the
Plaza de la Catedral, his songs becoming famous throughout Cuba:

Los caminos de mi Cuba	The roads of my Cuba
Nunca van a donde deben.	Never lead where they should.

Castro found himself increasingly critical of other groups: the
College of Lawyers he found too weak; the students (FEU) were
behaving badly; the main body of the Ortodoxo youth movement (led
by Max Lesnick and Omar Borges) had denounced Castro's movement
as destructive; he was furious that his wife, Mirta, should have accepted
a pension from the Ministry of Information, thanks to the influence of
her brother Rafael, under-secretary at the Ministry of the Interior.[44]
(Castro's marriage was clearly heading for breakdown, the test being his
instructions to his wife to withstand the pressure of her powerful and
politically successful family, while her husband was in prison.)

On 26 July 1954, a year after the attack on Moncada, Castro received
a visit from Hermida, Minister of the Interior, and two other *Batistiano*
ministers, Gastón Godoy and Marino López Blanco. Hermida said:

Castro, I want you to know that I am not your personal enemy, I am
simply an official filling the task of being Minister of the Interior.
You are here because the tribunals, not I, sentenced you. My task

---

[43] Sánchez was in gaol for the murder of the son of Joaquín Martínez Sáenz, who had been
killed by two gunmen hired by Sánchez in mistake for the father, whom Sánchez believed to be
the lover of his wife.
[44] Conte Agüero, *Cartas del Presidio*, 43 ff.

is simply to watch over the conduct of the prisons, always fulfilling the President's wishes . . . Batista is a very fair man, I have never in twenty years seen him insult anyone, nor even raise his voice: I realise I am not myself quite the same and people say I am a little brusque . . . Major [to the officer in attendance], treat them chivalrously, for they are gentlemen.

Castro listened in silence and said:

I, for my part, have never considered the struggle as a personal quarrel but a struggle against a ruling political system. [He added] I have been placed on the offensive by your declarations which leave my integrity in doubt. If an alleged intimate of mine is one of the high officials of the regime and these officials, without my wish or knowledge, make representations to this circumstance to attack my home and family . . .

The minister interrupted and said:

Look Castro, I know that the guilty one is Rafaelito[45] who always behaves as an irresponsible infant. I assure you on my honour that I have never had the intention of angering you and that the note you mention was altered and appeared in a different form from what I made. As for your name, what doubt can there be? There is no one in Cuba who has a more clearly defined position than you. Don't be impatient, I myself was a political prisoner in the years '30 and '31. I placed myself many times in the Country Club to make an assassination attempt on Machado or Ortiz. You are a young man, be calm, all these things will pass.

'Very well, Minister,' answered Castro, 'I accept your explanation . . . I recognize that you anyway have been very correct.'[46] When Castro's brother-in-law Díaz Balart heard of the visit, he violently criticized Hermida, protesting against such intercourse with the 'promoter of the murderous attack against the Army'. The letter was published, with the result that both Díaz Balart and Hermida had to resign.

In midsummer 1954 the Grau cause in the elections began to prosper when all but the most faithful Prío wing of the Auténticos began to support the old fox. People began to remember how ten years before they had taught their parrots to say *Viva Grau San Martín*, even in remote places.[47] The Ortodoxos were once again in difficulties. Raúl Chibás proved himself more ineffective than had been supposed and Márquez Sterling could not be prevented from entering to run in the

[45] i.e. Díaz Balart.
[46] Conte Agüero, *Cartas del Presidio*, 49–57.
[47] Nelson, 13.

election. Agramonte pursued private squabbles, challenging Aureliano Sánchez Arango to a duel for 'defaming the memory of Chibás'. Batista finally announced, as everyone expected, that he would himself run as president, taking Guas Inclán, son of old General Guas Pasquera of the war of independence, as his vice-president. These two were the 'unanimous' candidates of the four government parties (PAP, Liberals, Democrats, Radicals). He started off his election campaign by announcing that bonds reaching \$M350 would be issued to finance a huge public works programme. The situation seemed more and more like the days of Machado; for few doubted that this money would find its way into the hands of government members.

On 14 August Batista, as incumbent president, stepped down to run in the election campaign and his faithful secretary, Andrés Domingo took over temporarily with a cabinet similar to that before. The same day another letter came out of the Isle of Pines to Luis Conte Agüero from Fidel Castro: the tone was again different – as different from the letters in June as those were from the letters in December and the spring; Castro had evidently thought a good deal about the question of revolutionary leadership:

> I believe fundamentally that one of the biggest obstacles preventing the integration of the [opposition] . . . is the excessive number of *Personalismos* and the ambitions of groups and . . . *caudillos* . . . the [situation] . . . makes me remember the efforts of Martí to join all worthy Cubans in the struggle for independence . . . perhaps for this reason, the chapters I most admire in the history of Cuba are not so much the proud moments of battle . . . as that gigantic and heroic enterprise of uniting the Cubans for the struggle . . . I must in the first place organise the men of the 26th of July and unite, into an unbreakable bundle [*haz*], all the fighters, those in exile, those in prison, those free, who together amount to over eighty men implicated in the same historic day of sacrifice. The importance of such a perfectly disciplined nucleus contributes incalculable strength to the . . . formation of *cadres* of struggle for civil or insurrectional organisation. From then . . . a great civic-political movement must count on the necessary force to capture power, either by pacific or revolutionary paths, or run the risk of being beaten, like Ortodoxia, only two months before the election.[48]

This suggests that Castro was no longer regarding himself as an Ortodoxo; already he was contrasting his own behaviour with that of the Ortodoxos: he would not make Ortodoxia's mistakes: he could therefore not be an Ortodoxo. He continued:

[48] Conte Agüero, *Cartas del Presidio*, 60.

Conditions indispensable for the integration of a true civil movement are: ideology, discipline, leadership. All are desirable, but leadership is essential. I don't know if it was Napoleon who said that one bad general counts more in battle than twenty good ones. One cannot organise a movement in which everyone believes they have a right to make public declarations without consulting anyone. Neither can one expect anything of an organisation full of anarchic men who at the first difficulty take the path they think best, unsettling and destroying the vehicle. The organisation and propaganda apparatus must be so powerful that it implacably destroys anyone who tries to create splits, *camarillas*, schisms, or to rise against the movement . . . The programme must contain a full, concrete and acceptable exposition of the social and economic problems which face the country, so that a truly new and improving message can be taken to the masses. I know that not even God could create in a single day all the marvels of the world but from the first moment the masses must feel that the foundations of marvels exist. Above all . . . our energies must not be invested uselessly, improvising and amalgamating instead of creating and founding, a thing which . . . did not happen with Ortodoxia.[49]

It is clear from other letters that Napoleon, Julius Caesar ('a true revolutionary', in contrast with Cicero, the incarnation of oligarchy), and Plutarch's *Lives* were all on Castro's mind in 1954.[50] The overwhelming impression from his writings of this period is his desire to identify himself with the world historical process, his own position expressed in nineteenth-century romantic terms.

Batista was meanwhile staging a lavish electoral campaign, of which the most typical incident was the anecdote of how he had found a wounded crane in 1939, how he helped it and saved its life, but how it died after he went elsewhere; Cuba, said Batista, resembled this crane (*grulla*) and now he was bringing it back to life. The image caught on and the cry *Viva la grulla* was echoed everywhere by his supporters. He accumulated large sums of money given to him by companies and private supporters: according to his own youth leader Suárez Núñez, he personally made nearly $M12 out of the election.[51] The Communists continued to support Grau . . . Blas Roca later recalled: 'The meeting at Santiago [on 24 October 1954] was memorable . . . For twenty-four hours the party recovered its legality and, with the masses, became masters of the streets . . . Faced with the threat of an avalanche of

[49] *Ibid.*, 60–2.
[50] See Merle, 344–5.
[51] Suárez Núñez, 17.

negative votes, the Government found itself impelled to change the rules of the election and to call on Mujal to control the masses.'[52] The meeting in Santiago was however chiefly memorable for the fact that the crowd shouted Fidel Castro's name when Grau appeared.[53]

The government had in fact determined all along to control the election boards. Grau demanded equal representation with the government representatives. Refused, he demanded a postponement. This was not granted. Grau then withdrew from the election, to the annoyance of the Communists who accused him of surrendering to the pressure of 'Yankee imperialists'.[54] Batista accused Grau of being 'conspiratorial'. Agramonte praised him.[55] Batista next took what seemed the final step of outlawing the Communists completely; but in practice most Communists could carry on their work in the normal way: César Escalante thus continued to live at his wife's *crèche*; Carlos Rafael Rodríguez and Aníbal Escalante remained at large.

On 1 November the elections finally took place. Batista was returned as president without opposition, with only half the electorate voting, though to vote was nominally compulsory. Some Auténticos won seats in the House of Representatives and the Senate and so took the minority seats in the legislature – 18 out of 54 in the Senate, 16 out of 114 in the House of Representatives. Grau himself was understood to have received one out of six votes, even though he announced himself not to be taking part.

Castro's reaction to the election was blunted since his divorce from Mirta was then coming through, and, busy reading and studying, he allowed it to pass without comment. His chief anxiety was that his son had to sleep under the same roof as his in-laws, the Díaz Balarts, and 'receive on his innocent cheeks the kisses of these miserable Judases . . . I presume they know that for me to abandon this child they would have to kill me . . . I lose my head when I speak of these matters'.[56]

The new Congress assembled, with the Auténticos in their seats (only two of them accepted Grau's request to boycott it).[57] In February 1955 Batista was duly inaugurated, an event crowned with the capture and killing of a famous gangster of the old days, a friend of Prío's, Orlando León Lemus (*el Colorado*). There was a new ministry, though the names contained no surprises: Saladrigas was Foreign Minister and Jorge García Montes (vice-president of the Consultative

[52] Roca, VIIIth Congress, 35–6.
[53] Castro listened to the radio from prison. (Letter to his sister, in Conte Agüero, *Cartas del Presidio*, 63.)
[54] *Loc. cit.*
[55] Phillips, 241.
[56] Letter to his sister, in Conte Agüero, *Cartas del Presidio*, 65–6.
[57] HAR, February 1955. They were José Miguel Morales and Francisco Grau Alsina.

Assembly from 1953–5) was prime minister. Aurelio Fernández Concheso, a familiar face from the 1940s when he had been ambassador in
the U.S. (1940–4), cropped up as Minister of Education: in the interim
he had been a supreme court judge. One 'new' face was Raúl Menocal,
Minister of Commerce, son of the old president and mayor of Havana
during Batista's first period of office. The Interior Ministry was taken
by Santiago Rey, Minister without Portfolio since Moncada, a man who
had served Batista as he had served Prío before, opportunistically.
Santiago Verdeja, Minister of Defence, and chief therefore of the armed
forces except the police, was an ex-Menocalista; he was a doctor by
profession, had been a representative from 1917–25 and had spent many
months in La Cabaña in the last years of Machado: Ramón Vasconcelos,
the journalist who had been in Prío's cabinet and resigned, and had afterwards been Fidel Castro's sponsor on the newspaper *Alerta*, joined
Batista as Minister of Communications – a bizarre transformation of a
somewhat discredited politician who had begun his career as a diplomat
under Machado. The faithful provisional president, Andrés Domingo
y Morales del Castillo, returned to the secretaryship of the cabinet.
Ministers without Portfolio included Batista's old friend, the sugar chief
Amadeo López Castro, president of the Development Commission, and
Dr Jorge Barroso, the sugar stabilization board's chief.[58]

Constitutional government was now allegedly restored. Batista told
Congress, 'We want amnesty and we want peace,' though there could
be no amnesty while terrorism continued. There was still incessant
turmoil at the university, and bombs appeared sporadically all over
the island, placed either by Castro's friends or Prío's: the ex-mayor of
Santiago, Luis Casero, was arrested after a bomb explosion in late
February 1955 in Santiago. The Ortodoxos, seemingly uniting behind
Raúl Chibás, were less active than the Priístas. It was to Prío in Miami
that in March several congressmen of Batista's packed legislature,
Conrado Bécquer, a sugar workers' leader (an Auténtico opportunist),
with Jorge Cruz, Conrado Rodríguez, also of the sugar union, and
Alejandro Jiménez went to discuss the political situation, asking him
not to return without guarantees of pardon for all political prisoners.
But in April there was a growing feeling in all sections of opinion in
favour of an amnesty.

Batista believed that his position was so strong that he could afford

[58] Complete list: Prime Minister, Jorge García Montes; Minister of State, Saladrigas (C);
Education, Fernández Concheso; Labour, Suárez Rivas (J); Finance, Justo García Rayneri;
Agriculture, Fidel Barreto; Defence, Santiago Verdeja Neyra; Health, Armando Coro;
Interior, Santiago Rey; Justice, Camacho; Commerce, Raúl Menocal; Communications,
Ramón Vasconcelos; Public Works, Nicolás Arroyo; Transport, Mario Cobas; Ministers
without Portfolio: José Pardo Jiménez, Amadeo López Castro, Jorge L. Barroso, Julia Elisa
Consuegra, José Pérez González; Secretary of the Presidency, Andrés Domingo y Morales del
Castillo.

this: Justo Carrillo's Acción Libertadora, with Sánchez Arango's organization the only effective opposition group with links with the old regime, disintegrated at the end of 1954. There was an air of prosperity in Cuba, brought on after an agreement to sell reserve sugar in the U.S.S.R., sustained by the feeling that the elections had brought a period of uncertainty to an end. Cuban and U.S. promoters were discussing the idea of a cross-Cuba canal to cut the distance between Cuba and the Panama Canal – to spare ships a 'detour of 400 miles'. The plan was criticized by Liberals such as Mañach as likely to lead to still greater U.S. control over the economy, but the economic advantages seemed strong, and there appeared a good chance that the idea would prosper. A ferry from Key West to Cárdenas was opened, being immediately successful. Vice-President Nixon came to give the regime his blessing in February in the course of a Central American goodwill tour, and in April Allen Dulles of the CIA came to place his stethoscope to the Cuban 'security organization'. He said somewhat mysteriously that the U.S. was seriously preoccupied by the problem of Communism in Cuba.[59] Batista's public works programme was beginning and there was a great leap forward in private building in Vedado. A new organization for constitutional development, headed by Mañach, was formed with Luis Botifoll, Rufo López Fresquet, Justo Carrillo, Pardo Llada and Vicente Rubiera. A letter from Castro to Conte Agüero in March 1955 assured the democratic opposition that Castro and his group held to their principles. Even so, in mid-April Batista relaxed, and declared an amnesty. All political prisoners would come out in May. This was Batista's greatest error of judgement.

[59] Evidence of Allen Dulles.

CHAPTER LXXI

The Civic Dialogue

On 15 May 1955 Castro and his brother with eighteen followers left the Isle of Pines under the amnesty law. There were scenes of rejoicing at reunions with families, and Castro was welcomed by the National Committee of Ortodoxos. To *Bohemia* he announced:

> I do not have . . . the intention of creating a new political party. We do not abandon our plans of maintaining and cooperating with the (Ortodoxo) party . . . We consider it a good thing that Dr Raúl Chibás has been named as leader, though we cannot say that he has great political experience . . . All of us must unite under some flag . . . All [Ortodoxos] are necessary in this struggle, all have the same advanced ideological conception. And if there exists ideological unity, why need we continue divided? [He added] The amnesty is the result of an extraordinary popular mobilisation, backed splendidly by the Cuban press, which has gained the most glittering of victories.

To Agramonte and Raúl Chibas, Castro explained, 'What Cuba needs is decent politicians . . . Great economic and social reform is needed.'[1]

Castro repeated his opposition to any break with the Ortodoxos in an interview with Carlos Franqui, then a reporter on the periodical *Carteles*.[2] In his last weeks in prison, he had been preoccupied with the aim of getting representatives of the opposition youth (such as Conte Agüero) heard and seen on television.[3] In a letter to Conte Agüero himself, he argued that Christ's reply to the Pharisees as to the relation between God and Caesar was bound to make him unpopular with one of the two; 'thus today [the regime] is trying to ruin our prestige with the people or to leave us in prison.'[4] He appeared preoccupied with whether further armed action against Batista was desirable. He quoted Martí: 'Anyone is a criminal who promotes an avoidable war; and so is he who does not promote an inevitable civil war.' Compromise would always be rejected, though genuine constitutional guarantees could make violence unnecessary.[5] Castro saw his movement already as the

---

[1] *Bohemia*, 22 May 1955.
[2] Qu., Conte Agüero, *Cartas del Presidio*, 91.
[3] Letter to Mañach, 17 February 1955 (*Ibid.*, 71–3).
[4] *Ibid.*, 83.
[5] *Ibid.*, 85.

'spiritual sons of the Titan of Bronze' (that is, Maceo):[6] what room was there for him among the meek and mild Ortodoxos?

But where did Castro fit in? Not with some of the old members even of his own organization, such as the leader of the Bayamo attack in 1953, Martínez Arará, who saw him the day he returned; Castro criticized Martínez's relations with Carlos Prío;[7] nor with the students, who in the years since he had left the university had built up their own organization and their own leaders. Castro and his comrades, admittedly, were welcomed home formally by a meeting of students on 20 May at the university. The police moved in, led by two already notorious police captains, Colonel Carratalá and Lieutenant Esteban Ventura. The electricity of the university was cut off, and the police prevented the meeting being held in the famous *escalinata*, but it nevertheless continued.[8] Even so, the students did not need Castro as their leader: they already had their own, such as José Antonio Echevarría, the strongest candidate for the presidency of the FEU in the autumn, a youth from Cárdenas, a solid courageous and respectable character, though perhaps not of wide intelligence and gifts, known as '*Manzanita*' (little apple). He was an intellectual, later forced to play the role of a man of action, for which he was not fitted.[9] He was a Catholic and honest, and his arrival at the university had coincided with, or led to, a marked change in the moral attitude to politics in the university. Earlier in May he had been involved in riots at a meeting commemorating the death of Guiteras. He and four others had been wounded at Matanzas. The university had protested and been closed for two days.[10]

Castro had nothing directly to do with these events in the university. None of the university leaders were his followers, though Echevarría and Javier Pazos had links with the Ortodoxos. Of Echevarría, Castro later remarked:

Really between him and me there was always a great current of friendship, understanding, sympathy: he was a *muchacho* outstanding

---

[6] *Ibid.*, 86.

[7] Martínez Arará's evidence. The two met several times more between then and early July.

[8] *Bohemia*, 28 May 1955.

[9] Comment of Dr Herminio Portell Vilá.

[10] Echevarría's campaign for the presidency of FEU was the central question in the university in mid-1955. His opponent was Leonel Alonso, a Matancero of humble social origins who had worked his way to the university and was backed by the traditional Auténtico Priísta group, led by Hidalgo Peraza. Voting as usual was by faculties and the vote finally split 6 to 6. A progressive socialist group led by Javier Pazos, the son of Prío's director of the National Bank, moved over from Alonso to back Echevarría, securing a more extreme man, René Anillo, into the FEU as secretary. In the past, in the time of Castro, gangsterism would no doubt have settled the affair; one group would have bribed, kidnapped or even physically injured the other. The acute political crisis had led to the end of this bellicose and corrupt atmosphere within the university.

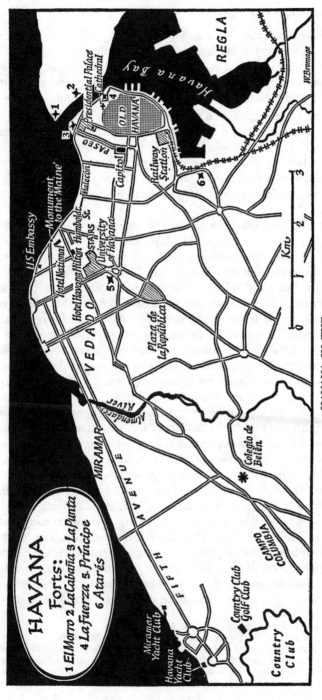

HAVANA
Forts:
1 El Morro 2 La Cabaña 3 La Punta
4 La Fuerza 5 Príncipe
6 Atarés

Miramar Yacht Club
Havana Yacht Club
Country Club Golf Club
Country Club
CAMPO COLUMBIA
Colegio de Belén
FIFTH AVENUE
MIRAMAR
Almendares River
VEDADO
Plaza de la República
US Embassy
Monument to the 'Maine'
Hotel National
Hotel Havana Hilton
University of Havana
Humboldt St.
STAIRS
Malecón
Capitol
PASEO
Presidential Palace
Cathedral
OLD HAVANA
Railway Station
Havana Bay
REGLA

W. Bromage

Km

HAVANA IN THE 1950s

in decisiveness, enthusiasm and valour . . . [but] we at that time would scarcely enter the University because there were some FEU leaders who thought that history was going to repeat itself and that they were going to be everything in the future, and only they: they believed themselves the eldest sons of the Revolution.[11]

But he had more success with the student leaders of the University of Santiago, a group of men evidently out of sympathy on personal grounds with those in Havana, and who had been for a time attached to García Barcena and then to one or two other minuscule groups.[12] Those men, Frank País and Pepito Tey (the president of the FEU in Oriente) went to Havana to meet Castro and reached an understanding with him.

The general atmosphere in Havana in mid-1955 was, however, anti-pathetic to Castro. Having staked all on the politics of action and, if need be, violence, the amnesty itself and the mood of compromise which it had created played against him. There was widespread feeling among Ortodoxos and middle-class professional Cubans that negotia-tions with Batista were both possible and really the only viable way ahead. Castro was temperamentally and psychologically opposed to this approach; nor could he forget, and his followers would not let him forget, the sixty-eight prisoners murdered after Moncada. Even with a moderate Catholic Action group which was prepared to counten-ance military action Castro could not cooperate since he wished to be the chief of any united movement.[13]

Within a fortnight of being let free Castro had published an article in *Bohemia* entitled, 'You Lie, Chaviano', a direct attack on the colonel in command in Santiago two years before,[14] making effective play with the sixteen-to-one proportion of killed to wounded, a proportion never obtained in wars of the past. Early in June Congressman Waldo Pérez Almaguer, Batista's governor in Oriente in 1953, followed with a denunciation in the newspaper *La Calle*, that Río Chaviano had defi-nitely himself ordered the execution of over thirty prisoners caught after Moncada. The editor of *La Calle*, Luis Orlando Rodríguez, Castro's new sponsor in the Cuban press, was taken into custody (on the orders, as it happened of Ramón Vasconcelos, the minister who had been Castro's previous sponsor in journalism before 1952), but even so, Chaviano was transferred, though he did make a response also in *La*

---

[11] Castro in his speech at Marquitos's trial, March 1964.

[12] These were Acción Libertadora and Acción Nacional Revolucionaria.

[13] Mario Llerena MSS, p. 18, describes the abortive negotiations between Castro on the one hand and Llerena (ex-member of García Barcena's MNR), Andrés Valdespino, and Amalio Fiallo – the last two being Catholic Action leaders. All of these collaborated eventually with Castro in the 26 July Movement, but went into exile afterwards.

[14] *Bohemia*, 29 May 1955.

Calle. A day or two later came a new murder: Jorge Agostini, ex-chief of the presidential secret police under Grau and Prío, had been in exile since 1952, and returned, hoping to profit under the amnesty. He was arrested. He was then either summarily shot or shot while trying to escape, more likely the first since twenty-one bullets were later found to have been fired, apparently under the orders of Julio Laurent, chief of Naval Intelligence.[15]

In a matter of weeks Castro decided to go to Mexico and to form there a trained and disciplined group to provide the backbone of a guerrilla troop to try to overthrow Batista by force – by, as he supposed then, some new dramatic strike. The police in Havana were probably preparing an attack on him, as became well known; according to one account, a car riddled with bullets already existed – ready for his body to be found within (killed 'fighting the police', as Agostini had been killed).[16] Castro's decision to go to Mexico appears to have been taken by him alone without consultation with the Ortodoxo leaders. His brother Raúl (who had recently been falsely accused of arson) had indeed preceded him. Before Castro left Havana he held a meeting on 19 July of his friends and supporters whom he would leave behind and it is perhaps appropriate to think of this meeting as inaugurating what afterwards became the 26 July Movement as an organization separate from Ortodoxia: for the time being, however, Castro refrained from defining his differences with the old movement of Chibás (anyway these were less differences of ideology or political aims than of method and tactics).[17]

The friends whom Castro left behind him consisted, first, of a few old comrades of the Moncada such as Haydée Santamaría, Pedro Miret and Lester Rodríguez, and one or two friends of these such as Aldo Santamaría, Haydée's brother, and the Ameijeiras brothers whose elder brother Juan Manuel had died after the Moncada attack: but these old comrades were in the minority. Most of the members of the 26 July Movement were new adherents of Castro, having until very recently been adherents of Professor García Barcena's Movimiento Nacional Revolucionario; they were looking for a new leader committed to the idea of revolutionary action against Batista now that the professor (who had also been released in the amnesty) had showed that he was no longer to be counted upon to this end. They included not only the leaders of the Santiago students, Pepito Tey and Frank País, the Baptist schoolmaster (with whom Lester Rodríguez, of the Moncada,

---

[15] See *Havana Post*, 22 February 1956; and for Castro's attack on the regime as a result, *La Calle*, 11 June 1955.

[16] Almeida in Franqui, 21; see *La Calle*, 4 June 1955, where Castro made the accusation at the time.

[17] René Ray Rivero, *Libertad y revolución* (1959), 11–12.

would work in Santiago), but also men such as Faustino Pérez – a Presbyterian chemist – Armando Hart, a law student who had defended García Barcena, and Enrique Oltuski, son of a Polish immigrant, who were to be the main organizers of the 26 July Movement in Cuba itself (for most of the years of struggle against Batista) until 1959. One new adherent at this time was at least for Castro an old acquaintance: this was Carlos Franqui, who had taken part in the abortive attack on the Dominican Republic in 1947 in the 'Cayo Confites' expedition. Franqui, an ex-Communist, was a journalist on the magazine *Carteles* and, having previously been the animator of several anti-Batista news-sheets, now organized the 26 July cyclostyled weekly, *Revolución*.[18]

Although Hart and Faustino Pérez became Castro's chief lieutenants later on, it was the Santiago group headed by Tey and País that seemed to count most with Castro at this moment, and Castro nominated País as his head of all 'action groups' in Cuba, when leaving the island himself.[19] This was chiefly because País already had, in the remains of the Oriente section of García Barcena's movement and of his own Acción Revolucionaria Oriente, the skeleton of an organization.

In Mexico Castro found a number of young Cubans together with some older exiles. One centre was the house in Pedregal de San Angel of Orquídea Pino, a beautiful Cuban singer married to a distinguished Mexican engineer, Alfonso Gutiérrez. There Castro and his friends began to prepare their next move and also to think more of their general ideology.

Mexico in 1955 was still run by the Institutional Revolutionary Party (PRI). The president, Adolfo Ruiz Cortines, was an austere book-keeper who attempted almost successfully to establish a thrifty government after the magnificences of his predecessor the expansionist, tireless and ambitious Miguel Alemán. Ruiz Cortines maintained the independence of Mexico in foreign affairs and the traditional hostility towards Fascism or any form of it, such as that expressed by Franco's Spain. Diplomatic relations with the exiled Spanish Republican government remained and there were many Spanish exiles and their families. The Communist party legally flourished, if without hope of gaining an electoral victory. Mexico City was a natural centre of political discussion and even conspiracy covering much of Latin America.

[18] Franqui had been a member of Juventud Socialista and afterwards worked for *Hoy* which 'seemed to him to deviate from the socialist line'. According to what he is believed to have told Mario Llerena (MSS, p. 5), he left the Communist party because of general disillusionment with their conduct and tactics.

[19] The 26 July committee left behind in Cuba were Aldo Santamaría, Manuel Cueto, Ricardo González, Maximo Reyes, Universo Sánchez, Ayán Rosell, Santiago Riera, Efraín Alfonso, Osvaldo Rodríguez, Haydée Santamaría, Carlos Franqui, Enrique Hart, Pedro Miret, Frank País, Vilma Espín, Carlos Chaín, Carlos Iglesias, and Quintín Pino (list in René Ray, 11–12).

In this volatile atmosphere Castro thrived. Under the influence of her *Batistiano* brother, his wife had now completed divorce proceedings so that he was now in a sense married only to the Revolution. He and his friends attached themselves early to Spanish Republicans such as the sculptor and frame-maker Víctor Trapote, a Catalan whose daughter married one of Castro's closest followers, Ramiro Valdés, a student from Artemisa and a Moncada veteran.[20] Trapote's studio became another centre of meetings for the 26 July Movement.[21] In August 1955 Castro sent back to Havana (by the hands of Ondina Pino, sister of Orquídea, in a hollowed-out copy of Garcilaso's *History of the Incas*) a document for the 'militants' of the Ortodoxo party entitled *Manifiesto No. 1.* Prefaced by quotations from Martí and Maceo, this followed roughly the line of *History will absolve me*, containing a fifteen-point programme of reforms to be carried out within the spirit of 'our advanced' Constitution of 1940. That old anarchist dream – 'distribution of land among peasant families' – reappeared as the first point; nationalization of public services, mass education, and industrialization figured importantly; but while there was an assurance that the 26 July Movement was led by 'new men without compromises with the past', Castro insisted that he was still an Ortodoxo and spoke of the pure principles of Chibás: 'We do not constitute a tendency within the party; we are the revolutionary apparatus of Chibásismo.'[22] Certainly all close followers of Castro appear still to have been Ortodoxos in outlook. Thus the early adherents in Mexico were Fernando Sánchez Amaya, who had been living there before Castro arrived; Pedro Miret, the ex-Moncadaista, engineering student and cartographer, who arrived from Havana; Juan Manuel Márquez, Ortodoxo ex-city counsellor for Marianao who had been beaten up by the police in Havana in June. The housing for these early Fidelistas was partly arranged by 'a Cuban long resident in Mexico', in a rather military style, all acknowledging the leadership of a *responsable de casa*. Five to ten people lived in each house. But as early as September 1955 Batista's secret service chief, Colonel Orlando Piedra,[23] arrived in Mexico, and a curious cat-and-mouse game of observation and betrayal began which was to last for over a year in Mexico City and its surroundings.

Back in Cuba the democratic mellowing of the regime continued. On 11 August 1955, Prío (who had been covered by the same amnesty as Castro) nerved himself to come home. Accompanied by much enthusiasm, he went first to the Hotel Nacional, then to his famous farm,

[20] Afterwards Minister of the Interior in Cuba.

[21] Discussion with Trapote, August 1962.

[22] *Manifiesto Numero 1 del 26 de Julio al Pueblo de Cuba*, August 1955. See Draper, *Castroism*, 10; and Conte Agüero, *Dos Rostros*, 104–7.

[23] Colonel Orlando Piedra Negueruela, chief of Buró de Investigaciones.

La Chata where a great rally of his supporters, old friends and place-men, assembled eagerly. There was a call for the mending of relations with Grau, and Prío said he would henceforth oppose Batista only through the ballot box. In September Prío was found working on 'a programme to attract the whole nation', although he said that he himself would not run in any election. On 1 October he addressed a large audience, perhaps 50,000, in the large square facing Havana's Ward Line piers. The critical point in his speech was a denunciation as illegal of all governmental acts carried out since 1952. Another big meeting followed in Santa Clara, but Prío failed to make much head-way in uniting the opposition, though he somewhat disturbed the government: 'The only solution with Prío is to kill him, kidnap him or expel him from Cuba,' General Tabernilla said to Batista, who knew better and said, 'Pancho, you know nothing about this sort of thing, you are mad.'[24]

The most favourable chance for uniting the opposition was a new movement formed specifically with that aim in view, the Sociedad de Amigos de la República (SAR: Society of Friends of the Republic). The moving spirit of this group was Cosme de la Torriente, then aged eighty-three, survivor of all the turbulent events in the history of the independent Cuban Republic; of the war against Spain; of Wood's and Estrada Palma's administrations; Foreign Minister under Menocal and Mendieta; leader of the Cuban delegation to the League, and, since 1938, retired, directing the Revista de la Habana.[25] In mid-October he sought an interview with Batista to try to persuade him there and then to hold elections. But Batista refused, on the grounds that De la Torriente had no status and no standing to make such demands. De la Torriente decided to hold a mass meeting in Prío's style, and, miraculously, the other opposition leaders decided to do nothing until then.[26]

The meeting was held on the waterfront on 19 November, the purpose being to force new elections during the course of 1956. All the opponents of Batista except the Communists were present. The crowd filled the space between the Alameda de Paula and the Customs House. The platform was remarkable for its catholicity. Apart from the venerable Don Cosme there was also present the young José Antonio Echevarría, newly elected president of the students (FEU); Raúl Chibás, president of the Ortodoxos; Carlos Prío; Grau San Martín; Dr Miró Cardona, president of the Bar Association; Pardo Llada, the radio commentator; Amalio Fiallo (of the Radical party), José Andreu (Democrat) and

[24] Suárez Núñez, 68.
[25] See Cosme de la Torriente, *Cuarenta años de mi vida* (1940).
[26] See the excellent summary of this period in *Hispanic American Report*, November–December 1955.

Rogelio Pina, the secretary of the newly formed SAR. The 26 July Movement did not take part and indeed had tried to dissuade the Ortodoxos from so doing.[27] The meeting marked a high point in the history of the democratic opposition. But afterwards nothing happened. Batista was secure in his palace, and amiably told newspapermen that such meetings were good for the country. He refused to discuss the idea of elections until 1958: though he would on the other hand be prepared to talk to Don Cosme.[28]

The renewed inaction brought new student riots, in both Santiago and Havana. Sorties against the police were made under the pretext of honouring martyrs. Many students were arrested, many wounded, some beaten up, some tortured; and on 10 December Raúl Cervantes, president of the Ortodoxo youth, was shot dead by police in Ciego de Avila. On 16 December the Rector of Havana University, Dr Clemente Inclán, a paediatrician, successfully persuaded the FEU to cease demonstrations and to return to work at least for a time. But the student leaders, headed by Echevarría, founded a new organization, the Directorio Revolucionario, whose aims were to gather together all interested in fighting against Batista – workers as well as students.[29] The end of student protest furthermore was followed almost immediately by protests from the sugar workers, for economic purposes. Wage agreements had for several years provided that if the average price of sugar exceeded the average for the preceding year, bonuses based on the excess would be paid. In 1955 prices were such that workers expected a small bonus at Christmas. But the Sugar Institute had included in their calculations a 350,000-ton allotment of reserve sugar withdrawn from current stocks for sale in 1956, at an artificially chosen price of 2·77 cents per pound. The sugar leaders claimed the ultimate price of 5 cents.

In consequence Cuba was faced in mid-December by a 500,000-man labour strike beginning on 26 December. This threatened to paralyse the entire sugar harvest due to begin on 1 January. The Communists and the newly formed Directorio Revolucionario (with as yet unknown membership) supported the strike, as well as some Mujalistas, and at least one Communist striker, Bernardo Carreras, was killed by the army with

[27] Raúl Chibás, Memoirs, MSS, p. 34.

[28] HAR, December 1955. Daniel James says that an attempt was made to break up this meeting by the Communist party. He cites Flavio Bravo, later a critical figure in Castro's regime, as a leading figure in this attempt. Of this there is no other evidence. (See James, 95.)

[29] The relationship between FEU and Directorio Revolucionario was described in a supplement to *Alma Mater* (undated): 'The FEU because of its special character is an academic organization ... The Directorio Revolucionario is the instrument created, inspired and originated by the FEU ... to vertebrate the student body in an organized manner in its typically revolutionary work.'

rifle butts at Palos.[30] Some members of Castro's organization left behind in Cuba also participated, at their head David Salvador, a sugar workers' leader in Las Villas who had joined the 26 July Movement in Santiago.[31] Salvador, like many of Castro's early supporters, had already had a chequered career having been a Communist from 1939 to 1946, an Auténtico and Ortodoxo, and a backer of Aureliano Sánchez Arango's Triple A (1952–5). He now became for a time co-ordinator of the 26 July Movement in Havana.

Batista finally decided in favour of Labour on 30 December. But several sugar union officials tried to use this opportunity to capture control of their Labour organization from José Luis Martínez, the sugar workers' leader, and indirectly from Mujal. They refused to order their followers back to work after Batista's settlement, and sought to hold a plenary meeting of sugar workers in opposition to the established leaders. The rebels were immediately suspended and Martínez took over their offices by force. The sugar leaders in Congress, Conrado Bécquer, Conrado Rodríguez, and Jorge Cruz, thereupon went on a hunger strike at the House of Representatives. This strike was only ended after 168 hours by the intervention of Cardinal Arteaga. Bécquer did not return to his post as vice-secretary-general of the FNTA, and radio programmes which backed his action were suspended.[32]

Faced with these industrial difficulties Batista finally agreed to see Don Cosme de la Torriente. He did so on 29 December and again on 10 January. In the meantime there were certain bomb explosions, presumably let off by students or by the 26 July Movement, in Santiago. Six people were injured. Newspapers such as *Diario de la Marina* and *Información* denounced these activities: 'A noble, generous and valiant people who love peace cannot at any moment nor under any circumstances give their backing to any infamous delinquent who places a bomb ... we must do everything possible to wipe out useless terrorism and terrorists' and 'We cannot permit the Martian gestures just started to fail without making ourselves accomplices of an unpardonable civil cowardliness'.[33] The Martian gestures were Don Cosme's offers at compromise.

Batista had now been in power again for nearly four years. In that time many people had become committed to him. He enjoyed the sympathy of many North Americans, not only the ambassador. The few bombs exploding in back streets and Castro's activity in Mexico seemed like freak hailstorms, disagreeable, inexplicable but unimportant

[30] Roca, VIIIth Congress, p. 24.
[31] David Salvador, born Ciego de Avila, 1923: secretary-general of the Cuban trade unions, 1959–60; in prison since 1960.
[32] *Havana Post*, 27 January 1956.
[33] 'Martian', of course, in Cuba means pertaining to José Martí.

and soon forgotten. Articles describing the health of the Cuban economy often appeared in the U.S. press: tourism in 1955 had been higher than ever before; the $M34 expansion of the U.S. government's Nicaro nickel plant was estimated as one quarter complete; car sales in 1955 were expected to be up 20% over 1954; Havana bank clearings on 1 December 1955 were 15% ahead of figures registered the previous year. Both national income and national output were 7% over 1954.[34] At the same time, a building boom was under way in Havana. Private building permits granted in 1955 in Havana province rose to 3,400 compared with 2,376 in 1952.[35] Many nineteenth-century houses in the Vedado were being torn down and in their place skyscrapers, such as the FOCSA apartment building and the Havana Hilton, were going up. Havana was being transformed. Another centre of new building was the Plaza de la República, on the south, inland side of Havana, where some ministries were being moved from the old city. Plans were under way for even more lavish and grandiose hotels such as the Capri and the Riviera. Gambling was taking on a new lease of life, with a large number of casinos opening. Pornographic films could now be seen in the Shanghai cinema. The *Havana Post* described Cuba as bidding for the title of 'The Las Vegas of Latin America'.[36] The old Hotel Nacional opened a casino in early 1956. Eartha Kitt, Maurice Chevalier, Lena Horne, and Nat King Cole appeared incessantly in Havana bars and night clubs. Fulgencio Batista, moving agreeably between the presidential palace and Campamento Columbia, with occasional visits to his old estate, Kuquine, handing out toys on the Día de Reyes, could have been forgiven if he concluded his position to be strong, and his crown firmly placed. 'The future looks fabulous for Havana,' said Wilbur Clark, a prince of croupiers, who had come from Las Vegas to operate a new casino at the Hotel Nacional.

When Batista saw Don Cosme on 10 January, he proposed that all future negotiations should be carried out by teams representing the two sides: Don Cosme agreed to consider this but, as Batista perhaps guessed would occur, he took a long time to consult everyone who wished to be consulted. Many tried to persuade Don Cosme that Batista was stalling and that he would in the end make no real concession, and certainly refuse any election in 1956. The Directorio Revolucionario, the new opposition force founded by the student leader Echevarría, in its first manifesto threw doubt on the political possibility of a real dialogue. The 26 July Movement did the same in more violent terms. The most persuasive force was nevertheless the writer (and ex-ABC

---

[34] See article by Ruth McCarthy, *Miami Herald*, 4 January 1956.
[35] U.S. Dept of Commerce, *Investment in Cuba* (1956), 98.
[36] See article, *Havana Post*, 19 January 1956.

member), Jorge Mañach, and he urged dialogue; and eventually at the end of January 1956 a committee representing each side was set up. Batista's men were the mayor of Havana, Pozo; the president of the Senate, Anselmo Alliegro; and various ministers (López Castro, Godoy, Álvarez, and Rey). Don Cosme's men were three Priístas (Tony Varona, Félix Lancís, Pablo Balbuena); and three Grauistas (Eduardo Suárez Rivas, Antonio Lancís and Miguel Hernández Bauzá). The Ortodoxos were Manuel Bisbé, Pelayo Cuervo and Dr Eduardo Corona. Others included the Movimiento de la Nación (Luis Botifoll, editor of *El Mundo*, José Pardo Llada and Enrique Huertas, a doctor); and various members of the amorphous Democratic party (Lincoln Rodón, Carlos Peláez, and Wilfredo Figueras).

The meetings began in March.

This *Diálogo Cívico* represented what turned out to be the last hope for Cuban middle-class democracy. But Batista clearly felt himself far too strong to have to make any concession. The *Havana Post*, expressing the attitude of the U.S. business community, after a survey of the four years of Batista's second reign, alluded to the disappearance of gangsterism and said: 'All in all, the Batista regime has much to commend it.'[37] But it was not only U.S. circles which backed the regime: all 'respectable' Cubans, such as read the *Diario de la Marina*, condemned student political militancy ('it is the university which is spoiling everything'). The opposition's demand for elections in 1956 was not acceptable; there could be nothing before November 1958.[38] On 11 March, in a radio and television speech, Batista publicly ridiculed Don Cosme's demands as absurd and on the 12th Don Cosme called a halt in all negotiations. A mood of doubt and depression swung over the political scene once more. Castro cleverly took the opportunity to issue from Mexico a new announcement separating himself from the Ortodoxos for good. This launched a catalogue of insults against the 'bad faith of the *políticos*', 'the intrigues of the incapable', 'the envy of the mediocre', 'the cowardice of the vested interests'. The latter suggested that under the guise of supporting the Constitution of 1940, Castro always had an inclination to break out of the bounds of normal democratic politics. Nevertheless he still held on to the father figure of Eddy Chibás. He broke with the Ortodoxo leaders but not the '*masas Chibásistas*'. He said that his movement was the 'revolutionary organization of the humble, for the humble, by the humble . . . the hope of renewal for the working class'. The 26 July Movement, he said, is a warm invitation to close ranks, extended

[37] *Ibid.*, Editorial, 19 March 1956, 4.
[38] Batista, *Cuba Betrayed*, 35, said that no decision was reached because of the opposition's demand for the immediate resignation of the government.

with open arms, to all the revolutionaries of Cuba, without petty party differences.[39]

His move was also prompted by a sudden revival of torturing and cruelty by the special police (SIM). In February there were three cases of atrocious police behaviour, firstly the case of a twenty-three-year-old student member of the Ortodoxos, Evélida González (a secretary of Castro's friend, Conte Agüero), secondly, that of a member of the Priísta youth organization, Antonio López Camejo; and thirdly, the case of José Carballo García who was beaten up in Las Villas. All were tortured by police agents to get information, the former on the interesting question of the relation between the 26 July Movement and the Ortodoxos. The revival of this behaviour by the *Batistiano* police left a dark stain and Batista's 'personal assurance' that the torturers would be discovered carried no conviction; the impression was that the police were out of control whenever they wished to be.[40]

[39] *Bohemia*, 1 April 1956.

[40] See *Havana Post*, 9–10 February, 1956, 12. Señorita González explained that her chief torturers were women, one black, one white.

CHAPTER LXXII

Castro in Mexico

Castro's movement in Mexico had had many ups and downs since its provisional establishment there the preceding summer. There were financial problems: Castro travelled to Miami and to New York in the autumn of 1955 in search of promoters, but his only big source of income was none other than ex-president Prío, always anxious to have his finger in almost any opposition activities. At the end of September, Castro met the ex-president of the Development Bank under Prío, Justo Carrillo, at Mérida, Yucatán; Carrillo was at this time working, as Castro must have known, with a group of left-wing officers to overthrow Batista by *golpe de estado*; and Castro asked him for the mayoralty of Havana after Batista's defeat if Carrillo should triumph.[1] Carrillo promised him instead 'a job in which you can apply all your energy, achieve a function of high usefulness and convert yourself into a constructive representative of your generation'.

Other sympathizers who gave money at this stage included Venezuelan exiles such as Romulo Betancourt, and some Mexicans. Castro also raised some money through appeals at meetings in the U.S., organized usually by Ortodoxo exiles. He appointed Juan Manuel Márquez as his representative in Miami, and from Miami brought back a military instructor in the shape of Miguel Sánchez, known as El Coreano, because, though a Cuban, he had fought in the U.S. army in the Korean war.[2] Another military instructor was an old Cuban-Spaniard, Alberto Bayo.

Bayo was born in Cuba, son of a Spanish officer and a mother from Camagüey, and joined first the Spanish army, and then its air section, sided with the Spanish Republic in the civil war and led the famous but unsuccessful expedition to Majorca in the summer of 1936: later he led guerrilla expeditions in Castille. A man of varied experience, he fought in the Moroccan wars as well as the civil war; he founded the first civil air school in Spain, and wrote books about whatever he had done, not to speak of novels, poetry and technical handbooks. Probably it was this considerable knowledge of the world and of past conflict

[1] Carrillo MSS, p. 7.
[2] F. Sánchez Amaya, *Diario del Granma* (1959).

that commended Bayo to Castro.[3] In the past he had been a Mason and a Socialist, and had been refused admittance to London by a prejudiced immigration officer.[4] Due to that and other accidents in the course of the Spanish Civil War he had developed a not unjustifiably hostile and jaundiced view of the role of England in contemporary international affairs.[5] Though he had begun the Spanish war as a Socialist of the Right, by the end he was to be found among Negrín's supporters, partly because he had been aide to Prieto in his most pessimistic period. Afterwards in Mexico, as director of the School of Military Aviation or as president of the Casa de la Democracia Española, Bayo had invariably taken a Popular Front line, and in the previous fifteen years at least once trained young Spanish Communists as *guerrilleros* to return to Spain.[6] Bayo was one of those whom the Spanish war had convinced that the Communists were often more resolute and brave than others;[7] but he had not kept his instructions for them, since he also helped to train a group of young anti-Communist fighters against the Somozas, the dictators of Nicaragua.

Bayo, El Coreano and a Cuban named José Smith began the preliminary military training of Castro's men in the autumn of 1955 at a firing range, Las Guamitas, in Santa Fe, a suburb of Mexico City. Castro attempted to establish military discipline, keeping the recruits in houses under the orders of a commander. But there came a serious setback when a number of the group (Cándido González, Montané, Máximo Celaya) were arrested for illegal holding of firearms and held in the Pocito prison, when they underwent the normal disagreeable, brutal treatment of Mexican prisons.[8]

The Mexican and *Batistiano* police[9] probably collaborated in this action: there was at least one attempt on Castro's life, no doubt by a Batista agent, in the style of Magriñats murder of Mella. A cache of arms which Castro kept in Sierra Madre Street, in the agreeable suburb of Lomas de Chapultepec, was confiscated. After this, Castro resolved to find a more remote place for training and set up a new base at the farm *Santa Rosa*, borrowed from a certain Señor Rivera (a survivor

[3] Castro first met Bayo in July 1955 (Alberto Bayo, *Mi Aporte a la Revolución Cubana* (1960), 15).

[4] See Bayo, *Mi Desembarcó en Mallorca* (1944), 298–9.

[5] e.g. the attempted espionage of the then Wing-Commander R. V. Goddard and Squadron Leader Pearson in 1938 (Bayo, *ibid.* 327–35).

[6] *Ibid.*, 352–3.

[7] 'I am not a Communist even though I admire them and I believe them to be admirable people' (Bayo, *Mi Desembarcó*, 126).

[8] See Oscar Lewis, *The Children of Sánchez* (1961); Sánchez Amaya, 16–17.

[9] Sánchez Amaya speaks of Colonels Cartaya and Maymir of the SIM as being on the trail. However, Colonel Cartaya, at least, suffered from too close contact with the revolutionaries, for on his return to Cuba he was submitted for eleven days to torture and left the 5th Police Station of Havana with six broken ribs. See his statement to *Revolución*, 24 January 1959, 8.

of Pancho Villa's army) on misleading assumptions,[10] in the Chalco district, twenty miles outside Mexico City. Here an even more rigid life was instituted. Passports were confiscated. Trainees were not allowed off the ranch except at specified hours. Sex life was controlled.[11] Letters to Cuba were kept to a minimum. Bayo successfully persuaded Castro to abandon the idea of frontal attack for guerrilla war – an idea which he had at first found repugnant. Discussion with unknown people was forbidden. The men of the 26 July Movement left *Santa Rosa* in batches. Early on, political instruction as well as military training began, though it seems that this was not much more than discussion led by certain prominent members of the group, such as the recorder of property, Dr Electro Pedrosa, Fernando Sánchez Tamayo, Universo Sánchez or Antonio López. None of these had either advanced or coherent political ideas. On the other hand, Bayo talked a great deal about the Spanish war, filling the minds of the young revolutionaries with heroic memories of past tragedies and betrayals.[12]

In the autumn of 1955 Castro was still empirical in what precisely his little force was striving for: for example he seems to have had conversations with some of the Cuban Communists in Mexico at that time, such as Joaquín Ordoqui, Lázaro Peña and Blas Roca. But a conversation is not a conversion. A number of his followers in the Moncada attack, such as Mario Dalmau, Calixto García and 'Ñico' López, had been in exile in Guatemala where some had worked with the revolutionary government until its overthrow in mid-1953 and therefore, when they arrived in Mexico, contributed a new bitterness and probably a new hostility to the U.S. More important from the point of view of what eventually occurred was Castro's meeting in late 1955 with Ernesto Guevara, known as 'Che'[13] Guevara, an Argentinian then aged twenty-six, a medical graduate of the University of Buenos Aires.[14]

Guevara came from a *bourgeois* family in Rosario, the second city of Argentina: his father, Ernesto Guevara Lynch, for a time ran a *mate* farm at Alta Gracia, near Córdoba, and both he and his wife Celia de la Serna (who owned the farm) were active in left-wing politics. His father had Irish blood through his mother, whilst his own mother was Spanish in origin. His family was Catholic but did not go to church

[10] See Bayo, 66–7.

[11] Daniel James says he saw receipts, etc., for budgets of this enterprise, covering, for example, $10,000 a month for training, $7,500 a month for food, $4,800 a month for propaganda, etc.

[12] *Cf.* Bayo, *passim.*

[13] 'Che' is the diminutive or affectionate for 'you' in Argentina, though he appears to have been called this from his middle twenties only, in Guatemala to begin with.

[14] In 1967 Castro said that he met Guevara in 'July or August 1955' (*Granma*, weekly edn, 29 October 1967), but this was probably a bit early. See Ricardo Rojo, *Che Guevara*, Paris, 1969, 66, where the meeting is described as late November. Guevara was born 14 July 1927.

much, though his sisters had been confirmed. Guevara *père* had taken part in anti-Perón plots and assisted Paraguayan revolutionaries.[15] Suffering from asthma from early in life, the son spent much time away from school, being educated partly by his mother and his four brothers and sisters. This goaded him into further study, at first in engineering. The family moved to Buenos Aires in 1944 but apparently went downhill financially.

Entering the university as an engineer, Guevara changed to medicine. An obituary notice remarked that 'interest in Baudelaire as well as sports tempered him both spiritually and physically'. Like Baudelaire, he had no ear for music. He worked for a while as assistant to Dr Salvador Pissani, an Argentinian heart specialist who specialized in allergies, with whom he was co-author of one or two scientific papers. As a student he travelled a good deal in Argentina, Peru and Chile, on bicycle and on foot, and he also visited Colombia and Venezuela. He seems to have had no contact with the Argentinian Communists[16] but his political interests appear to have been awoken by what he had seen in the rest of South America. Also, he had had several friends who were children of Spaniards exiled by or killed in the Spanish Civil War. The role of such politically aware children of Spain cannot be overestimated in discussing the Latin-American revolutionary experience. For a time he was engaged to a rich girl from Córdoba, but on graduation in March 1953, Guevara started again to travel, with a large library accompanying him; at first deciding to work in the Venezuelan leper hospital of Cabo Blanco where a student friend was already established, he was persuaded by an Ecuadorian lawyer, Ricardo Rojo, that 'Guatemala was the place to see' because of the revolutionary government there. On the way, he was arrested in Peru, and stayed some time in Ecuador and Panama where he wrote a number of semi-archaeological articles to pay his fare to Guatemala.

In Guatemala Guevara volunteered as a doctor in tropical diseases, in the jungle, but was unable to qualify quickly enough. He lived in Guatemala City and made his living 'selling things in rural areas'.[17] He met Antonio (Ñico) López, one of Castro's Moncada adherents and then an exile. Shortly, however, the Guatemalan govenment was overthrown as a result of the conspiracy of the U.S. Central Intelligence Agency and some right-wing Guatemalan officers. Guevara, taking refuge in the Argentinian Embassy, tried to be sent to the 'front' but

---

[15] Letter from him to Mario Llerena, Llerena MSS, 266–7.

[16] A friend of his youth, Fernando Barral, did join the Argentinian Communist Youth in 1946 but in an article in *Granma* (weekly edition, 29 October 1967), Barral said that it was precisely from then on that he ceased to see Guevara. Both Barral and Guevara were for a time attached to Guevara's cousin Negrita Córdoba, whose father was a *comunizante* poet.

[17] From an obituary by his first wife in *Granma*, 29 October 1967.

failed; but he apparently went on duty against air raids, tried to encourage the Guatemalans to fight, and by his own account 'saved lives and transported weapons'. He eventually left Guatemala for Mexico by means of the Argentine Embassy.

Guevara came out of his experience in Guatemala immensely hostile to the U.S., its final destroyer. He had not been to the U.S., but from that time regarded with suspicion anyone who had merely lived there for any length of time.[18]

In Mexico City Guevara worked as a street photographer, in company with another exile from Guatemala, 'El Patojo', Julio Cáceres,[19] whom he had met *en route*. Perhaps through the influence of Lombardo Toledano, Guevara got a job in Mexico City in the allergy ward at the general hospital: he also did some lecturing at the university. Afterwards, he went to work at the Institute of Cardiology, on the recommendation of Dr Concepción Palacios.

In late 1955 Guevara was a revolutionary but not necessarily a Marxist, if by that is understood simply a view that the changing means of production are the fathers to political change. On the other hand, he believed in the perfectibility of man, he despised the profit motive and thought that it could be quickly eradicated. According to a Cuban, Mario Dalmau, whom he met in Guatemala, he had 'read' everything written by Marx and Lenin, and had with him a complete library of their works. He was 'a complete Marxist'.[20] To his wife, Hilda Gadea, a Peruvian and an Aprista (whom he left behind in Lima), he appeared as a puritanical, intelligent and practical man who had already experienced one revolution and how it had failed: through the government failing to destroy the army and through the U.S. intervention from outside. He already believed in the purgative effects of revolution as such, believing (as he later put it) that 'revolution cleanses men, improving them as the experimental farmer corrects the defects of his plant'.[21] On the other hand, he was able to classify himself a few years later as a Trotskyist or an ex-Peronist and, though this was at a time when he was about to begin to use the Communists in Cuba, he may have been telling the truth.[22] Perhaps the explanation of his character is

[18] Seven years later, however, he apparently admitted that 'the model whom we must cite as closest [to] the man most resembling man of the future society [is] the North American . . . the product of a developed economy, of modern technology, of abundance . . . A revolutionary Cuban, Vietnamese, or Algerian of today [is] less like the man who is going to shape the Communist society than a Yankee . . . we men are children of the economic métier. But should this truth be told?' (S. Cazalis, *La República* (Caracas), February 1966).

[19] Ernesto (Che) Guevara, *Pasajes de la Guerra Revolucionaria*, 123; Hilda Gadea, article in *Granma*, 29 October 1967 (weekly edition).

[20] Mario Dalmau, *Granma*, 29 October 1967. This story about the books is borne out by the stories in *Bohemia*, July 1956, on the occasion of Guevara's arrest.

[21] Guevara, *op. cit.*, 124.

[22] To Luis Simón, in September 1958 (Luis Simón, MSS).

to be found in his ambiguous family, where extreme Lef
were combined with *haut-bourgeois* living, an extremely freqt
nomenon in Latin countries, and one which must greatly irritat
brought up in it; in addition the family was, though *bourgeois*, decli
and Guevara's mother was evidently a stronger influence than h
father.

In November 1955 Guevara met Castro, and the two talked for a
long time one night in the house of a Cuban exile, María Antonia
González de Paloma, in the Lomas de Chapultepec, whence, for a few
hours at dawn, Mount Popocatépetl can be seen.[23] Guevara saw Castro
as possessing the characteristics of a 'great leader', such as perhaps in
his wanderings he had been seeking.[24] In 1962 Guevara described himself as being from the first drawn to Castro as a romantic adventurer
who, however, had the courage to risk death for a noble cause.[25] He
enrolled in Castro's army, as a doctor and as a *guerrillero*. As such, he
was very successful at the *Santa Rosa* estate, far the most intelligent of
the pupils of Colonel Bayo,[26] though he was evidently always anti-
military in an orthodox sense.[27]

Perhaps under the influence of this new friendship Castro wrote an
article which appeared in *Bohemia* on 25 December 1955. This once
again criticized those who in Cuba 'did nothing' against Batista, denounced the Auténticos and proclaimed its author free of all public
corruption: '*Contra mundum*' seemed his battle-cry (though this was a
moment when there did, on the contrary, seem to be a chance of
negotiation between Batista and Don Cosme de la Torriente). In
February a Havana Urgency Court formally ordered Castro's arrest.[28]
Nevertheless Castro waited till the *Diálogo Cívico* had collapsed before
writing on 19 March a public resignation from the Ortodoxos. He also
announced the formation of the 26 July Movement as a separate one
from Ortodoxia, as it had in reality always been; and he denounced
the *Diálogo Cívico* as playing into Batista's hands. His own goals, he
said, remained the same: 'For the Chibásist masses, the 26 July Movement is not distinct from Ortodoxia'.[29]

[23] In his letter of farewell to Castro in 1965 Guevara recalled this meeting: 'At this moment
I remember many things – when I met you at María Antonia's house, when you suggested
my coming, all the tensions involved in the preparations.' (Castro speech, 3 October 1965,
Cuban Embassy, London, Inf. Bull. No. 97, p. 13.) The house is Amparán, No. 49.

[24] '*Tiene las características de gran conductor*' (*Verde Olivo*, 9 April 1961).

[25] *Bohemia*, 30 November 1962.

[26] 'Guevara overtook all the others because of his great learning and dedication to study
and observation.' (Bayo, 76.)

[27] Cf. his remark in 1963 to the journalist Cazalis at a detention camp at Guahanacabibes:
'No, no, not One! Two! Three! Four! Military discipline makes me vomit.' (*La República*,
Caracas, February 1966.)

[28] *Havana Post*, 4 February 1956.

[29] Du Bois, 121–4. See also Draper, *Castroism*, 10–11.

le that Castro had already decided on what
le gained power, since the capture of power
In early 1956 he was merely one among many
ion leaders, even if he was younger, more
tic and indeed more politically subtle than
illa tactics and the military training at the
d more on the experience of Spain than of
later said that he and his friends only knew of Mao's
book of guerrilla warfare after they had reached the Sierra Maestra,
and he later spoke of Bayo as '*el maestro*', so far as the guerrillas were
concerned. As for Castro himself, the older Cuban exile Teresa Casuso
described him as he seemed to her, a little later, on the edge of strife,
among a group in a prison yard in Mexico:

> Tall and clean-shaven, and with close-cropped chestnut hair, dressed
> soberly and correctly ... standing out from the rest by his look and
> his bearing ... He gave one the impression of being noble, sure,
> deliberate, like a big Newfoundland dog ... eminently serene ... He
> gave me a greeting of restrained emotion, and a handshake that was
> warm without being overdone. His voice was quiet, his expression
> grave, his manner calm, gentle ... he had a habit of shaking his head
> like a fine thoroughbred horse ... His basic point, the fixed star,
> was 'the People' ... Fidel showed that he had read a great deal of
> José Martí who seemed indeed to be the guiding spirit of his life ...
> The plans he revealed seemed beyond his reach and I felt a kind of
> pity for this aspiring deliverer who was so full of confidence and firm
> conviction and I was moved by his innocence ... [yet] I could not
> give myself up to the intense admiration which he inspired in his
> group of young men ... Fidel and his band of young men seemed to
> me to be a lost cause.[30]

Castro's letter of resignation from the Ortodoxos hardly had much
effect, for one reason above all: other plotters were at work. During the
early part of 1956 a series of conspiracies were made to overthrow
Batista, partly from Cuba itself, partly from the neighbouring dictatorship, the Dominican Republic, where Leonidas Trujillo, the Benefactor
on high heels, still ruled implacably as he had done for a quarter of a
century.

Cuban-Dominican relations had never been very good, at least since
the abortive Cayo Confites expedition of 1947. Batista tried to differentiate himself from his fellow dictator, and indeed there was a gap between them: Batista clearly was a dictator who wished always to be
loved, a democratically elected president: Trujillo did not mind being

[30] Casuso, 92 ff.

feared. Batista was less himself a torturer than a weak man surrounded by cruel ones whom he could not control. Bad relations between the two governments were exacerbated by the murder in Havana in January of a Dominican democratic exile, 'Pipi' Hernández, then a foreman at the Havana Hilton under construction in Vedado. It seemed clear that he had been murdered by agents of Trujillo, and, a few days later, several gangsters who had been associated earlier with the action groups of the 1940s were implicated. Among these was most important, a group led by N. Nasser, who had assaulted the Royal Bank of Canada, and Vizoso, an extortionist killed in a gun battle with the police.[31] In February counter-allegations began to implicate Batista's chief of staff and old friend General Tabernilla in plots against the Dominican Republic,[32] while the Ortodoxo chief, Pelayo Cuervo, in March accused other army leaders in Cuba of taking Trujillo's money and support in plotting against the government. On 12 March Trujillo carried out one of his biggest crimes – the kidnapping and eventual murder of Jesús Galíndez, leader of the Basque Nationalists in the Spanish Civil War and afterwards professor in Santo Domingo and in New York. Galíndez was kidnapped in New York, when preparing to publish an authoritative attack on Trujillo, and flown to Santo Domingo apparently by a young U.S. pilot, Gerald Murphy, a friend of various anti-Batista union leaders in Cuba such as Cálixto Sánchez.[33] The truth of this disgraceful affair has never been fully brought to light. There were various notes sent, rumours of war, complaints to the OAS, between Cuba and the Dominican Republic, and, in a jumpy mood, the SIM tried to round up all known enemies of the government, at least those on the right or gangster wing.

This nervousness on the part of the SIM was further encouraged by the appearance in Masferrer's journal, *Tiempo en Cuba*, on 18 March, of a report of a conspiracy led by Policarpo Soler, the Auténtico gangster who had been in Santo Domingo since 1952. Among those arrested were Cándido de la Torre, ex-city councillor; Hirigoyen, the bus workers' leader; Menelao Mora, an ex-Auténtico deputy; Echevarría, the student leader; and several Spanish exiles such as Carlos Gutiérrez Menoyo, Daniel Martín and Ignacio González. The SIM also made a bid to lay hands on several political gangsters such as the famous *el Extraño*. On 20 March a number of others involved with these plotters

[31] See *Havana Post*, 17 January 1956. One of the arrested murderers, Félix Oscar Gaveria Guerra, had been a policeman in De la Fé's ministry. Others involved were Ulises Sánchez Hinojosa and Rafael Eugenio Grafta (see *ibid.*, 28 February 1956). *El Caribe*, 12 August 1956, stated that Sánchez Hinojosa had returned from Cuba, after an 'intelligence mission', to rejoin the police in Santo Domingo.

[32] See *ibid.*, 15 February 1956.

[33] For the Galíndez case, see Ornes, *Pequeño Tirano del Caribe*; Bosch; Galíndez; and Basaldúa's tribute to Galíndez, Pedro de Basaldúa, *Jesús de Galíndez* (?1960).

were arrested, such as the head of the national lottery under Prío, Colonel Artigas, who had unwisely returned to Cuba; Prío's ex-secret service chief, Eufemio Fernández; and ex-congressman Esteva Lora.[34]

After these arrests a group of intelligent younger officers known as the *Puros*,[35] headed by the military attaché in Washington, Colonel Ramón Barquín, decided to make a long prepared strike against Batista. These men, though opposed to Batista and Batista's new establishment of officers, were not senior enough to have suffered in the general purge of the army of Prío's time. All had entered the army well after the revolution of 1933, were real professional men, and therefore had no hates or loyalties deriving from that time. Some of the *Puros* had been closely attached to the Ortodoxos before 10 March. Prío indeed had feared them, and by carefully removing them from central commands (it had been he who had appointed Barquín to Washington), had helped to make the way easier for Batista. Since then, the *Puros* had kept in touch with García Barcena and with the Ortodoxos. In April 1955 Barquín and Colonel Manuel Varela Castro, who commanded the Cuban tank regiment, took the lead of a number of young officers, among whom Majors Borbonnet and José Orihuela were prominent.[36] The plotters intended to take command of Campamento Columbia in orthodox *pronunciamiento* style. They planned not to kill Batista, but to put him on an aeroplane heading for the U.S.[37] They were, however, betrayed on 3 April 1956 by one of their number, the officer who was then the commander in La Cabaña and they and a large number of other officers only vaguely connected with them were arrested.[38]

This *golpe*, however unsuccessful, nevertheless marked a serious crisis for the Batista regime. Another group of army officers had taken shape with the nickname of *tanquistas*, men who wished to change Cuba from the limping democracy that it was even under Batista into the tougher totalitarian system which prevailed in the Dominican Republic. These were the men who had planned the *golpe* of 10 March, but had failed

---

[34] See *Havana Post*, 20 March 1956, and 21 March 1956.

[35] The name (signifying a cigar in Spanish and purer than pure in Cuban) was given to them contemptuously by Grau and it stuck.

[36] Others named were: Captains Ernesto Despaigne, Hugo Vázquez, José C. Ramos Avila, and Mateo Travieso (all of infantry); Lieutenants Manuel Villafaña and Réné Travieso (of the air force); and Lieutenant Guillermo J. Morales (*Havana Post*, 5 April 1956). See also Batista, *Cuba Betrayed*, 46. Barquín, *Bohemia* (8 February 1959), admitted that a number of Ortodoxos and like-minded men backed him: León Reduit, Vicente León, Justo Carrillo, Felipe Pazos, Diego Vicente Tejera, Fernando Leyva, Roberto Agramonte and Raúl Chibás. None of these was tried and only Carrillo was closely involved. He had been responsible for the selection of thirty-five to forty university trained young men to lead the police in Cuba after the success of the *golpe*.

[37] See Havana press, 10 and 11 April 1956, for trial report.

[38] Carrillo, MSS, p. 11.

to profit from it. In touch with Trujillo's army, they wanted to force Batista to carry through a totalitarian revolution, or else to abandon power to them. They were in touch too with Ernesto de la Fe and Senator Rolando Masferrer, the ex-leader of the MSR, and by now leader in Santiago of a large private army, *los Tigres*, trained (though inadequately) to carry out his merest whim. The *tanquistas'* plan was to stimulate disorder (even helping groups such as Castro's, which they hated) in order to justify their *golpe*, and their removal of constitutionalism. Batista would either have to be the figurehead or go. Thus the *tanquistas* spread a good many of Trujillo's arms about Cuba during early 1956, not really caring who had what, some going to Priístas, some to Castroists, while the *tanquistas* themselves held on to the tanks. But the defeat of the Puros' conspiracy not only revealed how badly the officers in Cuba were divided but gave such power to the Tabernillas that Batista was virtually their prisoner for the next two years. The *tanquistas* probably also helped *el Extraño* to get his hands on new caches of ammunition. But they clearly underestimated both the popularity of Batista in the rank and file of the army and the political guile of the dictator.[39]

Among the by now innumerable little groups in Cuba with gun-happy but patriotic and socially conscious *caudillos* was one surrounding Reynol García, an ambitious but unimportant Auténtico,[40] eager to make an attack on the government. What followed is hard to disentangle. Batista apparently prepared a trap for García in order to restrain the *tanquistas*. García was in his turn persuaded that if he arrived at the Goicuría barracks at Matanzas, the men would come over to him. He drove there with about a hundred men,[41] but he and nine others were killed, many wounded. At least one was killed after surrender[42] – a fact which was bitterly denounced. Prío, Varona and other Auténtico leaders were seized and questioned. Constitutional guarantees were suspended. Batista claimed that the opposition as a whole was now willing to kill innocent soldiers in its avid pursuit of power. He was thus able to assure the *tanquistas* that he was going to follow a tough policy at the same time as indicating that in difficult times like these it would be better to remain with the old leather-jacketed leader, the saviour of *la grulla*.[43] The suspension meant censorship, but in succeeding weeks the Cubans heard much in the press about captures of arms and further

[39] See the article by Javier Pazos, *Cambridge Opinion* (1963), 20.

[40] Ex-chauffeur to Aureliano Sánchez Arango.

[41] Some being Castro followers such as Israel Escalona, Julio César, Ernesto Carbonell, Casanova 'El guaguo'.

[42] See *Time*, 14 May 1956. *Life* magazine had photographs.

[43] Justo Carrillo, who was then with Castro in Yucatán, reports that Castro regarded this attack as opportunistic and irresponsible (MSS, p. 27). See *Havana Post*, 30 April 1956.

failures to catch *el Extraño*. Prío, blamed for Reynol García's attempt, was dispatched by Batista back to Miami, where he was nevertheless held before being allowed in[44] – administrative errors spoiling further the poor standing of the U.S. government with the Cuban opposition. It was not till June that Prío received permission to stay in the U.S.

The summer saw the climax of Batista's war of nerves with Trujillo. The Cuban Senate had empowered Batista to break relations with the Dominican Republic whenever he wanted. The Cuban police had claimed that Prío's contacts with Trujillo had been cemented by some of the men arrested in March, such as the Auténtico politician Menelao Mora, and Batista declared the Dominican minister *persona non grata*. Captain Esteban Ventura, the indefatigable police agent, found another cache of arms near Prío's farm. Policarpo Soler was charged with being concerned in June. Batista's aim was to implicate all his enemies with Trujillo, thereby making them seem, in the face of international public opinion, to be gangsters and gangsters based abroad, but this was difficult since it had already been his plan to involve Fidel Castro's group with the Communists. In late June yet another 'plot' was unearthed to kill Batista, this time affecting the Cuban matador, José Sánchez, again with the same old gangster names allegedly among his backers. Cuba, beneath a surface of prosperity, was a centre of warring gangs of gunmen, policemen, ex-ministers, officers, students, all out for 'supreme power', none collaborating genuinely with or 'implicated with' each other: thus, in Costa Rica, Eufemio Fernández's gang apparently betrayed some of Castro's supporters, and prevented them getting visas for Mexico, even though Fernández's backer Prío was then helping Castro.[45]

Castro's friends had now been training at the *Santa Rosa* farm for nine months. Castro himself kept in touch with all political groups; thus on 29 April he met Justo Carrillo in Tapachula, on the Guatemala-Mexican border, and while exchanging views about the *Puros'* plot, accepted $5,000 from him and the Montecristi movement. In addition Castro received money from López Vilaboy, president of Cubana Airways and a comrade of Batista – a gift he only accepted for lack of other help.[46] New waves of young men had come to join him, among them a group of ex-Moncada men from Costa Rica, where they had been in refuge. One of these was a well known gangster, Trujillo's

[44] *Havana Post*, 10 May 1956.

[45] Franqui, 23.

[46] Carrillo, MSS, 18–19. Carrillo criticized this and Castro replied that '*no tenía un centavo*' and therefore had had to. According to Carrillo, Castro spent some of the money he brought on a present for a girl: but, as Carrillo points out, Castro was usually forgiven for that sort of thing.

confidant, the hatchet-man Ricardo Bonachea; he turned out to be an informer. Probably in consequence the Mexican police, no doubt with Cuban police assistance, discovered their lair. Castro, Bayo, Guevara and twenty-one others were arrested on 24 July on charges of preparing an attack on another country.[47] A vast cache of arms was also captured. Mexican police, again in connivance with the Cuban SIM, apparently accused Castro of being in relation with the Communists in Mexico, saying that a visiting card of a Soviet official (Nikolai Leonov) had been found in his pocket and argued that he had had persistent contacts with the Cuban Communist Lázaro Peña, and with Lombardo Toledano. These allegations were reported in *Bohemia* in an article by a Spanish Mexican, Luis Dam. From prison on 3 July, Castro formally denounced the charges of being a Communist as 'absolutely fantastic'.[48] He also wrote a reply which appeared in the next week's issue of *Bohemia*. The whole incident, he charged, derived from a plot by the Batista regime and the U.S. Embassy. He added:

> What moral right on the other hand, does Señor Batista have to speak of communism when he was the presidential candidate of the Communist party in the elections of 1940, when his electoral slogans hid behind the Hammer and Sickle, when his photographs hung next to those of Blas Roca and Lázaro Peña, and when half a dozen of his present ministers and confidential collaborators were outstanding members of the Communist Party.[49]

To Justo Carrillo in April, Castro had said: 'The Communists will never be in a majority though their strength will grow in this struggle; afterwards ... you will be important in the government; you also, like I, will prevent them from dominating.'[50]

Castro continued to attack the Communists, and they attacked him in reply. Some time earlier a young Negro student, Walterio Carbonell, was expelled from the Communist party for sending a telegram congratulating Castro: the party added, for good measure, 'The

[47] They were: Ciro Redondo, Universo Sánchez, Ramiro Valdés, Cálixto García, Oscar Rodríguez, Celso Maragoto, Alberto Bayo (*fils*), Jimmy Hutzel, María Antonia González, Almeida, Rolando Santana, Ricardo Bonachea López, Arturo Chaumont, Reinaldo Benítez, Luis Crespo, Tomás Electo Pedrosa, Aguedo Aguiar, Eduardo Roig, José Raúl Vega, Horacio Rodríguez and Víctor Trapote (a Spanish-Mexican painter). (*Bohemia*, 8 July 1956.) Julio Díaz, Cándido González and Alfonso Celaya had already been arrested (*Bohemia*, 15 July 1956, 85).

[48] See *Havana Post*, 4 July.

[49] *Bohemia*, 15 July 1956. Draper rightly comments that it is hard to imagine a Communist, open or concealed, defending himself by reminding the Communists of their old friendship with the dictator. (See *Castroism*, 28 ff.) Batista himself said that rumours of ex-President Cárdenas's support for the plotters was absurd, since he and Cárdenas were great friends (see *Havana Post*, 20 September 1956).

[50] '*Ud. también, como yo, va a impedir que ellos dominen*' (Carrillo, MSS, p. 18).

party rejects this kind of adventurist action which serves only to immolate dozens of young people in ruin ... those who are attempting to involve the newspaper *Hoy* with a filthy provocation ... entangling it in the adventure of Castro and his group.'[51] Ironically, within a few weeks, Castro found himself having to write another letter of self-defence, this time against the argument that he was allied with Trujillo.[52]

On 24 July the Mexican police released Castro and his friends on the condition that they left Mexico.[53] Castro was now in fact anxious to return to Cuba to resume the conflict; he had already issued a promise to be either dead or back by the end of 1956. Final training now continued in Mexican apartments, not Santa Rosa, in the Lomas de Chapultepec, the house of the Cuban exile Teresa Casuso, widow of the poet de la Torriente Brau, killed in the Spanish war, which was used as an arms store.[54] In August, by arrangement with Teresa Casuso, Castro swam across the Río Grande to meet, on the advice of Justo Carrillo, the newly-exiled Prío at Reynolo near the border. Prío agreed to back Castro with $100,000, of which the first $50,000 arrived within a few weeks.[55] Castro's cause prospered more, since he now had money not only to buy arms but also to bribe the Mexican police to keep away,[56] although he was hard put to rival Batista's resources for the same activity. In September, Castro also reached an agreement of collaboration in the so-called 'pact of Mexico', with the students' president and leader of the Directorio, Echevarría, though when Castro apparently suggested an alliance with the Cuban Communists, Echevarría vigorously refused and the matter was dropped as was any suggestion that the Directorio should place itself under Castro's lead.[57] Both Echevarría and Castro renounced any collaboration with Trujillo. But Prío was financing another expedition (with Eufemio Fernández and others) in the Dominican Republic, and Castro had to work hard to get his own

[51] Qu., S. Casalis (Siquitrilla), *La República* (Caracas), 4 February 1965. Carbonell was later (1967) imprisoned by Castro for trying to organize a Cuban version of the Black Power movement.

[52] See Du Bois, 27-33.

[53] *Havana Post*, 25 July 1956. Twenty minor members were allowed out in early July: the last three to go out were Castro, Universo Sánchez and Ciro Redondo.

[54] Casuso, 105. Teresa Casuso describes how at this time Castro made a new offer of marriage to a beautiful Cuban, was accepted, but finally dropped – leaving Castro once more affianced only to Revolution. Teresa Casuso first met Castro and his friends in prison which she visited.

[55] Carrillo, MSS, p. 21. This was September. Present with Castro were Juan Manuel Márquez, Montané, Melba Hernández, and Rafael del Pino (Du Bois, 134). The other $50,000 was a long time coming.

[56] Casuso, 112.

[57] Evidence of Dr Primitivo Lima of the Directorio. There were 'other differences of a doctrinal character'. The Directorio undertook to kill an important member of Batista's regime but when they did so, Castro formally disassociated himself.

movement started first 'so as not to be confused with those others',[58] at a moment when Prío was in touch with him too.

Back in Havana, the *Diálogo Cívico* seemed to have foundered. Pardo Llada fended off a challenge to a duel from the Speaker of the House, Godoy. The usual animosities among the Ortodoxos persisted: Raúl Chibás resigned from the Ortodoxo leadership, out of disagreement with Emilio Ochoa over plans to commemorate the death of Eddy Chibás, and what power there was in the movement seemed now to lie with Luis Conte Agüero, the radio commentator and Castro's old friend, who had become Ortodoxo secretary-general. The 26 July Movement in Havana was busy not only with sabotage and occasional terrorism but also trying to work out a coherent dogma – a sure sign of intellectual ambiguity – by establishing a commission to this effect.[59] In union politics, Conrado Bécquer and Conrado Rodríguez defeated the Mujalistas in their election, though Mujal, becoming more and more a grand defender of the established order, himself retained control of the CTC. Batista seemed on top of the *tanquistas* and the Tabernillas on top of him. He had just received a new supply of arms from the U.S., 'to help democracy in Cuba', as part of the 1952 agreement and, in July and August with, first, examinations and then holidays, the students were relatively quiet – apart from an incident on 10 September when Echevarría's second-in-command at the university, Fructuoso Rodríguez, led a group of student gunmen (including Echevarría's old opponent Leonel Alonso) into the TV Channel 2 Station. However, in October, a gratuitous act of violence occurred in Santiago when a former police captain, Arsenio Escalona, who was believed to be in sympathy with the opposition, was beaten, tortured and thrown into Santiago Bay. The chief of naval intelligence, Captain Alejandro García Olayón, was accused, but left undisturbed. The clouds of barbarism seemed to be indeed gathering when, with this crime unpunished, an attack was launched by several students of Echevarría's group, led by Juan Pedro Carbó Serviá, a medical student who had become prominent in the campaign between Echevarría and Alonso, together with Rolando Cubela, another middle-class student. These two and others attacked a group of policemen and officers of Batista's army in the early hours of 28 October, a Sunday morning, as they left the night club Montmartre in the Vedado. Killed immediately was Colonel

---

[58] 113. See Salas Cañizares's statement, in *Havana Post* (11 August 1956). In September, meantime, a meeting occurred in Mexico of the Congress for Cultural Freedom. The Cuban delegation included the Ortodoxo, Mario Llerena, and Raúl Roa, professor at Havana, and one of the leaders of the generation of 1933, who was reluctant to meet Castro since he associated him with the UIR and MSR of the late 1940s.

[59] Mario Llerena, MSS (14). Llerena says that he and Oltuski were the main members of the commission which was also occasionally attended by Carlos Franqui and once by Armando Hart.

Blanco Rico, the thirty-six-year-old chief of military intelligence, and wounded were Colonel Marcelo Tabernilla (son of the chief of staff) and his wife. Another officer's wife was slightly injured. The bleeding and bejewelled women reeled into mirrors in the foyer which, in their fright, they took for open space.[60] Carbó Serviá and Cubela fled through the casino to escape through the service entrance.

This attack was made by the students in order to draw the attention of the Cuban-American Press Association, then meeting in Havana, to the existence of disorder. Ironically, alas, the gunmen chose to kill almost the only prominent member of Batista's police who opposed torture during interrogation. Also the attack seems to have been carried out almost by accident: Carbó and Cubela were anxious to kill any important functionary of the Batista government and they saw Blanco Rico by accident. Had he not recognized them, they might not have fired.[61]

The aftermath was bloody. The police naturally went to work to find the killers and at noon the next day General Salas Cañizares and Colonel Orlando Piedra, with some men, went to the Haitian Embassy in Miramar, for what reason never became clear. The Haitian ambassador and his staff were at lunch. Within the Embassy were a number of Cubans who had taken sanctuary there, on the normal understanding prevalent in Spanish America that they would receive sanctuary. Most had been present several days; the others had arrived at 4 a.m. that day. Carbó Serviá and Cubela were not there. The police knocked at the door and firing began: who fired first is not clear. The police then entered the Embassy, breaking the sanctuary rule, shooting dead several of the refugees, capturing others and killing them afterwards: ten were killed. The police lost nobody, though General Rafael Salas Cañizares was wounded, and died on 31 October, with Batista and the prime minister, García Montes, at his bedside, not to speak of his three brothers, two colonels and a lieutenant. Six of the ten civilians killed had apparently been Auténticos, who had taken part in the attack on the Goicuría barracks in April. Two others had been involved in an attempt on Masferrer in Santiago; the other two appear to have been students.[62] According to one source close to Batista, the death of Salas Cañizares did not much sadden the president since it enabled him to get his own hands on the ex-police chief's gambling protection income – reputedly $730,000 a month.[63]

[60] *Excelsior* (Mexico), article by Aldo Baroni. See *Havana Post*, 30 October 1956; *New York Times*, 29 October 1956.

[61] Private information. See *Havana Post*, 1 December 1956, for identification of these two, after their escape, by Armando de Cárdenas. He alleged that they had been helped to get away by Prío's nephew, Dr Fernando Prío.

[62] See *Havana Post*, 31 October 1956. Salas Cañizares was succeeded by Colonel Hernando Hernández.

[63] Suárez Núñez, 25.

Daily the press carried stories about the activities of Prío or Castro, Sánchez Arango, or the gangsters of Santo Domingo who, it was believed, were about to strike at any moment. An ugly consciousness of the imminence of violence settled over the island. In Castro's case these apprehensions were real. Having failed to obtain a Catalina flying boat or a U.S. naval crash boat, he had now procured a 58-foot yacht, the *Granma*, bought with Prío's money from an American couple named Ericson; it cost $15,000.[64] On to this he could place nearly one hundred people, and he could sail it from Tuxpan to Oriente, where sixty years before Martí had landed. On 2 November the newspaper *Alerta* published an exclusive interview with Castro in which he declared himself ready to enter Cuba at all costs – a fact interesting not only for itself, but for the suggestion it made that Castro still had some communication with his old friend the editor of *Alerta*, Ramón Vasconcelos, despite the fact that he had entered Batista's government.

In mid-November, just before the 26 July Movement was about to set off, a large cache of arms was captured by the Mexican police in Teresa Casuso's house. She, Pedro Miret and Ennio Leyva, who had been looking after these supplies, were arrested. Castro had this time apparently been betrayed by Rafael del Pino, his old companion at Bogotá, and one of his closest companions in the meantime; they had collaborated together in an attempt on Masferrer's life too, in the 1940s. Guilty or not, Del Pino had left the 26 July Movement before this disaster and was always blamed afterwards.[65] Batista, as a matter of fact, knew everything that was going on in Mexico, and according to one source he had turned down both an offer to murder Castro and to burn the boat in which he proposed to embark for Cuba.[66]

These events led Castro to move as quickly as possible on to Cuba. His organizer in Cuba, the Baptist school teacher Frank País, had come to Mexico a few weeks before to coordinate (and incidentally warn against) a rising in Santiago at the end of November, the moment when Castro planned to land (Melba Hernández had also returned from Cuba with the same message). On 21 November Castro himself was given three days by the Mexicans to leave Mexico City. He and most of his men did so, going to Vera Cruz, some leaving without training of any kind,[67] and only the leaders knowing exactly what they were going to do.

[64] Martínez Arará erroneously states it as $20,000.
[65] HAR, XII, 431. Goldenberg evidence *re* Masferrer; Du Bois, 13; Casuso, 117. After he was suspected, Del Pino was sent by Castro to Ciudad Victoria where a group of Cubans had been sent under Faustino Pérez. Del Pino stole a pistol and left for the U.S. whence he only returned in 1959 to lead an abortive expedition against Castro and to receive a thirty-year sentence.
[66] Suárez Núñez, 35.
[67] Bayo, *Mi aporte*, p. 163.

Before they left Castro had no time to prepare any new manifesto.[68] His ideas no doubt were much as they were when he wrote to Melba Hernández, on 4 October:

> The 26th of July [Movement] is constituted free of hate for anyone. It is not a political party, but a revolutionary movement. Its ranks are open to all Cubans who sincerely desire to re-establish political democracy and to implant social justice in Cuba. Its leadership is collective and secret, formed by new men of strong will who bear no responsibility for the past. The Cuban Revolution will achieve all reforms within the spirit and practice of our enlightened Constitution of 1940, without depriving anyone of what he legitimately possesses and indemnifying any interest that is injured . . . The Cuban Revolution will punish with a firm hand all acts of violence committed against the tyranny and will repudiate and repress all manifestations of ignoble vengeance inspired by hate or base passions.[69]

On 19 November Castro told a reporter from *Alerta* that he would be willing to desist from any invasion if Batista would accept a seven-point programme including Batista's own resignation, general elections within ninety days, a break of diplomatic relations with Trujillo, and amnesty for political prisoners.[70] One Havana intellectual who had met him in late summer 1956 thought that 'the possibility of [Castro] taking a too radical course did not cross my mind. On the contrary, my worry was that he might slide down the easy slope of traditional politics'.[71] In this mood, uncommitted, on 25 November the *Granma* sailed. Castro had crossed the Rubicon, emulating his hero Caesar as well as Martí. Ahead of him in Cuba, the only force making for peace, the Society of Friends of the Republic, remained inactive, due to the intransigence of Batista, and to the illness of Don Cosme de la Torriente. The future could hold only violence.

As often in the history of Cuban revolutions, this action contrasted with short-term prospects for prosperity. Ever since 1948 Cuba had made efforts not to maintain but to increase her share in the U.S. sugar market. These had failed. In 1956 the U.S. introduced new changes to her sugar law by which her domestic producers won most of the market created by enlarged demand in the U.S. (itself the product of increased population) and also shared out any deficit among them.

---

[68] The document dated November 1956 entitled *Nuestra Razón: Manifiesto-Programa*, was in fact not written (by Mario Llerena) until mid-1957. See Draper, *Castroism*, 12.

[69] As qu., James, 528.

[70] See *Havana Post*, 20 November 1956.

[71] Llerena, MSS, p. 27. Llerena adds, however, that he personally then told Castro that 'the 26th of July Movement . . . should let itself off from whatever ties it might still have with political organizations of the past'. Castro then said, 'We'll come to that . . . but at the beginning we cannot put every card on the table.'

But the immediate effects of this were overcome by the revision of the 1953 convention, in order to increase Cuban participation in the world market by 150,000 tons (though not her share, which dropped from 41·7% to 40·9%), and by the Suez crisis in October. The consequences of this were to raise sugar prices advantageously in the winter of 1956–7 and to promise well for 1957. There was also in this winter a drop in European and Russian beet production.[72] Thus Castro's revolution began in earnest at the moment when, as in 1895 at the time of Martí's landing in Cuba, the short-term prospects for Cuban sugar capitalism were promising.

[72] *Cf. Estudio,* 98–9.

CHAPTER LXXIII

The Granma and the Sierra Maestra

The *Granma* left Tuxpan, Mexico, in the night of 24–5 November 1956, with eighty-two men on board.[1] As at Moncada, the majority were white Cuban townsmen, though more of them had a higher education than at Moncada.[2] Twenty out of the eighty-two had taken part in the attack at Moncada or Bayamo in 1953. There were four non-Cubans on board – Guevara, from Argentina; Gino Doné, an Italian;[3] Guillén, a Mexican; and the pilot Ramón Mejías del Castillo ('Pichirilo'), a Dominican who had been on the abortive Cayo Confites expedition. One Guatemalan, Julio Cáceres, a friend of Guevara's, was turned down because Castro did not want a 'mosaic of nationalities'.[4]

Castro, supreme commander, took the rank of major. There were beneath him three platoons of twenty-two men each under 'captains' Raúl Castro, Juan Almeida and José Smith.[5] Guevara was in charge of health. The captain of the ship was an ex-captain in the Cuban navy, Onelio Pino, seconded by ex-Lieutenant Roberto Roque.[6]

The expedition set off in high spirits, though some friends in Mexico refused to take part on the grounds that it was doomed.[7] They had on board two anti-tank guns, thirty-five rifles with telescopic sights, fifty-five Mendoza rifles, three Thompson light machine guns and forty light hand machine gun pistols. The voyage took seven days due to ill-direction: sea-sickness and overcrowding lowered the euphoria, but by 1 December

[1] It is no doubt a misprint that caused Guevara to speak of '83' people on board (see *Geografía de Cuba*, 574), though it is an odd error to have made; the same error, rather curiously, was made by 'General' Bayo, in his enumerated list of men on the *Granma*; he reckoned the pilot, Mejías del Castillo, twice (*Mi Aporte a la Revolución Cubana*, 167–9). Photographs of most of the *Granma* men were published in *Revolución*, 2 December 1959.

[2] Guevara was misleading when he said in 1960 that 'none of the first group who arrived in the *Granma* . . . had a past of worker or peasant' (*Obra Revolucionaria*, No. 24, 16 September 1960, 21).

[3] Erroneously referred to by Guevara as 'Lino' in his book.

[4] Guevara, *Pasajes*, 122.

[5] Castro's headquarters was composed of: Juan Manuel Márquez, Faustino Pérez, Antonio López, Jesús Reyes, Cándido González, Onelio Pino, Roberto Roque, Jesús Montané, César Gómez, Ramón Mejías del Castillo, and Rolando Moya (Sánchez Amaya evidence, as qu., *Revolución*, 26 January 1959). The three platoons were divided into three sections commanded by a lieutenant and a sergeant.

[6] Pino was the brother of Orquidea Pino, married to the Mexican oil engineer, Alfonso Gutiérrez, in whose house, in El Pedregal de San Angel, Castro and his friends often met.

[7] e.g. The Spanish painter, Víctor Trapote, father-in-law to Ramiro Valdés.

when the *Granma* approached the south-west corner of Oriente province, enthusiasm returned. On 30 November the men on board heard by radio the news of the rising against Batista in Santiago, led by Frank País, to coordinate with the *Granma*'s arrival.[8] None of the force had had much to do with the Communist party except for 'Ñico' López who had visited Communist exiles in Mexico, such as Ordoqui.

Frank País, then aged twenty-four, assisted by several veterans of the Moncada attack, such as Haydée Santamaría and Lester Rodríguez, had prepared this rising with care and much intelligence. His organization in Santiago was far the best of the 26 July Movement's agencies in Cuba, and he had also had success in establishing cells in other nearby cities of Oriente.[9] He had had much success too in attracting the middle-class youth of Santiago to the revolutionary cause, including many girls, among them Vilma Espín, an engineering student, daughter of the Bacardi lawyer in the city, who on return from studying in the U.S. saw Castro in Mexico and acted as a messenger for the movement.[10] As has been seen, Frank País was actually opposed to a rising in Santiago or in Cuba generally at the end of November and, before he told Castro this, he had put his point of view to a meeting of the 26 July provincial leaders in Havana in August. But they, though disposing of less strength and less men than País, were more foolhardy than he and he was over-ruled.[11] Action being decided upon, País made every precaution and procured a great quantity of arms – some of them coming from Trujillo by, no doubt, an error on the part of Dr Eufemio Fernández who had a shipment of *matériel* landed in the wrong place in Oriente.

Despite, however, País's visit to Castro in early November, communications and orders for the coordination of the activities of the 26 July Movement were confused. Having heard that Castro would arrive '*una noche sin luna del mes de noviembre*', there was nearly a mobilization on 15 November, a very dark night. However, on 27 November Duque de Estrada, the propaganda secretary in Santiago, received a telegram from Mexico: 'Book you asked for is out of print. Editorial Divulgación.' This meant that the rising was to be timed seventy-two hours after this.

País and his organization now carried out far the most effective strike

---

[8] Sánchez Amaya, 35; Pablo Díaz, *Bohemia*, 3 December 1961, gives another account.

[9] The 26 July in Oriente was organized as follows: Treasurer, Dr María Antonia Figueroa; Propaganda, Gloria Cuadras; *Sección Obrera*, Ramón Alvarez; *Acción*, Frank País, with Pepito Tey his deputy; provincial co-ordinator, Lester Rodríguez; professionals, Dr Baudilio Castellanos; secretary of demonstrations and propaganda, Arturo Duque de Estrada. There were some ten cells in Santiago with eight or ten men in each (Arturo Duque de Estrada, *Revolución*, 30 July 1963).

[10] She later married Raúl Castro.

[11] Vicente Cubillas, 'Los Sucesos del 30 de Noviembre de 1956', *Bohemia*, 6 December 1959.

yet against the Batista regime:[12] País, an amateur soldier who had once desired to enter the military academy,[13] showed great talent for military leadership in arranging what was in effect a series of morale-raising commando raids. At dawn on 30 November 1956 perhaps three hundred young men in olive green uniforms with 26 July red and black armbands, attacked the police headquarters, the Customs House and the harbour headquarters. (They had got some of the arms by raiding the Shooting Club of Santiago, and some from the Triple A organization.) The Customs House was successfully set on fire, the other two captured.[14] At the same moment another group of *fidelistas* fell on the Boniato prison and freed several political prisoners there.[15] A number of policemen and soldiers were killed. País then withdrew, leaving the city in a state of panic. The next day he struck again, with eighty-six men,[16] setting fire to the harbour headquarters, capturing public buildings and bringing civil life to a standstill. Batista suspended guarantees in this and in three other provinces and sent reinforcements of 280 well-trained men by airlift to Santiago under Colonel Pedro Barrera, a career officer who had helped plan the *golpe* of 10 March. A small group of the 26 July men were eventually caught and isolated in the chief secondary school, but the rebels were allowed to escape through a back door; faced by absurd odds, the rebellion died. In fact, País had really controlled the city on 30 November and 1 December and perhaps a mortar differently directed would have led to the fall of Moncada.[17] At the same moment, a vigorous demonstration of exiled Cubans of the Club Patriótico paraded before the U.N. building in New York.[18] There were also successful commando raids in Guantánamo, where Julio Camacho had bought or stolen arms from the U.S. base. He and thirty men took the Ermita barracks without difficulty because there

[12] Much of this derives from evidence of his brother Agustín País, to Raúl Chibás, in Chibás MSS. According to Chibás, País rejected one man, Luis Clergé, from joining the 26 July Movement on the ground that he was a '*simpatizante comunista*' but when he insisted he was not, he was given '*tareas subalternas*'.

[13] According to Vilma Espín, *Revolución*, 17 January 1959, 16. She went on: 'His ideas were always revolutionary. In the system of Martí, he found a fertile inspiration. He was a complete Martían.' He had been a full-time revolutionary since January.

[14] The different columns were led by: Jorge Sotús and Antonio Roca (Policía Marítima); Pepito Tey and Otto Parellada, plus 45 men (Policía Nacional); Instituto de Santiago (50-100 men under Lester Rodríguez, veteran of Moncada); railway line – Enzo Infante, Tara Dimitro and Agustín País; 10-20 *francotiradores* under Emiliano Díaz, near the Moncada barracks; and other groups led by Agustín Navarrete, and the Céspedes brothers.

[15] These included Captain Braulio Coronú, an ex-enemy of Castro in 1953; Carlos Fonseca; and Orlando Benítez.

[16] The estimate of Representative Miguel de León Royas was 500. Chibás has 300 (MSS) for the first day. Robert Taber, *M26, The Biography of a Revolution* (1961), gives 86 (p. 75). (See *Havana Post*, 4 December 1956.)

[17] See Barrera Pérez, *Bohemia Libre*, 13 August 1961; Pazos, *Cambridge Opinion*, 21; Taber, 70-4; *Verde Olivo*, 16 December 1962.

[18] *Havana Post*, 4 December. Its leader was Arnaldo Barrón.

was no one there. They gave it up when the army arrived. The Labour leaders, Louit and Antonio Torres, carried out a twenty-four-hour general strike at the same time.[19]

The Santiago rising, however, brought three deaths among the Fidelistas – Pepito Tey (País's second-in-command and ex-president of the students in Oriente), Otto Parellada (telephone worker, who had tried unsuccessfully at the last minute to join in at Moncada), and Antonio Alomá (an office worker), but it had rubbed home to the army that basically the sons of the middle class were in opposition, and that their parents would, even if they had not taken part, at least not give them up.[20] Not only fathers but also strangers sheltered revolutionaries whom they had never seen before, and hid their guns.[21]

On 2 December, rather late for coordination, the *Granma* reached Cuba, though not before the naval second-in-command, ex-Lieutenant Roque, had fallen overboard and had to be picked up.[22] The omen was bad. The *Granma*, instead of beaching at Niquero at a good landing stage where waiting friends could immediately have assisted them (and where they were expected), was forced because of delays to hit land at the Playa de los Colorados, near Belic; and this was not land but swamp, overhung with thick undergrowth, swarming with little crabs. The men had been originally to land at dawn on 30 November at Niquero. The group would take Niquero and advance on Manzanillo, while the uprising broke out at Santiago. Then there would follow sabotage and agitation to culminate in a general strike.[23] None of this was now possible. It was even impossible to get all ammunition and weapons on land. The becalmed yacht was seen from the air by a fighter, a naval frigate appeared and there was some machine-gunning in the void. An 'irresponsible comrade' led them the wrong way.[24] At last, after three hours, the column reached hard ground. A peasant, Angel Pérez, invited the rebels to share his food, but when they were about to eat, they heard firing. They moved on inland and, on the first day after landing, did not eat at all.[25] One group became temporarily lost. Still they pressed on. They saw various peasants, some of whom gave blessings to the Virgen del Cobre for them.[26]

The next two days, 2 and 3 December, the little army pressed on towards the Sierra through cane fields attached to Julio Lobo's *central Niquero*. They lacked provisions, their boots were new, and they

[19] Vicente Cubillas, 'Los Sucesos del 30 de Noviembre', *Bohemia*, 6 December 1959.
[20] See León Rojas, *Havana Post, loc. cit.*
[21] Franqui, 155.
[22] Sánchez Amaya, 53–4; Guevara, *loc. cit.*
[23] Faustino Pérez, *Bohemia*, 11 January 1959.
[24] Guevara, *loc. cit.*
[25] Faustino Pérez's account in René Ray, *op. cit.*, 25.
[26] Sánchez Amaya, 54.

foolishly sucked cane stalks to combat thirst. The lost group rejoined the main body; where were they going, what were they going to do? To establish a base in the hills, as Castro had contemplated after the failure of Moncada? And then? Who knew? Meantime, Havana was full of rumours. It was said that Fidel Castro had landed with forty men, had been attacked and had been killed. The United Press correspondent in Havana, Francis McCarthy, reported Castro killed, and confirmed the error later by saying that this was clear from passport and documents found on the body.[27] Mario Llerena gave $5 to the presumed widow of Faustino Pérez.[28] Batista on the other hand publicly denied that Castro had left Mexico.[29]

The people in Havana were next told by their morning papers that rebels in the hills numbered anything from 'forty-nine to two hundred', and that one thousand troops were looking for them; but Castro's sisters, Emma and Lidia, in Mexico, with a carelessness and exuberance over figures that might have been envied by Las Casas, were claiming their brother was in Camagüey with over 50,000 men.[30] In fact, the government's reaction was that when the local commander at Manzanillo, Caridad Fernández, had informed the commander in Oriente, Díaz Tamayo, the latter had reported to Tabernilla in Havana, and Tabernilla, instead of sending locally based Oriente men against Castro, had sent a crony of his, Captain Juan González; González had at first confined himself to an effective defence of the barracks at Manzanillo, in the hope that they would be attacked.[31] There was then a confusion between Fernández and González, resulting in the death of some soldiers by accident and the appointment of Colonel Cruz Vidal to succeed González.

Castro was in fact betrayed. The party's guide left them on the morning of 5 December and went to the nearest rural guard post.[32] On that day none of the expedition could walk any further. All lay up in a canefield at a place named Alegría de Pío, not far from the Sierra.

At nearly four o'clock in the afternoon of 5 December the rebels were in consequence surprised on the edge of the canefield. Some aircraft had flown overhead and their noise concealed that of the army's aproach. Castro's men imagined that the shooting derived from one of their own patrols. The firing increased. A unit of the army under the command of Cruz Vidal was in fact less than a hundred yards away. The 26 July men returned fire. Great confusion followed, and Castro

[27] See *Havana Post*, 4 December 1956.
[28] Llerena, MSS, p. 35.
[29] *Loc. cit.*
[30] *Havana Post*, 5 December 1956.
[31] Barrera Pérez, *Bohemia Libre*, 16 August 1961.
[32] Guevara, *Pasajes*, 8.

and his headquarters' staff withdrew. Almeida, in command of one platoon, could not find anyone to give orders.[33] The withdrawal did not become general till about six o'clock. Castro attempted to re-group on the other side of the boundary line of the canefield, but too late. The army either set the canefield alight or it became alight due to incendiary bombing. Several men of the 26 July surrendered, to be immediately shot. Others were maltreated, though not as badly as were the prisoners of Moncada. A total of twenty-four seem to have been killed either in the fight or immediately after.[34] Some were captured but survived, to be tried later. Others escaped, some wounded, in separate little groups, all making for the jungle-covered mountains. They left apparently only one man killed on the other side.[35]

Two of the group who were taken prisoner, Mario Fuentes and José Díaz, gave to Colonel Ramón Cruz Vidal, the army commander, and then to the rest of Cuba, a description of the expedition:[36] the former even accused Castro of wounding him for wishing to surrender.

The men fleeing from Alegría de Pío found it hard to re-assemble. Some did not wish to do so; a peasant of the neighbourhood, Guillermo García, found some 'flying like rabbits'; one (unarmed) man wept, 'Why did I come?' (his wife was peacefully in Mexico).[37] Several groups made their way to safety for the time being; one was led by Guevara (wounded), and consisted of the mulatto Almeida, Ramiro Valdés, an older Spaniard 'veteran of the Spanish war', Rafael Chao, and Reinaldo Benítez;[38] Sánchez Amaya led another, consisting of six men.[39] Fidel Castro was with two others only, Universo Sánchez and Faustino Pérez.[40] Raúl Castro found himself with Efigenio Ameijeiras, Ciro Redondo and René Rodríguez.[41] Camilo Cienfuegos wandered round with 'Pancho' González and Pablo Hurtado.[42] Finally there was a group consisting of Calixto Morales, Calixto García, Carlos Bermúdez, Julio Díaz and Luis Crespo,[43] who later

[33] Sánchez Amaya, 65–73; Guevara, *Pasajes*, 9.
[34] *Cf.* the list in *Bayo*, 167.
[35] *Havana Post*, 7 December 1956.
[36] *Ibid.*, 8 December 1956.
[37] G. García to Franqui (Franqui, 71).
[38] Guevara, *Pasajes*, 10–11; Guillermo García speaks of finding Almeida, Che, Chao and 'Pancho' Gonzáles (Francqui, 71).
[39] Norberto Godoy, Enrique Camara, René Heinte, Mario Chaves, J. Capote and Raúl Suárez (Sánchez Amaya, 74 ff.).
[40] Faustino Pérez and René Ray, 28. *Cf.* U. Sánchez in Franqui, 39 ff.
[41] René Rodríguez, *Verde Olivo*, 2 December 1962. Ameijeiras said that a sixth member of this group was César Gómez; he gave himself up (Franqui, 3).
[42] Guevara, *Souvenirs de la Guerre Révolutionnaire*, 40 (this French edn, ed. Maspero, 1967, is more complete than the Havana edition of these memoirs, *Pasajes*). Guillermo García says that Cienfuegos came separately with Reinaldo Benítez and 'Aguilasta' (?) and another peasant who worked with him and later joined. Fajardo omitted Cienfuegos from the list.
[43] Faustino Pérez, *loc. cit.* Pérez actually said Raúl Díaz. See Crespo's account in *Revolución*, 23 July 1962.

joined Guevara. Thirteen men also gathered under Juan Manuel Márquez.

Of these groups, Sánchez Amaya and his friends wandered desperately in the forest for several days, thirsty and hungry, before reaching the sea; three gave themselves up and were killed; the other four made their way to Niquero and eventually to Havana.[44] Juan Manuel Márquez and his group gave themselves up and were mostly shot.[45] Despite napalm bombing of the forests, those still at large were facing the enemies of nature as much as Colonel Cruz Vidal. José Ponce drank his own urine.[46] Desperately, these survivors sought something edible among the trees, but found nothing except an occasional parasite plant, in which there was a residue of water. They ate herbs, occasional raw corn, or crabs.[47] Guevara attempted to draw water from a rock with his asthma apparatus and he and his group narrowly avoided asking for succour at a house where the health of Batista's army was being drunk.[48] Castro, alone with his two men, sucked cane stalks[49] and remained several days hidden in a cane field. They got some food from a peasant and carried enough away to keep them for a day or two. One peasant bought them food gratuitously and one of his sons, Guillermo García, joined them and led them towards the Sierra Maestra.[50] They were hidden for some days in the farms of Marcial Averiches and Mongo Pérez, brother of Cresencio Pérez, a lorry driver on Lobo's estate (uncle of García), who backed Castro, who had been looking for Castro for days and who now helped with his sons to gather together the remnants of the *Granma* men. Thus Raúl Castro's group of five men was able to meet with Castro on 17 December near the farm of Hermes Caldero.[51] Eventually, Almeida's group too discovered the whereabouts of Castro, and, leaving most of such arms as they had preserved, moved towards that place on 19 December. Guevara with his group were directed to Castro by several peasants, including an Adventist, Argelio Rosabal, Carlos Mas, and others.[52] The remaining Fidelistas in the

[44] Sánchez Amaya, *loc. cit.*

[45] Du Bois, 142–3.

[46] Franqui, 35.

[47] Guevara, in Núñez Jiménez, 575.

[48] Guevara, *Souvenirs*, 42.

[49] Universo Sánchez to Franqui, 42.

[50] To Lee Lockwood in 1965, Guillermo García (then a major) recalled 'I met Fidel for the first time on the twelfth of December ... Fidel said "Are we already in the Sierra Maestra?" I said, "yes." "Then the revolution has triumphed," he said.' (Lockwood, 52.)

[51] Franqui, 37, 75. Caldero is now a major in the Army. He was afterwards a guide in the Sierra.

[52] Guevara, *Souvenirs*, 43–4. Guevara's group consisted in the end of 'Pancho' González, Ramiro Valdés, Almeida, and himself, with Cienfuegos, Chao and Benítez following some way behind. Pablo Hurtado, who had originally been with Guevara, stayed behind ill at one of the peasants' houses being exhausted by the days of marching, and the hunger and thirst. He afterwards gave himself up.

Sierra thus came together. Cresencio Pérez was a curious figure to find later established as one of the founding fathers of the successful revolution, since he was a bandit more than a radical, a common criminal believed to have committed murder and reputedly father of eighty illegitimate children up and down the Sierra Maestra.

This re-assembly was chiefly due to the help of Cresencio Pérez and various men who worked with him, such as Guillermo García, and Manuel Fajardo, who also did much collecting together of rifles and other weapons. There were apparently fifteen of Castro's original followers together: Fidel and Raúl Castro, Guevara, Universo Sánchez, Faustino Pérez, Ramiro Valdés, Efigenio Ameijeiras, Camilo Redondo, Armando Rodríguez, René Rodríguez, Reinaldo Benítez, Calixto García, Calixto Morales, Chao ('veteran of the Spanish war') and Morán 'El Gallego'.[53] Castro then addressed these men, 'With the same vehemence which he would have done before a large political audience in the Central Park in Havana. He assured them that they had triumphed in the first stage of this adventure. He communicated to them that he did not have the least doubt that in the long run victory would be theirs . . . all left convinced of the strength of their position and the confidence of obtaining victory in a long run or the short . . .'[54]

---

[53] Carlos Bermúdez and 'Pancho' González seem to have dropped out at the last minute. It is remarkable how none of the participants who have written of these events agree on the exact names of those taking part. There may at one moment in early December have been only twelve men in the Sierra around Fidel Castro, as invariably argued since, no doubt to suggest Christ-like parallels, but this could only have been for a very short time before the survivors of the disaster at Alegría de Pío had caught up with one another. Camilo Cienfuegos in an interview published in *Revolución*, 4 January 1959, spoke of 'only eight men being left' after Alegría de Pío. Ameijeiras in another interview published 8 January 1959 said, 'of the eighty-two men who embarked on the *Granma* there remained not twelve – as Batista said – but nine' (*Revolución*, 8 January 1959). Castro himself spoke of twelve men several times in his speech of 8 January 1959 at Campamento Columbia (*Discursos para la Historia* (1959), 16) and this number crops up in the Circular de Organización by the National Directorate of the 26 July Movement of 18 March 1958. Castro also mentions it in his denunciation of the Miami group (see e.g. the version in Guevara's reminiscences, 227). Guevara in an account of the battles of the Sierra published in 1960, in the *Geografía de Cuba* by Antonio Núñez Jiménez (575), spoke of 'some seventeen' men reunited in early December and, a few lines later, a *quincena* – 'about fifteen'. Universo Sánchez, one of the men with Castro all the time after Alegría, repeated that there were twelve in 1963 (Franqui, 38). Faustino Pérez, in an account to René Ray, listed sixteen by name: these were Fidel and Raúl Castro, Guevara, Faustino Pérez, himself, Valdés, Sánchez, Ameijeiras, Armando Rodríguez, René Rodríguez, Cienfuegos, Almeida, Calixto García, Calixto Morales, Benítez and Julio Díaz (Ray, 28). To these however should be added the names of Redondo, Chao and Morán while that of Raúl Díaz should be omitted (see Guevara, *Pasajes*, 23). But the number of twelve has taken a firm hold over the Revolution's mythology and Carlos Franqui has even written a book, *Cuba: Le Livre de Douze*. In mid-February, at the time of the visit of Herbert Matthews, there probably were twelve *Granma* men for several weeks – since Faustino Pérez, René and Armando Rodríguez, Calixto García, Calixto Morales and Benítez had by then left; see below, p. 919. But several peasants were by then an integral part of the Movement.

[54] This is the account of Universo Sánchez as related to or by, Raúl Chibás (MSS), which I have preferred to other accounts of this occasion.

Back in Havana, the varying stories told of their fortunes in the Sierra had a curiously mixed effect. Was Castro dead or alive? Some Liberals, for instance a mother of four young sons in Havana, were secretly pleased at the United Press news that Castro was dead: sad for Cuba, she thought, but perhaps good for her and the lives of her sons.[55] The papers were as usual full of comforting statements by *Batistiano* businessmen and politicians describing good economic prospects: good production and investment levels everywhere.[56] Yet political confidence was weak: the death of the aged Don Cosme de la Torriente on 8 December symbolically removed, a week after Castro landed in Oriente, the strongest protagonist of a policy of compromise.[57] The regime and the opposition drifted daily further apart. During December the rumours that Castro was still alive began to trickle into Havana. A legend grew: Castro's survival from yet another terrible clash suggested a myth of immortality. As yet nothing was clearly known. The members of the 26 July Movement in Havana and Santiago knew nothing for certain, though they not unnaturally suspected that since the army had not exhibited Castro's body, he must be alive – a feeling of confidence which increased when Batista himself began to throw doubt on the idea that Castro had even left Mexico. Who therefore would not take the risk and go and join him: *Con Fidel en las montañas?*

Castro and his reunited followers had in truth moved further and further away from Alegría de Pío, being continually helped by Cresencio Pérez, another of whose cattlemen, Manuel Fajardo, joined Castro at this time, with the peasant Guillermo García.[58] According to one account Cresencio Pérez offered Castro a hundred men but Castro rejected them because they had no arms and accepted provisionally only fifteen, most of whom were for the time being only auxiliary or half-time helpers.[59] The slightly enlarged group marched at night and slept by day. Discussion was intense, Castro taking great interest in everything said and seen.[60] Guevara later recorded:

> Hunger, what is truly known as hunger, none of us had ever known before and then we began to know it . . . and so many things became very clear [i.e. about the condition of the peasants]. We who in the beginning punished severely anyone who took any animal from a rich farmer, one day took ten thousand head of cattle and we said

[55] A remark to me of Sra Sara de Pazos.
[56] See below, p. 909, for more detailed inquiry.
[57] Not long before he died, Haydée Santamaría, on behalf of Castro, had visited him and asked him for 'one more patriotic gesture' by committing suicide (evidence of Elena Mederos).
[58] Franqui, 77.
[59] Faustino Pérez, *Bohemia*, 11 January 1959.
[60] Guevara in *Geografía*, 576.

simply to the peasants, 'Eat.' And the peasants, for the first time in many years, and some for the first time in their lives, ate beef.[61]

This was therefore a formative period for the revolutionaries, and they learned much about the country where they had already begun a revolution. Before, Castro and his men

> ... did not know a single peasant in the Sierra Maestra and, further, the only information we had of [it] ... was what we had learnt in geography books ... [We] might have known that the [rivers] Cauto, Contramaestre and Yara rose there – but what we knew of the Yara was the song and nothing more ... [nevertheless] the bands of rebels immediately met with support from large numbers ...[62]

By now indeed the problem of food supplies was almost solved, since Cresencio Pérez and his comrades knew peasants who could sell or give a modest food supply, and who could tell them where to find water or where to get natural supplies.

> What did we meet in the Sierra Maestra? [Castro later went on in describing these days.] We met there the first peasants who wished to join us, some very scattered workers [*salteados*]. First the disappointments, the dispersion; some peasants helped us to regroup the remains of these forces. This group ... helped us meet each other in the Sierra ... What was the situation of the greater part of peasants at that moment? First, a great terror of the Army ... second, they could scarcely know that our group of badly dressed, hungry men, with very few arms, could defeat a force which moved in lorries, trains, aeroplanes ... We had often to move ... without being seen by the population ... because always in a township ... of 100 people ... there was a *Batistiano* ... and then the army would come in.[63]

---

[61] *Obra Revolucionaria*, No. 24 of 1960 (24 September 1960), 21.
[62] *Ibid.*, No. 46 of 1961, 17. The song runs:

> Por la orilla floreciente
> Que baña el río de Yara
> Donde dulce fresca y clara
> Se desliza la corriente
> Donde brilla el sol ardiente
> De nuestra abrasada zona
> Y un cielo hermoso corona
> La selva, el monte y el prado
> Iba un guajiro montado
> Sobre una yegua trotona.

[63] *Loc cit.*

It should be appreciated that it was clearly necessary for the rebels to buy the help of some of the peasants, and not inexpensively. Thus Faustino Pérez told Carrillo on 24 December 1956 that 'to attract peasants it was necessary to pay double the value of everything they bought from them . . .'[64]

The area of the Sierra Maestra is the wildest part of all Cuba. It includes the highest mountains of the island, including Pico Turquino, the Blue Mountain, which rises to 8,600 feet. It is an area of great beauty which has often inspired poets. Manuel Navarro Luna, for example, in his *Poemas Mambises* twenty-five years before, has written:

> The Blue Mountain
> And River Cauto!
> Sinews of the eternity
> Which begat us . . .
> The Mountain warms us with its great heart
> Splendid son of excellence and infinity . . .

This is the southernmost part of Cuba, and its vegetation and altitude resemble less Cuba than the other more hilly islands of the Antilles, of whose central range the Sierra Maestra is topographically the continuation; this range is indeed a contrast with the rest of the island. These mountains are wooded, the vegetation ranging from coarse cactus on the lower and dryer slopes to beautiful rain forests of tree ferns on the higher ones. The Sierra runs along the coast, to which its slopes descend precipitously, though interrupted by a curious natural terracing, each step being some 600 feet or more. The coast itself is indented, though without the offshore keys which lie off the north and south-west coasts of Cuba. The Sierra Maestra is about a hundred miles in length and twenty to thirty miles or so at its widest. The area is bounded by the sea in the south, the coastal plain of Niquero–Campechuela–Manzanillo in the west, and the central highway in the north and east, though in practice the mountains continue northwards as far as the Río Cauto and its valley. In the east also the mountains continue, becoming known as the Sierra del Cobre, the copper mountains, before falling to the central highway again and to Santiago and its bay.

The Sierra Maestra was a poor area. From time immemorial these lands had both belonged to a small group of families and had been neglected. Boundaries were obscure. Most of those who actually lived there were squatters without title or security to their land: these *precaristas* represented only 8 % to 10 % of the farmers of Cuba, but over

[64] Carrillo, MSS, p. 32.

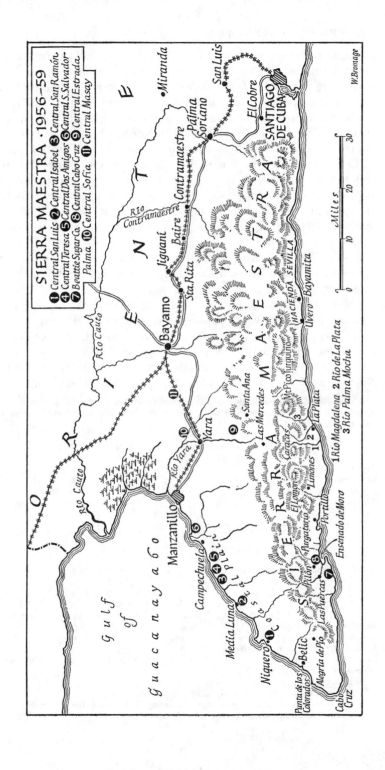

SIERRA MAESTRA · 1956–59

1 Central San Luis 2 Central Isabel 3 Central San Ramón.
4 Central Teresa 5 Central Dos Amigos 6 Central S. Salvador
7 Beattie Sugar Co. 8 Central Cabo Cruz 9 Central Estrada
Palma 10 Central Sofia 11 Central Masay

1 Rio Magdalena 2 Rio de La Plata
3 Rio Palma Mocha

Miles
0   10   20   30

W. Bromage

two-fifths of the *precaristas* were in Oriente.[65] Over half the population in the Sierra had had no education at all.[66] Few children of school age were going to school.[67] In all the area, the number of consensual marriages was nearly double the number of legal ones.[68] About half those in the rural parts of the area were illiterate, more especially at the western, Niquero end.[69] Unemployment, though high, apparently did not reach the levels found elsewhere in Oriente: 4% in Bayamo, 8% in El Cobre, only 1·4% in Jiguaní, but (because of the mills in the area and hence the seasonal opportunities and difficulties) in Niquero – 16%.[70] The majority of persons in the area were, of course, employed in agriculture. Nearly all the houses were *bohíos*, with earth floors; refrigerators, running water, baths and electric light were almost unknown.[71]

The area was increasing rapidly in population: thus the districts of Bayamo had grown between 1943 and 1953 by 60%, Cobre by 25%, Jiguaní by 35% and Niquero by over 30%.

The nearest towns to the Sierra Maestra were in the extreme east. First came Santiago with a population of 160,000; then there was El Cobre, founded by the Spaniards in 1558 as a centre for copper mining (hence the name) and known for its famous black wooden Virgin (allegedly found in the seventeenth century by two Indians and a Negro in the Bay of Nipe). In 1958, its population was only a little over

[65] Agricultural Census of 1946. See Draper for discussion, though the Census of 1953 suggests that 45·7% of those with houses in the country paid no rent for them. Thus in the total rural area the situation was:

	Total houses	Own houses Both house and land	Own houses House only	Rented	No rent	Others
Bayamo	15,999	5,890	3,704	772	5,461	172
El Cobre	6,576	1,850	1,247	83	3,067	329
Jiguaní	9,214	3,315	1,715	375	3,337	472
Niquero	8,598	736	7,069	221	374	198

Not declared

Bayamo	334
El Cobre	70
Jiguaní	99
Niquero	163

[66] Taken from census figures for Niquero, Jiguaní, El Cobre and Bayamo.

[67] Thus:

	Age 5–9 At school	Age 5–9 Not at school	Age 10–14 At school	Age 10–14 Not at school	Age 15–19 At school	Age 15–19 Not at school
Bayamo	5,591	17,290	8,813	11,192	1,943	12,849
El Cobre	1,737	5,654	2,558	3,991	531	3,989
Jiguaní	3,028	8,944	4,717	6,140	901	7,104
Niquero	1,430	10,161	2,369	7,360	445	6,559

(Census of 1953, 116–117.)

[68] Figures in *ibid.*, 50.

[69] Figures in *ibid.*, 150; i.e. those over 10.

[70] *Ibid.*, 168; i.e. many of these were employed during the harvest in the sugar mills.

[71] Figures in *ibid.*, 247; *ibid.*, 251–2 for rural houses.

2,500. Palma Soriano, with 25,500 people, had had in 1860 160 sugar mills, though in the 1950s there were merely three. Between these were Jiguaní, an eighteenth-century Indian foundation, with 7,000 people, and Baire, the starting point of the 1895 revolt, with 4,000. Bayamo, 50 miles west, had 20,000. Manzanillo, on the coast, 30 miles beyond Bayamo, had over 40,000. Niquero, with its sugar mill,[72] was an old town founded in 1571, down the coast towards the point where the *Granma* came ashore; it had a population of little more than 7,000. Campechuela, between Niquero and Manzanillo, had 5,000 people. A little to the north of Niquero was Media Luna with its sugar mill *Isabel*, employing 3,000, and controlling nearly 70,000 acres. The western coast of the Sierra broadened to a plain of about thirty miles in the Manzanillo–Bayamo area. Along that coast, in the two municipalities, there were in fact six sugar *centrales*. Along the south coast was Pilón, also with a sugar mill,[73] with 2,500 people, but otherwise in the area of the Sierra Maestra there was no other place with a population larger than 1,000. Communications in the Sierra Maestra were bad. They consisted chiefly of long forest paths which the sun never reached.

Race in the 1950s seems to have been fairly balanced between black and white.[74] Niquero, with nominally the most white people in the area, was oddly enough the least literate. At the same time, many of those in the northern part of the area, especially those living round Jiguaní, had Indian blood, or perhaps were entirely Indian: the Yara valley is the most strongly Indian area left in Cuba and, interestingly enough, it claims to be the least race conscious.[75]

The sugar mills in the Niquero district were Cuban-owned, *Niquero* and *Pilón* belonging to Julio Lobo. Much of the eastern section of the Sierra Maestra consisted of *latifundios* such as the huge Hacienda Sevilla, owned by the Lebanese Babun brothers, cement makers and exporters of cedar and mahogany.[76] Such cultivation as there was was confined to the line of the rivers. Coffee was extensively grown and there were a number of charcoal burners whose economic position was highly precarious. The lower stretches at the eastern end of the Sierra produced vast stores of honey. On the extreme west of the area, near

---

[72] It employed 4,000 workers.

[73] Employing 1,650, with lands of 136 caballería and milling another 377.

[74]

	White	Black	Mixed	Yellow
Bayamo	52,538	9,968	33,598	20
El Cobre	8,983	10,357	18,590	224
Jiguaní	35,239	3,362	15,379	15
Niquero	31,923	3,861	19,750	15

[75] See comments by Núñez Jiménez, *Geografía*, 562; visited by the author in 1961.

[76] *Cf.* evidence in Playa Girón trial given by sons of one of the Babuns, Omar, Lancelot and Santiago, who joined the invading force in 1961, having worked before 1959 in Guatemala (*Playa Girón: Derrota del Imperialismo*, 4 vols (1961), IV, 124–33). The Babuns sold this estate in late 1957 for $M1 (see Lazo, 138).

Cabo Cruz, there were estates belonging to the old Céspedes family. Large estates also belonged to the Beattie Sugar Company, to Lobo's big New Niquero Sugar Company, to various members of the Castillo family, and to the Cape Cruz Company (which controlled the *centra Pilón*). The large estates were run by *mayorales*, whose main task was to try to restrict the persistent diminution of these lands of their employers by the *precaristas* – a task which led to perpetual gunfights and occasional deaths; the *mayorales* might burn down the *precaristas'* house who in turn might respond by murder. Each side had its known leaders and gangs of followers. Many regarded the Sierra Maestra as the last refuge for escaping criminals and in many ways indeed it resembled the Wild West before the American Civil War.

Such was the region into whose most remote fastnesses Cresencio Pérez, for years a leader with his sons of the *precaristas*, began on 25 December 1956 to lead Castro's men. A few days before, one member of the party, the Baptist student Faustino Pérez, left the Sierra with two peasant guides (Quique Escalona and Rafael Sierra) for Havana to establish contact with and reorganize the town supporters of the movement, to confirm that Castro was in fact still living,[77] and to try to ensure that all available arms in Havana and other cities were in fact sent to the Sierra – an instruction upon which Castro had continually to insist but which was not quickly enacted.[78] He had arrived by Christmas.

[77] Faustino Pérez, in René Ray, *op. cit.* Faustino Pérez came from a Protestant lower middle-class family in Las Villas, and had been in charge of the dispensary next to the first Presbyterian church in Havana where he had stored explosives for the MNR movement before joining Castro. See also another Pérez account in *Bohemia*, 30 November 1962.

[78] See discussion in Régis Debray, *Révolution dans la Révolution?* (1967), 77–8.

CHAPTER LXXIV

Herbert Matthews goes to the Sierra

Christmas Day 1956 was greeted traditionally by Habaneros; newspapers were full of advertisements for presents from El Encanto, the big department store: for $36 flights to Miami ('55 minutes of sheer pleasure, 5 swift flights daily'). Rancho Luna Restaurant, 'typically Cuban country-style thatched *bohío*', told its sophisticated clients that 324,000 chickens had been eaten there in the last three years. Americans bade farewell to various 'integral' members of their community and their assiduous wives (active members of the American Club, Rovers' Club, Women's Club and the 'egregious Book and Thimble' society). The 'lovely family of Mr and Mrs John Albert Ferreira, Sr, of *central Agramonte*, would pass Christmas at the home of their son-in-law and daughter, Mr and Mrs Clarence Bonstra, in Country Club'. 'The Great Christmas Story of Old' was told anew in pageant to hundreds of Americans and Cubans. The *Havana Post*, recalling the crises of Suez and Hungary during 1956, alluded to 'revolutionaries in Oriente', whom the armed forces were 'hoping to dominate with a minimum of loss of life', and announced confidently that 'even if we are forced to a military decision with Communist Russia, our strength in the final analysis will be our faith in Christ'. *El Mundo* said that 'terrorism and sabotage are to be condemned at all times but even more so now at Christmas time'. 'Choose Irish linen as a lasting and lovely souvenir of your Cuban pleasant vacation' carolled one advertisement, and 'Greetings in the name of Hatuey, the finest Cuban beer', exclaimed another.

But the spirit of Christmas, over-worked ghost of affluent societies, was in truth weak. Faustino Pérez, arriving in Havana from the Sierra, received $1,000 from Justo Carrillo for the Movement on Christmas night.[1] The 26 July Movement planned to strike during the holiday and a number of bombs went off, causing a blackout on Christmas Eve in several towns of Oriente. Batista's army also struck: Colonel Fermín Cowley, commander at Holguín in northern Oriente, and, like so many of Batista's supporters, a cell member of ABC in the early 1930s,[2] gave orders for a number of reprisals. Twenty-two men accordingly were

---

[1] Justo Carrillo, MSS, p. 32.
[2] Phillips, 333. He had also been Batista's investigator in the case of corruption by Tabernilla, etc.

killed in different parts of Oriente, some members of the 26 July Movement, some Ortodoxos, some Auténticos – all members of the opposition.[3] Two were hanged and their bodies left on trees outside Holguín.

The scandal was great. Newspaper proprietors of leading papers called on all to 'preserve society', not excluding from condemnation the 'violent repression' of terrorism, and offering to mediate.[4] But this had no effect. New Year's Eve was the signal for further violence: the 26 July placed bombs in several public places; leading members of the 26 July Movement carefully laid bombs in the huge Tropicana night club, blowing off the arm of a seventeen-year-old girl, injuring the daughter of an ex-police chief, Martha Pino Donoso, and causing other damage.[5] Bombs were set off in Santiago. The army killed at least another three people in Oriente and two in Las Villas.[6]

At this time among the leaders of the 26 July Movement in Havana was Javier Pazos. He and others, children of the men of the revolution in 1933, such as Leila Sánchez and Raulito Roa (children of Aureliano Sánchez Arango and Raúl Roa), with others such as the surrealist painter Manuel Couzeiro, the law student leader Marcelo Fernández and Luis de la Cuesta, were prominent members of a group of young intellectuals in their twenties accustomed to meet in the committee rooms of the Cuban chapter of the Congress for Cultural Freedom, then headed by Mario Llerena, an older and more experienced political writer. The movement of these people towards Castro in 1956 had been one of the 26 July Movement's most important intellectual accretions to date.[7]

The tragic events of the New Year did not seem to trouble the mayor of New York, Robert Wagner, who passed the New Year in Havana. 'Such visits as yours contribute very substantially,' Batista assured him in English, 'to the good relations between our countries'. Mutual expressions of esteem and good jokes accompanied Mayor Wagner on his way to Varadero.[8] Isolated events of this sort might not have had much consequence, and even an accumulation of them, under the persuasion of Batista's public relations chief, Chester Arthur, are hard to pin down to any specific consequence. But they continued to give the impression that official North America was intimate with official Cuba: the enemies of the latter began easily to seem the enemies of the former. If Mayor Wagner seemed happy to receive the Order of Céspedes at the

[3] See names in *Havana Post*, 27 December 1956.
[4] See papers, 29 and 30 December.
[5] Evidence of Javier Pazos. See also *Havana Post*, 2 January 1957 and 4 January 1957.
[6] See *ibid.*, 2 January 1957.
[7] Llerena, MSS, 39–40; evidence of Javier Pazos.
[8] *Havana Post*, 2 January 1957.

hands of President Batista it seemed inevitable that Mayor Wagner should approve of President Batista. The U.S. assistant secretary of commerce, General Thomas Wilson, was happily present when Wagner received his decoration. The same point seemed hammered home even further with the award of the Cuban military medal to Colonel Isaacson, retiring head of the U.S. military mission. North Americans were not alone in these visits: Yael, daughter of General Dayan of Israel, had exchanged a Hebrew Bible for a pure silk Cuban flag with General Tabernilla in October 1956.[9]

The same moral applied when it became known that U.S. investment in late 1956 was on a high level; a total of $M357 new private investments were made in the years 1952 to 1957.[10] Texaco and Shell had invested in Cuba $M40 in 1956. Some such investments were made with joint Cuban and U.S. capital and as usual it was difficult sometimes to know which was which. Some Cuban firms had U.S. investors, some U.S. firms Cuban shareholders. Cuba still represented a far too tempting field for U.S. business: the Cuban economy in January 1957 was at record level, while the average Cuban income per head had risen to $400, or a total of $M2,400 – a near *per capita* maximum for Latin America. National credit stood high, due to recent prompt repayments of loans. Building in Havana and nearby, public and private, radiated its usual wild but unreliable air of well-being. North American investors did not observe that the political crisis had worsened while the dictatorship masked the effects of it. In January, furthermore, it seemed that the fears of the traditional weapon of cane-burning by Castro's men or others during the harvest had proved groundless. Gangsterism had declined, while U.S. brokers noted with satisfaction that Batista's relations with Trujillo had improved. The Cuban Minister of Agriculture even approvingly visited a livestock exhibition in Santo Domingo so there were fewer fears now of an invasion from gangsters based there. Castro's rebellion, if indeed it survived at all,[11] seemed, in Wall Street, in no way likely to pose an economic threat. U.S. business continued to hold conventions in Havana, the businessmen finding the high life, the brothels and the blue films even more exciting than what was available in Pittsburgh, and superficially more exciting than even the old days in Havana: the new hotels had an incomparably gilded luxury and splendour. Cuban ministers continued to be received in Washington: Santiago Rey, the Defence minister, went there in January 1957 as an official guest. He and other Cuban ministers absorbed without much

9 *Ibid.*, 3 January 1957.

10 HAR, January 1957. Britain too was involved. The *Board of Trade Journal* in January assured British investors that excellent opportunities lay ahead in Cuba.

11 The Mexican paper, *Ultimas Noticias*, stated that Castro had returned to Mexico on 5 January.

difficulty the most slipshod of U.S. politicians' stock denunciations of Communism, and denounced Castro, Prío, even Trujillo and other enemies, regularly as 'communistic'.[12]

But the Cuban police did not behave as if it had conquered its enemy. On 2 January, while the nation had still not digested the vile Christmas and New Year news, four youths – one of whom, William Soler, was only fourteen years old – were found killed in an empty building site in Santiago. They had apparently been arrested as suspects for the 26 July activities over the holidays and been tortured. In consequence, on 4 January a procession of five hundred women, headed by the mother of Soler, dressed in black, moved slowly through the streets of Santiago with a banner: '*Cesen los asesinatos de nuestros hijos!*', 'Stop the murders of our sons.' The press leaders' offers of mediation were supported by all varieties of persons – presidents of the coffee merchants, Rotarians, Freemasons, chambers of commerce, the Havana University Council – most of whom coupled their appeals for mediation with a denunciation of terrorism. However, the vice-president, Guas Inclán, rather spoiled the impression by welcoming the press bloc's attempt and saying that its chief, Cristóbal Díaz, was 'a successful businessman and a friend of President Batista'.[13]

Sporadic violence continued. Bombs were placed at least once a week somewhere in Cuba during January 1957. Arrests were frequently made and what happened to those held was not always clear. The house of Colonel Orlando Piedra, chief of the SIM, in 5th Avenue, Miramar, was fired on from a moving car on the night of 13 January. Castro's mother appears at this point to have appealed to Batista to save her son's life by letting him and his friends escape to an embassy.[14] On 15 January constitutional guarantees (already suspended in Oriente) were dropped throughout the island.[15]

Castro's force, regrouped in the Sierra, still about twenty men, now reappeared. On 14 January it had reached the river Magdalena, where the men washed and prepared for an attack on La Plata barracks at the mouth of the little river of that name.[16] At this point they apparently had twenty-three weapons – nine rifles with telescopic lenses, five semi-automatic rifles, four rifles with bolts, two Thompson machine guns,

[12] The *Havana Post*, a typical expression of the views of the U.S. colony in Cuba, reported as late as 16 February 1957 that 'McCarthy is a controversial figure but he is also a U.S. Senator and a patriotic citizen'.

[13] *Ibid.*, 6 January 1957. Cristóbal Díaz (born 1894) was an architect and owner of *El País*. He was also founder of Radio Habana.

[14] Army statement, 1 March 1957.

[15] This involved the appointment of censors to cover each paper. See list in press, 16 January 1957. The *Havana Post* and, one may assume, the U.S. colony in general approved, denouncing terrorism and saying that it must be Communist inspired and not the work of the known opposition leaders (see *Havana Post*, 16 January 1957).

[16] Guevara, 12.

two machine pistols and one 16-bore air gun.[17] Several more peasants had become loosely attached to them (Edward Díaz, Manuel and Sergio Acuña).[18] They had as a guide a peasant named Melquíades Elías. During the day they met two peasants, relations of the guide, one of whom as a precaution they held prisoner. On 15 and 16 January they carefully watched the barracks, and took two more prisoners, one of whom said that there were fifteen soldiers within. Another told them details of the local land-holding – how the Laviti family held a huge semi-feudal estate maintained against *precaristas* by three notorious tough *mayorales*.

Soon afterwards one of these agents, 'Chicho' Osorio, *mayoral* of the El Macho estate, approached on a mule, accompanied by a little black boy, and drunk.[19] Universo Sánchez called on Osorio to halt in the name of the rural guard: Osorio immediately answered 'Mosquito' – the password.[20] Castro was able to persuade him that he was himself colonel of the army looking for the rebels. Osorio told Castro how sluggardly the troops were in the barracks at La Plata and gave a good deal of other information, including the opinion that if Castro were caught he would be immediately murdered. Castro then placed his men ready for a night attack on 16–17 January, and divided his men into four groups, led respectively by Julio Díaz, Castro himself, Raúl Castro and Juan Almeida. At the moment the attack began, 2.40 a.m. on 17 January 1957, 'Chicho' Osorio, the unjust steward, was shot, still drunk.[21]

The principle of the attack was, in the dark, to fire a heavy volley from several sides and then to demand surrender. With the barracks surprised, this worked well: several houses at the side of the barracks were also set on fire by Guevara and Lucio Crespo. The Fidelistas afterwards stormed the place and the soldiers surrendered. Altogether 1,500 rounds had been fired.[22] The Batistianos had lost two dead, and five wounded; three prisoners were taken. Another crooked steward, Honorio, and the other soldiers fled. Castro lost no one. He ordered

---

[17] *Loc. cit.*

[18] Colonel Barrera, the Batistiano commander, later fairly accurately referred to the Acuñas as famous bandits, along with Julio Guerrero and Chico Mendoza, the latter being a semi-bandit leader and who however fought the *precaristas* on behalf of the proprietors.

[19] The accusation later lodged against Osorio was that he had used the government's anxiety after the landing of the *Granma* to dislodge various peasants on the pretext that they were Fidelistas (see Castro, *Discursos para la historia*, 25; Castro on Television, 9 January 1959).

[20] Franqui, *loc. cit.*

[21] This was the occasion of which Castro later spoke to the journalist Jules Dubois: 'When we arrived at the Sierra Maestra we executed a ranch foreman who had accused tenant farmers of being pro-rebel and who had increased holdings of his landlord from ten acres to four hundred by taking the land of those whom he denounced.' (Jules Dubois, *Fidel Castro: rebel – liberator or dictator?* (1959), 145). In a denunciation of the 26 July for 'atrocities', two farmers later spoke of 'Chicho' as an 'army guide'. (See *Havana Post*, 19 June 1957.)

[22] Guevara, 17. *Cf.* Franqui, 32–3.

the barracks to be burned. Three of the wounded soldiers died. The others were left behind in the care of prisoners when the Fidelistas returned to the jungle.

This victory enabled Castro to add to his supplies Springfield rifles, a new Thompson machine gun, a few thousand rounds, and various cartridge belts, firewood, clothes, food and knives. One of the prisoners later joined Castro's forces. Castro freed all the army's peasant prisoners and made off towards the next river, the Palma Mocha, a few kilometres nearer the Pico Turquino. On their way they observed the melancholy sight of an exodus of peasants from the hills. The previous day the overseer and the rural guard had told the *precaristas* of the region that the air force was going to bomb the Sierra in order to get rid of the rebels, and they should leave if they valued their lives. Since the government did not know that the Fidelistas were in the region and since there was no air attack the next day, this was evidently an attempt by the overseers to drive away the peasants in their own interests.[23]

> Almost every group of peasants whom we met [Castro recalled five years later] had some complaint. Naturally, we began a political attempt to win over the peasants ... They worked in the plain fifteen days, gathered fifteen or twenty pesos, bought salt and a little fat and then returned to their little coffee farms with them. The Agricultural Bank only gave money for credit to peasants who were already well off. When the rural guard passed by such peasants' houses you can be certain that at the very least he helped himself to a fine chicken; and the merchants who sold foods to the peasants sold dear. There were no schools.[24] These were the conditions that we met in the Sierra – the objective conditions ... [of revolution].

On 19 January, meanwhile, the press carried the false news that 'eight rebels and two members of the armed forces had been killed in a clash at La Plata'.[25] On 1 March, however, the army announced that in fact twelve men had been killed in this fight – while 'forty rebels' also had been killed, and twenty prisoners taken afterwards:[26] that is, rather more than double the total number of rebels at large were said to have been casualties – a useful criterion, no doubt, to judge the claims of other governments in similar wars.

Castro was in fact now heading northwards towards a small stream known as Arroyo del Infierno. Calculating that the army would pursue him, he prepared a simple ambush, though the effect was nearly spoiled by Guevara, who, wearing a Batistiano uniform captured at La Plata,

---

[23] Guevara, 17–18; Castro, 2 December 1961, *Obra Revolucionaria*, No. 46 of 1961, 22.
[24] This was definitely the case in respect of this area.
[25] *Havana Post*, 19 January 1957.
[26] *Ibid.*, 2 March 1957.

was fired on by Cienfuegos. Eventually a small troop of Batistianos, part of a patrol led by Lieutenant Sánchez Mosquera (as part of a recent new command of 100 men under Major Casillas) appeared, looking at two *bohíos* in the centre of a glade in which Castro's men had specifically avoided sheltering – remembering how Castro himself had been caught in a *bohío* after Moncada in 1953. Castro fired the first shot and killed one man, and three more Batistianos were also killed, one by Guevara. Afterwards both sides withdrew, the Fidelistas capturing one rifle, a Garand and a cartridge belt. This limited success taught Castro to attempt to attack vanguards of patrols, for 'without a vanguard there can be no army'.[27] The Fidelistas discovered later that Sánchez Mosquera had also shot a Negro peasant who had refused to act as their guide.[28]

Castro next returned south-west, to where they had been before La Plata, in the region of a densely wooded hill known as Caracas. They found the situation changed, for the army had since been through and Major Casillas had driven out many *precaristas*. Castro found only empty *bohíos*. He was rejoined at this point by a peasant, Eutimio Guerra, who had acted as a guide earlier, and after La Plata had gone down from the hills to visit his mother. In truth, he had been captured by the army and had agreed, for a fee of $10,000 and an army rank, to kill Castro. He was a well-known bandit leader, like Cresencio Pérez a defender of the *precaristas* against the *mayorales* and their henchmen.[29]

At this moment there was some despondency among the Fidelistas: various members of the party were demanding that they should be allowed to go into the cities. Castro announced a death penalty for insubordination, desertion and defeatism. Guevara drily commented that, as yet, the rebels lacked 'a spirit forged in struggle and ... a clear ideological conscience'.[30] All had been demoralized by the appearance over their heads the day before of a squadron of fighters which machine-gunned the forest close to them. They had not known that Eutimio Guerra was actually in one aeroplane, directing the attack.[31] In these circumstances, Castro took the critically dangerous but actually fundamental decision, in late January, to send René Rodríguez to Havana to tell his followers in the capital that he would be willing to see a

[27] Guevara, 91.

[28] *Ibid.*, 18–20; Núñez Jiménez, 576–7, for his earlier account. Barrera Pérez, on the other hand, then the commander in the Sierra Maestra, said that he lost no men during his time in command from 29 January to 16 April. This must be false.

[29] Barrera Pérez, *Bohemia Libre*, 20 August 1961. Barrera Pérez says that Guerra told Casillas that Castro's forces were divided into two – one led by the Castros, of 120 men, the other led by Guevara, of 80. Nothing could be further from the truth and Guerra probably helped Castro by this misinformation far more than he harmed him.

[30] Guevara, 24.

[31] Barrera Pérez confirms (*loc. cit.*).

foreign press correspondent, for with the Cuban press under censorship there would be no point in seeing a Cuban.[32]

The air attack had caused depression and dispersion of the Fidelistas. One peasant, Sergio Acuña, the bandit, abandoned the group, while his brother, Manuel, with Calixto García and Calixto Morales, became for a time separated from the main column. Fortunately, on the same day, 1 February, about ten new followers from Manzanillo led by Roberto Pesant successfully reached Castro. Surgical instruments and clothes were soon brought from Manzanillo, though one of the new men was quickly killed in some sporadic firing, from Sánchez Mosquera's forward patrol – the first death on Castro's side since Alegría de Pío. The column moved back towards the stream El Ají, seeking always territory which they knew, in order to establish contact with the *precaristas* and to be in a favourable position to receive help, men and supplies, from Manzanillo. Some more *precaristas* joined, among them a forty-five-year-old illiterate, Julio Zenón Acosta, who became what Guevara called the revolution's first pupil in education: Guevara taught him the alphabet.[33]

This group brought the news that Sergio Acuña, who had deserted a few days before, had returned to his home, had boasted of his activities as a *guerrillero* and had been betrayed. He had been beaten and then shot by Corporal Roselló, and his body hanged. This, commented Guevara, taught the column 'the value of cohesion and the uselessness of trying individually to flee the collective destiny'. There was afterwards a purge of the unreliable or exhausted, and the 'Spanish veteran', Chao, Reinaldo Benítez and Edward Díaz were sent away from the Sierra, while Ramiro Valdés and Ignacio Pérez, Cresencio's son (like his father a leader of *precaristas*), also went away temporarily to care for their wounds: Chao had lost faith in the enterprise, saying that the rebels had embarked on 'a phenomenal folly'.[34]

A curious little biblical story now occurred. The traitor Eutimio Guerra, back in the fold, claimed that he had known from a dream that an air raid on the woods was about to happen. A discussion followed as to whether dreams could in fact evoke the prediction of such events. Guevara, part of whose daily task was 'to make explanations of a political or cultural nature', patiently explained that it was impossible, but some – among them the illiterate Acosta – stuck firmly to a physiological interpretation. A few nights later Guerra made his bid to kill Castro. He complained he had no blanket, and asked Castro to lend him one (the nights at that time were cold). Castro replied that

[32] Matthews, 19, 21.
[33] Guevara, 31–2.
[34] Franqui, 71.

they had better share the same one. Castro and the traitor, armed with a 0·45 pistol, lay down then under the same blanket. But Castro was also guarded by three others and Eutimio Guerra spent the whole night fingering his pistol unable to make up his mind when to shoot.

Though vacillating in his mission, he was not, however, without audacity; the following day, he predicted, according to his famous dream foresight, that the Loma del Duro (to which Castro was now close) would be shot up by Batistiano aeroplanes. He was delighted when this turned out to be the case. The Castro supporters were dispersed for several days – the peasant Labrador, Armando Rodríguez and six of the last Manzanillo party were either lost or, despairing, abandoned their place. A day or so later a peasant boy was captured who said that he had talked with Eutimio at Captain Casillas's headquarters. Castro moved his camp, which only shortly afterwards was shot up, Acosta being killed. Suspicions about Eutimio Guerra grew, though nothing could be done, since for three days the Fidelistas were divided. Reunited on 12 February, but with some more losses, the Fidelistas still only numbered eighteen.[35] In the next day or so they moved towards the plain, and in the farm La Montería a meeting was held with representatives of some Fidelistas in the cities – Haydée Santamaría and Armando Hart from Havana, Frank País, Celia Sánchez and Vilma Espín from Santiago. (Women had been specially chosen for this rendezvous as it was supposed that they would have a better chance of getting through the army's barriers.)[36] País had previously been trying to persuade Castro to go abroad in order to rally the revolutionary forces there; but his mind was changed by Castro's determination, confidence and energy.[37]

It was a few days after this that Castro's rebellion became well known in North America. Castro was aware of the important part played by the North American press in the war of independence.[38] Certainly the request carried to Havana by René Rodríguez, for a foreign correspondent to go to the Sierra, was an intelligent one. The moment was propitious. The executions by the army at Christmas had tipped the balance among many professional people in Havana, including many Ortodoxos, who were increasingly prepared to take Castro seriously as a force maintaining the prestige of the opposition by actually fighting Batista. Typical Ortodoxos who changed their position included Raúl Chibás, until recently their nominal leader, who met Frank País in Santiago on

[35] See below, p. 919.
[36] Guevara, 37, 38. *Cf.* Haydée Santamaría and Celia Sánchez in Franqui, 60.
[37] Haydée Santamaría in *ibid.*
[38] This is suggested by Herbert Matthews, in quoting from Máximo Gómez, 'Without a press we shall get nowhere.'

28 January and returned to Havana to try and organize a 'Civic Resistance', on the model of that existing in Santiago, harking back to the cellular organization of the ABC in the struggle against Machado. Ignacio Mendoza, an Ortodoxo leader who had been leader of the bomb placers in the fight against Machado, and a member of a noted Havana legal and commercial family, became a leader in Havana of the struggle against Batista. Mendoza, a broker of respectability, seemed above suspicion.[39] The Civic Resistance was supposed to be an independent non-political secret organization composed of middle and upper-class people regardless of party; in fact, it was from the start a front organization for the 26 July Movement in the cities, and a means of getting supplies and money;[40] on the other hand many of those who worked in it thought that they were doing so in order to avoid actually joining the 26 July Movement which they judged too extreme.[41]

Enrique Oltuski, a youthful engineer, once a supporter of García Barcena, became the Havana head of the Civic Resistance; he had joined Castro in mid-1955.[42] Raúl Chibás found that within a month he had gained $1,000 mostly from persons contributing $1 each, as agreed, paying by cells of ten.[43] Another prominent man who began to collaborate with the 26 July Movement in these weeks was Felipe Pazos, Cuba's leading economist and a governor of the National Bank under Prío. His son had been active in the struggle against Batista from the end of 1955 and, as with many Cubans, the son apparently drove the father to enter the movement for which he was already risking his life. Like Mendoza, Pazos had been in the struggle against Machado, and a member of the Student Directorate in 1933. Although Pazos could not himself boast a large following, his acceptance of the 26 July Movement was indicative of the political development of the Cuban middle class.

The Pazos family had secured the success of Castro's request for a foreign journalist in the Sierra. Felipe Pazos went to the office of the *New York Times*, whose correspondent, the intrepid Mrs Ruby Hart Phillips, herself a veteran of the Machado struggle, arranged that Herbert Matthews, a senior editor on the *New York Times* experienced in Latin American affairs, who had extensively covered the Spanish Civil War, should come from New York to try to see Castro.[44] Though fifty-seven years old, he was intrepid: twenty years before, Hemingway

[39] *Cf.* Jules Dubois, 257.

[40] This was the description given of the Civic Resistance by Armando Hart to Mario Llerena (Llerena, MSS, p. 46).

[41] This was the comment of Raúl Chibás (MSS).

[42] *Revolución*, 20 January 1959.

[43] The system of the Civic Resistance was that no one knew more than ten members of the organization; each head of a cell only knew his superior, etc.

[44] Herbert Matthews (born 1900), in U.S. army 1918; with *New York Times*, 1922-66.

had described him as 'brave as a badger'. Matthews, with his wife for a cover, was escorted to Manzanillo by Javier Pazos and Faustino Pérez. Pazos himself said later, 'I must confess that within myself I had doubts about Fidel's presence in the Sierra until we saw him'.[45] Batista meantime on 12 January had announced that there was 'absolute peace throughout Cuba', except for a few bombs thrown by Communists whose 'identity had been perfectly defined'.[46]

Leaving his wife at the house of Pedro and Ena Saumell, two Manzanillo school teachers and supporters of Castro, Matthews set off into the Sierra on 15 February and met Castro at dawn on 17 February.

He had driven with Pazos and some others much of the way, but walked the last stretch.[47] He was much impressed: 'The personality of the man is overpowering. It was easy to see that his men adored him . . . Here was an educated, dedicated fanatic, a man of ideals, of courage and of remarkable qualities of leadership . . . one got a feeling that he is now invincible.' The significance of the interview was considerable. First, Matthews created for North Americans the legend of Castro, the hero of the mountains, 'of extraordinary eloquence', 'a powerful six-footer, olive-skinned, full-faced, with a shapely beard. He was dressed in an olive grey fatigue uniform and carried a rifle with a telescopic sight of which he was very proud . . .' 'a great talker who dealt fairly with the peasants, paying for everything they ate'. For the next three years Fidel Castro was, much to his surprise and even for a time his anger, a North American hero.

Second, the interview exaggerated the number under Castro's leadership. Castro said that Batista worked 'in columns of 200; we in groups of ten to forty', although 'I will not tell you how many we have, for obvious reasons . . .' 'They had had many fights and inflicted many losses,' Matthews reported; he described Castro as saying, 'We have been fighting for seventy-nine days now and are stronger than ever . . . the soldiers are fighting badly; their morale is low, ours could not be higher.' Matthews reported that Castro's men had over fifty telescopic rifles, while Castro left the clear impression that his original eighty-two of the *Granma* had been a hard core which since had been greatly added to: they had 'kept the government at bay while youths came in from other parts of Oriente'. In fact, Raúl Castro kept passing in front of Matthews with the same men, and the impression was left that Castro himself was 'in another camp' for much of the time;[48] Castro then had

[45] Matthews, *The Cuban Story*, 23.
[46] *Havana Post*, 12 January 1957.
[47] Matthews, *op. cit.*, 26, 27; Felipe Guerra (who accompanied the mission) wrote an account in *Bohemia*, 6 June 1964.
[48] Franqui, 59.

only eighteen followers.[49] Castro could, it is true, also rely on Cresencio Pérez, his sons and several other peasants such as Manuel Acuña, temporarily absent but who had at one time or another been with him.[50] Matthews specifically said that in Oriente 'thousands of men and women are heart and soul with Fidel Castro and the new deal for which they think he stands'; these were sympathizers, but sympathizers who might be called to arms. The truth was that Castro was increasingly gaining the confidence of *precaristas* and their leaders through such men as Pérez, against the large and small landowners, who believed that the presence of Batista's army and the existence of a war situation might help them to dispose of the *precaristas* for ever. This 'revolutionary' attitude on the part of the *precaristas* was increased when Lieutenant Casillas drove out the peasants from the region of Palma Mocha: the leaders of the *precaristas* found collaboration with the new force in the Sierra more and more necessary (Casillas was a thug; he kept a box full of human ears to show to favoured visitors; he liked fighting and once told a guest that after the battles were over in Cuba he would not stay in a land of peace but leave for Columbia and fight for Colonel Pérez Jiménez.)[51] Yet Castro so influenced Matthews both by his character and his energy that Matthews asked him 'about the report that he was going to declare a revolutionary government in the Sierra'. 'Not yet,' he replied, 'the time is not ripe. I will make myself known at the opportune moment.'[52]

Matthews's article on his visit to the Sierra was published on 24 February and immediately made of Castro an international figure. Since the censorship was by chance lifted in Cuba the very next day, the news that Castro was alive became known quickly in Cuba also. The imprecise overestimate of the size of Castro's forces helped to attract urban Cubans to his cause. It was supposed that Castro was winning, that Batista's reports could not any more be relied on, and that his side was therefore the right side to be on; Castro's morale was raised. The morale in Batista's army was further depressed, and afterwards, when the Minister of Defence, Santiago Rey, denied both that Matthews could have penetrated the army's ring round the Sierra and that Castro was alive, the government was made ridiculous, since Matthews next published a photograph that he had taken of himself with Castro.

[49] Raúl Castro, Ameijeiras, Redondo, Morán, Crespo, Almeida, Julio Díaz, Universo Sánchez, Cienfuegos and Guevara, of the original *Granma* group; Fajardo, Guillermo García and Ciro Frías of the *precaristas*; Pesant, Motolá, Yayo, Echevarría of the Manzanillo reinforcements; together with the treacherous guide Guerra.

[50] Soon after Matthews's visit, Morán, Raúl Díaz, Gil and Sotolongo rejoined (ex-*Granmaistas*).

[51] See Barrera Pérez, *Bohemia Libre*, 16 August 1961. For Casillas, the author has had private information.

[52] Qu. from Matthews's article in *New York Times*, 24–6 February 1957.

Castro deceived Matthews about the size of his forces but not much about his political aims. 'The 26th of July Movement talks of nationalism, anti-colonialism, anti-imperialism,' Matthews wrote. These views he must have heard from Javier Pazos and people like him whom he met in Havana. Also in Havana, he obtained the 26 July Movement's clandestine tabloid, *Revolución*, in which, in an article entitled 'Necessity of Revolution', the word 'socialism' appeared.[53] To Matthews, Castro, however, said: 'You can be sure that we have no animosity towards the United States and the American people ... we are fighting for a democratic Cuba and an end to the dictatorship. We are not anti-military ... for we know the men are good and so are many of the officers.' 'Anti-imperialism' and even 'democratic' might of course mean anything. It is clear that Matthews himself saw Castro as a social democrat; but it is not of course certain that that was how Castro saw himself. The precise nature of Castro's political purposes in February 1957 is indeed hard to estimate, since, as has been suggested, Castro himself has given so many discordant versions of his political education. It would be wisest to assume that this education was under way rather than complete. Guevara, the most politically sophisticated of the group suggests in his account of the campaign in the Sierra that even he was open to influence by outside people such as País, the Santiago leader; País, he tells us, was anyway instrumental in making him clean his rifle more efficiently.[54] Yet Guevara and Raúl Castro were, with Castro himself, the only ones in the Sierra at this moment who had had a higher education. Their influence must have been the dominant intellectual ones on Castro, while Castro himself, as we have seen, was not a man of fixed or coherent ideological point of view, or of firmly held opinions. Even so, it would be wrong to overestimate how far Guevara and Raúl Castro influenced Castro. The opportunities of political discussion were not limitless, and all three were preoccupied by problems of survival, battle and the search for food. Fidel Castro was without doubt the dominant individual in the Sierra. His childhood and youth had prepared him for this sort of struggle, perhaps indeed only for this sort of struggle. His programme as described in an early issue of *Revolución*, in February 1957, has the stamp of authenticity, both in its vagueness, its rhetoric and its yearning patriotism:

The Revolution is the struggle of the Cuban nation to achieve its

---

[53] Most of the article was taken from Mario Llerena's pamphlet, *Nuestra Razón* (p. 23), not yet published; but Franqui, who had commissioned the pamphlet, had changed 'social justice' to 'socialism'. This word, together with the use of the word by Castro in the Sierra, had led Matthews to argue that Castro never changed his mind (*The Cuban Story*, 79–80). The point was also seized on by W. A. Williams (*The U.S., Cuba and Castro*, 77–9).

[54] *Pasajes*, 38.

historic aims and realise its complete integration. This integration consists in the complete unity of the following elements: political sovereignty, economic independence, in particular a differentiated culture. The Revolution is not exactly a war and an isolated episode. It is a continuous historic process which offers distinct moments or stages. The conspiracies of the last century, the wars of '68 and '95, the repression of the 1930s and today the struggle against the Batista terror are parts of the same ... Revolution [which] ... is struggling for a total transformation of Cuban life, for profound modifications in the system of property, and for a change in institutions ... The Revolution is democratic, nationalist and socialist.[55]

As to the vexed and intriguing question of the relation between the 26 July Movement and Communism at this time, Blas Roca, the Communist secretary-general, said in 1960:

As soon as the first combat groups were established in the Sierra we tried to give them all possible aid. One outstanding, widely publicised case was a letter we sent to all the opposition parties shortly after the *Granma* landing, asking them to hold back the murderous hand of the government and prevent it from using superior force to exterminate Fidel Castro and his comrades.[56]

About six months later, in September 1957, the New York *Daily Worker*, the Communist paper of the U.S., was found complaining that the Cuban Communists were not getting enough credit for their support of the rebels.[57] But in reality, only four days after the publication of Castro's interview with Matthews, the Cuban Communist party made clear their 'radical disagreement with the tactics and plans' of Fidel Castro;[58] despite his 'valour and sincerity', they believed armed action to be wrong. They deplored terrorism, sabotage, and the burning of sugar cane. Though they admitted that the 26 July Movement 'came closest' to the Communists' 'strategic conception', it had not yet taken a strong enough line against 'imperialist domination' – that is, against the U.S. A month later Juan Marinello, then president of the Communists, wrote to Matthews, by then established on a pinnacle of fame as the interpreter of Cuba to North America, that the Communist party was opposed to the policy of 'the armed struggle' as such. It supported elections, forced on by such classic methods as strikes, popular demonstrations and civil protests. A Popular Front ought to be formed to

[55] Qu. Matthews, 79.
[56] Speech at 8th Congress of PSP.
[57] *Daily Worker*, 22 September 1957.
[58] *Carta del Comité Nacional del Partido Socialista Popular al Movimiento 26 de julio*, qu. Draper, *Castroism*, 29–30.

include not only workers and peasants but 'Cuban petty *bourgeoisie*' and 'national *bourgeoisie*'.[59] Thus, although the Communists might later claim that they had helped the 26 July Movement, at the time they differed from them upon a fundamental question of tactics; and, though tactical, it was the same sort of question which led to the open rift between Russia and China in 1959–60, or between Castro and the Latin American Communists in 1967.

There was clearly some dissension among the Communists. Both the youth movement, centred on Havana University, and some younger members of the party proper – particularly those such as Alfredo Guevara or Leonel Soto who had been university contemporaries of Castro – were doubtful of the desirability of placing all their bets on winning an electoral or constitutional struggle; already some such people saw in the Chinese road to power through armed struggle the only hope for triumph in Latin America; they were already distrustful of Soviet policies leading towards peaceful co-existence with the U.S. and the world of capitalism.[60]

The weeks after Matthews's report in the Sierra were not immediately successful for Castro. The false guide, Eutimio Guerra, was finally accused of treachery. He broke down, demanded to be killed, and only asked that his sons should be cared for; he was shot, a thunderstorm preventing the shot being heard.[61] Another dubious supporter, Morán, 'El Gallego', succeeded in leaving the group by shooting himself in the leg and so being allowed to stay behind.[62] Three old supporters of Castro, *Granma* men who had hidden, rejoined.[63] But the total force still numbered only about twenty, and morale was low. There was nothing to do till 5 March when they were due to meet new reinforcements being sent up from Santiago by Frank País. Guevara had a recurrence of asthma and had to be left behind for several days.[64] It rained heavily. Castro's boots were worn through. The force depended for food on purchases from a peasant named Emiliano and his son Hermes, in the valley Las Mercedes. Hermes was captured and gave Castro's position away. In a hurried escape, Guevara's asthma nearly prevented him leaving. Harsh days continued. A new attack at Altos de Merino followed, and a new dispersion – twelve men got away with Castro, six with Ciro Frías, who shortly was himself killed. On Batista's side, in yet another change of appointments, Major Barrera Pérez, the

[59] The letter is in Columbia University Library. See comments by Draper. *op. cit.*, 30–1; and Matthews, 51–2.
[60] Based on private discussions.
[61] Guevara, 40.
[62] Afterwards he joined Batista and was killed in Guantánamo.
[63] Raúl Díaz, Gil, Sotolongo.
[64] *Cf.* Ameijeiras, in Franqui, 119–20.

same who had established order in Santiago in November, was given the command in Oriente with 1,430 men, including a headquarters company, three infantry companies and one company of mountain troops with a battery of mountain artillery, an engineer corps, and a communications and transport group.[65]

Castro's group was late for its rendezvous with País's force but Jorge Sotús, the leader of that troop, consisting of some fifty men, managed nevertheless to get through alone to Castro and explain that he too was delayed, since Barrera Pérez had been holding the road too well. The rebels seemed in a tight corner and they could not even count on the support of all those *precaristas* whom they knew.[66] But some of the Batista forces were still incurring the further hatred and anger of the *precaristas* through arbitrary atrocities; in particular the navy (to whom part of the task of reducing Castro and re-establishing order had been allocated) was implicated. Thus the frigate *José Martí* was patrolling the coast from Cabo Cruz to Santiago; a lieutenant on board observed the naval intelligence chief, Laurent, and his henchman, García Olayón, in the act of burning the houses of peasants in the neighbourhood of Pilón. Some were drowned; countryside merchants met the same fate.[67]

These actions were opposed by the army colonel in charge, Barrera and his staff, and he and his aides sent a plan for an effective operation in the Sierra, which included a single command, the dismissal of the naval tyrants previously named and a rehabilitation scheme for the *precaristas*; as a consequence three of Batista's ministers, Dr Pardo Jiménez, Salas Humara and Fidel Barreto, arrived at the Sierra Maestra and a beginning was made: houses began to be built, medical services were embarked upon, and plans for schools laid, with a census of children. A free kitchen was set up at Colonel Barrera's command post where as many as three hundred persons a day were fed. Within a matter of weeks the army believed that it was beginning to wean away the affections of the *precaristas*, highly suspicious as most of them were at heart of both Castro and Batista.[68] By late March Barrera was in a position to contemplate the second part of his plan which was to construct an impenetrable line through which Castro's group could neither be reinforced nor supplied.

[65] After a survey by General Cantillo. The commanders were Barrera, chief of operations; Colonel Casasús, second in command; naval advisor, Major Rodríguez Alonso; legal advisor, Captain Evaristo Cordero; section 1, Captain Ricardo Grao; section 2, Major Joaquín Casillas Lumpuy; section 3, Captain Julio Castro Rojas; section 4, Lieutenant Fernando Ball Llovera.

[66] See Guevara in Núñez Jiménez's *Geografía*, 576. However, four new men did join in early March.

[67] Letters of Lieutenant Santa Cruz, U.S. Congressional Record, 20 March 1958, qu. Taber, 169. Also, see Barrera Pérez, *Bohemia Libre*, 13 August 1961, where he describes the interrogation of a survivor of one of the *noyades*.

[68] *Ibid.*, 20 August 1961; Suárez Núñez, 88-9.

CHAPTER LXXV

The Attack on the Palace

Even after the landing of the *Granma*, much of the sabotage outside the Sierra had been the work of people not part of Castro's movement. The Havana university students and the Directorio Revolucionario had been fairly active, despite some controversy over the use of violence between the latter's leader, Echevarría, and its 'intellectual leader', Jorge Valls, and despite the fact also that the university had been closed in late November. Also active had been a strong Priísta opposition group headed by Carlos Gutiérrez Menoyo, a thirty-three-year-old Spanish exile who had been in both the French resistance and the U.S. army. In 1957 he owned a grocer's shop in Havana. Associated with him in political gangsterism were several others of the same background, such as Ignacio González, also a Spaniard, who had been briefly arrested and then released in the preceding December. Though these were essentially Prío's men, they also had connections with the gangsters based on the Dominican Republic and through them even with Trujillo himself, from whom they got arms. Gutiérrez Menoyo had been a part of the famous Cayo Confites expedition. One man involved with them was Ricardo Olmedo, who had participated in a famous armed attack on the Royal Bank of Canada in 1948. Another, Ramón Alfaro, had had convictions for other than political activities.

These groups did not see eye to eye with Castro's 26 July Movement, although the Directorio Revolucionario had concluded an agreement with Castro in Mexico the previous summer,[1] and although, through its link with the Resistencia Cívica (in the process of formation by Raúl Chibás in Havana on the lines of País's movement in Santiago), the 26 July Movement's appeal was being widened. For some time anyway Gutiérrez, Menelao Mora, Echevarría and their friends had been actively but separately preparing an attack on Batista himself – a plan apparently devised in the first place by a comrade of Gutiérrez Menoyo, also a Spanish Republican, Daniel Martín Labandero, who had been caught and shot the previous autumn, escaping from the Principe prison.[2]

---

[1] See above, p. 888.

[2] According to Samuel B. Cherson, 'José Antonio Echevarría: Héroe y Mártir', *Bohemia*, March 1959, plans for the attack on Batista's life had been laid in 1955 and at least once in 1956.

The Directorio Revolucionario's links with Prío, meantime, grew closer during the winter of 1956–7, though Prío's money had also been made available to Castro. The decision to attack the palace was given extra weight by the publicity gained by Castro after his interview with Matthews: the other conspirators felt that time was no longer on their side.

At all events, in late February a plan even more dramatic than Castro's attack on the Moncada barracks was devised by the activist section of the Directorio, led by Echevarría, and Carlos Gutiérrez Menoyo, who broke relations with Prío and effectively joined Echevarría.[3] Another ex-Priísta, Menelao Mora, an ex-congressman in the Auténtico interest (earlier a member of the ABC), who had been president of the Havana bus company, Omnibus Aliados, also played a major part, bringing with him a number of personal followers. Menelao Mora had broken with Prío over the bus company, whose concession Prío, when still president, had given to Autobuses Modernos. Afterwards he joined Sánchez Arango for a time, but he always wished to strike out on his own and did so, having apparently organized 1,000 men in Havana in mid-1955.[4] Alberto, the son of Menelao Mora, then at the university, was a member of the Directorio, though a leftist one, while Menelao's brother Cándido had joined Batista and was now a representative in the assembly.[5] Some Auténticos involved, such as Segundo Ferrer, who had been in both Grau's and Prío's Secret Service, took this opportunity to join the Directorio.[6] The 26 July Movement was not at the beginning asked by anyone to help or to collaborate in any way. (It is of interest that, when the idea of an attempted assassination of Batista was put to Castro in 1955 by Justo Carrillo, he had vigorously opposed it: he was against personal attacks of that nature.[7]) The Communists were also aloof; they regarded the Directorio as 'a group of gangsters combined with elements of Prío, Aurelianismo and ... Trujillismo'.[8] The Directorio was indeed explicitly anti-Communist and specifically refused membership to those it thought 'red' – wisely, for at least one of those who applied was Marcos Armando Rodríguez, who, though a friend of Jorge Valls, was trying to ingratiate

---

[3] Cf. Taber, 104; and Faure Chomón in La Sierra y el Llano (Havana, 1960), 110.

[4] Enrique Rodríguez Loeches, Bohemia, 15 March 1959.

[5] In 1961 Cándido Mora would be one of the oldest members of the Bay of Cochinos expedition. See below, 1360. Alberto became a minister under Castro.

[6] Cuba, March 1964, 13.

[7] Carrillo, MSS, p. 25. This was at the Tapachula meeting. Castro explained his position on the grounds that 'It would not carry us to power but power would go to a reactionary military junta'.

[8] Letter from Marcos Armando Rodríguez to Joaquín Ordoqui, Hoy, 21 March 1964; César Gómez, in 1957 secretary of the Communist Youth, made play later with a photograph which showed a young Communist, Fulgencio Oroz, alongside Echevarría (ibid., 25 March 1964, 8).

himself with the Juventud Socialista, the Communist Youth, which he had also wished to join.[9] Faure Chomón,[10] one of the leaders of the Directorio, later claimed that its magazine, *Alma Mater*, 'often included quotations from Lenin',[11] and certainly its founder, Carlos Franqui, had been a Communist until the winter of 1946–7. But the general attitude of the Directorio was anti-Communist, democratic, middle class, and basically Catholic despite what has sometimes been suggested since.

The attack on Batista's palace was planned to be a shock attempt by about a hundred men to break through the presidential guards by sheer weight of numbers. They would shoot their way up to Batista's apartments on the first floor and kill the dictator. In the meantime José Antonio Echevarría and some others would capture Havana radio and announce the end of the tyranny. The detailed plans were worked out by Gutiérrez, with Menelao Mora and, for the Directorio, Faure Chomón and Fructuoso Rodríguez, who were too well known by the police to move freely.[12] On 9 March fifty men gathered in an apartment rented by Carlos Gutiérrez and awaited the call. The Russian poet Yevtushenko, in his autobiography, chose to write, having been told it by a Cuban:

> Each had his favourite occupation – one was reading, another writing poetry, others were playing chess. Among the revolutionaries were two painters, a realist and an abstract artist. They painted, arguing furiously (though, in view of the special conditions, in whispers) and very nearly came to blows. But when the final instructions arrived, both the realist and the abstract painters went to fight for the future of their country and were killed together.[13]

Of course, by no means all the men engaged in this assault were heroes or idealists; several were merely gun-happy men who relished the thought of a dramatic fight. The total force numbered nearly eighty, including most of the Directorio, except the pacifist Valls wing; several members of the 26 July Movement joined in of their own accord – some of them members of the original Artemisa Fidelistas of the days of the Moncada.[14] At the last minute on the morning of the attack, Javier Pazos, the 26 July leading representative in Havana, was asked if the

[9] This seems the only explanation of the conduct of this unhappy individual whose treachery and tragic end is chronicled later.

[10] Previously known as 'Chaumont'.

[11] *Hoy*, 21 March 1964.

[12] Evidence of Julio García Olivera, *Cuba*, March 1964.

[13] Yevtushenko, *A Precocious Autobiography*, 121. These were Luis Gómez Wangüemert and José Briñas – though in fact the first survived.

[14] See interview with Angel Eros, *Cuba*, March 1964. Eros, however, already called himself a member of the Directorio Revolucionario.

Fidelistas would join; he refused.[15] Castro apparently did not know what was going on. Listening to a wireless in the Sierra he could only tell his companions, 'Something big is going on in Havana.'[16] This was in fact a brave but rash frontal attack on the palace.

Since the forces were so large it was inconceivable that the plan would not be betrayed by someone; and in fact Batista had, on the 11th, got to know what was afoot through intercepted telephone calls.[17] His reaction, according to himself, was to ask the SIM chief, Colonel Piedra, to pass a message via Cándido Mora, the politician with the seat in the rump House of Representatives, to his brother, Menelao.[18] But this message was apparently not made explicitly clear. At all events, the rebels struck immediately after lunch on 13 March, with Batista's forces prepared for some sort of attack, though the details were not certain. Batista, whiling away the tedium of his tyranny reading *The Day Lincoln was Shot*, did not know on which day the attack would come and he had not imagined that it would be in broad daylight.[19]

The attack was in two waves. The first, led by Gutiérrez Menoyo, with Faure Chomón of the Directorio as his second-in-command, was composed of fifty men armed with sub-machine guns, twelve carbines, and a number of 0·45-calibre pistols. These men drove to the palace in a Buick sedan (four men), a Ford (four men) and a lorry labelled 'Fast delivery' (forty-two men).[20] All were in shirt sleeves, Batista having banned anyone going into the palace so dressed. The second wave was led by Ignacio González, with twenty-six men. Echevarría and Rodríguez Loeches, an ex-member of Masferrer's MSR, were to take over Radio Reloj, the somewhat absurd Havana radio station (which became very successful by broadcasting the time every minute, with news and advertisements in between), and announce that Batista was dead. As usual in Cuban revolutionary developments, the protagonists had a high sense of history: 'That morning we were Destiny,' recalled Chomón.[21] 'We knew that this attack ... was a highly historic enterprise which would free our people. We were going to give the world an impressive example.'

The first car arrived just before the palace at 3.20 p.m. Gutiérrez and three men[22] shot the traffic policeman[23] and, firing sub-machine

[15] Evidence of Javier Pazos.
[16] Ameijeiras, in Franqui, 131. On the other hand, Dr Lima says that he had known of, and encouraged, the attack in a letter to Echevarría before it occurred.
[17] Suárez Núñez, 72.
[18] Batista, *Cuba Betrayed*, 59.
[19] Batista to Edward Scott of the *Havana Post*, in *Havana Post*, 14 March 1957.
[20] *Cuba*, March 1964, 7.
[21] Franqui, 97.
[22] José Luis Goicoechea, José Castellanos, and Luis Almeida.
[23] Goicoechea to Franqui, 109.

guns, ran to the main entrance. About twelve surprised soldiers who were there fell dead, were wounded or fled. Though delayed by traffic, often a snag in street fighting in the twentieth century, the two other vehicles in the first wave arrived safely, but they were fired on from many quarters, including by a 0·30-calibre machine-gun on the church of San Angel. The men from the cars of the first wave ran to the palace; perhaps ten were shot down *en route*, but a group of nine men led by Menelao Mora reached the palace and quickly made their way up to the second floor of the palace on its left wing. Others kept on the ground floor. Gutiérrez, with four men, was on the left wing and destroyed the telephone switchboard with a grenade. They arrived at Batista's dining-room, and shot their way into the presidential offices, throwing grenades ahead of them and killing two men by Batista's desk. Not finding Batista, they realized that he had gone up to the 'presidential suite' on the next floor. Unfortunately for them they could not find the staircase upwards, though they had got from Prío careful plans of the palace.

The attackers then realized that Batista had concentrated his defences on the top floor, for from there rifle and machine-gun fire, directed by Batista himself, was beginning to dominate the courtyard and the forecourt of the palace. A telephone rang. Gómez Wangüemert answered: 'Yes it is true, the palace has fallen. Batista is dead. We are free.' Meantime some of Mora's group had become dispersed, while the whole second wave of the attack, under Ignacio González, had not arrived at all, since once the firing had begun, the palace was surrounded by a huge army of policemen and soldiers, almost giving the impression that it was they who were doing the attacking. Tanks even had begun to move towards the palace. Echevarría had captured the radio station and broadcast an excited message: 'People of Havana! The Revolution is in progress. The presidential palace has been taken by our forces and the Dictator has been executed in his den!' But after he had blown up the central control panel in the radio station, Echevarría was shot dead in the street by police. Meanwhile, the men on the second floor of the palace continued to fire and to throw grenades upwards, but, eventually, they retreated. Most (including Mora and Gutiérrez) were killed on the marble staircase. Only three of the men who had penetrated into Batista's offices actually escaped alive from the palace.[24] Firing continued much of the afternoon, soldiers shooting indiscriminately and wounding several bystanders. The little park near the palace seemed to run with blood. Most of the buildings nearby were chipped with bullets.

[24] This account derives chiefly from Luis Goicoechea. Goicoechea's story is graphically told in Taber, 110–22, and in *Cuba*, March 1965, where there are other stories by participants. See also Batista, *Cuba Betrayed*, 59.

In this contest, thirty-five rebels and five members of the palace guard were killed. One American tourist was accidentally killed. Afterwards, an unknown number of students, boys, odd suspects and members of the opposition, were rounded up and eventually shot – many, as usual, being tortured. The Ortodoxo ex-Senator Pelayo Cuervo, nominal president of the Ortodoxo party, was found murdered on the edge of a lake in the Country Club next morning. Apparently the police had thought, on the basis of papers found on Echevarría's body, that Cuervo would have become provisional president if the attack had succeeded, and had let themselves run riot. The executioner was Sergeant Rafael Linares.[25] Batista himself accused Prío of providing the arms, and told reporters that he had definite evidence that international Communism was heavily involved – though the Communists had held aloof.[26]

The attack on the palace was foolhardy. Castro was surely correct, if tactless, in saying that it constituted 'a useless expenditure of blood'. Its chances of success were remote. The third floor of the palace was only approachable by a lift, and therefore the attackers could never have got up there if the lift was, as it was, at the top. No provision had been made for the aftermath or for a successful hiding place for the attackers in the event of failure. If, however, the 'second wave' had arrived the attack might just have terrified the defenders into flight. Thus, as can be expected, the survivors felt full of rancour towards those who did not help them; they may have fought in the Spanish war but that was a long time ago, commented Chomón.[27] The 26 July Movement helped to pick up the wounded and Javier Pazos gave up to Chomón, Gutiérrez's second-in-command, his hiding place. The 26 July also captured a lorry-load of arms which had not been used and hid them in the apartment of a minor member of their movement, 'Barba Roja' Piñeiro, who was conveniently married to an American; they afterwards found their way to the Sierra.[28]

The aftermath of the attack on the palace had two characteristics; first, the sympathy which the business world, the upper classes in general, and foreign commercial interests showed towards Batista was remarkable. The leaders of all these communities called on Batista during the next few weeks to condemn the attack; so did the National Association of Sugar Mill Owners, the CTC (Mujal), the Veterans of

[25] Jules Dubois, 155.

[26] *Havana Post*, 14 March 1957. These days show Batista in the full flood of an anti-Communism which would have seemed extravagant even to McCarthy – verbally at least: on 9 March he has assured the Chicago journalist Dubois that the Communist Castro had killed six priests with his teeth at the Bogotazo.

[27] Franqui, 106.

[28] Javier Pazos's evidence. Piñeiro later became Castro's chief of counter-intelligence, afterwards vice-minister of the Interior. One member of the Directorio, Dr Lima, however, later accused the 26 July Movement of stealing the arms (Lima memorandum, p. 4).

The Moncada attack:
21a Fidel Castro (left) and other prisoners
 b The barracks afterwards

22a The Sierra Maestra
  b The Rebels in their stronghold: Raúl Castro, Juan Almeida, Fidel Castro,
    Ramiro Valdés, Ciro Redondo

the War of Independence, the Cuba Banking Association, the Insurance Companies, American and Spanish businessmen, property owners, coffee and cattle-breeders' associations, rice growers, cigarette and cigar manufacturers, even fishermen.[29] On 1 April the leading banks and bankers of Cuba, headed by Víctor Pedroso, Alex Roberts (Banco Caribe) and Martínez Sáenz, the president of the National Bank, called.

Most unsuccessful attempts at assassinations do good to the intended victim but in this case the advantage to the regime was enormous; Batista felt himself supported on every hand by all that was best in Cuban public and commercial life. He had never received such an overwhelming endorsement. A very large number greeted Batista on 7 April when he addressed the crowd – perhaps approaching the 250,000 which he claimed – in the square before the palace. The majority of these supporters no doubt regarded the attack on the palace as gangsterish as much as political, the latest in an endless series of outrages: to find Ricardo Olmedo, who had taken part in the attack on the Bank of Canada in 1948, among those involved, confirmed them in these views. The known participation of friends of Aureliano, Eufemio Fernández, the students and the 26 July Movement did not enhance, in public estimation, the reputation of any of these groups.[30]

The second consequence was heightened repression. The police maintained their search for the participants and made many arrests. On 19 April, Captain Esteban Ventura, of the police, and his men, were, due to the treachery of Marcos Armando Rodríguez, a university colleague of the students involved, able to corner and kill, in an apartment in Humboldt Street, four of the surviving leaders of the students: Fructuoso Rodríguez, who had succeeded Echevarría outside the radio station on 13 March;[31] José Westbrook, also 'a veteran of the radio station'; José Machado ('Machadito'); and Juan Pedro Carbó Serviá, who had been into the palace itself with Gutiérrez. Carbó had been one of the assassins of Colonel Blanco Rico in the night-club the previous autumn. The treachery of Rodríguez became afterwards a *cause célèbre* in revolutionary Cuba, due to his support afterwards by powerful Communist friends to whom he is believed later to have confessed the whole crime in Mexico.[32] At the time of his treachery, he was

[29] See Batista, *Cuba Betrayed*. Castro later commented bitterly on this 'contemptible procession of representatives of the upper classes ... all the *haute-bourgeoisie*, its lumpenist [!], gangsters, mujaliestas ... I assure you that none of this class visited the palace after the passage of a revolutionary law. None.' (*Obra Revolucionaria*, 1961, No. 46, p. 24).

[30] Though it might be argued, as Professor Dumont did of the Columbian banditry, that the gangsterism of Cuba '*se purifie en se politisant*' (*Cuba*, 9).

[31] It seems only too possible that, as Fructuoso Rodríguez's father told a judge later, the student leader was in fact alive when he reached the first aid post, and was afterwards killed. (See *Havana Post*, 27 April 1957.)

[32] The Communists were Joaquín Ordoqui and Edith García Buchaca, to whose house in Mexico Rodríguez often repaired when in exile 1957-9.

not, however, a Communist party member and his motives appear to have been primarily personal rather than political – a dislike of the activist wing of the Directorio, possibly a hatred of violence itself, probably jealousy, a desire to be important, and perhaps a continuing desire to try to please the Communist Youth leaders (who had continued to rebuff him even though he had been for a time their informer) by the destruction of their rivals who indeed might in the end have turned out anti-Communists.[33] It is clear that he did not do it for money and equally clear that the Communists to whom he later confessed did not take a very serious view of his treachery.

The burial of these four students, all Catholics, in the Colón cemetery, was attended by large crowds. Protests were widespread but it speaks harshly for the regime that four young men could be in effect executed without trial, without any reprimand for Captain Ventura and without much disapproval of him in the *haute-bourgeois* and commercial worlds. Imperceptibly Cuban society was disintegrating towards the same situation as occurred in the late 1920s and early 1930s, where police violence was condoned. The death of Dr Pelayo Cuervo served as a notice to all members of the opposition that they could count on no guarantees and made them more likely than ever to countenance Castro and the armed struggle.

The attack on the palace did not prevent new visits from distinguished North Americans; within a week Admiral Burke, chief of naval operations, came to receive an order of Cuban naval merit from Batista; Kansas businessmen continued to fly in for conventions. But 'normality' was increasingly absent; men were constantly arrested, for setting fire to canefields, for being suspected of bomb placing, even for collecting money in memory of José Antonio Echevarría. The secondary schools of Cuba were closed for one week by government order, and for another week after the deaths in Humboldt 7. In the continued atmosphere of agitation, Batista banned the half-term elections due for Congress in 1957, only permitting the establishment of a congressional committee to 'spend twenty days taking testimony from the political parties', including from the 26 July, and then 'work out a solution' for the future. This had little success though it heard a number of political opposition leaders such as Grau, Varona, Pardo Llada and Alonso Pujol.

The guerrilla 'war' might be the only heroic aspect of Cuban life in the spring of 1957, but there was nevertheless no revolutionary demand

---

[33] See the author's article in the *New Statesman*, 29 May 1964. The original police statement said that there were six students in the apartment and that Marquitos and Eugenio Pérez Cowley had been there and escaped (see *Havana Post*, 23 April 1957). Another account by one closely involved is *El Crimen de Humboldt 7*, by Enrique Rodríguez Loeches, *La Sierra y el Llano*, 143–65). Ventura, incidentally, in *his* book (p. 251) admitted that there was a betrayal but makes other accusations of identity.

from all sections of the nation. Thanks to the Suez crisis, sugar prices were high. The 1957 harvest was large, the crop had been declared free of control, and there was an unusual sale of 15,000 tons to the U.S.S.R. in April, causing much speculation which itself kept prices up. By April it was evident that there would be no difficulty in disposing of a substantial harvest, and the only question remaining was how much would be available, sixty-four mills having still to grind, and sixty-four having finished. Some cane was burned by Castro in Oriente but not enough to make an appreciable difference to the harvest. It was 1870–4 all over again. The guerrilla war and political activity was thus waged in the face of the economic situation in more ways than one, just as Martí's revolt against Spain had been: 1894 and 1957 were alike in being excellent years for the economy. 1957 also saw a number of important steps towards that reasonable diversification of the economy which had been urged for a long time by the World Bank and others: typical were the big paper mills established at the *central Trinidad* and at *central Morón*, using *bagasse*. A $M25 Shell oil refinery was inaugurated by Batista on 30 March. In April bulldozers were at work on a motorway to link the recently completed Via Blanca to Varadero with the Central Highway. A new suburb, Havana del Este, was taking shape. The *Hispanic American Report*, the best U.S. review of Latin American events at that time and usually criticized for its radical politics, commented:

> Economic stability and progress continued unabated. The Government continued heavy spending on public works, new buildings were going up everywhere, new investments . . . continued at an accelerated pace, *per capita* income was the highest ever recorded . . . government revenues were running $M21 ahead of the previous year.[34]

The only serious effect of the near-civil war was on the tourist trade,[35] but, even so, big hotels continued to be put up: the Havana Hilton was opened in April with a party attended by half of Batista's cabinet;[36] and the Capri and the Habana Riviera hotels, huge luxurious castles, were also under way – the Capri with a swimming pool on its roof on the twenty-fifth floor.

[34] HAR, May 1957.
[35] A protest appeared in *Havana Post*, 28 March 1957.
[36] *Ibid.*, 6 April 1957.

CHAPTER LXXVI

War in the Sierra (*March–May 1957*)

On 16 March Castro had received his first large reinforcement in the Sierra – fifty men from Santiago under Jorge Sotús.[1] These recruits seemed unpromising to those who had already lasted out in the Sierra for three months. Guevara complained that they were unused to having only one meal a day and that they brought with them all manner of useless things. All were exhausted from their journey from Manzanillo. Only thirty were armed, though they did have two old machine guns. They had been brought part of the way by a local rice grower, Hubert Matos, an important sympathizer who would figure in a *cause célèbre* two and a half years later. Sotús, who had led the attack on the Santiago Maritime police headquarters on 30 November 1956 had given himself the rank of captain; and he had named five lieutenants commanding ten men each.[2] Among this group were three young Americans – Charles Ryan, Victor Buchman and Michael L. Garney – sons of North Americans working in Guantánamo. They had set out in the hope of adventure, but two left before seeing action.

Relations between the new arrivals and the veterans of three months were bad. Sotús, a 'prosperous warehouse owner's son',[3] despite his eminent part in Frank País's battle of Santiago had not proved himself as a guerrilla leader and he had difficulties with Castro. The united force was reorganized in three companies under Sotús,[4] Raúl Castro[5] and Almeida,[6] while special vanguard and rearguard units were placed under Cienfuegos with four men and Ameijeiras with three men. A small headquarters unit under Castro himself comprised Ciro Redondo, Manuel Fajardo, Crespo, Guevara as doctor, and Universo Sánchez as chief of staff. This reorganization gave little responsibility in practice to the new recruits. A small inner council directed affairs, including Castro, the three company commanders, with Ciro Frías, Guillermo

---

[1] Taber gives 58 (p. 102); Guevara has 'about 50' (48).

[2] Hermo, Domínguez, René Ramos Latour ('Daniel'), 'Pedrín' Soto, who had escaped from the *débâcle* after the *Granma*, and a Santiago student named Peña.

[3] Taber, 72.

[4] Under Sotús were three lieutenants, Ciro Frías, Guillermo García and René Ramos Latour, who had come up with Sotús.

[5] Under Raúl Castro were three lieutenants, Julio Díaz, Ramiro Valdés (who rejoined, after his wound, after 24 March), and 'Naño' Díaz.

[6] Lieutenants Hermo, Guillermo, Domínguez and Peorín.

García, Cienfuegos, Fajardo and Guevara. Cooking, medicine, and provisioning was henceforth done in platoons rather than centrally. Already the outlines of an army were being drawn, about eighty strong though with rather fewer than that number of weapons. Each man was supposed to make for himself a hammock of sacking, though some canvas hammocks were also available. The company commanders sought to accustom the new recruits to the rigours of the mountains by marching and counter-marching, rather than, as suggested by the intemperate Guevara, attacking the nearest post to test them in the struggle.[7] They marched eastwards, finding as before among the peasants 'first a great terror of the army; [and] second, how it was [still] hard for them to realize how a badly dressed and badly armed group such as ourselves could defeat the army'.[8] Relations between the *precaristas* who had joined the column, and the people of the plain were not always good. For instance, the peasants were outraged one night by the eating of a horse.

On 30 March, meantime, Batista once more announced that Castro was not in the Sierra and that he had not been seen since 'he shot some soldiers sleeping' at La Plata. A few days later the army carried an aeroplane load of eighty journalists across the Sierra, to demonstrate that there was 'no one there'. Colonel Barrera's plans were now beginning to bear fruit; some of the *precaristas* had rallied to the army, though the scheme of attempting to insulate Castro from succour by a *'barrida'* was a somewhat defensive one: the field operation under Barrera having been placed under Major José Cañizares, with the mountain artillery, the naval units assigned, a squadron of bombers and a battalion of infantry.[9] This force was indeed perfectly adequate to keep the rebels from increasing their forces, though neither Cañizares nor Barrera supposed that Castro had so few men. By early April it seemed to them that their mission was completed, and Colonel Barrera, the inspiration of this stage of Batista's counter-offensive, could be recalled; according to him, he had lost only one man and that as a result of a shooting accident.[10] On return to Havana Barrera Pérez made a full report to Batista who congratulated him on his success. But this report did Barrera no good, since it immediately brought the jealousy of General Tabernilla's apparatus of intrigue and misrepresentation: it was put abroad by the chief of staff and his cronies that Barrera had attempted the rehabilitation of the *precaristas* in order to get in touch with the enemy: and that his failure to capture Castro was because he was secretly in

[7] Guevara, 49–51.

[8] Castro's speech, December 1961, *Obra Revolucionaria*, No. 46, p. 18.

[9] Composed of three companies under Captains Merob Sosa, Juan Chirino, and Raúl Sáenz de Calahorra. The air squadron was under Colonel Félix Catasús.

[10] He was recalled on 16 April (*Bohemia Libre*, 20 August 1961).

contact with him. For the time being Barrera successfully stood up to these insinuations in La Cabaña, while his activity in the Sierra, 'mopping up' the remains of the rebels, as it was supposed, was given over to the bloodthirsty Major Casillas, who had been in the area off and on since December. Before leaving, Barrera had in fact told the journalists who visited the Sierra that there was only a band of outlaws (not Castro) there, 'with harems of five women each'. The commander produced a number of *precaristas* who proclaimed themselves grateful to the army, and he said that, in addition to his 550 officers and men, he had at least 250 informers and government agents among the peasants and farmers of the area. He was accurate in his statement that there had been no action in the Sierra since 9 February,[11] but it was of course an error to withdraw the special troops which Barrera had with him, leaving the field to Casillas and conventionally trained men.

By mid-April 1957 the rebels had returned to the neighbourhood of the Pico Turquino. The *precaristas* García and Frías played a big part at this time, moving backwards and forwards across the jungle carrying news and food. The house of the priest of Manzanillo, Fr Antonio Albizú, became a rendezvous for messengers. There were still no engagements with the army. The rebels spent weeks establishing lines of contact with the peasants, identifying those who could be trusted, those who might serve as messengers, those who would give honest information and who would know places where permanent bases could be safely established and where food could be permanently provided or stored. This spring campaign – though it scarcely merits the name – was of the greatest importance in the future. One of Castro's followers from the plain was Celia Sánchez, daughter of a dentist on Lobo's plantation at Pilón.[12] From her the news came that (on the initiative of Hart and the 26 July organization in Havana) two new North American journalists, one with a television camera, were ready to visit the rebels. The idea was accepted by Castro, and Lalo Sardiñas, a commercial traveller from near the sugar mill *Estrada Palma*, transported into the hills Robert Taber and Wendell Hoffman, of the Columbia Broadcasting System.[13] With them came Marcelo Fernández, son of a Cárdenas grocer who had been president of the Engineering School at the University of Havana, as an English interpreter. The two Americans remained several days, and the

[11] See *Havana Post*, 13 April; E. Scott's column on 14 and 16 April; *cf.* Guevara, 54; HAR, September 1957.
[12] She was an eccentric woman in her thirties and Lobo had built her on the estate a dovecote where she could 'sleep, write or dream'. She later became Castro's secretary and his most faithful aide.
[13] A key part in the reception of these journalists was played by the Rev. Raúl Fernández Ceballos, pastor of the First Presbyterian Church in Havana, a preacher of predominantly left-wing views who afterwards remained in the 1960s a vigorous supporter of the revolution.

interview ultimately took place on top of the Pico Turquino. In the interview Castro gave an impression of moderation as strong as that he had given to Matthews: he said that he normally opposed bloodshed but that he wished to create an atmosphere where the government would have to fall; he requested that the U.S. should send no more arms to Batista; he was fighting for the restoration of the Constitution of 1940.[14] Shown in May, as 'The story of Cuba's Jungle Fighters', the film proved that, contrary to the statements of Colonel Barrera, Castro was certainly still in the Sierra. New recruits continued to arrive, some such as El Vaquerito, 'the little cowboy', from Morón (Camagüey), with no political ideas and the intention only of having a marvellous adventure – to whom Guevara, as political conscience of the group, had necessarily to give lessons; or the farm labourer and builder who had taken the bus from his home in Pinar del Río to join Castro to fight for a better world against the one which seemed to have so persecuted him.[15] The mere movement through the Sierra in these months was enough to show the revolutionary torch and, the legend being created, *precaristas*, after the brief Barrera experiment was over, once again began to approach the rebels as their friends. But treachery and the trial and afterwards execution of informers was still fairly frequent, as the guerrilla war became blended with older internecine blood feuds.

The experience of dealing with the peasants, with their ailments and their malnutrition, evidently affected the political views of the rebels. Guevara noted: 'In these activities there began to take shape in us the consciousness of the need for a definitive change in the life of the people. The idea of agrarian reform was born and that of communion with the people ceased to be theory, being converted into a definite part of our being.'[16] This may overstate the matter. Guevara had worked, if only for a short time, in the Guatemalan revolutionary Institute of Agrarian Reform. His experience was such that he needed less further education of this sort than he said; and his temperament was such that he preferred to teach others, rather than receive lessons, even from experience. Castro had been talking about the need for a radical change in society for a long time and, whatever importance is given to his later reinterpretation of his youth, he had clearly known of the existence of schemes to change society. But even Guevara's 'Marxism' was probably theoretical. Castro had said so many things, and had changed his mind so often, that, as with the Scriptures, almost any interpretation could have been based on them. Anything he had said would have been changed as a result of his experiences in the Sierra. But this does not

---

[14] See *Life*, 27 May 1957.
[15] This was the later Major Antonio Sánchez Díaz ('Piñares'). See his account in *Verde Olivo*, 12 May 1963. He was killed in Bolivia in 1967 with Guevara under the pseudonym 'Marcos'.
[16] Guevara, 65.

mean that his 'communion with the people' was not real and that it did not mark a definite change in the 'actualization' of his political activity. Guevara added: 'The guerrilla and the peasant became joined into a single mass, so that (and no one could say at which moment precisely of the long march it occurred) we became part of the peasants.' These judgements seem romantic, but they doubtless represent a true picture of what Guevara, the political teacher of new recruits, himself thought about the Sierra's importance.[17] In Guevara's conversations with a peasant named Banderas, afterwards killed, who fought in order to work with more land than he had, there were also clear foretastes of the revolution's own controversial socialization of land.[18]

The march eastwards continued and what happened in the next few weeks was a good illustration of the tactics of guerrilla action. At Pino del Agua, the rebels captured a mounted Batistiano corporal known to have many crimes to his discredit since the days of Machado. Castro resisted demands for his execution, since it was his policy to treat captives in the opposite manner to the way of the Batistianos. He and his horse were held prisoner by recruits, while the main body pressed on to see if an important cargo of arms had arrived at the appointed place despite the detention of the messenger.[19] But in fact the arms were brought in a yacht belonging to the Babun family, a large timber firm and ship-builders of Santiago – three machine guns on tripods, three Madison machine guns, nine MI carbines, ten Johnson automatic rifles, and 6,000 rounds.[20] The Babun family were great friends of Batista and the military leaders. but one of their employees, Enrique López, an old friend of the Castro brothers, was of some assistance to the rebels in getting food in this area. At this time, due to further recruitment of *precaristas*, and the return of various old friends such as Cresencio Pérez, total rebel numbers in the Sierra approached 150. But, due to the usual lack of physical preparation on some of the recruits' part, lack of persistence, or irritation with the horse-fly, many asked permission to return to their homes: 'Our struggle against lack of moral, ideological and physical preparation of the combatants was daily.' On 23 May Castro disbanded a whole squadron, leaving a total force of 127 men, eighty of whom were well armed, who were accompanied for a time by a U.S. journalist and secret agent, Andrew St George,[21] of Hungarian birth, who apparently returned to Washington to report that

[17] All this was still in respect of May 1957.

[18] See Guevara, 90.

[19] These were arms unused in the attack on the palace and sent up to the Sierra by Javier Pazos by means of a young Santiago recruit, Carlos Iglesias (known as 'Nicaragua').

[20] Guevara, 71.

[21] Mario Lazo, *Dagger in the Heart*, 235. Guevara regarded St George as a FBI spy, and, in a series of articles about Guevara's activities in Bolivia (*Sunday Telegraph*, 7 July 1968), St George was described as having done 'a spell in the U.S. military intelligence service'.

Castro was 'an ego-maniac and emotionally unstable but not a Communist'.

The 'guerrilla war' had still been quiet since February, and the irritation and even bewilderment of Batista and his officers at the worldwide interest in Castro can be readily understood. Now a new action was decided on: the discussion reveals the level at which events still were being enacted. Guevara merely desired, for instance, to capture a military lorry; Castro decided, however, on an attack on the military post of El Uvero, then ten miles away, placed similarly to the barracks of Plata, on the sea, and on the Babún brothers' estate. The rebels were helped greatly by Hermes Caldero, son-in-law of the administrator of the region. Two spies sent by Major Casillas were shot on 27 May; they had first revealed that the army knew of Castro's proximity to the post. A careful study was made of the surroundings. The rebels made the march to it at night down the roads built for their woodcutters by the Babuns. According to Colonel Barrera Pérez the employees of the region, on Castro's orders, gave a fiesta to the local soldiery the night before so that they would face an attack drunk and dazed; but of this no mention occurs in 'revolutionary history'.[22]

The orders for the attack were simply to surround the post on the three sides away from the sea, and then fire continuously at it. The living quarters where there were women and children were to be spared. The wife of the administrator of the estate knew of the imminent attack but did not leave because of not wishing to rouse suspicion. Rebel platoons commanded by Jorge Sotús, Guillermo García, Juan Almeida, Castro, Raúl Castro, Cienfuegos and Ameijeiras, got into position; Cresencio Pérez commanded the road towards Chivirico to prevent reinforcements. Guevara operated a machine gun. Eighty men entered into action, the remainder apparently staying in the hills.

The barracks were held by fifty-two men, commanded by Lieutenant Carrera, a somewhat aged officer in his fifties who had been in the army since 1922. The action, supposed to begin before dawn, began in fact only at daylight. Castro opened the firing, with his famous rifle with the telescopic lens; the barracks replied. One of the early shots broke the telephone exchange, and cut off the post from the possibility of communication. The advance then began, in bad conditions for the attackers, because of a lack of cover. Several men were wounded and some killed. Almeida overwhelmed the advance post in the direct path, with several wounded and one dead, and the ex-*precarista* Guillermo García did the same on the flank. The rebels prepared to storm the barracks after about three hours, with only some sporadic firing continuing. The rebels advanced, took over the living quarters

[22] Barrera Pérez, *Bohemia Libre*, 20 August 1961.

and captured the barracks' doctor, who showed himself incapable of action.[23]

In this contest, the fiercest which the rebels had yet fought, six attackers were killed – Julio Díaz (of the *Granma*); a guide, Eligio Mendoza; Moll; Emiliano Díaz (from the Santiago recruits), Vega and 'El Policía' an aide to Sotús. Two men were ¡very badly wounded. The army had fourteen killed, nineteen wounded (amongst them Lieutenant Carrera) and fourteen captured, while six escaped. One North American, Charles Ryan, fought for Castro.

After the contest, the rebels drew back to the mountains, carrying with them all possible supplies and medicaments in one of Babun's lorries. They took with them the fourteen prisoners, whom they later freed (after 'indoctrination', according to Colonel Barrera Pérez), and four of their own wounded, but left behind their two very badly wounded. It seemed impossible to move them, and the remaining Batistianos gave their word that they would be honourably treated. Leal, in fact, was sent to the Isle of Pines; Cilleros died on the way to Santiago. The other wounded men were escorted by Guevara in a column following behind the rest, going slowly and narrowly escaping capture, but aided by peasants and by a *mayoral* of the Peladero estate owned by a Santiago lawyer, José Pujol. The *mayoral* Sánchez was later caught and tortured brutally by the army, though he was, in the eyes of Guevara at least, an orthodox *mayoral*, faithful to his master, 'racist' and contemptuous of his peasants.[24]

This action heightened the morale of the rebels and gave them the feeling that they could master any of the little barracks near the Sierra.

Batista made no further attempt for the time being to cope with Castro in the only manner by which guerrilla forces can in fact be met, as suggested, for example, in the English campaign against guerrilla forces in Malaya in the 1950s, the most successful anti-guerrilla campaign of recent times. In Malaya the English decided on a full attempt to enmesh the Communist guerrillas of Chin Peng, blocked roads, and moved all scattered villagers into well-guarded compounds, echoing Weyler's camps, though they gave to those who were moved a new home and a new cash resettlement. Food was sealed, rationed and accounted for. These measures were accompanied by a general amnesty, a cash reward for surrender, and a rehabilitation programme including a monthly cash allowance during 'de-indoctrination' and preparation for a new job. There were also psychological appeals, protection against terrorism, generous aid for education, medical assistance and public

---

[23] See description of this battle in *Verde Olivo*, 2 June 1963, where the defeated Lieutenant Carrera exchanged memories with Ameijeiras; Guevara, 79, also has a rebel account.

[24] Guevara, 90. Sánchez was betrayed by peasants in August. *Cf. Havana Post*, 13 August 1957.

works. The English army in Malaya, interestingly enough, was smaller than Batista's in Cuba, consisting of 15,000 regular army and marines, but they were accompanied by 150,000 police and 250,000 volunteer home guards. The guerrilla forces were on the other hand far larger than Castro's at any stage, numbering 15,000 at their peak – and as Major Peterson of the U.S. marines thoughtfully put it, the rebellion was wiped out at a cost of £30,000 per guerrilla. Even so, some 1,000 or so guerrillas – more than Castro had at any stage in 1957 – were believed to be in action on the Thai border after the emergency was nominally declared at an end in 1960.

It would have been impossible for Batista to have emulated these methods completely, as men as intelligent as Barrera Pérez or Cantillo knew. His army of 40,000 was incomparably inferior to the English army of 15,000. So was his police. He could not rely on any organized voluntary help of any kind at any time. Maybe even allowing for the smaller number of rebels, £30,000 ($80,000) would have been too much per head though throughout 1957 with 150 rebels to destroy, this would have cost roughly only $M12, a sum which Batista could certainly have raised, perhaps out of his own pocket. But Batista certainly could not have attempted the mixture of toughness and magnanimity which characterized the approach of the English. Not only was he incapable of this, but the army was completely hamstrung by the evil genius of General Tabernilla and his cronies. Batista had never allowed himself to be influenced by the few intelligent officers who did exist in the Cuban army. The U.S. officers in Cuba as part of the military mission seem to have told him nothing. The small size of Castro's forces also placed Batista in a quandary: to concentrate an immense effort on the Sierra Maestra would explicitly contradict his argument that the rebels were being beaten. The problem of urban terrorism was also lacking in Malaya. In general, Batista's government showed itself incapable of dealing with a resolute, progressive revolutionary guerrilla force, with considerable peasant backing, once it had become firmly established.

These facts did not mean that by mid-1957 the regime was doomed to fall. Guerrilla forces had been maintained in China, Colombia or Guatemala for many years without achieving a national victory. The reasons for Batista's fall did not lie in the Sierra. The field of struggle was in Havana, and in Santiago, and in Washington as well. The role played by the government of the U.S. in the next eighteen months was ambivalent and extraordinary, even if in the end unsatisfactory both to Batista and to Castro.

CHAPTER LXXVII

The U.S. enters the Controversy

The attack on El Uvero came as a shock to Batista and, despite the protest of Tabernilla, it caused him to send back Colonel Barrera Pérez as field commander in the Sierra.[1] The month of May had been a time of difficulty: bombs went off incessantly. They were even set off in schools to try to keep children from taking their end of year examinations. Secondary schools spontaneously went on continuous strikes. There were frequent civilian casualties. On the day of the El Uvero attack itself, an immense explosion in Havana cut off telephone, electricity, gas and water for over fifty homes. The cost was $375,000, which the government was undecided whether to blame on Castro or their electoral enemies. Arrests also continued (among them Armando Hart and Carlos Franqui, of the Havana leadership). Captain Esteban Ventura, chief of police of the 5th Precinct, became in the public mind almost what Arsenio Ortiz had been in the era of Machado: a legendary death-dealer. Bombs were aimed to kill police chiefs, as in Machado's day. On 11 May, Batista met almost for the first time opposition from the law: at a trial in Santiago of a hundred Fidelistas, some survivors of the *Granma*, the presiding judge, Manuel Urrutia, declared that all should be acquitted. Batista, furious, foolishly allowed his Minister of Justice to enter a plaint against Urrutia (it was later dropped) and against the prosecutor, who had not asked for sentence. It was of small matter that the other two judges sent the *Granma* men to prison for varying periods of up to eight years: a judge had defied the government, and even the Conservative *Diario de la Marina*, which had always condemned terrorism, called on Batista to act according to the Constitution and hold elections. But Batista continued to refuse to put forward the date of elections any day before June 1958.

There was also trouble from the Electrical Workers' Union. Angel Cofiño, its leader, one of the few Cuban leaders who could have been regarded as a Social Democrat – he had been a Communist till 1941 – was dismissed in April, by Mujal, from his position on the executive of the CTC, on the suspicion that he was involved in sabotage against the government. Most electrical workers then went on strike to force Mujal to restore Cofiño. Many towns were partly or completely cut off from

[1] Barrera Pérez was nominated to go back on 9 June.

electricity or gas. The telephone union also walked out in sympathy. In consequence, Batista took the extreme step of temporarily nationalizing the electrical industry, and appointed an intervener, as Prío had done in the case of the railways in 1949. Several electrical union leaders were arrested. Cofiño then ordered his men back to work after deciding that the strike was not serving any useful end. He himself left Cuba, ostensibly to represent the country at the ILO in Geneva. Cofiño's conduct, however, as later became clear, was not irreproachable; his relations with Batista's government were far from unfriendly and those with the opposition were devious.[2]

The government's position meantime was curious. On the one hand Batista had the explicit and personal support of leaders of industry and of commerce, given at a series of ceremonies after his escape from assassination in March; and these men, and their U.S. colleagues so closely connected with them, continued to evince optimism about the state of the economy. The prosperity was indeed striking. Development seemed to be going ahead on every hand – a dry dock was planned for Havana; the Antilles Steel Company was expanding; the first quarter of 1957 showed new high levels of employment. Salaries were high, and reserves at $M476, were 9% higher than in 1956. The sugar chief Barreto explained that even the forty-five Oriente sugar mills (which then ground a fifth of the sugar in Cuba) had had a full harvest. The situation resembled 1870 more than 1895, though the old *Tinguaro* mill at Matanzas was seriously damaged on 26 May by a bomb, when it had only eight days more to grind, and the *Andorra* mill in Pinar del Río was similarly damaged, some sacks of sugar being destroyed. At the same time as the prosperity the threats to Batista grew daily. The movement towards sympathy with Castro mounted even among the opulent middle classes; and in the course of 1957 even the biggest sugar baron of all, Julio Lobo, gave the opposition $50,000.[3]

The constant attacks by the government leaders and their friends on Castro and the saboteurs as 'Communists' were beginning to have a life of their own: egged on by the BRAC,[4] Batista had for some months been sanctioning the dismissal of workers under a decree of 1955 if they proved to be Communists. In May 1957 he began, perhaps with reluctance, to take steps against Communist leaders – not because they had individually or as a party done anything to threaten him but because of the pressure of his own propaganda. Thus on 17 May Ursinio Rojas,

---

[2] See discussion of his case after the revolution, *Revolución*, 25 January 1959, 16.

[3] Carrillo MSS, p. 35. This money, obtained by Justo Carrillo and Rufo López Fresquet, was paid half to the 26 July Movement's treasurer Julio Duarte, and half to Carrillo's own, Montecristo movement. Lobo himself has, however, explained to the author that he never gave this money for Castro's movement.

[4] The Anti-Communist Bureau.

who had been the Communist secretary-general of the sugar workers till 1948, was arrested in Havana on the ground of helping Angel Cofiño and the electrical workers, a charge which scarcely carried weight since Cofiño and the Communists had been on atrocious terms since the former left the party in the 1940s. In this month also the Cuban Communist party, through its Havana City branch, and through Labour (particularly in the disturbed electrical union), began to make its first move towards the 26 July Movement – a gesture not reciprocated and which at the time led to very little. Yet within a few weeks, two members of Juventud Socialista, the Communist youth – Hiram Prats and Pablo Ribalta – were dispatched to the Sierra Maestra. Ribalta, a strong and handsome Negro, had worked for some years at the head-quarters of the International Union of Students in Prague and in October 1956 had visited China as a member of the delegation of the World Federation of Democratic Youth.[5] Prats, who had gone to the university in 1950, had been a member of Juventud Socialista since 1955; in 1957 he was president of the Young Communists' committee in the engineering school. These two joined Guevara – who formed a separate unit operating independently under Castro in July.[6] At the same time the Batistiano police began to treat Juventud Socialista more toughly than before, almost as much as it treated the 26 July and the Directorio: one member, Armando Mirabal, for instance, died after being beaten without revealing the names of his colleagues.[7]

The 26 July were, however, far from seeing eye to eye in these days with Juventud Socialista, at least outside the Sierra. Later in the year, Javier Pazos and Armando Hart shared a cell in prison, and the discussion turned to whether or not the Communist party should be allowed to function legally after the victory. Pazos thought yes; Hart the scion of a prominent Catholic family, thought no.[8]

From now on bombs and Molotov cocktails, arbitrary police executions and arrests leading to permanent disappearances were an essential part of the Cuban scene. Some of these bombs were laid by individuals wishing to assert themselves in the 'struggle'. Most were laid as part of the general programme of Civic Resistence, which had by this time abandoned its original policy of non-violence for sabotage, as a result

---

[5] Evidence of Carlos Zayas, a Spanish Democratic Socialist who was with him in China. After the Revolution, Ribalta became Cuban ambassador to Tanzania – a delicate post.

[6] *Hoy*, 25 March 1964 (Valdés Vivo's evidence at Marquito's trial; Hiram Prats's evidence.) Carlos Rafael Rodríguez in conversation with the author in June 1966 confirmed Ribalta's stay in the Sierra from 'late 1957'.

[7] *Ibid.*, Valdés Vivo evidence. Faure Chomón, no friend to the Communist party, referred to Mirabal in 1964 as 'a real Communist', who died fighting the tyranny.

[8] After the revolution, Pazos became an exile, and Hart became one of the eight-member Communist party politburo, secretary-general to the Latin American revolutionary organization and Minister of Education.

of a visit paid in mid-1957 by one of Castro's lieutenants, Iglesias ('Nicaragua').[9] Branches collected money, and distributed propaganda, flags and black and red arm bands. Sabotage was in the hands of a specific group in each branch, some of them being, like Ignacio González or Merced María Díaz Sánchez, veteran bomb layers of the 1930s; thus, when Señorita Díaz Sánchez, who worked in the Ministry of Public Works, was found injured in an explosion at the Havana Woolworth store in August, she was found to be an ex-member of Joven Cuba and to have laid bombs against Batista as early as 1936.[10] Manuel Ray, the architect, became chief of the Havana underground in mid-1957.

The bomb layers were of every age and every background; consider, for instance, the list of persons arrested on 15 August 1957: Francisco Pérez Rivas, aged twenty-seven, employee of Mendoza y la Torre, accused of distributing literature and placing bombs; María Urquiola Lechuga, aged forty-three, with no profession given, who owned the apartment where the bombs in this particular *cache* were found; Mercedes Urquiola Lechuga, her sister, aged twenty-seven, employed in the National Paper Company, accused of placing bombs and *petards*; José Manuel Alvárez Santa Cruz, student, aged seventeen, resident of the El Sevillano suburb, accused of placing bombs; Francisco Miares Fernández, aged eighteen, art student, resident of El Sevillano, accused of placing bombs given to him by two others; Manuel de Jesús Alfonso Gil, aged fifteen, resident of La Víbora, accused of selling 26 July bombs; Enrique Delgado Mayoral, aged eighteen, resident of the La Víbora suburb, employee of RCA laboratories, accused of bomb placing and bomb selling; Eliecer Cruz Cabrera, aged eighteen, student, accused of participating in a terrorist plot; Eladio and Ignacio Alfonso Carrera, aged sixteen and nineteen, accused of recruiting for the 26 July Movement; José Herrera León, aged sixteen, gardener, accused of placing bombs for a payment of $5; Ubaldo Fiallo Sánchez, aged twenty, a travelling drug salesman; Antonio Fernández Segura, aged thirty-five, dock employee; Jorge Alvarez Tagle, aged nineteen, employee of Richmond Company; Juan Fernández Segura, aged thirty-eight, labourer; Francisco Gómez Bermejo, aged seventeen, dock employee; Pastor Valiente Hernández, aged thirty-eight; Norberto Belanzoarán López, aged twenty-four. In the Señoritas Urquiola apartment were found: 15 *petards*, ready for action; two jars of phosphorus; one large time bomb; 24 Molotov cocktails; 15 gallons of gasoline mixed with oil; six 0·32-calibre Colt revolvers and ammunition.[11] The support given by

[9] For 'Nicaragua's' mission, see Llerena MSS, 58.
[10] *Havana Post*, 13 August 1957. Aged 53, she later died.
[11] *Ibid.*, 16 August 1957.

many teachers to the rebellion meant not only that their pupils followed them but that both had access in the science laboratories to the materials of explosion – as in the case of Eriberto Marbán, teacher at the Víbora Institute, who confessed on 27 August to having taught others to make weapons from materials in the laboratories.

A large number of Catholics and many priests in Oriente were now active members of the 26 July. In the course of the summer, Fr Guillermo Sardiñas climbed the Sierra to become, with permission of the coadjutor bishop of Havana, chaplain to the rebel army. Another priest, Fr Chelala, became treasurer of the movement in Holguín. The national treasurer, Enrique Canto, was a leading Catholic layman. Only the bishops and the regular clergy remained suspicious or divided, though both the bishops of Santiago and Matanzas never wavered in their hostility to the dictatorship. Protestant pastors such as the Rev. Fernández Ceballos were active in Havana. A labour organization depending on the Movement had also been founded, led at first by a bank workers' leader, Aguilera and then by David Salvador, the ex-Communist sugar worker from Las Villas.[12]

1957 was the first year of General Eisenhower's second term as president of the United States. It was a sluggish if, in retrospect, a happy time. The interviews between Castro and, first, Matthews and then Taber and Hoffman had created great interest in the U.S. Castro seemed a hero, a legend, a T. E. Lawrence of the Caribbean. The *New York Times* took a consistently interested and moderate position; for instance, a leader on the Humboldt 7 affair, doubtless written by Matthews, strongly denounced the 'harsh military dictatorship'. As in the 1870s, 1890s and 1930s, Cuban exiles were resourceful in demonstrations and in collecting money. From mid-1957 an agent of the 26 July operated in the Cuban Embassy in Washington, and a young economist, Ernesto Betancourt, was a registered 26 July agent in Washington. A similar organization existed in Mexico nominally headed by Pedro Miret and Gustavo Arcos, veterans of the Moncada attack, though, in the manner usually associated with exile movements, criticized by some other exiles, among them Castro's sisters who thought they were taking too much limelight. But the normal neighbourliness of U.S.–Cuban relations continued: *Time-Life* executives held their egregious conferences in Cuba; the Hedges family, half American, half Cuban, continued on excellent personal terms with the dictator, expressing in this intimacy the general approval felt by most American businessmen for the regime. Batista himself kept receiving U.S. honours of one kind or another – on

---

[12] See Carlos Rodríguez Quesada, *David Salvador*, 10. His deputies were Octavio Louit, a railwaymen's leader, and Reinol González, a bank employees' leader and a prominent member of the Catholic Workers' Youth.

18 May he became an honorary citizen of Texas. In return, he continued to distribute Cuban honours to resident or visiting U.S. officers or government officials. The U.S. military mission seemed to be frequent visitors to 'their Cuban opposite numbers'. Photographs showing U.S. colonels embracing General Tabernilla or Batista himself occurred often enough for the Cuban public to assume that the two countries were the close allies the statesmen of both said that they were.

The U.S. ambassador in Cuba, Arthur Gardner, had from the start closely identified himself with this position. He had suggested to Batista that the FBI or CIA should send up a man to the Sierra to kill Castro; Batista answered: 'No, no, we couldn't do that: we're Cubans.'[13] In his four years in Cuba Gardner had become a close friend of Batista's; he believed 'I don't think we ever had a better friend . . . It was regrettable, like all South Americans, that he was known – although I had no absolute knowledge of it – to be getting a cut . . . in almost all the things that were done. But . . . he was doing an amazing job.'[14]

In the spring the question of Gardner's replacement arose, not, so far as can be seen, from any dissatisfaction felt by the Secretary of State, John Foster Dulles, with his services, but because such a question was bound to arise after a new presidential term had begun. It was contemplated that one of the intellectual stars of the American foreign service, the admirable Charles Bohlen, then ambassador in Moscow, should go to Havana. It would have been a wise choice. Bohlen however went to Manila. Instead, the appointment in Havana went to Earl Smith, an investment broker, Yale 1926, colonel in the air force in the Second World War and on the War Production Board, then aged fifty-four, with no political experience of any sort. Gardner did not want to move: he went direct to Eisenhower, saying that 'Batista would be very upset as he, Gardner, was so close to Batista and that it would be a sign we were changing our policy towards Cuba and acknowledging the rightness of the criticism of himself.'[15] But Gardner had sent in a *pro forma* resignation after Eisenhower's re-election. This was taken out and accepted, to the ambassador's annoyance, on 14 May.

The ambassador returned to Washington. As in every other Cuban civil war, in 1868–78 and 1895–8, the situation there was critical. Gardner thought that the State Department had changed sides, and was supporting the cause of Castro against Batista. The assistant secretary in charge of the Latin American Department, Roy Rubottom, a

[13] Gardner to the author.
[14] Gardner evidence to Senate Internal Security Sub-Committee.
[15] Matthews, 68. Dulles told this to Herbert Matthews.

Texan ex-naval officer, had several times visited Havana during the Gardner era: 'My wife and I,' Gardner complained three years afterwards, 'would ask him questions whether he didn't agree with us and he would never answer ... He favoured Castro. There is no question about it.'[16] Rubottom, outside the easy-going, deceptively appealing Havana commercial belt which in the 1950s as in the 1850s had such a debilitating effect on all who experienced it, was disturbed at police torturing in Havana; as a Democrat, he had high hopes of the opposition. His chief, the ubiquitous U.S. diplomat of the 1940s and 1950s, Robert Murphy, took a stronger view; he believed Batista was a 'gorilla'.[17]

At the Caribbean desk in the State Department, meantime, a new appointment had been made: a man who later would, more than Rubottom, become a sacrificial scapegoat for U.S. anxiety in Cuba – William Wieland, then aged fifty, who had spent twelve years in Havana between 1925 and 1937. Wieland's father died young and his mother had married again, a Cuban, Manuel Montenegro, and for a time Wieland had gone under that name when a child. He had worked in Havana, first for the General Electric and Cuban Electric Companies, afterwards for the *Havana Post*, during the revolution of 1933. He met Sumner Welles and later, in 1941, 'when he had worked years for the Associated Press', Welles secured his entry into the State Department. Afterwards, he had been in various U.S. legations in Latin America, including that at Bogotá in 1947 during the Bogotazo. By experience he was thus well suited to the task of being the Cuban specialist in the State Department during a revolutionary period.

His views were, however, curiously difficult to estimate; granted that he was unjustly persecuted by the Senate Internal Security Sub-Committee and its special counsel J. G. Sourwine, Wieland appears to have changed his mind several times. 'I was never an admirer of Castro,' he told his taunters in 1960, 'I became convinced that he was a mentally sick man, completely obsessed with his own ego, and unscrupulously ambitious',[18] but at the same time William Pawley, another businessman ambassador, though of tougher mettle than Smith or Gardner, recalled that when they were both at Rio de Janeiro, he 'got him out [because] he was much too far to the Left'.[19] At the time of his appointment Wieland, like Murphy and Rubottom, was a firm opponent of Batista. This view was apparently shared by those members of the CIA in Washington who specialized on Cuba, such as Colonel J. C. King (later head of the CIA's Latin American section), and even

[16] Gardner evidence.
[17] So he told Gardner.
[18] *Communist Threat*, 670.
[19] *Ibid.*, 672.

more so by those who were in the Embassy at Havana, particularly its second-in-command.[20]

Such was the ambivalent atmosphere in Washington when Earl Smith took up his appointment as ambassador to Havana. Before going to Havana Smith consulted a fellow businessman and diplomat, Robert Hill, then concerned with the Department's relations with Congress, previously vice-president of Grace Shipping Lines and ambassador in Central America. Hill, who had just been appointed U.S. ambassador to Mexico, said to Smith, 'I am sorry you are going to Cuba ... You are assigned to Cuba to preside over the downfall of Batista. The decision has been made that Batista has to go.' Hill urged Smith to take with him to Havana a minister whom he could trust, and made some suggestions, but none would accept the job. One at least of them told Hill privately, 'I don't want to go to Havana because Castro is coming to power.' 'It was my judgement,' Hill said later, 'at that time that Castro was being assisted into power and that there had been some activity along the corridors of the Department to support his cause.'[21] But Smith persevered. Wieland suggested he should see Herbert Matthews – a sensible idea but one which later almost cost him his job.[22] Smith anyway saw Matthews, who told him that he thought Batista 'a ruthless and corrupt dictator ... who would soon fall, and that it would be in the best interest of Cuba and ... the world ... if Batista were removed'.[23] Matthews also urged Smith to travel in the rest of Cuba as soon as possible, and go outside Havana.

Smith, of good connections in the U.S., had known Cuba as a tourist for many years. Though he had had no diplomatic experience and owed his embassy to his contribution to Republican funds – he had been Republican leader in Florida since 1952 – he had 'long wanted' this job.[24] He was 'an old friend' of Cubans such as Raúl Menocal, then a minister, and Miguel Tarafa, a sugar king.[25] He was sworn as ambassador on 13 June. The wife of his Palm Beach companion, Senator John Kennedy of Massachusetts, was among the little group who attended the ceremony. But in order not to give the impression that his appointment would mean anything in the way of intervention by the U.S. or a change of policy he did not actually install himself in Cuba till mid-July. The stage was now set for a chapter bizarre even in the history of diplomacy.

[20] See Smith's testimony. For King see the testimony of Willauer and Gardner (ibid. 678). Lyman Kirkpatrick, *The Real CIA*, 157, describes how he secured Ambassador Gardner's reluctant agreement to allow the CIA to enter into contact with the opposition in 1956.

[21] Hill testimony, *Communist Threat*, 807–8.

[22] See Wieland, *ibid.*

[23] Smith testimony, *ibid.*, 682–3. Matthews notes in his book (71) this testimony to be accurate.

[24] Earl T. Smith, *The Fourth Floor* (1962), 4.

[25] *Havana Post*, 18 July 1957. See also, *ibid.*, 20 July 1957.

CHAPTER LXXVIII

Miami and Santiago

On 25 May 1957 a little group of men sailed out of Miami under the ex-leader of the Havana airport workers, Calixto Sánchez, who had been implicated in the attack on the palace in March and had apparently felt guilt at not having progressed further.[1] These were Prío's men. They had landed near Mayarí, in Oriente, Castro's home territory, and were swiftly tricked into surrender. Sixteen men, including Sánchez, were shot by the local lieutenant of police.[2] This was a serious setback to the hope Prío still cherished of putting forward an effective rival to Castro among the revolutionary opposition. A few days before, too, the most famous of Prío's gangster friends, El Extraño, had been arrested in Costa Rica with two companions, for planning to assassinate the democratic President Figueres; El Extraño said he had been offered $200,000 by Trujillo to kill Figueres. A case was mounted against him, he remained in prison, and one more Cuban gangster of the old time disappeared, at least for the time being. The ground was becoming clearer and clearer for the opposition to unite behind Castro in the Sierra.

In these circumstances and following the attack at El Uvero, Batista began a new policy towards the rebels. In June Colonel Barrera had been sent back to his battlefield of limited success earlier in the year, establishing a command post at the sugar mill *Estrada Palma*. He had devised a plan whereby he and his aides, Sánchez Mosquera, Moreno Bravo and Merob Sosa, would pursue the different rebel columns, when Díaz Tamayo was suddenly dismissed from command in Oriente and succeeded by an unconditional friend of General Tabernilla, Rodríguez Avila. He gave quite new orders for the evacuation of all the peasant families in the Sierra, so as to establish a zone which would be completely banned to all except the army. The army would shoot at sight without troubling to see whether the peasant concerned was a friend or a foe. The air force would also be able to bomb the jungle indiscriminately.

[1] Sánchez was an Auténtico who had joined Carrillo's Acción Libertadora and then Menelao Mora. On the day of the attack on the palace he did not appear and afterwards left Cuba with the help of Mujal, an old friend. In Miami he was regarded as a traitor and he gained the help of Prío to save his face (evidence of Suárez to Draper).

[2] Two members of the group, Lázaro Guerra Calderón and Mario Rodríguez Arenas, were captured and described how they had lived in the Dominican Republic till the attack.

At the same time, new plans had been decided upon by the 26 July Movement. June in the Sierra was passed in recuperation. The battle at El Uvero had been the first contest won by the rebels in which they had had serious casualties. The treatment of the wounded occupied a section of the force, under Guevara, for several weeks. Moving slowly back towards the heart of the Sierra, behind the main column, Guevara's force had gone up and down in size as different groups of peasants rallied to it and then dropped out; others came from the cities, and then returned there, unable to stand the hard conditions. Two Batistiano ex-soldiers joined Guevara but they significantly found the going too rough and went down again. It was not till late in June that the groups rejoined: the whole rebel force now reached about two hundred.[3] Batista's decision to change the nature of the war enlarged the area of free movement of the rebels. There was now almost a true *'territorio libre'* with a rough repair shop, a hospital, a shoe and leather factory, an armoury with an electric saw, and an ironmonger charged to refill brass grenades. There were bread ovens, and later, schools and a lecture hall. All such places were in danger from time to time, though several remote valleys such as that of La Mesa, were never reached and remained an invulnerable centre of these activities till the end of the war.[4]

If little new fighting occurred in the Sierra for a time, it was a period of much political manœuvring. Nearly every civic and social group in each province was writing to the government to protest against arbitrary arrests and against the continuance of military operations in the Sierra. Thanks to Suez and failures in the European and Russian beet fields the harvest had sold splendidly, and 1957 looked like being one of the best years of the Cuban economy. A meeting of the ecclesiastical hierarchy resulted in pleas for peace from Cardinal Arteaga, archbishop of Havana, and the bishop of Pinar del Río (Aurelio Díaz). Mgr Pérez Serantes, bishop of Santiago, made a similar plea.[5] The regular Ortodoxos and Auténticos dropped out of Batista's parliamentary commission, but the Congress nevertheless passed 'constitutional reforms' which included the provision for holding presidential elections on 1 June 1958, and the inauguration of a new president on 24 February 1959. Grau, Ochoa's branch of the Ortodoxos and four other groups of the centre opposition formed an alliance and proposed that the senior Supreme Court judge should take over as provisional president with elections within ninety days; but Grau also let it be known that he would take part in Batista's 1958 elections. Such ambivalence prevented any

[3] Guevara, 100.
[4] Núñez Jiménez, 577.
[5] *Havana Post*, 1 June 1957.

chance, always remote, that this new political alignment might be taken seriously.

Prío, damped by the failure of his last military expedition, that of the *Corinthia*, was reduced to the expedient of writing to Batista from Miami begging him to leave: Batista's answer was to stage a mass demonstration of parties backing him to open the 1958 election campaign in Santiago. But only about 5,000 came, most of these, it was thought, government employees, with sporadic rioting on the edges and some shooting. A similar meeting, by Senator Masferrer in Chivirico on the Sierra Maestra coast between Santiago and El Uvero, was also unsuccessful as a rallying point for the regime, though Masferrer, trying to outbid Castro, promised in a grandiose way to give land to the peasants.

Batista had several times said that he would not stand at the 1958 elections both because the Constitution forbade it and because he thought he had done his bit. Who would stand? The vice-president, Guas Inclán said that he hoped Castro would take part in the 1958 general elections. Ochoa, resident of the 'registered Ortodoxos', agreed to participate, as did Márquez Sterling, another dissident Ortodoxo. Both these ex-disciples of Chibás thereby dissociated themselves from the mass of his following, as from Castro. Various attempts began to be made to get these moderate opposition parties together with a single 'front'.

The 26 July Movement was also busy. In Mexico, a document described as a 'manifesto'[6] was published ostensibly containing Castro's views in November 1956; it had in fact been written by Mario Llerena, without direct contact with Castro. No doubt it reflected what many of the younger followers of Castro now believed: the Ortodoxos were no more 'than a curious psychological phenomenon lacking their own ideology and programme; only Chibás's personality had given them cohesion'; and Chibás was dead. The 26 July preferred to avoid abstract formulae or preconceived blueprints. 'The ideology of the Cuban Revolution must be born from Cuba's own roots and the condition of the people and of the race. It will not be . . . something imported from other latitudes.' But the 26 July Movement considered the 'Jeffersonian philosophy still valid' and subscribed fully to the 'Lincoln formula'. Yet it was also 'necessary to see that the dividends of the utilities, land and mines went to the country, not abroad'. Economic planning would free the nation from the evils of monoculture, such as the privileged monopolies, and the *latifundios*. (There was criticism of 'foreign bases' (such as Guantánamo).) A hopeful if mysterious sentence referred to the 26 July Movement's desire to reach a state of solidarity and harmony

---

[6] *Nuestra Razón: Manifiesto-Programa del Movimiento 26 de Julio. Cf.* Pedrero, 89–130. Llerena (MSS 93–5) discusses.

between capital and labour in order to raise productivity. Although the document did not mention the Constitution of 1940, there would be a representative government based on the genuine expression of popular will, and a new electoral code. The whole document might be regarded as roughly expressive of a social democratic movement in Europe, though it was more of a constitutional guide than an election programme.[7]

This and similar programmes caused more and more professional men to join the 26 July Movement, among them the outstanding young engineer, Manuel Ray, president of the Civil Engineers' Association. Ray, a graduate in 1946, had worked in the State Development Commission in the days of Prío and had recently been the engineer of the tunnel linking Vedado with Miramar in Havana. Sympathetic to the Ortodoxos, he nevertheless took a slightly different position; on 1 May 1957 he spoke with Raúl Chibás and then joined the Civic Resistance Movement. At that time he knew very little about Castro, as did most of that movement. He 'did not quite know Castro's programme' and had known Raúl Chibás 'only as a football leader at school'. Essentially non-political, he had wanted to become president of the Civil Engineers in order to destroy its corruption.[8]

So far Castro had avoided giving his name to any programme since he had arrived in the Sierra: indeed his remarks to Matthews, Taber and Andrew St George were all that had come out of the Sierra. He never commented on 'Nuestra Razón', and his lieutenants such as Hart and Marcelo Fernández avoided full endorsement of it. But having aroused expectation among the professional middle class this doctrinal silence could not last. In early July Raúl Chibás and Felipe Pazos, the titular Ortodoxo leader and the most distinguished economist in Cuba, made their way up to the Sierra. Chibás says that he went to the Sierra as a gesture, a commitment of maturity to the armed struggle.[9] On 12 July, after some days of discussions, a general manifesto was issued, signed by Castro, Chibás and Pazos. Most of it was written by Castro.[10] It called all Cubans to form a civic revolutionary front to 'end the regime of force, the violation of individual rights, and the infamous crimes of the police'; the only way to settle the peace of Cuba was free elections and a democratic government; the rebels were, the manifesto

---

[7] Llerena had, it appears, struck out of the text any mention of totalitarian Communism, on the suggestion of Faustino Pérez who had told him that some of those in the hills would find this unwelcome; he had included the radical section of the document on the advice of Marcelo Fernández (Llerena MSS, p. 44). Armando Hart wrote later that the document contained 'the thought of the Movement even though . . . it could be amplified' (letter, 15 October 1957).

[8] Evidence to the author of Manuel Ray, Puerto Rico, 1963.

[9] Chibás MSS.

[10] *Ibid.*

insisted, 'fighting for the fine ideal of a Cuba free, democratic and just'. There would be an absolute guarantee of press freedom and free elections in all the trade unions. A request to the U.S. was framed for a suspension of arms shipments in Cuba during the civil war, and also a rejection of foreign intervention or mediation. A military junta to replace Batista would be unacceptable. Instead, there would be an 'impartial' non-political provisional president, and a provisional government would hold elections within a year of getting office; elections would be held according to the Constitution of 1940 and the Electoral Code of 1943.

The economic side of the programme was written by Castro on the basis of notes taken by a young lawyer, Baudilio Castellanos, at Santiago, from lectures given by Pazos himself and his colleague, Regino Boti, a clever young economist, the son of a patriarchal poet of Guantánamo.[11] The proposals included a demand for the suppression of gambling and corruption; for agrarian reform, leading to the distribution among landless workers of uncultivated lands; for the increase of industrialization; and for the conversion of tenant farmers and squatters into proprietors. Existing owners would be compensated. There was nothing about nationalization of public utilities, nothing about the collectivization of land nor certainly of industry. It was a document somewhat less radical than that written by Llerena in Mexico, less radical also than Castro's own statements in Mexico, certainly less radical than the proposals in *History will absolve me*,[12] and less radical than Pazos's lectures themselves as embodied in a note current in Mexico in 1956 and worked on by Castro.[13] According to Guevara, Castro 'tried to make more explicit some of the declarations on agrarian reform' but he could not break the united front of the two others;[14] but the others present dispute the truth of this contention.[15]

Was this manifesto a deception? Guevara later commented explicitly:

> We were not satisfied with the compromise, but it was necessary; it was progressive at that moment. It could scarcely last beyond the moment when it marked a break in the development of the revolution[16] ... we knew it was a minimum programme, a programme which limited our effort, but ... we knew that it was not possible to realise our will from the Sierra Maestra and that we had to reckon,

[11] Pazos's evidence. Castellanos later became Cuban ambassador to France (1967).
[12] Text in Jules Dubois, 166–72.
[13] Guevara, 103.
[14] Llerena read this, but in the late summer of 1956 in Mexico City.
[15] Chibás (MSS), who says that Castro 'never tried to express different thoughts from those which we all signed in common'.
[16] *No podía durar más allá del momento en que significara una detención en el desarrollo revolucionario.*

MIAMI AND SANTIAGO · 955

during a long period, with a whole series of 'friends' who tried to use our military strength and the great confidence which the people already had in Fidel Castro, for their own macabre purposes, and ... to maintain the dominion of imperialism in Cuba, through its imported *bourgeoisie*, so tightly linked with North American masters ... This declaration for us was only a short pause in the journey,[17] we had to continue our fundamental task of defeating the enemy on the field of battle.[18]

Some of Castro's explanations of 1961 presumably apply to this epoch: 'It is undeniable that if when we began to be strong we had been known as people of very radical ideas, the social class which is now making war on us would have done so then' – that is, the professional middle class which afterwards turned in its majority away from Castro.[19]

In view of such remarks it would be appropriate to conclude that Castro's drafting and signature of the 'Pact of the Sierra' involved dissimulation; that probably as a result of his experiences in the Sierra itself and the influences to which he had been subject there (such as those of Guevara and his brother) he had already determined to attempt a more radical reconstruction of society than he had envisaged at the time of the Moncada attack or even the landing of the *Granma*; that although there was as yet no alliance, and scarcely actual contact with the Communist party of Cuba, nor even its youth movement, Fidel Castro, presumably through his brother Raúl, knew of the changing policies of those groups themselves which could later prepare the way for sympathy. But Castro's own thinking, like that even of Guevara, was in evolution; maybe he made in those days private commitments to Guevara and Raúl Castro, which he afterwards fulfilled; but he could have still deceived them or broken with them as he did others. In 1957 Castro was preoccupied with overthrowing Batista; and he did not seem particularly to care with whom he made an alliance, what he said, or what commitments he undertook to serve that end. The future, after the victory, could look after itself, an attitude held by nearly all combatants in nearly all wars.

That the 26 July Movement's political aims were in the process of change is shown by an article attributed (apparently falsely) to Castro in the magazine *Cuba Libre*, published in San José, Costa Rica, in August 1957, in which provisions for the nationalization of electricity and the telephone system and the 'final solution of the land problem' (including the expropriation of plots over 170 acres) were both included.

This manifesto of the Sierra signed, it was sent back to Havana by the

[17] *Un pequeño alto en el camino.*
[18] Guevara, 103–5.
[19] *Obra Revolucionaria*, 1961, No. 46, 17.

hands of a loyal peasant of the region, El Trolinero, and published in *Bohemia*. At the same time Castro's scheme for the establishment of a regular government in the Sierra foundered.[20] Two of the Ortodoxo splinter groups (those led by Manuel Bisbé in Havana, and Agramonte in Mexico) gave full support to it; two (those which followed Márquez Sterling and Ochoa) did not, nor did any other opposition group: 'What's the point of substituting one *de facto* government for another?' was their attitude.

Earl Smith meantime arrived in Havana on 15 July.[21] He found the capital calm, but outside the atmosphere was one of terror. There was near-open war in Santiago between the 26 July and the police. The plan of the 26 July Movement was to provoke universal disruption in the cities of Oriente and in the countryside by strikes and terrorism, and then to strike at the main public buildings in the cities, thereby winning control of the province. Jeeps and cars carrying soldiers or police were constantly attacked; and, always, a large percentage of those who were arrested turned out to be very young, even schoolboys. On 7 July an eight-year old girl was arrested placing a bomb in Guantánamo. The old gangsters of the days of Prío had thus given way to idealistic gunmen in their teens or even younger. It was as if delinquency had been articulated into street fighting, though sometimes 26 July Movement flags would appear on top of buildings rather than bombs beneath them – on the new FOCSA building in Vedado, or the television tower. But it was much harder to coordinate all these activities. Maybe there was some settling of private scores; what, for instance, really lay behind the murder of Daniel Sánchez, school bus driver of Santiago, found with the label 'Traitor to the 26 July' in the street on 6 July?

Batista tried to answer all this with pleas for 'electoralism'; the choice was between bloodshed and elections – his elections, that is, of 1958. He appealed to the 'genuine' opposition of Grau San Martín, Pardo Llada, and Ochoa, to continue to compete in his elections. On 4 July he issued a stirring statement recalling Jefferson and Washington. This had no effect save perhaps among the U.S. community who, once again, mouthed Roosevelt's old dictum about Trujillo. On 24 July Smith gave his first press conference: 'Our two nations I feel will always be the closest of friends and allies in the common fight against Communism.'[22] He also praised BRAC – unwisely, since BRAC had recently confounded Communists with all members of the opposition. But, he added, 'we have nothing substantial to make us believe', that Castro's

[20] See letter of refusal to countenance such an idea by Justo Carrillo, dated 27 June.
[21] Smith, *The Fourth Floor*, 8.
[22] *Ibid.*, 11–12.

movement 'is red-inspired'.[23] He came, he said, as an observer; and in this spirit he decided to follow Herbert Matthews's advice and get out of Havana as soon as he could, to see something of the country. The following week he announced that he would go to Oriente and visit Santiago, the U.S. base at Guantánamo and the U.S.-owned Moa Bay and Nicaro properties, the largest single U.S. concerns in the island.

Santiago had had a harsh July. There were even rumours that U.S. citizens were thinking of withdrawing altogether. 26 July Movement flags had often appeared. There had been much shooting. Schools had been burned. Molotov cocktails were used frequently by the 26 July Movement. On 26–27 July, the anniversary of the Moncada attack, the police were said to have arrested 200 people, many in Santiago. All this was, of course, a deliberate plan to destroy ordinary life in Oriente as much as possible prior to an attempted mass attack on public buildings. On 30 July, the day before Smith was due to set out, the main 26 July organizer in Santiago, Frank País, then still aged only twenty-three, was shot down in the Callejón del Muro in Santiago by the police chief of Santiago, Colonel José Salas Cañizares and one of his henchmen, 'Mano Negra'. País had been identified some weeks before as a main police quarry, and had been on the run, though remaining in the city. His brother José had been killed at the government demonstration in June. País had been hiding in the shop of Raúl Pujol, an ironmonger, who had been one of the chief suppliers of the rebels, and who was also killed.[24] One more political crime had been committed, one more execution without trial. The consequences were, however, unusual. The entire 26 July Movement of Santiago attended País's lying-in-state in the house of his *novia*, América Telebauta. The police refrained, however, from any action. The next day an immense demonstration of women gathered in the centre of Santiago to protest. Ostensibly arriving to shop, they gathered in the main square at the moment when Earl Smith, General Eisenhower's ambassador, was to be officially received.[25]

It was a successful demonstration. Smith drove into the city in an eight-car motorcade. Women dressed in black ran to greet him shouting 'Libertad! Libertad!' At the town hall huge crowds gathered. The Smiths went inside the hall and the police brought water hoses to press the women back, and arrested about forty. The main square was in confusion at the moment Smith came out. The police attempted desperately

[23] *Ibid.*
[24] Two men, a lieutenant of police and a soldier, Ortiz Guirado and Alvarez Echevarría, were tried for their part in the murder in July 1965 (*cf. Hoy*, 16 July 1965). Colonel Ventura, *Memorias*, 86, accused two prominent Castro followers Armando Hart and Haydée Santamaría, of betraying País to Colonel Faget of the BRAC but this is inconceivable.
[25] País was succeeded as 'national chief of the militias' by René Ramos Latour ('Daniel'), a worker in Nicaro, who had spent some time in the Sierra, and who had been active throughout Cuba raising money and collecting arms.

to beat back the women with a violence that outraged Smith. He saw women being knocked down and thrown into the police wagon. One woman successfully handed him a letter demanding a reconsideration of U.S. policy of support for Batista. In the afternoon, the ambassador gave a press conference and announced that 'excessive police action is abhorrent to me. I deeply regret that my presence in Santiago . . . may have been the cause of public demonstrations . . . I . . . trust that those held by the police have been freed.'[26] Afterwards, while País's body was escorted by a huge procession to the cemetery, Smith tactfully laid a wreath on Martí's grave.

These actions by Smith made an excellent impression among the Cuban opposition and on their friends in the U.S. The *New York Times* praised him. The friends of Batista denounced him, accusing him of undiplomatic behaviour. Against this charge Smith was defended by the Secretary of State, Dulles. Many now supposed that Smith would bring a new policy to Cuba: but in fact the State Department had merely instructed him 'to alter the prevailing notion in Cuba that the American Ambassador was intervening on behalf of the government of Cuba to perpetuate the Batista dictatorship'[27] – that is, he was to try to be neutral.

There was some coordination between the protests in Santiago and events in the Sierra. After the emissaries from the plain had left, Castro had reorganized his followers. Raúl Castro and Guevara both now commanded separate columns, with the rank of major. Guevara ceased to be doctor to the rebels, his place being taken by a new recruit from the plain, Dr Sergio del Valle. But these separate columns did not act in a new theatre of war; Castro resisted the demands from the plain that a 'second front' should be opened up – especially after the failure of a minor attempt to do so in the north near *central Miranda*.[28] The rebels were still troubled by desertions and one young peasant had recently been shot accordingly. On 26 July a group led by the peasant Guillermo García fell on the *central Estrada Palma*, the nearest sugar mill to the Sierra on the Manzanillo side, and withdrew after causing damage and casualties.[29] On 31 July Guevara's column tried to attack a small military post in the copper mining district, Bueycito, where he believed that Major Casillas would be found visiting a mistress. The column travelled in three lorries, fell on the barracks at night, and engaged in firing for only a few minutes before it surrendered; six Rural Guardsmen were wounded, one rebel killed and three wounded;

[26] Smith, *The Fourth Floor*, 21.
[27] *Ibid.*, 20.
[28] Guevara, 105–6.
[29] *Bohemia*, 30 July 1957. See also *Havana Post*, 29 July. In fact Guillermo García was after this disciplined for insufficient powers of command (see Chibás MSS).

the rebels burned the barracks, seized a Browning machine gun and other things useful to them, and took away as prisoners the sergeant in command and a spy named Orán, to act as hostages against reprisals in the village, but both were later freed. They also blew up a bridge, the dynamiter being a farmer in the village, Cristóbal Naranjo, who then joined the rebels. The village gave the rebels beer and fruit juices.[30]

On the plain, meantime, the País funeral procession was succeeded by a strike, long prepared, but only now enacted – following naturally from the closing of the shops in Santiago during the funeral and demonstrations. The police tried to force the shops to reopen, but the strike lasted five days. The Nicaro nickel plant was also closed. This was of course a part of the rebels' ambitious overall plan. The following week the strike spread through the island, in Havana affecting bus drivers and bank clerks. The government responded by arresting as many members of the 26 July Movement as they could. In Holguín, Colonel Cowley shot nine people in the streets during a power cut. There was, however, little coordination of the strikes and when Havana returned to work on 6 August, Oriente, licking its wounds, also went back. Constitutional guarantees were once more suspended. At least locally the Communists seem to have backed the strike where possible.[31]

From this time on it would be correct to assume that Cuba was in the same state of civil war as existed in, say, Cyprus or Malaya during the emergency, and the manner in which it was fought resembled the conditions whereby an imperial power attempted by the use of police methods to put down a revolt in which the rebels could count on the sympathy of large sections of the population of all classes. The police continued to kill men but each death created ten new supporters of the revolt. Beyond the horizon too there loomed the unpredictable power of the U.S., for so long the arbiter of Cuban destinies. It was inconceivable that the U.S. could remain merely an observer. Her army and navy continued to be ranged beside Batista, their white uniforms resplendent next to his in hundreds of photographs of innumerable friendly gatherings. Her businessmen continued only too friendly with the regime; the funeral of the textile and rayon magnate, Dayton Hedges, in June, had been attended by Batista and most of his cabinet; Hedges's sons, Dayton Jr. and Burke, were among Batista's closest friends. By late 1957 it seemed even to middle class professional men that the struggle not only resembled a struggle against an old imperial power but in fact *was* one; a few individuals, like the apparently

[30] See *Havana Post*, 3 August 1957.
[31] *Cf.* Blas Roca to the 8th Congress of the Communist Party (*The Cuban Revolution* (1961), 8).

progressive Earl Smith or Matthews[32] or enlightened men in the CIA
or State Department, could not atone for the silence of thousands of
businessmen, soldiers and tourists; silence surely meant commitment;
and commitment, enmity – an enmity which seemed bereft of disguise
in Oriente where the first battalion in search of Castro was composed
of men trained in the U.S. and which used 'the most modern U.S.
weapons'. Ambassador Gardner, when leaving in June, had announced
that the U.S. had no intention of intervening in Cuba; some newspapers
gave this statement a headline; Batista's hand went quickly to his
scabbard, denouncing the very idea that such a project could even be
considered and arguing that it was poor taste of the editors to use such
a headline from a remark by an old friend of Cuba out of context. But
clearly it suggested an anxiety not far below the surface: who would
provide the mediation, and when? For some weeks Batista and his
ministers implied that the opposition was seeking to do this. But more
extreme Americans accepted Batista's evaluation of Castro: thus
Spruille Braden, the ex-ambassador in Havana, progressive in the
1940s but now in the 1950s, through the turn of emotions during the
age of McCarthy, a member of the far Right, wrote in *Human Events* on
17 August 1957 that Castro 'is a fellow traveller, if not a member of the
Communist party and has been so for a long time . . .'.[33] The game of
accusations and counter-accusations had begun.

[32] Not surprisingly, Cuban journalists were annoyed at the ease with which U.S. journalists
seemed to have got to the Sierra, and they had not. See protest by the Cuban College of
Journalists, June 1957.

[33] Qu., *Communist in the Caribbean*, 248. Mario Lazo, the Cuban lawyer who advised the U.S.
Embassy in Havana, went to New York in August 1957 to try to get the *New York Times* to
stop supporting the rebels. At a discussion with the ex-ambassador to Cuba, Guggenheim, at
which Batista's ambassador to Washington, Arroyo, was present, Guggenheim explained,
'You must get Batista to call for elections before any change can be expected.' (Lazo, 116–17.)

CHAPTER LXXIX

The Naval Mutiny at Cienfuegos

Castro, Raúl Chibás and Pazos had denounced in the manifesto of the Sierra any idea that a section of the armed forces themselves might help towards the overthrow of Batista. They had criticized Barquín's *coup*. Of course if such a *coup* were to occur, it would prejudice Castro's own chances of attaining power. Thus Barquín was for Castro a dangerous rival. But in September a section of the navy in Cienfuegos made a serious attempt to overthrow the regime through the naval officers quartered there, in collaboration with the 26 July Movement, the Auténticos, and others.

The plan resembled most of those enacted by Cuban revolutionaries: a shock attack, surprise in overcoming numbers, afterwards improvisation. The situation in Cienfuegos favoured such action. But unlike the attack at Moncada, men inside the barracks played a key part in the attack; and again, unlike Moncada, the U.S. Embassy had been informed; indeed, according to the U.S. Ambassador, the second-in-command of the CIA (William Williamson) at the U.S. Embassy had told the conspirators that any government set up as a result of a successful rising would be recognized by the U.S.[1] Smith knew nothing of the CIA man's activities, though he did know of the projected revolt.

The 26 July Movement had had for some months a following among the younger officers of the navy, many of whom deeply resented the barbarous killer Laurent, chief of naval intelligence, and his henchmen. At the end of May a group of young civilian 26 July men in Cienfuegos had been arrested and tortured.[2] This was the signal for a new and ambitious plan to take over the naval base. The leader of the 26 July Movement in Cienfuegos, Emilio Aragonés, of a good family in the town, met Javier Pazos, temporarily head of the Havana underground. He co-ordinated the plan with Santiago and with Castro. Pazos took 'all the guns in Havana to Cienfuegos'. Aragonés, however, did not shine as an organizer and many of these were not used.[3] But the naval conspirators did not rely entirely on Castro's movement, since several had links with Carrillo's Montecristi, Prío and the Auténticos. Carrillo

---

[1] Smith testimony to Senate Internal Security Sub Committee; see Suárez Núñez, 75.
[2] René Ray, 33.
[3] Pazos's evidence.

had spent his share of Julio Lobo's $25,000 on this venture.[4] Nor was the scheme limited to Cienfuegos. The plan contemplated that as a key to the situation, the cruiser *Cuba* would be seized and with other ships then in Havana Harbour, would train her big guns on Campamento Columbia, and the Morrow and Príncipe castles, and then capture the city with naval manpower and the Havana underground. Other ports were implicated. In the pressure of conspiracy, men became committed to increasingly lavish schemes. Details were forgotten. The day before the attack was due, 5 September, the naval officers in Havana decided that they were not ready. An attempt was made to postpone all action, successfully in the case of Mariel and Santiago. But the 26 July Movement gave the order to go ahead in Cienfuegos.[5]

The attack on Cienfuegos was led by a cashiered naval lieutenant, Dionisio San Román, who had previously served in Cienfuegos and who in 1956 played a minor part in the Barquín conspiracy. Twenty-eight conspirators within the base were headed by Santiago Ríos, a petty officer. Their task was to capture the naval base at night, arrest the officers and open the gates to San Román and the Auténtico conspirators, led by Miguel Merino and Raúl Coll. Many of the married officers and men slept in the town, so that there were only about a hundred and fifty men sleeping at the base. At dawn, Ríos and four enlisted men took over the armoury and the main gatehouse. The sentry at the armoury and several of the men at the gate joined the rebellion, the others were locked up. All the inner security posts were also seized. By 5.30 a.m. the base was in rebel hands, though Colonel Roberto Comesañas, the commander, still slept. San Román came in from the town and woke and arrested the commander. A hundred and fifty members of the 26 July Movement arrived, with about fifty Auténticos. All received arms.

Officers and men began to arrive from the town. Each was quickly given the choice of being arrested or joining the rebellion. Six officers and most of the men took the second choice, while eighteen officers were arrested.

The rebellion was now led into the city; cries were heard of *Viva Cuba Libre! Viva la Revolución! Viva la marina de guerra! Viva San Román!* At 8 a.m. a rebellious lieutenant of the harbour police took over the maritime police headquarters and killed the superintendent, Major Cejas. The Cienfuegos military commander, Major Eugenio Fernández, was arrested at the headquarters of the Guardia Rural. All that remained was the police headquarters, which was surrounded by rebels. The

[4] Carrillo MSS, p. 35.

[5] Carrillo, who was involved in this from Havana, suggested that Faustino Pérez in Havana gave the order to go ahead knowing that there was only a slender chance of success – on the ground that Castro wished his possible rivals in the opposition, the Barquinistas, better dead.

Rebel Commanders:
23a Raúl Castro and 'Che' Guevara
  b Guevara later, as a Minister
  c Camilo Cienfuegos

The Honeymoon period,
abroad and at home:

24a Castro says goodbye to Vice-President Nixon, Washington, April 1959
  b The first cabinet after the fall of Batista: Robert Agramonte, Armando Hart, Cepero Bonilla, José Míro Cardona (Prime Minister), Luis Buch, Manuel Fernández, Angel Fernández, Manuel Ray, Faustino Pérez, Julio Martínez Páez

police commander, Major Ruiz, telephoned for help from Havana, and tried to cause delay. A cannonade followed. The police surrendered, and were all driven as prisoners to the naval base. By this time, of course, the city knew of the attack. But, though many shops were shuttered, the pavements and balconies were crowded with onlookers. Cienfuegos, except for the Guardia Rural base on the Santa Clara Road, had been captured. Many doubtful or hesitant supporters of the rebels put on the red and black 26 July arm bands or the orange Auténtico bands.

The freedom of Cienfuegos lasted only a morning. In the afternoon, Colonel Cándido Hernández drove in from Santa Clara at the head of motorized infantry. They were ambushed in the Parque Martí and many were killed or wounded – including the colonel, who was wounded and his son, who was killed. But, shortly, B-26 bombers, supplied by the U.S. as part of the U.S.–Cuban military programme, began to move over the city, dropping a few bombs and also machine-gunning the naval base and the rebels' defence posts. Tank and armoured regiments, also equipped with recent U.S. material, appeared from Havana. The city was given over to street fighting in which the rebels stood no chance. They should, no doubt, have withdrawn to the Sierra Escambray after their initial victories, but these had been too complete for such a course to be regarded as other than a retreat. The rebel commanders also had not anticipated such a heavy response, since they had assumed that there would also be fighting at Havana. The use of the tanks, armoured cars and B-26 bombers was technically a breach of the U.S.–Cuban arms understanding since it specifically forbade the use of these weapons except in agreement and in defence of the hemisphere. As a result there was no plan for a prolonged defence. Isolated groups fought on hopelessly throughout the evening and the night. By nightfall, however, the naval base was once more in government hands and by the next day the last rebels, holding out in the police headquarters, had been overwhelmed.

Sixty-seven rebels surrendered to the naval commander, Colonel Comesañas, and were later sent for trial. A few rebels, such as the 26 July chief, Aragonés, and naval lieutenant Julio Camacho, escaped from the city. Most prisoners were shot, including about thirty who surrendered in the police headquarters, and forty in the San Lorenzo school under one of the bravest of the rebels, Lieutenant Dimas Martínez. Naval intelligence, led by Captain García Olayón, searched houses; anyone who seemed to betray signs of having participated – possession of arms, wounds, blood on clothes and even, according to one allegation, the mere fact of youth – was dragged out and shot. San Román was captured, tortured for months, and killed – of course, without trial.[6] Allegations were later made by the secretary-general of the World Medical Association that two hundred wounded were buried alive;[7] though such figures are perhaps exaggerated, the reality was higher than the figures, of between forty and fifty, given by Batista himself. The armed forces had twelve men killed, according to the army.[8] Probably four hundred rebels in all took part in the action, and perhaps as many as three hundred were killed.[9] It was the largest action in the civil war so far. Cienfuegos was cut off for several days – but the press played down the part of the reinforcements: the average Cuban would have supposed that the rising had been defeated by the naval base itself.

There were important consequences. The government's use of the bombers, tanks and armoured cars could not be concealed from the U.S. Embassy or military mission; accordingly it was asked to explain. 'We did not get that satisfaction from them,' William Wieland said some years later. Further, in the coming weeks, 'the entire hemispheric defence unit supplied with U.S. grant equipment was eventually ... scattered in combat areas throughout the Eastern part of the island. This was done without seeking our prior agreement.'[10] As time passed with still no adequate explanation, the progressive group in the State Department, headed by Rubottom and Wieland, began to speculate whether this was not a reason for ending arms shipments to Batista. This move was being pressed strongly by supporters of Castro and Prío in the U.S. and during the winter it became the main question at issue in U.S.–Cuban relations.

The role of the new U.S. ambassador, Earl Smith, now became decisive. Smith's stand against police brutality in Santiago had won him great prestige among the opposition. The ABC colony disapproved and even condemned Smith's games of golf with such moderate members of the opposition as Luis Machado, Prío's ambassador to the U.S., or Joaquín Meyer, director of the Office of Economic Affairs under Prío and later a Cuban director of the World Bank. Batista's ex-prime minister, García Montes, refused to attend a dinner for Smith at the French Embassy. In fact Smith had little sympathy for the opposition. In his first weeks he may have been influenced by officials such as the political officer, John Topping, a Liberal, and by the CIA representatives – not only by the 'No. 2 man' (whose role at the Cienfuegos rising

[6] René Ray, 34–7.

[7] *Medical News*, January 1958; article by Dr Louis Bauer.

[8] *Havana Post*, 8 September 1957. The best account in English is that in Taber, 173–81. *Cf.* E. Morello, *New York World Telegram*, and Jules Dubois, *Chicago Tribune*, who were both there. See also the account by Carlos Franqui read on Radio Rebelde, 5 September 1958, and reprinted in *Revolución*, 26 January 1959, 11.

[9] This is the figure given by Smith, 31.

[10] Wieland evidence, *Communist Threat*, 541.

came out during the trial of the sixty-seven rebels) but also the head of the CIA in Havana, whom Smith regarded as a 'Fidelista'. Smith asked him to investigate Communist strength in Cuba, but he seems to have refused and, walking out of Smith's office, muttered: 'We don't care what you think.'[11] This man was shortly moved on but other members of the U.S. Embassy (many of them being new) remained hostile to Batista; and the question of arms deliveries hung on all winter, exacerbated by such incidents as the new arrest in Miami of Priístas with arms *caches*, and the feeling that, as even Grau had said, by merely recognizing Batista, the U.S. exercised a type of intervention. In general, however, the Embassy was wary of Castro himself. As Democrats, they would have liked an alternative to Castro as a successor to Batista; but, hostile to the idea of intervention, they shrank from any positive action to unseat Batista. The arms embargo seemed then the most positive form of negative action.

The belief (unsubstantiated, to be sure) that Castro, in pressing on with the rising in Cienfuegos, had been preoccupied by a treacherous desire to see his rivals, the Barquinistas, killed, led the leader of the Montecristi group, Carrillo – previously a supporter, though a sceptical one, of Castro – into an attempt to stage a *golpe de estado* on the Isle of Pines, where Barquín was still incarcerated.[12] Carrillo received a promise of help from the vice-president of Argentina, Admiral Rojas, and from the president of Honduras – neither of them fulfilled; the provisional president of Venezuela, Admiral Larrazábal, an old friend of Barquín's in Washington, also promised help.

In the Sierra the Cienfuegos affair was preceded by a clash at a hill known as Hombrito, between Guevara's column and an army group led by Major Merob Sosa, which was halted; and it was followed by an attack by Castro at Palma Mocha in the Cuevas zone where four veteran Fidelistas were killed but where fifty-seven Batistiano soldiers also died.[13] This attack was almost the last occasion when the Batistiano army entered the Sierra. By this time the able Colonel Barrera Pérez had once again been dismissed from his command as a result of intrigues of General Tabernilla and morale was low since he was replaced by none other than the incapable and cruel braggart Alberto del Río Chaviano of Moncada fame.[14]

Was there in fact a chance of a democratic solution without Castro?

[11] Smith, 34.
[12] Carrillo recorded, 'Here was revealed the aspiration of the 26th July Movement towards totalitarian power and the moral attitude of its leaders, capable of sending to their death hundreds of men to avoid the triumph of a different faction, with the result that the failure of the *golpe* of September produced the fall of tens of officials of the Army, the Navy and the Air Force.' (MSS, 37.)
[13] Guevara, 120. 'Veteran' means in this instance that they had been in the Sierra six months.
[14] Barrera Pérez, *Bohemia Libre*, 27 August 1961.

In purely political terms it seemed possible. Batista himself was no doubt genuine in his statement that he would not run in the 1958 elections. What he wanted now was less love from history but respectability before it. He wished to hand over his system to his successor so that eventually the whole opposition would be implicated in it. But who would be his successor? His brother Panchín? That would smack too much of the Dominican Republic, where Héctor Trujillo was now president while power remained with the general, his brother. López Castro, the development board chief? The prime minister Rivero Agüero? But these had no independent political backing without Batista himself. Such successors would have been swept away by either a Castro–Ortodoxo military victory or, more likely, a tougher military dictatorship under one of the generals or police chiefs. Elections were still, however, a year away and Batista resolutely refused to hold them earlier, partly because to do so would admit the illegality or provisional nature of the system, partly because if he were to consolidate the system he needed time. At this stage, in the early autumn of 1957, many people or parties were suggesting that they might still collaborate with him to the extent of taking part in his elections. Batista himself was making elections the main drive of his policy:

> Nothing will deprive the people of the path to the polls, [he said on 4 September] no one will make us back down ... the balance of bank clearings for the first six months of the year demonstrate the increasing economic power of the country. Foreign investors whom some have tried to scare away continue to announce new investments.

It was true. Hardly a day in early 1957 passed without some new investment by a large U.S. company. A heavy new programme of investment at Moa Bay was begun. In September Langbourne Williams, president of the Freeport Sulphur Co., the owner of Moa Bay, after an interview with Batista said that construction would begin immediately; Moa Bay was believed to represent the best source of new nickel in the free world,[15] cobalt being a specially high percentage.[16]

The question was now posed whether the 26 July Movement would make any compromise. Castro believed that he was strong enough to refuse to do so, and to ignore completely, for instance, the fact that Grau, the foremost opposition leader of the Centre, claimed to have 300,000 voters registered for him. In the autumn of 1957 there were a few minor actions in the Sierra such as that of Pino del Agua of 10 September,[17] but Castro was given all the time he needed to consolidate his position.

---

[15] HAR, October 1957 and May 1953.
[16] See *Havana Post*, July 1957.
[17] Guevara, *Souvenirs de la Guerre*, 148–9.

A few actions, such as the murder of fifty-three peasants at Oro de Guisa by the army, merely redounded to Batista's discredit.[18] Peasants began to feel that it was wiser to be in the Sierra with Castro than in their own homes and risk death from Río Chaviano.[19] Government and rebels, police and bomb-layers stepped up their war of nerves. Many peasants who had worked with Castro were betrayed by Leonardo Baró. An endless procession of young men followed each other into the underground and many into prison. A doctor, Jorge Ruiz Ramírez, was murdered after trying to treat a youth for gun wounds received in a clash with the police. The Cuban Medical Association made a new protest and more doctors became sympathetic to Castro merely by turning away from Batista. The assistant editor of Masferrer's *Tiempo en Cuba*, Luis Manuel Martínez, was shot in Havana by the 26 July Movement. In October bombs destroyed Radio Oriente. A curfew was imposed in Santiago and as usual on such occasions the bodies of several youths were found hanging. The whole of Oriente lay under military control, the army being responsible for the north, the navy for the south. Traffic was limited. A price of $100,000 was set on Castro's head. Earl Smith, becoming rapidly less inclined to believe the State Department or his own embassy advisers, telegraphed Allen Dulles, head of the CIA, recommending the placing of an agent with Castro in the Sierra 'to discover the extent of Communist control' in the 26 July Movement. Apparently this could not be done and anyway the CIA in Cuba itself remained favourable to, rather than opposed to, the 26 July,[20] even though relations with the rebels were not improved by the grant of the U.S. Legion of Merit to Colonel Carlos Tabernilla. A big assignment of arms went to Batista from New Jersey in November and a U.S. civilian agent arrested thirty-one Cubans in Florida, led by César Vega,[21] with arms for Castro. Various U.S. right-wing men urged that any embargo on arms to Batista would 'lead to Communist control'.[22] As if to answer such complaints, the *Daily Worker* argued that the Cuban Communists were not receiving adequate credit for their support of the rebels and that U.S. newspapers wanted to hide the fact.[23] In October the Soviet government made its first direct allusion to the struggle in Cuba, when its ECOSOC delegate attacked Batista's

[18] The army announced that fifty-three revolutionaries had been killed. Castro, on Radio Rebelde, 21 August 1958, qu. Jules Dubois, 297.
[19] The comment of Barrera Pérez, *Bohemia Libre*, 6 September 1961.
[20] Smith, 35. Lyman Kirkpatrick, however, implies that agents were successfully placed in the Sierra (*Real CIA*, 159), but perhaps he means simply Andrew St George, who was back in the U.S. by now.
[21] He was betrayed by an agent of Masferrer's, Ariel Ajo, later arrested in 1959 by the revolutionary government (*Revolución*, 26 January 1959, 31).
[22] e.g. Braden.
[23] See article by Harold Philbuch, *New York Tribune*, 22 September 1957.

as a 'terrorist government that strangles and tortures its people'.[24] This was certainly true; and however many Batistianos may have been killed by the rebels, there appear to have been no instances of torture by them.

Exile activity continued in the U.S. in the early winter, with uncertainty about Castro's plans; was the 26 July Movement simply an off-shoot of the Ortodoxo party? Had the Ortodoxo party merely joined the 26 July? Which, after the death of País, actually constituted the Central Committee of the 26 July Movement? Felipe Pazos, Lester Rodríguez (a Moncada man from Santiago), Mario Llerena and Luis Morán (a Santiago lawyer who had defended several *Granma* prisoners at their trial in May) spoke for the 26 July Movement at a general meeting of seven opposition groups, at Miami, in the house of Lincoln Rodón, who had been president of the Cuban House of Representatives until 1952. Present also, among others, were Agramonte and Bisbé for two of the Ortodoxo groups; Prío, Varona, Hevía and Carlos Maristany of the Auténticos;[25] Ramón Prendes for the remains of the FEU; Faure Chomón, second-in-command in the attack on the palace, for the Directorio Estudiantil, recently reformed separately from the FEU; and Angel Cofiño, with Hirigoyen, for the trade union opposition.[26] These men established what they called a council (junta) of National Liberation, including representatives of all the opposition except the Communists, Grau's Auténticos and those electionist Ortodoxos who followed Ochoa or Márquez Sterling. 'Tony' Varona, Prío's last premier (in exile since September), was named president, the Ortodoxo Bisbé became secretary, while the national committee consisted of all 26 July men – Mario Llerena (propaganda), Lester Rodríguez, Franqui (organization), and Raúl Chibás (finance) – the latter having now divested himself of the cloak of Ortodoxia. The new council declared first that the 'struggle' should be continued till democratic rule was restored, and that a general election should be held 'as soon as possible', in any case not more than eighteen months ahead. The Constitution of 1940 would be restored. The only economic point was that 'new sources of employment should be created, as well as higher standards of living'.[27] Since Prío financed not only the two Auténtico groups but the students, the Labour unionists and even to some extent the 26 July Movement, he was inevitably the centre of attention and reputed to be the main organizer.

---

[24] HAR, November 1957.

[25] Actually divided by now into two – the PRC or Auténtico party people; and the OA (Organización Auténtica), a more activist branch of the former, led by Maristany, who had been Prío's Minister of Communications.

[26] Directorio Obrero Revolucionario (DOR).

[27] Full text and commentary in Jules Dubois, 188–90, and Wieland, 579–86. *Cf.* Rodríguez Loeches, for the Directorio's point of view, 21.

This declaration had a good effect in the U.S. But Pazos and the two other 26 July men had not discussed these questions with Castro; indeed, Pazos had technically no real right to commit the 26 July Movement save that he was, with Chibás, now its best known backer. News of the Miami Pact reached Castro only through the *New York Times*. Comprehensibly, this infuriated Castro, less for its contents than for the fact that it was realized without himself. Nevertheless, to begin with, the National Directorate of the 26 July Movement responded with some caution to Pazos and Lester Rodríguez, saying that the agreement of Miami seemed to 'look like the clever political trickery of certain discredited leaders of the opposition'. It was only when the Junta in Miami reproduced all the familiar difficulties and confusions of democratic politics that the attitude of Castro hardened. At one point in November the letters from Armando Hart, the secretary of organization of the National Directorate, to Mario Llerena, representative of the 26 July Movement in Miami, seemed to be demanding the dissolution of the Miami Junta and its replacement by a national committee of non-partisan people: 'The military, the banks, big insurers, the sugar mill owners' would be canvassed for support of just such a body.[28] Llerena thought this impossible and, in a letter of 26 November to Hart he pointed to the necessity for the central committee to decide if they were going to break with the Junta or not. Finally, on 14 December, after a success by the rebels at Veguitas where a two-hundred-strong force inflicted a hundred and seventy casualties on a column of three hundred soldiers of Batista,[29] Castro dispatched a four thousand word letter to the Council of Liberation denouncing it:

> For those who are fighting against an Army incomparably greater in number and arms, with no support for a whole year apart from the dignity with which we are fighting for a cause which we love sincerely ... bitterly forgotten by fellow countrymen who, in spite of being well provided for, have systematically ... denied us their help, the Miami Pact was an outrage. The 26th of July had not authorised anyone to sign. Prío had refused them arms, how could they now sit down at a conference table with them?

Castro criticized the omission in the Miami Pact of any declaration against foreign intervention – 'clear evidence of a lax kind of patriotism and of a cowardice that are self-denouncing'.[30] He also denounced the omission of any consideration of the army: 'Let us have no military

---

[28] All this derives from Llerena's MSS. It has never been clear who precisely formed part of the Dirección Nacional but at this time it appears to have been Hart, Faustino Pérez and Castro.
[29] Taber, 197.
[30] The manifesto of the Sierra Maestra had included this.

junta ... let the people govern ... let the soldiers go back to their barracks.' Though there should be 'complete constitutional normality', the future president 'should not be limited in his free power of appointment'.[31] Cubans would, of course, have to fight 'other Caribbean dictators'. 'The new Government will be governed by the Constitution of 1940, will assure all the rights therein recognized and will stay clear of all political partisanships ...' Political parties would have only one right in the 'provisional period – freedom to organize, within the liberal framework of our Constitution and to take part in the general elections'. Finally, the provisional president would not be Pazos or anyone at Miami – but Judge Urrutia, the magistrate who had found that the *Granma* expeditionaries had behaved constitutionally in trying to overthrow Batista by force. This was a clever move: Urrutia had been on the Bench for thirty-one years, and was politically a moderate. He was put forward by Castro not as a strong man but deliberately as a man without qualities, who would prevent any more dangerous candidate (such as Pazos) from getting in instead.[32] Urrutia was at that time still in Cuba and, after discussions by letter with Mario Llerena, had been approached (only on 26 November) on Castro's behalf by Armando Hart and Luis Buch, who at that time could travel fairly easily between the U.S. and Cuba since his political activities were not well known. Hart and Buch asked Urrutia if he would take part in a five-man government of Cuba in exile. Urrutia agreed, asking 'time to obtain my retirement benefits' from the magistracy, and on 23 December arrived in Miami.[33] He had not had time to become absorbed in exile intrigues before. About Christmas time, Luis Buch and Raúl Chibás brought Urrutia a clear offer to be the 26 July candidate for the presidency, in the form of a letter from Armando Hart. (Hart himself had actually already said in a private letter to Llerena in Miami that he would really have preferred Castro himself as the provisional president.)[34]

Hart's letter was, as usual, couched in grandiose terms ('Destiny has reserved for me the honour of writing these lines'). The 26 July, he said, was 'a youthful movement which is sacrificing everything for the sole honour of being faithful to the tradition of Mambí'. Difficulties in Miami, that perennial problem in Cuban history, as yet made a

---

[31] It was presumably this phrase that struck the State Department Cuban chief, Wieland, as presenting a 'pretty hair-raising picture of a dictatorship' (Wieland, 579).

[32] Other candidates were Dr Gelasio Pérez, of the Cuban Medical Association, García Barcena and Carrillo. Urrutia, then aged 56, was born in Yaguajay (Las Villas), graduated 1923, judge of Jiguaní 1928. As a judge in Matanzas he had in 1933 saved the lives of two men pursued by Machado's police, and therefore himself had to hide in Havana. His father had been a major in the war of Independence. (*Revolución*, 4 January 1958.)

[33] Manuel Urrutia Lleó, *Fidel Castro & Company, inc.: Communist tyranny in Cuba* (1964), 7–10.

[34] Letter of Hart to Llerena, 19 November 1957.

government-in-exile 'inappropriate'. Nevertheless, Urrutia would remain 'the candidate of the people'. The 26 July Movement admitted that it might act alone and apart from the rest of the opposition: 'Alone we began and alone we may have to continue, because we must finish this crusade that represents the last historic possibility for Cuba to be preserved as a sovereign and independent nation.' Hart added:

> The struggle for national independence is more impassioned than ever before since, unless this process is successful, for small, politically disintegrated, socially immature and economically poor countries, perhaps one of the imperialisms now competing for the world will devour us completely and extinguish all hope of Cuba's occupying that position of which the liberators dreamed.[35]

Urrutia, flattered, believed that his acceptance would help the unification of the whole opposition. He did not appreciate that the old parties wanted other candidates. It is hard, on the other hand, to believe that he could have taken Hart's letter seriously: for the full realization of its terms implied a clash with the U.S., to which it is clear he was opposed. But it soon became obvious that, in the words of Mario Llerena to Marcelo Fernández in the Sierra in a letter in early January, the new president-elect was a man of 'unheard-of *naïveté*'.[36]

These developments had destructive effects. Castro (whose letter of 14 December arrived at Miami about 30 December)[37] demanded the withdrawal of the 26 July Movement from the Council of Liberation. Pelayo Cuervo's son Orlando resigned as chairman of the Miami 26 July group, expressing confidence in Pazos. The Ortodoxos, Bisbé and Agramonte, withdrew too. The council foundered. The reconstituted Directorio Estudiantil begged Castro to reconsider. So did Prío. Varona said that his group would accept Urrutia as provisional president but that they could not agree that the 26 July Movement should command the army and be responsible for order during the provisional period. That might mean continued military rule. Castro's reply was merely that his was the way to 'the destruction of tyranny'; Prío, he said, now counted for little in Cuba. Pazos and others left the 26 July, Chomón denounced Castro and prepared to organize his own invasion of Cuba, but the showdown increased rather than ended the fragmentation of the opposition; all over the U.S. and Central America were hundreds of groups and leaders each claiming to represent 'Fidel'.[38]

---

[35] Letter in Urrutia, 8–10. The translation has been modified.

[36] Llerena to Fernández, 6 January 1958, Llerena MSS.

[37] Llerena MSS, p. 160.

[38] Thus in New York there were three separate groups headed by the ex-*Granma* Negro, Pablo Díaz; by Angel Pérez Vidal; and by Arnaldo Barrón. In Miami Lester Rodríguez, Mario Llerena, Jorge Sotús and others were rivals for Fidel's affection more than his delegates.

Castro had already called for the destruction of the 1958 sugar harvest: 'Either Batista without *zafra* or *zafra* without Batista'; 'After the tyrant is in the tomb . . . we shall have a *zafra* of liberty.' A single-page pamphlet had been distributed to sugar workers, giving instructions for setting fire to cane, and including a suggestion for a rat to be tied to a gasoline-soaked sponge. Batista countered this scheme with a general permission for grinding to begin in December. More army units were dispatched towards the cane fields. Many fires did break out. The army was permitted to fire on all suspicious people. Mujal called on workers to 'stand guard against the torch'.

Arrests, deaths and bombs continued daily during November and December. The most sensational event was the assassination of the hated Colonel Fermín Cowley, commander in the Holguín district, in a hardware shop. He had been responsible for killing many 26 July men the previous December. His death predictably was followed by the murder of six men, all innocent, in reprisal, two weeks after. On 16 December the Auténtico Senator Conrado Rodríguez wrote to Godoy, president of the Senate, protesting against the deaths of five hundred Cubans in attempting to crush the opposition; Castro, calling in the hills for more personal assassinations such as that of Cowley, spoke of three thousand having been killed.[39] The unrest was spreading at last to Labour. A Mujalista dock workers' leader, Navea Arambarri, was found murdered, allegedly for anti-Communism. It was hardly surprising that in the course of this winter Mujal, still secretary-general of Labour, moved over more and more towards overt identification of the Labour movement with the regime. The Ministry of Labour announced that absenteeism would be regarded as an 'anti-government act'. Mujal tried to quell menaces of a general strike by the opposition with remarks that 'as long as I live there will be no general strike'. Union Labour had benefited from rising minimum wages, he trumpeted; what earthly need was there to strike?[40] And indeed, despite murder and bloodshed, 1957 had been a record year. Total income from sugar was $M680, $M200 more than in 1956 and higher than any sum achieved since 1952. New investments of foreign capital in 1957 totalled $M200. Bonuses for Christmas were numerous. Money flowed throughout the island. Professional gangsters swarmed the new hotels of Havana. The murder of the gangster Anastasia in Chicago was linked with an attempt by him to capture Meyer Lansky's gambling business in Havana.[41] It was also hard to separate [gangsterdom from revolutionary ardour; thus when in December Earl Smith, the U.S. ambas-

[39] HAR, January 1958.
[40] *Cf. ibid.*, November-December 1958.
[41] *Ibid.*, January 1957.

sador, received news through the U.S. Embassy in Ciudad Trujillo that 'Communist members of the Castro revolution were plotting my assassination', it was doubtful whether the Communists (who had shown hitherto little interest in violent action) or the Auténticos were really at the root of things. Smith himself was now no longer doubtful about the regime; Batista dined with him and his wife in December while the Democrat aspirant to the presidency, Senator John Kennedy, stayed in the embassy for Christmas.[42]

The size of Castro's forces was still being exaggerated by visitors, above all by North Americans. Thus Charles Ryan, who had gone up to the Sierra in March, had descended in October with the news that there were 1,000 men; a journalist for the *New York Herald Tribune*, Donald Hogan, spoke of 2,000 men, half of them well equipped.[43] None of these figures was true. At the end of the year Castro still had less than 300 men under arms.

[42] Smith, 222.
[43] *New York Herald Tribune*, 15 November 1957.

CHAPTER LXXX

The Arms Embargo

Castro had now been in the Sierra for over twelve months. Instead of being a hunted fugitive, he commanded a guerrilla army which could roam at will over nearly all the territory south and west of the *Carretera Central* in Oriente – almost 2,000 square miles. Within this region an elaborate system of maintenance and supply had been organized, based on the connivance of friendly peasants. Much merchandise came up on mules from Manzanillo, Bayamo and other places. There were also now quite elaborate factories in the heart of the Sierra: to the shoemakers and gun repairers a small cigar factory had been added, along with a butcher's shop, a bomb factory and hospitals. But there was still a great shortage of arms – only very few consignments got through, apart from the large quantity after the failure of the attack on the palace. Raids continued along the outlying areas, particularly near Manzanillo, farm machinery was destroyed, rice and cane fields were burned.[1] Westwards in Camagüey private aircraft were used to drop phosphorus on to cane fields.

In the Sierra itself the revolutionary army was increasingly preoccupied with what might be regarded as a second stage in its development: problems of discipline both in the army itself and among the peasants. Many of the latter, as Guevara later explained,[2] were alternatively suspicious and afraid, and also sometimes cynically opportunistic. Guevara commented: 'The execution of anti-social individuals who profited from the situation of force established in the country was, unhappily, not rare in the Sierra Maestra.'[3] There were numerous minor incidents, some causing unnecessary deaths, as when Captain Lalo Sardiñas shot an insubordinate peasant by mistake.[4] Numerous bandits took over sections of the so-called *territorio libre*. Shootings of treacherous peasants or bandits or marijuana smugglers (such as the Chinese bandit

---

[1] In one of these a *Granmaista*, Ciro Redondo, was killed, but, in general, casualties were slight.

[2] Guevara, 171 ff.

[3] *Ibid.*, 152.

[4] *Ibid.*, 154. On this occasion, Lalo Sardiñas was tried by majority vote: 70 voted for his death, 76 for a different punishment. 146 *guerrilleros* took part in this vote. Afterwards, several who were defeated in this vote withdrew.

Chang) were frequent, for the simple reason that the rebel army had no prison.[5]

In the big cities sabotage continued unabated, despite many arrests. Engineer Ray took over from Engineer Oltuski the leadership of the Havana Civic Resistance.[6] More than ever arrests resulted in the final disappearance of the man arrested – for instance, in Guanajay, Luis Enrique Álvarez was tortured so badly on 6 January, under the orders of Major Pérez Pantoja,[7] that he died. Some were thrown into the sea with weights – in the style of Machado.[8] The Esso gas storage depot was blown up in January, damaging the Havana water main. A building company was also attacked, and 280 lbs of dynamite with eighteen electric detonators disappeared. On 15 January a military bulletin from Campamento Columbia spoke of twenty-three rebels being killed in an 'encounter' at Los Hombritos; in fact they were prisoners taken from Boniato gaol and shot.[9] Two men fortunate to escape death were the prominent 26 July men of Havana, Javier Pazos and Armando Hart (arrested for the second time), along with Antonio Buch, information chief of the 26 July in Santiago. Typically, the Buch family – Luis Buch was chief of the Civic Resistance in Santiago – protested not to any Cuban institution, but to the *New York Times*; and that newspaper made a protest which may have helped stave off possible death.[10] The continual atrocities practised by the police did not, however, restrict the activities of the saboteurs; indeed, quite the contrary, they stimulated the desire for vengeance, and thrilled yet more and more young men and women anxious to recreate in reality the dangerous excitements of the cinema. The concept of 'revolution' rather than 'revolt' gathered more and more friends.

There were of course many who were anxious to end the increasingly acute political crisis, above all the North American business community, and the ABC colony in general. Prominent among these was Earl Smith. He held worried meetings with the nuncio, Mgr Centoz, and with other 'neutral' individuals, such as Guillermo Belt, ex-ambassador and ex-treasurer of ABC in the 1930s, or Luis Machado, ex-ambassador to the U.S.[11] But these neutral gentlemen were not in touch with the revolutionary forces. Machado, for instance, was the legal adviser

[5] An Auténtico lawyer, Humberto Sorí Marín, who had come to the Sierra after disputes on the plain, took part in these judgements. He later became Minister of Agriculture, quarrelled with Castro, fled to the U.S., returned as a conspirator and was shot in April 1961.

[6] *Revolución*, 20 January 1959. Oltuski (whose job had been transferred to Sta. Clara) went to Las Villas.

[7] Pérez Pantoja was himself executed after Batista's defeat.

[8] See letter of Luis Quintal Herrera, *ibid.*, 16 January 1959, 4.

[9] Taber, 199.

[10] Matthews, 62.

[11] Smith, *The Fourth Floor*, 31.

of Irénée du Pont, the millionaire of Varadero beach.[12] Such men would point out that, whatever the political situation, the economy could hardly be better. They were right. Smith was thus ill-prepared for the description of the economy made by Wieland in a State Department paper in early January which suggested that the country was in ruins. Wieland also proposed that the U.S. should put pressure on Batista's administration to speed its final downfall. Topping, head of the embassy's political division, helped Wieland prepare an Embassy memorandum with the same message. Smith set off angrily to Washington, paying his own fare since Assistant Secretary of State Rubottom, evidently reluctant to meet the ambassador, desperately said that the Department had no funds for the journey.

On arrival at Washington, Smith said that Batista would restore constitutional guarantees in Cuba, providing that, despite the misuse of grant-in-aid equipment at Cienfuegos, the U.S. assured him the delivery of twenty armoured cars which he had ordered. This arrangement was to be a secret, but since by this time Castro had an agent (the assistant military attaché Saavedra) in the Cuban Embassy in Washington, the news soon reached the Sierra Maestra in naturally more elaborate terms: Castro was thus found telling the journalist Homer Bigart (of the *New York Times*), that Batista had undertaken to restore civil liberties in return for U.S. action against revolutionary groups in the U.S.[13] But though Prío was indeed once again indicted before a Federal jury for planning an arms delivery to Cuba from Miami,[14] Castro's informant had garbled the information. He did, however, get accurate news of another development: Earl Smith gave a press conference in Washington in which he said that he did not think 'the U.S. government' would ever be able 'to do business with Fidel Castro', because Castro, he thought, would neither honour international obligations nor maintain law and order.[15] This naturally became known too.

Smith was not alone in making these judgements. Wieland was visited in Washington in January by General García Tuñón, one of the ablest of Batista's generals dismissed by Tabernilla, who tried to persuade the State Department that the best replacement for Batista would be a military junta composed of various officers, including himself, Barquín, and some of the more intelligent and humane of Batista's officers, such as Cantillo.[16] Wieland himself, however, in an unguarded

[12] Cf. *Bohemia*, 27 July 1952; *Havana Post*, 12 September 1957.
[13] *New York Times*, 25 February 1958. On 9 January Castro appointed Mario Llerena and Raúl Chibás as chairman and treasurer respectively of the Cuban Committee in exile which he recognized as the sole representatives of the 26 July in the U.S.
[14] This time he chose to go to gaol with his comrades, who could not raise bail.
[15] Smith, *The Fourth Floor*, 60.
[16] *Communist Threat*, 857-8.

moment, confided to a journalist[17] in words which afterwards haunted him:

> I know Batista is considered by many as a son of a bitch ... but American interests come first ... at least he is our son of a bitch,[18] he is not playing ball with the Communists ... On the other hand, Fidel Castro is surrounded by commies. I don't know whether he is himself a communist ... [But] I am certain he is subject to communist influences.[19]

Wieland's own comment later on was:

> Our problem ... was a desire to see an effective solution to Cuba's political strife that would ensure a democratic transition and the support of the ... bulk of the Cuban people [and] that would have eliminated any major threat from the violence which was at that time being waged by the Castro forces ... Castro at that time was still a small figure in the east ... We were not thinking of dictating on the type of government ...[20]

Batista himself was still keeping up his old programme – elections in the summer, with himself not a candidate. He did say, however, that he would afterwards be eligible to be chief of staff of the army. It was reasonable to suppose, therefore, that the presidency of Andrés Rivero Agüero (who would be the government candidate) would simply be a cover for a prolongation of the Batista era, a return to the era of the presidents *fainéants* of the 1930s. In February the Allied Professional Institute charged that the preparations being made for the elections included 'the most scandalous frauds in the history of Cuba', and argued that elections should not be held while Cuba was in civil war. These charges were the occasion for the withdrawal from the contest of Pardo Llada – 'never a serious candidate' – leaving only Grau and Márquez Sterling of the opposition in the running.

A bizarre proposal next came from Castro, sent through the Liberal congressman for Manzanillo, Manuel de Jesús León Ramírez. Castro undertook to agree to elections supervised by the OAS, provided Batista withdrew all military forces from Oriente. He also told Homer Bigart that after all he would not insist on Urrutia as president. This was news to Urrutia, who learned (at second hand) that the suggestion of his candidacy would only operate 'in the case of a revolutionary triumph'.[21] Batista regarded Castro's proposal as a sign of weakness, and rejected it.

[17] Shaffer, of *Newsweek*.
[18] This phrase of course echoes Roosevelt's about Trujillo.
[19] Wieland hearing, 1–4.
[20] *Ibid.*, 540–6.
[21] *Cf.* Urrutia, 12–18; and Meneses, *Fidel Castro*, 64.

A possible split in the 26 July Movement was therefore avoided; Raúl Chibás said that Castro's statements must have been misinterpreted because there could be 'no political solution where Batista presides over an election'.[22] Castro himself reaffirmed support for Urrutia,[23] in a letter to him on 9 March. But this modest gesture towards 'electoralism' was without doubt a possible opportunity for compromise and one rejected by the government.

Immediately afterwards, there was renewed activity on all sides, New guerrilla groups appeared in northern Oriente, and plans were made for the establishment of a second guerrilla force permanently in that region. On 16 February 1958, Castro destroyed a small garrison at Pino del Agua, killing ten, and capturing an officer,[24] an engagement which Guevara describes as marking the end of 'the long period of consolidation' of the *guerrilleros*. After this date it began to be evident to all the people of the hills that Castro and his men were there to stay and that therefore they had nothing to gain in the long run from working with Batista's army.[25] From all provinces there were reports of killing and sabotage, bodies being found hanging outside several towns. The presidents of the three student federations (Havana, Santiago and Las Villas) all declared that no students would go back to work until there was peace. Sabotage of railways reached such a pitch that timetables in East Cuba were changed daily and soldiers accompanied all trains. There were fires in harbours and warehouses, stores and schools. In Havana the 26 July Movement raided the central clearing bank and destroyed $M16 worth of cheques. On 23 February the Argentinian racing motorist, Fangio, was kidnapped from his hotel as propaganda to prevent him taking part in the race the next day. He was returned afterwards. At the race itself, a car skidded and, driving into the crowd, killed six and wounded fifty. The government accused the 26 July Movement of pouring oil on the course; the charge was denied, but the affair was never fully solved.[26] The leader of the kidnappers, Oscar Lucero, was later caught, tortured and murdered.[27]

Meantime a new expedition of guerrilla fighters composed of men of the Directorio had landed on the north coast of Cuba at Playa Santa Rita near Nuevitas, and made their way slowly south-west into the Escambray mountains; it had been a 'question of honour' for them to land before the first anniversary of the attack on the palace. Fifteen men and a woman left Miami on 31 January and arrived at 10.30 p.m.

[22] *Carteles*, 5 March 1958.
[23] Urrutia, 16.
[24] Taber, 207–8.
[25] Guevara, *Souvenirs*, 172–3.
[26] Batista, *Cuba Betrayed*, 70.
[27] *Revolución*, 19 January 1959.

on 8 February,[28] aiming to achieve, like Castro, what Chomón had called a 'mañana esplendorosa for our country'. Like Castro, they used a U.S. owned boat, the *Thor II*, which belonged to Alton Sweeting of Miami. They reached the Sierra on 13 February. (A number of anti-Batistianos of various political affiliations had been in these hills since mid-1957 – Rafael López Cárdenas, for instance.)[29] The Directorio had with them fifty Italian carbines, two English Sten machine guns, a Thompson, two Springheeds, one Garand, two M3s and one M1, with five Remington semi-automatic rifles with telescopic lenses.[30] Several local members joined, including Ramón Pando, the secretary of the Directorio in Las Villas. By 17 February there were already twenty-nine rebels in the second front of Escambray, in three columns; they had attacked a military post at Cacapual, Banao, and killed three men.[31] On 19 February, however, their advance guard met ten soldiers, and were dispersed. Pando, Edelmira and their guide were caught and murdered on the orders of Captain Mirabal, chief of police at Sancti Spiritus. After further skirmishes on the slopes of the hill Diana, they eventually moved on towards the site of the old Indian city of Cubanacán, where they stayed several days surrounded by rats. On 24 February they issued a new manifesto setting out their aims:

> We won't be . . . the people to make false promises . . . we are fighting to abolish in our country the idea of youth without education, men

[28] They were: Alberto Mora (son of the deputy Menelao Mora, killed in the attack on the palace), Eduardo García Lavandero, Carlos Montiel, Julio García, Faure Chomón, Alberto Blanco, Raúl Díaz Argüelles, Rolando Cubela, Antonio Castell, Enrique Rodríguez Loeches, Carlos Figueredo, Guillermo Jiménez, García Olivera, Luis Blanco, Ramón Pando (who joined them on arrival), Gustavo Martín and Esther Martín (Rodríguez Loeches, 50).

[29] *Revolución*, 15 January 1959.

[30] Also 11,000 cartridges for the carbines, 2,000 for the M1, 2,000 30·06 calibre and 5,000 calibre 0·45; three walkie-talkie sets, 65 uniforms, three tents, 'soda syphons, knapsacks, nylon pillows, lanterns, etc.' (Rodríguez Loeches.)

[31] The three columns were:

A	B	Advance Guard
Cubela	G. Lavandero	Ramón Pando
Darío Pedroso	Chomón	Willie Morgan (an American)
Pablo Machín	Luis Blanco	Artola
'Cárdenas'	Armando Fleites	Ramiro Camajuaní
Rodríguez Loeches	Eloy Gutiérrez Menoy (brother of	Edelmira
Carlos Figueredo	the leader of the 13 March	Faustinito (guide)
Julio García Clirera	attack)	
plus seven others	Ivan Rodríguez	
	Oscar Ruiz	

Of this group of young men, Cubela and Gutiérrez Menoyo were in years to come to be imprisoned for trying to murder Castro. Fleites fled to the U.S. in early 1961. Willie Morgan was shot for counter-revolutionary activities in 1961. Pando, Edelmira and Faustinito were killed within a month of their arrival. On the other hand, Chomón has been a Cuban minister since 1960; Machín is a major in charge of a factory and Rodríguez Loeches was an ambassador. Carlos Figueredo and Julio García both worked under Castro for the Ministry of the Interior.

without work ... We don't limit ourselves to re-establish ... the social guarantees systematically ignored by the dictatorship. We must ensure work to every Cuban, knowing that our country has the necessary conditions for economic development ... This proclamation, though specifically directed to Cuba, we extend to the American continent. The Directorio ... advocates the creation of a confederation of American Republics, such as demanded by Miranda and Bolívar ...[32]

But alas, matters went badly, the two groups became separated, and Chomón and his group went off for a time to Havana. Gutiérrez Menoyo held on grimly with a handful of men in Escambray,[33] and when Chomón returned he established himself independently in a different command.

Castro was being less histrionic. To Andrew St George, once again in the Sierra, he remarked in January: 'I have personally come to feel that nationalization is at best a cumbersome instrument. It does not seem to make the state stronger yet it enfeebles private enterprise ... foreign investments will always be welcome ... here.'[34] This was an appropriate thing to say to St George who on his own account was an agent of U.S. military intelligence. On 21 February Castro issued from the Sierra his first administrative decree, to apply a scheme of criminal jurisdiction to the *territorio libre* over which he now had control.[35] Henceforth he acted as if he were the *de facto* ruler of part of Oriente. Already he had a newspaper, *Cubano Libre*, run at first by two *guerrilleros*, and later by the Ortodoxo, Luis Orlando Rodríguez, and later still by Carlos Franqui. On 24 February a radio station began operating from the Sierra: *Aquí Radio Rebelde transmitiendo desde la Sierra Maestra en Territorio Libre de Cuba!*[36]

At this time, too, it appears that the cautious Cuban Communist party at long last also decided to support the idea of 'armed struggle' in cities and in the countryside – to back, that is, the very cause which they had previously denounced as Putschist.[37] A resolution supporting Castro seems to have been passed in February by the party leadership. Several

---

[32] Rodríguez Loeches, 72–84.

[33] *Ibid.*, 94–7.

[34] A Visit with a Revolutionary, *Coronet*, February 1958.

[35] Text in González Pedrero, 133–6.

[36] Jules Dubois, 212. Its news bulletins were written by Carlos Franqui, and others in the organization were Ricardo Martínez, Orestes Valera, Violeta Casals and Jorge Mendoza (René Ray, 60).

[37] Aníbal Escalante, *Fundamentos*, August 1959; Carlos R. Rodríguez, *Hoy*, 15 April 1959, 3. A decision was certainly taken but only after controversy. Carlos Rafael Rodríguez later said that he had personally got in touch with Haydée Santamaria, as representive of the 26 July Movement in Havana in August 1957 after the murder of Frank País in Santiago. See C. R. Rodríguez, *La Revolución y el transición*.

members of the Communist Youth (such as Prats[38] and Ribalta) had been in the Sierra in 1957. At least one peasant, a certain Conrado, who was a member of the Communist party, had been in contact with Guevara since mid-1957.[39] It is also clear from Guevara's writings that he had been in contact with the Communists in early 1958, for he tells us how he had upbraided a local party leader. 'You are capable of creating units who allow themselves to be martyred in the obscurity of a dungeon ... but not of creating units able to take a machine gun nest by assault.'[40] A member of the party proper, Osvaldo Sánchez Cabrera, visited Castro's headquarters as a go-between.[41] Carlos Rafael Rodríguez later spoke of 'public' instructions to Communist members to join Castro in February 1958.[42] However there was as yet no explicit alliance, only contact; and even that was lacking between the party on the one hand and, on the other, the Civic Resistance and the 26 July Movement in Havana.

It is possible indeed that the Communists would not have taken this decision had they not themselves begun to bear the brunt of attacks by Batista's police. The development of civil war and the propaganda need to identify the rebels as Communists, made it increasingly difficult for the regime to restrain itself from making attacks on known Communists – if not on the national leaders at least on local militants. Thus the police in Yaguajay, in the north of Las Villas, began wantonly to persecute various Communists. Over twenty members of the party in that area – the centre of three sugar mills (*Narcisa*, *Victoria*, *Nela*) – had their houses burned. Police ill-treatment occurred in other parts of the province. Yaguajay was, however, the most outrageous instance, chiefly because the Communists were specially strong in the union movement – they claimed 30% of the workers at the *central Narcisa* – and also among small farmers who had formed a league to resist dislodgement. The consequence was that the police literally drove the local Communists into a state of semi-rebellion, leading to the formation of a guerrilla group to which a Havana Communist, Félix Torres, was dispatched as commander. Another guerrilla group, an offshoot of the Directorio, refused the Communists entry, and, within a few months, Torres was leading his own Communist guerrilla force of fifty men, known as the Máximo Gómez column.[43]

At the same time that the Communists began to go over to the

[38] National organizer of Juventud Socialista.
[39] Guevara, p. 158.
[40] Guevara p. 178.
[41] *Verde Olivo*, 22 January 1961, and 2 July 1961; *Hoy*, 4 January 1964. (He was killed in an air crash in 1961.) *Cf.* comments by Draper, *Castroism*, 31.
[42] In *Hoy*, 15 April 1959. Suárez (58) discounts this.
[43] See letter of Félix Torres to Aldo del Valle, 9 January 1965, qu. *Hoy*, 20 July 1965.

revolutionary cause, another institution roused itself from an even stuffier lethargy: the Church decided at the end of February to take a hand in the Cuban political crisis. This derived from pressure from below: for instance, four young Catholics of the University of Villanueva were killed by the police on their way to join the rebel army.[44] On 10 February Father Angel Gaztelu, priest of the Church of the Holy Spirit in Havana, condemned the regime harshly in the course of a sermon. A similar statement was issued by Acción Católica, and the Catholic weekly *La Quincena* began also to denounce the regime. Conservative opponents of Batista had for some time hoped the Church would give leadership. The *Diario de la Marina*, the main Catholic paper, indeed attributed the political crisis to the decay of the upper class and of Catholic morality. On 1 March the Cuban bishops, headed by Cardinal Arteaga and the nuncio Mgr Centoz, called on the government to bring peace through the formation of a government of national unity, and on the revolutionaries to abandon sabotage and terrorism. A 'commission of harmony' was proposed, to consist of Raúl de Cárdenas, an aristocrat who, having been a deputy since 1911, had been vice-president both under Grau and in 1933; Gustavo Cuervo Rubio, vice-president and Foreign Minister during the Second World War, being now Señora Batista's gynaecologist; Víctor Pedroso, the bank president; and a Negro priest, Father Pastor González.

The government sought to prevent any publication of this unwelcome plan in the Havana press, but it soon transpired that some of the bishops, including Pérez Serantes of Santiago (who had instigated the scheme), had wanted a stronger call, including one to Batista to resign; others, such as the bishops of Camagüey and Cienfuegos, were opposed; the actual document therefore was a compromise such as Pérez Serantes, for one, did not really approve.[45]

It had, however, an immediate effect: On 3 March Batista's Foreign Minister, Dr Güell, told Earl Smith that his master would be pleased to invite the OAS, U.N. and the world's press to the Cuban elections. Batista also began to prepare a new ministry, selecting Dr Emilio Núñez Portuondo,[46] the ambassador at the U.N., to be at its head – a move clearly calculated to please the U.S. since Portuondo had been well known and popular there. Batista announced that he would be glad to see the Church's harmony group. This was nicely timed, since opinion in the U.S. government was hardening over the question of the supply of arms to Batista. The Cubans' use of grant-in-aid equipment against

[44] *Revolución*, 11 January 1959. Their re-burial in 1959 was attended by the Nuncio.
[45] See Dewart, 109–11. The letter was published by *Bohemia*, 18 January 1959.
[46] Emilio Núñez Portuondo (born 1898), son of the revolutionary General Núñez; lawyer and adviser to railways; Representative and Senator. He was brother to Ricardo Núñez Portuondo, the physician who was a presidential candidate in 1948.

the rebels was raised in the Senate Foreign Relations Committee on 5 March and Rubottom temporized.[47] The Embassy had in fact protested to Batista and received no quick answer. On 6 March it became clear that Núñez would only accept the premiership on the condition that the U.N. supervised the elections. The same day a full protest by thirteen judges against the regime of force showed the premier-designate the magnitude of the difficulties before the regime. Accordingly, he did not form a government after all, and on 12 March the old Foreign Minister, Dr Güell, took over with an administration scarcely different from its predecessor. On 9 March Castro, though tacitly acknowledging the bishops' good intent, had announced that he would not receive the Church's harmony commission because it was too much in favour of Batista – a fair comment on Cuervo and Pedroso, though not on Father González nor on Cárdenas.[48] Castro was now in the middle of what was described as a 'reunion of the National Directorate in the Sierra Maestra', taking place between 7 and 10 March discussing the persistent rumours in late February of a compromise with the regime. The National Directorate pointed out to all its provincial representatives that this – reflected in the interviews with Homer Bigart in the *New York Times* – was purely a 'tactical manœuvre'.[49]

The difficulties were now mounting on every side for Batista. On 11 March a courageous Havana magistrate, Alabau Trelles, agreed to indict police Colonel Ventura and the naval intelligence chief Laurent for the murder of four youths. A serious crisis could not be avoided. On 12 March Batista once again suspended civil rights and reimposed press and radio censorship. The indictment was quashed by the Minister of Justice and Alabau fled to the U.S. The hated Colonel Pilar García then became chief of police. The toughening up was everywhere evident. 75,000 secondary school children were now on strike. All schools were closed. Ambassador Earl Smith was visited by the only electoralist Ortodoxo, Márquez Sterling, along with Mario Lazo, the lawyer who inspired the Havana Hilton; both agreed that there was a case for the postponement of elections till November, with the inauguration of a new president in February 1959; Márquez Sterling confirmed Smith's own view when he agreed that 'Castro would be ten times worse than Batista'.[50]

Castro followed his rejection of the bishops' plan with a new manifesto

---

[47] Wieland, 541.

[48] Castro's reply in full was published in *Revolución*, 26 July 1962.

[49] *Circular de Organización*, dated Santiago de Cuba, 18 March 1958, which adds that both Castro and the National Directorate considered this to have been a mistake. But Raúl Castro left the Sierra Maestra for northern Oriente with his troop on 10 March.

[50] Smith, *The Fourth Floor*, 81. Lazo was always closely connected with the U.S. government and the CIA, as can be seen from Lyman Kirkpatrick's *The Real CIA*, 179.

from the Sierra[51]; there was mention of that ancient bludgeon, 'the general revolutionary strike, to be seconded ... by military action'. The 26 July Movement in Havana was in fact preparing such an action. Castro repeated (a warning to the U.S.) that strikes and war would be prolonged if a military junta should take over from Batista. Then came some confident demands: all highway and railway traffic should be halted throughout Oriente. As from 1 April payment of taxes to the State, provincial or municipal authorities, should be suspended. If payments were made, they would be declared null and void and have to be paid again to the new provisional government (headed by Urrutia). All those who remained after 5 April in offices of trust in the executive branch of the government would be judged guilty of treason. Officers and men who continued in the armed services after 5 April would be dismissed. Anyone who afterwards joined the armed services would be judged a criminal. Judges should resign if they wished to continue to practise after the victory of the revolution. The country as a whole should consider itself in a state of total war against the tyranny. Finally, 'Column 6 of the rebel forces under Major Raúl Castro ... had invaded the north part of Oriente [with fifty men][52] ... the whole nation is determined to be free or perish.'[53] At this point Castro had under his own command in fact only 100–120 men, excluding those with his brother and Almeida[54] – scarcely more that is than six months before. It is not clear how many supporters he had in the plain, but it is fairly evident that these far outdistanced that number: the organization being carefully established with sub-sections in all parts of Cuba[55] each with separate instructions for each month: thus in March action committees were supposed to unleash total war in Oriente, and extend armed action to Las Villas and Pinar del Río; the workers' committees were supposed to constitute a workers' front as 'flag of struggle'; and the resistance sections, whose tasks were to establish relations with Civic Resistance movements, had among other things to take action around the judicial persons to see that they resigned as demanded in the statement of 12 March.[56]

[51] Worked out by the National Directorate of the Movement, according to a letter of Marcelo Fernández to Mario Llerena of 30 March, and signed by Castro as 'Comandante jefe de las fuerzas armadas' and Faustino Pérez as 'delegado nacional'. Among those present was Major René Ramos Latour, who had succeeded País as chief of action in Santiago (See Verde Olivo, 10 May 1963, article by Major Lussón).

[52] Obra Revolucionaria, 1961, No. 46, 12. His mission was to harass transport and disrupt communications. A column under Almeida with 35 men had gone East.

[53] Tr. in Jules Dubois, 240.

[54] 'There remained forces which in conjunction were no more than 120 men. Less even. There were less than 100 men in the Sierra.'

[55] The sub-sections were Acción; Finanzas; Obreras; Propaganda; Resistencia; and Organización.

[56] From 'Plan de Trabajo para el mes de marzo', Circular de Organización, 18 March.

On 13 March Batista received Earl Smith at the Villa Kuquine. Seated in his study surrounded by its familiar busts of Lincoln, Batista told the ambassador he would accept 'all reasonable requests' by the Church's commission of harmony;[57] he would investigate allegations of brutality made against Captain Sosa Blanco and others; he would accept all suggestions for elections; and he could afford an amnesty to all revolutionaries providing they left their arms behind. He himself would stand down on 24 February 1959, and thereafter enjoy, as he hoped, an honourable retirement.[58] But the following day, Smith was assured by Raúl de Velasco, president of the Cuban Medical Association and chairman of the Civil Co-ordinating Committee (the most respectable of the civilian peace making groups), that elections would be no problem if Batista handed over to a neutral government; there could be no peaceful solution with Batista or his own designated successor in office.[59] As if to confirm that point of view, Raúl Menocal, Minister of Commerce until the recent cabinet reshuffle, narrowly escaped murder by the 26 July on 13 March: and even while Smith was speaking to Velasco, the most critical decision of the war had just been taken, symptomatically, in Washington: the U.S. suspended shipment of 1,950 Garand rifles due for shipment to Cuba and already on the New York dockside. This was in effect a U.S. embargo on arms to Batista; no more arms officially were sent except for some rockets in exchange for previously supplied defective items.[60]

No step by Castro could have so disheartened Batista. His old friends were seen to be deserting him. A position of neutrality, Batista complained to Smith, operated 'against the constitutional regime of Cuba'. The embargo in effect gave belligerent status to 'extremist groups'. Smith needed no persuasion on this subject. He bitterly opposed this embargo, and left no doubt even with Batista that he was convinced Castro's movement was 'infiltrated with communism'.[61] Very soon an emissary came to Smith from Mujal to say that if the U.S. attitude was changing towards Cuba, he, Mujal, would like to know, since he would not be likely to stand firm behind Batista: the trade unions were a non-party organization.

Smith, beset on all sides, said that the U.S. could not intervene and

[57] Bishop Müller of Matanzas had visited Batista after the compromise document had been issued and called on him to resign – an appeal which got nowhere.
[58] Smith, *The Fourth Floor*, 83.
[59] *Ibid.*, 86–7.
[60] Though Smith and others later blamed Wieland, there is no doubt that he was not alone in recommending the action; it was the general action of the Department. See Wieland evidence, 42. Urrutia, Raúl Chibás and Angel Santos Buch (later director of Civic Resistance, Havana) had called on Wieland just before (Urrutia, 17).
[61] Batista, *Cuba Betrayed*, 96.

he could not in any way anticipate his government's behaviour.[62] He asked the Department of State at least to deliver twenty armoured cars previously requested; the same day (18 March) he lunched with Herbert Matthews, prowling around Havana for the *New York Times*, and Matthews said that even the embassy's demands for elections constituted intervention.

Velasco's committee, meanwhile, encouraged, like all the opposition, by the U.S. action, issued a new call to Batista to resign, and for the formation of a neutral government which would annul all political condemnations since 1952. Miró Cardona, the lawyer, believed to be the author of this document, was forced to hide, disguised as a priest: from a sanctuary in the Uruguayan Embassy he wrote a report to the Havana Bar directors saying that, since Batista's regime was illegal, it could not call for elections.[63]

The inflammatory situation meant that Batista had little choice save to postpone elections, as Márquez Sterling had argued, from June until November. To save face he publicly also cancelled the order for armoured cars from the U.S. Smith begged the State Department that before banning all arms shipments he should at least suggest to Batista that he might merely absent himself during the elections, while a provisonal government and the army supervised the poll. Again, the State department refused Smith's recommendation as constituting intervention. Matthews, on the other hand, still in Havana, was now speaking of Castro, as St George and other journalists had before him, in heroic terms: 'The most remarkable and romantic figure . . . in Cuban history since José Martí.'[64] Castro needed this sort of backing then in propaganda almost as much as he needed arms; and the two matters were interconnected, since so much of his arms came from the U.S., bought with contributions from well-wishers in that country. Thus on 27 March the U.S. coastguards caught up with $20,000 worth of arms on a yacht, *El Orión* belonging to Arnaldo Barrón (one of the splinter group leaders of the 26 July Movement in New York), with thirty-six men 'bound for [Cuba';[65] such setbacks were compensated by the arrival of a large replenishment of arms brought by air from Costa Rica by a pilot, Pedro Díaz Lanz, who afterwards in 1959 would become briefly and sensationally head of the Cuban air force. The new government of Venezuela also made a gift of $50,000 to Urrutia for the 26 July Movement,[66] and the 26 July Movement in Santiago

[62] Smith, *The Fourth Floor*, 102.

[63] *Cf.* Jules Dubois, 229–33.

[64] Matthews, 70.

[65] He had been expelled from the 26 July and was perhaps hoping to work his passage back.

[66] Urrutia, 17. The dictator Jiménez had been overthrown in January.

had a considerable propaganda success in storming the Boniato barracks.[67]

The American ambassador now became, as at all previous moments of trouble in Cuba since 1902, the repository of confidences, hopes and fears; a Labour leader, Serafín Romualdo, told him he was afraid of being seen with Batista; the president of the Catholic university at Las Villas said that the Church urged U.S. intervention,[68] presumably occupation. At the Havana Biltmore Club, Smith told the British ambassador, Fordham,[69] that the U.S. hoped in a case of emergency that the two of them would act as if they were Siamese twins.[70] He hoped no doubt that the Anglo-Saxons would stand together.

[67] This operation was led by the then *jefe de acción* in Santiago, Belarmíno Castilla, one of the officers of the rebel army who did best in Cuba under the Revolution: he later (1966) became chief of staff and a member of the central committee of the Cuban Communist party.

[68] Smith, *The Fourth Floor*, 96–7, 103.

[69] Alfred Stanley Fordham (born 1907), married to a Peruvian; Eton and Trinity, Cambridge; previous posts, partly U.S. consular, partly Latin American, Stockholm and Warsaw, afterwards knighted.

[70] Smith, *The Fourth Floor*, 103.

CHAPTER LXXXI

The Strike of 9 April

Castro had publicly announced that a general strike would soon be called, but the government did not know when. Much was left to chance. The plan was that the 26 July Movement and Civic Resistance in Havana would call for the strike and, except in various concerns where they were strong, trust to luck that the call would be respected. The director and coordinator was Faustino Pérez, the member of the National Directorate who had survived from the *Granma* and gone down to Havana to assure Castro's supporters that all was well.[1] He did not, of course, have the backing of the bulk of the unions, nor of the Communists, the only opposition group with any real following in organized labour. The Communists had been prepared to join the strike committees, but they were rejected.[2] On 28 March Castro, however, wrote from the Sierra proposing that all groups of the opposition, including the Communists, should participate; the strike committee in Havana felt, however, that the idea was too difficult to achieve at that late hour.[3] There was already much doubt and suspicion between the rebels of the hills and those of the plain, many of whom regarded Castro as a would-be *caudillo* and his followers as militarists.[4] At the same time the organization of the strike was left entirely to the 26 July action committees, without any real contact with labour. The strike committee in Havana, the key area, was in the end composed of Pérez, Manuel Ray (the engineer), David Salvador (who had since mid-1957 been at the head of the 26 July's labour organization), Dr Fernández Ceballos (head of the Cuban evangelical churches), Carlos Lechuga (an Ortodoxo journalist), and Dr Eladio Blanco (a fashionable physician). None of these men was in favour of alliance with the Communists, less on doctrinal grounds than because of the damage such an alliance might have

[1] See above, p. 908. It is obscure whether Castro really wanted this strike, and it has been said, without evidence, that Faustino Pérez, then effectively in control of the 26 July Movement outside the Sierra, brought pressure on him to call it.

[2] Strike committees at national, provincial and municipal levels would consist of six people – a 26 July coordinator; an action and propaganda leader, both representatives of the 26 July Movement; a workers' representative, from the 26 July workers' front organization; and representatives of the Civic Resistance and of the students.

[3] Evidence of Manuel Ray; *cf.* Jules Dubois, 246, and Jacques Arnault, *Cuba et le Marxisme* (1963), 77. This was the first occasion that Castro showed himself willing to collaborate with the Communists.

[4] See Guevara, 180.

done to their cause among liberal opinion, which regarded the Communists of Cuba as not so much menacing as, in view of their past relation with Batista, simply untrustworthy. On 4 April Urrutia and Llerena (on behalf of the 26 July in exile) announced openly that they repudiated all collaboration with the Communists.[5]

The Communists themselves later extensively discussed this strike, saying:

> [It could] with armed support from the Sierra have led to the defeat of the tyranny, if it had been developed in the correct way ... The general strike was sabotaged by various elements [that is, the Civic Resistance], even though all elements were there for its ... triumph ... We had correctly planned in advance for the prospect that the masses would struggle on under the tyranny till they reached the phase of armed struggle ... But over a long period we did not take practical steps to promote these ends ... That was our failure.

The Communists nevertheless welcomed the strike 'as a step towards organization of the masses and away from excessive reliance on heroic but indecisive guerrilla warfare, futile bombing and sabotage'.[6] But Castro later castigated the 'premature' launching of the general strike due to 'an erroneous appreciation of the objective conditions'.[7]

The Civic Resistance's instructions for the strike read:

> As soon as you get the order to strike, sabotage your work and leave the place with your fellow workers ... Listen to the guidance given by 26 July radio stations. Do not use buses driven by police or strike-breakers. Proprietors of businesses which remain open will be considered as collaborators of the dictatorship. Block the streets with junk, garbage cans, bottles, etc.; assemble Molotov cocktails; Liberty or Death.

Faustino Pérez took the opportunity to assert publicly:

> [The] present revolutionary movement is far from being Communist ... We ... shall repeat as often as necessary that our leader [Castro] will not be part of the provisional Government ... The provisional Government will hold national elections within the shortest possible time ... We shall create a climate of confidence and security for the investment of national and foreign capital necessary for our industrial development.[8]

[5] Urrutia, 19.
[6] U.S. *Daily Worker*, 7 May 1958, qu. R. Scheer and M. Zeitlin, *Cuba: An American Tragedy*, rev. edn. (1964), 127.
[7] *Obra Revolucionaria*, 1961, No. 46, 12.
[8] Jules Dubois, 249.

The strike was in fact much more of an urban uprising than a with-drawal of labour and should be classed as such. Its leaders were men who were already somewhat suspicious of Castro and of his reliance on Guevara and Raúl Castro.

Batista seemed confident. He told a U.S. journalist, Skelly, that in any strike Castro did not have a chance of victory.[9] He was right. When 9 April came, there was a good deal of confused violence but most shops were open, as were most factories and the harbour. Neither the CTC nor the Communists took any notice of the 26 July's calls and the transport system therefore worked normally. Some electric com-panies were sabotaged, some buses overturned, two big shops were attacked, but the Havana electricity supply was left alone, though that had been supposed to signal the beginning of the strike. About twenty civilians were killed, as were three policemen, but probably another eighty revolutionaries were shot. There were rumours in Havana that the strike was a provocation by Batista to uncover strong-holds of opposition: and many workers who had struck in the morning went back to work in the afternoon. In Santiago, where a similarly abortive attempt was made, thirty were killed, many by Masferrer's private army of thugs, the rest by police. It was a bloody day but not a very successful one for the forces of protest.[10]

Afterwards came recriminations: the Communists blamed the 'uni-lateral call' of Faustino Pérez and the national directorate of the 26 July movement.[11] Carlos Rafael Rodríguez, the most intelligent of the Communist leaders, hoped that the failure of the strike would convince Castro of the need to include supporters of Grau and Prío in a future government and to subdue any anti-U.S. propaganda.[12] A few weeks later the Communists spoke of Castro's movement as com-posed of 'those who count on terroristic acts and conspiratorial *coups* as the chief means of getting rid of Batista'. Faustino Pérez did not mention the Communists in his explanation of the failure of the strike, but instead spoke of 'certain tactical factors inspired by our desire to avoid great torrents of blood so as not to add extra grief to what the people have already suffered . . .'[13]

The failure of this strike reduced Castro's prestige considerably. Sabotage and terrorism declined and in May even tourists began to return to Cuba.[14] Batista, cock-a-hoop, succeeded in getting five plane-

[9] *Miami News*, 4 April 1958. Skelly, who had lived in Oriente, knew the Castro family well as a child.

[10] *Cf.* Jules Dubois, 253; Taber, 238; Rodríguez Quesada, *Salvador*, 10.

[11] Draper, *Castro's Revolution* (1962), 12–13. Carlos Rafael Rodríguez, *France Nouvelle*, 17–22 July 1958.

[12] To Claude Julien of *Le Monde*; *cf.* Julien, *La Révolution cubaine* (1961).

[13] Qu. Jules Dubois, 258.

[14] HAR, June 1958.

loads of rifles from the Dominican Republic. Outside Havana there was little revolutionary activity. The statue of the patron of Artemisa, Saint Mark, was taken from its place in the church to avoid the holding of the carnival there in late April.[15] But few followed Castro's adjurations of March to public servants to break with the regime. Only twenty-six aircraft pilots resigned. Most people continued to pay as many taxes as they had ever done. The chief of the Central American Bureau of the CIA called on Ambassador Smith and comfortingly said that he quite agreed with the Ambassador's appreciation of Communist dangers in Cuba.[16] On the day that the Communists issued their denunciation of Faustino Pérez, Smith was busy noting more 'reports of Communist support for the 26 July'. The latest, he said, as if that settled the matter, came from J. Edgar Hoover.[17] Smith was also busy organizing the defence of the Guantánamo water supply, which was outside the base area. It was agreed that if Cuban troops had to withdraw (for use elsewhere) U.S. marines could step in. Smith's relations with Batista were never better.

Efforts to reach a compromise were still going on, but the bishops were the only optimists. The nuncio, Mgr Centoz, asked whether the U.S. could not intervene to force a truce. Smith said that was impossible. Could the U.S. provide Bishop Müller (the new coadjutor on his way to Oriente to try to see Castro) with a U.S. naval helicopter? That too would constitute intervention.[18] Bishop Müller nevertheless set off. At the end of the month (with little or no activity from Castro or anywhere else) the episcopacy demanded a specifically neutral government whose leaders would be ineligible for future office. The episcopacy would choose the prime minister. But Batista was now far less worried than he had been in March. The harvest was almost in: 4·5 million tons of sugar, and the effects of sabotage once more almost negligible. Substitutes for U.S. arms were being found. The 26 July Movement in Havana was hurt by the breaking of the strike. Faustino Pérez, though at large, was being hunted everywhere and went to the Sierra. He was replaced as national coordinator of the Movement by Marcelo Fernández. David Salvador was transferred from labour activities to reorganize the Havana underground. Ray remained head of the Civic Resistance.

The failure of the strike led directly to two separate developments. First Castro, as Carlos Rafael Rodríguez had hoped, went out of his way to issue soothing statements for the benefit of public opinion in the

---

[15] It was returned in January 1959, having been held by the cardinal archbishop of Havana. Cf. Revolución, 24 January 1959.

[16] Smith, The Fourth Floor, 34.

[17] J. Edgar Hoover (born 1895), born Washington; George Washington University; director of FBI since 1924; put his name on the cover of many books.

[18] Smith, The Fourth Floor, 126.

U.S. In mid-May he gave an interview to Jules Dubois in which he said:

> Never has the 26 July talked of Socialism or of nationalizing industries ... we have proclaimed from the first that we fought for the full enforcement of the Constitution of 1940 [whose provisions] establish guarantees, rights and obligations for all elements who have a part in production – including free enterprise and invested capital.[19]

He similarly began to promote discussions abroad for a new unification of the opposition, to take the place of the unhappy council of the previous November. This was helped by the establishment on 29 April of a direct radio telephone between the Sierra Maestra and Caracas, Venezuela. But also, and unknown to the rest of the opposition or to his own followers who were negotiating with other members of the opposition, he began to look with more sympathy on the idea of formal collaboration with the Communist party.

It is instructive that Castro took this new step at a time when his brother, the 'more radical' Raúl (as he later described him), was away in Northern Oriente. On 20 April Raúl Castro had written his first dispatch to his brother. He had been away then over a month, since 10 March, travelling partly by jeep, partly on foot. He was accompanied by Manuel Fajardo, Ciro Frías and Efigenio Ameijeiras of the old guard, though after a few days he had reached territory of Mayarí, which was familiar to him from childhood. He had with him a priest too, Fr Antonio Rivas, of Santiago, and indeed his good relations with the Church were such that Fr José Chabebé broadcast secret messages to him on his weekly radio programme from Santiago.[20] By 16 March Raúl Castro was in the Sierra Cristal. There he established relations with a number of other rebels – Captain Demetrio Montseny ('Villa'), Raúl Menéndez Tomasevich, whom he promoted to captain, and the 26 July leader in Guantánamo, 'Toto' Lara. Some of these previously existing units were Communists.[21] Raúl Castro also took over a group of some two hundred 'musketeers':[22]

> Good boys most of them from that zone, but living a fantasy of a revolution in various camps, with jeeps ... eating free in a farm with cooks and everything; the people provided everything for them and all they did was to drive like mad chickens with all the vehicles they

[19] Jules Dubois, 263.

[20] Dewart, 108.

[21] Aníbal Escalante, *Hoy*, 28 June 1959, notes, 'The communist campesinos...were of great help in the formation of the 2nd Front, Frank País.'

[22] These included Lieutenant Vicente Rudea, Sub-Lieutenant Jesús Alejandro Chuchú, Argelio Campos and Captain Julio Pérez.

had from side to side ... The *responsables* had among them 1,000 pesos in the treasury ... I told these gentlemen that we were staying there.[23]

Afterwards Raúl Castro purged this guerrilla band – though there were at least two other rebel groups in the area – two hundred men under Armando Castro (no relation), and thirty under ex-sergeant Wicho. Raúl Castro established in this remote area a public works corps (with tractors to make new roads), a bomb factory under Gilberto Cardero, with an American, Evans Russell, working beneath him, a health unit, headquarters, and even a temporary air base. Raúl Castro showed powers of organization not suspected by those who had previously seen him under the shadow of his brother. The steadily growing force was divided into companies led by Ameijeiras, Manuel Fajardo, and Frías, the first of these being attended by a bodyguard who, due to their wild appearance, were called Mau Maus. There was a successful attack on 8 April on the barracks of Ramón de las Yaguas.[24] Several villages were taken and though afterwards, as usual, most were evacuated, one or two such as Felicidad de Yateras remained permanently in their hands. They were soon joined by a mutinous group of Batista's soldiery under a Sergeant Zapata, and Lieutenant Carlos Lite ('Pepecito'). In this wild area there was almost total breakdown of law; had it indeed ever existed? The revolution caught all ages: one boy of ten killed a soldier, seized his rifle and then marched to the Sierra to place himself under Raúl Castro's orders.[25]

In mid-April Raúl Castro dispatched Ciro Frías with a small group of his followers – Company E – to the east of the city of Guantánamo.[26] But this force was beaten off and Frías killed in an attack on the barracks of Initas with a garrison of seventeen men, between Baracoa and Guantánamo, on the south-east coast. Immediately a new attack was ordered – Ameijeiras, with Félix Peña (who succeeded Frías) and Fajardo, would attack the barracks at Jamaica, in the Yateras area; Raúl Castro himself would attack the barracks at the *central Soledad*. These attacks also were unsuccessful. A third attack at the naval barracks at Caimanera did better. This brought the rebels close to the U.S. base at Guantánamo Bay. The essential achievement of Raúl Castro, however, was less in actual attacks, though this kept the army in a state of nerves, than in his success in unifying the many rebel bands who were at work

[23] See article by Lios Pavón, *Verde Olivo*, 24 March 1963.
[24] Raúl Castro, in *Revolución*, January 1959.
[25] *Ibid.*
[26] Captain Ciro Frías, Lieutenant Jesús Soto Mayor, Juan Carlos Borgés, Gerardo Reyes (Yayo) – all with Garands; Nano Pérez and Echevarría, with Johnsons; Floirán Piña with a *mirilla*; Conrado Díaz, with a Springfield; Moralitos, with a Browning machine rifle; and Labrada and Lite, with short arms. Frías was in command, Carlos Lite his second-in-command.

in the area, due to his possession of superior discipline and morale, with a civil organization including a legal adviser (Augusto Martínez Sánchez, a lawyer from Holguín), as well as a priest. By the end of April an Amazon group had been sent up from the city of Guantánamo, and supplies were also assured from that and other towns. All five companies were well organized over Eastern Oriente, with effective civilian backing.[27] Raúl Castro's headquarters lay at Monte Rus, two hours from Guantánamo. The regulations against pillage had almost abolished the incipient banditry of the region. By midsummer there were perhaps 1,000 ex-bandits or free rebels (*escopeteros*) over whom Raúl Castro had more or less established his leadership.[28]

If Castro was to draw nearer the Communists in mid-1958, he was also being more and more actively supported by the Church. Raúl Castro's contacts with the priests in Santiago were matched by chaplaincies held in both Fidel Castro's and Almeida's groups; Fidel Castro soon had a Protestant as well as a Catholic chaplain. In Havana a priest, Father Madrigal, had become treasurer of the 26 July; the church of Father Boza Masvidal became another centre of activity after the death of several young Catholics at police hands in April. The nuncio, Mgr Centoz, had taken a protest signed by many priests on that occasion to Batista, who, however, had refused to see him.[29] Lay Catholic leaders continued active on a far grander scale than the Communists.

Castro was by no means yet the only opponent in the field against Batista. His most formidable rival was Barquín, still in prison but with both his own group of officers (describing themselves as the 4 April Movement, from the date of their abortive *golpe* in 1957) and the Montecristi Movement, led by Justo Carrillo, working for his release by means of a *golpe* on the Isle of Pines. Carrillo had the promised support of the provisional president of Venezuela, Admiral Larrazábal, for his scheme;

[27] Company A: Menéndez Tomasevich – Alto Songo
Company B: Ameijeiras – Guantánamo
Company C: Julio Pérez – Sagua y Mayarí
Company D: Fajardo – Yateras
Company E: Peña – Baracoa, east of Guantánamo

[28] The source for this account, Raúl Castro's diary published in *Revolución*, 26–29 January 1959. See also the article by his aide, José Caussé, in *Verde Olivo*, 24 March 1963. A later reorganization placed all Raúl Castro's men in the columns led by Majors Lussón, Belarmino Castilla and Peña, and finally at the end of the war there was a fourth, under Major Iglesias ('Nicaragua'). Except for Peña who died suddenly in 1959, these remained the pillar of the revolutionary army in the 1960s. Thus these commanders and Captains Jiménez Lage, Filiberto Olivera, Colomé ('Furry') Pepito Cuza, Samuel Rodiles and Félix Lugano (Pilón), have in the main been the revolutionary commanders of the new Cuban army and of these commanders, seven (Lussón, Colomé, Jiménez Lage, Olivera, Fajardo, Menéndez Tomasevich and Ameijeiras) were on the first central committee of the new Cuban Communist party in 1965.

[29] *Bohemia*, 18 January 1959.

Venezuela would make available aircraft painted in the colours of the
Dominican Republic; but in order to receive this, Carrillo had to
secure the approval or the blind eye of the U.S. Carrillo then flew to
Washington where he saw General Darcey, chief of the U.S. delegation
on the Cuba–American Defence Board. Carrillo, still recalling what he
believed to be the treachery of the 26 July Movement over the Cienfuegos rising,[30] described to Darcey the situation which would face
the U.S. if Castro won, 'even without yet believing that Castro would
convert himself into a direct agent of Moscow'. He told Darcey: 'The
greater delay in the triumph of the revolution the more radical it would
be', that this radicalism would lead to some anti-Americanism, since the
U.S. arms embargo on Batista had been counter-balanced by the
maintenance of the military mission, by such things as U.S. decorations
to Tabernilla, or by the delivery of arms ordered before the embargo; he
added that if the army of Batista was quite overcome by Castro the
latter would substitute the Army of Cuba by the rebel army and that
the very least evil to befall the U.S. would be that in future, 'the U.S.
could not count on the Cuban Army . . . as she had been able to do in
the First and Second World Wars'.[31]

Darcey said that he could not possibly approve Carrillo's use of Venezuelan aeroplanes and that the U.S. desired to prevent rather than to
provoke disturbances in the Caribbean and advised Carrillo to try to
found a militant Catholic movement to fight Batista.[32] Thus Carrillo
was once more thwarted in his plan to free Barquín and create in him
a military counterweight to Fidel Castro in the ranks of the Cuban
opposition. Larrazábal eventually gave arms to the anti-Batista opposition in Cuba, but he did so only in November and then directly to the
26 July.[33]

[30] See above, 962 fn. 5.
[31] Carrillo MSS, 38–9.
[32] Loc. cit.
[33] Ibid. The arms were taken to the Sierra in the same aeroplane which carried Luis Buch
and 'President' Urrutia.

CHAPTER LXXXII

Batista's 'Big Push' of May 1958

On 24 May Batista launched against the Sierra Maestra the only major offensive of the war: *operación verano*. Seventeen battalions had been concentrated, each with a tank company; there was aerial and naval support; and the Rural Guard.[1] The commanders were Generals Cantillo and del Río Chaviano. These two officers were hardly on speaking terms and their personal animosity accounts for much of their subsequent failure. Their aim was to advance into the Sierra with an overwhelming mass of men, cut Castro off from supplies, and, by reducing the territory in which he operated to a few square miles, prepare the way for a final assault.

For weeks it was impossible to know what was going on. Even within the Sierra news was difficult to get at. The Batistiano army advanced with difficulty but sureness, along the foothills, mostly in the north of the front. Castro brought back all his men (until then grouped in little sub-columns), from the south.[2] The army columns were insistently ambushed and their losses were considerable, particularly from mines carefully laid by Castro, but for twenty-five days the officers drove their men on with energy and some zeal. Cantillo on the other hand had been somewhat dismayed by Batista's instruction that a quarter of the available men should be kept to guard the coffee crop and the sugar *centrales* of the region.[3]

Radio Rebelde appealed for doctors and some new ones rallied to the cause.[4] Castro later recalled that his difficulties were increased because he was now less mobile than before; he had a network of workshops and an elaborate system of communications. There was even a cigar factory.[5] 'We had therefore to reunite all our forces, except those in Santiago, to resist the enemy offensive; [but] we scarcely had three hundred

---

[1] Barrera Pérez, *Bohemia Libre*, 27 August 1961.
[2] Castro's commanders were previously: Column 3, Almeida (Cobre); Column 2, Cienfuegos (centre); Column 4, R. Valdés (E. Turquino); Column 7, Crecensio Pérez (east of Sierra); Column 8, Guevara; Column 1, H.Q., Castro himself. These were drawn back to guard along all the entrances to the Sierra (Núñez Jiménez, 582).
[3] Suárez Núñez, 96.
[4] *Cf.* interview with Dr Raúl Trilla Gómez, in *Revolución*, 26 January 1959, 8.
[5] Guevara, 176.

men, of whom sixty were very badly armed ...'[6] Almeida's column near Santiago and a patrol under Cienfuegos near Holguín were recalled.

In mid-June Batista's army was advancing in two directions, from the north and south, the latter being left unguarded. Two battalions under, respectively, Colonel Sánchez Mosquera and Major Menéndez Martínez, advanced from the mines of Bueycito, crossed the main range of the Sierra and moved on towards Santo Domingo. On 19 June these forces successfully reached Las Vegas de Jibacoa, Santo Domingo and Navajal. A day or two later they passed Gaviro and so surrounded the Sierra at the peak San Lorenzo. In north and south the army had penetrated in depth. Between the two advance guards there remained only four square miles of territory left undisputedly to Castro; 'Our territory was reduced and reduced until we could not reduce any further.'[7] But by this time the morale of the army was drooping. Many of the men, untrained for this sort of territory, were exhausted. There was a pause for consolidation at this extreme point of penetration; Navajal, where Major Quevedo had brought the 18th Battalion, advancing from the mouth of the River Plate,[8] and Merino, where Major Suárez Zoulet had penetrated with the 19th Battalion. On 29 June Sánchez Mosquera's 11th Battalion, which was resting in a valley at Santo Domingo, was surrounded on three sides by Castro's riflemen. Sánchez Mosquera had nearly 1,000 men, Castro still less than 300. But in the next three days' sporadic fighting, Sánchez Mosquera's force was decimated. Many prisoners were taken and barely a third escaped alive. Sánchez Mosquera was himself wounded and the short-wave radio equipment of one of his companies fell into Castro's hands, along with the army code and many arms.[9] The main reason was that the 'combat intelligence' of Castro's forces was immensely superior to that of the enemy – 'Batista's forces could not go a yard without a perspiring runner arriving a few minutes later to tell Castro of it.'[10]

The consequences of this setback were extraordinary. Batista's High Command, now a demoralized gaggle of corrupt, cruel and lazy officers without combat experience, began to fear total extinction from an enemy of whose numbers and whereabouts they knew nothing accurate,

[6] *Obra Revolucionaria*, 1961, No. 46, 12. On 9 January 1959 Castro said that he had 300 rifles (*Revolución*, 10 January 1959) but Guevara (*Souvenirs*, 197) says only 200 rifles in good condition. Taber comments that it was Castro's policy to lead Batista's army into the mountains 249).

[7] *Obra Revolucionaria*, 1961, No. 46, 12.

[8] La Plata.

[9] For all this, see Castro's own account on Radio Rebelde, 18 August 1958, qu. Núñez Jiménez, 578–82; Taber, 263–4.

[10] Dicky Chapelle in F. M. Osanka, ed., *Modern Guerrilla Warfare*, (1962), 320.

perhaps even believing some of their own communiqués which described hundreds of rebels being killed. The extent of Sánchez Mosquera's defeat was exaggerated. The advance was halted. At the same moment the rebel army launched a series of counter-attacks on all the exposed and most advanced positions; new combats followed at Merino, El Jigüe, Santo Domingo, Las Vegas de Jibacoa and Las Mercedes. To avoid being cut off the army attempted to withdraw. Some deserted (for instance, thirty out of eighty on 24 July at El Cerro). The air force failed to distinguish between Batistianos and rebels and some of the former were killed by napalm bombing. Fear of the rebels meant that instead of sending tanks forward to protect the infantry, the infantry was sent ahead to guard tanks and then mown down.

Within the next month almost the entire army withdrew from the Sierra Maestra. The High Command panicked. The withdrawal became so general that little resistance was offered. Minor advances were ordered, based on fallacious map-reading. Castro's capture of the enemy's code enabled him not only to discover army movements but even to give misleading orders (including to the air force).[11] Communications between the different columns barely existed. By the beginning of August, not merely Sánchez Mosquera's 11th Battalion but also Major Menéndez's 22nd Battalion and Major Suárez Zoulet's 19th had been destroyed as a fighting force. The 18th Battalion collapsed, partly due to lack of food and drink, partly because Castro entered into contact with Major Quevedo, whom he had known at the university and who afterwards joined the rebels. Several other units suffered serious losses. The gain in arms to the rebels was large: a 14-ton tank, twelve mortars, two bazookas, twelve machine guns on tripods and twenty-one rifle machine guns, 142 Garand rifles, 200 Cristóbal machine guns. Total rebel losses were 27 killed and about fifty wounded; those killed included five officers (nearly 20% – a high percentage, though in small-scale war of this sort not surprising). The rebels took 433 prisoners, of whom 422 were turned over to officials of the Red Cross and twenty-one to the army itself; none was maltreated.[12] 117 were wounded, of whom two died. The care with which these men were treated was exemplary even if that treatment served a political purpose, for it contrasted so strongly with treatment of prisoners captured by Batista that it inflicted another blow to army prestige. The army had till this point taken no prisoners at all. Castro justified this unusual but wise method:

War is not a mere question of rifles, bullets, cannon and aeroplanes. This belief has been many times one of the causes of the failure of

[11] The code was not changed till 25 July, being captured on 29 June. After that another code was also captured.
[12] See article on Red Cross, in *New York Times Magazine*, 25 August 1963.

tyrannies ... Since January 1957 ... some six hundred members of the armed forces ... have passed into our hands ... none have been killed ... while torture and death has been the certain fate awaiting every rebel, every sympathiser, even every suspect who fell into enemy hands. In many cases unhappy peasants have been assassinated to add to the number of bodies with which to justify the false news of the chief of staff ... more than six hundred defence-less citizens, in many cases far from any revolutionary activity, have been assassinated [by the army].[13] In these twenty months of campaign, killing has made nobody stronger. Killing has made *them* weak; refusing to kill has made *us* strong ... only cowards and thugs murder an enemy when he has surrendered ... the rebel army cannot carry out the same tactics as the tyranny which we fight ...'

It naturally cost the rebels less to send back the prisoners than to maintain them. Given, said Castro, the existing economic conditions and unemployment they would never lack men to fight for the army ... but 'victory depends on a minimum of men and a maximum of morale'.[14] This impression was confirmed by a clever U.S. journalist expert in guerrilla war, Dicky Chapelle, who later wrote that this handling of prisoners was an 'expression of utter contempt for the fighting potential of the defeated [which] had an almost physical impact'.[15]

News of these victories by Castro was concealed by the Batistiano High Command, and on two successive nights – 18 and 19 August – Castro broadcast on Radio Rebelde and gave as full details as he could of the encounters, in the eloquent accomplished language that became so familiar to Cuban audiences later: he paid special attention to the army, denouncing the High Command and General Cantillo, who he said belonged 'among the cowards who have contemplated with indifference – the rosary of corpses which his colleagues Chaviano, Ventura, Pilar García and others have left in the streets and cities of Cuba ...' In contrast, he stretched out his hand towards younger officers, 'who have in these months of war earned our gratitude. They are not corrupted, they love their career and their Service. For many of them, the War which has entangled them is absurd ... but they obey orders.' He cleverly contrasted them with the higher ranks, those who had made themselves millionaires by the exploitation of gaming, by vice protection and other crooked practices. He spoke of a possible *golpe* by the army; if this was the work of opportunist military men anxious to save their fortunes and to seek the best possible way out for the *camarilla* of the tyranny,

13 A guess no doubt.
14 Speech on Radio Rebelde, quoted in Núñez Jiménez, *Geografía*, 578–92.
15 Osanka, 329. Mrs Dicky Chapelle was killed in Vietnam.

We are resolutely against ... For ... the sacrifices *which have been made and the blood which has been shed cannot be made to leave things more or less as they were, so repeating the story which followed the fall of Machado.* If the military *golpe* is the work of honest men and has a sincerely revolutionary purpose, a peaceful solution will then be possible on just and beneficial bases. Between the armed forces and the Revolution, whose interests are not and never must be antagonistic, the problem of Cuba may be resolved. We are at war with the tyranny, not the armed forces ... The dilemma for the Army is clear ... either take a step forward, shaking off this corpse of the Batista regime ... or commit suicide as an institution. Those who today save the Army will not be able to save it within a few months. If war continues another six months the Army will totally disintegrate ...

Then Castro told the army what they could do to achieve peace: the arrest of Batista, of the politicians of the regime, and 'of all officers who have permitted torture. Afterwards there would be removal from the armed forces of all political issues so that they could never end up again as the instrument of any *caudillo* or political party.' There was also a quotation from Maceo ('The revolution will go on while a single injustice remains'), and a rousing peroration.[16] Batista on the other hand gave out an anodyne communiqué saying that army patrols had liquidated an enemy which then took to flight.[17]

Batista's offensive, important though it was for the war, was over-shadowed in the minds of many by the tactics of Raúl Castro on the northern coast of Cuba in June and July. The most serious incident of the summer had probably been the murder by the police of the two Giral sisters of Santiago, after an attempt on the Minister of Defence, Rey; and an attempt on Batista by a fifteen-year-old boy. On 26 June two hundred members of the 26 July under Raúl Castro came down from the Sierra Cristal on to Moa Bay and kidnapped ten U.S. citizens and two Canadians who were working there, including the head of the mineral engineering department at the University of Minnesota. Forty miles to the south Desmond Elsmore, field superin-tendent of the *Ermita* sugar mill, was also taken. On 27 June Richard Sargent, Canadian manager of the *Isabel* sugar mill, was captured, and twenty-seven U.S. sailors and marines were kidnapped when they were returning on a Cuban bus from an outing near Guantánamo. On 30 June the general manager and one other executive of Nicaro were kidnapped. The same day a letter reached Ambassador Smith from Raúl Castro saying that the captives would be released on the condition, first, that

[16] Qu. Núñez Jiménez, *Geografía*, 592-4.
[17] Suárez Núñez, 97.

the U.S. cease shipment of *all* military equipment to the government of Cuba – including spare and defective parts in previously supplied weapons; second, that the U.S. would cease assisting the Cuban government aircraft with fuel from the Guantánamo base; and third, that the U.S. would obtain an assurance from Batista that Cuba would not use U.S. military equipment against Castro.[18] Finally, in early July four United Fruit Company men and two officials were kidnapped.

These acts naturally angered the U.S. government. Senators Knowland and Styles Bridges demanded that if the men were not given up within forty-eight hours, 'effective help would be given to Batista'. John Foster Dulles told a press conference that the U.S. could 'not be blackmailed into helping the rebels'. The State Department denied that it was fuelling Cuban aircraft and that it was supplying arms to Batista, but made no reference to the third rebel demand.

Whatever the truth, Batista was now in considerable difficulties. He could not dislodge Castro, so he could not guarantee the return of the prisoners. Ambassador Smith believed that he would have allowed U.S. marines to land to do so. Smith, the navy and others in Washington also desired this: indeed the navy recommended 'an immediate intervention in Cuba of divisional size'. The State Department correctly argued that to enter Cuba would be much easier than leaving, while to intervene militarily might not save the lives of the marines.[19]

In the end, the prisoners were released with no concessions wrung from the U.S., save that the rebels in the Sierra Cristal would enjoy two or three weeks' freedom from air attack. The 26 July obtained maximum publicity for the release of the captives, who had been well treated, though subjected to long cross-examination by Vilma Espín, the young Santiago 26 July girl who had been in the Sierra Cristal since March. The effect of these kidnappings was to lose some of the good will that Castro had garnered in the U.S. But Castro won another victory when, in late July, Cuban troops were withdrawn from guarding the U.S. Guantánamo water supply at Yateras. U.S. troops took over. Castro protested. The U.S. withdrew and Cubans returned.[20]

While this important offensive and these kidnappings were continuing in the Sierra there had been a number of critical changes in the plain between the supporters of Castro and the rest of the anti-Batistiano opposition. After the strike of April there had been a time of relative calm in much of Cuba outside the Sierra. Ray and Faustino Pérez, directors of activity in Havana, had successfully evaded the police to

[18] Smith, *The Fourth Floor*, 142.
[19] R. D. Murphy, *Diplomat among Warriors* (1964), 456.
[20] *Ibid*, 458.

get to the Sierra in order to confer with Castro in mid-June, but on 17 June they received news that almost all of the executives of the Civic Resistance and 26 July in Havana had been arrested or had had to leave the country. Ray and Pérez returned quickly to Havana without seeing Castro. They found their organization almost leaderless, and many groups had lost touch with each other.[21] By this time the Communists in Havana, rebuffed by the Civic Resistance, had begun negotiating an agreement with the 26 July in the labour field. The 26 July Movement, for its part, knew from the experience of April that if it wanted any union or labour action, support would have to be obtained from some organization with strength there. The Communists were the only possibility.[22] On 5 June Carlos Rafael Rodríguez sent an article to *La France Nouvelle* (Paris) making clear that negotiations had at least begun:[23] Rodríguez also wrote that day to the French journalist Claude Julien explaining that the need was still to draw into the opposition alliance people such as Prío and Grau, forming a coalition that 'would go beyond the limits of anti-imperialism'.[24]

No important developments occurred for a few weeks and, presumably as a threat, the Communist party itself brightly came out on 28 June with an appeal for 'honest and democratic' elections – an apparent new retreat away from the policy of Castro. In consequence Ray, on behalf of the Civic Resistance, told the Communists that in these circumstances, they could contribute nothing to the struggle.[25] The Communists then began to organize new groups of partisans in Camagüey, Escambray and even Pinar del Río.[26] Raúl Castro kept in touch with the Communists in Havana, since at the end of June he sent 'Pepe' Ramírez, a Communist sugar workers' leader, to report to the Politburo in Havana in person about the kidnappings of U.S. businessmen, and early the following month Carlos Rafael Rodríguez, on behalf of the Communist central committee, made his way up first to see Raúl Castro in the Sierra Cristal and then to the Sierra Maestra.[27] For some days Fidel Castro (who appears not to have expected the visit) was either too busy, too preoccupied with the war or too cautious to see him. Rodríguez later recalled: 'In the Sierra Cristal, where Raúl Castro was in command, there was nothing but understanding for the Communists. But

[21] Ray to the author.
[22] Ursinio Rojas, Communist trade union leader, later said negotiations began in June and July (*Fundamentos*, March 1959).
[23] *La France Nouvelle*, No. 664, 17 July 1958.
[24] Julien, 123.
[25] Ray to the author.
[26] Arnault, 78.
[27] *Hoy*, 11 January 1959; Rodríguez confirmed to the author in June 1966 that he went up to the Sierra at that time. Rodríguez got his chance of going to the Sierra since Castro had invited all revolutionary parties to consult with him and only the Communists and Directorio took advantage of the opportunity.

when I got to Fidel in the Sierra Maestra, the understanding had changed to suspicion.'[28]

In Caracas, meantime, all opposition groups, apart from the Communists and the two 'electoral' parties (Grau's and Márquez Sterling's) met once more, and this time, on 20 July, a genuine pact was made by them with the 26 July Movement, all the organizations represented forming a 'Junta of Unity' or 'Frente Cívico Revolucionario Democrático'. Present were many men who had taken a personal part in the struggle and others who had always operated in exile, union leaders and students. The list was impressive: Prío, Miró Cardona (the lawyer of the Civic Dialogue); Varona; Rodríguez Loeches and Orlando Blanco (for the Directorio Revolucionario); David Salvador (26 July); Pascasio Linares, Lauro Blanco, José María Aguilera and Angel Cofiño – all trade union leaders, members of the United Labour Front; José Puente and Omar Fernández, leaders of the FEU; Gabino Rodríguez Villaverde, for the Barquinista officers (the 4 April Movement); Justo Carrillo, the economist now at the head of the Catholic Democratic Montecristi Movement; Lincoln Rodón, speaker of the House of Representatives in 1952, for the Democratic party; Angel María Santos Buch, the exiled leader of the Civic Resistance; and, finally, José Llanusa[29] on behalf of Fidel Castro, whose signature had been previously obtained and with whom contact was maintained by radio. It appears that Castro insisted on being paid another $44,000 by Prío before he would sign.[30] The pact demanded 'a common strategy to defeat the dictatorship by armed insurrection', a brief provisional government 'that will lead ... to full constitutional and democratic procedures; [and] a scheme to guarantee punishment of the guilty ... the rights of workers, the fulfilment of the international commitments ... as well as the economic and political progress of the Cuban people'.[31] The distinguished lawyer Miró Cardona was nominated to be coordinator of the Frente, and Castro was named commander-in-chief of the forces of the revolution. Judge Urrutia was designated 'President of Cuba in arms'.

This pact naturally gave a respectable and hopeful front to the opposition in general, but in reality it merely meant a temporary end to internecine squabbling, rather than a common strategy, and there was a good deal of quarrelling immediately afterwards, particularly over a 'theft' of

[28] See interview with Rodríguez by Gianni Corbi, in *L'Espresso* (Italy), 26 January–23 February 1964, and his evidence in the Marquitos trial, *Hoy*, 25 March 1964.

[29] Later chief of sports in Castro's revolutionary government and Minister of Education. Llanusa, pushed by Haydée Santamaría de Hart, began to be prominent in April.

[30] Evidence of Primitivo Lima (Directorio representative, Caracas). Prío promised another $6,000 to the Caracas pact alliance which was not paid.

[31] As qu. Jules Dubois, 280.

arms from the Directorio by the 26 July Movement: what had been intended for the Sierra Escambray, went to Raúl Castro in the Sierra Cristal.[32] Further, the nomination of Castro as commander-in-chief did not prevent the other groups maintaining their own operations, but it did enable Castro to demand more vigorously that those who wished for direct action should go and enrol themselves under his command in the Sierra Maestra.

[32] Evidence of Primitivo Lima. Gabino Rodríguez, the Barquinista representative, gave evidence that the money raised by the Frente was only enough to finance a small propaganda office and send a delegate to Geneva to the Red Cross (Gabino Rodríguez evidence).

CHAPTER LXXXIII

The Collapse

In August 1958, after the final withdrawal of the army, Castro fixed his headquarters near La Plata, some few miles inland from the sea, on a river of that name. Three new operations were planned. Castro and the main force would attempt the encirclement of Santiago; Guevara would set off westwards to the province of Las Villas with 148 men (Column No. 8, Ciro Redondo) to cut systematically all means of communication between the two ends of the island and to establish Castro's authority over those guerrillas still active in the Escambray – the Directorio being now once more under Faure Chomón, who had returned from Havana the previous month.[1] Cienfuegos with eighty-two men would move on to Pinar del Río (at the head of Column No. 2, Antonio Maceo). Castro appointed Guevara to be commander of all the opposition units in Las Villas (towns included) and gave him the power to collect taxes, apply the new Penal Code and inaugurate agrarian reform. It remained to be seen whether the Directorio would accept these impositions. Nor was the Directorio the only organization active in Escambray, since there was also a group of semi-gangsters who had split off from it, known as 'the Second Front of Escambray', apparently stimulated to do so by Prío. These were led by a brother of the Spaniard involved in the attack on the palace, Gutiérrez Menoyo.[2] Then there was also in Las Villas Félix Torres's 'Máximo Gómez' column of Communists, now sixty-five strong.[3]

Guevara and Cienfuegos left at the end of August, on foot, after their lorries had been destroyed in an air raid,[4] the former accompanied by an old Communist of Santa Clara, Armando Acosta, who, though he had left Santa Clara only a few weeks before, returned with the rank of captain and the pseudonym 'Rodríguez'.[5]

Meantime, from La Plata, Castro continued to negotiate both with

---

[1] See Guevara, in *Verde Olivo*, 5 October 1960. For Chomón's return, see Rodríguez Loeches, 99. The minutes of the Commissions of Cooperation and Coordination of the Caracas Frente (which I have seen) are full of quarrels as to the exact proportion between the effort to be spent on the Sierras de Escambray and Oriente.

[2] Primitivo Lima alleges that Prío encouraged the 'Second Front' to leave the Directorio.

[3] *Hoy*, 20 July 1965.

[4] Guevara, *Souvenirs*, 198.

[5] Evidence of Carlos Rafael Rodríguez to the author; memorandum of a 26 July leader in Las Villas, Joaquín Torres.

Communists and with all other members of the opposition. Carlos Rafael Rodríguez left the Sierra on 10 August,[6] with what he anyway later claimed was a verbal acceptance by Castro of the idea of unity between Fidelistas and Communists; and at least one more Communist, Luis Mas Martín, a member of Juventud Socialista when Castro had been at the university, came up to the Sierra and thereafter stayed at headquarters as the party's representative.[7] In 'the plain', that is, in Havana, Carlos Rafael Rodríguez met the local representatives of the parties which had signed the Caracas pact and told them, to their surprise, that Castro had become convinced that the Communists ought to join in with them, at least in the labour section which was designed to transform the opposition in that department. A meeting was held in Havana of the Caracas pact parties and all resisted the idea, the 26 July representative, Delio Gómez Ochoa, being specially hostile to the plan, despite Carlos Rafael Rodríguez's claims about Castro's views. Carlos Rafael Rodríguez then decided to go up again to the Sierra Maestra, as he was sure that Castro would disapprove what the Caracas junta had just done.[8] But then two further approaches by the Communists – this time by Marinello, the Communist president – were rejected, again with Gómez Ochoa intervening 'in an almost violent manner'.[9] Gómez Ochoa, who had left the Sierra for Havana on 23 May (that is, long before Carlos Rafael Rodríguez's first visit to the hills), was an Ortodoxo student of diplomatic law at the University of Havana, the son of a landowner, and a passionate anti-Communist and enemy of Raúl Castro. It cannot be quite excluded that Castro dispatched him as his representative in Havana to represent the right wing of the 26 July Movement at a moment when in fact he was himself opening negotiations with the Communist party.[10] Negotiations even over Labour unity with the Communists therefore remained incomplete, with Carlos Rafael Rodríguez again in the Sierra: this time however, he remained there,[11] establishing himself not at Castro's headquarters but in another camp nearby at Las Vegas. He was accompanied by a well-known Communist sugar workers' leader, Ursinio Rojas.

Shortly afterwards there was a definite agreement about the right of

[6] Evidence of Carlos Rafael Rodríguez to the author.

[7] *Hoy*, 15 January 1959.

[8] Letter from Angel del Cerro (Montecristi representative at these discussions) to Theodore Draper, 2 September 1962.

[9] Manuel Ledón evidence. This said, however, it is clear that some members of the 26 July Movement in Havana were in favour of an arrangement with the Communists – in particular Ricardo Alarcón, the leader of the students' branch of the 26 July Movement (in 1969 Cuban Ambassador to the U.N.).

[10] See Luis Simón (MSS, p. 254). Simón accompanied Gómez Ochoa from the Sierra to the plain in May and back again in October.

[11] Evidence of Carlos Rafael Rodríguez to the author, June 1966.

Communists to join the rebel army.[12] Delio Gómez Ochoa was then withdrawn from Havana to the Sierra and replaced by Marcelo Fernández, a more diplomatic spirit, and negotiations for an agreement on Labour unity went ahead faster. Fernández in later years was able to live down a strong conservative and anti-Communist period in 1959, to join in 1965 the new central committee of the Cuban Communist party. But relations between Castro and Rodríguez were not close. Rodríguez appears again to have been kept waiting for several days before being received by Castro,[13] and it seems improbable that any general political agreement, verbal or written, was reached between them as to the nature of Cuba after the victory. One member of the Directorio Revolucionario, Manuel Ledón, writing of the efforts made in Havana in August 1958 to achieve unity among the opposition groups in consequence of the Pact of Caracas, said that none now showed any concern with anything save getting rid of Batista: the clear assumption was that there would be a return to the Constitution of 1940, but no more.[14]

A critical meeting from the point of view of the negotiations on Labour unity occurred now in the zone controlled by Raúl Castro – the venue being selected because of the difficulties in getting to the Sierra Maestra. A large cortège of hardened Labour leaders – David Salvador, Jesús Soto, Octavio Louit (Cabrera), Conrado Bécquer and Ñico Torres – made the journey to the Sierra Cristal, where they were received by Raúl Castro, who harangued them on the need for unity with the Communists; and in the event such was the prestige of this young *guerrillero* that he got his way despite the fact that nearly all of these men had been for years rivals to and even enemies of the Communists.[15]

Castro, sensing victory, after the repulse of the army moved more and more into the role of a political rather than a guerrilla leader. Already in the early summer he had imposed a levy of 15 cents on each 250-pound bag of sugar produced in sugar mills. This levy was often paid, in Oriente, even by U.S. owned mills. In September came a request to the public to boycott fiestas, the lottery, and the newspapers, and to purchase only necessities. Castro also appealed to all to give any help to rebels that they could.

He now seemed for the first time to be giving thought to the nature of the future regime: the head of the Havana Civic Resistance, Manuel

[12] *Cf.* Blas Roca, VIIIth Congress speech, p. 38; *Hoy*, 11 January 1959.
[13] Ray to author.
[14] Manuel Ledón evidence.
[15] Memorandum of Joaquín Torres, of the 26 July Movement, also present. Present on Raúl Castro's side were the lawyers Martínez Sánchez ('a sort of major-domo') and Lucas Morán. The house where the meeting was held was nicknamed 'the Palace of Justice'.

Ray, visited him in September (meeting him for the first time). Castro asked Ray to work out a scheme for agrarian reform. Ray, impressed with Castro, agreed that the army should be purged after a victory and that the rebel army should take over its functions. But they disagreed over the size of the army – Castro being clearly interested, according to the recollection of Ray, in a large force.[16] Castro also wanted a boarding school for 20,000 rural children in each province. The Havana underground had been worried about the influence of Guevara and Raúl Castro in the Sierra, but at this time neither was with Castro. Raúl Castro had just completed another spectacular *coup*, by rescuing a prominent 26 July leader from Santiago, Carlos Iglesias ('Nicaragua'), from an Oriente train.[17]

Guevara had already on 7 September, with his column, crossed the Jobabo river into Camagüey and, moving along the south coast of the island, clashed with the army near Santa Cruz del Sur, where a captain under him, Marcos Borrero, was killed.[18] This expedition to Las Villas was carried out in conditions as bad as those of the early days in the Sierra: Cienfuegos, in a report written in October, spoke of:

> Forty days of march, often with the south coast and a compass as the only guide. During fifteen days we marched with water and mud up to the knees, travelling by night to avoid ambushes . . . during the thirty-one days of our journey across Camagüey we ate eleven times. After four days of famine we had to eat a mare . . . Almost all our animals were left in the marsh.[19]

As leader, Guevara showed himself as parsimonious and ascetic as any of his followers, thereby noticeably differentiating himself from Castro in the Sierra, who had usually lived well when he could.[20]

The two columns, Guevara's and Cienfuegos's, sometimes moved together in the earlier stages – as in their skirmish at Santa Cruz del Sur – afterwards separately, occasionally dispensing justice[21] or brushing with guards, but otherwise pressing on as fast as possible. Only one serious

---

[16] Ray to the author. Though Ray was pleased with these talks, the emphasis on a large army left a definite memory. Karl Meyer of the *Washington Post* recalls that in an interview in September Castro seemed preoccupied by the hemispheric significance of his struggle against the army. To stage a successful revolution against the army seemed to him, rightly, to be, not only remarkable from Cuba's point of view but from all Latin America's. (Meyer to author.)

[17] See the accounts by the attacking commander, Captain Raúl Menéndez Tomasevich and 'Nicaragua', in *Revolución*, 13 August 1962.

[18] Jules Dubois, 305.

[19] Report in Franqui, *L'Histoire des Douze*, 136–7; *Verde Olivo*, 29 October 1961.

[20] Luis Simón MSS, 279–80 (Simón encountered the columns near Manzanillo).

[21] Cienfuegos had two men, Máximo Quevedo and Edel Casañas, shot for looting. Franqui, 239.

setback occurred when, on 27 September, a group of Guevara's column under Captain Jaime Vega was caught and butchered by the army Sergeant Otaño.[22] Guevara received the assistance in Camagüey of the local Communists, who had offered him a mimeographical apparatus and propaganda leaflets: a member of the 26 July Movement, Joaquín Torres, told him at Guasimal, in the foothills of the Escambray mountains, that his organization could supply all this too. But Guevara, though appearing to accept these arguments, continued to use the Communists.[23]

Batista's government reacted slowly to the possibility, not yet of defeat, but of a prolongation of war. Like most Cuban rulers before him, Batista placed the blame on the U.S.; not only was the U.S. helping the rebels through denying him arms, but they were guilty of negligence in letting the rebels get arms.[24] In the U.S. itself the exiles were still, however, condemning the Eisenhower administration as committed to Batista; the military mission remained, for instance, necessitated by 'hemispheric defence'.[25] Further, in September, the U.S.'s ally, England, agreed to sell Batista fifteen Sea Fury fighters. Castro telegraphed the English prime minister, Harold Macmillan, in the name of liberty, to prevent the sale. Macmillan would not be drawn; there was no objection to the sale. When these were delivered, the rebel headquarters issued 'Law 4: against English aggression'. A plan was put forward to confiscate English companies' property; all good Cubans were asked to boycott English goods.

The situation in the cities was calmer but the police responded to what action there was with more savagery than ever. Thus, after two bombs exploded in Havana in August, seven youths were found hanging the next day. The inspector-general of the CIA, Kirkpatrick, complained to the Minister of Defence about the tortures practised by the BRAC, the anti-Communist bureau which was practically a branch of the CIA, but to no effect.[26] A little crisis involved the famous black Virgin of Regla, patron saint of sailors; two boys stole it and apparently dropped it in their flight. The rumour spread, however, that the police substituted a false, smaller one. The police became so disturbed that the traditional fiesta of 8 September was banned, while the rebels tried to keep the people away from all fiestas. In September there was sabotage at Havana airport of perhaps $M2 to $M3 worth of merchandise, and six

[22] The rumour is widespread in exile circles that the Batistiano local commander, Colonel Dueñas, was given $100,000 to permit Guevara to cross Camagüey on the condition that he crossed to the south.

[23] Memorandum of Joaquín Torres. (Not to be confused with the Communist Félix Torres.)

[24] In a note of 28 August. But on 9 September the U.S. seized the *Harpoon*, with one and a half tons of ammunition.

[25] *Cf.* Jules Dubois, 312–13.

[26] Kirkpatrick, *The Real CIA*, 175.

armed men set off a bomb destroying a transmitting station for Circuito Nacional Cubano at Havana, and also Radio Aeropuerto. Visitors to the cities continued to be amazed at the extent to which the middle classes, rotarians and professional people, were even more behind Castro, particularly in Santiago where smart residential districts such as Vista Alegre or the Country Club seemed embattled fortresses of the 26 July Movement.

At long last, indeed, in the autumn of 1958, the war began to make its mark on the economy.[27] By November there was a strong downward trend in all sales. Shop owners reduced their stock and turnover to a minimum.[28] There were many arrests, among them leaders of the 26 July such as Salvador and Louit in Havana, so that Manuel Ray was effectively in charge of all underground activity in the cities of the island. Two more kidnappings of Americans (Texaco employees) by Castro kept up the tense expectancy, even though they were quickly released. A U.S. transport took off fifty-five U.S. citizens from Nicaro, a confession of lack of trust in the Batista government's ability to keep order. The State Department mildly said that 'the U.S. might have to take action' if kidnapping did not cease, and Castro denounced Smith and Batista severally for trying to provoke U.S. intervention.[29] On 21 October a DC 3 with twelve passengers was hijacked when *en route* to Miami and forced to land in the Sierra Maestra.

Castro did not confine his activities to a war of nerves. In October the negotiations with the Communists for labour unity were concluded with the formation of a loose coalition, to be known as Frente Obrero Nacional de Unidad (FONU).[30] No one attributed much importance to this; it seemed merely a temporary tactical alliance. A member of the Montecristi Movement recalls that 'the Communists presented themselves with an exquisite urbanity and humility'. They asked to join the Frente but they agreed that they should be left to join the workers section. Here among the workers, they could count on 'some slight strength'.[31] Some old members of the Communist-dominated CTC (such as Alfredo Rancaño, of the waiters and 'gastronomic' workers, or José Miguel Espino, a railway leader) took positions in the new Labour organization. In fact, however, the FONU was scarcely in existence even by 1 January 1959 when Batista fell. More important seemed the text of a decree of agrarian reform to be applied after the victory – Law 1 of the Sierra Maestra. The essence of this law was that all those with

[27] See Batista, *Cuba Betrayed*, 76, for the president's reaction.
[28] HAR, December 1958.
[29] Smith, *The Fourth Floor*, 150-1.
[30] Apparently on 15 October (see article by Carlos Castañeda in *Bohemia Libre*, 16 October 1960).
[31] Andrés Suárez to Draper, 17 September 1962.

less than 150 acres would be guaranteed. All who had less than 60 acres would receive land, while those with large idle estates would be compensated if they were taken away. State land and Batista's lands would be divided up among peasants. There was thus no mention of cooperatives (as had been promised in *History will absolve me*) or indeed any effort at communal or collective holdings. The agrarian reform would be essentially the *repartimiento*, division of land, ancient ideal of the rural anarchists.[32] At the same time, a further law announced that those who took part in Batista's elections on 3 November would be sentenced to thirty years in prison or to death; and indeed within the next few weeks a prominent Batistiano politician in Camagüey, Aníbal Vega, was 'executed' by local 26 July men as an earnest of this intention.

A visit to Castro's camp in the Sierra in the autumn showed that the '*comandancia*' was now quite formally organized. Celia Sánchez, the dentist's daughter from Pilón, was firmly installed as Castro's secretary and she efficiently controlled his time and the people who visited him. The female group known as the 'battalion Mariana Grajales', led by Olga Guevara, served as the personal staff to the commander. Others in perpetual attendance included the organizers of Radio Rebelde (Franqui, Valera, Violeta Casals). Faustino Pérez lived in a nearby hut. Father Guillermo Sardiñas moved about as chaplain attempting on Castro's orders to regulate the inevitable sexual licence by marriages, without much success. Even a somewhat hostile observer, Luis Simón (who visited the '*comandancia*' in October), however, thought that this 'moral disintegration', as he called it, did not exceed the limits usually reached by regular armies.[33] Carlos Rafael Rodríguez and Luis Mas Martín, the two political representatives of the Communist party, did not play any military or indeed any other part in the activities of the Sierra; they behaved more as political refugees, like José Parda Llada (near whom they lived), than political organizers, who were being put up in the Sierra by Fidel Castro's permission. They had no hand in dealing with new recruits (Aldo Santamaría's responsibility); with the peasants, who preoccupied Faustino Pérez; or with economic matters, then principally dealt with by the Auditor-General, Sorí Marín. According to Luis Simón, Rodríguez 'read constantly a work of U.N. statistics and another by Raúl Presbisch.[34] He played chess badly but lost with elegance'.[35]

[32] Those consulted on this law in the Sierra were, apparently, Humberto Sorí Marín, Faustino Pérez, Angel M-Luis Rodríguez, Carlos Rafael Rodríguez, Luis Mas Martín, Carlos Franqui, Orestes Valera, Jorge Mendoza, Efrem González, and others (Luis Simón MSS, 150A).

[33] *Ibid.*, p. 265.

[34] The president of ECLA.

[35] Simón MSS, p. 266.

By the middle of October Guevara and Cienfuegos had arrived in the mountainous region of Las Villas.[36] Guevara had now 142 men in place of 148.[37] Aided by deserters from the army and by local 26 July men in the places which they passed, they travelled along much the same route as that followed by Maceo and Máximo Gómez in 1896. On arrival on 14 October in Las Villas, Cienfuegos linked forces with Félix Torres, the Communist commandant of the Yaguajay region who had taken the usual rank of major.[38] Félix Torres's sixty-five men were now organized into three platoons, but he immediately 'put himself at [Cienfuegos's] orders' and took part in an exchange of gunfire with an army group numbering perhaps 450.[39] Torres had also had further difficulties with a Directorio commander 'Diego', who had instructed the peasants with whom he came into contact not to help Torres since they were Communists – though one or two members of the 26 July Movement did in fact join Torres.[40] As elsewhere, women helped, above all with communications. Pastor González, shoemaker of Jarhaueca, was the centre of communication of arms, news, clothes and also men;[41] the priest of Yaguajay, Fr Modesto Amo, also assisted and even on occasion accompanied these forces.[42]

Guevara on arrival was also surprised to receive a letter from one of the leaders of the wilder Directorio splinter group, the Second Front of Escambray, Jesús Carreras, telling him that he could not go up into Escambray without first consulting him on his movements.[43] Guevara took no notice and advanced to the hills near Sancti Spiritus, establishing his base on the top of Monte del Obispo, and there waiting for new supplies of boots, that essential demand of guerrilla war. Guevara had an interesting, confused and unfriendly conversation with 'Major' Carreras, who was half drunk and therefore easy to mislead, and another with his colleague, 'Major' Peña, 'famous in the region for his forays behind cattle' who emphatically forbade Guevara to attack Guisa de Miranda, which 'was in his zone'. The 26 July coordinator in the province, Enrique Oltuski, came up from Trinidad to try to mediate and to meet Guevara, and went on to see Cienfuegos to the north. The Communists, Waldo Reina and Armando Acosta, also carried up a large cargo of provisions to Cienfuegos, and afterwards another Com-

[36] Guevara, *Souvenirs*, 201 (on October 16).

[37] *Revolución*, 15 January 1959.

[38] See *Obra Revolucionaria*, 1962, No. 10, 22; Guevara's interview in *O Cruzeiro Internacional*, 16 July 1964; Cienfuegos in Franqui, 136.

[39] *Revolución, Supplement* October 1961; *Hoy*, 8 October 1963.

[40] See Torres's letter to Del Valle, previously dated. Diego was 'Major' Víctor Manuel Paneque.

[41] See letter of Wilfredo Velázquez to Del Valle, *Hoy*, 21 July 1965.

[42] *Revolución*, 3 January 1959, commemorating this column's victorious entry into Havana.

[43] See Aldo Isidrón del Valle, *La Batalla de Santa Clara*, extracts in *Hoy*, 16 July 1965.

munist, Manuel del Peso, did the same.[44] Guevara also met some Directorio commanders including Chomón and Cubela though the former refused to make any agreement with the Communists in the province, since he recalled only too well their attacks upon him in the university as 'a gangster of the Revolution'. Chomón feared 'a trap of Castro's' to make him change his principles.[45] Guevara decided, wisely, that unity could only be effectively achieved by means of joint attacks on the enemy. Armando Acosta, becoming Guevara's chief aide, helped establish rebel headquarters on a peak known as Caballete de Casa. The work began of attempting to cut off the roads connecting the west with the east of the island. Some of the disaffected Directorio troops (under Gutiérrez Menoyo) were sent on one side. Major Víctor Bordón's group, which had been holding out in Matanzas since late 1956 and which had joined Guevara on arrival,[46] was purged by Guevara and Bordón was demoted to captain. Cienfuegos in the meantime busied himself with collective reading sessions, studying Martí's works and 'everything which related to General Maceo', these being read out by Cienfuegos himself in a deep voice.[47] He showed no eagerness to press on to Pinar del Río. More and more rallied to the cause, peasants, urban workers and women too. By November the agrarian reform was already being applied. Thus the lands of the farm *La Diana*, near Banao, belonging to the governor of Las Villas, Segundo Enríquez, were divided up among the peasants of the region, two cabs each.[48] Meanwhile, the local 26 July leaders had been increasingly angered by Guevara's reliance on Communists and complained through their own organization to the then national coordinator, Marcelo Fernández. Fernández, with Joaquín Torres and Oltuski, the Las Villas leaders, visited Guevara and made their complaints in no uncertain terms. Guevara replied that he was not obliged to insist on any political affiliation and that any Cuban could join his forces; finally, in the course of a heated argument, Guevara said that between him and the 26 July Movement there was a political chasm (*abismo político*) and that if in these moments they were united in the struggle against Batista, sooner or later they would end by going separate ways.[49] But, meantime, a first meeting had taken place

[44] In 1965 Cuban military attaché in Moscow.

[45] Evidence of Manuel Ledón. Chomón suggested a pact on a national level, causing '*un estallido de violencia*' in Fidel Castro.

[46] *Revolución*, 8 January 1959.

[47] Major Gálvez, in *Hoy*, 16 July 1965.

[48] *Hoy*, 16 July 1965.

[49] '*que si en esos momentos estábamos unidos en la lucha contra Batista, tarde o temprano terminaríamos per separarnos*' (memorandum of Joaquín Torres, present at this meeting). Of those present at this meeting, instructively, Marcelo Fernández was in 1968 a member of the central committee of the Cuban Communist party (and an opponent of Guevara's policies of excessive centralization); Oltuski worked still then in the Institute of Agrarian Reform; and Torres was in exile.

between the Directorio and the Communists in Havana: Alberto Mora, son of Menelao Mora who had been killed in the attack on the Palace, met Ramón Nicolau, a veteran Communist leader from Holguín.[50]

Batista's presidential election was duly held. On its eve Foster Dulles visited a Cuban Embassy reception in Washington, thereby giving his *imprimatur* to at least the process. But it had become clear that the only opposition candidate of any status, Márquez Sterling, had no hope – both through the certain knowledge that the ballots would be rigged and that he personally would not carry enough votes. There was a strong swing away from the electoral idea. The result was a foregone conclusion; Batista's candidate, Rivero Agüero, was elected. A self-made man who had come up with Batista – an orphan, he had worked in the fields at the age of seven[51] – his success might in normal times have been hailed as yet one more Horatio Alger success story, like Batista's own. These were not normal times. Few noticed his victory. Few believed that if he were to take over on 24 February as planned there would be any difference in the regime. Few believed that he would take over. He was not however fairly elected. The *New York Times* correspondent estimated that only 30% voted, and that in some places the poll was as low as 10%.[52] In fact, an entirely bogus set of election papers had been printed and marked by the army and distributed long before election by the air force, the printer receiving the sum of $40,000: it was one of the most perfectly executed frauds perpetrated, even in Cuba.[53] This fraud was the last straw even for Earl Smith who henceforth believed that Batista could not be allowed to remain and that every effort should be made by his government to find a replacement.[54] In west Cuba, the atmosphere was tense, but not violent. Well armed police and soldiers guarded the 8,500 polling stations. In Oriente there were massive abstentions, due to Castro's threats. In Las Villas, Guevara and Cienfuegos did their best to prevent the arrival of voting urns. Grau, who trailed third behind Rivero and Márquez Sterling, petitioned the Supreme Court to annul the elections because of fraud. The Cuban House of Representatives declared the elections

[50] Evidence of Guillermo Cabrera Infante who arranged the meeting, Mora arriving in an expensive *dril cien* suit, the veteran Communist expressing hatred for a recent Directorio terrorist attack in Mariano. The meeting was held in the beautiful house of Nicasio Silverio.

[51] Born Banes, Oriente; orphaned at ten; went aged 15 years to Santiago, illiterate; worked at night at University of Havana; afterwards lawyer; backed by Carlos Manuel de la Cruz; entered Ministry of Health, 1934; political secretary to Batista; director of Coffee Institute; sub-secretary of Agriculture; Minister of Agriculture, 1940; Minister of Education, 1952; prime minister, 1957-8. He was, though blue-eyed and fair-skinned, a half-brother of Castro's erstwhile Ortodoxo friend, Luis Conte Agüero, an octaroon.

[52] Phillips, 381.

[53] Suárez Núñez, 50.

[54] Evidence of Earl Smith, January 1969.

valid; again, few noticed. The fate of Cuba was being decided else-where.

Still, about 15 November Rivero Agüero, as president-elect, called on Ambassador Smith and told him that he was studying how to achieve a peaceful solution to Cuba's political problems, which would probably be supported by 90% of the people. He, like Smith, realized that Castro would oppose any peaceful formula, but thought he could gather support elsewhere. Ambassador Smith then went to the U.S. After giving a ball at the Waldorf Astoria – a charity occasion for the Florence Pritchett Smith scholarship for commercial design – he went to Washington on 23 November.[55] He urged the State Department to honour Rivero's appeal for U.S. backers. Rubottom and Wieland said that there was no solution possible in Cuba through U.S. aid. They did not wish to support or stimulate the Church's effort at reconciliation, and they did not think that any of the civil and military would associate themselves with the president-elect. Smith said that he had now realized that Batista could not last, since the economy was declining, bridges were being blown up, and so on. The Under-Secretary of State, Murphy, asked Smith if Castro's movement could be regarded as Communist and Smith said that he could convince any jury that it was.[56] In the end Smith went back to Havana, being told to ascertain if Rivero Agüero had any chance of devising a solution such as he had suggested, with the backing of the main elements of the opposition. But it transpired that Rivero had merely reverted to Batista's old position of an indefinite reliance on force.[57]

This failure did lead to new action in the U.S. A few days later a meeting was held in a house in Miami belonging to William Pawley, ex-ambassador and businessman (founder of Cubana Airlines in the 1920s). At this meeting there were present Deputy Assistant Secretary of State Snow,[58] Assistant Secretary Henry Holland,[59] and Colonel J. C. King, in command of the Latin American section of the CIA.[60] There was discussion: 'What do you do about this Cuban problem?' Pawley said that 'everything we were doing was wrong. I told them that we should now, to try to save the peace, see if we can go down there to get Batista to capitulate to a caretaker government unfriendly to him but satisfactory to us, whom we could immediately recognise and give military assistance to in order that Fidel Castro should not come to

[55] Smith, *The Fourth Floor*, 214.
[56] *Ibid.*, 160–1.
[57] Wieland evidence, 661–2, 545–7.
[58] Afterwards ambassador in Burma.
[59] He had been head of the Latin American division of the State Department in 1954 during the Guatemalan *coup*, to which he was privy, though he had opposed it.
[60] Pawley evidence to Senate Internal Security Sub-Committee, *Communist Threat*, 738.

power.' The next day they all went up to Washington and had talks at the CIA and Department of State. Pawley was then 'selected to go to Cuba to talk with Batista to see if I could convince him to capitulate, which I did'.[61]

But before Pawley arrived on this somewhat desperate and unconventional mission, events had begun to move fast. Though the activities of the resistance in Havana had been kept to a minimum, partly by the capture of the Auténtico representative in Havana (who gave away information under torture), partly by the insistence by Castro on the dispatch of arms to the Sierra, there had been some isolated incidents at the end of November, such as the seizure of yet another aeroplane, full of tourists bound for Varadero from Miami, by an unofficial Castro supporter, of whom nothing was known, resulting in the death of the crew and of ten passengers, which plunged into the Bay of Nipe. Castro, who had moved his headquarters to La Miel from La Plata,ǀ had planned an attack on the village of Bueycito, but the garrison withdrew before the attack; the rebels moved on towards Guisa, bypassing Bayamo, aiming to concentrate their forces over Santiago. An ex-schoolmaster and rice grower, Hubert Matos, with 245 men, and Almeida, with 350, began to invest that city. Rumours of an attack on the city were widespread, and there were innumerable bombings. There were also several minor clashes in the Guantánamo area.[62] At Guisa Castro faced 5,000 men of Batista's with 200 *guerrilleros*, of whom 100 were new to the combat.[63] Batista's commanders were beginning to despair: 'Our Army, tired and decimated by two years of fighting without relief, had completely lost its combat power. Desertions to the enemy increased daily. We lacked reserves and a great part of the officers confined in the barracks maybe [were] . . . in contact with the enemy.' The prospect of Batista's own abandonment of power in February caused further demoralization. Surrender of one or two officers such as Major Quevedo to Castro and two others (Villamil and Ulbino León) to Guevara, caused alarm out of all proportion to the damage caused. Several officers were arrested and gaoled by Batista for fear that they were about to act against him.[64] Raúl and Fidel Castro joined forces, but the different sections of Batista's kingdom seemed out of touch with each other, and all out of touch with Havana.[65] More and more people went to the Sierra Maestra and, often through

[61] *Ibid.*, 739; Kirkpatrick, *The Real CIA*, 178-9, refers.
[62] E.g. that described by Dicky Chapelle (*cf.* Osanka, *Modern Guerrilla Warfare*, 325).
[63] Debray, *Révolution dans la révolution*, 58.
[64] They were: Pedro Castro Rojas, José Rodríguez San Pedro, José Viamontes Jardines, Eugenio Menéndez, Félix Gutiérrez Fernández and José Robles Cortés.
[65] *Cf.* letter from General Silito Tabernilla to Batista, 13 February 1959, qu. Batista, *Cuba Betrayed*, 104-5, fn.

opportunism, effectively joined with the 26 July Movement even though until then they had been active in other organizations. Batista seemed to place all hope in an abrogation of arms embargo, but in an interview after his return from Washington, Smith left him in no doubt of the 'unpleasant' atmosphere in Washington.[66] About the beginning of December Smith saw a group of local business-men who mostly thought Batista could not last till the end of his term, perhaps not even past 1 January, unless the U.S. gave him support. These men argued that the 26 July was 'Communist-dominated', and the Esso representative, G. W. Potts, said that a recent 26 July statement seemed very similar to one by the Arbenz government in Guatemala. Everyone thought that the best idea was for the U.S. to support a military junta. Smith, reporting all this, suggested that Rivero Agüero should be persuaded to take over control immediately, with U.S. support for the formation of a national unity government.[67] On 5 December Kenneth Redmond, president of the United Fruit Company, telegraphed Dulles to help to save the sugar crop in Oriente: the rebels had cut off water to the United Fruit's *Preston* mill because of the company's refusal to pay 15 cents tax on every 250-pound bag of sugar.[68]

Batista made a number of desperate changes of command. Cantillo was named chief of operations in Oriente and Del Río Chaviano (whom he hated beyond reason and who had remained at the headquarters in Santiago) was transferred to Las Villas. Colonel Pérez Coujil took over in Camagüey from Colonel Dueñas. In Oriente Colonels Suárez Susquet and Sánchez Mosquera tried to keep their troops mobile. Even so more of the officers went over to Castro, particularly Captains Dinaz and Oquendo, who had been held in Jibacoa. Palma Soriano fell without a fight. By the beginning of December the government still held Santiago, Bayamo, Holguín and the other big towns; but outside these Castro seemed in control of southern Oriente. By 7 December the arrival of a transmitter had enabled him to be in radio communication with Cienfuegos in Las Villas. He could thus learn that on 1 December Guevara had finally reached a successful agreement with the Directorio; a pact signed by Guevara and Cubela (following conversations in which Chomón had also taken part for the Directorio and Ramiro Valdés for the 26 July) spoke of full agreement, full collaboration for military purposes, and agreement by the Directorio with Castro's agrarian reform.[69] But it did not speak of Guevara's or Castro's command over

[66] *Ibid.*, 96.
[67] Smith, *The Fourth Floor*, 162–3.
[68] HAR. It was a telegraph like this, perhaps also from Redmond, which alerted Dulles to the situation in Guatemala in 1954. Dulles had once been legal adviser to the United Fruit Company.
[69] *Cf. Hoy*, 17 July 1965.

the Directorio; that matter remained for later consideration. Meantime, the few representatives of the Directorio in Havana had received orders to go to Las Villas.[70] With this agreement behind them, the rebels put one army detachment to flight beyond Santa Lucia, so leaving Guevara free to blow up the bridge where the central highway crossed the River Tuinicú. By now Guevara's subordinate Captain José Silva controlled the road from Trinidad to Sancti Spiritus; the main railway was damaged at two points.

Pawley saw Batista for three hours on 9 December – Ambassador Smith (who was not informed) having flown to Washington. Pawley offered Batista the chance to live again at Daytona Beach. He suggested that a new provisional government for Cuba might be composed of Colonels Barquín and Borbonnet, General Díaz Tamayo and Pepe Bosch of the Bacardí family.[71] The trouble was, Pawley said, that he had no authority to say the U.S. would definitely carry out their side of the bargain, only that 'I will try to persuade the U.S. government'. Anyway, Batista refused, saying to an aide that he had had a mind to 'kick out this Pawley'.[72]

The following day Smith, in Washington, saw his State Department colleagues and Allen Dulles; he received instructions to disabuse Batista of any idea that Rivero Agüero might receive the backing of the U.S. government. So Smith went back once more to Havana and told the Foreign Minister, Dr Güell, 'It is my unpleasant duty to inform the President of the Republic that the U.S. will no longer support the present government of Cuba and that my government believes that the President is losing effective control'; Güell said that Batista would see Smith in a few days.[73]

At this point Batista made a last effort to rally his army. Ten companies of a hundred men each were sent to Santa Clara, reinforced by three battalions of 400 men each. Their mission was partly to prevent bridge destruction. The key point in this defence system was an armoured train prepared by Western Railways under Colonel Rosell y Leyva.[74]

About the middle of December Batista brought all the commanders of the armed services together to Ciudad Militar. It became clear that the president was contemplating some sort of desperate action. He told his followers: 'We should try and change the administration ... [and]

[70] Evidence of Manuel Ledón.
[71] Robert Murphy told Smith that Cantillo and Sosa would be part of the junta.
[72] *Communist Threat*, 739; Kirkpatrick, 179. Suárez Núñez, 105. Later Batista regretted not accepting Pawley's plan and said he would have done so if he had known that the U.S. government really backed the emissary (Lazo, 162–3).
[73] Smith, *The Fourth Floor*, 170.
[74] Batista, *Cuba Betrayed*, 99.

meet frequently, and discuss every new event.' Despite agreement on secrecy General Tabernilla, Batista's *bête noire*, and the real author of the army's defeat, talked to a large number of officers. Batista sent for him and Tabernilla said, 'The soldiers are tired and the officers do not want to fight. Nothing more can be done.' Already, in fact, General Cantillo, the commander in Oriente, on Tabernilla's instructions, was preparing for negotiations with Castro. General Tabernilla told his son, 'Silito' Tabernilla (still Batista's private secretary), to tell the president this news; 'Silito' could not bring himself to do so and merely pledged his loyalty to the president 'unto death'.[75] On 17 December Smith finally saw Batista and said on instructions that the State Department believed that Batista could no longer maintain effective control in Cuba and that it would avoid a great deal of bloodshed if he were to retire.[76] Batista replied that without him no military junta could survive; without him the army would collapse. Could the U.S. intervene to stop the fighting? Smith said that that was unthinkable. Batista asked if he could go to Florida to visit his home at Daytona Beach. Smith suggested Spain instead, and asked if he thought he could control the situation till February; Batista said it would be difficult since the U.S. had refused him arms in his hour of need. He ran through many possible solutions, as if distracted. No doubt by this date he had decided to leave Cuba;[77] and within forty-eight hours, anyway, he is found asking the head of the air force ('Wince', or Brigadier Carlos Tabernilla) how many seats he could ensure on an aeroplane at a moment's notice.[78] Smith afterwards regarded his action in this interview as being tantamount to an instruction to Batista to leave.[79] By this time even the business community in Havana seems to have agreed with Julio Lobo: 'We didn't care who overthrew Batista providing someone did.'[80]

Pawley's mission to Batista, however, was not the only activity in which the CIA was engaged in December 1958 so far as Cuba was concerned. Justo Carrillo was still hoping to realize his plan of achieving the release of Colonel Barquín and by now he and an aide, Dr Andrés Suárez, having failed to receive help from Argentina, Venezuela and Honduras, were at last in touch with the CIA – or rather one of its representatives named Beardsley in Havana, and Robert Rogers in Miami. This project was for once not rejected and must have been under consideration by the CIA in Washington while Pawley was in Havana.[81]

[75] Batista, *Cuba Betrayed*, 99.
[76] *Communist Threat*, 687.
[77] Smith, *The Fourth Floor*, 171–3.
[78] Suárez Núñez, 107. This was apparently on 20 December.
[79] Evidence of Earl Smith.
[80] Evidence of Julio Lobo.
[81] Justo Carrillo MSS, p. 44.

CHAPTER LXXXIV

How Batista Fell

The night after this interview with Smith, Batista met with his generals who, it transpired, were hoping to hear that the president was giving up the fight. Batista in fact wanted to make preparations to prevent the 'total disintegration of his troops'. The generals 'told me how strange it was that military units were being continually surrendered without combat to an enemy who, in number and military capacity, could not possibly possess the strength necessary to immobilize the army'.[1] Castro's forces were indeed operating at this time steadily but menacingly along the *Carretera Central*, upon which Contramaestre had been taken by Major Francisco Cabrera. This meant that Santiago was cut off by road – less an overwhelming strategic blow than a psychological one. The capture of this small town, the first place of over 1,000 persons to fall to the rebels, had a decisive effect upon Batista's administration. Refugees began to flee into Santiago, while Batista's air force with some reluctance and incompetence bombed the villages taken by Castro. Colonel Sánchez Mosquera was bogged down and all but surrounded. He himself was wounded. In Las Villas the army was if anything in an even greater disarray than in the east. Guevara's successes and the increasing demoralization of the enemy led to a decision to order Cienfuegos to remain with his column in Las Villas rather than, as was anticipated, to advance Maceo-like to Pinar del Río. Cienfuegos would aid Guevara to cut the island in half there and then. On 18 December Guevara captured Fomento, and on 21 December attacked Cabaiguán and Guayos to the east of that town some ten miles short of Sancti Spiritus;[2] Captain Bordón received the latter's surrender and on the 22nd, Cabaiguán surrendered too, to Major Cubela.[3] On 22 December Cienfuegos in the north of the province launched a full-scale attack on Yaguajay near the sea, while Guevara turned towards Havana to attack the road junction of Placetas, which, being almost deserted, he captured with its 30,000 inhabitants.[4]

[1] Batista, *Cuba Betrayed*, 103.

[2] Guevara, *Souvenirs*, 203.

[3] Bordón had been in the Sierra Escambray for almost two years before Guevara arrived there, in command of local 26 July forces operating *por la libre*. On Guevara's arrival he had been demoted but now was restored. Cubela was a leader of the Directorio.

[4] *Cf.* 'Diario de Guerra', in Núñez Jiménez, 500. In an interview in *Revolución* on January 4 1959 Cienfuegos said that he captured 250 men and 375 rifles.

All this military activity in the centre of the island took Batista completely unawares. The brilliance of Guevara's military leadership, with
the audacity of Castro's original strategic idea of sending him to the
centre of the island and not making himself known till then, was made
very clear. Batista later accused two of his officers, Major González
Finalés and Lieutenant Ubineo León, of letting Guevara pass through
their sectors for a cash payment.[5] But even if that were the case – for
which there is no evidence – it would hardly argue that the army was in
a fit state. On 20 December he refused an offer from Trujillo to land
2,000 'fresh men' in the Sierra Maestra and another 2,000 in Santa
Clara; 'I do not wish to treat with dictators,' he told Trujillo's emissary,
Colonel Estévez Maymir, the Cuban military attaché in St Domingo.[6]
    The last twitching reactions of Batista to what seemed the possi-
bility of defeat finally began. He appointed his oldest comrade, General
Pedraza, the chief of staff dismissed in 1940, to succeed Del Río Chaviano
in Las Villas, and transferred the latter to Oriente. But Tabernilla
persuaded the president that it would be best to have Pedraza at headquarters and so Colonel Casillas Lumpuy was brought back from the
Isle of Pines to the command in Santa Clara. From the nature of these
appointments it would seem that Batista was making a serious effort to
regain the initiative which he had incredibly lost to so small a group of
opponents. Meantime among his officers a *coup* was prepared to stave off
Castro's victory. The scheme was that General Cantillo would take over
in Oriente, while Commodore Carrera, General Del Río Chaviano and
Colonel Rosell, then in command nominally of the armoured train at
Santa Clara, would also take part. Colonel Barquín, still in prison, would
be approached to take over Las Villas, while the command at Campamento Columbia would be given to one of the officers associated with
him in his unsuccessful *golpe* of 1956. The military chiefs of Camagüey
and Holguín (Colonels Pérez Coujil and Ugalde Carrillo) would be captured or killed if they refused to join in. Batista would be put on to an
aeroplane to the U.S. along with the Tabernillas.[7] Barquín, who was
then in prison, apparently accepted, sending his graduation ring as
token of his agreement. It is evident that a number of officers, such as
Colonel Rosell, regarded Barquín not just as a man of compromise but
as the one officer who could defeat Castro. Action was planned for
26 December. Then General Del Río Chaviano decided that it would be
more appropriate to bring in the Tabernillas and inform them of the
role allotted to them. Meantime neither the U.S. Embassy nor Batista
was informed of what was happening. Batista himself was seeing his

[5] Batista, *Cuba Betrayed*, 86, fn.
[6] Suárez Núñez, 108.
[7] See Barrera Pérez, *Bohemia Libre*, 3 September 1961; and Colonel Rosell's *La Verdad*, 31 f.

usual group of bishops who told them that 'any sacrifice would be worth-while if it ended terrorism'; and indeed the civil war was far from lost, if only Batista could have brought himself to admit that a civil war, properly speaking, was in existence.

His generals still believed that they had the situation in control. Tabernilla, independently of Batista, dispatched General Cantillo to Oriente to try to discuss an armistice with Castro. Tabernilla had by then been told by Del Río Chaviano of the plan for a military *golpe*, and himself determined to try a modified version of it. During 22 December Batista, however, having received news of these moves, confronted Tabernilla and, in an interview that night, gave Cantillo permission to proceed to Oriente to do what he could with Castro; Cantillo, coming out of Batista's office, remarked to Batista's military secretary, still 'Silito' Tabernilla, 'Silito, every time I read a life of a great man, I skip the last pages because the end is always disagreeable.'[8] On 23 December at another meeting Tabernilla told Batista bluntly that he considered the war lost. He had received news that the city of Guantánamo was then surrounded by forces coming down from the hills under Juan Almeida, the mulatto singer who commanded what was described as the 'Tercera Frente Oriental'. The same day some of Guevara's forces, led by the Communist, Armando Acosta, reached the outskirts of Sancti Spiritus, upon which the 115,000-strong town surrendered without a battle. No spirit of resistance reigned in the city administration, and apart from the police there was no effective force there able to resist even a small number of men. In Oriente the next day (Christmas Eve), Cantillo (having given $10,000 each to Colonels Ugalde Carrillo and Jesús María Salas Cañizares, and $15,000 to Colonel Pérez Coujil)[9] successfully arranged through Father Guzmán, a priest of Santiago, a meeting with Castro at the Oriente sugar mill (which had once belonged to the Chibás family). Also present were Majors Sierra Talavera and José Quevedo. Cantillo, who arrived and left by helicopter, promised that the army would rise before 3 p.m. on 31 December and prevent Batista's escape.[10] According to one eye-witness of this meeting, every-thing was agreed between the two, except that Castro wished that the army officers of the Barquín group should be held in prison.[11] On Christmas Day Cantillo returned from Santiago by air to Havana. He was immediately confronted by Batista who carried out a clever inquiry

---

[8] This is Cantillo's and Suárez Núñez's account (p. 99), but Batista afterwards denied that he gave such permission to Cantillo. But the above appears to be correct.

[9] *Ibid.*, 110. As bribes to leave the country.

[10] Castro gave his account of this meeting in his speech of 2 January. (*Revolución*, 3 January 1959.) *Cf.* also *Discursos para la Historia*, 23. It is doubtful if Cantillo would agree with Castro's account.

[11] Carrillo evidence.

of him. Cantillo said that Tabernilla had insisted that he seek out Castro. Batista, not hearing exactly what had transpired at the meeting at the sugar mill, told Cantillo that he would be prepared to hand over power to a junta of officers headed by Cantillo as a gesture to the Cuban nation and to leave on 26 January. [12]

Castro passed Christmas with his brother Ramón at Marcané, near the *Alto Cedro* sugar mill; but Guevara was attacking Remedios near the north coast and commanding the main northern approach to Santa Clara, the capital of the province of Las Villas. Remedios fell on the 26th, its commander, Captain Guerrero, surrendering 150 large weapons. The same day Caibarién, a few miles further down the sea coast itself, also fell. The naval captain, Luis Aragon, who was in command there, offered no resistance. This cut off Santa Clara from reinforcement on the north and on the south.[13] Guevera moved next into position to attack Santa Clara. But perhaps an attack of this magnitude would not be needed. On the 28th Castro received an ambiguous note from Cantillo saying that, though 'the situation was developing favourably', it would be best to delay action till 6 January at least. Cantillo was vacillating. Castro said that it was impossible to wait, accused Cantillo of treachery, and continued his own build-up of forces around Santiago. But Castro did not expect Batista to collapse so fast as he now did.[14]

On 29 December Ambassador Smith, isolated by events whose direction he greatly disliked, apparently in ignorance of the intrigues which had been going on in the capital as of the battles elsewhere, was called on by the two Generals Tabernilla, father and son, together with Del Río Chaviano. Tabernilla *père* said that in his opinion the army would not fight any more and that the government could not last. He, Tabernilla, was anxious, however, to save Cuba from 'chaos, Castro and communism'. He proposed a military junta comprising Generals Cantillo, Sosa de Quesada (a Prústa officer), García Casones (an air force officer) and some naval officer; would the U.S. recognize such a government? Smith said that unfortunately he could only do business with Batista. He asked whether Tabernilla had talked with Batista? Yes, came the reply, but Batista had no plan. He had indeed asked Tabernilla to 'come up with a plan'. Smith sent back Tabernilla to talk again with Batista.[15]

Batista was, in fact, planning to leave, either as he had told Cantillo,

[12] Batista, *Cuba Betrayed*, has a slightly different version, but this is that of Colonel Barrera Pérez (*Bohemia Libre*, 3 September 1961).
[13] 'Diario', Núñez Jiménez, 500.
[14] So he admitted later in Washington to the ex-president of Ecuador, Galo Plaza whom both he and Batista had accepted as mediator earlier. (Evidence of Sr Galo Plaza.) See Castro speech, *Revolución*, 4 January 1959.
[15] *Communist Threat*, 709; Smith, *The Fourth Floor*, 177.

on 6 January or earlier. His children secretly left Havana on the 29th for the U.S. He had already burned much of his private correspondence and other documents.[16] He had arranged aeroplanes. In taking this decision Batista was thinking only of himself and a few close followers. He was making no provision for the thousands of Cubans who had worked with him and whose fortunes and in many cases whose lives depended on him. He had already a list of people who would be allowed to escape with him. Castro, meantime, had entered into correspondence by messenger with the commanding officer of Santiago, Colonel Rego, who had been part of Cantillo's conspiracy.[17] Guevara had already attacked Santa Clara. On the other hand most local political leaders and mayors had already abandoned their posts, and with their families were making essential journeys abroad for reasons of health.

Guevara travelled on 28 December from the coast at Caibarién along the road to Camajuaní and thence by small roads to reach the University of Santa Clara, on the outskirts of the town, at dusk. There he divided his forces (which numbered about 300)[18] into two. The southern column was the first to meet the defending forces (commanded for the last two or three days by Colonel Casillas Lumpuy). An armoured train, on which the colonel greatly relied, steamed along to the foot of the hill Capiro, at the north-east of the city, establishing there a command post. Guevara dispatched a small force under an eighteen-year-old, Captain Gabriel Gil, to capture the hill, using mostly hand grenades, and hidden from the train by the hill itself.[19] The defenders of the hill withdrew with surprising speed and the train was then withdrawn too towards the middle of the town. The morale of the defenders was shown to be very low. Guevara successfully mobilized the tractors of the School of Agronomy at the university to raise the rails of the railway. The train was therefore derailed. The officers within tumbled out and were immediately attacked. They asked for a truce. At this, the ordinary soldiers of the army began to fraternize with the rebels, saying that they were tired of fighting against their own people. Shortly afterwards the armoured train surrendered and its 350 men and officers were transported as prisoners. The train became a base for further attack. There was also fighting inside the city, between the police and the Civic Resistance. This grew in intensity during 31 December. Batista's air force – the usual B-26s and British Sea Furies – dropped bombs on the parts of the city occupied by Guevara, but only a few civilians were killed.

[16] Suárez Núñez, 116.

[17] Rego understood Castro's first note as a demand for surrender (see *Revolución*, 4 January 1959).

[18] Castro, on 18 October 1967 (*Granma*, weekly edition., 29 October 1967).

[19] Gabriel Gil had been in the *Granma*. Lost after Alegría de Pío, he had rejoined Castro in the Sierra in February 1957.

The Batistianos held out in five main centres – the Leoncio Vidal barracks; the central police station; the provincial government buildings; the Palace of Justice; and the Grand Hotel. The Palace of Justice was defended by two tanks. These were attacked by an eighteen-year-old rebel captain, Rogelio Acevedo.[20] Three men who stood beside the tanks were wounded. The Palace of Justice fell soon after, along with the provincial government and Grand Hotel. The police station was stormed by a suicide squadron led by the young rebel captain 'Vaquerito' ('the little cow-boy'),[21] who was killed in the assault. The commanding Batistiano, Colonel Cornelio Rojas, a septuagenarian, ordered resistance to the last man, but he was nevertheless captured and the police station fell.[22] Aeroplanes as ever moved in to attack the posts where the rebels triumphed, and night fell on the last day of 1958 with Colonel Casillas Lumpuy still holding half the city, with five hundred men, though many of them were contemplating desertion.[23] There were desperate telephone calls by Batista to Colonel Casillas in Santa Clara; and over the line also came news of disputes between Colonels Casillas and Fernández Suero, who had fallen back on military headquarters. 'The last time we spoke to them,' Batista recalled later, 'their words were practically unintelligible, they had become hoarse with yelling to make their orders understood above the tumult' – the noise being compounded by the shouting of 'undisciplined personnel' and indiscriminate shooting. The 'heroic defender of this redoubt', as Batista described Casillas, proceeded to arrest the 'seditious' Major Suárez Fowler who had urged the combatants to lay down their arms.[24] About 9 p.m. the chief of staff, General Rodríguez Avila, advised Batista that in his opinion Las Villas could not be held. At 10 p.m. General Cantillo advised the same in respect of Oriente. Batista, then at the Finca Kuquine, thereupon ordered his government and the military commanders to meet him at Campamento Columbia to say good-bye to the old year. This was normal and no one thought much of the invitation. Another meeting was at that same time being held in the

[20] Later one of the stalwart officers of the revolution. In 1965 member of the Central Committee of the Cuban Communist party.

[21] Roberto Rodríguez, of very small build, aged about twenty; he was a Camagüeyano from Morón. Guevara speaks of him as a youth of extraordinary '*alegría*', 'amazingly mendacious', who always decorated truth with fantasy, but who was nevertheless astoundingly brave.

[22] He was uncle to Masferrer, and was summarily tried and shot within forty-eight hours. He requested permission to command the firing squad; it was granted.

[23] Account in *Revolución*, 4 January 1959. Núñez Jiménez, 'Diario de Guerra', in *Geografía*, 502–3; Isidoro del Valle, *Hoy*, 18 July 1965. Somewhat unfortunately, as W. Lederer pointed out, *A Nation of Sheep* (1961), 138, Associated Press reported on 1 January from Havana that when the year had ended, the rebel threat had 'faded in a storm of Government firepower' and that Government troops 'hammered retreating rebel forces around Santa Clara . . . and drove them eastwards out of Las Villas'.

[24] Batista, 123.

Pentagon at Washington, at which Admiral Burke, chief of naval staff, with some support from Allen Dulles and Robert Murphy, argued that 'Castro was not the right man' for Cuba and that some action should be taken there to prevent him capturing power. The discussion lasted till 2 a.m., but nothing could be decided, and indeed what could have been at that late hour, other than an immediate intervention by the marines?[25]

The men of Batista's regime and their wives gathered at the military headquarters. In a confused gathering there were to be seen relations of Batista, military men, politicians, Batista's wife; José Luis del Pozo, mayor of Havana; ministers such as García Montes or Santiago Rey; Andrés Rivero Agüero, 'president-elect'; Anselmo Alliegro and Gastón Godoy, chairmen respectively of the Senate and of the House of Representatives. While most of these men nervously drank coffee, Batista saw the chiefs of staff in an inner room. These officers agreed that they could not last any longer and Batista went through a charade of handing over power to Cantillo who thus held in his hands the keys of incompatible intrigues, one with his brother officers, one with Castro, and both impossible to coordinate with one another. Afterwards, Batista came out and spoke to each group separately, saying he was resigning 'to avoid more bloodshed'. To the inner group of his intimate friends he proposed seats on aeroplanes which would leave for the U.S. or elsewhere in the course of the night. Meantime he asked Anselmo Alliegro, as president of the Senate, to designate the oldest judge on the Supreme Court (Carlos Manuel Piedra) as provisional president. Piedra, who was present, accepted, and General Cantillo took over from Rodríguez Avila as chief of staff. Batista then formally resigned and at 3 a.m. he flew out of the military airfield, accompanied by forty people, among them his wife and his son Jorge; Gonzalo Güell and his wife; Andrés Rivero Agüero; Gastón Godoy; Generals Rodríguez Avila, Rodríguez Calderón, and Rojas, and Colonels Orlando Piedra and Fernández Miranda. They headed not for the U.S. but for the Dominican Republic.[26] According to Castro, they took with them $M300 or $M400[27] but Batista and his followers already had money abroad and it does not appear that they had time to gather much cash. Batista's brother 'Panchín', governor of Havana, flew out of Havana with forty-six people later in the night, including ministers and police officers. Masferrer, warned by telephone, at the same time quietly left Santiago by yacht. Other flights followed, to New Orleans, or to Jacksonville (the Tabernillas and Pilar García).[28] Not only politicians fled, but also

[25] Admiral Burke to the author, 26 December 1962.
[26] Batista, *Cuba Betrayed*, 137.
[27] Speech, 1 January, *Revolución*, 4 January.
[28] Batista was afterwards refused permission to seek asylum in the U.S.

men such as Meyer Lansky, the gambler. Once the leading Batistianos had escaped, a message was passed to Radio Caracas in Venezuela, with whom they were on good relations and from that centre the world heard the news.

It is of course obscure to what extent Batista had enriched himself. His press secretary in exile and one who was for a time youth leader of his party estimated his fortune in 1958, as $M300, mostly invested abroad in Switzerland, Florida, New York or Mexico.[29] Certainly his income from protection money must have been quite considerable, though the estimated $M1·28 made each month out of this had to be divided among a lot of people.

Cantillo, now chief of staff, and on 1 January 1959 in effective command of the west of Cuba, then called a meeting of officers and told them the news, which rapidly spread throughout Havana and then the island. Cheering crowds came out into still dark streets. Judge Piedra, with other judges of the Supreme Court, and other prominent citizens such as Núñez Portuondo, Cuervo Rubio and Raúl de Cárdenas, read aloud in the presidential palace a cease-fire for the army and called upon Castro to do the same. But this shadow government had no backing. Pandemonium grew during the morning and supporters of Castro or of the Directorio began to appear in the streets, in uniform, announcing that they would keep order, as Batistiano officers and police disappeared, either flying abroad (aeroplanes continued to fly all morning), moving into foreign embassies or simply seeking other hiding. Most of the leaders of Batista's repression had escaped in the course of the morning. About noon the airport was declared closed for outgoing traffic, though by then most of the biggest targets for revolutionary revenge, such as the naval intelligence chief, Laurent, or Colonel Ventura of the political police, had escaped. Others, such as Major Jacinto Menocal, had killed themselves.[30] At Santa Clara meantime Colonel Casillas, the defender of the barracks, had learned the news of Batista's flight with fury. Quickly dressing in civilian clothes, he and Colonel Fernández Suero fled after handing over command to their subordinate, Colonel Hernández. At this moment, just after dawn, Guevara sent in a three-man peace mission demanding surrender.[31] The Batista soldiery once more demanded fraternization. Colonel Hernández asked for a truce. In the course of the discussion a telephone call came from Cantillo in Campamento Columbia. The peace mission refused to accept Cantillo as

[29] Suarez Nunez, 26. A more modest estimate was that given in the *Daily Mail*, 11 December, 1969: 'more than £40M'.

[30] *Revolución*, 4 January 1959.

[31] Núñez ménez, Rodríguez de la Vega, and Lieutenant Ríos Dr Núñez Jiménez, a distinguished geographer, had only joined Guevara on Christmas Eve. He was the author of a famous outline economic geography of Cuba.

chief of staff. It being then 1.30, p.m. they announced that hostilities would begin again, at 2.15. After discussions, the Batistiano army surrendered unconditionally in Santa Clara before that time. By then, Major Bordón had caught Colonel Casillas; afterwards he was shot, while trying (genuinely, it seems) to escape.[32] Santa Clara having fallen, Castro ordered Guevara to move on to Havana. He himself, who heard the news of Batista's escape at the *central América*,[33] was both furious and surprised. He placed the full blame on Cantillo, and ordered a general advance on Santiago. But an assault was not necessary. Colonel Rego had decided to surrender (the two communicated through a Baptist minister), and flew by helicopter to Castro's headquarters to do so. Castro spoke with Rego's officers, told them that he knew that not all the officers of Batista's army were assassins, and persuaded all either to join him or to give up their arms. Two frigates also surrendered. It appears that the commanders in Santiago thought that their attitude would save the army from dissolution,[34] and Castro also promised that Colonel Rego would become chief of staff of the Cuban army.

By that time however, Colonel Barquín, leader of the 'Liberal' officers of the 1956 *coup*, had reappeared in Havana, having been flown there by a Colonel Carrillo from prison in the Isle of Pines.[35] It appears that he owed his release to the somewhat delayed intervention of the CIA, who on 30 December had dispatched a man, with the backing of Justo Carrillo, to offer the head of the prison $100,000 to release this prisoner.[36] General Cantillo, realizing the impossibility of forming a junta of compromise, now handed over command to Barquín, with whom he had been in contact since 20 December. Barquín therefore proclaimed himself chief of the armed forces in Havana. He ordered some of his co-conspirators in 1956 to similar positions (Borbonnet to the first infantry division, Varela to La Cabaña, Villafaña to the air force, Andrés González to the navy). But being himself at this time a member of the 26 July Movement and therefore in touch with its leaders of the Havana underground, he also arrested Cantillo and telephoned Castro in Santiago to ask when Judge Urrutia should take over as head of state. He thus subordinated himself to the 26 July Movement and without an effort gave up what chance there was of a government of the centre.

---

[32] Núñez Jiménez, *Geografía*, 502-3. Some doubt hangs over the precise fate of Casillas, since, in *Revolución*, 5 January, it is reported he was shot after court martial.

[33] As he said in a speech at Camagüey, *Revolución*, 5 January.

[34] *Cf.* Castro's speech, *ibid.*, 4 January 1959.

[35] Not Justo Carrillo, but a cousin of his.

[36] Carrillo's negotiations with the CIA, begun in early December, had finally resulted in this rather than the more spectacular *golpe de estado* in the Isle of Pines which he had earlier designed. That this sum was offered to the prison commander is made quite clear from the Carrillo MSS, which describe the discussion between Carrillo and Willard Hubert Carr of the CIA on 30 December.

As he spoke, outside in the streets there was some looting. Casinos were invaded. The offices of Masferrer's *Tiempo en Cuba* were smashed. The newspaper *Alerta* was taken over by 26 July men. The Shell Petroleum headquarters was also smashed – the supposition being widespread that the president of the Cuban Shell office had been responsible for sending the Sea Furies and some tanks from England. Some parking meters (particularly unpopular because their profits had gone to a small group in the regime) and public telephones were broken. The houses of Ventura and Pilar García were sacked. The remaining officers and men in Havana who had belonged to Batista's army waited without knowing what would happen. Old residents in Havana wondered bitterly whether the bloody scenes at the overthrow of Machado would be repeated.[37] But Castro made an urgent broadcast from Santiago appealing to people not to take the law into their own hands, and with the 26 July men and the Directorio moving everywhere into police stations, there was a remarkable absence of such violence. Nevertheless, the general strike called by both Castro and the Communists persisted – the first success and indeed the first sign of life of FONU, the anti-Batistiano Labour front.

Colonel Barquín in Campamento Columbia probably could not have maintained himself apart from the 26 July Movement and Castro, nor did he seem seriously to have wanted to do so. Armando Hart and Quintín Pino of the 26 July Movement were with him at Campamento Columbia. Nevertheless, had Barquín so desired he could have made matters extremely difficult for Castro. But he soon found that the rebel army was in control of most of Cuba and in his first statement he recognized 'the heroic efforts of the Army of Liberation'. Nor apparently, and surprisingly, was there any attempt by the U.S. Embassy to try to persuade him to remain in command; he received only two telephone calls from Ambassador Smith in the course of his time at Colombia: the first asked for a safe-conduct for Trujillo's ambassador in Cuba, Porfirio Rubirosa; the second asked that the normal Latin American right of asylum in foreign embassies would be guaranteed.[38]

In the night of 1 to 2 January the decisive military event occurred.

Guevara arrived in Havana with his men, and went straight to La Cabaña and took over command from Colonel Varela at 4 a.m.[39]

[37] Phillips, *Cuban Dilemma*.

[38] Barquín to Meyer. Seventy-seven people took advantage of this last. They included politicians such as Miguel Angel Campa, Anselmo Alliegro, Santiago Rey, López Castro, Guas Inclán, Raúl Menocal, Carlos Saladrigas (Jun.,) Justo Luis Pozo, Octavio Montoro, Dámaso Sogo and Leopoldo Pío Elizalde; trade unionists such as Mujal; and some thugs such as Calviño (see list in *Revolución*, 10 January 1959, 11).

[39] Núñez Jiménez, 504; *Revolución*, 3 January 1959.

Camilo Cienfuegos, with Victor Bordón and about 700 men, entered Campamento Columbia and took over from Barquín.[40] Majors Cubela and Chomón, for the Directorio, occupied the presidential palace. In a less publicized military manœuvre Armando Acosta, who now suddenly appeared with the rank of 'Major', Guevara's Communist party aide from Escambray, took command at the old fort of La Punta, immediately opposite La Cabaña on the west side of the harbour of Havana. Meantime, Miró Cardona, the secretary of the alliance of the Caracas Pact, Agramonte, the Ortodoxo candidate in the 1952 general elections, with two members of the 26 July Movement (Llanusa and Haydée Santamaría), flew from Miami to Cuba, not to take over power in Havana but to an airport near the Sierra Maestra. On 2 January Havana members of the Directorio and 26 July followers patrolled the streets, and even Ambassador Smith gave a grudging cheer: 'Under the circumstances, they remained in remarkable control.'[41] No shot was fired, and here as elsewhere the 26 July and Batista's men were shortly seen fraternizing.

Castro had meantime arrived in Santiago, accepted the surrender of the town, and late on the night of 1–2 January, in a speech to a huge crowd, declared that Santiago, 'bulwark of liberty', would become the new capital of Cuba. He announced that 'the people had elected' Judge Urrutia provisional president; he spoke of the forthcoming revolution; and gave some account of his negotiations with Cantillo and Colonel Rego. To those members of the army not guilty of 'war crimes', he extended the hand of peace.[42] All over Cuba the local 26 July forces (or mixed 26 July and Directorio Estudiantil) were busy occupying administrative buildings, police and radio stations, telephone exchanges, barracks, and local trade union buildings. There was everywhere some looting of houses of Batista's officials, but no bloodbath. Symbolically, in view of the as usual ambivalent role played by the U.S. in Cuban revolutionary development, a U.S.-born major, Willie Morgan, of dubious antecedents at home, led Directorio forces to occupy Cienfuegos.[43]

On 2 January the 26 July Movement had called for a general strike to mark the end of the old regime, and in Havana and most cities this was fairly complete. In Havana the rebel trade union FONU, now in

[40] *Revolución*, 3 January, speaks of some 4,000!
[41] Smith, *The Fourth Floor*, 321.
[42] In *Revolución*, 3 and 4 January 1959.
[43] Cuban embassies abroad were also taken over; in Washington, for instance, the 26 July representatives, Ernesto Betancourt and Emilio Pardo (minister), took over from Batista's ex-minister Arroyo. Later in the day ex-ambassador to Cuba Arthur Gardner telephoned to enable Arroyo's belongings and dog to be taken away. Teresa Casuso took over in Mexico. Similar scenes occurred all over the world, though in some places (e.g. Germany) the ambassador (Adolfo Caval) immediately joined the Castro movement.

offices lent them by the Freemasons, formed with difficulty and Communist backing during the previous October, called for mass demonstrations. David Salvador came out of gaol to head it as secretary-general.[44] The rebel committees in all unions came out into the open. A meeting was held at the Parque Central addressed by a series of workers' leaders, some new, some old.[45] A *guaracha* dancer in the crowd sang:

> *Ya ya ya ya, te ganaste la guerra*
> *Gánate ahora la paz*
> *Que el que haya sido cruel*
> *Tenga su justicia honrada.*[46]

The old CTC leaders compromised with Batista, Mujal at their head, had fled to hiding, Mujal himself being in the Uruguayan Embassy. The speakers at the FONU meeting talked chiefly of freeing the CTC from corruption.

In the next few days all the unions reformed themselves with new leaders. Militants of the 26 July and Directorio took over as *de facto* police. Offices of newspapers which had backed Batista were occupied. Exiles began to return from Miami, Mexico and the rest of Latin America, including many Prústas, and Castro's nine-year-old son. Not all were well received; the old gangster González Cartas, 'El Extraño', went straight to La Cabaña. There was a little further shooting in Havana, one *miliciano* being shot up by a Ventura policeman.

Another inevitable process was, however, beginning. Hour by hour, ex-Batista soldiers, policemen, officers and *esbirros*, *políticos* and civil servants, were rounded up and jailed to await trial. Civic bodies from the Masons to the Spanish exile colony, the Chamber of Commerce and the sugar planters, all those who had so recently fawned on Batista, testified their support of the revolution. New rebel columns continued to arrive, some of them small groups who had held out for months as

---

[44] *Revolución*, 7 January, p. 2.

[45] Others on the first CTC executive were Wifredo Rodríguez, radio and television workers' leader; Alfredo Rancaño, the 26 July Movement's man in the gastronomic workers' union, but also a Communist; Octavio Louit, railway workers' leader from Guantánamo, who had been badly tortured by Batista; José Miguel Espino, transport workers' union, a Communist, probably since the 1930s; Orlando Blanco, of the Directorio, who also made a speech 'full of revolutionary concepts and generous human wisdom'; Rodrigo Lominchar, ex-Prústa congressman and sugar workers' leader, arrested in 1957 for planning the 'torch policy'; Jesus Soto, 26 July man from Escambray; and David Salvador, the 26 July Movement's general union chief (*Revolución*, 3 January 1959). These and other men established themselves in commissions controlling all the old CTC federations. The order calling off the strike on 5 January was signed by Livio Domínguez, Néstor Pinelo, Antonio Delgado, Patricio Durán, Alfredo Rancaño, Guido Guirado, Eduardo García, Narciso Sastre, Manuel Solaún and Carmen Martha Milla. (*Revolución*, 5 January 1959, p. 2.)

[46] Ya ya ya ya, you've won the war
Now you must win the peace;
He who has been so cruel
Let him have his just reward.

saboteurs in Havana or Matanzas, such as 'Majors' Sanjenís and
Paneque. The Directorio meantime was still in control of the presidential palace, and it began to be a question of whether they might not
refuse to move to make way for Urrutia. After all, they had attacked it
two years before. Now they felt it was theirs. Their secretary-general,
Faure Chomón, complained publicly that Castro had set up a provisional
government in Santiago without the consent or advice of the other
revolutionary groups. Cienfuegos, newly appointed by Urrutia chief of
the armed forces of land, sea and air in Havana province, glowered
from Columbia.

On 2 January the previously clandestine 26 July newspaper *Revolución*
appeared publicly. It was thought to be the voice of Castro, though for
a time it was merely the voice of the 26 July in Havana. On 5 January
it had been taken over from its clandestine directors by Carlos Franqui,
the director of Radio Rebelde in the Sierra, the ex-Communist who
had helped Castro in newspapers and radio since 1955. *Revolución*,
in these first days after Batista's flight, set the pace of things: on the 4th
a photograph of Castro was underwritten 'The Hero-Guide of Cuban
Reform. May God continue to illuminate him'. Across the pages of
Revolución, on television and on radio, and soon across the island, a
veritable series of legendary heroes, seemingly larger than life, were
made to stride across Cuba – the 'glorious Major Cienfuegos'; the
'incomparable Che'; 'Ramirito' (Ramiro Valdés), all referred to by
their Christian names. Here clearly was a nation which hungered at least
for heroism.

Castro himself was moving slowly up to Havana, delayed by cheering
crowds anxious to see him for the first time. He set off from Santiago
on 1 January but by the 4th he had only reached Camagüey. There
were speeches there, and at Holguín. No doubt he was consciously
keeping Havana waiting, to draw out their enthusiasm for as long as
possible, to win the rest of the country as if on an election tour; also, as
he explained in Camagüey, he had to 'organize the revolutionary forces'
on his way westwards – to make appointments, that is. He left his
brother Raúl in command of Oriente, along with a twenty-four-year-old
civilian aide, Carlos Chain. Guevara and Cienfuegos flew to confer with
Castro on 2 and 5 January. Castro's delay too helped create a public
for Cienfuegos. Hundreds of people saw him in person at Columbia,
thousands saw him on Havana Television. The easy manners of this
guerrilla chief made Batista's old barracks seem alive for the first time.
Cienfuegos let out parrots from their cages at Columbia, saying to the
reporters who were inevitably present, 'these also have a right to
liberty.'[47] Even Ambassador Smith, who had to visit Cienfuegos on

[47] *Revolución*, 5 January.

behalf of his old friends of the old regime, found him 'courteous if aloof'.[48] Bearded men went in and out of Cienfuegos's office, rifles tossed backwards and forwards. Guevara in La Cabaña, a formidable presence, allowed Cienfuegos the headlines and maintained a discreet silence while ordering a prescription. Cienfuegos symbolized the rebel warrior who, Havana found to its surprise, behaved impeccably. The *barbudos*, as they became known, did not drink, did not loot, conducted themselves as if they were saints. No army had ever behaved like this in Havana.

The spirit of dissension was kept alive by the Directorio Revolucionario. On 4 January the 26 July Movement had to make a formal request to the Directorio to leave the presidential palace before Urrutia arrived. Since their secretary-general, Chomón, was not there, they asked for more time. Cienfuegos contemplated reducing the Palace by force. Chomón came back and the palace was finally handed over to Urrutia (whom the Directorio accepted with shouts of 'Long Live the President'),[49] but on the 6 January Chomón was found telling a large meeting, with Urrutia present, on the famous *escalinata* of the university, that the Directorio felt itself profoundly preoccupied; unity had made the revolution and the triumph belonged to everyone not simply one group; but the Directorio had no jobs in the government. The question of the Directorio's future remained unresolved. They even began to accumulate and seize arms.

Castro finally arrived in Havana on 8 January. His triumph was complete. Havana went out to cheer. Television cameras covered the route of entry. Placards were inscribed: '*Gracias Fidel*'. Castro's column of cars, jeeps, tanks and lorries drove slowly in from the east, and stopped at the presidential palace. Castro talked to President Urrutia, and indeed to those old hands Prío and Varona, who had arrived from Miami. Behind him walked armed and bearded men, who were also cheered. Castro carried his famous rifle with the telescopic lens. He addressed the crowd from the palace terrace. Even Mrs Phillips, who had over a quarter of a century seen so many changes of government in Cuba, was moved: 'As I watched Castro I realised the magic of his personality . . . He seemed to weave a hypnotic net over his listeners, making them believe in his own concept of the functions of Government and the destiny of Cuba.'[50] He criticized the idea of having a presidential palace, though 'the Executive had to be somewhere' and, since there was no money for another palace, 'we are going to try to arrange that the people have an affection for this building . . . what however is the

[48] Smith, *The Fourth Floor*, 202.
[49] Urrutia, 31.
[50] Phillips, *Cuba Island of Paradox*, 406.

emotion of the leader of the Sierra on entering the palace? . . . exactly equal to what I feel on entering any other building in Cuba.' Afterwards he asked the crowd to open a file to let him pass through, without needing soldiers to help him do so.[51] He moved to Campamento Columbia, cheered all the way by crowds almost hysterically happy at seeing him. In this fortress he made a longer speech, with television in attendance.

It was not entirely a speech of rejoicing:

> Apparently peace has been won yet we ought not to feel ourselves so optimistic. While the people laugh today and are happy, we are preoccupied . . . Who can be 'the enemies of the revolution . . .' We ourselves the revolutionaries . . . who might turn out to be like the many revolutionaries of the past, who walked about with a 0·45 pistol and terrorised people. The worst part of the revolution against Machado was that afterwards gangs of revolutionaries roamed around fighting each other.

Castro half suggested that the Directorio Estudiantil (who had taken arms from Campamento Columbia two days before) was spoiling to be one of these gangs.[52] But this was perhaps the only precise statement in the speech. For the rest, it almost seemed as if William Jennings Bryan had returned. An Hispanic Bryan, a young strong tall no doubt military Bryan, but Bryan-like in his hypnotic effect on the immense audience, who on the other hand felt once more in their optimism that José Martí had really reappeared. As Castro began to speak two white doves were released by someone in the crowd; one of them alighted on Castro's shoulder: symbol and omen of peace.

[51] Text in *Discursos para la Historia*, tomo I, 5–6.
[52] Text in *ibid.*, 7–18.

BOOK IX

Victory : L'Illusion Lyrique *1959*

'The one thought that did not occur to anyone in the houses was that the Old World had not been crushed by its enemies but had killed itself.'

CESARE PAVESE, *The House on the Hill*

CHAPTER LXXXV

Springs of Victory

What had happened? A heroic epic? The band of hunted men in the Sierra at the end of 1956 seemed to have turned, two years later, into an army large enough to beat the army of the nation, to expel the tyrant, to set the people free. The rebels were apparently young men, their leader thirty-two, many of the others in their twenties or even younger, a generation unstained by previous political failure, steeled by war. Many of the new leaders (though not the most important of them) came from fairly humble origins. For an emotional, generous and optimistic people such as the Cubans, Castro's capture of power, with its air, self-conscious no doubt but irresistible, of re-enacting the wars of independence, redeeming Martí's failure and Céspedes's before that, gave a superb thrill of self-congratulation and pleasure. For much of both South and North America, weary of the seemingly endless if often worthy steppes of the Eisenhower era, Castro's victory also afforded a moment of romance, a splash of sunlight, the echo of an heroic age long before even Martí – the era of the conquistadors.[1] For a few weeks Castro was to Eisenhower's America what Lawrence of Arabia had been to England during the First World War. This popular success, national and international, helped Castro from the moment of victory to ignore his allies, to forget the 'pact of Caracas' and to let it be assumed that he alone had won the war.

Castro's hold over the Cubans was established within a few days of Batista's flight to such an extent that, while before 1 January he had only a handful of followers, within weeks many thousands believed that he could do no wrong. He was their liberator, not merely from Batista, but from all old evils. Mothers of men who had died in the struggle trooped to see him. Occasionally after years of struggle and disappointment, and for many reasons, peoples decide to place their collective will-power in the hands of a single man. Ever since the death of Martí, the Cubans had been searching for such an individual. Now they believed they had found one. This was not Caribbean Bonapartism. Rather it resembled the belief that so many had had a few years before in Clavelito, the miraculous broadcaster who cured disease by his voice,

---

[1] Thus *El Independiente* of Caracas, 'In truth Fidel Castro has revived with his glorious epic a concept of heroism little known in our time' (as qu. in *Revolución*, 26 January 1959).

Cuba is a country where politics, magic and religion are neighbouring provinces, sometimes without boundary lines. At the same time Victory inspired throughout society a spirit of civic virtue never previously encountered in Cuba. Cubans had had little to believe in. Customs and institutions which, in more stable countries, act as a brake on the ambitions of single men and on the emotional expectations of masses, in Cuba had scarcely existed either during modern industrial society or in the slave society which had preceded it.

Some of these judgements about Castro's movement were well based: Castro and his men had always been few and they had been brave. Most had social consciences. They had triumphed over overwhelming odds. Many of their comrades had been cut down or brutally tortured. Though many believed that they were living an epic, self-consciousness has often been the mark of real heroes. Let there be honour where honour is due. But the defeat of Batista was not due only to the vanquishing of the army in the field, and the exploits of Castro's rebel army: indeed, the only serious battles fought in the civil war were those of Santa Clara and those which led to the defeat of the army's offensive in the summer of 1958. But even here the scale of combat was small – six rebels being killed[2] in Guevara's army at Santa Clara, forty in the battles leading to the defeat of Batista's offensive in 1958. Such a dearth of pitched engagements is typical of guerrilla warfare, but in fact even the number of guerrilla engagements was small. The scale of operations was far smaller than, say, the Malayan conflict, though the Batista air force had attempted in late 1958 to destroy towns held by rebels such as Sagua de Tanamo. Castro operated as much as a politician seeking to influence opinion as he did as a guerrilla leader seeking territory. The Cuban civil war had been really a political campaign in a tyranny, with the campaigner being defended by armed men. His first concern had been to establish himself in an intractable territory; this he accomplished, though he had hardly really done so till early 1958.[3] At the same time and, perhaps more important, by the skilful use of the foreign press – no Cuban journalists went to the Sierra Maestra before mid-1957[4] – he established a name which became known in North and South America (but particularly North) as much as in Cuba itself. In January 1959 Guevara said, 'At that time the presence of a foreign journalist, American for preference, was more important for us than a military

[2] *Revolución*, 14 January 1959.

[3] A point made firmly by Régis Debray in *Révolution dans la Révolution*; which as earlier indicated was read and apparently revised by Castro: '*Ce n'est qu'au bout de 17 mois de combats continuels, en avril 1958, que les rebelles installèrent une base guérillera au centre de la Sierra Maestra*', (64).

[4] The first were Eduardo Hernández of the newsreel *Noticuba* and Agustín Alles of *Bohemia* (*cf. Revolución*, 14 January 1959).

victory.'[5] By early 1957 Castro had thus become a battle standard of opposition, a point of reference around which the opposition in the rest of the country and in exile could rally, even if from a distance.

Here Batista played into Castro's hands, though indeed the very forces which destroyed him (division and politicking in the army) had also brought him to power in 1952. The Cuban army and police – the two were closely connected at officer level – had greatly suffered from political division, ever since the Sergeants' Revolt of 1933. Batista's personal cronies, the men of 4 September 1933, headed by Tabernilla, who were kept out of most commands during the Auténtico period, returned in 1952. With their sons, brothers and other adherents, they kept all the commands to themselves. Not only the Auténtico officers (hardly a disadvantage to any armed forces)[6] but the younger career men, professionals without politics, had been thrust on one side; and even the supporters of Batista in 1952 were divided two years later; there were, for instance, those *tanquistas* who had wished to establish, with or without Batista, some sort of military authoritarian regime, possibly, similar to that in the Dominican Republic; there were also in Batista's regime several policemen, such as Carratalá or Ventura, who became commanders either in name or in fact, because of the nature of the armed civil war in the cities. There was social resentment among junior officers, especially those who wanted to go to senior officers' clubs and could not.[7]

Discipline among officers is bad if promotion derives overtly from favouritism. If there is indiscipline among officers, that of the ranks will be worse. Batistiano NCOs sought to ingratiate themselves with commanders by excess of zeal and brutality, knowing from experience that ingratiation with these officers led to results. Cowardly actions by privates led on occasion to promotions to corporalcies and sergeantcies. Officers regarded commands merely as means of enrichment by the use of intimidation. The army was rotten and became more so as time went on; at the same time there was an increasing gap between the reality of what was happening in Oriente and public announcements about it. Batista's officers, both of the police and of the armed services, spent their leisure at casinos or night clubs and enriched themselves by exacting protection money and other graft. Also, as during the first period of Batista's power, the army was the most favoured of institutions.

---

[5] Guevara's talk to *Nuestro Tiempo* Association, 27 January 1959, in *Oeuvres Révolutionnaires, 1959–1967* (1968), 25.

[6] They vanished from military or political life without a murmur, and with scarcely a trace (for example, see the list of senior officers in *Bohemia*, 3 August 1952), displaced by Batista's *madrugón*. Not one of them ever played a major part in politics again or indeed was ever heard of.

[7] e.g. Lieutenant Barrera to Ameijeiras, *Verde Olivo*, 12 May 1963.

New barracks for enlisted men, new clubs, new houses for officers, new military hospitals, were constantly built. In both periods, too, soldiers assumed many of the tasks normally conducted by the Ministries of Public Works, Health, Education, Labour, and the Interior; although rotten, the army was all-pervasive. Yet the ordinary soldier was ill-paid; he received a mere $30 a month; and by late 1958 it was almost impossible to secure recruits.

Batista's losses in the war against Castro were probably no more than 300 men.[8] But several officers (Villafaña, González Finales, Ubineo León, Quevedo, Oquendo, Durán Batista, Braulio Coronú) defected to Castro in late 1958. There was always some secret support for Castro in the armed services, particularly the navy, though, after the revolution of Cienfuegos, conspirators were somewhat cowed. One officer who had worked as second-in-command of Batista's military intelligence was a Castro spy.[9] By late 1958 the disillusion of junior officers with their leaders was widespread. Nor was the army well armed: the artillery batteries were the same make of Schneiders which defended Verdun; the coastal batteries were ancient Spanish, of Ordóñez make; the rifles were in many instances 1903 models.

Castro's task in the struggle was both to create in Cuba a situation of civil war, so that Batista's regime would become overtly identified with the army, and then to drive this army, forced into such prominence, to disintegrate or destroy itself through its own weaknesses, divisions, jealousies and errors. This he did and at the same time forced the Cubans to hate Batista, as a Cuban psychologist once commented;[10] this is doubtless a more explicit way of saying, as Guevara did in his subsequent manual on guerrilla warfare, 'one does not necessarily have to wait for a revolutionary situation: it can be created'.[11]

Morale in Batista's army declined further after the U.S. arms embargo. Until then, Batista could suggest in a hundred small ways that behind him stood if need be the armed might of the world's most powerful country. This impression was carefully fostered by visits from U.S. generals, admirals and politicians, and by frequent photographs in the press of officers of the U.S. military mission with Batista or Tabernilla. Batista's American press adviser, Edward Chester, assured these impressions wide currency. After the arms embargo, a pillar fell away from the *amour propre* of the regime; the government's dismay communicated itself to the army. A further blow was given to morale when in 1958, after much expectation, a Chief of Staff and central headquarters were

[8] Colonel Carrillo told a U.S. Senate Internal Security Sub-Committee in 1959 that his losses were 200 to 300 in fourteen months (*Communist Threat*, 361).
[9] Earl Smith, 202.
[10] To the author in 1961.
[11] Guevara, *Guerrilla Warfare*, 111. Trans. J. P. Morray (1961).

created. This supreme command was given to the discredited General Tabernilla, with promotions at the same time to a large number of other unpopular and discredited officers; when complaints became impossible to staunch, Batista resorted to promotions *en masse* of all officers.[12] Finally, Batista's own laziness and weakness damaged morale more than anything else: the president played canasta when he should have been making war plans; as his press secretary put it in exile, 'Canasta was a great ally of Fidel Castro'.[13] Quite apart from the issue of morale, Batista spent a lot of time dealing with his many private affairs, his foreign fortunes and their disposition, leaving himself too little time for affairs of state.[14] So too did Tabernilla: Julio Lobo relates that when Tabernilla billeted his men at the *central Pilón*, he was required to submit three invoices for goods supplied from the mill store, for the benefit of Tabernilla's private account.[15]

Castro's aim continued to be not to engage in combat but to maintain himself in being, occasionally raising morale in the cities and among his own men by some carefully planned and publicized assault on a well-selected outpost. The only way for the army to fight this elusive enemy would have been, as previously suggested, a painstaking system such as was constructed by the English in Malaya. Batista was incapable of this, and indeed any regular army, with traditions of discipline however bad, is always at a disadvantage compared with a little group such as Castro's. The small numbers of Castro's army was an advantage. When in midsummer 1958 Batista at last brought himself to admit the seriousness of the challenge to him and launched a major attack on the Sierra, the spirits of his comparatively large force were very low. Too many men were left to guard sugar mills. Officers showed themselves interested only in killing peasants. Different columns failed to communicate with others and let themselves be dealt with individually by Castro. The Cuban army, after all, had no experience, and therefore no traditions, of combat; the wars of independence had been fought by amateurs before the army was founded. No regiments had battle-honours, none had captured flags to flaunt in regimental chapels. Further, the army in 1957–8 was mostly untrained for jungle or guerrilla war while Castro's propaganda – both respecting his methods of war and his political aims – appealed strongly to the rank and file.

Guevara and Cienfuegos carried the war to Las Villas, where the Directorio Revolucionario had hung on through 1958 in conditions similar to Castro's in the Sierra Maestra the year before, though with less attractive and less gifted leaders. There were also the Communist

[12] Colonel Barrera Pérez, *Bohemia Libre*, 3 September 1961.
[13] Suárez Núñez, 11.
[14] *Ibid.*, 26.
[15] Evidence of Julio Lobo, 10 November 1968.

band led by Torres, an independent 26 July group under Víctor Bordón and the semi-banditry of the 'Second Front of Escambray'. These had done little before Guevara and Cienfuegos arrived in October 1958 – though almost as much as Castro had in his first six months in the Sierra. The new arrivals transformed the situation in Las Villas and indeed the war. Guevara's qualities of leadership turned out scarcely less than those of Castro himself, though they were more analytical and less intuitive. In addition, his arrival in Las Villas coincided with the adhesion of the Communist party to the revolutionary cause: this meant that the Communists of Las Villas, already under arms, were ready to give him every support. Perhaps they would have supported any leader of the 26 July – for instance, they backed Cienfuegos (who was less politically minded) as much as they did Guevara – but Guevara's political inclinations at the least helped effective collaboration. By December 1958 the province of Las Villas was in revolutionary tumult, a threat posed to communications with Oriente, the island perhaps cut in two; and in the middle of the month Guevara began his brilliant final campaign.

At the end of 1958 the rebel army was a heterogeneous group of about 3,000 at most, many of them civilian camp followers. In mid-1958 there had been a mere 300, and probably there were only about 1,500–2,000 persons in arms against Batista in early December, so that most of those who were in the fight at the end were recent recruits. Perhaps 200 were non-Cuban (North or South American); about 1 in 20 were women. The women were non-combatants except for the afterwards famous *Batallón Femenino*, which only suffered one casualty – one girl wounded.[16] These figures include those in Las Villas under Cienfuegos, Guevara and the Directorio. The youngest officer, Enrique Acevedo, was sixteen.[17]

The basic unit by late 1958 was a platoon of forty, commanded by a lieutenant, and the platoons, as usual, were grouped in companies led by captains. There were no formal NCOs, though some non-officers were given posts of responsibility. All could become officers. The highest ranked commanders were majors, of which by the end of 1958 there were perhaps forty. No one was paid.

By 1958 the rebels were usually fed regularly – usually rice with some

[16] Figure given by Castro in the third week of December 1958 to the U.S. correspondent Dicky Chapelle (Osanka, 327), and I have kept to it despite some claims to the contrary, e.g. Cienfuegos told *Revolución* (8 January 1959) that he reached Havana with about 7,000 men (*ibid.*, 13 January 1959). Goldenberg (*The Cuban Revolution and Latin America*, 162) says that he was told in February 1959 that there were 803 'officially recognized' soldiers of Castro in December. Javier Pazos prominent in the 26 July Movement in Havana and in the Sierra for a time, speaks of '2000, well-armed rebels' when Batista fled (*Cambridge Opinion*, February 1963). This is also Karol's (*Les Guerrilleros au pouvoir*, Paris 1970, 167 fn. 1).

[17] *Ibid.*, 7 January 1959.

beef; they had much better clothes, shoes and blankets than in 1957. Probably 85% of the weapons used had been captured[18] and indeed before April 1958 the quantity of arms brought to the Sierra from the cities was almost negligible: one large consignment after the failure of the attack on the palace, one flown in from Mexico in March. This was despite Castro's personal and constant insistence that the cities should dispatch arms to the Sierra as their first priority. By late 1958 the rebels had a few dozen jeeps, all captured, and some lorries.

At the end of the war, perhaps half the rebel army were squatters or field hands from coffee or sugar estates in the Sierra Maestra. Most of the others were town workers of some sort, though some were agricultural workers from other parts of Cuba.[19] Most of those who joined Castro in 1958 received some basic training in a remote part of the Sierra. All knew that if captured they would probably be killed, tortured, or both. This fear prevented them from going home while Batista continued in power. The leaders were exemplary. As well as Castro, Guevara, for instance, was regarded as first in the fight, first to help a wounded man, first to make sacrifices. The progressive views of the commanders were also a help to discipline: a Catholic, Israel Pérez Ríos, for instance, spoke of Guevara as an 'excellent man, a universal figure; his ideas are of such a wonderful humanity, and even though things have been said to attack his personality . . . I can assure you that his ideas derive from a generous heart'. Men felt the same of Cienfuegos: 'He was not a chief, he was a friend, a guide for us all; for the soldiers he was a father, teaching all, treating us with affectionate sincerity and teaching us to be human, so much so that he even insisted that prisoners should eat first.'[20]

The commander-in-chief (he signed himself as such on 1 January 1959) was of course Fidel Castro. His chief lieutenants were Guevara (in command in Las Villas) and Raúl Castro in command on the north coast of Oriente, based on the Sierra Cristal (the 'Second Front Frank País'). Camilo Cienfuegos, commander of the Antonio Maceo column in the north of Las Villas, was of equal rank, as was the mulatto Juan Almeida, commander of the Third Front (East) – that is, the region of Guantánamo. All these, including Castro, had the rank of major.

The rebel army by late 1958 was not only a fighting force. It included a large administration for the control of the *territorio libre* in Oriente: a secretariat, with branches in several different places; and sub-sections dealing with justice, health, education, even industry. In overall control of administration (with headquarters at La Plata) at the end of the

[18] Dicky Chapelle in Osanka, 334.

[19] For example, Universo Sánchez. Robin Blackburn in '*Prologue to the Cuban Revolution*' (*New Left Review*, October 1963), estimated 75% peasants.

[20] See reminiscences of these men in *Revolución*, 7 January 1959.

war was Faustino Pérez, the *Granma* medical student who before the unsuccessful strike of April had been commander of the 26 July underground movement in Havana and had afterwards come to the Sierra. The secretary-general of administration was René Ray, brother of the architect who commanded the civil resistance in Havana. The Justice Department was headed by Dr Humberto Sorí Marín. He, like Pérez and Ray, had worked in the Havana underground and previously had been an Auténtico. In command of the Health Department was Dr René Vallejo, a doctor from Manzanillo; of the Education Department, Rodolfo Fernández; of the Industry and Repair Department, José Pellón; and of personnel, Jorge Ribas, an engineer. In truth the rebel army, in its administration, its sheer size, and its varied activities was coming more and more to resemble a regular army and, in the end, no doubt, would have been compelled to fight in a regular style.

But as well as the war in Oriente and Las Villas, there was the civic resistance in the towns. These men and women suffered most from the repression. However many people were in truth killed in the civil war, the men or women, boys or girls of the cities accounted for most of the perhaps 1,500 to 2,000 casualties.[21] The significance of the Civic Resis-

[21] The numbers are not easy to estimate. In late 1957 Senator Conrado Rodríguez spoke of 300 being killed, promptly countered by Castro as being 5,000. In August 1958 Castro spoke of more than 6,000 being killed. Some time in late 1958, Grau San Martín spoke of 20,000 having been killed. The figure was quoted by the *New York Times* correspondent, but Batista denied it as grossly exaggerated. However, the number of 20,000 stuck and was afterwards widely used. It is doubtful if any of these estimates was more than a guess. The only list of the dead occurred in *Bohemia*, 11 January 1959 and afterwards in subsequent issues. This amounts to:

Rebels	429
Batistianos	153
In skirmishes killed by government	18
„ killed by rebels	85
„ killed by unknown	24
Terrorist bombs	25
Executed by 26 July (spies, etc.)	12
	746
Civilians killed, Santiago, July 1953	48
Attack on palace, March 1957	30
Naval revolt, Cienfuegos	62
Goicuría barracks, 1956	12
	152
GRAND TOTAL	898

My instinct is to suppose these figures roughly accurate. On the other hand they must ignore many peasants killed by the Army in Oriente – and that would probably raise the total by at least another few hundred. Definite figures will probably never be found but it is difficult to believe that more than 2,000 Cubans died between 1952 and 1958 as a direct consequence of the political crisis in Cuba and the Civil War. Nevertheless the figure 20,000 was being used within days of Batista's flight. *Revolución*, on 2 January, spoke of 'a hundred heroes and tens of thousands of dead'. *Cf.* Lazo, *Dagger in the Heart*, 124–5.

tance can hardly be exaggerated. No doubt it would not have got under way had it not been for Castro's presence in the hills. No doubt too the Civic Resistance by themselves could not have forced Batista to flee, but their continual activity and courage tied down police and soldiers and demoralized the government when they might have pooh-poohed the existence of Castro in the Sierra. The later contempt of Guevara and other revolutionaries[22] for these guerrillas of the plain (*llano*) was enormous, but scarcely just or appropriate, even though many of the leaders of the plain afterwards became politically eclipsed.[23]

Castro's presence in the hills, however, helped the disintegration of all other political opposition to Batista. Batista himself gave the *coup de grâce* in 1952 to the old political system of Cuba. Just as the 'system' of the early years of the Republic had been destroyed by one of its founders, General Machado, so the 'system' which arose out of the revolution of 1933 was destroyed in 1952 by Batista, the outstanding revolutionary of 1933, although the Auténtico failure to realize the promise of the system had helped it, like Batista's army, to die within itself.

The civil war of 1956–8 had polarized Cuba: by December 1958 the struggle resembled a single combat, between Batista and Castro. Auténticos such as Grau, Prío and Varona; Ortodoxos such as Ochoa, Agramonte, Bisbé and Márquez Sterling; Saladrigas or Martínez Sáenz, the old leaders of ABC, all these were pushed aside. Politicians of the older parties, such as Liberals (the first party of the early days of the Republic), who had in any way served Batista, were at the very least ruined. This ruin involved many politicians who had served Cuba, and themselves, during the previous twenty-five years. (Martínez Sáenz, who had served as president of the National Bank from 1952 to 1959 was soon arrested, along with Dr Ernesto Saladrigas and other politicians of Batista's days who had injudiciously remained in Cuba, such as Ernesto de la Fe, or Emeterio Santovenia.) In short, over the years, Batista had completed what administrative corruption, *gangsterismo*, mass unemployment and economic stagnation had begun: 'the Cuban people had completely lost faith in the men who had been ruling them but being a people of great vitality did not resign themselves to a mere vegetable life, and kept in their souls an enormous potential of faith and hope, afterwards mobilized by Castro'.[24]

[22] Such as Régis Debray, in *Révolution dans la Révolution*, 76 ff.
[23] *Cf.* Guevara, *Guerilla Warfare*. Debray's comments are concerned with the value of these experiences from the point of view of the future in South America. Experiences elsewhere, such as Aden, Cyprus, Ireland and the Resistance in Europe, would suggest that urban guerrillas may both be directed effectively from the city and be the decisive reason for the failure of the authorities against whom the rebellion is directed. Castro seemed to agree when in 1967 he encouraged Stokely Carmichael and the Negroes of North America to destroy the hearts of U.S. cities.
[24] Felipe Pazos, speech to Club de Leones, San Juan (Puerto Rico), 29 March 1961.

As with the Army, Castro had only to remain aloof, unbending, inscrutable in prison or in the hills, for the old political parties to kill themselves. Some Auténticos were discredited not only through the ill memory of their own days of power but because they had collaborated with Batista to a lesser or greater extent, as members of the official opposition with seats in the legislature, or as opposition candidates in the elections of 1954 or 1958. Grau was the most exposed in this respect, and indeed would figure in January among a list of professors of the university – he had retained his professorship in the medical faculty – to be purged. Others, through private squabbles, had lowered their prestige. Prío was the president whom Batista had displaced but he made no move to reassume power, to nominate himself as the legal president, and no one proposed the plan on his behalf. On 4 January he issued a declaration saluting the new revolutionary government and the revolution itself in 'this new era of democracy and liberty'.[25] He gave no support at all to the idea that the war had been won by a coalition in which he had played a part.

The Ortodoxos had also squabbled bitterly and fatally. In 1952 there had been one Ortodoxo party, loosely led by Eddy Chibás's lieutenant, Agramonte. Now in 1959 there were at least four such parties. While their divisions had weakened the old parties, so too had their failure to play a militant part in the physical struggle against Batista.

There had been, it is true, Auténticos in the attack on the palace, in the naval revolution at Cienfuegos, and of course in some of the attacks sponsored by Prío (such as Cándido González's attack on the north coast). But still the leaders had not been involved. Prío had sent expedition after expedition to its death in Cuba while himself remaining peacefully in Miami; Menelao Mora, the ex-Auténtico senator who died in the attack on the palace, had severed relations with Prío before the attack; while Ortodoxos who had taken part in the fight against Batista had rallied specifically to Castro's movement. Thus Felipe Pazos and Raúl Chibás were members of the 26 July, Chibás being now a 'major' and wearing a beard. Thus Agramonte was to become Foreign Minister in the first revolutionary government, Bisbé ambassador to the U.S.

Auténticos and others from older parties were discredited even if they had not taken part in Batista's regime. They were men who, like the country itself, had become adjusted to disorder and abnormality and the permanent political crisis of old Cuba. Many of them were excluded from participation in any future government by the decree of the Sierra (which now had the force of law) that banned all who had taken part in any of Batista's elections from public life for thirty years. The war

[25] *Ibid.*, 5 January 1959.

indeed not only destroyed the administration, it destroyed the system which had preceded the administration; and no one heard any more of the Pact of Caracas or other wartime agreements. A slogan of Castro's in 1958 had demanded a struggle against 'the 10th March [1952] without a return to the 9th': a slogan which, as will be seen, had plenty of backing.

CHAPTER LXXXVI

Castro and the Americas in 1959

What or who was the victor? Castro had, of course, influences around him. Those who had been with him through the struggle in the Sierra were those to whom he listened. These voices, however, did not all sing the same song. Some, such as those of Juan Almeida, of Celia Sánchez, the doctor's daughter from Pilón, or Efigenio Ameijeiras, the new police chief, felt loyalty to him as a leader *tout court* and would probably have followed whatever policy he decided on. Others had views of their own: Raúl Castro and Guevara doubtless put the extreme view, not necessarily that of Marxism or Communism but that the choice for Cuba lay between two extremes: either to permit the North-Americanized *bourgeoisie* (among whom would be classified most of the old Ortodoxo leaders) to spoil the prospects of social revolution, or institute a dictatorship of the proletariat. This choice was probably laid before Castro at the beginning of his time in office and the evidence suggests that beneath the rhetoric of those days he was coolly attempting to decide in which direction to go; the known comforts, and the possible intellectual corruption of the first alternative, the risky unknown of the second. Even in allegedly ideological matters such precise decisions are usually, where politicians are concerned, matters of calculation. But Guevara and Raúl Castro, as the most prominent commanders, had throughout had much influence on Castro. Their siren voices were balanced by neither the non-Communists nor anti-Communists. Yet even Guevara's voice in 1959 did not speak unambiguously. He was not a Communist and had never been a party member.[1] In 1964 he was asked whether in the Sierra Maestra he had foreseen that the Cuban Revolution would take so radical a direction as it by then had. Guevara answered:

Intuitively I felt it. Of course the direction, and the very violent development of the revolution could not have been foreseen. Nor was the Marxist-Leninist formulation foreseeable ... We had a more or less vague idea of solving problems which we clearly saw affected the

[1] See above, 879. Early in January he denied specifically again that he was a Communist (*Revolución*, 6 January 1959).

peasants who fought with us and the problems we saw in the lives of the workers.[2]

Somewhat earlier he had explained, 'We were only a group of combatants with high ideals and little preparation . . . we had to change the structures and we began the changes without a plan.'[3] A Spanish journalist present in the Sierra overheard Castro upbraiding Raúl Castro for exchanging letters with Guevara on political philosophy, the latter 'disagreeing with many of the premises of Marxism'.[4]

As to Castro's views in 1958–9, Guevara answered in 1964:

> I knew he was not a Communist but I believe I knew also that he would become a Communist, just as I knew then that I was not a Communist, but I also knew that I would become one within a short time and that the development of the Revolution would lead us all to Marxism-Leninism. I cannot say that it was a clear or conscious knowledge but it was an intuition, the consequence of a . . . careful assessment of the development of the attitude of the U.S. . . . and the way in which [the U.S.] acted at that time . . . in favour of Batista.[5]

This vague statement by an often candid politician is perhaps as close as it is possible to apprehend Guevara's state of mind about 1 January 1959. But at the end of that month Guevara, in a talk to the *Nuestro Tiempo* Association – an intellectual group in Havana partly composed of Communists – launched most of the ideas which he afterwards developed into a fairly consistent philosophy: he explained how the rebels in the Sierra had become converted by the needs of the peasants to the idea of agrarian reform; how the experience of the Sierra proved that 'a small group of resolute men' can conquer a regular army and how this offered an example to the rest of Latin America, whose other peoples should also seek to free themselves in the same way; and how the rebel army would henceforth be the main agent of social reform in Cuba ('our first instrument of struggle . . . the avant-garde of the Cuban people'); and how ultimately the entire Cuban people should transform themselves into a guerrilla army.[6] These thoughts were put forward less dogmatically than was afterwards Guevara's custom, and he recalled that the Constitution provided for agrarian reform, suggesting that here at least the aim of the revolution should be to fulfil the Constitution. Nevertheless, one must assume that it was of this sort of

---

[2] Lisa Howard, ABC Television interview, 22 March 1964 (interviewed in February).
[3] Speech in Algiers, 13 July 1963 (*Hoy*, 16 July 1963).
[4] Enrique Meneses, *Fidel Castro*, trans. J. Halcro Ferguson (1968), 62.
[5] Lisa Howard, ABC, 22 March 1964.
[6] In a lecture, 'Social Role of the Rebel Army', published in Guevara, *Oeuvres Révolutionnaires*, 22–32.

idea, couched presumably in more forthright style, that Guevara spoke to Castro in their many talks. The agrarian reform envisaged by Guevara at this stage seemed however to be less collectivist in principle than still based on the old idea of the division of large estates, coupled with some form of tariff policy which would encourage a large home market.

As for Raúl Castro it is true that he had been a member of the Communist Youth; but he had not been an orthodox one; he had always been influenced by his brother more than by his party friends; further, he had now acquired power in his own right and did not desire to share it. He was evidently an extremist but was not necessarily one subservient to any party line.[7] His apparent difference with Guevara over details of Marxism speaks for itself.

The only commander of the rebel army who rivalled Guevara and Raúl Castro in rank and fame was Cienfuegos; for a time, indeed, Cienfuegos (the son of Spanish anarchists), with his open, jovial manner and warm smile, bid fair to become almost as popular as Castro himself. Castro later spoke of him as 'a pure revolutionary soul, Communist timber ... as can be seen from his books, his writings, his unitary spirit, expressed in his letters where he speaks of Félix Torres [the Communist of Yaguajay], when he met him in Las Villas'.[8] Most people, however, had different judgements; 'definitely anti-Communist, not simply neutral';[9] 'a childlike fellow, always playing with guns'.[10] But Cienfuegos' influence on Castro was slight: and Castro said later that he might have been removed from his command because of his 'low political level'.[11] Cienfuegos came to prominence in the last three months of the war; his campaign in Las Villas had been far less well conducted than Guevara's. Guevara and Raúl Castro were more intimate comrades, though it is necessary to recall the former's delphic comment when, six years later, he left Cuba: 'My only serious failing was in not having confided more in you from the first moments in the Sierra Maestra and not having understood quickly enough your qualities as a leader and a revolutionary.'[12] It should also be recalled that Raúl Castro had been away from Castro's side in the Sierra almost since March 1958, and Guevara had been away since September.

[7] The conversation reported by R. López Fresquet, *My Fourteen Months with Castro* (1966), 162, is of interest here.

[8] *Obra Revolucionaria*, 1962 No. 10, 22 (26 March 1962).

[9] Evidence of Javier Pazos.

[10] Evidence of Raúl Chibás; López Fresquet, 58, calls him 'gay, happy-go-lucky, adventuresome'. Others point out that Cienfuegos was much under the influence of his brother Osmani, later an important figure during Cuba's Communist stage, who had been already in touch with Cuban Communists in Mexico.

[11] *Revolución*, 28 March 1962, 6.

[12] Letter to Castro of 1 April 1965. I assumed that this was genuine. For contrary comment see A. de la Carrera, in *The New Leader*, 25 October 1965, and S. Casalis, in *La República*.

Further, there was the paradox that the most anti-Communist of the 26 July members (such as the ex-Communist Franqui, the National co-ordinator Marcelo Fernández or Faustino Pérez in Havana) were also anti-U.S. and hostile to the Communists for being conservative, opportunistic, *embourgeoisé*, and insufficiently critical of the colossus of the north.

Castro's appeal as the rebel chief was heightened by his eloquence. This became apparent to a wide audience for the first time in his speech at Céspedes Park in Santiago on the night of 1 January. He spoke simply but romantically, in a classical manner, at immense length, and without notes. His tall figure and dignified, youthful, but grave face, regular features with a beard, was a commanding one to those who saw him speak in the flesh. The effect was scarcely less on the wider audiences of television. Even in this first speech he touched the later familiar note of the wise counsellor, the father as well as the rebel; the eloquence was warm, comprehensible, geared to sustain the heroic epic of the revolutionary war:

> What greater glory than the love of the people? What greater prize than these thousands of waving arms, so full of hope, faith and affection towards us? Never have we let ourselves be carried away by vanity or by ambition, because, as our Apostle [Martí] said, all the glories of the world vanish like a grain of maize; there is no satisfaction and no prize greater than that of fulfilling our duty, as we have been doing up to now, and as we shall always do, and in this I don't speak in my name, I speak in the name of the thousands and thousands [a perhaps pardonable exaggeration] of combatants who have made victory possible: I speak of the . . . respect due to our dead, the fallen, who will never be forgotten . . . this time it will not be possible to say, as on other occasions, that we will betray our dead, because this time the dead will continue in command. Physically, Frank País is not here, nor many others, but they are here spiritually – and only the satisfaction that their death was not in vain can compensate for the immense emptiness which they left behind them.[13]

Castro's political attitudes in January 1959 however were probably not quite clear even to himself. In a famous speech three years later he spoke surely a little too precisely on the subject:

> I believe absolutely in Marxism! Did I believe on 1 January [1959]? I believed on 1 January [1959] . . . Did I understand as well as today . . . no I did not . . . Could I call myself a faultless revolutionary on

[13] *Revolución*, 5 January 1959, 4.

1 January? No, I could not even then call myself an 'almost faultless revolutionary'.[14]

But which politician tells the truth three years later about his beliefs three years before? Can one demand greater consistency from revolutionaries than from liberals? When Castro spoke in this manner, he had engaged in a close alliance with the Communist party, by whom he was then in danger of being enveloped. For tactical reasons, he was seeking to prove his revolutionary worth. To Herbert Matthews in 1963 Castro said, 'At the time of the Moncada, I was a pure revolutionary but not a Marxist revolutionary. In my defence at my trial I outlined a very radical revolution but I thought then that it could be done under the Constitution of 1940 and within a democratic system. That was the time when I was a Utopian Marxist'.[15] Javier Pazos, an ex-Marxist ten years younger than Castro, and an urban plotter on Castro's staff in late 1957, commented in 1962: 'The Fidel Castro I knew in the Sierra Maestra ... was definitely not a Marxist. Nor was he particularly interested in social revolution. He was above all a political opportunist – a man with a firm will and an extraordinary ambition.'[16] A Spanish journalist recalled hearing Castro in the Sierra saying: 'I'm not breaking my neck fighting one dictatorship to fall into the hands of another', since he hated 'Soviet imperialism as much as Yankee imperialism'.[17] Other comments might be chosen, made by Castro himself and by others, to suggest the difficulty of making a judgement. On the other hand, several years later he was asked by an intimate how he would have managed in Cuba had it not been for the Soviet Union. He drew a cloud of smoke from his cigar and after due reflection remarked: 'I would have played with the national bourgeoisie for ten years but in the end it would have been the same thing'.[18] If Castro was already toying in January with taking Cuba into the Communist camp, his motives perhaps derived from a passion to enact the most difficult, heroic and independent role he could devise, rather than through conviction that the Marxist view of history was correct.

Those who knew Castro when young agree that he had always a

[14] *Obra Revolucionaria,* 1961 No. 46, 35.
[15] Herbert Matthews, *Return to Cuba,* 1964, 11. If words mean anything this suggests that Castro changed from 'pure revolutionary' to 'Utopian Marxist' between July and October 1953. But then, words do not always mean anything.
[16] *New Republic,* 2 November 1962.
[17] Meneses, 62.
[18] Reported by one who was there. Such *ex-post facto* remarks may not of course contain the truth. But Carlos Rafael Rodríguez, the experienced Communist representative with Castro in the Sierra Maestra later recalled a conversation with Castro in 1958, in the Sierra, during which Castro said that one of the defects of the Communist party's programme was that it defined too clearly the aims of the Revolution and so alerted the enemy. (C. R. Rodríguez, *La Revolución Cubana y el período de Transición,* Havana, mimeographed 1966, II, 37.)

passion for an historic role, for cutting a figure on the Latin American political scene which would echo the liberators Bolívar or San Martín. To cut a dash is so universal a desire in political life that no one should be surprised to discover it among the Cubans.

The experiences of the years of struggle, combined with Castro's own mercurial temperament, led him to see this role as that of the revolutionary leader *par excellence* – and the rebel of all America too: on 1 January in Santiago he explained that 'the eyes of all America' were on Cuba, that Cuba deserved to be one of the first countries of the world through its 'valour, intelligence and firmness'. What sort of revolution? Perhaps this was of less importance. Above all, 'the Revolution' had to be carried through to its most extreme point. Thus a letter in 1958 from Luis Buch (of the 26 July Movement in Santiago) to Armando Hart, then in prison, says: 'Justo Carrillo is a revolutionary and desires a moderate revolution: not what we are planning.'[19] 'The Revolution' would realize the dreams of Céspedes, Maceo and Martí, and, though many Cuban politicians had mouthed such aspirations before, Castro's personality, comparative youth and previous experiences made him psychologically insistent that this time there should be no compromise. 'The dead of the three wars of Independence will now mingle in their dust with those of 1956–9'. But times had changed, Martí's message might have to be re-interpreted. This was, after all, to be, according to Castro, 'a Revolution of the whole people'. The disillusions of the past, of 1898 and 1933, caused Castro, a link in a long chain, to be inevitably more radical. In the same first speech in Santiago on the night of 1 January he told his audience, 'The Revolution is now beginning. The Revolution will not be an easy task . . . but in this initial stage especially, full of danger.' But it would not be what happened in 1895–8, 'when the Americans intervened at the last minute and prevented Calixto García from being present at the fall of Santiago'. Nor would it be as in 1933 when first Carlos Manuel de Céspedes, then Batista, came to betray 'the Revolution', nor as in 1944 when 'those who arrived in power turned out to be thieves'. Judge Piedra, whom Cantillo had tried to make president, had also had the Christian names Carlos Manuel; but there would be 'no new Carlos Manuel'.[20] The revolution would not come in a day, but it would be achieved eventually. For the first time the Republic would be really free – 'the first time in four centuries'.[21]

What did 'the Revolution' mean? Members of the 26 July Movement

---

[19] Carrillo MSS (the letter was copied to the Montecristi movement).

[20] *Revolución*, 3 January 1959. The imagery of 1898 and 1933 was persistently used by other orators, for example Armando Hart, at the University on 6 January. At least once the 'betrayal' of the Spanish Republic, by Chamberlain, was cited in January as an example to avoid (28 January 1959).

[21] *Ibid.*, 4 January 1959.

always suggested that they were aware of the long 'revolutionary' past; they spoke of 'revolutionary obligations' and 'revolutionary duties' as if the adjective covered known and fully acceptable goals long ago worked out. But in his Santiago speech, Castro mentioned little specific save a plan for a school for 20,000 peasant children in the Sierra Maestra, a project which had been on his mind at least since he left Mexico.[22] On 5 January, in Camagüey, he said 'we have fought so that there will never again be censorship'[23] – a view to which he returned in Havana. On 6 January, at Matanzas, he was more explicit: 'We are going to attack illiteracy, graft, vice, gambling and disease'. The people of Cuba would save themselves morally.[24] In a letter from the prison of Principe in mid-1958, Armando Hart, who was of course pre-eminent in the 26 July Movement, had taken part in García Barcena's precursor, and who was furthermore of a Catholic, middle-class family, had written:

> I have here made concrete the two aspects of all revolutionary conduct: indoctrination of the *militancia* about where we are going, how we are going, and what we are, for the attainment of a greater integration and a full and comprehensible understanding of all the real forces which compose the community ... so that we all are able to play our proper role in the full development of the revolution ... if we do not triumph it will be because we do not have the right historical moment ... [The letter closed] without more than a revolutionary embrace to all the comrades.[25]

The opaque vagueness about aims concealed, however, resolution about methods. In 1961 Castro was asked by a journalist whether, when in the Sierra Maestra, he had imagined that the revolution 'would assume the aspect that it presently has'. Castro replied, 'We knew what kind of revolution we desired ... and that that revolution would advance as rapidly as the objective conditions of its development would permit. We wanted to give to our people the maximum of justice and well-being.'[26] From what Castro later said of his opinions in 1958-9, from his later views, and from consideration of his past, it is clear that Castro in January 1959 was a radical nationalist, willing or anxious to use 'revolutionary' methods to obtain his ends, but uncertain of the precise nature of those ends, of their practicality and of the wisest way of

[22] Llerena MSS, 30, recalls a conversation about 'school cities' in Mexico in 1956. This later matured as the City School Camilo Cienfuegos.

[23] *Revolución*, 5 January 1959.

[24] *Ibid.*, 7 January 1959.

[25] Letter to Quintín Pino, 25 July 1958 (Carrillo archives).

[26] *Revolución*, 13 May 1961. He added, 'we will continue advancing the revolution for as long a time as our forces and the circumstances permit us to do it.'

going about realizing them. He was more 'extreme' than he had made himself out to Herbert Matthews and Andrew St George in the Sierra Maestra and his experiences in the Sierra had deepened his self-confidence and his ambition. He was not a Communist in the sense of being a secret party member or a man much influenced by Marx's writings. On the contrary, he was already more 'revolutionary', genuinely nationalistic, unconventional, ambitious and audacious than the Cuban Communist party, which he regarded with almost the same suspicion that he looked on the other, rather similarly organized Communist parties of Latin America, during the late 1960s. Indeed, his ambition was too great, his temperament too quixotic to enable him to submit to the discipline and higher authority such as Communism regards as necessary; and the name, though not the policy, of his first political grouping in the late 1940s – *Unión Insurreccional Revolucionaria* – would have been quite appropriate for his inner group of followers in 1959.[27]

There was always in this undefined addiction to revolution for its own sake a certain Garibaldian romanticism as expressed particularly in the revolutionary slogans and catchwords – thus quite soon Castro ended his speeches with the slogan *Patria o Muerte* (in place of *Victoria o Muerte*), *Venceremos*! (Fatherland or Death, we shall conquer): a direct echo of the Risorgimento, even though they also echoed the epoch of the War of Independence (Mambí mottoes were *Independencia o Muerte* from 1895 to 1898 and *Patria y Libertad*, after 1902 – a slogan still seen on Cuban coins). It is almost as if Castro and his colleagues were in love with the concept of revolution, or with the word.[28] But then had this not been the tone of Cubans since at least 1895? Martínez Ortiz, in his history of the first years of Cuban independence, is found assuring his readers that the new municipal Council of Havana in 1899 was composed of 'revolutionaries of good stock', though these included Alfredo Zayas[29]; Horacio Ferrer, who was secretary of war in Céspedes's 'liberal' government in 1933, was described as 'a revolutionary who sweetens and enhances the significance of that word', in the preface to his autobiography.[30] Chibás described himself as a 'revolutionary' from his twentieth year and Grau had conceived his government in 1933 as such; 'we are the only pure revolutionaries in Cuba, doctor', Justo Carrillo had said of himself and the students to Grau in December 1933, when the latter's regime seemed to be crumbling.

[27] See the study of Castro by Carlos Diago in *Cambridge Opinion*, February 1963.

[28] *Cf.* Namier: 'The term was still current by force of ideological and linguistic survival; for ideas outlive the conditions which gave them birth and words outlast ideas.' (*England in the Age of the American Revolution*, 2nd edn, 4.)

[29] Martínez Ortiz, I, 35.

[30] Ferrer, *Con el rifle al hombro*, xi.

Indeed Chibás's use of the word explains much; he termed his demo-cratic Left organization 'Izquierda Revolucionaria'; and in an article in 1937 he explained that 'Revolution is not a synonym for violence. Terrorists and extremists have never made any Revolution in any part of the world but on the contrary have frustrated many'.[31]

Further, though it might seem to outsiders that the concept of 'Revolution' was immature or absurd, or both, it was evidently an indigenous one, unlike that of 'democracy' or 'constitution': it was a concept linking the Cuba of 1959 with that of 1868, comprehending the struggle for freedom by slaves, by *criollos* against Spaniards, by Cubans against the U.S.; 'nothing more idiotic can be imagined than the attempt to establish a liberal government under Spanish laws', General Wood had said; but nevertheless Cuba in the twentieth century was an old and quite different culture from that of the U.S., and however weak it might seem to Americans of Wood's generation, something of that culture survived – or at least people hoped it did, or hoped to make it do so. The North Americans' effort to impose their own values, however superior, on Cuban ones, however 'decadent' was almost certain to falter.[32] And, despite vagueness about what the revolution meant, the nation soon heard of counter-revolutionaries – for instance 'the Cantillo group'; listening to Castro's speech at Campamento Columbia, the Cubans heard of 'enemies of the revolution' for the first time.

But the concept of 'the Revolution', however explained, was funda-mental: people had talked of Revolution so much for twenty-five years that Castro was able ultimately to cause international upheaval by merely carrying out what his predecessors among reformist politicians in Cuba said they had already done themselves.[33] Before 1959 Castro had no ideology, even if perhaps he coveted one privately. All was vague, if heroic. Both he and the leaders of the 26 July generally had certain general ideas of nationalism and of social reform, but there was no explicit programme. When the revolution had to be defined, it divided.[34] Like all revolutions, its vision of the Utopian future was sustained by a view of the past.[35]

In fact by January 1959 Castro had already spoken of a number of goals. There had been the 'Fundamental laws' of the Moncada speech, and most recently the Caracas manifesto. There had been several other

[31] Conte Agüero, *Chibás*, 236.
[32] See Henry Wriston, in John Plank's *Cuba and the U.S.*, 38.
[33] Mario Llerena put this well, in *Bohemia Libre*, 20 January 1963: 'The people of Cuba were familiarized with the idea of the word 'Revolución'. . . . For thirty years they knew national-ist slogans and social achievements.'
[34] Thus Castro: 'As the Revolution becomes more defined, as the Revolution advances . . . progresses ideologically, the number of persons who can fit within the Revolution becomes reduced.' (Speech, *Revolución*, 11 November 1961).
[35] See C. A. M. Hennessy, 'The Roots of Cuban Nationalism', *International Affairs*, July 1963.

policy documents and many near-commitments to journalists, some dealing with personal matters, some public. None of these had been worked out in much detail, most were tactical compromises to gather more support. In 1961 Castro said to a North American:

Sometimes in the mountains, between fighting, I'd think of what would happen when we won, how we would have a new party and fight for the people's needs ... and it was all silly. Once we won, we had the power to do things; we didn't need party politics ... in the Sierra ... we could only think of politics in the old way, without realizing that it was not such a good way ... [He added] I'm a middle-class man with middle-class ideas, many ideas learned in school and never matched against life'.[36]

Castro told Karl Meyer in September 1958 that he personally was not interested in belonging to a revolutionary government.[37] He repeated this in a letter written to Colonel Rego Rubido on 31 December: 'Personally, power does not interest me.'[38] In his first speech at Santiago he said, 'Let no one think that I have pretensions to go above and beyond the President of the Republic', adding, 'fortunately we are immune to ambitions and vanities'.[39] These statements were either deceptions or self-deceptions, unless (which is not inconceivable, though improbable) he was so bowled over by the nature of his public backing in the next few weeks as to change his mind.[40]

If Castro coveted power, and if, once obtained, he like most other politicians would not give it up without a struggle, and if he was certain to use that power in a revolutionary style, the U.S. would inevitably be implicated. For so long the U.S. ambassador had been at least the second strongest man in Cuba. The U.S. regarded Cuba as in some ways her closest foreign friend. The economies of Cuba and the U.S. were really one. In 1959, the value of U.S. investment in Cuba was still greater than it was in any other Latin American country save for Venezuela, and, on a *per capita* basis, the value of U.S. 9nterprises in Cuba was over three times what it was anywhere else in Latin America. However, apart

[36] Carl Marzani, 'Fidel Castro: a Partisan View', *Mainstream*, May 1961.
[37] Evidence of Karl Meyer.
[38] *Revolución*, 4 January 1959.
[39] *Ibid.*, 5 January 1959.
[40] For instance, in April 1961 on a film for *Radio télévision française*, Castro said: 'I must admit that we [i.e. himself] really believed for a time that it would be possible to leave the power to others: we were a little ... utopian. In the first days after victory, we kept away from the government altogether and took no part in the decisions of the Council of Minis-ters ...' (qu. Dewart, 82). Celia Sánchez remarked to Herbert Matthews later 'we could not know that when victory came we and the 26 July Movement would be so strong and popular. We thought we would have to form a government with Auténticos, Ortodoxos and so forth. Instead, we found that we could be the masters of Cuba.' (Herbert Matthews, *Castro, A Political Biography*, London, 1969, 100.)

from sugar they were in utilities, and these were, or seemed to be, monopolies, and therefore also seemed to be identified with the government or at least regulated by it. These facts, combined with the U.S. Government's continued lease of the base at Guantánamo, meant that a political explosion was always near or could be made to be. They also meant that the U.S. businessmen, mill-owners and planters, would expect to appeal to the Embassy of the U.S.[41] The intimate association of U.S. and Cuban commercial interests made all Cuban governments of concern to the U.S. Castro was, however, determined from the start to avoid fitting into the familiar pattern of the progressive Latin American leader who, after a year or two of verbose power, becomes a docile puppet of Washington.[42] He was also, almost from the start, hostile to the grouping of 'Liberal' Caribbean leaders, such as Figueres of Costa Rica, Muñoz Marín of Puerto Rico, or Betancourt of Venezuela. Maybe it was a question of age. These men seemed to Castro, perhaps were, rather patronizing, in welcoming him as a junior member to the club which they had founded.

Eisenhower's America also expressed itself patronizingly. The difference in temperament between Eisenhower and Castro could hardly have been greater. But differences in temperament need not necessarily cause national quarrels. The two men themselves never met. The tension which later grew between Castro's Cuba and Eisenhower's U.S. had deeper roots. First, Castro's Cuba aspired to heroism and to an epic identity. Eisenhower's realm was comfortable. Castro's own temperament required tension, probably demanded an enemy; if possible a situation where he could pose, or remain, as the rebel chief embattled, surrounded by enemies (hence the very early allusions to enemies of the revolution, or counter-revolutionaries). Further, as two years later he himself suggested,[43] the kind of revolution which he had in mind, even in January 1959, had a definite use for an enemy, for an opponent who could be used, by playing on nationalism, to seal national differences. Thirdly, the relations of Cuba and the U.S., anyway since 1898, had been of a classic ambiguity.[44] Many Cuban intellectuals had looked forward for years to a day of reckoning. They read the books or lectures of Herminio Portell Vilá, Ramiro Guerra or Fernando Ortiz, castigating U.S. diplomacy or the sugar society which the U.S. seemed to sustain, and dreamed of vengeance. To choose to be free meant for

[41] See Leland Johnson, 'U.S. Business Interests in Cuba and the Rise of Castro', *World Politics*, April 1965. These matters are also explored below, on page 1172.

[42] See below, 1208.

[43] Two years later Castro stated baldly (*Obra Revolucionaria*, 25 January 1961, 6):, *Una Revolución que no fuese atacada, en primer lugar no sería, positivamente, una verdadera revolución. Además, una revolución que no tuviera delante un enemigo, correría el riesgo de adormecerse.'*

[44] 'Almost unbearable burdens' was the phrase of Theodore Draper, Castro's most intelligent critic in the U.S.

many Cubans, and above all for Castro, to act in a way most calculated to anger the U.S.[45]

Cuban intellectuals were also aware of the cultural threat of the U.S., just as Canadians had been a few years before, at the time of the Massey report, just as in the late 1960s other and grander countries, even in the Old World, became so. These feelings seem not to have been those of the mass: North Americans had always been more popular in Cuba than in Mexico or other countries. The revolutionaries, however, were suspicious of the U.S., not only because of the remote but also the recent past: the identification of the official U.S., through its ambassadors and its colonels of the military mission, with Batista; the use of U.S.-made bombs in the civil war; the failure of North Americans in Cuba to remark the police tortures and atrocities – precisely as had occurred in the days of Machado; all this assured that relations between the revolutionary and Eisenhower governments would be likely to be cool anyway at first. Castro only mentioned the U.S. once in his first, Santiago, speech (to point out their role in preventing the Cubans from getting the benefit of their 'victory' in 1898). He also said, gratuitously, that when 'the hour' came there would not be 4,000 but 400,000 Cubans ready to defend their liberties, if need be.[46] His silence on the subject was ominous, as was the extreme, exclusive nature of his patriotism: if Cuba had been unhappy in the past, who was more to blame than the U.S.? Revenge often plays a major part in the decisions of private life. Who can be surprised if it also does in public matters?

Many Cubans had in the past thought vaguely and disconnectedly about the U.S. as did Castro: in a sense, Castro made them live up to, or down to, these thoughts. Secondly, Castro had no plan.[47] If an opportunist, as Javier Pazos claimed, he was an inspired one, intuitively capable of seizing the right moment and wringing from it all the advantages. It is impossible to believe that in January 1959 his mind was made up to create, say, in Cuba a Communist state; impossible too not to believe that he was going to press far whatever he did. Like most Cubans, Castro did not seem to be personally anti-American; but he saw in a challenge to the U.S. one way to assert the idea at least of freedom; maybe the easiest way. To challenge the U.S. and withstand

---

[45] In 1969 the Communist leader, Carlos Rafael Rodríguez was asked: did the U.S. push Castro into Communism? 'No. Fidel always had a radical idea of the sort of revolution which he desired. But you might say that the U.S., by its actions, accelerated events in the Cuban Revolution.' Conversation with the author, January 1969.

[46] *Revolución*, 5 January 1959.

[47] These two last comments echo A. J. P. Taylor's comment on Hitler and the Germans in their relations to the Jews in *The Origins of the Second World War*. On the other hand it is doubtless true that, because of the much reduced economic role of the U.S. in Cuba since 1933, 'anti-imperialist tendencies in the upper and middle classes were weaker than they had been a generation before'. (Goldenberg, *The Cuban Revolution and Latin America*, 13.)

her rage: to avenge General Shafter's insult to General Calixto García in 1898; to avenge Sumner Welles's less studied insult to Grau San Martín in 1933; was not this the only way whereby, by antique instinct an honourable Cuban could find freedom?

The only real Cuba remained after all a rebel Cuba. Always in the past when rebels had captured power, they had become a new cause for protest. The only honourable national identity which the Cubans could disentangle from the last tumultuous hundred years was that of rebellion. Castro, the rebel incarnate who hardly ever again was seen dressed other than in the olive green uniform of the rebel of the Sierra, consciously or unconsciously appreciated that the only way of maintaining the integrity of both his rebellion and of the long tide of rebellions which preceded it, was to continue the rebellion, not now against Batista but against the ambiguous unpredictable colossus of authority who had been for so long Batista's friend, the U.S.: his first finance minister, López Fresquet, remarked, 'Castro planned to socialize Cuba. He believed that this would automatically alienate the U.S. He therefore gave up the hope of American friendship from the start.'[48] But did he not in fact desire first to 'alienate' the U.S. and then plan to socialize Cuba in consequence? Castro's desire to challenge the U.S., if not his hatred of it, appears deeply based.[49] In June 1958, Castro had written, after a bomb had dropped on a peasant's house, 'I swore to myself that the Americans were going to pay dearly for what they were doing. When this war is over, a much wider and bigger war will begin for me: the war that I am going to launch against them. I am saying to myself that is my true destiny.'[50]

The century-old anxiety was exacerbated by the contemporaneous one of the Eisenhower administration. Dulles was still Secretary of State in January 1959. For him and for the Administration generally, neutralist governments had been distrusted as much as outright enemies. Dulles and his brother Allen, still head of the CIA, had presided over the destruction of the Arbenz regime in Guatemala. Guevara had been present at the climax of that counter-revolution. He, Castro and their lieutenants knew that when it came to almost any reform there would be those in the U.S. who would demand 'action' (the marines or the CIA) to overthrow the Cuban government. He knew that 'Revolution', involving anything like the nationalization of U.S. property – an irresistibly attractive course for a Latin American revolutionary leader in power – would cause such voices to be widely listened to. He believed

[48] López Fresquet, 167.
[49] Cf. Philip Bonsal, 'Cuba, Castro and the U.S.', Foreign Affairs, January 1967: 'It was not Castro's predilection for Communism but his pathological hatred of the American power structure as he believed it to be ... in Cuba that led him eventually into the Communist camp.'
[50] Quoted Herbert Matthews, Castro, a political biography, 107.

perhaps that there was a risk of some sort of tension with the U.S. whatever he did in the direction of reform.

He was, as it happened, partly misinformed. The U.S. no longer opposed neutralism *tout court*. Conservatives in the State Department, in business, and in other government agencies were less well placed in 1959 than in 1954. Among many North American government employees (Wieland, Rubottom, Philip Bonsal, in particular) there was a strong desire to help a reforming government in Cuba. These men were critical of, even hostile to, the businessmen who had been ambassadors in Cuba since 1952. The U.S. had at the turn of 1958–9 no policy towards Cuba or really towards Latin America. Attacks on Vice-President Nixon had suggested that something was wrong, but it was unclear what. There were so many other problems. Castro, who had been for so long hidden from the world, did not know quite how untypical Ambassador Smith was. Ironically, Ambassador Smith was right in his judgement that the Castro regime would turn out to be Communist; a greater irony was that the tendency of men such as Gardner and Smith to see Communists behind every bush helped to make that regime welcome Communism.

There was one other no less important element in the argument. A strong democratic and constitutional regime would by the nature of things have received much support from the enlightened section in the government of the U.S.; aid, technical assistance, investment would have poured in; no doubt the Cuban standard of living would have gone up; no doubt most Cubans, above all most middle-class Cubans, but much of the working class too, would have enjoyed a better life; but it would not have been a Cuban life; it would have been a department of U.S. life, with all its *splendeurs et misères*. Perhaps Castro subconsciously appreciated that here was a last chance of affirming an insular individuality, partly hispanic, partly African, at all events not North American.

Was there any principle involved in the U.S. judgement of whether a regime in another country was good or bad at that time? Perhaps that would have been too strong a word, for the U.S., from habit, regarded the western hemisphere quite differently from the way it regarded Europe or Africa. There, one-party states, even Communist states might be tolerated, even traded with. Those countries were the sphere of influence of others, the Truman doctrine notwithstanding – though even there, in the first moments of the power of an ideologically reprehensible government, the U.S. government would not have 'stood idly by'. Latin America and the Caribbean were a different matter. Since the 1820s and the still far from musty Monroe doctrine, the notion of a state actively hostile to the U.S. in the western hemisphere was barely conceivable.

It was certainly something to be avoided at all costs. The principle of freedom was not the main one, unless that were defined as the system of economic free enterprise. Diplomacy was not dictated by the commercial interests of the U.S. in Latin America, though evidently, since those interests were large, that was a factor. Diplomacy was dictated by friendship or enmity, 'our son of a bitch' against their *enfant de miracle.*

Cuba was a special case. The long years of political, economic, social and cultural dominance of the U.S. in Cuba made many North Americans who went to Cuba – perhaps most of them – patronizing. Havana had been for so long the place for the good time, the prostitute, and the cigar, the blue film, the daiquirí at Sloppy Joe's or the Florida Bar, the quick win at the roulette table. 'Best place to get drunk', Errol Flynn wrote on a menu at the Bodeguita del Medio, a famous restaurant near the cathedral. So many North Americans indeed had had such a good time in Cuba that it never occurred to them that these associations could be humiliating to Cubans. In addition they knew nothing of the far from negligible intellectual life of Cuba. Their history books did not mention José Martí, nor even their encyclopaedias. For North Americans, the Cuban War of Independence was a forgotten prologue to the Spanish American War, and even historians believed that the U.S. Army doctors, Walter Reed and William Gorgas, had alone discovered the cause of yellow fever without help from the Cuban doctor, Carlos Finlay. In 1956 there were two major rows between the U.S. and Cuba even under Batista, one when the winner of the television game, the $64,000 question, won the prize for saying that Walter Reed and not Carlos Finlay had found the cure for yellow fever, one when the Hollywood film 'Santiago' made Martí and Maceo absurd. These tactless and ignorant attitudes resembled British views of Arab or Egyptian nationalism. They marked the conduct of U.S. politicians and diplomats as well as businessmen and tourists and were themselves reflected in Cuban intellectual life.[51]

Finally, and again this was peculiar to Cuba, the commercial relations between Cuba and the U.S. were open to every misunderstanding, and had so been since the Commercial Treaty of 1904, whose essential outlines were renewed in 1934: Cuba could indeed sell a great deal of sugar to the U.S. at very favourable prices. This arrangement not only made it more difficult for Cuba to diversify her production but also enabled U.S. companies to flood Cuba with a vast range of cheap and sometimes pointless goods, the sale of which by North American methods of advertising further debilitated the cultural life of the Cubans.

---

[51] See essay by D. C. Corbitt and José R. Machado, *The Vindication of Carlos Finlay as an element in U.S.-Cuban relations,* published in R. F. Smith, *Background to Revolution,* New York 1966, 74.

In the previous fifteen years the relations between the U.S. and Latin America had changed in many ways, but above all in the contrasts now even more sharply poised: U.S. power was the greatest in the whole world, not merely in the western hemisphere. Her standard of living was outrageously high in comparison with that in Latin America, which in some countries had even dropped in comparison with the 1920s. Her military forces were so well equipped and so numerous as to be quite out of the class of the other nations of the western hemisphere. The alliances which she had bilaterally made in the hemisphere had enabled some of the old successor nations of the Spanish empire to change their armies and police from ragged barefoot gangs of thugs into skilled and sophisticated twentieth-century praetorians, making governments stronger, and increasing the availability of weapons throughout the continent.[52] Unique source of firepower – no other nation in the Americas had an armament industry on anything like such a scale – the U.S. was also by now by far the greatest source of investment. Long past were the days when England could compete.

The wealth, though not necessarily the standard of living, of Latin America had increased. In Venezuela there were oil millionaires, but oil had not greatly improved the lives of workers in the Orinoco valley. During the 1950s, commodity prices had slumped so that the increase of production brought no help. In the same period the U.S. drew out of Latin America more profits than she invested – as was the case in respect of underdeveloped nations generally. Latin Americans also drew money out of their own countries faster than it was put in,[53] partly because of the well intentioned U.S. policy of encouraging social reform.

The general policy of the U.S. had perceptibly changed with the economic changes. Roosevelt's Good Neighbour policy, with its affirmation of non-intervention, had made for the U.S. many friends in Latin America. But now these friends were themselves old or dying. Radicals though they may have been in the 1930s, they were now preservers of the *status quo*; and that *status quo*, that definition of the relationship between the U.S. and Latin America, was more and more expressed less in living bonds, than in legal or diplomatic ones. 'Except for the Export-Import Bank,' Arthur Schlesinger noted, the Good Neighbour policy 'lacked an economic dimension'.[54] Yugoslavia, he pointed out, a Communist country, received more economic aid

---

[52] During the missile crisis of 1962 for instance, Castro castigated the U.S. for the fact that Batista's bombs were U.S.-made (*Obra Revolucionaria*, 1962, No. 31, 10). But the vast majority of arms in Latin America are U.S.-made. Certainly most of Castro's were in the Sierra Maestra, apart from a few old German and English guns.

[53] René Dumont (*Cuba, Socialisme et Développement* (1964)) estimated there was $M20,000 deposited in Latin American accounts in Switzerland.

[54] Schlesinger, *A Thousand Days* (English ed., 1967), 155.

between 1945 and 1960 than all South and Central America. There was another point: North American reformers, pragmatic, liberal and to a large extent successful, did not live in the same intellectual tradition as the rhetorical, schematic, romantic, system-loving hispanic Americans in the south. South Americans have been accustomed, like all patriarchal societies in decline, to see societies in terms of political clashes between classes; classifications of societies into landowners, capitalists, working class and peasants merely seem old-fashioned, even a trifle insulting in the North, which had never been patriarchal. Despite the new and sophisticated interest in Latin America in Washington since Vice-President Nixon's disastrous journey there in the spring of 1958, it was hard to see how the South could be for the North of America anything other than an enemy or a colony. At the same time, all Cuban intellectuals, in addition to their schematic view of their society, had at the back of their minds a large fund of anti-U.S. emotions, partly obsolete, partly superficial which, deriving from the era of the Platt Amendment or from Sumner Welles's Cuban posting in 1933, were nevertheless an important part of their rhetorical culture.

CHAPTER LXXXVII

L'Illusion Lyrique

'A decent moment': thus Ernest Hemingway with customary understatement on Cuba in January 1959, 'after a period of violent readjustment'. There would now, he added, be a peaceful government.[1] The flight of a tyrant, the defeat of his minions, the capture of power by young men, the miraculous culmination of a brave gesture, the attention of the world; an honest army guarding public buildings; great projects for reform ahead; young men ready for any job, any undertaking, whatever their experience or lack of it: these things gave Cuba in early 1959 an extraordinary mood of hope, confidence, enthusiasm, comradeship. Certain companies such as José Bosch's Bacardí Rum Company and the Hatuey Beer Company offered to pay their annual taxes in advance.

The new government was the first reason for enthusiasm. No one knew the provisional president, Judge Urrutia; but he appeared nevertheless the ideal chief magistrate, a good judge, conventional maybe but a man who, if a test came, would act decisively, even bravely. The prime minister, Miró Cardona, it seemed, was a man of much the same kidney; a respectable and intelligent lawyer who also had refused to bow to the dictator; as dean of the College of Lawyers he had been, with de la Torriente, the moving spirit of whose Civic Dialogue and he had been the secretary-general nominally supposed to co-ordinate the work of the Frente formed by the Pact of Caracas. The first cabinet of the Revolutionary Government (as it was named) was divided between men who were of the same age and background as these two and those who, much younger, were followers of Castro; in the first group, Agramonte, the Ortodoxo presidential candidate in 1952, became Foreign Minister; Rufo López Fresquet, an economist and tax expert who had been columnist on economics for the *Diario de la Marina*, technical adviser to the Finance Minister under Grau, and manager of the industrial division of the Development Bank under Prío, became Finance Minister;[2] Cepero Bonilla, also an economist and journalist, became Minister of Commerce; Angel Fernández, another middle-class lawyer,

---

[1] Hemingway (then in the U.S.) had lived off and on in Cuba for years, at Cojímar where he said twelve boys had been tortured and killed by Batista's police (*Revolución*, 23 January 1959).

[2] See López Fresquet, 8; López Fresquet had been in private practice under Batista and had worked in the Resistencia Cívica. He had been offered the Finance Ministry in early 1958.

friend of Urrutia's, became Minister of Justice, his under-secretary, Yabur, being an old collaborator of Manolo Castro in the university and a minor Ortodoxo politician; Luis Orlando Rodríguez, once secretary-general to the Auténtico Youth Movement, and the leader of the anti-Communist university group, familiarly known as El Bonche Universitario, and then an Ortodoxo, who had joined the 26 July Movement and gone to the Sierra to edit *Cubano Libre*, after his newspaper, *La Calle* (which had sponsored Castro in 1955), had been closed, became Minister of the Interior and henceforth wore a tailored uniform and shining boots; and Manuel Fernández, ex-follower of Guiteras in the 1930s, member of Joven Cuba, and in the 1950s of García Barcena's MNR, a romantic revolutionary, became Minister of Labour; a little younger was Regino Boti, an economist, son of a well-known patriarchal poet of Guatánamo, co-author with Felipe Pazos of the revolution's only existing economic plan, who returned from ECLA[3] to become Minister of Economics; while Elena Mederos, the only woman in the government, was a tireless social worker who became Minister of Social Welfare. Associated too with this group were other prominent men such as Felipe Pazos and Justo Carrillo, who returned to be presidents of the National and the Development Banks respectively, posts which they had held under Prío, and resigned at Batista's *golpe*. Pazos had gone through, in company with Raúl Chibás, the bizarre controversy with Castro at Miami: but in the euphoria of victory such events were temporarily forgotten. Emilio Menéndez, one of the few judges who had clean hands in the Batista era, took over as president of a new Supreme Court. Ernesto Dihigo, a noted lawyer and once Prío's Foreign Minister, became ambassador to the U.S. Manuel Bisbé, leader, like Agramonte, of one sect of the Ortodoxos, became ambassador to the U.N. The adherence of all these men made the government resemble, in one way, the sort of cabinet that Agramonte might have appointed had he been elected President in 1952: decent men, for the decent time.

Their '*bourgeois*' nature, however, hid the fact that they ruled over a vacuum. Foreign governments assumed that, since they were men of the middle class, their government would also be middle class; and Urrutia certainly settled in quickly to the agreeable tasks of a Cuban president in the old style, his day spent receiving journalists and old friends, the grand master of the Masonic Lodge, priests and bishops, ex-president Prío, and occasionally the new ministers. He used the language of revolution, but then so had others before him. Urrutia's own initiative, however, was limited to a proposal to end gambling and brothels.[4] He was not a hard-working man.

[3] The U.N. Economic Commission for Latin America.
[4] Proposed in a press conference at midnight on 7 January.

In contrast to Urrutia and the middle-aged ministers there were the Fidelistas and the active members of the rebel army or the Civic Resistance. Both leaders of the Civic Resistance in Havana became ministers – Faustino Pérez, the Baptist ex-medical student, with his long and varied work for the cause, from García Barcena's MNR and the *Granma* onwards, became the minister charged to look after property confiscated from Batista and his friends – such as the Villa Kuquine and the *central Washington* which had been Batista's, the Cubana and Q. Airlines which had belonged to José Villaboy and José Iglesias respectively; and Manuel Ray, the brilliant engineer of the Almendares tunnel who, never apprehended, led the campaign of sabotage in Havana in 1958, became Minister of Public Works and so was immediately responsible for the restoration of the bridges, railways, roads and other public enterprises which had been destroyed or harmed in the war, particularly in Oriente. The first national co-ordinator and organizer of the 26 July Movement, Armando Hart (son of a judge who was now Vice-President of the Supreme Court), who had first come to public notice when as a student he provoked a turmoil at a television programme on which Jorge Mañach was speaking, had been a member of García Barcena's MNR before joining Castro in 1955, and became at twenty-eight the new Minister of Education.[5] The new Ministers of Defence and Agriculture, Augusto Martínez Sánchez and Humberto Sorí Marín, had been lawyers and advocates advising respectively Raúl Castro and Fidel Castro in the Sierra Cristal and Sierra Maestra; the latter had been earlier an Auténtico. The Minister of Communications, Enrique Oltuski, son of Russian-Jewish refugees, had been organizer of the 26 July Movement in Las Villas; he, like Hart, was still in his twenties and had studied engineering in the University of Miami, Florida. The Minister of Health, Dr Martínez Páez, had directed one of the hospitals in the Sierra Maestra, while the Secretary to the Cabinet – always an important post – was Luis Buch, a lawyer of a Liberal Santiago family who had headed the Civic Resistance in Santiago, and who had acted innumerable times as a courier between Havana and Miami. All these seemed honest, intelligent, peaceful, literate and literary people such as have too seldom dignified the bloody scramble of hispanic politics.

Castro was a member of the government as commander-in-chief of the rebel army, but he did not come to cabinet meetings in early January. Yet from the start he acted as a kind of extra chairman of the government, his intimates in the cabinet, such as Hart and Martínez Sánchez, holding unofficial meetings with him in the suite at the

[5] His brother, Enrique, had been blown up by a bomb which he was making.

Havana Hilton, where he spent most of his time.[6] But few members of the cabinet, even those of the 26 July Movement, knew him well; Ray, for instance, had met him twice in the Sierra; Agramonte could only remember him from those ambivalent days in the Ortodoxo movement. With Sorí Marín and Martínez Páez, companions during part of 1958 in the Sierra, he was on distant terms. As for his own position before the possibilities of power, Castro told watchers of French television in 1961, 'We [or I, as others would have said] kept away from the government altogether and took no part in the decisions of the Council of Ministers. We had no doubt that the people responsible would take the elementary measures that the people were expecting.'[7]

To begin with, Castro's absence from the business of government had no consequences, beneficial or damaging. The cabinet sat most of the time, often till far into the night, attempting to establish continuity of administration. 'At no time,' the Finance Minister recalled, 'was a general government policy outlined ... the major part of each Cabinet session,' he added, 'was spent in the preparation of a new constitution.'[8] They had too to make many appointments. The upper ranks in most government departments had either fled or had to be purged. Heroes of the revolution took over everywhere as administrators, sometimes on their own insistence. But usually the new ministers managed to avoid the grossest follies: López Fresquet kept two-thirds of the old officials in the Treasury and managed to persuade Castro that a certain major who desired the job as director of motor taxes was unsuitable.[9] Ministers had vast patronage. Catholic ministers such as Sorí Marín appointed Catholics, rationalists appointed rationalists, men of steel named men of steel, Savonarolas named Savonarolas. At the same time each ministry was busy unearthing *botelleros*, the sinecures, and – it often turned out to be the same persons – the corrupt officials: 800 *botelleros* left the Treasury, 300 the customs department, 265 the transport commission, 580 the health department.[10] Doubtless many of these were ex-gangsters who had received jobs from Prío in an attempt to end

[6] Later, Castro remarked that at this time 'we were very ignorant of governmental problems. That is, we were ignorant about the governmental apparatus and how it functioned ... We saw the problems of the Revolution through a series of concepts and fundamental ideas'. (*Revolución*, 4 October 1961, 8.) López Fresquet, Minister of Finance, recalled (41) that these ministers, 'whenever presenting a project for consideration by the Cabinet, declared that they had previously discussed it with Castro.'

[7] Hervé Chaigne, OFM, in 'La Révolution Cubaine: Miroir de notre temps' (*Frères du Monde*, 1962 No. 3, qu. Dewart, 82). To Lockwood, Castro once again said, 'when we were fighting the Revolutionary war, and making plans for a government that would replace Batista, I didn't plan to occupy the office of Prime Minister or President or any similar position.' (*Castro's Cuba*, 172.)

[8] López Fresquet, 42.

[9] *Ibid.*, 75.

[10] *Revolución*, 19, 24, 26 January 1959.

gangsterismo. Each day in the press new accounts of graft were unearthed: cheques, shares, deals of all sorts belonging to Batista or his family and friends were published with relish by the revolutionary newspaper *Revolución*, followed by other newspapers – less enthusiastically, since the financial connections of many respectable journalists and newspapers with the old regime were also embarrassingly revealed. Thirty-six of the forty Supreme Court judges were dismissed and the newly appointed judges then purged the lower ranks of the judiciary: some 20% of the bench were in consequence dismissed for collaboration with the old regime, while one of the outstanding younger teachers, Mirta Rodríguez, who had played a big part in sabotage against Batista, demanded a full-scale purge of school teachers, employees of the Ministry of Education, and even of pupils. Purges were also demanded in the University, which did not therefore re-open immediately.

One problem which was solved more quickly than was supposed likely was that of the Directorio Revolucionario. There had been real fear of fighting between them and the 26 July Movement. On 9 January, the day after Castro's arrival in Havana, swayed by Castro's eloquence and by its success among the populace, they began to hand back arms. But Chomón, their leader, accompanied this gesture by saying that Castro had had no right to set up Santiago as the capital. Castro, in a television interview on the night of 9 January, replied by trying to divide Chomón from other leaders, such as Cubela, or from the ghost of the dead Echevarría; 'I always thought that the Revolution ought to make a single movement. Our thesis is that this group or that should not make a revolution, but the people.'[11] No one, however, wanted more bloodshed, at least not immediately. A group of Cuban mothers asked to be allowed to go to the university where the Directorio's arms were accumulated: they had had enough of fighting. This offer reached Castro when on television – a fact which raises doubt whether it was quite so spontaneous as it seemed. *Revolución* commented: 'Fidel inclined his head, shut his eyes briefly, shifted his position, opened his eyes and said: "this shows that public opinion is an irresistible force in a democracy"'.[12] On 13 January, Castro and the Directorio met, and after much argument, Castro, confident in the public backing that his rule enjoyed, soon persuaded the Directorio to lay down their arms. The Directorio bowed, essentially, to the pressure of events. In a few weeks their leading members accepted minor government posts – Cubela went to Prague as military attaché and much later, when Cuba restored diplomatic relations with the U.S.S.R., Chomón became

[11] *Discursos para la Historia*, 20.
[12] *Ibid.*, 22.

ambassador.[13] This difficulty was thus easily overcome; but the difficulty itself was one reason why even Miró Cardona the prime minister, fatally for himself, did not insist on calling a meeting of all those parties and groups who had taken part in the Pact of Caracas.

Revelation, accusation and punishment were the first business of the revolutionary government. True, there were many other promises, hopes, expectations and plans. Others besides President Urrutia hoped that the National Lottery would be converted into a national savings institute. Vice would certainly be eliminated – though the disappearance of Batista's police meant that much of its economic backing anyway collapsed. Plans for the eradication of illiteracy would be pressed. A plan for national industrialization would be prepared. The universities would reopen, though purged, just as the schools had already reopened. The government would surely cut electricity and telephone costs. There would be an agrarian reform, and even the Association of Sugar Colonos, hastily changing from their flattery of Batista, demanded that it should be really effective. Castro, it was true, had in the past mentioned so many separate schemes for agrarian reconstruction (and indeed one based on the idea of the *reparto*, or division of the large estates, had already begun to be applied in parts of Las Villas and Oriente) that it was unclear what precisely such a reform would be, but few doubted that it would convert small tenant farmers into proprietors;[14] that it would insist on the effective use of cultivable but uncultivated land; and that it would carry into effect strictures on *latifundios* contained in the 1940 Constitution. In consequence, embarrassing salutes to the revolution from all sections in society continued for many days. They read like comic epitaphs in old churches: 'To the glorious rebel army. Just as yesterday we were at your side in the mountains ... today we are with you to consolidate the fatherland. National Association of Coffee growers.' Freemasons and Veterans of 1898, department stores and textile firms, insurance companies and bankers saluted the revolutionary government with fervour. Men such as Víctor Pedroso, aristocrat, banker and insurer, gave his tribute to Urrutia as he had given it less than two years before to Batista, after the attempt on the palace. Many surprising people put on 26 July armbands. Meanwhile, early in January buildings and institutions began to be known by names of dead revolutionaries; the technological institute of Ceiba del Agua thus became the Escuela Tecnológica Juan Manuel Márquez.

But the government's main problem for the first weeks was that of

---

[13] The fate of these two was contrasting: Cubela, after being the agent responsible for the destruction of the University of Havana in 1960, was tried and imprisoned for thirty years in 1966 for planning to murder Castro; Chomón was a minister in Castro's government for many years, and in 1965 a member of the Secretariat of the Cuban Communist party.

[14] Castro's own words in January, *Discursos para la Historia*, 20.

arrest and retribution. How could this be done? Batista's leading policemen had either fled, or were in hiding, or had been arrested by the army. But by no means the entire police force was arrested. Those against whom no charges of murder, torture or other misconduct could be preferred, remained in their places: 'All who had a worthy and decorous record would be confirmed.' Over them, however, was quickly – that is, within a week of 1 January 1959 – laid a new skeleton of police command under, first, the leading organizer of sabotage ('Action Chief') in Havana, Aldo Vera and, after Castro arrived at the capital, under Castro's faithful friend of the *Granma* days, the 'hero of a hundred fights', the ex-chauffeur Efigenio Ameijeiras, two of whose brothers had died in the fight against Batista, one after Moncada.[15] Ameijeiras organized the system of police command to put it firmly under men of the 26 July, and he himself said plainly that he was acting under the orders not of Luis Orlando Rodríguez, the Minister of the Interior, traditional minister of police, but of the commander-in-chief, Castro himself.[16] At first Ameijeiras accepted the *status quo*, confirming as the new police in different districts those members of the underground who had actually occupied the various police headquarters; at the end of January, out of the nineteen police stations of Havana, however, only four remained in the same hands as at the beginning: the new commanders were chiefly Sierra Maestra combatants.[17] Ameijeiras was twenty-seven. He had a close personal relationship with Castro and, being without political ideology, was prepared to follow Castro anywhere. 'Capable and very brave, up to a certain point a born leader' was one judgement of him; 'he can treat his men fantastically well'.[18] The uniform of the police was quickly changed to remove the old image of the force so disastrously well-known previously. The police were also given a pay rise. Nevertheless, even in quite high ranks prominent members of the Batistiano police were still found: thus Colonel Ledón became chief of the traffic police in Havana.[19]

There was also the army. Castro began by continuing the line of his statements in the Sierra: apart from 'war criminals' the old army would be merged with the new. On 4 January Cienfuegos spoke to old

[15] According to Colonel Esteban Ventura, *Memorias* (1960), 35, Ameijeiras had been in gaol on a morals charge in 1955 and had had other criminal activities to his account, under the alias 'Jomeguía'.

[16] Castro, visiting national police headquarters on 9 January, assured journalists that the army would 'cease all police activities shortly'.

[17] *Cf.* lists in *Revolución*, 27 January. Among those who found themselves in command was Ricardo Olmedo (of the 11th station), who had taken part in the famous attack on the palace but before that in the even more famous assault on the Royal Bank of Canada in 1949.

[18] Javier Pazos to the author.

[19] *Revolución*, 28 January 1959, *tránsito*. Some police officers had secretly sided with the rebels – such as Gabriel Abay. According to J. P. Murray (*The Second Revolution in Cuba*, New York 1962, 35) some 1,100 'rebel soldiers' were brought into the police.

and new officers and men of both parties: 'We shall blend these two armies into one single army – the army which will in truth defend national interests, the army which will sustain our rights and the democracy of the nation.' The new government had no rancour against the old officers and men.[20] But two days later after a talk with Castro at Camagüey Cienfuegos had changed his tune: 'It is necessary to re-organize the armed forces with men loyal to the Revolution, and not accomplices of tyranny.'[21] On 9 January, Castro, in his first speech at Campamento Columbia, said that the president had specifically asked him 'to reorganize the army'.[22] Castro said that 'the country needed an army', because 'the enemy has taken millions of pesos which can be used against the Revolution', and because Trujillo has always had hostile sentiments against Cuba: 'The country cannot be left un-armed.' Castro, however, also said that he personally wished to com-mand 'the best column of the nation, that is the people'.[23] No one saw in this a foreshadowment of a militia. 'We have shown that ... it was false ... [to say] that a revolution could not be made against a modern army [and] without a total economic crisis.'[24] On 22 January he des-cribed a journalist who had asked him to abolish the army as an anarchist.[25] By this time, several officers of the intermediate school, democratic men of the old army, had been whisked to one side. The pivotal figure, Barquín, had become head of the military academies. Borbonnet, Barquín's chief follower who had been for a few hours in command at La Cabaña on 1 to 2 January, took over the nominal post of commander of tanks. Colonel Rego Rubido, the 'honourable' and 'worthy' commander in Santiago whom Urrutia actually made chief of the army staff, was appointed military attaché in Brazil. On 14 January, meanwhile, the first military-cultural school to 'raise the cultural level of the rebel army' was inaugurated at La Cabaña by Guevara.[26]

The provincial military commands of the island naturally went to trusted members of the rebel army – Raúl Castro in Oriente, Hubert Matos in Camagüey, Calixto Morales in Las Villas, Dermitio Escalona in Pinar del Río, and William Gálvez in Matanzas. Pedro Díaz Lanz, a commercial airline pilot who had flown arms into the Sierra from Central America, a less 'revolutionary' individual, became chief of the small air force; he was the son of an army officer tried by Machado. Colonel Rego Rubido's post as chief of army staff was taken by

[20] Ibid., 5 January.
[21] Ibid., 8 January.
[22] Discursos para la Historia, 16.
[23] Ibid., 20.
[24] Castro to journalists, Revolución, 23 January 1959, 13.
[25] Ibid., 23 January, 15.
[26] Ibid., 15 January. See below, 1082, for the significance of this.

Cienfuegos. Some of the soldiers of the old regime were freed, but few were integrated into the new army. With officers it was a little different: at headquarters Colonel Tomás Arias became director of personnel (G.1.); Major Quevedo became director of logistics (G.4); Captain Yañes Pelletier, the mulatto officer who saved Castro's life after Moncada, became his bodyguard.[27]

On the other hand, 145 ex-soldiers were imprisoned in the Príncipe Havana on 19 January, along with about 30 police and 25 civilians.

This new army soon appeared to be essentially the executive of the regime. Thus in Matanzas Major Gálvez settled a labour dispute in both the Rayon Works and the famous old *central Tinguaro*, which now belonged to Julio Lobo.

These forces of order, the new army, the half-new police, were the authority for the regime's policy of retribution, the vexed question of punishment for war crimes. The extent and horror of the Batista era became apparent only after it had ended. Bodies and skeletons, torture chambers and tortures, were discovered and photographed in the press. Those whose sons or brothers, husbands or *compañeros* had vanished came forward to demand revenge. Few of the assassins had taken steps to conceal their identify. Day after day after 1 January there were arrests. The laws dictating such steps were the decrees issued by Castro and his legal advisers in the Sierra Maestra: these had called on officers of the armed services to resign their commissions; on politicians to refuse collaboration with any elections; and had promised punishment of those who had committed crimes even on governmental orders. In that sense, therefore, the men of Batista's Cuba had been fully warned, and the law had been enacted prior to the offence; in that sense, too, as the advocates of the revolutionary regime, Castro included, pointed out, the Cuban war trials were legally superior to the Nuremberg trials: 'Those who applauded the Nuremberg tribunals cannot oppose our courts martial,' argued *Revolución* on 13 January.

There were other less legalistic arguments. The Foreign Minister, Agramonte, argued to the ambassadors and journalists who came to see him that the trials were dictated by the fear that relations of the dead or ill-treated would otherwise take the law into their own hands, as had occurred after the flight of Machado. Concern with the historical parallel was indeed an important point. There was anxiety lest, as had occurred in 1933–4, the successful revolution should spawn endless minor gangster forces roaming violently across the country. In the event, there was little private settling of scores, an almost unparalleled development in such situations in Cuba; and one has only to think of the end of the occupation of France to realize the extent of this achievement

[27] Significantly, however, old officers continued to draw their pensions.

by the Cubans, one of the most trigger-happy nations in the world. The only qualification that might be made to this judgement was the treatment of the hundred or so prisoners who seem to have been shot by Raúl Castro's men as soon as they reached Santiago.[28]

The ensuing trials of war criminals were conducted by tribunals composed of two or three members of the rebel army, an assessor, and perhaps a respected local citizen.[29] There was a prosecutor and a defence counsel. The trials conducted immediately after 1 January were drumhead courts martial, and perhaps one hundred or so officers or policemen suffered execution as a result up and down the country.[30] By 10 January however, regular tribunals had been set up, and from then on, as seems clear from the press accounts, the trials were fair in the sense that a genuine effort was made to establish the guilt or the innocence of the accused. A number confessed guilt. Once the truth was established, circumstances were not of course propitious for moderate sentences: every day new pictures of decomposed bodies or accounts of atrocities appeared in the newspapers. Even so, by no means all those who were convicted were shot; a first cousin of Batista's, Lieutenant Zaldívar, received a year and a half at Manzanillo for ill-treatment of prisoners.[31] Some got longer terms of imprisonment; others were released after examination without trial. By 20 January probably just over 200 men had been shot, all for murder of prisoners or for torture.[32] Some, such as the police agent Cara Linda, known for tortures in Caibarén, escaped after capture and lived on for some time a semigangster life in the country.[33] Many of those who were shot richly deserved it, by most criteria. Had they been imprisoned and afterwards let out, there would certainly have been some private acts of vengeance. Most of these men were corporals, sergeants or junior officers. General

[28] For what seems a genuine account see remarks of Father Jorge Bez, chaplain of the Catholic Youth in Santiago, to James Monahan and Kenneth Gilmore. (*The Great Deception*, New York, 1963, 27.)

[29] In *Santiago*: Major Belarmino Castilla; Captain Ayala and Captain Oriente Fernández, Dr Concepción Alonso and Jorge Serguera, Prosecutor. *Santa Clara*: Captain Orlando Pantoja (aide to Guevara in Escambray, ex-clerk in Contramaestra), Humberto Jorge Gómez, Delia Gayoso, Hornaldo Rodríguez, José Galbán del Río. *Havana* (Cabaña), investigations: Captain Antonio Llibre, Aníbal Sotolongo, José M. Duque de Estrada, Juan Rivero. Of these judges, Castilla became chief-of-staff of the Cuban army in 1966, Ayala was in 1962 chief interrogator of the political police (G.2.), Oriente Fernández a prominent aide of Castro's throughout the 1960s dealing with building projects, Serguera an ambassador and chief of radio and television in 1968, Pantoja was killed in Bolivia with Guevara, and Llibre was always on the General Staff.

[30] For instance, 'Judged in summary court martial, condemned and executed, were various agents of the SIM who tortured and murdered many people in Santa Clara – Montano, Alba Moya, Barroso, Sergeant la Rosa and a civilian spy named Villalta . . .' (*Revolución*, 4 January 1959).

[31] *Ibid.*, 22 January 1959.

[32] *Ibid.*, 19 January, speaks of 207 as having been shot.

[33] Cara Linda was not killed till 1962 (*ibid.*, 24 July 1962).

Cantillo, about to be shot without trial on 5 January for allowing Batista to escape, escaped death due to the intervention of Earl Smith and of the Brazilian ambassador, Vasco da Cunha.[34]

These trials were, however, unfair in the sense that as usual in such circumstances the powerful men got away and the little ones only were left to pay the price: Masferrer was in Florida – arriving on 6 January in his yacht with $M17, immediately impounded – but his chauffeur was awaiting trial in Santiago. The police chief, Colonel Ventura, too was in the U.S. but his private secretary was in Havana gaol. Some ex-ministers – including Santiago Rey the nominal chief, as Defence Minister, of all these men – were in foreign embassies, protected by the law of asylum, later to be escorted to flight by air, their last memory of Cuba the shouts of 'Traitor – thief – assassin' ringing from the crowd.

These Cuban war trials had scarcely opened than they began to be denounced in the U.S. Two important critics were Senator Wayne Morse and *Time* magazine. This led to a certain tension between Cuba and the U.S. when the revolutionary government was less than a fortnight old while the transcript of an exchange between Secretary of State Dulles and the Senate Foreign Relations Committee on 14 January shows that the State Department was thinking of some kind of pressure to bring on Cuba, 'to ensure a government of law and order and justice'.[35]

Ambassador Smith had by this time left Havana and resigned,[36] and the embassy was left with a *chargé d'affaires*; the U.S. recognized the new regime on 7 January, recalling no doubt the recriminations following their refusal to recognize Grau in 1933. Other countries followed suit.

Castro hardly mentioned the U.S. in his first speeches at Santiago or Havana. On 9 January he was asked if he knew that the U.S. had offered aid to reconstruct the country. All aid, he replied, would be welcome.[37] Did Castro know that the U.S. government was offering to withdraw her military mission? If the Cuban government asked for withdrawal, the mission would have to leave. That was not a prerogative of the U.S. but of Cuba. In addition, what use had the military mission been to Batista? Had they advised how to lose the war? 'If they are going to teach us that, it would be better that they teach us nothing.' Wars incidentally were won when one fought for a just and honourable cause.[38] On 13 January, Castro alluded to Senator Wayne Morse's castigation of the war trials:

[34] Earl Smith, 202–3.
[35] See discussion in W. A. Williams, *The United States, Cuba and Castro* (New York, 1962, 37).
[36] Under-Secretary Herter asked him to resign (Smith, 186).
[37] *Discursos para la Historia*, 27.
[38] *Revolución*, 10 January.

The Cuban revolution is already receiving criticisms ... from the U.S. ... There are interests, there are companies, who are afraid that some immoral concessions may be taken from them. The same with the military mission ... They cannot say that we are Communists, because, if so, they would have to say that the entire Cuban people is Communist. That would be absurd.[39]

In the same speech he said, 'The Platt Amendment is finished. I consider it an injustice to have imposed it on the generation who fought for independence.' But the *Daily News* of New York chose this moment to carry an article saying that the Platt Amendment should be restored.[40]

The criticisms of Senator Morse, in particular his suggestion that the U.S. should consider reprisals such as cutting off the sugar quota or freezing Cuban assets, caused great anger, backed by a wealth of historical allusion, evidently easily brought to Cuban lips: where had been the protests against Batista's atrocities? Had not the same occurred during 1895–8, when the 'interested neighbour' intervened at the point of Cuban victory, despite having been silent over Weyler's *reconcentrados*? And in 1933? Had not Batista strong links with the international press? So, this leading article of *Revolución* proclaimed, there would be a great public meeting, at five in the evening – the hour of García Lorca's death (another young man killed, the leader implied, due to external neglect) – to protest.[41] From this moment on Cubans heard daily in the press of an 'insidious campaign from abroad' against the revolution. The Associated Press was the special target of criticism, because of its past close relationship with Batista's government and the embarrassing revelation that its recent Havana correspondent, José Arroyo Maldonado, had been in receipt of a *botella* from the National Lottery of $71 a month. Castro said on television that he wanted the best relations with the U.S. but that he could not adopt an attitude of submission towards that country. 'I am not selling myself to the U.S., nor shall I receive orders from them.' Raúl Castro in Santiago said that he failed to see how the U.S. could complain about the executions when the U.S. had sold weapons to Batista 'to decimate the population of Cuba.'[42] Criticism began to be levied at Batista's concessions to the U.S. to develop Moa

[39] *Ibid.*, 14 January, 2.
[40] Qu., *ibid.*, 16 January, 14.
[41] *Ibid.*, 16 January 1959. The author was Guillermo Cabrera Infante, then just under thirty, and a man who later became one of the most successful modern Cuban novelists with *Así en la paz como en la Guerra*, and *Tres Tristes Tigres*. Cabrera was son of a Communist from Gibara who had worked on *Carteles* with Carlos Franqui in the 1950s and helped prepare the underground *Revolución*. From 1959 to 1961 he was director of the semi-independent *Lunes de Revolución* and afterwards was cultural attaché of the Cuban Embassy in Brussels. He now lives in London and is a prominent critic of the lack of intellectual freedom in Cuba.
[42] *Revolución*, 16 January, 8.

Bay. Worse, four members of the U.S. Embassy turned out to be honorary members of the hated SIM.[43] Nor was it simply Castro and his brother who spoke in uncompromising tones. President Urrutia said explicitly that he supported Castro in everything he had said.

Some slight efforts were made to heal these opening breaches. Paul Hellman, leader of the U.S. Chamber of Commerce, called on the Minister of Trade. The U.S. Embassy denied that the government had had anything to do with development at Moa. But information embarrassing to the U.S. continued to appear. The SIM were proved to have had special relations with the FBI and there were suggestions (never in fact sustained) that Ernesto de la Fe, Batista's first information minister in 1952, had even received a salary from the FBI. Several 'war criminals' – including the hated policemen Ventura, Pilar García and Carratalá – had taken refuge in the U.S. Castro demanded their extradition. In tones increasingly bitter, he told a group of U.S. journalists on 15 January that if the U.S. did not like what was being done in Cuba they could send the marines and then there would be '200,000 dead gringos'.[44] On 16 January at a speech by Chibás's grave he turned the metaphor upside down and said that if the marines came there would be six million dead Cubans.[45] In another speech the same day, he accused the U.S. of wishing to castrate the revolution: for the first time a Cuban government was in power which did not receive orders from abroad. Once more Castro gave his hearers some history, presented a little more harshly than before: the Platt Amendment had been 'a shame and a humiliation'; in 1933 the U.S. had bought Batista. The world had to know that Cuba 'knows how to defend herself. We are a small people but proud . . .' 'If they wish good relations with the people of Cuba, the first thing they must do is to respect our sovereignty. The criminals [during the civil war] were not the Cubans but those who did not speak a single word while the population of Cuba was being massacred.'[46] Guevara at La Cabaña went further: Wall Street always fought against peoples' struggles for freedom, as had occurred in the case of Guatemala. Similar aggression was being prepared against Cuba.[47] Swords, of course, were not yet drawn in January. Castro only mentioned U.S. economic interests, not the government. But yet, as he himself said, there was already tension, already the heavy air of imminent thunder. At the end of the month, the U.S. military mission would be finally withdrawn.

[43] See membership cards photographed, *loc. cit.*
[44] Phillips, *Cuban Dilemma*, 28.
[45] *Discursos para la Historia*, 30.
[46] *Revolución*, 17 January 1959.
[47] *Ibid.*, 20 January 1959.

First Shadows

Questions naturally arose quite early about the Communists. After all, the Cuban Communist party, if its prestige was not high, had at least survived the Batista era. On 2 January Guevara told a North American Communist, Joseph North, that in the new Cuba the Communist party would behave and conduct itself like all other parties.[1] Guevara, however, hotly denied to a journalist from his native Argentina that the 26 July Movement had anything to do with Communism;

> We are democratic men, our movement is democratic, of liberal conscience, and interested in all American cooperation. It is an old trick of dictators to call people Communists who refuse to submit to them. Within a year and a half a political force will be organized with the ideology of the 26 July Movement. Then there will be elections and the new party will compete with these other democratic ones.[2]

Guevara had in fact soon after arriving in Havana dispatched one of his officers, the geographer, Dr Núñez Jiménez, to capture the files and documents of the BRAC, the anti-Communist police and research bureau set up by Batista and U.S. Ambassador Gardner, and inspected and reorganized by Lyman Kirkpatrick of the CIA.[3] Its director, Colonel Faget, had escaped to Miami, but his deputy, Captain Castaño, was arrested.[4] On 6 January a decree abolished all political parties for the time being. The Communists officially were therefore just where the Auténticos were.[5] Little was heard of the Communists' role in

---

[1] Joseph North, *Cuba: hope of a hemisphere* (1961), 26.

[2] *Correo de la Tarde*, 5 January, qu. *Revolución*, 5 January. This would appear to have been one of the few lies told by Guevara: usually he was candid.

[3] Evidence of Máximo Ruiloba to the Senate Internal Security Committee, *Communist Threat*, 525.

[4] Castaño was later shot on the charge of having violated '*una dama revolucionaria*'. He was an able official who talked seven languages (see Barrera Pérez, *Bohemia Libre*, 3 September 1961).

[5] According to Daniel James, José Ignacio Rasco interviewed Castro on 6 January for *Información*, at Santa Clara. After an affectionate discussion of their schooldays together, Rasco asked about 'Communist infiltration'. Castro, furious, allegedly turned the question immediately aside and talked of 'Yankee imperialism' and how he, anyway, was not going to be 'another Yankee lackey'. Daniel James, *Cuba: The First Soviet Satellite in the Americas* (1961), 107.

the Sierra, or Las Villas, meagre though this had been: Félix Torres, Armando Acosta, Pablo Ribalta, Hirán Prats, did not figure among 'the heroes of the Revolution', though in fact they and others had played a certain limited part.[6] On 9 January Cienfuegos told a reporter that he personally had only known three men with Communist ideology in the Sierra but that the Communist party would have rights to organize themselves like all other democratic parties providing that they did not represent the interests of a foreign power.[7] Public anxiety about Guevara's politics was temporarily allayed by the arrival in Havana of Guevara's respectable parents, though Ernesto Guevara, Sr, said that the liberation of Cuba should be an example to other countries.[8]

The Communist party at the end of 1958 was indeed in an odd position. In the struggle against Batista it had played a less prominent part than the Catholic laity. As late as April 1958 it had been ready to act directly contrary to the 26 July Movement in the general strike. Afterwards the leadership had committed itself to an alliance with Castro, sending one of its most enlightened members, Carlos Rafael Rodríguez, to the Sierra. The party directorate in Las Villas established close relations with Guevara and Cienfuegos when it arrived there in October. The same month the party labour leaders had entered into an alliance with the 26 July labour section. All these were of course recent events and possibly only tactical arrangements which might not outlast the victory: indeed the labour arrangements did not do so. In November 1958 the party thought that the disunity of the opposition made the overthrow of Batista improbable in the near future and therefore was still hoping for 'a democratic coalition government'[9] while the actual party members who now began to appear among the clandestine groups of the opposition were 'friendly, humble almost suppliant and asked for nothing but the opportunity to be of assistance', since they believed that the rebellion led by Castro had 'an outside chance of succeeding – but no more than that'.[10] The Communist Youth Movement had sent two members to the Sierra to represent it with Castro in 1957, and there were other isolated individuals who joined the rebel cause. None of this amounted to much. It did, however, enable the Communist party to greet the victory with satisfaction and to come out from the era of the dictatorship not so discredited as it would have been had Batista fled, say, a year before. Its moral position, for instance, was somewhat

---

[6] Though on 9 January Major Torres's men gave up their arms (*Revolución*, 10 January, 3) and a feast was held on 12 January for Armando Acosta.

[7] *Revolución*, 10 January 1959.

[8] *Ibid.*

[9] Message to the Chilean Communist party, quoted Luis E. Aguilar, *Marxism in Latin America* (New York, 1968), 42–3.

[10] Alfredo Sánchez, *Cambridge Opinion*, February 1963. Sánchez was in 1958 in the Havana underground.

superior to that of the bishops, who as a body had not committed themselves either way before 1 January 1959.

The party thus survived intact. Since it had not been allowed to take part in any of Batista's elections it was not prevented from taking part in public activity by any decree of the Sierra. At the beginning of 1959 it was the only party with a well-established organization throughout the island: it had probably about 17,000 members.[11] If so, it was presumably exceeded in numbers by the 26 July Movement, but that was an amateurish movement without an ideology, an alliance more than a party,[12] an organization to which, in the month before Batista's final flight, large numbers of people nominally members of other political groups had attached themselves informally, by the mere fact of telling others or even themselves that they were members of the movement. Whatever happened, therefore, the Communist party of Cuba would be able to play a major part in post-Batista Cuba. In 1947, after all, it had won 120,000 votes and before that, for ten years, the Communists had run the unions with competence. In 1959, all their most prominent leaders had taken part in the Revolution of 1933.

Further, the discredit with which the Communist party had to cope can be exaggerated. Its collaboration with Batista in the war and with Grau was a long time ago. The party's passive line throughout most of Batista's second reign was in fact more damning during the heady days of victory. Where had most party secretaries been in the epic days of Moncada or the *Granma*? 'Under the bed,' as Castro said later.[13] To balance this they could only say that they had consistently opposed the U.S., Batista's chief backer, until near the end. They had some other assets. They could boast that alone of the old parties they were relatively honest.[14] The handsome Negro, Lázaro Peña, for instance, when secretary-general of the unions before 1947, had been reputed to hand back $500 out of his $600 monthly salary. Many of Cuba's best writers were either Communists or sympathizers, from Nicolás Guillén, an eloquent mulatto poet in the tradition of his friend García Lorca, to Manuel

[11] This was the estimate of General Cabell of the CIA in November 1959. Other evidence suggests the same. See above, 756. Other figures are discussed by Andrés Suárez (*Cuba: Castroism and Communism*, trans. J. Carmichael and E. Halperin (1967), 6), who believes that these figures were excessive. In 1946 the party had claimed 150,000 affiliates. Out of those who could be identified – admittedly a mere 77,000 – 64% were white and 36% black or mixed; 42% were industrial workers, 9% peasants, and 12% middle class people – artisans, merchants, professional men, employers or students.

[12] I have been unable to find any accurate figures or even estimates of members of the 26 July before 1959. In *Cuba et le Marxisme*, 103, Arnault says that there were 400 members in Havana. Andrés Suárez (33) thinks this an exaggeration. Carrillo says they had $M3 in their treasury on 1 January 1959.

[13] In his speech on 27 March 1962. See below, 1379.

[14] For instance, even Mario Lazo, a strongly anti-Communist lawyer, recorded the Communists he knew to be 'men of financial integrity, highly intelligent, and fanatically devoted to their Marxist beliefs' (Lazo, 241).

Navarro Luna, poet of Manzanillo. These men linked the Cuban Communists with the great international leftist cultural tradition, with the Spanish war (to which Guillén had gone, though as a 'cultural combatant'), with Pablo Neruda and Rafael Alberti and the rest. Some of their leaders, such as Rodríguez, or Fabio Grobart, were men of ability. Among their followers were many well-intentioned social reformers. All the leaders had a long experience of politics and probably the discredit which reflected on the party for its unswerving support of Moscow, including Stalin, for twenty-five years was balanced by the continuity of the leadership. Further, Blas Roca had successfully survived the crisis of 'de-Stalinization' in 1956; he had travelled to China in 1957 and experienced what he would refer to as 'the human qualities of Mao-Tse-tung' at first hand.[15] Rodríguez and Marinello had been members of the cabinet in the war, the first Latin American Communists to enter a cabinet. Finally, the fact that Batista had described his opponents as Communists assisted that party. They were given an importance to which they had perhaps never even aspired. On 8 February 1959 *Bohemia* published a long article by Francisco Parés (a Spanish Civil War exile in Cuba) which effectively pointed out that the Communists were 'the one [party] afloat'. He added, 'the Fidelismo of Fidel is not enough to ensure the survival of Fidelismo', an astute prediction.

Hoy, the Communist newspaper, meantime appeared again for sale publicly for the first time since 1953, with Carlos Rafael Rodríguez, one of the pentarchs of the Communist party during the era of Batista, as editor. On 1 January, the Havana Communists had moved into the old workers' palace, headquarters of the CTC, which they had built under Grau. They soon, however, gave way to the FONU. They also took over a number of small gambling places, broke the equipment, and hung signs outside saying that the Communist party branch had been set up there. In Havana, the Communists seized the political headquarters of Alberto Salas Amaro, a minor presidential candidate in 1958, as party headquarters there.[16] Meetings began to be held, though cautiously, and their first big gathering was in memory of the old poet-hero of 1933, Martínez Villena – always sure of sympathy beyond the ranks of party members. Indeed, the memory of Martínez Villena and of Mella was one of the party's strongest appeals. In all these weeks there was such confusion that Castro, at the very least, did not seem to care what the Communists did. But they were of course the only organized party, and the only group at all who bothered to publish in early January a new manifesto: that of 6 January, that is before Castro had reached Havana,

[15] See Roca's interview in *Hoy*, 6 May 1959, and his article of 4 September 1959, on Mao's *'calidad humana'*.
[16] Phillips, *The Cuban Dilemma*, 38–9.

which consisted of four points: to convert the rebel army into the nucleus of the army of the future; to promulgate nationally the agrarian reform decree of October; to seek new markets for Cuban goods in eastern Europe; and to restore the Constitution of 1940.[17]

Behind the scenes, the party was trying already to consolidate its position in one section of the army. Guevara had brought a number of Communists with him from Las Villas. Although no publicity was given to these men, one or two received, or seized, in the first confused moments of the breakdown of power, strategically sensitive posts; thus Armando Acosta, the Communist leader of Las Villas, who had been a right-hand man of Guevara's in the battle of Santa Clara and who had helped Cienfuegos with food, found himself commander of La Punta, the old fortress on the Havana side of the harbour, opposite El Morro and La Cabaña.[18] Such a post may have been no more than was due to Acosta as a man of ability, but that could hardly be said of some other appointments made under, or by, Guevara at La Cabaña; within a few weeks Marcos Armando Rodríguez, afterwards famous as the traitor of Humboldt 7, who had recently succeeded in joining the Communist party, appeared as 'an instructor' at La Cabaña.[19] Further, Acosta soon took over 'cultural activities' at La Cabaña, which meant that he was in control of military education and leisure, a post which he naturally filled with dogmatic enthusiasm. Several Communists found jobs under him, among them Alberto Lavandeyra, brought up in France and with experience of the Revolution in Guatemala, and Ramón Nicolau, commissar of the Cubans who fought in the Spanish Civil War and the 'contact' between the Communists and the Directorio in 1958. Without doubt, these appointments at La Cabaña were the beginning of Communist influence in the Rebel Army.[20] This was admittedly the beginning of a process, not its end; nor is it precisely clear whence the initiative came – presumably from Guevara. But it should be assumed that the Communists in the army, however few they were, took every opportunity, from the first day after the victory, to improve and extend their influence. From the beginning of January they praised the revolutionary victory. *Pravda* hailed the Cuban revolution on 3 January: 'The Cuban people have drunk the dregs of bitter suffering and cannot be frightened off. The patriots have the [task] ... of carrying the liberation through to the end.' But from another quarter there were already doubts: a U.S. diplomat, William Bowdler, second

---

[17] *Hoy*, 6 January 1959.
[18] *Revolución*, 5 January 1959.
[19] *Hoy*, 25 March 1964.
[20] Others who found jobs at La Cabaña at this time were intellectual friends of the Communists, such as the future propaganda film-maker, Santiago Alvarez, Antonio Massip (who had been director of *World Student News* in Prague) and Julio García Espinosa.

secretary at the embassy in Havana, had decided by 16 January 1959 that 'the Communists were being given a position everywhere',[21] and while the first Communist statement after Batista's flight, that of 6 January, was very moderate, the 'Theses on the Present Situation' published on 11 January seemed rather stronger.[22]

What happened in the army could have occurred in the unions. But here there was a tradition of anti-Communism. Everyone knew where they were. The 26 July Movement had a strong organization throughout organized labour. Hence by the end of January even the Communists who had been part of the Labour alliance (FONU), formed in October 1958, found themselves formally expelled from the FONU's new, smaller directorate.[23] They had not lost all following, since they controlled some unions – the dockworkers for instance, and the gastronomic workers – and since, as later transpired, some Labour leaders nominally neutral (such as Soto or Aguilera) were in fact willing to be sympathetic towards them. But they had nevertheless received a defeat and the new Minister of Labour, Manuel Fernández, was a known social democrat. Old Communist Labour leaders such as Lázaro Peña were either still in exile or needed time to readjust themselves to the circumstances.

On 16 January, before Chibás's grave, Castro himself formally denied that he was a Communist – an appropriate place since Chibás had always been an enemy of Communism.[24] His praise of Chibás seemed to confirm this. One man surely could not serve both Chibás and Marx. Castro repeated this denial on 22 January in a press conference.[25]

If Communists helped each other on to positions of influence, so too did the Catholics and others: thus the Minister of Agriculture, Sorí Marín, a Catholic ex-Auténtico, appointed young Catholics such as Manuel Artime and Rogelio González Corzo to command the Rural Commandos and to be Director of Agriculture.

On 9 January, the day after he arrived in Havana, Castro had said that elections would be held 'in a space of fifteen months, more or less':

> The political parties will be organized inside eight to ten months. In the first three months of the liberation it is a crime to thrust the

[21] Bowdler to the author in 1962.

[22] *Hoy*, 11 January 1959.

[23] This was composed of nine members, not twenty-one. These were José Pellón, Conrado Bécquer (previously treasurer of the sugar workers), Antonio Torres, José de Jesús Plana, Jesús Soto and José María Aguilera. Salvador's deputies in the underground, Octavio Louit and Reinol González, were secretary of organization and of international relations respectively. Antonio Torres had been Louit's aide in the general strike in Guantánamo on 30 November 1956.

[24] *Discursos para la Historia*, 30.

[25] *Revolución*, 23 January, 13.

people into politics. It is better to work furiously[26] to reconstitute the nation . . . Rarely in Latin America have there been revolutions which are not merely *coups d'état.*

Would the Constitution be adjusted? 'The moment a provisional president was put in power marked an adjustment.'[27] Two days later, Castro was interviewed again, this time by CBS television: would the Student Directorate take part in the forthcoming elections? 'Naturally,' said Castro, 'if we do not give liberty to all parties to organize themselves we will not be a democratic people. We have fought to give democracy and liberty to our people.' What guarantees were there that elections would be held? 'Public opinion . . . our word . . . our intentions . . . because we are disinterested . . . because it is obvious that we have nothing to gain in not having elections.'[28] It was, of course, already known that Castro wished to create 'a model people of America'.[29] At the Club de Leones on 13 January he was pressed a little on these topics; would there be any constituent assembly before the elections? 'The problem here was not of substituting the existing Constitution but of adjusting it; therefore it would be negative to speak of a constituent assembly.' Should there be a provisional legislative assembly to help with the heavy burdens of the Council of Ministers? 'The provisional government would be short-lived and would . . . put everyone to work. Our revolution is genuinely Cuban, genuinely democratic.'[30] Two days later the prime minister, Dr Miró Cardona, explained that the Constitution of 1940 had been 'actualized' by the revolution. This later seemed to mean, however, that several articles of the Constitution would be revised. For example, Article 21 causing penal laws to be retroactive if they favoured the accused was suspended to exclude collaborators of the 'tyrant'. Article 25 which banned the death penalty was amended to provide precisely that punishment for Batistianos and others. Confiscation of Batistianos' property was to be permitted.[31] These constitutional revisions were, of course, by decree. Only the prime minister, Miró, seems to have protested. But his request to be allowed to resign in protest against moves that he rightly considered had totalitarian implications was brushed aside by his colleagues, and he did not persevere.[32]

By this time the cabinet, sitting almost continuously and at all hours of the night, had approved, among other appointments, a minister to

[26] The word Castro used was *febrilmente.*
[27] *Discursos para la Historia*, 27.
[28] CBS, TV interview, 11 January, qu. Léo Sauvage, *L'Autopsie du Castroisme* (1962), 74.
[29] He said this in the national police headquarters on 10 January 1959.
[30] *Revolución*, 14 January 1959.
[31] *Ibid.*, 16 January.
[32] *Diario de la Marina* (Miami), 12 November 1960.

'consider the authority of the Laws of the Revolution' – that is, the nature of the Constitution.[33] This post went to Osvaldo Dorticós Torrado, a forty year-old Cienfuegos lawyer and from one of the families who had founded Cienfuegos, distantly linked by blood to the nineteenth-century millionaire Tomás Terry – and also, more closely, to an old Auténtico, Pedro López Dorticós, one of the officials of Batista's BANFAIC, recently arrested. Dorticós had had a flirtation with the Communist party in his youth and had once been private secretary to Juan Marinello, the literary president of the Communists. But that was long ago; Marinello was a figurehead; and now Dorticós, Commodore of the Cienfuegos Yacht Club, lawyer to big Cienfuegos companies, president of the National College of Lawyers, appeared the most *bourgeois* of the new ministers. His part in the 26 July Movement in Cienfuegos had been small.[34]

Those Liberals who were well placed in Urrutia's provisional government unfortunately could not sustain their high principles. Although this can be chiefly explained by the policy, the power and the character of Castro, they prepared the way for their destruction themselves. First, Urrutia agreed with Castro that there should be no elections for eighteen months. Until then there would be government by decree. This decision seems to have been contested by nobody. One of the first decrees issued by the cabinet was the dissolution of Batista's Congress. Another was the dissolution of all past criminal tribunals. A third was a decree abolishing political parties: thus, trumpeted *Revolución*:

> We finish with all the vices of the past, all the old political games. The triumph of the Revolution cannot give a green light to the petty interests of the opportunists of all time. Let the figureheads who did not participate in the revolutionary struggle ... not be permitted any opportunity to betray the Revolution with their capacious hypocrisy. Worthy men who belong to definite political parties already have posts in the ... provisional government ... The others ... would do better to be silent.[35]

A fourth decree banned all candidates in the elections of 1954 and 1958 from political life. Some, such as Dr Fidel Núñez Carrión or Alberto Salas, were arrested for venturing to take part in these elections: the former had aspired to be mayor of Havana in 1958, and the latter to be president. Other decrees of early January froze the bank accounts of all civil servants under Batista and stopped any outstanding large cheques

---

[33] This was on 10 January.
[34] See below.
[35] *Revolución*, 7 January 1959, 7.

drawn during the Batista era.[36] These decrees were concerned with the destruction of the past and the removal of corruption: the Batista bank accounts seemed outrageous to those who followed, and every form of state interference seemed desirable to prevent anyone who was believed to have robbed the State profiting from his thefts.

Yet why was it thought there should be no elections for eighteen months? Why did Agramonte and Urrutia, Pazos and Miró Cardona, accept this delay? Both Urrutia and Miró Cardona explained at the time that there would have to be changes in the Constitution of 1940 to take into account the change of power from illegality to legality.[37] Why did the rest of liberal Cuba accept that delay without thought, welcoming, with *Revolución*, the extinction of the political parties? Because, like Castro himself, and like, no doubt, the masses, if their views could have been effectively sounded, they were ready to reject politics. Even ex-President Prío and Agramonte, the Ortodoxo presidential candidate of 1952, seemed prepared, even anxious, to submit to a 'national guide and leader' such as Castro – already referred to as the '*máximo líder*' in January; they, too, wanted to purge Cuba, not rebuild the old institutions. All were happy in the 26 July Movement, which had never been and was never to become a political party.

Castro in these first days of victory was indeed almost the only person who dared to say that 'the right of dissent and to make opposition' was an inalienable right. 'We are not trying to make the 26 July Movement into a single totalitarian party,' he told listeners in Las Villas on 6 January.[38] In most of his statements however, he tried to place his revolution against the background of all Latin America: thus on 22 January, to an audience of journalists, some of them Latin American, he explained that 'a dream he had in his heart [*sic*] was that one day Latin America would be entirely united in a single force, because we have the same race, language, feelings [*sentimientos*].'[39] Nevertheless Castro was also a patriot of an extreme, almost extravagant kind: 'It would be difficult to find a people so noble, so sensitive, humane, as this; you cannot see a *corrida de toros* here, because the people would rise against it.'[40] When he said 'America', he meant South America too.

> We have above all the interests of our country and of our America . . .
> We are defending the interests of our peoples, we want political and
> economic independence and [desire] that exploitation cease and that

[36] Other decrees suspended for thirty days the guarantee against removal of the judiciary, expelled Barroso from the sugar stabilization institution, removed various state stipends given to journalists, etc.

[37] *Revolución*, 15 January 1959.

[38] *Ibid.*, 7 January 1959, 1.

[39] *Ibid.*, 23 January 1959, 14.

[40] *Ibid.*, 15. He said nothing of cockfights, which the people would doubtless rise up to keep. Some like cocks, some bulls.

regimes of social independence are established within the broadest frame of human liberties. This is the philosophy of the 26 July Movement ... the day [that liberty is no longer maintained] we shall resign ... The day the majority is against us we shall resign ...'[41]

All these themes were welded together in a series of speeches by Castro at the end of January. A huge meeting was held on 22 January in front of the presidential palace to support the government in its policy towards 'war crimes'. The crowd was, if anything, larger than that which greeted Castro on 8 January. Banners announced 'Cuban women demand execution of murderers'; 'For revolutionary justice'; and 'Extradite the lackeys of tyranny'. Some of these were in English, presumably for the benefit of the U.S. reporters who had hurried to Havana. Other banners recalled Nuremberg. Castro, on a specially constructed presidential tribune, was surrounded by most of his more prominent followers. His speech was essentially a denunciation of the U.S. for venturing to criticize the war trials when few had criticized the atrocities under Batista. But it was also a successful test of his strength. Thus he asked all who agreed with revolutionary justice to raise their arms: of course everyone did. Castro commented: 'Gentlemen of the diplomatic corps, gentlemen of the press of the whole continent, the jury of a million Cubans of all ideas and all social classes has voted.'[42]

Castro made eloquent play with the fear which had been expressed in the press that he might be assassinated: but 'the destiny of peoples cannot depend on one man ... because ... behind me come others more radical than I ... and [therefore] assassinating me would only fortify the revolution'. He thereupon named his brother, the mysterious, physically almost child-like Raúl, as second-in-command of the 26 July Movement, to succeed him if he should die. He demanded of the U.S. the extradition of war criminals who had gone there. He justified the executions by quoting, rather obviously perhaps, from the Bible: 'He who kills by the sword ...' He explained that the 26 July Movment had killed no innocent people, unlike the U.S. whose actions in Hiroshima and Nagasaki, as was well known, had been committed to save North American lives. Cuba had no hostile sentiment towards the U.S. but he believed that in the U.S. there were anti-Cuban interests, 'interests who fear the revolution'.[43] This speech suggested that Castro was either afraid of intervention by the U.S. or that he was already teasing himself and Cuba with the idea of it, to boost national morale and unity, a unity which would be behind himself and his victory. The criticisms of the war trials he attributed to an 'organized campaign of

[41] Remarks made on 23 January.
[42] Discursos para la Historia, 37.
[43] Ibid., 44.

criticism'; he left his hearers vague as to who was responsible, but suggested that they worked through AP or UPI.[44] He seemed also to be developing the idea of a fully independent Cuba, perhaps neutral internationally (though this idea had yet to be fully explored), and behind him was clearly the memory of Martí. To journalists, on the same day as this speech, he said explicitly that 'the interests' which were attacking the executions wished in fact to crush the revolution.[45] On 22 January a Mexican asked him what he would do if the U.S. were to impose an economic blockade on Cuba and whether the 'powerful U.S. interests' which were already attacking the Cuban revolution might decoy the 26 July Movement into the murderous morass of the cold war. Castro said firmly:

> We have to try at all costs to avoid world problems coming to convert our ideals into a scenario for that struggle. Certainly various mono-polistic interests . . . arrange matters by trying to obtain from govern-ments which they can suborn all manner of privileges, and some of them often can count on the backing of the public power of the U.S. . . .'

What would happen if such companies in the future tried to paralyse the revolution completely? The Cuban people would have to defend themselves as circumstances dictated. Castro's belief was that this situation was not going to occur. 'I really am not afraid of falling into the orbit of international Communism. What are we doing to defend the revolution? Have we sought support from Communism? No, we have sought the backing of public opinion of the peoples of America.'[46]

Faced with so many criticisms, the Cuban government decided to stage the first major war trial in Havana in public, in the large sports stadium. The accused were Major Jesús Sosa Blanco, Colonel Grau and Colonel Morejón; the council of war, Humberto Sorí Marín (Minister of Agriculture), Catholic lawyer and Advocate-General in the Sierra; Major Universo Sánchez (a Granmaista); and Raúl Chibás.[47] The sports stadium was unfortunately filled with a furious and yelling crowd, as well as three hundred Cuban and foreign journalists. The crowd inter-rupted evidence by shouting 'Bandit', 'assassin', 'thug'. Sosa Blanco, the first to be tried, conducted himself with cynicism, gaiety and some dignity before what he himself termed 'a Roman circus'. Careful examination of witnesses was impossible in that atmosphere. No doubt Sosa Blanco was guilty, as many people testified, of many deaths in Oriente province in 1957–8. He had burned 200 houses at Levisa, some

[44] Interview in *Revolución*, 23 January ,14.
[45] *Ibid.*, 23 January.
[46] *Ibid.*, 15.
[47] Of these it is worth noting that the first was later himself executed for treason within two years and the last is an exile. Universo Sánchez is an unimportant army officer (1970).

being full of people. He had killed nine members of the Argote de Céspedes family in El Oro de Guisa on 10 October 1957. The widow of a peasant swore that Sosa Blanco had shot her husband before her eyes. A man said he had seen Sosa Blanco shoot nineteen workers in Minas de Ocujal. That he had committed some, at least, probably most, of these crimes, seemed beyond question, though no evidence other than hearsay evidence was in fact produced. Some of the crimes had occurred before the first 'law' emanating from the Sierra Maestra, in February 1958, which promised justice to the members of Batista's army who carried out murders. But what was the status even of that law? These points were made by the defending counsel, Captain Aristides da Costa, who also said that in war these things did happen: one side killed the other. These points were dismissed, and Sosa Blanco was condemned to death.[48] This trial, intended to be a proof to the rest of the world of the integrity of revolutionary justice, was in fact the worst advertisement for it possible. The U.S. press agreed with the defendant that the trial was a circus.

On 22 January Castro left for Venezuela, to attend celebrations there on the first anniversary of the expulsion of the dictator, Pérez Jiménez, and to thank the 'sister republic' for her aid in the Cuban struggle. President-elect Betancourt was then still the hero of the Left in Venezuela as well as of the centre. A huge multitude greeted him, proving beyond doubt that he had a following on a continental scale. Castro replied by giving a victory sign in the style of Churchill.

Castro made a number of speeches in Caracas. Once more he denied that the revolution in Cuba was Communist. To the Venezuelan Congress, he gave the assurance: 'In Cuba we shall have also a congress within two years.' Visas between Cuba and Venezuela would be abolished. A Venezuelan military mission would be invited to instruct the new Cuban army. The Organization of American States would be filled with democrats, the dictators would be expelled.[49] A common market was possible in Latin America; perhaps a common passport; and 'the U.S. will have to adapt itself to Latin American politics, will not always be defending the interests of monopolies'. The 26 July Movement would of course become a political party, for political parties would not be permanently abolished in Cuba, new ones would be founded, though the old *politiqueros* would have to go. He, Castro, did not aspire to the presidency of Cuba. Indeed he was thinking of making a journey round South America, partly to stop 'the calumnies of some monopolistic sectors interested in maintaining their privileges in Cuba, partly to sow the seeds of unity in the countries of Latin America in

[48] A fairly full report of the trial appeared in *Revolución* in January 1959.
[49] *Discursos para la Historia*, 46–9.

defence of their common interests'. Castro left Caracas, undertaking that a mission would soon be sent to Venezuela to co-ordinate a common policy with President-elect Betancourt. So far so good.

In fact Castro had a somewhat bizarre conversation with President Betancourt. They talked alone, though surrounded at a distance by guards, in a large patio. Castro came straight to the point: he told Betancourt he was thinking of 'having a game with the gringos'. If necessary, would Betancourt help him out with a loan of $M300 and with oil? Betancourt, taken aback, gave a discouraging reply:[50] he was interested himself in evolution not revolution.[51]

At the same time the candid Guevara, still merely the commander at La Cabaña, was hinting that his own political programme would give serious reasons for disquiet to any capitalist as to his ultimate motives. In his speech on 27 January he was explaining that the rebel army, the 'vanguard of the Cuban people', was the 'primary instrument of struggle'; the entire nation should be turned into a guerrilla army.[52]

A lyric spirit survived in Cuba for many months after these remarks, and few foreigners left the island without being entranced by the nobility, the vigour and the charm of the revolutionaries; but from the very beginning of 1959 there were those who wondered precisely what would happen. To many people the month of January 1959 in Havana was a unique moment of history, golden in promise, the dawn of a new age; great projects had already been begun; however, in a way that most of them scarcely appreciated, it was also the end of an old world.

[50] Evidence to the author by Betancourt. See also Betancourt's article in *The Reporter*, 13 August 1964. As Mrs Phillips points out (*The Cuban Dilemma*), Castro used the word 'gringo' for North American on another occasion in January 1959, an odd usage by a Cuban; for Cubans usually say 'Yankee', and Castro did himself usually. It was presumably a calculated attempt to talk in the language of South Americans or.Mexicans.

[51] See Tad Szulc, 'Exporting the Cuban Revolution', in J. Plank, ed. *Cuba and the U.S., Long Range Perspectives* (1967), 78 and 88. This rebuff substantially affected Castro's attitude to Betancourt afterwards.

[52] Guevara's talk to the *Nuestro Tiempo* Association in Havana. For text, see Guevara, *Oeuvres Révolutionnaires*, 23–32, or Gregorio Selser, *La Revolución Cubana* (1960), 427 ff. As it happened, Roca chose 27 January also to expand on his 'New Theses' of 11 January. Reading between the lines it is evident that there was a clash between Guevara and the Communists, the latter being outflanked by the former.

BOOK X

Old Cuba at Sunset

'I don't understand why it should have been the Cubans. They are all so individualistic and they had the highest standard of living in Latin America.'

LUIS SOMOZA OF NICARAGUA TO NICHOLAS WOLLASTON

CHAPTER LXXXIX

The Island

There were now between six and six and a half million Cubans, about the same number as there were Englishmen at the time of Albemarle's capture of Havana in 1762, or North Americans during Jefferson's presidency.[1] At 132 to the square mile, the density of population was $2\frac{2}{3}$ times that of the U.S.,[2] and the fourth biggest in Latin America.[3] The population had doubled twice since 1899, when density had been 32 to the square mile, and was now growing at 2 to 3% a year – a high figure but substantially lower than say Brazil or Mexico, being close to the level of North West Europe in the 1880s. Most Cubans had been country-dwellers until about 1930; most lived in towns or villages afterwards.[4] The 'urban' population seems to have been 57% in 1953, 55% ten years before, 51% in the last years of Machado. Cuba was no longer primarily an agricultural country; but nor, in terms of workers, had it been so since the beginning of the century.[5]

In comparison with other countries nearby, Cuba was exceeded in population by Mexico (32 million), by Colombia (13 million), and of course by the U.S. while Venezuela, with more inhabitants than Cuba in 1900, was behind in 1958, at 6·3 million. The six central American states, lying between Mexico and Colombia, together totalled only 11 million.[6] Haiti and the Dominican Republic, the two republics on

[1] The last census was in 1953 when the population was said to have been 5,829,092. Estimates for 1958 vary from the National Bank's 6,136,000 to the National Economic Council's 6,563,000.

[2] (131·8), 1953 figures.

[3] Haiti, El Salvador and the Dominican Republic had more people per square mile.

[4] But a 'town' was a place only 150 people in size, according to census definition, and which had access to services such as electric light and medical service. Thus, by definition, the country was less well off than the town. The 1931–43 definition was whether one lived in a house with a number and in a street. 1899–1919 used to define a town as over '1,000 strong'. But 1931–43 gave much the same proportion as that of 1953.

[5] According to their respective censuses, Argentina has an urban population of 62·5% Canada 64%, Chile 62%, the U.S. 64%. Different criteria for these surveys make any absolute comparison impossible.

[6] Guatemala   3,546,000
El Salvador   2,434,000
Honduras   1,828,000
Nicaragua   1,378,000
Costa Rica   1,076,000
Panama   995,000
(Statistical Yearbook UN, 1961)

Hispaniola, numbered 3·5 million and 2·8 million, respectively. Puerto Rico had 2 million. The other islands of the Caribbean, French, Dutch, English and North American, did not together make up 4 million: the English islands totalled 3 million, the French, 500,000. The three Guianas reached 700,000, the Bahamas 45,000.

As for the rest of South America, Argentina, Brazil and Peru were of course all substantially larger than Cuba, having 20 million, 60 million, and 10 million people, respectively. Chile was only slightly larger (7 million). The others were smaller.[7] All Latin America and the Caribbean, Mexico included, comprised about 190,000 million, a figure only slightly above the U.S. In 1900 the U.S. had totalled 76 million; Latin America and the Caribbean under 30 million.

Within Cuba, the families in the country had usually more children than those in the town.[8] The size of families was slowly decreasing, but numbers were in fact still higher than in 1899–1907 when there had been so much more disease.[9] 80,000 women were believed to have had ten or more children,[10] and 660 had twenty or more children, of whom 250 lived in Oriente; interestingly enough, well over half these, nearly 400, were reckoned as white.[11]

The drop in the number of births during the war of independence between 1895–1898 could plainly be seen. No doubt in 1958 the virtual non-existence of men in their early sixties was a cause of extra instability in society: where would England be without those solid citizens, the elderly men in a hurry, retired from their professions, but still enthusiastic to bear responsibility, public and private, without payment?

The growth of Cuban towns in the twentieth century had been swift. In 1899 there were five cities with populations of over 25,000; in 1958, twenty-one. Cities with over 8,000 totalled sixteen in 1899, forty-six in 1958. The biggest rise was that of Havana's suburb-city Marianao, from the 'pretty little Cuban village' of a mere 5,000 (visited by Samuel Hazard) in 1899 to over 200,000 in 1958 – the second biggest city in

---

[7] Ecuador 4   million
   Uruguay 2·7   „
   Paraguay 1·7   „
[8] Census of 1953, xxix. 217 and 318, respectively per 100 women of 15 years or over, were the precise figures.
[9] *Size of families*: (Census of 1953, xxxvii; *ibid.*, 1919, 381):
   1899   4·8
   1907   4·8
   1919   5·7
   1931   5·20
   1943   5·18
   1953   4·86
[10] Census of 1953, 67. Precise figures, 81,430 and 2,000,106.
[11] Precise figures, 657,245 and 377.

Cuba, if reckoned separately from Havana. In 1958 Havana and Marianao together totalled over 1,000,000, compared with under 250,000 in 1899.

As in most of South America, big cities grew faster than small ones: under a quarter of the population in 1907 lived in cities of over 25,000;[12] in 1953, well over half.[13] In 1953 a third of the population lived in the four cities larger than 100,000.[14] Compared with Havana and its neighbour, the cities of Oriente increased less swiftly, but nevertheless continuously, especially Holguín and Guantánamo.

Agricultural families of course continued to live chiefly in separate farmsteads, not, as in Spain, in villages, for villages were places rather for merchants, wholesalers and professional people. Farmers and labourers would go to the village to get their letters, usually addressed care of a shopkeeper, since there was no free postal delivery: they went to 'town' in fact several times a week, for supplies or social activities, sometimes to take part in the nightly *paseo* up and down the squares with the town-dwellers.

The construction of the towns did not now follow the strict patterns of the conquistadors. Houses were often built along the main road, with only one or two back streets, usually not paved. All pavements were narrow. Houses might have a porch supported by pillars, Greek in inspiration if stone, square if they were frame houses. Most houses in towns were however made of wood with a tile or metal roof. Nearly all would be one storey high. The small towns of Cuba, without the charm of the cities, nor the excitement, but also without immediate access to the country, were in many ways the most depressed parts of the island.

By 1958 between a half and two-thirds[15] of the houses of Cuba had electric light, but only 9% of rural ones, compared with 87% of urban. Of all the houses or flats, between a third and a half had been built since 1945; about a third between 1920 and 1945; and the rest, less than a quarter, before 1920. About nine-tenths of the rural houses and about two-thirds of the urban ones had probably been built since 1920.[16] Over a quarter of the houses were said to have been built with

[12] 21·4%.
[13] 58%.
[14] 35%.
[15] 58% in 1953.
[16] In 1953, 34·5%, 39·8% and 25·7%; adjusted to take into account building since 1953. Figures in 1953 were:

312,382: before 1920
483,635: 1920–45
418,589: since 1945
41,988: undeclared

1,256,594

masonry and cement, though only 1% of those in the country. Two-thirds of the rural houses were still *bohíos* of palm and wood, with earth floors.[17] Though unhygienic, they were cool and, from the outside, beautiful. Half the Cuban houses had two to three rooms, 13% only one room, 17% five or more. 85% of rural houses had to use river water. 43% of urban houses, and only 3% of country ones had internal lavatories. Over half of the rural houses lacked all lavatory arrangements, giving a national fraction of just under a quarter. 15% of town houses, 1% of country houses, had baths.[18] All these low figures nevertheless represented marked advances over the situation fifty years before: in 1899, half the population had no lavatory arrangements. 1,300 houses in 1953 were declared worth $40,000, of which 1,100 were in Havana province. The average value was $1,000.[19] All houses were, of course, privately built, though the State had sometimes intervened in the regulation of rents and leases. Many members of the *bourgeoisie* had their savings invested in property; indeed, most of those who had savings had it so invested – a fact which affected all proposals of the revolutionary government of 1959 to cut rents. Rented houses added up to just over a third of the total houses – constituting the largest single source of revenue of the Cuban middle class.[20] A little under a quarter of the houses were lived in by squatters, or tied farmers, or in some other way occupied without payment of rent.[21] In towns, rented property amounted to over half the total,[22] but only 5% in the country, where nearly half were squatters,[23] compared with a tenth in the towns.[24]

In 1953 a sixth of the population lived in Havana.[25] It was a larger capital city in proportion to total inhabitants than any other in the world save the equally top-heavy London and Vienna.[26] Havana had sucked dry the province around it so that the density of population of those who lived on farms in the province of Havana was relatively small, in 1943 less than the national average.[27] Well over half[28] those

---

[17] Census of 1953, xliii.
[18] *Ibid.*, xliv–xv; c.f. *U.N. Demographic Yearbook 1958–9*;
[19] See Census of 1953 302. 1,306, 1,101 and $1,060 were the precise figures.
[20] 36·4%.
[21] 22·8%. 3·6% were unoccupied.
[22] 55%.
[23] 46%.
[24] 9%. Census, 253. In Pinar del Río, 70% of rural houses were occupied without rent, 65·6% in Matanzas, 62% in Camagüey. In 1943 statistics had been rather different. In towns, 124,931 families owned their houses; 4,240 were buying them on a mortgage; and 358,933 rented theirs. In the country, 129,926 owned their own farm; 2,097 had it on a mortgage; 227,403 rented it. (Census of 1943, 1010–11). 75,004 were unknown (squatters).
[25] Census of 1953.
[26] Census of 1943, 724.
[27] 22·9 national average; Havana in 1943, 18·4% (Census of 1943, 731).
[28] 221,455.

employed in services,[29] well over half[30] those employed in utilities,[31] and over half [32]of those employed in building were in Havana.[33] Sugar mills apart, perhaps three-quarters of the industrial investment in Cuba was in the region of Havana.

The traveller's first sight of Havana on arrival by sea remained what it had always been: a broad harbour, commanding buildings on either side, a multitude of ships, his views overlaid no doubt by the sentiment that Havana had been for longer than any city in the New World a centre of pleasure. To those who lived there, Havana cast a spell as great in the 1950s as in any earlier time, but now however there were at least four Havanas.

First, there was the old city, unchanged since the mid-nineteenth century, narrow streets, two-storey buildings, sometimes huge Spanish doors giving on to courtyards. Being near the docks, the old city remained the centre of business and it was, as always, the centre of restaurants, night life and brothels. The Presidential Palace remained in the old city, though other government departments had begun to be taken out of the centre to Batista's gaunt new buildings clustered round the Plaza de la República. The old city already had a serious traffic problem – exacerbated in the public mind by parking meters introduced in 1957 and which were, rightly, believed to be a means whereby various officials made money for themselves. The exodus of the richer families towards Miramar, on the North American model, lowered the rents, and the tone, of the old city. On the border of the old city was Chinatown, full of restaurants, more brothels and night clubs, some where blue films (since the mid 1950s) could be found cheaply. Some of the eighteenth-century palaces were crumbling, others were used by companies or embassies. In this respect, Havana resembled other Spanish-American capitals such as Lima or Mexico City. The prostitutes on the streets such as Virtudes or even the Prado were so numerous as to resemble a cattle market.[34] The Prado, with a double line of laurels, led up the centre of the old city, lined also with bootblacks, waiting taxis and beggars. These last were estimated to number about 5,000.[35] The gangster and brothel underworld of Havana under Batista was intimately connected with the police, and most night clubs paid protection money to some police officer or other. Most of this part of the city was held on leases which, though nominally monthly, were in

[29] Out of 395,904.
[30] 4,939.
[31] Out of 8,439.
[32] 34,617.
[33] Out of 65,292.
[34] One report estimated that in February 1958 11,500 in Havana earned their living as prostitutes (qu. Yves Guilbert, *La poudrière Cubaine: Castro l'infidèle* (1961), 35).
[35] W. MacGaffey and C. R. Barnett, *Twentieth-century Cuba* (1965), 144.

fact indefinite. Tenants who prospered might very well lay marble floors without any fear of being turned out. Rents could be raised but only within certain limits if the property in question was pre-1939.

The second Havana was Vedado, the fashionable suburb of the early years of the century but now the real centre of the city. Here Batista's building boom had had most effect. To the old Hotel Nacional, reconstructed after the battle in 1933 and redecorated in the 1950s, had been added several more glittering hotels such as the $M14, thirty-storey Havana Riviera, built by a group of North Americans apparently implicated in the murder of the Chicago gangster Anastasia; the $M5½ Capri, with a swimming pool on top of its twenty-two storeys; and the Havana Hilton, run by the Hilton chain on behalf of the Restaurant Workers' Union, which had invested $M24 of their pension funds in it. All these had casinos of astonishing luxury and splendour (being built by investors seeking gaming profits). All had several restaurants and bars. They were essentially an extension southwards of the plush hotels of Miami Beach. In them music was kept up endlessly over loud-speakers and, weekly, more and more well-known performers came from the U.S. to the cabarets. There were other new buildings, too, such as the even taller FOCSA building, a smart apartment block. Sheltering at the foot of these peaks lay many elegant villas, some embassies, some government departments, some still in the hands of the rich families who had built them during the early 1900s. It was in this part of Havana that the creeping 'Floridization' of the country was most visible.

A long broad avenue skirted the coast, the Malecón, which had begun to be built in the days of General Wood, offering splendid views, carrying the tourist or the gangster, the revolutionary or the sugar broker from the pillared arcades of old Havana past the remains of the old fort La Punta, as far as the Hotel Havana Riviera's bizarre blue pleasure-dome, passing on the way monuments to the students shot by the Spaniards in 1871, to the dead of the *Maine*, to Maceo and to Martí. The streets of Vedado, like the old city, were laid out on the gridiron pattern, but more irregularly, with variations due to ancient watercourses, paths or other boundaries.

Vedado had been extended on the west by a tunnel under the River Almendares, begun in 1950 by the engineer Manuel Ray, who showed his mastery also of conspiracy and sabotage in the year the tunnel was opened. The extension led to the most modern of the suburbs of Havana, Vedado's own successor as the home of the gracious, a huge area known as Miramar and, beyond, the even more gracious zone known as 'El Country Club'. This soft suburb had been constructed in the great days of *vacas gordas* during the 1920s and linked Havana with what had once been the separate township of Marianao. Miramar, and El Country Club even more, was a place of large comfortable houses, leafily set in their own grounds, to each house a royal palm and a hibiscus, with garages and outhouses, Havana's Wimbledon or Chevy Chase, though on a more exotic scale. The coastal frontier of Miramar was dotted with famous clubs and hotels with their private beaches – Havana Miramar Yacht Club, Hotel Commodore Yacht Club, Havana Biltmore Yacht Club, Copacabana Hotel Club. There stood too the 'largest theatre in the world', El Blanquita. El Country Club boasted above all, of course, the club after which it was named: there business men and politicians drank rum and Coca-cola (*Cuba Libre*), played golf, rode and behaved like gentlemen. Miramar or El Country Club was the home of the ABC colony, as Vedado had been thirty years before. It was the site of Tropicana, 'largest night club in the world', where Javier Pazos's famous bomb had exploded among the high heels on New Year's Eve, 1956. Not far, also, to the south-west of Miramar, lay the army head-quarters, Batista's favourite Campamento Columbia, with its airfield and its modern barracks. There was also the Colón cemetery where the marble vaults of the rich were fitted with lifts, air conditioning and telephones.[36]

The fourth and last Havana was the zone where most Habaneros lived, though there was not much remarkable about it. It was a large, dirty, dusty region behind Vedado and Old Havana, much of it slum, though most of it dating from the twentieth century, with some quarters, such as Pogolotti (called after the developer) conscious efforts at slum replacement by the creation of explicit working-class areas. None of this was picturesque; it was inadequately served by *guaguas*, full of frustration, steamily hot in summer, but noisy and animated at all times. It was a territory of crime, factories, tenements, small cinemas and cock-pits.[37]

Havana's several skins caused it to seem comparable to most cities of the rich and developed world rather than to the capitals of poor countries. There were a large number of little squares, most of them adorned with statues of Martí or some other hero. But contrasts were more extreme even than in Naples. Anxiety over traffic existed alongside beggars. There were eighteen daily papers, thirty-two radio stations, and five television centres; the city was so spread out as to demand car travel; air-conditioning had arrived on a large scale in hotels, businesses, restaurants, and many private houses, causing the breezy sections such as Vedado or Miramar to appear doubly enticing. But this contrasted with the slums, also doubly. Havana made other Caribbean capitals, such as Kingston, Jamaica, or San Juan, Puerto Rico, seem provincial:

[36] Robin Blackburn, *Prologue to the Cuban Revolution.*
[37] The nearby towns of Guanabacoa, Santiago de las Vegas, and Regla were also classified for administrative purposes in the metropolitan area of Havana. The first and last of these were centres of *santería*.

but the standard of living in the Cuban countryside lagged behind the levels in those islands.

Santiago, the second city of Cuba after Havana, with a population of 180,000, also contrasted with it. Its centre remained Spanish-colonial. No new North American architecture disturbed its agreeable symmetry. Its university, much less politically disturbed than Havana's, had almost as good a name. Its inhabitants regarded themselves as superior to those of Havana, and many were. It rejoiced in a tradition of rebellion. Its Spanish accent was specially eccentric, due to a mixture of bastard French deriving from the emigrants from Haiti, partly to the admixture of African words (some frenchified themselves). It had a pronounced black majority.[38]

A quarter of the people in Havana were born outside the province. In the other provinces the number of internal immigrants was negligible. For the first time in Cuban history too, immigration from abroad was no longer important. Over a million and a quarter immigrants, mostly Spaniards, had entered the island between 1902 and 1930, but afterwards the numbers were small.[39] By 1953 the number of persons born beyond Cuba was only 4% of the total (compared with 12% in 1919). Almost half of the 230,000 who were foreign-born lived in Havana province,[40] but many of these people had become nationalized and in 1953 only 150,000[41] were actually foreign citizens. Of these, men outnumbered women by over 50%[42] and half of these were Spanish.

The high percentage of 'foreigners' had dropped, due to lack of immigration during the depression and afterwards due to governmental nationalization policy, which caused the repatriation of many non-Cuban West Indians. Another factor was a change in the nationality law in 1940, whereby Cuba, following the U.S. in this as in everything, considered all those born in her territory, even from foreign parents, as Cuban, unless at twenty-one they renounced this and chose the nationality of the father.

Partly as a result there were now only half as many Spaniards in Cuba

---

[38] The population of other cities in 1953 were: Camagüey 110,000, Matanzas 64,000, Santa Clara 77,000, Cienfuegos 58,000, Guantánamo 64,000, Cárdenas 44,000, Pinar del Río 40,000, Sancti Spiritus 38,000.

[39] 1,280,000. *Investment in Cuba,* 177.

[40] Census of 1953, xxxiv. Foreigners (i.e. born abroad)

1953	230,431
1943	246,551
1931	436,897
1919	339,082
1907	228,741
1899	172,535

[41] 149,327.

[42] 102,612 men to 46,715 women. 74,561 were Spanish, 6,503 U.S., 27,543 Haitian (nearly all in Oriente or Camagüey), 14,421 'English' – mostly Jamaican, and also mostly in the east.

as there had been even ten years before. Many workers had gone back to Spain during the depression and then, due to Spain's own condition and Cuba's new nationalistic laws, there was no chance of return. Some immigration had derived from refugees of the Spanish Civil War – radicals, technicians, men of experience: these (and here Cuba resembled many South American countries) were an important and often explosive little group afterwards. There were a number of clubs for Spaniards, particularly the old regional ones such as the Centro Asturiano or *central Gallego* in old Havana, both founded in the 1880s. These were much the most effective co-operative bodies in Cuba, owning clinics and hospitals, whose separate identity had in the past indeed given rise to acute political tension. Spanish working class immigrants continued to be called Gallegos even though many did not come from Galicia. The Cubanization law of 1934 had driven many Spaniards out of industrial jobs to become taxi drivers, servants, waiters. Spaniards still dominated the Church, which was therefore the more ineffective.[43]

There were about 16,000 Chinese in Cuba, almost all male, as in the past: half were in Havana province, many of them market gardeners.[44] In Havana the Chinese had a monopoly over laundering, and there was also Chinatown. The Chinese population not surprisingly was decreasing, though Chinese marriages with white or black had been common and those half-yellow, half-white usually regarded themselves (and were so regarded) as white. The Chinese were held to be homosexual by many – again scarcely surprisingly.[45] There were several Chinese clubs, and the Kuomintang had a branch. The Chinese themselves, on the other hand emphasized the part played by Chinese in the war of independence and in other struggles.[46]

8,000 Jews were supposed to live in Cuba, 5,000 in Havana. Many came from East Europe after the First World War. About three-quarters were engaged in small retail trades. A Jewish Chamber of Commerce and other Jewish commercial associations existed in Havana, and the Havana Jews had been important during the formation of the Cuban Communist party.[47]

6,500 U.S. citizens were formally residents of Cuba but many more lived there for short periods. There were in addition a group of English and Canadian businessmen, all together forming an important community. Most were executives, others owned property inland. They lived at Vedado, Miramar, latterly in El Country Club, in attractive modern

[43] See below, 1127.
[44] Census of 1953, 89.
[45] Ortiz, *Negros Esclavos*, 12.
[46] See, for instance, Juan Jiménez Pastrana, *Los Chinos en las Luchas por la Liberación Cubana, 1847–1930*, a revolutionary account.
[47] See above, 577.

houses, almost always with servants. They would be seen most often at the Country Club itself, the Havana Yacht Club, the Miramar Club, centres of cocktails known by their English names. Many ABC women belonged to a Women's Club, concerned with good works, or the Mothers' Club, where there were tea dances for children. The Women's Club met at a building built by the Masons, where the Little Theatre and th Choral Society presented their productions.

The ABC colony exercised an influence disproportionate to its numbers. Because of the wealth of the countries from which they came, and their self-confidence, they set the tone of upper-class social life. The Cuban upper middle class was imitative and easily copied U.S. modes of behaviour. All rich Cubans had money in North America, most had been educated there or would send their children to be educated there, many looked on North America as their social guarantor: some were really more North American than Caribbean. In return, North Americans who lived in Cuba a long time became gradually Cubanized, their fates entangled with Cuba's.

The Cubans, however, modelled their eating habits on Europe, not the U.S.: two meals a day, one at noon, one at night. Small cups of delicious coffee were also drunk at all hours in offices, in little screws of paper. Mutton or lamb being unknown, the Cubans ate beef or veal, sometimes pork. Most meat was sold fresh without refrigeration and supplies were therefore unsteady. Native pigs gave pork, but little ham, bacon or lard. Cuban bread traditionally resembled Spanish, but by the 1950s the vile U.S. style was being introduced, particularly in the Havana district, where there was modern machinery, including meaningless wrapping equipment. There happily remained, however, many Cuban bakeries, since the old Cuban loaf was not easily mechanized.

The Cuban dishes *par excellence* were still chicken with rice (much rice was usually imported till the 1950s) and soup of black beans (also about half imported). Rice was in great demand, but since so much was imported from the U.S. (before the war, from the East) it was expensive. Plantains – banana vegetables – were used both green and ripe, sometimes cooked as chips. Other vegetables often used were sweet potato (*boniato*), malanga, yucca, yam and some ordinary potatoes. Green vegetables were mostly unknown and fruit was not much eaten.

The Cubans were fairly abstemious. The upper classes drank whisky, brandy and a little French or Spanish wine. The rest drank rum, *aguardiente* and local gin or beer. Coca-cola, Pepsi-cola, Canada Dry ginger ale, were as well-known in Cuba as in the U.S.: all these had Havana subsidiaries. Exquisite *refrescos* (pineapple juice, cane juice, even banana juice) were often drunk. More soft drinks were drunk in the 1950s than ever before. Bottled waters were popular because of vague inherited doubts about the purity of ordinary water, now rarely justified save in inland Oriente.

Cuba ate a good deal of sugar: her consumption per head of 50 kilos[48] a year was only exceeded by England, Australia and Denmark; it was higher than that of the U.S. (48 kilos). In comparison, Indians ate only 10 kg, Italy 15, Mexico 31, France 29. But only at rather low levels can consumption of sugar per head be regarded as an index of the standard of living.[49] In Cuba sugar was often eaten raw, before refining. Many rural families ate vast quantities of cane in the dead season, when they had no money to buy other food. The Cuban consumption of sugar was in 1958 not much above what it had been in 1938[50] and probably higher in the 1920s than in the 1950s.

Consumption of meat seems to have been about 65 lbs to 70 lbs a year, in comparison with 85 lbs in the late 1940s, and about half that of the U.S.[51] The average Cuban's daily consumption of 2,740 calories was adequate, but that did not take into account the high starch consumption and low share of the average person in lower-class Havana and Oriente.

By most criteria, Cuba was now one of the better off countries in Latin America. Income per head lay between $350 and $550 a year, probably nearer the higher figure.[52] The only Latin American countries which definitely exceeded these figures were Argentina and Venezuela.[53] These figures prove little; first they are probably inaccurate;[54] second, even if true they tell little of the nature of the country, its injustice or its poverty in the terms most people think of such matters. The English drank five and a half million bottles of champagne in 1963–4.[55] This could be held to mean that 'every other family had a bottle' whereas that would be an inaccurate picture of the champagne habits of the English. So it is with these Cuban figures. What point is

[48] 1956.
[49] Consumption figures of exporting countries are rather unreliable, but, according to Vitón and Pignalosa, Jamaica took only 33 kg per head, the Dominican Republic 24, and Brazil 36. Cuba clearly ate more sugar than any other major exporting country. Russian consumption figures are also high.
[50] 37 kg.
[51] *Investment in Cuba*, 74; Coléou, *L'élévage et les producteurs*, 68. H. T. Oshima, *A new estimate of the national income and product of Cuba in 1953* (Food research studies, Vol II, No. 3, Stanford, 1961), 219, said 66·1 lb.
[52] No statistics of underdeveloped countries are reliable. These statistics (precise figures being $433 and $544) are those of the National Bank of Cuba and those in Oshima (117). Felipe Pazos, director of the National Bank of Cuba 1950–52 and again in 1959, accepted Oshima's estimate (*Cambridge Opinion*, February 1963).
[53] U.N. Statistical Yearbook.
[54] The GNP figures from which these were obtained vary in different texts. Thus for 1958 Banco Nacional: $M2,738; Oshima: $M3,305; U.N. (Statistical Yearbook, 1961, 486): $M2,397.
[55] *Times*, 20 November 1965.

there in taking an average between the millionaire's income and the beggar's? Distribution of income is the test. However, even if these figures were accurate, they would mean that Cuba, richest pearl of the Antilles, was poorer than Greece, though probably richer than Spain, at that time. The U.S., Cuba's nearest neighbour (except for Haiti and Jamaica), probably had in 1957 an income per head of $2,572.[56] So it would be right to consider Cuba a poor country, indeed one where, though even supposing the national wealth was justly spread, poverty could be regarded as a dominant fact of life; not though in the same category of poverty as India, Mexico, Bolivia or Haiti.[57] Calculations about incomes also give inaccurate pictures of standards of living since they omit not only regional variation but questions such as leisure or climate, which are not only important but have financial implications.[58] At the same time, it does not seem that even by the debauched standards possible the national income rose much in the 1950s. Incomes, according to the National Bank, rose from $206 a year in 1945 to $344 in 1951, and with various ups and downs climbed to $356 by 1958. The average income between 1952 and 1958 must have been about $334; between 1947 (after which prices seem relatively stable) and 1951, $306. These facts indeed offer a good example of how easy it is to prove anything with figures: between 1947–50 and 1951–8 the average income might be said to have gone up 9%, and between 1951 and 1958 it perhaps went up 4% or under 0·5% a year. Supposing these figures correct, incomes in real terms were not much higher than they had been in the early 1920s. Admittedly, from 1929 till the war there had been a slump in sugar and other prices, and that had caused a severe drop in incomes.[59]

The general experience of the Cuban Republic indeed was that incomes were not expected to go up, but rather to remain the same, or maybe drop and then rise again; and that in terms of buying power the peak of all time was the end of the First World War.

These statistics are the explanation of Cuba's economic organization. Cuban society was less underdeveloped than stagnant. Fewer children proportionately of school age went to school in the 1950s than in the 1920s.[60]

[56] *Historical Statistics of the U.S.A.*, 139.

[57] Even if the highest of these figures is taken as accurate – $550 – then the last time the U.S. had such a figure was in 1934–5.

[58] See K. Silvert, 'A hemispheric perspective', in Plank, *op. cit.*, 132–4.

[59] The World Bank reported in 1950 (7): 'In the past decade *per capita* real income has risen 30%. But this [about $300] is only slightly above that of the early 1920s.' During the 1950s there was evidently a small superficial rise in real *per capita* incomes. (For comparison with 1929 figures, *c.f.* World Bank, 38; also, comment in D. Seers, ed., *Cuba, the economic and social revolution* (1964), 12 and 391, and Draper, *Castroism*, 99–100).

[60] See Ch. XCIII.

No new sugar mills had been built since the 1920s. (Admittedly, there had been too many founded very quickly before.)[61] The main income of the country depended therefore on a crop whose structure had been settled twenty-five years before. People talked as if they regarded over-coming the effects of the slump and returning to the *status quo* – just as, in the middle ages, men were fascinated by the vision of *Roma antiqua*, not of the future. Despite the modern buildings in Havana which caught the eye, Cuba was essentially an old society barely maintaining herself, and perhaps affected adversely by the knowledge that in existing world conditions her main product, sugar, could not hope to be sold to more countries than already bought it.[62] The consequences of economic stag-nation were greater since the population went up by 2·3% between 1943 and 1953, and the rate of increase was probably higher after 1953.

The difficulty of knowing who had what is the chief characteristic of most material on old Cuba at this, its sunset hour. Thus there was one physician per 1,000 people and one dentist per 3,000, compared with 1,900 and 20,000 respectively in Mexico.[63] But though the doctors in Cuba had increased in number by over 50% between 1943 and 1953, the history of the Republic suggests a greater proportion of doctors – in 1943 more than half – were in Havana or its neighbourhood.[64] Havana had also 600 dentists out of 1,000; 650 nurses out of 900; 400 chemists out of 660; and even 130 vets out of 200. Clustered round the capital, with high standards specially noticeable in serving the ABC colony, this relatively large number of doctors available to the better-off no doubt exacerbated rather than soothed social tension.

Statistics apart, however, the organization of health did make medicine available to most people except during very bad times. Each of the country's 126 *municipios* (roughly equivalent to counties in the U.S.) employed one doctor to give medical attention. He charged a nominal fee while attention at his clinic or in the hospital was free. In 1934 this worked out in the country as one physician for each 13,000 of the population and one free hospital bed for each 1,700. In comparison, in Havana there was in the same year one poor relief doctor for each 3,000 people and one hospital bed per 180 people: and these figures take no account of the many rich who sought private medicine. The discrepancy between town and country therefore could not be greater.[65]

[61] See Ch. XCIV.
[62] Explained more fully below, see Ch. XCIV.
[63] Draper, *Castroism*, 100, qu. *Statistical Abstract of Latin America, 1962*.
[64] i.e. province. 1943 was the last census year for which statistics were available by province.
[65] *Problems of the New Cuba*, 119.

Everything requires qualification. Many poor people would go to Havana, if they could, for medical attention. Bribery and influence secured prior attention in many municipal clinics. In very poor times, as during the depression, the indigent would be unable to afford the journey to the doctor or even his nominal fee if they got there. The debility of the public service, if less notable than in respect of education, affected the medicine services severely. Many poor people would go to herb-doctors or medicine men. The lunatic asylum at Mazorra near Havana was particularly scandalous, patients being treated callously while the Director was a political appointee interested primarily in his salary (under Batista the Director even seems to have made money by selling the land on which the asylum had been built). Equipment of every sort was lacking.

But all in all Cuban health steadily improved throughout the history of the Republic. The main killers of the past, tuberculosis, typhoid and malaria, decreased substantially. There was no smallpox epidemic after 1897 and no outbreak of yellow fever after 1905. Infant mortality had dropped enormously, even since the 1930s. Thus in 1958 the figure of infant deaths was about 35 per thousand, while in the five years 1928–32 it had been on the average 111: the equivalent, incidentally, to the present difference between the black population of South Africa and the whites. It was therefore appropriate that Aníbal Escalante, a Communist leader for many years and one who must have seen the changes for the better that had occurred since he entered politics, should write in 1961: 'Cuba is one of the countries (of Latin America) where the standard of living of the masses was particularly high', and went on to criticize the argument that Revolution is the more likely in countries where the misery is greatest.[66]

Cuba's proximity to the U.S. meant that it was easy for her citizens to lay hands on many items frequently regarded as indices of social advance. Thus Cuba had more telephones per head than any other Latin American country except Argentina and Uruguay;[67] more wirelesses than any except Uruguay;[68] and far more television sets than any other Latin American country:[69] Cuba indeed had more television sets per head than Italy, a dry statistic but through them Castro turned the country aflame. In respect of cars per head, she ranked above all Latin

---

[66] *Verde Olivo*, 30 July 1961.

[67] 26 per 1,000. *Cf.* Argentina 60, Uruguay 50, U.S. 381, U.K. 144.

[68] Cuba 194 per 1,000, Argentina 159 per 1,000, Uruguay 261 per 1,000, U.S. 945 per 1,000.

[69] Cuba 56 per 1,000, Argentina 19 per 1,000, Italy 43 per 1,000. In 1953 the census proclaimed that Cuba had 78,931 television sets; by 1959 these increased to about 360,000 to 400,000 (Census of 1953, 253; UNESCO, *Basic Facts*, 166). There appear to have been 4,500,000 television sets in Latin America in the early 1960s, so Cuba probably had a tenth of them, a larger share than any other country.

American countries except Venezuela.[70] Havana in 1954 is believed to have bought more Cadillacs than any other city in the world.[71] These interesting facts, however, merely show that for Cuba, unlike most of the rest of Latin America except Mexico, transport costs from the U.S. were small and there was no problem of foreign exchange. The dollar and peso remained interchangeable and Cuba's exports to the U.S. always covered her purchases. The existence of wirelesses and television sets on this scale, by laying the apparent facts of North America's faintly absurd riches before large and often neglected audiences, doubtless whetted appetite for change. Alas, no figures exist for the imports of guns and revolvers into Cuba; but, like other U.S. manufactured goods, they were in constant supply.

[70] i.e. passenger cars: 25 per 1,000 inhabitants, 29 in Venezuela. All these figures derive from *UN Statistical Year Book, 1960–3*. Draper, in a similar analysis, has slightly different figures, taken from *Statistical Abstract for Latin America, 1960*. Robin Blackburn pointed out (*loc. cit.*) that the television sets of Cuba compensated Castro for the lack of an organized party.

[71] Ruiz, *Cuba, The Making of a Revolution*, 9.

The Class Structure of Cuba

The structure of class in Cuba at the end of the 1950s was naturally stained by the hectic political events of the last three generations. The eighteenth-century *criollo* aristocracy had, during the golden age of sugar during the mid-nineteenth century, been largely displaced by adventurous capitalist immigrants from northern Spain. These in their turn had been wrecked in the 1880s and 1890s by the European sugar beet revolution, by the wars of independence, and by the challenge of technology made possible by North American capital. In the twentieth century, as has been seen, North Americans dominated the economic life of the country, despite a Cuban recovery of many sugar mills after 1934. These changes at the top of society, caused by the rapacious demands of sugar, brought shudders and cracks to the rest of the community, though in some ways the life of the sugar worker changed less than that of anyone else during the twentieth century: no new machinery was introduced which compared in its effect with the changes of the nineteenth century, and the life of the cane-cutter with his *machete* had changed much less than that of the Havana businessman, or even the Havana factory worker.

The size of the different sectors in Cuban society is not very easy to estimate, but at the bottom of the social scale there seem to have been some 200,000 families of peasants, of which 140,000 at least were very poor, owning, renting or 'squatting' on not much more than one *caballería* of land.[1] Some squatters (*precaristas*) became cane-cutters during the harvest. Many small farmers lived in very precarious circumstances, despite laws introduced since 1934, which were designed to help them – and in many cases did. In the Sierra Maestra, for instance, there was a state of half civil war long before Castro set up camp there in 1956, between landlord's agents and *precaristas* and, in disturbed times armies or landlords often treated peasants with complete callousness. Thus in the 1950s Benito Taboada Bernal, being friendly with Batista's president of the Senate, Anselmo Alliegro, took over with

---

[1] The size of the farm is not a good guide to wealth, since a tobacco grower with one *caballería* (33 acres) was of course rich in comparison with a farmer who planted a *caballería* of cane.

impunity over 1,000 *caballería* of land belonging to small farmers near Baracoa.[2]

Alongside this large peasant population, there were in Cuba some 600,000 rural workers, of whom well over half were cane-cutters, only employed fully during harvests. Some of these naturally had a few chickens and a little land of their own. Unlike the days of slavery, these workers were clearly differentiated from the 100,000 or so workers on sugar mills, the aristocrats of the labour force, well organized and dominant in the union system both under the Communists (before 1947) and with Mujal (after 1947). Next in social status came the 400,000 or so families of the Cuban urban proletariat, also well organized in unions. Alongside them were to be found perhaps 200,000 petty bourgeois families, street vendors, waiters, servants, dancers, parasitic in the sense that they lived off the rich or the tourists, uncertain in number since many were seasonally unemployed.

Finally, there was a large class of permanently or partially unemployed, half of them perhaps living in the shanty towns which were a characteristic of Havana or of Santiago as of most Latin American cities and perhaps one-half would-be rural workers, or at least countrymen. This group perhaps numbered 650,000, or a third of the labour force in some months of the year, such as May and June and September and October, though the figure may have dropped to about 400,000 or even below in the rest of the year.[3]

By the criteria used most often, Cuba had in the 1950s a large middle class: 53,000 persons had gained a university degree or diploma, just under 70% men; 86,000 were classified as professional or technical men – half that number being teachers;[4] another 90,000 were executives or directors of companies. There were 6,000 civil servants. As for what is usually referred to, inaccurately, slightingly, but nevertheless usefully, as 'the lower middle class', there were about 140,000 office workers and 120,000 salesmen.[5] In addition there were in the 1950s the enormous number of 185,000 officials, either national or local, 11% of the total population in employment, and most of

[2] Dr Carlos Rafael Rodríguez commented later that 'after 1952 all signs of legality vanished in the countryside' (Carlos Rafael Rodríguez, *La Revolución Cubana y el Período de Transición*, University of Havana mimeographed, folleto II). This is an excellent study, full of useful information.

[3] I have here largely followed the figures of Dr Carlos Rafael Rodríguez, *op. cit.* Slightly different figures are given by Robin Blackburn in *Prologue to the Cuban Revolution*. Both, however, base their estimates on the report of the *Consejo Nacional de Economía* of 1958. That document actually estimated overt unemployment at 361,000 unpaid workers (i.e. those who worked free for relations or parents) at 154,000, and partially unemployed (i.e. those who worked less than thirty hours a week) at 150,000.

[4] Census of 1953, 123–4.

[5] Census of 1953, 204–5.

them ill-paid, corrupt and the creatures of one or other of the leading politicians.[6]

To the size, intelligence and resilience of this Cuban middle class, many writers have paid special tribute.[7] That it was large is certain. But nevertheless, it had several unique characteristics which differentiated it from other middle classes in Latin America. First, it was not flanked by powerful landowners or by an upper class. The Cuban aristocracy had disintegrated during the sugar crisis between the two wars of independence. Old families such as the Calvos, Montalvos, and Pedrosos, remained, but not as latifundistas, the owners of half a province such as persisted in nearly all the rest of Latin America.[8] No descendant of an original grantee from the Spanish Crown owned a sugar mill in the 1950s. Instead, the largest and most productive estates were the property of companies, now mostly in name Cuban, but in the recent past mostly North American. Some aristocrats (Agramontes, Betancourts) held large cattle ranches in Camagüey, but these were not the greatest in the island. Others held cane *colonia*, sometimes being rich men: the list of big *colonos* in 1959 included a Zulueta, several Sotolongos, and an Iznaga. Others still more typically were in Havana, doubtless living well on stocks or high incomes, but essentially business men: such a one was Víctor Pedroso, president of the Bankers' Association and also of the Havana Yacht Club. Naturally, this section of society mixed extensively with the U.S. community: appropriately Elena Montalvo, descendant of all the oligarchy of the nineteenth century, married the elder son of Dayton Hedges, the textile millionaire; but if successful North Americans got their wives from the old Cuban families, the old Cuban families often got their standards, their dress, their drinks (as well, of course, as cars, telephones, radios and refrigerators) from the U.S. As the poet Pablo Armando Fernández put it to a North American traveller, 'Even our bad taste was imported'.[9] Other aristocrats had sunk rather lower: thus the Marqués de Almeiras was an employee at the Emergency Hospital, Havana.[10] In general, however, whereas, elsewhere in Latin America, rich business men made themselves landowners, in Cuba landowners made themselves, if they could, into businessmen. This is not to say that there were no rich in Cuba, of course; indeed, though it is hard to prove statistically, there were

[6] World Bank, 453. 80% of the national budget was spent on salaries in 1950, less later.

[7] Thus Gino Germani, in *Social Aspects of Economic Development in Latin America* (Paris UNESCO), 229, says Cuba had 22% in the middle and upper strata. Carlos María Raggi Ageo, *Materiales para el estudio de la clase media en la América Latina*, II, 79, said in 1950 that 33% (at least) of the economically active Cubans were middle class. Draper discusses the subject in *Castroism*, 76 ff., and Felipe Pazos, in *Cambridge Opinion*, February 1963.

[8] Except in Mexico and Bolivia.

[9] Warren Miller, *Ninety Miles from Home* (New York, 1961, 32).

[10] *Havana Post*, 15 September 1957. He was Abelardo de Zuazo.

probably more Cuban millionaires per head of population than any-where south of Dallas – millionaires in dollars, too, not Mexican *pesos* or Venezuelan *bolívares*. But they were rich as capitalists, not men of land, though they might buy country estates as symbols of prestige and keep them half uncultivated. They were men of Havana, not of the country – a fact which lessened the likelihood of regional hostility to-wards a government (one of the chief difficulties in other parts of Latin America: thus in Mexico even the left wing ex-President Cárdenas was the master of his own province). They had also been implicated in all the political and commercial booms and eclipses of the last fifty years; they had no Olympian prestige, no social standing beyond politics.[11] The foremost North American student of Cuban society before revolution indeed concluded that there was no national middle class in Cuba.[12] He was right, in the sense that they were 'upper' not 'middle'. His belief was that Cuban society, despite settlement of the island a century before permanent white settlement in North America, had never articulated itself. In fact, there had once been a certain society worthy of the name – that of the oligarchy of the early nineteenth century. This had been ruined by technological change, war and revolution. Also, though firm after its fashion, it had been based on slavery and, even more artificial, the slave trade. That world had vanished along with the *volante*, the liveried *calesero*, the fast slave ships with their raking masts, that had so entranced Theodore Canot in Havana harbour. The old order changed but gave place to nothing new. From the 1880s on-wards Cuba was a society of adventurers. Political independence brought interludes of hectic prosperity, never freedom from unrest. Wealth was made by speculation. North Americans burst into the country in the good times, and broke out again in the bad. Poor men became rich, the rich poor. The Dance of the Millions in 1920 and the depression of 1929–33 affected the Cuban middle class almost as severely as the collapse of the mark and the depression did the German middle class. Though the urban *bourgeoisie* of Havana was stratified into classes distinguished by numerous symbols of status, there was much social mobility. The more intelligent the observer, the more bewildered he became. Meantime, the bottom third of society, maybe the bottom half, was the unintegrated black or mulatto world, a world still half sub-consciously longing for the unobtainable 'Guiné', the dream world of Africa, where

All live happy
A-dancing in de patios

[11] This argument has also been developed in a contribution by the author, 'Middle Class Politics and the Cuban Revolution', in *The Politics of Conformity in Latin America*, ed. Claudio Véliz (Oxford University Press (1967).
[12] Lowry Nelson, 139.

Where all God's children
Ain't sol' fuh money.[13]

Perhaps the survival of the Negro world, the actual expansion of 'criminal anthropology' (as whites from Castile referred to Afro-Cuban ritual), exacerbated the tendency for two classes, one rich, one poor.

The second characteristic of the Cuban middle class was its peculiar frustration. Relatively prosperous, as was evident to any casual visitor to Havana, the middle class of the 1950s was strongly affected by the stagnation in the economy, so that everywhere there seemed a lack of opportunities – political, social, and also, partly because of the labour laws, economic. The frustration was specially strongly felt by young men just leaving the University, and indeed in some ways the middle class in Cuba felt more acutely frustrated than did the workers. Young men were specially pleased to find in the U.S. a kind of perfect scapegoat, while Batista's dictatorship, relatively kid-gloved to begin with, but becoming needlessly cruel and superficial, acted as a catalyst to all these feelings.

The shifting character of the middle class is well illustrated by the most unsteady rise in the number of servants: in 1899 there were over 40,000 servants.[14] Most were black;[15] over 6,000 were under fifteen; half the male servants and two-thirds of the women were illiterate. By 1907 (a lean year) the number of servants had fallen slightly.[16] Native Cubans were exceeded by white foreigners, mostly Spaniards.[17] Between a third and a half were in the city of Havana. By now half could read, and most of those in Havana could do so.[18] Twelve years later, in the golden days of sugar production just after the First World War, servants had doubled, to over 80,000.[19] Over half were now male, and now over half were white.[20] In 1943, after the depression, the servant force had dropped back to the same in numbers as in 1907 – a little over 40,000,[21] half being black or mulatto. The foreign white had dropped to about 3,500,[22] even though the Cubans' Alien Labour law had forced some Spaniards into domestic service. Over half were in

---

[13] Castro Alves, the 'poet of the slaves', qu. C. M. Lancaster, 'Gourds and Castanets', *Journal of Negro History*, vol. 28, 78 (January 1943).

[14] 41,464 according to the census.

[15] Census of 1899, 463: 11,289 male and 17,390 female, to 3,171 and 4,267 native white; 4,197 and 1,150 foreign.

[16] 39,312.

[17] Census of 1907, 545.

[18] *Ibid.*, 566.

[19] 83,157. Census of 1919, 145.

[20] Foreign whites (chiefly Spaniards) numbered 21,000 and Cuban white 25,000. 1,500 boys and 2,000 girls were under fifteen. Over half could read.

[21] 43,795.

[22] Census of 1943, 1114.

Havana.[23] The average wage was under $30 a month.[24] Ten years later, thanks to the post-war prosperity, servants again numbered over 70,000, an increase of well over half since 1943.[25]

The professional middle classes in Cuba were, as in most other places, less than half the total group who can be described as the *bourgeoisie*:[26] thus in 1953 there may have been about 20,000 schoolteachers together with about 40,000 others who could conceivably have been so regarded. The nearly 100,000 business men, merchants, bankers, other administrators or directors of enterprises had committed themselves deeply to Batista as they had to all previous regimes except Grau's. There was hardly a commercial body which had not visited the national palace in 1957 to express its congratulations to Batista on his escape from assassination at the hands of a group which, if not now precisely in power, was nevertheless closely associated with it.[27] In 1958, some prominent business men (such as Vilaboy, of Cubana Airways, or the Shell Manager) fled. Several were imprisoned, perhaps to be tried, perhaps not. Others changed their politics hastily and congratulated the revolutionary government, assuring them of their support in large advertisements in newspapers. But the business community was diminished in the public mind. Some rich men such as Pepín Bosch of Bacardí had supported Castro and others (along with the North American-owned Telephone Company) paid their taxes in advance to assist the new government. This availed them little. Along with news of atrocities[28] there also became known in January 1959 documentary evidence of all sorts of corrupt practices: most striking, perhaps, was the revelation of how some employees of the Telephone Company had managed to escape criticism when it raised prices in 1957:

There is a simple reason why the larger sections of the press are not complaining. They received their regular contribution ... in addition to the above-board advertising, thus getting paid more than double. So the only dissatisfaction came from *Bohemia*, the newspapers *Excelsior* and *El País*, and José Pardo Llada, the wireless commentator.[29]

[23] 23,260. *Ibid.*, 1120.

[24] *Ibid.*, 1205.

[25] 71,561. Thanks to the decline in the detail and quality of information given in the Census of 1953 in comparison with 1943, it is not clear how these were divided. Maybe I have shown excessive credibility in accepting these figures. They seem, however, *vraisemblable* in view of other evidence.

[26] e.g. in the U.S. professional, technical and kindred persons numbered five million; managers, officials and proprietors (except farmers) numbered 5·2 million (*Hist. Stat.*, 75).

[27] See above, 931.

[28] The exaggeration of the numbers killed had the political effect of blackening the regime of Batista and its collaborators even further – which was its intention: 'What were they doing when Batista was murdering our sons?' The exaggeration does not mean, of course, that the question was not pertinent.

[29] A photocopy of this document was printed *in extenso* in *Revolución*, 18 January 1959.

This clear alienation of the business world at the start of 1959 had a historical background. There had always been a tendency among Cuban captains of industry to regard politics and government as something to be left on its own, to be ignored as a creative force if at all possible; there were traces in this of the old Spanish situation where creoles were excluded by law from a leading part in government. Although sugar developers of the nineteenth century needed the Spanish government to guarantee the continuance of the slave system by force, no doubt they also found the Spanish regime useful, since it enabled them to abdicate political duties and responsibilities. For much of Cuban history under the Republic, the Cuban *entrepreneur* looked on politics rather as U.S. men of business did in the thirty years following the Civil War. In a sense, they were right. Cuban politics in the twentieth century were at least as poor-spirited as those of the U.S. in the age of Blaine. Julio Lobo refused the secretaryship of the Cuban Treasury under Grau San Martín on the ground that the administration was corrupt. If they could not keep out, business men tried simply to secure that government held the ring to enable them to prosper. Power, they appreciated, lay in New York, not Havana.

Many 'Cuban' business men were North Americans. Many merchants were still Spaniards, as they had been at the start of the century. Such 'foreigners' (as they were referred to in law, though everyone knew that that phrase meant North American or Spanish citizens) could not take part in politics. This in turn had counter-productive consequences. The holding of large sections of capital in a country by foreigners deprives that country of the effects of their power. They are powerful but they cannot as foreigners be responsible.[30]

Typical perhaps of the Cuban-U.S. relation was the Hedges family, already mentioned; the father, Dayton Hedges, son of a New York farmer and a small contractor in Long Island before 1914, came to Havana in the boom years, in 1919. He bought up electrical businesses, made a success of them and sold out to the Cuban Electrical Company in 1928. With the capital so adroitly gathered, he established a large cattle estate and his famous textile business. He also began to grow cotton, which had been neglected in Cuba for a century. He received various Cuban honours, such as the Order of Céspedes, and founded a golf tournament with his name – for the American and English Club. Grateful workers financed a bust of him in marble at the textile factory. In the 1940s he was rich enough to found a big rayon factory in Matanzas. One of his sons married Elena Montalvo, another had been twice

---

[30] Robin Blackburn therefore concluded (*Prologue to the Cuban Revolution*) that there was in Cuba no 'national bourgeoisie', alluding to the variety of racial and national origins of the major entrepreneurs.

president of the American Club, and a daughter had married a Cuban engineer working in her father's firm. The family were intimate friends of Batista. One village changed its name to Dayton Hedges, and Hedges also founded a model village for his workers where no rent was paid. He was followed as president of the Rayon and Textile Companies by his two sons. When Dayton Hedges died in 1957 his funeral was attended by Batista, most of his cabinet and the British and U.S. ambassadors; although Dayton's sons were in fact Cuban, one of *their* sons was nevertheless a U.S. marine and both were educated in U.S. schools. Later Burke Hedges, the younger son – 'Burkie Boy' to his friends – became Batista's ambassador to Brazil. The total Hedges fortune in Cuba amounted to $M35 in 1958-9.[31]

Cuba in general lacked, apart from the Spanish clubs, the solid voluntary institutions, the benevolent societies and the independent groups of middle-class worthies which characterize North America and Europe and help greatly in limiting executive power. But there were some professional groups of importance, such as the freemasons. The Havana Lodge was supposed to be the biggest in Latin America. It was a powerful and dignified group of business companions, perhaps 50,000 strong,[32] all more or less rationalist. Some of its leaders still believed that in being anti-Catholic they were being revolutionary. They recalled with complacency their *confrère*, Martí, and their heroic role as a division of the rationalists of Spain in the last days of the Inquisition. The Grand Master, Carlos Piñeiro, had founded a big technical college, the so-called Universidad José Martí, in Havana. Like the Baptists, their links with North America were close. There was an English-speaking lodge in Havana, founded during the U.S. military occupation. In the 1950s, the Masonic Temple held few secrets. Like the masons of continental Europe, they rejected the idea of 'The Grand Architect'. Their headquarters were of use even in the struggle against Batista: for instance, the group of Ortodoxo youth who provided the backbone of revolutionaries at Moncada had been wont to meet in the Freemason's Hall at Artemisa. In January 1959, the lodge Hijos de América demanded that the masons of the world unite to back the revolution,[33] but the masons, unlike the workers, had much to lose. This appeal signified merely an alignment with the *status quo*. They had not thereby saved themselves from charges of collaboration with the tyrant.

There were other professional associations. Any job demanding a university degree meant that the holder joined a special college (*colegio*) which tried to maintain standards. 203 colleges guaranteed middle-class

[31] *Havana Post*, 5 June 1957.
[32] H.A.R., xv, 805.
[33] *Revolución*, 26 January 1959.

professional practice with as much energy as they could. In the disturbed political atmosphere, which had lasted as long as anyone could remember, these colleges often became involved in politics. The College of Lawyers (of which Miró Cardona, the new prime minister, was Dean) and the College of Journalists were constantly asked to 'take a stand': so were the colleges of dentists, doctors, vets, architects, all men of good will. They often did, but they did not take to the hills. Since a policy of war had in 1959 conquered, the standing of these professional groups was automatically diminished. They had some heroes to offer in the new epic age now beginning but even a man such as Pelayo Cuervo, killed by the Country Club lake, was tarnished by the accusation of compromise with the old political parties and the belief that he would have accepted something short of Batista's unconditional surrender. 'All that was best in Cuban public life' died with Pelayo Cuervo; and the Country Club lake was a sadly appropriate spot for such a departure.

Black Cuba

In the 1950s the Negro or mulatto population was described as being under one-third of the total; an accurate figure is hard to give, since in 1953 the identification of this or that individual by the curious and misleading euphemism 'coloured' was left to the innumerators, whereas in previous censuses account was taken of the declarations made by the persons concerned. Presumably, therefore, the identification was inaccurate. At least one other published estimate suggested that as many as half of the total were 'Negroid' and another 20% really mulatto,[1] an estimate with which many intelligent observers would agree. These included Fernando Ortiz, the Afro-Cuban folklorist.[2]

OFFICIAL FIGURES FOR BLACK CUBA 1899–1953

		% of total population
1899	505,443	32·1
1907	608,967	29·7
1919	784,811	27·2
1931	1,179,106	27·2
1943	1,225,271	25·6
1953	{ 725,311 Negro 843,105 mulatto } 1,568,416 *Total*	27·2

However misleading the official figures may be, in comparison with whites there was a drop in the black or mulatto population between 1931 and 1943, due partly to the repatriation of over half the Jamaican or other West Indian labourers who had come to Cuba in the good times of the past,[3] partly to the effects of the depression which hit the poorest Cubans hardest (and probably more of these were black than white). The drop in the early years of the Republic was due to the Spanish immigration. The decline in that immigration, as well as the general recovery of prosperity after the Second World War, accounts

---

[1] MacGaffey and Barnett, 28. See also Goldenberg, 131.
[2] In conversation with the author, July 1966.
[3] 56%. Census of 1943, 741.

for the rise of the black or mulatto percentage between 1943 and 1953. On the other hand the official figures, which must represent something of the truth, suggest that the 'white' population increased four times, the black or mulatto population three times.

Again according to the official figures, the Negro population dropped from 15% of the total in 1899 to 10% in 1943, and rose again to 12% in 1953, whereas the mulatto population fell from 17% in 1899 to 14·1% in 1953.[4] These changes can scarcely be accurate, given the alterations in methods of examination, but they are all that exist. There was obviously intermarriage between black and white, but more usually between white men and black girls. The voluptuous mulatto remained a symbol for sexual desirability; but marriage between white girls and black or mulatto men was relatively rare. The social area where the races mixed most freely was that of prostitution, habitual criminality, drug trafficking, gambling and superstition.[5] The mixture of Chinese and *mulata* produced offspring of very special beauty.

At the beginning of the century, about twenty municipalities of Cuba had formally a black or mulatto majority of the population, and these remained apparently the most non-white areas. There was little change in fact in the general geographical distribution of the Negroes during the early history of the Republic. This immobility of the black population is one of the many aspects of the matter where Cuba contrasted with the U.S.: the U.S. Negro had little part in the great expansion to the west in the nineteenth century, but moved much in the twentieth.

On paper, even Oriente formally had a majority of white people. Havana province had a total of 350,000 Negro or mulatto people in 1953, or a fifth of the total number; three-fifths[6] of the black population as a whole were considered 'urban' – slightly more, that is, than the national percentage.[7] The birth rate appears to have been higher among whites than coloured. But mulattoes, in Cuba as elsewhere, sought to pass themselves off as 'white' once they got to the towns, and often succeeded, particularly if they became well off.

It is impossible to resolve exactly how (and if so to what extent) the black or mulatto population suffered economically in comparison with whites. In some districts with a theoretically mostly Negro population, the majority in all school ages did not go to school. But in the Oriente towns of Caney and Guantánamo, both of which had a black or mulatto majority, most of those aged ten to fourteen went to school, and

[4] See Census of 1953, 49. Negro population rose from 235,000 to 725,000; mulatto from 270,000 to 840,000.
[5] Ortiz, *Negros Esclavos*, 11.
[6] 943,983.
[7] 'White' figures were 2,365,759 (57·5%) to 1,878,197.

in Santiago a majority of those aged five to fourteen. Proximity to a city, more than race matters, determined this. There was little formal difference between predominantly Negro towns in Oriente and nearby mainly 'white' communities; while Santiago, a predominantly black city, resembled Camagüey, predominantly 'white', in the level of school attendance.[8] The only district even in Oriente which seems to have had an illiterate majority was Niquero, in the south-west, which was mainly white.[9] This was because many workers there were recently arrived sugar workers. Black and white illiteracy seems to have been much the same. In the late 1930s a quarter of students were black or mulatto – doubtless an underestimate.[10]

On paper, half the Cuban black or mixed population lived in Oriente,[11] the poorest province. They had not always done so, but then Oriente had not always been the province with the largest population, and it was natural that, in the early years of the century, the opening up of Oriente should attract a great immigration of labour. By the 1950s, however, the vast majority of Cubans were where they were because they had been born and brought up there.[12] Anyone, black or white, living in Oriente, had, again on paper, a less good chance of a good life than anyone living in Havana (schools, doctors, hospitals and so on being far less provided for), only 5,000 people out of the total population[13] having had any higher education. For educational and economic reasons alone it was not surprising to find black people poorly represented among the prestigious middle-class professions.[14] Even there, however, the situation had changed greatly since the beginning of the century. In 1943 there were 560 black or mulatto lawyers – a large number in comparison with the three or four in 1899–1907; 424 doctors were black or mulatto, a fifth of the total in the country, compared with 10 out of 1,000 in 1899–1907. There were also 3,500 teachers, compared with about 16,000 white teachers, though the black ones were more regular attenders than the whites. Negroes were well represented among musicians, painters and others involved in the arts. In 1943 workers on the average received less if black than if white: 46% of black workers got under $30 a month compared to 37% of white, while 43% of white got between $30 and $60 compared to 41·4% of black. There might be little in that but 6% of white workers got over $100 and only 2½% of black.

[8] See Census of 1953, 117–18.
[9] Though the sugar mill workers at Niquero from the manager down were all black or mulatto (evidence of Julio Lobo).
[10] *Problems of the New Cuba*, 32.
[11] 732,696 out of 1,568,416.
[12] See above, p. 1118.
[13] 1,797,606.
[14] We have to make do with 1943 statistics in these matters.

In some professions, the black or mulatto population was well established. As in the early part of the century, they dominated laundering, sewing, shoemaking, woodcutting, and tailoring. They were on a level with whites among barbers, bakers, carpenters, coopers, and blacksmiths. They held their own, in terms of their percentage of the population, among tobacco workers. They also represented a majority of the servant population, partly out of tradition, partly because those with servants liked to imitate the North American deep South. In unskilled work, the black or mulatto population did more than its fair share – 26% – of mining, building and industrial activities,[15] but had slightly less than its percentage in agriculture.[16] It would be correct to assume, no doubt, that as in 1900, racial distinction in the country was still the superficial visible symbol of a distinction which in reality was based on the ownership of property.[17]

The Constitution of 1940 barred all race discrimination. This worked reasonably well. The situation was described by Castro in a press conference on 23 January 1959 when he said, in reply to a North American journalist, that 'the colour question' in Cuba did not exist in the same way as it did in the U.S.; there was some racial discrimination in Cuba but far less; the revolution would help to eliminate these remaining prejudices; on this topic, Castro added delphically, 'Our thoughts are the thoughts of Martí.'[18] This was Castro's first comment of any sort on the question of race, though, later on, the Cuban revolution would emphasize race questions harshly. Castro might also have gone on to say that, in so far as it did exist, racial discrimination was chiefly a middle-class phenomenon. The Cuban middle class was always rather

[15] In 1943, the professional breakdown* of black or mulatto to white persons had been:

	Black or mulatto	White
Agriculture, cattle, fishing	23·0	77·0
Mining	33·0	67·0
Construction	44·2	55·8
Manufactures and mechanical industries	35·9	64·1
Transport and communications	22·9	77·1
Commerce	15·9	84·1
Banks and finance	9·2	90·8
Domestic and personal services	46·9	53·1
Recreation and other services	39·7	60·3
Professional services	14·5	85·5
Government	19·3	80·7
Various services	28·0	72·0
Industrial and commerce unclassified	26·5	73·5
Average	25·9	74·1

*Corrected from Census of 1943, 786

[16] The Agricultural Census of 1946 did not make any allusion to the question of colour, so we know nothing about the size of farms in this period.

[17] Williams, *Race Relations in Caribbean Society*, qu. above, p.431

[18] *Revolución*, 23 January 1959. Martí's views were expressed in the Manifesto of Montecristi.

conscious of North American habits. Such racial discrimination as there was appears to have been imitative of North America rather than to have sprung from anything special to Cuban circumstances. In the smarter hotels of Havana, frequented by the American business community,[19] racial prejudice was yet another example of the way that some Cubans were always exiles, even in Havana. There was a half racial, half class colour bar in those streets where the upper class walked in the evenings. In the tobacco industry Negroes were cigar-makers and strippers but not sorters or trimmers.[20] Segregation was most remarked in Camagüey, least so in Oriente. No doubt there was segregation in certain enterprises, and a committee for rights of Negroes had been set up in 1934. There were also clubs for mulattoes and Negroes alone, in addition to the religious groups.[21] Relations between Negroes and mulattoes were ambivalent: one proverb ran: 'One Negro may hurt another; a mulatto will do worse.' Fights between black and white on racial grounds were rare, though some seem to have occurred from time to time; for instance in Trinidad in 1934.[22] That racial prejudice in old Cuba was not overwhelming is suggested by the fact that Castro never mentioned the matter in any of his speeches or programmes before the revolution. To read *History will absolve me* would suggest that Castro was addressing a racially homogeneous nation.

This silence on Castro's part was in fact denounced by militant Cuban Negroes. Some years later, a Cuban Negro Communist of Chinese views, Carlos Moore, criticized Castro as an upholder of white Castilian upper-class ways, and claimed that Castro's alleged improvement in racial harmony was a fraud.[23] The question is more complicated. (One Negro commented in the mid-1960s, 'Before the Revolution the only time I remembered I was black was when I had a bath; now I am reminded of it every day'.[24]) In general, since the mysterious and unsuccessful 'Negro revolution' of 1912, Negroes had not played a prominent part in public life. One or two minor politicians had been mulatto, such as Vasconcelos (a minister under both Prío and Batista and Castro's earliest political sponsor) but none had been as prominent, in the second era of Cuba's history as a Republic, as Morúa Delgado or Juan Gualberto Gómez had been in the first. In Grau's time there were five black or mulatto senators out of fifty, twelve representatives out of 127.

[19] See above, p. 1101
[20] *Problems of the New Cuba* (1935), 32.
[21] Discussed below.
[22] Grant Watson dispatch, 12 January 1934. This was apparently a consequence of Negroes pushing their way into that section of Central Park, Trinidad, habitually reserved to whites.
[23] *Présence Africaine*, November 1965.
[24] Evidence of a Bayamés. On the other hand, Víctor Franco among others reports a comment, 'I wasn't a man before. I was a nigger.' (Víctor Franco, *The Morning After*, 63.) The author has met Cuban Negroes who have said or implied both.

Two prominent generals of Prío's day, Hernández Nardo and Querejeta, were Negroes. Locally, black or mulatto politicians were often successful: for instance, Justo Salas, a Negro, became mayor of Santiago
in the 1940s with votes from the (white) *bourgeois* district against black
votes for his white opponent. Negroes also rose to important positions in
the trade union movement, particularly among the Communist trade
unionists: Lázaro Peña, about to reappear on the political scene,
Aracelio Iglesias, the dockers' leader murdered in 1948, and Jesús
Menéndez, murdered in 1947, were the outstanding ones. The chief
exception was Batista, apparently a mulatto with Chinese blood. He
was the Cuban politician who appealed most to the black population,
precisely because he was a man from outside conventional politics, outside conventions, and because his lower-class origins, his apparent
sympathy with the masses, made him popular. Batista supported and
contributed to the *santería* and ñáñigo rites, whose initiates regarded him
as almost one of themselves, particularly in the city of Trinidad.[25] Indeed,
Batista paid 'out of his own money' for a big reunion in the summer
of 1958 for all the prominent *Santeros* (priests) of Guanabacoa, at which
many cocks and goats were sacrificed to appease the 'demons of war'.

Batista's army and police were full of Negroes and mulattoes. Yañes
Pelletier, the officer who arrested Castro in 1953 after Moncada, was
black. In 1943 (the latest year for which even doubtful statistics are
available), just under one-third of the army was allegedly black or
mulatto, just over what seems to have been the national proportion.[26]
In contrast, most active radicals or progressives were middle-class
whites. About a dozen of Castro's followers at Moncada were black or
mulatto,[27] but this was an exceptional event in Cuban revolutionary
history. Batista's soldiers openly said that it was a disgrace to follow a
white such as Castro against a *mestizo* such as Batista. When Captain
Yañes came on Castro hiding asleep in a *bohío*, it will be recalled that
the soldier who found them cried: '*Son blancos!*' 'They are white!'
Some Negroes even owed their lives at that time to the fact that they
were black.[28] It is not clear how many of the rebel army in the Sierra
were black but a majority certainly were not, and Almeida, a mulatto,
was the only officer of importance who was. The black population
as such never rallied to Castro before 1959. He appeared just another
middle-class white radical, with nothing to say to them.

The alienation of the black community from the revolutionaries and

[25] I am indebted for this comment to Sr Cabrera Infante.
[26] 4,039 Negroes or mulattoes to 14,637 white. There were 947 police of African origin to
5,492 hispanic.
[27] See analysis in appendix XI.
[28] *Cf.* Merle, *Moncada*, 264, 268. There seem to have been about a dozen Negroes or
mulattoes at Moncada.

conventional politics had really lasted throughout the Republic. Perhaps they were less without means to rise to higher goals, as Lowry Nelson says, than without aspirations to do so. Like all the Caribbean Africans, the Cuban Negroes were still coping, not always satisfactorily, with the heritage of the forced migration of their ancestors, and of slavery itself. This heritage had meant above all the destruction of the family, the substitution (in some cases) for many generations of the Master for the Father, except in his strictly biological function.[29] The Cuban Negroes were still in some respects demanding real emancipation. Their task of adjustment may have been made easier by the fact that African ceremonies and religions sometimes blended effectively with Catholic festivals,[30] though the task of self-articulation may have been more difficult than in the English West Indies, where the white population was insignificant. It was certainly different. Since race is so much a problem of noticeable physical attributes, the predominantly sallow-skinned Spaniards, with their strong draughts of Moorish and Jewish blood, probably blended more easily, at least with mulattoes, than did the pink or beige Anglo-Saxons, Celts, Germans and Slavs who constitute the majority in the U.S.[31] There was no Cuban society for the advancement of coloured people, though in the 1930s some Negro Communists had argued for an autonomous Negro state in Oriente.

Cuban Negroes were not, however, living in a private world of their own. Their world extended outwards to embrace, if not politics, at least painting and music. If a country is measured by its arts, Cuba was over half Negro. African rhythms, echoes of ceremonies forgotten or practised still in secrecy, dominated Cuban popular music and poetry. The dances, for which the Cubans were as famous internationally as their cigars or sugar, were mostly African: the conga, rumba, mambo and finally the pachanga, were all direct popularizations of religious dances. They were not, however, entirely African and in fact their blend of African and Spanish, with some North American and French influences, was their distinctive contribution. Much Cuban music derived from the 'love affair of African drums and Spanish guitar', as Fernando Ortiz put it, echoing the carnival dances of Negroes at Catholic festivals before they were banned. By 1958 the old white Spanish dances, such as the *habanera* or *bolero*, had almost vanished. The best Cuban musicians, such as Brindis de Salas or José María Jiménez, were black. Nicolás Guillén,[32] the best Cuban poet, himself a mulatto, tried to catch in his poetry the

[29] I am indebted to Dr Sherlock for this point.
[30] See above, p. 517, for further discussion.
[31] Even pure Castilians are of course darker than Anglo-Saxons.
[32] Born 1904 in Camagüey, published *Motivos de Son* (1930), *Sóngoro Cosongo* (1931), *West Indies Ltd* (1934), etc.

rhythm of the songs of Cuba as his master, García Lorca, did in Spain. Wilfredo Lam, half Chinese, half Negro,[33] in his jungle paintings, was partly an intellectual explorer but partly a mediator between a West already modishly searching for new dreams among primitive things and the African and West Indian worlds of green shadow and magic. The same sort of work was done in sculpture by Teodoro Ramos Blanco. Of course there were very few good Cuban artists who were untouched. The best Cuban novelist, probably the best novelist in South America, Carpentier, used *negrismo* in his *Ecue Yamba-O*, and his marvellous novel *The Kingdom of this World* is a brilliant evocation of Negro feelings during the Haitian revolution[34]. Guillén believed that in Cuba a real mulatto culture (which he named *negri-blanca*) was already, uniquely, in existence.

Artists in Cuba itself were in fact specifically mediators between black and white. So too were the folklorists, among whom Fernando Ortiz, the inspiration of Afro-Cuban studies for half a century and grand prosecutor of sugar monoculture, was the acknowledged master. His books too were an exploration: they awoke middle-class white Cubans to the beliefs, habits and myths of the African Cubans, weakening their fear and ignorance. It was hard to distinguish Afro-Cuban religion from lower-class Catholicism. Upper-class Catholics still referred to Afro-Cuban activities as witchcraft (*brujería*) – the word used by the Afro-Cuban population itself for bogus behaviour at rites. Other more timid writers described the development of Cuban Negroes as 'evolutionary disaster', or as inferior because their languages had no grammar.

The Africans introduced words as well as dances. A little Yoruba or Efik from Nigeria, some Fon from Dahomey, could be heard in Cuba, but the use of African languages was on the whole confined to religions, and, like the Sephardic Jews who lived so long in Arab countries, the Cuban Africans otherwise spoke the language of their adopted country, with different dialects.

The nature of Afro-Cuban religions appears to have become more closely identified than ever with Roman Catholicism since the Negro revolution of 1912. Catholicism was regarded by Africans increasingly as a Spanish version of the African *Santería*, the cult of *orishas*, dead great men. The black or mulatto middle class had become assimilated by white Spanish society except on the occasions of participation in

---

[33] Born 1902 in Sagua la Grande, son of Yam Lam and Serafina Castilla; educated at the Academia de S. Alejandro, Havana, and Spain; first exhibition Madrid, 1927; Paris, 1939; New York, 1942. Lived most of his life in Paris.

[34] Alejo Carpentier, born 1904, editor of *Carteles*, 1924–8, imprisoned by Machado; in Paris, 1933–9, and in Venezuela, 1945–59. He was the son of a French architect who went to Cuba in 1902.

Abakuá or *santería*, which therefore became more of a contrast with ordinary life. Changó, god of war, and St Barbara remained an uneasy identification, living in a ceiba tree of the acacia family (the only tree never uprooted by hurricanes), dressed alternately as man and woman; St Peter was still Elegua, destiny in a more malevolent dress, and also known as *El Dueño de los Caminos*, Master of the Paths. Destiny or Orumila, St Francis, was believed to have 200–300 *santeros* (*babalaôs*) in Havana alone – part-time, of course – ministering to his needs: white cocks and palm nuts at regular intervals and in special combinations. Madonnas as ever appeared sometimes with tribal marks. God himself, or Olofí, son of the Earth, a shadowy Holy Ghost rather than a Lord of Hosts, played little part. White people continued to go to these celebrations: senators, politicians and mayors would often make obeisance to these curious deities: '*Yo no creo pero lo repito*' ('I do not believe but I repeat the ritual') was a frequent explanation. One Cuban at least out of four had gone at one time or another to some such fiesta.[35]

There was much interchange between the different Africans, including the Cubans, Haitians and Jamaicans who had come for work in the 1920s or before and also in the 1940s. Some Yorubas, however, feared the Haitians' Voodoo. Haitians were thought to order Zombies to chase chosen victims 'at all hours, with a burning candle':[36] Voodoo had of course a nineteenth-century basis in Cuba as well. The ñáñigos were the most secretive of these groups: membership guaranteed a place in the next world only if kept secret. (They had been banned for a time after 1902 but Menocal allowed them to come back as part of an electoral deal.) Ñáñigos were feared by the whites: white nannies would explain to the children of the rich that, if they were bad, ñáñigos would come looking for little white boys.

The black population in Cuba therefore lived still partly in a mysterious dream world, hispanvariez or North Americanized to some extent, which whites could visit but never really incorporate into their own affluence or poverty. This went ill, inevitably, in a country where materialism had utterly displaced religion. The Communist party, despite its important following among Negroes, criticized the African cults as non-productive and anti-social, but without effect: it was true, however, that the African religions were fundamentally conservative and immobile, if vital: innovations in ceremony were rare except that it seems that during the twentieth century the stones upon which the cocks were sacrificed in Yoruba cults came to have greater and greater significance. These stones, hidden behind a curtain in the lower part of

---

[35] Catholic Action survey, 1958, qu. B. Macoin, *Latin America, the 11th Hour*, New York, 1962, 69.
[36] MacGaffey and Barnett, 209.

the altar, were supposed to have all sorts of magical powers once they had been baptized in blood. On the other hand, it is clear that this was not a wholly modern development since the most powerful stones, which were supposed to be able to walk, grow and bear children, were said to have been brought from Africa by the slaves.[37]

[37] See W. R. Banscom, 'The Focus of Cuban *Santería*', *South Western Journal of Anthropology*, VI, Spring 1950, quoted R. F. Smith, *Background to Revolution*, New York, 1966.

The Church

The Church emerged from the age of Batista with more credit than most supposed possible: Bishop Pérez Serantes was, of course, one of Castro's oldest friends, and the bishops had interceded for peace. Nevertheless the Church remained a Spanish institution with little hold among even white workers, less among black.[1] The Church was an institution of the upper class. The Negro transposition of African rituals and gods into Catholic guises left the Church as such by the way. The situation remained in 1958 as it was earlier in the century: there were few churches in the country; such country churches as there were were poor; attendance in the cities was confined to conventional white families of Spanish outlook, often women only;[2] there were many foreign (Spanish) priests, and a tradition, dating from the wars of independence, of siding with conservative opinion. Those wars had been so long as to make the Church's identification with Spain almost impossible to sever. The Spanish conservative newspaper, the old *Diario de la Marina*, was strongly clerical.

The separation of Church from State by the U.S. in 1900 had had the effect of alienating the Church still further from the country. When Spain fell the Church fell too, to be discredited so much as to be almost a laughing stock. The Church lost its subsidy from the government, losing still more revenue when civil marriage was made possible after 1902, and compulsory after 1918. Since the mid-nineteenth century, there had been no monastic lands. After the Second World War, several sugar mills began to assume the burden of paying priests' salaries and ordinary parish expenses. This subsidy from private enterprise further removed the Church from the masses, though the bishops themselves claimed they did not know of priests acting as agents of exploitation, only of their taking the side of strikers.[3]

Martí, a Mason and an agnostic, had been excommunicated. The

---

[1] The international church seemed to have been bowled over by Castro as much as North American opinion. Thus *Il Quotidiano*, whose views were syndicated throughout the world, assured its readers that Castro was 'not red', was a believer, and so could not have any indulgence towards an ideology of materialism (2 January 1959).

[2] Angel del Cerro, in *Ha Comenzado la Persecución Religiosa?* (supplement to *Cuadernos*, March–April 1961), estimated that 10% of the Cuban population practised Catholicism to some degree and 80% would accept it nominally: the latter figure is open to doubt.

[3] Open letter of the Cuban bishops to Castro, 4 December 1960.

fact that he was known as El Apóstol was an almost open insult. The Church was also thought to be corrupt. Its attraction for women caused it to be associated sometimes with effeminacy. Priests with mistresses were respected. Priests working in parishs theoretically numbered 784 in 1953, but may have been fewer in practice.[4] This meant that there were 7,500 Cubans to each priest, or much more than was the case in say Chile or Venezuela (2,750 and 4,350 to the priest respectively). Supposing all were working, however, this in proportion was less than forty years before.[5] The shortage of priests was acknowledged but nothing was done. About two-thirds were Spanish, though only two bishops (including the popular Pérez Serantes, of Santiago) were Spanish. The primate, Cardinal Arteaga, was a native of Camagüey. If those in religious orders were included, the proportion of Spaniards to Cubans rose to four to one. The social origin of the few Cuban priests was chiefly upper class. There were no seminaries or houses of study in Cuba. Hence, candidates went abroad. The Christian Brothers, established about 1900, were mostly French in origin.

If the Church itself was less influential than in many Latin American countries, it could not be shaken off altogether. It had been in Cuba too long; too many Cubans had been brought up nominally Catholic; it permeated attitudes, even of rationalists. Carnivals in honour of local saints persisted, as in Spain, even if the Negroes or mulattoes converted these occasions scandalously. Cities and citizens were called after saints. Religious instruction might be banned in State schools, but still the Church schools remained excellent – particularly (as in Spain) secondary schools. The Church sponsored many welfare efforts and for many years the Sisters of Charity ran the girls' reformatory with sensitivity and efficiency. The number of Catholic schools rose during the Republic. In 1946 a Catholic university – the only private university –

[4] Census of 1953, 204.

[5]

NUMBER OF PRIESTS IN CUBA

	Camagüey	Havana	City of Havana	Matanzas	Oriente	Pinar del Río	Santa Clara	Total
1899	16	117	89	44	36	20	50	283
1907	32	163	125	34	69	24	58	380
1919	100	374	269	81	165	34	126	880
1931	Not available							
1943	271	1,214		254	462	324	522	3,047*
1953	Not available							784

*Priests, social workers, etc.

(Compiled from Censuses of 1899, 1907, 1919, 1943, 1953.)

was founded: Santo Tomás de Villanueva. Catholic Action began to be active in the 1930s and in the 1940s a Christian Social Democrat movement was founded with an active youth movement.

In the 1950s the political crisis forced the Church to new activity. Neutrality became difficult, though not impossible. Batista continued to receive the tacit acceptance of bishops till the end, for reasons, it was argued, not totally unrelated to the justly famous largesse of Batista's second wife.[6] The revolutionaries of Castro's age criticized the Church as being Falangist, a charge true only in a few minor cases. The Church on the other hand had always denounced Communism; in early 1957 the Catholic *Diario de la Marina* said that 'the failure of religious conviction in general and the abandonment of Catholic principles in politics, economics and conduct is the underlying cause of the crisis' in Cuba. The *Diario* implied that the revolutionaries were Communists. But soon most of the Catholic laity backed Castro. Juventud Católica and other Catholic lay leaders took a strong line. Of the hierarchy Cardinal Arteaga congratulated Batista on taking power, and always preferred diplomacy to commitment, but himself did not escape a blow from a political policeman who afterwards went off with $30,000 in church funds. Of the other bishops, Cienfuegos supported Batista and, possibly sharing in the regime's spoils, fled to the U.S. on 1 January 1959; Matanzas (Alberto Martín Villaverde) was as vigorously opposed; Camagüey (Carlos Riu Anglés) thought it his and the Church's duty to be silent; Santiago (Pérez Serantes) had backed Castro from the beginning and indeed saved his life after Moncada: Pinar del Río was vacant and, as the diocesan administrator (Evelio Díaz) was also co-adjutor to the cardinal in Havana, he committed himself no further than his master.

The secular clergy almost all opposed Batista. Many were arrested. Some were tortured. Priests acted as treasurers to the 26 July Movement and at the very end of December several leading progressive priests were trying to get the hierarchy to issue a joint pastoral letter condemning the government. Was a Catholic renaissance now at hand?

Some thought so. The correspondent of *The Times* in Havana in January 1959 was persuaded that Castro was an ascetic and devout Catholic.[7] His deception was no doubt a mark of the time, possibly explained by a remark of Castro's that he favoured religious instruction in state schools.[8] Many churchmen reacted enthusiastically to Castro's triumph. Pérez Serantes appeared in public with Castro in Santiago. Mgr Roas of the Church of El Caney said, 'God has blessed this

[6] Dewart, 98.
[7] *Times*, 2 January 1959.
[8] Dewart, 143.

revolution, because its principles and ideals are in accord with God's word.'[9] The auxiliary bishop of Havana and Ignacio Biaín, the director of *La Quincena*, the leading church magazine (which had been attacking Batista since March 1958), supported the revolutionary tribunals.[10] Castro himself gravely said that the 'Catholics of Cuba have lent their most decided cooperation to the cause of liberty'.[11] So be it. The future therefore might not be dark.

Protestantism had a toe in Cuba too, perhaps 85,000 strong.[12] During the U.S. occupation of the turn of the century, forty Protestant denominations, from Southern Baptist to episcopal, swept in, establishing missions, schools, hospitals. Like the Communists, they depended at times on foreign support in order to survive. This enabled them to offer 'free religion', whereas the Catholics, with different financial arrangements depended on marriages and christenings for income. Even the Protestants concentrated on towns, though particularly on the less well off in Havana. Two North American writers argued that their activity in the country was hampered by the 'contrast between peasant living standards and even the humblest standard acceptable to a missionary accustomed to life in the U.S.'![13] The U.S. Baptists might be soldiers of Christ but they were not His *guerrilleros*. Nor did any Protestant fit in easily with any typical Cuban festival. Their relations with the U.S. were not, however, held much against them, and Protestants in general, with their high moral code and marmoreal concept of living, backed the revolution in the 1950s at least as much the Catholics did.

[9] *Revolución*, 15 January 1959, 15.
[10] *Ibid.*, 19 January 1957.
[11] *Bohemia*, 18 January 1959.
[12] *H.A.R.*, xvi, 257.
[13] MacGaffey and Barnett, 204.

Education

About a million Cubans or nearly a quarter of the population over ten were officially believed not to be able to read or write. Further, the proportion of illiterates in 1953 was even officially higher – 23·5 % instead of 22 % – than in 1943. The overall impression is that, while in the thirty years of the Republic there was a swift advance in education as in other matters, this had come to a full stop. Perhaps, however, illiteracy had fallen by 1958 to about 20 %;[1] it was higher among men than women,[2] though paradoxically school attendance was higher among boys than girls: perhaps this is explained by the fact that boys left school earlier than girls to begin work. Also, even working-class girls had more time than their brothers, for there was no tradition of labour in the fields or factory by girls. and rural illiteracy was undoubtedly much greater than the official figures.

Most other countries of Latin America had far less impressive figures. Haiti was almost 90 % illiterate, Bolivia and Guatemala nearly 70 %, Venezuela, Brazil and the Central American countries (except Costa Rica and Panama) about 50 % illiterate. Only Chile, Argentina and Uruguay were more literate than Cuba.

The great Constitution of 1940 had provided that education be compulsory for children between six and fourteen in the *escuela primaria elemental*.[3] At fourteen, children could if they desired, go to the *escuela primaria superior* for two years.[4] Like many other parts of the Constitution, this programme was not fulfilled. In 1953 44 % of the six to fourteen year olds (547,000 children) were reported as not going to school. In Oriente, non-attendance rose to 60 %, compared with 33 % in Havana province. Taking the 630,000 country children as a whole, under 40 % went to school; and in Oriente only just over a quarter of country children went. But nearly three-quarters of the town children (600,000 in total)_went to school.[5]

As for secondary schooling, in 1953, out of a total population (of those between fifteen and nineteen years of age) of 558,000, only 92,000 (17 %

---

[1] Estimate of *Estudio*, 826.
[2] 26% of men, 21% of women were illiterate.
[3] Grades 1 to 6.
[4] Grades 7 to 8.
[5] Census of 1953, 119.

or less) attended.[6] Thirty per cent of the teenage population of Havana might go to a secondary school, but only 7% of rural teenagers went to school.[7] For the twenty-one secondary schools were all in towns and there was no free transport. There were admittedly some state boarding schools but nothing like enough. All in all, only one in ten Cuban children between thirteen and eighteen went to school.

Primary school pupils customarily attended for four hours, either in the morning or the afternoon. In some places, this dropped to two hours.[8] Here the situation was worse in the 1950s than it had been sixty years before when 5½ hours' work was frequent, in one long and no doubt often distressing session.[9] Some of the syllabuses were absurdly North Americanized: 'What is the odd man out in this list: ROCKS, FOX, COCKS, SOCKS, LOCKS? The translation was direct: 'PEÑAS, ZORRO, GALLOS, CALCETINES, CERRAJAS'.[10] Nor was much attention paid to the special needs of rural areas. Children in the country usually got an urban education which was more than usually useless to them.[11]

Children who did not go to school spent their days running errands, carrying baskets, collecting salvage and stealing. Lowry Nelson in 1945 commented:

> Almost the entire childhood population in the lower-class urban families might be classified as 'neglected' in a better regulated society . . . [but] this underdeveloped urban group is necessary to the upper class. What the latter would do without them is hard to imagine. They would have difficulty surviving![12]

Many of those who were with Castro at Moncada probably came from this section of society.[13] Juvenile crime had been high throughout the history of the Republic, often with boys belonging to gangs led by older men who taught them to rob and who beat them, *à la* Dickens, if they brought back nothing.

The consequences of this worsening situation had led to an increase in private education. Thus in 1925–6 there were 30,000 pupils in

[6] This may be an exaggerated figure, since *El Mundo* in an estimate qu. by World Bank (p. 413) said at the end of 1950 the figure only reached 54,000, of whom 20,000 were in private schools.

[7] Census of 1953, xxxviii–xxxix. Detailed figures, *ibid.*, 99. See *ibid.* 1118 for discussion of Negro towns.

[8] E.g. the instance in Florida, qu. by World Bank, 415–18.

[9] Census of 1899, 581. The size of classes does not seem to have been so outrageous a problem as the others. Thus, though some teachers in the country might have 120 pupils, in towns 35 was common.

[10] Seen by the author in the Ministry of Education, 1962.

[11] Some schools had changed in this respect: for example the school at Florencia which had instruction in agriculture. But it all depended on the teacher.

[12] Nelson, 186–7.

[13] See below Appendix XI.

private primary schools, in 1950, 90,000. Due to the half-day session and the lack of confidence in teachers, even poor people had begun to stint themselves to put children in private schools. In the country itinerant private teachers often spent two hours or so at each of three different houses per day.[14] In a medium-sized municipality with a population of 50,000 such as Florida (Camagüey), there were 23 state schools (seven of them kindergartens) in the town area, and 25 schools, in the country with 27 teachers; there were also 35 to 45 private schools, only five of which were registered with the Ministry of Education, charging from 50 cents to $2 per pupil per month.

It would be a brave man who named the number of Cuban teachers, despite a formal enumeration of 36,000 in 1953.[15] Many of these, however – perhaps a quarter – were temporarily or permanently retired. In the years under Grau and his supremely corrupt Minister of Education, Alemán, the scandal of idle teachers grew. Grau and Alemán made a massive appointment of teachers simply for cash.

Education was excessively centralized. Though boards of education had once been elected – indeed, the first elections ever held in Cuba were for education boards – the minister now appointed provincial school superintendents, who named boards of education and teachers in each of the municipalities.[16] Books, supplies and salaries were dispatched monthly from the capital even to Santiago. A corps of inspectors also set out from Havana.[17] Maybe such centralization need not have been a source of bad education. But unfortunately the Constitution of 1940 had provided, out of good intentions, that the Education Ministry's budget should never be less than that of any other department, save in an emergency. This made the ministry a centre of graft second to none, exacerbated by the fact that teachers were appointed for life: another well-intentioned provision which led to corrupt practice, since they received full salaries whether teaching or not. There were 'specialists' in music or art or English with no knowledge. Inspectors were also often both incompetent and corrupt. Promotion depended on political patronage or seniority. This too increased the desire of teachers to go to Havana. One observer wrote:

If you take the early morning train from Havana to Matanzas you will notice well-dressed people who get off a few at a time, at each

14 The World Bank calculated $M8 to $M10 spent on private education per year in 1950 (415).
15 World Bank. By a ludicrous provision of the Constitution (art. 52), 'the annual salary of a primary teacher was not in any case to be less than one millionth part of the total national budget'.
16 World Bank. Out of 628 schools built under Grau, Sánchez Arango alleged that only 37 were placed according to need.
17 World Bank, 423.

stop all the way along the line. These are teachers living in Havana and going out by train to their teaching posts. They hate their jobs, hate the towns where they teach, hate the pupils and the parents. Whenever they can say they are ill they do not go. They do everything they can to get transferred to Havana.[18]

Few school buildings were owned by the State; most were given free by individuals, some were rented. This meant that most Cuban schools were not built as schools and that the State paid $240,000 annually for school buildings. Most buildings consisted of a single room, where the same teacher had to teach all classes. Only rarely did country schools serve as centres of community cooperation or do anything to meet the needs of any adult education. Of course variations abounded. We hear of children having to walk three miles to school, of teachers saying that in ten years they had received no books from the government, that the few in use were bought by them out of their own salary, that as supplies for the new school year, they had had twenty-four pencils and a small pad. Sometimes the initiative of parents was considerable; fathers might buy pencils or build roofs or provide furniture.[19] Many schools, however, were badly placed. Sanitation might be good, where schoolmasters made a strong personal effort and lived near the school; and many sugar mills built good schools.

The increasing emphasis on private education was one cause of increased social tension, reflecting the dilemma of 'private wealth and public squalor' also evident in the U.S. For some of the private schools, such as the Jesuit schools of Belén to which Chibás and Castro went, or the Ruston Academy in Havana, gave admirable educations.

Thus the overall situation of education in Cuba, about the time of Batista's *golpe*, was dispiriting. The sociologist Nelson, writing in 1945, thought that little progress had been made since 1907.[20] The World Bank, a rather conservative source, thought that Cuba's educational system had 'steadily deteriorated over a period of years'.[21] In 1925 Cuba had been at the top among Latin countries in percentage of children enrolled in school. By 1950 she had been surpassed by several. The Bank went on with a carefully calculated attribution of the blame to 'political influence and patronage', and gave the warning that unless

[18] See article by Gonzalo del Campo, *Trimestre*, VII, No. 1 (January–March 1949). A similar point was made to Lowry Nelson by the agricultural inspector of Cienfuegos: 'The chief obstacle is the teachers who are so young when called upon to teach in these (remote) places. They manoeuvre in order to be transferred, or abandon the schools for military service, since poor communication prevents them from going to town as frequently as they wish and they do not care to take up the rustic life.' (Nelson, 267.) Mr Max Nolf was told in 1962 that 6,000 teachers left Cuba between 1959 and 1962.

[19] World Bank, 421.
[20] Nelson, 238–9.
[21] World Bank, 403–4, 409.

this were removed there were 'grave doubts whether Cuba will be able to provide the soundly educated adaptable human reserves which are essential to the success of her future development'.

During the seven years of the second *Batistato* there were some administrative reforms: for instance, rural education was placed under a special division of the ministry. 500 new teachers were appointed for rural areas. About a thousand new schools were set up in the country. There were several new technical establishments. The Ministers of Education were less corrupt than Alemán, though they were inferior to Sanchez Arango. But after Batista fled, it was found that there were still a thousand *botelleros* in the Ministry of Education.[22] Twenty per cent of the educational budget was absorbed (in 1955) by the central administration.[23] There was talk of reorganization of the primary schools in 1956. But in general, Batista's achievements were modest. In 1958 as in 1953, according to Batista's census of that year, there had been over 700,000 children between five and fourteen who were at school, nearly 700,000 not.[24] In general, the educational situation in Cuba in 1958 was probably at least no better than in 1952: a social survey conducted in 1956[25] among peasant families suggested that in the whole country about 45% had never been to school and, of those who had been, nearly 90% had not got beyond the third grade. Batista was thus a good deal less successful than Machado in his schools policy.

The situation of Cuban education was further unbalanced since, while her primary school attendance record placed her below most countries of Latin America,[26] her secondary education record, if low in real terms, placed her among the leaders: 12% of those between fifteen to nineteen were at school in Cuba, and over 4% of those between twenty and twenty-four were engaged in higher education. Such statistics are typical. Cuban education was ambiguous. In some sections of society Cuba was as bad as Asia, in some good as New York. The shiftlessness and the drive by teachers to get to town, suggest that the educators were almost as rootless as those they taught. But Cuba could have afforded better than this. The position was bad enough to cause the parents of such children, themselves unschooled, to back any revolutionary cause which promised change.

[22] *Revolución*, 21 January, 1959.

[23] Seers, 173.

[24] Calculations from Census of 1953, 99. There is more than the usual amount of doubt about these figures. Ministry of Education files in Havana caused Richard Jolly to give state primary school attendance as 616,606, on 227 of *Cuban Economic and Social Revolution*, and 642,834 on 174. Private primary school attendance was 100,000 to 120,000. Of course 1958 was a troubled time.

[25] By the Agrupación Católica Universitaria, qu. Seers. *Cf.* Census of 1953.

[26] Argentina was 88%, Chile 85%, Uruguay 89%, Latin American average: 64%. UNESCO, *Projector Principal de Educación Boletín Trimestral*, No. 14 April–June 1962, 146, qu. Seers.

Cuba had now four universities – three state (Havana; Santiago, founded 1949; Las Villas, founded 1952) – and one private (Santo Tomás de Villanueva).[27] There had been no regular courses since November 1956. In 1953–5, 20,000 were enrolled in the state universities, 500 at Santo Tomás. The majority of undergraduates were preoccupied with arts or social subjects; out of 17,500 undergraduates at Havana, 1,500 only were involved in science. After the endless struggles of the 1920s and 1930s, Havana University was now autonomous and independent from ministerial control, like those of Mexico and other great Latin American institutions. The University of Havana had about 450 dons, most of whom had outside jobs as well or did journalism in order to supplement low salaries.

A Cuban of the old regime might argue that there was no point in learning to read in Cuba since there was little to read, and indeed very few books were published and most of those at the author's expense. Nor could the old Cuban press lift its head high in the weeks after January 1959. As earlier suggested, embarrassing revelations appeared frequently of dealings with the old regime, particularly over the Cuban Telephone Company's increase of prices. The only criticism had come from *Bohemia*, the newspapers *Excelsior* and *País*, and José Pardo Llada, the wireless commentator. Distributor of the bribes, it appeared, was Ichaso, of the *Diario de la Marina*, the oldest and most respectable of Cuban papers. Ichaso had been often a collaborator of *Bohemia* and was a member of the generation of 1923 at the university. More than fifty other journalists were quickly purged by the College of Journalists. But there was worse to come: on 29 January a full list was published of the most prominent journalists who were regularly bribed by the old regime, together with a list of their bribes. In effect these people received pay for non-existent government jobs. Nearly all the respectable newspapers had fatally compromised themselves, less by taking Batista's side than by at one time or another criticizing the politics of action: *Información*, *El Mundo*, and *Diario de la Marina*, all criticized 'terrorism'. One good source suggested that at the end of 1958 Batista was paying out to the press $450,000 a month for bribes.[28] Batista himself had bought the newspaper *Pueblo* and the weekly *Gente*, as well as the wireless chain Circuito Nacional Cubano, and the transmitter La Voz del Indio.[29]

Admittedly, Cuba had between sixty and seventy newspapers – eighteen well-established dailies in Havana alone – some of which were read daily (because of the good railways) throughout the island. The

---

[27] There were several private colleges and many technical schools and colleges including a school of agriculture in each province and schools of arts and crafts.
[28] Suárez Núñez, 30.
[29] *Loc. cit.*

twenty-eight main newspapers claimed a circulation of 580,000.[30] It is probable, however, that this figure was no higher, at least per head, than it had been in the 1950s.[31] Newspapers were exempt from corporate income tax and from duties on import of raw materials; and the government paid higher prices for advertisements than private business; and the papers concerned depended on the government more and more.

Several of the papers of the 1920s had vanished in the revolution of 1933, but the old *Diario de la Marina*, founded in 1832, remained, Catholic, Conservative, Spanish, and still in the hands of the Rivero family. *El Mundo*, founded in 1901, also survived – many of its shares being held by Prío, who in the 1950s sold them to Batista[32] – but both these two old papers were outstretched in circulation by recent foundations such as *El País, Prensa Libre* and *Excelsior*, which used subscription lotteries to boost circulation. Immediately after 1 January 1959, the Castroist *Revolución* and the old Communist paper *Hoy* reappeared. The American colony's *Havana Post* went on, though it was a superficial paper; there were many others catering for special interests such as the small anarchist group's *El Libertario*.

The magazines of Cuba were important. *Bohemia*, edited by a liberal, Miguel Angel Quevedo, had a circulation of 250,000,[33] much of it abroad: it was the most prominent weekly of hispanic America. It had been consistently hostile to Batista, and had given a platform to all Batista's opponents and greatly helped the revolutionary cause. Despite its consistently pro-U.S. line in matters such as the Cold War, it was the great liberal magazine of the Spanish Caribbean and helped too to persuade many people that Castro's cause was that of Jefferson.

[30] *Investment in Cuba*, 89.
[31] *Cf.* Chapera, 598.
[32] López Fresquet, 21.
[33] *Bohemia*, 1 November 1952.

Sugar

The world now ate[1] 50 million tons of sugar a year, twice as much as ten years before and six times as much as in 1900.[2] Since world population had barely doubled since 1900,[3] the average man thus ate three times as much sugar as in 1900.[4]

The increase of sugar eating in the ten years before 1958 had been greater than that of any other food. Most of this increase had been in Latin America, the Middle East and Africa, which were now reaching the levels attained by western Europe a century before, though England's consumption of sugar per head in 1858 was higher than the world average of 1958.[5] Latin America, without much rationing in the Second World War, increased its sugar eating a good deal between 1938 and 1948. After 1948 there was rapid growth in Africa and the Near East, and, after 1952, Asia began to go through the same experience, though starting from a level which was only half that of before the war, due to the spoliations of war in the Far East. China continued to have the lowest consumption per head – about 1 kilo per head of population before 1939, 1 kilo still in 1954, perhaps 1½ kilos in 1958. The advanced countries had, however, reached a plateau: thus U.S. consumption had not risen from its level of 50 kilos a head in the 1920s, though it had doubled in the first quarter of the century.

Prices were everywhere artificial. A bricklayer[6] would have to work

---

[1] Either directly or in manufactured food. The use of sugar industrially for products which did not end up as food was negligible. In low consumption countries the use of sugar in manufactured forms was negligible. In the U.S. and Great Britain, however, household consumption was respectively just under and just over 50% of the sugar consumed (Viton and Pignalosa, 15). But see the comment by Mr (now Sir) P. Runge in *ibid.*, 16, fn. 7.

[2] 1898–1900:   8,139,000 tons.
      1948–1950:   28,640,000 tons.
      1951–1958:   47,135,000 tons.
[3] 1898–1900:   1,470,000 tons.
      1948–1950:   2,440,000 tons.
      1951–1958:   2,800,000 tons.
[4] 1898–1900:   5·5 kg
      1948–1950:   11·7 kg
      1951–1958:   15·4 kg

(i.e. consumption had increased in 1958 64% since 1948–50. If China, Russia, Pakistan and India were left out, the average consumption would have been 26 kg.)

[5] England's sugar consumption in 1859 was 15·8 kg (*British Historical Statistics*, 356).

[6] Thought by the ILO to be the largest and most homogeneous group for wage statistics available in a large number of countries.

in England twenty minutes to earn enough for a kilo of sugar, in the U.S. four minutes only, in Thailand over two hours.[7] Factors other than price and income affect sugar consumption; but colder countries, contrary to myth, do not consume more sugar. In general, in 1958-9, the prospect was that tropical or semi-tropical countries would continue to demand more sugar; and within ten years the world seemed likely to need at least 70,000,000 tons or almost half as much again as in 1958.

Despite this unfolding market, the production of sugar in Cuba had been more or less static and was likely to remain so. First of all, at least eight important countries which had once imported all their sugar had begun their own production. Thus while in 1948 only five countries, apart from Cuba, produced over a million tons of sugar a year,[8] twelve did so in 1958.[9] Much of this increase was in beet sugar. The beet production in 1958 of the U.S., for instance, was two-thirds greater than it had been in 1948. U.S. cane, in Louisiana chiefly, had also slightly increased.[10] Puerto Rico had also greatly exceeded her quota of sales to the U.S. and had secured a permanent increase in her quota.

Cuba had already been shielded from the full effects of these developments. Hence the Korean crisis of 1950 caused the U.S. to buy an extra 600,000 tons at a time when there was a risk of a big surplus.[11] The Suez crisis had raised prices in 1957. Cuba continued to produce mostly 'raw sugar', that is, 96% pure sugar but with a thin layer of molasses and some other impurities. A few mills, however, did do their own refining, thus carrying the process from the cane to 100% pure sugar; much of this was sold in Cuba itself.

A further point was that the sugar market of the world was really by now rigidly divided into a number of consuming leagues, controlled respectively by the U.S., France, England and Russia. There was admittedly also a further 'free' world market outside these leagues, but this only constituted a fifth of the total production of sugar. An International Sugar Council, with headquarters in London, devotedly circulated statistical material, but did little more. The English, French and Russian consumers kept themselves to themselves. The U.S. league, however, was open to the English and French suppliers. Cuba was still far the largest exporting country, the U.S. the largest consuming one. The quota afforded the Cubans by the U.S. depended on, first, the previous estimate by the U.S. Secretary for Agriculture of the likely

[7] Viton and Pignatosa, 21.
[8] Brazil, India, Puerto Rico, Russia and the U.S.
[9] Argentina, Australia, Brazil, France, West Germany, India, Italy, Mexico, Philippines, Poland, Russia and the U.S.
[10] Figures in U.N. Statistical Yearbook for 1961, 195. *Cf.* W.B., 712.
[11] World Bank, 506.

CUBA

SUGAR
IN 1959

Mills—▲

PINAR DEL RIO
1. Andorra
2. Bahía Honda
3. El Pilar
*4. Galope
5. La Francia
6. Mercedita
7. Niágara
8. Orozco
9. San Cristóbal
10. San Ramón

HAVANA
11. Amistad
12. Fajardo
13. Gómez Mena
14. Havana
15. Hershey
16. Josefita
17. Mercedita
18. Occidente
19. Portugalete
20. Providencia
21. Rosario
22. San Antonio
23. Toledo

MATANZAS
24. Alava
25. Araújo
26. Australia
27. Carolina
28. Conchita
29. Cuba
30. Dolores
31. Dos Rosas
32. Elena
33. España
34. Guipuzcoá
*35. Limones
36. Mercedes
37. Por Fuerza
38. Progreso
39. Puerto
40. San Ignacio
41. Santa Amalia
42. Santa Rita
43. Santo Domingo
44. Soledad
45. Tinguaro
46. Triunfo
47. Zorrilla

SANTA CLARA
(ORLAS VILLAS)
48. Adela
49. Amazonas
50. Andreita
51. Caracas
52. Carmita
*53. Cieneguita
54. Constancia 'A'
55. Constancia 'E'
56. Corazón de Jesús
57. Covadonga
*58. Damují (antes)
    Palmira o Ferrer)
*59. Dos Hermanos 'C'
60. Escambray
61. Fe
*62. Fidencia
63. Hormiguero
64. La Vega
65. Macagua
66. Manuelita
67. Ma Antonia
*68. Ma. Luisa
*68. Ma. Luisa
69. Narcisa

70. Natividad
71. Nazábal
72. Nela
73. Parque Alto
74. Pastora
75. Perseverancia
76. Portugalete 'P'
77. Purio
78. Ramona
79. Reforma
80. Resolución
81. Resulta
82. Sn. Agustín 'L'
83. Sn. Agustín 'R'
84. San Francisco
85. Sn. Isidro
86. San José
87. San Pablo
*88. Sta. Catalina
89. Sta. Isabel
90. Sta. Lutgarda
91. Sta. María
92. Sta. Rosa
*93. Sta. Teresa
94. Soledad 'C'
95. Trinidad

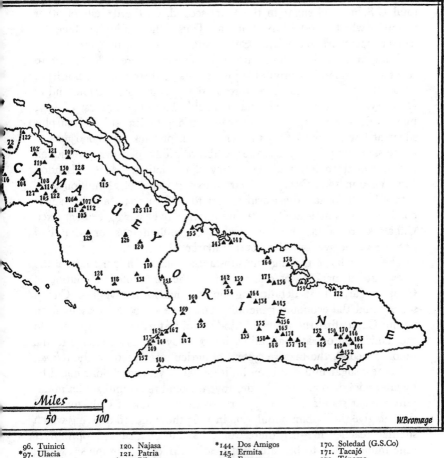

Miles
50   100

W.Bromage

96. Tuinicú
*97. Ulacia
98. Unidad
99. Vitoria
100. Washington
101. Zaza

CAMAGÜEY
102. Adelaida
*103. Agramonte
104. Algodones
105. Baraguá
*106. Camagüey
107. Céspedes
*108. Ciego de Avila
109. Cunagua
*110. Elia
111. Estrella
112. Florida
113. Francisco
*114. Jagüeyal
115. Jaronú
116. Jatibonico
117. Lugareño
117. Macareño
119. Morón

120. Najasa
121. Patria
*122. Pilar
123. Punta Alegre
124. Sta. Marta
125. Senado
126. Siboney
127. Stewart
*128. Velazco
129. Vertientes
130. Violeta

ORIENTE
131. Algodonal
*132. Almeida
*133. Altagracia
134. Alto Cedro
135. América
136. Báguanos
137. Borjita
138. Boston
139. Cacocúm
140. Cape Cruz
141. Chaparra
*142. Cupey
143. Delicias

*144. Dos Amigos
145. Ermita
146. Esperanza
147. Estrada Palma
*148. Hatillo
149. Isabel (Beattie)
*150. Isabel (Jamaica)
151. Jobabo
152. Los Caños
153. Mabay
154. Maceo
155. Manatí
156. Miranda
157. Niquero
158. Palma
159. Preston
160. Río Cauto
161. Romelié
162. Salvador
163. San Antonio
164. San Germán
165. Sta. Ana
166. Sta. Lucía
*167. San Ramón
168. Sta. Cecilia
169. Soffía

170. Soledad (G.S.Co)
171. Tacajó
172. Tánamo
*173. Teresa
*174. Unión

* did not grind since
  the Great Depression

total U.S. need of sugar in the year; second, on the deficits of other countries which also had fixed quotas. Thus if the Philippines failed to deliver their share to the U.S., Cuba had a chance of selling more.

From time to time international conferences were held to try to regulate the small but profitable jungle outside these leagues. But from 1944 till 1953 there had been no restriction of sugar production, and in Cuba every mill produced what it could. The huge harvest of 1952 marked the end of expansion. Instead of trying to dispose of the surplus sugar at low prices, Batista's government kept back 1,750,000 tons to try to save the prices. Thereafter, Cuba restricted her own production and accepted an international policy of restriction.[12] At the London conference in 1953 Cuba received an export quota of $2\frac{1}{4}$ million tons, rather less than half the world export total.[13] In 1958, another sugar conference was held at Geneva and another five-year agreement fixed Cuba's share of the 'free' market at 2·4 million tons, or what had become a little over one-third of that market.[14]

The difficulty of making any substantial increase in her share of the international market was one reason for the undoubted stagnation of Cuban sugar, with its debilitating consequences for the whole of Cuban society and the economy generally. But there were also reasons from within Cuba: first the artificial hindrances to further development, to mechanization or rationalization, imposed by law in deference to the unions; second, the bizarre system of agriculture based on the *colonos*.

No new sugar mill had been built for thirty years and none could be by law; nor could any mill be destroyed. Could the country even maintain present standards? In 1955 the National Bank of Cuba believed that, to give the Cuban population in 1965 the standard of living which she had reached in 1947, there would have to be a sugar crop of over nine million tons, to be valued at nearly $M800:[15] a prophecy which assumes importance when considering the actual achievements of Cuba in the 1960s.

The actual organization of the sugar industry in Cuba was indeed

---

[12] See above, 802 *Cf. Estudio*, 922.
[13] Or 41%. Others got:

Dominican Republic }	600,000 tons
Formosa	
Peru	280,000
Czechoslovakia	275,000
Indonesia	250,000
Poland	222,000
U.S.S.R.	200,000

(H.A.R., September 1953.) Cuba had asked for $2\frac{1}{2}$ million tons and might perhaps have got it if the organizations had not been in such a hurry.
[14] *Cf. Estudio*, 991–2. 1953–8 were referred to as 'years of restriction'. But in fact the years of real 'freedom' were far away, in the 1920s.
[15] Qu., *Investment in Cuba*, 7.

far from rational. Little had been done to develop the possible sugar industry by-products such as molasses (the residue containing no crystallizable sugar, used both in rough form as treacle and when refined as rum) or bagasse (cane waste) upon which industries could have been built. Bagasse can be used for hardboard, for paper-making, or for fencing, but most bagasse was used as fuel, often, once the harvest was under way, the main fuel. There had been little research into these matters, merely prophecy. The cane used in Cuba was now mostly of a variety brought from Java in the 1920s,[16] itself the successor of the old Crystallina, another Javanese plant,[17] and Otaheite. Cuba had never financed an effective national research station to breed varieties of cane which would be best for Cuban conditions. Only one interesting variety[18] had been bred in Cuba. An industry which had been for many years pre-eminent in the world should certainly have set aside the small percentage necessary for adequate national experiment. The Cuban Sugar Research Foundation at Jovellanos only received about $60,000 to $80,000 a year.[19] It still awaited payment of special taxes levied for its upkeep since 1941.[20] Yield of Cuban sugar per acre compared badly with most other countries. This was partly because, admittedly, the specially favourable soil in Cuba made it possible to rely on the same plant lasting longer than elsewhere though there was a big contrast in yields of sugar cane between first and later crops. (The first, plant, cane, often yielded thirty-five tons of sugar an acre, the second, ratoons, less, so that the average for all cane[21] was between sixteen and twenty tons.) This naturally compared ill with more intensively producing countries such as Hawaii (where research had always had a high priority), Peru and Indonesia,[22] but was somewhat compensated by the still relatively low price of land and by the high sugar content taken from the cane – at between 13 % and 15 %, the highest in the world.[23]

[16] Proefstation Oest Java (POJ), 2878.

[17] Crystallina, still used by 90% of Cuban cane planters in 1931.

[18] Media Luna 3/18 produced by Dr Ricardo Beattie at the *central Isabel*, Media Luna.

[19] 1½% of gross receipts would at the lowest reckoning have given an annual income of $M3·9.

[20] See more about this in Ch. CXVII.

[21] Say, 20% plant cane, 80% ratoons.

[22] Average yield respectively 206, 155, and 90 tons per hectare. Other yields in the 1950s were:

British Guiana:	90 tons	Jamaica:	59 ,,
Barbados:	87 ,,	Mexico:	55 ,,
Formosa:	70 ,,	U.S.A.:	53 ,,
South Africa:	70 ,,	Fiji:	47 ,,
Australia:	62 ,,	Trinidad:	47 ,,
Mauritius:	61 ,,	Brazil:	41 ,,
Puerto Rico:	61 ,,	Argentina:	34 ,,

(*FAO World Sugar Economy in Figures*).

[23] Núñez Jiménez, 227.

There had been some slight mechanization of the agricultural side of the sugar industry: for dragging cane to its point of shipment to the mill, the ox had now been largely replaced by the tractor.[24] Tractors were also used to weed and prepare land for cane. 'In some cases an operation with tractors is completed in ten days by ten workers when it took a hundred men three months to do it before.'[25] But further mechanization was made impossible by the law. Fertilization or fumigation by air were forbidden. The use of the continuous centrifugal by which the entire sugar-making operation might be made to work at the touch of a button (as occurred in Louisiana) was banned. Planting and cutting was still done by hand, mostly because of the hostility of unions to mechanization. Thus Julio Lobo had imported an experimental cane-cutting machine which remained in bond in the customs house for five years and eventually was returned to Louisiana when the authorities finally refused it entry.[26] But in nearly all Cuba except Oriente cutting of cane by machine was perfectly feasible – as indeed was shown during the 1968 sugar harvest when one-fifth of the total harvest was done by machine.[27] Loading at ports was also by hand – ten days being sometimes spent in work which probably could have been done in twenty hours with bulk shipping.[28]

The Institute of Sugar Stabilization had since 1931 been the directing force of the industry.[29] An autonomous institution, though always influenced by the government, it recommended the total amount of sugar to be produced each year and its division among the different mills. Its director, appointed by the president, was thus a powerful man, the maker and breaker of fortunes and often subornable by bribes. The Institute also regulated wages, the number of workers to be employed and whether any account should be taken of possible mechanization. Government was therefore much involved in this industry. Given its power, the institute could intervene, under a government willing to be corrupted, to create riches. One such example occurred during the record year in 1952. The sugar market in Cuba was then dominated by

[24] There were 1,888 tractors in Cuba in 1946, nearly 15,000 (all North American) in 1958 (*Estudio*, 1011). Over 90% of the cane land was prepared by tractor and 80% of cane carried in lorries.

[25] World Bank, 55.

[26] Evidence of Julio Lobo, Madrid, 9 November 1968.

[27] This admittedly is a controversial question. For the widespread use of the cane-cutting machine, doubtless much levelling of land and perhaps a less sinuous plant may be necessary. Castro in a speech on 2 January 1969 suggested that in the future cane would only be grown on flat land and during 1969–70 new items of machinery have begun to change the old picture.

[28] *Nuestra Industria*, qu. Reuters, Havana, 7 November 1962. Some attempt at bulk-shipping was imposed on the reluctant Cuban labour authorities since Tate & Lyle, a major shipper, had re-equipped their vessels for bulk-shipping. But the regulations even for this were highly restrictive.

[29] See above p. 562.

two big speculations: one by Francisco Blanco, administrator of Batista's mill *Washington*, an able and elderly man of experience, and the other by the great pluralist holder of many mills, Julio Lobo. Blanco had available between 300,000 and 150,000 tons of sugar, whose price was threatened by the decline in the world market. A national sugar-selling organization was appointed. It was finally agreed that $1\frac{3}{4}$ million tons of surplus sugar should be sold over the next five years and that the market would, in the meantime, be kept down.[30] At the International Sugar Council in 1953, the Cuban representatives were instructed to sign anything provided that they reached agreement fast, since Batista had this substantial surplus to dispose of himself; and these men did accept a figure for the quota considerably lower than might otherwise have been obtained.[31]

Despite stagnation of production, there had been two important changes in the industry during the quarter-century between the two revolutions of 1933 and 1959. First, there was an increase in the number of cane-growing *colonia*. Thus in 1899 there had been 15,000 cane *colonia*, feeding just over 200 *centrales* with cane;[32] in 1936, 28,000, or not quite twice as many: in 1950 there were 40,000, and in 1958 there were 68,000, or an increase of 50% in eight years.[33]

These changes, however, meant less of a revolution in land-holding than might appear: first, many separate *colonia* were in fact owned by the same man, family or company; for the sugar law of 1937 had intervened in favour of the *colono* against the *central*, giving him permanency of tenure, regulating his rights, compelling mill-owners to share both powers and profits with *colonos* and workers, increasing mill costs, and laying substantial taxes on 'administration cane', and so mill-owners themselves got round this law, buying land, perhaps from themselves, perhaps openly under their own name, or under the cover of nominees such as their wives or daughters.[34] Still, the number of real owners substantially increased, chiefly through subdivision among families, but also from the formation of new *colonia* during 'free' harvests, from the recognition of the right of sub-*colonos* to call themselves *colonos*, and perhaps most of all from the improved conditions for all following the law of 1937.

While in the past many *centrales* had depended on their own 'admini-

[30] See article by Pelayo Cuervo, in *Bohemia*, 1 December 1952.
[31] Evidence of Julio Lobo, 10 November 1968.
[32] 15,521 to be precise. The 1899 figure may be an underestimate, since the census did not take account of those who claimed title to estates.
[33] World Bank, 198, for 1950; *Anuario Azucarero* of 1959 for 1958, and *ibid.* of 1937 for 1936 (28,486 to be precise); Census of Cuba for 1899, 524. The Cuban agricultural census of 1946 (referring to facts of 1944) speaks of 29,100 farms devoted primarily to cane. The big expansion, as can be seen, came immediately after the war.
[34] Evidence *inter alia* of Julio Lobo.

stration cane', by the 1950s many depended only on *colonos*, some being tenants, others being proprietors.[35] This explains the drop in the land nominally owned by *centrales* between 1936 and 1958.[36] There were, however, some mills such as the *centrales Niquero* and *Cabo Cruz*, where the owner (in this case Lobo) did control all the lands, by dint however of buying up or out the *colonos*. These mills became technically very proficient, providing for several years the highest yields in Cuba and offering an example from which other mills began to profit.[37]

The *colonos* which were attached to the new mills of Oriente or Camagüey rented almost all their land at low rates; those in the old centre of sugar in Matanzas or Santa Clara might have once had mills on their land, or were perhaps the owners outright. Some *colonos* were rich. But only about a hundred produced over 500,000 arrobas each of cane (compared with nearly 1,200 who had so done in 1939).[38] The list included many names famous in the past history of the Cuban oligarchy who had given up grinding in the 1880s: thus a Céspedes sold cane to the *central Sofía* near Bayamo; Betancourts, Alfonsos, and Agramontes were active in central Cuba, an Iznaga still sold to Atkins's old mill *Soledad*, a Rionda operated at *Tuinicú*, and there were also Sotolongos, and Beltrans de la Cruz. But the largest *colonia* were companies.[39] In 1950, the World Bank Mission to Cuba had thought that 15% of *colonia* were owned by rich persons or firms, 70% by middle-class people, and another 15% by poor persons.[40] In the next eight years, the poor became more numerous.[41] Many of these last were nevertheless people of old families. Thus in Matanzas there were families who spoke impeccable Spanish and who were completely white but who nevertheless had never been as far as the main road.

The *colonos* still received in payment a percentage of the cane which they had delivered in sugar. This *arrobaje* varied from about 48% to 46% of the cane according to the average yield of the mill. Mills paid *colonos* at a ten-months' average price, not, as before 1948, a fifteen-day one. Payment also varied according to the tenure of the *colono*. Those who

[35] See Nelson, 121.

[36] In 1936, 236,437 cabs were controlled by *centrales*, of which 171,160 were owned; in 1958, the figures were 177, 427·5 and 124,667 respectively. (*Anuario Azucarero*; cf. figures in *Estudio*, 651, for 1939.) See *Problems of the New Cuba*, 269–80.

[37] Evidence of Julio Lobo.

[38] See list in *Anuario Azucarero* of 1959, 115 ff; for 1939, see Guerra, *La Industria Azucarera de Cuba*, 1940.

[39] Castro's family estate, run by his brother Ramón Castro, then had an *arrobaje* of 1,640,000 *arrobas* of cane delivered to the *central Miranda*.

[40] World Bank, 198.

[41] Census of 1943, 267. The larger *colonia* tended to be in the east part of the island, the smaller in the older areas of the west. Thus in the 1952 harvest the average *colono* in Camagüey produced 230,000 *arrobas* of cane, in Oriente 150,000 *arrobas*; in Matanzas, Havana and Las Villas the average was about 50,000. Well over half the *colonos* in 1952 (38,000 out of 62,000) produced under 30,000 *arrobas* of cane (*ibid.*, 1009).

rented their land from sugar *centrales* and those who owned land both used this system which, however theoretically fair, tied all *colonos* to their *central*, upon which they depended for transport for grinding, as well as, often, for credit. The system also meant that growers of good and bad cane received the same amount of sugar as each other; quantity, not quality, gave results.[42]

The whole system indeed was awkward and unprofitable. The *colonos* were one more hindrance against the introduction of mechanization. Their reluctance to collaborate also made scientific farming difficult, for example, to try to plant early and late maturing sugar cane in different places around the mill. *Colonos* were also reluctant even to invest in lorries to carry the cane to the mill. One experiment in re-organization was however carried out during the 1950s by Julio Lobo and other sugar mill owners in the province of Matanzas. Different *colonia* were exchanged between mill owners so that at least the most extreme illogicalities, whereby cane might have to be taken twenty miles to a traditional *central* instead of the nearest one, were avoided.[43] This rationalization worked well and began to be copied elsewhere. But this did not remove the *colono* completely, and it is difficult to avoid the conclusion that either the land had to be nationalized or most of it had to be bought up by the *central* for any improvement in agriculture to be possible – either capitalism or socialism was feasible, that is, but not neo-feudalism.

The second big change in the structure of Cuban sugar in the years since the depression was the relative U.S. withdrawal from ownership, primarily due to dislike of Cuban labour conditions but also to the general restrictions on expansion. This began with the sale in 1934 of the enormous Cuba Cane Corporation, which had been begun to exploit the favourable opportunities for sugar in the First World War. North American banks also gradually withdrew from the ownership of sugar mills. One businessman in 1950 commented that he and most of his colleagues 'admit that it is still worth operating in Cuba. But there is certainly far less scope for large profits'.[44] Batista's labour laws, the policy of Cubanization and the Sugar Law of 1937, had all done their work. The consequence was that even in mills nominally owned by U.S. companies, Cuban shareholders were sometimes prominent, some-times even pre-eminent.[45] Thus Lobo for a time had a controlling interest in Cuban Atlantic, and Batista also had a 10 % to 15 % share in that company.[46] Lobo had too a 25 % interest in the West Indies Sugar

[42] *Cf.* the details in *Estudio*, 648.
[43] Evidence of Julio Lobo.
[44] Qu., World Bank, 822.
[45] *Estudio*, 1273.
[46] Evidence of Julio Lobo, 10 November 1968.

Company and Falla Gutiérrez had substantial shares in Punta Alegre, both nominally U.S. companies.

The Cuban Atlantic Gulf Sugar Company, with nine mills in Las Villas, Camagüey and Matanzas, was now the biggest company in Cuba. Its total output in 1937 was almost half as much again as any other single company.[47] It later bought the big Hershey mill near Havana as well, and in the 1950s owned over 600,000 acres,[48] but sold off the Hershey estates in 1958 to Julio Lobo, a deal which was skilfully made operative on 31 December 1958, the day Batista left Cuba.[49] Lobo was at that time a passionate opponent of Batista and so had looked to the future with confidence.[50] (Cuban Atlantic had not known that they were selling to Lobo and they, in particular their manager Francisco Blanco, an old enemy of Lobo, were furious.)

Afterwards in importance came the Cuban-American Sugar Company, and then the famous United Fruit Company. The former had six mills including the huge *Chaparra* and *Delicias*, close to each other on the north coast of Oriente near Puerto Padre, where Columbus landed on his first voyage. *Chaparra*, begun in 1901 under the future President Menocal, had a capacity in 1958 of a tenth of the entire Cuban crop, due in part to its use of the first 12-roller mills, the most important recent technological improvement. Even larger so far as its use of labour was concerned was *Delicias*, built a few miles to the east in 1911. A short time later, Congressman Hawley, the founder of these mills, had bought and restored Diago's old mill, *Tinguaro*, and another Matanzas estate, *Merceditas*. Later still, the Apezteguía's record-breaking mill of the 1890s, *Constancia*, in Cienfuegos, also fell into the hands of Cuban-American who, by the 1950s, owned over 300,000 acres (though they sold off *Tinguaro* to Lobo).[51] The United Fruit Company owned only two mills, *Boston* and *Preston*, but also 280,000 acres; they were reckoned as being together worth $M38 and their annual Cuban payroll was $M10 and 40,000 men.[52]

The most obvious disadvantage, so far as Cuba was concerned, of this still substantial North American holding was that these mill owners would always vote, in the mill owners' association, according to the interests of their shareholders or banks rather than of Cuba.[53] On the other hand, a firm such as United Fruit did make available to employees

---

[47] 1,650,299 sacks. *Anuario Azucarero*, 1937, 45.
[48] 18,510 *caballería*. Núñez Jiménez, 235.
[49] See *Fortune*, April 1963. The broker was Loeb Rhodes.
[50] Evidence of Julio Lobo.
[51] 10,722 cabs. Núñez Jiménez, 235. See Jenks, *op. cit.*, 253, for Cuban-American.
[52] Ruby Hart Phillips, *The Cuban Dilemma*, New York, 1962, 185-8, and Mario Lazo, *The Dagger in the Heart*, 50. For their colonization scheme of 1928, when they moved some 14,000 Cubans from West Cuba to their estates, see *Problems of the New Cuba*, 285.
[53] Comment of their colleague Julio Lobo to the author.

high standards of education and health and entertainment, and such new technological improvements or chemical possibilities as were possible even to talk about in the curious state of Cuban labour relations.

Far the biggest Cuban concern was the large series of interests represented by Lobo, who possessed fourteen mills. Like Tomás Terry in the nineteenth century, Lobo was of Venezuelan origin, though the Lobos were originally Sephardic Jews from Curaçao.[54] In 1959 he was reckoned as controlling almost 1,000,000 acres.[55] Lobo had an admirable record for honesty (the revolutionary government confirmed it on minute examination of his books) and good treatment of his workers. He had, in 1959, as has been seen, only recently bought the large Hershey interests.[56] His efforts at rationalization and modernization were persistent if often thwarted.

Lobo had also in 1959 wide interests in hotels (he financed the building of the Capri and the Riviera hotels), banking, radio networks and shipping as well as his enormous sugar holdings. He was the largest art collector in Cuba and his collection of Napoleonic relics was the biggest outside France. His wealth derived partly from his father Heriberto who fled to Havana after the revolution in Venezuela in 1902 and entered into partnership in Havana with a Spaniard, Galbán, as a private banker and importer – much as the Drakes had started in the 1790s. Julio Lobo began to work in the firm in 1919, a graduate of Louisiana State University (then almost exclusively a sugar institute) and though Galbán retired, the Lobos and then Lobo alone kept the old name – the Galbán Lobo trading company – and the old offices in old Havana. The Lobos sold out most of their non-sugar interests in 1946, by which time (exactly as with the great merchants of the nineteenth century) Julio had moved into the sugar business himself, accumulating eleven mills by 1952, mostly bought from North Americans.[57] The Lobos had also done specially well during the Dance of the Millions when they had wisely sold at the right time. Julio Lobo survived an attempt on his life in 1946 by Eufemio Fernández and the ARG, who had unsuccessfully demanded $50,000 protection money from him. In the 1950s he again accumulated non-sugar interests of consequence. He lived partly in Havana and partly at his favourite mill *Tinguaro*, the Diagos' construction of the 1840s which he had re-equipped as well as he could, given the labour laws, and there his daughter – by a Montalvo – was

[54] For Lobo, see *Fortune*, November 1958, and *Life en Español*, 3 November 1958.

[55] 405,000 hectares, with a total production of 540,000 tons, valued at about $M50 a year. Of these however only about 200,000 acres were cultivated, or cultivable.

[56] He bought Hershey for $M25 on 31 December, 1958.

[57] Lobo bought his first mill in 1926 (*Escambray*), but entered more fully into mill ownership in 1939–40.

suitably christened in cane juice. There too he held literary parties in what he believed to be the 'Cliveden' of Cuba. Lobo, a genius in finance, was primarily non-political and believed 'we didn't care who overthrew Batista so long as someone did'.[58] He sold annually between 35 % and 50 % of Cuban sugar and 60 % of the refined sugar sold to the U.S. He also sold half the raw sugar produced by Puerto Rico, as well as much of the Philippine production. His position in the U.S., as in the Cuban sugar market, was dominant and feared. His fortune was estimated at $M85 in the 1950s by a knowledgeable New York banker.[59] He had contributed neither to Castro nor to Batista and the former had accordingly burned his cane fields.

Next after Lobo among the non-North Americans came the heirs, children and grandchildren, of the Spaniard Laureano Falla Gutiérrez, representing nearly 300,000 acres, under the name of Administración de Negocios Azucareros.[60]

Although sugar was still the industry *par excellence* of Cuba, and although Cubans had come back into the field as proprietors in the last few years, the sugar industry still seemed in some respects a foreign enterprise, a great international exhibition set up on Cuban soil, with foreign capital, foreign machinery and sometimes, as in the 1920s, even foreign workers. In the 1880s and 1890s foreign capital had reorganized Cuban sugar along its present lines. Even with the slow Cubanization of the twenty years before 1959, New York banks continued to finance the sugar warehouses in Cuba and the shipping of it to the U.S. not to speak of holding it in warehouses there, prior to sale.[61] The great U.S. *central*, a magnificent monument of capitalism on the surface, seemed indeed a representation of the 'Colossus of the North' itself, as in the poem by Agustín Acosta:

> While oxen slowly move on
> The old carts creak . . . creak
> They go towards the nearby colossus of steel
> They go towards the North American mill
> And as if complaining as they draw near
> The old carts creak . . . creak.[62]

[58] A remark to the author, 9 November 1968.
[59] *Fortune, op. cit.*
[60] This firm had invested about $M40 abroad for fear lest a revolution should come again as had occurred in 1933. Other important Cuban firms in the last period were Gómez Mena, previously Spanish, (with 6,312 cabs); Manuel Azpuru (2,579 cabs), Manuel Luzárraga (1,571), and García y Díaz (2,248). The Rionda family, still ran the *Manatí, Francisco, Tuinicú* and *Elia* sugar mills as well as extensive commercial interests; but technically these mills were considered U.S. and by now the Riondas were almost completely North American.
[61] W.B., 584.
[62] The author of this poem (written in 1926) afterwards became secretary to the presidency

The number of active mills remained much the same throughout the history of the Republic. A hundred out of the 161 mills existing in 1958 had been founded in the nineteenth century. Though the total number of mills had risen (during the First World War) for a time to almost 200, after the depression they never exceeded 161, a figure which stayed constant between 1946 and 1958. The twentieth-century mills in general survived, those that failed during the depression being chiefly the old ones of Matanzas and Santa Clara – only twelve new mills failed, compared with over 100 old ones.[63] The cane cut in Matanzas in 1959 was slightly less than that cut there a hundred years before.[64] The mills varied greatly in size – ranging in capacity from about 5,000 to 170,000 tons of sugar. Their total value was estimated in 1950 as between $M750 and $M1,000.[65] By any reckoning the big Cuban sugar mills constituted one of the most remarkable networks of capital investments in the world, with their great rollers which were fed in the harvest with a continous supply of cane day and night, and their great chimneys towering over the *batey*, the schools and chapels, the *barracones* for temporary workers, the shops, *bodegas*, houses for managers, and even sports grounds and golf courses.

Sugar was grown on a little over a quarter of all Cuban farms but only for 18% of the farmers was it the major source of income. These, however, were the biggest farms.[66] Two-thirds of agricultural incomes derived from sugar. Nearly half the irrigated area grew cane,[67] while cane covered over a quarter of the total area of the country, or $7\frac{1}{2}$ million acres. But probably not more than four million acres was in sugar production in any single year.[68] The rest was held in reserve. Half a million workers were employed by the industry in harvest time,

[63] In 1899 there were 62 mills in Matanzas, in 1939–58 only 23–4; in 1899 there were 73 mills in Santa Clara, after 1939 only 50. About half the old mills of Oriente collapsed but a nearly equal number of new ones were built there so that in 1899 there were 42 mills and in 1958, 40. In Camagüey 22 new mills had been founded, compared with only three in 1899 – of which one failed; there were thus 24 mills in that province in 1958.

[64] *Cf.* Moreno Fraginals, 65.

[65] World Bank, 795 and 194–5.

[66] Cane covered 60% of the cultivated area. These figures derived from the Agricultural Census of 1945, thirteen years old; but there is nothing else (W.B. 88, 104). Núñez Jiménez (*Geografía*, 226) speaks of 55% of the cultivated area.

[67] World Bank, 109: 45%.

[68] 3·9 million in 1953, 3 million in 1955 (*Investment in Cuba*, 32).

---

under Mendieta and a senator during the first Batista epoch for Matanzas. The labour laws, of course, favoured oxen against lorries.

> *Mientras lentamente los bueyes caminan*
> *Las viejas carretas rechinan ... rechinan*
> *Van hacia el coloso de hierro cercano*
> *Van hacia el ingenio norteamericano*
> *Y como quejandose cuando a él se avecinan*
> *Las viejas carretas rechinan ... rechinan.*

nearly 400,000 as cane cutters, the rest in the mills: this accounted for a third of those gainfully employed in the country.[69] The cane cutters were tough and professional and well-organized in unions. Their work though not heavy was tedious and in neglected fields exasperating.[70] Sugar mills operated a rail mileage almost double the public system, while, in 1950, 80% of the tonnage of the leading public railways derived from hauling cane. Half of Cuba's electric power generating capacity was controlled by sugar mills.

The precise role of sugar in the economy is elusive. Thus between a quarter and a third of national income derived from sugar: a high proportion, but still suggesting that Cubans did some other things.[71] These figures do not show how far the whole economy depended on exports, and exports of course did depend on sugar; thus in the forty years before Batista's final overthrow, sugar accounted for 82% of Cuban exports.[72] Also, in the years since the depression, Cuba had in some ways become more, not less, sensitive to price fluctuations deriving from sugar: several laws in the interests of humanity had tied the wages of many non-sugar workers, and also many ordinary prices, to the price of sugar. These covered railway freight rates, rents on sugar lands, taxes paid by the sugar industry, many leases and even interest rates on mortgage loans.[73] The improved labour conditions which had secured a more fair distribution of incomes since 1933 meant that any change in exports would be likely to cause greater changes in economic activity than before. Thus during the 1950s at least as much as in the past, 'all commitments made in Cuba – no matter how well the risk [seemed] . . . to be spread [were] in fact commitments which depended upon the fate of sugar in the international markets'.[74] When sugar prices were good, no other enterprise in Cuba was so rewarding. When they were bad, most other activities suffered at the same time. To many Cuban investors, other forms of investment seemed less attractive than sugar in good times and almost as risky in bad. Any investment in Cuba depended directly or indirectly on sugar; why not therefore invest

[69] *Cf.* Hugo Vivó, *El empleo y la población activa de Cuba* (1950). Carlos Rafael Rodríguez, April 1963, qu. *Hispanic American Report*, XVI, 349, said that the cane cutters never numbered less than 375,000. In the war years, 1941–3, the average sugar labour force was 500,000, getting probably $1·00 a day in 1941 in harvest time and 80 cents a day out of harvest; in 1942–3 these wages had risen to $1·53 in harvest and $1·00 out (Census of 1943, 261). But one must doubt whether there was any real fulfilment of the latter figure. According nevertheless to the official statistics, a total of $23,377,022 was paid in wages and salaries in the sugar industry in 1940, $27,191,091 in 1941, $40,472,169 in 1942.

[70] *Problems of the New Cuba*, 286.

[71] *Revista del Banco Nacional*, September 1955, qu. *Investment in Cuba*, 6.

[72] Núñez Jiménez, 227. Tobacco accounted for another 10%.

[73] The sugar law of 1937 provided that daily wages should be, in the harvest, the equivalent of 50 lbs of sugar; but they were not to exceed 96 cents and not to drop below a minimum of 80 cents. (Minimum wages rose to $2·88 a day by 1947.)

[74] World Bank, 571.

directly in it? The dominance of sugar was a leading reason why diversification was hard. Experience – the name which the Cubans gave to the two world wars, the depression, Korea, Suez – impressed on Cubans of all walks of life that good and bad times in Cuba depended on good and bad times in the world outside. War rather than peace still brought prosperity. Nothing which Cuba could do at home was so important to her economy as a variation of a cent or two in the price of sugar: thus, if there were sugar exports of three million tons, a one cent variation up or down made a difference of $M60 in Cuba's receipts.[75]

The Cuban sugar industry therefore in 1958 remained as dominant in the country's economy as it had always done since the collapse of coffee over a century before. Yet it was an old-fashioned industry, unable or unwilling to take advantage of an expanding world demand. Partly this was because of the very character of the world sugar condition, and partly also because the severity of the depression in Cuba had brought a protective series of laws which in the interests of humanity had sanctified both an archaic system of growing cane (the *colonia*) and a highly restrictive labour situation. Foreign investment was in decline and though this was welcomed for political reasons it expressed a lack of faith in an industry now apparently in its old age. Whereas in the 1850s Cuba had been the first to seize upon new ideas, in the 1950s she was the last.

What then should be done? No revolutionary leader in 1959 had any proposals for the sugar industry. In 1953, Castro had spoken of even more reforms to benefit the already pampered *colonos*; afterwards, silence. Enlightened economists such as Pazos or López Fresquet were primarily concerned with the industrialization of other sectors of the economy. In so far as the international sugar market was concerned, there was, in fact, little that Cuba could do within the boundaries of the existing system.

A resolute and united policy by all the cane-growing countries of the West Indies and South America could perhaps have secured slightly more progressive terms from the consumer countries. But the chances of such unity and of such resolution were remote. Cuba and Jamaica were almost within sight of one another, but their relations were negligible. There was no chance of Castro and Trujillo or of Cuba and Peru meeting to discuss common sugar policy. There were political rivalries based on generations of social and cultural differences. Politics apart, there was no precedent, before the UNCTAD conference in Geneva in 1965, for a group of primary producers to decide common policies. Had they been able to do so, the cane producers might have sought a settlement whereby the beet growers of the north at least did not expand

[75] *Ibid.*, 52.

their production. The cane producers might have argued that if the advanced countries really desired to assist unselfishly those less well off, they should in this, as in other ways, try to cease competition with tropical or sub-tropical countries in the crops that are those countries' life blood. The U.S. or the Soviet Union can grow wheat as well as beet; the Caribbean cannot.

But of course strategic fears of reliance on foreign trade in wars dictate European sugar policy, even though during and after both world wars the Great Powers of Europe needed Cuba more than she needed them. The difficulties of reaching a common agricultural policy even in the European Economic Communities suggest the complication likely to be met by Cuba and her cane-growing partners. Yet this would still have been the most creative policy for a Cuban government in 1959.

A second alternative seemed to be to accept things as they were: to sell between a third and a quarter of the harvest to the U.S., this proportion fractionally increasing over the years as the U.S. population rose, at the same time doing all possible to get the reversions from failures by other countries, within the U.S. league, to fulfil their quotas. Such failures might, however, have become rarer, and over the years other sugar producers of the Caribbean, such as the Dominican Republic would be bound to covet greater slices of the U.S. market. Still, if this policy had been accompanied by a really ruthless attempt at diversification of agriculture and industrialization, it might have been effective.

The third alternative for Cuba in these conditions of 'monoculture' was to seek to join another of the international sugar leagues: the English, the French or the Russian. The first two of these were out of the question, because of their limited size, and because of internal or imperial arrangements in England and France, not to speak of the English and French political arrangements with the U.S. The only possible new league, therefore, was the Russian. This was a desperate and, in the circumstances of 1959, apparently unreal plan. Russia, if not self-sufficient in sugar, was after all, herself a very large sugar producer. No one in Cuba had really thought of the Russian alternative in 1958 or 1959. Even the Cuban Communists seem to have presumed, even hoped, that somehow or other existing sugar marketing arrangements would be preserved.

Cuban radicals' inclination in 1959 was not to spend too much time on sugar, rather on diversification of agriculture and on industrialization. The great aim was to escape from the monoculture. The song of the 1950s of Carlos Puebla described sadly how

> The roads of old Cuba
> Lead nowhere.

Sugar had taken Cuba to an *impasse*. The revolutionary aim was to bring new roads, to rework the nickel mines, to grow tomatoes or avocados, to become self-sufficient in steel, to sell cigars to China: anything to avoid the production of sugar on the existing scale, much less an increased one.

Thus no one on the Left had a sugar policy. The sugar mills and estates were to be dragged into politics in the wake of the revolution's land reform and not as a part of sugar policy. Few stopped to think that one crop might work more effectively with one type of land reform than another: and that, doubtless, the concern should be first with the industrial structure of sugar, afterwards with the agricultural side. Quite apart from the gloomy long-term state of the international sugar market, the Cuban sugar industry needed reform. The low priority given to research; the static nature of an industry whose main capital investments, whatever the ownership, had been made over thirty years before; the incredibly complicated relations between *colonos* and mills; the nature of existing state involvement in the industry, quota-controlled and restricted, with regulations down to the last sugar bag – a state structure which really foreshadowed nationalization, though without any of its advantages; the fact that, with the restrictions and control which carried over even in years when harvests were theoretically 'free', competition between mills had virtually ceased; and the decline in the average yield per acre of Cuban sugar cane since 1938; all these facts suggested the need for reorganization.

The choice lay between greater freedom of mills to compete, and to modernize themselves, and the nationalization of the industrial side of the industry which would have been the logical continuation of the existing situation. The latter would have enabled the state to carry directly the responsibilities for welfare of large communities now borne by the sugar mills, and the closure where necessary of small or unproductive mills. It would have made possible the setting aside of at least 1 % of annual income for research which in its turn might have led to the discovery of some non-edible use for sugar which would (and still may) alter radically the lives of sugar producers.[77] It would have enabled modernization and mechanization to be brought in with maximum understanding between worker and employer. Given the uneasy state of relations between U.S.-owned sugar mills and workers, it would probably have improved labour relations. The large U.S. *centrales* dotted about Oriente and Camagüey undoubtedly had a debilitating effect on the country whatever their economic value. Nationalization, too, would have given the government direct responsibility for sugar policy in place of what had been anyway admitted for

[77] This is not so far fetched as it might seem, since sugar ($C_{12}H_{22}O11$) is 99·9% chemical.

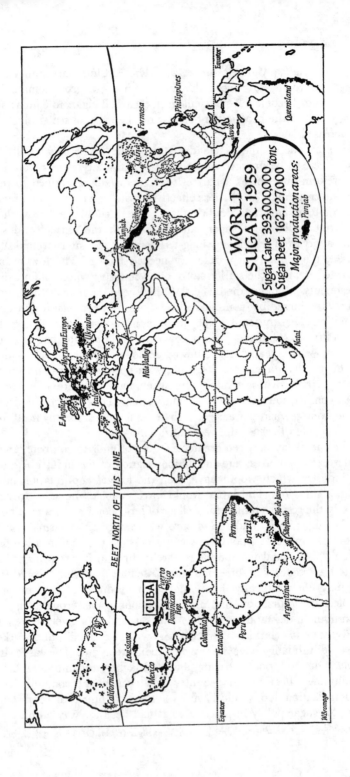

WORLD SUGAR · 1959

Sugar Cane 393,000,000 tons
Sugar Beet 162,727,000

Major production areas: Punjab

BEET NORTH OF THIS LINE

E.Anglia · Northern Europe · Ukraine · Italy · Nile Valley · Natal · Punjab · Ganges · India · China · Formosa · Phillipines · Java · Queensland · Equator

California · Louisiana · Mexico · CUBA · Puerto Rico · Dominican Rep. · Colombia · Ecuador · Peru · Pernambuco · Brazil · Rio de Janeiro · São Paulo · Argentina · Equator

W.Bromage

years to be indirectly theirs. It would give the government a control over the commanding heights of the economy with the minimum trouble. The industrial side of a sugar industry lends itself well to governmental direction. Combined with a flexible policy towards the sugar-growing estates, it might have been possible to get through the first years of a revolution without social upheaval and without the flight to Havana or abroad of administrators and technicians on the sugar mills. Nationalization of the mills (though not of the plantations) would have avoided the great customary temptations of favouritism, perhaps inevitable in the existing system. The possibilities indeed of corrupt practice were so great as to make state control desirable almost on those grounds alone. Nationalization might also have strengthened the hand of the government internationally by enabling Cuba to be represented by a delegation who did not represent a combination which included U.S. interests.

Such a policy towards the industrial side of the sugar industry could not have been adopted without consideration of the land where cane was grown. Thus perhaps the aim should been to encourage a reduction of the surface on which sugar was grown, credit being given for the import of cane cutters, with much national instruction for farmers about growing cane, while increasing yields through better drainage, fertilization and more frequent planting, and the national adoption of Lobo's rationalizing policies in Matanzas.

This policy, however, was not followed. When nationalization came, it came, like the treatment of agricultural lands, in the wake of other policies. In the early days of 1959, the revolutionary government desired to shake free of sugar rather than to saddle itself with running the industry; hence many follies and much frustration.

Tobacco and other Industries

The Cubans remained the greatest cigar-smokers in the world. A seventh of their cigars only were exported. The rest – 350 million or so in 1957 – were smoked by Cubans: fifty a head in the year, women and children included. But these were only half the cigars smoked in Cuba in 1918 when the figure reached well over 100 a head.[1] Cubans also smoked cigarettes in vast numbers.

There had been for many years now five well-defined tobacco-producing regions: of which Vuelta Abajo, the golden area at the west end of the island, was far the most important.

Tobacco had fallen behind cattle and beef products as the second biggest industry of the country, though it remained the second biggest export. Between two-thirds and three-quarters of Cuban tobacco was exported, mostly as leaf. Exports of cigars had greatly declined since the beginning of the century: 256 million cigars were exported in 1906; only about 40 million in the 1950s.[2] Still, the *douceur de vivre* so far as a good Havana cigar is concerned certainly ended in 1914. For tobacco growers in Cuba, this had been compensated by the increase in domestic demand, yet an immense quantity of cheap U.S. cigarettes was imported, perhaps 50% over and above 20,000 packets legally.[3] There was room of course for home manufacture of cheap cigarettes.

Tobacco production under Batista was consistent; a record production level of ninety million pounds in 1957 was the third highest ever (the highest was in 1950). But even here higher figures had been recorded (in 1926 the total reached ninety-five million pounds). Cubans were smoking slightly more cigarettes and cigars than in the past, but the difference was small.[4] Tobacco was grown on a quarter of Cuban farms, but was a primary source of income on only 14%, or between 20,000 and 25,000 farmers, who employed another 60,000 workers.[5] Three per cent of the cultivated area (110,000 acres) was

---

[1] *Estudio*, 499.

[2] Even this was better than in the 1940s when the figure dropped to 14 million. 1954 saw an export of 110 million cigars thanks to the relaxation of controls. But the figures soon slipped back.

[3] World Bank, 860–3. In 1958 there were only 15 cigarette factories.

[4] All figures here from *Anuario*, 1957, 147 ff.

[5] *Cf.* Núñez Jiménez, 322.

planted in tobacco.[6] Three-fifths of all tobacco farms were cultivated by sharecroppers[7] who, however, often owned some livestock and farm equipment. They got their tobacco seedlings and food on credit, many small farmers being thus perpetually in debt to shopkeepers.[8] Tobacco farms were, of course, small: the average was about 15 acres, except for the coarser region of Remedios, where it was 40 acres.[9]

The owners of tobacco land were often companies, sometimes North American such as the Cuban Land and Leaf Tobacco Company in Vuelta Abajo. This company for instance let land to eighty share-croppers,[10] who together employed over 3,000 wage workers. The company provided houses, irrigation, outhouses, a doctor, nurse and clinic, water, and allotments for vegetables. To producers of shade tobacco (grown under the artificial shade of cheesecloth on poles) the company also gave free manure and free credit for wages; they paid a third of all expenses such as fertilizers; and in return received half the crop.[11] Producers of sun tobacco – the biggest number – only gave to the company a quarter of the crop, but sharecroppers here had to pay more expenses – three-quarters of manure costs, and so on.[12] Other owners administered a part of their estates themselves and levied a variation of these charges on their tenants. The variations of holding were indeed infinite.[13] Thus often the wage workers grew tobacco themselves on land which they were allotted to grow vegetables or to keep cattle, thereby getting an extra income; and sometimes owners were exacting, demanding a full year's interest for the credit of a few months.

There seems to have been little change on these generally prosperous farms. On instances noted by Lowry Nelson, the same families had remained in the same place for over thirty years. Widows might take over active management from dead husbands.

A critical and controversial change had recently affected the cigar factories of Havana. These were still grouped together in Havana, great names well-known throughout the world (particularly at good dinner tables) – Romeo y Julieta, Ramon Allones, Larrañaga, Partagás, Montecristo, Menéndez Garcia (the biggest) – though there were about one thousand factories in the whole of Cuba.[14] These factories had always depended on hand labour. Elsewhere, cigar-rolling machines had been in

[6] 1949 figures (World Bank, 857), as estimated by U.S. Embassy, Havana.
[7] Seers.
[8] In 1950 90% of small farmers in the Remedios area were found to pay interest rates of 20% on loans from shopkeepers (World Bank, 593–4).
[9] Again these were 1946 figures.
[10] *Partidarios.*
[11] Shade tobacco might be necessary for say two-thirds of the wrappers of cigars.
[12] This instance was described by Nelson, 130–1.
[13] In Remedios there were sub-tenants of sharecroppers too (*cuartarios* and *terzedarios*), cf. loc cit.
[14] Núñez Jiménez, 322; *Investment in Cuba*, 82.

use for a long time. The Cuban cigar-makers, tightly organized and exclusive, had successfully resisted the introduction of machines since the first attempt to bring them to Cuba in 1925. This caused some lesser factories to incur losses and some had even moved to Florida, where they could supply the U.S. customer more cheaply – a bizarre event in a semi-developed country. But in 1950 a decree by Prío had permitted machine-made cigars. $40 a month was also provided for 900 workers who were consequently unemployed: this might not compare very satisfactorily with their previous $5 a day – $50 a fortnight – but was still a benevolent step, rare in the history of both North and South American labour relations.[15] Nor did this mean that all cigars were machine-made; the best cigars continued to be hand rolled. The number of cigars remained much the same. The number of different brands by now passed belief: Fernando Ortiz saw nearly 1,000 different types of cigar in a collection belonging to a Havana factory.[16]

The workers in tobacco factories in the 1950s numbered 35,000, compared with over 24,000 in 1899. In addition there were some 50,000 tobacco selectors and 8,000 twisters of leaf. Selection and stripping was seasonal work, lasting only a few weeks. 3,000 workers were occupied in Cuba's fifteen cigarette factories.[17] Probably 130,000 were working in the tobacco industry either on the agricultural or industrial side.[18]

The tobacco industry was better organized than sugar. It had a long tradition of honesty. One writer recalled in the old days 'seeing Negroes meet the train running from Villanueva to Batabanó on Thursdays with wheelbarrows loaded with sacks of gold doubloons, which were unloaded at Punta de Carta, Bailén and Cortés, and then carried on muleback through the tobacco country, leaving payment for the crop at each *vega*'.[19] Two commissions looked after the industry, one for prices, one for marketing. The former had an experimental station distributing better types of seed, compiling statistics and so on.

[15] *Cf. H.A.R.,* August 1951. It was partially paid for by a tax of $5 on each 1,000 machine-made cigars. The government had initially to suspend this law due to workers' protests.

[16] *Cuban Counterpoint*, 43. fn.

[17] Núñez Jiménez, 322.

[18] *Estudio*, 1103. Principal cigar factories in 1958 (*loc. cit.*):

Menéndez, García & Co.	$M2·58
Cifuentes & Co.	$M1·21
Tabacos Rey del Mundo	$M1·01
J. Palacio	$M0·97
Tabacalera Moya	$M0·74
Romeo y Julieta	$M0·59
José L. Piedra	$M0·48
Larrañaga	$M0·43

[19] 'Recuerdos Tabacaleros del Tiempo Viejo', in *Horizontes*, Havana, August 1936, qu. Ortiz, *Negros Esclavos*, 38.

The desirable reorganization in the tobacco industry was in agriculture. The sharecropping system led often to injustice; and most growers would have been more efficient had they been owners of their own land.

Fernando Ortiz, the chief chronicler of the Afro-Cuban tradition, contrasted sugar and tobacco, the two most noted Cuban products: the value of tobacco lay in its leaves, of sugar in its stalk; cane lived for years, tobacco for months; cane sought sunlight, tobacco shade; cane was without scent, could look after itself for months; tobacco was aromatic and needed constant care from skilled men. Above all, cane demanded seasonal mass labour, tobacco constant attention from a few experienced men. Cane was grown on large estates, tobacco on small holdings. All sugar was the same in the end, beet and cane sugar even producing the same element; no cigar is alike. Finally, sugar spelled slavery, tobacco freedom, and therefore Ortiz suggested Cuba should escape from sugar into tobacco production.[20]

Alas, despite the supreme quality of Cuban cigars, such an escape was not possible. Cuba can produce an indefinite amount of good tobacco. But so can every other island in the Caribbean, and many other countries. There was no chance that Cuban cigarette tobacco could ever displace the favourite suppliers of the main consumers. Her cigars were admittedly the best in the world. But the world cigar market has dropped sadly since the beginning of the century. Further, the great Cuban cigar came from tobacco which was grown only in a very small region of Cuba, the Vuelta Abajo, along the River Cuyaguateje. Here climate and soil combined, as along the great wine rivers of France, to produce the perfect conditions for the production of the great cigar. But the area was not large and in the nature of things could not be expanded to form an industry on which the whole island could live.

Cuba's railways and roads had been for many years better than in any country of the Americas save for the U.S. – perhaps even better than Canada's. But out of Cuba's 11,000 miles of railway, nearly 8,000 miles were private sugar lines; even the remaining 3,000 miles of public railway were dictated by the insatiable needs of the sugar industry, which was responsible for four-fifths of the freight tonnage in Cuba.

Four-fifths also of the public railways in Cuba belonged either to the U.S.-owned Consolidated Railways, operating east of Santa Clara, or to the Western Railroads of Cuba, bought in 1953 by the government from the English United Railways. Hershey & Co. ran a 100-mile railway in Matanzas. There were also sixteen small railways, chiefly in the east, with an average of under thirty miles each.

The Cuban roads were mixed. Those between big towns were

[20] Fernando Ortiz, *Cuban Counterpoint*, *passim*.

excellent; farm-to-market roads were bad. In 1955 the U.S. Embassy thought that only a fifth of Cuban farms had all-weather roads or railways to them.[21] Still, their general condition was so good that the decline of railway freight, since the opening of the Central Highway in 1931, had been as marked as it had been in the U.S. This did not make Cuba necessarily a modern country: it was simply another instance of the influence of a U.S. model. Bus transport similarly competed with railways, as did, in the 1950s, private cars on a popular scale. At the end of the 1940s, the government began a big new four-lane highway between Havana and Matanzas (the Vía Blanca), as well as other improvements on the Central Highway. Another highway linked Havana to the airport. In Havana in the 1950s, three modern tunnels eased the traffic flow. The Central Highway was, however, in need of improvement, since it was too narrow,[22] and had no shoulders.

The number of cars rose nearly 13 % a year in the 1950s – from 70,000 in 1950 to 160,000 in 1958.[23] An extraordinarily high proportion were taxis or cars for hire.[24] There were also an amazing number of Cadillacs and Oldsmobiles, but much inter-city traffic was still by bus, all owned by private companies. The largest was the Omnibus Aliados, with over half the buses, partly with rural services, mostly urban; and the Autobuses Modernos, founded in 1950–1 in Havana, after the removal of the old Havana Electric Railways, by William Pawley, the North American businessman (in Latin America) and ambassador (to Peru and Brazil).[25] The new company did not prosper. The government bought it out but sold it back to private enterprise in 1958. The bus service on the Central Highway was admirable, ten buses leaving Havana for Santiago every day, with good connections to towns on the north and south coasts.

Nineteen towns had airfields, and there were about a hundred other landing fields, many on sugar mills. North-east Oriente, with bad roads and railways, was almost as dependent on the air as was Alaska. The chief company was Cubana, a subsidiary of the U.S. Pan American Airways to begin with after its foundation in 1930, but bought[26] by a Cuban syndicate in 1953 headed by José López Vilaboy, a newspaper chief. Cubana flew to twenty places inland, and to Miami, Madrid, and other places abroad. Havana airport was also bought by Cubana at the same

[21] *Investment in Cuba*, 106.
[22] 21½ feet.
[23] UN Statistical Yearbook, 1963, 380. Mexico, Argentina, Brazil and Venezuela had more in South America.
[24] 22,000 compared with 10,000 in 1954. *Investment in Cuba*, 112. Lorries and commercial vehicles increased less fast, from 30,000 in 1950 to 50,000 in 1958.
[25] It was he who had been selected by the CIA to ask Batista to leave Cuba in December 1958.
[26] Pan American kept 25% of the shares.

time. Cubana had a fleet of chiefly English aeroplanes but was about to buy Boeing 707s at the time Batista fell.

There were still thirty shipping lines though, in the Cuba trade; they included regular sailings from New York and New Orleans and less frequent ones from Europe. With Palm Beach and Key West there were ferries. Havana accounted for two-thirds of the imports of Cuba but the sugar areas of the east exported more. Cuba's merchant marine was small: only about eighteen ocean-going ships out of a total number of 2,300 vessels.[27]

Cuba had been a leader in the scramble for instant communications. Havana was the first city in the world to have an automatic multi-exchange telephone. Wireless and television were also developed early. The telephone service became a permanent monopoly of the Cuban American Telephone Company, owned chiefly by IT & T, partly by the American Telephone and Telegraph Company.[28] It was, therefore, another utility entirely owned by North Americans.

Criticism of the telephone company had been persistent not only because of foreign control but because of bad management. There were still many unfilled orders.[29] The World Bank even reported that the company paid to its shareholders 'a good dividend on capital at expense of maintenance and replacement of equipment'.[30] The company, on the other hand, had wished for years to secure the revision of its contract so that it could raise rates which had remained the same since 1909. This was finally done in March 1957, the day after the attack on the palace, and with the customary distributions of bribes. The company then embarked on an expansion programme, with a huge new issue of stock, promising to install 60,000 new telephones by the end of 1960. This work was begun and, in 1958, there were just under 200,000 telephones, nearly all automatic. However, the telephone company had been marked from its birth by shady dealings by some of its personnel and was never free from corruption.[31]

The Cubans used the telephone phenomenally. The average Cuban subscriber seems to have made no less than fourteen to fifteen calls a day, compared with eight to nine in other parts of South America and five in the U.S. The load on existing equipment was thus heavy. Cubans also used the telephone a good deal for calls to the U.S.: 'Call up Miami for a spare wheel, and get it over by the next plane.'

[27] See below, Appendix XII for fisheries.
[28] The Cuban Telephone Company with the Cuban American Telephone and Telegraph Company, the Puerto Rico Telephone Company, and others, formed the basis of IT & T.
[29] The number of telephones, 60,000 in the 1920s, dropped to 30,000 in the depression and had risen again, to 110,000 in 1950 and 150,000 in 1955.
[30] World Bank, 340.
[31] López Fresquet, 26.

There were 160 wireless and four television stations, bringing messages of hope or gloom to over a million radio sets and nearly 500,000 television sets (all bought since 1950), and all made in the U.S.[32] These broadcasting companies were all Cuban, but the towns at least often gave the impression of being deluged with cheap North American music. There was one station for 'good music'. Already Cuba was dominated by television almost as much as the U.S. (at least in towns), more so than most European countries. No one had yet used it to effect for politics, though Chibás had shown the possibilities of wireless in 1949–51. Batista rarely appeared.

The Cuban industrial scene – excluding sugar and tobacco – had much changed since the depression and the tariffs of 1927. The last few years had shown a high rate of investment by foreign firms. Many new plants were begun. There was more diversification at the end of Batista's rule than at the start, though this was due partly at least to the industrial or agricultural bank founded under Prío.

Though many North Americans came to Cuba to found businesses in order to escape taxes at home, labour presented a serious problem. Recollection of the 1930s helped to keep workers organized, and made them terrified of further change. Industrialists thus customarily met 'a most insurmountable resistance to modernization'.[33] In 1950 the World Bank thought 'it is not easy to see how further investment in . . . Cuban industry could be made *less* attractive'.[34] Workers' resistance to mechanization of the cigar industry might be understood as an exceptional obstacle in a special business though, even there, costs had so risen as almost to price Cuban cigars out of their old markets. But some textile mills had been forced out of business and others had been saved only by government intervention. Where new methods had been successfully introduced, with the agreement of the workers, there had usually been a stipulation that the same size of labour force would be used as before; even that the new equipment should turn out no more products than the old.

All governments since 1945 had done what they could to encourage new industries; there were three-year exemptions from customs dues on new machinery or equipment, six-year exemptions from taxes on loan interests, ten-year exemptions from customs dues on imported raw materials; depreciation costs could be deducted, and so on. The trouble was that though several new industries were indeed set up, few of them used Cuban raw materials.

[32] *Investment in Cuba*, 116–18; *Estudio*, 1178–9.
[33] World Bank, 134–5.
[34] *Ibid.*, 135.

Under Batista, several of these hindrances were destroyed, by fair means or foul. The government made dismissals of labour possible and cut away red tape, and there is no reason to think that corruption in industry, though considerable, was on a larger scale than under Prío and Grau. (On the other hand, the corrupt practices of the army were much greater and often affected industry indirectly.) The Agricultural and Industrial Development Bank greatly helped too. The result was the expansion of the mid-1950s, causing industrial production to increase between 1955 and 1958 by 3·4% a year. Total investment perhaps increased from about $M2,800 in 1955 to $M3,300 in 1957.[35] In 1957 manufacturing was up by 12%, electricity by 30%, building by 25%: mining only was down, by 20%.[36] Even so, industrialization depended on imports of raw materials and many of the ridiculous sides of the Cuban economy survived: thus out of 11 million kilos of tomatoes exported annually, 9 million probably came back as sauce.[37] Further, the end of the negativeness of labour policy had only been achieved by the further implication of the leaders of trade unions into the system, and the corruption of some of them.[38]

One-third of the capital invested in Cuba was in sugar, followed in order of value by transport and communications, by mining and metallurgy, and by electricity.[39] The largest non-sugar plant in Cuba was the cotton-spinning Textilera Ariguanabo at Bauta, a few miles west of Havana, with 72,000 spindles, 2,000 looms, and employing 2,500. It had been founded in 1931 (before when all Cuban textiles had been imported) by Dayton Hedges of New York.[40] In 1948 Hedges founded a large and efficient rayon works at Matanzas, which employed 1,200. The Hedges's concerns dominated the Cuban textile business till 1958 when Burke Hedges, jr, after his father's death, sold the rayon business for a lavish sum to the state corporation, BANDES.[41] Ariguanabo had had incessant labour troubles in the late 1940s, when Hedges had desired to mechanize, and in fact actually laid off a third of its workers (with compensation), but the rayon works was from the beginning more modern

---

[35] *Estudio*, 1098.

[36] See Index of Industrial Activity, qu. *ibid.*, 1143.

[37] Industrialization was also slow in relation to human resources, and did not keep pace with the domestic savings and the possibilities offered by the general economy.

[38] Between 1945 and 1951, inclusive, annual industrial consumption of electricity hovered between 130,000 and 155,000 million kilowatts; between 1952 and 1956 it went faster, nearly by 10%. But the largest increase was, however, residential use, increasing between 1945 and 1956 from 77,993 million kilowatts to 383,544 million. In August 1957 residential consumption of electricity was nearly seven times what it had been eleven years before. (See *Anuario*, 1957, 205–9.)

[39] See 'Capital invested in Cuba', in table, *Investment in Cuba*, 116

[40] See above, p. 1114.

[41] The Economic and Social Development Bank.

with mechanical innovations, and there was no serious labour resistance to mechanization.[42]

After the Hedges's concerns the next largest non-sugar industrial plant was the Bacardí rum business at Santiago, which also made beer, and employed about 2,000. This manufacture was the only Cuban product about whose management the generally critical World Bank Mission reported that it 'could suggest no improvement'.[43] Strong cane brandy (*aguardiente*), and a little rather unsuccessful wine was made, from tropical fruits, and also some cheap domestic gin. There were five large modern breweries, including Bacardí's, producing excellent popular lager-type beers, demand for which (as in Europe at the same time) was rising fast. These manufactures employed some 10,000.[44] Coca-cola, Pepsi-cola, Canada Dry and Orange Crush, had Cuban dependencies.[45] Also in Cuba were three paper mills, with good chances of producing newsprint from bagasse in a fourth, opening experimentally in 1958, and ordinary paper from a fifth also from bagasse (W. R. Grace & Company).[46] Cuba had a rather advanced chemical sector producing, especially, sulphuric acid (from imported sulphur); and about forty good pharmaceutical laboratories, some of them U.S. owned. Annual sales of pharmaceutical goods were high – between $M60 and $M70 at retail prices – and indeed the World Bank found 'literally hundreds of Cuban enterprises producing patent medicines, home remedies, lotions, pomades, etc.'[47] About half the drugs and medicines sold were made in Cuba. Other plants – all developed since the depression – included canners, pasteurizing and cheese plants, butter factories and fifty-nine ice-cream plants.[48] The U.S.-owned Burrus Flour Mill at Regla opened in 1952 to lessen Cuba's reliance on imports of flour, which by 1955 had dropped to about 60% of total production.[49] There were some vegetable oil plants, chiefly U.S.-owned (Proctor and Gamble in 1931 had bought the old-established Sabatés & Co. and the Hershey Corporation's oil plant), but none made any impact on the Cuban demand for fats, which was almost entirely met by the U.S.[50] North Americans were also in the lead in other businesses – for example, paint, fertilizers and rubber (particularly tyres). The leather industry, on the other hand, was a contrast, being still a conglomeration of old small-scale concerns, providing, in the

[42] World Bank, 962.
[43] *Ibid.*, 979.
[44] Census of 1953.
[45] *Estudio*, 1110–13.
[46] Grace & Co. had been making paper from bagasse successfully in Peru since 1939.
[47] World Bank, *loc. cit.*
[48] *Investment in Cuba*, 76.
[49] *Ibid.*, 78.
[50] *Ibid.*, 81–2.

mid-1950s, about 7½ million pairs of shoes, coping with all but fancy demand.[51]

Cuba had no coal, few hydro-electric possibilities (because of sluggish rivers), and as yet inadequately developed oil resources. The main domestic fuel was bagasse.[52] Cuba's electricity consumption ranked high among countries of the Americas after the U.S.[53] The sugar mills made their own electricity, and all but a small percentage of the rest was distributed by the Cuban Electric Company, a subsidiary of the American and Foreign Power Company (itself a subsidiary of the vast Electric Bond and Share Company of New York) which had had a virtual electrical monopoly since the Machado days: Machado had himself sold his own smaller electrical supply business to Cuban Electric before being president of Cuba, and his chief financial backer, Henry Catlin, had been its president.[54] Most of Cuba had had electricity since the 1920s, at least in towns and large villages. Cuban Electric had an excellent record of growth, especially in the 1950s, as more and more businesses and private people modernized their lighting and air-conditioned their rooms. There were, however, many shortcomings: much equipment was old; there were frequent power shortages in the countryside; and rates were higher than those in the U.S.,[55] partly due at least to the need to bribe officials, from the president down. Scandals in the past had proliferated: government officials paid bills only when they felt like it; Havana city was years behind;[56] and in the industry there had been numerous semi-political strikes.[57]

The last years before the fall of Batista had been attended by numerous new projects: the French Compagnie Générale d'Enterprises Eléctriques had received a $M20 contract to construct a plant for the new development at East Havana; a hydro-electric project in Las Villas made use of the Habanilla river: such developments, admirable as they were, were however too late to save the tattered flag of private enterprise.[58]

Ever since a small strike at Bacuranao in 1914[59] a little oil had been known to exist in Cuba. An oil boom during the First World War had

[51] Shoe imports averaged 115,000 pairs between 1947 and 1953. *Cf. Investment in Cuba*, 97 and fn.

[52] The waste left behind after the sugar cane had been ground and the juice extracted.

[53] 103 watts of installed capacity *per capita* per year.

[54] See above, p. 570. For a description of Cuban Electric's remarkable adventures in 1933–4 see *Problems of the New Cuba*, 400

[55] The company said that they were not high in comparison with 'cost to consumer of generating his own power' and Cuban costs generally (*Investment in Cuba*, 105).

[56] Phillips, 126–7.

[57] Cuban Electric also operated the one small gas company.

[58] *Estudio*, 1169–72.

[59] Actually the Motembo oil field near Colón had been discovered in the late 1800s, Bacuranao in 1864, another near Cárdenas in 1890.

attracted some seventy companies, but only one well was found with commercial possibilities. The major oil companies began, however, to seek oil on a large scale after the Second World War, after the new boom in Venezuela. All save one had given up by 1954. In that year a rich strike was made at Jatibonico by the Tarabuca Group.[60] From May 1954 onwards 250 barrels a day flowed. Further exploration followed, backed by a generous credit policy by the Batista government which proclaimed it would pay up to 50 % of oil exploration. Another important strike followed at Jatibonico in 1956, and yet another at Yayajabos in Pinar del Río. In October 1957 the Pan American Land and Oil Royalty Company, with Texan interests, announced that they had bought three million acres in Cuba along with certain shares in other development projects. Between 1954 and 1958, investment in Cuban oil leapt from $M3 to $M44, producing from 57,000 to between 300,000 and 400,000 barrels.[61]

Thus the revolution found Cuban domestic oil quite promising though no clear knowledge existed of the size of the reserves. Meantime, most of Cuba's needs were met by imports. Rising use of cars greatly increased demand. Three-quarters of the petrol was imported from the U.S. or the British West Indies, and one-quarter was produced in local refineries from imported crude oil. Shell had just finished a big plant at Regla, with a capacity of 80,000 barrels. Also in 1956 Texaco finished a plant with 20,000 barrel capacity at Santiago.[62] Total new investment in the mid and late 1950s was about $M75.[63] A plan also existed to pipe oil from Campche in Mexico to South Cuba and thence to Florida.[64]

Cuba still had rich mineral resources, the large lateritic ore reserves of North Oriente being potentially one of the world's largest sources of nickel and of iron, an important producer of chrome, cobalt, copper and manganese, as well as some other minerals in small amounts – zinc, gold, silver and lead. 287 mines were open in Cuba in 1958, including 84 petrol explorers; the U.S. took 96 % of the output.

That Cuba had iron, mostly in northern Oriente, some in the south, had been known for centuries.[65] The latter began to be developed in the 1880s, the former in 1908 by Pennsylvania and, later, Bethlehem Steel. The south coastal operation persisted till 1945 (by then Bethlehem Steel controlled that too), the north only till 1917, but during the Second

[60] H.A.R., June 1954.
[61] Ibid., June 1958.
[62] Ibid., April 1956.
[63] Investment in Cuba, 95.
[64] H.A.R., October 1957. Edwin W. Pawley, a friend of Truman's, was involved in this.
[65] Columbus said in his diary, 25 November 1492, 'I saw on the beach many iron-coloured stones.'

World War the U.S. government, through the Freeport Sulphur Company, worked the iron at Mayarí in pursuit of nickel. All but 15% or so of the iron-producing regions were owned by U.S. companies and they or their parent companies had other and more easily worked sources of supply. For these companies, their Cuban sources were merely reserves. This was potentially inflammatory so far as Cuban interests were concerned but, in practice, resentment was confined to a few economists and to people who, like Castro, lived near the disused mineheads with heavy unemployment. There was not much public interest in iron or indeed any mineral resources in Cuba. The U.S. had been responsible for nearly all the exploration and mapping of resources (done chiefly because of shortages in the war). The World Bank Mission criticized Cubans as too often relying 'on future wars to stimulate further mineral development'.[66] But it was commercially out of the question for Cubans to work the small quantity of ore not controlled by U.S. interests: any expenditure of capital on mineral resources would so easily vanish with U.S. competition. Even so, the first Cuban steel plant had just been built at Cotorro in Havana in 1958 by the U.S. Republic Steel Company.

Nickel raised the question of Cuban mineral resources in its most acute form. Before the Second World War, all Cuban nickel resources were owned by Bethlehem Steel, and nothing was done. During the war the U.S. government built a large plant at Nicaro, fifteen miles east of Mayarí on the Bay of Levisa, at the huge cost of $M33·5. Employing 1,800 people, and therefore becoming the third largest industrial plant in Cuba in terms of workers[67] (with a payroll reaching $M13),[68] the Nicaro plant was operated by a subsidiary of the Freeport Sulphur Company (Nicaro Nickel). It began to work in 1943. In 1946 Cuba produced almost 10% of the nickel in the world. But the mill was closed in 1947.

Nicaro, still owned by the U.S. government (through a company in which the Administration held all the shares), was reopened in 1952 during the Korean War and kept open. It was now operated for the U.S. government by the Nickel Processing Corporation, a firm specially founded for the purpose by the National Lead Company (60% of the shares) and the Cía de Fomento de Minerales Cubana (Cuban shareholders, with 40% of the shares).[69] The Freeport Sulphur Company still retained an interest, since it provided most of what was used in the plant (through *its* subsidiary, Nicaro Nickel). An ex-U.S. ambassador, Robert Butler, was involved in this transaction, along with Inocente

[66] World Bank, 202.
[67] After Bacardí Rum and Dayton Hedges's textile mill at Ariguanabo, Nicaro was the most valuable plant in Cuba.
[68] World Bank, 998.
[69] But *cf. H.A.R.*, April 1952.

Alvarez, an Auténtico lawyer and Grau's foreign minister, to whom in fact Butler had been accredited,[70] which gave it a certain air of scandal. But rather more serious criticism attended the appointment of the General Service Administrator, Edward Mansure, an insurance man who, it turned out, allotted insurance to various political friends in Chicago who had recommended his appointment.[71] This return to the age of Mark Hanna did not, however, come out into the open till four years later, and meanwhile Mansure had announced a $M34 expansion programme at Nicaro: even this was attended by several serious doubts, since it later turned out that the Frederick Share Corporation gave $8,510 to the Republican party while seeking the contract which they afterwards gained.[72]

Nicaro having reopened, the Freeport Sulphur Company (which held a long-term contract to supply the U.S. government with nickel) announced that they were proposing to work the large nickel and cobalt deposits at Moa Bay, also on the Cuban north coast, about fifty miles east. The chairman of the Freeport Sulphur Company, Moa Bay, John Whitney,[73] said that Moa represented the best new source of nickel in the world. Once again all taxes were exempt for this U.S. concern. In March 1957 a processing plant costing $M120[74] was announced for Moa Bay, a result of a contract with the U.S. (government) General Services Administration by which the latter undertook to take all the nickel and cobalt which the company could produce till June 1965 – up to 270 million pounds of nickel and 29 million pounds of cobalt.[75] In the same month the Nicaro expansion project was completed.

Copper was the oldest and largest mining operation in the past history of Cuba, dating from 1530 at El Cobre, named after the mine.[76] The English ran the mine in the nineteenth century, selling out in the 1890s to a German-U.S. firm. In the twentieth century, however, the biggest and most efficient copper mine was at Matahambre, in the west of Pinar del Río, discovered in 1912, and after 1921 with a majority of stock owned by the U.S. Metal Company Ltd, the ore being refined by the U.S. Metal Refining Company, of Contact, New Jersey. The U.S. Metal Company withdrew in 1943 after labour troubles and low prices, and Cubans took over control. Matahambre had large deposits.

[70] *Fortune*, June 1953.

[71] *H.A.R.*, March 1956. Mansure (b. 1901, Chicago), chairman of E. L. Mansure Co.; president of Crime Prevention Inc., Cook County.

[72] *H.A.R.*, November 1956. Randall Cremer, ex-official of the company, told a committee of the House of Representatives that he felt 'naturally bound' by an agreement with the Republican party chairman, Hall.

[73] John Whitney (b. 1904), gentleman and financier; educated Oxford and Yale; owner of *New York Herald Tribune* and U.S. ambassador in London 1957–61.

[74] *H.A.R.*, February 1958.

[75] *Ibid.*, April 1957.

[76] See above, for nineteenth-century operations.

El Cobre had closed in 1918, but copper was found in all Cuban provinces. In 1950 the value of copper production exceeded that of all other metallic resources, though by the late 1950s it was overtaken by nickel. Nickel from Cuba still represented 40% of North American importation and Cuba was fourth among Latin American copper producers.[77] About 1,000 workers toiled away in Matahambre, the mine being connected to the little port of Santa Lucía by an aerial tramway.[78] The U.S. shareholders mostly sold out to Cubans after 1945. El Cobre was being exploited again in a small way.

Manganese and chrome also played a part. Cuba produced over half the world's chemical grade manganese, all being bought by the U.S. This metal, controlled, like iron, by Bethelehem Steel, had been mined since 1888 by U.S. companies and, as with other Cuban minerals, had had its best times during the world wars, when carriage was specially difficult between the U.S. and her normal providers in Africa or India. Rearmament in the 1950s kept the mines open and production in 1952–7 was about the same as during the Second World War.[79] Cuba was thus second to Brazil as manganese producer in the western hemisphere. She had been the major chrome producer for a while in the Second World War, but dropped a long way afterwards, though deposits remained large. Operations were partly in the main mineral areas, Mayarí to Baracoa, partly in north Camagüey. The old Caledonia mine at Mayarí, like Matahambre, had recently passed from Bethlehem Steel to Cuban interests.[80] Production in the 1950s was only about a third of what it had been in the four war years.

Non-metallic minerals such as marble, limestone or salt employed more than these mines and, of course, made a greater impact on the economy, since the effect of the former was nil. Limestone was found in nearly every province, and was extensively used in building and to make burned lime, to process sugar. Marble was the outstanding product of the Isle of Pines.

To be a 'reserve country' in all these ways was clearly infuriating. The mines were only worked when North America was waging war. Peace brought inactivity. It was the same story as in the sugar industry. U.S. ownership of the mineral fields meant that the Cuban economy could never be seen as a whole. Even those minerals which were exported were left unprocessed. On the other hand, those who believed that nickel

[77] Núñez Jiménez, 219.
[78] See *The Explosives Engineer* (Hercules Powder Company, Wilmington, Delaware), March-April 1955.
[79] Núñez Jiménez, 219–20; Jenks, 26; World Bank, 211, 980–3; *Investment in Cuba*, 64–5. *Cf.* Charles F. Park Jr., *The Manganese Depository of Cuba* (U.S. Department of the Interior (mimeographed), 1941); *Estudio*, 1077–9.
[80] See *Estudio*, 1079–81.

could be greatly developed reckoned without the knowledge that substitutes for it would be increasingly found in the 1960s.

The importance of Cuba to the U.S. will not be fully understood without realizing that the U.S. companies engaged in Cuba read 'like a *Who's Who* of American business': total U.S. investment stood at over $1 billion;[81] shareholding and commercial-political interest was widespread. Any action in Cuba which affected these interests would be bound to have widespread consequences. 160,000 workers, over 90% Cubans, were employed in North American firms in Cuba, and North American firms spent $M730 in Cuba, of which $M70 was in taxes – almost 20% of the Cuban budget. Many of these firms were Cuban subsidiaries of U.S. companies, dependent on the parent company for supplies. Any radical party in Cuba would have been driven to affect these interests since the U.S. business community dominated Cuban trade and even an outstanding Cuban capitalist like Julio Lobo was inclined to abdicate political responsibility to the U.S.[82]

[81] That is $M1,000. Estimates vary considerably of the exact amount invested in Cuba by the U.S. in 1959. Thus the U.S. Department of Commerce named investment in industry and public utilities as $M879 in 1957. J. Wilson Sandelson in Plank, *op. cit.*, 101, gave a total including agriculture of £M1,500. *Cuba Socialista* September 1962 had $M965.

[82] Lobo to the author (November 1968) complained that the U.S. should have alerted Cubans earlier to the realities of Castro's movement.

The Economy: Labour

The history of labour in Cuba had been curious. Before 1933, there had been a workers' accident compensation law only and certain social security measures for railway men and mineworkers. The government always took the side of employers in disputes with labour; under Machado, labour leaders had been murdered, strikes crushed by force, labour organizations banned. But the movement survived and, from the late 1930s, labour, because of its earlier struggles, was a major force. Successive governments, during Batista's first period of power, sought to placate labour with a series of advanced laws – providing an eight-hour day; a 44-hour week (with pay for 48 hours); a month's paid holiday; four further official holidays with pay; nine days' sick leave with pay; women workers to have six weeks' holiday before and after childbirth; some wages to be tied to the cost of living; and employers to be unable to move factories without government permission. Employees could only be dismissed with proof of cause. In *The Political and Social Thought of Fidel Castro*, a booklet published with Castro's approval in 1959, it was pointed out 'since 1933 Cuban distributive policy has (as the result of wage increases, the introduction of the eight-hour day, paid holidays, social insurance and so on) brought about a juster distribution of the national income [which] . . . used to flow into the pockets of the few and now reaches the hands of many.'[1]

It seemed indeed that the government almost intervened on the side of labour. By the 1950s in fact labour had almost a stranglehold over the government; and it would not be an exaggeration to say that Batista, during his second period of power, ran Cuba by means of an alliance with organized labour. In return for the support of labour, Batista underwrote the vast number of restrictive practices, the limitations on mechanization and the bans on dismissals, which were such a characteristic of the Cuban labour scene. The leaders of the union movement, such as Mujal, Hirigoyen and Linares, were Auténticos, once closely connected with that parliamentary party; there was also the dissident Communist leadership, which had run the central union structure from the time of its organization as a fairly respectable part of society about 1938 until 1948. They had left behind a tradition of

[1] English edition published Havana, 1959, 153.

étatisme which the Auténticos, being the party in the government as well, were happy to carry on. Thus organized labour was becoming an official trade union. Labour disputes were almost always settled by government decree. Collective bargaining was almost unknown, for one law provided that all disputes had to be discussed under the auspices of the Ministry of Labour if a majority of workers in the firm so desired. The Ministry of Labour had, however, only political appointees: and in the 1940s the unions packed the ministry with friends.

This situation was negative. 'Harder to get rid of a worker than of a wife' was a common joke by Cuban businessmen over daiquirís at the Havana Biltmore Yacht Club; 'Easier to get a new wife than a new job' the worker would doubtless have replied. Both workers and their leaders were obsessed with the past; they recalled not only the depression but how only recently the mill owner had power of life and death over the sugar worker (a mill owner might have a worker whipped or even killed by the rural guard); the memory of slavery, abolished only sixty-five years before, hung about the island like a dark cloud. Many union leaders, despite their friendship with Auténtico politicians, seemed motivated by revenge. But there was also insecurity about the future. Who knew how long the time of *vacas gordas* would last? Perhaps the 1950s were a mere interlude of calm before a new hurricane returned to blow away the forty-hour week, the holidays with pay, the social legislation, as if they had been unprotected coffee trees in a time of storm. If investors, industrialists and businessmen felt themselves gamblers, Cuban workers were a prey to all the anxieties which resulted from

> the instabilities, the stagnation and the chronic unemployment of the Cuban economy. They see all about them the fearsome consequences to workers and their families from loss of jobs. They lack confidence in the will or ability of employers, investors and the government to create new enterprises and new employment.[2]

There was the possibility of appeal to the courts over the Ministry of Labour. But this would be expensive, lengthy and perhaps settled ultimately by bribery, in which both employers and unions steeped themselves. Good friendships were anyway always at least as important as a good case (and such friendships ensured jobs, much more than did the themselves underemployed labour exchanges). The law was not always clear and was therefore much debated. Nor were the economic facts ever quite beyond dispute; how many were really unemployed, who were they, were any statistics honest? Different groups of workers developed into rigid, jealous, exclusive, essentially conservative castes of privilege, jobs passing from father to son.

[2] *Ibid.,* 358.

The tragedy was that, for all the enlightened labour legislation, there remained a large unemployed section of the population and an even larger partially employed one. Neither was usually incorporated in the union structure. The minimum unemployed during the five months of sugar harvest was about 8 % of the labour force; the maximum unemployed during the rest of the year might have been 32 %.[3] Probably in fact in an average year about one quarter of the labour force worked less than half the year, a tenth not at all. Thus the economy swung annually from a highly unsatisfactory but controllable situation (where a benevolent State might have been able to afford reasonably therapeutic measures) to a tragic one which in European or other advanced countries would have been regarded as intolerable: the only time that the U.S. approached such levels of unemployment was in 1933,[4] when there was doubt whether the State would endure. The Cuban State was not benevolent in the sense of providing unemployment benefits, and the Cuban unions turned a blind eye to unemployment much of the time – in the sugar mills, union power lay with the workers who had all-the-year-round jobs at the mill. The situation was partly saved in many families by the fact that it was unusual for all members to be out of work at the same time; many of those out of work were from the class of the 50,000 to 60,000 young men who annually reached the age of work, and perhaps most people by the age of thirty or so had found some solid all-the-year-round job. Many nominally unemployed sugar workers also had small plots of land which enabled them to grow something between harvests. The province with least unemployment was, not unexpectedly, Pinar del Río, which had the most diversified agriculture. The sugar areas on the other hand had the most unemployment.[5] These problems had also been specially acute since the depression, since, as has been seen, Cuba had a substantial increase in population between 1933 and 1958.

The fear of falling back into this melancholy group of the unemployed or underemployed naturally gripped the imaginations of all who had good jobs protected by unions and laws. Some labour leaders, for instance, favoured mechanization but, like labour leaders in most countries in such circumstances, they feared the inadequate creation of new jobs. Town workers, particularly casual ones who had come in from the country, sought to stay with a single employer for six months:

[3] The 1953 census found 173,811 during the 1953 harvest who were not working. See *Investment in Cuba*, 23, where this question is perceptively if conservatively discussed. *Cf. Estudio*, 804 ff. Felipe Pazos (*Cambridge Opinion*, February 1963) put the unemployment figure at 'seldom below 15%' and, in his speech to the Club de Leones, San Juan Puerto Rico, (29 March 1961) put the figure as between 300,000 and 400,000, never below the first.

[4] 12·8 million out of 51·8 million or 24·6% (*Historical Statistics*).

[5] *Estudio*, 815.

if they accomplished that, they would qualify for insurance protection and would be impossible to dismiss. Many failed, and did odd jobs washing cars, selling lottery tickets or begging: among all these categories there were internal social divisions, the better parts of Havana being most sought after, and so on, in reverse order.

These conditions made many labour leaders reactionary: the fact that workers could not be dismissed had a debilitating effect on them, depriving them of initiative; they had little to do except negotiate with a friendly Ministry of Labour. Driving around in ducktailed Cadillacs, the labour leaders, many of whom were involved in the graft and gangsterism associated with all pre-Revolutionary politics, made a deplorable impression on nearly all sections of society, particularly on the often nearly starving unemployed for whom they were supposed to be responsible. One example of corrupt practice related to the building of the Havana Hilton Hotel, which belonged to the pension fund of the Restaurant workers. So much money was wasted or stolen that even when going very well the hotel could not yield 1% return to the pension fund.[6]

The labour question obsessed businessmen in Cuba. Cuba's remarkable stagnation was attributed to it, though this was chiefly due to the prolonged crisis in the sugar industry. Many employers had constant and (in comparison with conditions of the past) unwonted trouble due to the overmanning of their enterprises. One employer made sixty appearances before the labour courts without one favourable decision. One company filed 200 applications for permission to sack workers for justifiable causes and failed each time. There was a famous instance of a disgruntled hosiery worker who became 'insubordinate'. On being warned, he wantonly cut up masses of cloth with his shears. He was dismissed and appealed. While waiting for the law to take its course, he came regularly to the factory and, according to the defence lawyers, 'outraged the female employees with depraved exhibitions'. The labour court supported the employer and the man found other work. Eight years later he appealed to the final Labour Court of Appeal, which decreed that the first factory would have to reinstate him and pay him back wages of $16,000. The employer appealed to President Prío who, acting for once like Solomon, cancelled the payment but ordered the worker reinstated.[7] These things contrived, with the existence of a large unemployed pool of labour, to give the impression to unthinking businessmen and others, not entirely falsely, that capitalist laws of supply and demand did not apply to Cuba. Some New York businessmen thought Cuba a country where an undesirable revolution had

[6] López Fresquet, 18.
[7] World Bank, 149.

already occurred. Certainly North American capital had often considered Cuba for new projects and had turned away because of the labour laws.[8]

In 1958 most cane cutters earned $3 to $4 a day.[9] In cane-cutting areas, wages were usually greater per household since every four households usually had seven workers – some, of course, being teenagers. The average industrial wage usually gave an income of about $1,600 a year.[10] All these wages were high – for those who received them – in comparison with what usually prevailed in Latin America, but they were only about half U.S. levels in 1950–1, although the average U.S. wage for all industries had been as low as $1,600 as recently as 1941–2.[11] Of course, Cuban prices were not directly comparable with those of the U.S. but the fact that U.S. manufactured goods could compete effectively with Cuban, often at higher prices than in the U.S., suggests the relative costs in the two countries. On the other hand, Cuban big estates were not feudal in character and were worked as large capitalist enterprises serving a national or world market and employing paid labourers. All big sugar estates had, of course, to collaborate with the state in respect of quantities of cane cut and even wages paid.

The rigidity of the Cuban labour scene was severely criticized in the World Bank's report on Cuba in 1951; partly in consequence, some successful efforts were then made to breach its reactionary side without, however, providing any compensating reorganization of society. Most important was the famous surrender by the cigar workers, enabling the mechanization of that industry.

Batista's government grasped the nettle of revising the right to dismiss workers, stopping short of it in terms of legislation but allowing it in several individual cases. Most labour leaders accepted this: for they had, like Mujal, transferred their loyalty directly from the Auténtico government to Batista's as if they had been impeccable civil servants. The consequences were, as has been seen, the late 1950s' rush of investment from abroad and a slight rise in unemployment, to something like 28 % in the dead season in late 1958;[12] this was despite such progress as had been made in agricultural diversification, particularly in rice and coffee – crops which are complementary to sugar, with harvests at different

[8] *Cf. H.A.R.*, May 1954.
[9] The average wage for ordinary or semi-skilled industrial labour was from $6 to $7 a day; builders got $7.50; crane operators $8.40; samplers in the sugar industry, $4.67; weighers, $7.15 to $7.69; general mechanics $10.71; welders, $11.12; foundrymen, $15.57; shop foremen, $12.47; chief electricians, $23.35 (W.B., 142). To each of these sums, 9.09% was added to convert their 44-hour week into one of 48 hours.
[10] Oshima's estimate.
[11] *Historical Statistics*, 94.
[12] *Primer Estudio Provisional del Balance de Recursos de Trabajo*, 23 July 1962.

times. This meant that fewer and fewer young people reaching fourteen found employment quickly. Still, the tendency gave alarm, scarcely affected by the increase in the minimum wage in February 1958 to $85 a week in Havana, $80 in other cities, and $75 in the country.[13]

The 1953 census suggested that a quite high percentage of Cubans – 25% of the labour force or about 450,000 – could be regarded as skilled. But Cuba always seemed short of foremen and inspectors. The census also showed that a sophisticatedly high proportion of the labour force was occupied in service activities, many with the railways and highways. A North American study of the Cuban economy published in July 1956[14] described the Cuban worker as having 'wider horizons than most Latin American workers and [expecting] more out of life in material amenities than many European workers ... His goal is to reach a standard of living comparable with that of the [North] American worker.' His imagination, that is, had been roused – he knew from television, films, or personal observation the kind of life lived by North Americans. At the same time it was clear that, unless a striking change occurred both in the sugar industry and in the place of sugar in the economy, this goal might move further away, not nearer. The workers feared that mechanization and improved methods of production would assist the capitalist, not the worker, and that neither government nor private initiative could create an expanding economy.

A million workers, or half the total labour force, belonged to a union in 1958.[15] The unions had been grouped together in the national confederation, the CTC, in 1938, which from then till 1947 had been run chiefly by the Communists, with the mulatto, Lázaro Peña, as secretary-general. The Auténticos had bludgeoned their way into control in 1947. First, Angel Cofiño, then Eusebio Mujal, was secretary-general. Almost half the total membership of the CTC consisted of the sugar workers who, under leaders such as Conrado Bécquer and Conrado Rodríguez, were much the most influential union for nearly all sugar workers, both

---

[13] *H.A.R.*, March 1958. These figures were not all fulfilled.

[14] *Investment in Cuba*, 24.

[15] Maybe up to 1,500,000, possibly only 800,000. In 1943 the labour force reached 1,520,851 or 46·84% of the total population over thirteen. Agriculture, including fishing and mining, accounted for 41·9% of the population – a drop of 7·2% since 1919. Ten years later, the Cuban labour force was estimated at just over two million (53·8% of those over fourteen); 60% of the labour force lived in places classified as urban (including the *bateys* of sugar mills); 17% of the labour force were women. Women only, as would be expected, were found more often in the town than the country – especially Havana, where over half the working women were (Census of 1953, xl–xli, 153 ff.). Over half the women (65%) who worked carried out various forms of 'service' jobs. The average age of the working force was 33·8, and of those seeking employment it was only 28·9. The economically active of these, 31%, lived in Havana province. 41% were in agriculture, and 18% lived as artisans or by helping operate machines (*ibid.*, xlii). This shows a surprising absence of drift from the land since 1943: in most developing countries the index of wealth is indeed the proportion of the working population who are not on the land.

in the mills and in the fields, were organized in the unions. There were, however, thirty-two industrial federations in all, with union organization, as might be expected, weak or non-existent in the very many smaller farms (other than those connected with sugar) and on cattle ranches or on coffee farms. Unions, like student politics, often led to political advancement – being obvious means of such for ambitious working-class men, especially Negroes or mulattoes. Most big unions had special committees on Negro questions. The Cadillac-mounted leaders of Mujal's group talked a lot about the class struggle, but few knew much about daily problems of workers. Mujal was believed to have accumulated a fortune of several millions. The port workers were the most obstructive union of all: though they had to cope with unemployment between October and January, they had secured laws which raised port costs in Havana so high as to discourage commerce. Communist-controlled even under Batista, they were the highest-paid workers in Cuba. Most were Negroes or mulattoes. They were backward, reactionary and lawless. Many were part-time smugglers, pimps or male prostitutes (the famous *negros bugarrones del muelle*). They were headquarters of *santería* or ñáñiguismo; the most famous Communist dock labour leader Aracelio Iglesias, murdered in 1948 in a brawl, was himself a santero.

It is clear, then, how at the same time friends of the old regime in Cuba were able to argue that the country had the most advanced labour laws and its enemies could say that the people were neglected. It is equally plain how the apparently strong institution of the Cuban trade unions was later incapable of providing resistance, moral or physical, to the pressure of revolution. The Cuban working class was in many respects exactly what Fanon called organized labour in the Third World in *Les Damnés de la Terre* – the 'pampered proletariat'.

The Economy: the Central Neurosis

Old societies out of joint usually demand overall solutions:

> [A reformer might] teach a farmer to grow tomatoes ... twice as big as his neighbour's, but then ... they lie rotting in the field because there is no market ... or because there are no lorries to take them to market or no roads. If the tomatoes ... get to market, it is so controlled that the farmer gets only a small return on his effort. When he seeks credit to invest in fertilizer ... he finds it ... non-existent. Once he has made his land useful, he may well find that his ownership is disputed and some faraway urban landlord may try to take it away from him. His local political representative is more than likely in cahoots with the urban landlord.[1]

In Cuba, the interlocking nature of the political and economical problems was at least as strong as elsewhere. There were two main economic anxieties: first, the anxiety of Cuban workers about employment generally, due to the memories of the 1930s, meant that costs of production were high, that efficiency was lowered and that foreign investment was discouraged. In 1950 the World Bank wrote:

> Unless this vicious circle is broken, all efforts at economic betterment in Cuba will be severely handicapped. Cubans of all classes will suffer by lower incomes, by fewer and inferior job opportunities and perhaps even by internal dangers to their cherished political freedoms.[2]

The warning was clear, and some slight changes for the better were introduced between then and 1952, when the 'cherished political freedoms' were indeed subverted. The Batistiano government afterwards attempted, like many other dictatorships, to seize the nettle of labour costs and, with the connivance of the corrupt unions, enabled manufacturers to cut costs by letting them lay off labour. After that, foreign investment increased considerably, but it did so, of course, in the unnatural scenery of Batista's arbitrary rule.

The second economic anxiety was also well described by the World Bank.

---

[1] G. C. Lodge, 'Revolution in Latin America', *Foreign Affairs*, January 1966.
[2] World Bank, 359.

Cuba enjoys a level of income and a standard of living among the highest in Latin America and probably the highest in any tropical country. However, the productive basis for this was mainly established before 1925 [that is, the industrial structure of the sugar industry]. Since then, the Cuban economy has made relatively little progress. Cuban incomes have fluctuated with the world market for sugar, [have been] affected strongly by trade cycles, tariffs, quotas and wars, but have shown little ... overall tendency to advance. At the same time, the Cuban economy suffers from a high degree of instability. Every year there is a long dead season when most of the sugar workers are unemployed and the most extensive capital equipment in the country lies idle ... instabilities from booms and depressions and political crises in the outside world quickly raise or lower the Cuban economic [picture] ... A stagnant and unstable economy with a high level of insecurity creates resistance to improvements in productive efficiency. And yet improvements in productive efficiency are the key to creating a more progressive, more stable economy ... [This is] the 'master circle' of all vicious circles that needs to be attacked.[3]

This 'master circle' lasted throughout the 1950s. The Sugar Agreement of 1953 inaugurated an era of permanent restriction of Cuba's main product. Apart from some changes in ownership of the mills, sugar remained stagnant. This affected much of the economy, despite the investment and building boom. Such efforts at diversification as the mechanization of rice-growing had brought small but not fundamental changes. It still seemed that diversification was 'almost beyond capitalist laws'. The spirit of lottery remained: for the grand capitalist, whatever might be won in the unpredictable international sugar market outshadowed all possible profits from less striking but constructive ventures of agricultural change.

The further problem was that Cuba had become a 'marginal supplier' in both the U.S. and the world markets. Except during the world wars and for some years afterwards, these markets had been so protected that further growth in sugar, the main industry of Cuba, seemed improbable. Thus the Cuban economy had lost the main expanding force which had impelled it since the late eighteenth century. Cuba produced 5·2 million tons of sugar in 1925; in 1955, 4·4 million tons. During that time the population had increased 70%, from 3½ million to 6 million,

---

[3] World Bank, 361. Felipe Pazos, Prío's Director of the National Bank (and Castro's), wrote in 1954: 'at bottom the major economic problems of Cuba in the last thirty years and many of the social, political and even moral problems, derive from this lack of growth in the basic industry.' (Felipe Pazos, *Dificultades y posibilidades de una política de industrialización en Cuba*, *Humanismo*, No 24, Mexico, 1954.)

giving an increase in the labour force of some 800,000. Of course, not all these men were out of work all the time, but 'the pressure of a growing population on a stagnant economy' continued to be the most severe problem.[4]

The word 'diversification' had therefore been on the lips of economists and politicians since the 1920s. Not much had really been done. Most capitalists were engaged in sugar. Available technology related to sugar. Sugar was so easily and effectively grown in Cuba. Until 1950 agricultural credit was only available for sugar or tobacco: the absence of farm-to-market roads hindered the development of other crops, but sugar had its own railways. Marketing facilities were good for sugar but for little else. Until 1950 governments had tried to keep down the prices of crops other than sugar to avoid rises in the cost of living. Freight rates too had favoured sugar till about 1950. True, since 1927 tariffs had stimulated home production, industrial and agricultural. But some government efforts had been self-defeating. Thus a law of 1942 obliged sugar mills to plant subsidiary crops such as beans or maize. This meant that at least part of non-sugar crops thereafter lay in the hands of those financially best equipped. But, by other legislation, sugar wage rates were to be paid for this activity. U.S. foods and manufactured products also entered Cuba only too easily. Hence, to secure diversification, sugar-men and cattle-men would have had to cooperate far more than they had ever showed any signs of being able to do.

The aim should have been clear: the expansion or creation of export industries or crops unconnected with sugar; and the concentration on sugar by-products for exports and the domestic market. But this could hardly be done without an economy planned more carefully than in the past and in more detail than, say, had been found possible in England or France.

One problem was that though Cuban capital had always been plentiful, there had been little desire to invest it in domestic industrial activity. There were definite improvements in this respect in the mid-1950s, partly due to the Agricultural and Industrial Development banks. In 1950 the World Bank argued that the 'investment atmosphere had become so unpleasant that foreigners did not care to bring industrial capital in . . . and Cubans themselves prefer to send theirs outside or to put it into real estate'.[5] Of course, conditions for a successful capital market cannot be created overnight and did not fully exist in any South American or Caribbean country. The Havana Stock Exchange,[6] the only Stock Exchange in Cuba, had only eighty members, and a

---

[4] Pazos, *loc. cit.*

[5] *Ibid.*, 136. Even during the prosperous days of 1947-9, the gross capital accumulation by Cubans absorbed only about 5% of the Gross National Product.

[6] Founded 1884.

small number of private shares were listed – less than sixty, and only about twelve actively traded. Few new issues came up. Most medium-sized enterprises were family companies in which outside shareholders were unwelcome. The money needed to expand a business was usually found among friends and relations. There were few brokers. The law governing the Stock Exchange was an old Spanish one. There was little supervision over market activities and high fees were paid to get securities onto the market. The consequence was that a small percentage only of the savings of Cubans went into new ventures. Saving as a proportion of the GNP was considerably less in the 1950s than in the 1940s. Repair, maintenance, acquisition and installation of capital equipment absorbed what savings there were, and in the 1950s a quarter went to building.

Recollection of past crashes, such as that of 1920 and that of New York in 1929, played a part. Cubans were very reluctant to invest in government issues, which were chiefly bought by banks, insurance companies and pension funds. In fact, most Cubans with money were interested first and foremost in having cash available. The nature of the economy made this necessary to meet the customary sudden swings of fortune. Available short-term funds were often put in New York or in bank deposits, sometimes (as in the case of many of Batista's associates) in U.S. currency in Cuban bank safety deposit boxes. Secondly, savers were interested in property, either in Havana or perhaps in Miami and New York City. In the 1950s building represented nearly 30% of capital formation, higher than between 1947 and 1949. Others with money invested in ordinary U.S. stock. Cubans had 'at least' $M150 invested in the U.S. in 1955,[7] probably over two-thirds in Florida. Prominent among these were Grau's crooked ex-Minister of Education's investments in the Alsina Corporation and Batista's large Florida investments.[8] The World Bank in 1950 found that a 'startling amount' of the larger denomination dollar bills returned to New York for collection from Florida had clearly originated in Cuba.[9] At least $M250 in the 1950s was deposited as nominally short-term assets in U.S. banks. Maybe in the mid-1950s Cuban investment in the U.S. had fallen off but by 1958 it had gone back at least to its former figure.[10] Again thanks to the improved financial conditions existing after the establishment of the National Bank, capital investment by Cubans increased during the 1950s.[11] Some investments by Cubans had been made

[7] *Investment in Cuba*, 15.
[8] World Bank, 519.
[9] *Ibid.*,
[10] *Cf. Investment in Cuba*, 15, fn. 25.
[11] According to the National Bank, investment between 1952 and 1957 was 12% of the gross product, fairly high, that is.

in Canada, Europe and some parts of South America (especially Venezuela).[12]

Foreign investment in Cuba greatly contrasted with Cubans' own investment. In 1900 foreign investment probably totalled $M50.[13] By 1913 it had risen to about $M400, of which about $M220 was U.S., the rest being English, French, Spanish or Canadian.[14] By 1929 U.S. investments reached about $M1,000,[15] the largest quantity of U.S. investment in Latin America – mostly in sugar mills, but also in utilities and tobacco. This figure fell during the depression and the Second World War, but rose again afterwards, to reach perhaps $M1200 in 1958.[16] By the 1950s utilities – electricity, telephone, railways – totalled more than their agricultural or sugar interests: about $M300 compared with $M270.[17] The rate of 'increase' of U.S. investment in Cuba had been slower than in any other Latin American country; but $M3,000 had been invested in Latin America by U.S. citizens in the first ten years after the Second World War, a third of that in oil.

English investment had dropped, and in 1958 consisted chiefly of a Shell refinery and a number of insurance companies. Canada had an important bank and some other minor businesses. France still had a sugar mill and the West Germans a supermarket chain, opened in 1955. Spaniards still had extensive holdings of property, while Cuban Spaniards sent home at least $M5 from Cuba.[18]

Cuba had about fifty banks with nearly two hundred branches, as well as the Postal Savings Bank and the National Bank, which had been moderately successful and remained the most prestigious economic body on the island, though its director under Batista, Martínez Sáenz, the old ABC leader, was inferior as an economist to Pazos, the director under Prío. But some good economists, such as Julián Alienes, had remained in Cuba throughout the *Batistato*.

As in the sugar industry, Cubans were gradually recovering control of banks since 1945. In 1939 foreign banks held over 80% of all deposits; in 1959 Cuban banks owned 60%. Still, the Royal Bank of Canada, the

---

[12] Even if a high figure of $M400 for total Cuban investment abroad is taken, this represents only a small percentage of the total amount of Latin American capital invested abroad—between $M5,000 and $M10,000 in 1963 according to Sir George Bolton (*Annual Review of BOLSA*, 1962–3, qu. *Manchester Guardian*, 8 April 1963), or between $M8,000 and $M10,000, according to *H.A.R.*, XV, 1174, in 1962. See also Dumont's figures, as described above.

[13] W. J. Clark, *Commercial Cuba: a book for business men* (1899) (excluding Spanish).

[14] Winkler, 275.

[15] Winkler had $M1,500, Paul Dickens $M1,000, Jenks $M1,150.

[16] Herbert Matthews in the *New York Times*, 26 April 1959, speaks of $M800, but in 1960 U.S. investments were reckoned at about $M1,000 (*New York Times*, 5 November 1962). Núñez Jiménez, *Geografía*, 294, speaks of $M800, following Matthews. See also figures of Sanderson, quoted above p. 1172.

[17] *Investment in Cuba*, 10.

[18] *Ibid.*, 120.

Bank of Nova Scotia, the National City, Chase Manhattan, and the First National Banks remained prominent and probably decisive. These and the other foreign banks (and for a long time the Cuban banks too) were marked by great reluctance to back anything but riskless ventures. Where labour remembered the depression, banks recalled the 'Dance of the Millions' of 1920. In contrast with most Latin American countries, banks were therefore a passive element in the Cuban economy. After 1950 the Cuban recovery was partly due to slightly less conservative attitudes to borrowing, to the influence of the National Bank, and to the change in 1951 from a monetary system based on the interchangeability of dollar and *peso* to one based on the *peso* alone (the *peso* remained however equal to the dollar). Bank deposits increased throughout the 1950s, showing no decline as the civil war continued, save for a brief drop in 1958 from 1957 levels, themselves high chiefly because of the successful harvest.[19]

The 1950s also saw the creation of new government credit institutions: to the Agricultural and Industrial Development Bank (BANFAIC) of 1951 was added a Mortgaging Insurance Institute in 1955, a National Finance Agency in 1953, the Cuban Foreign Trade Bank in 1954 and the Economic and Social Development Bank (BANDES) in 1955, all autonomous subsidiaries of the National Bank. BANFAIC had had much success, lending money for rice development, small credit associations, a Hanabanilla hydro-electric plant, and so on. The Mortgage Insurance Institute had the east Havana low cost housing project to its credit. The National Finance Agency had partly financed the expansion of Cuban Electric, a new Havana waterworks, and Marianao sewage. The Cuban Bank of Foreign Trade had carried out a sugar railway equipment arrangement with West Germany and had partly financed the Havana Hilton Hotel and the Havana harbour tunnel.

Taken as a whole U.S. capital had of course contributed greatly to Cuba's general development, though it had partly been responsible for the excessive emphasis on sugar. It had certainly brought living standards which could only be satisfied with plentiful supplies of American goods. As early as 1927, Leland Jenks had said that the U.S. had brought expensive techniques and heavy overhead charges and sought to compensate the consequent loss in personal relationships by housing improvements and welfare work. 'It finds that engineers from the [United] States will fill managerial positions more satisfactorily for $500 a month than Cubans for $250 . . . It has made it possible for irrevocable decisions affecting most of the Cuban population to be taken in Wall Street . . .'[20] These comments were as valid in 1958 as thirty years

---

[19] *Cf.* World Bank, 566; *Investment in Cuba,* 124; *Estudio,* 916.
[20] Jenks, 301–2.

before. Cuba might be the most highly capitalized tropical country[21] – that is, it had more capital per head than similar countries. But the phrase meant that it was more linked than any other country to the international capitalist system, however that itself might be changing, and the proximity of the north-east of the U.S., the richest region in the world, undoubtedly had a debilitating effect on the development of Cuban industries: goods from that area could be taken to Cuba cheaper than to Texas or California.

The tax system in Cuba meantime was full of contradictions, and for many years had been crying out for reform. Customs and purchase taxes gave half the total tax. Direct (income) taxes provided a mere quarter of total revenues. Nevertheless this fraction was much higher than it had been twenty years before. Budgetary revenues were anyway low – about 14% of the national income – since public works were usually financed out of loan issues, not taxation. Most of the taxes (64%) went on salaries. Throughout Batista's second period, a high proportion of revenues went to the armed forces, but in 1955 (before the beginning of the civil war), the proportion was perhaps about one quarter.[22] The provincial governments and municipalities lived from hand to mouth, depending on the national government.

Public debt increased throughout the 1950s. The debt outstanding in 1950 derived from past floating indebtedness and from various settlements of public works bills dating from the Machado era. In 1950 the Cuban government floated its first domestic issue of bonds. Between then and 1955, $M400 was raised, almost twice as much as Cuba had altogether previously borrowed. About a quarter was held by banks, a quarter by the Currency Stabilization Fund on behalf of U.S. banks, and the rest by other big insurance companies or pension funds. Between 1956 and 1958 the cost of political upheaval became evident. In 1958 total debt reached about $M800;[23] this, though high in comparison with what it had reached before, was hardly unbearable reckoned against the wealth of the nation, though some of the methods used in raising the money to pay it were questionable. But the bond issues almost all maintained their value at par.

In 1958 Cuba imported far more agricultural products from the U.S. than any other Latin American country did.[24] Of these most were goods which could have been grown at home – vegetables, oil, lard (the largest

[21] The phrase is H. C. Wallich's, *Monetary Problems of an Export Economy* (1950), of 1948. But it applies to 1958-9 too.

[22] Figure taken from *Investment in Cuba*, 121, adding 'National Defence' to 'Security and Justice'.

[23] *Cf. Estudio*, 850. The revolutionary regime accused Batista of leaving behind a debt of $M1,200. Batista's bank president, Martínez Sáenz, defended himself from gaol in *Por la Independencia de Cuba* (Havana, 1959).

[24] *Statistical Yearbook of UN, 1959*, qu. *Estudio*, 1145.

25 Peasants come to Havana to support the agrarian reform

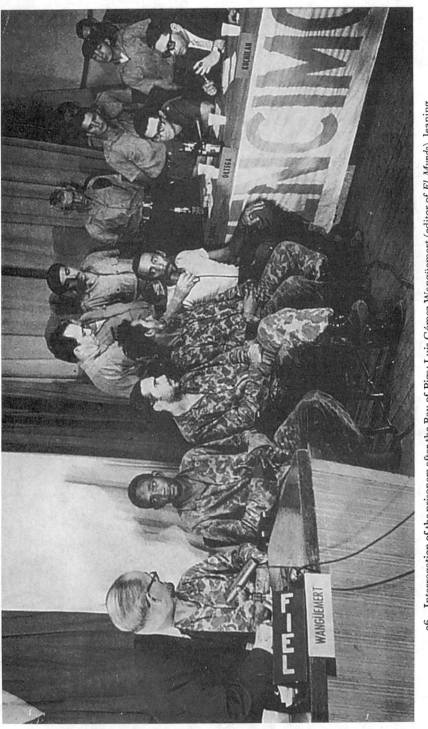

26 Interrogation of the prisoners after the Bay of Pigs: Luis Gómez Wangüemert (editor of *El Mundo*), leaning forward; the rebel commanders Oliva, Artime and Pérez San Roman, all sitting; Rafael Soler Puig, afterwards shot; Major Guillermo Jiménez and a journalist, Ortega

agricultural item). This figure was fairly constant.[25] But Cuba exported more or less twice the volume of agricultural goods that she consumed herself.

In the past Cuba had had an unfavourable balance of trade only rarely. This gave her a good name in international monetary circles. In the 1950s, however, there was usually a deficit in the balance of payments because of a fall in sugar prices and the increased import of North American goods. In the last months before the fall of Batista there was a considerable flight of capital, though it was difficult to know how large, for during the last years before 1958 Cuba lost much of her monetary resources for other reasons. To counteract the economic restrictions on sugar production, the government had embarked on a public works programme, backed by bonds. These expenditures further stimulated a demand for imports which (along with other expenses such as services, remission of profits, etc.) could not be met. Thus the resources in 1958 were actually below those of any year since 1947[26] and, in real terms (after subtracting further loans in foreign money etc.) were lower than any year since 1942. Even so, Cuba remained among the countries of Latin America with the largest gold reserves.[27]

Tourism developed considerably in the 1950s. In 1957 about 350,000 tourists[28] visited Cuba, bringing in $M62, compared with the 160,000 who arrived, on the average, ten years before, and who had brought only about $M17. Until 1956, however, the money that tourists spent in Cuba did not balance what Cubans spent abroad.[29] By 1958 there were many places apart from Havana and Varadero which offered good opportunities for the pleasure-bound traveller.

The importance of exports for the Cuban economy remained; so did the pattern. Exports made up between 30% and 40% of the national income, but the rest of the economy was still built up round exports. Between 1902 and 1945 four-fifths of Cuban exports went to the U.S., and after 1945 most Cuban exports still did, but the percentage nevertheless dropped to just over two-thirds in the 1950s due to increased sugar demand by other places.[30] This partly derived from a changed attitude to tariffs: before the Depression the Cuban government used the tariff primarily for revenue; afterwards, they used it to stimulate

[25] *Cf.* the rather confusing figures in *Estudio*, 1146–7.

[26] *Estudio*, 924.

[27] *Ibid.*, 931; *cf. H.A.R.*, February 1959, which quotes the National Bank as saying that the reserves had fallen $M424 to about $M373 between 1952 and 1959.

[28] Including excursionists who only stopped off there on a cruise.

[29] *Estudio*, 1126. Cubans abroad spent $M37·5 as tourists in 1958; there were about 33,000 Cubans supposed to be living abroad then. It is highly probable that the figures for tourist spending in Cuba was an underestimate. Certainly whole zones of Havana seemed laid out for tourist satisfaction on a bigger scale than these figures would suggest.

[30] *Investment in Cuba*, 135.

agricultural and industrial development, along with diversification, which gathered momentum after the Second World War.[31] From 1908 until the Depression Cuba had, incidentally, exported more to the U.S. than any other Latin American country. Since then, she was always second to Brazil.[32] What diversification there had been had not yet affected exports. Sugar represented the same proportion of exports after the Second World War as it did before the Depression,[33] in 1948 90% of exports, falling back afterwards towards 80%.

The decrease in Cuban exports to the U.S. had surprisingly little effect on Cuban imports from the U.S.; the U.S. supplied two-thirds of Cuban imports between 1911 and 1940, and about three-quarters since 1950. As ever since the eighteenth century, the most important import was food – nearly 30% of the whole between 1948 and 1954. How absurd that a country so promising for horticulture – no winter to speak of, good rain supply, good soil – should be importing from the U.S. nearly half its vegetables and fruit!

It is not easy to explain the remarkable debility of Cuban society in the middle of the twentieth century, to balance the considerable prosperity on the one hand against the psychological weaknesses on the other, the stifling labour laws and the stagnation, the reliance on sugar and the world market and the increased diversification. The weaknesses derive partly from the consequences of a long and destructive war of independence, in which most of the best men of the generation of 1895 died and in which the old Cuban society of the nineteenth century, already in decay, received a mortal blow. Afterwards, while Cuban politicians sought only personal profit from power, both Spaniards and Negroes, at the top and bottom of the social scale, in their separate ways chose to withdraw from responsibility; Spaniards remained Spaniards even in the second generation, they busied themselves with commerce and private life and, though for years economically dominant, they were politically inactive; Negroes recovered slowly from slavery, found *criollo* politics too hispanic to take an active part in them, and derived the most comfort from re-enacted African memories. Into the vacuum thus left strode the North Americans who, not always with enthusiasm, directed the economy and the foreign policy of Cuba for much of the twentieth century. In the 1920s Cuba had a *per capita* income about half that of the U.S. or two-thirds that of Britain, since she was an integral part of the U.S. economy. There was full employment. Naturally, patriotic Cubans worried about the political price paid for these benefits

[31] A general summary of the tariffs in Cuba in the mid-1950s can be seen in *ibid.*, 136.
[32] *Historical Statistics of the U.S.*
[33] *Investment in Cuba*, 140.

but that they were material benefits for the majority cannot be questioned. Cuban men of business came to regard the U.S. as 'the godfather of the island',[34] to whom they were ready to hand over responsibility. Though the Cubans had a currency of their own after 1914, the U.S. dollar bill was the only paper currency in general circulation until 1934.

The Depression and the Revolution of 1933 marked the political, social and economic system indelibly. As a consequence of her close relations with the U.S., Cuba probably suffered more from the former event than any other country. The Revolution of 1933 was conceived not simply as a means of overthrowing Machado but as a way of reconstructing a new world, worthy of Martí's patriotic dreams. In the event, the Revolution and what followed brought many important changes. The power of private capitalism was bridled. Much enlightened social legislation was introduced. The sugar planters received a new deal. Diversification of agriculture was encouraged. The Platt Amendment was abolished and the role of the U.S. in the economy reduced. Labour organized itself. A new constitution was prepared. But no political system was achieved and, instead of the 'decent men' of the Auténticos being responsible for these improvements, it was in fact Batista and the Communists. Further, the political life of the country remained feeble. The social changes did not prevent, indeed they increased, the stagnation in the country's main industry. Neither exports nor imports, nor educational figures, attained in the post-1945 world the levels of the 1920s. Both the population and the unemployed increased. Intellectuals sought scapegoats. The U.S., anyway partly responsible, was at hand.

Corruption and frivolity were doubtless the characteristics of old Cuba but it is pompous to condemn every manifestation of the latter as harshly as the former; the castle in the style of the Black Forest belonging to the Abreus, in the midst of the canefields of Matanzas, may shock Puritans but its absurdity is also an enchantment. Such follies may doom classes who construct them, but they nevertheless themselves survive to delight even those whom a more earnest purpose later dispatches there.[35]

[34] A remark to the author of Julio Lobo, 10 November 1968.
[35] This castle is now a workers' home.

BOOK XI

The Clash
1959 - 62

Castro in America

In the spring of 1959, the contenders for power in Cuba had already, it seemed, been reduced essentially to three groups: Castro and the rebel army; the Communists; and the liberal men of good will. The contenders did not, however, all recognize each other as such. The contenders did not as yet contend, nor were they so unified as they seemed: were the rebel army officers all so loyal? Had the liberals decided upon the determining point of their liberalism? What, after all, did it really mean to be loyal to Castro? In the battle for power, which, with hindsight, seems to have been inevitable, some never fought, however their loyalties may really have lain.

The reason lay partly in Castro's personality. A month after Batista's flight, Castro had established a personal hold over the Cuban masses such as no Latin American leader had ever had. Not even Perón at his peak had been so obviously and so universally loved. To those who had dreamed hopelessly for many years for a settled wage, for schools and medicine for their children, Castro represented a hope brighter than Grau in 1933 or 1944. Already he was the champion to whom multitudes desired to surrender their will, confident that he would not betray such expectations. After his return from Venezuela, Castro appeared so often on the television screen (the State Department was already beginning to curse the salesmen of those 400,000 sets) that he resembled less a De Gaulle or a Kennedy (others who used television to effect) than a kind of permanent confessor or a resident revolutionary medicine man. He roused the expectations of masses who, until January, had been torpid, despairing, cynical, lost 'ragged-trousered philanthropists', and anti-political. To the masses Castro, with his known unpunctuality, his volatility, his distrust of convention and law, his improvidence and talkativeness, seemed the most typical of themselves.[1] To the middle class he already seemed suspect: psychiatrists noted how he often spoke with two watches on his wrist.[2]

Television and radio were, of course, in private hands, including the two powerful national television networks, Channel 2, owned by

---

[1] *Cf.* Dewart, *Christianity and Revolution*, 33.

[2] See an attempt at a psychiatric explanation of Castro's behaviour and character by Oscar Sagredo Acebal, in *Bohemia Libre,* 17 September 1961.

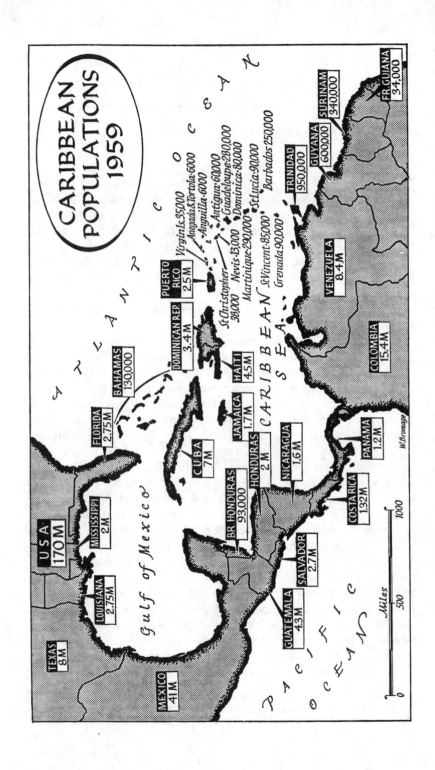

CARIBBEAN POPULATIONS 1959

TEXAS 8M
USA 170M
LOUISIANA 2.75M
MISSISSIPPI 2M
MEXICO 41M
FLORIDA 2.75M
BAHAMAS 130,000
DOMINICAN REP. 3.4M
PUERTO RICO 2.5M
Virgin Is. 35000
Angada&Tortola 6000
Anguilla 6000
St Christopher 38,000
Nevis 13,000
Antigua 60000
Guadeloupe 280,000
Dominica 80,000
Martinique 290,000
St Lucia 90000
St Vincent 85000
Barbados 250,000
Grenada 90,000
HAITI 4.5M
CUBA 7M
JAMAICA 1.7M
BR. HONDURAS 93,000
HONDURAS 2M
GUATEMALA 4.3M
SALVADOR 2.7M
NICARAGUA 1.6M
COSTA RICA 1.32M
PANAMA 1.2M
COLOMBIA 15.4M
VENEZUELA 8.4M
TRINIDAD 950,000
GUYANA 600000
SURINAM 340,000
FR. GUIANA 34,000

ATLANTIC OCEAN
CARIBBEAN SEA
Gulf of Mexico
PACIFIC OCEAN

Miles
0   500   1000

W.Bromage

the newpaper *El Mundo*, and CMQ Radio TV, belonging to the Mestre Brothers, but Castro never had any difficulty in appearing when he wanted, and several small stations, such as the Havana television company Channel 12, Radio Rebelde, Unión Radio and Radio Mambí, were from the beginning unconditional supporters of Castro.

Castro himself must always have had in his mind the suspicion sown by Guevara (with his experience of Guatemala) and by Raúl Castro that only an extreme solution could be victorious: either a dictatorship of the proletariat or the ruin of the revolution. To those of the middle class whose imaginations, from worthy motives or from base, were dominated with a vague desire for revenge on the U.S., Castro represented already, by the mere fact of his astounding victory, the spirit of challenge. '*Gracias Fidel*' was the placarded cry of thousands at public meetings throughout the spring: 'thanks' as yet for conquest and for further conquests ahead. Beyond Havana lay Latin America, her eyes on Cuba almost for the first time; beyond Cuba, the world. No Cuban had been so famous as Castro. Already shepherds in Spain and wool workers in Yorkshire had heard of 'Fidel'; he, a keen student of the international press, knew that they knew.

The speeches which Castro made now and which became so important part of his tenure of power were never carefully prepared. He would naturally consider the points which he wished to emphasize but found that

> If you try to give a definite shape to your ideas, to give them a prior form, when you begin to speak, you lose one of the finest influences that the public can exercise over the person who speaks, which is to transmit its ardour, its enthusiasm, its force, its inspiration through him. Often my speeches are conversations . . . with the public.[3]

The machinery of retribution against Batista's henchmen meantime ground on, imprisonments, trials and executions being reported from all over the island, with gory accounts being published of Batistiano tortures, along with documentary proof of the despoliations practised by the old regime.[4] The harvest ground on too, the 130th since Cuba first became the world's greatest sugar producer. The President decreed the 1959 sugar harvest should be 5·8 million tons, of which 350,000 tons were for the home market, 2·2 million tons for the U.S., 500,000 tons for the U.S. reserve, 1·5 million tons for the world market, the rest for various reserves.

[3] Lockwood, 178.

[4] It is curious to note that this ultra-nationalist regime should have employed as its chief executioner, at La Cabaña, a North American who joined Guevara in the Escambray, the farouche Captain Herman Marks, a native of Milwaukee with a criminal record.

But there were already discordant voices. In Washington, Wieland, still at the Caribbean desk in the State Department, wrote a memorandum arguing that 'if we strengthened the moderates in Cuba, Fidel could see that his own survival depended on the moderate wing and dissociate himself from the extremist wing'.[5] But the U.S., regardless whether they knew who or what that 'extremist wing' was, had little power to do anything just now. More important, inside Cuba, 6,000 employees of the Cuba Electric Company declared a slowdown in order to achieve a 20 % rise in wages, while 600 workers who had been dismissed by the company in 1957–8 began a strike in part of the presidential palace, demanding reinstatement. There were also hunger strikes by railway workers who had been left unemployed and by workers of a closed paper mill near Havana. 3,000 building workers left Moa Bay. The restaurant workers threatened to strike unless the casinos reopened. Twenty-one sugar mills were delayed in the harvest by wage demands. The revolution had aroused expectations, how were they to be satisfied? Castro spoke of his sympathy with the demands but appealed against strikes. In a speech to the Shell Oil workers he promised: 'We did not carry out the Revolution to defend the interests of the mighty but of the humble. Now it is the right strategy to avoid major conflicts, even if a sacrifice must be made, because a sacrifice now will be compensated by greater returns at another time.'[6] Yet it was obscure how these aims would be achieved.

More pointedly still, perhaps, Castro became involved in a dispute with the humorous paper *Zig Zag*, the *Canard Enchainé* of Cuba. *Zig Zag* made fun of him. Castro threatened to have it suppressed. Was the time for humour past? It began to be wondered, in intellectual circles only, to be sure, whether all had been solved. To the world Castro might seem a man of destiny. To intimates he seemed already more 'lost in the labyrinths of power'.[7] To the Shell workers Castro announced that the only sacrifice he would never make for the revolution would be 'to use force to carry through the revolution'. For the moment, he was believed.

On 7 February the cabinet had approved what was called a fundamental law of the Republic, a major abrogation of the Constitution of 1940. Legislative power was to be vested in the cabinet, which alone could change the fundamental law. Thus, even while liberals were still at least nominally in power, an autocratic measure perpetuated power in a self-perpetuating cabinet. It is difficult to believe that this was really, to democrats, justified by the 'exigencies of the Revolutionary

[5] Wieland, 649.
[6] *Discursos para la Historia*, 52.
[7] Casuso, 202.

Period', as President Urrutia put it.[8] Urrutia, however, was pre-occupied by one thing only: the suppression of gambling. Urrutia proposed compensation of employees. Castro on television slightingly said that 'from an air-conditioned office it is very easy to take bread from the mouths of casino employees'.[9] Urrutia wished to resign. He was persuaded to stay. This was Castro's first clash with the government which he had himself set up.

The next clash was not long in coming. The prime minister, the eminent lawyer, Dr Miró Cardona, had found his position false from the beginning. Like President Urrutia, he had already tried once to resign, in January, over the question of restoring the death penalty and making legal penalties retroactive.[10] But his lack of real power and Castro's lack of real responsibility, combined with his middle age in comparison with the youth of Castro and his friends, caused him now to resign absolutely, and to recommend that Castro should become premier in his stead.[11] Castro went to Urrutia with Luis Orlando Rodríguez. The latter, the ex-Auténtico youth leader, and now Minister of the Interior (though by no means an intimate of Castro's), told Urrutia that Castro should now become prime minister, since in that way 'the revolution would gain unity'. Castro said that 'he would accept the post of Prime Minister but, since he would be responsible for the policy of the Government, he would need sufficiently broad powers to enable him to act efficiently.'[12] That is, he did not want Urrutia to preside at cabinet meetings or even to be present at them. Urrutia said that he 'would be glad to have him become Prime Minister . . . with the broad prerogatives he required', and added that he, Urrutia, wanted to 'leave the Presidency to enter the Supreme Court'. Urrutia tendered his resignation to the cabinet, but several ministers, as well as Castro, begged him not to do so. The Minister of Public Works, Manuel Ray, was among them: 'Doctor, don't resign, you are the Revolution's last hope.'[13] Again, Urrutia agreed to stay; he was not thereafter present at cabinet meetings and retained only a nominal veto over decrees.

These were critical surrenders by the liberals. Miró wrote later: 'I resigned. Cuba did not protest; it accepted, it applauded.'[14] For Urrutia too, it was the beginning of the end. Had he been a man of greater energy, resolution and imagination, he might have done much. Unfortunately, he was no politician. He had been too long in the law

---

[8] Even when writing in exile (Urrutia, 35).

[9] *Revolución*, 1 February.

[10] *Diario de la Marina* (Miami), 12 November 1960.

[11] Lockwood, 176.

[12] Urrutia, 38.

[13] This is Urrutia's account, and Castro's account to Lee Lockwood initially confirms it (176) except of course for Ray's remark.

[14] *Diario de la Marina*, 12 November 1960.

courts. He was keen on having capital letters in the right places. He got up too late in the mornings. He never insisted that a day for elections should be swiftly announced.[15]

On assuming the prime ministership, Castro went out of his way to emphasize his moderation; he spoke of his 'lack of personal ambitions, loyalty to principles, unshakeable and profound democratic convictions'. He denied having ever wished a lowering of rents; and promised that the standard of living in Cuba would soon be raised above that in either the U.S. or Russia.[16] On the other hand, he also announced on 23 February that 'it would not be correct to organize elections now. We should get a crushing majority. It is in the public interest that elections are delayed till political parties are fully developed and their programmes clearly defined.'[17] Was this a declaration of intention, or a deception? If the latter, was it self-deception as well? Probably it was more valid a statement than Castro himself would have admitted later. By this time Castro had already appointed his 'more radical' brother Raúl as commander-in-chief of the armed forces. This meant evidently a step further to the Left in the army, for the Minister of Defence was Martínez Sánchez, Raúl Castro's advocate-general in the Sierra; the 'Second Front Frank País' appeared to control the army.[18]

On 16 February, the day that Castro attained the prime ministership, the national coordinator of the 26 July Movement referred to the revolution now 'under way' in somewhat mysterious terms as 'not an act, but a process' which would be characterized by a long series of socially conscious laws. These were summarized in sixteen points, which Castro himself did not formally acknowledge.[19] He did, however, often repeat the word 'process' in somewhat mystical style; and, in his first address to the cabinet, he said that it was necessary to 'begin . . . the

[15] In this paragraph I have benefited from discussion with Urrutia's secretary, Antonio de la Carrera.

[16] *Discursos para la Historia*, 32.

[17] *Revolución*, 24 February 1959.

[18] The other commanders were now Majors Cienfuegos (commander-in-chief); Belarminio Castilla, Hubert Matos, Ramiro Valdés, Calixto García, Antonio Duarte, Dermitio Escalona and Eddy Suñol, in command respectively of the military districts of Oriente, Camagüey, Las Villas, Matanzas, Havana, Pinar del Río and Holguín. Castilla shortly gave way to Manuel Piñeiro. Others of importance in the Army were Waldo Reina, commanding the infantry, Filiberto Oliviera, chief of the San Antonio air base, Abelardo Colomé, at the campamento de Managua, Demetrio Montseny, who was deputy to Guevara at La Cabaña, Antonio Lussón, director of operations, William Gálvez, inspector-general of the Army, Osmani Cienfuegos, head of army education, and René León, chief of the logistical section. Of these commanders, Suñol, Oliviera, Colomé, Montseny, Castilla, and Lussón had all been in Raúl Castro's column and, with the exception of Hubert Matos, all remained in prominent places during the whole of the 1960s. Piñeiro, Valdés, Calixto García, Suñol, Castilla, Oliviera, Colomé, Lussón and Osmani Cienfuegos were, along with Raúl Castro, members of the central committee of the (new) Cuban Communist party in 1965.

[19] *Revolución*, 16 February. See Suárez, 46–7, for a discussion of this stage of the evolution of Castro's thought.

revolution';[20] at the same time, he had begun to buy arms, light rifles and grenades from Belgium, ostensibly for fear of invasion by Trujillo.[21]

Many minor quarrels flickered between Communists and members of the 26 July Movement. Thus the chiefly 26 July police did nothing to prevent ex-saboteurs of the Civic Resistance from breaking into the offices of the Communist newspaper *Hoy*. Carlos Rafael Rodríguez, who had become the editor, remarked, 'If Fidel thinks that now the insurrection has won, we communists are going into a monastery he is making a mistake. The Revolution has not yet begun, and if he chooses the right road one day we shall all meet. But if not, it will be neither the first nor the last time that we shall go underground.'[22]

Castro's cabinets (which soon became weekly rather than almost daily occurrences) were, from the beginning, unusual gatherings. The cabinet might be due to assemble at three. Castro might not appear till three or more hours later, perhaps accompanied by Celia Sánchez and Guevara. At that point, the ministers would try to get the 'leader and guide' to speak to them on a special project. Castro might say that he needed sleep, since he had gone to bed at three, four or five the night before, and the meeting might be further delayed.[23]

There might be discussion, restricted to two or three people, at greater length on a subject dear to a particular minister's heart: such as Manuel Ray's plans for the much-needed secondary roads, opposed by Castro's preference for great highways. Ray himself had taken over in January, on his own initiative, all heavy equipment (steamrollers, bulldozers) which might be needed for development, and was probably the most active of all ministers in these weeks. His first plan was to finish all Batista's projects which were already begun. Castro agreed. But Ray disliked the East Havana project, which he thought involved too great an investment in housing. In such conversations, Ray, ex-leader of the underground in Havana, who had, however, only met Castro twice before 1 January, began to have doubts about Castro. Was Castro playing with them? On the other hand, Castro also impressed his colleagues as a good listener. His charm remained compelling, whether among two or three people, or two or three thousand.

At one of these meetings in February, Castro came up to a group of ministers and said: 'I have received an invitation from the American newspaper editors[24] to go to the U.S. Should I go?' 'Of course,' replied Pazos, the Bank Director, who, though not strictly a minister, was present. 'But suppose Eisenhower invites me to the White House?'

[20] López Fresquet, 47.
[21] *Ibid.*, 82–3. 25,000 F.A.L. light rifles, 50 million rounds and 100,000 grenades.
[22] Evidence of Guillermo Cabrera Infante, who was present when these remarks were made.
[23] This description derives from ministers now in exile: Elena Mederos, Pazos and Ray.
[24] ASNE – the American Society of Newspaper Editors.

'You should go,' said Pazos. Castro was evidently worried lest he lose prestige as a revolutionary leader, fearing that his Latin American admirers might suppose that he had sold out to North America, as so many other putatively radical leaders of Latin countries had done before; once more Castro and the slender cause of good Cuban-U.S. relations were the victims of the historic weaknesses of so many past leaders of the continent.[25]

Meantime, a new U.S. ambassador to Havana arrived: Philip Bonsal, with long experience of Spanish countries and of turbulent times with the Telephone Company in the 1920s. He had laid telephones through hundreds of Andalusian villages when the Spanish traditional Right regarded the telephone as the source of all their troubles. Latterly, he had been ambassador in Bolivia and Colombia. He had, too, been briefly vice-consul in Havana. The son of Stephen Bonsal, a journalist in the war of 1898, to experience he added a generally progressive and happily Whiggish frame of mind. 'On the basis of abundant though contradictory evidence' in Washington he had concluded before arriving that 'Castro was not a Communist'.[26]

The Cuban upper classes made things hard for Bonsal. Castro himself was obsessed, like many of those around him, with the recollection of Sumner Welles in Cuba in 1933; he later referred to the arrival of Bonsal as if in fact he had been Welles. The upper classes, he told an audience in 1961:

... never ceased to talk of the day when Bonsal would arrive. Three days before the radio and television ... began to talk about Bonsal's arrival, as if it were a really great event. The publicity was such that it began to be shocking for all revolutionaries or all men of honour even if not revolutionary ... Bonsal was treated as a proconsul.[27]

As a result, Castro avoided Bonsal for some time without a formal interview: doubtless he was actually uncertain as to what policy he wanted to follow towards the U.S. Anyway, while avoiding the U.S. ambassador, he nevertheless accepted the invitation to visit the U.S. newspaper editors in April.

Hitherto the revolution had been marked more by a mood, than deeds which positively alleviated the condition of the people. In March, however, the government took several overtly progressive steps: rents

[25] Pazos's evidence.
[26] Bonsal, 'Cuba, Castro and the U.S.', in *Foreign Affairs*, January 1967, 266. Philip Bonsal (b. 1903) educated St Pauls, Concord, and Yale. In Spain, Chile and Cuba with ITT, 1926-35. Vice-Consul, Havana, 1938, chief of division of American Republics, in State department, 1942-4, First Secretary, Madrid, 1944-7.
[27] *Obra Revolucionaria*, 46 of 1961, 24. Castro made the same allusion to Bonsal elsewhere. e.g. in the interview with Lee Lockwood: 'he came with the demeanour of a proconsul .. ; the reactionary press received him almost as if the Saviour had come' (p. 141).

for those who paid less than $100 a month were cut by half, raising thereby the purchasing power of the majority in the cities by perhaps a third (tenants who paid [more had rents cut by 30 % or 40 %). Owners of vacant sites would have to sell, either to the newly set up National Savings and Housing Institute (INAV) or to anyone who wanted to build and buy a house. INAV also took over all funds from the Lottery and, instead of lottery numbers, in future issued bonds: if these were kept for five years, they could be redeemed at 110%, if before at lesser rates. The government also took over the Telephone Company – nominally for the time being, it is true[28] – and cut its rates also, by means of an 'intervention', a tactic previously used by both Batista and Perón. Almost all labour contracts were re-negotiated between January and April, 1959. Licences and letters of credit would henceforth be needed for the import of about two hundred luxury goods. López Fresquet had already introduced measures to insist on less tax evasion, and a compromise had been reached whereby pre-1956 evasion was forgiven on condition of part repayment of 1956–8 taxes.[29] The property of Batista, of all his cabinet ministers since 1952, of all officers of the armed forces who had participated in the civil war, of all members of both houses of parliament, opposition and government, during the 1954–8 sessions, and of all who had sought any of these offices, all mayors and all provincial governors, was declared confiscated and was to pass to the State. In practice, this decree was not fully carried out. Thus Grau San Martín was permitted to live on in Cuba without interference, despite his collaboration in Batista's elections, perhaps because he was old, perhaps because he had known Castro in the past.

On 1 March Castro launched a large land distribution project in Pinar del Río, signing cheques himself, handing over land to peasants as if he were (though no one noticed the similarity) Machado or even Mussolini.[30] 25,000 acres had been bought up by the old Agricultural and Industrial Development Bank; 8,000 were handed out for pasture, 8,000 for tobacco. The government also announced that they were

---

[28] The Federation of Telephone Company Workers had undergone a palace revolution in February when the old leaders, headed by Vicente Rubiera, had been thrust aside by the 26 July Movement. (See Rubiera's evidence in James Monahan and Kenneth Gilmore, *The Great Deception*, 20–22.)

[29] López Fresquet, 86–7.

[30] 'I remember him, one day, during military manoeuvres, walking through a vast bare plain of yellow stubble surrounded by distant green hills ... peasants came running from all sides, red-faced, panting, to see him, touch him, shout to him. One of his Secretaries followed him with a leather envelope, the exact size of 1,000 lire bills to hand banknotes to the more miserable with the gesture of a gambler dealing out cards ... Nobody who saw it will ever forget the sight of city squares filled with mosaic, all eyes turned to one focal point, the balcony or stand from which he was speaking.' As this quotation about Mussolini from Barzini's *The Italians* (1964), 147, suggests, charismatic leaders have more in common with each other than with their own peoples.

going to develop the marshy and crocodile-ridden territory in the central south of the island, Cienaga de Zapata.

These measures increased the money supply without, however, much increasing production. Foreign trade fell off after the decree necessitating the licensing of luxury goods. People who in the past had lived by speculation in land prepared to abandon the country. More importantly, anxiety about the nature of the revolution was beginning to be widespread in Catholic circles. Andrés Valdespino, president of Juventud Católica, and Under-Secretary at the Treasury, wrote in *Bohemia* on 22 February that the radical reforms needed in Cuba could be enacted without Communism. Some young Catholics, such as Artime and González Corzo in the Ministry of Agriculture, were already, by March 1959, contemplating conspiracy.[31]

The trials of Batistianos were still going on, and on 3 March came a new and what seems, in retrospect, a decisive test of the regime's integrity. Forty-four Batista airmen, accused of war crimes, were found innocent in Santiago. The defence had argued that the pilots had not killed civilians but, on the contrary, that some had even dropped their bombs on unpopulated places. They claimed to have falsified their reports to their commanders. The bombing of Sagua de Tánamo was also found not to have occurred. The court found that the evidence was inadequate to prove the pilots' guilt and, despite speeches on the wireless by the prosecutor, acquitted them. This caused a storm of protest in Santiago. The pilots were not released. Then Castro announced on television in Havana that the acquittal had been an error, and called for a re-trial. The Minister of Defence, Martínez Sánchez, no less, replaced Lieutenant Sánchez Cejas as prosecutor, and a new court composed of safe revolutionaries was appointed. The president of the first court, Major Félix Peña, was found dead in his car in Campamento Columbia: suicide was presumed, but this death was never cleared up. He was replaced by a more reliable revolutionary, Major Piñeiro, who had been on Raúl Castro's staff and was now military commander in Santiago.[32] At the second trial all the airmen were convicted and sentenced to thirty, twenty or two years' imprisonment. The prosecutor concentrated on insulting the defence and produced no new evidence. Castro announced, 'Revolutionary Justice is based not on legal precepts, but on moral conviction . . . Since the airmen belonged to the air force of former president . . . Batista . . . they are criminals and must be punished.' The point, of course, was not that the men may have been guilty and the first judgement wrong; nor that all who served Batista in

[31] *Dos Héroes y un Ideal* (1962), 15.
[32] The other members of the new court were Majors Belarmino Castillo, Carlos Iglesias, Demetrio Montseny and Pedro Luis Díaz Lanz.

the air force were indeed more or less guilty men; but that the verdict of the first court was set aside for political and vengeful reasons. Several witnesses who had testified favourably to the defence were also goaled, and the defence lawyers lost their jobs.[33]

This proceeding was deplorable, but it did not, perhaps, in itself, mean that the regime was already committed to a permanently arbitrary path. Comparable events in France in 1944 did not in themselves doom the Fourth Republic. The political atmosphere was very heated. At all events, a crisis followed. The Minister of Health, Elena Mederos, one of the most principled of Cuban women, told Castro that she wished to resign: 'You don't want me in your government. I'm of a different generation to you and your friends. We are quite opposed to each other in spirit. I must resign.' Castro charmed her successfully: 'No, no,' he said, 'I need you. This train,' he added expansively, referring to the Revolution, 'knows where it is going. Your time to get off will be later.'[34]

But it was still doubtful whether the train did know where it was going. Even *Revolución* protested against the continuance of the trials. Castro told visiting U.S. newspapermen in mid-March that elections were going to be delayed for two years to enable the opposition to develop. On 6 March he told the national association of bankers that he desired their collaboration and added, to the correspondent of *U.S. News and World Report*, that he had no intention of nationalizing any industries. Castro held two large meetings of cabinet members, leaders of the 26 July Movement and army officers, to 'create a uniform policy'; but these were complete failures, the first ending in a riotous altercation as to who had been more effective in the struggle against Batista, the Sierra men or those of the city, the second discussing nepotism and the spread of bureaucracy.[35] On 4 March U.S. Ambassador Bonsal lunched with the Cuban Foreign Minister, Agramonte, and Castro, and had a 'very agreeable talk'. 'I thought there was a chance of working with him,' Bonsal later commented.[36] But then the pendulum seemed to swing back once more; on 13 March, at a ceremony to commemorate the dead killed two years before at the famous attack on the palace, both Castro and the old Directorio leader, Faure Chomón, made strong left-wing speeches, Chomón more extreme than Castro, suggesting even that the remains of the Directorio Revolucionario might be found to the left of the 26 July. The Directorio never again formally demanded elections as

[33] See 'The Case of the Airmen', in *Cuba and the Rule of Law* (International Commission of Jurists), 181–91.

[34] Evidence of Elena Mederos. After this event, it becomes harder and harder to know the truth of many things which have occurred in Cuba and perhaps this is where History may be said to have ended and contemporary politics begins.

[35] López Fresquet, 48–9.

[36] Bonsal to the author.

it had in January. Castro said that, were he not prime minister of Cuba, he would like to lead an expedition against Trujillo. It was also noticeable that the Communists took part in this rally as a participating sponsor, on the same level as the two other 'revolutionary organizations', the 26 July Movement and the Directorio. When, a few days later, on 22 March the ex-president of Costa Rica, José Figueres, a progressive friend of the Cuban opposition in the past, visited Cuba, this trend in Castro's speeches was repeated. At a great rally in Havana, Figueres allowed himself to give a lecture to the Cubans about representative democracy and to say that, in the event of war, Cuba should certainly stand with the U.S. and the West. David Salvador, the union chief of the revolution, an ex-Communist and anxious to work himself into membership of the revolutionary leadership, pulled the microphone away from Figueres and shouted that under no circumstances would Cuba support the U.S. in a new war. Within a few days, Castro was accusing Figueres of being a false friend; he added that the great trusts in their selfishness had killed ten times more Cubans than had the tyranny of Batista. The Revolution, he remarked, was confronted by an international conspiracy of vested interests. A significant conversation seems to have occurred in the cabinet, now, during discussion of the price of meat, which was usually raised in the dry season, when demand exceeded supply. Castro opposed the rise; the Minister of Commerce, Cepero Bonilla, said that the consequence would be the slaughtering of young steers and added that even the studs might be killed; Castro replied that that would not matter, since such a policy would leave him with a reputation of having given food to the people while if others took over they would have to raise prices. 'If we stay in power, we will import new studs.' Castro's attitude was approved, and his critics thought he was genuinely apprehensive of elections, for which surviving Auténticos such as Varona were calling vehemently.[37]

Still, not all Castro's accusations and anxieties were baseless. The first wave of exiles from Cuba, Batistianos and rightists, were already plotting. Even Colonel Artigas, lottery chief to Prío, called on Wieland in Washington with a plan to overthrow Castro by force. Wieland said firmly that Castro was not a Communist; there was no need at all to try to overthrow him.[38] Castro's ex-brother-in-law, Díaz Balart, Batista's youth leader, began in Miami to organize an opposition movement, the White Rose, to invade Cuba. Cubans never keep secrets and Castro was soon able to accuse the 'enemies of the Revolution' of buying arms in Miami, while apparently the U.S. authorities were not stopping them. Suddenly Castro's mood again changed – perhaps because of a change

[37] López Fresquet, 165.
[38] Communist Threat, 860.

in the advice of Guevara or Raúl Castro, perhaps out of conviction, perhaps from vacillation. He made another very calm speech. On 25 March came his first major allusion to the wish of the revolutionary government to end such racial discrimination as there was in Cuba, in jobs and in places of recreation; a speech which caused some anxiety among Conservatives in Cuba, but had no effect on foreign policy.[39] The alarm was confined to old Spanish white families, who saw in it a ghost of a slave revolt of the past. About the same time, the Minister of the Economy, Regino Boti, told his old economics master, Pazos, that the two of them, with the Finance Minister, López Fresquet, would be accompanying Castro on his visit to the U.S. the next month. Pazos said to Boti: 'This means negotiation?' Boti replied, 'Of course.' Pazos then said that the question of the amount of economic aid should be discussed. Boti, who was not an intimate of Castro's, said that Cuba should ask for $M500 worth of aid. In the following weeks, Pazos worked out various programmes for education, sanitation, housing, and so on, which might allow for this sum to be spent without definite strings attached. But there was no discussion between Pazos, Boti and Castro on the subject ¬ nor, indeed, on any subject, except vaguely on the political one of whether Cuba should or could be neutral and what neutrality meant.[40] This vagueness was in line with Castro's response to a hint by the State Department in February, that they would be fully prepared to give economic help to Cuba: this message was communicated to Justo Carrillo, the new vice-president of the National Bank, and José Antonio Guerra, on a visit to the IMF in February. On return, Carrillo went to a meeting of economic advisers, at which Castro was present: Castro received the good news and Carrillo was left waiting for further instructions, which never came. The impression was left with the economic advisers that Castro was simply uninterested in serious negotiations with the U.S. Publicly, however, Castro told a Cuban television audience on 2 April that he was going to the U.S. to secure credits perhaps from the World Bank, perhaps from the Export-Import Bank that 'will defend Cuba and the Revolution'.[41] Castro then authorized the dispatch of a memorandum to Washington listing themes for negotiation in economic matters.[42] BANFAIC, meantime, announced a plan for some forty new industries: a copper tube plant; a plastic plant; a light bulb plant. All these would secure cooperation from U.S. private business. Rhetoric and promises were thus not only the occupation of the govern-

[39] See comment by René Depestre, *Casa de las Americas*, vol. vi, No. 34, January 1966. This was Castro's first allusion to the racial question, and also, as Suárez points out (p. 50) the first occasion that the Communists published Castro's speech in full in *Hoy*.

[40] Pazos's evidence.

[41] *Revolución*, 3 April 1959.

[42] Justo Carrillo Memorandum.

ment. Still, the Cuban middle class was not comforted. On the contrary, Mrs Ruby Hart Phillips of the *New York Times* wrote in mid-April that they felt 'seriously hurt' by the reductions in rent, as well as by the forced sale of vacant sites. 'Nothing convinces them that this is not due to Communist influence.[43] The value of the *peso* also had fallen substantially since January, with world sugar prices at their lowest point since 1945. Nevertheless the measures enacted in March, along with the wage increases since January, did mean that the national income had been seriously and visibly redistributed, with real wages increasing perhaps over 15%, and the incomes of rentiers and entrepreneurs dropping accordingly. This remarkable political achievement, which gave such a large section of the populace a big stake in the Revolution, was accomplished by a drop in imports and by the reluctance of capitalists to invest or to increase prices.[44]

With Castro due to arrive in Washington on 15 April, a bizarre conference was now held by U.S. ambassadors in the Caribbean area. Nothing shows more clearly the extent to which the colossus of the north was uncertain as to how to react to the new phenomenon to its immediate south. There were clashes between Bonsal from Cuba, Robert Hill from Mexico, and Whiting Willauer from Costa Rica. Willauer, appointed ambassador to Honduras in 1954, because of 'years of experience in fighting Communism' (by his own account), had been one of the paladins of the defeat of the revolution in Guatemala.[45] The meeting of ambassadors turned out, in the view of Hill, to be 'designed to set the policy of patience and forbearance in dealing with Mr Castro. I took issue,' Hill later testified, 'with Ambassador Bonsal because I felt, despite his excellent presentation ... that patience and forbearance with a Communist would lead to disaster to the U.S.' Hill told the conference that 'the time to deal with Castro was there and then ... We had the instruments, if we wanted to resort to the Organisation of American States, to deal with the problem ... I believed that all evidence of Communism should be submitted to the OAS and that the U.S. request appropriate action ... I was unable to get that language adopted ... The only ambassador who supported me was Ambassador Willauer ...'

> Mr Bonsal's position [Hill went on] was that Castro was in power; that he had tremendous popular support; that there was considerable support in the hemisphere for Castro and Castroism, and that we ought to go slow in dealing with him ... despite the fact that he was

[43] *New York Times*, 24 April 1959.
[44] See Felipe Pazos, *Cambridge Opinion*, February 1963.
[45] See Allen Dulles's telegram congratulating him on his work over Guatemala, described in *Communist Threat*, Part 13, 865.

constantly insulting the U.S. and our President ... But Bonsal felt
that eventually Castro would see the light and return to the family of
Latin American nations. He said Cuba needed a revolution and Cuba
would then start to prosper and make its contribution to the Latin
American family ... The Ambassador pointed out that of course
Castro had Communist associates. However, he [thought] that Castro
made the decisions.[46]

Bonsal privately indeed told Ambassador Willauer that Castro 'wasn't
such a bad fellow; that he was, of course, eccentric, that he ... thought
he could probably be handled and he, Bonsal, could handle him if he
were left alone ... Castro was a terrific person, physically and mentally,
he was far from crazy, he was not living on pills [as some newspapers
had alleged] and he was not a Communist.'[47]
As always on such diplomatic occasions, the critical discussion was
about the communiqué. Hill and Willauer desired a firm statement of
U.S. criticisms of Castro. Bonsal thought that 'anything in the communiqué which cast any reflections upon Castro would make his job
very difficult'. Hill said, 'You are going to discourage every country in
Latin America that fears the Castro menace ... I cannot go along with a
communiqué that whitewashes Castro.' Bonsal said, 'If you cannot be a
team player why not resign?' Bonsal got his way, but both Willauer and
Hill made reports to Washington in dissent.[48] At the same time, it has
since become known that, on 26 March, two weeks before these exchanges, President Eisenhower was informed by the CIA that 'the
Castro regime was moving more and more towards an outright dictatorship'.[49]
The U.S., then, was essentially undecided about her policy. Some
diplomats, like some soldiers, wanted 'action'. But what sort of action
and on what grounds? Since Castro's own views seemed somewhat undecided, it was hard for the U.S. government to reach any decision
themselves. Could they not have acted differently so as to ensure that, if
and when Castro made up his mind, he would do so in such a way as not
to harm what were conventionally supposed to be U.S. interests – the
strategic balance in the Caribbean and the freedom of investment and
commercial exchange in Cuba itself? It is, perhaps, appropriate to
point out that while there were two opinions in Washington over
Castro, there were apparently two views inside the Communist party of
Cuba on the same subject; the one headed by Blas Roca, the party's

[46] Hill testimony in *Communist Threat*, Part 12,803.
[47] Willauer testimony, *Communist Threat*, 871.
[48] Hill testimony. Hill got no answer from Assistant Secretary of State, Rubottom (*ibid.*, 816).
[49] Eisenhower, 523.

secretary-general, the other by Carlos Rafael Rodríguez, the editor of *Hoy*. From March 1959 onwards, the latter seemed unable to contain his admiration for Castro, many articles testifying to Castro's integrity and patriotism and also attempting to prove that the Communists had done something for the rebel cause.[50]

The divisions in the U.S. were raised acutely during Castro's visit there in April. Before the expedition began, Ambassador Bonsal, whose optimistic and benign character can be observed clearly in the insults of his enemies, gave a reception which Castro attended. All was smiles. Grau San Martín took the opportunity of coming out of his ambiguously contrived retirement to demand elections. Elections were the only source of power. Castro had to reply. Elections, he replied, would follow when an Agrarian Reform was complete, when all could read and write, when all children went free to school and all had free access to medicine and doctors.

Castro left Havana for Washington on 15 April as the private guest of the U.S. newspaper editors. The Cuban ambassador in Washington, the worthy Ernesto Dihigo, had asked whether Castro required an official invitation from the U.S. government, and he had replied that he did not.[51] Still, maybe he would not have refused such an invitation had one been proffered. Had matters come to such a pass that the difference between an official invitation and a private one could decide the relations of nations? Such matters had done so in the remote past, but this, after all, was the age of rational man.

The public relations of Castro's journey to the U.S. were to be organized by Bernard Relling of New York. Relling proposed several alterations in the plans for the journey; Castro accepted all except the one that the men in his entourage should have their hair cut and another that those soldiers who went should, if possible, be those of a university background and should speak English.[52] North American institutions and clubs, meanwhile, sent innumerable invitations to Castro to include them on the journey. Unofficial North Americans indeed stretched out their hands to embrace a hero whom they had partly created, because of their own ardent demands for heroism.

About seventy people set off with Castro in two aeroplanes. Neither Raúl Castro nor Guevara went. Almost for the first time since January, Castro was wholly surrounded by people of social democratic instincts; almost for the first time, too, such people could get at him. Castro, however, made no concession to convention for the journey: he arrived

[50] Andrés Suárez (59) draws attention to the naming by Roca, in early April, of a new secretariat (himself, Luzardo, Aníbal Escalante) which did not include Rodríguez.

[51] Casuso, 207.

[52] *Ibid.,* 211.

at the airport two hours late 'in a worn and wrinkled uniform'.[53] On the aeroplane Castro passed the time talking to Pepín Bosch of Bacardí, who had been Prío's Finance Minister: Castro was arguing how much he thought the State could do for the economy, Bosch was describing the merits of private enterprise. Pazos, also on the aeroplane, had given Castro his list of projects for possible development and aid. But there was no discussion of these matters. Pazos did not insist. He regarded himself as a technician, not a politician.[54]

Castro was met at Washington Airport by Under-Secretary Rubottom. He broke away from guards to greet a large cheering crowd. At his first press conference in the U.S. he was asked if he came to seek foreign aid. Castro replied: 'No, we are proud to be independent and have no intention of asking anyone for anything.' Pazos, surprised, later asked Boti the meaning of this. Boti said, 'Yes, we have no intention of asking now, during Castro's visit, for aid, but you, Pazos, will return in a fortnight to make a request';[55] and, indeed, this theme was maintained throughout the visit: no economic discussions, no concessions to the U.S. Pazos and López Fresquet had discussions about money at the State Department and the International Monetary Fund. The State Department asked after the Cuban economy. It was magnificent, said López Fresquet. Did Pazos agree? Yes, replied the Bank Director, except that we have more *pesos* than dollars. No one asked for money and no one really offered it. No doubt, had it been asked for, it would have been offered; had it been offered, it might just possibly have been accepted. The progressive Rubottom went the furthest in asking about foreign aid, saying that the U.S. was very interested in Cuban projects. But each side, proud and suspicious, held back.[56]

The country, however, gave Castro a warm enough welcome. Everywhere he was followed by crowds. Everywhere his words were given close attention. To the newspaper editors at Washington, to Harvard and Princeton, at New York, he gave long and successful speeches,

---

[53] *Ibid.*

[54] Pazos's evidence; López Fresquet (106) has a similar account.

[55] Pazos's evidence; Castro had made the same point himself to López Fresquet. See López Fresquet, 105–6.

[56] Pazos's evidence; *cf.* López Fresquet, 108. To this frozen attitude Senator Kennedy alluded when, a year later, he publicly wondered whether 'Castro would have taken a less radical course' had the U.S. 'given the young rebel a warmer welcome in his hour of triumph, especially during his trip to this country' (J. F. Kennedy, *Strategy of Peace*, 1960). The view was often expressed by others more forcefully. Thus Dumont: '*Cette décade d'avril 1959, les Etats-Unis ont laissé passer une occasion inespérée dans leur histoire, de réviser leur politique vis-à-vis du sud de leur continent . . . Admettre la révolution cubaine, c'était en quelque sorte accepter une forme de décolonisation poussée . . .*' (*op. cit.*, 31). He added: '*Les chances d'établir un régime socialiste humaine assez indépendant de l'URSS, s'effondrent.*' Goldenberg is no doubt right in saying that the U.S. should have offered aid, and publicly, even if Cuba did not ask for it.

impressing his audiences by making jokes in English. Publicly, the visit was an unexampled success. Security guards, on the other hand, were put to great trouble.

There were other personal encounters: with Henry Luce of *Time* magazine; with Frank Bartholomew, president of United Press International; and with the Foreign Affairs Committee of the Senate. At some of these intimate meetings Castro appeared less confident than in the larger gatherings. Apart from a lunch with the Acting Secretary of State, Christian Herter, the only official meeting that Castro had with the U.S. government was with the vice-president, Richard Nixon. President Eisenhower was in Carolina, playing golf – a tactical and, perhaps, a tactless error, for Eisenhower could have seen Castro without losing dignity. Castro, like everyone else, might have found Eisenhower, the private man, more appealing than the public one.

On the other hand, according to Pazos, Castro had no desire to meet Eisenhower: a meeting could only have embarrassed him, while Eisenhower was 'more than irritated' that Castro was coming at all and would have liked to have refused him a visa.[57]

Nixon saw Castro at his office. Castro went there though he had previously demurred, thinking it too grand. The two men met alone. Nixon immediately took against Castro, apparently because the Cuban showed no interest in the files which the vice-president produced on Communism among Castro's supporters. Nixon also spoke of the bad impression made in the U.S. by the executions in Cuba. 'I simply confined myself', Castro said later, 'to ... explaining the realities of our country, which I believe were similar to those of the rest of Latin America, and to demonstrating that the measures we were going to take, some of which affected North American interests, were just.'[58] Afterwards, Nixon wrote: 'I was convinced Castro was either incredibly naïve about Communism or under Communist discipline and that we would have to treat him and deal with him accordingly.'[59] He also immediately suggested to his colleagues in the U.S. administration that a force of Cuban exiles should be armed immediately to overthrow Castro.[60] Nixon, that is, joined those Republican ambassadors for whom Castro was already an enemy, and one or two others, such as J. Edgar Hoover of the F.B.I. and Eisenhower's experienced trouble-shooter, William Pawley. Whilst hardly noticing it, therefore, the U.S. administration was falling back into an almost nineteenth-century position, echoing that of Polk's administration or Buchanan's, whereby active intervention from the U.S. mainland could not be excluded.

[57] Eisenhower, 523.
[58] Lockwood, 186.
[59] R. M. Nixon, *Six Crises* (1962), 351–2.
[60] See Draper, *Castro's Revolution*, 62.

Castro's reaction was different. He returned after his discussion with Nixon to the Cuban Embassy, where he slept in a room next to Ernesto Betancourt, an economic adviser, and Boti. He was noticeably reticent about his talk with Nixon, but thoughtfully said *à propos* of nothing in particular, 'What we have to do is stop the executions and the *infilitrado*'[61] – that is, the infiltration of Communists. This was, no doubt the high point of Castro's democratic phase. He later remarked that the North Americans whom he had met in the U.S. were unlike the planters and businessmen whom he had known in Cuba.[62] About the same time, Castro said to López Fresquet, 'Look, Rufo, I am letting all the Communists stick their heads out, so that I will know who they are. And when I know them, I will do away with them.'[63] López Fresquet thought that Castro had spoken 'with such frankness and honesty' that it had to be true.[64] Even more bizarre, Castro was prevailed on to meet the C.I.A.'s chief expert on Communism in Latin America, a Central European named Droller: the two talked privately for three hours, and afterwards Droller told López Fresquet, 'Castro is not only not a Communist, he is a strong anti-Communist fighter.'[65] Castro himself, in the U.S., was publicly explaining that he was not a Communist; nor, he said, were Raúl Castro or Vilma, his wife, Communists. If there were any Communists in the Cuban government (and he personally knew of none), they had no influence. Castro's heart was with the West in the cold war. Foreign investments would not only be respected, but encouraged. Yet the constant and obsessive concern of North Americans, public and private, with the single question of Communism irritated Castro and indeed others in his entourage: it was as if the U.S. did not care what Cuba was, provided it was not Communist. At the same time, it also seemed – no doubt the impression was erroneous – that the U.S. did not, for all its single-minded fear, quite appreciate what Communism was. An instructive and clearly well-informed article appeared on 26 April in the *New York Times*;[66] some U.S. officials thought that Cuba ought to be left to meet their economic difficulties before being forced to turn to the U.S. for help. Others believed that to wait too long risked a collapse of Castro's government, which would be followed either by a new right-wing dictatorship or, worse, the Communists. Such men

[61] Ernesto Betancourt's evidence. Betancourt later coined the phrase 'Alliance for Progress' (Schlesinger, 175). Castro later explained that the interview with Nixon was conducted in English, without an interpreter. He added 'My personal impressions were good' and said that Nixon never asked an impertinent question 'nor one that might have been regarded as any kind of inquisition about our politics' (*Hoy*, 16 May 1959, 4).

[62] At Princeton, to Betancourt.

[63] López Fresquet, 110.

[64] López Fresquet to James, *ibid.*, 124.

[65] *Ibid.*, 110. Droller later directed Cuban exile activities against Castro, under the name of Bender.

[66] By E. W. Kenworthy in Washington.

wanted the U.S. to take the initiative to help Cuba. But, in the face of conflicting views, there was indecision.

Yet, even while in North America, Castro was still under call from other voices. Raúl Castro, it seems, telephoned him tauntingly, saying that the Cuban press was reporting that the public success of his visit meant, in fact, a surrender to the U.S.[67] It was certainly a critical moment for the Communist cause in Cuba. On 15 April Hubert Matos, the rice grower who, as a commander, had led the advance into Santiago and who was now military governor of the province of Camagüey, made a speech which violently attacked Communism.[68]

Castro was due to go to Canada after the U.S. He also accepted a sudden invitation to go to Brazil and Argentina. Pazos argued that he should have refused, since there was so much to be done in Cuba. Boti told Pazos that it would be best to go, for otherwise Castro would be in Cuba on May Day, when he would be certain, if there, to make a violent speech. He added that Guevara would soon be sent off on a long journey and then receive an ambassadorship – a frequent consolation prize for Latin American extremists.[69]

The journey to Canada was a repetition of that to the U.S. But on the way from there to South America, Raúl Castro flew suddenly to meet his brother at the inappropriate rendezvous of Houston, Texas. It is not known what transpired then. It has been said that the beardless commander of the army adjured his elder brother to maintain his revolutionary integrity. It seems equally probable that the main discussion was about the theme of the speeches that Raúl Castro and Guevara would make on 1 May in Cuba; and they spoke, when the day came, of the need for 'unity'.[70] But afterwards, even on the journey south, Castro seems still to have kept up the moderate and confiding *persona* which he had shown in the U.S. To an old friend, José Ignacio Rasco, a leader of Cuba's few Christian democrats (he was a professor at the Catholic university of Santo Tomás de Villanueva and had been secretary of the 1957 National Liberation Movement), Castro confided, on the aeroplane, that he was not a Communist because 'Communism is the dictatorship of a single class and I . . . have fought all my life against dictatorship'; because 'Communism means hatred and class struggle and I am opposed to any form of hatred'; and because Communism 'Clashes with God and the Church and although I do not practise religion the way I learned it at secondary school, neither do I wish to have a quarrel with the Church'. He promised Rasco that, when he

[67] López Fresquet., 112–13, describes.
[68] See *Revolución*, 17 April, 1959.
[69] Pazos's evidence.
[70] On 22 March Castro had suggested that he would be making a speech on 1 May. In these circumstances, of course, this promise could not be fulfilled.

returned to Cuba, he would 'change, talk to businessmen, give up insulting the Nuncio'.[71] To another old friend, Conte Agüero, he admitted that 'you can't confide in the Communists'.[72]

The visits to Buenos Aires, Rio de Janeiro and Montevideo were also successful. At the former, Castro spoke at the second meeting of the committee of twenty-one Latin American countries.[73] There he proposed that the U.S. should give aid worth $M30,000 in public capital to Latin America over the next ten years. This proposal was dismissed in the U.S. as a ridiculously large sum, though when it came to the point the Alliance for Progress in the era of Kennedy spoke of $M20,000 of aid being needed.[74] Castro's speech reads as if sincerely intended: it pointed out that the U.S. had helped Europe on this scale, and that this sort of aid would actually benefit the U.S. in the long run. In this, of course, he was right. But actual economic contact between Cuba and the U.S., on 2 May, was confined to a U.S.-Cuban agreement under the Point 4 programme, concluded for technical cooperation in the development of agrarian reform.

Castro returned to Cuba on 7 May. He was met at the airport by Ambassador Bonsal, still the advocate of conciliation. The two men had a friendly talk. That, however, was the last that Bonsal was to see of Castro till June;[75] and between then and June decisive changes occurred.

Certain political shifts had, anyway, happened while Castro was away. The potentially dangerous Colonel Barquín had been ordered abroad as military attaché. Raúl Castro had appointed an old friend from the Moncada and Granma days, Ramiro Valdés, until now military commander in Matanzas, to the important post of chief of intelligence (G2) under the army. This post, which in the end made him head of Cuba's political police, had previously been filled by the less amenable Major Sanjenís. Attacks in Revolución and elsewhere had begun on the right-wing newspaper Avance. Some erstwhile traditional supporters of the revolution, such as Major Lorié, resigned. The outspoken Major Matos was certainly in contact with Díaz Lanz, the head of the air force, fearing and criticizing the Communist influence in the

[71] Rasco to James, James 131.

[72] Conte Agüero, Los Dos Rostros de Fidel Castro.

[73] This committee of the OAS had been set up in September 1958 in order to consider how 'Operation Panamerica', as proposed by President Kubitschek of Brazil, to try and raise the Latin American rate of economic growth, might be put into effect.

[74] Javier Pazos (New Republic, 12 January 1963), a Cuban delegate at the Buenos Aires conference, later recalled that Castro 'was very enthusiastic about his private Alliance for Progress scheme of $30 billion [i.e. English $M30,000]. My impression was that he was contemplating the possibility of staying on the American side of the fence as a sponsor of this . . . and as the leader of a Nasser-type revolution.' Castro also visited his uncle, Gonzalo Castro, an immigrant to Argentina.

[75] Bonsal to the author; see also Bonsal, Foreign Affairs, January 1967.

army. Meantime, sugar prices had fallen to their lowest point since 1944. The fall was at least partly due to Castro's airy talk of producing as much sugar as possible and of selling it below prevailing world market prices. On the other hand, the harvest for 1959 was nearly complete, and it was already clear that it would be higher than recent years. From North America, trumpets of alarm were beginning to blow: *Time* magazine on 11 May said: 'Fellow travellers work on the commission for the Revision of Cuban History Books'; in a television programme entitled 'Is Cuba going red?', a CBS correspondent, Stuart Norris, said that Cuba was becoming a Communist beachhead, a totalitarian dictatorship. There was a chorus of protests from Cubans in the U.S., headed by the respectable and elderly ambassador, Dihigo.[76]

The facts, however, were still ambiguous: Castro had, apparently, promised Major Matos that he would soon dismiss Communists or near-Communists such as his brother Raúl, Guevara, his old friend Alfredo Guevara (who had become head of the new film institute) and the geographer Núñez Jiménez, (Che Guevara's old aide at Santa Clara who had been helping to draft the agrarian reform law).[77]

In a speech on 9 May Castro continued to repeat the democratic phrases of his visit to the U.S.: the Cuban revolution, he said, was 'entirely democratic', and he explicitly denied that he had anything to do with Communism, for 'not only do we offer people food, but we also offer them freedom'.[78] So far so good: but about the same time, on 11 May, the University of Havana (having been closed since December 1956), finally reopened; and the first event of the new term was the setting up of a committee to purge the university of anti-revolutionaries. This news was less comforting. Some time early in May the journalist Cazalis met the Minister of Agriculture, Sorí Marín, who warned him, 'Fidel is going to take everything for himself. He knows no limits and it is impossible to know where we are going.'[79]

In the face of these conflicting pieces of dubious evidence, the only conclusion that it is possible to reach in respect of Cuba in May 1959 is that Castro was still vacillating between several tactics. Such 'intransigence' as the U.S. displayed could only have played a very small part, though the persistent questioning of whether Castro was or was not a Communist was more than an irritant, since it implied that, though Cuba was independent, she was not free to choose Communism.

[76] Bonsal, *loc. cit.*
[77] Daniel James, 150–1.
[78] *Revolución*, 10 May 1959.
[79] Cazalis, *La República* (Caracas), 4–10 February 1966.

Agrarian Reform: Politics and Crisis

A few days after his return from his travels Castro appeared before his cabinet in his Cojímar house with a draft agrarian reform law. The cabinet wanted, naturally, to read the law before promulgation, but Castro insisted it must be accepted as it was.[1] Otherwise, he said, the details would leak out and assist the opposition. Eventually, a sub-committee of three (headed by Castro's ex-adjutant-general, Sorí Marín, the Minister of Agriculture) examined the law. Sorí Marín (who despite his portfolio had hitherto had nothing to do with the law) showed the draft to the distinguished sugar economist, José Antonio Guerra, general manager of the National Bank, and Felipe Pazos, its director. Some amendments were suggested, but these were never accepted by Castro, because at the crucial moment Sorí Marín could not be found.[2] On 17 May the Agrarian Reform law was promulgated, in a formal ceremony in the Sierra Maestra, with all the cabinet attending.

This law was aimed less at the improvement of agriculture than at a change in the structure of land-holding. It had been mainly written by Guevara's aide, the geographer and economist Núñez Jiménez, with various others such as the economic editor of *Revolución*, Oscar Pino Santos, a man always associated with the Communists or the extreme left, though he had, nevertheless, till December 1958, been public relations director of Batista's National Economic Council. Núñez Jiménez, though always associated with the Left in the past, had decided to join Guevara from the University of Las Villas very late in the civil war – on 24 December 1958, to be precise: in consequence his beard was still less than perfect on the day of victory.

The first article of the law reflected the Constitution of 1940: the proscription of estates larger than 1,000 acres.[3] This maximum did not, however, apply to those sugar or rice plantations where the yields were more than half larger than the national average; in these instances, the maximum was 3,333 acres.[4] Foreign companies might hold land even over that limit, if the Cuban government deemed it in the national interest. The law affected directly only about 10% of the farms in the

---

[1] Evidence of Elena Mederos; López Fresquet (114) confirms.
[2] Evidence of Elena Mederos, Felipe Pazos and José Antonio Guerra.
[3] 30 cabs or 402·6 hectares.
[4] 100 cabs or 1,342 hectares.

country at the normal maximum of 1,000 acres (or 12,000 properties),[5] and much less than that at the special maximum. On the other hand, the law affected about 40% of the total land in farms. The law emphasized the role of the state and of collective undertakings much more than had been supposed likely; hence Castro's coyness to the cabinet the previous day. Even the Communists had supposed, if only as a tactic, that all land confiscated would be divided up; but by May they had accepted that the 'vigour of the Revolution and the support for it from the masses . . . made possible more radical measures.'[6]

Property over these limits would be expropriated, compensation being promised in twenty-year bonds, bearing an annual interest of 4·5%. Payments, as in the case of the agrarian law in republican Spain and in eastern European countries after 1919, would be on the assessed value of the land for tax purposes. Land expropriated would either be made into agricultural cooperatives, to be run for the time being by an Institute of Agrarian Reform (INRA), or would be distributed as individual holdings of 67 acres – the size of farm which was considered a 'life-providing minimum' for a family of five. *Precaristas*, sharecroppers and renters would have the first claim on the land which they had previously been working. If this turned out to be less than 67 acres, the rest of the plot would be made up as soon as possible, in so far as land was available. If cultivation were afterwards neglected, the land was supposed to be handed back to the state. Land once distributed could only be sold to the state, or with the state's agreement. It could not be divided.

The law also set out to free the sugar *colonos* from the mills. Companies would not, after the harvest of 1960, be allowed to run sugar plantations unless their shares were both registered and owned by Cubans; nor would anyone be able to have shares in sugar plantations if they were employees or owners of, or shareholders in, sugar mills. Land not given over to sugar could also be owned only by companies with their shares duly registered. Further, in future, land could be bought only by Cubans.

This law differed considerably from that promulgated in November 1958 by Law 3 of the Sierra Maestra. By that document, land was to be given to those who cultivated it. But now redistribution would form only a small part of the programme. Castro later explained that he 'already understood . . . that if you take, for example, a sugar plantation of 2,500 acres, where the land is good for sugar cane . . . and you divide it into

---

[5] There were probably a few more than 12,000 farms bigger than 1,000 acres, out of a total of 185,000.

[6] Carlos Rafael Rodríguez, *La Revolución Cubana*, Folleto II, 53.

two hundred portions of $12\frac{1}{2}$ acres each, ... the new owners will cut the production of sugar cane in half ... and ... raise for their own consumption a whole series of new crops.'[7] He added that his experience in the Sierra Maestra had suggested that, if large herds were divided up, the cows would be quickly eaten by their new owners, rather than kept for milk. 'This naturally fortified my conviction that the land of *latifundistas* should not be divided, but should be organized.' Still, the reform had more links with democratic models than, say, those of postwar eastern Europe. While no Cuban private estates could now be larger than 1,000 acres, in Poland and Bulgaria the maximum was between 50 and 120; and indeed many eastern European reforms of the 1920s went further than the Cuban ideas of 1959. The cooperatives presented a great contrast with Russian experience. The rates of interest proposed on the bonds were higher than General MacArthur's Agrarian Reform in Japan, and the time of repayment was shorter than the reform instituted in Formosa. The law was also obviously ambivalent in some ways: thus a tenant tobacco farmer in Pinar del Río would be doing much better, by the redistribution of land, than a tenant on the swamps of Las Villas. Further, the reform was in fact really political in intent rather than strictly economic, since it gave to the government a powerful instrument by which it could arbitrarily impoverish or ruin its enemies; and perhaps the reform was intended from the beginning as a first step towards further expropriation.[8]

INRA, the Agrarian Reform Institute, became quickly the main agency of the new government, for its task was not only to expropriate and redistribute land, but to organize road-building, health, education and housing in the country. INRA was also given a credit department, and it absorbed the old Sugar, Rice and Coffee Stabilization Institutes. It became, indeed, a kind of shadow government of its own. Under it, the country was divided into twenty-eight zones of different sizes, each commanded by an officer of the rebel army, who was responsible for carrying out the law, and who had much freedom in the interpretation of orders. Castro was the president of INRA, but the director in charge of day-to-day operations was the part-author of the law itself, Dr Núñez Jiménez. This appointment explained some of the errors of judgement committed in the next two years: Núñez Jiménez was, according to Professor Dumont (who was generally sympathetic to revolutionary Cuba), 'better fitted to organize a meeting or ride a horse, banners in the wind, to occupy the territory of the United Fruit

[7] Lockwood, 89.

[8] See for instance the doubtless sensationalized account of the second national congress of the Institute of Agrarian Reform by the then second-in-command of the district of Manzanillo, and future exile commander at the Bay of Cochinos, Manuel Artime (*Traición*, Miami, 1960, 53–63).

Company, than to organize, rationally, the socialist sector of agriculture.'[9] The assistant director, Oscar Pino Santos, had also helped draft the law but he was nevertheless a journalist by profession who had no experience of administration. Another odd appointment was Eduardo Santos Ríos, once Communist party leader in Oriente, who had been Batista's sub-director in BANFAIC, the Agricultural and Industrial Development Bank. The chief of the legal department was Waldo Medina, a judge sacked by Batista.

The co-operatives constituted the most unexpected part of the new law. Most people had expected simply the *reparto*, the division of land among the landless, the age-old, if vain, dream of all agricultural workers in Spain and Hispanic America. But in fact the co-operatives from the start did not ever signify what that word usually means; INRA appointed the manager of the enterprise, sometimes from among the workers. The workers were paid about $2·50 a day all the year round, supposedly an advance on the co-operatives' profits which would be added up at the end of the year. Any further profit, theoretically, would then be distributed. (Castro later explained that the idea of co-operatives had only been decided upon at the last minute, in the aircraft on the way to the signing of the law in the Sierra Maestra.[10])

INRA also had from the start some farms to run directly – the estates of Batista, his supporters, or others who had either fled, were dead or in prison. These were the prototypes of the state farms which later became the chief means of agricultural organization in revolutionary Cuba.

When the agrarian law was promulgated, the immediate consequence was a fall in the quotations of sugar companies on the New York Stock Exchange. Other Cuban stocks, such as utilities, unconnected with sugar, also dropped. In Cuba, the Sugar Mill Owners Association argued that the law would have 'grave economic repercussions' and asked Castro to postpone its enactment. They said that sugar cane could not be adequately prepared for harvest if the big land holdings were broken up while, if the *centrales* lost their administration cane, they would be unable to give credit to the *colonos*. The curious system of harvesting which had pertained since the 1880s was thus threatened at the roots. Tobacco growers in Pinar del Río also protested, though they did not seem to be much affected. The last of the Rionda family to have estates in Cuba, a Cuban-American now president of the Francisco Sugar Co., told his shareholders that he had made representations to

[9] Dumont, *Cuba*, 47. In view of this judgement it is entertaining to read the judgement before the U.S. Senate Internal Security Sub-Committee of an ex-Auténtico policeman, Silva, that Núñez Jiménez was a 'very dangerous man owing to his great talents' (*Communist Threat*, 534).
[10] *Revolución*, 22 December 1961.

27 U.2 photograph of missile base at San Cristóbal, West Cuba

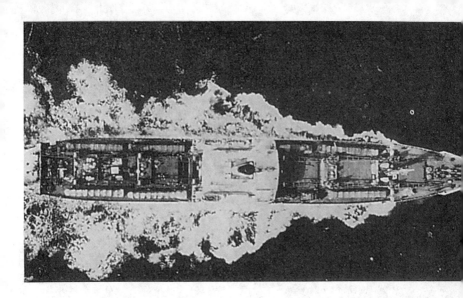

The withdrawal of the missiles:
28a The Soviet vessel *Fizik Kurchatov* at sea, showing six canvas-covered missile
   transporters with missiles on deck (7 November 1962)
  b The U.S. navy radar ship *Vesole* (left, foreground) alongside the Soviet vessel
   Volgoles, outbound from Cuba, with missiles on deck (11 November 1962)

the U.S. government over the law.[11] The Vertientes Sugar Co., with its huge mill, thought that its activities might soon be limited to the industrial side of sugar.[12] George Braga of the Manatí Sugar Co. sent a similar letter to his shareholders. A storm thus arose against the Agrarian Reform law and, because of the nature of land-holding in Cuba, it arose in New York as much as on the island. The theme of Communism in Cuba began more and more to appear in the U.S. press,[13] though most companies were merely uncertain of what provisions were applicable to them, and when.

Had such commentators looked closely, they would have observed that a clash between the revolution and the Communists seemed now to be under way in Cuba. Thus, on 8 May, the 26 July Movement's newspaper *Revolución* had denounced the Communist secretary-general, Blas Roca, for seeking to divide the Movement, 'that same Blas who made an agreement with Batista [in 1938] now denies the validity of Fidel's power'. The day before the launching of the Agrarian Reform law, *Revolución* denounced the Communist party as deviationist. Since Castro went to *Revolución* almost daily to check personally what was put into the paper, these attacks were obviously printed with his agreement. Perhaps in the quarrel between *Hoy* and *Revolución* in the middle of 1959 Castro merely let *Revolución* have its head in order to disprove accusations by U.S. journalists that the two papers were publishing identical headlines.[14] On 16 May *Revolución* anyway criticized a joint statement by a member of the 26 July Movement and the Communist party as an 'underhand political pact', which ignored both the 26 July national directorate and Fidel Castro. On 21 May Castro, in an interview on television, explained that his aim was a revolution different from capitalism ('which kills by hunger') and from Communism (which suppresses those liberties 'so dear to man'). The Cuban Revolution would be as autochthonous as Cuban music, and, being characterized by humanism, would be neither Left nor Right but 'one step forward'. It was, in colour, not red but olive green, the olive green of the rebel army uniform. As for the Communists, they were showing themselves 'anti-revolutionary' in their agitation for wage increases, and there were indeed certain coincidences between Communists and counter-revolutionaries. Were not the Communists responsible for

[11] Bernardo Rionda Braga, *ibid.*, 8 June, qu. Scheer and Zeitlin, 95–6. Bernardo Rionda was the nephew of Manuel and though, like him, born in Asturias, was now almost completely North American.

[12] Vertientes-Camagüey Company, Annual Report, January 1960 (*loc. cit.*).

[13] Scheer and Zeitlin (319) in their excellent analysis of the U.S. press of 1959–60, say that *Time* and *Newsweek* had only one article on the theme of Communism before 17 May. One can assume, therefore, that henceforth the public relations officers were very busy.

[14] See Lechuga's article in *Diario de la Marina*, 17 May 1959, in which he draws attention to the accusation and to the controversy.

unrest in San Luis, where peasants armed with stakes had attempted a spontaneous seizure of land?[15] On 22 May Castro appeared again on television: extremists, he said, had no place in the Cuban revolution. He also said – a hint, presumably, to his companions on his Washington journey – that soon Guevara would embark on a journey to Africa, Asia and Europe as his representative. The Communists' executive committee replied that they were appalled at Castro's 'unjust and unjustifiable attack',[16] while the secretary-general, Blas Roca, accused Castro of endangering the revolution by 'unleashing an anti-Communist campaign'.[17] But there was more trouble for them to come.

On 24 May the non-Communist union leaders formed a new labour alliance (the Frente Obrero Humanista) to support the 26 July Movement against Communism. Despite the short notice, this alliance successfully beat the Communists in all the major labour elections at the end of the month. The sugar workers, after re-electing by an immense majority (855 to 11) the ex-Senator Conrado Bécquer as their secretary-general, rather than the Communist Ursinio Rojas, denounced *Hoy* as propagating 'unfounded, defamatory and counter-revolutionary' statements against Bécquer. Bécquer himself pointed out that the 'Communists never helped the 26 July Movement before the 26 December 1958', that is, five days before Batista fled.[18] The Communist newspaper *Hoy* was censured by the Sugar Workers' Congress.

Thus, at the end of May all seemed to be going well for the liberal cause in Cuba. The law of Agrarian Reform, on analysis, turned out to be as modest as many other such laws in democracies. López Fresquet was bringing in a moderate tax reform law.[19] But, unfortunately, the liberals of Cuba themselves did not know how to direct their cause. They had no organized political following. Faced with the increasing evidence of Castro's immense talents as an orator and leader and his extraordinary popularity, those within the government felt themselves isolated. Elena Mederos at the Ministry of Health told her friend, the bank director Pazos, that they were both wasting their time, that they were simply being used, and that 'nothing was working'. Pazos assured her that 'things were going much better' and that he had recently secured that Castro came regularly week by week to the National Bank.[20] But, of course, such things were trivial in comparison with the importance of building a national movement to support the liberal cause. Further,

---

[15] *Revolución*, 22 May 1959. San Luis is a small town in Oriente, 15 miles north of Santiago. In 1961 Castro was to say that on this subject he had been misinformed (see speech of December 1 1961).

[16] *Hoy*, 23 May 1959.

[17] *H.A.R.*, xx, 266.

[18] Ruby Hart Phillips, *New York Times*, 30 May 1959.

[19] López Fresquet, 118.

[20] Elena Mederos's and Pazos's evidence.

even the liberals, including men such as Rufo López Fresquet, the Finance Minister, who later abandoned the revolution, were still many of them as mesmerized by Castro as was the nation itself.

The National Co-ordinator of the 26 July Movement was still Marcelo Fernández, who had filled this central position ever since the failure of the general strike in April 1958, in succession to Faustino Pérez. To him, presumably, and to others nominally in the direction of the 26 July, mostly ex-leaders of the Civic Resistance, would have fallen the task of its reorganization as a political party. Marcelo Fernández, though regarded in the university in the mid-1950s as a 'fellow traveller' (his candidacy for the presidency of the engineering school had been backed by the university Communists), was politically a moderate if an opportunist. The explanation why he did not, during 1959 establish a constitution and programme for the 26 July Movement, was simply that he could not get a clear directive from Castro. He seemed 'infuriated and worried that he never saw Fidel and that he never knew where he was'.[21] The 26 July Movement, of course, had evidently to depend on Castro, but Castro consistently refused to define its purpose. No doubt men such as Fernández, in the Movement's lower echelons, could have made some progress on their own. But they, like many others, were loyal to Castro. A word from him and their work, had they done it, would have been annulled. Thus their potentially powerful organization throughout the country remained a skeleton. The 26 July Movement seems to have had numerous interesting ideas about protecting Cuban industry from the U.S. Atlantic seaboard, nationalizing minerals, creating a hundred thousand new peasant proprietors who, in the tradition of the French Revolution rather than the Russian, would have been the backbone of a genuine national if limited revolution. But, as everyone really knew, the idea of Fidelismo without Fidel, or the 26 July Movement without Castro, was always fanciful.[22] Since Marcelo Fernández had been the organizer of the Movement since before January 1959, there could have been no question of his special appointment in order to destroy the Movement through inaction or ineptitude. Still, as in the years before the victory, the most anti-Communist group in the 26 July – Faustino Pérez, Carlos Franqui, Marcelo Fernández – was at the same time resolutely anti-American: dislike of the old Communists derived from memories of their persistent enthusiasm for the orthodox Communist line, not because of its violence or its revolutionary quality.

The Communists were now stronger than in January, with tentacles or sympathizers in every part of the state organization, especially in the new Agrarian Reform Institute (INRA), and with Guevara and Raúl

[21] The comment of Elena Mederos.
[22] See Javier Pazos, *Cambridge Opinion*, February 1963.

Castro, who were at least Marxists, as Castro's closest advisers. The controversy between *Revolución* and *Hoy* had been halted on Castro's explicit orders to *Revolución*.[23] In a country without political organization and without institutions the attractions for Castro of turning to the Communist party must have been strong, quite apart from his general alignment with the Communists on the subject of nationalism and on the U.S. On the other hand, the Communists had also shown, from their extremely prudent balance between articles in their press dealing with China as well as Russia that they too had their internal problems; not least because in respect of 'permanent revolution in the hemisphere', they were already outflanked by Guevara.[24]

At the end of May the Communists met again and worked out a theoretical basis for their policy towards Castro and the revolution. Blas Roca evidently had to contend with criticism not only from Carlos Rafael Rodríguez, the strongest supporter among the Communists of Castro's revolution (and therefore theoretically on the Right of the party), but also from among the Left. The consequence was a very moderate statement indeed, allocating a place in any revolution to the *petit bourgeoisie* as well as to the workers and peasants, and saying that, since the aims of the revolution were independence, land for the peasants, industrialization and 'strengthening democracy', it did not matter if Castro gave the name 'humanist' to the Movement which he directed. Blas Roca also denounced 'any leftist extremist tendency, any exaggerated measures', which reflected the dependence of Cuba upon imports and upon the geographical fact of proximity to the U.S.[25] This moderation was intended not only to pave the way towards permanent understanding with Castro, as Carlos Rafael Rodríguez desired, but also even to restrain him and Guevara.

With Castro vacillating, the latent forces of the opposition began to gather more coherently than they had done before, and perhaps it was this that decided him. The National Association of Cattlemen of Cuba thus declared firmly that the maximum limit of private property to 3,333 acres was inadequate to make business profitable. Caiñan Milanés, the cattlemen's president, pointed out that the land reform was more radical than the Communists' programme as it had been announced in 1956 – an accusation which, curiously, was confirmed by Carlos Rafael Rodríguez to Ruby Hart Phillips, though he said that the Communists were naturally participating in the revolution. Though there was some

[23] Private information.

[24] See description in Suárez, 55–7.

[25] '*Conclusiones del pleno del Comité Nacional del PSP, realizado en los días 25 al 28 de mayo de 1959*', *Hoy*, 7 June 1959. It is true that these conclusions had an appendix which described how the peculiarity of the Cuban revolution was supposed to be that the peasants, not the working class, were the chief factor in the overthrow of Batista.

coincidence between the Communists' programme of 1956 and Castro's, he thought that Castro was going too fast in providing for the take-over of administration caneland away from the sugar mills.[26] Landowners, meanwhile, bought time on the private radio stations to attack the law, and held rallies; it transpired that the Cattlemen's Association voted a fund of $500,000 to bribe newspapers to denounce the Reform.[27] Mgr Pérez Serantes, Castro's old friend at Santiago, had at first praised the Agrarian Reform law as 'necessary and human'; but he then changed his tune and cryptically said that 'certain groups in Cuba suspect that the authors of that law and the Communists have been drinking at the same spring'.[28] But the opposition did not, could not, rally round the Church, which was now divided, just as it had been in Batista's time: Mgr Evelio Díaz, for instance, had recently spoken of the agrarian law as fundamentally just.[29]

Nor could the opposition rally around any good Liberal either, since the good liberals were still in the government. The spokesman of protest thus became 'Tony' Varona, Prío's prime minister in 1950–2. Prío, on the other hand, publicly backed the law of Agrarian Reform. Varona's criticism of the law was to argue that the government should not distribute cultivated land and that state lands should be distributed first. Once again he called for elections.

On 11 June the U.S. government dispatched an official Note to Cuba on the subject of agrarian reform. This expressed 'concern', though it admitted both that Cuba had a legal right to expropriate foreign property and that land reform was a step towards social progress. The U.S. would insist, of course, on 'prompt, adequate and effective compensation', though they did not insist on specific amounts or valuation methods.[30] Some North American sympathizers of Castro later argued that this Note was of 'great significance in moulding the suspicions and arousing the ire of the Cuban revolutionaries'.[31] This is a little difficult to believe; no Cuban could have expected, realistically, that a law confiscating broad acres of property belonging to the United Fruit Company, the Pingree Ranch, or the King Ranch of Texas, could have been passed without protest in the U.S.

The point at issue was when compensation would be paid – 'promptly' or by bonds over twenty years – a serious matter, and one which would arise everywhere in Latin America after a land reform, for no country is

[26] Phillips, *The Cuban Dilemma*, 83.

[27] *Revolución*, 25 June 1959.

[28] *H.A.R.*, xii, 320.

[29] *Bohemia*, 29 May: 'Our present Land Reform in its noble purpose fully enters into the spirit and sense of Christian justice.'

[30] *New York Times*, 12 June 1959.

[31] Scheer and Zeitlin, 96.

ready to pay vast sums for compensation on the spot. The question was further complicated by the casual and wasteful manner in which the actual expropriations were carried out: thus when the Pingree Ranch was turned into a cooperative, a $20,000 breeding bull was killed by the army for a barbecue.[32] The expropriations were almost everywhere carried into effect by relatively inexperienced officers of the rebel army, who often simply took over what they thought worth confiscating. Only rarely were inventories made or receipts given. Thus in practice the details of the law were rather unsatisfactory in suggesting what actually happened.

Before the U.S. Note had in fact been delivered, Castro made a public proposal to the U.S. that they should increase purchase of Cuban sugar from three million tons a year to eight million.[33] Ultimately, no doubt, like the other advanced countries, the U.S. could have bought more tropical products if they had set about it generously; but an immediate increase of nearly 200% could not have been straight away practical. Soon after this, Bonsal saw Castro who agreed that:

[A big speech] was not the best way of attaining his expressed objective of underlining Cuba's ample and flexible historic potential as a supplier of sugar to the American market. He agreed with me that if he were to find it desirable to make this point again, he would exchange views with me as to the best way of doing so without indulging in empty gestures which could only discredit his awareness of the sugar situation ... These [Bonsal added later] were indeed the halcyon days of our relationship'.[34]

Bonsal did not, however, see Castro again till September.[35] In the meantime, the political situation radically changed. The day after the U.S. Note on Agrarian Reform, a cabinet meeting was held. Castro, as usual, was very late. He immediately made it clear that he proposed to dismiss several of the more moderate members, including Elena Mederos, who had reluctantly stayed 'on the train in March'.[36] Castro took a long time to come to the point and only indeed came into the open when Elena Mederos challenged him. She was succeeded as Minister of Social Welfare by her under-secretary, Raquel Pérez, a girl of no political experience. The Minister of the Interior, Luis Orlando Rodríguez, who had proved ineffective, was succeeded by the governor of Havana Province, José Naranjo, an ex-medical student who, though he had

[32] Lazo, 188.
[33] *Revolución*, 10 June 1959.
[34] Bonsal letter to Arthur Schlesinger, November 1962.
[35] Bonsal to the author.
[36] See above, p. 1203. This description of this cabinet meeting derives from Dr Mederos; see also López Fresquet, 50–1.

been with Echevarría in the Directorio, had also fought with Raúl Castro in Oriente. Due to their old friendship Castro promised Rodríguez a new job by letting him publish *La Calle* again. Dr Serafín Ruiz de Zárate, who had been doctor with Guevara in Las Villas, became Minister of Health. Angel Fernández, at the Ministry of Justice, was succeeded by his deputy, Yabur, a lawyer who had once been a friend of Manolo Castro in the university, of Syrian origin, an old enemy of Fidel Castro, but now an unconditional friend. Sorí Marín, the Minister of Agriculture who did not see the Agrarian Reform law before it reached the cabinet, was replaced by Pedro Miret, who had been with Castro at Moncada and in Mexico. Finally, Agramonte, the safe but ineffective Foreign Minister, was replaced by Dr Raúl Roa, for a long time Dean of the faculty of Social Sciences at the university, and since January ambassador to the OAS. All the outgoing members were known to oppose the Agrarian Reform in some particulars.

Roa was a characteristic example of a Latin American intellectual. At the university he was one of the first generation of revolutionary students, a law student associated with Mella, Martínez Villena, and De la Torriente Brau. He followed Mella into the Communist party in 1927[37] but later left. From his writings of the 1930s it is clear, however, that he was still close to Communism. But afterwards, his left-wing friends dead, he entered academic rather than political life; he married into a well-established commercial family of Syrian origin, the Kouris, became estranged from the Communists and, by the 1950s, seemed entirely literary, though not without occasional nostalgic articles about the heroic days of his youth. In 1955, when in Mexico on behalf of the Congress of Cultural Freedom (of which he was the Cuban representative), he had refused to meet Castro, on the grounds that he was a gangster.[38] In 1956 he had denounced the 'brutal methods of the Soviet army to repress the patriotic rising of the Hungarian people' by 'the lackeys of Moscow', and also 'the brain-washing and systematic engrossing of the sensibility' to which all are subject under 'Marxist Caesaro-papism'.[39] In 1959 he had adhered to the revolution, though during that summer he republished his denunciations of Communism with the introduction that the Cuban revolution had 'its own roots, programmes and course. It does not derive from Rousseau, George Washington or Marx'.[40]

Roa was thus an ambiguous minister. Ambiguous he remained, though remaining also Foreign Minister in a government whose leader

[37] Nicolas Guillén, himself a Communist, mentions Roa as a member of the party, in an interview with Joaquín Ordoqui, in *Hoy Domingo*, 14 August 1960.

[38] Casuso, 115. Llerena MSS, 33–4, also refers.

[39] Reprinted in 1959 in Havana, in *En Pie*, 217.

[40] Preface to *ibid.*

and some of whose ministers were twenty years younger than him.[41]

The spectre of opposition caused Castro to become more radical. Need he have done so? Was the fear in his mind the product of overworking fancy or were real enemies preparing machetes, guns and manifestos? Certainly he was meeting opposition, not only from the Cuban upper class and U.S. business interests, but also from the U.S. government. The situation was dangerous. Many remembered Guatemala. The counter-revolution might be weak but behind it, in the haunted minds of the reformers in Cuba, loomed the cloud of the U.S. with its hundreds of unofficial agencies and pressures, its power and its traditional reactions to defiance in the Caribbean region. Castro desired, anyway, to tease the U.S.[42] Doubtless he went a little further in anticipating a vigorous response before it had actually been aroused, and it seems that the leaders of the Revolution, from Guevara to Carlos Rafael Rodríguez, believed that the hostility of the landowners and the North American companies to the Agrarian reform was a fundamental reason forcing the Revolution towards more radical steps.[43]

On 13 June Castro violently attacked as traitors the critics of the Agrarian Reform law, saying that not a comma of it would be changed, and that the opposition was only preoccupied with their 'vested interests'. To the small group sitting in the television studio he rhetorically asked if they wanted elections. No, they hastily replied. Two days later Cuba formally rejected the U.S. Note of 11 June, saying that 'prompt' compensation was out of the question; the landowners would have to accept the bonds with $4\frac{1}{2}\%$ interest. The Cuban reply was, however, moderate in many ways, clearly being drafted in the Foreign Ministry. It conceded that the U.S. was a sincere supporter of land reform and had, in the past, helped Cuban economic growth; and it pointed out that, though the Constitution of 1940 had indeed provided for compensation for any expropriation in cash, Batista had ruined the Treasury and there was an unfavourable balance with the U.S. 'Powerful reasons'

[41] He is still Foreign Minister (1970). One of those law students who had known Roa well all his life wrote of him that he was intellectually a 'colonist', either of Sánchez Arango, or of his wife Ada Kouri, and ultimately of Castro (Carrillo MSS).

[42] See Betancourt conversation above, 1090. Carrillo, the old political warrior, who was now the vice-president of the National Bank, resigned on the ground that the INRA destroyed the autonomy of the National Bank. This was refused by Castro.

[43] See Carlos Rafael Rodríguez, *La Revolución Cubana* etc., Folleto II, 'the Revolution had to advance in order to survive'. Guevara said much the same in his speech in Algiers in late 1963: 'The great landowners, many of them North Americans, immediately sabotaged the law of Agrarian Reform. We were therefore face-to-face with a choice which comes to you more than once in your revolutionary life: a situation in which, once embarked, it is difficult to return to shore. But it would have been still more dangerous to recoil since that would have meant the death of the Revolution . . . the most just and the most dangerous course was to press ahead . . . and what we supposed to have been an agrarian reform with a bourgeois character was transformed into a violent struggle . . .' (As quoted *Révolution* (Paris), October 1963.)

justified the form of indemnities. This moderate response surely demanded a moderate counter-reply. At the same time, however, ominously, a
series of bombs were exploded in Havana – three during Castro's
speech of 13 June. Was it possible that the old cycle of violence was
about to begin again? Certainly the government feared so. Immediately
came a number of arrests, chiefly of ex-members of the Batistiano armed
forces. The Constitution of 1940 was quickly amended to permit a
death penalty for 'counter-revolutionaries', and a prominent right-wing
lawyer, Enrique Llaca Ortiz, was spirited out of his home by agents of
the Rebel Army intelligence, the DIER, and held for several days.

This event, reminiscent of happenings under so many Cuban
governments, brought a quick clash between the government and the
judiciary. The Audiencia of Havana ordered Llaca's release. The DIER
was ordered to obey Castro. Castro then ordered the Ministry of Justice
to proceed against the judges of the Audiencia (Gómez Calvo, Peñate and
Paprón). The Supreme Court stepped in. Mr Justice Alabau (the same
who, in 1958, had indicted Ventura and Laurent for the murder of four
boys) found that the judges had not exceeded their functions; he added,
'neither the Revolution nor the Revolutionary Government can repud-
iate *habeas corpus*,' since *habeas corpus* had been the banner of the revolution and 'only tyrants and despots discard *habeas corpus*.'

The Llaca case was an indication to Castro of how far he could legally
go against the opponents of the regime with the existing Constitution;
press further and he would have to jettison it. Yet while he was beginning
to act within Cuba – by instinct, impatience or ill-judgement – dicta-
torially (though there are democratic countries where people are held a
week without trial), internationally Castro still seemed the persecuted
outlaw in travail. He spoke as a man surrounded by enemies, struggling
among nameless conspiracies, as if still spiritually in the Sierra Maestra
with a handful of men, fighting his lonely battle against tyranny. From a
position of government, he remained a rebel. Other roles did not attract
him, or rather, he could not fill them and many Cubans, with their
long ambiguous unaroused hostility to the U.S., their memories of
Wood and Sumner Welles, their regard for their new leader, seem
scarcely to have wished him to. From this time onwards, Castro never
repeated the anti-Communism which had occasionally cropped up in
his speeches or in private conversation. Henceforth, he reserved his
criticism for those who were anti-Communists. While allowance should
be made for the irritation of Castro and his colleagues at being persistently questioned by U.S. and other journalists as to whether they
were Communists or not (with the assumption that they had no right
to be so in the Americas), it is difficult not to conclude that some critical
decisions must have been made now by Castro, Guevara and his brother

– and perhaps no one else; not necessarily the Cuban Communists themselves.

At this time, López Fresquet produced his comprehensive Tax Reform law for Castro to sign; he did so laughing, saying, 'Maybe when the time comes to apply the Law there won't be any tax-payers.'[44]

The Llaca case, meantime, would perhaps have been noticed more had it not been for its coincidence with an unsuccessful sally into foreign affairs. Many exiles from other Latin countries were now in Havana. An abortive attempt had already been made on Panamá. A force of volunteers was assembled to attack Trujillo, recalling the attack of 1947 on the Dominican Republic. Castro had always attacked Trujillo in his speeches; now he would do so physically, though not in person. Possibly the imminence of the invasion was a reason for Castro's evident decision in early June to reach a rapprochement with the Communists, whom he seems to have criticized in May.[45] There had been abortive plans for other attacks on nearby dictatorships – including Nicaragua and Guatemala – perhaps without the government's support. Now, with Castro's blessing, about two hundred Dominicans, with ten Cubans under a rebel army Officer, Delio Gómez Ochoa (who had gone to the Sierra in May 1957 from Santiago and had been an anti-Communist representative of the 26 July Movement in Havana in mid-1958), landed in two waves on the north coast of the Dominican Republic. Most were killed, however, immediately on landing. A few, including Gómez Ochoa, struggled inland, and were eventually captured. Most of these were tortured and shot, though not the commander. Afterwards, a group of young Dominicans formed a political movement inspired by the memory of the dead: the 14 June Movement, a group of generous young men who were brutally treated by successive regimes in the Dominican Republic, but nevertheless endured.

The Dominican invasion, intentionally or not, avoided extra attention being paid to what, with the Llaca affair, was a decisive turn for the revolutionary government. No doubt Castro had specifically desired the resignation of the liberal ministers before the take-over by the army, on behalf of the Agrarian Reform Institute as part of the Agrarian Reform law, of 131 large cattle ranches in Camagüey. Technically, the state 'intervened' in the running of the farms, just as they had in respect of the telephone company and as Prío had done in respect of the western railways. But intervention now meant permanent state direction. The total involved was between 250,000 and a third of a million acres. The

[44] López Fresquet, 164.
[45] This is argued by Andrés Suárez (66–7) not entirely convincingly, though it is clear that the idea of a venture against Trujillo did clash with their 'May conclusions'. Suárez's argument also is that the failure of the Dominican invasion led Castro to realign his entire politics.

ranches which were seized included North American estates such as the 26,000 acres recently bought by King Ranch of Texas and the Manatí Sugar Co., and other North American companies, along with large estates owned by the Betancourts, Agramontes and other famous Camagüeyan families. The army was meant to leave to each ranch 3,333 acres (100 cabs), though this stipulation was not always fulfilled.

The consequences were to give the government control of the beef supply. The ranchers, passing into open hostility to the revolution, predicted accurately that there would be excessive slaughtering and afterwards a beef shortage. This indeed had always occurred in revolutions.[46]

The cattle ranches of Camagüey were in fact the heart of counter-revolutionary Cuba, the home of conservative interests, whose predictable denunciations of agrarian reform alienated those members of the liberal centre, who were still attached to the regime. Meantime, the U.S. had officially still not answered the Cuban Note of 15 June. But, privately, U.S. businessmen were beginning to use the famous metaphor of the water melon: 'The more the Revolution is sliced, the redder it gets',[47] and on 22 June *Time* magazine told its seven million readers that Núñez Jiménez, the director of INRA, was 'a longtime Communist-liner', and prepared its readers for the news that Cuba's agrarian reform was inspired by the Devil. But this interpretation had not yet been decided by the Church in Cuba: a meeting of sixty-two representatives of the religious congregations inconclusively met at Belén at the end of June to discuss the matter.[48]

Within a week of the intervention of the large ranches, the government found itself under attack from another not unexpected quarter. The head of the air force, Díaz Lanz, had been increasingly fretful. Son of an army officer imprisoned by Machado and still only thirty-two, before the revolution he had been a commercial air line pilot for Q Airways. He had flown arms and ammunition to the Sierra Maestra from Florida. A good pilot, he was a man of limited intelligence. Though he had been a member of the notorious Second Tribunal which tried the Batistiano pilots at Santiago in March, he had refused to fly to Santo Domingo with the unsuccessful Dominican Republic expedition.[49] He had been for some time a conspirator against Communist influence in Cuba. In June he had complained at the 'indoctrination classes' in the air force, given by instructors sent by the commander-in-chief of the armed forces, Raúl Castro. This 'indoctrination' consisted of nationalistic versions of Cuban history, justification of governmental plans,

[46] e.g. in Spain when the anarchists took over in 1936.
[47] *Wall Street Journal*, 24 June 1959.
[48] See report in *Bohemia*, 4 July 1959.
[49] Evidence to Senate Internal Security Sub-Committee, 417.

particularly agrarian reform, and some elementary Marxism. The level of sophistication was low.

During June Díaz Lanz had, in fact, been ill with typhus. On his return to duty on 29 June, he gave a press conference, denied that, contrary to rumour, he had been kept a prisoner, and added, 'I am against every type of dictatorship, Trujillista, Batistiano, Communist ... especially the Communist system.' Castro immediately summoned him, upbraided him for giving such a declaration without his authorization and told him not to return to the air force. Díaz Lanz went home, prepared a letter of resignation and in the afternoon fled in a small boat with his family to Miami. In Havana Juan Almeida, the mulatto veteran of Moncada and the *Granma*, temporarily took Díaz Lanz's place.

Díaz Lanz was next attacked by Castro as the Benedict Arnold of the Cuban revolution. Even Felipe Pazos accused him of opportunism and of flying in the civil war as a mercenary. A purge of the air force followed. Officers thought to have been friendly with Díaz Lanz were dismissed, and a number of Venezuelans and Costa Ricans were brought to Cuba as replacements.

Next followed the final act in the political education of President Urrutia. Urrutia had already appeared in public with Major Matos with an anti-Communist speech in Camagüey of 8 June and had angered Castro by so doing. Having failed to resign with the liberal ministers on 12 June, Urrutia kept quiet until the end of the month when he was interviewed by Luis Conte Agüero in a television programme. Conte Agüero asked for his comments on the already weary question, were there Communists in the government? Urrutia said:

> In the ... Council of Ministers I know of no Communists. Dr Fidel Castro, you may be sure, is no Communist, and neither am I ... The Communists are fighting for the dictatorship of the proletariat, in which I do not believe ... It is essential that we prevent the frustration of the Revolution, this humanist Revolution of ours.[50]

Desperately, Urrutia was trying to use Castro's own language to attempt to describe his position. The Communists responded. On 30 June, Aníbal Escalante, for many years a member of the Communist leadership, denounced Urrutia: the president had abandoned his neutrality, had disloyally insulted the Communist party, thereby attacking the 'solidarity of the revolutionary camp in a difficult moment'.[51]

[50] Urrutia, 46. This was on 27 June.
[51] *Hoy*, 30 June 1959.

Castro now intervened. Alluding both to Urrutia and Díaz Lanz, he made this somewhat ambiguous reflection:

> I consider it not entirely honourable that if we are to avoid being called Communists, we must embark on campaigns against them and attack them ... This is not done by self-respecting men. We ... proclaim everyone's right to write as he thinks, from the *Diario de la Marina* to *Hoy*.[52]

The newspapers still continued, after all, though none now received a government subsidy, and some, having been always used to that assistance, found it, as a result, difficult to survive.

The next few days passed comparatively peacefully. Ominously, however, Guevara returned from his journey to the Middle East. Elsewhere, the clouds continued to mount; on 30 June, in Washington, a report prepared by 'the intelligence Community' under the chairmanship of the CIA argued that Castro was 'pro-Communist and his advisers either Communist or pro-Communist'.[53] The newspaper *Avance* meanwhile accused Urrutia of buying a luxurious villa, while *Revolución* published an affecting story whereby Castro made clear that he himself did not have enough money for a cabin even in the Zapata Swamp: 'Personally I neither have nor am I interested in having anything. Disinterest is a garment I wear everywhere', he remarked sententiously. On 12 July *Prensa Libre* hinted that Urrutia ought to follow Castro's example. On 13 July Conte Agüero again interviewed Urrutia (who in the meantime had issued a writ for libel against *Avance*). What were these rumours about Urrutia's difficulties with Castro? The president answered, 'I have absolutely no disagreement with Fidel Castro ... [who] sides with humanist democracy as do I.' But later he said: 'I believe that the Communists are inflicting terrible harm on Cuba ... The Communists in Cuba want to create a second front against the Cuban Revolution ... a front consisting of all those who side with Russia against the free world. I believe that this is criminal and harmful.' He recalled that the Communists in the time of Batista had criticized 'our policy of insurrection'; he recalled the Communists' curious behaviour in the Second World War; and he even ventured on a critique of Soviet society based on Marxist texts.[54]

Urrutia thus tried to drive a wedge between Castro and Communism, and he let it be known that he would continue his attacks on the latter. The next day, Díaz Lanz, the defecting air force commander,

---

[52] *Revolución*, 2 July.
[53] Raymond Leddy to Senate Internal Security Sub-Committee, *Communist Threat*, 849.
[54] See Urrutia, 49–53.

appeared in Washington at, no less, the Internal Security Sub-Committee of the U.S. Senate. Before Senators Eastland, Dodd, Olin, Johnston, Hruska and Keating, he gave a series of hair-raising if incoherent and inaccurate[55] accounts of life in Cuba, which greatly titillated these worried legislators – gossip, rumour, private speculation, some true statements, some false.

The achievement of Díaz Lanz, however, was to drive public and official opinion in the U.S. further into distrust of Cuba, and to weaken the liberal opposition in Cuba.[56] If the opponents of Castro were going to the U.S. to testify before a sub-committee known for its intemperance, then they would become traitors immediately, even in the eyes of moderate men. If Díaz Lanz acted thus, why should not Urrutia? Were all moderate men potential witnesses before the Senate? Further, how was it possible that the Senate Internal Security Sub-Committee should receive evidence from the defecting chief of the air force of a presumably friendly foreign country? Surely this suggested that the Senate did not regard Cuba as a foreign country. It followed, therefore, that if there were a persistent revolution in Cuba, the Senate would regard this as rebellion and recommend action accordingly.

The Senate, of course, was not the executive (as Castro acknowledged later), and the executive could not answer for what the legislature did (Eisenhower and Herter pointed out that they were not involved). But perhaps what the legislature thought today the executive might think tomorrow? In fluid political situations small things matter. The 'Díaz Lanz affair' had precisely the opposite effect to what Díaz Lanz probably wanted: the prevention of further radicalization of the regime. It gave Castro another opportunity to head leftwards with impunity.

Even Urrutia had to denounce Díaz Lanz, but it did not save him.[57] On 17 July he woke up to find that Castro had resigned. Going downstairs in the National Palace, he found the cabinet waiting, not knowing what to do. Urrutia tried unsuccessfully to telephone Castro. The cabinet assembled, Castro did not arrive, the ministers dispersed full of rumours. Conrado Bécquer, the sugar workers' leader, one of the many Vicars of Bray of the Cuban revolution, meantime publicly called for Urrutia's resignation. That night, Castro spoke on television. In a long and extraordinary speech he destroyed the president. It was less a speech than an execution. Urrutia 'complicated' government. Urrutia's appointments had been most disturbing. Then there was

[55] For instance, he called the Cuban Labour leader, Salvador, a Communist when he was plainly not.

[56] T. Szulc and K. E. Meyer, *The Cuban Invasion: the Chronicle of a Disaster* (1962), record one minister (perhaps Ray) as telling them, 'This shut us up.'

[57] He retracted this later. See his book, p. 67. On the 16th he had been due to speak again on television but he was told that the space had been sold.

Urrutia's house. There was Urrutia's salary of $40,000 a year, which, unlike that of ministers, had not been reduced; but most important was the blackmail of Communism. Urrutia was fabricating a legend of Communism in order to provoke aggression from abroad; he planned to abandon Cuba to return later and rule it along with a few North Americans. Urrutia was even responsible for removing the name of God from the fundamental law of the Republic. Castro then described himself as 'impotent' and 'defenceless'; 'even now we are hardly able to do any work, having been exhausted since Monday due to the fevered anti-Communist declaration that forced us into our present international position'. The purge of the judges was 'supposed to restore calm among the judiciary but because of rivalries and personal difficulties with a judge who was also his friend, Urrutia had decided on a guillotine'.

While Castro was speaking, messages in support of him began to arrive at the television station, while crowds gathered round the presidential palace, demanding Urrutia's resignation. All the ministers in the cabinet assembled and were prevented from leaving by Martínez Sánchez, the Defence Minister.[58] Urrutia's aide, Captain Aníbal Rodríguez, suggested a desperate resistance. Urrutia, however, thought better of it. He resigned, for the fourth time since January. This time no one stopped him from doing so. He left the palace.[59]

What moral is to be drawn? The assassination of Urrutia's character was merciless. But for thousands of Cubans, for the masses who supported the revolution tooth and nail, an obsessive interest in Communism seemed to involve an alignment with the U.S., the enemies of the revolution, and the friends of the old *status quo*. From now on in Cuba, the expression of anti-Communist views rendered the speaker liable to suspicion and even ultimately to arrest, trial and long-term imprisonment. By this time at least Castro must have decided, whatever sentimental views he may have had earlier, that, as he told Herbert Matthews four years later, the Cuban Communist party 'had men who were truly revolutionary, loyal, honest and trained. I needed them'.[60]

[58] López Fresquet, 125.
[59] Urrutia went to a friend's house, spent some time under house arrest and then took refuge in the Embassy of Venezuela, being permitted afterwards to leave the country with difficulty.
[60] Matthews, *Return to Cuba*, 11.

The Eclipse of the Liberals

Cuba now had no president and technically no prime minister. But Castro retained his hold on public opinion, the armed forces and INRA, and within hours a new president had been sworn. Castro had intended that Miró Cardona, the first premier after January 1959, should be asked to become president, but both Raúl Castro and Guevara thought that such an appointment would merely cause a new crisis within a few months.[1] A more amenable figure was Osvaldo Dorticós, the minister for law revision. He was abler than Urrutia, but of an equally *bourgeois* background: he came from one of the first families of Cienfuegos and was connected with the great Tomás Terry, who had married a great-aunt of his father's. For a time he had been a Communist and secretary to the president of the party, Marinello,[2] but afterwards he had sunk back into middle-class habits, becoming a prosperous lawyer, legal adviser to the Cienfuegos waterworks and commodore of the Cienfuegos Yacht Club. He discreetly worked with the 26 July Movement in Cienfuegos, though his Uncle Pedro, an old member of ABC and a senator, had worked for BANFAIC under Batista; he was now in prison.

Dorticós's colleagues regarded him as 'moderate'. Elena Mederos who sat next to him recalled that, in cabinet meetings, he would sweat with nervousness when Castro launched into an attack on the U.S.[3] Yet Dorticós was to prove invaluable as a nominal leader of the Cuban revolutionary regime. He gave it stability, continuity and formality on the occasions that such things were needed; 'bowing to Castro's every thought', he acted as secretary of the cabinet in an effort to find something to do. He became swiftly known as the one member of the Cabinet to keep office hours, and the only one indeed who was used to regular work.[4]

Castro, meantime, had announced that his political future would be submitted to 'all the people' on 26 July at a big meeting at the Plaza Cívica to commemorate the sixth anniversary of the storming of the

[1] This is Pazos's recollection based on contemporary hearsay.
[2] He had stood for the Communists in Cienfuegos in 1950.
[3] Evidence of Elena Mederos.
[4] López Fresquet, 52. Dorticós (b. 1919. Graduated Law School, 1941) remains (1970) president of Cuba.

Moncada barracks. In the intervening days peasants swarmed into Havana, many organized by INRA, many of their own volition. On 23 July a general strike organized by the CTC called for Castro's return to power. On the 26th came the great meeting in the Plaza Cívica, the *concentración campesina*. There was a public holiday. The army paraded. Residents of Havana fought with each other to lodge the countrymen. The huge audience, on the day, of countrymen and townsmen treated the occasion as one of entertainment. President Dorticós began the proceedings by announcing that in response to innumerable requests, Castro would resume as prime minister. The great crowd cheered for several minutes, sang, danced and called revolutionary slogans. Castro then spoke for four hours. He began with the sun high, and continued until after it had sunk behind his head. It was the first of many such occasions. The crowd was mesmerized. Castro, as usual, spoke clearly, without notes, often repeating his points to drive them home without ever quite repeating his phraseology. There were interruptions for dancing and singing as well as shouting '*Viva* Fidel!' There were men selling soft drinks, hats, sandwiches. This was 'direct democracy', the immediate communion between the 'maximum leader' and the people.

Castro had already suggested that his government would, at the very least, keep independent of U.S. diplomatic direction. Such a suggestion was irresistible. Idle to think that the unsophisticated or illiterate find such a policy unappealing. It appeals to the sophisticated and the unsophisticated, rich and poor, with consistent force. Only a few can escape the appeal of patriotism. Idle too, to say that patriotism is absurd for a small country demanding foreign markets and dominated by foreign capital. The absurd is often appealing too. Of course, Grau, even Batista, had promised much the same as Castro. Television and radio, however, gave to tens of thousands the impression that Castro was more determined than his predecessors.

By July, however, there seemed to be more positive changes as well. Castro had early announced a public works programme valued at $M134, to ease unemployment, now believed to be running at 700,000, or 10% of the total population. The Agrarian Reform Institute announced that it would spend $M100 in its first year. The Finance Minister, López Fresquet, announced his 3% income tax on all salaries, large and small, to help to finance the public works programme. The government ordered the oil refineries to raise the petrol price by 5 cents per gallon in order to finance a minimum wage of $85 a month for garage workers (as promised by Batista, though not realized by him). Then there was, of course, the agrarian reform itself. In August, some land began to be distributed to a few landless families. 100,000 families were supposed to receive plots of 67 acres within the next four months, all from large uncultivated estates.

But what did this add up to? If beneficial, of course, it mattered less what the process was called: socialism or democracy, Marxism or liberalism; general descriptions are more usually sought by defenders of ailing systems or their bitter opponents, than by their successful practitioners. Castro had launched the conception of humanism, to see it taken up as a banner by those who opposed Communism. He probably had toyed, however, perhaps was still toying, with remaining internationally neutral, a revolutionary nationalist 'Nasserite' position which, though its relations with the U.S. were distant, still remained far from an alignment with Russia.

There was further the question of the Communist party, which had organization, preparation, confidence and, at its back, a powerful if, as all those who had contact with Spanish Communists anyway knew, a not always predictable ally in Russia. Already the Communists had some position in the Cuban State, already they were Castro's followers, though he was not yet their leader. More positively, by July 1959, after years without a clear creed, Castro seems, under the influence of his brother and Guevara, to have felt increasingly drawn towards the idea of a complete explanation of politics, especially if its merits were constantly put to him by close and stern friends. There was the nagging anxiety that, unless he went to extremes, the *bourgeoisie* would spoil the revolution. Though some of the Communist leaders were, as U.S. critics alleged, wooden and without imagination, others were clever men; the central committee had a wide range of talent on which to draw. By this time, Castro might not have been able to dislodge the Communists even if he had tried. If he could not destroy them, perhaps the only choice was to join them.

Who now looked back with longing to parliamentary government? Apparently not even ex-President Prío. Tony Varona and Grau San Martín were still the only advocates of the democratic system and neither commanded much enthusiasm. If Cuba's liberals had been more united, more resolute and more forthcoming, Castro would have had to reckon with them. But liberals adopted Castro's language. For them, too, he was 'leader and guide'. They were devoted to 'the Revolution' which was after all such a personal achievement of Castro's. They could only be said to represent, at the best, the professional middle class – say 50,000 families, including school teachers, of whom many, especially some of the country school teachers, were hardly *bourgeois* people. They in no way represented the rest of the quite large Cuban middle class – the 100,000 businessmen, merchants, bankers, administrators or directors of enterprises and their families, many of whom were actually unable to distinguish social democracy from Communism, and who regarded Felipe Pazos as a man of the same kidney as Blas Roca. With one or two Whiggish exceptions (such as the Bacardí chief, Pepín Bosch, and the sugar baron, Lobo), they had viewed the revolution with distrust from the start. Castro could never count on them as allies in a great progressive democratic movement. He had, after all, in his speeches, already awakened the political imagination of the masses.

The suggestion that Castro had reached a decision on whether or how to work with the Communists by July 1959 may be exaggerated. But it could not have been long delayed.[5] In discussing all revolutions historians seek turning-points, moments of decision: students of Cuba endlessly seek the precise and dramatic point when all was lost for the liberal reforming cause. No simple moment can be so marked, since it was always unclear precisely how Castro did, in fact, work with the Communists. But it is equally evident that, at some time in the summer of 1959, Castro decided that he could afford to be authoritarian as well as radical, and also cast around for arms; thwarted of success in both Europe and the U.S., he began, at least now if not before, to contemplate an approach to the Soviet Union.

Meantime, after the meeting at the Plaza Cívica on 26 July 1959, the *guajiros* were reluctant to go home. Many of them had never before seen Havana. The shops, the girls, the extraordinary buildings, the ostentatious wealth, all the trappings of indolent living were too much for them. The radio and television implored them to assemble at certain points. Eventually they did so, with military help.

August 1959 began passively, with a plea for patience and understanding by Senator Fulbright in the conduct of U.S. relations with Cuba. Anxiety evidently existed in the minds of Cuban Communists because of the announcement of Khrushchev's visit to the U.S.; many times in that summer, the Cuban Communist paper, *Hoy*, assured its readers that Khrushchev's visit would halt the absurd ideological anti-Communism in the U.S. and so enable Cuba to embark peacefully on economic relations with Russia and other 'Socialist countries'. Another difficult moment occurred between the papers *Revolución* and *Hoy* when the latter accused the former of employing a Mujalista, Angel Cuiña,

[5] It is worthwhile noting that the first accusation, from an admittedly second-hand source, that Castro approached the Soviet Union through the French Embassy in Mexico, was dated July 1959. *Cf.* James, 237, who, on the alleged testimony of the ex-military attaché at the Cuban Embassy in Mexico, Captain Manuel Villafaña, says Ramiro Valdés came twice to Mexico this month. However, Valdés had excellent reasons for going to Mexico, since he was married to a Spanish-Mexican. A more likely emissary was the Communist president, Marinello, who returned to Cuba on 28 July after a visit to Russia, Poland and Czechoslovakia. Visitors to China in 1959 included Violeta Casals (July), Aníbal Escalante (October) and Chomón (November).

as labour editor; *Revolución* responded by accusing Marinello of having sent a copy of his poems to Santiago Rey, Batista's Minister of the Interior, and proving the matter by publishing the *dedication*. On 7 August *habeas corpus* was restored in Cuba; it had been suspended after Batista's fall. Lawyers began to file writs to free about five hundred people held prisoner as counter-revolutionaries, many of them arbitrarily arrested and most casually treated when in gaol.[6]

But this was premature. In mid-August, a plot by cattle farmers was unearthed in Las Villas. This had been devised partly by counter-revolutionaries of Camagüey and backed by Trujillo (it is just possible that the CIA were also involved). The conspirators approached Majors William Morgan, the U.S.-born liberator of Trinidad, and Eloy Gutiérrez Menoyo. Morgan had, since January, been running a frog farm near Trinidad. The plotters tried to bribe the two majors to help them, and both pretended to fall in with these schemes, though it cannot quite be excluded that both of them did indeed really side with the counter-revolution and then turn King's evidence.[7]

Morgan assembled fifty men at Trinidad Airport and dispatched a message to Trujillo saying, 'I hold the town and am fighting off government troops. Send me arms.' To maintain the illusion when the arms and men arrived, Morgan called on his men to shout, 'Down with Castro. Death to the Agrarian Reform', while Gutiérrez Menoyo asked Trujillo for a uniform comparable to *El Benefactor's* own. (Trujillo had asked for a country villa belonging to the editor of *Bohemia* as a price for his help.)[8] Morgan and Castro watched the plotters assembling from under a mango tree. All the invaders were then arrested and many others – perhaps as many as two thousand – were detained in other parts of Cuba. It seemed that a provisional government had been planned, with an ex-Labour minister of Prío's (Hernández Tellaheche) as president, the cattle chief Caíñan Milanés as vice-president, and another landowner, Mestre Gutiérrez, as prime minister. All these men and many others were arrested.[9]

That there was a conspiracy appears certain. That Trujillo was involved is equally clear. From this time on, however, the social benefits conferred by the revolution upon the poor and the landless were accompanied by imprisonments, delayed trials, occasional executions, more and more arbitrary seizures of land and overcrowded prisons. Castro's prisons were no doubt to begin with an improvement on those of

[6] For a description, see John Martino, *I was Castro's Prisoner* (1963).

[7] See Paul Bethel, *Cuba y los Estados Unidos*, 77–87, where the Information officer at the U.S. Embassy describes a meeting with Morgan before the failure of the plot.

[8] López Fresquet, 137–8.

[9] Morgan's U.S. citizenship was afterwards revoked. A recent biographer (R. D. Crassweller, *Trujillo*, 349–51) says that Morgan received $500,000 from Trujillo.

Batista. Torture was unusual, but thoughtlessness, overcrowding and humiliations frequent. The numbers in prison were also already higher than under Batista. Indeed, some who had supported Castro at an earlier stage were already now in gaol. Revolution, like Saturn, was beginning to devour its children.[10] As for the agrarian reform, estates of even medium size began to be taken over; cattle, machinery and even personal objects passed to INRA, which often did not give a receipt for what it took, much less compensation; peasants moving onto the land only gained for the time being *vales* or chits negotiable at the so-called people's stores.

Some days later a meeting of the Council of the Organization of American States was held in Santiago de Chile. Dr Roa was present, his first big conference as Cuban Foreign Minister, but at the last minute his thunder (always, it must be said, a pipe not a rumble) was stolen by the appearance of Raúl Castro, who made a curious figure, with his uniform and long hair in a bun, in comparison with the neat gentlemen of the council. His military aircraft arrived at Santiago without permission and was, for a time, held at the airport. He had come, he said, to 'give the boys a trip' and escort Dr Roa home. The only person pleased to see him, however, seemed to be the Chilean Socialist, Salvador Allende, along with crowds of enthusiastic lower-class Chileans. Other Latin American democrats, such as Betancourt, were chilly; Betancourt, indeed, was already telling friends privately that Castro was 'an evil influence in Latin America'.[11]

The conference concerned itself firstly with the problem of the Dominican Republic; the suggestion was made for an American peace commission to go there. Roa agreed; fearful of the precedent, Raúl Castro, however, said that the revolutionary government would certainly not admit any OAS investigation in Cuba. He added that in Cuba there would be a plebiscite within six months to decide when elections would be held. Elsewhere, the U.S. government remained at odds as to how to approach Cuba; for instance, an unedifying quarrel broke out between Wieland, still at his unenviable post on the Caribbean desk in the Department of State, who maintained that Castro was not a Communist, and the U.S. air attaché in Mexico, Colonel Glawe, who called Wieland himself 'either a fool or a Communist'.[12]

---

[10] Though it would be five years before Castro used this same metaphor and denied its applicability.

[11] Szulc and Meyer, 21.

[12] The whole curious incident can be read in *Communist Threat*, 845, 806–7, 797–98; and Wieland, *ibid.*, 602. This argument occurred in an aeroplane between Mexico and Mazatlán, during a 'briefing' for Dr Milton Eisenhower, the president's brother, a U.S. representative who had become a progressive influence on U.S. policy towards Latin America.

For the time being, however, these gyrations in the U.S. administration were not allowed to affect economic relations. Thus the U.S. Department of Agriculture, when revising the annual sugar quotas, gave Cuba a slightly increased tonnage along with the U.S. mainland producers. This was in the light of the still low sugar prices – world prices reached their lowest point in eighteen years in July (2·55 cents, whereas the minimum price for economic sugar farming in Cuba was thought to be 3·25 cents).

Inside Cuba, a group of small sugar planters petitioned the government to take over about a quarter of the 161 sugar mills, on the ground that they were behind in paying their debts to the *colonos*. But the low prices were of course adding to the mill owners' difficulties too: they could not even afford to pay for repairs. For the time being, the government only took over the *Macagua* mill, in addition to the eleven which they already ran because of their past ownership by Batista or his friends. The sugar industry limped onwards in bad shape, preparing for the second harvest of the revolution, to begin in January. The INRA production director, Pino Santos, comfortingly if meaninglessly, said that Cuba would follow an 'aggressive sugar policy'.

In September the government embarked anyway on an aggressive tariff policy: taxes on imports were laid – up to 30% on food, 40% on typewriters and office machines, 60% on cheap cars and some household items, and 80% on expensive cars. Import permits were henceforth generally required and foreign exchange restricted. The mood was to be one of austerity. Castro attacked alcoholism as 'a vice worse than all others combined', and imposed heavy taxes on drink. Yet at the same time, contradictorily, there was an attempt to revive tourism. Carlos Almoina, the head of the Tourist Institute,[13] announced a crash programme designed to boost investment in hotels, and a new jet airport, and plans were made for a big tourist conference the following month. Since, of course, nearly all tourists came from the U.S., this naturally meant an appeal for good relations.

In September indeed it was as if the regime, on the brink of drastic reconsideration of alliances, drew back, to allow moderate men such as Almoina to propose moderate plans. Euclides Vázquez Candela, the sub-director of *Revolución*, carried on a new polemic with the Communists.[14] Since June Castro had been attending, as prime minister, regular meetings of his economic advisers and economic ministers every Thursday – though he had always hitherto avoided any discussion of

---

[13] Almoina, a young intellectual of a *bourgeois* Spanish background, joined the U.S. army in the 1950s through disgust at the factionalism of the revolutionaries. (He later joined the opposition to Castro, was captured, condemned to death, reprieved and imprisoned.)

[14] *Cf. Revolución*, 10 September 1959, in which he argued that if Cantillo had formed his junta in mid-1958, the Communists would have supported him.

Cuba's economic relations with the U.S.[15] There was even an amiable meeting on 5 September between Bonsal and Castro. (Bonsal had forced the interview, after waiting since July, by saying that he was off to Washington for 'more than routine consultations'.) This meeting was relaxed and Bonsal left in a moderately hopeful mood; Castro said that the U.S. government should not pay too much attention to 'the propaganda excesses of young people working in an atmosphere of revolutionary enthusiasm'.[16] Relations between the two countries were held, however, at a nervous level by Admiral Burke, chief of naval operations, always one for tough action in the Caribbean: Soviet submarines, he announced, had been sighted in the Caribbean and the whole area was menaced by Communism. The admiral had indeed decided by now that Castro was a Communist, on the grounds that the Russians were interested in control of the world sea lanes such as Indonesia, Egypt, and now Cuba: 'the narrow places of the continents spelled danger.'[17]

In Cuba itself, López Fresquet, the Finance Minister, discussed for a long time with Hubert Matos the question of Communism and the revolution: unlike Burke, Matos did not think Castro a Communist. The Finance Minister and Matos thereupon agreed to work together 'to stop Communism, but devised no concrete plans'.[18] The same month Castro came down with his brother and Cienfuegos to Santa Clara and sacked the 26 July provincial leader (Joaquín Torres) and the heads of the army and of the INRA in the province (Demetrio Montseny and Suárez Gayol), substituting, not so much Communists, as unconditional supporters of themselves.[19] Matos, increasingly isolated in Camagüey, the most prominent and well placed of the army leaders willing to oppose Communism, had indeed done nothing before a new INRA chief, Captain Jorge Enrique Mendoza, was sent at the end of the month to increase the pace of agrarian reform in the province. Mendoza, an ex-law student and Ortodoxo, and a news reader on Radio Rebelde in the Sierra Maestra (who had first been appointed to INRA in Oriente), was, though not an old Communist, clearly not (as events were to show) a man to protest against the direction of the regime.[20]

Castro now, in the early autumn, seems to have tried vaguely to

[15] Evidence of Felipe Pazos.

[16] Bonsal, *Foreign Affairs*, January 1967.

[17] The admiral in conversation with the author, 26 December 1962.

[18] James, 167.

[19] These were, respectively, an old friend of Raúl Castro's, 'Nicaragua' (Carlos Iglesias), Orlando Puertas and Manuel Borgés (evidence of Joaquín Torres). All three of these were in Raúl Castro's column in the Sierra Cristal. Montseny remained in Cuba, Torres went into exile. Suárez Gayol, not the type of revolutionary ever to feel satisfied with the Revolution which he had achieved, went to Bolivia with Guevara where he was killed in 1967. He had been in touch with Matos earlier on.

[20] Mendoza later became editor of the government paper *Granma*, in 1967, and retains that post (1970).

reunite his followers: Cuba, he said, would have elections within four years. But to hold them sooner would only distract the Cubans from their main task of ending unemployment. He added that he would resign as soon as public opinion moved against him. At that time, however, he thought that 80 % of the population was with him. Doubtless there he was right.[21] But there is nothing to suggest the seriousness of his talk of elections. In September, thwarted in the search for arms from the U.S., Cuba asked England for seventeen Hunter jet fighters. Mr Selwyn Lloyd, the Foreign Secretary, was undecided. The U.S. apparently asked her ally not to sell and, after some weeks of further uncertainty, she agreed not to do so.[22] A pattern in Cuba similar to that which had occurred four years before in Egypt seemed about to develop and perhaps this was the really decisive moment for the history of the regime. Guevara, meantime, returned from his Afro-Asian tour, bearing rather unprofitable treaties with Egypt and Ceylon. Guevara praised most of the countries to which he had been except India, whose development, he thought, was kept back by 'cows and religion'. Yugoslavia, he added, was the country advancing fastest: a comment which some people thought significant. One journalist referred to him, prematurely, as a 'Titoist', but there is other evidence to suggest that Guevara had been greatly impressed by non-Communist countries during his tour – even by Japan, whose development he admired.[23] The Cuban Communists were back on a most moderate line: Blas Roca, at another plenary session of the party's central committee, spoke of the dangers of 'leftism', when the Cuban revolution depended more than other revolutions on the international situation and Cuba itself on imports. This was doubtless a reflection of the international mood set by Khrushchev's visit to the U.S.[24]

On 12 October the U.S. replied to the Cuban Note of 15 June on agrarian reform: Whatever the wrong-doings of the Batista regime, U.S. investors should not be penalized for actions for which they had no responsibility, nor did those actions provide the Cuban government with a valid reason for ignoring international law and the basic law of

[21] The last public opinion survey was held in late June. The cabinet was in session when the survey was made and the results were brought to Castro there, showing a decline from a February figure of 91·85% to 78·31%. The ministers seemed alarmed; Castro said 'we are still doing fine; at the end we will have only the children with us' (López Fresquet, 56).

[22] See discussion in the House of Lords, 2 December 1959. The Cuban government asked for a replacement of the 17 Sea Furies sold to Batista by an equal number of Hunter jet fighters. The British government rejected the request on the ground that 'the supply of jet aircraft . . . would introduce a new factor into a still very delicate situation'. The British government explicitly denied that the decision was reached after U.S. pressure.

[23] Luis Simón MSS, 286.

[24] Hoy, 7–8 October 1959. Khrushchev arrived in the U.S. on 15 September and the famous Camp David meeting, the high point perhaps of the era of co-existence, between Hungary and the U2 crisis of 1960, was on 25 September.

Cuba. The Japanese agrarian bonds had been used to pay Japanese landholders (Cuba had alluded to MacArthur's agrarian reform which provided compensation in bonds) and not foreign owners. The U.S. was, therefore, preparing to press her demands.

The exiles were also busy in early October, particularly carrying out flights over Cuba from Florida. On 11 October one aircraft dropped three bombs on a sugar mill in Pinar del Río, the first of many such occasions. Cuba protested to the U.S. Had the hard line won in Washington to such an extent that the government or the CIA were now prepared to help the exiles with arms, as Vice-President Nixon had proposed?[25] Despite the wealth of information which later flowed out of the U.S. on the subject of the administration's relations with the Cuban exiles, no evidence suggests that the U.S. government approved of CIA support for Cuban exiles before mid-March 1960.[26] But what if it did not approve? Agents of the CIA were sometimes prone to self-assertion even against the line of U.S. policy. What if someone in the administration nodded, either in sleep or silent approval, of limited support for the exiles? Possibly the CIA anticipated a decision which it felt certain would come. Among twenty men captured by the government in Pinar del Río two were U.S. pilots; the whole group had been supplied from Florida, no doubt unofficially, as the U.S. government said, but how unofficial was the CIA in Miami?[27] It is not possible yet to say for certain.

On 15 October, Martínez Sánchez, Raúl Castro's old advocate-general who had been Minister of Defence and as such had assisted the reorganization of the armed forces to give the key commands to Castro's faithful supporters, was moved to an equally sensitive post, the Ministry of Labour. Raúl Castro now joined the cabinet as Minister for the Armed Forces. At the same time, the moderate Minister of Labour, Manuel Fernández, dropped from sight, and on 17 October the Cuban ambassador in Washington plainly hinted for the first time in public that if Cuba were thwarted in her demands for arms from the British and the U.S. she might turn elsewhere – perhaps to Russia. On 15 October, too, there occurred the last of the regular Thursday meetings between Castro and his economic advisers and ministers: a recent meeting had spent itself entirely in an attempt by the advisers to persuade Castro to keep a dinner engagement which he had made a month before with a group of powerful businessmen. He excused himself, saying, 'for those people, I have no message';[28] succeeding events suggest that the die was now cast.

[25] Dewart thinks so, *Cf.* 45–6.

[26] But López Fresquet (136–7 and 168–9) says that the so-called Double Checker Corporation of Florida, which was used for the employ of U.S. pilots in the Bay of Pigs invasion and which had been incorporated on 14 May 1959, was already a CIA cover, and had been involved even in the Trujillo plot of June 1959. See *Miami Herald*, 5 March 1963.

[27] See *Time*, 26 October 1959.

[28] '*Es que para estos señores yo no tengo mensaje*' (Carrillo MSS).

The first major crisis in the regime since the scandal over Urrutia in July now came with the resignation of Matos, the military governor of Camagüey, on the ground that the revolution was being infiltrated by Communists. In his later trial he agreed that he had been talking of the need for a 'National Directory' of the 26 July Movement. Fourteen officers resigned with him. Matos took his decision because of Raúl Castro's appointment. He wrote on 19 October to Castro:

> I do not want to become an obstacle to the revolution and believe that, before choosing between adapting myself and resignation to avoid doing harm, it is honest and 'revolutionary' to leave. I think that, after the substitution of Duque[29] and others, whoever has had the frankness to speak to you of the Communist problem should do so. . . . I can conceive of the revolution's triumph only with the nation united. It is right, however, to recall to you that great men begin to decline when they cease to be just. I only organized the Cienaguilla expedition [in the Sierra] . . to defend the rights of the country. If after all, I am held to be ambitious or conspiratorial, it would be a reason not merely for leaving the Revolution but for regretting that I was not one of the many comrades who died in the struggle. I hope you will understand that my decision (which I have considered a long time) is irrevocable. Also I request you, speaking not as Major Matos, but simply as one of your comrades of the Sierra – you remember! – as one of those who set out determined to die in carrying out your orders, that you will agree to my request as soon as possible, allowing me to return home as a civilian, without having my sons afterwards learn in the street that their father is a traitor or a deserter. Wishing you every kind of success for yourself and in your revolutionary efforts for the country . . . I remain ever your comrade, Hubert Matos.[30]

This somewhat passive challenge (coinciding with another mysterious air raid from Florida) infuriated Castro, who denounced Matos in public. Perhaps Matos hoped to force Castro to make a clear declaration of his political aims. He apparently believed that Castro was unaware of the Communist conspiracy directed by Raúl Castro, who, he had told the Finance Minister, was ready to kill his brother, if need be.[31] The next day, anyway, Castro ordered the occupation of the city of Camagüey by the armed forces of the province. He perhaps feared an

---

[29] Mendoza's predecessor as INRA commander in Camagüey.

[30] Text in Guilbert, 127–8. The letter was published in *Prensa Libre* at the end of the month.

[31] López Fresquet, 130; López Fresquet and Matos had met on 5 September and Matos repeated the same to Andrés Valdespino on 6 September. On 29 September he had complained directly to Castro of the influence of communism. (B. Viera, *Bohemia Libre*, 11 December 1960.)

immediate U.S. invasion. Matos, sitting at his home, waited calmly for the storm. He penned another delphic communication, to be delivered to the country after his arrest:

> The risk I run does not matter. I believe that I have the courage and the serenity to face all contingencies . . . it is preferable to die rather than turn one's back on the values which animate the cause of truth, reason and justice. You spoke yesterday of my being in league with Díaz Lanz and God knows who, trying to stab the Revolution in the back . . . Very well, Fidel, I await calmly what you decide. You know I have the courage to pass twenty years in prison . . . I shall not order my soldiers . . . to open a single burst of fire against anyone, not even against the cut-throats you may send. I hope that History will give them their recompense, that History will judge, just as you once said that History will judge you too, Fidel . . .[32]

The courage of Matos was admirable, though his passivity well expresses the weakness of the liberal opponents of the new course. They could not bring themselves to desert the revolution; therefore, they could not desert Castro since Castro was the revolution.

On 20 October Castro came down to Camagüey with a group of followers to arrest Matos in person, as a 'traitor who had obstructed Agrarian Reform'. A great number of people came into the city that day as if to a carnival. Castro began speaking into a microphone the moment that he arrived at the airport, and marched towards Matos's headquarters. A crowd collected behind him. They arrived at the gates of the headquarters. Matos, waiting with his officers, could no doubt have shot them down. He did not do so. He went into captivity without a struggle. His officers followed too, though one, Manuel Fernández, later killed himself in despair.

Castro and Matos returned to Havana; Camilo Cienfuegos remained to take over Matos's command and broadcast a fiery denunciation of him. The following day the whole 26 July Movement executive in Camagüey resigned. The provincial coordinator, Joaquín Agramonte, was arrested. In the evening, apparently unconnected with the events at Camagüey, the ex-commander of the air force, Díaz Lanz, flew a two-engined B25 bomber from Florida over Havana and dropped thousands of leaflets signed by him, claiming that Castro was a Communist. A Cuban aircraft was sent up to shoot him down. Some bombs were thrown on the ground. In the confusion, it was thought that these had been dropped from the air. This is improbable. A Cuban frigate fired at the aircraft. Two people were killed, forty-five wounded, all no doubt as a result of the Cubans' own actions. Díaz Lanz's aircraft was one of several origin-

[32] This document was secretly circulated and is published in Guilbert, 128.

ally bought by Batista in the U.S. but never handed over to him; later it had been delivered by a U.S. sheriff to a Batistiano captain. The U.S. government afterwards admitted that it was a military aeroplane, though they argued that bombs could not be dropped from it. This, however, was never ascertained.[33] The Cuban Government published a pamphlet entitled *Havana's Pearl Harbor*, with a photograph on the title page purporting to show an air battle over the capital; this proved to be a *photomontage* and in fact it depicted U.S. C.54s over New Jersey in 1947.

Castro himself was in Havana at this time, addressing the Travel Agents' Conference. He went immediately to the television station to denounce the U.S. for at least passive complicity. A drunkard, Roberto Salas Hernández, tried unsuccessfully to kill him with a knife. Castro banned all night flights to Cuba, suspended *habeas corpus* once more and announced a plan to gather a volunteer army of workers – the origin of the later famous revolutionary militia. The travel agents remained at the Hilton Hotel, regally entertained. The president of ASTA, however, said: 'It is absolutely . . . no use to offer . . . tourists, splendid hotels, casinos, sumptuous night clubs, entertainments of all sorts . . . unless [he] . . . feels that he is coming to a place where he will be welcome.'[34] It was indeed hard to believe that this was the case when on 23 October *Revolución* came out with headlines as large as those which might have proclaimed a world war: 'THE AEROPLANES CAME FROM THE U.S.A.'

That day was one of travail for the surviving liberals in the cabinet. Felipe Pazos, the director of the National Bank, calling on President Dorticós for other reasons, said that, if Matos were being arrested for opposing Communism, so should he be; and was not too much fuss being paid to the pamphleteering raids? Dorticós replied that it might seem so, but they had to think of the rest of the world. Pazos said that he was not interested in the rest of the world but in Cuba. He also wished to resign. Dorticós said that he would raise the question in the cabinet.

Dorticós told the cabinet that Pazos had tried to recruit him to rebel against Castro. All the prominent Fidelistas thereupon demanded vigorous action against Pazos; Raúl Castro was in favour of execution. Pazos's supposed friends, the economists Boti and Cepero Bonilla, were silent. Eventually, on López Fresquet's initiative, it was decided to summon Pazos to the cabinet.[35] Pazos was undecided what to do. He

---

[33] See *New York Times*, 10 November 1959. The charge of bombs seems disposed of by the knowledge that, while they were supposed to be falling, Raúl Castro and Dorticós were watching a beautiful grass-skirted Hawaiian doing a belly dance in the Havana Hilton Hotel as part of the Travel Agents' Conference (see *Spectator* (London), 4 December 1959).

[34] *H.A.R.*, xii, 545.

[35] López Fresquet, 60–1.

thought of resigning due to ill-health and went to his doctor, who gave him a typhoid injection to give the appearance of fever.[36] In the cabinet, Matos's execution was also proposed. The leading moderates still in the cabinet – Ray, López Fresquet, Faustino Pérez – opposed this scheme. Castro insisted to the cabinet that he was an anti-Communist, and virtually succeeded in persuading his hearers that that was so. At least they did not resign. Castro put his arm round Ray's shoulders and said, 'Have confidence in me';[37] and, indeed, they did. Everyone contrived to confide in Castro. They believed him to be the arbiter, for he said different things to different people. Thus, to the board of the newspaper *Revolución* he said, 'What Che and Raúl have done in the Army [i.e. favouring Communists] borders on treason.'[38] Castro had by now got to know everyone's personal views and friendships so that he was able to play upon their sensitivities. On the other hand, cabinet meetings now became much more infrequent; indeed, there seem only to have been two more between November and late March 1960.[39] Decisions were taken elsewhere.

On 25 October Castro addressed half a million people brought by the labour unions to the front of the Presidential Palace: 'What reason have they for attacking Cuba? What crime have we committed? What has the Cuban people done to merit such attacks? . . . I ask the people if we have not achieved the most honest government in Cuba's history? . . . if they approve the execution of the war criminals . . . the abolition of sinecures?' . . . And so on. The cumulative effect of this rhetoric was overwhelming. The 'moderates' quivered. Pazos remained undecided, reflecting with Halifax that 'the angry buzz of a multitude is one of the bloodiest noises in the world'. But before a decision came on his fate, there was a new sensation: Camilo Cienfuegos, the man best loved in Cuba after Castro, the romantic cavalryman, the commander-in-chief of the army, the most loyal of the loyal, who had taken over from Matos in Camagüey, was lost over the sea in a flight to Havana. The country ceased work while an abortive search was carried out, but Cienfuegos was never found. Foul play was immediately suspected. Was not Cienfuegos anti-Communist? Had he been killed by Raúl Castro personally in a fit of jealousy? For these allegations, no evidence has been forthcoming. Castro certainly seemed upset and surprised when his brother brought the news to a cabinet meeting,[40] but then he was an excellent actor, and one observer who accompanied Castro on a search for Cienfuegos by air later recalled that Castro seemed in fact in no way

[36] All this derives from Pazos.
[37] Ray's evidence.
[38] *Ibid.*
[39] López Fresquet, 59.
[40] *Ibid.*, 58 and private information.

upset by the course of events and spent no time at all in the actual search. Cienfuegos had vigorously supported the arrest of Matos, at least in public. There is no evidence to suppose that he had any strong political views of any kind.[41] Indeed, Cienfuegos appears, on the contrary, to have been the leading member of that group of ex-officers of the Sierra who, without ideology and without any specially marked social origins, would always be loyal to Castro as a man through all his intellectual changes and accidents.

The search for Cienfuegos lasted several days. On the second day, false news came that he had been found. There was wild enthusiasm, and a holiday was proclaimed. But by early November the search was called off. Cienfuegos was presumed lost. He became a new martyr of the revolution. It was meantime understood that Matos would soon be tried. Revolutionary tribunals were reinstated and it was made clear that Pazos would be allowed to leave the bank for an embassy abroad.

The government of the U.S. had observed these developments with perplexity. It was no doubt harder for them to control flights to Cuba from Florida than Castro thought, though it was certainly easier than they had themselves at first said, as became clear when, on 27 October, they caused it to be a criminal act to leave the U.S. to further civil strife in any other nation and sent to Miami an extra hundred immigration agents. The Florida authorities sympathized generally with the exiles; and, though Díaz Lanz was soon arrested, a Miami judge refused to extradite him. At Havana, Bonsal and the embassy were still behaving with maximum caution, exchanging Notes with the Cuban foreign ministry over flights from Florida, Bonsal seeing Dorticós, though not Castro. On 27 October Bonsal had delivered a Note to Dorticós charging Cuba with deliberate efforts to 'replace traditional friendship with enmity'.[42] But this was a vague accusation. In Washington no one quite knew what to do: 'What is eating Premier Castro?' Eisenhower was asked at a press conference on 28 October. The president replied with no doubt genuine uncertainty:

> I have no idea of discussing possible motivations of such a man . . . certainly I am not qualified to go into such an abstruse and difficult

---

[41] Speculation about Cienfuegos' death has continued. The chief argument of those who allege foul play is that Cienfuegos's aide, Major Naranjo, was shortly afterwards killed and *his* assassin, Major Beatón, also killed in 1960. A nurse, later found insane, said in Miami in 1960 that she had nursed Cienfuegos in a Havana clinic. Roberto de Cárdenas, captain of the base from which Cienfuegos was supposed to have taken off, suggested that the flight was a put-up job, that no one saw Cienfuegos in the aeroplane, and that several others either killed themselves or were overpowered (see *La Vanguardia* (Lima) 16 August 1960). No doubt this is one of the many matters that history will elucidate, though, judging from such mysteries as to who killed General Prim in 1870 it is entirely possible that it will get no further than journalism.

[42] Department of State Memorandum, 27 October.

subject as that . . . here [after all] is a country that you believe, on the basis of our history, would be one of our real friends. . . . It would seem to be a puzzling matter to figure just exactly why the Cubans would now be, and the Cuban Government would be, so unhappy when, after all, their principal market is right here. . . .'[43]

By this time, the U.S. administration was already beginning to wonder whether to continue the sugar quota.[44] But a week after this press conference by Eisenhower, General Cabell, deputy director of the CIA, testified firmly to the Senate that the CIA gave evidence that

Castro is not a Communist . . . the Cuban Communists do not consider him a Communist party member or even a pro-Communist . . . It is questionable whether the Communists desire to recruit Castro into the Communist party, that they could do so if they wished or that he would be susceptible to Communist discipline if he joined.[45]

Though this comfortable news was not made generally known, on 13 November, Cuba, replying to the U.S. Note of 27 October, amicably described her desire to live in peace with the U.S. but adjured the U.S. not to identify herself with the financial interests of a few unrepresentative U.S. citizens and to stop the counter-revolutionary activities; the economic problem between Cuba and the U.S. was not just a matter of land reform: the 'historical reality of the present Revolution' had to be recognized and, in return, Cuba would recognize the historic reality of her links with the U.S.

The Note does not seem to have been answered. Had in fact the U.S. made its decision to oppose revolutionary Cuba *coûte que coûte*? Not yet. After all, there remained in Cuba many redoubts of *bourgeois* values. The most prominent, curiously enough, was the labour organization.

The condition of the Cuban unions had not changed during 1959; the leaders had consistently backed the government, but had boycotted those men known to be Communists. The unions were not, however, likely to make a vigorous challenge on behalf of the free system. The credit of many of the leaders was low because of past collaboration with Mujal or Batista. Some had only narrowly escaped being tried as Batistianos. Others were anxious through some new display of zeal to work their passage back to what now passed for respectability. The whole history of Cuban labour made such men likely to react defensively, selfishly and uncreatively to demands made on them by any progressive

[43] Qu. Szulc and Meyer, 39.
[44] D. D. Eisenhower, *Waging Peace* (1966), 524.
[45] *Communist Threat*, 162-3. General Charles Cabell (born 1903), director of plans, U.S. Strategic Air Force, 1944; director of operations, Mediterranean Allied Forces, 1944–45; deputy director of CIA since 1953.

government. If they had handed themselves over *en bloc* to Batista in 1952, it was not surprising that, despite their apparently strong position, they should, in 1959, be a rather easy prey for the Communists.

On 18 November 1959, the CTC held its Tenth Congress. Out of 3,000 delegates only about 260 were formally Communists. At the first session three Communists were included by the secretary-general, Salvador, on a list of thirteen nominees for the Executive Committee. Fights broke out everywhere. Castro had to be brought to restore order. No doubt this was contrived, though no one could have foreseen that the CTC would react quite like the madhouse to which Castro compared it. The Communists shouted 'Unity, Unity!', while the 26 July Movement replied with the accusation '*Melones, Melones!*' ('Melons'), the suggestion being that the Communists were pretending to be like the water melon, olive-green on the outside, the colour of the Fidelista uniforms, but red inside.[46] Castro explained that the Communists were included because of 'the needs of unity', But afterwards the CTC voted overwhelmingly against the three Communists, though Salvador supported them. Castro then instructed Salvador to draw up another list in the name of 'Unity'. The known Communists were excluded, but so too were well-known anti-Communists such as Reinol García, the Catholic Youth leader who had been international secretary of the CTC since January. The old Communist trade union leader of the 1940s, Lázaro Peña, reappeared in the corridors of the Congress and he and Raúl Castro did their best to discredit another secretariat member, Octavio Louit Cabrera, by privately showing around an old letter in which he asked Batista's police for release on the grounds that after torture he had adequately cooperated with them. Manolo Fernández, the anti-Communist secretary-general of the actors' union, was similarly discredited by the rather obvious trick of showing a photograph of him with a group of Batista officers.[47] Louit (who remained on the executive) was thus replaced as organization secretary by Jesús Soto, whose anti-Communism was later shown to be only skin-deep, and Gonzales, the international secretary, by Odón Alvarez de la Campa, a man similarly placed intellectually. Both these men appear to have been mesmerized by Raúl Castro.[48] The newspaper *Revolución*, the organ of the 26 July Movement, changed over and for good, during the course of these events, from a cautious hostility towards the Communists to an even more circumspect approval of their

[46] Two years later (both in 1959 and 1961), the Minister of Labour Martínez Sánchez, boasted, 'we will continue to be "*melones*" since we shall continue to be green outside and red within' (*Revolución*, 27 November 1961).

[47] Rodríguez Quesada, *Salvador*, 16. (Rodríguez Quesada was a delegate to the Congress.)

[48] The Executive was now composed of Octavio Louit, Conrado Bécquer, and José Pellón (thought to be all anti-Communists); and Soto, José María de Aguilera and Alvarez de la Campa, thought to be intellectually neutral. Aguilera, an opportunist, had always presented himself as 'a devout Catholic' (Andrés Valdespino, *Bohemia Libre*, 4 December 1960).

activities, and of the principle of 'revolutionary unity' with them. Castro seems himself not to have made any more hostile comments about them.

For the time being, however, it seemed that the Communists had been kept out. Indeed, the *New York Times* published its report of the Congress under the headline, 'Reds Frozen Out by Cuban Unions'. As a result, the Congress was ready to make a number of concessions to the Communists' point of view, an attitude anyway urged by Salvador in the name of nationalism. Thus the CTC withdrew from the American Labour Confederation (to which the AFL-CIO was affiliated), and proposed the creation of a new 'revolutionary confederation of Latin American workers'. This resolution was generally popular and strongly advocated by Salvador. Though few realized it at the time, the CTC was now half way towards recapture by the Communists, despite the fact that the party withdrew its delegates from most of the discussions and despite the castigation of the new executive (including 'such notorious Mujalistas as Octavio Louit Cabrera') by Lázaro Peña.[49] In fact, the executive excluded the stronger characters among the anti-Communists in the CTC and included a number of easily subornable bureaucrats.

At the end of the Congress, on 25 November, several more liberal ministers were dismissed from the cabinet, the issue really being the still unresolved matter of Hubert Matos, despite the fact that the minister involved, Faustino Pérez, denied it. Both Pérez and Manuel Ray had violent quarrels with Castro at the cabinet meeting, the latter saying that he doubted the truth of the accusation leading to Matos's arrest.[50] Manuel Ray then gave way at the Ministry of Public Works to Camilo Cienfuegos's brother Osmani (who had been chief of military education and was certainly very close to the Communist party), and went first to teach architecture at the university, afterwards to open opposition. Faustino Pérez, one of Castro's oldest followers, was replaced at the Ministry of Stolen Property by an ex-naval captain, Díaz Aztaraín, who had been discharged for conspiracy by Batista and whom Castro had made a captain of corvettes. He had married a sister of Raúl Castro's wife Vilma Espín de Castro, though nepotism could not be suspected as a cause of his promotion: at this moment the eldest of Castro's brothers, Ramón, who now ran the family estate, was engaged in a public quarrel with the regime. On 25 November, he had written a letter to *Prensa Libre*, denouncing the government and defending *Prensa Libre* itself, which had been accused of 'counter-revolutionary' views.

[49] *Hoy*, 25 November 1959.
[50] López Fresquet, 150–1, has an account. According to Ray (*Bohemia Libre*, 26 November 1960), Raúl Castro on this occasion said that the 26 July Movement had fulfilled its task in the fight with Batista and that there was no more need for it.

This third reorganization of government also confirmed the disappearance of Pazos from the National Bank to take up a nominal appointment as ambassador to the European Economic Community, and his substitution by Guevara, no less, who, since his return from his travels abroad, had directed the Industrial Development section of INRA. This change caused a financial panic and a run on the banks. Guevara announced, however, that he would follow Pazos's policies, and Castro blandly assured López Fresquet that Guevara would be more conservative than Pazos. But the consequences of Pazos's resignation were more serious for the regime than Castro could have imagined. Most of Pazos's best assistants, such as José Antonio Guerra and Ernesto Betancourt (the 26 July Movement's man in Washington before 1959), also left. (The vice-president, Justo Carrillo, Pazos's contemporary, had already gone.) Several of these officials stayed to hand over to Guevara and his aides, but their resignation – not all left Cuba – meant the disappearance of the liberal wing of the revolution, the genuine reformers who were also respected in Washington. For these and other reasons, it was now that Bonsal concluded that 'we could not expect to reach any sort of understanding' with Castro.[51]

The loss of so many technical advisers became immediately a source of anxiety to the government. After all, for Castro and his friends it was not a matter of running an existing society successfully but of changing society. A number of socialist or progressive advisers were brought in from the rest of Latin America, among them many Chileans, such as the economist, Jacques Chonchol, a Christian Democrat economist who acted as U.N. adviser to INRA, and Alban Lataste, a social economist who worked in the industrial section of INRA. But this was not enough, and the shortage of skilled administrators and planners was evidently an extra reason for a turn towards the East in search of aid.

Contact to this end must have been made in mid- or late November, for the Russian vice-president, Mikoyan,[52] was then in Mexico and was apparently called on by the sub-secretary of External Commerce, Héctor Rodríguez Llompart.[53]

On the surface, Cuba still had in late November 1959 several moderate ministers. Thus, of those appointed in January 1959, Boti was still at the Ministry of Economy, Hart at the Ministry of Education, López

[51] Letter to Schlesinger, previously cited.

[52] Anastas Ivanovich Mikoyan (b. 1895). Member of the Communist Party since 1915, and of the Central Committee of the Soviet Communist party since 1923. Member of the Praesidium 1935–66. In 1959 First Deputy Chairman of the USSR Council of Ministers.

[53] James, 249. Since Mikoyan arrived in Havana in February to conclude a commercial treaty, it is obvious that some negotiations with Russia must have been opened about two months earlier and this is the most suggestive occasion: at the time, indeed, *Revolución* made two pointed proposals for a visit by Mikoyan to Havana on 3 November and 17 November.

Fresquet at the Finance Ministry, Oltuski at the Ministry of Communications, Camacho at Transport, Luis Buch secretary to the cabinet and Cepero Bonilla at the Commerce Ministry. The Ministry of Justice was held by Alfredo Yabur, no revolutionary, and several of the other ministers such as Raquel Pérez de Miret (social welfare), or Serafín Ruiz de Zárate (health), could scarcely be regarded as dangerous by even the most suspicious. But ministers counted for little. Thus some of them, like Hart or Yabur, Dorticós or Raúl Roa, despite middle-class backgrounds, would follow Castro all through the 1960s. There were too other ministers more obviously revolutionary, apart from the Castro brothers, such as Guevara, Naranjo (the new Minister of the Interior), Martínez Sánchez, Miret and Osmani Cienfuegos.[54] The political police, the hated G.2, now almost as feared in *bourgeois* circles as Batista's SIM had been, was headed by Ramiro Valdés, of Moncada and the *Granma*, an intimate of Guevara's with whom he had been in Las Villas. The ordinary police was still under Ameijeiras, Castro's enthusiastic admirer. Of the even nominally leading members of the government, only López Fresquet now had serious qualms about the direction being taken by the regime, yet he was still as Castroist as Castro. Others were able to adapt themselves with surprising ease to the revolution and its consequences, even for instance to accept that at the end of November *habeas corpus* should finally and indefinitely be suspended; and there were many new arrests on suspicion of conspiracy at both ends of the island.

At the same time a number of new laws were directed against foreign firms. Foreign oil concessionaries thus had now to drill on their properties and not hold them against a distant future. Sixty per cent of their earnings had to go to the government (that is, slightly more than was the case in the Middle East). More cattle lands were seized. The King Ranch's big properties were triumphantly converted into a co-operative. Cattle feed was impossible to get except through INRA, so cattle had to be sold. Another law of November 1959 empowered the state to take over firms which found themselves in difficulties or tried to cut their losses by reducing production; this enabled the government to carry out many nationalizations, in particular of hotels. Land belonging to Bethlehem Steel and to International Harvester was also seized. Most of these seizures were outside the dictates of the agrarian reform, though the first land titles were handed out by Castro to the deserving small peasants on 9 December. Early in December, Núñez Jiménez was in Europe trying to negotiate a $M100 loan; he failed, perhaps because of U.S. pressure.[55] Perhaps had he been successful the pace of change in

---

[54] All these save Martínez Sánchez (who resigned after attempting suicide in 1965) were members of the Central Committee of the new Cuban Communist party in the late 1960s.
[55] *New York Times*, 5 December 1959.

Cuba might have slowed down. Among those upon whom he called in Europe was General Franco who, on being told that the Revolution was meeting difficulties because of the desire of the U.S. to be compensated for the expropriated *latifundios*, adjured him several times, 'Don't pay them a penny, not a penny'.[56] On 10 December Secretary of State Herter made vague threats as to what the U.S. 'might do to the Cuban sugar quota if Cuba doesn't calm down'.[57] In mid-December a Russian official, Alexander Alexayev, arrived in Havana as representative of the Tass agency.[58] Following five months of simple hostility to anti-Communism, the regime was now moving into a stage when preparations were being made for the complete realignment of her national and international posture.

[56] As reported by Núñez Jiménez on his return to Cuba, in the newspaper *Revolución* offices.

[57] *Wall Street Journal*, 11 December 1959.

[58] *Revolución*, 15 December 1959. Alexayev (b. 1913) had been First Secretary at the Russian Embassy in Argentina 1954–8 and in 1960 became head of the 'Latin' department of the Soviet Foreign Ministry. Alexayev became Russian ambassador to Cuba in 1962.

A Sword is Drawn

The trial of Hubert Matos and his brother officers, for 'uncertain, anti-patriotic and anti-revolutionary conduct' which, with their resignations was said to have provoked alarm and sedition in the forces under their command, began on 11 December. This trial later became of supreme importance for an evaluation of the integrity of the revolutionary government.

Matos was tried by a tribunal whose president, Major Sergio del Valle, was at the time commander-in-chief of the Cuban air force; Del Valle, a doctor in the Sierra Maestra, second-in-command to Cienfuegos in the journey west, later became chief of staff to the army and Minister of the Interior,[1] as well as a founder member of the central committee of the new Cuban Communist party. Other members of the tribunal were Dermitio Escalona, the military commander in Pinar del Río, Guillermo García, famous as the 'first peasant' to join Castro in the Sierra Maestra, and Juan María Puertas. The prosecutor, Jorge Serguera had been in Raúl Castro's column in the Sierra Cristal and, after being on the war crimes tribunals in Oriente was now Judge Advocate of the army, being previously a law student. Afterwards he was to become military commander in Matanzas province, Cuban ambassador to Algeria and finally director of radio and television in the late 1960s. As can be imagined, therefore, legal procedures did not play a decisive part in this trial. Both Raúl Castro and Fidel Castro made speeches at the trial, both full of irrelevant detail about the activities of Matos in the Sierra Maestra and the premier engaged in a series of undignified clashes with Matos and his counsel, Dr Lorié Bertot, who had had the misfortune not only to have been an attaché at the Cuban Embassy in Madrid under Prío but to have written a letter to Batista's secretary to ask if in 1952 he could keep his appointment, a fact which came out during the trial (Lorié Bertot had also written a fulsome article in praise of Batista in the Mexican press). All these circumstances militated against the possibility of Matos receiving a fair trial. No evidence against him was presented save reports of conversations during early 1959 that he had been critical of Communist influence in the revolution. A major argument of Raúl Castro's was that Matos received $120,000

[1] He retained this office in 1970.

from ex-President Urrutia; but in reply Matos claimed that this had been used for normal expenses and the presumed charge of corruption was not pursued. Possibly Matos had indeed done his best after mid-summer to slow down the process of agrarian reform in Camagüey (as argued by César Selema, the 26 July representative in the province in succession to the arrested Joaquín Agramonte); and doubtless he was indeed an anti-Communist in touch with others of similar views in the leadership of the revolutionary government. Perhaps too Matos had attempted to appoint non-Communist officials in Camagüey but that was not a crime. Both Matos and Napoleón Bécquer, another officer tried with him, were incidentally free-masons and members of the Man-zanillo lodge.[2] Matos's speech in his own defence at the end of the trial had to be made at six o'clock in the morning and lasted till almost eight o'clock; the text of this was not published in the revolutionary news-paper.[3]

In the end Matos received a sentence of twenty years and another twenty-one officers who had resigned with him received seven, three and two years of prison, respectively (the prosecutor had demanded the death penalty and the rumour was that Matos would have received this had it not been for the arguments of Faustino Pérez.[4] At all events one may be sure that the tribunal was not uninfluenced by the presence of the prime minister and the Minister of Defence as witnesses).[5]

Several other more genuine counter-revolutionaries, such as Rafael del Pino, were tried about the same time. Del Pino, for all his old friend-ship at Bogotá with Castro, received thirty years for trying to assist Batistianos to leave illegally. A number of North Americans received sentences too or were imprisoned indefinitely, for a variety of offences, some genuinely subversive, some not. Two men were executed for armed rebellion in Pinar del Río, many gaoled. Fifteen sailors were arrested in Santiago in connection with a plot to kill Castro. The atmosphere in Havana was one of suspicion and foreboding. Tourism had fallen off to a fifth of what it had been in 1958 and five major steamship lines cancelled their stops in Havana Bay. On 17 December Castro predicted that next year his followers would have to defend the revolution with weapons in hand, for a tremendous campaign against the revolution had been mounted; workers in bars, servants in private houses, should denounce to the police all remarks against the revolution; all ordinary

---

[2] Evidence of Manuel Bermúdez at the trial (*Revolución*, 15 December 1959, 12).

[3] See *Revolución*, 14, 15, 16 and 17 December 1959. The first two days of the trial were well reported, but not the last. Castro's speech was republished in a pamphlet, '*Y la luz se hizo*'.

[4] S. Casalis, *La República* (Caracas), February 1965.

[5] Matos remains in gaol (1970) but several of his fellow prisoners made a sensational escape from La Cabaña in 1960. In 1967, General Barrientos, the president of Bolivia, agreed to exchange Régis Debray, the French revolutionary, for Matos – an offer of which Castro did not take advantage.

men should become soldiers of the revolution: this was a step towards the creation of a militia.

The month of December 1959 therefore marks a critical stage in the revolutionary development of Cuba, when the government made plain that its enemies would not secure a fair trial. Matos's trial naturally shook the 26 July Movement to its roots – such as they were.

The consequent atmosphere of suspicion, however, did not yet extend beyond the upper-class suburbs of the big towns, though a mild sensation was caused by the arrival at Miami of two priests, Fr Ramón O'Farrill and Fr Eduardo Aguirre, saying that they had fled Cuba, since it was becoming Communist. The priests' superior, Mgr Díaz, confined himself to saying that the priests had left without his permission. Every visitor to Cuba meantime testified that Castro's popularity seemed in no way diminished among the majority of the population and, since North American democracy had itself degenerated into a popularity contest, this left Castro's critics with little to argue about. For the Cuban masses, Castro still represented not only hope, however, but achievement. The co-operatives on the land were exciting novelties. Some land was being distributed. The cuts in rents, telephone and electricity rates had increased purchasing power, and as yet the ensuing inflation had not at all caught up with wages. The tariffs against imports from the U.S. and the cuts in the travel allowance had hit the rich, not the poor. There had not been much change in rural unemployment, but free education and health for all was evidently now within reach, reducing the need for essential outlays by those who could least afford it. The law rumbled on ineffectively but at least, for the first time in Cuban history, not corruptly. The unfairness of treatment to counter-revolutionaries or suspected counter-revolutionaries seemed to the majority either justifiable, in an emergency, or perhaps a fair *quid pro quo* for generations of negligence, unthinking or conscious. The regime had already begun to make a special point of insisting on fair shares for Negroes, after Raúl Castro's speech commemorating Maceo's birthday in early December. This insistence later went further than the facts justified, a wary eye being cast towards the U.S. South. But as a rallying cry it could not fail to be popular and, even after the Matos affair, Castro retained his hold on nearly the whole population, apart from the upper class.

One remarkable occurrence in December 1959 was the abolition of Santa Claus. Santa Claus had been imported, along with Christmas trees, into Cuba during the 1930s, from the U.S., probably in consequence of the exile there, during the Machadato, of so many members of the *bourgeoisie*. This Protestant fantasy was abolished as 'imperialist'. Instead, there appeared the somewhat artificial figure of Don Feliciano, wearing a *guayabera*, a straw hat, a beard. This typical Cuban small farmer failed, however, to excite much affection or respect. Christmas trees were also banned from import. But the revolutionary government made a great fuss of the need to celebrate, and to give thanks, above all, of course to Castro. Prices for the traditional Christmas pig were cut. Money for the poor was collected in large quantities. Here, as before, the only people who were annoyed were the upper classes, who, in the last twenty-five years, had looked increasingly to the U.S. for their standards. The Church was not best pleased either, but many isolated Catholics still backed the regime: near the end of 1959 Fr Ignacio Biain was still praising the revolution in the pages of his journal, *La Quincena*, and he was still ready to criticize those who opposed it – even a man such as the Finance Minister, López Fresquet, who was voicing private doubts.[6] But a large Catholic layman's congress in Havana at the end of November became in effect a protest against Communism. Choruses of *'Caridad!'* (Charity) had been heard in the same rhythm which characterized the revolutionaries' cries of *'Paredón!'* (To the execution wall).

Each week brought a new vacillation and a new uncertainty between Cuba and the U.S., and between Cuba's internal politics and U.S. diplomacy. On 29 December President Dorticós thus called for a new commercial agreement with the U.S. to lead to better relations. This olive branch took Ambassador Bonsal back to Washington on 6 January 1960 for consultations. Would he return? Various anti-U.S. measures were decreed in his absence. Due to an increasing foreign exchange crisis, U.S.-owned sugar mills were banned from borrowing from Cuban banks and instructed to go to Wall Street. Cuban citizens who earned U.S. dollars were henceforth to convert them into *pesos*. Roa, the Foreign Minister, had recently said that foreign investment was welcome. But did these measures suggest that Roa could be discounted? Admittedly, Castro on 4 January declared publicly that he hoped relations with the U.S. would improve during 1960, while the Cuban Tourist Institute was still trying to find U.S. tourists, but by inviting Joe Louis as a guest for New Year they were evidently beginning to think now of black or poor North Americans rather than the old rash of businessmen. On 8 January INRA took over another 70,000 acres of U.S.-owned property, maybe worth a total of $M6. Bonsal, back in Havana by 10 January, protested, without receiving more than the usual reply that owners would be paid in bonds over twenty years with $4\frac{1}{2}\%$ interest. But as yet no one had seen any of these tantalizing documents. Did they exist at all? *Some* compensation, admittedly, had been paid: thus on 19 December INRA had taken over six U.S. sisal

6 López Fresquet, 164.

plantations for which it paid 50% in cash – $M1·3, promising the rest in bonds.[7] Still the U.S. government, in formally replying on 11 January to the most recent Cuban Note (of 13 November) on agrarian reform and related subjects, merely repeated its old position: cash compensation on the nail. The next day 'a spokesman for the Hershey sugar mill said that an unidentified plane dropped incendiary bombs on seven sugar cane fields north-east of Havana'.[8] The two events were, no doubt, unrelated in their inspiration; in their interpretation, they could, in Cuba, only be linked.

Two further campaigns were conducted by the government in January. The first was against alleged Mujalistas in the trade unions. After the December Congress, a purge committee had been set up composed of Salvador (increasingly doubtful now about the course upon which he was engaged); Soto, the ambiguous textile workers' leader, who seems to have willingly accepted the orders of his minister, Martínez Sánchez, to gain control of the union; Aguilera, the equally ambiguous bank employees' chief, a personal rival of Salvador's ever since being replaced by him in control of the 26 July Labour Front in 1957; and the doubly amputated Alvárez de la Campa. These men had an easy time discrediting several prominent union leaders such as the builders' leader (Rafael Estrada), the tobacco workers' leader (Luis Moreno), and the hardware workers' leader (Martínez Leiva). Their method was brutally simple; Luis Moreno, for instance, was summoned to a meeting to which only Communist members had been asked. He was denounced as a Mujalista, expelled and a new committee elected in his place. His successor, Faustino Calcines, had been a Communist for many years. On other occasions the democrats arrived at meetings half an hour after the Communists to find that all the decisions had been taken. This technique had been followed by Communist parties with equal success in eastern Europe, and was the main contribution by the Cuban Communists to the establishment of totalitarian government in Cuba; Blas Roca may have been correct when he pointed out in 1965 that the significance of the Cuban revolution was that 'socialism' had been achieved without the Communists being in the central place. But their role in destroying the old unions was very helpful.

The most prominent union leader of all did not have to be so treated. This was Conrado Bécquer, the secretary-general of the sugar workers. Either under pressure or because he saw which way the tide was flowing, he crossed over to the Communist group. He was a bureaucrat willing to work under Castro as under Prío, though he had, it will be remembered, carried out a hunger strike in 1957 against Batista's strike-breaking. Other unions were dealt with piecemeal. Thus the

[7] *New York Times*, 20 December 1959.
[8] *Ibid.*, 13 January 1960.

Theatre Artists dismissed Manolo Fernández as a counter-revolutionary (he took refuge in a foreign embassy) and replaced him by Violeta Casals, a well-known Communist actress though also a Radio Rebelde news reader in the Sierra. Armando Hernández, the Metallurgical Workers' Federation leader, was similarly replaced. The same process went on all over the country. One who complained about the Communists was (according to herself) Castro's sister Juana, until recently a strong backer of the revolution. Castro allegedly replied, 'Look, Juanita, we must use these people; we must be politicians. One must have a left hand.'[9] The CTC secretary-general, David Salvador, also complained to Castro, who replied that if it were not for the conflict with the U.S., he would get rid of the Communists, by February at latest. Word of this was purposely leaked to the 26 July Movement and the press. Salvador himself apparently believed that 'the only way the U.S. would accept the Cuban revolution' was 'international blackmail'; he accepted Castro's argument that the danger of a Communist capture of power was necessary for Cuba 'to have a lever' against the U.S. He was also still apparently transfixed, as were so many who afterwards entered opposition, by Castro's extraordinarily powerful personality.[10] Meantime the new labour leaders made appeals for the freezing of prices and for the abolition of the right to strike – appeals which the cabinet saw fit to answer immediately with legislation to those ends.

The difficulty now was that anyone who opposed this process indeed became a counter-revolutionary so far as Castro was concerned. Further, the only means of resisting was by force of arms. Small groups of people met, sought to get in touch with friends already in the U.S., perhaps tried illegally to go to the U.S., and finally were captured: if they had committed some act against the regime with arms they might be shot or would certainly be imprisoned for many years. Even those who were caught in the conspiratorial stage would be imprisoned – indefinitely, like most political prisoners, for the sentences were no guarantee of being either freed at the end of their term or of being kept till then. These proto-rebellions were never severe threats. But to Castro they no doubt seemed so. He continued to live in a disorganized way, to resist all suggestions for the formalization or institutionalization of the government or of his movement, rarely sleeping in the same house but sometimes in Cojímar, or in Celia Sánchez's apartment in Vedado or in the Havana Hilton. But even so, still he showed himself incessantly.

These matters were not allowed to remain without criticism from the

---

[9] In her sensationalist article published by *Life* and the *Sunday Telegraph* (London) in 1964.
[10] Rodríguez Quesada, *David Salvador*, 18. This must have been written after discussions later with Salvador himself.

non-revolutionary press. Throughout 1959 the *Diario de la Marina,* *Prensa Libre, Avance* and others had attacked the revolution or given space to its opponents. The government had been able to ignore such protests since they came from organs which had always been lukewarm towards the revolutionary experiment before 1 January and were consequently easy to discredit. The government also could rely on its own newspaper *Revolución* and the Communist paper *Hoy.* No controversy had shaken these papers or their relations with each other for months. But a crisis had been reached after the support given to Matos by the 26 July Movement's newspaper in Camagüey, *Adelante.* By January 1960 the old papers of Cuba were at full blast in denunciation of the revolution, led by the *Diario de la Marina.* At the same time both the College of Cuban journalists and the Union of Graphic Arts (that is, the printers) had been prepared to curry favour with them.[11] On 11 January, Castro gave the order that news cables should be accompanied by statements of 'clarification', put in by the printers' union, and nicknamed *coletillas* (little tails) by *Prensa Libre.* The newspapers in question denounced *coletillas* but were unable to prevent them. On 18 January Jorge Zayas, editor of *Avance,* sent down an editorial which the printers refused to set. Instead, the 'free press committee' demanded that the government take over *Avance.* A gang from the Graphic Arts Union invaded the building, led by its new Communist secretary-general, an old Communist newly appointed, Dagoberto Ponce. Zayas, who must have foreseen this clash (he had already sent his family to the U.S.) swiftly took asylum in the embassy of Ecuador. In a few days he left for Miami by aeroplane, where he later founded an exile newspaper, *El Avance Criollo,* with which to rouse the exiles to impotent fury for some months against the government of Castro. The Rivero family's *Diario de la Marina* and *Prensa Libre* – still run by that old revolutionary of the 1930s, Carbó – and some other lesser papers, continued to attack the government and to publish news discreditable to it. But since the government controlled the printers and the College of Journalists, it was quite clear that the days of these free journals were numbered; and at the same time, the regime was laying its hand over the remaining independent radio and television stations. Thus José Pérez, director of the second most important national television channel, Channel 12, was persistently obstructed by 'revolutionaries' on his staff and finally left his office to an 'intervenor' appointed by the government.

Two days after the collapse of *Avance* Castro once more appeared on his favourite television screen. His words were familiar:

[11] These were Baldomero Alvarez Ríos, Jorge Villar, and Tirso Martínez who became respectively President, Vice President and Secretary of the College of Journalists, and Pedro Souret, Dagoberto Ponce and Jesús Pullido of the Union of Graphic Arts.

International plot . . . insolent threats . . . war criminals . . . international oligarchies . . . state of siege . . . the only hope all counter-revolutionaries have ever had: to destroy the national revolution with the help of foreign forces . . . we are a small nation fighting alone . . . a small nation robbed of its reserves. . . . There is the threat to take away the sugar quota, to hold back part of the price of sugar, for they have begun giving the name of subsidy to the difference in price between the world market and that of the U.S. [which] . . . of course, is the result of U.S. sugar interests, who cannot produce at world market prices.

Castro then violently attacked both Ambassador Bonsal and the Spanish ambassador, Juan Pablo de Lojendio, Marqués de Vellisca, for helping counter-revolutionaries in Cuba, particularly Lojendio for helping Spanish priests (*curas falangistas*). It later transpired that, in fact, a meeting of all religious superiors (except that of the Christian Brothers) had been held in the Spanish Embassy to concert action against the regime.[12] Lojendio, however, immediately drove like one innocent to the television station, broke into the studio and demanded the microphone. Castro, who was still there, was for a moment taken aback and for once a Cuban television audience saw a genuine quarrel. The studio crowd shouted '*Fuera!*' 'Out', the picture faded, but the radio audience plainly heard the ambassador's imprecations, 'I have been slandered.' Castro then gave Lojendio twenty-four hours to leave Havana, which he did.[13] Next day, mobs paraded outside the Spanish Embassy and *Revolución* proclaimed: 'How debased are those who confide in Bonsal. What an inconceivable alliance – Bonsal, Lojendio, the war criminals, the great landowners, the thieves.' Bonsal had already, however, returned to the U.S. The argument that he should never return was pressed even harder. There had been no Cuban ambassador in Washington since November when Ernesto Dihigo had been withdrawn for indefinite consultations.

In succeeding days, it seemed that, at the least, diplomatic relations would be broken between the U.S. and Cuba. Senator Styles Bridges, chairman of the Republican party's policy committee, called for review of the sugar quota. Senator J. M. Butler said that the U.S. should re-examine Cuban policy, 'paying special attention to [Theodore] Roosevelt's . . . "Big stick".' For good measure in Havana, meantime, Amadeo Barletta, the proprietor of another opposition newspaper, *El Mundo*, was charged as a Batistiano; there was, perhaps, some truth

---

[12] See Fr G. Sardiñas, in *Bohemia*, 21 May 1961.
[13] He was not disgraced in Spain, for he went on to become ambassador to Switzerland. Lojendio (b. 1906) had been Ambassador in Havana since 1952.

in this allegation, for Barletta, an Italian by birth, had indeed a rather dubious international past. He owned forty-three businesses in Cuba, including until now Channel 12. But though he had not attacked Batista, he had not hitherto much criticized Castro and if he had indeed been a Batistiano, why had the government waited a full year before accusing him? At all events, *El Mundo* was taken over outright by the government on 22 January and after a while began to appear under the editorship of Luis Gómez Wangüemert, a journalist of Curaçao origin who had been working for Barletta for a number of years without previously having shown strongly radical views.

For those who desired a *rapprochement* between the U.S. and Cuba, some slight hope remained. On 26 January, Eisenhower made a fairly conciliatory speech on Cuba. By the end of the previous year, he said, the administration had indeed been 'discussing a change in the law that . . . [required] the U.S. to buy half of Cuba's sugar crop annually at premium prices'.[14] He was also being secretly advised to embark on other plans: Nixon and the chiefs of staff still wished 'to build up an anti-Castro force within Cuba itself. Some thought we should quarantine the island, arguing that if the economy declined . . . Cubans themselves might overthrow Castro'. But before the administration finally committed themselves to these tunnels of adventure, they did make one more effort to reach a compromise. The same day as Eisenhower's conciliatory speech, the U.S. minister in Havana (Bonsal still being away) called on the ambassador from Argentine, Julio Amoedo, and asked him to try to negotiate between the U.S. and Castro. The suggested basis for a compromise would be: an end to the campaign of television and press insults; Castro should receive Bonsal on his return and genuinely seek a way for differences to be solved; in return, the U.S. would finance Castro's agrarian reform as well as other economic and social problems.[15]

Amoedo saw Castro at midnight at the house of Celia Sánchez. Castro was at first negative and spoke of an editorial in the following day's *Revolución* which 'categorically and brutally' rejected the conciliatory message of Eisenhower of 26 January. This was, as it chanced, a critical moment in the Cuban revolution. A Soviet exhibition (which had also visited New York and Mexico) had opened in Havana.[16] Anastas Mikoyan was due to visit Cuba in early February and, though that fact

[14] Eisenhower, 524–5. Castro had also suggested in a speech at the national meeting of sugar workers that if the U.S. were to cut the quota, Cuba would nationalize the industry, (*Revolución*, 16 December 1959).
[15] For this and following, see letter from Amoedo in *New York Times*, 13 April 1964; article by T. Draper in the *New Leader*, 27 April 1964; and article by Amoedo, *ibid.*, 8–12. What 'finance' meant is obscure; presumably compensate the expropriated.
[16] This had been announced on 15 December.

was not generally known, it was known to the U.S. government:[17] Mikoyan indeed dined with Dulles on his way to Cuba and told him and Robert Murphy that he hoped to set up a trade mission. The State department 'kremlinologists' concluded that the trade mission would be a cover for 'clandestine and subversive operations throughout the hemisphere'.[18] Perhaps it seemed, in the long run, better to go out of the way to haul Cuba away from an alliance with Russia while risking the accusation of appeasement, than be held responsible, in this election year, for the loss of the island to Communism. No doubt, too, Eisenhower shrank from aggressive action against Cuba; apart from the objections on moral grounds which he may possibly have felt, if such action went wrong that also would scarcely enhance Republican electoral chances in November, for once again, as in 1956 over the Suez crisis, democratic electoral preoccupations cast a shadow over the integrity of diplomacy.

At all events, Castro relented; he permitted Amoedo to speak and cancelled the bitter editorial, ordering *Revolución* to call off the attacks on the U.S. (He thereby demonstrated himself to be in complete control of the press.) The next day, President Dorticós announced that differences between Cuba and the U.S. could be resolved by diplomacy, that the traditional friendship of Cuba and the U.S. was indestructible, and that the Cuban people desired to tighten diplomatic and economic relations with the U.S. The newspaper attacks ceased. Mgr Evelio Díaz, still coadjutor in Havana, chose Martí's birthday on 28 January to re-affirm support for the revolution – the last gesture, as it turned out, of a bishop towards the regime. Mikoyan's visit was, nevertheless, announced on 31 January.

Perhaps this was a moment when the drive towards open war between Cuba and the U.S. might have been avoided. Eisenhower did nothing about the plans for backing the counter-revolutionaries. Instead, he went on a short journey 'to see South America for himself'. But incendiary raids by exiles from Florida continued. The day after Dorticós's speech, incendiary bombs fell in Puerto Padre and upon several cane-fields in the north. There were other raids, one by a U.S.-built aircraft of Moroccan registration flown by an individual who was in the employ of Masferrer.[19] Then Mikoyan arrived in Havana.

The Russian attitude towards Cuba and towards Latin America was unclear. Did they even have a policy? They had given some support, often grudging, to the Communist parties of Latin America over the last

---

[17] Herter said that the Mikoyan visit had been arranged 'quite a long time ago' (*New York Times*, 1 February).

[18] Robert Murphy, *Diplomat among Warriors*, 537–8. (Murphy says the date was 1958 but this must be wrong.)

[19] *Bohemia*, 7 February 1960; see *New York Times*, 30 January 1960.

thirty-five years or so. Bombastic statements had exploded from Soviet publications from time to time: 'Latin America is a seething volcano. As in one country, so in another, outbursts are taking place which are sweeping away reactionary regimes and loosening the nooses which U.S. monopolies have thrown over their economies.'[20] Such exclamations did not necessarily mean that the Soviet government as such, preoccupied with problems of world power and survival, was enthusiastic about the capture of power by Communist parties in the New World. Clearly such achievements would embarrass the U.S. and presumably hinder any *modus vivendi* between the U.S. and the Soviet Union, which seemed then an important diplomatic aim. Stalin had a similar problem over Spain in 1936–9: a successful new Communist state in Spain would render more difficult any *rapprochement* with England and France, at the time the main drive of his diplomacy. A Communist Cuba was not, in short, a goal specially to be desired by the Soviet Union in the winter of 1959–60.

Russia had then only three diplomatic missions in Latin America – in Argentina, Mexico and Uruguay – though it had also consular or commercial representatives in Bolivia, Brazil, Chile and Colombia. China, North Korea and North Vietnam had no representation. Some eastern European countries had commercial agents. Tass had men in the three countries where there were Soviet embassies, while the Czechs had representation in Argentina. Quite recently, in December 1959, Russia had made a trade agreement with Brazil to buy $M200 worth of coffee – much their largest commitment in the New World.

Mikoyan had been to Mexico – the first Latin American visit by any major Russian politician – but in Cuba he found a different situation. Met at the airport by Castro and by the Cuban Communist leaders, he inaugurated the Soviet scientific exhibition and placed a wreath on Martí's statue – an intelligent gesture somewhat marred by the removal of the wreath by a group of Catholic students from the University of Villanova (Mgr Boza, the Rector, denied, somewhat half-heartedly, that he had cancelled lectures that day to permit this demonstration). Mikoyan toured Cuba and praised the agrarian reform. A concert was given in his honour at the auditorium of Havana at which, on his entrance, Raúl Castro and Guevara led the audience to clap: all save the Ministers of Finance and Agriculture, López Fresquet and Miret, did so.[21] Finally, an economic agreement was signed; Russia would buy 425,000 tons of sugar from Cuba in 1960 and a million tons a year in the next four years. Russia would also lend £M100 to Cuba for twelve

---

[20] *Kommunist*, October 1958.
[21] Evidence to Draper of Andrés Suárez, who was in López Fresquet's box. Miret stayed in Cuba, however, to become a member of the central committee of the Communist party in 1965.

years at $2\frac{1}{2}\%$ – the same sum which Núñez Jiménez had failed in December to raise in Europe. This would be used for new machinery and buildings. Russia would supply Cuba with crude and refined petrol and a variety of other products, such as wheat, pig iron, rolled steel, aluminium, newsprint, sulphur, caustic soda, and fertilizer. There would also be technical aid to build new factories and to drain swamps. Cuba would export fruit, juices, fibres, and hides to Russia. The agreement, signed with a flourish, was vague on many points, particularly on how much of each commodity Cuba was to import, what factories would be built and how many of what kind of technicians would come. It is not known whether, as seems likely, the question of arms was touched upon at this meeting; perhaps Castro put the question and perhaps Mikoyan referred it to Moscow.

So began the era of Cuban–Soviet economic arrangements. Other decisions were taken at this time, too – such as to establish a board for revolutionary propaganda for the rest of Latin America, the Asociación de América Latina Libre. Maybe too the establishment on 20 February of a central planning board under the Ministry of Economics owed something to Mikoyan's visit. Cuba began to be referred to in propaganda as *Territorio Libre de América*. The secretary of the Chinese journalistic association visited Havana and announced that a new Chinese daily would be set up, the type to come from Peking and the editorial offices to be at the Communist newspaper *Hoy*. These developments cannot all be exactly traced to the visit of Anastas Mikoyan, but they marked a change in the international status of Cuba. Admittedly, neutral countries such as Egypt had even closer relations with Russia, but the strategic geographical position of Cuba made it much less easy for her to remain neutral even with less close bonds with Russia. Further, it was evident that the new relations with Russia would be followed by elaborate dealings with other members of the Soviet *bloc*: even while Mikoyan was still in Cuba, an East German delegation arrived to reach a financial and commercial agreement.

The U.S. Embassy in Havana dutifully pointed out that Russia would now be buying Cuban sugar at world market prices, while the U.S. bought three times more at special prices. It was not the size of the Russian agreement but its style and accessories (and its promise of political arrangements) which gave it importance. The money involved for Russia was actually half that in the Brazilian coffee undertaking. Still, a commercial agreement with the USSR, even a military agreement, did not necessarily mean the acceptance of a Marxist or Marxist–Leninist ideology, with all the internal and external consequences which that involved. Russia perhaps would have preferred a neutral Castro to a committed one. If the latter did eventually occur, it was something which at all events cannot be attributed solely to Russia–perhaps not at all–and perhaps chiefly to Castro rather than the Cuban Communists. At the cabinet meeting which discussed the Mikoyan visit, Armando Hart had said, 'We don't need Russian Communism. If Marx and Engels had not existed, Fidel would have invented Communism anyway.'[22] The commercial agreement, on the other hand, was desirable, even essential, for, if Cuba were to achieve an outright break with the U.S., the Communist countries could provide an alternative market large enough to accept as much sugar as the U.S. customarily did.[23] Cuba had, after all, sold sugar to Russia in the past–over a million tons between 1955 and 1958.[24] The market was familiar to Cubans, and so were its opportunities. In November 1959 Russia had bought another 330,000 tons of sugar, but at the end of 1959, with sugar prices low, Cuba had a sugar surplus reaching to $1\frac{1}{2}$ million tons; while Russia had experienced a drought which harmed her own sugar beet crop.

What then had been the significance of Castro's calm in replying to the U.S. offer as transmitted by the Argentinian ambassador? As 'a dilatory tactic to diminish tension . . . while waiting for Mikoyan's arrival', as the ambassador himself thought? As something to fall back on if Mikoyan's visit proved a failure? It is unclear. Mikoyan's visit sharpened divisions in Cuba. 'Thank you,' said the *Diario de la Marina*, 'your visit has . . . defined the camps.' On 29 February Cuba sent a Note to the U.S. suggesting that negotiations should begin through diplomatic representatives with the one condition that, while these were going on, neither the U.S. government nor Congress should adopt any unilateral measures which might prejudice negotiations or cause damage to Cuba, her people or her economy. An *ad hoc* commission had already been appointed, ready to go to Washington, with full powers. On the 29th the U.S. said that the condition could not be accepted; the U.S. 'must remain free, in the exercise of its sovereignty, to take whatever steps it deems necessary'.[25] Viewed with the serenity that is possible in historical understanding, this reaction seems too strong; the condition seems reasonable, on the assumption, remote though it might be, that Cuba was sincere; on the other hand, Cuba could have spun out the negotiations indefinitely and insisted on the condition being upheld. Still, this was simply a matter to be tested, if negotiations were really desired.[26] Possibly, in Eisenhower's absence in South America, the mood

[22] López Fresquet, 162–3.
[23] Thus the *Wall Street Journal*, 5 February 1960: 'European and U.S. credit sources are cracking down on Cuba and the Cubans will have no other place to go than to Russia.'
[24] *Sugar y Azúcar*, April 1960.
[25] *New York Times*, 1 March 1960.
[26] It is unclear whether President Eisenhower was consulted in this matter: he had left Washington on 24 February for Brazil and was thereafter, till 29 February, in Argentina. His memoirs make no mention of the issue.

in Washington hardened against a *rapprochement*. Eisenhower himself was receiving some practical education in Latin American matters and, inasmuch as he had received a letter from the president of the Chilean students denouncing the U.S. as the friend of the rich and of the *status quo*, Eisenhower was beginning to realize that, as he himself put it, 'the private and public capital which had flowed bounteously into Latin America had failed to benefit the masses and ... upon my return ... I determined to begin planning ... for all the people of Latin America.'[27] Perhaps in consequence, the U.S. did nothing to alter its sugar legislation for six months.[28] Interestingly, Castro himself seemed relaxed and fit during such foreign contacts as occurred at this time – notably the visit of Jean-Paul Sartre and Simone de Beauvoir in late February and early March.

Whatever the U.S. had replied, and however unyielding they may have seemed, it is likely, nevertheless, that they had lost the friendship of Cuba by the end of February 1960. The Cuban government had, on 24 February, denied an anti-Communist demonstration the right to meet in Central Park, Havana and the old Communist president, Marinello, had explained that 'whoever raises in Cuba the flag of anti-Communism raises a traitor's flag'. Earlier in the month, 104 people, including the son of Batista's ex-mayor of Havana (Luis Pozo), were sentenced to between three and thirty years' imprisonment for their part in the Trujillo plot of 1959. The evening newspaper, *El País*, collapsed when its editor, Guillermo Martínez Márquez, resigned after refusing to print a *coletilla* at the foot of an anti-Communist article. INRA took over another fourteen sugar mills in February. A national militia, led by the youthful Captain Acevedo, was already being organized to replace some of the activities of the army whose loyalty was suspect.[29] (Acevedo, still under twenty-one, was typical of those on whom the Castro brothers were now increasingly relying: he had fought with Guevara in Las Villas and afterwards became instructor of the army recruits from secondary schools.) The last U.S. employee of the telephone company had been expelled. All commercial advertisements of foreign origin were banned on television or on the radio. All foreign-made chemical products were henceforth to be repackaged in Cuba before sale. The Church, too, was hardening its hostile position. The radical Mgr Díaz was in mid-February replaced as coadjutor to the archbishop in Havana by a tough anti-Communist, Mgr Boza Masvidal,

[27] *Waging Peace*, 530.
[28] Scheer and Zeitlin, 149, say that the U.S. administration had already decided to cut the quota. This is not borne out.
[29] Acevedo became (1965) a founder member of the central committee of the new Cuban Communist party.

who thereupon assumed the role of spokesman for the sick cardinal and sometimes for the hierarchy as such. The new bishop of Pinar del Río, Rodríguez Rozas, made one final declaration for the revolution. Afterwards, silence.[30] But still, however, the Communists were far from being on the most militant wing of the revolution; in a new report on 28 February Blas Roca denied that 'imperialism' was likely to launch an actual invasion of Cuba. Economic aggression was possible, but the U.S. needed Cuban sugar. It is true that this report did mention the 'increasing aggressiveness of the enemy and that the Revolution was advancing', but these statements were rather perfunctory.[31] It is difficult to see, therefore, that the Communist party, as such, could have been privy to Castro's private thoughts at this time.

On 3 March, *Revolución* announced that the U.S. reluctance to negotiate on the Cuban terms signified 'economic aggression', and the next day all chance of *rapprochement* between the U.S. and Cuba ended, probably by an accident. A French freighter, the *Coubre*, bringing 76 tons of war material (light rifles and grenades) from Belgium exploded in Havana harbour, in a manner reminiscent of the *Maine*. 75 Cuban dockers were killed and 200 injured. Many harbour installations were destroyed. A second munition ship was taken out of the danger zone. In one of his most memorable speeches, grave, resolved, but, as usual, in control of anger, Castro blamed the U.S. (though he admitted that he had no proof) for this 'sabotage', proclaimed twenty-four hours of mourning, and finally hurled at the U.S. the challenge of conflict: 'You will reduce us neither by war nor famine.' Secretary of State Herter naturally denied the accusation of responsibility. But immediately thereafter in the Cuban government press the attacks on the U.S. broke out anew.

As in the case of the *Maine*, the truth about this explosion has never been discovered. Cuban longshoremen and dock workers believed that it was an accident. Had inexperienced soldiers helped to unload, had dockers been seen smoking, or was it sheer incompetence? (Castro himself said that the dockers had been searched for matches.) Of course, the U.S. administration and, even more, the exiles in Miami, had a motive in preventing arms from reaching Cuba but, as in the case of the *Maine*, or the death of Prim, the accusation was not proven. One expert from Belgium, Dessard, admittedly, said that there was sabotage, but it was obscure how this could be so.[32] Meantime, Jean-Paul Sartre listened to this speech of Castro's about the *Coubre* and 'discovered the hidden face of all revolutions, their shaded face: the foreign menace

[30] Dewart, 158.
[31] *Hoy*, 1 March 1960.
[32] López Fresquet, 83.

felt in anguish. And I discovered the Cuban anguish because suddenly I shared it'.[33]

The administration in the U.S. had not even now decided what action it should take. On the other hand, they had introduced a bill into the Senate which gave President Eisenhower power to cut the Cuban sugar quota if there should be need. Eisenhower, on the 15th, said airily that this had not been intended as a reprisal against Cuba but as 'a way of assuring that the U.S. would get the sugar that it needed'. As some measure to appease the situation in Florida, a flight information centre had been set up at Miami to try to control pilots leaving from Florida, Alabama or Georgia. The Customs said that they would pay $5,000 for information leading to seizure of arms and the arrest of the guilty. Was this a last sop to Castro or a first step to ensure that what activity there was from the exiles was under effective U.S. organization? There was at least one more sop, however: in the first few days of March, the last of the liberals in the cabinet, Rufo López Fresquet, the Finance Minister, was approached by Mario Lazo, legal adviser to the U.S. Embassy and for years also to several large U.S. firms in Havana.[34] Lazo said that he believed that he could offer to Castro, on behalf of the U.S. government, new military planes and technical assistance (such as radar) to prevent exile aircraft coming from Florida. The U.S. would, perhaps, also be prepared to apologize for being unable to stop such incursions due to the many isolated airports. The gesture would mean 'an end to the quarrelling' and a new opening for talks.[35]

López Fresquet told Castro of this on 15 March at a reception at the Egyptian Embassy, supposing that it was a direct U.S. offer. Castro was 'curious'. 'What an interesting thing this international chess game is,' he commented and said that he would give an answer in forty-eight hours. But it is evident that the first two weeks of March had been of great moment for the regime. Thus on 1 March it had been announced by Blas Roca that 'imperialism' seemed unlikely to be going to invade Cuba; but on 16 March a resolution (said to have been adopted on 28 February) by the Communist party said that the Cubans needed arms from the friendly socialist countries, not just aid.[36] It seems possible therefore that Castro had seized on the *Coubre* disaster in order to justify an appeal to Russia for arms, an appeal which the Communists themselves, perhaps reluctantly, were now agreeing to support. Thus Lazo's

[33] J. P. Sartre, *Sartre on Cuba* (1961), 145. It is clear that Sartre accepted unquestioningly that the explosion was caused by sabotage; on the anniversary of the explosion on 4 March 1961, Castro also explicitly blamed the U.S. for the 'murder of these Cuban workers and soldiers' (*Obra Revolucionaria*, 4 March 1961, 10).

[34] Mario Lazo (born 1895), educated Pennsylvania and Cornell.

[35] López Fresquet to Draper, *New Leader*, 27 April 1969; *cf.* Lazo, 211, where Lazo implies this initiative was his own. See Andrés Suárez, 90, for further comment.

[36] *Hoy*, 16 March 1960.

idea came really too late. But, before any decision could be reached, the Cuban government made an apology for the remark of Castro's on 22 January suggesting that Bonsal was implicated in counter-revolutionary activities. The U.S. *chargé d'affaires*, Daniel Braddock, was also permitted to talk over problems of compensation with INRA. Ambassador Bonsal returned to Havana.[37] But on 17 March López Fresquet was summoned by President Dorticós, who said that Castro and he had decided not to accept the U.S. offer of the 15th. 'We don't trust the U.S.; we think that what they want us to do is to contradict ourselves. Once we admit publicly that they are on the level and that they are friendly to us, they will give Cuba nothing.' López Fresquet then told Dorticós that if Castro thought that no reconciliation with the U.S. was possible, he would himself resign; and that day he did so, later leaving for the U.S. He was the last of the liberal ministers,[38] and the last minister to defect from the Cuban revolutionary government, though many were later dismissed or transferred.

That same day in Washington, by chance, President Eisenhower accepted a recommendation of the Central Intelligence Agency to begin to arm and to train Cuban exiles.[39] This, of course, had for almost a year been pressed by Vice-President Nixon and by others such as Admiral Burke. The mind of the CIA was fixed on its successful operation in Guatemala five years before. Although for a long time only a 'support of [Cuban] guerrillas was envisaged',[40] the administration had now committed itself. Perhaps they thought that they could still draw back if need be, though President Eisenhower himself explained that the reason for the comparatively moderate size of operations was only because 'the Cubans living in exile had made no move to select . . . a leader whom we could recognize as the head of a government in exile'.[41] The U.S. sword was nevertheless now drawn against Cuba, the culmination of fifteen months of vacillation and of at least as many years of ambiguous feelings; and at the same time, appropriately, Blas Roca left Cuba for a visit to the Communist countries, doubtless to discover what his brother Communist leaders really thought of these developments.

[37] *New York Times*, 19 March.

[38] All this derives from a letter from López Fresquet to Draper, published in the *New Leader*, 27 April 1964.

[39] Eisenhower Press Conference at Cincinnati, 12 June 1961 (*New York Times*, 13 June 1961). Eisenhower confirms in his memoirs, *Waging Peace*, p. 533.

[40] The CIA Director of Plans, Richard Bissell, to the author, 14 January 1963.

[41] *Waging Peace*, 533. It would seem from Bonsal's article in *Foreign Affairs*, January 1967, 272, that he was not apprised of this decision.

The End of Capitalist Cuba

Yet having drawn a sword on 17 March, the U.S. had still not withdrawn the sugar quota. This now became the gauge in the conflict between the U.S. and Cuba. Agents of other countries interested in taking Cuba's sugar quota were active in Washington. Others still hoped that the U.S., by proceeding with kid gloves, could stave off or delay disaster in Cuba; among these was poor Ambassador Bonsal. But how far prized was the sugar quota in Cuba? On 21 March Guevara, the president of the National Bank, inaugurating a 'University of the Air' on television, denounced the quota as 'economic slavery' along with the U.S. premium which gave Cuba 5 cents per lb, or 2 cents above the world market. This premium had, he said, the effect of stimulating sugar to the point of enslaving Cuba with a permanent single crop economy, while forcing her to spend $1·15 on imports from the U.S. for every $1 earned.[1]

At the same time, Guevara also gave his listeners some inkling of his own philosophy:

To win something you have to take it away from somebody. . . . This something is the sovereignty of the country: it has to be taken away from that somebody who is called the monopoly, although monopolies in general have no country they have at least a common definition: all the monopolies which have been in Cuba which have made profits on Cuban land, have very close ties with the U.S.A. In other words, our economic war will be with the great power of the North.[2]

The U.S. government not unnaturally suggested that, if the quota was indeed 'enslaving', Cuba should renounce it. But other Cubans argued that any scheme to withdraw the quota was, in effect, 'a new Platt Amendment'. Bonsal, back in Havana, on 21 March tried to find out what in fact Cuba desired to do. This was difficult, since the

[1] Mario Lazo recounts a conversation with Guevara at this time in which the latter said, 'The higher sugar prices in the American market, limited by a unilaterally imposed quota, were a fiction'. Once the American quota is eliminated, he argued, 'and the sooner the better', Cuba would be master of the world market, able to dictate prices (*Dagger in the Heart*, 241). This conversation went on as Guevara's did later with Julio Lobo: 'The Castro regime and Yankee imperialism are engaged in a death struggle and we both know that one of the two must die.'

[2] *Revolución*, 22 March 1960.

Cuban government as a corporate unit itself did not know. Guevara probably wished to force a showdown with the U.S., hence his speech. But this did not necessarily apply to Castro – particularly at that moment while his position was still not impregnable at home.[3] Further, the U.S. did not really desire to cut off the quota (and so risk being accused of economic aggression by other countries of Latin America), Cuba would, perhaps, have preferred the U.S., by rough action, to appear in the ranks of aggressors.

The regime was still being attacked in several leading Cuban newspapers. Castro's old friend, the ex-secretary-general of the Ortodoxos, Luis Conte Agüero, violently denounced the government on television for its arbitrary behaviour but, on 25 March, he was physically prevented by an armed mob led by the deputy chief of the security police (G.2), Major Piñeiro ('Barbaroja'), from reading 'an open letter' to Castro on the main CMQ station.[4] On 27 and 28 March he received the full brunt of personal denunciation, first by Raúl Castro at an open-air meeting (with cries of '*Paredón*') and then by Fidel Castro on television, the new scourge of liberty. Conte Agüero wisely left for asylum at the Argentinian Embassy. This was a good example of the use of force to prevent free speech. On 28 March the chairman of the Havana hair-dressers' association, Raúl Ramón Proenza, was sentenced to three years' imprisonment for writing anti-Communist slogans on walls.

Such incidents led to the decision by the government to take over the CMQ station, the most important television centre in Havana. This occurred in a farouche manner. The bank accounts of about 400 Cubans were suddenly frozen on charges of collaborating with Batista: they were given fifteen days to prove their innocence or to accept the seizure of their accounts. Among those so effected were Abel and Goar Mestre, the owners of CMQ. Abel Mestre went on 30 March (the day after Conte Agüero's eclipse) to the bank with a number of salary cheques to be paid. But the clerk said that the bank employees' union did not wish to honour these. The following day, Abel Mestre entered the television studio just before the start of a popular programme, *Ante La Prensa* (on which Castro himself often appeared), locked the door behind him, announced that this week he himself would be the guest and delivered a tirade against Castro. Afterwards he went immediately into exile. Thereafter CMQ was a government station. There

---

[3] He alluded to the matter in a television speech in June 1960 and said of Guevara's declaration, 'We do not have to give any explanation.' (*Obra Revolucionaria*, 11 June 1960, 17.)

[4] Piñeiro, married to a North American, had been in Raúl Castro's column and afterwards became chief of the army in Oriente. He was one of the most faithful supporters of Castro and had entered the Ministry of the Interior in the course of the autumn of 1959.

had been several disputes between the government and the directors, because of the latter's reluctance to pay back salaries to employees who had gone to the Sierra. The only effective vocal opposition to the government could now come from the old newspapers, *Diario de la Marina* and *Prensa Libre*, and from the pulpit, since Channel 12, the other big television network, was under a government intervener and since all the small radio stations had by force or intimidation been grouped together in a new government-inspired corporation ironically known as FIEL (*Frente Independiente de Emisoras Libres*), under the virulent-voiced commentator Pardo Llada.

The unions by this time had their fangs drawn. The famous purge committee was still trying to expel all union officials who had voted against Communist candidates at the last Congress. But the purge committee itself was falling apart. Salvador, secretary-general of the Labour Confederation, was accused by his more militant comrade, Soto, of inadequate zeal, especially after the builders had refused to get rid of their leader Luis Peñelas and accept those proposed by the purge committee. Then Soto and the Minister of Labour dismissed Peñelas while Salvador was abroad in France to deliver compensation to the families of the French seamen killed in the *Coubre* disaster. Salvador went angrily to Castro who feigned surprise and denounced the Minister of Labour to his face. The latter refused to resign. Later Salvador learned that this scene had been a hoax and that the Communist executive had been ratified. Salvador then resigned, though for a time the matter was not made public.[5] Further, the extent to which he had often enthusiastically supported the government from the beginning of 1959 made it difficult for him to begin to contemplate joining the opposition – or even to imagine that he would be welcome there. The Ministry of Labour was anyway taking from the unions most of their *raisons d'être*; it alone negotiated with employers and it received authority to settle the labour controversies. In mid-April a new law required registration of all employers, employees and self-employed. Workers would not in future be able to seek work save through the ministry's offices and lists. Control of labour and relief of unemployment were conceived as irredeemably combined. The newly organized unions 'asked' their members for a loan of 4% from their salaries for the government's industrialization programme and kept also the old 1% membership fees, despite the fact that they no longer did their work.

There continued, at the same time, to be real rebellion in Cuba, explaining at least the severity of the measures undertaken by the regime against its enemies. About twenty men, including members of their chief's family, were for instance believed to be in the Sierra Maestra

[5] Rodríguez Quesada, 19.

under the ex-rebel, Captain Manuel Beatón. Beatón, whose talents were slight, had been passed over for good government positions in 1959, had taken to drink and, apparently in a personal quarrel, had murdered Major Cristóbal Naranjo, who had been charged to investigate Cienfuegos's disappearance. Beatón escaped from La Cabaña and set up as a bandit, raiding farms for food. Another little group was doing much the same in the Sierra Cristal, under Captain Higinio Díaz (Nino), an old but always undisciplined member of Raúl Castro's column, though he was a more serious opponent, being probably helped from Guantánamo (with which contact was still open) by the CIA.[6]

Díaz was also a member of a new group, the Movimiento de Rescate Revolucionario (MRR),[7] formed by several former followers of Castro, among them, Jorge Sotús, the 'prosperous warehouse owner's son' of Santiago who, after taking part in País's almost successful rising in that city on 30 November 1956, had led the first main group of reinforcements to Castro in March 1957; Sergio Sanjenís, who, after skirmishing about Matanzas in 1958 with Víctor Paneque, had been for a short while chief of military intelligence in Havana in 1959; and Manuel Artime, a professor at Havana Military Academy till November 1958, who, after a little fighting in the Sierra, had been for a while a zone chief of INRA. All these had abandoned the revolution because of its apparently Communist affiliations. Artime was a Catholic of a Spanish Conservative background.[8]

Artime was to be a specially important opponent of Castro. After the revolution he, with several others of similar views, had been in the Ministry of Agriculture under Sorí Marín.[9] He and the director of Agriculture, Rogelio González Corso, had begun to conspire against Castro as early as March 1959, and apparently made contact with Matos before his arrest. By April 1960 the MRR were Castro's best organized opponents, with a great many followers in the island, a clandestine newspaper, *Rescate*, and excellent connections in the U.S. After Eisenhower gave the CIA authority to support the exiles, the MRR was for a time the CIA's chief hope. Artime went on a speaking tour of Latin America, whilst Sanjenís and González Corso remained in Havana and Nino Díaz in the Sierra Cristal. The CIA (whose director in the anti-Castro operation was Frank Droller, the central European known to Cubans as 'Frank Bender', who had met Castro with such enthusiasm the previous year) busied itself with negotiating a centre for

[6] Szulc and Meyer, 59, suggest so.

[7] Movement of Revolutionary Rescue.

[8] See his political testament in *El Mundo* (Miami), 29 April 1961, and his somewhat hectic memoir, *Traición* (Mexico 1960).

[9] On 10 January 1959 he was found in charge of postal cheques and statistics at the Ministry of Posts, Telegraph and Radio.

training Cuban exiles in Guatemala (with the permission of the Guatemalan president, Ydigoras) at the coffee ranch Helvetia, near the Pacific coast, belonging to Roberto Alejo, brother of the Guatemalan ambassador to the U.S.[10] At the same time, a political front to this group began to be organized around the persons of Justo Carrillo, José Ignacio Rasco, professor at the university and a leader of the Cuban Christian Democrats, and Aureliano Sánchez Arango. All these were still in Havana, though living as private persons.

There were still, however, opponents of the revolution who were not connected directly or indirectly with the U.S. The most publicly active had been for some months a group of Catholic students led by Alberto Müller, a nephew of the bishop of Matanzas. His last protest had been an attempted demonstration at the doors of the CMQ television station during the Conte Agüero affair. In April his news sheet, *Trinchera*, was publicly burned, his friends mobbed by revolutionary students, and he himself forced to leave the university and take to underground activity. Other opposition was also being organized by Manuel Ray, until November Minister of Public Works, now teaching architecture at the university. Since he had been head of the underground against Batista not much more than a year before, he was returning to an activity which he knew well. By April he had already made contact with other progressive critics of the regime, including the Labour leader, Salvador, whose disillusion was setting in fast.[11]

Castro and the Cuban revolutionary government did not take long to discover the commitment of the U.S. to the exiles. The revolution had effective intelligence in Miami, and Cubans, Right as well as Left were bad at keeping secrets. Perhaps in order to forestall overt U.S. action with the exiles, as early as the end of March, Castro combined a warning to the U.S. that 'Cuba is not another Guatemala' with an offer to send back Ambassador Dihigo to Washington 'if they are readier to discuss things on a friendlier basis' – an allusion, no doubt, to López Fresquet's abortive offer of 17 March. There were other signs of a modification of Cuba's foreign policy in April: President Dorticós offered to send help to President Betancourt to put down a military rising in Venezuela – an offer which was refused. On 19 April Castro told a North American reporter, Richard Bates, on CBS television that:

[10] According to D. Wise and T. B. Ross, *The Invisible Government* (1965), 23, the CIA in Guatemala was represented by R. Kennard Davis. The CIA director of plans (Bissell), Droller's superior, denied to the author in 1963 that the CIA offered Ydigoras a *quid pro quo* of support for Guatemala's ambitions against British Honduras. But Ydigoras said in December 1961, and repeated in October 1962, that the 'U.S. had promised him assistance in his dispute over British Honduras in return for permitting the U.S. to use Guatemala as a training base for the invasion of Cuba' (See *New York Times*, 14 October 1962).

[11] Evidence of Ray.

Some similarity exists in the policy of the [U.S.] Government to that of Hitler and Mussolini in swearing that the revolution is a Communist plot: as Prime Minister I have been faithful to the Revolution. Cuba is going through a profound and genuine revolution and this is the main reason for the misunderstanding, which is due to many interests that will never be in agreement with a genuine and just revolution.

On 22 April he accused the U.S. of trying to create an international front against him. The next day President Ydigoras of Guatemala, who had already agreed to the use of the Helvetia coffee plantation for such dubious purposes, blandly accused Guevara of financing a revolution against Guatemala. But something of the truth about the CIA's activities quickly began to be known, since the Cuban news agency, *Prensa Latina* (run by an Argentinian protégé of Guevara's, Jorge Masetti), announced shortly that Ydigoras had made a secret pact against Cuba with his fellow dictator, Somoza, in Nicaragua, and that the proposed invasion had the backing of the State Department. Roa accused Ydigoras of planning a seaborne invasion in conjunction with the United Fruit Co. A breach of diplomatic relations followed on 25 April – the first with any country except the Dominican Republic. *Time* castigated Castro's concern with invasion by the adjective 'wacky';[12] but *Time* nevertheless itself had said on 29 February: 'Thoughts of Monroe and of intervention in Cuba were inevitably voiced in Washington.'

Cuba, however, still had many sympathizers, particularly in Europe, among the many intellectuals of the Left, who found no existing institutional framework but also no Utopia in Europe to satisfy them. Similarly, North American intellectuals, headed by such veteran globe-trotters as Carleton Beals and Waldo Frank, founded the Fair Play for Cuba Committee. A seven-column advertisement charged that the U.S. had over-dramatized Soviet–Cuban relations; 'many American republics, including the U.S., traded with Russia; the Communists [in Cuba] only numbered 16,000; give the reformers of Cuba "a fair hearing".' Controversy raged through the western hemisphere. After the Chilean students' letter to Eisenhower and his reply, there came a Chilean letter to Dorticós and his answer. Pablo Neruda finished a *Canción de Gesta* about Cuba in April. Cuba became for a time a catalyst of nationalistic emotions in several countries. The publication of a handbook on guerrilla warfare[13] by Guevara in April had an intoxicating effect on the articulate far Left throughout South America. Even in Spain students talked of taking to the hills, at the end of the summer term. Castro's

[12] *Time*, 23 May 1960.
[13] *La Guerra de Guerrillas.*

success in the Sierra, combined with the resolution of his revolutionary programme, thrilled students everywhere, loosening the bonds of young Communists with old party leaderships, creating in universities spontaneous alliances incongruous in all save the desire for action, struggle and gunfire. Nor was the enthusiasm confined to intellectuals. When Eisenhower went to Río de Janeiro he was greeted with signs saying 'We Like Ike, We Like Fidel, too'. The same happened during a visit to Latin America by Stevenson. An English film maker with a beard, even in Puerto Rico, was enthusiastically cheered, '*Viva* Fidel'.

In the U.S., apart from the Fair Play for Cuba group and other intellectuals, public and covert enmity was increasing. A baseball team decided not to play in Havana. A Foreign Aid bill passed with the provision that there should be no help to Cuba, unless conceived in the 'national . . . or hemisphere interest'. Farewell then to the third proposal in the compromise put to Castro through the ambassador of Argentina during the winter. In Havana, the U.S. Embassy delivered protest after protest at the arrest of U.S. citizens (many of them Cuban Americans), and note after note: and since the revolution was bringing not peace but a sword to the Caribbean, there could be no question of the sale of U.S. helicopters to Cuba. Cuba continued to protest about bombing raids, some bogus, some real, from Florida. But two events overshadowed local political responses: the imminence of the U.S. presidential election of 1960 and of the Summit Conference with Russia at Paris.

The fate of the latter was comic. Richard Bissell, the CIA director of operations, and an ex-Marshall Aid economist, who was now supervising the administration's scheme for setting the Cuban rebels at Castro, had, some years earlier, devised the incomparable U.2 photoespionage aircraft. The Russian destruction of the U.2 flown by Gary Powers (and his capture) wrecked any chance of an immediate thaw in diplomatic relations between the U.S. and Russia. Thereafter until the end of Eisenhower's administration, Russia was busy criticizing the U.S. with as much vituperation as in the days of Stalin. It may be that had it not been for this crisis with the U.S., Russia would have responded with less alacrity to the blandishments of Cuba, and Russian leaders would have thought more carefully about the consequences of sponsoring a close ally in the Caribbean.

The presidential election also cast its shadow on Cuban-American relations, though the matter played no part in the 'primaries'. Senator Kennedy treated the question with his customary wariness. Vice-President Nixon knew of the plan to arm the exiles; indeed, it was in a sense his plan, since he had urged it since April 1959. That made it hard for him to talk.

On 1 May a large parade of workers, brought as usual to Havana by free transport, assembled in the Plaza Cívica. There were also official representatives from Russia, China and eastern Europe. Fidel Castro once more addressed them. He denounced the electoral system, alleged that 'direct democracy' (such as he believed himself at that moment to be practising) was a thousand times more pure than 'these false democracies which use all means of corruption and fraud to betray the will of the people'. There were well publicized cries of '*Elecciones para qué?*' 'Elections what for?' It was noticeable that David Salvador, still nominally secretary-general of the CTC, was not present. Castro also told the crowds about 'invasion plots' from Guatemala. On this occasion the chant '*Cuba sí, Tanqui no*' was apparently first heard; it shortly became the chorus of a slight but entertaining jingle sung and played on gramophones all the summer, indeed until the records wore out.

Two days later, the Senate Internal Security Sub-Committee in Washington committed the imprudence of hearing evidence from Batista's ex-chief of staff, General Tabernilla, and from Colonel Ugalde Carrillo, who had commanded against Castro in the Sierra; the latter testified, on flimsy grounds, that a Soviet base was being built in the Ciénaga de Zapata for launching missiles.[14]

Despite the delusion of the colonel, the mere fact of his interrogation caused fury in Cuba. 'Flagrant intervention,' denounced Dr Roa. Nor was anyone in Cuba pleased by an AFL-CIO statement the next day that Castro was turning Cuba into a Russian outpost. Conrado Bécquer, the sugar leader, eager now to prove his staunchness, told his followers that AFL-CIO was directed by gangsters and that their views could be discounted.

On 7 May Cuba finally resumed diplomatic relations with Russia, and the Directorio leader Faure Chomón, who in the last year had moved at least as leftwards as Castro, was dispatched to Moscow as ambassador. Blas Roca, after visiting China and being enthusiastically received by Mao Tse-tung, was in Moscow in May and met Khrushchev for the first time; he wrote back a message of good cheer: 'Cuba cannot be blockaded economically by the U.S. imperialists. Our factories will not be paralysed from lack of oil, neither will our wives run short of bread if the U.S. monopolies decide to reduce the sugar quota and refuse to send what we need for our normal life.'[15] The first Russian ambassador to Cuba was Sergei Kudryatsev who had been prominent before in western circles as the director of the famous Canadian spy ring in the late 1940s; since he had diplomatic status, he had been expelled from Canada, not imprisoned.[16]

[14] See *Communist Threat*, 393.

[15] *Hoy*, 24 May 1960.

[16] Sergei Mikhaylovich Kudryatsev, b. 1915, Minister in France, 1959–60, Ambassador in Cuba 1960–62.

These moves merely met frontally the rumour of new U.S. measures against Cuba. Meantime, other travellers from Cuba followed Roca: the inspector-general of the army Major William Gálvez, to Peking, the director of agrarian reform, Núñez Jiménez, to Moscow. As yet no Russian arms seem to have been either promised or delivered, but it can be assumed that the question of arms must have been already in the air, and probably Núñez Jiménez discussed both sugar and oil with Russia. (Russian oil began to arrive in Cuba on 19 April.) In April Cuba had signed a major trade agreement with Poland; again, this was hardly open to complete condemnation – as Tad Szulc admitted in the *New York Times* on 2 April: 'Cuba's shortage of dollars . . . and the refusal by U.S. and most Western European exporters to grant credits leaves her with virtually no alternative.'

May saw the end of the free press. The *Diario de la Marina* had criticized the revolution with courage and consistent venom. On 11 May an article calling for free elections was organized and signed by 300 of the 450 employees. But the remaining minority brought in the strong men of the Graphic Arts Union under Dagoberto Ponce and the Journalists' Association under Tirso Martínez, who together broke up the plates from which the employees' letter was going to be printed. The secretary of the journalists who worked on the *Diario*, Pedro Hernández Lovio, called the police, but the local police captain said that he saw no sign of disorder: 'Show me a dead man and I will take action,' he said.[17] The editor, José Ignacio Rivero, protested and fled to the Peruvian Embassy. The *Diario de la Marina* was closed down. The following day *Prensa Libre*, the last of the free newspapers, with a circulation of 120,000, denounced the seizure of the *Diario* as a despoliation, an act of coercion and violence and a crime against freedom of expression. The same day, 12 May, Catholic students symbolically buried the *Diario* in a knoll at the university. On the 13 and 14 May *Prensa Libre* continued to denounce the government. A *coletilla* to a brave article by Luis Aguilar León boasted that for those who did not like 'totalitarian unity' there was always *paredón*, prison, exile or contempt. On the 15th, 80% of the employees at *Prensa Libre* signed a statement supporting the paper in 'these most burning controversies'. The following day, the signatories were taken before the CTC, presided over by David Salvador, who must have been in a difficult position, since he was already himself in contact with enemies of the revolution such as Ray. The employees were persuaded to recant and, in reward, they had an interview at one o'clock in the morning of 16 May with Castro. After further disturbances, the sub-editors Medrano and Ulises Carbó left the building and took refuge in the Embassy of Panamá. On the 16th *Prensa Libre* was taken

[17] Baran, 23.

over by the government on the grounds that it, like the *Diario de la Marina*, was attacking 'truth, justice and decency'. There did still remain one or two free independent newspapers of small circulation, which, however, refrained from criticism of anything, as well as two anarchist papers (*El Libertario* and *Solidaridad Gastronímica*) and a Trotskyist one (*Voz Proletaria*); while the weekly journal *Bohemia, Time,* the *New York Times* and other North American papers continued for the time being to be sold on news stands. The views of the government continued to be given in *Hoy, Revolución* and the new-style *El Mundo,* while the Directorio still nominally controlled an evening paper, *La Calle,* and there were several government papers in the provinces.

The fall of the free press in Cuba would have been more difficult to explain (or to bring about) had it not been for the fact that, like the union leaders, all these papers had not only collaborated with Batista but in many cases had actually received financial help from his government and those of his predecessors. This subsidization of the press had become so customary (as in Mexico still) that several newspapers completely relied on it.

About this time, the remaining non-Communist staunch and liberty-loving members of the 26 July, under its nominal leader Marcelo Fernández, seem to have met and drawn up an ultimatum to Castro demanding that he publicly reaffirm his hostility to Communism. The ultimatum was not presented, apparently because of the intervention of Carlos Franqui, the editor of *Revolución*. But Castro, as usual, got to know of these moves, and might perhaps have responded even so, had it not been for an opportune intervention by the Tass correspondent, A. Alexayev, a diplomat more than a journalist. Alexayev apparently gave Castro a direct message from Khrushchev, telling him that 'the Soviet Government wishes to express to you that it does not consider any party as an intermediary between it and you. Comrade Khrushchev . . . considers you to be the authentic leader of the Revolution'.[18] This suggested that Khrushchev was hoping to place Castro in the same position as Nasser or any leader of the third world, but not in that of a Gomulka or a satellite leader. He was helping Castro to assert himself as an individual leader without concern about the Cuban Communist party – a judgement presumably reached after he had talked matters over with Blas Roca. But to Castro, the letter had other implications: that he could take over the Communist party him-

[18] Casalis, *La República* (Caracas), 4 and 10 February 1966. S. Casalis was then a prominent journalist writing daily articles for *Revolución* and close to Guevara and Castro at this stage. His evidence may very well seem open to question, but the result nevertheless seems to give it much credence. Nicolás Rivero, who worked in the Foreign Ministry, thought that Alexayev did his best to persuade the Castro brothers to make fewer anti-U.S. rodomantades. (*Castro's Cuba,* 54.)

self and use it as if it were his bureaucracy. Thus the Cuban and Russian leaders were, for many months, at odds, paradoxically on the precise question of whether the Communists should take power in Cuba. For reasons of international politics, Russia probably would have desired a friendly neutral in Cuba more than a satellite: for reasons of national as well as international politics, and even psychological reasons, Castro himself seems to have preferred a more committed status. The Cuban Communist party probably believed that the U.S. would almost certainly intervene in Cuba rather than let them capture power. Javier Pazos, then still working under Boti in the Ministry of Economics, said later that many Communists 'privately admitted' that they hoped that this would occur, causing Cuba to become a kind of 'Hungary of the West', with repercussions throughout the continent.[19]

The destruction of the free press marked the beginning of a campaign against the revolution by the Church. Early in May a Mass held in the cathedral of Havana to commemorate the victims of Communism was broken up by militiamen singing the International. On 16 May, Mgr Pérez Serantes, archbishop of Santiago, finally laid aside neutrality and issued a pastoral letter denouncing the restoration of diplomatic relations with the Soviet Union: 'It can no longer be said that the enemy is at the gates, for in truth he is within, as if in his own domain.' He went on: 'The true Christian cannot live without freedom ... it has always seemed better to us to lose all, even to shed blood, than to renounce liberty.' Every home should, therefore, be turned into a domestic catechism class. But since there were few homes where the leaders of the family were qualified to fulfil this duty, he appealed to those who were to take the lead.[20] Too late, perhaps fifty years too late, the archbishop could do little: his warnings that Communism led to materialism caused a hollow laugh in such a city as Havana where capitalism had been more material than anywhere else. Still, the pastoral was read in the churches of Oriente and Havana, and published without comment in the two remaining independent papers, *Información* and *El Crisol*. The Communist Carlos Rafael Rodríguez replied in *Hoy* that nobody in Cuba was stopping anyone from the practice of religion: were there not hundreds of Catholics among the revolutionaries? Castro refrained from comment for the time being, reluctant for a full-scale clash when the tide of conspiracy seemed to be flowing high in the universities and among his old supporters. According to the *New York Times,* half the students were now neutral to the revolution – that is, potentially hostile. Perhaps against the will of the hierarchy, cautious against Castro as they had been cautious against Batista, the Catholic Church became

[19] Javier Pazos, *Cambridge Opinion*, February 1963, 25.
[20] A translation appeared in *Catholic Mind*, (January–February 1961), 1153.

inevitably a stronghold of opposition to the regime once the private schools began to be closed and independent youth and other organizations started to be banned.

It is difficult not to suppose that the government had this in mind when they dispatched 800 third-year students in May to the Sierra Maestra to help teach the peasants. Meantime, one of the few professors who still spoke openly, the ex-Auténtico minister, Sánchez Arango, already in contact with MRR, the exiles' political organization, was publicly accused of converting his classes into a counter-revolutionary political forum, and escaped to Miami through the embassy of Ecuador.

In Miami the CIA had by now practically persuaded the exiles' organizations to form themselves into a 'united front'. With the arrival of Sánchez Arango, this curiously named group became at last a reality, taking the title of Frente Revolucionario Democrático. This included the Auténtico prime minister under Prío, Tony Varona, who from the first had criticized Castro for his failure to hold elections; Rasco; Manuel Artime of the MRR; Justo Carrillo, the ex-chief of BANFAIC; and Aureliano Sánchez Arango. Artime was the military representative and the link with the CIA, but there were also connected with these men other Cuban soldiers, such as Colonel Martín Elena, an officer who had resigned his commission in 1952, when in command at Matanzas, in protest against Batista's *golpe*. A number of other Cubans, including various ex-officers of Batista's army, many of them linked with Barquín and his plot of April 1956,[21] had already set off for secret training in Guatemala and for a while some were at the U.S.'s own counter-guerrilla school at Panama. But this side of operations was still in an early stage. There were certainly under a hundred Cubans in training. The CIA was also active among other actual insurrectionaries in Cuba.

These new Cuban warriors were not precisely apprised of the fact that they were soldiers of the U.S., being told variously that their activities were paid for by 'a group of private U.S. businesses' or by 'a Cuban millionaire'. Few were deceived by this unsubtle posturing. But once these men had undertaken to work with the U.S. espionage organization they really surrendered freedom. So too did the politicians. Over the months these men, though they quarrelled with each other and with their benefactors, became in effect North Americans, relying on the U.S. to help them when things went wrong and regarding the U.S. president as their chief.

A steady flow of emigrants continued to come to the U.S., businessmen, ranchers, men of conspiracy, men with families, families without

---

[21] These included Manuel Blanco, Alejandro del Valle, Roberto, José and Miguel Pérez San Román, Miguel Orozco, Hugo Sueiro, Ramón J. Ferrer, 'Chiquí' García Martínez, Osvaldo Piedra and Alfonso Corsi.

fathers. The ease with which they were permitted to leave Cuba and to enter the U.S. was one of the factors which debilitated the opponents of the regime, causing almost each one of them to arrive in Miami, as it would seem, the leader of some new political organization, known by bombastic initials, but consisting of little more than the immediate family of that single exile. In this way Castro lost manpower but also many potentially dangerous opponents.

In Cuba the sugar harvest was now once more drawing to an end. A total of 5·8 million tons had been produced. But the harvest itself was less important than the fact that it had been the last one under the system of free enterprise which, with all its wastefulness and injustice, had made Cuba what she was. Immediately the harvest came to an end nearly all sugar land belonging to the mills, 2·7 million acres, was taken over by INRA. A thousand co-operatives were created on the plots thus made. Included in this immense seizure were the 275,000 acres belonging to the Cuban Atlantic, Cuban American, and the other grand U.S.-owned companies. In compensation, Cuba offered twenty-year bonds at $4\frac{1}{2}\%$, but in the case, for instance, of United Fruit, there was much doubt about the value: the company claimed its land was worth £M32, the government, £M6. With the estates there went, of course, machinery, shops, many buildings and labour: INRA ran many old shops as they were and opened new ones, so that by midsummer there were over 2,000 'people's shops', *tiendas del pueblo*. The mills themselves were not as yet touched and theoretically they could look forward to a harvest in 1961 where, outposts of private business, they would buy cane from co-operative planters as well as from the surviving *colonos*. Many mills doubted whether this arrangement could last. They were right to do so, since the whole system of private enterprise in Cuba was now menaced.

This train of events began when on 23 May the three large oil refineries in Cuba – Texaco, Royal Dutch and Standard Oil – were told by the government that a large consignment of Russian oil, in pursuance of the agreement of February, would soon arrive and that they would henceforth be asked to process 6,000 lbs of Russian crude oil a day. The capacity of the refineries was 85,000 lbs. These companies were already owed $M16 by Cuba for oil imports. The Cuban requirement would be detrimental to Venezuela. The companies hesitated. They were told that a fifth of Cuba's annual crude oil consumption would be supplied by Russia. This oil was anyway cheaper than that of Venezuela. The companies again hesitated.

Meantime, there was considerable coming and going in Havana. Sukarno paid a visit and according to one account took a careful look around Cuba and then, not entirely in jest, said to Castro, 'And you call this an under-developed country!' Dorticós went on a three-week tour of South America and, at the same time, Cuba invested in powerful short-wave radio equipment to broadcast to South America: and one observer dates Dorticós's journey as the beginning of the campaign by Castro to 'export his revolution to South America'.[22] Núñez Jiménez in Russia arranged for the purchase of some thirty new factories, along with technicians to run them in order to manufacture everything from steel to pencils. They would cost $M80 of which half would be paid for in goods. Castro tauntingly said that Cuba could produce more sugar were it not for the U.S. quota – his first apparent acceptance of Guevara's hard line of March.[23] In early June he formally abandoned the drive to bring in U.S. tourists. The State Department had recently said that all economic aid to Cuba would soon cease. But this was already limited anyway to two small programmes – six technicians at the agricultural experimental station and some others training Cubans in civil aviation – an annual cost of below $200,000. There was some tension in Havana over notices – prepared by the U.S. Embassy, for the use of businesses in the city – saying, 'This is the property of the U.S.', as if an invasion were about to follow. Bonsal, in a situation of increasing unhappiness as ambassador, being made to bear the brunt of humiliations intended for his predecessors, continued to send Note after Note criticizing slanders of his country, without avail. He did not know of the arming of the exiles; had he done so he could hardly have remained. In Cuba itself a group of students from the University of Santa Clara took to the hills; their leaders were captured and Plinio Prieto, a rebel army major, Porfirio Ramírez Ruiz (president of the Students' Federation of Las Villas) and Sinesio Walsh were shot, the first execution of students since January 1969.[24] David Salvador, still nominally the secretary-general of the unions, had gone underground in June, forming, with the ex-26 July leader in Camagüey, Joaquín Agramonte, the 30 November Movement – named after the day that Frank País had risen in 1956 in Santiago.[25] The wheel was indeed full circle. These students were regarded by the regime as much as bandits as Batista had regarded the men of the 26 July. They had not received much help from the peasants, and the leaders were in fact cornered in small towns buying food. More serious was the movement into active clandestine politics of Manuel Ray, the

[22] Tad Szulc, 'Exporting the Cuban Revolution', in Plank, *op. cit.*, 81.
[23] *Hoy*, 29 May 1960.
[24] Plinio Prieto had been in 1950 a teacher at a Havana night school and in 1952 he had joined Sánchez Arango's Triple A organization. In 1957 he joined the Directorio Revolucionario. He ran arms to Cuba from Florida in 1958 and on one occasion was lost in the Gulf of Mexico, spending ten days in an open boat without food.
[25] Rodríguez Quesada, 19.

ex-Public Works minister. By midsummer he had founded a new secret organization known as the Movimiento Revolucionario del Pueblo (MRP) which, unlike the MRR, had to begin with no relations with the U.S. Ray tried to gather all the old supporters of Castro who had now withdrawn their approval, inside and out of Cuba. Salvador joined him, the movement gained some followers, but it steadfastly refused collaboration with the CIA who, occupied with their own leaders, thought Ray was too far to the Left for them. Ray's slogan '*Fidelismo sin Fidel*' could, however, appeal only to the sophisticated, and to few even of them. To the masses, the phrase seemed an absurdity, as indeed, in a sense, it was. Meantime, rumours of invasion reached even the U.S. press: the well-informed *Wall Street Journal*, for instance, in early July published an article saying that 'there are government officials already engaged in considering just how Mr Castro's downfall might be hastened by promoting and discreetly backing opposition to him within Cuba if . . . his prestige . . . should . . . wane'.[26]

In the middle of 1960 freedom in the University of Havana was finally destroyed. That centre of learning had a long tradition of being domineered by a group of tough, often somewhat elderly students not averse to the use of firearms and kidnapping for the achievement of modest aims such as the presidency of the law students or the sub-secretaryship of the union. The students who engineered the collapse of university autonomy were in one sense therefore the apotheosis of an old if discreditable tradition. The men concerned – Rolando Cubela, a major in the Directorio; José Puente Blanco, one of Echevarría's successors; Angel Quevedo; and Omar Fernández – were to the government of Castro what the MSR of Manolo Castro had been to Grau San Martín: a *bonche*, prepared to use every means to secure mastery, which in this instance meant state control of the university. These four men, incidentally, had military ranks, and Omar Fernández, already administrator of customs, soon became Minister of Transport. Among some of these leaders, the policy demanded meant, as in the case of Cubela and Puente, a complete break with their past democratic political attitudes; others, such as Ricardo Alarcón (even as 26 July coordinator in the university in 1958), had always been in favour of collaboration with the Communists.[27] In 1959 these men had established themselves in the student federation, by political pressure, though even so Cubela had only beaten Pedro Luis Boitel, an opposition candidate for the Presidency of the FEU, by a narrow majority in an election in which intimidation was used. Similarly, Alarcón had only taken over the presidency

[26] Philip Geyelin, in *Wall Street Journal*, 11 July 1960.
[27] Fausto Masó (to Draper), who adds that Alarcón was used by Guevara as a '*punta de lanza*' within the 26 July Movement.

of the Law School by the 'promotion' of his chief rival, Amparo Victoria, to the post of Secretary of Embassy in Holland.[28]

The University was finally subverted by means of a carefully prepared incident in the Faculty of Civil Engineering. The professor of Hydraulics and one other teacher were quite unjustly denounced by a group of Fidelista students as being in breach of examination proceedings. The faculty board refused to dismiss these men. But the students then nominated two engineers as successors to them, one a brother-in-law of Guevara. The University Council backed the faculty board. On 15 July 1960 a large meeting of students (doubtless however a minority of the student body) and some teachers denounced the University Council and 'appointed' a new board of governors to direct the university: four professors and four students. The board then dismissed the council and the faculty boards.

Castro and Raúl Castro came to the university in pursuit of these demands; professors such as Portell Vilá, seeing how things were going, quickly made arrangements to leave the country. Two-thirds of the teachers at the university refused to accept the new board of governors and were dismissed by it. Dr Miró Cardona, ex-prime minister and still nominally an ambassador, a member of the law faculty, protested, but without success, before President Dorticós. The Rector of the University, Clemente Inclán, an opportunist of many years' standing, was after some months replaced by Dr Juan Marinello, for many years the president of the Cuban Communist party, a poet and well-known man of letters of the Left, though something of a figurehead; and, on 4 August, the government endorsed the board of governors as a policy-making body and approved a committee of University Reform to change the curriculum, the administrative procedures and policies of the University.[29]

The manner in which this ancient university lost its liberties was deplorable. Nevertheless, those liberties in the past had led so often to licence, its institutional fabric was so rotten with politics and gang warfare, that mere reform could arguably never have altered the fundamental disequilibrium. The political stranglehold over the FEU and its sub-committees held by perpetual students and the corruption and inefficiency of many teachers had given the University a terrible name. Like the press and the unions, this bastion of liberty had been often in disrepair. It is distressing to note that, after the radical revolution in the university, the new student leaders such as Cubela rode about in large cars, living the good life and bringing discredit even to the puritan revolution in which they had played an important part. The new board

[28] Professor Portell Vilá, in *Bohemia Libre*, 6, 13 and 20 November 1960.
[29] *Cuba and the Rule of Law*, 249–50; *Revolución*, 5 August 1960.

of governors began to scour the world for replacements for the dismissed academics, while admitting that for a time education would suffer. Meantime, other safeguards of political liberty were disappearing. Thus on 5 July a group of left-wing lawyers, some in militia uniform, entered the headquarters of the Havana Bar Association and took possession of its offices.

The great oil companies in mid-June at last replied that they would not process Russian oil, on the ground that this step would damage Venezuela.[30] The Cubans' case derived from a law of 1938 providing that foreign refineries were required to process Cuban crude oil – which the companies defined as oil taken from the Cuban soil. It seems that the secretary of the U.S. Treasury had strongly urged a refusal by the companies to process the oil, despite the companies' own reluctant inclination to agree.[31]

For a few days the Cuban government delayed its answer. Doubtless this situation necessitated a hasty consultation with Moscow. Raúl Castro left for Prague, presumably to discuss arms. The Havana Hilton and the Nacional hotels were taken over by the government. Nico Beatón and others of his gang in the Sierra Maestra were caught and shot. Two U.S. diplomats were expelled as counter-revolutionaries. U.S. policy specifically changed. 'Patience and forbearance' were openly dropped. A 50-kilowatt radio station on Swan Island, 400 miles southwest of Cuba, was built by the CIA to cover the Caribbean, first to attack Trujillo (the Church had turned against the 'benefactor' and the end of his evil regime was approaching) and then to attack Castro.[32] On 22 June Herter, Secretary of State, appeared before the Senate to plead for a bill authorizing Eisenhower to cut the sugar quota. The bill had been lying unattended since earlier in the month. 'This would be an appropriate time,' said Herter, 'for the U.S. to seek ways to diversify its sources of supply and reduce the dependence of its consumers on Cuban sugar.' This change of line was against the advice of Ambassador Bonsal who, despite his unexampled gloomy position in Havana, believed that the U.S. 'should have continued our policy of restraint longer than we did'.[33]

On 25 June came Castro's response: Herter's action proved everything that he had been saying. It was a declaration of economic war.

[30] 'Unexpectedly', *Wall Street Journal* stated on 13 June.

[31] Bonsal, *Foreign Affairs* (January 1967), 272, says that a Havana oil company representative present at the crucial meeting, so told him.

[32] Eisenhower, 534. Swan Island was set up under the cover of being the Gibraltar Steamship Corporation, owned by three prominent New York financiers, Thomas Dudley Cabot, Walter G. Lohr and Sumner Smith. The first of these had been president of the United Fruit Company.

[33] Letter to Schlesinger, 2.

Cuba must be prepared for months, even years, of hardship because of the policies undertaken by the U.S. Cuba would not starve, but even necessities would be lacking. There would no doubt be an armed attack. For every cut in the quota, however, a U.S. sugar mill would be expropriated.

The immediate consequences of these exchanges were that world sugar prices dropped to 2.85 cents a pound with the fear that excess Cuban sugar would be dumped on the market at a low price. Castro fixed his selling price of sugar hastily at 3 cents and the world price rose uneasily ten points to 2.95 cents. On 28 June the U.S. House of Representatives Committee on Agriculture, after a brief and, even to its undemanding members, unsatisfactory discussion, unanimously approved the bill on the sugar quota which enabled Eisenhower to reduce the quotas in 1960 or eliminate them altogether. The same day Castro signed the order saying that the Texaco oil refinery in Santiago had to refine Soviet crude oil or be expropriated. On 29 June, Cuban petroleum officials arrived at Texaco, Santiago, with two barges loaded with Soviet oil. The U.S. directors had already left. They had known what was coming. On 30 June the Esso and Shell refineries were taken over in Havana. The U.S. Senate passed the bill on 3 July, again scarcely without discussion.

Eisenhower delayed his signature on the sugar bill for a week. The State Department urged that, instead of a cut in the quota itself, the premium should be abolished, so that Cuba would thereafter simply be ranked with other producers without bonuses.[34] The ambassador in Cuba, Bonsal, still desired a small cut,[35] but Eisenhower decided to go the whole hog. On 6 July he reduced the quota for Cuba by 700,000 tons, the remaining unfulfilled slice of the Cuban share for 1960, and also by another 156,000 tons, the quantity that Cuba could have sent to the U.S. to make up for other countries' deficits. 'This action,' Eisenhower reflected, as he signed, 'amounts to economic sanctions against Castro. Now we must look ahead to other moves – economic, diplomatic, strategic.'[36]

Castro accused the U.S. of economic aggression and, for the first time, announced that arms would soon be available for the militia: presumably Raúl Castro had already reached an agreement in Czechoslovakia. On 9 July, over 600 U.S.-owned companies in Cuba were ordered to present sworn statements showing raw materials, spare parts, files, and so on, which were then in stock. This was an obvious foreshadowing of a complete nationalization of U.S. property. Perhaps they were not taken over there and then, for lack of technicians to run them rather than for

[34] According to Szulc and Meyer.
[35] Letter to Schlesinger.
[36] Eisenhower, 535. The total quota for 1960 had been 3,119,655 tons, of which over three-quarters had already been fulfilled.

any other reason, or perhaps because they relied primarily on importing raw materials from North America. Possibly, too, the Communist party attempted to draw Castro back. The same day, Khrushchev announced publicly that 'artillerymen' could defend Cuba, if need be with rockets.[37] Russia also would be prepared to take the 700,000 tons of sugar that the U.S. had spurned. Khrushchev added that the Monroe Doctrine was dead and 'the only thing you can do with anything dead is to bury it so that it will not poison the air'. Guevara remarked contentedly that Cuba was now defended by 'the greatest military power in history'; nuclear weapons were standing in the way of imperialism.[38] In the rising tide of charges and counter-charges, provocation and retaliation, neither side saw the end of the tunnel. A new attempt to mediate by the president of Argentina, Frondizi, met with no success.[39] The real significance of these events was that any idea that the Cuban Communists may have had that the U.S. could be provoked into a military intervention in the style of Hungary, in 1956, had now to be abandoned; Russia had given what passed for a guarantee; and therefore the party had no choice before them except to try and bring order and stability to the Cuban economy, which was now so disturbed by many arbitrary measures.

The regime in Cuba intended now to diversify her agriculture so that in a very short time – maybe by following the dicta of Professor Dumont – she need no longer rely on sugar. But this could not be achieved overnight. Meantime, the huge quantity of sugar which had previously gone to the U.S. had to be sold. For this reason alone Cuba would have wished to turn to Russia. By this time, too, Castro seems to have decided that for him freedom meant freedom to choose Communism if it could be arranged, or at the least freedom for close relations with the Soviet *bloc*,[40] and while these decisions were being taken, old comrades such as Marcelo Fernández, the national coordinator of the 26 July Movement, and Oltuski, the Minister of Communications, who had so impressed Sartre, dropped out from the government. The new line had need of new men.[41]

Having decided to escape from the sugar quota, Cuba's problem was

[37] 'In a figurative sense, if it became necessary, the Soviet military can support the Cuban people with rocket weapons.' Castro, commenting on this development from a hospital bed, but on television, said that the rockets were real not figurative and added insistently that the Russian offer had been 'absolutely spontaneous'. See Khrushchev's remarks to Carlos Franqui, in November 1960, quoted below, 1316 fn 17.

[38] Speech, 10 July 1960, *Obra Revolucionaria*, 26 July, 49.

[39] See *New York Times*, 6 July 1960, and *Hoy*, 30 July 1960; *cf.* Andrés Suárez, 95.

[40] The argument by Albert and Pearl Wohlstetter that Castro's motives towards the U.S. can be explained by his equally ambivalent relations towards his father seems ingenious if far-fetched.

[41] Both Fernández and Oltuski nevertheless stayed in Cuba and remain prominent servants of the Castro regime though both have had their difficulties with the security police, Oltuski even passing some time in gaol.

to derive the maximum benefit from U.S. abrogation of it. It was therefore desirable that the abrogation should have been unilateral and like an act of aggression. Eisenhower and Herter fulfilled these necessities to the letter. The abrogation caused much international sympathy for Castro. For years afterwards, ill-informed, if well-intentioned Liberals justified Castro's Communization of Cuba as a response to Eisenhower's sugar policy. But that policy enabled Castro to respond with a series of counter-measures which might not then have occurred (or just possibly might never have occurred) and anyway would have been more difficult to justify, even to the Cubans. These counter-measures led to the eclipse of all U.S. and most large Cuban private concerns within a few months, so weakening what chance there was of these giving backbone to further opposition. Thus apparently on Castro's own initiative alone and probably against both the wishes and the expectations of all his followers and of the Communists, on 6 August the Cuban Telephone Company, the Cuban Electric Company, the oil refineries and all the sugar mills which previously had only been 'intervened' were formally expropriated.[42]

No doubt these and other expropriations were carried out too quickly for economic success. Russian production had dropped in the early 1920s, partly because of the hasty nationalizations and the departure of technicians; China, learning this lesson, had proceeded in the late 1940s and 1950s at a slower pace. Seven years after the Chinese revolution a third of industry, two-thirds of commerce and most of agriculture were still in private hands.[43] Chinese production in consequence rose in the early years of the revolution. These lessons were lost on Cuba. Even some firms willing to collaborate with the regime were taken over. Certainly it would have been wiser to delay intervention until it was certain that the new responsibilities could be effectively borne.

These points of view were clearly put at the time by members of the Cuban Communist party: Blas Roca immediately explained that 'private enterprise that is not imperialistic ... is still necessary', and that some of the interventions 'could possibly have been avoided'.[44] Escalante urged at the eighth Congress that the revolution should try to keep the national *bourgeoisie* 'within the revolutionary camp'.[45] It does not seem, however, that Castro kept in close touch at this time with these sensible if elderly Communists.

During midsummer 1960, there were many statements of redefinition of what had occurred in Cuba: 'There are many similarities between

[42] See strong arguments to this effect by Andrés Suárez, 97.
[43] *Cf.* E.T. Luard and T.J. Hughes, *Economic Development of Communist China.*
[44] Blas Roca's report (English ed.), Eighth National Congress of PSP (1961), 105.
[45] Aníbal Escalante's report, *Hoy,* 19 August 1960.

the Cuban and the Chinese revolution,' remarked Odón Alvarez de la Campa, the armless trade unionist, to an audience in Peking; the unions themselves had acquired a 'revolutionary philosophy' as an organ of revolutionary indoctrination.[46] Cuba had now sold over $2\frac{1}{2}$ million tons of sugar to Communist countries in 1960, and only just over 2 million to the U.S. In August, the blunt-spoken Guevara, at the First Congress of Latin American Youth (whose mission was to rally the youth of Latin America against Yankee imperialism), said: 'If I were asked whether our Revolution is Communist, I would define it as Marxist. Our Revolution has discovered by its methods the paths that Marx pointed out.' A commercial and technical agreement had recently been signed with China. The Chinese State Opera as well as the Georgian Ballet made ceremonial visits. The important tenth Congress of the Cuban Communist party in August gave what seemed at least full support to the revolutionary government, though as usual Blas Roca spent much time castigating what he took to be a Leftist position, an even greater danger than imperialism. But he seemed completely to have passed over to the position held by his lieutenant, Dr Carlos Rafael Rodríguez, since in the course of his report to the Congress he gave full backing to Castro as the leader and guarantor of 'maximum unity'.[47] The editor of *Bohemia*, Miguel Angel Quevedo, who in June had published articles denouncing Hungary, Stalinism and concentration camps in Siberia, and who had been one of Castro's oldest supporters, sought asylum and suspended his journal saying:

> The deceit has been discovered. This is not the Revolution for which over 20,000 Cubans died. In order to carry out a purely national Revolution there was no need to submit our people to the hateful Russian vassalage. To carry out a profound social revolution, it was not necessary to install a system which degrades man to the condition of the State. . . . This is a revolution betrayed.[48]

He was followed into exile by Antonio Ortega, editor of *Carteles*. Several officials went at the same time, including the ex-Prime Minister, Miró.

But if Cuban society was being transformed along controlled and socialist lines, Castro remained a *caudillo*, a familiar figure in Latin America, but also an eccentric one, who remained restless, as it were on the run, still a rebel, still in jungle green uniform. Much depended upon him. In early July he was ill for a while, with an intestinal infection complicated by pleurisy in one lung. But by 26 July he was fit enough,

---

[46] The relations of Cuba with China as opposed to Russia are explored below, in the Epilogue to this book. Alvarez de la Campa defected from Cuba in 1964.

[47] See Blas Roca, Report, *op. cit.* The comments of Andrés Suárez, 101–2, are useful.

[48] He committed suicide in Caracas in 1969, leaving a note blaming the Revolution for his death.

along with perhaps not quite a million others, to 'rededicate the nation to the goals of the Revolution'. He also dedicated at this time the Camilo Cienfuegos mountain boarding school for children of peasants in the Sierra Maestra who lived in places too scattered for normal day school attendance to be possible. Belgian and Czech rifles were being bought to arm the new militia, which was now, he claimed, 200,000 strong.[49] But his main pledge was to make Cuba 'an example that can convert the Cordillera of the Andes into the Sierra Maestra of the Hemisphere'.

These thunderous cries were daily noted in Washington. So too was the fact that dealers in imported goods were now almost eliminated; in rural areas free enterprise was almost at an end, since the *tiendas del pueblo* sold goods at low prices with liberal credit. The upper classes had received increases in income tax and there were now much stricter regulations against evasion. Meantime, U.S. banks were refusing to change *pesos*, black market exchanges gave only 60 U.S. cents for a *peso* and in mid-July a Caribbean Rescue Committee was set up to assist and receive Cuban refugees into the U.S. (as well, technically, as refugees from the Dominican Republic, though there were many fewer of these).

In mid-August a special meeting of American foreign ministers of the OAS was held at San José, Costa Rica, on the proposal of both Cuba and the U.S. Christian Herter (who had succeeded Dulles) sought to persuade the conference to condemn Cuba for endangering the hemisphere. Many South Americans were prevented from agreeing, less by their consciences than by their knowledge of Castro's popularity among the public in their own countries. The Cuban representatives expressed themselves angry at having to leave their revolvers in the waiting-room. A committee was finally named to mediate between Cuba and the U.S., but the Cuban delegation had formally withdrawn. Castro, in Havana, predictably denounced the OAS as an organization in the pay of the U.S., and described President Eisenhower's recent proposal for a $M600[50] Latin American aid programme with contempt. But Eisenhower's proposal was the genuine plan of a perplexed president: 'We knew . . . that we could not indefinitely support governments that refused to carry out land and social reforms. We needed new policies that would reach the seat of the trouble.'[51] In the end, however, the U.S. were disappointed by what happened at San José; a resolution was passed which condemned all intervention in the Americas by non-American states and declared totalitarian states to be inconsistent with the continental system. But the

[49] *Revolución*, 27 July 1960.
[50] Of which $M100 was for earthquake relief in Chile.
[51] Eisenhower, 537.

State department had hoped for a condemnation of both Castro and Cuba, and neither were named.

Cuba's links with the U.S. were steadily growing fewer. No country was now supposed to buy Cuban sugar even with money lent by the U.S. Business consultants were busy trying to work out how credit terms abroad could be made to limit Cuban imports of spare parts. Companies predictably were trying to get their losses in Cuba written down as losses for tax purposes. The Standard Oil Co. sought to get oil tanker owners to refuse to carry Russian oil to Cuba. The Senate cut mutual security appropriations to any country which supplied military or even economic assistance to Cuba.

Cuban imports from the U.S. in the first five months of 1960 were thus 30% below 1959, and it was evident that for the last half of the year the pattern of trade would change completely. Meantime, the State Department were carefully removing those of their members who had been implicated in their time in softer relations with Cuba: Rubottom thus left Washington on 30 July to become ambassador in Argentina; Thomas Mann, a conservative Texan, took over as Assistant Secretary of State for Inter-American Affairs.[52] In Guatemala training continued, though on a small scale. Hatreds between ex-supporters of Castro and ex-Batistiano army officers smouldered. In Miami also there were quarrels. Manuel Artime, the CIA's choice as military commander, was unpopular. Meantime, on the other side of the sea several hundred Latin American students remained in Cuba after what was termed the First Latin American Youth Congress, in order to study not only farm techniques but also guerrilla and revolutionary activity.[53] The ranks in the Americas were closing.

In August a new pastoral letter, this time signed by Cardinal Arteaga and all the other Cuban bishops, formally denounced the Cuban regime. Mgr Díaz told the secretary to the presidency that the Church would be closed unless there were guarantees against riots; Dorticós gave them, 'despite all the provocations'. Castro responded more harshly against 'systematic provocations' by the Church, saying that 'whoever condemns a revolution such as ours betrays Christ and would be capable of crucifying Him again'. In the third week of August, six members of Juventud Católica, together with a Spanish Jesuit, Fr Manual Deboya, were captured after a gun battle in which two policemen were killed and the priest wounded. Deboya was charged with running an underground opposition cell. Finally, 2,000 members of Juventud Católica met at the Colegio Lasalle in Santiago, where the Castro brothers had

[52] Thomas Mann (b. 1912), had been a lawyer and since 1952 had been deputy chief of mission in Mexico.
[53] Tad Szulc, 'Exporting the Cuban Revolution', in Plank, 82.

been educated, and vigorously endorsed the pastoral letter, shouting '*Cuba sí, Comunismo no*'.[54]

Thus Castro seemed once more surrounded by trouble. In one of his most successful oratorical performances, on 2 September, he responded to the OAS 'Declaration of San José' with his new 'Declaration of Havana'. Cuba would accept Russia's offer of rockets in order to repel U.S. invasion. She would recognize Communist China. 'What have we done to deserve the Declaration of San José?' he demanded; the answer, 'Our people have done nothing more than break their chains.' He also issued a clarion call to the miserable of Latin America to throw off their chains too. This Declaration was said to have been approved by the National Assembly of the Cuban people – that is, the large crowd in the square. On 5 September the Economics minister, Boti, represented Cuba as the OAS's committee of 21, and denounced Eisenhower's aid plan: at least $M30,000 was necessary, as Castro had said in 1959 at Buenos Aires. Cuba would not sign the Declaration of San José and thereafter would cut herself off from all U.S. aid programmes for Latin America. Finally on 18 September Castro with a large entourage went to New York to attend the United Nations.

This second visit of Castro's to the U.S. contrasted with his first. This time there were no cheers. At best, there was silence, at worst, hostile demonstrations and sporadic brawls, in one of which a nine-year-old girl was killed. Squalid quarrels occurred over where the Cubans were to stay; having arrived at the Hotel Shelbourne, on the east side of New York, the delegation left in a hurry on the grounds that it was too expensive, and went to the Hotel Teresa in Harlem. Castro kept out of sight much of the time, visited the U.N. only twice, and was once a guest at the Russian delegation. His speech to the U.N. lasted four and a half hours, twenty-six minutes, the longest which had been delivered there. It was well-delivered, eloquent as usual, and dramatic, but failed to impress the U.S. press, who found it absurd and full of lies. But since this was the occasion of Khrushchev's public quarrels and table hitting, no friend of Russia could expect a good hearing – despite the fact that Khrushchev's motives should be interpreted in terms of his own struggles for power in Russia.[55] Castro left for Cuba on 28 September, on a Soviet airliner hastily borrowed when his own aeroplane was impounded under writs of attachment obtained in Miami against Cuban debts. He left behind over half his delegation. The visit had served little purpose.

While Castro was in New York, Cuba had begun to cast a shadow

[54] During August 1960, the North American sociologist, Wright Mills, was in Cuba to write the most famous of the early defences of the Revolution, *Listen Yankee*, (published in England as *Castro's Cuba*).

[55] See M. Tatu, *Power in the Kremlin*, trans. H. Katel (1969).

over the presidential election. Senator Kennedy for the Democrats began to speak of this issue as if it were yet another Republican failure. He once began to discuss the subject with his staff and said, 'All right but how would we have saved Cuba if we had the power?' Then he added, 'What the hell, they never told us how they would have saved China.'[56] In that spirit, he certainly succumbed to the temptation to use the matter very often. Thus on 23 September (Castro being still in New York) Kennedy said that he would have treated Cuba very differently during the last years of the Batista regime, 'but that now we must make clear our intention ... to enforce the Monroe doctrine ... and that we will not be content till democracy is restored to Cuba. The forces fighting for freedom in exile and in the mountains of Cuba should be sustained.' Nixon, who of course knew about the training of the exiles already under way, could not sound so vehement: 'We must recognize that there is "no quick or easy solution" to Castro's threat'; but 'given the opportunity and time the people of Cuba will find their own way back to freedom.'

Just at that moment, as it happened, the CIA's pursuit of that opportunity was heading for trouble: they now found the political front which they had constructed was turning out badly and desired, instead, a single leader. Richard Bissell had discovered the Cubans to be 'incorrigible, completely incapable of forming a front behind a single leader'.[57] One leader of the CIA's front, Sánchez Arango, admittedly a difficult man with whom to work, resigned with the accusation that the CIA had embarked on 'an incessant series of pressures and rebuffs'.[58] Justo Carrillo resigned from the Frente on 30 September on the grounds that 'the most sinister interests predominate'.[59] By this he meant that ex-Batistianos were receiving support within it. 'Tony' Varona became the formal coordinator of the exiles, but Artime remained the military leader (though staying in Miami).

The U.S. Embassy in Havana, an increasingly gloomy and solitary building, advised all nationals to leave Cuba as soon as possible. Castro made no bones about his troubles with the opposition: in the Sierra de Escambray about 1,000 rebels had gathered during October, now secretly supported by Castro's old friend, the North American Major Morgan, and by others who had fought in that district during the war with Batista. Strong forces of militiamen were moved into the foothills of the Escambray under Castro's own command, the peasants of the region being methodically evacuated to prevent them making food available. In Havana, and other cities, Ray's MRP also began to be active.

[56] Schlesinger, 202.
[57] Bissell to the author, 14 January 1963.
[58] Memorandum, qu. Draper, 71.
[59] Carrillo letter to Dr Miró Cardona.

In Escambray the fighting, which for a time seemed ominous, lasted a shorter time than had been thought likely. Starved of food, the rebels risked skirmishes and several of their leaders, ex-students or rebels, were killed or executed. Morgan and another Major, Jesús Carreras, of the Directorio, were captured (and executed some months later).[60] Some prisoners were condemned to twenty or thirty years' gaol. This important challenge to Castro was not apparently given much help by the CIA, who regarded the *guerrilleros* as lacking good security.

On 6 October at Cincinnati Kennedy specifically accused Eisenhower of creating in Cuba 'Communism's first Caribbean base'; the administration should have listened to Ambassadors Smith and Gardner (whose testimony to the Senate Internal Security Sub-Committee had just been released). Kennedy accused Eisenhower's administration of letting Castro get all the arms he needed for victory, while repeating his denunciation of the regime's support of Batista: 'We did nothing to persuade the people of Cuba and of Latin America that we wanted to be on the side of freedom.'

Perhaps as a result of these charges,[61] Eisenhower announced on 13 October a complete ban on all U.S. exports to Cuba, except medicine and some foodstuffs. The Secretary of Commerce, Muller, glibly said, 'If it pushes them into trade with the Communist *bloc*, that's just too bad. After all, we've been the ones that have been pushed around lately.'

The response in Cuba was swift. During the weekend of 14–15 October, Captain Núñez Jiménez at the head of INRA took over 382 large private enterprises in Cuba, including all the banks (except two Canadian ones), all the remaining private sugar mills, eighteen distilleries, sixty-one textile mills, sixteen rice mills, eleven cinemas and thirteen large stores. A second Urban Reform law followed which provided that no one should own more than one residence. Lessees of rented property became tenants of the state and, after a certain number of years, would become outright owners, while landlords would be compensated, though never at more than $350 a month.[62] On 25 October Castro nationalized another 166 U.S. enterprises. The Nicaro nickel plant and Woolworth; Sears Roebuck and General Electric Westinghouse; International Harvester, Remington Rand and Coca Cola; hotels and insurance companies: all the proudest names of U.S. international capitalism were silently and almost without protest overwhelmed. On 29 October Ambassador Bonsal was withdrawn for an

---

[60] See Martino, *I was Castro's Prisoner*, 142, an eye-witness description of Morgan's execution in La Cabaña.

[61] As suggested by the *Economist*. Eisenhower is silent on this topic in his memoirs.

[62] The cost of the building would be paid to the owner according to a specific value over a period of years, less the rent already paid. Mortgagees would receive 50% of their debt paid by new owners, the rest being paid to the government.

'extended period of consultation'. He never returned, though the U.S. Embassy itself remained in Havana till January 1961, when Castro told the Cubans that a U.S. invasion would occur before Eisenhower left the presidency on 20 January; he ordered a general mobilization, explaining that the excuse for the invasion would be the false accusation that Cuba was constructing rocket pads on her territory. He therefore demanded that the U.S. reduced their staff in the embassy to eighteen. Eisenhower then broke diplomatic relations. On neither 15 nor 25 October were the Communists any too pleased, Blas Roca and Carlos Rafael Rodríguez refraining from comment in *Hoy*. No doubt they had not been consulted.

One incident remains to be related marking the end of a stage in Cuban history. On 11 October 1960 Che Guevara, president of the National Bank, sent for Julio Lobo, the great sugar king, who had remained in Cuba despite disillusion with Castro for almost a year. He had lived quietly on his plantation, making plans for the emigration of his family. Up till then his sugar mills had functioned normally, though he had lost his land. When Guevara sent for him he supposed that he wanted to talk with him about certain moneys owing to him from the National Bank in connection with his building of the Hotels Capri and Riviera. But Guevara, with his customary candour, explained to Lobo that he and his aides had been examining Lobo's past accounts with morbid attention to detail and that they had not found any instance of irregularity. For this reason, Lobo had been 'left till the last', but now his time had come. 'We are Communists,' Guevara said, 'and it is impossible for us to permit you, who represent "the very idea" of capitalism in Cuba, to remain as you are.' Lobo had therefore to disappear or to 'integrate' with the revolution. Lobo pointed out that Khrushchev surely believed in the peaceful coexistence of two systems of production and peaceful competition between them. Guevara replied that that was all very well between nations but such a thing could not happen within the same one. Lobo asked how he could integrate himself with the revolution. In reply, Guevara proposed that he, Lobo, should become the general manager of the Cuban sugar industry under the revolutionary government, dealing with commerce, agriculture and industry. Guevara added that Lobo would, of course, lose his estates but he would be permitted the usufruct of *Tinguaro*, his favourite mill. Lobo, who in the past would have much liked the opportunity of rationalization and modernization that such an appointment could have given him, asked for time to consider the offer. Guevara agreed and Lobo undertook to tell his answer to Guevara or one of his aides (since Guevara was leaving shortly for Moscow) within a week. Lobo returned home and made immediate plans for flight. He instructed his secretary to take all she could from the banks and bury it in the old secret passage beneath his office in old Havana. But the next day his house was sealed and guarded. Lobo left for Miami on 13 October, leaving behind all his vast enterprises, his palaces, his El Greco and other splendid paintings, and his locks of Napoleon's hair.[63]

[63] Evidence of Julio Lobo, Madrid, 9 November 1968. Most of his skilled employees afterwards left Cuba but his general manager, Tomás Martínez, remained to direct the sugar industry of Cuba under the revolution, along with others who stayed, as usual, for a mixture of private and public motives.

The U.S. Prepares for Battle

During the culminating weeks of the campaign for the presidency of the U.S. in 1960, Cuba became for a few days the central topic. On 18 October, Nixon told an audience in Miami that the new Cuban regime was an intolerable cancer. 'Patience,' he said, 'is no longer a virtue.' The administration, he hinted broadly, was even then planning several steps to destroy this 'economic banditry'.[1] On 20 October Kennedy's staff put out a provocative statement about strengthening Cuban fighters for freedom. Nixon was annoyed. He had understood, he said later, that Kennedy had already been informed about the CIA's schemes during a general briefing on foreign affairs by Allen Dulles. But he was apparently misinformed.[2] Nixon assumed Kennedy was upbraiding the administration for not doing what in fact he knew they secretly were doing. Hence the somewhat bizarre discussion on the subject of Cuba in their fourth television electoral debate together; Nixon, to guard the security of his clandestine operations, accused Kennedy of 'dangerous irresponsibility' and of jeopardizing all U.S. friends in Latin America. Nixon said, 'What can we do? We can do what we did with Guatemala. There was a Communist dictator . . . the Guatemalan people themselves eventually rose up and they threw him out. . . .' Kennedy replied by arguing that mere economic quarantine was too little and too late.

This peculiar discussion led to even more peculiar results. Liberal editorials praised Nixon; columnists of the Right such as George Sokolosky praised Kennedy as speaking in the tones of Theodore Roosevelt and being closer to the national attitude of the Republican party than to the muddy internationalism of the Eisenhower administration. This would have an effect on Kennedy's Cuban policies later on.

There were, however, different democratic voices, notably that of Adlai Stevenson, then campaigning in North Carolina. On 25 October he made a speech which contradicted Kennedy's position, even attacking the economic embargo which, he thought, would drive Cuba further into the Soviet *bloc*. He also telephoned Kennedy to express his concern over the hard line which he had been employing and, probably in consequence, Kennedy for a time left the subject of Cuba alone,[3] definitely

---

[1] See Nixon, *Six Crises*, 352–3.
[2] *Cf. ibid.*, 354, fn; Schlesinger, 204; T. C. Sorensen, *Kennedy* (1965), 205.
[3] Adlai Stevenson to the author, 6 February 1963.

withdrawing from his most militant stand, to the relief in particular of the *New York Times*.

What was the reality? In Cuba, all believed an invasion inevitable. Castro talked of it all the time. But no one knew what type of invasion, above all what size, was likely. Florida, too, was in the same state of near ignorance as Havana. Miami might be full of Cuban refugees. Street signs and shops might have begun advertising in Spanish. But only a few people had friends or relations actually being trained in Guatemala, even though by November 1960 perhaps 60,000 people had already left Cuba since the coming of Castro, mostly by regular air flight, some by small boat, nearly half of them tourists without papers – probably half the whole professional group of the past in Cuba.

By now there were still only between 400 and 500 Cubans under training in Guatemala.[4] Yet the secret was out. On 30 October a Guatemalan paper, *La Hora*, published a front-page editorial by an eminent journalist, Clemente Marroquín Rojas, explaining that an invasion of Cuba was 'well under way, prepared not by our country, which is so poor and so disorganised, but implicitly by the U.S.A.' The Guatemalan Foreign Minister denied this, but the opposition demanded investigation. Few North Americans might read Guatemalan papers, but some did, among them Ronald Hilton, editor of an admirable monthly, the *Hispanic American Report*. He wrote an editorial in his November issue, explaining that Castro knew about the invasion plans even if public opinion in the U.S. did not.[5]

The purpose of the training in Guatemala was still to organize a guerrilla movement on the lines of what was already going on in the Escambray. Arms and supplies would be flown in from outside to assist guerrilla bands. Eisenhower had allotted $M13 to this scheme in August.[6] But already it had been proposed that it should be abandoned and in its place an invasion should take place, with air cover in U.S. planes (as in Guatemala in 1954) piloted by Cubans. This major change of policy had been agreed by early November. For it had been found more and more difficult to support what guerrilla activity there was; movement of information in and out of Cuba was increasingly complicated; and above all the Cubans had very bad security: this was 'the biggest single reason for this major policy decision'.[7] Apparently this decision was not put to the president, who later specifically said that no

---

[4] Schlesinger, 207. *Cf.* Haynes Johnson, *The Bay of Pigs* (1964), 55.

[5] It is curious that the only U.S. journal to pick up what was published in a Guatemalan paper was this semi-academic one.

[6] According to Schlesinger, 206.

[7] Bissell's evidence. (Bissell put this decision as early as December, but I think he must have made a mistake: *cf.* Haynes Johnson, 54; Schlesinger, 207; and Sorensen, 295.) Cuban exiles thought the major reason was the CIA's dislike of the guerrillas in Cuba, because these could be controlled.

plan for an invasion had been elaborated whilst he was in office.[8] Actually there was such a plan, but in the middle of the election it was not thought worthwhile telling him. Anyway, the CIA's guerrilla instructors left Guatemala and in their place came trainers for a conventional attack, with tanks, artillery and air support. Only some sixty *guerrilleros* continued, in the Counter Insurgency School in Panama. Recruiting for the Cuban operation began in Miami on a more sustained basis. But the invasion was envisaged as still requiring only about a thousand men at most.[9]

This was a strange decision. Partly, it rested on the assumption that the assault force had only to land for an army to spring up around it from the discontented people. In Guatemala in 1954, the CIA's aeroplanes had indeed merely arrived over the capital for the Arbenz regime to melt away. The CIA certainly had their success in Guatemala at the back of their minds, though they might perhaps have learned something from the erroneous Anglo-French anticipation of what would occur in Egypt in 1956, and from the fact that there were three clear differences between Cuba and Guatemala: firstly, the revolutionary regime in the latter country had never established its hold over the people to anything like such an extent as Castro had; secondly, Castro had destroyed the traditional army whereas Arbenz had not; and thirdly, Cuba was an island therefore more easily defended against a Duke of Brunswick than was Guatemala.

'The aim of the invading brigade,' Bissell said later, 'was specifically to establish a bridgehead . . . and *thereafter* to destroy Castro's air force [i.e. from an airstrip which they would have captured]. A government could have been established, which the U.S.A. could have recognised . . . We did not expect the "underground" to play a large part.'[10] It is difficult therefore to avoid the conclusion that the CIA hoped this government would be the recipient of substantial and open aid from the U.S. Indeed, the only logical explanation for a scheme to attack Cuba with about 800 to 900 men was that this would soon give the U.S. an opportunity to intervene.

There were, of course, further alarms. In November, just after Kennedy's election victory, a revolt in Guatemala nearly occurred, the very place where the new rebels were being trained. Eisenhower resolved 'that if we received a request from Guatemala for assistance, we would move in without delay'[11] – apparently the first clear decision by a

---

[8] Eisenhower said in 1962, 'We were more or less thinking of guerrilla type of action until we could get enough forces to do more . . . There was no specific strategical or tactical plan developed before I had left.' (H.A.R. v, xii, 33.)

[9] Recruits were paid up to $400 a month, additionally $175 for a wife, $50 for a first child, $25 for other children.

[10] Bissell to the author.

[11] *Waging Peace*, 612

government of the U.S. to intervene with its own troops since 1933. The administration also feared an attempt by Cuba to overthrow the Guatemalan or Nicaraguan governments, and, as a result, patrolled the Guatemalan and Nicaraguan coasts by sea and air, for some weeks.[12]

In November 1960 Manuel Ray escaped from Cuba, having left behind his MRP well organized and with its morale raised by a daring rescue from La Cabaña of several officers condemned at the same time as Matos. Ray's plans in Miami were the same as those which he had had in Cuba: to overthrow Castro from within Cuba and to continue politically the reforming work of the revolution as the liberals had envisaged it in 1959. But the CIA continued to distrust the Cuban underground, Bissell chiefly because of the Cubans' bad security arrangements, 'Frank Bender' perhaps because of their progressive aspirations. Ray's error doubtless was to have anything to do with the U.S. But the trouble was, as in the case of every revolt against authority in Cuba since the nineteenth century, that no Cuban rebel could bring himself to admit this. As it was, even Ray began to find himself increasingly expectant of the CIA, even though ranking himself as really in opposition among the exiles in Miami. Nor was Ray, though personally brave and appealing, able to establish himself as a major political leader of international importance.

On 17 November[13] Kennedy, president-elect, was for the first time told by Allen Dulles and Bissell about the plan for the invasion. Kennedy said that he was 'astonished by its magnitude and daring',[14] as well he might be, since it almost exactly reflected what he had demanded, perhaps with less than complete seriousness, during the electoral campaign. On 29 November, Allen Dulles gave Kennedy a more 'detailed briefing';[15] the president-elect listened with attention and then told Dulles to carry the work forward. 'The response was sufficiently affirmative,' says Schlesinger, 'for Dulles to take it as an instruction to expedite the subject.' But at the same time Kennedy 'had grave doubts from that moment on'.[16] Thus Kennedy, Hamlet-like, encouraged what he in fact mistrusted, perhaps already caught up by the dilemma between the policy which he had advocated during the campaign and what he thought wise – a dilemma which was to haunt him all the time in office. On 6 December Kennedy had his first meeting with Eisenhower, but, though Cuba was on the proposed agenda, the project of invasion does not seem to have been discussed.[17] Kennedy did not see Eisenhower

[12] *Ibid.*, 613.
[13] Or 18 November (*cf.* Schlesinger, 148, 210).
[14] Sorensen, 295.
[15] Schlesinger, 211.
[16] Sorensen, 295.
[17] See Eisenhower memorandum, *Waging Peace*, 712 ff.

again till 19 January, the day before his inauguration, and does not seem to have occupied himself with the matter before then.

In the meantime, much had happened. In early December the CIA's plans for invasion were presented to 'the secret inter-departmental committee charged with special operations', but apparently not formally approved.[18] The U.S. chiefs of staff as yet knew nothing of what was planned.[19] The fact of the forthcoming change of administration caused a certain confusion. Decisions took longer.

> The outgoing administration were reluctant to take responsibility for what they were not going to do themselves [recalled Bissell] and the people coming in were reluctant to take decisions before they saw the papers. And this was important because the situation in Cuba was getting more and more difficult.[20]

On 10 December, Willauer, the ambassador to Costa Rica and, as has been seen, one of the architects of the attack on Guatemala in 1954, was told by Secretary of State Herter, 'There are quite a lot of doubts whether this plan is correct, what the timing should be, various problems about putting the thing together.' Willauer was to investigate. With Under-Secretary Thomas Mann, he was convinced that the project 'should not be . . . undertaken unless there was practically no chance that it would fail'.[21] Eisenhower, meantime, was busy with political considerations; he wanted the Cuban exiles to elect a leader who would be recognized by the U.S. as the legal government of Cuba, if possible before the inauguration of Kennedy.[22] He had also made available $M1 for the resettlement of Cuban refugees, now numbered at 100,000.

By this time the news of the training at Guatemala was no longer secret. Following the *Hispanic American Report*, the *Nation* and then the *Los Angeles Mirror* and *St Louis Dispatch* were speaking of the secret camps. In Miami all Cubans knew where the recruiting centres were, especially after a visit at Christmas time by a group of the Guatemalan Cubans on a recruiting drive. These got on very badly with the politicians of the Frente, and indeed the Frente themselves were still squabbling. The CIA still desired to have no truck with Ray's group. Several of the latter were refused permission to join in the expedition, including at least one of the officers of Matos's group who had been rescued from La Cabaña in October. Recruitment was in the hands of Joaquín Sanjenís, brother of the MRR leader in prison in Cuba, and nephew of José Miguel Gómez's secretary; he seems to have favoured right-wing

---

[18] Schlesinger, 211.
[19] See Lazo, 251.
[20] Bissell to the author.
[21] Willauer to Senate, *Communist Threat*, 873–5.
[22] *Waging Peace*, 613–14.

recruits. Nor was he careful about the recruitment of Batistianos. The ensuing antagonisms seemed worse when they began to be generally known, as they did by 6 January, when *Time* reported that Ray was getting no funds from the U.S., while the Frente under Varona was being amply supplied – $135,000 a month regularly and $500,000 on occasion; on 10 January the *New York Times* even published a map of the Guatemalan base.

Eisenhower decided to do nothing about this. The rumours led Castro to a full general mobilization, enabling him to encourage the Russians to send yet more arms. Meantime the Guatemalan government announced that the camps were for training men to resist an impending Cuban attack. A group of U.S. reporters visited the Alejos coffee plantation base. The Cuban pilots were bidden for the visit.[23] In Europe such revelations as these about a government's intentions would have caused a storm. In the U.S. the constitutional organization of opposition was harder. Similarly, those who were prepared to criticize publicly an attack on Castro were few. They certainly could not be supposed to include Kennedy. From his television statements on 20 October, Nixon even might have been supposed the liberals' champion. But Nixon had his own problems at that time.

There were troubles too at the base in Guatemala. Some new arrivals from Miami were considered by the old commanders to be conspiring. These resigned, taking with them 230 men out of what was still only about 550. A CIA chieftain harangued the little army and persuaded all but forty to continue training. Twelve men considered incorrigible were held prisoner in a remote part of North Guatemala. But the mutiny rumbled on.[24]

It was in these circumstances that Kennedy took up the reins as president, on 20 January. Two days later, Allen Dulles and General Lemnitzer, representing the joint chiefs of staff, reviewed the invasion plans for members of the new administration – Rusk, McNamara and Robert Kennedy.[25] By this time the chiefs of staff had already become concerned with the Cuban plans, after having 'tacitly questioned' the prohibition on U.S. participation earlier in the month. CIA planners, however, were already looking at maps of south Cuba for possible sites for landing. On 26 January Kennedy had his first meeting on the subject of the invasion: he was 'wary and reserved'.[26] He allowed the CIA to continue its preparations, himself, meantime, being preoccupied with the articulation of the general plan for Latin American development of which he had already spoken in his campaign speech – an 'Alliance for

[23] Szulc and Meyer, 91.
[24] Haynes Johnson, 61.
[25] Schlesinger, 216; Willauer, 876, refers.
[26] Schlesinger, 216.

Progress'.[27] Had it not been for the Cuban issue, doubtless such a scheme would never have received any backing. At the same time the question of Cuba had revived for the first time for twenty-five years the controversy about U.S. intervention. One or two meetings were held in Washington in early February, and at least one of the people put to work on the project by the previous administration (Willauer) was unceremoniously dismissed.[28] But nothing more precise was done. Artime (taken out of his guerrilla training at Panamá), Varona and Antonio Maceo visited Guatemala, had various disputes with the officers there, patched them up and returned. A bigger recruiting drive began. Young men in Miami went to the recruiting base to avoid being left out of 'a major event' in their country's history. Not all went to Guatemala. Not all were accepted. Enquiries would be made about their political activity and background. Some were still taught guerrilla activity, since there were plans for diversionary work. One group of *guerrilleros* trained in Louisiana (some complained and said that they wanted 'a conventional war').[29]

Kennedy was undecided whether to go ahead with the invasion. One of his advisers, Schlesinger, advised against it on the simple grounds that it 'would fix a malevolent image of the new administration'.[30] The CIA leaders were, however, strongly in favour of going ahead;[31] Allen Dulles asked what could be done with the trained Cubans if not sent to war? Was there not a 'disposal problem'?[32] They would return disconsolate to Miami to complain, and U.S. prestige would be diminished; so would the cause of democracy. Bissell was an equally strong advocate: the morale of the brigade was high and had to be tested. Kennedy agreed that the 'simplest thing might be to let the Cubans go where they yearned to go to: Cuba', with the minimum risk to the U.S. There should, however, be no U.S. military intervention. Air strikes were too risky. The idea of landing at Trinidad, canvassed by Bissell, was rejected by Kennedy as too spectacular; the CIA suggested the Bay of Cochinos (or Bay of Pigs) as an alternative and the chiefs of staff agreed, though preferring Trinidad.[33] On 15 March Kennedy told the CIA to continue to plan on the assumption that the invasion would occur, but in such a way that it could still be called off twenty-four hours before it

[27] The phrase was apparently the joint responsibility of a Cuban liberal economist Ernesto Betancourt, and Karl Meyer of the *Washington Post*.

[28] *Communist Threat*, 875.

[29] Evidence of Antonio Campiña, Washington, 1962.

[30] Schlesinger, 218.

[31] 'Allen and Dick didn't just brief us . . . they sold us on it,' said a 'White House Adviser' to Stewart Alsop.

[32] Dulles appears to have first used this famous phrase on 11 March (Schlesinger, 219).

[33] This was a wily choice for it could give a well-defended beachhead, on which a provisional government could be easily landed.

was due to begin:[34] a somewhat desperate expedient, it would seem, by any standard. It now seemed that Kennedy was being persuaded to go ahead by the senior advisers inherited from Eisenhower, although he personally was against it.[35] But he was also caught up by the ideas which he had himself proposed the previous autumn. How could he abandon a policy which he had previously upbraided the Republicans for not embarking upon? There were, of course, risks to his general policies, with the Soviet Union, Latin America and Europe, interwoven with this scheme. But Kennedy seems to have made the curious error of supposing that this *amour* of his with the exiles could still be kept a secret from his bride, U.S. public opinion.

Kennedy compromised by telling the CIA to try to make the exile organization more liberal. They did this by bringing Manuel Ray's group into the Frente. On 18 March, the Frente chose Dr Miró Cardona, first premier under Castro, to be 'provisional president of Cuba' (he had reached Miami from Havana in the winter) out of a list of six presented by the CIA. The exiles' relations with the U.S. indeed increasingly resembled those of the Spanish kings with Rome over the election of bishops. On 22 March Ray signed an agreement with his old antagonist Varona, permitting Miró to found a 'Cuban Revolutionary Council' which would become the provisional government of Cuba after the success of the invasion. This body would retain most of its members in Cuba. It should give maximum priority to the aid of combatants already in Cuba. No one with 'a responsible position' under Batista would be able to join the new Cuban army. An agreement on the 'effective way of treating *latifundia*' was to be reached within two weeks.[36]

The council was merely the old Frente together with Ray. Droller-Bender insisted that Artime should be military commander. Prominent exiles rallied to support the council. Ray, according to Bissell, 'was quite eager to settle down after March'.[37] Back in Washington, Schlesinger prepared a white paper to prove that Castro had betrayed the revolution: the theme was to be that 'our objection', as Kennedy put it, 'isn't to the Cuban Revolution, it is to the fact that Castro has turned it over to the Communists.'[38]

There was, however, now a marked difference of view between the White House and the chiefs of staff on the one hand, and the CIA on the other. Both the former supposed that the latter was counting on the

[34] Schlesinger, 220.
[35] 'I used to come home from meetings supposing that only two persons – me and the president – were against the idea of invasion,' Schlesinger told the author (7 September 1962).
[36] Document qu. Draper, 96–8.
[37] Bissell to the author.
[38] Schlesinger, 222.

invasion being supported by large-scale risings inside Cuba, while the latter was thinking much more of 'an Anzio concept'. No special effort was being made to coordinate the movements of internal guerrilla forces, though the CIA apparently thought that there were then in Cuba 2,500 active militants in the army, 20,000 supporters in the towns and behind them a quarter of the Cuban population. The intelligence branch of the CIA did not know of the planned invasion, and the CIA failed to back up their own operators in Cuba.[39] The reason, as ever, was the lack of proper security among the Cubans. But this lack of faith in the Cuban guerrillas was not apparently communicated to Kennedy, who seems at best to have avoided knowing too much of the details and anyway seemed to be growing 'steadily more sceptical' as time went on. When Schlesinger gave Kennedy the text of his white paper, he asked, 'What do you think about this damned invasion?' 'As little as possible,' said Kennedy.[40]

A decision had now to be reached: should the invasion go on or not? Adlai Stevenson came to Washington and

> Expressed alarm at the press reports and asked [Kennedy] specifically what was going on . . . [Kennedy] said I could rest assured that whatever was being planned there would be no question of U.S. involvement. I said I was very greatly relieved at this ... I think at that time I did sense a very considerable degree of anxiety in Kennedy's mind as to whether he was in fact doing the right thing or not.[41]

A little afterwards, according to Stevenson, 'Tracy Barnes of the CIA came up and briefed us here on the Delegation [to the UN] . . . he assured us that this was simply a question of helping the exiles and that this was not in any way a U.S. operation. In the light of what happened, I suppose this can be regarded as less than candid.'[42] Others less loyal would perhaps have put it less politely.

The doubts voiced by Stevenson were put also by Senator Fulbright in a memorandum on 30 March: to let the exiles overthrow Castro would be generally denounced as an example of imperialism; the U.S.

---

[39] Szulc and Meyer, 125, report that the 'national co-ordinator' of the Cuban underground about 12–15 April was smuggled out of Cuba (?through Guantánamo) and sent back after discussions with Miró's group, with two tons of C4 plastic explosive. But he was in Miami when the invasion began.

[40] Schlesinger, 233.

[41] Stevenson to the author, 6 February 1963.

[42] *Ibid.* I imagine that this was the conference of 8 April referred to by Schlesinger, 245–6, though Stevenson did not mention Schlesinger's presence at it to the author. According to Schlesinger, Stevenson afterwards said he disapproved of the plan but would make out the best case for it.

would inevitably be tempted, if things went wrong, to use their own armed forces; he argued instead for containment: 'The Castro regime is a thorn in the flesh . . . not a dagger in the heart.'[43] On 31 March Chester Bowles, Assistant Secretary of State, opposed the invasion plan in a memorandum to Dean Rusk.[44] But, perhaps unfortunately, Kennedy spent Easter in Palm Beach, closer to the influence of the exiles and of his old friend, ex-ambassador Earl Smith. He returned more militant. On 3 April, Schlesinger's white paper was published: 'The present situation in Cuba confronts the western hemisphere and the Inter-American system with a grave and urgent challenge . . . [and] offers a clear and present danger to the authentic and autonomous revolution of the Americas.' On 4 April a decisive meeting was held. Dulles and Bissell repeated their well-known views in favour of action, with some new arguments. It was now or never to crush Castro; if the U.S. delayed Castro would have Soviet MiGs and trained pilots.[45] Provided the expedition was fully 'Cubanized' it would not matter much even if it failed. The survivors could quickly get to the Sierra Escambray – though, as no one apparently realized, those hills were nearly 100 miles away from the beachhead. Dulles had said that he thought the success would be easier than in Guatemala in 1954. A CIA emissary from Guatemala reported the brigade to be in good heart.[46] As for the Department of State, Rusk, who apparently distrusted the project, did not speak forcefully. His more forthright assistant, Thomas Mann, said that he would have opposed the plan at the start but now that the matter had proceeded so far, it should continue. McNamara favoured the invasion; he was swayed by the positive views of the joint chiefs of staff. A. A. Berle, jr, desired 'the men to be put into Cuba but did not insist on a major production',[47] whatever that may have meant. Only Fulbright openly opposed the invasion. Schlesinger, also fundamentally hostile, was too overawed to speak. How was he, 'a mere college professor', to intervene when the chiefs of staff and the secretaries of State and Defence approved? But, afterwards, he told Kennedy what he thought, and later said the same in a memorandum. Kennedy nevertheless decided to go ahead – apparently assuming that it was less an amphibious invasion than a large infiltration. Perhaps he too was overawed by his senior

[43] *Fulbright of Arkansas*, ed. Karl E. Meyer (1963), 194–205.

[44] Evidence of Chester Bowles, November 1962.

[45] This point of view was forcefully put by Allen Dulles in an interview in 'Meet the Press' on TV on 31 December 1961. Reston in the *New York Times* on 4 April said that between 100 and 200 Cuban airmen were in Czechoslovakia learning to fly MiGs and that this addition to Cuban air forces meant that only a full U.S. invasion could oust Castro. One can guess that this tale came from the CIA.

[46] Haynes Johnson and Bernard Gwertzman, *Fulbright the Dissenter*, London, 1969, 175; Sorensen, 296.

[47] Schlesinger, 228.

advisers – a sadly familiar development in the relation of politician and bureaucrat in democracies.

The Cuban Revolutionary Council was meantime preparing to return to Havana, though, to escape the feverish and reactionary attitude of Miami, they went first to New York. Two scholars from Harvard, Doctors John Plank and William Barnes, did their best. Schlesinger tried to persuade the Cubans to understand that the U.S. could not overtly support the invasion in any way. Kennedy publicly stated on 12 April that the U.S. would never intervene in a Cuban conflict. Whether the CIA chiefs thought this was the case seems unlikely; for Bissell was arguing strongly in favour of giving air cover, even though this might have led to U.S. intervention.[48] Afterwards the CIA kept the Cuban Revolutionary Council uninformed of their plans. Miró believed that the U.S. would one day intervene. A. A. Berle assured Miró that the U.S. would support the invaders with arms but not with any reinforcement of men.[49] Miró remained incredulous, though Kennedy had him told that, if he did not accept that there would be no U.S. intervention, there would be no invasion at all. Meanwhile, a U.S. marine colonel made a special report to Kennedy after a visit to Guatemala that the rebels were in a high state of elation, which he shared.

The atmosphere in Guatemala was indeed one of confidence. But this was at least partly because the officers had been led to believe that the U.S. would back them up in every way, including air and sea cover. Several CIA officers committed themselves to this effect.[50] Varona, for instance, was apparently told by a U.S. colonel that the Cubans would receive full air cover, and Ray was left with the same impression.[51] None of the leaders was told of the plan to head for the Escambray if things went wrong. All assumed that the sixteen B.26s which the CIA placed at the disposal of the exiles would be adequate to crush the – as it was assumed – disorganized and incompetent Cuban air force. The commanders in Guatemala had only a 'brigade' but they were apparently misled into thinking other units would be involved. They thought that their task was to establish a beachhead to which the provisional government would quickly come to ask help from the U.S. and elsewhere if need be.[52] The CIA advisers were so keen on the invasion that they urged the Cubans to go ahead even if it was cancelled in Washington. To do this they would even make a show of imprisoning

[48] Bissell to the author. See below, p. 1368 fn 38.
[49] Schlesinger, 239.
[50] See Haynes Johnson, 68.
[51] *H.A.R.*, V, xvi, 33; evidence of Ray.
[52] This was no doubt a reason for selecting the landing place at Girón and Cochinos Bay since it was easily defendable, given air superiority, by a small number of men; there were only three approach roads over the swamps.

the advisers,[53] including the operational chief, 'Frank'.[54] With this strange qualification the men of Brigade 2506 – so named after the serial number of one of its members who had died accidentally during training – were taken to Puerto Cabezas in Nicaragua. They set off on 14 April by sea, being seen off by Luis Somoza, the dictator of Nicaragua who asked them to bring him back some hairs from Castro's beard.[55] Like Narciso López's expeditions a hundred years before, they set out to fight for freedom, but under odd and ambiguous auspices; and the figure of the angry Somoza shaking his fist on the quayside was an appropriate mascot for them.

[53] Haynes Johnson, 76.
[54] His name was apparently William Freeman. His predecessor was William McQuaring – according to an exile in testimony in April 1961 (*Playa Girón, Derrota del Imperialismo*, 4 vols (1961), IV, *Los Mercenarios*, 333).
[55] Haynes Johnson, 77.

Cuba Socialista: I

As it happened, and as such zealous students of history as President Kennedy and that self-effacing 'college professor' Schlesinger must have realized, the very thing now needed by Castro to consolidate his regime was an unsuccessful attack from without, backed, though not to the hilt, by the U.S. Both the French and the Russian revolutions had been consolidated by invasions by exiles. Castro, like the Committee of Public Safety and the Bolsheviks, feared an invasion; Castro, like Miró Cardona (the Duke of Brunswick of Miami) could hardly believe that the 'illiterate millionaire', as he elegantly described Kennedy, would not, if it came to the pinch, back his protégés; but at least there would be a struggle, which surely would unite Cubans patriotically around the government against the old, and no doubt the final enemy, the Colossus of the North. At the time of the invasion, the Cuban revolutionary regime was in full economic crisis, characterized by confusion in both industry and agriculture, and Castro had had to admit in harsh contradiction with earlier boasts, 'for a country at the outset of such a fundamental revolution, it is particularly dangerous . . . to think that living standards can be substantially and immediately improved'[1].

But Castro made no concessions to try to avoid the dangers of invasion. Indeed, many passages in many speeches suggest that he was relieved that the last gloves, such as they had been, were off: 'The struggle of great interests is set forth, the inflamed struggle between Revolution and Counter-Revolution . . . war to the death between the forces was inevitable and in a revolution, the struggles are to the death'; and 'What is a Revolution? Is it perhaps a peaceful and tranquil process? Is it perhaps strewn with roses? Revolution is of all historic events, the most complex and convulsive.'[2] The prospects of actual gunfire would stimulate Castro on 16 April 1961 to his first public admission that Cuba was socialist: 'That is what they cannot forgive – that we should here . . . under their very nostrils, have made a socialist revolution.'[3] A month

---

[1] *Obra Revolucionaria*, 11, 26 March 1961.

[2] Speech, 4 January 1961 (*Obra Revolucionaria*, No. 1 of 1961, 22 and 24).

[3] Playa Girón, I, 75. This was of course a well-planned statement: Raúl Castro later said (*Revolución*, 24 July 1961) that the statement meant that the Revolution had fulfilled its national liberating phase (*etapa nacional liberadora*) as well as its anti-imperialist and anti-feudal agrarian stage.

earlier Faure Chomón, the olive-skinned ambassador to Russia, had, in Castro's presence, spoken of the revolutionary leaders as 'we Communists' at a ceremony commemorating the death four years before of his old leader, Echevarría (who had been far from being a Communist). At the time of the formation of the Directorio, Chomón had customarily been referred to by the university Communists as a gangster and he in turn had denounced them as 'patio revolutionaries'; while he had refused to agree in the Sierra Escambray to Guevara's demand that they should both ally with the local Communists under Torres. Now, doubtless through opportunism, he was the most zealous philo-Communist of all.[4] A month before that Castro, in an interview in the Italian Communist paper *L'Unitá*, had said of the Cuban Communists that they were:

> The only party that has always clearly proclaimed the necessity of a radical change in the structure of social relationships. It is also true that at first the Communists distrusted me and us rebels. It was a justified distrust, an absolutely correct position . . . because we of the Sierra . . . were still full of *petit bourgeois* prejudices and defects, despite Marxist reading . . . Then we came together, we understood each other and began to collaborate.[5]

One month previous even to that Aguilera, the propaganda secretary of the CTC, and Castro's chosen instrument in the trade unions, though another opportunist, had announced: 'It is time to state without fear, with unshaking knees, with untrembling voice and with our heads held high, that we are marching inexorably towards socialism in our Fatherland.'[6] The relations of Castro and his Communist allies were, however, still ambiguous, though the youth movement of the 26 July had merged with the Communist Youth. Castro himself made all the main decisions,[7] sustained probably by his personal backing from Khrushchev, and it is impossible to avoid the conclusion, judging from what happened later, that Castro was primarily interested in using the Communists, almost as Batista had used them, as a kind of bureaucracy to control the Labour movement and as much of the economy as he captured from private hands.

In December, nevertheless, Castro set up indoctrination schools of

[4] Manuel Ledón, one of Chomón's old comrades in the Directorio, recalled bitterly that in 1958 Chomón had tried to get help from the U.S. Embassy in Havana: his anti-imperialism, he commented, was indeed, 'eloquently modern'.

[5] *L'Unitá*, 1 February 1961. As Draper points out, this speech marked the beginning of an era of humbleness on Castro's part before the ideological purity of the Communists.

[6] *Revolución*, 7 November 1960. Andrés Suárez, 115, points out that *Hoy* did not publish this.

[7] e.g. the critical question of the establishment of State farms in place of co-operatives. *Cf.* Dumont, 57.

'revolutionary instruction' under his old Communist friend at the university, Leonel Soto, 'to train cadres for a united party'.[8] Soto was the first Communist party member to receive a major appointment under the regime and for a time he was alone. These schools (twelve in the provinces) gave courses lasting nine months, with students from the 26 July, the Communist party and some from the Directorio Revolucionario. They studied Marxist–Leninism in a primitive fashion; and the first course ended in April 1961. The national school was established in the Ministry of the Interior, in a large salon of the old Jesuit school of Belén which had been taken over for that branch of the administration. Here classes began at three in the afternoon, and continued till half-past ten at night; Blas Roca's *Fundamentos del Socialismo en Cuba* was the usual textbook in 1961. 'From three o'clock till five, Professor Carlos Rodríguez lectured on this work. At 5.15, after a coffee break, the group, of twenty-eight, divided into four seminars. At 7.30, there was a general discussion and Professor Rodríguez gave a final talk at nine o'clock'.

On the surface, Cuba seemed now firmly within the Communist alliance. On 1 January 1961 a parade in Havana had exhibited Russian tanks and other weapons, though not, as yet, MiGs. On 4 March, Castro had explained that he could draw on 'mountains on mountains of Communist arms' to defend Cuba if need be; the U.S. calculated that $M50 worth of Soviet weapons had arrived by April.[9] Even before the end of 1960, it had also become clear that Cuban embassies in South America were being used to deliver money to local Communist parties; and on 4 October 1960 the Cuban ambassador in Lima, Luis Ricardo Alonso, was discovered to have handed over $30,000 to various Peruvian Communists.[10] Similar occurrences were reported from El Salvador. Peru broke relations with Cuba in December. Prensa Latina offices were also closed, both there and in the Argentine. Cuba in November withdrew from the World Bank, arranging for the repurchase of her old shares of capital. Meantime, an ambassador had arrived in Havana from China, and from all the Communist countries. The western embassies on the other hand had become isolated oases of *bourgeois* society, eating black beans off gold plate. Internationally, Cuba was already recognized more as a part of the international Communist *bloc* than even of the nationalistic neutral world.

---

[8] *Cuba Socialista*, February 1963. Castro clearly was aware of the loaded nature of this activity, as can be seen from his speech of November 1961 when he explained, 'To indoctrinate is not a pleasant word . . . it makes you think that you are impressing knowledge on someone by force of repeating it innumerable times' (*Revolución*, 11 November 1961, 9).

[9] *White Paper on Cuba*, 22.

[10] The letter was discovered by anti-Communist Cubans who broke into the Embassy in November. Alonso later became ambassador in London, defected in 1965 and published an anti-revolutionary realistic novel.

Towards South America the Cuban leaders regarded themselves as having provided a 'catalyst';[11] for them, the Andes remained the Sierra Maestra of the continent, as Castro had described it in late 1960.

But from the very beginning of Cuba's relationship with the Communist world, Castro, Blas Roca and the others had to take into account the two factors of the development of the Chinese quarrel with Russia and the reluctance of Russia to make an explicit treaty committing her to defend Cuba if attacked. The Communist party of Cuba attempted a policy of neutrality in the Chinese dispute, thereby obliging itself to print both sides of every argument from the moment when the matter became acute after the meeting of the World Federation of Trade Unions in Peking and the Bucharest conference during June 1960. This neutrality was hard to maintain, particularly since there were evidently differences between Blas Roca, secretary-general of the party for so long, the representative of orthodoxy, and Carlos Rafael Rodríguez and those younger party members who sympathized more with Castro. This did not mean, however, that they were necessarily less extreme. On the contrary, though Rodríguez himself was by temperament and habit an anti-Stalinist, and a Khrushchevist first and foremost, many younger members of the Communist party, like some Fidelistas, were very favourably inclined towards the Chinese. In 1960 several Fidelistas, such as William Gálvez, the inspector-general of the army, visited China, while José María de la Aguilera and Vicente Cordero, for the CTC, were present in Peking during the first public clash there between China and Russia. Aguilera, as has been seen, seems to have been a person without any ideological foundation before 1959: yet the Cuban trade unionists in Peking gave general support to the Chinese position in July 1960.[12] The same month China and Cuba signed a commercial and tariff convention while, in September, Cuba and China entered upon diplomatic relations. These events were not much liked by either Blas Roca or Carlos Rafael Rodríguez, despite their own differences, and during the winter of 1960–1 therefore the Cuban-Chinese links on a governmental level were much superior to those between the Cuban and Chinese Communist parties. The 'international chess game' thus had its obscurer moments even on the left side of the Iron Curtain.[13]

The Cuban Communist party as such, however, made up its mind as to its general course of action in November and December 1960. Blas Roca, it will be recalled, had visited Mao in April with some approval. But in the early winter he and the rest of the party took a decisive turn

[11] Guevara, in honour of Guiterás, 15 May 1961, *Obra Revolucionaria*, 44.
[12] *Hoy*, 3 August 1960.
[13] These matters are discussed in Andrés Suárez, 104–6.

towards Moscow and this decision was rendered final at the meeting of Communist parties in Moscow in December. This occurred almost at the same time as Guevara (who a little earlier, after a successful commercial expedition to Prague, had stayed in Moscow several weeks without achieving much), was being received with enthusiasm in Peking. The enthusiasm was well-placed: at a banquet, Guevara had said that 'the great experience of the Chinese people in their twenty-two years of struggle in the backward countryside had revealed a new road for the Americas'.[14] In reply, Chou En-lai had spoken of the Cuban experience in glowing terms; and at the end of November, Cuba and China concluded an agreement whereby the Chinese would buy a million tons of sugar in 1961 and grant a credit of $M60 for equipment and technical aid. On leaving China, Guevara said: 'In general there was not a single discrepancy.'[15] Thenceforward, China spoke only of Castro, never of the Cuban Communists,[16] and Castro had for some years the backing of China as well as, through the Communist party and the Russian Embassy, of Russia.

For Chinese approval did not yet endanger that of Russia. In mid-December a new Russo-Cuban agreement was also signed. Russia would buy 2·7 million tons of sugar in 1961 at 4 cents a pound. Cuba expressed her fervent satisfaction. Russia expressed her willingness to defend Cuba 'against unprovoked aggressions', but made no new mention of missiles. Possibly Russian willingness to go even as far as this in a formal document would have been less easy to secure had it not been for China. Thereafter vessels sailed regularly to Cuba from the Communist ports of the old Hanse, and articles describing the beauties of East Europe appeared frequently in Cuban magazines such as the now revolutionary *Bohemia*, the army magazine *Verde Olivo*, or more glossy propaganda papers such as *Cuba* or *INRA*. Khrushchev gave another public promise to defend Cuba in case of aggression (but he admitted that the rockets which he had mentioned in July were 'symbolic').[17] In January Castro announced that 1,000 young Cubans would study agrarian collectives in Russia. In the spring of 1961 visitors to Cuba were received in Russian style with bouquets of flowers.

Cuba had already recognized Albania, Hungary, Outer Mongolia and North Vietnam, and embassies from these nations trundled across the world with great enthusiasm to Havana, which they found, with

---

[14] New China News Agency, 18 November 1960, qu. Andrés Suárez, 116.

[15] *Revolución*, 9 December 1960.

[16] This is Andrés Suárez's point, 117.

[17] Carlos Franqui (editor of *Revolución*): 'The imperialists contend that the statement of the Soviet Government concerning the possibility of rocket weapons in the event of an armed aggression against Cuba is purely symbolic. What do you think?' Khrushchev: 'I should like such statements to be really symbolic.'

surprise, enjoyed a living standard somewhat higher than they themselves aspired to. Fraternal solidarity was also pledged by Dr Núñez Jiménez in October with the FLN in Algeria and with Sekou Touré during his visit to Havana in October.

Cuba retained some non-Communist connections. Though she had withdrawn from the World Bank, Cuba naturally remained a member of the International Sugar Council[18] and of course of the U.N. Cuba exchanged sugar with Egypt in return for rice. She also remained on commercial terms with Canada, whose Conservative prime minister, Diefenbaker, bluntly refused to impose any embargo on Cuba. Through Canada, Cuba received some spare parts for cars, as for electrical and industrial appliances. Canadian businessmen were able to divest themselves of ideology more easily than those of the U.S. Canada was not a member of the OAS, and she was therefore excluded from the main institution through which the U.S. hoped to act. In return, Cuba compensated the Canadian banks (taken over in December) in cash, rather than in non-existent bonds.[19] There were still non-Communist 'technicians' in Cuba. Some Japanese for instance were making valiant efforts to grow rice in the impenetrable Zapata swamps, and an Irish company had been contracted to build a jute factory in Santa Clara.

In January 1961 too there even seemed a remote chance of reopening relations with the U.S. Both Castro and Blas Roca suggested in speeches that President Kennedy might in this respect be an improvement on President Eisenhower. On 21 January Castro said, 'For our part we are going to begin anew.' On 7 March he even proposed that 'if some day the U.S. wishes again to buy sugar from Cuba then we can discuss . . . indemnification'. Did the Cubans really now wish for an improvement? It is quite possible. Castro had purged at least something of his personal, national resentment against the U.S. But the sort of agreement which was remotely attainable with the U.S. would have been one to live and let live, leading eventually to U.S. acceptance of the regime, maybe to a certain modification of the most objectionable traits of the Cuban revolution, so far as the U.S. was concerned; and with the quarrelsome exiles swarming in Miami and Cuba's own inevitable identification with the – as it seemed – swelling revolutionary tide in Latin America, such a development was barely conceivable, even if the U.S. had been prepared to accept the humiliation of a socialist Cuba next door to them.

[18] The Mexico meeting of the Sugar Council in December concluded that in 1961 sugar available for the world market would be 16% above needs. As early as November Russia was in fact dumping Cuban sugar in the world market at less than prevailing prices.

[19] According to one unconfirmed source, the Royal Bank of Canada was enabled to withdraw its capital, unlike all the other banks.

What Russia thought of all this was still not clear, perhaps even to Russians. The Cuban revolution had not been planned by Russia. The swift developments there had taken the Russian government by surprise. Perhaps, as Khrushchev's letter transmitted through Alexayev seems to have suggested, Russia would still have preferred a neutral Cuba to a satellite one. But the Cuban cause had struck a definite note of enthusiasm in the Russian public. Poets and intellectuals thought that Cuba was enacting a genuine revolutionary struggle such as would perhaps give them new faith in their own system. Cuba had to be assisted and maintained now as well as ultimately to be made use of. Cuba represented a cause to which Khrushchev clearly responded and of which, once committed, he had to take care in his relation with his rivals. Thus Soviet (and eastern *bloc*) aid came in 1960 and 1961 in many ships, apparently without the cost being counted. Evidently Cuba could serve too as a centre of international Communist activity in South America, as well as a propaganda victory with which to taunt the U.S. (and perhaps China), and, who knew, giving some sort of military benefit as well. But this side of the matter seems not yet to have been discussed.

In return Russian technicians impressed Cubans as hard-working, but often 'their technical knowledge' seemed 'mediocre'. Many of them 'drank like Cossacks.' They lived in isolation, spent evenings on the beach playing basketball, never talking of politics, seeming 'a generous, watched-over, hard-working but poor people', a far from satisfactory representation of a 'future full of promise'. The Cubans found Czech technicians more human, but there were fewer of them. Chinese technicians were mercifully also few, and incomprehensible.[20]

Along with these international friendships, the old Communist leaders were certainly now always in public, at saluting bases and addressing workers and other groups, though they had no official status. Lázaro Peña, the old Labour chief, was to be seen at every gathering of the union but, apart from being referred to as the 'founder', he had no discernible profession. In the press the Communists were simply referred to as *dirigentes revolucionarios*, revolutionary leaders, a bland title with which however no one else was favoured. Of course, these men were not usually popular among the intimates of Castro. None of them as yet were members of the cabinet and, though they evidently had influence in some departments of State, their control over the army and INRA has been exaggerated. After January 1961 they never again made any pronouncement as a party upon any event in Cuba.

[20] *Cf.* the judgments in Casalis's articles, *La República* (Caracas), February 1966.

Between Fidelistas and Communists also there lurked one major antagonism: over the devious and far from heroic role that the party had played during the civil war. Even Guevara seems to have treated the Communist leaders personally with some scorn.[21] There also lurked scandal: thus among the old leaders of the Directorio Revolucionario such as Chomón (despite his identification of himself as a Communist), there still lurked the disagreeable affair of the betrayal of the four students in Calle Humboldt in 1957. Recently the presumed traitor, Marcos Armando Rodríguez, a young Communist, had been arrested in Prague and returned thence to Cuba;[22] he was under guard and interrogation in prison, but still protected by Communists such as Joaquín Ordoqui, a member of the Central Committee, and his *compañera*, Edith García Buchaca, once wife of their comrade Carlos Rafael Rodríguez.[23] At this time the old members of the Directorio were unable to force any action by the Communists to assist their pursuit of this enemy and this grumble behind the scenes was symptomatic of the anxieties within the revolution. Meanwhile the only effective group remotely opposed to the Communists from within the government seemed still those around Carlos Franqui and the newspaper *Revolución*, though Franqui himself had evidently undergone a serious change of mind since 1959.

There was, however, as yet no ideological identification between Castro and the Communists. The furthest that any of Castro's friends had gone in this direction was Guevara's argument that the Cuban revolutionaries were discovering Marxist laws by the practice of government: 'We, practical revolutionaries, initiating our struggle, merely fulfil laws foreseen by Marx the scientist.'[24] But Guevara, in conversation with René Dumont, had also said that his aim above all was to give workers 'a sense of responsibility', not of property, and Guevara was already critical of the Soviet Union's new emphasis on material encouragement to hard work. He refused to 'participate in Cuba in the creation' of 'a second North American society'.[25] Guevara envisaged thus already the perfectibility of man, a reliance only on loyalty to society, even before the second year of revolution was out. This, of course, suggested that Cuba was about to embark on all the difficulties, starting at the beginning, previously met in the socialist countries. Where the two groups, Fidelistas and Communists, could agree was in respect of the struggle against imperialism, assumed to be identical with

[21] See Luis Simón MSS.
[22] On 1 January 1961. He had been pursued consistently by Fructuoso Rodríguez's widow.
[23] All this came out in Rodríguez's trial in 1964.
[24] *Verde Olivo*, October 1960.
[25] Dumont, 54.

the counter-revolution; after all, even alleged leftist counter-revolutionaries such as Ray and Miró Cardona were now throwing in their lot with the CIA. For Castro and the Communists, to a slightly lesser extent, the 'Cuban national struggle' could now be seen primarily in terms of the struggle against the U.S.

One category of Cubans demands note though it elusively avoids analysis. These were those who, like Luis Orlando Rodríguez (ex-Minister of the Interior in 1959 and editor of *La Calle*, Grau's Director of Sports and leader of the university *bonche* in the 1940s), Marcelo Fernández (the old national co-ordinator of the 26 July Movement), José Pellón and Octavio Louit, had until 1959 been reckoned as not only non-Communists, but even '*enragé* anti-Communists',[26] and who now remained in Cuba, without breaking with the regime and indeed continuing to play minor parts in government. All these cases differ when it comes to the point; Luis Orlando Rodríguez apparently took the line of least resistance, having always perhaps been a little superficial, anti-Communist when it was fashionable and pro-Communist when that line too became profitable.[27] Others were bureaucrats prepared to serve anyone, particularly in the union movement. Others like Marcelo Fernández and Faustino Pérez are in perhaps the most interesting position of all: serious anti-Communists (despite a flirtation by the former with Communism when at the university), they lost their jobs in 1959 or 1960 for their hostility towards the old Communist party in Cuba. But they remained in Cuba, either mesmerized by Castro, or convinced that on balance it was wiser to remain and attempt in the long run to try to influence the regime towards what they conceived as moderate courses from within, or perhaps believing that whatever name was given to the practices of the government they were right. There were others such as Efigenio Ameijeiras or Juan Almeida, men of limited intellect but loyal to Castro as a leader and willing to follow him anywhere under any circumstances. Others still stayed because their families or friends desired to stay or because they themselves knew and loved the island too much to think of changing residences for mere political reasons. Others, again, found in the version of Communism applied in Cuba by Castro a surprisingly safe intellectual harbour after years moving from Catholicism to Ortodoxia to either García Barcena's or Aureliano Sánchez Arango's minor action groups; many had already shifted their political position so often that one more shift, even from liberalism to Communism, was a mere extra change almost as superficial as the others. Others still believed that with Castro

[26] As *El Mundo* (Miami Beach), 3 June 1961, put it about Luis Orlando Rodríguez.

[27] Rodríguez published anti-Communist articles in *La Calle* after it had been revived in 1959–60; the newspaper was closed and he became ambassador in Venezuela.

probably the choice of the Communist path was the final statement of freedom away from the U.S.: to replace the angry liberal father, the U.S. near at hand, with a distant one, however autocratic and narrow, appears to have been for many Cuban intellectuals an act of will second to none; and once Castro had personally established his control over the local Cuban Communist party, all their anxieties, such as they were, were at rest.

In its military organization Cuba was not yet a Communist state. After the Matos crisis the rebel army, with its doubtfully revolutionary and loyal political leadership, had been run down and re-organized. In its place now stood the militia, a volunteer army of about 150,000 men and women who, supporting the revolution, put on uniform and took up guns after their daily work, for about eight hours a week, and guarded public buildings and other installations of importance from the attacks of counter-revolutionaries. These amateur soldiers seemed everywhere in Cuba in 1961, sometimes obtrusive and officious, often lazing in rocking chairs in verandahs, their loaded rifles across their knees: 'We Cubans are an army people,' a heavily armed boy of fifteen remarked[28] in July 1961; it was true. The illusion of a nation in arms could not have been stronger under Carnot. Yet there remained among these dedicated gunmen a certain frivolity as well as charm which would have troubled Carnot or Trotsky. Perhaps this militia really embodied a return to the old national supposition that a regular army was pointless, since anyone could take up a rifle or a machete to defend his rights. The militia of course was organized by the army and army officers ran it, the commander being still the youthful Captain Rogelio Acevedo.[29] The head of the militias in the provinces was often the head of military intelligence, the so-called G.2, as well.

G.2 was now the main organization for the detection of counter-revolution being still under the direction of Castro's old *Granma* and Moncada colleague, Ramiro Valdés. Valdés organized (probably under Russian supervision) an efficient political police, though as yet it was in its early stages with, interestingly enough, prominent assistants being men of the supposedly once non-communist Directorio Revolucionario.[30] In the winter of 1960–1, some counter-revolutionaries captured in the Escambray had been tortured by the holding of their heads under water to get information and others were taken out to the execution wall and fired at with blank cartridges. Castro ceased this on the representations of some of his old followers. But in fact conditions in Cuban

[28] To the author.

[29] The militia was really the focus of the national defence effort until new 'revolutionary' officers' schools had produced a fully socialist generation.

[30] For instance Julio García Oliviera, José Abrahantes, Carlos Figueredo.

prisons from 1960 onwards once again, as under Batista or Machado, beggar description.[31]

Another disturbing development still had been a civilian branch of the militia, the Committees for the Defence of the Revolution (CDR), local citizens organized frankly as militant informers against possible counter-revolution.[32] The commander of these committees was an unknown, José Matar, a man without personal experience of command in the Sierra, and a young Communist of the old guard. Their activities extended to checking upon people who suddenly started disposing of their furniture: this would suggest that these people had decided to abandon Cuba and, being forbidden to take their possessions with them, wished to hand them over, for safe-keeping till counter-revolution or for ever, to friends, relations or western diplomats. These acts were illegal since a penalty for safe emigration was the gift to the State of all posses-sions save one suit of clothes and a few small objects (one ring, for instance).

The Agrarian Reform Institute (INRA) had by now absorbed all the old autonomous economic institutions such as the Coffee, Sugar, and Rice Stabilization bodies, and BANFAIC, the Bank for Economic and Social Development. Through INRA, indeed, the State controlled all the main capital equipment of the nation including, pre-eminently, sugar. The harvest of 1961 was the first *zafra del pueblo*, the people's harvest. Of course, this harvest had been sown in the bad old days and there had as yet been no reorganization whatever of the sugar mills – even though they had mostly been renamed, chiefly after heroes of the revolution or great dates in the international revolutionary tradition.[33] International revolutionary feast days indeed were now as many as those of the Church.

The harvest was successful, the figures by early April 1961 suggesting that the total would reach as high as any good average year before 1959. But the expressed goal of the revolution was still to enable the nation to escape from sugar. Work on this escape had been begun, so much so that, unless indeed diversification were quickly successful, the economy would inevitably decline, since a failure to replant in 1960 meant a fall

[31] See accounts in e.g. Martino, *I was Castro's Prisoner*, and *Cuba and the Rule of Law*. I have also benefited from discussions with several ex-prisoners among them Dr Joaquín Martínez Sáenz.

[32] *Revolución*, 29 September 1960.

[33] There were also some Communist heroes such as the sugar workers' leader, Jesús Men-éndez, murdered in 1947, who gave his name to what used to be the proud *Chaparra*; *España* became *España Republicana*; the first Communist to act as a go-between with Castro in the Sierra Maestra (and killed in early 1961 in an air crash), Osvaldo Sánchez, received in memory, Arango's *Providencia*; the United Fruit Company's *Preston* mill became *Guatemala*, after the abortive revolution; and *Natividad* became 7 *November* (1917).

in sugar production in 1963. By the spring of 1961, 33,000 peasants had become owners of land which they had previously cultivated as squatters, sharecroppers or tenants; just under a million acres had thus been 'distributed', nearly half in Oriente.[34] This accounted for between a third and a quarter of the farmers who in the past had suffered under this form of tenure. The land involved was not large; thus what was distributed even in Oriente amounted to only about 6% of the farmland (by 1946 estimates). Julio Lobo alone had this amount of land. But then, these farmers had in the past only held a small percentage of the total farm area. For those involved it nevertheless meant a revolution, less in their way of living, than in their view of society and their relations with it. It meant a freedom from indebtedness as well as from living outside the law. The agricultural co-operatives numbered about 900,[35] of which about 550 were devoted to crops, a few to livestock alone and 120 to mixed crops and livestock. Most were between 500 and 800 acres. They aimed to avoid the economic losses which would have followed had this land been divided up. But INRA never issued regulations for the management of the co-operatives, and their construction was loose. On the other hand, INRA did appoint managers, often members of the co-operative, who were supposed to keep in touch with the INRA zone chiefs. Co-operative members were usually paid $2.50 per eight-hour day, though there was no national scale. Wages were still held to be an advance on eventual profits to be divided at the end of the year, but these were not distributed either in 1959 or in 1960.

At the end of 1960 these co-operatives were about to die. The system seemed inequitable: some farms did well (for instance, forest co-operatives, because of the heavy demand for wood) and some badly, according to the wealth of the farm, rather than according to the deserts or the work of the labourer. However fair this might seem under capitalism where labour could be cut down or increased, it seemed unjust under socialism. The confusion was also unbelievable. Accounts were not kept properly. Even a sympathetic observer[36] noted: 'Everything happened *por la libre*. The most conscientious peasants in the co-operatives would fight against anarchy but the individual efforts were drowned in the

---

[34] Ownership titles granted and land distributed in Cuba, June 1959 to February 1961:

	Number of Titles	Hectares
Pinar del Río	5,536	53·4
Havana	2,669	37·7
Matanzas	3,057	33·1
Las Villas	4,508	58·3
Camagüey	2,524	27·1
Oriente	14,529	173·2
Total	32,823	382·8

[35] 881 in August 1960.
[36] Ania Francos, *La Fête Cubaine* (1962),

mass. It was often necessary to go to Havana to settle the smallest question.' Such errors were admitted by Castro: 'Certain administrators, with a vague conception of the Revolution . . . believed that the more goods they could hand out to farmers, the more revolutionary they were being.'[37] Another weakness was that very large pig and chicken farms were built, exposing the animals to epidemics. Castro himself seemed obsessed by hatred of *marabú* (the thorny tropical acacia which grows as a weed in the south) and had vast stretches cleared, while ignoring other places capable of producing much more at less cost.[38]

In the summer of 1960, after the harvest, sugar cane co-operatives were also set up and, by the spring of 1961, there were rather over 600 of them.[39] Most of the 120,000 members had previously been full-time agricultural workers at the sugar mills. Run with the same expectation as the other co-operatives (that they would eventually become commercially self-sufficient), they were in fact similarly under INRA, but more formally organized. There was thus a general assembly of all members of the co-operative able (though usually not anxious) to elect a directing board of seven to aid the manager, who was himself appointed by INRA. Their finances were centrally organized, with regional headquarters, technical staff accounts, machine repair workshops, and so on. INRA usually set up a *tienda del pueblo*, people's shop, where basic goods could be bought at reduced prices, perhaps 12% cheaper. Since rents were also abolished, these workers (paid $2.50 a day as were their colleagues in the other co-operatives) were in many respects a good deal better off than in the past – while there were any goods to buy. But on some occasions it is clear that co-operatives were founded against the desire of the workers concerned, who might be more interested in more wages than the sacrifices needed for the Revolution.[40] In late 1961 Castro himself complained that the small farmer of Mantanzas was 'allergic to co-operatives. He does not want to hear them mentioned. He is frightened by the mere word'.[41]

These 'pseudo-co-operatives',[42] however, afforded scant help in the amelioration of unemployment, even though seasonal workers could still be brought in for harvests, and they might one day be made permanent, providing diversification made it possible. Eventually it

[37] Castro, *Revolución*, 11 November 1961, 6.
[38] Dumont, 44–5.
[39] 622 to be precise. These figures were given in May, but they no doubt apply to March too. There had been 604 in August 1960. They covered 80,000 *caballería* (Castro, in speech, 10 November 1961, *Revolución* 11 November, 10.)
[40] See Agustín Souchy, *Testimonios sobre la Revolución Cubana*, Buenos Aires, 1960, 32.
[41] Castro, speech, 10 November 1961. Goldenberg (*op. cit*, 237) recalled an instance when former tenant farmers appeared before a dispossessed landlord and offered, out of fear for the future, to go on paying rent. Blas Roca, in a speech to the heads of schools for revolutionary instruction, made similar admissions.
[42] As Dumont called them, 44.

was expected that the manager would be elected, and that all profits would be distributed (though during the first five years four-fifths of profits were to be invested for schools, housing, roads, and so on). Diversification meant the cultivation of pangola grass, maize, rice and other crops on about a quarter of the total. The pangola would be used for feeding new herds of cattle. But most of these diversification areas (300,000 acres) were old cane ones and, by accident or inexperience, much good cane land was uprooted (by Castro among others), while bad land was often left to bear cane. The use of this excellent land was justified as a short-term measure to avoid the cost of clearing quite new land, but it brought trouble in the future. Nor to begin with were great efforts made to reap what could have been a great advantage of these arbitrary acts: there was no new scientific planting, little rationalization of the agricultural side of the industry. On the other hand, these measures did of course confirm the disappearance of all large *colonos* of the past, making possible improvements in the future.

The errors in administration partly derived from the fact that there were simply fewer men doing the work of management. In 1961 there was additionally a long drought. Weeding was ill-done, and drainage sometimes not kept up. On very many sugar estates, the precise character of diversification was left to the local manager, who did what he wished at his whim or his regional boss's. There was also a labour shortage, for better wages were to be had elsewhere, particularly in the new State farms which gave a chance of better housing. With other factors, these errors caused production in the cane co-operatives to be 10% lower in 1962 than in the surviving private plantations.[43] Planting was generally ignored in 1960 and 1961. In an historically comprehensible (if economically unwise) obsession to escape from sugar, the Cuban revolution neglected in fact the only crop which, like it or not, they could live on in totalitarian conditions; for sugar can be cut by an army or by machines and it is ground by an industrial proletariat, even though they may live in the country; and planting of course requires only the most modest agricultural knowledge.[44]

INRA had always since January 1959 administered some estates confiscated from Batistianos. After the Agrarian Reform others were added. By May 1960 INRA ran over 500 farms covering over two million acres. These had begun with the cattle estates, chiefly in

[43] See Carlos Rafael Rodríguez's speech to sugar workers, 18 July 1962. He said that land producing 40,000 to 50,000 *arrobas* of cane had been torn up, while some producing half this was left standing. (See comments in Seers, 130.)

[44] For this reason, the Cuban experience cannot be much of a guide for the agricultural development of other socialist countries nor, of course, for other Latin American territories, despite the Chilean Communist Juan Noyola's remark, 'I am one of the numerous Latin Americans who consider the Cuban Revolution as our common patrimony.' (Qu. Dumont, 18.)

Camagüey, and were later extended to rice plantations. Castro later explained:

> When we came to the case of the great cattle ranches, vast extensions of land where a few men managed thousands of head of cattle, the question arose, what should be done? Organize a co-operative ... with very few people ... rich [people]? I reached the conclusion that it was necessary to search for a superior form of social ownership of those lands.[45]

The decision not to divide up the rice plantations after the 1960 harvest was indeed a decisive one for the future of the regime. The state farms which were the result were, as it happens, not provided for under the agrarian reform but, by late 1960, they began to be regarded as the easiest method of running Cuban agriculture in the totalitarian circumstances then unavoidable. As early as August 1960 Castro told René Dumont that he desired to create large state farms for all agricultural production except sugar properties.[46] The following January, all the old non-sugar co-operatives were converted into state farms, and they and the cattle ranches were thenceforth known under the more resounding title of *granja del pueblo*.[47] This meant little more than the formalization of existing reality, since the co-operatives had not been allowed to work properly as such. By April 1961 there were 266 state farms, covering over five million acres, or an average of 20,000 acres[48] embracing every crop and being found all over the island – though Oriente and Camagüey together accounted for over half the total acreage. Many farms were divided into separated parcels of land, sometimes separated by miles, thus directly reproducing some aspects of the old system which were most in need of reform. These farms were administered directly by the State, without, as in the case of the still surviving cane co-operatives, any regional or local headquarters. They employed nearly 100,000 workers, mostly seasonal (70,000) and paid $2.11 a day (with free housing, medical care and education).

These farms bore obvious resemblances to the Russian *sovkhozy*. But the actual circumstances of Cuban agriculture helped to dictate the decision. Workers on the co-operatives were unused to taking individual

---

[45] Lockwood, 90.

[46] Dumont, 56. Dumont criticized them from the start, foreseeing some of the difficulties which they later encountered. He also thought that Castro had been too excessively influenced by his reading of Soviet literature, where the co-operative was described as an 'inferior form of property' and points out the personal nature of Castro's decision: Castro alone took the decision.

[47] However, the farms previously directly run by INRA continued to be so under different administration.

[48] The *Granma* farm in Oriente was over 100,000 acres, and there later came to be a farm of even over 250,000 acres.

initiatives, and the co-operatives themselves worked badly from the start. It seemed that a straightforward state system would assist both the diversification and the supply of food regularly to the cities. Sociologically, this had some success. Some workers on these farms for a time were happy to regard themselves as civil servants, serving a state which they themselves controlled; and Castro argued the system meant that land could be used 'in an optimum way, absolutely rationally, determining at each moment that whatever crop benefits the nation shall be produced'.[49]

But within a few months of their foundation, the sheer size of these state farms began to cause difficulties. The dispersion of the different parcels was another reason. The farms seemed, as Dumont had foreseen, to be little confederations, rather than a single unit. There was much disorganization, much folly: an observer in Pinar del Río found that the administrator of INRA for the province 'depended on the zone representatives who in turn depended on the co-operative administrators. The system was operating from the bottom upwards ... I doubt if any zone representative knew what he was responsible for.'[50] Passing by Santa Clara in May 1960 the French agronomist, Dumont, called on the provincial director of INRA, Luis Borges, an ex-student of dentistry. 'He vaunted himself before us to sign a little document every time he needed to acquire such and such an installation, factory, shop ... Clearly he carried out these expropriations without preconceived plan, on a whim, without seeing if it was really useful and above all if INRA was capable of running it.'[51] In the headquarters of INRA 'you could see ... not the prim, old-line functionaries ... but bearded rebels in uniform carrying arms. The working hours were not the 9 to 5 of the ordinary government workers [but] the irregular ... nocturnal hours ... of the guerrilla'.[52] Whether this was beneficial was doubtful. Meantime, no one thought of indemnification and everyone who coveted this was therefore driven to dream of, or plot, a change of government. Few received receipts for property which had been taken over. Many workers even on state farms sold goods privately and no one really knew how much land the state controlled or was supposed to.

Agricultural wages had probably gone up about a fifth since 1958. The people's shops, *tiendas del pueblo*, on the co-operatives had cut prices and increased buying power in the country. INRA claimed that meat consumption had gone up two-thirds in comparison with 1958; but this had been caused by extra slaughtering (made possible by increased demand in the towns) which soon led to shortages. In the early summer of

[49] Lockwood, 90.
[50] I. Pflaum, *American Universities Field Staff Reports Service*, V, No. 4, 38.
[51] Dumont, *Cuba*, 37.
[52] E. Boorstein, *Economic Transformation of Cuba* (1968), 48.

1960 Castro made several speeches in which he told workers in well organized unions such as the builders' or waiters' that the revolution was not for them primarily but for the unfortunate: workers too would have to make sacrifices for the revolution.[53]

Many, therefore, were the difficulties attendant on progress.

The most sympathetic criticism of the development of the agricultural programme of the revolution made in 1960 was that by Professor René Dumont, of the Sorbonne, who on 20 May gave a press conference giving constructive comment of several sorts, urging reflection, order and discipline.[54] No one, Dumont pointed out, had insisted that the cooperatives should keep accounts. The Agrarian Reform law had charged INRA to prepare the statutes of the co-operatives. But even here nothing had yet been done. The weaknesses of Dr Núñez Jiménez as chief of INRA were already patent but he nevertheless remained loaded with the full responsibility, rather than the Minister of Agriculture, Pedro Miret (preoccupied by reafforestation). Further, Dumont pointed out, on the large farms communications between plots might be non-existent. Difficulties of administration found in the cane co-operatives were redoubled. The manager was often merely a farmer with little or no experience of such large-scale farming, sometimes illiterate and ignorant of new crops and scientific training, often chosen because of his political reliability.[55] For this reform to have been successful, he should have been a master-farmer of vast knowledge. The state farm as constituted in April 1961 was not yet the answer to Cuban agriculture – though it had not yet been proved to be a failure.

These drawbacks to the state farms had not indeed been understood or admitted as early as the spring of 1961. The drive of Cuba's agricultural policy was in fact now in the direction of more and more of such large concerns. Few land titles were now granted to private peasants – only 200 new titles affecting 6,000 acres were distributed between February and December 1961.[56] The need for planning had now been generally admitted. Castro confessed at a later meeting that he had been 'one of the great promoters of action by impulse' but had been weaned away to 'planning' by Guevara, Carlos Rafael Rodríguez and Boti.[57]

[53] e.g. 'A pesar de ser la Revolución un proceso cuyo objetivo fundamental es la ayuda a los sectores más humildes del país, a los más necesitados, ocurrirá a veces de que alguna medida revolucionaria afectará también algún sector humilde . . .' (Obra Revolucionaria, 16 June 1960, 5).

[54] His report was partly published in the Études 1962 de Tiers Monde. René Dumont (b. 1904) is Director of Research at the Institut National Agronomique in Paris. His most famous book was False Start in Africa.

[55] Carlos Rafael Rodríguez, qu. Seers (from F. Castro, O. Dorticós, 68–72).

[56] No new titles at all were granted in Pinar del Río, Matanzas and Camagüey.

[57] 'I want the works begun "at will" to end, I want such haphazard ideas as works "by impulse" to end because they are now the antithesis of planning. Before, everything was "at will", but now everything must be planned.' (Obra Revolucionaria, 30 August 1961, 6).

By the spring of 1961 a little over a third of the farmland in Cuba was probably run by the State. Of the area now administered by the Agrarian Reform Institute, only 27 % had actually come to it in consequence of the original agrarian reform of May 1969; 7 % had come from gifts; 13 % from 'voluntary' sales; and 50 % derived from decrees of expropriation issued in the struggles of 1960, in July and October, land taken from great sugar mills and cattle estates as a result of political action.[58] The errors made in consequence of the State's capture of this large slice of the economy were many, since it was an unprecedented situation. Planning was inadequate in respect of seeds, fertilizers, insecticides, transport, and so on. Agricultural workers drifted into Havana or other cities to become semi-employed bureaucrats, while a labour shortage grew up behind them. Minor decisions continued to be referred to Havana. Too many tractors were bought, too few less sophisticated implements. INRA ceased, after the lyrical first days, to work in harmony with the armed forces. Transport became disorganized, because of the disappearance of spare parts, because of the new managers' inexperience, and because inadequate provision had been made both for the shipment of material and then for essential supplies. It was indeed extremely difficult to change fast from a system whereby many farms, some big, some small, produced a few individual crops, to one where a limited number of huge government estates tried to produce many crops. No individual had of course any economic interest in the success of these farms. There were bad estimates of the likely increase of demand for food caused by the rise in incomes after the earlier achievements of the revolution (such as cuts in rents and utilities). Estimates of production were also wildly wrong.[59] Accounts in the co-operatives were apparently not kept, and so prevented effective planning.[60] The Cubans had no traditions of sound book-keeping anyway. In this sense, they showed themselves an ex-colonial people who had left for too long to others their initiative and their invention. Used to extensive cultivation, all farms, big and small, found it hard to take full advantage of irrigation and drainage, even if these were established.

These vast changes in land tenure were also undertaken without even many of those trained and experienced managers who had existed in Cuba in the past. For by now the exodus to Miami included technicians from all over Cuba. Although many such persons were inevitably hostile to the new order, many more would have stayed if the regime had merely attempted one thing at a time. A breach with the U.S. was not necessary for a diversification of agriculture. It would doubtless have

[58] Gutelmann, qu. Dumont, 60–1.
[59] See Severo Aguirre, in *Cuba Socialista*, May 1962.
[60] Socialism cannot work without adequate statistics, for capitalism a guess is often as good (*cf.* Dumont, 100).

been wiser had it been possible, to have avoided the 'international chess game' while enacting agrarian reform.

Even without considering these matters, the government neglected all the large number of farmers still independent. True, farmers with estates smaller than 160 acres (as a result of the revolutionary redistribution or not) had begun since December to be linked together for purposes of planning, giving credit, machinery, distribution of output, in a new national co-operative association – Asociación Nacional de Agricultores Pequeños (ANAP).[61] By May 1961 about 85,000 farmers, with enterprises totalling about six million[62] acres and responsible for a quarter of the entire farmland, were part of ANAP and well within reach of INRA and the State.[63] Confusion, lack of wisdom and uncertainty of direction however took many of these farmers into the ranks of active counter-revolution and there were, in the winter of 1960–1961 many parts of Cuba where in consequence the writ of the government did not run.

A little over 40% of the land, almost 10 million acres, remained outside ANAP and in private hands, more than any single other category;[64] these were all now farmers with estates of between 150 and 1,500 acres, with probably few estates above 1,000 acres; that is, they were not exactly *latifundistas* though they nearly all employed several men. Maybe there were over 10,000 of them, and the total number of independent ones numbered 175,000, or far more than there had been in 1946.[65]

This whole category of private farmer was ignored by the regime. Banks being nationalized, transport and distribution being disrupted and INRA given all the advantages, they found it hard both to get supplies and to deliver their goods. These difficulties inevitably led many to a sulky reluctance to co-operate in any way with the new

[61] This had a general administrator appointed by INRA (José Ramírez, an old Communist and Raúl Castro's messenger in the Sierra), a network of people's stores, regional bureaucrats, etc. Farmers with larger estates could join providing they had a proved 'revolutionary background'. ANAP was, of course, a politically committed society. It had 1,400 tractors, or rather less than 10% of the total in Cuba.

[62] INRA'S 1961 report gave a total of 3½ million hectares in the hands of ANAP, obviously too high, as Seers says (p. 128), but his calculation that this is because there were 2·2 million hectares only in farms less than 67·1 hectares in 1946 does not take into account the increase in the number of small farms between 1946 and 1959.

[63] Within ANAP there were several other associations of peasants, devised to link the small private farmer to the national economy. By means of the Credit and Services Cooperative, farmers joined together to get credit and machinery and sell crops but cultivated land independently. These appear to have been confined to Las Villas and Oriente and to have numbered 220 or so by 1962. These were genuine co-operatives. Dumont, a strict critic, was impressed by one which he visited near Ciego de Avila in 1963. The president was elected by the members for a year, and an elected four-member council planned production (see Dumont, 89–90).

[64] Though over 40% of the land had been expropriated, including the land divided up.

[65] *Cuba Socialista*, May 1963, 15.

society, and to an increase in food shortages, especially in the towns (where over 60% of the population lived), as well as to the beginning of a black market. The only exception was among the sugar *colonos* who naturally took their cane to the mill as they had always done. The fact that the mill was now a state business made little difference. They continued to be paid in the same way, by *arrobaje*. But even some of them – perhaps 1,000 – refused in December 1960 to attend a pre-harvest rally, despite an attempt to persuade them to do so by Castro's brother Ramón, who opportunely seemed by now to have changed his views about the desirability of revolution.[66] It would seem unlikely that the regime wished to take over the properties of these farmers, but its policies were already, in early 1961, leading it to a position where it might have to do this in the name of simplification. Fear of this understandably was in the minds of many of these farmers, and exacerbated their plight.

In April 1961, if these farmers and those in ANAP are linked together, about 65 % of Cuban farm land was in private hands, including about two-thirds of the land in cane, three-quarters of the head of cattle, and most of the tobacco and coffee:[67] only rice among important crops was entirely in State hands.

The effects of the agricultural reform were by early 1961 hard to see, since reliable statistics were not published and, despite the appearance of some encouraging figures from the Government, it is doubtful if anyone really knew the truth. The production of the still surviving large private agricultural sector was quite impossible to know. Black market production was inestimable. One truth, however, was evident, whether it was a consequence of bad distribution or bad management or reluctance of private farmers to sell their produce: food was short from November 1960 in Cuba and became very short from the Spring of 1961 onwards.

On the other hand, in 1961 the main crop, sugar, gave a production of 6·8 million tons or higher than that of any year since the record-breaking crop of 1953 – in fact the second highest ever;[68] but the steps taken in 1960 meant that the crop for 1962 and thereafter would probably be down.[69] Cuba was obviously growing more cotton than before 1959, even if the 100,000 acres which the state claimed to be under cotton was probably an exaggeration. Among other crops, rice

[66] HAR *xiii*, 879.

[67] See calculations in Seers, 128.

[68] Of course, the *zafra del pueblo* was not finished till May–June but the signs were clear by the end of March that it would be a bumper year. This was partly because rainfall in 1960 had been exactly right.

[69] Also in 1961 the government decided for the first time to cut all the cane that had grown, not leaving any unharvested, as was usual: so 94% of cane was cut.

was stagnant[70] in 1961, but, so far as can be seen, every major crop, except coffee, returned higher figures in 1961 than in 1958.[71] Even rice was higher in 1961 than 1958. Any verdict on these figures is difficult; but if they were correct, it simply suggests that distribution must have been even worse than was usually admitted. The cattle situation somewhat resembled that of sugar: in the first quarter of 1961, 40,000 were slaughtered in Las Villas in place of 18,000 in the same months of 1959, that is, an increase of almost 40%. Havana's demands were three-fifths up in 1960 on 1958.[72] Similar increases existed in other provinces.[73] This meant a major reduction in beef reserves, so that from 1962 onwards the pinch would be severely felt. These inroads into reserves of food could have been prevented, since they were predictable.

While the land which was devoted to sugar, coffee and tobacco remained much as before, large tracts of new territory – over 440,000 acres, as reported in August 1961[74] – had been reclaimed from idleness or scrub, and planted with the crops of diversification, particularly rice, and also cotton and potatoes. This increase meant an increase in employment, though no doubt a less substantial one than that claimed by the Ministry of Labour. In all these crops there was also a substantial rise in the use of fertilizer and a modest increase in investment in agricultural machinery.[75] In 1959 and 1960, many landowners, including some who were later expropriated, tried to extend or to intensify their areas of cultivation, hoping thereby perhaps to postpone or (if Castro should change his mind or was overthrown) avoid reform.[76] Up till July 1960, after all, there had been relatively few expropriations. The increase of ownership among coffee and tobacco growers – mostly old tenants or share-croppers – helped morale in those departments. Meantime, the enthusiasm roused by the revolution stimulated farm managers to attempt impossibly high targets and even made workers, in 1959 and 1960, at least, in private estates, insist to their employers that high targets

---

[70] *Cuba Socialista*, May 1962, 57. INRA told Bianchi in 1962 that production fell but it did not give the magnitude.

[71]

	1957	1958	1959	1960	1961
Tobacco	41·7	50·6	35·6	45·3	52·3
Rice	256·8	225·9	282·1	304·2	230·0
Coffee	36·7	43·7	29·5	55·2	38·5
Potatoes	94·9	79·3	71·6	97·6	101·4
Maize		134			198

[72] INRA, *Un Año de Liberación Agraria*.

[73] *Cf.* Seers.

[74] *Obra Revolucionaria*, No. 30 of 1961, 78.

[75] *Cf.* Seers, 118. INRA said that $M81 had been spent on agricultural machinery by May 1961, of which $M35 had been spent in socialist countries. But had it arrived? According to the Banco Nacional Memorial for 1958 only $M17 had been spent on agricultural machinery between 1953–8. But of course the real value of these things had all changed. Much old machinery was falling apart.

[76] See comments by Felipe Pazos, in *Cambridge Opinion*, February 1963.

be named and pursued, on pain of denunciation before the INRA chief of the locality.[77] Cuba might pride herself on being the only country to have an agrarian reform and at the same time to raise production: but, as Dumont pointed out, even if this was true the comparison could only be made in comparison with socialist countries. Japan and Israel had enjoyed much more notable increases of production.[78]

Production and land tenure were not, of course, everything. Agrarian reform in addition meant better conditions of all sorts. Rural unemployment had almost ended. INRA's housing department had built by the end of 1960 fifty new small hospitals, sixty new schools, as well as the famous Camilo Cienfuegos primary boarding school in the Sierra Maestra, and about 10,000 new houses or apartments.[79] INRA also built many other new buildings, such as shops, clinics, clubs, warehouses, libraries – but, of course, no churches. There were about 2,000 *tiendas del pueblo* built by April 1961. No doubt some of these investments were economically rash; the quality of some of the new houses was much too high for mass production. Further, the Urban Reform of October 1960 not only ended private renting but virtually halted all private building. Castro said in 1962 that the Revolution could not in future build more than 10,000 to 12,000 houses a year, though 400,000 were needed.[80] Some roads which were built were also unnecessarily wide.[81]

The State's industrial reorganization had been at first under a department of INRA – the industries, that is, which had been confiscated from Batista's supporters. This department was run by Guevara for some weeks between his return from his travels and becoming president of the Bank. By July 1960 wholesale nationalization gave to this industrial department sixty companies worth $M800, including twenty sugar companies, the telephone and electric companies ($M80 and $M300 each) and three oil companies. In October INRA received a further 300 industrial establishments, including the remaining sugar mills and all the banks. By late 1960, INRA controlled over half the industrial structure of the island; and by February 1961 nearly three-quarters. In that month, the industrial undertakings were detached from INRA and made into a separate Ministry of Industries, under Guevara, with vice-ministries running different sections.[82]

[77] Cf. Felipe Pazos, '*Comentarios a dos Artículos sobre la Revolución Cubana*' (typescript).
[78] Dumont, *Cuba*, 62.
[79] 19,000 new houses a year were built in the period 1959–61, compared with 10,000 before 1958 (*ibid.*, 74, fn. 2). Most of these were in the country. In a number of speeches in 1961 Castro explained that housing would be far from a priority in revolutionary spending (e.g. speech at First Production Congress, 30 August 1961, *Obra Revolucionaria*, 6).
[80] *Revolución*, 22 June 1962.
[81] René Dumont and Julien Coléou, *La Ràforme Agraire é Cuba* (1962), 11.
[82] INRA kept the canneries and some other industries concerned with food.

Guevara's new empire employed 150,000 of whom 60,000 were in the sugar industry (at the mills or on its commercial side).[83] The ministry was highly centralized. All concerns sent to the ministry the proceeds of their sales, and were sent by the ministry the sums needed for their operation, though for the time being each business was responsible for its budget and its targets. No money was kept by separate enterprises. Credit was available at three months' call from the Finance Ministry. Guevara began to regroup the different industries[84] according to purpose, regardless of their success or efficiency: a fantasy of centralization which Guevara thought could be made to work, because of Cuba's small size, by telephone or aerial communication – 'a perfect mechanism of horology'.[85] Alas, the perfect mechanism, like the perfect socialist man, had not yet been found. Guevara, like King Ferdinand VII, found it impossible to keep even his clocks chiming in time with each other. As in agriculture, bureaucracy raised its head.

The problems incurred in the mere running of this ministry, with its multitudinous activities, were innumerable. Everyone underestimated the difficulties which Cuba would have in trying to organize herself alone, having been for so long an economic appendage of the U.S. However brilliant an economic imagination Guevara and some of his assistants might have, they had no experience of commercial administration. Guevara was then aged thirty-two. Some of his aides, such as the Chilean, Albán Lataste, the director of planning, or Angel Gutiérrez Paz, were older but they also had no experience of direction of industry.

[83] Ministry of Industry source in 1961
[84] These were:

Sugar mills	105
Distilleries	18
Manufactures of alcoholic drinks	6
Soap and scent factories	3
Factories of milk derivatives	5
Chocolate factories	2
Flour mills	1
Packaging or container factories	8
Paint factories	4
Chemical products factories	3
Basic metallurgy undertakings	6
Paper mills	7
Lamp factories	1
Textile and clothing factories	61
Rice mills	16
Food plants	7
Oil and grease plants	2
Coffee roasting plants	11
Printing presses	1
Building concerns	19
Electric plants	1
Total	287

[85] Guevara, *Révolution* (Paris), October 1963.

The only claim to fame indeed of the sub-secretary of the ministry, Orlando Borrego, was to have served with Guevara on the court which sentenced the BRAC commander, Captain Castaño, in 1959. Guevara complained of the difficulty of finding manpower to run these enterprises: 'we have to think hard where we can find 500 factory managers, and not a day passes when we don't have to sack one of them for incompetence'.[86]

It is difficult not to admire the energy, resolution and audacity with which Guevara and his companions faced their impossible task: impossible, since of course they had not only to run existing industries, or merely to raise their productive capacity – itself difficult in the unprecedented circumstances – but to lay down the lines for the further industrialization of Cuba, for those industries which would in the future, it was hoped, take over the burden of earning Cuba's international living from sugar. Thus elaborate plans were made to exploit the mineral deposits of Oriente, for making Cuba self-sufficient in steel, for shipyards capable of building large fishing boats, for machinery of all sorts, including mechanical cane cutters, for a new petrol refinery, for new electrical installations, for chemical expansion, for the production of paper from bagasse, hormones from cane wax, rubber from butane; indeed, many of Guevara's ideas derived from making the most use of the many rich by-products of the sugar industry. Since Cuba had such large reserves of nickel, should she not take her place as the second world producer? There were also projects for technological education – classes in statistics and lathe-turning, in industrial management and accountancy. A new plant might be needed and new refining methods might have to be learned. If the standard of living could be raised in the country, could not those who lived there be persuaded to buy things made in the towns?

Was this all a dream? In 1961 it did not entirely seem so. The first Cuban five-year plan had been presented in December. But serious problems were being met in running existing industry, much less expanding it; the spare parts which machines needed, like new slaves in the nineteenth century, had been brought across the sea – from Miami. No stocks had been kept in Cuba. Further, many existing industries had depended on the import of raw materials, all from the dollar area, to get started at all. Some factories, such as the Hedges's rayon factory, had for a while to be closed. Canada was a possible source of supply, but even there commerce needed foreign exchange. By the Spring of 1961, however, Guevara's ministry concentrated less on repairing machinery bought in the U.S. than on buying new stock from Russia or east Europe, and buying also ersatz raw materials from the same suppliers;

[86] Guevara, *Obra Revolucionaria*, 6 January 1961.

thus in May 1961 Guevara would inform Cuba that contracts for over a hundred factories had been signed with the eastern *bloc* including one for a steel mill, a petroleum refinery, and a motor car factory. There would be new flour mills from East Germany. Over a hundred technicians from the East were already in Cuba, apart from Chileans and other Latin Americans. The difficulties however of harnessing the country to a quite new technology were legion.

There were also, of course, difficulties about the possibility of expansion on the scale envisaged. Cuba still lacked indigenous sources of power. This meant a perpetual oil import and, unless the 'friendly countries of the East' changed their usual methods of commerce, a continuing challenge to the balance of payments. Food and other necessities would indefinitely have to be imported. All the essentials which Cuba had previously bought in the U.S., if not the luxuries, would have to be found from elsewhere. In December Russia had announced that she would buy in 1961 four million tons of sugar at 4 cents a pound; but would this continue? The central point was that, in order to escape from the sugar monoculture, Cuba would have to industrialize. But to industrialize she needed foreign currency, which could be earned, now as in the past, most easily by selling sugar. Cuba might have earned currency by selling market produce on a grand scale; would it be fanciful to see Cuba selling avocados as Israel did? But the obvious market for such expansion was the now closed North American one.

There were also difficulties with labour. Cuban workers often seemed to think that the revolution entitled them to work less, or at least to do so at their own pace.

The new state in industry, as in agriculture, ignored the surviving private sector and no effort was as yet made to organize within the State system the army of shoemakers, carpenters, small tobacco factories, garages, which probably exceeded 50,000 separate undertakings. The proprietors of these businesses were told by the government that there was no plan whatsoever for their capture by the State, but many were not reassured: they knew that governments break promises.[87]

The swift economic transformation of Cuba was, uniquely in the history of revolutions, brought about without a struggle. The State captured a series of concerns in prosperous working order. There was no problem of post-war reconstruction, as there had been in post-1945 Europe. Maybe peaceful transition actually hampered the success of socialism, since old ways and personnel had merely to be converted, not defeated.

[87] This did not happen till early 1968 in this instance.

The problems of organization and planning, combined with the co-ordination of town and country, led, in early 1961, to the formation of regional planning boards – *Juntas Unificadas de Coordinación Económica y Industrial* (the JUCEI). They marked the extinction of the revolution *por la libre* administered by optimistic ex-students. They were a praiseworthy attempt, inspired by Raúl Castro, to escape from excessive centralization. If they placed greater power in the hands of local bureaucrats, perhaps these would have a better chance of knowing what was happening than bureaucrats in Havana. These boards expressed the extent to which the old Communists (as they began to be known) expected to contribute to the new society. Thus in the JUCEI of Oriente, founded in March 1961 with Raúl Castro as its president, the secretary-general of the old Communist party of the province, Ladislao González Carvajal, appeared as the JUCEI secretary-general; and this identification of an established unofficial bureaucracy with a new official institution would be repeated throughout the island.[88] Of these Communists, only those who had chanced to be in Las Villas during Guevara's campaign there – such as Arnaldo Milián, secretary general of the Las Villas JUCEI – had done much in the fight against Batista.

Cuban Labour, the federation controlled by old Communists, had only one role to play in the development of the economy: to follow orders. In early 1960 Luis Simón, working in the State Electricity Company, had suggested to the minister, Martínez Sánchez, a new Labour charter; the latter had replied that 'the State imposes, it does not make contracts'.[89] Since then, the nationalization of the labour force had proceeded apace. In September 1960 the Ministry of Labour devised a 'crime against production', against persistent absentees – the only method of protest, now that strikes were unthinkable. During 1961 absenteeism would become a major problem for the revolution. A law in November 1960 enabled the Ministry of Labour to 'intervene' in any company where a labour dispute threatened production. In March 1961 new laws provided that workers should register with the ministry to qualify for a work permit, and gave the ministry authority to settle all labour disputes by means of a decree. Some degree of freedom of responsibility remained at a lower level: workers could elect advisory councils of their own which sometimes had limited local influence. But henceforth there were no disputes, only inarticulate hostility – particularly towards Lázaro Peña, the founder and now again secretary-general of the CTC(R). Nor was unemployment wiped out: if it

[88] Thus Ladislao's brother, José Luis, became secretary in Pinar del Río, Silvio Quintana in Havana, Leonides Calderio in Matanzas, Felipe Torres in Camagüey, and Arnaldo Milián in Las Villas.
[89] '*El estado impone, no conviena*' (Simón MSS, 299).

had decreased in the country (perhaps the average working year had increased from about 160 to 200 or 240 days,[90] it survived in the cities where there were perhaps 200,000 unemployed, excluding the under-employed who had increased because of the absence of tourists and North American goods to sell. Many hours were lost in military parades, meetings of all sorts and 'campaigns'.

As it was, economic breakdown was avoided by the challenge of invasion.

Note on statistics in Cuba 1959–61

During this time, the Cuban state took over very quickly much of the nation's means of production and services. Most trained Cuban statisticians, however, had gone into exile. The collection of statistics, therefore, in the first years of the Revolution was done in the most rudimentary way, despite the fact that in an economy which is to be planned, accuracy in this field is almost more important than anything else. In addition, many errors were made by officials who were both incompetent and anxious to please by exaggeration. The statistics of production from the (until 1963) large private agricultural sector were and, indeed, are still, very difficult to estimate. Finally, from 1960 onwards the Government itself was wont to regard statistics themselves as one more weapon in the fight against counter-revolution and 'imperialism'. Hence, with the best will in the world, it is impossible to regard the published figures for production between 1959 and 1961 as any more than 'indicative' (to use the graceful description of Professor Bettelheim). After 1961, other problems arise in respect of Cuban production figures, some of which are discussed in the Epilogue to this book. This whole matter has been explored in a masterly manner by Carmelo Mesa-Lago in his pamphlet, *Availability and Reliability of Statistics in Socialist Cuba*. Occasional Paper no. 1 (January 1970) of the Centre for Latin American studies at the University of Pittsburgh.

[90] Unemployment was in 1960–61 probably substantially higher than 1958 in industry, transport and building, lower in agriculture.

Cuba Socialista: II

1960 had been labelled as the 'year of agrarian reform', just as 1959 had been the year of 'liberation'. 1961 would be the year of 'education'. This meant not the expansion of education in general but a campaign against illiteracy. It was thought that there were nearly a million illiterates in Cuba, comprising half the rural population. Martí had said: 'To be literate is to be free.' This campaign, which (no doubt correctly from the point of view of strict economic priorities) had been given a low place in a list of necessities presented by Blas Roca at the Communist conference in August, represented the last fling (for the time being) of the romantic side of the revolution. Castro had promised at the U.N. that illiteracy would be stamped out within a year. Thousands of Cubans, whose faith in the revolution might otherwise have wavered, prepared in the spring of 1961 to throw themselves into a great campaign which would start in April. First, the illiterates would be found and named; by February 1961 412,000, by April 546,000.[1] In the towns volunteers who could read would teach those who could not. In the remote country districts teaching would be a full-time job. Who better for this task than secondary school children – by the nature of things, many of them middle class – who might, after all, learn from the experience of staying a few months in the poorer parts of the country? All secondary schools therefore would be closed after 15 April. Volunteers – and naturally the pressure to be a volunteer would be strong – would enrol as *brigadistas alfabetizadores* and, after instructions at Varadero beach, set out for the remote parts of their island, armed with a uniform, a hammock, a blanket, a paraffin lamp, a flag, a portrait of their patron, Conrado Benítez (a militiaman killed by the counter-revolution in the Sierra de Escambray) and two manuals: *¡ Venceremos!* and *¡ Alfabetizemos!*

The character of these manuals was scarcely objective: thus, exercise A of *¡ Alfabetizemos!* began: 'We are going to read *Organ-ización de Esta-dos Americ-anos*.' Illustrations showed happy labourers with their produce and children. *¡ Venceremos!* contained useful words and phrases such as 'Friends and Enemies'; 'The Revolution wins all battles'; and 'International Unity', as well as detailed instructions for the

[1] By August, when the campaign was well under way, 985,000 had been identified.

teacher. In the glossary at the end of *¡ Venceremos!* among the ten or so words or phrases beginning with B we hear of Bloqueo Económico: 'State of siege imposed by imperialism [which] . . . we have conquered thanks to the countries which trade with us.' Better no doubt a lively prejudice than a glum neutrality if one is going to learn to read fast. On the other hand, there was more rhetoric than sense in the incidental knowledge picked up during the illiteracy campaign.

Established now in Campamento Columbia, Batista's old military headquarters, Armando Hart, the Minister of Education, member of a Catholic but firmly revolutionary family – his father had recently become president of the Supreme Court – had also embarked on the reorganization of education. The Under-Secretary, Dulce María Escalona, a Communist, had been director of the Escuela Normal under Prío and Batista; she was a mathematician of intelligence, humanity and ability, who had been once interested in Dewey. The achievements of the revolution in education by 1961 were considerable: whereas, before 1959, over 40% of children between six and fourteen did not go to school, by 1961 probably all but 20% did. There were still however many who dropped out in the last two grades between eleven and fourteen. This achievement in primary education had been made possible by the increase of teachers in rural areas (about 5,000), in response to an appeal for volunteers. But enrolments had been faster and, partly due to the rise in population, the number of children per teacher was 37 in 1960–1, compared with 35 in 1956.[2] Most new teachers had been rather hastily trained at San Lorenzo in the Sierra Maestra. The old one-room primary school with several grades studying together naturally continued. The Camilo Cienfuegos City School in the Sierra was not yet ready for more than a handful of pupils. In addition, the formation of a children's revolutionary movement, socialist Boy Scouts and Guides, for children between seven and thirteen, the Unión de Rebeldes Pioneros,[3] based on the Russian youth movements of the same nature, headed by the 'youngest volunteer in the Sierra', Captain Joel Iglesias, gave the zealous something new to think about.[4] Most barracks had been turned into schools, but many schoolboys nevertheless seemed to be almost soldiers.

There was also some reorganization of secondary schools. Thus the old five-year *bachillerato* was abolished and replaced by courses designed specifically to increase the numbers of university students. University

[2] Seers, 114.

[3] Organized 10 May 1960. It merged with Juventud Socialista, the Communist Youth, October 1960.

[4] Iglesias, who was chief of the 10th police station, Havana, in January 1959, when aged hardly twenty, became a founder member of the Central Committee of the Cuban Communist Party in 1965.

entrance standards radically dropped. Most secondary schools remained in cities, while children who did not live there stayed in hostels, and many new boarding schools and technical colleges were established on nationalized estates or in luxury houses. Enrolment of pupils apparently increased by a third.

In the spring of 1961 all private schools had not been nationalized, though many had closed through lack of support. Some schools, such as Castro's old school, the Jesuit Belén, had been taken over. Foreign schools, such as the admirable Ruston's Academy of Havana, had also closed. Those private schools which did remain were unenthusiastic at the prospect of having to shut down on 15 April for the illiteracy campaign. They rightly realized that they had little chance of reopening. In March there had been riots, especially in Santiago and at Guantánamo, against the prospect of closing, but 15 April found all private schools, except a few nursery schools, ready to accept the inevitable.[5]

The universities, on the other hand, had not yet been formally reformed. But they were changing. Many teachers were in exile or had been removed. Heads of departments were all safe revolutionaries. In many departments foreign teachers had been recruited. In practice, the universities were Marxist-Leninist in bias by the spring of 1961. There had as yet been no radical revision of faculties to harness higher education to the needs of the economy (such as by abolition of arts courses) but the matter was already in the air. Students were far more strictly disciplined than ever before. Attendance at lectures was virtually compulsory, and those who did not wish to join the militia were in difficulties. 1,700 students had been sent in 1960 by the Ministry of Industries to study in the Soviet *bloc*. Teacher training colleges had been founded at Batista's old tubercular centre at Topes de Collantes in Escambray and in the Sierra Maestra at Minas del Frío. There were other educational projects, ranging from language courses to schools for sewing for peasants, schools for taxi drivers, shoemakers' classes, or rehabilitation classes for prostitutes.

The weakness of all these projects was the shortage of teachers. Many of those who taught were scarcely more than students or otherwise unqualified.

The revolution doubtless had increased the quantity of education; the quality of teaching had as probably declined. But access to education perhaps matters more than the wisdom of the educators. Even here, however, there had been much waste. Scholarship students were not all up to the work they were expected to do. Some did not work enough. There were still in 1961, as there were to be several years later, too many

[5] The education budget in 1961 was probably twice that of 1958, even taking into account the collapse of the value of the peso.

lawyers and artists and too few technicians. Standards in general were lowered at the university to meet the demands of new entrants.

The regime ran theatres, cinemas, television centres and musical activities, and sent the Havana state orchestra around the country. But the newspapers were now very dull. *Revolución* and *Hoy* differed only in that the latter presented a more solid and economically informed picture of events, under the editorship of Carlos Rafael Rodríguez, and the former, still under Carlos Franqui's editorship, with many of its staff secretly wretched at the way things were going, concentrated more on Castro's doings in the Sierra. The lively and heterodox literary supplement, *Lunes de Revolución*, had already excited the enmity of the orthodox communists. *Bohemia* under its new editors played the same role among magazines, while the army magazine, *Verde Olivo*, sold only a little less than *Bohemia* and remained the most dogmatically Communist.

ICAIC, the film institute of Cuba, directed by Castro's old Communist contemporary at the university, Alfredo Guevara, ran the cinemas, made new Cuban films, and dealt with the import of foreign films. Since the U.S. blockade in the autumn of 1960 and the shortage of foreign currency, few new U.S. or European films were shown, though some old ones were, of no special orthodoxy.[7] New films from the 'friendly countries' of the East also appeared, such as *A week in the Soviet Union* and *Life and Death of Ernst Thaelmann*.[8] The effort of two young filmmakers, Orlando Jiménez and Saba Cabrera, to shoot a specifically nonrealist film, *Pasado Meridiano* or *PM*, an impressionistic picture of an afternoon in January 1961, later brought up the whole question of commitment in the arts, leading in July to a famous discussion between Castro and selected intellectuals, afterwards to a cultural congress in August.[9] The ultimate consequence was the establishment of a Writer's Union directed by officials.

The revolutionary government also reconstructed the old National Council of Culture which eventually came under the direction of Edith García Buchaca, a veteran Communist, now *compañera* of Joaquín Ordoqui. This embarked on an ambitious sponsorship of painting and sculpture, concerts, music, dancing and theatre. These activities were dominated by insistence on a 'revolutionary conscience'. This did not necessarily mean a lowering of standards, since the best theatre company, Studio Theatre, run by Vicente Revueltas and his sister, was

---

[7] *The Sun also Rises, The Great Dictator*, etc. etc.

[8] The German Communist leader who died in Buchenwald.

[9] The film was not publicly shown; one reason was that it gave a free and easy impression of life in Havana at a time when the whole city was supposed to be alert and expecting an invasion. The only reviewer to praise it, Néstor Almendros, was sacked from his job on *Bohemia*. For a description, see Nicholas Wollaston, *Red Rumba*, 220.

already, even before 1959, Marxist in outlook; this flourished in 1960 and 1961, bringing Brecht and other European playwrights to the Cuban theatre for the first time with great success.

Publishing houses were now under the government, even though there had been none of any substance before. The difference no doubt was that in 1959 it would have been possible to publish, at one's own expense, a book attacking the regime in Cuba, whereas in 1961 it would not. The Imprenta Nacional directed by Alejo Carpentier had embarked on a vast expansion, mainly comprising speeches by Castro, Lenin, Marx, and Blas Roca's *Fundamentals of Socialism in Cuba*, but also more digestible wares, such as Jenks's *Our Cuban Colony*, along with Ramiro Guerra's *Azúcar y Población*, Tolstoy, *Don Quixote* and Voltaire. The Council of Culture published García Lorca and Cirilo Villaverde in large numbers. There was no purge of libraries: Orwell was still to be found in the National Library, though a new imprint of *Dr Zhivago* from Buenos Aires was apparently seized in early 1961 as counter-revolutionary literature.[10] Foreign newspapers and journals were by this time no longer sold and literature criticizing the regime or the system would usually not be displayed in bookshops. Much depended on who made the decisions: thus the director of the National Library, María Teresa Freyre de Andrade, an ex-Ortodoxo, and in the 1930s a member of the Jóvenes Revolucionarios Cubanos (in the 1950s she had taken refuge in the Mexican Embassy to avoid persecution), was a woman of intelligence and humanity.

Both television and radio continued to serve as a perpetual means of projection for the government. Even when there was no public occasion to celebrate, a record of one of Castro's speeches could be heard at one o'clock every day on the radio. Both mediums sounded, with their syncopation, as if they were revolutionary parodies of the U.S. system: '*Aquí Radio Progreso – la On-da de la Alegría*.'[11] The techniques of Madison Avenue (and the operators had themselves in some cases worked in New York or at least for New York companies) sold the revolution, the illiteracy campaign, and the struggle against the blockade. In the streets the revolutionary songs still, almost continuously, blared from gramophones, and, above all the *Hymn of the 26 July*, still jingled to their seaside rhythm. One of the best known voices of the revolution, however, Pardo Llada, the chief of the radio and television corporation FIEL, nicknamed the 'Minister of Hate', defected to Mexico late in March, screaming 'betrayal' in the same voice as he had until then screamed 'imperialism'.

[10] Fritz Allemann, *Der Monat*, April 1961. See discussion in Draper. The author saw an isolated copy of *Dr Zhivago* in a bookshop in Obispo Street in mid-1961.
[11] The Wave of Happiness.

Whether or not this government could be effectively labelled Communist, its achievements guaranteed it, even without the compelling oratory of Castro, the support of the vast majority of Cubans. The militant and conformist side of the regime, permanently on a war footing, troubled surprisingly few. The insistent intrusion of government into private lives, the call for volunteers for the militia, afterwards for the illiteracy campaign, a happy marching throng on the way to 'Unity', though intolerable to the *bourgeoisie*, caused at least a break from the unbelievable tedium which had marked many Cubans' lives in the past. Though Batista and the Auténticos had used propaganda, the Cubans had never experienced the massive doses of national propaganda that had been the lot of European nations during the World Wars. The majority, too, believed that for the first time the government, if intolerant, was at least not corrupt. It is tempting no doubt to dismiss this as an achievement comparable merely to Mussolini's in making Italian trains punctual.[12] But the break from corrupt officials, corrupt judiciary, corrupt politicians, corrupt unionists and corrupt men of business was, in the minds of the majority, a stark, extraordinary, maybe baffling but wonderful contrast. The sleazy world of prostitution, police protection rackets and clip joints had also almost vanished, and only prostitutes wholly regretted the disappearance of Uncle Sam. Gambling still continued, and sometimes on a grotesque scale: opponents of the revolution, many with passages booked to the U.S., knowing they could not take their money out of the country, went nightly into the still glittering and new casinos at the Havana Hilton (Habana Libre), the Riviera, the Nacional or the Capri hotels, sometimes placing counters on every square of a roulette board; in the background, behind the croupier's head, a huge notice proclaimed that 'To Save is to Make the Revolution'. Another, above the cashier, announced 'Lumumba will live for ever in the hearts of all free peoples'!

The anomaly of such gambling in a puritanical revolution was explained by the reluctance to increase unemployment by dismissing the croupiers. But it also served to keep some possible counter-revolutionaries from other temptations. These great hotels of Havana, built only two or three years previously, with their air-conditioning beginning to falter, the service and the food in decline, seemed like splendid ruins of a past civilization amid a new discordant one as yet unclearly defined. The Habana Libre presented the greatest contrast, since with its paintings by Wilfredo Lam, its ballroom, swimming pool and tinkling music, its several casinos, it had become the main international conference centre, the hotel for delegations from friendly socialist nations, for sym-

---

[12] As M. Leo Sauvage did, in an article in *The New Leader*, 8 November 1965, which criticized a review by the author in the *New York Times*.

pathetic Communists from the western hemisphere and fellow travellers from Europe. A bookstall in the foyer sold the latest revolutionary literature and the works of Marx and Martí. Through its revolving doors during 1961 would come delegation after delegation, revolutionary leaders of all generations, from all countries, from Ludwig Renn to General Lister, Francisco Juliao from Brazil, and the Leftist Perónist Cooke from Argentina, not to speak of journalists, cartoonists, spies, militiamen and militia girls, black, white, mulatto, in olive green uniforms, rifles at the trail, cigars in their mouths, as ready for a murderous attack as for the cha-cha-cha.

The majority of Cubans admittedly did not visit the Habana Libre, though from time to time whole floors of this and other palaces were given over to country people for courses in sewing or domestic hygiene. There would have been no difficulty in anyone going there if they had wished. Roof-top bars were now for the first time open to Negroes. This sense of social freedom was a further reason why, as all observers agreed, the majority backed the government, or rather were fascinated, even mesmerized by it. Most Cubans felt at least free from their landlord and the prejudices of the old master class. Social and national freedom went together. Cuban nationalism had been so aroused by Castro's speeches and the events of the last two years that the satisfaction at having shaken off the yoke of the U.S. went deep, among non-Communists as well as Communists. The government told the people so often that for the first time they could truly say 'This is my own, my native land' that, whether or not they required propaganda to make them think so, they believed it. Such reflections, on the other hand, were probably not shared by the old organized working class in the cities, whose standard of living dropped with the coming of the revolution.[13]

Much depended on Castro. His faults were evident: verbosity, carelessness of human life, xenophobia, egotism, a reluctance to delegate authority. But so too were his positive qualities: his energy, his audacity, his obsession to know what was going on, to see for himself the reality of how reforms were enacted. No one could accuse him, as Fanon in *Les damnés de la terre* did so many leaders of new states, of retiring to a palace and never visiting the country. On the contrary, Castro seemed never to be in the capital, always travelling by helicopter or jeep or Oldsmobile, always looking at some new project, always speaking, encouraging, threatening, denouncing, never indifferent. Simple and

---

[13] As admitted by Guevara: 'It is not a secret to anyone that our friends in petrol, for example, or of the telephone and electric companies, have not been directly benefited economically by the Revolution.' (*Revolución*, 29 November 1961, 3). For contrasting views of travellers to Cuba in the winter of 1960–61, see Warren Miller, *The Lost Plantation*, London 1961 (published in New York as *Ninety Miles from Home*), a sympathetic diary of a North American; and Nicholas Wollaston's *Red Rumba*, London 1962, 13–91, and 209–31.

sophisticated people alike still believed in him as their guide. How could he respond other than by dazzling them with his qualities? Castro had convinced his countrymen that he was a political genius and was recognized as such throughout the world. He had great talents. He was a superb orator. He was a dangerous enemy. Cubans and Latin Americans had been taught to respect force for too long under unjust governments of a different kidney for them to refuse admiration to a man of force of the Left.

Nationalism of course does not exist in the void but customarily springs from over-close experience of another nation which even xeno-phobia cannot quite shake off. To hear the literacy campaign pressed with jingles which were devised by advertising agents was to realize that North American habits had stretched far into the mind of the nation. In pursuing North America with such special venom, Cuba was now pursuing part of herself, as the continued counter-revolutionary activi-ties during the winter of 1960-1 suggested all too bluntly.

Communism, like Catholicism, owes its strength where it exists to a flexible adaptation to national character. Just as East Germany under Ulbricht has a Prussian priggishness, so Cuba under Castro retained a gaiety and even a superficiality which helped to make the revolution acceptable. Songs and jingles swept the island as much as ever, though now busloads of schoolgirls might be heard singing:

> *Somos Socialistas,*
> *Marxistas, Leninistas,*
> *Mañana seremos*
> *Tremendos Comunistas.*[14]

Even the shouts mechanically called by obedient throngs at mass meetings had sometimes a childish note:

> Pim – Pan – Pum
> Mao – Tse – tung.

A long speech by Castro might be interspersed by cheering, shouting, clapping and dancing, which would afford both the crowd and Castro a chance of rest though there would also be the more alarming cries of *Paredón, Paredón* (that is, to the execution) *Paredón* to the imperialists and the priests, though even this might turn into a bloodthirsty rumba

---

[14] I may have antedated this jingle somewhat; I heard it for the first time in July 1961. Another version runs:

> *Somos socialistas*
> *lo dijo el caballo*
> *y al que no le guste*
> *que lo pa ta un rayo.*

Castro figures in both revolutionary and counter-revolutionary myth as *caballo* (the horse).

(*Para los Curas, Paredón*). (Guevara once boasted that the Cuban Revolution was Revolution with Pachanga; but it also spelled execution, with the rumba.) Partly these effects were contrived, but they were really more spontaneous. Even to visitors who found the huge portraits of Marx and Castro unappealing, along with the posters of strong and sober workers with shovels poised, the strident cries of exhortation to unity, to patriotism, to work, Castro's appeals to the Cubans to become Spartans[15] and above all the ubiquitous guns, Cuba retained in 1961 some of its extraordinary charm, though most foreigners were as much excited by its paradoxes as by its achievements.

A major cause for anxiety was the law. Until the winter of 1960–1 the Supreme Court had remained much as it had been since the fall of Batista. The judges observed with dismay the increasing number of arbitrary arrests, the long sentences, and the political trials to which all opponents of the regime were subject, but this was not the concern of the ordinary judiciary; the revolutionary tribunals were outside their jurisdiction, just as the Urgency Courts first set up by Machado and used latterly by Batista to try political offenders fast, had also been.[16] Still, many of the judges were out of sympathy with the revolution. On 17 November 1960 the president of the Supreme Court, Emilio Menéndez, and his colleague Judge Morell Romero suddenly fled to the Argentinian Embassy. Their colleagues of the Court named them traitors, though nine of these dissented: within the week, these nine were themselves in exile. Menéndez was succeeded by Judge Enrique Hart, father of the Education minister and, as everyone thought, a good democrat and Catholic. But in December came a further purge of the court, now reduced to fifteen members. A government spokesman argued that the old Supreme Court included too many members pledged to un-revolutionary philosophies: in several cases involving the valuation of confiscated property, the court had even ruled in favour of plaintiffs. Castro explained that there was no need to have so many judges in Cuba, since litigation was no longer necessary. Henceforward, as this declaration might suggest, the revolution was a factor in all judicial procedure. It was not that, in the majority of criminal cases, guilt or innocence was prejudged but that, if guilt were decided, the services to the revolution of the person accused would exert a decisive influence over the sentence. Further, statements of the character and career of the accused were now

[15] '*Nosotros tenemos que ser un pueblo espartano . . . un pueblo luchador.*' (Speech to Milicias, *Obra Revolucionaria*, 20 January 1961, 16.)

[16] The thirty-two judges of the Supreme Court, which had been purged in January 1959, had, normally, life tenure and presided over five separate chambers. These dealt with civil and criminal appeals, administration and disputes over judicial and municipal appointments. The Court also dealt with such questions as the constitutionality or removal of local government officials, and in those and certain other circumstances sat all together.

made before the verdict. This politicization of law was doubtless inevitable in the unfolding violent revolutionary situation. The old legal system before whose tangles Generals Wood and Crowder had confessed themselves baffled, at long last snapped, like an old and rotten tree, the ancient rooks' nests still visible when it reached the ground.

There was also war in Cuba in 1960–1. All through the winter there had been small infiltrations, by the CIA and the exiles, rumours of invasion, emergencies, conspiracies and acts of violence. Militiamen had often to be kept from work, thereby adding to economic difficulties. Exile sources believed that 1,330 people had been shot by the government by October 1960, and by March more. The struggle in the Escambray between the counter-revolution and the government persisted all winter, but the latter gradually won by wearing down the *guerrilleros*, who lacked food and supplies and were not effectively sustained by the U.S. from the air. Many were shot, while among the dead on Castro's side was his personal physician, Luis Fajardo. The fighting continued till the spring, though more and more sporadically. Guevara thought that there were still 200 in arms in the Escambray in early 1961.[17] Several expeditions from Miami on the Cuban coast were broken up as soon as they arrived. The most serious failure was the escape of ex-captain Jorge Sotús, of the MRR and leader of Castro's first reinforcement in the Sierra; he escaped from the Isle of Pines in December 1960 by reaching a telephone in the prison, impersonating a superior officer in Havana and ordering his own release.[18] There was an attempt on Castro's life outside the Italian Embassy the same month, and occasionally militiamen were mysteriously murdered, one hanging on a tree, with the notice: 'Take this one down, we need the tree for others.'

In the winter of 1960, Rogelio González Corzo of the MRR directed a powerful campaign of sabotage and terrorism in Havana; many bombs were laid, letter boxes blown up, water mains destroyed, sugar and tobacco plantations set aflame. Mysterious posters assured Castro that his days were numbered. Ray's MRP also claimed responsibility for some of these acts, though Ray himself left secretly for Miami (MRP was thereafter directed in Cuba by Antonio Viciana, an accountant). A new companion, the ex-secretary-general of labour, David Salvador, founder of the 30 de Noviembre Movimiento was caught with Joaquín Agramonte as they tried to sail out of the River Jaimanitas near Havana in a yacht; Salvador was sent off to La Cabaña.[19] A bomb exploded on

[17] Ricardo Rojo, *Che Guevara*, Paris 1968, 91.
[18] He was, however, later killed by accident when embarking in Miami on a clandestine journey.
[19] He had $13,000 with him and he was at first accused of being in possession of foreign currency and of trying illegally to leave the country. See Rodríguez Quesada, 19–20. He was not tried till August 1962 when he was sentenced to thirty years.

6 December in the church of Our Lady of Charity, with the note '*Viva Khrushchev* – Down with priests' – probably a fraud. Sixteen people were later dispatched to gaol for periods of up to thirteen years. Seventeen students of *Juventud Católica* were arrested for placing a bomb at the University of Havana. Farm machinery was destroyed. The Havana–Santiago express was derailed near Santa Clara. Bands of rebels under Clodomiro Miranda and Benito Campa, both ex-combatants against Batista, roamed Pinar del Río and Matanzas. There was occasional hi-jacking of aeroplanes, bomb attacks on crowds, while big fires were lit, at the former Esso refinery in March and at the Hershey sugar mill, and the big Havana store of El Ecanto was destroyed in April.

One aim of the MRR and MRP was to stimulate government repression in the manner undertaken two years before by Batista. In this they were not successful. The consequence was more to drive the population apart into two increasingly hostile groups – the minority against the regime, the majority still for it. Among liberal intellectuals who had supported the regime in the beginning, a terrible crisis of conscience arose: should they not join the underground? Should they return to the life of sabotage and conspiracy. To try and dissuade them, there was a continuous parade of executions, including, in March, that of the North American Major Morgan and his old companion Major Carreras, who had tried to prevent Guevara from reaching the Sierra Escambray in 1958. On 18 March 1961 many of the most prominent leaders of the underground, including González Corso, were betrayed, arrested and later shot.[20] Among these were Sorí Marín and Rafael Díaz Hanscom who had tried to unite all the anti-Castro forces in Cuba.

Protests still admittedly occurred from within the regime, though the only open one was that emanating from the old thorn in the flesh of Batista, the Electrical Workers' Union, whose leader, Amaury Fraginals, had remained untouched by the purges. On 9 December a number of Cuban Electric employees[21] gathered in their headquarters at the Prado and marched to the Presidential Palace, shouting '*Cuba Sí, Rusia No*'. Fraginals was finally admitted to see Dorticós. He made his complaint. But four days later he went into hiding, and was immediately

[20] Lazo, 289.

[21] U.P. said 2,000; the Cuban Press, 200. Fraginals, aged 31, began to work for Cuban Electric in 1947. In 1956 he joined the 26 July Movement in Havana and worked for the action and sabotage group under Aldo Vera. He was in gaol from November 1957 until January 1959. He then was elected provisional secretary-general of his union, and confirmed in this position in May (Interview, *El Mundo*, Miami, 8 April 1961). Fraginals said: 'On 12 December we received an emissary who brought us an ultimatum: either we make declarations against the men who had taken part in the demonstrations or we would be put before the *paredón* . . . There was only one traitor, Abrahantes. The rest fled to different embassies and some of us stayed hidden.'

accused by Castro of organizing terrorism. The Electrical Workers' Union then expelled Fraginals dishonourably.[22] What seems more curious than these acts of defiance were acts of submission: how was it possible that an old Auténtico, anti-Communist trade union leader like Conrado Bécquer, senator even under Batista and collaborator of Mujal should be permitted to remain as secretary-general of the all important FNTA (sugar workers' union), or should permit himself to do so? Such anomalies can only be explained by the cynical opportunism built into the Cuban union system for so long: Bécquer moved from treasurer of the FNTA before 1959 to secretary-general afterwards.

The Church remained a privileged centre of opposition, since Castro and the Communists had decided to avoid meeting it head on. In August 1960 Blas Roca, the Communist secretary-general, had explained that, though the Church's influence was based on an existing division of classes, there were many Catholic workers who understood the desirability of social change. But in October, Mgr Boza Masvidal had attacked the government for 'passing the just limits of aid and vigilance' and of reaching for 'absolute control', making the individual into a mere piece of state machinery. Blas Roca in *Hoy* compared the bishop's article with the 'imperialistic' propaganda emanating from Swan Island. A priest who favoured the revolution, Father Germán Lence, denounced the hierarchy. In November a third pastoral by Mgr Pérez Serantes praised the U.S. for its stand against Communism, though added that it took an ideology to beat an ideology such as Communism; the real battle was between Rome and Moscow, not Washington and Moscow. The new United Youth Movement tried to prevent the reading of the pastoral in the cathedral of Santiago by singing revolutionary songs. On 4 December the hierarchy issued a final joint pastoral letter enjoining Castro to reject Communism, adding 'the Lord will illumine you'. Castro replied saying that the government did not have to answer the clergy, and committed himself to the view that to 'be anti-Communist is to be counter-revolutionary', explaining it was also 'counter-revolutionary to be anti-Catholic, anti-Protestant or anti-anything which divides Cubans'.[23] But there was little more protest. The churches remained open, if scarcely full, and Castro occasionally gave speeches criticizing, though not attacking, the Church.[24] The Church magazine *La Quincena* (the last independent paper) ceased. (The smaller independent papers such as *Información* and *El Crisol*, which had not suffered the political onslaught met by the *Diario de la Marina* and

[22] Fraginals was later captured but escaped to the U.S.

[23] *Revolución*, 17 December 1960.

[24] *Cf.* speech of 6 March 1961, where he alluded to the Indian Chief Hatuey's reluctance (in 1510) to go to the same heaven as the Spaniards.

Prensa Libre, had been forced out of circulation by the collapse of advertising, as well as by the absence of any government subsidy.)

In April 1960, just after Eisenhower had given his first blessing to the CIA's adventures, a reasonably fair poll – the last one up till this time – found that most Cuban town dwellers had believed themselves better off than in the past and that three-quarters of them thought that they would be even better off in another five years. Nearly half those living in towns were fanatically in favour of the regime, thinking Castro had 'the same ideas as Jesus Christ', and were longing 'to kiss the beard of Fidel Castro'. (Of these, half had had either no education or had not gone further than elementary school, while nearly half were in their twenties.) When asked about their desires, three-fifths of them said that they coveted above all an improved standard of living, one-third wanted jobs for all, one-third merely 'the success of the Revolution' as such. A quarter hoped for national unity and no more hatred. Few people apparently longed for a democratic government, measured by electoral processes – much fewer than those who demanded an honest government. Few feared Communism. When asked the question: 'What really matters in your own life, what are your wishes and hopes for the future, what would your life look like if you are to be happy?', somewhat over half[25] replied that they wanted good or improved health either for themselves or their family; when asked what were their worst personal fears, just under half[26] said ill-health. Public fears almost all concentrated on fear of a return to past conditions, of tyranny, police crime or oppression, violence, chaos.[27] These reactions were from town-dwellers, who probably by now numbered over 60% of the population; and no doubt the government of the revolution was even more popular in the countryside.

The worst side of the regime was, however, already its prisons. By this time there may have been 10,000 political prisoners in Cuba. Some had had something of a trial, some had not. Treatment by guards, food, sanitary arrangements, were all bad. There were far more prisoners now than Batista ever had and conditions were very bad. Some were held in old fortresses such as La Cabaña, or the Príncipe, and all the prisons were overcrowded. The revolutionary government fell back in this matter upon traditional Cuban authoritarian reactions. Many accounts of life in the prisons of Cuba under Castro were no doubt sensationalist, whilst other writers were driven to exaggerate. Still, the

[25] 52%.
[26] 49%.
[27] This derives from a public opinion survey conducted by Lloyd Free, Director of the Institute for International Social Research at Princeton, New Jersey, making use of a private Cuban research organization which was actually anti-government.

evidence suggests that the new regime was hardly an improvement on that of Batista in the matter of the treatment of enemies. The interrogation rooms of the G.2 might be more sophisticated than the torture chambers of Batista's SIM, but they were scarcely less vile.

The unhappiness, already the despair, of the Cuban middle or upper classes, was by this time undeniable, even supposing that they were not themselves in prison or conspiring, or closely related to those who were. Most of those who had anything to lose had by now lost their old confidence that society, being run by themselves, was on their side, however rotten it might be. All the predictable grooves of old Cuban behaviour were wearing down. Of course, one reason why the revolution was winning was that these grooves were in Cuba more superficially cut than elsewhere. Still, even under Batista, there had always been an established order of things of a certain kind, visits to clubs and hotels, cocktails and banquets, speculations and celebrations, journeys to the U.S.; now all those things, though not yet impossible, were difficult. Over most middle-class people brooded the question whether they should leave Cuba for the U.S., abandoning house, wealth, possessions, maybe for ever, or remain and become drawn into either the politics of counter-revolution or at least the contemplation of it. Long used to the acceptance of authority because they or their friends controlled it, it was impossible to accept that sanction when represented by a revolutionary group of wild, passionate, untidy, young, gun-happy soldiers.

For the majority, for nearly all the country-dwellers and for most of those who lived in towns, the reverse was true. For the first time they knew that authority was on their side, that justice could not be bought by their landlord or their employer; already they knew that, though unemployment might continue and that their lot might still be otherwise hard, the class which had bullied and patronized them was seriously menaced. Castro's tourist board, INIT, had taken over hotels, clubs, and, most important, beaches, and made them available to the general public. The Varadero International Hotel now cost $15 a day instead of $50, the marvellous sands and translucent blue water at the Havana Biltmore Yacht Club was open to all at 50 cents. Along miles of coast public bathing places were established. All this was done at great cost and within an arbitrary time fixed by Castro. The revolution had already increased opportunities for women and for the black or mulatto minority. The organizations of Cuban women played an essential part in co-ordinating mass support for the regime, even mass activity. (The illiteracy campaign of 1961 would be about half run by women or girls, and the cotton crop of 1962 harvested by women.)

Among the middle class, attitudes to the revolution were based chiefly on age: the young were mostly in favour, the old mostly against.

By now most of the well-known liberals had left the regime, and some had even left the country. But these good men were not willing to collaborate with disgruntled *rentiers* either in thought or in action. Curiously, almost for the first time in Cuban history, the only real contact between classes, between the old Cuba sliding away and the new one struggling to be born, was the Church, still somewhat undecided, though the hierarchy and the majority of priests and of leading laymen were now hostile to the government. But while two years before no detectable class interpretation could have been put upon the battle against Batista, there was now a class struggle in full spate in which both sides showed themselves intolerant.

The regime remained government by oratory. Castro's speeches and the size of his audiences were something new to the Americas, if not perhaps to Europe: Sartre wrote that 'this pedagogic eloquence, a little heavy sometimes, at other times vivid, gives the French listener the barely perceptible impression of listening to Péguy speak'.[28] Others recalled Mussolini. Castro himself, however, later argued:

> There is a great difference between our multitudes and the Fascist mobs . . . Our multitudes are not fanatical. Rather, very firmly-based convictions have been created on the basis of persuasion, of analysis, of reasoning. The Fascists brought together multitudes who seemed content. [But] their organisation and mobilisation of the masses was done by typically military means. They never had the character of spontaneity and, much less, the enthusiasm and the magnitude that our public meetings have . . . we offer facilities so that they can be brought to the meeting but absolutely nobody is required to come.[29]

By the time this remark was made – 1964 – there were certainly some classes of the population – the secondary school children for instance who were indeed required to go. But in 1960–1 enthusiasm was clearly real.

The contradictions and contrasts in Cuba in April 1961 were not well known in the U.S., despite the lavish sums spent on intelligence. Cuba was a country with just over a third of its agriculture and about a half of its industry in state hands, with political power concentrated in one man and his adherents. Castro's new allies, the Communists, and their powerful friends across the Atlantic had definite but ambiguous influence. Such was the challenge presented to Kennedy's U.S., a nation which, like Cuba, also fretted at mistakes of the previous ten years, but whose solid political structure could hardly be more different. Usually, the more men differ, the less they fight. In this instance, the two societies

[28] Sartre, *Sartre on Cuba*, 34.
[29] Lockwood, 179.

seemed incapable of living together. An invasion had indeed been mounted by one against the other which in its turn had done what it could to injure its rival's interests elsewhere in the Americas. They seemed about to fight for the simplest of reasons: they were enemies. It is therefore curious to recall not only that the U.S. base at Guantánamo Bay continued to employ daily some 2,000 Cubans from the city of the same name but that every day, even in April 1961, two aeroplanes filled with exiles, flew out of Havana to Miami in very large numbers considering that the air fares had to be paid for abroad. Perhaps 100,000 people had already left Cuba by the end of March 1961, mostly to the U.S. but also to Spain, Mexico and the rest of South America.[30] It remained indeed possible to telephone Miami from Havana and *vice versa*, and many calls were made, some concealing messages of espionage, most of affection; the international struggle between the U.S. and Cuba, and at its back that between the U.S. and Russia, was thus, at a personal level, simply a Cuban civil war, with the tragedy and inconvenience that faction customarily causes.

[30] The International Rescue Committee of New York estimated at the end of 1960 that as many as 30% were labourers and another 30% employees of one sort or another (Quoted Goldenberg, 210).

Battle of Cochinos Bay

'During the early hours of 15 [April 1961],' Castro later recalled,[1] 'because of certain news received from the province of Oriente we did not sleep. All the signs from one moment to another were that the invasion was going to take place. We were on guard.' He thought that the invasion would be in Oriente. Twelve battalions and batteries were sent to reinforce that coastline, though the most likely landing places – those which gave access to mountains – were already defended as well as possible. Castro had always assumed that the invasion would begin with an attack on his air force and, unlike Nasser in 1956 or 1967, he had dispersed his few planes, camouflaged them and surrounded them with batteries. For Cuba had then only a very small air force – fifteen B.26s, three T.33s, and six Sea Furies; the promised Russian MiGs had not yet arrived. These aircraft were separated one by one, while out-of-service aeroplanes were grouped together as bait to fool the attackers. Castro then went to military headquarters and ordered a general alert.

At 6 a.m. two B.26s with Cuban markings flew over the headquarters, dropping bombs. Six other B.26s bombed three other Cuban airfields (Santiago, San Antonio de los Baños, and Baracoa). The B.26s were, of course, U.S. aeroplanes, painted by the CIA, and flown from Nicaragua by exile pilots under the orders of Captain Villafaña who, a year previously, had still been military attaché in Mexico representing the government whose airfields he was now bombarding. At this time, the invasion fleet from Nicaragua had been twelve hours at sea and had another forty hours to go before it could reach Cuba itself. The rumour of landings in Oriente was a deliberately contrived feint by the U.S. navy, save that, near Guantánamo, a force of 168 Cuban exiles under Captain Nino Díaz was intended to land, though it failed to do so.[2]

The bombing caused much public panic in Havana and in the other cities. Apart from minor disturbances in the 1930s, Cuba like the

---

[1] In speech of 23 April.

[2] B.26s were chosen because, though they were old, slow Second World War survivals, they were possessed by many countries. The CIA thought that this would prevent identification with the U.S. (Sorensen, 301). Flying time between Nicaragua and Cuba meant that these machines on each flight could only have an hour at most over Cuba.

U.S. itself, had never previously been under the attention of this sophisticated warfare. The panic was natural, coming on top of months of rumours (*bolas*). But the military damage done was slight. There were no military aircraft at Havana. None of those was much damaged, though some decoys on the ground were blown up. At San Antonio de los Baños, one combat plane was destroyed; at Santiago, two. A few other aircraft were damaged. The other combat aircraft took to the air. The rebel aircraft made several sweeps over their targets, machine-gunning after they had dropped their bombs, before giving up when the anti-aircraft fire became too heavy. None of the attacking aeroplanes were shot down. On the ground seven people were killed, forty-four wounded, including two women.

Castro immediately struck against the underground. The police, led by Ameijeiras, ironically a strong anti-Communist though a devoted adherent of Castro, rounded up, during 15 April, all persons remotely suspected of hostility to the government, guilty or innocent, saboteurs and priests, men and women. The Blanquita Theatre, the moat of La Cabaña, the Príncipe Castle and the baseball park in Matanzas were all filled with detainees. The unsuccessful bombing raid gave Castro the occasion to smash all chances that the opposition underground might have to assist in the invasion. This did not matter to the CIA, who had discounted the importance of the underground and who did not even trouble to communicate effectively with their own paid agents.[3] During the day, exhortations were broadcast. Guevara ironically proclaimed: 'Our great master who teaches us most has always been imperialism. Every time that our soul flags, or that we think of resting, imperialism shows us, as today, that in a Revolution one can never rest.'[4]

Meantime, in Miami, a B.26 flown by Captain Mario Zúñiga had landed direct from Nicaragua; his aeroplane had been carefully dotted with bullet-holes to give the illusion of combat. He released the untruth that, being then a member of Castro's air force, he had decided to rebel, had bombed some Cuban airfields, and had flown to safety. His story was confused by the unplanned earlier arrival at Key West of a B.26 which had taken part in the bombing and which had made for Miami, not Nicaragua, after developing engine trouble. The story was further weakened by Zúñiga's refusal to give his real name; had his story been true, the Cuban government would presumably have

---

[3] Bissell told me: 'Our operations were *not* hampered by the arrest of so many people in Havana after the raids . . . we did not expect the underground to play a large part.' (Interview, January 1963.) Nevertheless, *cf.* the contradictory remark of Lyman Kirkpatrick, *The Real CIA*, 197, who says that these detentions were 'the first catastrophic blow to the . . . operation.'

[4] *Playa Girón*, I, 19.

quickly discovered the identity of the defector. But he was photographed. His wife in Miami recognized him and naturally wanted to get in touch, for she had not seen him since he had left, months ago, for Guatemala. Some sophisticated journalists also noticed that while Cuba's B.26s were known to have plexiglass noses, the Miami ones had opaque ones.[5] It seemed in addition curious that Dr Miró Cardona and the Cuban Revolutionary Council should be able to talk excitedly in the press in New York as if they knew all about what was going on: 'The Council has been in contact with and has encouraged these brave pilots,' said Miró, after asking reporters to gaze 'into these revolutionary eyes that have known little sleep at night'. Alas, poor Miró could not even in the teeth of reaction resist claiming that he was a revolutionary. Finally, the Cuban government announced that machine-gun ammunition used over Havana was made in the U.S.

The Cuban government were also internationally active. The diplomatic corps in Havana was summoned to the Foreign Ministry and shown some evidence of the foreign origins of the attack. The Foreign Minister, Roa, successfully raised the question of aggression at the U.N. Adlai Stevenson repeated the undertakings of Kennedy that the U.S. would not participate in action against Cuba and said that the pilots who arrived in Miami must be Cuban and that their aeroplanes were Cuban; he showed a photograph of these aeroplanes with the Cuban star upon them. The Guatemalan representative untruthfully denied that Cubans had been trained in his country. Stevenson's second-in-command, Harlan Cleveland,[6] had been assured by the CIA that the pilots who arrived in Miami were genuine defectors. Apparently, as it happened, Secretary of State Rusk confused the men of Miami with two genuine defectors, Roberto and Guillermo Verdaguer, air force officers who had arrived in Florida the previous day.[7] In fact, however, it was becoming clear that the 'cover story' would not hold either in the U.N. or in the eyes of an interested U.S. public opinion. Stevenson was later furious when he discovered that he had been lured into deceiving the world. It is odd that he did not resign.

At the same time, on board the attacking ships, the brigade was briefed by its officers. The officers were told by their CIA trainers that the bombing missions had been successful and that Castro's air force had been virtually destroyed.[8] That night the decoy mission under Nino

---

[5] Szulc and Meyer, 121.

[6] James Harlan Cleveland. Rhodes scholar and, when working on the Marshall Plan, inventor of the phrase 'Revolution rising expectations'.

[7] Schlesinger, 246. It is unclear from his excellent account whether the CIA deliberately lied to other sections of the government or whether the Intelligence Branch was itself ignorant.

[8] San Román to Johnson, in Haynes Johnson, 94.

Díaz off Oriente again failed to land, despite the direction of a CIA man on board.[9] The invaders sailed on oblivious that they would now land in very different circumstances to those which they had earlier contemplated.

It had been intended by the CIA that two further air strikes of B.26s would finish off the work done by the first, to coincide with the landings (to be at dawn on 17 April). They were to fly to an airstrip on the beach which would, it was hoped, then be occupied.[10] But Kennedy cancelled these further air attacks. The CIA directors, Bissell and General Cabell, were 'deeply disturbed', though not so much so that they insisted on seeing the president personally.[11] They merely gave the orders to their underlings in Nicaragua. Meantime, Kennedy had previously (at noon on Sunday, 16 April), authorized the expedition to continue to the beaches.

In Havana Castro addressed a large crowd at the funeral of the seven victims of those killed by the air attack the previous day. He recalled the incident of the *Coubre*, whose destruction he again attributed to the U.S. He alluded to the air attacks on canefields by aeroplanes based in the U.S.; and to Pearl Harbor, and how outraged the U.S. had been. He ironically read out dispatches by the United Press which had given the orthodox U.S. version of events. He ridiculed Kennedy and Stevenson. Cries of *Fuera*, Assassins, Cowards, *Patria o Muerte, Paredón*, interrupted the oration, as well as the jingles:

Pa'lante y Pa'lante	Forwards, forwards
Y al que no le guste	Let him who doesn't like it
Que tome purgante!	take a strong dose!
and *Fidel! Jrushchov!*	Fidel and Khrushchev
Estamos con los Dos![12]	We are with you both!

The first of these was shouted when Castro for the first time referred to the Cuban revolution as Socialist.

> Comrades, workers and peasants,
> This is the Socialist and Democratic Revolution of the humble, with the humble, for the humble ... The attack of yesterday was the prelude to aggression by the mercenaries. All units must now go to their battalions ... Let us form battalions and dispose

[9] Evidence of Antonio Campiña.

[10] General Cabell and Bissell to Mario Lazo (*Dagger in the Heart*, 256) confirmed that three air strikes were planned, not two as suggested by Schlesinger.

[11] They were partly misled by the belief that the first strike had destroyed more aircraft than in fact it had. Kennedy later decided this cancellation was an 'error, but not a decisive error' (Schlesinger, 266). Here he was probably wrong. See Lazo, 273 ff., and Lyman Kirkpatrick, 198 (who says that CIA representatives considered the change of plan 'criminally negligent').

[12] *Revolución* had formally rejected the U.S. spelling of Khrushchev in October 1960.

ourselves to sally out facing the enemy, with the National Anthem
. . . with the cry of 'To the fight' ['*Al combate*'], with the conviction that to die for our country is to live and that to live in chains
is to live under the yoke of infamy and insult . . . *Patria o Muerte,
venceremos.*[13]

With these words, Castro prepared for battle.

In the evening the invasion fleet made rendezvous thirty miles south
of Cienfuegos with landing craft dispatched from the U.S. naval air
base at Vieques.

The Revolutionary Council, the shadow organization referred to by
Castro as the 'Council of Worms' (*gusanos*), was meantime conferring in
New York. The council members, already shadow ministers of this and
that, Transport and Telegraphs, Education and Reconstruction, were told
by the CIA that they should prepare to return to Cuba, and accordingly
were flown to Miami under Bender-Droller, where they were given
dinner and uniforms. They waited. Their masters told them nothing.
Were they in fact prisoners? They went to bed in ignorance of the fact
that the expedition over which they were nominally in command would
begin while they were sleeping: the reason being 'security', the old
excuse which, often justifiably, the leading partners in any alliance give
to justify a deception of their allies.[14] The detention was not known to
Kennedy.[15]

The brigade was now ready to land. Its political chief was Manuel
Artime, the Catholic ex-inspector of INRA; the military commander
was José Pérez San Román. He and all the six battalion commanders –
the battalions were only 200 men each – had been army officers before
1959,[16] along with the second in command (Erneido Oliva), the chief of
staff (Ramón Ferrer), and the air force commander (Manuel Villafaña),
though many of these officers, being young, had had little to do with the
civil war. Several of them, including Pérez San Román and his brother,
had been vaguely associated with the *puros*, the rebel group of officers
who, under Colonel Barquín, had tried to overthrow Batista in 1956,
and were indeed held prisoner for a time in late 1958.[17] San Román, like
Artime, Oliva, Varela Canosa and Villafaña, had held jobs under

---

[13] *Playa Girón*, 1, 450–77. The penultimate sentence was a quotation from the Cuban
national anthem.

[14] Szulc and Meyer, 122; Schlesinger, 249.

[15] *Ibid.*, 257.

[16] Alejandro del Valle: 1st paratroop battalion
    Hugo Sueiro: 2nd infantry battalion
    Valentín Bacallao: 3rd armoured battalion
    Roberto Pérez S. Román: 4th heavy gun battalion
    Ricardo Montero Duque: 5th infantry battalion
    Francisco Montiel: 6th infantry battalion

[17] Suárez Núñez, 112.

Castro in 1959,[18] though Montero Duque, commander of the 5th battalion, had led a battalion fighting Castro in the Sierra Maestra and thus had fled the country in January 1959.[19]

The brigade was composed of predominantly middle-class and upper-class men, though there were too a hundred or so working-class Cubans. The average age was about thirty, though one man was sixty-one. There were about fifty Negroes and a few more mulattoes, including Oliva, the second-in-command. About 250 had been students and 135 had been soldiers at one time or another. Most of the brigade were Catholics and there were three priests among them, all Spaniards, one of them having been an officer in Franco's army in the civil war. The invaders wore shoulder patches in the shape of a shield bearing in the centre a Latin cross. The political views of the brigade varied from extreme right to centre. It did not include apparently anyone so far to the Left as Manuel Ray, or any member of his organization (the MRP). One or two people (such as Felipe Rivero,[20] of the family of the editors of the *Diario de la Marina*) regarded themselves as nationalists of the third position – Nasserites. One or two (such as José Manuel Gutiérrez) were there almost by chance, since their friends were joining in, others since they desired work. The sons of Miró Cardona, of Varona, of Raúl García Menocal, of 'Millo' Ochoa and of Alonso Pujol,[21] were there, as were Batista's president of the Assembly, Cándido Mora, uncle of the then Cuban minister for Foreign Trade, once a member of Masferrer's MSR, and brother of the dead leader of the attempted assassination of 17 March 1957; Batista's ambassador in Japan (García Montes); and, foolishly, both from the brigade's point of view and their own, several well known killers of Batista's time, including Ramón Calviño (nominally on the naval side) who had murdered personally twenty people after having been once a member of the 26 July Movement; José Franco Mira; Rafael Soler Puig, who personally had killed the Dominican exile, 'Pipi' Hernández, and the Communist dockers' leader, Aracelio Iglesias; and Jorge King Yun who, a common criminal, had murdered a militiaman in escaping from Cuba in 1960. This group had been allotted a sinister role if the invasion were to succeed: to deal with political opposition.[22] Castro's accountants later

[18] The two latter had been naval and air attachés in the Cuban Embassy in Mexico until early 1960. The pilots (operating from Nicaragua) included Captain Farias who had, when in command of the Camagüey air base, carried out an investigation into the death of Camilo Cienfuegos.

[19] His evidence when captured. *Cf. Playa Girón*, IV, 418. Other officers of Batista's army in the brigade were Captain Morales and Major Montero Díaz.

[20] Unfortunately for him his wife was a niece of Batista's minister Morales del Castillo, and had hidden his stamp collection in late December 1958.

[21] Prío's vice-president.

[22] Kennedy and his advisers at Washington seem not to have known of the inclusion of these men, which indeed was specifically against his orders. There were also several others with

reckoned that the 1,500 men of the brigade once had owned in Cuba a million acres of land, 10,000 houses, 70 factories, five mines, two banks, and ten sugar mills.[23] In fact, the invasion force contained a remarkably representative cross-section of those opposed to Castro.

The training of these men varied considerably. Some had had only one week, and some none at all. Others had been tramping the jungles of Guatemala for nearly a year. The majority could not have had more than two and a half months. Of the 160 or so who with Nino Díaz were supposed to land in Oriente and to stage a diversion and embark on guerrilla war, half had had only one week's training.[24]

In the baggage of one priest, Father Ismael de Lugo, a manifesto was later found proclaiming:

We come in the name of God, Justice and Democracy . . . We do not come out of hatred, but out of life . . . The Assault Brigade is composed of thousands [sic] of Cubans who are completely Catholic and Christian . . . Catholics of Cuba: our military might is crushing and invincible and even greater is our moral strength, our faith in God and in His protection and His help. Cuban Catholics: I embrace you on behalf of the soldiers of the liberating Army. Families, friends and relatives . . . soon you shall be re-united. Have faith, for victory is ours because God is with us and the Virgin of Charity cannot abandon her children. Catholics! Long Live Cuba, free, democratic and Catholic. Long live Christ the King!

Cheered by these and other statements, the invading army anchored 2,000 yards offshore, Pérez San Román off Playa Girón in the *Blagar* and the *Caribe*, Oliva off the Zapata swamp in the *Houston*, a sadly appropriate name for a Cuban exile troopship, with the *Barbara J.* Frogmen marked the landing places, the first men on shore, also appropriately, being North Americans: at Playa Girón, a CIA officer who went under the name of 'Gray'; at Playa Larga, at the top of the Bay of Cochinos, another agent known as 'Rip'. The frogmen mishandled the landing, and began to exchange shots with a patrolling jeep, while intense firing began on both beaches long before any substantial forces had landed. Landing was complicated by ignorance of the coral reefs lying offshore, which destroyed or delayed several landing craft. The *Blagar* began to pound the darkness with 75 mm shells. The pilot of the landing craft assigned to Oliva fell into the water. The landing craft engines themselves failed. Landing therefore was spread over

[23] *Playa Girón*, IV, 14.
[24] Evidence of Antonio Campiña.

dubious pasts, such as Rosendo Valdés, who had been a 'vigilante' at a notorious police station, and Mario Freyre, a landowner from Bayamo of a controversial reputation.

about six hours. At dawn, the supplies, the ammunition reserves and the whole 5th battalion were still on shipboard. One group, the so-called 3rd battalion, which was led by Valentín Bacallao, landed at Playa Girón and set out for the Girón airstrip. When they reached it they began to clear it ready for aircraft. Both Pérez San Román and Oliva, the commanders, also reached Playas Girón and Larga respectively.

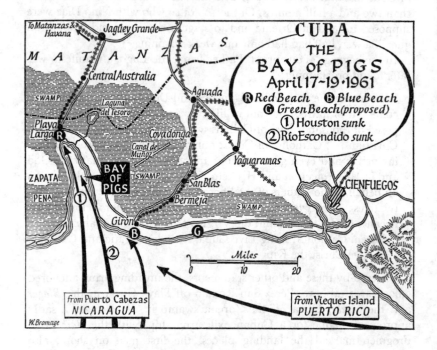

Castro heard of the invasion at 3.15 a.m. as a result of micro-wave transmission from militia units at Playas Girón and Larga, which were silenced about 4 o'clock. At this time, a battalion of the rebel army under Osmani Cienfuegos (Camilo's brother), the Minister of Public Works, was at the *central Australia*, twenty miles inland to the north of Playa Larga; there were platoons of armed charcoal workers in and around this very swampy land, based on Cayo Romano, north of Girón, to the south-west of Playa Larga and Buenaventura next to it. It was an area which had not been regarded as a likely point for invasion, because it was far from mountains and communications were difficult. Behind the woody region of hard soil stretching ten kilometres from the shore lay an impassable swamp, crossed, before the Revolution, only by two narrow-gauge railways, one a sugar line from Cochinos Bay to the *central Australia*, the other from Girón on the coast to the *central Covadonga.* It was an area where the revolution had certainly brought change to the 3,000 to 4,000 charcoal burners who previously had worked there as tenant farmers. Three roads had been built across the swamps, and tourist centres were being constructed at Girón, Larga and the Laguna del Tesoro. The standard of living in the region must have radically risen in the previous two years. Further, the region was actually being now used as a pilot for the great illiteracy campaign, and 200 adult teachers were at work there. 300 children from the swampland on the other hand were studying various trades in Havana – ceramics, tanning, carpentry.[25]

It would have been hard indeed to have found a region in Cuba in which a rebellion could have been less easily inspired among the local people. But then such a thing was not part of the CIA's purpose. Once established, however, the invaders would be hard to dislodge, for they could only be approached on land down three roads and not at all across the swamps. A provisional government could quickly have been established after the bridgehead. The swampland militia, further, was well equipped, particularly with the critical micro-wave radios. Castro was also assisted by luck and by the last-minute decision of Kennedy to abandon the second air strike.

Castro's first move was to place his air force on the alert and to order Cienfuegos's battalion at the *central Australia* to move south against the enemy. The militia of Matanzas province was mobilized to move south too. Castro himself flew to the *central Australia*. An able ex-regular officer Major José Fernández, 'el Gallego', was placed in overall field command. He showed himself much the coolest of Castro's officers in the following days, though little was made of him in heroic myth afterwards. He certainly seemed infinitely more competent as a commander than 'Major' Flavio Bravo, the young Communist contemporary of Castro's at the University, who was given command of the militia.[26]

At dawn, two Cuban Sea Furies, two T.33 jet trainers (quite forgotten by the U.S. planners) and a Cuban B.26 began to attack the landing craft and ships in Cochinos Bay. The B.26 was shot down but the confusion and damage caused at the last stage of the disembarkation was enormous. When the invading paratroops began to arrive at Playa Girón, their confused comrades fired on them as they made their drops. The 5th battalion, still in the *Houston*, the least experienced and least well-trained of the invading forces, then refused to disembark. The confusion was not staunched by the arrival of an invading B.26 from Nicar-

[25] Castro speech of 23 April, in *Playa Girón* 47.
[26] Evidence of a war correspondent on Castro's side who desires to remain anonymous. See also Ania Francos, *La Fête Cubaine*, which has an attractive picture of the fighting from the Cuban side.

agua – 3½ hours' flying time away – to provide cover for the invaders. Both the ships *Houston* and *Barbara J* were now under attack from the T.33 jets and a Sea Fury. The *Houston* was hit by a rocket from one of the former, and began to sink, laden with ammunition and oil supplies. The 5th battalion leapt into the sea, about thirty drowning, the rest gathering disconsolately on the beach looking for their commanders. Meantime at 9.30 a.m. in front of Playa Girón, the *Río Escondido*, with the main bulk of ammunition, oil, food and medical supplies, as well as the communications equipment, was also hit by a rocket from a Sea Fury. It blew up immediately, with a big explosion.[27] The remaining ships withdrew out of danger from the battle zone, their commanders promising the invading commander, Pérez San Román, that they would return at night to land the rest of the supplies. But for the rest of the day the brigade was left with little. The paratroops had lost most of their equipment in the swamp. Tanks had been effectively landed at Girón but they had not yet begun to establish contact between the two groups of invaders, under Pérez San Román and Oliva respectively.

At ten o'clock in the morning Oliva's forces at the head of the Bay of Cochinos at Playa Larga were in combat with the battalion of militia from the *central Australia*, though the strength of the paratroops was not adequate to force them to retreat far. In the east, at Girón, brigade paratroops had established road blocks on two of the roads across the swamp, while San Román protected the coast road from Cienfuegos. Within this perimeter, the invaders had captured two *pueblos*, San Blas and Girón, where a number of people threw in their lot with the invaders, helping them with food and water, five joining in as fighters.[28] Meantime, the Matanzas militia, accompanied by a well-trained and equipped force from the militia leaders' training school, was advancing southwards from *central Covadonga* towards the paratroop road blocks, and a battalion of infantry from Cienfuegos was also moving west along the coast road. About 150 militia had been taken prisoner, of whom a number – 50, according to the brigade – joined up with the invaders.

Back in the U.S. the Cuban Revolutionary Council had been surprised to hear at dawn the news of the invasion rhetorically issued in their name by a New York public relations firm, Lew Jones, which, as Arthur Schlesinger tells us sardonically, had once been used by Wendell Wilkie. They were furious. In Washington, at a press conference, Dean Rusk avoided direct questions on Cuba, on the grounds that a debate on the subject was being held at the U.N. There, Roa,

[27] The U.S. commission on the causes of the failure of the expedition (General Maxwell Taylor, Robert Kennedy, Admiral Burke, Allen Dulles) gave special emphasis to this (Sorensen, 297).
[28] Haynes Johnson, 115.

backed by Russia, was castigating the U.S. at the Security Council for countenancing aggression. Stevenson, very unhappy, did the best he could.

Castro was now moving against all opposition throughout the island in the most thorough and decisive fashion. Between the raids on 15 April and the evening of 17 April, perhaps 100,000 were arrested, including all the bishops (Pérez Serantes at Santiago was under house arrest), many journalists and the vast majority of the real underground, including most of the CIA's 2,500 agents and their 20,000 suspected counter-revolutionary sympathizers. Many North American journalists were held in overcrowded prisons. A number of imprisoned leaders of the counter-revolution such as Sorí Marín,[29] the advocate-general in the Sierra and Minister of Agriculture in 1959, Eufemio Fernández, Prío's police chief and ex-commander of Acción Revolucionaria Guiteras (ARG), Arturo Hernández Tellaheche, Prío's Labour minister and a leader of the 'Trujillo conspiracy' of 1959, and González Corso, the MRR saboteur, were shot. In these days what chance there was of any internal uprising in Cuba was ruined irreparably, perhaps for ever; but then the CIA had no regard for such a development. They had remained insistent that only invasion could lead to counter-revolution. Even men who had been sent in recent months into Cuba by the CIA as infiltrators were left without instructions. Some had heard mysterious messages broadcast from Radio Swan Island: 'Look well to the Rainbow' or 'The fish will rise very soon' or 'The fish is red'; but no one had been told what these meaningful words signified. One man reported, perhaps over-optimistically, that his 'men were in constant contact with one another and always ready for action but, unbelievably, they had never received the agreed signal from the U.S.'[30] In the late afternoon, the Lew Jones Agency issued an appeal in the name of the Revolutionary Council (still in virtual prison in Miami) for 'a coordinated wave of sabotage and rebellion'; by then there was almost no opponent of the regime left free in Cuba to answer either this spirited call or other more secret ones.

Back on the beaches, however, Oliva's battalions for a time held their own against their immediate opponents. The column of militia leaders from Matanzas coming along the road from the *central Australia* was badly damaged by the first coordinated air and land attack by the invaders.[31] At this time the Cuban forces had no air support, all available aeroplanes being occupied with attacking the invaders' ships. But in a few minutes the exile aeroplanes were shot down by a T.33 and a

[29] He had apparently made two efforts to kill Castro, on the first occasion being reprieved.
[30] Lazo, *Dagger in the Heart*, 26.
[31] Haynes Johnson implies that nearly all the 900 men in this battalion were killed. This was certainly an exaggeration.

Sea Fury. The T.33 jet trainer, far faster than the brigade's B.26s, was evidently becoming the major factor in the fight. Yet on both fronts the brigade had survived. They needed now their supply ships. But these had been pursued so successfully by the Cuban T.33s that they were already far away and reluctant to return. The *Caribe* had fled 218 miles south, the *Atlántico* 110 miles; the flagship *Blagar* and the *Barbara J* had also fled. The Cuban crew of the *Blagar* refused to go back unless the U.S. navy intervened, which of course they did not, though the U.S. officers on board wanted to return and doubtless had it not been for telecommunications and other modern equipment they would have done so: 'Nelson would never have won a victory if there had been a telex' an English admiral once remarked.[32]

The brigade was thus deserted by its supply ships, and so, instead of the night of 17–18 April being the occasion for reinforcement, it was one for renewed attack by the Cuban government forces who, under the able Major José Fernández, attacked first on the San Blas front with a consolidated advance of armoured cars and tanks. This was halted with bazookas and mortar fire by the invaders' paratroopers under Del Valle. Still, behind the tanks came four infantry battalions with howitzers and more tanks. They too were held up. A heavy attack was also mounted against the western, Playa Larga, position, using first 122 mm howitzers. The artillery fire caused alarm. When it ceased, Oliva attacked with brigade tanks. This coincided with a counter-attack by Castro's tanks, and brought no progress. Castro's forces, being inside the swamp, began to attempt an encircling movement on to Cape Ramona, at the same time pressing on remorselessly as far as possible with tanks by the direct route. Some 2,000 men were involved in Castro's attack – 1,600 militia, 300 regular soldiers, 200 police, 20 tanks. Both sides found their weapons equipped with surprising power, both sides believed they were fighting like heroes. But when day came and the Stalin tanks of the Government kept pressing on, the 2nd battalion of invaders panicked, though they were later rallied again by Oliva, who showed himself a competent and brave commander.

Now that the air-raids of 15 April had been shown to have failed utterly, the second strike (cancelled on Sunday) was reinstated. The B.26s of Nicaragua were supposed at dawn to strike again at San Antonio de los Baños, the airfield where the T.33s, so fatal to the *Houston* and the other B.26s themselves, were believed to be based; but fog prevented this. The pilots flew back to Nicaragua, disconsolate. An hour or so later, at 8.45 a.m., Oliva, commander of the Playa Larga section of the invasion, proposed at a meeting with the other commanders that, in

[32] Admiral Durnford-Slater in 1956. See Hugh Thomas, *The Suez Affair*, London, 1967, 158.

view of the large attack massing on his wing, the whole brigade should regroup and make for the Escambray mountains along the Cienfuegos road. This, the U.S.'s alternative scheme, was rejected by Pérez San Román, who had not heard of it before, as being too far, and since he supposed that the U.S. would, in the last resort, help the brigade out of their difficulties: in this illusion he was reinforced by a conversation with 'Gray' of the CIA[33] by radio telephone. 'Gray' assured him that 'We will never abandon you', offered to evacuate the force if need be and said that the 'jets are coming'. The illusion spread that the U.S. would in fact soon be intervening. Throughout the afternoon the brigade waited, once being cheered by the arrival of two U.S. Sabre jets which flew over the battlefield, but apparently did nothing.[34]

Meantime Castro's forces hesitated to strike a decisive and crippling blow due to their confusion about the numbers of their attackers. Only at about 6 p.m. did artillery begin to fire again, this time aiming at Girón and San Blas, followed by further attacks on land.

At about the same time, U.S. B.54s dropped supplies over Girón but, as an extra frustration, the wind blew these into the sea or the jungle. Much of them, however, was recovered, partly with the help of townspeople from Girón.[35] Meantime, the ships *Blagar*, *Barbara J* and *Atlántico* were some fifty miles south of the Bay of Pigs struggling with problems of their own: what was the U.S. government going to do? Would the crews return to the shore without adequate air cover? The CIA apparently cancelled the instructions to return to unload once more without consulting Washington.[36]

In Washington the recriminations had begun. In the morning Kennedy had had a letter from Khrushchev promising the Cubans 'all necessary assistance'. At midday Kennedy privately regretted that he had kept Allen Dulles as head of the CIA.[37] Neither Kennedy nor his advisers were deceived by Lew Jones's optimistic communiqués – 'peasants, workers and militia are joining the freedom front' – nor by the enthusiastic news in Miami newspapers (and even in one English paper) that Santiago had fallen and the Central Highway had been crossed at Colón. In the afternoon he and his advisers replied to

---

[33] Johnson, 142–3.
[34] This point is unclear. Castro said that U.S. jets at a great height attacked a column of his men and caused great damage and one of the invaders told Johnson that he saw signs of an attack. The jets might have come from the aircraft carrier *Essex*. But they had no orders to undertake this flight. 'Gray' of the CIA told San Román that the aircraft were specifically there to give protection against Cuban aircraft (*cf. ibid.*, 148). 'Gray' also implied to San Román that a large quantity of other aircraft was overhead.
[35] *Ibid.*, 149.
[36] Sorensen, 295.
[37] Schlesinger, 250.

Khrushchev's protest of the previous day with as much verve as they could summon: 'The great revolution in the history of man . . . is the revolution of those determined to be free.'

That night, as it became clear that the brigade was surrounded by 20,000 troops with artillery and tanks, large sections being already across the swamps into the hard forest land by the shore, Kennedy went to a ball. But he was interrupted. At midnight he was urged strongly by Bissell and Admiral Burke to make an air strike from the aircraft carrier *Essex* lying off Cuba, to knock out the T.33s and so free the tired pilots of the B.26s at Nicaragua to deal with Castro's tanks. These men were anxious to expand the conflict in order to save the brigade.[38]

This was the critical moment of the invasion. Had Kennedy agreed to let loose the aircraft from the *Essex*, the future might have turned out differently. But he only authorized six unmarked jets on the *Essex* to fly over the Bay of Cochinos at dawn the next day to cover a B.26 attack from Nicaragua and to help cover the landing of supplies from the *Blagar* and *Barbara J*. These aircraft were not to seek air or ground targets, a curiously ambiguous instruction which was rendered futile by a confusion over time with Nicaragua. The B.26s, two flown by U.S. pilots, arrived an hour early and were mostly shot down before the naval cover arrived. Some Cuban pilots in Nicaragua had refused to sally out again on what seemed to them a foolhardy mission. Four U.S. airmen were killed.[39] In these circumstances the *Essex* jets never set off at all and the ships never approached the beach even to try to unload their supplies.

At Miami in the morning the furious exiles' Revolutionary Council at last met Schlesinger and Berle, two members of Kennedy's administration upon whom they could at last pour out their anger and frustration. They had heard of the disasters from the front, they themselves wanted (they said) to go to the beaches, or at least to Nicaragua, they demanded air strikes and reinforcement. Alas, by the time that Schlesinger and Berle could retire to consult, the news from the beaches was too bad even to contemplate evacuation.

Ever since dawn Castro's forces had been closing around the beleaguered invaders. The paratroopers organized a counter-attack with the 3rd battalion, which faltered and became a retreat. At ten o'clock in the morning Castro's troops took San Blas, and at eleven reached the

---

[38] The author asked Bissell, 'In the end were you in favour of giving U.S. air cover?' Bissell: 'Yes, I was. Very strongly. When I saw that there would otherwise be a disaster I argued very strongly in favour of U.S. air intervention.' Hugh Thomas: 'Could this have led to U.S. [general] intervention?' Bissell: 'Yes.' (Discussion in Washington, 14 January 1963.)

[39] They were Wade C. Gray, Thomas Willard Ray, Riley W. Shlamberger and Lee F. Baker, the only U.S. casualties at Cochinos, though some other CIA men had taken part, e.g. 'Gray' and 'Rip' the frogmen. *Cf. New York Times*, 27 February 1963; *Birmingham* (Alabama) *News*, 4 May 1961; *Examiner* (Birmingham), 3 February 1963.

defences of Girón with tanks and militia. Both at Playa Girón and at Playa Larga the invaders were now falling back, becoming separated from each other. Pérez San Román was in contact with his battalion commanders only by messenger on a jeep, though he remained in desperate radio contact with 'Gray' of the CIA on the *Blagar*. But there was still no help forthcoming. For the time being the brigade had superior firepower but, after a while, the mere weight of numbers began to count. Castro's infantry persistently advanced, and the brigade mortars eventually used up all their ammunition. In the mid-afternoon the U.S. navy was permitted by Kennedy to approach the beaches to try to evacuate survivors, in company with the other invading ships. Of course they were too late. San Román explained by wireless that the Cuban tanks had reached Girón by 4.30 p.m. and announced that they were taking to the swamps. Between 4 and 5 o'clock on 19 April the invading forces destroyed their heavy equipment and dispersed as best they could, some[40] taking to the sea in small boats in the hope of rescue by the U.S. navy, most[41] taking to the swamps. The U.S. navy did not, however, take off survivors but, at the last, turned away, either given pause by artillery or by the knowledge that the invading forces had been dispersed. The disappearance of these ships caused anger: one invading soldier remarked, 'In the wake of that ship goes two hundred years of infamy.'[42]

Lew Jones in New York sought to save face, and announced: 'The recent landings in Cuba have been constantly although inaccurately described as an invasion. It was in fact a landing of supplies and support for the patriots who have been fighting in Cuba for months.' It was also put abroad that most of the invaders had successfully reached the Escambray.

Kennedy had by this time received the Cuban Revolutionary Council, and charmed them into acceptance of his decision not to salvage the invasion, whatever they or the actual fighters supposed that they had been told by the CIA. If the U.S. moved against Cuba, would not the USSR move against Berlin?[43]

Kennedy was thus wise to refuse to send in the full weight of U.S. military might at this point; no doubt a weaker or a more rash president would have done so.[44] Whatever the truth, or the constitutional position of the CIA's encouragement of the invaders to expect full U.S. aid, the

[40] Among them the paratroop commander Del Valle and the C-in-C's brother, Roberto.
[41] Including Artime, Pérez San Román, Ferrer, Oliva, the last separately, supposing that the first three had deserted.
[42] Haynes Johnson, 171.
[43] This obsession troubled Kennedy throughout his term.
[44] Nixon in *Readers' Digest*, November 1964, said that his advice to Kennedy on Cuba at this point had been to 'find a proper legal cover and . . . go on'.

U.S. government conducted itself badly in sending off a handful of men on a badly planned expedition to fight against overwhelming odds. Of course, the invaders deceived themselves, and no doubt difficulties of language and interpretation confused communications; maybe they made in their own minds explicit what had in those of others been either implicit or simply an encouragement. Perhaps the CIA thought that the brigade would fight better if they imagined that the U.S. would save them from disaster, even if it were not true. If so, they showed scant knowledge of psychology. It would seem certain that had the leaders of the invaders known the reality of U.S. policy – in so far as it had been defined – they would have planned a different battle in maybe a different place. But when Kennedy had said on 10 April that no U.S. forces would be involved in their attack, they imagined that this was for external consumption only. North American society seemed so bruised with advertisement and journalistic misinformation that it was impossible for even relatively honest politicians to be believed.

The U.S. government had also shown itself divided, ill-informed and careless of detail. Kennedy, like Eden over Suez, seems to have accepted the view of his advisers that his principal opponent was 'a hysteric'[45] and therefore incapable. Kennedy should have cancelled the scheme and listened to Fulbright and Schlesinger, the only men among his advisers who opposed it;[46] in allowing it to continue, though with his heart not in it, he showed himself less a man of destiny than a Hamlet, a prince whose courtiers were out of control. Meantime, waves of protest swept Latin America, doing more for the cause of Castro than all his propaganda campaigns and secret disbursement of money and pamphlets put together.

Castro's forces captured the surviving invaders in groups. Eventually there were 1,180 prisoners (1,297 had landed), including most of the leaders, disillusioned, bewildered and, as they thought, betrayed. One man at least, who had the brigade banner, reached Havana and the sanctuary of an embassy. The brigade lost 80 men in fighting and perhaps 30 to 40 in the disembarkation. Nine had died while *en route* to Havana in an overcrowded lorry; apart from these men, all the prisoners were well treated; Castro announced that his losses had been 87,[47] but the implication of his speech on 19 April was that the losses were greater than this: the chronicles of the invaders from the estimate of an unnamed Cuban doctor reckoned Cuban revolutionary losses as 1,250, with another 400 dying of wounds, and 2,000 wounded.[48] It is

---

[45] Schlesinger, 266.

[46] Apart from Chester Bowles, who had not been closely involved in the discussions. Schlesinger alone had opposed on the ground that it would not work, not that it was wrong.

[47] Speech of 23 April.

[48] Haynes Johnson, 129.

in fact hard not to believe that the Cuban revolutionary government did not lose many more men than they announced. The prisoners were not shot[49] but held, after public interrogation by Castro, Carlos Rafael Rodríguez and others, to be tried on television, imprisoned in distressing circumstances, and finally exchanged for medical supplies one and a half years later:[50] Oliva, Artime, Pérez San Román, were ransomed at $500,000 each; the others at $25,000, $50,000 and $100,000. Over half the brigade, including San Román and Oliva, later joined the U.S. army. The CIA estimated in early May that the invasion had cost $M45, a sum which they had not had to ask or account for to any authority.[51]

For Castro the defeat of the invasion was a triumph. After the defeat came the celebrations, the parading of prisoners on television, the jubilant announcement on 1 May, Workers' Day, that Cuba was a socialist state and that there would be no more elections. The revolution, he explained, was the direct expression of the will of the people; there was not an election every four years in Cuba but an election every day. Revolution, he added, had not given a vote to each citizen, it had given each citizen a rifle. The constitution of 1940 was too old and antiquated.[52] Castro placed special blame on Spanish priests, and only those who were not 'counter-revolutionary' would be allowed to stay in Cuba. All private schools would be nationalized. The prisons of Cuba remained full.

Kennedy, licking his wounds, blamed no one but himself, admitted himself in the wrong, and defiantly stated: 'The complacent, the self-indulgent, the soft societies are about to be swept away with the debris of history. Only the strong, only the industrious, only the determined, only the courageous, only the visionary, who determine the real nature of our struggle, can possibly survive.'[53] Ironically, the only other politician who might have made such a remark at this time was the one for whom Kennedy felt such special animosity: Castro. Kennedy went on quickly to approve the project of the U.S. Space Agency to land a man on the moon 'before this decade is out'; perhaps a victory for the U.S. in Cuba might have deprived mankind of that achievement in 1969.

---

[49] Except the Batista thugs, Calviño, Soler Puig and Jorge King Yun.

[50] Castro's original proposal for their exchange for 500 big tractors fell through after curious negotiations in the U.S. which reflected little credit on anyone; cf. Haynes Johnson, 229 ff., the brigade chronicler who blames domestic U.S. politics for the fact that the brigade was not exchanged in June 1961 for $M28 in credits, tractors and cash but for $M62 in December 1962.

[51] Their estimate in the Senate Foreign Relations Sub-Committee on Latin American Affairs (New York Times, 9 May 1961). To this might be added the $M62 which was eventually gathered to pay the prisoners' ransom.

[52] Obra Revolucionaria, 1 May 1961, 19–20. Russia, more circumspect, still officially referred to Cuba on 1 May as a sympathizer not as a member of the Socialist bloc. Castro's use of 'Socialism' was no doubt in the Russian sense of the word – a society en route to the perfect, but as yet unachieved, Communist society.

[53] New York Times, 21 April 1961.

Between the Crises

After the defeat of the invasion Cuba was driven towards full membership of the Communist alliance. Undecided Cubans, who had before April hesitated as to whether to join the underground or not, now naturally chose to support Castro rather than the right-wing invaders based in Florida. Castro himself remained the conductor of events, the resilient and indefatigable orator, apparently still the decisive voice in all political activities. The main nation-wide activity of 1961, the illiteracy campaign, was a project to which the Communists had given low priority and one which most evidently bore on it the marks of the earliest, original stage of the revolution – the redemption of Castro's promise to the U.N. in 1960. But, beneath Castro, his old followers of the early months dropped away from the limelight; in their place the Communist chiefs, familiar names in Cuban politics since the 1930s, middle-aged or even elderly men, came into their own, dogmatizing, explaining, directing: one wave of leaders was giving way to another. The Communist party, the Directorio Revolucionario, the 26 July Movement, the United Youth Movement and the Young Pioneers, casually began to be referred to as *organizaciones revolucionarias integradas*; then these words appeared in the press with capital letters – ORI; then by July it began to appear, without announcement, that the old Communist leaders (and only they) were always referred to as 'leaders, *dirigentes*, of the ORI'. Much play was made with the idea of a 'united movement'; indeed, to hear the enthusiasm at the ideas which were forthcoming at the great meeting, the 'Asamblea General Nacional', on 26 July 1961, in the presence of the cosmonaut, Major Yuri Gagarin, to commemorate the eighth anniversary of Moncada, it would have been supposed that that was indeed the magnificent prize an anxious nation was longing for. Castro, having worked up the crowd with his customary skill, rhetorically asked: '*Que levanten la mano los que apoyan la unión de todos los revolucionarios en el Partido Unico de la Revolución Socialista* (Will all who support the union of all revolutionaries in the united party of the Socialist Revolution raise their hands!).' 'At which everyone present including Dr Castro raised their hands giving cries of "Unity".'[1]

But no united party appeared. In his speech on 26 July Castro

[1] *Revolución*, 27 July 1961. The author was present.

limited himself to saying that the integration of the revolutionary parties would begin from below. On 6 November he explained that the 'true revolutionaries' would be 'a select and small party of the masses', while the masses, though they could support the revolution, could not call themselves revolutionaries.[2] Were there problems between the surviving Fidelistas and old Communists? If so, nothing appeared in the press. Aníbal Escalante, whose work as a Communist had begun even before the fall of Machado, began assiduously to organize the ORI as a model for this united party. An office of the ORI was set up in nearly every town, in fact merely the headquarters of the old Communist Party.[3] Its provincial secretaries were simply those who already had become secretaries of the planning boards (JUCEI)[4] and who had been in some cases for many years secretaries of the Communist party. Blas Roca said that there could be no better secretary-general of a future united party than Castro. Who could believe it? Castro's qualities were not secretarial. How long would he last? President Dorticós travelled to Belgrade to a conference of neutral countries, to Russia and to China, but seemed to resolve nothing. Nor did Blas Roca's visit to Moscow to the 22nd Congress of the Russian Communist party make clear to what extent the Cuban Communist party was abreast of events.

In early December some of these questions seemed to have been answered. Castro, hard pressed among his new bland allies, had to survive in order to conquer. On 2 December he explained to a somewhat surprised nation in a television speech that he had been for many years an apprentice Marxist–Leninist at least, even at the university, that he and his comrades had in the 1950s consciously disguised their radical views in order to gain power, and that, having become progressively more experienced, he had become a better Marxist and would be so until the day of his death.[5] It is not clear, however, whether the Communists or even Russia really relished the idea of Castro's socialism. It is improbable that Castro was telling the truth, and it is most likely that, being still rejected from full membership of the Communist *bloc*, he was making a bold bid for admission by battering on the front door while also claiming the leadership both of the Cuban and the Latin American Communist movement. So far as Cuba was concerned, government would in the future be by 'collective leadership'.

[2] Speech of Castro to the 1st National Congress of Responsables del Trabajo de Orientación Revolucionaria (*ibid.*, 11 November 1961, p. 9).

[3] Escalante said in October that the ORI had headquarters in 100 out of the 126 townships of the island (*Bohemia*, 6 October 1961).

[4] These were set up along the lines previously described (see above, p. 1337) in all provincial capitals by the end of July.

[5] There are several versions of the speech: two published in the first and second editions of *Revolución* on 2 December, one in *Bohemia* (abridged) on 10 December: one in *Obra Revolucionaria*.

Three months passed. The economic situation grew worse. The good figures for agriculture in 1961 were now seen to have been due to unrepeatable favourable factors. The lack of ordinary household goods caused much discontent. Houses were in short supply. There seemed to be much waste everywhere, especially in the ubiquitous armed forces. The National Conference of Production in August had revealed an 'infinite number of instances of bad management'. The U.S. market had been completely closed to Cuban goods since April and, in June, all U.S. goods had ceased going to Cuba – including lard and butter, basic food for Cubans. Public transport (on which so many depended to get to work) declined. Disorganization of production and distribution drove those with cars to travel many miles to find food in the country. INRA's sub-department, ACOPIO, received a monopoly of food distribution, but it lacked lorries or rolling stock to do this adequately. Professor Dumont thought that in 1961–2 only half the fruit and vegetables of the island were gathered.[6] Small farmers were supposed always to sell to ACOPIO, but this organization often could not organize the collection. Nor did ACOPIO make, to begin with, any distinction as to quality – which therefore, as might be expected, did not improve. Prices were held the same also all the year round. All decisions still depended on Havana. Even according to official figures, agricultural production fell in 1962. Cane replanting was 17 % behind – as much as 30 % in the cane co-operatives. Rice production would fall in 1962 from 300,000 tons to 200,000, the yield per hectare from 17 to 14 quintals. Yield also fell in respect of maize. The state farm production fell faster than that of the surviving private farms. 'The little *paysans routiniers* of Rancho Mundito [Pinar del Río] without irrigation or tractors, with poor soils on eroded hills, still harvest nearly seven tons of *taros* per hectare. On richer soils, with tractors and irrigation, the state farms only obtain a third of that, two to four tons.'[7] The State bought up most pigs belonging to small farmers; many died, chiefly from being too congested. The 'socialist chicken' was not a success either. Huge differences occurred in the produce of State farms according to the competence of the administration.

Industry was reorganized in about fifty consolidated businesses (*empresas consolidadas*), but Guevara did not give full direction to future development. Raw materials and equipment were bought by Guevara sometimes without much consideration of how they were to be used. He was, however, candid enough to admit that 'salaries cannot be raised; now we must simply work.'[8] Soviet and other Communist *bloc* aid amounted to $M570 in 1961–2, or $40 a head; in comparison U.S. aid

---

[6] Even in 1961, the author can remember seeing avocados lying uncollected under trees in Matanzas.

[7] Dumont, 70. But see note on p. 1338. Taros are cheap food plants.

[8] 'There are years of work ahead of us,' he went on (*Revolución*, 29 November 1961, 3).

to the rest of Latin America attained only about $2 a head. This $40, as Dumont pointed out, corresponded to the average total income of many parts of Africa. Yet the only bright spot in late 1961 was the successful end to the literacy campaign; and even there it seemed certain that much money had been lavished on a scheme of little immediate economic help and that some who had allegedly been taught to read would really not last as readers. Official statistics claimed that the percentage of illiterates had been reduced to 3·9% of the population, with at the end only 250,000 unable to read and write.

There was still no overt sign of the dissension in the State, though a speech by Castro revealed that he knew that there had been innumerable unnecessary arrests, with people being held for weeks without trial, and then returning to their houses to find their property had been stolen. He also said that after a speech of his in which he had adjured the nation to attack the *lumpenproletariat*, a police chief in Matanzas had given an order to arrest the *lumpenproletariat*, with the result that 200 homosexuals had been arrested in a single city.[9] The prolonged disappearance of Castro in February 1962 suggested that he was ill or even dead. He had told his audience on 2 December that as a student he had got to page 370 of *Das Kapital*: was he finishing it? His only sign of life were two pronouncements on foreign policy, in one of which he seemed to differentiate himself markedly from the Russian policy on coexistence between States of different social systems.[10] At the end of January Castro responded to the suspension of Cuba from the OAS (decided upon at Punta del Este[11]) by a most violent and revolutionary speech known thereafter as 'the Second Declaration of Havana', in which he appealed to the peoples of Latin America to rise against 'imperialism': 'the first and most important thing to understand is that it is not right or correct to distract the people with the vain and convenient illusion that they can triumph by legal means over the power that monopolies and oligarchies will defend with blood and fire'. Latin Americans should therefore adopt guerrilla warfare on the Cuban model. This speech may not have been very carefully thought out, but it certainly had resonance throughout the world. It was cheered as a call to permanent insurrection by China and

[9] *Revolución*, 11 November 1961.
[10] See interview with Russian editors in *Revolución*, 30 January 1962. *Cf.* the *Pravda* version reprinted in *ibid.*, 29 January 1962, and Andrés Suárez's comments, 144. The other pronouncement was 'Tres Años de Revolución', in *Cuba Socialista*, January 1962. To the editors he said: 'It is impossible for peaceful coexistence to exist between the exploited masses of Latin America and the Yankee monopolies . . . As long as imperialism exists international class war will exist between the exploited masses and the monopolies.'
[11] The U.S. once again sought a condemnation of Cuban communism but the conference merely resolved that Cuba had voluntarily placed herself outside the inter-American system. No measures against Cuba were specified and no sanctions taken, while the biggest Latin American countries, Brazil, Argentina, Mexico and Chile abstained from voting, along with Bolivia and Ecuador.

used by the militant wings of all revolutionary parties in Latin America as a manifesto. But it was not popular in Russia, though the Russian government did praise it as an expression of the intention of Cuba 'to base its relations with all nations on the principles of peaceful coexistence'.[12]

The disputes about the organization of the new united party in Cuba came to a head in January, but nothing was done. Aníbal Escalante gave tongue frequently and dogmatically about the future of the party. There were some foolish expropriations of peasants as a result of apparently real counter-revolutionary plotting, particularly in south Matanzas and south-east Las Villas.[13] Núñez Jiménez was dismissed as executive chief of INRA, Castro himself abandoned the presidency of that organization, and that major post as well as Núñez's was given to Carlos Rafael Rodríguez, the most flexible of the old Communists, Castro's oldest friend among them and a long-time critic, from within the party, of Blas Roca. This was the first important formal government post obtained by the Communists in Castro's regime. But the trouble in agriculture with the independent farmers, who still controlled over half the land, was such that a disaster was only avoided, according to Rodríguez, because of the 'prestige of the revolution' (or, should he have said, its power) and some small farmers' continued 'faith' in Castro. With this prestige strengthened rather than weakened by the events of the winter, Castro could decide that his quarrels (as they turned out to be) with the old guard of the Communists ought to come out into the open. Perhaps he was assisted in his now half-overt struggle against the Communists by the news, angrily communicated by Guevara in the March issue of *Cuba Socialista*, that henceforth Russian and east European raw materials would have to be paid for in foreign exchange earnings, not by Russian gifts or loans.[14] Nor, as can be imagined, despite Castro's intervention in their favour, were all the small-holders reconciled to the revolution; many 'drew back on themselves',[15] helping towards the decline of production in 1962. Guevara in addition had no love for the sort of disciplined party which seemed to be being built up by Escalante. For him it was already becoming a 'party of administration, not pioneering, a new élite which sought an easy life, with beautiful secretaries, Cadillacs, air-conditioning'.[16]

On 9 March the first official 'directorate of the ORI', evidently, as Escalante had said, a prototype for the future 'united party', was announced, a balanced compromise between old Communists and Fidelistas: in addition to Castro and his brother, there were thirteen Fidelistas

[12] *Revolución*, 19 February 1962.
[13] As explained by Carlos Rafael Rodríguez in *Cuba Socialista* May 1963, 14.
[14] *Cuba Socialista*, March 1962.
[15] Dumont, 87.
[16] Guevara in interview to *Al Thalia* (Cairo), published April 1965.

and ten old Communists. There was also Chomón, the sole representative of the Directorio, and President Dorticós. Admittedly the relations between at least four of the Fidelistas[17] and the old Communists before 1959 remained ambiguous. Still, there were on the list other Moncadistas or Granmaístas,[18] or veterans of the Sierra Maestra,[19] including three who had played some part in the 26 July Movement underground.[20] Of the Communists, eight had made their name before 1945,[21] one represented the Communist group who had been at the university with Castro,[22] and one had been until recently the Communist Youth leader.[23] Only one of the Fidelistas was a mulatto (Almeida), though three[24] of the rest were either mulatto or Negro.

There was too a greater crisis to come: in fact these nominations really only seem to have registered relative positions of power. The National Directorate was rarely heard of again. On 12 March Castro announced the formal beginning, on 19 March, of food rationing: Cubans were now entitled to two pounds of fat, six of rice and one and a half pounds of beans a month. In Havana and other cities, meat, fish, eggs, and milk were also rationed. Adults received three pounds of meat, one of fish, a quarter of a pound of butter, one of chicken meat and five eggs also each month. Children got a litre of milk a day. Malanga and other vegetables were also rationed. Ration cards were only issued to those who could prove that they had paid their rent. On 13 March, Castro gave a speech at the university commemorating the fifth anniversary of the attempt to kill Batista, in 1957. The testament of José Antonio Echevarría (president of the students, killed instead) was read out by a certain Ravelo. Then Castro spoke: 'And we,' he said, using the plural which he now always affected, less regally, presumably, than fraternally:

And we, while he was reading, were following the testament in a book . . . We noticed that he skipped the fourth paragraph . . . Out of curiosity we began to read what he had skipped and we saw what it said . . . *'We trust that the purity of our aims will attract the favour of God, to allow us to establish the rule of justice in our country.'* Now that is very interesting, 'I thought: "Caramba!" Did he intentionally omit these

[17] Raúl Castro, Osmani Cienfuegos (a rapidly rising star after the Bay of Pigs), Augusto Martínez Sánchez, and Guevara.

[18] Almeida, Ramiro Valdés, Haydée Santamaría and Guevara.

[19] García, 'the first peasant to join Castro'; the head of the air force, Sergio del Valle; and Osmani Cienfuegos.

[20] Hart, Emilio Aragonés, and Dorticós.

[21] Roca, C. R. Rodríguez, the Escalante brothers, Lázaro Peña, Severo Aguirre, Ordoqui and Manuel Luzardo, the only 'old Communist' already formally in the cabinet.

[22] Flavio Bravo.

[23] Ramón Calcines.

[24] Lázaro Peña, Ramón Calcines and Severo Aguirre.

three lines?' When he finished reading, I asked him. And he said: 'At the entrance they gave me instructions. I described what I was going to read and they told me to skip those three lines.'

Is this possible, comrades? Are we, so cowardly, so bigoted in mind, that we have to omit three lines from the testament of José Antonio Echevarría simply because . . . he believed in God? What sort of faith is this in truth? . . . And the tragedy is that the comrade who received the order to omit those lines is a poet, and in his own little book of verses (which I have here) is one which is entitled 'Prayer to the Unknown God'.[25]

Castro ended his speech with some mysterious allusions to the dangers of sectarianism – a word which was not often off his lips for months – and cited Lenin's pamphlet on left-wing Communism: 'an infantile disorder', a text often used by orthodox Communists when hectic dreamers of the Left are to be condemned. He also explained that the Young Rebels would soon be re-christened Young Communists – an event which occurred without much celebration in April.

On 16 March Guevara, who must have been specially close to Castro at this time, made a blistering attack on the revolutionary union leadership, concluding that the achievements of the revolution were 'confined to the establishment of a few small consumer goods factories and the completion of some factories begun under the dictatorship. He asked why it was that under the Revolution shoes lost their heels after one day's wear, and why the Revolution's Coca-cola tasted so vilely.' Does that sort of thing happen under capitalism? No. Then why should it happen under socialism? Because of the nature of socialism? No, that is a lie. It happens because of our own shortcomings, our lack of revolutionary vigilance, the inadequacy of our work.[26] On 17 March Castro told 'revolutionary instructresses' at the Conrado Benítez school that ORI secretaries up and down the country had imposed despotism on the country and were 'almost indistinguishable from Batista and his henchmen'.

Another ten days passed. Castro had clearly made a calculated bid for what affection he still could excite among what little remained of old Catholic Cuba and of the 26 July Movement; they would see surely that there was still a gap between himself and the Communist party of old. On 22 March the National Directorate of the ORI named a 'secretariat' which clearly would do all the work in the formation of the projected, 'united party'. It included Blas Roca but not Escalante, and the other members were Fidelistas. Roca himself took over as editor of

[25] *Obra Revolucionaria*, 1962 No. 13.
[26] Guevara, *Trabajo*, reported Goldenberg, 257.

Hoy, the party newspaper. On 24 March an old Communist, Manuel Luzardo, was brought into the cabinet as minister of (internal) Commerce, and Chomón, the one surviving Directorio leader, was brought back from Moscow as Minister of Communications. On 25 March the new INRA chief, Carlos Rafael Rodríguez, explained that the Russian and east European advisers had become critical of the economic administration of Cuba, while Raúl Castro was named vice-premier. On 27 March, finally, in a major television speech, Castro made a violent criticism of Aníbal Escalante, national organizer of the ORI, who had been dispatched the day before to Prague, being succeeded in his job at ORI by President Dorticós.

'Aníbal Escalante,' Castro told his listeners and watchers, 'was a Communist for many years:

> In our opinion he was a true Communist, an honest Communist . . . but Aníbal Escalante erred. Aníbal Escalante, a Communist, committed grave errors. The fact is that Communists also make mistakes! They are men, after all. Is this the only time that the Communists have made a mistake? No, Communists have made many mistakes. The history of the international Communist movement is studded with mistakes. Many apply Marxism wrongly. A man, after all, and only a man, and like every human being exposed to the temptation of error, Aníbal Escalante erred.

There followed specific charges: of organizing a party which would be in effect an apparatus following Escalante's own leadership; of creating a 'nest of privilege, of benefits, of a system of favours of all types'. Meantime, inside the Cuban administration, it had become impossible for a minister to remove any individual from one post to another without first asking the permission of the ORI. Things had got to such a pass that 'if a cat gave birth to four kittens, the ORI secretariat would have to be consulted'. *Sectarismo,* 'implacable, insatiable, incessant', had sprung up in every corner of the peninsula.

Castro turned to other instances of misbehaviour. There was Fidel Pompa, secretary of the ORI in a group of farms in Oriente: when the list of the national leaders of the ORI had been published, Pompa, 'with the mentality of a *gauleiter* rather than of a Marxist', had made insulting remarks about several Fidelistas (among them Guillermo García, the famous first peasant to join the revolution; Haydée Santamaría; Sergio del Valle; and Emilio Aragonés). How indeed, continued Castro, was Fidel Pompa to know who these people were and how much they had done in the civil war when, at the time, he had been hiding under his bed?

Castro finally asked: 'What should be our attitude towards the old

Communists? One of respect and recognition of their merits, and recognition for their past militancy. In my escort there are many old Communists and I am not going to dismiss them, since I have confidence in them. What on the other hand should be their attitude to us? One of modesty.'[27]

Castro chose to make this frank speech not discreetly, to a select body of the faithful (as Khrushchev had made his speech attacking Stalin), but before all the nation, on television screens – on no doubt 80% of the 500,000 Cuban television screens.

A few days later Castro went to Matanzas and spoke again, this time to the Provincial Committee of ORI in the town. The theme of his speech was advertised as being to 'complete and make precise' his remarks of 26 March.[28] He explained that rumours and suspicion had forced him to bring the whole Escalante affair into the open. He repeated the various charges against Escalante, though in harsher terms: Escalante had created a personal shrine, simply to satisfy his own desire for power. He had created a veritable parody of government; and 'it is not only Aníbal's fault – we have to distinguish between the things which are Aníbal's fault, those that are our own, and those that are the fault of five hundred Aníbals going free. The result anyway has been to create a divorce between masses and party.' He added: 'the masses saw all these problems: the transgressions of power, the arbitrary arrests, the wilfulnesses, the excesses, the whole policy of contempt towards a people!'

Castro then turned to the rules that ought to guide the revolution in future. The revolutionary caucus (*núcleo*) in factory or farm, office or anywhere else, must henceforth be composed of people who had gained this position through merit, not simply because they were old Communist militants. At the same time there should be no more arbitrariness, bureaucracy, anarchy, and no more drunkenness: 'Anthems, songs, we can have but no more congas for drunken dancing.'

In these two speeches Castro sought to make clear to the Cubans that he and not the old Communists were the masters of the Cuban revolution. But what now was he? He had taken the trouble to differentiate himself from the Communists. He continued to refer to himself as a Marxist–Leninist. But he remained an unusual one. Escalante was to be the scapegoat for the terror, as for the economic difficulties. The revolution over which Castro presided remained volatile. Partly this was

[27] *Obra Revolucionaria*, No. 10, 1962.

[28] No complete version of this statement was published, but an abbreviated version eventually appeared in the May issue of the small circulation monthly, *Cuba Socialista* and in *El Mundo* on 10 May. (This was the first time since 1959 that a major speech of Castro's was not published the day afterwards in the leading Cuban papers. The reason for this reticence was that the unabridged text was a good deal too personal.)

because of the threats from the exiles, the rumours of wars, the explosions and the landings, the arrests of spies and traitors. But even so the elusive united party of the revolution took a long time to appear. During the summer of 1962, workers in different enterprises made selections from among their members of 'model workers' from whom ultimately party members would be selected. This normally very democratic procedure had the effect of delaying the formation of the party indefinitely. Relations in the ministries and other organizations between the old Communists and the men of 1959 were very bad. Castro, not the old Communists, now made all the important theoretical speeches. Blas Roca, the theoretician of 1961, dropped back from the public eye in 1962, his main organizer over thirty years, Escalante, being in exile. Carlos Rafael Rodríguez kept to agrarian reform in place of his previous wide-ranging lectures on general policy and later in 1968 he would report to the central committee of the new Communist party that in his opinion in 1962 Escalante had been 'more abnormal than wicked' (this was at the time of Escalante's second bid for power in Cuba, in the mid 1960s). The only two other old Communists to retain national positions of the first importance were Manuel Luzardo at the Ministry of Commerce and Leonel Soto, Castro's old friend, at the school of revolutionary instruction. Many old Communists who had secured good positions through Escalante's backing were replaced, though César Escalante, Aníbal's brother, remained as theorist and intellectual director of the ORI, which itself remained in being as a shell for the 'new party'.

Russia accepted, doubtless without enthusiasm, the destruction of Escalante and, possibly in panic at the thought of losing Cuba to China, had greeted Cuba on 1 May as next in importance after the socialist *bloc* and before Yugoslavia: Cuba had evidently been promoted. In mid-May a new commercial treaty was signed between Cuba and Russia: by this, commercial exchange between the two would increase to $M750, and now apparently Russia agreed to buy two to three million tons of Cuban sugar in 1962.[29] Kudryatsev, the Soviet ambassador, left Cuba hastily, without being seen off at the airport; Castro later said that he had asked him to leave, but it is evident that he was the spokesman of an older stage of Cuban–Russian relations.[30] Castro himself remarked in the hearing of several people in the offices of *Revolución*, 'This Kudryatsev bores me more than Bonsal did'.[31] He was succeeded by Alexayev, who had been in Cuba off and on since 1959 and who had

---

[29] *Revolución*, 15 May 1962. Andrés Suárez's comments are interesting (155).

[30] Lisa Howard, *War/Peace Report*, September 1963. Chomón left Moscow on 5 May. His successor, Carlos Olivares, took some time to arrive. So both embassies had no heads of mission for a time.

[31] *Este Kudryatsev me tiene ya más cansado que Bonsal* (Evidence of Guillermo Cabrera Infante, then editor of *Lunes de Revolución*.)

once been in the Russian embassy in Buenos Aires. The Cuban newspapers were full of old stories of the Sierra (of the time, that is, before overt Communist support for Castro), and leaders until then discredited (such as Faustino Pérez, who had resigned over the Matos affair) were now once more favourably mentioned. Blas Roca in *Hoy* described Castro unequivocally as 'the best and most effective Marxist–Leninist of our country'.[32] In agriculture, a number of farms which had been wrongly expropriated in the February crisis were handed back to their owners by the new directorate at INRA. It was as if Castro had once more exhausted the usefulness of another wave of followers and was seeking out a new one still, perhaps composed of the flotsam of the past.

Diversification of agriculture and industrialization meantime went forward very slowly, though there were a number of further collectivizations – bakeries, clothing and bedding factories, distilleries – without apparently any special legislation. The consequences of the neglect of the sugar industry during 1960 and 1961 now became apparent. The 1962 sugar harvest was clearly falling behind all recent years, due to the rash cutting down of cane in the drive for diversification. 'We must simply recognize,' said Guevara who, as Minister of Industries, was still responsible for the manufacturing side of sugar, 'that this is a bad harvest.' He admitted there had been sabotage, bad work, indolence and shortage of hands.[33] He did not, however, admit that the 'volunteers, though unpaid, often cost more through their expenses of transport or errors of cutting than the regular day's pay of workers.'[34] Communications all over the island were breaking down for lack o spare parts. Food supplies were more and more irregular. ACOPIO, the monopoly food-purchase body, wallowed in disorder, peasants not knowing whether their produce would be bought or not. The shops were empty. Middle-class Cubans and now many from the working class also filled the Pan American flights to Miami; in this way more and more technically trained people left Cuba. Everyone complained: Russian and east European technicians about Cuban waste and inefficiency, a Polish journalist that he was longing to get back to the beaches of *bourgeois* Belgium;[35] Cuban officials complained about Russian intransigence and bad workmanship, and the reluctance of Russian technicians to leave their air-conditioned offices.[36] Cuban and Russian relations were very bad. There were some signs that Castro was anxious

[32] *Hoy*, 22 April 1962.
[33] At Asamblea Plenaria Azucarera Nacional, *H.A.R.*, XV, 318–19.
[34] Dumont, 81.
[35] To the author, in July 1962.
[36] This was certainly not always justified. In the summer of 1961 I stayed several days on a state farm near Manzanillo upon which four young Russian agronomists were working. They rose daily at 6.30 and returned at 4.30 p.m., sweating more, and more exhausted than any workers I have ever seen.

to start playing off Moscow against China which had also greeted the denunciation of Escalante with approval[37] and themselves like Russia concluded a new commercial treaty. Only with great difficulty, in addition, did the Polish Foreign Minister, Rapacki, secure mention of the word 'co-existence' in the joint communiqué with Cuba after his visit in May, while Raúl Castro gave a big speech on the North Korean national day – an occasion which customarily passes without enthusiasm in Warsaw or Budapest. Cuba also studiously avoided public condemnation of Albania, China's only ally in Europe. On 3 June Khrushchev gave a reply to these implicit criticisms and upbraided Cuba at a celebration bidding goodbye to about a thousand Cubans who had been training in Russia. Khrushchev compared Cuba's economic position with that of Russia after the civil war. He said that Lenin had then brought in the New Economic Policy which made concessions to capitalists within Russia, in order ultimately to strengthen socialism. Such things might be necessary in Cuba (*Hoy* said much the same for a time, without avail). It would take more than arms and heroism to get over the food shortages. Khrushchev promised to send 'arms and other things' to Cuba, but the road to socialism meant a high degree of consciousness, intelligence and work.[38]

After this lecture a *rapprochement* began. With his old knapsack and rifle, Castro went first for a new tour of the Sierra Maestra telling Cuban Communists that he had 'once more raised the banner of rebellion' – against whom was left unexplained.[39] At the end of June, however, Castro, with unusual humility, at another celebration, bade goodbye this time to Soviet technicians with the words:

We know our deficiencies, we know of inexperienced administrators who in some cases lack political intelligence and in others lack a sense of hospitality. We know that a [Russian] technician who went to a state farm run by an experienced and hospitable comrade . . . would be very well treated. But we know that there was no lack of places where the administration received them coldly or with indifference . . . or when the administration did not make use of the knowledge of the technicians . . . [Some] thought that the way to treat the technicians well was to take them out, or even to offer them girls.

He ended up with a sudden new enthusiasm for 'the Soviet people, led by the at all times glorious Communist party of the Soviet Union . . . and by the great and dearly loved friend of Cuba, Nikita Khrushchev'.[40] Blas Roca made a speech in Montevideo which accepted blame for

[37] Andrés Suárez, 156.
[38] *Revolución*, 4 June 1962,
[39] *Ibid.*, 16 June 1962.
[40] *Ibid.*, 1 July 1962.

having not seen earlier that guerrilla war was the correct means of struggle against Batista.[41] But it was clear that something else had occurred which made it worthwhile, even necessary, to mend matters with Russia. This was partly of course the knowledge that now Cuba could not do without Russian economic aid. China might be a heroic example but still only Russia could provide Cuba with cane-cutting machines, credit, technical assistance, and, above all, a market for her sugar: the Chinese could have eaten the sugar but could not have paid for it. It had become obvious that the harvest would not top five million tons. This marked a return to the figures of the controlled low harvests of the mid 1950s, so that Cuba would not even have been able to deliver the $4\frac{3}{4}$ million tons contracted to Russia.[42] Meantime, nearly 3,000 Cubans a week were leaving their country for exile, mostly for the U.S., but many also for Spain or the rest of South America: by midsummer over 200,000 exiles had left the island since the beginning of 1959, or almost 3% of the population – already one of the largest exoduses on record. Further, they were from all sections of the community, with the exception of the countryside.[43] Many of these were people who had previously sympathized with the Castro regime. The climax of disorder in the Cuban economy after the revolution was probably attained in mid-1962. In the face of these economic and social difficulties it seems evident that a military decision of the first importance had been taken by the Cuban and Russian governments.

[41] *Cuba Socialista*, July 1962.
[42] As agreed under their 1961 economic pact.
[43] R. R. Fagen, R. A. Brody and Thomas J. O'Leary, *Cubans in Exile: Disaffection and the Revolution* (1968), 17; see also *The Cuban Immigration 1959–1966 and its impact on Miami-Dade County, Florida* (Coral Gables, Florida, 1967).

The Missile Crisis: I

In the months since the humiliation at Cochinos Bay, the government of President Kennedy had had many matters to treat of other than
Cuba: the Congo; the steel magnates; the Alliance for Progress; Laos
and Vietnam; the Negro question; Berlin; and Khrushchev at Vienna.
Kennedy had travelled. But Cuba had remained a dominant (though
not a predominant) concern. Cuba had been suspended from the OAS
in January. Personally, Kennedy felt responsibility for the still imprisoned members of Brigade 2506: those men were in confinement because of his personal decisions or indecisions a year before – the first clear
intimation of the bitterness of power to one who previously had only
known of its delights.[1] Publicly, he was not allowed by his Republican
opponents to forget Cuba. A new electoral campaign, the half-term
legislative elections of November 1962, was at hand. Kennedy would
no doubt be reproached for allowing Cuba to remain Communist, just
as he had himself reproached the Republicans in 1960. Further, there
were still the Cuban exiles, still the Cuban Revolutionary Council, still
the latter's president, the ex-prime minister, Miró Cardona. The
shadow president of Cuba and the actual president of the U.S. met
several times and, on 10 April 1962, Miró took away the impression that
Kennedy was anxious to re-form an exile army: 'I left the White House
with the assurance that the liberation of Cuba would follow soon with
Cubans as the vanguard in the battle.'[2] But Kennedy merely expressed
the hope that one day soon Cuba would be free and, knowing that
whatever he said would be passed quickly to Miami, did not make any
pledge. Miró had misunderstood A. A. Berle in the week before
Cochinos Bay; once again he was confused.[3] But at all events during the
spring of 1962 the enthusiasm of the exiles, dampened after Cochinos,
began to mount. The U.S. press published articles about the size of

[1] The prisoners of the Bay of Pigs were not tried until March 1962 (except for five executed
as war criminals for their part during the struggle against Batista and a few others condemned
for political crimes apart from the Cochinos battle). At the trial, only Ulises Carbó, son of
Sergio, and Alonso Pujol, son of Prío's vice-president, denounced the U.S.

[2] Miró Cardona's article, published in *S.P.* (Madrid), 1 May 1963.

[3] Evidence of Richard Goodwin in letter, 12 May 1969. Perhaps also Miró was involved in a
justification of his own authority and continued working relations with the U.S. government.

forces required to overthrow Castro: six divisions, a figure which Miró said Kennedy had mentioned to him, were thought necessary.

Doubtless these rumours reached Castro. The Cubans in Miami were less discreet even than usual when they scented victory. During the trial in March of the men of Cochinos Bay, a message had been passed to Castro through President Goulart of Brazil, by Richard Goodwin, that if the invaders were shot, opinion in the U.S. would be so roused as to make invasion inevitable.[4] During late April a huge marine man-oeuvre was carried out by the U.S. in the Caribbean, followed by further raids by exile groups – notably 'Alpha 66'.[5] Such Miami rumours and the general atmosphere of hostility and tension must have caused Castro to fear an invasion.

In Cuba itself, meantime, while the economy slackened, discontent clearly grew. On 16 June demonstrations occurred in the city of Cárdenas. Housewives marched into the streets beating pots and pans. Tanks were dispatched by the heavy-handed Major Jorge Serguera, the provincial military commander, to overawe them. Dorticós arrived to make a speech, blaming the 'imperialist blockade' as well as 'our errors' for shortages and denouncing the housewives' protest as 'a miserable and counter-revolutionary provocation'.[6] Afterwards, demon-strations occurred at Santa Clara[7] and at El Cano near Havana, where one young militiaman was killed and another wounded by the police in a confused incident. The government reacted as if terrified by what further crises they might encounter: the shops at El Cano were confi-scated, the inhabitants lost all their cars, telephones and lorries, and were forced into unemployment and submission.[8] The local militia, which had proved notably inadequate in this trial, was purged and reorganized.

These events, combined with the economic dislocation, made Castro more nervous than ever of the effects of a possible invasion, which he began to regard as more difficult to withstand than at any previous time. Was the militia loyal? How would it react if faced with the marines?[9] Surely, as the U.S. election campaign continued, there would be greater call for the U.S. to 'solve' the Cuban question, if need be by force? What, after all, if Miró really had a commitment from Kennedy as he, Miró, himself believed – and as Castro doubtless by this time had learned? There were other suggestions of invasion, some

[4] Haynes Johnson, 274–5.
[5] *Cf. Le Monde,* 11 May.
[6] See *Revolución,* 17 June and 18 June 1962.
[7] As the author discovered, in the course of a visit there in July.
[8] El Cano later became the site of an experimental farm.
[9] Those over forty years old were really no more than a reserve; those under forty were used to guard public buildings etc.

false, such as Rusk's routine interviews with Latin American ambassadors.[10]

Thus on 1 July, only a few days after the El Cano incident, Raúl Castro set out for Moscow to secure a promise of more protection for Cuba from Russia. As a result of the discussions between Raúl Castro and Khrushchev and others, Russia agreed to send an increased military force to Cuba, modern equipment, a number of short-range surface-to-air (SAM) missiles used for defence, similar to those which had been given by Russia to Indonesia and Iraq, and also some medium- and intermediate-range missiles capable of delivering nuclear and thermonuclear warheads on the U.S. and other targets in the Americas.

There seems, however, little doubt that the decision to send missiles to Cuba must have been taken by the Russians some time before this, possibly in April,[11] at all events before Khrushchev's lecture to the returning Cubans on 2 June. If the decision were taken in April, at, for instance, as seems likely, the Soviet Party Praesidium meeting held between 22 and 25 April, it may not have been communicated to the Cubans before mid-June, though perhaps there was some preliminary discussion during Khrushchev's talks with the Cuban Minister for Public Works, Osmani Cienfuegos, and the Cuban ambassador to Moscow on 28 April and 5 May, respectively. Perhaps the visit to Cuba of Rashidov, a Soviet Praesidium Alternate and secretary-general of the Uzbek Communist party, at the head of the delegation to 'study irrigation problems', was important; Rashidov spent an unusually long time is Moscow on his return before going back to Uzbekistan.[12] Doubtless, at an early stage of their decision-making, in April or May, the Russians kept their ideas very much to themselves.

The reason for the decision to send missiles to Cuba, however, is not entirely clear. Cuba, fearing invasion, had a desire for extra defence against the U.S. Superficially missiles would afford this. Cuba also had a

[10] See *Política Internacional*, No. 1, 181–2, and Joxe, *loc. cit.* It is possible that Castro also learned of a second planned 'manœuvre' for late October in which the marines were supposed to overthrow a tyrant named Ortsac in a Caribbean island.

[11] This is the argument of Michel Tatu, *Power in the Kremlin*, 233, on the basis of analysis of hardening statements by Russians from then on, and from changes in the command structure of the Russian armed forces. Castro himself in a speech in 1963 spoke of conversations beginning on the matter in June (*Revolución*, 20 April 1963), and this is the interpretation of Roger Hillsman, *To Move a Nation* (1967), 159. A contrary view is expressed by H. M. Pachter, *Collision Course* (1963), 6–7, where it is suggested that the decision was not taken till Guevara's visit to Moscow in August. Good Cuban sources have described to me what sound without doubt to have been equipment connected with the missiles as having been transported by road at night by heavily guarded Russian lorries on 22 May.

[12] Tatu, 335. Andrés Suárez, 160, also points to Rashidov's visit as important. Sharif Rashidovich Rashidov (born 1917) had been chairman of the Uzbek Writers' Union before becoming chairman of the Praesidium of the Uzbek Republic. He had headed the Soviet delegation to the Cairo conference on Afro-Asian solidarity in 1957 and was to be Russia's representative at the famous Tricontinental Conference in Havana in January 1966.

desire that Russia should be 'highly compromised' in her fate. But this extra security could probably have been afforded by extending the guarantees under the Warsaw Pact to Cuba, or by a more explicit and formal commitment by Khrushchev to declare war in case of aggression against her ally. Yet for Russia the installation of, say, sixty missiles, some with the range of 1,000 miles,[13] a few of 1,500 to 2,000 miles,[14] would in fact have doubled the capacity of Russia to strike the U.S. This would still have left Russia with only half the means of striking her enemy that the U.S., with its bombers and missiles, had to strike Russia. But these weapons placed in Cuba would (because of their approach from the South) escape the U.S. early warning system, thus upsetting plans for retaliation. So the missile installation would have been naturally a move which would have been pressed vigorously by some Russian military chiefs – though possibly not by all of them: thus perhaps Marshal Moskalenko, who in the spring of 1962 was in charge of strategic rockets, may have been unhappy at shipping such valuable weapons to so exposed a situation, for he was replaced in April.[15] But legally or illegally, right or wrong, the installation of missiles would evidently have political consequences out of proportion to the strategic advantage gained. Of course, Khrushchev did not desire to use the weapons. But he knew that, if successfully established, they could be a means of exerting diplomatic pressure on Kennedy: either, as the U.S., and indeed most commentators, have assumed, over Berlin; or in order to achieve a guarantee against a U.S. invasion of Cuba. Khrushchev's own position was at that time exposed within the Communist camp so far as Berlin was concerned and he coveted a prestigious victory.[16]

If Cuba had agreed or had asked for offensive missiles, Russia was of course legally entitled to send them. But this was an affair outside legality. It was not clear how the U.S. would react. Yet the legal rights of Cuba would not determine that reaction. So much must have been clear to Khrushchev, who naturally realized that the U.S. knew that Russia had never before established missiles in the territory of an ally, and that the tradition of Russian diplomacy had always been to refuse to over-extend her lines of communication. Khrushchev must therefore have expected the U.S. to be surprised at this new move.

On the Communist side, those involved in this drama have told various and contradictory stories. Thus Khrushchev, in a television interview in 1967, said, 'When we learned that a new socialist state had appeared not far from American shores, I understood that it would not last long if we didn't help it . . . And so I decided, after consulting my

[13] Medium range missiles (MRBM).
[14] Intermediate range (IRBM).
[15] Tatu, 23.
[16] See ibid., 232 ff.

colleagues, to send some rocket units to Cuba.'[17] This indeed cuts a long story very short. For in 1962 itself Khrushchev told both Kennedy (in his letter of 27 October) and the Supreme Soviet:[18] 'we carried weapons there at the request of the Cuban government . . . including . . . twenty Russian IRBMs[19] . . . These were to be in the hands of Russian military men . . . Our aim was only to defend Cuba.'[20] But those who establish bases abroad customarily say that they do so at the request of the governments concerned. Russia would gain strategically from setting up missiles in Cuba providing that Khrushchev and the Kremlin were indeed able to maintain control of the situation, that Castro would not be able to force events, and that the local Soviet technicians would always under all circumstances, even a U.S. invasion of Cuba, be able to communicate with home. If the U.S. were to invade Cuba, the missiles would have failed, so far as Cuba was concerned; and Russia would have to go to war with the U.S. But the central Russian gain by which the whole matter would be judged was the change it would make in the global balance of strengths. This was so considerable as to make the idea tempting for that reason alone. After all, it seems likely that Russia had always desired a neutral in Cuba more than a satellite; but if satellite she had become, with all its consequent risks, then one *quid pro quo* would be to make her a strategically profitable satellite.

For President Kennedy and his Secretary of Defence, McNamara, had sought to maintain superiority of nuclear weapons and systems of delivery on a scale sufficient to destroy Russia's nuclear striking power at all known or suspected bases,[21] hopefully leaving enough force left over to threaten all large Russian cities with destruction if there chanced to be any nuclear striking force left intact – for example, in submarines. Even after a surprise attack by Russia, the U.S. hoped to be able to bring to bear as much as, or more, destructive power than Russia had been able to use first. The U.S. second strike was to be as great as the Russian first strike.[22] McNamara had explained, in a speech at Ann Arbor (University of Michigan), that this apparently wasteful policy enabled him to escape from the doctrine of massive retaliation against Russian cities advocated by Dulles and Nixon in the 1950s. Of course, 'counterforce', as McNamara's policy was known, could theoretically be employed in reply to a nuclear attack against cities, but it would be more likely to be used as a first strike aroused by a major conventional attack. The policy necessitated a vast stockpile of nuclear weapons.

---

[17] As reported, verbatim text, in *Sunday Times* (London), 16 July 1967.
[18] On 12 December 1962.
[19] Intermediate range ballistic missiles.
[20] Speech of 12 December.
[21] U.2 photographs had made all Russian missile bases generally evident.
[22] Gilpatrick at Hot Springs, 21 October 1961.

Thus the U.S. in November 1962 had probably between 200 and 220 ICBMs, while Russia probably had only between 50 and 75. By 1964, when the programme would be complete, the U.S. would have 1,000.

Russia had pursued a less grandiose policy. In 1962 she had probably five times fewer nuclear delivery weapons than the U.S. She had about 350 to 700 shorter-range missiles, but these could not reach the U.S. from Russia, only Europe.[23] Russia had only 200 intercontinental bombers compared with 600 U.S. They had about 1,000 medium-range bombers each. About 130 to 150 missiles were established on U.S. Polaris submarines. It is possible, therefore, that during early 1962 Russian planners were desperate, especially if a U.S. invasion of Cuba was liable to force them to redeem Khrushchev's pledge to defend that (to them) remote island. After all, the world balance of nuclear power had recently been upset. If anything could be done to prevent an invasion and therefore to neutralize Cuba, enabling it to survive, the opportunity should be seized.

Cuba was, of course, an attractive advertisement for the world Communist movement. But militarily speaking Cuba must have been an embarrassment for Russia. The best thing to do, in the face of a Cuban desire for protection, would be to guarantee Cuba completely against U.S. invasion, while retaining all power of military decision in Cuba for the Russian command. Though the Warsaw Pact guarantees would have formally given Cuba security, they would not do so if war actually came: for it could not be defended by conventional means. In one sense, therefore, the installation of missiles in Cuba was a more conservative step than it seemed to North Americans. Since 1961 there had been no equilibrium, only uneasy imbalance. Khrushchev himself apparently explained to Kennedy in his 'secret' letter of 26 October that the missiles had been sent to Cuba because of the Bay of Cochinos, when Cuba had been attacked.[24]

[23] This was a received view in Washington in 1963: cf. Mark Frankel, in the *New York Times*, 13 December 1963, quoting from a Rand information analysis which criticized the idea that the missiles were put into Cuba to defend the island; and Arnold L. Horelick, 'The Cuban Missile Crisis', in *World Politics*, April 1963. It is impossible to agree with his view that medium-range missiles would alone have served the Russo–Cuban purpose, since, though they would have hit southern U.S. cities, the real point of the 'deterrent' is to expose the capital to fire; quite apart from the fact that the U.S. missile sites in Montana or North Dakota were also outside the range of either T.1s, T.2s or T.4s established in Cuba. The Wohlstetters appear wrong ('Controlling the risks in Cuba', *Adelphi Papers* (1965)), 12, in suggesting that 2,200 miles could cover all the U.S. from Cuba. Half Montana, for instance, would be out of range.

[24] As summarized by Elie Abel, *The Missiles of October* (1967), 180. See below, 1412. fn. 31 For this paragraph, see Sir Basil Liddell Hart, in *Quick* (Germany), 11 November 1962, who pointed out that Khrushchev's 'best chance of destroying the nuclear balance was to put a large number of IRBMs into Cuba, the only place from which such intermediate-range weapons could reach the principal targets in the U.S.' He concluded, however, that the adverse change in the nuclear balance was a 'basic curb to Russian cold war activities' since it hindered (them) pressing threats to near the brink.

Castro later gave several explanations for the installation of the missiles in Cuba. He told the Cubans (in January 1963) that the Russians had desired them, and repeated this explanation to Claude Julien of *Le Monde*: 'We had thought among ourselves of the possibility of asking Russia for missiles. But we had not reached any decision when Moscow proposed them. It was explained to us that in accepting them we would reinforce the Socialist camp.'[25] To Lisa Howard, a sympathetic listener from the American Broadcasting Company, Castro explained (in May 1963) that the decision involved 'simultaneous action on the part of both governments'. To Herbert Matthews, Castro (in October 1963) said that the Cubans asked for the missiles from Russia; he and his friends in early 1962 'felt almost sure that the U.S. were preparing a military invasion of Cuba'. They had been strengthened in this belief after Aleksei Adzubei, Khrushchev's son-in-law and editor of *Izvestia*, had reported to that effect after an interview with Kennedy – a judgement which, like Miró's conclusion, seems to have been erroneous.[26] Castro added that Russia thought that the U.S. would attack him and that 'the idea of installing the nuclear weapons was his, not [that of] the Russians''.[27]

But, soon after, Castro changed his tack again. To another Frenchman, Jean Daniel of *L'Express* (in November 1963), he said: 'Now, I'll tell you something that nobody knows about. I have never spoken of it before[!][28] But . . . the world has a right to know the true story of the missiles.' Six months before the crisis, at the time of Miró's interview with Kennedy, Castro explained, Cuba received the news that the CIA was preparing a new invasion. Castro and his advisers were uncertain what Kennedy personally was thinking. Adzubei then visited Kennedy and, as Castro told Matthews, derived the impression that the president believed that the balance of world forces had been disrupted by the Communist capture of Cuba: 'Kennedy reminded the Russians that the U.S. had not interfered in Hungary.' Though Adzubei apparently did not then think that the U.S. was about to attack, he and Khrushchev decided that that was possible when they heard of Castro's earlier information. (According to Pierre Salinger, Kennedy had mentioned Hungary on this occasion but not 'in the context' that Castro placed the remarks.)[29] Russia, said Castro, was after this 'reluctant to install

[25] *Le Monde*, 22 March 1963. The interview was in January.

[26] The State Department denied it. The subject is ignored by both Schlesinger and Sorensen.

[27] Herbert Matthews, *Return to Cuba* (1964), 16.

[28] *Cf.* the version in *L'Express*, 14 December 1963. The versions in the *New York Times*, *Observer* (London) and *New Republic* are all shorter, and the *Observer*'s version is badly transcribed.

[29] *New York Times*, 13 December 1963. Adzubei asked Kennedy directly whether there would be an invasion of Cuba and Kennedy said no. If Adzubei desired to know the import-

conventional weapons' since the U.S. might then still risk an invasion, and then Russia would have to retaliate and a world war would be inevitable. So, in June, Raúl Castro and Guevara went to Russia to discuss the installation of missiles. . . .' Jean Daniel said further that Castro told him:

> The only thing we asked the Russians to do was to make it clear to the U.S. that an attack on us was an attack on the Soviet Union. We had extensive discussion before arriving at the proposal of installing guided missiles, *a proposal which surprised us at first and gave us great pause*.[30] We finally went along with the Soviet proposal because, on the one hand, the Russians convinced us that the U.S. would not let itself be intimidated by conventional weapons and secondly because it was impossible for us not to share the risks which the Soviet Union was taking to save us.[31]

But oddly enough, even this was not Castro's last account. On 7 January 1964 Castro told Matthews that Daniel's 'journalistic version' was inaccurate; it had been the Cubans who had put forward the idea of missiles. He repeated this to Matthews 'at least four times'.[32] Castro suggested to another correspondent[33] that he personally had desired the missiles so that the U.S., if they invaded Cuba, would have to confront the possibility of thermo-nuclear war. In October 1964 Castro did not answer adequately a question on this subject when put to him by another representative of the *New York Times*, Cyrus Sulzberger: 'Both Russia and Cuba participated,' he tautologically replied. Again, in July 1965, Castro said that 'we made the decision at a moment when we thought that concrete measures were necessary to paralyse the plans of aggression of the United States and *we posed this* necessity *to the Soviet Union*.'[34] Finally, in 1967 Castro gave yet another account to Herbert Matthews: 'we felt ourselves in danger from the U.S. We consulted with the Russians, when they suggested the missiles, we immediately said "Yes by all means".'[35]

Of these differing accounts, that given to Jean Daniel was the most complete but also the most troublesome. If the minor errors are ignored as deriving from Daniel's or Castro's bad memory (Raúl Castro and Guevara did not go to Moscow together, neither went in

[30] Author's italics.
[31] *New Republic*, 21 December 1963.
[32] Herbert Matthews, *Return to Cuba*, 16.
[33] B. Collier, *New York Herald Tribune*, 17 August 1964.
[34] To Lee Lockwood, 200.
[35] Herbert Matthews, *Castro*, 196.

ance of Cuba to the U.S. he could compare it to the importance of Hungary to the USSR: an unfortunate parallel from which Khrushchev may have drawn an obvious moral. Karol (*op. cit.* 263) argues that Khrushchev knew all along that the U.S. would not invade Cuba.

June), there would seem one major discrepancy of timing: Adzubei's discussion with Kennedy in Washington was on 30 January 1962, while he is supposed to have gone some time *after* the reports about the CIA's new invasion activities. Yet these were said to have come only six months before the installation of the missiles, that is, in April 1962 – a likely date, since it was then that Miró Cardona left the White House for Miami with the 'certitude' that Cuba would soon be freed.

These accounts by Castro should not, however, obscure two central points: first, that however honestly the Cubans and the Russians may have believed that the U.S. were planning an invasion of Cuba, they were wrong: Kennedy, like Theodore Roosevelt in 1906, did not desire a military occupation of Cuba. Secondly, whether or not Castro took the initiative over the missiles – a most improbable eventuality, in the direct sense of the word – he must have been delighted to have them and probably had always coveted them, at the very least since Khrushchev's first mention of the matter in 1960 when it will be recalled that the Russian leader first announced that 'in a figurative sense' his artillery-men could support Cuba with rocket fire. Guevara, it will be recalled, immediately gave a very tough, Cuban interpretation of these words, even claiming that in consequence, Cuba was, by force of circumstance, 'the arbiter of world peace'.[36] Perhaps Castro had been scheming, as one impressed above all from the earliest age by weapons, to lay hold of missiles ever since 1960 and that he had seized on the apparent U.S. threat, however genuine he judged it to be, as an excuse to get what he wanted.[37]

Doubtless Kennedy's inaction, which had led to the defeat of Cochinos Bay persuaded Khrushchev (who had met Kennedy in Vienna) that he would not now act. Maybe some Russians thought that the brazen display of Communist might in the American hemisphere would bring home to Latin America not only the possibility of an open challenge to the U.S. but the clear advantage of Russian over Chinese policies.[38]

So much for the origins of this celebrated gamble by Russia in the Caribbean. In practice the plan provided for, first, the protection of Cuba by a powerful ring of defences – twenty-four batteries of surface-to-air missiles, with 25 miles' radius, a hundred MiG fighters, nuclear defence missiles and ship-to-ship missiles. Ilyushin 28 bombers and ballistic missiles would also be established, along with four battle groups of special ground troops with tactical nuclear weapons. The ballistic

---

[36] Guevara, *Hoy*, 12 July 1960.
[37] Andrés Suárez (163–4) argues this strongly.
[38] Leon Lipson, 'Castro and the Cold War', in Plank, 194.

missiles were to be at San Cristóbal (3 battalions of MRBMs), Guana-jay (2 battalions of IRBMs), Remedios (2 battalions of IRBMs) and Sagua la Grande (3 battalions of MRBMs). All these needed many special vehicles and personnel. Over a hundred ships were needed to bear this material to Cuba:[39] as lavish an armada as had ever set off across the Atlantic for an armed encounter in the Caribbean.

[39] Hillsman, 159.

The Missile Crisis: II

The crisis which now unfolded was a drama in the course of which the population of the northern hemisphere was closer to extinction than at any previous time. Cuba, the agent of the crisis, at last dragged her ambitions and anxieties to be free to inspire for the first time in 200 years a world conflict and also the risk of cataclysm. Yet, in the course of the crisis, the island of Cuba itself slid from view: the protagonists became the United States and Russia. Cuba observed events with impatience from the wings.

On 26 July 1962, at the annual celebration of the foundation of his movement, Castro explained to the thousands gathered at Santiago that a direct U.S. invasion was now all that Cuba need fear. As he spoke, Russian arms and men in large numbers began to arrive at the small harbour of Mariel and other ports. At this time survey work was certainly being done for the future missile sites. In August Cuba took several steps more away from romantic agriculture to Russian methods; a 'labour book', which all had to have to obtain work, was introduced; rises in wages were prohibited; the cane co-operatives became state farms, on the vote, it was said, of all but three of the 1,380 *cooperativistas* gathered at the conference: the *cooperativistas* had complained that they received only half the wage of state farm workers, and that there had been no attempt to convert the co-operatives into genuine or self-sufficient concerns.[1] The *cooperativistas* themselves had apparently been unable to make any attempt whatever to reproduce in Cuba the self-reliant and successful co-operative societies of Israel or even of North America. Many workers had left agriculture for the towns. The cane co-operative had produced less in 1962 than in 1961.[2] The government seems to have concentrated its energies on the state farms. This rationalizing move, of course, did not solve the problem of agriculture. Carlos Rafael Rodríguez remarked, 'The negative factors still outweigh the positive.'[3]

That same day in the U.S., 23 August, the director of the CIA, McCone, was telling President Kennedy that, from exile reports and

---

[1] According to Dumont, *Cuba*, 52, the three were the only co-operatives to have made a profit in the last two years.

[2] *Hoy*, 21 September 1962.

[3] *Ibid.*, 23 August 1962. These *granjas de la caña* were not merged with the *granjas del pueblo*, so that, with the farms directly run by INRA since 1959, there were now three separate types of state direction.

aerial photographs, he thought that Russia was preparing to place 'offensive missiles' in Cuba.[4] Perhaps the French intelligence officer, Thiraud de Vosjoly, the celebrated hero of Leon Uris's thriller *Topaz*, brought him eye-witness information. No one believed McCone, though it seems he had first put forward the idea as early as 10 August.[5] It was anyway a presentiment of his, not a judgement.

On 24 August Kennedy at his press conference stated firmly: 'I am not for invading Cuba at this time.' The sentence, while it did not satisfy those in the U.S. who pressed for 'Action', was scarcely reassuring in Cuba either. The same day Roger Hillsman, director of Intelligence at the State Department, told the Washington press corps 'off the record' the news that the recent armaments which had been observed to have arrived in Cuba might include surface-to-air missiles (SAM).[6] On 29 August a U.2, flying over Pinar del Río, discovered evidence of SAMs in position.[7] McCone rightly calculated that this meant that offensive missiles would be installed, on the argument that the only use for SAMs would be to protect offensive missiles; but he was on a honeymoon in France.[8] Two days later, possibly in consequence of leakage of information from the CIA, Senator Keating announced that the Russian build-up was 'deliberately designed' to enable Russia to build missile sites.

On 2 September, meantime, a Russian communiqué at the end of Guevara's discussions in Moscow announced that Cuba had asked for more military help and that Russia would supply it because of threats from the U.S. Russia would also build for Cuba a new steel mill and a $M13 fishing port. Two days later, Kennedy publicly announced that the U.S. had seen the Cuban SAMs. He added that the U.S. would have to act if 'offensive ground-to-ground missiles' were introduced into Cuba. He thus clearly distinguished between SAMs and MRBMs, both of which were in reality already being provided for in Cuba; both had either already arrived or were on the way there. Thus while Kennedy was committing his prestige to the maintenance of one position, Russia and Cuba were already committed to another.[9]

---

[4] Abel, 18. Hillsman, 172, confirms. Maybe, as Abel says (40), Kennedy was still distrustful of the CIA because of its role in the previous Cuban fiasco. Anyway there remained in Washington a general belief that Russia would not take this step, and McCone did not press his opinion.

[5] See Arthur Krock, *Memoirs* (1968), 378, and Patrick Seale and Maureen McConville, 'Is there a "Philby" near de Gaulle?', *Observer*, 14 April and 21 April 1968.

[6] Hillsman, 170. These were the weapons which had brought down the U.2 of Gary Powers.

[7] Sorensen, 670. These were missiles similar to the U.S. Nike. Of course, all U.2 flights over Cuba were technically an illegal violation of Cuban airspace.

[8] *Ibid.*, McCone sent three telegrams on 7, 10 and 13 September, to the CIA giving his views but these were not distributed to Kennedy.

[9] Robert Kennedy, 'Thirteen Days', *Sunday Times*, 27 October 1968, suggests that this statement was made on his advice, itself tendered after a talk with the Soviet ambassador, Dobrynin, on that day.

On 7 September Kennedy formally asked for, and Congress agreed to, the mobilization of 150,000 reserves. This was evidently a request made with one eye on the Cuban situation. Castro's reaction was typical: Cuba did not require instructions from Washington about the steps which it would take to defend its sovereignty. Raúl Castro said that an attack on Cuba would mark the demise of imperialism. Construction work meantime on the Guanajay IRBM site would doubtless have been begun by then.[10] It was incidentally also on 7 September that Khrushchev had his famous conversation with Robert Frost and suggested that the western democracies were too old to fight – a clear indication of a new hard Russian line.[11] A statement by Tass on 11 September attacked the U.S. almost hysterically, and said: 'One cannot now attack Cuba and expect that the aggressor will be free from punishment,' though this document misleadingly added that there was no need to shift nuclear weapons 'for the repulsion of aggression . . . to any other country, for instance, to Cuba.'[12] Some time in the next few days, however, Khrushchev sent a personal message to assure Kennedy that under no circumstances would surface-to-surface missiles be sent to Cuba – a directly false message.[13] What Castro had called, two years before, the 'international chess game' was thus already far advanced in early September. It is fair to add that this summer and autumn of 1962 were characterized by further radical measures of liberalization and destalinization in Russia; this was the time when Khrushchev assured Bukharin's widow that her husband had been innocent and when Yevtushenko's *Stalin's Heirs* and Solzhenitsyn's *One Day in the Life of Ivan Denisovich* were published: Khrushchev was in fact pressing ahead on all fronts ambitiously.

On 8 and 15 September respectively two large Russian freighters, the *Omsk* and the *Poltava*, built for the lumber trade, with large hatches, riding high in the water, arrived in Havana, with lorries on the top deck, and a number of medium-range ballistic missiles beneath.[14] They were apparently unloaded at night by Russians and moved out by convoys between 9 September and 20 September.[15]

The die was now cast.

[10] Hillsman, 184.

[11] Not 'too liberal', as Frost later said. See discussion in Schlesinger, *A Thousand Days* (London edn.), 702, fn.

[12] *Pravda*, 12 September 1962. The jumbled wording of this statement suggests that it was written by Khrushchev. See Tatu, 240. The Cubans treated this as an explicit commitment to defend Cuba if attacked. Thus *Revolución* had huge headlines afterwards announcing 'Rockets for the U.S. if Cuba is attacked.'

[13] Robert Kennedy, 'Thirteen Days', *Sunday Times*, 27 October 1968.

[14] Hillsman, 184. The arrival of these odd vessels was noted by the U.S. but it was thought that a shortage of ships had led to their use. *Cf.* Abel, 42, and Hillsman, 187.

[15] *Ibid.*, 184. *Cf.* Roberta Wohlstetter, 'Cuba and Pearl Harbor: Hindsight and Foresight', *Foreign Affairs*, July 1965, qu. McNamara press conference.

On 13 September Kennedy, however, again stated that if Cuba were to gather an 'offensive military capacity for the Soviet Union', the U.S. would do 'whatever must be done'. This far from explicit statement was intended for U.S. opinion at home as much as for Castro and Khrushchev, perhaps mostly for Senator Keating, who was making strong speeches up and down the U.S. in the Republican interest alleging that offensive missiles were already established in Cuba and denouncing any exchange of 'Berlin for Cuba'.[16] But there had been so many rumours about missiles in Cuba: even in 1959, when the Russians had yet to send any weapons at all to Cuba, the U.S. government's Cuban missile file was five inches thick.[17] The government of the U.S. had so firmly decided that it would be both foolish and against all expected Russian behaviour to send this war material to Cuba that hints from exiles, agents in Cuba and others were neglected.[18]

By 18 to 21 September secret reports began to arrive of mysterious activities in the San Cristóbal area, a thickly wooded, mountainous and beautiful region about half-way between Pinar del Río and Havana.[19] But these were not reliable reports, and despite the fact that construction on the San Cristóbal and Remedios missile sites was almost certainly begun between 15 and 20 September, this was not noticed by the U.2 flight of 17 September.[20] On 19 September the U.S. Intelligence Board formally concluded that Russia would not send offensive missiles to Cuba.[21] Even so, a report reached the CIA two days later from an agent inside Cuba that sixty-foot missiles, twice as large as SAMs, were in the island.[22] But this news was taken even by the CIA with a pinch of salt, out of 'pure scepticism', according to Hillsman.[23] 'Wolf' had been cried too often by too many people. Construction on the fourth Cuban IRBM site seems to have been begun at Sagua la Grande between 25

[16] *New York Times*, 10 September 1962.
[17] Hillsman, 169.
[18] *Cf.* Roberta Wohlstetter on this, in *Foreign Affairs*, July 1965.
[19] Secretary of Defence McNamara, in testimony, 7 February 1963, to the House Appropriations Committee. The author remembers a climb in this region as late as July 1962 to a mountain top from which an endless landscape of royal palms stretched to the horizon and to the sea, the beauty of the scene disturbed only by an occasional vulture.
[20] According to Sorensen, 672, flights were held up after 5 September because of bad weather. This is incorrect; see Hillsman, 171, McNamara (qu. Roberta Wohlstetter (*op. cit.*)) and Schlesinger, *A Thousand Days*, 684. The flight on the 5th over west Cuba had been negative, according to McNamara. Some caution was shown because the U.S. lost a U.2 over China on 9 September. The U.2s could cover all Cuba in one flight, given normal weather but usually two were used.
[21] Hillsman, 170; Robert Kennedy, 'Thirteen Days', *op. cit.* McCone was still away and still thinking differently but according to Arthur Krock (*op. cit*) his views were cut out of the report by his deputy, General Carter.
[22] Abel, 24; confirmed by Hillsman, 174–5, who says that the report referred to movements on 12 September.
[23] Hillsman, 186.

September and 30 September,[24] and on 28 September, meantime, the Cuban Student Directorate in exile circulated a mimeographed letter stating that fifteen guided missile sites were being built.[25]

The arms increase in Cuba had meantime inspired xenophobia of rare proportions in the U.S. press. The *U.S. News and World Report* in its first September issue[26] specifically said that Cuba was getting 'Soviet rockets with a range of up to 400 miles'. The arrival of Russian troops in Cuba appeared to be the first time that a non-American power had established itself in the Americas since Napoleon III's ill-fated expedition to Mexico. Cuba became consequently the central issue in the congressional election campaign, with Republican politicians upbraiding the president for his inaction. In their issue of 21 September *Time* published a portrait of President Monroe on the cover and described the details of his doctrine, forgetting that, whatever its validity, it did not apply to Cuba, but arguing nevertheless that Russian action in Cuba called for U.S. action under it.[27] In an issue of the *U.S. News and World Report*, dated 17 September a retired general described the military methods of crushing the Cuban regime: a sea blockade and a land invasion. Six divisions, he confirmed, would be needed.

Of course, there were dissentient voices, but not in politically critical places. The Department of Defence announced that Cubans enrolled in the U.S. army could be used against Cuba. The *U.S. News and World Report*[28] then published another excitable article headlined, 'Is Blockade of Cuba on the Way?'. It added: 'A decision to blockade, if made, will have to follow a fuller build-up of Soviet power in Cuba.' A week later, Mrs Henry Luce wrote a long article in *Life* pointing out the contrast between Kennedy's toughness on Cuba during the elections of 1960 and his current 'calm'. She was full of dire if fashionable predictions: 'Time is running out in Latin America and the cold war is still being lost there.' She demanded action: 'What is now at stake in the decision for intervention or non-intervention in Cuba is the question not only of American prestige but of American survival.'[29] In the first week of October Richard Rovere, in the *New Yorker*, published an ominous article about 'a war party' in Washington, which he argued was no less active than the group which engineered war in 1898.[30]

All this meant pressure on the administration at an election time. Even so, there was no suggestion that Kennedy was going to surrender

[24] *Ibid.*, 184.
[25] *New York Times*, 24 October 1962.
[26] Dated 10 September.
[27] The conclusion of the article put the case negatively by destroying the administration argument against direct action to oust Castro.
[28] In an issue distributed 24 September – 1 October.
[29] *Life*, 5 October 1962, 56.
[30] *New Yorker*, 10 October 1962.

to it, as McKinley had done sixty years before. U.2 reconnaissance flights were made over east Cuba on 5 and 7 October and revealed nothing. On 10 October Senator Keating said that he had '100% reliable' evidence from exiles that six intermediate-range missile sites were under construction.[31] Two days earlier it seemed that President Dorticós of Cuba almost admitted the truth when, at the U.N., he had said that the threat of U.S. invasion had led Cuba to acquire armaments which 'it had not wanted and [which it] hoped it would not have to use'.[32] On 10 October Kennedy authorized a new U.2 flight over west Cuba.[33] This was carried out on Sunday 14 October by the U.S. air force (not the CIA), the flight having been delayed a day or two by Hurricane Daisy. Photographs showed that, in an area not covered by U.2 flights since 5 September, sites for a battalion of mobile medium-range 1,000-mile ballistic missiles were being constructed at San Cristóbal.[34] From other excavations it seemed that hard permanent sites for IRBMs of 2,000-mile radius were also being prepared.[35] McCone of the CIA, therefore, as Kennedy later had to admit, was 'right all along'.[36]

Between 16 October and 21 October, the U.S. government confirmed this information. Much time was spent on determining the reasons for the Soviet-Cuban action. Prominent among the theories put forward was that Khrushchev, after the U.S. elections in November, would at the U.N. personally reveal the existence of the missiles and propose the exchange of Berlin for withdrawing the missiles.[37] Others thought that Khrushchev might wish to trade the Cuban missiles for the U.S. ones in Turkey and Italy,[38] or that he desired to prove that the U.S. was too weak to risk nuclear war, thereby permitting further Russian penetration into South America and encouraging even European allies to make

[31] After the crisis he said that he had secured this remarkably precise information from a government official, doubtless from the CIA. For discussion of this claim, see Hillsman, 177–9.

[32] *Revolución*, 9 October 1962. Dorticós met Gromyko at New York and it is of course likely that they exchanged views on the major problem about to engulf their two nations.

[33] Schlesinger, *A Thousand Days*, 684. Sorensen, 672, says 9 October. The plan was suggested on 4 October, according to both Schlesinger and Hillsman (p. 175), because (according to Hillsman) of U.S. naval photographs of Soviet ships at sea on 28 September – which seemed to suggest that Russia was sending Ilyushin bombers to Cuba. (Hillsman, 167.)

[34] *Ibid.*, 166.

[35] See Chronology in the *New York Times*, 6 November 1962, which says that Ilyushins were observed in a photograph taken on 28 September. These bombers had a range of about 900 miles, a speed of 500 mph. But the photographs were not evaluated properly until 9 October, the information made available on the 10th.

[36] Krock, 380. It will be remembered that, according to Krock, McCone had guessed that offensive missiles were being placed in Cuba as early as 5 August.

[37] This view was taken by the U.S. ambassador in Moscow, Thompson (Abel, 48; *cf.* Sorensen, 677, on 'Theory 4'). Khrushchev had said earlier that he would postpone bringing up the Berlin question until after the U.S. elections. It is also the basic argument in Tatu's *Power in the Kremlin*.

[38] Actually they were due anyway to be removed by the U.S., as will be seen.

accommodation with Russia.[39] Others speculated that, to disprove the Chinese view, Russia desired the U.S. to invade Cuba – thereby dividing the west and enabling Khrushchev incidentally to move in Berlin.[40] Some certainly thought that the missiles were merely for the defence of Cuba, as well as that the new deployment doubled Russian first-strike capacity – which if it did not really alter profoundly the strategic balance, might nevertheless seem to do so. It seemed to others that whatever the precise reason or reasons for the Soviet action, Khrushchev must have gambled that the U.S. president would be unable to decide on a firm course of action so close to the time of the election.

Kennedy in the end reached the rather lame explanation that Khrushchev's conduct could be explained by a desire to prove the U.S. weak before the world, believing that the defence of Cuba and an increase of missile power were 'likely but insufficient' causes of this new Russian action.[41] The information obtained on 14 October was confirmed by more U.2 flights: twenty (in place of two) occurred in the next six days. Three incomplete IRBM fixed sites and six actual mobile MRBM sites were discovered.[42] All were guarded and manned by Russians, not Cubans. The U.S. counted 30 to 35 missiles, though there were apparently 42.[43]

What was to be done? Complete inactivity was ruled out as being likely to confirm 'the fears of De Gaulle and others that the U.S. could not be depended upon to meet threats even farther from our shores', while in Latin America a 'failure to intervene would bring a Castro-Communist trend', even in countries where non-intervention was a 'religion'.[44] McNamara nevertheless 'pointed out . . . we had long lived within range of Soviet missiles, we expected Khrushchev to live with our missiles nearby, and, by taking this addition calmly, we could prevent him from inflating its importance'.[45] Kennedy rejected this

[39] Apparently the view of the U.S. Ambassador to France, a Russian expert, Charles Bohlen (Sorensen, 677), as well as to some extent that of the president.

[40] Sorensen, 677

[41] In conversation with Schlesinger, on 21 October, Kennedy however attributed the Russian action to a desire to draw Russia and China together or at least to strengthen Russia's name in the international revolutionary movement by standing up for Cuba; to a desire to develop a stronger position in Berlin negotiations; and simply to 'deal the U.S. a blow' (Schlesinger, 693).

[42] They could be dismantled and reassembled, within six days. They were really movable rather than mobile, being about 55 to 60 feet long and liquid-fuelled (cf. *Washington Post*, 26 October 1962, 48).

[43] 'We never knew how many missiles were brought to Cuba. The Soviets said there were forty-two. We counted forty-two going out. We saw fewer than forty-two going in.' (R. Gilpatrick, on ABC Television, 11 November 1962.) But Russia probably intended 48 MRBMs and 16 IRBMs. None of the latter seems to have arrived.

[44] Sorensen, 681.

[45] *Loc. cit.*, Hillsman, 195. See Abel, 52, for confirmation. Incidentally most of those involved in the decisions changed their position, sometimes several times, in the course of the discussions.

policy because of the international political effects – not, apparently, because of the strategic consequences. He thought that 'the Soviet move had been undertaken so swiftly, so secretly and with so much deliberate deception . . . that it presented a provocative change in the delicate *status quo*'. He considered too that missiles on Soviet territory or submarines were different from missiles in the western hemisphere, particularly because of their political and psychological effect on Latin America. Such a step, if accepted, he thought would be clearly followed by further steps. His September pledges of action had clearly regarded this step as unacceptable. 'He was not willing to let the U.N. debate and Khrushchev equivocate while the missiles became operational.'[46] He 'knew he would have to act' just as if he had been slapped in the face: it was a challenge more than a threat[47] and, given his vulnerable position in U.S. politics over Cuba, he believed that he had to respond.

Thus Kennedy had also, in rejecting the 'do nothing' approach, rejected any idea for mere diplomatic action as argued by some of his advisers.[48] This decision also seems to have been taken more because of national than international politics (as perhaps Khrushchev's had been as well). In retrospect, however, it is curious that Kennedy did not choose first to present the Russians with his evidence in secrecy. The president chose to react strongly and outside existing methods of arbitration and existing alliances: partly from fear that once, for instance, the English or French governments were told, leakages were more likely.[49] If the European allies had been told, the countries of South America, who believed themselves entitled by treaties to close consultation where American events were concerned, would have also to be be brought into the story. But in addition to the problem of keeping the secret, the European allies might make light of the crisis: 'Most Europeans cared nothing about Cuba and thought we were over-anxious about it. They had long accustomed themselves to living next door to Soviet missiles. Would they support our risking a world war (for such seemed to be the case even at the beginning) . . . because we now had a dozen hostile missiles nearby?'[50] Further, the British and French might

[46] Sorensen, 683. Dillon told Abel that Kennedy's first reaction 'was that one simply could not accept the fact of Soviet missiles in Cuba trained on the U.S.' (Abel, 48).

[47] This is the reading of Robert Kennedy's record (*Sunday Times*, 27 October 1968). Kennedy later thought that he 'would have been impeached' if he had not acted in some way. See also Ronald Steel, 'Endgame', *New York Review of Books*, 13 March 1969.

[48] Abel, 53. Bohlen, Stevenson and Bundy seem to have thought diplomacy best.

[49] A point impressed on the author by Bundy in conversation (January 1963).

[50] Sorensen, 681. The same point was in Nitze's mind: 'We could expect the British to take a different view. The Allies generally had failed to appreciate why the presence of missiles in Cuba [if they were placed there] . . . would be intolerable to the U.S.' (Abel, 33). Pachter, 16, bluntly commented that the reason 'above all' why the Allies were not consulted was 'the doubt whether they would go along with the chosen style of action'. This was to be an American showdown with the Soviet Union and it had to be carried out by the American president in his own way.

point out with bitterness how generous the U.S. had been in the past with advice to them as to how to cope calmly with nationalism.[51]

The U.S. government thus advanced into the crisis distrusting their allies but willing nevertheless to embark on a policy which might bring ruin, even if victory, to them all.[52] For though NATO was not informed or consulted as such, NATO bases in Italy and Turkey were fully prepared. Kennedy was not prepared to allow Harold Macmillan or General de Gaulle to play the restraining role played over the Suez crisis by General Eisenhower in 1956. The idea of consulting the U.N. was indeed as abhorrent to Kennedy as it had been in 1956 to Eden; for, as a Chilean long ago pointed out, so far as the rest of the Americas was concerned, the U.S. cared 'as much about international law as about a radish'.[53] No doubt the OAS could be brought into the picture, as indeed it later was, but the OAS were told, not consulted, as were the U.N. and NATO.[54]

This failure to consult the Allies was scarcely commented upon at the time, since the Allies concerned felt it wiser not to give the impression that they had been slighted: this neglect was later criticized, however, in Europe and, curiously, defended by the leading U.S. political commentator, Lippman: 'The command of nuclear power to balance Soviet nuclear power cannot be shared . . . only one can sit at the wheel.'[55]

By 17 October Kennedy and his government were divided on the comparatively simple choice as to whether to instigate an immediate attack by air on the Cuban missile sites or whether to blockade Cuba roughly along the lines proposed three weeks before in the *U.S. News and World Report*. Dean Acheson and the chiefs of staff favoured the former policy;[56] it was ultimately rejected, since it was thought it would expand the conflict and kill thousands of Cubans and Russians, in a surprise attack resembling Pearl Harbour, so blackening 'the name of the U.S.

[51] As Raymond Aron pointed out in his article, 'A European Perspective', in Plank, 141.

[52] Ormsby Gore, the British ambassador, was told of the crisis at noon on 21 October, before any other ally.

[53] Manuel Foster Recabarren; I am indebted to Mr Raymond Carr for this quotation.

[54] The U.S. Congress was also in the dark, as was the cabinet formally until 4 p.m. on 22 October. Kennedy was acting by executive order, presidential proclamation and 'inherent powers'. . . He had earlier rejected all suggestions of reconvening Congress' (Sorensen, 701–2). He even seems to have been annoyed that congressional leaders (whom he met at 5 p.m. that day) should argue the toss with him.

[55] Address to the Anglo-American Association in Paris, qu. *New Republic*, 22 November 1962. The leading French political commentator, Raymond Aron, replied, '*Must we have blind faith*? When Lippman asks Europeans to hand over the wheel of the car, he is really asking them to abdicate after a fashion . . . the combination of an American/nuclear/monopoly and non-consultation with its allies reduces the European countries . . . to the status of protectorate nations.' De Gaulle criticized Kennedy, in his press conference of 14 January 1963.

[56] Robert Kennedy, *Sunday Times*, 27 October 1968.

in the pages of history', leading to 'our indictment in the court of history'.[57]

A decision was therefore ultimately made to establish a naval blockade to prevent the further arrival of offensive weapons, missiles or bombers. The advantage of this was that it began the 'escalation' of the crisis at its lowest rung – it left a large number of possible alternatives open for the future, and it did not in itself risk anyone's death. Kennedy was probably strengthened in making this decision by intelligence reports that Russia was not at all ready for a nuclear war and perhaps the information of Russian unreadiness given by the spy, Penkovsky (arrested incidentally in Moscow on 22 October), played a part here.[58]

While the implications of this recommendation were being worked out by Kennedy's advisers, Kennedy was personally assured in Washington by the Russian Foreign Minister, Gromyko, that Russia would never give offensive weapons to Cuba.[59] This assurance amazed and angered Kennedy and probably contributed to the bitterness of his first public speech on the missiles. Khrushchev had assured the U.S. ambassador in Moscow of the peaceful nature of his intentions on 16 October.[60] But Gromyko perhaps supposed that the U.S. had already discovered the existence of missiles in Cuba and was already speculating about Russia's response.[61] It remains odd that Kennedy did not tax Gromyko directly with the U.S. discoveries in Cuba: Robert Kennedy suggested that this was because U.S. policy had not been quite decided.

The impending crisis had been well concealed, though the British Embassy got wind of matters by 17 October.[62] Troop and aircraft movements to Florida had been remarked by the press, though on Kennedy's

---

[57] The words of Robert Kennedy (Sorensen, 684–5; cf. Schlesinger, A Thousand Days, 689); he told his brother, 'I now know how Tojo felt when planning Pearl Harbour.' For all this, see Sorensen, and Robert Kennedy, 'Thirteen Days', op. cit. The decision for the blockade was made on 18 October, but some discussion of alternatives continued, for the joint chiefs of staff still preferred an air strike or an invasion. An invasion would however have been much more difficult then than in 1961. Thus, Cuba now had probably 22 anti-aircraft guided missile bases, and two more being built (guide line missiles); surface-to-surface 'cruise' missiles, comparable to the U.S. Maces and Matadors; 100 MiG fighters; 20 Ilyushin 28 light bombers; and some Komar class, Russian P.T. boats carrying missiles (Washington Post, 26 October 1962, 18). At the same time the commander-in-chief of the tactical air force told Kennedy that even a major surprise air attack could not have eliminated without fail all the offensive missiles.

[58] Oleg Penkovsky, The Penkovsky Papers (1965), 323.

[59] Most of their talk was about Berlin. Kennedy later made much of this apparent deception by Gromyko but though (unlike the Russian ambassador in Washington) it must be assumed Gromyko knew of the existence of missiles in Cuba, doubtless he regarded himself within his rights as calling them 'defensive' just as Rusk would have referred to the U.S. Jupiters in Turkey by that useful adjective. Given the tortuous and unsatisfactory nature of international diplomacy, Gromyko's remarks do not now seem specially heinous.

[60] Hillsman, 166.

[61] Cf. ibid., 167.

[62] General Strong, director of the Joint Intelligence Bureau, noticed signs of unusual activity in the Pentagon on this day (Abel, 60).

request the *New York Times* did not publish an article on the subject.[63]
Long-prepared naval manœuvres off Vieques caused both Moscow and
Havana to become apprehensive.[64] Even so, Kennedy's announcement

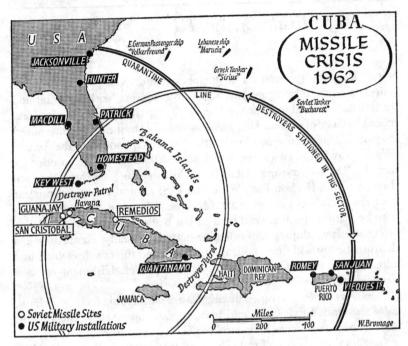

of his decision was delayed until 22 October, to give time to his advisers
to inform the Allies in Europe and South America, not to speak of
Congress. The little criticism there was from Congress was that an air
strike or an invasion of Cuba would be more appropriate: even the often
pacific Fulbright supported this idea on the grounds that a blockade
would pit Russian ships against U.S. armed forces and hence risk war
more easily.[65]

[63] Schlesinger, *A Thousand Days*, 692. Sorensen, 698, describes the incident in a different
style. Abel says the *Washington Post* also 'patriotically abandoned its metier'. Hillsman says the
New York Times simply kept quiet.

[64] See *Revolución*, 19 October.

[65] Johnson and Gwertzman, 182; Robert Kennedy, *Sunday Times*, 27 October 1968.

The Missile Crisis: III

Kennedy's speech on 22 October made seven points: offensive missile sites were being prepared in Cuba, an area 'with a special and historical relationship with the U.S.A.' These sites altered the international balance of power. This was unacceptable to the U.S., and indeed constituted 'aggressive conduct' of the sort which had led to the Second World War in the 1930s and which should then have been stopped by Britain. The longer-range IRBMs would threaten everything between Lima and the Hudson Bay. While the U.S. naturally opposed nuclear war, she would not shrink from it if need be. A 'quarantine' would therefore be instituted – the word seemed less bellicose than 'blockade' – to prevent further shipment of offensive material. Finally, Kennedy asked Khrushchev to withdraw both the bombers and the missiles which had already arrived in Cuba and to abandon the establishment of their launching sites.[1]

Kennedy's speech avoided linking Castro with Russia on the, perhaps, false assumption that Cuba had been imposed upon; there was no hint that Cuba was going to be invaded or Castro overthrown.

The legal justification for this 'quarantine' was formally less the U.N. Charter than the Charter of the OAS, which entitled member states to take 'collective measures to guard the security of the Americas'. The approval of the OAS was sought on 23 October and obtained by 19 votes too, with Uruguay abstaining, though only because her ambassador in Washington had received no instructions. All the other ambassadors were overawed by the solemnity of Dean Rusk's appeal to them. A U.S. resolution to the U.N. Security Council also called for the dismantling of the offending sites and the removal of both the missiles and the jet bombers, and for the establishment of a U.N. Observer Corps to visit Cuba in order to guarantee this.

The quarantine itself comprised sixteen destroyers, three cruisers, an anti-submarine aircraft carrier and six utility ships[2] disposed in an arc from Florida to beyond Puerto Rico,[3] with orders to inspect, stop and, if

---

[1] *New York Times*, 23 October 1962.

[2] Sorensen, 708.

[3] The line was drawn 500 miles from Cuba, rather than 800 as at first envisaged, on the suggestion of the English ambassador to give more time to Russian ships actually approaching to get instructions (Schlesinger, *A Thousand Days*, 699, and Robert Kennedy, *op. cit.*).

necessary, disable (rather than sink) those Russian vessels *en route* for Cuba which were capable of carrying nuclear warheads, air-to-surface or surface-to-air missiles, bombers, or any equipment to support that material. By including surface-to-air weapons, Kennedy was extending the quarantine to cover the most dangerous sort of defensive weapons. Kennedy also told his ambassadors in Guinea and Senegal, where Russian aircraft stopped on their way to Cuba, to ask the governments of those countries to refuse landing rights to Russia during the crisis, so as to avoid the dispatch of warheads by air; both agreed – even Sékou Touré, a friend of Castro's, on the grounds that he opposed bases on foreign soil.[4]

The world then waited with some apprehension for the Russian response. From the U.S. there was general though not unanimous approval. The *New York Times* showed a certain lack of enthusiasm by saying that Kennedy 'could not have done much less'.[5] The *New York Post* criticized the lack of consultation of the U.N. and OAS. On succeeding days the *New York Times* published critical letters. In London, Macmillan told Kennedy that Europe, used to living under the 'nuclear gun', might wonder what all the fuss was about; his view was that Khrushchev would try to 'trade Cuba for Berlin'.[6] Adenauer seemed initially 'rather agitated'.[7] Gaitskell in England questioned the legality of the quarantine and urged Macmillan to fly to Washington.[8] Diefenbaker in Canada wavered. The English government, like other allies, nevertheless gave support, though (a fact which passed unnoticed) this was the first time that England had given formal approval to someone else's blockade at sea. The torch had indeed passed on.[9] As some of Kennedy's advisers had predicted, the English newspapers were the most critical. Thus *The Times* wondered if there really were missiles in Cuba, *The Guardian* thought that Khrushchev was showing to the U.S. 'the meaning of U.S. bases close to the Soviet frontier', and even the *Daily Mail* called the blockade an 'act of war' and suggested that Kennedy was being led by 'popular emotion'. *The Daily Telegraph* was also critical. Bertrand Russell announced to the world in general: 'Within a week you will all be dead to please American madmen,' and telegraphed Kennedy: 'Your action desperate. Threat to survival.' He appealed as well to Khrushchev to be cautious.[10]

[4] Abel, 136–9.
[5] *New York Times*, 23 October, 36.
[6] Schlesinger, *A Thousand Days*, 698.
[7] Abel, 128.
[8] Statement by Labour Party National Executive, which also deplored the lack of consultation.
[9] Lloyd's suspended fixed insurance for risks in shipping to London.
[10] Lord Russell, *Unarmed Victory* (1963), 29. On 23 October over six million shares changed hands in the U.S. (*Washington Post*, 24 October 1962). Prices for 'commodity futures' recorded

Bad news also came from the east where the Indo-Chinese border quarrel had burst out again. On 23 October China (who had presumably been informed by Russia of her Cuban action) lifted all restraints on invasion in North India and authorized her troops to advance as far as they could: she was taking advantage of an opportunity – not, of course, coordinating an attack, though Russia gave her full support for a week.[11]

In Cuba itself, two medium-range missiles were ready to operate by 23 October.[12] There were about 20,000 Russian troops in Cuba in four units of about 5,000 men each – two units near Havana, one in central Cuba, one in the east. They had modern Russian ground fighting armaments including rocket launchers like the U.S. 'Honest John'.[13] These facts were not yet publicly admitted in Cuba, though Kennedy's speech had been listened to and most of it was published by *Revolución*.[14] The general supposition was not only that Cuba was about to be invaded but that it would be subject to nuclear bombardment. This, of course, was irrational, though obviously, in a full war, Havana might very well have been destroyed, by conventional or other means. Castro, however, must have known that his most likely danger was a U.S. invasion by sea or an aerial bombardment of the missile sites. On 23 October, anyway, he called for general mobilization. Red posters depicting a man holding a machine-gun called the population to arms. Raúl Castro moved down the island to take command in Santiago, and we catch a glimpse of him on 25 October surrounded by old comrades such as Calixto García, Armando Acosta, Faustino Pérez, Luis Mas Martín and Abilio Cortina (secretary of the Oriente JUCEI) under the slogan *Listos para Vencer*, ready to conquer.[15] According to one observer: 'It was as if a long-contained tension relaxed, as if the whole country had said as one, "at last". The long wait for the invasion, the war of nerves, the sneak attacks, the landing of spies, the blockade. All this was past.'[16] The discipline, the absence of panic and the dedication were impressive. Castro himself spoke

---

[11] China was later reproached for this advance, by Suslov at the plenum of the Central Committee of Russia on 14 February 1964, published April 1964.

[12] Sorensen, 709.

[13] According to Wohlstetter, *Foreign Affairs*, July 1965, these were not seen by the U.S. U.2s, only by the low level photography which followed.

[14] *Revolución*, 26 October.

[15] *Ibid*.

[16] Adolfo Gilly, *Inside the Cuban Revolution* (trans. Félix Gutiérrez, 1964), 48. Gilly was a Trotskyist who later turned against Castro. Ironically, precisely similar words could be found among U.S. reporters. Thus: 'A sense of relief from frustration has rolled across the Mid-Western prairies following the President's action [*sic*] on Cuba.' (*New York Times*, 25 October 1962, 22, New York edn.)

---

their biggest jump since the Korean war – including curiously sugar which exceeded the daily limit of ½ cent per pound on 23 October. On 24 October Khrushchev's reply to Bertrand Russell led to a buying spree.

briefly (one hour and twenty minutes) to the Cubans on 23 October condemning Kennedy's 'piracy', and said that anyone who wished to inspect Cuba should come prepared to fight. 'We refuse all inspection: Cuba is not the Congo . . . Our arms are not offensive.' He compared Kennedy to the pirate Sir Henry Morgan, in contrast to Drake, who 'had undoubted qualities'. Did the satiated shark, the U.S., really think Cuba a little sardine?[17] But the 'international chess game' was now at last out of Castro's hands. He was in the dark as to what would happen. He was apparently not consulted by Khrushchev but, like De Gaulle, merely informed. For Castro, too, his alliances were never the same again. For ordinary Cubans, however, the most important part of the crisis was the indefinite suspension of flights by Pan American to Miami: this twice-weekly air service, which had carried perhaps 250,000 refugees to the U.S., was not resumed till 1965 and then under quite different conditions.

The Russian response to the demands of Kennedy was, like Kennedy's own decisions, made in the dark so far as their opponents' real intentions were concerned. Russia seems to have seen the quarantine as intended to prevent the coming of the IRBMs. But the jet Ilyushin bombers had been in Cuba for some time. Was the U.S. merely seeking to avoid the arrival of 'offensive' weapons or were they in fact hoping to crush Castro too? Of course, reaction in the Moscow press was violent: 'America's ruling class has at last dropped its mask . . . seldom has any country committed so uncouth and treasonable an aggression.' The first official Russian response, like Castro's, was to announce on 23 October that all their weapons in Cuba were defensive and that the quarantine was an act of piracy. At the U.N. the Russian ambassador, Zorin, left presumably without instructions, unwisely accused the U.S. of inventing the evidence. Contrariwise, the Russian press officer at the U.N. told his U.S. colleague that New York would probably be blown up the next day.[18] Dobrynin, the Soviet ambassador in Washington seemed, like Zorin, without instructions and out of touch.[19] Khrushchev then wrote Kennedy a letter echoing the public messages, and was promptly answered with a private restatement of the U.S. public position.[20]

It was known in Washington from aerial reconnaissance that twenty-five Russian cargo ships, five of them with large hatches (and therefore suitable for carrying missiles), were then heading for Havana.[21] On the evening of 23 October U.S. newspapers proclaimed: 'Showdown can come

[17] Text in *Revolución*, 24 October. He did not actually admit the existence of missiles.
[18] Abel, 133.
[19] Schlesinger, *A Thousand Days*, 699; Kennedy, *Sunday Times*, 27 October 1968, confirms.
[20] Sorensen, 709.
[21] *New York Times*, 24 October 1962, 1.

tonight.'[22] This was an exaggeration, for the quarantine did not come into being until the following morning, Wednesday, 24 October, when at 10 a.m. Russian submarines were reported to be following the cargo ships, like the long sharks which for so many years used to pursue slave ships on the same route. 'Sea Clash Near' was then the headline of the *Washington Daily News* on 24 October. This was for most people, including for Kennedy and his government, a harsh moment.[23]

During the course of the morning the Russian ships altered course or drew to a halt at sea: 'Some Red ships turning back', the *Washington Evening Star* announced prematurely. The news came to Kennedy and his advisers at a morning meeting. The Pentagon thought that the ships might be aiming to rendezvous at sea with the submarines behind them and so force their way through. At the same time Khrushchev, answering Bertrand Russell in a publicly announced missive, suggested a new summit conference, and pledged that his government would not be reckless and would 'do everything in our power to prevent war'.[24] The use by Khrushchev of the aged Russell in his house in North Wales as an intermediary was the most bizarre aspect of these days. It caused what now seems to have been the first step backwards in the Russian position to be somewhat overlooked. U Thant, a more conventional go-between, proposed a Russian suspension of arms shipments and a U.S. delay in imposing the quarantine. But Kennedy brushed this aside to say that the missiles already in Cuba had to be removed before the quarantine could be suspended.[25] Khrushchev, on the other hand, in his answer to U Thant, showed his willingness to accept negotiation, even with the blockade – a further sign of a retreat.[26] In the afternoon Khrushchev saw a U.S. businessman, William Knox of Westinghouse International.[27] The conversation was ambiguous. Khrushchev seemed weary: the missiles, he said, were defensive; Kennedy was risking a world war; and Russian submarines would soon be sinking U.S. ships if they tried to halt Russian ships. Some in the U.S. administration saw in Knox's report of this talk a Russian desire to negotiate and a need to give Khrushchev a way of escape.[28] At the least, he had now admitted it was true, though privately, that the missiles in Cuba existed. In the Pentagon, meantime, McNamara was quarrelling with the chief of naval staff, Admiral Anderson, about the precise physical consequences of stopping a Russian ship: the admiral, a brave successor to Admiral

---

[22] *Washington Daily News.*
[23] Robert Kennedy, *Sunday Times*, 27 October 1968.
[24] Qu. *Washington Evening Star*, 24 October (Stocks Final), 1.
[25] Sorensen, 709–10.
[26] Tatu, 265.
[27] Schlesinger, 702–3.
[28] *loc. cit.*

Schley, said that he needed no guidance, since the navy had 'always known how to conduct a blockade'.[29]

On 25 October, a Russian tanker (the *Bucharest*) and an East German passenger ship (the *Völkerfreund*) were allowed through the quarantine without being searched, on the grounds that they could not possibly be carrying missiles or other equipment similar. Twelve of the Russian ships on the way to Cuba had by then halted.

The blockade or quarantine seemed therefore to have worked. There remained the U.S. demands for the removal of existing missiles and bombers. The medium-range missiles were now believed to be ready for use within a few days and the intermediate-range ones within a month. Kennedy and his advisers discussed the possibility of extending the blockade to cover oil, of further low-level flights, of a direct approach to Castro, and again, as before the crisis, at an air strike or an invasion. U.S. newspapers began to publish lists of 'approved fall-out shelters'. There were, meantime, more signs of Russian concern to avoid war. Gromyko made a speech in Berlin without mentioning Cuba. Russian diplomats tried to persuade intermediaries everywhere to try to tempt allied governments to intercede.[30] Adlai Stevenson in the U.N. was making the best publicity out of the Russian representative's obvious lack of knowledge and instruction, while Zorin still denied that any Russian missiles were in Cuba, a point of view which Stevenson found easy to ridicule with a famous public show of the photographs, thereby making up for some of the ignominy which had come to him in 1961. U Thant, ignored the previous day by Kennedy, sent a further plea to both parties to avoid 'confrontation' in the Caribbean.

On Friday, 26 October, there was no change in the Russian or Cuban position and Kennedy ordered a 'crash programme on civil government in Cuba . . . after the invasion'. Work on the missile sites seemed indeed to be continuing apace. The inspection at sea was enacted for the first time on the *Manuela*, a Panamanian vessel, bound for Cuba under Russian charter. The boarding party allowed it to sail on. But *Pravda*'s headline that morning had been remarkably pacific and, in the middle of the day, the Russians made their first positive proposal for a compromise, through the curious intermediary of Aleksander Fomin of their Washington Embassy (doubtless an intelligence officer) and a well-connected Washington television reporter, John Scali of ABC News: would the U.S. be interested in a promise not to invade Cuba in return for a Russian withdrawal of the missiles under U.N. inspection? Scali consulted Hillsman and Rusk and reported later to Fomin that the U.S. saw 'real possibilities' in the idea. A little afterwards, a letter for Ken-

---

[29] *Cf.* description in Abel.
[30] Including grotesquely the ill-fated Stephen Ward of the Profumo case.

nedy arrived from Khrushchev making much the same proposal in evidently sincere though confused terms, while Zorin made the same proposal to U Thant, with the Cuban delegation in New York in support.[31] This letter was emotional, apparently in Khrushchev's own style, being full of recollections of the horrors of war. Russia, said Khrushchev, had sent missiles to Cuba because of the Bay of Cochinos; they were defensive; and a U.S. pledge not to invade Cuba would remove the need for them.

Before Kennedy had time to reply to this letter, another one from the Kremlin on Saturday, 27 October, altered the thrust of the bargain by taking up an idea launched by *The Times* (of London) and echoed by Walter Lippman[32] in the *New York Herald Tribune* on 25 October, for the evacuation of the U.S. missile bases from Turkey.[33] Khrushchev also assured Kennedy that the missiles already in Cuba were completely under Russian control.[34] This letter confused the U.S. (though in it Russia publicly admitted that there were missiles in Cuba), while the proposal contained in it was not acceptable to Kennedy.[35] Was Khrushchev still in control? The two letters resembled the different telegrams sent from Berlin to Vienna in the crisis of July 1914 which had led to the First World War. 'Who rules in Berlin?' had asked General Conrad von Hötzendorf; and indeed there was doubtless serious dissension at this time between the Russian leaders as to the course to be followed.[36]

The arrival of the second letter was followed by the news that a U.2 aeroplane had been shot down over Cuba by a SAM missile and that another U.2 had accidentally strayed over Russia in the far east, maybe,

[31] Sorensen, 712; Schlesinger, *A Thousand Days*, 706–7. Schlesinger implies that the bargain offered in it was more categorical than does Sorensen. Unlike Khrushchev's other letters, this important one was not published in Moscow. It was thought by some that this suggests that Khrushchev wrote it behind the praesidium's back. Abel quotes a passage from it (181), but it has not otherwise been made public.

[32] Lippman had written that in both World Wars the U.S. 'suspended diplomacy when the guns began to shoot. In both wars as a result we achieved a great victory but we could not make peace. There is a mood in this country today which could easily cause us to make the same mistake again.' Thus, Kennedy had suspended diplomacy when he had seen Gromkyo, when he should have given him a chance to save face. He also suggested that Turkey was comparable to Cuba and an exchange over the two might be a 'way out of the tyranny of automatic and uncontrollable events'. (*Washington Post*, 25 October 1962.)

[33] Marshal Malinovsky had alluded to Cuba and Turkey in the same breath on 23 October. The Russians may have thought that Lippman was speaking for Kennedy.

[34] The Russians may have had electronic locks, possibly even controlled in Russia, on these missiles, as the U.S. had over their overseas missiles since July of the same year. (Roberta and Albert Wohlstetter, 8, suggest that the real reason for the 20,000 Russian troops was to guard the missiles from the Cubans, not from the marines.)

[35] Although U.S. plans had already been made for the removal of the missile sites from Turkey, already obsolete, as Khrushchev no doubt knew.

[36] Tatu, 270, suggests that Khrushchev was out-voted that day in the praesidium and was not responsible for any of the actions taken then, but later gave (on 21 December 1962) to the Supreme Soviet, a speech describing not what did happen but what should have happened.

as Khrushchev later said, risking confusion with a nuclear bomber. 'Would the Russians view this as a final reconnaissance in preparation for a nuclear attack? ... There was a moment of frightening grimness.'[37] Castro has since maintained that it was he who was responsible for bringing the U.2 down, suggesting that the missiles in Cuba were not all under central Moscow control.[38] Though Kennedy did not order (as had been provided for) any response to the destruction of the U.2 over Cuba, all the U.S. nuclear and conventional forces throughout the world were now made ready for action, while a huge invasion force was massed in Florida: 'Our little group seated around the Cabinet table in continuous session that Saturday felt nuclear war to be closer on that day than at any time in the nuclear age.'[39] Perhaps Russia desired a war. The chiefs of staff once again recommended an air strike, to be followed by an invasion: both to occur on the Monday.[40]

On the brilliant, rather feminine suggestion of his brother, President Kennedy decided that his most promising line of action would now be to ignore the most recent of Khrushchev's letters and to reply to the penultimate one, by accepting a direct exchange of a promise not to invade Cuba for a withdrawal of the missiles.[41] The withdrawal of the missiles, however, would have to be under U.N. observation. It does not seem as if anyone considered that this was a substantial concession, for none seriously desired to invade Cuba. Robert Kennedy personally took a copy of this letter (which he and Sorensen had drafted) to the Russian ambassador in Washington and added that, unless the U.S. 'received assurances within twenty-four hours', the president would take 'military action' on 30 October.[42] An invasion of Cuba would have probably followed on that day. 'If the Russians were ready to go to nuclear war over Cuba, they were ready to go to nuclear war, and that was that,' Robert Kennedy said afterwards.[43] The Russian ambassador, however, had told Robert Kennedy that he personally thought that Khrushchev was too deeply committed to his present policy to accept Kennedy's letter. Meantime, the Cuban exiles in Miami and elsewhere

[37] Schlesinger, *A Thousand Days*, 708.

[38] Castro in 1964 *Hoy*, 2 May 1964, qu. Andrés Suárez, 70.

[39] Sorensen, 706.

[40] Robert Kennedy, *The Times*, 30 October 1968.

[41] *Ibid.*, 31 October 1968. Hillsman, 223, refers to this as 'the Trollope ploy' after a scene in Barsetshire where the girl interprets a squeeze of hand as a proposal of marriage. See also Sorensen, 714, and Schlesinger, *A Thousand Days*, 709; Pachter, 67–8, argued that the 'first' letter had been written second but, since it was more personal and probably Khrushchev's unaided work, arrived first. Sorensen dismisses this interpretation (712, fn); Schlesinger seems to accept it.

[42] Robert Kennedy, *The Times*, 31 October 1968, has a longer account. He added that he thought the missiles in Turkey would anyway soon be removed though not under duress. Schlesinger, *A Thousand Days*, 709; Sorensen, 715.

[43] Schlesinger, *A Thousand Days*, 710.

all supposed that the moment of liberation of Cuba was at hand. They were, needless to say, not consulted by the Kennedys in the new plan.

While Washington slept – 'Saturday night was about the blackest of all'[44] – Russia had to react. He had 'received information', Khrushchev later told the Supreme Soviet, 'that the invasion would be carried out in the next two or three days . . . Immediate action was necessary.'[45] Despite, probably, opposition from Kozlov and perhaps Brezhnev, during the night of 27–28 October, Khrushchev confirmed that his 'first letter' contained a real plan by which he was prepared to stand. He gave immediate orders for the cessation of work on the missile sites, for their dismantlement and their return to Russia. Washington discussed the news in the early morning. Kennedy, with magnanimity, welcomed Khrushchev's 'statesmanlike decision', and discouraged any mention of 'capitulation' or 'humiliation', as well he might, since, of course, the promise not to invade Cuba was a *quid pro quo*, if a slight one so far as Russia was concerned. Castro was not consulted by Khrushchev and heard the news while talking with Guevara; he swore, kicked the wall and broke a looking glass in his fury.[46]

So ended the famous crisis over Cuba of October 1962, in the course of which the world was acutely threatened. Yet, like most dramas, this event had a muffled ending. Khrushchev, Kennedy and the world relaxed, but many North Americans and nearly all Cuban exiles thought Kennedy should have gone further, while the Cuban government and many Cubans, at least, were furious with Russia. 'They betrayed us as [they did] in Spain', was one typical reaction.[47] In a famous 'private' speech at the University, Castro accused Khrushchev of lack of *cojones* (balls) and the meeting ended with the students singing a new song,

Nikita, Nikita!	Nikita, Nikita,
Lo que se da	What you give away
No se quita.	You shouldn't take back

The notion of a private bargain between Kennedy and Khrushchev was repugnant to Castro. Publicly, Carlos Rafael Rodríguez drew parallels with Munich, and Castro himself spoke of a 'certain displeasure' after 'misunderstandings' which had arisen with Russia. Castro's own terms for ending the crisis were more elaborate: they included an end not only of the blockade, but of all harassments, raids by exiles, and overflights, as well as a U.S. withdrawal from Guantánamo. These conditions were not accepted by the U.S. In this way Castro formally avoided the conclusion of any bargain binding him. The

[44] *Ibid.*

[45] See Tatu, 269, for a convincing explanation of the ambiguities of this speech of 12 December.

[46] Guevara to Ricardo Rojo, in Rojo, *Che Guevara*, 130.

[47] Gilly, 54.

Russians, admittedly, dismantled the missile sites and returned both the missiles and the jet bombers to Russia, demurring, since these last were now supposed to be Cuban property. The Cuban government, however, refused to permit any U.N. observation. China backed Cuba: Khrushchev, they said, had followed his 'adventurism' by 'capitulationism'. But still, as Faustino Pérez found out in a mission to Peking in December, China could offer little in the way of credits.

Since the withdrawal of the missiles occurred without U.N. inspection, the government of the U.S. (though withdrawing the quarantine) did not in the end give a public promise never to invade Cuba. They were able to check that the Russians had indeed done what they said they would do by means of the U.2. Yet, despite their formal freedom to do so, the U.S. did not invade Cuba and it seems that, in further exchanges with Russia, they did give Russia an assurance that they had no intention of doing so. Kennedy, however, felt strong enough to promise the assembly of returned veterans from the Bay of Cochinos, on 30 December 1962, that one day a free Cuba would be restored by force of arms.

It thus seemed to many that Kennedy had gained a great victory, and even those who had doubted his wisdom during the testing time turned afterwards to felicitate him, if only for the restraint which he showed in not pressing his advantage to the point of humiliating Khrushchev or overthrowing Castro. For several years afterwards, Russian foreign policy was reserved and unadventurous. Khrushchev, it is true, also claimed a victory and told the Supreme Soviet on 12 December that socialism in Cuba had been preserved by his skill. Nevertheless, this was evidently a statement directed at the First Secretary's enemies in Russia, and it is clear that in internal Russian policy the Cuban crisis was a turning point. Khrushchev had to face serious difficulties in early 1963, and these contributed to his fall in October 1964. Against a modest gain obtained in respect of Cuba itself, Khrushchev had lost much internationally. He had lost much internally also, and from then on the 'liberal' cause in Russia and the cause of destalinization declined. This was an unexpected and unwelcome consequence of Kennedy's sternness.

Kennedy's motives in the crisis, despite the quantity of information published about them, are still not quite clear: was he perhaps not more concerned by the apparent increase in Russian power, and its political effects, or by the challenge apparently made personally and politically to his administration, than by real military considerations? He was concerned with the line which he had drawn on 4 September and 13 September between offensive and defensive missiles. Of course, he might not have made those statements if it had not been for the election campaign and the pressure of the Republicans. Once they had been made, he clearly had to act if the line was crossed, so as to avoid another humiliation over Cuba.[48] The trouble was that the Russian decision to cross the line had already been taken by the time the statements were made. Kennedy appreciated that the establishment of the missiles in Cuba would assist the Russians though, unlike McNamara, he did not seem to measure their precise significance in doubling the Russian striking force; had he done so, he might have noticed the provocative character of the U.S.'s own missile policy under his rule. Indeed, it is difficult to see why Kennedy and McNamara, having reached a point so far ahead of Russia, were not prepared for precisely this response. Many of the things said by Kennedy, as by Khrushchev, during the crisis were intended primarily for propaganda: in this way must be judged the president's allusion to the cities of Lima and Mexico as becoming within range of nuclear attack: for they were, and are, of course, within range of attack by long-range Russian missiles. Kennedy's appeal to Khrushchev to 'abandon this course of world domination' is more ambiguous; was he talking now to Khrushchev genuinely or to his own public opinion? Thus, puzzles remain.

Kennedy was admirably concerned in the crisis with details, down to the lowest level of administrative action, to ensure that the force used was no more than he had intended and that nothing might get out of control.[49] It is possible to take issue with the policy, and indeed a European might well be tempted to suppose that McNamara's policy of inaction or Stevenson's diplomatic approach would have been wiser. A less proud statesman than Kennedy might have first taken the question to Russia or Cuba, secretly, and left a public challenge to a last resort. But one can only compare Kennedy's mastery and knowledge of his resources, and the subtlety and sophistication with which he approached the 'appalling risks' which he was taking (in the words of the *New Statesman*), regardless of principles, with the hectic way in which Sir Anthony Eden conducted the Suez affair in 1956.

Kennedy acted during the crisis with restraint but afterwards used the power his restraint had given him with some freedom; for instance, he abruptly told Macmillan at Nassau that England could not have a missile of her own at U.S. expense. Europe, shortly afterwards, was admonished; Canada humiliated; and the Western Alliance has never been the same again. To save his position over Cuba, Kennedy therefore began the dismantlement of U.S. links with Europe – a dismantlement likely, under his successors, to go much further. On the other hand, the test ban treaty, implying Russian acceptance of U.S. nuclear

---

[48] Pachter commented (p. 13): 'Were he humiliated for a second time over Cuba, Kennedy would lose all hopes for a stable world peace'.

[49] *Cf.* Senator H. M. Jackson, *Los Angeles Times*, 29 January 1963; and *Administration of National Security*, published in 1963 by the Senate.

supremacy was one undoubted consequence of Kennedy's restraint during and after the crisis.

Kennedy's action was taken in the full understanding that despite any favourable intelligence assessments that he might have received, nuclear war might be the consequence. The chances that Russia would 'go all the way to war', he later said, seemed to him 'somewhere between one out of three and evens'.[50] McNamara, a scarcely sentimental politician, at one point wondered 'how many more sunsets he was destined to see'.[51] Other advisers to Kennedy made plans for the evacuation of the capital. Before Kennedy spoke on 22 October, all U.S. missile crews had been placed on 'maximum alert', 800 B.47 bombers were prepared, with their bomb bays closed, and dispersed, along with 550 similarly loaded B.52s and 70 B.58s (Hustlers). 90 B.52s carrying 25 to 50 megaton H-bombs were in the air over the Atlantic, while 100 Atlas, 50 Titan and 12 Minutemen ICBMs were ready on their launching pads. All missiles and bombers were also ready on land bases abroad, on aircraft carriers and on submarines. The smaller, though similar, forces available to Russia were doubtless also primed. James Reston in the *New York Times* on 23 October stated authoritatively[52] that the government would use all means necessary to force a withdrawal of the missile sites, and that if this led to Soviet retaliation such as a counter blockade of Berlin, 'the U.S. is prepared to risk a major war to defend its present position'.[53] Nervous jokes about the chances of survival were recorded by members of the U.S. administration as by most ordinary men; Robert Kennedy spoke of the possible 'end of mankind'.[54] Cuban reactions were apparently not dissimilar: Guevara was busy writing an article which (published posthumously six years later) evidently took the question of nuclear war in its stride: 'What we affirm is that we must proceed along the path of liberation even if this costs millions of atomic victims'; he envisaged the Cuban people 'advancing fearlessly towards the hecatomb which signifies final redemption'.[55]

[50] Sorensen, 705. He evidently repeated this assessment to several people, as the author learned at the time.

[51] Abel, 201.

[52] 'On the highest authority' was his source. No doubt this was Kennedy himself.

[53] *New York Times*, 23 October 1962, 1. All major commands were in a state of 'DEFCON 2', the symbol for the last step short of DEFCON 1, war. *Cf. Newsweek*, 28 October 1963.

[54] Robert Kennedy, *Times*, 27 October 1968.

[55] *Verde Olivo*, 6 October 1968. It would seem that it was Castro's apparent willingness to take the risk of possible nuclear war that so greatly impressed Guevara and is the explanation of his otherwise somewhat mysterious comment in his letter to Castro of 1965: 'At your side I have felt the pride of belonging to our people during those radiant yet sad days of the Caribbean crisis. Not often has a statesman acted more brilliantly than you did during those days and I am also proud of having followed you unhesitatingly . . .'

The Cuban missile crisis, or the Caribbean crisis, as it has been called by the Cubans, brought to an end exactly two hundred years of often intimate relations between North America and Cuba. At first, from the time of the English expedition until the end of the Napoleonic Wars, Anglo-Saxon businessmen sought commerce in Havana. From the 1820s until the 1890s, far-sighted North Americans supposed that in the long run Cuba would follow Texas, California and New Mexico, into the Union. Between the 1890s and 1962, the Government of the U.S. had, for a variety of political, strategic and economic reasons, regarded the complexion of the Cuban administration as ultimately her affair. But in 1962, President Kennedy, though gaining a propaganda victory over Cuba's new ally, Russia, acquiesced in the *fait accompli* of a Cuban nationalist Communist regime which had been constructed out of, and driven by, virulent hostility towards the U.S. and her part in two hundred years of Cuban history. Was this acquiescence caused by the fact that U.S. economic and even strategic interests in Cuba were slighter than they once had been; that a stagnant Cuban sugar industry was becoming more and more a Cuban concern in the 1940s and 1950s, while nuclear weapons were rendering archaic U.S. preoccupations with the Caribbean and the approach to the Panamá Canal (and indeed the Panamá Canal itself)? At all events, the crisis of 1962, the most severe one in the history of the world, was certainly primarily a matter of prestige, propaganda, and politics, rather than a test of economic and strategic interests.

In 1962 Cuba had a newly established and still somewhat unstable totalitarian government, which controlled all the heavy industry and two-thirds of the agriculture of the country. The economy was in a state of great confusion and civil liberties as understood in North America and Western Europe were non-existent. Most Cubans who believed in the liberal virtues were either in gaol or in exile. But the Cuban Government was nevertheless popular among the masses, either because they admired what the Government had already done, because they coveted what it was promising them for the future or simply because they were spellbound by Castro. It was natural that President Kennedy and his circle, reared in the lap of a supremely self-confident and successful society, should find Castro's arbitrary, inefficient, often cruel and always rhetorical regime utterly intolerable. But Castro had created in Cuba a system which was deliberately the very opposite of everything which the U.S. stood for, or at least of what he thought the U.S. stood for. If there is to be blame for 'what happened in Cuba', the fault lay at least as much in Washington and New York as in Havana or Santiago. Some years later, a historian from North America remarked complacently, 'If our performance in Cuba had been flawless, it might still have proved futile because of Cuban unwisdom'.[56] True, no doubt, but there was such a long record of North American unwisdom in Cuba as to render the comment absurd; leaving aside matters of recent history, during the second Batistato, it is obvious that the recognition of Grau San Martín by Roosevelt in 1933 would have saved Roosevelt's heirs no end of trouble. The folly of the Platt Amendment was made clear by Senator Foraker before it was made law.[57] The dispatch of General Crowder to Havana in 1921 without consultation with the Cuban Government was an act with few parallels even in the history of British imperial relations with the decrepit Moguls of Delhi. It would also have been better if General Leonard Wood had kept his scorn for the Latin race as a whole to himself and if both he and General Crowder had brought themselves to learn a little Spanish. Indeed, it is still difficult not to believe that if the U.S. were going to exert the sort of political control over Cuba that they did between 1902 and 1933, it would have been better if they had taken over the island altogether.

Had the crisis of 1962 turned into the Third World War, as indeed it might have done, these matters would perhaps already be being analysed by those historians who would have survived it. Some, no doubt, would quite ignore the role of Cuba in the development of the drama of 1962. Others might regard the crisis as the final showdown between the Anglo-Saxon and Latin races, with Cuba an appropriate firing point of a most destructive international conflict. It is indeed in some ways fitting that Cuba, for so long the victim of the policies of the great rich powers and their sugar-eating populaces, should have one day almost got her own back and threatened to drag the great powers down with her. In the end, however, both Cubas were in 1962 deceived: Kennedy did not liberate the island from Castro and Khrushchev took away the missiles. Small powers can often begin a world crisis, great powers always end them.

[56] Henry Wriston, in John Plank, *Cuba and the U.S.*
[57] See above p. 453.

Epilogue

'At first sight, a very correct country.'
MAYAKOVSKY, ON A VISIT TO CUBA IN 1924.

NOTE TO EPILOGUE

Events in Cuba since 1962

1963	April–May	Castro's first visit to Russia
		Change back to emphasis on sugar
	October	Second Agrarian Reform
	November	Compulsory Military Service
1964	January	Castro's second visit to Russia
		Russo–Cuban sugar agreement
		Leyland bus agreement
	March	Trial of Marcos Armando Rodríguez
	November	Havana conference of Latin American Communists
	December	Attempted suicide of Martínez Sánchez
	December–March (1965)	Guevara's tour of Afro-Asian countries
1965	March	Castro's attack on Sino–Soviet dispute
		Guevara disappears
		Drive against homosexuality in the University
	April	Civil war in Santo Domingo
	June	Castro's speech emphasizing agriculture
	October	Formation of Cuban Communist party and central committee
		Gromyko's visit to Cuba
		Renewal of emigration to the U.S.A. at first by boat then by air
1966	January	Tricontinental conference
		Formation of AALAPSO
	February	Castro's row with China
	March	Cubela case
		Quarrel between Venezuelan communists and guerrillas
1967	January	Publication of Debray's *Revolution in the Revolution*
	June	Kosygin's visit to Havana
	August	OLAS conference Havana supports armed struggle
	October	Guevara killed Bolivia
1968	February	Escalante and microfaction trial
	March	Revolutionary offensive closes 50,000 small businesses
	October	Padilla Case
1969	July	Opening of the ten million ton harvest.

The Utopians

The purpose of the Revolution in Cuba was put most clearly by Guevara: 'we are seeking something new which will permit a perfect identification between the government and the community as a whole, adapted to the special needs of socialism and avoiding to the utmost the commonplaces of bourgeois democracy (such as houses of parliament) ... We have been greatly restrained by the fear that any formalization might make us lose sight of the ultimate and most important revolutionary aspiration: to see man freed from alienation.'[1]

These designs were admittedly not mentioned as being the purpose of the Revolution in the late 1950s or even in the early 1960s, but no one should be surprised that the policies of revolutionary governments, like those of more orthodox administrations, should change. The reason why these radical plans came to dominate the Revolution has been discussed earlier. They are ambitious, if not entirely new, schemes, and, since ten years is a short time to judge a social upheaval such as that caused by the Revolution in Cuba, it would scarcely seem odd if they have not yet been achieved. Nor are they self-evidently correct: Guevara's contempt for bourgeois democracy seems to be obsessive; his use of the word 'socialism' suggests a single body of revealed truth, whereas by now it should be obvious that there are as many types of, as there are roads to, that dogma. Nor is the word 'alienation' free from ambiguity, particularly when many of those held to be alienated are agricultural rather than city workers. Nevertheless, it is legitimate now to ask to what extent these grand plans have been realized in the years since the missile crisis of 1962, and how far they are likely to be achieved in the immediate future. Perhaps the extent of their fulfilment so far will throw light not only on their validity as a programme but also on their wisdom and justice.

Since 1962 many changes have occurred in the health, education, and in the way of living and thinking of the whole population in Cuba; and a large new bureaucracy and political movement have been constructed to persuade, cajole and, on occasion, force the people to carry out the policies which are expected to further and to finance the social

[1] Guevara, *El socialismo y el hombre en Cuba*, Havana, Ediciones R, 1965. This essay has often been reprinted and translated.

changes: for it is certainly not yet possible to identify government and community completely, despite the fact that there is virtually no work other than for the community and despite propaganda which persuades many people that they are living an epic and are, if not always materially better off, at least much more virtuous than they were before.

Cubans now probably all have enough to eat, but only just enough. The strict rationing means that cereals, sugar and fats provide two-thirds of the calories in most people's diet: in 1964, a Czech economist, Selucky, thought that the Cubans received about 'the same quantity of fats, oils, rice, beans, sugar and beef as we got in the last years of the war'[2] – and the year 1964 was a better time than five years later. The queues for items temporarily off the ration (such as – in early 1969 – bread) and outside restaurants suggest that most people would like to eat much more than they do. The distribution of food has been erratic. Still, few die of malnutrition and, in the country, particularly in Oriente province, the very poor peasants must be fed better and more regularly than before the revolution: and nearly everyone has better meals than they did during the terrible years of the depression which lasted so long in Cuba.[3]

Two qualifications must be made: first, high officials, foreign technicians (not to speak of foreign visitors) and all persons in power are able to live better than ordinary people; they have the right to go to special shops where goods can actually be bought. There may be no discrimination against Negroes in the old grand hotels, but none save the powerful get, for instance, into *La Torre*, a restaurant in Havana where there is always excellent food. Most of the leaders of the Revolution seem quite austere and simple men but many officials have not been able to resist the pleasures of power, and enjoy themselves. It should also be recalled that during the twentieth, and indeed the nineteenth, century, Cuba was not a country of famine (nor, since 1900, of plague). For this reason, as for many others, Cuba in the past resembled an unequally developed province of a rich country, a West Virginia, more than a typical part of the under-developed or third world.

The shortages have an effect on the quality of life for all but the highest officials. When the day's work is over, much time has to be spent on queueing for food and other essentials. Militia or other voluntary service for the state also occupies time. It must be said that the Cubans,

[2] Radoslav Selucky, Spotlight on Cuba, *East Europe*, v. 13, No. 10, October 1964, quoted Mesa-Lago, *Labour Sector and Socialist Distribution in Cuba*, p. 159.

[3] Rationing seems (1969/1970) to be: *meat*, ¾ pound a week in Havana, ½ pound outside; *fish*, ¼ pound a week; *butter*, 2 ounces a month; *eggs*, 3 a week; *coffee*, 1½ ounces a week; *bread*, 4 ounces a day; *rice*, 3 pounds a month; *sugar*, 6 pounds a month; *cooking oil*, 12 ounces a month; *chicken*, offered only to minors or aged on production of a medical certificate. Other items such as *clothes* (two pairs of trousers and one shirt a year) and *toothpaste* (one tube a month per family) are also rationed.

who are by nature cheerful, seem to accept these things with remarkably good grace, even if they criticize them.

The strict rationing is caused by, first, the absence of the large amount of food imported before 1960 from the U.S.; second, the decline in agricultural production in the early years of the Revolution[4]; and third, the very high percentage – perhaps 30% to 35% – of the national production which is 'saved or invested'.[5] Most traditional Cuban products, such as fruit, vegetables and beef, are shipped off to East Europe and Russia to help pay for Cuba's debts in those countries. Efforts to get the Cubans to change their traditional diets – to eat more fish, for example – have not been very successful. Cubans with memories therefore must recall with cynicism Castro's promise, when food began to be short in November 1960: 'Remember what I am telling you! The foodstuffs which will be available once more by December will never disappear again.'[6] The provision of a network of ice cream restaurants with fifty-four flavours scarcely compensates for the disappearance of regular square meals. Other consumer goods such as minor pharmaceutical or stationery articles are also lacking.

To balance this, unemployment has undoubtedly fallen, despite the new use in the economy of many once housebound women and girls. This is partly because of the emigration of such a large percentage of the population[7]; partly because of the drift to the cities during the first years of the Revolution, in particular to government, party agencies and the armed forces[8]; and partly because of the increase in the number of children who go to school or colleges. The gangs of children hanging around doing nothing, which was such a characteristic of old Cuba, have almost disappeared, except in parts of Havana, along with the 'dead season'. Many former sugar cane cutters have been absorbed in one capacity or another in 'revolutionary tasks' in the ministries or on

---

[4] Recent figures are not conclusive, but FAO statistics up to 1965 suggest a per capita decline in agricultural production since 1958 of 31% (FAO *Monthly Bulletin of Statistics*, April 1965 pp. 17–20). Since 1965 agricultural production has doubtless increased but not for the benefit of the consumer.

[5] Estimate of Wassily Leontief, 'A Visit to Cuba', *New York Review of Books*, 21 August 1969.

[6] *Obra Revolucionaria* no. 28, 9 November 1960.

[7] See below, p. 1482.

[8] It is difficult to know for certain what this rural population which drifted into the cities actually did. Goldenberg (who left Cuba in July 1960) thought that 'many factories employed more workers than they really needed; the civil service was greatly inflated; there were many ways of getting a state scholarship to some school or other; although militia service was unpaid for, it was sometimes possible to live on it; finally the system of *botellas* had reappeared' (Goldenberg, 260). *Bohemia* (2 March 1962) commented 'Cuba has a sector called supplementary reserve. Here we have thousands of men and women who do nothing except receive a salary from the state . . . They sit at home and wait till they can collect their cheque at the end of the month. Many would like to do something with their time, others fill their heads with bad ideas.'

the state farms, which have been too inefficient to organize their workers economically. There has even been a shortage of skilled labour, particularly in the sugar industry. But observation suggests that there is substantial underemployment even in sugar mills. This may increase if the present programme of mechanization is successful. It also seems that the 'revolutionary offensive' of 1968[9] which closed so many small businesses, from bars to fruit-sellers, must have led to much unemployment, particularly in Havana and among both the owners of, and workers in, the many surviving small factories and workshops (*chinchales*), employing two or three people, and shops, even though emigration has accounted for some of them.

The Revolution has in many ways improved Cuban health. The general teaching hospitals, the specialist hospitals and the specialist institutes are well maintained by a new generation of Cuban doctors with 'a high level of understanding and ability'.[10] Everywhere there has been a marked increase in hygiene and sanitation. The availability of medicine has been much more fairly spread throughout the country. Preventive medicine has been much emphasized and many clinics have been established in rural areas. Deaths from tuberculosis, malaria and typhoid have been much reduced and as elsewhere polio seems to have been eliminated by mass vaccination. One admirable achievement is the Mazorra lunatic asylum, imaginatively directed by Doctor Bernabé Ordaz, once an establishment of nightmares, today serene – it has become deservedly a part of every approved tour of the country for foreign visitors.[11] On the other hand, doctors, though now slightly more numerous than in the past, have probably been less well trained.[12] Some of the best doctors in Cuba have emigrated. Medicine and other equipment has often been lacking or irregularly supplied, since most of it comes from Russia or East Europe. Prejudice, masquerading as ideology, has perhaps sometimes hampered the best treatment: one doctor in Santiago refused to use North American equipment on Cuban patients even if he had none other.[13] Nurses and dentists remain short. Gastroentiritis, syphilis and hepatitis seem to have increased recently.

---

[9] See below, p. 1445.

[10] The comment of Dr David Spain, director of the department of pathology at Brookland Hospital Centre, Brooklyn, qu. Leo Huberman and Paul Sweezy, Socialism in Cuba, *Monthly Review Press*, New York, 1969, 58.

[11] I could not help wondering, during a visit to the asylum in 1969, how many of the well-kept patients whom I saw were there in direct or indirect consequence of political events since 1959.

[12] There are now about 8,000 doctors in Cuba, in comparison with 7,200 in 1958. Of these about 2,500 left Cuba between 1959 and 1965, and they are still leaving at the rate of four a month. See Willis Butler, 'Cuba's Revolutionary Medicine,' *Ramparts*, May 1969. Taking into account the increase in population, doctors per head probably number much the same as in 1958.

[13] To the author, in 1961, admittedly a tense time.

Infant mortality, at forty per thousand live births seems at the very least to have remained static and, if still low in comparison with the rest of Latin America, remains higher than for most of the Caribbean and is almost double that of the U.S. and Western Europe.[14]

Cuba has no population policy and no worries about population. Her growth rate, at about 2·7%, is lower than that of most of her neighbours and, as Castro himself suggested, Cuba could, if her economy were well organized, feed a population three times her present size. On the other hand, Cuba's food production since 1959 has not kept pace with the population increase and the annual rate of population increase is going up. Her present density of population of about seventy per square kilometre is thus likely to be double that within thirty years or less. That will bring her not far short of the congestion on the smaller Caribbean islands. There are admittedly birth control clinics in most large Cuban hospitals and the *anillo*, a variety of intra-uterine loop, is offered free to all women after their first child (if they are in hospital, which most now are) but, despite advertisements drawing attention to this service, it does not seem to be much used, probably because of male opposition on the grounds that it would make infidelity easier. In these important respects, therefore, socialist Cuba is rather less 'revolutionary' than, say, capitalist Japan, which halved its birth rate in ten years between 1947 and 1957.

Education in Cuba has undergone a rebirth since the Revolution, though some qualifications are necessary. In numbers, the changes seem immensely beneficial: half the children of primary school age had no education before 1959. Today they all receive some teaching, so that primary schools have nearly 1½ million pupils instead of 720,000 in 1958. There are 50,000 primary school teachers in place of scarcely 17,000 before 1958. A much bigger percentage of children also go as state scholars (*becados*) to secondary schools than in the past – about 180,000 out of 400,000 of the appropriate age group; while, since 1967, nearly all infants go to kindergarten (*círculos infantiles*) from their 45th day onwards under the administration of an old Communist, Clementina Serra. In 1964–5 the Ministry of Education reported an enrolment in adult education of 484,000.[15]

Many children, however, are taken away from home to go to the secondary boarding schools against their wills, and all teaching is

[14] The figure of 40 per thousand was given in a speech by the Minister of Health, Helidoro Martínez Junco, at the close of the first national forum for paediatric standards, November 1969 (*Granma*, 23 November 1969). Government investment in health, though evidently high, is hard to estimate, given the ambiguous value of money. Thus, on paper, the Government spent ten times in 1967 what was spent ten years before ($M260 in place of $M20) but this takes no account of what was spent on private medicine in the past nor of the complete and incalculable change in the value of money.

[15] Leo Huberman, 'A Revolution Revisited' *Nation*, 2 August, 1965.

carried out under the shadow of the regime's slogan for youth – *Estudio, Trabajo, Fusil* (Study, Work, the Rifle). Children from six years upwards have to play a part in 'productive labour' in some branch of agriculture during the week-ends and in the holidays, as a part of 'socialist education'. From the names of schools to the examples given in learning grammar, much attention is paid to revolutionary heroes, in particular to Guevara, the model revolutionary without fear and above reproach. Religion, of course, plays no part. There also remain serious shortages of books, of teachers and of school rooms, so much so that, as the Minister of Education, José Llanusa, explained in 1968, these shortcomings probably would not be overcome until 1980. Finally, the content of education in revolutionary Cuba seems, despite a veneer of modernity, to be old-fashioned: there is learning by rote, and rules and examples; while the emphasis given to physical fitness in recent years (particularly under Llanusa, a former national director of Cuban tourism and of sports) is curiously reminiscent of the English public school, the 'team spirit' being, in Cuba as in Wessex, a good corrective to suspect 'intellectualism' and the spirit of inquiry. Also, as a North American favourable to the Revolution remarked, 'Pictures, slogans, the names given to state farms . . . all teach young Cubans to think of their lives as intimately related to Revolution elsewhere:'[16] an imperial education through the looking-glass.

These qualifications apply even more strongly to higher education. At first sight, the achievements have been remarkable. There were 30,000 technical school pupils and 40,000 full-time students in 1969, compared with 6,250 and 25,000 respectively in 1958 and, if the increase of university places has been relatively slight, it is obviously salutary in an agricultural country to increase technical education at the cost of law students and historians. There have also been some magnificent achievements, such as Ricardo Porro's splendid if unfinished school of Fine Arts in the old Country Club golf course.[17] On the other hand, all students have to take a year's course in dialectical materialism; spend fifteen days a year in a military camp; play their part, like school children, during the vacations, in 'productive labour'; and serve a number of hours a week in the militia. Most available textbooks are direct translations of Russian texts. The teaching in some departments is mostly done by last year students. University autonomy has come to an end and, though students nominally participate in the running of the institutions in which they work, these are in all important respects tied to the needs of the economy, not the desires of the student. The Communist

[16] Elizabeth Sutherland, *The Youngest Revolution, a Personal Report on Cuba*, New York, 1969, p. 59.
[17] Porro afterwards went into exile, in Paris.

Party of Cuba, here as in other sections of society, plays the decisive part: for instance, it was certainly not spontaneous disgust but national politics that caused a national assembly of students in 1967 to insist that homosexuals should publicly confess their shortcomings,[18] and in 1965 to demand a purge of all students suspected of a lack of enthusiasm for the Revolution.[19]

Long-term prospects for the Universities in Cuba are scarcely encouraging. After observing in December 1966 that university students had less 'revolutionary consciousness' than middle-grade agronomists, Castro denounced 'the wall of theory and abstractionism', and two years later, in December 1968, was found looking forward to a time when all Cuban universities could be abolished, since only a few exceptional activities would then require higher studies. Normal education would always include technical education in the last years and most people would then enter agriculture or industry as trained technicians: 'in future, practically every factory, every agricultural zone, every hospital, every school will be a university'; and, it might be added, looking at the children marching to meals in military formation, and at the proliferation of uniforms (grey shirts and green trousers for secondary school pupils – *becados*, pink shirts and blue trousers for girls doing domestic or technical training), every school a regiment.

Already there have been a number of minor troubles in the university: some students have disliked the undemocratic organization of the students' union, the compulsory militia service, the occasional unequal treatment of men and women, the forty-five days of agricultural work and the disapproval of tight trousers and miniskirts. The possibility of active dissent is, of course, closed, and Llanusa has told students 'we shall not have a Czechoslovakia here'.[20]

The revolutionary regime, needing the labour and the enthusiasm of the young, has given them in return benefits and rewards. The proportion of the population below fifteen years old must be close to the world average of 45%. Visitor after visitor to Cuba marvels at young Cubans' dedication, vitality and sense of responsibility at an early age. The Isle of Pines was in 1966 renamed the Isle of Youth, and became the centre for experimental agriculture carried out without pay and without expenses by an ever increasing number of Cubans from the age of twelve

[18] See below, p.1435. According to one account to me, one student was expelled from the University on this occasion on the ground that he had not lifted up his hand to vote with the majority.

[19] See an account by C. K. McClatchy, *Cuba Revisited*, 1967, McClatchy Newspapers, Sacramento, California. McClatchy was told by one student that only devoted revolutionaries should be permitted to get a university education, regardless of academic ability.

[20] The Ministry of Education at one point decreed that skirts should be two inches above the knee.

to twenty-seven.[21] Will this new generation be ready in the future to hand over the torch to fresh generations? Or will, as happened with the first generation of Komsomol enthusiasts in Russia and East Europe, the present generation of youth leaders turn with the passing of the years into apparatchiks, suspicious of new changes, the 'conservative' target therefore for criticism or hatred by a new wave of 'liberals', 'abstractionists', or 'humanists'?

The latter eventuality is surely the more probable, as is suggested by a 'hippie' cult and its repression in late 1968, and from the high percentage of young people among criminals in the crime wave of 1968–9[22] and among those who would clearly like to leave Cuba but cannot do so except illegally.[23] Unless the community and the government are indeed one by that time, more and more people in future will regard with scepticism Castro's paternalistic dictum 'Work is Youth's best pedagogue' and begin to question the theory that 'taking part in agricultural tasks will not only deepen the revolutionary conscience of the young but will serve to give them new human values'. Indoctrination is 'a double-edged sword'.[24] After Savanarola, the Medicis returned; and, in the end many people, perhaps most people usually come round to the view that private ease and entertainment are worth more than all the creeds in the world and that scepticism is more productive than enthusiasm.

The Revolution's treatment of health and education gives several hints as to the real character of this regime: we see dedicated men working with bad equipment, children evidently enjoying themselves marching to the adult sound of trumpets, uniformity parading as patriotism. But nothing is quite as clear cut as it sounds in the speech, say, of a Cuban delegate to UNESCO. Such ambiguity also appears when the status under the Revolution of both women and of Negroes is considered.

'The true feminine struggle,' a Cuban girl in her late twenties told Elizabeth Sutherland, an astute North American observer, 'is the rejection of all those childhood teachings, all those family pressures during

[21] For a description see (*inter alia*) James Higgins, 'The New Men of Cuba', *Nation*, 12 February 1968. The Isle of Youth now has a population of perhaps 50,000 in place of 8,000 in 1953. It is a kind of permanent summer camp for voluntary workers, with all essentials provided free.

[22] See below, page 1459.

[23] At present no young man between 14 and 28 – that is, potentially of a military age, is permitted to apply for an exit visa to emigrate from Cuba. The most famous escapee to get round the law in recent years was Armando Socorrás Ramírez who, aged 22, successfully stowed away in June 1969 in the wheel carriage of a jet aircraft travelling between Havana and Madrid; the youngest, Rafael Sánchez Reinel, who swam to the U.S. base at Guantánamo aged 13.

[24] Remark by Josué León Fuentes, a graduate of the Casa Blanca secondary school, Havana, who later went into exile (Paul Bethel, *Terror and Resistance in Communist Cuba*, Citizens' Committee for a Free Cuba, 1964, 20).

adolescence and even the dominant social thinking which affects her as an adult . . . the ideal of femininity, of womanhood, as meaning the dedication of one's life to finding and keeping a companion, generally at the price of being his satellite.'[25] Though this battle is not yet over, the role of women has certainly much changed since the Revolution. First, the family has altered considerably. Civil marriages are free (held in marriage palaces, on the Russian model, such as that in Havana in the old building of the Spanish Club) and honeymoon couples get reduced rates and priority treatment at what used to be smart hotels at beaches or in the country.[26] Children are encouraged to go to kindergartens from very early in their lives, so leaving women free for 'productive work'. The consequence has been that, whereas before 1959 women were only exceptionally involved in agriculture (as, for example, in the cane-fields of Pinar del Río) in the late 1960s much of the coffee-planting, particularly in Havana province, was done by women, and women have also directed cane collection centres.[27] In late 1967, the Labour Minister Jorge Risquet (an old Communist who had been education officer in Raúl Castro's column in the Sierra Cristal) explained that in future 'the chief task of women will be to replace in the factories those workers who have gone off (voluntarily) to the sugar harvest'. An injunction by the Cuban Federation of Women, at the time of Castro's destruction of small businesses, adjured women to maintain a 'militant combative attitude everywhere: at home, at school, in the neighbourhood, at work, in recreation centres, in shopping queues and on buses'[28]: an indication of the large number of activities with which women are supposed to be able to juggle. Certainly, women played a large part in the Committees for the Defence of the Revolution. The proportion of girls among university students has increased, girls have taken over as traffic police in Havana, while the sewing schools and other handicraft courses of peasant girls have doubtless been genuinely revolutionary in their effects.

On the other hand, the goal of incorporating a million women into economic activity will probably not be reached by 1970. The new independence of women has not always commended itself to men, however radical they may otherwise be, and women have evidently borne the brunt of rationing and shortages of ordinary goods, from clothes to soap. They often now work as well as keep house. Even in 1962 women were noticeably more hostile than men to the revolution,[29]

[25] Sutherland, p. 90.

[26] They also seem to be virtually compulsory for those living together in consentual unions.

[27] *Bohemia* of 29 March 1968 described a cane collection centre run by women as a 'tribute to the revolutionary activity of womankind'.

[28] *Granma* weekly edition 20 March 1968.

[29] Zeitlin, pp. 126–7.

and probably over half of those who have gone into exile since 1959 have been women. Women have not really been prominent in politics[30] and it is possible to doubt whether they have truly been happier with their publicly committed status in modern Cuba than they were in the past. The cult of virility or *machismo*, may have almost vanished, along with prostitution (and sexual habits have somewhat changed too) but in most Cuban households in the past women in fact reigned supreme. Outside the house men rode about in Oldsmobiles or Buicks with machine guns, became gangsters, spoke of Liberty and Destiny, frequented bars, brothels and casinos, but perhaps that was all only theatre and in real life women ruled. Now the gap between reality and imagination has closed but possibly real feminine power is less, given that in personal relations Cubans still seem conservative: thus, though both marriage and divorce have much increased, in 1967 a survey in *Juventud Rebelde* suggested that 50% even of *habaneros* thought virginity a prerequisite to marriage.

As with women, so with Negroes: if material conditions are alone considered, at first sight both Negroes and mulattoes must be better off in Cuba today than before the Revolution. The provision of title deeds to squatters, the increase of attractive rural housing, the illiteracy campaign, the increase of education, sanitation, hygiene and health in the countryside (particularly in Oriente province) must have benefited Negroes and mulattoes in particular. In 1962, in the last reasonably independent survey of opinion made in Cuba, the North American sociologist Maurice Zeitlin found that 80% of Negroes were wholly in favour of the Revolution, as opposed to 67% whites.[31] Perhaps many Negroes still see Castro as a kind of national *santero* in an Afro–Cuban ritual, the strong man who is exorcising evil (many had the same view of Batista and Machado). Yet some Negroes suffer from greater self-consciousness now and the Afro–Cuban fiestas, symbols of continuing separate loyalties, have, because of the difficulty of getting cocks and other items necessary, became less frequent. Yet they survive, whites attending as in the past, and doubtless *santería* and *ñáñigo* will outlive Castro as they have outlived other captains-general of Cuba[32]: 'Abakuá will last in Cuba as long as there are drums'.[33] In addition, older racial

[30] Out of 100 central committee (or central committee commissions and politburo) members in 1965, five only were women, and of these, four must have owed their importance to their proximity to male leaders of the revolution – Celia Sánchez being Castro's secretary since the Sierra Maestra, Elena Gil being secretary to Dorticós, Vilma Espín (President of the Federation of Women) being wife to Raúl Castro and Haydée Santamaría being wife to Armando Hart, the party's Secretary of Organization. The other woman, Clementina Serra, an old Communist, is Director-General of Infant schools.
[31] Zeitlin, *Revolutionary Politics and the Cuban working class*, Princeton, 1967, p. 77.
[32] See my article on a Congolese *fiesta de palo* in January 1969 (*The Times* 1 March 1969).
[33] *'Hay abakuá pa rato! Habrá abakuá mientras haya tambor'*, said in 1959 the Cuban composer Ignacio Pineiro.

prejudices and habits, attitudes of subservience by Negroes as of arrogance by whites, seem to continue. Neither Marx nor Martí, the two prophets of the Revolution, understood race as it is apprehended in the second half of the twentieth century, and the works of neither seem adequate to resolve the anxieties that evidently characterise Cubans as well as other 'Afro–Americans': are they to support assimilation or integration, hispanization or assertion of Africa, and will old myths (of black sexual superiority, for instance) disappear, along with blond dolls?[34]

All these issues were brought into the domain of controversy by a black Cuban communist, Carlos Moore, in a famous article in *Présence Africaine*, a Paris Maoist journal, in 1965. He argued that the Cuban revolution was simply a victory of the white national bourgeoisie, that prejudice continued, that the size of the Negro population in Cuba continued to be falsified in statistics, along with the contribution of Negroes to the history of Cuba, and that Cuban Negroes played no greater part in Cuban politics than they had before 1958 – if anything less.[35] It is true that only a tenth of the central committee of the Cuban Communist party as constituted in 1965 seems to have black blood, and that the regime has evidently laboured its tolerance towards Negro susceptibilities in order to contrast itself with North American practice (Castro, it will be remembered, never mentioned the Negro question in any speech or statement of intentions before he came to power). The advantages gained by the Cuban Negroes since 1959 at Castro's hands have certainly been less far-reaching than those obtained in the last ten years of Spanish colonial rule by mulatto publicists such as Juan Gualberto Gómez or Martín Morúa Delgado.

It is possible that Castro's overt support for the black power movement in the U.S. (particularly since the visit of Stokely Carmichael to Havana in 1967) will cause difficulties in Cuba itself. Thus Walterio Carbonell, a Negro Communist who, in 1953, defended Castro's policies against the orthodox Communist Party in Cuba, has already spent some time in a camp of rehabilitation[36] on the ground that his folkloric investigations had racist overtones. Some exiled North American Negro militants from Robert Williams to the Black Panthers have

[34] See an excellent chapter by Elizabeth Sutherland, *The Youngest Revolution*, pp. 62–78. Jan Carew, a Guyanan, asked in 1963 a Negro from Oriente 'what it's like to be a Negro in revolutionary Cuba', to receive the answer 'we are still black and a minority and the Revolution does not invent soap to wash you white . . . they free us on paper but there is a lot of separateness in our lives still . . . and we're not like the Yankee Negro, we're not trying to be like the white Cuban . . . the white Cuban is one of the most boring human beings God ever made, they're heroic . . . they will defy the white world and you will applaud them and admire them but you'll never like them . . . I wouldn't want [my daughter] to get involved with one of those dull sanctimonious bearded white idiots' (*Topolski's Chronicle*, vol. XI, Nos. 17–20, 1963).

[35] Carlos Moore, *Présence Africaine*, October 1965.

[36] See below, p.1461.

encountered what they have taken to be prejudice,[37] and several counter-revolutionary guerrilla leaders, such as 'Cara Linda' and 'Machetero', were Negroes.

Cuba is still, of course, the largest and most populous of the islands of the Caribbean, even though, for reasons of language, the Revolution has had little effect upon the English, French and Dutch islands and only a limited effect on Puerto Rico (save, perhaps, for the contra-productive one of the arrival there of some 15,000 Cuban exiles). Castro has affirmed Cuba's cultural Spanish and Spanish–American links, rather than her economic Caribbean ones and in many respects the Cuban Revolution is primarily cultural. Yet in the long run it is hard to see how any of the islands of the Antilles can ever achieve political freedom unless they do so in common with each other, and here the black and African tradition in Cuba is certain to be the most resilient, in contrast with the endless rhetoric of the Spanish-American revolutionary heritage.

Social revolution as complete as that which has occurred in Cuba usually frees people from many crusty habits, however little that may have been the original aim of the social reformers. But Cuba was always one of the freest places so far as sex was concerned and the Revolution has had a strong puritanical element. The consequence has therefore been ambiguous.

Thus as before 1959 *posadas*, or *casas non-sanctas*, for brief encounters at a modest cost, continue despite attempts to suppress them in the first, liberal years of the Revolution.[38] There is evidently in Cuba, in consequence of the Revolution, an inquisitive mood of experiment affecting all sides of personal and family behaviour – with one qualification: the experimenters must be heterosexual. Homosexuals have been less favoured; and there is no reason to suppose that the Cuban homosexual population is any less than in the rest of the world, indeed under persecution it may be growing.[39] In 1965, a national campaign was

[37] Carlos Moore was Williams' interpreter. Williams, after several years of exile in Cuba (where he ran a radio station named Radio Free Dixie), went to China and from there denounced the Cuban Revolution in his newsheet, *Crusader*: 'The Negro is becoming again a pathetic victim to race prejudice and discrimination . . . Afro–Cubans are beginning to feel the pinch of subtle but fast returning racism' (*Crusader*, Vol. 8 No. 43, March 1967). Later, he argued that the Cuban counter-espionage police (G2) was infiltrated by the CIA (*Ibid*, May 1967). Williams wrote a long letter to Castro in August 1966 complaining of his treatment. In mid 1969, the Black Panthers, including Eldridge Cleaver, in Havana, were encountering difficulties and even arrests. (*See International Herald Tribune*, 26 June 1969.)

[38] In the first months of the Revolution César Blanco, an ex-Lutheran minister, chief of public order to the first Minister of the Interior, used to go to *posadas* in Havana and surround them with lights and loudspeakers. He would then announce on the latter, 'You have five minutes from now to abandon these vicious antics'. But this period of puritanism did not last and the *posadas* were nationalized by Llanusa when director of tourism. Blanco left Cuba for the U.S. in October 1960.

[39] See José Yglesias, Cuban Report: their hippies, their squares, *New York Times Magazine*, 12 January 1969.

launched against this minority, homosexuality being declared incompatible with revolutionary attitudes. Several prominent homosexuals lost their jobs, in, for instance, the film institute ICAIC, and in the university they were made to confess publicly their 'vices', were expelled from their courses and in some cases dispatched to work on the land. Though this disagreeable campaign was afterwards abandoned – on Castro's initiative, it was said, though the whole affair could not have been begun without his encouragement – an English writer could still find in 1968 a boy who, believing that he was homosexual, wished that he had died at birth, since in Cuba 'homosexuals are regarded as worse than beasts'.[40]

The regime has other phobias. Thus, after various attacks in earlier years of the Revolution on those who sought a soft life, Castro, on 28 September 1968, in a speech commemorating the 8th anniversary of the foundation of the Committees for the Defence of the Revolution, denounced young Cubans who had taken to living in an 'extravagant manner': long hair and fancy clothes, he said, spelled moral degeneracy and would ultimately lead to political and economic sabotage. A week later, a well-known commentator, Guido García Inclan, denounced not only exotic clothes and long hair but those who played guitars, smoked marijuana and 'danced madly to epileptic music'. These were the sort of people who 'hung about listening to imperialist jukeboxes' in small bars but (after so many of these had been closed) were now organizing themselves in 'bands of schizophrenics' with names like 'los Beats' or 'los Chicos Melenudos' (the long-haired boys), with special initiation ceremonies and oaths of loyalty. This had led to such 'incredible acts' as the desecration of the national flag and of portraits of Guevara. There followed mass shavings of long-haired men and the departure of miniskirted girls, who were said to have made 'passionate love in their school uniforms', to forced labour camps in the countryside. The campaign is bizarre in a country supposedly 'liberated' by bearded men ten years before.

[40] Michael Frayn, *Observer*, 12 January 1969.

The 'Ten Million Ton Harvest' and its Implications

The political revolution following the capture of power in 1959 was to have been accompanied by, first, an immediate increase in standards of living; second, a rapid industrialization; and third, a switch away from that emphasis on sugar which had played for so long such a large and, as many thought, destructive part in Cuban society. None of these things occurred: Guevara in 1960 spoke of a future in which Cuba would be self-sufficient in steel, while by 1965 industrialisation had been indefinitely postponed: in 1960 Castro was explaining how improvements in living standards would come faster than in any other country which had undergone a revolution but two years later the standards of life in the cities had collapsed while at the end of the 1960s most Cubans were living in a very Spartan manner. Finally, while between 1960 and 1962 the role of sugar in the economy was denigrated, sugar has if anything since 1963 played a larger part than before 1959.[1] The 'year of the Decisive Endeavour', 1969–70,[2] was indeed specially geared to the production of ten million tons of sugar, a goal which, because of the innate unwisdom of relying on the production of a large quantity of an already far from scarce commodity, would once have seemed so foolish as to be absurd. In order to expand the capacity of the sugar industry to produce ten million tons of sugar, it was necessary to invest a new $M1,000, a figure which exceeded the total assets of the sugar industry in 1965.[3] With a rigidly controlled economy, however, and the emigration of many technicians, it was obviously easier to concentrate all energies upon this well-tried crop than to launch successfully into other enterprises, at least as a matter of central concentration. In this

---

[1] It was on 10 August 1963, before the Institute of Hydraulic Resources, in the Havana Libre Hotel, Havana, that Castro announced, 'we are going to develop the cane fields primarily and then the cattle. These are going to be pillars of the economy until 1970.'

[2] The years since 1959 have each received a name from the government to suggest the national theme. Thus, 1959 was the year of Liberation, 1960 of Agrarian Reform, 1961 of Education, 1962 of Planning, 1963 of Organization, 1964 of the Economy, 1965 of Agriculture, 1966 of Solidarity with the Underdeveloped World, 1967 of Heroic Vietnam, 1968 of the Heroic Guerrilla. As with many things in Cuba, the labelling of years was systematized, not invented, by Castro: thus the year 1953 had been described by Batista as the 'year of the centenary of the Apostle' (that is, of Martí's birth).

[3] Michel Gutelman, *L'Agriculture Socialisée à Cuba* (Maspero, Paris 1967, 205).

respect, the Revolution has been fundamentally regressive, and it must have occurred to many Cubans to ask whether it would not have been more beneficial to have achieved a less profound social change if thereby it had been easier to achieve economic diversification.

Despite the special and grand emphasis laid on sugar since 1964, however, harvests have usually been well below the figures achieved in the 1950s and the yield from the cane has also been smaller.[4] These failures are partly attributable to bad weather, but bad management, delay in getting the cane from the field to the mill,[5] neglect of the industry in the early years, sabotage, shortage of machinery, and even shortage of labour have also been responsible. For a variety of reasons, (among them retirement) the professional cane cutters of the 1950s have almost disappeared and voluntary labour, however energetic, has often been less satisfactory. The harvest of 1969 was described by Castro as 'the country's agony', and totalled $4\frac{1}{2}$ million tons only. But the goal of reaching ten million tons in the harvest of 1970 was proclaimed for such a long time and such stress had been laid on this goal in propaganda ('What are you doing towards the ten million?') that it almost seemed as if the regime would stand or fall by the extent to which this target was fulfilled.

Nevertheless, in the middle of May 1970 Castro bitterly admitted that this target could not after all be achieved and that nine million would be the maximum possible. Even this, however, represents less of a real achievement than it will seem at first sight, since much of the sugar came from cane left over from 1969 or prematurely cut from the harvest of 1971. It is also unfortunately conceivable that the figures were falsified and, providing that Russia assists in the deception (by, for instance, announcing she has bought from Cuba seven million tons), there is no means of checking the truth of the announcement.[6] Further, even if the ten million tons had been achieved, Cuba would still have been producing less sugar per head of population than she was in 1925, while the long-term costs of this grand Potemkin-type harvest cannot easily be measured.

It was a bizarre undertaking: the news that this harvest of 1970 would

[4] The yield from the cane averaged 10·85% in 1969 in comparison with 12·62% in 1958. In 1969 Castro was speaking of a yield of 12·05% as quite exceptional (interview, 20 December 1969, published *Granma* weekly edition, 28 December 1969).

[5] Cane loses sucrose by easily calculated percentages if there is a prolonged delay between canefield and mill. Cane which reaches the mill seven days after being cut has lost 25% of the sugar it would have had if it reached it immediately. In the first part of the harvest, of 1969–70, this seems to have happened quite often.

[6] It is true that the faking of statistics is a little more difficult than it might seem, particularly when the separate achievements of the individual mills are all announced and indeed followed by the press during the course of the grinding. But since 1964 Cuba has followed a policy of secrecy about sugar statistics to 'impede . . . enemies of the Revolution'.

begin on 26 July 1969 (with a *zafra chica*) and that Christmas Eve 1969 would be celebrated, because of the activities on the cane fields, in July 1970, are among the most notable surrealistic contributions to Cuban political life. Meantime, a delegation from North Vietnam, not to speak of the Soviet Minister of Defence, Marshal Grechko, and the entire Cuban cabinet have all done their time in the canefields, while government propaganda has spoken of the harvest as if it were a military challenge: 'Every worker should act as he would in the face of an enemy attack, should feel like a soldier in a trench with a rifle in his hand.'[7]

A commercial agreement with Russia signed in January 1964, and the International Sugar Agreement of 1968 (in force for five years from 1 January 1969), assures Cuba of markets in the short term: the Russians agreed to buy an annually increasing amount of Cuban sugar at 6 cents a pound up to 7 million tons by 1970, though in fact Cuba was on a number of occasions unable to meet her part of the bargain.[8] The International Sugar Agreement gave Cuba a quota of 2·15 million tons.[9] But even leaving aside the political consequences of so close a commercial friendship with Russia,[10] the long-term consequences of reliance on sugar in a world able to produce increasing quantities of it are discouraging, particularly when the Cuban sugar industry seems less efficient and competitive than it was even in the 1950s – not to speak of the last century, when it was in the van of technical experiment (Cuba was even overtaken by Brazil as the largest sugar cane producer in 1966).

There is, however, one important recent development: the beginning of mechanization of the sugar harvest. There were admittedly many early difficulties. Thus despite the construction with the help of Czech and Russian technicians, and parts, of 100 cane-cutting and stripping machines from Russia in 1965 and about 5,000 machines for lifting the cane when it is cut, most of the harvest of sugar in 1969–70 was still being both cut and loaded by hand.[11] For the Russian machines, the *Libertadoras*, often broke down, could only work eight hours a day and when there was

---

[7] Castro's speech at the opening of the main stage of the harvest, 27 October 1969 (*Granma* weekly edition, 2 November 1969).

[8] Russia agreed to take 2·1 million tons of sugar in 1965, 3 million tons in 1966, 4 million tons in 1967 and 5 million tons in 1968–9. China blamed Russia for forcing Cuba to continue to emphasise sugar in her economy (See *People's Daily*, 22 February 1966).

[9] The total sugar available for sale on the 'free market' was conceived as 9·4 million tons, of which 7·7 million were basic exports and 1·65 re-exports from the Communist countries (some Cuban sugar included, doubtless). Other large quotas included Australia, 1·1 million; British West Indies and Guyana, 200,000 and Brazil, 500,000

[10] See below, page 1474.

[11] See P. Sakun, *URSS*, July 1968, figure for imported cane-cutters. The most frequently used variety of cane, incidentally, remains that used before 1959 – the Javanese POJ 2878, but recently successful experiments have been made with a Barbados variety.

no dew, and were useless in the rain or on bumpy ground. In 1968, Castro nevertheless explained that mechanization would be complete by 1975, when the Revolution would 'have secured one of its most humane achievements, having changed over for ever from working conditions fit for animals to those which are truly humane' – that is, to complete mechanization.[12] In the following years, several new combine cane harvesters, of Cuban manufacture, for cutting cane, were used, and the harvest of 1969–70 will apparently use over 200 of these *Hendersons* (called after Robert Henderson, its English-American inventor who had been before the Revolution general manager of the United Fruit Company's mill, *the Preston* – a curious hero for the Revolution but undoubtedly a real one).[13]

Since 1962, the structure of agriculture, industry and labour have all been transformed, so that the still partially bourgeois society which was threatened in the Missile Crisis no longer exists.

In October 1963, a second agrarian reform nationalized all private holdings larger than 167 acres (five *caballería*). Many of these larger proprietors who had been left out of the earlier agrarian reform were said to be leaving their land uncultivated, presumably since they did not see the point of producing anything if they were only able to sell at the low prices offered by the Institute of Agrarian Reform (INRA). But the private sector of agriculture generally had fulfilled its obligations in respect of production more efficiently than had the state farms or co-operatives, so that the second agrarian reform law was a political rather than an economic measure. Many of these private farmers in the middle range were among the opponents of the regime and had taken to the hills, particularly in the Escambray, Matanzas and the north of Las Villas, during mid-1963, in sporadic revolts.[14]

Some 11,000 farms were thereby added to the state domain, which was in consequence responsible for a little over two-thirds of Cuban agriculture.[15] Though the actual acts of state intervention were often carried out callously, there was no widespread fighting, and no deaths seem to have been reported. All expropriated farmers who were not actual opponents of the regime were compensated, at the rate of $15 a month per

[12] Speech, 5 July 1968.
[13] The *Hendersons* are cutters assembled (apparently at Santa Clara) on top of bulldozers imported from Russia. They need a cane collection centre where the leaves of the cane are stripped off before being dispatched to the mill. Some 300 of these were planned for 1971.
[14] Carlos Rafael Rodríguez, *La Revolución Cubana y el Periodo de Transición*, Folleto 2, 12.
[15] The second agrarian reform expropriated 6,062 farms between 5 and 10 *caballería* (a total of 608,000 hectares), 3,105 between 10 and 20 *caballería* (610,000 hectares), 1,456 between 20 and 30 *caballería* (508,000 hectares) and 592 larger than 30 *caballería* (377,000 hectares).

caballería confiscated, up to a total of $250, for a period of ten years. In addition, some private farms remain with up to about 900 acres, mostly estates farmed by a single family.

Even after this reform, however, there remained between 150,000 and 200,000 small farmers in Cuba, or almost 80% of the farmers of the country before the Revolution.[16] These, despite alarms, remained in being at the beginning of the 1970s. About a quarter of these farms, or 40,000, are so small that they produce only for the farm family, with no surplus for sale. These include many of those 35,000 who received title deeds of land shared out under the terms of the unfulfilled first agrarian reform.[17] Some of these farmers remain relatively rich men. But all private farmers are free only up to a certain point. Thus they are members of the state-directed Association of Private Farmers,[18] are allowed to grow certain crops only, and can sell their produce only to the state purchasing agency (ACOPIO). These farmers can also only sell their estates, if they wish to do so, to the state, and the regime apparently thinks that in the long run, all these private estates will by sale come into state hands.[19] Not unnaturally, therefore, there has been considerable anxiety, particularly among those farmers who might seem to come within the next category, 100 to 150 acres.[20]

The small farmers still make a big contribution to the revolution's agricultural programme. They grow most (70%) of the fruit in Cuba, nearly all the coffee and tobacco (90%), own almost half of the livestock and still grow about 25% of the cane. (Tobacco is grown by about 40,000 private farmers, though the manufacture of cigars and cigarettes is controlled by the government.) It would be a serious mistake if ideological preconceptions were to cause any further state intervention in a department of the economy which, despite many discouragements, is still very productive.

Since 1964 agriculture has been the centre of the regime's attention and has naturally benefited substantially. 25% of the Gross National Product is invested in agriculture.[21] There have been huge imports of tractors from Russia and Czechoslovakia, many irrigation projects, the building of fertilizer plants – one by the English firm of Simon-Carves, costing £M14 near Cienfuegos[22] – several experimental cattle projects

[16] According to the Agricultural Census of 1946 – and there is no later source – farms smaller than 150 acres constituted over 80% of the farms in Cuba.

[17] Only 35,000 deeds were distributed under the terms of the regime's promise in 1959 to give 100,000 land titles.

[18] *Asociación nacional de agricultores privados.*

[19] Castro's speech to the 3rd congress of ANAP, May 1967.

[20] Dumont, p. 87.

[21] There were 35,000 tractors in 1967 in comparison with 9,200 in 1960 (Castro speech of 2 January 1968).

[22] Simon-Carves of Stockport had built chemical or fertilizer plants in other Communist countries before (see Ian Ball, *Daily Telegraph*, 3 February 1967).

(including an Institute of Animal Science[23]) to increase the quality of animals, directed by the English agronomist, Dr Thomas Preston of Aberdeen, greater care of grasses, and much greater use of fungicides and pesticides. Castro's own interests in agriculture have been continuous. The nationalization of most of the cane land, though it has carried with it familiar disadvantages, has at least made possible on a national scale the rational planning of planting and harvesting. The large investment which the Revolution has made in agriculture could certainly assure Cuba of being one of the most modern and prosperous agricultural countries in the world by 1975–80, assuming that wise decisions are made politically. In particular, the future of Cuban rice and of cattle, especially beef cattle, seems promising. Livestock figures are now apparently well over those of 1959, despite the heavy slaughtering which went on during 1959–60.[24] Land under cultivation is said to have increased by 50%.[25] Except for wheat, fats and oils, Cuba could supply all her basic foods, and, in the long run, home-grown cotton and other fibres could presumably supply the domestic clothing industry. But there are dark sides to the situation. Thus, despite efforts to decentralise since 1965, there remains much inefficiency, and the planning powers of JUCEI, the planning boards, and INRA, though much reduced in functions, continue to hamper local managers, even if it is no longer the case, as occurred before 1965, that small items such as nails had to be ordered from Havana. Castro's own obsession with agriculture and his unchallenged position in the country is not an unmixed blessing for agricultural administrators. Thus since 1965 special farms have been assigned to the personal attention of Castro and these have received absolute priority in respect of equipment, often to the cost of other farms. These farms have so multiplied since 1968 that René Dumont, after a prolonged visit in 1969, described the Cuban countryside as 'now divided up in a series of special giant enterprises given over to single crops'.[26] This is a complete reversal of what occurred before 1965, when each People's Farm diversified and grew twenty-five to thirty-five different crops.

There have also been continuous difficulties with the agricultural workers. In 1966 there had to be a nationwide campaign against the

[23] See the *Informe Anual* of the *Instituto de Ciencia Animal*, 1966.

[24] According to one (Cuban) estimate, cattle numbers about 7 million head of cattle, well above the 1959 figure of 5·8 million. The aim is to raise numbers of cattle to 12 million by 1975, permitting an annual slaughter of 4 million and the daily production of 30 million litres of milk (Gutelman, *L'Agriculture socialisée à Cuba*, 79). However, it is fair to doubt whether these targets will be achieved and whether Castro is right in predicting a rice surplus by 1970. Russia, it will be remembered, has not fulfilled a single one of her agricultural plans since 1929.

[25] According to Castro, on 2 January 1968, land cultivation in 1958 in Cuba was 2·3 million hectares. In 1967 this had risen by 56% to 3·7 million hectares.

[26] René Dumont, Les Cubains trouvent le temps long, *Le Monde*, 9 December 1969.

withholding by workers on state farms of small plots of land for themselves; 'even the paths between state farms' had been privately sown, state irrigation had been diverted to secret private plots and private cultivation and the keeping of livestock around state workers' houses had begun at an alarming rate. In precisely the same way, the slaves of the past had developed their own *conucos* around their barracoons. It does not seem as if the twentieth-century authoritarian state has in the long run been any more successful than the nineteenth-century private capitalist in preventing agricultural labourers from self-help. How much agricultural time and labour is 'wasted' in this way is impossible to predict.

Finally, agricultural production, particularly if it is intended to be internationally competitive, is increasingly the consequence of a huge combined economic system in which efficiency depends upon industry, science and commerce as much as upon the farmer. Most competitive agricultural countries, such as Denmark or Britain (since 1945), are serviced by a large number of 'para-agricultural workers'.[27] Thus it is not really feasible to concentrate on agricultural development regardless of its implications, and it must be a matter of serious doubt whether Cuba's continued reliance on Russian and East European industry for the tools of her agricultural undertakings promises well, since this industry has in the past been so unsuccessful in serving her own agricultures.

There is also a black market. As early as 1963 the black market was supposed to give food prices at between three and ten times the official figures. For a long time, the regime turned a blind eye to the large number of townspeople who would drive out of the cities at week-ends to buy food direct from peasants and indeed, with the rationing of petrol from the beginning of 1967, and the lack of buying power of all money, along with the virtual disappearance of all goods from the shops, this activity has more or less come to an end. It was replaced by a system of barter, by which hats, for instance, would be exchanged for chickens, or coffee for a barrel of beer, though one instance was reported in 1969 of a pig for a party being bought for $600.

It is fairly clear that agriculture will dominate Cuban life for the foreseeable future, perhaps forever. Castro appears to bank on likely world food shortages to secure for Cuba permanently a market for increased agricultural production.[28] On the other hand, Castro's politics have changed often and other Cuban leaders still seem to expect more tradi-

[27] René Dumont and Bernard Rosier, *The Hungry Future*, André Deutsch, London, 1969, 38.

[28] Perhaps this at least he has learned from Professor René Dumont, many of whose other suggestions have been unwisely spurned.

29 Castro speaks in the Plaza de la Revolución, 1964

30a Castro cuts cane, 1965
b   Castro explains a new dam

tionally that agriculture in the long run will 'create exports so as to allow us to enter upon industrialization'.[29] In either event, the social consequences are likely to be considerable, since the Cuban regime evidently hopes, at the moment, to reverse the customary drift of labour into the cities characteristic of the rest of the world and preserve, or even expand, the rural population – so attempting to disprove the conventional wisdom that progress and industrialization are synonyms. This romantic plan is not likely to succeed.

The control of the immense bureaucracy created by the Revolutionary intervention in every sphere of the national life, in all departments, but particularly in agriculture, has been one of the government's most difficult tasks. This began to be appreciated at least as early as 1963. Castro's speeches in the following twelve months were full of scorn for many of the cogs in the machine which he had created: 'the place where I was born and brought up, which was a latifundia, had one or two office clerks; now it is a state farm and has twelve clerks';[30] 'We have accomplished nothing if previously we worked for the capitalists and now we work for another type of person who is not a capitalist but who consumes much and produces nothing';[31] 'capitalists threw away money in luxuries, in entertainment, but did not waste money in the work centres and managed their businesses well. And we, the socialists, are we going to stop the capitalist waste and still throw away the fruits of the peoples' labour? The people benefit not at all if the money that the capitalists spent in one way we socialists spend in another . . . what difference is there between a stingy rich man and a squandering revolutionary? That the former impoverishes some to enrich himself, while the revolutionary impoverishes everybody without enriching anybody';[32] and 'a spendthrift in an important position equals the harm done by 10,000 counter-revolutionaries.'[33]

In 1966 'the struggle against bureaucracy' had become a 'prime task' for the Cuban Communist Party. Sometimes, the regime insisted that bureaucracy was an unpleasant residue of capitalism and by no means a fault inherent in socialism. But Castro was found complaining, in a speech to the Cuban women's federation in December 1966, that even

[29] Dr Carlos Rafael Rodríguez, in an interview to the author in January 1969, said 'we hope that whereas sugar now accounts for 80% of Cuban exports, the percentage will drop to some 25%, with coffee, beef and minerals accounting for some 70%: in particular, coffee, in the past a derisory export, should account for 25% of Cuban exports in the future.' Castro made the same prediction in a speech on 4 November 1969, but in an earlier speech (27 October 1969) promised that production of sugar cane would be doubled again by 1980. (*Granma*, 2 November 1969.)

[30] Fidel Castro, *Obra Revolucionaria*, September 1964 No. 23, pp. 9–20.

[31] Fidel Castro, at Matanzas, *Revolución*, 15 November 1964.

[32] Fidel Castro, *Obra Revolucionaria*, October 1964 No. 28, p. 33.

[33] Fidel Castro at Matanzas, *Revolución*, 15 November 1964.

the 'struggle against bureaucracy committees' had become 'bureau-cratized' and admitted that they would continue to be so for 'several more years'. Many workers in banks and offices, meantime, were 'ra-tionalized' or dismissed and, in a speech in early 1967, Castro regretted that he had not in 1959 transferred the capital from Havana to the small town of Guáimaro.

The New Men

Industry has also undergone a structural change since 1962, for in March 1968 the government destroyed the last vestiges of private enterprise, during the so-called 'revolutionary offensive' which closed without compensation 50,000 small businesses, from fruit sellers in the street to cockpits, pawn shops, music schools, laundries and garages. This campaign evidently owed much to the example of the cultural revolution in China and was certainly embarked upon only after much deliberation. Since then, apart from fishermen and farmers, the only private undertakings in Cuba are a few medical practices. Many famous bars and restaurants were closed, some for good, some to open sporadically thereafter on the initiative of the local Committee for the Defence of the Revolution.[1] For seven years, the small businessmen had in fact lived in a twilight society, constituting more a safety valve than an economic enterprise, since the state was the only big customer (for the manufacturers, for example, of machinery or clothing) and the only provider of raw materials. As early as 1962, many shops, restaurants, and groceries had been taken over without special decrees and, in December of that year, most enterprises using hired labour were nationalized. This revolutionary offensive was described by Dr Carlos Rafael Rodríguez as the 'logical consequence of the deepening of the Revolution', which until then had 'left behind in the cities a still large *petit bourgeoisie* of small traders and speculators. This . . . was a persistent threat to the type of socialist man whom we desire to create. In practice it became a centre of opposition . . . [giving] special favours to the remains of the rentier class . . . who thereby received the best of what was being produced by the community.'[2] In a speech at the time, when opening a school at Boca de Jaruco, Castro argued that private business is basically immoral and that material incentives of any sort mar the character of the new man. Castro described the bar owners, hot-dog stallholders and night club proprietors whom he was destroying, as 'drones in perfect physical condition who put up a stand and earn fifty dollars a day while they watch the lorries go by filled with women on their way to work in Havana's Green Belt' (95·1 % of hot dog stallholders, he assured the

[1] See below, p. 1457.
[2] Interview, 13 January 1969.

country, with surely an excess of precision, were counter-revolutionaries or 'small spongers').

In the succeeding months, Castro began to develop at greater length the concept of the free 'new man' who would, as Guevara had hoped, be no longer alienated from society, unsullied by contact with the profit motive, but conscious, like Alain's peasant, of the country rather than the corrupt city, and living for the community from the cradle to the grave. (Castro seems first to have spoken of this at length at the congress of small farmers – ANAP – in May 1967; he described how in the future 'we shall do away with the vile intermediary, money' and how then men would work from habit, though there would be an abundance of everything and a free distribution of goods.)[3] But even in 1965 he was saying that 'from an early age [man] must be discouraged from every egotistic feeling in the enjoyment of material things, such as the sense of individual property',[4] though he had avoided taking sides in the controversy over material incentives for labour, sometimes seeming to favour moral rewards, as did Guevara, and sometimes material ones, as did the more traditional old Communists. Indeed, some of Castro's remarks on this matter conflict as strongly with his later views as any other change of face; for instance, in the summer of 1965, the year of Guevara's disappearance from the Cuban political scene,[5] he is found telling a meeting of cane cutters that 'we cannot choose idealistic methods that conceive all men to be guided by duty, because in actual life, that is not so . . . it would be absurd to expect that the great masses of men who earn their living cutting cane will make a maximum effort just by being told that it is their duty, whether they earn more or less. That would be idealistic.'[6]

At all events, Cuba in the late 1960s was committed to an industrial attitude long since discarded in Eastern Europe. Overtime pay was abolished. So too was 'socialist emulation', the scheme whereby, as in Russia, workers receive extra pay for more work and a penalty for failing to fulfil their targets. (This had been used in various forms between 1962 and 1967; abolition was doubtless a relief to all, since some first-prize workers had shown an embarrassing preference for material goods – a refrigerator or a motor bicycle – rather than a holiday in Russia.)[7] National work heroes in the style of Stakhanov were also

[3] Speech at the conference of small farmers, May 1967.
[4] Lockwood, 126.
[5] See below, p. 1469.
[6] Fidel Castro, '*Discurso en el Acto de Entrega de diplomas a las Trabajadores que mas se distinguieron en la V zafra del pueblo*', El Mundo, 25 July 1965.
[7] The first 'festival of socialist emulation' was held in April 1962, and later that year 45 prize houses were distributed to the first winners – fourteen, incidentally, to soldiers. In 1965, 1,500 refrigerators and 100 motor cycles, 500 journeys to Russia and East Europe and 2,000 holidays at Varadero beach were offered, but only 80 journeys to Russia were taken up. In

abolished, since it was found that they caused jealousy, not admiration. (There were also doubts: did the National Hero of Labour for 1964, Rafael Cuevas, really lay 2,190 bricks in four hours, and did his predecessor in 1963, Reinaldo Castro, really cut a daily average of 1,280 *arrobas* of cane – a figure which certainly compared well with the 150 *arrobas* which was the daily average for the cane cutter before 1959?)

In place of these discredited methods, Castro since 1968 attempted to institute 'Communism and yet more Communism'.[8] He repeatedly said that in the long run he desired to abolish money completely, and indeed by 1969 several things, such as sport, cinemas and local telephone calls, were available in 'a Communist way', that is, free. An article in the government daily newspaper *Granma* put the matter clearly: 'since we were small we were taught to ask "how much have you got? How much are you worth?" Then we learned that money was unnecessary ... already in Cuba those six letters (*dinero*) mean less. The new generation does not believe in all the old myths about money.' Further, voluntary labour or voluntary overtime has become more and more the typical solution of the regime to labour problems, though it is hard to make a true estimate of the value, or cost, of this to the economy. Castro was thus attempting to create, from above, a gigantic kibbutz, as it were, out of Cuba, though at the same time seeking the target of a monstrously big sugar crop in 1969–70.

Doubtless in some ways this new policy seeks to make, and indeed successfully makes, a virtue out of necessity, seeking a philosophical justification for economic hardship. There is little point after all in material incentives in the form of money if there are no goods to buy. On the other hand, it seems that this attempt to achieve the stage of Communism at the same time as building socialism, to differentiate Cuba from the more comfortable regimes of Eastern Europe and Russia (lands at least mildly responsive to the 'philosophy of the full shop window', which Castro has mocked), responds to a puritanical, anarchic and individualistic strain in Castro's own character and also in the character of Cuban society which, in the past, knew so much about money and so much more than the previously largely agrarian Communist countries already in existence.

Moral incentives have not yet triumphed entirely. In September 1969, wages for sugar workers were raised by a third, specifically in order to try and avoid a further drift of experienced men from the

[8] Castro, speech, 19 April 1968.

1966,100 private cars were among the prizes. Meanwhile, César Escalante, secretary for the 'commission of revolutionary orientation' of the PURS, had complained that 'very few workers actually participate in emulation . . . only a third of workers attend emulation meetings . . . brotherly competition has not yet been understood by the masses' (*Hoy*, 18 October 1964).

industry.[9] There remains much absenteeism – the Cuban workers' only effective protest and occasional sabotage – and it is doubtful whether what the then secretary-general, Miguel Martín, described in 1967 as a 'morass of indiscipline, irresponsibility and superficiality' (to characterize labour attitudes) has really much changed,[10] and whether, despite such experiments as the Isle of Youth (where a moneyless society has got further than on the main island), these policies have really brought Cuban workers nearer to ideal Communism than the more tolerant policies of, say, Dubček or Tito. Can Communism as defined by Marx, after all, triumph in an atmosphere of 'liberalism, no, softening, no'?[11] Is not the disappearance of the state also a necessity?[12] And, despite the understandable revulsion felt by many Cubans, after four centuries of corruption, from the seamier side of the money economy, is that revulsion quite so strong as to cause Cubans as a whole to react in a quite different way from the rest of humanity? It is impossible to believe it, or even to think that what Leo Huberman and Paul Sweezy call the 'de-automobilization' of Cuba is much liked.[13] Societies have to take into account good and bad people alike. What if the perfect man were to turn out to be a tragic delusion? It is indeed difficult to believe that these ideas would last long were it not for Castro's unique skill in presenting them in their most attractive light.

The increasing emphasis on sugar in Cuba since 1964 has meant that there has scarcely been any new industrialization. On the other hand, serious efforts have been concentrated on various existing undertakings, particularly nickel, where the two old U.S. plants at Moa and Nicaro, on the north shore of Oriente province, on top of one of the largest nickel deposits in the world, have pressed ahead, with production well above that of the 1950s.[14] Nickel has now surpassed tobacco as the country's second most valuable export, after sugar.

Batista's regime was sustained in the 1950s by an alliance of the Army with the highly organized and powerful trade unions. Both were

[9] Speech by Jorge Risquet, Minister of Labour, 6 June 1969. He added that it was 'logical' for a worker, even 'of complete revolutionary outlook', to be concerned about the family budget.

[10] *Bohemia* (12 September 1969) published an inquiry into labour difficulties at a railway workshop at Camagüey. This showed that in April 1969 only five men out of 1,600 had responded to an appeal to cut cane without pay, that each worker did less than half an hour's voluntary overtime, and that 4,611 man days were lost through absenteeism.

[11] Castro, speech, 28 September 1968.

[12] In an interview on 13 January 1969, I suggested to Dr Rodríguez that Marx had thought that the Communist society could not be achieved until after the disappearance of the state (scarcely a possibility at the moment in Cuba). He replied sharply: 'Marx wrote little about the nature of Communist society.'

[13] Sweezy & Huberman, *Socialism in Cuba*, 95. Anyone who has seen those Cubans who still drive cars look after these prized possessions would doubt it.

[14] Production of nickel reached 35 million tons in 1967, in comparison with 18 million in 1958.

corrupt, and the unions were also restrictive, preventing the modernization of agriculture and industry – in particular of the sugar industry.

The Revolution, by converting the unions basically into a department of state, had smashed both the corruption and also the past restrictive hostility to change which characterized this system. A number of
unproductive sugar mills have thus been abandoned and, as has been
seen, a beginning has been made to both mechanization and the
rational planning of the sugar crop, along the lines vainly advocated by
Lobo in the 1950s (carried out, ironically, by Tomás Martínez, the
Revolution's chief sugar manager, and Lobo's general manager in the
past). Bulk handling of the sugar crop at the ports has also been possible
with the end of the old union of dock labourers. Some, doubtless, would
hesitate before regarding these activities as among the benefits of the
Revolution, but they are so nevertheless, despite the troubles and even
misery which they have actually brought to certain well-established
working-class communities.

But there is nothing else very imaginative about the Cuban labour and
industrial scene under the Revolution. There is no workers' control. A
sugar mill, for instance, is run by an Administrator appointed by the
state, advised by chemists and technicians as in the past – often the same
men who did the job before 1959 and who have remained in Cuba for a
variety of reasons, some idealistic, some personal. The cane is cut, and
carried, by the same men who worked for Lobo or Gómez Mena –
apart from the armies of voluntary workers, whose activities are perhaps
less economic than educative or political in intent. Except that there is
no chance to protest save by absenteeism, sabotage or exile, and that
even on the dirtiest wall there are likely to be posters adjuring patriotism, there has been less change in life at the mill than would have been
thought possible: and as late as 1969 the Minister of Labour, Risquet,
was admitting that there was still a 'marked difference' between the
income of workers during the harvest and after it.[15]

The unions, reduced to fourteen in 1966, and with free elections un-
heard of since 1961, are now primarily methods of organization. In
September 1963 there seems to have been a major challenge to the
regime by the old Construction Workers, but it was heavily repressed.[16]

[15] Speech of 6 June 1969. He added that, in the dead season, some workers still looked elsewhere than in the sugar industry for employment and, if they found it, would not come back.

[16] According to exile sources, at the meeting of the equipment union (a constituent of the
Construction Workers' Federation) on 11 September 1963, resolutions were passed demanding
full pay for 'lay-offs' when equipment was being repaired (a frequent occurrence), regular
hourly wages for heavy equipment workers when re-assigned to common labour during break-
downs in machinery, and publication in the press of a manifesto incorporating the union's
demands. Lázaro Peña, the secretary-general of the CTC(R), tried to address the meeting
but he was drowned by shouts of 'we are hungry! we want freedom! we want work!' The
leaders of this protest were afterwards punished. (Paul Bethel, *Terror and Resistance in Communist Cuba*, 41.)

In June 1968, the secretary-general of the Labour confederation, Miguel Martín (who had succeeded the 'founder' Lázaro Peña), gave a regional meeting in Camagüey the familiar explanation that since 'the working class is in power', the general collective interest as defined by the government was 'the criterion for all judgements'. New faces may now be seen among the union leaders, but none of them is an independent spirit, and indeed their manner of election precludes any but 'vanguard workers' or 'exemplary workers'. From August 1969, every Cuban worker has had to possess a 'control card' and a 'labour dossier' upon which all absences and other shortcomings are marked.

The economic planning of Cuba has stayed much the same since the early 1960s. Thus the JUCEPLAN, the Cuban version of the Russian GOSPLAN, remains, despite reforms, as do the local boards, the JUCEI, founded in 1961 as rough equivalents of the Russian regional Economic Councils. In industry, all plants producing the same item are integrated in a single combined *empresa* or corporation while, in agriculture, state farms are grouped regionally under INRA. Domestic trade is controlled by the Ministry of Internal Trade, foreign trade by its respective ministry. The methods, of course, closely resemble Russian practice, as do the economic plans; and the first Cuban Five Year Plan was reduced to a four-year one so that it would end at the same time as those in other socialist countries. In Cuba, the JUCEPLAN prepares the national plan, which is then referred to the Ministries, then to the *empresas* and finally to the farms and factories, where production meetings are held and where, in theory, workers can propose alterations. The plan then retraces its steps upwards to JUCEPLAN to be approved by Ministers, being thereafter sent back down the channel of production in the form of definite goals for definite plants. The consultative process is an illusion; to the workers, one reporter quite sympathetic to the Revolution wrote, the whole process is a 'complete abstraction'; they showed 'little interest in discussing it'.[17] In November 1968, a new secretary-general of the CTC(R), Héctor Ramos Latour,[18] boasted how a million workers had discussed a new social security law, in a 'parliament of the working masses', but he presented no news as to whether or not a single amendment had in consequence been introduced.

The Cuban Revolutionary Government, like all socialist administrations, has also had persistent difficulties in establishing standards. Thus some years ago it was said that the 'establishment of the *norms system* has brought to light deficiencies in the work of the local trade unions, who

---

[17] Adolfo Gilly, *The Monthly Review*, October 1964. See also the remarks of Lázaro Peña, then secretary-general of the CTC(R) in September 1962, quoted Mesa-Lago.

[18] He succeeded Miguel Martín as secretary-general in November 1968.

do not yet understand the importance of production and baulk when faced with any measure of reorganization which may change old working habits, the remains of capitalism'.[19] Wages in Cuba are paid according to skill, and fairly wide differences still exist in consequence between eight separate grades in four occupational sectors,[20] though some information on this subject has been kept secret. There is a minimum wage of $85 a month and a maximum one of $450. Pensions are $60 a month. These rules mirror Russian practice, though the ratio between the highest paid technician and the lowest paid industrial worker is higher than in Russia,[21] while leading technicians in Cuba as elsewhere in the Communist world get all sorts of advantages such as free cars, special meals and journeys.

For those who find the demands made upon them under the present system of labour organization excessive, there is 'labour justice'. This copes with such matters as nonfulfilment of schedules, absenteeism, damage to state machinery and negligence, and imposes a variety of penalties, including deduction of wages, transfer from place of work, dismissal and also commitment to forced labour camps; thus among the thirty-two reasons in 1962 for committal to the camp at Guanahacabibes in West Cuba were 'negligence or ignorance which causes a standstill in production and hampering output standards'.[22]

Apart from the isolated incident of the builders' protest in 1963, there is, however, little overt evidence of hostility of workers towards the revolutionary regime. In 1962 far more workers told the sociologist Zeitlin that they thought that they had more influence on the government than before 1959 while most workers believed that there was no call for any election. Quite obviously most workers thought that nationalization meant that they now worked for themselves and not for the boss.[23] Skilled workers seemed more inclined to support the revolution than unskilled ones. On the other hand, there has been no serious inquiry since. No one knows to what extent, for instance, Escalante and the old Communists enjoyed support in 1968.[24]

It is impossible to say precisely to what extent the low productivity of the Cuban economy since the Revolution is due to poor wage scales, and to what extent it has been the consequence of bad management, lack of spare parts, absence of technicians, the U.S. blockade, excessive

[19] Martínez Sánchez, *La implantación del sistema salarial*, 16, qu. Mesa-Lago, 71.

[20] Agricultural labourers, administrative employees, industrial workers, technicians and executive officials.

[21] The ratio in 1968 was 1:11 in Cuba and 1:6.8 in Russia.

[22] '*Reglamento del Centro de Rehabilitación de Uvero Quemado*', *Nuestra Industria*, March 1962.

[23] Zeitlin, *Revolutionary Politics*, 38, 206. The figures were in the first matter 170 to 8 with 17 thinking that they had the influence as before 1959 and 7 having no opinion; Zeitlin's sampling method is open to question.

[24] See below, p. 1469, for the Escalante affair.

expenditure on the social services and so on. Nevertheless, it is clear that, quite apart from failing to increase production in the more important sectors of the economy such as, in particular, sugar, the mixture of material and moral incentives has not increased the quality of products: in the early years of the Revolution, glue did not dry, matches broke their heads, toothpaste turned to stone after a few months. There were numerous conferences on 'quality' but in 1966 President Dorticós was still describing the matter as 'alarming'. Cursory inquiries in 1969 (rendered difficult by the almost total absence of material goods in the shops) suggest that this has certainly not much changed, and productivity per working day, although greater than in 1963–4, is still probably lower than before the Revolution.

The shortage of statistics and the unreliability of those that do exist naturally make it difficult to speak of general production figures for the years between 1960 and 1970 in Cuba. But it seems likely that whereas between 1959 and 1961 there was probably a rise in Gross National Production, and between 1961 and 1963 at least nothing worse than stagnation, since 1963 there has been a drop amounting to at least an average of 0.5% a year.[25] Considering that the Government has, according to its own statistics, failed to ensure much more than an average four-hour day of work from its citizens,[26] it is perhaps surprising that the fall of production has not been greater still.

[25] See Mesa-Lago, *Availability and Reliability of Statistics in Socialist Cuba*, Centre for Latin American studies, University of Pittsburgh, 1970, p. 51.
[26] As quoted K. S. Karol, *Les Guérrilleros au Pouvoir*, Paris 1970, 424.

The Guardians

If Cuban society is as yet far from the Utopia coveted by Guevara, and now by Castro, the political machine constructed to create it has become elaborate. Castro himself, it is true, remains the curiously described 'maximum leader', prime minister, first secretary of the Cuban Communist Party, commander-in-chief of the armed forces, and Minister–President of the Institute for Agrarian Reform. It is evident that, even more than in the years during which the Revolution consolidated its hold, he takes all the decisions, gives what emphasis and explanations he judges right for the policies undertaken and, by the continuing use of television, press and radio, as well as personal appearances before both large and small crowds, sustains and justifies the regime, at the same time upholding the enthusiasm of his own followers.

The main political change since 1962 has been the eclipse of the old Communist leaders who, because of their many years of experience both of political organization and of the world Communist scene, played such an important part in the establishment of the 'socialist' character of the Cuban Revolution in the years 1960 and 1961. The surviving members of Castro's 26 July Movement are in power, though nevertheless they call themselves formally Communists. Aníbal Escalante's ORI (*organizaciones revolucionarias integradas*), which set out to be an amalgamation of the 26 July Movement and the old Communist Party, on the latter's terms, disappeared during 1963 without ceremony, while its successor, the PURS (*Partido Unificado de la Revolución Socialista*), appeared without inauguration. This movement was soon recognized by the Russian Communists as a 'fraternal party' but, in 1965, the PURS in its turn gave way to a new 'Communist Party of Cuba'.

This, as usual in communist states, was controlled by a central committee with a politburo and a secretariat superior to it, which, totalling a hundred members in all, remained, despite a few expulsions and deaths much the same until the end of the 1960s.[1] Of this one hundred,

[1] Efigenio Ameijeiras, Armando Acosta, Ramón Calcines and José Matar were expelled in 1966, 1967, 1968 and 1969 respectively. Three members of the 1965 central committee were killed with Guevara in Bolivia in 1967 – Major Juan Vitalio Acuña, Antonio Sánchez Díaz and Captain Eliseo Reyes.

sixty-eight were formally military men, although the actual military role of some of them in the Sierra or elsewhere was slight.[2] (Provincial committees of the new party were also from the start full of army men.) Twenty-one of the hundred were apparently members of the old Cuban Communist Party before 1959, ranging from men grown grey in the service of the party (such as Fabio Grobart, Blas Roca and Juan Marinello) to younger contemporaries of Castro at the University (such as Flavio Bravo and Leonel Soto)[3]. Nevertheless, no old Communist was on the politburo or on the secretariat,[4] which was dominated by the two Castros and their followers from the first days of the struggle against Batista.[5] The fact that the ideological director of the Revolution (*Responsable Nacional de Ideología*) is the ex-Catholic, ex-Minister of Education, Armando Hart, a man more of ambition than of intellectual distinction, means that the ideological director of the regime is firmly under the control of the Castros. Though only ten of the central committee and its bodies had been at the Moncada or on the

[2] Thus Major Flavio Bravo, an old Communist of Castro's generation at the University, is not known to have fought much; while *Comrade* Marcelo Fernández and *Comrade* Armando Hart probably did as much as Major Faustino Pérez. The military contingent in the Central Committee formally consisted of 58 majors, 9 captains and a lieutenant, major being still the highest Cuban army rank.

[3] This was in contrast with the old party representation on the 24-member national committee of the PURS. There, the old Communists had 11 members, with the 26 July Movement 12 and the Directorio Revolucionario 1. Old party members were in 1965 Blas Roca, Carlos Rafael Rodríguez, Armando Acosta, Severo Aguirre, Flavio Bravo, Ramón Calcines, Joel Domenech, Fabio Grobart, Secundino Guerra, Manuel Luzardo, Isidoro Malmierca, Juan Marinello, Miguel Martín, José Matar Franye, Arnaldo Milián, Lázaro Peña, José Ramírez, Ursinio Rojas, Clementina Serra, and Leonel Soto. Blas Roca was chairman of a commission to draw up a constitution for Cuba, a project of which nothing much has been heard. Carlos Rafael Rodríguez, though no longer President of the Institute for Agrarian Reform (a post he held from 1962 to 1964), has remained on the central committee's economic commission and, as a frequent spokesman for the regime both in Cuba and abroad, exerts more influence on policy-making than any other old Communist – possibly, at times, more than anyone else, apart from Castro (with whom he seems to be on excellent terms) a remarkable career for an ex-member of Batista's cabinet during the Second World War.

[4] Perhaps it is worth adding that all save three of the Communist Party presidium elected at its last independent congress in 1960 were in 1965 members of the central committee or its branches (the three were Aníbal Escalante and Joaquín Ordoqui, who were disgraced, and César Escalante, who was dead). Two out of six members of the National Committee elected in 1960 also found places in 1965 (Arnaldo Milián and Felipe Torres, but not Ladislao and José Luis González Carvajal, Leonidas Calderio and Silvio Quintana), along with the youth leader of 1960 – Isidoro Malmierca, who became first editor of the new party newspaper, *Granma*.

[5] Thus of the eight men who constitute the politburo and the secretariat, four were both in the Moncada attack and on the *Granma* (the two Castros, Ramiro Valdés and Juan Almeida). Armando Hart was a prominent organizer of the 26 July Movement from early on, and Guillermo García was the 'first peasant to join Castro' in the Sierra (one may doubt whether his presence in such a high political role in 1965 is much more than honorific, despite his military responsibilities). Sergio de Valle, chief of the army staff and afterwards Minister of the Interior, succeeded Guevara as chief doctor in the Sierra in 1957. The eighth member was Osvaldo Dorticós, the President of the Republic, whose role in the struggle against Batista was slight.

Granma[6] and only four seem to have been ex-members of the Directorio Revolucionario,[7] most of the military members, and therefore a majority of the whole committee, must have been in the Sierra Maestra in one role or another.

The regime has sought to ignore all these old differences, and the Revolution has often depended on even newer men: the ex-shop assistants, clerks and factory workers of 1958 who perhaps trained as teachers were, within months, found to be 'able, dynamic and revolutionary', and so became directors of sugar mills by 1961 – a living suggestion of the lack of opportunity in the old society.[8] These opportunists of the system were typified by Captain Jorge Enrique Mendoza and Major Jorge Serguera, who by 1969 were in charge respectively of the national newspaper *Granma* and of the mass media; by Major Piñeiro, the head of counter-espionage, Major Acevedo, the first commander of the militia, and Major Iglesias, the first commander of the united youth movement. Equally interesting has been the continuing adherence to the regime of men such as Major René de los Santos, chief of army intelligence (DIER) in 1959, and described even by Manuel Artime as 'non-Communist and above reproach',[9] yet he remained in Cuba to be a founder member of the central committee of the new Cuban Communist Party in 1965.

Most of these men, who are often courageous, energetic and dedicated, were still at the end of the 1960s only in their thirties and may consequently be expected, in default of a counter-revolution, to want many more years of power. Leaving aside the old Communists, the average age of the central committee of 1965 could scarcely have been more than thirty-six. On the other hand, at lesser levels, the Revolutionary government has been much assisted by the survivors of other important generations in left-wing Cuban politics; survivors on the one hand from the political gangster age of the late 1940s[10] and, on the other, from the old Left generation at the University in the 1920s and 1930s. True, many of these ex-students were even by 1944 far from radical, as the experience of Dr Grau San Martín's administration showed. But others, such as those who had sided with Ala Izquierda Estudiantil in their

[6] The two Castros, Almeida, Ramiro Valdés, Calixto García and Jesús Montané were both at Moncada and on the *Granma*; Pedro Miret and Haydée Santamaría were in addition at the first, but not on the second, and Efigenio Ameijeiras and Faustino Pérez were on the *Granma* but not at Moncada.

[7] Chomón, José Abrantes, Julio García Olivera and José Naranjo.

[8] *Bohemia* 15 January 1961, quoted Goldenberg, 212.

[9] (*Hombre intachable y no comunista*, Artime, 78).

[10] Thus of those who were with Castro at Cayo Confites in 1948, Carlos Franqui was for a long time editor of the 26 July Movement's newspaper *Revolución* (and afterwards was understood to have been working on Castro's 'memoirs'); Eduardo Corona and Enrique Rodríguez Loeches have been ambassadors; and Feliciano Maderne a deputy judge of the Supreme Court.

youth, had remained so, at least nominally, and could be counted upon to support revolutionary action in the 1960s, which they had long advocated without perhaps ever thinking (or perhaps in the end desiring) that it would actually happen.[11]

Castro has, in short, been uniquely able to harness to revolutionary nationalism a contrasting galaxy of energies, including not only reformers and idealists but also the 'social outcasts always in the van of every revolution or counter-revolution'.[12] Many who in the late 1960s worked as bureaucrats went through the most diverse political, and politically active, experiences in the late 1940s and 1950s, and now at last have found an intellectual or emotional haven.[13] Castro was able brilliantly to profit from the incandescent situation in Cuba in the 1940s and 1950s, to create a single movement from several 'generations' of men who were idealistic, frustrated and willing to commit violence. (Perhaps this had its drawbacks once the Revolution was firmly in power, since the brave señorito does not always make a good manager; thus Castro complained in 1963 that there were 3,000 candidates to be diplomats, only 100 to be agronomists). But it is with some relief that a liberal historian must note that none of those primarily responsible for the destruction of the free press, such as Dagoberto Ponce or Tirso Martínez, for the subversion of the university, such as Rolando Cubela or Omar Fernández, or the conversion of the unions into a department of state, such as Jose María Aguilera or Octavio Louit, has done particularly well under the regime which they did so much to establish.

The Cuban Communist Party was in 1969 about 70,000 in size, proportionally the smallest per head of the population among Communist countries.[14] The process of selection of members was original: after a purge of the ORI (and the expulsion of those old Communists who took part in the elections of 1958), the central committee of the ORI appointed commissions to select new members. These commissions analysed all places of work and arranged for the selection of certain 'exemplary workers' as party members, who further had to meet general assemblies of workers. This method, devised for the old PURS between 1962 and

[11] For a 'generational' interpretation of the Cuban Revolution, see Roberto Retamar's 'Les Intellectuels dans la Révolution', in Partisans (Paris), April–June 1967.

[12] See Dennis Mack Smith, Italy, A Modern History (Ann Arbor 1959), 16; those who in Italy 'from the condottiere to the Carbonari and the fascist squadristi have been the most combustible and explosive elements in Italian society'. Perhaps General Wood, for all his New England priggishness, was right when he said of Cuba in 1900, 'generations of misrule and duplicity have produced a type of man whose loyalty is always at the disposal of the man on top, whoever or whatever he may be' (Hagedorn, vol. 1, 282).

[13] For instance, the chief of the Foreign Press department of the Foreign Ministry during my visit to Cuba in 1969 had been before the Revolution an accountant at the big department store, El Encanto.

[14] In 1951, there were allegedly about 50,000 members of the then Communist Party.

1965, seems also to have been put into effect for the Communist Party since then. Most party members attended one of the schools of revolutionary instruction set up in 1961 to make sure that revolutionaries learned the principles of Marxism–Leninism (though these were closed in 1968). The first congress of the Cuban Communist Party, despite Castro's assertions that it would be in 1966, 1967 and so on, has been indefinitely postponed. There have also been inordinate delays in the selection of party members in the Ministries.

As important as the Party in organizing the country and stimulating the public have been the neighbourhood 'Committees for the Defence of the Revolution' (CDRs). Every street has one and everyone may join, so that it is not surprising that on paper there are over three million members (out of a total Cuban population, including children, of about eight million), organized hierarchically (with a central committee in Havana), not only for vigilance and snooping but for putting educational, medical or other campaigns into national effect, and holding regular seminars on 'revolutionary instruction'. The CDRs report on suspicious counter-revolutionaries, list possessions of those who have asked to leave Cuba, organize everything from fiestas to volunteers to work in the country, and interfere in all private life for the public good– ensuring the 'life of the open book', as José Yglesias put it in his sympathetic study of life in Mayarí in Oriente.[15] The anniversary of their foundation, on 28 September 1960, is one of the main revolutionary feast days, accompanied by dancing, poetry reading, beauty contests and a mass rally in the Plaza de la Revolución, with a speech by Castro. Being organized on a geographical basis the CDRs are the centre of 'revolutionary activity' for many who do not work in factories or farms, and hence have a high percentage of women among their membership. One of their campaigns, the Social Rehabilitation Front, was launched in September 1969 with the broad aim to 'counteract all behaviour detrimental to the social system'. These committees are really the core of the new Cuban society, creating a new culture of propaganda, participation, conformity and labour in a country which in the past was such a curious mixture of private endeavour and private suffering. But the precise measure of participation is quite slight and all major matters of, for instance, town planning or economic policy are decided at the summit, and not at the roots, of the political structure.[16]

The Party, the Committees for the Defence of the Revolution and, of

---

[15] José Yglesias, *In the Fist of the Revolution*, 274–307. The now extinct theoretical journal *Cuba Socialista* described the CDRs as 'system of collective revolutionary vigilance, in which everyone knows who everyone is, what each person in each block does, what relations he had with the tyranny . . . . whom he meets . . .' Qu. Zeitlin, 100.

[16] For a study of the CDRs see Richard R. Fagen, *The Transformation of Political Culture in Cuba*, Stanford University Press (1969), 69 ff.

course, the armed forces control the country. Besides them, the 294 municipal councils of Cuba rather surprisingly survive, but their power is slight and candidates for those bodies have to fulfil Party conditions, while the Party appoints the presidents. In an effort to reinvigorate local life and escape the most stultifying bureaucratism, 'local government delegates' were elected with much fanfare in 1967–8 by public assemblies, but once again 'safe revolutionaries' dominated among those successful, and in many respects their essentially parish pump activities duplicated those of the CDRs.

The armed forces, with (since 1 March 1964) their two and a half to three years of compulsory service and their $259M. expenditure, total 200,000[17] – by far the largest military undertaking in Latin America. The Cubans have 300 tanks and 165 combat aircraft, with 24 surface-to-air missile installations. Most of the regular soldiers, including officers, have been recruited since 1959. Since many of them were previously unemployed members of the lumpenproletariat, bootblacks or washers of cars, they owe everything to the Revolution and, apart from the curious occasion in 1967 when certain unnamed senior officers were supposed to be showing themselves susceptible to 'Chinese propaganda', their loyalty seems to have been absolute. Among the top commanders, many served under Raúl Castro in the Sierra Cristal in 1958, and Raúl Castro has throughout remained Minister of Defence (though he once was absent for several months, taking a course in Russia). The armed forces, it should be added, are the backbone of the regime in more than one way, since they spend a great deal of time in agricultural tasks, for which the government has to pay only the military wage of $7 a month rather than the national wage. In 1969–70, the armed forces were 'mobilized for the sugar harvest as they would have been in case of war', with about 80,000 men from the forces involved, being responsible for an estimated 18% of the harvest.[18]

Justice in revolutionary Cuba is a part of the governmental system, as in other Communist countries. This means that with conventional crimes or misdemeanours the law works adequately, relatively quickly and free from bribery, if often brutally or arbitrarily. In the case of political crimes, there is no rule of law. *Habeas corpus* has not existed since 1959 and people can be, and are, held for interrogation for weeks or indefinitely without trial. There is no way of appealing against, or even drawing attention to, these abuses.

At major political trials, such as those of Matos in 1959, Marcos Armando Rodríguez in 1964 and of Aníbal Escalante and his friends

[17] Separate services total: Army 175,000; Navy, 7,000; Air Force, 12,000. Reserves total 85,000. Military services can be extended beyond three years, even more if needed for agricultural tasks.

[18] Castro, speech of 4 November 1969 (*Granma* 16 November 1969)

in 1968[19], Fidel Castro and other revolutionary leaders have played important parts, Castro acting as prosecutor as well as witness and judge.[20] The speech of the public prosecutor, Dr Santiago Cuba, initiating the judicial term of 1961–2, set the tone by criticizing 'ancient themes about the separation of powers and about the independence and political neutrality' of the judiciary.[21] Political trials have all been marked by irregularity of procedure; this began during the trial of the Batistiano pilots in March 1959 and of the 'Trujillo conspirators' in June of the same year (when the noise was such that the defence could not be heard). In the trial of Rodríguez only the confession of the accused proved guilt; and in the case of Escalante, the accused were merely found guilty of a pro-Russian political attitude which, if inconvenient to Castro, had been virtually government policy a year or so before.[22] Other trials of those accused of counter-revolutionary activities or espionage have been similarly unfair. Some trials have had admittedly to occur in conditions close to war. But neither that fact nor the frequent guilt of the accused excuses the indignity which has characterized these occasions. In the early days, defence lawyers and witnesses were themselves arrested. Latterly, defence lawyers have been appointed by the government and defence witnesses have not given evidence.

At lower levels and in non-political trials, reasonably serious efforts seem to be made to establish the guilt or innocence of accused persons but, when sentences are delivered, these are likely to be heavy or light in respect of the 'revolutionary qualities' of the persons concerned. There is clearly much casualness in minor cases, particularly in the *Tribunales Populares*, the grass roots courts which meet in the evenings to deal with brawls, minor labour disputes and problems of public order. On these, which numbered 366 at the end of 1968,[23] legal training by judges is limited to a ten-day course; they only have to be 'good Communists' and to have reached the sixth grade in education. They are the Cuban Revolution's version of English justices of the peace. These judges – three sitting together – can impose $500 fines, six months' gaol, house arrest, or internment in a 'rehabilitation farm'.[24] More serious offences are dealt with by the *Audiencias*, as in the past. In 1968–9, there was a big crime wave, apparently a consequence of the 'revolutionary offensive' of March 1968: and, in the spring of 1969, a number of exemplary sentences were imposed. Sergio del Valle, the ex-doctor of the Sierra

[19] See below, page 1468.

[20] The speeches of Raúl Castro and Fidel Castro in the Escalante case were in fact at the Central Committee of the Party, but they were nevertheless judicial in effect.

[21] Quoted *Cuba and the Rule of Law*, p. 65.

[22] See *Granma* (weekly edition) 11 February 1968. There seems, however, no reasonable doubt that Marcos Armando Rodríguez was guilty. See below, 1467.

[23] *Verde Olivo*, 10 November 1968.

[24] See an account by Michael Frayn, *Observer*, 10 January 1969.

and second-in-command to Camilo Cienfuegos in 1958, who had become Minister of the Interior, explained that crimes against property had recently risen (after a big drop since 1959), that the use of the death penalty for a wide variety of crimes would be desirable, and that inveterate criminals should be 'eliminated mercilessly'. (Death penalties for robberies had occasionally been invoked in 1962.)[25] He was especially alarmed that over half the murders in Havana should have been carried out by members of religious (particularly Afro–Cuban) sects.[26] On the whole, however, the crime rate has dropped by half since before the Revolution, though it is still four times the English rate.[27] There is practically no drunkenness and very little prostitution.

Numbers of persons killed or imprisoned under the Revolution are impossible to estimate fairly: Castro himself admitted the existence of 20,000 political prisoners in 1965;[28] a pessimist might well suspect the figure to be closer to the 40,000 named by the exiles, if those in forced labour or 'rehabilitation' camps are included. The total number of executions by the Revolution probably reached 2,000 by early 1961, perhaps 5,000 by 1970.[29] But who can be certain of figures in this realm? Further, accounts by ex-prisoners of appalling conditions during interrogation or in Cuban political prisons in La Cabaña, the Príncipe or (until 1965) the Isle of Pines are too numerous to be discounted.[30] It is true that most accounts of inhumanity date back to 1960–61, when invasion was daily expected, but no good regime should be capable, even under any provocation, of such malign behaviour to its opponents. The history of other totalitarian states suggests that such conditions might recur if there are no safeguards against them. As it is, malevolent operators of the Ministry of the Interior live like successful bull-fighters, in silk suits and grand houses, and showing themselves no improvement on

[25] Lieut. Pedro Pupo Pérez, Deputy Minister of Public Order, on Channel 6 of the national television network, 5 May 1969. The death penalty has also been applied for rape of minors, and to people guilty of trying to sabotage the harvest.

[26] Speech during the National Forum on Internal Order, 24–9 March 1969.

[27] In 1960 there were 198,107 crimes; in 1968, 96,693; in 1960 there were 230 murders; in 1967, 88 – or 1·14 per 100,000 inhabitants. This is still about four times the English murder rate and four times the English crime rate.

[28] Interview with Lee Lockwood, Lockwood, 205. Castro said then that 'at least half' of these prisoners were in 'some form of rehabilitation plan'.

[29] In 1963 the Cuban exile newsheet, *Cuban Information Service*, with an accuracy that does not command confidence, estimated that 2,875 people had been executed by order of Revolutionary Tribunals, 4,245 executed without trial, 2,962 killed fighting against Castro forces and 613 missing (*Cuban Information Service*, 1 June 1963). A later estimate, by a Spanish diplomat in Havana, with access to cemetery statistics, was 22,000 Cubans killed or died in gaol; 2,000 drowned attempting to escape; 24,000 Cubans now in concentration camps, 7,000 in gaol, 7,200 on penal farms and 17,231(!) held by the security police. (Jaime Caldevilla, Spanish information officer in Havana, as reported in *The Daily Telegraph*, 28 April 1969.)

[30] For the descriptions of Cuban prisons, admittedly in the early years, see Carlos Rodríguez Quesada, *David Salvador*, 20; John Martino, *I was Castro's prisoner*, passim; *Cuba and the Rule of Law* (International Commission of Jurists); and Haynes Johnson, *The Bay of Pigs*.

Colonel Ventura or Pilar García, while in gaol the long list of political prisoners is headed by Hubert Matos, David Salvador, Alberto Müller, Pedro Luis Boitel, Gustavo Arcos and Carlos Almoina, all 26 July men of the early days, of whose condition nothing for certain is known.[31]

For several years perhaps the most odious creation of the Revolution was the rehabilitation camps known as Military Units for Aid to Production (UMAP). These camps were set up to house large numbers of civil servants, homosexuals, ex-members of the bourgeoisie or potential, rather than overt, opponents of the regime. Many officials suspected of leading a soft life in Havana were dispatched to the camps on suspicion and the Committees for the Defence of the Revolution also sent unenthusiastic revolutionaries there. There they worked in the fields for often many months in prison conditions. These camps were ultimately brought to an end but they seem to survive in a different form.

For all except a few prisoners there is, however, a 'rehabilitation' programme, by which those willing to be 'rehabilitated' move progressively from one stage of re-education to another, until their conditional release, when the ominously named Department for the Prevention of Social Evils allocates them to a suitable centre of work. But dangerous enemies of the state are not offered these choices and many resilient prisoners have refused to take advantage of them.

The Cuban government has never deigned to answer the requests for information about political prisoners put by, for instance, Amnesty International or other international bodies. Few political trials have been observed by foreign journalists or outsiders and while, in the late 1960s, Castro has acknowledged many errors of economic policy, he has yet to admit a single mistake in the treatment of his opponents. The regime, like those of Eastern Europe, thus has on its conscience the bloody character of its establishment, innumerable searches of houses without warrant, thefts of property of suspected persons, lengthy interrogations in secret police buildings and callous infliction of indignities on prisoners and their visitors ('Go away and wear a black dress since you are a widow,' Major William Gálvez briefly told one visitor to the Isle of Pines).[32] In 1968, Castro refused the proposal of the Bolivian President, Barrientos, to exchange Hubert Matos for Régis Debray, and offered in reply '100 counter-revolutionaries' for the bones of Guevara: but the latter were already consumed.

[31] Nor indeed whether these men will not suffer in consequence of any publicity given internationally to their cause.

[32] *Cuba and the Rule of Law*, 225. Gálvez, a prominent army officer in the early 1960s, was Inspector-General of the Army in 1960. His sense of humour was always macabre: as military governor of Matanzas in 1959 his first act was to polish the shoes of the bootblacks in the Parque Marta Abreu, the city's main square.

On the other hand, conditions in ordinary prisons for common criminals have certainly improved since 1959, with serious efforts being made at re-education.

The instruments of control used by the government have, of course, included censorship, but also the positive use of television, radio, films and the press, the first of these in a truly revolutionary way, sombre presage perhaps of tyrannies of the future, not only enabling Castro to destroy his enemies in the first years of the revolutionary regime but also sustaining the new system during its many difficulties and changes of policy. Much is made of the years of revolutionary struggle against Batista and the average Cuban who has remained in the island must have a very curious view of the old days by this time, whatever attitude he may have to the Revolution. Street and city names have not been changed, nor have statues been built to living men; however, this is not the age of stone or marble, but of celluloid, and there are everywhere pictures of Castro, along with Martí, Marx and Lenin, while Guevara's dour but stirring visage has been seen even more often now that he has reached Parnassus. The names of hospitals and sugar mills, schools and factories, usually commemorate some dead hero of the recent past, such as Abel Santamaría (killed at Moncada), Conrado Benítez (the young literacy teacher killed in mysterious circumstances in early 1961), or Camilo Cienfuegos. Older heroes, of the 1930s, such as Guiteras or Martínez Villena, are also commemorated. The innumerable epigrams of Martí, some good, some bad, are written in huge letters on hoardings to prove some point or another for a political system of which he would doubtless have fallen foul. The whole propaganda projects of the Revolution are, indeed, a good example of Sorel's myth in action – 'a complex of remote goals, tense moral moods and expectations of apocalyptic success'[33] – sustained by memories of past skirmishes extravagantly made epic, as well as by regular mass rallies on national holidays such as the anniversaries of the flight of Batista, of the attack on Moncada barracks and of the foundation of the Committees for the Defence of the Revolution. The propaganda of the Cuban regime has consistent aims: to replace the mentality of the lottery with that of nationalism, in order to make sacrifices bearable;[34] and to distort the real history of the recent past. One young architect described a hard day's work in the canefields and then saw how a few hundred yards away a cutting machine had done the same work in a few minutes; 'it was then,' he said, 'that I realized what it meant to be underdeveloped, how close, in spite of Havana's modernity, we were to Africa.'[35]

[33] E. A. Shils' introduction to Georges Sorel, *Reflections on Violence* (Glencoe, The Free Press, 1950), 20–21.
[34] Cf. Goldenberg, 301.
[35] André Schiffren, *The New Republic*, 29 June 1968.

A more inaccurate description of Cuba's predicament could scarcely be imagined.

Newspapers are in consequence tedious. *Granma*, the 'official organ of the central committee of the Communist Party of Cuba', is less a newspaper than an exhortation sheet, reporting Castro's speeches in full, with little news and occasional snippets of inspiring history. Its editor, the mulatto, Jorge Enrique Mendoza, who was once the chief of agrarian reform in Camagüey who clashed with Matos, is best known for his curious assertion in 1967 that the Israeli army in the Six-Day War was commanded by Nazis. There are no other national daily papers except for an evening version of *Granma*, *Juventud Rebelde*. The director of television and broadcasting, Major Jorge Serguera, also curiously has a link with the Matos case since he was then, as a Judge-Advocate of the Rebel Army, the chief prosecutor. He was for a time military governor of Matanzas, a post he lost after unwisely sending for tanks to use against housewives in the bread riot of Cárdenas in 1962. The last columnist who ventured a joke about the Revolution, Segundo Cazalis, was savagely attacked by Castro in March 1964 and his column, *Siquitrilla*, was abruptly brought to an end. Compared with the Cuban press, that of Spain might be considered sparkling. Any cartoon such as that which appeared in 1900 in *Discusión*, during the U.S. military occupation, depicting poor Cuba crucified between two thieves, would doubtless earn the artist more than the twenty-four hours' gaol intemperately handed out by General Wood.

The censorship has been candidly defended by Castro: 'The Revolution is the first to lament that individual guarantees cannot be granted – ... the Revolution explains that to concede those guarantees would serve that powerful enemy who has tried to destroy the Revolution and to drown it in the blood of the people.'[36] During the *Siquitrilla* affair, Castro explained: 'These gentlemen who write "truth never hurts", I don't know whether they conceive of truth as an abstract entity. Truth is a concrete entity in the service of a noble cause.' (So, it might be added, is untruth, from time to time.) Cazalis, the journalist in question, incidentally, had earlier received an order not to attack in his column the government of Spain, with whom Cuba was then undertaking commercial relations.

The history of the arts under the revolution has naturally been unsteady and, in innumerable personal instances, tragic. Thus the first flush of national self-confidence which was a characteristic of 1959 and expressed in particular by the Monday supplement to the newspaper *Revolución*, was succeeded by increasing disillusion during the years

[36] Speech at 1st national congress of *Responsables del Trabajo de Orientación Revolucionaria*, *Revolución*, 11 November 1961.

1961–62, particularly during the months when Aníbal Escalante was busy setting up the ORI. *Lunes de Revolución* was banned, films such as the famous PM (which had no revolutionary content) were attacked, the main means of self-expression came under the control of men who worked safely for the regime: thus Alfredo Guevara, an old Communist (if relatively young), took over the direction of the promising film institute (ICAIC); and Nicolás Guillén, an admirable poet but politically an instrument of the Communist Party, became President of the Writers Union. Even before the missile crisis, independent spirits began either to abandon Cuba, or to keep silent, or to take jobs as cultural attachés in Cuban embassies abroad; while others made their peace with the regime, reached compromises, and either allowed themselves to be censored or censored themselves; others still, moving into positions of cultural power, began to regard as part of their job the passing of judgement on the works of their contemporaries. Some work of note continued to be done and, in terms of quantity of output (novels, plays, films, poems), the Revolution's achievement has been remarkable, but the most distinguished Cuban artists are still those who, like the novelists Alejo Carpentier (now Cuban cultural minister in France)[37] and José Lezama Lima, or the painters, René Portocarrero[38] and Wilfredo Lam (who has lived in Paris since the late 1940s), were well established before the Revolution, or those who, like Severo Sarduy or Guillermo Cabrera Infante (once the director of *Lunes de Revolución*), are now in exile. Against this should be set the fact that the regime has spent a great deal on artistic promotion, and it can fairly claim to have brought poetry, ballet, music, travelling libraries and theatre to the countryside of Cuba. Some of the historical work on Cuba in the last century, particularly that by Manuel Moreno Fraginals and Juan Pérez de la Riva, has been of a high standard.[39] The two main literary and artistic magazines, *Unión* and *Casa de las Américas*, are good. But new popular music seems to have died and Cuba which, during the 'bad old days', was for so long a source of new music and dances, from the conga, rumba, mambo and habanera to the chachachá, has not had any new rhythms to which to dance or to export.

Restrictions on liberty have been quite flexibly interpreted so far as painting is concerned despite, admittedly, efforts by Blas Roca and other old Communists to force down the throats of the Cubans the realist standards of their Mexican friends, such as David Alfaro Siqueiros. Thus Castro explained in 1963 that when 'Russia's satellites in Havana' (pre-

[37] Surprisingly, considering the sceptical tone of such books as *The Kingdom of this World*.

[38] Portocarrero enjoys a favoured position since, though he lives and works in Cuba, he is able to exhibit and sell abroad, and spends what he wants.

[39] Moreno Fraginals is known for his excellent study of the nineteenth-century sugar mill, *El Ingenio*. Pérez de la Riva is editor of the scholarly *Revista de la Biblioteca Nacional*.

sumably Escalante) had asked him to ban an abstract painting, as Khrushchev had done in Russia, he had replied: 'Our enemies are capitalism and imperialism, not abstract painting.'[40] Guevara in 1965, in *Socialism and Man*, described social realist art rather surprisingly as the 'corpse of nineteenth-century bourgeois painting'. But Castro's 'Address to the Intellectuals' in 1961 had included the aphorism: 'everything within the Revolution, nothing against the Revolution', while the declaration of principles at the foundation of the Union of Writers and Artists included the remark 'we regard it as absolutely essential that all writers and artists, regardless of individual aesthetic differences, should take part in the great work of defending and consolidating the Revolution. By using severe self-criticism we shall purge our means of expression to become better adapted to the needs of the struggle.'[41]

'Our principal idea has been full freedom for those who support the Revolution, nothing for those who are opposed,' President Dorticós remarked rather sourly in 1964[42] and, in 1965, Castro was explaining that his view of art had much in common with his view of Truth: 'Art is not an end in itself. Man is the end. Making men happier, better.'[43] In 1966, admittedly, José Lezama Lima published a major novel, *Paradiso*, which not only had no concern whatever for the Revolution but, in its famous Chapter XI, dealt mainly with homosexual practices. But it turned out that the novel had only passed the censor because it was so long and difficult to read, no second impression appeared and soon a much harder note was set by the editor of the young Communist paper, *El Caimán Barbudo*, Jesús Díaz, in an article entitled *Towards a Militant Culture*.[44] In 1967, a big exhibition of modern paintings was held in Havana: no socialist realist paintings admittedly were exhibited but Castro's own contribution was ominous: an anti-aircraft gun, a bull and seven cows.

The test of the regime came, however, as might be expected, in literature. In 1966, the great Chilean poet, Pablo Neruda, was roundly criticized in a letter signed by many of the Cuban regime's most faithful writers for suggesting, after a meeting with President Belaúnde of Peru, that there could be an end to the 'cold war in culture'. At a conference in 1967, Cuban writers unanimously accepted a proposal by Castro that copyright should no longer be respected and that royalties should not be paid, even to foreigners. One writer, Jaime Suretsky, argued that 'non-payment enabled the author to realize himself as a human being' (though writers have earned royalties abroad which they have not been

[40] Interview with Claude Julien, *Le Monde*, 23 March 1963.
[41] *Hoy*, 23 August 1961, quoted Goldenberg, 254.
[42] Dorticós to Mark Schleiffer, *Monthly Review* April 1964, p. 655.
[43] Lockwood, p. 207
[44] *Para una cultura militante*, *Bohemia*, 26 September 1966.

able to touch). Finally, in a famous case in 1968, the young poet
Heberto Padilla, gained the Writers' Union annual poetry prize from
an international jury, but was never permitted to receive it from the
Cuban Writers' Union on the grounds that one of his poems, *Fuera de
Juego*, was insufficiently committed. In fact, his early criticisms of the
stifling atmosphere of the Cuban cultural scene in the Young Communist periodical, *El Caimán Barbudo*, had already caused his denunciation by
Lisandro Otero, the editor of *Cuba* and a prominent conformist novelist.[45] In 1969 Haydée Santamaría, the Moncada veteran who had become literary *apparatchik* as President of the Casa de las Americas, explained to the juries who were to judge the latter's annual prize that no
artist could remain non-political since that itself implied a political
stand,[46] while later in 1969 the Padilla affair was apparently repeated in
the case of Pablo Armando Fernández who also won a prize, delivered
himself of some critical remarks about the Cuban cultural scene on
television, and had the prize withdrawn. (But, in this case, Castro intervened and insisted on the return of the award.)

Perhaps the most disagreeable side of these developments has been
the increased role of the armed forces through their organ, *Verde Olivo*,
in the establishment of cultural standards: It was *Verde Olivo* which
first attacked Padilla and other writers 'whose spinelessness is matched
only by their pornography and counter-revolutionism'.[47]

The reason for these events is as much the existence of a by now well
entrenched literary bureaucracy (as in all Communist countries) as
national political developments. Thus the Union of Writers and
Artists (UNEAC) directs the main Cuban publishing house. All writers
have to belong to it. The bureaucrats attached to this institution, as to
the centre for the dissemination of Cuban culture, the Casa de las
Américas, or the 'committee of revolutionary orientation' (or censor-

[45] Nevertheless, Padilla afterwards lived peaceably. Associated with Padilla was Antón
Arrufat. See *Times Literary Supplement*, 11 July, 22 August and 14 November 1968, *Le Monde*,
5 November 1968, and David Gallagher, *New York Review of Books*, 23 May 1968. Even more
disagreeable, Leopoldo Avila, in *Verde Olivo* (8 November, 1968), falsely accused Padilla of
having swindled the Cuban foreign trade agency and having been dismissed. The cause for
Padilla's explosion in *El Caimán Barbudo* was that journal's inquiry into the attitudes of
prominent Cuban writers to Otero's novel *Pasión de Urbino*. Since Otero is a powerful apparatchik, all save Padilla were adulatory. Padilla raised the question of why so much fuss was
made about Otero's novel when the brilliant apolitical interpretation of Havana in the last
years of Batista, *Tres Tristes Tigres*, by the exiled Guillermo Cabrera Infante, had not been
considered. After these exchanges, the editors of *El Caimán Barbudo* were speedily changed,
even though one of them, Jesús Díaz, was the author of *Towards a Militant Culture*.
[46] *Bohemia*, 24 January 1969. Not surprisingly, therefore, the novel prize went to *La Canción
de la Crisalida* by Renato Prado Oropesa about Guevara in Bolivia and the essay prize to the
Peruvian guerrillero, Héctor Béjar. This was a change from Haydée Santamaría's speech in
1968 on the same occasion, when she had said that there was no more reason for a book jacket
to have political content than the trousers of the critics.
[47] Quoted 'Commentary', *Times Literary Supplement*, 14 November 1968.

ship board), founded by César Escalante, have undoubtedly used their power to further their own not always distinguished careers, at the cost of less conventional spirits. For the present, admittedly, these things have perhaps scarcely got beyond the condition of scandal and have not yet reached outrage. So far as numbers are concerned, book production has much increased, fifteen million being produced in 1969 – mostly textbooks, and about 70 % distributed free.

Since 1962, there have been only a few political crises. Thus the Minister of Labour, Augusto Martínez Sánchez, the lawyer from Holguín who presided over the destruction of the free unions in 1959–60, tried unsuccessfully to kill himself in 1964 when he was dismissed, partly for mismanagement, partly apparently since he sought to flirt with all political groups. Eighteen months later, early in 1966, Rolando Cubela, who, as President of FEU, had done similar hatchet work in destroying the university in 1960, was sentenced to twenty-five years' imprisonment for taking part in an attempted assassination of Castro, in connivance with the CIA.[48] He joined in gaol, therefore, Pedro Luis Boitel, the democratic student leader whom he helped to ruin. At the same time, Efigenio Ameijeiras, Castro's first chief of police in 1959, and at the time a Vice-Minister of the Armed Forces, was imprisoned and dismissed from the central committee of the Cuban Communist Party for 'moral offences' and there was a national purge of corrupted elements. Armando Acosta, for a long time the Communist boss of Oriente, was also dismissed with some fanfare in 1967 after failing with the slogan 'more sugar from less cane' (or, according to one informant, for holding a specially lavish party to celebrate his daughter's fifteenth birthday). But the most serious crises were those which led to the final discrediting and discomfiture of the two most prominent old Communists after Blas Roca and Carlos Rafael Rodríguez: namely, Joaquín Ordoqui and Aníbal Escalante.

Ordoqui – a Communist since 1927 – and his *compañera*, Edith García Buchaca, lost their jobs (as respectively Vice-Minister of the Armed Forces and President of the Council of Culture) when it became known that, in exile in Mexico in 1957–8 and afterwards in Havana, they had protected the young Communist Marcos Armando Rodríguez, who confessed to having betrayed the four students killed by Ventura and Batista's police in Humboldt Street in 1957.[49] Rodríguez was finally shot after his two trials had shaken the unity of the revolutionary

---

[48] Cubela, who had not done very well for himself during the Revolution, was apparently approached by Manuel Artime, the exile leader, on behalf of the CIA, when he was an attaché at the Cuban embassy in Madrid. The plot was unearthed by a skilful Cuban spy in exile circles in Miami. Cubela escaped death only after a 'personal appeal for clemency' by Castro.

[49] See above, p. 931.

government,[50] and Ordoqui and Edith García Buchaca were kept under house arrest indefinitely.

The second instalment of the Escalante affair shook the government even more than the case of Marcos Armando Rodríguez. Aníbal Escalante, the old communist leader who had been main organizer of the ORI and discredited publicly in 1962, returned to Cuba from Prague in 1964. He was given an honorary post as administrator of the farm *Dos Hermanos*. Far from learning from his past errors, however, he apparently re-embarked on an attempt to recover his lost position by playing on the discontents of 'old militants' of the old Communist Party, who, like himself, had failed to establish themselves in the new Castroist party. Among these were two members of the Communist Central Committee constituted in 1965, José Matar, the first chief of the important Committees for the Defence of the Revolution and afterwards Cuban ambassador in Budapest, and Ramón Calcines, the sugar workers' leader from Las Villas, who, after being the Communist Youth leader in 1960, was practically Minister of Foreign Affairs from January 1961 to March 1962 while he was part of the Foreign Relations Commission of the ORI; later, he had run the fruit export section in the Institute of Agrarian Reform. A series of luncheons and dinners were held at *Dos Hermanos* and other places. Heretical speeches were also said to have been made at funerals. Escalante and this 'microfaction' (as he and his friends were described by their enemies) seem to have disapproved of armed struggle in Latin America, and to have considered the guerrilla war in Venezuela an 'adventure'. They allegedly said 'No one understands Fidel: he is mad', and argued that Guevara was a Trotskyist (and that his departure was to be welcomed). The microfaction was accused later of having criticized voluntary labour in agriculture, desired to re-introduce material incentives, suggested that the revolutionary leadership was petty bourgeois and represented a 'leftist adventurist deviation', and that a change of leadership would improve relations with Russia.[51] Escalante was charged with establishing a group of personal followers in several sections of the Cuban communist party and with gathering documents on the economy and passing them to Russian officials; particularly, as befitted one who had spent a lifetime in

---

[50] See *Liborio* (Chile) No. 1, and Hugh Thomas, 'Murder in Havana', *New Statesman*, 29 May 1964. For a semi-fictional treatment of this extraordinary case, see *Utiles despues de muertos*, by Carlos Manuel Pellecer (Barcelona 1969), an ex-Communist from Guatemala who lived for some time in Cuba. The main point never cleared up was whether in fact Rodríguez, as he claimed, had confessed his betrayal to Edith García Buchaca; and how it was that Rodríguez could have been warned, when in Prague in 1961, of his impending arrest, by a Brazilian diplomat.

[51] The microfaction also took a strong line on the question of the elimination of the bus conductor, since they believed this 'would lead to more conflicts in the buses'. (Raúl Castro's speech, *Granma*, 11 February 1968.)

a communist party, to Russian security officials.[52] Needless to say, these activities could not be concealed, the Cuban public began to hear in speeches about the 'microfaction' (depicted in cartoons as microbes) in mid-1967, and eventually Escalante and thirty-six followers were tried. Many curious activities were unearthed: for example, Félix Fleitas, chief of security of the ORI in 1961-2, had recalled to his discredit the fact that he had once run a *bordello* for Soviet technicians; Escalante had approached Russian, East German and Czech officials whom he thought had access to Russian leaders in order to create an opinion in the Soviet Union in favour of his position – among them, Dr Frantisek Kriegel, a Czech adviser to the Ministry of Health,[53] and Emilio de Quesada, an old Communist who openly admitted, in his trial, that 'we came to wish for a certain degree of political pressure to secure changes'.[54]

The consequence was that Escalante and his friends were imprisoned for varying periods, and that Calcines and Matar lost their places on the Central Committee.

Finally, among the major political crises of the regime, Guevara resigned in 1965 from his post as Minister of Industries after what seems to have been a quarrel with Castro,[55] fought in the Congo with the Kinshasa rebels, and died, aged thirty-nine, two years later in Bolivia, betrayed, like the Italian nationalist, Pisacane, in the nineteenth century, by the peasants whom he had hoped to free: killed with him, as has been seen, were several members of the Central Committee of the Cuban Communist Party.[56] Guevara was shot by the Bolivian army after his capture.

Guevara was a brave, sincere and determined man who was also

[52] Raúl Castro explained in his speech to the Central Committee of the Communist Party that 'a very small number of advisers, journalists and secretaries of foreign embassies participated in the activities of the microfaction'.

[53] Kriegel had fought in the Spanish War and in 1968, as a member of the Praesidium of the Czechoslovak Communist Party, became one of the most prominent liberalizers in the Dubček regime. He was arrested with Dubček on 21 August 1968 and has since been discredited.

[54] *Granma* (weekly edition) 11 February 1968 contains speeches.

[55] This is clearly the implication of Ricardo Rojo's life (*Che Guevara*, French edition, 168). Guevara returned from an extended world tour on 14 March 1965, and on 16 March wrote to his mother in Buenos Aires that he was going to spend a month cutting cane and then five years directing a nationalized industry. In fact, for a variety of reasons Guevara left Cuba at the end of July 1965 for the Congo. Castro ordered him to leave the Congo because of the worsening of Cuban–Chinese relations and, in March 1966, Guevara was again in Cuba. He left for Bolivia in September 1966.

[56] See above, p. 1453. In addition to these (Juan Vitalio Acuña, Antonio Sánchez Díaz and Eliseo Reyes) ten other Cubans were killed in Bolivia (Major Ricardo Gustavo Machín, Orlando Pantoja, Israel Reyes, Jesús Suárez Gayol, Manuel Hernández, Octavio de la Concepción, José María Martínez, René Martínez, Fernández Montes de Oca and Carlos Coello); three Cubans escaped from Bolivia via Chile (Daniel Alarcón, Harry Villegas and Leonardo Tamayo). Six of these men had been with Guevara on the road to Santa Clara in 1958, and all but two had been members of the 26 July Movement.

obstinate, narrow and dogmatic. At the end of his life, he seems to have become convinced of the virtues of violence almost for its own sake: 'How close could we look into a bright future should two, three or many Vietnams flourish throughout the world with their share of deaths and their intense tragedies . . . [with] imperialism impelled to disperse its forces under the . . . increasing hatred of all peoples of the world.'[57] Hatred, for Guevara, was indeed a praiseworthy emotion which could transform man into 'an effective, violent, selective and cold killing machine'.[58] Guevara became in his last years a man for whom the sweetest music was openly the 'staccato singing of the machine guns and new battle cries of war and victory'.[59] In an article written during the missile crisis but published posthumously, he even remarked 'we must proceed along the path of liberation, even if that costs millions of atomic victims'.[60]

In Cuba, Guevara too had shown other dogmatism: he was worsted in the controversy with Marcelo Fernández, his successor as President of the National Bank as to the extent to which state corporations should or should not be autonomous. Guevara took the narrowest centralist line. His airy predictions in 1960–61 that Cuba would be able swiftly to industrialize came to naught. The many half completed or empty factories, 'standing like sad memories of the conflict between pretension and reality', as the Yugoslav journal *Borba* put it in 1965, were his memorial.[61] He was not a merciful spirit. A Cuban lawyer defending a woman accused of having had relations with the previous government recalled that Guevara had in 1959 said: 'I do not know how you dare take an interest in this person . . . I will have her shot . . . if any person has a good word for the previous government that is enough for me to have him shot.'[62] He seems to have assumed in the most *simpliste* way also that the high wages gained by the European working classes were inevitably paid for by the 'millions of exploited peasants and workers of Latin America, Africa and Asia'.[63] He was dogmatic: in 1961 he was

[57] Guevara's message to the journal, *Tricontinental*, June 1967, published *Granma*, 17 April 1967.

[58] *Ibid.*

[59] *Ibid.*

[60] *Verde Olivo*, 6 October 1968. It is surely impossible that Guevara's elevated thoughts on the dignity of war (reminiscent of Theodore Roosevelt, who also suffered from asthma) would have been ventured by anyone other than a native of a continent which, for all its palace coups and gangsterism, has been less exposed to the consequences of conflict and violence than any other during the last century. Blas Roca incidentally is also 'not afraid of nuclear weapons' (see Anthony Sylvester, Cuba's Lesson for Latin America, *Daily Telegraph*, 11 June 1965).

[61] See Guevara's speech at the first National Production Conference, 1961, pp. 110–12. For a veiled attack on Guevara's economics, see also the speech of President Dorticós, in *Cuba Socialista*, March 1966, p. 26–42.

[62] *Cuba and the Rule of Law* (International commission of Jurists, Geneva, 1962), 158.

[63] Remarks to Marc Schleifer, *Monthly Review* (April 1964), 652.

credited with the old-fashioned view that 'we must arrive at 100 % state ownership', since even small properties were unproductive and disturbing to the entire country.[64] Yet he was candid and, on the whole, he deceived neither himself nor others. His quarrel with the Soviet Union and the, as he thought, increasingly *embourgeoisé* Communist parties of East Europe, was expressed without much care for his own future. He believed that both the law of value, which still characterizes even inter-socialist trade, and material incentives, used then in Cuba as in East Europe, were immoral. His influence over Castro, always strong, for good or evil, has grown after his death, for Castro has since taken up many of his views. As in the case of Martí, or Lawrence of Arabia, failure has brightened, not dimmed, the legend.[65]

Since 1962, opposition in Cuba has been sporadic. The last bid by the 'liberals' was a promise by Manuel Ray to land in Cuba with an army of liberation by 20 May 1964. But though he set off from Puerto Rico, he landed in the Bahamas, not Oriente, and his star has since sunk. He and most other prominent anti-Castro Cuban politicians have been integrated into North American life. Manuel Artime apparently organized a new exile army in Costa Rica in 1963–4, with CIA money, but without an invasion.[66] Several assassination attempts, on the other hand, are said to have been inspired in North America, notably that of Rolando Cubela in March 1966, perhaps the last fling of the *señorito* in Cuban politics.[67] Minor guerrilla skirmishing has gone on most of the time in Oriente and other mountainous districts in an unsung war; rumours abound but probably at least 4,000 *guerrilleros* have been killed since 1962.[68] A special 'organization for the struggle against "banditry"'

[64] *Revolución*, 29 November 1961.

[65] Lives of Guevara have begun to appear. For a sympathetic and favourable study by a friend, see *Che Guevara, Vie et Mort d'un ami* by Ricardo Rojo (Paris 1969); and, for a hostile study, see Horacio Rodríguez, *Che Guevara, Mythe ou Réalité* (Paris 1969).

[66] See Al Burt, 'The Mirage of Havana', *Nation*, 25 January 1965. According to Burt, the Costa Rican government brought this adventure to an end on the ground that it was being used as a base for smuggling. Of past Cuban politicians, Batista lives on in Spain in comfort, protected by his millions; Grau San Martín died in Havana in 1969; Prío, Masferrer, Ventura, Varona, Sánchez Arango, Raúl Chibás, Felipe Pazos and Javier Pazos – Batistianos, Ortodoxos, Auténticos, ex-members of the 26 July Movement – live on in the U.S. or elsewhere. Julio Lobo is in Madrid. Other exiles are to be found all over South America and in Paris – a diaspora as large and perhaps in the long run as fruitful as that of the Spanish Republicans after 1939.

[67] The end of those dapperly dressed youths, in the words of Carleton Beals, with 'long fine hands, white skins, sleek plastered black hair, . . . capable of facing the firing squad or directing a Santa Clara sugar plantation' (Carleton Beals, *The Crime of Cuba*, 70) – capable of only these two things perhaps.

[68] Raúl Castro (22 July 1967) spoke of 3,591 'bandits' and 500 Cuban soldiers killed since. He said between $500 million and $800 million had been used solely to destroy 'armed bandits'. In 1965 Fidel Castro had spoken of 2,005 bandits and 295 Cuban soldiers killed (Speech of 26 July 1965).

(LCB) has been founded under an old associate of Raúl Castro's in the Sierra Cristal, Major Menéndez Tomassevich. In 1968 there was a big wave of sabotage, including arson in ships, factories and farms, with several shot or imprisoned in consequence. Of this secret war little has been written – perhaps never will be. One story, however, was published in Cuba of how a Haitian *santero* named Baldomero, aged seventy-five, took to the hills with a group of voodoo followers. The disciples were captured, but Baldomero was never found. Rumours in the Sierra Maestra were that he had made himself invisible, or had changed himself into a serpent, or a stone, or a tree; once, indeed, a peasant, surprised by a snake, shouted, in the hearing of others, 'Quick, quick, kill him, it might be Baldomero'. The legend of Baldomero lives on.[69]

The regime's relations with the Church quietened after the crises of 1960–61. The churches stayed open, and the Papal Delegate, Mgr. Cesare Zacchi (later also Bishop of Havana), has also remained, along with the Cuban diplomatic mission to the Vatican. At one time the police made lists of those who went to church, but this practice has been stopped. On the other hand, religion plays no part in schools and no new rural settlement has a church. Priests and pastors have to do military service. No practising Catholic can become a Communist. Holy Week was in 1965 rechristened 'Playa Girón Week' and devoted to mass manual voluntary labour (it has since become extended to 'Playa Girón Month'). In 1966, streets near churches were turned into play-grounds at the times of services, the noise of children drowning the Mass. Licences to repair churches have, it seems, sometimes been refused and, in consequence, the buildings can be closed as dangerous. In early 1969, there were attacks on religion as such in the magazine of the armed services, *Verde Olivo*. This organ criticized the 'spirit of resignation' implicit in religion, its 'blind faith' in the supernatural and its search for truth through prayer; for 'religion divided the popular forces' and helps to delay the appearance of the New Man, who, of course, should be as free from superstition as from ambition.[70] Jehovah's Witnesses were accused by Castro in 1963 of being a counter-revolutionary sect and, in 1969, their pacifism, their refusal to swear by the national flag, to work on Sundays and 'to give adequate attention to weapons' were all condemned. Two-thirds of the ministers at the Western Baptist convention were also arrested in April 1965, tried, and found guilty of espionage. The Protestant churches have, however, suffered consider-

[69] Orlando Reyes, *Mitos y Leyendas de las Villas*, Colección folklórico Cubano, ediciones de la Universidad Central de las Villas, 1965.
[70] *Verde Olivo*, 2 February 1969.

ably since the emigration of so many North American pastors and seem to have retreated into at best political neutrality.[71]

More recently, the Cuban hierarchy appealed in a pastoral letter in the spring of 1969 for an end to the U.S. economic boycott, and the Cuban government applauds the socially conscious Catholics and priests of South America – providing that they are 'militant' like the Camilo Torres Movement, which believes that 'the armed struggle is the duty of the Christian conscience in Latin America' and that the 'guerrilla's love of violence is basically a sublime love of truth'.[72] In 1968 Castro noted the presence of a group of revolutionary priests at the Cultural Congress of Havana and compared the orthodox Communists of Latin America to them: 'When we see sectors of the clergy becoming revolutionary, how shall we resign ourselves to seeing sectors of Marxism becoming ecclesiastical?'[73]

[71] See C. Alton Robertson, *The Political Role of the Protestants in Cuba*, in Occasional Bulletin of the Missionary research library, New York, Vol. xviii, Nos. 2 and 3 (February and March 1967).

[72] *Punto Final*, Santiago de Chile, 25 February 1969. Camilo Torres, a radical Colombian priest, was killed by the Colombian army in 1966.

[73] Castro's closing speech to the Congress, 1968.

New Friends and Old

The extent to which the Cuban Revolutionary Government has allowed its internal policies to be dictated since 1962 by the desires of its main commercial and military ally, Russia, is naturally still obscure. But it is obvious, on the one hand, that, despite the close relations between the two countries, Castro, because of his own temperament and because of Cuba's geographical position, has often been at least verbally an unsteady ally; on the other hand, that in a number of matters of real importance to Russia, he has had to follow Russian ideas most closely. Thus Castro, unlike, for instance, the Communist Party of Italy, supported the Russian invasion of Czechoslovakia in 1968; and Russian influence probably secured that Cuba turned her main economic attention back from the heady ideas of swift industrialization to continued emphasis on the production of sugar. By the Russo–Cuban sugar agreement of January 1964 Cuba indeed agreed to sell to Russia, at the fixed price of 6 cents a pound (then well above the world market price), increasing proportions of her sugar crop between then and 1970. Russia, therefore, is the father of Cuba's continuing monoculture – though, despite Khrushchev's talk about an 'international division of labour' within the socialist world, both Russian and Czechoslovak sugar beet production has continued to increase and Russia has re-sold much Cuban sugar on the world market.

Leaving aside military assistance, which appears to be free, Russia and the East European communist countries must be owed by Cuba many hundreds of million dollars on both current and capital account. Thus between 1965 and 1969, Soviet civilian aid seems to have amounted to $M300 a year, and maybe more than that in 1969–70.[1] Of Cuban

---

[1] In 1968 the rough equivalent of $M327 was an estimate of the figure. For 1965, see P. J. Wiles *Communist International Economics*, Basil Blackwell, Oxford, 1969, p. 403. Wiles estimated this as follows:

sugar subsidy	95 M roubles
exports to Cuba f.o.b.	338
imports from Cuba f.o.b.	277
balance	61
freight services rendered to Cuba	34
salaries and technical advisers less Cuba contribution	3
	808 M roubles

i.e. approximately $M308

Revolutionary Diplomacy:
31a Castro in Russia, 1964: (*L to R*) Mikoyan, Brezhnev, Podgorny, Castro, Malinovsky, Khrushchev, Grechko, Alexiev (Soviet Ambassador to Cuba)
  b Castro with the Deputy Prime Minister of North Vietnam, Le Thanh Nghi, 1967

imports from Russia, oil is doubtless the largest item, apart from machinery, with over 150 tankers arriving from Russia a year.[2] All Cuba's wheat comes from Russia and Cuba has imported from her or from her satellites some 40,000 tractors and 2,000 combine harvesters, not to speak of innumerable spare parts for old North American machines. Cuban exports to Russia were apparently valued at 281 million roubles in 1961, and 372 million in 1968; Cuban imports have also risen consistently.[3] Russia has re-equipped sugar mills, built electricity plants, hospitals, factories, irrigation plants and roads. Numerous Russian technicians are at work in Cuba, and many Cuban students have by now had extensive technical education in Russia. As Castro put it in 1969, Russia's aid has been 'inestimable and decisive'. The U.S. Government guesses that the Cuban capital debt to Russia approaches $1·5 billion.[4] On the other hand, figures mean little in this field: Castro himself in 1967 spoke of his foreign commerce as being 'practically on a barter basis, with so-called exchange money, almost worthless except in the country in which the agreement is held'.[5] Russia has probably done well out of her sugar dealings with Cuba, given the apparently high cost of producing sugar from beet in Russia itself.[6] It is also obvious that the disbursement of a million or so dollars a day to Cuba is not a very large expenditure measured alongside Russia's other spending abroad.

Thus Russia plays almost as great a part in Cuban politics as the U.S. did in the past: she is Cuba's main market for her main product; she supplies Cuba with the weapons (and doubtless the intelligence and espionage technology) without which the regime might not have been able to survive; she takes most of even Cuba's secondary products such as fruit and vegetables; she is her only supplier of both wheat and oil. A Russian embassy official, Rudolf Shliapnikov, apparently told Aníbal Escalante in 1967, referring to Russia's hold over the Cuban economy, 'We have only to say that repairs are being held up at Baku for three weeks and that's that'.[7] Castro has publicly admitted that he knows only too well 'the bitterness of having to depend to a considerable degree on

[2] 167 tankers docked in Havana in 1967, or one every 54 hours (Castro's speech of 2 January 1968).

[3] Sakun P., *URSS*, July 1968. According to P. Sakun, Russian commercial attaché in Cuba from 1960 till 1968, the figures were (in million roubles):

	1959	1960	1961	1962	1963	1964	1965	1966	1967	1968
Total	6·7	160	539	541	508	591	646	689	842	914
Russian exports to Cuba	—	67	258	330	360	331	338	432	507	542
Russian imports from Cuba	6·7	93	281	211	148	260	308	257	335	372

[4] U.S. department of commerce, *Survey of Agriculture in Cuba*, 1969, 15. A good diplomatic source in Havana early in 1969 put this figure much higher.

[5] Castro speech, 10 August 1967 (at the end of the OLAS conference).

[6] See discussion in Gutelmann, 215, where it is suggested that Russian costs must be three times as great as those in Cuba.

[7] Speech of Raúl Castro to the Central Committee, reported *Granma*, February 1968.

things which come from outside and how that can become a weapon and at least create the temptation to use it' :[8] at least, the U.S. in the past paid in convertible currency, not in goods of dubious appeal or efficacy. Doubtless, therefore, the desire to escape from Russian economic control was one reason for the imposition of petrol rationing (though only in January 1968), as for the conclusion of a $M30 credit agreement with Rumania for oil drilling equipment in March 1968. Every effort has recently been made to save fuel, even to produce sugar 'without a single drop of oil'. But for the moment, Cuba under socialism could no more do without Russia as a market and as a supplier of essential fuel than she could do without the U.S. under capitalism. It is thus remarkable that Cuba has ventured so often so far away from Russia's policies as she has. Even Castro's support for Russia over Czechoslovakia may not have been so reluctant as might be supposed since, as his speech on the occasion made clear, however much he might deplore the use of force by one big country against another small one, he also much disliked the tolerant character of socialism under Dubček.

The main area where Russia and Cuba have fallen out, however, has been over the question of whether or not the policy of the armed struggle is the only way to achieve revolution in Latin America.

Castro's attitudes to this matter have varied often in the eight years following the Second Declaration of Havana which pledged Cuban support for the 'liberation' of the continent. These changes have occurred partly because of some unforeseeable event in the world outside, such as the retirement of Khrushchev, the Vietnam war and its repercussions within the U.S., partly because of Guevara's expedition to Bolivia, the Russo–Chinese dispute, and difficulties within the Communist parties of South America themselves (in particular the Communist Party of Venezuela). Thus, despite the undoubted annoyance felt by Castro with Russia after the missile crisis in 1962, Cuban–Russian relations remained very good for two years – chiefly because of Castro's close friendship with Khrushchev (to whom perhaps he even felt, after his two visits to Russia in 1963 and 1964, a species of loyalty), partly perhaps because of a reluctance to embark upon any further entanglements while the Cuban Communist Party itself was still far from united. Until late 1965, at least, Castro seemed ready to accept the view, strongly held by Russia and by the orthodox leadership of the Latin American Communist parties, that the question as to whether the road to socialism should be peaceable or by means of an 'armed struggle' (*lucha armada*) was one to be settled by the 'struggling peoples themselves'.[9] Castro also avoided, in his speeches

---

[8] Castro speech, 13 March 1968.

[9] As stated in the communiqué at the end of Castro's first visit to Moscow in May 1964.

or simply in newspaper reports, any mention, of any sort, of the difficulties between Russia and China, with almost as many articles continuing to appear in the Cuban press about the latter as the former. This cautious attitude was internationally approved in November 1964 at a secret conference of Latin American Communist parties at Havana.[10]

But this caution was never very popular in Cuba, and Guevara (before he disappeared in March 1965) and Raúl Castro went some way to differentiate themselves on the matter from Fidel Castro in some of their statements. Castro began to find himself described by the Chinese as a revisionist, while radical revolutionaries in the rest of Latin America, though still looking to Cuba as the capital of Revolution and knowing that, for the simple reason of having survived, the underprivileged of South America regarded Castro as a saviour, began to doubt the purity of Castro's ideology. 1965 nevertheless was a good time for Russo–Cuban relations. During that summer, after Guevara had left, Castro criticized harshly the ideal of moral incentives which he afterwards adopted, while the conversion of the old PURS (previously ORI) into the Cuban Communist Party, with its militarily-orientated Central Committee, was completed.

Castro's cautious attitude came to an end at the first Tricontinental Conference, held in Havana, in January 1966, when the Afro–Asian Solidarity Organization, previously held together by the Egyptians and the Russians, was turned into AALAPSO (Afro-Asian and Latin American Peoples' Solidarity Organization) and, much to the Russians' surprise, was captured by Castro, who then gave a wild promise that any revolutionary movement anywhere in the world could count on Cuba's unconditional help. AALAPSO established its headquarters thereafter in Havana, and the familiar figure of Osmani Cienfuegos, previously not much known for his international activities or interests, became the new secretary-general. The presence of a remarkable number of radical guerrilla leaders from the rest of Latin America gave drama to the conference, and naturally these men quite overshadowed the representatives of the orthodox Communist parties whom the Russians had hoped would dominate the scene. Admittedly, Castro did treat the conference to a spectacular attack on China which had recently gone back on the terms of its rice agreement with Cuba – an attack which he followed up in March by describing Mao Tse Tung as 'senile, barbarous and no longer competent to stay in office'. The Chinese, he said, had confused Communism with Fascism, and Mao's regime was

[10] See D. Bruce Jackson, *Castro, the Kremlin and Communism in Latin America,* Johns Hopkins University, Baltimore, 1969, 28–31. The conference was a complete success for the Russians. The Chinese, who had expected much of the occasion, were later very angry – perhaps showing Castro the extent of Chinese–Russian rivalry for the first time.

worse than an absolute monarchy.[11] But this did not compensate the Russians for their diplomatic defeat in seeing the Tricontinental Conference endorse the idea of the armed struggle with no holds barred. This change of front by Castro was caused partly by a desire to resume leadership of the world's militant revolutionaries, partly because of increased scepticism about the 'peaceful way' after the failure of the Socialist–Communist alliance in the elections of 1964 in Chile, partly as a result of the deepening of the war in Vietnam, where Cuba had close relations with the North Vietnamese, as befitted, it seemed, two small and isolated countries fighting the U.S.[12]

Cuba's relations with the rest of the Communist world have since that time been dogged by controversy. Castro and the orthodox Communists have violently attacked each other, Castro criticizing in particular the Venezuelan Communists, whom he accused of having betrayed the Venezuelan freedom fighters led by Douglas Bravo. AALAPSO divided, and no new conference has been held, though the Latin American delegates at that conference formed themselves into a new organization – OLAS (Latin American Solidarity Organization) – which held its conference at Havana in August 1967, to 'coordinate and give impetus to the struggle against U.S. imperialism'. Influenced by the reappearance, in Bolivia, of Guevara (who was elected President of the conference in his absence), the meeting unanimously echoed his appeal for the creation of 'many Vietnams' in the Western Hemisphere. Castro used the occasion to launch a specially violent attack on the 'pseudo-revolutionaries' of the bourgeois Communist parties, not simply the Venezuelans: the Yugoslavs, for instance, were by this time almost inured to being referred to by Cubans as 'opportunists and traitors'.

Guevara was killed in October 1967, but despite the consequent failure of his plans, the guerrilla movement in Latin America received much publicity in the world press. Castro felt strong enough therefore to send only a very minor representative to the celebrations in Moscow for the fiftieth anniversary of the Russian Revolution, Dr Machado Ventura, the Minister of Health (he it was therefore who heard Brezhnev give his own attack on 'pseudo-revolutionary theories divorced from life' – by which he meant different people from Castro). The controversy continued in innumerable Communist Party journals, in literary weeklies and in *Pravda*. Guevara began to be attacked by orthodox Communists, on the one hand, as having been a 'Bakuninist' and, on the other, as having refused to accept the leadership of the Bolivian Communist Party. The publication of Guevara's Bolivian diaries, though

[11] Castro speech of 13 March 1966.

[12] Cuba is also the only country to have diplomatic relations with the NLF in Vietnam, the 'Ambassador' being Raúl Valdés Vivó, who before the Revolution was secretary-general of the Communist Youth movement.

exciting interest in his fate, did not enhance his reputation, and the Russian edition of that work contained a long critique of his military tactics. Castro, in an introduction to the Cuban edition, however, accused the Bolivian Communist leadership of having betrayed Guevara, just as he had accused the Venezuelan Communists of having betrayed Douglas Bravo.

Large numbers of South Americans and Africans have meantime received guerrilla training in Cuba. Cuba is reputed to have helped the Republic of Congo (Brazzaville) put down a revolt in 1966, to have advised El Fatah in Jordan and, in 1964, to have helped to overthrow the Sultan of Zanzibar. Cuba continues to broadcast to Latin America many hours of propaganda and encouragement to subversion in Quechua, Aymará, Guaraní and other tongues, as well as in Spanish. The 'armed struggle' itself, however, remains an elusive part of South American life, exaggerated by both the Cubans and also by the South American governments, the latter in order to be in a good position to receive new arms supplies from the U.S. In the Cuban press, the South American continent continues to seem 'one vast battle front', seething with violence, the revolutionaries 'thrashing government troops' and about to enter in triumph the Miraflores Palace in Caracas or, like Zapata's men in Mexico, Sanborn's restaurant.[13]

In 1969 Castro's militancy somewhat declined. Concentrating on the herculean efforts needed to harvest the famous ten million tons of sugar, Castro made little reference to the 'armed struggle' in his speeches.[14] In early 1970 Bravo, the Venezuelan guerrilla leader, publicly broke with Castro, accusing him of being a tool of the Soviet Union.[15] But the old quarrels smoulder and neither revolution nor the principles of the Alliance for Progress have made much headway.

The discussion on the disputed desirability of the armed struggle has distorted Cuban history. The combat urged by Guevara in his last writings (and supported by Régis Debray) somewhat facilely envisaged a battle of *ultras*, with no compromise with the bourgeoisie and none with the liberal establishment in the U.S. Yet Castro's own struggle in the hills was different; he fought as a political leader driven to take up

[13] This criticism was made of the Cuban Press in 1965 by the Guatemalan Communist Manuel Galich (See *Revolución*, 1 April 1965).
[14] A speech of Carlos Rafael Rodríguez to the Central Committee of the Cuban Communist Party in 1968 made clear that the Sino–Soviet controversy was not to be a subject of argument; Manuel Bravo Chapman was indeed attacked for trying to turn the INRA supply department into a centre of political debate on this matter (*Granma*, 11 February 1968). In 1969 a Cuban defector, Orlando Castro Hidalgo, who had worked in intelligence, claimed that in May 1968 Castro made a secret agreement with Russia committing Cuba to a pro-Soviet line in Latin America in return for continued economic aid (*Christian Science Monitor*, 16 July 1969). This apparently did not exclude continued training in Cuba for guerrillas for the rest of the underdeveloped world, for example the Eritrean liberation army.
[15] *Le Monde*, 15 January 1970.

arms but always willing to make concessions and gestures to all. As in previous Cuban civil wars, liberal North Americans helped the Cuban rebels to the best of their considerable ability. By seeking to fight under purer colours, even without compromise with the local Communist parties, the South American rebels of the late 1960s may possibly preserve the integrity of their ideals (though even that is not certain, since desperate circumstances need cynicism as well as heroism); but they will not be fighting as did Castro, who was more economical in lives than Guevara presumably would have been had he achieved his 'two, three or more Vietnams'. Castro is evidently aware of these paradoxes: in 1961 he explained 'Naturally, if we had stood on the top of Pico Turquino when we were only a handful of men and said that we were Marxist–Leninists, we might never have got down to the plain'[16]; and Carlos Rafael Rodríguez once sagely remarked 'who could conceive Matthews' articles in the *New York Times* in favour of a Communist guerrilla?'[17]

The Cubans are in an unusual position in comparison with the rest of Latin America so far as the 'armed struggle' is concerned; the Cuban wars of independence, 1868–78 and 1895–98, were far more destructive in terms of lives and social consequences than the wars of independence of the early nineteenth century in the other parts of the old Spanish Empire. Indeed, those Cuban wars, by completing the ruin of the old Cuban oligarchy, opened the way to the dominance of Cuban society by North America – an outcome which would be the most likely consequence of a long armed struggle in any large Latin American country in the 1970s – an eventuality which is certainly possible. On the other hand, the Cuban revolutionary war of 1956–58 was infinitely milder than say the Mexican revolution or the long period of violence which has characterized Colombia since 1948.

The Cuban Revolution, a Garibaldiesque challenge to North America as much as an attempt to resolve Cuba's own problems, indeed remains perhaps more menacing to North than to South America, for it was to begin with a reproach to the greed of affluence and the standards of North America which, because of improved communications, were introduced into Cuba at so great a pace in the 1950s. The Cuban revolution is thus as much a part of a North American revolution as one of the South: a fact more and more evident as Florida continues to throng with exiles, becoming once more what she administratively was for a time in the late eighteenth century: *la jurisdicción de la Habana ultramar*; while Cuba herself, by a bizarre inverse historical repetition, is now again cut off from the rest of Spanish America as she was before

[16] Speech of 20 December 1961.
[17] Carlos Rafael Rodríguez, *La revolución cubana y el período de transición*, II, 41.

1762, with Russia playing the role of imperial mother once played by Spain.

North American policy has not much changed since the missile crisis. The last statement menacing Cuba by a U.S. president was Kennedy's at the Orange Bowl, Miami, on 29 December 1962, when he welcomed back the prisoners from the Bay of Pigs and promised that, one day, the Brigade's flag (which he agreed to keep safely) would be returned to it in a free Havana.[18] Afterwards, however, Kennedy sought passivity rather than war and it is just possible that his murder in November 1963 prevented reconciliation.[19]

The policy of President Johnson towards Cuba was conservative. Preoccupied by Asia, the administration concentrated on the maintenance of the economic embargo and on the isolation of Cuba from the hemisphere, and largely succeeded. The base at Guantánamo was retained. Cuban adventures abroad, such as Guevara's attempted guerrilla war in Bolivia, were crushed,[20] but Cuba herself was left alone.[21] Meantime, those who lost money in Cuba kept their files open,[22] and private investment in Latin America slowly began to increase again, after the years when it dropped substantially because of fears of revolution.[23] In 1969 there was discussion again of a possible U.S. *rapprochement* with Cuba. Castro told a North American banker that the new U.S. administration seemed more courteous and cautious than its predecessor. Nevertheless, it would seem that during the present stage of his intellectual development Castro has said too often, 'We have no contact with the U.S. and we don't want any' – the embargo notwithstanding – for there to be any real possibility of understanding.[24] The embargo after all, has its political uses and it has probably helped Castro more than it has hurt him.

[18] *New York Times*, 30 December 1962.

[19] See Jean Daniel's article in *New Republic*, 14 December 1963; also William Attwood, *The Reds and the Blacks* (Hutchinson, London 1967), 144.

[20] For an interesting argument that the CIA never lost trace of Guevara (but pretended to), that his re-appearance in Bolivia was immediately analysed in Washington and that the CIA did not desire Guevara killed, see Andrew St George, 'How the U.S. got Che', *True*, April 1969.

[21] To say therefore with Saverio Tutino (*Partisans*, April–June 1962) that in Cuba '*C'est la vie quotidienne qui est directement menacée*' seems romantic.

[22] The Foreign Claims Settlement Commission fixed U.S. claims to Cuba at $M2,700, of which $M400 were individual claims by separate people and the rest 948 corporation claims (*New York Times*, 24 May 1967).

[23] Private investment in Latin America was estimated at $1 billion in 1957 and dropped to $M200 in 1961 (*New York Herald Tribune*, 10 June 1962, 7). The slump of private investment in Latin America, by Latin Americans themselves and by U.S. citizens, with the transfer of much capital elsewhere (to Europe for instance), was one major consequence of the Revolution in Cuba.

[24] Interview with K. S. Karol, *New Statesman*, 22 September 1967.

After the missile crisis, the U.S. suspended Pan American flights from Havana to Miami and for three years the only flights out of Cuba to the Western world were via Mexico or Madrid. The number of exiles to leave Cuba was therefore small. But since December 1965, an air service has been established whereby 3,000–4,000 'gusanos'[25] leave Cuba each month on airliners chartered by the U.S. Government. This safety valve, both merciful and wise, has since 1965 taken 200,000 Cubans to Florida; but the waiting list at the Swiss Embassy of those who desire to leave is believed to exceed another 200,000, while all males between fifteen and twenty-seven, as well as those who 'will reach that age in the next few years' are banned from leaving. (Many technicians also cannot leave.) With the 300,000 or so who left Cuba between 1959 and 1962, a tenth of the population has abandoned Cuba or desires to do so. The possibility of flight is admittedly a better alternative than the policies practised by Stalin during the 1930s and 1940s, when a similar proportion of the Russian population was in concentration camps.[26] But comparison with Stalin is scarcely the best criterion and the waiting list is itself a cause of terrible chagrin, since an application to leave Cuba opens the would-be exile to difficulties and humiliations, including the loss of professions and possessions. Those who apply to leave Cuba place themselves at the disposal of the Government and, even if all goes well and the applicants are given a place in the queue, the usual practice is that they work on farms for a minimum wage, usually for two years or even more, before they receive their permission to leave, their tickets (paid in foreign currency), and their visas to enter the U.S. or Spain. They live in special constructed barracks, *albergues*, with earth floors, much resembling indeed the *barracones* of slaves in the last century. In consequence, many still seek to leave Cuba illegally, by boat or through Guantánamo, often to die in the attempt, perhaps eaten by sharks, or caught and shot.[27]

[25] *Gusano*, literally maggot or earthworm, the Revolution's name for those who oppose it.

[26] The regime's 'permissiveness' to those who desired to leave Cuba was among the grounds for criticism by Escalante's 'microfaction'. Out of the 38,000 Chinese (that is, born in China) in Cuba in 1953, only about 5,000 remain, according to one investigator. So far as anyone knows, these arrangements will last forever.

[27] Estimates of numbers of Cuban exiles now abroad vary very much. With children born in exile, the total may now be something close to 800,000.

The Pursuit of Freedom

Cuba in the 1960s has thus presented a tragedy for a large minority of her citizens, especially for the many of them who, through no fault of their own but because of the accumulation of social history, seemed previously too frivolous for drama: so many families have been divided or broken, so much personal unhappiness has been caused for political reasons and, leaving aside the leaders, so many also, on both sides, doctors and educationalists in Havana as well as democratic exiles in the U.S., believe that they have acted for the best, yet nevertheless despise and hate each other. Most distressing, perhaps, is 'the internal conflict, almost impossible to convey, of the individual who is convinced of the correctness of his analysis of the "betrayed revolution" and yet is constantly wary of abetting . . . another "enemy camp" that was and still is abhorrent to his values.'[1] There is also the tragedy of a political movement which began by harnessing generous emotions from all kinds of people and has become, at the least, intolerant; and there is the tragedy of innumerable Cubans who die in exile far from the land which they love.

The Cuban Revolution, therefore, gives a lesson in politics. Those who admire the social advances made under the Revolution must consider the brutality of the gaolers, the arbitrary character of an unpredictable but ubiquitous tyranny, the tedium of an inefficient bureaucratic state and the melancholy of a society where eccentricity and private experiment ('the sad colouring of submission,' as Segundo Cazalis put it), much less private enterprise, is damned. Those who abhor the tyranny need to be reminded of the evident integrity of many of the leaders, that a minimum wage, and universal schooling and medicine did not obtain before (but could have done so), and that rural poverty is much reduced. The lovers of the Revolution, sometimes dazzled, as was Columbus, by the beauty of the Cuban vegetation and the charm of the people (as by the restricted view of the country they sometimes get through the windows of the black ICAP car[2]), also perhaps

[1] Carlos Luis, *Notes of a Cuban Revolutionary in exile*; see also the novel by the former Cuban Ambassador in London, Luis Ricardo Alonso, *Territorio Libre* (Peter Owen, London, 1966).

[2] ICAP, the Cuban Institute of Friendship with the Peoples is the official body which looks after visitors and ensures that they see the best of Cuba. ICAP's budget is generous and seems always able to afford cigars, daiquiris and good meals to reliable visitors.

need to recall that health and education are only aids to the good life and that in Cuba as elsewhere in the Communist world, where it is often supposed that the ends justify the means, the ends themselves seem forgotten. The end of even Marx's political ambitions was a society where human beings are not regarded as objects or part of an inscrutable historical process and where the smallest minority can dissent even on trumpery matters. The multitudes in uniform are surely supposed to be marching to a spot where they can disband. For a historian, the good life is a society where Truth is not abused and where the study of history, even recent history, can be pursued without interference – a society much like that which Fidel Castro described in his first famous speech, *History Will Absolve Me*, and which he said that Batista had destroyed in 1952: 'Once upon a time there was a Republic. It had its constitution, its laws, its civil rights, its President, a Congress, and law courts. Everyone could assemble, associate, speak and write with complete freedom . . . There existed a public opinion both respected and heeded.'[3] This was rather an exaggeratedly favourable description by Castro of Cuba under Carlos Prío; it bears no relation to life under Castro himself.

Of course, Castro and his government may have been popular, perhaps with most of the people most of the time, though, with the absence of elections or even opinion polls since 1960, there has been no knowing this for sure, and it is impossible to distinguish, in a totalitarian system, between, as Boris Goldenberg put it, 'spontaneous enthusiasm and enforced or opportunistic conformity'.[4] But even if it could be statistically proved that more Cubans still loved Castro than hated him, that would only be one factor. Given the power which autocratic governments can now have over the mass media to control discussion as they like, it becomes less and less interesting to say of such and such a regime that it is popular. Was it ever so? General Crowder was doubtless right when in 1927 he told Secretary of State Kellogg that 'most Cubans favoured a second term for Machado'.[5] Even in relatively free societies, polls are wayward. Maxime du Camp at Naples in 1860 heard people in the streets shout 'Long Live Italy' with enthusiasm and then ask their neighbour what the word 'Italy' meant. Who are they, how many are they, these masses who, throughout the 1960s, have shouted 'Yankees, Remember Girón!', or *'Estoy con Fidel'*, *'Venceremos'*, *'Paredón'*, *'Fuera'*, *'Unidad'*, *'Fidel, seguro a los Yankees darle duro'*, *'Somos socialistas, palant'y palant'y'*, *'Viva el socialismo chachachá'*, *'Ni un paso atrás'*, *'viva la internacional proletaria'*, *'Patria o Muerte'*, or other of the innumerable

---

[3] *History Will Absolve Me*, 16.
[4] Goldenberg, 236.
[5] Robert F. Smith, 116.

slogans of Revolutionary Cuba? Were some the same men and women who in 1950 suggested, in a poll taken by the Esso Standard Oil Company, that most Cubans would prefer to work for a U.S. company than the Cuban Government[6] – a thought difficult to coordinate with the attitudes of the thousands who cheered Castro's tirades against the 'illiterate millionaire', Kennedy, in the early 1960s? It is doubtless so.

Castro's magnetism and oratory have enabled him to direct Cuban society since 1959 very much according to his own designs. He has successfully persuaded many people that the absence of goods in the shops is a sign of virtue, that the market economy such as exists even in East Europe is an evil, that cities are vicious and that the countryside is noble.[7] His oratory has persuaded many to accept even the ideas of abolishing Christmas and to welcome the fact that the harvest of the year 1969–70 will last eighteen months; similarly, in the past there were eloquent slave owners able to explain why there should be a Sunday only every ten days, and yet still be loved. Castro's elevation of violence, his harping on the theme of conflict, his use of the rifle as a symbol, attracts the nation and probably panders to the latent *macho* spirit which has perhaps suffered a set-back in private life.[8] Strong and intolerant governments are often much more popular than easy-going and tolerant ones, just as war is not universally hated.

Further, Castro has done many things which have been popular even if they have been unjust to minorities or even if they have been at least partly designed to achieve popularity. Revolutionary Cuba has throughout enjoyed a quite new national spirit deriving from the heady experience of social revolution and international adventure. Castro's own personality, undoubtedly fortunate, apparently heroic, certainly indefatigable and formidable, is itself a phenomenon in which many

[6] See *Public opinion survey in Cuba prepared for Esso Standard Oil Company* (Cuba), September 1950, by International Public Opinion Research Inc., of New York. 'About 1 out of 3 people give first preference to an American Company and very few voice a desire to work for the Cuban Government.'

[7] Perhaps here as in so many matters, an epigram of Martí's paved the way: *La ciudad extravía el juicio, el campo lo ordena y acrisola* ('The city distorts the judgement, the country orders and refines it').

[8] Castro's charm also has played a part. From whom else would Jean-Paul Sartre have accepted the remark: 'If someone asked me for the moon it would be because someone needed it'.? After this, Sartre said in 1960, Castro became one of his 'few friends'. It is remarkable how Castro's willingness to use violent language unthinkable in a bourgeois democracy has also enthralled many foreign visitors. The most curious comment is from Clive Jenkins who visited Cuba in 1961 and asked a militiaman: 'Do you want elections?' He looked at me and shook his machine gun, 'We've got these,' he said. At this point in time, I found this a convincing reply.' (The militiaman's remark was an echo of Castro's speech of 1 May 1961.) Introduction to *Cuba and Fidel*, by Norman Lewis, Union of Democratic Control London, 1961.

Cubans can take pride.[9] The educational and health reforms of the Revolution are immensely popular in a nation which coveted them in the past more than formal democracy; the armies of children hanging round the tenement or the bohío were of course in the past a constant reproach to the parents, as well as an anxiety. Finally, the ruin of the old master class, the end of corruption and of *gangsterismo*, the abolition of social discrimination and of the subservient attitudes to North America have certainly given many Cubans much pleasure; while the Revolution's earliest and internationally most famous achievement – the opening of the private beaches to the masses – symbolizes one side of the achievement of the last ten years which the most resolute friends of pure political liberty have to take into account.

The question, therefore, whether these achievements have been worth the candle is likely to be subjective. Depending on temperament as much as on riches or class, there are those, in Cuba as elsewhere, who believe that 'if a more just economic system is only attainable by closing men's minds against free inquiry . . . the price [is] too high'.[10] The facts are clear; there is no constitution in Cuba and, though a commission of the Central Committee of the Communist Party is said to be preparing one, nothing suggests that such a thing would change matters, any more than the Soviet constitution of 1935 did in Russia. Castro's government, therefore, remains what it has been since 1959 – a good example of Halévy's definition of dictatorship – 'a group of armed men, moved by a common faith, seize power, and decree that they are the state'.[11] To some Cubans it must indeed seem as if one of the idealistic political gangster groups of the late 1940s – the most idealistic as well as the most ruthless – had finally seized the public buildings and now monopolize the big cars and the machine guns.

Without doubt, also, this system of government, as well as being oppressive, is also often inefficient. Governments desirous of economic development naturally wish to ride roughshod over local interests. How tedious to have to have an inquiry over the siting of a new airport! But in the long run the discussion of policy before it is decided upon is of course profitable. In Cuba, according to Segundo Cazalis, bad news, in the classic style, is often not taken to Castro, since he associates the bearer with the intelligence.[12] Castro's personality is a complicated one and certainly not fully known even to himself: what is clear is that he does not find it easy to surround himself with constructive critics. 'Yes-men'

---

[9] It has been assumed that in the event of a free election Castro would win (see for example the assertion to this effect by Professor Roger Fisher, Professor of Law at Harvard, in *The New Republic*, 15 June 1963). How anyone can know this is obscure.

[10] Bertrand Russell, *The Practice and Theory of Bolshevism* (Allen & Unwin, London 1920), 8.

[11] Élie Halévy, *The Era of Tyrannies* (Allen Lane, The Penguin Press, 1967), 215.

[12] Cazalis, *La República* (Caracas), 14 February 1965.

clearly abound. A free press in Cuba might have prevented the neglect of the sugar industry during 1960–63, the numerous wasteful industrial projects, the still controversial coffee campaign of the late 1960s, or the sad neglect of the beautiful city of Havana (which, whether Castro likes it or not, is one of Cuba's prides), and even the Ten Million Ton harvest of 1969–70. Is it necessary to point out, so late in the day, that Liberty is a convenience as well as a principle? There is also, in an arbitrary system always the possibility of further distortion, as occurred in Germany under the stress of war in the early 1940s, or in Russia under that of agrarian change in the 1930s; whereas parliamentary democracy, for all its faults, has the virtue of being a good way of settling internal disputes without violence.

The Cuban Revolutionary Government is hence an experiment whose moral, not whose example, needs to be borne in mind by others: Cuba's standard of living measured by most gauges was always higher than most countries of the so-called underdeveloped world. Cuba's social misery in the past was due to an extreme form of that public meanness and private affluence that characterizes North America as well as South. Cuba, before 1959, certainly needed reform and more than most countries. It should be possible to stand back and welcome such changes that are incontestably benevolent; to question those which seem of uncertain merit; to denounce those which have been unjust or mistaken; to criticize tyrannical methods even if these have resulted in some good being done; and not to despair that, in other circumstances or in other countries, the means may match the ends. Socialism, after all, was intended by those who first thought of it to be a system of society in which not only the common good was given priority but in which each individual would be treated with the respect that human beings deserve.

Castro in 1963 expressed surprise that North Americans should seek to differentiate Castroism and Communism,[13] and at first sight Revolutionary Cuba clearly owes much to the Communist system as practised in Russia or East Europe. The organization of the party, of labour, and of planning, reflects orthodox Communist ideas as practised in well-established Communist states; in particular, of the party within the Army and the police.

There are obviously characteristics of the Cuban system which distinguish it from the 'friendly socialist countries', as they are known in Havana. These include some institutions (if that is not perhaps too strong a word) such as the Committees for the Defence of the Revolution and the militia. It also seems that, despite the frequent incompetence of

[13] '*No sé por que establecén esta diferencia*', *Hoy*, 24 February 1963. '*Entre esos mil milones,*' Guevara once remarked, the Cuban Communists were '*una gota pero uno gota diferenciable* (a drop but a recognizable drop).

the huge bureaucracy that the state has bred in Cuba, the functionaries carry out their duties with somewhat greater respect for individuals than has been the case in other Communist countries. The state is still able to count on the enthusiasm of many, particularly children and young people. Perhaps, however, this also is a subjective judgement, since many with experience of Cuban prisons would think differently.

The national temperament and climate of Cuba, along with the most recent historical experience of Cuba, has most affected the character of the system. For example, Castro on the one hand had no tradition of competent officialdom to assist him, as was the case in Communist countries of Eastern Europe and in Russia; nor was the Cuban Communist system built, as was the case in every other country where the theory has caught hold, upon a people which had suffered the ravages of a prolonged and bloody war. The Cuban civil war which brought Castro to power was quite modest in its scope and the dictatorship of Batista, although vulgar and brutal – and the brutalities were specially easy to publicize – cannot be compared with the tyranny of the Nazi new order in Europe and in West Russia in the early 1940s.

It is also obvious that any dictatorship in a country with an equable climate such as Cuba, where there is no need for winter fuel nor for winter clothing, is easier to bear and therefore itself assumes a somewhat more benevolent identity. Thus it is possible to excuse some of the abuses of Communism in Russia by the explanation that it is Russian; and some of the attractions – for so they are to many – of Communism in Cuba by the explanation that it is Cuban.

The Cuban revolutionary state is also to be differentiated from other Communist systems because of Castro's own claims to be able to decide for himself the direction and the timing of his interpretation of Marxist–Leninism. Castro's temperament, the manner in which he came to power – through his own efforts, like Mao or Tito, that is, and not on the coat-tails of the Red Army – and Cuba's geographical situation, have given him an independent position. Castro has used this to argue that it is possible to build Socialism and Communism at the same time (Lenin and Marx would have considered this view heretical, superficial, infantilist or Bakuninist) and that 'battle is the best school of Marxism'. Castro supports 'revolutionaries, with or without parties', or any revolutionary process in any Latin American country – even if those who have prompted that revolution are a group of military leaders, considering that 'in most countries the [orthodox] Communist movement is too narrow and dogmatic to contain all . . . revolutionary energies'.[14]

[14] These remarks were made by Castro respectively to K. S. Karol (*New Statesman*, 22 September 1967), on 29 August 1969, *à propos* of the 'pseudo-revolutionary' Venezuelan Communist party; on 14 July 1969, at Puerto Padre, in respect of the Peruvian military government; and again, to K. S. Karol, in 1967.

Never has Castro admitted that war is an evil. Once again, in 1970, as in 1959, it would seem that the name of his first political group, the UIR (*Unión Insurreccional Revolucionaria*) which he joined as a student, is in many ways the best label for his political position.

Perhaps this is just to say that Castro, a revolutionary before he was a Communist, had a temperamental preference for youth and for heroic, action rather than for age, study (of Marx or anyone else)[15] and caution and is therefore inevitably critical of the older generation of Communist party leaders in Latin America – the old contemporaries of Blas Roca, Escalante, or Ordoqui. On the other hand, perhaps this, like the view that it is possible to build Socialism and Communism at the same time, is a transient, not a firmly worked out, philosophy. Once the fashion in Cuba was for material incentives, now (when there is nothing to buy) it is for moral ones; but will this last for ever? The 'new man' may turn out to have old passions. Castro's views on the armed struggle were less heroic between 1962 and 1966 (and, indeed, have been slightly less heroic since 1969). It is reasonable enough to suppose that Castro will always prefer 'the most competent, the most able, the most audacious' people, as he told the North American, Lee Lockwood[16], but in those terms the perfect revolutionary sounds much the same as the perfect capitalist. Castro and the railway builder, Percival Farquhar, probably would see eye to eye.

When it comes to the point, Castro's changing moods more than any firmly organized body of principles seem most characteristic of him; thus there was a remarkably short space between the time he was saying with, as some of his later enemies would admit, apparent sincerity, 'Neither I nor the movement are Communist' (on 13 January 1959) or 'the only sacrifice which I am not prepared to make . . . would be to use force to further the revolution' (6 February 1959) to the famous remarks of 1961: 'I shall be a Marxist–Leninist for the rest of my life' (on 2 December 1961). What, therefore, characterized the Cuban Revolution is that on top of a familiarly organized Communist system, there has been an elevation of Castro's role as 'maximum leader', and the articulation of this personal power through frequent and skilfully managed personal appearances, culminating in great speeches. All major decisions have been taken in Cuba since 1959 by Castro, sometimes paying heed to those pressure groups which exist even in a closed society (such as the

---

[15] Castro must be the first Marxist–Leninist leader who had scarcely read much of the works of the Master and who scarcely allows more than a few words and few expressions taken from Marxism to enter his vocabulary. In his speech on 4 November 1969, encouraging the armed forces to do their best in the great sugar harvest of 1969–70, he announced that he and his followers were to be the standard bearers of '*the best* of Marx's ideas and of the best of Lenin's ideas' – which, of course, might mean anything.

[16] Lockwood, 190.

Army or the old Communists), sometimes not. In public, 'the Revolution', that irresistible movement of men and spirits towards Utopia, is
made to resemble an African deity, whose needs, sometimes wayward
and inscrutable, are interpreted by Castro as *santero*, a worthy successor
to others who aspired to fulfil this role in Cuba, from Carlos Manuel de
Céspedes and Martí onwards. (Grau San Martín was, of course, a false
prophet, but, is it permissible to say, a prophet all the same?) The
waywardness of Castro can be seen in his odd admission that 'capitalism
digs two graves – one for itself, one for the society which comes after
capitalism'.[17]

It is tempting to compare the distinctive colouring which Castro
has given to Cuban communism with fascism[18]; there is Castro's evident
belief, with Chibás but also with Mosley or Hitler, that political power
lies in 'the response of a large audience to a stirring speech'.[19] There is
the willingness of large sections of the population, including intelligent
and humane people, to surrender their individuality to Castro as men
did to Fascist leaders. There is the persistent elevation of the principle
of violence and the appeals to martial reactions in the regime's propaganda; and there is the cult of leadership, the emphasis on physical
fitness in the education system, and the continual denigration of bourgeois democracies. The very statement of Guevara's in *Socialism and
Man* which defines the drives of Cuban socialism shares with fascism,
as with expressionism, 'the urge to recapture the "whole man" who
seems atomized and alienated by society',[20] a man who could not find
himself among the 'commonplaces of bourgeois democracy', as Guevara
put it. The 'New Man', held to be typified by Guevara, a hero, and
man of action, will and character, would have been admired by French
fascists such as Brasillach or Drieu or by D'Annunzio, of the wild demagogic epoch of the Republic of Fiume, who himself has seemed to at
least one commentator to have been Castro's intellectual precursor.[21]
Castro's moralizing and his desire to break with all material aims reflects
fascist regenerationism; and his presentation of himself as the thoughtful and benevolent father resembles Mussolini. In fact, of course, the
fascist revolutions of the 1930s cannot be understood (any more than
Castro's can) if observed wholly negatively, or if it is forgotten that even
the Nazi revolution 'satisfied a deeply felt need for activism combined
with identification [with] . . . a classless society'.[22] Fascism was a heresy

[17] Speech in Camagüey, *Hoy*, 15 May 1962.
[18] See above, pp. 1037, 1051, 1086–7.
[19] R. Skidelsky's phrase in referring to Mosley, in *European Fascism*, ed. by S. J. Woolf
(1968), 236.
[20] George Mosse, 'The Genesis of Fascism', in *Journal of Contemporary History*, No. 1, 1966.
[21] Cf. Richard Lowenthal, 'Unreason and Revolution', in *Encounter*, November 1969.
[22] Mosse, *loc. cit.*

of the international socialist movement and several fascist leaders had once been men of the Left: it is possible to imagine Castro moving in time (or, more probably, at a certain time) from extreme Left to what passes for extreme Right. The charismatic leader, both left and right, after all, lives against an artificial background. As George Kennan put it, 'He creates [the background] for himself; but he believes in it implicitly and in part he generally succeeds in making it seem real to others as well. And his role, as he plays it, may be none the less heroic and impressive for this artificiality of the scenery.'[23] Of no one is this percipient comment more true than of Castro who is also, of course, the heir of the Latin American continent's tradition of *caudillismo*.

But the main deviations from the international Communist movement which have characterized the Cuban Revolution have really derived from the history of Cuba itself. Revolutionary governments are driven by pictures of the past as much as by visions of the future. For at least a generation Cuban politicians have been passionately in love with the word 'Revolution'.[24] The abuses of capitalism in Cuba created the Revolution in its own image. Cubans have also been equally in love with the word 'liberty'; slaves sought liberty from masters, merchants from Spanish laws, romantics from the Spanish Army, twentieth-century intellectuals from the strait-jacket of sugar. Now Castro considers that he has redeemed these past desires by creating the first *territorio libre* of America, though several hundred thousands of Cubans have defined freedom as exile.

Castro frequently described the Revolution as a 'process', beginning with the first Cuban war of independence, and the propaganda of the regime always so depicts it. Thus 1968 was celebrated as the culmination of a 'hundred years of struggle': 'the Revolution of 1868,' wrote the novelist, Lisandro Otero, in the glossy propaganda magazine *Cuba* of which he is the editor, 'was continued in 1895, rendered more profound in 1933, reborn in 1953, and was triumphant if not consummated in 1959' (the history of Cuba might also be written as the history of the prisoner in La Cabaña, or the exile of Miami, where the statue of José Martí stands next to that of Bolívar and where Maceo's grandson in 1961 formed part of a council to overthrow Castro). Though history has been distorted since 1959, Castro's Revolution was the culmination of three generations of 'revolutionary activity', verbal violence, extravagant hopes of redemption and further embroidery on the idea of

---

[23] George Kennan, *Russia and the West under Lenin and Stalin*.
[24] See above, pp.1053–7. But this is true even of exiles: thus Castro's sister, Juanita, in her attacks in the U.S. and elsewhere on her brother, still speaks of the need for a 'true Revolution' to create 'a totally new Cuba . . . a Cuba which has nothing to do with the past or the present' (Interview in Miami, 21 October 1969, on Radioemisora WFAB).

freedom: 'When the news reached my encampment . . . it provoked an unimaginable delirium . . . we considered ourselves definitely free,' wrote Orestes Ferrara, a colonel in the rebel army in 1898.[25] The news in question was that of the intervention of the U.S. who then seemed to proffer freedom, just as in 1960 it seemed proffered by Russia.

Yet the obsession with freedom creates its own bondage, and is there not doubt whether in any real sense even Castro is a free man? He imposes his personality on Cuba but, like all Cuban rulers, he is at the mercy of the sugar markets as of the twenty-year relative stagnation in the Cuban economy which he has not arrested. In part, too, he is the creation of the dreams of Cubans for a revolutionary leader of epic stature, just as he is the articulate expression of a nation whose 'authentic qualities' include what is usually known as 'gaiety' – such as, for instance, responsiveness to rhythm – as well as cruelty: a country which, if it has never had a good civil service, has usually had a bloody police. The long shadows of past habits stretch across the most radical reforms, either blacking them out or giving them quite different colours. In 1959, Castro was in much the same position *vis-à-vis* the U.S. as was the Spanish prime minister Sagasta in 1898 at the beginning of the Spanish–American war. But Castro could call Russia into the lists to sell him arms (and to buy his sugar) where Sagasta could not call on, say, Britain or Germany: the cold war, that is, 'provided Castro with alternatives denied previous rulers of Cuba'.[26] It is possible that the 'liberals', the only alternative in 1959 to Castro and the Communists, would in effect have repeated, if they had had the chance, what their grandfathers did in 1898 (denying it, of course, with a show of nationalistic rhetoric) and swung Cuba into an ever closer alliance with the U.S., the island benefiting from U.S. aid and technology, so as to make Cuba materially better off than she could ever have been under Castro, though culturally submissive. Castro has in contrast created a strong, ruthless but original and popular despotism, with many remarkable social reforms to its credit and which, whatever label is given to it, represents a serious challenge to the liberal society. It would be an even more serious one if the totalitarian side of the system were dismantled and if free discussion and criticism were to be encouraged. This, however, is not likely since the regime depends so much on fanaticism and dogmatism, and fanatics are seldom humane.

In the two centuries since the English captured Havana in 1762, the Cuban population increased fifty-fold, from 150,000 to over seven million. As in the case of the U.S. the growth derived from immigra-

---

[25] In a letter to me sixty-six years later from Rome, 28 April 1964.
[26] Ruiz, *Cuba, The Making of a Revolution*, 5.

tion, rather than natural increase. So big a change in population meant that the island, including scenery and even climate – because of the felling of the great forests – has changed. But 'authentic Cuban' situations repeat themselves: American presidents under electoral pressure – Polk, McKinley, Kennedy – adopt strong measures; exiles gather in Miami (especially in the 1890s, the 1930s, the 1950s, but never so much as in the 1960s); revolutionary 'bandits' raise the flag of liberty in the hills and are shot as thieves; and, as Castro should be warned, political rebellions occur at economically prosperous times – in 1868, 1895 and 1956. The next rebellion will probably occur after, not before, the Revolutionary Government has achieved its economic goals, and the population has time to speculate on their purpose.

The history of Cuba since the late eighteenth century, when the country began to produce sugar on a lavish scale for the world market, has been like the history of the world seen through the eyes of a child: an invention in Silesia, a plague in Africa, a war or a prosperous time in England or in France – these apparently unconnected events beyond Cuba's control have determined the lives of Cubans who, despite their tropical innocence, were the only links between them. The island was never isolated. All great events, from the Napoleonic wars to the Suez crisis, dictated to Cuba; and the history of the Revolution of Castro is the history of what was itself self-consciously a great event whose purpose was to escape the bondage of geographical as well as economic circumstances. But iron historical laws, which are a limitation even on the greatest powers and the greatest men, naturally impose themselves on Cuba and Castro: starting out in 1959 like Talleyrand at the Congress of Vienna, representative of small states wishing to be heard, she desired to be exemplary. But, alas, 'poor Cuba always hopeful, always deceived!'[27] The future of Cuba continues to depend on circumstances beyond her control. Dr Grau San Martín told Sumner Welles that 'Cuba could get along without the regulation of foreign powers and even without foreign commercial interchanges'; Eddy Chibás wanted Cuba 'free from the economic imperialism of Wall Street and the political imperialism of Moscow, Rome and Berlin.' But still the only alternative market to Russia in 1970 for Cuba's sugar production is the U.S. just as Russia was the only alternative in 1960 to the U.S. With economic diversification further away than ever, and the whole island turned into a single sugar plantation, Cuba has no hope of escaping the politics of its customers or its investors. The eighteenth-century problem of obtaining slaves from across the sea from other countries has been exactly reproduced by the problem of obtaining oil; the Russian embassy official

[27] Luis Estévez y Romero, *Desde el Zanjón hasta Baire*, 41.

Shliapnikov who boasted how a delay at Baku could strangle the Cuban economy is a twentieth-century South Sea Company factor. Perhaps even Cubans for all their gifts, cannot escape Goethe's dictum: 'In vain will undisciplined spirits strive to achieve pure freedom. For the Master first reveals himself in limitation and only Law can give us liberty.'

AFTERWORD

To summarize the history of Cuba during the 26 years since the publication of the first edition of this book in 1971 is at first sight remarkably straightforward. Unlike what has occurred in every other country in the world, the all-powerful president of Cuba remains much as he was in 1970. Castro, that is, survives, and that fact still determines the political life of the country. The wishes of that one individual continue to be transmuted into strategies. His brother Raúl also remains—as he has for nearly forty years—heir to the throne and minister of defense. In 1993 the number of candidates for the national elections was still the same as the number of parliamentary seats. There remains only one national newspaper, *Granma*, the official publication of the Communist party of Cuba, a thin tabloid that appears only five days a week. For a government that once seemed interested in causing upheavals in every country in Latin America except Mexico, the stability of Cuba is astounding.

The character of the economy has not changed much either, in that sugar is still the main export commodity. The level of production, expected to be about four million tons in 1997–1998, has also remained much the same as it was in the last years before 1959. Even though the mechanization of the sugar industry had brought far more plentiful harvests in the late 1970s and '80s, in the 1990s the harvests fell to pre-revolutionary levels when the Soviet Union abandoned its subsidies to Cuba. And, if tourism now runs close to sugar as an earner of foreign exchange, that impetus is like a step backwards in time to the promising, but undeveloped, pleasure industry of the 1950s. True, that last emphasis, with its remarkable revival of prostitution in a country which boasted that it had eradicated the profession by 1964, would have seemed a sad concession to capitalism to the revolutionaries of the 1970s, but the scale of Cuba's economic collapse in the 1990s—brought on by the disintegration of the USSR—meant that they had few alternatives.

It is true that the international winds of economic change have caused the Cuban government to reexamine such delicate matters as the benefits of the profit-motive and the occasional ill effects of socialism. But that reexamination has not taken Cuba very far. The government still directs the economy as much as it can.

Nor has the policy of the United States changed noticeably. The strength of the Cuban exile community in Miami has grown, mobilizing an extremely effective and vociferous "lobby" (based on the Israeli model) that pays substantial sums to both Republican and Democratic parties to ensure the maintenance of the U.S. embargo. The Florida vote is an essential one in all presidential elections, to such an extent that the embargo is sometimes described as a domestic issue. The Helms-Burton law of 1996 (Cuban Liberty and Democratic Solidarity Act) actually tightened the embargo, making any foreign business, or individual, which, or who, carried on trade with any enterprise in Cuba that derived from a confiscated U.S. company, liable to have its (or his) assets in the United States confiscated. The law created maximum difficulties, not only with Mexico and Canada, substantial trade partners with Cuba since 1990, but with the European Union, whose foreign trade commissioner, Leon Brittan, eventually reached an agreement with the United States to delay action on the matter. But the law did not alter anything substantial in the U.S. government's long-standing strategy. The U.S. government continues a policy towards Cuba that it has long abandoned against even North Vietnam.

To understand why requires a brief discussion of the three distinct eras in Cuba's history since 1970. First, there was the age of aggressive involvement in the affairs of Latin America and Africa—and not only in the region of Angola, but in a score of countries in that continent.

Second, there was the period when, under the administration of President Reagan in the United States, Cuban expansionism on behalf of the Soviet Union was effectively stayed.

Third, there has been the unforseeable time when, after the collapse of the Soviet Union, Communist Cuba has lived as an increasingly isolated nation, barely surviving an economic collapse between 1989 and 1993 of between 35 and 50 percent, and reviving in 1995.[1]

[1]It seems that the Cuban economy grew 7.8 percent in 1996.

The first of the three eras was quite alarming. Castro had always sought to turn the Andes into the Sierra Maestra of the continent. He had said so himself in the so-called Second Declaration of Havana in 1960. He was not a man content to confine himself to the small dimensions of an island, even a large and beautiful one such as Cuba. From early on, his government, in collaboration with the Soviet Union, had inspired, or at least assisted, guerrilla movements both in Africa and in Latin America. Had not Cuban troops been seen as early as 1961 in Zanzibar at the time of the coup d'état there? Were there not Cuban troops ready to act in the war between Morocco and Algeria in 1962? Did not Cuba play a major part in inspiring a civil war in Betancourt's Venezuela? In those heady days Castro was seeking a world role, not just an American one, much less a Caribbean one. He offered himself as the Soviet Union's most reliable ally, more dependable than East Germany or Bulgaria, and showed how Cuba was able to send out tens of thousands of troops in the cause of revolution, thereby making possible the astounding event of a sizeable quantity of Cuban infantry arriving in Angola to support the MPLA, the Soviet protégés in that country. No Western intelligence service had predicted this move, no political analyst understood it, for those who knew the Soviet Union had not bothered to study Cuba, while the rare specialists in Cuban affairs knew nothing of Russia. By the time the CIA had made its analyses, Cuban troops were already in action against Savimbi's UNITA movement and causing that assembly of anti-Communists to seek the almost open support of South Africa. For the second time in two decades Castro had inspired a major world crisis.

From the beginning it seemed clear that—though the financing and the infrastructure of the Cuban adventure in Angola was supported by the Soviet Union—the idea was Castro's. In the days of Brezhnev the Soviet system did not easily conceive such breathtakingly audacious acts of international intervention. Whether Castro deliberately willed it or not, his move had the immediate effect of ending the attempted rapprochement with Cuba by Gerald Ford's administration which Dr. Henry Kissinger had skillfully embarked upon when secretary of state.

Within months, the shadow of Castro and Cuba seemed to be extending all over central and southern Africa. *Cambio 16*, the important Spanish magazine that did so much to assist the process of transition in Spain, published a photograph of the "maximum leader" standing up in a jeep, smoking a cigar and looking dreamily, if covetously, across some savannah land in central Angola. Where did the limits of Castro's ambition lie? Windhoek? Johannesburg? Capetown? Would the Cuban army, equipped with Soviet weapons and acting as Soviet "surrogates"—the word of the time—steal the minerals of South Africa for Moscow? Would the "liberation" of the former mean that the strategically important base at the tip of the continent would henceforth serve the global strategies of Moscow? We all assumed that the Soviet Union had a world plan. Suddenly, the Cubans seemed to be the effective agents of that ambition everywhere. Within a short time another branch of the Cuban army was to be found assisting, in conventional formation, the Marxist regime of Colonel Mengistu in Ethiopia.

The fact that many of the rank and file of these Cuban troops were black Cubans facilitated their commitment. The greater part of the African slave population of Cuba were, in essence, immigrants—involuntary immigrants but immigrants all the same—of the nineteenth century. A young Cuban corporal in 1980 might easily have had an ancestor who had been born in Angola or the Congo, and carried across the Atlantic in one of Julián Zulueta's slave-trading steamships. The role of *santería*—in 1997 more important, it seems, than ever—made Cuba much closer to Africa than to the United States. Soviet troops would have stood out in cities like Luanda or Addis Abbaba almost as much as American soldiers would have. But boys from Santiago de Cuba or Matanzas fitted easily into the landscape.

Nor was it only a matter of Africa. At long last in 1979 a second Marxist regime was established in the Americas. This was, of course, in Nicaragua, where the Sandinistas, a group of Cuba-trained and Cuba-supported guerrillas, came to power in the wake of the discredited old dictator Anastasio Somoza, courtesy of a bitter and untidy guerrilla war. Michael Manley's strongly socialist first government in Jamaica also counted on Cuban guidance in its security arrangements. Finally, the Cubans were, of course, deeply involved in the coup d'état that led directly to the United States' involvement in Grenada in the autumn of 1982.

It is not altogether easy now to recall, from the relative tranquillity of the late '90s, the mood of those days in the late '70s and early '80s. But, at the time, this era of aggression seemed a volatile and dangerous one. It led directly to the second phase in Cuba's recent past: the need to stand firmly against a "darkening world horizon," which played a significant part in the electoral victories of Margaret Thatcher in 1979 and of Ronald Reagan in 1980. Some people might joke: "Why is Cuba the largest country in the world?" Answer: "Because its army is in Africa, its population is in Florida, and its government is in Moscow." But the Soviet "threat" was no joke, and the Cubans played a part in it—a dangerous part, actually, since Cuban soldiers seemed ready to go anywhere and do anything, and since the island of Cuba itself played an essential role in Soviet military tactics: in wartime B20 bombers could be expected to fly over the United States to drop their bombs on Boston, New York, and Washington, before landing happily in Havana.

Thus, Castro had converted his island into exactly what he had always wanted: a place not in the sun, but in the eye of the storm. Perhaps he dreamed of one day playing a direct role in Soviet policy. Even if he did not, the *guerrillero* with "twelve men" in the Sierra Maestra in 1956 might have been at first a pawn in the international chess game but, as in chess, pawns can transform themselves into queens if they reach the end of the board. The Cuban leader seemed already to have the range of that masterly piece.

The Soviet Union maintained its support for Castro under Andropov and Chernenko. Then suddenly, and amazingly, the game collapsed. With Gorbachev "the international contradictions" of Soviet policies, to use the expression that Marxists had always enjoyed using in respect to capitalism, became increasingly intolerable. Soviet diplomats began to distance themselves from Castro, who seemed increasingly old-fashioned, and whose visits to Moscow became more and more infrequent. Then Gorbachev started to dismantle the legacy of his predecessors in Eastern Europe. A Soviet diplomat met Cuban exiles in Miami. Peace was made in Angola, the Cuban army went home; its generals were accused of plotting against their government, and one or two such military men (headed by General Emilio Ochoa) lost their lives when they were betrayed. Long before, Eddie Seaga had defeated Manley in elections in Jamaica. Next, the persistent and popular opposition leader Violeta Chamorro defeated the Sandinistas in Nicaragua. The whole house of cards of Soviet-Cuban aggrandizement fell to pieces. Before long, the Soviet Union itself began to disintegrate. Gorbachev was overthrown and later rescued, only to lose power when the Soviet Communist party was declared illegal. Leningrad became Saint Petersburg, and a new era for Russia began. So did a new era for Cuba.

Every year in the last of these three eras—Cuba's period of isolation—there have been external voices (rather like that of the allegorical figure Rumour in a Shakespeare play) who prophesied doom for the regime. It seemed a logical and inevitable development as all of Soviet Russia's allies in Eastern Europe, as well as her puppets in Africa, collapsed, often in a dramatic manner. But all those who have made such prophesies have had to eat their words, for the end has never come. For the most part, Cuban exiles in Spain or the United States (especially if, as so many have, they have encountered success in their new homes outside the island) now seem to accept that they will never go home to live, even if they have in their minds the perfectly reasonable idea of recovering lost property. If their family once owned a lovely house in the district near *el country club* or in Miramar, they will, of course, hope to recover it from the North Koreans, say, who have used the place as their embassy for so long. But whether the former owners themselves will return to live in those gilded halls is another matter.

Havana remained, however, Havana. Castro—his international wings certainly clipped, his dreams of global activity and power turned to dust—publicly expressed not only astonishment but deep regret regarding the changes that had transformed his Russian benefactor. But he insisted that he continued to believe in Marxism-Leninism as well as in Communism in general. The fair-weather flight to neo-capitalism was not for him. His words were still surprisingly persuasive to many people. Senator Claiborne Pell of Rhode Island, for example, brought himself to say that he thought Castro would carry out his own *perestroika*, or restructuring. A change in the economy began—even if the pace was slow. Only tourism represented a real initiative, but many Spanish and European tourists set off with appreciation. Markets, private restaurants, *paladares* (sometimes approved officially, sometimes condemned), and foreign investment followed: Spain's investment alone in Cuba in 1996 totalled over eleven million dollars.

Then Castro began to court the Roman Catholic Church. It was a dramatic change in a country where for many years Catholics had to conceal their faith. For a generation, those known to be Christians found their children mocked at school and their jobs threatened. But in 1997 Pope John Paul II, who had been booed in Sandinista Nicaragua ten years earlier, agreed to visit the island in January 1998.

By that time, the Church had become a major participant in Cuban politics for the first time in history. The second national ecclesiastical conference, *el segundo encuentro national eclesial*, in 1996 generously, and bravely, favored national reconciliation and dialogue between the two Cubas. "To favor the path of reconciliation," the bishops' conference declared in March 1996 at the shrine of El Cobre, "with the active participation of all those implicated and interested, inside and outside our country, seems to constitute the unique opportunity possible for the future of the Cuban nation." The elevation in 1994 of the Archbishop of Havana, Jaime Ortega Alamino, to be Cuba's second cardinal in history coincided with the beginning of a new epoch in the history of the Church.

Churches have begun to hold daily, instead of weekly, masses, and some have re-opened their doors for the first time in many years, often to packed congregations. The Virgin of El Cobre was taken on "a pilgrimage of blessing" to all the churches, and open-air masses have been widely held. Castro himself, who held a meeting with the Pope in January 1997, asked Protestant and Jewish religious leaders to pray for the future of the island. He told one audience that his meeting with the Pope had been "a miracle."

This new epoch has not been wholly a political development, but there are, however, political consequences. *Juventud Rebelde*, the review for the Communist youth, tried to anticipate a new Catholic-Communist "front against capitalism and imperialism" by stating that the Pope's visit was intended "to be interpreted as sympathy for Cuba against the United States blockade." In the editorial view of *Juventud Rebelde* the Pope, in numerous speeches, "has taken the same view as does Cuba of capitalism and its neo-liberal arrangements."[2] The Pope's visit would allow Cuban society to display its firm attitudes against drugs, child prostitu-

---

[2]Cited in *The Economist*, December 6, 1996.

tion, and other social evils on which matters Castro and the Pope were held to see eye to eye.

But political immobility continued. There were efforts, to be sure, to try and persuade Castro to move towards democracy. Here the government of Spain played a positive part. Felipe González, the long-lasting prime minister in Madrid, was, after all, a socialist, if a democratic one. Yet even he failed to persuade the Cuban leader to move an inch towards what was becoming more and more the norm of Latin American political practice. What Manuel Fraga, the right-wing president of the Spanish autonomous government of Galicia, said to Castro is not quite clear, but the two did establish good relations together. But Fraga was no more able to effect any political change in Cuba than was his socialist compatriot. Castro attended the Olympic games in Barcelona and the "Expo" in Seville, as well as the meetings of the heads of Spanish-speaking countries in Guadalajara, Mexico and Margarita, Venezuela. But, though there were several changes towards a more open economy, political reform remained far from Castro's agenda, as he confronted Cuba's precarious future.

For the first time in its history—or at least since 1510—the island is really on its own. Cuba was a Spanish colony for nearly four centuries. After 1898 she was a semi-dependent client of the United States, which had enabled her to escape from Spain. Then she was a near-subject of the Soviet Union, which had enabled her to escape from the United States. Now Cuba has no master, not even a godfather. Further, no one is actively seeking to be her godfather. She has relations with the other countries of Latin America, but depends on none of them; and, indeed, in this new age of neo-liberalism, so close to "the end of history," her political structure is quite different from any of theirs. Cuba has attained this position of isolation *faute de mieux*, no doubt, against the desires of her still restive president, who would have preferred to retain an intimacy with the Soviet Union, had it survived, and an influential role in the Soviet world system. In much the same way that Columbus believed Cuba to be part of the mainland (he called it Fernandina after King Ferdinand the Catholic) and persuaded his sailors to sign a declaration agreeing with that eccentric geographical definition, Castro's faith in his own imaginative "sitings" have been shown to be equally mistaken.

A question mark must remain over the future of an island that insists on maintaining a small controlled economy in a world where interdependence and globalization are the watchwords, even in large countries. Many are now finding that they suffer if they insist on preserving their emotionally satisfying bureaucratic sovereignties.

Cuba has one of the few surviving nineteenth-century economies. Seldom have other countries changed so little. The old cotton plantations in the Mississippi delta, for example, have vanished completely, as have the mills where their product was turned into fine thread. How ironic it is that Cuba in the 1950s sought to create a diversified economy! The first, and now the only, socialist republic of the Americas has distinguished itself by preserving the fabric of a society that Karl Marx would have recognized. Cuba is marked by out-of-date machinery, rusting iron rather than new bright plastic, ancient automobiles, and old-fashioned music and dress. "I've seen the future and it works," said the journalist Lincoln Steffens on his return from Russia in 1930; "I've seen the past and it doesn't work" might be a similar comment on Russia's last love child in 1998.

By chance, if not design, Cuba's isolation in 1998 is a fulfillment at last of what the first advocates of independence desired. Martí wanted to be free from Spain, but he definitely did not wish for Cuba to become involved with the "monster," the United States, inside whose belly he had, as he told us, lived. All intelligent observers know by now that to maintain sovereignty *pur et dur*, as the French revolutionaries would have put it, is to limit prosperity. No self-respecting nation wants to be governed by foreigners, but to make money and to prosper in the modern world requires some surrender of sovereignty. Britain is learning that hard lesson in respect to the European Monetary Unit [EMU]; Mexico has learned it in respect to the North American Free Trade Agreement [NAFTA]. Two Cuban exile friends of mine, one living in London, the other in Paris, regularly exchange faxes on the subject of whether a liberated Cuba should join NAFTA.

At the moment the most that can be said for Cuba's political and economic isolation is that it has been chiefly responsible for maintaining her living standards at less than half of that which would probably otherwise be possible. Most of us remember approximately where Cuba stood in the league of Latin American countries in 1959 as measured by the standard of living: was it second or third? Certainly higher than fifth. Nowadays the question is whether the island ranks at the bottom in such a listing. Lower than Haiti? It seems possible. Of course, the failure of the Communist system has as much to do with the economic failure as it does with the consequences of depending for so long and so absolutely on the Soviet Union. The rigid assertion of full economic sovereignty in a nation of eleven million—with no private initiatives even now permitted to seek business abroad—has also played its negative part in ensuring that modern Cuba is characterized by shortages verging on famine and by destitution on a scale that places it below its standard of living in 1895.

There are those who argue, actually, that the transitional period in Cuba has begun. Thus, Jorge Domínguez of Harvard University, the most sensitive of modern observers of the Cuban scene, has said that the Cuban state "has begun to lose the control which it used to have over national life." This loss of control, suggests Domínguez, is especially evident in the field of economics, where the illegal, or informal, economy has begun to flourish, just as it did in the Soviet Union before the transformative events of 1989. But it can also be seen in the fact that there is now a new status—"*semi-exilio*"—of thousands of writers and artists who never broke with the regime but who nevertheless only reside in Cuba during family holidays.

Cuba's artistic life has flourished better in these last years than its politics or economics. Guillermo Cabrera Infante, from his London command post, has continued to write ambitiously and brilliantly in Cuban Spanish, as shown in his last work, *Mi Música Extremada*. Tomás Gutiérrez Alea established an international name as a filmmaker, especially with his *Fresa y Chocolate* (*Strawberries and Chocolate*), before his early death. With his series of books after his masterly *El Ingenio* Manuel Moreno Fraginals has earned a claim as Cuba's best living historian. One has only to skim through the new journal *Encuentro*, published by Cubans in Madrid, to observe the wealth of talent.

Given this intellectual vitality, it is unsurprising that in the last ten years the most important political challenge to Castro's regime was the Declaration of Ten Intellectuals in May 1991. The ten poets, novelists, journalists, and broadcasters requested a "civic dialogue" between the regime and the opposition; the election of the members of the national assembly by secret vote;

the liberation of all political prisoners; the abandonment of the arrangements that prevent Cubans from either leaving or returning to the country; and the reestablishment of free agricultural markets in order to attempt to increase the supply of food. The official newspaper *Granma* denounced the declaration as "a new maneuver of the CIA," and its authors as "ideological heirs of annexationism," who were collaborating ideologically with "the historic enemies of the Cuban people." All but one of the signatories left Cuba within five years. Most other Cuban intellectuals signed (or were falsely said to have signed) a counterdeclaration condemning the Ten; those who refused (for example, the writer Alberto Batista Reyes) lost their employment.[3]

Another stagnation is visible in the position of blacks in Cuba. The population now seems to be about a third black, a third white, and a third mulatto. The regime has always boasted of its tolerance towards the black section of society. All the same, photographs of members of the central committee of the Cuban Communist party suggest that the majority are of pure Spanish or European blood. In this respect, too, little has changed between 1971 and 1997.

Although certain aspects of Cuba's present may appear uncannily similar to the 1970s, the word "revolution" becoming curiously close to stagnation,[4] our understanding of many historical persons and events has changed in light of new evidence. It is not simply that biographies of Castro (for example, Quirk's) or Che Guevara (for example, Castaneda's) abound. Even our view of the sinking of the *Maine* in 1898 has been changed forever by a meticulous study prepared in the 1970s by U.S. Admiral Hyman Rickover, at the time commander of the U.S. nuclear submarine fleet. In the intervals between his duties on the ocean bed, he carried out a new enquiry of naval records and gave a categorical explanation that heat from a fire in a coal bunker adjacent to the reserve magazine destroyed the *Maine*. He pointed out, much as the 1898 Spanish report by del Peral and de Salas had done, that the coal bunkers were then usually on the sides of warships, the munitions in the middle, with a metal bulkhead separating them, so that in an attack the coal would act as a buffer. The coal on the *Maine* was bituminous; it burned better

[3]For a vivid account of the suffering of one of the original signatories see Manuel Díaz Martínez's excellent article "La Carta de los Diez" in *Encuentro* 2, autumn 1996.
[4]As it did in Mexico for so long.

than the anthracite that had been considered as an alternative. Evidence indicated that the coal on the *Maine* had not been inspected for nearly twelve hours.

This conclusion, of course, exonerates Spain and makes the United States' report look distinctly discreditable. Rickover speculated as to how it was possible that the distinguished naval court of enquiry in 1898 was not told of the coal bunker fires on so many U.S. naval ships. (In 1897 Theodore Roosevelt, as assistant secretary for the Navy, had even recommended an enquiry to investigate the benefits and disadvantages of various types of coal and the causes of the spontaneous combustion that sometimes occurred.) Admiral Rickover drily commented that "the natural tendency to look for reasons which did not reflect upon the navy might have been a predisposing factor in the court's findings"; an adverse report would have cast doubt on the design of the ship. Rickover concluded, "Had the ship blown up in an American or a friendly foreign port . . . it is doubtful that an enquiry would have laid the blame on a mine."

Rickover's excellent work was published by the Naval Institute Press of Annapolis, which perhaps explains why more attention was not paid to the book. It never made its way into the mainstream of studies on the causes of the Spanish-American War of 1898. Everyone in the U.S. government in Washington in the 1960s and 1970s knew Rickover to be a highly intelligent man but he was also thought of as a nuisance, so it was easier for them to ignore the implications of his findings.

The "missile crisis" of 1962, discussed so amply in this book, is another fine example. We have learned a great deal more about that epic clash over Cuba between the Soviet Union and the United States, most recently as a result of the publication of the verbatim transcripts of the contemporary conversations between President Kennedy and his advisers in the White House. The consequence of these "revelations" is to appreciate that more than a mere agreement not to invade Cuba formed part of the settlement between the United States and the Soviet Union; the United States also agreed to withdraw their (actually out-of-date) Jupiter missiles in Turkey, provided, however, that the Soviet Union did not publicize the scheme.

A careful reading of the tapes shows, too, that President Kennedy was the most moderate of those who made the decisions in the White House; had he accepted the advice of his chiefs of staff, there would have been an invasion of Cuba by the United States that almost certainly, the editors suggest, would have led to a worldwide nuclear war. It would not be inaccurate to contrast McKinley's surrender to his advisers and an enraged public opinion in 1898 to President Kennedy's stance in 1962.

Consider the other revelations that have emerged from the 1970s onwards about U.S.-approved efforts in the early 1960s to overthrow the regime of Fidel Castro and even kill its leader. The first wave of such information occurred as a direct consequence of the U.S. Congress' Church Committee on CIA Operations in the 1960s. All manner of remarkable plots against Fidel Castro were disclosed during the proceedings. Incompetence and surrealism seem to have characterized the world's most famous intelligence agency in its heydey. In the 1990s we are still hearing of the wild plans of the past: "Operation Bingo," intended to fake an attack by Cuba on the U.S. base at Guantánamo Bay, providing a pretext for a devastating U.S. military assault on Havana; "Operation Good Times," which would have distributed photographs of an obese Castro carousing with two ladies at a banquet; "Remember the Maine," a scheme to "blow up a U.S. warship in Guantánamo Bay and blame Cuba," as one memorandum ran; and an idea whereby the United States would develop a fraudulent terrorist campaign in Washington to justify an assault. The chiefs of staff apparently endorsed these ideas as "suitable for planning purposes" on March 13, 1962.[5] We know too, thanks to the biographies of Castro by Tad Szulc and Robert Quirk, and of Che Guevara by Jorge Castaneda, much more about the conversations in early 1959 between the old Communists and the leaders of the new government, which resulted in a globally active, instead of a neutralist, Communist government.

In Cuba, history continues to play a part in the island's present as well as its immediate future. For example, in a report to the fifth plenum of the Central committee of the Communist party of Cuba in March 1996, Raúl Castro, the minister of defense, spent a good deal of time talking about the attack on the Moncada barracks, the events of 1958, and the thwarted Bay of Pigs invasion, as if they were the most recent events in the politics of the island. He even compared his and his brother's vic-

---

[5]*The New York Times*, November 19, 1997, p. A25.

tory in 1958 to Thermopylae: "During centuries," he said, "the Battle of Thermopylae has been the great legend: three hundred Spartans, even though they knew how to die heroically, could not conquer the more numerous and better-armed Persians. With the commander-in-chief [Castro], in order to defeat the last offensive of tyranny in the summer of 1958, a mere 300 rebels resisted 10,000 soldiers armed with tanks, with good artillery, and with the entire aviation and fleet of the country—and knew how to achieve a victory! The centuries will pass and even though our enemies continue to deny it, people will continue to talk of it as they do of the battle of the pass of Thermopylae, with the difference that the Spartans died heroically and lost everything, while the 300 rebels under our commander-in-chief conquered!"

In due time a full account of the years covered in this afterword will be required. For the moment, though, it seems likely that recovering a knowledge of the past may play just as crucial a part in the history of Cuba as it did in Russia before the fall of the Soviet Union. Modern Cubans need to know how Castro and his comrades gained and manipulated power, but it will also be useful—dare I say desirable—to remember the prosperous times in Cuba's past. The Cuban colony was certainly slave-powered in the 1830s, but slavery in Cuba was a more nuanced institution than in the United States. At the time of writing this afterword, it is hard to be optimistic about the future of Cuba in the short term. But in the long run Cuban history, tragic as it has been, shows that nothing is to be excluded as impossible.

HUGH THOMAS
January 1998

Appendices

     I The Cuban Oligarchy
    II Cuban Governors and Presidents
   III Who were the Cuban Indians?
    IV Kennion's Slave Concession
     V Estimated Cuban Slave Imports
    VI Outfit of a Slave Ship, 1825
   VII Slave Ships from Havana, 1825
  VIII Affidavit of Lieutenant Nott
    IX Chinese Imports to Cuba, 1847–73
     X The Last Slave Journey across the Atlantic, 1865
    XI The Attack on Moncada and Bayamo
   XII The State of Agriculture in 1959
  XIII Cuban and World Sugar Production, 1770–1970
   XIV World Raw Sugar Prices, 1900–1962

The Cuban Oligarchy

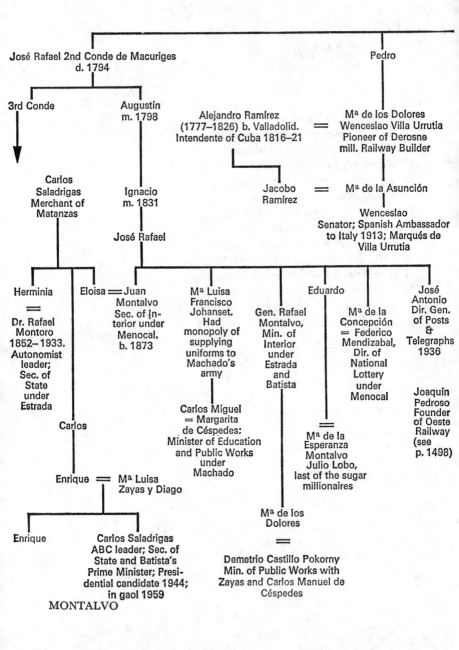

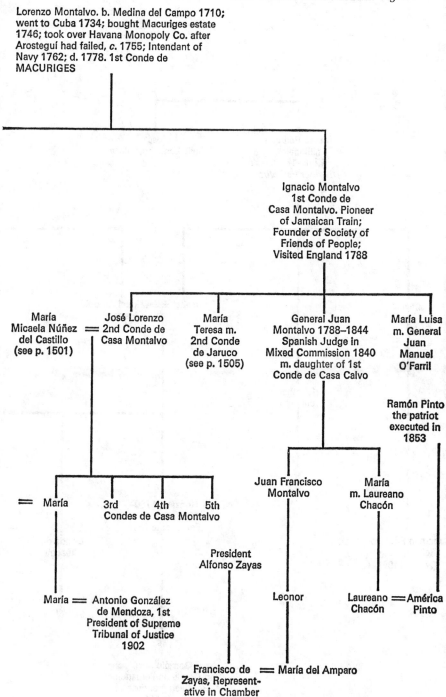

Lorenzo Montalvo. b. Medina del Campo 1710; went to Cuba 1734; bought Macuriges estate 1746; took over Havana Monopoly Co. after Arostegui had failed, c. 1755; Intendant of Navy 1762; d. 1778. 1st Conde de MACURIGES

Ignacio Montalvo 1st Conde de Casa Montalvo. Pioneer of Jamaican Train; Founder of Society of Friends of People; Visited England 1788

María Micaela Núñez del Castillo (see p. 1501) = José Lorenzo 2nd Conde de Casa Montalvo

María Teresa m. 2nd Conde de Jaruco (see p. 1505)

General Juan Montalvo 1788–1844 Spanish Judge in Mixed Commission 1840 m. daughter of 1st Conde de Casa Calvo

María Luisa m. General Juan Manuel O'Farril

Ramón Pinto the patriot executed in 1853

= María

3rd 4th 5th Condes de Casa Montalvo

Juan Francisco Montalvo

María m. Laureano Chacón

President Alfonso Zayas

María = Antonio González de Mendoza, 1st President of Supreme Tribunal of Justice 1902

Leonor

Laureano Chacón = América Pinto

Francisco de Zayas, Representative in Chamber = María del Amparo

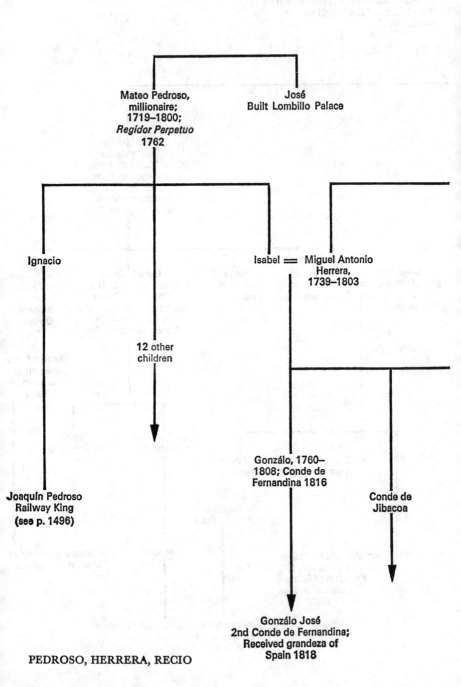

Mateo Pedroso,
millionaire;
1719–1800;
Regidor Perpetuo
1762

José
Built Lombillo Palace

Ignacio

Isabel ═ Miguel Antonio
Herrera,
1739–1803

12 other
children

Joaquín Pedroso
Railway King
(see p. 1496)

Gonzálo, 1760–
1808; Conde de
Fernandina 1816

Conde de
Jibacoa

Gonzálo José
2nd Conde de Fernandina;
Received grandeza of
Spain 1818

PEDROSO, HERRERA, RECIO

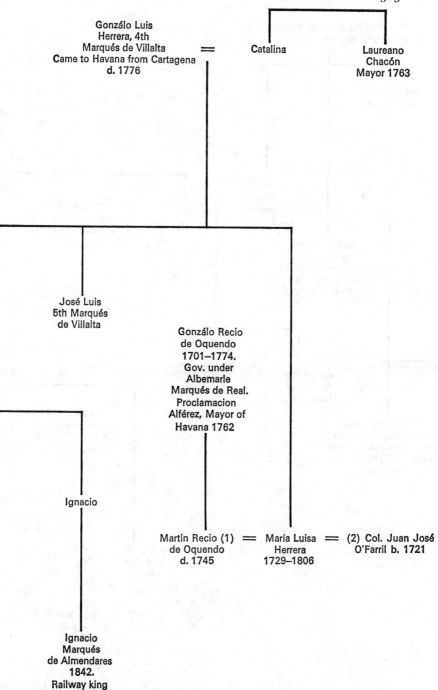

Gonzálo Luis
Herrera, 4th
Marqués de Villalta
Came to Havana from Cartagena
d. 1776

Catalina

Laureano
Chacón
Mayor 1763

José Luis
5th Marqués
de Villalta

Gonzálo Recio
de Oquendo
1701–1774.
Gov. under
Albemarle
Marqués de Real.
Proclamacion
Alférez, Mayor of
Havana 1762

Ignacio

Martín Recio (1)
de Oquendo
d. 1745

María Luisa
Herrera
1729–1806

(2) Col. Juan José
O'Farril b. 1721

Ignacio
Marqués
de Almendares
1842.
Railway king

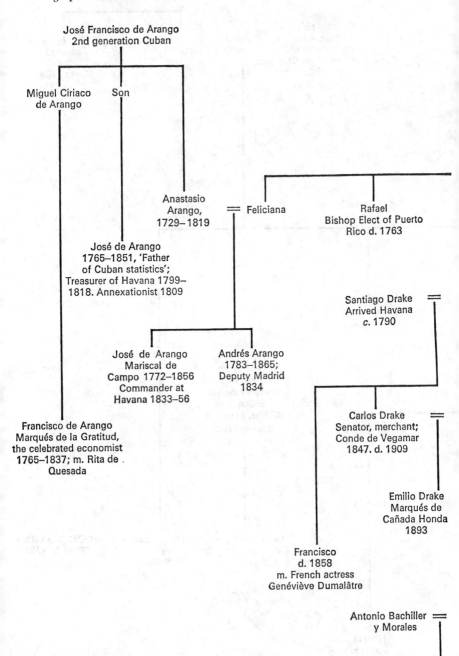

ARANGO, NÚÑEZ DE CASTILLO

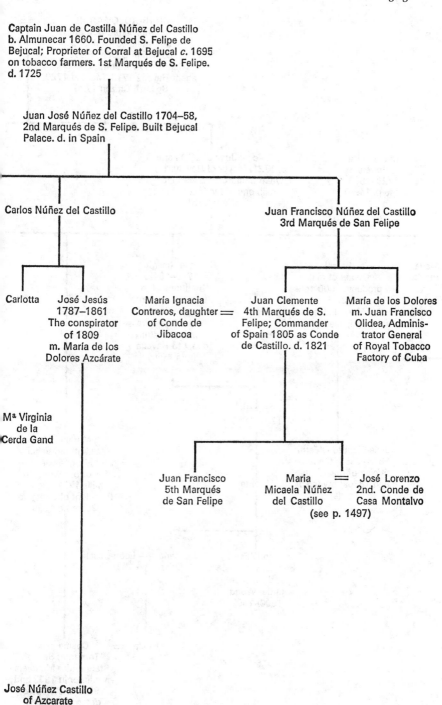

Captain Juan de Castilla Núñez del Castillo
b. Almunecar 1660. Founded S. Felipe de
Bejucal; Proprieter of Corral at Bejucal c. 1695
on tobacco farmers. 1st Marqués de S. Felipe.
d. 1725

Juan José Núñez del Castillo 1704–58,
2nd Marqués de S. Felipe. Built Bejucal
Palace. d. in Spain

Carlos Núñez del Castillo

Juan Francisco Núñez del Castillo
3rd Marqués de San Felipe

Carlota

José Jesús
1787–1861
The conspirator
of 1809
m. María de los
Dolores Azcárate

María Ignacia
Contreros, daughter =
of Conde de
Jibacoa

Juan Clemente
4th Marqués de S.
Felipe; Commander
of Spain 1805 as Conde
de Castillo. d. 1821

María de los Dolores
m. Juan Francisco
Olidea, Adminis-
trator General
of Royal Tobacco
Factory of Cuba

Mª Virginia
de la
Cerda Gand

Juan Francisco
5th Marqués
de San Felipe

Maria   =
Micaela Núñez
del Castillo

José Lorenzo
2nd. Conde de
Casa Montalvo

(see p. 1497)

José Núñez Castillo
of Azcarate

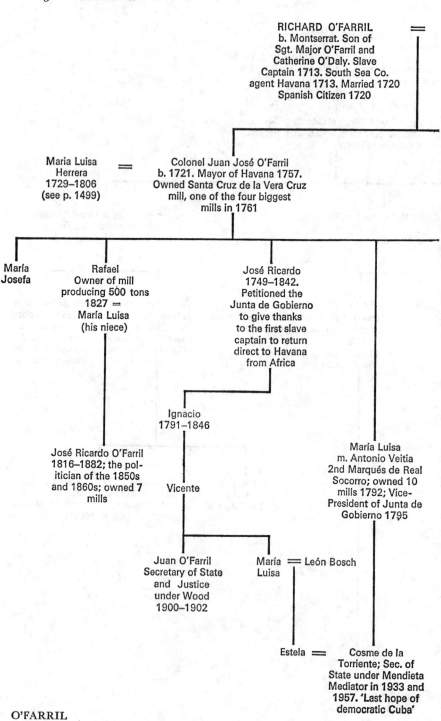

RICHARD O'FARRIL
b. Montserrat. Son of
Sgt. Major O'Farril and
Catherine O'Daly. Slave
Captain 1713. South Sea Co.
agent Havana 1713. Married 1720
Spanish Citizen 1720

Maria Luisa
Herrera
1729–1806
(see p. 1499)

Colonel Juan José O'Farril
b. 1721. Mayor of Havana 1757.
Owned Santa Cruz de la Vera Cruz
mill, one of the four biggest
mills in 1761

María
Josefa

Rafael
Owner of mill
producing 500 tons
1827 =
María Luisa
(his niece)

José Ricardo
1749–1842.
Petitioned the
Junta de Gobierno
to give thanks
to the first slave
captain to return
direct to Havana
from Africa

Ignacio
1791–1846

José Ricardo O'Farril
1816–1882; the pol-
itician of the 1850s
and 1860s; owned 7
mills

Vicente

María Luisa
m. Antonio Veitia
2nd Marqués de Real
Socorro; owned 10
mills 1792; Vice-
President of Junta de
Gobierno 1795

Juan O'Farril
Secretary of State
and Justice
under Wood
1900–1902

María Luisa = León Bosch

Estela = Cosme de la
Torriente; Sec. of
State under Mendieta
Mediator in 1933 and
1957. 'Last hope of
democratic Cuba'

O'FARRIL

María Josefa de
Arriola

Catalina 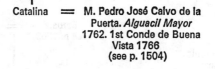 M. Pedro José Calvo de la
Puerta. *Alguacil Mayor*
1762. 1st Conde de Buena
Vista 1766
(see p. 1504)

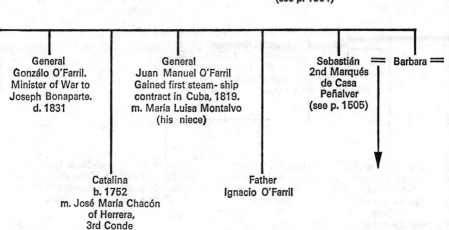

General
Gonzálo O'Farril.
Minister of War to
Joseph Bonaparte.
d. 1831

General
Juan Manuel O'Farril
Gained first steam- ship
contract in Cuba, 1819.
m. María Luisa Montalvo
(his niece)

Sebastián 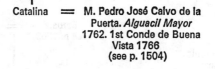 Barbara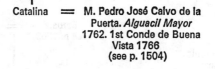
2nd Marqués
de Casa
Peñalver
(see p. 1505)

Catalina
b. 1752
m. José María Chacón
of Herrera,
3rd Conde
de Casa Bayona

Father
Ignacio O'Farril

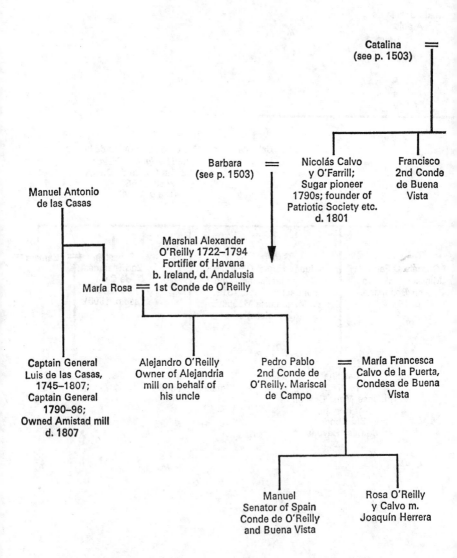

CALVO, PEÑALVER, O'REILLY, LAS CASAS

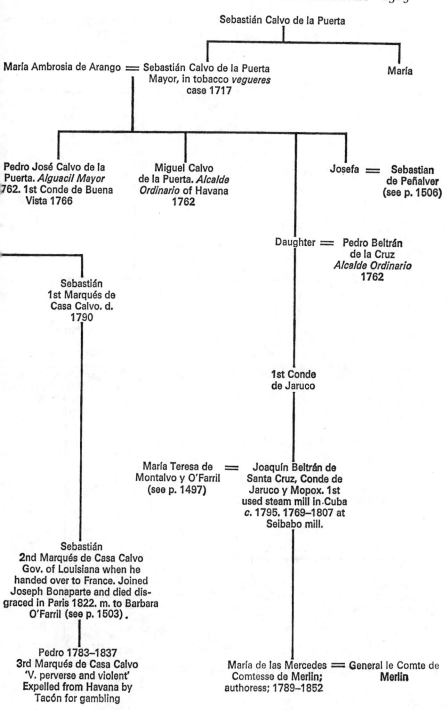

Sebastián Calvo de la Puerta

María Ambrosia de Arango ══ Sebastián Calvo de la Puerta Mayor, in tobacco *vegueres* case 1717

María

Pedro José Calvo de la Puerta. *Alguacil Mayor* 762. 1st Conde de Buena Vista 1766

Miguel Calvo de la Puerta. *Alcalde Ordinario* of Havana 1762

Josefa ══ Sebastian de Peñalver (see p. 1506)

Daughter ══ Pedro Beltrán de la Cruz *Alcalde Ordinario* 1762

Sebastián 1st Marqués de Casa Calvo. d. 1790

1st Conde de Jaruco

María Teresa de Montalvo y O'Farril (see p. 1497) ══ Joaquín Beltrán de Santa Cruz, Conde de Jaruco y Mopox. 1st used steam mill in Cuba *c.* 1795. 1769–1807 at Seibabo mill.

Sebastián 2nd Marqués de Casa Calvo Gov. of Louisiana when he handed over to France. Joined Joseph Bonaparte and died disgraced in Paris 1822. m. to Barbara O'Farril (see p. 1503).

Pedro 1783–1837 3rd Marqués de Casa Calvo 'V. perverse and violent' Expelled from Havana by Tacón for gambling

María de las Mercedes ══ General le Comte de Comtesse de Merlin; authoress; 1789–1852

Merlin

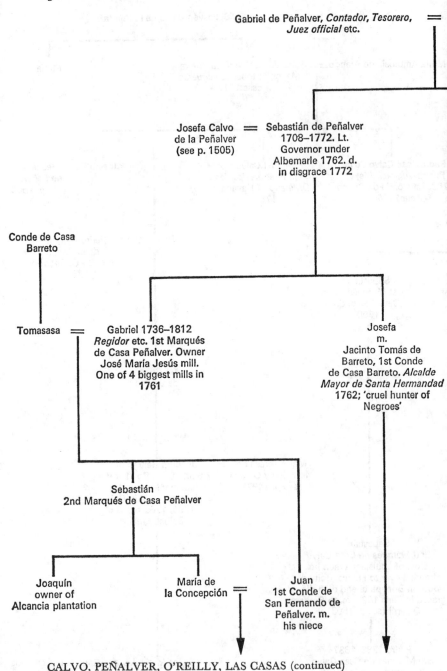

Gabriel de Peñalver, *Contador, Tesorero, Juez official* etc.

Josefa Calvo de la Peñalver (see p. 1505) = Sebastián de Peñalver 1708–1772. Lt. Governor under Albemarle 1762. d. in disgrace 1772

Conde de Casa Barreto

Tomasasa = Gabriel 1736–1812 *Regidor* etc. 1st Marqués de Casa Peñalver. Owner José María Jesús mill. One of 4 biggest mills in 1761

Josefa m. Jacinto Tomás de Barreto, 1st Conde de Casa Barreto. *Alcalde Mayor de Santa Hermandad* 1762; 'cruel hunter of Negroes'

Sebastián 2nd Marqués de Casa Peñalver

Joaquín owner of Alcancia plantation

María de la Concepción = Juan 1st Conde de San Fernando de Peñalver. m. his niece

CALVO, PEÑALVER, O'REILLY, LAS CASAS (continued)

Maria Calvo de la
Puerta (see p. 1505)

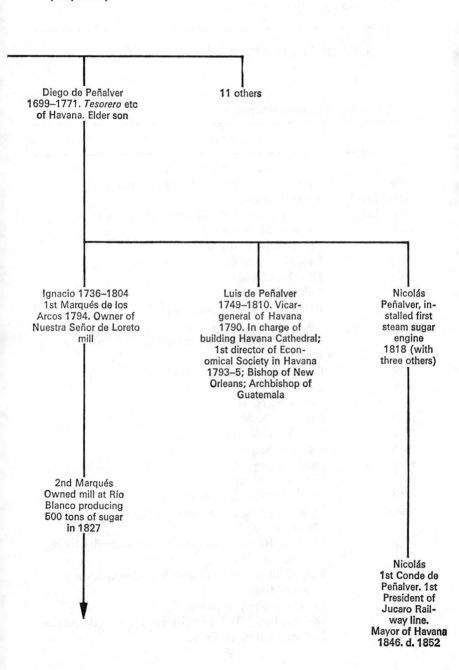

Diego de Peñalver
1699–1771. *Tesorero* etc
of Havana. Elder son

11 others

Ignacio 1736–1804
1st Marqués de los
Arcos 1794. Owner of
Nuestra Señor de Loreto
mill

Luis de Peñalver
1749–1810. Vicar-
general of Havana
1790. In charge of
building Havana Cathedral;
1st director of Econ-
omical Society in Havana
1793–5; Bishop of New
Orleans; Archbishop of
Guatemala

Nicolás
Peñalver, in-
stalled first
steam sugar
engine
1818 (with
three others)

2nd Marqués
Owned mill at Río
Blanco producing
500 tons of sugar
in 1827

Nicolás
1st Conde de
Peñalver. 1st
President of
Jucaro Rail-
way line.
Mayor of Havana
1846. d. 1852

Cuban Governors and Presidents

SPANISH GOVERNORS OF CUBA

Date	Name
1761	Juan de Prado Portocarrero
1762	Ambrosio Villapando, Conde de Ricla
1765 (June)	Diego Manrique
1765 (July)	Pascual Jiménez de Cisneros, provisional
1766	Antonio M. Bucarely
1771	Marqués de la Torre
1777	Diego J. Navarro
1781	Juan M. Cagigal
1782	Luis de Unzaga, provisional
1785	Bernardo Troncoso, provisional
	José Ezpeleta, provisional
	Domingo Cabello, provisional
(Dec)	José Ezpeleta
1789	Domingo Cabello, provisional
1790	Luis de las Casas
1796	Juan Bassecourt
1799	Salvador de Muro
1812	Juan Ruiz de Apodaca
1816	José Cienfuegos
1819	Juan M. Cagigal
1821	Nicolás de Mahy
1822	Sebastián Kindelán, provisional
1823	Dionisio Vives. Given absolute authority by royal decree of 1825
1832	Mariano Rocafort. Given absolute authority by royal decree of 1825
1834	Miguel Tacón. Given absolute authority by royal decree of 1825
1838	Lt-Gen. Joaquín Ezpeleta
1840	Lt-Gen. Pedro Telles de Girona, Príncipe de Anglona
1841	Lt-Gen. Gerónimo Valdés

Date	Name
1843 (Sept)	Lt-Gen. Francisco Javier de Ulloa, provisional
1843 (Oct)	Lt-Gen. Leopoldo O'Donnell, Count of Lucena
1848	Lt-Gen. Federico Roncali, Count of Alcoy
1850	Lt-Gen. José Gutiérrez de la Concha
1852	Lt-Gen. Valentín Canedo
1853	Lt-Gen. Juan de la Pezuela, Marqués de la Pezuela
1854	Lt-Gen. José Gutiérrez de la Concha, Marqués de la Habana, 2nd time
1859	Lt-Gen. Francisco Serrano, Duque de la Torre
1862	Lt-Gen. Domingo Dulce
1866 (May)	Lt-Gen. Francisco Lersundi
1866 (Nov)	Lt-Gen. Joaquín del Manzano
1867 (Sep)	Lt-Gen. Blas Villate, Conde de Valmaseda
1867 (Dec)	Lt-Gen. Fransisco Lersundi
1869 (Jan)	Lt-Gen. Domingo Dulce, 2nd time
1869 (2 June)	Lt-Gen. Felipe Genovés del Espinar, provisional
1869 (28 June)	Lt-Gen. Antonio Fernández y Caballero de Rodas
1870	Lt-Gen. Blas Villate, Conde de Valmaseda
1872	Lt-Gen. Francisco Ceballos
1873 (Apr)	Lt-Gen. Cándido Pieltaín
1873 (Nov)	Lt-Gen. Joaquín Jovellar
1874	Lt-Gen. José Gutiérrez de la Concha, Marqués de la Habana, 3rd time
1875 (May)	Lt-Gen. Buenaventura Carbó, provisional
1875 (June)	Lt-Gen. Blas Villate, Conde de Valmaseda
1876 (Jan)	Lt-Gen. Joaquín Jovellar, under Martínez Campos, gen. in chief
1876 (Oct)	Lt-Gen. Arsenio Martínez Campos
1879 (Feb)	Lt-Gen. Cayetano Figueroa, provisional
1879 (Apr)	Lt-Gen. Ramón Blanco
1881	Lt-Gen. Luis Prendergast, Marqués de la Victoria de las Tunas
1883 (Aug)	Gen. of Division Tomás y Regna, provisional
1883 (Sept)	Lt-Gen. Ignacio María del Castillo
1884	Lt-Gen. Ramón Fajardo
1886	Lt-Gen. Emilio Calleja
1887	Lt-Gen. Sabas Marín
1889	Lt-Gen. Manuel Salamanca
1890 (Feb)	Gen. José Sánchez Gómez, provisional
1890 (Apr)	Lt-Gen. José Chinchilla

Date	Name
1890 (Aug)	Lt-Gen. Camilo Polavieja
1892	Lt-Gen. Alejandro Rodríguez Arias
1893 (July)	Gen. Jose Arderius, provisional
1893 (Sept)	Lt-Gen. Emilio Calleja
1895	Capt. Gen. Arsenio Martínez Campos
1896 (Jan)	Lt-Gen. Sabas Marín y González
1896 (Feb)	Lt-Gen. Valeriano Weyler
1897	Lt-Gen. Ramón Blanco
1898	Lt-Gen. Adolfo Jiménez Castellanos

U.S. MILITARY GOVERNORS

Date	Name
1899 (Jan)	General John Brooke
1899 (Dec)	General Leonard Wood

CUBAN PRESIDENTS

Date	Name
1902	General Tomás Estrada Palma
1906 (Sept)	William Howard Taft; provisional U.S. Governor
1906 (Oct)	Charles E. Magoon; provisional U.S. Governor
1909	General José Miguel Gómez
1913	General Mario García Menocal
1921	Alfredo Zayas
1925	General Gerardo Machado
1933 (Aug)	Carlos Manuel de Céspedes
1933 (3 Sept)	The 'Pentarquía' (Dr Ramón Grau San Martín, Porfirio Franco, José Miguel Irisarri, Sergio Carbó, Guillermo Portela)
1933 (10 Sept)	Dr Ramón Grau San Martín
1934 (16 Jan)	Carlos Hevia
1934 (17 Jan)	Colonel Carlos Mendieta
1936 (May)	Miguel Mariano Gómez
1936 (12 Dec)	José Antonio Barnet
1936 (24 Dec)	Federico Laredo Bru
1940	Fulgencio Batista
1944	Dr Ramón Grau San Martín
1948	Dr Carlos Prío
1952	Fulgencio Batista
1959 (Jan)	Manuel Urrutia
1959 (July)	Dr Osvaldo Dorticós

Who were the Cuban Indians?

(i)

The Indians, native-born pre-Columbian inhabitants of the island, played a part in the development of modern Cuba, as well as Spaniards and Negroes. Their contributions are found in language (particularly place names) and also in habits. Thus many common Spanish-Cuban words have an Indian origin: most of the common words beginning 'Gua' are Indian in origin, such as *guajiro*, the Cuban word for an independent farmer, probably the Indian word for a common man. Most of these words refer to agricultural techniques. Havana (or la Habana) is merely 'savanna' or plain, the S and H being interchangeable in the Indian language. Other place names have the same origin. Similarly, the most typical Cuban house throughout its history is the Indian *bohío*, and known as such. Certain Indian agricultural methods are also inherited, such as the continued use of the *guayo*, or cassava grater, made by driving sharp flints into a wooden slab. The mute dogs which so impressed Columbus have some descendants among the wild pariah dogs of Oriente; and tobacco, the principal source of pleasure of the Indians, has also been taken over by the Cubans, as by the world.

The Cuban Indians were for a long time thought to have been destroyed by their Spanish conquerors in the sixteenth century. It would, however, be more accurate to think of them as absorbed. When Columbus appeared off the north coast of Cuba, the island seemed, like other Caribbean islands, fully occupied. Seventy years later, the Indians had almost disappeared – so much so that it is sometimes suggested that they were almost totally destroyed in this period. The matter has been seriously distorted. The population of Cuba in 1492 was probably not 300,000, as suggested by the Indians' chief propagandist, Father Bartolomé de Las Casas (himself one of the first conquistadors in Cuba from 1511 to 1514). Las Casas' figures, even though those of a near eyewitness, were always liable to exaggeration and were often intended as hyperbolic: thus, in a famous passage, he described how 10 Spaniards on horseback 'could despatch 100,000 Indians without 100 escaping'. Las Casas could only guess;[1] he was less well equipped than future genera-

---

[1] Like most brilliant Spaniards of his generation, he was a converted Jew at a time when the Spaniards were treating the Jews badly – one reason why his estimate of Spanish illiberalism tinged towards the Indians may be tempered with exaggeration.

tions to make a guess, since they have archaeological findings to help them; his guess is no more likely to be accurate than those who say, looking at a mass meeting in the Plaza Cívica, Havana, in 1970, that a million people are present. In the sixteenth century, exaggeration was anyway frequent. Even Oviedo, Las Casas' critic and antagonist over the question of the treatment of Indians, alleged that there were in Cuba only 500 Indians in 1548, there having been a million or more in 1492.[2] A more recent estimate is 60,000, accepted by Cuban historians of the first rank such as Ramiro Guerra and Emeterio Santovenia. The lowest estimate and the one to which I incline is 16,000.[3]

Another unknown factor is the number of Spaniards who had children by Indian women; their offspring was regarded as in no way racially different from the Spaniards. In the rest of the Spanish Empire the same situation prevailed; a recent student of Mexican population of the sixteenth century speculated that in Mexico 'it may well be that a majority of the so-called Spanish were really *mestizos*'.[4] This was probably at least as true of Cuba, where the Indians did not constitute such a large element of the population as in Mexico. Such *mestizos* lived as Spaniards – imperial-born Spaniards certainly, and therefore, from the beginning, socially inferior to the *peninsulares* who came out from Spain itself, but not different from those of pure Spanish blood born in Cuba or elsewhere in the Empire. There are few references to this subject in the long list of Spanish decrees affecting the government of the Indies, apart from an instruction by Ferdinand in respect of mixed marriages in Hispaniola: if a Spaniard took an Indian wife, her relations were 'understandably' not to be granted to that particular Spaniard for service on his *encomienda*,[5] while Columbus was allowed to take to Haiti only one woman for every ten emigrants.[6]

The archaeologist who has done the most field work on the Cuban Indians on the spot, the North American M. R. Harrington, certainly believed that a majority of the Cuban 'Spaniards' of the late sixteenth century were the off-spring of marriages between Spaniards and Indians and that intermarriage contributed to the apparent extinction of the original inhabitants.[7] It certainly appears likely, from the mere fact of

[2] *Historia General*, qu. *Documents of West Indian History*, p. 111.

[3] The highest estimate of population of pre-Columbian Cuba was 600,000 (*Handbook of the South American Indians* IV p. 542).

[4] Borah, W., *New Spain's Century of Depression*, p. 6; see also Cook, The Mexican Population in 1793 'Human Biology' XVI, December 1942, pp. 500–504.

[5] Quoted *Documents of West Indian History*.

[6] Morison, *Admiral of the Ocean Sea* II, p. 57.

[7] Harrington, *Cuba before Columbus*, p. 140. (No. 17 of the publications of the Museum of the American Indians). Here Harrington is following the speculation of Francisco Vidal y Carete, *Estudio de las Razas Humanas*, pp. 81–93. The neglect of that book is doubtless explained by the fact that it was published in Madrid in the middle of the Spanish–American war, in 1897. Irving Rouse, *Handbook of the South American Indians*, p. 519, makes the same point.

the immense numbers of Indian words which have survived into contemporary Cuban Spanish, that the Indian blood which continued in Cuba was stronger than is usually supposed.[8]

Even if the most gloomy figures for the Indians are accepted and it is supposed that the Indians had sunk to about 5,000 in 1550,[9] this number was still greatly superior to the number of Spaniards, who could not have been more than 700[10] in that year. Here Cuba was in contrast with the other major Spanish colonies of the Caribbean – Hispaniola, the Bahamas, Jamaica and Puerto Rico.

The Cuban population in general appears to have developed as follows: in 1535 the Indians allegedly numbered 5,000, the Spaniards 300, the Negroes 1,000; the population in 1602 was probably 20,000, of whom 13,000 were in Havana, but there is no evidence of racial differences. In 1662 the population was probably 30,000 – whites numbering a little more than Negroes; the pure-bred Indians were then estimated as between 3,000 and 4,000.

Accepting some anyway of these figures as accurate, how the Cuban population moved from 5,700 in 1550 (5,000 Indians plus 700 Spaniards) to 20,000 in 1602 we do not know. But what seems likely is less that the Indian population disappeared than that the habit of reckoning Indians separately from Spaniards disappeared. Surely here exists one of those examples of 'inspired reality' which is such a feature of Spanish history.

Curiously enough, Cuba almost alone of Spanish colonies in the New World seems to have increased its population between about 1550 and 1600. Owing partly to two catastrophic epidemics in 1545–6 and 1576–9, Mexico declined from perhaps $6\frac{1}{2}$ million in 1540 to about $2\frac{1}{2}$ million in 1597 – declining still further in all probability to only $\frac{1}{2}$ million in 1650; and probably the rest of the Empire also dropped. Haiti and Puerto Rico barely kept going at all. Cuba increased because of the large shifting population centred on Havana. Spain herself underwent a demographic as well as an economic decline from 1575 since, bad though economic conditions were, food was still more abundant in the Empire than in Spain herself.[11]

[8] This subject is not discussed at any length in Guerra & Santovenia etc, whose *Historia de Cuba* simply says: 'Don Diego Velázquez and a few conquerors arrived in Cuba with Spanish women, creating families temporarily domiciled in the island, while others settled down with Indians; but the larger part of the masculine population . . . did not get as far as founding a home or creating much of a family. Later however . . . many married men had illegitimate children, distance and isolation making for the break-up of social morals, making '*la barraganía*' the most general type of union before 1555' (I, p. 235).

[9] According to Guerra, *Manual de Historia de Cuba*, p. 25. I. A. Wright, *The Early History of Cuba*, says, 2,000 only. The most recent work of Guerra's (with others) sticks to 'not more than 5,000 in 1555'.

[10] This figure given by Rouse in *Handbook of the South American Indians*, p. 519.

[11] Braudel estimates the population of Spain at 3,089,894 in 1530; 4,004,730 in 1541; 6,031,440 in 1594. Then came the terrible epidemic of 1599–1600. Between 1594 and 1694 Spanish

If it is true that most of the earliest settlers in Cuba came from Andalusia – and this seems to be the case – then that might be an added reason for thinking intermarriage likely. For many Andalusians in the early sixteenth century already had mixed blood, partly Jewish, partly Moorish; while the ruinous controversy in Spain over purity of blood, which might even have led these mixed groups into an intolerance of their own if faced with a new subject people, did not get under way until the 1520s at the earliest.

To sum up, the Cuban white population was first constituted by the 300 or so followers of Velázquez. Shortly afterwards this was increased by other colonists from Spain or elsewhere. Some of these moved on with Cortés, or later to Peru. From about 1530 until 1562 the white Spanish population remained roughly constant, emigration from Spain being then almost exclusively directed to the mainland. Some Canary islanders and some officials came to Cuba while the sons of some officials stayed. By 1560 it would seem there existed a new native generation, some pure Spanish, some Indian–Spanish, more Indians still than either; of the first two groups, this generation were far more locally minded than their fathers – having had no formal education, no education in wars, and no education of the world, and knowing nothing save the island. From 1562 until 1607, on the other hand, there was a great increase above all in transient persons (*forasteros*) in contrast with *vecinos* – men who had houses.

This argument is not to deny the cruelty practised by the Spaniards when they first reached Cuba, nor to say that this cruelty was not a large factor in the loss of population suffered by the Indians. Much of Las Casas' denunciations of his own countrymen have the irresistible stamp of authenticity. As in Haiti, the Cuban Indians were divided up into work-shifts of 50 to 100 to be at the service of the Spaniards, who were formally obliged to instruct the Indians in Christianity in return. This famous so-called system of *encomienda* (commendation), an institution used by the Crown in medieval Castille to make temporary grants of territory reclaimed from the Moors to noblemen, was considered a distinct advance on any system of simple slavery or mere division – both of which had been practised to begin with in Haiti. But in reality there was little difference.

What really broke the Indians in the Caribbean, however, was perhaps less the drudgery than the destruction of the old customs and

cities lost half their population; Burgos was in ruins, Segovia a desert. Between 1600 and 1650 Spain lost *en gros* one quarter of her population, mostly in the centre, not the periphery. Braudel also speaks of '*les quelque cent mille Espagnols qui ont quittés l'Espagne*' (Braudel, p. 355–8; see also Earl Hamilton in *Economic History Review*, May 1935, p. 169).

community life. The Laws of Burgos of 1512 explicitly forbade dancing, painting bodies, or getting drunk, and provided that (as in Johannesburg in the 1950s) the old dwellings of the Indians were to be burned 'so that they might lose the longing to return to them, although [it was allowed] in the removal violence should not be used but much gentleness'.[12]

Yet in fact what might have been a tolerable though harsh royal attitude was made intolerable by the way it was carried out. Las Casas described how, in 1511–14, the Indian men were taken off to the gold mines while their wives were left behind to till the soil: 'Husband and wives were never together nor did they see each other in eight or ten months or in a whole year and when, at the end of this time . . . they were together again, the men were so tired . . . from hunger and work and the women no less, that they had no interest in love and so ceased to have children.' Infant mortality was very high 'because the mothers . . . had no milk'. The agriculture of the Indians in Cuba meantime needed constant attention and, when neglected, there was simply not enough food.[13] Sometimes as many as a hundred killed themselves, by drinking poisonous sap from the cassava fruit 'by way of amusement', the historian Oviedo noted, apparently without irony.[14] It does seem that the decline of the Indian population derived as much from the collapse in living standards after the conquest – the new diseases and the disruption of the natural economy (the same reasons which caused the collapse of the Mexican population)[15] – as from straightforward massacre or overwork. In addition, Cortés took some 3,000 Cuban Indians to Mexico and Narváez after him. Some Indians fled to Florida.[16]

These attitudes were normal in respect of all the Indians of the Caribbean during the years 1493–1515. Spanish activity was, however, worse in Haiti and Puerto Rico than in Cuba. The sober judge of Haiti, Alonso de Zuazo, estimated that the population of that island had dropped from an estimated 1,130,000 in 1492 to 11,000 in 1518[17] – which if, as usual, a likely exaggeration must at least indicate something of the shock caused. Oviedo, no friend of the Indians, believed that the population of Hispaniola sank from over a million in 1492 to 500 in 1548.[18] The Haitian Indians were certainly more numerous than those in Cuba and they bore the full brunt of the gold rush in its early days. But the story is the

---

[12] 'El Texto de Las Leyes de Burgos de 1512', *Revista de Historia de América* (1938, No. 4, pp. 5–79), qu. Hanke, *The Spanish Struggle for Justice in the New World*, p. 24.
[13] Loven, *Origins of Tainan Culture*, p. 497.
[14] Oviedo, *Historia General*, qu. *Documents*, p. 111.
[15] Borah, *New Spain's Century of Depression*, p. 3.
[16] *Handbook of the South American Indians*.
[17] Letter, 22 January 1518, qu. *Documents*, p. 84.
[18] Oviedo, qu. *Documents of West Indian History*, p. 111.

same too of the other two Spanish settlements of the region, Puerto Rico and Jamaica.[19]

To justify this destruction the Spaniards devised many charges against the Indians. They were said to be homosexual and promiscuous, shiftless, with other vices 'so ugly that many are too obscure to be listened to'. They were cannibals, had no system of justice, were lazy, cowardly, went about shamelessly naked, told lies, gloried in getting drunk and, worse still, got drunk on 'fumes and certain herbs', taking more pride in going off to the woods and eating roots, spiders and other filth than in the Spanish way of life. They were inattentive in Church, forgot the teachings of the faith which they had just learned, saying that they wished to change neither their customs nor their gods. In addition, they were 'ungrateful'.[20] Some Spaniards even complained that the Indians gave away objects for nothing and that their skulls were so thick that the Europeans had to take care in fighting not to strike them on the head lest their swords were blunted.[21]

If these charges seem obviously false or absurd, it would also appear that the Indians were less than the angelic and kind people described by Las Casas and Columbus. Columbus, in a passionately enthusiastic note on his first voyage, described the Cubans' houses as 'quite the most lovely' that he had seen, 'well-swept and clean and their furnishings very well arranged . . . [full of] images made like women and many heads like masks, very well worked. There were (and this is an observation he specially emphasized) dogs that never barked; wild animals kept in the houses (as pets, not beasts of burden); and wonderful outfits of nets and hooks and fishing tackle.'[22]

(ii)

There were three Indian races in Cuba – the Tainos, the Ciboneys and the Guanajatabeyes – of whom the most important were the Tainos, though the earliest inhabitants of Cuba were the Guanajatabeyes. The Tainos were a branch of the Arawak race which had dominated all the Antilles the previous generation – but only the preceding generation. Their language, common to all the Arawaks in the Antilles and the

[19] Captain Juan Melgarejo, Governor of Puerto Rico, reported on 1 January 1582 that Puerto Rico (settled in 1512) had had a population of 5,500 Indians in 1514. By 1582 there were none left. (*Documents*, p. 85.) There are a remarkable abundance of pre-Columbian sites and remains in Puerto Rico to substantiate a high figure, and Adolf de Hortos, in the *Handbook of the South American Indians*, estimates that 200,000 was an accurate figure (*op. cit.*, p. 540).

[20] It was Oviedo (*Historia General* IV, ch. iii, vol. i, pp. 142–6) who made the charge of ingratitude. For other charges see *Report of the Jeronomite Commission* to Cardinal Cisneros, 1516, cited Tapia y Rivera, *Biblioteca Histórica*, p. 208–24, and quoted *Documents*, p. 134; the speech of Fray Ortiz before the Council of the Indies, 1512, is quoted *Documents*, p. 108–9.

[21] Hanke, *The Spanish Struggle for Justice*, p. 11.

[22] Columbus' Journal.

Bahamas, was Amazonian in origin.[23] They evidently came in two waves from South America, the first, referred to sometimes as 'sub-Tainos' about 1400, the second, Tainos proper, about 1460. They were of medium height, broad-headed, strong-boned, with high cheekbones, high brows, flat noses, bad teeth, lips not too full, straight hair, copper skins, lithe and supple bodies. They were somewhat lethargic but intelligent and emotional.[24]

They could count up to ten, but had no writing system.

Archaeological evidence has greatly increased our knowledge of these people.[25] Some of the furnishings observed by Columbus have been recovered: chairs with four legs and carved backs; a hammock (*hamaca*) to sleep in, six to eight feet long, made of cotton or string-work: clay bowls for mixing food and wooden bowls for eating from, also calabashes for drinking and for bailing boats. The houses themselves were the *bohíos*, a version of which can still be seen in Cuba, made from palm and bamboo, but big enough for twenty people. They had no floors, and their roofs had to be renewed every two or three years. But the structures were strongly built, adequate to withstand hurricanes. There were two entrances – one for men, one for women – but no doors. These buildings were not laid out in streets but were built higgledy-piggledy all over the town.

Strictly speaking, however, under the Indians, only a chief's house was called a *bohío*, these being rectangular, and gabled, while commoners' houses (*cañayos*) were smaller, circular, and with a conical roof. The Indians had fire, obtained by hollowing a piece of dry *guagiona* wood. The powder of the wood rubbed off finally caught fire. They also got fire by tying two sticks tightly together and forcing a third between them.

There was not much gold in Cuba, as the Spaniards were to find to their disgust – much less than in Haiti. Some gold was washed out of the rivers. More had been imported, chiefly for decoration, from Haiti and also Yucatan, in both nuggets and in plate form. Some copper was also mined, near the surface. Stone beads were worn, and shells (including snail shells) were used as necklaces, sometimes worked into figurines, or human faces, or birds.

The extent of private property is uncertain. What there was, was handed on through the mother, or as gifts at death or marriage. Perhaps food and other material was held in common.

Mothers washed their babies in the sea or in rivers, immediately after birth. Bridegrooms had to pay a bride price, perhaps in the form of work, possibly in a form of hire purchase (in beads or plate of copper

[23] *Handbook of the South American Indians*, p. 507.
[24] *Op.cit.*, p. 522.
[25] See particularly M. R. Harrington, *op. cit*; S. Loven, *op. cit*; and Seward, *Handbook of the South American Indians*, IV, '*The Caribbean Tribes*', p. 495–546.

alloy) over the engagement period of one month. During this time, the bride remained secluded. Then came the wedding festival, the bride's hair was cut, and there was dancing and eating: the bride's father would give beads to the groom.

The diet of the Tainos was quite elaborate. They fished, hunted, and grew vegetables and fruits. They fished directly for molluscs with their hands diving for them if necessary. Even lobsters were caught by hand. Big fish were shot with arrows and harpoons, and also poisoned with the herb *conani*. They used a small sucking fish, *remora*, to draw up turtles and even sharks, on hooks of sharp twigs (they envied the European hooks immediately). Fish weirs were built on rivers. Inland, the Cubans used baskets and nets. The fish when caught were placed in ponds along with turtles, for use when necessary.

Hunting was more primitive. They beat up game with their dumb dogs. Of the birds killed, the *biaya* got off the ground only with difficulty and was tired out by the Indians running after it. There was the *guaniguanaje*, a small rodent who died out very quickly after the arrival of European dogs. The Indians also hunted the *hutias* (another small rodent) at night by the light of *cocuyos*. Ducks and geese were caught by huntsmen who hid under calabashes in rivers, floating as if naturally; one duck would be attracted and dragged down, and others would gather to investigate and also be caught. (These also would be kept, in corrales.) Iguanas were reserved for the feasts of chiefs, being caught first by being irritated, and so forced to show their teeth: the huntsman would force a stick in the mouth, capture the animal and tie him to a tree until the time came to go back home. A more unusual dish was the *megaloccus*, a form of giant sloth which also died out quickly after the arrival of the Europeans.[26] The Tainos also caught parrots, luring them by holding a parrot already caught and then lassoing them; they were not eaten but traded as pets or decoration: the Spaniards were said to have seized 10,000 parrots at Sagua la Grande.[27]

The Tainos skinned what they caught but did not take out the entrails except those of the iguana. Meat and fish were roasted on spits. A large pot of pepper existed in which meat could be kept for several days after the hunt.

They worked the soil with fire-hardened sticks (*coa*), their only tool being the dibble. Their agricultural technique consisted of building mounds of earth to loosen the ground underneath, to protect roots of plants and to be ready for a form of ash compost from burnt trees. Urine was also used to fertilize the ground. (Irrigation was used in south-west Haiti). They grew beans, peanuts, a type of maize, fruit trees and yucca –

[26] Harrington, II, p. 257.
[27] Navarrete, I, p. 31. Doubtless, the figure is still exaggerated.

a heavy vegetable still used in the twentieth century. Their staple food was the cassava manioc, a root from which – and this must have been an economic achievement of great importance – they successfully drained the poisonous juice. They scraped skin off the root with flint, shredded it on a board covered with smaller flints and drained the juice through a cotton or woven stocking: one end of the stocking was hung from a branch, the other weighted with a stone; or else a woman would stand on a cross bar attached to the stocking. A cake was made from the shreds and baked on a clay griddle set on three stones over the fire.[28] Their maize was grown on hillsides, planted twice a year during a new moon and when it was raining. Children kept birds away, standing on platforms in trees. Grain was ground between two stones, or maybe wooden mortars. It was used both for soup and also apparently for a type of beer. Cassava was planted twice a year. Every few years the Tainos changed fields. They also used peppers (for the preservation of meat) and cinnamon and an aromatic fruit for use as soap.[29] They appear to have eaten three or four times a day. After the third meal, they often took an emetic and were sick in the river. Then they went back and danced, took snuff and tobacco and ate their last meal. Las Casas noted they had food in hand (in Camagüey) for 5–8 days.[30] Cakes were stored in dry leaves.

This raises the question of tobacco and snuff. The first Spaniards in Cuba had been struck by one curious habit of the Indians: 'many people going backwards and forwards to their villages, men and women, and the men always carried a firebrand in their hands and certain plants which have been dried . . . and [which] they light at one end and at the other they suck or chew or draw in with their breath . . . [and] it intoxicates them and in this way they say they do not feel tired.'[31] This tobacco – the word derived from a tubular instrument for inhaling snuff (*cahoba*) – originally had a partly religious, partly medicinal use.[32] But by the conquest it had become popular, though it was still also used for religious purposes.[33] Snuff was used to get in touch with the spirit world[34] and its inhalation obviously had disturbing effects: the Tainos often sank into sleeps in which they saw visions.[35] Cigars were wrapped up in leaves of trees, or perhaps in maize leaves. Pipes do not seem to have been used.

No one cultivated any crop in order to exchange it for profit or other crops. But pottery was made on an open hearth, chiefly

[28] *Handbook*, p. 523.
[29] See Loven's analysis, *op. cit.*, p. 404–7.
[30] Las Casas, vol 65, cap. 17.
[31] Las Casas, *Historia de las Indias*, I, ch. 45, (LL) Vol. 62, p. 332.
[32] See Fernando Ortiz, *Cuban Counterpoint: Tobacco and Sugar*, p. 119 ff.
[33] Loven, p. 396.
[34] *Ibid*, p. 388.
[35] Oviedo, I, p. 131.

into gourds and bowls. The Tainos carved, made baskets, spun cloth –
in one building the Spaniards claimed to have seen over fifty-five
tons of cloth. The technique may have been one of netting rather
than weaving. Cord was made from hemp, cotton, grass or magüey
fibre.

Men went about naked. Girls over the age of puberty wore a small
cloth and married women wore a longer skirt hanging from their waists –
the longer it was, the grander the woman. Both sexes painted themselves, men usually red, the women usually white, though they also used
other colours, apparently not only during festivals or at war. The Tainos
deliberately tried to lengthen the heads of their race by elaborate
treatment of the skulls of children: these were pressed against boards and
cushions. Hair was fastened in a band. Men were beardless. Ears were
pierced for rings. When it rained, they carried palm shoots. They pol-
ished stone into knives and axes but had not developed the wheel. They
were therefore far more mobile by water than by land and few of their
settlements were far from the sea. Their (unpainted) canoes (*canoas*)
were powerful and swift, more so than Spanish rowboats.[36] Columbus saw
one canoe made from a cedar trunk which could carry 150 persons, presumably intended for very long journeys, with a reserve crew and food
supplies.[37] Such journeys might cover the 100 miles to Jamaica, the 120
miles to Yucatan, or to the Bahamas. The largest canoe which Columbus
saw at sea had seventy to eighty oarsmen.[38] The paddles used were about
three feet long, sharpened to a point, with a crossbar handle at the top,
enabling each stroke to be as long as possible.[39] The canoes were made
from cedar or cotton wood. The Tainos rowed rhythmically and very
fast, without stops apparently even on long journeys. Such skill made up
for a certain backwardness in boat design, such as taking in water and
turning over easily.

The Tainos believed in a Supreme Being, invisible, living in the
sky, whose name was Yocahu Vagua Maorcoti.[40] He was of a passive
nature. It is uncertain if he was regarded as the Prime Mover, and he
was not supposed to be responsible for rain. He was identified with
harvest and fruitfulness and his name, Yocahu, had probably a connection with the word Yucca, the Cuban vegetable.[41] He had a mother with
five names and a maternal uncle. It was believed that man originally came from two caves in Haiti named Cacibaginagua and Amiau-

[36] Oviedo, I, p. 171, qu. Loven, p. 416.
[37] Navarrete, I, p. 224; Las Casas, vol 62, cap. 354.
[38] Navarrete, I, p. 335; Loven, p. 416. Both Columbus and Las Casas speak of honeycombs
in Cuba which could only have come from Yucatan (Loven, p. 59).
[39] See illustration Harrington, I, fig. 50.
[40] Las Casas, *Apol. Hist*, (Serrano y Sanz ed.), p. 321.
[41] Loven, p. 563.

ba, guarded by Yocahu's son, Marocael.[42] Marocael one night left the door unguarded; the first human beings escaped. Most people came out of Cacibaginagua, but a few, ancestors of the upper class, came out of Amiauba. Marocael hastened back and was turned to stone. There were legends that the women were then taken by a certain Guaguiona to the island of Matinino, and the children to Ganin, where they turned into frogs through lack of food. Guaguiona went back to the island of Matinino, where he had various adventures with women and caught syphilis. The other men, meantime, on Haiti, found a substitute for women in a neutral group of beings whom they found in trees and who were given female genitals by woodpeckers. The Sun and Moon were believed to have come from another cave, Gionoucua.

The Tainan religion was dominated less by Yocahu than by a series of *zenus* (gods) represented by idols. Everyone had at least one and often up to ten *zenus*. The chief often gave his *zenus* a special house but ordinary people kept theirs at home. Most *zenus* were in the shape of grotesque beings, but also animals and vegetables. They were made of cotton, wood, stone, shell, and gold. Some were geometric. Others, such as ancestors' bones, needed no preparation. The powers of *zenus* varied: when people desired to use their *zenus*, they would place snuff on their head and sniff it up through a forked tube, so inducing visions. Some people fasted, or were sick, before communicating with their *zenus*. Their views were also revealed by medicine men or sometimes by chiefs. *Zenus* were treated as if they were human beings needing food and drink, being bathed with yucca juice or cassava bread. Sometimes they were put in caverns such as the enormous, hot, bat-ridden and cockroach-laden underground chambers near Maisi.[43] Such shrines often had drawings on the stones in them. *Zenus* were consulted most often during illnesses, in respect of treatment and chances of cure. If medicine men were later found to have been mistaken, and ill-intent was proved, they were killed.

The Tainos also believed that human beings had spirits, those of live people being called *goetz* and of dead ones *opia*. After death, *opia* went to a paradise named Coalbai, said to be a beautiful valley in Haiti. Sometimes at night *opia* were understood to return and receive a Cuban fruit which they had liked. They were thought evil and people travelled in groups in order to avoid them. Tainan women often felt for the navel of their partners to make sure that an *opia* (who were known never to have navels) was not trying to rape them.

There were three classes among the Tainos in Cuba before Columbus:

[42] Real caves in the Sierra de Caonao. The similarity between the names Caonao and Canaan may have caused the bizarre seventeenth-century rumour that the Caribbean Indians were really Jewish.

[43] Harrington, *op. cit.*, p. 1.

chiefs, commoners and a middle class of free men who formed a kind of officer corps (*nitaynos*). These classes apparently did not inter-marry. The chief (*cacique*, a word which passed later into Spanish) was a despot. He arranged the daily routine of hunting and tilling; and had powers of life and death. Such powers were delegated to sub-chiefs or headmen of villages. Chiefs inherited through the eldest sons of their eldest sister, unless there were no sisters – in which case the sons in-herited. Women seem also to have been able to inherit. The chief wore a gold crown and usually had a big canoe with its bows painted. Subsidi-ary or lesser chiefs wore feather head-dresses, though this seems only to have applied to Haiti. Cuban chiefs are believed to have had *jus primae noctis*.[44] The *nitaynos* supervised communal work and acted gener-ally as the chief's aides. They and the chiefs attended *cahoba* meetings at which snuff was taken, to decide major issues of war and peace. They had certain judicial duties. Las Casas says he often saw chiefs eating from the same dish as everyone else. But on any critical occasion the chiefs kept apart and consulted the *zenus* whose idols they had in their house. The commoners did the work of the village, but not as slaves; it is likely that many of the latter (*naboria*) were Ciboneys (that is, earlier inhabitants) who had been captured, or who willingly preferred to live where they had always done rather than emigrate north or far westward.

It appears that, in all classes, promiscuity but not polygamy was the rule. Only the chiefs had more than one wife. Divorce was probably rare, though Las Casas reached this conclusion only by observing that couples often seemed old. Promiscuity seems to have taken the form of a kind of hospitable prostitution. There were also homosexuals who dressed as women, even though female dress consisted of such a small cloth.[45] The tasks of women were, of course, to prepare the food, but they also shared in the cultivation with digging sticks. Fathers apparently taught their children all they needed to know of conventions, religion and politics.

The most notable disease in pre-Columbian Cuba was syphilis, ap-parently a mild form which when caught by the Spaniards turned out more serious. That syphilis was taken back to Spain from Cuba and the other West Indian islands by Columbus seems certain.[46] The Tainos had had syphilis for so long that they had developed elaborate methods of treating it and their myths often featured heroic oarsmen rowing thousands of miles in search of therapeutic herbs.

Medicine men fasted before visiting the sick. They blackened their faces with soot, and consulted their *zenu*. In the sick man's presence he

[44] *Handbook*, IV, p. 543.
[45] Las Casas, *Historia*, vol. 63, p. 57.
[46] Oviedo (vol i, p. 85–6) says that Spaniards contracted syphilis on Columbus's first voyage. For a discussion see Loven; and Morison, *Admiral of the Ocean Sea*.

took a herb called *gioia* which made him sick. He lit a torch and began to sing, shaking a rattle. He sucked the body of the patient, and drew off an imaginary object, throwing it outside, sometimes showing a real stone and pretending it was this which caused the illness. Such stones were later regarded as *zenus*. Medicine men knew various herbs which genuinely helped the sick. When patients became incurably ill, euthanasia was allowed (on the agreement of the chief). The sick were then either strangled or were left to die in a hammock slung between two trees, food and water being left nearby. Burial customs differed, chiefs' bodies being occasionally cut up, sometimes placed in caves or wooden graves, sometimes with food and weapons. In some cases, a favourite wife was buried with a chief, or even two of them, and a hole would then be left open in the grave and any wife who wished to would crawl in within a given period. Very often, heads were dried. No doubt these differing customs signify differences in special tribes' behaviour, but the key has not yet been found.[47]

The festivals of the Tainos had the customary mixture among American Indians of formality and abandon. The most elaborate were held at harvest, usually in the square in front of the chief's house. The chief beat the drum, led the singing and greeted the people. There were separate dances for men and women, the men singing stories of heroic deeds by ancestors; songs might last from three to four hours, drums and jingling snail shells being the accompaniment. There was also a primitive kind of metal castanet and a rattle made with a gourd full of stones. Conch shells were sometimes used as trumpets, and the Tainos may also have had bone flutes. Dances were usually at night, in the cool. Sometimes the dancers were given corn beer, on which they might become drunk. Both sexes wore grass wreaths or floral wreaths and necklaces of snail shells, and there was much painting of bodies. In large festivals there were gladiatorial contests, as occurred in Haiti when four men were killed before Columbus's brother Bartolomé. The Tainos had an excellent ball game, *batey*, played with a rubber ball of *gutta percha*. This originated in Mexico and took place along with festivals in the open place in front of the chief's house. The rules resembled those of badminton, but it was played by twenty or thirty people using specific parts of their body (shoulder, head, back, thighs, elbows, not hands or feet) instead of rackets. Men and women both played, but separately, though young men sometimes took on the girls. There were sometimes games between two nearby communities.[48] Spectators watched from slabs of stone, chiefs from wooden chairs.

The Tainos were generous. The chief acted as host to travellers

[47] For all this see Loven, p. 536–50.
[48] McNutt, *De Orbe Novo*, II, p. 252; Oviedo, I, p. 166.

(though presumably they were few), brought them to his house and gave them food, and offered women of the village. The Tainos exchanged gifts and even names. They placed their hands on the heads of those they wished to honour.

The Tainos did not apparently clash much among themselves – Las Casas noted that he did not recall noticing a single occasion of fights among them. Stealing was also apparently rare (partly doubtless because of the almost total absence of small personal possessions) but, when it occurred, it was punished very harshly – by death, being pierced by a sharp stick or left to die impaled on a branch. Adultery was also punished by death.[49] There was no military caste and wars were rare, hence the extreme military unpreparedness in face of the Spaniards. Perhaps, too, the comparatively tame landscape of Cuba (the absence of natural pests) caused a certain flaccidity. When they did fight, the Tainos threw spears as weapons, though they relied most on clubs (*macanas*), swung with two hands, in close combat. They had bows and arrows but only of fifty to sixty yards' range and therefore not much used save in hunting. The tactics of the Tainos in combat were usually defensive, fighting as from an ambush. They practised dodging missiles. They had no war music, and began battle merely with a war-cry, though they painted themselves red. In all these military respects they were far behind the Caribs and the natives of South America. To the Spaniards they not unnaturally seemed very feeble; even Spanish greyhounds wreaked havoc. But they were not cowardly. Hatuey, the last representative of 'free Cuba', showed great courage in rejecting execution by the sword in return for baptism, instead of being burned to death if he refused a christening, saying that he had no wish to go to Heaven since he understood that he might there meet his Spanish conquerors.

(iii)

Of the Ciboneys less is known.[50] Their relation to the Tainos (or where they were to be found) is not precisely established. Probably they were concentrated on the keys north and south of Cuba known now as Los Jardines de los Reyes, and also in south-west Haiti. Though it is possible that the Ciboneys preceded the Tainos in their migration north along the Antilles, it is more likely that they came down from Florida and North America (for instance, their use of hermatite for painting their skins resembles the usages of the North American Indians, while

[49] Oviedo, I, p. 139, 144.
[50] This is primarily because of delay in excavation. Archaeology is not yet advanced enough to know how far for instance, the Tainos got in their journey west across Cuba.

their shell culture resembles that of Florida).[51] They evidently used shells for many purposes, and had flints for cutting and stone hammers, but they lacked pottery and axes. They were fish-eaters like the Tainos, particularly liking molluscs.[52] They lacked cultivated crops, relying for food on hunting, wild fruits and vegetables. They seem to have ground up the vegetables, but did not perhaps cook their food, though they had fire. They occasionally cremated their dead[53] but usually buried them,[54] and stone balls are found in their burial sites, suggesting that they believed in a life after death.[55] They are regarded as palaeolithic while the Tainos were neolithic.[56] The word Cuba appears to be of Ciboney origin[57] but it is also often thought that the Ciboney language, though unintelligible to the Tainos, was in fact close to Tainan. It also seems likely that the Ciboney were concentrated in Pinar del Río, when Columbus came, or in the south of Cuba. Much of central Cuba was at that time covered with impassable forest (like most of the West Indies), and it is hard to know where the Tainos ceased their influence.

Less still is known of the Guanajatabeyes, the supposed earliest inhabitants of Cuba. In the early period no Spaniard ever saw one.[58] Possibly they did later when a number of Indians shot bows and arrows at cattle in the extreme west of the island. Spanish myth suggested that they had tails. The Tainos thought they were cave-dwellers who fled from any contact, even with other Indians, with 'the swiftness of a deer'.[59] But probably they lived in huts. Their identity is obscure and they might perhaps be merely a sub-category of earlier Ciboneys.[60] The western part of Cuba was not colonized by the Spaniards until the early seventeenth century and some of these intractable people possibly survived into the nineteenth century.

(iv)

What judgement then, if any, can be passed on the Cuban Indians? To describe them, as Columbus did, as 'very free from wickedness . . .

[51] *Handbook 4*, p. 497.

[52] Cosculluela, J. A., *Nuestro Pasado Ciboney* (Havana, 1925), p. 16.

[53] Loven, p. 558.

[54] *Handbook 4*, p. 499.

[55] *Handbook 4*, p. 505.

[56] Harrington's identification of various objects with geometric designs as Ciboney (p. 348–55, p. 398–9) has since been questioned by Irving Rouse, who has proved some other pre-Columbian art to be in fact Taino.

[57] See Loven's analysis (*op. cit.*, p. 464–7). No other traces of the language of Ciboney survive. The word Ciboney itself apparently derives from the Taino (Arawak) *siba* (rock) and *eyeri* (man).

[58] This is Loven's assertion (*op. cit.*, p. 3), following Dr García Valdés.

[59] McNutt, F. A., *De Orbe Novo, The Eight Decades of Peter Martyr D'Anghera*, p. 1380, qu. Loven, p. 4

[60] See *Handbook*, p. 500.

who would all become good Christians given good missionaries', or in the highly ethical colours of Las Casas, seems naïve. They were clearly hospitable, kind in their innocent reaction to strangers, and evidently peaceful. They lacked any of the reflective pity or irony which in the sixteenth century characterized West Europeans, even the Spaniards. Their cruelty (towards thieves, for instance, or the sick) has something remorselessly mechanical about it. But they had a high level of living, better perhaps than their conquerors were used to. Their emphasis on a fish diet was suggestive of dietary possibilities generally unrealized in the Caribbean and South America even in the twentieth century. In snuff and tobacco they had civilized drugs. Their administrative system was less elaborate but very much less stifling than that of the Aztecs or Incas. Unlike the Caribs, they were not cannibals.

The Indians, of course, suffered under the Spaniards. Even before Cuba had been invaded, in 1511, the Dominican Fray Antonio de Montesinos had made his famous sermon in Santo Domingo criticizing the Spanish treatment of Indians. The colonists complained, and the Dominican order condemned the friar, who was summoned home to Spain and there reproved by his superior. However, the scandal was enough to cause the Crown to pass the Laws of Burgos respecting treatment of the Indians and, though these were both inadequate and unfulfilled, the protest was continued in 1514 by Bartolomé de Las Casas, son of a profiteer from Columbus' second journey and who had himself for a time ruled Indians as an *encomendero* in Cuba on the Animao river.

The consequence was an elaborate controversy lasting until the middle of the century over the proper treatment of the Indians. The discussion continued in a theoretical fashion along four lines: (1) Could the Indians live like Christians? (2) Could the New World be colonized with Spanish farmers? (3) Could the faith be spread by peaceful means alone? (4) Could the *encomienda* system be abolished? Several curious experiments were begun to try and answer these questions, including many in Cuba: in 1526 the King (Charles V, the Emperor) ordered the Franciscan provincial in Haiti, Pedro Mexía, to go to Cuba 'where there is a greater need than in other places'. He was to free all Indians without masters (*encomenderos*) as well as those whose masters died in the next six months. Twelve of the most capable Indians were to be sent to Spain for education as missionaries. But the agents of these fine plans were incapable, and nothing transpired. A little later, Governor Guzmán gave a hundred Indians freedom near Bayamo and attached them to a supervisor, Francisco Guerrero, whose job was specifically to teach them to live like Christian peasants in Castile (naturally this included tithe and tax payments). The Indians were to be allowed to dance, but not with paint or masks. But Guerrero visited the village rarely, and used the

Indians as servants and one of them as a mistress. In 1532 a new governor, Manuel Rojas, sent a new supervisor to the village. Many Indians had died, others fled. Another experiment began. This also came to nothing. In 1535 the Governor reported to Spain that the Indians were incapable of living by themselves. A royal decree on his recommendation then announced that liberty could be given to the Indians only if they had proved their ability to use it wisely. A number of Indians applied for liberty and were interviewed. Some were found deficient in religious instruction, others in political ability. One Indian was found sound on all counts but his wife was rejected and he did not choose to be free alone.[61] Meantime, there had been several Indian revolts, particularly one in 1529 which had been put down repressively by a Spanish governor whose strength had been greatly weakened since the departure for Mexico in 1519 of the mayor of Santiago, Hernán Cortés, and 600 able Spaniards.

Work continued in the mines till 1539.[62] In that year the Spanish finally realized that gold was not one of Cuba's main resources (84,500 ounces only had been obtained since 1511).[63] In 1535 meantime the Bull *Sublimis Deus* proclaimed the American Indians to be really human beings, whose souls had to be won for the Church.[64] No *encomiendas* were granted in Cuba after 1536, and they were formally wound-up in 1542 (though on the mainland, where Indian questions were different, they were revived in some places and lasted until the eighteenth century). In the late sixteenth century, after the public change of policy by the Spaniards, several villages were founded exclusively with Indians[65] – a device to save them from being enslaved which was used throughout the Spanish Empire. (These were El Cobre, near Santiago, Guanabacoa, near Havana, and Pueblo Viejo, near Bayamo.) These villages survived and prospered. They established farms and traded with the outside.[66] In the eighteenth century at least one new town, Jiguaní, was founded by Indians in East Cuba.[67] In the nineteenth century, people of evident pure Indian origin were found in five towns of Oriente: Yara, near Bayamo; Dos Brazos, between Baracoa and Yateras; La Guira, near Yateras; El Caney near Santiago; and Jiguaní. Guanabacoa was still considered Indian. By 1900 it appeared that some 400 pure Indians survived, at Yara, Doz Brazos and La Guira, but by then intermarriage and mixture of cultures had become the rule.[68] In the Baracoa region, and

[61] This account is based on Lewis Hanke's *Social Experiments in America*, p. 49–71.
[62] The royal fifth was not recorded after that date.
[63] Guerra y Santovenia, *Historia de Cuba*, I, p. 295. The value was 1½ M pesos.
[64] Text in Documents, p. 85.
[65] See above, p. 21.
[66] *Handbook*, p. 519.
[67] *Loc. cit.*
[68] *Loc. cit.* See also Pezuela. An early anthropologist, Dr Carlos de la Torre, found an Indian village with parish records going back to 1690, in El Caney.

in Yateras and Yara to a lesser extent, persons of strongly Indian features survive to this day, and elsewhere it often seems that Indian features can be discerned, but they are normally mixed with Spanish.[69]

These Indians have been allowed to lose their identity in the rest of the Cuban nation, to which they have no doubt made an important contribution, taken as a whole. No census ever made a separate mention of Cuban Indians,[70] and they have been usually classed as white. In the twentieth century, nationalistic or revolutionary movements have ignored the Indians almost completely, not wishing (unlike the Mexican revolutionaries) to hark back to the pre-Columbian world, even for myths. Cuban social anthropology has concentrated almost exclusively on the Negro contribution, owing to the superb studies of Fernando Ortiz. The neglect of the Indian connection has to some extent led to a misunderstanding by the Cubans of their own national identity, which in its turn has led to a specially strident, Hispanic nationalism, and which, in the twentieth century, has been driven to assert itself primarily in terms of its relations to the United States. But perhaps the ferocity of Cuban nationalism during the Revolution of 1959 would not have occurred in quite the same way if it had been based on a rediscovery of the indigenous Indian past, as happened in Mexico, rather than on a passionate rejection of North America.[71]

The history of the Indians in Cuba differs from that in other Spanish territories. In the other Caribbean islands, as has been seen, they vanished faster and more completely than in Cuba. The Caribs succeeded, however, in holding out in the Lesser Antilles, though they were ultimately beaten down in later colonial wars. About 600 remain in the island of Dominica and there are several thousand more, mostly mixed with Negroes, on the mainland.[72]

When the mainland was conquered in the decade after the conquest of Cuba, the scandal of the Caribbean labour camps had become too widely known for a similar policy to be followed. Besides, the Indians of Mexico and Peru were too many to be destroyed. Many consciences

[69] See the illustrations in Harrington and the *Handbook* (plates 96 & 97). Mixture with Negro features appears rarer than it is, since the African strain seems to obliterate Indian features even more than white.

[70] Except in the *Cuadro Estadístico de la Siempre Fiel Isla de Cuba* (1846), where the information is incomplete.

[71] One of the most popular of the books of the Revolution, Núñez Jiménez' *Geografía de Cuba*, discusses the subject fairly accurately thus: 'According to Fray Bartolomé de las Casas, the population of Cuba reached 300,000, a fact which appears exaggerated from the poor economic development of our archipelago in those pre-Columbian times. Spanish barbarism submitted the Indians to a limitless exploitation, almost finished them off. There only remained a few reduced groups of Indian communities which little by little were mixed, until becoming absorbed by the African and European influx. Today it is only possible to meet with a few mixed Indians in the wildest region of the Sierra Maestra and the Baracoa mountains.' (*Geografía*, p. 176.)

[72] See Irving Rouse's article on them in the *Encyclopaedia Americana*, V, p. 608.

had been aroused, and a genuine 'struggle for justice' began which, if never completely successful, certainly enables the Catholic Church to look on the first century of its domination of Latin America with some pride. The legal treatment of the Indians continued as a major subject of controversy till the late sixteenth century.[73] As a result, most continental countries of Latin America have an 'Indian problem', whereas Cuba and the Caribbean does not. There remain perhaps twenty million pure-bred Indians in Latin America, comprising a majority in several countries, many of whom cannot speak Spanish and remain quite unassimilated.

Archaeology in Cuba

The earliest serious investigator was Miguel Rodríguez Ferrer, who carried out various inquiries in the late 1840s. His findings, however, were not published till 1876. In 1882 Antonio Bachiller published an important book on the Tainan language and its survival in Cuba.[74] The next serious investigator was Dr Carlos de la Torre of the University of Havana, active from the 1890s; he wrote a brief account of his conclusions which was included in a manual of Cuban history for schools published in 1901. His chief errors were to suppose the Caribs reached Cuba and that the Ciboneys were Tainan; hence the overworking of the word Ciboney in most twentieth-century Cuban suppositions about their more remote past.

North Americans were responsible for the beginning of a scientific knowledge of old Cuba. The first names in a long list of patient enquirers were Dr Walter Fawkes (1904) and Stewart Cullin (1901) and, later, more important, M. R. Harrington of the Museum of the American Indian, New York, who was active in Cuba from 1913 to 1920.[75] His work was continued by Irving Rouse in the 1940s, though the most detailed analysis of the results of archaeology, alongside the records of the first Spaniards, was carried out by a Swede, Sven Loven, whose work was first published in the 1920s and then revised and translated into English in the 1930s.[76]

[73] See Hanke, *op. cit.*, and the enlarged version in *La lucha por justicia en la conquista de América* (Buenos Aires). As he points out, however ineffective and unreal this may seem to be alongside contemporary humanitarianism, there were few instances of such questions even arising where the Anglo-Saxons were concerned. Roger Williams of Rhode Island did question the right of Plymouth to Indian lands unless attested by just sale, but he later agreed to withdraw the idea in agreement with Governor Winthrop.

[74] Antonio Bachiller y Morales, *Cuba Primitiva* (1882).

[75] See *Handbook*, vol. IV, p. 497–546.

[76] Loven, *Origins of the Tainan Culture* (Gotenburg, 1935).

Kennion's Slave Concession

By George Earl of Albemarle, Viscount Bury, Baron of Ashford, one of His Majesty's most Honourable Privy Council, Captain, Keeper and Governor of the Island of Jersey, Colonel of the King's own regiment of Dragoons, Lieutenant General of His Majesty's forces, and Commander in Chief of a Secret Expedition.

Whereas a number of Negro Slaves are wanted to support the annual decrease of this Island and to maintain the Plantations and Settlements in the same State and Condition they were in before it became subject to the Crown of Great Britain and Whereas in order to prevent many Wiles and Abuses that would arise from an unrestrained Importation it is absolutely necessary to limit the number annually to be introduced. And whereas it might become hurtfull and prejudicial to His Majesty's other Sugar Colonies not to confine in the strictest manner the number of Negroes to be admitted into this Island and the better to ascertain such Limitations it has been an invariable Custom to grant by Licence to particular Person or Persons the sole importation of Negroes for Sale.

I do hereby grant unto John Kennion Esq. or His certain agent or attorney the sole Licence and Liberty of importing Negroes into the Island of Cuba during the present war with the Crown of Spain or to such farther Time as his Majesty may be pleased to allow according to the following regulations – Viz:

That all the said Negroes so imported shall be brought into the Harbour or City of Havanna to be sold.

That the number of Negroes to be imported annually shall not exceed Two Thousand. Viz:

Fifteen Hundred Males   &
Five Hundred Females.

And I do hereby strictly forbid any other Person or Persons whatsoever upon Pain of Confiscation of their Effects and imprisonment of their Persons to buy or sell, or by any means to introduce into the Island of Cuba from the day of the Date hereof any Negro or other Slaves during the War or to such farther Period of Time as aforesaid except what is meant and understood to be imported by the said John Kennion His

certain attorney or agent according to the Tenor hereof of the said John Kennion paying a Duty upon each Negro sold of Forty Dollars for each Man or Woman and Twenty Dollars for each Girl or Boy.
Given under my Hand and Seal this 23rd of October 1762 By His Majesty's Command

(Liverpool papers Add. 38201 folio 299)

Estimated Cuban Slave Imports[1]

AIMES			SACO	
Date	Number		Date	Number
1512– 1763	60,000		1512– 1740	52,000
1763– 1789	30,875		1740– 1789	40,000

AIMES and SACO	
Date	Number
1790	2,534
1791	8,498
1792	8,528
1793	3,777
1794	4,164
1795	5,832
1796	5,711
1797	4,552
1798	2,001
1799	4,919
1800	4,145
1801	1,659
1802	13,832
1803	9,671
1804	8,923
1805	4,999
1806	4,395
1807	2,565
1808	1,607
1809	1,162
1810	6,672
1811	6,349
1812	6,081
1813	4,770
1814	4,321
1815	9,111
1816	17,737
1817	25,841
1818	19,902
1819	15,147
1820	17,194

[1] These are estimates made by prominent historians of Cuba, the North American Aimes and the Cuban Salo (for whom see above, p. 295). Aimes's table is in his *History of Slavery in Cuba*, p. 269. British Foreign Office estimates (published in Lloyd, *The Navy and the Slave Trade*, p. 275–6) derive from Parliamentary Papers 1847–48, vol. xxii, 4th Report, p. 3 and 1865, vol. v, p. 465.

AIMES and SACO	
Date	Number
1821	6,415
1822	2,500
1823	3,000
1824	3,000
1825	7,000
1826	3,500
1827	3,500
1828	4,500
1829	7,500
1830	9,000
1831	9,000
1832	6,750
1833	6,750
1834	8,250
1835	9,500
1836	10,750
1837	12,240
1838	10,495
1839	9,350
1840	10,104
1841	6,300
1842	2,500
1843	1,500
1844	3,000
1845	950
1846	500
1847	1,450
1848	1,950
1849	3,500
1850	2,500
1851	3,600
1852	4,500
1853	2,000
1854	6,000
1855	9,000
1856–	9,000
1857–	9,000
1858–	9,000
1859	9,000
1860	3,000
1861	2,000
1862	600
1863	1,000
1864	1,000
1865	400
TOTAL	527,828

British Foreign Office Estimates for Spanish Colonies (i.e. Cuba & Puerto Rico)	
1825	39,000
1826	
1827	NOT
1828	AVAILABLE
1829	
1830	40,500
1831	
1832	NOT
1833	AVAILABLE
1834	
1835	40,000
1836	29,000
1837	28,000
1838	28,000
1839	25,000
1840	14,470
1841	11,857
1842	3,150
1843	8,000
1844	10,000
1845	1,350
1846	1,700
1847	1,500
1848	–
1849	8,700
1850	3,100
1851	5,000
1852	7,924
1853	13,900
1854	13,900
1855	6,408
1856	7,304
1857	10,431
1858	16,992
1859	30,973
1860	24,995
1861	23,964
1862	11,254
1863	7,507
1864	6,807
1865	–

Outfit of a Slave Ship bound for Africa from Guadaloupe, 1825[1]

Invoice of Merchandize put on Board the Schooner "L'Oiseau," Captain Blais, and consigned to him, to wit:—

	$	Cts
1158 Gallons of Rum[2] .... at 36 Cents a pint	416	88
80 Barrels of Powder of 25lb ....2000lb at 25 Cents per barrel	500	—
6 Tierces[3] of Rice ....3600 at 5 Cents per tierce	180	—
220 Muskets ....at 5 Dol. each	1100	—
110 Bars of Iron of 15 to 16lb. ....3600 at 6 Cents each	216	—
220 Kettles ....1320 at 8 Cents each	105	60
220 Ruffles at 2½ Dol. per dozen	45	84
220 Cases of Gin, at 2¼ Dol. each	495	—
220 Pieces Guinea Blue[4] ....at 4 Dol. each	880	—
220 Ditto ditto White[4] ....at 3 Dol. each	660	—
220 Ditto ditto Limeneas[4] ....at 3½ Dol. each	770	—
3309 Ells to be divided into 220 pieces Nicanes[4]	377	26
220 Pieces Chacelats[4] ....at 3¼	715	—
220 Handkerchiefs, Romales 15 in the piece at $2	440	—
220 Ditto – – Kermitches 10 ditto ......at $2	440	—
220 Ditto – – Blue – 10 ditto ......at $2	440	—
220 Ditto – – Madrasses, Red and Blue, assorted ....at $1½	360	—
45 Pieces of striped Silk of 20 yards to be divided into small pieces	180	—
10 Dozen Razors ....at $4	40	—
9 Ditto ditto ....at $3¼	29	25
20 Ditto Padlocks	26	—
1 Barrel of Flints	10	—
2524 Pounds of Tobacco ....at 6½ Cents	164	6
24 Mirrors ....at $8½ p.doz.	19	47
60 Bundles of Necklaces and small Necklaces in form of a pipe	16	—
	8626	36

EXPENSES

Duties	100	—
Expences of Negroes for sewing the Bales	20	—
	8746	36

Pointe à Pitre, 17th September 1825.   (Signed)   J. LAFOSSE.

[1] Parliamentary papers on the Slave Trade, 1826, vol. xxix, p. 309.
[2] i.e. Rum at 36 cents a pint.
[3] A measure equivalent to ⅓ of a pipe, itself equivalent to ½ tun (i.e., 105 imperial gallons).
[4] Various Cloths.

APPENDIX VII

Slave Ships from Havana, 1825[1]

RESULT of the Voyages of 32 Vessels which sailed from the Port of Havannah for the Coast of Africa, during the Year 1825, as far as can be ascertained.

CLASS	NAME	RESULT OF VOYAGE
Schooner – –	Fingal – –	Captured by H.M.S. Ferret, and condemned at Havannah.
Brig – –	San José Aquila – –	Returned 9th Nov. 1825, after landing Negroes.
Schooner – –	Iris – – –	Returned 16th Sept. – ditto – ditto.
Ditto – –	Joaquina – –	Returned 29th Dec. – ditto – ditto.
Ditto – –	Ninfa – – –	Returned 29th July – ditto – ditto.
Ditto – –	Jacinta – – –	Returned 2d Dec. – ditto – ditto.
Brig –	Conquistador –	Returned 15th Dec. – ditto – ditto.
Ditto – –	Aníbal – –	Returned 27th Dec. – ditto ditto.
Schooner – –	Segunda Gallega	Said to be captured, and carried to Sierra Leone.
Ditto – –	Clarita – – –	Said to have been lost on the coast of Africa after capture.
Ditto – –	Buenaventura –	Returned 29th Dec. 1825, after landing Negroes.
Ditto – –	Paulita – – –	Returned 10th Dec. – ditto – ditto.
Ditto – –	Amazona. – –	
Ditto – –	Barbarita.	
Brig – –	Mágico – – –	Captured by H.M.S. Union, and condemned at Havannah.
Schooner – –	Ninfa Habanera	Said to be captured, and carried to Sierra Leone.
Ditto – –	Matilde – –	Returned 10th Dec. 1825, after landing Negroes.
Brig	Asdrubal	
Schooner – –	Anfitrite – –	Returned 6th Dec. – ditto – ditto.
Ditto – –	Teagenes – –	Returned 27th May 1829 ditto – ditto.
Ditto – –	Iberia – – –	Said to be captured, and carried to Sierra Leone.
Ditto – –	Carlota – – –	Returned 14th June 1826, after landing Negroes.

[1] Report of British Commissioners, Havana, 1 Jan, 1827.

CLASS	NAME	RESULT OF VOYAGE
Brig – –	Orestes – – –	Lost on the Bahama bank; the Negroes taken on board H.M. schooner Speedwell, and emancipated at Havannah.
Ditto	Sirius – – –	Said to be lost on the coast of Africa.
Schooner – –	Intrépida	
Ditto – –	Minerva	
Ditto – –	Ismenia	
Brigantine – –	Teresa – – –	Said to be captured, and carried to Sierra Leone.
Schooner – –	Iris – – –	Destroyed by her crew, after landing Negroes at Escondido.
Ditto – –	Nicanor	
Ditto – –	Flecha	
Ditto – –	Micaela	

Affidavit of Lieutenant Nott

Statement of Occurrences relative to the Detention of the "Mexicano" Steam Packet, off the Havannah, by His Majesty's Sloop "Pylades."[1]

On the 20th of August 1826, about 6 A.M., the Ship being then at least 4 miles from the Moro Fort, I was ordered by Captain Jackson to proceed, under the command of Lieutenant Hast, and examine the Steam Packet "Mexicano", apparently on her passage to Matanzas, to discover, by diligent search, whether she was in any manner engaged in the illicit conveyance of slaves from one Port in the Spanish Possessions to another, as most expressly forbid by Article 7, which he pointed out to me, in the Treaty between Their Catholick and Most Christian Majesties The Kings of Spain and Great Britain.

Accordingly, on boarding the "Mexicano," by direction of Lieut. Hast, I demanded of the Master his Licence from the Government of Havannah, to convey the Negroes to Matanzas, which I knew, from positive information, were then on board. He denied having any Negroes, and, consequently, the necessity of a Passport of this description; calling out, at the same time, in junction with the Passengers, to return to the Havannah, and ordering the helm to be altered for that purpose, which I immediately prevented by taking the tiller from the helmsman, and placing a guard over it. Lieut. Hast then stated his orders to search the Vessel, which the Master intimated he should not do, again denying the presence of any Negroes on board, except the Servants of the Passengers, who were all on the deck. Lieut. Hast then dispatched a Boat to the "Pylades" for additional force and instructions; and, in the mean time, we both proceeded among those Blacks assembled on the fore-part of the deck; and I am ready to make Oath, that they were not to be identified with, nor did in any manner, except form and colour, resemble those Negroes afterwards discovered secreted in the hold.

On ordering the fore-hatches to be lifted, several of the Crew jumped on them, and refused to be moved, unless by force. The generality of the Passengers began now to be vehemently clamorous, desiring the Master,

[1] From Parliamentary papers, 1826, Vol. xxix, p. 339

if he had any Negroes on board, to produce them, that the Vessel might be liberated, and permitted to return to the Havannah. But amongst the foremost of those who opposed this, and contributed to disturbance, both at this time and during the succeeding passage, was one Henry Stondon, calling himself Merchant of Havannah, and who eventually proved to be so; another of the Passengers mentioned that the Mate, on perceiving me in one of the Boats, approaching the "Mexicano," to board her, had exclaimed, 'There is the Officer who boarded the "Minerva," he is coming to pay us off for that business, I suppose.' My conviction now became stronger that Negroes were positively on board, contrary to the existing Laws.

On the arrival of orders from Captain Jackson to search, let what would occur, with a sufficient force to compel compliance, the Master of the "Mexicano" signified his intent to offer no further opposition, and declared that he considered himself, from that moment, no longer in charge of the Vessel. Lieut. Hast and myself then proceeded to the forehold, into which we descended, and became satisfied that no Person was openly visible, though sufficient light was conveyed through the hatchway, both the hatches being off; but on ordering some chairs and other furniture to be removed from between the bulk-heading, which separated the steam-boilers from the Vessel's side, 14 male Negroes were discovered stowed beneath these articles, and exposed to the intense heat produced by the lighted stoves. The general idea which seemed to pervade the minds of these poor wretches was, that their throats would be instantly cut, and they besought us, by the most supplicating signs and gestures, to spare them from the horrid fate they seemed to anticipate. On comprehending, from our assurances, that deliverance, not destruction, was intended, their joy became unbounded, and one, more intelligent than the rest, pointed to the fore-peak, where, after diligent investigation, 6 females were found underneath rope sails and a hawser, the whole of which must have been deliberately coiled upon them, for the purpose of concealment. The greater part of these unfortunate beings, both male and female, were afflicted with severe ophthalmia, and, at the time of discovery, nearly deprived of sight, from the quantity and nature of the discharge, encrusted from want of attention of the eyes and upper part of the face.

I further observed that they were all shaved, similar to the Negroes landed from the "Minerva," and I have no hesitation in affirming; from their total ignorance of any European language or custom; from the newness of their clothes, and the awkward mode in which they used them evidently considering them as a novelty; and from the disinclination they evinced to European provision, as well as their general manner and appearance, that they had been very recently imported from Africa, though, on the subsequent Trial before the Mixed Commission, the Owner, (a Spanish Marquis) and several other people of respectability, swore to their having been above 9 Months on the Island of Cuba, which assertions afterwards became the publick joke of Havannah, and were decidedly considered, in general opinion, as deliberate falsehoods. Indeed, from the conversations of the Passengers, who, far from concealing, rather openly conversed on the subject of their being part of the cargo of the "Minerva," as well as from the circumstance of Mr Wade, Master of the "Mary Brade," Liverpool Merchant Brig, having recognised one of the women (very remarkable in her appearance,) as being landed from that Schooner, on the Evening of the 16th August, I firmly believe that the 20 Negroes secreted in the hold of the "Mexicano," were part of those landed in Havannah, from the "Minerva" Spanish Schooner previously chased in by the "Pylades."

After a strict investigation in every part of the "Mexicano," the Master was informed, that if he possessed a Permission from the Government of Havannah, authorising him to convey Negroes who were slaves, from one Port in the Spanish Possessions to another, his Vessel would be immediately liberated, and on his stating, that he was only provided with one Paper, which proved to be a Licence for himself and Crew to run the Steam packet "Mexicano," between Havannah and Matanzas, for 30 days, she was taken possession of by His Majesty's Officers, and sail made, in company with the "Pylades," the Engineer having refused, at the instance of the Master, to put the machinery in motion, which resolution was, however, overruled by the Passengers on the following day; and by great exertion the "Pylades" and the "Mexicano" arrived in the Havannah, on Monday Night, the 21st.

On the Passengers leaving the Vessel, 47, out of 53, produced, and had their Passports registered, the remaining 6, being General Traders between the 2 Ports, had not supposed it necessary to provide such Document; but I am ready to swear, that all the Negroes on board, with the exception of the 20 secreted in the hold, were either furnished with separate Passports, or included in that of the Master.

One of the Owners of the "Mexicano," after the liberation of the Vessel, unguardedly confessed to me, in conversation, that the Negroes in question had been embarked from the Church of St. Francisco (the Place where I had previously observed part of the Cargo of the "Minerva" landed) on the Morning of the 20th, for conveyance to Matanzas.

Of all the circumstances here related, except this last, Lieut. Hast must be perfectly aware, and I have no doubt, in conjunction with myself, is ready to make Oath to the truth of.

Signed by me, in Port Royal Harbour, on the 27th day of September 1826.

(Signed)   JOHN NEALE NOTT, Acting Lieutenant.

P.S. In the conversations mentioned in the foregoing Statement, I either spoke in French, when it was understood, or had the assistance of an Interpreter, who spoke Spanish and English.

(Signed)   JOHN NEALE NOTT.

Chinese Imports to Cuba: 1847-73[1]

TABLE A

Statement of the Number of Chinese Coolies imported into Cuba yearly since 1847.

Year	Vessels		Chinese		
	Number	Tonnage	Shipped	Died at Sea	Landed
1847	2	979	612	41	571
1853	15	8,349	5,150	843	4,307
1854	4	2,375	1,750	39	1,711
1855	6	6,544	3,130	145	2,985
1856	15	10,677	6,152	1,182	2,970
1857	28	18,940	10,101	1,554	8,547
1858	33	32,842	16,411	3,027	13,384
1859	16	13,828	8,539	1,332	7,207
1860	17	15,104	7,227	1,008	6,219
1861	16	15,919	7,212	290	6,922
1862	1	759	400	56	344
1863	3	2,077	1,045	94	951
1864	7	5,513	2,664	532	2,132
1865	20	12,769	6,810	407	6,403
1866	43	24,187	14,169	1,126	13,043
1867	42	26,449	15,661	1,247	14,414
1868	21	15,265	8,400	732	7,668
1869	19	13,692	7,340	1,475	5,864
1870	3	2,300	1,312	63	1,249
1871	5	2,825	1,827	178	1,649
1872	20	12,886	8,914	766	8,148
1873	6	4,786	3,330	209	3,121
Total	342	249,065	138,156	16,346	121,810

[1] Estimates by the British Consulate-General

TABLE B

Chinese imports by nationality of importer

Flag	Vessels		Chinese			Percent-age of Deaths
	Number	Tonnage	Embarked	Landed	Died at Sea	
British	35	27,815	13,697	11,457	2,240	16.31
United States ..	34	40,576	18,206	16,419	1,787	9.80
Austrian	3	1,377	936	864	72	7.70
Belgian	3	2,482	1,199	1,182	17	1.42
Chilian	4	1,702	926	743	183	19.76
Danish	1	1,022	470	291	179	38.
Dutch	19	14,906	8,113	7,132	981	12.09
French	104	64,664	38,540	33,795	4,745	12.31
German	8	4,207	2,176	1,932	244	11.21
Italian	5	5,586	2,832	2,505	327	11.20
Norwegian ..	5	2,296	1,366	1,104	262	19.18
Peruvian	6	4,979	2,609	1,999	610	23.38
Portuguese ..	21	15,847	8,228	7,266	962	11.70
Russian	12	9,857	5,471	5,093	378	6.90
Spanish	78	47,604	31,356	28,085	3,271	10.43
San Salvador ..	4	4,145	2,031	1,943	88	4.33
Total	342	249,065	138,156	121,810	16,346	11.83

(Signed)   JOHN V. CRAWFORD, *Acting Consul-General.*
British Consulate-General, Havana,
    September 1, 1873.

The Last Slave Journey across the Atlantic, 1865

The following report from the British Commissary Judge, Havana, to the Foreign Secretary (Lord Stanley) in London appears to record the last known shipment of slaves from Africa to the New World.

My Lord,   *Havana, September 30, 1866.*

I HAVE the honour to inclose the Annual Statement of Landings of African Negroes which have been effected in this island since the 30th of September last.

My predecessor, in his Report of last year, has given to General Dulce the credit which that Governor so well deserved for his exertions in putting down the Slave Trade in this island.

No sooner had General Lersundi arrived, than rumours were rife of landings of Negroes in all parts of the island, and the details of some of these pretended landings were given to me with such apparent accuracy and exactitude that it was almost impossible not to place faith in them. But I found, on inquiring closely into the matter, that the evidence broke down in every single instance, and I am at present under the belief that no landing has taken place during the present Captain-General's administration. Of course, however, I may be mistaken, and landings may have been effected without my knowledge or that of the Captain-General; but this, though just possible, is barely so. Intelligence can hardly be kept back from the Consulate-General, and still less easily from the Supreme Government, and General Lersundi always communicates to me any information which he receives bearing upon this question. I have had the honour of reporting to your Lordship the General's repeated assurances of his determination to put the law in force to the uttermost, and to punish with the greatest severity any persons who may be found attempting to carry on the Slave Trade in this Colony; and from General Lersundi's character, I cannot doubt the perfect sincerity and good faith of his intentions.

I think that, altogether, there is fair reason for supposing that the Cuban Slave Trade is virtually almost at an end. I do not, of course, mean to say that until Spain declares the Traffic to be piracy, and those engaged in it to be guilty of a capital offence, attempts and even successful attempts will not be made to introduce slaves into this island. On the contrary, in spite of the many dangers and obstacles now thrown in the way of the Traffic, there will always be men found ready to run heavy risks for heavy profits; and the very desperation of the game, so far from deterring some of the more daring slave-dealers, will only add to the zest with which they ply their horrible trade.

But not only do the Spanish Government and the present Captain-General appear honestly determined to carry out the laws, but the state of public feeling among the Cubans is very different from what it was a few years ago. The more enlightened among them earnestly deprecate the importation of more slaves into the island, and are turning their attention to that problem so difficult to be solved, viz., how slavery can be abolished so prudently, so safely, and so gradually, as to benefit the whites as well as the blacks; to strengthen instead of weakening the material prosperity of the country; and to elevate instead of depressing the moral tone of the community. In this respect the experience of neighbouring countries furnishes them with many a warning of evil to be avoided, but I fear with few examples to be followed.

With regard to the Negroes captured in March last near Cape San Antonio, I regret to say that I have as yet been able to obtain no information in regard to their ultimate disposal, though within the last few days I have again addressed General Lersundi on the subject. I also begged the Captain-General to inform me what are the measures he proposes to adopt for the amelioration of the condition of the emancipados, as the African Negroes captured by the Spanish authorities are called. Hitherto the condition of these poor people has been almost as bad, in some cases even worse, than that of the slaves themselves. Hired out nominally for a period of years, and ostensibly under the protection of the Government, they are carried off to the plantations, whence they seldom return, and are hardly ever known to regain the liberty to which they are legally entitled. General Lersundi told me that the abuses to which these poor creatures are subject had made a great impression on his mind, and had shocked him extremely. He said that he was determined to put a stop to these abuses; and I hope soon to be able to report to your Lordship that he has done so effectually.

I have, &c.
(Signed)   W. W. FOLLETT SYNGE.

INCLOSURE IN THE ABOVE

STATEMENT of the Number of Slaves reported to have been Landed in Cuba, from October 1, 1865, to September 30, 1866.

Date of Landing.	Where Landed or Captured.	Number of Slaves.		Remarks.
		Landed.	Captured	
1865 Sept. 18	Pinar del Río ..	143	143	This cargo was brought by a Spanish brigantine, and is supposed to have come from Ambrizette. It is possible that a larger number of Negroes were brought, and that part of the expedition succeeded in evading the vigilance of the authorities.
October	Pan de Azúcar ..	600	..	This cargo belonged to the late Don Fco. Marty, and was landed at his estate, Pan de Azúcar. The landing is denied by the authorities, but the fact was publicly known at the time.
1866 April 5	Cape Antonio ..	700	275	The capture was made by the Spanish gunboat "Neptuno," together with another lot of 100, which were subsequently released as not being Bozals. This cargo belonged to the same owners as that which was seized at Pinar del Río. The rest of the expedition was taken to Pan de Azúcar, or distributed in the Vuelta de Abajo.
		1,443	418	

Havana, September 30, 1866.
(Signed)   W.W. FOLLETT SYNGE, *Commissary Judge.*

Social origins of the men and women involved in the attack on Moncada and Bayamo, 26 July 1953

NUMBER OF PEOPLE IDENTIFIED

154

COLOUR

White 60
Mulatto 3 and ? 11
Negro 4
Mestizo ? 3
Indian–Negro 1
Indian Features 1

PLACE OF WORK

Artemisa 20
Bolondrón (Matanzas) 1
Caibarién 1
Calabazar 3
Cienfuegos 1
Colón 3
El Cotorro (Havana) 1
Florida 1
Guanajay 5
Havana 46
Havana province 1
La Lisa (Marianas) 1
Marianao 6
Nueva Paz 6
Palma Soriano 2
Pijirigua (Vinales) 1
Pinar del Río 1
San José de los Ramos 1
Santiago 2

AGE

Under 20 28
20–29 36
30–39 14
Over 40 9

PROFESSIONAL STATUS

Accountants 3 (of whom 1 assistant)
Agricultural workers 10
Bakers 2
Bank Workers 1
Barmen 2
Builders 10 (of whom 3 classified as 'masilleros'[1])
Bus workers 1
Business men 1
Bookshop attendants 1
Butchers 1
Carretilleros de tejar[2] 1
Carpenters 3
Chapisteros[3] 1
Chimney sweeps 1
Cattle Breeders 1
Commercial travellers 3
Cooks 2
Dentists 1
Dockers 1
Engineers 1
Factory workers 13 (of whom 3 in textile factories, 2 each in milk, beer and shoe factories, and 1 each respectively in a drink factory, a refrigeration works and an electricity company. 1 unclassified)
Farmers 2
Flower sellers 1
Funeral attendants 1
"Gastronomic workers" 1
Lawyers 1
Lorry drivers 6 (including 1 ice-deliverer)

Mechanics 3
Milkmen (*Traseguero de leche*) 1
Messenger 1
Nurses 1 (Male)
Office workers 1
Oyster sellers 1
Parking attendants 2
Photographers 2
Pharmaceutical laboratory assistants 1
Plumbers 1
Porters 1 (market porter)
Printers 1
Sailors 1 (at Havana Biltmore Yacht Club)
Schoolboys 1
Shoemakers 1
Shop assistants 9 (ironmonger's 2, chemist's, confectioner's, electrician's, haberdasher's, shoeshop, 2 unclassified)
Stonecutters 1
Students 6 (of whom 1 a teacher trainee, and 4 dropped out on the morning)
Sugar workers 3 (1 a harvest worker only, 1 worked in a refinery and 1 a mechanic)
Tailors 4
Tanners 1
Teachers 1
Turners 1
Unemployed 1
Others 23 (their professions not yet clarified)
(NOTE: Some changed their jobs often, some are described as having two jobs.)

Notes

[1] Putty-layer
[2] Carrier of tiles
[3] Mechanic

General Note

This analysis has been compiled out of such newspapers and anecdotal information as I have been able to discover. It accounts for some 90 % of those involved, the total participants numbering 170.

The State of Agriculture in 1959

In 1946, 70% of the Cuban farms were smaller than 60 acres, occupying 11% of the farm land. Most of these were single family farms without paid labour – subsistence farms, with periods of under-employment. In contrast, 70% of the farm land was run by 8% of the farmers: and less than 1% of the farmers ran 36% of the land in farms.

Statistics like this can be found for many countries. In Cuba the situation had changed for the better during the previous half-century: in 1899, 93% of the farms were smaller than 30 acres. But, in terms of relative shares, less had changed; in 1899 70% of the cultivated area had been run by 16% of the farmers; 1.2% of the farmers ran 36% of the cultivated area.[1] The biggest group actually thus increased their share of land because of the opening up of the east of Cuba.

Most farmers lived on their farms rather than, as in Spain, in villages. Most relied on hand labour and on oxen. Even a cart was found only on a small number of farms. Everyone had a machete in a leather scabbard, often used for hoeing as for harvesting, the 'cutlass à tout faire'.[2] There were few buildings, except in the tobacco industry or the dairy district near Havana. Work was very rarely done by women.

The land in farms had increased enormously: from 30% in 1899, the percentage had gone up to 80% of the whole territory. The cultivated land – that is, not pasture or woodland – had increased even more: from 3% in 1899 to 22%. Of course, 1899 was a black year, just after the war, but even before, in 1895, the cultivated area was still under 5% of the land. The increase was most in Oriente and Camagüey, the old virgin forest lands of the east, but even Havana and Matanzas increased their land in farms by nearly a half and Las Villas by over three times. On the other hand, the average size of farms decreased by nearly half; from 7.8 caballería to between $4\frac{1}{4}$ and $4\frac{1}{3}$ caballería – about 140 acres. This statistic means less than it seems. The 1899 average was unduly high because of the abnormal size in those days of the average ranch in the cattle area of Camagüey; Camagüey apart, the average would have been about the same as in 1946.[3] While the farm area expanded, so did

---

[1] Census of 1899, p. 545; Agricultural Census of 1946, qu. WB, p. 88. Such figures are not exactly comparable, since definitions of farms change.

[2] *Cf.* Dumont, *Cuba*, p. 26.

[3] The 1899 census got its average wrong (see p. 543).

the number of farms: the number went up $1\frac{1}{8}$ times, the total farm area by $1\frac{1}{2}$. Chiefly this was due to subdivision among families; but partly to immigration, to the increase of squatters (*precaristas*), especially in the days of confusion following the fall of Machado, and to the encouragement given by the state (by the Law of 1937 and other statutes) to sugar *colonos*, who numbered nearly 40,000 in 1946.[4] Further, the new areas opened up brought no great changes in land-holding; there were as many tenant farmers as in the west. Land was opened up often by companies who then sought tenants.

These figures refer to a time twelve or thirteen years before the coming of Castro; in the intervening period, the number of sugar *colonos* increased by a half, so that, though there are no better guides than those of 1946, there were certainly more farms in 1959 than in 1946; probably there were now 200,000, with not much more land.[5] The average farm probably decreased somewhat, perhaps being under four caballería, or 120 acres. Most of the land in farms was, of course, not cultivated (21·7%), but was in pasture (43%).

There was little change in tenure of farms since 1899. After the war with Spain, 28% of the farmers owned their land;[6] in 1946 the figure had only risen to 30.5%.[7] The aggregate number of owners had admittedly increased three times,[8] and if farms run by administrators were added to the owners the total would increase to 36%. But this is not suggestive of progress; renters had more than doubled.[9] The situation was thus much as it had been at the beginning of the century. In some places, disputes arising from the original *mercedes* still survived; thus huge communal farms survived in some parts of Oriente with the coheirs, though utterly impoverished, unable to dispose of their own tract at will and with many acres uncultivated in consequence.[10]

Most Cuban farms were thus on various sorts of rents, either direct lease, sub-lease, or sharecropping. If some leases were worked fairly, many were not. Further, in one way the situation was worsening: in the last years before the revolution, the lowest group of farmers (*precaristas*) without tenure or lease, numbered 8% of the total.[11]

Over half those who owned their farms had been living there more than fifteen years, over a third (36%) more than twenty-five years; at

[4] *Cf.* Comments in Estudio, p. 1379.
[5] Castro speech, *Revolución*, 1 Nov 1961, p. 10.
[6] Census of 1899, p. 544.
[7] Agricultural Census of 1946.
[8] From just under 17,000 to just under 48,000 (Census, p. 555; Agricultural Census, p. 413).
[9] From 40,984 to 86,099.
[10] D.C. Corbitt, Mercedes and Realengos, HAHR 1939, p. 277.
[11] Even if all those classified as "other" in the 1899 Census are regarded as being comparable, this would only total 4%, or 2,737, compared with the 13,700 *precaristas* of the late 1940s.

the other end of the scale, 44% of the *precaristas* had been there less than five years. Of the large army of renters, well over half the sharecroppers had been in their farms less than ten years, and only 90% had been there over twenty-five years. Length of stay in fact varied in exact proportion to security of tenure.[12] In the years between 1946 and 1958, this pattern was preserved, with perhaps the plight of *precaristas* becoming more acute.

Of course, these divisions were not precise. There were rich sharecroppers, even rich squatters, and poor owners. Sharecropping was most frequent in tobacco. Ownership was most usual in dairy and mixed farming and least in tobacco. In coffee, sharecropping and cash-renting were equally common but in sugar cash-renting was to be expected. There were many large owner-operators or managers among the cattle estates of Camagüey. Cash tenancy was more common in Havana, Matanzas and Las Villas, squatting in Oriente. Written agreements were more frequent among cash-renters than sharecroppers.[13] All these different forms of tenure, however, did not conceal the fact that most farmers in Cuba were far from free; on the contrary, the large number of sugar *colonos* were tied by a 'triple bond to the mill: they were dependent upon it for the land to rent, for the milling of the cane and for credit.'[14] Other farmers were tied to their landlords by other credit arrangements.

Those working on the land numbered under half the working population: 42% in 1953. This was few for a country which still depended for its lifeblood on agricultural products. But, again, this situation had not changed much in fifty years. The 'drift away from the land', in so far as that famous phenomenon had occurred in Cuba, was chiefly the consequence of the terrible misery during the depression. People went into the towns, knowing that it was possible at least to beg there, and never returned. The proportion of the labour force working on the land remained much the same during the first quarter of the twentieth century (about 49%); it dropped to 41·9% by 1943, and remained there till 1953, if anything increasing by a fraction to ′42%. This stagnation obviously reflects the static condition of the sugar industry. For, of course, at least half those who got their living from the land were involved in sugar, either growing it or helping to grind it during the harvest.

It was unclear what proportion of land workers was black or mulatto

[12] *Censo Agrícola*, p. 92. The *Estudio* (p. 1381) errs in saying that from this table it can be seen that 47% of the *precaristas* had been *in situ* over ten years – the figure is 32%. Nor does this table give the lie to Castro's arguments that there had been rural dislodgements on a large scale, since these occurred in the 1950s. *Cf.* Nelson, p. 172–3.
[13] *Cf.* Nelson, p. 166–7.
[14] W.B. p. 92.

in the years immediately before the revolution; but in 1943 less than one-sixth were – 107,000 – or a good deal less than the national proportion of just under a third.[15] This proportion had remained static since the start of the century, though in 1919 the figure had risen to 130,000. Probably many of those who went into the towns in the depression were black or mulatto.

Many of the total number of agricultural workers, in particular the sugar workers, were accustomed to organized and disciplined employment. The most striking fact, however, about the agricultural labouring population was its migratory and seasonal nature. The Agricultural Census of 1946 reported that for the 432,690 farm wage-earners, the average time of employment in the year was four months – that is, during the harvest. During this period, the workers received reasonable wages, though they might have to go a long way from home to get them, probably without their families. Sometimes they might be paid by piece-work (such as the 26 cents per can of coffee beans noted by Lowry Nelson on the San Blas farm), sometimes by the month, sometimes supplemented with food and a room during the picking season. During the rest of the year, they were not employed. During the moderately prosperous year 1943, for instance, 665,000 were reported either unemployed in the dead season, or having no known occupation.[16] The number without work dropped during the autumn, as activity began in tobacco, moved on to coffee, and finally reached sugar. But even during the sugar harvest about 9% of the total labour force was unemployed. Unemployment rose again in the summer and, after the end of the sugar harvest there was only maintenance in the sugar mills and some planting. In those months employment also fell in transport, trade, shipping and other industries, as domestic consumption fell.[17] Between August and October the unemployment rate may have been about 21%.[18] In general, only 6% of agricultural workers seem to have been employed for nine months or more.[19]

The effects of unemployment may have been greater in the 1950s than before the war, except for the appalling years 1931–3. In, say, 1939, the sugar harvest might actually last a shorter time than ten or fifteen years later but there were more odd agricultural jobs to be picked up, so that the average cane-cutter might expect to find work for two-thirds of the *tiempo muerto*. In the 1950s mechanization was beginning to cut such jobs by perhaps half. According to some reports, perhaps a fifth of the

---

[15] 106,595 out of 575,637 *agricultores*.
[16] *Cf.* comment by W. B., p. 3; Nelson, p. 44. This was the time of the Agricultural Census of that year.
[17] This describes 1957.
[18] *Cf. Symposium de Recursos Nacionales de Cuba,* qu. Seers.
[19] W. B., p. 44.

rural people did not have steady work even during the harvest.[20] 'Even at the height of the *zafra* there are at least two hundred men without steady work against six hundred . . . at the mill . . .' Certainly, too, in the sugar industry itself, mechanization – replacing ox-carts with motor-lorries – had caused unemployment. Nor was there an outlet for surplus labour as, for instance, Puerto Rico and Jamaica had at least at that time. Most sugar workers probably had a small area of ground to cultivate, on which they kept chickens, and grew some elementary vegetables. But mostly they lived on credit, competing for occasional public works jobs which might arise.

The condition of farming was poor. Only 7% of the cultivated acreage was fertilized, most of it in sugar farms, and most of it in Pinar del Río, the least good sugar area. Not even the large North American companies had taken the trouble to analyse their soils for specific deficiencies[21] as a guide to the fertilizer needed. What fertilizer there was derived from imported raw materials, made up chiefly at one of two companies, both owned by U.S. firms.[22] Irrigation was infrequent too, and the restriction of the sugar crop in 1953 actually made it uneconomic in sugar: but in rice much was done in the 1950s. The total use of fertilizers increased by 100% between 1955 and 1957.[23]

Crop storage was inadequate except in the case of sugar. Several cold storage warehouses were built in important producing areas in 1945 at the cost of $1½M, but the operation of these was not good, control being in Havana, and at one such place the World Bank mission could not find anybody who understood the temperature instruments.[24]

There was only one manufacturer of farm machinery in Cuba;[25] the rest came from the U.S., at prices inflated 18% above U.S. prices by government tariffs and even higher by dealers: thus a Ford tractor in 1950 cost $1,290 in the U.S., $1,750 in Cuba; a milking machine $76 in the U.S., $134 in Cuba; one dealer was selling a chicken incubator at $239 instead of $89 in the U.S.[26] There were few repair shops and fewer machine sheds. Only eight coffee farms in Cuba had mechanical equipment for bean processing. Bad roads meant continued reliance on horses: in 1946 38% of Cuban farms were unable to use motor-transport at any time, and another 31% could not use it during the rainy season.[27] But there had been changes in the 1950s here also. Some rice planters

[20] A proprietor of a retail general store; W. B., p. 56.
[21] W. B., p. 106.
[22] The American Agricultural Chemical Company and the Aman Company (*cf.* W.B., p. 938–40).
[23] *Estudio*, p. 1131.
[24] W. B., p. 116.
[25] W. B., p. 973.
[26] W. B., p. 99.
[27] *Censo Agrícola*, qu. *Investment in Cuba*, p. 49.

used aeroplanes; and there were perhaps 23,000 tractors in use in 1958, compared with 1,200 in 1945.[28] The thriving rice production was mostly mechanized. But, as has been seen, such innovations were difficult in sugar and Lobo's machine cane-cutter, which remained in bond and then had to be sent back, was typical of the conditions of Cuba.

The import of machinery raised the question of its effect on jobs in all spheres. Workers were torn by the desire to make their work easier and by their fear of losing it altogether as a result.

Few small farmers could buy equipment. There was justified mistrust of the idea of shared ownership of machinery, for that meant no single person had an incentive to take responsibility for its care.

There was little co-ordination between government and farmers. The 219 inspectors appointed by the Ministry of Agriculture to distribute seed, literature, and information, were badly paid, and so spent only half their time at their jobs, maybe otherwise operating farms of their own. Some inspectors did not receive travelling expenses. The Government knew how to manage tariffs, but not agricultural economics. The Ministry's agricultural research station at San Antonio de los Baños was in poor shape. Research programmes were planned, but little was done. Nobody was prepared to carry on with his predecessor's work. In the days of Grau and Prío, a change of administration was thought a good reason for abandoning any project. Funds were short, too, at both the sugar and experimental station at Jovellanos and the coffee one at Palma Soriano; in 1950 the former had not received any of the funds for which special sugar taxes had been levied since 1940.[29] The coffee station was situated on bad ground. No one kept farms in touch with these centres or with the agricultural education department at the University of Havana. The Ministry maintained small agricultural secondary schools in each of the Cuban provinces, for the sons of farmers. But few of those who went returned to farm; and why should only farmers' sons be allowed to go?[30]

Some improvement, admittedly, had come from the agricultural section of the industrial and agricultural bank (BANFAIC). Set up in December 1950, it had hardly had a chance before Prío fell. Still it continued, though its activities became increasingly involved with

[28] This is a controversial matter. In 1955, the U.S. Embassy (*Investment in Cuba*) thought there were about 13,000 tractors in use. Import in the next four years 1955–8 may have been about 2,000 a year which would lead to a figure of 21,000. But the Colegio Nacional de Ingenieros Agrónomos y Azucareros de Cuba en el Exilio speak of 25,000, and so did International Harvester. The question becomes important when the Revolution's handling of agriculture is considered (*cf. Estudio*, p. 1149). The committee in the U.S. dealing with Castro's proposal for the exchange of the 1,200 prisoners after Cochinos Bay for 500 tractors thought there were 22,500 wheel tractors then in Cuba, and 3,000 caterpillars (*cf.* Haynes Johnson, p. 238).

[29] W. B., p. 120–21.

[30] W. B., p. 119.

politics and favouritism. BANFAIC provided several worthwhile long-term loans for irrigation, buildings, stock and property; and some short-term loans for annual costs. It organized a number of rural credit schemes. It made possible the mechanization of rice production and supported coffee and maize prices.[31] In the 1950s credit could be got for other things than sugar growing.

In 1958, cane accounted for probably 36.5% of the value of the Cuban agricultural production. Beef followed, bringing in 15.5%, with milk at 10%, and tobacco only equal with rice at 6%. Coffee was even lower, at a mere 4%. Tobacco had dropped back in the last fifteen years, but otherwise the pattern had remained much the same. Diversification existed on a small scale; 70% of farms reported some income from cereals and beans, 66.7% from root crops, and 61% from livestock products.[32]

Home production accounted for 70% of Cuba's food.[33] Chief imports were rice, lard, pulses and flour; also some eggs, potatoes, some fruit and vegetables, tinned goods and condensed milk.

Cattle-rearing had a longer history in Cuba even than sugar. Most ranches were in the east of the island, particularly the big cattle district of Camagüey. These ranches resembled those of the North American mid-west. Many cattle estates were run by managers: in Camagüey, indeed, it was normal. About three-quarters of all the farms of Cuba had some livestock, but only 18% realized the major section of farm income from livestock, about half of them large ranches, and half small farms.[34] There were about the same number of head of cattle in Cuba in the 1950s as in the 1920s;[35] from being an exporter of beef Cuba had indeed become an importer. The cattle per head of population was far less than in 1894. The number of pigs had roughly kept up with the population, though the climate was against pig breeding – hence the reliance on U.S. lard. Still, the native pig survived, usually left to root for himself. Imports of lard went up by a third in the 1950s.[36]

This was an unhappy situation. Cuba had many possibilities as a cattle-raising country. Pasture was always available on natural grasses, and occupied between 35% and 45% of the whole country. Certainly,

[31] Sugar:	$M 266.6
Beef:	$M 112
Milk:	$M 72
Tobacco:	$M 45.2
Rice:	$M 45.5
Coffee:	$M 31.5
TOTAL (with others)	$M 731

(Estimate by INRA Production Department, qu. Sears.)

[32] *Censo Agricultura*, qu. *Investment in Cuba*.
[33] *Investment in Cuba*, p. 29.
[34] See *Censo Ganadero de 1952*.
[35] About 4.5 million in 1955, 5.0 million in 1930, 5.3 million in 1920.
[36] *Investment in Cuba*, p. 48. Beef: $M9 in 1958.

the sub-tropical climate required selection of breeds and perhaps helped keep the cattle birth rate down to only two-thirds of that in the U.S. But grass was managed badly, though there was complete dependence on pasture feeding.[37] Some new strains of cattle had been brought in, however. Cattle farming employed about 100,000.[38] Perhaps 70 % of the land was occupied by cattle farms,[39] and most of the cattle were in the hands of owner-farmers rather than tenants. There were some small cattle farmers who undoubtedly found life hard, often being forced to sell at low prices.

It is obscure how many cattle ranches in Cuba were owned by North Americans, but the figure (unlike sugar) was on the increase: thus King Ranch of Texas was about to buy a series of huge new estates, in conjunction with the Rionda sugar interests.[40]

Dairy farming had improved in the last thirty years out of all proportion. In 1927 Havana had to import most of its milk and eggs. In the 1950s there were 2,000 specialized dairy farms, concentrated around the main cities. But still most milk came from beef herds, so that the average production per cow was very low – only two litres.[41] Eggs but not chickens were imported, though chickens had been before 1927.

Coffee production had recovered. For the first thirty years of the century, the coffee crop had been usually inadequate. Coffee had had to be imported. In 1927 a heavy tariff was imposed, and the depression followed. Domestic demand fell. By the late 1930s, coffee had even begun to be exported again. After 1945 domestic demand rose again and, in some years, coffee was once more imported. Harvests fluctuated wildly; that of 1949–50 was 43% higher than the year before; in 1956 Cuba exported 46 million pounds of coffee, in 1952 she imported 70 million. But in general, the old bad days of complete reliance on the import of coffee had come to an end.[42]

Nearly all Cuba's 9,000–10,000 coffee farms (*cafetales*) were in southeast Oriente, and that region produced 85–90 % of the total.[43] The number of farms had not much increased since the 1930s.[44] The area given over to coffee remained the same. Most coffee land was owned by people

---

[37] *Cf.* Dumont (*Cuba*, p. 26) who remarked:
'*En plantant de la pangola dont la production s'étale sur neuf mois de l'année, au lieu de quatre avec la Guinée, on atteint la valeur de 30 à 40 q ha de grains. En la fertilisant rationellement, on double à peu près, 60 à 70 q. Si on ajoute l'irrigation et le pâturage rationné, on peut presque doubler à nouveau, et on a déjà noté 130 à 140 q : soit 27 fois plus que les prés négligés.*'
[38] Núñez Jiménez, p. 323.
[39] Núñez Jiménez has 68%.
[40] Núñez Jiménez, p. 327–8.
[41] *Investment in Cuba. Cf. Estudio*, p. 1106–7.
[42] *Cf.* W. B., p. 826; Péñez de la Riva, p. 233–44.
[43] These were those who reported coffee as their main source of income. Another 10,000 had some coffee plants.
[44] There were supposed then to have been 8,041 farms.

who did not operate it, for coffee farmers were usually tenants, maybe only with eight-year agreements – and coffee trees only bear after four or five years. Perhaps afterwards a new agreement might be drawn up whereby the tenant became sharecropper and handed over to the land-lord a third of the crop. Even owner-operators were often victimized by those to whom they sold the crop. They might be charged 20 % interest on all credit, accompanied by a demand for the transfer of the property as guarantee. If, as sometimes happened in Oriente, the creditor was a wholesale grocer, he could force the farmer to buy from him (and at a high price) all the food that he required. Sometimes owners might aban-don their estate. While all coffee growers needed credit, few were credit-worthy. The grocer might borrow from banks. If so, he would re-lend to the coffee grower at a high rate, sometimes up to 25 %, or its equivalent in coffee, at low cost. In general, even after the coming of BANFAIC, there were few means of supplying farmers with the five to six years' credit which they needed to enlarge or to improve coffee tree standards.[45]

Coffee picking, in October to December, was usually done by family labour backed on larger farms by a varying number of migratory work-ers, perhaps moving in gangs from one farm to another, possibly from far away, probably returning to the same place each year. Such workers would stay during the harvest in a large *bohío*, specially built, having meals at the family table.

Coffee farmers had neither knowledge nor money to get the best out of their trees. There was little effort to make terraces to avoid erosion, little attention to selection of plants, little fertilization, and usually primitive means for the drying of beans for the market. This was chiefly due to the character of the tenure. In 1945 there were only eight *cafetals* with mechanical preparation plants. Also, all forms of communication with coffee growers were bad. Most farms were isolated, scattered in re-mote mountains, reached only by mule or on foot. It cost $4.00 per quintal (101.41 lbs) to get coffee from remote farms to Guantánamo. In the rainy season it was almost impossible to get there at all.

Thanks presumably to the soil and climate, Cuban coffee remained among the best in the world. It was sad to see it so ill-regarded. Coffee growers, were, unlike sugar manufacturers and tobacco growers, all Cuban – even if Cuban of remote French blood.

Rice production had been a success of the last ten years, though for most of the twentieth century it had supplied less than 10 % of Cuba's large demands.[46] Large-scale mechanization and irrigation radically altered the situation and by 1953 produced a third of the demand. Where

[45] W. B., p. 593; Nelson, p. 128–9.
[46] Consumption amounted to between 110 and 132 lbs per head a year between 1945 and 1955.

there were 50,000 acres of ricefields before 1940, by the mid-1950s there were over 200,000. Rice was now grown chiefly in Pinar del Río and in Oriente (particularly around Manzanillo). This was BANFAIC's chief success, being realized in Batista's day, if planned under Prío, and had been one of the main recommendations of the World Bank in 1950.[47] This rice expansion brought a new type of large farm. In the 1950s, as before, large rice growers controlled small ones – particularly in the region near Manzanillo – for they acted as banks for them, charging interest of 10% on loans or on credit for equipment.[48] Despite this, Cuba continued to import more rice than any other Latin American country, nearly all from the U.S.

Other successful products were henequen (for rope or twine), in which Cuba and Mexico accounted for almost the whole world production. Most was exported raw to the U.S. Cotton was grown intermittently, but not now commercially.

The great old forests of Cuba had disappeared. Forest occupied only 15% of the land surface, in place of 40% in 1899. But probably only a small proportion of even this reduced area was really covered by old hardwood forests. The pines of Pinar del Río had all gone. The worst destruction had however come after the First World War in Oriente. No one worried much about these changes, despite a law preventing the felling of trees without permission, and it seemed likely that the remaining land in forest would vanish, save in remote mountainous regions. Much of it went for fuel. Plywood, most of the cooperage needs of the country, wooden crates, all these were imported.[49] Cuban mahogany, once greatly prized, was so scarce that exports had been prohibited in 1946.[50] But funds obtained by tax for reafforestation had been diverted under Grau to private gain.

Cuba had done little to develop its fishing. The yearly catch varied between fifty and sixty million pounds a year, much the same as just before 1939. Bad fishing technique, refrigeration and marketing was responsible for failure even to satisfy the undeveloped demand. Cuba imported almost half its fish. The most common fish caught was in the Gulf of Mexico, the Red grouper – *cherna del alto* – a kind of salmon.

The fishermen of the big fleet at Havana numbered about ten or twelve to a boat, receiving two-thirds of the catch, while the owner got the rest. Food and supplies were advanced by the owner, and paid back by the men out of their profits from the catch. Expeditions might last an average of 24 days. Most of Cuba's 7,000 fishing boats were small sailing boats or rowing boats. Except for two big fleets based on Havana and

[47] W.B., p. 556.
[48] *Cf.* W. B., p. 594; and Chonchol.
[49] *Investment in Cuba*, p. 54; W. B., p. 903–13.
[50] See Earl E. Smith *The Forests of Cuba* (María Mons Cabot Foundation), 1954.

Batabanó owned by Julio Lobo, they were disorganized. The industry was so badly organized that the whole Havana fishing fleet sometimes returned at the same time. Then there would be far too much fish, and boats would have to stay in harbour with their catch aboard, maybe causing the whole catch to rot before it could be sold.[51]

It seemed unlikely that communal effort was the key to progress. In 1946 Grau's government had set up a fishing co-operative at Batabanó and given one big boat for tuna fishing and some smaller boats. But the fishermen were unable to co-operate. The big boat was used by private operators. The co-operative turned out a fiasco.[52] The same thing had occurred at Caribarén on the north coast, in an attempt to handle sales. But such examples of fishing co-operatives as there have been are not those imposed or even suggested by governments, but those which were spontaneously developed, as in Israel or Catalonia before 1936.[53]

Some improvements came to fishing in the 1950s. BANFAIC, in January 1952, set up a new marine biology research centre.[54] Batista's government created a fishermen's association and a national fish institute. In 1953 a new floating refrigerator capable of taking 500,000 lbs was built. In 1954 a fish distribution terminal began to be built with capacity for 60,000 lbs of fish per eight hours and refrigeration for a million pounds.[55] Still, in 1958, 35 million pounds of fish were imported, just over the apparent value of fish produced by Cubans.[56]

In Cuba, as elsewhere, only with large or at least medium-sized farms could the advantages of modern farming be effectively run. Excessive division of land leads to as many problems as excessive concentration – as in Galicia or Haiti. Rearrangements of land ownership, however progressive, will probably fail unless accompanied by great educational efforts by the Government concerned, and by more just and better credit and marketing arrangements, the former demanding the distribution of a vast quantity of brochures describing in language simple enough for ordinary farmers to understand the method of developing new products. In addition, efficient agriculture depended on a national plan which would concentrate dairy and vegetable produce near the great cities and remove from those zones the main sources of raw material; sugar, for example, could effectively be taken away from Havana.

Despite the increase in the area of farms, agriculture still held to the pattern of the age of slavery: a few huge estates, centering around sugar, upon which the national wealth depended, including *colonos* and wage

[51] W.B., p. 917.
[52] W.B., p. 918.
[53] See Langdon Davies, *Behind the Spanish Barricades*.
[54] HAR, February 1952.
[55] *Estudio*, p. 1032 ff.
[56] 33.7 million lbs in 1957 (Núñez Jiménez, p. 337).

earners, the latter being the grandchildren of the slaves of the past, and equally well disciplined. They were factory workers in a sense, whether they worked in the mill or mechanically cutting in the field, and hence were unlike most 'peasants' in the rest of Latin America.[57] 'Agrarian reform' was the solution suggested by most Latin American economists to the problem of their continent. The view was shared by many North American liberals. There were already some coffee co-operatives.[58] But to carry out major reform with compensation was immensely expensive. In 1961, the first evaluation of land in the Colombian agrarian reform gave an estimate twenty times larger than the annual budget. In a liberal society no doubt the solution to the 'agrarian problem' of Cuba would have been the movement of many workers to new work in industry in cities or in the U.S.A. But this was not to be.

[57] Probably 60% of the agricultural labour force worked for wages.

[58] Pérez de la Riva, *El Café*, p. 230: for instance the *Caficultores de Cumanayagua* (Cienfuegos), or the *Bloc Agrícola* in Palma Soriano.

Sugar Tables[1]

CUBAN AND WORLD SUGAR PRODUCTION
1770–1970[2]
(All figures in tons)

| Year | WORLD PRODUCTION | | | CUBAN PRODUCTION |
	Cane	Beet	Total	Total
1770–8				10,000
1786				12,654
1787				12,248
1788				13,844
1789				13,825
1790	ESTIMATES			15,577
1791				17,003
1792	NOT	NIL		18,571
1793				17,594
1794	AVAILABLE			20,726
1795				14,086
1796				24,075
1797				23,613
1798				26,974
1799				33,120
1800				28,419
1801				31,968
1802				40,881
1803				31,615
1804				38,791
1805				34,909

[1] The above table has been constructed as follows: Noel Deerr THE HISTORY OF SUGAR for Cuban figures to 1900 and world figures to 1941; *Anuario Azucarero de Cuba* (1959) for Cuban figures from 1900 to 1959; F. A. O. handbook for world figures from 1942 to 1959; World Sugar Council for all figures since 1960.

[2] Many figures have been corrected to the nearest thousand, hence some apparent discrepancies in the World Total column.

	WORLD PRODUCTION			CUBAN PRODUCTION
Year	Cane	Beet	Total	Total
1806				31,302
1807				36,254
1808				25,175
1809		NOT		57,786
1810				37,334
1815				42,822
1816				40,097
1817				43,415
1818				41,476
1819				38,548
1820				43,119
1821				47,333
1822		AVAILABLE		52,359
1823				60,042
1824				49,065
1829				73,200
1836				164,885
1838				147,000
1839	781,716	38,602	820,318	130,200
1840	788,000	48,198	830,198	160,891
1841	829,000	50,919	879,919	162,425
1842	840,000	41,240	881,240	
1843	909,000	46,911	955,911	NOT
1844	961,000	53,458	1,014,458	AVAILABLE
1845	1,003,000	60,857	1,063,857	
1846	1,017,000	80,004	1,097,004	
1847	1,067,000	96,346	1,163,346	
1848	1,008,000	79,885	1,087,885	
1849	1,070,000	110,737	1,180,737	
1850	1,043,000	159,435	1,202,435	223,145
1851	1,186,000	163,757	1,349,757	263,999
1852	1,167,000	202,810	1,369,810	251,609
1853	1,284,000	194,893	1,478,893	322,000
1854	1,301,000	176,210	1,477,210	374,000
1855	1,243,000	246,856	1,489,856	392,000
1856	1,195,000	276,702	1,471,702	348,000
1857	1,220,000	370,004	1,590,004	355,000
1858	1,358,000	409,614	1,767,614	385,000

	WORLD PRODUCTION			CUBAN PRODUCTION
Year	Cane	Beet	Total	Total
1859	1,438,000	387,539	1,825,539	536,000
1860	1,376,000	351,602	1,727,602	447,000
1861	1,466,000	413,671	1,879,671	446,000
1862	1,363,000	474,719	1,857,719	525,000
1863	1,334,000	457,146	1,791,146	507,000
1864	1,333,000	474,719	1,837,719	575,000
1865	1,506,000	680,685	2,195,685	620,000
1866	1,544,000	671,810	2,215,810	612,000
1867	1,499,000	687,281	2,186,281	597,000
1868	1,759,000	760,025	2,519,025	749,000
1869	1,728,000	821,141	2,549,141	726,000
1970	1,662,000	939,096	2,601,096	726,000
1871	1,697,000	976,915	2,673,915	547,000
1872	1,805,000	1,128,918	2,933,918	690,000
1873	1,848,000	1,198,463	3,046,463	775,000
1874	1,883,000	1,284,586	3,167,586	681,000
1875	1,816,000	1,377,336	3,193,336	718,000
1876	1,792,000	1,085,204	2,877,204	590,000
1877	1,770,000	1,358,828	3,128,828	520,000
1878	1,873,000	1,615,934	3,488,934	533,000
1879	1,908,000	1,459,385	3,367,385	670,000
1880	1,883,000	1,857,000	3,740,000	530,000
1881	1,806,000	1,832,000	3,638,000	493,000
1882	2,079,000	2,173,000	4,252,000	595,000
1883	2,210,000	2,323,000	4,533,000	460,000
1884	2,225,000	2,550,000	4,775,000	559,000
1885	2,300,000	2,172,000	4,472,000	631,000
1886	2,400,000	2,687,000	5,087,000	732,000
1887	2,541,000	2,367,000	4,908,000	647,000
1888	2,359,000	3,556,000	5,915,000	657,000
1889	2,138,000	3,537,000	5,675,000	NOT AVAILABLE
1890	2,597,000	3,680,000	6,277,000	632,000
1891	3,502,000	3,481,000	6,983,000	817,000
1892	3,040,000	3,381,000	6,421,000	976,000
1893	3,561,000	3,833,000	7,394,000	816,000
1894	3,531,000	4,726,000	8,257,000	1,054,000
1895	2,840,000	4,221,000	7,061,000	1,004,000
1896	2,842,000	4,802,000	7,644,000	225,000

| Year | WORLD PRODUCTION | | | CUBAN PRODUCTION |
	Cane	Beet	Total	Total
1897	2,869,000	4,695,000	7,564,000	212,000
1898	2,995,000	4,690,000	7,685,000	306,000
1899	2,881,000	5,411,000	8,292,000	336,000
1900	5,253,000	6,006,000	11,259,000	300,000
1901	5,763,000	6,881,000	12,643,000	636,000
1902	5,844,000	5,700,000	11,544,000	850,000
1903	6,035,000	6,067,000	12,101,000	1,000,000
1904	6,265,000	4,920,000	11,185,000	1,045,000
1905	6,729,000	7,274,000	14,003,000	1,173,000
1906	7,124,000	7,245,000	14,349,000	1,231,000
1907	6,643,000	7,063,000	13,706,000	1,431,000
1908	7,372,000	6,986,000	14,358,000	970,000
1909	8,042,000	6,648,000	14,690,000	1,536,000
1910	8,156,000	8,668,000	16,824,000	1,843,000
1911	8,571,000	6,947,000	15,518,000	1,465,000
1912	8,969,000	9,039,000	18,008,000	1,913,000
1913	9,661,000	9,054,000	18,715,000	2,442,000
1914	9,902,000	8,312,000	18,213,000	2,615,000
1915	10,611,000	6,110,000	16,721,000	2,609,000
1916	11,173,000	5,865,000	17,038,000	3,034,000
1917	11,710,000	5,153,000	16,863,000	3,063,000
1918	11,452,000	4,428,000	15,880,000	3,473,000
1919	11,862,000	3,350,000	15,213,000	4,012,000
1920	11,925,000	4,906,000	16,831,000	3,742,000
1921	12,740,000	5,130,000	17,870,000	3,983,000
1922	12,500,000	5,357,000	17,857,000	4,035,000
1923	13,520,000	6,059,000	19,579,000	3,646,000
1924	14,906,000	8,295,000	23,201,000	4,113,000
1925	15,141,000	8,618,000	23,759,000	5,189,000
1926	15,315,000	7,896,000	23,211,000	4,932,000
1927	15,953,000	9,164,000	25,118,000	4,509,000
1928	17,188,000	9,613,000	26,801,000	4,042,000
1929	17,382,000	9,249,000	26,730,000	5,156,000
1930	15,942,000	11,911,000	27,853,000	4,671,000
1931	16,216,000	8,782,000	24,997,000	3,121,000
1932	14,742,000	7,994,000	22,736,000	2,604,000
1933	15,113,000	9,159,000	24,272,000	1,994,000
1934	14,842,000	9,792,000	24,634,000	2,256,000

| | WORLD PRODUCTION | | | CUBAN PRODUCTION |
Year	Cane	Beet	Total	Total
1935	16,598,000	10,430,000	27,029,000	2,538,000
1936	18,416,000	10,233,000	28,649,000	2,557,000
1937	18,782,000	11,194,000	29,975,000	2,975,000
1938	18,451,000	10,225,000	28,676,000	2,976,000
1939	19,395,000	11,116,000	30,511,000	2,724,000
1940	19,255,000	11,244,000	30,499,000	2,779,000
1941	19,225000	9,373,000	28,598,000	2,407,000
1942	15,874,000	8,466,000	24,340,000	3,345,000
1943	14,449,000	8,588,000	23,037,000	2,842,000
1944	14,757,000	7,375,000	22,132,000	4,171,000
1945	13,016,000	6,346,000	19,362,000	3,454,000
1946	12,815,000	5,370,000	18,185,000	3,940,000
1947	15,451,000	7,282,000	22,733,000	5,677,000
1948	17,109,000	7,485,000	24,594,000	5,877,000
1949	18,045,000	10,065,000	28,110,000	5,074,000
1950	18,449,000	10,711,000	29,160,000	5,395,000
1951	19,568,000	13,372,000	33,566,000	5,589,000
1952	22,168,000	13,919,000	36,087,000	7,012,000
1953	21,613,000	13,372,000	34,985,000	5,007,000
1954	22,402,000	16,369,000	38,771,000	4,753,000
1955	23,510,000	14,844,000	38,354,000	4,404,000
1956	23,954,000	15,751,000	39,705,000	4,605,000
1957	25,586,000	16,058,000	41,644,000	5,506,000
1958	25,335,000	18,085,000	44,420,000	5,614,000
1959	28,840,000	20,766,000	49,606,000	5,788,000
1960	29,372,000	22,719,000	52,091,000	5,862,000
1961	31,445,000	23,303,000	54,749,000	6,707,000
1962	29,971,000	21,615,000	51,586,000	4,815,000
1963	30,317,000	22,321,000	52,637,000	3,821,000
1964	32,821,000	27,327,000	60,148,000	4,590,000
1965	37,525,000	27,567,000	65,091,000	6,082,000
1966	36,366,000	27,823,000	64,189,000	4,867,000
1967	37,762,000	28,924,000	66,686,000	6,236,000
1968	37,175,000	29,717,000	66,892,000	5,315,000
1969*	38,100,000	30,900,000	70,000,000	4,700,000
1970*	42,500,000	30,000,000	72,500,000	9,000,000†

* Estimates
† Cuban Government Estimate

World Raw Sugar Prices

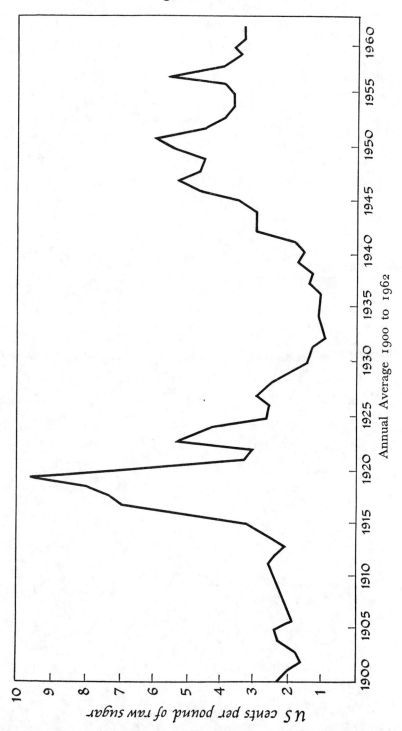

Annual Average 1900 to 1962

US cents per pound of raw sugar

Glossary
Bibliographical Note
General Bibliography
Index

Glossary

ABAKUÁ   Secret Society of Afro-Cubans based on Efik legend. Members were known as Ñáñigos.

AGUARDIENTE   Cane Brandy

APAPA   Haussa Negro from Nigeria

ARROBA   Spanish measure, approximately equal to 25lbs or 1/90 of a ton

BAGASSE   Cane waste

BATEY   The group of buildings around a sugar mill, including living quarters

BARRIL (OF MOLASSES) $5\frac{1}{2}$ U.S. gallons (nineteenth century)

BOCOY   1) Hogshead in which was put mascabado sugar; might have added up to anything between 40–60 *arrobas*, more usually 50–54 *arrobas* or a little over $\frac{1}{2}$ ton of sugar (1000–1500 lbs)
2) Hogshead of 25 to 33 barrels of molasses (nineteenth century)

BOSONGO, BA-SONGO   Angolan Negro tribe

BOX OF SUGAR (CAJA)   From 17 to 22 *arrobas* (in nineteenth century)

BOZAL   Negro born in Africa, who could not talk Spanish. After the end of the slave trade became synonym for tough. (Do not confuse with *bozal*, meaning piece of pork given as a reward for good conduct to horses, nor again *bozal*, meaning, in Aragon and Murcia (Spain), a kind of muzzle for dogs)

CABALLERÍA   Cuban measure equivalent to 330 acres or 130 hectares

CABILDO   1) Town Council
2) Club, especially Negro club

CACHIMBO   Old fashioned sugar mill of very small size

CALESERO   Coachman of the *volante* era

CARABALÍ   Corruption of Calbary. Native of Calabar, Nigeria

CENTRAL   Modern sugar mill acting as 'centre' for grinding of cane

CHINCHAL   Small business

CHINO   Child of a mulatto and Negress or vice-versa. The word fell out of use when real Chinese began to be imported, though these were officially referred to as 'Asiáticos'

CIMARRÓN   Escaped slave (*cf.* Maroon, a corruption)

COLONO   Sugar planter, owner of a *Colonia*, who sells cane to a *Central*

CONTRAMAYORAL   Subordinate to Mayoral

CORRAL   Small farm, granted in the sixteenth century to breed pigs, one league in radius, but later also polygonal with 72 or 120 sides, making up 421 cabs and 36,625 cordeles. Division always practised by communal vote – after 1819. Now used to describe any circular farm, even if cattle in them, and also any space where escaped animals are held

CRIOLLO   1) Any Spaniard born in the Empire rather than in the homeland (See *Peninsular*)

2) A Negro slave born in the Americas (*cf. Bozal, Ladino*)

CUCURUCHO   Very dark rough sugar from the bottom of the cane, in contrast to *Blanco* and *Quebrado*

DIEZMO   Tithe

ESQUIFACIÓN   Clothing for slaves

ESTANCIA   Farm, usually about 12 to 125 acres, and usually concentrating on sweet potato, *ñame*, platanos, lettuce, fodder (*maloja*) or market gardening and dairy stuff

FINCA   Medium- or large-sized Cuban farm

GARRAFÓN   25 bottles of wine

GOLPE, GOLPE DE ESTADO   *Coup d'état*

GUAJIRO   Countryman, i.e. farmer or peasant

GUARAPO   Cane juice

HACENDADO   Proprietor of farm

HACIENDA   Farm

HATO   Large farm, with pasture, for cattle breeding. Originally either circular or with 72 sides, with a central point designated by a big heavy wooden post known as *Bramadero*. When circular it was 2 leagues in radius, i.e. an area of 1684 cabs and 144 cordeles, 4 times the size of a *corral*. See also *potrero*

HORMA   Cone in which sugar was put in the Casa de Purga (eighteenth and nineteenth centuries)

INGENIO   Sugar mill. Used usually to describe sugar mill of the past, pre-*Central* era

ISLEÑO   Canary islander

LADINO   A Negro slave brought from Africa who could talk Spanish. Earlier, an African slave who had been two or more years in Spain and Portugal

LIBORIO   Symbolic name for a Cuban, e.g. John Bull, Uncle Sam, Juan Chapín (Guatemala), el Concho Primo (Dominican Republic), El Charro Mejicano

LUCUMÍ   African Negro from West Africa; yorubas

MASCABADO   Rough sugar not placed in cones but in *bocoyes*

MAESTRO DE AZÚCAR   Sugar chemist

MAMBÍ   is a word which ironically seems to have come from the Dominican Republic, probably of African origin meaning child of an ape or vulture: it seems to have been first used by the Spaniards to describe the rebels, who then assumed it themselves. That it is an African word is suggested by the fact that it has two plurals (*Mambies* and *Mambises*) and an odd feminine (*Mambisa*)

MANDINGO African Negro tribe established between Senegal and Liberia, and inland

MAYORAL Overseer

MERCED A grant, therefore a grant by the Spanish Crown. It has come to mean one of the circular grants given in the sixteenth and eighteenth centuries

MIEL Molasses

MONTERO Mounted cattle herd (see *Sabanero*)

MULECÓN, MULECÓ A male slave older than an infant, younger than puberty. Usually 7 to 10 years

MULEQUE 1) Adjective form Mulecón: *Dar muleque* – to die
2) Also Bozal slave from 6 to 14 years

ÑÁÑIGO Member of the Abakuá cult

PENINSULAR A person of Spanish blood born in Spain

POTRERO A small farm with pasture for cattle breeding. Originally circular. Hence *potrerero*

PIEZA DE INDIAS A Negro slave aged between 18 and 35. Also, *any* Negro slave

QUEBRADO (or Terciado) Brown-yellow sugar from the middle of the cone, lying between *Blanco* and *Cucurucho*

RANCHEADOR Man who pursued escaped slaves

RASPADURA Crude sweet sugar

REALENGO Royal or Crown territory. Used in colonial Cuba to describe the area left between the *mercedes* (grants to individuals). The word is still in use in respect of special areas: e.g. Realengo 18, an area in Oriente where there was a famous revolution in the 1930s

SABANERO Cattle herd (on foot). See *Montero*

SANTERO A priest, or impressario, of Afro-Cuban cults. Hence, *Santería*

SITUADO Subsidy

TRAPICHE The mill or the millhouse in which sugar was ground; in Cuba, came to be used to refer to old-fashioned and relatively unmechanized sugar mills in contrast to the *Ingenio* and the *Central*; i.e. therefore, sugar mills which only make *raspadwia* and *miel*

TREN Train; i.e. Jamaican train of cauldrons for use in evaporation stage of sugar manufacture

TASAJO Jerked (i.e. dried) beet

VEGA Plantation dedicated to tobacco

VOLANTE Old-fashioned Cuban coach and two horses (or one), with large wheels

YOLOF Senegalese Negro brought to Cuba in large numbers

Bibliographical Note

A list of the more important books and articles consulted in the preparation of this study is appended. This note suggests further reading.

GENERAL HISTORIES OF CUBA: The ten volume *Historia de la Nación Cubana* (Havana, 1952) by Ramiro Guerra and others is indigestible and often unreadable. Ramiro Guerra's *Manual de Historia de Cuba* is a useful but somewhat out-of-date general introduction (up till 1868). Jorge Ibarra's *Historia de Cuba* (published by the Cuban armed services, 1968) is a good, clear, modern account, which tails off after 1898. Willis Fletcher Johnson's *The History of Cuba* (5 vols, New York, 1920) still has much in it worth reading.

ECONOMIC HISTORIES: The chapters by Julio Le Riverend in Guerra, etc. (above), are always worth reading. The classic study is Heinrich Friedländer's *Historia Económica de Cuba* (Havana, 1944), but it is also out of date. The *Estudio Sobre Cuba* produced by José R. Alvarez Díaz and a team at the University of Miami (1963) is an invaluable if controversial source book. Useful material can still be found in old works by Humboldt, Pezuela, de la Sagra and García de Arboleya, but all have to be used with much care, especially the last.

THE SUGAR INDUSTRY: Nöel Deerr's *History of Sugar* (2 vols, London, 1948) is an excellent source book which should be brought up to date and reprinted. Ramiro Guerra's *Azúcar y Población en las Antillas* (many editions, including an abridged English translation as *Sugar and Society in the Caribbean*, Yale, 1964) is a famous introductory essay. Manuel Moreno Fraginals' *El Ingenio* (Vol. 1, Havana, 1964) is a magnificent piece of scholarship which has transformed our knowledge of this industry in the late eighteenth and early nineteenth centuries. Roland Ely's *Cuando Reinaba su Majestad El Azúcar* (Buenos Aires, 1963) is an admirable social history, though its technical sections should be used with caution.

These two books render out-of-date many of the older works by Ramiro Guerra or even Fernando Ortiz on this theme, though the latter's *Cuban Counterpoint: Tobacco and Sugar* (New York, 1947) remains attractive reading. Nothing of much value has been written on the sugar industry during the twentieth century.

BLACK CUBA: The best books here are those of Fernando Ortiz, particularly *Los Negros Esclavos* (Havana, 1916), and his disciple Lydia Cabrera (especially her study of the Ñáñigos, *La Sociedad Secreta Abakuá* (Havana, 1958)). Interesting general information can be found in the books of anthropologists such as Roger Bastide (e.g. *Les Amériques Noires*, Paris, 1967). On slavery there is Miguel Barnet's transcription of Esteban Montejo's memoirs (*The Autobiography of a Runaway Slave* London, 1968), the Cuban chapters of *Slavery in the Americas* by Hubert Klein (Oxford 1967) and Arthur Corwin's study of abolitionism, *Spain and the Abolition of Slavery in Cuba* (Texas, 1968).

THE ECONOMY: Apart from the general economic studies suggested above, much valuable information on the Cuban economy of the past can be found in the World Bank's *Report on Cuba* (Baltimore, 1952) and in *Investment in Cuba*, a study prepared by the U.S. Department of Commerce in 1955 for U.S. businessmen. Julián Alienes's *Características Fundamentales de la Economía Cubana* (Havana, 1950) and Henry Wallich's *Monetary Problems of an Export Economy* (Cambridge, Massachussetts, 1950) are useful. Captain Núñez Jiménez's *Geografía de Cuba* (Havana, 1960) is a useful, if slanted, compendium.

SOCIAL HISTORY: There is little to recommend here apart from Lowry Nelson's *Rural Cuba* (Minneapolis, 1950). A general survey can be found in Wyatt Macgaffey and Clifford Barnett's *Twentieth Century Cuba* (New York, 1965). The various Censuses (of 1899, 1907, 1919, 1943 and 1953) are all invaluable documents, particularly the first.

NINETEENTH-CENTURY HISTORY: Apart from the important works of Moreno Fraginals and Ely listed above, there are some useful political studies. Outstanding here is Herminio Portell Vilá's *Historia de Cuba en sus Relaciones con los Estados Unidos y España* (4 vols, Havana, 1938) though this carries twentieth-century grievances far back into the last century. Philip Foner's *History of Cuba and its Relations with the U.S.* (Vols 1 and 2, New York, 1961 and 1962) covers much the same ground for the English reader and has an excellent chapter on the tobacco industry. Juan Pérez de la Riva's edition of the letters of Captain General Tacón, *Correspondencia Reservada* (Havana, 1963) is a monument of patient scholarship. The best study of the Ten Year War remains Antonio Pirala's *Anales de la Guerra de Cuba* (Madrid, 1896), though it emphazises the Spanish point of view. The best short account of the second War of Independence is that contained in Vol. 2 of Melchor Fernández Almagro's *Historia Política de la España Contemporánea* (Madrid, 1959), though once again it is pro-Spanish. From the Cuban side, useful accounts appear in the big *Historia de la Nación Cubana* and in Jorge Ibarra's history, though this is not a war about which any Cuban has been able to write with objectivity, despite the vast bibliography. There is unfortunately as yet no first-class biography of José Martí.

Many of the nineteenth-century travellers to Cuba left invaluable accounts, as will be seen from the use made of them in this book. (A useful bibliography appears in Ely's work, above-mentioned.) Among the most helpful are those by Samuel Hazard (*Cuba with Pen and Pencil*, Hartford, 1871), Edwin Atkins (*Sixty Years in Cuba*, Cambridge, Massachussetts, 1926) and the Comtesse Merlin's *La Havane* (3 vols, Paris, 1844).

THE SPANISH-AMERICAN WAR AND THE OCCUPATION: The classic debunking book is Warren Millis's *The Martial Spirit* (New York, 1931). An excellent study of the press in 1895–1898 in the U.S. is Joseph Wisan's *The Cuban Crisis as Reflected in the New York Press* (reprinted by Octagon, New York, 1965). North American political attitudes are very well discussed in John Grenville and George Berkeley Young's *Politics, Strategy and American Diplomacy* (Yale, 1967). A more old-fashioned study, but admirably written, is Margaret Leech's *In the Days of McKinley* (New York, 1959). The first U.S. military occupation of Cuba is described by David Healey (*The U.S. and Cuba* 1898–1902, Madison, 1963) and the second by Allan Reed Millett (*The Politics of Intervention*, Ohio, 1968), which unfortunately appeared while that section of the present book was already complete. The first volume of Hubert Hagedorn's life of General Leonard Wood (New York, 1931) is revealing.

THE CUBAN REPUBLIC 1902–1952: The best study of the first twenty years of the Cuban Republic remains that by G. E. Chapman (*A History of the Cuban Republic*, New York, 1927). R. Martínez Ortiz's *Cuba: Los Primeros Años de Independencia* (2 vols, Paris, 1921) is good up to 1909. Leland Jenks's entertaining economic study, *Our Cuban Colony* (New York, 1928) is still excellent up to about 1925. The compilation of facts in León Primelles's two volumes of *Crónica Cubana* (Havana, 1955 and 1957) is useful. A. Sanjenis's study of José Miguel Gómez (*Tiburón*, Havana, 1915) is entertaining.

From 1925 till 1952 the material is scant indeed. Robert F. Smith's *The U.S. and Cuba* (New York, 1960) is an excellent study of U.S. – Cuban commercial relations in the 1920s. There is, however, no study of either Machado, the first *Batistato* (1933–44), nor of the era of Grau and Prío. Even the Revolution of 1933 has been neglected. *Faute de mieux*, useful for this period are Gonzalo de Quesada's *En Cuba Libre* (Havana, 1938), Ricardo Adam y Silva's *La Gran Mentira* (Havana,

1947) and Alberto Lamar Schweyer's *Comó Cayó el Presidente Machado* (Madrid, 1934). The early chapters of Ruby Hart Phillips's *Cuba, Island of Paradox* (New York, 1959) are excellent as a general guide to the atmosphere of the Revolution of 1933. I also found the dispatches of the British Minister in Havana at the time, Mr Grant Watson (now available in the Public Record Office, London), very helpful, as well, of course, as the reports from Mr Sumner Welles, the U.S. Ambassador (in the 1933 volume of the Foreign Relations of the U.S.) Luis Conte Agüero's *Eduardo Chibás* (Mexico, 1955) illuminates the short history of the Ortodoxo movement. The memoirs of Raúl Roa (*Retorno a la Alborada*, Santa Clara, 1964) contain much interesting material on the late 1920s.

THE SECOND BATISTATO: Again there is no general study. The following books are of value in piecing together the history of the regime: Batista's own apologia, *Respuesta* (Mexico, 1960); José Suárez Núñez's *El Gran Culpable* (Caracas, 1963) and Florentino Rosell's *La Verdad* (Miami, 1960). Ambassador Earl Smith's *The Fourth Floor* (New York, 1962) contains useful information despite its attacks on the State Department.

THE REVOLUTION: On the Castro movement in the 1950s there is no shortage of material. The best general study of the struggle against Batista remains Robert Taber's *M-26, The Biography of a Revolution* (New York, 1963), despite the haste with which it was written. Theodore Draper's two books of essays, *Castro's Revolution* (New York, 1962) and *Castroism: Theory and Practice* (New York, 1968) still contain much that is useful. Guevara's *Pasajes de la Guerra Revolucionaria* (Havana, 1963, many foreign editions) is excellent for the war in the Sierra up to the end of 1957. Other memoirs of more or less use include Raúl Castro's campaign diaries, originally published in *Revolución*, January 1959 and republished in *La Sierra y el Llano* (Havana, 1959); Rufo López Fresquet's *My Fourteen Months with Castro* (New York, 1966); Manuel Urrutia's *Fidel Castro & Co* (New York, 1964); Fernando Sánchez Amaya's *Diario del Granma* (Havana, 1959); and René Ray Rivero's *Libertad y Revolución* (Havana, 1959).

The best general analysis of what happened to the regime after 1959 and why is Andrés Suárez's *Cuba: Castroism and Communism* (Cambridge, Massachusetts, 1967). The most interesting picture of Castro is given in Lee Lockwood's long interview, in *Castro's Cuba, Cuba's Fidel* (New York, 1967). A good introduction to Cuba's development in relation to the hemisphere appears in Boris Goldenberg's *The Cuban Revolution and Latin America* (London, 1965) while the chapters on Cuba itself are fair and well-balanced. Biographies of Castro include Herbert Matthews's enthusiastic *Castro* (London, 1969) and Luis Conte Agüero's hostile polemic, *Los dos rostros de Fidel Castro* (Mexico, 1960). The Guevara bibliography grows daily.

The best introduction to the economic changes of the revolution is given in Dudley Seers (ed.), *Cuba, the economic and social revolution* (Chapel Hill, 1964), though it only goes up to 1962–3. René Dumont's *Cuba, Socialisme et Développement* (Paris, 1964) is a sound introduction to the history of agriculture under Castro. There are many journalists' impressions of Cuba, particularly of the early days: C. Wright Mills's *Listen Yankee* (New York, 1960) has a period interest, as has Jean Paul Sartre's impressions (*Sartre on Cuba*, New York, 1961). A sympathetic picture of the crisis in Cuban society in late 1960 was given by Warren Miller's *Sixty Miles from Home* (New York, 1961).

North American reactions to Castro are analysed in Manuela Semidei's *Les États-Unis et la Révolution Cubaine* (Paris, 1968) and in the well-known works of Theodore Sorensen (*Kennedy*, London, 1965), Arthur Schlesinger Jr. (*A Thousand Days*, London, 1965) and Roger Hillsman (*To Move a Nation*, New York, 1967). The story of the Bay of Pigs is well told, from the point of view of the invaders, by Haynes Johnson (*The Bay of Pigs*, New York, 1964). Much useful information can be found in the hearings of the sub-committee of the U.S. Senate Judiciary Committee published as *The Communist Threat to the U.S. Through the Caribbean* (Washington, 1960–63).

On Cuba and power politics since 1962, there is D. Bruce Jackson's *Castro, the Kremlin and Latin America* (Baltimore, 1969). Recent U.S. policy to Cuba is also well discussed by a number of writers in John Plank's *Cuba and the U.S., Long Range Perspectives* (Washington, 1967). Two studies by Carmelo Mesa-Lago (*The Labor Sector and Socialist Distribution in Cuba*, New York 1968, and *Availability and Reliability of Statistics in Socialist Cuba*, Pittsburgh 1969) illuminate many dark corners. An interesting study of Castro's relationship to communism, both before coming to power and after, has been made by K. S. Karol, *Les Guérrilleros au pouvoir*, Paris 1970, which appeared after this book was in proof.

General Bibliography

I BOOKS AND PAMPHLETS

(Works of particular value are starred)

ABBOT, WILLIS J., *Watching the world go by* (Boston, 1933)

*ABEL, ELIE, *The missiles of October* (New York, 1967)

ABRIL AMORES, EDUARDO, *El plan trienal del coronel Batista; la redención de un pueblo y la inmortalidad de un hombre* (Havana, 1937)

Actas de las asembleas de represents y del consejo de Gobierno durante la guerra de independencia, 3 vols (Havana, 1930)

ACUÑA, JUAN ANTONIO, *Cuba: revolución frustrada? Que el pueblo juzgue!* (Montevideo, 1960)

*ADAM Y SILVA, RICARDO, *La gran mentira, 4 de Septiembre de 1933* (Havana, 1947)

ADAMS, BROOKS, *America's economic supremacy* (New York, 1900)

ADAMS, FREDERICK UPHAM, *Conquest of the tropics; the story of the creative enterprises conducted by the United Fruit Company* (New York, 1914)

ADAMS, JOHN QUINCY, *Memoirs of John Quincy Adams*, ed. C. F. Adams (1874)

Writings of John Quincy Adams, ed. Worthington Chauncey Ford (New York, 1913)

*AIMES, HUBERT H. S., *A history of slavery in Cuba, 1511–1868* (New York and London, 1907)

ALBEMARLE, see Keppel, G. T.

ALDEREGUÍA, GUSTAVO, *En esta hora sombria*, 2nd edn (Havana, 1957)

*ALEXANDER, R. J., *Communism in Latin America* (New Brunswick, 1957)

ALGER, RUSSELL ALEXANDER, *The Spanish-American War* (New York and London, 1901)

ALIENES UROSA, JULIÁN, *Características fundamentales de la economía cubana* (Havana, 1950)

AMPÈRE, JEAN JACQUES, *Promenade en Amérique. Etats-Unis, Cuba, Mexique*, 2 vols (Paris, 1855)

ANDRESKI, STANISLAV, *Parasitism and subversion: The case of Latin America* (London, 1966)

APTHEKER, HERBERT, *American negro slave revolts* (New York, 1944)

ARANGO Y PARREÑO, FRANCISCO, *Obras*, 2 vols (Havana, 1952)

ARCINIEGAS, GERMÁN, *El estudiante de la mesa redonda* (Bogotá, 1933)

ARMIÑÁN PÉREZ, LUIS DE, *Weyler, el gran capitán* (Madrid, 1946)

ARANDA, SERGIO, *La Revolución agraria en Cuba* (Mexico, 1968)

ARNAULT, JACQUES, *Cuba et le Marxisme* (Paris, 1963)

ARTIME BUESA, MANUEL, *Traición!* (Mexico, 1960)

*ATKINS, EDWIN F., *Sixty years in Cuba* (Cambridge, Mass, 1926)

ATTWOOD, WILLIAM, *The Reds and the Blacks* (London, 1967)

AZCARATE ROSELL, RAFAEL, *Nicolás Azcárate el reformista* (Havana, 1939)

AZCUY Y CRUZ, ARACELIO, *Cuba: campo de concentración* (Mexico, 1954)

BACHILLER Y MORALES, ANTONIO, *Cuba: monografía histórica que comprende desde la perdida de la Habana hasta la restauración española* (Havana, 1883)

BAEZA FLORES, ALBERTO, *Las cadenas vienen de lejos* (Mexico, 1960)

BALLOU, MATURIN MURRAY, *Due South; or, Cuba past and present* (Boston and New York, 1885)

BARAN, PAUL A., *Reflections on the Cuban revolution* (New York, 1961)

BARBARROSA, ENRIQUE, . . . *El proceso de la república; análisis de la situación política y económica de Cuba bajo el gobierno presidencial de Tomás Estrada Palma y José Miguel Gómez, con datos e informaciones estadísticas* (Havana, 1911)

BARINETTI, CARLO, *A Voyage to Mexico and Havana including some general observations on the U.S.* (New York, 1841)

BARONI, ALDO, *Cuba, país de poca memoria* (Mexico, 1944)

BASTIDE, ROGER, *Les Amériques noires* (Paris, 1967)

BATISTA, FULGENCIO, *Cuba betrayed* (New York, 1962)

——, *Estoy con el pueblo* (Havana, 1939)

——, *Piedras y leyes* (Mexico, 1961)

——, *Respuesta* (Mexico, 1960)

BAYO, ALBERTO, *Mi aporte a la revolución cubana* (Havana, 1960)

——, *Mi Desembarcó en Mallorca* (Mexico, 1944)

BEALE, HOWARD K., *Theodore Roosevelt and the rise of America to World Power* (Baltimore, 1956)

BEALS, CARLETON, *The crime of Cuba* (Philadelphia and London, 1933)

——, *Rifle rule in Cuba* (New York, 1935)

BEER, THOMAS, *Hanna* (New York, 1929)

BEER, THOMAS, *Stephen Crane, a study in American letters* . . . (London, 1924)

BEMIS, SAMUEL FLAGG, ed., *The American secretaries of state and their diplomacy* (New York, 1927–9)

BENHAM, F., and H. A. HOLLEY, *The economy of Latin America* (Oxford, 1960)

BERNSTEIN, HARRY, *Origins of Inter-American Interest, 1700–1812* (1945)

BETHEL, PAUL D., *Cuba y los Estados Unidos* (Barcelona, 1962)

——, *Terror and Resistance in Communist Cuba* (Miami, 1964)

BLASIER, STEWART COLE, *The Cuban and Chilean communist parties, instruments of Soviet policy, 1935–48* (Ann Arbor, 1956) (Ph.D thesis, unpublished)

BLEYER, WILLARD GROSVENOR, *Main currents in the history of American journalism* (Boston, 1927)

BLUNT, REGINALD, ed., *Mrs Montague . . . her letters and friendships from 1762 to 1800* (1923)

BOLÍVAR, SIMÓN, *Cartas del Libertador (1799–1830)* (Caracas, 1929)

BONSAL, STEPHEN, *The fight for Santiago* (London, 1899)

BOORSTEIN, EDWARD, *The Economic transformation of Cuba* (New York and London, 1968)

BOSCH, JUAN, *Cuba, la isla fascinante* (Santiago de Chile, 1955)

BOWERS, CLAUDE, *Beveridge and the progressive era* (Cambridge, Mass, 1932)

BRENNAN, RAY, *Castro, Cuba and justice* (New York, 1959)

BRODY, RICHARD A., with R. R. Fagen and T. J. O'Leary, see Fagen, Richard R.

BROWNE, PATRICK, *The civil and natural history of Jamaica, etc.* (London, 1756)

BRUGUERA, F. G., *Histoire contemporaine d'Espagne* (Paris, 1953)

BRYSON, LYMAN, ed., *Social change in Latin America today* (New York, 1960)

BUCHANAN, JAMES, *The works of James Buchanan* (Philadelphia, 1908–11)

BUENO, SALVADOR, *Historia de la literatura cubana* (Havana, 1954)

BUNAU-VARILLA, PHILIPPE, *The great adventure of Panamá* (London, New York, 1920)

BURNS, SIR ALAN CUTHBERT MAXWELL, *History of the British West Indies* (London, 1954)

BUXTON, SIR THOMAS, *The African slave trade* (London, 1839)

CABRERA, JOSÉ M. PÉREZ, with Ramiro Guerra and others, see Guerra, Ramiro

CABRERA, LYDIA, *El Monte* (Havana, 1954)

——, *La Sociedad secreta Abakuá narrada por viejos adeptos* (Havana, 1958)

*CABRERA, RAIMUNDO, *Mis malos tiempos* (Havana, 1920)

——, *Cuba y sus jueces* (Havana, 1887)

*CALCAGNO, FRANCISCO, *Diccionario biográfico cubano* (New York, 1878)

CALDERÓN DE LA BARCA, FRANCES, *The Attaché in Madrid; or Sketches of the court of Isabella II* (New York, 1856)

CALDWELL, ROBERT GRANVILLE, *The López expeditions to Cuba, 1848–1851* (Princeton, 1915)

CALLAHAN, JAMES MORTON, *Cuba and international relations* (Baltimore, 1899)

CAMBA ANDREU, FRANCISCO, *Fernando Villaamil* (Madrid, 1944)

CANOT, THEODORE, *Revelations of a slave trader; or, twenty years' adventures of Captain Canot* (New edition, London, 1954)

*CANTERO, JUSTO G., *Los ingenios* (Havana, 1857)

CARBONELL Y RIVERO, MIGUEL ANGEL, *Antonio Maceo* (Havana, 1935)

——, *Juan Gualberto Gómez* (Havana, 1938)

——, *Sanguily* (Havana, 1938)

*CARR, RAYMOND, *Spain 1808–1939* (Oxford, 1966)

CARRERA PUJAL, JAIME, *Historia política y económica de Cataluña. Siglos XVI al XVIII* (Barcelona, 1946, 1947)

*CARRILLO, JUSTO, Papers, memoirs, etc. (manuscripts deposited in the Hoover Library of War, Revolution and Peace)

CARRILLO, SANTIAGO, *Cuba 68* (Paris, 1968)

CASA DE LAS AMÉRICAS (Havana), *Cuba: transformación del hombre* (Havana, 1961)

——, *La sierra y el llano* (Havana, 1961)

*CASTRO, FIDEL, *Discursos para la historia* (Havana, 1959)

——, *Guía del pensamiento político económico de Fidel* (Havana, 1959)

*——, *History will absolve me* (New York, 1961)

——, *La revolución cubana* (Buenos Aires, 1960)

*——, *26 cartas del presidio* (Havana, 1960)

——, Speeches in *Obra Revolucionaria, Revolución* and *Granma* (Havana, 1960)

*CASUSO, TERESA, *Cuba and Castro* (New York, 1961)

*Census of Cuba, 1899, 1907, 1919, 1931, 1943, 1953; for 1899, see U.S. Government: War Department; for 1907, see U.S. Government: Bureau of the Census; for 1919, 1931, 1943 and 1953, see Cuba

CÉSPEDES, CARLOS MANUEL DE, *Cartas a su esposa Ana de Quesada* (Havana, 1964)

CHADWICK, FRENCH ENSOR, *The relations of the United States and Spain. Diplomacy (the Spanish-American War)*, 3 vols (New York, 1909, 1911)

*CHAPMAN, CHARLES EDWARD, *A history of the Cuban republic* (New York, 1927)

CHAUNU, HUGUETTE et PIERRE, *Séville et L'Atlantique (1504–1650)* (Paris, 1956)
*CHESTER, EDMUND A., *A sergeant named Batista* (New York, 1954)
CHEVALIER, FRANÇOIS, *La Formation des grands domaines au Mexique* (Paris, 1952)
*CHIBÁS, RAÚL, Memoirs (manuscripts)
Cinco diarios del sitio de la Habana, Departamento de colección cubana (Havana, 1963)
CLAIBORNE, JOHN FRANCIS, *Life and correspondence of John A. Quitman, major-general, U.S.A. and governor of the state of Mississippi* (New York, 1860)
CLARK, WILLIAM JARED, *Commercial Cuba. A book for business men* (London and New York, 1899)
COBLENTZ, EDMOND DAVID, ed., *William Randolph Hearst* (1952)
COLLAZO, ENRIQUE, *Desde Yara hasta el Zanjón* (Havana, 1893)
COLUMBUS, CHRISTOPHER, *THE JOURNAL, 1492–3* (London, 1893)
**Communist Threat to the U.S.A. through the Caribbean*, Hearings of the Internal Security Sub-Committee, U.S. Senate (Washington, D.C., 1959–62)
CONCAS Y PALAU, VÍCTOR MARÍA, *The Squadron of Admiral Cervera* (Washington, 1900)
Constituciones de la República de Cuba (Havana, 1952)
CONTE AGÜERO, LUIS, *América contra el comunismo* (Miami, 1961)
——, **Eduardo Chibás, el adalid de Cuba* (Mexico, 1955)
——, *Los dos rostros de Fidel Castro* (Mexico, 1960); (second edition: *Fidel Castro – psiquiatría y política* (Mexico, 1968))
CORBETT, SIR JULIAN, *England in the seven years' war.* 2 vols (London, 1907)
Correspondencia diplomática de la delegación cubana en Nueva York, 1895–1898, 5 vols (Havana, 1946)
CORWIN, ARTHUR F., *Spain and the abolition of slavery in Cuba* (Texas, 1968)
CRASSWELLER, ROBERT D., *Trujillo, the life and times of a Caribbean dictator* (New York, 1966)
CREELMAN, JAMES, *On the great highway* (London, 1901)
CRUZ BASTILLO, ULISES, *El Mensaje a García* (Havana, 1943)
Cuba, una revolución en su marcha (Paris, 1967)
*——, *Census of the Republic of Cuba, 1919* (Havana, 1922)
——, *Census of 1931* (Havana, 1938–9)
——, *Censo de 1943* (Havana, 1945)
——, *Censo de 1953* (Havana, 1955)
Cuba and the Rule of Law (International Commission of Jurists, Geneva 1962)
Cuban Immigration 1959–1966 and its impact on Miami-Dade County, Florida (Florida, 1967)
CURTIS, WILGUS H., *The Caribbean: its political problems* (Gainesville, 1956)
CUST, EMMELINE MARY ELIZABETH (Mrs Henry), *Wanderers: episodes from the travels of Lady Emmeline Stuart-Wortley and her daughter Victoria 1849–1855* (London, 1928)

DANIELS, JOSEPHUS, *Shirt-Sleeve Diplomat* (Chapel Hill, 1947)
*DAVIS, DAVID BRION, *The Problem of Slavery in Western Culture* (New York, 1966)
DAVIS, J. MERLE, *The Cuban Church* (New York, 1942)
*DEBRAY, RÉGIS, *Révolution dans la révolution? Lutte armée et lutte politique en Amérique Latine* (Paris, 1967)
*DEERR, NOËL, *The history of sugar*, 2 vols (London, 1949, 1950)
DE LA TORRIENTE, COSME, *Cuarenta años de ma vida* (Havana, 1940)
DE LA TORRIENTE, LOLO, *Mi casa en la tierra* (Havana, 1956)

DÉLANO, LUIS ENRIQUE, *Cuba 66* (Santiago de Chile, 1966)

DEMAGNY, RENÉ, *Cuba, l'exil et la ferveur* (Paris, 1962)

DEROSNE Y CAIL, C. M., *De la elaboración del azúcar en las colonias* (Havana, 1844; Madrid, 1925)

*DEWART, LESLIE, *Cuba, church and crisis; Christianity and politics in the Cuban revolution* (London and New York, 1964)

DEWEY, GEORGE, *Autobiography of George Dewey* (London and New York, 1913)

DIKE, KENNETH, *Trade and politics in the Niger delta, 1830–1885* (Oxford, 1956)

Documentos de Carlos Baliño (Havana, 1964)

Documentos de la revolución cubana (Montevideo, 1967)

Documentos inéditos sobre la toma de la Habana por los Ingleses en 1762 (Havana, 1963)

Documents of West Indian History, vol. I, 1492–1655, ed. Eric Williams (Trinidad, 1963)

DODD, WILLIAM E., *Robert James Walker, Imperialist* (Chicago, 1913)

La Dominación Inglesa en la Habana, Libro de Cabildos, 1762–1763 (Havana, 1962)

*DONNAN, ELIZABETH, *Documents illustrative of the Slave Trade to America*, 4 vols (Washington, 1930; reprint, New York, 1965)

Dos heroes y un ideal (Miami, 1962)

DOW, GEORGE FRANCIS, *Slave ships and slaving*, 15 vols (Salem, 1927)

*DRAPER, THEODORE, *Castroism: theory and practice* (London, 1965)

*DRAPER, THEODORE, *Castro's revolution: myths and realities* (London and New York, 1962)

DUBOIS, JULES, *Fidel Castro: rebel – liberator or dictator?* (Indianapolis, 1959)

DU BOIS, WILLIAM EDWARD BURGHARDT, *The suppression of the African slave-trade to the United States of America 1638–1870*, vol. I (Cambridge, Mass, 1896)

DUGGAN, LAURENCE, *The Americas. The search for hemisphere security* (New York, 1949)

DULLES, FOSTER RHEA, *America's rise to world power, 1898–1954* (New York, 1955)

——, *Prelude to world power: American diplomatic history 1860–1900* (New York, 1965)

*DUMONT, RENÉ, *Cuba, socialisme et développement* (Paris, 1964)

——, and COLÉOU, JULIEN, *La réforme agraire à Cuba: ses conditions de réussite* (Paris, 1962)

——, and ROSIER, BERNARD, *The Hungry Future* (London, 1969)

DUMUR, JEAN, *Cuba* (Lausanne, 1962)

DUVERGIER DE HAURANNE, ERNEST, *Huit mois en Amérique, lettres et notes de voyage, 1864–1865*, 2 vols (Paris, 1866)

EDWARDS, BRYAN, *The history, civil and commercial of the British colonies in the West Indies*, 3 vols (London, 1793–1801)

*EISENHOWER, DWIGHT DAVID, *Waging peace* (London, 1966)

ELIZALDE, LEOPOLDO PÍO, *Defamation* (Mexico D.F., 1961)

——, *La tragedía de Cuba* (Mexico, 1959)

ELKINS, STANLEY, *Slavery* (Chicago, 1953)

ELLIOTT, J. H., *Imperial Spain, 1469–1716* (London, 1963)

ELLIS, HOWARD S., *Economic development for Latin America* (London, 1961)

*ELY, ROLAND T., *Cuando reinaba su majestad el azúcar* (Buenos Aires, 1963)

——, *La economía Cubana entre las dos Isabelas, 1492–1832*, 3rd edn (Bogotá, 1962)

ENGLAND: Departments of State: Board of Trade, *Report of the privy council on the African trade 1788*, 6 pts (London, 1789)

ENTICK, JOHN, *The general history of the late war* . . ., 5 vols (London, 1763)

ERENCHUN, FÉLIX, *Anales de la isla de Cuba*, 3 vols (Havana, 1856)

ESTEVEZ Y ROMERO, LUIS, *Desde el Zanjón hasta Baire* (Havana, 1899)

*Estudio sobre Cuba (Miami, 1963)

ETTINGER, AMOS, *The mission to Spain of Pierre Soulé, 1853–1855* (London, 1932)

EUSTIS, FREDERIC, *Augustus Hemenway 1805–1876* (Salem, 1955)

EVTUSHENKO, EVGENY, *A Precocious Autobiography* (London, 1963)

FAGEN, RICHARD R., with Richard A. Brody and Thomas J. O'Leary, *Cubans in Exile: Disaffection and the Revolution* (Stanford, 1968)

——, *The Transformation of the Political Culture in Cuba* (Stanford, 1969)

FAGG, JOHN EDWIN, *Cuba, Haiti and the Dominican Republic* (New York, 1965)

FANON, FRANTZ, *Les damnés de la terre* (Paris, 1961)

FERNÁNDEZ, CRISTÓBAL C. M. F., *El confesor de Isabel II y sus actividades en Madrid* (Madrid, 1964)

FERNÁNDEZ ALMAGRO, MELCHOR, *Cánovas. Su vida, su política* (Madrid, 1951)

——, **Historia política de la España contemporanea*, 2 vols (Madrid, 1959)

FERNÁNDEZ DURO, CESÁREO, *La armada española desde la unión de los reinos de Castilla y de León*, 9 vols (Madrid, 1895–1903)

FERNÁNDEZ RETAMAR, ROBERTO, *La poesía contemporanea en Cuba 1927–1953* (Havana, 1954)

FERRARA, ORESTES, *Mis relaciones con Máximo Gómez* (Havana, 1942)

FERRER, HORACIO, *Con el rifle al hombro* (Havana, 1950)

FIELD, MAUNSELL B., *Memories of many men and some women* (London, 1874)

FIGUEREDO, JOSÉ MARÍA, *La revolución de Yara* (c. 1880)

FIGUEROA Y TORRES, Álvaro de, CONDE DE ROMANONES, *Doña María Cristina de Habsburgo Lorena, la discreta Regente de España*. . ., 2nd edn (Madrid, 1934)

FITZGIBBON, RUSSELL, ed., *The constitutions of the Americas* (Chicago, 1948)

FITZGIBBON, RUSSELL, *Cuba and the United States, 1900–1935* (Menasha, 1935)

FLACK, HORACE EDGAR, *Spanish-American diplomatic relations preceding the War of 1898* (Baltimore, 1882)

**FONER, PHILIP, *A history of Cuba and its relations with the U.S.*, vols I and II (1962, 1963)

FORAKER, JOSEPH BENSON, *Notes of a busy life*, 2 vols (Cincinnati, 1916)

FORDE, CYRIL DARYLL, ed., *Efik traders of old Calabar* (London, 1956)

FOREIGN RELATIONS OF THE U.S. (F.R.) See U.S. government

FORTESCUE, HON. SIR JOHN WILLIAM, *A history of the British army*, 13 vols (London and New York, 1899–1930)

F. R. See U.S. Government

FRANCO, JOSÉ LUCIANO, *Antonio Maceo, Apuntes para una historia de su vida*, 3 vols (Havana, 1951–7)

FRANCO, JOSÉ LUIS, *La batalla por el dominio del Caribe y el golfo de México*, 3 vols (Havana, 1964, 1965, 1968)

——, *La conspiración de Aponte* (Havana, 1963)

——, *Placido y otros ensayos* (Havana, 1964)

FRANCO, VÍCTOR, *La révolution sensuelle* (Paris, 1962)

FRANCOS, ANIA, *La fête cubaine* (Paris, 1962)

FRANQUI, CARLOS, *Le livre des douze* (Paris, 1965)

FRANK, WALDO, *Cuba: prophetic island* (New York, 1961)

*FRIEDLÄNDER, HEINRICH, *Historia económica de Cuba* (Havana, 1944)

FROUDE, JAMES ANTHONY, *The English in the West Indies* (London, 1888)

FYFE, CHRISTOPHER, *A history of Sierra Leone* (London, 1962)

GAILLARDET, F., *L'aristocratie en Amérique* (Paris, 1883)

GALÍNDEZ, JESÚS de, *La era de Trujillo* (Santiago de Chile, 1956)

GALLEGO, TESIFONTE, *La insurrección cubana* (Madrid, 1897)

GALLENGA, ANTONIO, *The pearl of the Antilles* (London, 1873)

GARCÍA DE ARBOLEYA, JOSÉ, *Manual de la Isla de Cuba* (Havana, 1859)

GARCÍA CARRAFFA, ALBERTO Y ARTURO, *Enciclopedia heráldica y genealógica hispano-Americana* (Madrid and Salamanca, 1919–30)

GARCÍA DE POLAVIEJA Y DEL CASTILLO, Camilo Marquis de Polavieja, *Relación documentada de mi política en Cuba* (Madrid, 1898)

GARCÍA GALLÓ, GASPAR M. JORGE, *Biografía del tabaco habano*, 2nd edn (Havana, 1961)

GARRIGO, ROQUE E., *Historia documentada de la conspiración de los soles y rayos de Bolívar* (Havana, 1927)

GAULD, CHARLES A., *The last titan: Percival Farquhar, american entrepreneur in Latin America* (Stanford, 1964)

GEERLIGS, H. C. PRINSEN, *Cane sugar and its manufacture* (Altrincham, 1909)

GENOVESE, EUGENE D., *The political economy of Slavery* (London, 1966)

GILLY, ADOLFO, *Inside the cuban revolution* (New York, 1964)

*GOLDENBERG, BORIS, *The Cuban revolution and Latin America* (London, 1965)

GÓMEZ, MÁXIMO, *Diario de campaña* (Havana, 1940)

GONZÁLEZ, EDELMIRA, *La revolución en Cuba; memorias del Coronel Rosendo Collazo* (Havana, 1934)

GONZÁLEZ, MANUEL PEDRO, *José Martí, epic chronicler of the U.S. in the eighties* (North Carolina, 1953)

GRAY, RICHARD BUTLER, *José Martí, Cuban patriot* (Gainesville, 1962)

*GRENVILLE, JOHN and YOUNG, GEORGE, *Politics, strategy and American diplomacy* (Yale, 1967)

GRIEVE, AVERIL MACKENZIE, *The last years of the English slave trade, Liverpool, 1750–1807* (London, 1941)

GROBART, FABIO, *XV Años de lucha (en el aniversario del partido comunista)* (Havana, 1940)

*GUERRA, RAMIRO, *Azúcar y población en las Antilles*, 5th edn (Havana, 1961)

——, **Manual de historia de Cuba*, 2nd edn (Havana, 1964)

——, *Mudos Testigos* (Havana, 1948)

——, with José M. Pérez Cabrera, Juan J. Remos and Emeterio S. Santovenia, *Historia de la nación cubana*, 10 vols (Havana, 1952)

——, **Guerra de los diez años, 1868–1878*, 2nd edn (Havana, 1960)

——, *La industria azucarera en Cuba* (Havana, 1940)

——, *Teodoro Roosevelt* (Havana, 1958)

GUEVARA, ERNESTO (Che), *Guerrilla warfare* (New York, 1961)

*——, *Ecrits, oeuvres révolutionnaires, 1959–1967* (Paris, 1968)

*——, *Pasajes de la guerra revolucionaria* (Havana, 1963) (translations in French and English)

——, *The complete Bolivian diaries of Che Guevara: Bolivian diary* (London, 1968)

*——, *Venceremos: the speeches and writings of Ernesto Che Guevara* (London, 1968)

GUGGENHEIM, H. F., *The U.S. and Cuba* (New York, 1933)

GUILBERT, YVES, *La poudrière cubaine; Castro l'infidèle* (Paris, 1961)

GURNEY, JOSEPH JOHN, *A winter in the West Indies* (London, 1840)

*GUTELMAN, MICHEL, *L'agriculture socialisée à Cuba* (Paris, 1967)

GWYNN, STEPHEN, *Letters and friendships of Sir Cecil Spring Rice*, 2 vols (London, 1929)

*HAGEDORN, HERMANN, *Leonard Wood*, 2 vols (New York, 1931)

HAMILTON, EARL, *War and prices in Spain 1651–1800* (Cambridge, Mass, 1947)

HARING, C. H., *The buccaneers in the West Indies in the 17th Century* . . . (London, 1910)

——, *Trade and navigation between Spain and the Indies in the time of the Hapsburgs* (Cambridge, Mass, 1918)

*HARRINGTON, MARK RAYMOND, *Cuba before Columbus* (New York, 1921)

HAWTHORNE, JULIAN, *Nathaniel Hawthorne and his wife*, 2 vols (London, 1885)

*HAZARD, SAMUEL, *Cuba with pen and pencil* (Hartford, 1871)

*HEALY, DAVID F., *The U.S. in Cuba, 1898–1902* (Madison, 1963)

HEMMENT, JOHN C., *Cannon and camera* (New York, 1898)

HENNESSY, C. A. M., *The federal republic in Spain* (Oxford, 1962)

HENRIQUEZ I CARVAJAL, FEDERICO, *El mensajero*, vols I and II (Havana, 1964)

HERR, RICHARD, *The eighteenth-century revolution in Spain* (Princeton, 1958)

HERRERA DE LA SERNA, NILDA, *Montoro, su vida y obra* (Havana, 1952)

*HERRING, HUBERT, *A history of Latin America*, 2nd edn (New York, 1961)

HILL, H. C., *Roosevelt and the Caribbean* (Chicago, 1927)

HILLSMAN, ROGER, *To move a nation* (New York, 1967)

HIRSCHMAN, ALBERT D., *Journeys towards progress. Studies of economic policy-making in Latin America* (New York, 1963)

HOFSTADTER, RICHARD, *The paranoid style in American politics* (New York, 1967)

HOLBROOK, STEWART HALL, *Lost men of American history* (New York, 1947)

HOLLEY, H. A. and F. BENHAM. See Benham, F.

HORREGO ESTUCH, LEOPOLDO, *Juan Gualberto Gómez* (Havana, 1954)

——, *Martín Morúa Delgado, Vida y Mensaje* (Havana, 1954)

HOWARD, WARREN STARKIE, *American slavers and the federal law, 1837–1862* (Berkeley and Los Angeles, 1963)

HUBERMAN, LEO and PAUL M. SWEEZY, *Cuba: anatomy of a revolution* (New York, 1961)

——, *Socialism in Cuba* (New York, 1969)

HUGHES, TREVOR JONES, and E. LUARD, see Luard, Evan

HULL, CORDELL, *The memoirs of Cordell Hull*, 2 vols (London, 1948)

HUMBOLDT, FRIEDRICH HEINRICH ALEXANDER VON, *Essai politique sur le royaume de Nouvelle Espagne*, 2 vols (1811)

*——, *The island of Cuba* (New York, 1856)

——, *Personal narrative of travels to the equinoctial regions of the new continent, 1799–1804*, 3 vols (Bohn, 1852–3)

IBARRA, JORGE, *Historia de Cuba* (Havana, 1968)

ICKES, HAROLD L., *The secret diary of Harold L. Ickes* (New York, 1955)

INSTITUTE FOR INTERNATIONAL SOCIAL RESEARCH. Lloyd A. Free, *Attitudes of the Cuban people toward the Castro regime in the late spring of 1960* (New Jersey, 1960)

*INTERNATIONAL BANK FOR RECONSTRUCTION AND DEVELOPMENT, *Report on Cuba* (Baltimore, 1952) (Referred to in this book as 'World Bank')

*Investment in Cuba, see U.S. Department of Commerce

JACKSON, D. BRUCE, *Castro, The Kremlin and communism in Latin America* (Baltimore, 1969)

JAMES, DANIEL, *Cuba: the first Soviet satellite in the Americas* (New York, 1961)

JAMES, PRESTON E., *Latin America*, 3rd edn (New York, 1959)

JAMESON, ROBERT FRANCIS, *Letters from the Havanna, during the year 1820* . . . (London, 1820)

JANES, HURFORD, and SAYERS, H. J., *The story of Czarnikow* (London, 1963)

JAY, W. M. L., Mrs (*pseud.*, i.e. Julia L. M. Woodruff), *My winter in Cuba* (New York and Hartford, Conn., 1871)

JEFFERSON, THOMAS, *The writings of Thomas Jefferson*, 10 vols (New York, 1893–9)

*JENKS, LELAND, . . . *Our Cuban colony, a study in sugar* (New York, 1928)

JESSUP, PHILIP, *Elihu Root*, 2 vols (New York, 1938)

JIMÉNEZ PASTRANA, JUAN, *Los Chinos en las lucha por la liberación Cubana 1847–1930* (Havana, 1963)

JINESTA, CARLOS, *José Martí en Costa Rica* (San José, 1933)

*JOHNSON, HAYNES, *The Bay of Pigs; the leaders' story of brigade 2506* (New York, 1964)

——, (with Bernard Gwertzman) *Fulbright the dissenter* (London, 1969)

JOHNSON, WILLIS FLETCHER, *The history of Cuba*, 5 vols (New York, 1920)

JOLLY, RICHARD, *Cuba. The economic and social revolution*. See Seers, Dudley. G.

JULIEN, CLAUDE, *La révolution cubaine* (Paris, 1961)

*KAROL, K. S., *Les Gúerrilleros au pouvoir* (Paris, 1970)

KENNEDY, ROBERT F., *Thirteen days* (New York, 1969) (References in this book are to the *Times* serialization (London, 1968)

KENNAN, GEORGE, *American diplomacy, 1900–1950* (Chicago, 1951)

KEPNER, CHARLES DAVID, and SOOTHILL, JAY HENRY, *The banana empire* (New York, 1935)

KEPPEL, GEORGE THOMAS (Earl of Albemarle), *Memoirs of the Marquis of Rockingham and his contemporaries*, 2 vols (London, 1852)

KIERNAN, V. G., *The Spanish revolution of 1854* (London, 1966)

KIRKPATRICK, LYMAN B., *The real CIA* (London, 1968)

*KLEIN, HERBERT S., *Slavery in the Americas. A comparative study of Cuba and Virginia* (London, 1967)

KROCK, ARTHUR, *Memoirs. Sixty years on the fighting line* (New York, 1968)

KUCZYNSKI, ROBERT RÉNÉ, *Population movements* (Oxford, 1936)

LAFEBER, WALTER, *The new empire* (Ithaca, 1963)

*LAMAR SCHWEYER, ALBERTO, *Cómo cayó el presidente Machado; una pagina oscura de la diplomacia norteamericana* (Madrid, 1934; English trans., Havana, 1938)

LAMBERT, FRANCIS, 'The Cuban Question in Spanish Restoration Politics' (unpublished Ph.D. Thesis, Oxford, 1968)

*LAZO, MARIO, *Dagger in the heart* (New York, 1968)

LEARNED, HENRY BARRETT, in BEMIS, SAMUEL F., *The American secretaries of state*, vol. 6 (1927)

——, *William Learned Marcy, secretary of state* (1928)

LEDERER, WILLIAM J., *A nation of sheep* (New York, 1961)

*LEECH, MARGARET, *In the days of McKinley* (New York, 1959)

LEMA, MARQUÉS DE, *Mis Recuerdos, 1880–1901* (Madrid, 1930)

LEQUERICA VÉLEZ, FULGENCIO, *600 Dias con Fidel* (Bogotá, 1961)
LE RIVEREND, JULIO, *Historia económica de Cuba* (Havana, 1965)
——, *La república dependencia y Revolución* (Havana, 1966)
LEWIS, GORDON, *Puerto Rico, freedom and power in the Caribbean* (London, 1963)
LISTER, ENRIQUE, *Nuestra guerra* (Paris, 1966)
LIZASO, FÉLIX, *Martí, místico del deber* (Buenos Aires, 1952)
*LLERENA, MARIO, Memoir (unpublished MSS)
——, 'Nuestra Razon' (unpublished pamphlet)
LLOYD, CHRISTOPHER, *The navy and the slave trade* (London, 1949)
*LOCKMILLER, DAVID, *Magoon in Cuba, 1906–1909* (Chapel Hill, 1938)
——, *Enoch H. Crowder* (Missouri, 1955)
*LOCKWOOD, LEE, *Castro's Cuba: Cuba's Fidel* (New York, 1967)
LONG, JOHN DAVIS, *America of yesterday* (Boston, 1923)
——, *The new American navy*, 2 vols (London and Cambridge, Mass., 1904)
*LÓPEZ FRESQUET, RUFO, *My fourteen months with Castro* (New York, 1966)
LÓPEZ SÁNCHEZ, JOSÉ, *Tomás Romay and the origin of science in Cuba* (Havana, 1967)
*LOVEN, S., *Origins of the Tainian culture, West Indies* (Göteborg, 1935)
LOZANO CASADO, MIGUEL, *La Personalidad del General José Miguel Gómez* (Havana, 1913)
LUARD, EVAN, and HUGHES, TREVOR JONES, *Economic development of communist China, 1949–1958* (London, 1959)
LUNDBERG, FERDINAND, *Imperial Hearst* (New York, 1937)
LUZARDO, MANUEL, with B. ROCA and others, see Roca, Blas

MCCULLOH, JOHN RAMSAY, *A dictionary, practical, theoretical and historical of commerce and commercial navigation* (London, 1840)
*MACGAFFEY, WYATT, and BARNETT, CLIFFORD ROBERT, *Twentieth-century Cuba: the background of the Castro revolution* (New York, 1965)
MADÁN, CRISTÓBAL F., *Llamamiento de la isla de Cuba a la nacion española* (New York, 1855)
MADARIAGA, SALVADOR DE, *Fall of the Spanish empire* (London, 1947)
MADDEN, RICHARD ROBERT, *The island of Cuba* (London, 1849)
MAHAN, ALFRED THAYER, *The interest of America in sea power, present and future* (London and Cambridge, Mass., 1897)
MALLIN, JAY, *Fortress Cuba, Russia's American base* (Chicago, 1965)
MAÑACH, JORGE, *Martí, Apostle of freedom . . .* (New York, 1950)
MARINELLO, JUAN, *Contemporaneos* (Havana, 1964)
——, *Cuba en su puesta* (Havana, 1944)
MARTÍ, JOSÉ, *Obras completas* (Havana, 1931)
MARTIN, GASTON, *Histoire de l'esclavage dans les colonies françaises* (Paris, 1948)
*MARTÍNEZ ORTIZ, RAFAEL, *Cuba: los primeros años de independencia*, 2 vols, 2nd edn (Paris, 1921)
MARTÍNEZ SÁENZ, JOSÉ, *Por la independencia de Cuba* (Havana, 1959)
MARTINO, JOHN, *I was Castro's Prisoner* (New York, 1963)
Martires del Moncada (Havana, 1965)
MASSÉ, ETIENNE MICHEL, *L'isle de Cuba et L'Havane* (Paris, 1825)
MATHIESON, WILLIAM LAW, *British slave emancipation, 1838–1849* (London, 1932)
——, *Great Britain and the slave trade, 1839–1865, etc.* (London, 1929)
MATTHEWS, HERBERT L., *Castro: A political biography* (London, 1969)

——, *The Cuban story*, (New York, 1961)

——, *Return to Cuba* (pamphlet)

MAURA GAMAZO, GABRIEL (Duke of Maura), *Historia crítica del reinado de Don Alfonso XIII*, 2 vols (Barcelona, 1919)

*MAY, ERNEST, *Imperial democracy. The emergence of America as a great power* (New York, 1961)

MELGAR, CONDE FRANCISCO, *Veinte años con Don Carlos* (Madrid, 1940)

MELLA, JULIO A., *Documentos para su vida* (Havana, 1964)

MENESES, ENRIQUE, *Fidel Castro: siete años de poder* (Madrid, 1966)

MERINO (BERNARDO) and IBARZAZAL, FEDERICO, *La revolución de Febrero*, 2nd edn (Havana, 1918)

*MERLE, ROBERT, *Moncada, premier combat de Fidel Castro, 26 juillet 1953* (Paris, 1965)

MERLIN, MERCEDES, COUNTESS, *La Havane*, 3 vols (Paris, 1844)

MESA-LAGO, CARMELO, *The labour sector and socialist distribution in Cuba* (New York, 1968)

MEYER, KARL E. (ed), *Fulbright of Arkansas* (Washington, 1963)

——, and T. SZULC, see Szulc, Tad

MILLER, WARREN, *90 miles from home; the face of Cuba today* (Boston, 1961)

*MILLETT, ALLAN REED, *The politics of intervention; the military occupation of Cuba, 1906–1909* (Columbus, 1968)

*MILLIS, WALTER, *The Martial spirit* (New York, 1931)

MILLS, C. WRIGHT, *Listen, Yankee; the revolution in Cuba* (New York, 1960)

MINER, DWIGHT CARROLL, *The fight for the Panama route* (New York, 1940)

MONAHAN, JAMES and GILMORE, KENNETH, *The great deception* (New York, 1963)

MONROE, JAMES, *The writings of James Monroe*, 7 vols (New York, 1898–1903)

MONTEJO, ESTEBAN, *The autobiography of a runaway slave* (London, 1968)

MONTERO RIOS, EUGENIO, *El tratado de Paris* (Molina, 1952; Ortega, 1953)

MORALES Y MORALES, VIDAL, *Iniciadores y primeros martires de la revolución Cubana*, 3 vols (Havana, 1931)

*MORENO FRAGINALS, MANUEL, *El Ingenio*, Tomo I, 1760–1860 (Havana, 1964)

MORGAN, H. WAYNE, *William McKinley and his America* (New York, 1962)

MORISON, SAMUEL ELIOT, *Admiral of the ocean sea*, 2 vols (Boston, 1942)

MOROTE, LUIS, *Sagasta; Melilla; Cuba* (Paris, 1908)

MOSES, BERNARD, *The Spanish dependencies in South America* (London, 1914)

MUNRO, DANA, *Intervention and dollar diplomacy* (Princeton, 1964)

MURPHY, ROBERT DANIEL, *Diplomat among warriors* (London, 1964)

MUSGRAVE, GEORGE CLARKE, *Under three flags in Cuba* (London and Cambridge, Mass, 1899)

National agrarian census (Havana, 1946)

*NELSON, LOWRY, *Rural Cuba* (Minneapolis, 1950)

*NEVINS, JOSEPH ALLAN, *Hamilton Fish* (New York, 1937)

NIÑO, ALBERTO, *Antecendentes y secretos del 9 del Abril* (Bogotá, 1949)

NIXON, RICHARD M., *Six crises* (London, 1962)

——, *The speeches of Vice-President Richard M. Nixon: Presidential campaign, 1960* (Washington, 1961)

NORTH, JOSEPH, *Cuba: hope of a hemisphere* (New York, 1961)

Nuestra Razón: Manifiesto – programa del movimiento 26 de julio
Nuevos papeles sobre la toma de la Habana por los Ingleses en 1762 (Havana, 1951)
*NÚÑEZ JIMÉNEZ, ANTONIO, *Geografía de Cuba*, 2nd edn (Havana, 1961)

O'BRIEN, FRANK MICHAEL, *The story of 'The Sun', New York, 1833–1928* (New York and London, 1928)
O'KELLY, JAMES J., *The Mambi-Land, or adventures of a Herald correspondent in Cuba* (London and Philadelphia, 1874)
O'LEARY, THOMAS. J., with R. R. FAGEN and R. A. BRODY, see Fagen, Richard R.
OLIVAR BERTRAND, RAFAEL, *El caballero Prim*, 2 vols (Barcelona, 1952)
*ORTIZ, FERNANDO, *Cuban counterpoint: tobacco and sugar* (New York, 1947)
——, *Hampa Afro-Cubana: Los negros brujos* (Madrid, 1917)
——, *Hampa Afro-Cubana: Los negros esclavos* (Havana, 1916)
——, *La africania de la musica folklorica de Cuba* (Havana, 1950, 1965)
——, *La decadencia cubana* (Havana, 1924)
——, *Los bailes y el teatro de los negros en el folklore de Cuba* (Havana, 1951)
——, *Los cabildos Afrocubanos* (Havana, 1921)
OSANKA, FRANKLIN MARK (ed), *Modern Guerrilla Warfare* (New York, 1962)
OTERO, LISANDRO, *Cuba* (Havana, 1960)

PACHTER, HENRY MAXIMILIAN, *Collision course* (London, 1963)
Papeles sobre la toma de la Habana por los Ingleses en 1762 (Havana, 1948)
PARES, RICHARD, *War and trade in the West Indies* (New York, 1963)
PARK, CHARLES F., *Manganese deposits of Cuba* (Washington, 1942)
*PARRY, J. H., and SHERLOCK, P. M., *A short history of the West Indies*, 2nd edn (London, 1963)
PELIFER, CHARLES M., *Tomorrow in Cuba* (New York, 1899)
PERAZA, C. G., *Machado, Crimenes y horrores de un regimen* (Havana, 1933)
*PÉREZ DE LA RIVA, FRANCISCO, *El café, historia de su cultivo y exploración en Cuba* (Havana, 1944)
——, *Origen y régimen de la propriedad territorial en Cuba* (Havana, 1946)
PÉREZ DE LA RIVA, JUAN, ed., see Tacón, *Correspondencia*
PERKINS, DEXTER, *The Monroe doctrine 1867–1907* (Baltimore, 1937)
PERKINS, HOWARD CECIL (ed), *Northern editorials on secession*, 2 vols (1942)
*PEZUELA, JACOBO DE LA, *Diccionario geográfico, estadístico, histórico, de la isla de Cuba*, 4 vols (Madrid, 1859)
——, *Ensayo histórico de la Isla de Cuba* (New York, 1842)
——, *Sitio y Rendición de la Habana en 1762* (Madrid, 1859)
PFLAUM, IRVING P., *Reports on Cuba: American universities field staff reports service*, vol. 4 (1960)
PHILALETHES, DEMOTICUS, *Yankee travels through the island of Cuba* (New York, 1856)
PHILLIPS, RUBY HART, *Cuba, island of paradox* (New York, 1959)
——, *Cuban sideshow* (Havana, 1935)
——, *The Cuban dilemma* (New York, 1962)
PHILLIPS, ULRICH BONNELL, *American Negro slavery: a survey* (London and New York, 1918)
PICHARDO MOYA, FELIPE, *Los Indios de Cuba en sus tiempos históricos* (Havana, 1945)
PINO SANTOS, OSCAR, *El imperialismo norteamericano en la economía de Cuba* (Havana, 1961)

——, *La Estructura Económica de Cuba y la reforma agraria* (Havana, 1959)

*PIRALA, ANTONIO, *Anales de la guerra de Cuba*, 3 vols (Madrid, 1896)

PIRON, HIPPOLYTE, *L'île de Cuba* (Paris, 1876)

PLANK, JOHN, ed., *Cuba and the U.S.: long range perspectives* (Washington, 1967)

PLASENCIA, ALEIDA, ed., *Recuerdos de las guerras de Cuba, 1868–1871* (Havana, 1963)

PLAYA GIRÓN, *Derrota del imperialismo*, 4 vols (Havana, 1961)

POLK, JAMES KNOX, *The diary of James K. Polk during his presidency, 1845–1849* (Chicago, 1910)

POPE-HENNESSY, JAMES, *Sins of the fathers* (London, 1967)

PORTELL VILÁ, HERMINIO, *Céspedes, el padre de la patria Cubana* (Madrid, 1931)

——, **Historia de Cuba en sus relaciones con los Estados Unidos y España*, 4 vols (Havana, 1938)

PORTER, ROBERT, *Industrial Cuba* (New York and London, 1899)

PRATT, JULIUS, *Expansionists of 1898* (Baltimore, 1936)

PRESCOTT, WILLIAM H., *History of the Conquest of Mexico*, 2 vols, 4th edn (London, 1849)

*PRIMELLES, LEON, *Crónica Cubana*, 2 vols (Havana, 1955, 1957)

Primer Estudio Provisional del Balance de Recursos de Trabajo (July, 1962)

PRINGLE, H. F., *Life and Times of William Howard Taft*, 2 vols (New York, 1939)

——, *Theodore Roosevelt* (London, 1932)

**Problems of the New Cuba* (New York, 1935)

El PSP (Havana, 1944)

Public Opinion Survey in Cuba, prepared by Esso Standard Oil Company (typescript, New York, 1950)

QUESADA Y MIRANDA, GONZALO DE, *En Cuba Libre!* (Havana, 1938)

RAMÓN DE SAN PEDRO, J. M., *Don José Xifre Casus* (Barcelona, 1956)

RASHED, ZENAB ESMAT, *The peace of Paris, 1763* (Liverpool, 1951)

*RAUCH, BASIL, *American interest in Cuba: 1848–1855* (New York, 1948)

RAVINES, EUDOCIO, *La gran estafa* (Mexico, 1952)

RAY RIVERO, RENÉ, *Libertad y revolución: Moncada, Gramma, Sierra Maestra* (1959)

*REBELLO, CARLOS, *Estados relativos a la producción Azucarera de la Isla de Cuba* (1860)

REED, WILLIAM HOWELL, *Reminiscences of Elisha Atkins* (Cambridge, Mass, 1890)

Reply to the U.S. state department white paper on Cuba (Havana, 1961)

REYES, ORLANDO, *Mitos y Leyendas de las Villas* (Santa Clara, 1965)

REYNOSO, ÁLVARO, *Ensayo sobre el cultivo de la caña de azúcar*, 5th edn (Havana, 1954)

RHODES, JAMES FORD, *The McKinley and Roosevelt administrations, 1897–1909* (New York, 1922)

RICHARDSON, JAMES DANIEL, *A compilation of the messages and papers of the presidents, 1789–1897* (1896, etc.)

RICHARDSON, LEON BURR, *William E. Chandler, republican* (New York, 1940)

RIPPY, JAMES FRED, *British investments in Latin America, 1822–1949* (Minneapolis, 1959)

*RIVERO MUÑIZ, JOSÉ, *Tabaco: su historia en Cuba*, vol. I (Havana, 1964)

ROA, RAÚL, *En pié* (Santa Clara, 1959)

——, *Retorno a la alborada*, 2 vols (Havana, 1964)

——, *Rubén Martínez Villena; La Pupila Insomne* (Havana, c. 1960)

1606 GENERAL BIBLIOGRAPHY

ROBERTS, W. ADOLPHE, *Havana: portrait of a city* (New York, 1953)

ROBINSON, ALBERT GARDNER, *Cuba and the intervention*, 2nd edn (New York, 1910)

ROCA, BLAS, *Al combate!* (Havana, 1946)

——, *Balance de la labor del partido desde la última asamblea nacional y el desarrollo de la Revolución* (Havana, 1960); trans. (New York, 1961)

——, *Contra la reacción sediciosa* (Havana, 1940)

——, *El socialismo cubano y la Revolución de Fidel* (Lima, 1961)

——, *En defensa del pueblo* (Havana, 1945)

——, *Las experiencias de Cuba* (Havana, 1939)

——, **Los fundamentos del socialismo en Cuba* (Havana, 1961)

——, *Por la consolidación de la república democratica y las avances obtenidas* (Havana, 1939)

——, *Por la defensa nacional y el progreso de Cuba* (Havana, 1941)

——, *29 artículos sobre la Revolución Cubana* (Havana, 1960)

*RODRÍGUEZ, CARLOS RAFAEL, 'La Revolución Cubana y el Periodo de Transición', 2 folios (typescript, Havana, 1966)

RODRÍGUEZ, JOSÉ IGNACIO, *Vida del Presbitero Don Félix Varela* (Havana, 1944)

RODRÍGUEZ, HORACIO, *Che Guevara, mythe ou réalité* (Paris, 1969)

RODRÍGUEZ ALTUNAGA, RAFAEL, *El General Emilio Núñez* (Havana, 1958)

RODRÍGUEZ LOECHES, ENRIQUE, *Rumbo a Escambray* (Havana, 1960)

RODRÍGUEZ MOREJÓN, G., *Fidel Castro: biografía* (Havana, 1959)

RODRÍGUEZ QUESADA, CARLOS, *David Salvador* (Miami, 1961)

ROIG DE LEUCHSENRING, EMILIO, *La Habana, apuntes históricos*, 3 vols, 2nd edn (Havana, 1964)

——, *Los Estados Unidos contra Cuba republicana*, 2 vols (Havana, 1964)

ROJO, RICARDO, *Che Guevara, vie et mort d'un ami* (Paris, 1969)

ROOSEVELT, FRANKLIN D., *The public papers and addresses of Franklin D. Roosevelt*, 13 vols (New York, 1938)

ROOSEVELT, THEODORE, *Autobiography* (New York, 1913)

——, *Addresses and presidential messages of Theodore Roosevelt, 1902–1904* (New York and London, 1904)

——, *Selections from the correspondence of Theodore Roosevelt and Henry Cabot Lodge. 1884–1918* (New York and London, 1925)

*——, *The letters of Theodore Roosevelt*, 8 vols (Cambridge, Mass, 1951–4)

——, *The works of Theodore Roosevelt*, 20 vols (New York, 1926)

ROSELL, FLORENTINO E., *La verdad* (Miami, 1960)

ROSS, THOMAS BERNARD, and D. WISE, see Wise, David

ROWAN, ANDREW, and RAMSEY, MARATHON, *The island of Cuba* (London, 1898)

ROY, L. F. LE, and GAZTELN, MGR A., *Fray Gerónomo Valdés* (Havana, 1963)

*RUBENS, HORATIO SEYMOUR, *Liberty: the story of Cuba* (New York, 1932)

RUIZ, RAMÓN EDUARDO, *Cuba: the making of a revolution* (Mass., 1968)

RUSSELL, BERTRAND, *Unarmed victory* (1963)

SACO, JOSÉ ANTONIO, *Contra La Anexión* (Paris, 1846)

*——, *Colección de papeles*, 3 vols (1960–63)

*——, *Historia de la esclavitud de la raza africana en el nuevo mondo y en especial en los paises américo-híspanos*, vol. I (Barcelona, 1879)

SAGRA, RAMÓN DE LA, *Historia Económica-política y estadística de la isla de Cuba* (Havana, 1831)

——, *Cuba en 1860 ó sea cuadro de sus adelantos en la población, la agricultura, el comercio y las rentas publicas* (Paris, 1863)

SÁNCHEZ AMAYA, FERNANDO, *Diario del Gramma* (Havana, 1959)

*SANJENÍS, AVELINO, *Tiburón* (Havana, 1915)

SANTOVENIA, E., with RAMIRO GUERRA and others, see Guerra, Ramiro

——, *Prim, el Caudillo Estadista* (Madrid, 1933)

SAN MARTÍN, RAFAEL, *El grito de la Sierra Maestra* (Buenos Aires, 1960)

SARTRE, JEAN-PAUL, *Sartre in Cuba* (New York, 1961)

SATINEAU, MAURICE, *Histoire de la Guadeloupe sous l'ancien régime, 1635–1789* (Paris, 1928)

SAUVAGE, LÉO, *L'autopsie du castrisme* (Paris, 1962)

SAYERS, H. J., and H. JANES, see Janes, Hurford

SCHEER, ROBERT and ZEITLIN, MAURICE, *Cuba: An American Tragedy*, rev. edn (1964)

*SCHLESINGER, ARTHUR, *A thousand days. John F. Kennedy in the White House* (London, 1967)

SCOTT, JAMES B., *Outline of the rise and progress of freemasonry in Louisiana* (New Orleans, 1925)

*SEERS, DUDLEY (ed), *Cuba, the Economic and Social Revolution* (Chapel Hill, 1964)

SEITZ, DON CARLOS, *Joseph Pulitzer: his life and letters* (London, 1926)

SELSER, GREGORIO, *La Revolución Cubana* (Buenos Aires, 1960)

SEMIDEI, MANUELA, *Les Etats-Unis et la révolution cubaine, 1959–1964* (Paris, 1968)

*SERVIAT, P., *40 anniversario de la fundación del partido comunista* (Havana, 1965)

SHAFER, ROBERT JONES, *Economic societies in the Spanish world (1763–1821)* (1958)

SHERLOCK, P. M., and J. H. PARRY, see Parry, J. H.

La Sierra y el Llano. See Casa de las Americas

SIGSBEE, CHARLES DWIGHT, *The 'Maine': an account of her destruction in Havana harbor, etc.* (London and New York, 1899)

SIMÓN, LUIS, manuscript (in Hoover Library of War, Revolution and Peace)

*SMITH, EARL E. T., *The fourth floor* (New York, 1962)

*SMITH, ROBERT F., *The U.S. and Cuba, 1917–1960* (New York, 1960)

SOOTHILL, JAY HENRY, and C. O. KEPPNER, see Keppner, Charles David

SORENSEN, THEODORE C., *Kennedy* (London, 1965)

SORIA, GEORGES, *Cuba à l'heure Castro* (Paris, 1961)

SOUCHY, AGUSTIN, *Testimonios sobre la revolución cubana* (Buenos Aires, 1960)

SOULSBY, H. G., *The right of search and the slave trade in Anglo-American relations, 1814–1862* (Baltimore, 1933)

SOUZA, B., *Biografía de un regimiento mambí: el regimiento Calixto García* (Havana, 1899)

——, *Máximo Gómez, el generalísimo* (Havana, 1936)

STAPLETON, EDWARD J., *Some official correspondence of George Canning*, 2 vols (London, 1887)

STEIN, EDWIN C., *Cuba, Castro and communism* (New York, 1962)

STEPHENSON, NATHANIEL WRIGHT, *Nelson W. Aldrich. A leader in American politics* (New York, 1930)

*SUÁREZ, ANDRÉS, *Cuba: Castroism and communism* (1967)

SUÁREZ NÚÑEZ, JOSÉ, *El gran culpable* (Caracas, 1963)

SUÁREZ RIVAS, EDUARDO, *Un pueblo crucificado* (Miami, 1964)

*SUTHERLAND, ELIZABETH, *The youngest revolution: A personal report on Cuba* (New York, 1969)

SWANBERG, W. A., *Citizen Hearst* (London, 1962)

SWEEZY, PAUL M., and LEO HUBERMAN, see Huberman, Leo

SWERLING, BORIS CYRIL, *International control of sugar 1918–41* (Stanford, 1949)

SZULC, TAD and MEYER, KARL E., *The Cuban invasion: the chronicle of a disaster* (New York, 1962)

*TABER, ROBERT, *M26: The biography of a revolution* (New York, 1961)

*TACÓN, Y ROSIQUE, GENERAL MIGUEL, *Correspondencia reservada, 1834–1836*, ed. Juan Pérez de la Riva (Havana, 1963)

Taft-Bacon report (Washington, 1906)

TANNENBAUM, FRANK, *Slave and citizen: the Negro in the Americas* (New York, 1947)

TATU, MICHEL, *Power in the Kremlin* (London, 1969)

TAUSSIG, CHARLES W., *Some notes on sugar and molasses* (New York, 1910)

TAYLOR, JOHN GLANVILLE, *The United States and Cuba* (London, 1851)

THAYER, THOMAS PRENCE, *Chrome resources of Cuba* (Washington, 1942)

TITHERINGTON, RICHARD H., *A history of the Spanish-American War* (New York, 1900)

TOUZEAU, JAMES, *The rise and progress of Liverpool from 1551–1835*, 2 vols (Liverpool, 1910)

TRELLES, CARLOS MANUEL, *El Progreso (1902–1905) y el retroceso (1906–1922) de la República de Cuba* (Havana, 1923)

TROLLOPE, ANTHONY, *The West Indies and the Spanish Main* (London, 1862)

TUÑÓN DE LARA, MANUEL, *La España en el siglo XIX, 1808–1914* (Paris, 1961)

*TURNBULL, DAVID, *Travels in the West* (London, 1840)

URRUTIA LLEÓ, MANUEL, *Fidel Castro and Company, Inc.* (New York, 1964)

U.S. GOVERNMENT, *A Survey of Agriculture in Cuba* (Washington, 1969)

——, '*The White Paper on Cuba*' (Washington, 1961)

——, *Investment in Cuba* (Washington, 1956)

——, *Report on the census of Cuba 1899* (Washington, 1900)

——, *Statement of the secretary of the navy of expenditures under the navy department in the island of Cuba from January 1, 1899, to April 30, 1900* (Washington, 1900)

——, *Summary of the labor situation in Cuba* (Washington, 1956)

——, Bureau of the census: *Cuba: population, history, resources, 1907*

——, War department, *Annual report for 1899, 1900, 1901 and 1902* (Washington, 1900, 1901, 1902, 1903)

VARONA, ENRIQUE, *De la colonia a la república* (Havana, 1919)

VEGA COBIELLAS, ULPIANO, *Los doctores Ramón Grau San Martín y Carlos Saladrigas Zayas* (Havana, 1944)

VELA, DAVID, *Martí en Guatemala* (Guatemala City, 1954)

VÉLIZ, CLAUDIO, ed., *The politics of conformity in Latin America* (London, 1967)

VENTURA NOVO, ESTEBAN, *Memorias* (Mexico, 1961)

VICENS VIVES, JAIME, *Manual de historia económica de España* (Barcelona, 1969)

VILAVERDE, CIRILO, *Cecilia Valdés* (Havana, 1941)

*VITON, A., and PIGNALOSA, F., *Trends and forces of world sugar consumption* (Rome, 1961)

VIVÓ, HUGH, *El empleo y la población activa de Cuba* (Havana, 1950)

*WALLICH, HENRY CHRISTOPHER, *Monetary problems of an export economy; the Cuban experience, 1914–1947* (Cambridge, Mass, 1950)

WARD, WILLIAM ERNEST FRANK, *A history of Ghana*, 2nd edn (London, 1958)

WELLES, SUMNER, *Naboth's vineyard*, 2 vols (New York, 1928)

——, *The time for decision* (London and New York, 1944)

WEYL, NATHANIEL, *Red star over Cuba, the Russian assault on the western hemisphere* (New York, 1960)

WEYLER, GENERAL, *Mi mando en Cuba*, 6 vols (Madrid, 1910)

WHITAKER, ARTHUR P., *The U.S. and the independence of Latin America 1800–1830*, 2nd edn (New York, 1964)

WHITWORTH, SIR CHARLES, *State of trade of Great Britain in its imports and exports progressively from the year 1697*, 2 pts (London, 1776)

WILKERSON, LOREE A., *Fidel Castro's political programs from reformism to Marxism-Leninism* (Gainesville, 1965)

WILKERSON, MARCUS MANLEY, *Public opinion and the Spanish-American war* (Louisiana, 1932)

WILLIAMS, ERIC, *Capitalism and slavery*, 2nd edn (London, 1964)

WILLIAMS, GOMER, *History of the Liverpool privateers and letter of marque, with an account of the Liverpool slave trade* (London, 1897)

WILLIAMS, WILLIAM APPLEMAN, *The U.S., Cuba and Castro* (New York, 1962)

*WISAN, JOSEPH E., *The Cuban crisis as reflected in the New York press (1895–1898)* (New York, 1965)

WISE, DAVID, and ROSS, THOMAS BERNARD, *The invisible government* (London, 1965)

*WOOD, BRYCE, *The making of the good neighbour policy* (New York, 1961)

WOODRUFF, JULIA LOUISA MATILDA, see Jay, W. M. L. (*pseud.*)

WORLD BANK, *Report on Cuba* (Washington, 1951)

*WRIGHT, IRENE ALOHA, *Cuba* (New York, 1910)

——, *The early history of Cuba* (New York, 1916)

WRIGHT, PHILIP GREEN, *The Cuban situation and our treaty relations* (Washington, D.C., 1931)

WRIGHT, ROBERT, *The life of Major-General James Wolfe* (London, 1864)

YGLESIAS, JOSÉ, *In the fist of the revolution* (New York, 1968)

Y la Luz se Hizo: declaraciones del comandante Fidel Castro . . . en el juicio contra el ex-comandante Hubert Matos (Havana, 1959)

ZEITLIN, MAURICE, and R. SCHEER, see Scheer, Robert

——, *Revolutionary Politics and the Cuban Working Class* (Princeton, 1967)

ZULUETA, PEDRO DE, *Trial of Pedro de Zulueta (on a charge of slave trading) at the Old Bailey (1843)* (British and Foreign Anti-Slavery Society, 1843)

II ARTICLES

(Some of the more useful articles on Cuba in the period covered by this book)

AIMES, H. S., 'Coartación', *Yale Review*, vol. 17 (February 1909)

AUXIER, G. W., 'Propaganda activities of the Cuban junta', *Hispanic American Historical Review*, vol. 19 (1939)

BAKER, RAY STANNARD, 'How the beet sugar industry is growing', *Review of Reviews*, vol. 22 (March 1901)

BERLE, A. A., 'The Cuban crisis', *Foreign Affairs*, vol. 39, No. 1, 40–55 (October 1960)

BLACKBURN, ROBIN, 'Prologue to the Cuban revolution', *New Left Review* (October 1963)

BONSAL, PHILIP, 'Cuba, Castro and the U.S.', *Foreign Affairs* (January 1967)

BURT, A. L., 'The Mirage of Havana', *Nation* (25 January 1965)

BUTLER, WILLIS P., 'Cuba's revolutionary medicine', *Ramparts* (May 1969)

Cambridge Opinion, articles by Felipe Pazos, Carlos Diago, etc. (January 1963)

CASTRO, JUANA, 'My brother is a tyrant', *Sunday Telegraph* (30 August and 5 September 1964)

CASTRO, RAÚL, 'Diario de Campaña', *Revolución* (January 1959)

CAZALIS, SEGUNDO, contributor to *La República,* Caracas (4, 5, 7, 8, 9, 10 February 1966)

CORBITT, D. C., 'Immigration in Cuba', *Hispanic American Historical Review*, vol. 22 (1942)

——, 'Mercedes and realengos', *Hispanic American Historical Review*, vol. 19 (1939)

——, 'El primer ferrocarril construido', *Revista Bimestre Cubana*, vol. 12 (April–June 1938)

COX, ISAAC, 'The Pan-American policy of Jefferson and Wilkinson', *Mississippi Valley Historical Review*, vol. 1.

CRONON, EDMUND DAVID, 'Interpreting the new good neighbour policy: the Cuban crisis of 1933', *Hispanic American Historical Review*, vol. 39, No. 4, 558–67 (1959)

CUBILLAS, VICENTE, 'Los Sucesos del 30 de Noviembre de 1956', *Bohemia* (6 December 1959)

DEERR, NOËL, and ALEXANDER BROOKS, 'The early use of steam power in the Cane sugar industry', the *Newcomen Society, Transactions*, vol. 21, 1940–1

DEL VALLE, ALDO ISIDRÓN, 'La batalla de Santa Clara', *Hoy* (16 July 1965)

DRAPER, THEODORE, 'Castro and communism', *Reporter* (17 January 1963)

DUMONT, RENÉ, 'Les Cubains trouvent le temps long', *Le Monde* (9 December, 1969)

FITZGIBBON, R. H., and H. M. MEALEY, 'The Cuban elections of 1936', *American Political Science Review* (August 1936)

FRAYN, MICHAEL, 'Michael Frayn in Cuba', *Observer* (12, 19, 26 January 1969)

GOLDENBERG, BORIS, 'La revolución agraria cubana', *Cuadernos*, 48–56 (February 1962)

GRAHAM, JAMES D., 'The slave trade, depopulation and human sacrifice in Benin History', *Cahiers d'Etudes Africaines*, vol. 5, Bk 2 (1965)

GRENVILLE, J. A., 'American naval preparations for war with Spain 1896–1898', *American Studies*, vol. 2, No. 1

HENNESSY, C. A. M., 'The roots of Cuban nationalism', *International Affairs* (July 1963)

HILL, LAURENCE F., 'Abolition of the African slave trade to Brazil', *Hispanic American Historical Review*, vol. 11 (May 1931)

HORELICK, L., 'The Cuban missile crisis', *World Politics* (April 1963)

HORREGO ESTUCH, LEOPOLDO, 'El alzamiento del doce', *Bohemia*, No. 25 (23 June 1967)

JOHNSON, JOHN J., 'Political change in Latin America. The emergence of the middle sectors', *Stanford Studies in History, Economics and Political Science*, vol. 15 (1965)

JOHNSON, LELAND L., 'U.S. business interests in Cuba and the rise of Castro', *World Politics* (April 1965)

JOXE, ALAIN, 'La *crise* cubaine de 1962', *Strategie*, No. 1 (1964)

JULIEN, CLAUDE, 'Sept heures avec M. Fidel Castro', *Le Monde* (22 and 23 March 1963)

KHRUSHCHEV, NIKITA, 'My memories of power', *Sunday Times* (16 July 1967)

KLING, MERLE, 'Cuba: a case study of a successful attempt to seize political power by the application of unconventional warfare', *American Academy of Political and Social Science Annals* (May 1962)

LANCASTER, C. M., 'Gourds and castanets', *Journal of Negro History* (January 1943)

LEON, RUBÉN DE, 'Los sucesos de Septiembre 1933', *Bohemia* (18 March 1934)

LEONTIEF, WASSILY, 'A visit to Cuba', *New York Review of Books* (21 August 1969)

LIDDELL HART, B. H., 'Why did Khrushchev try to put missiles in Cuba?', *Quick Magazine* (11 November 1962)

LINCOLN, FREEMAN, 'Julio Lobo, colossus of sugar', *Fortune*, vol. 58, No. 3 (September 1958)

LUIS, CARLOS, 'Notes of a Cuban Revolutionary in Exile', (? 1965)

MCNEILL, HARRY, 'No "curse" on the Negro', *Negro World Digest*, vol. 1 (1940)

MANZANI, CARL, 'Fidel Castro: a partisan view', *Mainstream* (May 1961)

MARSHALL, C. E., 'Birth of the mestizo in New Spain', *Hispanic American Historical Review*, vol. 14 (1934)

MARTIN, PERCY A., 'Slavery and abolition in Brazil', *Hispanic American Historical Review*, vol. 13 (1933)

MESA-LAGO, CARMELO, 'Availability and reliability of statistics in Socialist Cuba', *Latin American Research Review*, Spring and Summer 1969

MOORE, CARLOS, *Présence Africaine* (October 1965)

MOSES, DAVID, 'Diego Martínez in the bight of Benin', *Journal of African History*, vol. 6 (1965)

NEASHAM, V. AUBREY, 'Spain's emigrants to the New World', *Hispanic American Historical Review*, vol. 19 (1918)

O'BRIEN, EDNA, 'Look at Cuba', *Sunday Times* (1 December 1968)

O'CONNOR, JAMES, 'The foundations of Cuban socialism', *Studies on the Left* (1963)

PAZOS, FELIPE, 'Dificultades y posibilidades de una política de industrialización de Cuba', *Humanismo*, No. 24 (October 1954)

PAZOS, JAVIER, 'Long live the revolution', *New Republic* (3 November 1962)

PÉREZ DE LA RIVA, JUAN, 'Documentos para la historia de las gentes sin historia; el tráfico de culíes chinos', *Revista de la Biblioteca José Martí*, Año 6, No. 2

——, 'Demografía de los Culíes chinos en Cuba', *Revista de la Biblioteca Nacional*, Año 57, No. 4

PIERSON, W. W., 'Francisco Arango', *Hispanic American Historical Review*, vol. 16 (1936)

PORTELL VILÁ, HERMINIO, 'Cuban students and Machado's bloody tyranny', *Cuban Information Service* (1932)

PRATT, J. W., 'Origin of manifest destiny', *American Historical Review*, vol. 32 (July 1927)

PRICHARD, WALTER, 'Effects of the civil war on the Louisiana sugar industry', *Journal of Southern History*, vol. 5 (August 1939)

RETAMAR, ROBERTO, 'Les Intellectuels dans la révolution', *Partisans* (April–June 1967)

ROBERTSON, C. ALTON, 'The political role of protestants in Cuba', *Occasional Bulletin Missionary Research Library*, vol. 18, Nos 1 and 2 (January, February 1967)

ST GEORGE, ANDREW, 'A visit with a revolutionary', *Coronet* (February 1958)

——, 'Secrets of the Guevara diaries', *Sunday Telegraph* (7, 14, 21 and 28 July 1968)

SAKUN, P., contributor to *U.R.S.S.* (July 1968)

SCHIFFREN, ANDRÉ, 'Cuba's Fourth World' (29 June 1968)

SCROGGS, W. O., 'William Walker's designs on Cuba', *Mississippi Valley Historical Review*, vol. 1

SEALE, PATRICK, and MCCONVILLE, MAUREEN, 'Is there a "Philby" near de Gaulle?', *Observer* (14 and 21 April 1968)

SHAFTER, GENERAL, 'Cuba with Shafter', *Century Magazine* (January 1899)

SHAW, BEN B., 'Building a railway in unusual circumstances', *Railway Age* (31 October 1925)

SHERIDAN, R. B., 'The wealth of Jamaica in the 18th Century: a rejoinder', *Economic Historical Review*, 2nd series, vol. 21, No. 1 (April 1968)

SIMÓN, LUIS, 'Mis relaciones con el "Che" Guevara', *Cuadernos* (May 1962)

STERN, DANIEL J., 'Defensive reactions to political anxiety; the American anti-communist liberal and the invasion of Cuba', *Studies on the Left*, vol. 2, No. 2, 3–29 (1961)

STOKES, W. S., 'The Cuban parliamentary system in action 1940–1947', *Journal of Politics* (1 May 1949)

——, 'National and local violence in Cuban politics', *Southwestern Social Science Quarterly* (September 1953)

TEICHERT, PEDRO C. M., 'Latin America and the socio-economic impact of the Cuban revolution', *Journal of Inter-American Studies*, vol. 4, 105–20 (January 1962)

THOMAS, HUGH, 'Castro and communism', *Listener* (16 January 1964)

——, 'Murder in Havana', *New Statesman* (29 May 1964)

——, 'Origins of the Cuban revolution', *World Today* (October 1963)

——, 'The Origins of the Cuban revolution', *Listener* (9 January 1964)

THOMAS, R. P., 'The Sugar colonies of the old empire: profit or loss for Great Britain', *Economic History Review*, 2nd series, vol. 21, No. 1 (April 1968)

TUTHILL, R. L., 'An independent farm in Cuba', *Economic Geography*, vol. 25, No. 3, 201–10 (July 1949)

VÉLIZ, CLAUDIO, 'Cuba', *Topolski's Chronicle*, vol. XI, Nos. 17–20, 1963

VILLAREJO, DONALD, 'American investment in Cuba', *New University Thought*, vol. 1, No. 1 (Spring 1960)

WOHLSTETTER, ROBERTA, 'Cuba and Pearl Harbor: hindsight and foresight', *Foreign Affairs* (July 1965)

——, and WOHLSTETTER, ALBERT, 'Controlling the risks in Cuba', *Adelphi Papers* (April 1965)

WRONG, DENNIS H., 'The American left and Cuba', *Commentary*, 93–103 (February 1962)

YGLESIAS, JOSÉ, 'Cuban Report: their hippies, their squares', *New York Times* (12 January 1969)

Index

AAA, 797, 855

Abárzuza, Buenaventura de (1841–1910), Spanish Minister for Overseas Territories, 307 n. 41; succeeds Maura, 304; Cuban reform, 307, 308, 348

ABC, foundation and membership, 594 and n. 46, 683; programme and methods, 594–5; bomb outrages, 595–6; and Vázquez Bello's murder, 598; secret organ *Denuncia*, 605; favours intervention, 605; denounced as 'fascist', 606; and de la Torriente as negotiator, 609; and Welles, 610, 611; and Machado's overthrow, 613–14, 617; and 1933 general strikes, 615; starts the revolution, 625; pursuit of *porristas*, 628; membership of new government, 629, 644; American outlook, 629; denounced by Communists, 651; and Batista, 651, 652; part of joint action, 655; and Hotel Nacional, 659; breaks with Directorio, 663; and November conspiracies, 666, 667, 669; and Mendieta's presidency, 678; revolutionary character, 681, 750; and 1939 elections, 718; and Smith, 964, 975

ABC Colony, and El Country Club, 1099, 1101–2; composition, 1101–2; medical provision, 1105; and racism, 1121

ABC Radical, 784; announces Machado's resignation, 624; ignored by Welles, 629, 632; and Batista, 637; and Hotel Nacional battle, 660; splinter group, 663; ceases to back government, 663, 674 n. 36, 678; revolutionary character, 681; and Batista's Army, 695

Abd-el-Krim, 76 and n. 18

Aberdeen, George Hamilton Gordon, Earl of, and Cuban slave trade, 203, 204, 206

Abolitionism and abolitionists, ignored by Cuba, 75; attitude of industrialists, 84 n. 55; preached in Cádiz, 88; international proposals, 93–4; coffee farmers and, 133; effect on slave conditions, 164–5; and African economy, 166–7, 167 n. 54; assist independent communities, 184 n. 1; effect of Negro conspiracy, 206; Cuban reformers and, 233–4, 235, 239

Abrahantes, José, and G.2, 1321 n. 30, 1349; and new Communist party, 1455 and n. 7

Acción Católica, 866 and n. 13, 982, 1129

Acción Libertadora, 802, 862, 866 n. 12

Acción Nacional Revolucionaria, 866 n. 12

Acción Republicana, 718

Acción Revolucionaria Guiteras (ARG), 741, 742, 746 n. 21, 817 n. 71; and Grau, 749, 754; and 1948 elections, 757; bribed with official posts, 763

Acción Revolucionaria Oriente, 868

Acevedo, Enrique, 1042

Acevedo, General Guillermo, 508

Acevedo, Capt. Rogelio, at Santa Clara, 1025; later career, 1025 n. 20, 1268 n. 29; militia commander, 1268, 1321, 1455

Achard, Franz Carl (1753–1821), and sugar loaf from beet, 125 and n. 66

Acheson, Dean (1893–), 1403

ACOPIO, INRA sub-department, 1374, 1382, 1440

Acosta family, 503

Acosta Agustín, 1150 and n. 62

Acosta, Major Armando, Cuban communist, 1005, 1408; assists Cienfuegos, 1012–13, 1079; aide to Guevara, 1013, 1030, 1082; and surrender of Sancti Spiritus, 1022; commander of La Punta, 1082; expulsion from party, 1453 n. 1, 1467; and PURS, 1454 n. 3

Acosta, Facundo, 237

Acosta, Félix José de, 45 n. 14

Acosta, Julio Zenón, 916; death, 917

Acosta Rubio, Dr Raúl, ousted by Tabernilla, 852

Acuña, Manuel, *Fidelista* bandit, 913 and n. 18, 916, 920

Acuña, Sergio, *Fidelista* bandit, 913 and n. 18, 916, 920

Adams, John (1735–1826), U.S. President, 66–7

Adams, John Quincy (1767–1848), U.S. President, and annexation of Cuba, 100–1

Adenauer, Konrad, 1407

Adzubei, Aleksei, 1391 and n. 29, 1393

AFL-CIO, 1251; statement on Castro, 1279

Africa, effect of abolition of slave trade, 95–6, 166–7; increasing population, 96; slave trade, 158, 183, 204, 284; origin of yellow fever, 460 n. 79; origin of Cuban place-names, 519; influence on Cuban art, 1123; sugar consumption, 1138

Africa, West, slave trade, 3 n. 16, 52, 71, 158, 166–7, 282; Portuguese zone, 31; price of slaves, 50–1, 51 n. 39, 95, 96, 167; Cuban expeditions to, 83, 136, 156; Spanish preference for its slaves, 86; export of palm oil, 93, 95–6, 159; economic crisis after abolition, 95–6, 166–7; coffee plant (*liberica*), 128 and n. 2; Courts of Arbitration, 157; Europeans and the interior, 160; last slave export, 169–70; religious survival in Cuba, 177, 517; R.N. Squadron, 215

Africans, dealings with slave merchants, 159–60; and ban on slave trade, 201; and sale of slaves, 283; survivors in U.S. of slave trade, 283

Africans, Cuban, and Catholic religious practices, 39, 48 n. 20; their *cofradías*, 39–40; the *Día de los Reyes*, 40; ban on religious ceremonies, 206, 517; transculturation of saints, 517–18, 519; *see also* Negroes

Agostini, Jorge, 797, 867

Agramonte family, 749 and n. 35, 772, 1110, 1146, 1229

Agramonte, Ignacio (1868), 245, 247, 260; death, 261–2

Agramonte, Joaquín, 1245; arrest, 1256; and 30 November Movement, 1285; attempted escape, 1348

Agramonte, Roberto, 754 n. 48, 766, 884 n. 36; and elections, 772, 773, 858, 1086; career, 772; SIM and, 792; arrest, 799; and Ochoa, 800; open letter to Batista, 800; accused of *colaboracionismo*, 802; Ortodoxo splinter group, 956, 968, 971, 1030; Foreign Minister, 1046, 1065, 1068, 1203; and war trials, 1073; dismissal, 1225

Agrarian Reform law, 1215–17, 1220; political intent, 1217; protests against, 1218–19, 1222–3; U.S. official note, 1223, 1226–7; payment of compensation, 1223–4, 1226, 1239, 1258, 1284; expropriations, 1224, 1228–9, 1239, 1258; opposition, 1226 and n. 43; Castro and, 1226; implementation, 1235–6, 1284, 1323; (2nd) aimed at larger proprietors, 1439 and n. 15

Agricultural and Industrial Development Bank (BANFAIC), 789, 914, 1185; Prío and, 768, 775–6, 1164; presidency, 768, 784, 1066; and industrial expansion, 1165, 1182, 1205; land purchase, 1201; absorption, 1322; loans for improvements, 1553–4, 1556; and rice-growing, 1557; marine biology research, 1558

Agriculture, race and, 425 and n. 46, 429–31; reduced livestock (1899), 428 and n. 58; numbers occupied in, 429 and n. 59, 515 n. 6, 1096, 1109 and n. 3, 1178 n. 15; U.S. economic aid, 726; in Sierra Maestra, 906; Castro and agrarian reform, 1010–11; Guevera and, 1049–50; living conditions of workers, 1095–6; class structure, 1108–9; based on *colonos* system, 1142, 1153; income from sugar, 1151; and unemployment, 1175; need for diversification, 1189, 1290, 1325, 1327, 1329, 1332, 1382, 1554; numbers of co-operatives, 1323, 1395; lack of scientific planning, 1325, 1329, 1441; 1961 drought, 1325; expenditure on machinery, 1332 and n. 35; fall in production (1962), 1374, 1376, 1425 and n. 4; Russian technicians, 1382 and n. 36, 1383; and Russian methods, 1395; employment of children, 1428; nationalization of private

Agriculture – *Cont.*
holdings over five *caballería*, 1439 and
n. 15; contribution of small farmers,
1440; benefits from Revolutionary
regime, 1440; import of machinery,
1440; dependence on wise political
decisions, 1441; increase in land
cultivated, 1441 and n. 25; system of
barter, 1442; domination of Cuban
life, 1442; bureaucratic control, 1443;
use of armed forces, 1458; neglect of
fertilization, 1552; amount of mechanization, 1553 and n. 28; % composition of Cuban production (1958),
1554 and n. 31; pig breeding, 1555;
improved dairy farming, 1555; surviving relics of slavery, 1558–9
Agrupación Católica Universitaria, 767
Agrupación Comunista, founding members, 576; sección Hebrea, 577, 1578;
work of first Congress, 577
Agrupación Revolucionaria pro Ley y
Justicia, 600, 662, 681, 743 n. 9; and
1933 Revolution, 629 and n. 17; and
rebel sergeants, 635, 638; outbreak of
violence, 670; and Batista's army, 695
Aguiar, Luis José de, 45 n. 14, 48 and n.
21, 53 n. 52
Aguilar Léon, Luis, 808 n. 23, 1280
Aguilera, José María de, Labour leader,
946, 1240 n. 48, 1259; and FONU,
1003, 1083 n. 23; and communism,
1313; in Peking, 1315; and new
regime, 1456
Aguinaldo, General, 385, 407; self-
proclaimed President of Philippines,
402; surrenders Manila, 404, 406;
prepares to resist U.S., 409
Aguirre, Severo, communist, 846, 1377
n. 21; and PURS, 1454 n. 3
Aguirre Cerda, President of Chile, 714
Ainciart, Machado's police chief, 617,
620, 628
Air force, Cuban, trial of Batistiano
pilots, 1202–3, 1459; 'indoctrination
classes', 1229–30; Díaz Lanz and,
1229–30; purge of, 1230; and Battle
of Cochinos Bay, 1355, 1356, 1363–4
Air force, U.S., and Cuban invasion,
1367 and n. 34
Airfields, 1162, 1355–6
Ala Izquierda Estudiantil, 592, 650,
1455; membership, 592 n. 35; imprisonment, 594 n. 43; and rebel

sergeants, 635, 639; student involvement, 685, 696, 707; and Mella, 685;
organ *Linea*, 685; Communist domination, 707, 750 n. 38; controls
University, 743 n. 9
Alarcón, Daniel, escape from Bolivia,
1469 n. 56
Alarcón, Ricardo, 1006 n. 9, 1286 and
n. 27, 1286–7
Alaska, purchased by U.S., 211, 250
Albemarle, Arnold Joost van Keppel,
2nd Earl of, 2 n. 5, 3 n. 11
Albemarle, George, 3rd Earl of (1724–
72), commander-in-chief Havana expedition, 1 and n. 3, 2, 5–6; lands in
Cuba, 6, 18; sickness, 7, 10, 49 n. 26,
56; surrender terms, 10; prize money,
43, 56, 57; governor-general of Cuba,
43–4; and the *cabildo*, 44; demands
tribute from the Church, 48; and an
English church, 48 n. 20; casualties,
48–9; gives Kennion slave monopoly,
49–50, 50 n. 32; purchase of slaves,
50 and n. 38; effect of his expedition
on Cuba, 52–3; abolishes cash
presents, 53; leaves Havana, 53;
subsequent career, 56 and n. 63; buys
Quidenham, 56–7
Aldama family, 141; and railways, 122;
sugar mills (*Armonía, Concepción Union*),
122 and n. 49; hierarchical position,
153, 154; and white labour, 184; and
Saco, 199
Aldama, Miguel de (1821–88), son of
the above, 240; Havana palace, 146,
148, 203, 211, 229, 248; sugar mills,
154, 207 n. 5; use of Basque labour,
185; and '*anexionismo*', 207, 208, 232,
241; slave revolt, 207–8; reform
policy, 232; slave strike, 236, 239;
and Independence War (1868), 246,
259, 270; death in poverty, 270
Aldereguía, Gustavo, 593, 594 and n.
43, 639
Aldrich, Senator Nelson, 288, 336 n.
32
Alegría de Pío, 898–9, 901 n. 53, 916
Alejos training base, 1305
Alemán, José, Sec. of War, 351, 456 n.
56; Education Minister, 743, 754,
756, 758, 812, 845, 1133; expedition
against Trujillo, 754; acquired fortune, 758, 765; indictment of his
widow, 768

Alemán, Miguel, President of Mexico, 868

Alexayev, Alexander (1913–), 1254 n. 58; Tass representative, 1254, 1281, 1318; Russian ambassador, 1381–2

Alfaro, Eloy, President of Ecuador, 333

Alfonso XII, King of Spain (1857–85), 263

Alfonso XIII, King of Spain (1886–1941), 298

Alfonso family, and railways, 122; mill-ownership, 122, 152, 153, 205, 1146; and white labour, 184; and Saco, 199

Alfonso, Gonzalo, Havana Railway president, 122; sugar mill, 122

Alfonso, José Luis, Havana Railway vice-president and mill-owner, 122 and n. 49, 208

Alfonso, José Ramón de, Marqués de Montelo, 142, 238; in Madrid, 236

Alger, Senator Russell (1836–1907), Sec. of War, 374 and n. 40; on McKinley, 379–80, 380 n. 54; and U.S.-Spanish War (1898), 383, 384, 397–9; and army recall, 405; supports Wood, 439 and n. 17

Algeria, FLN, 1317

Alliance for Progress, 1213 and n. 74, 1305–6, 1306 n. 27

Alliegro, Dr Anselmo, Prime Minister, 1026, 1029 n. 38, 1108; and 1952 elections, 776; alleged conversation with Prío, 776–7; member of diálogo cívico, 874

Allwood, Philip, interest in Cuba, 69 and n. 45; and slave trade, 71; new cane variety, 80; expulsion, 82

Almagro, Luis, Sec. of Justice, 674 n. 36, 675–6

Almeida, Juan, mulatto, 828 n. 24, 887 n. 47, 1122; Moncadista, 835, 836; in Granma, 894, 1455 n. 6; in Cuba, 899 and n. 38, 900 and n. 52; in the Sierra, 901 n. 53, 913, 920 n. 49; his group, 934 and n. 6, 939, 984 and n. 52; chaplaincy, 994; and operación verano, 996 n. 2, 997; invests Santiago, 1016; and Guantánamo, 1022, 1043; commander Third Front, 1043; and Castro, 1048, 1320; succeeds Díaz Lanz, 1230; politics of, 1320; and ORI, 1377 n. 18; and new Communist party, 1454 n. 5

Almendares, Marqués de, mill-ownership (Gran Antilla, Serafina), 152, 427

Alonso, Leonel, 889; and FEU presidency, 864 n. 10

Alonso, Luis Ricardo, ambassador in Lima, 1314 and n. 10

Alpízar, Félix, 595, 631, 634

Alvarado, Dr O., 843 n. 1

Alvarez, Alberto Inocento, Minister of Commerce, 592 n. 33, 743 n. 10, 748, 874; Sec. of State, 751; and Nicaro Nickel, 1170–1

Alvarez, Santiago, 638; at La Cabaña, 1082 n. 20

Alvarez de la Campa, Odon, and CTC, 1250 and n. 4, 1259, 1291–2; defection, 1292 n. 46

Alvarez Fuentes, German, 743 n. 10, 796

Alvarez Santa Cruz, José Manuel, bomb placer, 945

Alvarez Tagle, Jorge, 945

Amadeo, King of Spain, Duke of Aosta, 155; nominated by Prim, 258; his rule, 259; abdication, 261

Ambriz, Slave factory, 203

Ameijeiras brothers, 867, 1071

Ameijeiras, Efigenio, Fidelista, 899 and n. 41, 901 and n. 53, 1048, 1071; in the Sierra, 901 n. 53, 920 n. 49, 934, 939, 940 n. 23; accompanies Raúl, 992, 993, 994 n. 27; police command, 1071, 1253, 1467; alias 'Jomeguía', 1071 n. 15; anti-communist, 1320; rounds up underground, 1356; expulsion from party, 1453 n. 1; and new Communist party, 1455 n. 6; dismissed for moral offences, 1467

Americans, North, in Cuba: sugar and coffee plantation owners, 131–2, 140–1, 499, 503, 600, 601, 1164; hoteliers, 145; treatment of Cubans during occupation, 417–18, 687; racism, 418–19; sugar consumption, 469, 500; Cuban residents, 500, 648 n. 45, 909, 1101–2; 'Vedado' set, 500; investment in Cuba, 534, 909, 1114, 1164, 1166; return of tourists (1919) 541; fear of Communism, 632; and sergeants' revolt, 640; Guevara and, 880 n. 18; Club activities, 909; visit Batista, 932; in Santiago, 957; and political crisis, 975; kidnapped at Moa Bay, 1000, 1010; and Cuban

Americans – *Cont.*
embassy, 1058; ignore police violence, 1059; patronising attitude to Cuba, 1062; compared with S. Americans, 1064; dominate economic life, 1108, 1111; *bourgeoisie*, 1113 n. 26; effect on foreign policy, 1188–9; state take-over of cattle ranches, 1228–9; advised to leave Cuba, 1296

Amiel, Col., 668

Amodeo, Julio, Argentine ambassador, 1263, 1264, 1276

Ampère, Jean Jacques, in U.S., 218

Anarchism and anarchists, in Spain, 249, 291, 298, 304, 350 n. 56; in Cuba, 291–2, 350, 442; Baliño and, 302; Chicago riots (1886), 317; Martí and, 317; strikes, 506 n. 7, 569; trade unions, 534; attracted by Communist state, 575–6; Latin-American, 578–9; deportations, 580; persecuted by Machado, 580, 596; and control of CNOC, 580, 596; Castro's affinity, 828; idea of *repartimiento*, 831; *El Libertario*, 1137, 1281; *Solidaridad Gastronímica*, 1281

Anarcho-syndicalism, in Cuba, 291, 574; in Spain, 408, 574

Anderson, Admiral, 1410–11

Anderson, General, 402, 404

André, Armando, murder of, 574, 681

Andreu, José, and Prío's cabinet, 775 n. 1; at anti-Batista meeting, 870

Angiolillo, Miguel, 350

Anglo-American War (1812–14), 85, 87

Angola, 50–1, 183

Angulo, Capt. Andrés, 614

Anson, Admiral George, 2, 5 and n. 27

Anti-Imperialist League, 578

Anti-Slavery Society, 201

Antonio de Montesinos, and Cuban Indians, 1526

Apezteguía family, 153

Apezteguía, Julio, Marqués de, and *central Constancia*, 290 and n. 36, 330, 1148

Apezteguía, Martín Felipe, 290 n. 36, 303

Aponte, General Carlos, 700

Aponte, José Antonio, 91

APRA, 714, 880

Aragón, Capt. Luis, 1023

Aragón, Dr, 611

Aragonés, Emilio, 961, 963, 1377 n. 20

Arambarri, Navea, 972

Aran, Capt., 653

Arana, Sabino de, 298, 409

Aranda, Conde de, 72 n. 2; and Independence War (1895), 319

Arango family, mill and estate ownership, 152 and n. 80; social position, 154; *central Tuinicú*, 538

Arango, Augusto, 248

Arango, Francisco de (1765–1839), and sugar industry, 72 and n. 1, 79, 80, 82; studies England's slave trade, 72, 75 and n. 13; and liberalism, 73, 74; and use of land, 80; belief in white domination, 81; and Humboldt, 82 n. 46; sugar mill, *La Ninfa*, 82 and n. 47; monopoly of wheat import, 85; attitude to abolition, 91, 93–4, 167; Marqués de la Gratitud, 167

Arango, José de, treasurer of Havana, 88; and slave trade commission, 206

Arango, Miguel, and Cuba Cane, 538, 548

Arbenz, Col., President of Guatemala, overthrown by U.S., 855, 1060, 1302

Arce, José, 564

Arcos, Gustavo, 946, 1461

Arcos, Marqués de los, 82 n. 47, 427

Arévalo, Juan, 547 n. 18, 575 n. 24; socialist group, 707; at Miami, 748

Arguelles, 91

Argüelles, Col., governor of Colón, 234

Ariás, Col. Tomás, 1073

Aricos, Gustavo, Moncadista, 824 n. 3, 836 n. 15, 837, 854 and n. 23

Armando Fernández, Pablo, literary award, 1466

Armed forces, and full employment, 1425 and n. 8; control of country, 1458; compulsory service, 1458; under Revolution, 1458 and n. 17; armaments, 1458; agricultural tasks, 1458; and cultural standards, 1466; organ *Verde Oliva*, 1466, 1472

Armengol Rodríguez, 666

Army, Cuban Republic, Magoon's foundations, 490, 680; numbers and postings (1907), 490 n. 42; political unrest, 508; Communists and, 581; relations with Machado, 582–3, 591, 595, 614, 622 and n. 29, 623, 624, 630, 631, 680–1; structure in 1920s, 583; Sergeants' revolt, 583, 634 ff., 646 and n. 37, 682, 721, 1039;

Army, Cuban Republic – *Cont.*
attempted uprising, 588; the NCOs, 631, 634, 682, 702, 1039; and Céspedes, 634; Enlisted Men's Club, 634, 635; fear of salary cuts, 634–5; and Hotel Nacional, 644, 659, 679; reorganizations, 646, 745–6, 784, 791–2; and Batista, 657, 658–9, 658 n. 1, 724–5, 778 and n. 7, 779–83, 1039; and students, 658; and November revolt, 666, 679; purge of 1933, 673 and n. 27; only effective political unit, 679, 680, 691–2, 778; state in 1933, 680 ff.; lack of camaraderie in Officer Corps, 681–2; absence of colour bar, 683; ends 1935 strike, 699; extension of power, 702; schoolteachers, 702; under Prío, 763; political complexion, 778, 1039; and new government, 785, 798; state of intrigue, 798; and Moncada attack, 838–9, 840, 841, 844; indiscipline, 841, 852, 1039; *puros* and *tanquistas* plots against Batista, 884 and n. 36, 885, 1039; student attacks on, 889–90; and Castro, 898–9, 999–1000, 1008 and n. 16, 1017, 1020, 1021, 1022, 1040, 1041, 1071 ff.; and 26 July reprisals, 909–10; La Plata attack, 914, 923–4; in the Sierra, 914–15, 920, 935–6, 939, 950, 965, 967 and n. 18, 1041; and *precaristas*, 924; defence of Palace, 929; defence of El Uvero, 939–40; and guerrilla warfare, 941, 1041; and U.S. officers, 947; and peasants, 950; *operación verano*, 996–7; demoralization, 997–8, 1016; withdrawal, 998, 1005; treatment of prisoners, 998, 999; changes in command, 1017; Santa Clara expedition, 1018; and Batista, 1020, 1039 and n. 6, 1041; fraternizes with rebels, 1024, 1027; surrender, 1028; favoured institution, 1039–40; poor pay and armaments of soldiers, 1040; effect of U.S. arms embargo, 1040; creation of supreme command, 1040–1; lack of *esprit de corps*, 1041; executive of new regime, 1073–; consolidation of Communists, 1082

Army, Revolutionary (1959), main columns, 994 n. 28; Castro's plans, 1008, 1198; advantage of smallness, 1041; heterogeneous character, 1042,

1043; numbers, 1042 and n. 16; organization and equipment, 1042–3, 1043–4; character of leaders, 1043; administration of *territorio libre*, 1043; overall control, 1043–4; civilian casualties, 1044 and n. 21; Communist influence, 1082; Guevara and, 1090; commanders, 1198 and n. 18; takeover cattle-ranches, 1228–9; reorganization, 1321; replaced by militia, 1321

Army, Spanish (Cuban), 307; Havana garrison, 12, 110; Negroes and mulattos, 65–6, 66 n. 24, 172, 205; defeat in S. America, 103; and law and order in Cuba, 110; and Independence War (1868), 248, 252, 254; supplemented by volunteers and *guerrilleros*, 254; tactics against guerrilla warfare, 259; lack of direction, 260; reinforced by Campos, 265–6; crushes the *Guerra Chiquita*, 269, 294; and Independence War (1895), 317, 319, 325, 329, 335; Weyler and, 328, 331; behaviour of commanders, 335; protests against, 358; hatred of U.S., 363; and war with U.S. (1898), 382–3, 388–9, 393–4, 399; at San Juan, 393, 394

Army, United States, and War with Spain (1898), 384, 385, 387–8; Cuban landing, 388–9, 390–1; battle of San Juan, 393–4; camp conditions, 398, 399; prisoners and booty, 401 n. 34; occupation of Cuba, 403; losses from disease, 404–5; demands recall, 405

Aróstegui, Martín Esteban de, plot to recapture Havana, 48

Arrate, José Martín Félix de, 4, 45 n. 14, 73

Arrieta family, 154, 277, 428

Arrieta, Joaquín de, 208, 278, 427

Arroyo, Nicolás, 861 n. 58; ambassador in Washington, 960 n. 33, 1030 n. 43

Arteaga, Cardinal, Archbishop of Havana, 1128; and Batista, 793, 1129; ends hunger strike, 872; plea for peace, 951, 982

Arteaga, Senator Emilio, bill limiting land purchase, 658

Artemesa, 591, 595; Batista and, 637; foundation, 824; Castro stronghold, 824, 825, 927; statue of patron saint,

Artemesa – *Cont.*
991 and n. 15; Freemasons' Hall, 1115
Artesiano, Mario, 769
Arthur, Chester, 910
Artigas, Jesús, 791
Artigas, Col. Ricardo, lottery chief, 782; and army plot, 782–3; and Castro, 783 n. 17, 1204; arrest, 884
Artime, Manuel, 1275 and n. 9, 1455; and Rural Commandos, 1083; and Manzanillo, 1217 n. 8; in exile, 1217 n. 8, 1467; opponent of Castro, 1275 and n. 9, 1283; CIA link, 1283, 1296, 1467 n. 48, 1471; unpopularity, 1294; in Guatemala, 1306; and Brigade, 2506, 1359, 1369 n. 41; new exile army, 1471 and n. 66
Asbert, Col. Ernesto, 526, 534; Liberal leader, 475, 484 n. 18, 528; supports Menocal, 509, 527
Asociación Nacional de Agricultores Pequeños (ANAP), creation and membership, 1330; organization, 1330 nn. 61, 62; inclusion of peasant organizations, 1330 n. 63; land ownership, 1330 and n. 62, 1331; addressed by Castro, 1446 and n. 3
Astor, John Jacob (1864–1912), 385 and n. 16
Atarés Barracks, 623, 849; Castle, 668
Atarés, Conde de, governor of Havana, 63 n. 13
Atkins, Edwin (1850–1926), 114 n. 11, 348, 365, 409; and *Soledad* mill, 114, 288, 302 n. 27, 321, 322, 1146; and Independence War (1895), 321, 322–3, 330, 343; favours Cuban autonomy, 332; sugar baron, 336, 457, 468, 537; lobbies for peace, 373; and mayoral election, 472; opposes sugar tariff, 552 and n. 42, 553
Atkins, Elisha, 137 n. 9, 141 n. 21, 146
Atkins, Robert, son of Edwin, 537
Auténticos (Authentic Revolutionary Movement), 743, 843 n. 41; reorganized by Grau, 706, 710, 714, 737; and elections (1939), 718, (1944), 735–6, (1948), 756–7, (1962), 772, 774 and n. 36, (1954), 857, 860; and Grau's presidency, 744, 749; use of gunmen, 744, 753; and Communists, 744, 747, 748, 752, 753, 772–3, 853; pensions plan, 747; Chibás and, 749, 750, 751;

effect of cold war, 752; and Trujillo expedition, 755; in Prío's government, 764, 768 n. 20; in disrepute for gangsterism, 775; and *Batistato*, 792, 796, 800, 951; and Ortodoxos, 800, 802; in Congress, 860; attack on Goicuría barracks, 890; and Directorio, 926; supports naval mutiny, 961, 962, 963; division into PRA and OA, 968 and n. 25; capture of Havana representative, 1016; and army under Batista, 1039 and n. 6; and Civil War, 1045, 1046; Youth Movement, 1066; and union movement, 1173–4; and CTC, 1178; calls for elections, 1204
Autobuses Modernos, 926, 1162
Autonomists, 268, 351; Martí and, 296, 298, 304; distrusted in Spain, 297–8, 303; dwindling influence, 300; and first home rule government, 356, 357, 359; message to McKinley, 377; and Spanish-American War, 381; dissolves itself, 412; dependence on U.S., 413–14
Averhoff, Octavio, Sec. of Treasury, 611; escapes by air, 625
Averiches, Marcial, 900
Avila, Capt., 755
Ayacucho, defeat of Spanish army, 103, 408
Ayala, Antonio Ignacio de, and the *cabildo*, 45 n. 14
Ayan Rosell, 868
Ayesterán, Joaquín de, 75 n. 11; introduces 'centrifugal' machine, 118, 136 n. 2; railways and, 122, 123; plantation, *Amistad*, 122, 278; outstanding debt, 136 n. 2; sugar mills, 153
Azcárate, Nicolás de, 269, 296; Liceo headmaster, 237; in Madrid, 238; peace negotiator, 258
Azcárate Rosell, Carlos, 743 n. 10
Azcárraga, General, 406

Babcock, General, 253
Babst, Earl (1870–1967), 532
Babun Bros., Hacienda Sevilla, 907 and n. 76, 939; carry armaments, 938
Bacallao, Valentín, and Brigade 2506, 1359 n. 16; Cuban landing, 1362
Bacardí, Emiliano, mayor of Santiago, 411

Bacardí, Emilio (c. 1860), describes the *tumba*, 177–8; *Via Crucis*, 177, 178 n. 51

Bacon, Anthony, 67 n. 29, 84 n. 55

Bacon, Robert (1860–1919), Ass. Sec. of State, 477 n. 22; sent to Havana, 477; and Liberal revolutionaries, 477–8

Baeza, Ramiro, 785 n. 24, 794, 802

Baker (Bécquer), J. W., sugar plantation, *San José*, 140 and n. 18; Gentleman of the Bedchamber, 143; house decoration, 148

Baker, Peter, shipbuilder and slave trader, 168 and n. 36, 69, 71; and a new monopoly contract, 69–70, 72 n. 1

Bakunin, Mikhail (1814–76), 249, 302

Balán, Major, 655

Balbuena, Pablo, and CTC, 783; and *diálogo cívico*, 874

Balcarres, Alexander, Earl of, use of Cuban mastiffs, 38, 81 n. 44

Baliño, Carlos (1848–1926), Tampa socialist, 302 and n. 23; anarchism, 302, 305, 575; and communism, 576, 577 and n. 36

Ball Llovera, Lieut., Fernando, in Oriente, 924 n. 65

Ballou, Mathew, 165 and n. 45

Banco Nacional, foundation, 545 and n. 5, 546, 600, 1066; and 1920 crisis, 545; bought by Poté López, 545; Merchant and, 545, 549; closes its doors, 549–50; and sugar crop, 1142; Presidency, 1470

Banderas, 938

Banderas, Quintín, 323, 346; death, 348–9

Banks, in Cuba, 136, 1184; U.S. Export-Import, 691 and n. 2, 716 and n. 2; loans and credits, 726–7, 730; freezing of accounts, 1085–6, 1273; take-over by INRA, 1297

Baralt, Luis, 611

Barba, Alvaro, and army plot, 781, 782, 785 n. 24; and Batista, 794, 795; and *Acción Libertadora*, 802

Barceló, Gabriel, 750 n. 38, 592 n. 33

Barceló, José, 620

Barletta, Amadeo, 1262–3

Barnes, Tracy, of CIA, 1308

Barnes, Dr William, 1310

Barnet, José Antonio, 701

Baró, José Luis, 234, 538 n. 11; planter (*Luisa*) and slave trader, 137, 141, 157–8; social position, 153; slave revolt, 204

Baró, Juan Pedro, 538 and n. 11, 601

Baró, Leonardo, 967

Barquín, José, 650, 651

Barquín, Major Ramón, 763, 778–9, 1018; leader of *puros*, 784, 884, 1359; plot against Batista, 884, 961, 962 and n. 5, 1021, 1283; appointed to Washington, 884; imprisonment, 965, 994, 1021; planned release, 994–5, 1019, 1021, 1028; arrival in Havana, 1028; submission to *Fidelistas*, 1029, 1030; and new army, 1072; sent abroad, 1213

Barraqué, Jesús María, Sec. of Justice, 574

Barreiro, Alejandro, 576, 577 and n. 36

Barrera, Juan de la, 38

Barrera Pérez, Lieut. (Major), 840, 896, 1023 n. 12; and army conspiracy (1952), 779 n. 11; and Castro, 779 n. 11; commander in Sierra, 915 nn. 28, 29, 935–6, 939, 940; in Oriente, 923–4, 924 n. 65; plan for Sierra Maestra, 924; rehabilitation of *precaristas*, 924, 925; recalled, 935 and n. 10, 965; returned to Sierra, 942 and n. 1, 950

Barreras, Alberto, 529, 620

Barreras del Castillo, Luis, 641 n. 22

Barreto, Fidel, 861 n. 58, 924; sugar chief, 943

Barrientos, José, Lieut. of Aviation, 666, 667

Barrientos, General, president of Bolivia, 1256 n. 5, 1461

Barrieta, Dina, 275

Barrón, Arnaldo, 896 n. 18, 971 n. 38, 986 and n. 65

Barroso, Dr Jorge, Sugar Board chief, 800, 861 and n. 58, 1086 n. 36

Bartholomew, Frank, 1210

Bassecourt, Juan, captain-general of Cuba, 85 and n. 3

Bastarrica, Fr, denounces Batista's *golpe*, 793

Bastide, Roger, 517

Bates, Richard, CBS, 1276

Bathurst, Richard, 48 and n. 24

Batista, Belisario, 635, 636

Batista, Sergeant Fulgencio (afterwards General) (born 1901), menacing funeral oration, 631, 634, 637; and Céspedes as president, 648; AND ARMY CONSPIRACY OF 1933, 634–5; future government, 634 n. 1; family and early life, 635–6; as *mulato lindo*, 636 and n. 7; joins army, 636; and ABC, 636–7; character and abilities, 637, 678–9; and Welles, 640, 655–6, 659 n. 4, 661; AND ATTACK ON HOTEL NACIONAL, 646, 659 and n. 5, 660; AS CHIEF OF STAFF AND COLONEL, 646, 647; strengthens his hold, 651, 655; antagonists, 652; desire to be president, 654; conflict with old officers, 657; treatment of prisoners, 660; and students, 661, 674–5; relations with Grau, 662, 664, 672, 674, 709; weakening position, 663; a warning to the army, 666; and November conspirators, 667, 668; AND THE FALL OF GRAU, 671, 673, 676, 691; REAL CENTRE OF POWER AFTER JANUARY 1934, 678, 679, 680, 691; intentions and achievements, 679–80; corrupt practices, 692, 800, 859; use of violence, 695–6; backed by upper classes, 696, 699, 703; in complete control, 699, 706; heroic speeches, 700; popularity with masses, 701, 709, 712, 798; and Menocal, 701, 721; educational moves, 702, 704; amnesty for political exiles, etc., 703, 708, 862; marriages, 703 n. 36, 845 and n. 1; and sugar trade, 704, 707–8; programme for 'new' government, 706; three-year plan, 707, 709; unearths 'revolutionary' plot, 709–10; attitude towards Communism, 710–13, 718, 846, 855, 930 and n. 26, 943; in U.S., 711–12; in Mexico, 713; and elections (1939), 718 and n. 12; (1944), 735; (1948), 757; (1952), 768, 773, 776, 779; (1954), 845, 852, 853, 858, 859–60; (1958), 952, 956, 966, 977, 982, 986; ELECTION AS PRESIDENT (1940), 718, 721, 722, 726; relations with U.S., 722–3, 726–8, 889, 910–11, 946–7, 956, 959, 960, 964, 965, 967, 1009; popularity, 724, 736; cabinets, 724, 783 and n. 41, 860–1; attitude to ex-comrades, 724–5; M. 25 loan negotiations, 730; and World War II, 734; legacy to Cuba, 736 and nn. 54, 55; assassination attempts, 756 n. 52, 926, 1000; denounces Prío's proposed loan, 762–3, 764; conspiracy to put him in power, 778 and n. 8, 779–83; manifesto, 784; new constitutional code, 790, 799–800, 852–3; changed personality, 791; opposition to, 792–5, 799, 801, 870–1; self-justification, 795–61; insecurity, 798; and attack on Kuchilán, 799; press opposition, 800; *central Washington*, 800, 1067; meeting with Castro, 817–18, 818 n. 73; SECOND COUP D'ETAT (1952), 823, 824, 882, 884–6, 889, 925 and n. 2; and BRAC, 828 n. 23; and Moncada attack, 839, 843; and army misuse of power, 840–1, 843; children, 845 n. 1; and Negroes, 851; improved position, 851–2; general approval of, 872–3, 874; compared with Trujillo, 882–3; and Castro's activities, 891, 898, 902, 919, 920, 935; ATTACK ON HIS PALACE, 927–31, 938 n. 19, 943; bans Congress elections, 932; and El Uvero, 939; and guerrilla warfare, 941; opposed by judiciary, 942; and nationalization, 943; new policy towards rebels, 950, 951; Church opposition, 982; prepares new ministry, 982 and n. 46; suspends civil rights, 983; and U.S. arms embargo, 985; and general strike, 990–1; offensive against Sierra, 996 ff.; bogus presidential election, 1014; refuses Pawley's advice, 1018 and n. 72; meeting with Smith, 1019, 1020; reorganizes army commands, 1021; and Castro-Cantillo meeting, 1022–3; plans to leave Cuba, 1023–4, 1026; and defence of Santa Clara, 1025; Campamento Columbia meeting, 1025, 1026; RESIGNATION AND FLIGHT (1 JANUARY 1959), 1026; refused asylum in U.S., 1026 n. 28; personal enrichment, 1027 and n. 29; destructive forces, 1039; neglect of public affairs, 1041; destroys old political system (1952), 1045; completes *gangsterismo*, 1045; use of U.S. bombs (1962), 1063 n. 52; confiscation of his property, 1067, 1201; horrors of his regime, 1073; general acceptance, 1113; exaggeration of atrocities, 1113 and n. 28; mulatto-Chinese origin,

Batista, Sergeant Fulgencio – *Cont.*
1122; bribes the press, 1136; public debt legacy, 1186 n. 23; sustained by army and trade unions, 1448–9; survival in Spain, 1471 n. 66

Batista, Fr Diego, 242

Batista, 'Panchín', brother of Fulgencio, Governor of Havana, 764, 784; misappropriations investigation, 764–5; flight from Cuba, 1026

Bayamo, contraband market, 22–3; tobacco growing, 24; sugar production 81; masonic lodges, 242; character and origin, 242; revolutionary movement, 242–4; betrayal, 244; and Independence War (1868), 245, 248, 256; proclaims abolition, 247; *central Mabay*, 653; *Sofia*, 1146; attack on barracks, 828, 835, 854, 894, 1546–7; failure and aftermath, 838; Agricultural Census (1946), 906 n. 65; population, 907 and n. 74; maintenance of Castro, 974

Bayo, Alberto, military instructor, 876, 878; career, 876–7, 877 n.; and Communists, 877 and n. 7; Guevera and, 881, 882; arrest, 887; and *Granma's* complement, 894 n. 1

Beach, Moses Yale, career and inventions, 211 n. 21; and annexation of Cuba, 211–12; ed. *New York Sun*, 211

Beal, Capt. Walter, on burning of plantations, 323; on rebel forces, 323; on El Mejicano, 324; sugar *colono*, 330; on Cuba in mid-war, 334–6

Beals, Carleton, 1277; *The Crime of Cuba*, 1471 n. 67

Beardsley, CIA representative, 1019

Beatón, Major Manuel, assassin, 1248 n. 41; banditry, 1275; execution, 1288

Beaulac, Willard, U.S. *chargé d'affaires*, 719; ambassador, 719 n. 15, 771; recognizes Batista, 789; apprised of army *coup*, 790 n. 4

Beaupré, Arthur Matthias (1853–1919), 510 n. 6; and Zapata swamp affair, 510; and Gómez' proposed loan, 510–11

Beauvoir, Simone de, 1268

Becerra, Manuel, 253, 303

Beckford family, 33

Beckford, William (1709–70), 55 n. 60, 183

Bécquer, Conrado, Auténtico, 861; sugar leader (FNT), 872, 1083 n. 23, 1178, 1350; hunger strike, 872, 1259; trade unionist, 889, 1007, 1259; and FONU, 1083 n. 23; re-elected Sec. Gen., 1220; and Urrutia, 1232; and CTC, 1250; and Communists, 1259, 1279

Bécquer, José, 678

Bécquer, Capt. Napoleon, tried with Matos, 1256

Behn, Sosthenes, 586

Béjar, Hector, essay prize-winner, 1466

Belanzoarán López, Nirberto, terrorist, 945

Belaúndé Terry, Fernando, president of Peru, 1465

Belknep, Commodore, 529–30

Bell, General, 490

Bell, Richard, English merchant, 141

Belmont, August, 465 n. 7; and purchase of Cuba, 228 and n. 50

Belt, Dr Guillermo, ABC leader, 624, 710, 975; and committee of complaints, 613; member of new government, 629; ambassador in Bogotá, 816

Beltrán de Santa Cruz, Pedro, 32 n. 22, 47; magistrate, 44 and n. 13; and the *cabildo*, 44, 45 n. 14; ennobled in Spain, 61 n. 1

Ben, Otero, 768

Bender, Frank, *see* Droller

Benítez, Conrado, 1339; death, 1462

Benítez, Capt. Manuel, and attack on Hotel Nacional, 658, 660; police chief, 725

Benítez, Reinaldo, *Fidelista*, 887 n. 47, 899 and n. 42, 900 n. 52, 901 and n. 53, 916

Bentinck, Lord George, proposes seizure of Cuba, 212

Berle, Adolf A., Jr (born 1895), U.S. Brains Trust member, 632 n. 29; in Cuba, 598, 632, 653, 654, 687, 723 n. 28; and invasion plan, 1309, 1310, 1385

Bermúdez, Carlos, *Fidelista*, 899, 901 n. 53

Bermúdez, Roberto, bandit, 320

Berris, Col., 351

Bessemer, Sir Henry, steel process, 273, 279

Betances, Dr Ramón Emetério, and Cánovas' murder, 350

Betancourt family, 32, 208 n. 11, 422; mill and estate owners, 152, 241, 1110, 1146, 1229; impoverishment, 241

Betancourt, Ernesto, 26 July agent in U.S., 946, 1030 n. 43, 1211; 'Alliance for Progress', 1211 n. 61, 1306 n. 27; leaves National Bank, 1252

Betancourt, Manduley, 687

Betancourt, Romulo, Communist, 579; president-elect of Venezuela, 761 n. 7, 814, 816 n. 67, 1058, 1089, 1276; and Castro, 876, 1090 and nn. 50, 51, 1239

Beveridge, Senator Albert (1862–1927), on U.S. expansionism, 311–13; and Cuba, 482

Biaín, Fr Ignacio, director of *La Quincena*, 1130, 1258

Biddle, Nicholas, and Isle of Pines, 503

Bigart, Homer, U.S. journalist, 976, 977, 983

Bilbatúa, takes over barracks, 782

Bisbé, Manuel, 751, 754 n. 48, 764, 874; SIM and, 792; Ortodoxo group, 956, 968, 971, 1066; ambassador to U.S., 1046; to U.N., 1066

Bissell, Richard, director CIA, 1278, 1296; his U.2, 1278, 1389 n. 21; advocate of invasion, 1306, 1309; and U.S. air cover, 1310, 1368 and n. 38; and underground movements, 1356 n. 3

Blaine, James Gillespie (1830–93), 288, 297, 301 n. 22, 1114; effect of monetary proposals, 627

Blakely, U.S. consul, imprisonment, 86

Blanco, Dr Eladio, member of strike committee, 988

Blanco, Francisco, manager of *central Washington*, 800, 1145, 1148; sugar speculation, 1145

Blanco, Lauro, trade unionist, and Junta of Unity, 1003

Blanco, Luis, *Fidelista*, 979 and nn. 28, 31

Blanco, Manuel, ex-cooper, 148–9, 275 n. 18

Blanco, Orlando, and Junta of Unity, 1003; CTC, 1031 n. 45

Blanco, Pedro, slave factory, 137 and n. 6, 160, 202; slave ships, 157 and n. 5; Barcelona stockbroker, 157 and n. 6

Blanco, General Ramón, captain-gen-eral, 269; and Philippine war, 347, 353, 373, 378; succeeds Weyler, 353, 370; alliance offer, 378; call to arms, 381–2; and U.S.–Spanish war, 395; surrender terms, 399, 400

Blanco and Carballo, slave traders, sailing instructions, 158

Blanco Rico, Col., chief of military intelligence, 890, 931

Blénac, Admiral Jean Courbon, Comte de (1710–66), in W. Indies, 6

Bliss, General Tasker (1853–1930), 422 n. 27; controller of customs, 422, 431

Bohlen, Charles, Russian expert, U.S. ambassador in Manila, 947; in France, 1401 n. 39; and missile crisis, 1402 n. 48

Boitel, Pedro Luis, and FEU presidency, 1286; unknown fate, 1461, 1467

Bolivia, 278; Communist party, 578–9, 1478; Guevara and, 842 n. 40, 937 n. 15, 938 n. 21, 1241 n. 19, 1469 and n. 55, 1478–9, 1481; illiteracy, 1131; U.S.S.R. and, 1265, U.S. and, 148

Bolívar, Simón (1783–1830), 213, 408, 568; and independence, 101, 105 and n. 47; defeats Spanish army, 103; proposed Mexican-Colombian ex-pedition, 104–5

Bonachea, Ricardo, hatchet man, 887

Bonaparte, Joseph (1768–1844), and Spanish throne, 87, 88

Bonny, slave centre, 158, 160

Bonsal, Philip (1903–), U.S. ambassa-dor, career, 1200 and n. 26; relations with Castro, 1200 and n. 27, 1203, 1208, 1213, 1224, 1241, 1252, 1262, 1271; at Caribbean meeting, 1206–7; and Dorticós, 1248, 1258; and take-over of U.S. property, 1258; returns to U.S., 1262, 1297–8; back in Havana, 1271, 1272–3, 1285, 1288; and sugar quota bill, 1289

Bonsal, Stephen (1865–1951), 728 n. 19, 1200; *The Fight for Santiago*, 440 and n. 21

Borbonnet, Lieut., 763

Borbonnet, Major, *puros*, 884, 1018, 1028; and new army, 1072

Bordón, Major Víctor, joins Guevara, 1013, 1020 and n. 3, 1028, 1030; 26 July group, 1042

Borges, Luis, and INRA, 1327

Borges, Omar, 856

Borges, Admiral Pedro Pascual, 778

Borrego, Orlando, and Ministry of Industry, 1335

Borrel, José, sugar mill, *Guaimaro*, 119; slave trader, 137

Borrero, Capt. Marcos, death, 1008

Bosch, José, Bacardí Rum Co., 1065

Bosch, Juan, 754–5; and expedition against Trujillo, 755–6, 756 n. 52, 812 n. 48; quarrel with Paniagua, 766; resignation, 768; and Castro, 812 n. 48

Bosch, Col. Pepe, 1018, 1113; and Castro's U.S. visit, 1209

Boti, Regino, economist, 954; Minister of Economics, 1066, 1246, 1282; to visit U.S., 1205, 1209, 1211; denounces aid plan, 1295

Botiful, Luis, ed. *El Mundo*, 862, 874

Botiful, Major, chief of police, 637

Bowdler, William, U.S. diplomat, fear of Communism, 1082–3

Bowles, Chester, opposes invasion plan, 1309, 1370 n. 46

Boyer, President, 220

Boza, Mazvidal, Mgr, Rector Villanova University, 994, 1265, 1268–9, 1350

Bozales, 162, 429; price of, 89 n. 25, 131, 170, 174

Braddock, Daniel, U.S. *chargé d'affaires*, 1271

Braden, Spruille (1894–), U.S. ambassador, 730 and nn. 32, 33, 731; and Cuban central bank, 731–2; and 1942 sugar harvest, 732; and Castro, 960

Braga, George, Manatí Sugar Co., 1219

Bravo, Chapman, Manuel, 1479

Bravo, 'Major' Flavio, and Castro's regime, 871 n. 28, 1454 n. 2; commander of militia, 1363; and ORI, 1377 n. 22; and new Communist party, 1454; and PURS, 1454 n. 3

Bravo, Moreno, *Batistiano*, 950

Brazil, 200, 218; sugar mills, 28 n. 9; the *malungo*, 37 n. 33; and slavery, 78, 95 n. 9, 158, 159, 161, 167; and abolition, 99, 231 and n. 64, 279, 518; sugar production, 126, 1143 n. 22, 1438; coffee production, 131 and n. 16, 1139 and n. 89; and *emancipados*, 182; and right of search, 201; *centrales* and *engenhos*, 277; survival of African cults, 518 and n. 21, 520; anarchist paper, *A Plebe*, 578; Com-

munist party, 578, 697; population figures, 1093, 1094; sugar imports, 1103 n. 49; illiteracy, 1131; U.S.S.R. and, 1265; sugar quota 1438 n. 9

Brezhnev, 1478

Bridges, Senator Styles, 1001, 1262

Brigade 2506, 1481; taken to Puerto Cabenza, 1311; invasion fleet, 1357; troops and commanders, 1359 and n. 16, 1360; composition, 1360 and n. 22, 1361; Cuban landing, 1361–2, 1363–4; meets militia, 1365; deserted by supply ships, 1366; anticipates U.S. aid, 1367; surrounded in swamps, 1368–9; casualties, 1370; treatment of prisoners, 1370, 1371 and n. 50, 1385 and n. 1, 1386

Bristowe, John, sells Quidenham, 56–7

Broderick, Sir John, and Cuba (1933), 605

Bronson, L. E., 546

Brooke, General John Rutter (1838–1926), 420 n. 19; military governor of Cuba, 420, 422, 441; object of his rule, 421; and financial aid to Cuba, 436; and the law, 437; bans Cuban celebrations, 437; disagreements with Wood, 439, 441; retirement, 443; and sugar trade, 458

Brooks, Santiago Esteban, 580

Brouzon, Claudio, murder, 587

Browder, Earl, Sec. Gen. of U.S. Communist party, 697, 744; and Latin-American area, 697

Brown, Albert Gallatin, and slavery, 229

Bru, Col. Frederico Laredo (1875–), 568 n., 629, 769 n. 23; and Las Villas rising, 568, 701; vice-president, 701; *président fainéant*, 705, 706, 712, 713, 718; and 1942 elections, 719; signs Casanova bill, 723

Bruce, James, U.S. emissary to Machado, 592–3

Brussels, 'Anti-Imperialist' Conference, 588

Bruzon, José, 268

Bryan, William Jennings (1860–1925), 337, 1034; and intervention, 372, 482; on Nebraska volunteers, 405 n. 18

Buch, Antonio, 975

Buch, Luis, 970, 975, 995 n. 33, 1053; Secretary to Cabinet, 1067, 1253

Buchanan, James (1791–1868), U.S. president, 211 n. 23, 228; and Mexican war, 211–12; and purchase of Cuba, 213–14, 225, 228–9, 230, 367 n. 1; Sec. of State, 225; adds threats to money, 225 and n. 32; Democratic candidate, 225; and expansionism, 228

Buchman, Victor, U.S. *Fidelistas*, 934

Bullitt, William C., U.S. ambassador in Paris, 346 n. 51

Bundy, and missile crisis, 1402 nn. 48, 49

Burgess, John, and expansionism, 311

Burke, Admiral, 1364 n. 27; and Batista, 932; and Castro, 1206, 1241, 1271; fear of Communism, 1241; favours U.S. air cover, 1368

Burnham, James, U.S. sugar planter, 141

Burnett, Francis Hodgson, 352

Buró de Represión a las Actividades Comunistas (BRAC), foundation, 828 n. 23, 855, 1078; and dismissal of Communists, 943; Batista and, 956–7; use of torture, 1009; Guevera and, 1078

Burón, slave factory owner, 204

Burriel, General, and *Virginius* incident, 263 and n. 37

Bustamente, Gutierre de Hevia y (1720–72), admiral in command Havana, 7 and n. 35

Bustamente, Sánchez, 587

Bute, John Stuart, Earl of (1713–92), 4, 42; Prime Minister, 53–4

Butler, Robert, U.S. ambassador, and Nicaro Nickel, 1169–70

Butler, Senator J. M., 1262

Buttari, Edgardo, student, 592 n. 33; and Prío's cabinet, 775 n. 1; and Grau, 852 n. 30

Buxton, Sir Thomas (1786–1845), and slave trade, 163 n. 39, 215

Byng, Admiral John (1704–57), 3 n. 11, 5 n. 28

Caballero, Gustavo, Liberal leader, 529; murder, 530, 571

Caballero de Rodas, General, captain-general, 252, 257, 259

Cabell, General Charles (1903–), CIA, 1080 n. 11, 1249 n. 45; denies

Castro's Communism, 1249; and invasion, 1358

cabildo, the, 30, 37; cattle ranchers and, 23; Albemarle's deputies, 43–4; definition, 44 n. 12; weekly meetings, 44; inter-related membership, 44–5, 45 n. 14; accepts English occupation, 48; and mayoral election, 53 and n. 52; and new Spanish government, 61; loses responsibility to *intendentes*, 65; and U.S. annexation, 88, 90; coterminous with municipality, 109; increase in nineteenth century, 180; preserve African religion, 180, 517, 518–19

Cabrera, Carlos Rafael (d. 1961), Communist, 981 and n. 41

Cabrera, Major Francisco, *Fidelista*, 1020

Cabrera, Raimundo, Liberal, 268; and 1917 revolt, 528

Cabrera, General Ruperto, succeeds Damera, 763, 778; attempted murder, 771; and (1952) army conspiracy, 779, 780–1

Cabrera, Saba, and *Pasada Meridano*, 1342

Cabrera Infante, Guillermo, novelist, 1076 n. 41, 1199 n. 22, 1464; at Mora Communist meeting, 1014 n. 50; protest against U.S., 1076; *Tres Tristes Tigres*, 1466 n. 45

Cabrera, rebel leader, 321

Cáceres, Julio ('El Patojo'), 880, 894

cafetales, see Coffee farms

Caffery, Jefferson, successor to Welles, 643, 670, 672 n. 22; interview with Cintas, 614 and n. 34; and Grau's régime, 661, 673–4, 674 and n. 33, 685; attempted assassination, 695; accepts Batista, 696; and strike movement (1935), 699; and sugar tax bill, 704; subsequent career, 710 n. 14

Caibarién, 1074; fall of, 1023, 1024; fishing co-operative, 1558

Caiñan Milanés, Roberto, criticism of land reform, 1222; counter-revolutionary, 1238

Calcines, Faustino, 1259

Calcines, Ramón, 1377 n. 23, 1453 n. 1, 1468–9; and PURS, 1454 n. 3

Calderio, Francisco, *see* Roca, Blas

Caldero, Hermes, 900 and n. 51, 939

Calderon, Baica, de la, 223

Calhoun, John Caldwell, Sec. of War, 100, 209

Calhoun, William J., 343

Calleja, Lt-Gen. Emilio, captain-general, and Independence War (1895), 307, 309

Calviño, Ramón, gangster, 1029 n. 38 and Brigade 2506, 1360; shot, 1371 n. 49

Calvo de la Puerta family, 152, 153, 1110; entitled Marqués de Buena Vista and Casa Calvo, 143

Calvo de la Puerta, Manuel, 132, 153, 155, 252, 258

Calvo de la Puerta, Miguel, and the *cabildo*, 45 and n. 4

Calva de la Puerta, Nicolás (d. 1802), liberal economist, 73; model sugar mill, 79 and n. 37; new cane variety, 80; and Humboldt in Cuba, 82 n. 46; and O'Farrills, 84

Calvo de la Puerta, Pedro José, 32, 47; Havana magistrate, 44; and the *cabildo*, 45 and n. 14; ennobled in Spain, 61 n. 1

Calvo Herrera, Capt. Miguel, police chief, 595

Camacho, Julio, 896, 963, 979 n. 31; Minister of Transport, 1253

Camagüey, 47, 349, 807, 982, 1021; sugar mills, 241, 469, 531, 537, 1151 n. 63, (plate), 1141; abolitionists, 249–50; and Independence War (1868), 264; censuses, 424 n. 38; farming areas, 425 n. 44, 1548; per cent white population, 429; armed forces, 490; U.S. marine station, 548, 551, 554, 686; railroad, 557; and Menocal 571; CNOC Congress, 576–7; private aircraft, 974; Communist group, 1002, 1009; Guevara and, 1008, 1009 and n. 22; Castro and, 1032, 1054; housing, 1096 n. 24; population figures, 1100 n. 38; cattle ranchers, 1110, 1548, 1550, 1554; Negro population, 1119; segregation, 1121; priesthood, 1128 n. 5; cane production, 1146 n. 41; take-over of cattle ranches, 1228–9; anti-Castro plot, 1238; military occupation, 1244–5; and Matos' arrest, 1245; peasant land ownership, 1323 n. 34, 1328 n. 56; state farms, 1326

Cameron, Senator James, 368; Resolution on Cuba, 339 n. 4, 340

Camilo Cienfuegos City School, 1054 n. 22, 1340; dedication, 1293

Campa, Benito, 1349

Campa, Miguel Angel (1882–), Sec. of State, 717 and n. 7, 1029 n. 38; and Batista's government, 783, 784, 789

Campamento Columbia, 622, 623, 962, 1021; and sergeants' revolt, 635, 651; Batista and 637, 651, 675, 702, 725, 1099; under Rodríguez, 663, 664; November revolt, 666; plan to capture, 667; Grau and, 745; and 1952 conspiracy, 780; raided by MNR, 801; Castro's speech (8.1.59), 901 n. 53, 1034, 1072; meeting of Batistianos, 1025, 1026, 1027; take-over by Guevara, 1030; Ministry of Education, 1340

Campbell, Robert Blair (1809–62), U.S. consul in Havana, and annexation, 212

Campo Florida, Marqués de, mill-ownership, 152

Cancio, Leopoldo (1851–1927), 547 and n. 15

Canelejas, José, Prime Minister, 359 n. 25; ed. *El Heraldo*, 359; murder, 359 n. 25

Canning, George, 101, 103

Canosa, Col. Varela, and Brigade 2506, 1359–60; in Mexico, 1360 n. 18

Canot, Theodore, slave trader, 160, 1111

Cánovas del Castillo, Antonio (1828–97), Spanish Prime Minister, 266, 267, 308, 377; Minister of the Colonies, 238 and n. 25; flight from Madrid, 239; Cuban policy, 267, 289, 308–9, 327, 333, 348; murder, 350 and nn. 56, 57, 363

Cantero, Justo, sugar plantations (*Buena Vista, Guinia de Soto*), 118 n. 32, 141; Gentleman of the Bedchamber, 143; Trinidad Place, 146–7, 171 n. 14; social position, 153; *Los Ingenios*, 141

Cantillo, General, 941, 976; commander *operación verano*, 996; relations with Castro, 999, 1019, 1022 and n. 8, 1023; chief of army in Oriente, 1017, 1025; and officers' *coup*, 1021; centre of intrigue, 1026; chief of staff, 1027–8; hands over to Barquín, 1028; escapes death, 1075

Canto, Enrique, 840–1; 26 July treasurer, 946

Capablanca, Ramiro, 641 n. 23; and Grau's cabinet, 652

Capote, Corporal, and Sergeants' revolt, 635

Carballo García, José, 875

Carbó, Ulises, and *Prensa Libre*, 1280; trial, 1385 n. 1

Carbó, Sergio, 593, 1261; director *La Semana*, 635, 638, 664; and Batista, 638, 647, 658, 675 n. 39; prepares 'Proclamation of the Revolutionaries', 638; and a new government, 639, 658; and reorganization of the army, 646; meeting with Welles, 658–9; and attack on Hotel Nacional, 658–9; and student meetings, 664, 674 n. 36, 675

Carbo Servía, Juan Pedro, attacks army, 889–90, 890 n. 61, 931; death, 931

Carbonell, Walterio, expelled from Communist party, 887–8; Black Power movement, 888 n. 51; in rehabilitation camp, 1433

Cárdenas family, 321; mill and estate ownership, 152

Cárdenas, Joaquín de, estate ownership, 152

Cárdenas, General Lázaro, President of Mexico, 713 n. 32, 1111; agrarian reform, 709; and Batista, 713, 887 n. 49; and Communism, 715, 829

Cárdenas, Raúl de, 624; member of new government, 629; and 'commission of harmony', 982; calls for cease-fire, 1027

Cardero, Gilberto, bomb factory, 993

Cardozo, Manuel, slave merchant, 156

Caribbean islands, importance of Havana, 1; sugar production, 27, 28, 537 ff.; purchase of male slaves, 31; population statistics, 52, 503, 1094 (plate), 1194; trading activity, 64; effect of American Revolution, 67; first successful slave revolt, 75; U.S. (South) and annexation, 210; common factors, 232; U.S. ambitions, 253, 476; future of Africans, 283–4; German activities, 343 and n. 32, 731, 735; and yellow fever, 460; Communist party, 697; Castro and

'Liberal' leaders, 1058; meeting of U.S. ambassadors, 1206; U.S. reaction to defiance, 1226; Soviet submarines, 1241; effect of Cuban Revolution, 1434; treatment of Indians, 1514 ff.

Carleton, Guy (later Lord Dorchester), and Havana expedition, 5 and n. 26, 16

Carlos, Don (1848–1909), claimant to throne, 244, 247, 385–6; raises Carlist flag (1872), 260; Weyler and, 353 and n. 69; demands war, 377

Carmichael, Stokely, Castro and, 1045 n. 23; visits Havana, 1433

Caro, Col., 6

Carpentier, Alejo (1904–), Negro novelist, 1124 and n. 34, 1464; and Imprenta Nacional, 1343; *The Kingdom of this World*, 1124, 1464 n. 37

Carpentier family, in Cuba, 133

Carratalá, Col., police chief, 864, 1039; asylum in U.S., 1077

Carrera, Eladio and Ignacio, 945

Carrera, Lieut., *Batistiano*, 939, 940 n. 23; and officers' *coup*, 1021

Carreras, Bernado (d. 1955), Communist, 871

Carreras, Major Jesús, 'second front' leader, 1012; capture and death, 1297, 1349

Carreras, José, slave trader, 234

Carrero Justiz, Francisco, 487 and n. 29; Sec. of Presidency, 674 n. 36; Min. of Communications, 674 n. 36, 783 n. 20; and Batista, 793

Carrero Justiz, Pablo, 839

Carrillo, Justo, 884 n. 36, 956 n. 20; student, 592 n. 38, 638 and n. 13, 641 n. 22; Bank president, 768, 784, 802, 1205, 1252; and Batista, 789, 876; *Acción Libertadora*, 862; and Castro, 876, 885 n. 43, 886 and n. 46; and 26 July, 909, 943 n. 3, 965 n. 12; and attempted murder of Batista, 926; Montecristo movement, 943 n. 3, 961, 965, 994–5, 1053 and n. 20; and naval mutiny, 961–2; Isle of Pines *golpe*, 965 and n. 12, 994, 1028 n. 36; presidential candidate, 970 n. 32; and Barquín's release, 994–5, 1019, 1028 and n. 36; fails to get U.S. support, 995; revolutionary, 1055–6; and new government (1959), 1066; and U.S.

Carrillo, Justo – *Cont.*
economic aid, 1205; resignation, 1226 n. 42; centre of anti-Castroism, 1276, 1283; resignation from *Frente*, 1296
Carrillo, Col. Ugalde, and SIM, 839, 840; casualties, 1040 n. 8; at Holguín, 1021; bribed to leave, 1022; interviewed by U.S., 1279
Carroll, Dr James, 461
Casa Barreto, Condes de, 38
Casa Bayona, Conde de, 152
Casa Calvo, Marqués de, 87, 180–1; 197
Casa Enrile, Marqués de, 68
Casa Montalva, Conde de, 79 n. 37, 84, 202; estate at Macuriges, 63; visits England, 72, 75 and n. 13; liberal economist, 73; labour-saving pioneer, 79
Casalis, Secundio, 1483; on Castro, 1215; column *Siquitrilla*, 1463; *La Republica*, 1486 n.
Casals, Violeta, Communist, 980 n. 36, 1011, 1260; in China, 1237 n. 5
Casanova, Senator José María, 676, 762
Casas, Alvaro and Baldomero, 796
Casas, César, Minister of Commerce, 751
Casasaús, Col., *Batistiano*, in Oriente, 924 n. 65
Casaseca, José Luis, 117 and n. 25
Casero, Luis (1902–), 843 n. 41; and Prío's cabinet, 768 and n. 21, 775 n. 1; arrest, 861
Casillas, Capt., murders Menéndez, 761; in the Sierra, 915 and n. 29, 936, 939; treatment of peasants, 920; succeeds Barrera, 936
Cassilis Lumpuy, Major Joaquín, 924 n. 65; and Santa Clara, 1021, 1024, 1025; flight, 1027; shooting of, 1028 and n. 32
Cass, Senator Lewis, 212 and n. 28, 214
Castanón, Gonzálo, 259
Castaño, Capt., 1078 and n. 4, 1335
Castelar, Emilio, 261
Castellanos, Dr Baudilio, 895 n. 9, 954 and n. 11
Castellanos, Nicolás, 764, 768, 773, 784, 791
Castilla, Belarmino, raids Boniato barracks, 987 and n. 67; and Communist party, 987 n. 67; in revolutionary army, 994 n. 28, 1198 n. 18, 1202 n.

32; and war trials, 1074 n. 29; chief of staff (1966), 1074 n. 29
Castillo, Capt., 623
Castillo, General Demetrio, 403, 484 n. 18, 630
Castillo Duany, arrest, 475
Castillo Pokorny, Demetrio, member of new government, 629 and n. 15; American outlook, 629
Castro, Angel, father of Fidel, 803 and n. 3, 840; antipathy to N. Americans, 803; and United Fruit Co., 803, 804, 809; his farm (Manacas), 804 and n. 15, 805 and n. 16; living conditions, 805 and n. 14, 806; marriages and children, 805–6; character, 807, 809; relations with his children, 808; war experiences, 809
Castro, Armando, rebel group, 993
Castro, Emma, 806, 898
Castro, Fidel (b. 1927), 634 n. 1, 755 n. 51, 761 n., 7, 803 n. 2; guerrilla warfare, 330, 807, 867, 882, 932, 974, 978, 1038; first international political figure, 563; accuses Prío in speech before Tribunal de Cuentes, 764 n. 12, 820–1; ATTACK ON MONCADA BARRACKS, 803, 824 n. 3, 828, 833, 837 ff.; character, 803, 808, 819, 821, 822 and n. 102; early life and experiences, 803 ff.; parentage, 806, 826 and n. 17; education, 807, 826 and n. 17; imprisonment (1954), 809, 847; early political activity, 810, 820, 821–3; 886; on his university career, 810–11, 818; and revolutionary organizations, 810, 811, 819; and gang warfare, 811, 813; expedition against Dominican Republic, 812; accused of Manolo's murder, 812–13; implication in *Bogotazo*, 814–17, 816 n. 67; Latin American ambitions, 814 and n. 57, 1086–7, 1285, 1293, 1295, 1315; marriages, 817, 821, 856; Ortodoxo, 817, 819, 820, 827, 847, 856, 858, 863, 874, 881, 882; doctor of law, 817, 818, 819; and Batista, 817–18, 821, 822, 823, 824, 848–9, 867, 881, 955; and elections (1952), 820, (1954), 856, 860 and n. 3, (1958), 977, (post-1959), 1083–4, 1085, 1198, 1203, 1204, 1208, 1242, 1279, 1371; contributions to *Alerta*, 820; manifestos, etc., *Zarpazo*, 821 and n. 92, *El*

Castro, Fidel – *Cont.*

Acusador, 827; Revolutionary proclamation, 829; 'Pact of the Sierras', 953–5, 955–6; Sierra manifesto, 983–4; Second Declaration of Havana, 1375–6; and Communism, 822, 828, 842, 887, 955, 988 and n. 3, 992, 994, 1002–3, 1005, 1010, 1051, 1052 nn. 15, 18, 1055 and n. 28, 1059, 1060 n. 50, 1076, 1088, 1313 and n. 5, 1489; composition of his followers, 824 and nn. 2, 3, 825–7, 827 n. 18, 867–8, 903; and Sino-Soviet breach, 827 n. 19; five revolutionary laws, 830 and n. 29, 831–2; in hiding, 841, 844; capture, 841, 887, trial, 843; use of royal 'we', 847 n. 6; pamphlet embodying defence plea (1954), 847–8, 848 n. 8, 849–51, 855; attack on Cuban society, 851; letters from prison, 853–4, 855–6, 858; on revolutionary leadership, 858–9; divorce, 860, 869; released under amnesty law, 863; speech to Ortodoxos, 863–4; and Marquitas' trial, 864, 866; denounces Chaviano, 866; in Mexico, 867, 868; 26 July Movement (*see under*) financial resources, 876, 878 n. 11, 886 and n. 46, 888, 918; and Bayo, 877 and n. 3; military training of his followers, 877, 882, 888; farm base Santa Rosa, 877–8, 881, 886; meets Guevara, 878 and n. 14, 881 and n. 23; and Pact of Mexico, 888; procures the *Granma*, 891, 892, 894; AND INVASION OF CUBA, 891–2; betrayal, 898; Sierra Maestra gathering, 901 and nn. 53, 54, 902, 912 ff. (*see under*); and the peasants, 903, 914, 916–17, 920, 935; armaments, 912–13, 914, 919, 938 and n. 19, 974, 986; need for foreign press, 915–16, 917 and n. 38, 918; describes his aims and programme, 921–2; AND ATTACK ON PALACE, 928, 930, 931 n. 29; reinforced from Santiago, 934; press interview, 937; and social problems, 937–8; mounting support, 943, 950; reorganizes his followers, 958; and naval mutiny, 961, 965; price on his head, 967; denounces Miami Pact, 969–70, 971; and Urrutia as president, 970, 971, 977, 978; fragmentation of *Fidelistas*, 971 and n. 38; orders destruction of sugar harvest, 972; attempted murders, 979 n. 31, 1246, 1348, 1365 n. 29; decree on *territorio libre*, 980; press (*Cubra Libre*), 980; radio station (Radio Rebelde), 980 and n. 36, 999, 1017; and 'commission of harmony', 983; reunion of National Directorate, 983 and n. 49; his numbers, 984 and n. 54, 996–7, 997 n. 6; and a general strike, 988 and n. 1, 989, 990, 991–2, 1029; wish to unify opposition, 992; and the Church, 994, 1212–13, 1294, 1350, 1473; rival groups, 994–5; defence against *operación verano*, 996 ff.; captures enemy code, 998 and n. 11; treatment of prisoners, 998–9; and Junta of Unity, 1003, 1004; encircles Santiago, 1005; moves from *guerrillero* to politician, 1007; and future regime, 1007–8; law against English aggression, 1009; middle class support, 1010; organization of his *Commandancia*, 1011; joined by Raúl, 1016; in control Oriente, 1017; meeting with Cantillo, etc., 1022 and n. 10; and Batista's collapse, 1023 and n. 14; flight, 1027, 1028; *central América*, 1028; TRIUMPHAL PROGRESS TO HAVANA, 1032, 1033, 1083; hold over Cubans, 1037–8, 1045, 1051, 1193, 1235, 1251, 1345–6; use of foreign press, 1038–9; task in civil war, 1040, 1041; and Revolution, 1054, 1055–6, 1059 n. 45, 1069, 1198–9, 1203, 1214, 1219, 1312, 1328, 1371, 1490–1; later aspects of his character and personality, 1054, 1060, 1193, 1220, 1227, 1231, 1247, 1260, 1345–6; speaks of his goals, 1056–7, 1057 n. 40; relations with U.S., 1057, 1058, 1059–60, 1075–7, 1087, 1199–1200, 1205, 1209, 1224, 1289, 1317, 1481; contrasted with Eisenhower, 1058; hatred of U.S., 1061 and n. 49, 1061, 1078 n. 5; slogans, 1047, 1055; eloquence, 1051, 1485 and n. 8; member of 1959 government, 1067–8, 1068 and nn. 6, 7; and agrarian reform, 1070, 1208, 1215; and the police, 1071 and n. 16; and the army, 1071–3, 1198; and war crimes, 1073, 1075–6, 1087, 1195; denies he's a Communist, 1083, 1089, 1211, 1212, 1247; '*máximo líder*', 1086, 1235,

Castro, Fidel – *Cont.*

1489–90; in Venezuela, 1089–90, 1193; use of term 'gringo', 1090 n. 50; on colour question, 1120, 1205 and n. 39; use of television, 1193–5, 1462; unprepared speeches, 1195, 1224; PRIME MINISTER, 1197, 1198, 1235, 1240–1, 1243; cabinet meetings, 1199, 1203, 1204; land distribution project, 1201; and Justice, 1202–3, 1227, 1347–8; efforts to achieve unity, 1203, 1241–2; moves to the Left, 1203, 1226, 1232; plots against, 1204, 1238; in the U.S., 1208–12; on Communists, 1211, 1212, 1219–20, 1227; journey to S. America, 1213; drawn towards Communism, 1222, 1227, 1231, 1233, 1236, 1290, 1291, 1314; resignation, 1232; denounces Urrutia, 1232–3; PLAZA CIVICA MEETING, 1234–5; public works programme, 1235; and the Soviet Union, 1237 and n. 5, 1383, 1474, 1475–6, 1479; popularity poll, 1242 and n. 21; and Matos, 1244, 1245, 1255–6, 1256 n. 3; orders occupation of Camagüey, 1244–5; addresses labour union, 1247; and Cienfuegos' death, 1247–8; and CTC Congress, 1250; and counter-revolutionaries, 1262, 1350; and U.S. conciliatory message, 1263, 1264, 1267, 1276; and *Coubre* explosion; 1269, 1270 n. 33, 1270; organized opponents, 1274–6, 1285–6, 1296–7; international approval, 1277–8; addresses May 1 Parade, 1278–9; ultimatum to non-Communists, 1281; interpretation of Khrushchev's message, 1281–2; and U.S.S.R. rocket defence, 1290 n. 37, 1295; denounces OAS, 1293; 'Declaration of Havana', 1295; reception at N. York meeting of UN, 1295; AND INVASION, 1312, 1355, 1358, 1362, 1363, 1365, 1386–7, 1395, 1397, 1408; admits Cuba's Socialism, 1312 and n. 3; indoctrination schools, 1313–14, 1314 n. 8; creates state farms, 1326 and n. 46, 1327, 1328; and 'action by planning', 1328 and n. 57; and Havana underground, 1356 and n. 3; victory celebration, 1371; remains decisive political force, 1372, 1380–1, 1453; declares himself a Marxist-Leninist, 1373 and n. 5,

1380, 1488–9; pronouncement on peaceful co-existence, 1375 and n. 10; clashes with old Communist guard, 1376, 1379–80; director ORI, 1376, 1378, 1379–80; and Echevarría's testament, 1377–8; denounces Escalante, 1379, 1380; and Russian missiles, 1387, 1391–2, 1393; orders general mobilization, 1408–9, 1298, 1305; and shooting of U.2, 1413; anger at Khrushchev's decision, 1414; terms for ending crisis, 1414; and nuclear war threat, 1417 n. 55; unfulfilled promises, 1425, 1436; and abolition of Universities, 1429; scepticism regarding his 'indoctrination', 1430; destruction of small businesses, 1431, 1445–6; pre-Revolution silence on Negro question, 1433; support for U.S. Black Power movement, 1433; and homosexuals, 1435; denounces youthful extravagances, 1435; and 10 million-ton harvest, 1436, 1437, 1438 and n. 7, 1479; and mechanization of sugar industry, 1439; continuing interest in agriculture, 1441; scorn for bureaucrats, 1443–4; concept of free 'new man', 1446, 1448, 1489; changing ideas on material incentives, 1446; desire to abolish money, 1447; creation of single movement from diverse elements, 1456 and n. 12; and political trials, 1459 and n. 20; defends censorship, 1463; and the arts, 1464–5; 'Address to the Intellectuals', 1465; and abolition of copyright, 1464; foreign commerce, 1475; visits to Russia, 1476 and n. 9; venerated by S. America, 1477; and AALAPSO, 1477; attack on China, 1477–8; and other Communist parties, 1478–9; decreased militancy, 1479; nature of his struggle, 1479–80; view of Republic under Prío, 1484; is he still popular?, 1485–6; governmental dictatorship, 1486; and armed struggle, 1489; and rural dislodgement, 1550 n. 12; proposed exchange of prisoners for tractors, 1553 n. 28 SPEECH (of 11.11.61), 819 and n. 80, 955; confessional speech (2.12.61), 818, 819, 832 and n. 32; speech in self-defence (*History will absolve me*) 843 and n. 43, 847, 848 and n. 8, 853,

Castro, Fidel – *Cont.*
855, 869, 954, 1484; speech to Ortodoxos, 163–4; speech at Campamento Columbia (8.1.59), 901 n. 53; speech in Santiago, 1030, 1051, 1053, 1054, 1057, 1059, 1075; later speeches 1353, 1358–9, 1372–3, 1375, 1380 and n. 28; *Political and Social Thought of Fidel Castro*, 1173, 1174, 1462

Castro, Fidelito, son of Fidel, 821; in the Sierra, 901 and n. 53

Castro, Juana, sister of Fidel, 806, 1260 and n. 9, 1491 n. 24; on Fidel, 808 n. 26

Castro, Lidia, son of Fidel, 805, 898

Castro, Lidia Ruz de, mother of Fidel Castro, 805–6; character, 807; mariage, 807 and n. 20

Castro, 'Manolo', (d. 1948), gunman, 742, 755, 1066; murder, 742 n. 8, 761, 762, 812–13; and *El Bonche*, 743 n. 9; and FEU, 812

Castro, Panchin, 966

Castro, Pedro Emilio, brother of Fidel, 805, 808

Castro, Ramón, brother of Fidel, 806, 1023, 1331; education, 807; and family estate, 1146 n. 39, 1251; quarrels with regime, 1251

Castro, Raúl, brother of Fidel, 806, 824 n. 3, 1234; education, 807, 826 n. 11; on Fidel, 808; and Communism, 826 and n. 10, 955, 992, 1050, 1214; childhood, 826 n. 11; and 26 July, 826, 1251 n. 50; part in Moncada attack, 836, 837; in Mexico, 867; in *Granma*, 894; marriage, 895 n. 10; joins Fidel, 900, 901, 990, 1016; in the Sierra, 901 and n. 53, 913, 919; influence on Fidel, 921, 1195; his group, 934 and n. 5, 939, 958; in Oriente, 983 n. 49, 984 and n. 52, 992, 1032, 1043, 1072; and the Church, 992; group of 'musketeers', 992 and n. 22, 993; attacks *central Soledad*, 993; unifies rebel bands in Sierra Cristal, 993–4; reorganization of his columns, 994 n. 28; tactics in N. Cuba, 1000, 1005, 1008–9; and Labour unity, 1007; rescues 'Nicaragua', 1008; and Cuba's future, 1048; as a leader, 1050, 1250; shooting of prisoners, 1074; and war trials, 1076; named as Fidel's successor, 1087; commander-in-chief armed forces, 1198, 1229; and

Castro in U.S., 1212; and speech of 1 May, 1212; 'indoctrination classes', 1229–30; in Chile, 1239; in Santa Clara, 1241; Minister for Armed Forces, 1243, 1458; Communist conspiracy, 1244; and Pazos, 1246; and Matos' trial, 1255–6; and Aguero, 1273; in Prague, 1288, 1289; and Cuba's Socialism, 1344 n. 3; forms JUCEI, 1337; and ORI, 1376, 1377 n. 17; vice-premier, 1379, 1383; seeks aid from U.S.S.R., 1387; and missile crisis, 1397, 1408; and new Communist party, 1454, 1455 n. 6; and Escalante's trial, 1459 n. 20; on 'microfaction', 1469 n. 52

Castro Alves, 1111–12, 1112 n. 13

Castro Hidalgo, Orlando, defector, 1479 n. 14

Casuso, Teresa (Tete), 760; on Castro, 882, 888 n. 54; arms cache, 891; *Cuba and Castro*, 539 and n. 17; in Mexico, 1030 n. 43

Catholics, 1129–30; anxiety over Revolution, 1202; back regime, 1258; anti-Communist protest, 1258; student anti-Castroists, 1276; burn *Diario*, 1280; in Brigade 2506, 1360

Catlin, Henry, C., and Havana Electric, 570, 581, 804, 1167

Cavada, General Féderico, invasion plan, 260

Cavala, Féderico, rebel leader, 256

Cayo Confites island, 755, 825, 868, 894, 925, 1455

Ceballos, General Francisco de, captain-general, 259, 262

Cejas, Major, police chief, 962

Celaya, Máximo, arrest in Mexico, 877

Centoz, Mgr, 975, 982, 994; and U.S. intervention, 991

centrales, emergence of, 275, 276; and *colonos*, 1145–6; conversion from large mills, 278; U.S. machinery, 289; wartime foundations, 537, 539; effect of foreign investment, 541–2; paper mills, 933; drop in land ownership, 1146 and n. 36; *Alava*, 428; *Borjita*, 537 n. 7; *Constancia*, 290; *La Vega*, 537 n. 7; *Mabay*, 653; *Miranda*, 805; 809 and n. 30; *Morón*, 933; *Santa Teresa*, 290; *Soledad*, 323; *Trinidad*, 933; *Ulacio*, 537 n. 7

Cepero, Manuel, ABC murder, 598

Cepero Bonilla, Minister of Commerce, 1065, 1204, 1246, 1253

Cervantes, Raúl, student, murder, 871

Cervera, Admiral Pascual (1839–1909), 382 n. 6, 408; at Cape Verde Islands, 382; Antilles, 383, 385; Admiralty telegram, 383; at Santiago, 386, 389, 395; and the battle, 396

Céspedes, Carlos Manuel de (1819–74), 347, 812; revolutionary activity, 243; sugar farm (*La Demajagua*), 243 and n. 40, 245; and War of Independence (1868), 245, 249, 250, 260; and slavery, 245, 246, 247, 248, 250; destroys sugar plantations, 255–6; encourages slave revolt, 256; killed in ambush, 260.

Céspedes, Carlos Miguel, 584; and Ports Company, 506, 507, 573; Minister of Public Works, 573, 581; and Central Highway, 583; acting-president, 621, 623; his new government, 627, 628, 629, 1055; American outlook, 629; Cuban expectations, 630–1; restores 1902 Constitution, 631; and sergeants' revolt, 638, 640, 645, 682; offered presidency, 646; asylum in Brazil, 651

Céspedes, Javier de, 243

Céspedes, Lt-Col. Miguel Angel, 660 n. 11, 783 and n. 20

Céspedes, Ricardo, 422

Chaumón, Major Faure, and MSR, 742; and Directorio, 927, 968, 1005; and attack on Palace, 927, 928, 930; and Mirabal, 944 n. 7; in Miami, 968; denounces Castro, 971; N. Cuba landing, 979 nn. 28, 31, 980; Cuban Minister, 979 n. 31, 1069–70, 1070 n. 13, 1379; and Communists, 1013 and n. 45, 1070 n. 13; and Directorio, 1017, 1030, 1033, 1313; and Castro government, 1032, 1203; and Santiago as capital, 1069; leftist tendencies, 1203, 1279; in China, 1237 n. 5; ambassador in Moscow, 1279, 1313, 1381 n. 30; adopts Communism, 1313; and ORI, 1377

Chabebé, Fr José, 992

Chacón family, 32

Chacón, Laureano, and the *cabildo*, 45 n. 14; elected mayor, 53 and n. 52

Chadbourne, Thomas, 561, 707; and sugar restrictions, 562

Chadwick, Capt., emissary to Shafter, 398–9

Chaffee, Col., 421, 422–3, 441; succeeds Brooke, 447 n. 23

Chain, Carlos, and 26 July Committee, 868 n. 19; in Oriente, 1032

Chamberlain, Sam, and Hearst's papers, 352 and n. 63

Chang, drug smuggler, 974–5

Chanler, Lewis and Winthrop, gun-runners, 364 and n. 51

Chanler, William Astor (1867–1934), 364 and nn. 48, 51; and 1898 War, 385

Chao, Rafael, *Fidelista*, 899 and n. 38, 900 n. 52; in the Sierra, 901 and n. 53; loses faith, 916

Chapelle, Dicky, U.S. journalist, 999, 1042 n. 16; his wife, 999 n. 15

Chapman, Prof. Charles, on Cuba (1926), 584, 740–1

Chaves, Mario, and Castro, 899

Chelala, Fr, 26 July priest, 946

Chenard, Fernando, and Castro, 826

Chester, Edward, U.S. press adviser, 1040

Chibás, Eduardo, 537 n. 8, 592 n. 33, 641 n. 22, 649, 653; member of new government, 629; American outlook, 629; and press relations, 639; owner *central Oriente*, etc., 749 and n. 35

Chibás, Eduardo (1907–), son of above, 706, 721, 736 n. 55, 796, 953, 1493; and Grau's cabinet, 650, 651, 663, 674 n. 36, 750; student backing, 696, 750; arrest, 699, 750; denounces Roca, 714, 751; and elections, 722, 757; and Grau's corruption, 739, 751, 753; family background and education, 749, 807; revolutionary activities, 750, 752, 1055–6; and Machado, 750; oratory, 750, 751, 766–7; advocate of Grau, 750–1, 752; growing intransigence, 751; character, 752; opposed to Communism, 752, 767, 1083; his Ortodoxos, 754, 756, 757, 869, 952; attacks on Prío's government, 761, 763, 764, 766–7, 768–9; attempted murder in gaol, 762; denounces MSR, 766; use of radio, 766–7, (*el Adalid*), 769–70, 1164; and agrarian reform, 767, 830, 831; clashes with Arango, 769; suicide,

Chibás, Eduardo – *Cont.*
770 and n. 25, 799; Castro and, 817, 869, 874, 1083

Chibás, Raúl, arrest, 799; Ortodoxos president, 853, 857, 861, 863, 870, 884 n. 36, 952; resignation, 889; accepts Castro, 917–18; and Civic Resistance, 918 n. 41, 925, 953; and Castro manifesto, 953–4, 954 n. 15, 961; and Nat. Liberation Council, 968; and 26 July, 969, 976 n. 13, 1046; war trials adjudicator, 1088; in exile, 1088 n. 47, 1471

Chile, Communist party, 579, 714–15, 1079 n. 9; Popular Front, 747 n. 28; González's presidency, 753 n. 44; population figures, 1093 n. 5, 1094; priesthood, 1128; U.S.S.R. and, 1265, students denounce U.S., 1268, 1277; failure of Socialist-Communist alliance, 1478

China, 944 and n. 5; and slave replacement, 110, 186; Boxer rebellion, 447 and n. 20; implication in Cuban history, 447; breach with Russia (1959–60), 923, 1315, 1476; guerrilla forces, 941; sugar consumption, 1138; Cuban newspaper, 1266; private enterprise, 1291; Cuban relations, 1292, 1314, 1315, 1415, 1469; Communist party and, 1315–16; and Castro, 1316, 1375–6, 1477–8; to buy Cuban sugar, 1316; technicians in Cuba, 1318; approves Escalante's denunciation, 1383; reaction to 'quarantine' line, 1408 and n. 11; and emphasis on sugar, 1438 n. 8; influence of her cultural revolution, 1445; return of exiles, 1482 and n. 26

Chonchol, Jacques, Chilean economist, 1252

Chorro, Lieut., 795

Chou En-lai, and Cuba, 1316

Church, Roman Catholic, and slave legislation, 35, 63; attitude to slavery, 39, 151; adaptation of African religious rites, 39–40, 48 n. 20, 281, 1123, 1127; poverty of clergy, 40, 150–1; lose influence on slaves, 74; profits from sugar boom, 74; loss of tithe rights (*Diezmos*), 82–3, 151; mill ownership, 83; position of lower clergy, 91, 150, 287, 1128; impositions in Cuba, 102; excuse for fiestas,

150, 152, 286; in nineteenth-century Cuba, 150–2, 286–7; mulatto priests, 172; religious instruction in schools, 285–6, 1128; and Independence War (1895), 320; and American-Spanish War, 372; severed from new state, 439; confiscation of lands, 462 and n.; capital assets, 462 n. 86; relations with the State, 462, 1127; purchase of her property, 492, 1127; weakness as an influence, 683, 684 n. 7; Spanish personnel, 683 and n. 4, 1101, 1127, 1128; social importance, 683; town-centred life, 683 and n. 5, 1127; poor quality priesthood, 683–4; and Batista, 793, 1129; and the Directorio, 927; membership of 26 July, 946, 1129; condemns regime, 982; 'commission of harmony', 982, 983, 985; and U.S. intervention, 987, 991; supports Castro, 994, 1127 and n. 11, 1129; and Revolutionary Government, 1080; and Afro-Cuban activities (*Brujería*), 1124; removed from the people, 1127; number of priests, 1128 and n. 5; denounces Communism, 1129, 1350; division over Castro, 1223, 1258; and agrarian reform, 1229; hardens against regime, 1268–9; campaign against revolution, 1282–3, 1294; centre of opposition, 1350, 1353; bridge between classes, 1353; priests in Brigade 2506, 1360, 1361; post-Revolution position, 1472; absence in rural areas, 1472; treatment of priests, 1472

CIA (Central Intelligence Agency), 1078; overthrows Guatemala government, 855; 879; and Communism in Cuba, 862, 991; and Cuba, 948, 949 n. 20, 961, 964–5, 967, 1016; suggested agents in Sierra, 967 and n. 20; and BRAC tortures, 1009; and Barquín's release, 1028 and n. 36; and Batista, 1162 n. 25; and Castro's regime, 1207; argues his communism, 1231; supports Cuban exiles, 1243 and n. 26, 1271, 1275; and MRR., 1275; Guatemala training school, 1275–6, 1277, 1283; in Miami, 1283; and Cuban insurrectionists, 1283; Swan Island radio station, 1288 and n. 32; wish for a single leader, 1296; and *guerrilleros*, 1297, 1301 n. 7, 1303,

CIA – *Cont.*
1308; and Arbenz's overthrow, 1302; invasion plan, 1302, 1304, 1305, 1307, 1310–10, 1365; rebel expectancy, 1303; and MRP, 1304; proposed presidency, 1307; and Revolutionary Council, 1310; and U.S. air cover, 1310; infiltration into Cuba, 1348, 1365 and n. 2; and the underground, 1356; arrest of Cuban agents, 1365; and U.S. aid to invaders, 1367, 1369–70; cost of invasion, 1371 and n. 51; and missile sites, 1398; and attempted assassination of Castro, 1467 and n. 48; and Guevara in Bolivia, 1481 n. 20

Cidra, 322

Ciego de Avila, 465, 536, 871, 1330 n. 63

Cienfuegos, Bishop, supports Batista, 1129

Cienfuegos, Camilo, *Fidelista*, 899 and n. 42, 900 n. 52, 1241; in the Sierra, 901 n. 53, 915, 920 n. 49, 934, 935, 939; and *operación verano*, 996 n. 2, 997; Las Villas operation, 1005, 1008–9, 1012, 1020, 1041–2, 1050; reading sessions, 1013; attack on Yaguajay, 1020, and Castro's takeover, 1030; chief of armed forces, 1032; revolutionary hero, 1032–3, 1247, 1462; as a leader, 1043; and Communism, 1050, 1079; character, 1050 and n. 10; and new army, 1071–3, 1198 n. 18; denounces Matos, 1245, 1248; death over sea, 1247–8; speculation over, 1248 and n. 41, 1275, 1360 n. 18; mountain boarding school dedication, 1293, 1333

Cienfuegos, Osmani, and Communism, 1050 n. 10; and army education, 1198 n. 18; Minister of Public Works, 1251, 1253; and Cuban invasion, 1362; at *central Australia*, 1362, 1363, 1364; and ORI, 1377 n. 17; in Moscow, 1387; and AALAPSO, 1477

Cintas, Oscar, Cuban ambassador to U.S., 614 n. 34; interview with Caffery, 614 and n. 34; and Machado, 618; Roosevelt and, 620; and Welles, 621

Cirugeda, Major, 339

Cisneros, Evangelina, 351–2

Cisneros, Gaspar Betancourt (pseudonym *El Lugareño*, 208 n. 11) (1803–66), 208 n. 11; and *anexionismo*, 208, 209, 212, 215; ed. *La Verdad*, 212

Cisneros, Miguel Angel, 629

Cisneros Betancourt, Salvador, Marqués de Santa Lucía, 306; President of rebel government, 260; arrest, 307; succeeds Martí, 318–19; delegate to Constitutional Convention, 449, 456 n. 56

Claiborne, John F. H., and annexation of Cuba, 215–16

Claret, Archibishop San Antonio María (1807–70), 150, 151 and n. 72; abolitionist, 221; attempted assassination, 233 n. 7

Clark, J. Reuben, under-Sec. of State, and Machado, 589

Clark Diaz, Sergio, 743 n. 10, 764 n. 13; seizes radio station, 757

Clark, Wilbur, croupier, 873

Clavelito, broadcast singer, 798, 1037

Clay, Henry (1777–1852), Sec. of State, 104 n. 45, 104–5

Cleaver, Eldridge, Black Panther exile, 1434 n. 37

Cleveland, Grover (1837–1908), U.S. president, 313 n. 13a; bellicose speech, 325 and n. 27; Cuban policy, 332, 333, 336, 337, 339, 343, 459; opposed to war, 374–5

Cleveland, James Harlan, and Cuban invasion, 1357 and n. 6

Clubs, Havana, 207, 211, 498, 516, 540

coartación, legal right of slaves, 35, 36 and n. 30, 171; price of, 171; per cent embarking on, 171 n. 18; price of *coartado*, 172; frequency in cities, 180

Cobden, Richard (1804–65), freetrader, 204, 231 n. 64

Cobián, Ricardo, and November revolt, 667

Cochin, Augustin, 62 and n. 6

Cochinos, Bay of, 926 n. 5, 1217 n. 8; invasion plan and, 1306, 1310 n. 52

Cochinos Bay, Battle of, 1243 n. 26, 1355 ff.; Cuban defences, 1355, 1363; air strikes, 1355–6, 1358, 1360, 1365–6; U.S. navy and, 1357–8, 1359, 1366; landing parties, 1361–2, 1363–4; capture of *pueblos*, 1364; Cuban defectors, 1364; use of government forces, 1366; expected U.S. air cover,

Cochinos Bay, Battle of – *Cont.*
1367–8; victory of Castro's forces, 1368–9, 1370–1; cost of, 1371 and n. 51; invading ships used, *Caribe, Houston, Barbara J., Blagar, Río Escondido, Atlántico*, 1361–8 *passim*

Codovilla, Victorio, Argentinian Communist, 588 n. 11, 697

coffee, 27, 273; consumption, 38; French immigrants and, 78, 129, 133; Cuban production, 97, 131 and n. 16, 132, 425, 1555; and her wealth, 109; total investment in, 120, 123; climax and decline in crop, 128, 129, 132; grown for beauty, 129, 130; exempt from taxes, 129; export figures, 129 and n. 6; wrecked by hurricanes, 131, 133; world production, 131 n. 16; disposition of crop, 132; slaves employed, 168; U.S. duty, 194; black or mulatto production, 431; production figures, 1957–61, 1332 n. 71; share-cropping and cash-renting, 1550; payment for piece work, 1551; credit system, 1556; labour used in picking, 1556

coffee farms (*cafetales*), numbers of, 129 and n. 7, 1555; land occupation, 129 and n. 8, 132, 1555; value of, 129; favoured areas, 129, 1555; groups of buildings, 130; *casa de vivienda*, 130; the *mayoral*, 130, 131; paralleled to sugar growing, 130; slaves employed, 130–1, 132 and n. 17; capital invested, 130 and n. 12; decline in numbers, 130, 131, 132; typical appearance, 130–1; cost of slaves, 131; given over to sugar, 131; ownership, 131–2, 1555–6; life of slaves, 179–80; cemeteries, 180; employment of women, 1431; lack of expertise and mechanization, 1556; effect of isolated conditions, 1556

Cofiño, Angel, and CTC, 753, 1178; dismissal, 942–3; questionable conduct, 943 and n. 2; and Communism, 944; in Miami, 968; and Junta of Unity, 1003

Coll, Raúl, 962

Collado, Luis, 745

Collazo, Lt. Faustino, 666

Collazo, Col., 529, 591, 668

Collazo, General Enrique, 386

Collazo, Natalia, 593

Colombia, Army of Independence, 101–3; Roosevelt and, 418 and n. 7, 468 n. 26; population figures, 503, 1093; Communist party, 579; sergeants' revolt, 638; Pan-American Conference, 1948, 814–16; guerrilla warfare, 941; Cienfuegos and, 1032–3; U.S.S.R. and, 1265; *violencia*, 1480; agrarian reform, 1559

Colorado, Manuel, 487; and new Cuban army, 994 n. 28

Comellas, Guillermo, 763

Comesañas, Col. Roberto, 962, 963

Comillas, Antonio López, Marqués de, 155, 347

Communism, 291 n. 42; newspaper *Hoy*, 400 n. 33; changes in international movement, 696–8; U.S. stock denunciations, 912 and n. 12; scapegoat for violence, 912 n. 15, 919, 956, 981; 26 July and, 922, 1051; Castro's leaders and, 1048–52, 1078–9; a lever against U.S., 1260; comparison between Cuba and Eastern Europe, 1487–91

Communists, and ill-treatment of Negroes, 524 n. 35; import revolutionary literature, 575; socialist origins, 579; and control of CNOC, 580, 596 and n. 54; persecution under Machado, 587–9; lower middle classes and, 596; organized sugar strike, 598, 605–6; denounce ABC, 606; ignored by Welles, 629; plot against Céspedes, 631 and n. 22; and Grau's regime, 651; welcome Mella's ashes, 656; revolutionary character, 681; Congresses, 692 and n. 5, 959 n. 31; U.S.–Cuban relationship, 692; student following, 696; attack U.S., 765; and 'Bogotazo', 814, 815–16; movement of youth towards, 825–6; and Moncada plan, 842 and n. 40; and rebel army, 1007, 1012–13; meeting with Directorio, 1014; and new government (1959), 1078–9, 1204; and literature, 1080–1; at La Cabaña, 1082 and n. 20; 'Thesis on the Present Situation', 1083; union control, 1083; Negro, 1123, 1125; and 26 July, 1199; publish a speech of Castro's, 1205 n. 39; two views of Castro, 1207; crisis in Cuba, 1212; and land reform, 1216, 1222–3; clash with Revolution,

Communists – *Cont.*
1219–21; increased strength, 1221; and establishment of totalitarianism, 1259; and control of Cuba, 1282; and U.S. intervention, 1290; *dirigentes revolucionarios*, 1318, 1372; and *Fidelistas*, 1319, 1372; old and new society, 1337; first formal government post, 1376; and ORI, 1376, 1377 and nn.; and idea of reward for labour, 1446; and disappearance of the State, 1448 and n. 12

Concás, Víctor, 396

Confederación Nacional del Trabajo (CNT), 408, 575 n. 22, 766

Confederación Nacional Obrera Cubana (CNOC), 575, 578; union membership, 578; affiliation to Profintern, 578; struggle for its control, 580; organized strikes, 590, 598, 605–6, 618, 653, 677; and Machado, 605–6; protest against Spanish shops, 673; revolutionary conclusions (1934), 674; Communist controlled, 696; disappearance, 713

Confederación de Trabajadores de Cuba (CTC), establishment, 713; and Batista, 718, 785, 930; given official status, 733, 744; XIth National Congress, 748; government take-over of headquarters, 754, 756; and army plot, 1952, 783 and n. 19; and general strikes, 783, 990; and FONU, 1010, 1031 and n. 45; executive membership, 1031 n. 5; trade union grouping, 1178; and Communists, 1178, 1250, 1251; sugar-workers' membership, 1178; and Castro as prime minister, 1235; proposes confederation of Latin American workers, 1251; and dissident journalists, 1280; propaganda secretary, 1313

Conte Agüero, Luis, and Chibás, 751, 754 n. 48; arrest, 799; and Castro, 847 and n. 6, 858, 863, 889, 1014 n. 51, 1213; interviews Urrutia, 1230–1; ruin, 1273

Contreras Labarca, Chilean Communist, 727, 747 n. 28

Cooke, J. W., 1345

Coolidge, Calvin, U.S. president, receives Machado, 586; in Havana, 587

Corcho, Rigoberto, 837 n. 20, 838 and n. 22

Cordero, Vicente, C. T. C., 1315

Cordobés, Capt. Isidro, 667

Coro, Dr Eduardo, 874; and Chibás, 767; ambassador, 1455 n. 10

Corominas, María, 611

Coronu, Capt. Braulio, political defector, 896 n. 15; defector, 1040

Correa, General, Minister of War, 382

Cortés, Hernán (1485–1547), 27, 1514, 1515

Cortina, Abilio, JUCEI, 1408

Cortina, Estanislao, mayor of Havana, 629

Cortina, José Maneul (1880–), Sec. of State, 724 and n. 2

Cortina, José María ('El Dinámico'), 573

Corunna, 64 and n. 18

Corzo, Artime, 1202

Cossío Betancourt, Capt., 659

Cossío del Pino, Alejo, shooting of, 774

Costa, mayor of Marianao, Liberal rebel, 528

Costa Rica, 302, 759, 886, 950; coffee production, 131 n. 16; under protection of U.K., etc., 228 n. 49; declares war on Nicaragua, 228; Communist party, 579; arms from, 986; population figures, 1093 n. 6, and Artime's exile army, 1471 and n. 66

Costales Latatu, Manuel, 652

Cotoño, Manuel, 587, 592 n. 33

cotton, Cuban production, 70, 1331, 1557; replaces slaves, 93; U.S. boom, 165; Catalonian boom, 279

Couzeiro, Manuel, 910

Cowley, Col. Fermín (d. 1957), and government misuse of power, 840, 909 n. 2; commander at Holguín, 909, 959; reprisals against 26 July, 909–10; assassination and reprisals, 972

Craig, General Malin, 712 and n. 24

Craigie, R. R., and U.S. intervention, 660 n. 10; and Welles, 671 n. 19

Crawford, Acting Consul-General, 247 n. 4; and slave landings, 235 n. 14

Creelman, James, *World* correspondent, 336 and n. 27, 340 and n. 14, 391; at San Juan, 394

Crespo, General, 259

Crespo, Lucio, 913, 920 n. 49, 934

Crespo, Luis, 887 n. 47, 899

Creswell, John, 251 and n. 16

Criollos, 40, 71 n. 55; and post of *peninsulares*, 47 and n. 18, 300; make peace with Spain, 61; oligarchy, 72 n. 1, 194, 278; law and government and, 109; excluded from professions, 111; occupations, 111; women, 145; excluded from public life, 149, 1114; Tacón and, 194; and Pinillos, 196; and *anexionismo*, 208; and Independence War (1868), 246; and Republican party, 474; displaced by capitalist immigrants, 1108; as *latifundistas*, 1110

Crittenden, Col., and López's expedition, 217

Crombet, Flor, deportation, 300; and Independence War (1895), 306, 309, 772 n. 28; death, 316

Crowder, General Enoch (1859–1932), 486 and n. 27, 571, 587; and law reform, 487–8, 535; and elections, 489, 549; return to Cuba, 534–5, 548–9, 686, 687, 1418; political power, 550; and financial crisis, 553; reform programme, 554, 555; 'Honest Cabinet', 555, 743 n. 10; ambassador, 555–6, 584; on Machado, 584

Cruz, Jorge, 861; 872

Cruz Cabrera, Eliecer, terrorist, 945

Cruz Vidal, Col. Ramón, 634 and n. 1, 780, 792 and n. 10, 898, 899

Cuba, Spanish possession, 1, 12, 27, 96, 102; English landing and occupation, 6, 12, 43, 48; population figures, 12 and n. 1, 18–19, 171, 172, 1513–14, 1528 n. 71; mixed blood people, 13 and n. 5; architectural features, 13, 16–17, 17 n. 10; virgin countryside, 17–18; flora and fauna, 18, 1518; physical features, 18; country people, 18–19; asked for a land survey, 20–1; Spanish-Indian miscegenation, 21 and n. 21; place-name origin, 22; smaller crops and products, 24; first industrial revolution, 32, 97; dependence on imports, 40, 125; office of captain-general, 45, 46, 110, 111; creole estates, 46–7; arrival of English merchants, 49; effect of import of cheap labour, 52–3; fortunes made in, 57, 61; causes of her prosperity, 61–6; administrative changes, 65; dependence on world market, 66, 74; N.

American traders and, 66, 67, 68; exports, 70 and n. 47; international slave market, 70; financial system, 73; beginning of free education, 75; effect of slave revolution, 77; enriched by free slave trade, 83; intimations of nationalism, 85, 89; reliance on U.S. food supplies, 87; trade relations with U.S., 87 n. 11, 97, 194 and n. 4, 208, 209, 287–91; effect of England's abolition, 87, 99; and independence, 88–9, 101, 103–5; and mainland movements, 90–1; royalist refugees, 91; and abolition, 94, 96, 98, 170, 173, 279; drop in white immigrants, 96; influx of foreign merchants after 1815; proposed annexation to U.S. (*anexionismo*), 99–100, 103–4, 111, 207–9, 215, 218, 227, 240–1, 251–2; flight of Liberals, 102–3; under martial law, 103, 105; role of the army, 110; official corruption, 111, 299; U.S. influence on her development, 133, 270, 313, 379, 413, 419; tobacco smoking, 134, 148; hotels, 141; titled families, 143; lack of law and order, 149; isolated position, 173–4; new sources of labour, 185–8, 1541; increase in 'white' population, 188; increased slave imports (1859–61), 188–9, 189 n. 23; social conditions in nineteenth century, 193; and emancipation, 196, 221, 223; exempt from 1812 Constitution, 198; constitutional reform, 233 ff., 238, 267–8, 303; ban on political parties, 235; first elections, 238; national anthem, 245; revolutionary House of Representatives, 250, 260; political parties, 268; new mortgage law, 272; North Americanization, 273, 275, 278, 289, 298; source of capital, 275; social changes from sugar crisis, 278–9; fall in economic growth, 279; standard of living in nineteenth century, 284–5, 287; working-class organizations, 291–2; racial integration, 293; promulgation of Spanish Constitution, 294; political banditry, 302–3, 319; and world financial crisis (1893), 303; condition during (1896) war, 334–5, 357; payment of Spanish debts, 351; under U.S. occupation,

Cuba, Spanish possession – *Cont.*
410–11, 420–1, 437; end of Spanish rule, 412; Spanish achievements, 412–3; decline of black race, 419; post-war condition, 422; indebtedness, 434 and n. 97; labour troubles, 422; presidential elections, 459–60; becomes independent, 460; electoral system (1900), 461–2; U.S. trading sharks, 463; reciprocity treaty with U.S., 468–9, 536; an unequally developed province, 1424; archaeological studies, 1529

Cuba (Republic), political independence, 471; periods of prosperity, 471, 526, 533–4, 600, 739, 746, 765; Congressional scandals, 47; elections, (1902), 472–3, (1905), 473–4, (1908), 489 and n. 40, (1912), 509; position of U.S. legation, 474; Liberal revolt, 475–9; without a government, 479; U.S. intervention, 479–80m 481; revival of *anexionismo*, 489; state in 1909, 497 ff.; Spanish immigration, 497, 514; country houses, 499; high cost of living, 501; population statistics, 503, 1093 and n. 1, 1094, 1105, 1181–2, 1492–3; political corruption, 505, 740; absence of racism, 514, 515; survival of African religion, 518; disregard for Afro-Cuban culture, 524; declares war on Germany, 530, 601; goes money mad, 534; and economic crisis (1919), 536, 537, 562–3; U.S. investment, 536, 540, 599–600, 911, 966, 1057–8; eastward expansion of sugar lands, 537, 539–40, 600–1, 1465; social problems caused by foreign investment, 542, 600–1; 'dance of the millions', 543, 544 ff., 601, 687, 1111, 1149, 1185; financial crisis, 544 ff.; anti-Americanism, 555; financial and political bankruptcy (1930s), 593, 605–6, 615, 688; failure to create a political system, 599, 605–6; national identification with Negroes, 601–2; reign of violence, 607, 886, 944–5, 956, 975, 1348–9; three-day hurricane, 632, 638; spread of disorder, 653, 656–7; political disintegration, 655, 656, 679, 684, 770–1; per cent of foreigners (1907–31) 684 and nn. 10, 11; survival of Spanish influence, 683–4; desire for reform and stability, 691; U.S.-Japanese competition, 693; commercial relations with U.S., 693–4, 717–18, 729; mood of despair, 696; slow economic improvement, 700; fall in exports, 716; revaluation bill, 716 and n. 4; declares war on Japan, Germany and Italy, 729; diplomatic relations with U.S.S.R., 731, 1279, 1282; war organization, 731; black market, 749; collapse of public morality, 764–5, 768, 786; military agreement with U.S., 771; commemoration of 50th anniversary, 795; health of economy under Batista, 872–3, 909, 911, 933, 943, 972; reaction to Castro's landing, 902, 911, 920; rise in *per capita* income, 911; suspension of constitutional guarantees, 912 and n. 15; increased repression, 931–2; state of civil war, 959, 972, 981, 1010; U.S. arms embargo, 985; and Batista's flight, 1027; revolutionary heroes, 1032; and Castro's victory, 1037–8, 1065; future choice, 1049; concept of Revolution, 1055–6, 1056 n. 33; effect of U.S. patronage and domination, 1061, 1062; town and country dwellers, 1093; birthrate, 1094; 'Floridization', 1098; immigrant population, 1100 and n. 40; U.S. citizens, 1101; comparative poverty, 1103, 1104; economic stagnation, 1105, 1142, 1180–2; class structure, 1108–11; millionaires, 1111; *entrepreneurs*, 1114 and n. 30; newspapers, 1136–7; shipping lines, 1163; instant communications, 1163; shoe imports, 1167 and n. 51; foreign investment in, 1184 and n. 12; recovery after 1950, 1185; imports from U.S., 1186–7, 1188; balance of payments, 1187; gold reserves, 1187 and n. 27; redistribution of national income, 1206; restoration and suspension of *habeas corpus*, 1238, 1246, 1253; changed international status, 1266; opposition to government, 1274–5; end of free press, 1280–1; threat to free enterprise, 1284, 1293; eclipse of U.S. and private concerns, 1291; relations with China, 1292; lessening links with U.S., 1294; and threat of

Cuba (Republic) – *Cont.*

invasion, 1301, 1308; compared with Guatemala, 1302; underground co-ordination, 1308 n. 39; part of Communist *bloc*, 1314, 1372; recognition of embassies, 1316–17; place of anti-Communists, 1320–1; exodus of technicians, 1329, 1382; improved social conditions, 1333; industrial problems, 1336–6, 1382; need for foreign currency, 1335, 1336, 1376; retains its charm, 1346–7; worsened economic position, 1374, 1382, 1384; suspended from OAS, 1375; dominated by '*sectarismo*', 1379; complaints of, 1382 and n. 36; growing discontent, 1386; an embarrassment to U.S.S.R., 1390; part in missile crisis, 1395, 1408; fear of nuclear bombardment, 1408; reaction to invasion threat, 1408–9; anger at Russian withdrawal, 1414; social changes since 1962, 1423 ff.; food rationing, 1424; continuance of brothels (*posadas* or *Casas non-Sanctas*), 1434; anticipated economic improvements, 1436; commercial agreement with Russia, 1438, 1474; first Five Year Plan, 1450; low productivity in economy, 1451–2; political changes since 1962, 1453–4; opportunists of new system, 1455; controlling forces, 1457–8, 1462; crime rates, 1460 and n. 27; use of death penalty, 1460; commemoration of live and dead heroes, 1462; lack of opposition, 1471; wave of sabotage, 1472; relations with the Church, 1472–3; debts to E. European *bloc*; Soviet civilian aid, 1474 and nn. 1, 3; imports to and from Russia, 1475 and nn. 3, 4; admired by South America, 1477; and Vietnam, 1478 and n. 12; and rest of Communist world, 1478–9; trains foreign guerrillas, 1479; compared with South America, 1479–80; exiles leaving for Florida, 1482 and n. 25; lesson of the Revolution, 1483; is the regime still popular?, 1484 ff.; new national spirit, 1485; governmental inefficiency, 1486–7; standard of living, 1487; debt to Russian Communism, 1487; huge bureaucracy, 1488; differentiation from other Com-

munists systems, 1488–91; culmination of Revolutionary activity, 1491–2; uncontrollable destiny, 1493; drift from the land, 1550; disappearance of forests, 1557

Cuban Communist Party, on Magoon, 485 n. 22; Havana foundation, 574, 575, 1081; membership of Comintern, 578; group organizations, 581; murder of students, 587; attracts lower middle classes, 596; membership, 596 and n. 53, 1080 and n. 11; internal divisions, 597, 923; Jewish group, 597; agreement with Machado, 605–6, 618, 632, 683; and 1933 strikes, 615, 618, 718; and U.S. intervention, 618, 1282, 1290; weak strategic position, 632, 683; and Grau, 672, 710, 744, 745, 747 and n. 26, 748, 752, 753, 756; in control of CNOC, 696; relations with Batista, 706, 710, 711, 712, 716, 721, 724, 728–9, 736, 785, 793, 846–7, 855, 870, 871 n. 28, 942; and elections, 718, 722, 756–7, 772–3, 774 n. 36, 853, 859, 860; approves 1940 Constitution, 720–1; denounces Germany, 727; enters cabinet, 733; closeness to Marxism, 734; co-operation with UN and U.S., 734; supports Saladrigas, 735; effect of cold war, 752; moves into opposition, 756; and Ortodoxos, 757, 772–3; and Prío's presidency, 764, 843 n. 41; attacks on offices, 766; and the University, 767 n. 19; accusations against CTC, 770; denounces Batista's *coup*, 785 and n. 23, 792; and Moncada barracks, 828, 842 and n. 40, 843 n. 44; outlawed, 846; five-man Junta, 846 and n. 5; supports sugar strikers, 871; attitude to Castro, 922–3, 980 and n. 37, 981–2, 1207–8; and the Directorio, 926; and Palace attack, 930 and n. 26; moves towards 26 July, 944, 1002 and n. 22, 1006; Castro and, 1052, 1055, 1078 n. 5, 1222 and n. 25, 1233, 1236, 1298, 1319; and Santiago strike, 959 and n. 31; attacked by police, 981; guerrilla groups, 981; and a general strike, 988–9, 990, 1029, 1079; denounces Pérez, 990, 991; and Second Front, 992 n. 21; formation of FONU, 1010; joins revolutionary

Cuban Communist Party – *Cont.*
cause, 1042, 1078; position in 1958, 1079–80; assets, 1080–1; reappearance of *Hoy*, 1081; new manifesto, 1081–2; and the army, 1082; and Negro cults, 1125; denounces *Revolución*, 1219; internal problems, 1222; wide range of talents, 1236; and Khrushchev's U.S. visit, 1237; and totalitarian government, 1259; defends private enterprise, 1291; 10th Congress, 1292; neutrality in Sino-Russian quarrel, 1315; and relations with China, 1315; at public gatherings, 1318; membership (1951), 1456 n. 14; activities of 'microfaction', 1468 and n. 51; accusations against, 1468–9, 1469 n. 53

Cuban Communist Party (new), first Central Committee membership (1965), 994 n. 28, 1007, 1013 n. 49, 1025 n. 20, 1198, 1253 and n. 54, 1265 n. 21, 1273 n. 4, 1381; founder members, 1255, 1268 and n. 29, 1340 n. 4, eclipse of old leaders, 1453 and n. 1; succeeds PURS, 1453; control of, 1453 and n. 1; military members, 1454 and n. 2, 1455; members of 'old' party, 1454 and nn. 3, 4; *Moncadaist*, 1454 and n. 5; *Granmaista*, 1454 and n. 5, 1455 and n. 6; domination by Castro and *Fidelista*, 1454; average age, 1455; membership, 1969, 1456; selection for membership, 1456–7; and schools of revolutionary instruction, 1457; delay in Ministerial appointments, 1457; and municipal appointments, 1458; official organ, 1463; purge of corrupted elements, 1467, 1468–9; members of new formation, 1468; military-orientated Central Committee, 1477; characteristics, 1487–91

Cuban Constitution (1902), 449–56; and judiciary, 471–2; and provincial self-government, 472, 486–7; begins to crack, 508; restored by Céspedes, 631

Cuban National Bank, 639, 759 n. 2, 789; postponement, 732; establishment, 760, 764, 775; presidency, 760, 784, 931, 1226 n. 42, 1470; and *per capita* incomes, 1104 and n. 59; appointment of Guevara, 1252

Cuban Revolutionary Council, foundation, 1307; to return to Havana, 1310; and invasion, 1357, 1359, 1364, 1368; flown to Miami, 1359, 1368; detention, 1359; Kennedy and, 1369, 1385

Cuban Revolutionary Party, lists 'Bases', 301–2; Martí and, 305; provisional cabinet (*consejo de Gobierno*), 319–20, 322; elects new government, 351, 359; contact with Janney, 359; and U.S., 363, 403–4, 409, 437; and Spanish-American War, 381, 398; post-war behaviour, 409; criticisms of its army, 410; ignored by U.S. occupiers, 437

Cubans, Spanish-Indian origins, 21 and n. 21; Africanization of *fiestas*, 40; and slave trade, 68 and n. 33, 83, 98–9; and mainland independence movements, 90–1; become landowners, 95; enmity with Spain, 111; social life, 146–7, 148, 254–5, 277–8, 1102; aristocracy, 149, 278; and cock-fighting, 150; and religious observance, 152, 1127 and n. 2, 1128; hierarchical groups, 152–4; inaccurate names for African tribes, 183 n. 72; enrichment under captains-general, 193; attitude to *anexionismo*, 209, 215, 218, 221, 448; social changes after sugar crisis (1880s), 277–8; concern with complete independence, 301–2, 357; and civil administration under U.S., 403, 421–2, 437, 438; lack of U.S. consultation, 410, 437; in Wood's cabinet, 444 and n. 1; and U.S. constitutional demands, 452; and Magoon's law reforms, 487; hostile feelings towards U.S., 501–2, 1058–9, 1064, 1227, 1233, 1235, 1320, 1321; and Castro's triumph, 1040; anti-imperialism, 1059 n. 47; identification with rebellion, 1060; and war criminals, 1073–4; town- and country-dwellers, 1093, 1094, 1095, 1351 and n. 27; influence of U.S., 1102, 1110; eating and drinking habits, 1102–3; sugar consumption, 1103 and n. 49; standard of living, 1103–4; income *per capita*, 1103, 1104, 1104 n. 59, 1188; evidence of social advance, 1106–7, 1106 nn., 1107 n.; class structure, 1108 ff.; intermarriage, 1110; tobacco

Cubans – *Cont.*

smoking, 1158; use of telephone, 1163; employment in U.S. firms, 1172; employment fears, 1180; investment habits, 1182 ff.; and control of banks, 1184–5; money spent abroad, 1187 and n. 29; debilitated society, 1188; fate of anti-Communists, 1233, 1320 and n. 26, 1321; U.S. emigrants, 1283–4; poor security arrangements, 1301, 1303, 1308; opinion of Russian technicians, 1318; support revolutionary government, 1344, 1349; use of *Habana Libre*, 1344–5; post-revolution class struggle, 1353; effect of invasion, 1372; food rationing, 1377, 1424 and n. 3, 1425; general exodus, 1382, 1384; provoked to defend Cuba, 1397 and n. 12; and Russian withdrawal, 1414; improved life since 1962, 1424; emigration figures, 1425; drift into cities, 1425; position of youth, 1429; conservatism in personal relations, 1432; knowledge of money, 1447, 1448; ability to commit violence, 1456 and n. 13; end of the *Señorita*, 1471 and n. 67; and the armed struggle, 1480; tragic position in 1960s, 1483 ff.; problematical attitude to regime, 1484; love of 'Liberty' and 'Revolution', 1491 and n. 24; cause of Hispanic nationalism, 1528

Cubela, Rolando, attacks police and army, 889–90, 890 n. 61; N. Cuba landing, 979 nn. 28, 31; attempt on Castro's life, 979 n. 31, 1070 n. 13, 1467 and n. 48; and Guevara, 1013, 1017; leader of Directorio, 1020 and n. 3, 1030, 1069; military attaché, 1069; and Havana University, 1070 n. 13, 1286, 1287, 1456, 1467; imprisonment, 1070 n. 13, 1467; attempted assassination, 1471

Cuervo, Orlando, 971

Cuervo, Dr Pelayo, 761, 831, 874, 883; and Grau, 768; attempted murder, 778; and Batista's corruption, 800, 801; arrest, 802; murder, 930, 932 1116

Cuevas, Rafael, National Hero of Labour, 1447

Cuina, Angel, Mujalista, 1237–8

Cumberland, William Augustus, Duke

of, 2 and nn. 5, 7, 3 n. 11, 42, 43, 56

Cunha, Vasco da, 1075

Cuna Reis, slave merchants, 157

Cunliffe, Sir Ellis, M.P. for Liverpool, 56

Curti, Segundo, 674 n. 36; Minister of Interior, 743 n. 10, 780; and army plot (1952), 782; leaves with Prío, 785

Curtis, Charles, U.S. *chargé d'affaires*, 590

Cushing, Caleb, and expansionism, 222; Cuban policy, 264

Czolgosz, Leon, shoots McKinley, 457

da Costa, Capt. Aristides, defence counsel, 1089

Da Silva, Brazilian Communist, 697

Da Souza, Francisco Félix, slave merchant career, 159; Whydah cargoes, 203

Dady, Michael, 463

Dallas, Commander, 198

Dallas, George Mifflin, U.S. vice-president, and annexation of Cuba, 209–10, 213

Dalrymple, Judge, and Mixed Commission, 202

Dam, Luis, journalist, 887

Dana, Charles Anderson, *Sun*, 296, 313, 314, 331, 337, 348, 358; *World*, 313, 333, 338, 358; and *Maine*, 362, 363; and Spanish war, 368 and n. 6, 369, 385

Daniel, Jean, 1391, 1392

Daniels, Josephus, U.S. ambassador in Mexico, 664 and n. 27

Darcey, General, interview with Carrillo, 995

Darío, Rubén, 'The Triumph of Caliban', 417 and n. 2

Darthez and Brothers, slave traders, 157

Davidson, George, expulsion, 199

Davis, Charles W., 223

Davis, Senator Jefferson, U.S. Sec. at War, and annexation of Cuba, 212, 219, 222; López and, 214; leader of the South, 230; president of confederate states, 230–1

Davis, Norman H. (1878–1944), 507 n. 8; organizes Ports Co., 506–7, 686; and bank crisis, 548; and a Cuban loan, 551, 553; U.S. involvement, 686; at Sugar Conference, 686 n. 16

Davis, Richard Harding, journalist in

Davis, Richard Harding – *Cont.*
Cuba, 340 and n. 8, 388, 390, 502; *Does our Flag Protect Women?*, 340-1

Dawson, Capt. James, privateer, 68 n. 36; and slave trade, 69 and n. 37, 71; and a new monopoly contract, 69-70, 70 n. 46, 72 n. 1

Day, William Rufus (1849-1923), Ass. Sec. of State, 341 and n. 23; and *Maine*, 358, 362; and de Lôme, 360; peace protagonist, 374

Dayan, Yael, 911

de Castro, Alejandro, 239, 240

de Gaulle, General, 1401, 1403 and n. 55

de la Cruz, Carlos Eduardo, Minister of Justice, 743 n. 10

de la Cruz, Carlos Manuel, and Mendieta's cabinet, 678

de la Cuesta, Luis, and 26 July, 910

de la Fe, Ernesto, and Batista's cabinet, 783 n. 20, 789, 799, 840; and *tanquistas*, 885; arrest, 1045; and FBI, 1077

de la Luz Caballero, José (1800-62), and College of San Francisco, 205 and n. 28

de la Peña, Lucilo, student, 593, 664, 674 n. 36, 674 n. 39

de la Rosa, Carlos, mayor of Matanzas, vice-president, 571

de la Sagra, Ramón, and census of 1791 and 1792, 89, 90

de la Torre, Cándido, arrest, 883

de la Torre, Carlos, Rector of Havana University, 564 and n. 2; and FEU, 565

de la Torre, Oscar, 638 n. 13, 663; and Batista's government, 783 n. 20, 784

De la Torriente family, ruination at *Carlota* mill, 274

De la Torriente, Cosme (1872-1957), 306, 676, 710, 892; Judge in Santa Clara, 422; approached by Welles, 609, 610; accepted as negotiator, 610, 611, 623; in hiding, 646; and Grau, 671; Sec. of Presidency, 677, 678; and SAR, 870; and Batista, 870, 872, 873; and *diálogo cívico*, 873-5, 1065; death, 902 and n. 57

De la Torriente, Ramón and Esteban, 141-2, 293; social position, 153; and Independence War (1868), 249, 256; shippers and merchants, 274

de la Torriente Brau, Pablo, 695, 1225; and Spanish Civil War, 703, 888

de Lôme, Enrique Dupuy (1851-1904),

Spanish Minister, 343, 359; and the Junta, 359-61; resignation, 360, 361

de Wolf, James, U.S. slave trader, 71, 84 n. 55

Deboya, Fr Manuel, S. J., in gun battle, 1294

Debray, Régis, revolutionary, 1256 n. 5, 1461, 1479; contempt for *llano*, 1045 and nn. 22, 23

Decker, Karl, reporter, rescues Miss Cisneros, 352; sent to Havana (1897), 365

de los Santos, Major René, chief of DIER, 1455

del Cerro, Angel, 793

del Cueto, José Antolín (1854-1929), interim Rector, 565

del Peso, Manuel, Communist, 1013; in Moscow, 1013 n. 44

del Pino, Rafael, 888 n. 55; and UIR, 814, 817 n. 71; in Bogotá, 814-16; alleged betrayal of Castro, 891 and n. 65; tried with Matos, 1256

del Pozo, José Luis, mayor of Havana, 1026

Del Pozo, Justo Luis, 591

del Rio Balmaseda, Joaquin, 652, 669

del Rio Chaviano, Col. Alberto, commander Moncada barracks, 839 and n. 28, 840 and n. 31, 842; career, 841-2; hostility towards, 844, 852; denouncement, 866; replaces Pérez in the *Sierra*, 965, 967; commander *operación verano*, 996; and Las Villas, 1017, 1021; and officers' *coup*, 1021, 1022

del Valle, Alejandro, anti-Castroist, 1283 n. 21; member Brigade 2506, 1359 n. 16, 1366, 1369 n. 40

del Valle, Dr Sergio, 958; commander-in-chief air force, 1255; and Matos' trial, 1255; Minister of Interior, 1255 and n. 1, 1454 n. 5, 1460; and ORI, 1377 n. 19; and use of death penalty, 1459-60

Delgado, Col. Erasmo, dissident officer, 623, 624, 625

Delgado, Esteban, 588

Delgado, Josefa A., sugar mill, *S. Felipe*, 427

Delgado Mayoral, Enrique, 945

Del Monte, Domingo (1804-53), sugar planter (*Ceres*), 207 n. 1; in exile, 206, 207; Cuban poet, 207 n. 1; his *tertulias*, 207 n. 1

Denman, Capt., 202, 204

Derosne, Charles (1780–1846), sugar technician, 154; new vacuum boiler, 117; and 'centrifugal' machine, 118, 136 n. 3, 274 n. 15; Cuban sales, 120; cost of, 121, 174

Despaigne, Manuel, member of 'Honest Cabinet', 555 and n. 55, 567, 651; and Grau's cabinet, 651, 662

Dessalines, Jean-Jacques, emperor of Haiti, 76

Desvernine, Pablo, under new U.S. government, 421; and Farquhar, 464; First Sec. (Wood's) Treasury, 464; Foreign Minister, 534 n. 35

Dewey, Commodore (later Admiral), 355; Roosevelt and, 365; and Spanish American War, 385 n. 17; at Manila, 396, 402, 406

Diago family, 117, 123, 141; sugar estates, 123, 153, 268, 1148; and railways, 122, 123; social position, 153; and technological advances, 154; use of Chinese labour, 186; reduced circumstances, 277, 428

Diago, Fernando, 136

Diago, Francisco, 427

Diago, Pedro, 97 and n. 19, 117

Díaz, Aurelio, Bishop of Pinar del Río, peace plea, 951

Díaz Cristóbal (1894–), press chief, 912 and n. 13

Díaz, Edward, 913, 916

Díaz, Emiliano, and 26 July, 896 n. 14; death, 940

Díaz, Mgr Evelio, diocesan administrator, 1129, 1268, 1294; and Agrarian law, 1223 and n. 29; supports Revolution, 1264

Díaz, Capt. Higinio ('Nino'), bandit group, 1275; leader Cuban exiles, 1355; failure to land, 1357–8, 1361

Díaz, Jesús, Towards a Militant Culture, 1465, 1466 n. 45

Díaz, José, prisoner, 899

Díaz, Julio, 887 n. 47, 899; in the Sierra, 901 n. 53, 913, 920 n. 49; under Raúl, 934 n. 5; death, 940

Díaz, Lieut, chief of police, murder, 595

Díaz, Lomberto, 768

Díaz, Corporal Oscar, and sergeants' revolt, 635; rated 2nd Lieut, 646 n. 37

Díaz, Don Porfirio, Mexican dictator, 313, 582; and Cuban rebellion, 333

Díaz Aztaraín, Rolando, Minister of Stolen Property, 1251

Díaz Balart, Mirta, wife of Castro, 817, 856; divorce, 860

Díaz Balart, Rafael, 817, 818, 821 n. 96, 835 n. 3, 857 and n. 45; Sub.-Sec. for Interior, 835, 856; Transport Minister, 843 n. 41; youth leader, 845; resignation, 857; opposition movement (White Rose), 1204

Díaz Calderón, Sergeant Arturo, 648; rated Lieut, 646 n. 37

Díaz Cartaya, Agustín, 'Hymn of 26 July', 833 and n. 36, 834

Díaz Hanscom, Rafael, execution, 1349

Díaz Lanz, Pedro, airline pilot, 986, 1229; chief of air force, 1072, 1202 n. 32, 1213; career, 1229; and 'indoctrination classes', 1229–30; antidictatorship speech, 1230; resignation and flight, 1230; before U.S. Senate, 1231–2, 1232 n. 55; bombs Havana with leaflets, 1245; his aircraft, 1245–6, 1246 n. 33; arrest, 1248

Díaz Sánchez, Mercedes María, bomb layer, 945

Díaz Sánchez, Señorita, bomb layer, 945

Díaz Tamayo, in Oriente, 898, 1018; and army conspiracy, 780; dismissal, 950

Diefenbaker, Canadian Prime Minister, 1317; and missile crisis, 1407

Dihigo, Ernesto, Foreign Minister, 764 n. 13; ambassador to U.S., 1066 1208, 1214, 1243, 1276; withdrawn, 1262

Dimitrov, Georgi Mihailov (1882–1949), Communist chief, 697, 745

Dinaz, Capt., defector, 1017

Dingley Tariff Act, 1897, 457

Directorio Estudiantil, membership, 592 and n. 33, 674 n. 36, 683, 733, 750, 784, 968; and sergeants' revolt, 638, 639, 654; revolutionary statement, 640–1, 681; elects grau president, 649; and U.S. ambassador, 651; supports Grau, 652; and old politicians, 653, 655; and Batista, 661, 663; breaks with ABC, 663; in disorder, 663; dissolution, 665

Directorio Revolucionario (DR), 968 n. 26; foundation, 871; relationship to FEU, 871 n. 29; anti-Batista aims,

Directorio Revolucionario (DR) – *Cont.*
871, 873, 888 n. 57; supports sugar strike, 871; and Castro, 888, 925, 1029, 1030, 1069; sabotage activity, 925; links with Prío, 926; and Palace attack, 926; anti-Communism, 926–7; guerrilla landing, 978–80; armaments, 979 and n. 30; manifesto, 979–80; and Junta of Unity, 1003; meeting with Communists, 1014; occupy palace, 1032, 1033; problematical future, 1033, 1069, 1203–4; *La Calle*, 1281; and betrayal of students, 1319; integrated into ORI, 1372; and [PURS], 1454 n. 3; membership new Communist Party, 1455 and n. 7

Dobrynin, A., Soviet ambassador in U.S., 1396 n. 9, 1409

Dodd, Senator, 1232

Dodge, General Augustus, 226

Dolz, Dr Eduardo, 356–7

Dolz, Ricardo, 459, 473

Domínguez, Capt. Felipe, and November revolt, 668

Dominican Republic, 609, 850 n. 24; circular land grants, 20 n. 16; free ports, 64; Cuban immigrants, 271 n. 6; Communist party, 579 and n. 43, 697; U.S. rule, 626 and n. 4; Cabrals-Trujillo friendship, 703 n. 35; England buys sugar harvest, 729; expedition against Trujillo, 754–6, 756 n. 52, 812, 868; plots against Batista, 882–3; relations with Cuba, 886, 990–1; political gangsters, 925; Cuban refugees, 1026; population figures, 1093 n. 3, 1093–4; sugar import, 1103 n. 49; quota, 1142 n. 13; attacked by Castro, 1228 and n. 45, 1229; subsequent imprisonment 1268

Doné, Gina, in *Granma*, 894

Doroeto, mulatto slave, 'emperor' of Cuba, 265

Dorta Duque, Dr, 611

Dorticós, Andres, Fr, immigrant, 98

Dorticós, Osvaldo (born 1919), President of Cuba, 98 n. 24, 1085, 1234, 1235, 1465; social position, 1085; value to revolutionary regime, 1234; and Pazos, 1246; and Cuban–U.S. relations, 1258, 1264, 1271, 1276; in S. America, 1285; in Europe, 1373; and ORI, 1377 and n. 20, 1379;

denounces demonstrations, 1386; statement at U.N. on invasion threat, 1400 and n. 32; and new Communist party, 1454 n. 5

Dos Amigos, African slave merchant, 159

Dos Riós, 316

Douglas, Commodore James, and Jamaica, 5 and n. 28; and Havana expedition, 5–6

Douglas, Senator Stephen Arnold, urges purchase of Cuba, 212; Democratic candidate, 219

Drake family, 127; credit bankers, 118, 122, 141; and railways, 122; sugar mills, 122, 123; recovery of debts, 136 n. 2, 140; rise of, 141; become counts (Vega Mar), 142; foreign investments, 148; and *anexionismo*, 207, 208

Drake, Carlos, 141

Drake, Emilio, 141

Drake, Capt. Philip, assumes name Don Felipe Drax, 93, 137; and slave trade, 93, 95 n. 9, 137; visits slave-breeding farm, 170 n. 10

Dreir, John, U.S. ambassador to OAS, 789 n. 3

Droller (Bender), Frank, 1303; CIA expert on Communism, 1211 and n. 65; anti-Castro operation, 1275, 1307

Duarte family, and Isle of Pines, 503

Dubois, Jules, 930 n. 26, 992; and execution of Osorio, 913 n. 21

Duclos, Jacques, attacks Browder (*Cahiers du Communisme*), 744–5

Dudley, Major Edgar, Judge Advocate, 423, 461

Dueñas, Col., *Batistiano*, 1009 n. 22, 1017

Duggan, Lawrence, 688 and n. 26, 723 and n. 28, 728 n. 19

Duggan, Thomas, plantation inventory, 112–13

Dulce, Domingo, captain-general, 237, 248 and n. 6; and Reformers, 234, 235, 248; and rebel volunteers, 248, 249, 252; war aims, 252; resignation, 252

Dulles, Allen, 529 n. 10, 1026, 1260 n. 45, 1389; director CIA, 855, 862, 1060, 1367; and invasion plan, 1303, 1305, 1364 n. 27; advocates invasion, 1306 and n. 31, 1309; and 'disposal

Dulles, Allen – *Cont.*
problem', 1306 and n. 32; television interview, 1309 n. 45
Dulles, John Foster, 529 n. 10, 530 n. 14, 533, 947, 1001, 1014; Batista and, 855; defends Smith, 958; and Guatemala, 1017 n. 68; Sec. of State, 1060, 1075
Dumas, Alexandre Père, and Soulé, 219 n. 9, 221
Dumont, U.S. consul-general, 670
Dumont, Prof. René, 1328 n. 54, 1442 n. 28; on Nuñez Jiménez, 1217–18; his 'pseudo-co-operatives', 1324 and n. 42; criticism of co-operatives, 1326 and n. 46, 1327, 1328, 1330 n. 63, 1382, 1395; on Cuban countryside, 1441
Dupont, Admiral, 362
Dupont, Irénée, 538 n. 13, 976
Dupotey, Hugo, murder, 742
Duque, Félix, INRA commander, 1244 and n. 29
Duquesne, Marqués de la, and abolition, 234
Durán Batista, defector, 1040
Durutty, Sir Eduardo, 731

Eastland, Senator, 1232
Echevarría, Corporal Angel, 634, 646 n. 37
Echevarría, José Antonio (1815–85), 233 and n. 2, 238, 239
Echevarría, José Antonio ('*Manzanita*'), student of 1950s, 785 n. 24; and FEU presidency, 864 and n. 10, 870; Castro on, 864; at election meeting, 870; and Directorio, 871; arrest, 883; and 'pact of Mexico', 888; *Fidelista*, 920 n. 49; and use of violence, 925; and Palace attack, 926, 927, 928; death, 929, 930, 932; testament, 1377–8
Edelman, Chief Justice, 676
Edelmira (d. 1958), 979 and n. 31
Eden, Sir Anthony, 1416
education, 147–8, 307; Economic Society and, 73, 75, 285; primary, 75, 1135; encouraged by prosperity, 85–6; responsibility of Captain-general, 110; use of U.S. facilities, 209. 1102; nineteenth century, 285–6; co-ordination of Cuban and Spanish, 285; illiteracy figures, 432 and n. 90, 1112, 1131, 1339 and n. 1, 1372, 1375; school attendance, 432–3, 1131, 1135 and n. 24; Magoon's policy, 492; and rural areas, 702, 1132, 1135; Castro's proposed reforms, 831; of black population, 1118–19; becomes compulsory, 1131; increase in private sector, 1132–33, 1134; centralization, 1133, 1135; Ministry budget, 1133, 1135, 1341 n. 5; ministerial graft, 1133; cause of social tension, 1134; deterioration under Batista, 1134–5; administrative reforms, 1135; adult, 1136 and n. 27, 1427; achievements of Revolution, 1340–1, 1427–8, 1430; remains old-fashioned, 1428; achievements in 'higher' sector, 1428; Castro's vision, 1429; *see also* Schools
Edwards, James H., 632
Eisenhower (1890–1969), U.S. President, 845, 1232; second term, 946, 947, 1009, 1060, 1207; contrasted with Castro, 1058; and Cuban affairs, 1210, 1248–9, 1262, 1264, 1267 n. 26, 1270, 1297, 1298, 1304; in S. America, 1264, 1267–8, 1278; agrees to arm Cuban exiles, 1271; and sugar quota bill, 1288, 1289, 1291; Latin American aid programme, 1293, 1295; and guerrilla training, 1301–2, 1302 n. 8; and Guatemala revolt, 1302–3; and CIA, 1351; and Suez, 1403
Elias, Melquíddes, peasant *Fidelista*, 913
Eliott, General George (Lord Heathfield) (1717–90), and Havana expedition, 3 and n. 3; captures Guanabacoa, 7
Elsmore, Desmond, 1000
emancipation, 180, 241–2, 245
England, and with Spain, 1, 87, 231; and slave trade, 31, 33, 34, 39, 87 n. 12, 157, 161, 183, 215; and scientific farming, 32; occupation of Havana, 39, 42, 47 ff.; Cuban imports, 49; and sugar trade, 54, 68, 70, 208; W. Indians in House of Commons, 55 n. 59; and Cuban prosperity, 62; and abolition, 75 and n. 13, 83, 87, 93, 99, 161, 215, 231; and Saint Domingue, 76; fall in exports to Africa, 95–6; accepts U.S. slave-grown cotton, 99; and U.S. annexation of Cuba, 100, 101; sugar consumption, 126, 1103, 1138 n. 5; arrival of coffee, 128, 131

England – *Cont.*
n. 16; cigar smoking, 134; and Africa's economy, 166–7; labour conditions in 19th century, 181, 283; and *emancipados*, 182; frees slaves, 196 and n. 61; 'right of search', 203. 231; rumoured seizure of Cuba, 207; first labour organization, 236 n. 17; steel production, 273; ban 'truck' system, 276; average annual death rate, 284 n. 9; trade dealings with Cuba, 287; investment in Cuba, 510, 1184; and sugar, 532, 536, 537; sells Batista fighters, 1009, 1029; sugar consuming league, 1139; asked for arms, 1242; and missile crisis in U.S., 1402 and n. 50, 1403 and n. 52, 1404, 1407 and nn. 8, 9; press comments, 1407

Enríquez, Segundo, Governor of Las Villas, 1013

Enríquez Ravena, Enrique, chief of secret police, murder, 746 and n. 21

Erice, Pedro Juan de, 82

Escalante, Aníbal ('Cid'), and Communism, 597, 846, 860; ed. *Hoy*, 710, 770, 795; attempted murder, 770–1; on Cuba, 1106; attacks Urrutia, 1230; in China, 1237 n. 5; and the *bourgeoisie*, 1291; and ORI, 1373 and n. 3, 1376, 1377 and n. 21, 1464, 1468; denounced by Castro, 1379, 1380, 1383; in exile, 1381; bid for power, 1381, 1468; disgraced, 1454 n. 4, 1468–9; trial, 1458–9; accusations against, 1468–9

Escalante, César, Communist, 597 and n. 58, 795, 860, 1446 n. 7, 1467; and ORI, 1381; death, 1454 n. 4

Escalona, Arnaldo, 798 and n. 23

Escalona, Arsenio, 889

Escalona, Víctor, 838

Escalona, Dermitio, commander in Pinar del Río, 1072, 1198; and Matos' trial, 1255

Escalona, Dulce María, Under-Sec. of Education, 1340

Escalona, Quique, 908

Escalona Almeida, Rafael, 592 n. 34, 655

Escario, Col., in Santiago, 398; and peace terms, 400

Escobar, Chilean Communist, 727

Escoto, Gustavo, and de Lôme, 359–60; discharged, 492

Escuela Superior de Guerra, 797

Espalza, Pablo de, Banco de Bilbao, 155

Espartero, General, 203, 224

Espeleta, captain-general, 202 n. 12

Espín, Vilma, and 26 July Committee, 868 n. 19, 895 and n. 10; on País, 896 n. 13; in the Sierra, 917, 1001; wife of Raúl, 1251; post-Revolution position, 1432 n. 30

Espiño, José Miguel, Communist, and FONU, 1010; CTC, 1031 n. 45

Espiño, Juan, 122, 187

Estenoz, Evaristo, 514; defeat, 523

Estévez, Juan, 634

Estévez, Marqués de, and slave trade commission, 206

Estévez, Pedro, 302

Estevez Maymir, Col., 1021

Estrada, Arturo, Duque de, 895 and n. 9

Estrada, Pedro, 47

Estrada, Rafael, 1259

Estrada Palma, Tomás, 'president' of rebel republic, 265, 314, 453, 459, 516; capture, 266; and Cuban Junta in N. York, 314, 319, 326, 359; and U.S. recognition of belligerents, 323; resignation, 339, 479; letter to Calixto García, 349; and Cánovas' murder, 350 n. 57; and de Lôme, 360; and 1898 War, 381, 404; and presidential elections (1901), 459–60; (1905), 473, 474; first Cuban president, 460, 471; and Liberal revolt, 475, 477, 479–80; asks for U.S. help, 476–8, 687; and U.S. naval bases, 502; vetoes restoration of lottery, 511–12

Estrampes, Francisco, 227

Evans, Col. de Lacy, 101

exiles, Cuban, in N. York, 242, 250; and Cuba's future, 287; organize *Tuinicú* Cane Sugar Co., 290; and a new revolutionary movement, 294, 300, 301; *La Liga de Instrucción*, 300; Bases of Manresa, 301; league of pro-Cuban citizens, 314–15; and Roosevelt's election, 598; 26 July agents, 946; officers of Cuban Committee, 976 n. 13; and Civil War, 1009; flights over Cuba, 1243, 1264, 1270, 1271; infiltrate into Cuba, 1348; pilots and Battle of Cochinos Bay, 1355, 1385; raids by 'Alpha 66'

exiles – *Cont.*
1386; and missiles in Cuba, 1400, 1413–14 *see also* Junta Cubana

Faber (mulatto) family, 161
Fabregat, Luis, 547 n. 18, 575 n. 24
Facciolo, Eduardo, 218–19, 259 n. 19
Faget, Col. of BRAC, 957 n. 24, 1078
Fajardo, Lieut, 396–7
Fajardo, Dr Luis, 1348
Fajardo, Manuel, aids Castro, 901, 902, 920 n. 49; in the Sierra, 934, 935; accompanies Raúl, 992, 993, 994 n. 27
Falcon, Christopher, 228
Falla Gutiérrez, Laureano, sugar mill owner, 573, 1148, 1150
Famel, Franklin, 290
Fanelli, 249, 302
Fangio, racing motorist, 978
Farley, Archbishop of N. York, 486
Farquhar, Perceval, 444 n. 2, 466, 804, 1489; and electrification of Havana, 463–4, 465 n. 7, 600; railway project, 464, 465
Feijoo de Sotomayor, Camilo, 427
Feito, Armando, 699
Feria, Vasco Porcayo de Figueroa, Duke of, 46–7
Fernández, Lieut Abelardo, 659
Fernández, Angel, Minister of Justice, 1065–6; dismissal, 1225
Fernández, Cáridad, 898
Fernández, Conchita, sec. to Chibás, 751
Fernández, Enrique, 699
Fernández, Dr Eufemio, 755, 888, 1149; chief of secret police, 757, 760, 768, 886, 931; arrest, 883; death, 1365
Fernández, Major Eufemio, 962
Fernández, Major José (El Gallego), 1363, 1366
Fernández, Manolo, and CTC, 1250, 1260
Fernández, Manuel, and MNR, 801 n. 28, 1066; Minister of Labour, 1066; social democrat, 1083; drops out, 1243
Fernández, Marcelo, student leader, 910, 936, 953 and n. 7; national co-ordinator, 991, 1221; anti-Communist period, 1007, 1051, 1221, 1320; and Labour unity, 1007; member Central Committee Communist Party, 1013 n. 49, 1454; opponent of

Guevara, 1013 and n. 49; failure to reorganize 26 July, 1221; drops out, 1290 and n. 41; Guevara and, 1470
Fernández, Omar, 1286, 1003, 1456
Fernández, Pablo Armando, poet, 1110
Fernández, Col. Rigoberto, 528, 529
Fernández, Rodolfo, 1044
Fernandez, Senator Wilfredo, 612, 687
Fernández Bramosio, Antonio (d. 1878), 233 and n. 6
Fernández Cabral, Sergeant, attack on, 817 and n. 70
Fernández Ceballos, Rev. Raúl, *Fidelista*, 936 n. 13, 946, 988
Fernández Concheso, Aurelio, Cuban ambassador, 641 n. 22; in Washington, 730; received by Stalin, 731; Minister of Education, 861 and n. 58
Fernández de Batista, Marta, 791; 2nd wife of Fulgencio, 845 and n. 1, 1026; in Washington, 845
Fernández de Castro, Autonomist, 357, 456 n. 56
Fernández de Castro, José Antonio, 566 n. 11, 567 n. 13
Fernández Mascaró, Guillermo, 573
Fernández Ortega, Dr Eufemio, 741
Fernández Sánchez, Leonardo, 589, 751 n. 39, 820
Fernández Suero, Col., 1025; flight, 1027
Fernández Supervielle, Manuel, Minister of Finance, 743 n. 10; mayor of Havana, 749, 753; suicide, 753–4
Fernandina Herrera, Gonzalo José, Conde de, grandee, 32 n. 22, 63 n. 15, 143, 202, 206, 427
Ferrara, Orestes, 422, 1492 and n. 25; Liberal rebel, 475, 528; and Ports Co., 506; law of 'National Defence', 508; in Washington, 528, 559–60; and sugar crisis, 547–8; ed. *Heraldo de Cuba*, 555, 628; and Machado, 570, 572–3, 623, 624, 679; and Sumner Welles, 606, 609, 619–20, 621; in London, 608; his proposals, 621, 622; escapes by air, 625; joins officers, 653; and anti-Americanism, 687; returns, 708
Ferrer, Col. Horacio, dissident officer, 623, 675 n. 39; war minister, 629 n. 15, 638; and Céspedes, 640, 1055; and Welles, 645; asks for U.S. intervention, 651

GGG

Ferrer, Ramón, 1359, 1369 n. 41
Ferrer, Capt. Raimundo, 658
Ferrer, Segundo, 926
Fesser, Eduardo, 123
Fiallo, Amalio, 866 n. 13, 870
Fiallo, René, 781
Fiallo Sánchez, Ubaldo, 945
Figueras, Wilfredo, 874
Figueredo, Carlos, 979 nn. 28, 31; and
    G.2, 1321 n. 30
Figueredo, Dr Félix, 267
Figuerdo, Pedro (Perucho), 242, 245
Figueredo, Luis, 243
Figueres, President of Costa Rica, 759,
    950, 1058, 1204
Figuero, Sotero, 301
Finlay, Carlos (1833–1915), 641 n. 23;
    and source of yellow fever, 46 and n.
    80, 1062
Finlay, Carlos, son of above, 650, 661
Fish, Hamilton (1808–93), Sec. of
    State, 250 n. 12, 261; Cuban policy,
    250, 251, 253, 257, 261, 264, 270; on
    anti-slavery law, 257
Fish, Hamilton, grandson of above,
    390
Fiske, John, 311
Fleitas, Felix, and Escalante, 1469
Fleming, Robert, 466
Flores Magón, Enrique, Mexican Com-
    munist, and Camagüey meeting, 577
Fomin, Aleksander, 1411
Fonseca, Carlos, 896 n. 15
Font, Antonio, 157
Font, Ernesto, 351
Foraker, Senator J. B., and rebel
    government, 375–6; amendment to
    Army Bill, 438–9, 463, 464; and U.S.
    occupation, 443; and Platt Amend-
    ment, 453, 1419; and Cuba, 482
    criticism of his law, 600
Forbes, Paul, 251, 252–3
Forcade, Pedro, 137, 157
Forcade, Tina, 624
Ford, James W., 712
Fordham, (Sir) Alfred Stanley (1907–),
    British ambassador, 987 and n. 69
Fordney, Joseph, 553
Forsyth, John, 199 and n. 15
Fortescue, Sir John, and Saint Dom-
    ingue, 76 and n. 19
Fortuny, Mario, 852
Foster, John, 289
Fowler family, 140

Fraginals, Amaury, union leader, 1349
    n. 21; anti-Castro protest, 1349 and
    n. 21; expelled from union, 1350;
    capture and escape, 1350 n. 22
Franca, Porfirio, and Banco Nacional,
    549; and sergeants' revolt, 638–9,
    642; resignation, 647; and Grau, 655
Franco, General Francisco (1892–), 328,
    868, 1254
Frank, Waldo, 1277
Franklin, Benjamin, 211; and fall of
    Havana, 42–3
Franqui, Carlos, and Carteles, 863, 868,
    1076 n. 41; Fidelistas, 868 and nn. 18,
    19, 889 n. 59, 901 n. 53; organizes
    Revolución, 868, 1032, 1076 n. 41,
    1281, 1342, 1455 n. 10; and 'social-
    ism', 921 n. 53; Communist, 927;
    arrest, 942; and Nat. Liberation
    Council, 968; ed. Cubano Libre, 980;
    radio news reader, 980 n. 36, 1011;
    and Law I, 1011 n. 32; and Com-
    munism, 1051, 1221, 1319
Freeman, Frederick, 141 and n. 21
Freeman, William ('Frank'), 1311 and
    n. 54
Frente Cívico Revolucionaria Demo-
    crático (Junta of Unity), founder
    members, 1003, 1030, 1065; demands,
    1003; combines opposition, 1003–4;
    financial resources, 1004 n. 32;
    dissensions, 1005 n. 1; Havana
    meeting, 1006; and union with
    Communists, 1006
Fresquet, Rufo López, 862, 943 n. 3; on
    Cienfuegos, 1050 n. 10; on Castro's
    plans, 1060; Finance Minister, 1065
    and n. 2, 1068 and n. 6, 1221, 1252–3,
    1270; and tax evasion, 1201; in U.S.,
    1029; tax reform law, 1220, 1228,
    1235; and Communism in Cuba,
    1241; and Pazos, 1246–7; and the
    regime, 1253, 1258; and Lazo's offer
    of planes, etc., 1270–1; resignation,
    1271
Frexas, Pablo, 159
Freyre, Fernando, 812 and n. 45, 814 n.
    57, 819 n. 79
Freyre de Andrade, General Fernando
    (1863–1929), judge in Havana, 422;
    and Gómez, 438; and 1905 elections,
    473
Freyre de Andrade, María Teresa,
    director National Library, 1343

Frías, Lieut Ciro, 920 n. 49, 934 n. 4, 936, 992, 993; death, 923, 993 and n. 26

Frías, Francisco de, Conde de Pozos Dulces, 208 n. 10; and *anexionismo*, 208; conspiracy against Spain, 218–19; his 'Order of the Lone Star', 219

Frondízi, President of Argentina, 1290

Frost, Robert, 1397 and n. 11

Froude, James Anthony (1818–94), in Cuba, 286 and n. 15, 413

Frye, Alexis, and Wood's school reforms, 446–7

Fuentes, Justo, 761–2, 762 n. 8, 813, 817

Fuentes, Mario, 899

Fuertes, Carlos María, 592 n. 35; murder, 607

Fuertes, Juan Luis, 592 and n. 35

Fuertes, Manuel, 595

Fulbright, Senator, and U.S.-Cuban relations, 1237; opposes invasion plan, 1308–9, 1309, 1370

Gadea, Hilda, 880

Gagarin, Major Yuri, 1372

Gaitán, Jorge Eliécer, 815 and n. 59, 816

Gaitskell, Hugh, and missile crisis, 1407

Galarza, Vicente de (later Conde), 268 n. 11, 303; follower of Campos, 268

Galich, Manuel, and Cuban press, 1479 n. 13

Galíndez, Major Ignacio, rated 2nd Lieut, 646 n. 37; and November revolt, 667; in command Columbia, 725; replaced, 745

Galíndez, Jesús, Basque Nationalist, murder, 833

Gallenga, *Times* correspondent, 181, 187, 262 and n. 34; and slave imports and prices, 235 n. 14, 236

Galván, General Jesús, president of rebel republic, 267

Gálvez, José María, prime minister of home rule government, 356, 381

Gálvez, William, commander at Matanzas, 1072, 1461 and n. 32; inspector-general, 1198 n. 18; in Peking, 1280, 1315

Gans, Oscar, Cuban ambassador in U.S., 762; in Prío's cabinet, 764 n. 13, 775

Gaona, Antonio, 580

García, Antonio, 130

García, Bernardo, police chief, 724–5

García, Calixto, 1408, 1455 n. 6; in Mexico, 878, 887 n. 47; in Cuba, 899, 901; in the Sierra, 901 n. 53, 916, 936; commander in Matanzas, 1198 n. 18

García, General Calixto, leads fresh rising, 269, 306; and Independence War (1895), 319, 339, 345–7, 351, 398; refuses truce offer, 378; U.S. negotiations, 386, 388; and U.S. landing, 391; and peace terms, 400; and U.S. occupation, 403, 410; hands over to shadow government, 404; in N. York, 412; death, 412; state funeral 421

García, Guillermo, and Castro, 899 and nn. 38, 42, 900 and n. 50, 901, 902, 920 n. 49; Lieut under Sotús, 934 n. 4, 935; at El Uveró, 939; attacks *Estrada Palma*, 958 and n. 29; and Matos' trial, 1255; and ORI, 1377 n. 19; and new Communist party, 1454 n. 5

García, Manuel, 302 and n. 27, 303; death, 319

García, Menéndez, 1159

García, Col. Pilar, 840 n. 31; chief of police, 983; flight from Cuba, 1026, 1029; asylum in U.S., 1077

García, Reynol, anti-Batista plot, 885; excluded from CTC, 1250

García, General Vicente, and peace terms, 266; commander-in-chief, 267

García Agüero, Salvador, and PUR, 706–7; senator, 747

García Bárcena, Rafael, 754 n. 48, 822, 1054; student, 592 n. 35, 638; forms MNR, 796–7, 825, 866 n. 13, 867, 1320; arrest, torture, etc., 801 and n. 28; presidential candidate, 970 n. 32

García Buchaca, Edith, Communist, 931 n. 32, 1319; and Council of Culture, 1342, 1467; and Rodríguez, 1467, 1468 n. 50; house arrest, 1468

García Capote, Domingo, sugar mill, *Santo Domingo*, 427

García Casones, General (air force), 1023

García de Arboleya, 168 n. 3, 169, 174 n. 30

García Inclan, Guido, radio commentator, 1435

García Kohly, 487

García Lorca, 1076, 1080, 1124, 1343
García Montes, Jorge, and Machado's
debts, 716; and Batista, 790, 1026;
prime minister, 860–1, 861 n. 58, 890;
and Smith, 964
García Montes, Oscar, 731; in Washington, 723 n. 34, 728, 730; and
Batista's cabinet, 724; vice-president,
790
García Olayón, Capt. Alejandro, chief
of naval intelligence, 889, 924; and
naval mutiny, 963
García Pedroso, Sergeant Gonzalo,
rated Lieut, 646 n. 37; head of
police, 667
García Sierra, Carlos, 595
García Tuñón, General, protests to
Batista, 785; in Chile, 839; proposes
military junta, 976
García Tuñón, Capt. Jorge, and army
conspiracy, 779
García Vélez, General Carlos, 484 n.
18; protest movement, 567, 568
Gardner, Arthur, U.S. ambassador, and
Alemán, 758 n. 60, 845; and Batista,
845, 947; treatment of Communists,
846; and BRAC, 855 1078; replace-
ment, 947; in Washington, 947–8,
1030 n. 43; and CIA, 949 n. 20; and
intervention, 960; fear of Commun-
ism, 1061; evidence to Security Sub-
committee, 1297
Garibaldi, Giuseppe, 220, 306, 1055
Garney, Michael L., 934
Gaudí, Antonio, 498
Gaunauro, Julio, 593
Gaztelu, Fr Angel, 982
Gelabert, José, and 'Hope of Asabiaca'
coffee, 128 and n. 3
Ghezo, King of Dahomey, slave trade
income, 159
Ghioldi, Rodolfo, Argentine Com-
munist, 697
Gibson, Hugh, U.S. chargé d'affaires,
510
Gil, Arturo, 751 n. 39, 920 n. 50, 923 n.
63
Gil, Capt. Gabriel, 1024 and n. 19
Gil, Manuel de Jesús Alfonso, 945
Gill, Wilson, 447
Gilly, Adolfo, 1408 and n. 16
Gimperly, Col, military attaché, 614,
618, 628
Ginjaume, José de Jesús, 817 nn. 70, 71

Giral sisters, 1000
Gispert, Francisco, 427
Glawe, Col, U.S. military attaché, and
Wieland, 1239 and n. 12
Godínez, Elisa, wife of Batista, 636, 703
n. 36; divorce, 845 n. 1
Godkin, E. L., ed. Evening Post, 313,
356, 366, 450; on de Lôme, 361; and
Cuban independence, 450
Godoy, Gastón, 856, 874, 889, 1026
Goicuría, Domingo (1804–70), 226 n.
43; expedition to Cuba, 226, 257; and
Civil War, 226 n. 43; and independ-
ence, 227; and Walker, 227, 228;
capture and death, 257
Goicoechea, Fermín, 542
Goldenbert, Boris, 1484; and MSR,
741–2, 754, 769; and gangsterism,
769; and full employment, 1425 n. 8
Goliat, Gilberto, 752
Gómez, César, 894 n. 5, 899 n. 41; sec.
Communist Youth, 926 n. 8
Gómez, Francisco, 344, 345
Gómez, Joaquín, 132, 136 n. 1, 137,
154, 156; Royal Bank director, 136 n.
1, 156, 195; sugar mills, 136 n. 1,
156; mason, 156; and Tacón, 195,
199; and slave trade commission, 206
Gómez, General José Miguel (1858–
1921), 448 n. 24, 456 n. 56, 526, 569,
686; civil governor Santa Clara, 422,
473; Republican leader, 447; supports Palma, 459; and elections, 473,
489–90, 527, 547, 549; and Platt
Amendment, 474; and Liberal revolt,
475, 528, 529, 682; hostility towards
Zayas, 484, 509; and law reform, 487;
succeeds Magoon, 497, 504; presidency, 504, 559, 701; issue of illegal
contracts, 504–5; presidential palace,
505; use of graft (chivo), 505; public
works scandals, 506–7, 510–11; revival of violence under, 507–9;
allocates Zapata privileges, 509–10;
and Negro revolt (1912), 510; legacy
to Cuba, 511–13; compared with
Menocal, 525; capture, 529; release,
534; and sugar crisis, 547–8; death,
551; and the army, 680
Gómez, Juan Gualberto (1854–1930),
mulatto, 293 n. 3, 448 n. 24, 524,
1121, 1433; and racial questions, 293,
303 n. 32, 419; and Independence
War (1895), 306, 307, 309, 316, 321;

Gómez, Juan Gualberto – *Cont.*
and Maximo, 438; demands Wood's recall, 452; denounces Platt Amendment, 454, 456 n. 56; and railways, 465; and 1902 Congressional elections, 473; and Liberal revolt, 475; and Negro revolutionaries, 522, 523; and Menocal, 571; *Por Qué Somos Separatistas*, 303

Gómez, Leonel, 811–12

Gómez, Maximo (1836–1905), 448 n. 24; outstanding rebel leader, 255 and n. 7, 256, 258, 267, 339, 345, 347; invasion plan, 260, 264; and Maceo's defamation, 265; and a new rising (1879), 269, 294; relations with Martí, 297; commander new revolutionary war (1895), 302, 305, 306; and Maura's scheme, 304; general-in-chief, 319, 320, 321, 326, 328; after Weyler's arrival, 331, 333–4, 337, 339, 344, 345–6; and Maceo's death, 344; war aims, 344–5; loss of following, 349; in Remedios, 351; and Spanish amnesty, 353; refuses Blanco's alliance, 378–9; welcomes U.S. intervention, 379; in charge of army, 412; entry into Havana, 421; ignored by U.S. occupiers, 437; proposed deposition, 438; Wood and, 445; and Nationalist Party, 447; and constitutional convention, 449, 453; and elections (1901), 459; death, 473 n. 2

Gómez, Miguel Mariano (son of José Miguel Gómez), president, accepts Welles' mediation, 610; Machado and, 612; and Grau, 642, 654, 655; mayor of Havana, 671, 678, 679; election, 701–2; and military character of schools, 702, 704; presidency, 702–4; character, 703; dismisses military reservists, 703–4

Gómez Brothers, and Castro, 825 and n. 8.

Gómez Bermejo, Francisco, terrorist, 945

Gómez Calvo, Judge, 1227

Gómez Calvo, Jesús, takes over navy, 725

Gómez de Criado, Francisco, 427

Gómez Ochoa, Delio, *Fidelistas* and Ortodoxo, opposes union with Communists, 1006, 1007; Dominican landing, 1228

Gómez Wangüermert, Luis, 927 n. 13, 929; ed. *El Mundo*, 1263

Gonzales, William, U.S. Minister, 527 and n. 7, 533

González, Andrés, 1028

González, Angel Anselmo, naval chief of staff, 725

González, Sergeant Basilio, 669

González, Cándido, 877 and n. 47, 894 n. 5, 1046

González, Cecilio, 264

González, Evélida, 875 and n. 40

González, Fernández y, 238

González, Ignacio, political gangster, 883, 925, 945; and Palace attack, 928, 929

González, Marqués, 10

González, Pastor, shoemaker, 1012

González, Fr Pastor, 982, 983

González, 'Pancho', 899 and n. 38, 900 n. 52, 901 n. 53

González Comejo, Luciano, Communist, 826

González Cartas, Jesús (El Extraño), and ARG, 741, 746 n. 21; 754; political gangster, 883, 885, 886, 1031; arrest, 950; returns to Cuba, 1031

González Carvajal, Ladislao, Communist, University control, 743 n. 9; and JUCEI, 1337

González Corzo, Rogelio, Mgr; Director of Agriculture, 1083, 1275; anti-Castro conspirator, 1275; terrorist campaign, 1348; betrayal and death, 1349, 1365

González Finales, Major, 1021; defection, 1040

González Lanoza, José Antonio, 421–2, 422 n. 26

González Larriñaga, 82, 134, 1159

González Llorente, Pedro, 449, 456 n. 56

González de Paloma, María Antonio, Cuban exile, 881 and n. 23, 887 n. 47

González y Torstall, 185

Goodwin, Richard, 1385 n. 3, 1386

Gordon, Capt. Nathaniel, 231 and n. 61

Gorki, Maxim, 578

Gosham, Major, 12–13, 17, 46

Goulart, President of Brazil, 1386

Govín, Antonio, 356

Govín, Félix, 294

Govín, Rafael, 466

Gramero, Francisco, 660
Granados, Dr, 655
Granados, María García, Martí and (*La Niña de Guatemala*), 296 and n. 9
Grangham, E., 545
Granma, the, 925; purchase of, 891; sails from Tuxpan, 892, 894; complement and armaments, 894 and n. 1; off Oriente, 895; Cuban landing, 897; Grant, (Sir) Alexander, 49 n. 31, 56
Grant, General Ulysses (1822–85), U.S. president, 250, 261; Cuban policy, 251, 253, 257, 270, 367 n. 1; and annexation of Santo Domingo, 253; and Monroe doctrine, 627
Grau, Francisco, 729 n. 3, 753
Grau San Martín, Dr Ramón (1887–1969), Dean of Medical Faculty, 638; and sergeants' revolt, 638, 639, 654; and a new government, 640, 642; and the presidency, 647, 648, 650–1; character and appearance, 650; cabinet, 650, 651–2, 661, 664, 743 and n. 10, 744; and Welles, 654–5; rapprochement with Batista, 662, 664; and Caffery, 674 n. 34; proposed resignation, 674–6; leaves for Mexico, 677, 695; communist condemnation, 697–8; in exile, 706, 711; a threat to Batista, 709; and elections, 718 and n. 12, 722, 735–6, 756–7, 773, 852, 853, 857, 860, 951, 956, 966, 977, 1014; corrupt presidency, 737, 739 ff., 757–8, 759; and revolutionary groups, 741, 743, 1055; reorganizes the army, 745–6; attempted assassination, 746; acts of spoilage, 747, 761; wins Congress majority, 748–9; growing apprehension, 753; accusations against, 761, 764, 796; indictment, 768; leader of Auténticos, 800–1; and anti-Batista meeting 870; and the *puros*, 884 n. 35; estimate of casualties, 1044 n. 21; subject of purge, 1046; black senators, 1121; after Revolution, 1201, 1208; pro-democracy, 1236; not recognized by U.S., 1419; death in Havana, 1471 n. 66
Grau, Col., 1088
Grau, Paulina Alsina de, sec. to the Presidency and sister-in-law and mistress of Grau, 739 and n. 3; influence, 743

Grechko, Marshal, in Cuba, 1438
Greeley, Horace, 220, 257
Green, William, 585
Greene, General, 404
Greene, Gardiner, 131–2
Gregson, William, 4 n. 17, 84 n. 55
Grindberg, Yotshka, 577 and n. 36
Grobart, Fabio, Communist, 577, 633 n. 36, 692, 1081; link with Comintern, 578; arrest and imprisonment, 597; leaves Cuba, 846 and n. 4; and new Communist party, 1454 and n. 3
Gromyko, Andrey, in N. York, 1400 n. 32; assurances to Kennedy, 1404 and n. 59; and missile crisis, 1411
Guadeloupe, 49, 116; and slave trade, 50 n. 35, 51 and n. 43, 52 n. 47, 53 n. 49, 55 n. 57; and sugar, 54, 120 n. 39; retains French law, 55; English and N. American imports, 55; free ports, 64; British conquest, 85
Guantánamo Bay, U.S. base, 449 n. 29, 502, 728, 992, 1354
Guardia, Vicente de la, 427
Guas Inclán, Rafael, 1029 n. 38; and Batista's cabinet, 8, 13 n. 41; and vice-presidency, 858; and the peers, 912; and 1958 elections, 952
Guas Pasquerra, General, 858
Guasimal, 1009
Guatemala, railway, 466, 467 n. 18, 769, 1228; population figures, 503, 1093 n. 6; Communist party, 579; and U.S. intervention, 644 n. 31; overthrow of Arbenz's government, 855, 879, 1015 n. 59, 1060, 1206 and n. 45, 1302, 1304; Cuban exiles, 878, 1276; Guevara and, 879–80, 937; guerrilla warfare, 941; illiteracy, 1131; CIA, 1276 and n. 10; guerrilla training 1283, 1294, 1301, 1302 and n. 9, 1304, 1305; publishes news of invasion, 1301; rebel elation, 1310; criticism of Cuban press, 1479 and n. 13
Güell, Dr, Foreign Minister, 982; premier, 983; leaves Cuba, 1026
Güell y Ferrer, Juan, and Catalan cotton industry, 155
Guerra, Benjamín, 315, 381
Guerra, Eutimio, traitor, 915, 916–17, 920 n. 49; peasant bandit, 915; shot, 923
Guerra, Faustino, *see* Pino Guerra

Guerra, Félix Oscar, gangster, 883 and n. 31

Guerra, José Antonio (son of Ramiro Guerra), student, 592 n. 35, 641 n. 22; and IMF, 1205; and Agrarian Reform law, 1215; leaves National Bank, 1252

Guerra, Col. Miguel, in command Campo Columbia, 666, 667

Guerra, Ramiro, 592 n. 35, 1058; on Magoon, 483; backs Machado, 570, 622; and his resignation, 624, 625; *Azúcar y Población*, 1343

Guerrero, Capt., surrenders Remedios, 1023

Guerrero, Francisco, and Indians, 1526-7

Guerrilla warfare, effective policy against, 329-30, 940-1; struggles of 1950s, 842 n. 40; training for, 877, 878, 882 (*see also* Guatemala); and older blood feuds, 937; Sierra tactics, 938, 939; Communist group, 981; place of civic resistance, 1045 and n. 23; and Latin America, 1294, 1375; post-Revolution activity, 1471; death of *guerrilleros* since 1962, 1471 and n. 68; training of foreign recruits, 1478; *see also* Sierra Maestra

Guevara, Alfredo, Communist, 822, 1214; at Havana University, 810, 814, 817, 923; director ICAIC, 1342, 1464

Guevara, Ernesto ('Che') (1927-67), 634 n. 1, 878 n. 13, 1234, 1436, 1477, 1487 n. 13; meets Castro, 878 and n. 14, 881 and n. 23; family background, 878-9, 880-1; education, 879; political beginnings and philosophy, 879, 880, 1049, 1094, 1272, 1319; in Guatemala, 878-80, 1060, 1195; and the U.S., 880 and n. 18, 1077, 1272 and n. 1, 1273, 1285; in Mexico, 880; arrest, 880 n. 20, 887; *guerrillero*, 881 and n. 26; and *Granma's* complement, 894 and nn. 1, 2; in Cuba, 899 and n. 38, 900 and n. 52; with Castro in Sierra, 901 and n. 53, 902-3, 913, 914-16, 920 n. 49, 921, 939, 958, 974, 987, 996 n. 2; influence on him, 921, 955, 990, 1048, 1195, 1471; asthma, 923, 1470 n. 60; and new recruits, 934, 935, 937, 938; temperament and character, 937, 1008, 1042, 1043, 1319; at El Uvero, 939, 940; and

Castro's manifesto, 954-5; attack on Bueyceto, 958-9; contact with Communists, 981, 1009; and *operación verano*, 997 n. 6; Las Villas expedition, 1005, 1008, 1012, 1013, 1020, 1041-2; and 26 July, 1013; pact with Directorio, 1017; captures Placetas, 1020 and n. 4; and Remedios, 1023; brilliant strategy, 1021, 1042; demands surrender, 1027-8; in command Havana, 1029; revolutionary 'hero', 1032, 1033, 1428, 1471, 1490; and Communism and Communists, 1048 and n. 1, 1049, 1078, 1082, 1090 and n. 52, 1214, 1222, 1319; and Agrarian Reform, 1049, 1252, 1272; new military-cultural school, 1072; in Escambray, 1195 n. 4; Algerian speech on the Revolution (1963), 1226 and n. 43; world tour, 1231, 1242, 1469 n. 55; on Cuban Revolution, 1292, 1319, 1378, 1423; ultimatum to Lobo, 1298-9; in Prague, 1316; Peking reception, 1316; and Ministry of Industries, 1333-5, 1374, 1382; lesson from imperialism, 1356; dislike of Escalante's party, 1376; and ORI, 1377 n. 17; in Moscow, 1396; and nuclear war threat, 1417 and n. 55; obsessive hatred of bourgeois democracy, 1423; use of word 'socialism', 1423; and the 'new man', 1446, 1490; disappearance from political scene, 1446, 1469 and n. 55; death, 1469, 1478; quarrel with Castro, 1469 and n. 55; in Bolivia, 1453 n. 1, 1469 n. 55, 1476, 1478, 1481; assessment, 1469-71; and use of violence, 1470 and n. 60, 1479; economic dogmatisms, 1470-1; attacked by Orthodox Communists, 1478; publication of Bolivian diaries, 1478-9; and Vietnam, 1480; *Guerrilla Warfare*, 1040 and n. 11, 1045 n. 23, 1277; *El socialismo y el hombre en Cuba*, 1423 and n. 1, 1465, 1490

Guevara Lynch, Ernesto, father of 'Che', 878, 1079

Guevara, Olga, 1011

Guggenheim, Harry F. (1890-), U.S. ambassador in Cuba, 590 and n. 22, 591; and Machado, 595; attacked by *Alma Mater*, 605; and Batista, 960 n. 33

Guillén, Nicolás, Communist mulatto poet, 1080, 1123 and n. 22, 1124, 1225 n. 37; and Spanish Civil War, 703, 1081; president 'Writers' Union', 1464

Guillén, in *Granma*, 894

'Guillermon', 254

Guisa de Miranda, 1012, 1016

Guitart, Renato, 836 n. 9, 837 and n. 20

Guiteras, Antonio, 592 n. 33, 658; and Grau's cabinet, 650, 661, 671, 675; background and character, 650; accuses government, 664, 676; growing strength, 665; organizes general strike, 676; leaves for Oriente, 677; bomb incidents, 691; Jove Cuba, 695, 699–700, 741, 750; Communist condemnation, 697–8; death, 700, 736, 754, 793; vengeance for, 700; revolutionary hero, 1462

Gullón, Pío, Spanish Foreign Minister, 367; reply to U.S. note, 354; and peace efforts, 369, 372, 377

'Guralsky', 697

Gurbich, Félix, 577

Gurney, Joseph, 161 and n. 27

Gutiérrez, Alfonso, 868, 894 n. 6

Gutiérrez, Gonzalo, 595

Gutiérrez, José Manuel, signs Montreal document, 802 n. 29, 843 n. 41; and Brigade 2506, 1360

Gutiérrez, Mestre, 1238

Gutiérrez, Juan, 596

Gutiérrez, Dr Viriato, sugar proposals, 561, 542 n. 11; and Machado's cabinet, 573; denounces Cuban-U.S. sugar deal, 730

Gutiérrez de la Concha, captain-general, 226, 263; and Pinto's conspiracy, 226–7, 227 n. 45; and slave trade, 227; military cadres, 248

Gutiérrez Fernández, Félix, and Batista, 1016 n. 64

Gutiérrez Menoyo, Carlos, Spanish exile; arrest, 883; opposition group, 925; and Palace attack, 926, 927, 928, 929, 979 n. 31, 1005; death, 929

Gutiérrez Menoyo, Eloy, and N. Cuba landing, 979 n. 31; 980; attempt to murder Castro, 979 n. 31; leader of 'second Front', 1005; in Las Villas, 1013; and anti-Castro plot, 1238

Guziñan, Eduardo, 475

Guzmán, Fr, 1022

Guzmán, Governor, frees Indians, 1526

Haiti, 448 and n. 25, 1124, 1558; slave leaders, 76; revolution, 76, 89, 91, 104; sugar trade, 76–8, 87 n. 11, 729; immigrants from, 129, 131, 241 and n. 37, 431, 524, 525, 540, 684; coffee production, 131 n. 16; and annexation to U.S., 291; Luders case, 343 n. 32; Communist party, 579, 697; U.S. rule, 626; raid on Mirama embassy, 890; population figures, 1093 n. 3, 1093–4, 1513; practice of voodoo, 1125, illiteracy, 1131; primitive Indians, 1515, 1520, 1523, 1524, 1526

Hanna, Lieut, new public school, 446, 460

Hanna, Mark, 352, 421, 445, 456, 1170

Harding, Warren G., U.S. president, 548, 551

Hardwicke, Philip Yorke, 1st Earl of, 42

Hart, Armando, and MNR, 801 n. 28, 1067, 1432 n. 30; and 26 July, 868, 889 n. 59, 957 n. 24, 1067, 1454 n. 5; in the Sierra, 917; and Civic Resistance, 918 v. 40; attitude to Communism, 944 and n. 8, 1267; and *Nuestra Razon*, 953 and n. 7; and Miami Pact, 969; and Urrutia as president, 970–1; arrest, 975; and Barquín, 1209; imprisonment, 1053, 1054; use of 1898 and 1933 imagery, 1053 n. 20; Minister of Education, 1067, 1252, 1253, 1340; reorganizes education, 1340; and ORT, 1377 n. 20; ideological director of Revolution, 1454

Hart, Enrique, 868 n. 19, 936; arrest, 942; death, 1066 n. 5

Hart, Judge Enrique (father of the above and Armando Hart), succeeds Menéndez, 1347

Hast, Lieut., and HMS *Pylades*, 1537

Hatuey, Chief, 1350 n. 24, 1524

Havana, used by Spanish treasure ships, 1, 12 and n. 2, 64; strategic importance, 1; population figures, 1, 12 and n., 109 n. 3, 136, 144, 424, 429, 497, 1095, 1096–7; English expedition, 1–2, 5 and n. 27, 6–7, 10–11; commercial activities, 12; cosmopolitan, semi-criminal character, 12; mixed blood inhabitants, 12–13, 16 n. 5; architectural features, 13, 143, 146, 433, 873; religious buildings, 13, 16,

Havana – *Cont.*
71; grandees' houses and palaces, 17, 146; dirt and disease, 17, 146; place-name origin, 22 and n. 23, 1511; and sugar industry, 27, 30–1; resident merchant class, 30; decline of ship-yard, 31 n. 16, 64; sacked by slaves, 38; English occupation, 39, 42, 47–8, 56; extent of jurisdiction, 48 and n. 23; arrival of English merchants and goods, 49, 55–64, 95 n. 11; involve-ment in slave trade, 49–50, 51, 69, 95 n. 11, 95, 161, 170, 176, 200, 201; ships entering, 51, 136; disposition of English imports, 53 and n. 50; election of mayor (*alcaldes ordinarios*), 53, 149; land prices, 63; refortifica-tion, 63, 67; trade with Spanish ports, 64 and n. 18; becomes a bishopric, 71 and n. 55; intellectual activity, 72, 73 and n. 5; influx of capital and foreign merchants, 80–1, 98; and abolition, 94; decline in sugar plantations, 118 n. 32; railway warehouses, 123; hotels and restaurants, 141, 145–6, 340, 343, 498, 500, 933, 1098, 1344, 1424; street names, 143–4; city life, 144–5, 287, 288, 498; street life, 146; the lottery (*see under*), 150 and n. 62; oligarchic families, 152, 1110; bar-racoons, etc., 65–6; outbreak of violence, 193, 194, 293; construction of the Paseo, 195; tobacco factory (*El Figaro*), 237; in charge of volunteer forces, 252; death-rate, 284 n. 6; schools, 286 n. 13; beggars, 287; brothels and prostitutes, 287, 1097 and n. 34; seediness in 1890s, 299; rebel numbers (1895), 324; and Independence War, 329, 330, 339, 345, 357; first home rule government, 356; opposes autonomy, 358, 363; post-war conditions, 422–3, 437; armed forces (1907), 490 n. 42; American influences and residents, 497–8, 500–1; and Negro rising (1912), 523; in World War I, 532; anti-Machado demonstrations, 617; under Grau, 653, 664; November revolt, 667, 669; town and gown violence, 698; conference on World War II, 723 and n. 28; effect of new wealth, 765; reaction to Castro, 866, 898, 932; Palace attack, 926–32;

professional gangsters, 972, continu-ing sabotage, 975, 978, 1009–10; 9 April strike, 990; arrest of 26 July members, 1010; resistance activities, 1016, 1097–8; after Batista's flight, 1028–9; behaviour of *barbudos*, 1033; arrival of Castro, 1033–4; old city, 1097; Pogolotti quarter, 1099; im-migrant numbers, 1100; medical and dental services, 1105, 1106; priest-hood, 1128 n. 5; newspapers, 1136; airport, 1162–3; port workers, 1179; Plaza Cívica meeting (1959), 1234–5, 1237; leaflet bombing, 1245–6; Soviet exhibition, 1263; arrest of Americans, 1278; Western embassies, 1314; posi-tion of *Habana Libre*, 1344–5; U.S. bombing, 1355–6; Castro's speech, 1358; unemployment, 1426; Cultural Congress, 1968, 1473; Second Declar-ation, 1476

Havemeyer, Henry Osborne, 289 n. 31, 464; his sugar group, 289–90, 336

Havemeyer, Horace, 552

Hawley, Congressman R. B., sugar mill, *Chaparra*, 467–8; and Cuban Ameri-can, 532, 549; buys *Tinguaro* and *Mercedita*, 1148

Hawley-Smoot tariff (1929), 561, 694

Hay, John (1838–1905), Sec. of State, 404 and n. 13, 417; letter to Roose-velt, 404; Colombian plan 468 n. 26

Haya de la Torre, Víctor, his APRA, 566, 579

Hayes, Rutherford (1822–93), U.S. President, 272

Hazard, Samuel, 124, 133, 146, 150, 1094

Hearst, William Randolph (1863–1951), *N.Y. Journal* and Cuban War, 313, 326, 331, 333, 337, 351–2, 356; ideology, 313; and atrocity stories, 331, 336, 341, 351; Cuban rep-resentatives, 340; and rescue of Miss Cisneros, 353; and Spanish War, 358, 361, 365–6, 368–9, 371, 374, 379, 384–5; and de Lôme, 360, 361; and sinking of *Maine*, 361–2, 363, 366, 371; senatorial expedition to Cuba, 366, 369; in Cuba, 391–2; at San Juan, 394, 397; and Cuban atrocity, 398; accuses Pulitzer, 406 and n. 19; imperialism, 419

Hedges family, 946, 959, 1114–15

Hedges, Burke, 1115, 1165

GGG*

Hedges, Dayton, 1110, 1114, 1165
Hellman, Paul, 1077
Hemenway, Augustus, sugar mill, *San Jorge*, 140 and n. 16
Hemingway, Ernest, on Matthews, 918–19; in Cuba (1959), 1065 and n. 1; 'The Shot', 742 n. 8
Hendel, sergeant Matías, 646
Henderson, Robert, cane harvester, 1439 and n. 13
Heredia y Campuzano, José María de (1803–39), Cuban poet, 102 and n. 40, 207 n. 1; Tacón and, 197; *Ode to Niagara*, 102 n. 40
Herick, Myron, 367
Hermida, Ramón, student, 592 n. 33; and Batista, 778, 783 and n. 20, 784; Tabernilla and, 839; visits Castro in prison, 856–7; resignation, 857
Hernández, Armando, 1260
Hernández, Col Blas, and Batista, 637, 849; bandit army, 655, 656, 681; and November revolt, 668; death, 669
Hernández, Col, 1027
Hernández, Col Cándido, 963
Hernández, Col Charles, 386
Hernández, José, 300
Hernández, José Elias, 226 and n. 44
Hernández, Mariana, 427
Hernández, Mario Alfonso, 634; rated Lieut, 646 n. 37; and November revolt, 669
Hernández, Melba, 827 n. 18, 836, 838, 847, 848 n. 8, 888 n. 55, 891
Hernández, Lieut Miguel, 667
Hernández, Dr Nicolás ('Colacho'), and army conspiracy, 779 n. 11, 784; and Batista's government, 783 n. 20, 798; Tabernilla and, 839
Hernández, 'Pipi', 883, 1360
Hernández Bauzá, Miguel, member of *diálogo cívico*, 874
Hernández Cartaya, 567
Hernández Lovio, Pedro, and *Diario*, 1280
Hernández Nardo, General, 1122
Hernández Tellaheche, Arturo, 843 n. 41; counter-revolutionary, 1238; shot, 1365
Herrera family, *cafetal* and sugar mill owners, *La Gratitud*, *Sansom* and *Union*, 132, 152, 153; entitled Marqués de Almendares and Villalta, Condes de Jibacoa and Fernandina, 143

Herrera, General, 617; Machado and, 572; at Welles' mediation talks, 611; and his new plan, 621–2; president elect, 623–4; in hiding, 625; murder, 670
Herrera, Miguel Angel de, 246, 247
Herrera, Ramón, 303, 304
Herrera de Morales, Francisca, sugar mill, *El Libano*, 427
Herrera y Roig, Capt. José, 66
Hershey, Milton, 538 n. 15, 560, 1166; buys *San Juan Bautista*, 538; and Havana-Matanzas railway, 541, 1161; Lobo and, 1149 and n. 56
Herter, Christian, 1210, 1232, 1264 n. 17; threats to Cuba, 1254; and *Coubre* explosion, 1269; and sugar quota bill, 1288, 1291; at OAS meeting, 1293
Hervey, Capt. Augustus (Earl of Bristol), and Havana expedition, 6 and n. 30, 10, 42
Hevia, Aurelio, 593, 675, 968
Hevia, Carlos, son of above, 593, 638 n. 13; Sec. of Agriculture, 669, 675; compromise candidate, 675–6; president, 676, 772; resignation, 676, 775 n. 1; and 1952 elections, 772 and n. 29, 773, 778, 790; imprisonment, 797; signs Montreal document, 802 n. 29
Hidalgo, José, 781
Hidalgo, Fr Miguel, 91
Hidalgo Peraza, José, 785 n. 24, 864 n. 10
Hill, Robert, U.S. ambassador to Mexico, 949, 1206; advice to Smith, 1206; and Castro, 1206–7
Hillsman, Roger, 1396
Hilton, Ronald, 1301 and n. 5, 1304
Hirigoyen, Marco Antonio, and ARG, 741, 754 and n. 46; and CTC, 783, 1173; arrest, 797–8; in Miami, 968
Hoar, Senator George Frisbie, anti-expansionist, 407
Hobson, Lieut, 387
Hoffman, Wendell, U.S. journalist, 936–7, 946
Hogan, Donald, 973
Holland, 93, 562
Holland, Henry, U.S. Ass. Sec. of State, 1015 n. 59; and Miami meeting, 1015
Hollins, H. B., 466
Holmes, John, 105

Honduras, 33 n. 25; rights of baymen, 55; Communist party, 579; U.S. marine landing, 626; population figures, 1093 n. 6

Hoover, Herbert, 531 n. 17, 560; and Food Board, 531; and U.S. loan, 553

Hoover, J. Edgar, 991 and n. 17; and Castro, 1210

Hormaza, Raimondo, and abolitionism, 81

Hosier, Admiral Francis, 38

Houston, General Samuel, 222

Howard, Edward, his 'vacuum pan', 116 and nn. 19, 20, 117

Howard, Lisa, and ABC, 1391

Howe, Julia Ward (1819–1910), 352

Howell, B. H., 552

Howland, Samuel Shaw, 131–2

Hruska, Senator, 1232

Hudicourt, Max, 697

Huertas, Dr Enrique, 874

Hughes, Charles Evans, U.S. Sec. of State, 550, 551, 554; and a Cuban loan, 553

Hull, Cordell (1871–1955), and legal corruption in Cuba, 423; opposes tariff increase, 560; secretary of state (1933), 607; instructions to Welles, 607 and n. 9, 608, 620, 640, 642, 644; and intervention, 645; and Grau's government, 661; lobbyist for Lakin 686; and Mendieta, 691; bilateral treaties, 694; lost interest in Cuba, 696 n. 17; and Batista, 712; and 1940 Cuban elections, 719; in Havana, 723

Humara, Salas, 924

Humbert-Droz, Jules, Comintern Latin Sec. gen., 578 and n. 37, 579, 596 nn. 53, 56; replaced by Togliatti, 596 and n. 56

Humboldt, Baron Friedrich Alexander von (1769–1859), 82 n. 48; on Cuba, 12, 17 and n. 14, 33 and n. 80, 208; and merchant class, 82; and the Census (1791 and 1792), 89; judgement on slavery, 281 and n. 1

Hurtado, Pablo, and Castro, 899, 900 n. 52

Ichaso, Francisco, 566 n. 11; and *Bohemia*, 1136

Iglesias, Aracelio, Negro unionist, murder, 1122, 1179, 1360

Iglesias, Major Carlos ('Nicaragua'), 1202 n. 32; and 26 July Committee, 868 n. 19, 1241 n. 19; in the Sierra, 938 n. 19, 1241 n. 19; his mission, 945 and n. 9; column in revolutionary army, 994 n. 28; rescue of, 1008

Iglesias, Capt. Joel, 1340 and n. 4, 1455

Iglesias, José, 1067

Iglesias Diaz, Aracelio, murder, 761

Inclan, Dr Clemente, 871, 1287

Indians, primitive, 19, 36, 907, 1511–29; responsibility for syphilis, 21 and n. 19, 1521, 1522 and n. 46; diminution from famine and disease, 21, 1515; absorption into Spanish families, 21 and n. 21, 22, 1511, 1512–13; tobacco and snuff smoking and cultivation, 22 and n. 24, 1511, 1519, 1522; crop cultivation, 24, 1518–19; revolts against *conquistadores*, 38, 1527; 'black legend' of, 46–7; revolt in Lower Creek, 77; and coffee growing, 133; the *bohío*, 1511, 1517; agricultural methods, 1511, 1515; alleged disappearance, 1511; probable population, 1511–12, 1512 n. 3, 1513–14; inter-marriage with Spaniards, 1512–13; position of *mestizos*, 1512; treatment by Spaniards, 1514–16, 1526–27; system of *encomienda*, 1527; destruction of old life, 1514–15; accusations against, 1516 and n. 20; Cuban races, 1516 ff.; language, 1516–17, 1525 and n. 57; S. American origin, 1517; social customs, 1517–18; characteristics, 1525; controversy over treatment, 1526–7; papal Bull *Sublimes Deus* and, 1527; exclusive villages, 1527; later survival, 1527–8; lose their identity, 1528; ignored by nationalists, 1528

Institute of Agrarian Reform (INRA), 1216; agency for new law, 1217; task, 1217; second national congress, 1217 n. 8; and co-operatives, 1218, 1284, 1323, 1324, 1395; Communist sympathisers, 1221; spending budget, 1235; appropriations, 1239, 1258, 1268, 1284, 1332; UN adviser, 1252; lack of compensation, 1258–9, 1284; 'people's shops', (*tiendas del pueblo*), 1284, 1293, 1324, 1327, 1333; takeover of private enterprises, 1297, 1322; and sugar equipment, 1322; administration of estates, 1325, 1326

Institute of Argrarian Reform – *Cont.*
n. 47, 1327, 1329; and ANAP, 1330
and n. 61, 62; housing achievements,
1333; and industrial reorganization,
1333 and n. 82; new directorate,
1382; *granjas del pueblo* and *granjas del
cana*, 1395 n. 3; hampering effect on
local managers, 1441; in control of
state farms, 1450; fruit export section,
1468
Irisarri, José María, Radical lawyer,
and Batista, 638 n. 13, 639, 647; and
Grau, 655, 664
Irisarri; Martínez, 228, 784
Irving, Washington, U.S. Minister in
Madrid, 207
Isaacson, Col, U.S. military mission,
911
Isle of Pines, 143, 153, 295, 351;
acquires a capital, 110; belief in gold,
206; question of status, 502; *de facto*
Cuban territory, 502; U.S. citizens,
502 and n. 11, 503; disappearance of
oligarchy, 503; model prison, 574,
660, 847, 940, 1028, 1348; Carillo's
golpe, 965, 994, 1028 n. 36; source of
marble, 1171; renamed Ise of Youth,
1429; voluntary agricultural experiments, 1429–30; population, 1430 n.
21; political prisoners, 1460
IT and T, composition, 1163 and n. 28;
Bonsal and, 1200 and n. 26
Iturralde, rebel officer, 588
Iturralde, Dr Rafael, 668
Ivonet, 514
Iznaga, family of Trinidad, 33, 208,
290; fortune from slave trading, 83,
137; sugar mills, 119, 137, 152;
declining fortunes, 275
Iznaga, José Aniceto, and *anexionismo*,
208
Iznaga, Pedro, 141, 290 n. 33, 152
Iznaga, Carlos, 275
Izquierda Revolucionaria, 706, 750,
1056

Jackson, Andrew (1767–1845), U.S.
president, 199
Jackson, Capt, and detention of *Mexi-
cana*, 1537
Jacksonville, Cuban refugees, 1026
Jamaica, 5 n. 27, 76, 119; and sugar
trade, 4, 64, 290, 1103 n. 49, 1143 n.
22; Negro contingent, 5; sugar
production, 27, 28 nn. 7, 9, 30, 54, 61
n. 3; absentee landlords, 32 55; and
slave trade, 33, 34, 63, 65, 169, 183;
slave-white proportions, 34 and n. 27,
66 n. 25; trade with Cuba, 53 and n.
50; declining prosperity, 54; and
English acquisition of Cuba, 54, 55;
free ports, 64; planters' indebtedness,
66; import of ackee and mango trees,
67; English pioneers and, 75; slave
revolts, 77–8, 81 n. 44, 203; massacre
by Coromantee slaves, 78; introduction of coffee, 128; largest plantation,
153–4; hours of work, 175; tax on
crop land, 184 n. 1; after emancipation, 184; rebel refugees, 260, 269;
ban on immigrants from, 431, 524,
540; repatriation of labourers, 1117
James, Daniel, 871 n. 28, 878 n. 11
Janney, Samuel, banker, and Cuba's
debt to Spain, 351, 356; to cajole
Spaniards out of Cuba, 359; and
Teller Amendment, 376 and n. 45
Jaruco y Mopax, Joaquín, Conde de
(1769–1807), 84; steam-powered mill,
79; wheat import monopoly, 85
Jarvis, Samuel, 545 and n. 5
Jefferson, Thomas (1743–1826), U.S.
President, Embargo Act, 87; willingness to purchase Cuba, 88, 100, 101 n.
35; and abolition, 165
Jenks, Prof. Leland, describes Mer-
chant, 545; on Cuba in 1926, 584
and n. 58; and U.S. capital in
Cuba (1902–27), 600 and n. 74,
1185
Jérez, Rodrigo de, and tobacco smok-
ing, 22 and n. 24
Jews, university restrictions, 13; and
Spanish ventures, 22 and n. 24; exiles
in Cuba, 47, 1101; emigration
restrictions, 47; Communist group,
576, 597, 697; Hitler and, 1059 n. 47
numbers in Cuba, 1101; and Cuban
Communist party, 1101
Jiménez, Alejandro, 861
Jiménez, Col José Antonio, 625
Jiménez, José María, 1123
Jiménez, Capt. Lage, and new Cuban
army, 994
Jiménez, Orlando, *Pasado Meridiano*
(*PM*), 1342 and n. 9
Jiménez Castellanós, captain-general,
420

Johnson, Cane, Attorney-general, opposes annexation of Cuba, 213
Johnson, Senator, 1232
Johnston, President, Cuban policy, 1481
Jones, Capt. and frigate *Vestal*, 198
Jordan, General Thomas, 313
Jordan, Reinaldo, 592 n. 33, 641 n. 22; Sub. Sec. of Education, 674 n. 36
Jorro, Miguel, 258–9
Jovellar, General Joaquín (1819–92), 262 n. 32; captain-general, 262, 265, 266
Juan Hernandez Bay, 528
Juara y Soler, Tomás de, 123 n. 54, 427
Juarez, Benito, President of Mexico, 251
Judah, R., U.S. ambassador, 589
Juliao, Francisco, 1345
Julien, Claude, 1002, 1391 and n. 25
Junco, Sandalio, Negro Communist, expulsion, 597 and n. 60; and Auténticos, 714
Juventud Católica, 793, 1129, 1202, 1250; attacks regime, 1294–5, 1349
Juventud Socialista, 800, 801, 868 n. 18, 927, 1340 n. 3; and Castro, 825, 847, 944, 981 and n. 38; banned, 846; in the Sierra, 981, 1006

Keating, Senator, 1232; and Cuban missile sites, 1396, 1398, 1400 and n. 31
Keith, Minor, 467 n. 18; and United Fruit, 466; Nipe Bay purchase, 467
Kellog, Frank Billings, Sec. of State, 626 and n. 4
Kelly, Hugh, 290
Kennan, George, 420 and n. 17; on the charismatic leader, 1491 and n. 23
Kennedy, of Mixed Commission, 202
Kennedy, John (1917–63), U.S. president, Senator, 949; in Cuba, 973; and Castro, 1209 n. 56, 1418; and presidential election, 1278, 1296, 1300; and Cuban issue, 1296, 1297, 1300, 1385; and Eisenhower, 1297, 1303–4; and invasion plan, 1303, 1305, 1306–7, 1308, 1309–10; takes up office, 1305; and Latin American development, 1305–6, 1307; publicly denies intervention, 1310, 1357; orders and behaviour during operation, 1358 and n. 11, 1363, 1367–8, 1369–70, 1369 n. 43, 1370; ignorance of Brigade 2506, 1360 n. 22; approves moon-landing project, 1371; domestic problems, 1385; post-invasion Cuban affairs, 1385, 1393, 1396; and nuclear weapon superiority, 1389; correspondence with Khrushchev, 1389, 1390, 1409, 1413; distrust of CIA, 1396 n. 4; announcement on introduction of missiles, 1396, 1398, 1402; mobilizes reserves, 1397; authorizes U.2 flight, 1400 and n. 33; theory of Russian-Cuban action, 1401 and nn. 39, 41; rejects policy of non-intervention, 1401–2, 1402 nn. 46, 47; need to act, 1402; rejects arbitration and diplomacy, 1402, 1412 n. 32; fails to consult allies, 1403; choice of action, 1403–4, 1404–5, 1406; deceived by Gromyko, 1404 and n. 59; speech justifying 'quarantine', 1406, 1408, 1410; and extension of blockade, 1411; accepts compromise suggestion, 1413; welcomes Khrushchev's withdrawal, 1414; debatable motives during crisis, 1415–16, 1416 n. 48; subsequent conduct, 1416; breaks U.S.–European links, 1416; faces threat of nuclear war, 1417 and n. 50; approves nationalist Communist Cuba, 1418; post-missile Cuban policy, 1481
Kennedy, Robert, 1396 n. 9; and invasion plan, 1305, 1364 n. 27; and missile crisis, 1404 and n. 57, 1413
Kennion, John (1726–85), 84 n. 55; contractor for Havana expedition, 3 and n. 15, 51; slave-trade activities, 3 and n. 16; Jamaica estates, 4 and n. 19, 56, 57 and n. 65, 64; slave import monopoly, 49–50; numbers sold, 50 and n. 34; subsequent career, 57 and nn. 65, 66
Keppel, Commodore Augustus (Admiral, Viscount) (1725–86), and expedition to Havana, 1–2, 3; career, 2 and n. 10, 57; prize money, 43; and Jamaica squadron, 53; captures Gorée, 54
Keppel, Frederick (1729–77), Bishop of Exeter, marriage, 56 n. 63
Keppel, General William, and expedition to Havana, 2; career, 3 and n. 11, 57; storms El Morro, 10; prize money, 43; military governor of Havana, 53

Khrushchev, Nikita (born 1894), visits U.S., 1237, 1242 and n. 24; meets Roca, 1279, 1281; and Castro, 1281, 1313, 1318, 1383; and rocket defence of Cuba, 1290 and n. 37, 1316 and n. 17, 1390, 1393; at U.N. meeting (1960), 1295; Cuban followers, 1315; and the invasion, 1367–8; attacks Stalin, 1380; and Cuba's road to socialism, 1383; address to returning Cubans, 1383, 1387; and missile aid to Cuba, 1387, 1388–9, 1390; need for a prestige victory, 1388; conversation with Frost, 1397 and n. 11; false message to Kennedy, 1397; liberal programme, 1397; and Berlin question, 1400 and n. 37, 1404 n. 59; declares peaceful intentions, 1404; reply to Russell, 1407 n. 10, 1410; response to Kennedy's demands, 1409; suggests Summit Conference, 1410; signs of retreat, 1410, 1411–12; compromise proposal letter, 1412 and n. 31, 1413 n. 41; orders dismantlement and return of missiles, 1414; loss of national and international prestige, 1415; friendship with Castro, 1476

Kimball, Lieut W.W., war plan against Spain, 336 n. 34, 342 n. 29

King, Col J. C., and Cuban affairs, 948–9; and CIA, 1015

Kirkpatric, Lyman, 949 n. 20, 967 n. 20; and BRAC, 1009, 1078

Knowland, Senator, 1001

Knowles, Sir Charles, and defence of Havana, 5 n. 17; and her houses, 17

Knox, Philander (1835–1921), 508 n. 12; threat of intervention, 508–9; 'preventive policy', 509–11, 523, 608 n. 10; and Negro rising (1912), 523

Knox, William, 1410

Kossuth, Louis, Hungarian patriot, 220 n. 12; in New Orleans, 216; in London, 220 n. 12, 221

Kriegel, Dr Frantisek, and Escalante, 1469 and n. 53

Kruger, Alfred, and Havana railway, 122

Kubitschek, President of Brazil, 1213 n. 73

Kuckilán, Mario, attack on, 799

Kudryatsev, Sergei Mikhaylovich (born 1915), ambassador to Cuba, 1279 and n. 16; hasty withdrawal, 1381 and n. 30

La Plata barracks, attack on, 912–14; Castro's headquarters, 1005–6, 1043–4

labour, social structure, 1108; situation in Cuba, 1153, 1173, 1177; resistance to modernization, 1164, 1178; Batista and, 1165; relations with governments, 1173, 1249–50, 1274; laws giving social advances, 1173; problems of dismissal, 1174, 1176; fear of future, 1174; fear of unemployment, 1175, 1180; Court of Appeal, 1176; skilled force, 1178; envy of U.S. standards, 1178; union membership, 1178 and n. 15, 1249; per cent of population, 1178 n. 15; average age, 1178 n. 15; increased numbers, 1182; absenteeism, 1337, 1448 and n. 10; and reward incentives, 1446–7 1448; use of voluntary work, 1447, 1448 n. 10, 1449; indifference to economic planning, 1450; pension rates, 1451; lack of hostility to regime, 1451

Labour movements, 5341 anarcho-syndicalists, 574–5, 575 n. 22; and Batista, 713, 791, 972, 1177; and Communism, 714–15; and 26 July, 947, 1002, 1007, 1079; spread of unrest, 972; need for unity 1007; formation of FONU, 1010; and unemployment, 1175; reactionary character, 1176; graft among leaders, 1176

Laborde, Pedro, buys central Pilar, 542

Labourdette, Mario, head of police, 662–3, 674 n. 36

Labra, Rafael María de (1841–1918), 240 n. 29; and abolitionist movement, 240; leader of Republican party, 367

Lacoste, Perfecto, on sugar trade decline, 458

Lago Pereda, Roberto, 592 n. 34, 638 n. 13, 641 n. 22

Lagos, 159, 183, 231

Laine, Col Honoré, war correspondent, 398

Lajas, Negro cabildas, 140

Lakin, Herbert C., and Cuban railways, 466 n. 11, 554, 560, 686; and sugar tariff, 560, 561

Lam, Wilfredo (born 1902), Chinese-Negro artist, 1124 and n. 33, 1344, 1464

Lamarr, Hortensia, 611, 624

Lamb, Frederick James (Lord Melbourne), and illegal slave traffic, 200

Lambia, Col, military attaché, Costa Rica, 839

Lamont, Thomas, and Machado, 586

Lancís, Antonio, and *diálogo cívico*, 874

Lancís, Félix, prime minister, 743 n. 10, 775; and *diálogo cívico*, 874

Lancís Castillo, Ricardo, member of 'Honest Cabinet', 555 and n. 55

land, circular grants by Spanish Crown, 19 and n. 15, 20, 95, 149; enticements to settlers, 19; effect on Cuban geography, 20; disposal of *realengos*, 20, 95; monastic ownership, 40, 102, 110; *intendentes* and, 65; liberating decrees, 95; total in cultivation, etc., 112; prices *c.* 1800–*c.* 1863, 119 and n. 36, 120; clearance for sugar fields, 119 and n. 36; litigation concerning, 149; rise in price, 185, 307 n. 43, 471; cost of leasing, 307 n. 43; effect of Spanish-American War, 424–5; effect of confusion in surveys and titles, 499; increase in squatters, 499; foreign ownership, 499, 687; purchased by N. Americans, 503, 600, 601; Prío's new law, 760; freedom of owners under Batista, 796; Castro's proposed reforms, 830–1, 955, 1010–11, 1017, 1070; Guevera and its socialisation, 938; implementation of reforms, 1013; peasant ownership, 1108, 1323 and n. 23, 1328; rural workers, 1109; wealth and ownership, 1111; Castro's distribution project, 1201; halt in drift from, 1178 n. 15; the co-operatives, 1218, 1224, 1257, 1323, 1325; state seizure, 1253; source of its ownership, 1329; private ownership, 1331; acres reclaimed and crops cultivated, 1332; increase in farming, 1464, 1548; occupancy by farmers (1946), 1548; numbers working on, 1550; task faced by Revolution, 1558–9

Landeira, Col Lázaro, and army conspiracy, 779

Lansing, Robert, U.S. Sec. of State, 529 and n. 10, 533; sends Crowder to Cuba, 548

Lansky, Meyer, gambling business, 972; flight from Cuba, 1027

Lara, 'Toto', 26 July leader, 992

Larrazabal, Admiral, President of Venezuela, 965; supports Montecristi movement, 994–5

Las Casas, Fr Bartolomé, 1511 n. 1, and Indians, 1511, 1514, 1515, 1519, 1522

Las Casas, Luis de (1745–1807), 81 n. 44, 90; captain-general, 72 and n. 2; and England's slave trade, 72; founds Liberal institutions, 73, 110; social benefits, 73; sugar mills, *Amistad, Alejandria*, 74–5, 75 n. 11, 122; death in poverty, 79 n. 34

Lataste, Alban, Chilean economist, 1252; and Ministry of Industry, 1334

Laurent, Capt. Emilio, anti-Machado rising, 593; chief of police, 637 and n. 13

Laurent, Julio, Chief of Naval Intelligence, 867, 924, 961; indicted for murder, 983, 1227; flight, 1027

Lavandeyra, Alberto, 1082

Lavastida, Capt. Manuel, 508; and SIM, 839, 842

Laviti family, 913

Law, the, 461; and slaves, 35; and sugar industry, 54, 1142, 1144, 1182; coterminous with government, 109; and land titles, 149; both dear and corrupt, 149–50; and killing of Negroes, 176; and compulsory education, 286; and racial integration, 293; abolishes *Cabotaje*, 300 n. 20; electoral, 300 n. 20; tariff reform, 300 n. 20; U.S. reorganization, 423, 437, 439; right to *tanteo*, 463; Magoon's revisions, 486–8, 490; under Machado, 596; numbers engaged in, 821 n. 95; and war crimes, 1073; change relating to nationality, 1100, 1101; Cubanization, 1934, 1101; absence in countryside, 1109 n. 2; black and mulatto practitioners, 1119; and foreign firms, 1253; registration of employees, 1274; Urban Reform, 1297 and n. 62; and labour disputes, 1337; position of Supreme Court, 1347 and n. 16; revolutionary factors, 1347; administration under Revolution, 1458–60; conduct of political

Law – *Cont.*
trials, 1458–9; sentences imposed, 1459–60; use of death penalty, 1460 and n. 25; number of executions, 1460 and n. 29; *see also* Judiciary

Law, George, and U.S. Mail Steamship [Co.] 219 and n. 6; and annexationism, 219

Laws of Burgos, 1515, 1526

Lawton, General (d. 1899), 390 n. 2; and Cuban landing, 390, 391; and battle of San Juan, 393; and peace terms, 400; Governor of Oriente, 403, 405 n. 14; in the Philippines, 410 n. 35

Lay, Col of Europa Hotel, 141; Santa Isabel Hotel, 145

Lazear, Dr Jesse, death from yellow fever, 461

Lazo, María, lawyer to U.S. embassy, 960 n. 33, 983, 1270 n. 34; and CIA, 983 n. 50; on Communists, 1080 n. 14; offer to Castro, 1270 and n. 35; and Guevara, 1272 n. 1

Leal, Antonio, prison reader, 237

Leal, 940

Lechuga, Carlos, 988

Ledón, Manuel, and Batista's removal, 1007; chief of traffic police, 1071; and Chomón's 'anti-imperialism', 1313 n. 4

Lee, General Fitzhugh (1834–1905), 343 n. 34, 353; consul-general in Havana, 343; and war with Spain, 343, 1384; warns of anti-American conspiracy, 356, 358; and destruction of *Maine*, 362; and U.S. citizens in Havana, 373; military governor of Havana, 421, 439 n. 14, 441; and U.S. occupation, 442–3, 448

Lee, General Robert E., 214, 343

Léger, Antoine, 159

Leiva, Martínez, 1259

Lema, Marqués de, 367

Lemnitzer, General, 1305

Lemus, José Francisco (d. 1832), independence movement, 101–2, 102 n. 39

Lence, Fr Germán, pro-Castroist, 1350

León, Rubén de, revolutionary, 595, 649, 672, 674 n. 36, 755; attacks Batista, 674–5; and Mendieta, 675; and Almagro, 676; and Prío's cabinet, 762, 775 and n. 1; presidential candidate, 769

León, Ulbino, surrenders to Guevara, 1016, 1021; defection, 1040

Léon Lemus, Orlando (El Colorado), gang leader, 761–2, 763; capture and death, 860

Leonard, Major, 668

Leonov, Nikolai, 887

Lerroux, Alejandro, Spanish Radical, 662 and n. 20

Lersundi, General Francisco, captain-general, reactionary policy, 240 and n. 31; and Bayamo revolutionaries, 244; and Cuban War (1868), 245, 247; replaced, 248; and slave shipments, 1543–4

Lesnick, Max, 812 n. 49, 814 n. 56, 856

Leyland, Thomas, 71, 84 n. 55, 86 and n. 8

Leyva, Ennio, 891

Leyva Rosell, Col, 1018, 1021, 1024

Lezama, José, 549–50

Lezama Lima, José, 1464; and homosexuality (*Paradiso*), 1465

Liberals (Cuban), and sugar industry, 72; social institutions, 73; and pursuit of wealth, 73–4, 75; and slavery, 74, 75; reaction to Haiti revolt, 80; belief in white domination, 81; and Morales' demands, 81; flight abroad, 102; Havana cafés, 129; dismantle monasteries, 197; extinction in E. Cuba, 197

Liberals, National, 599; and elections, 472–4, 489, 548, 549, 570–1, 774, 853 n. 32, 858; revolt against Congress, 475–80; Taft on, 478; under Magoon, 484 and n. 18, 486; amnesty for rebels, 485, 492; nominate Zayas, 509; division amongst, 526, 527; plan revolution against Menocal ('*La Chambelona*'), 528–31, 531 n. 15, 569; destruction, 531; amnesty for prisoners, 534 and n. 35; and Machado's overthrow, 618, 620, 679, 682, 714; and Mendieta, 692; oppose Batista, 714; and Communists, 989; ruined by Civil War, 1045; in Urrutia's government, 1085; and Castro's government, 1220, 1223, 1232, 1236; middle-class representation, 1236–7; crisis among intellectuals, 1349

Liberals, Spanish, anti-clerical, 240

Lightburn, Mrs, mulatto, slave trader, 161

Lilinokalani, Queen of Hawaii, deposed by U.S., 312

Lima, Dr, knowledge of Palace attack, 928 n. 16, 930 n. 28

Linares, General Arsenio, and Maceo, 330–1; and U.S. landing, 389; and condition of troops, 399–400

Linares, Sergeant Rafael, murders Cuervo, 930

Lincoln, Abraham, U.S. president, 230; and annexation of Cuba, 230; concedes British right of search, 231 and n. 60; crushes New York slave traffic, 231; emancipation proclamation, 235; death, 235

Lister, General Enrique, Spanish Communist, in Cuba, 589 and n. 15, 1345

Lite, Lieut Carlos ('Pepecito'), 993 and n. 26

Litvinov, Maxim, opens Havana Soviet Embassy, 731

Lindra, Cara, 1074 and n. 33

Lippman, Walter, and command of nuclear power, 1403 and n. 53; and missile crisis, 1412; and U.S. suspension of diplomacy, 1412 n. 32

Llaca Ortiz, Enrique, 1227, 1228

Llanusa, José, and Junta of Unity, 1003; Minister of Education, 1003 n. 29, 1428, 1429; and Castro's triumph, 1030; nationalised posadas, 1434 n. 38

Llerena, Mario, and MNR, 797, 801 n. 28, 866 n. 13; in Mexico, 889 n. 58, 952, 954 n. 14; and 26 July Commission, 889 n. 59, 892 n. 71; and Congress for Cultural Freedom, 910; in Miami, 968; and National Liberation Council, 968; opinion of Urrutia, 971; rival for Castro's affection, 971 n. 38; 26 July representative in U.S., 976 n. 13, 989; repudiates collaboration with Communists, 989; Nuestra Razon, 892 n. 68, 921 n. 53, 952 and n. 6, 953 and n. 7, 954

Lloyd, Selwyn, 1242

Lobé, Mr, Dutch consul-general, 162

Lobo, Heriberto, father of Julio, 1149

Lobo, Julio, 798, 1147, 1237; centrales Niquero, 897, 900, 907, 1146; Tinguaro, 1073, 1149–50; Cabo Cruz, 1146; Sugar Co., 908, 1147, 1148; Pilón

plantation, 936; supports opposition, 943 and n. 3, 962; and Batista's removal, 1019, 1148, 1150; and Tabernilla, 1041; refuses Treasury secretaryship, 1114; cane-cutting machine, 1144, 1449; sugar speculation, 1145, 1150; mill ownership, 1148, 1149 and n. 57; family background, 1149; land ownership, 1149 and n. 55; murder attempt upon, 1149; financial genius, 1150; and Castro, 1172 and n. 82; Guevara's ultimatum, 1298; leaves Cuba, 1298–9; survival in Madrid, 1471

Lodge, William Cabot, 314 n. 19, 338, 342, 365 n. 61; and annexation of Cuba, 314, 481; and Puerto Rico, 388; and Philippines, 407; his imperialism, 418, 419; and Wood, 443

Lojendio, Juan Pablo de, Marqués de Vellisca, Spanish ambassador, 1262 and n. 13

Long, Boaz, U.S. minister, 548, 550; and electoral fraud (1920), 548

Long, John Davis, Naval Secretary, 342 and n. 25; and Maine, 358, 362; and war with Spain, 365, 366, 374, 384, 387, 397–8

López, Alfrédo, secretary CNOC, 575; movement towards sindicatos, 575–6; murder, 580

López, José Luis, 826

López, 'Nico' (Antonio), 825, 878, 879; and 26 July, 878, 894 n. 5; in exile, 879, 895

López, General Narciso (1798–1851), 213 n. 33, 305; proposed Cuban revolution, 212–13, 214, 215–17, 248; betrayal, 213 and n. 36; links with U.S. extremists, 215–16, captured and garrotted, 217

López Blanco, Marino, and Batista's government, 783 n. 20, 843 n. 41, 856

López Camejo, Antonio, tortured by police, 875

López Cardenas, Rafael, anti-Batistiano, 979 and n. 31

López Castro, Amadeo, Secretary of Agriculture, 705; Sugar Law, 708; in Washington, 723 n. 34, 730; and Batista's cabinet, 724, 790, 800, 861 and n. 58, 874

López Castro, Amadeo, 966, 1029 n. 38

López Dorticós, Pedro, and BANFAIC, 1085, 1234; imprisonment, 1234

López Ferrer, Spanish ambassador, 621

López Migoya, Sergeant (later General) Manuel, 764 n. 36, 725; and army conspiracy (1933), 634; chief of staff, 634 n. 1, 725; rated Capt., 646 n. 37; replaced, 745, 778

López Querralta, Col, 305

López Rodríguez, José ('Pote'), 538; and Miramar, 540, 545; sugar mill, España, 542; overdraft at Banco Nacional, 545, 546; and financial crisis, 547; death, 549

López Valiñas, José Agustín, Mexican gunman, 588 and n. 13

Lora, Esteva, 884

Lorenzo, General Manuel, 197–8

Lorié, Major, 1213

Lorié Bertot, Dr, counsel to Matos, 1255

Loti, Pierre, 382 and n. 4

Loutit, Octavio, Labour leader, 897, 946 n. 12, 1007; arrest, 1010; CTC, 1031 n. 45, 1250 and n. 48, 1251; and FONU, 1083 n. 23; anti-Communist, 1320; and new regime, 1456

Loynaz del Castillo, 322, 475

Lozovsky, Alexander, and capitalism, 578

Luce, Henry, and Time, 1210

Luce, Mrs Henry, and missile crisis (Life), 1399

Lucero, Oscar (d. 1958), kidnapper, 978

Ludlow, General William (1843–1901), 421 n. 22; military governor in Havana, 421, 441, 448, 463, 629; president War College Board, 463 n. 1

Lugo, Fr Ismael de, and Brigade 2506, 1361

Luque, Angel de, director El Globe, 308 and n. 46

Luthringer, and Cuban central bank, 732

Luz, Cipriano de la, postmaster-general, 18; and the cabildo, 45 n. 14; mayor, 53 and n. 52; plantation, Santa Ana de Aguiar, 151, 178

Luz, Ramón de la, independence movement, 88–9, 91

Luzardo, Manuel, Communist, 846; and ORI, 1377 n. 21; Minister of Commerce, 1379, 1381

Lyman, U.S. military attaché, 551

MacArthur, General, in the Philippines, 404; Agrarian Reform, 1242–3

McBain, Howard Lee, 610 and n. 17

McCabe, Bishop (Methodist), 366

McCarthy, Francis, 778 n. 8, 898

McCarthy, Senator, and Communism, 912 n. 12, 930 n. 26, 960

McCleary, Major, mayor of Oriente, 410

McClernand, Edward John, at Santiago, 397 and n. 24

McCone, director CIA, and offensive missiles in Cuba, 1395–6, 1396 nn. 4, 8; 1398 n. 21, 1400 and n. 36

McCook, John James, 351 n. 60; and Cuban debt to Spain, 351

Maceo, Antonio (1848–96), mulatto rebel captain, 255 and n. 6, 256, 258, 264, 294, 363, 796; the 'Titan of Bronze', 255 n. 6, 267, 864; defamation, 264–5; and peace terms. 266; interview with Campos, 267; betrayal, 269; returns to Cuba, 300; revolutionary activity, 300, 302; deportation, 300; and Independence War (1895), 306, 307, 309, 316, 319, 321, 326, 328, 1012; Negro columns, 324; Weyler and, 329, 330–1, 335, 339; guerrilla campaign, 331, 334; death, 339; U.S. reaction, 339, 340; destruction of towns, 424; successor, 444 n. 1

Maceo, Antonio (grandson of the above), rebel group, 1005, 1043; in Guatemala, 1306

Maceo, Francisco, Bayamo, revolutionary, 242; frees slaves, 250

Maceo, José (brother of Antonio Maceo), nationalist, 306; and Independence War (1895), 309, 316, 321; death, 339

Machado, Eduardo, 176, 266, 593

Machado, General Gerardo (1871–1939), Cuban president, 509 and n. 14, 568 n. 19, 1045; Liberal, 526, 527, 528, 568, 569; buys Carmita, 538; character and criminal origins, 569, 570; mayor of Santa Clara, 569 and n. 2; business deals, 569–70; and the presidency, 570–1, 572–3, 599; 'victory train', 571; in U.S., 572, 582; public works programme, 572–3, 581–2; cabinet, 573–4; continuing corruption, 574, 581; labour troubles, 574, 1173; and party political move-

Machado, General Gerardo – *Cont.*

ments, 580; army-based power, 582, 595, 623, 681; extension of power without election, 585, 587, 588; murderous policy, 587–8, 590; character of his enemies, 587, 590, 593–4, 681; secures U.S. loan, 588 and n. 10, 590, 673; and Mella's murder, 588; supported by U.S. business, 589 and n. 20, 590; student opponents, 591; attempt to overthrow, 593; ABC and, 594–6; payment of his debts, 597, 708–9, 716, 722; opposes intervention, 599; and F. D. Roosevelt, 605; agreement with Communists, 605–6; organizes violence (*La Porra*), 607; negotiations with Welles, 608, 609–14, 616, 617–18, 620, 622; and the opposition, 609; obstructs constitutional change, 612; amnesty law, 612, 613; speech to Congress, 612–13; events leading to his fall, 615–16; decision to resign, 619, 622; *pronunciamiento* against, 622; escapes to Nassau, 623–5; his family, 625 n. 36; in exile, 679, 708; and Veterans' Association, 687–8; Urgency Courts, 1347

Machado, José ('Machadito'), death, 931

Machado, Luis, opposition member, 964, 975–6

Macías, Antonio, and PUR, 707

Macías, Domingo, and sugar tax bill, 704

McKinley, William (1834–1901), U.S. president, 288 n. 24, 299, 336 n. 31; tarriff reforms, 288–9, 307, 336; Republican candidate, 336, 337; Cuban policy, 336, 356, 436, 443, 451–2; and war with Spain, 342, 353–4, 364–5, 367–8, 374 and n. 5; and Roosevelt's appointment, 342; his administration, 343; and Canova's proposed reforms, 348; supports Sagasta's plan, 355; sends *Maine* to Havana, 358; criticized by de Lôme, 360; and *Maine* explosion, 362, 368, 371, 407; peace proposals, 367, 402; appeals for money, 368; meets European ambassadors, 373; message to Congress, 375–6; signs ultimatum to Spain, 376, 380 n. 54; calls up National Guard, 384; and the Philip-

pines, 385, 407 and n. 23, 443; and Shafter, 398; and army recall, 405; address to U.S. Commissioners, 406; in the South, 417; and Wood, 440, 456; signs Platt Amendment, 454, 456; and Post Office scandal, 456; murder, 457

Maclean, Governor, 165

Macmillan, Harold, Prime Minister of Britain, 1403, 1416; and Castro, 1009; and missile crisis, 1407

McNamara, Robert (born 1916), Secretary of Defence, and invasion plan, 1305, 1309; and nuclear weapon superiority, 1389; 'counterforce' policy, 1389, 1416; and Cuban missile sites, 1398 nn. 19, 20; and U.S. intervention, 1401, 1410–11; faces threat of nuclear war, 1417

Macuriges, Montevideo estate, 47, 63

Madan Cristóbal, sugar planter, *Rosa*, 208; and *anexionismo*, 208, 211, 215; and railways, 208

Madariaga, Lorenzo de, 48

Madden, Richard Robert (1798–1886), career, 150 n. 61, 162 n. 37, 182 and n. 67; and the lottery, 150; and the Church, 151; and abolition in Jamaica, 162 n. 37; and *Amistad* case, 173 n. 21; and *emancipados*, 182

Madrigal, Fr, 994

Magoon, Charles (1861–1920), 404 n. 10, 687; informs Palma of cease-fire, 403–4, 484; sent to Cuba, 482 ff.; accusations against, 482–5, 492–3, 493 n. 53; career, 483–4; issues U.S. contracts, 485–6, 506; law reforms, 486–8, 490–1; founds the army, 490, 680; his armed force, 490 and n. 43; occasions of political violence, 491; and cigar workers' strike, 491–2; educational policy, 492; assessment, 492

Magriñat, José, 571; murderer of Mella, 588 and n. 13, 633

Mahan, Alfred Thayer (1840–1914), 312 n. 13, 343, 397; and influence of sea power on history, 310; and a U.S. naval base in Cuba, 419

Maine, the, ordered to Key West, 356, 358; Havana reception, 359; blown up in harbour, 36–2, 1269; enquiries into, 362–3; alternative responsibility, 363–4; report, 371; interview with relatives, 374

Maldonado, José Arroyo, 1076
Mañach, Jorge, 566 n. 11, 695, 754 n. 48, 772, 852; ABC programme, 594, 1066; and Batista, 795, 796, 874; and constitutional development, 862
Mann, Dudley, 224
Mann, Thomas (born 1912), Ass. Sec. of State, 1294 and n. 52; and invasion plan, 1304, 1309
'Mano Negra', 957
Mansure, Edward, 1170 and n. 71
Mantes, Pedro, 162
Mantoux, Pierre, 563 and n. 15
Manuilsky, D., 697
Manzano, 206
Mao Tse-tung (born 1893), 882, 1081, 1279; attacked by Castro, 1477–8
Marban, Eriberto, 946
Marcy, William Learned, Sec. of State, 220; and purchase of Cuba, 223 and n. 22, 225
María Cristina (1806–78), queen of Spain (mother of Queen Isabella II), 137 and n. 8, 203; sugar mills, Santa Susana, San Martín, 137, 153, 427; company group La Gran Azucarera, 154, 221 and n. 18, 278, 427; slave traffic, 156, 214; Carlist rebellion against, 194; and purchase of Cuba, 213, 221–3; in 1854 revolution, 224; and McKinley, 359; and peace proposals, 367, 369, 377
'Mariana Grajales batallion', 1011
Mariategui, José Carlos, 566, 579
Marimán, José, 550, 554
Marinello, Juan (1898–), 566 n., 567 n. 13, 706 and n. 3, 793, 1085, 1234, 1268; and PUR, 706; praises Batista, 728–9; enters cabinet, 733, 1081; on party's task, 733; vice-president of Senate, 747, 1081; Communist candidate, 757, 1006; and 26 July, 922–3; in E. Europe, 1237 n. 5; attacked by Revolución, 1238; Rector Havana University, 1287; and new Communist party, 1454; and PURS, 1454 n. 3
Maristany, Carlos, Minister of Communications, 762; Auténticos, 968 and n. 25
Marmol, Donato, 248, 265
Marquéz, Juan Manuel, and 26 July, 869, 888 n. 55, 900; in Miami, 876, 894 n. 5

Marquéz Sterling, Carlos, 792 and n. 9; and Batista, 796; and 1958 elections, 983, 1014
Marquéz Sterling, Manuel (1872–1934) 792 n. 9, 956; founder of Heraldo de Cuba, 652 n. 6; and Grau's cabinet, 652, 674; proposed president, 676; Ortodoxo group, 968; and 1958 elections, 952, 977
Marroquín Rojas, Clemente, and Le Hora, 1301
Marshall, General, and OAS, 814; at Bogotá, 815
Martí, José (1853–95), 256, 566; independence leader, 255, 296, 317; on Independence War, 269; leader of U.S. Cuban exiles, 294; parentage, 295; schooling, 295; founds Patria Libre, 295, 301; imprisonment and exile, 295, 296; in Mexico, 295–6; literary achievements, 296, 317; teacher in Guatemala, 296; marriage, 296; in U.S., 296–7, 301, 311; newspaper contributions, 296–7; and U.S. way of life, 297, 310, 311; consulship, 297, 300; and annexation, 298, 363; school for revolutionaries, 300; condemns bimetallism, 301; 'Bases' of his Party, 301–2; anarchist and socialist support, 302, 305; denounces Maura's reforms, 303; and Independence War, 305–6, 309, 316; illness, 305; distrust of U.S. expansionism, 310, 317, 417; lands in Cuba, 316; death, 316; appeal to Cubans, 317; his 'fatherland', 417–18; lack of spiritual heir, 678; unachieved revolution, 686; surviving influence, 828, 829; Castro and, 833, 863, 882, 1088; U.S. ignorance of, 1062; Manifesto of Montecristi, 1120 and n. 18; excommunicated, 1127–8; misunderstanding of 'race', 1433; revolutionary hero, 1462; Amistad funesta, 297; Amor con amor se paga, 296; 'The White Rose', 317; on Whitman, 297
Martí, Manuel, 636
Martín, Daniel, 883
Martín Castellano, Dr Negro, 611, 721 and n. 20
Martín Labandero, Daniel, 925
Martín Villaverde, Alberto, Bishop of Matanzas, 1129
Martínez, Diego, 159

Martínez, Lieut Dimas, 963
Martínez José Luis, 872
Martínez, Luis Manuel, 967
Martínez, Raúl, 854 and n. 34
Martínez, Ricardo, Profintern representative, 579; and Radio Rebelde, 980 n. 36
Martínez, Saturnino, founder of *La Aurora*, 237; campaigns for prison readers, 237–8; directs a strike, 239; struggle with Roig, 291; abandons Labour movement, 292
Martínez, Tirso, 1261 n. 11, 1280, 1456
Martínez Arará, Raúl, 829; commander Bayamo attack, 835 and nn. 2, 3, 836 n. 9, 838 and n. 25; and Castro on release, 864 and n. 7
Martínez de Campos, General Arsenio (1831–1900), brings reinforcements, 265–6, 266 n. 5; peace terms, 266, 267, 299; and Maceo, 267; captain-general, 267, 308, 309, 321; conciliatory followers, 267–8; prime minister of Spain, 269, 279; abolishes slavery in Cuba (1888), 279; in Morocco, 304, 308; and Independence War (1895), 309, 316, 320, 311, 368; advice to Canovas, 320–1, 327; resignation, 326–7
Martínez de Campos, Nicolás, Conde de Santovenia, 142
Martínez de Pinillos, Barnabé, money-lender, 82
Martínez Fraga, Pedro (1889–), Cuban ambassador, 717 n. 5, 716–17, 719
Martínez Irujo, Carlos, 85
Martínez Iznardi, José, 85
Martínez Junco, Helidoro, 1427 and n. 14
Martínez Marquéz, Guillermo, 566 n. 11; ed. *El País*, 1268
Martínez Ortiz, 1055; on Magoon, 483; bill to restore lottery, 512
Martínez Paez, Dr, Minister of Health, 1067, 1068
Martínez Sáenz, Joaquín, 611, 634; a founder of ABC, 594, 611, 613; and Machado's overthrow, 624; member of new government, 629, 642; in hiding, 646; dictator of ABC, 652; flight to Miami, 663, 666; and Mendieta's government, 678, 691 n. 2, 695; and Batista's government, 784; murder, 856 n. 43; President of National Bank, 931, 1184; arrest, 1045; in gaol, 1186 n. 23
Martínez Sánchez, Augusto, legal adviser to Raúl, 994, 1007, 1067; Minister of Defence, 1067, 1198, 1202, 1233; Minister of Labour, 1243, 1250 n. 46, 1259, 1337, 1467; attempted suicide, 1253 n. 54, 1467; and ORI, 1377 n. 17
Martínez Villena, Rubén (d. 1934), 580, 656 n. 19, 692, 1081, 1225; 'protest of the 13', 566 and n. 11, 567 and n. 12; protest movements, 567, 568; imprisonment, 568; moves towards Communism, 589; in the Caucasus, 597 and n. 57; secret return, 615; replaced by Blas Roca, 632; last speech, 656
Marty y Torrens, Francisco, slave merchant, 156, 181, 186, 195, 235
Marx, Karl (1813–83), 302, 566, 592, 734, 1433; view of society, 1484; *Das Kapital*, 818, 1375
Marxism, Castro and, 817, 818–19, 829, 850, 1051–2, 1266, 1373; Guevara and, 880, 937, 1292
Marxism-Leninism, 1457, 1488; Castro's interpretation, 1488, 1489 and n. 15
Mas, Carlos, 900
Mas Martín, Luis, Communist, in the Sierra, 1006, 1011 and n. 32
Masetti, Jorge, 1277
Masferrer, Rolando (El Cojo), anti-Communist, and Spanish Civil War, 704, 741; founder of MSR, 741, 742, 754, 755, 756 n. 52, 763, 811, 928; expedition against Trujillo, 755; activities of, 761, 792; challenges Chibás, 766; and 1952 elections, 769; attempted murder of, 771, 890; and army plot, 783; and Batista, 792; journal, 883; private army, *los Tigres*, 885, 990; and 1958 elections, 952; flight from Cuba, 1026, 1075; survival in exile, 1471 n. 66
Masó, Bartolomé, Cuban nationalist, 306, 316; president of House of Representatives, 319; vice-premier, 319, 321; and presidency, 351, 459–60, 473–4; proclaims Cuban-U.S. alliance, 379; passive role in 1898 war, 381; Wood and, 445
Masó, Col Blas, 588
Mason, Vice-consul, 400

Mason, John Y., Sec. U.S. Navy, approves annexation of Cuba, 213

Matar, José, commander of CDR, 1322, 1468; expulsion from party, 1453 n.; and PURS, 1454 n. 3; ambassador in Budapest, 1468

Matienzo, Juan, and Peruvian administration, 39

Matos, Hubert, 934, 1251; trial, 831 n. 94, 1244, 1255–6, 1256 nn., 1458; invests Santiago, 1011; commander in Camagüey, 1072, 1198 n. 18, 1212; anti-Communism, 1212, 1213, 1230, 1241, 1244; replacement, 1241; explains his resignation, 1244 and n. 31, 1245; arrested by Castro, 1245; proposed execution, 1247; tribunal, 1255; sentence, 1256 and n. 5; effect of unfair trial, 1257; press support, 1261; unknown fate, 1461

Matos, Tuerto, bandit, 320

Matson, Capt., destroys barracoons, 203

Matthews, Herbert (born 1900), 918 and n. 44, 1233; on Magoon, 483; in Cuba, 901 n. 53, 946, 960, 986, 1052, 1391, 1392; and the press, 917 n. 38; creates Castro legend, 919, 920, 946, 986; and numbers of *Fidelista*, 919–20, 921; and 26 July, 921; and Ambassador Smith, 949, 957, 986

Matthews, H. Freeman, deputy to Caffery, 672 and n. 23

Maura, Antonio, 303 n. 30; suggested reforms, 303–4, 380

Mederos, Elena, Minister of Social Welfare, 1066; in exile, 1199 n. 23; and Castro, 1203, 1220; dismissal, 1224; and Dorticós, 1234

Medina, Pedro, 71

Medina, Waldo, 1218

Meíjas del Castillo, Ramón ('Pichirilo'), 894 nn. 1, 5

Mejía, Gustavo Adolfo, 763 and n. 11

Mejías, Sergio, 843 n. 41; and Prío's cabinet, 775 n. 1, 781, 855

Melgarejo, Capt. Juan, Governor of Puerto Rico, 1516 n. 19

Mella, Julio Antonio (1905–29), 565 n. 6, 650, 1081; and FEU, 564 n. 3, 565; career and personality, 565–6; student protest, 568; joins Havana Communists, 576, 577 and n. 36, 580, 1225; murder in Mexico, 588 and n. 3, 633; return of his ashes, 656

Mella, Vazquez de, Carlist, 327, 337, 386

Menchaca Torre, Matías, 187

Méndez Capote, Professor Domingo (1863–1933), 421 n. 24, 571; vice-president revolutionary government, 351; *Gobernación*, 421; and Platt Amendment, 454, 455, 456 n. 56; supports Palma, 459; resignation, 479

Méndez Penate, 676; accepts Welles as mediator, 610; returns to Cuba, 631; Minister of Justice, 677, 678; suicide, 692

Mendieta, Col Carlos (1873–1960), Cuban president, 534 n. 33, 567, 641; Unionist Liberal, 526, 527, 528, 678; condemns Menocal, 534, 678; presidential candidate, 570; and Machado, 572, 590–1, 593, 678; attempted arrest, 591; supports Welles, 610; return to Cuba, 631; in hiding, 646; and Grau's regime, 651, 654, 663, 671, 674; asked to take over, 663–4, 671; assumes presidency, 676–7, 678; U.S. recognition, 677, 691; character and career, 678; cabinet, 678; Union Nacional, 682; and Cuba Cane, 687; suspends constitutional guarantees, 691–2, 696, 699; achievements, 698; postpones elections, 701; resignation, 701

Mendive, Rafael María, 295

Mendizábal, Liberal Spanish government, 197, 462

Mendoza, Antonio González de, lawyer, *pronunciamiento* against Machado, 622; *politícos* representative, 656

Mendoza, Eligio, 940

Mendoza, Ignacio, 918

Mendoza, Ignacio González de, 592 n. 35, 595–6

Mendoza, Jorge, 980 n. 36, 1011 n. 32, 1241 n. 20, 1244 n. 29, 1463; ed. *Granma*, 1241 n. 20, 1455, 1463

Mendoza, Ramón, 540

Menéndez, Emilio, President of Supreme Court, 1066; in exile, 1347

Menéndez, Jesús (d. 1947), leader of sugar workers, 756, 761, 1322 n. 33; death, 761

Menéndez Martínez, Major, and *operación verona*, 997, 998

Menéndez Tomasevich, Capt. Raúl, rebel, 992, 1008 n. 17; group leader, 994 n. 27; organizer of LCB, 1472

Menocal, Major Jacinto, 1027

Menocal, General Mario García (1866–1941), 351, 467 n. 22; president of Cuba, 507, 509, 525, 531; military career, 467–8, 680; and sugar mill, *Chaparra*, 468, 475, 523, 525, 528, 532; *Palma*, 532, 542; and Liberal revolt, 475; leader of Conservative Party, 489, 568; annuls Ports Co., 507, 525; and the lottery, 513, 526; and Negro rising (1912), 523; committed to bribery and corruption, 525, 526, 529, 533; compared with Gómez, 525; achievements, 525, 526; fraud election campaign, 526–7, 530; Liberal revolt against, 528–9; receives U.S. support, 529, 530, 531; in World War I, 531; offers U.S. training grounds, 533; buys Asbert's palace, 534; invites Crowder to Cuba, 534–5; and 1920 financial crisis, 545, 546–7; and Zayas' corrupt election, 547 and n. 17; and 1921 election, 549; electoral tour (1924), 571; and André's murder, 574; and Machado, 590, 591, 593; in Miami, 610, 671, 679, 696; opposes intervention, 611, 612; returns to Cuba, 631, 646; ABC and, 652, 654; part of common front, 655; the army and, 680; waits in the wings, 696, 706; 'Democratic' candidate, 701; and 1940 elections, 719, 721–2; Batista and, 721

Menocal, Raúl García, 727, 730, 949, 1029 n. 38; and *Santa Marta* sugar mill, 727 n. 15; and Batista's cabinet, 861 and n. 58; escapes murder, 985

mercedes, circular land grants, 19 and n. 15, 20; forbidden, 95

Merchant, W., 554; and *Banco Nacional*, 545–6; described by Jenks, 545; financial crisis, 547; escapes abroad, 550

Merino, 997, 998

Merino, Miguel, 962

Merrick and Sons, Philadelphia, 115

Merritt, General, 385

Meruelos, Rolando, 741

Messersmith, George, U.S. ambassador, 722, 727–8; and 1940 elections, 721; and military affairs, 723; and U.S. loan to Cuba, 723

Mestre Brothers, 1195, 1273

Mestre, Armando, 851

Mestre, José Manuel, 233 n. 7; and reform, 233; backs 1868 rebellion, 246

Mexia, Fr Pedro, 1526

Mexico, 1, 13, 278; circular land grants, 20 n. 16; position of Cuba *vis-à-vis*, 43, 45, 73, 111; post of viceroy, 45; trading monopoly, 68; wax imports, 70 n. 47; post of *oidor*, 73 n. 6; treatment of slaves, 75 n. 15; popular rising, 1810, 89; *intendentes*, 90; becomes independent, 99; Junta for Cuba's liberation, 103–4; sugar machine, 120 n. 39; cost of free Indian labourers, 181, 188; acquired by U.S., 210 and n. 16, 232; Martí and, 295–6; under dictatorship, 313; Communist party, 577, 579, 588 and n. 13, 765, 868, 931 and n. 32; Mella and, 588 and n. 13; pursuit of Pancho Villa, 626 n. 1; French intervention, 627; and intervention in Cuba, 644 and n. 31; rural schools, 702 and n. 32; land law, 709; U.S. Peace Congress, 763; Castro and, 854, 867, 868–9, 876 ff., 911 n. 11, 1054 and n. 22; and 26 July, 868, 869, 946, 952, 1030 n. 43; School of Military Aviation, 877; treatment of prisoners, 877; Communist exiles, 878; return of exiles from, 1031; population figures, 1093; sugar consumption, 1103; medical services, 1105; sugar production, 1139 and n. 9, 1145 n. 22; Soviet diplomatic mission, 1265; Revolution, 1480; inter-marriage with Indians, 1512; population decline, 1513, 1515; primitive Indians, 1528

Meyer, Karl, U.S. journalist, talks with Castro, 1008 n. 16, 1057; and 'Alliance for Progress', 1306 n. 27

Meyer, Joaquín, 964

Miares Fernández, Francisco, 945

Michie, William, 49

middle classes, opposition group (ABC), 594–6; and Revolution (1959), 605, 1237, 1352–3; secret societies (OCRR), 609; and intervention, 642; fear of Communism, 642; and Batista, 1709, 1113; last democratic hope, 874; and Santiago

middle classes – *Cont.*

rising, 897; and Castro, 943, 955, 1010, 1193, 1195, 1206; and Civil War, 959–60; property investment, 1096; numbers and occupations, 1110–11; and economic stagnation, 1112; servants, 1112 and nn.; and the professions, 1113, 1115–16; *bourgeoisie*, 1113; corrupt commercial practices, 1113; attitude to politics, 1114; lack of voluntary institutions, 1115; lack of black members, 1119; and racial discrimination, 1120–21; and Liberalism, 1236–37; alrernative choices, 1352; attacked by 'Revolutionary offensive', 1445

Mikoyan, Anastas Ivanovich (1895–), 1252 n. 52; in Mexico, 1252, 1265; in Cuba, 1252 n. 53, 1263–4, 1265–6, 1267

Miles, General Nelson, 384 n. 13; commander of U.S. army (1898), 387 and n. 25; at Siboney, 399; and surrender terms, 399, 400; and Puerto Rico, 401, 402

Militia, the, origin, 1246, 1257; organization, 1268, 1321 and n. 29; and Communism, 1282; arms for, 1289, 1293; and anti-Castro rebels, 1296, 1348; replaces rebel army, 1321; student recruitment, 1341; murder of, 1348; and invasion, 1363, 1364; at *central Covadonga*, 1364; air attacks on, 1365; doubts concerning, 1386 and n. 9; unpaid service, 1425 n. 8; compulsory service, 1429

Miller, George, U.S. journalist, description of Cuba, 673

Mills, Wright, *Listen Yankee*, 1295 n. 54

Minas de Ojujal, 1089

Minor, Bob, U.S. Communist, 692

Mira, José Franco, and Brigade 2506, 1360

Mirabal, Armando, police victim, 944 and n. 7

Mirabal, Capt., chief of police, 979

Miranda, Clodomiro, rebel band, 1349

Miranda, ex-Capt. Fernández, 779 and n. 11, 780; leaves Cuba, 1026

Miret, Pedro, at Moncada, 824 n. 3, 867, 1544 n. 6; and 26 July Committee, 868 n. 19; in Mexico, 869, 946; arrest, 891; Minister of Agriculture, 1225, 1265 and n. 21

Miret, General Vicente, denounces Gómez' government, 508

Miró, General, 445

Miró Cardona, Dr, president Bar Association, 870, 1116; and Batista's resignation, 986; and Junta of Unity, 1003, 1030; prime minister, 1065, 1070, 1197, 1234; and Constitutional revisions, 1084; and elections, 1086; resignation, 1197; and University reform, 1287; in exile, 1292, 1357, 1358; provisional president, 1307; and U.S. intervention, 1310, 1344, 1385–6, 1393; and CIA, 1320; and Cuban invasion, 1357, 1393; in Miami, 1393

Miró Argenter, José, 306

Missiles, Russian, 1387 and n. 11, 1388 and nn. 13, 14, 1390 and n. 23, 1394, 1401; repercussions, 1389; Castro's explanations, 1391–2; Russian plan, 1393–4; transport needed, 1394, 1397; survey of sites, 1395; arrival in Havana, 1397 and n. 14, 1398; Ilyushin bombers, 1400 n. 35; numbers, 1401 and n. 43, 1404 n. 57; orders of 'quarantine' fleet, 1406–7; Russian explanations, 1409, 1410, 1412; U.S. demands their removal, 1411; under Russian control, 1412 and n. 34; withdrawal from Cuba, 1415

Missile crisis (1962), use of U.S. bombs, 1063 n. 52; main protagonists (U.S. and U.S.S.R.), 1395, 1396, 1402 n. 50, 1403; discovery of Cuban sites, 1398; influence on election campaign, 1399, 1401; the Press and, 1399; U.S. theories on Soviet–Cuban action, 1400–1; Kennedy's involvement, 1401–2, 1403–4, 1403 n. 54, 1404 n. 57, 1406; U.S. 'quarantine' line, 1406 and n. 3, 1406–7, 1410; approach of Russian ships, 1409–11; Russian compromise proposal, 1411–12; U.S. assembles nuclear and invasion forces, 1413, 1417; Khrushchev orders withdrawal of weapons, 1414; U.S. at 'maximum' alert, 1417 and n. 53; threat to *bourgeois* society, 1439; Castro's annoyance with Russia, 1476

Mitchell, José Miguel, freed Negro, 204

Miyar, Ramón, student, 592 n. 34, 641 n. 22; and Pentarquía meeting, 648–9

Miyares, Carmen, Martí and, 296
Modesto Amo, Fr, 1012
Modotti, Tina, *compañera* of Mella, 588
Moncada barracks, Castro's attack on, 803, 824 n. 3, 835 ff.; composition of his followers, 824 and nn. 3, 4, 825, 836, 984; its purpose, 828; armaments and finance, 835 and n. 7, 836; casualties, 838 and nn.; aftermath, 838, 841, 843; trial of rebels, 838 n. 27, 843; savagery of repression, 838–9, 840–1; judges at trial, 843 n. 44; public opinion of, 843–4; denunciation of Chaviano, 866; País and, 896; social and geographical origins of those involved, 1546–7
Monroe Doctrine, 627, 1290, 1399
Monroe, James, 101 n. 35; 'Doctrine', 103, 104, 228, 449; U.S. defence, 627
Montall, Lieut of Aviation, 667
Montalvo family, 152, 262, 278, 1110; entitled Condes de Macuriges and Casa Montalvo, 142; in decay, 153; sugar estates, *La Holanda*, 176; *Andreita*, 278; *Concepción*, 278
Montalvo, Elena, marriage, 1110, 1114
Montalvo, Juan, and Mixed Commission, 202
Montalvo, Lorenzo, *Comisario* of the navy, 46, 47; Cuban estate, 47 and n. 17
Montalvo, General Rafael, army commissions, 692; career, 703; *Batistiano*, 703, 705
Montané, Jesús, 888 n. 55, 894 n. 5; *Moncadaist*, 824 n. 3, 825, 836, 1455 n. 6; arrest in Mexico, 877
Montoas, Francisco, and emancipation, 235 and n. 11
Monteagudo Fleites, Capt., 783
Monteagudo, General José de Jesús, 345, 456 n. 56; arrest, 475; Liberal, 484 n. 18; commander of rural guards, 490, 680; succeeds Guerra, 508; supports Menocal, 509; and Negro rising, 523
Montejo, Esteban, 142, 515; and hours of work, 175; and Chinese, 188; and the *colonia*, 177; and Independence War (1895), 319; post-war Havana, 422; *Autobiography of a Runaway Slave*, 140 n. 14, 142, 151, 302 n. 27, 410
Montenegro, Carlos, and MSR, 741
Montero Castillo, Manuel, 797–8
Montgomery, Cora, 212

Montoro, Rafael, 487; leader of Conservative party, 489
Montseny, Capt. Demetrio ('Villa'), rebel, 992; at La Cabaña, 1198, 1202 n. 32; dismissal, 1241 and n. 19
Moore, Carlos, Communist, and Castro's racial policy, 1121; and Williams, 1434 n. 37; *Présence Africaine*, 1433
Mora, Alberto, and Directorio, 926 and n. 5, 979 n. 28, 1014 and n. 50
Mora, Antonio, Mutual Aid Society, 236
Mora, Cándido, uncle of Alberto, *Batistiano*, 926 and n. 5, 928
Mora, Manuel, Communist, 579
Mora, Menelao, brother of Cándido, arrest, 883, 886; anti-Batista movement, 925, 950 n. 1; and Palace attack, 926, 927, 928, 929; death, 929, 979 n. 28, 1014, 1046
Morales, Calixto, *Fidelista*, 899, 901; in the Sierra, 901 n. 53, 915; commander in Las Villas, 1072
Morales, José María, banker, 118 and n. 29; and Lopez's expedition, 217
Morales, Leonardo, 584
Morales, Lieut, and Major, *Moncadaists*, 837, 844, 852; accuse Chaviano, 852
Morales, Nicolás, Negro conspirator, 81, 91
Morales Lemus, José (1810–71), 233 n. 4, 240, 242; and reform, 233; election, 238; and annexation, 241; backs 1868 rebellion, 246; U.S. government and, 250; in New York, 259, 264; loss of wealth, 270
Moran, Luis, in Miami, 968
Morán 'El Gallego', *Fidelistas*, 901; in the Sierra, 901 n. 53, 920 n. 49; desertion, 923 and n. 62
Moré, José Eugenio, Conde de Casa Moré, 268 and n. 12; benefactions, 278
Morejón, Col, 1088
Morell de Santa Cruz, Pedro Augustín (1644–1768), bishop of Havana, 48 n. 19; defies Albemarle, 47–8; encourages African-Catholic practices, 40–1, 48 n. 20, 518
Morell Romero, José, student, 592 n. 34, 638 n. 13, 641 n. 22; in Prío's cabinet, 764 n. 13; judge, in exile, 1347
Moreno, Gustavo, and Grau's cabinet, 651

Moreno, Luis, 1259
Moreno de la Torre, Andrés, 351
Moreno Fraginals, Manuel, 1464 and n. 39
Moret, Segismundo (1838–1913), Minister of the Colonies, new abolition law, 257–8, 279; and Cuban autonomy, 351, 367, 369; accepts Weyler's resignation, 352–3; announces amnesty, 353; reformed constitution, 354; and Spanish-American War, 377
Morgan, J. P. (1867–1943), 526, 545, 546, 586; and a Cuban loan, 547, 550, 551, 553, 555, 586
Morgan, Senator, 453
Morgan, U.S. Minister in Cuba, 474 and n. 8
Morgan, Stokeley, 584
Morgan, William (d. 1961), U.S. Fidelistas, and N. Cuba landing, 979 n. 31; occupies Cienfuegos, 1030; liberator of Trinidad, 1238; and anti-Castro plot, 1238 and nn. 7, 9, 1296; capture and death, 1297 and n. 60, 1359
Morillas, Pedro José, 184
Moriones, General, 261
Morote, Luis, and Gómez, 344–5, 345 n. 41
Morris, Robert (1734–1806), financier of N. American revolution, 67 and n. 29; and Cuba, 67
Morrow, Dwight, 553, 555
Morse, Senator Wayne, 1075, 1076
Morúa Delgado, Martín, mulatto, 294 n. 6, 456 n. 56, 459, 1121, 1433; lottery re-establishment act, 511; and colour bar, 516
Moskalenko, Marshal, and strategic rockets, 1388
Movimiento Nacional Revolucionaria (MNR), formation, 797, 866 n. 13; 'electoralists' and 'insurrectionists', 801 n. 27; collapse, 801; ex-members, 867
Movimiento Revolucionaria del Pueblo (MRP), foundation, 1286; activity, 1296, 1348; La Cañana rescue, 1303; brought into Frente, 1307
Moviemiento de Rescate Revolucionaria (MRR), 1275 and n. 7; U.S. support, 1275; newspaper (Rescate), 1275

Movimiento Socialista Revolucionaria (MSR); membership, 741–2; gunmen, 753; expedition against Trujillo, 755, 812; bribed with official posts, 763
Mujal, Eusebio (b. 1915), 770, 950 n. 1, 1029 n. 38; joins Communist party, 596 and nn. 52, 54; sec. gen. Joven Cuba, 699–700, 700 n. 26; joins Auténticos, 714, 748, 753, 1173; and exclusion of Communists from unions, 748; and army conspiracy, 783 and n. 19, 784; boss of CTC, 785, 792, 872, 889, 942, 972, 1178; and Batista's regime, 972, 1177; flight to Uruguay, 1031; private fortune, 1179
mulattoes, university restrictions, 13; free population, 36, 65 n. 23; majority in population, 52, 168; mill ownership, 63; Cuban numbers (Census), 65 and n. 23, 66, 81 and n. 43, 109, 169, 173, 429 and nn., 514 and n. 3, 515 and nn., 117–18; and African slave trade, 159, 160, 161; numbers and per cent freemen (1774–1861), 172; purchase of equality, 172; poets and writers, 172 and n. 20a; origins, 173; increase in numbers freed, 173; as contract workers, 185–6; and racism, 292; and Independence War (1895), 306; owner-managers of colonos, 428 and n. 57; location, 429 n. 66, 430; crops produced, 431; livestock possessions, 431 and n. 8; in the professions, 432 and n. 89, 1119, 1120 and n. 15; and 1900 elections, 461; intermixture with whites, 516; illiteracy rate, 517; and African ceremonies, 519; in Batista's army, 679; few churchmen, 683 and n. 4; and domestic service, 1112, 1120; intermarriage, 1118; pass as white, 1118; schooling, 118–19; wages; occupations, 1120 and n. 15; relations with Negroes, 1221; and public life, 1121–22, 1122–3; and unions, 1122; in army and police, 1122; Fidelista, 1122; culture negri-blanca, 1124; in Brigade 2506, 1360; improved material conditions since Revolution, 1432; and agriculture, 1559
Müller, Bishop of Matanzas, 985 n. 57, 991, 1276

Müller, Alberto, anti-Castroist, 1276; news sheet *Trinchera*, 1276; unknown fate, 1461

Müller, Sec. of Commerce, 1297

Muñoz, Dr, *Moncadaist*, 824 n. 3, 836

Muñoz, García, Liberal Governor of Oriente, 529

Muñoz Marín, Luis, Governor of Puerto Rico, 1058

Munroe, F. Adair, president Cuba Co., 608-9

Murillo, Consuelo, sec. to Chibás, 751

Murphy, Gerald, U.S. pilot, 883

Murphy, Robert, U.S. diplomat, and Castro, 948, 1015, 1026

Mussolini, Benito, 1490; Machado and, 573, 580; charismatic leadership, 1201 n. 30; and Pontine marshes, 1344

Naranjo, Cristóbal, 959; murder, 1248 n. 41, 1275

Naranjo, José, Minister of the Interior, 1224-5, 1253, 1455 and n. 7

Narváez, General, 239, 240

Narváez, Pánfilo de, 242, 1515

Nationalism, first intimations, 85; its heroes, 255 and nn. 6, 7; engendered by Independence War (1868), 270; demands independence, 332-3; after Spanish-American War, 442, 447; and U.S., 554, 684; Machado and, 605; and surviving Spanish influence, 684-5; student political philosophy, 685; Castro and, 818, 822, 1222; Cuba's catalyst position, 1277; aroused in Cubans, 1345, 1346

Nationalization, movement towards, 558; Blas Roca and, 734; Castro and, 955, 1203, 1253, 1289-90, 1297, 1371; U.S. and, 1060; foreshadowed in sugar industry, 1155-6; and Russian oil production, 1291; acquisitions of INRA, 1333; rapid increase, 1337; of private schools, 1341; of agriculture, 1349-40, 1441; bureaucracy created by, 1443; of small businesses, 1445

NATO, and missile crisis, 1403

Navajal, 997

Navarro Luna, Manuel, 904, 1080-1

Navy, Cuban, composition (1933), 659 n. 7; fires on Hotel Nacional, 659;

barrack mutiny, 664; and November revolt, 668; and Batista, 725; war losses, 731; sinks German submarine, 731; and Castro, 924; and Sierra war, 935; Cienfuegos mutiny, 961-3; 26 July sympathizers, 961, 962; and *operación verano*, 996, 1000, 1001; secret *Fidelistas*, 1040

Ships: *Cuba*, 659, 668, 962; *Harpoon*, 1009 n. 24; *Manuel Rionda*, 725; *Martí*, 924; *Patria*, 668

Neely, Charles, 445-6, 457

Negrete, Lieut, 780, 781

Negrín López, Juan, 877

Negroes, at defence of Havana, 7; free population, 13, 36, 65 n. 23, 66, 172, university restrictions, 13; the *carabelas*, 37 and n. 33; and suicide, 37 and n. 35, 284; and Spanish *fiestas*, 40; merger of Catholic and African religious cults, 39, 48 n. 20, 177, 281, 517-18; price of (Gold Coast), 51; mill ownership, 63; Census numbers, 65 and n. 23, 81 and n. 43, 109 n. 3, 169, 429 and nn., 514 n. 3, 515 and nn.; slave revolts, 77-8, 81, 91, 510, 512, 522-3; as *mayoral*, 130; and tobacco farms, 134; *cabildos*, 140, 147, 205; *bailes de tambor*, 147, 255; house servants, 147; lack of Church ministration, 151; majority in population, 168; purchase of freedom, 169, 171-2, 279; trade occupations, 169; and the arts, 172, 205, 206, 1119, 1123-4; freedom to kill them, 176; tribal origins, 183 and n. 72; cultural influences, 183 and n. 72; as wage-paid workers, 184 n. 1, 185-6, 242; involvement in craft work, 186, 515; relations with Chinese, 188; conspiracy of 1844, 205-6; punishments (*La Escalera*), 205, 206; destruction of *bourgeoisie*, 205-6; and Lincoln, 235; Mutual Aid Societies, 236-7; and Independence War (1868), 247, 265; (1895), 306, 323, 324; results from freedom, 280, 293; varying treatment, 281; and Martí, 300; decline in numbers, 419; in U.S. army in Cuba, 420 and n. 20; owner-managers of *colonos*, 428 and n. 57; numbers in agriculture, 429; Cuban-and African-born, 429, 517 and n. 15; location, 429 n. 66, 430; crops

Negroes – *Cont.*

produced, 431; livestock possessions, 431 and n. 88; in the professions, 432 and n. 89, 515, 1119 and n. 15; and franchise, 449, 461; illiteracy, 461, 517; growing feeling against whites, 474; contribution to Liberal revolt, 514; plan a revolution, 514; source of their difficulties, 515 ff.; peculiar form of 'delinquency', 516–17; illegitimacy rate, 517 and n. 14; evade ban on religious ceremonies, 517; transculturation of saints, 517–18, 519; literary tournaments and improvisations, 521; lack of outstanding politicians, 524; and of political solidarity, 524, 1188; wartime immigrants, 540 and n. 22; source of Cuban national identity, 601–2; contribution to folklore, 602; Machado and, 606, 683; in Batista's army, 679; ignored by political parties, 683; Church membership, 683 and n. 4; and Communism, 692; preference for urban work, 805 n. 12; bottom layer of society, 1111–12; as servants, 1112, 1120; population in 1950s, 1117–18; inter-marriage, 1118; geographical immobility, 1118; schooling, 1118–19; wages, 1119; occupations, 1120 and n. 15; racism and, 1120–1; relations with mulattoes, 1121; denounce Castro's silence on racism, 1121; and public life, 1121–22, 1122–23; and unions, 1122; and Batista, 1122; and army and police, 1122 and n. 8; descendants of forced migrants, 1123; Afro-Cuban religion, 1124–6; racial interchange, 1125; port workers, 1179; political inactivity, 1188; use of rooftop bars, 1345; in Brigade 2506, 1360; improved conditions since Revolution, 1432; image of Castro, 1432; survival of older prejudices, 1432–4; on White Cubans, 1433 n. 34; and agriculture, 1550–1

Efors and Efiks, 160 and n. 23, 524, 1124; secret society (*Abakuá*), 521

Ibos, 52, 160, 283

Yorubas, 52, 160, 177, 183 and n. 72, 283, 1124, 1125; transculturation of saints, 517; Afro–Cuban religious ceremonies, 518; dominant influence in Cuba, 519; religious manifestation in Cuba, 520–1; African and American *santería*, 520, 522; initiation of women, 520; nature of Obatala (Christ), 520; identification of Our Lady with Odudúa, 520; cult patrons, 520–1

Nelson, Hugh, U.S. Minister in Spain, 100 and n. 34, 104

Nelson, Lowry, on the lottery, 513 and n. 26; and Cuban marriage, 684 and n. 8; and children, 1132; and education, 1133–4, 1134 and n. 18; San Blas farm, 1551; *Rural Cuba*, 513 n. 26

Neruda, Pablo, 1465; *Canción de Gesta* on Cuba, 1277

Nervo, Padilla, Mexican chargé d'affaires, 644 and n. 31

Newcastle, Sir Thomas Pelham-Holles, Duke of (1693–1768), and Havana expedition, 4, 5, 42

Nicaragua, 417, 579, 589 n. 17, 1228; invasion of, 227; under protection of U.K., 228 n. 49; restoration of slavery, 228; U.S. intervention, 626 and nn. 4, 5, 668; population figures, 1093 n. 6; feared Cuban overthrow, 1303; arrival of rebels, 1311; base for Cuban invasion, 1355, 1360 n. 18, 1363–4, 1366, 1368

Nicolau, Ramón, Communist, at La Cabaña, 1082

Nicolson, South Sea Co. factor, 24 n. 28, 31–2

Niger Delta, slave trade, 159, 160, 183, 521

Niño, Colombian chief of police, 816

Nivernais, Duc de, and fall of Havana, 42 and n. 1

Nixon, Richard (born 1913), U.S. president, vice-president, 862, 1061, 1389; in Latin America, 1064; meets Castro, 1210; and Cuban exiles, 1243, 1271, 1278, 1296, 1300, 1305; clashes with Kennedy, 1300; and support for invasion, 1369 n. 44

Norris, Stuart, CBS, 1214

North, Joseph, 1078

Nott, Lieut, detains *Mexicano* off Havana, 1537

Nozzolino, Caefano, 159

Núñez, General Emilio, 456 n. 56, 459, 508; vice-president, 526, 531; and 1916 elections, 526–7

Núñez, Suárez, 859
Núñez Carrión, Dr Fidel, 1085
Núñez del Castillo, Carlos, Director Havana Savings Bank, 207; and *anexionismo*, 207, 208
Núñez del Castillo, José, 207
Núñez del Castillo family, 32, 47, 122, 141
Núñez Jiménez, Dr Antonio, geographer, Guevara peace envoy, 1027 and n. 31; and BRAC, 1078; and Agrarian Reform, 1214, 1215, 1328; director of INRA, 1217, 1229, 1297, 1376; judgements of, 1217–18, 1218 n. 9; efforts to raise a loan, 1253–4; buys Russian factories, 1285; take-over of private enterprise, 1297; and FLN, 1317; and primitive Indians, 1528 n. 21
Núñez Portuondo, Emilio (1898–), 982 n. 46; to head new ministry, 982, 983; calls for cease-fire, 1027
Núñez Portuondo, Ricardo, and 1948 elections, 757, 982 n. 46
Núñez y Estrada, his *Political Economy*, 238
Nurse, Capt., 203

O'Donnell, Leopoldo (1808–67), later Duke of Tetuan, captain-general of Cuba, government policy, 204, 206; and Negro conspiracy (1844), 205 and n. 24, 206; slave trading profits, 206; popular revolution (1854), 224; premier, 238; dismissal, 239
O'Farrill family, aggrandisement by marriage, 83–4; mill and slave owning fortunes, 84, 152; outstanding debts, 136 n. 2, 140; public benefactions, 153, 278; social position, 154; and abolition, 234
O'Farrill, General Gonzalo, 88 n. 17; Spanish Minister of War, 84, 88
O'Farrill, José Ricardo, 233 n. 5; liberal economist, 73, 79 n. 37; and reform, 233; and emancipation, 235; indebtedness, 235 and n. 12; sugar mill, *Esperanza*, 235
O'Farrill, Brig. Gen. Juan, 32 n. 22; first steam-boat licence, 84, 121; and slave trade Commission, 206
O'Farrill, Fr Ramón, refugee, 1257
O'Kelly, J. J., 254–5
O'Reilly family, 152; in decay, 153;

lose cattle-slaughtering monopoly, 423
O'Reilly, Marshal Alejandro (1725–94), 75 n. 11; fortification expert, 63 and n. 14, 72 n. 2
O'Reilly, Conde, 153, 234
O'Sullivan, John L. (1813–95), ed. *Democratic Review*, 211, 224; and racism, 210–11, 211 n. 20 ('Manifest Destiny'); and purchase of Cuba, 211; and Young America, 220 n. 12
Obregón, José Enrique, 581, 593
Ochoa, Emilio, 754 n. 48, 782, 843 n. 41, 956; and Chibás, 767, 889; arrest 799; and Agramonte, 800; agreement with Prío, 802; and 1958 elections, 951, 952, 956; Ortodoxo group, 968
Olin, Senator, 1232
Oliva, Erneldo, and Brigade 2506, 1359, 1361; beach landing, 1362, 1364, 1365; under attack, 1366–7; late career, 1371
Olmedo, Ricardo, political gangster, 925, 931; new police command, 1071 n. 17
Olney, Richard (1835–1917), Sec. of State, 332 n. 11; and Cuban affairs, 332, 335–6, 338 and n. 48, 340
Oltuski, Enrique, and 26 July, 868, 889 n. 59, 918, 1067; and Civic Resistance, 918, 975 and n. 6; and Guevara, 1012; and Inst. of Agrarian Reform, 1013 n. 49; Minister of Communications, 1067, 1253; drops out, 1290 and n. 41
Operación verano, 996–8
Oquendo, Capt., 1017, 1040
Ordaz, Dr Bernarbé, director Mazorra asylum, 1426
Ordoqui, Joaquín, Communist, 597 and n. 59, 895, 930 n. 32, 1319, 1342; denounces Guiteras and Grau, 697; and Spanish Civil War, 703; confers with Batista, 711, 878; sporting weekly, 765; and ORI, 1377 n. 21; disgraced, 1454 n. 4, 1467, 1468
Orense, 224
Organization of American States (OAS) (Pan American Union), 301 n. 22, 883, 977, 1206; asked for help, 789 and n. 3; and 1958 elections, 982; Castro and, 1089; Latin American committee, 1213 and n. 73; meeting

Organization of American States – *Cont.*
in Santiago de Chile, 1239; 'Declaration of San José', 1293, 1295; suspension of Cuba, 1375 and n. 11, 1385; and missile crisis, 1403, 1406

Organizaciones Revolucionarias Integradas (ORI), old Communist leaders, 1372, 1373, 1468; headquarters, 1373 and n. 3; Communist–*Fidelistas* directorate, 1376–7, 1377 n. 17; mulattoes and Negroes, 1377 and n. 24; promotion of a 'united party', 1378–9; dominates political appointments, 1379; shell for 'new party', 1381; disappearance in 1963, 1453; purge of, 1456; selection of new members, 1456

Orihuela, Lieut José, *puros*, 763, 884

Ormond, John (Mungo John), African slave merchant, 161; and Río Pongo, 160 and n. 24

Oro de Guisa, murder of peasants, 967 and n. 18

Orozco, 579

Ortega, Antonio, ed. *Carteles*, 1291

Ortega, Nila, 795

Ortiz, Major Arsenio (d. 1949), 598, 609, 634, 681, 743

Ortiz, Fernando, 524, 532, 1058, 1117, 1123, 1528; on Havana 'delinquency', 516–17; use of prefix Afro-, 519 n. 22, 1124; and *Abakuá*, 521; draft law for university autonomy, 565; draft protest, 567; and Cuban folklore, 602 and n. 75, 1124; contrasts tobacco and sugar, 1161

Ortiz Faes, Gustave, 762; career, 761 n. 7, 813 n. 53

Ortodoxos, 754, 843 n. 41, 930; Communists and, 757; attack the regime, 761; and Chibas' oratory, 767 and elections, 773–4, 774 n. 36, 853, 857; hopes placed in, 775–6; and Batista, 785, 789 and n. 3, 792, 796, 951; co-operation with Auténticos, 800, 802; raid Prío's villa, 820; welcome Castro, 863, 917–18; distinguished from 26 July, 867, 881; Castro's *Manifesto No. 1*, 869; and the *puros*, 884 and n. 36; internal dissension, 889; splinter groups, 956 968, 1046; and Civil War, 1045

Ortodoxo Youth, 814 n. 56, 824, 856, 1115

Osorio, 'Chicho', shot at La Plata, 913 and nn. 19, 21

Otaño, Sergeant, 1009

Otero, Lisandro, ed. *Cuba*, 1491; denounces *Padilla*, 1466; *Pasión de Urbino*, 1466 n. 45

Ovares, Enrique, 767 n. 19, 814

Ovares, Lieut José, 668

Pacheco, Abelard, 590

Pacheco, Pedro, 715

Pact of Caracas, 1003–4, 1007, 1065, 1070

Padilla, Herberto, and Writers' Union prize, 1466 and n. 45

Paez, General, 104

País, Frank, 801 n. 28; and Castro, 866, 867; head of 'action groups', 868 and n. 19, 891; Santiago rising, 895, 1275; commando raids, 896; revolutionary character, 896 n. 13; in the Sierra, 917, 923; shot by police, 957, 968; alleged betrayal, 967 n. 24; 'Second Front', 1043, 1198; controls the army, 1198

Palacios, Dr Concepción, and Guevara, 880

Palau, Félix, murder, 752

Pallas, Paulino, anarchist, 304

Palmerston, Henry Temple, Viscount, 201; and Turnbull in Cuba, 203; freetrader and abolitionist, 215; and enforcement of abolition, 231

Paneque, 'Major' Victor Manuel ('Diego'), 1032, 1275; and Torres, 1012 and n. 40

Paniagua, Julio, 766, 768

Pantoja, Capt. Orlando, 1074 n. 29; death in Bolivia, 1074 n. 29, 1469

Pantoja, Major Pérez, 975 and n. 7

Paprón, Judge, 1227

Para, Domingo de, 571

Pardo Jiménez, José, *Batistiano*, 861 n. 58, 924

Pardo Llada, José, radio writer, 822, 854 and n. 35, 862, 874, 889, 1113, 1136, 1274; SIM and, 792; arrest, 801; signs Prío-Ochoa agreement, 802 n. 29; at anti-Batista meeting, 870; and 1958 elections, 956, 977; in the Sierra, 1011; defects to Mexico, 1343

Paredes, Dr Ricardo, Communist, 579

Parejo, Antonio, agent to Queen Mother, 154, 156, 214, 221; planter, *Santa Susana*, and slave trader, 137 and n. 8; funeral, 147

Parellada, Otto, and 26 July, 896 n. 14; death, 897

Parés, Francisco, on Communists, 1081

Parker, Vice-Admiral Hyde (1784–1854), off Havana, 203

Parra, 'General' Masó, bandit, 491 and n. 44

Partido Obrero Socialista, foundation, 575

Partido Revolucionario Cubano Auténtico; *see* Auténtico

Partido Socialista Popular (PSP), new name of URC, 733, 747; slogan, 733; membership goal, 734; Roca and, 745 and n. 16

Partido Socialista Radical, foundation, 547 n. 18, 575 and n. 24

Partido Unificado de la Revolución (PURS), Escalante and, 1446 n. 7, 1453; succeeds ORI, 1453, 1477; succeeded by 'new' Communist party, 1453, 1477; old party representation, 1454 n. 3; selection of members, 1456–7

Partido Unión Revolucionaria (PUR), organization, 706–7, 710; Communist front, 707, 712

Pastor, Antonio (later Count), 137, 156–7

Pastor, Luis María, 239

Pastor, Manuel, 195, 199

'Patachula', 824 n. 3, 825

Patterson, R., 193 and n. 3

Pauncefote, Sir Julian, British ambassador, 373

Pavía, General, captain-general in Puerto Rico, 244, 248 n. 6, 261, 263

Pawley, William (1896–), U.S. ambassador, 815 n. 60, 1162 and n. 25 1210; in Bogotá, 815–16; in Rio de Janeiro, 948; and Batista-Castro problem, 1015–16, 1018, 1162 n. 25; suggests new government, 1018

Payne, Senator E., 460

Pazos, Felipe, economist, 641 n. 22, 759 n. 2, 831, 864 n. 10, 884 n. 36, 1066, 1230; student, 592 n. 34, 759, 918; proposes president, 649, 656; and Prío, 759; President National Bank, 760, 918, 1181 n. 3, 1184, 1199–1200,

1215, 1220, 1252; resignation, 784, 1246; and Batista, 789; and 26 July, 918, 968, 971, 1046; and Castro's political manifesto, 953–4, 961; and naval mutiny, 961; and Miami Pact, 969, 1066; escapes death, 975; accepts election delay, 1086; in exile, 1199 n. 23; and U.S. economic aid, 1205; and U.S. visit, 1209; summoned to cabinet, 1246–7; leaves Cuba, 1248; and EEC, 1252; in exile, 1471 n. 66

Pazos, Javier, son of above, and FEU presidency, 964 and n. 10; and 26 July, 921, 1042 n. 16; and Castro, 910, 919, 1052, 1213 n. 74; and Palace attack, 927–8, 930, 938 n. 19; attitude to Communism, 944; in exile, 944 n. 8, 1471 n. 66; and Ministry of Economics, 1282

Pearcy, S. H., 502

Pedraza, Sergeant (afterwards General) José Eleuterio, and army plot, 634, 635; in Batista's government (1940), 634 n. 1; rated Capt., 646 n. 37; military governor of Havana, 699; and Batista as president, 725–6; imprisonment, 746

Pedraza, General, and Batista, 1021

Pedroso family, 187, 278, 1110; commercial origins, 136; mill and estate ownership, 152; reduced circumstances, 277, 428

Pedroso, Carlos, Conde de Casa Pedroso, 142

Pedroso, Dr Electro, 878

Pedroso, José, attorney-general, 47; Havana house, 17 and n. 13, 30 n. 14

Pedroso, Martín, 186

Pedroso, Mateo (1719–1800), *regidor perpetuo*, 17 n. 13, 45; Havana merchant, 30 and n. 14, 32, 33; capital resources, 33, 66

Pedroso, Pablo, 30 n. 14, 33

Pedroso, Víctor, banker, 1110; and Batista, 931; and 'commission of harmony', 982, 983; praises Urrutia, 1070

Peláez, Carlos, 874

Pellón, José, 1044; and FONU, 1083 n. 23; and CTC, 1250 n. 48, 1320

Peña, Félix, 993, 994 nn. 27, 28, 1202

Peña, Lázaro, 756, 765–6, 842, 843 n. 41, 846; Negro Sec. Gen. of CTC, 713, 734, 744, 1080, 1122, 1178, 1250,

Peña, Lázaro – *Cont.*
1251, 1318, 1449 n. 16, 1450; Grau opposes his elections, 753 and n. 44; Castro and, 878, 887; hostility towards, 1337; Sec. CTC(R), 1337; and ORI, 1377 n. 21; and PURS, 1454 n. 3

Peña, 'Major', in Sierra Escambray, 1012

Peña, Col Rafael, and Mendieta's cabinet, 678

Peña Vilaboa, José, and Communism, 576, 577 n. 34; first Sec. Gen., 577 and n. 36

Peñalver family, 32, 47, 152; entitled Marqués de Arcos and de Casa Peñalver, Conde de San Fernando and Peñalver, 143; inbreeding, 204 n. 21

Peñalver, Gabriel, son of Sebastián, 44; and the *cabildo*, 45 n. 14; ennobled in Spain, 61 n. 1; slave losses, 87 and n. 15

Peñalver, Ignacio, *see* Arcos, Marqués de

Peñalver, Joaquín, sugar mill revolt, 204

Peñalver, Luis (1749–1810), episcopal preferment, 71 and n. 55; and Economical Society, 73

Peñalver, Nicolás, Conde de, son of above, 123 and n. 53; use of Chinese labour, 186

Peñalver, Sebastián de (1708–82), 44 n. 10; deputy to Albermarle, 43–4, 44 n. 11; *regidor*, 45 and n. 14; death in disgrace, 61

Peñate, Judge, 1227

Pendás, Porfirio, 592 nn. 33, 35, 744

Peñelas, Luis, 1274

Peninsulares, 43, 91; and English occupation, 47; and technology, 154; and Independence War (1868), 246, 248; military cadres, 248; Madrid representative, 258; in Constitutional Union party, 268; in reduced circumstances, 277; predominance in elections, 294; relations with *criollos*, 300

Pentarquía, the, nominations, 639; alleged Communist interest, 644; and Céspedes, 646; and election of president, 647; breaks with Batista, 648

Penzoldt, 'centrifugal' machine, 118

Perdomo, Col, 646, 663

Pereda, Manuel, 187

Pérez, Caldwell, 806

Pérez, Crecencio, helps Castro, 900, 901, 902, 903, 908; in the Sierra, 915, 938, 996 n. 2

Pérez, Emma, 741

Pérez, Faustino, Baptist student, 898, 899, 962 n. 5, 1408, 1455 n. 6; and MNR, 801 n. 28, 908 n. 77; and 26 July, 868, 891 n. 65, 894 n. 5, 988 n. 1; in the Sierra, 901 and n. 53, 904, 1001–2, 1011, 1044; leaves for Havana, 908 and n. 77, 909, 988; and Matthews, 919; and *Nuestra Razón*, 953 n. 7; plan for general strike, 988 and n. 1, 989, 990, 991, 1044; replaced by Fernandez, 991; and Law I, 1011 n. 32; controls army administration, 1043–4; anti-U.S. and Communist, 1051, 1221, 1320; and new government (1959), 1067, 1247; and Matos, 1251, 1256; reinstatement, 1382

Pérez, Senator Gonzalo, 512

Pérez, Ignacio, 916

Pérez, José, 1261

Pérez, José Miguel, 576, 577 and nn. 33, 35

Pérez, Mongo, 900

Pérez Almaguer, Waldo, Governor of Oriente, 839 and n. 28; denounces Chaviano, 886

Pérez Chaumont, Capt. ('Ojos Bellos'), commander Moncada barracks, 839, 842

Pérez Coujil, Col, 1017, 1021; bribed to leave, 1022

Pérez Damera, Major, promoted general, 745–6, 755; and Trujillo expedition, 755; deposition, 763, 778; attempted assassination, 774

Pérez de la Riva, Demetrio, 268

Pérez de la Riva, Juan, 1464 and n. 39

Pérez de Miret, Raquel, Minister of Social Welfare, 1224, 1253

Pérez Galdos, Juan, 275

Pérez Jiménez, Venezuelan dictator, 1089

Pérez Leiva, Emiliano, 666

Pérez Rivas, Francisco, bomb layer, 945

Pérez San Román, José, anti-Castroist, 1283 n. 21; and Brigade 2506, 1359 and n. 16

Pérez San Román, Roberto, and Brigade 2506, 1359 and n. 16, 1361, 1367; beach landing, 1362, 1364; expects U.S. aid, 1367, 1369; and defeat, 1369 n. 41; ransomed, 1371

Pérez Santisteban, Roberto, 741, 754

Pérez Serantes, Enrique, Bishop of Camagüey, afterwards Archbishop of Santiago, 807, 1128; and treatment of Moncada prisoners, 840, 841, 844; peace plea, 951, 982; and Castro, 1127, 1129; criticizes Agrarian Reform, 1223; denounces Communism, 1282, 1350; praises U.S., 1350; house arrest, 1365

Perón, Juan Domingo (born 1895), Argentinian dictator, 880, 1193; and Cuban students, 814 and n. 56; and Falkland Islands, 814

Peru, 16, 566, 846, 1166 n. 46, 1488 n. 14, 1528; treatment of slaves, 39; position of viceroy, 45; *intendentes*, 90; declared independent, 99; *central* system, 277; oligarchic rule, 278; Communist party, 579, 697, 714, 1314 and n. 10; population figures, 1094; sugar quota, 1142 n. 13; breaks with Cuba, 1314

Pesant, Roberto, 916, 920 n. 49

Pezuela, Jacopo de la, 221 n. 14; and 1792 census, 90; and Church capital, 462 n. 86

Pezuela, Juan Manuel, Marqués de la Pezuela (1810–75), captain-general, 220–1, 221 n. 14; abolitionist, 221, 222; decree freeing *emancipados*, 221; opens sugar plantations to investigation, 222; decree ordering annual registration of slaves, 223; dismissal, 226

Phillips, Ruby Hart, of *New York Times*, on student shooting, 607 and n. 8; on strikes, 616; Cuban Revolution, 630, 631 n. 22; Grau, 652–3; Mendieta, 676; Cubans in Spain, 703 n. 34; Batista, 845; secures Matthews for Cuba, 918; and Castro, 1033 n. 50, 1206

Phillips, James Doyle, of *New York Times*, and sergeants' revolt, 637, 639; and Grau, 650; and surrender of Atarés, 669; and military clique, 704

Phinney family, 141

Pidal, Pedro, Spanish Foreign Minister, 214

Piedra, Judge Carlos Manuel, pro-

visional president, 1026, 1053; calls for cease-fire, 1027

Piedra, Col Orlando, chief of Buró de Investigaciónes, 869 and n. 23; in Mexico, 869; reprisals on students, 890; and SIM, 912, 928; leaves Cuba, 1026

Pieltaín, General Cándido (1822–88), captain-general, 261 n. 31; war policy, 261–2

Pierce, Franklin (1804–69), U.S. president, 219, 220 n. 12, 381 n. 1; and annexationism, 222; and *Black Warrior* affair, 222–3; bans private expeditions, 224; loses control of Congress, 225; and Nicaragua, 227–8

Pierson, Warren, President Import-Export Bank, 716 and n. 2, 727

Pigs, Bay of, *see* Cochinos, Bay of

Pin, General, 335, 343, 363

Pina, Rogelio, 871

Piñeiro, Carlos, Grand Master, 1115

Piñeiro, Major Manuel ('Barba Roja'), 930, 1273 n. 4; chief of counter-intelligence, 930 n. 28, 1198 n. 18 1202, 1273, 1455

Pino, Ondina, 869

Pino, Capt. Onelio, in *Granma*, 894 and n. 5

Pino, Orquídea, 868, 894 n. 6

Pino, Quintín, 868 n. 19, 1029

Pino Donoso, Martha, 910

Pino Guerra, Col, 474–5, 475 n. 9, 526; Liberal revolt, 475, 528; Liberal, 484 n. 18; commander new army, 490, 680; resignation, 508; and presidential election, 570

Pino Santos, Communist, 1215, 1218, 1240

Pinto Ramón, 226–7, 227 n. 45, 233 n. 4

Pio Élizalde, Leopalda, 817, 1029 n. 38

Pissani, Dr Salvador, 879

Pitt, William, Earl of Chatham, 4; and Havana expedition, 5; and Caribbean colonies, 55 and n. 60

Pitt, William (the younger), 76

Pittucks, Philip, 153–4

Pi y Margall, 253, 298, 327, 385; and Cuban independence, 348

Plank, Dr John, 1310

Platt, Senator Orville H., 453

Platt Amendment, 359 n. 23, 453, 470 500, 507, 1064; becomes law, 453, 454; accepted by Cuban Convention,

Platt Amendment – *Cont.*
455; possible ending, 586, 615; Machado and, 586, 588; U.S. and, 591, 688; effect of, 593; Communists and, 615; Batista and, 679; student repudiation, 686; abrogation in 1934, 694–5, 695 n. 14, 1189; use of word *plattista*, 695; Castro and, 1076, 1077; folly of, 1419

Playa Girón, invasion landings, 1361, 1362, 1363, 1369; militia, 1362; 'Week' and 'Month', 1472

Pocock, Sir George (1706–92), Admiral in charge Havana expedition, 3 and n. 12, 5–6; prize money, 43; casualties, 48–9; subsequent career, 57

Poey, Juan, railway vice-president, 122 and n. 50

Poey and Hernández, slave traders, 87, 83, 122

Poinsett, Joel, 100

Polavieja, General Camilo García de (1838–1914), aide to Campos, 267, 408; and Cuban independence, 299 and n.16; and Philippine war, 347, 348

Police force, 110; Tacón and, 194; numbers, races, etc., 490 n. 42, 515 and n. 7; use of murder and brutality, 591, 595, 598, 607, 700, 768, 875, 890, 912, 931, 932 and n. 23, 975, 1009; ABC and, 595; lack of colour bar, 683; under Batista, 791–2, 1039; and Negro Communists, 846 n. 5; and Castro's release, 864, 867; student attacks on, 889–90; raid Haitian Embassy, 890; and 26 July, 912; defence of Havana Palace, 929, 930; and Juventud Socialista, 944; part in Civil War, 959; attack Communists, 981; *de facto* 26 July and Directorio, 1031; under Revolutionary Government, 1071 and nn.; protection racket, 1097; under Castro, 1253; infiltrated by CIA, 1434 n. 37

Police, political (G. 2), 1253, 1273; and counter-revolutionaries, 1321–2; civilian branch, 1322; interrogations, 1352

Political prisoners, trial of, 1458–9, 1461; their numbers, 1460 and nn. 28, 29; unknown fate, 1460–1, 1461 n. 31; rehabilitation programme, 1461

Polk, James Knox (1795–1849), U.S. president, 211; and Mexican War,

211–12; and purchase of Cuba, 212, 213, 219, 367 n. 1

Polo de Bernabé, Admiral José (1821–95), and *Virginius* incident, 262 and n. 36

Pompa, Fidel, sec. ORI, 1379

Ponce, Dagobert, 1261 and n. 11, 1280, 1456

Ponce, José, 836 n. 10, 900

Ponce de Léon, Nestor, 587–8

Pons, Angel, 666

Pontifex and Wood, 117

Porra, Pizzi de, 668

Porristas, 682, 695; killing of, 628, 632

Porro, Ricardo, 1428 and n. 17

Portela, Guillermo, 638 n. 13, 639, 647, 655, 664

Portell Vila, Professor Herminio, 754 n. 48, 1058; on López, 214 n. 42, 217; calls for Machado's resignation, 591; at Montevideo, 671 n. 17; and Chibás' suicide, 770 n. 25; and the radio, 793; member Havana Municipal Council, 795; tutor to Castro, 803, 809, 819; and University Reform, 1287

Portocarrero, Jesús, and Batista's government, 783 and n. 20

Portocarrero, René, painter, 1464 and n. 38

Portuondo, Bartolomé, Marqués de las Delicias, Judge of Mixed Court, 142

Portuondo, José Antonio, 2nd Marqués de las Delicias, 195

Potts, G. W., Esso representative, 1017

Powers, Gary, 1278, 1396 n. 6

Pozo, Justo Luis, 1029 n. 38; Mayor of Havana, 784, 1268; member of *diálogo cívico*, 874

Pozos Dulces, Conde de, progressive planter, 213; and reform, 233; and abolition, 234; ed. *El Siglo*, 235; election, 238; and white immigrants, 275–6

Prado, Juan de (1716–c. 1770), captain-general, 6 and n. 34, 44; defence of Havana, 7, 10–11, 46; death in disgrace, 11, 43

Prats, Hiram, 944, 981 and n. 38, 1079

Pratt, Congresswoman Ruth, 560–1

Prendes, Ramón, 968

Prendes Fernández, Segundo, 774

Prebisch, Raúl, President ECLA, 1011 and n. 34

Presno, Dr José Antonio, 629 and n. 14; proposed president, 649; Minister of Health, 743 n. 10

Press, Cuban, 1136–7; and repression of violence, 910, 912 and n. 15; Castro and, 915–16, 917, 918; visits Sierra, 935, 936–7, 938–9, 960 n. 32, 973, 976, 1038 and n. 4; condemns regime, 982, 1273; corruption and bribery, 1136; criticises Castro, 1260–1; end of freedom, 1261, 1262–3, 1268, 1280; attacks on U.S., 1269; dullness under Revolution, 1463

Prestes, Luis Carlos, Brazilian Communist, 697

Preston, Andrew, 546 and n. 8

Preston, Dr Thomas, agronomist, 1441

Preston, William, 228 n. 51; and purchase of Cuba, 228, 229

Prieto, Indalecio, 877

Prieto, Major Plinio, rebel, execution, 1285 and n. 24

Prim, General Juan, 243 and n. 43; and Cuban rebellion, 247; U.S.–Cuba negotiations, 251, 253, 257; prime minister, 252, 253; denunciation, 253; nominates a king for Spain, 258; and a Cuban peace, 258–9; murder, 259 and n. 22, 1248 n. 41

Primo de Rivera, General Fernando, 347

Primo de Rivera, José Antonio, influence on Castro, 807–8, 822 and n. 101

Prío, Antonio, 780; and Havana mayoralty, 760, 764

Pío Socorrás, Carlos (born 1903), 759 n. 1; student, 592 n. 38, 595, 638 n. 13, 641 n. 22, 759; and presidency, 649, 759, 780; and La Cabaña gaol, 660; at Montevideo, 671 n. 17; Auténtico, 744, 1046; and elections (1940), 722; (1948), 757; (1952), 773; Minister of Labour, 753, 756; takes over CTC headquarters, 754; gangster bodyguard, 757; love of money, 759; character, 759–60; farm La Chata, 760, 869–70; law against gangsterismo, 760, 761; cabinet, 760, 764, 775 and n. 1; establishes Central Bank, 760, 1164; breaks with Grau, 761; public works programme, 762; and army discontent, 763; 'Pact of grupos', 763; accusations against Grau 764, 767; labour troubles, 766; opens CMQ television station, 766 n. 17;

and political chaos, 770; alleged coup d'état plan, 776, 780; denies conservation with Alleigro, 776–7; and army conspiracy, 781–3, 785–6; abandons struggle, 784; leaves for Mexico, 785–6; assessment, 786; agreement with Ochoa, 803; arrest in Florida, 852; political discussions, 861; returns to Cuba, 869–70, 1033, 1046; attempts to unite opposition. 870; and Castro, 876, 888; and the Puros, 884; in Miami, 886, 968; in the U.S., 886; second expedition to Dominican Republic, 888–9; opposition group, 925, 950, 952, 971; links with Directorio Revolucionario, 926; and naval mutiny, 961; organizer Nat. Lib. Council, 968; indicted for planning arms delivery, 976 and n. 14; and Junta of Unity, 1003 and n. 30; and Escambray 'Second Front', 1005 and n. 2; return of supporters, 1031; and Civil War, 1046, decree authorizing machine-made cigars, 1160; backs Agrarian Reform, 1223; survival in exile, 1471 n. 66

Pro-Dignidad Estudiantil movement, 767 and n. 19

Pro Ley y Justicia, see Agrupación Revolucionaria

Proctor, Senator Redfield, 369 n. 13; on autonomy in Cuba, 369

Proenza, Raúl Ramón, 1273

Profintern ('Red Union'), 578, 579

Puebla, Carlos, 856, 1154

Puente, José, 1003

Puente, Orlando, 775 n. 1, 780

Puente Blanco, José, and Havana University, 1286

Puertas, Juan María, 1255

Puertas, Orlando, 1241

Puerto Cabezas, Brigade 2506 and, 1311

Puerto Padre, 1148, 1264

Puerto Rico, 27, 33 n. 25, 64, 76, 104, 194, 289, 353; convict colony, 33; sugar production, 126, 457 and n. 64, 1139 and n. 8, 1143 n. 22; coffee production, 131 n. 16, 457; reforming majority, 238; Madrid representative, 239; proposes abolition, 239; revolutionary activity, 243, 244, 248 n. 6; and Independence War (1868), 263; liberated slaves, 279; franchise reform, 303; proposed reformed Consti-

Puerto Rico – *Cont.*
  tution, 264; U.S. and, 388 and n. 30,
  402, 406, 420, 502; exempt from
  sugar tariff, 550, 560; Communist
  movement, 579, 697; population
  figures, 1094, 1513; Telephone Co.,
  1163 n. 28; point of 'quarantine' line,
  1406; Cuban exiles, 1434; primitive
  Indians, 1515, 1516 and n. 19
Puig Jordan, Argelio, 598
Pujol, Col Eduardo, 529, 530
Pujol, José, 940
Pujol, Raúl, 957 and n. 24
Pulitzer, Joseph (1847–1911), 314, 331;
  ed. *World*, 340, 406 n. 19; and war
  with Spain over Cuba, 341, 406; and
  Canovas' reforms, 348; steals Hearst's
  news, 406; hires Crane as correspondent, 406 n. 20; war fund for 71st New
  York Regiment, 406 n. 20

Querejeta, General, 1122
Quero, Col, police commander, 571
Quesada, Emilio de, and Escalante, 1469
Quesada, Gonzalo de, 333, 456 n. 56,
  459; and New York Junta, 315;
  deposition, 438; representative in
  Washington, 477; ABC, 570, 571 n. 9,
  615
Quesada, Col Héctor de, 646
Quesada, General Manuel de, and
  Revolutionary War (1868), 245, 250
Quesalta, Rafael de, sugar mill,
  Desengano, 427
Quevedo, Angel, and Havana Uni-
  versity, 1286
Quevedo, José, at Cantillo-Castro meet-
  ing, 1022
Quevedo, Major, and *operación verano*,
  997, 998; surrenders to Castro, 1016;
  director of logistics, 1073
Quevedo, Miguel Angel (d. 1969), ed.
  Bohemia, 741, 1137; condemns the
  Revolution, 1292 and n. 48
Quiñones, Col, and Liberal revolt, 528
Quintana, Silvio, 1454 n. 4; and
  JUCEI, 1337 n. 88
Quitman, John Anthony, Governor of
  Mississippi, 215 and n. 49, 216;
  backs López, 216; and Frías' con-
  spiracy against Spain, 218; proposed
  expedition to Cuba, 220, 221, 222,
  224–5, 226, 227; and preservation of
  slavery, 220; resignation, 227

radio, Cuba and, 766 n. 18, 1163,
  1164; used by Chibás, 766–7; and
  Palace attack, 928, 929; destruction
  in Oriente, 967; bomb outrages, 1010;
  Castro and, 1195, 1235; government
  control, 1261, 1268, 1270, 1343;
  influence of U.S., 1343: Circuito
  Nacional Cubano, 1136; COCO,
  817; FIEL, 1274, 1343; La Voz del
  Indio, 1136; Radio Aeropuerto, 1010;
  Radio Free Dixie, 1434 n. 37;
  Radio Mambí, 1195; Radio Rebelde,
  980, 996, 1011, 1032, 1195; Radio
  Reloj, 928; Radio Unión, 798,
  1195
railways, 110, 121–3, 208, 464, 1161;
  and sugar, 41, 121, 123, 234, 273,
  1152, 1161; Havana plans, 121–2,
  197, 464, 541, 1349; cost and extent,
  122; source of stock, 122 and n. 48;
  control of, 122; establishment of
  warehouses, 123; English investment,
  201; slave revolt, 204; effect of cheap
  rails, 273, 279; private boom, 274;
  building of, 431; American developers, 464, 541; Arsenal Lands scandal,
  506; Nuevitas-Caibarién affair, 510;
  survival of private operators, 557,
  558; decline in freightage, 1162;
  workers' strike, 1196
Ramírez, Alejandro (1777–1821), *intendente*, 94 and n. 6, 117 n. 26
Ramírez, José ('Pepe'), and ANAP,
  1002, 1330 n. 61
Ramírez, Manuel de Jesús Léon, 977
Ramírez, Trinidad, 244
Ramírez Ruiz, Porfirio, 1285
Ramos, Adolfo, 236
Ramos, Domingo, 646
Ramos, García, 618
Ramos Blanco, Teodoro, Negro sculp-
  tor, 1124
Ramos Latour, Hector, 1450
Ramos Latour, René ('Daniel'), *Fidel-
  istas*, 934 n. 2, 957 n. 25; Lieut under
  Sotús, 934 n. 4; succeeds País, 957 n.
  25, 984 n. 51
Ramousse, Fr Jean Marie, 808
Rampola, Cardinal, 371
Rancaño, Alfredo, Communist, member
  FONU, 1010, 1031 n. 45
Randolph, Col Archibald, 723
Rapacki, Polish Foreign Minister, 1383
Rasco, Col Federico, 636, 681

Rasco, José Ignacio, talks with Castro, 1078 n. 5, 1212; political anti-Castroist, 1276; in Miami, 1283

Rashidov, Sharif, and Uzbec Communist party, 1387 and n. 12

Rathbone, Albert, 547

Rathbone, Estes, 421, 445-6, 456-7

Ravines, Eudocio, 697

Rawlins, John Aaron, backs Cuban rebels, 251 and n. 15, 253; death, 253 and n. 26

Ray, Manuel, President Civil Engineers' Association, and Havana underground, 945, 1001, 1010, 1067, 1276; joins 26 July, 953; and Castro, 953, 1007-8, 1008 n. 16, 1068, 1197, 1199, 1251 and n. 50; head of Civic Resistance, 975, 991, 1044; member of strike committee, 988; in the Sierra, 1001-2; Minister of Public Works, 1067, 1068, 1247, 1276; Almendares Tunnel, 1067, 1098; in exile, 1199 n. 23; roadway plans, 1199; in opposition, 1251, 1276, 1280; forms MRP, 1286, 1296, 1304, 1305, 1248; in Miami, 1303, 1346; and Castro's overthrow, 1303; failure as international leader, 1303; and Varona, 1307; and U.S. air cover, 1310; and CIA, 1320; and a Cuban invasion, 1471

Ray, René, 1044

Real Proclamación, Marqués de la, 123; and abolition, 234

realengos, land grants, 20 and n. 16; squatters, 20; royal ban on, 29 n. 13; redistributed, 276; Batista and, 709

Recabarren, Manuel Foster, 1403 and n. 53

Recios family, 17, 32

Recio, López, civil governor of Puerto Príncipe, 422

Recio de Oquendo, Gonzalo (1701-73), 44 n. 11, 47; deputy to Albemarle, 44; and the *cabildo*, 45 n. 14; and English occupation, 48; entitled in Spain, 61

Redmond, Kenneth, 1017

Redono, Ciro, 887 n. 47, 888 n. 53, 899; in the Sierra, 901 and n. 53, 920 n. 49, 934, 1005; death, 974 n. 1

Reed, Thomas Brackett ('Tsar') (1839-1902), 373

Reed, Dr Walter, 461, 1062

Rego, Capt., 330

Rego, Col, 1024 and n. 17, 1028

Rego, José, 576 n. 26, 577 n. 33

Rego Rubido, Col, 1072

Reguero, Dr Alfredo, 710

Reid, Whitelaw, 313-14

Reina, Waldo, 1012, 1198 n. 18

religious cults, African, multiracial occasions, 516; transculturation of saints, 517-18, 519, 1125; American and African manifestations, 520; value to Negroes, 524; blend with Catholic festivals, 1123, 1125

Relling, Bernard, 1208

Remington, Frederick, cartoonist, 340 n. 7; in Cuba, 340, 365

Remos, Dr Juan, 776 n. 3; Minister of Education, 705, 776; visits Batista, 776

Renn, Ludwig, 1345

Rentería, Léon, 752

Reston, James, 1417

Reunión, Conde de, Royal Bank director, 136 n. 1; sugar mills, *Concepción, Dos Hermanos*, 136 n. 1, 427; and abolition, 234

Revolutionaries and Revolutionary groups, 688; student, 592; ABC, 594-5, 681; variety, 681; continued demands, 691; and Batista, 703; semi-gangster, 741-3, 763; and Grau, 749, 754; bribed with official posts, 763; Castro's proclamation, 829, 1054, 1055; role of Spanish Civil War exiles, etc., 879; concept in 1959, 1051-2; and sugar industry, 1155; consolidated by invasion, 1344

Revueltas, Vicente, 1342-3

Rey, Santiago, 1029 n. 38, 1238; and Batista's cabinet, 843 n. 41, 861 and n. 58, 874, 1026; in Washington, 911-12; and Castro, 920; attempted murder, 1000; escapes judgement, 1075

Reijnolo, 888

Reynoso, Alvaro, 153, 185 and n. 4

Ribalta, Pablo, 944 and n. 5, 981, 1079

Ribas, Jorge, 1044

Ricafort, Mariano, captain-general, 193 and n. 1; succeeded by Tacón, 194

Rice plantations, left undivided, 1326; State ownership, 1331; production figures, 1332 and n. 71, 1374; future of, 1441 and n. 24; mechanization of, 1552-3, 1554, 1556; consumption, 1556 and n. 46; import of grain, 1557

Ricla, Ambrosio de Funes, Conde de, captain-general, 63 and n. 13; Governor, 63 n. 13; imposes new taxes, 65

Ridruejo, Dionisio, 317

Riera Medina, Judge, 768

Riesgo, Alfonso Bernal del, 754

Riesgo, Capt., 96

Rillieux, Norbert, 117 and n. 22, 154

Rionda, Bernardo, 1218–19, 1219 n. 11

Rionda, Manuel, 600, 1219 n. 11; and Cuba Cane, 532, 538, 541, 549, 560; and Vendendor Unico, 561

Ríos, Lieut, 1027 and n. 31

Ríos, Santiago, 962

Risquet, Jorge, Labour minister, 1431, 1447–8, 1448 n. 9, 1449 and n. 15

Ríu Anglés, Carlos, Bishop of Camagüey, 1129

Riva, General Armando, 526

Rivas, Fr Antonio, 992

Rivera, Diego de, 579, 588 and n. 13

Rivero family, 1137, 1261

Rivero, Felipe, 1360; editor *Jorobemos*, 713–14

Rivero, José Ignacio, 1280

Rivero, Nicolás, 500, 1281 n. 18

Rivero Agüero, Andrés, Minister of Education, 783 n. 20; presidential candidate, 977; prime minister elect, 966, 1014 and n. 15, 1015, 1026; leaves Cuba, 1026

Roa, Raúl, 592 n. 35, 889 n. 58, 910; and Marxism, 592, 594 n. 43, 1225–6; Foreign Minister, 592, 1225–6, 1226 n. 41, 1258; imprisonment, 594 n. 43, 597; and revolutionary government, 639, 1253; and U.S., 685; and student murders, 763 n. 11; career and personality, 1225–6, 1226 n. 41; at OAS meeting, 1239; and Ydigoras, 1277; alleges foreign aggression, 1277

Roa, Raúlito, 910

Roa Sierra, Juan, 815 and n. 59

Roas, Mgr, 1129–30

Roberts, Alex, 931

Robertson, W. H., 208 n. 7, 223

Robledo, Orestes, 785 n. 24, 794

Robles Cortés, José, mayor of Santiago, 1016 n. 64, 1527

Roca, Blas (Francisco Calderio), 597 and n. 59, 632, 692, 714, 748, 752–3, 842, 1259; and Communist Party, 697, 699, 711, 744, 846, 922; and Batista, 710, 711, 736, 773, 785 n. 23; demands new constitution, 710–11, 711 n. 18; visits U.S., 711; on Cuban party programme, 712–13; and Grau's victory, 718; on 1940 Constitution, 720–1; and co-operation with England and U.S., 734; denounces Teheran and Yalta, 745; 'negative vote', 853, 860; in Mexico, 878; and 26 July, 922; in China, 1081, 1279; his 'new Theses', 1090 n. 52; and Castro, 1207–8, 1220; denounced by *Revolución*, 1219; anti-Americanism, 1222, 1269; moderate line, 1242, 1292; denies 'imperialistic' invasion of Cuba, 1269, 1270, 1279; meets Khrushchev, 1279; defends private enterprise, 1291; at 10th Congress, 1292; and relations with China, 1315–16; and the Church, 1350; favours a united party, 1373; in Moscow, 1373; and ORI, 1377 n. 21, 1378; ed. *Hoy*, 1378–9, 1382; drops out, 1381; in Montevideo, 1383–4; and 'new' Communist party, 1454; and PURS, 1454 n. 3; and a new constitution for Cuba, 1454 n. 3; and the arts, 1464; and nuclear weapons, 1470 n. 60; *Los Fundamentos del Socialismo*, 851, 1314, 1343

Rockingham, Marquis of, 56

Rodney, George, Admiral (later Lord), 7 n. 36, 65; W. Indian fleet, 1 and nn. 2, 3; captures Martinique, 5; and American revolution, 67

Rodó, José Enrique, 417

Rodón, Lincoln, 674 n. 36, 874; Miami meeting, 968; and Junta of Unity, 1003

Rodríguez, Capt. Aníbal, 1233

Rodríguez, Armando, 901 and n. 53, 917

Rodríguez, Carlos Rafael (born 1913), 944 n. 6, 1109 n. 2, 1319, 1443 n. 29, 1448 n. 12; career, 733 and n. 44; enters Batista's cabinet, 733, 734, 1081; role in university, 743 n. 9; ignorance of Moncada plan, 842 and n. 39; and Communism, 846, 860, 981, 1002, 1006, 1052 n. 18, 1199; and strike failure, 990, 991; visits Castro in the Sierra, 1002 and n. 27, 1003, 1006, 1011, 1079; relations with him, 1007, 1197, 1199 and n. 22,

Rodríguez, Carlos Raphael – *Cont.*
1222, 1292, 1315; and Law I, 1011
n. 32; and Castro's Communism,
1059 n. 45; Minister of the Interior,
1197; ed. *Hoy*, 1199, 1208 and n. 50,
1282, 1342; and land reform, 1222;
radicalism, 1226 n. 43; replies to
Pérez Serantes, 1282; at indoctrination school, 1314; and relations with
China, 1315; speech to sugar workers,
1325 n. 43; post-invasion fate, 1371
and n. 50; President INRA, 1376,
1379, 1381, 1395; and ORI, 1377 n.
21; and missile crisis, 1414; on
'revolutionary offensive', 1445; and
PURS, 1454 n. 3; continuing influence, 1454 n. 3; and Sino-Soviet
controversy, 1479; on a Communist
guerrilla, 1480

Rodríguez, Senator Conrado, 972;
member of sugar union, 861, 872,
889, 1178; hunger strike, 872; estimate of casualties, 1044 n. 21

Rodríguez, Fructuoso, student gunman,
889; and Palace attack, 927; death,
931 and n. 31, 1319 n. 22

Rodríguez, Homoboro, and November
revolt, 666; execution, 669

Rodríguez, Corporal Julio, 666

Rodríguez, Laureano, 357

Rodríguez, Lester, 824 n. 3, 854 and n.
34, 867–8, 895 and n. 9, 896 n. 14,
968, 969, 971 n. 38

Rodríguez, Luis Orlando, and *El
Bonche*, 743 n. 9; career, 743 n. 9,
1066; and Chibás, 751, 754 n. 48;
SIM and, 792; arrest, 799, 866; ed.
La Calle, 866, 1066, 1225, 1320 n. 27;
ed. *Cubano Libre*, 980, 1066; Minister
of Interior, 1066, 1071; dismissal,
1224–5; anti-Communist, 1320 and
n. 27

Rodríguez, Marcos Armando ('Marquitos'), trial (1964), 597 n. 58, 846
n. 5; Castro's speech, 864, 866 and
n. 11; police raid and, 932 n. 33;
Directorio and, 926–7, 1082, 1319;
traitor (of Calle Humbert 7), 931–2,
1082, 1319; Communists and, 931 and
n. 32; instructor at La Cabaña, 1082;
arrest in Prague, 1319, 1468 n. 50;
interrogation, trial and execution,
1319 and n. 23, 1458, 1459, 1467–8;
guilt, 1459 and n. 22

Rodríguez, Mayía, 306
Rodríguez, Mirta, 1069
Rodríguez, Sergeant Pablo (*oficinista*),
634, 646 n. 37, 658, 663, 674 n. 36,
675, 682
Rodríguez, René, 899, 901 and n. 53,
915–16
Rodríguez, Roberto ('Vaquerito'), 1025
and n. 21
Rodríguez Avila, General, 950, 1025,
1026; leaves Cuba, 1026
Rodríguez Calderón, ex-Capt., 779 n.
11, 780, 1026
Rodríguez de la Vega, Guevara peace
envoy, 1027 and n. 31
Rodríguez Llompart, Héctor, 1252
Rodríguez Loeches, Enrique, and
Palace attack, 928; N. Cuba landing,
979 nn. 28, 31; and Junta of Unity,
1003; ambassador, 1455 n. 10
Rodríguez Miranda, Augusto, and
PUR, 707 and n. 4
Rodríguez Rozas, Bishop of Pinar del
Río, 1269
Rodríguez Villaverde, Gabino, 4 April
Movement, 1003, 1004
Rodríguez San Pedro, José, 1016 n.
64

Rogers, Robert, 1019
Roig, Enrique (d. 1889), 291
Roja, Ricardo, 879
Rojas, Admiral, vice-president Argen-
tina, 965
Rojas, Col Cornelio, 1025 and n. 22
Rojas, Governor Manuel, and Indians,
1527
Rojas, Ursino, Communist, 1002 n. 22;
arrest, 943–4; in the Sierra, 1006;
election defeat, 1220; and PURS,
1454 n. 3
Rojas González, Capt. Juan, 898, 779
n. 11
Rojas Pinilla, Gustavo, 771
Roller, Arnold, 579
Roloff, General Carlos, rebel leader,
265 and n. 3, 306, 349; Sec. for War,
319, 322
Román, musician, 205
Romero Robledo, Francisco, 303, 308
and n. 49; and peace offer, 406
Romualdo, Serafín, 987
Roncaldi, Federico, Conde de Alcoy,
captain-general, 214
Roosevelt, Elliott, 789

Roosevelt, Franklin Delano (1882–1945), U.S. president, election, 598; Brains Trust membership, 598, 687; implication in Cuba, 598, 608, 693, 696 and n. 17; and Welles in Cuba, 606, 610 and n. 18, 617, 618, 620, 621, 644, 645, 648; knowledge of Latin America, 627; joint statement with Welles, 669–70; and sugar bill, 704; Good Neighbour policy, 711, 1063–4; meeting with Batista, 712; suspends sugar quotas, 717; 'last call' speech, 727; death, 745

Roosevelt, Theodore (1858–1919), U.S. president, 311 n. 4, 338, 418; and expansionism, 311; 'Chilean Volunteer', 312; and prospect of war, 325, 342, 356, 364, 365 and n. 63; Ass. Sec. of Navy, 342, 355; imperial ambitions, 342–3, 418, 419; and sinking of *Maine*, 361, 364, 371; refuses a command, 384; in Tampa, 387, 388; in Cuba, 390–1, 401; in command Rough-Riders, 391 n. 6, 393; at San Juan, 393 and n. 18, 394–5; Governor New York State, 417 and n. 1, 439; attitude to backward races, 418 and n. 7; and Wood as Governor of Cuba, 439, 440, 441, 443, 447 n. 20, 457; and Wilson, 441 n. 26; succeeds McKinley, 457; and sugar tariff, 459, 468; reciprocatory treaty with Cuba, 468–9; Panama Canal project, 468 n. 26, 476; and foreign intervention in Caribbean, 476, 478; 'Corollary' to Monroe Doctrine, 476 and n. 16; sends Taft and Baron to Havana, 476–7; and intervention in Cuba, 477, 478, 481–2, 489; letter to Estrada, 478–9; his presidency, 481; sends Magoon to Cuba, 482, 485; date for withdrawal, 489 and n. 37; and Gómez' presidency, 504; and Cuban finance, 686; *Autobiography*, 390 and n. 4, 393 n. 18

Root, Elihu, 444 n. 2, 446, 557; and Cuban suffrage, 448; and Cuban – U.S. relationship, 449–52, 459, 460; and Platt Amendment, 455–6

Ros, Leonardo, mayor of Santiago, 403
Ros, Leopoldo Fernando, 607
Rosabel, Angelio, 900
Roselló, Corporal, *Batistiano*, 916

Roussel, José, 234
Rousseau family, in Cuba, 133
Rovere, Richard, 1399
Rowan, Lieut Andrew, 386 and n. 21
Rubens, Horatio, Junta's lawyer, 305, 315 n. 23, 360; and Cuban independence, 376; and tariff hearings, 552, 558; director Consolidated Railways 557 and n. 1
Rubiera, Vicente, 752, 862, 1201 n. 28
Rubio, López, 595
Rubio Padilla, Juan Antonio, student, 592 n. 34, 638 and n. 13, 641 n. 22, 649; at Montevideo, 671 n. 17; and Prío's cabinet, 775 n. 1
Rubirosa, Porfirio, 1029
Rubottom, Roy, U.S. Ass. Sec., pro-Castro, 947–8; progressive group, 964; and arms and aid for Cuba, 983, 1015; and Cuban reform, 1061; and Castro's visit, 1209; ambassador in Argentina, 1294
Rius Rivera, General Juan, civil governor of Havana, 422; and Wood's cabinet, 444 n. 1, 445
Ruíz, Fabio, 963
Ruíz, Fabio, chief of police, and ARG, 741, 742, 754
Ruiz, José, revolt, 162
Ruiz Cortines, Adolfo, President of Mexico, and Spain, 868
Ruiz Meza, R., 611
Ruíz Ramírez, Dr Jorge, 967
Ruíz de Zarate, Dr Serafín, Minister of Health, 1225, 1253
Rusk, Dean, 1305, 1309, 1357, 1364; and missile crisis, 1406
Russell, Betrand, 1407, 1410
Russell, Evans, 993
Russell, Lord John, 215
Rustán, Policarpo, 265
Ryan, Charles, 934, 940
Ryan, Thomas, 465 n. 7, 465–6, 466 n. 13, 973

Saavedra, ass. military attaché, 976
Saco, José Antonio (1797–1879), abolitionist, 207, 239–40; expulsion from Cuba, 195 and n. 6, 196, 199; and *Revista Bimestre Cubana*, 195; distrust of African race, 195; compares free and slave labour, 196 and n. 10; exiled in Paris, 196–7, 206, 238; and

Saco, José Antonio – *Cont.*
an annexation war, 209; election, 238; *La Supresión del Trafico*, 206

Sacroacia, oligarchic families, 152, 153 and n. 81

Sáenz Yañez, Adolfo, 422

Ságaro, Bartolomé, 588

Sagastes, Praxedes (1827–1903), Liberal, prime minister, 303, 351, 1492; abandons Maur's reforms, 304; gives way to Cánovas, 308; accepts Weyler's resignation, 352–3; and Cuban autonomy, 353–5; diplomatic efforts, 377–8, 381; and peace terms, 406

St George, Andrew, journalist and secret agent, 938 and n. 21, 939, 967 n. 20, 980, 1055

Salabarria, Mario, 812, 817 n. 70; and MSR, 742, 754; chief of secret police, 742; gangster battle, 755

Saladrigas, Carlos, 790; and ABC, 594, 613, 666, 790; and Machado's resignation, 624; member of new government, 629, 642; in Hotel Nacional, 646; attempted arrest, 646 n. 37; and November revolt, 666, 667; and Mendieta's cabinet, 692, 727; premier, 724, 731; and 1941 elections, 735, 790; Batista's president, 790, 793; Foreign Minister, 860, 861 n. 58

Saladrigas, Enrique, 783 n. 20, 784

Saladrigas, Dr Ernesto, 1045

Salamanca, General, captain-general, 299 and n. 15

Salas, Brindis de, 1123

Salas, Justo, Negro mayor of Santiago, 1122

Salas Amaro, Alberto, 1181

Salas Cañizares, Major José, *Batistiano* commander, 935; police chief, 957; bribed to leave, 1022

Salas Cañizares, Brig. Rafael, police chief, 780, 791, 794, 798, 799, 819, 840; reprisals on students, 890; death, 890; gambling protection income, 890 and n. 63

Salas Hernández, Roberto, attempts to murder Castro, 1246

Salas Humara, 924

Salmerón, Nicolás, 367, 385

Salvador, David (born 1923), 872 and n. 31, 946 and n. 12, 1232 n. 55; member strike committee, 988; and

Junta of Unity, 1003, 1007; arrest, 1010; sec. gen. FONU, 1031 and n. 45, 1083 n. 23, 1274, 1348; and Figueres, 1204; and CTC, 1250, 1280; uncertainty of regime, 1259, 1260, 1276; resignation, 1274; in contact with anti-Castroists, 1280; forms 30 November movement, 1285; joins MRP, 1286, 1348; sent to La Cabaña, 1348 and n. 19; trial, 1348 n. 19

Salvador, Santiago, 304

Salvo, Alberto, 1085

Salvoechea, Fermín, 305

Sampson, Capt. (later Admiral), blockade of Havana, 377, 386; character, 386; at Santiago Bay, 387, 388, 389, 395, 396; interviewed by Hearst, 391–3; hatred of Schley, 396, 397

San Cristóbal de la Habana, 22 n. 23; planned nuclear weapons, 1394; missile sites, 1398 and n. 19, 1400

San Felipe, Marqués and Marquésa de, 32, and n. 22, 81 n. 44, 141, 143; *see also* Núñez del Castillo

San Martín, Luis, 1408

San Miguel, 500

Sanabria, Antonio, 588 and n. 13

Sánchez, Alberto, 697

Sánchez, Alejo, 666

Sánchez, Bernabé, 100

Sánchez, Calixto, 783, 883; and Batista, 791; and *Acción Libertadora*, 802, 950 n. 1; and Palace attack, 950 and n. 1; in Miami, 950 and n. 1; death, 950

Sánchez, Capt., 357–8

Sánchez, Celia, *Fidelistas*, 936 n. 12; in the Sierra, 917, 936, 1011; and Castro, 936 n. 12, 1011, 1048, 1199, 1263; and victory, 1057 n. 40; post-Revolution position, 1432 n. 30

Sánchez, Daniel, 956

Sánchez, Diego Julián, 274–5

Sánchez, José, 886

Sánchez, Leila, 910

Sánchez, Miguel (El Coreano), 876

Sánchez, Universo, 868 n. 19, 878, 887 n. 47, 888 n. 53, 889, 901 and n. 53, 913, 920 n. 49, 943, 1043 n. 19, 1088 and n. 47

Sánchez Agramonte, Armando, mayor of Puerto Príncipe, 422

Sánchez Arango, Aureliano, 639, 799, 822, 858, 862, 885 n. 40, 910, 926,

Sánchez Arango, Aureliano – *Cont.*
931; student, 592 nn. 33, 38, 769 n.
32; Minister of Education, 760, 761,
852, 1135; clashes with Chibás, 769,
770; Foreign Minister, 775 and n. 1;
and army plot, 782; leaves with
Prío, 785; and Triple A (AAA), 797,
855, 872, 1285 n. 24, 1320; exiled,
855; anti-Castroist, 1276, 1283; survival in exile, 1471 n. 66
Sánchez Amaya, Fernando, 869, 877 n.
9, 899, 900
Sánchez Cejas, Lieut, 1202
Sánchez del Monte, Enrique, imprisonment, 856 and n. 43
Sánchez Díaz, Major Antonio ('Piñares', 'Marcos'), 937 n. 15; death in
Bolivia, 937 n. 15, 1453 n. 1, 1469 n.
56
Sánchez Iznaga, Sáturnino, mayor of
Trinidad, 422
Sánchez Mosquera, Col, 915, 916, 950,
997, 998, 1017, 1020
Sánchez Tamayo, Fernando, and 26
July, 878
Sánchez y Iznaga, José María, and
anexionismo, 208, 213
Sanders, Romulus M., U.S. Minister
in Madrid, and purchase of Cuba,
213–14; and Young America, 220 n.
12
Sandino, 'General', (d. 1934), 626 and
n. 5
Sandoval, Col Ximénes, 316
Sanguily ('Sanguilito'), Col Julio (son
of Manuel Sanguily), 631; meetings
with Welles, 622, 623, 624; and
Machado's departure, 625; in com-
mand of officers, 653, 659
Sanguily, 'General' Manuel, 459, 567;
nationalist, 304; arrest, 307; and
Gómez' deposition, 438; and consti-
tutional convention, 449, 456 n. 56
Sanjenís, Joaquín, 1304–5
Sanjenís, 'Major', 1032, 1213
Sanjenís, Sergio, 1275 and n. 8, 1304
Santa Colona, Boris, 836, 838
Santa Cruz, Marquésa de, 203
Santa Cruz de Oviedo, Esteban, 171
Santemaría, Abel, 825, 828–9, 835 and
n. 7, 836 and n. 9, 837, 838, 1462
Santamaría, Aldo, 867, 868 n. 19,
1011
Santamaría, Haydée, and Castro, 828,

827 and n. 18, 833, 867, 957 n. 24;
and Moncada, 838, 1455 n. 6; and 26
July Committee, 868 n. 19, 1230;
Santiago rising, 895; and de la
Torriente, 902 n. 57; in the Sierra,
917, 1003 n. 29; and ORI, 1377 n.
18; post-Revolution position, 1432 n.
30, 1455 n. 6; political commitment
of artists, 1466 and n. 46
Santander, General, 103
Santiago de Cuba, 121, 158, 262 and n.
35, 288, 799, 1100; seat of bishopric,
13, 16, 71 n. 55; slave revolt, 38;
appointment of governor, 46; creole
houses, 47; maintains Spanish flag,
48; free entry of slaves, 69; archbishopric, 71 n. 55; Economic Society,
73 n. 5; St Dominic exiles 77; sugar
production, 81; foreign merchants,
98, 141; copper-miners, 99; coffee
growing, 129; French club, 133; bullfighting, 150; *regidor decano*, 142;
Negro traders, 169; and 1836 elections, 197–8, 859–60, 952; and
Independence Wars, 256, 324; public
and private schools, 286 n. 13; U.S.
advance on, 390–4; internal conditions, 395, 403; handed over to U.S.,
400; Wood as governor, 411; population figures, 424, 906, 1100; farming
areas, 425 n. 44; ban on Negro
import, 431, 439; yellow fever epidemics, 460; Church party, 462;
Negro or mulatto majority, 515 and
n. 8, 100; Liberal revolt, 528; attack
on Moncada barracks, 803, 828,
835–8, 843–4, 854 nn.; 26 July,
867–8, 917–18, 975, 986–7, 1010;
bomb outrages, 872, 910; Masferrer
and, 885; and Castro, 895–7, 934,
1010; population, 906; police conflicts, 912, 956, 957; trial of *Fidelista*,
942; and País's murder, 957, 959;
strike, 959; and naval mutiny, 961;
Civic Resistance, 975; 9 April strike,
990; investment, 1016, 1020; influx of
refugees, 1020; surrender, 1028;
proclaimed 'new' capital, 1030; Spanish influence, 1100; Negro population,
1119; trial of airmen, 1202–3; bombing of airfield, 1355, 1356; College
Dolores, 749, 807; La Salle College,
807, 808
Santocildes, General, 321

Santos Buch, Angel María, director of Civic Resistance, 985 n. 60, 1003; and Junta of Unity, 1003

Santos Carrera, Isidro, 523

Santos Jiménez, Dr Rafael, Liberal, 611; member of new government, 629 and n. 15; and Mendieta's cabinet, 678

Santos Ríos, Eduardo, 1218

Santovenia, Conde de, Royal Bank director, 136 n. 1; sugar mills, 136 n. 1, 427

Santovenia, Emeterio, 790, 1045

Saraleguí, Midshipman, 397

Sardiñas, Fr Guillermo, 946, 1011

Sardiñas, Lalo, 936, 974 and n. 4

Sarduy, Severo, in exile, 1464

Sargent, Richard, 1000

Sarriá family, 274 and n. 16, 275

Sarriá, Claudio, 323, 437 n. 9

Sarriá, Domingo, I and II, 274

Sarriá, Juan, 176, 274; death, 274

Sarriá, Lieut, 839, 841, 851

Sartorius, Manuel and Ricardo, 303

Sartre, Jean-Paul, 1268, 1269–70, 1270 n. 33, 1353, 1485 n. 8

Sauce, Mme, 141

Saumell, Ena and Pedro, 919

Savisky, Silvestro, 579

Scali, John, 1411

Schlesinger, Arthur Meier, Jnr (born 1917), special assistant to President Kennedy, advises against invasion, 1306, 1307 n. 35, 1309, 1370 and n. 46; white paper on Castro, 1307, 1308, 1309; and Stevenson, 1308 n. 42; and exiles, 1310

Schley, Commodore, character, 386; reaches Santiago, 387; commands the battle, 396, 466 n. 13

Schneider, Mr, 609

Schoenvich, Judge, Otto, 484 and nn. 17, 32

Schweyer, Alberto Lamar, 566 n. 11, 612, 620 n. 21, 264, 625

Scovel, Sylvester, 340 and n. 10, 400, 422

Segura, Antonio and Juan Fernández, 945

Seigle, Octavio, 703

Selema, César, 1256

Semjovich, Yunger, see Grobart, Fabio

Serguera, Major Jorge, and war trials, 1074 n. 29; and television, etc., 1074

n. 29; prosecutor Matos' trial, 1255; later career, 1255, 1386, 1455, 1463

Serra, Clementina, 1427, 1432 n. 30

Serra, Rafael, 300

Serrano, General Francisco (1810–85), 237; slave trade negotiations, 229–30; Reformers and, 235; exiled, 239; and 1868 Revolution, 243; and Cuban rebellion, 247–8; regent, 252; and sale of Cuba, 252–3

Seward, William Henry, 230

Shafter, Brig.-Gen. Rufus (1835–1906), 387 n. 26, 412, 417, 1060; ordered to Cuba, 384; and landing party, 387, 388, 389, 390, 391 and n. 6; at San Juan, 394, 395; at Santiago, 397, 398–9; and surrender terms, 399, 400; advises removal of troops, 405

Shaler, William, U.S. consul in Havana, 88 and n. 21

Shattuck, Edwin, 552, 560

Sheffield Peace Conference, 765

Sherman, Senator John (1832–1900), 256–7, 313 n. 15; and annexation of Cuba, 313, 332; Sec. of State, 341; and war with Spain, 341; and Cánovas' reforms, 348; protest note to Spain, 349–50, 355 n. 78; senility, 374 n. 36

Shlyaprikov, Rudolf, 1475, 1494

Sickles, Daniel (1825–1914), and expansionism, 220 n. 12; U.S. Minister to Spain, 251, 252; career, 251–2; and Cuba negotiations, 252–3

Sierra, Gervasio, 534

Sierra, Rafael, 908

Sierra Talavera, Major, 1022 and n. 10

Sierra Escambray, 18, 256, 963, 1004; 1960–1 war, 330 and n. 5; guerrilla forces, 978–9 and n. 28, 979 n. 31; manifesto, 979–80; Guevara and, 1020 n. 3, 1313; anti-Castro rebels, 1296–7

Sierra Maestra, 18, 254; coffee growing, 129, 907; Castro and, 634 n. 1, 762 n. 8, 779 n. 11, 844, 882, 900 and n. 50, 903, 912 ff., 934, 1038; meeting of *Fidelista*, 900–1, 901 n. 53, 902–4, 912; *precaristas*, 904, 906, 908, 913 and n. 18, 914, 915, 916, 920 and n. 49, 924, 935, 937, 1108; terrain, 904; education statistics, 906 and nn. 66, 67; social conditions, 906; population, 906; towns, 906–7; racial balance,

Sierra Maestra – *Cont.*

917 and n. 74; *latifundios*, 907; estates, 907–8; *mayorales*, 908, 913, 115, 940; food supplies, 923, 935; incidence of treachery, 937, 967, 974–5; numbers of *Fidelista*, 938; '*territorio libre*', 951, 974, 980; Chibás-Pazos-Castro meeting, 953; proposed government, 956; hombrito clash, 965; army organization, 974; disciplinary problems, 974; behaviour of peasants, 974; second guerrilla force, 978–80; radio station, 980 and n. 36; radio telephone to Venezuela, 992; *operación verano*, 996–1003; issue of Law I, etc., 1010–11; organization of '*commandancia*', 1011; decrees, 1046, 1073, 1089; anti-Revolutionary group, 1274–5; Minas del Frio training college, 1341; *centrales, Estrada Palma, Isabel, Miranda,* 907, 950, 958; legend of Baldomero, 1472

Sigsbee, Charles Dwight (1845–1923), 358 n. 14; commander of *Maine*, 358, 361; and the explosion, 362

Sigur, Laurence, 216

Silva, Capt. José, 1018

Silva, Lieut, 591

Silva, Manuel, 351

Silvela, Francisco, 383 and n. 7, 408 and n. 25

Silverio, Dr Nicasio, 611; member of new government, 629 n. 20, 1011; and State Electricity Co., 1337

SIM (special police), 634 n. 1, 762, 792, 842; and Moncada prisoners, 839; revival of torture, 875; reaction to gangsterism, 883, 887; and Palace attack, 928; executions after war trials, 1074 n. 30; U.S. membership, 1077

Simón, Luis, and Ochoa, 1006 n. 10; in the Sierra, 1008

Simon-Carves of Stockport, 1440 and n. 22

Simonovich, Gregorio, 767

Siqueiros, David Alfaro, 579

Skelly, John, 990 and n. 9

Skelton (mulatto), 161

slave merchants, African, effects of abolition, 95 and n. 13; dealings with kings, 156; nationalities, 159; trading, profits, 159; racial domination by Aros and Efiks, 160; dealings with

middlemen, 160; semi-criminal character, 160, 167

slave merchants, Havana (*negreros*), 194, 195; Spanish connections, 156; displaced foreigners, 156; representatives of foreign firms, 157; involvement in piracy, 160–1; justification of slavery, 181

Slave trade, Liverpool merchants, M.P.s, etc., 3–4; Cuban merchants and, 31, 33, 136; legal and illegal agencies, 33; monopoly companies, 33 and n. 25, 49; capture of Havana and, 49–50; disappointment with profits, 50; triangular route, 51 n. 43; effect on Cuban imports, 51 n. 43; effect of American Revolution, 67, 68–9; increased Spanish activity, 68–9; freeing of, 1790, 83; links with manufacturers, 84 and n.; fears of abolition, 89, 90, 91, 93–4; continuance after abolition, 93, 98–9, 105, 109, 164–5, 166, 167, 193, 209; compensation paid, 94; direct routes, 137; and social position, 154; Courts of Arbitration, 157, 201; reliance on U.S., 161; financial interests, 165; and piracy, 166; increased profits, 206; purview of the rich, 234, 236

Slave Trade Acts, prosecutions under, 231 n. 61

Slave Trading Company, 68 n. 33

Slavery, holds Cuba together, 109; delays labour-saving agriculture, 184–5; purpose of *anexionismo*, 208–9, 219; condition in American South, 210; reformists and, 233–4, 235, 239; revolutionaries and, 243, 249–50, 250–1; Moret's law and, 257–8; Spain and abolition, 258, 262; contribution to Cuban society, 273, 287; assessment, 281 ff.; and family life, 281–2, 516, 1123; and Africa's population, 283–4; an African monocrop, 284; effect on racism, 515, 516; its social results, 516–17, 1113; and survival of African cults, 518, 520; basis of Cuban oligarchy, 1111

slaves, 6; at defence of Havana, 7; university restrictions, 13; escaped, 19, 21, 37; smuggling of, 23; and sugar production, 28, 29, 30, 168–9; price and cost of, 31 and n. 18, 50 and n. 31, 68 and n. 36, 69, 95, 96, 98, 109,

Slaves – *Cont.*

118, 124, 163 and n. 39, 170, 172, 174 and nn. 24, 25, 185, 189, 206, 234, 236, 256, 279; preference for males, 31, 171, 283; credit buying, 32–3; Cuban population, 33–4, 52 and nn. 45, 46, 65 and n. 23, 89–90, 168 and n. 2, 169, 170 and n. 11, 172; treatment of, 34, 74, 75 n. 15, 176, 281; legislation concerning, 34–5, 109; right of *coartación*, 36, 169, 171–2; emancipation (*emancipados*), 35, 94, 122, 172, 181–2, 183, 201, 206; position in cities, 36–7; revolts by, 37, 38, 75, 77–8, 140, 204–6; import duties, 49; exchange for goods in Africa, 51 and n. 43; and Cuban prosperity, 63, 74, 89 and n. 90, 109; employment tax, 69, 70; new slave code (1789), 74, (1842), 204; numbers per mill, 82 and n. 47, 112; post-abolition position, 87, 94, 95; arrivals after 1820, 98–9, 99 n. 26, 169 and n. 6; varied nationality, 114; and Havana railway, 122; and coffee growing, 130–1; fear of their Revolution, 148, 173; and gambling, 150; nicknames, 156; methods of purchase, 156, 159–60; source of supply, 158, 160; U.S. imports, 161–2; marriage figures, 168 n. 2; other occupations, 169, 170; breeding from, 170–1; purchase of equality, 172; imprisonment on arrival, 173; effect of mechanization, 174, 176; hours of work, 174–5; and the harvest, 175, 181; death rate, 175 and n. 35; punishment, 175–6; revenge by, 176; belief in charms, 176 and n. 44; leave of absence, 176–71; plantation folklore, 177; maintenance and renewal costs, 178–9; medical care, 179; housing and clothing, 179; burial, 179–80; town and country, 180, 185; loyalty to employers, 180–1; care of old and sick, 181; and drinking (*aguardiente*), 181; domestic workers, 183; strikes by, 236; hired out for wages, 241; and Independence War (1868), 247, 256; position of *liberto*, 250; *patronato* on liberation, 279; after freedom, 195, 278–80, 293; stricter regulations, 206; fall in standard of living, 280; total numbers in transatlantic trade, 282 and n. 3; possible improved condition, 283 and n. 4; Cuban imports, 1790–1865, 1532–3; numbers landed, 1865–6, 1545; *see also* Negroes

Slaves, women, 31, 69, 70 and n. 49; obligatory import, 86; drop in numbers, 90; lack of, 140; comparative numbers, 168 and n. 2, 169, 429 and n. 66; per cent age-grouping, 168 n. 2; treatment of mothers, 171 and n. 15; mistresses of white men, 173

slaveships, numbers entering Havana, 51 and n. 43; joint stock enterprises, 156; nationality, 158; right of search, 158, 231 and n. 60; sailing instructions, 158; merchandize carried, 150 and n. 19; and piracy, 160–1; Baltimore clippers, 161 and n. 26, 163, 215; insurance after abolition, 162; insurrections in, 162; financing of, 162–3; mortality *en passage*, 163, 282 n. 3; building of, 163; treatment of slaves, 163–4 (voyage of the *Rodeur*), 230 and n. 57; secret and illegal landings, 164–5, 165 n. 45, 200, 235 n. 14; denunciation of, 173; after abolition, 200, 230; carry U.S. colours, 203; last recorded voyage to Cuba, 235 and n. 14, 1543–5; numbers leaving Havana for Africa, 1825, 1535–6

Sleeper, James, U.S. chargé d'affaires, 475, 476–7

Slidell, Senator John, 228 n. 50, 229, 230

Smith, Earl T., U.S. ambassador to Cuba, 947, 949 and n. 20, 1075, 1309; career, 949; and Havana atmosphere, 956; press conferences, 956–7, 958; official reception, 957–8; Cuban policy, 958, 960, 964; and naval mutiny, 961; stand against police brutality, 964; Embassy attitude to Castro, 965; and Communism in 26 July, 967, 991; threatened assassination, 972–3; and Batista, 973, 985, 991, 1015, 1017, 1019, 1023; and political crisis, 975; in Washington, 976; judgement on Castro, 976, 983, 1016; and 1958 elections, 983, 986, 1014, 1015; and U.S. arms embargo, 985–6; receives ransom terms, 1000–1; and U.S. intervention, 1001; and Barquín, 1029; praises 1959 takeover, 1030; and Cienfuegos, 1032–3;

Smith, Earl T. – *Cont.*
  untypicality, 1061; fear of Communism, 1061; resignation, 1075 and n. 36; evidence to Security Sub-committee, 1297
Smith, José, military instructor, 877; in *Granma*, 894
Smith, Robert, U.S. representative in Cuba, 67
Smith, Robert A. C., 464
Smith, William, Purser of *Crescent City*, 219
Smoot, Senator, 551–2, 553, 560, 561
Snow, Ass. Sec. of State, 1015 and n. 58
Snuff, 22, 23, 24, 64; mills, 22, 24, 25, 134; primitive Indians and, 1519
Soca Llanes, General Rogelio, 780
Socialism and socialists, trade unions, 298; support Martí, 301; scarcity in Cuba, 575; move towards Communism, 576, 579; use of word by *Fidelista*, achieved by Revolution, 1259, 1344, 1336, 1358; need of statistics, 1329 n. 60; acclaimed by Castro, 1358–9, 1371 n. 52; use of word by Guevara, 1423; original purpose, 1487
Sociedad de Amigos de la República (SAR), formation, 870, 892
Sogo, Capt. Damaso (Soguito), 1029 n. 38; and army conspiracy, 780; provincial commander, 840 n. 31
Sokolosky, George, 1300
Soler, Policarpo, assassin, 762 n. 8, 771; action group, 763–4; leaves Cuba, 792; conspiracy in exile, 883, 886
Soler, William, 912
Soler Puig, Rafael, 1306, 1371 n. 49
Someruelos, Marqués de, captain-general, 88 and n. 18
Somoza, Luis, 1277, 1311
Sonthonax, 76
Sorí Marín, Dr Humberto, lawyer, career, 975 n. 5, 1044, 1067; and Law I, 1011 n. 32; Auditor-General, 1011; and Justice Dept., 1044; Minister of Agriculture, 1067, 1068, 1215, 1225, 1275; Catholic appointments, 1083; war trials adjudicator, 1088; execution, 1088 n. 47, 1349, 1365
Sosa, Capt. Merob, 935 n. 9, 950, 965
Sosa Blanco, Major Jesús, alleged brutality, 985; war trial, 1088–9
Sosa de Quesada, General, 1023

Soto, Hernando de, 16
Soto, Jesús, 1007, 1031 n. 45, 1083 n. 23, 1250 n. 48, 1259, 1274
Soto, Leonel, Communist, 1454 and n. 4; at Havana University, 810, 817, 923, 846 n. 5; 'revolutionary' instructor, 1314, 1381
Soto, Oscar, 567
Soto, 'Pedrin', 934 nn. 2, 6
Sotolongo family, 17, 32, 1146
Sotús, Jorge, and 26 July, 896 n. 14, 934; in the Sierra, 924, 934 and n. 1; his group, 934 and n. 2, 939, 940; personal relations, 934, 971 n. 38; and MRR, 1275, 1348; escape from prison, 1348; death, 1348 n. 18
Soulé, Pierre (1801–70), Minister to Spain, career, 219 and n. 9, 220; and annexation, 219 and n. 10; in Madrid, 221–2; offers $M130 for Cuba, 223; and Spanish Revolution, 224; at London conference, 224–5; use of threats, 225 and n. 32; resignation, 225–6
Sourwine, J. G., 948
Spain, at war with England, 1; defence of Cuba, 6–11; influence on Cuban architecture, 17; labour shortages, 19, 38; tobacco growing, 23; sugar production, etc., 27 and n. 4, 62 and n. 5; and slave trade, 31, 34, 99, 156, 166, 226, 257–8; increasing population, 38–9; emigration to Americas, 47 and n. 16; and Peace of Paris, 56; and Cuban prosperity, 62; extended trading rights, 64 and n. 18; gains Louisiana, 65 and nn. 19, 20; increased revenue from Havana, 65 and n. 22; and American Revolution, 67; Economic Societies, 73 and n. 5; goods for African trade, 81; relationship with England, 85, 87; reimposes foreign trade ban, 85; trade relations with U.S., 86, 131, 133 and n. 21, 196; collapse of imperial system, 87; and abolition, 91, 94, 99, 200, 240, 279; and emigrant (Catholic) labour, 94; revolutions (1820), 96, (1854), 224, (1868), 243–4; collapse of constitutional government, 102; at peace with ex-colonies, 105; relative stagnation, 109; preeminence of army, 110; gap between her and Cuba, 111; railway development,

Spain – *Cont.*

123; lack of commercial banks, 136; planters from, 141; grandees, 143; state of the Church, 150; influence of Cuban millionaires, 155; slaveships, 158, 161; and emancipation, 182; attraction of Cuban wages, 185; civil war (Carlist), 194, 198, 201, 260, 261; breakdown of Restoration settlement, 194; orders Cuban elections, 197; quicksilver mines, 217; debts to Britain, etc., 228; and Cuban constitutional reform, 238, 239; revolt in San Gil barracks, 239; reaction to Cuban war, 247, 270; acceptance of volunteer forces, 249; forewarnings of anarchism, 249; growth of Republican Federalism, 259; army disaffection, 261; restoration of monarchy, 263, 265; sugar beet industry, 272 and n. 11; white immigrants from, 276 and n. 23; increased prosperity, 278–9; trade relations with Cuba, 287–8, 288 n. 23, 289; anarcho-syndicalism, 291; failure of Cuban policy, 298; rise of separatism, 298, 304; and Independence War (1895), 307–8, 309, 326, 327; and U.S. intervention in Cuba, 333, 336, 337, 347; and Cánovas's murder, 350–1; and Cuban autonomy, 353, 354, 380; sends *Vizcaya* to New York, 358; and sinking of *Maine*, 363, 370; and war with U.S., 369 ff., 380, 381; and Manila defeat, 385; peace terms, 402; to evacuate Cuba and the Philippines, 407; aftermath of peace, 408, 417; revolutionary literature, 575; Communist movements, 578, 579; recognition of Grau, 662; Constitution of 1931, 719, 720; practice of corruption, 738; *integristas*, 803 n. 4; first civil air school, 876; influence on Cuban music, 1123; Stalin and, 1265; demographic changes, 1513 and n. 11

Spaniards, immigrants in Cuba, 471, 497, 540, 541, 1100 and n. 42, 1101, 1117; and union organization, 541; return to Spain, 553, 1101; deportation of anarchists, 580, 596; Communist leaders, 589 and n. 16; accept 1959 Revolution, 1031; clubs for, 1101; use of term Gallegos, 1101

Spaniards (Cuban), and tobacco growing, 22–3, 134; refortify Havana, 63; exit from Florida, 65 and n. 21; advance loans in English islands, 66; and slave trade, 68–71, 83, 183; dominant merchant class, 141–2, 499–500, 601, 684–5; the *ayacuchos*, 142; and abolition, 165; treatment of slaves, 182, 281; of Chinese labourers, 187–8; and annexationism, 219, 409; and Independence War (1868), 246, 248, 256; brutal behaviour, 256, 257, 259; followers of Campos, 268; favoured by captains-general, 299–300; and Americans, 410; evacuate Cuba, 410; Cuba's debt to, 412–14; under U.S. occupation, 442; in civil service, 484, 508 and n. 11, 509; mill ownership, 541, 708; and 1933 revolts, 620; effect of 'fifty-per-cent' law, 670, 673, 702; town-centred life, 683 and n. 5; Cuba- and Spain-born, 684 n. 11; Cuban hostility towards, 685, 686; effect of Cubanization law, 1101; and domestic service, 1112; and business, 1114; blend with mulattoes, 1123; property holdings, 1184; political irresponsibility, 1188; and primitive Indians, 1511, 1512, 1514–16, 1526–7

Spanish-American War of Independence, 1810, 89 ff.

Spanish-American War, 1896–98, 336 and n. 34, 340–1, 355 n. 79, 803; efforts to avoid, 367–8; preliminary moves, 368–77; declaration of war, 377; U.S. motives, 379, 381; Spanish forces, 382–3; U.S. preparations, 383–5; invasion of Cuba, 385, 387; negotiations with rebels, 386; at Santiago Bay, 386–8; Cuban landing, 388–9, 390–1; Battle of San Juan, 392–4; of Santiago Bay, 395–7; truce, 397; U.S. camp conditions, 397, 398; surrender demand, 398–9; peace terms, 400, 402; aftermath, 404–6; cost to Spain, 413; influence on U.S., 417, 420; rebel position under U.S. administration, 403, 410, 420; payment and disbanding of troops, 412, 420–1; part played by U.S. intervention, 413; effect on population numbers, 423–4; ruin caused by, 424–5, 428

Spanish Civil War, 577, 588 n. 13, 918, 1469 n. 53; exiles from, 579 n. 43,

Spanish Civil War – *Cont.*
1101; outbreak, 703; Cuban fighters, 703 and n. 34, 741, 1082, 1360; Battle of Jarama, 703 n. 34; of the Ebro, 741; Bayo and, 876, 877, 878; role of children of exiles, 879; murder of Galíndez, 883; link with Cuban Communists, 1081

Spooner, Senator, 419

Sprechels, Claus, 290

Spring-Rice, Sir Cecil, and Roosevelt, 312

Squiers, U.S. Minister to Cuba, 419, 474 and n. 8, 502

Stalin, Joseph, 597 n. 60, 731, 744, 846, 1081, 1315, 1482

Steinhart, Frank (1864–1938), Consul-general, 431, 475 n. 11; and Liberal revolt, 475–6; Speyer representative, 485, 506; and Havana Electric Railway, 485–6, 550; relations with Magoon, 486, 686; and Crowder, 550; Machado and, 687

Stephens, Senator Alexander, 226 and n. 2, 230–1

Sterling, Domingo, 239

Stevenson, Adlai (1900–65), in S. America, 1278; and 1960 presidential election, 1300; and Cuban affairs, 1300–1; and Invasion plan, 1308 and n. 42, 1365; denies U.S. intervention, 1357; and missile crisis, 1402 n. 48, 1411

Stewart, 'Don Guillermo', 140

Stewart, John, 79

Stimson, Henry, 560, 590, 591, 626, 688

Stirner, Alfred, 579

strikes, 442, 579–80, 698–9; dockers, 442; cigar workers, 491–2, 575; anarchist-led, 506 n. 7, 569, 575; by CNOC, 590; doctors, 691; Aliados Omnibus Co., 766; sugar workers, 871–2; hunger, 872; electrical workers, 942; schoolchildren, 983; committee membership, 988 and n. 2; sparked off by Revolution, 1196; made illegal, 1260; general, 615, 631–2, 653, 676, 677, 692, 766, 783, 959, 988, 1030

Strong, Josiah, 311

Students Federation (FEU), 564 and n. 3, 743, 767 n. 19, 810, 811, 856, 871, 968; presidency election, 864 and n. 10, 1286; relationship to Directorio

Revolucionario, 871 n. 29; strike for peace, 978; and Junta of Unity, 1003; political stranglehold, 1286, 1287; post-Revolution undemocratic organization, 1429

students, University, demonstrate against corruption, 564, 566; demands and achievements, 564–5; murders of, 587–8; opponents of Machado, 591–2, 685; political parties, 591–2, 594; oppose U.S. intervention, 599; and 1933 Revolution, 605, 625, 685; and Welles, 611, 629; demand a *revolutionary* government, 631, 639, 640–1; and Batista, 637, 654, 658, 695, 793–5, 801; and Grau, 655, 656, 674–5, 685; vote against Directorio, 665; and nationalism, 685; their ages, 685; anti-Americanism, 685–6; collaboration with Guiteras, 695; division between, 696; initiate strike protest movement, 698–9; and gangster-ridden groups, 741–4, 763; and Fuentes' murder, 762; and army conspiracy, 781–2, 785; protest celebrations, 795, 796, 801; expedition to Manzanillo, 812; and Castro, 824 and n. 3, 864; and Moncada attack, 837; renewed rioting and violence, 871, 889–90; sabotage work, 925, 945; black and mulatto, 1119; hostility to revolution, 1282; sent to teach Sierra peasants, 1283; renewed executions, 1285; increased discipline, 1341; sent to study in Soviet *bloc*, 1341, 1475; post-Revolution conditions, 1428–9, 1429 n. 19; public confessions of homosexuality, 1429 and n. 18; dress prohibitions, 1429 and n. 20; increased proportion of women, 1431

Suárez, Dr Andrés, 1019

Suárez, José, 824; Moncadaist, 837 n. 20

Suárez Argudin, José, 170–1

Suárez Fernández, Miguel, 756, 757, 766

Suárez Fowler, Major, 1025

Suárez Gayol, Jesús, dismissal from INRA, 1241; death in Bolivia (1967), 1469 n. 56

Suárez Rivas, Eduardo, 747–8, 775 n. 1, 800, 802 n. 29, 861 n. 58, 874

Suárez Susquet, Col, in Oriente, 1017

Suárez Zoulet, Major, 997, 998

Subirats, Judge, 841
sugar (cane), S. Pacific origin, 27 and n. 2; variations in quality, 28, 41, 112; Cuban process, 40–1; comparative costs, 54; exports, 61 and n. 2, 119; price variations, 55, 62 and nn. 4, 5, 85, 126, 189, 272, 273, 307, 469 and n. 30, 526, 531–2, 537, 539, 544, 717, 738 n. 2, 748, 760–1, 1214, 1240, 1267, 1289; new Santa Cruz variety, 80 and n. 39; dependence on slave labour, 109; golden age of production, 111, 182, 193; the *maestro de azúcar*, 115; expert technicians, 115; merging of grinding and evaporation, 116, 117; new refining process, 117; iridescent white variety, 117, 124; total investment in (1830), 120; disorganized production, 121; varying types of *cana*, 121, and n. 40, 124; transport costs, 121, 123; attempts to standardize, 124; marketing of, 124; challenge of beet, 125; increased demands, 126; world consumption, 126 and n. 70, 1103, 1138 and nn., 1139; abolitionists and its import, 215; reformists and its manufacture, 234; packeted, granulated, 274 n. 15; place of small peasant, 275–6; *colono* production (*see under*), 276; produced by white population, 430; Cuban monopoly of U.S. market, 536, 537; technological changes, 536; English sales, 537; price-fixing, 539, 728, 729; end of price control, 542–3; crisis of 1920, 544; outstanding loans, 546; revival of refining, 547–8; disposal of 1921 crop, 551, 553; effect of U.S. internal policy, 557, 707; crop limitation 559, effect of international depression, 562; and of U.S. recognition of Mendieta, 677; Batista and, 679; U.S. and a 'new deal' for Cuba, 691; new tax on, 707; U.S. quota (1941), 726; Cuban–U.S. deals, 729–30, 748; source of Cuban wealth, 739, 740; *per capita* consumption, 740; Castro and, 830, 831; new Convention allocations, 846, 893; Castro-Batista counter-orders, 972; Cuban consumption, 1003; artificial prices, 1138–40; Javanese variety, 1143; yield per acre, 1143 and n. 22; use of cutting machine, 1144 and n. 27;

bulk-shipping, 1144 and n. 28; as a source of income, 1151–2; role in the economy, 1152–3; per cent of exports, 1152, 1188; world production areas (1959) (plate), 1156; contrasted with tobacco, 1161; capital investment, 1165; U.S. and the quota, 1262–3, 1268 and n. 28, 1270, 1272–3, 1288; Cuban surplus, 1267, 1290–1, 1292; drop in world prices, 1289; sale of U.S. quota, 1290–1, 1292; first *zafra del pueblo* (1961 harvest), 1322, 1331 and n. 68; co-operatives, 1324 and n. 39, 1325, 1326; suitability for Cuba, 1325; crop in 1962, 1331, and n. 69, 1374, 1382, 1384; use of by-products, 1335; increased role in economy after Revolution, 1436 and n. 1, 1438, 1474; lower average yield from cane, 1437 and n. 4; cause of loss of sucrose, 1437 and n. 5; disappearance of cane-cutter, 1437; possible faking of statistics, 1437 and n. 6; total available on free market, 1438 n. 9; use of Russian and Czech technicians and machinery, 1438–9; per cent of Cuban exports, 1443 n. 29; increased emphasis on since 1964, 1448; Russo-Cuban agreement, 1474; harvest: time spent on, 175; daily work of slaves, 175; their enjoyment, 181; main event of year, 501; financial repercussions, 501; political implications, 672–3; 94 per cent cut, 1331; events of 1970, 1331 and n. 68 (*zafra del pueblo*); use of cane-cutters, 1425–6, 1438 and n. 11, 1439; mechanization, 1438 and n. 11, 1449
Sugar Agreement, 1953, 1181
Sugar Co-ordination Law (1937), 1145, 1147; implications, 708; and wages, 1152 n. 73
Sugar Defence Commission, 559
sugar industry, source of imperial wealth, 4, 57; dependence on slave labour, 30–1; accompanying home industries, 39; effect of import of cheap labour, 52–3; legalization of markets, 62; rapid development, 72, 73–4, 125; decline after slave revolt, 77; effects of mechanization, 124, 189, 1144 and n. 27; abolition of English tariffs, 208; U.S. involvement, 272, 289 and n. 31, 290, 466, 468, 552–3,

sugar industry – *Cont.*
558, 561, 892–3; Wood and its revival, 457, 458–9; lack of capital, 458; pre- and post-world development, 536 ff.; formation of combines, 541; end of price control (1921), 542–3; decline in 1920s, 557 ff.; state involvement, 558–9, 1144–5; need for a policy, 561–2, 1153–5; Cuban share of U.S. market, 562; high involvement of foreigners, 684, 1150; effect of Jones-Cooligan Act, 692–3, 692 n. 7; effect of World War II, 717; golden era of expansion, 738; in the doldrums, 771; effect of Suez crisis, 933, 951; and Cuba's economic stagnation, 1105, 1142, 1176, 1181, 1189; and her class structure, 1108; controlling leagues, 1139, 1142, 1154; international policy, 1142, 1153; 'years of restriction', 1142 n. 14; Cuban organization, 1142 ff.; lack of research, 1143, 1155; U.S. withdrawal, 1147; workers employed, 1151–2, 1152 n. 69; dominance in Cuba's economy, 1153, 1182; future policies, 1154–5; prospects of nationalization, 1155; unemployment, 1175, 1551–2; importance of by-products, 1182; under Castro, 1240; numbers employed, 1334; shortage of skilled labour, 1426, 1436; geared to produce 10 million tons, 1436–7; decreased efficiency, 1438; static condition, 1550

sugar mills, machinery, 28 and n. 9, 29, 41; setting, 29; limited working period, 29; merchant owners, 32 and n. 22; protective device, 33; increased size and labour force, 62–3; Negro and mulatto ownership, 63; held in plurality, 63, 152–3, 708 n. 9; degenerate into prisons, 74; French innovations, 78 and n. 30; use of *bagasse* as fuel, 78, 116, 121 n. 40; removal of duty on imported machinery, 78; introduction of 'Jamaica train', 78–9, 79 n. 33, 97, 115; use of steam power, 79, 97 and n. 19, 112, 115–16, 241; introduction of *volvedora*, etc., 79, 115; foundation of new mills, 80–1; production per mill, 97, 124; use of oxen, 112, 116, 119, 123, 1144; variation in technical advance, 114;

varied labour force, 114, 115; technological revolution, 115–17, 154, 274 n. 15, 536; movement towards total capitalization, 117–18; location of modern buildings, 118–19; spread of investment in (*c.* 1830), 120; use of camels, 123; numbers, 123–4, 425, 426, 427, 428, 605, (plate), 1140–1; construction in 1860, 124; the *Casa de Purga*, 124; main Cuban sites (*c.* 1860), 138–9; 'Sundays', 151–2; social groupings, 152–4; company ownership, 154, 1110; built on slave fortunes, 154; attachment for debt, 154–5, 271; investment in slaves, 174 n. 24; work of slaves, 175; use of white labour, 184; ruined in Ten Years' War, 271; need to mechanize and cut costs, 273; effect of cheap steel rails, 273; mechanical essentials, 274 n. 15; Spanish ownership, 499–500, 541; U.S. ownership, 541–2, 687, 708 and n. 9; hit by disaster, 544, 546, 551, 688; new investment (*Vertientes*), 551–2; CNOC organized strike, 598, 605–6, 613, 631–2, 652, 656; occupation by workers, 632, 653, 656, 657; Grau's policy, 673; lack of churches, 683; Batista and, 707–8; Castro's levy, 1007; lack of new buildings, 1105, 1142; nature of labour force, 1109, 1152 ar.d n. 69; pay priests' salaries, 1127; and refining process, 1139; use of tractors, 1144 and n. 24; withdrawal of U.S. support, 1147; first 12-rollers, 1148; acreage covered, 1151 and n. 66; cane-cutters, 1152; uneasy labour relations, 1155; Owners Association, 1218; government land take-over, 1240, 1268, 1283; renamed after Revolution, 1322 and n. 33; underemployment, 1426; effect of mechanization, 1426, 1449; organization under Revolution, 1449

sugar planters, capital requirements, 32–3, 66 and n. 26, 82; state of indebtedness, 66 and n. 26, 82, 136, 271; treatment of slaves, 75 n. 15; dependence on merchants, 82–4, 136, 271; and annexation, 99–101, 105, 208, 221; fail to implement anti-slavery, 109; and the militia, 110; measures to increase production, 115;

sugar planters – *Cont.*

transport costs, 121; control of railways, 122; commercial activities, 136; and slave trading, 136–40; foreign immigrants, 140–2; social life, 142, 148; town and overseas houses, 142, 148; demoralized rich society, 142; purchase of titles, 142–3; and Negro entertainments, 147; foreign investments and travel, 148; and miscegenation, 148; inbreeding, 148, 153; lack of public spirit, 149; hierarchical grouping, 152–4; oligarchic families, 152–3; self-made immigrants, 153–4; and attachment for debt, 154–5; and slave breeding, 170–1; Negro mistresses, 173; use of white labour, 184; new sources of labour, 185; rent slaves as day workers, 188; restock after cholera epidemic, 201; effect of Negro conspiracy, 206; resell *emancipados*, 206; fear of abolition, 207; and López's failure, 217; seek constitutional reform, 233 ff.; position of smaller estates, 241 and n. 35, 428 and nn.; rebellion in the East, 242–4, 260; need to placate the west, 269; financial position in 1880s, 271–2; lack of second crop, 273; and the *colonato*, 276; continued style of life, 277–8; employ contract labour, 279; and reform, 293; and Independence War (1895), 322–3, 324, 330, 343, 424; encouraged to borrow, 546; financial crisis, 546, 553; bankruptcy, 551; New York orientation, 684; and 1937 Sugar Law, 1145

sugar plantations, 19; Cuban numbers, 27–8, 28 n. 7, 97, 111–12, 277 land cultivation, 29, 41, 62, 66, 119; land prices, 29, 63; buildings and outhouses, 29, 114; agricultural timetable, 29; cost of slaves, 30 and n. 15, 31 and n. 18; dependence on their labour, 31, 52, 66, 68, 73–4, 282; concentration camp analogy, 35 n. 29; application of scientic agriculture 80; extension in area, 80–1; cost of, *c.* 1800, 83; effect of England's abolition, 87; average size and production, 112; acreage in use, 112, 129 n. 8; average inventory, 112–13; the *casa de vivienda*, 114, 129; boundary hedges, 114; white salaried workers,

114 and n. 14; the overseer (*mayoral*), 114 and n. 11; other workers, 115 and n. 14; ten-slave *trapiches*, 119 and n. 33, 124; move eastwards, 119, 537, 805; money investment, 123 and n. 59, 130 and n. 11; land ownership, 123 n. 59; centre of activity, 124; state of roads, 149; absorption of slaves, 168 and n. 3, 170, 174; investment in slaves, 174 and nn. 24, 25, 30; cemeteries, 180; first slave strike, 236, 239; comparison between east and west, 241, 254; destruction of, 255–6, 264; emergence of the *central*, 275, 276 (*see under*); power of master, 282; U.S. infiltration, 289–90; INRA take-over, 1284; cash-renting, 1550

Sugar Stabilization Act, 1930, 562, 717, 861

Sulzberger, Cyrus, 1392

Sumner, General, 393

Superunda, Conde de, viceroy of Peru, 6–7

Suretsky, Jaime, and copyright, 1465

Surí Castillo, Emilio, 752, 756

Sutherland, Elizabeth, 1430–1, 1433 n. 34

Sweeting, Alton, 979

Syme Muir, 187

Synge, W. W. Follett, 1544, 1545

Szulc, Tad, in *New York Times*, 1280

Tabarés, Diego de, 6–7

Taber, Robert, 936–7, 946, 997 n. 6

Tabernas, Juan Bautista, 129

Tabernilla, Brig. Carlos ('Wince'), 1019, 1021, 1023

Tabernilla, General Francisco, 911; and army conspiracy, 779 n. 11, 780; disillusionment, 798; intrigues against Batista, 839–40, 852; promotes his sons, 839–40; and Prío, 870; accused of plots against Domingo, 883; and Castro's landing, 898; maligns Barrera, 935–6; evil genius of army, 941, 965, 1019, 1039, 1041; awarded U.S. Legion of Merit, 967; and army's defeat, 1019, 1021, 1022, 1023; and officers' *coup*, 1021, 1022; proposes military Junta, 1023; flight from Cuba, 1026; in supreme command (1958), 1041; interviewed by U.S., 1279

Tabernilla, Col Marcelo, attack on, 890

Tabernilla, General 'Silito', 1019; promoted by his father, 839–40; ousts Rubio as sec. to Batista, 852, 1019, 1022

Tabernilla Dolz, ex-General, 745, 798; and army conspiracy, 779 n. 11

Tacón, Miguel (1775–1855), captain-general, 144, 145, 149, 180, 194 n. 5; apportionment of slave costs, 109 n. 1; and *emancipados*, 181, 182; and Chinese labour, 186; career and character, 194, 199; cut from slave trade, 194; administrative reforms, 194–5; expels Saco, 195, 196; opposes Havana railway, 197; and Villanueva, 197; ignores election order (1836), 197–8; ordered to expel archbishop of Santiago, 198; attempted assassination, 199; encouragement of African cultural ideas, 199; returns to Spain entitled, 199, 202; reputation, 199

Taft, Henry W., 485, 506, 686

Taft, Senator William Howard, 342; U.S. president, 477 n. 22, 485 n. 25; sent to Havana, 477; and Liberal revolutionaries, 477–9; on Estrada, 478; proclaims Provisional Government, 479; 'preventive policy', 509–11; 'dollar diplomacy', 511

Tallet, José Z., poet, 566 and n. 11

Tamayo, Capt., 839

Tamayo, Diego, 444 n. 1, 455, 456 n. 56

Tapachula, Castro-Carrillo meeting, 886, 926 and n. 7

Tarafa, Col Josefa Mariana, 290 n. 36; and northern Railroad, 557; and crop limitation, 559 and n. 7

Tarafa, Col Miguel, 614 n. 34, 949; army pay scandal, 471

Tasende, José Luis, 825, 836 n. 9, 837 n 20

Taussig, Charles, 598, 686–7

Taylor, J. G., 140–1, 150, 231 n. 64

Taylor, Zachary (1784–1850), U.S. president, 212, 214; and López' proposed revolution, 214 and n. 42

Tejera, Diego Vicente, 302, 884 n. 36, 781, 782

Teller, Henry Moore, 376 n. 43; his amendment, 376, 409; and Platt Amendment, 453

Terradas, Pércz, 588

Terry, Emilio, 268, 335

Terry, Francisca, 322

Terry, Tomás, 235 n. 12; slave merchant, 98 and n. 24, 137, 140, 141, 170; railway backer, 123; sugar mill, *Caracas*, 137, 278; financial achievements, 140 and n. 13, 148, 238 n. 26, 240, 1085; reputation, 140 and n. 14; social position, 153, 1234; election, 238

Tetuán, Duque de, 349–50

Tey, José ('Pepito'), 866, 867, 868, 895 n. 9, 896 n. 14; death, 897

30 November Movement, formation, 1285, 1348

Thomas, Samuel, 464, 465

Thrasher, John S., 208

Thurston, Senator, 371 and n. 20

Tillman, Senator, 453

Tirgale, Baltasar Ricaud de, technician, 10

Tizol, Ernesto, 825, 836 n. 9

tobacco, import figures, 4 n. 20; farmers, 19, 23–4, 80, 133, 1159; Cuban origin, 21, 22; Indian cultivation and smoking, 22 and n. 24, 1519; Spanish cultivation, 22–3, 24; land needs, 23, 134; the Crown and, 23–4, 133; smuggling of, 23–4; for cigars, 24, 134, 1158 and n. 2; Cuban process, 25–6; conversion to sugar production, 32, 77 n. 26; Spanish ban on export, 70; ruination after slave revolt, 77, 80; end of import duty on machinery, 78; abolition of monopoly, 94, 133; money invested in (1860), 123; increased production, 133; free trade in, 133; value of land and slaves, 133, 134; number of farms (*vegas*), 133, 134, 291; value of total product, 134; quantity smoked in Cuba, 134, 1158; export figures, 134, 135, 1158 and n. 2; effect of U.S. tariff, 135; smoking in Havana, 145, 148, 193, 288, 541; only secondary crop, 273; trade with U.S., 289; effect of Ten Years' War, 291; ban on leaf-export, 334; white-controlled production, 430, 434; state of the industry (1898), 434–5; crop and exports (1892–1900), 434–5; strikes, 691, (*Huelga de la Moneda*), 491; U.S. controlled trade, 466; 1907 slump, 491, 493; effect of World War II, 728; Castro's cigar factory, 996; per cent of exports, 1152 n. 72; cigar smoking, 1158; producing regions,

Tobacco – *Cont.*
1158, 1161; cigar exports, 1158 and n. 2; cigarette factories, 1158 n. 3, 1160; production figures, 1158, 1332 n. 71; area cultivated, 1158–9; use of sharecroppers, 1159, 1161, 1550; company-owned lands, 1159; shade-variety, 1159 and n. 11; cigar names, 1159; factories, 1160 and n. 18; organization of industry, 1160–1; contrasted with sugar, 1161; drop in world market, 1161; resistance to modernization, 1164; grown by private farmers, 1440

tobacco factories, private, 134–5; mutual aid societies, 236–7; prison-reading scheme, 237–8; destruction in Ten Years' War, 291; employment of women, 291 and n. 41; racial discrimination, 1121; and mechanization, 1159–60, 1164, 1177; labour force, 1160; government control of production, 1440

Tobacco Stabilization Board, 784

Togliatti, Palmiro, 596, 697

Toledano, Lombardo, 714 and n. 37, 715, 880, 887

Topping, John, 964, 976

Toral, General Juan José (1832–1904), at Santiago, 397 and n. 25, 398–9; and surrender terms, 399, 400; at Vigo, 408

Torres, Antonio, Labour leader, 897; and FONU, 1083 n. 23

Torres, Major Félix, Communist, guerrilla group, 981, 1005, 1109 n. 23, 1042, 1079; joins Cienfuegos, 1012, 1050

Torres, Joaquín, 1007 n. 15, 1009 and n. 23, 1013 and n. 49, 1241 and n. 19

Torres, Nico, 1007

Torres Menier, Capt., 635

Touchet, Samuel, 49 n. 31, 54 n. 54, 84 n. 55

Touré, Sekou, 1317, 1407

Toussaint Louverture, 76

trade unions and organizations, 249; tobacco factories, 236; Spanish, 298; Anarchist, 291, 534, 575 and n. 22; primitive character, 491; influence of Spanish immigrants, 541; craft (*gremios*) and factory (*sindicatos*), 575–6; dissolution by Mendieta, 692; declared illegal, 699; increased power

in 1930s, 702, 1173; Batista and, 711, 716, 791, 1175; CTC, 713, 1178; importance of 1933 Congress, 714; and Communists and Communism, 733, 748, 756, 855, 981, 1083, 1173, 1249, 1250, 1259–60; well-established, 736; government control, 754; sugar union and, 872; strikes, 942, 988; and Revolution, 1031 and n. 45, 1179; rural workers, 1109; resistance to technological advances, 1142, 1144, 1164; relations with governments, 1173; obsessed with past, 1174; and unemployment, 1175; Labour membership, 1178 and n. 15; and political advancement, 1179; industrial federations, 1179; weakness in rural areas, 1179; and Negro question, 1179; corruption, 1180; back the government, 1249; purge of 'Mujalistas', 1259, 1274; usurped by Ministry of Labour, 1274; in China, 1315

Trapote, Victor, 869, 887 n. 47, 894 n. 7

Travel Agents' Conference, 1246 and n. 33

Treaty of Guadeloupe Hidalgo, 210

Treaty of Paris (1783), 67–8, 451, 452, 457 n. 60

Trejo, Dr Rafael, 674 n. 36, 782

Trejo, Rafael, 591, 592 n. 38, 597, 695, 759

Trelles, Alabau, 983

Trelles, Carlos (1866–), 567 n. 15; on Magoon, 483; denunciatory pamphlet, 567

Tribunales Populares, offences dealt with, 1459

Tricontinental Conference, 1966, 1387 n. 12; Castro and, 1477; presence of Latin American guerrilla leaders, 1477; Russia and China and, 1477 n. 10, 1478

Trinidad, 33, 48, 222; sugar mills (*Guinia de Toto*), 81, 118 n. 32, 179; foreign merchants, 98; sugar exports, 119; yield per acre, 1143 n. 22; Cantero Palace, 147; tax on crop land, 184 n. 1; Chinese labourers, 186; in decay, 278; rebel numbers, 324; Yoruba traditions, 519 n. 21; *Chango*, 520; Negro-white violence, 673, 1121 and n. 22; and Batista, 1122; suggested landing place, 1306 and n. 33

Trist, Nicolas, U.S. Consul, 199, 210 n. 16

Tro, Emilio, chief of police, 742, 755, 774, 811, 812

Trollope, Anthony, 144, 145, 148, 149, 150

Trope, Miguel de la, 492

Trotsky, Leon, 714

Trotskyism, 588 n. 13, 741, 880, 1281

Trujillo, Hector, President of Dominican Republic, 966

Trujillo, General Leonidas (d. 1961), President of Dominican Republic, 609, 626, 735, 759, 882, 925, 950, 1199, 1288; acceptance by Cabrals, 703 n. 35; expedition against, 754–6; relations with Cuba, 882, 911; compared with Castro, 882–3; kidnaps Galíndez, 883; his army, 885; Roosevelt and, 977 n. 18; offer to Batista, 1021; attacked by Castro, 1228 and n. 45; backs anti-Castro plot, 1238 and n. 19, 1243 n. 26; trial of conspirators, 1459

Truman, Harry S. (born 1884), 845, 1061; imperialistic tendencies, 745; and military aid for Greece and Turkey, 753 n. 44; and Trujillo expedition, 755

Tugwell, Rexford, 598, 687

Turnbull, David, British Consul in Havana, 201; and slave costs, 109 and n. 1; and slave ships, 158; efforts to end trade, 165, 203; and mulatto population, 173; abolitionist, 201–2; expulsion, 203–4; and Negro conspiracy, 205; and British slave dealings, 231 n. 64

Tuxpan, 894

26 July Movement, inauguration, 867, 881; membership, 867–8, 1080 and n. 12; Santiago group, 868, 895, 902; Cuban Committee, 868 n. 19; Mexican centre, 869, 952; manifestoes, 869, 984 n. 51; and democratic opposition, 871; supports sugar strike, 872; Havana group, 872, 895, 902, 936, 981, 984, 991, 1002, 1010; and Batista, 873; invitation to revolutionaries, 874–5; military training, 877–8; establishes a commission, 889 and n. 59; prepares for invasion, 891; Castro on, 892 and n. 71; lack of coordination, 895, 897; Cuban landing,

897–901; Circular de Organizacion (8.3.58), 901 n. 53; financial resources, 909; reprisals against, 909–10; bomb outrages, 910; young intellectual adherents, 910; attack on La Plata barracks, 912–14; 'atrocity' denunciations, 913 n. 21; mood of despondency, 915, 923; air attacks, 915, 916, 917; purge of malcontents, 916; numbers, 917, 919–20, 923; Sierra rendezvous, 917 ff.; lack of higher education, 921; relationship to and with Communism, 922–3, 944 and n. 8, 953 n. 7, 1002 and n. 22, 1006 and n. 9, 1007 and n. 15, 1051, 1078, 1219–22, 1221, 1313; allied groups, 925; and Palace attack, 927–31; police murders in Humboldt St., 931–2, 932 and n. 33, 1082, 1318; numbers in Sierra army, 934–5, 937, 938, 951, 973; communication with peasants, 936, 937; at El Uvero, 939–40; U.S. attitude, 946, 968; political activities, 952, 955, 966; statement of ideology, 952–3; recruitment of professional classes, 953; terrorist activity, 956, 957, 978; and naval mutiny, 961, 995; reaction to Miami Pact, 969; concept of the revolutionary, 975, 1053; U.S. representatives and groups, 976 n. 13, 1221; reunion of National Directorate, 983 and n. 49; sub-sections and duties, 984 and n. 55; Venezuelan gift, 986, 995 and n. 33; and a general strike, 988 and n. 2, 989, 990, 1030–1; Church support, 994; and kidnappings, 1001; pact with opposition groups, 1003; anger at Guevara's Communism, 1013; joined by other organizations, 1016–17; Barquín and, 1028; takes over Alerta, 1029; and Castro's triumph, 1030, 1033; public issue of Revolución, 1032; resignation of Camagüey executive, 1245; and 10th Congress of CTC, 1250; effect of Matos' trial, 1257; integrated with ORI, 1372; and organized labour, 1083, 1201 n. 28; position after Revolution, 1086, 1203, 1204, 1221; and the Revolution, 1198; surviving members, 1453; and PURS, 1454 n. 3; Nuestra Razon, 892 n. 68, 921 and n. 53, 952 and n. 6, 953 and n. 7, 954; see also Sierra Maestra

U Thant, 1410, 1411, 1412
Unión de Rebeldes Pioneros, formation, 1340 and n. 3
Unión Democratica, and elections, 447–8, 718
Unión General de Trabajadores (UGT), 298, 408, 442
Unión Insurrecional Revolucionaria (UIR), membership, 742, 755 and n. 51; use of violence, 742–3, 753, 761, 774; bribed with official posts, 763; Castro and, 811, 812, 813, 817, 1055, 1489; sick humour, 813
Unión Militar Revolucionaria, 634 and n. 1, 651
Unión Nacionalista, 611, 629, 651, 655; short survival, 682
Union of Workers and Artists (UNEAC), declaration of principles, 1465; annual prize awards, 1466 and nn. 45, 46; control of publishers, 1466–7
Unión Revolucionaria Comunista (URC), 721; Executive Committee, 720 n. 19, 729 n. 25; changes name, 733
Unionist Party, 526, 527
U.S.S.R., 542; relations with U.S., 381, 1265, 1278; attacked by Germany, 727; and Cuban sugar, 728, 862, 935, 1316, 1317 n. 18, 1336, 1381, 1384; diplomatic relations with Cuba, 731, 793, 967, 1265–6; beet sugar production, 893; breach with China (1959/61), 923; Castro and, 1052, 1281–2, 1314; and Cuban Revolution, 1082, 1318; sugar production, 1139 and nn. 8, 9; quota, 1142 n. 13; rumoured submarines in Caribbean, 1241; Havana exhibitions, 1263, 1265, 1314; Latin-American policy, 1264–5, 1266; diplomatic and consular representatives, 1265; economic relations with Cuba, 1265–6, 1381, 1384; sends arms and aid to Cuba, 1314, 1318; willingness to defend her, 1316 and n. 17, 1384; purchase of stock and factories from, 1335–6, 1376; promised Migs, 1355; references to Cuba and Socialist bloc, 1371 and n. 52, 1381; and Castro's 'Declaration of Havana', 1376; complaints concerning their technicians, 1382; promised equipment, 1387,

1396; and missiles for Cuba, 1387 and n. 11, 1388–9; nuclear weapon policy, 1390; plan for defence of Cuba, 1393–4; programme of liberalization and destalinization, 1397; protagonist in missile crisis, 1395 ff.; troops in Cuba, 1408; reaction to Kennedy's demand, 1409; concern to avoid war, 1410, 1411; ships passing 'quarantine' line, 1411; compromise proposals, 1411–12; internal disagreement, 1412 and n. 36; effect of missile decision, 1415; use of text-books in Cuban universities, 1428; purchase of Cuban sugar, 1438 and n. 8, 1474, 1475; industrial system, 1446, 1447, 1451; GOSPLAN, 1450; Guevara and, 1471; relations with Cuban Republic, 1474; civilian aid, 1474 and n. 1; exports to Cuba, 1475 and n. 1; technicians in Cuba, 1475; education of her students, 1475; part played in her politics, 1475
United States, gains Louisiana, 65 n. 20; ambassadors to Cuba, 67; and slave trade, 71, 80, 86, 96, 161, 165, 166, 204, 238; treatment of slaves, 75 n. 15; and Cuban sugar, 85, 87 n. 11, 126, 457, 558, 728 and n. 21, 729–30, 732–3, 748, 771, 1103, 1138, 1150, 1272–3, 1288, 1289; exports to and imports from Cuba, 87 n. 11, 1187–8, 1425; proposed purchase of Cuba, 88, 90, 199, 211 and n. 22, 212–17, 225, 251, 228–32, 252–3, 351, 367; and abolition, 93, 170, 207; commercial relations with Cuba, 97, 194 and n. 4, 287–90, 693–4, 717–18, 729, 1062; recognizes S. American independence, 99; and 'annexationism', 99–100, 103–4, 111, 209 ff.; influence on Cuba's development, 104–5, 133, 270, 599, 602, 719, 726–8, 1185–6, 1346; tariff on coffee, 131, on tobacco, 135; tonnage duty on Spanish ships, 131, 133 and n. 21, 194; coffee consumption, 131 n. 16; immigrant cigar workers, 135; Cuban investments, 148, 275, 290 and n. 38, 466–70, 509, 511, 536, 537, 599–600, 911, 1057–8, 1183, 1184; slaveships, 158, 161; insurance, 162 and n. 36; refuses Britain right of search, 201 and n. 7, 203; acquires New Mexico and

United States – *Cont.*

California, 210; expansionist sentiment 'manifest destiny', 211 and n. 20, 310–15, 325; and López's expedition, 214, 217; *Black Warrior* episode, 222–3, 226; propaganda weapon 'Africanization', 223–4; threats to Spain, 225; and recognition of Cuba's belligerency, 251, 253, 256–7, 260–1, 264, 270, 323, 332, 337, 339–40; recognises Spanish Republic, 261; steel production, 273, 311; enters Cuban economic field, 274; travellers in Cuba, 288; numbers working on farms and in cities, 310 and n. 3; arrival of immigrants, 311; population figures, 311 and n. 7, 1093 and nn. 2, 5; industrial power, 311–12; and imperialism, 312 and n. 13, 379, 402, 407, 419; failure to solve Negro problem, 312–13; Press battles, 313; proposed intervention in Spanish-Cuban affairs, 332, 353–4, 359 and n. 23, 379; and 1896 elections, 335–6; reaction to *Maine* incident, 364–6; and war with Spain (*see under*); absorbs Philippines, 407; part in world affairs, 417–20, 1063; behaviour as occupiers, 420–3, 436 ff.; constitutional relations with China, 449–556; and beet sugar, 458 and n. 69, 560–1; sugar tariff affairs, 459, 550, 552 and n. 42, 558; mining concessions, 466; reciprocity treaty with Cuba, 468–9, 536; intervention in her affairs, 476–9, 482–9, 489 n. 39, 508–9 (1933), 607 ff., 627, 641, 644, 646–7, 638, 941, 986, 991, 1001; Cuban bases, 502; and racism, 516; loss of African culture, 519; and Negro rising (1912), 523; understanding of Cuban corruption, 527–8; condemns Liberal revolt, 529; and 1914–18 War, 530; postwar combines, 541; and Cuban finance, 546–7, 550–1, 553, 554, 555, 686–7, 723 and n. 34, 728; and (1920) electoral fraud, 548–50; change in Cuban policy, 576–7; base for Cuban rebels, 587; policy of non-intervention, 589 and n. 17; and Machado's corrupt rule, 589–90; instances of foreign intervention, 626; and recognition of Grau's government, 627, 651, 654,

655, 661, 662, 670, 672, 673–4; recognizes Mendieta's regime, 677; student accusations, 685–6; influence of Japan, 693; and Machado's debts, 716; military talks with Batista, 722–3, 771; enters 1939–45 War, 729; and Peña's election to CTC, 753 n. 44; obsession with Communism, 765, 1211, 1214, 1219 and n. 13, 1227; Congressional Mission, 771–2; and Batista's, 789–90, 874, 959, 964, 967, 982–3, 985, 1059; and Castro, 876, 911, 946–7, 958, 1037, 1058, 1208 ff.; and Cuba's Civil War, 959–60, 1015–16, 1026; knowledge of naval mutiny, 961, 963; arms embargo, 985–6, 995, 1040; and rebel kidnappings, 1001, 1010; position of Cuban embassy, 1058; relations with Castro's Cuba, 1058, 1196, 1207, 1226, 1229, 1232, 1258, 1262–3, 1264, 1267–71; threat to culture, 1059, 1062; attitude to neutralism, 1061; relations with Latin America, 1061, 1063; armaments supplier, 1063 and n. 52; denounces war trials, 1075–6, 1087–8, 1089; Cuban investment in, 1102, 1148–9, 1172 and n. 81; *per capita* income, 1104; sugar production, etc., 1139 and nn. 8, 9, 1143 n. 22; controlling interest in Cuban industries, 1164–72 *passim*; unemployment, 1175; wage levels, 1177; possible economic aid, 1205, 1209 and n. 56, 1211–12, 1213, 1240, 1258, 1294, 1295; exchange of notes on Agrarian Reform, 1223, 1226, 1229, 1242–5, 1259; heightened mistrust of Cuba, 1232, 1278; Camp David meeting, 1242 n. 24; and Cuban exiles, 1243, 1283–4, 1293; source of Lanz's aircraft, 1245–6; and flights to Cuba, 1248; and Cuban-Soviet relations, 1264, 1267 n. 23; accused of *Coubre* explosion, 1269, 1270 n. 33; Castro sympathizers, 1277; presidential election campaign (1960), 1278, 1296, 1300; Summit Conference with U.S.S.R., 1278; and counter-revolutionaries, 1283; nationalization of her Cuban companies, 1289–90, 1291, 1297; invasion plans, 1301 ff.; 1354, 1355–6; revival of 'intervention', 1306; opposing views on invasion, 1307–8; ignorance of

United States – *Cont.*

Cuban contrasts, 1353; public ignorance of involvement in invasion, 1357, 1364-5; Commission on its failure, 1364 n. 27; government mismanagement, 1369-70; closed market to Cuba, 1374; and her Communism, 1375 n. 11; Congressional election campaign (1962), 1385, 1386, 1399; and missiles in Cuba, 1388, protagonist in missile crisis, 1395 ff.; approval of 'quarantine' decision, 1407; long association with Cuba, 1418; unwise behaviour towards her, 1418-19; exiled Negro militants, 1433-4; alleged assassination attempts, 1471; supplies arms to Latin America, 1479; domination of Latin America and Cuba, 1480, 1493; threat of Cuban Revolution, 1480; and Bolivian guerrilla war, 1481; private investment in Latin America, 1481 and n. 23; blockade of Cuba, 1481; suspension of Miami flights, 1482; chartered air service for exiles, 1482; supplies Cuban farm machinery, 1552

United States, Southern, slave trade, 161, 210, 231, 280 n. 24; attitude to slavery, 184 n. 3, 210, 218 and n. 4, 230; cotton boom, 165, 210; and economic expansion, 210, 310; racism, 210; and López's expedition, 215-16, 217; possible secession, 220 n. 12; and acquisition of Cuba, 222, 229, 230, 231, 232; reconstruction, 252; tribal origins of Negroes, 519

U.S.-Mexican War, 210, 211 n. 21, 212, 214, 245

U.S. Military government (mission) (1899-1902), to recast Cuban society, 436; attack on U.S. soldiers, 437 and n. 9; imposition of military government, 437 ff.; numbers of servicemen, 438 and n. 10; planned withdrawal, 460; numbers (1902-9), 490 and n. 43; bans religious festivals, 517; relations with Cuban officers, 947; use of bombers and tanks at Cienfuegos, 963, 964; remains in Cuba, 1009; Castro and, 1075, 1077; withdrawal, 1077

U.S. Senate, Internal Security Committee, 947 n. 14, 948, 1218 n. 9, 1297; Foreign Relations Committee, 1075

Universidad Popular José Martí, 566, 589; foundation, 1115

universities, numbers of pupils, 286 n. 13; *colegios*, 1115-16; numbers of, 1136; drop in entrance standards, 1340-1, 1342; slow changes under Revolution, 1341; Marxist-Leninist bias, 1341; post-Revolution, 1428-9; future prospects, 1429; and homosexuals, 1435

University of Havana, 79 n. 37, 1136; exclusions from, 13; anatomy course, 86; philosophy professor, 96 n. 18; in 1899, 433; reinaugurated, 447; reform movement, 564; closed by Machado, 591, 1214; student political parties, 591-2, 594, 810; opposes intervention, 599; and sergeants' revolt, 637-8, 641 and n. 23; constitutional role, 641; membership of Grau's cabinet, 650, 651; achieves autonomy, 698; occupied by soldiers, 699; and gangster-ridden groups, 743, 763, 811; amunition stores, 762; anti-government movement, 767; closed on election day (1949), 767 n. 19; and army plot, 783; opposes *Batistato II*, 793-5, 801; closure, 801; Castro and, 809-11; elections, 811; end of gangsterism, 864 n. 10; Communist Youth movement, 923; destruction, 1070 n. 13; purged of anti-revolutionists, 1214; destruction of freedom, 1286-7; corrupt and inefficient reputation, 1287; Agricultural education department, 1553

Uppman family, 134, 546

Uría, General Quirino, 780

Uris, Leon, *Topaz*, 1396

Urquiola Lechuga, María and Mercedes, bomb placers, 945

Urria, Marquésa de, 427

Urrutia, Manuel, Judge, acquits *Fidelistas*, 942, 970; proposed president, 970-1, 977, 978, 995 n. 33, 1003, 1065; career, 970 n. 32; repudiates collaboration with Communists, 989, 1230, 1231; Castro and, 1030, 1033, 1197, 1231; occupies Palace, 1033; as president, 1066, 1070, 1077, 1086, 1197, 1230; and suppression of gambling, 1197; efforts to resign,

Urrutia, Manuel – *Cont.*
1197–8; libel writ against *Avance*, 1231; denounces Lanz, 1232; destroyed by Castro, 1232–3; resignation and departure, 1233 and n. 59

Valdés, Gabriel de la Concepción (Placido) (1809–44), 172 and n. 20, 205

Valdés, Geronimo (1784–1855), 202, 203, 213

Valdés, Joaquín, 589

Valdés, Ramiro, 1017, 1032, 1455 n. 6; and Castro, 826, 869, 887 n. 47, 899, 900 n. 52; Moncadaist, 837 n. 20; Minister of Interior, 869 n. 20; in the Sierra, 901 and n. 53, 916, 996 n. 2; Lieut under Castro, 934 n. 5; commander in Las Villas, 1198; head of intelligence (G.2), 1213, 1253, 1321; in Mexico, 1237 n. 5; and ORI, 1377 n. 18; and new Communist party, 1454 n. 5

Valdés Daussá, José Antonio, 607

Valdés Daussá, Ramiro, 592 n. 34, 595, 629, 635, 638 and n. 13, 641 n. 22, 742, 743

Valdés Vivó, Raúl, ambassador to S. Vietnam, 944 nn. 6, 7, 1478 n. 12

Valdés Rodríguez, Fermín, 300

Valdés Rodríguez, José Manuel, 614

Valdéspino, Andrés, 793, 866 n. 13, 1202

Valera, Jesús Rolando, 798

Valero, Agustín, 782, 785 n. 24

Valiente, Col Francisco, 411

Valiente, Pablo José (1740–1818), *intendente*, 73 and n. 6; sugar mill, *La Ninfa*, 82 and n. 47; ignores trade bans, 85

Valiente Hernández, Pastor, 945

Valladolid, Archbishop of, 348

Valle, Col P. A. del, 723

Vallejo, Dr René, 1044

Valls, Jorge, 925, 926, 927

Valmaseda, General, 248, 252, 259, 265

Van Horne, Sir William (1843–1915), 464 n. 6; Cuban railway project, 444 n. 2, 464–6, 466 n. 11, 569 n. 2, 600

Vanderbilt, 'Commodore' Cornelius (1794–1877), 227

Varela, Carlos Enrique Alfonso, 855

Varela, Col, 1028, 1029

Varela, Fr Félix (1788–1853), 86, 96 and n. 18, 102

Varela Canosa, Col, and Brigade 2506, 1359–60; in Mexico, 1360 n. 18

Varela Castro, Col Manuel, and the *puros*, 884

Varona, Antonio ('Tony'), student leader, and Grau, 655, 744; Prío's prime minister, 762, 764, 782, 792, 802, 968, 1223; member *diálogo cívico*, 874; in Miami, 968, 1283; and presidential candidate, 971; and Agrarian Reform, 1223; advocate of democracy, 1236; co-ordinator of exiles, 1296; in Guatemala, 1306; and U.S. air cover, 1310; survival in exile, 1471 n. 66

Varona, Barnabé, rebel general, 262

Varona, Enrique (d. 1925), 580

Varona, Enrique José (1849–1933), man of letters, 333 and n. 18, 444 n. 1, 505, 567–8, 591, 687; approves U.S. intervention 479; heads Students' Federation, 564–5; and Junta of Unity, 1003

Varona, Col Miguel, 530

Vasconcelos, José, 702 and n. 32

Vasconcelos, Ramón, mulatto, resigns from cabinet, 760; ed. *Alerto*, 820, 861, 866, 891; and Machado, 820 n. 87, 861; Minister of Commerce, 846, 861 and n. 58

Vázquez Bello, Clemente, electoral manager, 570; assassination, 597–8, 607

Vázquez Candela, Euclides, and Communists, 1240 and n. 14

Vega, Aníbal, 1011

Vega, César, 967 and n. 21

Vega, Capt. Jaime, 1009

Vega, José Raúl, 887 n. 47, 940

Velasco, Fernández, 674 n. 36, 675

Velasco, Raúl de, 985, 986

Velázquez, Diego de, arrival in Cuba, 1513 n. 8, 1514

Vendedor Unico, 561, 800

Venezuela, 33 n. 25, 98, 137, 213 and n. 33, 503; trading monopoly, 68; British Guiana boundary dispute, 325; Communist party, 579, 1476, 1478, 1488 n. 14; Castro's speech (1959), 821 n. 93; Cabo Blanco leper hospital, 879; gift to Urrutia, 986 and n. 66; radio telephone to Sierra, 992; aids Montecristi movement, 994–5; Radio Caracas, 1027; U.S. and,

Venezuela – *Cont.*
1057; oil millionaires, 1063; population figures, 1093; standard of living, 1103, 1107 and n.; priesthood, 1128; illiteracy, 1131; 1902 Revolution, 1149; oil boom, 1168; Cuban investment, 1184; military rising, 1276

Ventura, Col Esteban, 756 n. 52; police chief, 864, 886, 957 n. 24, 1039; student murders in Humbolt St, 931, 932 and n. 33; upper class approval, 932; legendary death-dealer, 942; indicted for murder, 983, 1227; flight, 1027, 1029, 1075; and Ameijeiras, 1071 n. 15; asylum in U.S., 1077, 1471 n. 66

Ventura, Dr Machado, in Moscow, 1478

Vera, Aldo, 1071, 1349 n. 21

Verdaguer, Roberto and Guillermo, 1357

Verdeja, Santiago, 861 and n. 58

Viadenibule, Orosman, 613

Viciana, Antonio, 1348

Victoria, Ampado, 1287

Vieques, U.S. navy and, 1405

Vieta, Drangel, 783 and n. 18

Vietnam War, 1476, 1478 and n. 12

Vignier, Dr A., 768

Vilaboy, López, 886, 1113, 1162

Vilar, César, and CNOC, 580, 581, 696; secret visit to Machado, 605–6, 711; offer to call off strike, 618; senator, 747

Vilasuso, José, 576

Villa, Pancho, 877–8

Villa-Urrutia, Wenceslao, 117 and n. 26, 141, 153

Villaboy, José, 1067

Villacampa, Brig., 298

Villafaña, Lieut Manuel, *Batistiano*, 884 n. 36; and air force, 1028; defection, 1040; in Mexico, 1237 n. 5, 1355, 1360 n. 18; and Nicaragua air base, 1355; commander Brigade 2506, 1359

Villalta, Marqués de, 53 n. 52, 63

Villamil, 1016

Villanueva, Claudio Martínez Pinillos, Conde de (1782–1853), *intendente*, 111 and n. 6, 143, 144, 196 n. 11; and Havana railway, 121–3, 197; sets up Royal Bank, 136 n. 1; and Saco's expulsion, 196; disagreements with Tacón, 197–8; and his resignation, 199; opposes emancipation, 203

Villanueva, José Pico, 52

Villaverde, Cirilo (1802–94), 807, 1343; compares coffee and sugar plantation cemeteries, 179–80; condemned to *vile garrotte*, 213; *Cicilia Valdes*, 213 and n. 37

Villuendas, Enrique, 473

Vitalio Acuña, Major Juan, death in Bolivia, 1453 n. 1, 1469 n. 56

Vitoria de las Tunas, Menocal and, 351, 468, 534

Vives, General Francisco Dionisio (1735–1840), captain-general, 102 102 and n. 38, 105, 193; given '*facultades omnimodas*', 102; and illegal slave trade, 105, 193; at siege of Gerona, 110; life and character, 193

Vivó, Jorge Antonio, Communist sec. gen., 596, 597, 721 and n. 20

Vizoso, 883

Vollmern, August, 573–4

Vosjoly, Thiraud de, 1396

Wagner, Robert, 910–11

Walker, Jimmy, 586

Walker, Robert, 213

Walker, William, 227–8, 227 n. 47

Walsh, Sinesio, 1285

Warsaw Pact, and Cuba, 1388, 1390

Watson, Grant, British Minister, and 1933 Revolution, 628; on Cuban disorder, 657; and battle of Hotel Nacional, 659–60; and recognition of Grau's government, 671 and n. 18; on Grau, 677

Webster, Daniel, 207

Weinberg, Albert, 311

Welles, Sumner (1892–1962), 549 n. 29, 717; characteristics of a Cuban president, 549; and a Cuban loan, 551, 730; ambassador in Havana, 606–7, 1064; *Naboth's Vineyard*, 607; instructions from Hull, 607–8; negotiations concerning Machado, 608, 609–10, 613–14, 615, 616, 621–2, 624–5; accepted as mediator, 610–12, 613; and bomb incident, 611 and n. 21; committee of complaints, 613; Communists' protests, 615; five-point plan, 616, 617–18; and U.S. intervention, 619, 621, 642, 644, 645, 648, 651, 662; threatened assassination, 620; and a president-elect,

Welles, Sumner – *Cont.*
623–4; misunderstanding of conditions, 627–8, 629; loses faith in Céspedes, 631; asks to be replaced, 632; panic at sergeants' revolt, 639–40, 649 n. 49; conversations with Hull, 642; with Caffery, 643; asks for protection, 643–4; at Hotel Nacional, 648, 652; and Grau's regime, 651 and n. 5, 1060; meeting with Directorio, 653; with Grau, 654; and Batista, 661, 712; accusations against, 662, 665; and a provisional government, 662, 663; ignorance of ideologies, 664; deputation from officers, 665; ignorance of November Revolution (1933), 666; joint statement with Roosevelt, 669–70; hostility to Grau, 671, 672, 685, 688; leaves Havana, 671 and n. 19, 672, 674; and U.S.-Cuba commercial treaty, 694; lost interest in Cuba, 696 n. 17; and an alliance with S. America, 727

West Indies, 13; and slave trade, 3 n. 16, 75–6, 78; and sugar, 4 n. 20, 126; slave-white proportions, 34 and n. 27; free black population, 36; comparative social conditions, 38; import and export figures, 51 n. 43; 'comparative economic successes', 54; dependence on home backing, 74; first railway, 122; and coffee, 128, 131 n. 16; import of labour from, 540, 684; absence of Communist organization, 697; repatriation of labour, 1117

West Indies, British, comparative slave-white population, 34 and n. 27, 66 and n. 25; and N. American Revolution, 67, 89 n. 24; and sugar, 68, 126, 127, 208–9, 290; and slavery, 69, 75 n. 15, 203; declining prosperity, 93, 99, 127; position of *emancipados*, 94, 182; use of contract labour, 184 and n. 1; exit of planters to India, 184 n. 2; social and economic disasters, 184 and n. 2; compensation for slave owners, 196 n. 9; source of labour, 467; lack of African cults, 519 n. 19; population figures, 1094; sugar quota, 1438 n. 9

West Indies, Dutch, population, 1094
West Indies, French, comparative white-slave population, 34 and n. 27; overtakes British colonies, 64; N.

American traders and, 66; treatment of slaves, 75 n. 15; collapse of sugar trade, 77; and emancipation, 214–15; population figures, 1094

West Indies, Spanish, 104, 402
Westbrook, José, death, 931
Westcott, Senator, justifies annexation of Cuba, 212
Weyler, General Valeriano, Marqués de Tenerife (1838–1930), succeeds Martínez Campos, 320, 327, 328; character and policy, 328–9; 'military areas', 329, 940; plan against guerrillas, 329–30; bans export of tobacco leaf, etc., 334; areas of concentration, 335; U.S. vilification, 336–7, 352; bans reporters, 340; and sugar harvest, 343–4; tactics against Gómez, 344; pacifies some provinces, 345; attacked by Madrid Press and government, 347; hopes of ending war, 348–9; and Cánovas' murder, 351; resignation, 352, 376; U.S. reputation, 353; Carlists and, 353 and n. 69; bomb incident, 574, 681
Wheeler, General Joseph (1836–1906), 384, 390 n. 3, 417; at Cuban landing, 390, 391; at San Juan, 393, 394; and peace terms, 400
White, Francis, Ass. Sec. of State, and (1920) electoral fraud, 548; and Machado's corruption, 589
White, Harry Dexter, 723 n. 28, 728, 731
Whites (Cuban born), population figures, 429, 1094 and n. 11, 1118; in control of sugar and tobacco farms, 430; wish to increase their numbers, 431; intermixture with coloured people, 516, 1118; wages compared with blacks, 1119; attendance at African fiestas, 1125
wheat, import monopoly scandal, 85 and n. 2
Whitney, John, 1170 and n. 73
Wicho, ex-sergeant, 993
Widener and Elkins, 465 n. 7, 645–6
Wieland, William, ed. *Havana Post*, 948; Welles and, 611 n. 23, 948; career, 948; and Cuban affairs, 948, 970 n. 31, 976, 1015, 1061; anti-Batista, 948, 949; and use of U.S. equipment, 964; judgement on Castro and Batista, 976–7; and arms embargo,

Wieland, William – *Cont.*
  985 n. 60; and Castro, 1196, 1204;
  argument with Glawe, 1239 and n. 12
Wilkinson, General James, 88 n. 19;
  and purchase of Cuba, 88
Willauer, Whiting, U.S. ambassador to
  Costa Rica, and Castro, 1206–7; and
  attack on Guatemala, 1206, 1304;
  and invasion plan, 1304; dismissal,
  1306
Williams, Longbourne, 966
Williams, Robert, exiled U.S. Negro,
  1433–4
Williamson, Harold, U.S. chargé
  d'affaires, 587
Williamson, William, 961
Wilson, Earl, 748 and n. 31
Wilson, General James, in Cuba, 421
  and n. 23, 448; Governor of Matanzas, 440–1; possible governor of Cuba,
  441 and n. 26, 447 and n. 23
Wilson, General Thomas, U.S. assistant
  sec., 911
Wilson, T. W. (1856–1924), U.S.
  president, 542; on Wood, 439;
  election, 528; asked to intervene in
  elections, 528, 529; fourteen points,
  532; and Liberal revolt, 534 n. 35;
  democratic principles, 626
Wilson-Gorman tariff, 290–1, 307
Wolfe, General James (1727–59), 2, 5
Wood, Leonard (1860–1927), 387 n. 27,
  1056; leader of Rough-Riders, 387,
  388, 390; at Cuban landing, 390, 391
  n. 6; Governor of Santiago, 403, 405,
  421, 439; work as Governor of
  Oriente, 410–12; disagreement with
  Brooke, 439, 440, 441; Wilson on,
  439; possible Governor of Cuba,
  439–40; hopes for Cuban reform, 440,
  442, 443, 444–5, 450–1; succeeds
  Brooke as Governor, 443, 444; new
  cabinet, 444 and n. 1; and annexation, 444, 445, 460; contempt for
  Cubans, 445, 1419; reorganizes educational system, 446–7, 460; quarrels
  with Frye, 447; and independence,
  447; national electoral system, 448;
  in sole control, 448–9, 449 n. 29; and
  a new constitution, 448–57, 472;
  revival of sugar industry, 457; and
  Cuba's economic needs, 458, 468–9;
  orders presidential elections (1901),
  459; hands over to Palma, 460; and

conquest of yellow fever, 461; and
  Church lands, 462; and U.S. trading
  sharks, 463; and railways, 465;
  imposes U.S. constitution, 472; abolishes cock-fighting, etc., 511; presidential nominee, 548–9
Woodbury, Mrs, 141
Woodford, Stewart Lyndon (1853–
  1913), 354 n. 72; envoy to Spain,
  353–4, 355 n. 78; Maria Cristina and,
  367; and autonomy, 367–8, 369; and
  sale of Cuba, 369–70; three-point
  offer, 370; peace efforts, 372, 373;
  and outbreak of war, 376, 377
Woodin, William H., 558 and n. 2, 586,
  614 n. 34, 686
Woodville, William, 70 and n. 50
working classes, first organizations,
  291–2; and Communism, 579; and
  sergeants' revolt, 638; source of army
  officers, 679; and Batista, 785; *Fidelistas*, 824 and n. 2; a 'pampered
  proletariat', 1179; lowered standards
  after Revolution, 1345 and n. 13
World War I (1914–18), effect on sugar
  trade, 526, 531–2, 537–8; U.S. entry,
  528; Cuba and, 530, 531–3; and
  Cuban expansion, 600
World War II (1939–45), and sugar
  trade, 717–18, 726, 728, 740; and
  Cuba, 722, 734–5; U.S. and aggression against Latin America, 722–3;
  fall of France, 726; liberation of
  Europe and N. Africa, 738
Wounded Knee, massacre of, 1890, 310,
  420
Wright, Chester, 584–5
Wright, Irene, *Cuba*, 419, 498, 500, 501,
  503, 513, 517
Wright, J. Butler (1877–1939), 710 and
  n. 13, 716, 717, 719 n. 15

Xifré, José, his fortune from Cuban
  trade, 155

Yabur, Alfredo, 1066; Minister of
  Justice, 1225, 1253
Yalob, Noske, 587
Yalta Conference, 745
Yañes Pelletier, Capt., 1073, 1122
Ydigoras, president of Guatemala, 1276
  and n. 10; accuses Guevara, 1277
Yglesias, José, and CDRs, 1457 and n.
  15

Young, General, 391 n. 6, 394, 410

Zacchi, Mgr Cesare, Bishop of Havana, 1472
Zaldo, Carlos, 268, 546
Zaldo, Teodoro de, 465
Zalvidar, Lieut, 1074
Zamora, Dr Zénon, 705
Zapata, Escuela Emiliano, 588
Zapata, Sergeant, 993
Zaragoza, 272, 351
Zayas, Alfredo (1861–1934), 456 n. 56, 459, 473 n. 3, 599 n. 69, 636, 1055; imprisonment, 471; vice-president, 473, 509; and Liberal party, 477, 478, 526–7, 528, 568; hostility towards Gómez, 484, 509; and law reform, 487; and elections, 489, 549; Santa Clara convent project, 505; nominated for president, 509, 547 and n. 18; founds Popular Party, 534; and Crowder, 550, 554; reforms, 550, 554; personal expenses, 550; and a U.S. loan, 550–1, 553, 555; and Menocal's contracts, 551; work of his 'Honest Cabinet', 555; personal enrichment, 555–6, 568; receives student delegation, 565; protests against, 566–8; supports Machado, 571; final frauds, 572; in retirement, 574
Zayas, Alfredo, Jnr, 554, 555
Zayas, Dr Francisco, 356
Zayas, Jorge, 1261
Zayas Bazán, Carmen, wife of Martí, 296
Zayas Bazán Cristóbal, and the cabildo, 45 and n. 14
Zayas Bazán, Rogelio, Governor of Camagüey, 571; as Minister of Interior, 575
Zayas Bazán, Lieut, aviation corps radio, 623, 624
Zaydin, Dr, premier, 732; and Prío's cabinet, 775 n. 1
Zeitlin, Maurice, 1432
Zenea, Juan Clemente (1832–71), poet, 259 and n. 19; shooting of, 259 n. 19
Zequeira, Carmen, 427
Zequeira, Felipe José de, and the cabildo, 45 n. 14; ennobled in Spain, 61 and n. 1
Zorin, Russian ambassador to U.N., 1409; and missile crisis, 1409, 1411, 1412
Zorilla, 186
Zuaznavar, Fidel, 427
Zuaznavar, Santiago, 427
Zuazo, Alonse de, 1515
Zubizarreta, Octavio, Sec. of Interior, 598
Zulueta, Julián de (1814–78), afterwards Marqués de Alava, 136 n. 3, 141, 234; mill ownership, Alava, Habana, Vizcaya, 136 and n. 3, 137, 153, 236, 262, 278, 427; social position, 153, 154, 157, 262; slave trader, 157, 214; use of Chinese labour, 186; slave strike, 236; and Independence War (1868), 246, 247, 248, 249, 252; new mill Zaza burnt, 264
Zulueta, Pedro de, cousin of the above, African merchant, 137 and n. 6; and slave trade, 157, 231 n. 64
Zuñiga, Capt. Mario, alleged defection, 1356–7